Bill James Handbook 2003

Baseball Info Solutions

Published by ACTA Publications

Cover by Tom Wright

Cover Photo by Scott Jordan Levy

First Edition: June, 2003

Published by: ACTA Publications, 4848 N. Clark Street, Chicago, IL 60646 (800-397-2282) www.actapublications.com

ISBN 0-87946-257-4

Printed in the United States of America

Acknowledgments

If you want a perspective of just how many numbers can be produced from a baseball game, try putting out a book like this. It's a monumental task, especially from a company in its infancy.

What hasn't already been said - probably a thousand times - about Bill James in the Acknowledgments sections of books like this? When Bill talks, people listen. We couldn't be more pleased and grateful to have him lend his name and work to our humble new endeavor.

John Dewan is a legend in the sports statistical industry and Baseball Info Solutions is his latest venture. John provided the framework for BIS and is always available for critical consulting decisions and original ideas.

Damon Lichtenwalner is the master of the BIS database. His effort and self-sacrifice are quite simply amazing. Mike Canter isn't employed by BIS, but if he hadn't taken on this book as a side project, it never would have happened. Like John, Mike is definitely "old school" in the sports statistics game. Ryan Galla is still fairly new, but is proving to be a fast learner with the kind of passion for baseball (and perhaps more importantly, sabermetric baseball) that can't be taught. Thanks also to Andy Bausher and Bob Vaughan, who helped get things going our first year.

We also very much appreciate the efforts of Greg Pierce and the rest of ACTA Publications, for taking on an unusual publication for them (their business is Christian books), but bestowing instant credibility upon us in the publishing world.

Without our fantastic group of helpers, collecting the immense amount of data we do would be impossible. Thanks to: Mark Alcaro, Bryce Babcock, Kevin Barge, Mike Brodhead, Darin Brown, Brad Burrow, John Coleman, Dennis Crowley, David Dick, Craig Fritz, Hal Fullman, Zack Fullman, Paul Galgon, Greg Gambler, Joe Glandon, Russ Goddard, Jared Haydt, Scott Hickman, David Houck, John Hunt, Wes Koser, Vinay Kumar, Paulina Kuo, Chippy Lichtenwalner, Randy Lillard, George Lindholm, Eugene Linger, Gene McCaffrey, Al Melchior, John Menna, Mike Mihalik, Gus Papadopoulos, Scott Pianowski, Pat Quinn, Todd Radcliffe, Daryl Ravani, Gary Read, Tim Reyes, Joe Ritzo, Bob Routier, Kenn Ruby, Bob Schaeffer, Kyle Schmidt, Erik Siegrist, Karen Thomas, Scott Thurston, Jon Vrecsics, John Wagner, Ian Waldraff, Dustin Webb, Mike Webber, Trace Wood and Todd Zola.

A special thanks to Durward Hamil, who provided some extra editing help.

And finally, thanks to Greg Ambrosius, Steve Greenberg, Peter Kreutzer, Rob Neyer, Mat Olkin, Ron Shandler and Rick Wolf, industry professionals who have helped spread the early good word about Baseball Info Solutions.

-- Steve Moyer
   President

Dedication

This book is dedicated to everyone who helped breathe life into Baseball Info Solutions. Long may we stand!

Table of Contents

Introduction

The King is dead. Long live the King!

The news that STATS, Inc., had discontinued publication of the *Major League Handbook* (the "red book" as it was affectionately called) left the baseball world with an empty space on its bookshelf. But for Baseball Info Solutions it also presented a great opportunity. After consulting with our old friend, Bill James, we decided to produce our own all-new, in-depth book of baseball statistics, the *Bill James Handbook*.

The 2003 edition you have in your hands is a prototype for the future. We plan this to be an annual publication, with future editions coming out within weeks of the end of the baseball season. For 2004, Bill plans to add sections on "fielding tendencies" and "manager tendencies" and other great features with new designs and useful data. We also hope to add "projections of performance" based on past statistics.

You may also notice our Alfred Hitchcockian "Where's Bill James?" exercise in this and future editions. We'll let you figure that game out yourself.

Certainly, there are other baseball statistical publications that have value in their own right. No one has yet published the be-all, end-all annual review of baseball stats that includes absolutely everything every single fan wants to know. (I'm not sure anyone would want to carry around such a monster anyway!) However, I think you will find this book to be the one you will use the most - whether you are a professional sports researcher, a rabid fantasy league participant or just someone who wants to get your baseball statistics accurately and easily.

Hardcore fans know the difference.

I hope you'll agree.

Steve Moyer
President
Baseball Info Solutions

2002 Team Statistics

2002 American League Standings

Overall

East

Team	W-L	Pct	GB	D1	LD1	LLd
New York Yankees	103-58	.640	0.0	106	9/29	10.5
Boston Red Sox	93-69	.574	10.5	72	6/27	5.0
Toronto Blue Jays	78-84	.481	25.5	2	4/2	0.0
Baltimore Orioles	67-95	.414	36.5	2	4/2	0.0
Tampa Bay Devil Rays	55-106	.342	48.0	4	4/5	0.5

Central

Team	W-L	Pct	GB	D1	LD1	LLd
Minnesota Twins	94-67	.584	0.0	161	9/29	17.0
Chicago White Sox	81-81	.500	13.5	15	5/26	1.0
Cleveland Indians	74-88	.457	20.5	18	4/19	4.0
Kansas City Royals	62-100	.383	32.5	0	-	0.0
Detroit Tigers	55-106	.342	39.0	0	-	0.0

West

Team	W-L	Pct	GB	D1	LD1	LLd
Oakland Athletics	103-59	.636	0.0	47	9/29	4.0
Anaheim Angels*	99-63	.611	4.0	13	9/18	1.0
Seattle Mariners	93-69	.574	10.0	131	8/22	6.5
Texas Rangers	72-90	.444	31.0	1	3/31	0.0

* Clinched Wild Card Birth on 9/26. Division Clinch Dates: Minnesota 9/15, New York 9/21, Oakland 9/27.
D1 = Number of days a team had at least a share of first place of their division; LD1 = Last date the team had at least a share of first place; LLd = The largest number of games that a team led their division

East Division

Tm	AT		VERSUS						CONDITIONS				GAME			MONTHLY						ALL-STAR	
	Home	Road	East	Cent	West	NL	LHS	RHS	Day	Night	Grass	Turf	1-Rn	5+Rn	XInn	Apr	May	June	July	Aug	Sep	Pre	Post
NYY	52-28	51-30	46-29	29-7	17-15	11-7	25-11	78-47	32-26	71-32	90-49	13-9	21-21	35-13	6-7	17-10	19-9	14-12	17-8	17-11	19-8	55-32	48-26
Bos	42-39	51-30	51-25	19-17	18-14	5-13	24-12	69-57	30-20	63-49	76-64	17-5	13-23	34-19	3-5	16-7	20-8	10-16	17-12	12-15	18-11	52-33	41-36
Tor	42-39	36-45	41-35	16-16	12-24	9-9	16-24	62-60	33-25	45-59	32-34	46-50	23-21	23-18	4-8	8-16	10-17	15-12	13-14	13-17	19-8	34-52	44-32
Bal	34-47	33-48	26-50	18-14	14-22	9-9	16-28	51-67	14-30	53-65	56-81	11-14	22-25	22-24	9-5	12-14	12-14	14-13	11-14	14-16	4-24	42-43	25-52
TB	30-51	25-55	25-50	13-19	10-26	7-11	8-21	47-85	14-27	41-79	22-44	33-62	17-28	10-33	9-10	9-15	9-19	10-17	7-20	11-18	9-17	28-57	27-49

Central Division

Tm	AT		VERSUS						CONDITIONS				GAME			MONTHLY						ALL-STAR	
	Home	Road	East	Cent	West	NL	LHS	RHS	Day	Night	Grass	Turf	1-Rn	5+Rn	XInn	Apr	May	June	July	Aug	Sep	Pre	Post
Min	54-27	40-40	15-17	50-25	19-17	10-8	23-29	71-38	25-24	69-43	34-36	60-31	29-16	35-13	6-7	16-11	15-13	15-12	19-7	15-14	14-10	52-33	42-34
CWS	47-34	34-47	18-14	40-36	15-21	8-10	17-24	64-57	30-28	51-53	72-70	9-11	15-21	39-27	3-2	16-10	12-16	12-16	11-15	14-13	16-11	42-46	39-35
Cle	39-42	35-46	19-17	37-39	12-20	6-12	23-23	51-65	25-21	49-67	66-78	8-10	16-17	19-26	4-4	12-13	13-15	11-15	10-16	12-16	15-13	39-47	35-41
KC	37-44	25-56	10-22	33-43	14-22	5-13	15-23	47-77	23-31	39-69	55-89	7-11	14-27	14-32	7-12	8-16	13-14	10-17	13-16	11-18	7-19	33-52	29-48
Det	33-47	22-59	11-25	29-46	9-23	6-12	12-22	43-84	15-37	40-69	54-91	1-15	23-23	7-37	5-6	8-17	12-15	7-20	13-14	10-19	5-21	31-54	24-52

West Division

Tm	AT		VERSUS						CONDITIONS				GAME			MONTHLY						ALL-STAR	
	Home	Road	East	Cent	West	NL	LHS	RHS	Day	Night	Grass	Turf	1-Rn	5+Rn	XInn	Apr	May	June	July	Aug	Sep	Pre	Post
Oak	54-27	49-32	23-22	32-9	32-26	16-2	35-16	68-43	35-16	68-43	96-54	7-5	32-14	29-20	10-4	15-11	10-17	21-7	15-12	24-4	18-8	50-38	53-21
Ana	54-27	45-36	28-13	30-15	30-28	11-7	30-16	69-47	23-12	76-51	89-58	10-5	31-22	30-12	10-5	11-13	19-7	17-12	16-10	18-11	18-10	51-35	48-28
Sea	48-33	45-36	25-20	23-18	34-24	11-7	27-18	66-51	25-20	68-49	84-63	9-6	24-25	27-19	11-6	18-8	16-11	17-11	15-12	13-15	14-12	55-33	38-36
Tex	42-39	30-51	25-16	18-27	20-38	9-9	15-31	57-59	15-22	57-68	65-85	7-5	18-26	23-24	6-12	10-15	11-16	14-14	10-17	15-12	12-16	39-47	33-43

Team vs. Team Breakdown

	EAST					CENTRAL					WEST			
	NYY	Bos	Tor	Bal	TB	Min	CWS	Cle	KC	Det	Oak	Ana	Sea	Tex
New York Yankees	-	10	10	13	13	6	4	6	5	8	5	4	4	4
Boston Red Sox	9	-	13	13	16	3	2	5	4	5	6	4	4	4
Toronto Blue Jays	9	6	-	15	11	1	2	3	4	6	6	2	3	1
Baltimore Orioles	6	6	4	-	10	5	3	1	7	2	4	2	5	3
Tampa Bay Devil Rays	5	3	8	9	-	2	3	2	2	4	1	1	4	4
Minnesota Twins	0	3	6	1	5	-	11	11	14	14	3	5	5	6
Chicago White Sox	2	4	4	4	4	8	-	9	11	12	2	3	5	5
Cleveland Indians	3	4	3	5	4	8	10	-	9	10	2	3	3	4
Kansas City Royals	1	2	3	0	4	5	8	10	-	10	1	3	3	7
Detroit Tigers	1	4	0	4	2	4	7	9	9	-	1	1	2	5
Oakland Athletics	4	3	3	5	8	6	7	5	8	6	-	11	8	13
Anaheim Angels	3	3	7	7	8	4	6	6	6	8	9	-	9	12
Seattle Mariners	5	5	4	5	5	4	4	4	6	5	11	10	-	13
Texas Rangers	3	4	8	6	5	3	4	5	2	4	6	7	7	-

(read wins across and losses down)

2002 National League Standings

Overall

EAST							CENTRAL							WEST					
Team	W-L	Pct	GB	D1	LD1	LLd	Team	W-L	Pct	GB	D1	LD1	LLd	Team	W-L	Pct	GB	D1	LD1	LLd
Atlanta Braves	101-59	.631	0.0	133	9/29	21.5	St Louis Cardinals	97-65	.599	0.0	114	9/29	13.0	Arizona Diamondbacks	98-64	.605	0.0	128	9/29	9.0
Montreal Expos	83-79	.512	19.0	23	5/2	2.0	Houston Astros	84-78	.519	13.0	2	4/4	0.0	San Francisco Giants*	95-66	.590	2.5	33	5/15	3.0
Philadelphia Phillies	80-81	.497	21.5	3	4/7	0.0	Cincinnati Reds	78-84	.481	19.0	57	6/17	5.0	Los Angeles Dodgers	92-70	.568	6.0	29	7/15	3.5
Florida Marlins	79-83	.488	23.0	14	5/16	2.0	Pittsburgh Pirates	72-89	.447	24.5	18	4/25	2.5	Colorado Rockies	73-89	.451	25.0	0	-	0.0
New York Mets	75-86	.466	26.5	41	5/29	2.0	Chicago Cubs	67-95	.414	30.0	1	4/3	0.0	San Diego Padres	66-96	.407	32.0	0	-	0.0
							Milwaukee Brewers	56-106	.346	41.0	2	4/3	0.0							

* Clinched Wild Card Birth on 9/28. Division Clinch Dates: Atlanta 9/9, St Louis 9/20, Arizona 9/28.
D1 = Number of days a team had at least a share of first place of their division; LD1 = Last date the team had at least a share of first place; LLd = The largest number of games that a team led their division

East Division

	AT		VERSUS						CONDITIONS				GAME			MONTHLY							ALL-STAR	
Tm	Home	Road	East	Cent	West	AL	LHS	RHS	Day	Night	Grass	Turf	1-Rn	5+Rn	XInn	Apr	May	June	July	Aug	Sep	Pre	Post
Atl	52-28	49-31	47-28	24-12	15-16	15-3	14-9	87-50	33-17	68-42	87-52	14-7	28-17	26-17	7-8	12-15	18-10	21-5	18-8	16-11	16-10	56-32	45-27
Mon	49-32	34-47	37-39	21-15	13-19	12-6	18-18	65-61	22-21	61-58	28-40	55-39	30-22	20-12	13-6	16-10	11-17	15-11	11-16	13-15	17-10	46-41	37-38
Phi	40-40	40-41	34-41	22-14	14-18	10-8	16-20	64-61	24-29	56-52	37-35	43-46	22-24	11-16	11-7	9-18	12-14	15-11	14-13	18-10	12-15	39-47	41-34
Fla	46-35	33-48	36-40	18-18	15-17	10-8	19-23	60-60	21-25	58-58	66-71	13-12	24-20	14-30	5-12	13-13	13-16	15-11	11-15	14-13	13-15	45-43	34-40
NYM	38-43	37-43	35-41	20-15	10-22	10-8	18-21	57-65	21-33	54-53	66-75	9-11	27-26	23-17	5-9	16-10	13-15	11-15	15-11	6-21	14-14	43-44	32-42

Central Division

	AT		VERSUS						CONDITIONS				GAME			MONTHLY							ALL-STAR	
Tm	Home	Road	East	Cent	West	AL	LHS	RHS	Day	Night	Grass	Turf	1-Rn	5+Rn	XInn	Apr	May	June	July	Aug	Sep	Pre	Post
Stl	52-29	45-36	11-19	57-33	21-9	8-4	21-16	76-49	33-26	64-39	93-63	4-2	22-19	28-18	5-5	12-14	18-10	12-12	17-9	17-14	21-6	47-38	50-27
Hou	47-34	37-44	16-14	49-41	14-16	5-7	21-16	63-62	35-26	49-52	82-74	2-4	18-25	22-19	5-8	11-14	13-15	12-14	18-9	18-11	12-15	41-45	43-33
Cin	38-43	40-41	12-18	50-40	14-16	2-10	17-21	61-63	30-28	48-56	76-80	2-4	26-23	18-30	12-6	16-9	16-13	11-15	12-14	11-18	12-15	46-41	32-43
Pit	38-42	34-47	16-13	43-47	10-20	3-9	19-16	53-73	23-27	49-62	70-85	2-4	27-24	14-25	4-4	14-10	11-19	11-15	13-14	11-18	12-13	38-49	34-40
ChC	36-45	31-50	12-18	36-54	13-17	6-6	15-24	52-71	38-50	29-45	65-92	2-3	18-36	16-18	5-9	8-16	13-16	12-14	11-15	12-18	11-16	35-51	32-44
Mil	31-50	25-56	7-23	35-55	12-18	2-10	9-23	47-83	17-37	39-69	55-98	1-8	14-28	14-28	3-10	8-18	13-16	11-16	9-17	10-18	8-19	33-55	23-51

West Division

	AT		VERSUS						CONDITIONS				GAME			MONTHLY							ALL-STAR	
Tm	Home	Road	East	Cent	West	AL	LHS	RHS	Day	Night	Grass	Turf	1-Rn	5+Rn	XInn	Apr	May	June	July	Aug	Sep	Pre	Post
Ari	55-26	43-38	21-11	23-13	43-33	11-7	28-22	70-42	36-21	62-43	96-60	2-4	23-20	30-17	9-3	16-10	18-10	14-12	17-10	19-9	14-13	51-36	47-28
SF	50-31	45-35	17-14	23-13	47-29	8-10	21-18	74-48	35-30	60-36	91-61	4-5	28-22	31-11	8-1	15-11	15-12	15-12	14-13	18-10	18-8	49-38	46-28
LA	46-35	46-35	20-12	20-16	40-36	12-6	24-15	68-55	29-26	63-52	86-66	6-4	33-15	20-16	7-4	16-10	15-13	19-8	10-16	18-10	14-13	54-34	38-36
Col	47-34	26-55	18-14	17-19	31-45	7-11	16-26	57-63	28-28	45-61	71-82	2-7	18-19	19-30	5-5	10-16	19-10	10-17	9-16	13-16	12-14	42-46	31-43
SD	41-40	25-56	16-16	13-23	29-47	8-10	19-25	47-71	22-31	44-65	61-91	5-5	18-25	16-31	4-11	14-12	11-18	9-18	11-14	13-15	8-19	35-53	31-43

Team vs. Team Breakdown

	EAST					CENTRAL						WEST				
	Atl	Mon	Phi	Fla	NYM	Stl	Hou	Cin	Pit	ChC	Mil	Ari	SF	LA	Col	SD
Atlanta Braves	-	13	11	11	12	5	3	4	3	4	5	3	3	2	4	3
Montreal Expos	6	-	11	9	11	3	3	5	3	3	4	2	4	2	2	3
Philadelphia Phillies	7	8	-	9	10	4	3	4	2	4	5	3	3	3	3	2
Florida Marlins	8	10	10	-	8	4	3	1	4	2	4	1	4	3	2	5
New York Mets	7	8	9	11	-	3	2	4	1	5	5	2	0	2	3	3
St Louis Cardinals	1	3	2	2	3	-	13	11	11	12	10	4	4	4	4	5
Houston Astros	3	3	3	3	4	6	-	11	11	11	10	3	1	3	3	4
Cincinnati Reds	2	1	2	5	2	8	6	-	11	12	13	0	2	4	3	5
Pittsburgh Pirates	3	3	4	2	4	6	6	7	-	9	15	2	2	2	2	2
Chicago Cubs	2	3	2	4	1	6	6	8	10	-	7	2	3	2	4	2
Milwaukee Brewers	1	2	1	2	1	7	8	6	4	10	-	2	1	1	3	5
Arizona Diamondbacks	3	4	4	5	5	2	3	6	4	4	4	-	8	9	14	12
San Francisco Giants	3	2	3	3	6	2	5	4	4	3	5	11	-	11	11	14
Los Angeles Dodgers	4	5	4	3	4	2	3	2	4	4	5	10	8	-	12	10
Colorado Rockies	3	4	3	5	3	2	3	3	4	2	3	5	8	7	-	11
San Diego Padres	3	4	4	1	4	1	2	1	4	4	1	7	5	9	8	-

(read wins across and losses down)

American League Batting

Tm	G	AB	H	2B	3B	HR	(Hm	Rd)	TB	R	RBI	TBB	IBB	SO	HBP	SH	SF	ShO	SB	CS	SB%	GDP	LOB	Avg	OBP	Slg
NYY	161	5601	1540	314	12	223	(108	115)	2547	897	857	640	48	1171	72	23	41	3	100	38	.72	150	1191	.275	.354	.455
Bos	162	5640	1560	348	33	177	(77	100)	2505	859	810	545	39	944	72	22	53	7	80	28	.74	139	1175	.277	.345	.444
CWS	162	5502	1475	289	29	217	(132	85)	2473	856	819	555	17	952	49	48	53	7	75	31	.71	111	1085	.268	.338	.449
Ana	162	5678	1603	333	32	152	(71	81)	2456	851	811	462	42	805	74	49	64	8	117	51	.70	105	1165	.282	.341	.433
Tex	162	5618	1510	304	27	230	(132	98)	2558	843	806	524	45	1055	62	34	65	12	62	34	.65	129	1155	.269	.338	.455
Sea	162	5569	1531	285	31	152	(64	88)	2334	814	771	629	62	1003	51	41	72	7	137	58	.70	123	1239	.275	.350	.419
Tor	162	5581	1457	305	38	187	(102	85)	2399	813	771	522	30	1142	53	17	57	6	71	18	.80	130	1104	.261	.327	.430
Oak	162	5558	1450	279	28	205	(116	89)	2400	800	772	609	37	1008	68	20	36	6	46	20	.70	128	1197	.261	.339	.432
Min	161	5582	1518	348	36	167	(68	99)	2439	768	731	472	30	1089	56	34	52	6	79	62	.56	121	1124	.272	.332	.437
Cle	162	5423	1349	255	26	192	(95	97)	2232	739	706	542	35	1000	56	39	39	8	52	37	.58	149	1066	.249	.321	.412
KC	162	5535	1415	285	42	140	(88	52)	2204	737	695	524	27	921	52	44	51	13	140	65	.68	106	1092	.256	.323	.398
TB	161	5604	1418	297	35	133	(63	70)	2184	673	640	456	29	1115	58	44	36	14	102	45	.69	116	1132	.253	.314	.390
Bal	162	5491	1353	311	27	165	(92	73)	2213	667	636	452	25	993	64	40	49	15	110	48	.70	128	1037	.246	.309	.403
Det	161	5406	1340	265	37	124	(61	63)	2051	575	546	363	22	1035	64	30	57	10	65	44	.60	125	1029	.248	.300	.379
AL	1132	77788	20519	4218	433	2464	(1269	1195)	32995	10892	10371	7325	488	14233	851	499	710	118	1236	579	.68	1760	15791	.264	.331	.424

American League Pitching

Tm	G	CG	Rel	IP	BFP	H	R	ER	HR	SH	SF	HB	TBB	IBB	SO	WP	Bk	W	L	Pct.	ShO	Sv-Op	Hld	OAvg	OOBP	OSlg	ERA
Ana	162	7	400	1452.1	6097	1345	644	595	169	27	59	49	509	24	999	52	7	99	63	.611	14	54-71	66	.247	.314	.392	3.69
Oak	162	9	408	1452.0	6158	1391	654	593	135	50	42	62	474	45	1021	40	9	103	59	.636	19	48-69	86	.252	.315	.384	3.68
Bos	162	5	338	1446.0	6049	1339	665	603	146	30	52	84	430	29	1157	31	6	93	69	.574	17	51-68	40	.246	.308	.385	3.75
NYY	161	9	334	1452.0	6159	1441	697	625	144	38	41	48	403	44	1135	59	2	103	58	.640	11	53-69	46	.256	.309	.395	3.87
Sea	162	8	343	1445.1	6117	1422	699	654	178	39	48	49	441	34	1063	43	3	93	69	.574	12	43-64	57	.257	.315	.410	4.07
Min	161	8	435	1444.2	6133	1454	712	662	184	30	41	45	439	24	1026	62	3	94	67	.584	9	47-65	83	.261	.318	.421	4.12
Bal	162	8	407	1450.2	6258	1491	773	719	208	20	38	54	549	34	967	54	1	67	95	.414	3	31-46	58	.266	.336	.435	4.46
CWS	162	7	423	1423.0	6131	1422	798	716	190	41	43	60	528	31	945	54	6	81	81	.500	7	35-46	60	.260	.330	.423	4.53
Tor	162	6	461	1438.1	6338	1504	828	767	177	42	52	71	590	56	991	57	4	78	84	.481	6	41-70	69	.269	.344	.431	4.80
Cle	162	9	421	1424.2	6271	1508	837	777	142	39	66	57	603	38	1058	52	8	74	88	.457	4	34-53	51	.274	.348	.423	4.91
Det	161	11	372	1414.0	6221	1593	864	774	163	44	53	62	463	34	794	59	5	55	106	.342	7	33-54	32	.285	.343	.455	4.93
Tex	162	4	487	1439.2	6446	1528	882	824	194	38	40	76	669	32	1030	84	11	72	90	.444	4	33-66	65	.272	.351	.451	5.15
KC	162	12	421	1441.0	6386	1587	891	834	212	47	69	52	572	48	909	68	6	62	100	.383	6	30-54	40	.281	.349	.463	5.21
TB	161	12	306	1440.1	6424	1567	918	846	215	35	57	94	620	24	925	62	10	55	106	.342	3	25-46	24	.279	.357	.463	5.29
AL	1132	115	5556	20164.0	87182	20592	10862	9989	2457	520	701	863	7290	497	14020	777	85	1129	1135	.499	122	558-841	777	.265	.332	.424	4.46

American League Fielding

Team	G	Inn	PO	Ast	OFAst	E	(Throw	Field)	TC	DP	GDP	SB	CS	SB%	CPkof	PPkof	PB	UER	UERA	FPct
Minnesota	161	1444.2	4333	1415	26	74	(29	45)	5822	124	112	57	27	.68	0	9	5	50	0.31	.987
Anaheim	162	1452.1	4357	1560	26	87	(41	46)	6004	147	126	78	51	.60	4	1	7	49	0.30	.986
Baltimore	162	1450.2	4351	1711	27	91	(42	49)	6153	164	145	103	44	.70	0	12	22	54	0.34	.985
Seattle	162	1445.1	4334	1508	22	88	(34	54)	5930	131	119	66	35	.65	1	2	7	45	0.28	.985
Texas	162	1439.2	4318	1677	29	99	(49	48)	6094	150	131	74	28	.73	9	2	11	58	0.36	.984
Chicago	162	1423.0	4270	1586	27	97	(45	50)	5953	154	137	99	38	.72	1	3	9	82	0.52	.984
Oakland	162	1452.0	4356	1786	14	102	(51	50)	6244	139	127	68	46	.60	1	0	9	61	0.38	.984
Boston	162	1446.0	4335	1633	27	104	(45	59)	6072	135	120	118	50	.70	1	4	20	62	0.39	.983
Toronto	162	1438.1	4316	1600	31	107	(48	59)	6023	152	131	107	41	.72	0	3	18	61	0.38	.982
Cleveland	162	1424.2	4273	1648	29	113	(53	59)	6034	154	131	126	59	.68	0	4	15	60	0.38	.981
Tampa Bay	161	1440.1	4321	1551	38	125	(63	59)	5997	163	140	92	53	.63	1	5	13	72	0.45	.979
Kansas City	162	1441.0	4322	1696	38	130	(68	62)	6148	151	138	90	36	.71	0	4	8	57	0.36	.979
New York	161	1452.0	4355	1515	17	127	(59	67)	5997	115	100	92	39	.70	1	6	10	72	0.45	.979
Detroit	161	1414.0	4241	1705	49	142	(60	80)	6088	143	119	72	34	.68	3	4	23	90	0.57	.977
American League	1132	20164.0	60482	22591	400	1486	(687	787)	84559	2022	1776	1242	581	.68	22	59	177	873	0.39	.982

National League Batting

Tm	G	AB	H	2B	3B	HR	(Hm	Rd)	TB	R	RBI	TBB	IBB	SO	HBP	SH	SF	ShO	SB	CS	SB%	GDP	LOB	Avg	OBP	Slg
Ari	162	5508	1471	283	41	165	(83	82)	2331	819	783	643	58	1016	50	62	53	10	92	46	.67	130	1211	.267	.346	.423
Stl	162	5505	1475	285	26	175	(88	87)	2337	787	758	542	77	927	67	83	49	10	86	42	.67	123	1160	.268	.338	.425
SF	162	5497	1465	300	35	198	(72	126)	2429	783	751	616	103	961	65	68	52	7	74	21	.78	136	1241	.267	.344	.442
Col	162	5512	1508	283	41	152	(97	55)	2329	778	750	497	40	1043	56	49	50	7	103	53	.66	133	1094	.274	.337	.423
Hou	162	5503	1441	291	32	167	(88	79)	2297	749	719	589	57	1120	59	64	37	6	71	27	.72	144	1177	.262	.338	.417
Mon	162	5479	1432	300	36	162	(85	77)	2290	735	695	575	85	1104	46	108	42	10	118	64	.65	123	1158	.261	.334	.418
LA	162	5554	1464	286	29	155	(73	82)	2273	713	693	428	50	940	53	67	44	13	96	37	.72	140	1087	.264	.320	.409
Phi	161	5523	1428	325	41	165	(79	86)	2330	710	676	640	70	1095	53	67	39	3	104	43	.71	129	1260	.259	.339	.422
Cin	162	5470	1386	297	21	169	(85	84)	2232	709	678	583	66	1188	66	95	40	8	116	52	.69	119	1169	.253	.330	.408
Atl	161	5495	1428	280	25	164	(82	82)	2250	708	669	558	68	1028	54	67	49	7	76	39	.66	147	1185	.260	.331	.409
ChC	162	5496	1351	259	29	200	(99	101)	2268	706	676	585	52	1269	44	78	19	10	63	21	.75	117	1173	.246	.321	.413
Fla	162	5496	1433	280	32	146	(66	80)	2215	699	653	595	69	1130	61	59	49	13	177	73	.71	129	1190	.261	.337	.403
NYM	161	5496	1409	238	22	160	(81	79)	2171	690	650	486	46	1044	63	75	30	7	87	42	.67	142	1111	.256	.322	.395
SD	162	5515	1393	243	29	136	(59	77)	2102	662	627	547	42	1062	30	45	41	16	71	44	.62	132	1158	.253	.321	.381
Pit	162	5330	1300	243	20	142	(61	81)	2029	641	610	537	44	1109	73	68	41	15	86	49	.64	97	1149	.244	.319	.381
Mil	162	5415	1369	269	18	139	(62	77)	2113	627	597	500	37	1125	55	79	34	15	94	50	.65	144	1086	.253	.320	.390
NL	1294	87794	22753	4482	488	2595	(1260	1335)	35996	11516	10961	8921	964	17161	895	1134	689	157	1514	703	.68	2085	18609	.259	.331	.410

National League Pitching

Tm	G	CG	Rel	IP	BFP	H	R	ER	HR	SH	SF	HB	TBB	IBB	SO	WP	Bk	W	L	Pct.	ShO	Sv-Op	Hld	OAvg	OOBP	OSlg	ERA
Atl	161	3	469	1467.1	6131	1302	565	511	123	74	32	42	554	63	1058	40	4	101	59	.631	15	57-71	79	.240	.313	.364	3.13
SF	162	10	417	1437.1	6056	1349	616	566	116	72	43	36	523	44	992	36	2	95	66	.590	13	43-60	70	.251	.319	.372	3.54
LA	162	4	423	1457.2	6139	1311	643	598	165	71	38	46	555	45	1132	33	3	92	70	.568	15	56-71	78	.242	.315	.387	3.69
Stl	162	4	472	1446.1	6135	1355	648	595	141	70	56	60	547	39	1009	40	2	97	65	.599	9	42-63	82	.251	.323	.386	3.70
Ari	162	14	423	1447.2	6070	1361	674	630	170	44	37	54	421	30	1303	48	11	98	64	.605	10	40-59	59	.247	.305	.397	3.92
Hou	162	2	480	1445.0	6205	1423	695	643	151	76	48	55	546	78	1219	38	3	84	78	.519	11	43-58	70	.260	.330	.410	4.00
NYM	161	9	451	1442.2	6212	1408	703	624	163	74	42	55	543	75	1107	22	7	75	86	.466	10	36-51	62	.256	.327	.403	3.89
Mon	162	9	437	1453.0	6246	1475	718	641	165	79	39	46	508	80	1088	51	5	83	79	.512	3	39-59	78	.265	.329	.421	3.97
Phi	161	5	450	1449.2	6222	1381	724	671	153	66	34	70	570	54	1075	68	5	80	81	.497	9	47-71	78	.252	.328	.421	4.17
Pit	161	2	458	1412.2	6131	1447	730	664	163	60	35	55	572	93	920	34	5	72	89	.447	7	47-66	96	.268	.342	.423	4.23
ChC	162	11	390	1441.1	6236	1373	759	687	167	85	57	58	606	53	1333	44	2	67	95	.414	9	23-48	32	.253	.331	.407	4.29
Fla	162	11	461	1456.1	6340	1449	763	706	151	73	45	58	631	46	1104	55	7	79	83	.488	12	36-55	68	.262	.341	.415	4.36
Cin	162	2	462	1453.2	6296	1502	774	690	173	62	43	56	550	63	980	52	2	78	84	.481	8	42-57	67	.269	.338	.426	4.27
SD	162	5	458	1435.1	6330	1522	815	738	177	64	58	66	582	61	1108	51	4	66	96	.407	10	40-62	59	.274	.346	.442	4.63
Mil	162	7	446	1432.1	6339	1468	821	752	199	93	45	62	666	82	1026	64	8	56	106	.346	4	32-42	52	.268	.352	.442	4.73
Col	162	1	506	1426.2	6345	1554	898	825	225	49	47	64	582	49	920	42	6	73	89	.451	8	43-59	78	.277	.349	.466	5.20
NL	1294	99	7203	23105.0	99433	22680	11546	10541	2602	1112	699	883	8956	955	17374	718	76	1296	1290	.501	153	666-952	1108	.258	.331	.410	4.11

National League Fielding

Team	G	Inn	PO	Ast	OFAst	E	(Throw	Field)	TC	DP	GDP	SB	CS	SB%	CPkof	PPkof	PB	UER	UERA	FPct
Houston	162	1445.0	4335	1656	34	83	37	45	6074	147	115	104	36	.74	3	6	5	52	0.32	.986
Philadelphia	161	1449.2	4349	1695	27	88	41	46	6132	153	134	74	34	.69	0	4	12	53	0.33	.986
Los Angeles	162	1457.2	4374	1676	29	90	44	44	6140	129	114	110	53	.67	4	1	12	45	0.28	.985
San Francisco	162	1437.1	4311	1619	33	90	30	60	6020	161	138	87	36	.71	0	4	7	50	0.31	.985
Arizona	162	1447.2	4338	1497	17	89	33	55	5924	110	95	77	43	.64	1	6	13	44	0.27	.985
St Louis	162	1446.1	4337	1660	34	102	46	55	6099	162	133	86	34	.72	3	4	9	53	0.33	.983
Milwaukee	162	1432.1	4290	1628	24	103	52	50	6021	152	130	109	49	.69	0	3	12	60	0.43	.983
Florida	162	1456.1	4367	1624	33	106	40	64	6097	154	134	93	61	.60	1	2	6	57	0.35	.983
Atlanta	161	1467.1	4401	1806	24	114	45	67	6321	169	155	96	55	.64	2	6	12	54	0.33	.982
Pittsburgh	161	1412.2	4237	1885	39	115	45	69	6237	145	145	94	44	.68	2	11	12	66	0.42	.982
Colorado	162	1426.2	4278	1683	34	112	41	69	6073	156	136	87	23	.79	0	8	12	73	0.46	.982
Chicago	162	1441.1	4325	1496	22	114	49	64	5935	138	117	112	54	.67	0	3	15	72	0.45	.981
Cincinnati	162	1453.2	4359	1765	38	120	46	74	6244	163	140	67	42	.61	2	9	28	84	0.52	.981
San Diego	162	1435.1	4307	1669	32	127	58	69	6103	155	135	76	40	.66	0	3	14	77	0.48	.979
Montreal	162	1453.0	4389	1788	43	139	61	75	6286	158	132	85	44	.66	1	5	12	77	0.48	.978
New York	161	1442.2	4326	1617	28	144	65	79	6087	134	114	151	53	.74	0	1	11	79	0.49	.976
National League	1294	23105.0	69293	26764	491	1736	733	985	97793	2409	2067	1508	701	.68	19	76	192	1005	0.39	.982

Career Register

Beyond the obvious:

Age is seasonal age as of June 30, 2003.

For pitchers, BFP is batters facing pitcher; TBB is total walks; IBB is intentional walks; Op is save opportunities; Hld is holds.

New additions to the traditional Career Register section are runs created (RC) for batters and component ERA (ERC) for pitchers. Runs created (RC) is a method of measuring every facet of a hitter's strengths and weaknesses and combining those factors into one production number. It was invented by Bill James many years ago and he has revised the formula several times. Component ERA (ERC) estimates what a pitcher's ERA should have been based upon his raw pitching stats, such as Hits, Home Runs and Walks Allowed, etc. It gives a good indication of whether or not a pitcher "deserved" his ERA, whether he was saved or deserted by pitchers that followed him, etc. ERC was also invented by Bill James. You can find complete definitions and formulas for each in the Glossary.

Players who have appeared in fewer than three major league seasons have full minor league stats included. Other 2002 major leaguers who spent time in the minors last year have just their 2002 minor league totals included (indicated by an asterisk).

When a player led the league in a particular category, his register total will be in boldface.

Finally, there are some advantages to printing this type of book late. We were able to include the following players who did not play in the major leagues in 2002, some of whom were spring training surprises and others who may not appear in any of the other popular statistical guides. These players are:

Erick Almonte, Jason Anderson, Steve Avery, Luis Ayala, Rocco Baldelli, Rod Beck, Nick Bierbrodt, Jeremy Bonderman, Kiko Calero, Ron Calloway, D. J. Carrasco, David Cone, Enrique Cruz, R.A. Dickey, Darren Dreifort, Scott Elarton, Cal Eldred, Jesse Foppert, John Franco, Jody Gerut, Jeremi Gonzalez, Andy Good, Robby Hammock, Ken Harvey, Tim Laker, Chris Latham, Curtis Leskanic, Allan Levrault, Doug Linton, Carlton Loewer, Aquilino Lopez, Javier Lopez, Al Martin, Hideki Matsui, Seth McClung, Billy McMillon, Gil Meche, Trever Miller, Xavier Nady, Mike Neu, Lance Painter, Tommy Phelps, Horacio Ramirez, Stephen Randolph, Carlos Reyes, Matt Roney, Scott Service, Kyle Snyder, Russ Springer, Josh Stewart, Mark Teixeira, Kevin Tolar, Billy Traber, Chase Utley, Jose Valverde, Claudio Vargas, Oscar Villarreal, Brandon Webb, Todd Wellemeyer, Turk Wendell, Jerome Williams, Dontrelle Willis and Kevin Witt.

Paul Abbott

Pitches: R **Bats:** R **Pos:** SP-5; RP-2   **Ht:** 6'3" **Wt:** 204 **Born:** 9/15/67 **Age:** 35

Year Team	Lg	G	GS	CG	GF	IP	BFP	H	R	ER	HR	SH	SF	HB	TBB	IBB	SO	WP	Bk	W	L	Pct	ShO	Sv-Op	Hld	ERC	ERA
2002 Sn Brnardino*	A+	1	1	0	0	5.0	19	3	0	0	0	1	0	0	2	0	5	0	0	0	0	-	0	0--	-	1.59	0.00
2002 Tacoma*	AAA	2	2	0	0	8.2	41	13	10	6	3	0	0	0	3	0	8	0	0	0	1	.000	0	0--	-	8.98	6.23
1990 Minnesota	AL	7	7	0	0	34.2	162	37	24	23	0	1	1	1	28	0	25	1	0	0	5	.000	0	0-0	0	5.53	5.97
1991 Minnesota	AL	15	3	0	1	47.1	210	38	27	25	5	7	3	0	36	1	43	5	0	3	1	.750	0	0-0	0	4.42	4.75
1992 Minnesota	AL	6	0	0	5	11.0	50	12	4	4	1	0	1	1	5	0	13	1	0	0	0	-	0	0-0	0	5.10	3.27
1993 Cleveland	AL	5	5	0	0	18.1	84	19	15	13	5	0	0	0	11	1	7	1	0	0	1	.000	0	0-0	0	6.28	6.38
1998 Seattle	AL	4	4	0	0	24.2	105	24	11	11	2	0	1	0	10	0	22	3	0	3	1	.750	0	0-0	0	3.85	4.01
1999 Seattle	AL	25	7	0	8	72.2	298	50	31	25	9	3	4	0	32	3	68	2	0	6	2	.750	0	0-2	3	2.65	3.10
2000 Seattle	AL	35	27	0	2	179.0	766	164	89	84	23	1	4	5	80	4	100	3	0	9	7	.563	0	0-0	4	4.09	4.22
2001 Seattle	AL	28	27	1	0	163.0	710	145	79	77	21	3	5	7	87	5	118	11	0	17	4	.810	0	0-0	0	4.33	4.25
2002 Seattle	AL	7	5	0	0	26.1	137	40	36	35	5	1	4	0	20	0	22	2	0	1	3	.250	0	0-0	0	9.89	11.96
9 ML YEARS		132	85	1	17	577.0	2522	529	316	297	71	16	20	15	309	14	418	29	0	39	24	.619	0	0-2	7	4.39	4.63

Brent Abernathy

Bats: R **Throws:** R **Pos:** 2B-116; PR-2   **Ht:** 6'1" **Wt:** 191 **Born:** 9/23/77 **Age:** 25

Year Team	Lg	G	AB	H	2B	3B	HR	(Hm	Rd)	TB	R	RBI	RC	TBB	IBB	SO	HBP	SH	SF	SB	CS	SB%	GDP	Avg	OBP	Slg
1997 Hagerstown	A	99	379	117	27	2	1	(-	-)	151	69	26	56	30	0	32	6	6	2	22	13	.63	6	.309	.367	.398
1998 Dunedin	A+	124	485	159	36	1	3	(-	-)	206	85	65	80	44	0	38	1	12	6	35	13	.73	11	.328	.381	.425
1999 Knoxville	AA	136	577	168	42	1	13	(-	-)	251	108	62	90	55	1	47	6	5	7	34	15	.69	11	.291	.355	.435
2000 Durham	AAA	27	91	24	6	0	1	(-	-)	33	14	15	15	11	0	11	4	3	5	9	2	.82	0	.264	.351	.363
2000 Syracuse	AAA	92	358	106	21	2	4	(-	-)	143	47	35	46	26	1	32	1	3	3	14	13	.52	7	.296	.343	.399
2001 Durham	AAA	61	252	76	20	0	4	(-	-)	108	45	23	38	16	0	23	2	3	2	11	4	.73	3	.302	.346	.429
2001 Tampa Bay	AL	79	304	82	17	1	5	(3	2)	116	43	33	39	27	1	35	0	3	1	8	3	.73	3	.270	.328	.382
2002 Tampa Bay	AL	117	463	112	18	4	2	(2	0)	144	46	40	47	25	0	46	6	8	2	10	4	.71	8	.242	.288	.311
2 ML YEARS		196	767	194	35	5	7	(5	2)	260	89	73	86	52	1	81	6	11	3	18	7	.72	11	.253	.304	.339

Bobby Abreu

Bats: L **Throws:** R **Pos:** RF-148; CF-18; PH-3   **Ht:** 6'0" **Wt:** 195 **Born:** 3/11/74 **Age:** 29

Year Team	Lg	G	AB	H	2B	3B	HR	(Hm	Rd)	TB	R	RBI	RC	TBB	IBB	SO	HBP	SH	SF	SB	CS	SB%	GDP	Avg	OBP	Slg
1996 Houston	NL	15	22	5	1	0	0	(0	0)	6	1	1	1	2	0	3	0	0	0	0	0	-	1	.227	.292	.273
1997 Houston	NL	59	188	47	10	3	3	(3	0)	70	22	26	25	21	0	48	1	0	0	7	2	.78	0	.250	.329	.372
1998 Philadelphia	NL	151	497	155	29	6	17	(10	7)	247	68	74	101	84	14	133	0	4	4	19	10	.66	6	.312	.409	.497
1999 Philadelphia	NL	152	546	183	35	11	20	(13	7)	300	118	93	131	109	8	113	3	0	4	27	9	.75	13	.335	.446	.549
2000 Philadelphia	NL	154	576	182	42	10	25	(14	11)	319	103	79	130	100	9	116	1	0	3	28	8	.78	12	.316	.416	.554
2001 Philadelphia	NL	162	588	170	48	4	31	(13	18)	319	118	110	125	106	11	137	1	0	9	36	14	.72	13	.289	.393	.543
2002 Philadelphia	NL	157	572	176	50	6	20	(8	12)	298	102	85	115	104	9	117	3	0	6	31	12	.72	11	.308	.413	.521
7 ML YEARS		850	2989	918	215	39	116	(61	55)	1559	532	468	628	526	51	667	9	4	26	148	55	.73	56	.307	.409	.522

Jose Acevedo

Pitches: R **Bats:** R **Pos:** SP-5; RP-1   **Ht:** 6'0" **Wt:** 185 **Born:** 12/18/77 **Age:** 25

Year Team	Lg	G	GS	CG	GF	IP	BFP	H	R	ER	HR	SH	SF	HB	TBB	IBB	SO	WP	Bk	W	L	Pct	ShO	Sv-Op	Hld	ERC	ERA
1997 Chrlstn - WV	A	15	8	0	3	57.1	245	61	29	25	8	2	1	5	9	0	34	4	1	3	3	.500	0	0--	-	4.03	3.92
1998 Chrlstn - WV	A	25	25	2	0	158.2	668	169	74	69	9	4	3	6	40	132	6	0	9	9	9	.500	0	0--	-	2.41	3.91
1999 Clinton	A	24	24	1	0	133.2	553	119	65	56	14	2	3	0	43	0	136	5	3	8	6	.571	1	0--	-	3.21	3.77
2000 Dayton	A	25	23	0	2	141.0	610	135	74	61	16	1	4	6	53	0	123	6	0	11	5	.688	0	0--	-	3.97	3.89
2001 Chattanooga	AA	16	11	0	1	78.0	319	68	34	32	6	5	1	3	25	1	82	2	0	4	4	.500	0	0--	-	3.11	3.69
2002 Louisville	AAA	23	23	0	0	154.2	631	146	61	55	16	7	4	3	34	0	128	1	0	12	7	.632	0	0--	-	3.20	3.20
2001 Cincinnati	NL	18	18	0	0	96.0	417	101	61	58	17	6	3	3	34	2	68	4	0	5	7	.417	0	0-0	0	4.84	5.44
2002 Cincinnati	NL	6	5	0	0	23.2	112	28	21	19	8	2	0	2	12	0	14	1	0	4	2	.667	0	0-0	0	7.81	7.23
2 ML YEARS		24	23	0	0	119.2	529	129	82	77	25	8	3	5	46	2	82	5	0	9	9	.500	0	0-0	0	5.39	5.79

Juan Acevedo

Pitches: R **Bats:** R **Pos:** RP-65   **Ht:** 6'2" **Wt:** 228 **Born:** 5/5/70 **Age:** 33

Year Team	Lg	G	GS	CG	GF	IP	BFP	H	R	ER	HR	SH	SF	HB	TBB	IBB	SO	WP	Bk	W	L	Pct	ShO	Sv-Op	Hld	ERC	ERA
1995 Colorado	NL	17	11	0	0	65.2	291	82	53	47	15	4	2	6	20	2	40	2	1	4	6	.400	0	0-0	1	6.65	6.44
1997 New York	NL	25	2	0	1	47.2	215	52	24	19	6	2	5	4	22	2	33	0	1	3	1	.750	0	0-4	3	5.34	3.59
1998 St Louis	NL	50	9	0	29	98.1	394	83	30	28	7	8	1	4	29	2	56	3	0	8	3	.727	0	15-16	3	2.87	2.56
1999 St Louis	NL	50	12	0	21	115.1	467	115	71	67	17	4	6	4	48	3	52	5	0	6	8	.429	0	4-6	4	5.78	5.89
2000 Milwaukee	NL	62	0	0	18	82.2	347	77	38	35	11	1	1	1	31	9	51	3	2	3	7	.300	0	0-2	7	3.74	3.81
2001 Col-Fla	NL	58	0	0	20	60.1	282	68	35	28	6	3	3	2	35	9	47	1	0	2	5	.286	0	0-5	4	5.34	4.18
2002 Detroit	NL	65	0	0	48	74.2	314	68	33	22	4	5	5	5	23	3	43	2	0	1	5	.167	0	28-35	1	3.12	2.65
2001 Colorado	NL	38	0	0	14	32.0	153	37	24	20	4	2	1	1	19	6	26	0	0	0	2	.000	0	0-5	3	5.62	5.63
2001 Florida	NL	20	0	0	6	28.1	129	31	11	8	2	1	2	1	16	3	21	1	0	2	3	.400	0	0-0	1	5.04	2.54
7 ML YEARS		327	34	0	140	531.2	2300	545	284	246	66	27	23	26	208	30	322	16	4	27	35	.435	0	47-68	23	4.51	4.16

Terry Adams

Pitches: R Bats: R Pos: RP-27; SP-19   Ht: 6'3" Wt: 215 Born: 3/6/73 Age: 30

Year Team	Lg	G	GS	CG	GF	IP	BFP	H	R	ER	HR	SH	SF	HB	TBB	IBB	SO	WP	Bk	W	L	Pct	ShO	Sv-Op	Hld	ERC	ERA
1995 Chicago	NL	18	0	0	7	18.0	86	22	15	13	0	0	0	0	10	1	15	1	0	1	1	.500	0	1-1	0	4.95	6.50
1996 Chicago	NL	69	0	0	22	101.0	423	84	36	33	6	7	3	1	49	6	78	5	1	3	6	.333	0	4-8	11	3.20	2.94
1997 Chicago	NL	74	0	0	39	74.0	341	91	43	38	3	1	2	1	40	6	64	6	0	2	9	.182	0	18-22	11	5.49	4.62
1998 Chicago	NL	63	0	0	15	72.2	330	72	39	35	7	3	3	1	41	3	73	4	3	7	7	.500	0	1-7	13	4.55	4.33
1999 Chicago	NL	52	0	0	38	65.0	277	60	33	29	9	1	3	0	28	2	57	6	0	6	3	.667	0	13-18	3	4.00	4.02
2000 Los Angeles	NL	66	0	0	18	84.1	369	80	42	33	6	3	0	0	39	0	56	5	0	6	9	.400	0	2-7	15	3.77	3.52
2001 Los Angeles	NL	43	22	0	10	166.1	708	172	84	80	9	6	0	3	54	1	141	7	2	12	8	.600	0	0-1	4	3.74	4.33
2002 Philadelphia	NL	46	19	0	10	136.2	590	132	76	66	9	10	2	3	58	5	96	8	0	7	9	.438	0	0-1	12	3.77	4.35
8 ML YEARS		431	41	0	159	718.0	3124	713	368	327	49	31	13	9	319	24	580	42	6	44	52	.458	0	39-65	69	3.98	4.10

Jeremy Affeldt

Pitches: L Bats: L Pos: RP-27; SP-7   Ht: 6'4" Wt: 215 Born: 6/6/79 Age: 24

Year Team	Lg	G	GS	CG	GF	IP	BFP	H	R	ER	HR	SH	SF	HB	TBB	IBB	SO	WP	Bk	W	L	Pct	ShO	Sv-Op	Hld	ERC	ERA
1997 Royals	R	10	9	0	0	40.0	171	34	24	20	3	2	3	5	21	0	36	4	2	2	0	1.000	0	0--	-	4.17	4.50
1998 Lansing	A	6	3	0	0	17.0	90	27	21	18	1	0	1	0	12	0	8	2	0	0	3	.000	0	0--	-	8.46	9.53
1998 Royals	R	12	9	0	0	56.0	241	50	24	18	1	3	0	8	24	0	67	7	0	4	3	.571	0	0--	-	3.61	2.89
1999 Chrlstn - WV	A	27	24	2	1	143.1	637	140	78	61	4	9	4	8	80	0	111	14	4	7	7	.500	1	0--	-	4.28	3.83
2000 Wilmington	A+	27	26	0	0	147.1	656	158	87	67	7	8	5	10	59	0	92	17	1	5	15	.250	0	0--	-	4.35	4.09
2001 Wichita	AA	25	25	0	0	145.1	621	153	74	63	9	6	5	10	46	0	128	3	1	10	6	.625	0	0--	-	4.11	3.90
2002 Wichita	AA	3	3	0	0	6.0	21	1	1	1	0	0	0	1	3	0	3	2	0	0	0	-	0	0--	-	0.90	1.50
2002 Kansas City	AL	34	7	0	4	77.2	353	85	41	40	8	2	1	3	37	4	67	5	2	3	4	.429	0	0-1	1	4.97	4.64

Benny Agbayani

Bats: R Throws: R Pos: LF-47; PH-14; RF-3; PR-2; CF-1; DH-1   Ht: 6'0" Wt: 225 Born: 12/28/71 Age: 31

Year Team	Lg	G	AB	H	2B	3B	HR	(Hm	Rd)	TB	R	RBI	RC	TBB	IBB	SO	HBP	SH	SF	SB	CS	SB%	GDP	Avg	OBP	Slg
2002 Co Springs*	AAA	43	147	40	8	1	11	(-	-)	83	28	32	32	28	0	32	2	0	2	1	0	1.00	3	.272	.391	.565
2002 Pawtucket*	AAA	5	17	3	1	0	0	(-	-)	4	1	2	1	3	0	6	0	0	0	0	0	-	1	.176	.300	.235
1998 New York	NL	11	15	2	0	0	0	(0	0)	2	1	0	0	1	0	5	0	0	0	0	2	.00	1	.133	.188	.133
1999 New York	NL	101	276	79	18	3	14	(10	4)	145	42	42	50	32	4	60	3	0	3	6	4	.60	8	.286	.363	.525
2000 New York	NL	119	350	101	20	1	15	(9	6)	168	59	60	66	54	2	68	7	0	3	5	5	.50	6	.289	.391	.480
2001 New York	NL	91	296	82	14	2	6	(4	2)	118	28	27	41	36	0	73	5	1	1	4	5	.44	11	.277	.364	.399
2002 Col-Bos		61	154	35	6	0	4	(1	3)	53	15	27	20	16	1	40	0	0	1	1	0	1.00	5	.227	.298	.344
2002 Colorado	NL	48	117	24	5	0	4	(1	3)	41	10	19	13	10	0	35	0	0	1	1	0	1.00	4	.205	.266	.350
2002 Boston	AL	13	37	11	1	0	0	(0	0)	12	5	8	7	6	1	5	0	0	0	0	0	-	1	.297	.395	.324
5 ML YEARS		383	1091	299	58	6	39	(24	15)	486	145	156	177	139	7	246	15	1	8	16	16	.50	31	.274	.362	.445

Kurt Ainsworth

Pitches: R Bats: R Pos: SP-4; RP-2   Ht: 6'3" Wt: 192 Born: 9/9/78 Age: 24

Year Team	Lg	G	GS	CG	GF	IP	BFP	H	R	ER	HR	SH	SF	HB	TBB	IBB	SO	WP	Bk	W	L	Pct	ShO	Sv-Op	Hld	ERC	ERA
1999 Salem-Keizer	A-	10	10	1	0	44.2	187	34	18	8	1	3	2	3	16	0	64	3	0	3	3	.500	0	0--	-	2.53	1.61
2000 Shreveport	AA	28	28	0	0	158.0	667	138	67	58	12	4	5	3	63	3	130	7	1	10	9	.526	0	0--	-	3.25	3.30
2001 Fresno	AAA	27	26	0	0	149.0	634	139	91	84	22	4	6	7	54	1	157	10	0	10	9	.526	0	0--	-	4.06	5.07
2002 Fresno	AAA	20	19	1	0	116.0	477	101	49	44	7	4	2	3	43	0	119	5	1	8	6	.571	0	0--	-	3.16	3.41
2001 San Francisco	NL	2	0	0	2	2.0	12	3	3	3	1	0	0	1	2	0	3	0	0	0	0	-	0	0-0	0	16.26	13.50
2002 San Francisco	NL	6	4	0	0	25.2	108	22	7	6	1	2	0	1	12	0	15	1	0	1	2	.333	0	0-0	0	3.34	2.10
2 ML YEARS		8	4	0	2	27.2	120	25	10	9	2	2	0	2	14	0	18	1	0	1	2	.333	0	0-0	0	4.08	2.93

Izzy Alcantara

Bats: R Throws: R Pos: PH-9; RF-5; 1B-2; LF-2   Ht: 6'2" Wt: 210 Born: 5/6/73 Age: 30

Year Team	Lg	G	AB	H	2B	3B	HR	(Hm	Rd)	TB	R	RBI	RC	TBB	IBB	SO	HBP	SH	SF	SB	CS	SB%	GDP	Avg	OBP	Slg
2002 Indianapolis*	AAA	110	410	110	21	2	27	(-	-)	216	61	65	72	51	2	88	1	0	1	9	3	.75	13	.268	.350	.527
2000 Boston	AL	21	45	13	1	0	4	(1	3)	26	9	7	9	3	0	7	0	0	0	0	0	-	0	.289	.333	.578
2001 Boston	AL	14	38	10	1	0	0	(0	0)	11	3	3	3	3	0	13	0	0	0	1	0	1.00	3	.263	.317	.289
2002 Milwaukee	NL	16	32	8	1	0	2	(0	2)	15	3	5	2	0	0	6	0	0	0	0	1	.00	0	.250	.250	.469
3 ML YEARS		51	115	31	3	0	6	(1	5)	52	15	15	14	6	0	26	0	0	0	1	1	.50	3	.270	.306	.452

Antonio Alfonseca

Pitches: R Bats: R Pos: RP-66   Ht: 6'5" Wt: 250 Born: 4/16/72 Age: 31

Year Team	Lg	G	GS	CG	GF	IP	BFP	H	R	ER	HR	SH	SF	HB	TBB	IBB	SO	WP	Bk	W	L	Pct	ShO	Sv-Op	Hld	ERC	ERA
1997 Florida	NL	17	0	0	2	25.2	123	36	16	14	3	1	0	1	10	3	19	1	0	1	3	.250	0	0-2	0	6.41	4.91
1998 Florida	NL	58	0	0	27	70.2	316	75	32	32	10	7	6	3	23	9	46	1	0	4	6	.400	0	8-14	9	4.96	4.08
1999 Florida	NL	73	0	0	49	77.2	325	79	28	28	4	3	1	4	29	6	46	1	0	4	5	.444	0	21-25	5	3.96	3.24
2000 Florida	NL	68	0	0	62	70.0	311	82	35	33	7	3	1	1	24	3	47	0	2	5	6	.455	0	45-49	0	4.79	4.24
2001 Florida	NL	58	0	0	52	61.2	268	68	24	21	6	5	1	5	15	3	40	2	0	4	4	.500	0	28-34	0	4.24	3.06
2002 Chicago	NL	66	0	0	55	74.1	330	73	34	33	5	4	3	3	36	3	61	1	0	2	5	.286	0	19-28	0	4.12	4.00
6 ML YEARS		340	0	0	247	380.0	1673	413	169	161	35	23	12	17	147	27	259	6	2	20	29	.408	0	121-152	14	4.53	3.81

Edgardo Alfonzo

Bats: R **Throws:** R **Pos:** 3B-134; PH-5   **Ht:** 5'11" **Wt:** 187 **Born:** 11/8/73 **Age:** 29

Year Team	Lg	G	AB	H	2B	3B	HR	(Hm	Rd)	TB	R	RBI	RC	TBB	IBB	SO	HBP	SH	SF	SB	CS	SB%	GDP	Avg	OBP	Slg
1995 New York	NL	101	335	93	13	5	4	(0	4)	128	26	41	37	12	1	37	1	4	4	1	1	.50	7	.278	.301	.382
1996 New York	NL	123	368	96	15	2	4	(2	2)	127	36	40	38	25	2	56	0	9	5	2	0	1.00	8	.261	.304	.345
1997 New York	NL	151	518	163	27	2	10	(4	6)	224	84	72	91	63	0	56	5	8	5	11	6	.65	4	.315	.391	.432
1998 New York	NL	144	557	155	28	2	17	(8	9)	238	94	78	85	65	1	77	3	2	3	8	3	.73	11	.278	.355	.427
1999 New York	NL	158	628	191	41	1	27	(11	16)	315	123	108	121	85	2	85	3	1	9	9	2	.82	14	.304	.385	.502
2000 New York	NL	150	544	176	40	2	25	(13	12)	295	109	94	122	95	1	70	5	0	6	3	2	.60	12	.324	.425	.542
2001 New York	NL	124	457	111	22	0	17	(6	11)	184	64	49	62	51	0	62	5	1	5	5	0	1.00	1	.243	.322	.403
2002 New York	NL	135	490	151	26	0	16	(8	8)	225	78	56	89	62	8	55	7	0	3	6	0	1.00	5	.308	.391	.459
8 ML YEARS		1086	3897	1136	212	14	120	(52	68)	1736	614	538	645	458	15	498	29	25	40	45	14	.76	68	.292	.367	.445

Luis Alicea

Bats: B **Throws:** R **Pos:** 2B-32; 3B-31; PH-25; DH-15; 1B-2; SS-1; LF-1; RF-1   **Ht:** 5'9" **Wt:** 175 **Born:** 7/29/65 **Age:** 37

Year Team	Lg	G	AB	H	2B	3B	HR	(Hm	Rd)	TB	R	RBI	RC	TBB	IBB	SO	HBP	SH	SF	SB	CS	SB%	GDP	Avg	OBP	Slg
1988 St Louis	NL	93	297	63	10	4	1	(1	0)	84	20	24	20	25	4	32	2	4	2	1	1	.50	12	.212	.276	.283
1991 St Louis	NL	56	68	13	3	0	0	(0	0)	16	5	0	4	8	0	19	0	0	0	0	1	.00	0	.191	.276	.235
1992 St Louis	NL	85	265	65	9	11	2	(2	0)	102	26	32	32	27	1	40	4	2	4	2	5	.29	5	.245	.320	.385
1993 St Louis	NL	115	362	101	19	3	3	(2	1)	135	50	46	53	47	2	54	4	1	7	11	1	.92	9	.279	.362	.373
1994 St Louis	NL	88	205	57	12	5	5	(3	2)	94	32	29	36	30	4	38	3	1	3	4	5	.44	1	.278	.373	.459
1995 Boston	AL	132	419	113	20	3	6	(0	6)	157	64	44	61	63	0	61	7	13	6	13	10	.57	10	.270	.367	.375
1996 St Louis	NL	129	380	98	26	3	5	(4	1)	145	54	42	55	52	10	78	5	4	6	11	3	.79	4	.258	.350	.382
1997 Anaheim	AL	128	388	98	16	7	5	(2	3)	143	59	37	61	69	3	65	8	4	2	22	8	.73	4	.253	.375	.369
1998 Texas	AL	101	259	71	15	3	6	(1	5)	110	51	33	44	37	0	40	5	4	3	4	3	.57	1	.274	.372	.425
1999 Texas	AL	68	164	33	10	0	3	(0	3)	52	33	17	17	28	0	32	0	3	1	2	1	.67	4	.201	.316	.317
2000 Texas	AL	139	540	159	25	8	6	(4	2)	218	85	63	80	59	1	75	5	7	7	1	3	.25	13	.294	.365	.404
2001 Kansas City	AL	113	387	106	16	4	4	(1	3)	142	44	32	44	23	0	56	4	3	1	8	6	.57	6	.274	.320	.367
2002 Kansas City	AL	94	237	54	8	2	1	(0	1)	69	28	23	25	32	1	34	1	3	0	2	3	.40	5	.228	.322	.291
13 ML YEARS		1341	3971	1031	189	53	47	(20	27)	1467	551	422	532	500	26	624	48	49	45	81	50	.62	74	.260	.346	.369

Chad Allen

Bats: R **Throws:** R **Pos:** LF-3; RF-1; PH-1; PR-1   **Ht:** 6'1" **Wt:** 195 **Born:** 2/6/75 **Age:** 28

Year Team	Lg	G	AB	H	2B	3B	HR	(Hm	Rd)	TB	R	RBI	RC	TBB	IBB	SO	HBP	SH	SF	SB	CS	SB%	GDP	Avg	OBP	Slg
2002 Rochester*	AAA	8	32	7	2	1	0	(-	-)	11	1	1	2	0	0	6	0	0	0	0	0	-	2	.219	.219	.344
2002 Buffalo*	AAA	70	279	84	20	1	10	(-	-)	136	45	62	42	15	0	34	2	0	1	0	1	.00	10	.301	.340	.487
1999 Minnesota	AL	137	481	133	21	3	10	(4	6)	190	69	46	61	37	1	89	2	1	2	14	7	.67	10	.277	.330	.395
2000 Minnesota	AL	15	50	15	3	0	0	(0	0)	18	2	7	6	3	0	14	1	0	1	0	2	.00	1	.300	.345	.360
2001 Minnesota	AL	57	175	46	13	2	4	(1	3)	75	20	20	23	19	1	37	0	0	1	1	2	.33	7	.263	.333	.429
2002 Cleveland	AL	5	10	1	1	0	0	(0	0)	2	0	0	0	0	0	2	0	1	0	0	0	-	1	.100	.100	.200
4 ML YEARS		214	716	195	38	5	14	(5	9)	285	91	73	90	59	2	142	3	2	4	15	11	.58	19	.272	.329	.398

Luke Allen

Bats: L **Throws:** R **Pos:** PH-4; RF-3   **Ht:** 6'2" **Wt:** 208 **Born:** 8/4/78 **Age:** 24

Year Team	Lg	G	AB	H	2B	3B	HR	(Hm	Rd)	TB	R	RBI	RC	TBB	IBB	SO	HBP	SH	SF	SB	CS	SB%	GDP	Avg	OBP	Slg
1997 Great Falls	R+	67	258	89	12	6	7	(-	-)	134	50	40	48	19	1	53	0	1	0	12	11	.52	3	.345	.390	.519
1998 Sn Brnardino	A+	105	399	119	25	6	4	(-	-)	168	51	46	58	30	0	93	3	7	4	18	11	.62	4	.298	.349	.421
1998 San Antonio	AA	23	78	26	3	1	3	(-	-)	40	9	10	14	6	1	16	0	1	0	1	2	.33	0	.333	.381	.513
1999 San Antonio	AA	137	533	150	16	12	14	(-	-)	232	90	82	77	44	0	102	1	2	2	14	8	.64	8	.281	.336	.435
2000 San Antonio	AA	90	339	90	15	5	7	(-	-)	136	55	60	46	40	3	71	1	0	5	14	5	.74	10	.265	.340	.401
2001 Jacksonville	AA	125	486	141	32	6	16	(-	-)	233	74	73	80	42	3	111	1	1	5	13	3	.81	5	.290	.345	.479
2001 Las Vegas	AAA	2	9	2	1	0	0	(-	-)	3	1	0	0	0	0	0	0	0	0	0	0	-	1	.222	.222	.333
2002 Las Vegas	AAA	137	501	165	28	3	12	(-	-)	235	85	78	89	56	3	77	2	0	5	4	6	.40	12	.329	.395	.469
2002 Los Angeles	NL	6	7	1	1	0	0	(0	0)	2	2	0	1	2	0	3	0	0	0	0	0	-	0	.143	.333	.286

Armando Almanza

Pitches: L **Bats:** L **Pos:** RP-51   **Ht:** 6'3" **Wt:** 240 **Born:** 10/26/72 **Age:** 30

Year Team	Lg	G	GS	CG	GF	IP	BFP	H	R	ER	HR	SH	SF	HB	TBB	IBB	SO	WP	Bk	W	L	Pct	ShO	Sv-Op	Hld	ERC	ERA
2002 Jupiter*	A+	6	5	0	0	6.2	23	1	0	0	0	0	0	0	3	0	6	0	0	0	0	-	0	0--	-	0.49	0.00
1999 Florida	NL	14	0	0	2	15.2	64	8	4	3	1	1	1	1	9	1	20	0	1	0	1	.000	0	0-0	3	2.09	1.72
2000 Florida	NL	67	0	0	8	46.1	216	38	27	25	3	2	2	2	43	6	46	1	0	4	2	.667	0	0-4	13	4.79	4.86
2001 Florida	NL	52	0	0	8	41.0	178	34	24	22	8	1	3	0	26	1	45	2	0	2	2	.500	0	0-2	12	4.73	4.83
2002 Florida	NL	51	0	0	10	45.2	191	36	22	22	8	3	3	0	23	1	57	2	1	3	2	.600	0	2-4	12	3.83	4.34
4 ML YEARS		184	0	0	28	148.2	649	116	77	72	20	7	9	3	101	9	168	5	2	9	7	.563	0	2-10	40	4.19	4.36

Carlos Almanzar

Pitches: R **Bats:** R **Pos:** RP-7; SP-1   **Ht:** 6'2" **Wt:** 200 **Born:** 11/6/73 **Age:** 29

Year Team	Lg	G	GS	CG	GF	IP	BFP	H	R	ER	HR	SH	SF	HB	TBB	IBB	SO	WP	Bk	W	L	Pct	ShO	Sv-Op	Hld	ERC	ERA
2002 Louisville*	AAA	21	0	0	18	23.0	91	21	7	7	0	0	0	1	5	0	19	0	0	1	0	1.000	0	11--	-	2.55	2.74
1997 Toronto	AL	4	0	0	2	3.1	12	1	1	1	1	0	0	0	1	0	4	0	0	0	1	.000	0	0-0	0	1.39	2.70
1998 Toronto	AL	25	0	0	8	28.2	129	34	18	17	4	1	0	1	8	2	20	0	0	2	2	.500	0	0-3	1	4.85	5.34
1999 San Diego	NL	28	0	0	11	37.1	173	48	32	31	6	2	1	3	15	2	30	2	0	0	0	-	0	0-0	0	6.54	7.47
2000 San Diego	NL	62	0	0	11	69.2	308	73	35	34	12	2	3	4	25	2	56	2	0	4	5	.444	0	0-3	8	4.83	4.39

Year Team	Lg	G	GS	CG	GF	IP	BFP	H	R	ER	HR	SH	SF	HB	TBB	IBB	SO	WP	Bk	W	L	Pct	ShO	Sv-Op	Hld	ERC	ERA
2001 New York	AL	10	0	0	7	10.2	46	14	4	4	2	1	1	0	2	1	6	0	0	0	1	.000	0	0-2	0	5.63	3.38
2002 Cincinnati	NL	8	1	0	4	11.2	45	6	4	3	0	0	2	0	5	1	7	1	0	0	1	.000	0	0-0	0	1.26	2.31
6 ML YEARS		137	1	0	43	161.1	713	176	94	90	25	6	7	8	56	6	123	5	0	6	10	.375	0	0-8	9	4.87	5.02

Erick Almonte

Bats: R **Throws:** R **Pos:** SS   **Ht:** 6'2" **Wt:** 180 **Born:** 2/1/78 **Age:** 25

Year Team	Lg	G	AB	H	2B	3B	HR	(Hm	Rd)	TB	R	RBI	RC	TBB	IBB	SO	HBP	SH	SF	SB	CS	SB%	GDP	Avg	OBP	Slg
1997 Yankees	R	52	180	51	4	4	3	(-	-)	72	32	31	26	21	1	27	0	1	2	8	2	.80	5	.283	.355	.400
1998 Greensboro	A	120	450	94	13	0	6	(-	-)	125	53	33	26	29	0	121	3	7	2	6	2	.75	17	.209	.260	.278
1999 Tampa	A+	61	230	59	8	2	5	(-	-)	86	36	25	26	18	0	49	2	5	2	3	1	.75	6	.257	.313	.374
1999 Yankees	R	9	30	9	2	0	2	(-	-)	17	5	9	6	3	0	10	0	0	2	1	0	1.00	1	.300	.343	.567
2000 Norwich	AA	131	454	123	18	4	15	(-	-)	194	56	77	66	35	0	129	3	12	2	12	2	.86	9	.271	.326	.427
2001 Columbus	AAA	97	345	99	19	3	12	(-	-)	160	55	55	57	44	1	90	2	7	2	4	5	.44	7	.287	.369	.464
2001 Norwich	AA	3	12	3	0	0	0	(-	-)	3	2	0	1	1	0	6	0	0	0	1	0	1.00	0	.250	.308	.250
2002 Columbus	AAA	66	221	52	10	1	9	(-	-)	91	25	28	26	15	0	60	0	2	2	2	1	.67	2	.235	.282	.412
2002 Norwich	AA	53	187	45	7	0	8	(-	-)	76	28	33	27	30	2	59	0	3	2	10	2	.83	6	.241	.342	.406
2001 New York	AL	8	4	2	1	0	0	(0	0)	3	0	0	2	0	0	1	0	0	0	2	0	1.00	0	.500	.500	.750

Roberto Alomar

Bats: B **Throws:** R **Pos:** 2B-147; PH-3   **Ht:** 6'0" **Wt:** 185 **Born:** 2/5/68 **Age:** 35

Year Team	Lg	G	AB	H	2B	3B	HR	(Hm	Rd)	TB	R	RBI	RC	TBB	IBB	SO	HBP	SH	SF	SB	CS	SB%	GDP	Avg	OBP	Slg
1988 San Diego	NL	143	545	145	24	6	9	(5	4)	208	84	41	68	47	5	83	3	16	0	24	6	.80	15	.266	.328	.382
1989 San Diego	NL	158	623	184	27	1	7	(3	4)	234	82	56	85	53	4	76	1	17	8	42	17	.71	10	.295	.347	.376
1990 San Diego	NL	147	586	168	27	5	6	(4	2)	223	80	60	76	48	1	72	2	5	5	24	7	.77	16	.287	.340	.381
1991 Toronto	AL	161	637	188	41	11	9	(6	3)	278	88	69	106	57	3	86	4	16	5	53	11	.83	5	.295	.354	.436
1992 Toronto	AL	152	571	177	27	8	8	(5	3)	244	105	76	109	87	5	52	5	6	2	49	9	.84	8	.310	.405	.427
1993 Toronto	AL	153	589	192	35	6	17	(8	9)	290	109	93	121	80	5	67	5	4	5	55	15	.79	13	.326	.408	.492
1994 Toronto	AL	107	392	120	25	4	8	(4	4)	177	78	38	67	51	2	41	2	7	3	19	8	.70	14	.306	.386	.452
1995 Toronto	AL	130	517	155	24	7	13	(7	6)	232	71	66	84	47	3	45	0	6	7	30	3	.91	16	.300	.354	.449
1996 Baltimore	AL	153	588	193	43	4	22	(14	8)	310	132	94	126	90	10	65	1	8	12	17	6	.74	14	.328	.411	.527
1997 Baltimore	AL	112	412	137	23	2	14	(10	4)	206	64	60	78	40	2	43	3	7	7	9	3	.75	10	.333	.390	.500
1998 Baltimore	AL	147	588	166	36	1	14	(7	7)	246	86	56	87	59	3	70	2	3	5	18	5	.78	11	.282	.347	.418
1999 Cleveland	AL	159	563	182	40	3	24	(12	12)	300	138	120	131	99	3	96	7	12	13	37	6	.86	13	.323	.422	.533
2000 Cleveland	AL	155	610	189	40	2	19	(8	11)	290	111	89	111	64	4	82	6	11	6	39	4	.91	19	.310	.378	.475
2001 Cleveland	AL	157	575	193	34	12	20	(7	13)	311	113	100	130	80	5	71	4	9	9	30	6	.83	9	.336	.415	.541
2002 New York	NL	149	590	157	24	4	11	(4	7)	222	73	53	74	57	4	83	1	6	1	16	4	.80	12	.266	.331	.376
15 ML YEARS		2183	8386	2546	470	76	201	(104	97)	3771	1414	1071	1453	959	59	1032	46	133	88	462	110	.81	185	.304	.375	.450

Sandy Alomar Jr.

Bats: R **Throws:** R **Pos:** C-88; PH-3   **Ht:** 6'5" **Wt:** 235 **Born:** 6/18/66 **Age:** 37

Year Team	Lg	G	AB	H	2B	3B	HR	(Hm	Rd)	TB	R	RBI	RC	TBB	IBB	SO	HBP	SH	SF	SB	CS	SB%	GDP	Avg	OBP	Slg
2002 Charlotte*	AAA	3	8	1	0	0	0	(-	-)	1	0	0	0	0	0	0	0	0	0	0	0	-	1	.125	.125	.125
1988 San Diego	NL	1	1	0	0	0	0	(0	0)	0	0	0	0	0	0	1	0	0	0	0	0	-	0	.000	.000	.000
1989 San Diego	NL	7	19	4	1	0	1	(1	0)	8	1	6	2	3	1	3	0	0	0	0	0	-	1	.211	.318	.421
1990 Cleveland	AL	132	445	129	26	2	9	(5	4)	186	60	66	60	25	2	46	2	5	6	4	1	.80	10	.290	.326	.418
1991 Cleveland	AL	51	184	40	9	0	0	(0	0)	49	10	7	10	8	1	24	4	2	1	0	4	.00	8	.217	.264	.266
1992 Cleveland	AL	89	299	75	16	0	2	(1	1)	97	22	26	26	13	3	32	5	3	0	3	3	.50	7	.251	.293	.324
1993 Cleveland	AL	64	215	58	7	1	6	(3	3)	85	24	32	32	11	0	28	6	1	4	3	1	.75	3	.270	.318	.395
1994 Cleveland	AL	80	292	84	15	1	14	(4	10)	143	44	43	48	25	2	31	2	0	1	8	4	.67	7	.288	.347	.490
1995 Cleveland	AL	66	203	61	6	0	10	(4	6)	97	32	35	30	7	0	26	3	4	1	3	1	.75	8	.300	.332	.478
1996 Cleveland	AL	127	418	110	23	0	11	(3	8)	166	53	50	44	19	0	42	3	2	2	1	0	1.00	20	.263	.299	.397
1997 Cleveland	AL	125	451	146	37	0	21	(9	12)	246	63	83	78	19	2	48	3	6	1	0	2	.00	16	.324	.354	.545
1998 Cleveland	AL	117	409	96	26	2	6	(3	3)	144	45	44	43	18	0	45	3	5	3	0	3	.00	15	.235	.270	.352
1999 Cleveland	AL	37	137	42	13	0	6	(4	2)	73	19	25	23	4	0	23	0	1	2	0	1	.00	4	.307	.322	.533
2000 Cleveland	AL	97	356	103	16	2	7	(5	2)	144	44	42	45	16	1	41	4	4	4	2	2	.50	9	.289	.324	.404
2001 Chicago	AL	70	220	54	8	1	4	(1	3)	76	17	21	20	12	1	17	2	3	2	1	2	.33	6	.245	.288	.345
2002 CWS-Col		89	283	79	14	1	7	(5	2)	116	29	37	29	9	0	33	1	1	2	0	0	-	11	.279	.302	.410
2002 Chicago	AL	51	167	48	10	1	7	(5	2)	81	21	25	22	5	0	14	1	1	2	0	0	-	5	.287	.309	.485
2002 Colorado	NL	38	116	31	4	0	0	(0	0)	35	8	12	7	4	0	19	0	0	0	0	0	-	6	.267	.292	.302
15 ML YEARS		1152	3932	1081	217	10	104	(48	56)	1630	463	517	476	189	13	440	38	37	29	25	24	.51	118	.275	.312	.415

Moises Alou

Bats: R **Throws:** R **Pos:** LF-122; PH-6; RF-4; DH-2; CF-1   **Ht:** 6'3" **Wt:** 220 **Born:** 7/3/66 **Age:** 36

Year Team	Lg	G	AB	H	2B	3B	HR	(Hm	Rd)	TB	R	RBI	RC	TBB	IBB	SO	HBP	SH	SF	SB	CS	SB%	GDP	Avg	OBP	Slg
2002 Daytona*	A+	2	8	5	1	0	0	(-	-)	6	0	2	3	1	0	1	0	0	0	0	0	-	0	.625	.667	.750
1990 Pit-Mon	NL	16	20	4	0	1	0	(0	0)	6	4	0	1	0	0	3	0	1	0	0	0	-	1	.200	.200	.300
1992 Montreal	NL	115	341	96	28	2	9	(6	3)	155	53	56	53	25	0	46	1	5	5	16	2	.89	5	.282	.328	.455
1993 Montreal	NL	136	482	138	29	6	18	(10	8)	233	70	85	79	38	9	53	5	3	7	17	6	.74	9	.286	.340	.483
1994 Montreal	NL	107	422	143	31	5	22	(9	13)	250	81	78	92	42	10	63	2	0	5	7	6	.54	7	.339	.397	.592
1995 Montreal	NL	93	344	94	22	0	14	(4	10)	158	48	58	52	29	6	56	9	0	4	4	3	.57	9	.273	.342	.459
1996 Montreal	NL	143	540	152	28	2	21	(14	7)	247	87	96	81	49	7	83	2	0	7	9	4	.69	15	.281	.339	.457
1997 Florida	NL	150	538	157	29	5	23	(12	11)	265	88	115	97	70	9	85	4	0	7	9	3	.75	11	.292	.373	.493
1998 Houston	NL	159	584	182	34	5	38	(19	19)	340	104	124	130	84	11	87	5	0	6	11	3	.79	14	.312	.399	.582
2000 Houston	NL	126	454	161	28	2	30	(9	21)	283	82	114	104	52	4	45	2	0	9	3	3	.50	21	.355	.416	.623
2001 Houston	NL	136	513	170	31	1	27	(15	12)	284	79	108	104	57	14	57	3	0	8	5	1	.83	18	.331	.396	.554
2002 Chicago	NL	132	484	133	23	1	15	(7	8)	203	50	61	58	47	4	61	0	0	3	8	0	1.00	15	.275	.337	.419

Year Team	Lg	G	AB	H	2B	3B	HR	(Hm Rd)	TB	R	RBI	RC	TBB	IBB	SO	HBP	SH	SF	SB	CS	SB%	GDP	Avg	OBP	Slg
1990 Pittsburgh	NL	2	5	1	0	0	0	(0 0)	1	0	0	0	0	0	0	0	0	0	0	0		1	.200	.200	.200
1990 Montreal	NL	14	15	3	0	1	0	(0 0)	5	4	0	1	0	0	3	0	1	0	0	0		0	.200	.200	.333
11 ML YEARS		1313	4722	1430	283	30	217	(113 104)	2424	746	895	851	493	74	639	33	9	61	89	33	.73	127	.303	.368	.513

Juan Alvarez

Pitches: L **Bats:** L **Pos:** RP-52　　　　　　　　　　　**Ht:** 6'0" **Wt:** 175 **Born:** 8/9/73 **Age:** 29

		HOW MUCH HE PITCHED						WHAT HE GAVE UP										THE RESULTS						
Year Team	Lg	G	GS	CG	GF	IP	BFP	H	R	ER	HR	SH	SF	HB	TBB	IBB	SO	WP	Bk	W	L	Pct	ShO	Sv-Op	Hld	ERC	ERA
2002 Tulsa*	AA	2	0	0	0	1.2	7	1	0	0	0	0	0	0	0	0	0	0	0	0	0	-	0	0--	-	0.65	0.00
2002 Oklahoma*	AAA	15	0	0	3	17.1	78	19	7	7	1	2	1	1	9	1	13	2	0	0	0	-	0	1--	-	4.98	3.63
1999 Anaheim	AL	8	0	0	1	3.0	14	1	1	1	0	1	0	0	4	0	4	1	0	0	1	.000	0	0-0	1	3.04	3.00
2000 Anaheim	AL	11	0	0	3	6.0	38	14	9	9	3	0	0	1	7	1	2	1	0	0	0	-	0	0-0	0	21.26	13.50
2002 Texas	AL	52	0	0	12	39.2	173	35	22	21	7	2	2	3	21	0	30	0	1	0	4	.000	0	0-4	10	4.83	4.76
3 ML YEARS		71	0	0	16	48.2	225	50	32	31	10	3	3	3	32	1	36	2	1	0	5	.000	0	0-4	11	6.38	5.73

Tony Alvarez

Bats: R **Throws:** R **Pos:** CF-6; PH-4; LF-2; PR-2; RF-1　　　　　**Ht:** 6'1" **Wt:** 200 **Born:** 5/10/79 **Age:** 24

		BATTING																	BASERUNNING				AVERAGES		
Year Team	Lg	G	AB	H	2B	3B	HR	(Hm Rd)	TB	R	RBI	RC	TBB	IBB	SO	HBP	SH	SF	SB	CS	SB%	GDP	Avg	OBP	Slg
1998 Pirates	R	50	190	47	13	1	4	(- -)	74	27	29	25	13	1	24	3	1	5	19	1	.95	4	.247	.299	.389
1999 Williamsport	A-	58	196	63	14	1	7	(- -)	100	44	45	47	21	1	36	16	1	6	38	9	.81	2	.321	.418	.510
2000 Hickory	A	118	442	126	25	4	15	(- -)	204	75	77	75	39	2	93	15	0	8	52	21	.71	8	.285	.357	.462
2001 Lynchburg	A+	25	93	32	4	0	2	(- -)	42	10	11	16	7	0	11	0	0	0	7	3	.70	2	.344	.390	.452
2001 Altoona	AA	67	254	81	16	1	6	(- -)	117	34	25	39	9	0	30	7	2	0	17	11	.61	6	.319	.359	.461
2002 Altoona	AA	125	507	161	37	1	15	(- -)	245	79	59	85	27	1	71	9	2	3	29	18	.62	6	.318	.361	.483
2002 Pittsburgh	NL	14	26	8	2	0	1	(0 1)	13	6	2	4	3	0	5	0	1	0	1	0	1.00	0	.308	.379	.500

Victor Alvarez

Pitches: L **Bats:** L **Pos:** RP-3; SP-1　　　　　　　　　**Ht:** 5'10" **Wt:** 150 **Born:** 11/8/76 **Age:** 26

		HOW MUCH HE PITCHED						WHAT HE GAVE UP										THE RESULTS						
Year Team	Lg	G	GS	CG	GF	IP	BFP	H	R	ER	HR	SH	SF	HB	TBB	IBB	SO	WP	Bk	W	L	Pct	ShO	Sv-Op	Hld	ERC	ERA
1997 Great Falls	R+	12	8	0	3	48.1	212	49	30	18	0	0	4	3	17	0	50	2	3	4	1	.800	0	0--	-	3.44	3.35
1999 Vero Beach	A+	12	12	1	0	73.0	280	56	21	16	4	1	1	2	16	0	57	1	1	4	4	.500	0	0--	-	2.12	1.97
1999 San Antonio	AA	9	9	0	0	56.1	234	58	27	23	5	3	1	2	10	0	43	1	0	4	3	.571	0	0--	-	3.44	3.67
2000 Vero Beach	A+	4	4	0	0	22.2	94	17	14	13	6	0	0	0	11	0	20	1	0	1	1	.500	0	0--	-	4.15	5.16
2000 San Antonio	AA	11	8	0	0	48.1	218	44	27	21	3	5	3	7	30	1	43	0	0	0	3	.000	0	0--	-	4.74	3.91
2001 Jacksonville	AA	8	8	0	0	45.0	163	27	6	6	1	1	0	1	7	0	40	2	0	2	0	1.000	0	0--	-	1.19	1.20
2001 Las Vegas	AAA	20	20	0	0	118.0	502	115	63	56	12	4	2	6	41	0	94	4	5	7	4	.636	0	0--	-	3.97	4.27
2002 Las Vegas	AAA	34	15	0	8	122.2	526	132	69	64	11	5	4	3	39	1	106	4	1	10	7	.588	0	3--	-	4.23	4.70
2002 Los Angeles	NL	4	1	0	1	10.1	40	9	5	5	1	0	0	0	2	0	7	0	0	0	1	.000	0	0-0	0	2.70	4.35

Wilson Alvarez

Pitches: L **Bats:** L **Pos:** RP-13; SP-10　　　　　　　　**Ht:** 6'1" **Wt:** 245 **Born:** 3/24/70 **Age:** 33

		HOW MUCH HE PITCHED						WHAT HE GAVE UP										THE RESULTS						
Year Team	Lg	G	GS	CG	GF	IP	BFP	H	R	ER	HR	SH	SF	HB	TBB	IBB	SO	WP	Bk	W	L	Pct	ShO	Sv-Op	Hld	ERC	ERA
2002 Orlando*	AA	2	2	0	0	8.0	29	6	1	1	0	0	0	0	2	0	7	0	0	1	0	1.000	0	0--	-	1.87	1.13
1989 Texas	AL	1	1	0	0	0.0	5	3	3	3	2	0	0	0	2	0	0	0	0	0	1	.000	0	0-0	0	-	-
1991 Chicago	AL	10	9	2	0	56.1	237	47	26	22	9	3	1	0	29	0	32	2	0	3	2	.600	1	0-0	0	4.09	3.51
1992 Chicago	AL	34	9	0	4	100.1	455	103	64	58	12	3	4	4	65	2	66	2	0	5	3	.625	0	1-1	3	5.61	5.20
1993 Chicago	AL	31	31	1	0	207.2	877	168	78	68	14	13	6	7	122	8	155	2	1	15	8	.652	1	0-0	0	3.69	2.95
1994 Chicago	AL	24	24	2	0	161.2	682	147	72	62	16	6	3	0	62	1	108	3	0	12	8	.600	1	0-0	0	3.49	3.45
1995 Chicago	AL	29	29	3	0	175.0	769	171	96	84	21	6	5	4	93	4	118	1	2	8	11	.421	0	0-0	0	4.66	4.32
1996 Chicago	AL	35	35	0	0	217.1	946	216	106	102	21	5	2	4	97	3	181	2	0	15	10	.600	0	0-0	0	4.26	4.22
1997 CWS-SF		33	33	2	0	212.0	896	180	97	82	18	10	6	4	91	4	179	5	1	13	11	.542	1	0-0	0	3.30	3.48
1998 Tampa Bay	AL	25	25	0	0	142.2	624	130	78	75	18	1	2	9	68	0	107	4	0	6	14	.300	0	0-0	0	4.30	4.73
1999 Tampa Bay	AL	28	28	1	0	160.0	703	159	92	75	22	3	3	6	79	1	128	3	0	9	9	.500	0	0-0	0	4.87	4.22
2002 Tampa Bay	AL	23	10	0	3	75.0	338	80	47	44	13	2	3	4	36	3	56	2	0	2	3	.400	0	1-1	2	5.48	5.28
1997 Chicago	AL	22	22	2	0	145.2	613	126	61	49	9	6	5	3	55	1	110	4	0	9	8	.529	1	0-0	0	3.05	3.03
1997 San Francisco	NL	11	11	0	0	66.1	283	54	36	33	9	4	1	1	36	3	69	1	1	4	3	.571	0	0-0	0	3.86	4.48
11 ML YEARS		273	234	11	7	1508.0	6532	1404	759	675	166	52	35	40	744	26	1130	26	4	88	80	.524	4	2-2	5	4.23	4.03

Alfredo Amezaga

Bats: B **Throws:** R **Pos:** PR-7; SS-5; DH-1　　　　　　　**Ht:** 5'10" **Wt:** 165 **Born:** 1/16/78 **Age:** 25

		BATTING																	BASERUNNING				AVERAGES		
Year Team	Lg	G	AB	H	2B	3B	HR	(Hm Rd)	TB	R	RBI	RC	TBB	IBB	SO	HBP	SH	SF	SB	CS	SB%	GDP	Avg	OBP	Slg
1999 Butte	R+	8	34	10	2	0	0	(- -)	12	11	5	6	5	0	5	1	0	0	6	2	.75	0	.294	.400	.353
1999 Boise	A-	48	205	66	6	4	2	(- -)	86	52	29	36	23	2	29	5	3	1	14	3	.82	7	.322	.402	.420
2000 Lk Elsinore	A+	108	420	117	13	4	4	(- -)	150	90	44	68	63	0	70	4	5	5	73	21	.78	4	.279	.374	.357
2001 Arkansas	AA	70	285	89	10	5	4	(- -)	121	50	21	45	22	1	55	4	3	0	24	15	.62	0	.312	.370	.425
2001 Salt Lake	AAA	49	200	50	5	4	1	(- -)	66	28	16	20	14	1	45	3	2	1	9	6	.60	2	.250	.307	.330
2002 Salt Lake	AAA	128	518	130	25	7	6	(- -)	187	77	51	57	45	0	100	8	6	6	23	14	.62	15	.251	.317	.361
2002 Anaheim	AL	12	13	7	2	0	0	(0 0)	9	3	2	6	0	0	1	0	0	0	1	0	1.00	1	.538	.538	.692

Brady Anderson

Bats: L **Throws: L** **Pos:** CF-16; LF-15; PH-8; RF-1; DH-1   **Ht:** 6'1" **Wt:** 202 **Born:** 1/18/64 **Age:** 39

								BATTING												BASERUNNING				AVERAGES		
Year Team	Lg	G	AB	H	2B	3B	HR	(Hm	Rd)	TB	R	RBI	RC	TBB	IBB	SO	HBP	SH	SF	SB	CS	SB%	GDP	Avg	OBP	Slg
1988 Bos-Bal	AL	94	325	69	13	4	1	(1	0)	93	31	21	25	23	0	75	4	11	1	10	6	.63	3	.212	.272	.286
1989 Baltimore	AL	94	266	55	12	2	4	(2	2)	83	44	16	30	43	6	45	3	5	0	16	4	.80	4	.207	.324	.312
1990 Baltimore	AL	89	234	54	5	2	3	(1	2)	72	24	24	28	31	2	46	5	4	5	15	2	.88	4	.231	.327	.308
1991 Baltimore	AL	113	256	59	12	3	2	(1	1)	83	40	27	33	38	0	44	5	11	3	12	5	.71	1	.230	.338	.324
1992 Baltimore	AL	159	623	169	28	10	21	(15	6)	280	100	80	115	98	4	98	9	10	9	53	16	.77	2	.271	.373	.449
1993 Baltimore	AL	142	560	147	36	8	13	(2	11)	238	87	66	92	82	4	99	10	6	6	24	12	.67	4	.263	.363	.425
1994 Baltimore	AL	111	453	119	25	5	12	(7	5)	190	78	48	75	57	3	75	10	3	2	31	1	.97	7	.263	.356	.419
1995 Baltimore	AL	143	554	145	33	10	16	(10	6)	246	108	64	99	87	4	111	10	4	2	26	7	.79	3	.262	.371	.444
1996 Baltimore	AL	149	579	172	37	5	50	(19	31)	369	117	110	140	76	1	106	22	6	4	21	8	.72	11	.297	.396	.637
1997 Baltimore	AL	151	590	170	39	7	18	(8	10)	277	97	73	113	84	6	105	19	2	1	18	12	.60	1	.288	.393	.469
1998 Baltimore	AL	133	479	113	28	3	18	(7	11)	201	84	51	77	75	1	78	15	4	1	21	7	.75	7	.236	.356	.420
1999 Baltimore	AL	150	564	159	28	5	24	(10	14)	269	109	81	118	96	7	105	24	1	7	36	7	.84	6	.282	.404	.477
2000 Baltimore	AL	141	506	130	26	0	19	(9	10)	213	89	50	87	92	5	103	8	5	7	16	9	.64	4	.257	.375	.421
2001 Baltimore	AL	131	430	87	12	3	8	(4	4)	129	50	45	44	60	4	77	8	2	1	12	4	.75	3	.202	.311	.300
2002 Cleveland	AL	34	80	13	4	0	1	(0	1)	20	4	5	7	18	2	23	2	0	1	4	0	1.00	5	.163	.327	.250
1988 Boston	AL	41	148	34	5	3	0	(0	0)	45	14	12	15	15	0	35	4	4	1	4	2	.67	2	.230	.315	.304
1988 Baltimore	AL	53	177	35	8	1	1	(1	0)	48	17	9	10	8	0	40	0	7	0	6	4	.60	1	.198	.232	.271
15 ML YEARS		1834	6499	1661	338	67	210	(96	114)	2763	1062	761	1083	960	59	1190	154	74	50	315	100	.76	65	.256	.362	.425

Brian Anderson

Pitches: L **Bats: R** **Pos:** SP-24; RP-11   **Ht:** 6'1" **Wt:** 183 **Born:** 4/26/72 **Age:** 31

		HOW MUCH HE PITCHED						WHAT HE GAVE UP												THE RESULTS						
Year Team	Lg	G	GS	CG	GF	IP	BFP	H	R	ER	HR	SH	SF	HB	TBB	IBB	SO	WP	Bk	W	L	Pct	ShO	Sv-Op	Hld	ERC	ERA
1993 Anaheim	AL	4	1	0	3	11.1	45	11	5	5	1	0	0	2	0	4	0	0	0	0	0	-	0	0-0	0	3.08	3.97
1994 Anaheim	AL	18	18	0	0	101.2	441	120	63	59	13	3	6	5	27	0	47	5	5	7	5	.583	0	0-0	0	5.05	5.22
1995 Anaheim	AL	18	17	1	0	99.2	433	110	66	65	24	5	5	3	30	2	45	1	3	6	8	.429	0	0-0	0	5.37	5.87
1996 Cleveland	AL	10	9	0	0	51.1	215	58	29	28	9	2	3	0	14	1	21	2	0	3	1	.750	0	0-0	1	4.96	4.91
1997 Cleveland	AL	8	8	0	0	48.0	199	55	28	25	7	0	5	0	11	0	22	1	0	4	2	.667	0	0-0	0	4.71	4.69
1998 Arizona	NL	32	32	2	0	208.0	845	221	100	100	39	8	3	4	24	2	95	3	6	12	13	.480	1	0-0	0	3.99	4.33
1999 Arizona	NL	31	19	2	4	130.0	549	144	69	66	18	4	0	1	28	3	75	0	2	8	2	.800	1	1-2	1	4.23	4.57
2000 Arizona	NL	33	32	2	0	213.1	876	226	101	96	38	6	6	1	39	7	104	1	4	11	7	.611	0	0-0	0	4.15	4.05
2001 Arizona	NL	29	22	1	1	133.1	571	156	93	77	25	7	4	1	30	2	55	2	1	4	9	.308	0	0-1	0	5.00	5.20
2002 Arizona	NL	35	24	0	1	156.0	659	174	86	83	23	6	8	1	32	3	81	2	5	6	11	.353	0	0-0	1	4.28	4.79
10 ML YEARS		218	182	8	9	1152.2	4833	1275	640	604	197	41	40	18	237	20	549	17	26	61	58	.513	2	1-3	3	4.48	4.72

Garret Anderson

Bats: L **Throws: L** **Pos:** LF-137; CF-14; DH-10; PH-1   **Ht:** 6'3" **Wt:** 228 **Born:** 6/30/72 **Age:** 31

								BATTING												BASERUNNING				AVERAGES		
Year Team	Lg	G	AB	H	2B	3B	HR	(Hm	Rd)	TB	R	RBI	RC	TBB	IBB	SO	HBP	SH	SF	SB	CS	SB%	GDP	Avg	OBP	Slg
1994 Anaheim	AL	5	13	5	0	0	0	(0	0)	5	0	1	2	0	0	2	0	0	0	0	0	-	0	.385	.385	.385
1995 Anaheim	AL	106	374	120	19	1	16	(7	9)	189	50	69	63	19	4	65	1	2	4	6	2	.75	8	.321	.352	.505
1996 Anaheim	AL	150	607	173	33	2	12	(7	5)	246	79	72	68	27	5	84	0	5	3	7	9	.44	22	.285	.314	.405
1997 Anaheim	AL	154	624	189	36	3	8	(5	3)	255	76	92	80	30	6	70	2	1	5	10	4	.71	20	.303	.334	.409
1998 Anaheim	AL	156	622	183	41	7	15	(4	11)	283	62	79	88	29	8	80	1	3	3	8	3	.73	13	.294	.325	.455
1999 Anaheim	AL	157	620	188	36	2	21	(10	11)	291	88	80	92	34	8	81	0	0	6	3	4	.43	15	.303	.336	.469
2000 Anaheim	AL	159	647	185	40	3	35	(20	15)	336	92	117	95	24	5	87	0	1	9	7	6	.54	21	.286	.307	.519
2001 Anaheim	AL	161	672	194	39	7	28	(13	15)	321	83	123	97	27	4	100	0	0	5	13	6	.68	12	.289	.314	.478
2002 Anaheim	AL	158	638	195	56	3	29	(13	16)	344	93	123	111	30	11	80	0	0	10	6	4	.60	11	.306	.332	.539
9 ML YEARS		1206	4817	1432	300	23	164	(79	85)	2270	623	756	696	220	51	649	4	12	45	60	38	.61	122	.297	.326	.471

Jason Anderson

Pitches: R **Bats: L** **Pos:** RP   **Ht:** 6'0" **Wt:** 170 **Born:** 6/9/79 **Age:** 24

		HOW MUCH HE PITCHED						WHAT HE GAVE UP												THE RESULTS						
Year Team	Lg	G	GS	CG	GF	IP	BFP	H	R	ER	HR	SH	SF	HB	TBB	IBB	SO	WP	Bk	W	L	Pct	ShO	Sv-Op	Hld	ERC	ERA
2000 Staten Island	A-	15	15	0	0	80.0	342	84	41	36	1	2	2	5	25	0	73	5	4	6	5	.545	0	0--	-	3.68	4.05
2001 Greensboro	A	23	19	1	3	124.0	530	127	68	52	9	3	8	3	40	1	101	8	0	7	9	.438	0	1--	-	3.80	3.77
2001 Staten Island	A-	7	7	0	0	48.0	184	32	9	9	2	0	4	0	12	0	56	1	1	5	1	.833	0	0--	-	1.87	1.69
2002 Tampa	A+	12	3	0	3	24.1	102	27	13	11	2	1	2	0	3	0	22	2	1	4	2	.667	0	1--	-	3.43	4.07
2002 Norwich	AA	16	0	0	10	19.1	72	14	2	2	1	1	0	0	5	1	21	3	0	1	1	.500	0	2--	-	1.94	0.93
2002 Columbus	AAA	26	0	0	25	34.1	138	26	13	12	3	2	1	1	11	0	28	0	1	5	1	.833	0	7--	-	2.55	3.15

Jimmy Anderson

Pitches: L **Bats: L** **Pos:** SP-25; RP-3   **Ht:** 6'1" **Wt:** 218 **Born:** 1/22/76 **Age:** 27

		HOW MUCH HE PITCHED						WHAT HE GAVE UP												THE RESULTS						
Year Team	Lg	G	GS	CG	GF	IP	BFP	H	R	ER	HR	SH	SF	HB	TBB	IBB	SO	WP	Bk	W	L	Pct	ShO	Sv-Op	Hld	ERC	ERA
1999 Pittsburgh	NL	13	4	0	2	29.1	127	25	15	13	2	2	1	1	16	2	13	4	0	2	1	.667	0	0-0	0	3.62	3.99
2000 Pittsburgh	NL	27	26	1	0	144.0	648	169	94	84	13	5	3	7	58	2	73	6	0	5	11	.313	0	0-0	0	5.21	5.25
2001 Pittsburgh	NL	34	34	1	0	206.1	922	232	123	117	15	11	9	11	83	14	89	6	1	9	17	.346	0	0-0	0	4.69	5.10
2002 Pittsburgh	NL	28	25	1	1	140.2	636	167	91	85	20	5	4	5	63	5	47	4	0	8	13	.381	0	0-0	0	5.84	5.44
4 ML YEARS		102	89	3	3	520.1	2333	593	323	299	50	23	17	24	220	23	222	20	1	24	42	.364	0	0-0	0	5.08	5.17

Marlon Anderson

Bats: L Throws: R Pos: 2B-143; PH-4   Ht: 5'11" Wt: 200 Born: 1/6/74 Age: 29

		BATTING																			BASERUNNING				AVERAGES		
Year Team	Lg	G	AB	H	2B	3B	HR	(Hm	Rd)	TB	R	RBI	RC	TBB	IBB	SO	HBP	SH	SF	SB	CS	SB%	GDP	Avg	OBP	Slg
1998 Philadelphia	NL	17	43	14	3	0	1	(1	0)	20	4	4	7	1	0	6	0	0	1	2	0	1.00	0	.326	.333	.465
1999 Philadelphia	NL	129	452	114	26	4	5	(4	1)	163	48	54	49	24	1	61	2	4	2	13	2	.87	6	.252	.292	.361
2000 Philadelphia	NL	41	162	37	8	1	1	(1	0)	50	10	15	12	12	0	22	0	0	0	2	2	.50	5	.228	.282	.309
2001 Philadelphia	NL	147	522	153	30	2	11	(7	4)	220	69	61	72	35	5	74	2	10	5	8	5	.62	12	.293	.337	.421
2002 Philadelphia	NL	145	539	139	30	6	8	(4	4)	205	64	48	52	42	14	71	5	2	4	5	1	.83	16	.258	.315	.380
5 ML YEARS		479	1718	457	97	13	26	(17	9)	658	195	182	192	114	20	234	9	16	12	30	10	.75	39	.266	.313	.383

Matt Anderson

Pitches: R Bats: R Pos: RP-12   Ht: 6'4" Wt: 190 Born: 8/17/76 Age: 26

		HOW MUCH HE PITCHED						WHAT HE GAVE UP											THE RESULTS						
Year Team	Lg	G	GS	CG	GF	IP	BFP	H	R	ER	HR	SH	SF	HB	TBB	IBB	SO	WP	Bk	W	L	Pct	ShO	Sv-Op	Hld	ERC	ERA
1998 Detroit	AL	42	0	0	10	44.0	194	38	16	16	3	6	3	2	31	4	44	2	0	5	1	.833	0	0-4	6	4.38	3.27
1999 Detroit	AL	37	0	0	9	38.0	180	33	27	24	8	0	2	1	35	1	32	3	0	2	1	.667	0	0-2	3	6.34	5.68
2000 Detroit	AL	69	0	0	27	74.1	324	61	44	39	8	2	6	3	45	4	71	4	0	3	2	.600	0	1-1	9	4.02	4.72
2001 Detroit	AL	62	0	0	41	56.0	239	56	33	30	2	1	2	0	18	4	52	9	1	3	1	.750	0	22-24	9	3.19	4.82
2002 Detroit	AL	12	0	0	8	11.0	58	17	13	11	1	1	2	2	8	1	8	1	0	2	1	.667	0	0-2	0	9.52	9.00
5 ML YEARS		222	0	0	95	223.1	995	205	133	120	22	10	15	8	137	14	207	19	1	15	6	.714	0	23-33	27	4.49	4.84

Shane Andrews

Bats: R Throws: R Pos: 3B-4; 1B-2; LF-1; PH-1   Ht: 6'1" Wt: 220 Born: 8/28/71 Age: 31

		BATTING																			BASERUNNING				AVERAGES		
Year Team	Lg	G	AB	H	2B	3B	HR	(Hm	Rd)	TB	R	RBI	RC	TBB	IBB	SO	HBP	SH	SF	SB	CS	SB%	GDP	Avg	OBP	Slg
2002 Pawtucket*	AAA	116	390	100	19	1	22	(-	-)	187	61	63	64	52	1	123	3	0	3	1	1	.50	9	.256	.346	.479
1995 Montreal	NL	84	220	47	10	1	8	(2	6)	83	27	31	21	17	2	68	1	1	2	1	1	.50	4	.214	.271	.377
1996 Montreal	NL	127	375	85	15	2	19	(8	11)	161	43	64	48	35	8	119	2	0	2	3	1	.75	2	.227	.295	.429
1997 Montreal	NL	18	64	13	3	0	4	(2	2)	28	10	9	7	3	0	20	0	0	0	0	0	-	0	.203	.232	.438
1998 Montreal	NL	150	492	117	30	1	25	(12	13)	224	48	69	68	58	3	137	0	2	7	1	6	.14	10	.238	.314	.455
1999 Mon-ChC	NL	117	348	68	12	0	16	(9	7)	128	41	51	37	50	3	109	1	0	5	1	1	.50	10	.195	.295	.368
2000 Chicago	NL	66	192	44	5	0	14	(7	7)	91	25	39	28	27	1	59	2	0	1	1	1	.50	9	.229	.329	.474
2002 Boston	AL	7	13	1	1	0	0	(0	0)	2	2	0	0	1	0	3	1	0	0	0	0	-	0	.077	.200	.154
1999 Montreal	NL	98	281	51	8	0	11	(5	6)	92	28	37	25	43	2	88	0	0	4	1	1	1.00	6	.181	.287	.327
1999 Chicago	NL	19	67	17	4	0	5	(4	1)	36	13	14	12	7	1	21	1	0	1	0	1	.00	4	.254	.329	.537
7 ML YEARS		569	1704	375	76	4	86	(40	46)	717	196	263	209	191	17	515	7	3	19	7	10	.41	35	.220	.298	.421

Kevin Appier

Pitches: R Bats: R Pos: SP-32   Ht: 6'2" Wt: 200 Born: 12/6/67 Age: 35

		HOW MUCH HE PITCHED						WHAT HE GAVE UP											THE RESULTS						
Year Team	Lg	G	GS	CG	GF	IP	BFP	H	R	ER	HR	SH	SF	HB	TBB	IBB	SO	WP	Bk	W	L	Pct	ShO	Sv-Op	Hld	ERC	ERA
1989 Kansas City	AL	6	5	0	0	21.2	106	34	22	22	3	0	3	0	12	1	10	0	0	1	4	.200	0	0-0	0	8.72	9.14
1990 Kansas City	AL	32	24	3	1	185.2	784	179	67	57	13	5	9	6	54	2	127	6	1	12	8	.600	3	0-0	0	3.34	2.76
1991 Kansas City	AL	34	31	6	1	207.2	881	205	97	79	13	8	6	2	61	3	158	7	1	13	10	.565	3	0-0	1	3.32	3.42
1992 Kansas City	AL	30	30	3	0	208.1	852	167	59	57	10	8	3	2	68	5	150	4	0	15	8	.652	0	0-0	0	2.41	2.46
1993 Kansas City	AL	34	34	5	0	238.2	953	183	74	68	8	3	5	1	81	3	186	5	0	18	8	.692	1	0-0	0	2.25	2.56
1994 Kansas City	AL	23	23	1	0	155.0	653	137	68	66	11	9	7	4	63	7	145	11	1	7	6	.538	0	0-0	0	3.31	3.83
1995 Kansas City	AL	31	31	4	0	201.1	832	163	90	87	14	3	3	8	80	1	185	5	0	15	10	.600	1	0-0	0	3.01	3.89
1996 Kansas City	AL	32	32	5	0	211.1	874	192	87	85	17	7	4	5	75	2	207	10	1	14	11	.560	1	0-0	0	3.41	3.62
1997 Kansas City	AL	34	34	4	0	235.2	972	215	96	89	24	4	4	4	74	2	196	14	1	9	13	.409	1	0-0	0	3.37	3.40
1998 Kansas City	AL	3	3	0	0	15.0	69	21	13	13	3	0	1	1	5	1	9	1	0	1	2	.333	0	0-0	0	7.33	7.80
1999 KC-Oak	AL	34	34	1	0	209.0	926	230	131	120	27	7	5	7	84	4	131	10	1	16	14	.533	0	0-0	0	4.99	5.17
2000 Oakland	AL	31	31	1	0	195.1	884	200	109	98	23	5	6	0	102	10	129	6	0	15	11	.577	0	0-0	0	4.89	4.52
2001 New York	NL	33	33	1	0	206.2	856	181	89	82	22	6	7	15	64	4	172	12	0	11	10	.524	1	0-0	0	3.38	3.57
2002 Anaheim	AL	32	32	0	0	188.1	795	191	89	82	23	1	8	7	64	2	132	7	0	14	12	.538	0	0-0	0	4.29	3.92
1999 Kansas City	AL	22	22	1	0	140.1	613	153	81	76	18	5	3	6	51	3	78	5	0	9	9	.500	0	0-0	0	4.83	4.87
1999 Oakland	AL	12	12	0	0	68.2	313	77	50	44	9	2	2	1	33	1	53	5	1	7	5	.583	0	0-0	0	5.32	5.77
14 ML YEARS		389	377	34	2	2479.2	10437	2298	1091	1005	211	66	71	71	887	47	1937	98	6	161	127	.559	12	0-0	1	3.51	3.65

Alex Arias

Bats: R Throws: R Pos: 3B-4; SS-1; PH-1   Ht: 6'3" Wt: 202 Born: 11/20/67 Age: 35

		BATTING																			BASERUNNING				AVERAGES		
Year Team	Lg	G	AB	H	2B	3B	HR	(Hm	Rd)	TB	R	RBI	RC	TBB	IBB	SO	HBP	SH	SF	SB	CS	SB%	GDP	Avg	OBP	Slg
2002 Rochester*	AAA	16	52	7	2	0	0	(-	-)	9	2	3	0	5	0	11	0	0	0	0	0	-	3	.135	.211	.173
2002 Columbus*	AAA	61	211	56	16	0	1	(-	-)	75	32	22	24	16	0	15	2	2	1	3	2	.60	4	.265	.322	.355
1992 Chicago	NL	32	99	29	6	0	0	(0	0)	35	14	7	13	11	0	13	2	1	0	0	0	-	4	.293	.375	.354
1993 Florida	NL	96	249	67	5	1	2	(1	1)	80	27	20	29	27	0	18	3	1	3	1	1	.50	5	.269	.344	.321
1994 Florida	NL	59	113	27	5	0	0	(0	0)	32	4	15	8	9	0	19	1	1	1	0	1	.00	1	.239	.298	.283
1995 Florida	NL	94	216	58	9	2	3	(2	1)	80	22	26	27	22	1	20	2	3	3	1	0	1.00	3	.269	.337	.370
1996 Florida	NL	100	224	62	11	2	3	(1	2)	86	27	26	30	17	1	28	3	1	1	2	0	1.00	8	.277	.335	.384
1997 Florida	NL	74	93	23	2	0	1	(0	1)	28	13	11	9	12	0	12	3	4	0	0	1	.00	6	.247	.352	.301
1998 Philadelphia	NL	56	133	39	8	0	1	(1	0)	50	17	16	19	13	3	18	1	1	1	2	0	1.00	1	.293	.358	.376
1999 Philadelphia	NL	118	347	105	20	1	4	(4	0)	139	43	48	50	36	6	31	4	1	2	2	2	.50	12	.303	.373	.401
2000 Philadelphia	NL	70	155	29	9	0	2	(1	1)	44	17	15	13	16	2	28	3	3	1	1	0	1.00	1	.187	.271	.284
2001 San Diego	NL	70	137	31	9	0	2	(0	2)	46	19	12	15	17	1	22	1	1	2	1	0	1.00	3	.226	.312	.336
2002 New York	AL	6	7	0	0	0	0	(0	0)	0	0	0	0	1	0	1	0	0	0	0	0	-	0	.000	.125	.000
11 ML YEARS		775	1773	470	84	6	18	(10	8)	620	203	196	213	181	14	211	23	17	16	10	5	.67	47	.265	.338	.350

Tony Armas Jr.

Pitches: R Bats: R Pos: SP-29   Ht: 6'4" Wt: 215 Born: 4/29/78 Age: 25

Year Team	Lg	G	GS	CG	GF	IP	BFP	H	R	ER	HR	SH	SF	HB	TBB	IBB	SO	WP	Bk	W	L	Pct	ShO	Sv-Op	Hld	ERC	ERA
1999 Montreal	NL	1	1	0	0	6.0	28	8	4	1	0	0	1	0	2	1	2	0	0	0	1	.000	0	0-0	0	4.53	1.50
2000 Montreal	NL	17	17	0	0	95.0	403	74	49	46	10	7	3	3	50	2	59	3	0	7	9	.438	0	0-0	0	3.49	4.36
2001 Montreal	NL	34	34	0	0	196.2	851	180	101	88	18	15	6	10	91	6	176	9	1	9	14	.391	0	0-0	0	3.95	4.03
2002 Montreal	NL	29	29	0	0	164.1	705	149	87	81	22	6	2	7	78	12	131	14	2	12	12	.500	0	0-0	0	4.19	4.44
4 ML YEARS		81	81	0	0	462.0	1987	411	241	216	50	28	12	20	221	21	368	28	3	28	36	.438	0	0-0	0	3.94	4.21

Rolando Arrojo

Pitches: R Bats: R Pos: RP-21; SP-8   Ht: 6'4" Wt: 236 Born: 7/18/68 Age: 34

Year Team	Lg	G	GS	CG	GF	IP	BFP	H	R	ER	HR	SH	SF	HB	TBB	IBB	SO	WP	Bk	W	L	Pct	ShO	Sv-Op	Hld	ERC	ERA
2002 Red Sox*	R	1	1	0	0	3.0	9	4	0	0	0		0	0	0	0	1	0	0	0	0	0	--	0	0--	--	5.40	0.00
2002 Sarasota*	A+	1	0	0	0	2.0	7	2	0	0	0	0	0	0	0	0	2	0	0	0	0	--	0	0--	--	2.31	0.00
1998 Tampa Bay	AL	32	32	2	0	202.0	853	195	84	80	21	5	3	19	65	2	152	3	1	14	12	.538	2	0-0	0	4.03	3.56
1999 Tampa Bay	AL	24	24	2	0	140.2	630	162	84	81	23	5	3	14	60	2	107	2	0	7	12	.368	0	0-0	0	6.09	5.18
2000 Col-Bos		32	32	0	0	172.2	771	187	118	108	24	4	7	16	68	6	124	4	2	10	11	.476	0	0-0	0	5.14	5.63
2001 Boston	AL	41	9	0	11	103.1	438	88	44	40	8	6	2	12	35	4	78	2	0	5	4	.556	0	5-7	3	3.25	3.48
2002 Boston	AL	29	8	0	4	81.1	348	83	47	45	7	4	3	6	27	1	51	2	0	4	3	.571	0	1-4	4	4.15	4.98
2000 Colorado	NL	19	19	0	0	101.1	470	120	77	68	14	3	7	12	46	6	80	1	2	5	9	.357	0	0-0	0	6.08	6.04
2000 Boston	AL	13	13	0	0	71.1	301	67	41	40	10	1	0	4	22	0	44	3	0	5	2	.714	0	0-0	0	3.88	5.05
5 ML YEARS		158	105	4	15	700.0	3040	715	377	354	83	24	18	67	255	15	512	13	3	40	42	.488	2	6-11	7	4.59	4.55

Bronson Arroyo

Pitches: R Bats: R Pos: RP-5; SP-4   Ht: 6'5" Wt: 194 Born: 2/24/77 Age: 26

Year Team	Lg	G	GS	CG	GF	IP	BFP	H	R	ER	HR	SH	SF	HB	TBB	IBB	SO	WP	Bk	W	L	Pct	ShO	Sv-Op	Hld	ERC	ERA
2002 Nashville*	AAA	22	21	3	0	143.0	574	126	57	47	10	6	3	2	28	1	116	5	0	8	6	.571	2	0--		2.54	2.96
2000 Pittsburgh	NL	20	12	0	1	71.2	338	88	61	51	10	5	2	4	36	6	50	3	1	2	6	.250	0	0-0	0	6.18	6.40
2001 Pittsburgh	NL	24	13	1	1	88.1	390	99	54	50	12	4	6	4	34	6	39	4	1	5	7	.417	0	0-0	2	5.09	5.09
2002 Pittsburgh	NL	9	4	0	1	27.0	123	30	14	12	1	1	1	0	15	3	22	0	0	2	1	.667	0	0-0	1	4.64	4.00
3 ML YEARS		53	29	1	3	187.0	851	217	129	113	23	10	9	8	85	15	111	7	2	9	14	.391	0	0-0	3	5.44	5.44

Miguel Asencio

Pitches: R Bats: R Pos: SP-21; RP-10   Ht: 6'2" Wt: 160 Born: 9/29/80 Age: 22

Year Team	Lg	G	GS	CG	GF	IP	BFP	H	R	ER	HR	SH	SF	HB	TBB	IBB	SO	WP	Bk	W	L	Pct	ShO	Sv-Op	Hld	ERC	ERA
1999 Phillies	R	9	5	0	3	28.2	137	35	24	19	1	0	4	2	16	0	14	1	0	1	4	.200	0	0--	-	5.71	5.97
2000 Clearwater	A+	5	5	0	0	33.0	132	22	10	10	2	0	0	0	17	0	24	1	1	2	1	.667	0	0--	-	2.58	2.73
2000 Batavia	A-	7	7	1	0	39.2	165	32	23	22	3	1	1	3	17	0	28	2	0	2	2	.500	0	0--	-	3.32	4.99
2001 Clearwater	A+	28	21	2	1	155.1	649	124	62	49	7	3	6	2	70	1	123	9	2	12	5	.706	1	0--	-	2.86	2.84
2002 Kansas City	AL	31	21	0	7	123.1	557	136	73	70	17	2	6	3	64	2	58	7	0	4	7	.364	0	0-0	0	5.55	5.11

Andy Ashby

Pitches: R Bats: R Pos: SP-30   Ht: 6'1" Wt: 202 Born: 7/11/67 Age: 35

Year Team	Lg	G	GS	CG	GF	IP	BFP	H	R	ER	HR	SH	SF	HB	TBB	IBB	SO	WP	Bk	W	L	Pct	ShO	Sv-Op	Hld	ERC	ERA
1991 Philadelphia	NL	8	8	0	0	42.0	186	41	28	28	5	1	3	3	19	0	26	6	0	1	5	.167	0	0-0	0	4.54	6.00
1992 Philadelphia	NL	10	8	0	0	37.0	171	42	31	31	6	2	2	1	21	0	24	2	0	1	3	.250	0	0-0	0	6.17	7.54
1993 Col-SD	NL	32	21	0	3	123.0	577	168	100	93	19	6	7	4	56	5	77	6	3	3	10	.231	0	1-1	0	7.10	6.80
1994 San Diego	NL	24	24	4	0	164.1	682	145	75	62	16	11	3	3	43	12	121	5	0	6	11	.353	0	0-0	0	2.82	3.40
1995 San Diego	NL	31	31	2	0	192.2	800	180	79	63	17	10	4	11	62	3	150	7	0	12	10	.545	2	0-0	0	3.60	2.94
1996 San Diego	NL	24	24	1	0	150.2	612	147	60	54	17	6	2	3	34	1	85	3	0	9	5	.643	0	0-0	0	3.50	3.23
1997 San Diego	NL	30	30	2	0	200.2	851	207	108	92	17	13	6	5	49	2	144	3	0	9	11	.450	0	0-0	0	3.59	4.13
1998 San Diego	NL	33	33	5	0	226.2	939	223	90	84	23	8	5	7	58	8	151	7	0	17	9	.654	1	0-0	0	3.55	3.34
1999 San Diego	NL	31	31	4	0	206.0	862	204	95	87	26	10	1	7	54	4	132	6	0	14	10	.583	3	0-0	0	3.78	3.80
2000 Phi-Atl	NL	31	31	3	0	199.1	867	216	124	109	29	18	10	6	61	9	106	6	1	12	13	.480	0	0-0	0	4.52	4.92
2001 Los Angeles	NL	2	2	0	0	11.2	49	14	5	5	2	0	0	0	1	0	7	0	0	2	0	1.000	0	0-0	0	4.42	3.86
2002 Los Angeles	NL	30	30	0	0	181.2	771	179	85	79	20	7	6	8	65	3	107	2	0	9	13	.409	0	0-0	0	4.10	3.91
1993 Colorado	NL	20	9	0	3	54.0	277	89	54	51	5	3	3	3	32	4	33	2	3	0	4	.000	0	1-1	0	9.06	8.50
1993 San Diego	NL	12	12	0	0	69.0	300	79	46	42	14	3	4	1	24	1	44	4	0	3	6	.333	0	0-0	0	5.58	5.48
2000 Philadelphia	NL	16	16	1	0	101.1	455	113	75	64	17	11	9	5	38	5	51	4	0	4	7	.364	0	0-0	0	5.20	5.68
2000 Atlanta	NL	15	15	2	0	98.0	412	103	49	45	12	7	1	1	23	4	55	2	1	8	6	.571	0	0-0	0	3.84	4.13
12 ML YEARS		286	273	21	3	1735.2	7367	1766	880	787	197	92	49	58	523	47	1130	53	4	95	100	.487	7	1-1	0	3.99	4.08

Pedro Astacio

Pitches: R Bats: R Pos: SP-31   Ht: 6'2" Wt: 210 Born: 11/28/69 Age: 33

Year Team	Lg	G	GS	CG	GF	IP	BFP	H	R	ER	HR	SH	SF	HB	TBB	IBB	SO	WP	Bk	W	L	Pct	ShO	Sv-Op	Hld	ERC	ERA
1992 Los Angeles	NL	11	11	4	0	82.0	341	80	23	18	1	3	2	2	20	4	43	1	0	5	5	.500	4	0-0	0	2.78	1.98
1993 Los Angeles	NL	31	31	3	0	186.1	777	165	80	74	14	7	8	5	68	5	122	8	1	14	9	.609	2	0-0	0	3.24	3.57
1994 Los Angeles	NL	23	23	3	0	149.0	625	142	77	71	18	6	5	4	47	4	108	4	0	6	8	.429	1	0-0	0	3.71	4.29
1995 Los Angeles	NL	48	11	1	7	104.0	436	103	53	49	12	5	3	4	29	5	80	5	0	7	8	.467	1	0-1	2	3.76	4.24
1996 Los Angeles	NL	35	32	0	0	211.2	885	207	86	81	18	11	5	9	67	9	130	6	2	9	8	.529	0	0-0	0	3.69	3.44
1997 LA-Col	NL	33	31	2	2	202.1	862	200	98	93	24	9	7	9	61	0	166	6	3	12	10	.545	1	0-0	0	3.92	4.14
1998 Colorado	NL	35	34	0	0	209.1	938	245	160	145	39	12	3	17	74	0	170	2	0	13	14	.481	0	0-0	0	5.91	6.23
1999 Colorado	NL	34	34	7	0	232.0	1008	258	140	130	38	6	10	11	75	6	210	5	0	17	11	.607	0	0-0	0	5.08	5.04

15

Year Team	Lg	G	GS	CG	GF	IP	BFP	H	R	ER	HR	SH	SF	HB	TBB	IBB	SO	WP	Bk	W	L	Pct	ShO	Sv-Op	Hld	ERC	ERA
2000 Colorado	NL	32	32	3	0	196.1	875	217	119	115	32.	7	4	15	77	5	193	8	0	12	9	.571	0	0-0	0	5.42	5.27
2001 Col-Hou	NL	26	26	4	0	169.2	733	181	101	96	22	6	5	13	54	3	144	2	0	8	14	.364	1	0-0	0	4.68	5.09
2002 New York	NL	31	31	3	0	191.2	828	192	106	102	32	8	7	16	63	5	152	1	2	12	11	.522	1	0-0	0	4.57	4.79
1997 Los Angeles	NL	26	24	2	2	153.2	654	151	75	70	15	9	5	4	47	0	115	4	3	7	9	.438	1	0-0	0	3.67	4.10
1997 Colorado	NL	7	7	0	0	48.2	208	49	23	23	9	0	2	5	14	0	51	0	0	5	1	.833	0	0-0	0	4.72	4.25
2001 Colorado	NL	22	22	4	0	141.0	617	151	91	86	21	5	4	10	50	3	125	2	0	6	13	.316	1	0-0	0	4.94	5.49
2001 Houston	NL	4	4	0	0	28.2	116	30	10	10	1	1	1	3	4	0	19	0	0	2	1	.667	0	0-0	0	3.43	3.14
11 ML YEARS		339	296	30	9	1934.1	8308	1990	1043	974	250	80	59	105	635	46	1518	48	16	115	107	.518	11	0-1	2	4.37	4.53

Rich Aurilia

Bats: R **Throws:** R **Pos:** SS-131; PH-2   **Ht:** 6'1" **Wt:** 185 **Born:** 9/2/71 **Age:** 31

Year Team	Lg	G	AB	H	2B	3B	HR	(Hm	Rd)	TB	R	RBI	RC	TBB	IBB	SO	HBP	SH	SF	SB	CS	SB%	GDP	Avg	OBP	Slg
1995 San Francisco	NL	9	19	9	3	0	2	(0	2)	18	4	4	7	1	0	2	0	1	1	1	0	1.00	1	.474	.476	.947
1996 San Francisco	NL	105	318	76	7	1	3	(1	2)	94	27	26	29	25	2	52	1	6	4	4	1	.80	1	.239	.295	.296
1997 San Francisco	NL	46	102	28	8	0	5	(1	4)	51	16	19	16	8	0	15	0	1	2	1	1	.50	3	.275	.321	.500
1998 San Francisco	NL	122	413	110	27	2	9	(5	4)	168	54	49	54	31	3	62	2	5	2	3	3	.50	3	.266	.319	.407
1999 San Francisco	NL	152	558	157	23	1	22	(9	13)	248	68	80	79	43	3	71	5	3	5	2	3	.40	16	.281	.336	.444
2000 San Francisco	NL	141	509	138	24	2	20	(12	8)	226	67	79	74	54	2	90	0	4	4	1	2	.33	15	.271	.339	.444
2001 San Francisco	NL	156	636	206	37	5	37	(15	22)	364	114	97	124	47	2	83	0	3	3	1	3	.25	14	.324	.369	.572
2002 San Francisco	NL	133	538	138	35	2	15	(4	11)	222	76	61	61	37	0	90	4	3	7	1	2	.33	15	.257	.305	.413
8 ML YEARS		864	3093	862	164	13	113	(47	66)	1391	426	415	444	246	12	465	12	26	26	14	15	.48	68	.279	.332	.450

Brad Ausmus

Bats: R **Throws:** R **Pos:** C-129; PH-3   **Ht:** 5'11" **Wt:** 200 **Born:** 4/14/69 **Age:** 34

Year Team	Lg	G	AB	H	2B	3B	HR	(Hm	Rd)	TB	R	RBI	RC	TBB	IBB	SO	HBP	SH	SF	SB	CS	SB%	GDP	Avg	OBP	Slg
1993 San Diego	NL	49	160	41	8	1	5	(4	1)	66	18	12	19	6	0	28	0	1	0	2	0	1.00	2	.256	.283	.413
1994 San Diego	NL	101	327	82	12	1	7	(6	1)	117	45	24	36	30	12	63	1	6	2	5	1	.83	8	.251	.314	.358
1995 San Diego	NL	103	328	96	16	4	5	(2	3)	135	44	34	49	31	3	56	2	4	4	16	5	.76	6	.293	.353	.412
1996 SD-Det		125	375	83	16	0	5	(2	3)	114	46	35	32	39	1	72	5	6	2	4	8	.33	8	.221	.302	.304
1997 Houston	NL	130	425	113	25	1	4	(1	3)	152	45	44	51	38	4	78	3	6	6	14	6	.70	8	.266	.326	.358
1998 Houston	NL	128	412	111	10	4	6	(2	4)	147	62	45	51	53	11	60	3	3	1	10	3	.77	18	.269	.356	.357
1999 Detroit	AL	127	458	126	25	6	9	(5	4)	190	62	54	69	51	0	71	14	3	5	12	9	.57	11	.275	.365	.415
2000 Detroit	AL	150	523	139	25	3	7	(3	4)	191	75	51	68	69	0	79	6	4	2	11	5	.69	19	.266	.357	.365
2001 Houston	NL	128	422	98	23	4	5	(4	1)	144	45	34	38	30	6	64	1	6	2	4	1	.80	13	.232	.284	.341
2002 Houston	NL	130	447	115	19	3	6	(4	2)	158	57	50	42	38	3	71	6	2	3	2	3	.40	30	.257	.322	.353
1996 San Diego	NL	50	149	27	4	0	1	(0	1)	34	16	13	6	13	0	27	3	1	0	1	4	.20	1	.181	.261	.228
1996 Detroit	AL	75	226	56	12	0	4	(2	2)	80	30	22	26	26	1	45	2	5	2	3	4	.43	4	.248	.328	.354
10 ML YEARS		1171	3877	1004	179	27	59	(33	26)	1414	499	383	455	385	40	642	41	40	23	80	41	.66	123	.259	.331	.365

Jeff Austin

Pitches: R **Bats:** R **Pos:** RP-10   **Ht:** 6'0" **Wt:** 185 **Born:** 10/19/76 **Age:** 26

Year Team	Lg	G	GS	CG	GF	IP	BFP	H	R	ER	HR	SH	SF	HB	TBB	IBB	SO	WP	Bk	W	L	Pct	ShO	Sv-Op	Hld	ERC	ERA
1999 Wilmington	A+	18	18	0	0	112.1	473	108	52	47	10	5	3	2	39	0	97	5	0	7	2	.778	0	0- -	-	3.68	3.77
1999 Wichita	AA	6	6	0	0	34.1	155	40	19	17	1	0	1	2	11	1	21	4	0	3	1	.750	0	0- -	-	4.27	4.46
2000 Wichita	AA	6	6	1	0	43.0	168	33	16	14	3	0	2	5	4	0	31	2	0	2	2	.500	0	0- -	-	2.02	2.93
2000 Omaha	AAA	23	19	1	1	126.2	551	150	85	63	16	3	7	4	35	1	57	8	1	7	9	.438	1	0- -	-	4.99	4.48
2001 Omaha	AAA	28	8	0	9	70.2	319	89	56	54	14	3	2	4	27	1	55	5	2	3	7	.300	0	2- -	-	6.65	6.88
2002 Omaha	AAA	39	0	0	13	52.1	226	54	24	19	2	0	4	2	15	2	44	11	1	4	0	1.000	0	2- -	-	3.42	3.27
2001 Kansas City	AL	21	0	0	6	26.0	117	27	17	16	4	1	2	1	14	2	27	3	0	0	0	-	0	0-0	1	5.31	5.54
2002 Kansas City	AL	10	0	0	6	11.0	52	14	6	6	0	0	2	0	6	1	6	1	0	0	0	-	0	0-0	0	5.24	4.91
2 ML YEARS		31	0	0	15	37.0	169	41	23	22	4	1	4	1	20	3	33	4	0	0	0	-	0	0-0	1	5.30	5.35

Bruce Aven

Bats: R **Throws:** R **Pos:** LF-5; CF-1; RF-1; PH-1   **Ht:** 5'9" **Wt:** 180 **Born:** 3/4/72 **Age:** 31

Year Team	Lg	G	AB	H	2B	3B	HR	(Hm	Rd)	TB	R	RBI	RC	TBB	IBB	SO	HBP	SH	SF	SB	CS	SB%	GDP	Avg	OBP	Slg
2002 Buffalo*	AAA	35	119	34	5	0	5	(-	-)	54	17	16	20	14	1	21	3	0	0	1	0	1.00	4	.286	.375	.454
2002 Scrtn/WlksBr*	AAA	59	205	50	11	0	8	(-	-)	85	26	42	33	36	2	35	8	0	2	3	1	.75	7	.244	.375	.415
1997 Cleveland	AL	13	19	4	1	0	0	(0	0)	5	4	2	1	1	0	5	0	0	0	0	1	.00	0	.211	.250	.263
1999 Florida	NL	137	381	110	19	2	12	(3	9)	169	57	70	65	44	1	82	9	0	6	3	0	1.00	6	.289	.370	.444
2000 Pit-LA	NL	81	168	42	11	0	7	(4	3)	74	20	29	19	8	0	39	0	0	0	2	3	.40	4	.250	.284	.440
2001 Los Angeles	NL	21	24	8	2	0	1	(1	0)	13	3	2	5	0	0	5	2	0	0	0	0	-	0	.333	.385	.542
2002 Cleveland	AL	7	17	2	0	0	0	(0	0)	2	1	0	0	4	0	4	0	0	0	1	0	1.00	0	.118	.286	.118
2000 Pittsburgh	NL	72	148	37	11	0	5	(4	1)	63	18	25	15	5	0	31	0	0	0	2	3	.40	4	.250	.275	.426
2000 Los Angeles	NL	9	20	5	0	0	2	(0	2)	11	2	4	4	3	0	8	0	0	0	0	0	-	0	.250	.348	.550
5 ML YEARS		259	609	166	33	2	20	(8	12)	263	85	103	90	57	1	135	11	0	6	6	4	.60	10	.273	.343	.432

Steve Avery

Pitches: L **Bats:** L **Pos:** RP   **Ht:** 6'4" **Wt:** 205 **Born:** 5/11/70 **Age:** 33

Year Team	Lg	G	GS	CG	GF	IP	BFP	H	R	ER	HR	SH	SF	HB	TBB	IBB	SO	WP	Bk	W	L	Pct	ShO	Sv-Op	Hld	ERC	ERA
1990 Atlanta	NL	21	21	1	1	99.0	466	121	79	62	7	14	4	2	45	2	75	1	3	3	11	.214	1	0-0	0	5.26	5.64
1991 Atlanta	NL	35	35	3	0	210.1	868	189	89	79	21	8	4	3	65	0	137	4	1	18	8	.692	1	0-0	0	3.25	3.38
1992 Atlanta	NL	35	35	2	0	233.2	969	216	95	83	14	12	8	0	71	3	129	7	3	11	11	.500	2	0-0	0	3.02	3.20
1993 Atlanta	NL	35	35	3	0	223.1	891	216	81	73	14	4	8	0	43	5	125	3	1	18	6	.750	1	0-0	0	2.92	2.94

HOW MUCH HE PITCHED / **WHAT HE GAVE UP** / **THE RESULTS**

Year Team	Lg	G	GS	CG	GF	IP	BFP	H	R	ER	HR	SH	SF	HB	TBB	IBB	SO	WP	Bk	W	L	Pct	ShO	Sv-Op	Hld	ERC	ERA
1994 Atlanta	NL	24	24	1	0	151.2	628	127	71	68	15	4	6	4	55	4	122	5	2	8	3	.727	0	0-0	0	3.12	4.04
1995 Atlanta	NL	29	29	3	0	173.1	724	165	92	90	22	6	4	6	52	4	141	3	0	7	13	.350	1	0-0	0	3.73	4.67
1996 Atlanta	NL	24	23	1	0	131.0	567	146	70	65	10	7	3	4	40	8	86	5	0	7	10	.412	0	0-0	0	4.22	4.67
1997 Boston	AL	22	18	0	1	96.2	453	127	76	69	15	1	4	2	49	0	51	4	0	6	7	.462	0	0-0	1	7.01	6.42
1998 Boston	AL	34	23	0	4	123.2	546	128	74	69	14	3	0	4	64	0	57	7	0	10	7	.588	0	0-1	1	5.06	5.02
1999 Cincinnati	NL	19	19	0	0	96.0	426	75	62	55	11	3	6	1	78	0	51	4	1	6	7	.462	0	0-0	0	4.69	5.16
10 ML YEARS		278	261	14	6	1538.2	6538	1510	789	713	143	70	47	26	562	26	974	47	9	94	83	.531	6	0-1	2	3.85	4.17

Luis Ayala

Pitches: R **Bats:** R **Pos:** RP   **Ht:** 6'2" **Wt:** 170 **Born:** 1/2/78 **Age:** 25

Year Team	Lg	G	GS	CG	GF	IP	BFP	H	R	ER	HR	SH	SF	HB	TBB	IBB	SO	WP	Bk	W	L	Pct	ShO	Sv-Op	Hld	ERC	ERA
1997 Saltillo	AAA	37	2	0	0	62.1	269	76	37	32	3	1	7	3	21	4	30	2	1	7	5	.583	0	0--	-	4.99	4.62
1998 Saltillo	AAA	47	4	0	0	83.1	381	105	52	50	2	10	1	4	45	13	29	3	0	7	8	.467	0	7--	-	5.65	5.62
1999 Saltillo	AAA	61	0	0	0	79.0	287	54	17	15	1	3	0	3	22	5	28	3	0	7	3	.700	0	41--	-	1.76	1.71
2000 Saltillo	AAA	55	0	0	52	65.1	269	69	22	20	4	4	0	3	13	1	38	1	0	5	3	.625	0	25--	-	3.59	2.76
2001 Salem	A+	33	0	0	33	40.0	164	34	11	9	2	3	2	0	11	0	34	0	0	1	2	.333	0	21--	-	2.47	2.03
2001 Saltillo	AAA	13	0	0	12	13.1	61	19	10	6	0	1	0	2	5	0	10	2	1	0	1	.000	0	7--	-	6.67	4.05
2002 Saltillo	AAA	49	0	0	43	53.2	225	43	16	10	2	2	0	7	15	0	43	0	0	3	5	.375	0	23--	-	2.60	1.68
2002 Ottawa	AAA	6	0	0	3	7.2	32	7	3	3	1	0	0	0	4	0	6	0	0	0	0	-	0	0--	-	4.48	3.52

Manny Aybar

Pitches: R **Bats:** R **Pos:** RP-15   **Ht:** 6'1" **Wt:** 177 **Born:** 5/4/72 **Age:** 31

Year Team	Lg	G	GS	CG	GF	IP	BFP	H	R	ER	HR	SH	SF	HB	TBB	IBB	SO	WP	Bk	W	L	Pct	ShO	Sv-Op	Hld	ERC	ERA
2002 Fresno*	AAA	45	0	0	42	50.1	216	46	24	21	6	4	3	2	18	1	53	3	0	1	4	.200	0	24--	-	3.63	3.75
1997 St Louis	NL	12	12	0	0	68.0	295	66	33	32	8	7	4	4	29	0	41	1	1	2	4	.333	0	0-0	-	4.40	4.24
1998 St Louis	NL	20	14	0	1	81.1	369	90	58	54	6	4	1	2	42	1	57	2	0	6	6	.500	0	0-0	-	5.04	5.98
1999 St Louis	NL	65	1	0	22	97.0	430	104	67	59	13	4	3	4	36	3	74	1	2	4	5	.444	0	3-5	12	4.68	5.47
2000 Col-Cin-Fla	NL	54	0	0	20	79.1	349	74	42	38	11	5	4	2	35	3	45	7	1	2	2	.500	0	0-1	1	4.08	4.31
2001 Chicago	NL	17	1	0	1	22.2	113	28	19	16	5	1	1	2	17	0	16	2	0	2	1	.667	0	0-0	2	8.38	6.35
2002 San Francisco	NL	15	0	0	4	14.1	63	16	6	4	1	0	0	1	3	2	11	0	1	1	0	1.000	0	0-0	1	3.71	2.51
2000 Colorado	NL	1	0	0	0	1.2	10	5	3	3	1	0	0	0	0	0	0	0	0	0	1	.000	0	0-0	0	21.12	16.20
2000 Cincinnati	NL	32	0	0	10	50.1	226	51	31	27	7	4	3	2	22	2	31	7	1	1	1	.500	0	0-0	1	4.57	4.83
2000 Florida	NL	21	0	0	10	27.1	113	18	8	8	3	1	1	0	13	1	14	0	0	1	0	1.000	0	0-1	0	2.53	2.63
6 ML YEARS		183	28	0	48	362.2	1619	378	225	203	44	21	13	15	162	9	244	13	5	17	18	.486	0	3-6	16	4.75	5.04

Brandon Backe

Pitches: R **Bats:** R **Pos:** RP-9   **Ht:** 6'0" **Wt:** 190 **Born:** 4/5/78 **Age:** 25

Year Team	Lg	G	GS	CG	GF	IP	BFP	H	R	ER	HR	SH	SF	HB	TBB	IBB	SO	WP	Bk	W	L	Pct	ShO	Sv-Op	Hld	ERC	ERA
1998 Princeton	R+	1	0	0	1	2.0	9	0	0	0	0	0	0	0	2	0	3	0	0	0	0	-	0	0--	-	0.84	0.00
2001 Chrlstn - SC	A	16	0	0	15	24.2	98	17	8	8	2	2	0	4	7	1	20	2	0	2	1	.667	0	7--	-	2.51	2.92
2001 Bakersfield	A+	17	0	0	12	24.2	97	13	7	3	1	0	2	0	8	0	33	2	0	1	0	1.000	0	3--	-	1.27	1.09
2001 Orlando	AA	14	0	0	1	22.0	94	20	14	14	1	0	0	4	11	0	20	2	0	1	0	1.000	0	0--	-	4.49	5.73
2002 Orlando	AA	20	14	3	4	92.1	400	91	58	48	9	2	1	5	37	1	45	9	0	4	6	.400	0	2--	-	4.19	4.68
2002 Tampa Bay	AL	9	0	0	4	13.0	61	15	10	10	3	0	0	2	7	0	6	0	0	0	0	-	0	0-0	0	7.37	6.92

Mike Bacsik

Pitches: L **Bats:** L **Pos:** SP-9; RP-2   **Ht:** 6'3" **Wt:** 190 **Born:** 11/11/77 **Age:** 25

Year Team	Lg	G	GS	CG	GF	IP	BFP	H	R	ER	HR	SH	SF	HB	TBB	IBB	SO	WP	Bk	W	L	Pct	ShO	Sv-Op	Hld	ERC	ERA
1996 Burlington	R+	13	13	1	0	69.2	276	49	23	17	2	0	2	1	14	0	61	3	1	4	2	.667	0	0--	-	1.58	2.20
1997 Columbus	A	28	28	0	0	139.0	622	163	94	84	16	7	3	9	47	1	100	12	2	4	14	.222	0	0--	-	5.18	5.44
1998 Kinston	A+	27	27	1	0	165.2	667	147	64	53	17	5	4	4	37	3	128	4	0	10	9	.526	0	0--	-	2.92	2.88
1999 Akron	AA	26	26	1	0	149.1	647	164	84	77	24	5	5	4	47	0	84	4	0	11	11	.500	0	0--	-	4.96	4.64
2000 Kinston	A+	11	11	0	0	65.0	269	72	36	33	4	1	2	2	8	0	56	0	0	3	6	.333	0	0--	-	3.48	4.57
2000 Akron	AA	11	11	0	0	71.1	287	61	23	22	3	4	1	3	15	0	44	3	0	7	1	.875	1	0--	-	2.41	2.78
2000 Buffalo	AAA	5	5	0	0	29.0	124	31	20	18	7	0	2	0	7	0	9	0	0	0	3	.000	0	0--	-	4.73	5.59
2001 Buffalo	AAA	21	20	2	0	121.1	501	115	47	44	13	2	0	3	25	0	81	0	0	12	5	.706	0	0--	-	3.16	3.26
2001 Akron	AA	4	4	1	0	27.1	104	21	7	6	2	0	0	0	3	0	19	0	0	1	1	.500	1	0--	-	1.72	1.98
2002 Norfolk	AAA	25	14	1	3	108.1	467	134	48	45	13	4	1	4	25	0	75	1	0	5	5	.500	1	0--	-	5.17	3.74
2001 Cleveland	AL	3	0	0	0	9.0	45	13	10	9	0	0	1	1	3	1	4	0	0	0	0	-	0	0-0	0	5.56	9.00
2002 New York	NL	11	9	1	1	55.2	247	63	29	27	8	5	1	4	19	3	30	0	0	3	2	.600	0	0-0	0	5.13	4.37
2 ML YEARS		14	9	1	1	64.2	292	76	39	36	8	5	2	5	22	4	34	0	0	3	2	.600	0	0-0	0	5.20	5.01

Carlos Baerga

Bats: B **Throws:** R **Pos:** PH-32; DH-29; 2B-17; 3B-1; PR-1   **Ht:** 5'11" **Wt:** 215 **Born:** 11/4/68 **Age:** 34

BATTING / **BASERUNNING** / **AVERAGES**

Year Team	Lg	G	AB	H	2B	3B	HR	(Hm	Rd)	TB	R	RBI	RC	TBB	IBB	SO	HBP	SH	SF	SB	CS	SB%	GDP	Avg	OBP	Slg
1990 Cleveland	AL	108	312	81	17	2	7	(3	4)	123	46	47	36	16	2	57	4	1	5	0	2	.00	4	.260	.300	.394
1991 Cleveland	AL	158	593	171	28	2	11	(9	2)	236	80	69	81	48	5	74	6	4	3	2	.60	12	.288	.346	.398
1992 Cleveland	AL	161	657	205	32	1	20	(9	11)	299	92	105	103	35	10	76	13	2	9	10	2	.83	15	.312	.354	.455
1993 Cleveland	AL	154	624	200	28	6	21	(8	13)	303	105	114	104	34	7	68	6	3	13	15	4	.79	17	.321	.355	.486
1994 Cleveland	AL	103	442	139	32	2	19	(8	11)	232	81	80	74	10	1	45	6	3	8	2	.80	10	.314	.333	.525
1995 Cleveland	AL	135	557	175	28	2	15	(7	8)	252	87	90	87	35	6	31	3	0	5	11	2	.85	15	.314	.355	.452
1996 Cle-NYM		126	507	129	28	0	12	(5	7)	193	59	66	51	21	0	27	9	2	5	1	1	.50	23	.254	.293	.381
1997 New York	NL	133	467	131	25	1	9	(4	5)	185	53	52	53	20	1	54	3	3	5	2	6	.25	13	.281	.311	.396

Year Team	Lg	G	AB	H	2B	3B	HR	(Hm	Rd)	TB	R	RBI	RC	TBB	IBB	SO	HBP	SH	SF	SB	CS	SB%	GDP	Avg	OBP	Slg
1998 New York	NL	147	511	136	27	1	7	(3	4)	186	46	53	51	24	6	55	6	3	7	0	1	.00	21	.266	.303	.364
1999 SD-Cle		55	137	33	1	0	3	(2	1)	43	10	10	12	10	1	24	2	2	1	2	1	.67	5	.241	.300	.314
2002 Boston	AL	73	182	52	11	0	2	(1	1)	69	17	19	17	7	1	20	2	1	6	6	0	1.00	6	.286	.316	.379
1996 Cleveland	AL	100	424	113	25	0	10	(5	5)	168	54	55	47	16	0	25	7	2	4	1	1	.50	15	.267	.302	.396
1996 New York	NL	26	83	16	3	0	2	(0	2)	25	5	11	4	5	0	2	2	0	1	0	0	-	8	.193	.253	.301
1999 San Diego	NL	33	80	20	1	0	2	(1	1)	27	6	5	9	6	0	14	2	1	0	1	0	1.00	2	.250	.318	.338
1999 Cleveland	AL	22	57	13	0	0	1	(1	0)	16	4	5	3	4	1	10	0	1	1	1	1	.50	3	.228	.274	.281
11 ML YEARS		1353	4989	1452	257	17	126	(52	74)	2121	676	705	669	260	40	531	60	24	63	58	23	.72	141	.291	.330	.425

Danys Baez

Pitches: R **Bats:** R **Pos:** SP-26; RP-13   **Ht:** 6'3" **Wt:** 225 **Born:** 9/10/77 **Age:** 25

Year Team	Lg	G	GS	CG	GF	IP	BFP	H	R	ER	HR	SH	SF	HB	TBB	IBB	SO	WP	Bk	W	L	Pct	ShO	Sv-Op	Hld	ERC	ERA
2000 Kinston	A+	9	9	0	0	49.2	221	45	29	26	5	3	1	6	20	0	56	4	1	2	2	.500	0	0--	-	3.92	4.71
2000 Akron	AA	18	18	0	0	102.2	426	98	46	42	6	5	6	5	32	0	77	7	0	4	9	.308	0	0--	-	3.46	3.68
2001 Buffalo	AAA	16	0	0	8	25.1	100	18	9	9	2	0	1	0	9	0	30	0	1	2	0	1.000	0	3--	-	2.32	3.20
2001 Akron	AA	1	0	0	0	2.0	7	1	0	0	0	0	0	0	0	0	2	0	0	0	0	-	0	0--	-	0.54	0.00
2001 Cleveland	AL	43	0	0	8	50.1	202	34	22	14	5	0	1	3	20	4	52	3	0	5	3	.625	0	0-1	14	2.51	2.50
2002 Cleveland	AL	39	26	1	9	165.1	726	160	84	81	14	2	8	9	82	5	130	6	1	10	11	.476	0	6-8	0	4.35	4.41
2 ML YEARS		82	26	1	17	215.2	928	194	106	95	19	2	9	12	102	9	182	9	1	15	14	.517	0	6-9	14	3.90	3.96

Jeff Bagwell

Bats: R **Throws:** R **Pos:** 1B-153; DH-4; PH-1   **Ht:** 6'0" **Wt:** 215 **Born:** 5/27/68 **Age:** 35

Year Team	Lg	G	AB	H	2B	3B	HR	(Hm	Rd)	TB	R	RBI	RC	TBB	IBB	SO	HBP	SH	SF	SB	CS	SB%	GDP	Avg	OBP	Slg
1991 Houston	NL	156	554	163	26	4	15	(6	9)	242	79	82	95	75	5	116	13	1	7	7	4	.64	12	.294	.387	.437
1992 Houston	NL	162	586	160	34	6	18	(8	10)	260	87	96	96	84	13	97	12	2	13	10	6	.63	17	.273	.368	.444
1993 Houston	NL	142	535	171	37	4	20	(9	11)	276	76	88	102	62	6	73	3	0	9	13	4	.76	20	.320	.388	.516
1994 Houston	NL	110	400	147	32	2	39	(23	16)	300	104	116	121	65	14	65	4	0	10	15	4	.79	12	.368	.451	.750
1995 Houston	NL	114	448	130	29	0	21	(10	11)	222	88	87	89	79	12	102	6	0	6	12	5	.71	9	.290	.399	.496
1996 Houston	NL	162	568	179	48	2	31	(16	15)	324	111	120	144	135	20	114	10	0	6	21	7	.75	15	.315	.451	.570
1997 Houston	NL	162	566	162	40	2	43	(22	21)	335	109	135	142	127	27	122	16	0	8	31	10	.76	10	.286	.425	.592
1998 Houston	NL	147	540	164	33	1	34	(20	14)	301	124	111	125	109	8	90	7	0	5	19	7	.73	14	.304	.424	.557
1999 Houston	NL	162	562	171	35	0	42	(12	30)	332	143	126	148	149	16	127	11	0	7	30	11	.73	18	.304	.454	.591
2000 Houston	NL	159	590	183	37	1	47	(28	19)	363	152	132	144	107	11	116	15	0	7	9	6	.60	19	.310	.424	.615
2001 Houston	NL	161	600	173	43	4	39	(21	18)	341	126	130	130	106	5	135	6	0	5	11	3	.79	20	.288	.397	.568
2002 Houston	NL	158	571	166	33	2	31	(16	15)	296	94	98	109	101	8	130	10	0	9	7	3	.70	16	.291	.401	.518
12 ML YEARS		1795	6520	1969	427	28	380	(191	189)	3592	1293	1321	1445	1199	145	1287	113	3	92	185	70	.73	182	.302	.414	.551

Cory Bailey

Pitches: R **Bats:** R **Pos:** RP-37   **Ht:** 6'1" **Wt:** 210 **Born:** 1/24/71 **Age:** 32

Year Team	Lg	G	GS	CG	GF	IP	BFP	H	R	ER	HR	SH	SF	HB	TBB	IBB	SO	WP	Bk	W	L	Pct	ShO	Sv-Op	Hld	ERC	ERA
2002 Omaha*	AAA	18	0	0	16	19.2	77	13	4	4	0	0	0	0	10	0	17	1	0	1	0	1.000	0	9--	-	2.19	1.83
1993 Boston	AL	11	0	0	5	15.2	66	12	7	6	0	1	1	0	12	3	11	2	1	0	1	.000	0	0-0	0	3.29	3.45
1994 Boston	AL	5	0	0	2	4.1	24	10	6	6	2	0	0	0	3	1	4	0	0	0	1	.000	0	0-1	0	18.76	12.46
1995 St Louis	NL	3	0	0	0	3.2	15	2	3	3	0	0	0	0	2	1	5	1	0	0	0	-	0	0-0	0	1.37	7.36
1996 St Louis	NL	51	0	0	12	57.0	251	57	21	19	1	2	1	1	30	3	38	3	0	5	2	.714	0	0-1	10	3.97	3.00
1997 San Francisco	NL	7	0	0	4	9.2	45	15	9	9	1	0	1	0	4	0	5	0	0	0	0	-	0	0-0	0	7.87	8.38
1998 San Francisco	NL	5	0	0	1	3.1	13	2	1	1	1	0	0	0	1	0	2	0	0	0	0	-	0	0-0	0	2.70	2.70
2001 Kansas City	AL	53	0	0	13	67.1	283	57	28	26	3	3	3	0	33	2	61	4	0	1	1	.500	0	0-1	12	3.20	3.48
2002 Kansas City	AL	37	0	0	14	46.0	211	53	24	21	5	3	2	2	31	7	24	1	1	3	4	.429	0	1-7	5	6.30	4.11
8 ML YEARS		172	0	0	51	207.0	908	208	99	91	13	9	8	3	116	17	150	11	2	9	10	.474	0	1-10	27	4.47	3.96

Paul Bako

Bats: L **Throws:** R **Pos:** C-76; PH-11; PR-3   **Ht:** 6'2" **Wt:** 205 **Born:** 6/20/72 **Age:** 31

Year Team	Lg	G	AB	H	2B	3B	HR	(Hm	Rd)	TB	R	RBI	RC	TBB	IBB	SO	HBP	SH	SF	SB	CS	SB%	GDP	Avg	OBP	Slg
1998 Detroit	AL	96	305	83	12	1	3	(2	1)	106	23	30	34	23	4	82	0	1	4	1	1	.50	3	.272	.319	.348
1999 Houston	NL	73	215	55	14	1	2	(2	0)	77	16	17	26	26	3	57	0	3	3	1	1	.50	4	.256	.332	.358
2000 Hou-Fla-Atl	NL	81	221	50	10	1	2	(2	0)	68	18	20	20	27	10	64	1	1	1	0	0	-	6	.226	.312	.308
2001 Atlanta	NL	61	137	29	10	1	2	(0	2)	47	19	15	15	20	2	34	0	0	0	1	0	1.00	6	.212	.312	.343
2002 Milwaukee	NL	87	234	55	8	1	4	(2	2)	77	24	20	19	20	3	46	0	3	0	0	2	.00	4	.235	.295	.329
2000 Houston	NL	1	2	0	0	0	0	(0	0)	0	0	0	0	0	0	1	0	0	0	0	0	-	0	.000	.000	.000
2000 Florida	NL	56	161	39	6	1	0	(0	0)	47	10	14	16	22	7	48	1	1	1	0	0	-	4	.242	.335	.292
2000 Atlanta	NL	24	58	11	4	0	2	(2	0)	21	8	6	4	5	3	15	0	0	0	0	0	-	2	.190	.254	.362
5 ML YEARS		398	1112	272	54	5	13	(8	5)	375	100	102	114	116	22	283	1	8	8	3	4	.43	20	.245	.314	.337

Rocco Baldelli

Bats: R **Throws:** R **Pos:** CF   **Ht:** 6'4" **Wt:** 187 **Born:** 9/25/81 **Age:** 21

Year Team	Lg	G	AB	H	2B	3B	HR	(Hm	Rd)	TB	R	RBI	RC	TBB	IBB	SO	HBP	SH	SF	SB	CS	SB%	GDP	Avg	OBP	Slg
2000 Princeton	R+	60	232	50	9	2	3	(-	-)	72	33	25	19	12	0	56	5	2	0	11	3	.79	3	.216	.269	.310
2001 Chrlstn - SC	A	113	406	101	23	6	8	(-	-)	160	58	55	50	23	0	89	11	5	6	25	9	.74	7	.249	.303	.394
2002 Bakersfield	A+	77	312	104	19	1	14	(-	-)	167	63	51	63	18	2	63	7	4	1	21	6	.78	2	.333	.382	.535
2002 Orlando	AA	17	70	26	3	1	2	(-	-)	37	10	13	15	5	0	11	2	0	3	3	2	.60	1	.371	.413	.529
2002 Durham	AAA	23	96	28	6	1	3	(-	-)	45	13	7	11	0	0	23	0	2	0	2	5	.29	1	.292	.292	.469

James Baldwin

Pitches: R **Bats:** R **Pos:** SP-23; RP-7 **Ht:** 6'3" **Wt:** 235 **Born:** 7/15/71 **Age:** 31

Year Team	Lg	G	GS	CG	GF	IP	BFP	H	R	ER	HR	SH	SF	HB	TBB	IBB	SO	WP	Bk	W	L	Pct	ShO	Sv-Op	Hld	ERC	ERA
1995 Chicago	AL	6	4	0	0	14.2	81	32	22	21	6	0	0	0	9	1	10	1	0	0	1	.000	0	0-0	0	16.49	12.89
1996 Chicago	AL	28	28	0	0	169.0	719	168	88	83	24	2	3	4	57	3	127	12	1	11	6	.647	0	0-0	0	4.17	4.42
1997 Chicago	AL	32	32	1	0	200.0	879	205	128	117	19	3	6	5	83	3	140	14	3	12	15	.444	0	0-0	0	4.28	5.27
1998 Chicago	AL	37	24	1	3	159.0	712	176	103	94	18	3	5	10	60	2	108	5	1	13	6	.684	0	0-1	0	4.89	5.32
1999 Chicago	AL	35	33	1	1	199.1	886	219	119	113	34	4	7	7	81	1	123	11	1	12	13	.480	0	0-0	0	5.33	5.10
2000 Chicago	AL	29	28	2	0	178.0	758	185	96	92	34	6	5	8	59	3	116	4	1	14	7	.667	1	0-0	0	4.91	4.65
2001 CWS-LA	AL	29	28	2	0	175.0	764	191	95	86	25	7	7	7	63	1	95	7	0	10	11	.476	1	0-0	0	4.94	4.42
2002 Seattle	AL	30	23	0	4	150.0	662	179	95	88	26	4	2	7	49	2	88	1	0	7	10	.412	0	0-0	0	5.70	5.28
2001 Chicago	AL	17	16	2	0	95.2	431	109	56	49	15	3	5	4	38	0	42	4	0	7	5	.583	1	0-0	0	5.44	4.61
2001 Los Angeles	NL	12	12	0	0	79.1	333	82	39	37	10	4	2	3	25	1	53	3	0	3	6	.333	0	0-0	0	4.35	4.20
8 ML YEARS		226	200	7	8	1245.0	5461	1355	746	694	186	29	34	48	461	16	807	55	7	79	69	.534	2	0-1	0	4.98	5.02

Brian Banks

Bats: B **Throws:** R **Pos:** PH-11; RF-5; LF-3; 1B-1; 3B-1 **Ht:** 6'3" **Wt:** 210 **Born:** 9/28/70 **Age:** 32

Year Team	Lg	G	AB	H	2B	3B	HR	(Hm	Rd)	TB	R	RBI	RC	TBB	IBB	SO	HBP	SH	SF	SB	CS	SB%	GDP	Avg	OBP	Slg
2002 Calgary*	AAA	130	439	136	38	3	19	(-	-)	237	90	89	97	73	2	77	6	0	7	10	5	.67	-	.310	.410	.540
1996 Milwaukee	NL	4	7	4	2	0	1	(0	1)	9	2	2	4	1	0	2	0	0	1	0	0	-	0	.571	.625	1.286
1997 Milwaukee	NL	28	68	14	1	0	1	(0	1)	18	9	8	4	6	0	17	0	0	1	0	1	.00	1	.206	.267	.265
1998 Milwaukee	NL	24	24	7	2	0	1	(0	1)	12	3	5	5	4	0	7	0	0	0	0	0	-	0	.292	.393	.500
1999 Milwaukee	NL	105	219	53	7	1	5	(4	1)	77	34	22	26	25	5	59	1	3	2	6	1	.86	2	.242	.317	.352
2002 Florida	NL	20	28	9	1	0	1	(1	0)	13	3	4	4	1	0	6	0	0	0	0	0	-	0	.321	.345	.464
5 ML YEARS		181	346	87	13	1	9	(5	4)	129	51	41	43	37	5	91	0	3	3	6	2	.75	3	.251	.321	.373

Willie Banks

Pitches: R **Bats:** R **Pos:** RP-29 **Ht:** 6'1" **Wt:** 195 **Born:** 2/27/69 **Age:** 34

Year Team	Lg	G	GS	CG	GF	IP	BFP	H	R	ER	HR	SH	SF	HB	TBB	IBB	SO	WP	Bk	W	L	Pct	ShO	Sv-Op	Hld	ERC	ERA
2002 Pawtucket*	AAA	6	4	0	0	26.0	103	20	14	13	2	0	0	1	9	0	15	1	0	1	2	.333	0	1--	-	2.75	4.50
1991 Minnesota	AL	5	3	0	2	17.1	85	21	15	11	1	0	0	0	12	0	16	3	0	1	1	.500	0	0-0	0	6.02	5.71
1992 Minnesota	AL	16	12	0	2	71.0	324	80	46	45	6	2	5	2	37	0	37	5	1	4	4	.500	0	0-0	0	5.30	5.70
1993 Minnesota	AL	31	30	0	1	171.1	754	186	91	77	17	4	4	3	78	2	138	9	5	11	12	.478	0	0-0	0	4.90	4.04
1994 Chicago	NL	23	23	1	0	138.1	598	139	88	83	16	5	2	2	56	3	91	8	1	8	12	.400	1	0-0	0	4.27	5.40
1995 ChC-LA-Fla	NL	25	15	0	2	90.2	430	106	71	57	14	6	3	2	58	7	62	9	1	2	6	.250	0	0-1	1	6.43	5.66
1997 New York	AL	5	1	0	2	14.0	57	9	3	3	0	2	0	1	6	0	8	0	0	3	0	1.000	0	0-1	0	1.96	1.93
1998 NYY-Ari		42	0	0	13	58.0	265	54	37	31	6	6	1	2	37	4	40	5	1	2	3	.400	0	1-2	5	4.59	4.81
2001 Boston	AL	5	0	0	1	10.2	42	5	4	1	0	0	0	0	4	0	10	1	0	0	0	-	0	0-0	0	1.06	0.84
2002 Boston	AL	29	0	0	18	39.0	162	32	15	14	5	0	1	3	14	0	26	1	0	2	1	.667	0	1-1	0	3.45	3.23
1995 Chicago	NL	10	0	0	2	11.2	73	27	23	20	5	1	1	0	12	4	9	3	0	1	0	1.000	0	0-1	1	18.75	15.43
1995 Los Angeles	NL	6	6	0	0	29.0	138	36	21	13	2	1	1	1	16	2	23	4	1	0	2	.000	0	0-0	0	5.82	4.03
1995 Florida	NL	9	9	0	0	50.0	219	43	27	24	7	4	1	1	30	1	30	2	0	2	3	.400	0	0-0	0	4.42	4.32
1998 New York	AL	9	0	0	5	14.1	77	20	16	16	4	2	0	1	12	2	8	1	0	1	1	.500	0	0-0	0	9.74	10.05
1998 Arizona	NL	33	0	0	8	43.2	188	34	21	15	2	4	1	1	25	2	32	4	1	1	2	.333	0	1-2	5	3.14	3.09
9 ML YEARS		181	84	1	40	610.1	2717	632	370	322	65	25	16	15	302	16	428	41	10	33	39	.458	1	2-5	6	4.76	4.75

Rod Barajas

Bats: R **Throws:** R **Pos:** C-68; PH-6; 1B-1 **Ht:** 6'2" **Wt:** 229 **Born:** 9/5/75 **Age:** 27

Year Team	Lg	G	AB	H	2B	3B	HR	(Hm	Rd)	TB	R	RBI	RC	TBB	IBB	SO	HBP	SH	SF	SB	CS	SB%	GDP	Avg	OBP	Slg
2002 Tucson*	AAA	5	16	7	1	0	1	(-	-)	11	2	1	5	1	0	2	0	0	0	0	0	-	0	.438	.471	.688
1999 Arizona	NL	5	16	4	1	0	1	(1	0)	8	3	3	2	1	0	1	0	1	0	0	0	-	0	.250	.294	.500
2000 Arizona	NL	5	13	3	0	0	1	(1	0)	6	1	3	1	0	0	4	0	0	0	0	0	-	0	.231	.231	.462
2001 Arizona	NL	51	106	17	3	0	3	(2	1)	29	9	9	4	4	0	26	0	0	0	0	0	-	0	.160	.191	.274
2002 Arizona	NL	70	154	36	10	0	3	(1	2)	55	12	23	16	10	4	25	3	2	3	1	0	1.00	3	.234	.288	.357
4 ML YEARS		131	289	60	14	0	8	(5	3)	98	25	38	23	15	4	56	3	3	3	1	0	1.00	4	.208	.252	.339

Lorenzo Barcelo

Pitches: R **Bats:** R **Pos:** RP-4 **Ht:** 6'4" **Wt:** 220 **Born:** 8/10/77 **Age:** 25

Year Team	Lg	G	GS	CG	GF	IP	BFP	H	R	ER	HR	SH	SF	HB	TBB	IBB	SO	WP	Bk	W	L	Pct	ShO	Sv-Op	Hld	ERC	ERA
2002 Charlotte*	AAA	2	1	0	0	5.1	23	5	4	4	1	0	0	0	1	0	1	0	0	0	0	-	0	0--	-	3.22	6.75
2000 Chicago	AL	22	1	0	5	39.0	157	34	17	16	5	0	1	0	9	1	26	1	0	4	2	.667	0	0-1	0	2.90	3.69
2001 Chicago	AL	17	0	0	3	21.0	96	24	13	11	1	1	1	1	8	2	15	1	0	0	1	.000	0	0-0	1	4.33	4.71
2002 Chicago	AL	4	0	0	0	6.0	28	9	6	6	1	0	0	0	1	0	1	0	0	0	0	.000	0	0-0	1	6.43	9.00
3 ML YEARS		43	1	0	8	66.0	281	67	36	33	7	1	2	1	18	3	42	2	0	5	3	.625	0	0-1	2	3.65	4.50

Josh Bard

Bats: B **Throws:** R **Pos:** C-24 **Ht:** 6'3" **Wt:** 215 **Born:** 3/20/78 **Age:** 25

Year Team	Lg	G	AB	H	2B	3B	HR	(Hm	Rd)	TB	R	RBI	RC	TBB	IBB	SO	HBP	SH	SF	SB	CS	SB%	GDP	Avg	OBP	Slg
2000 Salem	A+	93	309	88	17	0	2	(-	-)	111	40	25	40	32	1	33	1	1	2	3	1	.75	6	.285	.352	.359
2000 Co Springs	AAA	4	17	4	0	0	0	(-	-)	4	0	1	1	0	0	2	0	0	0	0	0	-	0	.235	.235	.235
2001 Carolina	AA	35	124	32	13	0	1	(-	-)	48	14	24	18	19	1	23	1	1	1	0	1	.00	1	.258	.359	.387
2001 Mahning Vl	A-	13	44	12	4	0	2	(-	-)	22	7	8	8	6	0	2	1	0	0	0	1	.00	1	.273	.373	.500
2001 Akron	AA	51	194	54	11	0	4	(-	-)	77	26	25	26	16	1	27	2	1	1	0	0	-	4	.278	.338	.397

Year Team	Lg	G	AB	H	2B	3B	HR	(Hm	Rd)	TB	R	RBI	RC	TBB	IBB	SO	HBP	SH	SF	SB	CS	SB%	GDP	Avg	OBP	Slg
2001 Buffalo	AAA	1	4	0	0	0	0	(-	-)	0	0	0	0	0	0	1	0	0	0	0	0	-	0	.000	.000	.000
2002 Buffalo	AAA	94	344	102	26	2	6	(-	-)	150	36	53	46	20	0	45	0	3	3	0	0	-	13	.297	.332	.436
2002 Cleveland	AL	24	90	20	5	0	3	(2	1)	34	9	12	7	4	0	13	0	1	0	0	0	-	6	.222	.255	.378

Kevin Barker

Bats: L **Throws:** L **Pos:** 1B-6; PH-1   **Ht:** 6'3" **Wt:** 205 **Born:** 7/26/75 **Age:** 27

								BATTING												BASERUNNING				AVERAGES		
Year Team	Lg	G	AB	H	2B	3B	HR	(Hm	Rd)	TB	R	RBI	RC	TBB	IBB	SO	HBP	SH	SF	SB	CS	SB%	GDP	Avg	OBP	Slg
2002 Portland*	AAA	113	390	98	14	1	14	(-	-)	156	54	48	51	46	2	70	3	0	3	1	1	.50	10	.251	.333	.400
1999 Milwaukee	NL	38	117	33	3	0	3	(1	2)	45	13	23	16	9	1	19	0	0	1	1	0	1.00	0	.282	.331	.385
2000 Milwaukee	NL	40	100	22	5	0	2	(0	2)	33	14	9	14	20	0	21	1	0	1	1	0	1.00	1	.220	.352	.330
2002 San Diego	NL	7	19	3	0	0	0	(0	0)	3	0	0	0	1	0	6	0	0	0	1	0	1.00	1	.158	.200	.158
3 ML YEARS		85	236	58	8	0	5	(1	4)	81	27	32	30	30	1	46	1	0	2	3	0	1.00	2	.246	.331	.343

Michael Barrett

Bats: R **Throws:** R **Pos:** C-110; 1B-6; PH-6   **Ht:** 6'2" **Wt:** 200 **Born:** 10/22/76 **Age:** 26

								BATTING												BASERUNNING				AVERAGES		
Year Team	Lg	G	AB	H	2B	3B	HR	(Hm	Rd)	TB	R	RBI	RC	TBB	IBB	SO	HBP	SH	SF	SB	CS	SB%	GDP	Avg	OBP	Slg
1998 Montreal	NL	8	23	7	2	0	1	(0	1)	12	3	2	5	3	0	6	1	0	0	0	0	-	0	.304	.407	.522
1999 Montreal	NL	126	433	127	32	3	8	(5	3)	189	53	52	59	32	4	39	3	0	1	0	2	.00	18	.293	.345	.436
2000 Montreal	NL	89	271	58	15	1	1	(0	1)	78	28	22	19	23	5	35	1	0	1	0	1	.00	7	.214	.277	.288
2001 Montreal	NL	132	472	118	33	2	6	(3	3)	173	42	38	46	25	2	54	2	4	3	2	1	.67	14	.250	.289	.367
2002 Montreal	NL	117	376	99	20	1	12	(4	8)	157	41	49	49	40	7	65	1	6	5	6	3	.67	14	.263	.332	.418
5 ML YEARS		472	1575	409	102	7	28	(12	16)	609	167	163	178	123	18	199	8	11	10	8	7	.53	53	.260	.315	.387

Miguel Batista

Pitches: R **Bats:** R **Pos:** SP-29; RP-7   **Ht:** 6'2" **Wt:** 195 **Born:** 2/19/71 **Age:** 32

					HOW MUCH HE PITCHED					WHAT HE GAVE UP										THE RESULTS						
Year Team	Lg	G	GS	CG	GF	IP	BFP	H	R	ER	HR	SH	SF	HB	TBB	IBB	SO	WP	Bk	W	L	Pct	ShO	Sv-Op	Hld	ERC	ERA
1992 Pittsburgh	NL	1	0	0	1	2.0	9	4	2	2	1	0	0	0	3	0	1	0	0	0	0	-	0	0-0	0	20.26	9.00
1996 Florida	NL	9	0	0	4	11.1	49	9	8	7	0	3	0	0	7	2	6	1	0	0	0	-	0	0-0	0	2.77	5.56
1997 Chicago	NL	11	6	0	2	36.1	168	36	24	23	4	4	4	1	24	2	27	2	0	0	5	.000	0	0-0	0	5.09	5.70
1998 Montreal	NL	56	13	0	12	135.0	598	141	66	57	12	7	5	6	65	7	92	6	1	3	5	.375	0	0-0	3	4.70	3.80
1999 Montreal	NL	39	17	2	3	134.2	606	146	88	73	10	8	11	7	58	2	95	6	0	8	7	.533	1	1-1	0	4.62	4.88
2000 Mon-KC		18	9	0	2	65.1	310	85	68	62	19	1	2	2	37	2	37	4	0	2	7	.222	0	0-2	0	8.37	8.54
2001 Arizona	NL	48	18	0	6	139.1	581	113	57	52	13	9	3	10	60	2	90	6	0	11	8	.579	0	0-0	4	3.43	3.36
2002 Arizona	NL	36	29	1	2	184.2	790	172	99	88	12	5	8	6	70	3	112	9	2	8	9	.471	0	0-0	2	3.45	4.29
2000 Montreal	NL	4	0	0	0	8.1	49	19	14	13	2	1	1	2	3	0	7	0	0	0	1	.000	0	0-2	0	14.73	14.04
2000 Kansas City		14	9	0	2	57.0	261	66	54	49	17	0	1	0	34	2	30	4	0	2	6	.250	0	0-0	0	7.50	7.74
8 ML YEARS		218	92	3	32	708.2	3115	706	412	364	71	37	33	32	324	20	460	34	3	32	41	.438	1	1-3	9	4.42	4.62

Tony Batista

Bats: R **Throws:** R **Pos:** 3B-154; DH-7   **Ht:** 6'0" **Wt:** 205 **Born:** 12/9/73 **Age:** 29

								BATTING												BASERUNNING				AVERAGES		
Year Team	Lg	G	AB	H	2B	3B	HR	(Hm	Rd)	TB	R	RBI	RC	TBB	IBB	SO	HBP	SH	SF	SB	CS	SB%	GDP	Avg	OBP	Slg
1996 Oakland	AL	74	238	71	10	2	6	(1	5)	103	38	25	37	19	0	49	1	0	2	7	3	.70	2	.298	.350	.433
1997 Oakland	AL	68	188	38	10	1	4	(0	4)	62	22	18	14	14	0	31	2	3	0	2	2	.50	8	.202	.265	.330
1998 Arizona	NL	106	293	80	16	1	18	(9	9)	152	46	41	46	18	0	52	3	0	4	1	1	.50	7	.273	.318	.519
1999 Ari-Tor		142	519	144	30	1	31	(10	21)	269	77	100	87	38	4	96	6	3	7	4	0	1.00	12	.277	.330	.518
2000 Toronto	AL	154	620	163	32	2	41	(25	16)	322	96	114	94	35	1	121	6	0	3	5	4	.56	15	.263	.307	.519
2001 Tor-Bal	AL	156	579	138	27	6	25	(14	11)	252	70	87	70	32	1	113	4	0	7	5	2	.71	9	.238	.280	.435
2002 Baltimore	AL	161	615	150	36	1	31	(14	17)	281	90	87	80	50	9	107	11	0	6	5	4	.56	13	.244	.309	.457
1999 Arizona	NL	44	144	37	5	0	5	(1	4)	57	16	21	21	16	3	17	2	0	2	2	0	1.00	1	.257	.335	.396
1999 Toronto	AL	98	375	107	25	1	26	(9	17)	212	61	79	66	22	1	79	4	3	5	2	0	1.00	11	.285	.328	.565
2001 Toronto	AL	72	271	56	11	1	13	(9	4)	108	29	45	27	13	1	66	4	0	3	0	1	.00	2	.207	.251	.399
2001 Baltimore	AL	84	308	82	16	5	12	(5	7)	144	41	42	43	19	0	47	0	0	4	5	1	.83	7	.266	.305	.468
7 ML YEARS		861	3052	784	161	14	156	(73	83)	1441	439	472	428	206	15	569	33	6	29	29	16	.64	66	.257	.308	.472

Rick Bauer

Pitches: R **Bats:** R **Pos:** RP-55; SP-1   **Ht:** 6'6" **Wt:** 212 **Born:** 1/10/77 **Age:** 26

					HOW MUCH HE PITCHED					WHAT HE GAVE UP										THE RESULTS						
Year Team	Lg	G	GS	CG	GF	IP	BFP	H	R	ER	HR	SH	SF	HB	TBB	IBB	SO	WP	Bk	W	L	Pct	ShO	Sv-Op	Hld	ERC	ERA
1997 Bluefield	R+	13	13	0	0	72.1	294	58	31	23	1	0	4	4	20	0	67	8	0	8	3	.727	0	0- -	-	2.24	2.86
1997 Delmarva	A	1	0	0	0	2.0	7	0	0	0	0	0	0	0	1	0	2	0	0	0	0	-	0	1- -	-	0.27	0.00
1998 Delmarva	A	22	22	1	0	118.0	505	127	69	62	11	5	2	8	44	0	81	6	0	5	8	.385	1	0- -	-	4.79	4.73
1999 Frederick	A+	26	26	4	0	152.0	662	159	85	77	17	3	11	12	54	2	123	11	1	10	9	.526	0	0- -	-	4.57	4.56
2000 Bowie	AA	23	23	1	1	129.0	583	154	89	76	16	3	3	12	39	1	87	4	0	6	8	.429	0	1- -	-	5.31	5.30
2000 Frederick	A+	3	3	0	0	19.0	79	20	13	11	1	0	1	0	6	0	15	2	0	0	1	.000	0	0- -	-	3.83	5.21
2001 Bowie	AA	9	9	2	0	61.0	247	52	27	24	8	1	2	5	10	0	34	1	0	2	6	.250	0	0- -	-	2.88	3.54
2001 Rochester	AAA	19	18	1	0	113.1	493	119	63	49	10	5	3	4	28	0	89	4	0	10	4	.714	1	0- -	-	3.70	3.89
2002 Rochester	AAA	1	1	0	0	4.0	18	4	4	3	2	0	1	0	2	0	1	0	0	0	1	.000	0	0- -	-	7.30	6.75
2001 Baltimore	AL	6	6	0	0	33.0	143	35	22	17	7	0	1	1	9	0	16	0	0	0	5	.000	0	0-0	0	4.74	4.64
2002 Baltimore	AL	56	1	0	17	83.2	358	84	41	37	12	2	2	4	36	4	45	4	0	6	7	.462	0	1-5	12	4.78	3.98
2 ML YEARS		62	7	0	17	116.2	501	119	63	54	19	2	3	5	45	4	61	4	0	6	12	.333	0	1-5	12	4.78	4.17

Danny Bautista

Bats: R **Throws:** R **Pos:** RF-37; CF-5; PH-1   **Ht:** 5'11" **Wt:** 204 **Born:** 5/24/72 **Age:** 31

Year Team	Lg	G	AB	H	2B	3B	HR	(Hm	Rd)	TB	R	RBI	RC	TBB	IBB	SO	HBP	SH	SF	SB	CS	SB%	GDP	Avg	OBP	Slg
1993 Detroit	AL	17	61	19	3	0	1	(0	1)	25	6	9	8	1	0	10	0	0	1	3	1	.75	1	.311	.317	.410
1994 Detroit	AL	31	99	23	4	1	4	(1	3)	41	12	15	9	3	0	18	0	0	0	1	2	.33	1	.232	.255	.414
1995 Detroit	AL	89	271	55	9	0	7	(3	4)	85	28	27	18	12	0	68	0	6	0	4	1	.80	6	.203	.237	.314
1996 Det-Atl		42	84	19	2	0	2	(1	1)	27	13	9	8	11	0	20	1	0	0	1	2	.33	4	.226	.323	.321
1997 Atlanta	NL	64	103	25	3	2	3	(1	2)	41	14	9	11	5	1	24	1	2	1	2	0	1.00	4	.243	.282	.398
1998 Atlanta	NL	82	144	36	11	0	3	(2	1)	56	17	17	15	7	0	21	0	3	2	1	0	1.00	4	.250	.281	.389
1999 Florida	NL	70	205	59	10	1	5	(2	3)	86	32	24	25	4	0	30	1	0	1	3	0	1.00	5	.288	.303	.420
2000 Fla-Ari	NL	131	351	100	20	7	11	(5	6)	167	54	59	54	25	4	50	3	4	5	6	2	.75	11	.285	.333	.476
2001 Arizona	NL	100	222	67	11	2	5	(0	5)	97	26	26	31	14	1	31	1	2	0	3	2	.60	7	.302	.346	.437
2002 Arizona	NL	40	154	50	5	2	6	(4	2)	77	22	23	26	11	2	21	0	0	1	4	2	.67	1	.325	.367	.500
1996 Detroit	AL	25	64	16	2	0	2	(1	1)	24	12	8	8	9	0	15	0	0	0	1	2	.33	1	.250	.342	.375
1996 Atlanta	NL	17	20	3	0	0	0	(0	0)	3	1	1	0	2	0	5	1	0	0	0	0	-	3	.150	.261	.150
2000 Florida	NL	44	89	17	4	0	4	(1	3)	33	9	12	8	5	0	20	0	0	0	1	0	1.00	1	.191	.234	.371
2000 Arizona	NL	87	262	83	16	7	7	(4	3)	134	45	47	46	20	4	30	3	4	5	5	2	.71	10	.317	.366	.511
10 ML YEARS		666	1694	453	78	15	47	(19	28)	702	224	218	205	93	8	293	7	17	11	28	12	.70	48	.267	.306	.414

Steve Bechler

Pitches: R **Bats:** R **Pos:** RP-3   **Ht:** 6'2" **Wt:** 239 **Born:** 11/18/79

Year Team	Lg	G	GS	CG	GF	IP	BFP	H	R	ER	HR	SH	SF	HB	TBB	IBB	SO	WP	Bk	W	L	Pct	ShO	Sv-Op	Hld	ERC	ERA
1998 Orioles	R	9	9	0	0	49.2	209	51	22	15	4	1	1	1	8	0	39	4	1	2	4	.333	0	0--	-	3.17	2.72
1999 Delmarva	A	26	26	1	0	152.1	642	137	69	60	12	5	2	4	58	0	139	9	0	8	12	.400	1	0--	-	3.42	3.54
2000 Frederick	A+	27	27	2	0	162.0	712	179	98	87	19	3	1	6	57	1	137	6	0	8	12	.400	0	0--	-	4.75	4.83
2001 Frederick	A+	13	13	1	0	83.1	330	73	24	21	3	3	4	2	22	0	71	3	0	5	2	.714	1	0--	-	2.69	2.27
2001 Rochester	AAA	2	2	0	0	7.1	44	14	14	13	4	0	0	0	5	0	6	2	0	1	1	.500	0	0--	-	14.39	15.95
2001 Bowie	AA	12	12	2	0	79.0	306	63	31	27	14	0	0	1	15	0	58	3	0	3	5	.375	0	0--	-	2.78	3.08
2002 Bowie	AA	4	4	0	0	23.2	100	28	11	9	2	1	0	1	6	0	13	3	0	2	1	.667	0	0--	-	4.77	3.42
2002 Rochester	AAA	24	24	2	0	149.2	648	154	78	68	15	6	6	2	52	2	77	5	0	6	11	.353	1	0--	-	4.03	4.09
2002 Baltimore	AL	3	0	0	0	4.2	25	6	7	7	3	0	0	1	4	0	3	0	0	0	0	-	0	0-0	0	13.72	13.50

Rod Beck

Pitches: R **Bats:** R **Pos:** RP   **Ht:** 6'1" **Wt:** 235 **Born:** 8/3/68 **Age:** 34

Year Team	Lg	G	GS	CG	GF	IP	BFP	H	R	ER	HR	SH	SF	HB	TBB	IBB	SO	WP	Bk	W	L	Pct	ShO	Sv-Op	Hld	ERC	ERA
1991 San Francisco	NL	31	0	0	10	52.1	214	53	22	22	4	4	2	1	13	2	38	0	0	1	1	.500	0	1-1	1	3.52	3.78
1992 San Francisco	NL	65	0	0	42	92.0	352	62	20	18	4	6	2	2	15	2	87	5	2	3	3	.500	0	17-23	4	1.44	1.76
1993 San Francisco	NL	76	0	0	71	79.1	309	57	20	19	11	6	3	1	13	4	86	4	0	3	1	.750	0	48-52	0	2.05	2.16
1994 San Francisco	NL	48	0	0	47	48.2	207	49	17	15	10	3	3	0	13	2	39	0	0	2	4	.333	0	28-28	0	4.17	2.77
1995 San Francisco	NL	60	0	0	52	58.2	255	60	31	29	7	4	3	0	21	3	42	2	0	5	6	.455	0	33-43	0	4.20	4.45
1996 San Francisco	NL	63	0	0	58	62.0	248	56	23	23	9	0	2	1	10	2	48	1	0	0	9	.000	0	35-42	0	2.95	3.34
1997 San Francisco	NL	73	0	0	66	70.0	281	67	31	27	7	1	0	2	8	2	53	1	0	7	4	.636	0	37-45	1	2.84	3.47
1998 Chicago	NL	81	0	0	70	80.1	349	86	33	27	11	2	5	2	20	4	81	2	0	3	4	.429	0	51-58	1	4.05	3.02
1999 ChC-Bos		43	0	0	27	44.0	196	50	29	29	5	2	2	1	18	3	25	1	0	2	5	.286	0	10-15	3	4.99	5.93
2000 Boston	AL	34	0	0	8	40.2	169	34	15	14	2	2	0	2	12	1	35	1	0	3	0	1.000	0	0-3	7	2.59	3.10
2001 Boston	AL	68	0	0	28	80.2	342	77	42	35	15	3	2	3	28	6	63	5	1	6	4	.600	0	6-11	15	4.25	3.90
1999 Chicago	NL	31	0	0	19	30.0	141	41	26	26	5	2	2	0	13	3	13	1	0	2	4	.333	0	7-11	1	6.75	7.80
1999 Boston	AL	12	0	0	8	14.0	55	9	3	3	0	0	0	1	5	0	12	0	0	0	1	.000	0	3-4	2	1.79	1.93
11 ML YEARS		642	0	0	479	708.2	2922	651	283	258	85	33	24	19	171	31	597	22	3	35	41	.461	0	266-321	32	3.18	3.28

Josh Beckett

Pitches: R **Bats:** R **Pos:** SP-21; RP-2   **Ht:** 6'5" **Wt:** 216 **Born:** 5/15/80 **Age:** 23

Year Team	Lg	G	GS	CG	GF	IP	BFP	H	R	ER	HR	SH	SF	HB	TBB	IBB	SO	WP	Bk	W	L	Pct	ShO	Sv-Op	Hld	ERC	ERA
2000 Kane County	A	13	12	0	0	59.1	232	45	18	14	4	5	0	2	15	0	61	1	1	2	3	.400	0	0--	-	2.26	2.12
2001 Brevard Cnty	A+	13	12	0	0	65.2	238	32	13	9	0	2	1	0	15	0	101	1	1	6	0	1.000	0	0--	-	0.90	1.23
2001 Portland	AA	13	13	0	0	74.1	286	50	16	15	8	0	1	4	19	0	102	1	1	8	1	.889	0	0--	-	2.17	1.82
2002 Jupiter	A+	1	1	0	0	6.0	24	4	0	0	0	0	0	0	1	0	12	0	0	1	0	1.000	0	0--	-	1.18	0.00
2002 Marlins	R	1	1	0	0	4.0	13	5	2	2	0	0	0	0	1	0	7	1	0	0	0	-	0	0--	-	5.82	4.50
2001 Florida	NL	4	4	0	0	24.0	99	14	9	4	3	0	0	1	11	0	24	1	0	2	2	.500	0	0-0	-	2.36	1.50
2002 Florida	NL	23	21	0	0	107.2	454	93	56	49	13	5	3	1	44	2	113	5	0	6	7	.462	0	0-0	-	3.50	4.10
2 ML YEARS		27	25	0	0	131.2	553	107	65	53	16	5	3	2	55	2	137	6	0	8	9	.471	0	0-0	-	3.28	3.62

Erik Bedard

Pitches: L **Bats:** L **Pos:** RP-2   **Ht:** 6'1" **Wt:** 186 **Born:** 3/6/79 **Age:** 24

Year Team	Lg	G	GS	CG	GF	IP	BFP	H	R	ER	HR	SH	SF	HB	TBB	IBB	SO	WP	Bk	W	L	Pct	ShO	Sv-Op	Hld	ERC	ERA
1999 Orioles	R	8	6	0	1	29.0	117	20	7	6	1	0	0	0	13	0	41	3	0	2	1	.667	0	0--	-	2.25	1.86
2000 Delmarva	A	29	22	1	2	111.0	466	98	48	44	2	1	0	10	35	0	131	14	0	9	4	.692	1	2--	-	2.91	3.57
2001 Frederick	A+	17	17	0	0	96.1	382	80	27	23	4	3	1	9	26	0	130	3	0	9	2	.818	0	0--	-	2.09	2.15
2001 Orioles	R	2	2	0	0	6.0	25	4	2	2	0	0	0	2	3	0	7	0	0	1	0	1.000	0	0--	-	3.36	3.00
2002 Bowie	AA	13	12	0	1	68.2	282	43	18	15	0	2	3	3	30	0	66	6	0	6	3	.667	0	0--	-	1.79	1.97
2002 Baltimore	AL	2	0	0	0	0.2	4	2	1	1	0	0	0	0	0	0	1	0	0	0	0	-	0	0-0	0	14.52	13.50

Joe Beimel

Pitches: L **Bats:** L **Pos:** RP-45; SP-8   **Ht:** 6'3" **Wt:** 215 **Born:** 4/19/77 **Age:** 26

Year Team	Lg	G	GS	CG	GF	IP	BFP	H	R	ER	HR	SH	SF	HB	TBB	IBB	SO	WP	Bk	W	L	Pct	ShO	Sv-Op	Hld	ERC	ERA
1998 Erie	A-	17	6	0	3	47.0	220	56	39	33	6	3	1	5	22	0	37	3	1	1	4	.200	0	0--	-	6.11	6.32
1999 Hickory	A	29	22	0	3	130.0	570	146	81	64	12	4	5	12	43	0	102	10	2	5	11	.313	0	0--	-	4.89	4.43
2000 Lynchburg	A+	18	18	2	0	120.2	515	111	49	45	6	7	6	8	44	1	82	2	0	10	6	.625	1	0--	-	3.39	3.36
2000 Altoona	AA	10	10	1	0	62.2	279	72	38	29	8	0	2	6	21	0	28	1	3	1	6	.143	0	0--	-	5.30	4.16
2001 Pittsburgh	NL	42	15	0	9	115.1	511	131	72	67	12	3	1	6	49	4	58	3	0	7	11	.389	0	0-0	0	5.24	5.23
2002 Pittsburgh	NL	53	8	0	8	85.1	391	88	49	44	9	7	3	4	45	12	53	2	0	2	5	.286	0	0-1	5	4.65	4.64
2 ML YEARS		95	23	0	17	200.2	902	219	121	111	21	10	4	10	94	16	111	5	0	9	16	.360	0	0-1	5	4.98	4.98

Kevin Beirne

Pitches: R **Bats:** L **Pos:** RP-9; SP-3   **Ht:** 6'4" **Wt:** 210 **Born:** 1/1/74 **Age:** 29

Year Team	Lg	G	GS	CG	GF	IP	BFP	H	R	ER	HR	SH	SF	HB	TBB	IBB	SO	WP	Bk	W	L	Pct	ShO	Sv-Op	Hld	ERC	ERA
2002 Las Vegas*	AAA	22	22	0	0	125.2	538	129	64	58	12	4	4	9	41	0	88	4	0	10	3	.769	0	0--	-	4.24	4.15
2002 Vero Beach*	A+	1	0	0	0	2.0	7	1	0	0	0	0	0	0	0	0	2	0	0	0	0	-	0	0--	-	0.54	0.00
2000 Chicago	AL	29	1	0	8	49.2	220	50	41	37	9	1	5	4	20	1	41	1	0	1	3	.250	0	0-1	0	4.97	6.70
2001 Toronto	AL	5	0	0	2	7.0	40	13	10	10	1	1	0	0	6	1	5	0	0	0	0	-	0	0-0	0	11.51	12.86
2002 Los Angeles	NL	12	3	0	5	29.0	127	26	11	11	4	1	1	2	17	2	17	4	0	2	0	1.000	0	0-1	0	4.75	3.41
3 ML YEARS		46	4	0	15	85.2	387	89	62	58	14	3	6	6	43	4	63	5	0	3	3	.500	0	0-2	0	5.39	6.09

David Bell

Bats: R **Throws:** R **Pos:** 3B-139; 2B-12; PH-7; SS-3; 1B-2   **Ht:** 5'10" **Wt:** 195 **Born:** 9/14/72 **Age:** 30

Year Team	Lg	G	AB	H	2B	3B	HR	(Hm	Rd)	TB	R	RBI	RC	TBB	IBB	SO	HBP	SH	SF	SB	CS	SB%	GDP	Avg	OBP	Slg
1995 Cle-Stl		41	146	36	7	2	2	(1	1)	53	13	19	14	4	0	25	2	0	1	1	2	.33	0	.247	.275	.363
1996 St Louis	NL	62	145	31	6	0	1	(1	0)	40	12	9	9	10	2	22	1	0	1	1	1	.50	3	.214	.268	.276
1997 St Louis	NL	66	142	30	7	2	1	(1	0)	44	9	12	11	10	2	28	0	2	1	1	0	1.00	6	.211	.261	.310
1998 Stl-Cle-Sea		132	429	117	30	2	10	(2	8)	181	48	49	53	27	4	65	2	1	5	0	4	.00	11	.273	.315	.422
1999 Seattle	AL	157	597	160	31	2	21	(11	10)	258	92	78	87	58	0	90	2	3	7	7	4	.64	7	.268	.331	.432
2000 Seattle	AL	133	454	112	24	2	11	(4	7)	173	57	47	54	42	0	66	6	6	4	2	3	.40	11	.247	.316	.381
2001 Seattle	AL	135	470	122	28	0	15	(7	8)	195	62	64	58	28	1	59	3	5	4	2	1	.67	8	.260	.303	.415
2002 San Francisco	NL	154	552	144	29	2	20	(7	13)	237	82	73	79	54	2	80	9	6	7	1	2	.33	18	.261	.333	.429
1995 Cleveland	AL	2	2	0	0	0	0	(0	0)	0	0	0	0	0	0	0	0	0	0	0	0	-	0	.000	.000	.000
1995 St Louis	NL	39	144	36	7	2	2	(1	1)	53	13	19	14	4	0	25	2	0	1	1	2	.33	0	.250	.278	.368
1998 St Louis	NL	4	9	2	1	0	0	(0	0)	3	0	0	1	0	0	3	0	0	0	0	0	-	0	.222	.222	.333
1998 Cleveland	AL	107	340	89	21	2	10	(2	8)	144	37	41	41	22	4	54	2	1	5	0	4	.00	8	.262	.306	.424
1998 Seattle	AL	21	80	26	8	0	0	(0	0)	34	11	8	11	5	0	8	0	0	0	0	0	-	3	.325	.365	.425
8 ML YEARS		880	2935	752	162	12	81	(34	47)	1181	375	351	365	233	11	435	25	23	30	15	17	.47	60	.256	.313	.402

Jay Bell

Bats: R **Throws:** R **Pos:** PH-20; 3B-6; 1B-5; 2B-2; SS-2   **Ht:** 6'0" **Wt:** 184 **Born:** 12/11/65 **Age:** 37

Year Team	Lg	G	AB	H	2B	3B	HR	(Hm	Rd)	TB	R	RBI	RC	TBB	IBB	SO	HBP	SH	SF	SB	CS	SB%	GDP	Avg	OBP	Slg
2002 Tucson*	AAA	7	22	5	3	0	0	(-	-)	8	4	2	3	4	0	1	0	0	0	0	0	-	1	.227	.346	.364
2002 Lancaster*	A+	7	20	4	1	0	1	(-	-)	8	4	7	3	4	0	6	0	0	0	0	0	-	1	.200	.333	.400
1986 Cleveland	AL	5	14	5	2	0	1	(0	1)	10	3	4	4	2	0	3	0	0	0	0	0	-	0	.357	.438	.714
1987 Cleveland	AL	38	125	27	9	1	2	(1	1)	44	14	13	12	8	0	31	1	3	0	2	0	1.00	5	.216	.269	.352
1988 Cleveland	AL	73	211	46	5	1	2	(2	0)	59	23	21	17	21	0	53	1	1	2	4	2	.67	3	.218	.289	.280
1989 Pittsburgh	NL	78	271	70	13	3	2	(1	1)	95	33	27	27	19	0	47	1	10	2	5	3	.63	9	.258	.307	.351
1990 Pittsburgh	NL	159	583	148	28	7	7	(1	6)	211	93	52	71	65	0	109	3	39	6	10	6	.63	14	.254	.329	.362
1991 Pittsburgh	NL	157	608	164	32	8	16	(7	9)	260	96	67	84	52	1	99	4	30	3	10	6	.63	15	.270	.330	.428
1992 Pittsburgh	NL	159	632	167	36	9	9	(5	4)	248	87	55	79	55	0	103	4	19	2	7	5	.58	12	.264	.326	.383
1993 Pittsburgh	NL	154	604	187	32	9	9	(3	6)	264	102	51	102	77	6	122	6	13	1	16	10	.62	16	.310	.392	.437
1994 Pittsburgh	NL	110	424	117	35	4	9	(3	6)	187	68	45	64	49	1	82	3	8	3	2	0	1.00	15	.276	.353	.441
1995 Pittsburgh	NL	138	530	139	28	4	13	(8	5)	214	79	55	69	55	1	110	4	3	1	2	5	.29	13	.262	.336	.404
1996 Pittsburgh	NL	151	527	132	29	3	13	(7	6)	206	65	71	67	54	5	108	5	6	6	4	6	.40	10	.250	.323	.391
1997 Kansas City	AL	153	573	167	28	3	21	(10	11)	264	89	92	97	71	2	101	4	3	9	10	6	.63	13	.291	.368	.461
1998 Arizona	NL	155	549	138	29	5	20	(11	9)	237	79	67	83	81	3	129	7	5	3	3	5	.38	14	.251	.353	.432
1999 Arizona	NL	151	589	170	32	6	38	(21	17)	328	132	112	121	82	2	132	4	4	9	7	4	.64	9	.289	.374	.557
2000 Arizona	NL	149	565	151	30	6	18	(9	9)	247	87	68	89	70	0	88	3	6	5	7	3	.70	7	.267	.348	.437
2001 Arizona	NL	129	428	106	24	1	13	(6	7)	171	59	46	62	65	3	79	4	8	4	0	1	.00	9	.248	.349	.400
2002 Arizona	NL	32	49	8	1	0	2	(0	2)	15	3	11	6	5	0	9	1	0	1	0	0	-	2	.163	.250	.306
17 ML YEARS		1991	7282	1942	393	67	195	(95	100)	3054	1112	857	1054	831	24	1405	55	158	57	91	60	.60	161	.267	.344	.419

Rob Bell

Pitches: R **Bats:** R **Pos:** SP-15; RP-2   **Ht:** 6'5" **Wt:** 225 **Born:** 1/17/77 **Age:** 26

Year Team	Lg	G	GS	CG	GF	IP	BFP	H	R	ER	HR	SH	SF	HB	TBB	IBB	SO	WP	Bk	W	L	Pct	ShO	Sv-Op	Hld	ERC	ERA
2002 Oklahoma*	AAA	12	11	2	1	75.1	312	70	36	34	10	0	2	2	25	0	55	3	0	5	0	1.000	2	0--	-	3.81	4.06
2002 Tulsa*	AA	1	1	0	0	8.0	26	4	0	0	0	0	0	0	0	0	5	0	0	1	0	1.000	0	0--	-	0.58	0.00
2000 Cincinnati	NL	26	26	1	0	140.1	625	130	84	78	32	8	7	3	73	6	112	11	0	7	8	.467	0	0-0	0	4.98	5.00
2001 Cin-Tex		27	27	0	0	149.2	670	176	115	111	32	3	9	7	64	1	97	9	0	5	10	.333	0	0-0	0	6.40	6.67
2002 Texas	AL	17	15	0	0	94.0	425	113	69	65	16	1	6	1	35	0	70	7	0	4	3	.571	0	0-0	0	5.67	6.22
2001 Cincinnati	NL	9	9	0	0	44.1	188	46	28	27	9	0	1	3	17	1	33	1	0	0	5	.000	0	0-0	0	5.43	5.48
2001 Texas	AL	18	18	0	0	105.1	482	130	87	84	23	3	8	4	47	0	64	8	0	5	5	.500	0	0-0	0	6.82	7.18
3 ML YEARS		70	68	1	0	384.0	1713	419	268	254	80	12	17	9	172	7	279	27	0	16	21	.432	0	0-0	0	5.69	5.95

Mark Bellhorn

Bats: B **Throws:** R **Pos:** 2B-77; 3B-36; 1B-22; PH-22; SS-12; PR-2   **Ht:** 6'1" **Wt:** 205 **Born:** 8/23/74 **Age:** 28

Year Team	Lg	G	AB	H	2B	3B	HR	(Hm	Rd)	TB	R	RBI	RC	TBB	IBB	SO	HBP	SH	SF	SB	CS	SB%	GDP	Avg	OBP	Slg
1997 Oakland	AL	68	224	51	9	1	6	(3	3)	80	33	19	29	32	0	70	0	5	0	7	1	.88	1	.228	.324	.357
1998 Oakland	AL	11	12	1	1	0	0	(0	0)	2	1	1	1	3	0	4	1	0	0	2	0	1.00	0	.083	.313	.167
2000 Oakland	AL	9	13	2	0	0	0	(0	0)	2	2	0	1	2	0	6	0	0	0	0	0	-	0	.154	.267	.154
2001 Oakland	AL	38	74	10	1	2	1	(1	0)	18	11	4	3	7	0	37	0	1	0	0	0	-	1	.135	.210	.243
2002 Chicago	NL	146	445	115	24	4	27	(15	12)	228	86	56	80	76	3	144	6	2	0	7	5	.58	6	.258	.374	.512
5 ML YEARS		272	768	179	35	7	34	(19	15)	330	133	80	114	120	3	261	7	8	0	16	6	.73	8	.233	.342	.430

Ronnie Belliard

Bats: R **Throws:** R **Pos:** 2B-49; 3B-42; PH-26; PR-9   **Ht:** 5'8" **Wt:** 197 **Born:** 4/7/75 **Age:** 28

Year Team	Lg	G	AB	H	2B	3B	HR	(Hm	Rd)	TB	R	RBI	RC	TBB	IBB	SO	HBP	SH	SF	SB	CS	SB%	GDP	Avg	OBP	Slg
1998 Milwaukee	NL	8	5	1	0	0	0	(0	0)	1	0	0	0	0	0	0	0	0	0	0	0	-	0	.200	.200	.200
1999 Milwaukee	NL	124	457	135	29	4	8	(5	3)	196	60	58	72	64	0	59	0	6	4	4	5	.44	16	.295	.379	.429
2000 Milwaukee	NL	152	571	150	30	9	8	(4	4)	222	83	54	81	82	4	84	3	4	7	7	5	.58	12	.263	.354	.389
2001 Milwaukee	NL	101	364	96	30	3	11	(7	4)	165	69	36	56	35	2	65	5	4	2	5	2	.71	5	.264	.335	.453
2002 Milwaukee	NL	104	289	61	13	0	3	(0	3)	83	30	26	14	18	0	46	1	6	3	2	3	.40	8	.211	.257	.287
5 ML YEARS		489	1686	443	102	16	30	(16	14)	667	243	174	223	199	6	254	9	20	16	18	15	.55	41	.263	.341	.396

Clay Bellinger

Bats: R **Throws:** R **Pos:** 1B-1; PH-1   **Ht:** 6'3" **Wt:** 215 **Born:** 11/18/68 **Age:** 34

Year Team	Lg	G	AB	H	2B	3B	HR	(Hm	Rd)	TB	R	RBI	RC	TBB	IBB	SO	HBP	SH	SF	SB	CS	SB%	GDP	Avg	OBP	Slg
2002 Salt Lake*	AAA	89	324	83	17	5	13	(-	-)	149	45	41	41	13	0	87	2	1	0	4	2	.67	8	.256	.289	.460
1999 New York	AL	32	45	9	2	0	1	(1	0)	14	12	2	3	1	0	10	0	0	0	1	0	1.00	1	.200	.217	.311
2000 New York	AL	98	184	38	8	2	6	(2	4)	68	33	21	21	17	1	48	5	1	2	5	0	1.00	1	.207	.288	.370
2001 New York	AL	51	81	13	1	1	5	(2	3)	31	12	12	5	4	0	23	1	1	1	1	2	.33	2	.160	.207	.383
2002 Anaheim	AL	2	1	0	0	0	0	(0	0)	0	0	0	0	0	0	1	0	0	0	0	0	-	0	.000	.000	.000
4 ML YEARS		183	311	60	11	3	12	(5	7)	113	57	35	29	22	1	82	6	2	3	7	2	.78	4	.193	.257	.363

Carlos Beltran

Bats: B **Throws:** R **Pos:** CF-149; DH-12; PH-1   **Ht:** 6'1" **Wt:** 190 **Born:** 4/24/77 **Age:** 26

Year Team	Lg	G	AB	H	2B	3B	HR	(Hm	Rd)	TB	R	RBI	RC	TBB	IBB	SO	HBP	SH	SF	SB	CS	SB%	GDP	Avg	OBP	Slg
1998 Kansas City	AL	14	58	16	5	3	0	(0	0)	27	12	7	9	3	0	12	1	0	1	3	0	1.00	2	.276	.317	.466
1999 Kansas City	AL	156	663	194	27	7	22	(12	10)	301	112	108	100	46	2	123	4	0	10	27	8	.77	17	.293	.337	.454
2000 Kansas City	AL	98	372	92	15	4	7	(4	3)	136	49	44	43	35	2	69	0	2	4	13	0	1.00	10	.247	.309	.366
2001 Kansas City	AL	155	617	189	32	12	24	(7	17)	317	106	101	118	52	2	120	5	1	5	31	1	.97	7	.306	.362	.514
2002 Kansas City	AL	162	637	174	44	7	29	(10	19)	319	114	105	120	71	1	135	4	3	7	35	7	.83	12	.273	.346	.501
5 ML YEARS		585	2347	665	123	33	82	(42	40)	1100	393	365	390	207	7	459	14	6	27	109	16	.87	50	.283	.341	.469

Francis Beltran

Pitches: R **Bats:** R **Pos:** RP-11   **Ht:** 6'5" **Wt:** 220 **Born:** 11/29/79 **Age:** 23

Year Team	Lg	G	GS	CG	GF	IP	BFP	H	R	ER	HR	SH	SF	HB	TBB	IBB	SO	WP	Bk	W	L	Pct	ShO	Sv-Op	Hld	ERC	ERA
1997 Cubs	R	16	0	0	5	23.2	111	27	18	9	1	1	1	3	8	0	17	3	2	0	1	.000	0	1--	-	4.49	3.42
1998 Cubs	R	12	5	0	3	35.2	165	49	23	22	1	4	2	2	14	1	26	1	1	1	1	.500	0	0--	-	5.96	5.55
1999 Cubs	R	7	0	0	6	10.2	38	5	3	0	0	0	0	1	1	0	8	0	0	0	1	.000	0	2--	-	0.78	0.00
1999 Eugene	A-	16	0	0	7	28.0	142	41	32	26	2	0	1	3	14	0	28	6	0	0	2	.000	0	0--	-	7.34	8.36
2000 Lansing	A	16	0	0	11	17.2	97	24	22	19	0	0	3	4	19	0	16	4	0	1	1	.500	0	0--	-	9.24	9.68
2000 Eugene	A-	25	0	0	13	43.2	180	28	16	13	1	1	1	1	20	2	52	6	0	2	2	.500	0	8--	-	1.93	2.68
2001 Daytona	A+	21	18	0	0	95.1	424	93	62	53	10	1	4	9	40	1	72	4	0	6	9	.400	0	0--	-	4.35	5.00
2002 W Tennesse	AA	39	0	0	35	41.2	171	28	14	12	2	3	1	2	19	2	43	3	2	2	2	.500	0	23--	-	2.34	2.59
2002 Chicago	NL	11	0	0	4	12.0	65	14	11	10	2	3	1	0	16	1	11	2	0	0	0	-	0	0-0	0	9.45	7.50

Adrian Beltre

Bats: R **Throws:** R **Pos:** 3B-157; PH-2   **Ht:** 5'11" **Wt:** 170 **Born:** 4/7/79 **Age:** 24

Year Team	Lg	G	AB	H	2B	3B	HR	(Hm	Rd)	TB	R	RBI	RC	TBB	IBB	SO	HBP	SH	SF	SB	CS	SB%	GDP	Avg	OBP	Slg
1998 Los Angeles	NL	77	195	42	9	0	7	(5	2)	72	18	22	20	14	0	37	3	2	0	3	1	.75	4	.215	.278	.369
1999 Los Angeles	NL	152	538	148	27	5	15	(6	9)	230	84	67	84	61	12	105	6	4	5	18	7	.72	4	.275	.352	.428
2000 Los Angeles	NL	138	510	148	30	2	20	(7	13)	242	71	85	85	56	2	80	2	3	4	12	5	.71	13	.290	.360	.475
2001 Los Angeles	NL	126	475	126	22	4	13	(4	9)	195	59	60	60	28	1	82	5	2	5	13	4	.76	9	.265	.310	.411
2002 Los Angeles	NL	159	587	151	26	5	21	(7	14)	250	70	75	74	37	4	96	4	1	6	7	5	.58	17	.257	.303	.426
5 ML YEARS		652	2305	615	114	16	76	(29	47)	989	302	309	323	196	19	400	20	12	20	53	22	.71	47	.267	.327	.429

Marvin Benard

Bats: L **Throws:** L **Pos:** PH-33; RF-20; LF-14; CF-6   **Ht:** 5'9" **Wt:** 191 **Born:** 1/20/71 **Age:** 32

Year Team	Lg	G	AB	H	2B	3B	HR	(Hm	Rd)	TB	R	RBI	RC	TBB	IBB	SO	HBP	SH	SF	SB	CS	SB%	GDP	Avg	OBP	Slg
1995 San Francisco	NL	13	34	13	2	0	1	(0	1)	18	5	4	7	1	0	7	0	0	0	1	0	1.00	1	.382	.400	.529
1996 San Francisco	NL	135	488	121	17	4	5	(2	3)	161	89	27	57	59	2	84	4	6	1	25	11	.69	8	.248	.333	.330
1997 San Francisco	NL	84	114	26	4	0	1	(0	1)	33	13	13	11	13	0	29	2	0	1	3	1	.75	2	.228	.315	.289

Year Team	Lg	G	AB	H	2B	3B	HR	(Hm	Rd)	TB	R	RBI	RC	TBB	IBB	SO	HBP	SH	SF	SB	CS	SB%	GDP	Avg	OBP	Slg
1998 San Francisco	NL	121	286	92	21	1	3	(2	1)	124	41	36	51	34	1	39	2	4	1	11	4	.73	3	.322	.396	.434
1999 San Francisco	NL	149	562	163	36	5	16	(9	7)	257	100	64	93	55	2	97	6	1	1	27	14	.66	5	.290	.359	.457
2000 San Francisco	NL	149	560	147	27	6	12	(6	6)	257	102	55	81	63	0	97	6	2	2	22	7	.76	4	.263	.342	.396
2001 San Francisco	NL	129	392	104	19	2	15	(3	12)	172	70	44	56	29	2	66	4	1	3	10	5	.67	3	.265	.320	.439
2002 San Francisco	NL	65	123	34	9	2	1	(0	1)	50	16	13	14	7	0	26	1	0	0	5	1	.83	3	.276	.321	.407
8 ML YEARS		845	2559	700	135	20	54	(22	32)	1037	436	256	370	261	7	445	25	14	9	104	43	.71	29	.274	.345	.405

Alan Benes

Pitches: R **Bats:** R **Pos:** SP-7

Ht: 6'5" **Wt:** 235 **Born:** 1/21/72 **Age:** 31

Year Team	Lg	G	GS	CG	GF	IP	BFP	H	R	ER	HR	SH	SF	HB	TBB	IBB	SO	WP	Bk	W	L	Pct	ShO	Sv-Op	Hld	ERC	ERA
2002 Iowa*	AAA	28	19	0	3	113.0	512	130	79	71	17	5	5	4	53	0	85	5	1	10	9	.526	0	0- -	-	5.80	5.65
1995 St Louis	NL	3	3	0	0	16.0	76	24	15	15	2	1	0	1	4	0	20	3	0	1	2	.333	0	0-0	0	6.84	8.44
1996 St Louis	NL	34	32	3	1	191.0	840	192	120	104	27	15	9	7	87	3	131	5	1	13	10	.565	1	0-0	0	4.76	4.90
1997 St Louis	NL	23	23	2	0	161.2	666	128	60	52	13	5	4	4	68	3	160	9	2	9	9	.500	0	0-0	0	3.01	2.89
1999 St Louis	NL	2	0	0	2	2.0	7	2	0	0	0	0	0	0	0	0	2	0	0	0	0	-	0	0-0	0	2.31	0.00
2000 St Louis	NL	30	0	0	16	46.0	214	54	33	29	7	2	1	2	23	2	26	5	0	2	2	.500	0	0-1	2	5.96	5.67
2001 St Louis	NL	9	1	0	4	14.2	68	14	12	12	5	0	0	0	12	0	10	0	0	2	0	1.000	0	0-0	0	7.55	7.36
2002 Chicago	NL	7	7	0	0	39.1	167	42	22	19	3	1	2	0	12	1	32	2	0	2	2	.500	0	0-0	0	3.91	4.35
7 ML YEARS		108	66	5	23	470.2	2038	456	262	231	57	24	16	14	206	9	381	24	3	29	25	.537	1	0-1	2	4.30	4.42

Andy Benes

Pitches: R **Bats:** R **Pos:** SP-17; RP-1

Ht: 6'6" **Wt:** 245 **Born:** 8/20/67 **Age:** 35

Year Team	Lg	G	GS	CG	GF	IP	BFP	H	R	ER	HR	SH	SF	HB	TBB	IBB	SO	WP	Bk	W	L	Pct	ShO	Sv-Op	Hld	ERC	ERA
2002 Memphis*	AAA	4	4	0	0	17.1	72	17	7	6	2	1	1	1	4	0	8	0	0	1	1	.500	0	0- -	-	3.67	3.12
2002 Potomac*	A+	1	1	0	0	7.0	34	8	7	7	2	2	0	0	6	0	3	0	0	0	0	-	0	0- -	-	8.54	9.00
1989 San Diego	NL	10	10	0	0	66.2	280	51	28	26	7	6	2	1	31	0	66	0	3	6	3	.667	0	0-0	0	3.12	3.51
1990 San Diego	NL	32	31	2	1	192.1	811	177	87	77	18	5	6	1	69	5	140	2	5	10	11	.476	0	0-0	0	3.40	3.60
1991 San Diego	NL	33	33	4	0	223.0	908	194	76	75	23	5	4	4	59	7	167	3	4	15	11	.577	1	0-0	0	2.92	3.03
1992 San Diego	NL	34	34	2	0	231.1	961	230	90	86	14	19	6	5	61	6	169	1	1	13	14	.481	2	0-0	0	3.33	3.35
1993 San Diego	NL	34	34	4	0	230.2	968	200	111	97	23	10	6	4	86	7	179	14	2	15	15	.500	2	0-0	0	3.25	3.78
1994 San Diego	NL	25	25	2	0	172.1	717	155	82	74	20	11	1	1	51	2	189	4	0	6	14	.300	1	0-0	0	3.21	3.86
1995 SD-Sea		31	31	1	0	181.2	809	193	107	96	18	4	8	6	78	5	171	5	0	11	9	.550	1	0-0	0	4.59	4.76
1996 St Louis	NL	36	34	3	1	230.1	963	215	107	98	28	2	6	6	77	7	160	6	0	18	10	.643	1	1-1	0	3.69	3.83
1997 St Louis	NL	26	26	0	0	177.0	727	149	64	61	9	6	7	5	61	4	175	7	0	10	7	.588	0	0-0	0	2.80	3.10
1998 Arizona	NL	34	34	1	0	231.1	979	221	111	102	25	11	8	6	74	3	164	9	1	14	13	.519	0	0-0	0	3.64	3.97
1999 Arizona	NL	33	32	0	0	198.1	886	216	117	106	34	6	3	4	82	3	141	10	0	13	12	.520	0	0-0	0	5.18	4.81
2000 St Louis	NL	30	27	1	1	166.0	719	174	95	90	30	9	8	1	68	0	137	1	0	12	9	.571	0	0-0	1	5.05	4.88
2001 St Louis	NL	27	19	0	3	107.1	500	122	92	88	30	3	4	6	61	0	78	1	0	7	7	.500	0	0-1	0	7.27	7.38
2002 St Louis	NL	18	17	1	0	97.0	417	80	39	30	10	5	5	5	51	3	64	0	0	5	4	.556	0	0-0	0	3.78	2.78
1995 San Diego	NL	19	19	1	0	118.2	518	121	65	55	10	3	4	4	45	3	126	3	0	4	7	.364	1	0-0	0	4.05	4.17
1995 Seattle	AL	12	12	0	0	63.0	291	72	42	41	8	1	4	2	33	2	45	2	0	7	2	.778	0	0-0	0	5.66	5.86
14 ML YEARS		403	387	21	6	2505.1	10645	2377	1206	1106	289	102	74	55	909	52	2000	63	16	155	139	.527	9	1-2	1	3.81	3.97

Armando Benitez

Pitches: R **Bats:** R **Pos:** RP-62

Ht: 6'4" **Wt:** 229 **Born:** 11/3/72 **Age:** 30

Year Team	Lg	G	GS	CG	GF	IP	BFP	H	R	ER	HR	SH	SF	HB	TBB	IBB	SO	WP	Bk	W	L	Pct	ShO	Sv-Op	Hld	ERC	ERA
1994 Baltimore	AL	3	0	0	1	10.0	42	8	1	1	0	0	0	1	4	0	14	0	0	0	0	-	0	0-0	0	2.71	0.90
1995 Baltimore	AL	44	0	0	18	47.2	221	37	33	30	8	2	3	5	37	2	56	3	1	1	5	.167	0	2-5	6	5.06	5.66
1996 Baltimore	AL	18	0	0	8	14.1	56	7	6	6	2	0	1	0	6	0	20	1	0	0	1	1.000	0	4-5	1	1.78	3.77
1997 Baltimore	AL	71	0	0	26	73.1	307	49	22	20	7	2	4	1	43	5	106	1	0	4	5	.444	0	9-10	20	2.92	2.45
1998 Baltimore	AL	71	0	0	54	68.1	289	48	29	29	10	3	2	4	39	2	87	0	0	5	6	.455	0	22-26	3	3.63	3.82
1999 New York	NL	77	0	0	42	78.0	312	40	17	16	4	0	0	0	41	4	128	2	0	4	3	.571	0	22-28	17	1.69	1.85
2000 New York	NL	76	0	0	68	76.0	304	39	24	22	10	2	1	0	38	2	106	0	0	4	4	.500	0	41-46	3	2.08	2.61
2001 New York	NL	73	0	0	64	76.1	320	59	32	32	12	2	1	1	40	6	93	5	0	6	4	.600	0	43-46	0	3.67	3.77
2002 New York	NL	62	0	0	52	67.1	275	46	20	17	8	3	2	3	25	0	79	1	0	1	0	1.000	0	33-37	5	2.55	2.27
9 ML YEARS		495	0	0	333	511.1	2126	333	184	173	61	14	14	15	273	21	689	13	1	26	27	.491	0	176-203	47	2.89	3.04

Mike Benjamin

Bats: R **Throws:** R **Pos:** 3B-60; PH-22; PR-17; SS-15; 2B-11; 1B-1; RF-1

Ht: 6'0" **Wt:** 172 **Born:** 11/22/65 **Age:** 37

Year Team	Lg	G	AB	H	2B	3B	HR	(Hm	Rd)	TB	R	RBI	RC	TBB	IBB	SO	HBP	SH	SF	SB	CS	SB%	GDP	Avg	OBP	Slg
1989 San Francisco	NL	14	6	1	0	0	0	(0	0)	1	6	0	0	0	0	1	0	0	0	0	0	-	0	.167	.167	.167
1990 San Francisco	NL	22	56	12	3	1	2	(2	0)	23	7	3	5	3	1	10	0	0	0	1	0	1.00	0	.214	.254	.411
1991 San Francisco	NL	54	106	13	3	0	2	(0	2)	22	12	8	3	7	2	26	2	3	2	3	0	1.00	3	.123	.188	.208
1992 San Francisco	NL	40	75	13	2	1	1	(0	1)	20	4	3	4	4	1	15	0	3	0	1	0	1.00	1	.173	.215	.267
1993 San Francisco	NL	63	146	29	7	0	4	(3	1)	48	22	16	12	9	2	23	4	6	0	0	0	-	3	.199	.264	.329
1994 San Francisco	NL	38	62	16	5	1	1	(1	0)	26	9	9	10	5	1	16	3	5	0	5	0	1.00	1	.258	.343	.419
1995 San Francisco	NL	68	186	41	6	0	3	(1	2)	56	19	12	14	8	3	51	1	7	0	11	1	.92	3	.220	.256	.301
1996 Philadelphia	NL	35	103	23	5	1	4	(0	4)	42	13	13	13	12	5	21	2	1	0	3	1	.75	2	.223	.316	.408
1997 Boston	AL	49	116	27	9	1	0	(0	0)	38	12	7	7	4	0	27	1	1	1	2	3	.40	2	.233	.262	.328
1998 Boston	AL	124	349	95	23	0	4	(2	2)	130	46	39	39	15	1	73	6	13	2	3	0	1.00	11	.272	.312	.372
1999 Pittsburgh	NL	110	368	91	26	7	1	(1	0)	134	42	37	40	20	3	90	2	11	3	10	1	.91	7	.247	.288	.364
2000 Pittsburgh	NL	93	233	63	18	2	2	(0	2)	91	28	19	28	12	0	45	3	6	1	5	4	.56	2	.270	.313	.391
2002 Pittsburgh	NL	108	120	18	2	1	0	(0	0)	22	7	3	0	7	0	31	1	1	1	0	4	.00	5	.150	.202	.183
13 ML YEARS		818	1926	442	109	15	24	(10	14)	653	227	169	177	106	19	429	25	57	10	44	14	.76	38	.229	.277	.339

Gary Bennett

Bats: R **Throws:** R **Pos:** C-90; PH-1   **Ht:** 6'0" **Wt:** 208 **Born:** 4/17/72 **Age:** 31

Year Team	Lg	G	AB	H	2B	3B	HR	(Hm	Rd)	TB	R	RBI	RC	TBB	IBB	SO	HBP	SH	SF	SB	CS	SB%	GDP	Avg	OBP	Slg
1995 Philadelphia	NL	1	1	0	0	0	0	(0	0)	0	0	0	0	0	0	1	0	0	0	0	0	-	0	.000	.000	.000
1996 Philadelphia	NL	6	16	4	0	0	0	(0	0)	4	0	1	1	2	1	6	0	0	0	0	0	-	0	.250	.333	.250
1998 Philadelphia	NL	9	31	9	0	0	0	(0	0)	9	4	3	4	5	0	5	0	0	1	0	0	-	1	.290	.378	.290
1999 Philadelphia	NL	36	88	24	4	0	1	(0	1)	31	7	21	7	4	0	11	0	0	2	0	0	-	0	.273	.298	.352
2000 Philadelphia	NL	31	74	18	5	0	2	(0	2)	29	8	5	12	13	0	15	2	0	0	0	0	-	7	.243	.371	.392
2001 Phi-NYM-Col	NL	46	131	32	6	1	2	(2	0)	46	15	10	15	12	4	24	1	2	2	0	0	-	1	.244	.308	.351
2002 Colorado	NL	90	291	77	10	2	4	(2	2)	103	26	26	28	15	2	45	6	2	0	1	3	.25	10	.265	.314	.354
2001 Philadelphia	NL	26	75	16	3	1	1	(1	0)	24	8	6	7	9	1	19	0	1	1	0	0	-	1	.213	.294	.320
2001 New York	NL	1	1	1	0	0	0	(0	0)	1	0	0	1	0	0	0	0	0	0	0	0	-	0	1.000	1.000	1.000
2001 Colorado	NL	19	55	15	3	0	1	(1	0)	21	7	4	7	3	3	5	1	1	1	0	0	-	0	.273	.317	.382
7 ML YEARS		219	632	164	25	3	9	(4	5)	222	60	66	67	51	7	107	9	4	5	1	3	.25	19	.259	.321	.351

Joaquin Benoit

Pitches: R **Bats:** R **Pos:** SP-13; RP-4   **Ht:** 6'3" **Wt:** 205 **Born:** 7/26/77 **Age:** 25

Year Team	Lg	G	GS	CG	GF	IP	BFP	H	R	ER	HR	SH	SF	HB	TBB	IBB	SO	WP	Bk	W	L	Pct	ShO	Sv-Op	Hld	ERC	ERA
1997 Rangers	R	10	10	1	0	44.0	177	40	14	10	0	1	0	1	11	0	38	1	0	3	3	.500	0	0--	-	2.53	2.05
1998 Savannah	A	15	15	1	0	80.0	339	79	41	34	8	3	1	3	18	0	68	3	1	4	3	.571	0	0--	-	3.41	3.83
1999 Charlotte	A+	22	22	0	0	105.0	483	117	67	62	5	1	7	11	50	0	83	3	2	7	4	.636	0	0--	-	5.03	5.31
2000 Tulsa	AA	16	16	0	0	82.1	346	73	40	35	6	0	4	4	30	0	72	6	0	4	4	.500	0	0--	-	3.34	3.83
2001 Tulsa	AA	4	4	0	0	21.2	94	23	8	8	1	0	0	1	6	0	23	2	0	1	0	1.000	0	0--	-	3.69	3.32
2001 Oklahoma	AAA	24	24	1	0	131.0	566	113	63	61	14	2	4	4	73	0	142	7	0	9	5	.643	1	0--	-	4.13	4.19
2002 Oklahoma	AAA	16	16	0	0	98.2	412	74	42	39	8	1	4	7	37	0	103	6	0	8	4	.667	0	0--	-	2.75	3.56
2002 Charlotte	A+	1	1	0	0	5.0	20	1	0	0	0	0	0	0	3	0	8	0	0	0	0	-	0	0--	-	0.76	0.00
2001 Texas	AL	1	1	0	0	5.0	26	8	6	6	3	0	1	0	3	0	4	0	0	0	0	-	0	0-0	0	13.11	10.80
2002 Texas	AL	17	13	0	2	84.2	405	91	51	50	6	4	3	5	58	2	59	7	0	4	5	.444	0	1-1	0	5.52	5.31
2 ML YEARS		18	14	0	2	89.2	431	99	57	56	9	4	4	5	61	2	63	7	0	4	5	.444	0	1-1	0	5.91	5.62

Kris Benson

Pitches: R **Bats:** R **Pos:** SP-25   **Ht:** 6'4" **Wt:** 200 **Born:** 11/7/74 **Age:** 28

Year Team	Lg	G	GS	CG	GF	IP	BFP	H	R	ER	HR	SH	SF	HB	TBB	IBB	SO	WP	Bk	W	L	Pct	ShO	Sv-Op	Hld	ERC	ERA
2002 Nashville*	AAA	4	4	0	0	17.2	69	8	4	3	1	0	1	0	8	0	25	0	0	0	2	.000	0	0--	-	1.41	1.53
2002 Altoona*	AA	1	1	0	0	7.0	25	5	1	1	0	0	1	0	0	0	7	0	0	1	0	1.000	0	0--	-	2.09	1.29
1999 Pittsburgh	NL	31	31	2	0	196.2	840	184	105	89	16	6	7	6	83	5	139	2	1	11	14	.440	0	0-0	0	3.78	4.07
2000 Pittsburgh	NL	32	32	2	0	217.2	936	206	104	93	24	7	6	10	86	5	184	5	0	10	12	.455	1	0-0	0	3.97	3.85
2002 Pittsburgh	NL	25	25	0	0	130.1	575	152	76	68	18	5	3	3	50	8	79	3	1	9	6	.600	0	0-0	0	5.32	4.70
3 ML YEARS		88	88	4	0	544.2	2351	542	285	250	58	18	16	19	219	18	402	10	2	30	32	.484	1	0-0	0	4.21	4.13

Jason Bere

Pitches: R **Bats:** R **Pos:** SP-16   **Ht:** 6'3" **Wt:** 225 **Born:** 5/26/71 **Age:** 32

Year Team	Lg	G	GS	CG	GF	IP	BFP	H	R	ER	HR	SH	SF	HB	TBB	IBB	SO	WP	Bk	W	L	Pct	ShO	Sv-Op	Hld	ERC	ERA
2002 Iowa*	AAA	1	1	0	0	5.0	20	2	1	1	0	0	0	0	3	0	3	0	0	1	0	1.000	0	0--	-	1.32	1.80
1993 Chicago	AL	24	24	1	0	142.2	610	109	60	55	12	4	2	5	81	0	129	8	0	12	5	.706	0	0-0	0	3.46	3.47
1994 Chicago	AL	24	24	0	0	141.2	608	119	65	60	17	4	4	1	80	0	127	2	0	12	2	.857	0	0-0	0	4.03	3.81
1995 Chicago	AL	27	27	1	0	137.2	668	151	120	110	21	4	7	6	106	6	110	8	0	8	15	.348	0	0-0	0	6.63	7.19
1996 Chicago	AL	5	5	0	0	16.2	93	26	19	19	3	1	1	0	18	1	19	2	0	0	1	.000	0	0-0	0	11.16	10.26
1997 Chicago	AL	6	6	0	0	28.2	123	20	15	15	4	1	1	3	17	0	21	1	0	4	2	.667	0	0-0	0	3.86	4.71
1998 CWS-Cin	AL	27	22	0	2	127.1	588	137	91	80	17	4	7	3	78	0	84	8	0	6	9	.400	0	0-0	0	5.73	5.65
1999 Cin-Mil	NL	17	14	0	0	66.2	322	79	52	45	9	6	2	2	50	3	47	6	0	5	0	1.000	0	0-0	0	7.00	6.08
2000 Mil-Cle		31	31	0	0	169.1	767	180	107	103	25	12	6	5	89	7	142	5	1	12	10	.545	0	0-0	0	5.34	5.47
2001 Chicago	NL	32	32	2	0	188.0	801	171	99	90	24	7	6	1	77	7	175	6	0	11	11	.500	0	0-0	0	3.75	4.31
2002 Chicago	NL	16	16	0	0	85.2	379	98	63	54	13	3	7	3	28	1	65	5	0	1	10	.091	0	0-0	0	5.09	5.67
1998 Chicago	AL	18	15	0	0	83.2	404	98	71	60	14	4	5	2	58	0	53	7	0	3	7	.300	0	0-0	0	6.90	6.45
1998 Cincinnati	NL	9	7	0	2	43.2	184	39	20	20	3	0	2	1	20	0	31	1	0	3	2	.600	0	0-0	0	3.65	4.12
1999 Cincinnati	NL	12	10	0	0	43.1	220	56	37	33	6	5	1	2	40	3	28	2	0	3	0	1.000	0	0-0	0	8.60	6.85
1999 Milwaukee	NL	5	4	0	0	23.1	102	23	15	12	3	1	1	0	10	0	19	4	0	2	0	1.000	0	0-0	0	4.26	4.63
2000 Milwaukee	NL	20	20	0	0	115.0	515	115	66	63	19	12	3	1	63	7	98	3	1	6	7	.462	0	0-0	0	5.06	4.93
2000 Cleveland	AL	11	11	0	0	54.1	252	65	41	40	6	0	3	4	26	0	44	2	0	6	3	.667	0	0-0	0	5.94	6.63
10 ML YEARS		209	201	4	2	1104.1	4959	1090	691	631	145	46	43	29	624	25	919	51	1	71	65	.522	0	0-0	0	4.95	5.14

Dave Berg

Bats: R **Throws:** R **Pos:** 2B-52; 3B-20; SS-13; 1B-10; RF-10; DH-8; PH-7; LF-3   **Ht:** 5'11" **Wt:** 196 **Born:** 9/3/70 **Age:** 32

Year Team	Lg	G	AB	H	2B	3B	HR	(Hm	Rd)	TB	R	RBI	RC	TBB	IBB	SO	HBP	SH	SF	SB	CS	SB%	GDP	Avg	OBP	Slg
1998 Florida	NL	81	182	57	11	0	2	(1	1)	74	18	21	32	26	1	46	0	4	3	3	0	1.00	1	.313	.393	.407
1999 Florida	NL	109	304	87	18	1	3	(1	2)	116	42	25	39	27	0	59	2	3	0	2	2	.50	7	.286	.348	.382
2000 Florida	NL	82	210	53	14	1	0	(1	0)	72	23	21	26	25	0	46	5	1	0	3	0	1.00	5	.252	.340	.343
2001 Florida	NL	82	215	52	12	1	4	(2	2)	78	26	16	22	14	0	39	2	2	2	0	1	.00	3	.242	.292	.363
2002 Toronto	AL	109	374	101	26	2	4	(3	1)	143	42	39	47	26	1	57	5	4	5	0	2	.00	6	.270	.322	.382
5 ML YEARS		463	1285	350	81	5	14	(8	6)	483	151	122	166	118	2	247	14	14	14	8	5	.62	22	.272	.337	.376

Brandon Berger

Bats: R **Throws:** R **Pos:** RF-21; LF-14; DH-9; PH-7; CF-3; 1B-1; PR-1   **Ht:** 5'11" **Wt:** 205 **Born:** 2/21/75 **Age:** 28

								BATTING												BASERUNNING				AVERAGES		
Year Team	Lg	G	AB	H	2B	3B	HR	(Hm Rd)	TB	R	RBI	RC	TBB	IBB	SO	HBP	SH	SF	SB	CS	SB%	GDP	Avg	OBP	Slg
1996 Spokane	A-	71	283	87	12	1	13	(- -)	140	46	58	52	31	0	64	2	1	3	17	5	.77	7	.307	.376	.495
1997 Lansing	A	107	393	115	22	6	12	(- -)	185	64	73	69	42	1	79	7	0	4	13	1	.93	8	.293	.368	.471
1998 Wilmington	A+	110	338	75	18	3	8	(- -)	123	53	50	43	53	1	94	5	7	5	13	3	.81	11	.222	.332	.364
1999 Wilmington	A+	119	450	132	27	4	16	(- -)	215	73	73	83	45	0	93	8	6	6	29	7	.81	3	.293	.363	.478
2000 Wichita	AA	27	86	14	2	0	3	(- -)	25	9	8	6	7	0	27	2	1	1	6	1	.86	2	.163	.240	.291
2000 Wilmington	A+	102	379	108	18	4	15	(- -)	179	63	71	68	40	2	71	17	4	3	12	4	.75	8	.285	.376	.472
2001 Wichita	AA	120	454	140	28	3	40	(- -)	294	98	118	106	43	2	91	14	1	3	14	6	.70	9	.308	.383	.648
2002 Omaha	AAA	68	261	76	16	1	13	(- -)	133	34	47	49	25	0	43	5	0	1	11	2	.85	4	.291	.363	.510
2001 Kansas City	AL	6	16	5	1	1	2	(1 1)	14	4	2	5	2	0	2	0	0	0	0	0	-	0	.313	.389	.875
2002 Kansas City	AL	51	134	27	5	1	6	(5 1)	52	16	17	16	8	2	32	2	0	1	1	0	1.00	2	.201	.255	.388
2 ML YEARS		57	150	32	6	2	8	(6 2)	66	20	19	21	10	2	34	2	0	1	1	0	1.00	2	.213	.270	.440

Peter Bergeron

Bats: L **Throws:** R **Pos:** CF-31; PR-1   **Ht:** 6'0" **Wt:** 190 **Born:** 11/9/77 **Age:** 25

								BATTING												BASERUNNING				AVERAGES		
Year Team	Lg	G	AB	H	2B	3B	HR	(Hm Rd)	TB	R	RBI	RC	TBB	IBB	SO	HBP	SH	SF	SB	CS	SB%	GDP	Avg	OBP	Slg
2002 Ottawa*	AAA	104	340	99	9	4	1	(- -)	119	51	29	46	39	1	65	1	11	2	7	7	.50	1	.291	.364	.350
1999 Montreal	NL	16	45	11	2	0	0	(0 0)	13	12	1	6	9	0	5	0	1	0	0	0	-	0	.244	.370	.289
2000 Montreal	NL	148	518	127	25	7	5	(3 2)	181	80	31	58	58	0	100	0	14	2	11	13	.46	4	.245	.320	.349
2001 Montreal	NL	102	375	79	11	4	3	(1 2)	107	53	16	28	28	2	87	5	8	0	10	7	.59	5	.211	.275	.285
2002 Montreal	NL	31	123	23	3	2	0	(0 0)	30	24	7	14	22	0	44	0	3	0	10	3	.77	0	.187	.310	.244
4 ML YEARS		297	1061	240	41	13	8	(4 4)	331	169	55	106	117	2	236	5	26	2	31	23	.57	9	.226	.305	.312

Lance Berkman

Bats: B **Throws:** L **Pos:** CF-122; LF-76; RF-12; PH-2   **Ht:** 6'1" **Wt:** 220 **Born:** 2/10/76 **Age:** 27

								BATTING												BASERUNNING				AVERAGES		
Year Team	Lg	G	AB	H	2B	3B	HR	(Hm Rd)	TB	R	RBI	RC	TBB	IBB	SO	HBP	SH	SF	SB	CS	SB%	GDP	Avg	OBP	Slg
1999 Houston	NL	34	93	22	2	0	4	(2 2)	36	10	15	12	12	0	21	0	0	1	5	1	.83	2	.237	.321	.387
2000 Houston	NL	114	353	105	28	1	21	(10 11)	198	76	67	76	61	1	73	1	0	7	6	2	.75	6	.297	.388	.561
2001 Houston	NL	156	577	191	55	5	34	(13 21)	358	110	126	144	92	5	121	13	0	6	7	9	.44	8	.331	.430	.620
2002 Houston	NL	158	578	169	35	2	42	(20 22)	334	106	128	131	107	20	118	4	0	3	8	4	.67	10	.292	.405	.578
4 ML YEARS		462	1601	487	120	8	101	(45 56)	926	302	336	363	267	26	333	18	0	17	26	16	.62	26	.304	.406	.578

Adam Bernero

Pitches: R **Bats:** R **Pos:** RP-17; SP-11   **Ht:** 6'4" **Wt:** 205 **Born:** 11/28/76 **Age:** 26

		HOW MUCH HE PITCHED						WHAT HE GAVE UP												THE RESULTS						
Year Team	Lg	G	GS	CG	GF	IP	BFP	H	R	ER	HR	SH	SF	HB	TBB	IBB	SO	WP	Bk	W	L	Pct	ShO	Sv-Op	Hld	ERC	ERA
2002 Toledo*	AAA	9	9	2	0	57.0	225	46	13	10	2	2	2	2	13	0	49	2	0	2	2	.500	1	0--	-	2.21	1.58
2000 Detroit	AL	12	4	0	4	34.1	141	33	18	16	3	2	3	1	13	1	20	1	0	0	1	.000	0	0-0	1	3.94	4.19
2001 Detroit	AL	5	0	0	4	12.1	56	13	13	10	4	0	1	1	4	0	8	1	0	0	0	-	0	0-0	0	5.79	7.30
2002 Detroit	AL	28	11	0	5	101.2	459	128	74	70	17	3	5	6	31	1	69	5	1	4	7	.364	0	0-0	0	5.95	6.20
3 ML YEARS		45	15	0	13	148.1	656	174	105	96	24	5	9	8	48	2	97	7	1	4	8	.333	0	0-0	1	5.46	5.82

Angel Berroa

Bats: R **Throws:** R **Pos:** SS-20   **Ht:** 6'0" **Wt:** 175 **Born:** 1/27/78 **Age:** 25

								BATTING												BASERUNNING				AVERAGES		
Year Team	Lg	G	AB	H	2B	3B	HR	(Hm Rd)	TB	R	RBI	RC	TBB	IBB	SO	HBP	SH	SF	SB	CS	SB%	GDP	Avg	OBP	Slg
1999 Athletics	R	46	169	49	11	4	2	(- -)	74	42	24	29	16	0	26	7	0	2	11	4	.73	1	.290	.371	.438
1999 Midland	AA	4	17	1	1	0	0	(- -)	2	3	0	0	0	0	2	0	0	0	0	0	-	0	.059	.059	.118
2000 Visalia	A+	129	429	119	25	6	10	(- -)	186	61	63	60	30	1	70	10	2	3	11	9	.55	10	.277	.337	.434
2001 Wilmington	A+	51	199	63	18	4	6	(- -)	107	43	25	44	9	1	41	14	3	3	10	6	.63	7	.317	.382	.538
2001 Wichita	AA	80	304	90	20	4	8	(- -)	142	63	42	53	17	0	55	22	6	3	15	6	.71	6	.296	.373	.467
2002 Omaha	AAA	77	297	64	11	4	8	(- -)	107	37	35	29	15	0	84	11	4	2	6	4	.60	5	.215	.277	.360
2001 Kansas City	AL	15	53	16	2	0	0	(0 0)	18	8	4	6	3	0	10	0	0	0	2	0	1.00	2	.302	.339	.340
2002 Kansas City	AL	20	75	17	7	1	0	(0 0)	26	8	5	8	7	1	10	1	0	0	3	0	1.00	1	.227	.301	.347
2 ML YEARS		35	128	33	9	1	0	(0 0)	44	16	9	14	10	1	20	1	0	0	5	0	1.00	3	.258	.317	.344

Jason Beverlin

Pitches: R **Bats:** L **Pos:** RP-4; SP-3   **Ht:** 6'5" **Wt:** 220 **Born:** 11/27/73 **Age:** 29

		HOW MUCH HE PITCHED						WHAT HE GAVE UP												THE RESULTS						
Year Team	Lg	G	GS	CG	GF	IP	BFP	H	R	ER	HR	SH	SF	HB	TBB	IBB	SO	WP	Bk	W	L	Pct	ShO	Sv-Op	Hld	ERC	ERA
1994 W Michigan	A	17	1	0	9	41.0	168	32	12	8	1	2	1	1	14	0	48	3	4	3	2	.600	0	1--	-	2.24	1.76
1995 W Michigan	A	22	14	0	1	89.0	392	76	51	40	4	3	3	8	40	0	84	5	5	3	9	.250	0	0--	-	3.33	4.04
1995 Greensboro	A	7	7	1	0	51.0	198	49	15	15	1	0	0	6	6	0	31	4	0	2	4	.333	1	0--	-	2.41	2.65
1996 Tampa	A+	25	1	0	6	46.1	194	43	22	18	5	1	1	1	17	2	38	4	1	2	0	1.000	0	1--	-	3.67	3.50
1996 Norwich	AA	8	4	0	1	16.0	81	25	21	15	2	0	2	0	6	1	17	0	0	0	3	.000	0	0--	-	7.11	8.44
1997 Norwich	AA	25	0	0	8	41.2	203	50	38	36	10	0	0	6	24	0	42	3	0	1	0	1.000	0	0--	-	7.70	7.78
1997 Tampa	A+	7	6	0	0	41.1	167	37	26	22	4	2	2	4	13	1	24	6	0	1	3	.250	0	0--	-	3.67	4.79
1998 Tampa	A+	7	5	0	0	32.0	142	37	23	20	2	0	4	1	16	2	15	2	1	1	3	.250	0	0--	-	5.28	5.63
1998 Norwich	AA	25	9	0	8	81.0	343	68	34	33	5	2	4	3	38	0	86	6	1	3	5	.375	0	1--	-	3.36	3.67
1999 Norwich	AA	28	27	1	0	173.1	743	153	91	71	16	6	7	6	81	0	147	10	1	15	9	.625	0	0--	-	3.78	3.69
2000 Columbus	AAA	3	3	0	0	6.2	45	13	14	14	1	0	0	0	14	0	6	1	0	0	3	.000	0	0--	-	19.53	18.90
2000 Norwich	AA	24	24	1	0	143.2	618	110	61	45	7	3	4	10	87	2	100	6	0	8	9	.471	0	0--	-	3.49	2.82
2001 Salt Lake	AAA	19	12	1	0	83.0	350	82	41	39	9	0	2	4	29	0	74	2	2	6	2	.750	0	0--	-	4.14	4.23
2001 Arkansas	AA	6	6	0	0	39.1	164	36	15	12	4	0	1	3	11	0	30	4	0	4	2	.667	0	0--	-	3.47	2.75

HOW MUCH HE PITCHED								WHAT HE GAVE UP												THE RESULTS							
Year Team	Lg	G	GS	CG	GF	IP	BFP	H	R	ER	HR	SH	SF	HB	TBB	IBB	SO	WP	Bk	W	L	Pct	ShO	Sv-Op	Hld	ERC	ERA
2002 Buffalo	AAA	23	20	1	2	118.2	497	107	55	51	11	6	7	4	39	1	106	8	0	10	8	.556	1	0--	-	3.33	3.87
2002 Toledo	AAA	4	3	0	0	18.2	77	17	5	4	0	0	1	0	6	0	13	1	0	3	0	1.000	0	0--	-	2.66	1.93
2002 Cle-Det	AL	7	3	0	1	19.2	95	27	22	19	3	0	0	0	9	0	16	2	0	0	3	.000	0	0-0	-	6.81	8.69
2002 Cleveland	AL	4	0	0	1	7.1	35	9	7	6	1	0	0	0	4	0	9	1	0	0	0	-	0	0-0	-	6.16	7.36
2002 Detroit	AL	3	3	0	0	12.1	60	18	15	13	2	0	0	0	5	0	7	1	0	0	3	.000	0	0-0	-	7.21	9.49

Rocky Biddle

Pitches: R **Bats:** R **Pos:** RP-37; SP-7 **Ht:** 6'3" **Wt:** 230 **Born:** 5/21/76 **Age:** 27

HOW MUCH HE PITCHED								WHAT HE GAVE UP												THE RESULTS							
Year Team	Lg	G	GS	CG	GF	IP	BFP	H	R	ER	HR	SH	SF	HB	TBB	IBB	SO	WP	Bk	W	L	Pct	ShO	Sv-Op	Hld	ERC	ERA
2002 Charlotte*	AAA	2	2	0	0	7.0	27	4	1	1	0	0	0	1	1	0	9	0	0	0	0	-	0	0--	-	1.20	1.29
2000 Chicago	AL	4	4	0	0	22.2	105	31	25	21	5	0	2	0	8	0	7	2	0	1	2	.333	0	0-0	0	7.01	8.34
2001 Chicago	AL	30	21	0	1	128.2	571	137	87	77	16	4	3	8	52	3	85	6	0	7	8	.467	0	0-3	1	4.85	5.39
2002 Chicago	AL	44	7	0	9	77.2	339	72	42	35	13	0	1	5	39	4	64	5	0	3	4	.429	0	1-3	4	4.78	4.06
3 ML YEARS		78	32	0	10	229.0	1015	240	154	133	34	4	6	13	99	7	156	13	0	11	14	.440	0	1-6	5	5.03	5.23

Nick Bierbrodt

Pitches: L **Bats:** L **Pos:** SP **Ht:** 6'5" **Wt:** 214 **Born:** 5/16/78 **Age:** 25

HOW MUCH HE PITCHED								WHAT HE GAVE UP												THE RESULTS							
Year Team	Lg	G	GS	CG	GF	IP	BFP	H	R	ER	HR	SH	SF	HB	TBB	IBB	SO	WP	Bk	W	L	Pct	ShO	Sv-Op	Hld	ERC	ERA
1996 Diamndbcks	R	8	8	0	0	38.0	147	25	9	7	1	0	0	0	13	0	46	2	0	1	1	.500	0	0--	-	1.74	1.66
1996 Lethbridge	R+	3	3	0	0	18.0	72	12	4	1	0	0	1	1	5	0	23	1	0	2	0	1.000	0	0--	-	1.57	0.50
1997 South Bend	A	15	15	0	0	75.2	340	77	43	34	4	3	1	9	37	0	64	6	1	2	4	.333	0	0--	-	4.67	4.04
1998 High Desert	A+	24	23	1	0	129.2	560	122	66	49	7	3	6	7	64	0	88	9	0	8	7	.533	0	0--	-	4.06	3.40
1999 El Paso	AA	14	14	2	0	76.0	341	78	45	39	3	2	1	8	37	0	55	5	0	5	6	.455	0	0--	-	4.55	4.62
1999 Tucson	AAA	11	11	0	0	43.1	213	57	42	35	9	4	0	3	30	0	43	3	0	1	4	.200	0	0--	-	8.58	7.27
2000 Tucson	AAA	4	3	0	0	18.2	77	13	10	10	3	0	0	2	14	0	11	0	0	2	1	.667	0	0--	-	5.03	4.82
2000 Diamndbcks	R	4	3	0	0	8.0	34	4	4	4	0	0	0	1	5	0	10	1	0	0	0	-	0	0--	-	2.03	4.50
2000 El Paso	AA	7	7	0	0	35.1	166	37	30	28	1	2	1	3	24	0	36	5	0	1	3	.250	0	0--	-	5.22	7.13
2001 El Paso	AA	4	4	0	0	19.2	76	13	3	3	1	0	0	0	6	0	18	0	0	2	1	.667	0	0--	-	1.77	1.37
2001 Tucson	AAA	7	6	0	0	45.1	185	48	15	11	0	3	1	1	9	1	56	1	0	4	1	.800	0	0--	-	3.09	2.18
2002 Chrlstn - SC	A	1	1	0	0	5.0	23	5	4	2	0	0	0	0	2	0	2	1	0	0	0	-	0	0--	-	3.11	3.60
2001 Ari-TB		16	16	0	0	84.1	389	100	59	52	17	0	2	4	39	1	73	3	0	5	6	.455	0	0-0	0	6.37	5.55
2001 Arizona	NL	5	5	0	0	23.0	108	29	21	21	6	0	1	0	12	0	17	0	0	2	2	.500	0	0-0	0	7.43	8.22
2001 Tampa Bay	AL	11	11	0	0	61.1	281	71	38	31	11	0	1	4	27	1	56	3	0	3	4	.429	0	0-0	0	5.99	4.55

Larry Bigbie

Bats: L **Throws:** R **Pos:** PH-8; LF-6; RF-6; CF-1 **Ht:** 6'4" **Wt:** 190 **Born:** 11/4/77 **Age:** 25

BATTING															BASERUNNING				AVERAGES		
Year Team	Lg	G	AB	H	2B	3B	HR	(Hm Rd)	TB	R	RBI	RC	TBB	IBB	SO	HBP	SH	SF	SB	CS	SB%	GDP	Avg	OBP	Slg
1999 Bluefield	R+	8	30	8	0	0	0	(- -)	8	3	4	2	3	0	8	1	0	1	1	3	.25	1	.267	.343	.267
1999 Delmarva	A	43	165	46	7	3	2	(- -)	65	18	27	26	29	0	42	0	0	3	3	1	.75	4	.279	.381	.394
2000 Frederick	A+	55	201	59	11	0	2	(- -)	76	33	28	29	23	2	34	0	1	4	3	3	.70	3	.294	.360	.378
2000 Bowie	AA	31	112	27	6	0	0	(- -)	33	11	5	10	11	0	28	0	1	0	3	0	1.00	3	.241	.309	.295
2001 Bowie	AA	71	262	77	13	3	8	(- -)	120	41	33	46	40	1	54	0	0	1	10	7	.59	5	.294	.386	.458
2001 Rochester	AAA	10	42	13	4	0	1	(- -)	20	5	2	7	3	0	8	0	0	0	1	1	.50	0	.310	.356	.476
2002 Rochester	AAA	98	348	105	23	2	2	(- -)	138	42	35	49	35	7	79	1	0	4	7	3	.70	9	.302	.363	.397
2001 Baltimore	AL	47	131	30	6	0	2	(0 2)	42	15	11	14	17	1	42	0	1	0	4	1	.80	2	.229	.318	.321
2002 Baltimore	AL	16	34	6	1	0	0	(0 0)	7	1	3	1	1	0	11	0	0	1	1	0	1.00	1	.176	.194	.206
2 ML YEARS		63	165	36	7	0	2	(0 2)	49	16	14	15	18	1	53	0	1	1	5	1	.83	3	.218	.293	.297

Craig Biggio

Bats: R **Throws:** R **Pos:** 2B-142; PH-2; LF-1 **Ht:** 5'11" **Wt:** 185 **Born:** 12/14/65 **Age:** 37

BATTING															BASERUNNING				AVERAGES		
Year Team	Lg	G	AB	H	2B	3B	HR	(Hm Rd)	TB	R	RBI	RC	TBB	IBB	SO	HBP	SH	SF	SB	CS	SB%	GDP	Avg	OBP	Slg
1988 Houston	NL	50	123	26	6	1	3	(1 2)	43	14	5	11	7	2	29	0	1	0	6	1	.86	1	.211	.254	.350
1989 Houston	NL	134	443	114	21	2	13	(6 7)	178	64	60	64	49	8	64	6	6	5	21	3	.88	7	.257	.336	.402
1990 Houston	NL	150	555	153	24	2	4	(2 2)	193	53	42	68	53	1	79	3	9	1	25	11	.69	11	.276	.342	.348
1991 Houston	NL	149	546	161	23	4	4	(0 4)	204	79	46	79	53	3	71	2	5	3	19	6	.76	2	.295	.358	.374
1992 Houston	NL	162	613	170	32	3	6	(3 3)	226	96	39	95	94	9	95	7	5	2	38	15	.72	5	.277	.378	.369
1993 Houston	NL	155	610	175	41	5	21	(8 13)	289	98	64	105	77	7	93	10	4	5	15	17	.47	10	.287	.373	.474
1994 Houston	NL	114	437	139	44	5	6	(4 2)	211	88	56	94	62	1	58	8	2	2	39	4	.91	5	.318	.411	.483
1995 Houston	NL	141	553	167	30	2	22	(6 16)	267	123	77	116	80	1	85	22	11	7	33	8	.80	6	.302	.406	.483
1996 Houston	NL	162	605	174	24	4	15	(9 6)	251	113	75	105	75	0	72	27	8	8	25	7	.78	10	.288	.386	.415
1997 Houston	NL	162	619	191	37	8	22	(7 15)	310	146	81	139	84	6	107	34	0	7	47	10	.82	0	.309	.415	.501
1998 Houston	NL	160	646	210	51	2	20	(10 10)	325	123	88	135	64	0	113	23	1	4	50	8	.86	10	.325	.403	.503
1999 Houston	NL	160	639	188	56	0	16	(10 6)	292	123	73	117	88	9	107	11	5	6	28	14	.67	5	.294	.386	.457
2000 Houston	NL	101	377	101	13	5	8	(2 6)	148	67	35	63	61	3	73	16	7	5	12	2	.86	10	.268	.388	.393
2001 Houston	NL	155	617	180	35	3	20	(10 10)	281	118	70	109	66	4	100	28	0	6	7	4	.64	11	.292	.382	.455
2002 Houston	NL	145	577	146	36	3	15	(7 8)	233	96	58	73	50	2	111	17	9	2	16	2	.89	15	.253	.330	.404
15 ML YEARS		2100	7960	2295	473	49	195	(83 112)	3451	1401	869	1373	963	62	1257	214	73	63	381	112	.77	108	.288	.377	.434

Casey Blake

Bats: R **Throws:** R **Pos:** 3B-5; 1B-3; PR-2; DH-1; PH-1   **Ht:** 6'2" **Wt:** 205 **Born:** 8/23/73 **Age:** 29

Year Team	Lg	G	AB	H	2B	3B	HR	(Hm Rd)	TB	R	RBI	RC	TBB	IBB	SO	HBP	SH	SF	SB	CS	SB%	GDP	Avg	OBP	Slg
2002 Edmonton*	AAA	126	482	149	25	3	19	(- -)	237	87	58	89	54	1	78	6	0	4	24	9	.73	11	.309	.383	.492
1999 Toronto	AL	14	39	10	2	0	1	(0 1)	15	6	1	4	2	0	7	0	0	0	0	0	-	1	.256	.293	.385
2000 Minnesota	AL	7	16	3	2	0	0	(0 0)	5	1	1	2	3	0	7	1	0	1	0	0	-	0	.188	.333	.313
2001 Min-Bal	AL	19	37	9	1	0	1	(0 1)	13	3	4	5	4	1	12	0	0	0	3	0	1.00	0	.243	.317	.351
2002 Minnesota	AL	9	20	4	1	0	0	(0 0)	5	2	1	1	2	0	7	0	0	0	0	0	-	0	.200	.273	.250
2001 Minnesota	AL	13	22	7	1	0	0	(0 0)	8	1	2	4	3	1	8	0	0	0	1	0	1.00	0	.318	.400	.364
2001 Baltimore	AL	6	15	2	0	0	1	(0 1)	5	2	2	1	1	0	4	0	0	0	2	0	1.00	0	.133	.188	.333
4 ML YEARS		49	112	26	6	0	2	(0 2)	38	12	7	12	11	1	33	1	0	1	3	0	1.00	2	.232	.304	.339

Hank Blalock

Bats: L **Throws:** R **Pos:** 3B-46; PH-3; PR-2   **Ht:** 6'1" **Wt:** 195 **Born:** 11/28/80 **Age:** 22

Year Team	Lg	G	AB	H	2B	3B	HR	(Hm Rd)	TB	R	RBI	RC	TBB	IBB	SO	HBP	SH	SF	SB	CS	SB%	GDP	Avg	OBP	Slg
1999 Rangers	R	51	191	69	17	6	3	(- -)	107	34	38	42	25	4	23	1	0	5	3	2	.60	1	.361	.428	.560
1999 Savannah	A	7	25	6	1	0	1	(- -)	10	3	2	3	1	0	3	1	0	1	0	0	-	0	.240	.286	.400
2000 Savannah	A	139	512	153	32	2	10	(- -)	219	66	77	85	62	3	53	5	0	11	31	8	.79	14	.299	.373	.428
2001 Charlotte	A+	63	237	90	19	1	7	(- -)	132	46	47	53	26	7	31	1	0	4	7	4	.64	6	.380	.437	.557
2001 Tulsa	AA	68	272	89	18	4	11	(- -)	148	50	61	59	39	1	38	2	0	2	3	3	.50	5	.327	.413	.544
2002 Oklahoma	AAA	95	387	119	32	1	8	(- -)	177	63	62	62	34	1	61	1	1	2	2	1	.67	9	.307	.363	.457
2002 Texas	AL	49	147	31	8	0	3	(2 1)	48	16	17	14	20	1	43	1	2	2	0	0	-	2	.211	.306	.327

Henry Blanco

Bats: R **Throws:** R **Pos:** C-79; PH-2   **Ht:** 5'11" **Wt:** 220 **Born:** 8/29/71 **Age:** 31

Year Team	Lg	G	AB	H	2B	3B	HR	(Hm Rd)	TB	R	RBI	RC	TBB	IBB	SO	HBP	SH	SF	SB	CS	SB%	GDP	Avg	OBP	Slg
1997 Los Angeles	NL	3	5	2	0	0	1	(0 1)	5	1	1	2	0	0	1	0	0	0	0	0	-	0	.400	.400	1.000
1999 Colorado	NL	88	263	61	12	3	6	(3 3)	97	30	28	32	34	1	38	1	3	2	1	1	.50	4	.232	.320	.369
2000 Milwaukee	NL	93	284	67	24	0	7	(3 4)	112	29	31	33	36	6	60	0	0	4	0	3	.00	9	.236	.318	.394
2001 Milwaukee	NL	104	314	66	18	3	6	(4 2)	108	33	31	30	34	6	72	2	5	2	3	1	.75	10	.210	.290	.344
2002 Atlanta	NL	81	221	45	9	1	6	(4 2)	74	17	22	16	20	5	51	1	2	5	0	2	.00	5	.204	.267	.335
5 ML YEARS		369	1087	241	63	7	26	(14 12)	396	110	113	113	124	18	222	4	10	13	4	7	.36	28	.222	.300	.364

Willie Bloomquist

Bats: R **Throws:** R **Pos:** LF-7; 2B-4; PR-2; PH-1   **Ht:** 5'11" **Wt:** 180 **Born:** 11/27/77 **Age:** 25

Year Team	Lg	G	AB	H	2B	3B	HR	(Hm Rd)	TB	R	RBI	RC	TBB	IBB	SO	HBP	SH	SF	SB	CS	SB%	GDP	Avg	OBP	Slg
1999 Everett	A-	42	178	51	10	3	2	(- -)	73	35	27	29	22	0	25	1	0	1	17	5	.77	1	.287	.366	.410
2000 Lancaster	A+	64	256	97	19	6	2	(- -)	134	63	51	59	37	2	27	0	1	1	22	12	.65	3	.379	.456	.523
2000 Tacoma	AAA	51	191	43	5	1	1	(- -)	53	17	23	13	7	0	28	0	4	3	5	0	1.00	3	.225	.249	.277
2001 San Antonio	AA	123	491	125	23	2	0	(- -)	152	59	28	46	28	0	55	1	7	4	34	9	.79	11	.255	.294	.310
2002 Tacoma	AAA	104	337	91	14	3	6	(- -)	129	47	47	44	29	1	44	3	9	3	20	10	.67	5	.270	.331	.383
2002 Seattle	AL	12	33	15	4	0	0	(0 0)	19	11	7	10	5	0	2	0	0	0	3	1	.75	0	.455	.526	.576

Geoff Blum

Bats: B **Throws:** R **Pos:** 3B-104; PH-21; LF-9; RF-3; SS-2; 1B-1; 2B-1; PR-1   **Ht:** 6'3" **Wt:** 200 **Born:** 4/26/73 **Age:** 30

Year Team	Lg	G	AB	H	2B	3B	HR	(Hm Rd)	TB	R	RBI	RC	TBB	IBB	SO	HBP	SH	SF	SB	CS	SB%	GDP	Avg	OBP	Slg
1999 Montreal	NL	45	133	32	7	2	8	(0 8)	67	21	18	22	17	3	25	0	3	0	1	0	1.00	3	.241	.327	.504
2000 Montreal	NL	124	343	97	20	2	11	(5 6)	154	40	45	50	26	2	60	3	3	4	1	4	.20	4	.283	.335	.449
2001 Montreal	NL	148	453	107	25	0	9	(6 3)	159	57	50	49	43	8	94	10	3	5	9	5	.64	12	.236	.313	.351
2002 Houston	NL	130	368	104	20	4	10	(6 4)	162	45	52	61	49	5	70	1	1	2	2	0	1.00	8	.283	.367	.440
4 ML YEARS		447	1297	340	72	8	38	(17 21)	542	163	165	182	135	18	249	14	10	11	13	9	.59	27	.262	.336	.418

Hiram Bocachica

Bats: R **Throws:** R **Pos:** CF-30; PH-29; LF-20; PR-10; RF-6; 2B-2; DH-1   **Ht:** 5'11" **Wt:** 165 **Born:** 3/4/76 **Age:** 27

Year Team	Lg	G	AB	H	2B	3B	HR	(Hm Rd)	TB	R	RBI	RC	TBB	IBB	SO	HBP	SH	SF	SB	CS	SB%	GDP	Avg	OBP	Slg
2000 Los Angeles	NL	8	10	3	0	0	0	(0 0)	3	2	0	1	0	0	2	0	0	0	0	0	-	0	.300	.300	.300
2001 Los Angeles	NL	75	133	31	11	1	2	(2 0)	50	15	9	15	9	0	33	1	0	0	4	1	.80	0	.233	.287	.376
2002 LA-Det		83	168	37	7	0	8	(2 6)	68	26	17	14	10	0	41	0	1	0	3	3	.50	3	.220	.264	.405
2002 Los Angeles	NL	49	65	14	3	0	4	(1 3)	29	12	9	7	5	0	19	0	0	0	1	1	.50	1	.215	.271	.446
2002 Detroit	AL	34	103	23	4	0	4	(1 3)	39	14	8	7	5	0	22	0	1	0	2	2	.50	2	.223	.259	.379
3 ML YEARS		166	311	71	18	1	10	(4 6)	121	43	26	30	19	0	76	1	1	0	7	4	.64	4	.228	.275	.389

Brian Boehringer

Pitches: R **Bats:** B **Pos:** RP-70   **Ht:** 6'2" **Wt:** 190 **Born:** 1/8/70 **Age:** 33

Year Team	Lg	G	GS	CG	GF	IP	BFP	H	R	ER	HR	SH	SF	HB	TBB	IBB	SO	WP	Bk	W	L	Pct	ShO	Sv-Op	Hld	ERC	ERA
1995 New York	AL	7	3	0	0	17.2	99	24	27	27	5	0	1	1	22	1	10	3	0	0	3	.000	0	0-1	0	11.86	13.75
1996 New York	AL	15	3	0	0	46.1	205	46	28	28	6	3	1	1	21	2	37	1	0	2	4	.333	0	0-1	4	4.42	5.44
1997 New York	AL	34	0	0	11	48.0	210	39	16	14	4	3	2	0	32	6	53	2	0	3	2	.600	0	0-3	5	3.74	2.63
1998 San Diego	NL	56	1	0	18	76.1	347	75	38	37	10	5	1	4	45	4	67	1	0	5	2	.714	0	0-1	7	5.06	4.36

Year Team	Lg	G	GS	CG	GF	IP	BFP	H	R	ER	HR	SH	SF	HB	TBB	IBB	SO	WP	Bk	W	L	Pct	ShO	Sv-Op	Hld	ERC	ERA
		HOW MUCH HE PITCHED						**WHAT HE GAVE UP**												**THE RESULTS**							
1999 San Diego	NL	33	11	0	8	94.1	409	97	38	34	10	6	4	1	35	1	64	2	0	6	5	.545	0	0-2	3	4.12	3.24
2000 San Diego	NL	7	3	0	1	15.2	74	18	15	10	4	0	1	0	10	0	9	0	0	0	3	.000	0	0-1	0	7.15	5.74
2001 NYY-SF		51	0	0	17	69.0	311	67	35	28	7	2	4	5	29	5	60	0	0	0	4	.000	0	2-2	3	4.02	3.65
2002 Pittsburgh	NL	70	0	0	20	79.2	328	65	30	30	5	6	3	2	33	6	65	1	0	4	4	.500	0	1-6	28	2.92	3.39
2001 New York	AL	22	0	0	8	34.2	155	35	15	12	3	1	2	3	12	0	33	0	0	0	1	.000	0	1-1	1	4.03	3.12
2001 San Francisco	NL	29	0	0	9	34.1	156	32	20	16	4	1	2	2	17	5	27	0	0	0	3	.000	0	1-1	2	4.01	4.19
8 ML YEARS		273	21	0	76	447.0	1983	431	227	208	51	25	19	14	227	28	365	10	0	20	27	.426	0	3-17	50	4.39	4.19

Jeremy Bonderman

Pitches: R Bats: R Pos: SP **Ht: 6'2" Wt: 210 Born: 10/28/82 Age: 20**

Year Team	Lg	G	GS	CG	GF	IP	BFP	H	R	ER	HR	SH	SF	HB	TBB	IBB	SO	WP	Bk	W	L	Pct	ShO	Sv-Op	Hld	ERC	ERA
		HOW MUCH HE PITCHED						**WHAT HE GAVE UP**												**THE RESULTS**							
2002 Modesto	A+	25	25	1	0	144.2	627	129	77	58	15	6	7	5	55	1	160	9	3	9	8	.529	0	0--	-	3.45	3.61
2002 Lakeland	A+	2	2	1	0	12.0	49	11	8	8	3	1	0	2	4	0	10	1	0	0	1	.000	0	0--	-	5.42	6.00

Barry Bonds

Bats: L Throws: L Pos: LF-135; DH-5; PH-4 **Ht: 6'2" Wt: 228 Born: 7/24/64 Age: 38**

Year Team	Lg	G	AB	H	2B	3B	HR	(Hm	Rd)	TB	R	RBI	RC	TBB	IBB	SO	HBP	SH	SF	SB	CS	SB%	GDP	Avg	OBP	Slg
		BATTING																		**BASERUNNING**				**AVERAGES**		
1986 Pittsburgh	NL	113	413	92	26	3	16	(9	7)	172	72	48	64	65	2	102	2	2	2	36	7	.84	4	.223	.330	.416
1987 Pittsburgh	NL	150	551	144	34	9	25	(12	13)	271	99	59	92	54	3	88	3	0	3	32	10	.76	4	.261	.329	.492
1988 Pittsburgh	NL	144	538	152	30	5	24	(14	10)	264	97	58	97	72	14	82	2	0	2	17	11	.61	3	.283	.368	.491
1989 Pittsburgh	NL	159	580	144	34	6	19	(7	12)	247	96	58	91	93	22	93	1	1	4	32	10	.76	9	.248	.351	.426
1990 Pittsburgh	NL	151	519	156	32	3	33	(14	19)	293	104	114	121	93	15	83	3	0	6	52	13	.80	8	.301	.406	.565
1991 Pittsburgh	NL	153	510	149	28	5	25	(12	13)	262	95	116	113	107	25	73	4	0	13	43	13	.77	8	.292	.410	.514
1992 Pittsburgh	NL	140	473	147	36	5	34	(15	19)	295	109	103	134	127	32	69	5	0	7	39	8	.83	9	.311	.456	.624
1993 San Francisco	NL	159	539	181	38	4	46	(21	25)	365	129	123	155	126	43	79	2	0	7	29	12	.71	11	.336	.458	.677
1994 San Francisco	NL	112	391	122	18	1	37	(15	22)	253	89	81	105	74	18	43	6	0	3	29	9	.76	3	.312	.426	.647
1995 San Francisco	NL	144	506	149	30	7	33	(16	17)	292	109	104	125	120	22	83	5	0	4	31	10	.76	12	.294	.431	.577
1996 San Francisco	NL	158	517	159	27	3	42	(23	19)	318	122	129	148	151	30	76	1	0	6	40	7	.85	11	.308	.461	.615
1997 San Francisco	NL	159	532	155	26	5	40	(24	16)	311	123	101	140	145	34	87	8	0	5	37	8	.82	13	.291	.446	.585
1998 San Francisco	NL	156	552	167	44	7	37	(21	16)	336	120	122	141	130	29	92	8	1	6	28	12	.70	15	.303	.438	.609
1999 San Francisco	NL	102	355	93	20	2	34	(16	18)	219	91	83	85	73	9	62	3	0	3	15	2	.88	6	.262	.389	.617
2000 San Francisco	NL	143	480	147	28	4	49	(25	24)	330	129	106	139	117	22	77	3	0	7	11	3	.79	6	.306	.440	.688
2001 San Francisco	NL	153	476	156	32	2	73	(37	36)	411	129	137	191	177	35	93	9	0	2	13	3	.81	5	.328	.515	.863
2002 San Francisco	NL	143	403	149	31	2	46	(19	27)	322	117	110	161	198	68	47	9	0	2	9	2	.82	4	.370	.582	.799
17 ML YEARS		2439	8335	2462	514	73	613	(300	313)	4961	1830	1652	2102	1922	423	1329	74	4	82	493	140	.78	131	.295	.428	.595

Jung Bong

Pitches: L Bats: L Pos: SP-1 **Ht: 6'3" Wt: 175 Born: 7/15/80 Age: 22**

Year Team	Lg	G	GS	CG	GF	IP	BFP	H	R	ER	HR	SH	SF	HB	TBB	IBB	SO	WP	Bk	W	L	Pct	ShO	Sv-Op	Hld	ERC	ERA
		HOW MUCH HE PITCHED						**WHAT HE GAVE UP**												**THE RESULTS**							
1998 Braves	R	11	10	0	0	48.1	181	31	9	8	2	1	1	6	14	0	56	7	3	1	1	.500	0	0--	-	2.10	1.49
1999 Macon	A	26	20	0	2	108.2	484	111	61	48	8	5	1	11	50	0	100	9	4	6	5	.545	0	1--	-	4.67	3.98
2000 Macon	A	20	19	0	0	112.2	500	119	65	53	4	5	3	14	45	0	90	10	2	7	7	.500	0	0--	-	4.44	4.23
2000 Myrtle Beach	A+	7	6	0	0	41.1	163	33	14	10	1	1	0	5	7	0	37	4	0	3	1	.750	0	0--	-	2.21	2.18
2001 Myrtle Beach	A+	28	28	0	0	168.0	677	151	67	56	7	6	3	4	47	0	145	7	1	13	9	.591	0	0--	-	2.87	3.00
2002 Greenville	AA	27	17	0	4	122.0	533	136	59	44	6	5	5	3	45	1	107	8	1	7	8	.467	0	2--	-	4.35	3.25
2002 Atlanta	NL	1	1	0	0	6.0	27	8	5	5	0	0	0	0	2	0	4	0	0	0	1	.000	0	0-0	-	5.03	7.50

Aaron Boone

Bats: R Throws: R Pos: 3B-154; SS-16; PH-5 **Ht: 6'2" Wt: 200 Born: 3/9/73 Age: 30**

Year Team	Lg	G	AB	H	2B	3B	HR	(Hm	Rd)	TB	R	RBI	RC	TBB	IBB	SO	HBP	SH	SF	SB	CS	SB%	GDP	Avg	OBP	Slg
		BATTING																		**BASERUNNING**				**AVERAGES**		
1997 Cincinnati	NL	16	49	12	1	0	0	(0	0)	13	5	5	3	2	0	5	0	1	0	1	0	1.00	1	.245	.275	.265
1998 Cincinnati	NL	58	181	51	13	2	1	(2	0)	74	24	28	27	15	1	36	5	3	2	6	1	.86	5	.282	.350	.409
1999 Cincinnati	NL	139	472	132	26	5	14	(7	7)	210	56	72	70	30	2	79	8	5	5	17	6	.74	6	.280	.330	.445
2000 Cincinnati	NL	84	291	83	18	0	12	(5	7)	137	44	43	50	24	1	52	10	2	4	6	1	.86	5	.285	.356	.471
2001 Cincinnati	NL	103	381	112	26	4	14	(10	4)	184	54	62	63	29	1	71	8	3	6	6	3	.67	6	.294	.351	.483
2002 Cincinnati	NL	162	606	146	38	2	26	(14	12)	266	83	87	86	56	4	111	10	9	4	32	8	.80	9	.241	.314	.439
6 ML YEARS		562	1980	536	122	11	68	(38	30)	884	266	297	299	156	9	354	41	23	21	68	19	.78	33	.271	.333	.446

Bret Boone

Bats: R Throws: R Pos: 2B-153; PH-2; DH-1 **Ht: 5'10" Wt: 190 Born: 4/6/69 Age: 34**

Year Team	Lg	G	AB	H	2B	3B	HR	(Hm	Rd)	TB	R	RBI	RC	TBB	IBB	SO	HBP	SH	SF	SB	CS	SB%	GDP	Avg	OBP	Slg
		BATTING																		**BASERUNNING**				**AVERAGES**		
1992 Seattle	AL	33	129	25	4	0	4	(2	2)	41	15	15	7	4	0	34	1	1	0	1	1	.50	4	.194	.224	.318
1993 Seattle	AL	76	271	68	12	2	12	(7	5)	120	31	38	35	17	1	52	4	6	4	2	3	.40	6	.251	.301	.443
1994 Cincinnati	NL	108	381	122	25	2	12	(5	7)	187	59	68	65	24	1	74	8	5	5	3	4	.43	10	.320	.368	.491
1995 Cincinnati	NL	138	513	137	34	2	15	(6	9)	220	63	68	70	41	0	84	6	5	5	5	1	.83	14	.267	.326	.429
1996 Cincinnati	NL	142	520	121	21	3	12	(7	5)	184	56	69	50	31	0	100	3	5	9	3	2	.60	9	.233	.275	.354
1997 Cincinnati	NL	139	443	99	25	1	7	(4	3)	147	40	46	42	45	4	101	4	4	5	5	5	.50	11	.223	.298	.332
1998 Cincinnati	NL	157	583	155	38	1	24	(13	11)	267	76	95	80	48	3	104	4	4	4	6	4	.60	23	.266	.324	.458
1999 Atlanta	NL	152	608	153	38	1	20	(9	11)	253	102	63	77	47	0	112	5	1	2	14	9	.61	11	.252	.310	.416
2000 San Diego	NL	127	463	116	18	2	19	(8	11)	195	61	74	63	50	7	97	5	0	7	8	4	.67	11	.251	.326	.421
2001 Seattle	AL	158	623	206	37	3	37	(19	18)	360	118	141	126	40	5	110	9	5	13	5	5	.50	11	.331	.372	.578
2002 Seattle	AL	155	608	169	34	3	24	(13	11)	281	88	107	96	53	4	102	6	2	6	12	5	.71	11	.278	.339	.462
11 ML YEARS		1385	5142	1371	286	20	186	(93	93)	2255	709	784	711	400	25	970	55	51	61	64	43	.60	121	.267	.323	.439

Pedro Borbon

Pitches: L **Bats:** L **Pos:** RP-72   **Ht:** 6'1" **Wt:** 230 **Born:** 11/15/67 **Age:** 35

			HOW MUCH HE PITCHED						WHAT HE GAVE UP										THE RESULTS							
Year Team	Lg	G	GS	CG	GF	IP	BFP	H	R	ER	HR	SH	SF	HB	TBB	IBB	SO	WP	Bk	W	L	Pct	ShO	Sv-Op	Hld	ERC	ERA
1992 Atlanta	NL	2	0	0	2	1.1	7	2	1	1	0	0	0	0	1	1	1	0	0	0	1	.000	0	0-0	0	5.90	6.75
1993 Atlanta	NL	3	0	0	0	1.2	11	3	4	4	0	1	0	0	3	0	2	0	0	0	0	—	0	0-0	0	14.26	21.60
1995 Atlanta	NL	41	0	0	19	32.0	143	29	12	11	2	3	1	1	17	4	33	0	1	2	2	.500	0	2-4	6	3.61	3.09
1996 Atlanta	NL	43	0	0	19	36.0	140	26	12	11	1	4	0	1	7	0	31	0	0	3	0	1.000	0	1-1	4	1.64	2.75
1999 Los Angeles	NL	70	0	0	11	50.2	220	39	23	23	5	0	3	0	29	1	33	1	0	4	3	.571	0	1-2	15	3.45	4.09
2000 Toronto	AL	59	0	0	6	41.2	213	45	37	30	5	2	7	5	38	5	29	0	0	1	1	.500	0	1-1	12	6.91	6.48
2001 Toronto	AL	71	0	0	14	53.1	217	48	24	22	8	2	2	4	12	3	45	0	0	2	4	.333	0	0-5	13	3.44	3.71
2002 Tor-Hou		72	0	0	9	50.1	232	53	32	30	10	3	6	3	25	8	50	1	0	4	4	.500	0	1-5	17	5.36	5.36
2002 Toronto	AL	16	0	0	6	12.2	60	12	8	7	3	0	1	1	6	3	11	1	0	1	2	.333	0	0-2	1	4.61	4.97
2002 Houston	NL	56	0	0	3	37.2	172	41	24	23	7	3	5	2	19	5	39	0	0	3	2	.600	0	1-3	16	5.63	5.50
8 ML YEARS		361	0	0	80	267.0	1183	245	145	132	31	15	19	15	132	22	224	2	1	16	15	.516	0	6-18	67	4.12	4.45

Joe Borchard

Bats: B **Throws:** R **Pos:** LF-10; CF-5; RF-3; PR-2; PH-1   **Ht:** 6'5" **Wt:** 220 **Born:** 11/25/78 **Age:** 24

								BATTING												BASERUNNING				AVERAGES		
Year Team	Lg	G	AB	H	2B	3B	HR	(Hm	Rd)	TB	R	RBI	RC	TBB	IBB	SO	HBP	SH	SF	SB	CS	SB%	GDP	Avg	OBP	Slg
2000 White Sox	R	7	29	12	4	0	0	(-	-)	16	3	8	7	4	0	4	0	0	0	0	0	—	0	.414	.485	.552
2000 Winstn-Salm	A+	14	52	15	3	0	2	(-	-)	24	7	7	10	6	0	9	2	0	1	0	0	—	0	.288	.377	.462
2000 Birmingham	AA	6	22	5	0	1	0	(-	-)	7	3	3	2	3	0	8	0	0	1	0	0	—	1	.227	.308	.318
2001 Birmingham	AA	133	515	152	27	1	27	(-	-)	262	95	98	97	67	1	158	10	0	5	5	4	.56	13	.295	.384	.509
2002 Winstn-Salm	A+	2	3	0	0	0	0	(-	-)	0	1	0	2	6	0	0	0	0	0	0	0	—	0	.000	.667	.000
2002 Charlotte	AAA	117	438	119	35	2	20	(-	-)	218	62	59	72	49	2	139	4	0	2	2	4	.33	11	.272	.349	.498
2002 Chicago	AL	16	36	8	0	0	2	(0	2)	14	5	5	5	1	0	14	0	0	0	0	0	—	0	.222	.243	.389

Pat Borders

Bats: R **Throws:** R **Pos:** C-2; DH-2; PH-2   **Ht:** 6'2" **Wt:** 200 **Born:** 5/14/63 **Age:** 40

								BATTING												BASERUNNING				AVERAGES		
Year Team	Lg	G	AB	H	2B	3B	HR	(Hm	Rd)	TB	R	RBI	RC	TBB	IBB	SO	HBP	SH	SF	SB	CS	SB%	GDP	Avg	OBP	Slg
2002 Tacoma*	AAA	92	317	84	16	1	12	(-	-)	138	42	27	38	11	0	47	0	2	1	3	2	.60	6	.265	.289	.435
1988 Toronto	AL	56	154	42	6	3	5	(2	3)	69	15	21	18	3	0	24	0	2	1	0	0	—	5	.273	.285	.448
1989 Toronto	AL	94	241	62	11	1	3	(1	2)	84	22	29	22	11	2	45	1	1	2	2	1	.67	7	.257	.290	.349
1990 Toronto	AL	125	346	99	24	2	15	(10	5)	172	36	49	48	18	2	57	0	1	3	0	1	.00	17	.286	.319	.497
1991 Toronto	AL	105	291	71	17	0	5	(2	3)	103	22	36	26	11	1	45	1	6	3	0	0	—	8	.244	.271	.354
1992 Toronto	AL	138	480	116	26	2	13	(7	6)	185	47	53	52	33	3	75	2	1	5	1	1	.50	11	.242	.290	.385
1993 Toronto	AL	138	488	124	30	0	9	(3	6)	181	38	55	46	20	2	66	2	7	3	2	2	.50	18	.254	.285	.371
1994 Toronto	AL	85	295	73	13	1	3	(3	0)	97	24	26	25	15	0	50	0	1	0	1	1	.50	7	.247	.284	.329
1995 KC-Hou		63	178	37	8	1	4	(1	3)	59	15	13	14	9	2	29	0	0	0	0	0	—	3	.208	.246	.331
1996 Stl-Ana-CWS		76	220	61	7	0	5	(3	2)	83	15	18	23	9	0	43	0	5	0	0	2	.00	4	.277	.306	.377
1997 Cleveland	AL	55	159	47	7	1	4	(0	4)	68	17	15	21	9	0	27	2	0	0	0	2	.00	5	.296	.341	.428
1998 Cleveland	AL	54	160	38	6	0	0	(0	0)	44	12	6	11	10	0	40	2	2	1	0	2	.00	3	.238	.289	.275
1999 Cle-Tor		12	34	9	0	1	1	(1	0)	14	3	6	4	1	0	5	0	0	1	0	0	—	3	.265	.286	.412
2001 Seattle	AL	5	6	3	0	0	0	(0	0)	3	1	0	1	0	0	1	0	1	0	0	0	—	0	.500	.500	.500
2002 Seattle	AL	4	4	2	1	0	0	(0	0)	3	0	1	1	0	0	1	0	0	0	0	0	—	0	.500	.500	.750
1995 Kansas City	AL	52	143	33	8	1	4	(1	3)	55	14	13	14	7	1	22	0	0	0	0	0	—	3	.231	.267	.385
1995 Houston	NL	11	35	4	0	0	0	(0	0)	4	1	0	0	2	1	7	0	0	0	0	0	—	2	.114	.162	.114
1996 St Louis	NL	26	69	22	3	0	0	(0	0)	25	3	4	7	1	0	14	0	1	0	0	1	.00	1	.319	.329	.362
1996 Anaheim	AL	19	57	13	3	0	2	(2	0)	22	6	8	5	3	0	11	0	1	0	0	1	.00	1	.228	.267	.386
1996 Chicago	AL	31	94	26	1	0	3	(1	2)	36	6	6	11	5	0	18	0	3	0	0	0	—	2	.277	.313	.383
1999 Cleveland	AL	6	20	6	0	1	0	(0	0)	8	2	3	2	0	0	3	0	0	1	0	0	—	0	.300	.300	.400
1999 Toronto	AL	6	14	3	0	0	1	(1	0)	6	1	3	2	1	0	2	0	0	0	0	0	—	3	.214	.267	.429
14 ML YEARS		1010	3056	784	156	12	67	(36	31)	1165	267	328	312	149	12	508	10	27	18	6	13	.32	88	.257	.292	.381

Mike Bordick

Bats: R **Throws:** R **Pos:** SS-117   **Ht:** 5'11" **Wt:** 175 **Born:** 7/21/65 **Age:** 37

								BATTING												BASERUNNING				AVERAGES		
Year Team	Lg	G	AB	H	2B	3B	HR	(Hm	Rd)	TB	R	RBI	RC	TBB	IBB	SO	HBP	SH	SF	SB	CS	SB%	GDP	Avg	OBP	Slg
1990 Oakland	AL	25	14	1	0	0	0	(0	0)	1	0	0	0	1	0	4	0	0	0	0	0	—	0	.071	.133	.071
1991 Oakland	AL	90	235	56	5	1	0	(0	0)	63	21	21	17	14	0	37	3	12	1	3	4	.43	3	.238	.289	.268
1992 Oakland	AL	154	504	151	19	4	3	(3	0)	187	62	48	69	40	2	59	9	14	5	12	6	.67	9	.300	.358	.371
1993 Oakland	AL	159	546	136	21	2	3	(2	1)	170	60	48	59	60	2	58	11	10	6	10	10	.50	9	.249	.332	.311
1994 Oakland	AL	114	391	99	18	4	2	(1	1)	131	38	37	43	38	1	44	3	3	5	7	2	.78	9	.253	.320	.335
1995 Oakland	AL	126	428	113	13	0	8	(2	6)	150	46	44	50	35	2	48	5	7	3	11	3	.79	8	.264	.325	.350
1996 Oakland	AL	155	525	126	18	4	5	(2	3)	167	46	54	52	52	0	59	1	4	5	5	6	.45	8	.240	.307	.318
1997 Baltimore	AL	153	509	120	19	1	7	(5	2)	162	55	46	39	33	1	66	2	12	4	0	2	.00	23	.236	.283	.318
1998 Baltimore	AL	151	465	121	29	1	13	(10	3)	191	59	51	60	39	0	65	10	15	4	6	7	.46	13	.260	.328	.411
1999 Baltimore	AL	160	631	175	35	7	10	(3	7)	254	93	77	82	54	1	102	5	8	10	14	4	.78	25	.277	.334	.403
2000 Bal-NYM		156	583	166	30	1	20	(9	11)	258	88	80	84	49	0	99	3	4	5	9	6	.60	16	.285	.341	.443
2001 Baltimore	AL	58	229	57	13	0	7	(2	5)	91	32	30	29	17	1	36	6	2	3	9	3	.75	4	.249	.314	.397
2002 Baltimore	AL	117	367	85	19	3	8	(6	2)	134	37	36	40	35	0	63	3	6	2	7	4	.64	9	.232	.302	.365
2000 Baltimore	AL	100	391	116	22	1	16	(6	10)	188	70	59	62	34	0	71	1	2	5	6	5	.55	12	.297	.350	.481
2000 New York	NL	56	192	50	8	0	4	(3	1)	70	18	21	22	15	0	28	2	2	0	3	1	.75	4	.260	.321	.365
13 ML YEARS		1618	5427	1406	239	28	86	(45	41)	1959	637	572	624	467	10	740	61	97	53	93	57	.62	137	.259	.322	.361

Toby Borland

Pitches: R Bats: R Pos: RP-15   Ht: 6'6" Wt: 210 Born: 5/29/69 Age: 34

		HOW MUCH HE PITCHED						WHAT HE GAVE UP													THE RESULTS						
Year Team	Lg	G	GS	CG	GF	IP	BFP	H	R	ER	HR	SH	SF	HB	TBB	IBB	SO	WP	Bk	W	L	Pct	ShO	Sv-Op	Hld	ERC	ERA
2002 Calgary*	AAA	56	0	0	38	70.0	295	55	24	23	2	1	2	7	30	3	75	9	0	5	2	.714	0	14--	-	2.86	2.96
1994 Philadelphia	NL	24	0	0	7	34.1	144	31	10	9	1	1	0	4	14	3	26	4	0	1	0	1.000	0	1-1	0	3.50	2.36
1995 Philadelphia	NL	50	0	0	18	74.0	339	81	37	31	3	3	2	5	37	7	59	12	0	1	3	.250	0	6-9	11	4.62	3.77
1996 Philadelphia	NL	69	0	0	11	90.2	399	83	51	41	9	4	1	3	43	3	76	10	0	7	3	.700	0	0-2	10	3.89	4.07
1997 NYM-Bos		16	0	0	5	16.2	89	17	14	14	2	0	0	3	21	0	8	3	0	0	1	.000	0	1-2	1	8.72	7.56
1998 Philadelphia	NL	6	0	0	3	9.0	39	8	5	5	1	1	0	0	5	0	9	2	0	0	0	-	0	0-0	1	4.17	5.00
2001 Anaheim	AL	2	0	0	1	3.1	19	8	5	4	1	1	0	0	1	0	0	0	0	0	1	.000	0	0-1	0	14.71	10.80
2002 Florida	NL	15	0	0	3	13.2	62	14	8	8	3	0	2	3	5	0	11	2	0	1	0	1.000	0	0-0	0	5.85	5.27
1997 New York	NL	13	0	0	5	13.1	65	11	9	9	1	0	0	1	14	0	7	3	0	0	1	.000	0	1-2	1	5.68	6.08
1997 Boston	AL	3	0	0	0	3.1	24	6	5	5	1	0	0	2	7	0	1	0	0	0	0	-	0	0-0	0	23.38	13.50
7 ML YEARS		182	0	0	48	241.2	1091	242	130	112	20	10	5	18	126	13	189	33	0	10	8	.556	0	8-15	23	4.61	4.17

Joe Borowski

Pitches: R Bats: R Pos: RP-73   Ht: 6'2" Wt: 240 Born: 5/4/71 Age: 32

		HOW MUCH HE PITCHED						WHAT HE GAVE UP													THE RESULTS						
Year Team	Lg	G	GS	CG	GF	IP	BFP	H	R	ER	HR	SH	SF	HB	TBB	IBB	SO	WP	Bk	W	L	Pct	ShO	Sv-Op	Hld	ERC	ERA
1995 Baltimore	AL	6	0	0	3	7.1	30	5	1	1	0	0	0	0	4	0	3	0	0	0	0	-	0	0-0	0	2.32	1.23
1996 Atlanta	NL	22	0	0	8	26.0	121	33	15	14	4	5	0	1	13	4	15	1	0	2	4	.333	0	0-0	1	6.46	4.85
1997 Atl-NYY		21	0	0	9	26.0	123	29	13	12	2	1	0	0	20	5	8	0	0	2	3	.400	0	0-0	2	5.74	4.15
1998 New York	AL	8	0	0	6	9.2	42	11	7	7	0	0	0	0	4	0	7	0	0	0	1	.000	0	0-0	0	4.27	6.52
2001 Chicago	NL	1	1	0	0	1.2	13	6	6	6	1	1	0	0	3	0	1	0	0	0	1	.000	0	0-0	0	39.91	32.40
2002 Chicago	NL	73	0	0	25	95.2	391	84	31	29	10	5	3	1	29	6	97	1	0	4	4	.500	0	2-6	12	3.05	2.73
1997 Atlanta	NL	20	0	0	8	24.0	111	27	11	10	2	1	0	0	16	4	6	0	0	2	2	.500	0	0-0	1	5.51	3.75
1997 New York	AL	1	0	0	1	2.0	12	2	2	2	0	0	0	0	4	1	2	0	0	0	1	.000	0	0-0	1	8.25	9.00
6 ML YEARS		131	1	0	51	166.1	720	168	73	69	17	12	3	2	73	15	131	2	0	9	12	.429	0	2-6	15	4.24	3.73

Ricky Bottalico

Pitches: R Bats: L Pos: RP-30   Ht: 6'1" Wt: 215 Born: 8/26/69 Age: 33

		HOW MUCH HE PITCHED						WHAT HE GAVE UP													THE RESULTS						
Year Team	Lg	G	GS	CG	GF	IP	BFP	H	R	ER	HR	SH	SF	HB	TBB	IBB	SO	WP	Bk	W	L	Pct	ShO	Sv-Op	Hld	ERC	ERA
1994 Philadelphia	NL	3	0	0	3	3.0	13	3	0	0	0	0	0	1	0	0	3	0	0	0	0	-	0	0-0	0	3.05	0.00
1995 Philadelphia	NL	62	0	0	20	87.2	350	50	25	24	7	3	1	4	42	3	87	1	0	5	3	.625	0	1-5	20	2.17	2.46
1996 Philadelphia	NL	61	0	0	56	67.2	269	47	24	24	6	4	2	2	23	2	74	3	0	4	5	.444	0	34-38	0	2.29	3.19
1997 Philadelphia	NL	69	0	0	61	74.0	324	68	31	30	7	1	2	2	42	4	89	3	0	2	5	.286	0	34-41	0	4.29	3.65
1998 Philadelphia	NL	39	0	0	28	43.1	206	54	31	31	7	1	2	1	25	5	27	2	0	1	5	.167	0	6-7	3	6.63	6.44
1999 St Louis	NL	68	0	0	40	73.1	347	83	45	40	8	3	0	3	49	1	66	6	0	3	7	.300	0	20-28	8	5.16	4.91
2000 Kansas City	AL	62	0	0	50	72.2	319	65	40	39	12	3	1	2	41	3	56	5	1	9	6	.600	0	16-23	1	4.65	4.83
2001 Philadelphia	NL	66	0	0	18	67.0	281	58	31	29	11	7	4	4	25	2	57	5	0	3	4	.429	0	3-7	22	3.88	3.90
2002 Philadelphia	NL	30	0	0	6	27.1	128	33	16	14	3	2	1	1	13	2	24	2	0	0	3	.000	0	0-1	15	5.80	4.61
9 ML YEARS		460	0	0	282	516.0	2237	461	243	231	61	24	13	20	261	22	483	27	1	27	38	.415	0	114-150	69	4.12	4.03

Micah Bowie

Pitches: L Bats: L Pos: RP-13   Ht: 6'4" Wt: 210 Born: 11/10/74 Age: 28

		HOW MUCH HE PITCHED						WHAT HE GAVE UP													THE RESULTS						
Year Team	Lg	G	GS	CG	GF	IP	BFP	H	R	ER	HR	SH	SF	HB	TBB	IBB	SO	WP	Bk	W	L	Pct	ShO	Sv-Op	Hld	ERC	ERA
1994 Braves	R	6	5	0	1	29.2	124	27	14	10	1	0	2	1	5	0	35	1	0	0	3	.000	0	0--	-	2.34	3.03
1994 Danville	R+	7	5	0	0	32.2	141	28	16	13	4	2	3	3	13	1	38	2	0	3	1	.750	0	0--	-	3.69	3.58
1995 Macon	A	5	5	0	0	27.2	104	9	8	7	1	0	0	3	11	0	36	1	0	4	1	.800	0	0--	-	1.10	2.28
1995 Durham	A+	23	23	1	0	130.1	561	119	65	52	8	13	3	8	61	3	91	4	3	4	11	.267	0	0--	-	3.82	3.59
1996 Durham	A+	14	13	0	0	66.1	283	55	29	27	4	6	3	7	33	0	65	2	0	3	6	.333	0	0--	-	3.70	3.66
1997 Durham	A+	9	6	0	0	39.1	167	29	16	16	2	0	2	0	27	0	44	2	0	2	2	.500	0	0--	-	3.46	3.66
1997 Greenville	AA	8	7	0	0	43.2	193	34	19	17	3	1	2	3	26	1	41	2	0	3	2	.600	0	0--	-	3.54	3.50
1998 Greenville	AA	30	29	1	0	163.0	676	132	73	63	12	7	2	6	64	0	160	7	3	11	6	.647	0	0--	-	3.00	3.48
1999 Richmond	AAA	13	13	0	0	73.0	288	65	24	24	4	2	2	0	14	0	82	2	0	4	4	.500	0	0--	-	2.49	2.96
2000 Iowa	AAA	9	9	0	0	45.1	220	59	44	40	9	3	1	1	31	3	35	2	0	1	7	.125	0	0--	-	7.99	7.94
2000 W Tennessee	AA	18	18	1	0	117.1	481	91	47	45	6	7	1	3	48	1	106	1	0	7	6	.538	1	0--	-	2.71	3.45
2001 Sacramento	AAA	38	10	1	9	116.0	506	123	68	65	13	2	2	5	44	1	102	1	0	6	8	.429	1	3--	-	4.61	5.04
2002 Sacramento	AAA	46	0	0	15	54.2	229	40	21	19	2	1	3	2	24	2	64	1	1	3	2	.600	0	4--	-	2.43	3.13
1999 Atl-ChC	NL	14	11	0	2	51.0	265	81	60	58	9	3	3	2	34	2	41	4	2	2	7	.222	0	0-0	0	9.69	10.24
2002 Oakland	AL	13	0	0	4	12.0	55	12	2	2	1	0	0	1	8	1	8	0	0	2	0	1.000	0	0-0	3	5.26	1.50
1999 Atlanta	NL	3	0	0	2	4.0	23	8	6	6	1	0	0	0	4	0	2	0	0	0	1	.000	0	0-0	0	15.43	13.50
1999 Chicago	NL	11	11	0	0	47.0	242	73	54	52	8	3	3	2	30	2	39	4	2	2	6	.250	0	0-0	0	9.23	9.96
2 ML YEARS		27	11	0	6	63.0	320	93	62	60	10	3	3	3	42	3	49	4	2	4	7	.364	0	0-0	3	8.79	8.57

Brian Bowles

Pitches: R Bats: R Pos: RP-17   Ht: 6'5" Wt: 220 Born: 8/18/76 Age: 26

		HOW MUCH HE PITCHED						WHAT HE GAVE UP													THE RESULTS						
Year Team	Lg	G	GS	CG	GF	IP	BFP	H	R	ER	HR	SH	SF	HB	TBB	IBB	SO	WP	Bk	W	L	Pct	ShO	Sv-Op	Hld	ERC	ERA
1995 Blue Jays	R	8	0	0	2	15.0	70	18	12	4	2	0	1	1	3	0	11	2	1	0	1	.000	0	0--	-	4.58	2.40
1996 Medicine Hat	R+	24	0	0	7	39.2	193	53	35	28	5	1	3	5	21	1	29	9	0	2	2	.500	0	1--	-	7.37	6.35
1997 Hagerstown	A	4	0	0	1	10.1	49	14	10	8	2	0	0	0	5	0	9	1	0	1	0	1.000	0	0--	-	7.93	6.97
1997 Dunedin	A+	7	1	0	3	14.1	68	20	14	12	2	0	1	0	7	1	9	3	1	0	2	.000	0	0--	-	7.07	7.53
1997 St.Catharines	A-	16	16	0	0	78.2	351	76	53	44	6	0	3	11	35	0	64	4	1	5	8	.385	0	0--	-	4.42	5.03
1998 Dunedin	A+	9	2	1	0	27.0	126	32	13	10	2	1	1	1	16	0	17	1	1	1	2	.333	0	0--	-	5.94	3.33
1998 Hagerstown	A	31	4	0	9	67.2	306	80	41	34	4	2	3	9	18	1	48	6	0	2	4	.333	0	0--	-	4.73	4.52
1999 Hagerstown	A	48	1	0	22	79.1	355	73	41	35	4	4	3	12	39	3	80	9	0	6	2	.750	0	3--	-	4.12	3.97
2000 Tennessee	AA	49	0	0	12	81.2	343	64	31	27	1	2	3	8	36	1	72	11	0	4	4	.500	0	0--	-	2.84	2.98

Year Team	Lg	G	GS	CG	GF	IP	BFP	H	R	ER	HR	SH	SF	HB	TBB	IBB	SO	WP	Bk	W	L	Pct	ShO	Sv-Op	Hld	ERC	ERA
2001 Syracuse	AAA	66	0	0	24	77.1	338	56	30	25	3	5	1	7	44	4	81	14	3	3	5	.375	0	6- -	-	2.98	2.91
2002 Syracuse	AAA	59	0	0	46	59.0	259	46	24	22	4	5	1	8	32	5	53	3	1	4	7	.364	0	14- -	-	3.53	3.36
2001 Toronto	AL	2	0	0	0	3.2	15	4	0	0	0	0	0	0	1	0	1	4	1	0	0	-	0	0-0	-	3.55	0.00
2002 Toronto	AL	17	0	0	7	20.0	89	13	11	9	0	0	1	3	14	1	19	5	1	2	1	.667	0	0-1	1	3.00	4.05
2 ML YEARS		19	0	0	7	23.2	104	17	11	9	0	0	1	3	15	1	23	6	1	2	1	.667	0	0-1	1	3.09	3.42

Jason Boyd

Pitches: R Bats: R Pos: RP-23   Ht: 6'3" Wt: 173 Born: 2/23/73 Age: 30

Year Team	Lg	G	GS	CG	GF	IP	BFP	H	R	ER	HR	SH	SF	HB	TBB	IBB	SO	WP	Bk	W	L	Pct	ShO	Sv-Op	Hld	ERC	ERA
2002 Portland*	AAA	19	0	0	6	26.0	105	19	4	3	2	2	0	1	7	0	22	2	0	0	1	.000	0	4- -	-	2.16	1.04
2002 Pawtucket*	AAA	9	0	0	4	16.0	71	13	7	7	3	0	0	1	9	0	15	1	0	1	0	1.000	0	1- -	-	4.44	3.94
1999 Pittsburgh	NL	4	0	0	0	5.1	24	5	2	2	0	0	1	1	2	0	4	1	0	0	0	-	0	0-0	-	3.53	3.38
2000 Philadelphia	NL	30	0	0	11	34.1	161	39	28	25	2	3	0	1	24	4	32	1	0	0	1	.000	0	0-1	2	5.71	6.55
2002 San Diego	NL	23	0	0	6	28.1	131	33	29	25	6	3	3	0	15	1	18	3	0	1	0	.000	0	0-3	4	6.35	7.94
3 ML YEARS		57	0	0	17	68.0	316	77	59	52	8	6	4	2	41	5	54	5	0	1	1	.500	0	0-4	6	5.81	6.88

Chad Bradford

Pitches: R Bats: R Pos: RP-75   Ht: 6'5" Wt: 203 Born: 9/14/74 Age: 28

Year Team	Lg	G	GS	CG	GF	IP	BFP	H	R	ER	HR	SH	SF	HB	TBB	IBB	SO	WP	Bk	W	L	Pct	ShO	Sv-Op	Hld	ERC	ERA
1998 Chicago	AL	29	0	0	8	30.2	125	27	16	11	0	0	0	0	7	0	11	1	1	2	1	.667	0	1-3	9	2.16	3.23
1999 Chicago	AL	3	0	0	0	3.2	24	9	8	8	1	0	0	0	5	0	1	0	1	0	0	-	0	0-0	0	21.34	19.64
2000 Chicago	AL	12	0	0	5	13.2	52	13	4	3	0	0	0	0	1	1	9	0	0	1	0	1.000	0	0-0	2	2.01	1.98
2001 Oakland	AL	35	0	0	19	36.2	154	41	12	11	6	1	0	1	6	0	34	0	0	2	1	.667	0	1-4	4	4.36	2.70
2002 Oakland	AL	75	0	0	14	75.1	311	73	29	26	2	2	2	5	14	5	56	0	1	4	2	.667	0	2-5	24	2.77	3.11
5 ML YEARS		154	0	0	46	160.0	666	163	69	59	9	3	2	6	33	6	110	2	2	9	4	.692	0	4-12	39	3.24	3.32

Milton Bradley

Bats: B Throws: R Pos: CF-94; PR-5; PH-2; DH-1   Ht: 6'0" Wt: 190 Born: 4/15/78 Age: 25

Year Team	Lg	G	AB	H	2B	3B	HR	(Hm Rd)	TB	R	RBI	RC	TBB	IBB	SO	HBP	SH	SF	SB	CS	SB%	GDP	Avg	OBP	Slg
2002 Buffalo*	AAA	6	23	6	0	0	0	(- -)	6	3	3	2	3	0	5	0	0	2	2	1	.67	0	.261	.321	.261
2002 Akron*	AA	3	11	3	1	0	0	(- -)	4	1	1	1	1	0	1	0	0	0	0	1	.00	0	.273	.333	.364
2000 Montreal	NL	42	154	34	8	1	2	(1 1)	50	20	15	14	14	0	32	1	1	1	2	1	.67	3	.221	.288	.325
2001 Mon-Cle		77	238	53	17	3	1	(0 1)	79	22	19	21	21	0	65	1	2	0	8	5	.62	7	.223	.288	.332
2002 Cleveland	AL	98	325	81	18	3	9	(4 5)	132	48	38	40	32	2	58	0	1	0	6	3	.67	12	.249	.317	.406
2001 Montreal	NL	67	220	49	16	3	1	(0 1)	74	19	19	20	19	0	62	1	2	0	7	4	.64	6	.223	.288	.336
2001 Cleveland	AL	10	18	4	1	0	0	(0 0)	5	3	0	1	2	0	3	0	0	0	1	1	.50	1	.222	.300	.278
3 ML YEARS		217	717	168	43	7	12	(5 7)	261	90	72	75	67	2	155	2	4	1	16	9	.64	22	.234	.301	.364

Darren Bragg

Bats: L Throws: R Pos: PH-46; RF-36; CF-18; LF-12; PR-8; DH-3   Ht: 5'9" Wt: 180 Born: 9/7/69 Age: 33

Year Team	Lg	G	AB	H	2B	3B	HR	(Hm Rd)	TB	R	RBI	RC	TBB	IBB	SO	HBP	SH	SF	SB	CS	SB%	GDP	Avg	OBP	Slg
2002 Richmond*	AAA	22	75	22	5	0	1	(- -)	30	15	8	15	20	0	15	0	1	0	4	2	.67	0	.293	.442	.400
1994 Seattle	AL	8	19	3	1	0	0	(0 0)	4	4	2	1	2	1	5	0	0	0	0	0	-	0	.158	.238	.211
1995 Seattle	AL	52	145	34	5	1	3	(1 2)	50	20	12	19	18	1	37	4	1	2	9	0	1.00	2	.234	.331	.345
1996 Sea-Bos	AL	127	417	109	26	2	10	(7 3)	169	74	47	66	69	4	74	4	2	7	14	9	.61	5	.261	.366	.405
1997 Boston	AL	153	513	132	35	2	9	(3 6)	198	65	57	65	61	5	102	3	5	4	10	6	.63	16	.257	.337	.386
1998 Boston	AL	129	409	114	29	3	8	(3 5)	173	51	57	58	42	0	99	6	4	5	5	3	.63	16	.279	.351	.423
1999 St Louis	NL	93	273	71	12	1	6	(4 2)	103	38	26	41	44	1	67	3	5	0	3	0	1.00	5	.260	.369	.377
2000 Colorado	NL	71	149	33	7	1	3	(3 0)	51	16	21	16	17	1	41	0	0	3	4	1	.80	5	.221	.296	.342
2001 NYM-NYY		23	61	16	7	0	0	(0 0)	23	5	5	8	4	0	24	1	1	0	3	2	.60	0	.262	.318	.377
2002 Atlanta	NL	109	212	57	15	2	3	(2 1)	85	34	15	27	24	0	52	2	1	1	5	2	.71	4	.269	.347	.401
1996 Seattle	AL	69	195	53	12	1	7	(4 3)	88	36	25	35	33	4	35	2	1	4	8	5	.62	2	.272	.376	.451
1996 Boston	AL	58	222	56	14	1	3	(3 0)	81	38	22	31	36	2	39	2	1	3	6	4	.60	3	.252	.357	.365
2001 New York	NL	18	57	15	6	0	0	(0 0)	21	4	5	7	4	0	23	1	1	0	3	2	.60	0	.263	.323	.368
2001 New York	AL	5	4	1	1	0	0	(0 0)	2	1	0	1	0	0	1	0	0	0	0	0	-	0	.250	.250	.500
9 ML YEARS		765	2198	569	137	12	42	(23 19)	856	307	242	301	281	15	501	23	19	21	53	23	.70	51	.259	.346	.389

Russell Branyan

Bats: L Throws: R Pos: LF-66; PH-27; 3B-24; 1B-18; DH-5; PR-2; RF-1   Ht: 6'3" Wt: 195 Born: 12/19/75 Age: 27

Year Team	Lg	G	AB	H	2B	3B	HR	(Hm Rd)	TB	R	RBI	RC	TBB	IBB	SO	HBP	SH	SF	SB	CS	SB%	GDP	Avg	OBP	Slg
1998 Cleveland	AL	1	4	0	0	0	0	(0 0)	0	0	0	0	0	0	2	0	0	0	0	0	-	0	.000	.000	.000
1999 Cleveland	AL	11	38	8	2	0	1	(0 1)	13	4	6	4	3	0	19	1	0	0	0	0	-	0	.211	.286	.342
2000 Cleveland	AL	67	193	46	7	2	16	(13 3)	105	32	38	34	22	1	76	4	0	1	0	0	-	2	.238	.327	.544
2001 Cleveland	AL	113	315	73	16	2	20	(11 9)	153	48	54	50	38	1	132	3	0	5	1	1	.50	3	.232	.316	.486
2002 Cle-Cin		134	378	86	13	1	24	(5 19)	173	50	56	49	51	3	151	2	0	4	4	3	.57	5	.228	.320	.458
2002 Cleveland	AL	50	161	33	4	0	8	(1 7)	61	16	17	14	17	0	65	0	0	2	1	2	.33	3	.205	.278	.379
2002 Cincinnati	NL	84	217	53	9	1	16	(4 12)	112	34	39	35	34	3	86	2	0	2	3	1	.75	2	.244	.349	.516
5 ML YEARS		326	928	213	38	5	61	(29 32)	444	134	154	137	114	5	380	10	0	10	5	4	.56	9	.230	.317	.478

Dewon Brazelton

Pitches: R **Bats:** R **Pos:** SP-2   **Ht:** 6'4" **Wt:** 205 **Born:** 6/16/80 **Age:** 23

		HOW MUCH HE PITCHED						WHAT HE GAVE UP												THE RESULTS						
Year Team	Lg	G	GS	CG	GF	IP	BFP	H	R	ER	HR	SH	SF	HB	TBB	IBB	SO	WP	Bk	W	L	Pct	ShO	Sv-Op	Hld	ERC	ERA
2002 Orlando	AA	26	26	1	0	146.0	620	129	69	54	7	5	3	10	67	1	109	10	2	5	9	.357	0	0--	-	3.61	3.33
2002 Durham	AAA	1	1	0	0	5.0	20	5	0	0	0	0	0	0	1	0	6	0	0	1	0	1.000	0	0--	-	2.76	0.00
2002 Tampa Bay	AL	2	2	0	0	13.0	51	12	7	7	3	0	0	2	6	0	5	0	0	0	1	.000	0	0-0	-	6.29	4.85

Juan Brito

Bats: R **Throws:** R **Pos:** C-9   **Ht:** 5'11" **Wt:** 205 **Born:** 11/7/79 **Age:** 23

		BATTING																			BASERUNNING				AVERAGES		
Year Team	Lg	G	AB	H	2B	3B	HR	(Hm	Rd)	TB	R	RBI	RC	TBB	IBB	SO	HBP	SH	SF	SB	CS	SB%	GDP	Avg	OBP	Slg
1997 Royals	R	25	70	22	4	0	3	(-	-)	35	14	15	12	5	1	5	1	1	0	0	0	-	3	.314	.368	.500
1998 Lansing	A	63	212	52	7	0	0	(-	-)	59	16	22	17	17	0	41	2	1	2	2	2	.50	6	.245	.305	.278
1999 Wilmington	A+	14	46	13	1	0	0	(-	-)	14	3	1	4	1	0	11	0	0	0	0	0	-	1	.283	.298	.304
1999 Chrlstn - WV	A	61	208	50	6	0	0	(-	-)	56	14	19	13	11	0	37	1	3	0	1	2	.33	8	.240	.282	.269
1999 Omaha	AAA	2	7	2	2	0	0	(-	-)	4	1	0	1	0	0	2	0	0	0	0	0	-	0	.286	.286	.571
1999 Wichita	AA	4	11	1	0	0	0	(-	-)	1	0	0	0	2	0	3	0	0	0	0	0	-	2	.091	.231	.091
2000 Wichita	AA	34	105	27	2	0	0	(-	-)	29	9	10	9	11	2	15	1	0	2	2	1	.67	4	.257	.328	.276
2000 Wilmington	A+	22	54	12	4	0	0	(-	-)	16	4	9	5	8	0	7	0	0	1	1	0	1.00	2	.222	.317	.296
2000 Omaha	AAA	17	49	14	1	0	1	(-	-)	18	8	2	6	3	0	10	0	1	0	1	1	.50	0	.286	.327	.367
2001 Wichita	AA	70	236	63	10	0	4	(-	-)	85	22	28	24	17	0	29	0	7	1	3	3	.50	9	.267	.315	.360
2002 Omaha	AAA	3	9	2	1	0	0	(-	-)	3	1	1	1	1	0	1	0	0	0	0	0	-	0	.222	.300	.333
2002 Wichita	AA	89	302	77	11	0	7	(-	-)	109	40	38	31	21	1	46	1	5	3	1	1	.50	9	.255	.303	.361
2002 Kansas City	AL	9	23	7	2	0	0	(0	0)	9	1	1	0	0	0	3	0	0	0	0	0	-	2	.304	.304	.391

Chris Brock

Pitches: R **Bats:** R **Pos:** RP-22   **Ht:** 6'0" **Wt:** 185 **Born:** 2/5/71 **Age:** 32

		HOW MUCH HE PITCHED						WHAT HE GAVE UP												THE RESULTS						
Year Team	Lg	G	GS	CG	GF	IP	BFP	H	R	ER	HR	SH	SF	HB	TBB	IBB	SO	WP	Bk	W	L	Pct	ShO	Sv-Op	Hld	ERC	ERA
2002 Bowie*	AA	1	1	0	0	5.0	21	6	2	2	2	0	0	1	0	0	2	0	0	0	0	-	0	0--	-	6.73	3.60
1997 Atlanta	NL	7	6	0	1	30.2	144	34	23	19	2	3	4	0	19	2	16	2	1	0	0	-	0	0-0	-	5.10	5.58
1998 San Francisco	NL	13	0	0	4	27.2	120	31	13	12	3	2	0	1	7	1	19	0	0	0	0	-	0	0-0	-	4.11	3.90
1999 San Francisco	NL	19	19	0	0	106.2	479	124	69	65	18	5	3	4	41	2	76	8	2	6	8	.429	0	0-0	-	5.59	5.48
2000 Philadelphia	NL	63	5	0	17	93.1	403	85	48	45	21	1	2	3	41	0	69	4	1	7	8	.467	0	1-3	16	4.71	4.34
2001 Philadelphia	NL	24	0	0	6	32.2	147	35	16	15	6	2	1	2	15	2	26	2	0	3	0	1.000	0	0-1	3	5.50	4.13
2002 Baltimore	AL	22	0	0	3	44.0	192	52	24	23	6	0	2	1	14	1	21	0	0	2	1	.667	0	0-0	-	5.19	4.70
6 ML YEARS		148	30	0	31	335.0	1485	361	193	179	56	13	12	10	137	8	227	16	4	18	17	.514	0	1-4	19	5.12	4.81

Troy Brohawn

Pitches: L **Bats:** L **Pos:** RP-11   **Ht:** 6'1" **Wt:** 190 **Born:** 1/14/73 **Age:** 30

		HOW MUCH HE PITCHED						WHAT HE GAVE UP												THE RESULTS						
Year Team	Lg	G	GS	CG	GF	IP	BFP	H	R	ER	HR	SH	SF	HB	TBB	IBB	SO	WP	Bk	W	L	Pct	ShO	Sv-Op	Hld	ERC	ERA
1994 San Jose	A+	4	4	0	0	16.2	80	27	15	13	2	1	0	2	5	0	13	1	0	0	2	.000	0	0--	-	8.38	7.02
1995 San Jose	A+	11	10	0	1	65.1	246	45	14	12	4	1	1	1	20	0	57	5	1	7	3	.700	0	0--	-	2.09	1.65
1996 Shreveport	AA	28	28	0	0	156.2	668	163	99	80	30	7	3	6	49	0	82	8	3	9	10	.474	0	0--	-	4.80	4.60
1997 Shreveport	AA	26	26	1	0	169.0	695	148	57	48	10	3	1	2	64	0	98	4	3	13	5	.722	1	0--	-	3.16	2.56
1998 Fresno	AAA	30	19	0	4	121.2	528	144	75	71	18	11	5	3	36	1	87	8	0	10	8	.556	0	0--	-	5.24	5.25
1999 Tucson	AAA	3	2	0	0	4.0	16	5	1	0	0	0	0	0	1	0	6	0	0	0	0	-	0	0--	-	4.62	0.00
2000 Diamndbcks	R	3	3	0	0	4.0	16	5	1	0	0	0	0	0	1	0	6	0	1	0	0	-	0	0--	-	4.62	0.00
2000 Tucson	AAA	11	1	0	2	16.2	71	18	7	7	5	1	2	1	5	0	16	0	1	0	0	-	0	0--	-	5.95	3.78
2001 Tucson	AAA	2	0	0	1	3.1	13	1	0	0	0	0	0	0	1	0	4	0	0	0	0	-	0	0--	-	0.52	0.00
2002 Fresno	AAA	56	0	0	14	69.0	300	71	31	28	7	3	1	4	21	2	55	5	1	3	3	.500	0	1--	-	4.00	3.65
2001 Arizona	NL	59	0	0	10	49.1	220	55	27	27	5	2	4	1	23	2	30	2	0	2	3	.400	0	1-3	10	5.07	4.93
2002 San Francisco	NL	11	0	0	2	5.2	25	5	4	4	1	0	0	2	1	0	3	0	0	0	1	.000	0	0-0	3	4.37	6.35
2 ML YEARS		70	0	0	12	55.0	245	60	31	31	6	2	4	3	24	2	33	2	0	2	4	.333	-	1-3	13	5.00	5.07

Ben Broussard

Bats: L **Throws:** L **Pos:** LF-32; PH-5; 1B-4; DH-1; PR-1   **Ht:** 6'2" **Wt:** 220 **Born:** 9/24/76 **Age:** 26

		BATTING																			BASERUNNING				AVERAGES		
Year Team	Lg	G	AB	H	2B	3B	HR	(Hm	Rd)	TB	R	RBI	RC	TBB	IBB	SO	HBP	SH	SF	SB	CS	SB%	GDP	Avg	OBP	Slg
1999 Billings	R+	38	145	59	11	2	14	(-	-)	116	39	48	55	34	2	30	4	0	1	1	0	1.00	4	.407	.527	.800
1999 Clinton	A	5	20	11	4	1	2	(-	-)	23	8	6	10	3	0	4	0	0	1	0	0	-	1	.550	.609	1.150
1999 Chattanooga	AA	35	127	27	5	0	8	(-	-)	56	26	21	17	11	1	41	3	0	0	1	0	1.00	0	.213	.291	.441
2000 Chattanooga	AA	87	286	73	8	4	14	(-	-)	131	64	51	60	72	3	78	6	0	2	15	2	.88	6	.255	.413	.458
2001 Mudville	A+	30	102	25	5	0	5	(-	-)	45	14	21	17	16	0	31	4	0	3	0	0	-	2	.245	.360	.441
2001 Chattanooga	AA	100	353	113	27	4	23	(-	-)	209	81	69	87	61	5	69	8	0	3	10	3	.77	5	.320	.428	.592
2002 Louisville	AAA	57	187	51	14	1	11	(-	-)	100	31	30	40	31	2	50	9	0	3	4	1	.80	4	.273	.396	.535
2002 Buffalo	AAA	42	153	37	8	0	5	(-	-)	60	30	21	23	24	2	30	3	1	1	0	0	-	1	.242	.354	.392
2002 Cleveland	AL	39	112	27	4	0	4	(2	2)	43	10	9	9	7	1	25	1	0	0	0	0	-	3	.241	.292	.384

Jim Brower

Pitches: R **Bats:** R **Pos:** RP-52   **Ht:** 6'3" **Wt:** 215 **Born:** 12/29/72 **Age:** 30

		HOW MUCH HE PITCHED						WHAT HE GAVE UP												THE RESULTS						
Year Team	Lg	G	GS	CG	GF	IP	BFP	H	R	ER	HR	SH	SF	HB	TBB	IBB	SO	WP	Bk	W	L	Pct	ShO	Sv-Op	Hld	ERC	ERA
1999 Cleveland	AL	9	2	0	1	25.2	113	27	13	13	8	1	1	1	10	1	18	0	0	3	1	.750	0	0-0	0	5.96	4.56
2000 Cleveland	AL	17	11	0	1	62.0	293	80	45	43	11	1	0	2	31	1	32	3	0	2	3	.400	0	0-0	0	6.95	6.24
2001 Cincinnati	NL	46	10	0	13	129.1	559	119	65	57	17	9	3	5	60	5	94	5	1	7	10	.412	0	1-2	2	4.21	3.97
2002 Cin-Mon	NL	52	0	0	23	80.1	344	77	40	39	7	2	1	4	32	2	57	1	0	3	2	.600	0	0-1	6	3.94	4.37

33

Year Team	Lg	G	GS	CG	GF	IP	BFP	H	R	ER	HR	SH	SF	HB	TBB	IBB	SO	WP	Bk	W	L	Pct	ShO	Sv-Op	Hld	ERC	ERA
2002 Cincinnati	NL	22	0	0	11	39.1	158	38	18	17	2	1	1	0	10	1	24	0	0	2	0	1.000	0	0-0	0	3.08	3.89
2002 Montreal	NL	30	0	0	12	41.0	186	39	22	22	5	1	0	4	22	1	33	1	0	1	2	.333	0	0-1	6	4.79	4.83
4 ML YEARS		124	23	0	38	297.1	1309	303	163	152	43	13	5	12	133	9	201	9	1	15	16	.484	0	1-3	8	4.82	4.60

Adrian Brown

Bats: B **Throws:** R **Pos:** CF-64; PH-28; RF-9; PR-4   **Ht:** 6'0" **Wt:** 200 **Born:** 2/7/74 **Age:** 29

Year Team	Lg	G	AB	H	2B	3B	HR	(Hm	Rd)	TB	R	RBI	RC	TBB	IBB	SO	HBP	SH	SF	SB	CS	SB%	GDP	Avg	OBP	Slg
2002 Nashville*	AAA	51	184	62	7	1	3	(-	-)	80	36	16	35	23	0	18	0	6	1	22	6	.79	3	.337	.409	.435
1997 Pittsburgh	NL	48	147	28	6	0	1	(0	1)	37	17	10	10	13	0	18	4	2	1	8	4	.67	3	.190	.273	.252
1998 Pittsburgh	NL	41	152	43	4	1	0	(0	0)	49	20	5	16	9	0	18	0	4	0	4	0	1.00	3	.283	.323	.322
1999 Pittsburgh	NL	116	226	61	5	2	4	(2	2)	82	34	17	31	33	2	39	1	6	1	5	3	.63	5	.270	.364	.363
2000 Pittsburgh	NL	104	308	97	18	3	4	(2	2)	133	64	28	53	29	1	34	0	2	1	13	1	.93	5	.315	.373	.432
2001 Pittsburgh	NL	8	31	6	0	0	1	(0	1)	9	3	2	2	3	0	3	0	0	0	2	1	.67	1	.194	.265	.290
2002 Pittsburgh	NL	91	208	45	10	2	1	(0	1)	62	20	21	16	19	0	34	1	3	1	10	6	.63	5	.216	.284	.298
6 ML YEARS		408	1072	280	43	8	11	(4	7)	372	158	83	128	106	3	146	6	17	4	42	15	.74	18	.261	.330	.347

Dee Brown

Bats: L **Throws:** R **Pos:** LF-8; DH-5; PH-3; PR-1   **Ht:** 6'0" **Wt:** 225 **Born:** 3/27/78 **Age:** 25

Year Team	Lg	G	AB	H	2B	3B	HR	(Hm	Rd)	TB	R	RBI	RC	TBB	IBB	SO	HBP	SH	SF	SB	CS	SB%	GDP	Avg	OBP	Slg
2002 Omaha*	AAA	121	458	126	23	1	17	(-	-)	202	66	75	68	44	2	111	6	0	4	10	4	.71	12	.275	.344	.441
1998 Kansas City	AL	5	3	0	0	0	0	(0	0)	0	2	0	0	0	0	1	0	0	0	0	0	-	0	.000	.000	.000
1999 Kansas City	AL	12	25	2	0	0	0	(0	0)	2	1	0	0	2	0	7	0	0	0	0	0	-	0	.080	.148	.080
2000 Kansas City	AL	15	25	4	1	0	0	(0	0)	5	4	4	1	3	0	9	0	0	0	0	0	-	0	.160	.250	.200
2001 Kansas City	AL	106	380	93	19	0	7	(4	3)	133	39	40	34	22	4	81	1	1	2	5	3	.63	12	.245	.286	.350
2002 Kansas City	AL	16	51	12	3	1	1	(0	1)	20	5	7	4	4	0	20	0	0	0	0	0	-	0	.235	.291	.392
5 ML YEARS		154	484	111	23	1	8	(4	4)	160	51	51	39	31	4	118	1	1	2	5	3	.63	12	.229	.276	.331

Kevin Brown

Pitches: R **Bats:** R **Pos:** SP-10; RP-7   **Ht:** 6'4" **Wt:** 200 **Born:** 3/14/65 **Age:** 38

Year Team	Lg	G	GS	CG	GF	IP	BFP	H	R	ER	HR	SH	SF	HB	TBB	IBB	SO	WP	Bk	W	L	Pct	ShO	Sv-Op	Hld	ERC	ERA
2002 Las Vegas*	AAA	2	2	0	0	9.2	36	6	2	2	0	0	0	0	3	0	7	1	0	1	0	1.000	0	0- -	-	1.46	1.86
1986 Texas	AL	1	1	0	0	5.0	19	6	2	2	0	0	0	0	0	0	4	0	0	1	0	1.000	0	0-0	0	3.25	3.60
1988 Texas	AL	4	4	1	0	23.1	110	33	15	11	2	1	0	1	8	0	12	1	0	1	1	.500	0	0-0	0	6.33	4.24
1989 Texas	AL	28	28	7	0	191.0	798	167	81	71	10	3	6	4	70	2	104	7	2	12	9	.571	0	0-0	0	3.02	3.35
1990 Texas	AL	26	26	6	0	180.0	757	175	84	72	13	2	7	3	60	3	88	9	2	12	10	.545	2	0-0	0	3.54	3.60
1991 Texas	AL	33	33	0	0	210.2	934	233	116	103	17	6	4	13	90	5	96	12	3	9	12	.429	0	0-0	0	4.92	4.40
1992 Texas	AL	35	35	11	0	265.2	1108	262	117	98	11	7	8	10	76	2	173	8	2	21	11	.656	1	0-0	0	3.34	3.32
1993 Texas	AL	34	34	12	0	233.0	1001	228	105	93	14	5	3	15	74	5	142	8	1	15	12	.556	3	0-0	0	3.55	3.59
1994 Texas	AL	26	25	3	1	170.0	760	218	109	91	18	2	7	6	50	3	123	7	0	7	9	.438	0	0-0	0	5.49	4.82
1995 Baltimore	AL	26	26	3	0	172.1	706	155	73	69	10	5	2	9	48	1	117	3	0	10	9	.526	1	0-0	0	3.03	3.60
1996 Florida	NL	32	32	5	0	233.0	906	187	60	49	8	4	4	16	33	2	159	6	1	17	11	.607	3	0-0	0	2.00	1.89
1997 Florida	NL	33	33	6	0	237.1	976	214	77	71	10	5	1	14	66	7	205	7	1	16	8	.667	2	0-0	0	2.92	2.69
1998 San Diego	NL	36	35	7	0	257.0	1032	225	77	68	8	13	3	10	49	4	257	10	0	18	7	.720	3	0-0	1	2.35	2.38
1999 Los Angeles	NL	35	35	5	0	252.1	1018	210	99	84	19	7	1	7	59	1	221	4	1	18	9	.667	1	0-0	0	2.51	3.00
2000 Los Angeles	NL	33	33	5	0	230.0	921	181	76	66	21	13	4	9	47	1	216	4	0	13	6	.684	1	0-0	0	2.30	2.58
2001 Los Angeles	NL	20	19	1	0	115.2	465	94	41	34	8	5	0	2	38	2	104	3	1	10	4	.714	0	0-0	0	2.71	2.65
2002 Los Angeles	NL	17	10	0	0	63.2	277	68	36	34	9	2	0	5	23	1	58	2	0	3	4	.429	0	0-0	0	4.98	4.81
16 ML YEARS		419	409	72	1	2840.0	11788	2656	1168	1016	178	80	50	124	791	39	2079	91	14	183	122	.600	17	0-0	2	3.18	3.22

Kevin L Brown

Bats: R **Throws:** R **Pos:** C-2; PH-1   **Ht:** 6'2" **Wt:** 231 **Born:** 4/21/73 **Age:** 30

Year Team	Lg	G	AB	H	2B	3B	HR	(Hm	Rd)	TB	R	RBI	RC	TBB	IBB	SO	HBP	SH	SF	SB	CS	SB%	GDP	Avg	OBP	Slg
2002 Durham*	AAA	6	20	3	0	0	2	(-	-)	9	4	4	2	2	0	6	0	0	1	0	0	-	1	.150	.227	.450
2002 Pawtucket*	AAA	70	226	55	13	1	6	(-	-)	88	29	21	26	18	0	60	0	1	0	0	0	-	4	.243	.299	.389
1996 Texas	AL	3	4	0	0	0	0	(0	0)	0	1	1	1	2	0	2	1	0	1	0	0	-	0	.000	.375	.000
1997 Texas	AL	4	5	2	0	0	1	(0	1)	5	1	1	2	0	0	0	0	0	0	0	0	-	0	.400	.400	1.000
1998 Toronto	AL	52	110	29	7	1	2	(1	1)	44	17	15	15	9	0	31	2	3	4	0	0	-	1	.264	.320	.400
1999 Toronto	AL	2	9	4	2	0	0	(0	0)	6	1	1	1	0	0	3	0	0	0	0	0	-	0	.444	.444	.667
2000 Milwaukee	NL	5	17	4	3	0	0	(0	0)	7	3	1	2	1	0	5	0	0	0	0	0	-	0	.235	.278	.412
2001 Milwaukee	NL	17	43	9	0	1	4	(0	4)	23	7	12	6	2	0	18	1	0	0	0	0	-	1	.209	.261	.535
2002 Boston	AL	2	1	0	0	0	0	(0	0)	0	0	0	0	0	0	0	0	0	0	0	0	-	0	.000	.000	.000
7 ML YEARS		85	189	48	12	2	7	(1	6)	85	30	31	28	14	0	59	4	3	5	0	0	-	2	.254	.311	.450

Roosevelt Brown

Bats: L **Throws:** R **Pos:** PH-50; LF-48; CF-13; RF-4; DH-1; PR-1   **Ht:** 5'10" **Wt:** 205 **Born:** 8/3/75 **Age:** 27

Year Team	Lg	G	AB	H	2B	3B	HR	(Hm	Rd)	TB	R	RBI	RC	TBB	IBB	SO	HBP	SH	SF	SB	CS	SB%	GDP	Avg	OBP	Slg
1999 Chicago	NL	33	64	14	6	1	1	(0	1)	25	6	10	6	2	0	14	0	3	1	1	0	1.00	2	.219	.239	.391
2000 Chicago	NL	45	91	32	8	0	3	(1	2)	49	11	14	18	4	0	22	1	0	2	0	1	.00	0	.352	.378	.538
2001 Chicago	NL	39	83	22	6	1	4	(3	1)	42	13	22	13	7	0	12	1	0	1	0	0	-	3	.265	.326	.506
2002 Chicago	NL	111	204	43	12	0	3	(2	1)	64	14	23	21	23	0	50	3	0	1	2	2	.50	4	.211	.299	.314
4 ML YEARS		228	442	111	32	2	11	(6	5)	180	44	69	58	36	0	98	5	3	5	3	3	.50	9	.251	.311	.407

Brian Buchanan

Bats: R Throws: R Pos: RF-38; PH-31; DH-16; 1B-15; PR-1   Ht: 6'4" Wt: 230 Born: 7/21/73 Age: 29

Year Team	Lg	G	AB	H	2B	3B	HR	(Hm	Rd)	TB	R	RBI	RC	TBB	IBB	SO	HBP	SH	SF	SB	CS	SB%	GDP	Avg	OBP	Slg
2002 Edmonton*	AAA	1	3	0	0	0	0	(-	-)	0	0	0	0	0	0	0	0	0	0	0	0	.00	0	.000	.000	.000
2000 Minnesota	AL	30	82	19	3	0	1	(1	0)	25	10	8	6	8	0	22	1	0	2	0	2	.00	3	.232	.301	.305
2001 Minnesota	AL	69	197	54	12	0	10	(7	3)	96	28	32	33	19	0	58	2	0	1	1	1	.50	2	.274	.342	.487
2002 Min-SD		92	227	61	10	1	11	(7	4)	106	31	28	28	15	0	59	3	0	0	2	2	.50	6	.269	.322	.467
2002 Minnesota	AL	44	135	34	5	1	5	(3	2)	56	19	15	11	6	0	33	2	0	0	2	1	.67	4	.252	.294	.415
2002 San Diego	NL	48	92	27	5	0	6	(4	2)	50	12	13	17	9	0	26	1	0	0	0	1	.00	2	.293	.363	.543
3 ML YEARS		191	506	134	25	1	22	(15	7)	227	69	68	67	42	0	139	6	0	3	3	5	.38	11	.265	.327	.449

Mike Buddie

Pitches: R Bats: R Pos: RP-25   Ht: 6'3" Wt: 212 Born: 12/12/70 Age: 32

Year Team	Lg	G	GS	CG	GF	IP	BFP	H	R	ER	HR	SH	SF	HB	TBB	IBB	SO	WP	Bk	W	L	Pct	ShO	Sv-Op	Hld	ERC	ERA
2002 Ottawa*	AAA	29	0	0	11	42.0	183	34	21	19	2	5	2	1	23	3	18	5	0	4	4	.500	0	2--	-	3.15	4.07
1998 New York	AL	24	2	0	8	41.2	180	46	29	26	5	1	1	3	13	1	20	2	1	4	1	.800	0	0-0	0	4.80	5.62
1999 New York	AL	2	0	0	2	2.0	9	3	1	1	0	0	1	0	1	0	1	0	0	0	0	-	0	0-0	0	8.13	4.50
2000 Milwaukee	NL	5	0	0	2	6.0	27	8	3	3	0	1	0	0	1	1	5	0	0	0	0	-	0	0-0	0	3.91	4.50
2001 Milwaukee	NL	31	0	0	6	41.2	174	34	20	18	2	0	2	4	17	2	22	3	0	0	1	.000	0	2-2	2	3.09	3.89
2002 Milwaukee	NL	25	0	0	6	39.2	185	46	23	20	5	5	1	1	21	7	28	3	0	1	2	.333	0	0-2	2	5.44	4.54
5 ML YEARS		87	2	0	23	131.0	575	137	76	68	13	7	4	8	52	11	76	8	1	5	4	.556	0	2-4	4	4.44	4.67

Mark Buehrle

Pitches: L Bats: L Pos: SP-34   Ht: 6'2" Wt: 200 Born: 3/23/79 Age: 24

Year Team	Lg	G	GS	CG	GF	IP	BFP	H	R	ER	HR	SH	SF	HB	TBB	IBB	SO	WP	Bk	W	L	Pct	ShO	Sv-Op	Hld	ERC	ERA
2000 Chicago	AL	28	3	0	6	51.1	225	55	27	24	5	1	0	3	19	1	37	0	0	4	1	.800	0	0-2	3	4.56	4.21
2001 Chicago	AL	32	32	4	0	221.1	885	188	89	81	24	9	4	8	48	2	126	1	5	16	8	.667	2	0-0	0	2.79	3.29
2002 Chicago	AL	34	34	5	0	239.0	984	236	102	95	25	9	3	3	61	7	134	6	1	19	12	.613	2	0-0	0	3.53	3.58
3 ML YEARS		94	69	9	6	511.2	2094	479	218	200	54	19	7	14	128	10	297	7	6	39	21	.650	4	0-2	3	3.30	3.52

Ryan Bukvich

Pitches: R Bats: R Pos: RP-26   Ht: 6'3" Wt: 237 Born: 5/13/78 Age: 25

Year Team	Lg	G	GS	CG	GF	IP	BFP	H	R	ER	HR	SH	SF	HB	TBB	IBB	SO	WP	Bk	W	L	Pct	ShO	Sv-Op	Hld	ERC	ERA
2000 Spokane	A-	10	0	0	8	14.0	56	5	1	1	0	1	0	1	9	0	15	1	0	0		1.000	0	2--	-	1.44	0.64
2000 Chrlstn - WV	A	11	0	0	9	14.1	57	6	3	3	0	2	0	1	7	0	17	1	0	0	0	-	0	4--	-	1.29	1.88
2000 Wilmington	A+	2	0	0	0	2.0	15	3	4	4	0	1	0	1	5	2	3	1	0	0	1	.000	0	0--	-	14.54	18.00
2001 Wilmington	A+	37	0	0	29	57.2	248	41	16	11	1	0	2	4	31	0	80	5	1	0	1	.000	0	13--	-	2.68	1.72
2001 Wichita	AA	7	0	0	3	12.0	47	6	5	5	2	0	0	0	2	0	14	2	0	0	0	-	0	2--	-	2.26	3.75
2002 Wichita	AA	23	0	0	18	34.1	134	17	8	5	0	2	0	0	15	1	47	0	0	1	1	.500	0	8--	-	1.26	1.31
2002 Omaha	AAA	12	0	0	11	13.2	50	4	0	0	0	0	0	0	7	0	17	0	0	0		1.000	0	8--	-	0.91	0.00
2002 Kansas City	AL	26	0	0	2	25.0	121	26	19	17	2	4	3	1	19	3	20	1	0	1	0	1.000	0	0-1	5	5.39	6.12

Dave Burba

Pitches: R Bats: R Pos: SP-21; RP-14   Ht: 6'4" Wt: 240 Born: 7/7/66 Age: 36

Year Team	Lg	G	GS	CG	GF	IP	BFP	H	R	ER	HR	SH	SF	HB	TBB	IBB	SO	WP	Bk	W	L	Pct	ShO	Sv-Op	Hld	ERC	ERA
2002 Akron*	AA	1	1	0	0	4.2	16	2	0	0	0	0	0	0	1	0	1	0	0	0	0	-	0	0--	-	0.76	0.00
1990 Seattle	AL	6	0	0	2	8.0	35	8	6	4	0	2	0	1	2	0	4	0	0	0	0	-	0	0-0	0	3.19	4.50
1991 Seattle	AL	22	2	0	11	36.2	153	34	16	15	6	0	0	0	14	3	16	1	0	2	2	.500	0	1-1	0	3.97	3.68
1992 San Francisco	NL	23	11	0	4	70.2	318	80	43	39	4	2	4	2	31	2	47	1	1	2	7	.222	0	0-0	0	4.71	4.97
1993 San Francisco	NL	54	5	0	9	95.1	408	95	49	45	14	6	3	3	37	5	88	4	0	10	3	.769	0	0-0	10	4.44	4.25
1994 San Francisco	NL	57	0	0	13	74.0	322	59	39	36	5	3	1	6	45	3	84	3	0	3	6	.333	0	0-3	11	3.80	4.38
1995 SF-Cin	NL	52	9	1	7	106.2	451	90	50	47	9	4	1	0	51	3	96	5	0	10	4	.714	1	0-1	5	3.38	3.97
1996 Cincinnati	NL	34	33	0	0	195.0	849	179	96	83	18	5	**12**	2	97	9	148	9	1	11	13	.458	0	0-0	0	3.89	3.83
1997 Cincinnati	NL	30	27	2	1	160.0	706	157	88	84	22	6	3	9	73	10	131	6	0	11	10	.524	0	0-0	0	4.57	4.73
1998 Cleveland	AL	32	31	0	0	203.2	870	210	100	93	30	3	10	7	69	4	132	6	0	15	10	.600	0	0-0	0	4.50	4.11
1999 Cleveland	AL	34	34	1	0	220.0	940	211	113	104	30	2	3	8	96	3	174	13	0	15	9	.625	0	0-0	0	4.45	4.25
2000 Cleveland	AL	32	32	0	0	191.1	848	199	99	95	19	5	5	2	91	2	180	7	0	16	6	.727	0	0-0	0	4.62	4.47
2001 Cleveland	AL	32	27	1	4	150.2	684	188	112	104	16	5	7	3	54	2	118	6	0	10	10	.500	0	0-0	0	5.43	6.21
2002 Tex-Cle	AL	35	21	1	2	145.1	645	155	91	84	16	2	3	9	57	3	95	9	1	5	5	.500	0	0-2	1	4.69	5.20
1995 San Francisco	NL	37	0	0	7	43.1	191	38	26	24	5	3	1	0	25	2	46	2	0	4	2	.667	0	0-1	5	4.07	4.98
1995 Cincinnati	NL	15	9	1	0	63.1	260	52	24	23	4	1	0	0	26	1	50	3	0	6	2	.750	1	0-0	0	2.93	3.27
2002 Texas	AL	23	18	1	2	111.1	499	125	71	67	13	2	2	7	40	3	70	9	1	4	5	.444	0	0-0	0	4.90	5.42
2002 Cleveland	AL	12	3	0	0	34.0	146	30	20	17	3	0	1	2	17	0	25	0	0	1	0	1.000	0	0-1	1	4.01	4.50
13 ML YEARS		443	232	6	53	1657.1	7229	1665	902	833	189	45	56	52	717	49	1313	70	3	110	85	.564	1	1-7	27	4.42	4.52

John Burkett

Pitches: R Bats: R Pos: SP-29   Ht: 6'3" Wt: 215 Born: 11/28/64 Age: 38

Year Team	Lg	G	GS	CG	GF	IP	BFP	H	R	ER	HR	SH	SF	HB	TBB	IBB	SO	WP	Bk	W	L	Pct	ShO	Sv-Op	Hld	ERC	ERA
2002 Pawtucket*	AAA	1	1	0	0	2.1	11	4	3	3	0	0	0	0	1	0	2	0	0	0	1	.000	0	0--	-	8.25	11.57
1987 San Francisco	NL	3	0	0	1	6.0	28	7	4	3	2	1	0	1	3	0	5	0	0	0	0	-	0	0-0	0	8.25	4.50
1990 San Francisco	NL	33	32	2	1	204.0	857	201	92	86	18	6	5	4	61	7	118	3	3	14	7	.667	0	1-1	0	3.56	3.79
1991 San Francisco	NL	36	34	3	0	206.2	890	223	103	96	19	8	8	**10**	60	2	131	5	0	12	11	.522	1	0-0	0	4.22	4.18
1992 San Francisco	NL	32	32	3	0	189.2	799	194	96	81	13	11	4	4	45	6	107	0	0	13	9	.591	1	0-0	0	3.37	3.84

Year Team	Lg	G	GS	CG	GF	IP	BFP	H	R	ER	HR	SH	SF	HB	TBB	IBB	SO	WP	Bk	W	L	Pct	ShO	Sv-Op	Hld	ERC	ERA
1993 San Francisco	NL	34	34	2	0	231.2	942	224	100	94	18	8	4	11	40	4	145	1	2	22	7	.759	1	0-0	0	3.07	3.65
1994 San Francisco	NL	25	25	0	0	159.1	676	176	72	64	14	12	5	7	36	7	85	2	0	6	8	.429	0	0-0	0	4.03	3.62
1995 Florida	NL	30	30	4	0	188.1	810	208	95	90	22	10	0	6	57	5	126	2	1	14	14	.500	0	0-0	0	4.53	4.30
1996 Fla-Tex		34	34	2	0	222.2	934	229	117	105	19	12	6	5	58	4	155	0	0	11	12	.478	1	0-0	0	3.68	4.24
1997 Texas	AL	30	30	2	0	189.1	828	240	106	96	20	4	7	4	30	1	139	1	0	9	12	.429	0	0-0	0	4.72	4.56
1998 Texas	AL	32	32	0	0	195.0	854	230	131	123	19	7	5	8	46	1	131	3	0	9	13	.409	0	0-0	0	4.55	5.68
1999 Texas	AL	30	25	0	1	147.1	656	184	95	92	18	5	3	3	46	1	96	4	0	8	8	.529	0	0-0	0	5.44	5.62
2000 Atlanta	NL	31	22	0	4	134.1	603	162	79	73	13	8	5	4	51	2	110	2	0	10	6	.625	0	0-1	0	5.28	4.89
2001 Atlanta	NL	34	34	1	0	219.1	902	187	83	74	17	6	7	6	70	13	187	5	1	12	12	.500	1	0-0	0	2.86	3.04
2002 Boston	NL	29	29	1	0	173.0	760	199	93	87	25	5	4	8	50	5	124	2	1	13	8	.619	1	0-0	0	4.95	4.53
1996 Florida	NL	24	24	1	0	154.0	645	154	84	74	15	11	4	3	42	2	108	0	0	6	10	.375	0	0-0	0	3.64	4.32
1996 Texas	AL	10	10	1	0	68.2	289	75	33	31	4	1	2	2	16	2	47	0	0	5	2	.714	1	0-0	0	3.76	4.06
14 ML YEARS		413	393	20	7	2466.2	10539	2664	1266	1164	237	103	63	81	653	58	1659	30	8	154	127	.548	6	1-2	1	4.07	4.25

Ellis Burks

Bats: R **Throws:** R **Pos:** DH-127; LF-6; PH-5 **Ht:** 6'2" **Wt:** 205 **Born:** 9/11/64 **Age:** 38

Year Team	Lg	G	AB	H	2B	3B	HR	(Hm	Rd)	TB	R	RBI	RC	TBB	IBB	SO	HBP	SH	SF	SB	CS	SB%	GDP	Avg	OBP	Slg
1987 Boston	AL	133	558	152	30	2	20	(11	9)	246	94	59	84	41	0	98	2	4	1	27	6	.82	1	.272	.324	.441
1988 Boston	AL	144	540	159	37	5	18	(8	10)	260	93	92	97	62	1	89	3	4	6	25	9	.74	8	.294	.367	.481
1989 Boston	AL	97	399	121	19	6	12	(6	6)	188	73	61	69	36	2	52	5	2	4	21	5	.81	8	.303	.365	.471
1990 Boston	AL	152	588	174	33	8	21	(10	11)	286	89	89	91	48	4	82	1	2	2	9	11	.45	18	.296	.349	.486
1991 Boston	AL	130	474	119	33	3	14	(8	6)	200	56	56	60	39	2	81	6	2	3	6	11	.35	7	.251	.314	.422
1992 Boston	AL	66	235	60	8	3	8	(4	4)	98	35	30	32	25	2	48	1	0	2	5	2	.71	5	.255	.327	.417
1993 Chicago	AL	146	499	137	24	4	17	(7	10)	220	75	74	76	60	2	97	4	3	8	6	9	.40	11	.275	.352	.441
1994 Colorado	NL	42	149	48	8	3	13	(7	6)	101	33	24	36	16	3	39	0	0	0	3	1	.75	3	.322	.388	.678
1995 Colorado	NL	103	278	74	10	6	14	(8	6)	138	41	49	49	39	0	72	2	1	1	7	3	.70	7	.266	.359	.496
1996 Colorado	NL	156	613	211	45	8	40	(23	17)	392	142	128	147	61	2	114	6	3	2	32	6	.84	19	.344	.408	**.639**
1997 Colorado	NL	119	424	123	19	2	32	(17	15)	242	91	82	82	47	0	75	3	1	2	7	2	.78	17	.290	.363	.571
1998 Col-SF	NL	142	504	147	28	6	21	(10	11)	250	76	76	89	58	1	111	5	6	9	11	8	.58	12	.292	.365	.496
1999 San Francisco	NL	120	390	110	19	0	31	(16	15)	222	73	96	84	69	2	86	6	0	0	4	5	.58	11	.282	.394	.569
2000 San Francisco	NL	122	393	135	21	5	24	(15	9)	238	74	96	94	56	5	49	1	0	8	5	1	.83	10	.344	.419	.606
2001 Cleveland	AL	124	439	123	29	1	28	(15	13)	238	83	74	85	62	2	85	5	0	9	5	1	.83	16	.280	.369	.542
2002 Cleveland	AL	138	518	156	28	0	32	(16	16)	280	92	91	105	44	3	108	6	1	1	2	3	.40	13	.301	.362	.541
1998 Colorado	NL	100	357	102	22	5	16	(8	8)	182	54	54	60	39	0	80	2	2	5	3	7	.30	10	.286	.355	.510
1998 San Francisco	NL	42	147	45	6	1	5	(2	3)	68	22	22	29	19	1	31	3	4	4	8	1	.89	2	.306	.387	.463
16 ML YEARS		1934	7001	2049	391	62	345	(181	164)	3599	1220	1177	1280	763	31	1286	56	29	62	178	83	.68	166	.293	.364	.514

A.J. Burnett

Pitches: R **Bats:** R **Pos:** SP-29; RP-2 **Ht:** 6'4" **Wt:** 229 **Born:** 1/3/77 **Age:** 26

Year Team	Lg	G	GS	CG	GF	IP	BFP	H	R	ER	HR	SH	SF	HB	TBB	IBB	SO	WP	Bk	W	L	Pct	ShO	Sv-Op	Hld	ERC	ERA
1999 Florida	NL	7	7	0	0	41.1	182	37	23	16	3	1	3	0	25	2	33	0	0	4	2	.667	0	0-0	0	4.00	3.48
2000 Florida	NL	13	13	0	0	82.2	364	80	46	44	8	6	3	2	44	3	57	2	0	3	7	.300	0	0-0	0	4.45	4.79
2001 Florida	NL	27	27	2	0	173.1	733	145	82	78	20	6	8	7	83	3	128	7	1	11	12	.478	1	0-0	0	3.76	4.05
2002 Florida	NL	31	29	7	0	204.1	844	153	84	75	12	9	4	9	90	5	203	14	0	12	9	.571	5	0-1	0	2.77	3.30
4 ML YEARS		78	76	9	0	501.2	2123	415	235	213	43	22	18	18	242	13	421	23	1	30	30	.500	6	0-1	0	3.47	3.82

Jeromy Burnitz

Bats: L **Throws:** R **Pos:** RF-140; PH-18; PR-2; DH-1 **Ht:** 6'0" **Wt:** 213 **Born:** 4/15/69 **Age:** 34

Year Team	Lg	G	AB	H	2B	3B	HR	(Hm	Rd)	TB	R	RBI	RC	TBB	IBB	SO	HBP	SH	SF	SB	CS	SB%	GDP	Avg	OBP	Slg
1993 New York	NL	86	263	64	10	6	13	(6	7)	125	49	38	42	38	4	66	1	2	2	3	6	.33	2	.243	.339	.475
1994 New York	NL	45	143	34	4	0	3	(2	1)	47	26	15	17	23	0	45	1	1	0	1	1	.50	2	.238	.347	.329
1995 Cleveland	AL	9	7	4	1	0	0	(0	0)	5	4	0	2	0	0	0	0	0	0	0	0	-	0	.571	.571	.714
1996 Cle-Mil		94	200	53	14	0	9	(5	4)	94	38	40	37	33	2	47	0	0	2	4	1	.80	4	.265	.377	.470
1997 Milwaukee	NL	153	494	139	37	8	27	(18	9)	273	85	85	100	75	8	111	5	3	0	20	13	.61	8	.281	.382	.553
1998 Milwaukee	NL	161	609	160	28	1	38	(17	21)	304	92	125	102	70	7	158	4	1	7	7	4	.64	9	.263	.339	.499
1999 Milwaukee	NL	130	467	126	33	2	33	(12	21)	262	87	103	104	91	7	124	16	0	6	7	3	.70	11	.270	.402	.561
2000 Milwaukee	NL	161	564	131	29	2	31	(12	19)	257	91	98	94	99	10	121	14	0	9	6	4	.60	12	.232	.356	.456
2001 Milwaukee	NL	154	562	141	32	4	34	(16	18)	283	104	100	97	80	9	150	5	0	4	0	4	.00	8	.251	.347	.504
2002 New York	NL	154	479	103	15	0	19	(12	7)	175	65	54	48	58	5	135	10	1	2	10	7	.59	11	.215	.311	.365
1996 Cleveland	AL	71	128	36	10	0	7	(4	3)	67	30	26	27	25	1	31	2	0	0	2	1	.67	3	.281	.406	.523
1996 Milwaukee	NL	23	72	17	4	0	2	(1	1)	27	8	14	10	8	1	16	2	0	2	2	0	1.00	1	.236	.321	.375
10 ML YEARS		1147	3788	955	203	23	207	(100	107)	1825	641	658	643	567	52	957	60	8	32	58	43	.57	67	.252	.356	.482

Pat Burrell

Bats: R **Throws:** R **Pos:** LF-157; PH-3 **Ht:** 6'4" **Wt:** 222 **Born:** 10/10/76 **Age:** 26

Year Team	Lg	G	AB	H	2B	3B	HR	(Hm	Rd)	TB	R	RBI	RC	TBB	IBB	SO	HBP	SH	SF	SB	CS	SB%	GDP	Avg	OBP	Slg
2000 Philadelphia	NL	111	408	106	27	1	18	(7	11)	189	57	79	69	63	2	139	1	0	2	0	0	-	5	.260	.359	.463
2001 Philadelphia	NL	155	539	139	29	2	27	(10	17)	253	70	89	86	70	7	162	5	0	4	2	1	.67	12	.258	.346	.469
2002 Philadelphia	NL	157	586	165	39	2	37	(18	19)	319	96	116	105	89	9	153	3	0	6	1	0	1.00	16	.282	.376	.544
3 ML YEARS		423	1533	410	95	5	82	(35	47)	761	223	284	260	222	18	454	9	0	12	3	1	.75	33	.267	.361	.496

Sean Burroughs

Bats: L **Throws:** R **Pos:** 3B-48; 2B-13; PH-10   **Ht:** 6'2" **Wt:** 200 **Born:** 9/12/80 **Age:** 22

Year Team	Lg	G	AB	H	2B	3B	HR	(Hm	Rd)	TB	R	RBI	RC	TBB	IBB	SO	HBP	SH	SF	SB	CS	SB%	GDP	Avg	OBP	Slg
1999 Fort Wayne	A	122	426	153	30	3	5	(-	-)	204	65	80	94	74	7	59	14	2	5	17	15	.53	10	.359	.464	.479
1999 R Cucamnga	A+	6	23	10	3	0	1	(-	-)	16	3	5	7	3	0	3	1	0	0	0	1	.00	1	.435	.519	.696
2000 Mobile	AA	108	392	114	29	4	2	(-	-)	157	46	42	60	58	6	45	3	4	4	6	8	.43	10	.291	.383	.401
2001 Portland	AAA	104	394	127	28	1	9	(-	-)	184	60	55	68	37	2	54	4	4	0	9	2	.82	13	.322	.386	.467
2002 Portland	AAA	50	179	54	16	2	2	(-	-)	80	29	23	30	21	0	16	3	0	2	1	0	1.00	5	.302	.380	.447
2002 San Diego	NL	63	192	52	5	1	1	(0	1)	62	18	11	14	12	1	30	1	1	0	2	0	1.00	6	.271	.317	.323

Homer Bush

Bats: R **Throws:** R **Pos:** 2B-34; PH-23; PR-6; SS-4   **Ht:** 5'10" **Wt:** 185 **Born:** 11/12/72 **Age:** 30

Year Team	Lg	G	AB	H	2B	3B	HR	(Hm	Rd)	TB	R	RBI	RC	TBB	IBB	SO	HBP	SH	SF	SB	CS	SB%	GDP	Avg	OBP	Slg
1997 New York	AL	10	11	4	0	0	0	(0	0)	4	2	3	1	0	0	0	0	0	0	0	0	-	0	.364	.364	.364
1998 New York	AL	45	71	27	3	0	1	(1	0)	33	17	5	13	5	0	19	0	2	0	6	3	.67	1	.380	.421	.465
1999 Toronto	AL	128	485	155	26	4	5	(2	3)	204	69	55	73	21	0	82	6	8	3	32	8	.80	9	.320	.353	.421
2000 Toronto	AL	76	297	64	8	0	1	(1	0)	75	38	18	17	18	0	60	5	4	1	9	4	.69	10	.215	.271	.253
2001 Toronto	AL	78	271	83	11	1	3	(2	1)	105	32	27	37	8	1	50	6	2	4	13	4	.76	2	.306	.336	.387
2002 Tor-Fla		63	132	30	2	0	1	(1	0)	35	16	7	6	5	0	25	2	2	0	4	1	.80	2	.227	.266	.265
2002 Toronto	AL	23	78	18	2	0	1	(1	0)	23	9	2	4	2	0	12	2	1	0	2	0	1.00	2	.231	.268	.295
2002 Florida	NL	40	54	12	0	0	0	(0	0)	12	7	5	2	3	0	13	0	1	0	2	1	.67	0	.222	.263	.222
6 ML YEARS		400	1267	363	50	5	11	(7	4)	456	174	115	147	57	1	236	19	18	8	64	20	.76	24	.287	.325	.360

Brent Butler

Bats: R **Throws:** R **Pos:** 2B-72; 3B-33; SS-13; PH-12; PR-4   **Ht:** 6'0" **Wt:** 180 **Born:** 2/11/78 **Age:** 25

Year Team	Lg	G	AB	H	2B	3B	HR	(Hm	Rd)	TB	R	RBI	RC	TBB	IBB	SO	HBP	SH	SF	SB	CS	SB%	GDP	Avg	OBP	Slg
1996 Johnson City	R+	62	248	85	21	1	8	(-	-)	132	45	50	50	25	1	29	2	1	2	8	1	.89	11	.343	.404	.532
1997 Peoria	A	129	480	147	37	2	15	(-	-)	233	81	71	89	63	6	69	4	0	5	6	4	.60	9	.306	.388	.485
1998 Prnc William	A+	126	475	136	27	2	11	(-	-)	200	63	76	68	39	2	74	9	2	7	3	4	.43	12	.286	.347	.421
1999 Arkansas	AA	139	528	142	21	1	13	(-	-)	204	68	54	58	26	0	47	6	0	5	0	4	.00	16	.269	.308	.386
2000 Co Springs	AAA	122	438	128	35	1	8	(-	-)	189	73	54	65	44	1	46	4	7	9	1	3	.25	15	.292	.356	.432
2001 Co Springs	AAA	65	272	91	20	3	7	(-	-)	138	51	38	46	15	0	26	4	3	2	4	2	.67	13	.335	.375	.507
2002 Co Springs	AAA	24	105	35	9	1	2	(-	-)	52	20	17	18	6	1	12	1	0	0	0	0	-	3	.333	.375	.495
2001 Colorado	NL	53	119	29	7	1	1	(0	1)	41	17	14	11	7	0	7	1	2	1	1	1	.50	4	.244	.287	.345
2002 Colorado	NL	113	344	89	18	4	9	(7	2)	142	55	42	42	10	3	40	5	4	4	2	6	.25	6	.259	.287	.413
2 ML YEARS		166	463	118	25	5	10	(7	3)	183	72	56	53	17	3	47	6	6	6	3	7	.30	10	.255	.287	.395

Mike Bynum

Pitches: L **Bats:** L **Pos:** RP-11; SP-3   **Ht:** 6'4" **Wt:** 200 **Born:** 3/20/78 **Age:** 25

Year Team	Lg	G	GS	CG	GF	IP	BFP	H	R	ER	HR	SH	SF	HB	TBB	IBB	SO	WP	Bk	W	L	Pct	ShO	Sv-Op	Hld	ERC	ERA
1999 Idaho Falls	R+	5	3	0	0	17.0	60	7	0	0	1	0	0	0	4	0	21	0	0	1	0	1.000	0	0--	0	0.73	0.00
1999 R Cucamnga	A+	7	7	0	0	38.1	159	35	17	14	1	1	1	2	8	0	44	2	2	3	1	.750	0	0--	0	2.57	3.29
2000 R Cucamnga	A+	21	21	0	0	126.0	517	101	55	42	4	3	5	8	51	0	129	7	1	9	6	.600	0	0--	0	2.88	3.00
2000 Mobile	AA	6	6	0	0	34.0	144	31	12	11	2	1	2	2	16	0	27	1	1	3	1	.750	0	0--	0	3.91	2.91
2001 Mobile	AA	16	15	0	0	84.1	368	90	53	47	14	4	3	3	35	0	69	0	0	2	7	.222	0	0--	0	5.23	5.02
2002 Mobile	AA	6	5	0	0	33.0	123	17	5	3	0	0	0	3	7	0	29	2	0	4	0	1.000	0	0--	0	1.10	0.82
2002 Portland	AAA	7	7	0	0	41.0	167	36	19	16	6	3	1	0	7	0	35	0	0	3	2	.600	0	0--	0	3.10	3.51
2002 San Diego	NL	14	3	0	3	27.1	130	33	16	16	3	3	2	3	15	2	17	2	0	1	0	1.000	0	0-0	0	6.31	5.27

Marlon Byrd

Bats: R **Throws:** R **Pos:** CF-8; RF-2   **Ht:** 6'0" **Wt:** 225 **Born:** 8/30/77 **Age:** 25

Year Team	Lg	G	AB	H	2B	3B	HR	(Hm	Rd)	TB	R	RBI	RC	TBB	IBB	SO	HBP	SH	SF	SB	CS	SB%	GDP	Avg	OBP	Slg
1999 Batavia	A-	65	243	72	7	6	13	(-	-)	130	40	50	49	28	1	70	5	0	3	8	2	.80	3	.296	.376	.535
2000 Piedmont	A	133	515	159	29	13	17	(-	-)	265	104	93	105	51	0	110	10	1	5	41	5	.89	7	.309	.379	.515
2001 Reading	AA	137	510	161	22	8	28	(-	-)	283	108	89	110	52	3	93	11	2	7	32	5	.86	7	.316	.386	.555
2002 Scrtn/WlksBr	AAA	136	538	160	37	7	15	(-	-)	256	103	63	95	46	2	98	11	2	5	15	1	.94	5	.297	.362	.476
2002 Philadelphia	NL	10	35	8	2	0	1	(1	0)	13	2	1	0	1	0	8	0	0	0	0	2	.00	0	.229	.250	.371

Paul Byrd

Pitches: R **Bats:** R **Pos:** SP-33   **Ht:** 6'1" **Wt:** 185 **Born:** 12/3/70 **Age:** 32

Year Team	Lg	G	GS	CG	GF	IP	BFP	H	R	ER	HR	SH	SF	HB	TBB	IBB	SO	WP	Bk	W	L	Pct	ShO	Sv-Op	Hld	ERC	ERA
1995 New York	NL	17	0	0	6	22.0	91	18	6	5	1	0	2	1	7	1	26	1	2	2	0	1.000	0	0-0	3	2.53	2.05
1996 New York	NL	38	0	0	14	46.2	204	48	22	22	7	1	1	0	21	4	31	3	0	1	2	.333	0	0-2	4	4.67	4.24
1997 Atlanta	NL	31	4	0	9	53.0	236	47	34	31	6	2	2	4	28	4	37	3	1	4	4	.500	0	0-0	5	4.15	5.26
1998 Atl-Phi	NL	9	8	2	0	57.0	233	45	19	17	6	2	1	0	18	1	39	2	0	5	2	.714	1	0-0	0	2.62	2.68
1999 Philadelphia	NL	32	32	1	0	199.2	872	205	119	102	34	5	6	17	70	2	106	11	3	15	11	.577	0	0-0	0	4.87	4.60
2000 Philadelphia	NL	17	15	0	0	83.0	371	89	67	60	17	3	1	3	35	2	53	1	0	2	9	.182	0	0-0	0	5.42	6.51
2001 Phi-KC		19	16	1	1	103.1	444	120	54	51	12	4	6	2	26	1	52	2	0	6	7	.462	0	0-0	0	4.62	4.44
2002 Kansas City	AL	33	33	7	0	228.1	935	224	111	99	36	2	13	7	38	1	129	3	1	17	11	.607	2	0-0	0	3.55	3.90
1998 Atlanta	NL	1	0	0	0	2.0	11	4	3	3	0	0	0	0	0	0	1	0	0	0	0	-	0	0-0	0	9.72	13.50
1998 Philadelphia	NL	8	8	2	0	55.0	222	41	16	14	6	2	1	0	17	1	38	2	0	5	2	.714	1	0-0	0	2.41	2.29

Year Team	Lg	G	GS	CG	GF	IP	BFP	H	R	ER	HR	SH	SF	HB	TBB	IBB	SO	WP	Bk	W	L	Pct	ShO	Sv-Op	Hld	ERC	ERA
2001 Philadelphia	NL	3	1	0	1	10.0	45	10	9	9	1	2	2	4	4	0	3	1	0	0	1	.000	0	0-0	0	4.36	8.10
2001 Kansas City	AL	16	15	1	0	93.1	399	110	45	42	11	2	4	1	22	1	49	1	0	6	6	.500	0	0-0	0	4.65	4.05
8 ML YEARS		196	108	11	30	793.0	3386	796	432	387	119	19	32	34	243	16	473	26	7	52	46	.531	3	0-2	7	4.21	4.39

Eric Byrnes

Bats: R **Throws:** R **Pos:** LF-52; PR-25; RF-22; PH-11; CF-10; DH-3   **Ht:** 6'2" **Wt:** 210 **Born:** 2/16/76 **Age:** 27

Year Team	Lg	G	AB	H	2B	3B	HR	(Hm	Rd)	TB	R	RBI	RC	TBB	IBB	SO	HBP	SH	SF	SB	CS	SB%	GDP	Avg	OBP	Slg
2002 Sacramento*	AAA	31	119	31	7	0	4	(-	-)	50	16	16	15	7	0	15	0	0	0	5	1	.83	2	.261	.302	.420
2000 Oakland	AL	10	10	3	0	0	0	(0	0)	3	5	0	1	0	0	1	1	0	0	2	1	.67	0	.300	.364	.300
2001 Oakland	AL	19	38	9	1	0	3	(2	1)	19	9	5	7	4	0	6	1	0	0	1	0	1.00	0	.237	.326	.500
2002 Oakland	AL	90	94	23	4	2	3	(2	1)	40	24	11	10	4	0	17	3	1	2	3	0	1.00	3	.245	.291	.426
3 ML YEARS		119	142	35	5	2	6	(4	2)	62	38	16	18	8	0	24	5	1	2	6	1	.86	3	.246	.306	.437

Jolbert Cabrera

Bats: R **Throws:** R **Pos:** CF-16; RF-14; PH-9; LF-8; 2B-4; 3B-3; PR-3; DH-1   **Ht:** 6'1" **Wt:** 190 **Born:** 12/8/72 **Age:** 30

Year Team	Lg	G	AB	H	2B	3B	HR	(Hm	Rd)	TB	R	RBI	RC	TBB	IBB	SO	HBP	SH	SF	SB	CS	SB%	GDP	Avg	OBP	Slg
2002 Buffalo*	AAA	23	91	26	5	0	0	(-	-)	31	16	7	11	9	0	10	1	2	1	4	2	.67	3	.286	.353	.341
2002 Las Vegas*	AAA	27	102	35	8	1	2	(-	-)	51	22	11	20	14	2	18	1	0	3	2	3	.40	3	.343	.417	.500
1998 Cleveland	AL	1	2	0	0	0	0	(0	0)	0	0	0	0	0	0	1	0	0	0	0	0	-	0	.000	.000	.000
1999 Cleveland	AL	30	37	7	1	0	0	(0	0)	8	6	0	2	1	0	8	1	0	0	3	0	1.00	1	.189	.231	.216
2000 Cleveland	AL	100	175	44	3	1	2	(2	0)	55	27	15	16	8	0	15	2	1	1	6	4	.60	1	.251	.290	.314
2001 Cleveland	AL	141	287	75	16	3	1	(1	0)	100	50	38	32	16	0	41	6	1	2	10	4	.71	4	.261	.312	.348
2002 Cle-LA		48	84	12	2	0	0	(0	0)	14	8	8	3	7	0	15	1	1	1	1	1	.50	3	.143	.215	.167
2002 Cleveland	AL	38	72	8	1	0	0	(0	0)	9	5	7	1	5	0	13	1	0	1	1	1	.50	3	.111	.177	.125
2002 Los Angeles	NL	10	12	4	1	0	0	(0	0)	5	3	1	2	2	0	2	0	1	0	0	0	-	0	.333	.429	.417
5 ML YEARS		320	585	138	22	4	3	(3	0)	177	91	61	53	32	0	80	10	3	4	20	9	.69	9	.236	.285	.303

Jose Cabrera

Pitches: R **Bats:** R **Pos:** RP-39; SP-11   **Ht:** 6'0" **Wt:** 180 **Born:** 3/24/69 **Age:** 34

Year Team	Lg	G	GS	CG	GF	IP	BFP	H	R	ER	HR	SH	SF	HB	TBB	IBB	SO	WP	Bk	W	L	Pct	ShO	Sv-Op	Hld	ERC	ERA
1997 Houston	NL	12	0	0	6	15.1	57	6	2	2	1	3	0	0	6	0	18	0	0	0	0	-	0	0-1	2	1.16	1.17
1998 Houston	NL	3	0	0	1	4.1	19	7	4	4	0	0	0	0	1	1	5	0	0	0	0	-	0	0-0	0	6.28	8.31
1999 Houston	NL	26	0	0	11	29.1	119	21	7	7	3	0	3	0	9	2	28	4	0	4	0	1.000	0	0-1	6	2.12	2.15
2000 Houston	NL	52	0	0	22	59.1	266	74	40	39	10	3	3	3	17	2	41	1	1	2	3	.400	0	2-3	5	5.72	5.92
2001 Atlanta	NL	55	0	0	23	59.1	253	52	24	19	5	2	6	2	25	4	43	3	1	4	7	.636	0	2-8	6	3.38	2.88
2002 Milwaukee	NL	50	11	0	8	103.1	474	131	84	78	23	8	4	9	36	9	61	3	0	6	10	.375	0	0-1	3	6.64	6.79
6 ML YEARS		198	11	0	71	271.0	1188	291	161	149	42	13	19	14	94	18	192	11	2	19	17	.528	0	4-14	22	4.77	4.95

Orlando Cabrera

Bats: R **Throws:** R **Pos:** SS-153; PH-1   **Ht:** 5'10" **Wt:** 185 **Born:** 11/2/74 **Age:** 28

Year Team	Lg	G	AB	H	2B	3B	HR	(Hm	Rd)	TB	R	RBI	RC	TBB	IBB	SO	HBP	SH	SF	SB	CS	SB%	GDP	Avg	OBP	Slg
1997 Montreal	NL	16	18	4	0	0	0	(0	0)	4	4	2	0	1	0	3	0	1	0	1	2	.33	1	.222	.263	.222
1998 Montreal	NL	79	261	73	16	5	3	(2	1)	108	44	22	34	18	1	27	0	5	1	6	2	.75	6	.280	.325	.414
1999 Montreal	NL	104	382	97	23	5	8	(6	2)	154	48	39	42	18	4	38	3	4	0	2	2	.50	9	.254	.293	.403
2000 Montreal	NL	125	422	100	25	1	13	(7	6)	166	47	55	49	25	3	28	1	3	3	4	4	.50	12	.237	.279	.393
2001 Montreal	NL	162	626	173	41	6	14	(7	7)	268	64	96	85	43	5	54	4	4	7	19	7	.73	15	.276	.324	.428
2002 Montreal	NL	153	563	148	43	1	7	(3	4)	214	64	56	62	48	4	53	2	9	4	25	7	.78	16	.263	.321	.380
6 ML YEARS		639	2272	595	148	18	45	(25	20)	914	271	270	266	153	17	203	10	26	15	57	24	.70	59	.262	.309	.402

Miguel Cairo

Bats: R **Throws:** R **Pos:** PH-70; LF-19; 2B-18; 3B-7; SS-6; RF-5; 1B-3; DH-3; CF-1; PR-1   **Ht:** 6'1" **Wt:** 200 **Born:** 5/4/74 **Age:** 29

Year Team	Lg	G	AB	H	2B	3B	HR	(Hm	Rd)	TB	R	RBI	RC	TBB	IBB	SO	HBP	SH	SF	SB	CS	SB%	GDP	Avg	OBP	Slg
1996 Toronto	AL	9	27	6	2	0	0	(0	0)	8	5	1	2	2	0	9	1	0	0	0	0	-	1	.222	.300	.296
1997 Chicago	NL	16	29	7	1	0	0	(0	0)	8	7	1	3	2	0	3	1	0	0	0	0	-	0	.241	.313	.276
1998 Tampa Bay	AL	150	515	138	26	5	5	(3	2)	189	49	46	58	24	0	44	6	11	2	19	8	.70	9	.268	.307	.367
1999 Tampa Bay	AL	120	465	137	15	5	3	(1	2)	171	61	36	57	24	0	46	7	7	5	22	7	.76	13	.295	.335	.368
2000 Tampa Bay	AL	119	375	98	18	2	1	(0	1)	123	49	34	42	29	0	34	2	6	5	28	7	.80	4	.261	.314	.328
2001 ChC-Stl	NL	93	156	46	8	1	3	(2	1)	65	25	16	23	18	1	23	0	7	1	2	1	.67	4	.295	.366	.417
2002 St Louis	NL	108	184	46	8	2	2	(1	1)	65	28	23	18	13	2	36	3	6	2	1	1	.50	5	.250	.307	.353
2001 Chicago	NL	66	123	35	3	1	2	(1	1)	46	20	9	17	16	1	21	0	7	1	2	1	.67	3	.285	.364	.374
2001 St Louis	NL	27	33	11	5	0	1	(1	0)	19	5	7	6	2	0	2	0	0	0	0	0	-	1	.333	.371	.576
7 ML YEARS		615	1751	478	79	15	14	(7	7)	629	224	157	203	112	3	195	20	37	15	72	24	.75	39	.273	.321	.359

Kiko Calero

Pitches: R **Bats:** R **Pos:** RP   **Ht:** 6'1" **Wt:** 185 **Born:** 1/9/75 **Age:** 28

Year Team	Lg	G	GS	CG	GF	IP	BFP	H	R	ER	HR	SH	SF	HB	TBB	IBB	SO	WP	Bk	W	L	Pct	ShO	Sv-Op	Hld	ERC	ERA
1996 Spokane	A-	17	11	0	3	75.0	318	77	34	21	5	0	6	3	18	0	61	2	2	4	2	.667	0	1--	-	3.51	2.52
1997 Wichita	AA	23	22	2	0	127.2	541	120	70	63	15	4	6	4	44	0	100	2	2	11	9	.550	0	0--	-	3.76	4.44
1998 Lansing	A	4	4	0	0	16.2	76	19	7	7	1	0	0	2	7	0	10	1	1	1	0	1.000	0	0--	-	5.15	3.78

Year Team	Lg	G	GS	CG	GF	IP	BFP	H	R	ER	HR	SH	SF	HB	TBB	IBB	SO	WP	Bk	W	L	Pct	ShO	Sv-Op	Hld	ERC	ERA
1998 Wilmington	A+	17	17	0	0	97.2	409	74	33	31	7	1	3	7	51	1	90	6	0	7	3	.700	0	0- -	-	3.36	2.86
1998 Wichita	AA	3	3	0	0	14.0	72	23	16	15	2	1	0	1	6	0	5	0	0	1	0	1.000	0	0- -	-	8.68	9.64
1999 Wichita	AA	26	23	1	1	129.1	579	143	67	59	14	2	2	6	57	3	92	7	2	9	3	.750	1	1- -	-	5.07	4.11
2000 Wichita	AA	28	25	0	0	153.2	648	141	74	62	16	7	3	10	66	2	130	7	1	10	7	.588	0	0- -	-	4.11	3.63
2001 Wichita	AA	27	19	0	1	124.1	531	110	57	46	10	3	6	7	51	1	94	7	1	14	5	.737	0	0- -	-	3.54	3.33
2002 Wichita	AA	5	2	0	0	16.0	64	10	5	4	2	0	1	0	5	0	15	1	0	1	0	1.000	0	0- -	-	1.93	2.25
2002 Omaha	AAA	20	18	0	0	125.2	510	112	52	48	11	5	7	4	35	1	109	6	1	7	7	.500	0	0- -	-	3.11	3.44

Mickey Callaway

Pitches: R Bats: R Pos: SP-6 **Ht: 6'2" Wt: 200 Born: 5/13/75 Age: 28**

Year Team	Lg	G	GS	CG	GF	IP	BFP	H	R	ER	HR	SH	SF	HB	TBB	IBB	SO	WP	Bk	W	L	Pct	ShO	Sv-Op	Hld	ERC	ERA
2002 Salt Lake*	AAA	17	14	1	0	91.1	370	79	26	17	7	1	1	1	22	0	75	5	2	9	2	.818	0	0- -	-	2.65	1.68
1999 Tampa Bay	AL	5	4	0	0	19.1	99	30	24	16	2	0	1	0	14	1	11	1	0	1	2	.333	0	0-0	0	8.89	7.45
2001 Tampa Bay	AL	2	0	0	2	5.0	20	3	4	4	2	0	0	0	2	0	2	0	0	0	0	-	0	0-0	0	3.65	7.20
2002 Anaheim	AL	6	6	0	0	34.1	147	31	20	16	4	1	0	3	11	0	23	2	0	2	1	.667	0	0-0	0	3.63	4.19
3 ML YEARS		13	10	0	2	58.2	266	64	44	36	8	1	1	3	27	1	36	3	0	3	3	.500	0	0-0	0	5.26	5.52

Ron Calloway

Bats: L Throws: L Pos: LF **Ht: 6'1" Wt: 210 Born: 9/4/76 Age: 26**

Year Team	Lg	G	AB	H	2B	3B	HR	(Hm	Rd)	TB	R	RBI	RC	TBB	IBB	SO	HBP	SH	SF	SB	CS	SB%	GDP	Avg	OBP	Slg
1997 Lethbridge	R+	43	148	37	5	0	0	(-	-)	42	23	9	12	14	0	29	3	0	2	5	8	.38	4	.250	.323	.284
1997 South Bend	A	9	25	7	1	0	0	(-	-)	8	3	1	3	2	0	8	0	0	0	1	0	1.00	1	.280	.333	.320
1998 High Desert	A+	44	156	44	8	2	3	(-	-)	65	30	27	21	12	0	38	2	2	2	2	4	.33	3	.282	.337	.417
1998 South Bend	A	69	251	66	12	2	3	(-	-)	91	29	33	31	25	1	50	2	1	3	7	5	.58	3	.263	.331	.363
1999 High Desert	A+	60	196	62	14	1	3	(-	-)	87	41	23	38	30	0	34	2	2	0	22	7	.76	3	.316	.412	.444
1999 El Paso	AA	11	32	7	0	0	0	(-	-)	7	4	1	3	7	0	7	0	0	0	1	2	.33	0	.219	.359	.219
1999 Jupiter	A+	54	211	57	8	4	3	(-	-)	82	30	25	23	15	0	45	2	4	0	5	6	.45	9	.270	.325	.389
2000 Jupiter	A+	135	530	147	24	6	6	(-	-)	201	78	65	71	55	3	89	4	1	6	34	14	.71	13	.277	.346	.379
2001 Harrisburg	AA	74	279	92	22	4	9	(-	-)	149	48	47	58	24	2	46	3	5	3	25	7	.78	2	.330	.385	.534
2001 Ottawa	AAA	61	239	63	12	0	10	(-	-)	105	27	35	34	16	2	64	6	2	2	11	1	.92	5	.264	.323	.439
2002 Ottawa	AAA	128	447	118	21	5	14	(-	-)	191	72	60	59	44	3	89	6	4	5	16	12	.57	18	.264	.335	.427

Mike Cameron

Bats: R Throws: R Pos: CF-155; PR-5; PH-3 **Ht: 6'2" Wt: 195 Born: 1/8/73 Age: 30**

Year Team	Lg	G	AB	H	2B	3B	HR	(Hm	Rd)	TB	R	RBI	RC	TBB	IBB	SO	HBP	SH	SF	SB	CS	SB%	GDP	Avg	OBP	Slg
1995 Chicago	AL	28	38	7	2	0	1	(0	1)	12	4	2	3	3	0	15	0	3	0	0	0	-	0	.184	.244	.316
1996 Chicago	AL	11	11	1	0	0	0	(0	0)	1	1	0	0	1	0	3	0	0	0	0	1	.00	0	.091	.167	.091
1997 Chicago	AL	116	379	98	18	3	14	(10	4)	164	63	55	63	55	1	105	5	2	5	23	2	.92	8	.259	.356	.433
1998 Chicago	AL	141	396	83	16	5	8	(5	3)	133	53	43	39	37	0	101	6	1	3	27	11	.71	6	.210	.285	.336
1999 Cincinnati	NL	146	542	139	34	9	21	(12	9)	254	93	66	96	80	2	145	6	5	3	38	12	.76	4	.256	.357	.469
2000 Seattle	AL	155	543	145	28	4	19	(5	14)	238	96	78	91	78	0	133	9	7	6	24	7	.77	10	.267	.365	.438
2001 Seattle	AL	150	540	144	30	5	25	(7	18)	259	99	110	96	69	3	155	10	1	13	34	5	.87	13	.267	.353	.480
2002 Seattle	AL	158	545	130	26	5	25	(7	18)	241	84	80	80	79	3	176	7	4	5	31	8	.79	4	.239	.340	.442
8 ML YEARS		905	2994	747	154	31	113	(46	67)	1302	493	434	468	402	9	833	43	23	35	177	46	.79	49	.249	.343	.435

Jay Canizaro

Bats: R Throws: R Pos: 2B-30; 3B-8; PH-2; PR-1 **Ht: 5'9" Wt: 178 Born: 7/4/73 Age: 29**

Year Team	Lg	G	AB	H	2B	3B	HR	(Hm	Rd)	TB	R	RBI	RC	TBB	IBB	SO	HBP	SH	SF	SB	CS	SB%	GDP	Avg	OBP	Slg
2002 Edmonton*	AAA	66	247	71	11	2	14	(-	-)	128	43	37	45	30	0	46	3	0	1	6	3	.67	7	.287	.370	.518
1996 San Francisco	NL	43	120	24	4	1	2	(1	1)	36	11	8	7	9	0	38	1	1	1	0	2	.00	5	.200	.260	.300
1999 San Francisco	NL	12	18	8	2	0	1	(0	1)	13	5	9	6	1	0	2	0	0	0	1	0	1.00	0	.444	.474	.722
2000 Minnesota	AL	102	346	93	21	1	7	(2	5)	137	43	40	42	24	0	57	1	0	0	4	2	.67	8	.269	.318	.396
2002 Minnesota	AL	38	112	24	8	1	0	(0	0)	34	14	11	10	10	0	22	1	1	2	0	1	.00	1	.214	.280	.304
4 ML YEARS		195	596	149	35	3	10	(3	7)	220	73	68	65	44	0	119	3	2	3	5	5	.50	14	.250	.303	.369

Javier Cardona

Bats: R Throws: R Pos: C-14; PH-2 **Ht: 6'1" Wt: 210 Born: 9/15/75 Age: 27**

Year Team	Lg	G	AB	H	2B	3B	HR	(Hm	Rd)	TB	R	RBI	RC	TBB	IBB	SO	HBP	SH	SF	SB	CS	SB%	GDP	Avg	OBP	Slg
2002 Portland*	AAA	20	63	18	1	2	1	(-	-)	26	7	6	8	2	0	12	1	0	1	0	0	-	1	.286	.313	.413
2000 Detroit	AL	26	40	7	1	0	1	(1	0)	11	1	2	1	0	0	9	1	0	1	0	0	-	0	.175	.190	.275
2001 Detroit	AL	46	96	25	8	0	1	(0	1)	36	10	10	9	2	1	12	1	2	1	0	1	.00	2	.260	.280	.375
2002 San Diego	NL	15	39	4	1	0	0	(0	0)	5	2	2	2	2	0	10	0	0	1	0	0	-	4	.103	.143	.128
3 ML YEARS		87	175	36	10	0	2	(1	1)	52	13	14	10	4	0	31	2	2	3	0	1	.00	4	.206	.228	.297

Chris Carpenter

Pitches: R Bats: R Pos: SP-13
Ht: 6'6" **Wt:** 215 **Born:** 4/27/75 **Age:** 28

Year Team	Lg	G	GS	CG	GF	IP	BFP	H	R	ER	HR	SH	SF	HB	TBB	IBB	SO	WP	Bk	W	L	Pct	ShO	Sv-Op	Hld	ERC	ERA
2002 Tennessee*	AA	5	5	0	0	18.2	88	26	18	17	5	2	1	0	8	0	9	2	0	0	1	.000	0	0--	-	7.96	8.20
2002 Syracuse*	AAA	1	1	0	0	6.0	28	8	3	3	1	1	0	0	2	0	6	1	0	0	1	.000	0	0--	-	6.14	4.50
1997 Toronto	AL	14	13	1	1	81.1	374	108	55	46	7	1	2	2	37	0	55	7	1	3	7	.300	1	0-0	0	6.38	5.09
1998 Toronto	AL	33	24	1	4	175.0	742	177	97	85	18	4	5	5	61	1	136	5	0	12	7	.632	1	0-0	0	4.12	4.37
1999 Toronto	AL	24	24	4	0	150.0	663	177	81	73	16	4	6	3	48	1	106	9	1	9	8	.529	1	0-0	0	4.90	4.38
2000 Toronto	AL	34	27	2	1	175.1	795	204	130	122	30	3	1	5	83	1	113	3	0	10	12	.455	0	0-0	0	6.04	6.26
2001 Toronto	AL	34	34	3	0	215.2	930	229	112	98	29	3	1	16	75	5	157	5	0	11	11	.500	2	0-0	0	4.82	4.09
2002 Toronto	AL	13	13	1	0	73.1	327	89	45	43	11	1	4	4	27	0	45	3	0	4	5	.444	0	0-0	0	5.91	5.28
6 ML YEARS		152	135	12	6	870.2	3831	984	520	467	111	16	19	35	331	8	612	32	2	49	50	.495	5	0-0	0	5.16	4.83

Giovanni Carrara

Pitches: R Bats: R Pos: RP-62; SP-1
Ht: 6'2" **Wt:** 235 **Born:** 3/4/68 **Age:** 35

Year Team	Lg	G	GS	CG	GF	IP	BFP	H	R	ER	HR	SH	SF	HB	TBB	IBB	SO	WP	Bk	W	L	Pct	ShO	Sv-Op	Hld	ERC	ERA
1995 Toronto	AL	12	7	1	2	48.2	229	64	46	39	10	1	2	1	25	1	27	1	0	2	4	.333	0	0-0	0	7.43	7.21
1996 Tor-Cin		19	5	0	4	38.0	188	54	36	34	11	1	0	2	25	3	23	1	0	1	1	.500	0	0-1	0	9.71	8.05
1997 Cincinnati	NL	2	2	0	0	10.1	49	14	9	9	4	1	0	0	6	1	5	0	0	0	1	.000	0	0-0	0	9.47	7.84
2000 Colorado	NL	8	0	0	2	13.1	72	21	19	19	5	0	1	1	11	2	15	0	0	0	1	.000	0	0-1	0	12.21	12.83
2001 Los Angeles	NL	47	3	0	2	85.1	348	73	30	30	12	6	1	1	24	3	70	0	0	6	1	.857	0	0-3	9	3.10	3.16
2002 Los Angeles	NL	63	1	0	13	90.2	387	83	34	33	14	6	2	6	32	4	56	1	0	6	3	.667	0	1-6	14	3.97	3.28
1996 Toronto	AL	11	0	0	3	15.0	76	23	19	19	5	0	0	0	12	2	10	1	0	0	1	.000	0	0-1	0	11.46	11.40
1996 Cincinnati	NL	8	5	0	1	23.0	112	31	17	15	6	1	0	2	13	1	13	0	0	1	0	1.000	0	0-0	0	8.62	5.87
6 ML YEARS		151	18	1	23	286.1	1273	309	174	164	56	15	6	11	123	14	196	3	0	15	11	.577	0	1-11	23	5.45	5.15

D.J. Carrasco

Pitches: R Bats: R Pos: RP
Ht: 6'2" **Wt:** 190 **Born:** 4/12/77 **Age:** 26

Year Team	Lg	G	GS	CG	GF	IP	BFP	H	R	ER	HR	SH	SF	HB	TBB	IBB	SO	WP	Bk	W	L	Pct	ShO	Sv-Op	Hld	ERC	ERA
1998 Watertown	A-	13	1	0	6	31.2	145	36	23	19	3	1	0	2	14	0	38	1	0	1	1	.500	0	2--	-	5.20	5.40
1999 Williamsport	A-	18	4	0	6	51.2	212	43	20	17	2	1	3	3	23	0	49	7	4	4	2	.667	0	0--	-	3.27	2.96
1999 Lynchburg	A+	2	0	0	0	5.2	29	9	8	4	0	1	0	0	3	0	4	0	0	1	0	1.000	0	0--	-	7.15	6.35
2000 Hickory	A	27	0	0	25	40.1	176	35	10	6	0	0	1	0	7	20	1	40	2	0	5	4	.556	0	6--	-	3.66	1.34
2000 Lynchburg	A+	8	0	0	6	10.1	45	16	5	4	1	1	0	0	8	0	10	1	0	1	0	1.000	0	2--	-	10.96	3.48
2000 Altoona	AA	9	0	0	3	14.0	68	16	14	13	0	0	0	1	13	0	10	1	0	1	1	.500	0	0--	-	6.73	8.36
2001 Lynchburg	A+	22	0	0	11	36.0	141	18	7	6	0	1	0	2	14	1	40	1	2	4	0	1.000	0	7--	-	1.29	1.50
2001 Altoona	AA	27	1	0	11	37.0	169	34	22	17	2	2	0	0	25	2	35	2	0	2	2	.500	0	1--	-	4.17	4.14
2002 Lynchburg	A+	55	0	0	44	72.2	286	52	18	13	1	4	4	0	18	1	83	2	0	4	4	.500	0	29--	-	1.86	1.61

Jamey Carroll

Bats: R Throws: R Pos: 3B-13; SS-3; 2B-1
Ht: 5'10" **Wt:** 175 **Born:** 2/18/75 **Age:** 28

Year Team	Lg	G	AB	H	2B	3B	HR	(Hm	Rd)	TB	R	RBI	RC	TBB	IBB	SO	HBP	SH	SF	SB	CS	SB%	GDP	Avg	OBP	Slg
1996 Vermont	A-	54	203	56	6	1	0	(-	-)	64	40	17	25	29	0	25	0	3	2	16	11	.59	1	.276	.363	.315
1997 W Palm Bch	A+	121	407	99	19	1	0	(-	-)	120	56	38	41	43	0	48	4	8	4	17	11	.61	4	.243	.319	.295
1998 Jupiter	A+	55	222	58	5	0	0	(-	-)	63	40	14	25	24	1	26	5	2	1	11	4	.73	2	.261	.345	.284
1998 Harrisburg	AA	75	261	66	11	3	0	(-	-)	83	43	20	34	41	0	29	5	5	0	11	5	.69	4	.253	.365	.318
1999 Harrisburg	AA	141	561	164	34	5	5	(-	-)	223	78	63	78	48	2	58	5	5	4	21	10	.68	13	.292	.351	.398
2000 Ottawa	AAA	91	349	97	17	2	2	(-	-)	124	53	23	43	33	1	32	2	6	2	6	3	.67	9	.278	.342	.355
2000 Harrisburg	AA	45	169	49	5	3	0	(-	-)	60	23	18	20	12	0	13	0	1	1	8	2	.80	5	.290	.335	.355
2001 Ottawa	AAA	83	267	64	8	2	0	(-	-)	76	26	16	19	18	1	41	2	2	1	5	5	.50	8	.240	.292	.285
2002 Harrisburg	AA	3	9	4	0	0	0	(-	-)	4	1	1	3	3	0	0	0	0	0	0	0	-	0	.444	.583	.444
2002 Ottawa	AAA	117	421	118	19	2	8	(-	-)	165	57	49	54	37	1	39	3	7	1	6	10	.38	8	.280	.342	.392
2002 Montreal	NL	16	71	22	5	3	1	(1	0)	36	16	6	12	4	0	12	0	4	0	1	0	1.00	1	.310	.347	.507

Lance Carter

Pitches: R Bats: R Pos: RP-8
Ht: 6'1" **Wt:** 190 **Born:** 12/18/74 **Age:** 28

Year Team	Lg	G	GS	CG	GF	IP	BFP	H	R	ER	HR	SH	SF	HB	TBB	IBB	SO	WP	Bk	W	L	Pct	ShO	Sv-Op	Hld	ERC	ERA
1994 Eugene	A-	8	7	0	1	26.1	118	28	17	16	2	1	3	1	15	0	23	4	3	1	0	1.000	0	0--	-	5.19	5.47
1994 Royals	R	5	5	0	0	31.0	110	19	1	1	1	0	0	0	3	0	36	1	0	3	0	1.000	0	0--	-	1.10	0.29
1995 Springfield	A	27	24	1	0	137.2	584	151	77	61	14	2	4	8	22	0	118	11	1	9	5	.643	1	0--	-	3.89	3.99
1996 Wilmington	A+	16	12	0	3	65.1	292	81	50	46	8	1	0	2	17	2	49	3	0	3	6	.333	0	0--	-	5.08	6.34
1998 Lansing	A	15	2	0	10	40.1	158	34	6	3	0	1	1	0	9	1	37	0	0	3	1	.750	0	2--	-	2.02	0.67
1998 Wilmington	A+	28	1	0	11	52.0	217	50	21	19	5	5	3	4	14	1	61	4	0	1	4	.200	0	5--	-	3.65	3.29
1999 Wichita	AA	44	0	0	33	69.2	282	49	10	6	1	1	1	2	27	5	77	3	0	5	2	.714	0	13--	-	1.96	0.78
2000 Omaha	AAA	34	6	0	13	76.1	321	88	46	42	13	2	2	1	18	1	51	0	1	2	8	.200	0	5--	-	4.95	4.95
2002 Durham	AAA	33	18	2	2	132.0	498	111	43	41	15	1	1	1	12	0	90	0	0	12	2	.857	1	1--	-	2.29	2.80
1999 Kansas City	AL	6	0	0	3	5.1	21	3	3	3	2	0	0	0	3	0	3	0	0	0	0	.000	0	0-0	0	4.22	5.06
2002 Tampa Bay	AL	8	0	0	7	20.1	79	15	3	3	2	0	0	0	5	1	14	0	0	2	0	1.000	0	2-2	0	2.12	1.33
2 ML YEARS		14	0	0	10	25.2	100	18	6	6	4	0	0	0	8	1	17	0	0	2	1	.667	0	2-2	0	2.52	2.10

Mike Caruso

Bats: L Throws: R Pos: SS-5; 2B-4; 3B-2; PR-2　　　　Ht: 6'1" Wt: 172 Born: 5/27/77 Age: 26

Year Team	Lg	G	AB	H	2B	3B	HR	(Hm Rd)	TB	R	RBI	RC	TBB	IBB	SO	HBP	SH	SF	SB	CS	SB%	GDP	Avg	OBP	Slg
2002 Chattanooga*	AA	3	14	5	0	0	1	(- -)	8	4	4	3	1	0	0	0	1	0	1	0	1.00	0	.357	.400	.571
2002 Omaha*	AAA	60	219	67	3	2	3	(- -)	83	28	23	31	12	1	14	4	3	2	10	3	.77	1	.306	.350	.379
1998 Chicago	AL	133	523	160	17	6	5	(3 2)	204	81	55	68	14	0	38	7	8	3	22	6	.79	8	.306	.331	.390
1999 Chicago	AL	136	529	132	11	4	2	(0 2)	157	60	35	40	20	0	36	3	11	1	12	14	.46	6	.250	.280	.297
2002 Kansas City	AL	12	20	2	0	0	0	(0 0)	2	3	0	0	1	0	2	0	0	0	0	0	-	0	.100	.143	.100
3 ML YEARS		281	1072	294	28	10	7	(3 4)	363	144	90	108	35	0	76	10	19	4	34	20	.63	14	.274	.302	.339

Raul Casanova

Bats: B Throws: R Pos: C-30; PH-5　　　　Ht: 6'0" Wt: 216 Born: 8/23/72 Age: 30

Year Team	Lg	G	AB	H	2B	3B	HR	(Hm Rd)	TB	R	RBI	RC	TBB	IBB	SO	HBP	SH	SF	SB	CS	SB%	GDP	Avg	OBP	Slg
2002 Indianapolis*	AAA	14	43	12	4	0	0	(- -)	16	2	8	4	3	0	8	0	0	2	0	0	-	3	.279	.313	.372
1996 Detroit	AL	25	85	16	1	0	4	(1 3)	29	6	9	5	6	0	18	0	0	0	0	0	-	0	.188	.242	.341
1997 Detroit	AL	101	304	74	10	1	5	(5 0)	101	27	24	29	26	1	48	3	0	1	1	1	.50	10	.243	.308	.332
1998 Detroit	AL	16	42	6	2	0	1	(1 0)	11	4	3	3	5	0	10	1	0	0	0	0	-	0	.143	.250	.262
2000 Milwaukee	NL	86	231	57	13	3	6	(4 2)	94	20	36	31	26	1	48	4	2	2	1	2	.33	3	.247	.331	.407
2001 Milwaukee	NL	71	192	50	10	0	11	(7 4)	93	21	33	28	12	2	29	1	0	3	0	0	-	3	.260	.303	.484
2002 Mil-Bal		33	88	16	1	0	1	(0 1)	20	3	8	3	10	4	19	1	0	1	0	0	-	3	.182	.270	.227
2002 Milwaukee	NL	31	87	16	1	0	1	(0 1)	20	3	8	3	10	4	18	1	0	1	0	0	-	3	.184	.273	.230
2002 Baltimore	AL	2	1	0	0	0	0	(0 0)	0	0	0	0	0	0	1	0	0	0	0	0	-	0	.000	.000	.000
6 ML YEARS		332	942	219	37	4	28	(18 10)	348	81	113	99	85	8	172	10	2	7	2	3	.40	27	.232	.301	.369

Sean Casey

Bats: L Throws: R Pos: 1B-109; PH-11; DH-1　　　　Ht: 6'4" Wt: 225 Born: 7/2/74 Age: 28

Year Team	Lg	G	AB	H	2B	3B	HR	(Hm Rd)	TB	R	RBI	RC	TBB	IBB	SO	HBP	SH	SF	SB	CS	SB%	GDP	Avg	OBP	Slg
2002 Louisville*	AAA	2	8	4	0	0	1	(- -)	7	2	3	3	1	1	0	0	0	0	0	0	-	0	.500	.556	.875
1997 Cleveland	AL	6	10	2	0	0	0	(0 0)	2	1	1	1	1	0	2	1	0	0	0	0	-	0	.200	.333	.200
1998 Cincinnati	NL	96	302	82	21	1	7	(3 4)	126	44	52	45	43	3	45	3	0	3	1	1	.50	11	.272	.365	.417
1999 Cincinnati	NL	151	594	197	42	3	25	(11 14)	320	103	99	119	61	13	88	9	0	5	0	2	.00	16	.332	.399	.539
2000 Cincinnati	NL	133	480	151	33	2	20	(9 11)	248	69	85	91	52	4	80	7	0	6	1	0	1.00	16	.315	.385	.517
2001 Cincinnati	NL	145	533	165	40	0	13	(6 8)	244	69	89	86	43	8	63	9	0	3	3	1	.75	16	.310	.369	.458
2002 Cincinnati	NL	120	425	111	25	0	6	(3 3)	154	56	42	44	43	6	47	5	0	3	2	1	.67	11	.261	.334	.362
6 ML YEARS		651	2344	708	161	6	71	(31 40)	1094	342	368	386	243	34	325	34	0	20	7	5	.58	69	.302	.373	.467

Kevin Cash

Bats: R Throws: R Pos: C-7　　　　Ht: 6'0" Wt: 185 Born: 12/6/77 Age: 25

Year Team	Lg	G	AB	H	2B	3B	HR	(Hm Rd)	TB	R	RBI	RC	TBB	IBB	SO	HBP	SH	SF	SB	CS	SB%	GDP	Avg	OBP	Slg
2000 Hagerstown	A	59	196	48	10	1	10	(- -)	90	28	27	27	22	1	54	1	1	1	5	3	.63	7	.245	.323	.459
2001 Dunedin	A+	105	371	105	27	0	12	(- -)	168	55	66	60	43	2	80	8	4	1	4	3	.57	11	.283	.369	.453
2002 Syracuse	AAA	67	236	52	18	0	10	(- -)	100	27	26	30	25	0	72	2	2	1	0	1	.00	3	.220	.299	.424
2002 Toronto	AL	7	14	2	0	0	0	(0 0)	2	1	0	0	1	0	4	0	0	0	0	0	-	1	.143	.200	.143

Scott Cassidy

Pitches: R Bats: R Pos: RP-58　　　　Ht: 6'2" Wt: 175 Born: 10/3/75 Age: 27

Year Team	Lg	G	GS	CG	GF	IP	BFP	H	R	ER	HR	SH	SF	HB	TBB	IBB	SO	WP	Bk	W	L	Pct	ShO	Sv-Op	Hld	ERC	ERA
1998 Medicine Hat	R+	15	14	0	0	81.1	325	71	31	22	4	2	3	5	14	0	82	2	0	8	1	.889	0	0--	-	2.50	2.43
1999 Hagerstown	A	27	27	1	0	170.2	694	151	78	62	13	2	1	21	30	0	178	3	2	13	7	.650	0	0--	-	2.95	3.27
2000 Dunedin	A+	14	13	1	1	88.0	342	53	15	13	4	3	2	3	34	2	89	4	0	9	3	.750	0	0--	-	1.82	1.33
2000 Tennessee	AA	8	7	0	0	42.2	190	48	30	28	7	1	4	4	15	0	39	3	0	2	2	.500	0	0--	-	5.49	5.91
2001 Tennessee	AA	16	15	4	0	96.2	394	78	45	37	10	3	0	7	27	0	81	1	0	6	6	.500	3	0--	-	2.90	3.44
2001 Syracuse	AAA	11	11	0	0	63.0	276	60	24	19	6	0	1	6	26	0	48	1	0	3	3	.500	0	0--	-	4.18	2.71
2002 Syracuse	AAA	3	2	0	1	9.0	33	8	4	4	2	0	0	0	4	0	4	1	0	1	0	1.000	0	0--	-	2.79	4.00
2002 Toronto	AL	58	0	0	17	66.0	282	52	42	42	12	4	5	7	32	3	48	2	0	1	4	.200	0	0-7	-	4.17	5.73

Vinny Castilla

Bats: R Throws: R Pos: 3B-139; PH-5　　　　Ht: 6'1" Wt: 205 Born: 7/4/67 Age: 35

Year Team	Lg	G	AB	H	2B	3B	HR	(Hm Rd)	TB	R	RBI	RC	TBB	IBB	SO	HBP	SH	SF	SB	CS	SB%	GDP	Avg	OBP	Slg
1991 Atlanta	NL	12	5	1	0	0	0	(0 0)	1	1	0	0	0	0	2	0	1	0	0	0	-	0	.200	.200	.200
1992 Atlanta	NL	9	16	4	1	0	0	(0 0)	5	1	1	2	1	1	4	1	0	0	0	0	-	0	.250	.333	.313
1993 Colorado	NL	105	337	86	9	7	9	(5 4)	136	36	30	34	13	4	45	2	0	5	2	5	.29	10	.255	.283	.404
1994 Colorado	NL	52	130	43	11	1	3	(1 2)	65	16	18	22	7	1	23	0	1	3	2	1	.67	3	.331	.357	.500
1995 Colorado	NL	139	527	163	34	2	32	(23 9)	297	82	90	94	30	2	87	4	4	6	2	8	.20	15	.309	.347	.564
1996 Colorado	NL	160	629	191	34	0	40	(27 13)	345	97	113	110	35	7	88	5	0	4	7	2	.78	20	.304	.343	.548
1997 Colorado	NL	159	612	186	25	2	40	(21 19)	335	94	113	110	44	9	108	8	0	4	2	4	.33	17	.304	.356	.547
1998 Colorado	NL	162	645	206	28	4	46	(26 20)	380	108	144	122	40	7	89	6	0	6	5	9	.36	24	.319	.362	.589
1999 Colorado	NL	158	615	169	24	1	33	(20 13)	294	83	102	93	53	7	75	1	0	5	2	3	.40	15	.275	.331	.478
2000 Tampa Bay	AL	85	331	73	9	1	6	(2 4)	102	22	42	22	14	3	41	3	0	6	1	2	.33	9	.221	.254	.308
2001 TB-Hou		146	538	140	34	1	25	(12 13)	251	69	91	70	35	3	108	4	0	4	1	4	.20	22	.260	.308	.467
2002 Atlanta	NL	143	543	126	23	2	12	(5 7)	189	56	61	36	22	4	69	7	0	6	4	1	.80	22	.232	.268	.348

Year Team	Lg	G	AB	H	2B	3B	HR	(Hm	Rd)	TB	R	RBI	RC	TBB	IBB	SO	HBP	SH	SF	SB	CS	SB%	GDP	Avg	OBP	Slg
2001 Tampa Bay	AL	24	93	20	6	0	2	(2	0)	32	7	9	7	3	0	22	1	0	0	0	0	-	3	.215	.247	.344
2001 Houston	NL	122	445	120	28	1	23	(10	13)	219	62	82	63	32	3	86	3	0	4	1	4	.20	19	.270	.320	.492
12 ML YEARS		1330	4928	1388	232	21	246	(142	104)	2400	665	805	715	294	48	739	41	6	49	28	39	.42	157	.282	.324	.487

Alberto Castillo

Bats: R **Throws:** R **Pos:** C-14; PH-1 \
Ht: 6'0" **Wt:** 200 **Born:** 2/10/70 **Age:** 33

							BATTING													BASERUNNING				AVERAGES		
Year Team	Lg	G	AB	H	2B	3B	HR	(Hm	Rd)	TB	R	RBI	RC	TBB	IBB	SO	HBP	SH	SF	SB	CS	SB%	GDP	Avg	OBP	Slg
2002 Columbus*	AAA	30	91	25	7	0	0	(-	-)	32	7	8	11	9	0	8	2	1	1	1	0	1.00	3	.275	.350	.352
1995 New York	NL	13	29	3	0	0	0	(0	0)	3	2	0	0	3	0	9	1	0	0	1	0	1.00	0	.103	.212	.103
1996 New York	NL	6	11	4	0	0	0	(0	0)	4	1	0	1	0	0	4	0	0	0	0	0	-	0	.364	.364	.364
1997 New York	NL	35	59	12	1	0	0	(0	0)	13	3	7	3	9	0	16	0	2	1	0	1	.00	3	.203	.304	.220
1998 New York	NL	38	83	17	4	0	2	(0	2)	27	13	7	7	9	0	17	1	6	0	0	2	.00	1	.205	.290	.325
1999 St Louis	NL	93	255	67	8	0	4	(2	2)	87	21	31	29	24	1	48	2	5	4	0	0	-	6	.263	.326	.341
2000 Toronto	AL	66	185	39	7	0	1	(1	0)	49	14	16	14	21	0	36	0	2	3	0	0	-	3	.211	.287	.265
2001 Toronto	AL	66	131	26	4	0	1	(0	1)	33	9	4	7	7	0	30	3	5	0	1	1	.50	2	.198	.255	.252
2002 New York	AL	15	37	5	1	1	0	(0	0)	8	3	4	1	1	0	12	0	3	0	0	0	-	2	.135	.158	.216
8 ML YEARS		332	790	173	25	1	8	(3	5)	224	66	69	60	74	1	172	7	23	8	2	4	.33	17	.219	.289	.284

Frank Castillo

Pitches: R **Bats:** R **Pos:** SP-23; RP-13 \
Ht: 6'1" **Wt:** 198 **Born:** 4/1/69 **Age:** 34

		HOW MUCH HE PITCHED						WHAT HE GAVE UP											THE RESULTS							
Year Team	Lg	G	GS	CG	GF	IP	BFP	H	R	ER	HR	SH	SF	HB	TBB	IBB	SO	WP	Bk	W	L	Pct	ShO	Sv-Op	Hld	ERC	ERA
1991 Chicago	NL	18	18	4	0	111.2	467	107	56	54	5	6	3	0	33	2	73	5	1	6	7	.462	0	0-0	0	3.04	4.35
1992 Chicago	NL	33	33	0	0	205.1	856	179	91	79	19	11	5	6	63	6	135	11	0	10	11	.476	0	0-0	0	3.02	3.46
1993 Chicago	NL	29	25	2	0	141.1	614	162	83	76	20	10	3	9	39	4	84	5	3	5	8	.385	0	0-0	0	4.98	4.84
1994 Chicago	NL	4	4	1	0	23.0	96	25	13	11	3	1	0	0	5	0	19	0	0	2	1	.667	0	0-0	0	4.09	4.30
1995 Chicago	NL	29	29	2	0	188.0	795	179	75	67	22	11	3	6	52	4	135	3	1	11	10	.524	2	0-0	0	3.49	3.21
1996 Chicago	NL	33	33	1	0	182.1	789	209	112	107	28	4	5	8	46	4	139	2	1	7	16	.304	1	0-0	0	4.87	5.28
1997 ChC-Col	NL	34	33	0	0	184.1	830	220	121	111	25	17	2	8	69	4	126	3	0	12	12	.500	0	0-0	0	5.51	5.42
1998 Detroit	AL	27	19	0	4	116.0	531	150	91	88	17	2	6	5	44	0	81	0	0	3	9	.250	0	1-1	0	6.32	6.83
2000 Toronto	AL	25	24	0	1	138.0	576	152	58	55	18	5	2	5	56	0	104	0	0	10	5	.667	0	0-0	0	3.42	3.59
2001 Boston	AL	26	26	0	0	136.2	580	138	72	64	14	3	6	5	35	2	89	3	1	10	9	.526	0	0-0	0	3.68	4.21
2002 Boston	AL	36	23	0	2	163.1	711	174	101	92	19	1	11	7	58	6	112	1	2	6	15	.286	0	1-2	0	4.51	5.07
1997 Chicago	NL	20	19	0	0	98.0	446	113	64	59	9	11	0	4	44	1	67	0	0	6	9	.400	0	0-0	0	5.23	5.42
1997 Colorado	NL	14	14	0	0	86.1	384	107	57	52	16	6	2	4	25	3	59	2	0	6	3	.667	0	0-0	0	5.83	5.42
11 ML YEARS		294	267	10	7	1590.0	6845	1655	873	804	190	71	46	59	500	32	1097	33	9	82	103	.443	3	2-3	0	4.21	4.55

Luis Castillo

Bats: B **Throws:** R **Pos:** 2B-144; PH-3 \
Ht: 5'11" **Wt:** 190 **Born:** 9/12/75 **Age:** 27

							BATTING													BASERUNNING				AVERAGES		
Year Team	Lg	G	AB	H	2B	3B	HR	(Hm	Rd)	TB	R	RBI	RC	TBB	IBB	SO	HBP	SH	SF	SB	CS	SB%	GDP	Avg	OBP	Slg
1996 Florida	NL	41	164	43	2	1	1	(0	1)	50	26	8	19	14	0	46	0	2	0	17	4	.81	0	.262	.320	.305
1997 Florida	NL	75	263	63	8	0	0	(0	0)	71	27	8	21	27	0	53	0	1	0	16	10	.62	6	.240	.310	.270
1998 Florida	NL	44	153	31	3	2	1	(0	1)	41	21	10	14	22	0	33	1	1	0	3	0	1.00	1	.203	.307	.268
1999 Florida	NL	128	487	147	23	4	0	(0	0)	178	76	28	78	67	0	85	0	6	3	50	17	.75	3	.302	.384	.366
2000 Florida	NL	136	539	180	17	3	2	(1	1)	209	101	17	95	78	0	86	0	9	0	62	22	.74	11	.334	.418	.388
2001 Florida	NL	134	537	141	16	10	2	(1	1)	183	76	45	67	67	0	90	1	4	3	33	16	.67	6	.263	.344	.341
2002 Florida	NL	146	606	185	18	5	2	(1	1)	219	86	39	80	55	4	76	2	4	1	48	15	.76	7	.305	.364	.361
7 ML YEARS		704	2749	790	87	25	8	(2	6)	951	413	155	374	330	4	469	4	27	7	229	84	.73	34	.287	.364	.346

Juan Castro

Bats: R **Throws:** R **Pos:** SS-25; PH-19; 2B-17; PR-3; 1B-1; 3B-1 \
Ht: 5'11" **Wt:** 195 **Born:** 6/20/72 **Age:** 31

							BATTING													BASERUNNING				AVERAGES		
Year Team	Lg	G	AB	H	2B	3B	HR	(Hm	Rd)	TB	R	RBI	RC	TBB	IBB	SO	HBP	SH	SF	SB	CS	SB%	GDP	Avg	OBP	Slg
2002 Louisville*	AAA	5	17	3	0	0	0	(-	-)	3	2	2	0	1	0	3	0	1	0	0	0	-	0	.176	.222	.176
1995 Los Angeles	NL	11	4	1	0	0	0	(0	0)	1	0	0	1	1	0	1	0	0	0	0	0	-	0	.250	.400	.250
1996 Los Angeles	NL	70	132	26	5	3	0	(0	0)	37	16	5	8	10	0	27	0	4	0	1	0	1.00	3	.197	.254	.280
1997 Los Angeles	NL	40	75	11	3	1	0	(0	0)	16	3	4	2	7	1	20	0	2	0	0	0	-	0	.147	.220	.213
1998 Los Angeles	NL	89	220	43	7	0	2	(0	2)	56	25	14	12	15	0	37	0	9	2	0	0	-	5	.195	.245	.255
1999 Los Angeles	NL	2	1	0	0	0	0	(0	0)	0	0	0	0	0	0	1	0	0	0	0	0	-	0	.000	.000	.000
2000 Cincinnati	NL	82	224	54	12	2	4	(1	3)	82	20	23	20	14	1	33	0	4	2	0	2	.00	9	.241	.283	.366
2001 Cincinnati	NL	96	242	54	10	0	3	(0	3)	73	27	13	16	13	2	50	0	4	0	0	0	-	9	.223	.261	.302
2002 Cincinnati	NL	54	82	18	3	0	2	(0	2)	27	5	11	11	7	0	18	0	1	1	0	0	-	1	.220	.278	.329
8 ML YEARS		444	980	207	40	6	11	(1	10)	292	96	70	70	67	4	187	0	24	7	1	2	.33	28	.211	.260	.298

Ramon Castro

Bats: R **Throws:** R **Pos:** C-37; PH-26; DH-1 \
Ht: 6'3" **Wt:** 235 **Born:** 3/1/76 **Age:** 27

							BATTING													BASERUNNING				AVERAGES		
Year Team	Lg	G	AB	H	2B	3B	HR	(Hm	Rd)	TB	R	RBI	RC	TBB	IBB	SO	HBP	SH	SF	SB	CS	SB%	GDP	Avg	OBP	Slg
1999 Florida	NL	24	67	12	4	0	2	(0	2)	22	4	4	6	10	3	14	0	0	1	0	0	-	1	.179	.282	.328
2000 Florida	NL	50	138	33	4	0	2	(0	2)	43	10	14	14	16	7	36	1	0	2	0	0	-	1	.239	.318	.312
2001 Florida	NL	7	11	2	0	0	0	(0	0)	2	0	1	0	1	0	1	0	0	0	0	0	-	0	.182	.250	.182
2002 Florida	NL	54	101	24	4	0	6	(4	2)	46	11	18	14	14	3	24	0	1	3	0	0	-	4	.238	.322	.455
4 ML YEARS		135	317	71	12	0	10	(4	6)	113	25	37	34	41	13	75	1	1	6	0	0	-	6	.224	.310	.356

Frank Catalanotto

Bats: L **Throws:** R **Pos:** LF-25; 2B-23; 1B-15; PH-9; DH-8; PR-3 **Ht:** 5'11" **Wt:** 195 **Born:** 4/27/74 **Age:** 29

Year Team	Lg	G	AB	H	2B	3B	HR	(Hm	Rd)	TB	R	RBI	RC	TBB	IBB	SO	HBP	SH	SF	SB	CS	SB%	GDP	Avg	OBP	Slg
2002 Tulsa*	AA	4	16	2	0	1	0	(-	-)	4	1	3	0	1	0	1	1	0	0	0	0	-	3	.125	.222	.250
1997 Detroit	AL	13	26	8	2	0	0	(0	0)	10	2	3	4	3	0	7	0	0	0	0	0	-	0	.308	.379	.385
1998 Detroit	AL	89	213	60	13	2	6	(3	3)	95	23	25	30	12	1	39	4	0	5	3	2	.60	4	.282	.325	.446
1999 Detroit	AL	100	286	79	19	0	11	(6	5)	131	41	35	42	15	1	49	9	0	5	3	4	.43	5	.276	.327	.458
2000 Texas	AL	103	282	82	13	2	10	(6	4)	129	55	42	49	33	0	36	6	3	2	6	2	.75	5	.291	.375	.457
2001 Texas	AL	133	463	153	31	5	11	(4	7)	227	77	54	88	39	3	55	8	1	1	15	5	.75	5	.330	.391	.490
2002 Texas	AL	68	212	57	16	6	3	(2	1)	94	42	23	39	25	0	27	8	3	2	9	5	.64	3	.269	.364	.443
6 ML YEARS		506	1482	439	94	15	41	(21	20)	686	240	182	252	127	5	213	35	7	15	36	18	.67	22	.296	.362	.463

Roger Cedeno

Bats: B **Throws:** R **Pos:** LF-131; PH-19; PR-3; CF-1 **Ht:** 6'1" **Wt:** 205 **Born:** 8/16/74 **Age:** 28

Year Team	Lg	G	AB	H	2B	3B	HR	(Hm	Rd)	TB	R	RBI	RC	TBB	IBB	SO	HBP	SH	SF	SB	CS	SB%	GDP	Avg	OBP	Slg
1995 Los Angeles	NL	40	42	10	2	0	0	(0	0)	12	4	3	3	3	0	10	0	0	1	1	0	1.00	1	.238	.283	.286
1996 Los Angeles	NL	86	211	52	11	1	2	(0	2)	71	26	18	26	24	0	47	1	2	0	5	1	.83	6	.246	.326	.336
1997 Los Angeles	NL	80	194	53	10	2	3	(3	0)	76	31	17	31	25	2	44	3	3	2	9	1	.90	1	.273	.362	.392
1998 Los Angeles	NL	105	240	58	11	1	2	(2	0)	77	33	17	27	27	2	57	0	3	1	8	2	.80	1	.242	.317	.321
1999 New York	NL	155	453	142	23	4	4	(4	0)	185	90	36	82	60	3	100	3	7	2	66	17	.80	5	.313	.396	.408
2000 Houston	NL	74	259	73	2	5	6	(3	3)	103	54	26	42	43	0	47	0	2	1	25	11	.69	6	.282	.383	.398
2001 Detroit	NL	131	523	153	14	11	6	(4	2)	207	79	48	76	36	1	83	2	6	5	55	15	.79	5	.293	.337	.396
2002 New York	NL	149	511	133	19	2	7	(2	5)	177	65	41	59	42	1	92	2	5	2	25	4	.86	10	.260	.318	.346
8 ML YEARS		820	2433	674	92	26	30	(17	13)	908	382	206	346	260	9	480	11	28	14	194	51	.79	29	.277	.348	.373

Matt Cepicky

Bats: L **Throws:** R **Pos:** PH-17; LF-16; RF-1 **Ht:** 6'2" **Wt:** 215 **Born:** 11/10/77 **Age:** 25

Year Team	Lg	G	AB	H	2B	3B	HR	(Hm	Rd)	TB	R	RBI	RC	TBB	IBB	SO	HBP	SH	SF	SB	CS	SB%	GDP	Avg	OBP	Slg
1999 Vermont	A-	74	323	99	15	5	12	(-	-)	160	50	53	52	20	1	49	1	0	0	10	9	.53	6	.307	.349	.495
2000 Jupiter	A+	131	536	160	32	7	5	(-	-)	221	61	88	72	24	4	64	2	1	5	32	13	.71	9	.299	.328	.412
2001 Harrisburg	AA	122	459	121	23	8	19	(-	-)	217	59	77	60	21	2	97	2	2	4	5	12	.29	5	.264	.296	.473
2002 Harrisburg	AA	109	419	116	25	2	16	(-	-)	193	54	76	61	33	4	94	2	1	8	7	1	.88	14	.277	.327	.461
2002 Montreal	NL	32	74	16	3	0	3	(2	1)	28	7	15	8	4	1	21	0	0	0	0	0	-	0	.216	.256	.378

Jaime Cerda

Pitches: L **Bats:** L **Pos:** RP-32 **Ht:** 6'0" **Wt:** 175 **Born:** 10/26/78 **Age:** 24

Year Team	Lg	G	GS	CG	GF	IP	BFP	H	R	ER	HR	SH	SF	HB	TBB	IBB	SO	WP	Bk	W	L	Pct	ShO	Sv-Op	Hld	ERC	ERA
2000 Pittsfield	A-	20	1	0	7	47.0	176	33	6	3	0	2	0	0	6	0	51	2	0	4	1	.800	0	5--	-	1.28	0.57
2001 St.Lucie	A+	28	0	0	15	55.2	213	40	8	6	3	3	1	1	12	0	56	0	0	2	1	.667	0	6--	-	1.83	0.97
2001 Binghamton	AA	12	0	0	9	20.1	82	17	7	7	1	1	1	1	6	0	22	2	0	1	0	1.000	0	3--	-	2.72	3.10
2001 Norfolk	AAA	3	0	0	1	4.2	18	2	2	2	0	0	0	0	2	0	4	1	0	0	0	-	0	0--	-	1.08	3.86
2002 Binghamton	AA	14	0	0	5	31.2	121	21	8	8	0	1	1	0	10	0	33	2	0	5	1	.833	0	0--	-	1.59	2.27
2002 Norfolk	AAA	12	0	0	4	21.0	77	10	2	1	0	0	0	0	7	1	17	0	0	0	0	-	0	1--	-	1.03	0.43
2002 New York	NL	32	0	0	7	25.2	114	22	7	7	0	0	3	1	14	0	21	0	1	0	0	-	0	0-0	4	3.19	2.45

Shawn Chacon

Pitches: R **Bats:** R **Pos:** SP-21 **Ht:** 6'3" **Wt:** 212 **Born:** 12/23/77 **Age:** 25

Year Team	Lg	G	GS	CG	GF	IP	BFP	H	R	ER	HR	SH	SF	HB	TBB	IBB	SO	WP	Bk	W	L	Pct	ShO	Sv-Op	Hld	ERC	ERA
1996 Rockies	R	11	11	0	0	56.1	241	46	17	10	1	0	2	4	15	0	64	3	2	1	2	.333	0	0--	-	2.22	1.60
1996 Portland	A-	4	4	0	0	19.2	92	24	18	15	1	0	0	1	9	0	17	5	0	0	2	.000	0	0--	-	5.75	6.86
1997 Asheville	A	28	27	1	0	162.0	701	155	80	70	13	5	3	14	63	1	149	15	1	11	7	.611	0	0--	-	3.99	3.89
1998 Salem	A+	12	12	0	0	56.0	258	53	35	33	5	3	2	6	31	0	54	8	1	0	4	.000	0	0--	-	4.61	5.30
1999 Salem	A+	12	12	0	0	72.0	316	69	44	33	3	1	3	2	34	0	66	5	0	5	5	.500	0	0--	-	3.78	4.13
2000 Carolina	AA	27	27	4	0	173.2	739	151	71	61	10	4	2	9	85	1	172	16	0	10	10	.500	3	0--	-	3.65	3.16
2001 Co Springs	AAA	4	4	0	0	24.0	98	18	6	6	3	3	0	1	7	0	28	0	0	2	0	1.000	0	0--	-	2.62	2.25
2002 Co Springs	AAA	4	4	0	0	20.2	93	23	12	11	3	1	1	2	10	0	15	0	1	2	0	1.000	0	0--	-	5.95	4.79
2001 Colorado	NL	27	27	0	0	160.0	711	157	96	90	26	6	3	10	87	10	134	6	0	6	10	.375	0	0-0	0	5.22	5.06
2002 Colorado	NL	21	21	0	0	119.1	537	122	84	76	25	5	2	7	60	3	67	0	1	5	11	.313	0	0-0	0	5.63	5.73
2 ML YEARS		48	48	0	0	279.1	1248	279	180	166	51	11	5	17	147	13	201	6	1	11	21	.344	0	0-0	0	5.40	5.35

Endy Chavez

Bats: L **Throws:** L **Pos:** CF-35; PH-2; PR-2 **Ht:** 6'0" **Wt:** 165 **Born:** 2/7/78 **Age:** 25

Year Team	Lg	G	AB	H	2B	3B	HR	(Hm	Rd)	TB	R	RBI	RC	TBB	IBB	SO	HBP	SH	SF	SB	CS	SB%	GDP	Avg	OBP	Slg
1997 Mets	R	33	119	33	6	3	0	(-	-)	45	26	15	18	20	0	10	0	0	1	1	2	.33	2	.277	.379	.378
1997 Kingsport	R+	19	73	22	4	0	0	(-	-)	26	16	4	12	13	0	10	0	2	0	5	2	.71	2	.301	.407	.356
1998 Kingsport	R+	33	114	33	8	4	0	(-	-)	49	26	16	20	17	0	17	0	0	3	10	5	.67	1	.289	.373	.430
1999 Capital City	A	73	253	64	8	1	0	(-	-)	74	40	15	27	34	0	36	0	2	1	20	12	.63	3	.253	.340	.292
1999 St.Lucie	A+	45	183	57	8	3	2	(-	-)	77	33	18	30	22	2	22	0	2	1	9	3	.75	5	.311	.383	.421
2000 St.Lucie	A+	111	433	129	20	2	1	(-	-)	156	84	43	62	47	4	48	0	7	3	38	16	.70	3	.298	.364	.360
2001 Wichita	AA	43	168	50	6	1	1	(-	-)	61	27	13	23	16	0	13	0	3	3	11	6	.65	1	.298	.353	.363
2001 Omaha	AAA	23	104	35	6	0	0	(-	-)	41	18	4	13	0	0	13	0	1	0	4	3	.57	1	.337	.333	.394
2002 Ottawa	AAA	103	405	139	28	5	4	(-	-)	189	67	41	70	33	2	37	0	10	1	21	13	.62	8	.343	.392	.467

Year Team	Lg	G	AB	H	2B	3B	HR	(Hm	Rd)	TB	R	RBI	RC	TBB	IBB	SO	HBP	SH	SF	SB	CS	SB%	GDP	Avg	OBP	Slg
								BATTING												BASERUNNING				AVERAGES		
2001 Kansas City	AL	29	77	16	2	0	0	(0	0)	18	4	5	2	3	0	8	0	0	0	0	2	.00	3	.208	.238	.234
2002 Montreal	NL	36	125	37	8	5	1	(0	1)	58	20	9	14	5	0	16	0	7	1	3	5	.38	0	.296	.321	.464
2 ML YEARS		65	202	53	10	5	1	(0	1)	76	24	14	16	8	0	24	0	7	1	3	7	.30	3	.262	.289	.376

Eric Chavez

Bats: L **Throws:** R **Pos:** 3B-143; DH-9; LF-1; PH-1   **Ht:** 6'1" **Wt:** 206 **Born:** 12/7/77 **Age:** 25

Year Team	Lg	G	AB	H	2B	3B	HR	(Hm	Rd)	TB	R	RBI	RC	TBB	IBB	SO	HBP	SH	SF	SB	CS	SB%	GDP	Avg	OBP	Slg
								BATTING												BASERUNNING				AVERAGES		
1998 Oakland	AL	16	45	14	4	1	0			20	6	6	7	3	1	5	0	0	0	1	1	.50	1	.311	.354	.444
1999 Oakland	AL	115	356	88	21	2	13	(8	5)	152	47	50	50	46	4	56	0	0	0	1	1	.50	7	.247	.333	.427
2000 Oakland	AL	153	501	139	23	4	26	(15	11)	248	89	86	86	62	8	94	1	0	5	2	2	.50	9	.277	.355	.495
2001 Oakland	AL	151	552	159	43	0	32	(14	18)	298	91	114	99	41	9	99	4	0	7	8	2	.80	7	.288	.338	.540
2002 Oakland	AL	153	585	161	31	3	34	(17	17)	300	87	109	105	65	13	119	1	0	2	8	3	.73	8	.275	.348	.513
5 ML YEARS		588	2039	561	122	10	105	(54	51)	1018	320	365	347	217	35	373	6	0	14	20	9	.69	32	.275	.344	.499

Raul Chavez

Bats: R **Throws:** R **Pos:** C-2   **Ht:** 5'11" **Wt:** 210 **Born:** 3/18/73 **Age:** 30

Year Team	Lg	G	AB	H	2B	3B	HR	(Hm	Rd)	TB	R	RBI	RC	TBB	IBB	SO	HBP	SH	SF	SB	CS	SB%	GDP	Avg	OBP	Slg
								BATTING												BASERUNNING				AVERAGES		
2002 New Orleans*	AAA	111	373	85	10	0	3	(-	-)	104	24	36	25	21	2	50	7	5	5	3	4	.43	11	.228	.278	.279
1996 Montreal	NL	4	5	1	0	0	0	(0	0)	1	1	0	0	1	0	1	0	0	0	1	0	1.00	1	.200	.333	.200
1997 Montreal	NL	13	26	7	0	0	0	(0	0)	7	0	2	2	0	0	5	0	0	1	1	0	1.00	0	.269	.259	.269
1998 Seattle	AL	1	1	0	0	0	0	(0	0)	0	0	0	0	0	0	0	0	0	0	0	0	-	0	.000	.000	.000
2000 Houston	NL	14	43	11	2	0	1	(0	1)	16	3	5	3	3	2	6	0	0	1	0	0	-	5	.256	.298	.372
2002 Houston	NL	2	4	1	1	0	0	(0	0)	2	1	0	1	1	0	0	1	0	0	0	0	-	0	.250	.500	.500
5 ML YEARS		34	79	20	3	0	1	(0	1)	26	5	7	6	5	2	12	1	0	2	2	0	1.00	6	.253	.299	.329

Bruce Chen

Pitches: L **Bats:** L **Pos:** RP-49; SP-6   **Ht:** 6'2" **Wt:** 210 **Born:** 6/19/77 **Age:** 26

Year Team	Lg	G	GS	CG	GF	IP	BFP	H	R	ER	HR	SH	SF	HB	TBB	IBB	SO	WP	Bk	W	L	Pct	ShO	Sv-Op	Hld	ERC	ERA
			HOW MUCH HE PITCHED							WHAT HE GAVE UP												THE RESULTS					
1998 Atlanta	NL	4	4	0	0	20.1	91	23	9	9	3	1	0	1	9	1	17	0	0	2	0	1.000	0	0-0	0	5.55	3.98
1999 Atlanta	NL	16	7	0	3	51.0	214	38	32	31	11	1	1	2	27	3	45	0	0	2	2	.500	0	0-0	0	4.07	5.47
2000 Atl-Phi	NL	37	15	0	4	134.0	559	116	54	49	18	8	3	2	46	4	112	4	1	7	4	.636	0	0-0	0	4.75	3.29
2001 Phi-NYM	NL	27	27	0	0	146.0	634	146	96	79	29	4	7	1	59	4	126	5	0	7	7	.500	0	0-0	0	5.99	4.87
2002 NYM-Mon-Cin	NL	55	6	0	9	77.2	360	85	53	48	16	2	3	2	43	5	80	4	0	2	5	.286	0	0-0	4	5.99	5.56
2000 Atlanta	NL	22	0	0	4	39.2	176	35	15	11	4	3	2	1	19	2	32	0	1	4	0	1.000	0	0-0	0	3.62	2.50
2000 Philadelphia	NL	15	15	0	0	94.1	383	81	39	38	14	5	1	1	27	2	80	4	0	3	4	.429	0	0-0	0	3.22	3.63
2001 Philadelphia	NL	16	16	0	0	86.1	381	90	53	48	19	2	4	1	31	4	79	2	0	4	5	.444	0	0-0	0	4.87	5.00
2001 New York	NL	11	11	0	0	59.2	253	56	37	31	10	2	3	0	28	0	47	3	0	3	2	.600	0	0-0	0	4.58	4.68
2002 New York	NL	1	0	0	0	0.2	3	1	0	0	0	0	0	0	0	0	0	0	0	0	0	-	0	0-0	0	4.47	0.00
2002 Montreal	NL	15	5	0	4	37.1	179	47	29	29	9	0	0	1	23	3	43	3	0	2	3	.400	0	0-0	0	7.69	6.99
2002 Cincinnati	NL	39	1	0	5	39.2	178	37	24	19	7	2	3	1	20	2	37	1	0	0	2	.000	0	0-0	4	4.55	4.31
5 ML YEARS		139	59	0	16	429.0	1858	408	238	216	77	16	14	8	184	17	380	13	1	20	18	.526	0	0-0	4	4.47	4.53

Chin-Feng Chen

Bats: R **Throws:** R **Pos:** PH-2; LF-1   **Ht:** 6'1" **Wt:** 189 **Born:** 10/28/77 **Age:** 25

Year Team	Lg	G	AB	H	2B	3B	HR	(Hm	Rd)	TB	R	RBI	RC	TBB	IBB	SO	HBP	SH	SF	SB	CS	SB%	GDP	Avg	OBP	Slg
								BATTING												BASERUNNING				AVERAGES		
1999 Sn Brnardino	A+	131	510	161	22	10	31	(-	-)	296	98	123	119	75	6	129	5	0	7	31	7	.82	7	.316	.404	.580
2000 San Antonio	AA	133	516	143	27	3	6	(-	-)	194	66	67	70	61	3	131	3	1	3	23	15	.61	7	.277	.355	.376
2001 Vero Beach	A+	62	235	63	15	3	5	(-	-)	99	38	41	37	28	2	56	6	0	1	2	0	1.00	3	.268	.359	.421
2001 Jacksonville	AA	66	224	70	16	2	17	(-	-)	141	47	50	54	41	4	65	2	1	1	5	4	.56	7	.313	.422	.629
2002 Las Vegas	AAA	137	511	145	26	4	26	(-	-)	257	90	84	85	58	1	160	0	0	7	1	0	1.00	19	.284	.352	.503
2002 Los Angeles	NL	3	5	0	0	0	0	(0	0)	0	1	0	0	1	0	3	0	0	0	0	0	-	0	.000	.167	.000

Scott Chiasson

Pitches: R **Bats:** R **Pos:** RP-4   **Ht:** 6'3" **Wt:** 200 **Born:** 8/14/77 **Age:** 25

Year Team	Lg	G	GS	CG	GF	IP	BFP	H	R	ER	HR	SH	SF	HB	TBB	IBB	SO	WP	Bk	W	L	Pct	ShO	Sv-Op	Hld	ERC	ERA
			HOW MUCH HE PITCHED							WHAT HE GAVE UP												THE RESULTS					
1998 Royals	R	13	0	0	6	24.1	111	24	17	13	2	2	1	5	11	0	26	10	0	2	0	1.000	0	1- -	-	4.86	4.81
1999 Sth Oregon	A-	15	13	0	1	69.0	318	80	52	40	6	3	2	5	39	0	51	3	0	2	5	.500	0	0- -	-	5.98	5.22
2000 Visalia	A+	31	23	0	4	156.0	666	146	66	53	17	3	2	6	57	2	150	8	1	11	4	.733	0	2- -	-	3.76	3.06
2001 W Tennesse	AA	52	0	0	45	61.1	247	43	15	12	2	4	1	4	20	4	62	7	0	3	4	.429	0	24- -	-	1.99	1.76
2001 Iowa	AAA	11	0	0	10	12.0	49	11	3	3	1	0	0	2	0	0	14	0	0	0	0	-	0	10- -	-	2.59	2.25
2002 Iowa	AAA	27	0	0	17	28.1	132	34	26	25	9	1	3	3	13	1	26	2	1	1	4	.200	0	7- -	-	7.67	7.94
2002 W Tennesse	AA	3	0	0	0	3.0	17	5	2	1	0	0	0	1	1	0	5	0	0	0	0	-	0	0- -	-	5.95	3.00
2001 Chicago	NL	6	0	0	3	6.2	28	5	2	2	2	0	0	1	2	0	6	1	0	1	1	.500	0	0-0	1	4.13	2.70
2002 Chicago	NL	4	0	0	0	4.2	31	11	12	12	2	0	0	0	6	1	3	0	0	0	0	-	0	0-0	0	20.56	23.14
2 ML YEARS		10	0	0	3	11.1	59	16	14	14	4	0	0	1	8	1	9	1	0	1	1	.500	0	0-0	1	10.25	11.12

Matt Childers

Pitches: R Bats: R Pos: RP-8

Ht: 6'5" Wt: 195 Born: 12/3/78 Age: 24

Year Team	Lg	G	GS	CG	GF	IP	BFP	H	R	ER	HR	SH	SF	HB	TBB	IBB	SO	WP	Bk	W	L	Pct	ShO	Sv-Op	Hld	ERC	ERA
1997 Helena	R+	14	10	0	1	61.0	285	81	49	42	5	2	4	0	24	0	19	1	0	1	4	.200	0	1- -	-	5.75	6.20
1998 Helena	R+	2	2	1	0	14.0	53	9	1	1	0	0	0	0	4	1	4	0	0	1	0	1.000	1	0- -	-	1.39	0.64
1998 Beloit	A	14	12	3	0	67.0	303	89	55	38	5	3	2	4	20	0	49	2	0	3	7	.300	0	0- -	-	5.71	5.10
1999 Beloit	A	20	19	0	0	100.0	448	129	72	66	9	1	5	5	30	1	52	0	2	3	10	.231	0	0- -	-	5.54	5.94
2000 Beloit	A	12	12	1	0	73.0	300	64	33	22	4	0	0	1	17	0	47	2	1	8	2	.800	1	0- -	-	2.52	2.71
2000 Mudville	A+	15	15	0	0	85.1	388	103	59	45	10	2	2	3	32	0	43	3	2	3	9	.250	0	0- -	-	5.41	4.75
2001 High Desert	A+	20	20	0	0	117.1	529	155	95	84	19	3	7	6	29	0	76	5	0	6	11	.353	0	0- -	-	6.03	6.44
2001 Huntsville	AA	7	7	0	0	39.1	172	41	19	15	3	1	1	5	12	0	21	3	0	2	2	.500	0	0- -	-	4.27	3.43
2002 Huntsville	AA	35	10	0	24	82.0	374	103	47	41	6	6	5	2	27	0	57	2	0	2	5	.286	0	12- -	-	5.09	4.50
2002 Indianapolis	AAA	3	0	0	1	5.0	18	1	0	0	0	0	0	0	2	0	4	0	0	0	0	-	0	0- -	-	0.50	0.00
2002 Milwaukee	NL	8	0	0	2	9.0	48	13	12	12	2	1	0	1	8	1	6	0	0	0	0	-	0	0-0	0	10.39	12.00

Randy Choate

Pitches: L Bats: L Pos: RP-18

Ht: 6'1" Wt: 180 Born: 9/5/75 Age: 27

Year Team	Lg	G	GS	CG	GF	IP	BFP	H	R	ER	HR	SH	SF	HB	TBB	IBB	SO	WP	Bk	W	L	Pct	ShO	Sv-Op	Hld	ERC	ERA
2002 Columbus*	AAA	31	0	0	7	36.2	150	25	8	7	0	1	0	2	15	1	32	2	0	3	2	.600	0	1- -	-	1.97	1.72
2000 New York	AL	22	0	0	6	17.0	75	14	10	9	3	0	1	1	8	0	12	1	0	1	0	1.000	0	0-0	2	3.99	4.76
2001 New York	AL	37	0	0	13	48.1	207	34	21	18	0	2	1	9	27	2	35	3	0	3	1	.750	0	0-0	3	3.03	3.35
2002 New York	AL	18	0	0	11	22.1	101	18	18	15	1	0	0	3	15	0	17	4	0	0	0	-	0	0-0	4	4.13	6.04
3 ML YEARS		77	0	0	30	87.2	383	66	49	42	4	2	2	13	50	2	64	8	0	3	2	.600	0	0-0	5	3.51	4.31

Hee Seop Choi

Bats: L Throws: L Pos: 1B-22; PH-3; PR-1

Ht: 6'5" Wt: 235 Born: 3/16/79 Age: 24

Year Team	Lg	G	AB	H	2B	3B	HR	(Hm	Rd)	TB	R	RBI	RC	TBB	IBB	SO	HBP	SH	SF	SB	CS	SB%	GDP	Avg	OBP	Slg
1999 Lansing	A	79	290	93	18	6	18	(-	-)	177	71	70	70	50	0	68	2	0	2	2	1	.67	8	.321	.422	.610
2000 Daytona	A+	96	345	102	25	6	15	(-	-)	184	60	70	66	37	5	78	6	0	5	4	1	.80	7	.296	.369	.533
2000 W Tennessee	AA	36	122	37	9	0	10	(-	-)	76	25	25	30	25	0	38	0	0	1	3	1	.75	5	.303	.419	.623
2001 Iowa	AAA	77	266	61	11	0	13	(-	-)	111	38	45	36	34	1	67	0	0	4	5	1	.83	5	.229	.313	.417
2002 Iowa	AAA	135	478	137	24	3	26	(-	-)	245	94	97	102	95	4	119	6	0	7	3	2	.60	6	.287	.406	.513
2002 Chicago	NL	24	50	9	1	0	2	(1	1)	16	6	4	2	7	0	15	0	0	-	0	0	-	2	.180	.281	.320

McKay Christensen

Bats: L Throws: L Pos: LF-2; CF-1; PH-1; PR-1

Ht: 5'11" Wt: 180 Born: 8/14/75 Age: 27

Year Team	Lg	G	AB	H	2B	3B	HR	(Hm	Rd)	TB	R	RBI	RC	TBB	IBB	SO	HBP	SH	SF	SB	CS	SB%	GDP	Avg	OBP	Slg
2002 Norfolk*	AAA	97	377	107	23	6	5	(-	-)	157	52	30	53	26	0	72	7	4	0	20	13	.61	4	.284	.341	.416
1999 Chicago	AL	28	53	12	1	0	1	(1	0)	16	10	6	4	4	0	7	0	1	2	2	1	.67	1	.226	.271	.302
2000 Chicago	AL	32	19	2	0	0	0	(0	0)	2	4	1	0	2	0	6	1	0	0	1	1	.50	0	.105	.227	.105
2001 CWS-LA		35	53	17	2	0	1	(1	0)	22	7	7	10	3	0	12	4	0	0	3	2	.60	0	.321	.400	.415
2002 New York	NL	4	3	1	0	0	0	(0	0)	1	1	0	1	1	0	1	0	0	0	0	0	-	0	.333	.500	.333
2001 Chicago	AL	7	4	1	0	0	0	(0	0)	1	0	0	0	0	0	2	1	0	0	0	0	-	0	.250	.400	.250
2001 Los Angeles	NL	28	49	16	2	0	1	(1	0)	21	7	7	9	3	0	10	3	0	0	3	2	.60	0	.327	.400	.429
4 ML YEARS		99	128	32	3	0	2	(2	0)	41	22	14	15	10	0	26	5	1	2	6	4	.60	1	.250	.324	.320

Ryan Christenson

Bats: R Throws: R Pos: CF-16; LF-6; PR-5

Ht: 6'0" Wt: 191 Born: 3/28/74 Age: 29

Year Team	Lg	G	AB	H	2B	3B	HR	(Hm	Rd)	TB	R	RBI	RC	TBB	IBB	SO	HBP	SH	SF	SB	CS	SB%	GDP	Avg	OBP	Slg
2002 Indianapolis*	AAA	67	260	66	17	2	5	(-	-)	102	38	30	31	18	0	28	2	3	1	11	5	.69	5	.254	.306	.392
2002 Brewers*	R	4	10	4	2	0	0	(-	-)	6	1	2	2	0	0	2	0	0	1	0	0	-	0	.400	.364	.600
1998 Oakland	AL	117	370	95	22	2	5	(2	3)	136	56	40	45	36	0	106	1	10	4	5	6	.45	1	.257	.321	.368
1999 Oakland	AL	106	268	56	12	1	4	(2	2)	82	41	24	26	38	0	58	1	8	4	7	5	.58	6	.209	.305	.306
2000 Oakland	AL	121	129	32	2	2	4	(3	1)	50	31	18	18	19	0	33	1	4	0	1	2	.33	1	.248	.349	.388
2001 Oak-Ari		26	8	1	1	0	0	(0	0)	2	4	1	1	1	0	2	0	0	0	1	0	1.00	0	.125	.222	.250
2002 Milwaukee	NL	22	58	9	4	0	1	(0	1)	16	5	3	1	5	0	13	0	3	0	0	0	-	1	.155	.222	.276
2001 Oakland	AL	7	4	0	0	0	0	(0	0)	0	1	0	0	0	0	1	0	0	0	0	0	-	0	.000	.000	.000
2001 Arizona	NL	19	4	1	1	0	0	(0	0)	2	3	1	1	1	0	1	0	0	0	1	0	1.00	0	.250	.400	.500
5 ML YEARS		392	833	193	41	5	14	(7	7)	286	137	86	91	99	0	212	3	25	8	14	13	.52	9	.232	.313	.343

Jason Christiansen

Pitches: L Bats: R Pos: RP-6

Ht: 6'5" Wt: 241 Born: 9/21/69 Age: 33

Year Team	Lg	G	GS	CG	GF	IP	BFP	H	R	ER	HR	SH	SF	HB	TBB	IBB	SO	WP	Bk	W	L	Pct	ShO	Sv-Op	Hld	ERC	ERA
1995 Pittsburgh	NL	63	0	0	13	56.1	255	49	28	26	5	6	3	3	34	9	53	4	1	1	3	.250	0	0-4	12	3.89	4.15
1996 Pittsburgh	NL	33	0	0	9	44.1	205	56	34	33	7	2	3	1	19	2	38	4	1	3	3	.500	0	0-2	5	6.19	6.70
1997 Pittsburgh	NL	39	0	0	9	33.2	154	37	11	11	2	0	0	0	17	3	37	4	0	3	0	1.000	0	0-2	8	4.80	2.94
1998 Pittsburgh	NL	60	0	0	19	64.2	269	51	22	18	2	5	1	0	27	7	71	3	0	3	3	.500	0	6-10	15	2.39	2.51
1999 Pittsburgh	NL	39	0	0	17	37.2	158	26	17	17	2	2	1	2	22	4	35	0	0	2	3	.400	0	3-5	7	2.85	4.06
2000 Pit-Stl	NL	65	0	0	19	48.0	210	41	29	27	3	4	1	2	27	5	53	3	0	3	8	.273	0	1-4	22	3.60	5.06
2001 Stl-SF	NL	55	0	0	11	36.1	149	29	13	13	5	1	3	1	15	1	31	4	0	2	1	.667	0	3-4	11	3.41	3.22
2002 San Francisco	NL	6	0	0	2	5.0	21	6	3	3	1	0	0	0	2	0	1	0	0	1	0	1.000	0	0-0	0	6.48	5.40
2000 Pittsburgh	NL	44	0	0	17	38.0	164	28	22	21	2	3	1	0	25	4	41	3	0	2	8	.200	0	1-3	13	3.11	4.97
2000 St Louis	NL	21	0	0	2	10.0	46	13	7	6	1	1	0	2	2	1	12	0	0	1	0	1.000	0	0-1	9	5.64	5.40

Year Team	Lg	G	GS	CG	GF	IP	BFP	H	R	ER	HR	SH	SF	HB	TBB	IBB	SO	WP	Bk	W	L	Pct	ShO	Sv-Op	Hld	ERC	ERA
2001 St Louis	NL	30	0	0	8	19.1	83	15	10	10	4	0	1	1	10	1	19	0	0	1	1	.500	0	3-3	4	4.12	4.66
2001 San Francisco	NL	25	0	0	3	17.0	66	14	3	3	1	1	2	0	5	0	12	4	0	1	0	1.000	0	0-1	7	2.62	1.59
8 ML YEARS		360	0	0	99	326.0	1421	295	157	148	27	20	12	11	163	31	319	22	2	17	22	.436	0	13-31	77	3.77	4.09

Alex Cintron

Bats: B **Throws:** R **Pos:** 2B-18; 3B-9; SS-8; PH-6; PR-2   **Ht:** 6'2" **Wt:** 185 **Born:** 12/17/78 **Age:** 24

								BATTING										BASERUNNING				AVERAGES		
Year Team	Lg	G	AB	H	2B	3B	HR	(Hm | Rd)	TB	R	RBI	RC	TBB	IBB	SO	HBP	SH	SF	SB	CS	SB%	GDP	Avg	OBP	Slg
1997 Diamndbcks	R	43	152	30	6	1	0	(- | -)	38	23	20	11	21	0	32	2	3	1	1	4	.20	3	.197	.301	.250
1997 Lethbridge	R+	1	3	1	0	0	0	(- | -)	1	0	0	0	0	0	1	0	1	0	0	0	-	0	.333	.333	.333
1998 Lethbridge	R+	67	258	68	11	4	3	(- | -)	96	41	34	30	20	0	32	2	3	2	8	4	.67	8	.264	.319	.372
1999 High Desert	A+	128	499	153	25	4	3	(- | -)	195	78	64	62	19	0	65	3	17	4	15	8	.65	14	.307	.333	.391
2000 El Paso	AA	125	522	157	30	6	4	(- | -)	211	83	59	64	29	0	56	2	13	7	9	9	.50	22	.301	.336	.404
2001 Tucson	AAA	107	425	124	24	3	3	(- | -)	163	53	35	49	15	1	48	2	20	6	9	6	.60	12	.292	.315	.384
2002 Tucson	AAA	85	351	113	22	3	4	(- | -)	153	53	26	50	11	0	33	2	10	1	9	5	.64	8	.322	.345	.436
2001 Arizona	NL	8	7	2	0	1	0	(0 | 0)	4	0	0	1	0	0	0	0	0	0	0	0	-	0	.286	.286	.571
2002 Arizona	NL	38	75	16	6	0	0	(0 | 0)	22	11	4	5	12	2	13	0	3	0	0	0	-	2	.213	.322	.293
2 ML YEARS		46	82	18	6	1	0	(0 | 0)	26	11	4	6	12	2	13	0	3	0	0	0	-	2	.220	.319	.317

Jeff Cirillo

Bats: R **Throws:** R **Pos:** 3B-141; 1B-11; PH-4; PR-1   **Ht:** 6'1" **Wt:** 190 **Born:** 9/23/69 **Age:** 33

								BATTING										BASERUNNING				AVERAGES		
Year Team	Lg	G	AB	H	2B	3B	HR	(Hm | Rd)	TB	R	RBI	RC	TBB	IBB	SO	HBP	SH	SF	SB	CS	SB%	GDP	Avg	OBP	Slg
1994 Milwaukee	NL	39	126	30	9	0	3	(1 | 2)	48	17	12	14	11	0	16	2	0	0	0	1	.00	4	.238	.309	.381
1995 Milwaukee	NL	125	328	91	19	4	9	(6 | 3)	145	57	39	55	47	0	42	4	1	4	7	2	.78	8	.277	.371	.442
1996 Milwaukee	NL	158	566	184	46	5	15	(6 | 9)	285	101	83	105	58	0	69	7	6	6	4	9	.31	14	.325	.391	.504
1997 Milwaukee	NL	154	580	167	46	2	10	(4 | 6)	247	74	82	91	60	0	74	14	4	3	4	5	.57	13	.288	.367	.426
1998 Milwaukee	NL	156	604	194	31	1	14	(6 | 8)	269	97	68	103	79	3	88	4	5	2	10	4	.71	26	.321	.402	.445
1999 Milwaukee	NL	157	607	198	35	1	15	(6 | 9)	280	98	88	111	75	4	83	5	3	7	7	4	.64	15	.326	.401	.461
2000 Colorado	NL	157	598	195	53	2	11	(9 | 2)	285	111	115	108	67	4	72	6	1	12	3	4	.43	19	.326	.392	.477
2001 Colorado	NL	138	528	165	26	4	17	(9 | 8)	250	72	83	89	43	6	63	5	1	9	12	2	.86	15	.313	.364	.473
2002 Seattle	AL	146	485	121	20	0	6	(2 | 4)	159	51	54	51	31	0	67	9	13	6	8	4	.67	12	.249	.301	.328
9 ML YEARS		1230	4422	1345	285	19	100	(51 | 49)	1968	678	624	727	471	17	574	56	34	52	55	33	.63	126	.304	.374	.445

Brady Clark

Bats: R **Throws:** R **Pos:** PH-39; LF-15; RF-9; CF-5; PR-2   **Ht:** 6'2" **Wt:** 195 **Born:** 4/18/73 **Age:** 30

								BATTING										BASERUNNING				AVERAGES		
Year Team	Lg	G	AB	H	2B	3B	HR	(Hm | Rd)	TB	R	RBI	RC	TBB	IBB	SO	HBP	SH	SF	SB	CS	SB%	GDP	Avg	OBP	Slg
2002 Louisville*	AAA	25	109	33	7	0	1	(- | -)	43	17	17	13	3	0	9	2	1	2	0	2	.00	3	.303	.328	.394
2000 Cincinnati	NL	11	11	3	1	0	0	(0 | 0)	4	1	2	1	0	0	2	0	0	0	0	0	-	0	.273	.273	.364
2001 Cincinnati	NL	89	129	34	3	0	6	(4 | 2)	55	22	18	21	22	1	16	1	4	1	4	1	.80	6	.264	.373	.426
2002 Cin-NYM	NL	61	78	15	4	0	0	(0 | 0)	19	9	10	6	7	2	11	1	1	0	1	2	.33	2	.192	.267	.244
2002 Cincinnati	NL	51	66	10	3	0	0	(0 | 0)	13	6	9	4	6	2	9	1	1	0	1	2	.33	2	.152	.233	.197
2002 New York	NL	10	12	5	1	0	0	(0 | 0)	6	3	1	2	1	0	2	0	0	0	0	0	-	0	.417	.462	.500
3 ML YEARS		161	218	52	8	0	6	(4 | 2)	78	32	30	28	29	3	29	2	5	1	5	3	.63	8	.239	.332	.358

Howie Clark

Bats: L **Throws:** R **Pos:** DH-8; LF-4; 1B-1; PH-1   **Ht:** 5'11" **Wt:** 180 **Born:** 2/13/74 **Age:** 29

								BATTING										BASERUNNING				AVERAGES		
Year Team	Lg	G	AB	H	2B	3B	HR	(Hm | Rd)	TB	R	RBI	RC	TBB	IBB	SO	HBP	SH	SF	SB	CS	SB%	GDP	Avg	OBP	Slg
1992 Orioles	R	43	138	33	7	1	0	(- | -)	42	12	6	13	12	2	21	2	1	0	1	2	.33	2	.239	.309	.304
1993 Albany	A	7	17	4	0	0	0	(- | -)	4	2	1	1	0	0	3	0	0	0	1	0	1.00	1	.235	.235	.235
1993 Bluefield	R+	58	180	53	10	1	3	(- | -)	74	29	30	30	26	0	34	4	1	4	2	2	.50	4	.294	.388	.411
1994 Albany	A	108	353	95	22	7	2	(- | -)	137	56	47	53	51	3	58	7	4	1	5	4	.56	7	.269	.371	.388
1994 Frederick	A+	2	7	1	1	0	0	(- | -)	2	1	0	0	0	0	2	0	0	0	0	0	-	0	.143	.143	.286
1995 High Desert	A+	100	329	85	20	2	5	(- | -)	124	50	40	42	32	0	51	4	3	3	12	6	.67	4	.258	.329	.377
1996 Bowie	AA	127	449	122	29	3	4	(- | -)	169	55	52	61	59	1	54	2	10	7	2	8	.20	8	.272	.354	.376
1997 Bowie	AA	105	314	90	16	0	9	(- | -)	133	39	37	47	32	2	38	1	1	3	2	2	.50	5	.287	.351	.424
1998 Bowie	AA	88	276	79	16	0	9	(- | -)	122	37	45	43	29	2	42	3	0	1	1	1	.50	7	.286	.359	.442
1998 Rochester	AAA	30	95	22	4	1	3	(- | -)	37	13	8	10	9	0	11	0	0	0	1	2	.33	2	.232	.298	.389
1999 Rochester	AAA	79	279	82	19	4	6	(- | -)	127	33	28	45	34	2	24	1	1	2	1	2	.33	8	.294	.370	.455
1999 Bowie	AA	39	126	37	6	0	2	(- | -)	49	14	9	20	10	0	12	3	0	0	2	0	1.00	0	.294	.360	.389
2000 Bowie	AA	13	53	18	6	0	1	(- | -)	27	11	9	10	3	0	6	1	0	1	0	0	-	1	.340	.379	.509
2000 Rochester	AAA	54	189	54	10	0	3	(- | -)	73	25	21	29	26	0	14	1	1	1	3	1	.75	4	.286	.373	.386
2001 Yucatan	Mex	121	493	164	42	7	5	(- | -)	235	68	64	86	43	3	47	2	4	5	5	4	.56	12	.333	.385	.477
2001 Chico	IND	4	15	8	0	1	0	(- | -)	10	3	0	5	1	0	1	0	0	0	0	0	-	0	.533	.563	.667
2002 Rochester	AAA	108	418	129	21	4	7	(- | -)	179	57	43	64	41	2	28	2	2	5	3	4	.43	11	.309	.369	.428
2002 Baltimore	AL	14	53	16	5	0	0	(0 | 0)	21	3	4	7	3	0	6	2	0	0	0	0	-	5	.302	.362	.396

Tony Clark

Bats: B **Throws:** R **Pos:** 1B-85; PH-7; DH-3   **Ht:** 6'7" **Wt:** 245 **Born:** 6/15/72 **Age:** 31

								BATTING										BASERUNNING				AVERAGES		
Year Team	Lg	G	AB	H	2B	3B	HR	(Hm | Rd)	TB	R	RBI	RC	TBB	IBB	SO	HBP	SH	SF	SB	CS	SB%	GDP	Avg	OBP	Slg
1995 Detroit	AL	27	101	24	5	1	3	(0 | 3)	40	10	11	11	8	0	30	0	0	0	0	0	-	2	.238	.294	.396
1996 Detroit	AL	100	376	94	14	0	27	(17 | 10)	189	56	72	55	29	1	127	0	0	6	0	1	.00	2	.250	.299	.503
1997 Detroit	AL	159	580	160	28	3	32	(18 | 14)	290	105	117	107	93	13	144	3	0	5	1	3	.25	11	.276	.376	.500
1998 Detroit	AL	157	602	175	37	0	34	(18 | 16)	314	84	103	107	63	5	128	3	0	5	3	3	.50	16	.291	.358	.522
1999 Detroit	AL	143	536	150	29	0	31	(12 | 19)	272	74	99	94	64	7	133	6	0	3	2	1	.67	14	.280	.361	.507

Year Team	Lg	G	AB	H	2B	3B	HR	(Hm	Rd)	TB	R	RBI	RC	TBB	IBB	SO	HBP	SH	SF	SB	CS	SB%	GDP	Avg	OBP	Slg
2000 Detroit	AL	60	208	57	14	0	13	(6	7)	110	32	37	35	24	2	51	0	0	0	0	0	-	10	.274	.349	.529
2001 Detroit	AL	126	428	123	29	3	16	(7	9)	206	67	75	74	62	10	108	1	0	6	0	1	.00	14	.287	.374	.481
2002 Boston	AL	90	275	57	12	1	3	(1	2)	80	25	29	18	21	0	57	1	0	1	0	0	-	11	.207	.265	.291
8 ML YEARS		862	3106	840	168	8	159	(79	80)	1501	453	543	501	364	38	778	14	0	26	6	9	.40	85	.270	.347	.483

Royce Clayton

Bats: R Throws: R Pos: SS-109; PH-2; PR-1   **Ht: 6'0" Wt: 185 Born: 1/2/70 Age: 33**

Year Team	Lg	G	AB	H	2B	3B	HR	(Hm	Rd)	TB	R	RBI	RC	TBB	IBB	SO	HBP	SH	SF	SB	CS	SB%	GDP	Avg	OBP	Slg
1991 San Francisco	NL	9	26	3	1	0	0	(0	0)	4	0	2	0	1	0	6	0	0	0	0	0	-	1	.115	.148	.154
1992 San Francisco	NL	98	321	72	7	4	4	(3	1)	99	31	24	25	26	3	63	0	3	2	8	4	.67	11	.224	.281	.308
1993 San Francisco	NL	153	549	155	21	5	6	(1	5)	204	54	70	64	38	2	91	3	8	7	11	10	.52	16	.282	.331	.372
1994 San Francisco	NL	108	385	91	14	6	3	(1	2)	126	38	30	40	30	2	74	3	3	2	23	3	.88	7	.236	.295	.327
1995 San Francisco	NL	138	509	124	29	3	5	(2	3)	174	56	58	53	38	1	109	3	4	3	24	9	.73	7	.244	.298	.342
1996 St Louis	NL	129	491	136	20	4	6	(6	0)	182	64	35	56	33	4	89	1	2	4	33	15	.69	13	.277	.321	.371
1997 St Louis	NL	154	576	153	39	5	9	(5	4)	229	75	61	67	33	4	109	3	2	5	30	10	.75	19	.266	.306	.398
1998 Stl-Tex		142	541	136	31	2	9	(2	7)	198	89	53	62	53	1	83	3	6	5	24	11	.69	16	.251	.319	.366
1999 Texas	AL	133	465	134	21	5	14	(6	8)	207	69	52	71	39	1	100	4	9	3	8	6	.57	6	.288	.346	.445
2000 Texas	AL	148	513	124	21	5	14	(9	5)	197	70	54	54	42	1	92	3	12	3	11	7	.61	21	.242	.301	.384
2001 Chicago	AL	135	433	114	21	4	9	(6	3)	170	62	60	50	33	2	72	3	9	7	10	7	.59	16	.263	.315	.393
2002 Chicago	AL	112	342	86	14	2	7	(4	3)	125	51	35	37	20	0	67	3	7	4	5	1	.83	7	.251	.295	.365
1998 St Louis	NL	90	355	83	19	1	4	(1	3)	116	59	29	37	40	1	51	2	3	2	19	6	.76	10	.234	.313	.327
1998 Texas	AL	52	186	53	12	1	5	(1	4)	82	30	24	25	13	0	32	1	3	3	5	5	.50	6	.285	.330	.441
12 ML YEARS		1459	5151	1328	239	45	86	(49	37)	1915	659	534	579	386	21	955	31	65	45	187	83	.69	140	.258	.311	.372

Roger Clemens

Pitches: R Bats: R Pos: SP-29   **Ht: 6'4" Wt: 235 Born: 8/4/62 Age: 40**

Year Team	Lg	G	GS	CG	GF	IP	BFP	H	R	ER	HR	SH	SF	HB	TBB	IBB	SO	WP	Bk	W	L	Pct	ShO	Sv-Op	Hld	ERC	ERA
2002 Tampa*	A+	1	1	0	0	5.0	21	5	3	3	1	0	0	0	2	0	6	0	0	1	0	1.000	0	0--	-	4.93	5.40
2002 Norwich*	AA	1	1	0	0	7.0	26	5	1	1	0	0	0	0	0	0	7	1	0	0	1	.000	0	0--	-	1.04	1.29
1984 Boston	AL	21	20	5	0	133.1	575	146	67	64	13	2	3	2	29	3	126	4	0	9	4	.692	1	0-0	0	3.81	4.32
1985 Boston	AL	15	15	3	0	98.1	407	83	38	36	5	1	2	3	37	0	74	1	3	7	5	.583	1	0-0	0	2.96	3.29
1986 Boston	AL	33	33	10	0	254.0	997	179	77	70	21	4	6	4	67	0	238	11	3	24	4	.857	1	0-0	0	2.03	2.48
1987 Boston	AL	36	36	18	0	281.2	1157	248	100	93	19	6	4	9	83	4	256	4	3	20	9	.690	7	0-0	0	2.94	2.97
1988 Boston	AL	35	35	14	0	264.0	1063	217	93	86	17	6	3	6	62	4	291	4	7	18	12	.600	8	0-0	0	2.36	2.93
1989 Boston	AL	35	35	8	0	253.1	1044	215	101	88	20	9	5	8	93	5	230	7	0	17	11	.607	3	0-0	0	3.13	3.13
1990 Boston	AL	31	31	7	0	228.1	920	193	59	49	7	7	5	7	54	3	209	8	0	21	6	.778	4	0-0	0	2.33	1.93
1991 Boston	AL	35	35	13	0	271.1	1077	219	93	79	15	6	8	5	65	12	241	6	0	18	10	.643	4	0-0	0	2.23	2.62
1992 Boston	AL	32	32	11	0	246.2	989	203	80	66	11	5	5	9	62	5	208	3	0	18	11	.621	5	0-0	0	2.38	2.41
1993 Boston	AL	29	29	2	0	191.2	808	175	99	95	17	5	7	11	67	4	160	3	1	11	14	.440	1	0-0	0	3.53	4.46
1994 Boston	AL	24	24	3	0	170.2	692	124	62	54	15	2	5	4	71	1	168	4	0	9	7	.563	1	0-0	0	2.72	2.85
1995 Boston	AL	23	23	0	0	140.0	623	141	70	65	15	2	3	14	60	0	132	9	0	10	5	.667	0	0-0	0	4.67	4.18
1996 Boston	AL	34	34	6	0	242.2	1032	216	106	98	19	4	7	4	106	2	257	8	1	10	13	.435	2	0-0	0	3.52	3.63
1997 Toronto	AL	34	34	9	0	264.0	1044	204	65	60	9	5	2	12	68	1	292	4	0	21	7	.750	3	0-0	0	2.17	2.05
1998 Toronto	AL	33	33	5	0	234.2	961	169	78	69	11	8	2	7	88	0	271	6	0	20	6	.769	3	0-0	0	2.27	2.65
1999 New York	AL	30	30	1	0	187.2	822	185	101	96	20	10	5	9	90	0	163	8	0	14	10	.583	1	0-0	0	4.59	4.60
2000 New York	AL	32	32	1	0	204.1	878	184	96	84	26	1	2	10	84	0	188	2	1	13	8	.619	0	0-0	0	3.93	3.70
2001 New York	AL	33	33	0	0	220.1	918	205	94	86	19	4	4	5	72	1	213	14	0	20	3	.870	0	0-0	0	3.43	3.51
2002 New York	AL	29	29	0	0	180.0	768	172	94	87	18	5	5	7	63	6	192	14	0	13	6	.684	0	0-0	0	3.72	4.35
19 ML YEARS		574	573	116	0	4067.0	16775	3478	1573	1425	297	92	83	136	1321	51	3909	120	19	293	151	.660	45	0-0	0	2.95	3.15

Matt Clement

Pitches: R Bats: R Pos: SP-32   **Ht: 6'3" Wt: 213 Born: 8/12/74 Age: 28**

Year Team	Lg	G	GS	CG	GF	IP	BFP	H	R	ER	HR	SH	SF	HB	TBB	IBB	SO	WP	Bk	W	L	Pct	ShO	Sv-Op	Hld	ERC	ERA
1998 San Diego	NL	4	2	0	0	13.2	62	15	8	7	0	2	0	0	7	1	13	2	0	2	0	1.000	0	0-0	0	4.14	4.61
1999 San Diego	NL	31	31	0	0	180.2	803	190	106	90	18	7	6	9	86	2	135	11	0	10	12	.455	0	0-0	0	4.89	4.48
2000 San Diego	NL	34	34	0	0	205.0	940	194	131	117	22	12	5	16	125	4	170	23	0	13	17	.433	0	0-0	0	4.87	5.14
2001 Florida	NL	31	31	0	0	169.1	760	172	102	95	15	14	3	15	85	2	134	15	0	9	10	.474	0	0-0	0	4.84	5.05
2002 Chicago	NL	32	32	3	0	205.0	858	162	84	82	18	11	4	6	85	7	215	7	0	12	11	.522	2	0-0	0	2.96	3.60
5 ML YEARS		132	130	3	0	773.2	3423	733	431	391	73	46	18	46	388	16	667	58	0	46	50	.479	2	0-0	0	4.32	4.55

Pasqual Coco

Pitches: R Bats: R Pos: RP-2   **Ht: 6'1" Wt: 180 Born: 9/24/77 Age: 25**

Year Team	Lg	G	GS	CG	GF	IP	BFP	H	R	ER	HR	SH	SF	HB	TBB	IBB	SO	WP	Bk	W	L	Pct	ShO	Sv-Op	Hld	ERC	ERA
1997 St. Ctharines	A-	10	8	0	1	46.0	199	48	32	25	5	0	4	2	16	1	44	6	1	1	4	.200	0	0--	-	4.33	4.89
1998 St. Ctharines	A-	15	15	1	0	81.2	353	62	52	29	4	2	1	9	32	0	84	10	3	3	7	.300	0	0--	-	2.72	3.20
1999 Hagerstown	A	14	14	0	0	97.2	384	67	29	24	4	1	1	8	25	1	83	2	0	11	1	.917	0	0--	-	1.90	2.21
1999 Dunedin	A+	13	13	2	0	75.0	338	81	50	47	7	3	3	6	36	0	59	7	2	4	6	.400	0	0--	-	5.16	5.64
2000 Tennessee	AA	27	26	2	0	167.2	723	154	83	70	16	1	4	17	68	0	142	6	3	12	7	.632	0	0--	-	4.03	3.76
2001 Tennessee	AA	3	3	0	0	16.0	65	13	7	7	3	0	0	0	5	0	13	1	0	1	0	1.000	0	0--	-	3.28	3.94
2001 Syracuse	AAA	22	22	0	0	121.2	529	128	67	63	11	1	7	8	50	0	82	9	3	8	6	.571	0	0--	-	4.70	4.66
2002 Syracuse	AAA	30	23	1	2	141.0	621	145	91	78	17	0	10	9	57	0	98	6	1	4	9	.308	0	0--	-	4.65	4.98
2000 Toronto	AL	1	1	0	0	4.0	23	5	4	4	1	0	0	1	5	0	2	1	0	0	0	-	0	0-0	0	11.69	9.00
2001 Toronto	AL	7	1	0	3	14.1	63	12	8	7	0	1	1	2	6	0	9	0	0	1	0	1.000	0	0-0	0	3.00	4.40
2002 Toronto	AL	2	0	0	1	1.0	10	4	2	2	0	0	0	0	3	1	0	0	0	0	1	.000	0	0-0	0	34.64	18.00
3 ML YEARS		10	2	0	4	19.1	96	21	14	13	1	1	1	3	14	1	11	1	0	1	1	.500	0	0-0	0	5.86	6.05

Dave Coggin

Pitches: R **Bats:** R **Pos:** RP-31; SP-7   **Ht:** 6'4" **Wt:** 205 **Born:** 10/30/76 **Age:** 26

		HOW MUCH HE PITCHED					WHAT HE GAVE UP											THE RESULTS							
Year Team	Lg	G	GS	CG	GF	IP	BFP	H	R	ER	HR	SH	SF	HB	TBB	IBB	SO	WP	Bk	W	L	Pct	ShO	Sv-Op	Hld	ERC	ERA
2000 Philadelphia	NL	5	5	0	0	27.0	126	35	20	16	2	2	0	1	12	0	17	1	0	2	0	1.000	0	0-0	0	5.95	5.33
2001 Philadelphia	NL	17	17	0	0	95.0	415	99	46	44	7	4	3	5	39	6	62	3	0	6	7	.462	0	0-0	0	4.30	4.17
2002 Philadelphia	NL	38	7	0	7	77.0	339	65	42	40	4	1	2	4	51	3	64	11	0	2	5	.286	0	0-0	1	4.05	4.68
3 ML YEARS		60	29	0	7	199.0	880	199	108	100	13	7	5	10	102	9	143	15	0	10	12	.455	0	0-0	1	4.42	4.52

Mike Colangelo

Bats: R **Throws:** R **Pos:** LF-14; PR-6; RF-5; PH-2; CF-1   **Ht:** 6'1" **Wt:** 185 **Born:** 10/22/76 **Age:** 26

		BATTING																	BASERUNNING				AVERAGES		
Year Team	Lg	G	AB	H	2B	3B	HR	(Hm	Rd)	TB	R	RBI	RC	TBB	IBB	SO	HBP	SH	SF	SB	CS	SB%	GDP	Avg	OBP	Slg
2002 Sacramento*	AAA	70	217	46	9	0	0	(-	-)	55	22	22	16	33	0	36	7	4	3	3	3	.50	16	.212	.331	.253
1999 Anaheim	AL	1	2	1	0	0	0	(0	0)	1	0	0	1	1	0	0	0	0	0	0	0	-	0	.500	.667	.500
2001 San Diego	NL	50	91	22	3	3	2	(1	1)	37	10	8	11	8	0	30	1	0	0	0	0	-	3	.242	.310	.407
2002 Oakland	AL	20	23	4	1	0	0	(0	0)	5	2	0	0	1	0	2	1	1	0	0	0	-	0	.174	.240	.217
3 ML YEARS		71	116	27	4	3	2	(1	1)	43	12	8	12	10	0	32	2	1	0	0	0	-	3	.233	.305	.371

Greg Colbrunn

Bats: R **Throws:** R **Pos:** 1B-40; PH-26; 3B-5; DH-3; PR-1   **Ht:** 6'0" **Wt:** 212 **Born:** 7/26/69 **Age:** 33

		BATTING																	BASERUNNING				AVERAGES		
Year Team	Lg	G	AB	H	2B	3B	HR	(Hm	Rd)	TB	R	RBI	RC	TBB	IBB	SO	HBP	SH	SF	SB	CS	SB%	GDP	Avg	OBP	Slg
2002 Tucson*	AAA	6	25	9	3	0	2	(-	-)	18	6	7	7	3	0	3	0	0	0	0	0	-	1	.360	.429	.720
1992 Montreal	NL	52	168	45	8	0	2	(1	1)	59	12	18	18	6	1	34	2	0	4	3	2	.60	1	.268	.294	.351
1993 Montreal	NL	70	153	39	9	0	4	(2	2)	60	15	23	17	6	1	33	1	1	3	4	2	.67	1	.255	.282	.392
1994 Florida	NL	47	155	47	10	0	6	(3	3)	75	17	31	25	9	0	27	2	0	2	1	1	.50	3	.303	.345	.484
1995 Florida	NL	138	528	146	22	1	23	(12	11)	239	70	89	71	22	4	69	6	0	4	11	3	.79	15	.277	.311	.453
1996 Florida	NL	141	511	146	26	2	16	(7	9)	224	60	69	68	14	0	76	14	0	5	4	5	.44	22	.286	.333	.438
1997 Min-Atl		98	271	76	17	0	7	(3	4)	114	27	35	32	10	1	49	2	1	2	1	2	.33	8	.280	.309	.421
1998 Col-Atl		90	166	51	11	2	3	(1	2)	75	18	23	26	10	0	34	4	0	0	4	3	.57	1	.307	.361	.452
1999 Arizona	NL	67	135	44	5	3	5	(2	3)	70	20	24	26	12	0	23	4	0	2	1	1	.50	3	.326	.392	.519
2000 Arizona	NL	116	329	103	22	1	15	(6	9)	172	48	57	66	43	2	45	10	0	3	0	1	.00	13	.313	.405	.523
2001 Arizona	NL	59	97	28	8	0	4	(1	3)	48	12	18	16	9	0	14	4	0	0	0	0	-	5	.289	.373	.495
2002 Arizona	NL	72	171	57	16	2	10	(3	7)	107	30	27	34	13	1	19	0	0	1	0	0	-	5	.333	.378	.626
1997 Minnesota	AL	70	217	61	14	0	5	(2	3)	90	24	26	25	8	1	38	1	0	2	1	2	.33	7	.281	.307	.415
1997 Atlanta	NL	28	54	15	3	0	2	(1	1)	24	3	9	7	2	0	11	1	1	0	0	0	-	1	.278	.316	.444
1998 Colorado	NL	62	122	38	8	2	2	(1	1)	56	12	13	19	8	0	23	1	0	0	3	3	.50	1	.311	.359	.459
1998 Atlanta	NL	28	44	13	3	0	1	(0	1)	19	6	10	7	2	0	11	3	0	0	1	0	1.00	0	.295	.367	.432
11 ML YEARS		950	2684	782	154	11	95	(44	51)	1243	329	414	399	165	11	423	49	2	26	29	20	.59	77	.291	.341	.463

Lou Collier

Bats: R **Throws:** R **Pos:** PH-4; LF-3; CF-3; PR-3; 2B-2; 3B-1; RF-1   **Ht:** 5'10" **Wt:** 191 **Born:** 8/21/73 **Age:** 29

		BATTING																	BASERUNNING				AVERAGES		
Year Team	Lg	G	AB	H	2B	3B	HR	(Hm	Rd)	TB	R	RBI	RC	TBB	IBB	SO	HBP	SH	SF	SB	CS	SB%	GDP	Avg	OBP	Slg
2002 Ottawa*	AAA	89	307	97	26	6	6	(-	-)	153	48	52	59	37	1	69	6	1	5	5	2	.71	9	.316	.394	.498
1997 Pittsburgh	NL	18	37	5	0	0	0	(0	0)	5	3	3	0	1	0	11	0	0	0	1	0	1.00	1	.135	.158	.135
1998 Pittsburgh	NL	110	334	82	13	6	2	(1	1)	113	30	34	35	31	6	70	6	3	5	2	2	.50	8	.246	.316	.338
1999 Milwaukee	NL	74	135	35	9	0	2	(2	0)	50	18	21	17	14	0	32	0	1	2	3	2	.60	2	.259	.325	.370
2000 Milwaukee	NL	14	32	7	1	0	1	(0	1)	11	9	2	4	6	0	4	0	0	0	0	0	-	1	.219	.333	.344
2001 Milwaukee	NL	50	127	32	8	1	2	(1	1)	48	19	14	19	17	0	30	1	1	2	5	1	.83	5	.252	.340	.378
2002 Montreal	NL	13	11	1	1	0	0	(0	0)	2	3	0	0	1	1	3	1	1	0	0	0	-	0	.091	.231	.182
6 ML YEARS		279	676	162	32	7	7	(4	3)	229	82	74	75	70	7	150	8	6	10	11	5	.69	12	.240	.314	.339

Jesus Colome

Pitches: R **Bats:** R **Pos:** RP-32   **Ht:** 6'4" **Wt:** 205 **Born:** 12/23/77 **Age:** 25

		HOW MUCH HE PITCHED						WHAT HE GAVE UP												THE RESULTS						
Year Team	Lg	G	GS	CG	GF	IP	BFP	H	R	ER	HR	SH	SF	HB	TBB	IBB	SO	WP	Bk	W	L	Pct	ShO	Sv-Op	Hld	ERC	ERA
1998 Athletics	R	12	11	0	0	56.2	229	47	27	20	1	0	1	6	16	0	62	5	3	2	5	.286	0	0- -	-	2.66	3.18
1999 Modesto	A+	31	22	0	2	128.2	564	125	63	48	7	1	6	9	60	2	127	13	2	8	4	.667	0	1- -	-	4.05	3.36
2000 Midland	AA	20	20	0	0	110.1	478	99	62	44	10	4	4	5	50	0	95	6	1	9	4	.692	0	0- -	-	3.80	3.59
2000 Orlando	AA	3	3	0	0	14.2	72	18	12	11	2	1	0	2	7	0	9	0	0	1	2	.333	0	0- -	-	6.35	6.75
2001 Durham	AAA	13	0	0	3	17.1	79	22	13	12	1	1	1	2	6	0	18	3	0	0	3	.000	0	0- -	-	5.65	6.23
2002 Durham	AAA	18	0	0	5	29.0	116	18	8	7	1	1	0	0	13	0	30	4	0	2	2	.500	0	1- -	-	1.91	2.17
2001 Tampa Bay	AL	30	0	0	9	48.2	209	37	22	18	8	2	2	2	25	4	31	2	0	2	3	.400	0	0-0	6	3.62	3.33
2002 Tampa Bay	AL	32	0	0	15	41.1	205	56	41	38	6	4	1	2	33	5	33	5	0	2	7	.222	0	0-5	3	8.53	8.27
2 ML YEARS		62	0	0	24	90.0	414	93	63	56	14	6	3	4	58	9	64	7	0	4	10	.286	0	0-5	9	5.72	5.60

Bartolo Colon

Pitches: R **Bats:** R **Pos:** SP-33   **Ht:** 6'0" **Wt:** 235 **Born:** 5/24/73 **Age:** 30

		HOW MUCH HE PITCHED						WHAT HE GAVE UP												THE RESULTS						
Year Team	Lg	G	GS	CG	GF	IP	BFP	H	R	ER	HR	SH	SF	HB	TBB	IBB	SO	WP	Bk	W	L	Pct	ShO	Sv-Op	Hld	ERC	ERA
1997 Cleveland	AL	19	17	1	0	94.0	427	107	66	59	12	4	1	3	45	1	66	5	0	4	7	.364	0	0-0	0	5.53	5.65
1998 Cleveland	AL	31	31	6	0	204.0	883	205	91	84	15	10	2	3	79	5	158	4	0	14	9	.609	2	0-0	0	3.87	3.71
1999 Cleveland	AL	32	32	1	0	205.0	858	185	97	90	24	5	4	7	76	5	161	4	0	18	5	.783	1	0-0	0	3.68	3.95
2000 Cleveland	AL	30	30	2	0	188.0	807	185	81	81	21	2	3	4	98	4	212	4	0	15	8	.652	1	0-0	0	3.97	3.88
2001 Cleveland	AL	34	34	1	0	222.1	947	220	106	101	26	8	4	2	90	2	201	4	1	14	12	.538	0	0-0	0	4.24	4.09
2002 Cle-Mon		33	33	8	0	233.1	966	219	85	76	20	19	6	2	70	5	149	4	0	20	8	.714	3	0-0	0	3.29	2.93

Year Team	Lg	G	GS	CG	GF	IP	BFP	H	R	ER	HR	SH	SF	HB	TBB	IBB	SO	WP	Bk	W	L	Pct	ShO	Sv-Op	Hld	ERC	ERA
2002 Cleveland	AL	16	16	4	0	116.1	467	104	37	33	11	6	3	2	31	1	75	3	0	10	4	.714	2	0-0	0	3.09	2.55
2002 Montreal	NL	17	17	4	0	117.0	499	115	48	43	9	13	3	0	39	4	74	1	0	10	4	.714	1	0-0	0	3.48	3.31
6 ML YEARS		179	177	19	0	1146.2	4888	1099	531	491	118	48	20	21	458	22	947	25	1	85	49	.634	7	0-0	0	3.93	3.85

Clay Condrey

Pitches: R **Bats:** R **Pos:** RP-6; SP-3 **Ht:** 6'3" **Wt:** 195 **Born:** 11/19/75 **Age:** 27

Year Team	Lg	G	GS	CG	GF	IP	BFP	H	R	ER	HR	SH	SF	HB	TBB	IBB	SO	WP	Bk	W	L	Pct	ShO	Sv-Op	Hld	ERC	ERA
1998 Padres	R	5	0	0	4	5.1	26	6	4	2	0	0	0	0	5	1	4	1	1	0	0	.000	0	0--	-	5.82	3.38
1998 Idaho Falls	R+	18	0	0	17	24.2	111	31	12	7	2	1	1	1	4	0	19	3	0	2	1	.667	0	5--	-	4.45	2.55
1999 Fort Wayne	A	42	0	0	39	47.2	202	40	24	20	5	0	2	0	19	4	47	4	1	2	3	.400	0	20--	-	3.04	3.78
1999 R Cucamnga	A+	6	0	0	1	7.1	29	4	3	3	1	0	0	0	3	0	9	0	0	0	0	-	0	0--	-	1.98	3.68
2000 R Cucamnga	A+	18	0	0	9	20.2	85	18	9	8	1	1	0	2	7	0	21	2	1	1	1	.500	0	4--	-	3.26	3.48
2000 Mobile	AA	35	0	0	19	43.2	195	41	27	26	4	3	2	5	20	0	25	1	0	2	2	.500	0	8--	-	4.29	5.36
2001 Mobile	AA	27	0	0	23	33.2	144	33	23	17	1	4	2	0	15	4	21	0	0	2	2	.500	0	12--	-	3.49	4.54
2001 Portland	AAA	39	0	0	13	53.0	231	63	37	28	7	4	3	4	13	1	45	2	0	1	3	.250	0	2--	-	5.11	4.75
2002 Portland	AAA	25	23	0	0	133.2	552	128	56	52	12	6	3	5	40	1	73	2	3	10	4	.714	0	0--	-	3.60	3.50
2002 San Diego	NL	9	3	0	2	26.2	106	20	7	5	1	2	2	2	8	1	16	1	1	1	2	.333	0	0-0	3	2.29	1.69

David Cone

Pitches: R **Bats:** L **Pos:** SP **Ht:** 6'1" **Wt:** 200 **Born:** 1/2/63 **Age:** 40

Year Team	Lg	G	GS	CG	GF	IP	BFP	H	R	ER	HR	SH	SF	HB	TBB	IBB	SO	WP	Bk	W	L	Pct	ShO	Sv-Op	Hld	ERC	ERA
1986 Kansas City	AL	11	0	0	5	22.2	108	29	14	14	2	0	0	1	13	1	21	3	0	0	0	-	0	0-0	0	6.48	5.56
1987 New York	NL	21	13	1	3	99.1	420	87	46	41	11	4	3	5	44	1	68	2	4	5	6	.455	0	1-1	2	3.87	3.71
1988 New York	NL	35	28	8	0	231.1	936	178	67	57	10	11	5	4	80	7	213	10	10	20	3	.870	4	0-0	1	2.34	2.22
1989 New York	NL	34	33	7	0	219.2	910	183	92	86	20	6	4	4	74	6	190	14	4	14	8	.636	2	0-0	0	2.89	3.52
1990 New York	NL	31	30	6	1	211.2	860	177	84	76	21	4	6	1	65	1	233	10	4	14	10	.583	2	0-0	0	2.87	3.23
1991 New York	NL	34	34	5	0	232.2	966	204	95	85	13	13	7	5	73	2	241	17	1	14	14	.500	2	0-0	0	2.85	3.29
1992 NYM-Tor		35	34	7	0	249.2	1055	201	91	78	15	6	9	12	111	7	261	12	1	17	10	.630	5	0-0	0	3.05	2.81
1993 Kansas City	AL	34	34	6	0	254.0	1060	205	102	94	20	7	9	10	114	2	191	14	2	11	14	.440	1	0-0	0	3.25	3.33
1994 Kansas City	AL	23	23	4	0	171.2	690	130	60	56	15	1	5	7	54	0	132	5	1	16	5	.762	3	0-0	0	2.57	2.94
1995 Tor-NYY	AL	30	30	6	0	229.1	954	195	95	91	24	2	3	6	88	2	191	11	1	18	8	.692	2	0-0	0	3.34	3.57
1996 New York	AL	11	11	1	0	72.0	295	50	25	23	3	1	5	2	34	0	71	4	1	7	2	.778	0	0-0	0	2.48	2.88
1997 New York	AL	29	29	1	0	195.0	805	155	67	61	17	3	2	4	86	2	222	14	2	12	6	.667	0	0-0	0	3.15	2.82
1998 New York	AL	31	31	3	0	207.2	866	186	89	82	20	4	4	15	59	1	209	6	0	20	7	.741	0	0-0	0	3.31	3.55
1999 New York	AL	31	31	1	0	193.1	827	164	84	74	21	5	6	11	90	2	177	7	1	12	9	.571	1	0-0	0	3.76	3.44
2000 New York	AL	30	29	0	0	155.0	733	192	124	119	25	6	8	9	82	3	120	11	0	4	14	.222	0	0-0	0	6.72	6.91
2001 Boston	AL	25	25	0	0	135.2	614	148	74	65	17	2	6	10	57	4	115	9	0	9	7	.563	0	0-0	0	5.06	4.31
1992 New York	NL	27	27	7	0	196.2	831	162	75	63	12	6	6	9	82	5	214	9	1	13	7	.650	5	0-0	0	3.04	2.88
1992 Toronto	AL	8	7	0	0	53.0	224	39	16	15	3	0	3	3	29	2	47	3	0	4	3	.571	0	0-0	0	3.08	2.55
1995 Toronto	AL	17	17	5	0	130.1	537	113	53	49	12	0	1	2	41	2	102	6	1	9	6	.600	2	0-0	0	3.12	3.38
1995 New York	AL	13	13	1	0	99.0	417	82	42	42	12	0	1	1	47	0	89	5	0	9	2	.818	0	0-0	0	3.63	3.82
16 ML YEARS		445	415	56	9	2880.2	12099	2484	1209	1102	254	75	82	106	1124	41	2655	149	32	193	123	.611	22	1-1	3	3.33	3.44

Jeff Conine

Bats: R **Throws:** R **Pos:** 1B-103; DH-7; LF-6; PH-1 **Ht:** 6'1" **Wt:** 220 **Born:** 6/27/66 **Age:** 37

Year Team	Lg	G	AB	H	2B	3B	HR	(Hm	Rd)	TB	R	RBI	RC	TBB	IBB	SO	HBP	SH	SF	SB	CS	SB%	GDP	Avg	OBP	Slg
1990 Kansas City	AL	9	20	5	2	0	0	(0	0)	7	3	2	2	2	0	5	0	0	0	0	0	-	1	.250	.318	.350
1992 Kansas City	AL	28	91	23	5	2	0	(0	0)	32	10	9	10	8	1	23	0	0	0	0	0	-	1	.253	.313	.352
1993 Florida	NL	162	595	174	24	3	12	(5	7)	240	75	79	83	52	2	135	5	0	6	2	2	.50	14	.292	.351	.403
1994 Florida	NL	115	451	144	27	6	18	(8	10)	237	60	82	84	40	4	92	1	0	4	1	2	.33	8	.319	.373	.525
1995 Florida	NL	133	483	146	26	2	25	(13	12)	251	72	105	93	66	5	94	1	0	12	2	0	1.00	13	.302	.379	.520
1996 Florida	NL	157	597	175	32	2	26	(15	11)	289	84	95	99	62	1	121	4	0	7	1	4	.20	17	.293	.360	.484
1997 Florida	NL	151	405	98	13	1	17	(7	10)	164	46	61	55	57	3	89	2	0	2	2	0	1.00	11	.242	.337	.405
1998 Kansas City	AL	93	309	79	26	0	8	(4	4)	129	30	43	40	26	1	68	2	0	6	3	0	1.00	6	.256	.312	.417
1999 Baltimore	AL	139	444	129	31	1	13	(7	6)	201	54	75	64	30	0	40	3	1	7	0	3	.00	12	.291	.335	.453
2000 Baltimore	AL	119	409	116	20	2	13	(6	7)	179	53	46	58	36	1	53	2	0	4	3	3	.57	12	.284	.341	.438
2001 Baltimore	AL	139	524	163	23	2	14	(5	9)	232	75	97	89	64	6	75	5	0	8	12	8	.60	12	.311	.386	.443
2002 Baltimore	AL	116	451	123	26	4	15	(12	3)	202	44	63	61	25	6	66	2	0	10	8	0	1.00	10	.273	.307	.448
12 ML YEARS		1361	4779	1375	255	25	161	(82	79)	2163	606	757	738	468	30	861	27	1	66	35	22	.61	121	.288	.350	.453

Jason Conti

Bats: L **Throws:** R **Pos:** CF-28; RF-28; LF-21; PH-4; PR-3 **Ht:** 5'11" **Wt:** 175 **Born:** 1/27/75 **Age:** 28

Year Team	Lg	G	AB	H	2B	3B	HR	(Hm	Rd)	TB	R	RBI	RC	TBB	IBB	SO	HBP	SH	SF	SB	CS	SB%	GDP	Avg	OBP	Slg
2000 Arizona	NL	47	91	21	4	3	1	(1	0)	34	11	15	10	7	2	30	1	0	0	3	0	1.00	2	.231	.293	.374
2001 Arizona	NL	5	4	1	0	0	0	(0	0)	1	1	0	1	1	0	2	0	0	0	0	0	-	0	.250	.400	.250
2002 Tampa Bay	AL	78	222	57	15	2	3	(2	1)	85	26	21	25	18	1	55	1	4	0	4	2	.67	5	.257	.315	.383
3 ML YEARS		130	317	79	19	5	4	(3	1)	120	38	36	36	26	3	87	2	4	0	7	2	.78	7	.249	.310	.379

Aaron Cook

Pitches: R Bats: R Pos: SP-5; RP-4   **Ht: 6'3" Wt: 175 Born: 2/8/79 Age: 24**

Year Team	Lg	G	GS	CG	GF	IP	BFP	H	R	ER	HR	SH	SF	HB	TBB	IBB	SO	WP	Bk	W	L	Pct	ShO	Sv-Op	Hld	ERC	ERA
1997 Rockies	R	9	8	0	0	46.0	208	48	27	16	1	2	0	5	17	0	35	3	3	1	3	.250	0	0- -	-	3.94	3.13
1998 Portland	A-	15	15	1	0	79.1	364	87	50	43	8	1	1	7	39	0	38	7	0	5	8	.385	0	0- -	-	5.35	4.88
1999 Asheville	A	25	25	2	0	121.2	561	157	99	87	17	2	1	9	42	0	73	15	0	4	12	.250	0	0- -	-	6.17	6.44
2000 Asheville	A	21	21	4	0	142.2	579	130	54	47	10	1	0	16	23	0	118	5	0	10	7	.588	2	0- -	-	2.97	2.96
2000 Salem	A+	7	7	1	0	43.0	196	52	33	26	4	1	1	7	12	0	37	3	0	1	6	.143	0	0- -	-	5.39	5.44
2001 Salem	A+	27	27	0	0	155.0	649	157	73	53	4	5	1	7	38	0	122	6	1	11	11	.500	0	0- -	-	3.24	3.08
2002 Carolina	AA	14	14	2	0	95.0	370	73	24	15	4	3	1	5	19	0	58	5	0	7	2	.778	2	0- -	-	2.04	1.42
2002 Co Springs	AAA	10	10	1	0	64.1	275	67	40	27	6	0	0	3	18	0	32	7	1	4	4	.500	0	0- -	-	3.97	3.78
2002 Colorado	NL	9	5	0	1	35.2	154	41	18	18	4	0	0	2	13	0	14	0	0	2	1	.667	0	0-0	1	5.31	4.54

Dennis Cook

Pitches: L Bats: L Pos: RP-37   **Ht: 6'3" Wt: 190 Born: 10/4/62 Age: 40**

Year Team	Lg	G	GS	CG	GF	IP	BFP	H	R	ER	HR	SH	SF	HB	TBB	IBB	SO	WP	Bk	W	L	Pct	ShO	Sv-Op	Hld	ERC	ERA
2002 R Cucamnga*	A+	4	3	0	0	3.2	20	8	7	7	3	0	0	0	1	0	5	1	0	0	1	.000	0	0- -	-	18.02	17.18
1988 San Francisco	NL	4	4	1	0	22.0	86	9	8	7	1	0	3	0	11	1	13	1	0	2	1	.667	1	0-0	0	1.29	2.86
1989 SF-Phi	NL	23	18	2	1	121.0	499	110	59	50	18	5	2	2	38	6	67	4	2	7	8	.467	1	0-0	1	3.60	3.72
1990 Phi-LA	NL	47	16	2	4	156.0	663	155	74	68	20	7	7	2	56	9	64	6	3	9	4	.692	1	1-2	4	4.06	3.92
1991 Los Angeles	NL	20	1	0	5	17.2	69	12	3	1	0	1	0	0	7	1	8	0	0	1	0	1.000	0	0-1	1	1.79	0.51
1992 Cleveland	AL	32	25	1	1	158.0	669	156	79	67	29	3	3	2	50	2	96	4	5	5	7	.417	0	0-0	0	4.28	3.82
1993 Cleveland	AL	25	6	0	2	54.0	233	62	36	34	9	3	2	2	16	1	34	0	1	5	5	.500	0	0-2	2	5.21	5.67
1994 Cleveland	AL	38	0	0	8	33.0	143	29	17	13	4	3	0	0	14	3	26	0	1	3	1	.750	0	0-1	3	3.40	3.55
1995 Cle-Tex	AL	46	1	0	10	57.2	255	63	32	29	9	4	5	2	26	3	53	1	0	2	0	.000	0	2-2	6	5.36	4.53
1996 Texas	AL	60	0	0	9	70.1	298	53	34	32	2	3	5	7	35	7	64	0	0	5	2	.714	0	0-2	11	2.85	4.09
1997 Florida	NL	59	0	0	12	62.1	272	64	28	27	4	1	1	2	28	4	63	0	0	1	2	.333	0	0-2	13	4.22	3.90
1998 New York	NL	73	0	0	18	68.0	286	60	21	18	5	3	3	3	27	4	79	1	1	8	4	.667	0	1-5	25	3.35	2.38
1999 New York	NL	71	0	0	12	63.0	262	50	27	27	11	1	2	1	27	1	68	0	0	10	5	.667	0	3-6	19	3.60	3.86
2000 New York	NL	68	0	0	15	59.0	269	63	35	35	8	0	0	5	31	4	53	3	2	6	3	.667	0	2-8	10	5.49	5.34
2001 NYM-Phi	NL	62	0	0	14	45.2	194	43	24	23	8	3	1	2	14	3	38	3	1	1	1	.500	0	0-3	6	3.93	4.53
2002 Anaheim	AL	37	0	0	5	24.0	100	21	9	9	2	0	2	1	10	0	13	0	0	1	1	.500	0	0-1	7	3.58	3.38
1989 San Francisco	NL	2	2	1	0	15.0	58	13	3	3	1	0	0	0	5	0	9	1	0	1	0	1.000	0	0-0	0	3.12	1.80
1989 Philadelphia	NL	21	16	1	1	106.0	441	97	56	47	17	5	2	2	33	6	58	3	2	6	8	.429	1	0-0	1	3.66	3.99
1990 Philadelphia	NL	42	13	2	4	141.2	594	132	61	56	13	5	5	2	54	9	58	6	3	8	3	.727	1	1-2	3	3.57	3.56
1990 Los Angeles	NL	5	3	0	0	14.1	69	23	13	12	7	2	2	0	2	0	6	0	0	1	1	.500	0	0-0	1	9.43	7.53
1995 Cleveland	AL	11	0	0	1	12.2	62	16	9	9	3	1	0	1	10	2	13	0	0	0	0	-	0	0-0	1	8.80	6.39
1995 Texas	AL	35	1	0	9	45.0	193	47	23	20	6	3	5	1	16	1	40	1	0	2	0	.000	0	2-2	5	4.49	4.40
2001 New York	NL	43	0	0	11	36.0	148	28	18	17	6	1	1	1	10	1	34	3	1	1	1	.500	0	0-2	6	2.83	4.25
2001 Philadelphia	NL	19	0	0	3	9.2	46	15	6	6	2	2	0	1	4	2	4	0	0	0	0	-	0	0-1	2	8.88	5.59
15 ML YEARS		665	71	6	116	1011.2	4298	950	486	440	130	37	38	31	390	49	739	23	16	64	46	.582	3	9-35	106	3.94	3.91

Mike Coolbaugh

Bats: R Throws: R Pos: 3B-4; PH-1   **Ht: 6'1" Wt: 190 Born: 6/5/72 Age: 31**

Year Team	Lg	G	AB	H	2B	3B	HR	(Hm	Rd)	TB	R	RBI	RC	TBB	IBB	SO	HBP	SH	SF	SB	CS	SB%	GDP	Avg	OBP	Slg
1990 Medicine Hat	R+	58	211	40	9	0	2	(-	-)	55	21	16	9	13	0	47	1	1	2	3	2	.60	8	.190	.238	.261
1991 St. Ctharines	A-	71	255	58	13	2	3	(-	-)	84	28	26	23	17	0	40	3	4	4	4	5	.44	1	.227	.280	.329
1992 St. Ctharines	A-	15	49	14	1	1	0	(-	-)	17	3	2	5	3	0	12	0	2	0	0	2	.00	1	.286	.327	.347
1993 Hagerstown	A	112	389	94	23	1	16	(-	-)	167	58	62	49	32	5	94	3	4	4	4	3	.57	9	.242	.301	.429
1994 Dunedin	A+	122	456	120	33	3	16	(-	-)	207	53	66	60	28	3	94	7	3	4	3	4	.43	14	.263	.313	.454
1995 Knoxville	AA	142	500	120	32	2	9	(-	-)	183	71	56	51	37	3	110	11	4	3	7	11	.39	13	.240	.305	.366
1996 Charlotte	A+	124	449	129	33	4	15	(-	-)	215	76	75	72	42	4	80	8	0	3	8	10	.44	10	.287	.357	.479
1996 Tulsa	AA	7	23	8	3	0	2	(-	-)	17	6	9	7	2	0	3	2	0	0	1	0	1.00	1	.348	.444	.739
1997 Huntsville	AA	139	559	172	37	2	30	(-	-)	303	100	132	106	52	3	105	7	2	8	8	3	.73	17	.308	.369	.542
1998 Co Springs	AAA	108	386	107	35	2	16	(-	-)	194	62	75	59	32	0	93	1	2	4	0	3	.00	13	.277	.331	.503
1999 Columbus	AAA	114	391	108	31	2	15	(-	-)	188	65	66	62	38	0	112	2	2	4	5	7	.42	5	.276	.340	.481
2000 Columbus	AAA	117	387	105	28	0	23	(-	-)	202	63	61	60	68	7	96	3	3	3	6	3	.67	5	.271	.380	.522
2001 Indianapolis	AAA	94	347	93	24	3	10	(-	-)	153	49	50	52	39	1	92	5	6	4	3	2	.60	10	.268	.347	.441
2002 Memphis	AAA	116	411	100	20	1	29	(-	-)	209	62	75	72	51	2	126	9	1	3	9	3	.75	4	.243	.338	.509
2001 Milwaukee	NL	39	70	14	6	0	2	(2	0)	26	10	7	6	5	0	16	2	0	0	0	0	-	3	.200	.273	.371
2002 St Louis	NL	5	12	1	0	0	0	(0	0)	1	0	0	0	1	0	3	0	1	0	0	0	-	1	.083	.154	.083
2 ML YEARS		44	82	15	6	0	2	(2	0)	27	10	7	6	6	0	19	2	1	0	0	0	-	4	.183	.256	.329

Ron Coomer

Bats: R Throws: R Pos: 3B-26; 1B-11; PH-10; DH-9; PR-3   **Ht: 6'0" Wt: 215 Born: 11/18/66 Age: 36**

Year Team	Lg	G	AB	H	2B	3B	HR	(Hm	Rd)	TB	R	RBI	RC	TBB	IBB	SO	HBP	SH	SF	SB	CS	SB%	GDP	Avg	OBP	Slg
1995 Minnesota	AL	37	101	26	3	1	5	(2	3)	46	15	19	12	9	0	11	1	0	0	0	1	.00	9	.257	.324	.455
1996 Minnesota	AL	95	233	69	12	1	12	(5	7)	119	34	41	38	17	1	24	0	0	3	3	0	1.00	10	.296	.340	.511
1997 Minnesota	AL	140	523	156	30	2	13	(4	9)	229	63	85	70	22	5	91	0	0	5	4	3	.57	11	.298	.324	.438
1998 Minnesota	AL	137	529	146	22	1	15	(6	9)	215	54	72	57	18	1	72	0	0	8	2	2	.50	22	.276	.295	.406
1999 Minnesota	AL	127	467	123	25	1	16	(6	10)	198	53	65	57	30	1	69	1	0	3	2	1	.67	16	.263	.307	.424
2000 Minnesota	AL	140	544	147	29	1	16	(3	13)	226	64	82	66	36	2	50	4	0	5	2	0	1.00	25	.270	.317	.415
2001 Chicago	NL	111	349	91	19	1	8	(3	5)	136	25	53	37	29	1	70	2	0	6	0	0	-	23	.261	.316	.390
2002 New York	AL	55	148	39	7	0	3	(2	1)	55	14	17	13	6	1	23	0	1	1	0	0	-	8	.264	.290	.372
8 ML YEARS		842	2894	797	147	8	88	(31	57)	1224	322	434	350	167	12	410	8	1	31	13	7	.65	124	.275	.314	.423

Brian Cooper

Pitches: R **Bats:** R **Pos:** SP-2   **Ht:** 6'1" **Wt:** 185 **Born:** 8/19/74 **Age:** 28

Year Team	Lg	G	GS	CG	GF	IP	BFP	H	R	ER	HR	SH	SF	HB	TBB	IBB	SO	WP	Bk	W	L	Pct	ShO	Sv-Op	Hld	ERC	ERA
2002 Syracuse*	AAA	27	25	1	1	155.2	671	176	98	88	19	0	9	7	46	1	71	5	0	9	9	.500	0	0- -	0	4.81	5.09
1999 Anaheim	AL	5	5	0	0	27.2	124	23	15	15	3	0	1	4	18	0	15	0	0	1	1	.500	0	0-0	0	4.79	4.88
2000 Anaheim	AL	15	15	1	0	87.0	396	105	66	57	18	4	4	2	35	1	36	1	0	4	8	.333	1	0-0	0	6.17	5.90
2001 Anaheim	AL	7	1	0	5	13.2	55	10	5	4	2	0	1	0	4	0	7	0	0	0	1	.000	0	0-0	0	2.51	2.63
2002 Toronto	AL	2	2	0	0	8.1	41	14	13	13	5	1	1	0	4	0	3	1	0	0	1	.000	0	0-0	0	13.71	14.04
4 ML YEARS		29	23	1	5	136.2	616	152	99	89	28	5	7	6	61	1	61	2	0	5	11	.313	1	0-0	0	5.88	5.86

Alex Cora

Bats: L **Throws:** R **Pos:** SS-61; 2B-40; PH-38; PR-1   **Ht:** 6'0" **Wt:** 180 **Born:** 10/18/75 **Age:** 27

| | | | | | | | BATTING | | | | | | | | | | | | | BASERUNNING | | | | AVERAGES | | |
Year Team	Lg	G	AB	H	2B	3B	HR	(Hm	Rd)	TB	R	RBI	RC	TBB	IBB	SO	HBP	SH	SF	SB	CS	SB%	GDP	Avg	OBP	Slg
1998 Los Angeles	NL	29	33	4	0	1	0	(0	0)	6	1	0	1	2	0	8	1	2	0	0	0	-	0	.121	.194	.182
1999 Los Angeles	NL	11	30	5	1	0	0	(0	0)	6	2	3	0	0	0	4	1	0	0	0	0	-	1	.167	.194	.200
2000 Los Angeles	NL	109	353	84	18	6	4	(2	2)	126	39	32	38	26	4	53	7	6	3	4	1	.80	6	.238	.302	.357
2001 Los Angeles	NL	134	405	88	18	3	4	(2	2)	124	38	29	30	31	6	58	8	3	2	0	2	.00	16	.217	.285	.306
2002 Los Angeles	NL	115	258	75	14	4	5	(4	1)	112	37	28	46	26	4	38	7	2	0	7	2	.78	3	.291	.371	.434
5 ML YEARS		398	1079	256	51	14	13	(8	5)	374	117	92	115	85	14	161	24	13	4	11	5	.69	26	.237	.306	.347

Francisco Cordero

Pitches: R **Bats:** R **Pos:** RP-39   **Ht:** 6'2" **Wt:** 200 **Born:** 5/11/75 **Age:** 28

Year Team	Lg	G	GS	CG	GF	IP	BFP	H	R	ER	HR	SH	SF	HB	TBB	IBB	SO	WP	Bk	W	L	Pct	ShO	Sv-Op	Hld	ERC	ERA
2002 Oklahoma*	AAA	11	1	0	8	12.1	62	15	14	8	2	0	0	1	7	1	21	2	0	0	2	.000	0	2- -	0	6.36	5.84
1999 Detroit	AL	20	0	0	4	19.0	91	19	7	7	2	2	4	0	18	2	19	1	0	2	2	.500	0	0-0	6	6.19	3.32
2000 Texas	AL	56	0	0	13	77.1	365	87	51	46	11	2	6	4	48	3	49	7	0	1	2	.333	0	0-3	4	6.15	5.35
2001 Texas	AL	3	0	0	2	2.1	12	3	1	1	0	0	0	0	2	1	1	1	0	0	1	.000	0	0-0	1	5.73	3.86
2002 Texas	AL	39	0	0	25	45.1	177	33	12	9	2	0	0	2	13	1	41	1	0	2	0	1.000	0	10-12	1	2.11	1.79
4 ML YEARS		118	0	0	44	144.0	645	142	71	63	15	4	10	6	81	7	110	10	0	5	5	.500	0	10-15	12	4.77	3.94

Wil Cordero

Bats: R **Throws:** R **Pos:** PH-33; LF-28; 1B-11; RF-5; DH-2   **Ht:** 6'2" **Wt:** 200 **Born:** 10/3/71 **Age:** 31

| | | | | | | | BATTING | | | | | | | | | | | | | BASERUNNING | | | | AVERAGES | | |
Year Team	Lg	G	AB	H	2B	3B	HR	(Hm	Rd)	TB	R	RBI	RC	TBB	IBB	SO	HBP	SH	SF	SB	CS	SB%	GDP	Avg	OBP	Slg
1992 Montreal	NL	45	126	38	4	1	2	(1	1)	50	17	8	17	9	0	31	1	1	0	0	0	-	3	.302	.353	.397
1993 Montreal	NL	138	475	118	32	2	10	(8	2)	184	56	58	55	34	8	60	7	4	1	12	3	.80	12	.248	.308	.387
1994 Montreal	NL	110	415	122	30	3	15	(5	10)	203	65	63	74	41	3	62	6	2	3	16	3	.84	8	.294	.363	.489
1995 Montreal	NL	131	514	147	35	2	10	(2	8)	216	64	49	72	36	4	88	9	1	4	9	5	.64	11	.286	.341	.420
1996 Boston	AL	59	198	57	14	0	3	(2	1)	80	29	37	24	11	4	31	2	1	1	2	1	.67	8	.288	.330	.404
1997 Boston	AL	140	570	160	26	3	18	(11	7)	246	82	72	75	31	7	122	4	0	4	1	3	.25	11	.281	.320	.432
1998 Chicago	AL	96	341	91	18	2	13	(5	8)	152	58	49	47	22	0	66	3	1	4	2	1	.67	7	.267	.314	.446
1999 Cleveland	AL	54	194	58	15	0	8	(3	5)	97	35	32	34	15	0	37	6	0	2	2	0	1.00	7	.299	.364	.500
2000 Pit-Cle		127	496	137	35	5	16	(8	8)	230	64	68	70	32	1	76	7	0	1	1	2	.33	18	.276	.328	.464
2001 Cleveland	AL	89	268	67	11	1	4	(2	2)	92	30	21	28	22	2	50	4	2	3	0	0	-	8	.250	.313	.343
2000 Pittsburgh	NL	89	348	98	24	3	16	(8	8)	176	46	51	55	25	1	58	4	0	1	1	2	.33	11	.282	.336	.506
2000 Cleveland	AL	38	148	39	11	2	0	(0	0)	54	18	17	15	7	0	18	3	0	0	0	0	-	7	.264	.310	.365
2002 Cleveland	AL	6	18	4	0	0	0	(0	0)	4	1	1	0	0	0	3	0	0	0	0	0	-	1	.222	.222	.222
2002 Montreal	NL	66	143	39	9	0	6	(2	4)	66	21	29	27	17	0	26	2	0	4	2	0	1.00	3	.273	.349	.462
11 ML YEARS		1061	3758	1038	229	19	105	(49	56)	1620	522	487	523	270	29	652	51	12	27	47	18	.72	97	.276	.331	.431

Marty Cordova

Bats: R **Throws:** R **Pos:** LF-72; DH-54; PH-7   **Ht:** 6'0" **Wt:** 206 **Born:** 7/10/69 **Age:** 33

| | | | | | | | BATTING | | | | | | | | | | | | | BASERUNNING | | | | AVERAGES | | |
Year Team	Lg	G	AB	H	2B	3B	HR	(Hm	Rd)	TB	R	RBI	RC	TBB	IBB	SO	HBP	SH	SF	SB	CS	SB%	GDP	Avg	OBP	Slg
1995 Minnesota	AL	137	512	142	27	4	24	(16	8)	249	81	84	88	52	1	111	10	0	5	20	7	.74	10	.277	.352	.486
1996 Minnesota	AL	145	569	176	46	1	16	(10	6)	272	97	111	97	53	4	96	8	0	9	11	5	.69	18	.309	.371	.478
1997 Minnesota	AL	103	378	93	18	4	15	(4	11)	164	44	51	47	30	2	92	3	0	2	5	3	.63	13	.246	.305	.434
1998 Minnesota	AL	119	438	111	20	2	10	(6	4)	165	52	69	52	50	3	103	5	0	6	3	6	.33	14	.253	.333	.377
1999 Minnesota	AL	124	425	121	28	3	14	(9	5)	197	62	70	68	48	2	96	9	0	6	13	4	.76	22	.285	.365	.464
2000 Toronto	AL	62	200	49	7	0	4	(3	1)	68	23	18	21	18	0	35	3	0	0	3	2	.60	6	.245	.317	.340
2001 Cleveland	AL	122	409	123	20	2	20	(9	11)	207	61	69	68	23	0	81	8	0	2	3	0	.00	9	.301	.348	.506
2002 Baltimore	AL	131	458	116	25	2	18	(11	7)	199	55	64	63	47	3	111	3	2	3	1	6	.14	17	.253	.325	.434
8 ML YEARS		943	3389	931	191	18	121	(68	53)	1521	475	536	504	321	15	725	49	2	33	56	36	.61	109	.275	.343	.449

Bryan Corey

Pitches: R **Bats:** R **Pos:** RP-1   **Ht:** 6'0" **Wt:** 170 **Born:** 10/21/73 **Age:** 29

Year Team	Lg	G	GS	CG	GF	IP	BFP	H	R	ER	HR	SH	SF	HB	TBB	IBB	SO	WP	Bk	W	L	Pct	ShO	Sv-Op	Hld	ERC	ERA
1995 Jamestown	A-	29	0	0	28	28.0	116	21	14	12	2	0	1	1	12	1	41	4	0	2	2	.500	0	10- -	-	2.74	3.86
1996 Fayetteville	A	60	0	0	53	82.0	315	50	19	11	2	4	6	2	17	3	101	6	2	6	4	.600	0	34- -	-	1.26	1.21
1997 Jacksonville	AA	52	0	0	36	68.0	298	74	42	36	8	5	3	1	21	3	37	4	0	3	8	.273	0	9- -	-	4.25	4.76
1998 Tucson	AAA	39	10	0	14	87.2	401	116	61	53	14	1	2	6	24	0	50	2	2	4	6	.400	0	2- -	-	6.19	5.44
1999 Toledo	AAA	48	0	0	17	69.1	303	63	27	22	6	4	1	2	34	4	36	2	1	5	2	.714	0	2- -	-	3.81	2.86
2000 Sacramento	AAA	47	6	0	16	85.0	362	88	43	40	11	4	3	2	29	2	55	2	1	8	3	.727	0	4- -	-	4.42	4.24
2001 Portland	AAA	47	12	0	25	106.0	455	124	55	55	12	3	5	3	31	3	66	1	1	8	7	.533	0	6- -	-	4.90	4.67

Year Team	Lg	HOW MUCH HE PITCHED						WHAT HE GAVE UP										THE RESULTS						
		G	GS	CG	GF	IP	BFP	H	R	ER	HR	SH	SF	HB	TBB	IBB	SO	WP	Bk	W	L	Pct	ShO	Sv-Op	Hld	ERC	ERA
2002 Las Vegas	AAA	37	0	0	10	53.2	251	79	31	26	5	3	1	2	18	1	33	0	0	5	4	.556	0	1- -		6.79	4.36
1998 Arizona	NL	3	0	0	2	4.0	20	6	4	4	1	1	0	1	2	0	1	0	0	0	0	-	0	0-0	0	10.40	9.00
2002 Los Angeles	NL	1	0	0	1	1.0	3	0	0	0	0	0	0	0	0	0	0	0	0	0	0	-	0	0-0	0	0.00	0.00
2 ML YEARS		4	0	0	3	5.0	23	6	4	4	1	1	0	1	2	0	1	0	0	0	0	-	0	0-0	0	7.06	7.20

Mark Corey

Pitches: R **Bats:** R **Pos:** RP-26   **Ht:** 6'3" **Wt:** 210 **Born:** 11/16/74 **Age:** 28

Year Team	Lg	HOW MUCH HE PITCHED						WHAT HE GAVE UP										THE RESULTS						
		G	GS	CG	GF	IP	BFP	H	R	ER	HR	SH	SF	HB	TBB	IBB	SO	WP	Bk	W	L	Pct	ShO	Sv-Op	Hld	ERC	ERA
1995 Princeton	R+	4	2	0	0	14.2	61	12	7	6	1	0	0	0	6	0	8	0	0	1	1	.500	0	0- -		2.92	3.68
1997 Chrlstn - WV	A	26	26	1	0	136.0	602	169	87	69	7	8	5	4	42	3	97	14	0	8	13	.381	0	0- -		4.87	4.57
1998 Burlington	A	20	20	6	0	140.0	577	125	55	38	9	3	3	6	36	0	109	10	1	12	6	.667	2	0- -		2.88	2.44
1998 Chattanooga	AA	6	6	0	0	26.1	127	32	25	24	6	1	2	2	16	1	6	0	0	0	4	.000	0	0- -		7.50	8.20
1998 Indianapolis	AAA	1	1	1	0	6.0	24	4	3	3	1	1	0	0	3	0	2	0	0	0	1	.000	0	0- -		3.20	4.50
1999 Binghamton	AA	29	27	0	0	155.0	698	175	108	93	18	4	1	9	64	0	111	1	1	7	13	.350	0	0- -		5.22	5.40
2000 Binghamton	AA	14	2	0	2	25.2	101	15	5	3	0	1	1	0	11	0	19	2	0	0	0	-	0	0- -		1.55	1.05
2000 Norfolk	AAA	20	11	0	2	63.2	303	80	52	48	11	2	3	8	29	1	43	4	0	3	7	.300	0	1- -		6.88	6.79
2001 Binghamton	AA	25	0	0	23	35.0	137	23	10	7	1	2	0	1	12	0	50	2	0	1	2	.333	0	17- -		1.83	1.80
2001 Norfolk	AAA	28	0	0	21	36.2	147	24	7	6	1	3	0	0	22	0	42	0	0	8	2	.800	0	10- -		2.63	1.47
2002 Norfolk	AAA	25	0	0	21	26.1	100	14	3	3	1	3	0	1	7	1	37	0	0	3	1	.750	0	7- -		1.24	1.03
2002 St.Lucie	A+	1	0	0	1	2.0	6	0	0	0	0	0	0	0	0	0	3	0	0	0	0	-	0	0- -		0.00	0.00
2001 New York	NL	2	0	0	0	1.2	13	5	3	3	0	0	0	0	3	1	3	0	0	0	0	-	0	0-0	0	21.72	16.20
2002 NYM-Col	NL	26	0	0	8	12.0	114	32	23	21	9	1	0	3	16	2	21	1	0	0	3	.000	0	0-0	1	11.75	8.59
2002 New York	NL	12	0	0	5	10.0	48	10	7	5	2	0	0	1	8	1	9	1	0	0	3	.000	0	0-0	0	6.76	4.50
2002 Colorado	NL	14	0	0	3	12.0	66	22	16	16	7	1	0	2	8	1	12	0	0	0	0	-	0	0-0	1	16.43	12.00
2 ML YEARS		28	0	0	8	23.2	127	37	26	24	9	1	0	3	19	3	24	1	0	0	3	.000	0	0-0	1	12.51	9.13

Rheal Cormier

Pitches: L **Bats:** L **Pos:** RP-54   **Ht:** 5'10" **Wt:** 187 **Born:** 4/23/67 **Age:** 36

Year Team	Lg	HOW MUCH HE PITCHED						WHAT HE GAVE UP										THE RESULTS						
		G	GS	CG	GF	IP	BFP	H	R	ER	HR	SH	SF	HB	TBB	IBB	SO	WP	Bk	W	L	Pct	ShO	Sv-Op	Hld	ERC	ERA
1991 St Louis	NL	11	10	2	1	67.2	281	74	35	31	5	1	3	2	8	1	38	2	1	4	5	.444	0	0-0	0	3.41	4.12
1992 St Louis	NL	31	30	3	1	186.0	772	194	83	76	15	11	3	5	33	2	117	4	2	10	10	.500	0	0-0	0	3.42	3.68
1993 St Louis	NL	38	21	1	4	145.1	619	163	80	70	18	10	4	4	27	3	75	6	0	7	6	.538	0	0-0	0	4.13	4.33
1994 St Louis	NL	7	7	0	0	39.2	169	40	24	24	6	1	2	3	7	0	26	2	0	3	2	.600	0	0-0	0	3.80	5.45
1995 Boston	AL	48	12	0	3	115.0	488	131	60	52	12	6	2	3	31	2	69	4	0	7	5	.583	0	0-2	9	4.56	4.07
1996 Montreal	NL	33	27	1	1	159.2	674	165	80	74	16	4	8	9	41	3	100	8	0	7	10	.412	1	0-0	0	3.93	4.17
1997 Montreal	NL	1	1	0	0	1.1	9	4	5	5	1	0	0	0	1	0	0	0	0	1	0	1.000	0	0-0	0	27.46	33.75
1999 Boston	AL	60	0	0	7	63.1	275	61	34	26	4	1	3	5	18	2	39	1	0	2	0	1.000	0	0-3	15	3.33	3.69
2000 Boston	AL	64	0	0	12	68.1	293	74	40	35	7	5	2	0	17	2	43	1	0	3	3	.500	0	0-2	9	3.86	4.61
2001 Philadelphia	NL	60	0	0	16	51.1	222	49	26	24	5	3	0	4	17	4	37	1	0	5	6	.455	0	1-6	12	3.67	4.21
2002 Philadelphia	NL	54	0	0	7	60.0	268	61	38	35	6	0	2	4	32	6	49	4	0	5	6	.455	0	0-3	9	4.85	5.25
11 ML YEARS		407	108	7	52	957.2	4070	1016	505	452	95	42	29	39	232	25	593	33	3	53	54	.495	1	1-16	54	3.91	4.25

Nate Cornejo

Pitches: R **Bats:** R **Pos:** SP-9   **Ht:** 6'5" **Wt:** 240 **Born:** 9/24/79 **Age:** 23

Year Team	Lg	HOW MUCH HE PITCHED						WHAT HE GAVE UP										THE RESULTS						
		G	GS	CG	GF	IP	BFP	H	R	ER	HR	SH	SF	HB	TBB	IBB	SO	WP	Bk	W	L	Pct	ShO	Sv-Op	Hld	ERC	ERA
1998 Tigers	R	5	0	0	2	14.1	58	12	2	2	0	0	0	1	2	0	9	1	0	1	0	1.000	0	1- -		1.89	1.26
1999 W Michigan	A	28	28	4	0	174.2	750	173	87	72	4	10	9	12	67	0	125	11	5	9	11	.450	1	0- -		3.72	3.71
2000 Lakeland	A+	12	12	1	0	77.0	322	67	37	26	5	0	1	4	31	0	60	2	1	5	5	.500	0	0- -		3.39	3.04
2000 Jacksonville	AA	16	16	0	0	91.2	389	91	52	47	6	3	3	4	43	1	60	1	1	5	7	.417	0	0- -		4.39	4.61
2001 Erie	AA	19	19	3	0	124.1	519	107	47	37	12	3	0	7	41	0	105	4	0	12	3	.800	1	0- -		3.24	2.68
2001 Toledo	AAA	4	4	0	0	29.2	113	24	8	7	1	1	0	0	7	0	22	1	0	4	0	1.000	0	0- -		2.20	2.12
2002 Toledo	AAA	21	20	1	0	132.1	576	163	72	65	11	4	2	8	31	1	86	1	2	9	8	.529	0	0- -		4.93	4.42
2001 Detroit	AL	10	10	0	0	42.2	217	63	38	35	10	2	0	3	28	4	22	1	0	4	4	.500	0	0-0	0	9.48	7.38
2002 Detroit	AL	9	9	1	0	50.0	230	63	33	28	6	1	1	2	18	0	23	2	0	1	5	.167	0	0-0	0	5.69	5.04
2 ML YEARS		19	19	1	0	92.2	447	126	71	63	16	3	1	5	46	4	45	3	0	5	9	.357	0	0-0	0	7.37	6.12

Humberto Cota

Bats: R **Throws:** R **Pos:** C-7; PH-1   **Ht:** 6'0" **Wt:** 205 **Born:** 2/7/79 **Age:** 24

Year Team	Lg	BATTING																			BASERUNNING				AVERAGES		
		G	AB	H	2B	3B	HR	(Hm	Rd)	TB	R	RBI	RC	TBB	IBB	SO	HBP	SH	SF	SB	CS	SB%	GDP	Avg	OBP	Slg
1997 Devil Rays	R	44	133	32	6	1	2	(-	-)	46	14	20	17	17	0	27	3	1	3	3	1	.75	1	.241	.333	.346
1997 Hudson Val	A-	3	9	2	0	0	0	(-	-)	2	0	2	0	0	0	1	0	0	0	0	0	-	0	.222	.222	.222
1998 Princeton	R+	67	245	76	13	4	15	(-	-)	142	48	61	54	32	1	59	6	1	3	4	4	.50	3	.310	.399	.580
1999 Chrlstn - SC	A	85	336	94	21	1	9	(-	-)	144	42	61	44	20	1	51	2	1	5	1	1	.50	9	.280	.320	.429
1999 Hickory	A	37	133	36	11	2	2	(-	-)	57	28	20	23	21	1	20	0	0	2	3	1	.75	0	.271	.365	.429
2000 Altoona	AA	112	429	112	20	1	8	(-	-)	158	49	44	45	21	1	80	3	1	5	6	4	.60	8	.261	.297	.368
2001 Nashville	AAA	111	377	112	22	2	14	(-	-)	180	61	72	62	25	1	74	8	1	3	7	2	.78	8	.297	.351	.477
2002 Nashville	AAA	118	404	108	27	1	9	(-	-)	164	51	54	49	31	1	106	5	0	8	5	8	.38	11	.267	.321	.406
2001 Pittsburgh	NL	7	9	2	0	0	0	(0	0)	2	0	1	0	0	0	5	0	0	0	0	0	-	0	.222	.222	.222
2002 Pittsburgh	NL	7	17	5	1	0	0	(0	0)	6	2	0	1	1	1	4	0	0	0	0	0	-	0	.294	.333	.353
2 ML YEARS		14	26	7	1	0	0	(0	0)	8	2	1	1	1	1	9	0	0	0	0	0	-	0	.269	.296	.308

Craig Counsell

Bats: L Throws: R Pos: 3B-94; SS-22; 2B-13; PH-1; PR-1　　　　**Ht: 6'0" Wt: 175 Born: 8/21/70 Age: 32**

Year Team	Lg	G	AB	H	2B	3B	HR	(Hm	Rd)	TB	R	RBI	RC	TBB	IBB	SO	HBP	SH	SF	SB	CS	SB%	GDP	Avg	OBP	Slg
1995 Colorado	NL	3	1	0	0	0	0	(0	0)	0	0	0	0	1	0	0	0	0	0	0	0	-	0	.000	.500	.000
1997 Col-Fla	NL	51	164	49	9	2	1	(1	0)	65	20	16	24	18	2	17	3	3	1	1	1	.50	5	.299	.376	.396
1998 Florida	NL	107	335	84	19	5	4	(2	2)	125	43	40	48	51	7	47	4	8	1	3	0	1.00	5	.251	.355	.373
1999 Fla-LA	NL	87	174	38	7	0	0	(0	0)	45	24	11	12	14	0	24	0	5	2	1	0	1.00	2	.218	.274	.259
2000 Arizona	NL	67	152	48	8	1	2	(0	2)	64	23	11	25	20	0	18	2	1	1	3	3	.50	4	.316	.400	.421
2001 Arizona	NL	141	458	126	22	3	4	(4	0)	166	76	38	61	61	3	76	2	6	6	6	8	.43	9	.275	.359	.362
2002 Arizona	NL	112	436	123	22	1	2	(0	2)	153	63	51	63	45	3	52	1	4	3	7	5	.58	10	.282	.348	.351
1999 Florida	NL	37	66	10	1	0	0	(0	0)	11	4	2	1	5	0	10	0	2	0	0	0	-	1	.152	.211	.167
1999 Los Angeles	NL	50	108	28	6	0	0	(0	0)	34	20	9	11	9	0	14	0	3	2	1	0	1.00	1	.259	.311	.315
7 ML YEARS		568	1720	468	87	12	13	(7	6)	618	249	167	233	210	15	234	12	27	14	21	17	.55	35	.272	.353	.359

Steve Cox

Bats: L Throws: L Pos: 1B-110; DH-35; PH-3　　　　**Ht: 6'4" Wt: 225 Born: 10/31/74 Age: 28**

Year Team	Lg	G	AB	H	2B	3B	HR	(Hm	Rd)	TB	R	RBI	RC	TBB	IBB	SO	HBP	SH	SF	SB	CS	SB%	GDP	Avg	OBP	Slg
1999 Tampa Bay	AL	6	19	4	1	0	0	(0	0)	5	0	0	0	0	0	2	0	0	0	0	0	-	2	.211	.211	.263
2000 Tampa Bay	AL	116	318	90	19	1	11	(7	4)	144	44	35	54	46	2	47	4	0	1	1	2	.33	9	.283	.379	.453
2001 Tampa Bay	AL	108	342	88	22	0	12	(3	9)	146	37	51	45	24	0	75	10	0	2	2	2	.50	11	.257	.323	.427
2002 Tampa Bay	AL	148	560	142	30	1	16	(4	12)	222	65	72	63	60	5	116	7	0	6	5	0	1.00	15	.254	.330	.396
4 ML YEARS		378	1239	324	72	2	39	(14	25)	517	146	158	162	130	7	240	21	0	9	8	4	.67	37	.262	.340	.417

Carl Crawford

Bats: L Throws: L Pos: LF-63　　　　**Ht: 6'2" Wt: 219 Born: 8/5/81 Age: 21**

Year Team	Lg	G	AB	H	2B	3B	HR	(Hm	Rd)	TB	R	RBI	RC	TBB	IBB	SO	HBP	SH	SF	SB	CS	SB%	GDP	Avg	OBP	Slg
1999 Princeton	R+	60	260	83	14	4	0	(-	-)	105	62	25	38	13	0	47	1	1	3	17	3	.85	5	.319	.350	.404
2000 Chrlstn - SC	A	135	564	170	21	11	6	(-	-)	231	99	57	87	32	1	102	3	9	1	55	9	.86	1	.301	.342	.410
2001 Orlando	AA	132	537	147	24	3	4	(-	-)	189	64	51	62	36	2	90	4	6	2	36	20	.64	3	.274	.323	.352
2002 Durham	AAA	85	353	105	17	9	7	(-	-)	161	59	52	55	20	5	69	2	4	4	26	8	.76	5	.297	.335	.456
2002 Tampa Bay	AL	63	259	67	11	6	2	(1	1)	96	23	30	34	9	0	41	3	6	1	9	5	.64	0	.259	.290	.371

Joe Crede

Bats: R Throws: R Pos: 3B-53　　　　**Ht: 6'2" Wt: 195 Born: 4/26/78 Age: 25**

Year Team	Lg	G	AB	H	2B	3B	HR	(Hm	Rd)	TB	R	RBI	RC	TBB	IBB	SO	HBP	SH	SF	SB	CS	SB%	GDP	Avg	OBP	Slg
2002 Charlotte*	AAA	95	359	112	21	0	24	(-	-)	205	57	65	70	26	1	48	4	0	7	0	1	.00	8	.312	.359	.571
2000 Chicago	AL	7	14	5	1	0	0	(0	0)	6	2	3	2	0	0	3	0	0	1	0	0	-	0	.357	.333	.429
2001 Chicago	AL	17	50	11	1	1	0	(0	0)	14	1	7	4	3	0	11	1	0	1	1	0	1.00	1	.220	.273	.280
2002 Chicago	AL	53	200	57	10	0	12	(7	5)	103	28	35	31	8	0	40	0	0	1	0	2	.00	1	.285	.311	.515
3 ML YEARS		77	264	73	12	1	12	(7	5)	123	31	45	37	11	0	54	1	0	3	1	2	.33	2	.277	.305	.466

Doug Creek

Pitches: L Bats: L Pos: RP-52　　　　**Ht: 6'0" Wt: 227 Born: 3/1/69 Age: 34**

Year Team	Lg	G	GS	CG	GF	IP	BFP	H	R	ER	HR	SH	SF	HB	TBB	IBB	SO	WP	Bk	W	L	Pct	ShO	Sv-Op	Hld	ERC	ERA
1995 St Louis	NL	6	0	0	1	6.2	24	2	0	0	0	0	0	0	3	0	10	0	0	0	0	-	0	0-0	0	0.83	0.00
1996 San Francisco	NL	63	0	0	15	48.1	220	45	41	35	11	1	0	2	32	2	38	2	0	0	2	.000	0	0-1	7	5.80	6.52
1997 San Francisco	NL	3	3	0	0	13.1	64	12	12	10	1	0	0	0	14	0	14	0	0	1	2	.333	0	0-0	0	5.94	6.75
1999 Chicago	NL	3	0	0	2	6.0	32	6	7	7	1	0	1	0	8	1	6	1	0	0	0	-	0	0-0	0	8.01	10.50
2000 Tampa Bay	AL	45	0	0	8	60.2	265	49	33	31	10	2	3	2	39	3	73	3	0	1	3	.250	0	1-3	2	4.50	4.60
2001 Tampa Bay	AL	66	0	0	16	62.2	279	51	34	30	7	1	3	4	49	5	66	4	0	2	5	.286	0	0-3	15	4.84	4.31
2002 TB-Sea	AL	52	0	0	17	55.2	262	57	37	36	10	1	1	7	35	2	56	4	0	3	2	.600	0	0-2	5	6.19	5.82
2002 Tampa Bay	AL	29	0	0	6	37.1	172	39	27	26	8	0	0	3	21	1	37	2	0	2	1	.667	0	0-2	4	6.15	6.27
2002 Seattle	AL	23	0	0	11	18.1	90	18	10	10	2	1	1	4	14	1	19	2	0	1	1	.500	0	0-0	1	6.22	4.91
7 ML YEARS		238	3	0	59	253.1	1146	222	164	149	40	5	8	15	180	13	263	14	0	7	14	.333	0	1-9	29	5.23	5.29

Cesar Crespo

Bats: B Throws: R Pos: LF-6; PH-5; PR-5; 2B-4; 3B-4; SS-1; CF-1; RF-1　　　　**Ht: 5'11" Wt: 170 Born: 5/23/79 Age: 24**

Year Team	Lg	G	AB	H	2B	3B	HR	(Hm	Rd)	TB	R	RBI	RC	TBB	IBB	SO	HBP	SH	SF	SB	CS	SB%	GDP	Avg	OBP	Slg
1998 Capital City	A	116	428	108	18	4	6	(-	-)	152	61	48	54	44	1	114	3	7	1	47	14	.77	6	.252	.326	.355
1999 Brevard Cnty	A+	115	427	122	17	2	6	(-	-)	161	63	40	66	62	2	86	1	7	2	22	8	.73	9	.286	.376	.377
2000 Portland	AA	134	482	124	21	6	9	(-	-)	184	96	60	72	77	3	118	2	8	5	41	15	.73	8	.257	.359	.382
2001 Portland	AAA	78	273	71	18	3	8	(-	-)	119	46	29	46	39	1	66	1	5	1	23	3	.88	4	.260	.354	.436
2002 Portland	AAA	92	322	83	17	2	9	(-	-)	131	43	37	51	50	2	78	3	3	0	21	7	.75	5	.258	.363	.407
2001 San Diego	NL	55	153	32	6	0	4	(0	4)	50	27	12	17	25	0	50	0	1	0	6	2	.75	2	.209	.320	.327
2002 San Diego	NL	25	29	5	2	0	0	(0	0)	7	5	0	0	3	0	6	0	1	0	3	2	.60	0	.172	.250	.241
2 ML YEARS		80	182	37	8	0	4	(0	4)	57	32	12	17	28	0	56	0	2	0	9	4	.69	2	.203	.310	.313

Jack Cressend

Pitches: R Bats: R Pos: RP-23   **Ht: 6'1" Wt: 185 Born: 5/13/75 Age: 28**

Year Team	Lg	G	GS	CG	GF	IP	BFP	H	R	ER	HR	SH	SF	HB	TBB	IBB	SO	WP	Bk	W	L	Pct	ShO	Sv-Op	Hld	ERC	ERA
2002 Twins*	R	3	3	0	0	6.1	21	10	7	5	0			1	1	0	8	1	0	0	0	-	0	0--	-	9.42	7.11
2002 Fort Myers*	A+	3	1	0	0	5.0	21	4	2	2	0	0	0	0	2	0	5	0	0	1	0	1.000	0	0--	-	2.31	3.60
2000 Minnesota	AL	11	0	0	4	13.2	61	20	8	8	0	0	0	0	6	0	6	0	0	0	0	-	0	0-0	0	6.65	5.27
2001 Minnesota	AL	44	0	0	9	56.1	232	50	24	23	6	2	2	1	16	0	40	2	0	3	2	.600	0	0-2	5	3.13	3.67
2002 Minnesota	AL	23	0	0	4	32.0	154	40	25	21	6	1	2	1	19	4	22	1	0	0	1	.000	0	0-0	0	6.92	5.91
3 ML YEARS		78	0	0	17	102.0	447	110	57	52	12	3	4	2	41	4	68	3	0	3	3	.500	0	0-2	5	4.70	4.59

Coco Crisp

Bats: B Throws: R Pos: CF-31; LF-2   **Ht: 6'0" Wt: 185 Born: 11/1/79 Age: 23**

Year Team	Lg	G	AB	H	2B	3B	HR	(Hm	Rd)	TB	R	RBI	RC	TBB	IBB	SO	HBP	SH	SF	SB	CS	SB%	GDP	Avg	OBP	Slg
1999 Johnson City	R+	65	229	59	5	4	3	(-	-)	81	55	22	39	44	0	41	2	8	2	27	6	.82	0	.258	.379	.354
2000 New Jersey	A-	36	134	32	5	0	0	(-	-)	37	18	14	15	11	0	22	1	5	0	25	3	.89	1	.239	.301	.276
2000 Peoria	A	27	98	27	9	0	0	(-	-)	36	14	7	15	16	0	15	0	4	0	7	3	.70	1	.276	.377	.367
2001 Potomac	A+	139	530	162	23	3	11	(-	-)	224	80	47	82	52	6	64	1	7	1	39	21	.65	8	.306	.368	.423
2002 New Haven	AA	89	355	107	16	1	9	(-	-)	152	61	47	56	36	1	56	0	5	1	26	10	.72	6	.301	.365	.428
2002 Akron	AA	7	32	13	1	0	1	(-	-)	17	9	4	8	3	1	3	0	1	0	4	0	1.00	0	.406	.457	.531
2002 Buffalo	AAA	4	21	5	1	0	0	(-	-)	6	3	2	1	0	0	2	0	0	0	1	0	1.00	2	.238	.238	.286
2002 Cleveland	AL	32	127	33	9	2	1	(1	0)	49	16	9	19	11	0	19	0	3	2	4	1	.80	2	.260	.314	.386

Mike Crudale

Pitches: R Bats: R Pos: RP-48; SP-1   **Ht: 6'0" Wt: 205 Born: 1/3/77 Age: 26**

Year Team	Lg	G	GS	CG	GF	IP	BFP	H	R	ER	HR	SH	SF	HB	TBB	IBB	SO	WP	Bk	W	L	Pct	ShO	Sv-Op	Hld	ERC	ERA
1999 Johnson City	R+	24	0	0	8	33.0	142	29	15	12	1	1	0	1	14	0	36	5	0	0	1	.000	0	1--	-	3.09	3.27
2000 Peoria	A	38	0	0	14	50.2	209	40	17	13	2	5	0	3	16	3	45	4	0	6	1	.857	0	5--	-	2.37	2.31
2000 Potomac	A+	21	0	0	9	25.2	120	31	17	13	3	2	2	1	11	1	28	0	0	2	4	.333	0	2--	-	5.49	4.56
2001 New Haven	AA	62	0	0	30	80.1	338	76	42	29	7	2	2	0	22	4	85	7	0	4	9	.308	0	9--	-	3.08	3.25
2002 Memphis	AAA	13	0	0	13	14.2	57	10	3	3	1	0	0	0	5	1	16	2	0	1	0	1.000	0	7--	-	2.00	1.84
2002 St Louis	NL	49	1	0	14	52.2	213	43	11	11	3	3	6	1	14	2	47	3	0	3	0	1.000	0	0-1	6	2.35	1.88

Deivi Cruz

Bats: R Throws: R Pos: SS-147; PH-9; 1B-1   **Ht: 6'0" Wt: 184 Born: 11/6/72 Age: 30**

Year Team	Lg	G	AB	H	2B	3B	HR	(Hm	Rd)	TB	R	RBI	RC	TBB	IBB	SO	HBP	SH	SF	SB	CS	SB%	GDP	Avg	OBP	Slg
1997 Detroit	AL	147	436	105	26	0	2	(0	2)	137	35	40	31	14	0	55	0	14	3	3	6	.33	9	.241	.263	.314
1998 Detroit	AL	135	454	118	22	3	5	(5	0)	161	52	45	42	13	0	55	3	5	2	3	4	.43	11	.260	.284	.355
1999 Detroit	AL	155	518	147	35	4	13	(9	4)	221	64	58	64	12	0	57	4	14	5	1	4	.20	10	.284	.302	.427
2000 Detroit	AL	156	583	176	46	5	10	(1	9)	262	68	82	74	13	2	43	4	8	7	1	4	.20	25	.302	.318	.449
2001 Detroit	AL	110	414	106	28	1	7	(2	5)	157	39	52	42	17	0	46	4	1	2	4	1	.80	13	.256	.291	.379
2002 San Diego	NL	151	514	135	28	2	7	(3	4)	188	49	47	40	22	2	58	3	3	5	2	3	.40	20	.263	.294	.366
6 ML YEARS		854	2919	787	185	11	44	(20	24)	1126	307	324	293	91	4	314	18	45	24	14	22	.39	88	.270	.294	.386

Enrique Cruz

Bats: R Throws: R Pos: SS; 2B   **Ht: 6'1" Wt: 180 Born: 11/21/81 Age: 21**

Year Team	Lg	G	AB	H	2B	3B	HR	(Hm	Rd)	TB	R	RBI	RC	TBB	IBB	SO	HBP	SH	SF	SB	CS	SB%	GDP	Avg	OBP	Slg
1999 Mets	R	54	183	56	14	2	4	(-	-)	86	34	24	35	28	0	41	1	0	1	0	0	-	3	.306	.399	.470
2000 Capital City	A	49	157	29	12	0	1	(-	-)	44	19	12	13	25	1	44	1	1	1	3	3	.25	1	.185	.299	.280
2000 Kingsport	R+	63	223	56	14	0	9	(-	-)	97	35	39	34	26	1	56	3	4	2	19	7	.73	3	.251	.335	.435
2001 Capital City	A	124	438	110	20	2	9	(-	-)	161	60	59	62	59	0	106	6	3	3	33	7	.83	7	.251	.346	.368
2002 St.Lucie	A+	124	467	136	21	2	6	(-	-)	179	69	45	57	32	2	76	2	3	5	33	16	.67	15	.291	.336	.383

Ivan Cruz

Bats: L Throws: L Pos: PH-12; 1B-7   **Ht: 6'2" Wt: 219 Born: 5/3/68 Age: 35**

Year Team	Lg	G	AB	H	2B	3B	HR	(Hm	Rd)	TB	R	RBI	RC	TBB	IBB	SO	HBP	SH	SF	SB	CS	SB%	GDP	Avg	OBP	Slg
2002 Memphis*	AAA	125	461	129	27	0	35	(-	-)	261	83	100	86	49	7	96	3	0	5	0	0	-	14	.280	.349	.566
1997 New York	AL	11	20	5	1	0	0	(0	0)	6	0	3	2	2	0	4	0	0	0	0	0	-	0	.250	.318	.300
1999 Pittsburgh	NL	5	10	4	0	0	1	(1	0)	7	3	2	2	0	0	2	0	0	0	0	0	-	0	.400	.400	.700
2000 Pittsburgh	NL	8	11	1	0	0	0	(0	0)	1	0	0	0	0	0	8	0	0	1	0	0	-	1	.091	.091	.091
2002 St Louis	NL	17	14	5	0	0	1	(0	1)	8	2	3	4	1	0	3	0	0	0	0	0	-	1	.357	.400	.571
4 ML YEARS		41	55	15	1	0	2	(1	1)	22	5	8	8	3	0	17	0	0	0	0	0	-	1	.273	.310	.400

Jacob Cruz

Bats: L Throws: L Pos: DH-15; RF-9; 1B-4; PH-4; PR-4; LF-3   **Ht: 6'0" Wt: 210 Born: 1/28/73 Age: 30**

Year Team	Lg	G	AB	H	2B	3B	HR	(Hm	Rd)	TB	R	RBI	RC	TBB	IBB	SO	HBP	SH	SF	SB	CS	SB%	GDP	Avg	OBP	Slg
2002 Toledo*	AAA	11	43	7	1	1	0	(-	-)	10	6	5	3	8	0	14	1	0	1	1	0	1.00	3	.163	.302	.233
1996 San Francisco	NL	33	77	18	3	0	3	(3	0)	30	10	10	10	12	0	24	2	1	0	0	1	.00	2	.234	.352	.390
1997 San Francisco	NL	16	25	4	1	0	0	(0	0)	5	3	3	3	3	0	4	0	0	1	0	0	-	3	.160	.241	.200
1998 SF-Cle		4	4	0	0	0	0	(0	0)	0	0	0	0	0	0	3	0	0	0	0	0	-	0	.000	.000	.000

Year Team	Lg	G	AB	H	2B	3B	HR	(Hm Rd)	TB	R	RBI	RC	TBB	IBB	SO	HBP	SH	SF	SB	CS	SB%	GDP	Avg	OBP	Slg
1999 Cleveland	AL	32	88	29	5	1	3	(3) (3)	45	14	17	14	5	0	13	1	1	1	0	2	.00	4	.330	.368	.511
2000 Cleveland	AL	11	29	7	3	0	0	(0) (0)	10	3	5	5	5	0	4	1	0	1	1	0	1.00	0	.241	.361	.345
2001 Cle-Col		72	144	31	5	0	4	(2) (2)	48	19	18	13	15	0	50	4	1	2	0	4	.00	4	.215	.303	.333
2002 Detroit	AL	35	88	24	3	1	2	(0) (2)	35	12	6	11	13	0	20	3	1	2	3	1	.75	2	.273	.377	.398
1998 San Francisco	NL	3	3	0	0	0	0	(0) (0)	0	0	0	0	0	0	2	1	0	0	0	0	-	0	.000	.000	.000
1998 Cleveland	AL	1	1	0	0	0	0	(0) (0)	0	0	0	0	0	0	1	0	0	0	0	0	-	0	.000	.000	.000
2001 Cleveland	AL	28	68	15	4	0	3	(2) (1)	28	12	11	7	5	0	23	3	0	0	0	2	.00	0	.221	.303	.412
2001 Colorado	NL	44	76	16	1	0	1	(0) (1)	20	7	7	6	10	0	27	1	1	2	0	2	.00	1	.211	.303	.263
7 ML YEARS		203	455	113	20	2	12	(8) (4)	173	61	59	53	53	0	118	11	4	7	4	8	.33	15	.248	.337	.380

Jose Cruz

Bats: B **Throws:** R **Pos:** LF-56; RF-47; CF-21; PH-3; DH-2   **Ht:** 6'0" **Wt:** 210 **Born:** 4/19/74 **Age:** 29

Year Team	Lg	G	AB	H	2B	3B	HR	(Hm Rd)	TB	R	RBI	RC	TBB	IBB	SO	HBP	SH	SF	SB	CS	SB%	GDP	Avg	OBP	Slg
1997 Sea-Tor	AL	104	395	98	19	1	26	(11) (15)	197	55	68	63	41	2	117	0	1	5	7	2	.78	5	.248	.315	.499
1998 Toronto	AL	105	352	89	14	3	11	(4) (7)	142	59	42	55	57	3	99	0	1	4	11	4	.73	6	.253	.354	.403
1999 Toronto	AL	106	349	84	19	3	14	(8) (6)	151	63	45	57	64	5	91	0	1	0	14	4	.78	6	.241	.358	.433
2000 Toronto	AL	162	603	146	32	5	31	(15) (16)	281	91	76	91	71	3	129	2	2	3	15	5	.75	11	.242	.323	.466
2001 Toronto	AL	146	577	158	38	4	34	(15) (19)	306	92	88	101	45	4	138	1	2	2	32	5	.86	8	.274	.326	.530
2002 Toronto	AL	124	466	114	26	5	18	(7) (11)	204	64	70	72	51	1	106	0	1	4	7	1	.88	8	.245	.317	.438
1997 Seattle	AL	49	183	49	12	1	12	(7) (5)	99	28	34	31	13	0	45	0	1	1	1	0	1.00	3	.268	.315	.541
1997 Toronto	AL	55	212	49	7	0	14	(4) (10)	98	31	34	32	28	2	72	0	0	4	6	2	.75	2	.231	.316	.462
6 ML YEARS		747	2742	689	148	21	134	(64) (70)	1281	424	389	439	329	18	680	3	7	18	86	21	.80	38	.251	.330	.467

Juan Cruz

Pitches: R **Bats:** R **Pos:** RP-36; SP-9   **Ht:** 6'2" **Wt:** 165 **Born:** 10/15/78 **Age:** 24

Year Team	Lg	G	GS	CG	GF	IP	BFP	H	R	ER	HR	SH	SF	HB	TBB	IBB	SO	WP	Bk	W	L	Pct	ShO	Sv-Op	Hld	ERC	ERA
1998 Cubs	R	12	5	0	0	41.1	210	61	48	28	2	1	5	3	14	0	36	8	3	2	4	.333	0	0--	-	6.12	6.10
1999 Eugene	A-	15	15	0	0	80.1	374	97	59	53	11	1	4	9	33	0	65	4	0	5	6	.455	0	0--	-	6.05	5.94
2000 Lansing	A	17	17	2	0	96.0	423	75	50	35	6	1	0	13	60	0	106	8	1	5	5	.500	1	0--	-	4.01	3.28
2000 Daytona	A+	8	7	1	0	44.1	182	30	22	16	5	0	0	3	18	0	54	4	0	3	0	1.000	0	0--	-	2.71	3.25
2001 W Tennesse	AA	23	23	0	0	121.1	534	107	56	54	6	6	2	16	60	0	137	4	0	9	6	.600	0	0--	-	3.93	4.01
2001 Chicago	NL	8	8	0	0	44.2	185	40	16	16	4	2	0	2	17	1	39	0	0	3	1	.750	0	0-0	0	3.59	3.22
2002 Chicago	NL	45	9	0	14	97.1	431	84	56	43	11	7	8	8	59	4	81	1	0	3	11	.214	0	1-4	3	4.49	3.98
2 ML YEARS		53	17	0	14	142.0	616	124	72	59	15	9	8	10	76	5	120	1	0	6	12	.333	0	1-4	3	4.20	3.74

Nelson Cruz

Pitches: R **Bats:** R **Pos:** RP-38; SP-5   **Ht:** 6'1" **Wt:** 185 **Born:** 9/13/72 **Age:** 30

Year Team	Lg	G	GS	CG	GF	IP	BFP	H	R	ER	HR	SH	SF	HB	TBB	IBB	SO	WP	Bk	W	L	Pct	ShO	Sv-Op	Hld	ERC	ERA
2002 New Orleans*	AAA	6	0	0	2	8.0	31	4	4	4	2	0	0		4	0	8	0	0	0	1	.000	0	1--	-	2.81	4.50
1997 Chicago	AL	19	0	0	5	26.1	116	29	19	19	6	1	0	0	9	1	23	3	0	0	2	.000	0	0-0	6	5.21	6.49
1999 Detroit	AL	29	6	0	10	66.2	295	74	44	42	11	2	4	3	23	1	46	2	0	2	5	.286	0	0-0	4	5.09	5.67
2000 Detroit	AL	27	0	0	12	41.0	172	39	14	14	4	0	2	3	13	3	34	2	0	5	2	.714	0	0-1	2	3.69	3.07
2001 Houston	NL	66	0	0	16	82.1	342	72	41	38	11	3	2	9	24	4	75	0	1	3	3	.500	0	2-4	10	3.59	4.15
2002 Houston	NL	43	5	0	11	78.1	360	90	44	39	12	5	3	6	29	4	61	4	0	2	6	.250	0	0-2	1	5.31	4.48
5 ML YEARS		184	11	0	54	294.2	1285	304	162	152	44	11	11	21	98	13	239	11	1	12	18	.400	0	2-7	23	4.53	4.64

Mike Cuddyer

Bats: R **Throws:** R **Pos:** RF-24; 3B-9; PH-7; 1B-6; PR-2   **Ht:** 6'2" **Wt:** 190 **Born:** 3/27/79 **Age:** 24

Year Team	Lg	G	AB	H	2B	3B	HR	(Hm Rd)	TB	R	RBI	RC	TBB	IBB	SO	HBP	SH	SF	SB	CS	SB%	GDP	Avg	OBP	Slg
1998 Fort Wayne	A	129	497	137	37	7	12	(- -)	224	82	81	81	61	3	107	10	0	4	16	7	.70	13	.276	.364	.451
1999 Fort Myers	A+	130	466	139	24	4	16	(- -)	219	87	82	88	76	0	91	10	2	6	14	4	.78	20	.298	.403	.470
2000 New Britain	AA	138	490	129	30	8	6	(- -)	193	72	61	66	55	2	93	12	6	2	5	4	.56	16	.263	.351	.394
2001 New Britain	AA	141	509	153	36	3	30	(- -)	285	95	87	108	75	3	106	6	0	3	5	9	.36	16	.301	.395	.560
2002 Edmonton	AAA	86	330	102	16	9	20	(- -)	196	70	53	69	36	1	79	3	0	3	12	7	.63	9	.309	.379	.594
2001 Minnesota	AL	8	18	4	2	0	0	(0 0)	6	1	1	2	2	0	6	0	0	0	1	0	1.00	1	.222	.300	.333
2002 Minnesota	AL	41	112	29	7	0	4	(2 2)	48	12	13	14	8	0	30	1	1	1	2	0	1.00	3	.259	.311	.429
2 ML YEARS		49	130	33	9	0	4	(2 2)	54	13	14	16	10	0	36	1	1	1	3	0	1.00	4	.254	.310	.415

Will Cunnane

Pitches: R **Bats:** R **Pos:** RP-16   **Ht:** 6'1" **Wt:** 205 **Born:** 4/24/74 **Age:** 29

Year Team	Lg	G	GS	CG	GF	IP	BFP	H	R	ER	HR	SH	SF	HB	TBB	IBB	SO	WP	Bk	W	L	Pct	ShO	Sv-Op	Hld	ERC	ERA
2002 Iowa*	AAA	43	0	0	7	73.2	301	67	23	18	3	1	1	2	23	3	69	1	0	4	1	.800	0	2--	-	2.97	2.20
1997 San Diego	NL	54	8	0	16	91.1	430	114	69	59	11	1		5	49	3	79	3	0	6	3	.667	0	0-2	4	6.48	5.81
1998 San Diego	NL	3	0	0	1	3.0	14	4	2	2	1	0	0	0	1	1	1	0	0	0	0	-	0	0-0	0	6.84	6.00
1999 San Diego	NL	24	0	0	2	31.0	130	34	19	18	8	2	0	0	12	3	22	3	0	2	1	.667	0	0-0	5	5.87	5.23
2000 San Diego	NL	27	3	0	4	38.1	169	35	21	18	2	1	1	1	21	0	34	1	0	1	1	.500	0	0-0	1	3.90	4.23
2001 Milwaukee	NL	31	1	0	6	51.2	238	66	34	31	6	7	1	2	22	6	37	0	0	0	3	.000	0	0-0	1	5.93	5.40
2002 Chicago	NL	16	0	0	2	26.1	115	27	16	16	5	1	0	1	13	1	30	1	0	1	1	.500	0	0-1	1	5.49	5.47
6 ML YEARS		155	12	0	31	241.2	1096	280	161	144	33	12		9	118	14	203	8	0	10	9	.526	0	0-3	12	5.76	5.36

Jack Cust

Bats: L **Throws:** R **Pos:** PH-20; LF-18   **Ht:** 6'1" **Wt:** 205 **Born:** 1/16/79 **Age:** 24

| | | | | | | | | BATTING | | | | | | | | | | | | BASERUNNING | | | | AVERAGES | | |
Year Team	Lg	G	AB	H	2B	3B	HR	(Hm Rd)	TB	R	RBI	RC	TBB	IBB	SO	HBP	SH	SF	SB	CS	SB%	GDP	Avg	OBP	Slg
1997 Diamndbcks	R	35	121	37	11	1	3	(- -)	59	26	33	27	31	0	39	0	0	0	2	0	1.00	4	.306	.447	.488
1998 South Bend	A	16	62	15	3	0	0	(- -)	18	5	4	5	5	1	20	0	0	1	0	1	.00	0	.242	.294	.290
1998 Lethbridge	R+	73	223	77	20	2	11	(- -)	134	75	56	73	86	3	71	4	0	2	15	8	.65	3	.345	.530	.601
1999 High Desert	A+	125	455	152	42	3	32	(- -)	296	107	112	124	96	2	145	2	0	3	1	4	.20	5	.334	.450	.651
2000 El Paso	AA	129	447	131	32	6	20	(- -)	235	100	75	103	117	12	150	2	0	2	12	9	.57	10	.293	.440	.526
2001 Tucson	AAA	135	442	123	24	2	27	(- -)	232	81	79	97	102	3	160	5	0	5	6	3	.67	10	.278	.415	.525
2002 Co Springs	AAA	105	359	95	24	0	23	(- -)	188	74	55	78	83	4	121	5	0	3	6	3	.67	5	.265	.407	.524
2001 Arizona	NL	3	2	1	0	0	0	(0 0)	1	0	0	1	1	0	0	0	0	0	0	0	-	0	.500	.667	.500
2002 Colorado	NL	35	65	11	2	0	1	(0 1)	16	8	8	6	12	0	32	0	0	1	0	1	.00	3	.169	.295	.246
2 ML YEARS		38	67	12	2	0	1	(0 1)	17	8	8	7	13	0	32	0	0	1	0	1	.00	3	.179	.309	.254

Eric Cyr

Pitches: L **Bats:** R **Pos:** RP-5   **Ht:** 6'4" **Wt:** 200 **Born:** 2/11/79 **Age:** 24

| | | HOW MUCH HE PITCHED | | | | | | WHAT HE GAVE UP | | | | | | | | | | | | THE RESULTS | | | | | | | |
Year Team	Lg	G	GS	CG	GF	IP	BFP	H	R	ER	HR	SH	SF	HB	TBB	IBB	SO	WP	Bk	W	L	Pct	ShO	Sv-Op	Hld	ERC	ERA
1999 Padres	R	11	5	0	1	38.2	159	34	19	14	2	2	1	1	15	0	39	0	0	2	1	.667	0	0--	-	3.23	3.26
1999 Idaho Falls	R+	1	1	0	0	5.0	19	5	1	1	0	0	0	0	1	0	3	1	0	1	0	1.000	0	0--	-	2.93	1.80
2000 Fort Wayne	A	9	6	0	0	32.2	140	28	18	17	2	0	1	4	15	0	31	1	0	2	2	.500	0	0--	-	3.77	4.68
2000 Padres	R	2	1	0	1	3.0	14	4	1	1	0	0	0	0	2	0	4	0	0	0	0	-	0	0--	-	6.62	3.00
2001 Lk Elsinore	A+	21	16	0	0	100.2	399	68	28	18	1	3	0	3	24	0	131	1	0	7	4	.636	0	0--	-	1.49	1.61
2002 Mobile	AA	14	14	0	0	72.1	311	62	37	26	6	2	3	6	34	0	65	0	2	4	6	.400	0	0--	-	3.78	3.24
2002 Portland	AAA	9	2	0	2	14.1	69	14	6	5	0	0	0	2	10	0	11	3	0	0	0	-	0	0--	-	4.73	3.14
2002 San Diego	NL	5	0	0	0	6.0	29	6	7	7	0	1	1	0	6	1	4	0	0	0	1	.000	0	0-0	0	5.34	10.50

Omar Daal

Pitches: L **Bats:** L **Pos:** SP-23; RP-16   **Ht:** 6'3" **Wt:** 204 **Born:** 3/1/72 **Age:** 31

| | | HOW MUCH HE PITCHED | | | | | | WHAT HE GAVE UP | | | | | | | | | | | | THE RESULTS | | | | | | | |
Year Team	Lg	G	GS	CG	GF	IP	BFP	H	R	ER	HR	SH	SF	HB	TBB	IBB	SO	WP	Bk	W	L	Pct	ShO	Sv-Op	Hld	ERC	ERA
1993 Los Angeles	NL	47	0	0	12	35.1	155	36	20	20	5	2	2	0	21	3	19	1	2	2	3	.400	0	0-1	7	5.29	5.09
1994 Los Angeles	NL	24	0	0	5	13.2	55	12	5	5	1	1	0	0	5	0	9	1	1	0	0	-	0	0-0	3	3.24	3.29
1995 Los Angeles	NL	28	0	0	0	20.0	100	29	16	16	1	1	1	1	15	4	11	0	1	4	0	1.000	0	0-1	0	7.85	7.20
1996 Montreal	NL	64	6	0	9	87.1	366	74	40	39	10	2	9	3	37	3	82	1	1	4	5	.444	0	0-4	9	3.44	4.02
1997 Mon-Tor		42	3	0	6	57.1	270	82	48	45	7	7	1	2	21	3	44	2	0	2	3	.400	0	1-3	3	6.76	7.06
1998 Arizona	NL	33	23	3	4	162.2	664	146	60	52	12	9	6	3	51	3	132	0	1	8	12	.400	1	0-0	1	3.12	2.88
1999 Arizona	NL	32	32	2	0	214.2	895	188	92	87	21	4	7	7	79	3	148	3	2	16	9	.640	1	0-0	0	3.39	3.65
2000 Ari-Phi	NL	32	28	0	1	167.0	775	208	128	114	26	6	6	9	72	11	96	0	2	4	19	.174	0	0-0	0	6.17	6.14
2001 Philadelphia	NL	32	32	0	0	185.2	801	199	100	92	26	7	5	5	56	3	107	0	3	13	7	.650	0	0-0	0	4.45	4.46
2002 Los Angeles	NL	39	23	0	3	161.1	668	142	73	70	20	11	4	4	54	3	105	0	0	11	9	.550	0	0-0	1	3.42	3.90
1997 Montreal	NL	33	0	0	6	30.1	150	48	35	33	4	5	1	2	15	3	16	1	0	1	2	.333	0	1-3	3	8.60	9.79
1997 Toronto	AL	9	3	0	0	27.0	120	34	13	12	3	2	0	0	6	0	28	1	0	1	1	.500	0	0-0	0	4.85	4.00
2000 Arizona	NL	20	16	0	1	96.0	460	127	88	77	17	3	5	7	42	11	45	0	1	2	10	.167	0	0-0	0	6.78	7.22
2000 Philadelphia	NL	12	12	0	0	71.0	315	81	40	37	9	3	1	2	30	0	51	0	1	2	9	.182	0	0-0	0	5.37	4.69
10 ML YEARS		373	147	5	40	1105.0	4749	1116	582	540	129	50	34	32	411	36	753	8	13	64	67	.489	2	1-9	28	4.22	4.40

Jeff D'Amico

Pitches: R **Bats:** R **Pos:** SP-22; RP-7   **Ht:** 6'7" **Wt:** 250 **Born:** 12/27/75 **Age:** 27

| | | HOW MUCH HE PITCHED | | | | | | WHAT HE GAVE UP | | | | | | | | | | | | THE RESULTS | | | | | | | |
Year Team	Lg	G	GS	CG	GF	IP	BFP	H	R	ER	HR	SH	SF	HB	TBB	IBB	SO	WP	Bk	W	L	Pct	ShO	Sv-Op	Hld	ERC	ERA
1996 Milwaukee	NL	17	17	0	0	86.0	367	88	53	52	21	3	3	0	31	0	53	1	1	6	6	.500	0	0-0	0	5.11	5.44
1997 Milwaukee	NL	23	23	1	0	135.2	585	139	81	71	25	4	4	8	43	2	94	3	1	9	7	.563	1	0-0	0	4.69	4.71
1999 Milwaukee	NL	1	0	0	1	1.0	4	4	0	0	0	0	0	0	0	0	1	0	0	0	0	-	0	0-0	0	1.95	0.00
2000 Milwaukee	NL	23	23	1	0	162.1	667	143	55	48	14	10	3	6	46	5	101	5	0	12	7	.632	0	0-0	0	3.01	2.66
2001 Milwaukee	NL	10	10	0	0	47.1	216	60	42	32	11	2	1	1	16	4	32	2	0	2	4	.333	0	0-0	0	6.30	6.08
2002 New York	NL	29	22	1	1	145.2	621	152	84	80	20	8	4	3	37	8	101	0	0	6	10	.375	1	0-0	0	3.96	4.94
6 ML YEARS		103	95	3	2	578.0	2460	583	315	283	91	27	15	18	173	19	382	11	2	35	34	.507	3	0-0	0	4.19	4.41

Johnny Damon

Bats: L **Throws:** L **Pos:** CF-151; PH-2; DH-1; PR-1   **Ht:** 6'2" **Wt:** 190 **Born:** 11/5/73 **Age:** 29

| | | | | | | | | BATTING | | | | | | | | | | | | BASERUNNING | | | | AVERAGES | | |
Year Team	Lg	G	AB	H	2B	3B	HR	(Hm Rd)	TB	R	RBI	RC	TBB	IBB	SO	HBP	SH	SF	SB	CS	SB%	GDP	Avg	OBP	Slg
1995 Kansas City	AL	47	188	53	11	5	3	(1 2)	83	32	23	29	12	0	22	1	2	3	7	0	1.00	2	.282	.324	.441
1996 Kansas City	AL	145	517	140	22	5	6	(3 3)	190	61	50	64	31	3	64	3	10	5	25	5	.83	4	.271	.313	.368
1997 Kansas City	AL	146	472	130	12	8	8	(3 5)	182	70	48	63	42	2	70	3	6	1	16	10	.62	3	.275	.338	.386
1998 Kansas City	AL	161	642	178	30	10	18	(11 7)	282	104	66	98	58	4	84	4	3	6	26	12	.68	4	.277	.339	.439
1999 Kansas City	AL	145	583	179	39	9	14	(5 9)	278	101	77	108	67	5	50	3	3	4	36	6	.86	13	.307	.379	.477
2000 Kansas City	AL	159	655	214	42	10	16	(10 6)	324	136	88	129	65	4	60	1	8	12	46	9	.84	7	.327	.382	.495
2001 Oakland	AL	155	644	165	34	4	9	(2 7)	234	108	49	79	61	1	70	5	5	4	27	12	.69	7	.256	.324	.363
2002 Boston	AL	154	623	178	34	11	14	(5 9)	276	118	63	100	65	5	70	6	3	5	31	6	.84	4	.286	.356	.443
8 ML YEARS		1112	4324	1237	224	62	88	(40 48)	1849	730	464	670	401	24	490	26	40	37	214	60	.78	44	.286	.348	.428

Vic Darensbourg

Pitches: L **Bats:** L **Pos:** RP-42   **Ht:** 5'8" **Wt:** 170 **Born:** 11/13/70 **Age:** 32

		HOW MUCH HE PITCHED						WHAT HE GAVE UP											THE RESULTS						
Year Team	Lg	G	GS	CG	GF	IP	BFP	H	R	ER	HR	SH	SF	HB	TBB	IBB	SO	WP	Bk	W	L	Pct	ShO	Sv-Op	Hld	ERC	ERA
1998 Florida	NL	59	0	0	10	71.0	287	52	5	29	5	3	3	6	30	6	74	4	0	0	7	.000	0	1-2	13	2.47	3.68
1999 Florida	NL	56	0	0	5	34.2	180	50	36	34	3	5	2	5	21	1	16	1	3	0	1	.000	0	0-1	10	7.90	8.83
2000 Florida	NL	56	0	0	17	62.0	274	61	32	28	7	3	6	2	28	1	59	0	0	5	3	.625	0	0-1	4	4.33	4.06
2001 Florida	NL	58	0	0	19	48.2	202	52	24	23	4	1	2	1	10	6	33	0	0	1	2	.333	0	1-3	11	3.52	4.25
2002 Florida	NL	42	0	0	13	48.1	233	61	34	33	10	2	3	2	26	4	33	0	0	1	2	.333	0	0-0	3	6.98	6.14
5 ML YEARS		271	0	0	64	264.2	1176	276	131	147	29	14	16	10	115	18	215	6	3	7	15	.318	0	2-7	40	4.53	5.00

Brian Daubach

Bats: L **Throws:** R **Pos:** 1B-60; LF-35; DH-28; PH-15; RF-13   **Ht:** 6'1" **Wt:** 233 **Born:** 2/11/72 **Age:** 31

		BATTING																	BASERUNNING				AVERAGES		
Year Team	Lg	G	AB	H	2B	3B	HR	(Hm	Rd)	TB	R	RBI	RC	TBB	IBB	SO	HBP	SH	SF	SB	CS	SB%	GDP	Avg	OBP	Slg
1998 Florida	NL	10	15	3	1	0	0	(-	-)	4	0	3	1	1	0	5	1	0	0	0	0	-	0	.200	.294	.267
1999 Boston	AL	110	381	112	33	3	21	(11	10)	214	61	73	74	36	0	92	3	0	0	0	1	.00	5	.294	.360	.562
2000 Boston	AL	142	495	123	32	2	21	(10	11)	222	55	76	70	44	2	130	6	0	4	1	1	.50	6	.248	.315	.448
2001 Boston	AL	122	407	107	28	3	22	(11	11)	207	54	71	71	53	7	108	5	1	6	1	0	1.00	0	.263	.350	.509
2002 Boston	AL	137	444	118	24	2	20	(11	9)	206	62	78	76	51	4	126	7	0	4	2	1	.67	10	.266	.348	.464
5 ML YEARS		521	1742	463	118	10	84	(43	41)	853	232	301	292	185	13	461	22	1	14	4	3	.57	31	.266	.341	.490

Jeff DaVanon

Bats: B **Throws:** R **Pos:** PH-6; CF-4; RF-4; LF-2; DH-2; PR-2   **Ht:** 6'0" **Wt:** 185 **Born:** 12/8/73 **Age:** 29

		BATTING																	BASERUNNING				AVERAGES		
Year Team	Lg	G	AB	H	2B	3B	HR	(Hm	Rd)	TB	R	RBI	RC	TBB	IBB	SO	HBP	SH	SF	SB	CS	SB%	GDP	Avg	OBP	Slg
2002 Angels*	R	5	15	10	6	1	0	(-	-)	18	5	4	10	5	0	2	0	0	1	2	0	1.00	0	.667	.714	1.200
2002 Salt Lake*	AAA	25	100	33	10	1	5	(-	-)	60	21	18	25	17	0	24	1	1	1	5	3	.63	1	.330	.429	.600
1999 Anaheim	AL	7	20	4	0	1	1	(1	0)	9	4	4	2	2	0	7	0	0	0	1	0	1.00	1	.200	.273	.450
2001 Anaheim	AL	40	88	17	2	1	5	(3	2)	36	7	9	9	11	0	29	0	0	1	1	3	.25	1	.193	.280	.409
2002 Anaheim	AL	16	30	5	3	0	1	(0	1)	11	3	4	4	2	0	6	0	1	0	1	0	1.00	0	.167	.219	.367
3 ML YEARS		63	138	26	5	2	7	(4	3)	56	14	17	15	15	0	42	0	1	1	2	4	.33	1	.188	.266	.406

Tom Davey

Pitches: R **Bats:** R **Pos:** RP-19   **Ht:** 6'7" **Wt:** 230 **Born:** 9/11/73 **Age:** 29

		HOW MUCH HE PITCHED						WHAT HE GAVE UP											THE RESULTS						
Year Team	Lg	G	GS	CG	GF	IP	BFP	H	R	ER	HR	SH	SF	HB	TBB	IBB	SO	WP	Bk	W	L	Pct	ShO	Sv-Op	Hld	ERC	ERA
1999 Tor-Sea	AL	45	0	0	15	65.0	298	62	41	34	5	1	2	7	40	1	59	6	0	2	1	.667	0	1-1	4	4.87	4.71
2000 San Diego	NL	11	0	0	2	12.2	50	12	1	1	0	0	0	0	2	0	6	1	0	2	1	.667	0	0-1	2	2.33	0.71
2001 San Diego	NL	39	0	0	8	38.0	169	41	22	19	3	0	0	1	17	3	37	3	1	2	4	.333	0	0-4	12	4.53	4.50
2002 San Diego	NL	19	0	0	2	21.0	97	23	14	13	2	0	3	3	11	1	21	1	0	1	0	1.000	0	0-1	2	5.63	5.57
1999 Toronto	AL	29	0	0	10	44.0	198	40	28	23	5	1	2	3	26	0	42	6	0	1	1	.500	0	1-1	3	4.65	4.70
1999 Seattle	AL	16	0	0	5	21.0	100	22	13	11	0	0	0	4	14	1	17	0	0	1	0	1.000	0	0-0	1	5.28	4.71
4 ML YEARS		114	0	0	27	136.2	614	138	78	67	10	1	5	11	70	5	123	11	1	7	6	.538	0	1-7	20	4.63	4.41

Ben Davis

Bats: B **Throws:** R **Pos:** C-77; PH-9; 1B-3; PR-2   **Ht:** 6'4" **Wt:** 214 **Born:** 3/10/77 **Age:** 26

		BATTING																	BASERUNNING				AVERAGES		
Year Team	Lg	G	AB	H	2B	3B	HR	(Hm	Rd)	TB	R	RBI	RC	TBB	IBB	SO	HBP	SH	SF	SB	CS	SB%	GDP	Avg	OBP	Slg
1998 San Diego	NL	1	1	0	0	0	0	(0	0)	0	0	0	0	0	0	0	0	0	0	0	0	-	0	.000	.000	.000
1999 San Diego	NL	76	266	65	14	1	5	(1	4)	96	29	30	27	25	3	70	0	0	2	2	1	.67	9	.244	.307	.361
2000 San Diego	NL	43	130	29	6	0	3	(1	2)	44	12	14	13	14	1	35	0	3	1	1	1	.50	1	.223	.297	.338
2001 San Diego	NL	138	448	107	20	0	11	(3	8)	160	56	57	54	66	5	112	4	1	7	4	4	.50	13	.239	.337	.357
2002 Seattle	AL	80	228	59	10	1	7	(1	6)	92	24	43	32	18	1	58	2	1	4	1	1	.50	6	.259	.313	.404
5 ML YEARS		338	1073	260	50	2	26	(6	20)	392	121	144	126	123	10	275	6	5	14	8	7	.53	30	.242	.320	.365

Doug Davis

Pitches: L **Bats:** R **Pos:** SP-10   **Ht:** 6'4" **Wt:** 190 **Born:** 9/21/75 **Age:** 27

		HOW MUCH HE PITCHED						WHAT HE GAVE UP											THE RESULTS						
Year Team	Lg	G	GS	CG	GF	IP	BFP	H	R	ER	HR	SH	SF	HB	TBB	IBB	SO	WP	Bk	W	L	Pct	ShO	Sv-Op	Hld	ERC	ERA
2002 Oklahoma*	AAA	9	9	0	0	61.1	257	70	38	34	7	1	1	3	11	0	48	0	0	4	3	.571	0	0- -	-	4.39	4.99
1999 Texas	AL	2	0	0	0	2.2	20	12	10	10	3	0	0	0	3	0	3	0	0	0	0	-	0	0-0	0	41.42	33.75
2000 Texas	AL	30	13	1	4	98.2	450	109	61	59	14	6	4	3	58	3	66	5	1	7	6	.538	0	0-3	2	5.93	5.38
2001 Texas	AL	30	30	1	0	186.0	828	220	103	92	14	4	6	3	69	1	115	7	2	11	10	.524	1	0-0	0	4.90	4.45
2002 Texas	AL	10	10	1	0	59.2	262	67	36	33	7	3	3	3	22	0	28	2	2	3	5	.375	1	0-0	0	5.05	4.98
4 ML YEARS		72	53	3	4	347.0	1560	408	210	194	38	13	13	9	149	4	212	14	5	21	21	.500	1	0-3	2	5.41	5.03

J.J. Davis

Bats: R **Throws:** R **Pos:** PH-5; RF-4   **Ht:** 6'5" **Wt:** 250 **Born:** 10/25/78 **Age:** 24

		BATTING																	BASERUNNING				AVERAGES		
Year Team	Lg	G	AB	H	2B	3B	HR	(Hm	Rd)	TB	R	RBI	RC	TBB	IBB	SO	HBP	SH	SF	SB	CS	SB%	GDP	Avg	OBP	Slg
1997 Pirates	R	45	165	42	10	2	1	(-	-)	59	19	18	18	14	2	44	2	0	3	0	0	-	4	.255	.315	.358
1997 Erie	A-	4	13	1	0	0	0	(-	-)	1	1	0	0	0	0	4	0	0	0	0	0	-	0	.077	.077	.077
1998 Augusta	A	30	106	21	6	0	4	(-	-)	39	11	11	7	3	0	24	0	0	0	1	1	.50	4	.198	.220	.368
1998 Erie	A-	52	196	53	12	2	8	(-	-)	93	25	39	32	20	1	54	2	0	2	4	1	.80	5	.270	.341	.474
1999 Hickory	A	86	317	84	26	1	19	(-	-)	169	58	65	59	44	3	99	4	0	2	2	5	.29	3	.265	.360	.533

		BATTING																		BASERUNNING				AVERAGES		
Year Team	Lg	G	AB	H	2B	3B	HR	(Hm Rd)	TB	R	RBI	RC	TBB	IBB	SO	HBP	SH	SF	SB	CS	SB%	GDP	Avg	OBP	Slg
2000 Lynchburg	A+	130	485	118	36	1	20	(- -)	216	77	80	68	52	2	171	4	0	4	9	4	.69	11	.243	.319	.445
2001 Altoona	AA	67	228	57	13	3	4	(- -)	88	21	26	27	21	0	79	2	0	1	2	5	.29	1	.250	.317	.386
2001 Pirates	R	4	17	8	1	0	2	(- -)	15	3	6	6	1	0	2	0	0	0	0	0	-	1	.471	.500	.882
2002 Altoona	AA	101	348	100	17	3	20	(- -)	183	51	62	63	33	0	101	3	0	3	7	4	.64	3	.287	.351	.526
2002 Pittsburgh	NL	9	10	1	0	0	0	(0 0)	1	1	0	0	0	0	4	1	0	0	0	0	-	1	.100	.182	.100

Jason Davis

Pitches: R **Bats:** R **Pos:** SP-2; RP-1   **Ht:** 6'6" **Wt:** 195 **Born:** 5/8/80 **Age:** 23

		HOW MUCH HE PITCHED						WHAT HE GAVE UP											THE RESULTS						
Year Team	Lg	G	GS	CG	GF	IP	BFP	H	R	ER	HR	SH	SF	HB	TBB	IBB	SO	WP	Bk	W	L	Pct	ShO	Sv-Op	Hld	ERC	ERA
2000 Burlington	R+	10	10	0	0	45.0	201	48	27	22	5	3	3	5	16	0	35	5	1	4	4	.500	0	0--	-	4.77	4.40
2001 Columbus	A	27	27	1	0	160.0	677	147	72	48	9	2	2	14	51	1	115	5	2	14	6	.700	1	0--	-	3.35	2.70
2002 Kinston	A+	17	17	1	0	99.2	442	107	64	46	7	7	3	8	31	2	68	6	0	3	6	.333	1	0--	-	4.13	4.15
2002 Akron	AA	10	10	0	0	59.0	250	63	26	23	2	1	1	5	16	0	45	3	2	6	2	.750	0	0--	-	3.90	3.51
2002 Cleveland	AL	3	2	0	0	14.2	60	12	3	3	1	1	0	0	4	0	11	0	1	1	0	1.000	0	0-0	0	2.40	1.84

Kane Davis

Pitches: R **Bats:** R **Pos:** RP-16   **Ht:** 6'3" **Wt:** 194 **Born:** 6/25/75 **Age:** 28

		HOW MUCH HE PITCHED						WHAT HE GAVE UP											THE RESULTS						
Year Team	Lg	G	GS	CG	GF	IP	BFP	H	R	ER	HR	SH	SF	HB	TBB	IBB	SO	WP	Bk	W	L	Pct	ShO	Sv-Op	Hld	ERC	ERA
2002 Norfolk*	AAA	1	0	0	0	1.0	4	1	0	0	0	0	0	0	0	0	2	0	0	0	0	-	0	0--	-	1.95	0.00
2000 Cle-Mil		8	2	0	1	15.0	85	27	24	21	4	0	0	2	13	0	4	0	1	0	3	.000	0	0-0	0	13.77	12.60
2001 Colorado	NL	57	0	0	6	68.1	301	66	36	33	11	2	4	1	32	4	47	4	0	2	4	.333	0	0-5	9	4.50	4.35
2002 New York	NL	16	0	0	5	14.0	70	15	11	11	2	2	1	1	11	2	24	1	0	1	1	.500	0	0-0	1	6.19	7.07
2000 Cleveland	AL	5	2	0	0	11.0	61	20	21	18	3	0	0	1	8	0	2	0	1	0	3	.000	0	0-0	0	12.94	14.73
2000 Milwaukee	NL	3	0	0	1	4.0	24	7	3	3	1	0	0	1	5	0	2	0	0	0	0	-	0	0-0	0	16.04	6.75
3 ML YEARS		81	2	0	12	97.1	456	108	71	65	17	4	5	4	56	6	75	5	1	3	8	.273	0	0-5	10	5.99	6.01

Gookie Dawkins

Bats: R **Throws:** R **Pos:** SS-21; PH-8; PR-4; 2B-3   **Ht:** 6'1" **Wt:** 180 **Born:** 5/12/79 **Age:** 24

		BATTING																		BASERUNNING				AVERAGES		
Year Team	Lg	G	AB	H	2B	3B	HR	(Hm Rd)	TB	R	RBI	RC	TBB	IBB	SO	HBP	SH	SF	SB	CS	SB%	GDP	Avg	OBP	Slg
2002 Chattanooga*	AA	40	155	42	10	1	1	(- -)	57	21	12	20	25	0	28	0	2	0	5	5	.50	8	.271	.372	.368
2002 Louisville*	AAA	47	167	42	5	2	0	(- -)	51	14	8	14	12	2	34	1	0	2	2	3	.40	5	.251	.302	.305
1999 Cincinnati	NL	7	7	1	0	0	0	(0 0)	1	1	0	0	0	0	4	1	0	0	0	0	-	0	.143	.250	.143
2000 Cincinnati	NL	14	41	9	2	0	0	(0 0)	11	5	3	2	2	1	7	0	1	0	0	0	-	3	.220	.256	.268
2002 Cincinnati	NL	31	48	6	2	0	0	(0 0)	8	2	0	1	6	0	21	0	1	0	2	1	.67	1	.125	.222	.167
3 ML YEARS		52	96	16	4	0	0	(0 0)	20	8	3	3	8	1	32	1	2	0	2	1	.67	4	.167	.238	.208

Joey Dawley

Pitches: R **Bats:** R **Pos:** RP-1   **Ht:** 6'4" **Wt:** 205 **Born:** 9/19/71 **Age:** 31

		HOW MUCH HE PITCHED						WHAT HE GAVE UP											THE RESULTS						
Year Team	Lg	G	GS	CG	GF	IP	BFP	H	R	ER	HR	SH	SF	HB	TBB	IBB	SO	WP	Bk	W	L	Pct	ShO	Sv-Op	Hld	ERC	ERA
1993 Bluefield	R+	20	0	0	15	30.2	143	34	20	12	1	2	1	1	14	3	30	3	1	3	1	.750	0	3--	-	4.18	3.52
1994 Bluefield	R+	11	0	0	5	23.2	110	20	18	15	2	0	1	1	18	0	18	4	0	2	2	.333	0	2--	-	4.55	5.70
1994 Albany	A	5	0	0	4	7.1	37	7	6	5	0	0	1	1	7	1	4	1	0	0	0	-	0	0--	-	5.28	6.14
1995 Frederick	A	24	0	0	8	32.2	163	41	28	23	4	1	1	3	22	1	29	5	1	1	2	.333	0	1--	-	7.14	6.34
1995 Palm Spring	IND	15	0	0	4	28.0	128	28	14	12	2	0	1	2	9	0	20	1	1	1	0	1.000	0	0--	-	3.58	3.86
1996 Palm Spring	IND	27	0	0	18	33.2	146	26	14	6	3	0	0	1	18	1	29	2	1	2	1	.667	0	4--	-	3.27	1.60
1997 Chico	IND	41	0	0	35	41.1	196	42	24	20	2	0	2	2	18	2	51	2	1	1	4	.200	0	14--	-	3.70	4.35
1998 Chico	IND	45	0	0	41	43.0	196	43	22	16	2	2	2	0	27	2	36	5	0	2	4	.333	0	26--	-	4.44	3.35
1999 Greenville	AA	26	11	0	2	91.2	387	76	54	41	5	3	4	3	37	3	89	3	2	5	3	.625	0	0--	-	2.91	4.03
1999 Richmond	AAA	7	7	1	0	40.0	174	43	26	23	5	3	2	0	12	0	31	4	0	3	0	.000	0	0--	-	4.20	5.18
2001 Myrtle Beach	A+	5	0	0	2	10.0	34	4	2	2	1	0	0	0	0	0	16	0	0	1	0	1.000	0	0--	-	0.35	1.80
2001 Richmond	AAA	3	0	0	1	6.1	22	3	2	2	1	0	0	0	1	0	5	1	0	0	0	-	0	0--	-	1.23	2.84
2001 Greenville	AA	22	21	1	0	127.1	518	95	50	43	15	6	4	4	46	0	130	3	1	7	5	.583	0	0--	-	2.82	3.04
2002 Richmond	AAA	24	23	1	1	140.1	564	113	44	41	10	5	4	5	36	0	136	3	1	9	7	.563	1	0--	-	2.48	2.63
2002 Atlanta	NL	1	0	0	1	0.1	1	0	0	0	0	0	0	0	0	0	1	0	0	0	0	-	0	0-0	0	0.00	0.00

Zach Day

Pitches: R **Bats:** R **Pos:** RP-17; SP-2   **Ht:** 6'4" **Wt:** 185 **Born:** 6/15/78 **Age:** 25

		HOW MUCH HE PITCHED						WHAT HE GAVE UP											THE RESULTS						
Year Team	Lg	G	GS	CG	GF	IP	BFP	H	R	ER	HR	SH	SF	HB	TBB	IBB	SO	WP	Bk	W	L	Pct	ShO	Sv-Op	Hld	ERC	ERA
1996 Yankees	R	7	5	0	1	33.2	139	41	26	21	3	0	0	4	3	0	23	0	0	5	2	.714	0	0--	-	4.71	5.61
1997 Oneonta	A-	14	14	0	0	92.0	372	82	26	22	2	2	4	1	23	0	93	3	0	7	2	.778	0	0--	-	2.50	2.15
1998 Tampa	A+	18	17	0	0	100.0	479	142	89	61	5	3	2	6	32	4	69	5	0	5	8	.385	0	0--	-	5.86	5.49
1998 Greensboro	A	7	6	1	0	36.0	155	35	22	11	1	2	1	3	6	0	37	4	0	2	2	.333	0	0--	-	2.75	2.75
1999 Yankees	R	5	4	0	0	16.2	74	20	10	7	1	0	1	0	4	0	17	0	0	1	1	.500	0	0--	-	4.47	3.78
1999 Greensboro	A	2	2	0	0	8.0	42	14	11	6	2	0	1	1	1	0	6	3	0	1	0	1.000	0	0--	-	6.62	6.75
2000 Greensboro	A	13	13	1	0	85.1	343	72	29	18	6	0	0	1	31	0	101	11	1	9	3	.750	1	0--	-	3.05	1.90
2000 Tampa	A+	7	7	0	0	34.1	150	33	22	16	2	0	0	2	15	1	36	1	0	2	4	.333	0	0--	-	3.73	4.19
2000 Akron	AA	8	8	0	0	46.0	192	38	20	18	1	4	0	3	21	0	43	4	0	4	2	.667	0	0--	-	3.13	3.52
2001 Akron	AA	22	22	2	0	136.2	572	123	57	47	8	3	1	4	45	1	94	7	0	9	10	.474	0	0--	-	3.08	3.10
2001 Buffalo	AAA	1	1	0	0	6.0	22	3	1	1	0	0	0	0	4	0	1	0	0	2	0	1.000	0	0--	-	0.80	1.50
2001 Ottawa	AAA	5	4	0	0	26.2	120	38	23	22	2	0	1	2	8	0	15	3	0	2	2	.500	0	0--	-	6.59	7.43
2002 Ottawa	AAA	17	16	1	0	90.0	373	77	38	35	5	3	1	4	32	0	68	7	0	5	6	.455	0	0--	-	3.03	3.50
2002 Montreal	NL	19	2	0	5	37.1	153	28	18	15	2	0	1	1	15	2	25	1	0	4	1	.800	0	1-2	2	2.66	3.62

Luis de los Santos

Pitches: R **Bats:** R **Pos:** SP-3 **Ht:** 6'2" **Wt:** 216 **Born:** 11/1/77 **Age:** 25

				HOW MUCH HE PITCHED				WHAT HE GAVE UP											THE RESULTS								
Year Team	Lg	G	GS	CG	GF	IP	BFP	H	R	ER	HR	SH	SF	HB	TBB	IBB	SO	WP	Bk	W	L	Pct	ShO	Sv-Op	Hld	ERC	ERA
1995 Yankees	R	2	0	0	1	5.0	23	5	2	0	0	0	0	1	2	0	6	0	0	0	0	-	0	0--	-	3.99	0.00
1996 Greensboro	A	7	6	0	0	31.2	141	39	17	17	4	0	1	0	11	0	21	0	0	4	1	.800	0	0--	-	5.44	4.83
1996 Oneonta	A-	10	10	3	0	58.0	240	44	28	24	3	0	3	3	21	0	62	2	1	4	4	.500	2	0--	-	2.51	3.72
1997 Greensboro	A	14	14	1	0	88.2	377	91	45	30	3	3	6	7	13	0	62	4	0	5	6	.455	0	0--	-	3.03	3.05
1997 Tampa	A+	10	10	0	0	61.2	240	49	19	16	4	0	3	2	8	0	39	0	1	5	0	1.000	0	0--	-	1.96	2.34
1997 Norwich	AA	4	4	0	0	25.0	104	23	9	7	4	1	1	0	7	0	15	0	1	1	1	.500	0	0--	-	3.53	2.52
1998 Norwich	AA	13	13	2	0	79.0	360	97	49	43	4	1	3	7	23	2	51	4	0	2	6	.250	0	0--	-	4.82	4.90
1998 Tampa	A+	10	10	1	0	66.2	280	69	40	31	2	3	2	3	11	0	33	5	1	4	2	.667	0	0--	-	3.03	4.19
1999 Columbus	AAA	12	12	0	0	66.0	299	81	42	35	11	1	0	4	24	0	45	1	0	6	3	.667	0	0--	-	6.05	4.77
1999 Yankees	R	2	2	0	0	8.0	28	5	0	0	0	0	0	1	0	0	7	0	0	0	0	-	0	0--	-	1.11	0.00
2000 Yankees	R	4	3	0	0	15.0	64	15	5	5	0	0	0	0	6	0	19	0	1	2	0	1.000	0	0--	-	3.40	3.00
2002 Durham	AAA	24	16	1	2	115.1	453	105	38	31	8	4	2	5	21	0	68	2	0	9	2	.818	1	0--	-	2.86	2.42
2002 Tampa Bay	AL	3	3	0	0	14.0	71	24	19	18	5	0	2	3	4	0	7	0	0	0	3	.000	0	0-0	0	11.49	11.57

Valerio de los Santos

Pitches: L **Bats:** L **Pos:** RP-51 **Ht:** 6'2" **Wt:** 206 **Born:** 10/6/72 **Age:** 30

				HOW MUCH HE PITCHED				WHAT HE GAVE UP											THE RESULTS								
Year Team	Lg	G	GS	CG	GF	IP	BFP	H	R	ER	HR	SH	SF	HB	TBB	IBB	SO	WP	Bk	W	L	Pct	ShO	Sv-Op	Hld	ERC	ERA
2002 Indianapolis*	AAA	2	0	0	0	2.0	8	1	0	0	0	0	0	0	1	0	5	0	0	1	0	1.000	0	0--	-	1.41	0.00
1998 Milwaukee	NL	13	0	0	3	21.2	75	11	7	7	4	0	0	0	2	0	18	1	0	0	0	-	0	0-0	0	1.25	2.91
1999 Milwaukee	NL	7	0	0	3	8.1	43	12	6	6	1	0	0	1	7	0	5	1	0	0	1	.000	0	0-0	0	9.65	6.48
2000 Milwaukee	NL	66	2	0	15	73.2	320	72	43	42	15	2	1	1	33	7	70	3	1	2	3	.400	0	0-1	9	4.79	5.13
2001 Milwaukee	NL	1	0	0	0	1.0	5	1	1	1	0	0	0	0	1	0	1	0	0	0	0	-	0	0-0	0	5.48	9.00
2002 Milwaukee	NL	51	0	0	12	57.2	237	42	21	20	4	3	7	2	26	3	38	1	0	2	3	.400	0	0-0	7	2.70	3.12
5 ML YEARS		138	2	0	33	162.1	680	138	78	76	24	5	8	4	69	10	132	6	1	4	7	.364	0	0-1	16	3.71	4.21

Kory DeHaan

Bats: L **Throws:** R **Pos:** LF-6; PR-3; CF-2; PH-2; RF-1 **Ht:** 6'2" **Wt:** 187 **Born:** 7/16/76 **Age:** 26

								BATTING											BASERUNNING				AVERAGES		
Year Team	Lg	G	AB	H	2B	3B	HR	(Hm	Rd)	TB	R	RBI	RC	TBB	IBB	SO	HBP	SH	SF	SB	CS	SB%	GDP	Avg	OBP	Slg
1997 Erie	A-	58	205	49	8	6	1	(-	-)	72	43	18	28	38	2	43	2	6	4	14	9	.61	4	.239	.357	.351
1998 Augusta	A	132	475	149	39	8	8	(-	-)	228	85	75	96	69	3	114	8	8	7	33	13	.72	4	.314	.404	.480
1999 Lynchburg	A+	78	295	96	19	5	7	(-	-)	146	55	42	60	36	3	63	4	4	1	32	10	.76	4	.325	.405	.495
1999 Altoona	AA	47	190	51	13	2	3	(-	-)	77	26	24	24	11	0	46	2	5	3	14	6	.70	3	.268	.311	.405
2000 R Cucamnga	A+	4	14	3	1	0	1	(-	-)	7	2	1	2	1	0	4	0	0	0	0	0	-	0	.214	.267	.500
2000 Las Vegas	AAA	10	41	12	4	0	0	(-	-)	16	7	3	6	2	0	11	1	1	1	3	0	1.00	1	.293	.333	.390
2001 Portland	AAA	87	304	77	9	5	7	(-	-)	117	35	28	34	20	1	71	2	1	1	12	9	.57	4	.253	.303	.385
2001 Mobile	AA	42	159	47	8	2	4	(-	-)	71	29	23	29	22	1	27	2	2	3	12	4	.75	2	.296	.382	.447
2002 Portland	AAA	120	442	125	31	14	2	(-	-)	190	64	39	67	31	2	96	9	2	4	23	9	.72	2	.283	.340	.430
2000 San Diego	NL	90	103	21	7	0	2	(1	1)	34	19	13	7	5	0	39	0	1	1	4	2	.67	2	.204	.239	.330
2002 San Diego	NL	12	11	1	0	0	0	(0	0)	1	1	0	0	0	0	6	0	0	0	0	0	-	0	.091	.091	.091
2 ML YEARS		102	114	22	7	0	2	(1	1)	35	20	13	7	5	0	45	0	1	1	4	2	.67	2	.193	.225	.307

Mike DeJean

Pitches: R **Bats:** R **Pos:** RP-68 **Ht:** 6'4" **Wt:** 219 **Born:** 9/28/70 **Age:** 32

				HOW MUCH HE PITCHED				WHAT HE GAVE UP											THE RESULTS								
Year Team	Lg	G	GS	CG	GF	IP	BFP	H	R	ER	HR	SH	SF	HB	TBB	IBB	SO	WP	Bk	W	L	Pct	ShO	Sv-Op	Hld	ERC	ERA
1997 Colorado	NL	55	0	0	15	67.2	295	74	34	30	4	3	1	3	24	2	38	2	0	5	0	1.000	0	2-4	13	4.29	3.99
1998 Colorado	NL	59	1	0	14	74.1	307	78	29	25	4	4	4	1	24	1	27	3	0	3	1	.750	0	2-3	11	3.92	3.03
1999 Colorado	NL	56	0	0	17	61.0	288	83	61	57	13	3	3	2	32	8	31	3	0	2	4	.333	0	0-4	9	7.77	8.41
2000 Colorado	NL	54	0	0	15	53.1	235	54	31	29	9	3	1	0	30	6	34	5	0	4	4	.500	0	0-4	7	5.22	4.89
2001 Milwaukee	NL	75	0	0	19	84.1	371	75	31	26	4	1	4	9	39	7	68	8	0	4	2	.667	0	2-4	8	3.56	2.77
2002 Milwaukee	NL	68	0	0	60	75.0	326	66	28	26	7	4	2	2	39	8	65	7	0	1	5	.167	0	27-30	0	3.74	3.12
6 ML YEARS		367	1	0	135	415.2	1822	430	214	193	41	18	15	17	188	32	263	28	0	19	16	.543	0	33-49	48	4.55	4.18

Carlos Delgado

Bats: L **Throws:** R **Pos:** 1B-140; DH-3 **Ht:** 6'3" **Wt:** 230 **Born:** 6/25/72 **Age:** 31

								BATTING											BASERUNNING				AVERAGES		
Year Team	Lg	G	AB	H	2B	3B	HR	(Hm	Rd)	TB	R	RBI	RC	TBB	IBB	SO	HBP	SH	SF	SB	CS	SB%	GDP	Avg	OBP	Slg
1993 Toronto	AL	2	1	0	0	0	0	(0	0)	0	0	0	0	1	0	0	0	0	0	0	0	-	0	.000	.500	.000
1994 Toronto	AL	43	130	28	2	0	9	(5	4)	57	17	24	20	25	4	46	3	0	1	1	1	.50	5	.215	.352	.438
1995 Toronto	AL	37	91	15	3	0	3	(2	1)	27	7	11	5	6	0	26	0	0	2	0	0	-	1	.165	.212	.297
1996 Toronto	AL	138	488	132	28	2	25	(12	13)	239	68	92	83	58	2	139	9	0	8	0	0	-	13	.270	.353	.490
1997 Toronto	AL	153	519	136	42	3	30	(17	13)	274	79	91	94	64	9	133	8	0	4	0	3	.00	6	.262	.350	.528
1998 Toronto	AL	142	530	155	43	1	38	(20	18)	314	94	115	117	73	13	139	11	0	6	3	0	1.00	8	.292	.385	.592
1999 Toronto	AL	152	573	156	39	0	44	(17	27)	327	113	134	121	86	7	141	15	0	7	1	1	.50	11	.272	.377	.571
2000 Toronto	AL	162	569	196	57	1	41	(30	11)	378	115	137	164	123	18	104	15	0	4	0	1	.00	12	.344	.470	.664
2001 Toronto	AL	162	574	160	31	1	39	(13	26)	310	102	102	126	111	22	136	16	0	3	3	0	1.00	9	.279	.408	.540
2002 Toronto	AL	143	505	140	34	2	33	(17	16)	277	103	108	118	102	18	126	13	0	8	1	0	1.00	1	.277	.406	.549
10 ML YEARS		1134	3980	1118	279	10	262	(133	129)	2203	698	814	848	649	93	990	90	0	43	9	6	.60	73	.281	.390	.554

Wilson Delgado

Bats: B **Throws:** R **Pos:** SS-8; PH-4; PR-1   **Ht:** 5'11" **Wt:** 165 **Born:** 7/15/72 **Age:** 30

Year Team	Lg	G	AB	H	2B	3B	HR	(Hm	Rd)	TB	R	RBI	RC	TBB	IBB	SO	HBP	SH	SF	SB	CS	SB%	GDP	Avg	OBP	Slg
2002 Memphis*	AAA	98	365	95	19	2	7	(-	-)	139	31	35	41	23	4	54	3	5	1	2	5	.29	6	.260	.309	.381
1996 San Francisco	NL	6	22	8	0	0	0	(0	0)	8	3	2	4	1	0	5	2	0	0	1	0	1.00	0	.364	.440	.364
1997 San Francisco	NL	8	7	1	1	0	0	(0	0)	2	1	0	0	0	0	2	0	1	0	0	0	-	0	.143	.143	.286
1998 San Francisco	NL	10	12	2	1	0	0	(0	0)	3	1	1	1	1	0	3	0	0	0	0	0	-	0	.167	.231	.250
1999 San Francisco	NL	35	71	18	2	1	0	(0	0)	22	7	3	7	5	0	9	1	1	0	1	0	1.00	0	.254	.312	.310
2000 NYY-KC	AL	64	128	33	2	0	1	(0	1)	38	21	11	12	11	0	26	0	0	2	2	1	.67	2	.258	.312	.297
2001 Kansas City	AL	14	25	3	0	0	0	(0	0)	3	1	1	0	3	0	10	0	0	1	0	0	-	1	.120	.214	.120
2002 St Louis	NL	12	20	4	2	0	2	(2	0)	12	2	5	2	0	0	6	0	1	0	0	0	-	0	.200	.200	.600
2000 New York	AL	31	45	11	1	0	1	(0	1)	15	6	4	5	5	0	9	0	0	1	1	0	1.00	1	.244	.314	.333
2000 Kansas City	AL	33	83	22	1	0	0	(0	0)	23	15	7	7	6	0	17	0	0	1	1	1	.50	1	.265	.311	.277
7 ML YEARS		149	285	69	8	1	3	(2	1)	88	36	23	26	21	0	61	3	3	2	4	1	.80	5	.242	.299	.309

David Dellucci

Bats: L **Throws:** L **Pos:** RF-45; PH-35; LF-20; DH-3; PR-3; CF-2   **Ht:** 5'11" **Wt:** 198 **Born:** 10/31/73 **Age:** 29

Year Team	Lg	G	AB	H	2B	3B	HR	(Hm	Rd)	TB	R	RBI	RC	TBB	IBB	SO	HBP	SH	SF	SB	CS	SB%	GDP	Avg	OBP	Slg
2002 Tucson*	AAA	4	15	2	1	0	0	(-	-)	3	2	1	1	2	0	4	0	0	0	0	0	-	0	.133	.235	.200
1997 Baltimore	AL	17	27	6	1	0	1	(0	1)	10	3	3	3	4	1	7	1	0	0	0	0	-	2	.222	.344	.370
1998 Arizona	NL	124	416	108	19	12	5	(1	4)	166	43	51	51	33	2	103	3	0	1	3	5	.38	6	.260	.318	.399
1999 Arizona	NL	63	109	43	7	1	1	(0	1)	55	27	15	24	11	0	24	3	0	0	2	0	1.00	3	.394	.463	.505
2000 Arizona	NL	34	50	15	3	0	0	(0	0)	18	2	2	6	4	0	9	0	0	0	0	2	.00	1	.300	.352	.360
2001 Arizona	NL	115	217	60	10	2	10	(5	5)	104	28	40	36	22	4	52	2	0	0	2	1	.67	2	.276	.349	.479
2002 Arizona	NL	97	229	56	11	2	7	(2	5)	92	34	29	26	28	5	55	1	0	3	2	4	.33	7	.245	.326	.402
6 ML YEARS		450	1048	288	51	17	24	(8	16)	445	137	140	146	102	12	250	10	0	4	9	12	.43	21	.275	.344	.425

Ryan Dempster

Pitches: R **Bats:** R **Pos:** SP-33   **Ht:** 6'3" **Wt:** 215 **Born:** 5/3/77 **Age:** 26

Year Team	Lg	G	GS	CG	GF	IP	BFP	H	R	ER	HR	SH	SF	HB	TBB	IBB	SO	WP	Bk	W	L	Pct	ShO	Sv-Op	Hld	ERC	ERA
1998 Florida	NL	14	11	0	1	54.2	272	72	47	43	6	5	6	9	38	1	35	5	0	1	5	.167	0	0-1	0	8.14	7.08
1999 Florida	NL	25	25	0	0	147.0	666	146	77	77	21	3	6	6	93	2	126	8	0	7	8	.467	0	0-0	0	5.49	4.71
2000 Florida	NL	33	33	2	0	226.1	974	210	102	92	30	4	5	5	97	7	209	4	0	14	10	.583	1	0-0	0	4.04	3.66
2001 Florida	NL	34	34	2	0	211.1	954	218	123	116	21	15	7	10	112	5	171	5	0	15	12	.556	1	0-0	0	4.91	4.94
2002 Fla-Cin	NL	33	33	4	0	209.0	915	228	127	125	28	9	6	10	93	2	153	2	0	10	13	.435	0	0-0	0	5.35	5.38
2002 Florida	NL	18	18	3	0	120.1	521	126	66	64	12	7	3	7	55	1	87	0	0	5	8	.385	0	0-0	0	4.95	4.79
2002 Cincinnati	NL	15	15	1	0	88.2	394	102	61	61	16	2	3	3	38	1	66	2	0	5	5	.500	0	0-0	0	5.90	6.19
5 ML YEARS		139	136	8	1	848.1	3781	874	476	453	106	36	30	40	433	17	694	24	0	47	48	.495	2	0-1	0	5.07	4.81

Sean DePaula

Pitches: R **Bats:** R **Pos:** RP-5   **Ht:** 6'4" **Wt:** 220 **Born:** 11/7/73 **Age:** 29

Year Team	Lg	G	GS	CG	GF	IP	BFP	H	R	ER	HR	SH	SF	HB	TBB	IBB	SO	WP	Bk	W	L	Pct	ShO	Sv-Op	Hld	ERC	ERA
2002 Buffalo*	AAA	34	0	0	18	57.0	244	55	26	25	6				18	0	53	4	0	2	3	.400	0	9- -			3.95
1999 Cleveland	AL	11	0	0	4	11.2	45	8	6	6	0	2	0	0	3	0	18	0	0	0	0	-	0	0-0	3	1.50	4.63
2000 Cleveland	AL	13	0	0	3	16.2	83	20	11	11	3	0	1	0	14	2	16	0	0	0	0	-	0	0-2	2	7.49	5.94
2002 Cleveland	AL	5	0	0	1	6.1	33	11	9	9	3	0	0	0	3	0	8	0	0	1	1	.500	0	0-2	1	12.28	12.79
3 ML YEARS		29	0	0	8	34.2	161	39	26	26	6	2	1	0	20	2	42	0	0	1	1	.500	0	0-4	6	5.94	6.75

Mark DeRosa

Bats: R **Throws:** R **Pos:** 2B-32; SS-19; PH-17; RF-5; 3B-4; LF-2; PR-2   **Ht:** 6'1" **Wt:** 205 **Born:** 2/26/75 **Age:** 28

Year Team	Lg	G	AB	H	2B	3B	HR	(Hm	Rd)	TB	R	RBI	RC	TBB	IBB	SO	HBP	SH	SF	SB	CS	SB%	GDP	Avg	OBP	Slg
2002 Richmond*	AAA	16	55	14	3	0	0	(-	-)	17	9	6	5	5	0	2	2	0	0	2	0	1.00	4	.255	.339	.309
2002 Myrtle Beach*	A+	2	7	0	0	0	0	(-	-)	0	0	0	0	1	0	1	0	0	0	0	0	-	0	.000	.125	.000
1998 Atlanta	NL	5	3	1	0	0	0	(0	0)	1	2	0	0	0	0	1	0	0	0	0	0	-	0	.333	.333	.333
1999 Atlanta	NL	7	8	0	0	0	0	(0	0)	0	0	0	0	0	0	2	0	0	0	0	0	-	0	.000	.000	.000
2000 Atlanta	NL	22	13	4	1	0	0	(0	0)	5	9	3	2	2	0	1	0	0	0	0	0	-	0	.308	.400	.385
2001 Atlanta	NL	66	164	47	8	0	3	(3	0)	64	27	20	22	12	6	19	5	1	2	2	1	.67	3	.287	.350	.390
2002 Atlanta	NL	72	212	63	9	2	5	(3	2)	91	24	23	27	12	3	24	3	2	3	2	3	.40	5	.297	.339	.429
5 ML YEARS		172	400	115	18	2	8	(6	2)	161	62	46	51	26	9	47	8	3	5	4	4	.50	8	.288	.339	.403

Delino DeShields

Bats: L **Throws:** R **Pos:** 2B-41; PH-22; PR-6; RF-1   **Ht:** 6'1" **Wt:** 180 **Born:** 1/15/69 **Age:** 34

Year Team	Lg	G	AB	H	2B	3B	HR	(Hm	Rd)	TB	R	RBI	RC	TBB	IBB	SO	HBP	SH	SF	SB	CS	SB%	GDP	Avg	OBP	Slg
1990 Montreal	NL	129	499	144	28	6	4	(3	1)	196	69	45	75	66	3	96	4	1	2	42	22	.66	10	.289	.375	.393
1991 Montreal	NL	151	563	134	15	4	10	(3	7)	187	83	51	74	95	2	151	2	8	5	56	23	.71	6	.238	.347	.332
1992 Montreal	NL	135	530	155	19	8	7	(1	6)	211	82	56	79	54	4	108	3	9	3	46	15	.75	10	.292	.359	.398
1993 Montreal	NL	123	481	142	17	7	2	(2	0)	179	75	29	79	72	3	64	3	4	2	43	10	.81	6	.295	.389	.372
1994 Los Angeles	NL	89	320	80	11	3	2	(1	1)	103	51	33	42	54	0	53	0	1	1	27	7	.79	9	.250	.357	.322
1995 Los Angeles	NL	127	425	109	18	3	8	(2	6)	157	66	37	60	63	4	83	1	3	1	39	14	.74	6	.256	.353	.369
1996 Los Angeles	NL	154	581	130	12	8	5	(3	2)	173	75	41	52	53	7	124	1	2	5	48	11	.81	12	.224	.288	.298
1997 St Louis	NL	150	572	169	26	14	11	(6	5)	256	92	58	98	55	1	72	3	7	6	55	14	.80	5	.295	.357	.448
1998 St Louis	NL	117	420	122	21	8	7	(3	4)	180	74	44	70	56	2	61	0	4	4	26	10	.72	6	.290	.371	.429
1999 Baltimore	AL	96	330	87	11	2	6	(4	2)	120	46	34	41	37	0	52	1	5	1	11	8	.58	5	.264	.339	.364

Year Team	Lg	G	AB	H	2B	3B	HR	(Hm	Rd)	TB	R	RBI	RC	TBB	IBB	SO	HBP	SH	SF	SB	CS	SB%	GDP	Avg	OBP	Slg
2000 Baltimore	AL	151	561	166	43	5	10	(4	6)	249	84	86	94	69	2	82	1	3	9	37	10	.79	16	.296	.369	.444
2001 Bal-ChC		126	351	82	17	5	5	(3	2)	124	55	37	49	59	1	77	1	4	2	23	2	.92	8	.234	.344	.353
2002 Chicago	NL	67	146	28	6	1	3	(1	2)	45	20	10	14	21	2	38	0	6	1	10	1	.91	0	.192	.292	.308
2001 Baltimore	AL	58	188	37	8	2	3	(1	2)	58	29	21	21	31	1	42	1	1	1	11	1	.92	3	.197	.312	.309
2001 Chicago	NL	68	163	45	9	3	2	(2	0)	66	26	16	28	28	0	35	0	3	1	12	1	.92	5	.276	.380	.405
13 ML YEARS		1615	5779	1548	244	74	80	(36	44)	2180	872	561	827	754	31	1061	20	57	42	463	147	.76	99	.268	.352	.377

Elmer Dessens

Pitches: R Bats: R Pos: SP-30   Ht: 6'0" Wt: 187 Born: 1/13/72 Age: 31

Year Team	Lg	G	GS	CG	GF	IP	BFP	H	R	ER	HR	SH	SF	HB	TBB	IBB	SO	WP	Bk	W	L	Pct	ShO	Sv-Op	Hld	ERC	ERA
1996 Pittsburgh	NL	15	3	0	1	25.0	112	40	23	23	2	3	1	0	4	0	13	0	0	0	2	.000	0	0-0	3	6.77	8.28
1997 Pittsburgh	NL	3	0	0	1	3.1	13	2	0	0	0	0	0	1	0	0	2	0	0	0	0	-	0	0-0	1	1.31	0.00
1998 Pittsburgh	NL	43	5	0	8	74.2	332	90	50	47	10	4	3	0	25	2	43	1	0	2	6	.250	0	0-1	6	5.19	5.67
2000 Cincinnati	NL	40	16	1	6	147.1	640	170	73	70	10	12	7	3	43	7	85	4	0	11	5	.688	0	1-1	1	4.31	4.28
2001 Cincinnati	NL	34	34	1	0	205.0	862	221	103	102	32	7	7	1	56	1	128	4	1	10	14	.417	1	0-0	0	4.49	4.48
2002 Cincinnati	NL	30	30	0	0	178.0	737	173	70	60	24	7	1	7	49	8	93	3	1	7	8	.467	0	0-0	0	3.82	3.03
6 ML YEARS		165	88	2	16	633.1	2696	696	319	302	78	33	19	12	177	18	364	12	2	30	35	.462	1	1-2	10	4.40	4.29

Matt DeWitt

Pitches: R Bats: R Pos: RP-5   Ht: 6'3" Wt: 225 Born: 9/4/77 Age: 25

Year Team	Lg	G	GS	CG	GF	IP	BFP	H	R	ER	HR	SH	SF	HB	TBB	IBB	SO	WP	Bk	W	L	Pct	ShO	Sv-Op	Hld	ERC	ERA
2002 Portland*	AAA	2	2	0	0	9.0	34	5	1	1	1	0	1	0	2	0	7	0	0	1	0	1.000	0	0- -		1.72	1.00
2000 Toronto	AL	8	0	0	4	13.2	68	20	13	13	4	0	0	2	9	0	6	1	0	0	1	.000	0	0-0	0	10.93	8.56
2001 Toronto	AL	16	0	0	9	19.0	87	22	8	8	2	1	0	1	10	5	13	2	0	0	2	.000	0	0-0	0	5.34	3.79
2002 San Diego	NL	5	0	0	4	7.1	30	6	2	1	1	0	1	0	3	0	5	0	0	1	0	1.000	0	0-0	0	3.43	1.23
3 ML YEARS		29	0	0	17	40.0	185	48	23	22	7	1	1	3	22	5	24	3	0	1	3	.250	0	0-0	0	6.71	4.95

Einar Diaz

Bats: R Throws: R Pos: C-100; PR-3; PH-1   Ht: 5'10" Wt: 190 Born: 12/28/72 Age: 30

Year Team	Lg	G	AB	H	2B	3B	HR	(Hm	Rd)	TB	R	RBI	RC	TBB	IBB	SO	HBP	SH	SF	SB	CS	SB%	GDP	Avg	OBP	Slg
1996 Cleveland	AL	4	1	0	0	0	0	(0	0)	0	0	0	0	0	0	0	0	0	0	0	0	-	0	.000	.000	.000
1997 Cleveland	AL	5	7	1	1	0	0	(0	0)	2	1	1	0	0	0	2	0	0	0	0	0	-	0	.143	.143	.286
1998 Cleveland	AL	17	48	11	1	0	2	(1	1)	18	8	9	5	3	0	2	2	0	3	0	0	-	0	.229	.286	.375
1999 Cleveland	AL	119	392	110	21	1	3	(2	1)	142	43	32	46	23	0	41	5	6	1	11	4	.73	10	.281	.328	.362
2000 Cleveland	AL	75	250	68	14	2	4	(2	2)	98	29	25	30	11	0	29	8	6	0	4	2	.67	7	.272	.323	.392
2001 Cleveland	AL	134	437	121	34	1	4	(0	4)	169	54	56	53	17	0	44	16	8	0	1	2	.33	11	.277	.328	.387
2002 Cleveland	AL	102	320	66	19	0	2	(1	1)	91	34	16	14	17	1	27	6	6	2	0	1	.00	13	.206	.258	.284
7 ML YEARS		456	1455	377	90	4	15	(6	9)	520	169	139	148	71	1	145	37	26	6	16	9	.64	43	.259	.309	.357

Juan Diaz

Bats: R Throws: R Pos: PH-2; 1B-1; DH-1   Ht: 6'2" Wt: 228 Born: 2/19/74 Age: 29

Year Team	Lg	G	AB	H	2B	3B	HR	(Hm	Rd)	TB	R	RBI	RC	TBB	IBB	SO	HBP	SH	SF	SB	CS	SB%	GDP	Avg	OBP	Slg
1997 Savannah	A	127	460	106	24	2	25	(-	-)	209	63	83	63	48	2	155	4	1	4	2	2	.50	10	.230	.306	.454
1997 Vero Beach	A+	1	3	2	0	0	1	(-	-)	5	2	3	2	0	0	1	1	0	0	0	0	-	0	.667	.750	1.667
1998 Vero Beach	A+	67	250	73	12	1	17	(-	-)	138	33	51	47	21	2	52	4	0	3	1	2	.33	4	.292	.353	.552
1998 San Antonio	AA	56	188	50	13	0	13	(-	-)	102	26	30	32	15	1	45	2	0	0	0	0	-	4	.266	.327	.543
1999 San Antonio	AA	66	254	77	21	1	9	(-	-)	127	42	52	46	26	1	77	3	0	4	0	0	-	4	.303	.369	.500
2000 Sarasota	A+	14	51	14	2	1	4	(-	-)	30	7	12	10	4	0	15	1	0	1	0	0	-	1	.275	.333	.588
2000 Trenton	AA	50	198	62	14	1	17	(-	-)	129	36	53	40	10	0	56	0	0	2	0	0	-	6	.313	.343	.652
2000 Pawtucket	AAA	13	43	12	0	0	7	(-	-)	33	11	17	11	6	0	9	0	0	2	1	0	1.00	2	.279	.353	.767
2001 Pawtucket	AAA	74	279	75	17	1	20	(-	-)	154	45	51	46	17	2	85	6	0	1	0	0	-	10	.269	.323	.552
2002 Pawtucket	AAA	104	389	101	14	0	20	(-	-)	175	47	53	48	24	2	105	3	0	3	0	0	-	17	.260	.305	.450
2002 Boston	AL	4	7	2	1	0	1	(0	1)	6	2	2	3	1	0	2	0	0	0	0	0	-	0	.286	.375	.857

R.A. Dickey

Pitches: R Bats: R Pos: RP   Ht: 6'3" Wt: 205 Born: 10/29/74 Age: 28

Year Team	Lg	G	GS	CG	GF	IP	BFP	H	R	ER	HR	SH	SF	HB	TBB	IBB	SO	WP	Bk	W	L	Pct	ShO	Sv-Op	Hld	ERC	ERA
1997 Charlotte	A+	8	6	0	2	35.0	162	51	32	27	8	0	0	6	12	1	32	5	3	1	4	.200	0	0- -		7.71	6.94
1998 Charlotte	A+	57	0	0	54	60.0	260	58	31	22	9	4	1	0	22	3	53	3	2	1	5	.167	0	38- -		3.94	3.30
1999 Tulsa	AA	35	11	0	21	95.0	419	105	60	48	13	1	4	2	40	1	59	9	0	6	7	.462	0	10- -		5.16	4.55
1999 Oklahoma	AAA	6	2	0	1	22.2	99	23	12	11	1	3	0	1	7	1	17	2	0	2	2	.500	0	0- -		3.43	4.37
2000 Oklahoma	AAA	30	23	2	2	158.1	680	167	83	79	13	4	9	7	65	1	85	5	2	8	9	.471	0	1- -		4.60	4.49
2001 Oklahoma	AAA	24	24	3	0	163.0	687	164	77	68	14	7	2	7	45	1	120	3	0	11	7	.611	0	0-0	0	3.71	3.75
2002 Oklahoma	AAA	37	19	1	8	154.0	664	176	81	70	8	7	9	4	47	5	109	5	0	8	7	.533	0	0- -		4.27	4.09
2001 Texas	AL	4	0	0	1	12.0	53	13	9	9	3	0	0	0	7	1	4	1	0	0	1	.000	0	0-0	0	6.57	6.75

Mike DiFelice

Bats: R **Throws:** R **Pos:** C-61; PH-12   **Ht:** 6'2" **Wt:** 205 **Born:** 5/28/69 **Age:** 34

Year Team	Lg	G	AB	H	2B	3B	HR	(Hm	Rd)	TB	R	RBI	RC	TBB	IBB	SO	HBP	SH	SF	SB	CS	SB%	GDP	Avg	OBP	Slg
1996 St Louis	NL	4	7	2	1	0	0	(0	0)	3	0	2	1	0	0	1	0	0	0	0	0	-	0	.286	.286	.429
1997 St Louis	NL	93	260	62	10	1	4	(1	3)	86	16	30	23	19	0	61	3	6	1	1	1	.50	11	.238	.297	.331
1998 Tampa Bay	AL	84	248	57	12	3	3	(1	2)	84	17	23	19	15	0	56	1	3	2	0	0	-	12	.230	.274	.339
1999 Tampa Bay	AL	51	179	55	11	0	6	(5	1)	84	21	27	29	8	0	23	3	0	1	0	0	-	1	.307	.346	.469
2000 Tampa Bay	AL	60	204	49	13	1	6	(4	2)	82	23	19	21	12	0	40	0	5	2	0	0	-	8	.240	.280	.402
2001 TB-Ari		60	170	32	5	1	2	(0	2)	45	14	10	10	8	0	49	4	3	2	1	1	.50	3	.188	.239	.265
2002 St Louis	NL	70	174	40	11	0	4	(3	1)	63	17	19	17	17	3	42	1	2	3	0	0	-	4	.230	.297	.362
2001 Tampa Bay	AL	48	149	31	5	1	2	(0	2)	44	13	9	10	8	0	39	3	2	2	1	1	.50	3	.208	.259	.295
2001 Arizona	NL	12	21	1	0	0	0	(0	0)	1	1	1	0	0	0	10	1	1	0	0	0	-	0	.048	.091	.048
7 ML YEARS		422	1242	297	63	6	25	(14	11)	447	108	130	120	79	3	272	12	19	11	2	2	.50	39	.239	.289	.360

Ben Diggins

Pitches: R **Bats:** R **Pos:** SP-5   **Ht:** 6'7" **Wt:** 230 **Born:** 6/13/79 **Age:** 24

| | | | | HOW MUCH HE PITCHED | | | | WHAT HE GAVE UP | | | | | | | | | | THE RESULTS | | | | | | | |
Year Team	Lg	G	GS	CG	GF	IP	BFP	H	R	ER	HR	SH	SF	HB	TBB	IBB	SO	WP	Bk	W	L	Pct	ShO	Sv-Op	Hld	ERC	ERA
2001 Wilmington	A+	21	21	0	0	105.2	446	88	49	42	5	2	0	3	48	0	79	10	0	7	6	.538	0	0--	-	3.13	3.58
2002 Vero Beach	A+	20	19	0	0	114.0	487	103	54	46	8	3	1	10	41	1	101	10	0	6	10	.375	0	0--	-	3.50	3.63
2002 Huntsville	AA	7	7	0	0	37.2	151	26	13	8	0	6	2	3	15	0	34	2	1	2	1	.667	0	0--	-	2.16	1.91
2002 Milwaukee	NL	5	5	0	0	24.0	118	28	24	23	4	3	2	1	18	1	15	3	1	0	4	.000	0	0-0	0	7.08	8.63

Brendan Donnelly

Pitches: R **Bats:** R **Pos:** RP-46   **Ht:** 6'3" **Wt:** 200 **Born:** 7/4/71 **Age:** 31

| | | | | HOW MUCH HE PITCHED | | | | WHAT HE GAVE UP | | | | | | | | | | THE RESULTS | | | | | | | |
Year Team	Lg	G	GS	CG	GF	IP	BFP	H	R	ER	HR	SH	SF	HB	TBB	IBB	SO	WP	Bk	W	L	Pct	ShO	Sv-Op	Hld	ERC	ERA
1992 White Sox	R	9	7	0	1	41.2	191	41	25	17	0	0	2	8	21	0	31	6	0	0	3	.000	0	1--	-	4.35	3.67
1993 Geneva	A-	21	3	0	7	43.0	198	39	34	30	4	1	1	6	29	0	29	7	3	4	0	1.000	0	1--	-	5.15	6.28
1994 Ohio Valley	IND	10	0	0	1	13.2	59	13	5	4	1	0	0	3	4	0	20	1	0	1	1	.500	0	1--	-	4.10	2.63
1995 Chrlstn - WV	A	24	0	0	22	30.1	112	14	4	4	0	1	2	1	7	1	33	1	0	1	1	.500	0	12--	-	0.85	1.19
1995 Winstn-Salm	A+	23	0	0	14	35.1	138	20	6	4	1	2	0	2	14	2	32	0	1	1	2	.333	0	2--	-	1.63	1.02
1995 Indianapolis	AAA	3	0	0	2	2.2	18	7	8	7	2	0	1	1	2	0	1	2	0	1	1	.500	0	0--	-	26.41	23.63
1996 Chattanooga	AA	22	0	0	10	29.1	133	27	21	18	4	0	1	4	17	2	22	1	0	1	2	.333	0	0--	-	4.52	5.52
1997 Chattanooga	AA	62	0	0	21	82.2	359	71	43	30	6	4	3	4	37	4	64	9	0	6	4	.600	0	6--	-	3.34	3.27
1998 Chattanooga	AA	38	0	0	35	45.1	203	43	16	15	4	1	1	3	24	5	47	8	0	2	5	.286	0	13--	-	4.24	2.98
1998 Indianapolis	AAA	19	1	0	6	37.1	157	29	16	11	3	1	0	3	16	3	39	2	0	4	1	.800	0	0--	-	3.03	2.65
1999 Nashua	IND	3	0	0	3	3.0	11	1	1	1	1	0	0	0	3	0	4	0	0	0	0	-	0	0--	-	5.16	3.00
1999 Durham	AAA	37	1	0	10	62.0	247	53	23	21	5	0	4	4	18	61	5	0	0	5	5	.500	0	2--	-	1.64	3.05
1999 Altoona	AA	2	0	0	2	2.1	12	4	2	2	0	1	2	0	2	0	0	0	0	0	0	-	0	1--	-	10.22	7.71
1999 Syracuse	AAA	5	0	0	2	9.1	39	8	4	3	1	2	0	0	4	1	9	1	0	0	1	.000	0	0--	-	3.31	2.89
2000 Syracuse	AAA	37	0	0	7	42.2	203	47	34	26	5	4	1	1	27	2	34	1	0	4	6	.400	0	0--	-	5.62	5.48
2000 Iowa	AAA	9	0	0	3	16.2	83	25	19	14	3	0	1	2	6	1	14	2	0	0	3	.000	0	1--	-	7.85	7.56
2001 Arkansas	AA	27	0	0	24	29.0	120	21	8	8	2	0	1	1	13	1	37	1	0	4	1	.800	0	12--	-	2.66	2.48
2001 Salt Lake	AAA	29	0	0	12	41.1	165	38	11	11	4	1	1	0	8	0	50	2	0	5	1	.833	0	1--	-	2.88	2.40
2002 Salt Lake	AAA	25	0	0	17	33.2	142	27	13	13	5	1	1	0	11	0	42	2	1	4	0	1.000	0	6--	-	3.18	3.48
2002 Anaheim	AL	46	0	0	11	49.2	199	32	13	12	2	3	1	2	19	3	54	1	0	1	1	.500	0	1-3	13	1.89	2.17

Chris Donnels

Bats: L **Throws:** R **Pos:** PH-53; 3B-25; PR-3; 1B-1   **Ht:** 6'0" **Wt:** 185 **Born:** 4/21/66 **Age:** 37

Year Team	Lg	G	AB	H	2B	3B	HR	(Hm	Rd)	TB	R	RBI	RC	TBB	IBB	SO	HBP	SH	SF	SB	CS	SB%	GDP	Avg	OBP	Slg
2002 Tucson*	AAA	4	10	3	1	0	0	(-	-)	4	3	0	3	2	0	3	2	0	0	0	0	-	0	.300	.500	.400
1991 New York	NL	37	89	20	2	0	0	(0	0)	22	7	5	8	14	1	19	0	1	0	1	1	.50	0	.225	.330	.247
1992 New York	NL	45	121	21	4	0	0	(0	0)	25	8	6	7	17	0	25	0	1	0	1	0	1.00	1	.174	.275	.207
1993 Houston	NL	88	179	46	14	2	2	(0	2)	70	18	24	22	19	0	33	0	0	1	2	0	1.00	6	.257	.327	.391
1994 Houston	NL	54	86	23	5	0	3	(2	1)	37	12	5	14	13	0	18	0	0	0	1	0	1.00	1	.267	.364	.430
1995 Hou-Bos		59	121	32	2	2	2	(0	2)	44	17	13	14	12	2	24	0	0	0	0	0	-	2	.264	.328	.364
2000 Los Angeles	NL	27	34	10	3	0	4	(3	1)	25	8	9	8	6	1	7	0	0	0	0	0	-	3	.294	.390	.735
2001 Los Angeles	NL	66	88	15	2	0	3	(2	1)	26	8	8	7	12	2	25	1	0	0	0	0	-	3	.170	.277	.295
2002 Arizona	NL	74	80	19	4	1	3	(1	2)	34	5	16	11	10	1	14	0	0	3	0	0	-	2	.238	.312	.425
1995 Houston	NL	19	30	9	0	0	0	(0	0)	9	4	2	3	3	2	6	0	0	0	0	0	-	1	.300	.364	.300
1995 Boston	AL	40	91	23	2	2	2	(0	2)	35	13	11	11	9	0	18	0	0	1	0	0	-	1	.253	.317	.385
8 ML YEARS		450	798	186	36	5	17	(8	9)	283	83	86	91	103	7	165	1	2	6	5	1	.83	17	.233	.319	.355

Octavio Dotel

Pitches: R **Bats:** R **Pos:** RP-83   **Ht:** 6'0" **Wt:** 200 **Born:** 11/25/73 **Age:** 29

| | | | | HOW MUCH HE PITCHED | | | | WHAT HE GAVE UP | | | | | | | | | | THE RESULTS | | | | | | | |
Year Team	Lg	G	GS	CG	GF	IP	BFP	H	R	ER	HR	SH	SF	HB	TBB	IBB	SO	WP	Bk	W	L	Pct	ShO	Sv-Op	Hld	ERC	ERA
1999 New York	NL	19	14	0	1	85.1	368	69	52	51	12	3	5	6	49	1	85	3	2	8	3	.727	0	0-0	0	4.30	5.38
2000 Houston	NL	50	16	0	25	125.0	563	127	80	75	26	7	8	7	61	3	142	6	0	3	7	.300	0	16-23	0	5.47	5.40
2001 Houston	NL	61	4	0	20	105.0	438	79	35	31	5	2	2	2	47	2	145	4	0	7	5	.583	0	2-4	14	2.62	2.66
2002 Houston	NL	83	0	0	22	97.1	376	58	21	20	7	3	7	4	27	2	118	2	0	6	4	.600	0	6-10	31	1.61	1.85
4 ML YEARS		213	34	0	68	412.2	1745	333	188	177	50	15	22	19	184	8	490	15	2	24	19	.558	0	24-37	45	3.48	3.86

Sean Douglass

Pitches: R Bats: R Pos: SP-8; RP-7   Ht: 6'6" Wt: 198 Born: 4/28/79 Age: 24

Year Team	Lg	G	GS	CG	GF	IP	BFP	H	R	ER	HR	SH	SF	HB	TBB	IBB	SO	WP	Bk	W	L	Pct	ShO	Sv-Op	Hld	ERC	ERA
1997 Orioles	R	9	1	0	5	17.2	80	20	14	12	2	4	0	2	9	0	10	1	0	1	3	.250	0	0--	-	6.03	6.11
1998 Bluefield	R+	10	10	0	0	53.0	210	45	20	19	6	0	1	0	14	0	62	3	0	2	2	.500	0	0--	-	2.91	3.23
1999 Frederick	A+	16	16	1	0	97.2	425	101	48	36	9	4	3	5	35	0	89	3	0	5	6	.455	0	0--	-	4.25	3.32
2000 Bowie	AA	27	27	1	0	160.2	687	155	79	72	17	3	2	5	55	1	118	5	0	9	8	.529	0	0--	-	3.78	4.03
2001 Rochester	AAA	27	27	0	0	162.1	710	160	79	63	13	5	4	5	61	0	156	6	0	8	9	.471	0	0--	-	3.81	3.49
2002 Rochester	AAA	14	13	0	1	66.2	299	66	39	35	4	1	3	2	35	0	71	3	0	4	6	.400	0	0--	-	4.29	4.73
2001 Baltimore	AL	4	4	0	0	20.1	94	21	12	12	3	0	1	1	11	0	17	1	1	2	1	.667	0	0-0	0	5.27	5.31
2002 Baltimore	AL	15	8	0	2	53.1	245	58	41	36	10	2	1	2	35	2	44	3	0	0	5	.000	0	0-0	0	6.56	6.08
2 ML YEARS		19	12	0	2	73.2	339	79	53	48	13	2	2	3	46	2	61	4	1	2	6	.250	0	0-0	0	6.19	5.86

Darren Dreifort

Pitches: R Bats: R Pos: SP   Ht: 6'2" Wt: 211 Born: 5/3/72 Age: 31

Year Team	Lg	G	GS	CG	GF	IP	BFP	H	R	ER	HR	SH	SF	HB	TBB	IBB	SO	WP	Bk	W	L	Pct	ShO	Sv-Op	Hld	ERC	ERA
1994 Los Angeles	NL	27	0	0	15	29.0	148	45	21	20	0	3	0	4	15	3	22	1	0	0	5	.000	0	6-9	3	7.39	6.21
1996 Los Angeles	NL	19	0	0	5	23.2	106	23	13	13	2	3	1	0	12	4	24	2	1	1	4	.200	0	0-2	1	3.84	4.94
1997 Los Angeles	NL	48	0	0	15	63.0	265	45	21	20	3	5	2	1	34	2	63	3	1	5	2	.714	0	4-7	9	2.72	2.86
1998 Los Angeles	NL	32	26	1	0	180.0	752	171	84	80	12	11	6	10	57	2	168	9	0	8	12	.400	1	0-0	0	3.50	4.00
1999 Los Angeles	NL	30	29	1	0	178.2	773	117	105	95	20	8	2	7	76	2	140	9	4	13	13	.500	1	0-0	0	4.39	4.79
2000 Los Angeles	NL	32	32	0	0	192.2	842	175	105	89	31	9	0	12	87	1	164	17	3	12	9	.571	1	0-0	0	4.40	4.16
2001 Los Angeles	NL	16	16	0	0	94.2	416	89	62	54	11	7	1	6	47	0	91	10	0	4	7	.364	0	0-0	0	4.50	5.13
7 ML YEARS		204	103	3	35	761.2	3302	725	411	371	79	46	12	40	328	14	672	51	9	43	52	.453	3	10-18	13	4.14	4.38

Ryan Drese

Pitches: R Bats: R Pos: SP-26   Ht: 6'3" Wt: 220 Born: 4/5/76 Age: 27

Year Team	Lg	G	GS	CG	GF	IP	BFP	H	R	ER	HR	SH	SF	HB	TBB	IBB	SO	WP	Bk	W	L	Pct	ShO	Sv-Op	Hld	ERC	ERA
1998 Watertown	A-	9	9	0	0	42.0	179	40	21	19	1	0	2	3	14	0	40	4	0	2	5	.286	0	0--	-	3.30	4.07
1999 Kinston	A+	15	15	1	0	69.1	310	46	47	38	2	3	1	10	52	0	81	7	1	5	4	.556	0	0--	-	3.55	4.93
1999 Mahning VI	A-	5	5	0	0	17.0	66	8	6	5	1	0	2	1	7	0	26	0	1	0	2	.000	0	0--	-	1.53	2.65
1999 Columbus	A	2	2	0	0	12.0	49	9	6	6	2	0	0	4	4	0	15	3	0	0	2	.000	0	0--	-	2.86	4.50
2000 Kinston	A+	1	1	0	0	2.1	9	2	1	1	0	1	0	0	1	0	4	1	0	0	1	.000	0	0--	-	3.03	3.86
2001 Akron	AA	14	13	1	1	86.0	340	64	34	32	4	7	1	6	29	0	73	4	0	5	7	.417	1	0--	-	2.51	3.35
2001 Buffalo	AAA	11	10	0	0	60.2	255	60	28	27	7	2	1	6	17	0	52	1	1	5	1	.833	0	0--	-	4.12	4.01
2002 Buffalo	AAA	3	3	0	0	22.0	86	16	4	4	1	1	0	0	4	0	16	0	0	1	0	1.000	0	0--	-	1.61	1.64
2001 Cleveland	AL	9	4	0	2	36.2	149	32	15	14	2	1	0	1	15	2	24	0	0	1	2	.333	0	0-0	0	3.27	3.44
2002 Cleveland	AL	26	26	1	0	137.1	635	176	104	100	15	3	9	6	62	1	102	11	0	10	9	.526	0	0-0	0	6.26	6.55
2 ML YEARS		35	30	1	2	174.0	784	208	119	114	17	4	9	7	77	3	126	11	0	11	11	.500	0	0-0	0	5.59	5.90

J.D. Drew

Bats: L Throws: R Pos: RF-118; PH-22; CF-6; PR-2   Ht: 6'1" Wt: 195 Born: 11/20/75 Age: 27

Year Team	Lg	G	AB	H	2B	3B	HR	(Hm	Rd)	TB	R	RBI	RC	TBB	IBB	SO	HBP	SH	SF	SB	CS	SB%	GDP	Avg	OBP	Slg
1998 St Louis	NL	14	36	15	3	1	5	(4	1)	35	9	13	12	4	0	10	0	0	1	0	0	-	4	.417	.463	.972
1999 St Louis	NL	104	368	89	16	6	13	(8	5)	156	72	39	58	50	0	77	6	3	3	19	3	.86	4	.242	.340	.424
2000 St Louis	NL	135	407	120	17	2	18	(11	7)	195	73	57	80	67	4	99	6	5	1	17	9	.65	3	.295	.401	.479
2001 St Louis	NL	109	375	121	18	5	27	(15	12)	230	80	73	92	57	4	75	4	3	4	13	3	.81	6	.323	.414	.613
2002 St Louis	NL	135	424	107	19	1	18	(9	9)	182	61	56	65	57	4	104	8	3	4	8	2	.80	4	.252	.349	.429
5 ML YEARS		497	1610	452	73	15	81	(44	37)	798	295	238	307	235	12	365	24	14	13	57	17	.77	21	.281	.378	.496

Tim Drew

Pitches: R Bats: R Pos: RP-6; SP-1   Ht: 6'1" Wt: 195 Born: 8/31/78 Age: 24

Year Team	Lg	G	GS	CG	GF	IP	BFP	H	R	ER	HR	SH	SF	HB	TBB	IBB	SO	WP	Bk	W	L	Pct	ShO	Sv-Op	Hld	ERC	ERA
2002 Buffalo*	AAA	15	15	2	0	96.1	402	96	43	35	6	3	4	4	23	1	43	3	2	8	4	.667	2	0--	-	3.34	3.27
2002 Ottawa*	AAA	13	13	0	0	84.2	348	77	31	27	5	7	2	3	24	2	29	0	0	6	3	.667	0	0--	-	3.00	2.87
2000 Cleveland	AL	3	3	0	0	9.0	51	17	12	10	1	0	2	1	8	0	5	0	0	1	0	1.000	0	0-0	0	12.94	10.00
2001 Cleveland	AL	8	6	0	0	35.0	173	51	39	31	9	1	2	4	16	0	15	5	0	2	0	.000	0	0-0	0	8.95	7.97
2002 Montreal	NL	7	1	0	3	16.0	64	12	8	5	1	1	1	0	2	0	10	0	0	1	0	1.000	0	2-3	1	1.57	2.81
3 ML YEARS		18	10	0	3	60.0	288	80	59	46	11	2	5	5	26	0	30	5	0	2	2	.500	0	2-3	1	7.16	6.90

Travis Driskill

Pitches: R Bats: R Pos: SP-19; RP-10   Ht: 6'0" Wt: 225 Born: 8/1/71 Age: 31

Year Team	Lg	G	GS	CG	GF	IP	BFP	H	R	ER	HR	SH	SF	HB	TBB	IBB	SO	WP	Bk	W	L	Pct	ShO	Sv-Op	Hld	ERC	ERA
1993 Watertown	A-	21	8	0	0	63.0	276	62	38	29	4	3	6	5	21	0	53	6	0	5	4	.556	0	3--	-	3.70	4.14
1994 Columbus	A	62	0	0	59	64.1	267	51	25	18	2	5	2	1	30	4	88	6	0	5	5	.500	0	35--	-	2.75	2.52
1995 Kinston	A+	15	0	0	9	23.0	90	17	7	7	2	0	3	1	5	1	24	1	0	0	2	.000	0	0--	-	2.11	2.74
1995 Cantn-Akrn	AA	33	0	0	22	46.1	200	46	24	24	3	1	1	1	19	1	39	0	1	3	4	.429	0	4--	-	3.89	4.66
1996 Cantn-Akrn	AA	29	24	4	0	172.0	732	169	89	69	8	6	6	3	63	0	148	10	2	13	7	.650	2	0--	-	3.56	3.61
1997 Buffalo	AAA	29	24	1	1	147.0	645	159	86	76	22	2	6	3	60	0	102	15	1	8	7	.533	0	0--	-	5.06	4.65
1998 Akron	AA	5	4	0	1	26.1	109	27	12	10	4	0	1	1	7	0	16	0	0	3	0	1.000	0	0--	-	4.31	3.42
1998 Buffalo	AAA	1	1	0	0	6.0	28	9	6	6	0	0	0	0	1	0	5	0	0	0	0	-	0	0--	-	5.13	9.00
1999 Buffalo	AAA	31	18	0	3	132.1	561	146	78	71	21	5	6	6	32	2	90	4	0	9	8	.529	0	0--	-	4.67	4.83
2000 New Orleans	AAA	28	28	2	0	179.1	774	201	101	92	15	5	3	7	45	0	113	6	0	12	11	.522	1	0--	-	4.20	4.01

Year Team	Lg	G	GS	CG	GF	IP	BFP	H	R	ER	HR	SH	SF	HB	TBB	IBB	SO	WP	Bk	W	L	Pct	ShO	Sv-Op	Hld	ERC	ERA
2001 New Orleans	AAA	28	28	1	0	178.2	735	175	83	75	21	6	5	6	33	2	145	5	1	11	5	.688	0	0--	-	3.36	3.78
2002 Rochester	AAA	4	4	1	0	22.0	86	17	8	4	1	0	0	1	1	0	15	0	0	2	2	.500	1	0--	-	1.53	1.64
2002 Baltimore	AL	29	19	0	6	132.2	589	150	78	73	21	2	2	8	48	1	78	6	0	8	8	.500	0	0-0	0	5.36	4.95

Eric DuBose

Pitches: L **Bats:** L **Pos:** RP-4   **Ht:** 6'3" **Wt:** 231 **Born:** 5/15/76 **Age:** 27

Year Team	Lg	G	GS	CG	GF	IP	BFP	H	R	ER	HR	SH	SF	HB	TBB	IBB	SO	WP	Bk	W	L	Pct	ShO	Sv-Op	Hld	ERC	ERA
1997 Sth Oregon	A-	3	1	0	0	10.0	39	5	0	0	0	0	0	0	6	0	15	0	0	1	0	1.000	0	0--	-	1.71	0.00
1997 Visalia	A+	10	9	0	0	38.1	194	43	37	30	4	2	0	5	28	0	39	6	3	1	3	.250	0	0--	-	6.46	7.04
1998 Visalia	A+	17	10	0	4	72.0	307	56	34	27	5	1	2	5	35	0	85	8	2	6	1	.857	0	1--	-	3.24	3.38
1998 Huntsville	AA	14	14	1	0	83.1	363	86	37	25	2	3	4	7	34	1	66	4	0	7	6	.538	1	0--	-	4.10	2.70
1999 Midland	AA	21	14	0	3	77.0	361	89	57	47	10	2	4	7	44	1	68	8	0	4	2	.667	0	1--	-	6.32	5.49
2000 Midland	AA	18	0	0	1	26.1	131	25	16	13	1	0	0	3	18	2	20	2	0	5	1	.833	0	0--	-	4.36	4.44
2000 Visalia	A+	5	0	0	2	10.2	46	8	2	2	0	0	0	1	5	1	12	1	0	0	1	.000	0	1--	-	2.45	1.69
2002 Rochester	AAA	1	0	0	0	0.1	5	1	2	1	0	0	0	0	2	0	0	0	0	0	0	-	0	0--	-	35.68	27.00
2002 Bowie	AA	41	0	0	13	64.2	263	46	21	18	2	4	2	3	21	0	66	3	0	5	3	.625	0	3--	-	2.02	2.51
2002 Baltimore	AL	4	0	0	2	6.0	25	7	2	2	1	0	0	1	1	0	4	0	0	0	0	-	0	0-0	0	5.59	3.00

Brandon Duckworth

Pitches: R **Bats:** R **Pos:** SP-29; RP-1   **Ht:** 6'2" **Wt:** 185 **Born:** 1/23/76 **Age:** 27

Year Team	Lg	G	GS	CG	GF	IP	BFP	H	R	ER	HR	SH	SF	HB	TBB	IBB	SO	WP	Bk	W	L	Pct	ShO	Sv-Op	Hld	ERC	ERA
1998 Piedmont	A	21	21	5	0	147.2	577	116	58	46	10	1	5	7	24	0	119	8	2	9	8	.529	3	0--	-	2.10	2.80
1998 Clearwater	A+	9	9	0	0	53.0	235	64	25	22	2	2	1	1	22	0	46	4	0	6	2	.750	1	0--	-	5.05	3.74
1999 Clearwater	A+	27	17	0	1	132.0	602	164	84	71	13	5	7	5	40	0	101	10	1	11	5	.688	0	1--	-	5.12	4.84
2000 Reading	AA	27	27	1	0	165.0	688	145	70	58	17	5	2	7	52	0	178	6	3	13	7	.650	0	0--	-	3.27	3.16
2001 Scrtn/WlksBr	AAA	22	20	2	1	147.0	584	122	46	43	14	7	3	2	36	2	150	5	0	13	2	.867	1	0--	-	2.79	2.63
2001 Philadelphia	NL	11	11	0	0	69.0	289	57	29	27	7	3	6	2	29	5	40	2	0	3	2	.600	0	0-0	0	2.98	3.52
2002 Philadelphia	NL	30	29	0	0	163.0	725	167	103	98	26	7	3	7	69	5	167	10	0	8	9	.471	0	0-0	0	4.80	5.41
2 ML YEARS		41	40	0	0	232.0	1014	224	132	125	28	14	6	13	98	10	207	12	0	11	11	.500	0	0-0	0	4.25	4.85

Matt Duff

Pitches: R **Bats:** R **Pos:** RP-7   **Ht:** 6'1" **Wt:** 192 **Born:** 10/6/74 **Age:** 28

Year Team	Lg	G	GS	CG	GF	IP	BFP	H	R	ER	HR	SH	SF	HB	TBB	IBB	SO	WP	Bk	W	L	Pct	ShO	Sv-Op	Hld	ERC	ERA
1997 Springfield	IND	14	12	2	1	79.2	334	70	33	24	3	2	6	3	27	1	76	3	0	7	4	.636	0	0--	-	2.88	2.71
1997 Augusta	A	2	1	0	1	6.0	26	6	1	1	0	0	0	1	2	0	6	0	0	1	0	1.000	0	0--	-	3.79	1.50
1998 Augusta	A	10	0	0	9	9.0	42	8	3	3	1	0	0	1	4	0	12	0	0	1	0	1.000	0	3--	-	3.83	3.00
1998 Lynchburg	A+	40	0	0	25	62.2	257	52	26	23	4	3	3	1	20	2	61	4	0	4	5	.444	0	10--	-	2.64	3.30
1999 Lynchburg	A+	7	7	0	0	39.0	169	41	22	22	6	1	1	0	13	0	40	0	1	3	2	.400	0	0--	-	4.43	5.08
1999 Altoona	AA	44	0	0	29	57.2	241	43	19	18	5	4	2	2	35	4	59	4	1	2	4	.333	0	12--	-	3.52	2.81
2000 Altoona	AA	47	0	0	22	55.0	253	50	31	24	1	4	2	1	36	9	61	2	1	0	4	.000	0	6--	-	3.60	3.93
2001 St.Paul	IND	22	0	0	16	32.0	146	38	23	17	1	1	0	1	11	0	41	1	0	0	3	.000	0	3--	-	4.41	4.78
2001 Sioux Falls	IND	17	0	0	14	21.0	84	16	5	4	0	2	0	0	6	0	29	2	0	4	0	1.000	0	7--	-	1.82	1.71
2002 Potomac	A+	4	0	0	4	4.1	18	4	0	0	0	0	0	0	1	0	3	0	0	0	0	-	0	4--	-	2.34	0.00
2002 New Haven	AA	47	0	0	22	65.0	255	38	12	10	3	4	2	1	21	2	91	5	0	11	1	.917	0	4--	-	1.49	1.38
2002 Memphis	AAA	4	0	0	1	4.2	19	2	1	1	1	0	0	0	4	0	3	0	0	0	0	-	0	1--	-	3.65	1.93
2002 St Louis	NL	7	0	0	1	5.2	28	3	3	3	0	0	0	0	8	2	4	0	0	0	0	-	0	0-0	0	3.63	4.76

Courtney Duncan

Pitches: R **Bats:** L **Pos:** RP-2   **Ht:** 6'0" **Wt:** 190 **Born:** 10/9/74 **Age:** 28

Year Team	Lg	G	GS	CG	GF	IP	BFP	H	R	ER	HR	SH	SF	HB	TBB	IBB	SO	WP	Bk	W	L	Pct	ShO	Sv-Op	Hld	ERC	ERA
1996 Williamsport	A-	15	15	1	0	90.1	360	58	28	22	6	3	0	5	34	0	91	8	0	11	1	.917	0	0--	-	2.16	2.19
1997 Daytona	A+	19	19	1	0	121.2	489	90	35	22	3	6	1	8	35	0	120	8	1	8	4	.667	0	0--	-	2.09	1.63
1997 Orlando	AA	8	8	0	0	45.0	196	37	28	17	2	1	2	1	29	5	45	4	0	2	2	.500	0	0--	-	3.56	3.40
1998 W Tennessee	AA	29	29	0	0	162.2	730	141	89	77	7	9	7	14	108	5	157	9	2	7	9	.438	0	0--	-	4.23	4.26
1999 W Tennessee	AA	11	8	0	2	41.2	210	44	42	33	3	2	6	2	42	4	42	8	0	1	7	.125	0	0--	-	6.58	7.13
1999 Daytona	A+	15	11	1	3	65.0	300	70	60	40	6	3	2	4	34	1	48	5	0	4	5	.444	1	1--	-	5.10	5.54
2000 W Tennessee	AA	61	0	0	41	73.1	307	57	32	25	2	4	3	0	33	2	72	3	0	5	4	.556	0	25--	-	2.53	3.07
2001 Iowa	AAA	7	0	0	1	8.1	36	7	3	3	1	0	0	0	5	1	15	0	0	1	0	1.000	0	0--	-	3.94	3.24
2002 Iowa	AAA	55	0	0	22	62.2	295	67	35	30	6	3	3	0	33	1	64	6	0	3	5	.375	0	6--	-	4.28	3.99
2001 Chicago	NL	36	0	0	15	42.2	193	42	24	24	5	1	3	2	25	3	49	2	0	3	3	.500	0	0-2	7	4.91	5.06
2002 Chicago	NL	2	0	0	1	2.1	10	2	0	0	0	0	0	0	1	0	1	0	0	0	0	-	0	0-0	0	2.67	0.00
2 ML YEARS		38	0	0	16	45.0	203	44	24	24	5	1	3	2	26	3	50	2	0	3	3	.500	0	0-2	7	4.79	4.80

Adam Dunn

Bats: L **Throws:** R **Pos:** LF-113; 1B-44; RF-17; PH-4; DH-1   **Ht:** 6'6" **Wt:** 240 **Born:** 11/9/79 **Age:** 23

Year Team	Lg	G	AB	H	2B	3B	HR	(Hm	Rd)	TB	R	RBI	RC	TBB	IBB	SO	HBP	SH	SF	SB	CS	SB%	GDP	Avg	OBP	Slg
1998 Billings	R+	34	125	36	3	1	4	(-	-)	53	26	13	22	22	1	23	3	0	1	4	2	.67	3	.288	.404	.424
1999 Rockford	A	93	313	96	16	2	11	(-	-)	149	62	44	62	46	3	64	10	0	3	21	10	.68	6	.307	.409	.476
2000 Dayton	A	122	420	118	29	1	16	(-	-)	197	101	79	92	100	4	101	12	0	6	24	5	.83	10	.281	.428	.469
2001 Chattanooga	AA	39	140	48	9	0	12	(-	-)	93	30	31	39	24	3	31	3	1	0	6	3	.67	1	.343	.449	.664
2001 Louisville	AAA	55	210	69	13	0	20	(-	-)	142	44	53	60	38	3	51	5	0	1	5	1	.83	1	.329	.441	.676

Year Team	Lg	G	AB	H	2B	3B	HR	(Hm	Rd)	TB	R	RBI	RC	TBB	IBB	SO	HBP	SH	SF	SB	CS	SB%	GDP	Avg	OBP	Slg
2001 Cincinnati	NL	66	244	64	18	1	19	(8	11)	141	54	43	51	38	2	74	4	0	0	4	2	.67	4	.262	.371	.578
2002 Cincinnati	NL	158	535	133	28	2	26	(13	13)	243	84	71	97	128	13	170	9	1	3	19	9	.68	8	.249	.400	.454
2 ML YEARS		224	779	197	46	3	45	(21	24)	384	138	114	148	166	15	244	13	1	3	23	11	.68	12	.253	.391	.493

Shawon Dunston

Bats: R **Throws:** R **Pos:** PH-26; RF-22; LF-18; CF-9; DH-3; PR-2; 1B-1; SS-1   **Ht:** 6'1" **Wt:** 180 **Born:** 3/21/63 **Age:** 40

Year Team	Lg	G	AB	H	2B	3B	HR	(Hm	Rd)	TB	R	RBI	RC	TBB	IBB	SO	HBP	SH	SF	SB	CS	SB%	GDP	Avg	OBP	Slg
1985 Chicago	NL	74	250	65	12	4	4	(3	1)	97	40	18	31	19	3	42	0	1	2	11	3	.79	3	.260	.310	.388
1986 Chicago	NL	150	581	145	37	3	17	(10	7)	239	66	68	64	21	5	114	3	4	2	13	11	.54	5	.250	.278	.411
1987 Chicago	NL	95	346	85	18	3	5	(3	2)	124	40	22	32	10	1	68	1	0	2	12	3	.80	6	.246	.267	.358
1988 Chicago	NL	155	575	143	23	6	9	(5	4)	205	69	56	55	16	8	108	2	4	2	30	9	.77	6	.249	.271	.357
1989 Chicago	NL	138	471	131	20	6	9	(3	6)	190	52	60	59	30	15	86	1	6	4	19	11	.63	7	.278	.320	.403
1990 Chicago	NL	146	545	143	22	8	17	(7	10)	232	73	66	67	15	1	87	3	4	6	25	5	.83	9	.262	.283	.426
1991 Chicago	NL	142	492	128	22	7	12	(5	7)	200	59	50	59	23	5	64	4	4	11	21	6	.78	5	.260	.292	.407
1992 Chicago	NL	18	73	23	3	1	0	(0	0)	28	8	2	9	3	0	13	0	0	0	2	3	.40	0	.315	.342	.384
1993 Chicago	NL	7	10	4	2	0	0	(0	0)	6	3	2	2	0	0	1	0	0	0	0	0	-	0	.400	.400	.600
1994 Chicago	NL	88	331	92	19	0	11	(2	9)	144	38	35	42	16	3	48	2	5	2	3	8	.27	4	.278	.313	.435
1995 Chicago	NL	127	477	141	30	6	14	(8	6)	225	58	69	68	10	3	75	6	7	3	10	5	.67	8	.296	.317	.472
1996 San Francisco	NL	82	287	86	12	2	5	(3	2)	117	27	25	38	13	0	40	1	5	1	8	0	1.00	6	.300	.331	.408
1997 ChC-Pit	NL	132	490	147	22	5	14	(10	4)	221	71	57	69	8	0	75	3	5	5	32	8	.80	9	.300	.312	.451
1998 Cle-SF		98	207	46	13	3	6	(2	4)	83	36	20	21	6	0	28	4	1	3	9	4	.69	3	.222	.255	.401
1999 Stl-NYM	NL	104	243	78	11	3	5	(4	1)	110	35	41	34	2	0	39	5	3	2	10	4	.71	8	.321	.337	.453
2000 St Louis	NL	98	216	54	11	2	12	(6	6)	105	28	43	26	6	0	47	3	4	2	3	1	.75	11	.250	.278	.486
2001 San Francisco	NL	88	186	52	10	3	9	(6	3)	95	26	25	28	2	0	32	2	2	1	3	1	.75	2	.280	.293	.511
2002 San Francisco	NL	72	147	34	5	0	1	(0	1)	42	7	9	9	3	0	33	1	1	1	1	0	1.00	0	.231	.250	.286
1997 Chicago	NL	114	419	119	18	4	9	(7	2)	172	57	41	52	8	0	64	3	3	4	29	7	.81	7	.284	.300	.411
1997 Pittsburgh	NL	18	71	28	4	1	5	(3	2)	49	14	16	17	0	0	11	0	2	1	3	1	.75	2	.394	.389	.690
1998 Cleveland	AL	62	156	37	11	3	3	(1	2)	63	26	12	18	6	0	18	1	0	3	9	2	.82	2	.237	.265	.404
1998 San Francisco	NL	36	51	9	2	0	3	(1	2)	20	10	8	3	0	0	10	3	1	0	0	2	.00	1	.176	.222	.392
1999 St Louis	NL	62	150	46	5	2	5	(4	1)	70	23	25	21	2	0	23	3	2	1	6	3	.67	4	.307	.327	.467
1999 New York	NL	42	93	32	6	1	0	(0	0)	40	12	16	13	0	0	16	2	1	1	4	1	.80	4	.344	.354	.430
18 ML YEARS		1814	5927	1597	292	62	150	(76	74)	2463	736	668	713	203	44	1000	41	56	49	212	82	.72	98	.269	.296	.416

Todd Dunwoody

Bats: L **Throws:** L **Pos:** LF-1; RF-1   **Ht:** 6'1" **Wt:** 205 **Born:** 4/11/75 **Age:** 28

Year Team	Lg	G	AB	H	2B	3B	HR	(Hm	Rd)	TB	R	RBI	RC	TBB	IBB	SO	HBP	SH	SF	SB	CS	SB%	GDP	Avg	OBP	Slg
2002 Buffalo*	AAA	102	363	97	31	4	7	(-	-)	157	57	29	45	12	1	62	4	7	0	8	3	.73	9	.267	.298	.433
1997 Florida	NL	19	50	13	2	2	2	(0	2)	25	7	7	9	7	0	21	1	0	0	2	0	1.00	1	.260	.362	.500
1998 Florida	NL	116	434	109	27	7	5	(2	3)	165	53	28	47	21	0	113	4	3	0	5	1	.83	6	.251	.292	.380
1999 Florida	NL	64	186	41	6	3	2	(1	1)	59	20	20	15	12	0	41	1	0	1	3	4	.43	1	.220	.270	.317
2000 Kansas City	AL	61	178	37	9	0	1	(1	0)	49	12	23	11	8	0	42	1	2	6	3	0	1.00	4	.208	.238	.275
2001 Chicago	NL	33	61	13	4	0	1	(0	1)	20	6	3	5	3	0	14	0	0	0	0	1	.00	0	.213	.250	.328
2002 Cleveland	AL	2	6	0	0	0	0	(0	0)	0	0	0	0	0	0	3	0	1	0	0	0	-	0	.000	.000	.000
6 ML YEARS		295	915	213	48	12	11	(4	7)	318	98	81	87	51	0	234	7	6	7	13	6	.68	12	.233	.277	.348

Erubiel Durazo

Bats: L **Throws:** L **Pos:** 1B-56; PH-17; DH-5; RF-2   **Ht:** 6'3" **Wt:** 240 **Born:** 1/23/74 **Age:** 29

Year Team	Lg	G	AB	H	2B	3B	HR	(Hm	Rd)	TB	R	RBI	RC	TBB	IBB	SO	HBP	SH	SF	SB	CS	SB%	GDP	Avg	OBP	Slg
2002 Tucson*	AAA	7	22	7	2	1	1	(-	-)	14	5	3	4	0	0	2	1	0	0	0	0	-	1	.318	.348	.636
2002 El Paso*	AA	5	14	7	3	0	2	(-	-)	16	5	7	7	4	0	1	0	0	0	0	0	-	1	.500	.611	1.143
1999 Arizona	NL	52	155	51	4	2	11	(4	7)	92	31	30	38	26	1	43	1	0	3	1	1	.50	1	.329	.422	.594
2000 Arizona	NL	67	196	52	11	0	8	(3	5)	87	35	33	34	34	2	43	1	0	2	1	0	1.00	3	.265	.373	.444
2001 Arizona	NL	92	175	47	11	0	12	(4	8)	94	34	38	36	28	1	49	2	0	2	0	0	-	1	.269	.372	.537
2002 Arizona	NL	76	222	58	12	2	16	(11	5)	122	46	48	46	49	2	60	2	0	3	0	1	.00	1	.261	.395	.550
4 ML YEARS		287	748	208	38	4	47	(22	25)	395	146	149	154	137	6	195	6	0	10	2	2	.50	6	.278	.390	.528

Chad Durbin

Pitches: R **Bats:** R **Pos:** SP-2   **Ht:** 6'2" **Wt:** 200 **Born:** 12/3/77 **Age:** 25

Year Team	Lg	G	GS	CG	GF	IP	BFP	H	R	ER	HR	SH	SF	HB	TBB	IBB	SO	WP	Bk	W	L	Pct	ShO	Sv-Op	Hld	ERC	ERA
2002 Omaha*	AAA	1	1	0	0	1.2	9	4	2	2	0	0	0	0	0	0	2	0	0	0	1	.000	0	0- -		10.16	10.80
2002 Royals*	R	3	3	0	0	6.0	19	4	0	0	0	0	0	0	1	0	5	0	0	0	0	-	0	0- -		1.49	0.00
2002 Wichita*	AA	3	1	0	0	5.1	26	5	4	3	1	1	0	0	4	0	6	0	0	0	0	-	0	0- -		5.44	5.06
1999 Kansas City	AL	1	0	0	0	2.1	9	1	0	0	0	0	0	0	1	0	3	1	0	0	0	-	0	0-0	0	1.08	0.00
2000 Kansas City	AL	16	16	0	0	72.1	349	91	71	66	14	1	3	0	43	1	37	7	0	2	5	.286	0	0-0	0	7.05	8.21
2001 Kansas City	AL	29	29	2	0	179.0	777	201	109	98	26	2	7	11	58	0	95	6	0	9	16	.360	0	0-0	0	5.15	4.93
2002 Kansas City	AL	2	2	0	0	8.1	43	13	11	11	3	0	0	1	4	0	5	0	0	0	1	.000	0	0-0	0	10.58	11.88
4 ML YEARS		48	47	2	0	262.0	1178	306	191	175	43	3	10	12	106	1	140	14	0	11	22	.333	0	0-0	0	5.77	6.01

Ray Durham

Bats: B **Throws:** R **Pos:** 2B-103; DH-43; PH-4   **Ht:** 5'8" **Wt:** 180 **Born:** 11/30/71 **Age:** 31

Year Team	Lg	G	AB	H	2B	3B	HR	Hm	Rd	TB	R	RBI	RC	TBB	IBB	SO	HBP	SH	SF	SB	CS	SB%	GDP	Avg	OBP	Slg
1995 Chicago	AL	125	471	121	27	6	7	(1	6)	181	68	51	57	31	2	83	6	5	4	18	5	.78	8	.257	.309	.384
1996 Chicago	AL	156	557	153	33	5	10	(3	7)	226	79	65	87	58	4	95	10	7	7	30	4	.88	6	.275	.350	.406
1997 Chicago	AL	156	634	172	27	5	11	(3	8)	242	106	53	83	61	0	96	6	2	8	33	16	.67	14	.271	.337	.382
1998 Chicago	AL	158	635	181	35	8	19	(10	9)	289	126	67	110	73	3	105	6	6	3	36	9	.80	5	.285	.363	.455
1999 Chicago	AL	153	612	181	30	8	13	(7	6)	266	109	60	103	73	1	105	4	3	2	34	11	.76	9	.296	.373	.435
2000 Chicago	AL	151	614	172	35	9	17	(5	12)	276	121	75	110	75	0	105	7	5	8	25	13	.66	13	.280	.361	.450
2001 Chicago	AL	152	611	163	42	10	20	(9	11)	285	104	65	97	64	3	110	4	6	6	23	10	.70	10	.267	.337	.450
2002 CWS-Oak	AL	150	564	163	34	6	15	(11	4)	254	114	70	96	73	1	93	7	10	5	26	7	.79	15	.289	.374	.450
2002 Chicago	AL	96	345	103	20	2	9	(6	3)	154	71	48	61	49	0	59	5	8	4	20	5	.80	13	.299	.390	.446
2002 Oakland	AL	54	219	60	14	4	6	(5	1)	100	43	22	35	24	1	34	2	2	1	6	2	.75	2	.274	.350	.457
8 ML YEARS		1200	4698	1306	263	57	112	(49	63)	2019	827	506	733	508	14	792	50	44	43	225	75	.75	80	.278	.352	.430

Jayson Durocher

Pitches: R **Bats:** R **Pos:** RP-39   **Ht:** 6'3" **Wt:** 195 **Born:** 8/18/74 **Age:** 28

Year Team	Lg	G	GS	CG	GF	IP	BFP	H	R	ER	HR	SH	SF	HB	TBB	IBB	SO	WP	Bk	W	L	Pct	ShO	Sv-Op	Hld	ERC	ERA
1993 Expos	R	7	7	3	0	39.0	150	32	23	15	0	2	0	3	13	0	21	3	1	2	3	.400	0	0--	--	2.74	3.46
1994 Vermont	A-	15	15	3	0	99.0	422	92	40	34	0	0	3		44	1	74	11	1	9	2	.818	1	0--	--	3.24	3.09
1995 Albany	A	24	22	1	0	122.0	526	105	67	53	5	4	11	5	56	1	88	11	1	3	7	.300	0	0--	--	3.24	3.91
1996 W Palm Bch	A+	23	23	1	0	129.1	557	118	65	48	5	4	3	7	44	0	101	15	3	7	6	.538	1	0--	--	3.08	3.34
1997 W Palm Bch	A+	25	17	0	2	87.0	385	84	58	37	6	3	3	4	39	0	71	10	2	6	4	.600	0	0--	--	3.96	3.83
1998 Jupiter	A+	23	0	0	12	36.1	162	47	21	17	3	1	2	1	8	0	27	4	0	2	1	.667	0	5--	--	4.99	4.21
1998 Harrisburg	AA	10	0	0	4	11.1	48	10	8	5	0	1	1	0	6	0	12	1	0	0	1	.000	0	1--	--	3.29	3.97
1999 Harrisburg	AA	29	1	0	11	51.2	224	44	29	20	5	2	2	6	25	1	36	3	1	1	3	.250	0	4--	--	4.00	3.48
1999 Ottawa	AAA	17	0	0	6	35.2	146	17	12	6	2	3	1	1	20	2	22	3	0	1	3	.250	0	4--	--	1.71	1.51
2000 Las Vegas	AAA	31	0	0	18	40.0	187	44	25	22	2	2	2	3	25	3	38	6	0	3	5	.375	0	7--	--	5.33	4.95
2000 Mobile	AA	27	0	0	23	30.1	132	26	7	7	4	2	1	3	12	1	43	3	0	1	1	.500	0	14--	--	3.74	2.08
2001 Tulsa	AA	3	0	0	2	3.2	15	0	0	0	0	0	0	0	3	0	4	2	0	0	0	-	0	0--	--	1.10	0.00
2001 Oklahoma	AAA	31	0	0	20	39.2	176	34	25	22	5	3	0	1	23	1	52	1	0	4	1	.800	0	6--	--	4.41	4.99
2002 Indianapolis	AAA	20	0	0	9	26.1	115	19	9	8	3	0	0	2	15	0	39	2	0	1	0	1.000	0	2--	--	3.51	2.73
2002 Milwaukee	NL	39	0	0	10	48.0	189	27	13	10	3	0	1	2	21	2	44	1	0	1	1	.500	0	0-1	3	1.88	1.88

Jermaine Dye

Bats: R **Throws:** R **Pos:** RF-111; DH-19; PH-3   **Ht:** 6'5" **Wt:** 220 **Born:** 1/28/74 **Age:** 29

Year Team	Lg	G	AB	H	2B	3B	HR	Hm	Rd	TB	R	RBI	RC	TBB	IBB	SO	HBP	SH	SF	SB	CS	SB%	GDP	Avg	OBP	Slg
2002 Sacramento*	AAA	4	16	3	2	0	0	(-	-)	5	3	1	1	2	0	2	0	0	0	0	0	-	1	.188	.278	.313
2002 Modesto*	A+	2	8	4	3	0	0	(-	-)	7	1	2	3	0	0	0	0	0	0	0	0	-	-	.500	.500	.875
1996 Atlanta	NL	98	292	82	16	0	12	(4	8)	134	32	37	36	8	0	67	3	0	3	1	4	.20	11	.281	.304	.459
1997 Kansas City	AL	75	263	62	14	0	7	(3	4)	97	26	22	26	17	0	51	1	1	1	2	1	.67	6	.236	.284	.369
1998 Kansas City	AL	60	214	50	5	1	5	(3	2)	72	24	23	17	11	2	46	1	0	4	2	2	.50	8	.234	.270	.336
1999 Kansas City	AL	158	608	179	44	8	27	(15	12)	320	96	119	106	58	4	119	1	0	6	2	3	.40	17	.294	.354	.526
2000 Kansas City	AL	157	601	193	41	2	33	(15	18)	337	107	118	125	69	6	99	3	0	6	0	1	.00	12	.321	.390	.561
2001 KC-Oak	AL	158	599	169	31	1	26	(16	10)	280	91	106	99	57	6	112	7	1	11	9	1	.90	8	.282	.346	.467
2002 Oakland	AL	131	488	123	27	1	24	(13	11)	224	74	86	71	52	2	108	10	0	5	2	0	1.00	15	.252	.333	.459
2001 Kansas City	AL	97	367	100	14	0	13	(8	5)	153	50	47	54	30	3	68	6	1	6	7	1	.88	2	.272	.333	.417
2001 Oakland	AL	61	232	69	17	1	13	(8	5)	127	41	59	45	27	3	44	1	0	5	2	0	1.00	6	.297	.366	.547
7 ML YEARS		837	3065	858	178	13	134	(69	65)	1464	450	511	480	272	20	602	26	2	36	18	12	.60	77	.280	.340	.478

Damion Easley

Bats: R **Throws:** R **Pos:** 2B-84; PR-1   **Ht:** 5'11" **Wt:** 187 **Born:** 11/11/69 **Age:** 33

Year Team	Lg	G	AB	H	2B	3B	HR	Hm	Rd	TB	R	RBI	RC	TBB	IBB	SO	HBP	SH	SF	SB	CS	SB%	GDP	Avg	OBP	Slg
2002 Toledo*	AAA	8	26	3	1	0	0	(-	-)	4	5	0	0	5	0	0	1	0	0	0	2	.00	1	.115	.281	.154
1992 Anaheim	AL	47	151	39	5	0	1	(1	0)	47	14	12	14	8	0	26	3	2	1	9	5	.64	2	.258	.307	.311
1993 Anaheim	AL	73	230	72	13	2	2	(0	2)	95	33	22	37	28	2	35	3	1	2	6	6	.50	5	.313	.392	.413
1994 Anaheim	AL	88	316	68	16	1	6	(4	2)	104	41	30	28	29	0	48	4	4	2	4	5	.44	8	.215	.288	.329
1995 Anaheim	AL	114	357	77	14	2	4	(1	3)	107	35	35	30	32	1	47	6	6	4	5	2	.71	11	.216	.288	.300
1996 Ana-Det	AL	49	112	30	2	0	4	(1	3)	44	14	17	16	10	0	25	1	5	1	3	1	.75	0	.268	.331	.393
1997 Detroit	AL	151	527	139	37	3	22	(12	10)	248	97	72	88	68	3	102	16	4	5	28	13	.68	18	.264	.362	.471
1998 Detroit	AL	153	594	161	38	2	27	(19	8)	284	84	100	94	39	2	112	16	0	2	15	5	.75	8	.271	.332	.478
1999 Detroit	AL	151	549	146	30	4	20	(12	8)	238	83	65	82	51	0	124	19	2	7	11	3	.79	15	.266	.346	.434
2000 Detroit	AL	126	464	120	27	2	14	(5	9)	193	76	58	69	55	1	79	11	4	4	13	4	.76	11	.259	.350	.416
2001 Detroit	AL	154	546	137	31	7	11	(4	7)	214	77	65	72	52	3	90	13	4	4	10	5	.67	10	.250	.323	.376
2002 Detroit	AL	85	304	68	14	1	8	(4	4)	108	29	30	29	27	3	43	11	1	3	1	3	.25	4	.224	.307	.355
1996 Anaheim	AL	28	45	7	1	0	2	(1	1)	14	4	7	4	6	0	12	0	3	0	0	0	-	0	.156	.255	.311
1996 Detroit	AL	21	67	23	1	0	2	(0	2)	30	10	10	12	4	0	13	1	2	1	3	1	.75	0	.343	.384	.448
11 ML YEARS		1191	4189	1066	223	21	119	(63	56)	1688	583	506	559	399	17	731	103	33	31	105	52	.67	92	.254	.332	.403

Adam Eaton

Pitches: R **Bats:** R **Pos:** SP-6   **Ht:** 6'2" **Wt:** 190 **Born:** 11/23/77 **Age:** 25

Year Team	Lg	G	GS	CG	GF	IP	BFP	H	R	ER	HR	SH	SF	HB	TBB	IBB	SO	WP	Bk	W	L	Pct	ShO	Sv-Op	Hld	ERC	ERA
2002 Lk Elsinore*	A+	3	3	0	0	13.1	54	10	7	4					3	0	19	0	0	0	0	-	0	0--	-	1.57	2.70
2002 Portland*	AAA	2	2	0	0	12.1	50	9	9	4	3	0	1	1	3	0	6	0	0	1	1	.500	0	0--	-	3.16	2.92
2000 San Diego	NL	22	22	0	0	135.0	583	134	63	62	14	1	3	2	61	3	90	3	0	7	4	.636	0	0-0	-	4.34	4.13

			HOW MUCH HE PITCHED						WHAT HE GAVE UP										THE RESULTS					
Year Team	Lg	G	GS	CG	GF	IP	BFP	H	R	ER	HR	SH	SF	HB	TBB	IBB	SO	WP	Bk	W	L	Pct	ShO	Sv-Op	Hld	ERC	ERA
2001 San Diego	NL	17	17	2	0	116.2	499	108	61	56	20	3	2	5	40	3	109	3	0	8	5	.615	0	0-0	0	4.01	4.32
2002 San Diego	NL	6	6	0	0	33.1	142	28	20	20	5	2	2	2	17	0	25	2	0	1	1	.500	0	0-0	0	4.28	5.40
3 ML YEARS		45	45	2	0	285.0	1224	270	144	138	39	6	7	9	118	6	224	8	0	16	10	.615	0	0-0	0	4.20	4.36

Angel Echevarria

Bats: R **Throws:** R **Pos:** PH-22; 1B-13; RF-11; LF-8; PR-2   **Ht:** 6'4" **Wt:** 235 **Born:** 5/25/71 **Age:** 32

							BATTING													BASERUNNING				AVERAGES		
Year Team	Lg	G	AB	H	2B	3B	HR	(Hm	Rd)	TB	R	RBI	RC	TBB	IBB	SO	HBP	SH	SF	SB	CS	SB%	GDP	Avg	OBP	Slg
2002 Iowa*	AAA	63	217	64	12	3	13	(-	-)	121	40	45	41	17	2	48	4	0	0	0	0	-	4	.295	.357	.558
1996 Colorado	NL	26	21	6	0	0	0	(0	0)	6	2	6	3	2	0	5	1	0	2	0	0	-	0	.286	.346	.286
1997 Colorado	NL	15	20	5	2	0	0	(0	0)	7	4	0	2	2	0	5	0	0	0	0	0	-	0	.250	.318	.350
1998 Colorado	NL	19	29	11	3	0	1	(1	0)	17	7	9	6	2	0	3	2	0	0	0	0	-	0	.379	.455	.586
1999 Colorado	NL	102	191	56	7	0	11	(5	6)	96	28	35	30	17	0	34	3	0	0	1	3	.25	11	.293	.360	.503
2000 Col-Mil	NL	41	51	10	2	0	1	(1	0)	15	3	6	5	7	0	11	0	0	0	0	0	-	0	.196	.293	.294
2001 Milwaukee	NL	75	133	34	11	0	5	(3	2)	60	12	13	18	8	0	29	3	0	1	0	1	.00	2	.256	.310	.451
2002 Chicago	NL	50	98	30	7	0	3	(3	0)	46	14	21	15	8	0	17	1	0	4	0	0	-	2	.306	.351	.469
2000 Colorado	NL	10	9	1	0	0	0	(0	0)	1	0	2	0	0	0	2	0	0	0	0	0	-	0	.111	.111	.111
2000 Milwaukee	NL	31	42	9	2	0	1	(1	0)	14	3	4	5	7	0	9	0	0	0	0	0	-	1	.214	.327	.333
7 ML YEARS		328	543	152	32	0	21	(13	8)	247	70	90	79	46	0	104	10	0	7	1	4	.20	22	.280	.343	.455

Eric Eckenstahler

Pitches: L **Bats:** L **Pos:** RP-7   **Ht:** 6'7" **Wt:** 220 **Born:** 12/17/76 **Age:** 26

				HOW MUCH HE PITCHED						WHAT HE GAVE UP										THE RESULTS					
Year Team	Lg	G	GS	CG	GF	IP	BFP	H	R	ER	HR	SH	SF	HB	TBB	IBB	SO	WP	Bk	W	L	Pct	ShO	Sv-Op	Hld	ERC	ERA
2000 Oneonta	A-	8	0	0	4	11.0	46	7	3	2	0	0	1	2	3	0	13	1	0	0	0	-	0	0- -	-	1.71	1.64
2000 W Michigan	A	10	3	0	4	18.2	89	21	15	12	4	1	1	1	11	0	22	0	1	0	2	.000	0	1- -	-	6.58	5.79
2001 Lakeland	A+	4	0	0	2	6.0	22	3	1	1	0	0	0	1	2	0	7	2	0	1	0	1.000	0	1- -	-	1.54	1.50
2001 Erie	AA	46	0	0	18	64.2	289	65	32	28	7	1	1	3	31	4	73	3	1	4	2	.667	0	4- -	-	4.52	3.90
2002 Toledo	AAA	52	0	0	17	67.0	287	57	37	33	8	4	1	3	35	1	69	1	0	2	4	.333	0	0- -	-	4.06	4.43
2002 Detroit	AL	7	0	0	2	8.0	39	14	5	5	1	0	0	0	2	0	13	0	0	1	0	1.000	0	0-0	0	8.30	5.63

David Eckstein

Bats: R **Throws:** R **Pos:** SS-147; DH-3; PH-2   **Ht:** 5'8" **Wt:** 170 **Born:** 1/20/75 **Age:** 28

							BATTING													BASERUNNING				AVERAGES		
Year Team	Lg	G	AB	H	2B	3B	HR	(Hm	Rd)	TB	R	RBI	RC	TBB	IBB	SO	HBP	SH	SF	SB	CS	SB%	GDP	Avg	OBP	Slg
1997 Lowell	A-	68	249	75	11	4	4	(-	-)	106	43	39	48	33	1	29	12	8	1	21	5	.81	2	.301	.407	.426
1998 Sarasota	A+	135	503	154	29	4	3	(-	-)	200	99	58	97	87	3	51	22	1	2	45	16	.74	8	.306	.428	.398
1999 Trenton	AA	131	483	151	22	5	6	(-	-)	201	109	52	100	89	0	48	25	13	5	32	13	.71	6	.313	.440	.416
2000 Pawtucket	AAA	119	422	104	20	0	1	(-	-)	127	77	31	52	60	0	45	20	9	4	11	8	.58	8	.246	.364	.301
2000 Edmonton	AAA	15	52	18	8	0	3	(-	-)	35	17	8	16	9	0	1	6	1	0	5	3	.63	0	.346	.485	.673
2001 Anaheim	AL	153	582	166	26	2	4	(3	1)	208	82	41	80	43	0	60	21	16	2	29	4	.88	11	.285	.355	.357
2002 Anaheim	AL	152	608	178	22	6	8	(3	5)	236	107	63	90	45	0	44	27	14	8	21	13	.62	7	.293	.363	.388
2 ML YEARS		305	1190	344	48	8	12	(6	6)	444	189	104	170	88	0	104	48	30	10	50	17	.75	18	.289	.359	.373

Jim Edmonds

Bats: L **Throws:** L **Pos:** CF-139; PH-10   **Ht:** 6'1" **Wt:** 212 **Born:** 6/27/70 **Age:** 33

							BATTING													BASERUNNING				AVERAGES		
Year Team	Lg	G	AB	H	2B	3B	HR	(Hm	Rd)	TB	R	RBI	RC	TBB	IBB	SO	HBP	SH	SF	SB	CS	SB%	GDP	Avg	OBP	Slg
1993 Anaheim	AL	18	61	15	4	1	0	(0	0)	21	5	4	4	2	1	16	0	0	0	0	2	.00	1	.246	.270	.344
1994 Anaheim	AL	94	289	79	13	1	5	(3	2)	109	35	37	38	30	3	72	1	1	1	4	2	.67	3	.273	.343	.377
1995 Anaheim	AL	141	558	162	30	4	33	(16	17)	299	120	107	100	51	4	130	5	1	5	1	4	.20	10	.290	.352	.536
1996 Anaheim	AL	114	431	131	28	3	27	(17	10)	246	73	66	88	46	2	101	4	0	2	4	0	1.00	8	.304	.375	.571
1997 Anaheim	AL	133	502	146	27	0	26	(14	12)	251	82	80	90	60	5	80	4	0	5	5	7	.42	8	.291	.368	.500
1998 Anaheim	AL	154	599	184	42	1	25	(9	16)	303	115	91	104	57	7	114	1	1	1	7	5	.58	16	.307	.368	.506
1999 Anaheim	AL	55	204	51	17	2	5	(3	2)	87	34	23	30	28	0	45	0	0	1	5	4	.56	3	.250	.339	.426
2000 St Louis	NL	152	525	155	25	0	42	(22	20)	306	129	108	126	103	3	167	6	1	8	10	3	.77	5	.295	.411	.583
2001 St Louis	NL	150	500	152	38	1	30	(16	14)	282	95	110	113	93	12	136	4	1	10	5	5	.50	8	.304	.410	.564
2002 St Louis	NL	144	476	148	31	2	28	(17	11)	267	96	83	102	86	14	134	8	0	6	4	3	.57	9	.311	.420	.561
10 ML YEARS		1155	4145	1223	255	15	221	(117	104)	2171	784	709	795	556	51	995	33	5	39	45	35	.56	71	.295	.380	.524

Joey Eischen

Pitches: L **Bats:** L **Pos:** RP-59   **Ht:** 6'0" **Wt:** 210 **Born:** 5/25/70 **Age:** 33

				HOW MUCH HE PITCHED						WHAT HE GAVE UP										THE RESULTS					
Year Team	Lg	G	GS	CG	GF	IP	BFP	H	R	ER	HR	SH	SF	HB	TBB	IBB	SO	WP	Bk	W	L	Pct	ShO	Sv-Op	Hld	ERC	ERA
2002 Ottawa*	AAA	11	0	0	9	14.0	55	8	4	0	0	0	0	3	3	0	15	0	0	1	0	1.000	0	4- -	-	1.51	0.00
1994 Montreal	NL	1	0	0	0	0.2	7	4	4	4	0	0	0	1	0	0	1	0	0	0	0	-	0	0-0	0	47.92	54.00
1995 Los Angeles	NL	17	0	0	8	20.1	95	19	9	7	1	0	0	2	11	1	15	1	0	0	0	-	0	0-0	1	3.97	3.10
1996 LA-Det	NL	52	0	0	14	68.1	308	75	36	32	7	3	2	4	34	7	51	4	0	1	2	.333	0	0-2	2	5.15	4.21
1997 Cincinnati	NL	1	0	0	0	1.1	7	2	1	1	0	0	0	0	1	0	2	1	0	0	0	-	0	0-0	0	7.52	6.75
2001 Montreal	NL	24	0	0	7	29.2	131	29	17	16	4	1	0	1	16	1	19	1	0	0	1	.000	0	0-2	4	4.89	4.85
2002 Montreal	NL	59	0	0	18	53.2	217	43	11	8	1	3	2	2	18	5	51	6	1	6	1	.857	0	2-3	11	2.31	1.34
1996 Los Angeles	NL	28	0	0	11	43.1	198	48	25	23	4	3	1	4	20	4	36	1	0	1	0	1.000	0	0-0	1	5.07	4.78
1996 Detroit	AL	24	0	0	3	25.0	110	27	11	9	3	0	1	0	14	3	15	3	0	1	1	.500	0	0-2	1	5.30	3.24
6 ML YEARS		154	0	0	47	174.0	765	172	79	68	13	7	4	10	80	14	139	13	1	7	4	.636	0	2-7	16	4.16	3.52

Scott Elarton

Pitches: R **Bats:** R **Pos:** SP   **Ht:** 6'8" **Wt:** 240 **Born:** 2/23/76 **Age:** 27

Year Team		HOW MUCH HE PITCHED						WHAT HE GAVE UP											THE RESULTS					
	Lg	G	GS	CG	GF	IP	BFP	H	R	ER	HR	SH	SF	HB	TBB	IBB	SO	WP	Bk	W	L	Pct	ShO	Sv-Op	Hld	ERC	ERA
1998 Houston	NL	28	2	0	7	57.0	227	40	21	21	5	1	1	1	20	0	56	1	0	2	1	.667	0	2-3	2	2.35	3.32
1999 Houston	NL	42	15	0	8	124.0	524	111	55	48	8	7	4	4	43	0	121	3	0	9	5	.643	0	1-4	5	3.16	3.48
2000 Houston	NL	30	30	2	0	192.2	855	198	117	103	29	5	7	6	84	1	131	8	0	17	7	.708	0	0-0	0	4.82	4.81
2001 Hou-Col	NL	24	24	0	0	132.2	595	146	105	104	34	7	2	6	59	2	87	5	0	4	10	.286	0	0-0	0	6.21	7.06
2001 Houston	NL	20	20	0	0	109.2	499	126	88	87	26	7	2	6	49	1	76	5	0	4	8	.333	0	0-0	0	6.42	7.14
2001 Colorado	NL	4	4	0	0	23.0	96	20	17	17	8	0	0	0	10	1	11	0	0	0	2	.000	0	0-0	0	5.18	6.65
4 ML YEARS		124	71	2	15	506.1	2201	495	298	276	76	20	14	17	206	3	395	17	0	32	23	.582	0	3-7	7	4.44	4.91

Dave Elder

Pitches: R **Bats:** R **Pos:** RP-15   **Ht:** 6'0" **Wt:** 180 **Born:** 9/23/75 **Age:** 27

Year Team		HOW MUCH HE PITCHED						WHAT HE GAVE UP											THE RESULTS					
	Lg	G	GS	CG	GF	IP	BFP	H	R	ER	HR	SH	SF	HB	TBB	IBB	SO	WP	Bk	W	L	Pct	ShO	Sv-Op	Hld	ERC	ERA
1997 Pulaski	R+	20	0	0	17	32.1	127	18	8	7	2	1	0	1	12	0	57	4	0	2	2	.500	0	6--	-	1.56	1.95
1999 Charlotte	A+	24	1	0	16	44.1	186	33	15	14	2	4	0	2	25	0	42	4	0	4	2	.667	0	4--	-	3.16	2.84
1999 Tulsa	AA	3	0	0	1	6.2	32	8	7	6	0	0	0	0	6	1	7	0	0	1	0	1.000	0	0--	-	6.37	8.10
2000 Tulsa	AA	33	21	0	8	116.2	554	121	80	64	9	4	4	4	88	0	104	11	0	7	6	.538	0	3--	-	5.63	4.94
2001 Tulsa	AA	13	13	0	0	72.0	308	64	28	24	1	0	3	2	43	0	78	3	0	4	6	.400	0	0--	-	3.83	3.00
2001 Oklahoma	AAA	15	8	0	3	57.2	266	54	36	32	4	2	0	4	43	0	56	4	1	5	4	.556	0	0--	-	5.15	4.99
2002 Akron	AA	23	1	0	18	36.0	142	19	8	8	1	1	0	0	18	2	42	1	0	2	1	.667	0	9--	-	1.59	2.00
2002 Buffalo	AAA	22	1	0	15	34.0	145	32	11	10	1	1	1	0	14	0	42	2	0	3	1	.750	0	5--	-	3.31	2.65
2002 Cleveland	AL	15	0	0	3	23.0	100	18	10	8	1	1	2	1	14	3	23	0	0	0	2	.000	0	0-0	3	3.22	3.13

Cal Eldred

Pitches: R **Bats:** R **Pos:** RP   **Ht:** 6'4" **Wt:** 235 **Born:** 11/24/67 **Age:** 35

Year Team		HOW MUCH HE PITCHED						WHAT HE GAVE UP											THE RESULTS					
	Lg	G	GS	CG	GF	IP	BFP	H	R	ER	HR	SH	SF	HB	TBB	IBB	SO	WP	Bk	W	L	Pct	ShO	Sv-Op	Hld	ERC	ERA
1991 Milwaukee	NL	3	3	0	0	16.0	73	20	9	8	2	0	0	0	6	0	10	0	0	2	0	1.000	0	0-0	0	5.57	4.50
1992 Milwaukee	NL	14	14	2	0	100.1	394	76	21	20	4	1	0	2	23	0	62	3	0	11	2	.846	1	0-0	0	1.94	1.79
1993 Milwaukee	NL	36	36	8	0	258.0	1087	232	120	115	32	5	12	10	91	5	180	2	0	16	16	.500	1	0-0	0	3.62	4.01
1994 Milwaukee	NL	25	25	6	0	179.0	769	158	96	93	23	5	7	4	84	0	98	2	0	11	11	.500	0	0-0	0	3.97	4.68
1995 Milwaukee	NL	4	4	0	0	23.2	104	24	10	9	4	1	0	1	10	0	18	1	1	1	1	.500	0	0-0	0	4.91	3.42
1996 Milwaukee	NL	15	15	0	0	84.2	363	82	43	42	8	0	4	6	38	0	50	1	0	4	4	.500	0	0-0	0	4.33	4.46
1997 Milwaukee	NL	34	34	1	0	202.0	885	207	118	112	31	4	6	9	89	0	122	5	0	13	15	.464	1	0-0	0	5.00	4.99
1998 Milwaukee	NL	23	23	0	0	133.0	602	157	82	71	14	5	3	4	61	3	86	6	0	4	8	.333	0	0-0	0	5.54	4.80
1999 Milwaukee	NL	20	15	0	2	82.0	392	101	75	71	19	2	3	1	46	0	60	8	1	2	8	.200	0	0-0	0	7.13	7.79
2000 Chicago	AL	20	20	2	0	112.0	492	103	61	57	12	3	2	5	59	0	97	4	0	10	2	.833	1	0-0	0	4.36	4.58
2001 Chicago	AL	2	2	0	0	6.0	34	12	9	9	1	0	0	1	3	1	6	0	0	0	1	.000	0	0-0	0	14.25	13.50
11 ML YEARS		196	191	19	2	1196.2	5195	1172	644	607	150	26	37	43	510	9	789	32	2	74	68	.521	4	0-0	0	4.39	4.57

Mark Ellis

Bats: R **Throws:** R **Pos:** 2B-85; SS-8; 3B-7; PR-3; PH-2   **Ht:** 5'11" **Wt:** 180 **Born:** 6/6/77 **Age:** 26

Year Team		BATTING																	BASERUNNING				AVERAGES		
	Lg	G	AB	H	2B	3B	HR	(Hm | Rd)	TB	R	RBI	RC	TBB	IBB	SO	HBP	SH	SF	SB	CS	SB%	GDP	Avg	OBP	Slg
1999 Spokane	A-	71	281	92	14	0	7	(- | -)	127	67	47	59	47	3	40	3	5	4	21	7	.75	1	.327	.424	.452
2000 Wilmington	A+	132	484	146	27	4	6	(- | -)	199	83	62	86	78	0	72	7	4	3	25	7	.78	11	.302	.404	.411
2000 Wichita	AA	7	22	7	1	0	0	(- | -)	8	4	4	4	5	0	5	0	0	0	1	0	1.00	0	.318	.444	.364
2001 Sacramento	AAA	132	472	129	38	6	0	(- | -)	197	71	53	70	54	4	78	5	5	5	21	7	.75	13	.273	.351	.417
2002 Sacramento	AAA	21	84	25	10	1	0	(- | -)	37	14	5	15	6	0	13	4	0	0	4	0	1.00	1	.298	.372	.440
2002 Oakland	AL	98	345	94	16	4	6	(6 | 0)	136	58	35	54	44	1	54	4	8	3	4	2	.67	3	.272	.359	.394

Robert Ellis

Pitches: R **Bats:** R **Pos:** RP-3   **Ht:** 6'5" **Wt:** 220 **Born:** 12/15/70 **Age:** 32

Year Team		HOW MUCH HE PITCHED						WHAT HE GAVE UP											THE RESULTS					
	Lg	G	GS	CG	GF	IP	BFP	H	R	ER	HR	SH	SF	HB	TBB	IBB	SO	WP	Bk	W	L	Pct	ShO	Sv-Op	Hld	ERC	ERA
2002 Las Vegas*	AAA	29	28	1	0	172.2	753	195	100	80	17	12	4	13	37	0	110	12	2	9	7	.563	0	0--	-	4.31	4.17
1996 Anaheim	AL	3	0	0	3	5.0	19	0	0	0	0	0	0	0	4	0	5	1	0	0	0	—	0	0-0	0	0.64	0.00
2001 Arizona	NL	19	17	0	1	92.0	413	106	61	59	12	6	7	4	34	2	41	3	2	6	5	.545	0	0-0	0	5.17	5.77
2002 Los Angeles	NL	3	0	0	0	2.2	13	6	3	3	1	0	0	0	0	0	0	0	0	0	1	.000	0	0-0	0	13.68	10.13
3 ML YEARS		25	17	0	4	99.2	445	112	64	62	13	6	7	4	38	2	46	4	2	6	6	.500	0	0-0	0	5.04	5.60

Alan Embree

Pitches: L **Bats:** L **Pos:** RP-68   **Ht:** 6'2" **Wt:** 190 **Born:** 1/23/70 **Age:** 33

Year Team		HOW MUCH HE PITCHED						WHAT HE GAVE UP											THE RESULTS					
	Lg	G	GS	CG	GF	IP	BFP	H	R	ER	HR	SH	SF	HB	TBB	IBB	SO	WP	Bk	W	L	Pct	ShO	Sv-Op	Hld	ERC	ERA
1992 Cleveland	AL	4	4	0	0	18.0	81	19	14	14	3	0	2	0	8	0	12	1	1	0	2	.000	0	0-0	0	5.25	7.00
1995 Cleveland	AL	23	0	0	8	24.2	111	23	16	14	2	2	2	0	16	0	23	1	0	3	2	.600	0	1-1	6	4.51	5.11
1996 Cleveland	AL	24	0	0	2	31.0	141	30	26	22	10	1	3	2	21	3	33	3	0	1	1	.500	0	0-0	1	6.58	6.39
1997 Atlanta	NL	66	0	0	15	46.0	190	36	13	13	1	4	1	2	20	2	45	3	1	3	1	.750	0	0-0	16	2.66	2.54
1998 Atl-Ari	NL	55	0	0	16	53.2	237	56	32	25	7	4	1	1	23	0	43	3	0	4	2	.667	0	1-3	12	4.71	4.19
1999 San Francisco	NL	68	0	0	13	58.2	244	42	22	22	6	3	2	3	26	2	53	1	0	3	2	.600	0	0-3	22	2.86	3.38
2000 San Francisco	NL	63	0	0	21	60.0	263	62	34	33	4	4	5	3	25	2	49	1	0	3	5	.375	0	2-5	9	4.24	4.95
2001 SF-CWS	AL	61	0	0	17	54.0	245	65	47	44	14	0	6	3	17	2	59	3	1	1	4	.200	0	0-3	9	6.20	7.33
2002 SD-Bos	NL	68	0	0	20	62.0	251	47	19	14	6	1	2	1	20	3	81	1	0	4	6	.400	0	2-7	18	2.48	2.03
1998 Atlanta	NL	20	0	0	5	18.2	87	23	14	9	2	1	1	0	10	0	19	0	0	1	0	1.000	0	0-1	6	6.06	4.34
1998 Arizona	NL	35	0	0	11	35.0	150	33	18	16	5	3	0	1	13	0	24	3	0	3	2	.600	0	1-2	6	4.03	4.11

Year Team	Lg	G	GS	CG	GF	IP	BFP	H	R	ER	HR	SH	SF	HB	TBB	IBB	SO	WP	Bk	W	L	Pct	ShO	Sv-Op	Hld	ERC	ERA
2001 San Francisco	NL	22	0	0	7	20.0	106	34	26	25	7	0	3	2	10	2	25	1	0	0	2	.000	0	0-1	0	11.29	11.25
2001 Chicago	AL	39	0	0	10	34.0	139	31	21	19	7	0	3	1	7	0	34	2	0	1	2	.333	0	0-2	9	3.61	5.03
2002 San Diego	NL	36	0	0	13	28.2	118	23	7	3	2	0	0	0	9	2	38	1	0	3	4	.429	0	0-2	10	2.38	0.94
2002 Boston	AL	32	0	0	7	33.1	133	24	12	11	4	1	2	1	11	1	43	0	0	1	2	.333	0	2-5	8	2.56	2.97
9 ML YEARS		432	4	0	112	408.0	1763	380	223	201	53	19	24	14	176	14	398	19	2	22	25	.468	0	6-22	93	4.09	4.43

Juan Encarnacion

Bats: R **Throws:** R **Pos:** RF-93; CF-71; PH-3   **Ht:** 6'3" **Wt:** 215 **Born:** 3/8/76 **Age:** 27

							BATTING													BASERUNNING				AVERAGES		
Year Team	Lg	G	AB	H	2B	3B	HR	(Hm	Rd)	TB	R	RBI	RC	TBB	IBB	SO	HBP	SH	SF	SB	CS	SB%	GDP	Avg	OBP	Slg
1997 Detroit	AL	11	33	7	1	1	1	(1	0)	13	3	5	4	3	0	12	2	0	0	3	1	.75	1	.212	.316	.394
1998 Detroit	AL	40	164	54	9	4	7	(4	3)	92	30	21	31	7	0	31	1	0	3	7	4	.64	2	.329	.354	.561
1999 Detroit	AL	132	509	130	30	6	19	(6	13)	229	62	74	64	14	1	113	9	4	2	33	12	.73	12	.255	.287	.450
2000 Detroit	AL	141	547	158	25	6	14	(4	10)	237	75	72	76	29	1	90	7	3	4	16	4	.80	15	.289	.330	.433
2001 Detroit	AL	120	417	101	19	7	12	(4	8)	170	52	52	48	25	1	93	6	5	4	9	5	.64	9	.242	.292	.408
2002 Cin-Fla	NL	152	584	158	22	5	24	(8	16)	262	77	85	74	46	0	113	4	3	7	21	9	.70	18	.271	.324	.449
2002 Cincinnati	NL	83	321	89	11	2	16	(6	10)	152	43	51	42	26	0	63	1	3	3	9	4	.69	7	.277	.330	.474
2002 Florida	NL	69	263	69	11	3	8	(2	6)	110	34	34	32	20	0	50	3	0	4	12	5	.71	11	.262	.317	.418
6 ML YEARS		596	2254	608	106	29	77	(27	50)	1003	299	309	297	124	3	452	29	15	20	89	35	.72	57	.270	.314	.445

Mario Encarnacion

Bats: R **Throws:** R **Pos:** LF-2; PH-1   **Ht:** 6'2" **Wt:** 187 **Born:** 9/24/75 **Age:** 27

							BATTING													BASERUNNING				AVERAGES		
Year Team	Lg	G	AB	H	2B	3B	HR	(Hm	Rd)	TB	R	RBI	RC	TBB	IBB	SO	HBP	SH	SF	SB	CS	SB%	GDP	Avg	OBP	Slg
1996 W Michigan	A	118	401	92	14	3	7	(-	-)	133	55	43	43	49	0	131	5	4	0	23	8	.74	12	.229	.321	.332
1997 Modesto	A+	111	364	108	17	9	18	(-	-)	197	70	78	70	42	1	121	6	0	1	14	11	.56	7	.297	.378	.541
1998 Huntsville	AA	110	357	97	15	2	15	(-	-)	161	70	61	61	60	1	123	4	3	1	11	8	.58	9	.272	.382	.451
1999 Midland	AA	94	353	109	21	4	18	(-	-)	192	69	71	70	47	4	86	1	0	2	9	9	.50	6	.309	.390	.544
1999 Vancouver	AAA	39	145	35	5	0	3	(-	-)	49	18	17	11	6	0	44	2	0	2	5	4	.56	7	.241	.277	.338
2000 Sacramento	AAA	81	301	81	16	3	13	(-	-)	142	51	61	49	36	2	95	3	1	5	15	7	.68	8	.269	.348	.472
2000 Modesto	A+	5	15	3	0	0	0	(-	-)	3	1	1	0	1	0	4	0	0	0	0	0	-	2	.200	.250	.200
2001 Sacramento	AAA	51	186	53	8	2	12	(-	-)	101	29	33	33	17	2	61	4	0	1	4	3	.57	5	.285	.356	.543
2001 Co Springs	AAA	16	45	17	5	0	2	(-	-)	28	8	10	11	4	0	8	1	0	0	0	1	.00	1	.378	.440	.622
2002 Iowa	AAA	61	200	56	9	0	7	(-	-)	86	24	28	27	17	0	61	3	0	2	0	2	.00	7	.280	.342	.430
2001 Colorado	NL	20	62	14	1	0	0	(0	0)	15	3	3	3	5	0	14	0	0	0	2	1	.67	3	.226	.284	.242
2002 Chicago	NL	3	7	0	0	0	0	(0	0)	0	0	0	0	2	0	3	0	0	0	0	0	-	0	.000	.222	.000
2 ML YEARS		23	69	14	1	0	0	(0	0)	15	3	3	3	7	0	17	0	0	0	2	1	.67	3	.203	.276	.217

John Ennis

Pitches: R **Bats:** R **Pos:** SP-1   **Ht:** 6'5" **Wt:** 220 **Born:** 10/17/79 **Age:** 23

		HOW MUCH HE PITCHED						WHAT HE GAVE UP												THE RESULTS							
Year Team	Lg	G	GS	CG	GF	IP	BFP	H	R	ER	HR	SH	SF	HB	TBB	IBB	SO	WP	Bk	W	L	Pct	ShO	Sv-Op	Hld	ERC	ERA
1998 Braves	R	8	2	0	2	25.1	113	30	16	13	0	1	0	2	6	1	18	1	0	0	3	.000	0	0--	-	3.91	4.62
1999 Danville	R+	13	13	0	0	65.2	296	71	46	37	7	3	2	9	21	0	60	3	2	4	3	.571	0	0--	-	4.73	5.07
2000 Macon	A	18	16	0	0	98.2	403	77	37	28	5	2	1	6	25	0	105	3	0	7	4	.636	0	0--	-	2.27	2.55
2001 Myrtle Beach	A+	25	25	1	0	138.1	569	111	63	55	12	4	5	7	45	0	144	2	3	6	8	.429	0	0--	-	2.84	3.58
2002 Greenville	AA	26	26	0	0	148.2	625	131	79	69	7	11	5	7	62	0	103	6	0	9	9	.500	0	0--	-	3.35	4.18
2002 Atlanta	NL	1	1	0	0	4.0	18	5	2	2	0	1	0	0	3	0	1	0	0	0	0	-	0	0-0	0	6.70	4.50

Morgan Ensberg

Bats: R **Throws:** R **Pos:** 3B-43; PH-6; PR-1   **Ht:** 6'2" **Wt:** 210 **Born:** 8/26/75 **Age:** 27

							BATTING													BASERUNNING				AVERAGES		
Year Team	Lg	G	AB	H	2B	3B	HR	(Hm	Rd)	TB	R	RBI	RC	TBB	IBB	SO	HBP	SH	SF	SB	CS	SB%	GDP	Avg	OBP	Slg
1998 Auburn	A-	59	196	45	10	1	5	(-	-)	72	39	31	33	46	1	51	6	0	2	15	3	.83	5	.230	.388	.367
1999 Kissimmee	A+	123	427	102	25	2	15	(-	-)	176	72	69	66	68	0	90	9	1	3	17	6	.74	9	.239	.353	.412
2000 Round Rock	AA	137	483	145	34	0	28	(-	-)	263	95	90	104	92	3	107	8	3	6	9	12	.43	15	.300	.416	.545
2001 New Orleans	AAA	87	316	98	20	0	23	(-	-)	187	65	61	69	45	0	60	3	0	4	6	3	.67	12	.310	.397	.592
2002 New Orleans	AAA	83	292	84	12	3	7	(-	-)	123	50	37	51	50	1	56	7	1	3	9	5	.64	9	.288	.401	.421
2000 Houston	NL	4	7	2	0	0	0	(0	0)	2	0	0	1	0	0	1	0	0	0	0	0	-	0	.286	.286	.286
2002 Houston	NL	49	132	32	7	2	3	(2	1)	52	14	19	13	18	0	25	3	0	0	2	0	1.00	8	.242	.346	.394
2 ML YEARS		53	139	34	7	2	3	(2	1)	54	14	19	14	18	0	26	3	0	0	2	0	1.00	8	.245	.344	.388

Scott Erickson

Pitches: R **Bats:** R **Pos:** SP-28; RP-1   **Ht:** 6'4" **Wt:** 230 **Born:** 2/2/68 **Age:** 35

		HOW MUCH HE PITCHED						WHAT HE GAVE UP												THE RESULTS							
Year Team	Lg	G	GS	CG	GF	IP	BFP	H	R	ER	HR	SH	SF	HB	TBB	IBB	SO	WP	Bk	W	L	Pct	ShO	Sv-Op	Hld	ERC	ERA
1990 Minnesota	AL	19	17	1	1	113.0	485	108	49	36	9	5	2	5	51	4	53	3	0	8	4	.667	0	0-0	0	4.07	2.87
1991 Minnesota	AL	32	32	5	0	204.0	851	189	80	72	13	5	7	6	71	3	108	4	0	20	8	.714	3	0-0	0	3.36	3.18
1992 Minnesota	AL	32	32	5	0	212.0	888	197	86	80	9	7	9	8	83	3	101	6	1	13	12	.520	3	0-0	0	3.75	3.40
1993 Minnesota	AL	34	34	1	0	218.2	976	266	138	126	17	10	13	10	71	1	116	5	0	8	19	.296	0	0-0	0	5.05	5.19
1994 Minnesota	AL	23	23	2	0	144.0	654	173	95	87	15	3	4	9	59	0	104	10	0	8	11	.421	1	0-0	0	5.61	5.44
1995 Min-Bal	AL	32	31	7	1	196.1	836	213	108	105	18	3	5	6	67	0	106	3	2	13	10	.565	2	0-0	0	4.48	4.81
1996 Baltimore	AL	34	34	6	0	222.1	968	262	137	124	21	5	5	11	66	4	100	1	0	13	12	.520	0	0-0	0	4.90	5.02
1997 Baltimore	AL	34	33	3	0	221.2	922	218	100	91	16	3	4	5	61	5	131	11	0	16	7	.696	2	0-0	0	3.40	3.69
1998 Baltimore	AL	36	36	11	0	251.1	1102	284	125	112	23	7	2	13	69	4	186	4	0	16	13	.552	2	0-0	0	4.40	4.01
1999 Baltimore	AL	34	34	6	0	230.1	995	244	127	123	27	7	6	11	99	4	106	10	0	15	12	.556	3	0-0	0	4.97	4.81
2000 Baltimore	AL	16	16	1	0	92.2	446	127	81	81	14	3	5	4	48	0	41	0	0	5	8	.385	0	0-0	0	7.50	7.87
2002 Baltimore	AL	29	28	3	0	160.2	719	192	109	99	20	2	7	8	68	2	74	5	0	5	12	.294	0	0-0	0	5.80	5.55

Year Team	Lg	G	GS	CG	GF	IP	BFP	H	R	ER	HR	SH	SF	HB	TBB	IBB	SO	WP	Bk	W	L	Pct	ShO	Sv-Op	Hld	ERC	ERA
1995 Minnesota	AL	15	15	0	0	87.2	390	102	61	58	11	2	1	4	32	0	45	1	0	4	6	.400	0	0-0	0	5.29	5.95
1995 Baltimore	AL	17	16	7	1	108.2	446	111	47	47	7	1	2	1	35	0	61	2	2	9	4	.692	2	0-0	0	3.84	3.89
12 ML YEARS		355	350	51	2	2267.0	9842	2473	1235	1136	211	63	65	96	813	30	1226	65	3	140	128	.522	17	0-0	0	4.58	4.51

Darin Erstad

Bats: L **Throws:** L **Pos:** CF-143; 1B-5; DH-4; PH-3   **Ht:** 6'2" **Wt:** 220 **Born:** 6/4/74 **Age:** 29

								BATTING												BASERUNNING				AVERAGES		
Year Team	Lg	G	AB	H	2B	3B	HR	(Hm	Rd)	TB	R	RBI	RC	TBB	IBB	SO	HBP	SH	SF	SB	CS	SB%	GDP	Avg	OBP	Slg
1996 Anaheim	AL	57	208	59	5	1	4	(1	3)	78	34	20	26	17	1	29	0	1	3	3	3	.50	3	.284	.333	.375
1997 Anaheim	AL	139	539	161	34	4	16	(8	8)	251	99	77	92	51	4	86	4	5	6	23	8	.74	5	.299	.360	.466
1998 Anaheim	AL	133	537	159	39	3	19	(9	10)	261	84	82	94	43	7	77	6	1	3	20	6	.77	2	.296	.353	.486
1999 Anaheim	AL	142	585	148	22	5	13	(7	6)	219	84	53	64	47	3	65	1	1	3	17	7	.65	16	.253	.308	.374
2000 Anaheim	AL	157	676	240	39	6	25	(11	14)	366	121	100	145	64	9	82	1	2	4	28	8	.78	6	.355	.409	.541
2001 Anaheim	AL	157	631	163	35	1	9	(3	6)	227	89	63	79	62	7	113	10	1	7	24	10	.71	8	.258	.331	.360
2002 Anaheim	AL	150	625	177	28	4	10	(2	8)	243	99	73	73	27	4	67	2	5	4	23	3	.88	9	.283	.313	.389
7 ML YEARS		935	3801	1107	202	24	96	(41	55)	1645	610	468	573	311	35	555	24	17	30	134	45	.75	51	.291	.346	.433

Felix Escalona

Bats: R **Throws:** R **Pos:** SS-26; 2B-25; 3B-4; PR-4; PH-3   **Ht:** 6'0" **Wt:** 196 **Born:** 3/12/79 **Age:** 24

								BATTING												BASERUNNING				AVERAGES		
Year Team	Lg	G	AB	H	2B	3B	HR	(Hm	Rd)	TB	R	RBI	RC	TBB	IBB	SO	HBP	SH	SF	SB	CS	SB%	GDP	Avg	OBP	Slg
1996 Astros	R	28	75	11	2	0	1	(-	-)	16	8	9	4	8	0	31	4	1	1	1	2	.33	0	.147	.261	.213
1997 Astros	R	51	189	39	9	0	1	(-	-)	51	27	9	17	20	0	49	3	4	0	11	3	.79	1	.206	.292	.270
1997 Kissimmee	A+	3	9	2	0	0	0	(-	-)	2	6	0	2	1	0	2	3	0	0	0	0	-	0	.222	.462	.222
1998 Kissimmee	A+	3	4	0	0	0	0	(-	-)	0	0	0	0	0	0	1	0	0	0	0	0	-	0	.000	.000	.000
1998 Auburn	A-	51	149	31	5	0	1	(-	-)	39	22	17	11	11	0	33	6	1	4	4	2	.67	4	.208	.282	.262
1999 Michigan	A	116	396	114	29	4	6	(-	-)	169	78	47	61	29	0	60	17	7	3	7	7	.50	4	.288	.360	.427
2000 Michigan	A	64	251	65	14	1	6	(-	-)	99	42	35	34	22	1	49	4	3	2	7	0	1.00	4	.259	.326	.394
2000 Kissimmee	A+	42	143	36	5	1	0	(-	-)	43	19	8	14	9	0	21	6	3	1	5	3	.63	3	.252	.321	.301
2001 Lexington	A	130	536	155	42	2	16	(-	-)	249	92	64	88	30	2	85	16	5	5	46	12	.79	8	.289	.342	.465
2002 Tampa Bay	AL	59	157	34	8	2	0	(0	0)	46	17	9	12	3	0	44	7	3	1	7	2	.78	2	.217	.262	.293

Kelvim Escobar

Pitches: R **Bats:** R **Pos:** RP-76   **Ht:** 6'1" **Wt:** 210 **Born:** 4/11/76 **Age:** 27

									HOW MUCH HE PITCHED			WHAT HE GAVE UP										THE RESULTS					
Year Team	Lg	G	GS	CG	GF	IP	BFP	H	R	ER	HR	SH	SF	HB	TBB	IBB	SO	WP	Bk	W	L	Pct	ShO	Sv-Op	Hld	ERC	ERA
1997 Toronto	AL	27	0	0	23	31.0	139	28	12	10	1	2	0	0	19	2	36	0	0	3	2	.600	0	14-17	1	3.68	2.90
1998 Toronto	AL	22	10	0	2	79.2	342	72	37	33	5	0	3	0	35	0	72	0	0	7	3	.700	0	0-1	5	3.41	3.73
1999 Toronto	AL	33	30	1	2	174.0	795	203	118	110	19	2	8	10	81	2	129	6	1	14	11	.560	0	0-0	0	5.62	5.69
2000 Toronto	AL	43	24	3	8	180.0	794	186	118	107	26	5	4	3	85	3	142	4	0	10	15	.400	1	2-3	3	4.94	5.35
2001 Toronto	AL	59	11	0	15	126.0	517	93	51	49	8	2	5	3	52	5	121	2	0	6	8	.429	1	0-0	13	2.54	3.50
2002 Toronto	AL	76	0	0	68	78.0	355	75	39	37	10	1	0	5	44	6	85	4	0	5	7	.417	0	38-46	3	4.77	4.27
6 ML YEARS		260	75	5	118	668.2	2942	657	375	346	69	12	20	21	316	18	585	16	1	45	46	.495	2	54-67	22	4.36	4.66

Bobby Estalella

Bats: R **Throws:** R **Pos:** C-37; PH-1   **Ht:** 6'1" **Wt:** 213 **Born:** 8/23/74 **Age:** 28

								BATTING												BASERUNNING				AVERAGES		
Year Team	Lg	G	AB	H	2B	3B	HR	(Hm	Rd)	TB	R	RBI	RC	TBB	IBB	SO	HBP	SH	SF	SB	CS	SB%	GDP	Avg	OBP	Slg
2002 Co Springs*	AAA	23	79	23	9	0	6	(-	-)	50	16	20	18	11	0	20	0	0	1	0	0	-	0	.291	.374	.633
1996 Philadelphia	NL	7	17	6	0	0	2	(0	2)	12	5	4	4	1	0	6	0	0	0	1	0	1.00	0	.353	.389	.706
1997 Philadelphia	NL	13	29	10	1	0	4	(1	3)	23	9	9	9	7	0	7	0	0	0	0	0	-	2	.345	.472	.793
1998 Philadelphia	NL	47	165	31	6	1	8	(3	5)	63	16	20	15	13	0	49	1	0	3	0	0	-	4	.188	.247	.382
1999 Philadelphia	NL	9	18	3	0	0	0	(0	0)	3	2	1	1	4	0	7	0	0	0	0	1	.00	0	.167	.318	.167
2000 San Francisco	NL	106	299	70	22	3	14	(6	8)	140	45	53	52	57	9	92	2	0	3	3	0	1.00	4	.234	.357	.468
2001 SF-NYY		32	97	19	5	1	3	(2	1)	35	12	10	10	12	2	30	2	0	0	0	0	-	2	.196	.297	.361
2002 Colorado	NL	38	112	23	8	0	8	(6	2)	55	17	25	18	14	0	33	0	0	4	0	1	.00	1	.205	.285	.491
2001 San Francisco	NL	29	93	19	5	1	3	(2	1)	35	11	10	10	11	2	28	1	0	0	0	0	-	2	.204	.295	.376
2001 New York	AL	3	4	0	0	0	0	(0	0)	0	1	0	0	1	0	2	1	0	0	0	0	-	0	.000	.333	.000
7 ML YEARS		252	737	162	42	5	39	(18	21)	331	106	122	109	108	11	224	5	0	10	4	2	.67	13	.220	.320	.449

Shawn Estes

Pitches: L **Bats:** R **Pos:** SP-29   **Ht:** 6'2" **Wt:** 200 **Born:** 2/18/73 **Age:** 30

									HOW MUCH HE PITCHED			WHAT HE GAVE UP										THE RESULTS					
Year Team	Lg	G	GS	CG	GF	IP	BFP	H	R	ER	HR	SH	SF	HB	TBB	IBB	SO	WP	Bk	W	L	Pct	ShO	Sv-Op	Hld	ERC	ERA
1995 San Francisco	NL	3	3	0	0	17.1	76	16	14	13	2	0	0	1	5	0	14	4	0	0	3	.000	0	0-0	0	3.37	6.75
1996 San Francisco	NL	11	11	0	0	70.0	305	63	30	28	3	5	0	2	39	3	60	4	0	3	5	.375	0	0-0	0	3.78	3.60
1997 San Francisco	NL	32	32	3	0	201.0	849	162	80	71	12	13	2	8	100	2	181	10	2	19	5	.792	2	0-0	0	3.28	3.18
1998 San Francisco	NL	25	25	1	0	149.1	661	150	89	84	14	15	4	5	80	6	136	6	1	7	12	.368	1	0-0	0	4.71	5.06
1999 San Francisco	NL	32	32	1	0	203.0	914	209	121	111	21	14	3	5	112	2	159	15	1	11	11	.500	1	0-0	0	4.96	4.92
2000 San Francisco	NL	30	30	4	0	190.1	829	194	99	90	11	7	6	3	108	1	136	11	0	15	6	.714	2	0-0	0	4.75	4.26
2001 San Francisco	NL	27	27	0	0	159.0	693	151	78	71	11	5	9	5	77	7	109	10	2	9	8	.529	0	0-0	0	3.96	4.02
2002 NYM-Cin	NL	29	29	1	0	160.2	713	171	94	91	13	7	6	9	83	9	109	3	1	5	12	.294	1	0-0	0	5.00	5.10
2002 New York	NL	23	23	1	0	132.2	580	133	70	67	12	7	4	5	66	9	92	2	1	4	9	.308	1	0-0	0	4.51	4.55
2002 Cincinnati	NL	6	6	0	0	28.0	133	38	24	24	1	0	2	4	17	0	17	1	0	1	3	.250	0	0-0	0	7.52	7.71
8 ML YEARS		189	189	10	0	1150.2	5040	1116	605	559	87	66	30	38	604	30	904	63	7	69	62	.527	7	0-0	0	4.36	4.37

Johnny Estrada

Bats: B **Throws:** R **Pos:** C-10; PH-1

Ht: 5'11" **Wt:** 209 **Born:** 6/27/76 **Age:** 27

Year	Team	Lg	G	AB	H	2B	3B	HR	(Hm	Rd)	TB	R	RBI	RC	TBB	IBB	SO	HBP	SH	SF	SB	CS	SB%	GDP	Avg	OBP	Slg
1997	Batavia	A-	58	223	70	17	2	6	(-	-)	109	28	43	34	9	1	15	1	2	5	0	0	-	9	.314	.336	.489
1998	Piedmont	A	77	303	94	14	2	7	(-	-)	133	33	44	40	6	1	19	5	0	3	0	1	.00	11	.310	.331	.439
1998	Clearwater	A+	37	117	26	8	0	0	(-	-)	34	8	13	8	5	0	7	0	2	2	0	0	-	2	.222	.250	.291
1999	Clearwater	A+	98	346	96	15	0	9	(-	-)	138	35	52	40	14	3	26	2	6	8	1	0	1.00	12	.277	.303	.399
2000	Reading	AA	95	356	105	18	0	12	(-	-)	159	42	42	49	10	2	20	4	2	0	1	0	1.00	8	.295	.322	.447
2001	Scrtn/WlksBr	AAA	32	131	38	13	0	0	(-	-)	51	13	16	15	5	0	6	1	0	1	0	0	-	5	.290	.319	.389
2002	Scrtn/WlksBr	AAA	118	434	121	27	0	11	(-	-)	181	49	67	54	26	7	53	5	0	7	1	0	1.00	19	.279	.322	.417
2001	Philadelphia	NL	89	298	68	15	0	8	(7	1)	107	26	37	25	16	6	32	4	2	4	0	0	-	15	.228	.273	.359
2002	Philadelphia	NL	10	17	2	1	0	0	(0	0)	3	0	2	0	2	1	2	0	0	0	0	0	-	0	.118	.211	.176
	2 ML YEARS		99	315	70	16	0	8	(7	1)	110	26	39	25	18	7	34	4	2	4	0	0	-	15	.222	.270	.349

Adam Everett

Bats: R **Throws:** R **Pos:** SS-34; PR-7

Ht: 6'0" **Wt:** 156 **Born:** 2/2/77 **Age:** 26

Year	Team	Lg	G	AB	H	2B	3B	HR	(Hm	Rd)	TB	R	RBI	RC	TBB	IBB	SO	HBP	SH	SF	SB	CS	SB%	GDP	Avg	OBP	Slg
1998	Lowell	A-	21	71	21	6	2	0	(-	-)	31	11	9	13	11	0	13	3	1	1	2	1	.67	2	.296	.407	.437
1999	Trenton	AA	98	338	89	11	0	10	(-	-)	130	56	44	52	41	0	64	10	9	4	21	5	.81	3	.263	.356	.385
2000	New Orleans	AAA	126	453	111	25	2	5	(-	-)	155	82	37	64	75	0	100	11	4	4	13	4	.76	6	.245	.363	.342
2001	New Orleans	AAA	114	441	110	20	8	5	(-	-)	161	69	40	59	39	0	74	16	9	4	24	5	.83	4	.249	.330	.365
2002	New Orleans	AAA	88	345	95	16	7	2	(-	-)	131	51	25	46	24	1	59	6	7	3	12	3	.80	3	.275	.331	.380
2001	Houston	NL	9	3	0	0	0	0	(0	0)	0	1	0	0	0	0	1	0	0	0	1	0	1.00	0	.000	.000	.000
2002	Houston	NL	40	88	17	3	0	0	(0	0)	20	11	4	6	12	1	19	1	2	0	3	0	1.00	1	.193	.297	.227
	2 ML YEARS		49	91	17	3	0	0	(0	0)	20	12	4	6	12	1	20	1	2	0	4	0	1.00	1	.187	.288	.220

Carl Everett

Bats: B **Throws:** R **Pos:** RF-39; CF-32; LF-18; DH-18; PH-7; PR-1

Ht: 6'0" **Wt:** 215 **Born:** 6/3/71 **Age:** 32

Year	Team	Lg	G	AB	H	2B	3B	HR	(Hm	Rd)	TB	R	RBI	RC	TBB	IBB	SO	HBP	SH	SF	SB	CS	SB%	GDP	Avg	OBP	Slg
2002	Charlotte*	A+	1	4	2	0	1	0	(-	-)	4	1	1	2	0	0	1	0	0	0	0	0	-	0	.500	.500	.500
1993	Florida	NL	11	19	2	0	0	0	(0	0)	2	0	0	0	1	0	9	0	0	0	1	0	1.00	0	.105	.150	.105
1994	Florida	NL	16	51	11	1	0	2	(2	0)	18	7	6	5	3	0	15	0	0	0	4	0	1.00	0	.216	.259	.353
1995	New York	NL	79	289	75	13	1	12	(9	3)	126	48	54	41	39	2	67	2	1	0	2	5	.29	11	.260	.352	.436
1996	New York	NL	101	192	46	8	1	1	(1	0)	59	29	16	21	21	2	53	4	1	1	6	0	1.00	4	.240	.326	.307
1997	New York	NL	142	443	110	28	3	14	(11	3)	186	58	57	58	32	3	102	7	3	2	17	9	.65	3	.248	.308	.420
1998	Houston	NL	133	467	138	34	4	15	(5	10)	225	72	76	76	44	2	102	3	3	2	14	12	.54	11	.296	.359	.482
1999	Houston	NL	123	464	151	33	3	25	(11	14)	265	86	108	105	50	5	94	11	2	8	27	7	.79	5	.325	.398	.571
2000	Boston	AL	137	496	149	32	4	34	(17	17)	291	82	108	106	52	5	113	8	0	5	11	4	.73	4	.300	.373	.587
2001	Boston	AL	102	409	105	24	4	14	(6	8)	179	61	58	59	27	3	104	13	0	4	9	2	.82	3	.257	.323	.438
2002	Texas	AL	105	374	100	16	0	16	(11	5)	164	47	62	59	33	4	77	6	1	4	2	3	.40	7	.267	.333	.439
	10 ML YEARS		949	3204	887	189	20	133	(73	60)	1515	490	545	530	302	26	736	54	11	22	93	42	.69	48	.277	.347	.473

Scott Eyre

Pitches: L **Bats:** L **Pos:** RP-67; SP-3

Ht: 6'1" **Wt:** 210 **Born:** 5/30/72 **Age:** 31

			HOW MUCH HE PITCHED						WHAT HE GAVE UP										THE RESULTS						
Year	Team	Lg	G	GS	CG	GF	IP	BFP	H	R	ER	HR	SH	SF	HB	TBB	IBB	SO	WP	Bk	W	L	Pct	ShO	Sv-Op	Hld	ERC	ERA
1997	Chicago	AL	11	11	0	0	60.2	267	62	36	34	11	1	2	1	31	1	36	2	0	4	4	.500	0	0-0	0	5.37	5.04
1998	Chicago	AL	33	17	0	10	107.0	491	114	78	64	24	2	3	2	64	0	73	7	0	3	8	.273	0	0-0	0	6.31	5.38
1999	Chicago	AL	21	0	0	8	25.0	129	38	22	21	6	0	1	1	15	2	17	1	0	1	1	.500	0	0-0	1	9.23	7.56
2000	Chicago	AL	13	1	0	3	19.0	93	29	15	14	3	0	2	1	12	0	16	0	0	1	1	.500	0	0-0	0	9.49	6.63
2001	Toronto	AL	17	0	0	5	15.2	66	15	6	6	1	0	1	1	7	2	16	2	0	1	2	.333	0	2-3	3	3.96	3.45
2002	Tor-SF		70	3	0	3	74.2	333	80	41	37	4	2	4	0	36	8	58	5	0	2	4	.333	0	0-1	18	4.26	4.46
2002	Toronto	AL	49	3	0	3	63.1	283	69	37	35	4	2	4	0	29	7	51	4	0	2	4	.333	0	0-1	12	4.32	4.97
2002	San Francisco	NL	21	0	0	3	11.1	50	11	4	2	0	0	0	0	7	1	7	1	0	0	0	-	0	0-0	6	3.91	1.59
	6 ML YEARS		165	32	0	32	302.0	1379	338	198	176	49	5	13	6	165	13	216	17	0	12	20	.375	0	2-4	22	5.88	5.25

Jorge Fabregas

Bats: L **Throws:** R **Pos:** C-52; PH-16

Ht: 6'3" **Wt:** 220 **Born:** 3/13/70 **Age:** 33

Year	Team	Lg	G	AB	H	2B	3B	HR	(Hm	Rd)	TB	R	RBI	RC	TBB	IBB	SO	HBP	SH	SF	SB	CS	SB%	GDP	Avg	OBP	Slg
1994	Anaheim	AL	43	127	36	3	0	0	(0	0)	39	12	16	11	7	1	18	0	1	0	2	1	.67	5	.283	.321	.307
1995	Anaheim	AL	73	227	56	10	0	1	(1	0)	69	24	22	18	17	0	28	0	3	1	0	2	.00	9	.247	.298	.304
1996	Anaheim	AL	90	254	73	6	0	2	(1	1)	85	18	26	27	17	3	27	0	3	5	0	1	.00	7	.287	.326	.335
1997	Ana-CWS	AL	121	360	93	11	1	7	(1	6)	127	33	51	33	14	0	46	1	6	4	1	1	.50	16	.258	.285	.353
1998	Ari-NYM	NL	70	183	36	4	0	2	(0	2)	46	11	20	10	14	1	32	1	1	2	0	0	-	4	.197	.255	.251
1999	Fla-Atl	NL	88	231	46	10	2	3	(1	2)	69	20	21	19	26	6	27	2	4	5	0	0	-	9	.199	.280	.299
2000	Kansas City	AL	43	142	40	4	0	3	(2	1)	53	13	17	17	8	1	11	0	2	0	1	0	1.00	6	.282	.320	.373
2001	Anaheim	AL	53	148	33	4	2	2	(0	2)	47	9	16	9	3	0	15	0	4	2	0	0	-	5	.223	.235	.318
2002	Ana-Mil		65	155	28	4	0	3	(0	3)	41	13	22	12	8	1	13	0	2	2	0	0	-	5	.181	.216	.265
1997	Anaheim	AL	21	38	3	1	0	0	(0	0)	4	2	3	2	3	0	3	0	2	0	0	0	-	2	.079	.146	.105
1997	Chicago	AL	100	322	90	10	1	7	(1	6)	123	31	48	33	11	0	43	1	4	4	1	1	.50	14	.280	.302	.382
1998	Arizona	NL	50	151	30	4	0	1	(0	1)	37	8	15	9	13	1	26	1	0	2	0	0	-	3	.199	.263	.245
1998	New York	NL	20	32	6	0	0	1	(0	1)	9	3	5	1	1	0	6	0	1	0	0	0	-	1	.188	.212	.281
1999	Florida	NL	82	223	46	10	2	3	(1	2)	69	20	21	19	26	6	27	2	4	5	0	0	-	7	.206	.289	.309
1999	Atlanta	NL	6	8	0	0	0	0	(0	0)	0	0	0	0	0	0	0	0	0	0	0	0	-	2	.000	.000	.000
2002	Anaheim	AL	35	88	17	1	0	0	(0	0)	18	8	8	2	6	1	6	0	2	0	0	0	-	3	.193	.245	.205
2002	Milwaukee	NL	30	67	11	3	0	3	(0	3)	23	5	14	3	2	0	7	0	0	4	0	0	-	2	.164	.178	.343
	9 ML YEARS		646	1827	441	56	5	23	(6	17)	576	153	211	149	114	13	217	4	26	23	4	5	.44	61	.241	.284	.315

Jeff Farnsworth

Pitches: R **Bats:** R **Pos:** RP-44 **Ht:** 6'2" **Wt:** 190 **Born:** 10/6/75 **Age:** 27

Year Team	Lg	G	GS	CG	GF	IP	BFP	H	R	ER	HR	SH	SF	HB	TBB	IBB	SO	WP	Bk	W	L	Pct	ShO	Sv-Op	Hld	ERC	ERA
1996 Everett	A-	10	7	0	1	39.1	158	33	19	18	4	0	1	0	13	0	42	6	5	3	3	.500	0	0- -	-	3.03	4.12
1997 Lancaster	A+	5	5	0	0	20.2	93	24	20	16	2	1	1	3	8	0	18	2	0	1	1	.500	0	0- -	-	5.64	6.97
1999 Lancaster	A+	26	9	0	6	72.0	351	91	61	52	7	1	10	15	43	1	43	10	0	3	6	.333	0	3- -	-	7.43	6.50
2000 New Haven	AA	39	8	0	6	101.1	414	91	40	39	6	2	2	9	25	1	70	3	1	9	3	.750	0	2- -	-	3.05	3.46
2001 San Antonio	AA	27	27	0	0	155.1	688	182	92	75	10	4	3	8	47	0	113	3	3	11	10	.524	0	0- -	-	4.60	4.35
2002 Detroit	AL	44	0	0	15	70.0	331	100	47	45	6	3	1	2	29	8	28	6	1	2	3	.400	0	0-1	2	6.52	5.79

Kyle Farnsworth

Pitches: R **Bats:** R **Pos:** RP-45 **Ht:** 6'4" **Wt:** 235 **Born:** 4/14/76 **Age:** 27

Year Team	Lg	G	GS	CG	GF	IP	BFP	H	R	ER	HR	SH	SF	HB	TBB	IBB	SO	WP	Bk	W	L	Pct	ShO	Sv-Op	Hld	ERC	ERA
2002 Iowa*	AAA	2	0	0	2	3.0	11	3	2	2	1	0	0	0	0	0	2	0	0	0	1	.000	0	0- -	-	4.18	6.00
1999 Chicago	NL	27	21	1	1	130.0	579	140	80	73	28	6	2	3	52	1	70	7	1	5	9	.357	1	0-0	0	5.39	5.05
2000 Chicago	NL	46	5	0	8	77.0	371	90	58	55	14	4	4	4	50	8	74	3	0	2	9	.182	0	1-6	6	6.72	6.43
2001 Chicago	NL	76	0	0	24	82.0	339	65	26	25	8	2	2	1	29	2	107	2	2	4	6	.400	0	2-3	24	2.76	2.74
2002 Chicago	NL	45	0	0	17	46.2	213	53	47	38	9	2	5	1	24	7	46	1	0	4	6	.400	0	1-7	6	5.89	7.33
4 ML YEARS		194	26	1	50	335.2	1502	348	211	191	59	14	13	9	155	18	297	13	3	15	30	.333	1	4-16	36	5.06	5.12

Sal Fasano

Bats: R **Throws:** R **Pos:** C-2 **Ht:** 6'2" **Wt:** 254 **Born:** 8/10/71 **Age:** 31

Year Team	Lg	G	AB	H	2B	3B	HR	(Hm	Rd)	TB	R	RBI	RC	TBB	IBB	SO	HBP	SH	SF	SB	CS	SB%	GDP	Avg	OBP	Slg
2002 Durham*	AAA	31	101	26	6	0	6	(-	-)	50	11	9	19	12	0	29	9	0	0	0	1	.00	1	.257	.385	.495
2002 Indianapolis*	AAA	34	97	20	9	0	1	(-	-)	32	5	11	8	3	0	24	6	0	1	0	0	-	2	.206	.271	.330
2002 Salt Lake*	AAA	22	76	21	3	0	5	(-	-)	39	13	10	14	7	0	24	2	0	1	1	0	1.00	0	.276	.349	.513
1996 Kansas City	AL	51	143	29	2	0	6	(1	5)	49	20	19	13	14	0	25	2	1	0	1	1	.50	3	.203	.283	.343
1997 Kansas City	AL	13	38	8	2	0	1	(0	1)	13	4	1	2	1	0	12	0	0	0	0	0	-	1	.211	.231	.342
1998 Kansas City	AL	74	216	49	10	0	8	(4	4)	83	21	31	26	10	1	56	16	3	2	1	0	1.00	4	.227	.307	.384
1999 Kansas City	AL	23	60	14	2	0	5	(2	3)	31	11	16	12	7	0	17	7	0	1	0	1	.00	1	.233	.373	.517
2000 Oakland	AL	52	126	27	6	0	7	(4	3)	54	21	19	16	14	0	47	3	0	1	0	0	-	3	.214	.306	.429
2001 Oak-KC-Col	AL	39	85	17	5	0	3	(3	0)	31	12	9	10	5	0	31	4	2	0	0	0	-	3	.200	.277	.365
2002 Anaheim	AL	2	1	0	0	0	0	(0	0)	0	0	0	0	0	0	1	0	0	0	0	0	-	0	.000	.000	.000
2001 Oakland	AL	11	21	1	0	0	0	(0	0)	1	2	0	0	1	0	12	1	0	0	0	0	-	0	.048	.130	.048
2001 Chicago	AL	3	1	0	0	0	0	(0	0)	0	0	0	0	0	0	0	0	0	0	0	0	-	0	.000	.000	.000
2001 Colorado	NL	25	63	16	5	0	3	(3	0)	30	10	9	10	4	0	19	3	2	0	0	0	-	1	.254	.329	.476
7 ML YEARS		254	669	144	27	0	30	(14	16)	261	89	95	79	51	1	189	32	6	4	2	2	.50	15	.215	.300	.390

Jeff Fassero

Pitches: L **Bats:** L **Pos:** RP-73 **Ht:** 6'1" **Wt:** 200 **Born:** 1/5/63 **Age:** 40

Year Team	Lg	G	GS	CG	GF	IP	BFP	H	R	ER	HR	SH	SF	HB	TBB	IBB	SO	WP	Bk	W	L	Pct	ShO	Sv-Op	Hld	ERC	ERA
1991 Montreal	NL	51	0	0	30	55.1	223	39	17	15	1	6	0	1	17	1	42	4	0	2	5	.286	0	8-11	7	1.75	2.44
1992 Montreal	NL	70	0	0	22	85.2	368	81	35	27	1	5	2	2	34	6	63	7	1	8	7	.533	0	1-7	12	3.10	2.84
1993 Montreal	NL	56	15	1	10	149.2	616	119	50	38	7	7	4	0	54	0	140	5	0	12	5	.706	0	1-3	6	2.48	2.29
1994 Montreal	NL	21	21	1	0	138.2	569	119	54	46	13	7	2	1	40	4	119	6	0	8	6	.571	0	0-0	0	2.82	2.99
1995 Montreal	NL	30	30	1	0	189.0	833	207	102	91	15	19	7	2	74	3	164	7	1	13	14	.481	0	0-0	0	4.43	4.33
1996 Montreal	NL	34	34	5	0	231.2	967	217	95	85	20	16	5	3	55	3	222	5	2	15	11	.577	1	0-0	0	3.00	3.30
1997 Seattle	AL	35	35	2	0	234.1	1010	226	108	94	21	7	10	3	84	6	189	13	2	16	9	.640	1	0-0	0	3.60	3.61
1998 Seattle	AL	32	32	7	0	224.2	954	223	115	99	33	8	8	10	66	2	176	12	0	13	12	.520	0	0-0	0	4.10	3.97
1999 Sea-Tex	AL	37	27	0	2	156.1	751	208	135	125	35	2	7	4	83	3	114	9	0	5	14	.263	0	0-0	2	7.69	7.20
2000 Boston	AL	38	23	0	4	130.0	577	153	72	69	16	7	2	1	50	2	97	2	0	8	8	.500	0	0-0	5	5.25	4.78
2001 Chicago	NL	82	0	0	30	73.2	308	66	31	28	6	1	2	1	23	5	79	3	0	4	4	.500	0	12-17	25	2.97	3.42
2002 ChC-Stl	NL	73	0	0	18	69.0	315	81	43	41	9	7	1	3	27	5	56	2	1	8	6	.571	0	0-3	13	5.25	5.35
1999 Seattle	AL	30	24	0	1	139.0	669	188	123	114	34	1	6	4	73	3	101	7	0	4	14	.222	0	0-0	2	8.02	7.38
1999 Texas	AL	7	3	0	1	17.1	82	20	12	11	1	1	1	0	10	0	13	2	0	1	0	1.000	0	0-0	0	5.21	5.71
2002 Chicago	NL	57	0	0	17	51.0	240	65	37	35	5	6	1	3	22	5	44	2	1	5	6	.455	0	0-1	6	5.79	6.18
2002 St Louis	AL	16	0	0	1	18.0	75	16	6	6	4	1	0	0	5	0	12	0	0	3	0	1.000	0	0-2	7	3.70	3.00
12 ML YEARS		559	217	17	116	1738.0	7491	1739	857	758	177	92	50	31	607	40	1461	75	7	112	101	.526	2	22-41	70	3.89	3.93

Carlos Febles

Bats: R **Throws:** R **Pos:** 2B-115; PR-4; PH-2; SS-1 **Ht:** 5'11" **Wt:** 185 **Born:** 5/24/76 **Age:** 27

Year Team	Lg	G	AB	H	2B	3B	HR	(Hm	Rd)	TB	R	RBI	RC	TBB	IBB	SO	HBP	SH	SF	SB	CS	SB%	GDP	Avg	OBP	Slg
2002 Omaha*	AAA	13	54	12	2	1	1	(-	-)	19	10	5	5	4	0	5	1	0	1	2	1	.67	1	.222	.283	.352
1998 Kansas City	AL	11	25	10	1	2	0	(0	0)	15	5	2	7	4	0	7	0	0	0	2	1	.67	0	.400	.483	.600
1999 Kansas City	AL	123	453	116	22	9	10	(5	5)	186	71	53	63	47	0	91	9	12	3	20	4	.83	16	.256	.336	.411
2000 Kansas City	AL	100	339	87	12	1	2	(2	0)	107	59	29	39	36	1	48	10	13	1	17	6	.74	10	.257	.345	.316
2001 Kansas City	AL	79	292	69	9	2	8	(6	2)	106	45	25	30	22	0	58	1	1	0	5	2	.71	7	.236	.291	.363
2002 Kansas City	AL	119	351	86	16	4	4	(2	2)	122	44	26	44	41	0	63	7	5	0	16	5	.76	8	.245	.336	.348
5 ML YEARS		432	1460	368	60	18	24	(15	9)	536	224	135	183	150	1	267	27	31	5	60	18	.77	41	.252	.332	.367

Pedro Feliciano

Pitches: L Bats: L Pos: RP-6   Ht: 5'10" Wt: 185 Born: 8/25/76 Age: 26

Year Team	Lg	G	GS	CG	GF	IP	BFP	H	R	ER	HR	SH	SF	HB	TBB	IBB	SO	WP	Bk	W	L	Pct	ShO	Sv-Op	Hld	ERC	ERA
1995 Great Falls	R+	6	0	0	3	6.2	43	12	12	10	0	0	0	0	7	1	9	4	2	0	0	-	0	0- -	-	9.44	13.50
1996 Great Falls	R+	22	1	0	10	41.0	206	50	36	26	1	0	5	3	26	2	39	4	3	2	3	.400	0	3- -	-	5.62	5.71
1997 Savannah	A	36	9	1	8	105.2	437	90	45	31	11	3	3	1	39	0	94	6	4	3	7	.300	0	4- -	-	3.24	2.64
1997 Vero Beach	A+	1	0	0	0	2.0	7	3	1	1	1	0	0	0	0	0	1	0	0	0	0	-	0	0- -	-	10.61	4.50
1998 Vero Beach	A+	22	10	0	8	68.1	300	68	44	35	8	0	1	2	30	1	51	2	0	2	5	.286	0	2- -	-	4.39	4.61
2000 Vero Beach	A+	25	2	0	7	61.1	289	76	31	26	4	4	4	5	24	1	48	3	0	4	5	.444	0	0- -	-	5.32	3.82
2000 San Antonio	AA	9	0	0	3	9.1	37	7	2	2	0	1	0	1	4	1	11	0	2	0	0	-	0	2- -	-	2.59	1.93
2000 Albuquerque	AAA	1	0	0	1	1.0	9	3	3	2	2	0	0	0	1	0	2	0	0	0	0	-	0	0- -	-	34.63	18.00
2001 Jacksonville	AA	54	0	0	38	60.1	229	41	14	13	3	4	0	3	11	1	55	2	0	5	4	.556	0	17- -	-	1.62	1.94
2001 Las Vegas	AAA	6	0	0	1	8.2	49	16	11	7	2	1	0	1	5	1	5	1	0	0	1	.000	0	0- -	-	11.36	7.27
2002 Chattanooga	AA	28	0	0	14	38.2	160	33	14	11	1	4	1	3	11	1	26	0	0	2	1	.667	0	4- -	-	2.62	2.56
2002 Louisville	AAA	20	0	0	6	26.2	116	35	10	9	3	1	3	1	4	0	19	0	1	1	1	.500	0	0- -	-	5.17	3.04
2002 Norfolk	AAA	5	0	0	3	9.0	41	14	7	7	1	0	1	0	1	0	11	1	0	0	0	-	0	2- -	-	6.26	7.00
2002 New York	NL	6	0	0	3	6.0	26	9	5	5	0	0	0	0	1	0	4	0	0	0	0	-	0	0-0	0	5.56	7.50

Pedro Feliz

Bats: R Throws: R Pos: 3B-44; PH-25; SS-1; LF-1; PR-1   Ht: 6'1" Wt: 205 Born: 4/27/77 Age: 26

Year Team	Lg	G	AB	H	2B	3B	HR	(Hm	Rd)	TB	R	RBI	RC	TBB	IBB	SO	HBP	SH	SF	SB	CS	SB%	GDP	Avg	OBP	Slg
2000 San Francisco	NL	8	7	2	0	0	0	(0	0)	2	1	0	1	0	0	1	0	0	0	0	0	-	0	.286	.286	.286
2001 San Francisco	NL	94	220	50	9	1	7	(3	4)	82	23	22	20	10	2	50	2	3	3	2	1	.67	5	.227	.264	.373
2002 San Francisco	NL	67	146	37	4	1	2	(1	1)	49	14	13	12	6	1	27	0	0	1	0	0	-	2	.253	.281	.336
3 ML YEARS		169	373	89	13	2	9	(4	5)	133	38	35	33	16	3	78	2	3	4	2	1	.67	7	.239	.271	.357

Jared Fernandez

Pitches: R Bats: R Pos: SP-8; RP-6   Ht: 6'2" Wt: 225 Born: 2/2/72 Age: 31

Year Team	Lg	G	GS	CG	GF	IP	BFP	H	R	ER	HR	SH	SF	HB	TBB	IBB	SO	WP	Bk	W	L	Pct	ShO	Sv-Op	Hld	ERC	ERA
1994 Utica	A-	21	1	0	15	30.0	144	43	18	12	4	0	0	0	8	2	24	0	1	1	1	.500	0	4- -	-	5.94	3.60
1995 Utica	A-	5	5	1	0	38.0	148	30	11	8	2	0	1	1	9	1	23	1	0	3	2	.600	0	0- -	-	2.22	1.89
1995 Trenton	AA	11	10	1	0	67.0	290	64	32	29	4	3	1	5	28	1	40	2	0	5	4	.556	0	0- -	-	3.90	3.90
1996 Trenton	AA	30	29	3	0	179.0	798	185	115	101	19	5	9	10	83	5	94	10	0	9	9	.500	0	0- -	-	4.74	5.08
1997 Trenton	AA	21	16	1	4	121.1	560	138	90	73	12	2	2	0	66	0	73	14	0	4	6	.400	0	0- -	-	5.40	5.41
1997 Pawtucket	AAA	11	11	0	0	60.2	281	76	45	39	7	2	2	5	28	1	33	4	0	3	0	.000	0	0- -	-	6.34	5.79
1998 Trenton	AA	36	7	0	10	118.1	527	132	80	69	8	8	3	3	51	3	70	15	1	3	7	.300	0	1- -	-	4.69	5.25
1998 Pawtucket	AAA	5	2	0	2	24.2	107	26	16	13	5	0	2	3	7	0	15	4	0	1	1	.500	0	0- -	-	5.19	4.74
1999 Trenton	AA	7	0	0	4	18.2	80	18	9	7	4	0	0	0	8	0	10	1	0	3	0	1.000	0	1- -	-	4.82	3.38
1999 Pawtucket	AAA	27	20	3	2	163.1	687	172	88	77	20	7	5	5	39	0	76	3	1	12	9	.571	0	0- -	-	4.04	4.24
2000 Pawtucket	AAA	31	9	2	17	113.1	464	103	51	38	10	4	4	5	36	0	65	11	1	10	4	.714	0	4- -	-	3.44	3.02
2001 Louisville	AAA	33	28	4	2	196.1	843	218	105	90	24	3	1	9	54	0	118	20	0	10	9	.526	1	0- -	-	4.60	4.13
2002 Louisville	AAA	26	18	1	4	128.1	547	151	63	56	14	2	2	1	31	1	80	7	1	12	5	.706	0	1- -	-	4.77	3.93
2001 Cincinnati	NL	5	2	0	2	12.1	57	13	9	6	1	0	0	2	6	0	5	1	0	1	0	1.000	0	0-0	0	5.21	4.38
2002 Cincinnati	NL	14	8	0	2	50.2	232	59	31	25	5	1	2	3	24	1	36	3	0	1	3	.250	0	0-0	0	5.54	4.44
2 ML YEARS		19	10	0	4	63.0	289	72	40	31	6	1	2	5	30	1	41	4	0	1	4	.200	0	0-0	0	5.48	4.43

Mike Fetters

Pitches: R Bats: R Pos: RP-65   Ht: 6'4" Wt: 239 Born: 12/19/64 Age: 38

Year Team	Lg	G	GS	CG	GF	IP	BFP	H	R	ER	HR	SH	SF	HB	TBB	IBB	SO	WP	Bk	W	L	Pct	ShO	Sv-Op	Hld	ERC	ERA
1989 Anaheim	AL	1	0	0	0	3.1	16	5	4	3	1	0	0	0	1	0	4	2	0	0	0	-	0	0-0	0	8.14	8.10
1990 Anaheim	AL	26	2	0	10	67.2	291	77	33	31	9	1	0	2	20	0	35	3	0	1	1	.500	0	1-1	1	4.88	4.12
1991 Anaheim	AL	19	4	0	8	44.2	206	53	29	24	4	1	0	3	28	2	24	4	0	2	5	.286	0	0-1	0	6.44	4.84
1992 Milwaukee	NL	50	0	0	11	62.2	243	38	15	13	3	5	2	7	24	2	43	4	1	5	1	.833	0	2-5	8	2.13	1.87
1993 Milwaukee	NL	45	0	0	14	59.1	246	59	29	22	4	5	3	2	22	4	23	0	0	3	3	.500	0	0-0	8	3.89	3.34
1994 Milwaukee	NL	42	0	0	31	46.0	202	41	16	13	0	2	3	1	27	5	31	3	1	1	4	.200	0	17-20	3	3.36	2.54
1995 Milwaukee	NL	40	0	0	34	34.2	163	40	16	13	3	2	1	0	20	4	33	5	0	0	3	.000	0	22-27	2	5.27	3.38
1996 Milwaukee	NL	61	0	0	55	61.1	268	65	28	23	4	0	4	1	26	4	53	5	0	3	3	.500	0	32-38	1	4.24	3.38
1997 Milwaukee	NL	51	0	0	20	70.1	298	62	30	27	4	6	4	1	33	3	62	2	1	1	5	.167	0	6-11	11	3.41	3.45
1998 Oak-Ana	AL	60	0	0	28	58.2	264	62	34	28	5	4	2	1	25	2	43	6	0	2	8	.200	0	5-9	11	4.29	4.30
1999 Baltimore	AL	27	0	0	10	31.0	151	35	23	20	5	1	0	2	22	2	22	1	1	1	0	1.000	0	0-3	2	6.66	5.81
2000 Los Angeles	NL	51	0	0	20	50.0	201	35	18	18	7	3	0	2	25	2	40	3	0	6	2	.750	0	5-7	11	3.34	3.24
2001 LA-Pit	NL	54	0	0	21	47.1	223	49	32	29	7	1	3	4	26	1	37	7	0	3	2	.600	0	9-12	14	5.37	5.51
2002 Pit-Ari	NL	65	0	0	22	55.0	252	53	31	25	4	0	2	3	37	6	53	8	0	3	3	.500	0	0-2	16	4.75	4.09
1998 Oakland	AL	48	0	0	22	47.1	214	48	26	21	3	4	2	1	21	2	34	3	0	1	6	.143	0	5-8	10	3.93	3.99
1998 Anaheim	AL	12	0	0	6	11.1	50	14	8	7	2	0	0	0	4	0	9	3	0	1	2	.333	0	0-1	1	5.95	5.56
2001 Los Angeles	NL	34	0	0	7	29.2	139	33	23	20	6	1	3	1	13	0	26	6	0	2	1	.667	0	1-3	14	5.53	6.07
2001 Pittsburgh	NL	20	0	0	14	17.2	84	16	9	9	1	0	0	3	13	1	11	1	0	1	1	.500	0	8-9	0	4.58	4.58
2002 Pittsburgh	NL	32	0	0	13	30.1	134	25	13	11	3	0	1	1	18	1	29	2	0	1	0	1.000	0	0-1	11	3.86	3.26
2002 Arizona	NL	33	0	0	9	24.2	118	28	18	14	1	0	1	2	19	5	24	6	0	2	3	.400	0	0-1	5	5.91	5.11
14 ML YEARS		592	6	0	284	692.0	3024	674	338	289	60	31	26	29	336	37	503	53	4	31	40	.437	0	99-136	88	4.28	3.76

Robert Fick

Bats: L **Throws:** R **Pos:** RF-140; DH-6; PH-3 **Ht:** 6'1" **Wt:** 200 **Born:** 3/15/74 **Age:** 29

Year Team	Lg	G	AB	H	2B	3B	HR	(Hm	Rd)	TB	R	RBI	RC	TBB	IBB	SO	HBP	SH	SF	SB	CS	SB%	GDP	Avg	OBP	Slg
1998 Detroit	AL	7	22	8	1	0	3	(0	3)	18	6	7	6	2	0	7	0	0	0	1	0	1.00	1	.364	.417	.818
1999 Detroit	AL	15	41	9	0	0	3	(1	2)	18	6	10	6	7	0	6	0	0	1	1	0	1.00	1	.220	.327	.439
2000 Detroit	AL	66	163	41	7	2	3	(0	3)	61	18	22	21	22	2	39	1	0	2	2	1	.67	4	.252	.340	.374
2001 Detroit	AL	124	401	109	21	2	19	(8	11)	191	62	61	62	39	3	62	4	0	4	0	3	.00	10	.272	.339	.476
2002 Detroit	AL	148	556	150	36	2	17	(12	5)	241	66	63	71	46	4	90	7	0	5	0	1	.00	17	.270	.331	.433
5 ML YEARS		360	1183	317	65	6	45	(21	24)	529	158	163	166	116	9	204	12	0	12	4	5	.44	33	.268	.336	.447

Nate Field

Pitches: R **Bats:** R **Pos:** RP-5 **Ht:** 6'2" **Wt:** 200 **Born:** 12/11/75 **Age:** 27

Year Team	Lg	G	GS	CG	GF	IP	BFP	H	R	ER	HR	SH	SF	HB	TBB	IBB	SO	WP	Bk	W	L	Pct	ShO	Sv-Op	Hld	ERC	ERA
1998 Vermont	A-	25	0	0	16	35.0	150	21	16	12	1	1	0	3	11	0	39	5	1	3	1	.750	0	2--	-	1.52	3.09
1999 Cape Fear	A	42	0	0	21	65.0	300	75	49	39	8	2	3	7	22	2	55	4	0	4	8	.333	0	2--	-	5.12	5.40
1999 Ottawa	AAA	2	0	0	1	3.0	16	4	1	1	0	0	0	0	4	0	4	0	0	0	0	-	0	0--	-	9.50	3.00
2000 Sioux City	IND	11	0	0	3	23.1	100	17	10	5	1	1	1	0	15	3	19	3	0	3	0	1.000	0	0--	-	2.91	1.93
2000 Chrlstn - WV	A	17	0	0	4	36.1	152	28	10	9	2	4	1	2	15	0	31	3	1	1	2	.333	0	0--	-	2.79	2.23
2001 Wichita	AA	52	0	0	44	73.0	300	61	16	12	3	3	2	2	18	3	67	5	0	4	2	.667	0	19--	-	2.27	1.48
2002 Omaha	AAA	18	0	0	17	16.1	81	22	10	6	0	0	0	0	8	0	13	0	0	1	0	1.000	0	7--	-	5.37	3.31
2002 Columbus	AAA	21	2	0	5	38.2	180	46	30	29	6	0	7	1	21	1	25	1	0	2	1	.667	0	0--	-	6.28	6.75
2002 Kansas City	AL	5	0	0	0	5.0	26	8	5	5	2	1	0	0	3	1	3	2	0	0	0	-	0	0-0	0	10.82	9.00

Chone Figgins

Bats: B **Throws:** R **Pos:** PR-10; 2B-8; PH-3 **Ht:** 5'9" **Wt:** 155 **Born:** 1/22/78 **Age:** 25

Year Team	Lg	G	AB	H	2B	3B	HR	(Hm	Rd)	TB	R	RBI	RC	TBB	IBB	SO	HBP	SH	SF	SB	CS	SB%	GDP	Avg	OBP	Slg
1997 Rockies	R	53	210	59	5	6	1	(-	-)	79	41	23	35	34	0	50	3	0	2	30	12	.71	2	.281	.386	.376
1998 Portland	A-	69	269	76	9	3	1	(-	-)	94	41	26	37	24	0	56	2	6	1	25	4	.86	3	.283	.345	.349
1999 Salem	A+	123	444	106	12	3	0	(-	-)	124	65	22	40	41	0	86	3	14	2	27	13	.68	5	.239	.306	.279
2000 Salem	A+	134	522	145	26	14	3	(-	-)	208	92	48	77	67	0	107	1	6	5	37	19	.66	7	.278	.358	.398
2001 Carolina	AA	86	332	73	14	5	2	(-	-)	103	41	25	37	40	2	73	2	6	2	27	8	.77	0	.220	.306	.310
2001 Arkansas	AA	39	138	37	12	2	0	(-	-)	53	21	12	19	14	0	26	0	3	3	7	2	.78	0	.268	.329	.384
2002 Salt Lake	AAA	125	511	156	25	18	7	(-	-)	238	100	62	95	53	1	83	0	6	6	39	8	.83	0	.305	.364	.466
2002 Anaheim	AL	15	12	2	1	0	0	(0	0)	3	6	1	1	0	0	5	0	0	0	2	1	.67	1	.167	.167	.250

Nelson Figueroa

Pitches: R **Bats:** R **Pos:** RP-19; SP-11 **Ht:** 6'1" **Wt:** 155 **Born:** 5/18/74 **Age:** 29

Year Team	Lg	G	GS	CG	GF	IP	BFP	H	R	ER	HR	SH	SF	HB	TBB	IBB	SO	WP	Bk	W	L	Pct	ShO	Sv-Op	Hld	ERC	ERA
2002 Indianapolis*	AAA	6	6	0	0	39.2	170	39	18	16	2	1	2	0	13	0	25	1	0	5	0	1.000	0	0--	-	3.31	3.63
2000 Arizona	NL	3	3	0	0	15.2	68	17	13	13	4	1	2	0	5	0	7	2	0	0	1	.000	0	0-0	0	5.31	7.47
2001 Philadelphia	NL	19	13	0	1	89.0	393	95	40	39	8	4	0	7	37	3	61	2	0	4	5	.444	0	0-0	0	4.76	3.94
2002 Milwaukee	NL	30	11	0	4	93.0	412	96	59	52	18	11	5	4	37	6	51	5	0	1	7	.125	0	0-0	1	4.94	5.03
3 ML YEARS		52	27	0	5	197.2	873	208	112	104	30	16	7	11	79	9	119	9	0	5	13	.278	0	0-0	1	4.89	4.74

Jeremy Fikac

Pitches: R **Bats:** R **Pos:** RP-65 **Ht:** 6'2" **Wt:** 185 **Born:** 4/8/75 **Age:** 28

Year Team	Lg	G	GS	CG	GF	IP	BFP	H	R	ER	HR	SH	SF	HB	TBB	IBB	SO	WP	Bk	W	L	Pct	ShO	Sv-Op	Hld	ERC	ERA
1998 Idaho Falls	R+	12	0	0	6	20.0	82	11	6	5	0	0	1	0	8	1	19	1	0	2	0	1.000	0	1--	-	1.27	2.25
1999 R Cucamnga	A+	40	6	0	13	85.0	381	94	50	48	7	0	2	4	43	0	75	8	2	8	3	.727	0	0--	-	5.26	5.08
2000 R Cucamnga	A+	61	0	0	43	75.0	298	46	19	15	2	4	1	4	24	0	101	6	0	5	3	.625	0	20--	-	1.61	1.80
2001 Mobile	AA	53	0	0	33	68.2	276	54	16	15	3	4	2	3	20	4	75	3	0	6	0	1.000	0	18--	-	2.30	1.97
2001 Portland	AAA	1	0	0	0	3.0	13	3	1	1	0	0	0	0	1	0	3	0	0	0	0	-	0	0--	-	3.05	3.00
2002 Mobile	AA	3	0	0	3	3.0	11	5	1	1	0	0	0	0	0	0	3	0	0	1	0	1.000	0	1--	-	7.06	3.00
2001 San Diego	NL	23	0	0	5	26.1	99	15	6	4	2	2	0	1	5	1	19	0	0	2	0	1.000	0	0-2	6	1.33	1.37
2002 San Diego	NL	65	0	0	15	69.0	318	74	50	42	13	2	2	3	34	8	66	6	1	4	7	.364	0	0-6	12	5.39	5.48
2 ML YEARS		88	0	0	20	95.1	417	89	56	46	15	4	2	4	39	9	85	6	1	6	7	.462	0	0-8	18	4.07	4.34

Bob File

Pitches: R **Bats:** R **Pos:** RP-5 **Ht:** 6'4" **Wt:** 215 **Born:** 1/28/77 **Age:** 26

Year Team	Lg	G	GS	CG	GF	IP	BFP	H	R	ER	HR	SH	SF	HB	TBB	IBB	SO	WP	Bk	W	L	Pct	ShO	Sv-Op	Hld	ERC	ERA
1998 Medicine Hat	R+	28	0	0	26	32.0	124	24	7	5	1	1	2	2	5	0	28	1	0	2	1	.667	0	16--	-	1.77	1.41
1999 Dunedin	A+	47	0	0	42	53.0	203	30	13	10	2	3	0	4	14	0	48	1	1	4	1	.800	0	26--	-	1.46	1.70
2000 Tennessee	AA	36	0	0	32	34.2	153	29	20	12	1	2	1	2	13	0	40	0	1	4	3	.571	0	20--	-	2.67	3.12
2000 Syracuse	AAA	20	0	0	11	19.1	69	14	2	2	1	0	0	1	2	0	10	0	0	2	0	1.000	0	8--	-	1.71	0.93
2001 Tennessee	AA	3	0	0	3	3.0	10	3	1	1	1	0	0	0	0	0	2	0	0	0	0	-	0	1--	-	4.65	3.00
2001 Syracuse	AAA	2	0	0	1	4.0	14	1	0	0	0	0	0	2	0	0	3	0	0	0	0	-	0	0--	-	0.81	0.00
2002 Dunedin	A+	4	3	0	0	3.2	23	13	9	7	0	0	0	0	3	0	1	0	1	0	2	.000	0	--	-	11.92	11.12
2002 Syracuse	AAA	33	0	0	12	36.1	168	39	29	24	2	1	1	6	15	1	23	1	0	0	0	-	0	2--	-	4.72	5.94
2001 Toronto	AL	60	0	0	18	74.1	299	57	28	27	6	3	1	7	29	8	38	2	0	5	3	.625	0	0-2	6	2.98	3.27
2002 Toronto	AL	5	0	0	0	3.1	20	8	7	7	0	1	0	0	2	0	2	0	0	0	1	.000	0	0-0	1	13.02	18.90
2 ML YEARS		65	0	0	21	77.2	319	65	35	34	6	4	1	7	31	8	40	2	0	5	4	.556	0	0-2	7	3.33	3.94

Chuck Finley

Pitches: L Bats: L Pos: SP-32

Ht: 6'6" Wt: 226 Born: 11/26/62 Age: 40

Year Team	Lg	G	GS	CG	GF	IP	BFP	H	R	ER	HR	SH	SF	HB	TBB	IBB	SO	WP	Bk	W	L	Pct	ShO	Sv-Op	Hld	ERC	ERA
										HOW MUCH HE PITCHED →			**WHAT HE GAVE UP** →								**THE RESULTS** →					
1986 Anaheim	AL	25	0	0	7	46.1	198	40	17	17	2	4	0	1	23	1	37	2	0	3	1	.750	0	0-0	1	3.36	3.30
1987 Anaheim	AL	35	3	0	17	90.2	405	102	54	47	7	2	2	3	43	3	63	4	3	2	7	.222	0	0-2	0	5.07	4.67
1988 Anaheim	AL	31	31	2	0	194.1	831	191	95	90	15	7	10	6	82	7	111	5	8	9	15	.375	0	0-0	0	4.03	4.17
1989 Anaheim	AL	29	29	9	0	199.2	827	171	64	57	13	7	3	2	82	0	156	4	2	16	9	.640	1	0-0	0	3.19	2.57
1990 Anaheim	AL	32	32	7	0	236.0	962	210	77	63	17	12	3	2	81	3	177	9	0	18	9	.667	2	0-0	0	3.17	2.40
1991 Anaheim	AL	34	34	4	0	227.1	955	205	102	96	23	4	3	8	101	1	171	6	3	18	9	.667	2	0-0	0	3.94	3.80
1992 Anaheim	AL	31	31	4	0	204.1	885	212	99	90	24	10	10	3	98	2	124	6	0	7	12	.368	1	0-0	0	4.91	3.96
1993 Anaheim	AL	35	35	13	0	251.1	1065	243	108	88	22	11	7	6	82	1	187	8	1	16	14	.533	2	0-0	0	3.60	3.15
1994 Anaheim	AL	25	25	7	0	183.1	774	178	95	88	21	9	6	3	71	0	148	10	0	10	10	.500	2	0-0	0	4.10	4.32
1995 Anaheim	AL	32	32	2	0	203.0	880	192	106	95	20	4	5	7	93	1	195	13	1	15	12	.556	1	0-0	0	4.13	4.21
1996 Anaheim	AL	35	35	4	0	238.0	1037	241	124	110	27	7	9	11	94	5	215	17	2	15	16	.484	1	0-0	0	4.38	4.16
1997 Anaheim	AL	25	25	3	0	164.0	690	152	79	77	20	3	4	5	65	0	155	10	2	13	6	.684	1	0-0	0	3.99	4.23
1998 Anaheim	AL	34	34	1	0	223.1	976	210	97	84	20	3	5	6	109	1	212	8	0	11	9	.550	1	0-0	0	4.10	3.39
1999 Anaheim	AL	33	33	1	0	213.1	913	197	117	101	23	7	3	8	94	2	200	15	0	12	11	.522	0	0-0	0	4.03	4.43
2000 Cleveland	AL	34	34	3	0	218.0	936	211	108	101	23	5	4	2	101	3	189	9	0	16	11	.593	0	0-0	0	4.26	4.17
2001 Cleveland	AL	22	22	1	0	113.2	495	131	78	70	14	2	5	2	35	0	96	1	0	7	7	.533	0	0-0	0	4.85	5.54
2002 Cle-Stl	NL	32	32	2	0	190.2	809	183	97	87	13	7	6	1	78	6	174	3	0	11	15	.423	1	0-0	0	3.68	4.15
2002 Cleveland	AL	18	18	1	0	105.1	456	114	56	52	6	3	5	0	48	3	91	1	0	4	11	.267	0	0-0	0	4.49	4.44
2002 St Louis	NL	14	14	1	0	85.1	351	69	41	36	7	4	1	1	30	3	83	2	0	7	4	.636	1	0-0	0	2.74	3.80
17 ML YEARS		524	467	63	24	3197.1	13638	3069	1517	1366	304	104	85	76	1332	36	2610	130	22	200	173	.536	15	0-2		4.00	3.85

Steve Finley

Bats: L Throws: L Pos: CF-144; PH-10; PR-1

Ht: 6'2" Wt: 195 Born: 3/12/65 Age: 38

Year Team	Lg	G	AB	H	2B	3B	HR	(Hm	Rd)	TB	R	RBI	RC	TBB	IBB	SO	HBP	SH	SF	SB	CS	SB%	GDP	Avg	OBP	Slg
1989 Baltimore	AL	81	217	54	5	2	2	(0	2)	69	35	25	23	15	1	30	1	6	2	17	3	.85	3	.249	.298	.318
1990 Baltimore	AL	142	464	119	16	4	3	(1	2)	152	46	37	47	32	3	53	2	10	5	22	9	.71	8	.256	.304	.328
1991 Houston	NL	159	596	170	28	10	8	(0	8)	242	84	54	80	42	5	65	2	10	6	34	18	.65	8	.285	.331	.406
1992 Houston	NL	162	607	177	29	13	5	(5	0)	247	84	55	93	58	6	63	3	16	2	44	9	.83	10	.292	.355	.407
1993 Houston	NL	142	545	145	15	13	8	(1	7)	210	69	44	64	28	1	65	3	6	3	19	6	.76	8	.266	.304	.385
1994 Houston	NL	94	373	103	16	5	11	(4	7)	162	64	33	54	28	0	52	2	13	1	13	7	.65	3	.276	.329	.434
1995 San Diego	NL	139	562	167	23	8	10	(4	6)	236	104	44	90	59	5	62	4	4	2	36	12	.75	8	.297	.366	.420
1996 San Diego	NL	161	655	195	45	9	30	(15	15)	348	126	95	117	56	5	87	4	1	5	22	8	.73	20	.298	.354	.531
1997 San Diego	NL	143	560	146	26	5	28	(5	23)	266	101	92	84	43	2	92	3	2	7	15	3	.83	10	.261	.313	.475
1998 San Diego	NL	159	619	154	40	6	14	(8	6)	248	92	67	76	45	0	103	3	3	4	12	3	.80	9	.249	.301	.401
1999 Arizona	NL	156	590	156	32	10	34	(17	17)	310	100	103	105	63	7	94	3	2	5	8	4	.67	4	.264	.336	.525
2000 Arizona	NL	152	539	151	27	5	35	(17	18)	293	100	96	104	65	7	87	8	2	9	12	6	.67	9	.280	.361	.544
2001 Arizona	NL	140	495	136	27	4	14	(8	6)	213	66	73	71	47	9	67	1	2	3	11	7	.61	8	.275	.337	.430
2002 Arizona	NL	150	505	145	24	4	25	(14	11)	252	82	89	95	65	7	73	3	1	3	16	4	.80	10	.287	.370	.499
14 ML YEARS		1980	7327	2018	353	98	227	(99	128)	3248	1153	907	1103	646	58	993	41	78	57	281	99	.74	118	.275	.335	.443

Tony Fiore

Pitches: R Bats: R Pos: RP-46; SP-2

Ht: 6'4" Wt: 210 Born: 10/12/71 Age: 31

Year Team	Lg	G	GS	CG	GF	IP	BFP	H	R	ER	HR	SH	SF	HB	TBB	IBB	SO	WP	Bk	W	L	Pct	ShO	Sv-Op	Hld	ERC	ERA
2002 Edmonton*	AAA	2	2	0	0	13.0	53	15	6	6	2	0	0	0	2	0	6	0	0	2	0	1.000	0	0--		4.49	4.15
2000 Tampa Bay	AL	11	0	0	3	15.0	74	21	16	14	3	0	0	2	9	2	8	1	0	1	1	.500	0	0-1	0	8.74	8.40
2001 TB-Min	AL	7	0	0	0	9.2	41	9	6	6	0	0	0	1	3	0	1	1	0	0	1	.000	0	0-0	0	3.07	5.59
2002 Minnesota	AL	48	2	0	11	91.0	385	74	32	32	10	4	2	5	43	4	55	2	0	10	3	.769	0	0-0	5	3.57	3.16
2001 Tampa Bay	AL	3	0	0	3	3.1	15	4	2	2	0	0	0	1	1	0	3	1	0	0	0	-	0	0-0	0	5.47	5.40
2001 Minnesota	AL	4	0	0	2	6.1	26	5	4	4	0	0	0	0	2	0	5	0	0	0	1	.000	0	0-0	0	2.01	5.68
3 ML YEARS		66	2	0	19	115.2	500	104	54	52	13	4	2	8	55	6	71	4	0	11	5	.688	0	0-1	5	4.11	4.05

Brian Fitzgerald

Pitches: L Bats: L Pos: RP-6

Ht: 5'11" Wt: 175 Born: 12/26/74 Age: 28

Year Team	Lg	G	GS	CG	GF	IP	BFP	H	R	ER	HR	SH	SF	HB	TBB	IBB	SO	WP	Bk	W	L	Pct	ShO	Sv-Op	Hld	ERC	ERA
1996 Everett	A-	21	1	0	8	39.0	181	56	36	28	2	1	1	0	8	0	31	1	2	1	2	.333	0	1--	-	5.31	6.46
1997 Wisconsin	A	41	0	0	28	69.2	281	63	16	15	4	1	0	0	19	2	68	2	1	3	1	.750	0	10--	-	2.82	1.94
1998 Lancaster	A+	41	0	0	18	70.2	315	79	39	33	5	2	1	2	24	2	48	1	0	1	2	.333	0	1--	-	4.28	4.20
1998 Orlando	AA	2	0	0	1	4.1	18	5	1	1	0	0	0	0	1	0	4	0	0	0	0	-	0	1--	-	3.69	2.08
1999 Lancaster	A+	6	6	0	0	24.0	153	50	35	27	3	0	2	0	4	0	23	1	0	1	3	.250	0	0--	-	8.10	10.13
1999 New Haven	AA	29	1	0	13	54.0	228	58	24	23	2	2	1	0	18	0	37	0	0	2	2	.500	0	3--	-	3.96	3.83
2000 New Haven	AA	44	2	0	18	79.0	331	84	33	31	7	1	1	3	19	0	62	1	1	6	4	.600	0	4--	-	3.94	3.53
2001 San Antonio	AA	30	0	0	10	41.1	174	33	10	9	0	3	0	3	16	4	26	1	0	4	1	.800	0	1--	-	2.39	1.96
2001 Tacoma	AAA	20	1	0	9	34.2	153	40	19	15	5	0	0	0	11	0	26	2	0	2	1	.667	0	0--	-	4.90	3.89
2002 Tacoma	AAA	29	0	0	11	48.1	222	57	36	30	4	1	2	0	23	1	37	0	1	2	3	.400	0	2--	-	5.19	5.59
2002 Co Springs	AAA	7	0	0	2	9.0	37	8	4	4	1	0	1	0	3	0	4	0	0	1	1	.500	0	0--	-	3.32	4.00
2002 Seattle	AL	6	0	0	3	6.1	36	11	8	6	2	0	1	1	2	0	3	0	0	0	0	-	0	0-0	1	9.86	8.53

John Flaherty

Bats: R Throws: R Pos: C-75; PH-1

Ht: 6'1" Wt: 196 Born: 10/21/67 Age: 35

Year Team	Lg	G	AB	H	2B	3B	HR	(Hm	Rd)	TB	R	RBI	RC	TBB	IBB	SO	HBP	SH	SF	SB	CS	SB%	GDP	Avg	OBP	Slg
1992 Boston	AL	35	66	13	2	0	0	(0	0)	15	3	2	3	3	0	7	0	1	1	0	0	-	0	.197	.229	.227
1993 Boston	AL	13	25	3	2	0	0	(0	0)	5	3	2	1	2	0	6	1	1	0	0	0	-	0	.120	.214	.200
1994 Detroit	AL	34	40	6	1	0	0	(0	0)	7	2	4	1	1	0	11	0	2	1	0	1	.00	1	.150	.167	.175

Year Team	Lg	G	AB	H	2B	3B	HR	Hm	Rd	TB	R	RBI	RC	TBB	IBB	SO	HBP	SH	SF	SB	CS	SB%	GDP	Avg	OBP	Slg
1995 Detroit	AL	112	354	86	22	1	11	(6	5)	143	39	40	39	18	0	47	3	8	2	0	0	-	8	.243	.284	.404
1996 Det-SD		119	416	118	24	0	13	(8	5)	181	40	64	53	17	2	61	3	4	4	3	3	.50	13	.284	.314	.435
1997 San Diego	NL	129	439	120	21	1	9	(4	5)	170	38	46	52	33	7	62	0	2	2	4	4	.50	11	.273	.323	.387
1998 Tampa Bay	AL	91	304	63	11	0	3	(1	2)	83	21	24	17	22	0	46	1	4	3	0	5	.00	9	.207	.261	.273
1999 Tampa Bay	AL	117	446	124	19	0	14	(3	11)	185	53	71	54	19	0	64	6	1	10	0	2	.00	14	.278	.310	.415
2000 Tampa Bay	AL	109	394	103	15	0	10	(7	3)	148	36	39	41	20	2	57	0	2	2	0	0	-	11	.261	.296	.376
2001 Tampa Bay	AL	78	248	59	17	1	4	(3	1)	90	20	29	22	10	1	33	1	5	1	1	0	1.00	9	.238	.269	.363
2002 Tampa Bay	AL	76	281	73	20	0	4	(4	0)	105	27	33	32	15	0	50	1	2	4	2	2	.50	6	.260	.296	.374
1996 Detroit	AL	47	152	38	12	0	4	(2	2)	62	18	23	17	8	1	25	1	3	1	1	0	1.00	5	.250	.290	.408
1996 San Diego	NL	72	264	80	12	0	9	(6	3)	119	22	41	36	9	1	36	2	1	3	2	3	.40	8	.303	.327	.451
11 ML YEARS		913	3013	768	154	3	68	(36	32)	1132	282	354	314	160	12	444	16	32	30	10	17	.37	82	.255	.293	.376

Darrin Fletcher

Bats: L Throws: R Pos: C-36; PH-11; DH-3

Ht: 6'2" Wt: 210 Born: 10/3/66 Age: 36

Year Team	Lg	G	AB	H	2B	3B	HR	Hm	Rd	TB	R	RBI	RC	TBB	IBB	SO	HBP	SH	SF	SB	CS	SB%	GDP	Avg	OBP	Slg
1989 Los Angeles	NL	5	8	4	0	0	1	(1	0)	7	1	2	3	1	0	0	0	0	0	0	0	-	0	.500	.556	.875
1990 LA-Phi		11	23	3	1	0	0	(0	0)	4	3	1	0	1	0	6	0	0	0	0	0	-	0	.130	.167	.174
1991 Philadelphia	NL	46	136	31	8	0	1	(1	0)	42	5	12	9	5	0	15	0	1	0	1	1	.00	2	.228	.255	.309
1992 Montreal	NL	83	222	54	10	2	2	(1	0)	74	13	26	19	14	3	28	2	2	4	0	2	.00	8	.243	.289	.333
1993 Montreal	NL	133	396	101	20	1	9	(5	4)	150	33	60	49	34	2	40	6	5	4	0	0	-	7	.255	.320	.379
1994 Montreal	NL	94	285	74	18	1	10	(4	6)	124	28	57	40	25	4	23	3	0	12	0	0	-	6	.260	.314	.435
1995 Montreal	NL	110	350	100	21	1	11	(3	8)	156	42	45	51	32	1	33	4	1	2	0	1	.00	15	.286	.351	.446
1996 Montreal	NL	127	394	105	22	0	12	(7	5)	163	41	57	50	27	4	42	6	1	3	0	0	-	13	.266	.321	.414
1997 Montreal	NL	96	310	86	20	1	17	(10	7)	159	39	55	50	17	3	35	5	0	2	1	1	.50	6	.277	.323	.513
1998 Toronto	AL	124	407	115	23	1	9	(3	6)	167	37	52	50	25	7	39	6	1	7	0	0	-	19	.283	.328	.410
1999 Toronto	AL	115	412	120	26	0	18	(10	8)	200	48	80	63	26	0	47	6	0	4	0	1	.00	16	.291	.339	.485
2000 Toronto	AL	122	416	133	19	1	20	(10	10)	214	43	58	73	20	3	45	5	0	4	1	0	1.00	8	.320	.355	.514
2001 Toronto	AL	134	416	94	20	0	11	(4	7)	147	36	56	35	24	4	43	6	1	6	0	1	.00	18	.226	.274	.353
2002 Toronto	AL	45	127	28	6	0	3	(0	3)	43	8	22	14	4	0	13	0	1	3	0	0	-	4	.220	.239	.339
1990 Los Angeles	NL	2	1	0	0	0	0	(0	0)	0	0	0	0	0	0	1	0	0	0	0	0	-	0	.000	.000	.000
1990 Philadelphia	NL	9	22	3	1	0	0	(0	0)	4	3	1	0	1	0	5	0	0	0	0	0	-	0	.136	.174	.182
14 ML YEARS		1245	3902	1048	214	8	124	(61	63)	1650	377	583	506	255	31	399	49	13	51	2	6	.25	122	.269	.318	.423

Jose Flores

Bats: R Throws: R Pos: PR-5; 2B-2; SS-1; PH-1

Ht: 5'11" Wt: 180 Born: 6/28/73 Age: 30

Year Team	Lg	G	AB	H	2B	3B	HR	Hm	Rd	TB	R	RBI	RC	TBB	IBB	SO	HBP	SH	SF	SB	CS	SB%	GDP	Avg	OBP	Slg
1994 Batavia	A-	68	229	58	7	3	0	(-	-)	71	41	16	33	41	0	31	6	2	3	23	8	.74	3	.253	.378	.310
1995 Clearwater	A+	49	185	41	4	3	1	(-	-)	54	25	19	16	15	0	27	4	7	1	12	5	.71	4	.222	.293	.292
1995 Piedmont	A	61	186	49	7	0	0	(-	-)	56	22	19	20	24	0	29	3	5	4	11	8	.58	6	.263	.350	.301
1996 Scrtn/WlksBr	AAA	26	70	18	1	0	0	(-	-)	19	10	3	8	12	0	10	2	1	1	0	1	.00	2	.257	.376	.271
1996 Clearwater	A+	84	281	64	6	5	1	(-	-)	83	39	39	29	34	0	42	3	5	1	15	2	.88	6	.228	.317	.295
1997 Scrtn/WlksBr	AAA	71	204	51	14	1	1	(-	-)	70	32	18	26	28	1	51	2	5	2	3	1	.75	2	.250	.343	.343
1998 Scrtn/WlksBr	AAA	98	345	104	18	2	6	(-	-)	144	53	34	58	49	1	45	2	7	2	12	6	.67	1	.301	.389	.417
1999 Scrtn/WlksBr	AAA	64	228	56	6	2	0	(-	-)	66	35	18	30	37	1	43	7	4	0	13	3	.81	1	.246	.368	.289
1999 Tacoma	AAA	42	143	44	6	1	3	(-	-)	61	33	15	32	37	1	23	5	2	2	4	3	.57	2	.308	.460	.427
2000 New Haven	AA	12	38	7	3	0	0	(-	-)	10	5	1	4	7	0	5	2	1	0	0	0	-	0	.184	.340	.263
2000 Tacoma	AAA	91	328	93	14	4	3	(-	-)	124	53	30	53	53	0	44	5	1	3	19	7	.73	6	.284	.388	.378
2001 Co Springs	AAA	100	316	93	21	5	2	(-	-)	130	61	36	55	48	1	57	3	4	1	8	2	.80	1	.294	.391	.411
2002 Sacramento	AAA	95	363	111	19	1	2	(-	-)	138	64	38	59	56	1	53	3	7	6	16	4	.80	11	.306	.397	.380
2002 Oakland	AL	7	3	0	0	0	0	(0	0)	0	2	0	0	1	0	0	1	0	0	1	1	.50	0	.000	.400	.000

Randy Flores

Pitches: L Bats: L Pos: RP-26; SP-2

Ht: 6'0" Wt: 180 Born: 7/31/75 Age: 27

Year Team	Lg	G	GS	CG	GF	IP	BFP	H	R	ER	HR	SH	SF	HB	TBB	IBB	SO	WP	Bk	W	L	Pct	ShO	Sv-Op	Hld	ERC	ERA
1997 Oneonta	A-	13	13	2	0	74.2	308	64	32	27	3	0	1	4	23	1	70	5	1	4	4	.500	1	0- -	-	2.77	3.25
1998 Tampa	A+	5	5	0	0	23.2	115	28	23	17	2	2	2	1	16	2	15	0	4	1	2	.333	0	0- -	-	6.07	6.46
1998 Greensboro	A	21	20	2	0	130.2	535	119	48	38	6	2	3	7	33	0	139	2	4	12	7	.632	1	0- -	-	2.92	2.62
1999 Tampa	A+	21	20	1	1	135.0	555	118	56	43	4	4	4	7	38	0	99	5	0	11	4	.733	1	0- -	-	2.71	2.87
1999 Norwich	AA	4	4	0	0	25.0	120	32	20	18	0	2	0	1	11	1	19	1	1	1	0	1.000	0	0- -	-	4.97	6.48
2000 Norwich	AA	31	20	3	3	141.0	601	138	64	46	8	4	2	5	59	1	97	8	1	10	9	.526	0	1- -	-	3.92	2.94
2001 Columbus	AAA	4	4	0	0	23.1	117	43	24	19	3	0	0	0	7	0	16	1	1	1	2	.333	0	0- -	-	9.21	7.33
2001 Columbus	AAA	3	0	0	1	5.2	23	5	4	3	2	0	0	0	2	0	4	1	0	1	0	1.000	0	0- -	-	5.04	4.76
2001 Norwich	AA	25	25	3	0	158.2	677	156	64	49	13	5	3	1	63	0	115	3	3	14	6	.700	2	0- -	-	3.90	2.78
2002 Oklahoma	AAA	15	0	0	6	20.1	89	22	13	13	1	1	0	1	5	1	16	1	0	1	1	.500	0	1- -	-	3.59	5.75
2002 Co Springs	AAA	7	7	0	0	35.2	156	36	15	13	1	0	2	2	18	0	27	0	0	2	2	.500	0	0- -	-	4.32	3.28
2002 Tex-Col		28	2	0	9	29.0	140	40	26	24	7	2	2	3	16	3	14	4	0	0	2	.000	0	1-2	2	8.69	7.45
2002 Texas	AL	20	0	0	5	12.0	52	11	7	6	2	1	2	0	8	2	7	3	0	0	0	-	0	1-2	2	5.07	4.50
2002 Colorado	NL	8	2	0	4	17.0	88	29	19	18	5	1	0	3	8	1	7	1	0	0	0	.000	0	0-0	0	11.52	9.53

Cliff Floyd

Bats: L Throws: R Pos: RF-66; LF-54; DH-20; PH-8

Ht: 6'4" Wt: 260 Born: 12/5/72 Age: 30

Year Team	Lg	G	AB	H	2B	3B	HR	Hm	Rd	TB	R	RBI	RC	TBB	IBB	SO	HBP	SH	SF	SB	CS	SB%	GDP	Avg	OBP	Slg
1993 Montreal	NL	10	31	7	0	0	0	(0	1)	10	3	2	2	0	0	9	0	0	0	0	0	-	0	.226	.226	.323
1994 Montreal	NL	100	334	94	19	4	4	(2	2)	133	43	41	46	24	0	63	3	2	3	10	3	.77	3	.281	.332	.398
1995 Montreal	NL	29	69	9	1	0	1	(1	0)	13	6	8	2	7	0	22	1	1	0	3	0	1.00	1	.130	.221	.188
1996 Montreal	NL	117	227	55	15	4	6	(3	3)	96	29	26	35	30	1	52	5	1	3	7	1	.88	2	.242	.340	.423

Year Team	Lg	G	AB	H	2B	3B	HR	(Hm	Rd)	TB	R	RBI	RC	TBB	IBB	SO	HBP	SH	SF	SB	CS	SB%	GDP	Avg	OBP	Slg
1997 Florida	NL	61	137	32	9	1	6	(2	4)	61	23	19	23	24	0	33	2	1	1	6	2	.75	3	.234	.354	.445
1998 Florida	NL	153	588	166	45	3	22	(10	12)	283	85	90	92	47	7	112	3	0	3	27	14	.66	10	.282	.337	.481
1999 Florida	NL	69	251	76	19	1	11	(4	7)	130	37	49	45	30	5	47	2	0	2	5	6	.45	8	.303	.379	.518
2000 Florida	NL	121	420	126	30	0	22	(13	9)	222	75	91	88	50	5	82	8	0	9	24	3	.89	4	.300	.378	.529
2001 Florida	NL	149	555	176	44	4	31	(16	15)	321	123	103	121	59	19	101	10	0	5	18	3	.86	9	.317	.390	.578
2002 Fla-Mon-Bos		146	520	150	43	4	28	(13	15)	277	86	79	95	76	19	106	10	0	3	15	5	.75	6	.288	.388	.533
2002 Florida	NL	84	296	85	20	0	18	(7	11)	159	49	57	65	58	18	68	7	0	1	10	5	.67	0	.287	.414	.537
2002 Montreal	NL	15	53	11	2	0	3	(3	0)	22	7	4	2	3	1	10	1	0	0	1	0	1.00	0	.208	.263	.415
2002 Boston	AL	47	171	54	21	0	7	(3	4)	96	30	18	28	15	0	28	2	0	2	4	0	1.00	5	.316	.374	.561
10 ML YEARS		955	3132	891	225	17	132	(64	68)	1546	510	508	549	347	56	627	44	4	29	115	37	.76	47	.284	.361	.494

Josh Fogg

Pitches: R **Bats:** R **Pos:** SP-33   **Ht:** 6'0" **Wt:** 202 **Born:** 12/13/76 **Age:** 26

Year Team	Lg	G	GS	CG	GF	IP	BFP	H	R	ER	HR	SH	SF	HB	TBB	IBB	SO	WP	Bk	W	L	Pct	ShO	Sv-Op	Hld	ERC	ERA
1998 White Sox	R	2	0	0	0	4.0	13	0	0	0	0	1	0	0	1	0	5	1	0	1	0	1.000	0	0--	-	0.07	0.00
1998 Hickory	A	8	8	0	0	41.1	173	36	14	10	4	1	0	1	13	0	29	1	1	1	3	.250	0	0--	-	3.08	2.18
1998 Winstn-Salm	A+	1	0	0	1	1.0	6	2	2	0	0	0	0	0	0	0	2	1	0	1	0	1.000	0	0--	-	6.14	0.00
1999 Winstn-Salm	A+	17	17	1	0	103.1	441	93	44	34	3	1	1	11	33	0	109	2	0	10	5	.667	1	0--	-	3.12	2.96
1999 Birmingham	AA	10	10	0	0	55.0	249	66	37	36	8	1	2	5	18	0	40	2	1	3	2	.600	0	0--	-	5.65	5.89
2000 Birmingham	AA	27	27	2	0	192.1	787	190	68	55	7	5	4	6	44	2	136	9	1	11	7	.611	0	0--	-	3.10	2.57
2001 Charlotte	AAA	40	16	0	19	114.2	498	129	68	61	19	6	1	4	30	1	89	4	0	4	7	.364	0	4--	-	4.81	4.79
2001 Chicago	AL	11	0	0	4	13.1	53	10	3	3	0	0	1	1	3	1	17	0	0	0	0	-	0	0-0	2	1.73	2.03
2002 Pittsburgh	NL	33	33	0	0	194.1	832	199	102	94	28	6	3	8	69	12	113	2	0	12	12	.500	0	0-0	-	4.46	4.35
2 ML YEARS		44	33	0	4	207.2	885	209	105	97	28	6	4	9	72	13	130	2	0	12	12	.500	0	0-0	2	4.27	4.20

Jesse Foppert

Pitches: R **Bats:** R **Pos:** SP   **Ht:** 6'6" **Wt:** 210 **Born:** 7/10/80 **Age:** 22

Year Team	Lg	G	GS	CG	GF	IP	BFP	H	R	ER	HR	SH	SF	HB	TBB	IBB	SO	WP	Bk	W	L	Pct	ShO	Sv-Op	Hld	ERC	ERA
2001 Salem-Keizer	A-	14	14	0	0	70.0	264	35	18	15	7	0	3	5	23	0	88	4	3	8	1	.889	0	0--	-	1.65	1.93
2002 Shreveport	AA	11	11	1	0	61.1	249	44	22	19	3	3	1	3	21	0	74	3	0	3	3	.500	0	0--	-	2.24	2.79
2002 Fresno	AAA	14	14	0	0	79.0	337	71	37	35	12	3	5	3	35	0	109	7	1	3	6	.333	0	0--	-	4.23	3.99

Brook Fordyce

Bats: R **Throws:** R **Pos:** C-55; PH-1   **Ht:** 6'0" **Wt:** 190 **Born:** 5/7/70 **Age:** 33

Year Team	Lg	G	AB	H	2B	3B	HR	(Hm	Rd)	TB	R	RBI	RC	TBB	IBB	SO	HBP	SH	SF	SB	CS	SB%	GDP	Avg	OBP	Slg
1995 New York	NL	4	2	1	1	0	0	(0	0)	2	1	0	1	1	0	0	0	0	0	0	0	-	0	.500	.667	1.000
1996 Cincinnati	NL	4	7	2	1	0	0	(0	0)	3	0	1	2	3	0	1	0	0	0	0	0	-	0	.286	.500	.429
1997 Cincinnati	NL	47	96	20	5	0	1	(1	0)	28	7	8	8	8	1	15	0	0	1	2	0	1.00	0	.208	.267	.292
1998 Cincinnati	NL	57	146	37	9	0	3	(3	0)	55	8	14	16	11	3	28	0	1	0	0	1	.00	2	.253	.306	.377
1999 Chicago	AL	105	333	99	25	1	9	(5	4)	153	36	49	52	21	0	48	3	3	2	2	0	1.00	5	.297	.343	.459
2000 CWS-Bal	AL	93	302	91	18	1	14	(8	6)	153	41	49	51	17	0	50	4	2	5	0	0	-	4	.301	.341	.507
2001 Baltimore	AL	95	292	61	18	0	5	(0	5)	94	30	19	23	21	1	56	3	3	1	1	2	.33	7	.209	.268	.322
2002 Baltimore	AL	56	130	30	8	0	1	(1	0)	41	7	8	11	9	0	19	3	0	1	1	0	1.00	5	.231	.301	.315
2000 Chicago	AL	40	125	34	7	1	5	(3	2)	58	18	21	18	6	0	23	2	2	1	0	0	-	1	.272	.313	.464
2000 Baltimore	AL	53	177	57	11	0	9	(5	4)	95	23	28	33	11	0	27	2	0	4	0	0	-	3	.322	.361	.537
8 ML YEARS		461	1308	341	85	2	33	(18	15)	529	130	148	164	91	5	217	14	12	9	6	3	.67	23	.261	.314	.404

Casey Fossum

Pitches: L **Bats:** B **Pos:** RP-31; SP-12   **Ht:** 6'1" **Wt:** 165 **Born:** 1/6/78 **Age:** 25

Year Team	Lg	G	GS	CG	GF	IP	BFP	H	R	ER	HR	SH	SF	HB	TBB	IBB	SO	WP	Bk	W	L	Pct	ShO	Sv-Op	Hld	ERC	ERA
1999 Lowell	A-	5	5	0	0	14.1	56	6	2	2	1	0	0	2	5	0	16	0	4	1	0	1.000	0	0--	-	1.43	1.26
2000 Sarasota	A+	27	27	3	0	149.1	623	147	71	57	7	2	6	7	26	0	143	3	0	9	10	.474	3	0--	-	2.92	3.44
2001 Trenton	AA	20	20	0	0	117.2	483	102	47	37	5	0	0	12	28	0	130	2	0	3	7	.300	0	0--	-	2.78	2.83
2002 Pawtucket	AAA	5	3	1	1	25.0	111	34	15	11	1	0	1	3	6	0	28	2	0	3	0	.000	0	0--	-	5.78	3.96
2001 Boston	AL	13	7	0	3	44.1	197	44	26	24	4	0	1	6	20	1	26	1	1	3	2	.600	0	0-0	0	4.70	4.87
2002 Boston	AL	43	12	0	13	106.2	461	113	56	41	12	2	4	4	30	0	101	3	0	5	4	.556	0	1-1	3	4.14	3.46
2 ML YEARS		56	19	0	16	151.0	658	157	82	65	16	2	5	10	50	1	127	4	1	8	6	.571	0	1-1	3	4.30	3.87

John Foster

Pitches: L **Bats:** L **Pos:** RP-5   **Ht:** 6'0" **Wt:** 200 **Born:** 5/17/78 **Age:** 25

Year Team	Lg	G	GS	CG	GF	IP	BFP	H	R	ER	HR	SH	SF	HB	TBB	IBB	SO	WP	Bk	W	L	Pct	ShO	Sv-Op	Hld	ERC	ERA
1999 Danville	R+	18	0	0	7	39.0	148	28	10	6	0	5	0	2	6	0	36	4	0	4	1	.800	0	1--	-	1.51	1.38
2000 Myrtle Beach	A+	38	0	0	17	48.2	204	48	13	10	2	4	2	2	14	4	46	4	0	2	1	.667	0	3--	-	3.22	1.85
2001 Greenville	AA	50	0	0	21	68.2	303	71	30	23	6	11	3	2	33	7	63	5	0	8	7	.533	0	7--	-	4.47	3.01
2002 Richmond	AAA	55	0	0	25	62.0	277	67	30	29	5	4	1	1	28	8	48	3	0	8	4	.667	0	8--	-	4.41	4.21
2002 Atlanta	NL	5	0	0	0	5.0	28	6	6	6	3	0	0	1	6	0	6	0	0	1	0	1.000	0	0-0	0	14.44	10.80

Keith Foulke

Pitches: R **Bats:** R **Pos:** RP-65 **Ht:** 6'0" **Wt:** 210 **Born:** 10/19/72 **Age:** 30

Year Team	Lg	G	GS	CG	GF	IP	BFP	H	R	ER	HR	SH	SF	HB	TBB	IBB	SO	WP	Bk	W	L	Pct	ShO	Sv-Op	Hld	ERC	ERA
1997 SF-CWS		27	8	0	5	73.1	326	88	52	52	13	3	1	4	23	2	54	1	0	4	5	.444	0	3-6	5	5.68	6.38
1998 Chicago	AL	54	0	0	18	65.1	267	51	31	30	9	2	2	4	20	3	57	3	1	3	2	.600	0	1-2	13	2.95	4.13
1999 Chicago	AL	67	0	0	31	105.1	411	72	28	26	11	3	0	3	21	4	123	1	0	3	3	.500	0	9-13	22	1.80	2.22
2000 Chicago	AL	72	0	0	58	88.0	350	66	31	29	9	5	2	2	22	2	91	1	0	3	1	.750	0	34-39	3	2.28	2.97
2001 Chicago	AL	72	0	0	69	81.0	322	57	21	21	3	4	1	8	22	1	75	1	0	4	9	.308	0	42-45	0	2.06	2.33
2002 Chicago	AL	65	0	0	35	77.2	306	65	26	25	7	2	0	2	13	2	58	1	0	2	4	.333	0	11-14	10	2.38	2.90
1997 San Francisco	NL	11	8	0	0	44.2	209	60	41	41	9	2	0	4	18	1	33	1	0	1	5	.167	0	0-1	0	7.41	8.26
1997 Chicago	AL	16	0	0	5	28.2	117	28	11	11	4	1	1	0	5	1	21	0	0	3	0	1.000	0	3-5	5	3.27	3.45
6 ML YEARS		357	8	0	216	490.2	1982	399	189	183	52	19	6	23	121	14	458	8	1	19	24	.442	0	100-119	53	2.68	3.36

Andy Fox

Bats: L **Throws:** R **Pos:** SS-112; PH-14; 2B-7; 3B-4; RF-1 **Ht:** 6'4" **Wt:** 202 **Born:** 1/12/71 **Age:** 32

Year Team	Lg	G	AB	H	2B	3B	HR	(Hm	Rd)	TB	R	RBI	RC	TBB	IBB	SO	HBP	SH	SF	SB	CS	SB%	GDP	Avg	OBP	Slg
1996 New York	AL	113	189	37	4	0	3	(1	2)	50	26	13	15	20	1	28	1	9	0	11	3	.79	5	.196	.276	.265
1997 New York	AL	22	31	7	1	0	0	(0	0)	8	13	1	3	7	0	9	0	2	0	2	1	.67	1	.226	.368	.258
1998 Arizona	NL	139	502	139	21	6	9	(5	4)	199	67	44	74	43	0	97	18	0	1	14	7	.67	2	.277	.355	.396
1999 Arizona	NL	99	274	70	12	2	6	(4	2)	104	34	33	38	33	10	61	9	1	3	4	1	.80	4	.255	.351	.380
2000 Ari-Fla	NL	100	250	58	8	2	4	(2	2)	82	29	20	25	22	4	53	3	0	0	10	4	.71	2	.232	.302	.328
2001 Florida	NL	54	81	15	0	1	3	(3	0)	26	8	7	9	15	1	17	2	0	0	1	0	1.00	1	.185	.327	.321
2002 Florida	NL	133	435	109	14	5	4	(3	1)	145	55	41	57	49	6	94	10	5	3	31	7	.82	9	.251	.338	.333
2000 Arizona	NL	31	86	18	4	0	1	(1	0)	25	10	10	5	4	1	16	0	0	0	2	1	.67	1	.209	.244	.291
2000 Florida	NL	69	164	40	4	2	3	(1	2)	57	19	10	20	18	3	37	3	0	0	8	3	.73	1	.244	.330	.348
7 ML YEARS		660	1762	435	60	16	29	(18	11)	614	232	159	221	189	21	359	43	17	7	73	23	.76	22	.247	.333	.348

Chad Fox

Pitches: R **Bats:** R **Pos:** RP-3 **Ht:** 6'3" **Wt:** 206 **Born:** 9/3/70 **Age:** 32

Year Team	Lg	G	GS	CG	GF	IP	BFP	H	R	ER	HR	SH	SF	HB	TBB	IBB	SO	WP	Bk	W	L	Pct	ShO	Sv-Op	Hld	ERC	ERA
2002 Huntsville*	AA	3	0	0	0	5.1	21	5	1	0	0	0	0	0	2	0	7	0	0	0	1	.000	0	0--	-	3.21	0.00
1997 Atlanta	NL	30	0	0	8	27.1	120	24	12	10	4	0	0	0	16	0	28	4	0	1	0	1.000	0	0-1	1	4.44	3.29
1998 Milwaukee	NL	49	0	0	12	57.0	242	56	27	25	4	6	0	1	20	0	64	5	0	1	4	.200	0	0-2	20	3.66	3.95
1999 Milwaukee	NL	6	0	0	2	6.2	36	11	8	8	1	0	0	0	4	0	12	1	1	0	0	-	0	0-0	1	9.96	10.80
2001 Milwaukee	NL	65	0	0	9	66.2	287	44	16	14	6	2	1	5	36	7	80	5	1	5	2	.714	0	2-4	20	2.75	1.89
2002 Milwaukee	NL	3	0	0	0	4.2	25	6	3	3	0	1	0	0	5	1	3	0	0	1	0	1.000	0	0-0	5	7.03	5.79
5 ML YEARS		153	0	0	31	162.1	710	141	66	60	15	9	1	7	81	8	187	15	2	7	7	.500	0	2-7	48	3.71	3.33

John Franco

Pitches: L **Bats:** L **Pos:** RP **Ht:** 5'10" **Wt:** 185 **Born:** 9/17/60 **Age:** 42

Year Team	Lg	G	GS	CG	GF	IP	BFP	H	R	ER	HR	SH	SF	HB	TBB	IBB	SO	WP	Bk	W	L	Pct	ShO	Sv-Op	Hld	ERC	ERA
1984 Cincinnati	NL	54	0	0	30	79.1	335	74	28	23	3	4	4	2	36	4	55	2	0	6	2	.750	0	4-9	1	3.58	2.61
1985 Cincinnati	NL	67	0	0	33	99.0	407	83	27	24	5	11	1	1	40	8	61	4	0	12	3	.800	0	12-15	11	2.86	2.18
1986 Cincinnati	NL	74	0	0	52	101.0	429	90	40	33	7	8	3	2	44	12	84	4	2	6	6	.500	0	29-38	1	3.30	2.94
1987 Cincinnati	NL	68	0	0	60	82.0	344	76	26	23	6	5	2	0	27	6	61	1	0	8	5	.615	0	32-41	0	3.10	2.52
1988 Cincinnati	NL	70	0	0	61	86.0	336	60	18	15	3	5	1	0	27	3	46	1	2	6	6	.500	0	39-42	0	1.82	1.57
1989 Cincinnati	NL	60	0	0	50	80.2	345	77	35	28	3	7	3	0	36	8	60	3	2	4	8	.333	0	32-39	0	3.42	3.12
1990 New York	NL	55	0	0	48	67.2	287	66	22	19	4	3	1	0	21	2	56	7	2	5	3	.625	0	33-39	0	3.24	2.53
1991 New York	NL	52	0	0	48	55.1	247	61	27	18	2	3	0	1	18	4	45	6	0	5	9	.357	0	30-35	0	3.73	2.93
1992 New York	NL	31	0	0	30	33.0	128	24	6	6	1	0	2	0	11	2	20	0	0	6	2	.750	0	15-17	0	2.00	1.64
1993 New York	NL	35	0	0	30	36.1	172	46	24	21	6	4	1	1	19	3	29	5	0	4	3	.571	0	10-17	5	6.62	5.20
1994 New York	NL	47	0	0	43	50.0	216	47	20	15	2	2	1	1	19	0	42	1	0	1	4	.200	0	30-36	0	3.27	2.70
1995 New York	NL	48	0	0	41	51.2	213	48	17	14	4	4	1	0	17	2	41	0	0	5	3	.625	0	29-36	0	3.26	2.44
1996 New York	NL	51	0	0	44	54.0	235	54	15	11	4	4	1	0	21	0	48	2	0	4	3	.571	0	28-36	0	3.53	1.83
1997 New York	NL	59	0	0	53	60.0	244	49	18	17	3	5	1	1	20	2	53	0	0	5	3	.625	0	36-42	0	2.57	2.55
1998 New York	NL	61	0	0	54	64.2	289	66	28	26	4	4	5	4	29	7	59	2	0	0	8	.000	0	38-46	0	4.11	3.62
1999 New York	NL	46	0	0	34	40.2	182	40	14	13	1	3	1	2	19	1	41	0	0	0	2	.000	0	19-21	1	3.77	2.88
2000 New York	NL	62	0	0	14	55.2	239	46	24	21	6	3	0	2	26	6	56	2	0	5	4	.556	0	4-4	20	3.36	3.40
2001 New York	NL	58	0	0	16	53.1	232	55	25	24	8	2	1	2	19	2	50	4	1	6	2	.750	0	2-7	17	4.50	4.05
18 ML YEARS		998	0	0	741	1150.1	4880	1062	414	351	70	79	28	19	449	72	907	50	9	88	76	.537	0	422-520	51	3.31	2.75

Julio Franco

Bats: R **Throws:** R **Pos:** 1B-95; PH-45; DH-2 **Ht:** 6'1" **Wt:** 188 **Born:** 8/23/58 **Age:** 44

Year Team	Lg	G	AB	H	2B	3B	HR	(Hm	Rd)	TB	R	RBI	RC	TBB	IBB	SO	HBP	SH	SF	SB	CS	SB%	GDP	Avg	OBP	Slg
1982 Philadelphia	NL	16	29	8	1	0	0	(0	0)	9	3	3	2	2	1	4	0	1	0	0	2	.00	1	.276	.323	.310
1983 Cleveland	AL	149	560	153	24	8	8	(6	2)	217	68	80	62	27	1	50	2	3	6	32	12	.73	21	.273	.306	.388
1984 Cleveland	AL	160	658	188	22	5	3	(1	2)	229	82	79	72	43	1	68	6	1	10	19	10	.66	23	.286	.331	.348
1985 Cleveland	AL	160	636	183	33	4	6	(3	3)	242	97	90	78	54	2	74	4	0	9	13	9	.59	26	.288	.343	.381
1986 Cleveland	AL	149	599	183	30	5	10	(4	6)	253	80	74	76	32	1	66	0	0	5	10	7	.59	28	.306	.338	.422
1987 Cleveland	AL	128	495	158	24	8	8	(5	3)	212	86	52	81	57	2	56	3	0	3	32	9	.78	23	.319	.389	.428
1988 Cleveland	AL	152	613	186	23	6	10	(3	7)	251	88	54	89	56	4	72	2	1	4	25	11	.69	17	.303	.361	.409
1989 Texas	AL	150	548	173	31	5	13	(9	4)	253	80	92	93	66	11	69	1	0	6	21	3	.88	27	.316	.386	.462
1990 Texas	AL	157	582	172	27	1	11	(4	7)	234	96	69	94	82	3	83	2	2	2	31	10	.76	12	.296	.383	.402
1991 Texas	AL	146	589	201	27	3	15	(7	8)	279	108	78	113	65	8	78	3	0	2	36	9	.80	13	.341	.408	.474
1992 Texas	AL	35	107	25	7	0	2	(2	0)	38	19	8	12	15	2	17	0	1	0	1	1	.50	3	.234	.328	.355
1993 Texas	AL	144	532	154	31	3	14	(6	8)	233	85	84	83	62	4	95	1	5	7	9	3	.75	16	.289	.360	.438

Year Team	Lg	G	AB	H	2B	3B	HR	(Hm	Rd)	TB	R	RBI	RC	TBB	IBB	SO	HBP	SH	SF	SB	CS	SB%	GDP	Avg	OBP	Slg
1994 Chicago	AL	112	433	138	19	2	20	(10	10)	221	72	98	87	62	4	75	5	0	5	8	1	.89	14	.319	.406	.510
1996 Cleveland	AL	112	432	139	20	1	14	(7	7)	203	72	76	79	61	2	82	3	0	3	8	8	.50	14	.322	.407	.470
1997 Cle-Mil		120	430	116	16	1	7	(5	2)	155	68	44	58	69	4	116	1	1	4	15	6	.71	17	.270	.369	.360
1999 Tampa Bay	AL	1	1	0	0	0	0	(0	0)	0	0	0	0	0	0	1	0	0	0	0	0	-	0	.000	.000	.000
2001 Atlanta	NL	25	90	27	4	0	3	(2	1)	40	13	11	14	10	1	20	1	0	0	0	0	-	0	.300	.376	.444
2002 Atlanta	NL	125	338	96	13	1	6	(3	3)	129	51	30	38	39	3	75	1	2	3	5	1	.83	13	.284	.357	.382
1997 Cleveland	AL	78	289	82	13	1	3	(2	1)	106	46	25	37	38	2	75	0	1	0	8	5	.62	13	.284	.367	.367
1997 Milwaukee	NL	42	141	34	3	0	4	(3	1)	49	22	19	21	31	2	41	1	0	4	7	1	.88	4	.241	.373	.348
18 ML YEARS		2041	7672	2300	352	48	150	(77	73)	3198	1168	1022	1131	802	54	1101	35	17	71	265	102	.72	271	.300	.366	.417

Matt Franco

Bats: L **Throws:** R **Pos:** 1B-51; PH-29; LF-2; RF-2   **Ht:** 6'1" **Wt:** 210 **Born:** 8/19/69 **Age:** 33

Year Team	Lg	G	AB	H	2B	3B	HR	(Hm	Rd)	TB	R	RBI	RC	TBB	IBB	SO	HBP	SH	SF	SB	CS	SB%	GDP	Avg	OBP	Slg
2002 Richmond*	AAA	47	173	50	11	0	6	(-	-)	79	24	28	27	14	0	19	3	0	2	1	0	1.00	6	.289	.349	.457
1995 Chicago	NL	16	17	5	1	0	0	(0	0)	6	3	1	2	0	0	4	0	0	0	0	0	-	0	.294	.294	.353
1996 New York	NL	14	31	6	1	0	1	(0	1)	10	3	2	2	1	0	5	1	0	1	0	0	-	0	.194	.235	.323
1997 New York	NL	112	163	45	5	0	5	(3	2)	65	21	21	21	13	4	23	1	0	0	1	0	1.00	4	.276	.330	.399
1998 New York	NL	103	161	44	7	2	1	(1	0)	58	20	13	20	23	6	26	1	1	1	0	1	.00	8	.273	.366	.360
1999 New York	NL	122	132	31	5	0	4	(0	4)	48	18	21	17	28	3	21	0	0	1	0	0	-	9	.235	.366	.364
2000 New York	NL	101	134	32	4	0	2	(1	1)	42	9	14	15	21	3	22	0	0	1	0	0	-	3	.239	.340	.313
2002 Atlanta	NL	81	205	65	15	4	6	(3	3)	106	25	30	39	27	2	31	0	0	1	1	0	1.00	5	.317	.395	.517
7 ML YEARS		549	843	228	38	6	19	(8	11)	335	99	102	116	113	18	132	2	2	5	2	1	.67	30	.270	.356	.397

Ryan Franklin

Pitches: R **Bats:** R **Pos:** RP-29; SP-12   **Ht:** 6'3" **Wt:** 165 **Born:** 3/5/73 **Age:** 30

		HOW MUCH HE PITCHED						WHAT HE GAVE UP											THE RESULTS						
Year Team	Lg	G	GS	CG	GF	IP	BFP	H	R	ER	HR	SH	SF	HB	TBB	IBB	SO	WP	Bk	W	L	Pct	ShO	Sv-Op	Hld	ERC	ERA
2002 Everett*	A-	1	1	0	0	2.2	10	2	1	0	0	0	0	0	0	1	1	0	0	0	0	-	0	0- -	-	1.13	0.00
1999 Seattle	AL	6	0	0	2	11.1	51	10	6	6	2	0	0	1	8	1	6	0	0	0	0	-	0	0-0	1	5.52	4.76
2001 Seattle	AL	38	0	0	14	78.1	335	76	32	31	13	1	2	4	24	4	60	2	0	5	1	.833	0	0-1	5	4.08	3.56
2002 Seattle	AL	41	12	0	10	118.2	495	117	62	53	14	5	5	5	22	1	65	0	0	7	5	.583	0	0-1	3	3.40	4.02
3 ML YEARS		85	12	0	26	208.1	881	203	100	90	29	6	7	10	54	6	131	2	0	12	6	.667	0	0-2	9	3.76	3.89

Wayne Franklin

Pitches: L **Bats:** L **Pos:** SP-4   **Ht:** 6'2" **Wt:** 205 **Born:** 3/9/74 **Age:** 29

		HOW MUCH HE PITCHED						WHAT HE GAVE UP											THE RESULTS						
Year Team	Lg	G	GS	CG	GF	IP	BFP	H	R	ER	HR	SH	SF	HB	TBB	IBB	SO	WP	Bk	W	L	Pct	ShO	Sv-Op	Hld	ERC	ERA
2002 New Orleans*	AAA	29	27	1	1	179.0	733	153	68	62	14	5	8	11	59	2	141	2	1	13	9	.591	0	0- -	-	3.16	3.12
2000 Houston	NL	25	0	0	4	21.1	103	24	14	13	2	0	2	4	12	1	21	0	1	0	0	-	0	0-0	8	6.61	5.48
2001 Houston	NL	11	0	0	3	12.0	60	17	9	9	4	0	0	0	9	0	9	0	0	0	0	-	0	0-0	1	10.43	6.75
2002 Milwaukee	NL	4	4	0	0	24.0	103	16	8	7	1	1	0	0	17	1	17	0	0	2	1	.667	0	0-0	0	2.96	2.63
3 ML YEARS		40	4	0	7	57.1	266	57	31	29	7	1	2	4	38	2	47	0	1	2	1	.667	0	0-0	9	5.47	4.55

Kevin Frederick

Pitches: R **Bats:** L **Pos:** RP-8   **Ht:** 6'1" **Wt:** 208 **Born:** 11/4/76 **Age:** 26

		HOW MUCH HE PITCHED						WHAT HE GAVE UP											THE RESULTS						
Year Team	Lg	G	GS	CG	GF	IP	BFP	H	R	ER	HR	SH	SF	HB	TBB	IBB	SO	WP	Bk	W	L	Pct	ShO	Sv-Op	Hld	ERC	ERA
1998 Elizabethton	R+	17	0	0	10	29.2	130	28	21	14	4	1	0	0	10	1	46	4	0	1	4	.200	0	1- -	-	3.53	4.25
1999 Twins	R	2	0	0	0	2.1	14	6	5	4	0	0	1	0	1	0	3	0	0	0	0	-	0	0- -	-	13.44	15.43
2000 Quad City	A	27	0	0	11	46.0	193	34	17	12	1	3	1	4	23	4	51	4	0	5	0	1.000	0	4- -	-	2.74	2.35
2000 Fort Myers	A+	19	0	0	7	30.0	123	20	11	9	0	1	1	1	14	1	37	4	2	2	1	.667	0	3- -	-	2.02	2.70
2001 Fort Myers	A+	9	0	0	4	18.0	65	9	2	2	1	0	0	0	3	1	19	0	0	2	0	1.000	0	1- -	-	0.94	1.00
2001 New Britain	AA	44	0	0	18	82.2	331	56	17	15	5	6	2	8	28	7	109	4	0	6	2	.750	0	7- -	-	2.19	1.63
2002 Edmonton	AAA	46	2	0	38	55.0	246	63	31	28	8	1	4	2	21	1	47	4	0	3	6	.333	0	22- -	-	5.29	4.58
2002 Minnesota	AL	8	0	0	3	11.2	56	13	13	13	3	0	0	0	10	0	5	2	0	0	0	-	0	0-0	0	8.14	10.03

Travis Fryman

Bats: R **Throws:** R **Pos:** 3B-113; PH-8   **Ht:** 6'1" **Wt:** 195 **Born:** 3/25/69 **Age:** 34

Year Team	Lg	G	AB	H	2B	3B	HR	(Hm	Rd)	TB	R	RBI	RC	TBB	IBB	SO	HBP	SH	SF	SB	CS	SB%	GDP	Avg	OBP	Slg
1990 Detroit	AL	66	232	69	11	1	9	(5	4)	109	32	27	36	17	0	51	1	1	0	3	3	.50	3	.297	.348	.470
1991 Detroit	AL	149	557	144	36	3	21	(8	13)	249	65	91	75	40	0	149	3	6	6	12	5	.71	13	.259	.309	.447
1992 Detroit	AL	161	659	175	31	4	20	(9	11)	274	87	96	85	45	1	144	6	5	6	8	4	.67	13	.266	.316	.416
1993 Detroit	AL	151	607	182	37	5	22	(13	9)	295	98	97	112	77	1	128	4	1	6	9	4	.69	8	.300	.379	.486
1994 Detroit	AL	114	464	122	34	5	18	(10	8)	220	66	85	73	45	1	128	5	1	13	2	2	.50	6	.263	.326	.474
1995 Detroit	AL	144	567	156	21	5	15	(9	6)	232	79	81	90	63	4	100	3	0	7	4	2	.67	18	.275	.347	.409
1996 Detroit	AL	157	616	165	32	3	22	(10	12)	269	90	100	86	57	2	118	4	1	10	4	3	.57	18	.268	.329	.437
1997 Detroit	AL	154	595	163	27	3	22	(9	13)	262	90	102	85	46	5	113	5	0	11	16	3	.84	15	.274	.326	.440
1998 Cleveland	AL	146	557	160	33	2	28	(16	12)	281	74	96	91	44	0	125	3	0	4	10	8	.56	12	.287	.340	.504
1999 Cleveland	AL	85	322	82	16	2	10	(6	4)	132	45	48	37	25	1	57	1	0	2	2	1	.67	13	.255	.309	.410
2000 Cleveland	AL	155	574	184	38	4	22	(9	13)	296	93	106	112	73	2	111	1	0	10	1	5	.50	15	.321	.392	.516
2001 Cleveland	AL	98	334	88	15	0	3	(3	0)	112	34	38	36	30	1	63	3	0	3	1	2	.33	8	.263	.327	.335
2002 Cleveland	AL	118	397	86	14	3	11	(4	7)	139	42	55	46	40	1	82	2	0	0	0	0	-	12	.217	.292	.350
13 ML YEARS		1698	6481	1776	345	40	223	(115	108)	2870	895	1022	953	602	19	1369	41	15	78	72	38	.65	154	.274	.336	.443

Brian Fuentes

Pitches: L Bats: L Pos: RP-31 **Ht: 6'4" Wt: 220 Born: 8/9/75 Age: 27**

Year Team	Lg	G	GS	CG	GF	IP	BFP	H	R	ER	HR	SH	SF	HB	TBB	IBB	SO	WP	Bk	W	L	Pct	ShO	Sv-Op	Hld	ERC	ERA
1996 Everett	A-	13	2	0	3	26.2	114	23	14	13	2	0	1	0	13	0	26	5	0	0	1	.000	0	0--	-	3.47	4.39
1997 Wisconsin	A	22	22	0	0	118.2	486	84	52	47	6	3	3	8	59	0	153	11	3	6	7	.462	0	0--	-	2.88	3.56
1998 Lancaster	A+	24	24	0	0	118.2	541	121	73	55	8	1	6	9	81	0	137	14	2	7	7	.500	0	0--	-	5.51	4.17
1999 New Haven	AA	15	14	0	0	60.0	272	53	36	33	5	2	5	11	46	0	66	1	1	3	3	.500	0	0--	-	5.71	4.95
2000 New Haven	AA	26	26	1	0	139.2	610	127	80	70	7	4	7	13	70	0	152	14	0	7	12	.368	0	0--	-	4.00	4.51
2001 Tacoma	AAA	35	0	0	13	52.0	205	35	19	17	4	3	1	6	25	0	70	3	0	3	2	.600	0	6--	-	3.13	2.94
2002 Co Springs	AAA	41	0	0	5	48.2	224	44	25	20	0	4	5	4	32	1	61	3	2	3	3	.500	0	1--	-	3.98	3.70
2001 Seattle	AL	10	0	0	3	11.2	47	6	6	6	2	0	1	3	8	0	10	1	0	1	1	.500	0	0-1	1	4.39	4.63
2002 Colorado	NL	31	0	0	9	26.2	118	25	14	14	4	0	2	3	13	0	38	1	0	2	0	1.000	0	0-0	0	4.91	4.73
2 ML YEARS		41	0	0	12	38.1	165	31	20	20	6	0	3	6	21	0	48	2	0	3	1	.750	0	0-1	1	4.76	4.70

Brad Fullmer

Bats: L Throws: R Pos: DH-93; 1B-29; PH-11 **Ht: 6'0" Wt: 220 Born: 1/17/75 Age: 28**

Year Team	Lg	G	AB	H	2B	3B	HR	(Hm	Rd)	TB	R	RBI	RC	TBB	IBB	SO	HBP	SH	SF	SB	CS	SB%	GDP	Avg	OBP	Slg
1997 Montreal	NL	19	40	12	2	0	3	(1	2)	23	4	8	8	2	1	7	1	0	0	0	0	-	0	.300	.349	.575
1998 Montreal	NL	140	505	138	44	2	13	(3	10)	225	58	73	70	39	4	70	2	0	1	6	6	.50	12	.273	.327	.446
1999 Montreal	NL	100	347	96	34	2	9	(4	5)	161	38	47	47	22	6	35	2	0	3	2	3	.40	14	.277	.321	.464
2000 Toronto	AL	133	482	142	29	1	32	(16	16)	269	76	104	86	30	3	68	6	0	6	3	1	.75	14	.295	.340	.558
2001 Toronto	AL	146	522	143	31	2	18	(8	10)	232	71	83	73	38	4	88	6	0	7	5	2	.71	13	.274	.326	.444
2002 Anaheim	AL	130	429	124	35	6	19	(9	10)	228	75	59	73	32	6	44	15	0	3	10	3	.77	7	.289	.357	.531
6 ML YEARS		668	2325	655	175	13	94	(41	53)	1138	322	374	357	163	28	312	32	0	20	26	15	.63	60	.282	.335	.489

Aaron Fultz

Pitches: L Bats: L Pos: RP-43 **Ht: 6'0" Wt: 200 Born: 9/4/73 Age: 29**

Year Team	Lg	G	GS	CG	GF	IP	BFP	H	R	ER	HR	SH	SF	HB	TBB	IBB	SO	WP	Bk	W	L	Pct	ShO	Sv-Op	Hld	ERC	ERA
2002 Fresno*	AAA	17	0	0	14	22.2	95	18	8	8	1	2	1	0	11	2	22	2	0	1	3	.250	0	4--	-	2.78	3.18
2000 San Francisco	NL	58	0	0	18	69.1	299	67	38	36	8	7	6	3	28	0	62	0	2	5	2	.714	0	1-3	7	4.19	4.67
2001 San Francisco	NL	66	0	0	17	71.0	300	70	40	36	9	3	4	1	21	3	67	1	0	3	1	.750	0	1-2	12	3.75	4.56
2002 San Francisco	NL	43	0	0	12	41.1	185	47	22	22	4	2	1	3	19	3	31	1	0	2	2	.500	0	0-1	4	5.36	4.79
3 ML YEARS		167	0	0	47	181.2	784	184	100	94	21	12	11	7	68	6	160	2	2	10	5	.667	0	2-6	23	4.28	4.66

Rafael Furcal

Bats: B Throws: R Pos: SS-150; 2B-4; PR-2 **Ht: 5'10" Wt: 165 Born: 10/24/77 Age: 25**

Year Team	Lg	G	AB	H	2B	3B	HR	(Hm	Rd)	TB	R	RBI	RC	TBB	IBB	SO	HBP	SH	SF	SB	CS	SB%	GDP	Avg	OBP	Slg
2000 Atlanta	NL	131	455	134	20	4	4	(1	3)	174	87	37	78	73	0	80	3	9	2	40	14	.74	2	.295	.394	.382
2001 Atlanta	NL	79	324	89	19	0	4	(3	1)	120	39	30	41	24	1	56	1	4	6	22	6	.79	5	.275	.321	.370
2002 Atlanta	NL	154	636	175	31	8	8	(4	4)	246	95	47	79	43	0	114	3	9	2	27	15	.64	8	.275	.323	.387
3 ML YEARS		364	1415	398	70	12	16	(8	8)	540	221	114	198	140	1	250	7	22	10	89	35	.72	15	.281	.347	.382

Mike Fyhrie

Pitches: R Bats: R Pos: RP-12; SP-4 **Ht: 6'2" Wt: 205 Born: 12/9/69 Age: 33**

Year Team	Lg	G	GS	CG	GF	IP	BFP	H	R	ER	HR	SH	SF	HB	TBB	IBB	SO	WP	Bk	W	L	Pct	ShO	Sv-Op	Hld	ERC	ERA
2002 Sacramento*	AAA	13	13	0	0	77.1	317	61	22	20	4	1	1	5	23	0	68	0	1	7	2	.778	0	0--	-	2.50	2.33
1996 New York	NL	2	0	0	0	2.1	14	4	4	4	0	0	0	0	3	0	0	0	0	0	1	.000	0	0-0	0	11.30	15.43
1999 Anaheim	AL	16	7	0	5	51.2	235	61	32	29	8	0	1	0	21	1	26	0	0	0	4	.000	0	0-0	1	5.45	5.05
2000 Anaheim	AL	32	0	0	7	52.2	220	54	14	14	4	1	3	0	15	4	43	0	0	0	0	-	0	0-0	2	3.53	2.39
2001 ChC-Oak	AL	18	0	0	5	20.0	81	18	7	7	1	0	0	0	8	0	11	0	0	0	2	.000	0	0-0	5	3.34	3.15
2002 Oakland	AL	16	4	0	2	48.2	212	46	25	24	3	1	0	4	20	1	29	1	1	2	4	.333	0	0-0	1	3.81	4.44
2001 Chicago	NL	15	0	0	4	15.0	64	16	7	7	1	0	0	0	7	0	6	0	0	0	2	.000	0	0-0	5	4.67	4.20
2001 Oakland	AL	3	0	0	1	5.0	17	2	0	0	0	0	0	0	1	0	5	0	0	0	0	-	0	0-0	0	0.67	0.00
5 ML YEARS		84	11	0	19	175.1	762	183	82	78	16	2	4	4	67	6	109	1	1	2	11	.154	0	0-0	9	4.23	4.00

Eric Gagne

Pitches: R Bats: R Pos: RP-77 **Ht: 6'2" Wt: 195 Born: 1/7/76 Age: 27**

Year Team	Lg	G	GS	CG	GF	IP	BFP	H	R	ER	HR	SH	SF	HB	TBB	IBB	SO	WP	Bk	W	L	Pct	ShO	Sv-Op	Hld	ERC	ERA
1999 Los Angeles	NL	5	5	0	0	30.0	119	18	8	7	3	1	0	0	15	0	30	1	0	1	1	.500	0	0-0	0	2.42	2.10
2000 Los Angeles	NL	20	19	0	0	101.1	464	106	62	58	20	5	3	3	60	1	79	4	0	4	6	.400	0	0-0	0	5.97	5.15
2001 Los Angeles	NL	33	24	0	3	151.2	649	144	90	80	24	6	8	16	46	1	130	3	1	6	7	.462	0	0-0	0	4.22	4.75
2002 Los Angeles	NL	77	0	0	71	82.1	314	55	18	18	6	3	2	2	16	4	114	1	0	4	1	.800	0	52-59	1	1.60	1.97
4 ML YEARS		135	48	0	74	365.1	1546	323	178	163	53	15	13	21	137	6	353	9	1	15	15	.500	0	52-59	1	3.85	4.02

Andres Galarraga

Bats: R **Throws:** R **Pos:** 1B-89; PH-24 **Ht:** 6'3" **Wt:** 250 **Born:** 6/18/61 **Age:** 42

Year Team	Lg	G	AB	H	2B	3B	HR	(Hm	Rd)	TB	R	RBI	RC	TBB	IBB	SO	HBP	SH	SF	SB	CS	SB%	GDP	Avg	OBP	Slg
1985 Montreal	NL	24	75	14	1	0	2	(0	2)	21	9	4	4	3	0	18	1	0	0	1	1	.33	0	.187	.228	.280
1986 Montreal	NL	105	321	87	13	0	10	(4	6)	130	39	42	42	30	5	79	3	1	1	6	5	.55	8	.271	.338	.405
1987 Montreal	NL	147	551	168	40	3	13	(7	6)	253	72	90	86	41	13	127	10	0	4	7	10	.41	11	.305	.361	.459
1988 Montreal	NL	157	609	184	42	8	29	(14	15)	329	99	92	110	39	9	153	10	0	3	13	4	.76	12	.302	.352	.540
1989 Montreal	NL	152	572	147	30	1	23	(13	10)	248	76	85	79	48	10	158	13	0	3	12	5	.71	12	.257	.327	.434
1990 Montreal	NL	155	579	148	29	0	20	(6	14)	237	65	87	70	40	8	169	4	0	5	10	1	.91	14	.256	.306	.409
1991 Montreal	NL	107	375	82	13	2	9	(3	6)	126	34	33	30	23	5	86	2	0	0	5	6	.45	6	.219	.268	.336
1992 St Louis	NL	95	325	79	14	2	10	(4	6)	127	38	39	33	11	0	69	8	0	3	5	4	.56	8	.243	.282	.391
1993 Colorado	NL	120	470	174	35	4	22	(13	9)	283	71	98	102	24	12	73	6	0	6	2	4	.33	9	.370	.403	.602
1994 Colorado	NL	103	417	133	21	0	31	(16	15)	247	77	85	82	19	8	93	8	0	5	8	3	.73	10	.319	.356	.592
1995 Colorado	NL	143	554	155	29	3	31	(18	13)	283	89	106	90	32	6	146	13	0	5	12	2	.86	14	.280	.331	.511
1996 Colorado	NL	159	626	190	39	3	47	(32	15)	376	119	150	130	40	3	157	17	0	8	18	8	.69	14	.304	.357	.601
1997 Colorado	NL	154	600	191	31	3	41	(21	20)	351	120	140	126	54	2	141	17	0	3	15	8	.65	16	.318	.389	.585
1998 Atlanta	NL	153	555	169	27	1	44	(16	28)	330	103	121	124	63	11	146	25	0	5	7	6	.54	18	.305	.397	.595
2000 Atlanta	NL	141	494	149	25	1	28	(14	14)	260	67	100	88	36	5	126	17	0	1	3	5	.38	15	.302	.369	.526
2001 Tex-SF		121	399	102	28	1	17	(8	9)	183	50	69	56	31	2	117	12	0	3	1	3	.25	12	.256	.326	.459
2002 Montreal	NL	104	292	76	12	0	9	(7	2)	115	30	40	35	30	6	81	9	0	3	2	2	.50	8	.260	.344	.394
2001 Texas	AL	72	243	57	16	0	10	(5	5)	103	33	34	30	18	1	68	9	0	1	1	0	1.00	6	.235	.310	.424
2001 San Francisco	NL	49	156	45	12	1	7	(3	4)	80	17	35	26	13	1	49	3	0	2	0	3	.00	3	.288	.351	.513
17 ML YEARS		2140	7814	2248	429	32	386	(196	190)	3899	1158	1381	1287	564	105	1939	175	1	58	127	78	.62	169	.288	.347	.499

Ron Gant

Bats: R **Throws:** R **Pos:** LF-78; PH-24; RF-5; DH-4; CF-1 **Ht:** 6'0" **Wt:** 195 **Born:** 3/2/65 **Age:** 38

Year Team	Lg	G	AB	H	2B	3B	HR	(Hm	Rd)	TB	R	RBI	RC	TBB	IBB	SO	HBP	SH	SF	SB	CS	SB%	GDP	Avg	OBP	Slg
1987 Atlanta	NL	21	83	22	4	0	2	(1	1)	32	9	9	8	1	0	11	0	1	1	4	2	.67	3	.265	.271	.386
1988 Atlanta	NL	146	563	146	28	8	19	(7	12)	247	85	60	78	46	4	118	3	2	4	19	10	.66	7	.259	.317	.439
1989 Atlanta	NL	75	260	46	8	3	9	(5	4)	87	26	25	20	20	0	63	1	2	1	9	6	.60	0	.177	.237	.335
1990 Atlanta	NL	152	575	174	34	3	32	(18	14)	310	107	84	107	50	0	86	1	1	4	33	16	.67	8	.303	.357	.539
1991 Atlanta	NL	154	561	141	35	3	32	(18	14)	278	101	105	99	71	8	104	5	0	5	34	15	.69	6	.251	.338	.496
1992 Atlanta	NL	153	544	141	22	6	17	(10	7)	226	74	80	74	45	5	101	7	0	6	32	10	.76	10	.259	.321	.415
1993 Atlanta	NL	157	606	166	27	4	36	(17	19)	309	113	117	105	67	2	117	2	0	7	26	9	.74	14	.274	.345	.510
1995 Cincinnati	NL	119	410	113	19	4	29	(12	17)	227	79	88	87	74	5	108	3	1	5	23	8	.74	11	.276	.386	.554
1996 St Louis	NL	122	419	103	14	2	30	(17	13)	211	74	82	77	73	5	98	3	1	4	13	4	.76	6	.246	.359	.504
1997 St Louis	NL	139	502	115	21	4	17	(11	6)	195	68	62	63	58	3	162	1	0	1	14	6	.70	2	.229	.310	.388
1998 St Louis	NL	121	383	92	17	1	26	(14	12)	189	67	67	64	51	2	92	2	0	2	8	0	1.00	6	.240	.331	.493
1999 Philadelphia	NL	138	516	134	27	5	17	(6	11)	222	107	77	86	85	0	112	1	0	3	13	3	.81	6	.260	.364	.430
2000 Phi-Ana		123	425	106	19	3	26	(12	14)	209	69	54	70	56	1	91	1	1	4	6	6	.50	7	.249	.335	.492
2001 Col-Oak		93	252	65	13	3	10	(7	3)	114	46	35	42	35	2	80	0	2	3	5	1	.83	6	.258	.345	.452
2002 San Diego	NL	102	309	81	14	1	18	(9	9)	151	58	59	50	36	1	59	2	1	5	4	6	.40	8	.262	.338	.489
2000 Philadelphia	NL	89	343	87	16	2	20	(9	11)	167	54	38	53	36	1	73	1	1	3	5	4	.56	7	.254	.324	.487
2000 Anaheim	AL	34	82	19	3	1	6	(5	1)	42	15	16	17	20	0	18	0	0	1	1	2	.33	0	.232	.379	.512
2001 Colorado	NL	59	171	44	8	2	8	(6	2)	80	31	22	29	24	2	56	0	2	2	3	1	.75	0	.257	.345	.468
2001 Oakland	AL	34	81	21	5	1	2	(1	1)	34	15	13	13	11	0	24	0	0	1	2	0	1.00	6	.259	.344	.420
15 ML YEARS		1815	6408	1645	302	50	320	(166	154)	3007	1076	1004	1027	768	38	1402	32	12	56	243	102	.70	97	.257	.337	.469

Rich Garces

Pitches: R **Bats:** R **Pos:** RP-26 **Ht:** 6'0" **Wt:** 250 **Born:** 5/18/71 **Age:** 32

Year Team	Lg	G	GS	CG	GF	IP	BFP	H	R	ER	HR	SH	SF	HB	TBB	IBB	SO	WP	Bk	W	L	Pct	ShO	Sv-Op	Hld	ERC	ERA
2002 Red Sox*	R	2	2	0	0	4.0	12	1	1	0	0	0	0	0	0	0	5	0	0	0	0	-	0	0--	-	0.16	0.00
1990 Minnesota	AL	5	0	0	3	5.2	24	4	2	1	0	0	0	0	4	0	1	0	0	0	0	-	0	2-2	0	2.99	1.59
1993 Minnesota	AL	3	0	0	1	4.0	18	4	2	0	0	0	0	0	2	0	3	0	0	0	0	-	0	0-0	0	3.63	0.00
1995 ChC-Fla	NL	18	0	0	7	24.1	108	25	15	12	1	1	0	0	11	2	22	0	0	0	2	.000	0	0-1	1	3.81	4.44
1996 Boston	AL	37	0	0	9	44.0	205	42	26	24	5	0	5	0	33	5	55	0	0	3	2	.600	0	0-2	4	5.04	4.91
1997 Boston	AL	12	0	0	4	13.2	66	14	9	7	2	0	1	1	9	0	12	0	0	1	0	.000	0	0-2	1	5.70	4.61
1998 Boston	AL	30	0	0	11	46.0	201	36	19	17	6	2	1	2	27	3	34	1	1	1	1	.500	0	1-3	6	3.83	3.33
1999 Boston	AL	30	0	0	4	40.2	164	25	9	7	1	0	0	0	18	1	33	0	0	5	1	.833	0	2-3	2	1.75	1.55
2000 Boston	AL	64	0	0	9	74.2	309	64	28	27	7	1	4	1	23	5	69	3	0	8	1	.889	0	1-5	17	2.85	3.25
2001 Boston	AL	62	0	0	5	67.0	284	55	32	29	6	3	1	4	25	1	51	2	1	6	1	.857	0	1-2	17	3.09	3.90
2002 Boston	AL	26	0	0	7	21.1	97	21	20	18	4	2	3	3	12	2	16	0	0	0	1	.000	0	0-0	5	5.78	7.59
1995 Chicago	NL	7	0	0	4	11.0	46	11	6	4	0	0	0	0	3	0	6	0	0	0	0	-	0	0-0	1	2.92	3.27
1995 Florida	NL	11	0	0	3	13.1	62	14	9	8	1	1	0	0	8	2	16	0	0	0	2	.000	0	0-1	1	4.58	5.40
10 ML YEARS		287	0	0	60	341.1	1476	290	162	142	32	9	15	11	164	19	296	6	2	23	10	.697	0	7-20	53	3.51	3.74

Freddy Garcia

Pitches: R **Bats:** R **Pos:** SP-34 **Ht:** 6'4" **Wt:** 235 **Born:** 6/10/76 **Age:** 27

Year Team	Lg	G	GS	CG	GF	IP	BFP	H	R	ER	HR	SH	SF	HB	TBB	IBB	SO	WP	Bk	W	L	Pct	ShO	Sv-Op	Hld	ERC	ERA
1999 Seattle	AL	33	33	2	0	201.1	888	205	96	91	18	3	6	10	90	4	170	12	3	17	8	.680	1	0-0	0	4.46	4.07
2000 Seattle	AL	21	20	0	0	124.1	538	112	62	54	16	6	1	2	64	4	79	4	2	9	5	.643	0	0-0	0	4.20	3.91
2001 Seattle	AL	34	34	0	0	238.2	971	199	88	81	16	8	5	5	69	6	163	3	1	18	6	.750	3	0-0	0	2.61	3.05
2002 Seattle	AL	34	34	1	0	223.2	955	227	110	109	30	4	8	6	63	3	181	8	1	16	10	.615	0	0-0	0	3.98	4.39
4 ML YEARS		122	121	7	0	788.0	3352	743	356	335	80	21	20	23	286	17	593	27	7	60	29	.674	4	0-0	0	3.70	3.83

Jesse Garcia

Bats: R **Throws:** R **Pos:** 2B-21; PR-9; PH-7; SS-5; LF-2; RF-2   **Ht:** 5'10" **Wt:** 171 **Born:** 9/24/73 **Age:** 29

						BATTING														BASERUNNING				AVERAGES		
Year Team	Lg	G	AB	H	2B	3B	HR	(Hm	Rd)	TB	R	RBI	RC	TBB	IBB	SO	HBP	SH	SF	SB	CS	SB%	GDP	Avg	OBP	Slg
2002 Richmond*	AAA	58	230	69	12	1	6	(-	-)	101	29	17	34	16	0	32	2	2	1	9	5	.64	5	.300	.349	.439
1999 Baltimore	AL	17	29	6	0	0	2	(1	1)	12	6	2	3	2	0	3	0	3	0	0	0	-	1	.207	.258	.414
2000 Baltimore	AL	14	17	1	0	0	0	(0	0)	1	2	0	0	2	0	2	0	0	0	0	0	-	0	.059	.158	.059
2001 Atlanta	NL	22	5	1	0	0	0	(0	0)	1	3	0	0	0	0	1	0	1	0	6	2	.75	0	.200	.200	.200
2002 Atlanta	NL	39	61	12	1	0	0	(0	0)	13	6	5	3	0	0	14	0	0	0	0	1	.00	1	.197	.197	.213
4 ML YEARS		92	112	20	1	0	2	(1	1)	27	17	7	6	4	0	20	0	4	0	6	3	.67	2	.179	.207	.241

Karim Garcia

Bats: L **Throws:** L **Pos:** RF-49; CF-3; LF-2; PH-2   **Ht:** 6'0" **Wt:** 195 **Born:** 10/29/75 **Age:** 27

						BATTING														BASERUNNING				AVERAGES		
Year Team	Lg	G	AB	H	2B	3B	HR	(Hm	Rd)	TB	R	RBI	RC	TBB	IBB	SO	HBP	SH	SF	SB	CS	SB%	GDP	Avg	OBP	Slg
2002 Columbus*	AAA	74	288	78	16	3	12	(-	-)	136	44	49	41	20	3	48	0	0	0	1	5	.17	2	.271	.316	.472
2002 Buffalo*	AAA	23	91	36	7	2	3	(-	-)	56	16	22	22	9	2	14	0	0	0	0	1	.00	1	.396	.450	.615
1995 Los Angeles	NL	13	20	4	0	0	0	(0	0)	4	1	0	0	0	0	4	0	0	0	0	0	-	0	.200	.200	.200
1996 Los Angeles	NL	1	1	0	0	0	0	(0	0)	0	0	0	0	0	0	1	0	0	0	0	0	-	0	.000	.000	.000
1997 Los Angeles	NL	15	39	5	0	0	1	(0	1)	8	5	8	2	6	1	14	0	0	1	0	0	-	0	.128	.239	.205
1998 Arizona	NL	113	333	74	10	8	9	(4	5)	127	39	43	31	18	1	78	0	0	3	5	4	.56	6	.222	.260	.381
1999 Detroit	AL	96	288	69	10	3	14	(4	10)	127	38	32	36	20	1	67	0	0	1	2	4	.33	2	.240	.288	.441
2000 Det-Bal	AL	16	33	3	0	0	0	(0	0)	3	1	0	0	0	0	10	0	0	1	0	0	-	0	.091	.091	.091
2001 Cleveland	AL	20	45	14	3	0	5	(1	4)	32	8	9	11	3	0	13	1	0	1	0	0	-	1	.311	.360	.711
2002 NYY-Cle	AL	53	202	60	8	0	16	(7	9)	116	30	52	35	6	0	41	0	0	2	0	3	.00	6	.297	.314	.574
2000 Detroit	AL	8	17	3	0	0	0	(0	0)	3	1	0	0	0	0	4	0	0	0	0	0	-	1	.176	.176	.176
2000 Baltimore	AL	8	16	0	0	0	0	(0	0)	0	0	0	0	0	0	6	0	0	1	0	0	-	0	.000	.000	.000
2002 New York	AL	2	5	1	0	0	0	(0	0)	1	1	0	0	0	0	1	0	0	0	0	0	-	0	.200	.200	.200
2002 Cleveland	AL	51	197	59	8	0	16	(7	9)	115	29	52	35	6	0	40	0	0	2	0	3	.00	6	.299	.317	.584
8 ML YEARS		327	961	229	31	11	45	(16	29)	417	122	144	115	53	3	228	1	0	8	7	11	.39	16	.238	.277	.434

Luis Garcia

Bats: R **Throws:** R **Pos:** PH-3; PR-2; CF-1; RF-1   **Ht:** 6'3" **Wt:** 208 **Born:** 9/22/75 **Age:** 27

						BATTING														BASERUNNING				AVERAGES		
Year Team	Lg	G	AB	H	2B	3B	HR	(Hm	Rd)	TB	R	RBI	RC	TBB	IBB	SO	HBP	SH	SF	SB	CS	SB%	GDP	Avg	OBP	Slg
1995 White Sox	R	45	161	37	5	2	0	(-	-)	46	33	12	16	20	1	29	0	3	3	9	3	.75	3	.230	.310	.286
1996 Hickory	A	76	289	79	18	3	3	(-	-)	112	31	38	32	14	2	41	2	1	0	9	6	.60	8	.273	.311	.388
1996 South Bend	A	58	221	48	9	1	1	(-	-)	62	23	16	12	9	2	29	1	0	1	3	4	.43	5	.217	.250	.281
1997 Winstn-Salm	A+	130	498	128	29	7	13	(-	-)	210	55	81	54	16	0	93	0	4	5	4	8	.33	9	.257	.277	.422
1998 Winstn-Salm	A+	106	389	105	29	1	10	(-	-)	166	49	58	48	13	1	68	3	2	5	8	5	.62	6	.270	.295	.427
1999 Tigres	Mex	56	239	88	18	3	8	(-	-)	136	38	54	50	13	3	22	0	0	5	13	5	.72	6	.368	.393	.569
2000 Tigres	Mex	120	477	169	27	2	22	(-	-)	266	89	81	100	39	5	91	2	0	8	33	9	.79	15	.354	.399	.558
2001 Tigres	Mex	98	368	122	25	5	19	(-	-)	214	73	82	75	38	3	51	3	0	3	16	6	.73	20	.332	.396	.582
2002 Rochester	AAA	89	339	82	14	2	4	(-	-)	112	23	31	23	7	0	45	2	1	2	1	1	.50	15	.242	.260	.330
2002 Baltimore	AL	6	3	1	0	0	0	(0	0)	1	0	0	0	0	0	1	0	0	0	0	0	-	0	.333	.333	.333

Reynaldo Garcia

Pitches: R **Bats:** R **Pos:** RP-3   **Ht:** 6'3" **Wt:** 170 **Born:** 4/15/74 **Age:** 29

		HOW MUCH HE PITCHED					WHAT HE GAVE UP										THE RESULTS							
Year Team	Lg	G	GS	CG	GF	IP	BFP	H	R	ER	HR	SH	SF	HB	TBB	IBB	SO	WP	Bk	W	L	Pct	ShO	Sv-Op	Hld	ERC	ERA
1999 Rangers	R	12	11	0	0	64.0	268	55	30	23	3	2	4	0	26	0	42	4	3	4	4	.500	0	0- -	-	2.98	3.23
2000 Savannah	A	49	2	1	35	97.0	410	87	37	29	6	2	4	5	33	1	82	8	0	6	7	.462	0	14- -	-	3.19	2.69
2001 Charlotte	A+	35	16	0	9	116.1	499	107	62	46	7	6	4	8	45	3	111	8	1	5	10	.333	0	4- -	-	3.52	3.56
2002 Tulsa	AA	18	9	0	1	68.1	294	63	36	28	11	3	2	3	30	1	54	4	1	5	1	.833	0	0- -	-	4.39	3.69
2002 Oklahoma	AAA	25	0	0	10	31.2	135	23	12	10	2	1	2	2	14	1	33	2	0	2	2	.500	0	4- -	-	2.64	2.84
2002 Texas	AL	3	0	0	2	2.0	14	7	7	7	3	0	0	0	1	0	2	1	0	0	0	-	0	0-0	0	39.83	31.50

Nomar Garciaparra

Bats: R **Throws:** R **Pos:** SS-154; PH-3   **Ht:** 6'0" **Wt:** 190 **Born:** 7/23/73 **Age:** 29

						BATTING														BASERUNNING				AVERAGES		
Year Team	Lg	G	AB	H	2B	3B	HR	(Hm	Rd)	TB	R	RBI	RC	TBB	IBB	SO	HBP	SH	SF	SB	CS	SB%	GDP	Avg	OBP	Slg
1996 Boston	AL	24	87	21	2	3	4	(3	1)	41	11	16	13	4	0	14	0	1	1	5	0	1.00	0	.241	.272	.471
1997 Boston	AL	153	684	209	44	11	30	(11	19)	365	122	98	122	35	2	92	6	2	7	22	9	.71	9	.306	.342	.534
1998 Boston	AL	143	604	195	37	8	35	(17	18)	353	111	122	117	33	1	62	8	0	7	12	6	.67	20	.323	.362	.584
1999 Boston	AL	135	532	190	42	4	27	(14	13)	321	103	104	105	51	7	39	8	0	4	14	3	.82	11	.357	.418	.603
2000 Boston	AL	140	529	197	51	3	21	(7	14)	317	104	96	127	61	20	50	2	0	7	5	2	.71	8	.372	.434	.599
2001 Boston	AL	21	83	24	3	0	4	(3	1)	39	13	8	13	7	0	9	1	0	0	0	1	.00	1	.289	.352	.470
2002 Boston	AL	156	635	197	56	5	24	(10	14)	335	101	120	115	41	4	63	6	0	11	5	2	.71	17	.310	.352	.528
7 ML YEARS		772	3154	1033	235	34	145	(65	80)	1771	565	564	632	232	34	329	31	3	37	63	23	.73	66	.328	.375	.562

Lee Gardner

Pitches: R **Bats:** R **Pos:** RP-12   **Ht:** 6'0" **Wt:** 219 **Born:** 1/16/75 **Age:** 28

		HOW MUCH HE PITCHED					WHAT HE GAVE UP										THE RESULTS							
Year Team	Lg	G	GS	CG	GF	IP	BFP	H	R	ER	HR	SH	SF	HB	TBB	IBB	SO	WP	Bk	W	L	Pct	ShO	Sv-Op	Hld	ERC	ERA
1998 St.Pete	A+	3	0	0	1	4.0	15	3	0	0	0	0	0	0	1	0	2	0	0	0	0	-	0	0- -	-	1.79	0.00
1998 Chrstn - SC	A	28	0	0	13	35.2	154	38	18	16	3	2	0	1	4	0	55	1	0	0	3	.000	0	3- -	-	3.14	4.04
1999 Orlando	AA	1	0	0	0	2.0	9	3	2	2	0	0	0	0	1	0	1	0	0	0	0	-	0	0- -	-	7.26	9.00
1999 St.Pete	A+	20	0	0	13	23.0	96	20	7	5	1	1	1	2	5	0	22	0	0	2	0	1.000	0	7- -	-	2.60	1.96
2000 Orlando	AA	36	0	0	24	45.0	186	34	19	17	0	4	3	2	14	1	48	6	0	3	2	.600	0	12- -	-	1.93	3.40

Year Team	Lg	G	GS	CG	GF	IP	BFP	H	R	ER	HR	SH	SF	HB	TBB	IBB	SO	WP	Bk	W	L	Pct	ShO	Sv-Op	Hld	ERC	ERA
2000 Durham	AAA	21	0	0	9	18.2	75	12	7	7	1	1	0	0	9	1	8	1	0	1	0	1.000	0	5--	-	2.18	3.38
2001 Orlando	AA	1	0	0	0	1.2	4	0	0	0	0	0	0	0	0	0	0	0	0	0	0	-	0	0--	-	0.00	0.00
2001 Durham	AAA	56	0	0	18	76.0	324	76	27	23	10	3	2	2	23	2	55	4	0	5	2	.714	0	2--	-	3.95	2.72
2002 Durham	AAA	45	0	0	35	49.2	207	50	14	13	1	1	0	0	15	3	52	0	0	2	1	.667	0	25--	-	3.14	2.36
2002 Tampa Bay	AL	12	0	0	3	13.1	65	12	11	6	3	1	2	3	8	0	8	0	0	1	1	.500	0	0-2	1	5.86	4.05

Jon Garland

Pitches: R **Bats:** R **Pos:** SP-33 **Ht:** 6'6" **Wt:** 205 **Born:** 9/27/79 **Age:** 23

Year Team	Lg	G	GS	CG	GF	IP	BFP	H	R	ER	HR	SH	SF	HB	TBB	IBB	SO	WP	Bk	W	L	Pct	ShO	Sv-Op	Hld	ERC	ERA
2000 Chicago	AL	15	13	0	1	69.2	324	82	55	50	10	0	2	1	40	0	42	4	0	4	8	.333	0	0-0	1	6.26	6.46
2001 Chicago	AL	35	16	0	8	117.0	510	123	59	48	16	2	5	4	55	2	61	3	0	6	7	.462	0	1-1	2	5.16	3.69
2002 Chicago	AL	33	33	1	0	192.2	827	188	109	98	23	3	4	9	83	1	112	5	0	12	12	.500	1	0-0	-	4.46	4.58
3 ML YEARS		83	62	1	9	379.1	1661	393	223	196	49	5	11	14	178	3	215	12	0	22	27	.449	1	1-1	3	4.99	4.65

Chris George

Pitches: L **Bats:** L **Pos:** SP-6 **Ht:** 6'2" **Wt:** 200 **Born:** 9/16/79 **Age:** 23

Year Team	Lg	G	GS	CG	GF	IP	BFP	H	R	ER	HR	SH	SF	HB	TBB	IBB	SO	WP	Bk	W	L	Pct	ShO	Sv-Op	Hld	ERC	ERA
1998 Royals	R	5	4	0	0	15.2	65	14	9	5	1	1	0	0	4	0	10	0	0	0	1	.000	0	0--	-	2.67	2.87
1999 Wilmington	A+	27	27	0	0	145.0	618	142	65	58	8	3	4	5	53	0	142	6	1	9	7	.563	0	0--	-	3.67	3.60
2000 Wichita	AA	18	18	0	0	97.1	429	92	41	34	8	3	6	6	51	1	80	2	2	8	5	.615	0	0--	-	4.37	3.14
2000 Omaha	AAA	8	8	0	0	44.2	194	47	29	24	8	0	1	1	20	0	27	1	1	3	2	.600	0	0--	-	5.36	4.84
2001 Omaha	AAA	20	20	0	0	117.1	489	103	54	46	14	2	1	1	51	0	84	0	1	11	3	.786	0	0--	-	3.78	3.53
2002 Omaha	AAA	22	21	1	0	127.1	580	145	86	83	15	3	2	3	65	0	94	7	0	6	12	.333	0	0--	-	5.58	5.87
2001 Kansas City	AL	13	13	1	0	74.0	313	83	48	46	14	3	4	0	18	0	32	3	2	4	8	.333	0	0-0	0	4.82	5.59
2002 Kansas City	AL	6	6	0	0	27.1	124	37	17	17	2	0	1	1	8	0	13	1	0	0	4	.000	0	0-0	0	5.70	5.60
2 ML YEARS		19	19	1	0	101.1	437	120	65	63	16	3	5	1	26	0	45	4	2	4	12	.250	0	0-0	0	5.06	5.60

Esteban German

Bats: R **Throws:** R **Pos:** 2B-8; PR-1 **Ht:** 5'9" **Wt:** 165 **Born:** 1/26/78 **Age:** 25

Year Team	Lg	G	AB	H	2B	3B	HR	(Hm	Rd)	TB	R	RBI	RC	TBB	IBB	SO	HBP	SH	SF	SB	CS	SB%	GDP	Avg	OBP	Slg
1998 Athletics	R	55	202	62	3	10	2	(-	-)	91	52	28	44	33	0	43	4	2	1	40	8	.83	1	.307	.413	.450
1999 Modesto	A+	128	501	156	16	12	4	(-	-)	208	107	52	100	102	0	128	5	5	7	40	16	.71	3	.311	.428	.415
2000 Midland	AA	24	75	16	1	0	1	(-	-)	20	13	6	10	18	0	21	2	2	0	5	3	.63	1	.213	.379	.267
2000 Visalia	A+	109	428	113	14	10	2	(-	-)	153	82	35	72	61	0	86	5	4	2	78	8	.91	4	.264	.361	.357
2001 Midland	AA	92	335	95	20	3	6	(-	-)	139	79	30	64	63	0	66	12	4	0	31	11	.74	6	.284	.415	.415
2001 Sacramento	AAA	38	150	56	8	0	4	(-	-)	76	40	14	36	18	0	20	6	2	1	17	2	.89	4	.373	.457	.507
2002 Sacramento	AAA	121	458	126	16	4	2	(-	-)	156	72	43	68	78	1	66	8	7	0	26	14	.65	7	.275	.390	.341
2002 Oakland	AL	9	35	7	0	0	0	(0	0)	7	4	0	2	4	0	11	1	0	0	1	0	1.00	0	.200	.300	.200

Franklyn German

Pitches: R **Bats:** R **Pos:** RP-7 **Ht:** 6'4" **Wt:** 265 **Born:** 1/20/80 **Age:** 23

Year Team	Lg	G	GS	CG	GF	IP	BFP	H	R	ER	HR	SH	SF	HB	TBB	IBB	SO	WP	Bk	W	L	Pct	ShO	Sv-Op	Hld	ERC	ERA
1998 Athletics	R	14	12	0	0	54.1	249	69	43	37	5	1	5	7	18	0	46	5	3	2	1	.667	0	0--	-	5.90	6.13
1999 Sth Oregon	A-	15	15	0	0	73.2	344	89	52	49	10	0	4	4	45	1	58	4	0	3	5	.375	0	0--	-	6.83	5.99
2000 Modesto	A+	17	14	0	2	72.0	333	88	55	44	4	0	3	6	37	0	52	7	2	5	5	.500	0	0--	-	5.94	5.50
2000 Vancouver	A-	9	2	0	2	20.1	86	13	4	4	0	0	0	1	10	0	20	4	0	1	0	1.000	0	0--	-	1.99	1.77
2001 Visalia	A+	53	0	0	45	63.1	294	67	34	28	7	3	2	2	31	1	93	11	0	2	4	.333	0	19--	-	4.75	3.98
2002 Midland	AA	37	0	0	28	41.1	174	28	14	14	0	0	3	2	27	2	59	7	0	1	1	.500	0	16--	-	2.56	3.05
2002 Toledo	AAA	23	0	0	21	22.2	88	15	4	4	0	0	1	0	7	0	31	1	1	1	1	.500	0	13--	-	1.54	1.59
2002 Detroit	AL	7	0	0	1	6.2	25	3	0	0	0	2	0	1	2	1	6	0	0	1	0	1.000	0	1-1	1	1.09	0.00

Jody Gerut

Bats: L **Throws:** L **Pos:** CF **Ht:** 6'0" **Wt:** 190 **Born:** 9/18/77 **Age:** 25

Year Team	Lg	G	AB	H	2B	3B	HR	(Hm	Rd)	TB	R	RBI	RC	TBB	IBB	SO	HBP	SH	SF	SB	CS	SB%	GDP	Avg	OBP	Slg
1999 Salem	A+	133	499	144	33	11	11	(-	-)	232	80	63	85	61	4	65	3	1	3	25	12	.68	10	.289	.367	.465
2000 Carolina	AA	109	362	103	32	3	3	(-	-)	150	48	57	65	76	2	54	2	1	7	18	11	.62	9	.285	.405	.414
2002 Buffalo	AAA	55	183	59	7	2	1	(-	-)	73	31	21	28	23	0	20	1	0	0	3	5	.38	6	.322	.401	.399
2002 Akron	AA	65	256	72	15	2	9	(-	-)	118	44	39	42	34	3	30	1	0	0	17	8	.68	7	.281	.368	.461

Jason Giambi

Bats: L **Throws:** R **Pos:** 1B-92; DH-63 **Ht:** 6'3" **Wt:** 235 **Born:** 1/8/71 **Age:** 32

Year Team	Lg	G	AB	H	2B	3B	HR	(Hm	Rd)	TB	R	RBI	RC	TBB	IBB	SO	HBP	SH	SF	SB	CS	SB%	GDP	Avg	OBP	Slg
1995 Oakland	AL	54	176	45	7	0	6	(3	3)	70	27	25	27	28	0	31	3	1	2	2	1	.67	4	.256	.364	.398
1996 Oakland	AL	140	536	156	40	1	20	(6	14)	258	84	79	88	51	3	95	5	1	5	0	1	.00	15	.291	.355	.481
1997 Oakland	AL	142	519	152	41	2	20	(14	6)	257	66	81	91	55	3	89	6	0	6	0	1	.00	11	.293	.362	.495
1998 Oakland	AL	153	562	166	28	0	27	(12	15)	275	92	110	103	81	7	102	5	0	9	2	2	.50	16	.295	.384	.489
1999 Oakland	AL	158	575	181	36	1	33	(17	16)	318	115	123	132	105	6	106	7	0	8	1	1	.50	11	.315	.422	.553
2000 Oakland	AL	152	510	170	29	1	43	(23	20)	330	108	137	152	**137**	6	96	0	0	8	2	0	1.00	9	.333	**.476**	.647

Year Team	Lg	G	AB	H	2B	3B	HR	(Hm	Rd)	TB	R	RBI	RC	TBB	IBB	SO	HBP	SH	SF	SB	CS	SB%	GDP	Avg	OBP	Slg
2001 Oakland	AL	154	520	178	**47**	2	38	(27	11)	343	109	120	**153**	**129**	24	83	13	0	9	2	0	1.00	17	.342	**.477**	**.660**
2002 New York	AL	155	560	176	34	1	41	(19	22)	335	120	122	140	109	4	112	15	0	5	2	2	.50	18	.314	.435	.598
8 ML YEARS		1108	3958	1224	262	8	228	(121	107)	2186	721	797	886	695	53	714	63	2	54	11	8	.58	101	.309	.416	.552

Jeremy Giambi

Bats: L **Throws:** L **Pos:** LF-42; PH-34; 1B-21; RF-18; DH-10   **Ht:** 5'11" **Wt:** 216 **Born:** 9/30/74 **Age:** 28

Year Team	Lg	G	AB	H	2B	3B	HR	(Hm	Rd)	TB	R	RBI	RC	TBB	IBB	SO	HBP	SH	SF	SB	CS	SB%	GDP	Avg	OBP	Slg
1998 Kansas City	AL	18	58	13	4	0	2	(0	2)	23	6	8	7	11	0	9	0	0	1	0	1	.00	3	.224	.343	.397
1999 Kansas City	AL	90	288	82	13	1	3	(2	1)	106	34	34	41	40	5	67	3	1	4	0	0	-	7	.285	.373	.368
2000 Oakland	AL	104	260	66	10	2	10	(3	7)	110	42	50	37	32	2	61	3	3	4	0	0	-	7	.254	.338	.423
2001 Oakland	AL	124	371	105	26	0	12	(5	7)	167	64	57	64	63	1	83	4	3	2	0	1	.00	13	.283	.391	.450
2002 Oak-Phi		124	313	81	17	0	20	(12	8)	158	58	45	59	79	2	94	4	1	0	0	1	.00	5	.259	.414	.505
2002 Oakland	AL	42	157	43	7	0	8	(6	2)	74	26	17	24	27	0	40	3	0	0	0	0	-	4	.274	.390	.471
2002 Philadelphia	NL	82	156	38	10	0	12	(6	6)	84	32	28	35	52	2	54	1	1	0	0	1	.00	1	.244	.435	.538
5 ML YEARS		460	1290	347	70	3	47	(22	25)	564	204	194	208	225	10	314	14	8	11	0	3	.00	35	.269	.381	.437

Jay Gibbons

Bats: L **Throws:** L **Pos:** RF-92; 1B-30; DH-12; PH-5   **Ht:** 6'0" **Wt:** 200 **Born:** 3/2/77 **Age:** 26

Year Team	Lg	G	AB	H	2B	3B	HR	(Hm	Rd)	TB	R	RBI	RC	TBB	IBB	SO	HBP	SH	SF	SB	CS	SB%	GDP	Avg	OBP	Slg
1998 Medicine Hat	R+	73	290	115	29	1	19	(-	-)	203	66	98	84	37	1	25	3	0	9	2	1	.67	7	.397	.457	.700
1999 Hagerstown	A	71	292	89	20	2	16	(-	-)	161	53	69	56	32	1	56	1	0	5	3	0	1.00	12	.305	.370	.551
1999 Dunedin	A+	60	212	66	14	0	9	(-	-)	107	34	39	40	25	0	38	0	0	1	2	1	.67	4	.311	.382	.505
2000 Tennessee	AA	132	474	152	38	1	19	(-	-)	249	85	75	98	61	5	67	10	0	7	3	1	.75	10	.321	.404	.525
2001 Baltimore	AL	73	225	53	10	0	15	(9	6)	108	27	36	31	17	0	39	4	0	0	0	1	.00	7	.236	.301	.480
2002 Baltimore	AL	136	490	121	29	1	28	(17	11)	236	71	69	72	45	3	66	2	0	4	1	3	.25	9	.247	.311	.482
2 ML YEARS		209	715	174	39	1	43	(26	17)	344	98	105	103	62	3	105	6	0	4	1	4	.20	16	.243	.307	.481

Benji Gil

Bats: R **Throws:** R **Pos:** 2B-26; SS-14; PH-11; 1B-10; DH-5; PR-2   **Ht:** 6'2" **Wt:** 210 **Born:** 10/6/72 **Age:** 30

Year Team	Lg	G	AB	H	2B	3B	HR	(Hm	Rd)	TB	R	RBI	RC	TBB	IBB	SO	HBP	SH	SF	SB	CS	SB%	GDP	Avg	OBP	Slg
2002 Salt Lake*	AAA	6	24	10	5	1	2	(-	-)	23	4	6	8	1	0	4	0	0	0	0	2	.00	0	.417	.440	.958
1993 Texas	AL	22	57	7	0	0	0	(0	0)	7	3	2	0	5	0	22	0	4	0	1	2	.33	1	.123	.194	.123
1995 Texas	AL	130	415	91	20	3	9	(5	4)	144	36	46	36	26	0	147	1	10	2	2	4	.33	5	.219	.266	.347
1996 Texas	AL	5	5	2	0	0	0	(0	0)	2	0	1	1	1	0	1	0	1	0	0	1	.00	0	.400	.500	.400
1997 Texas	AL	110	317	71	13	2	5	(3	2)	103	35	31	26	17	0	96	1	6	4	1	2	.33	3	.224	.263	.325
2000 Anaheim	AL	110	301	72	14	1	6	(4	2)	106	28	23	33	30	0	59	5	5	2	10	6	.63	7	.239	.317	.352
2001 Anaheim	AL	104	260	77	15	4	8	(6	2)	124	33	39	38	14	0	57	0	2	2	3	4	.43	6	.296	.330	.477
2002 Anaheim	AL	61	130	37	8	1	3	(2	1)	56	11	20	19	5	0	33	0	2	2	2	1	.67	0	.285	.307	.431
7 ML YEARS		542	1485	357	70	11	31	(20	11)	542	146	162	153	98	0	415	7	30	12	19	20	.49	21	.240	.288	.365

Geronimo Gil

Bats: R **Throws:** R **Pos:** C-125   **Ht:** 6'2" **Wt:** 195 **Born:** 8/7/75 **Age:** 27

Year Team	Lg	G	AB	H	2B	3B	HR	(Hm	Rd)	TB	R	RBI	RC	TBB	IBB	SO	HBP	SH	SF	SB	CS	SB%	GDP	Avg	OBP	Slg
1996 Savannah	A	79	276	67	13	1	7	(-	-)	103	29	38	26	8	3	69	5	1	3	0	2	.00	4	.243	.274	.373
1997 Vero Beach	A+	66	213	53	13	1	6	(-	-)	86	30	24	26	15	0	41	4	1	0	3	0	1.00	5	.249	.310	.404
1998 San Antonio	AA	75	241	70	17	3	6	(-	-)	111	27	29	34	15	0	43	0	2	2	2	1	.67	8	.290	.329	.461
1999 San Antonio	AA	106	343	97	26	1	15	(-	-)	170	47	59	60	49	1	58	2	0	4	2	0	1.00	15	.283	.372	.496
2000 San Antonio	AA	100	352	100	19	1	11	(-	-)	154	42	58	53	33	3	65	6	1	5	3	2	.60	8	.284	.351	.438
2000 Albuquerque	AAA	15	50	19	5	0	2	(-	-)	30	9	22	12	5	0	8	0	0	1	0	1	.00	1	.380	.421	.600
2001 Las Vegas	AAA	82	281	83	15	0	9	(-	-)	125	40	40	39	16	1	56	2	0	3	0	1	.00	9	.295	.334	.445
2001 Rochester	AAA	23	82	22	6	1	2	(-	-)	36	7	14	10	0	0	23	1	0	2	0	0	-	1	.268	.271	.439
2001 Baltimore	AL	17	58	17	2	0	0	(0	0)	19	3	6	7	5	0	7	2	1	0	0	0	-	1	.293	.369	.328
2002 Baltimore	AL	125	422	98	19	0	12	(5	7)	153	33	45	33	21	1	88	1	5	1	2	2	.50	17	.232	.270	.363
2 ML YEARS		142	480	115	21	0	12	(5	7)	172	36	51	40	26	1	95	3	6	1	2	2	.50	18	.240	.282	.358

Brian Giles

Bats: L **Throws:** L **Pos:** LF-152; CF-3; PH-2   **Ht:** 5'10" **Wt:** 202 **Born:** 1/20/71 **Age:** 32

Year Team	Lg	G	AB	H	2B	3B	HR	(Hm	Rd)	TB	R	RBI	RC	TBB	IBB	SO	HBP	SH	SF	SB	CS	SB%	GDP	Avg	OBP	Slg
1995 Cleveland	AL	6	9	5	0	0	1	(0	1)	8	6	3	3	0	0	1	0	0	0	0	0	-	0	.556	.556	.889
1996 Cleveland	AL	51	121	43	14	1	5	(2	3)	74	26	27	29	19	4	13	0	0	3	3	0	1.00	6	.355	.434	.612
1997 Cleveland	AL	130	377	101	15	3	17	(7	10)	173	62	61	66	63	2	50	1	3	7	13	3	.81	10	.268	.368	.459
1998 Cleveland	AL	112	350	94	19	0	16	(10	6)	161	56	66	66	73	8	75	3	1	3	10	5	.67	7	.269	.396	.460
1999 Pittsburgh	NL	141	521	164	33	3	39	(24	15)	320	109	115	127	95	7	80	3	0	8	6	2	.75	14	.315	.418	.614
2000 Pittsburgh	NL	156	559	176	37	7	35	(16	19)	332	111	123	139	114	13	69	7	0	8	6	0	1.00	15	.315	.432	.594
2001 Pittsburgh	NL	160	576	178	37	7	37	(18	19)	340	116	95	117	90	14	67	4	0	4	13	6	.68	10	.309	.404	.590
2002 Pittsburgh	NL	153	497	148	37	5	38	(15	23)	309	95	103	131	135	24	74	7	0	5	15	6	.71	10	.298	.450	.622
8 ML YEARS		909	3010	909	192	26	188	(92	96)	1717	581	593	692	589	72	429	25	4	38	66	22	.75	72	.302	.416	.570

Marcus Giles

Bats: R **Throws:** R **Pos:** 2B-52; PH-9; 3B-8; PR-2   **Ht:** 5'8" **Wt:** 180 **Born:** 5/18/78 **Age:** 25

Year Team	Lg	G	AB	H	2B	3B	HR	(Hm	Rd)	TB	R	RBI	RC	TBB	IBB	SO	HBP	SH	SF	SB	CS	SB%	GDP	Avg	OBP	Slg
1997 Danville	R+	55	207	72	13	3	8	(-	-)	115	53	45	49	32	0	47	3	1	3	5	2	.71	4	.348	.437	.556
1998 Macon	A	135	505	166	38	3	37	(-	-)	321	111	108	129	85	4	103	10	0	3	12	5	.71	15	.329	.433	.636
1999 Myrtle Beach	A+	126	497	162	40	7	13	(-	-)	255	80	73	96	54	5	89	4	0	5	9	6	.60	9	.326	.393	.513
2000 Greenville	AA	132	458	133	28	2	17	(-	-)	216	73	62	86	72	6	71	2	0	1	25	5	.83	11	.290	.388	.472
2001 Richmond	AAA	67	252	84	19	1	6	(-	-)	123	48	44	47	22	1	48	2	0	3	13	5	.72	4	.333	.387	.488
2002 Richmond	AAA	31	115	37	6	0	3	(-	-)	52	25	16	21	13	0	15	0	0	2	3	0	1.00	1	.322	.385	.452
2001 Atlanta	NL	68	244	64	10	2	9	(5	4)	105	36	31	33	28	0	37	0	1	0	2	5	.29	8	.262	.338	.430
2002 Atlanta	NL	68	213	49	10	1	8	(4	4)	85	27	23	22	25	3	41	2	1	1	1	1	.50	5	.230	.315	.399
2 ML YEARS		136	457	113	20	3	17	(9	8)	190	63	54	55	53	3	78	2	2	1	3	6	.33	13	.247	.327	.416

Keith Ginter

Bats: R **Throws:** R **Pos:** 3B-25; PH-2; SS-1; PR-1   **Ht:** 5'10" **Wt:** 190 **Born:** 5/5/76 **Age:** 27

Year Team	Lg	G	AB	H	2B	3B	HR	(Hm	Rd)	TB	R	RBI	RC	TBB	IBB	SO	HBP	SH	SF	SB	CS	SB%	GDP	Avg	OBP	Slg
2002 New Orleans*	AAA	121	435	115	28	1	12	(-	-)	181	70	54	67	56	0	97	12	0	2	3	4	.43	7	.264	.362	.416
2000 Houston	NL	5	8	2	0	0	1	(1	0)	5	3	3	2	1	0	3	0	0	0	0	0	-	0	.250	.300	.625
2001 Houston	NL	1	1	0	0	0	0	(0	0)	0	0	0	0	0	0	0	0	0	0	0	0	-	0	.000	.000	.000
2002 Hou-Mil	NL	28	81	19	9	0	1	(1	0)	31	7	8	13	17	0	15	1	0	0	0	0	-	0	.235	.374	.383
2002 Houston	NL	7	5	1	1	0	0	(0	0)	2	1	0	1	2	0	1	1	0	0	0	0	-	0	.200	.500	.400
2002 Milwaukee	NL	21	76	18	8	0	1	(1	0)	29	6	8	12	15	0	14	0	0	0	0	0	-	0	.237	.363	.382
3 ML YEARS		34	90	21	9	0	2	(2	0)	36	10	11	15	18	0	18	1	0	1	0	0	-	0	.233	.364	.400

Matt Ginter

Pitches: R **Bats:** R **Pos:** RP-33   **Ht:** 6'1" **Wt:** 220 **Born:** 12/24/77 **Age:** 25

	HOW MUCH HE PITCHED						WHAT HE GAVE UP									THE RESULTS						
Year Team	Lg	G	GS	CG	GF	IP	BFP	H	R	ER	HR	SH	SF	HB	TBB	IBB	SO	WP	Bk	W	L	Pct	ShO	Sv-Op	Hld	ERC	ERA
2002 Charlotte	AAA	13	0	0	7	16.0	74	20	8	7	3	0	0	0	10	1	9	1	0	1	0	1.000	0	0-0	0	7.35	3.94
2000 Chicago	AL	7	0	0	3	9.1	52	18	14	14	5	0	1	0	7	0	6	1	0	1	0	1.000	0	0-1	0	16.24	13.50
2001 Chicago	AL	20	0	0	7	39.2	167	34	23	23	2	0	3	7	14	2	24	2	0	1	0	1.000	0	0-0	0	3.44	5.22
2002 Chicago	AL	33	0	0	15	54.1	236	59	34	27	6	0	2	1	21	0	37	2	0	1	0	1.000	0	1-1	0	4.72	4.47
3 ML YEARS		60	0	0	25	103.1	455	111	71	64	13	0	6	8	42	2	67	5	0	3	0	1.000	0	1-2	0	5.07	5.57

Charles Gipson

Bats: R **Throws:** R **Pos:** LF-56; PR-24; RF-13; CF-5; 3B-4; PH-3; DH-1   **Ht:** 6'1" **Wt:** 195 **Born:** 12/16/72 **Age:** 30

Year Team	Lg	G	AB	H	2B	3B	HR	(Hm	Rd)	TB	R	RBI	RC	TBB	IBB	SO	HBP	SH	SF	SB	CS	SB%	GDP	Avg	OBP	Slg
1998 Seattle	AL	44	51	12	1	0	0	(0	0)	13	11	2	4	5	1	9	1	0	0	2	1	.67	1	.235	.316	.255
1999 Seattle	AL	55	80	18	5	2	0	(0	0)	27	16	9	6	6	0	13	1	2	0	3	4	.43	2	.225	.287	.338
2000 Seattle	AL	59	29	9	1	1	0	(0	0)	12	7	3	4	4	0	9	0	0	0	2	3	.40	1	.310	.394	.414
2001 Seattle	AL	94	64	14	2	2	0	(0	0)	20	16	5	5	4	0	20	2	1	1	1	1	.50	2	.219	.282	.313
2002 Seattle	AL	79	72	17	5	2	0	(0	0)	26	22	8	7	9	0	14	1	2	0	4	0	1.00	3	.236	.329	.361
5 ML YEARS		331	296	70	14	7	0	(0	0)	98	72	27	26	28	1	65	5	5	1	12	9	.57	9	.236	.312	.331

Joe Girardi

Bats: R **Throws:** R **Pos:** C-88; PR-3   **Ht:** 5'11" **Wt:** 200 **Born:** 10/14/64 **Age:** 38

Year Team	Lg	G	AB	H	2B	3B	HR	(Hm	Rd)	TB	R	RBI	RC	TBB	IBB	SO	HBP	SH	SF	SB	CS	SB%	GDP	Avg	OBP	Slg
1989 Chicago	NL	59	157	39	10	0	1	(0	1)	52	15	14	15	11	5	26	2	1	1	2	1	.67	4	.248	.304	.331
1990 Chicago	NL	133	419	113	24	2	1	(1	0)	144	36	38	40	17	11	50	3	4	4	8	3	.73	13	.270	.300	.344
1991 Chicago	NL	21	47	9	2	0	0	(0	0)	11	3	6	3	6	1	6	0	1	0	0	0	-	0	.191	.283	.234
1992 Chicago	NL	91	270	73	3	1	1	(1	0)	81	19	12	24	19	3	38	1	0	1	0	2	.00	6	.270	.320	.300
1993 Colorado	NL	86	310	90	14	5	3	(2	1)	123	35	31	42	24	0	41	3	12	1	6	6	.50	6	.290	.346	.397
1994 Colorado	NL	93	330	91	9	4	4	(1	3)	120	47	34	35	21	1	48	2	6	2	3	3	.50	13	.276	.321	.364
1995 Colorado	NL	125	462	121	17	2	8	(6	2)	166	63	55	47	29	0	76	2	12	1	3	3	.50	15	.262	.308	.359
1996 New York	AL	124	422	124	22	3	2	(1	1)	158	55	45	55	30	1	55	5	11	3	13	4	.76	11	.294	.346	.374
1997 New York	AL	112	398	105	23	1	1	(1	0)	133	38	50	37	26	1	53	2	5	2	2	3	.40	14	.264	.311	.334
1998 New York	AL	78	254	70	11	4	3	(1	2)	98	31	31	27	14	1	38	2	8	1	2	4	.33	10	.276	.317	.386
1999 New York	AL	65	209	50	16	1	2	(1	1)	74	23	27	15	10	0	26	0	8	2	1	1	.75	16	.239	.271	.354
2000 Chicago	NL	106	363	101	15	1	6	(4	2)	136	47	40	45	32	3	61	3	6	3	1	0	1.00	12	.278	.339	.375
2001 Chicago	NL	78	229	58	10	1	3	(2	1)	79	22	25	25	21	4	50	0	2	1	0	1	.00	2	.253	.315	.345
2002 Chicago	NL	90	234	53	10	1	1	(0	1)	68	19	13	16	16	3	35	0	5	1	1	0	1.00	10	.226	.275	.291
14 ML YEARS		1261	4104	1097	186	26	36	(20	16)	1443	453	421	426	276	34	603	25	81	23	44	31	.59	135	.267	.316	.352

Doug Glanville

Bats: R **Throws:** R **Pos:** CF-117; PH-23; PR-8   **Ht:** 6'2" **Wt:** 174 **Born:** 8/25/70 **Age:** 32

Year Team	Lg	G	AB	H	2B	3B	HR	(Hm	Rd)	TB	R	RBI	RC	TBB	IBB	SO	HBP	SH	SF	SB	CS	SB%	GDP	Avg	OBP	Slg
1996 Chicago	NL	49	83	20	5	1	1	(1	0)	30	10	10	9	3	0	11	0	2	1	2	0	1.00	0	.241	.264	.361
1997 Chicago	NL	146	474	142	22	5	4	(2	2)	186	79	35	60	24	0	46	1	9	2	19	11	.63	9	.300	.333	.392
1998 Philadelphia	NL	158	678	189	28	7	8	(3	5)	255	106	49	86	42	1	89	6	5	4	23	6	.79	7	.279	.325	.376
1999 Philadelphia	NL	150	628	204	38	6	11	(5	6)	287	101	73	112	48	1	82	6	5	5	34	2	.94	9	.325	.376	.457
2000 Philadelphia	NL	154	637	175	27	6	8	(3	5)	238	89	52	75	31	1	76	2	12	7	31	8	.79	11	.275	.307	.374
2001 Philadelphia	NL	153	634	166	24	3	14	(6	8)	238	74	55	70	19	1	91	4	10	7	28	6	.82	7	.262	.285	.375
2002 Philadelphia	NL	138	422	105	16	3	6	(3	3)	145	49	29	34	25	4	57	2	8	3	19	2	.90	5	.249	.292	.344
7 ML YEARS		948	3556	1001	160	31	52	(23	29)	1379	508	303	446	192	8	452	21	51	29	156	35	.82	48	.281	.320	.388

Troy Glaus

Bats: R Throws: R Pos: 3B-156; SS-2; PH-1

Ht: 6'5" Wt: 245 Born: 8/3/76 Age: 26

Year Team	Lg	G	AB	H	2B	3B	HR	(Hm	Rd)	TB	R	RBI	RC	TBB	IBB	SO	HBP	SH	SF	SB	CS	SB%	GDP	Avg	OBP	Slg
1998 Anaheim	AL	48	165	36	9	0	1	(0	1)	48	19	23	13	15	0	51	0	0	2	1	0	1.00	3	.218	.280	.291
1999 Anaheim	AL	154	551	132	29	0	29	(12	17)	248	85	79	84	71	1	143	6	0	3	5	1	.83	9	.240	.331	.450
2000 Anaheim	AL	159	563	160	37	1	47	(24	23)	340	120	102	129	112	6	163	2	0	1	14	11	.56	14	.284	.404	.604
2001 Anaheim	AL	161	588	147	38	2	41	(22	19)	312	100	108	114	107	7	158	6	0	7	10	3	.77	16	.250	.367	.531
2002 Anaheim	AL	156	569	142	24	1	30	(13	17)	258	99	111	100	88	4	144	6	0	8	10	3	.77	12	.250	.352	.453
5 ML YEARS		678	2436	617	137	4	148	(71	77)	1206	423	423	440	393	18	659	20	0	21	40	18	.69	54	.253	.359	.495

Tom Glavine

Pitches: L Bats: L Pos: SP-36

Ht: 6'0" Wt: 185 Born: 3/25/66 Age: 37

Year Team	Lg	G	GS	CG	GF	IP	BFP	H	R	ER	HR	SH	SF	HB	TBB	IBB	SO	WP	Bk	W	L	Pct	ShO	Sv-Op	Hld	ERC	ERA
1987 Atlanta	NL	9	9	0	0	50.1	238	55	34	31	5	2	3	3	33	4	20	1	1	2	4	.333	0	0-0	0	5.70	5.54
1988 Atlanta	NL	34	34	1	0	195.1	844	201	111	99	12	17	11	8	63	7	84	2	2	7	17	.292	0	0-0	0	3.74	4.56
1989 Atlanta	NL	29	29	6	0	186.0	766	172	88	76	20	11	4	2	40	3	90	2	0	14	8	.636	4	0-0	0	2.99	3.68
1990 Atlanta	NL	33	33	1	0	214.1	929	232	111	102	18	21	2	1	78	10	129	8	1	10	12	.455	1	0-0	0	4.24	4.28
1991 Atlanta	NL	34	34	9	0	246.2	989	201	83	70	17	7	6	2	69	6	192	10	2	20	11	.645	1	0-0	0	2.47	2.55
1992 Atlanta	NL	33	33	7	0	225.0	919	197	81	69	6	2	6	2	70	7	129	5	0	20	8	.714	5	0-0	0	2.61	2.76
1993 Atlanta	NL	36	36	4	0	239.1	1014	236	91	85	16	10	2	2	90	7	120	4	0	22	6	.786	2	0-0	0	3.70	3.20
1994 Atlanta	NL	25	25	2	0	165.1	731	173	76	73	10	9	6	1	70	10	140	8	1	13	9	.591	0	0-0	0	4.02	3.97
1995 Atlanta	NL	29	29	3	0	198.2	822	182	76	68	9	7	5	5	66	0	127	3	0	16	7	.696	1	0-0	0	3.14	3.08
1996 Atlanta	NL	36	36	1	0	235.1	994	222	91	78	14	15	2	0	85	7	181	4	0	15	10	.600	0	0-0	0	3.29	2.98
1997 Atlanta	NL	33	33	5	0	240.0	970	197	86	79	20	11	6	4	79	9	152	3	0	14	7	.667	2	0-0	0	2.80	2.96
1998 Atlanta	NL	33	33	4	0	229.1	934	202	67	63	13	6	2	2	74	2	157	3	0	20	6	.769	3	0-0	0	2.93	2.47
1999 Atlanta	NL	35	35	2	0	234.0	1023	259	115	107	18	22	10	4	83	14	138	2	0	14	11	.560	0	0-0	0	4.31	4.12
2000 Atlanta	NL	35	35	4	0	241.0	992	222	101	91	24	9	5	4	65	6	152	0	0	21	9	.700	2	0-0	0	3.19	3.40
2001 Atlanta	NL	35	35	1	0	219.1	929	213	92	87	24	5	8	2	97	10	116	2	0	16	7	.696	1	0-0	0	4.21	3.57
2002 Atlanta	NL	36	36	2	0	224.2	936	210	85	74	21	12	6	8	78	8	127	2	0	18	11	.621	1	0-0	0	3.61	2.96
16 ML YEARS		505	505	52	0	3344.2	14030	3174	1388	1252	247	166	84	50	1140	110	2054	59	7	242	143	.629	22	0-0	0	3.42	3.37

Ross Gload

Bats: L Throws: L Pos: PH-23; 1B-4; LF-2

Ht: 6'0" Wt: 185 Born: 4/5/76 Age: 27

Year Team	Lg	G	AB	H	2B	3B	HR	(Hm	Rd)	TB	R	RBI	RC	TBB	IBB	SO	HBP	SH	SF	SB	CS	SB%	GDP	Avg	OBP	Slg
1997 Utica	A-	68	145	64	15	2	3	(-	-)	92	28	43	44	28	0	57	2	0	5	1	1	.50	5	.441	.522	.634
1998 Kane County	A	132	501	157	41	3	12	(-	-)	240	77	92	88	58	7	84	3	2	3	7	6	.54	13	.313	.386	.479
1999 Brevard Cnty	A+	133	490	146	26	3	10	(-	-)	208	80	74	78	53	3	76	5	2	5	3	1	.75	8	.298	.369	.424
2000 Portland	AA	100	401	114	28	4	16	(-	-)	198	60	65	66	29	3	53	2	3	4	4	1	.80	4	.284	.333	.494
2000 Iowa	AAA	28	104	42	10	2	14	(-	-)	98	24	39	37	9	1	13	1	0	1	1	1	.50	2	.404	.452	.942
2001 Iowa	AAA	133	475	141	32	10	15	(-	-)	238	70	93	79	35	3	88	3	4	7	9	7	.56	8	.297	.344	.501
2002 Co Springs	AAA	104	442	139	28	6	16	(-	-)	227	69	71	76	18	0	59	1	1	6	9	4	.69	4	.314	.338	.514
2000 Chicago	NL	18	31	6	0	1	1	(0	1)	11	4	3	3	3	0	10	0	0	1	0	0	-	1	.194	.257	.355
2002 Colorado	NL	26	31	8	1	0	1	(1	0)	12	4	4	3	3	0	7	0	0	0	0	0	-	0	.258	.324	.387
2 ML YEARS		44	62	14	1	1	2	(1	1)	23	8	7	6	6	0	17	0	0	1	0	0	-	1	.226	.290	.371

Gary Glover

Pitches: R Bats: R Pos: SP-22; RP-19

Ht: 6'5" Wt: 205 Born: 12/3/76 Age: 26

Year Team	Lg	G	GS	CG	GF	IP	BFP	H	R	ER	HR	SH	SF	HB	TBB	IBB	SO	WP	Bk	W	L	Pct	ShO	Sv-Op	Hld	ERC	ERA
1999 Toronto	AL	1	0	0	1	1.0	3	0	0	0	0	0	0	0	1	0	0	0	0	0	0	-	0	0-0	0	1.26	0.00
2001 Chicago	AL	46	11	0	10	100.1	429	98	61	55	16	2	2	4	32	3	63	4	0	5	5	.500	0	0-1	7	4.12	4.93
2002 Chicago	AL	41	22	0	10	138.1	604	136	86	80	21	6	2	7	52	1	70	6	0	7	8	.467	0	1-1	2	4.39	5.20
3 ML YEARS		88	33	0	21	239.2	1036	234	147	135	37	8	4	11	85	4	133	10	0	12	13	.480	0	1-2	9	4.26	5.07

Wayne Gomes

Pitches: R Bats: R Pos: RP-20

Ht: 6'2" Wt: 225 Born: 1/15/73 Age: 30

Year Team	Lg	G	GS	CG	GF	IP	BFP	H	R	ER	HR	SH	SF	HB	TBB	IBB	SO	WP	Bk	W	L	Pct	ShO	Sv-Op	Hld	ERC	ERA
2002 Nashville*	AAA	6	1	0	1	9.1	57	21	16	16	1	1	1	0	12	1	7	5	0	0	2	.000	0	0- -		17.34	15.43
2002 Pawtucket*	AAA	42	0	0	12	71.2	306	61	30	21	8	6	2	4	28	2	54	1	0	5	2	.714	0	4- -		3.43	2.64
1997 Philadelphia	NL	37	0	0	13	42.2	191	45	26	25	4	2	0	1	24	0	24	2	0	5	1	.833	0	0-1	3	5.16	5.27
1998 Philadelphia	NL	71	0	0	16	93.1	408	94	48	44	9	5	1	3	35	4	86	6	0	9	6	.600	0	1-8	13	4.00	4.24
1999 Philadelphia	NL	73	0	0	58	74.0	341	70	38	35	5	5	3	2	56	2	58	3	1	5	5	.500	0	19-24	9	5.00	4.26
2000 Philadelphia	NL	65	0	0	26	73.2	324	72	41	36	6	7	4	3	35	3	49	10	0	4	6	.400	0	7-11	4	4.20	4.40
2001 Phi-SF	NL	55	0	0	16	63.0	285	72	37	37	7	6	4	1	29	6	52	4	0	6	3	.667	0	1-5	10	5.11	5.29
2002 Boston	AL	20	0	0	8	21.1	99	20	11	11	2	1	0	3	12	2	15	0	0	1	2	.333	0	1-1	2	4.59	4.64
2001 Philadelphia	NL	42	0	0	12	48.0	215	51	23	23	4	4	3	1	22	4	35	2	0	4	3	.571	0	1-5	9	4.43	4.31
2001 San Francisco	NL	13	0	0	4	15.0	70	21	14	14	3	2	1	0	7	2	17	2	0	2	0	1.000	0	0-0	1	7.50	8.40
6 ML YEARS		321	0	0	137	368.0	1648	373	201	188	33	26	12	13	191	17	284	25	1	30	23	.566	0	29-50	41	4.59	4.60

Alexis Gomez

Bats: L **Throws:** L **Pos:** RF-2; PH-2; PR-1   **Ht:** 6'2" **Wt:** 180 **Born:** 8/6/80 **Age:** 22

					BATTING														BASERUNNING				AVERAGES		
Year Team	Lg	G	AB	H	2B	3B	HR	(Hm	Rd)	TB	R	RBI	RC	TBB	IBB	SO	HBP	SH	SF	SB	CS	SB%	GDP	Avg	OBP	Slg
1999 Royals	R	56	214	59	12	1	5	(-	-)	88	44	31	35	32	0	48	1	1	1	13	5	.72	1	.276	.371	.411
2000 Wilmington	A+	121	461	117	13	4	1	(-	-)	141	63	33	46	45	1	121	2	7	1	21	10	.68	8	.254	.322	.306
2001 Wilmington	A+	48	169	51	8	2	1	(-	-)	66	29	9	22	11	2	43	1	2	0	7	3	.70	4	.302	.348	.391
2001 Wichita	AA	83	342	96	15	6	4	(-	-)	135	55	34	46	27	1	70	4	1	4	16	10	.62	4	.281	.337	.395
2002 Wichita	AA	114	461	136	21	8	14	(-	-)	215	72	75	73	45	5	84	3	2	4	36	24	.60	9	.295	.359	.466
2002 Kansas City	AL	5	10	2	0	0	0	(0	0)	2	0	0	0	0	0	2	0	0	0	0	0	-	0	.200	.200	.200

Chris Gomez

Bats: R **Throws:** R **Pos:** SS-130; PH-1   **Ht:** 6'1" **Wt:** 185 **Born:** 6/16/71 **Age:** 32

					BATTING														BASERUNNING				AVERAGES		
Year Team	Lg	G	AB	H	2B	3B	HR	(Hm	Rd)	TB	R	RBI	RC	TBB	IBB	SO	HBP	SH	SF	SB	CS	SB%	GDP	Avg	OBP	Slg
1993 Detroit	AL	46	128	32	7	1	0	(0	0)	41	11	11	12	9	0	17	1	3	0	2	2	.50	2	.250	.304	.320
1994 Detroit	AL	84	296	76	19	0	8	(5	3)	119	32	53	39	33	0	64	3	3	1	5	3	.63	8	.257	.336	.402
1995 Detroit	AL	123	431	96	20	2	11	(5	6)	153	49	50	43	41	0	96	3	3	4	4	1	.80	13	.223	.292	.355
1996 Det-SD		137	456	117	21	1	4	(2	2)	152	53	45	52	57	1	84	7	6	2	3	3	.50	16	.257	.347	.333
1997 San Diego	NL	150	522	132	19	2	5	(2	3)	170	62	54	52	53	1	114	5	3	3	5	8	.38	16	.253	.326	.326
1998 San Diego	NL	145	449	120	32	3	4	(3	1)	170	55	39	58	51	7	87	5	7	1	1	3	.25	11	.267	.346	.379
1999 San Diego	NL	76	234	59	8	1	1	(1	0)	72	20	15	23	27	3	49	1	2	1	1	2	.33	6	.252	.331	.308
2000 San Diego	NL	33	54	12	0	0	0	(0	0)	12	4	3	4	7	0	5	0	1	1	0	0	-	1	.222	.306	.222
2001 SD-TB		98	301	78	19	0	8	(5	3)	121	37	43	36	17	0	38	2	6	5	4	0	1.00	5	.259	.298	.402
2002 Tampa Bay	AL	130	461	122	31	3	10	(2	8)	189	51	46	52	21	0	58	7	6	3	1	3	.25	8	.265	.305	.410
1996 Detroit	AL	48	128	31	5	0	1	(1	0)	39	21	16	13	18	0	20	1	3	0	1	1	.50	5	.242	.340	.305
1996 San Diego	NL	89	328	86	16	1	3	(1	2)	113	32	29	39	39	1	64	6	3	2	2	2	.50	11	.262	.349	.345
2001 San Diego	NL	40	112	21	3	0	0	(0	0)	24	6	7	4	9	0	14	0	2	2	1	0	1.00	5	.188	.244	.214
2001 Tampa Bay	AL	58	189	57	16	0	8	(5	3)	97	31	36	32	8	0	24	2	4	3	3	0	1.00	4	.302	.332	.513
10 ML YEARS		1022	3332	844	176	13	51	(25	26)	1199	374	359	371	316	12	612	34	40	23	26	25	.51	90	.253	.322	.360

Alex Gonzalez

Bats: R **Throws:** R **Pos:** SS-42; PR-1   **Ht:** 6'0" **Wt:** 200 **Born:** 2/15/77 **Age:** 26

					BATTING														BASERUNNING				AVERAGES		
Year Team	Lg	G	AB	H	2B	3B	HR	(Hm	Rd)	TB	R	RBI	RC	TBB	IBB	SO	HBP	SH	SF	SB	CS	SB%	GDP	Avg	OBP	Slg
2002 Marlins*	R	5	12	2	1	0	0	(-	-)	3	0	1	0	0	0	5	0	0	1	0	0	-	1	.167	.154	.250
1998 Florida	NL	25	86	13	2	0	3	(1	2)	24	11	7	5	9	0	30	1	2	0	0	0	-	2	.151	.240	.279
1999 Florida	NL	136	560	155	28	9	14	(7	7)	241	81	59	69	15	0	113	12	1	3	3	5	.38	13	.277	.308	.430
2000 Florida	NL	109	385	77	17	4	7	(5	2)	123	35	42	26	13	0	77	2	5	2	7	1	.88	7	.200	.229	.319
2001 Florida	NL	145	515	129	36	1	9	(5	4)	194	57	48	56	30	6	107	10	3	3	2	2	.50	13	.250	.303	.377
2002 Florida	NL	42	151	34	7	1	2	(1	1)	49	15	18	14	12	1	32	4	3	2	3	1	.75	2	.225	.296	.325
5 ML YEARS		457	1697	408	90	14	35	(19	16)	631	199	174	170	79	7	359	29	14	10	15	9	.63	37	.240	.284	.372

Alex S Gonzalez

Bats: R **Throws:** R **Pos:** SS-142   **Ht:** 6'0" **Wt:** 200 **Born:** 4/8/73 **Age:** 30

					BATTING														BASERUNNING				AVERAGES		
Year Team	Lg	G	AB	H	2B	3B	HR	(Hm	Rd)	TB	R	RBI	RC	TBB	IBB	SO	HBP	SH	SF	SB	CS	SB%	GDP	Avg	OBP	Slg
1994 Toronto	AL	15	53	8	3	1	0	(0	0)	13	7	1	2	4	0	17	1	1	0	3	0	1.00	2	.151	.224	.245
1995 Toronto	AL	111	367	89	19	4	10	(8	2)	146	51	42	47	44	1	114	1	9	4	4	4	.50	7	.243	.322	.398
1996 Toronto	AL	147	527	124	30	5	14	(3	11)	206	64	64	61	45	0	127	5	7	3	16	6	.73	12	.235	.300	.391
1997 Toronto	AL	126	426	102	23	2	12	(4	8)	165	46	35	50	34	1	94	5	11	2	15	6	.71	9	.239	.302	.387
1998 Toronto	AL	158	568	136	28	1	13	(7	6)	205	70	51	56	28	1	121	6	13	3	21	6	.78	13	.239	.281	.361
1999 Toronto	AL	38	154	45	13	0	2	(1	1)	64	22	12	23	16	0	23	3	0	0	4	2	.67	4	.292	.370	.416
2000 Toronto	AL	141	527	133	31	2	15	(5	10)	213	68	69	64	43	0	113	4	16	1	4	4	.50	14	.252	.313	.404
2001 Toronto	AL	154	636	161	25	5	17	(9	8)	247	79	76	72	43	0	149	7	7	10	18	11	.62	16	.253	.303	.388
2002 Chicago	NL	142	513	127	27	5	18	(13	5)	218	58	61	59	46	7	136	3	4	2	5	3	.63	11	.248	.312	.425
9 ML YEARS		1032	3771	925	199	25	101	(50	51)	1477	465	411	434	303	10	894	35	68	25	90	42	.68	88	.245	.306	.392

Jeremi Gonzalez

Pitches: R **Bats:** R **Pos:** SP   **Ht:** 6'0" **Wt:** 220 **Born:** 1/8/75 **Age:** 28

		HOW MUCH HE PITCHED						WHAT HE GAVE UP											THE RESULTS						
Year Team	Lg	G	GS	CG	GF	IP	BFP	H	R	ER	HR	SH	SF	HB	TBB	IBB	SO	WP	Bk	W	L	Pct	ShO	Sv-Op	Hld	ERC	ERA
1992 Rockies	R	14	7	0	1	45.0	238	65	59	39	0	0	6	10	22	0	39	11	1	0	5	.000	0	0--	-	6.82	7.80
1993 Huntington	R+	12	12	1	0	67.2	319	82	59	47	6	1	2	5	38	0	42	5	2	3	9	.250	0	0--	-	6.23	6.25
1994 Peoria	A	13	13	1	0	71.1	325	86	53	44	4	2	3	7	32	0	39	5	2	1	7	.125	0	0--	-	5.64	5.55
1994 Williamsport	A-	16	12	1	2	80.2	357	83	46	38	6	3	3	10	29	0	64	4	1	4	6	.400	1	1--	-	4.37	4.24
1995 Rockford	A	12	12	1	0	65.1	297	63	43	37	4	1	4	8	28	0	36	8	1	4	4	.500	0	0--	-	4.05	5.10
1995 Daytona	A+	19	2	0	7	44.1	178	34	15	6	0	1	2	1	13	1	30	4	2	5	1	.833	0	4--	-	1.92	1.22
1996 Orlando	AA	17	14	0	2	97.0	415	95	39	36	6	1	2	4	28	1	85	2	0	6	3	.667	0	0--	-	3.36	3.34
1997 Iowa	AAA	10	10	1	0	62.0	249	47	27	24	8	1	1	1	21	0	58	2	0	2	2	.500	0	0--	-	2.83	3.48
1999 Daytona	A+	2	2	0	0	4.2	16	2	0	0	0	0	0	0	0	0	4	0	0	0	0	-	0	0--	-	0.40	0.00
1999 W Tennesse	AA	3	3	0	0	10.1	46	7	2	2	0	1	0	1	9	0	12	0	0	0	1	.000	0	0--	-	3.76	1.74
1999 Iowa	AAA	3	3	0	0	10.0	45	10	8	5	1	1	0	1	6	0	10	1	0	0	1	.000	0	0--	-	5.40	4.50
2002 Oklahoma	AAA	46	5	0	0	92.0	400	86	40	34	8	4	3	8	39	5	93	1	2	6	5	.545	0	14--	-	3.97	3.33
1997 Chicago	NL	23	23	1	0	144.0	613	126	73	68	16	4	5	2	69	5	93	1	1	11	9	.550	1	0-0	0	3.79	4.25
1998 Chicago	NL	20	20	1	0	110.0	493	124	72	65	13	5	2	3	41	5	70	2	3	7	7	.500	1	0-0	0	4.80	5.32
2 ML YEARS		43	43	2	0	254.0	1106	250	145	133	29	9	7	5	110	10	163	3	4	18	16	.529	2	0-0	0	4.22	4.71

Juan Gonzalez

Bats: R **Throws:** R **Pos:** RF-62; DH-8; PH-1   **Ht:** 6'3" **Wt:** 220 **Born:** 10/16/69 **Age:** 33

Year Team	Lg	G	AB	H	2B	3B	HR	(Hm	Rd)	TB	R	RBI	RC	TBB	IBB	SO	HBP	SH	SF	SB	CS	SB%	GDP	Avg	OBP	Slg
1989 Texas	AL	24	60	9	3	0	1	(1	0)	15	6	7	2	6	0	17	0	2	0	0	0	-	4	.150	.227	.250
1990 Texas	AL	25	90	26	7	1	4	(3	1)	47	11	12	14	2	0	18	2	0	1	0	1	.00	2	.289	.316	.522
1991 Texas	AL	142	545	144	34	1	27	(7	20)	261	78	102	81	42	7	118	5	0	3	4	4	.50	10	.264	.321	.479
1992 Texas	AL	155	584	152	24	2	43	(19	24)	309	77	109	90	35	1	143	5	0	8	0	1	.00	16	.260	.304	.529
1993 Texas	AL	140	536	166	33	1	46	(24	22)	339	105	118	116	37	7	99	13	0	1	4	1	.80	12	.310	.368	**.632**
1994 Texas	AL	107	422	116	18	4	19	(6	13)	199	57	85	60	30	10	66	7	0	4	6	4	.60	18	.275	.330	.472
1995 Texas	AL	90	352	104	20	2	27	(15	12)	209	57	82	61	17	3	66	0	0	0	0	0	-	15	.295	.324	.594
1996 Texas	AL	134	541	170	33	2	47	(23	24)	348	89	144	119	45	12	82	3	0	3	2	0	1.00	10	.314	.368	.643
1997 Texas	AL	133	533	158	24	3	42	(18	24)	314	87	131	100	33	7	107	3	0	10	0	0	-	12	.296	.335	.589
1998 Texas	AL	154	606	193	**50**	2	45	(21	24)	382	110	**157**	128	46	9	126	6	0	11	2	1	.67	20	.318	.366	.630
1999 Texas	AL	144	562	183	36	1	39	(14	25)	338	114	128	121	51	7	105	4	0	12	3	3	.50	10	.326	.378	.601
2000 Detroit	AL	115	461	133	30	2	22	(8	14)	233	69	67	73	32	3	84	2	0	1	1	2	.33	13	.289	.337	.505
2001 Cleveland	AL	140	532	173	34	1	35	(22	13)	314	97	140	108	41	5	94	6	0	**16**	1	0	1.00	18	.325	.370	.590
2002 Texas	AL	70	277	78	21	1	8	(4	4)	125	38	35	38	17	1	56	1	0	1	2	0	1.00	11	.282	.324	.451
14 ML YEARS		1573	6101	1805	367	23	405	(185	220)	3433	995	1317	1111	434	72	1181	57	2	76	25	17	.60	171	.296	.344	.563

Luis Gonzalez

Bats: L **Throws:** R **Pos:** LF-146; PH-3   **Ht:** 6'2" **Wt:** 195 **Born:** 9/3/67 **Age:** 35

Year Team	Lg	G	AB	H	2B	3B	HR	(Hm	Rd)	TB	R	RBI	RC	TBB	IBB	SO	HBP	SH	SF	SB	CS	SB%	GDP	Avg	OBP	Slg
1990 Houston	NL	12	21	4	2	0	0	(0	0)	6	1	0	2	2	1	5	0	0	0	0	0	-	0	.190	.261	.286
1991 Houston	NL	137	473	120	28	9	13	(4	9)	205	51	69	64	40	4	101	8	1	4	10	7	.59	9	.254	.320	.433
1992 Houston	NL	122	387	94	19	3	10	(4	6)	149	40	55	41	24	3	52	2	1	2	7	7	.50	6	.243	.289	.385
1993 Houston	NL	154	540	162	34	3	15	(8	7)	247	82	72	90	47	7	83	10	3	**10**	20	9	.69	9	.300	.361	.457
1994 Houston	NL	112	392	107	29	4	8	(3	5)	168	57	67	57	49	6	57	3	0	6	15	13	.54	10	.273	.353	.429
1995 Hou-ChC	NL	133	471	130	29	8	13	(6	7)	214	69	69	72	57	8	63	6	1	6	6	8	.43	16	.276	.357	.454
1996 Chicago	NL	146	483	131	30	4	15	(6	9)	214	70	79	75	61	8	49	4	1	6	9	6	.60	13	.271	.354	.443
1997 Houston	NL	152	550	142	31	2	10	(4	6)	207	78	68	73	71	7	67	5	0	5	10	7	.59	12	.258	.345	.376
1998 Detroit	AL	154	547	146	35	4	23	(15	8)	260	84	71	89	57	7	62	8	0	8	12	7	.63	9	.267	.340	.475
1999 Arizona	NL	153	614	**206**	45	4	26	(10	16)	337	112	111	129	66	6	63	7	1	5	9	5	.64	13	.336	.403	.549
2000 Arizona	NL	**162**	618	192	47	2	31	(14	17)	336	106	114	128	78	6	85	12	2	12	2	4	.33	12	.311	.392	.544
2001 Arizona	NL	**162**	609	198	36	7	57	(26	31)	419	128	142	164	100	24	83	14	0	5	1	1	.50	14	.325	.429	.688
2002 Arizona	NL	148	524	151	19	3	28	(11	17)	260	90	103	113	97	8	76	5	0	7	9	2	.82	12	.288	.400	.496
1995 Houston	NL	56	209	54	10	4	6	(1	5)	90	35	35	26	18	3	30	3	1	3	1	3	.25	8	.258	.322	.431
1995 Chicago	NL	77	262	76	19	4	7	(5	2)	124	34	34	46	39	5	33	3	0	3	5	5	.50	8	.290	.384	.473
13 ML YEARS		1747	6229	1783	384	54	249	(111	138)	3022	968	1020	1097	749	95	846	84	10	76	110	76	.59	135	.286	.366	.485

Raul Gonzalez

Bats: R **Throws:** R **Pos:** CF-18; PH-14; LF-12; RF-4   **Ht:** 5'9" **Wt:** 190 **Born:** 12/27/73 **Age:** 29

Year Team	Lg	G	AB	H	2B	3B	HR	(Hm	Rd)	TB	R	RBI	RC	TBB	IBB	SO	HBP	SH	SF	SB	CS	SB%	GDP	Avg	OBP	Slg
1991 Royals	R	47	160	47	5	3	0	(-	-)	58	24	17	21	19	0	21	0	1	2	3	4	.43	4	.294	.365	.363
1992 Appleton	A	119	449	115	32	1	9	(-	-)	176	82	51	64	57	1	58	2	4	6	13	5	.72	4	.256	.339	.392
1993 Wilmington	A+	127	461	124	30	3	11	(-	-)	193	59	55	69	54	1	58	4	1	4	13	5	.72	8	.269	.348	.419
1994 Wilmington	A+	115	414	108	19	8	9	(-	-)	170	60	51	56	45	2	50	2	2	4	0	4	.00	8	.261	.333	.411
1995 Wichita	AA	22	79	23	3	2	2	(-	-)	36	14	11	14	8	0	13	0	0	0	4	0	1.00	1	.291	.356	.456
1995 Wichita	A+	30	100	30	5	2	3	(-	-)	48	13	7	14	14	3	34	2	3	7	6	4	.60	3	.292	.320	.481
1996 Wichita	AA	23	84	24	5	1	1	(-	-)	34	17	9	10	5	0	12	1	0	0	1	2	.33	3	.286	.333	.405
1997 Wichita	AA	129	452	129	30	4	13	(-	-)	206	66	74	67	36	0	52	2	3	8	12	8	.60	12	.285	.335	.456
1998 Wichita	AA	118	455	148	31	1	17	(-	-)	232	84	86	87	58	3	53	2	1	4	12	8	.60	15	.325	.401	.510
1999 Trenton	AA	127	505	169	33	4	18	(-	-)	264	80	103	100	51	3	71	3	1	7	12	3	.80	14	.335	.394	.523
2000 Iowa	AAA	69	241	64	13	1	4	(-	-)	91	35	33	28	21	1	20	2	0	1	5	5	.50	6	.266	.328	.378
2001 Louisville	AAA	142	539	161	39	1	11	(-	-)	235	90	66	82	64	2	70	1	0	5	6	8	.43	20	.299	.371	.436
2002 Louisville	AAA	114	432	144	27	2	13	(-	-)	214	91	69	84	61	4	59	4	1	6	9	8	.53	15	.333	.416	.495
2000 Chicago	NL	3	2	0	0	0	0	(0	0)	0	0	0	0	0	0	2	0	0	0	0	0	-	0	.000	.000	.000
2001 Cincinnati	NL	11	14	3	0	0	0	(0	0)	3	0	0	1	1	0	3	0	0	0	0	0	-	0	.214	.267	.214
2002 Cin-NYM	NL	40	104	27	3	0	3	(1	2)	39	13	12	13	6	0	22	0	0	1	4	2	.67	3	.260	.297	.375
2002 Cincinnati	NL	10	23	6	1	0	0	(0	0)	7	4	1	2	2	0	5	0	0	0	2	0	1.00	1	.261	.320	.304
2002 New York	NL	30	81	21	2	0	3	(1	2)	32	9	11	11	4	0	17	0	0	1	2	2	.50	2	.259	.291	.395
3 ML YEARS		54	120	30	3	0	3	(1	2)	42	13	12	14	7	0	27	0	0	1	4	2	.67	3	.250	.289	.350

Wiki Gonzalez

Bats: R **Throws:** R **Pos:** C-54; PH-2   **Ht:** 5'11" **Wt:** 203 **Born:** 5/17/74 **Age:** 29

Year Team	Lg	G	AB	H	2B	3B	HR	(Hm	Rd)	TB	R	RBI	RC	TBB	IBB	SO	HBP	SH	SF	SB	CS	SB%	GDP	Avg	OBP	Slg
2002 Lk Elsinore*	A+	19	53	18	8	0	1	(-	-)	29	10	6	14	12	0	3	4	0	1	0	0	-	2	.340	.486	.547
1999 San Diego	NL	30	83	21	2	1	3	(1	2)	34	7	12	7	1	0	8	1	0	0	0	0	-	5	.253	.271	.410
2000 San Diego	NL	95	284	66	15	1	5	(1	4)	98	25	30	30	30	4	31	3	1	1	1	2	.33	6	.232	.311	.345
2001 San Diego	NL	64	160	44	6	0	8	(5	3)	74	16	27	25	11	1	28	4	0	1	2	0	1.00	3	.275	.335	.463
2002 San Diego	NL	56	164	36	8	1	1	(1	0)	49	16	20	17	27	3	24	1	0	2	0	0	-	10	.220	.330	.299
4 ML YEARS		245	691	167	31	3	17	(8	9)	255	64	89	79	69	8	91	9	1	4	3	2	.60	23	.242	.317	.369

Andy Good

Pitches: R Bats: R Pos: SP   Ht: 6'1" Wt: 209 Born: 9/19/79 Age: 23

		HOW MUCH HE PITCHED						WHAT HE GAVE UP											THE RESULTS							
Year Team	Lg	G	GS	CG	GF	IP	BFP	H	R	ER	HR	SH	SF	HB	TBB	IBB	SO	WP	Bk	W	L	Pct	ShO	Sv-Op	Hld	ERC	ERA
1998 Diamndbcks	R	9	8	0	0	33.2	152	46	25	16	1	0	1	2	7	0	25	3	0	1	3	.250	0	0--	-	5.13	4.28
1998 South Bend	A	2	0	0	1	6.0	28	7	4	2	0	0	0	2	1	0	6	0	1	0	1	.000	0	0--	-	4.53	3.00
1999 South Bend	A	27	27	0	0	153.2	662	160	80	70	9	3	9	9	42	0	146	7	0	11	10	.524	0	0--	-	3.72	4.10
2001 Lancaster	A+	19	18	0	0	101.1	454	108	63	54	12	6	4	13	27	0	104	5	0	8	6	.571	0	0--	-	4.43	4.80
2001 El Paso	AA	10	9	0	0	56.2	270	79	44	37	2	1	2	3	20	0	46	3	0	2	3	.400	0	0--	-	5.80	5.88
2002 El Paso	AA	28	27	2	0	178.0	730	170	89	70	21	5	6	7	26	0	128	3	0	13	6	.684	1	0--	-	3.09	3.54

Tom Goodwin

Bats: L Throws: R Pos: LF-28; CF-22; PH-21; PR-10; RF-7   Ht: 6'1" Wt: 175 Born: 7/27/68 Age: 34

							BATTING													BASERUNNING				AVERAGES		
Year Team	Lg	G	AB	H	2B	3B	HR	(Hm	Rd)	TB	R	RBI	RC	TBB	IBB	SO	HBP	SH	SF	SB	CS	SB%	GDP	Avg	OBP	Slg
2002 Fresno*	AAA	17	62	14	3	1	0	(-	-)	19	11	7	6	8	0	8	0	1	0	3	2	.60	1	.226	.314	.306
1991 Los Angeles	NL	16	7	1	0	0	0	(0	0)	1	3	0	0	0	0	0	0	0	0	1	1	.50	0	.143	.143	.143
1992 Los Angeles	NL	57	73	17	1	1	0	(0	0)	20	15	3	6	6	0	10	0	0	0	7	3	.70	0	.233	.291	.274
1993 Los Angeles	NL	30	17	5	1	0	0	(0	0)	6	6	1	1	1	0	4	0	0	0	1	2	.33	1	.294	.333	.353
1994 Kansas City	AL	2	2	0	0	0	0	(0	0)	0	0	0	0	0	0	1	0	0	0	0	0	-	0	.000	.000	.000
1995 Kansas City	AL	133	480	138	16	3	4	(2	2)	172	72	28	64	38	0	72	5	14	0	50	18	.74	5	.288	.346	.358
1996 Kansas City	AL	143	524	148	14	4	1	(0	1)	173	80	35	65	39	0	79	2	21	1	66	22	.75	3	.282	.334	.330
1997 KC-Tex	AL	150	574	149	26	6	2	(0	2)	193	90	39	65	44	1	88	3	11	3	50	16	.76	7	.260	.314	.336
1998 Texas	AL	154	520	151	13	3	2	(2	0)	176	102	33	74	73	0	90	2	10	3	38	20	.66	2	.290	.378	.338
1999 Texas	AL	109	405	105	12	6	3	(1	2)	138	63	33	49	40	0	61	0	7	3	39	11	.78	7	.259	.324	.341
2000 Col-LA	NL	147	528	139	11	9	6	(4	2)	186	94	58	74	68	2	117	1	5	4	55	10	.85	7	.263	.346	.352
2001 Los Angeles	NL	105	286	66	8	5	4	(1	3)	96	51	22	29	23	0	58	0	1	2	22	8	.73	3	.231	.286	.336
2002 San Francisco	NL	78	154	40	5	2	1	(0	1)	52	23	17	21	14	0	25	0	3	0	16	2	.89	5	.260	.321	.338
1997 Kansas City	AL	97	367	100	13	4	2	(0	2)	127	51	22	42	19	0	51	2	11	1	34	10	.77	5	.272	.311	.346
1997 Texas	AL	53	207	49	13	2	0	(0	0)	66	39	17	23	25	1	37	1	0	2	16	6	.73	2	.237	.319	.319
2000 Colorado	NL	91	317	86	8	8	5	(4	1)	125	65	47	54	50	2	76	1	5	4	39	7	.85	3	.271	.368	.394
2000 Los Angeles	NL	56	211	53	3	1	1	(0	1)	61	29	11	20	18	0	41	0	0	0	16	3	.84	4	.251	.310	.289
12 ML YEARS		1124	3570	959	107	39	23	(10	13)	1213	599	269	448	346	3	605	13	72	16	345	113	.75	40	.269	.334	.340

Tom Gordon

Pitches: R Bats: R Pos: RP-34   Ht: 5'10" Wt: 190 Born: 11/18/67 Age: 35

				HOW MUCH HE PITCHED				WHAT HE GAVE UP												THE RESULTS							
Year Team	Lg	G	GS	CG	GF	IP	BFP	H	R	ER	HR	SH	SF	HB	TBB	IBB	SO	WP	Bk	W	L	Pct	ShO	Sv-Op	Hld	ERC	ERA
2002 Daytona*	A+	2	2	0	0	2.2	12	1	1	1	0	0	0	0	2	0	3	1	0	0	0	-	0	0--	-	1.42	3.38
2002 Iowa*	AAA	2	0	0	1	1.2	9	1	4	3	0	0	0	0	3	0	1	0	0	0	0	-	0	1--	-	6.15	16.20
1988 Kansas City	AL	5	2	0	0	15.2	67	16	9	9	1	0	0	0	7	0	18	0	0	0	2	.000	0	0-0	2	4.22	5.17
1989 Kansas City	AL	49	16	1	16	163.0	677	122	67	66	10	4	4	1	86	4	153	12	0	17	9	.654	1	1-7	3	2.97	3.64
1990 Kansas City	AL	32	32	6	0	195.1	858	192	99	81	17	8	2	3	99	1	175	11	0	12	11	.522	1	0-0	0	4.37	3.73
1991 Kansas City	AL	45	14	1	11	158.0	684	129	76	68	16	5	3	4	87	6	167	5	0	9	14	.391	0	1-4	4	3.67	3.87
1992 Kansas City	AL	40	11	0	13	117.2	516	116	67	60	9	2	6	4	55	4	98	5	2	6	10	.375	0	0-2	0	4.17	4.59
1993 Kansas City	AL	48	14	2	18	155.2	651	125	65	62	11	6	6	1	77	5	143	17	0	12	6	.667	0	1-6	2	3.18	3.58
1994 Kansas City	AL	24	24	0	0	155.1	675	136	79	75	15	3	8	3	87	3	126	12	1	11	7	.611	0	0-0	0	4.04	4.35
1995 Kansas City	AL	31	31	2	0	189.0	843	204	110	93	12	7	11	4	89	4	119	9	0	12	12	.500	0	0-0	0	4.59	4.43
1996 Boston	AL	34	34	4	0	215.2	998	249	143	134	28	2	11	4	105	5	171	6	1	12	9	.571	1	0-0	0	5.50	5.59
1997 Boston	AL	42	25	2	16	182.2	774	155	85	76	10	3	4	3	78	1	159	5	0	6	10	.375	1	11-13	0	3.08	3.74
1998 Boston	AL	73	0	0	69	79.1	317	55	24	24	2	2	2	0	25	1	78	9	0	7	4	.636	0	46-47	0	1.72	2.72
1999 Boston	AL	21	0	0	15	17.2	82	17	11	11	2	0	0	1	12	2	24	0	0	0	2	.000	0	11-13	1	5.04	5.60
2001 Chicago	NL	47	0	0	40	45.1	187	32	18	17	4	0	0	1	16	1	67	2	0	1	2	.333	0	27-31	5	2.27	3.38
2002 ChC-Hou	NL	34	0	0	10	42.2	181	42	19	16	3	3	0	1	16	3	48	0	0	1	3	.250	0	0-0	6	3.71	3.38
2002 Chicago	NL	19	0	0	7	23.2	104	27	12	9	1	1	0	1	10	1	31	0	0	1	1	.500	0	0-0	2	4.75	3.42
2002 Houston	NL	15	0	0	3	19.0	77	15	7	7	2	2	0	0	6	2	17	0	0	0	2	.000	0	0-0	4	2.53	3.32
14 ML YEARS		525	203	18	208	1733.0	7510	1590	872	792	140	45	57	30	839	40	1546	93	4	106	101	.512	4	98-123	18	3.83	4.11

Jason Grabowski

Bats: L Throws: R Pos: LF-4   Ht: 6'3" Wt: 200 Born: 5/24/76 Age: 27

							BATTING													BASERUNNING				AVERAGES		
Year Team	Lg	G	AB	H	2B	3B	HR	(Hm	Rd)	TB	R	RBI	RC	TBB	IBB	SO	HBP	SH	SF	SB	CS	SB%	GDP	Avg	OBP	Slg
1997 Pulaski	R+	50	174	51	14	0	4	(-	-)	77	36	24	36	40	2	32	0	1	1	6	1	.86	2	.293	.423	.443
1998 Savannah	A	104	352	95	13	6	14	(-	-)	162	63	52	60	57	0	93	1	0	1	16	9	.64	7	.270	.372	.460
1999 Charlotte	A+	123	434	136	31	6	12	(-	-)	215	68	87	85	65	3	66	5	1	2	13	10	.57	6	.313	.407	.495
1999 Tulsa	AA	2	6	1	0	0	0	(-	-)	1	1	0	1	2	1	2	0	0	0	0	0	-	0	.167	.375	.167
2000 Tulsa	AA	135	493	135	33	5	19	(-	-)	235	93	90	90	88	1	106	4	0	7	8	7	.53	12	.274	.383	.477
2001 Tacoma	AAA	114	394	117	32	3	9	(-	-)	182	60	58	71	61	5	94	2	0	5	7	4	.64	8	.297	.390	.462
2002 Sacramento	AAA	73	265	78	22	3	12	(-	-)	142	50	52	52	39	2	56	1	0	0	6	4	.60	8	.294	.387	.536
2002 Oakland	AL	4	8	3	1	1	0	(0	0)	6	3	1	3	3	0	1	0	0	0	0	0	-	0	.375	.545	.750

Mark Grace

Bats: L Throws: L Pos: 1B-98; PH-34   Ht: 6'2" Wt: 200 Born: 6/28/64 Age: 39

							BATTING													BASERUNNING				AVERAGES		
Year Team	Lg	G	AB	H	2B	3B	HR	(Hm	Rd)	TB	R	RBI	RC	TBB	IBB	SO	HBP	SH	SF	SB	CS	SB%	GDP	Avg	OBP	Slg
1988 Chicago	NL	134	486	144	23	4	7	(0	7)	196	65	57	73	60	5	43	0	4	5	3	3	.50	12	.296	.371	.403
1989 Chicago	NL	142	510	160	28	3	13	(8	5)	233	74	79	94	80	13	42	0	3	3	14	7	.67	13	.314	.405	.457
1990 Chicago	NL	157	589	182	32	1	9	(4	5)	243	72	82	93	59	5	54	5	1	8	15	6	.71	10	.309	.372	.413
1991 Chicago	NL	160	619	169	28	5	8	(5	3)	231	87	58	84	70	7	53	3	4	7	3	4	.43	6	.273	.346	.373
1992 Chicago	NL	158	603	185	37	5	9	(5	4)	259	72	79	100	72	8	36	4	2	8	6	1	.86	14	.307	.380	.430
1993 Chicago	NL	155	594	193	39	4	14	(5	9)	282	86	98	104	71	14	32	1	1	9	8	4	.67	25	.325	.393	.475

Year Team	Lg	G	AB	H	2B	3B	HR	(Hm Rd)	TB	R	RBI	RC	TBB	IBB	SO	HBP	SH	SF	SB	CS	SB%	GDP	Avg	OBP	Slg
1994 Chicago	NL	106	403	120	23	3	6	(5 1)	167	55	44	61	48	5	41	0	0	3	0	1	.00	10	.298	.370	.414
1995 Chicago	NL	143	552	180	51	3	16	(4 12)	285	97	92	110	65	9	46	2	1	7	6	2	.75	10	.326	.395	.516
1996 Chicago	NL	142	547	181	39	1	9	(4 5)	249	88	75	94	62	8	41	1	0	6	2	3	.40	18	.331	.396	.455
1997 Chicago	NL	151	555	177	32	5	13	(6 7)	258	87	78	104	88	3	45	2	1	8	2	4	.33	18	.319	.409	.465
1998 Chicago	NL	158	595	184	39	3	17	(7 10)	280	92	89	109	93	8	56	3	0	7	4	7	.36	17	.309	.401	.471
1999 Chicago	NL	161	593	183	44	5	16	(8 8)	285	107	91	110	83	4	44	2	0	10	3	4	.43	14	.309	.390	.481
2000 Chicago	NL	143	510	143	41	1	11	(3 8)	219	75	82	92	95	11	28	6	2	8	1	2	.33	7	.280	.394	.429
2001 Arizona	NL	145	476	142	31	2	15	(6 9)	222	66	78	87	67	6	36	4	1	5	1	0	1.00	7	.298	.386	.466
2002 Arizona	NL	124	298	75	19	0	7	(4 3)	115	43	48	44	46	6	30	1	0	3	2	0	1.00	5	.252	.351	.386
15 ML YEARS		2179	7930	2418	506	45	170	(74 96)	3524	1166	1130	1359	1059	112	627	34	16	96	70	48	.59	186	.305	.385	.444

Tony Graffanino

Bats: R **Throws:** R **Pos:** 3B-35; 2B-25; SS-8; PH-8   **Ht:** 6'1" **Wt:** 190 **Born:** 6/6/72 **Age:** 31

Year Team	Lg	G	AB	H	2B	3B	HR	(Hm Rd)	TB	R	RBI	RC	TBB	IBB	SO	HBP	SH	SF	SB	CS	SB%	GDP	Avg	OBP	Slg
1996 Atlanta	NL	22	46	8	1	1	0	(0 0)	11	7	2	3	4	0	13	1	0	1	0	0	-	0	.174	.250	.239
1997 Atlanta	NL	104	186	48	9	1	8	(5 3)	83	33	20	29	26	1	46	1	3	5	6	4	.60	3	.258	.344	.446
1998 Atlanta	NL	105	289	61	14	1	5	(3 2)	92	32	22	22	24	0	68	2	1	1	1	4	.20	7	.211	.275	.318
1999 Tampa Bay	AL	39	130	41	9	4	2	(0 2)	64	20	19	23	9	0	22	1	2	0	3	2	.60	1	.315	.364	.492
2000 TB-CWS	AL	70	168	46	6	1	2	(1 1)	60	33	17	23	22	0	27	2	1	1	7	4	.64	2	.274	.363	.357
2001 Chicago	AL	74	145	44	9	0	2	(1 1)	59	23	15	22	16	0	29	1	4	1	4	1	.80	4	.303	.370	.407
2002 Chicago	AL	70	229	60	12	4	6	(4 2)	98	35	31	34	22	1	38	2	4	2	2	1	.67	2	.262	.329	.428
2000 Tampa Bay	AL	13	20	6	1	0	0	(0 0)	7	8	1	2	1	0	2	1	0	0	0	0	-	1	.300	.364	.350
2000 Chicago	AL	57	148	40	5	1	2	(1 1)	53	25	16	21	21	0	25	1	1	1	7	4	.64	1	.270	.363	.358
7 ML YEARS		484	1193	308	60	12	25	(14 11)	467	183	126	156	123	2	243	10	15	13	23	16	.59	19	.258	.329	.391

Danny Graves

Pitches: R **Bats:** R **Pos:** RP-64; SP-4   **Ht:** 6'0" **Wt:** 185 **Born:** 8/7/73 **Age:** 29

Year Team	Lg	G	GS	CG	GF	IP	BFP	H	R	ER	HR	SH	SF	HB	TBB	IBB	SO	WP	Bk	W	L	Pct	ShO	Sv-Op	Hld	ERC	ERA
1996 Cleveland	AL	15	0	0	5	29.2	129	29	18	15	2	0	1	0	10	0	22	1	0	2	0	1.000	0	0-1	0	3.37	4.55
1997 Cle-Cin		15	0	0	3	26.0	134	41	22	16	2	3	2	0	20	1	11	1	0	0	0	-	0	0-0	1	9.10	5.54
1998 Cincinnati	NL	62	0	0	35	81.1	340	76	31	30	6	2	5	2	28	4	44	4	0	2	1	.667	0	8-8	6	3.38	3.32
1999 Cincinnati	NL	75	0	0	56	111.0	454	90	42	38	10	5	2	2	49	4	69	3	0	8	7	.533	0	27-36	0	3.25	3.08
2000 Cincinnati	NL	66	0	0	57	91.1	388	81	31	26	8	6	4	3	42	7	52	3	1	10	5	.667	0	30-35	0	3.64	2.56
2001 Cincinnati	NL	66	0	0	54	80.1	337	83	41	37	7	3	2	4	18	6	49	2	1	6	5	.545	0	32-39	0	3.59	4.15
2002 Cincinnati	NL	68	4	0	54	98.2	412	99	37	35	7	3	6	3	25	9	58	5	0	7	3	.700	0	32-39	1	3.33	3.19
1997 Cleveland	AL	5	0	0	2	11.1	56	15	8	6	2	0	1	0	9	0	4	0	0	0	0	-	0	0-0	0	8.52	4.76
1997 Cincinnati	NL	10	0	0	1	14.2	78	26	14	10	0	3	1	0	11	1	7	1	0	0	0	-	0	0-0	1	9.52	6.14
7 ML YEARS		367	4	0	264	518.1	2194	499	222	197	42	22	22	14	192	31	306	19	2	35	21	.625	0	129-158	7	3.67	3.42

Shawn Green

Bats: L **Throws:** L **Pos:** RF-156; DH-1; PH-1   **Ht:** 6'4" **Wt:** 200 **Born:** 11/10/72 **Age:** 30

Year Team	Lg	G	AB	H	2B	3B	HR	(Hm Rd)	TB	R	RBI	RC	TBB	IBB	SO	HBP	SH	SF	SB	CS	SB%	GDP	Avg	OBP	Slg
1993 Toronto	AL	3	6	0	0	0	0	(0 0)	0	0	0	0	0	0	1	0	0	0	0	0	-	0	.000	.000	.000
1994 Toronto	AL	14	33	3	1	0	0	(0 0)	4	1	1	0	1	0	8	0	0	0	1	0	1.00	1	.091	.118	.121
1995 Toronto	AL	121	379	109	31	4	15	(5 10)	193	52	54	61	20	3	68	3	0	3	1	2	.33	4	.288	.326	.509
1996 Toronto	AL	132	422	118	32	3	11	(7 4)	189	52	45	64	33	3	75	8	0	2	5	1	.83	9	.280	.342	.448
1997 Toronto	AL	135	429	123	22	4	16	(10 6)	201	57	53	70	36	4	99	1	1	4	14	3	.82	1	.287	.340	.469
1998 Toronto	AL	158	630	175	33	4	35	(21 14)	321	106	100	108	50	2	142	5	1	3	35	12	.74	6	.278	.334	.510
1999 Toronto	AL	153	614	190	45	0	42	(20 22)	361	134	123	132	66	4	117	11	0	5	20	7	.74	13	.309	.384	.588
2000 Los Angeles	NL	162	610	164	44	4	24	(15 9)	288	98	99	107	90	9	121	8	0	6	24	5	.83	18	.269	.367	.472
2001 Los Angeles	NL	161	619	184	31	4	49	(19 30)	370	121	125	134	72	10	107	5	0	5	20	4	.83	10	.297	.372	.598
2002 Los Angeles	NL	158	582	166	31	4	42	(18 24)	325	110	114	108	93	22	112	5	0	5	8	5	.62	26	.285	.385	.558
10 ML YEARS		1197	4324	1232	270	24	234	(115 119)	2252	731	714	784	461	57	850	46	2	33	128	39	.77	91	.285	.358	.521

Todd Greene

Bats: R **Throws:** R **Pos:** C-15; 1B-15; PH-11; DH-4; LF-1; PR-1   **Ht:** 5'10" **Wt:** 208 **Born:** 5/8/71 **Age:** 32

Year Team	Lg	G	AB	H	2B	3B	HR	(Hm Rd)	TB	R	RBI	RC	TBB	IBB	SO	HBP	SH	SF	SB	CS	SB%	GDP	Avg	OBP	Slg
2002 Las Vegas*	AAA	32	125	44	12	0	11	(- -)	89	27	41	29	3	0	21	3	0	3	0	0	-	5	.352	.373	.712
2002 Oklahoma*	AAA	39	152	46	9	0	6	(- -)	73	21	29	25	9	0	27	1	1	3	2	0	1.00	2	.303	.339	.480
1996 Anaheim	AL	29	79	15	1	0	2	(1 1)	22	9	9	4	4	0	11	1	0	0	2	0	1.00	1	.190	.238	.278
1997 Anaheim	AL	34	124	36	6	0	9	(5 4)	69	24	24	22	7	1	25	0	0	0	2	0	1.00	1	.290	.328	.556
1998 Anaheim	AL	29	71	18	4	0	1	(0 1)	25	3	7	7	2	0	20	0	0	0	0	0	-	0	.254	.274	.352
1999 Anaheim	AL	97	321	78	20	0	14	(7 7)	140	36	42	35	12	0	63	3	0	2	1	4	.20	8	.243	.275	.436
2000 Toronto	AL	34	85	20	2	0	5	(2 3)	37	11	10	9	5	0	18	0	0	4	0	0	-	4	.235	.278	.435
2001 New York	AL	35	96	20	4	0	1	(1 0)	27	9	11	5	3	0	21	1	0	0	0	0	-	4	.208	.240	.281
2002 Texas	AL	42	112	30	5	0	10	(6 4)	65	15	19	12	2	0	23	1	1	2	0	0	-	4	.268	.282	.580
7 ML YEARS		300	888	217	42	0	42	(22 20)	385	107	122	94	35	1	181	6	1	4	5	4	.56	24	.244	.277	.434

Rusty Greer

Bats: L **Throws:** L **Pos:** LF-22; DH-22; RF-6; PH-2; 1B-1   **Ht:** 6'0" **Wt:** 195 **Born:** 1/21/69 **Age:** 34

Year Team	Lg	G	AB	H	2B	3B	HR	(Hm	Rd)	TB	R	RBI	RC	TBB	IBB	SO	HBP	SH	SF	SB	CS	SB%	GDP	Avg	OBP	Slg
2002 Tulsa*	AA	6	17	7	2	0	0	(-	-)	9	4	1	5	5	1	3	0	0	0	0	0	-	0	.412	.545	.529
1994 Texas	AL	80	277	87	16	1	10	(3	7)	135	36	46	57	46	2	46	2	2	4	0	0	-	3	.314	.410	.487
1995 Texas	AL	131	417	113	21	2	13	(7	6)	177	58	61	64	55	1	66	1	2	3	3	1	.75	9	.271	.355	.424
1996 Texas	AL	139	542	180	41	6	18	(9	9)	287	96	100	113	62	4	86	3	0	10	9	0	1.00	9	.332	.397	.530
1997 Texas	AL	157	601	193	42	3	26	(18	8)	319	112	87	125	83	4	87	3	1	2	9	5	.64	11	.321	.405	.531
1998 Texas	AL	155	598	183	31	5	16	(8	8)	272	107	108	103	80	1	93	4	0	9	2	4	.33	18	.306	.386	.455
1999 Texas	AL	147	556	167	41	3	20	(10	10)	274	107	101	109	96	2	67	5	0	5	2	2	.50	5	.300	.405	.493
2000 Texas	AL	105	394	117	34	3	8	(5	3)	181	65	65	67	51	1	61	3	0	5	4	1	.80	14	.297	.377	.459
2001 Texas	AL	62	245	67	23	0	7	(2	5)	111	38	29	38	27	1	32	1	1	5	1	2	.33	5	.273	.342	.453
2002 Texas	AL	51	199	59	9	2	1	(1	0)	75	24	17	27	19	0	17	0	0	1	1	0	1.00	5	.296	.356	.377
9 ML YEARS		1027	3829	1166	258	25	119	(61	58)	1831	643	614	703	519	16	555	22	6	44	31	15	.67	91	.305	.387	.478

Seth Greisinger

Pitches: R **Bats:** R **Pos:** SP-8   **Ht:** 6'3" **Wt:** 200 **Born:** 7/29/75 **Age:** 27

Year Team	Lg	G	GS	CG	GF	IP	BFP	H	R	ER	HR	SH	SF	HB	TBB	IBB	SO	WP	Bk	W	L	Pct	ShO	Sv-Op	Hld	ERC	ERA
1997 Jacksonville	AA	28	28	1	0	159.1	710	194	103	92	29	3	6	3	53	0	105	12	2	10	6	.625	0	0--	-	5.78	5.20
1998 Toledo	AAA	10	10	0	0	58.2	247	50	21	19	5	1	5	2	22	0	37	3	2	3	4	.429	0	0--	-	3.42	2.91
1999 Lakeland	A+	1	1	0	0	4.2	17	2	2	2	1	0	0	1	1	0	2	0	0	0	0	-	0	0--	-	1.34	3.86
1999 Toledo	AAA	2	2	0	0	7.2	34	9	5	5	0	1	0	0	3	0	4	1	0	0	1	.000	0	0--	-	4.30	5.87
2002 Erie	AA	4	4	0	0	21.0	86	12	4	3	1	0	1	1	9	0	21	0	0	2	0	1.000	0	0--	-	1.79	1.29
2002 Toledo	AAA	3	3	0	0	15.1	63	15	8	7	0	0	0	2	7	0	11	1	0	1	1	.500	0	0--	-	4.31	4.11
1998 Detroit	AL	21	21	0	0	130.0	562	142	79	74	17	2	5	4	48	2	66	3	0	6	9	.400	0	0-0	0	4.89	5.12
2002 Detroit	AL	8	8	0	0	37.2	168	46	26	26	4	1	1	1	13	2	14	0	0	2	2	.500	0	0-0	0	5.23	6.21
2 ML YEARS		29	29	0	0	167.2	730	188	105	100	21	3	6	5	61	4	80	3	0	8	11	.421	0	0-0	0	4.97	5.37

Ben Grieve

Bats: L **Throws:** R **Pos:** RF-118; DH-16; PH-3   **Ht:** 6'4" **Wt:** 216 **Born:** 5/4/76 **Age:** 27

Year Team	Lg	G	AB	H	2B	3B	HR	(Hm	Rd)	TB	R	RBI	RC	TBB	IBB	SO	HBP	SH	SF	SB	CS	SB%	GDP	Avg	OBP	Slg
1997 Oakland	AL	24	93	29	6	0	3	(3	0)	44	12	24	18	13	1	25	1	1	0	0	0	-	1	.312	.402	.473
1998 Oakland	AL	155	583	168	41	2	18	(5	13)	267	94	89	101	85	3	123	9	0	1	2	2	.50	18	.288	.386	.458
1999 Oakland	AL	148	486	129	21	0	28	(13	15)	234	80	86	81	63	2	108	8	0	1	4	0	1.00	17	.265	.358	.481
2000 Oakland	AL	158	594	166	40	1	27	(13	14)	289	92	104	95	73	2	130	3	0	5	3	0	1.00	32	.279	.359	.487
2001 Tampa Bay	AL	154	542	143	30	2	11	(5	6)	210	72	72	82	87	2	159	8	0	1	7	1	.88	15	.264	.372	.387
2002 Tampa Bay	AL	136	482	121	30	0	19	(7	12)	208	62	64	69	69	5	121	8	0	2	8	2	.80	15	.251	.353	.432
6 ML YEARS		775	2780	756	168	5	106	(46	60)	1252	412	439	446	390	15	666	37	1	11	24	5	.83	96	.272	.368	.450

Ken Griffey Jr.

Bats: L **Throws:** L **Pos:** CF-54; PH-19; LF-1; RF-1   **Ht:** 6'3" **Wt:** 205 **Born:** 11/21/69 **Age:** 33

Year Team	Lg	G	AB	H	2B	3B	HR	(Hm	Rd)	TB	R	RBI	RC	TBB	IBB	SO	HBP	SH	SF	SB	CS	SB%	GDP	Avg	OBP	Slg
1989 Seattle	AL	127	455	120	23	0	16	(10	6)	191	61	61	64	44	8	83	2	1	4	16	7	.70	4	.264	.329	.420
1990 Seattle	AL	155	597	179	28	7	22	(8	14)	287	91	80	101	63	12	81	2	0	4	16	11	.59	12	.300	.366	.481
1991 Seattle	AL	154	548	179	42	1	22	(16	6)	289	76	100	112	71	21	82	1	4	9	18	6	.75	10	.327	.399	.527
1992 Seattle	AL	142	565	174	39	4	27	(16	11)	302	83	103	102	44	15	67	5	0	3	10	5	.67	15	.308	.361	.535
1993 Seattle	AL	156	582	180	38	3	45	(21	24)	359	113	109	137	96	25	91	6	0	7	17	9	.65	14	.309	.408	.617
1994 Seattle	AL	111	433	140	24	4	40	(18	22)	292	94	90	107	56	19	73	2	0	2	11	3	.79	9	.323	.402	.674
1995 Seattle	AL	72	260	67	7	0	17	(13	4)	125	52	42	49	52	6	53	0	0	2	4	2	.67	4	.258	.379	.481
1996 Seattle	AL	140	545	165	26	2	49	(26	23)	342	125	140	131	78	13	104	7	1	7	16	1	.94	7	.303	.392	.628
1997 Seattle	AL	157	608	185	34	3	56	(27	29)	393	125	147	142	76	23	121	8	0	12	15	4	.79	12	.304	.382	.646
1998 Seattle	AL	161	633	180	33	3	56	(30	26)	387	120	146	136	76	11	121	7	0	4	20	5	.80	14	.284	.365	.611
1999 Seattle	AL	160	606	173	26	3	48	(27	21)	349	123	134	132	91	17	108	7	0	2	24	7	.77	8	.285	.384	.576
2000 Cincinnati	NL	145	520	141	22	3	40	(18	22)	289	100	118	111	94	17	117	9	0	8	6	4	.60	7	.271	.387	.556
2001 Cincinnati	NL	111	364	104	20	2	22	(12	10)	194	57	65	69	44	6	72	4	1	4	2	0	1.00	5	.286	.365	.533
2002 Cincinnati	NL	70	197	52	8	0	8	(4	4)	84	17	23	26	28	6	39	3	0	4	1	2	.33	6	.264	.358	.426
14 ML YEARS		1861	6913	2039	370	35	468	(250	218)	3883	1237	1358	1419	913	199	1212	63	7	72	176	66	.73	130	.295	.379	.562

Jason Grimsley

Pitches: R **Bats:** R **Pos:** RP-70   **Ht:** 6'3" **Wt:** 205 **Born:** 8/7/67 **Age:** 35

Year Team	Lg	G	GS	CG	GF	IP	BFP	H	R	ER	HR	SH	SF	HB	TBB	IBB	SO	WP	Bk	W	L	Pct	ShO	Sv-Op	Hld	ERC	ERA
2002 Wichita*	AA	1	1	0	0	1.0	5	1	1	1	0	0	0	0	1	0	0	0	0	0	0	-	0	0--	-	5.48	9.00
1989 Philadelphia	NL	4	4	0	0	18.1	91	19	13	12	2	1	0	0	19	1	7	2	0	1	3	.250	0	0-0	0	6.86	5.89
1990 Philadelphia	NL	11	11	0	0	57.1	255	47	21	21	1	2	1	2	43	0	41	6	1	3	2	.600	0	0-0	0	3.98	3.30
1991 Philadelphia	NL	12	12	0	0	61.0	272	56	34	33	4	3	2	3	41	3	42	1	0	1	7	.125	0	0-0	0	4.39	4.87
1993 Cleveland	AL	10	6	0	1	42.1	194	52	26	25	3	1	0	1	20	1	27	2	0	3	4	.429	0	0-0	1	5.57	5.31
1994 Cleveland	AL	14	13	1	0	82.2	368	91	47	42	7	4	2	6	34	1	59	6	1	5	2	.714	0	0-0	0	4.89	4.57
1995 Cleveland	AL	15	2	0	2	34.0	165	37	24	23	4	1	2	2	32	1	25	7	0	0	0	-	0	1-1	0	7.37	6.09
1996 Anaheim	AL	35	20	2	4	130.1	620	150	110	99	14	4	5	13	74	5	82	11	0	5	7	.417	1	0-0	0	5.98	6.84
1999 New York	AL	55	0	0	25	75.0	336	66	39	30	7	3	3	4	40	5	49	8	0	7	2	.778	0	1-4	8	3.73	3.60
2000 New York	AL	63	4	0	18	96.1	428	100	58	54	10	2	6	5	42	1	53	16	0	3	2	.600	0	1-4	4	4.63	5.04
2001 Kansas City	AL	73	0	0	24	80.1	327	71	32	27	8	2	1	2	28	5	61	4	0	1	5	.167	0	0-7	26	3.34	3.02
2002 Kansas City	AL	70	0	0	26	71.1	310	64	32	31	4	1	0	1	37	8	59	8	0	4	7	.364	0	1-3	13	3.51	3.91
11 ML YEARS		362	72	3	100	749.0	3366	751	436	397	64	24	22	39	410	31	505	84	2	33	41	.446	1	4-19	52	4.71	4.77

Marquis Grissom

Bats: R **Throws:** R **Pos:** CF-72; LF-36; PH-25; RF-2; PR-1   **Ht:** 5'11" **Wt:** 188 **Born:** 4/17/67 **Age:** 36

Year Team	Lg	G	AB	H	2B	3B	HR	(Hm	Rd)	TB	R	RBI	RC	TBB	IBB	SO	HBP	SH	SF	SB	CS	SB%	GDP	Avg	OBP	Slg
1989 Montreal	NL	26	74	19	2	0	1	(0	1)	24	16	2	10	12	0	21	0	1	0	1	0	1.00	1	.257	.360	.324
1990 Montreal	NL	98	288	74	14	2	3	(2	1)	101	42	29	37	27	2	40	1	4	1	22	2	.92	3	.257	.320	.351
1991 Montreal	NL	148	558	149	23	9	6	(3	3)	208	73	39	71	34	0	89	1	4	0	76	17	.82	8	.267	.310	.373
1992 Montreal	NL	159	653	180	39	6	14	(8	6)	273	99	66	96	42	6	81	5	3	4	78	13	.86	12	.276	.322	.418
1993 Montreal	NL	157	630	188	27	2	19	(9	10)	276	104	95	103	52	6	76	3	0	8	53	10	.84	9	.298	.351	.438
1994 Montreal	NL	110	475	137	25	4	11	(4	7)	203	96	45	73	41	4	66	1	0	4	36	6	.86	10	.288	.344	.427
1995 Atlanta	NL	139	551	142	23	3	12	(5	7)	207	80	42	68	47	4	61	3	1	4	29	9	.76	8	.258	.317	.376
1996 Atlanta	NL	158	671	207	32	10	23	(11	12)	328	106	74	111	41	6	73	3	4	4	28	11	.72	12	.308	.349	.489
1997 Cleveland	AL	144	558	146	27	6	12	(5	7)	221	74	66	69	43	1	89	6	6	9	22	13	.63	12	.262	.317	.396
1998 Milwaukee	NL	142	542	147	28	1	10	(2	8)	207	57	60	59	24	2	78	2	2	2	13	8	.62	12	.271	.304	.382
1999 Milwaukee	NL	154	603	161	27	1	20	(9	11)	250	92	83	81	49	4	109	0	4	5	24	6	.80	12	.267	.320	.415
2000 Milwaukee	NL	146	595	145	18	2	14	(4	10)	209	67	62	59	39	2	99	0	2	4	20	10	.67	9	.244	.288	.351
2001 Los Angeles	NL	135	448	99	17	1	21	(9	12)	181	56	60	41	16	0	107	2	0	2	7	5	.58	12	.221	.250	.404
2002 Los Angeles	NL	111	343	95	21	4	17	(10	7)	175	57	60	56	22	2	68	2	0	4	5	1	.83	6	.277	.321	.510
14 ML YEARS		1827	6989	1889	323	51	183	(81	102)	2863	1019	783	934	489	39	1057	28	31	51	414	111	.79	126	.270	.318	.410

Buddy Groom

Pitches: L **Bats:** L **Pos:** RP-70   **Ht:** 6'2" **Wt:** 207 **Born:** 7/10/65 **Age:** 37

		HOW MUCH HE PITCHED						WHAT HE GAVE UP											THE RESULTS						
Year Team	Lg	G	GS	CG	GF	IP	BFP	H	R	ER	HR	SH	SF	HB	TBB	IBB	SO	WP	Bk	W	L	Pct	ShO	Sv-Op	Hld	ERC	ERA
1992 Detroit	AL	12	7	0	3	38.2	177	48	28	25	4	3	2	0	22	4	15	0	1	0	5	.000	0	1-2	0	6.20	5.82
1993 Detroit	AL	19	3	0	8	36.2	170	48	25	25	4	2	4	2	13	5	15	2	1	0	2	.000	0	0-0	1	5.72	6.14
1994 Detroit	AL	40	0	0	10	32.0	139	31	14	14	4	0	3	2	13	2	27	0	0	0	1	.000	0	1-1	11	4.25	3.94
1995 Det-Fla		37	4	0	11	55.2	274	81	47	46	8	2	2	2	32	4	35	3	0	2	5	.286	0	1-3	0	8.05	7.44
1996 Oakland	AL	72	1	0	16	77.1	341	85	37	33	8	2	0	3	34	3	57	5	0	5	0	1.000	0	2-4	10	5.00	3.84
1997 Oakland	AL	78	0	0	7	64.2	285	75	38	37	9	0	4	0	24	1	45	3	0	2	2	.500	0	3-5	12	5.18	5.15
1998 Oakland	AL	75	0	0	13	57.1	251	62	30	27	4	1	3	1	20	1	36	1	0	3	1	.750	0	0-6	16	4.12	4.24
1999 Oakland	AL	76	0	0	6	46.0	196	48	29	26	1	2	0	1	18	5	32	2	1	3	2	.600	0	0-3	27	3.71	5.09
2000 Baltimore	AL	70	0	0	14	59.1	260	63	37	32	5	5	5	0	21	2	44	1	0	6	3	.667	0	4-11	27	4.01	4.85
2001 Baltimore	AL	70	0	0	35	66.0	265	64	28	26	4	0	1	1	9	0	54	2	0	1	4	.200	0	11-13	16	2.75	3.55
2002 Baltimore	AL	70	0	0	17	62.0	239	44	11	11	4	0	1	2	12	3	48	0	0	3	2	.600	0	2-4	19	1.73	1.60
1995 Detroit	AL	23	4	0	6	40.2	203	55	35	34	6	2	2	2	26	4	23	3	0	1	3	.250	0	1-3	0	7.54	7.52
1995 Florida	NL	14	0	0	5	15.0	71	26	12	12	2	0	0	0	6	0	12	0	0	1	2	.333	0	0-0	0	9.52	7.20
11 ML YEARS		619	15	0	140	595.2	2597	649	324	302	55	17	25	14	218	30	408	19	3	25	27	.481	0	25-52	139	4.42	4.56

Mark Grudzielanek

Bats: R **Throws:** R **Pos:** 2B-147; PH-2; DH-1   **Ht:** 6'1" **Wt:** 185 **Born:** 6/30/70 **Age:** 33

		BATTING																		BASERUNNING				AVERAGES		
Year Team	Lg	G	AB	H	2B	3B	HR	(Hm	Rd)	TB	R	RBI	RC	TBB	IBB	SO	HBP	SH	SF	SB	CS	SB%	GDP	Avg	OBP	Slg
1995 Montreal	NL	78	269	66	12	2	1	(1	0)	85	27	20	24	14	4	47	7	3	0	8	3	.73	7	.245	.300	.316
1996 Montreal	NL	153	657	201	34	4	6	(5	1)	261	99	49	90	26	3	83	9	1	3	33	7	.83	10	.306	.340	.397
1997 Montreal	NL	156	649	177	54	3	4	(1	3)	249	76	51	75	23	0	76	10	3	3	25	9	.74	13	.273	.307	.384
1998 Mon-LA	NL	156	589	160	21	1	10	(5	5)	213	62	62	64	26	2	73	11	8	7	18	5	.78	18	.272	.311	.362
1999 Los Angeles	NL	123	488	159	23	5	7	(4	3)	213	72	46	76	31	1	65	10	2	3	6	6	.50	13	.326	.376	.436
2000 Los Angeles	NL	148	617	172	35	6	7	(4	3)	240	101	49	80	45	0	81	9	2	3	12	3	.80	16	.279	.335	.389
2001 Los Angeles	NL	133	539	146	21	3	13	(8	5)	212	83	55	66	28	0	83	11	3	5	4	4	.50	9	.271	.317	.393
2002 Los Angeles	NL	150	536	145	23	0	9	(5	4)	195	56	50	52	22	4	89	3	1	4	4	1	.80	17	.271	.301	.364
1998 Montreal	NL	105	396	109	15	1	8	(3	5)	150	51	41	47	21	1	50	9	5	4	11	5	.69	11	.275	.323	.379
1998 Los Angeles	NL	51	193	51	6	0	2	(2	0)	63	11	21	17	5	1	23	2	3	3	7	0	1.00	7	.264	.286	.326
8 ML YEARS		1097	4344	1226	223	24	57	(33	24)	1668	576	382	527	215	14	597	70	23	28	110	38	.74	103	.282	.324	.384

Kevin Gryboski

Pitches: R **Bats:** R **Pos:** RP-57   **Ht:** 6'5" **Wt:** 235 **Born:** 11/15/73 **Age:** 29

		HOW MUCH HE PITCHED						WHAT HE GAVE UP											THE RESULTS						
Year Team	Lg	G	GS	CG	GF	IP	BFP	H	R	ER	HR	SH	SF	HB	TBB	IBB	SO	WP	Bk	W	L	Pct	ShO	Sv-Op	Hld	ERC	ERA
1995 Everett	A-	25	0	0	14	36.0	156	27	18	14	2	3	1	3	18	2	25	3	0	1	5	.167	2	2- -	-	2.95	3.50
1996 Wisconsin	A	32	21	3	5	138.2	630	146	90	73	7	9	6	12	62	2	100	12	0	10	5	.667	1	1- -	-	4.44	4.74
1997 Lancaster	A+	21	15	0	4	67.1	332	113	82	74	13	2	4	1	26	0	41	7	0	0	7	.000	0	0- -	-	9.20	9.89
1998 Lancaster	A+	37	3	0	17	85.0	351	75	35	25	4	1	2	4	31	1	73	3	0	5	5	.500	0	8- -	-	3.18	2.65
1998 Orlando	AA	2	0	0	0	5.0	23	8	5	5	1	0	0	0	1	0	4	2	0	0	0	-	0	0- -	-	7.85	9.00
1999 New Haven	AA	47	0	0	32	62.1	267	67	27	20	5	5	2	3	20	4	41	3	0	2	5	.286	0	10- -	-	4.19	2.89
2000 New Haven	AA	16	0	0	14	18.0	78	15	5	5	0	1	0	1	8	1	20	4	0	1	1	.500	0	9- -	-	2.71	2.50
2000 Tacoma	AAA	31	0	0	18	41.0	181	45	23	22	3	2	0	0	23	4	35	7	0	2	2	.500	0	2- -	-	5.07	4.83
2001 Tacoma	AAA	58	0	0	50	60.0	256	64	29	26	8	5	1	0	19	2	50	2	0	2	5	.286	0	22- -	-	4.33	3.90
2002 Richmond	AAA	7	0	0	6	7.0	29	7	1	1	0	0	0	0	1	0	5	1	0	1	0	1.000	0	3- -	-	2.41	1.29
2002 Macon	A	2	1	0	0	2.0	8	1	0	0	0	0	0	1	0	0	1	0	0	0	0	-	0	0- -	-	3.21	0.00
2002 Atlanta	NL	57	0	0	10	51.2	238	50	20	20	6	1	0	5	37	5	33	2	0	2	1	.667	0	0-2	11	5.58	3.48

Eddie Guardado

Pitches: L **Bats:** R **Pos:** RP-68   **Ht:** 6'0" **Wt:** 194 **Born:** 10/2/70 **Age:** 32

		HOW MUCH HE PITCHED						WHAT HE GAVE UP											THE RESULTS						
Year Team	Lg	G	GS	CG	GF	IP	BFP	H	R	ER	HR	SH	SF	HB	TBB	IBB	SO	WP	Bk	W	L	Pct	ShO	Sv-Op	Hld	ERC	ERA
1993 Minnesota	AL	19	16	0	2	94.2	426	123	68	65	13	1	3	1	36	2	46	0	0	3	8	.273	0	0-0	0	6.18	6.18
1994 Minnesota	AL	4	4	0	0	17.0	81	26	16	16	3	1	2	0	4	0	8	0	0	0	2	.000	0	0-0	0	7.01	8.47
1995 Minnesota	AL	51	5	0	10	91.1	410	99	54	52	13	6	5	0	45	2	71	5	1	4	9	.308	0	2-5	5	5.20	5.12
1996 Minnesota	AL	83	0	0	17	73.2	313	61	45	43	12	6	4	3	33	4	74	3	0	6	5	.545	0	4-7	18	3.81	5.25
1997 Minnesota	AL	69	0	0	20	46.0	201	45	23	20	7	2	1	2	17	2	54	2	0	0	4	.000	0	1-1	13	4.23	3.91

Year Team	Lg	HOW MUCH HE PITCHED						WHAT HE GAVE UP												THE RESULTS						
		G	GS	CG	GF	IP	BFP	H	R	ER	HR	SH	SF	HB	TBB	IBB	SO	WP	Bk	W	L	Pct	ShO	Sv-Op	Hld	ERC	ERA
1998 Minnesota	AL	79	0	0	12	65.2	286	66	34	33	10	3	6	0	28	6	53	2	0	3	1	.750	0	0-4	16	4.42	4.52
1999 Minnesota	AL	63	0	0	13	48.0	197	37	25	25	6	2	1	2	25	4	50	0	0	2	5	.286	0	2-4	15	3.63	4.69
2000 Minnesota	AL	70	0	0	36	61.2	262	55	27	27	14	3	2	1	25	3	52	1	1	7	4	.636	0	9-11	8	4.34	3.94
2001 Minnesota	AL	67	0	0	26	66.2	270	47	27	26	5	5	3	1	23	4	67	4	0	7	1	.875	0	12-14	14	2.13	3.51
2002 Minnesota	AL	68	0	0	62	67.2	270	53	22	22	9	2	2	1	18	2	70	0	0	1	3	.250	0	**45**-51	0	2.66	2.93
10 ML YEARS		573	25	0	198	632.1	2716	612	341	329	92	31	29	11	254	29	545	17	2	33	42	.440	0	75-97	89	4.22	4.68

Vladimir Guerrero

Bats: R **Throws:** R **Pos:** RF-161   **Ht:** 6'3" **Wt:** 210 **Born:** 2/9/76 **Age:** 27

Year Team	Lg	BATTING																		BASERUNNING				AVERAGES		
		G	AB	H	2B	3B	HR	(Hm	Rd)	TB	R	RBI	RC	TBB	IBB	SO	HBP	SH	SF	SB	CS	SB%	GDP	Avg	OBP	Slg
1996 Montreal	NL	9	27	5	0	0	1	(0	1)	8	2	1	1	0	0	3	0	0	0	0	0	-	1	.185	.185	.296
1997 Montreal	NL	90	325	98	22	2	11	(5	6)	157	44	40	51	19	2	39	7	0	3	3	4	.43	11	.302	.350	.483
1998 Montreal	NL	159	623	202	37	7	38	(19	19)	367	108	109	124	42	13	95	7	0	5	11	9	.55	15	.324	.371	.589
1999 Montreal	NL	160	610	193	37	5	42	(23	19)	366	102	131	127	55	14	62	7	0	2	14	7	.67	18	.316	.378	.600
2000 Montreal	NL	154	571	197	28	11	44	(25	19)	379	101	123	137	58	23	74	8	0	4	9	10	.47	15	.345	.410	.664
2001 Montreal	NL	159	599	184	45	4	34	(21	13)	339	107	108	116	60	24	88	9	0	3	37	16	.70	**24**	.307	.377	.566
2002 Montreal	NL	161	614	**206**	37	2	39	(20	19)	**364**	106	111	125	84	**20**	70	6	0	5	40	**20**	.67	20	.336	.417	.593
7 ML YEARS		892	3369	1085	206	31	209	(113	96)	1980	570	623	681	318	108	431	44	0	22	114	66	.63	104	.322	.386	.588

Wilton Guerrero

Bats: B **Throws:** R **Pos:** PH-64; 2B-17; PR-8; SS-7; 3B-5; CF-5; LF-4; RF-3   **Ht:** 6'0" **Wt:** 175 **Born:** 10/24/74 **Age:** 28

Year Team	Lg	BATTING																		BASERUNNING				AVERAGES		
		G	AB	H	2B	3B	HR	(Hm	Rd)	TB	R	RBI	RC	TBB	IBB	SO	HBP	SH	SF	SB	CS	SB%	GDP	Avg	OBP	Slg
1996 Los Angeles	NL	5	2	0	0	0	0	(0	0)	0	1	0	0	0	0	2	0	0	0	0	0	-	0	.000	.000	.000
1997 Los Angeles	NL	111	357	104	10	9	4	(2	2)	144	39	32	41	8	1	52	0	13	2	6	5	.55	7	.291	.305	.403
1998 LA-Mon	NL	116	402	114	14	9	2	(0	2)	152	50	27	47	14	0	63	1	6	3	8	2	.80	4	.284	.307	.378
1999 Montreal	NL	132	315	92	15	7	2	(0	2)	127	42	31	40	13	0	38	2	10	0	7	6	.54	4	.292	.324	.403
2000 Montreal	NL	127	288	77	7	2	2	(2	0)	94	30	23	30	19	0	41	0	6	1	8	1	.89	6	.267	.312	.326
2001 Cincinnati	NL	60	142	48	5	1	1	(1	0)	58	16	8	20	3	0	17	0	2	0	5	2	.71	1	.338	.352	.408
2002 Cin-Mon	NL	103	140	31	2	1	0	(0	0)	35	12	5	8	7	1	32	0	9	0	7	1	.88	2	.221	.259	.250
1998 Los Angeles	NL	64	180	51	4	3	0	(0	0)	61	21	7	18	4	0	33	1	3	2	5	2	.71	3	.283	.299	.339
1998 Montreal	NL	52	222	63	10	6	2	(0	2)	91	29	20	29	10	0	30	0	3	1	3	0	1.00	1	.284	.313	.410
2002 Cincinnati	NL	59	78	19	1	1	0	(0	0)	22	9	4	7	6	0	13	0	5	0	2	1	.67	1	.244	.298	.282
2002 Montreal	NL	44	62	12	1	0	0	(0	0)	13	3	1	1	1	1	19	0	4	0	5	0	1.00	1	.194	.206	.210
7 ML YEARS		654	1646	466	53	29	11	(5	6)	610	190	126	186	64	2	245	3	46	6	41	17	.71	24	.283	.310	.371

Aaron Guiel

Bats: L **Throws:** R **Pos:** RF-60; PH-10; DH-2; CF-1   **Ht:** 5'10" **Wt:** 190 **Born:** 10/5/72 **Age:** 30

Year Team	Lg	BATTING																		BASERUNNING				AVERAGES		
		G	AB	H	2B	3B	HR	(Hm	Rd)	TB	R	RBI	RC	TBB	IBB	SO	HBP	SH	SF	SB	CS	SB%	GDP	Avg	OBP	Slg
1993 Boise	A-	35	104	31	6	4	2	(-	-)	51	24	12	25	26	1	21	4	2	0	3	0	1.00	1	.298	.455	.490
1994 Cedar Rpds	A	127	454	122	30	1	18	(-	-)	208	84	82	79	64	2	93	6	5	3	21	7	.75	7	.269	.364	.458
1995 Lk Elsinore	A+	113	409	110	25	7	7	(-	-)	170	73	58	68	69	0	96	7	4	4	7	6	.54	7	.269	.380	.416
1996 Midland	AA	129	439	118	29	7	10	(-	-)	191	72	48	71	56	0	71	10	2	1	11	7	.61	6	.269	.364	.435
1997 Midland	AA	116	419	138	37	7	22	(-	-)	255	91	85	102	59	3	94	18	2	3	14	10	.58	9	.329	.431	.609
1997 Mobile	AA	8	26	10	2	0	1	(-	-)	15	9	9	8	5	0	4	1	0	0	1	0	1.00	6	.385	.500	.577
1998 Las Vegas	AAA	60	183	57	15	4	5	(-	-)	95	33	31	39	28	2	51	4	1	2	5	1	.83	4	.311	.410	.519
1998 Padres	R	8	16	8	3	1	1	(-	-)	16	8	6	9	5	1	5	3	0	0	1	1	.50	0	.500	.667	1.000
1999 Las Vegas	AAA	84	257	63	25	2	12	(-	-)	128	46	39	46	44	3	86	5	0	3	5	4	.56	6	.245	.362	.498
2000 Omaha	AAA	73	258	74	15	2	13	(- | -)	132	47	40	52	35	0	54	6	0	1.00	0	6	0	1.00	8	.287	.389	.512
2001 Omaha	AAA	121	442	118	27	3	21	(-	-)	214	78	73	75	51	3	92	13	1	6	6	4	.60	12	.267	.355	.484
2002 Omaha	AAA	61	215	76	11	1	9	(-	-)	116	44	50	51	29	3	34	8	0	3	8	1	.89	4	.353	.443	.540
2002 Kansas City	AL	70	240	56	13	0	4	(4	0)	81	30	38	33	19	1	61	4	2	4	1	5	.17	3	.233	.296	.338

Carlos Guillen

Bats: B **Throws:** R **Pos:** SS-130; DH-3; PH-2; PR-1   **Ht:** 6'1" **Wt:** 202 **Born:** 9/30/75 **Age:** 27

Year Team	Lg	BATTING																		BASERUNNING				AVERAGES		
		G	AB	H	2B	3B	HR	(Hm	Rd)	TB	R	RBI	RC	TBB	IBB	SO	HBP	SH	SF	SB	CS	SB%	GDP	Avg	OBP	Slg
1998 Seattle	AL	10	39	13	1	1	0	(0	0)	16	9	5	7	3	0	9	0	0	0	2	0	1.00	0	.333	.381	.410
1999 Seattle	AL	5	19	3	0	0	1	(0	1)	6	2	3	1	1	0	6	0	1	0	0	0	-	0	.158	.200	.316
2000 Seattle	AL	90	288	74	15	2	7	(3	4)	114	45	42	36	28	0	53	2	7	3	1	3	.25	6	.257	.324	.396
2001 Seattle	AL	140	456	118	21	4	5	(2	3)	162	72	53	56	53	0	89	1	7	6	4	1	.80	9	.259	.333	.355
2002 Seattle	AL	134	475	124	24	6	9	(4	5)	187	73	56	57	46	4	91	1	3	3	4	5	.44	8	.261	.326	.394
5 ML YEARS		379	1277	332	61	13	22	(10	12)	485	201	159	157	131	4	248	4	18	12	11	9	.55	24	.260	.328	.380

Jose Guillen

Bats: R **Throws:** R **Pos:** RF-60; PH-22; LF-6; PR-3; CF-2; DH-1   **Ht:** 5'11" **Wt:** 195 **Born:** 5/17/76 **Age:** 27

Year Team	Lg	BATTING																		BASERUNNING				AVERAGES		
		G	AB	H	2B	3B	HR	(Hm	Rd)	TB	R	RBI	RC	TBB	IBB	SO	HBP	SH	SF	SB	CS	SB%	GDP	Avg	OBP	Slg
2002 Co Springs*	AAA	5	17	7	3	0	0	(-	-)	10	2	5	4	1	0	2	1	0	0	0	1	.00	1	.412	.474	.588
2002 Louisville*	AAA	8	29	9	4	0	2	(-	-)	19	4	8	5	0	0	5	0	0	0	0	0	-	1	.310	.310	.655
1997 Pittsburgh	NL	143	498	133	20	5	14	(5	9)	205	58	70	56	17	0	88	8	0	3	1	2	.33	16	.267	.300	.412
1998 Pittsburgh	NL	153	573	153	38	2	14	(10	4)	237	60	84	68	21	0	100	6	1	4	3	5	.38	7	.267	.298	.414
1999 Pit-TB		87	288	73	16	0	3	(1	2)	98	42	31	28	20	2	57	7	1	2	1	0	1.00	16	.253	.315	.340
2000 Tampa Bay	AL	105	316	80	16	5	10	(5	5)	136	40	41	43	18	1	65	13	2	0	1	1	.75	6	.253	.320	.430
2001 Tampa Bay	AL	41	135	37	5	0	3	(0	3)	51	14	11	15	6	2	26	3	0	1	2	3	.40	2	.274	.317	.378
2002 Ari-Cin	NL	85	240	57	7	0	8	(5	3)	88	25	31	16	14	1	43	3	1	0	4	5	.44	13	.238	.287	.367

Year Team	Lg	G	AB	H	2B	3B	HR	(Hm	Rd)	TB	R	RBI	RC	TBB	IBB	SO	HBP	SH	SF	SB	CS	SB%	GDP	Avg	OBP	Slg
1999 Pittsburgh	NL	40	120	32	6	0	1	(0	1)	41	18	18	12	10	1	21	0	1	1	1	0	1.00	7	.267	.321	.342
1999 Tampa Bay	AL	47	168	41	10	0	2	(1	1)	57	24	13	16	10	1	36	7	0	1	0	0	-	9	.244	.312	.339
2002 Arizona	NL	54	131	30	4	0	4	(3	1)	46	13	15	7	7	1	25	2	0	1	3	4	.43	7	.229	.277	.351
2002 Cincinnati	NL	31	109	27	3	0	4	(2	2)	42	12	16	9	7	0	18	1	1	0	1	1	.50	6	.248	.299	.385
6 ML YEARS		614	2050	533	102	12	52	(26	26)	815	239	268	226	96	6	379	40	5	11	14	16	.47	60	.260	.305	.398

Mark Guthrie

Pitches: L **Bats:** R **Pos:** RP-68   **Ht:** 6'4" **Wt:** 215 **Born:** 9/22/65 **Age:** 37

Year Team	Lg	G	GS	CG	GF	IP	BFP	H	R	ER	HR	SH	SF	HB	TBB	IBB	SO	WP	Bk	W	L	Pct	ShO	Sv-Op	Hld	ERC	ERA
1989 Minnesota	AL	13	8	0	2	57.1	254	66	32	29	7	1	5	1	21	1	38	1	0	2	4	.333	0	0-0	0	5.02	4.55
1990 Minnesota	AL	24	21	3	0	144.2	603	154	65	61	8	6	0	1	39	3	101	9	0	7	9	.438	1	0-0	0	3.69	3.79
1991 Minnesota	AL	41	12	0	13	98.0	432	116	52	47	11	4	3	1	41	2	72	7	0	7	5	.583	0	2-2	5	5.45	4.32
1992 Minnesota	AL	54	0	0	15	75.0	303	59	27	24	7	4	2	0	23	7	76	2	0	2	3	.400	0	5-7	19	2.43	2.88
1993 Minnesota	AL	22	0	0	2	21.0	94	20	11	11	2	1	2	0	16	2	15	1	3	2	1	.667	0	0-1	8	5.20	4.71
1994 Minnesota	AL	50	2	0	13	51.1	234	65	43	35	8	2	6	2	18	2	38	7	0	4	2	.667	0	1-3	12	5.95	6.14
1995 Min-LA		60	0	0	14	62.0	272	66	33	29	6	4	0	2	25	5	67	5	1	5	5	.500	0	0-2	15	4.44	4.21
1996 Los Angeles	NL	66	0	0	16	73.0	302	65	21	18	3	4	4	1	22	2	56	1	0	2	3	.400	0	1-3	12	2.73	2.22
1997 Los Angeles	NL	62	0	0	18	69.1	305	71	44	41	12	10	3	0	30	6	42	2	1	1	4	.200	0	1-4	13	4.69	5.32
1998 Los Angeles	NL	53	0	0	11	54.0	234	56	26	21	3	5	0	2	24	1	45	2	0	2	1	.667	0	0-1	8	4.20	3.50
1999 Bos-ChC		57	0	0	15	58.2	254	57	38	35	10	2	3	2	24	5	45	3	0	1	3	.250	0	2-2	14	4.45	5.37
2000 ChC-TB-Tor		76	0	0	15	71.1	315	70	41	37	8	4	4	2	37	9	63	13	0	3	6	.333	0	0-4	10	4.44	4.67
2001 Oakland	AL	54	0	0	11	52.1	225	49	29	26	7	1	3	4	20	1	52	3	0	6	2	.750	0	1-3	12	4.17	4.47
2002 New York	NL	68	0	0	13	48.0	190	35	13	13	3	0	1	1	19	3	44	4	0	5	3	.625	0	1-2	17	2.48	2.44
1995 Minnesota	AL	36	0	0	7	42.1	181	47	22	21	5	2	0	1	16	3	48	3	1	5	3	.625	0	0-2	10	4.89	4.46
1995 Los Angeles	NL	24	0	0	7	19.2	91	19	11	8	1	2	0	1	9	2	19	2	0	0	2	.000	0	0-0	5	3.54	3.66
1999 Boston	AL	46	0	0	15	46.1	207	50	32	30	9	0	3	2	20	3	36	2	0	1	1	.500	0	2-2	12	5.42	5.83
1999 Chicago	NL	11	0	0	0	12.1	47	7	6	5	1	2	0	0	4	2	9	1	0	0	2	.000	0	0-0	2	1.46	3.65
2000 Chicago	NL	19	0	0	3	18.2	82	17	11	10	1	2	3	1	10	4	17	4	0	2	3	.400	0	0-0	3	3.61	4.82
2000 Tampa Bay	AL	34	0	0	7	32.0	145	33	18	16	4	1	0	0	18	5	26	7	0	1	1	.500	0	0-3	4	4.77	4.50
2000 Toronto	AL	23	0	0	5	20.2	88	20	12	11	3	1	1	1	9	0	20	2	0	0	2	.000	0	0-1	3	4.68	4.79
14 ML YEARS		700	43	3	158	936.0	4024	949	475	427	95	48	36	19	359	49	754	60	5	49	51	.490	1	14-34	145	4.12	4.11

Ricky Gutierrez

Bats: R **Throws:** R **Pos:** 2B-93; DH-1; PH-1   **Ht:** 6'1" **Wt:** 190 **Born:** 5/23/70 **Age:** 33

Year Team	Lg	G	AB	H	2B	3B	HR	(Hm	Rd)	TB	R	RBI	RC	TBB	IBB	SO	HBP	SH	SF	SB	CS	SB%	GDP	Avg	OBP	Slg
1993 San Diego	NL	133	438	110	10	5	5	(5	0)	145	76	26	50	50	2	97	5	1	1	4	3	.57	7	.251	.334	.331
1994 San Diego	NL	90	275	66	11	2	1	(1	0)	84	27	28	25	32	1	54	2	2	3	2	6	.25	8	.240	.321	.305
1995 Houston	NL	52	156	43	6	0	0	(0	0)	49	22	12	16	10	3	33	1	1	1	5	0	1.00	4	.276	.321	.314
1996 Houston	NL	89	218	62	8	1	1	(1	0)	75	28	15	29	23	3	42	3	4	1	6	1	.86	4	.284	.359	.344
1997 Houston	NL	102	303	79	14	4	3	(0	3)	110	33	34	30	21	2	50	3	0	0	5	2	.71	17	.261	.315	.363
1998 Houston	NL	141	491	128	24	3	2	(1	1)	164	55	46	54	54	5	84	6	3	7	13	7	.65	20	.261	.337	.334
1999 Houston	NL	85	268	70	7	5	1	(1	0)	90	33	25	31	37	4	45	2	3	1	2	5	.29	9	.261	.354	.336
2000 Chicago	NL	125	449	124	19	2	11	(7	4)	180	73	56	72	66	0	58	7	16	4	8	2	.80	10	.276	.375	.401
2001 Chicago	NL	147	528	153	23	3	10	(7	3)	212	76	66	74	40	0	56	10	17	11	4	3	.57	13	.290	.345	.402
2002 Cleveland	AL	94	353	97	13	0	4	(2	2)	122	38	38	39	20	0	48	7	3	1	0	1	.00	14	.275	.325	.346
10 ML YEARS		1058	3479	932	135	25	38	(25	13)	1231	461	346	420	353	20	567	46	50	30	49	30	.62	106	.268	.341	.354

Cristian Guzman

Bats: B **Throws:** R **Pos:** SS-146; PH-4; PR-2   **Ht:** 6'0" **Wt:** 195 **Born:** 3/21/78 **Age:** 25

Year Team	Lg	G	AB	H	2B	3B	HR	(Hm	Rd)	TB	R	RBI	RC	TBB	IBB	SO	HBP	SH	SF	SB	CS	SB%	GDP	Avg	OBP	Slg
1999 Minnesota	AL	131	420	95	12	3	1	(1	0)	116	47	26	29	22	0	90	3	7	4	9	7	.56	5	.226	.267	.276
2000 Minnesota	AL	156	631	156	25	20	3	(3	5)	245	89	54	76	46	1	101	2	4	3	28	10	.74	5	.247	.299	.388
2001 Minnesota	AL	118	493	149	28	14	10	(7	3)	235	80	51	79	21	0	78	5	8	0	25	8	.76	6	.302	.337	.477
2002 Minnesota	AL	148	623	170	31	6	9	(6	3)	240	80	59	61	17	2	79	2	8	6	12	13	.48	12	.273	.292	.385
4 ML YEARS		553	2167	570	96	43	28	(17	11)	836	296	190	245	106	3	348	12	30	14	74	38	.66	28	.263	.299	.386

Luther Hackman

Pitches: R **Bats:** R **Pos:** RP-37; SP-6   **Ht:** 6'4" **Wt:** 195 **Born:** 10/10/74 **Age:** 28

Year Team	Lg	G	GS	CG	GF	IP	BFP	H	R	ER	HR	SH	SF	HB	TBB	IBB	SO	WP	Bk	W	L	Pct	ShO	Sv-Op	Hld	ERC	ERA
1999 Colorado	NL	5	3	0	0	16.0	84	26	19	19	5	2	0	0	12	0	10	0	0	1	2	.333	0	0-0	0	11.65	10.69
2000 St Louis	NL	1	0	0	0	2.2	17	4	3	3	0	2	0	1	4	1	0	0	0	0	0		0	0-0	0	11.43	10.13
2001 St Louis	NL	35	0	0	8	35.2	149	28	18	17	7	1	2	2	14	0	24	1	1	1	2	.333	0	1-3	5	3.71	4.29
2002 St Louis	NL	43	6	0	9	81.0	366	90	42	37	7	3	6	4	39	3	46	7	1	5	4	.556	0	0-1	1	5.09	4.11
4 ML YEARS		84	9	0	17	135.1	616	148	82	76	19	8	6	7	69	4	80	8	2	7	8	.467	0	1-4	6	5.54	5.05

Travis Hafner

Bats: L **Throws:** R **Pos:** DH-13; PH-7; 1B-3   **Ht:** 6'3" **Wt:** 240 **Born:** 6/3/77 **Age:** 26

Year Team	Lg	G	AB	H	2B	3B	HR	(Hm	Rd)	TB	R	RBI	RC	TBB	IBB	SO	HBP	SH	SF	SB	CS	SB%	GDP	Avg	OBP	Slg
1997 Rangers	R	55	189	54	14	0	5	(-	-)	83	38	24	32	24	1	45	3	0	0	7	2	.78	3	.286	.375	.439
1998 Savannah	A	123	405	96	15	4	16	(-	-)	167	62	84	61	68	2	139	6	0	5	7	3	.70	8	.237	.351	.412
1999 Savannah	A	134	480	140	30	4	28	(-	-)	262	94	111	97	67	6	151	11	0	5	5	4	.56	11	.292	.387	.546
2000 Charlotte	A+	122	436	151	34	4	22	(-	-)	253	90	109	107	67	2	86	18	0	7	5	4	.00	7	.346	.447	.580

Year Team	Lg	G	AB	H	2B	3B	HR	(Hm Rd)	TB	R	RBI	RC	TBB	IBB	SO	HBP	SH	SF	SB	CS	SB%	GDP	Avg	OBP	Slg
2001 Tulsa	AA	88	323	91	25	0	20	(- -)	176	59	74	67	59	5	82	4	0	3	3	1	.75	10	.282	.396	.545
2002 Oklahoma	AAA	110	401	137	22	1	21	(- -)	224	79	77	100	79	4	76	12	0	0	2	1	.67	9	.342	.463	.559
2002 Texas	AL	23	62	15	4	1	1	(0 1)	24	6	6	7	8	1	15	0	0	0	0	1	.00	0	.242	.329	.387

Jerry Hairston Jr.

Bats: R **Throws:** R **Pos:** 2B-119; PH-2; PR-2   **Ht:** 5'10" **Wt:** 175 **Born:** 5/29/76 **Age:** 27

								BATTING											BASERUNNING				AVERAGES		
Year Team	Lg	G	AB	H	2B	3B	HR	(Hm Rd)	TB	R	RBI	RC	TBB	IBB	SO	HBP	SH	SF	SB	CS	SB%	GDP	Avg	OBP	Slg
1998 Baltimore	AL	6	7	0	0	0	0	(0 0)	0	2	0	0	0	0	1	0	0	0	0	0	-	0	.000	.000	.000
1999 Baltimore	AL	50	175	47	12	1	4	(1 3)	73	26	17	24	11	0	24	3	4	0	9	4	.69	2	.269	.323	.417
2000 Baltimore	AL	49	180	46	5	0	5	(2 3)	66	27	19	22	21	0	22	6	5	0	8	5	.62	8	.256	.353	.367
2001 Baltimore	AL	159	532	124	25	5	8	(5 3)	183	63	47	57	44	0	73	13	9	4	29	11	.73	12	.233	.305	.344
2002 Baltimore	AL	122	426	114	25	3	5	(2 3)	160	55	32	54	34	0	55	7	8	4	21	6	.78	5	.268	.329	.376
5 ML YEARS		386	1320	331	67	9	22	(10 12)	482	173	115	157	110	0	175	29	26	8	67	26	.72	27	.251	.320	.365

John Halama

Pitches: L **Bats:** L **Pos:** RP-21; SP-10   **Ht:** 6'5" **Wt:** 210 **Born:** 2/22/72 **Age:** 31

			HOW MUCH HE PITCHED						WHAT HE GAVE UP										THE RESULTS						
Year Team	Lg	G	GS	CG	GF	IP	BFP	H	R	ER	HR	SH	SF	HB	TBB	IBB	SO	WP	Bk	W	L	Pct	ShO	Sv-Op Hld	ERC	ERA
2002 Tacoma*	AAA	2	2	0	0	14.2	62	19	11	10	0	1	0	1	1	1	9	1	0	0	1	.000	0	0- -	3.97	6.14
1998 Houston	NL	6	6	0	0	32.1	147	37	21	21	0	3	4	0	13	0	21	2	1	1	1	.500	0	0-0	4.34	5.85
1999 Seattle	AL	38	24	1	7	179.0	763	193	88	84	20	5	9	7	56	3	105	4	0	11	10	.524	1	0-0 1	4.47	4.22
2000 Seattle	AL	30	30	1	0	166.2	736	206	108	94	19	4	6	2	56	0	87	4	1	14	9	.609	1	0-0 0	5.42	5.08
2001 Seattle	AL	31	17	0	6	110.1	485	132	66	58	18	3	4	6	26	0	50	2	0	10	7	.588	0	0-0 1	5.21	4.73
2002 Seattle	AL	31	10	0	12	101.0	438	112	45	40	9	3	2	1	33	5	70	2	1	6	5	.545	0	0-0 0	4.29	3.56
5 ML YEARS		136	87	2	25	589.1	2569	680	331	297	66	18	25	18	184	8	333	14	3	42	32	.568	2	0-0 2	4.84	4.54

Bill Hall

Bats: R **Throws:** R **Pos:** SS-13; PR-5; 3B-2; PH-1   **Ht:** 6'0" **Wt:** 175 **Born:** 12/28/79 **Age:** 23

								BATTING											BASERUNNING				AVERAGES		
Year Team	Lg	G	AB	H	2B	3B	HR	(Hm Rd)	TB	R	RBI	RC	TBB	IBB	SO	HBP	SH	SF	SB	CS	SB%	GDP	Avg	OBP	Slg
1998 Helena	R+	29	85	15	3	0	0	(- -)	18	11	5	3	9	0	27	1	1	0	5	5	.50	2	.176	.263	.212
1999 Ogden	R+	69	280	81	15	2	6	(- -)	118	41	31	38	15	1	61	2	2	1	19	8	.70	6	.289	.329	.421
2000 Beloit	A	130	470	123	30	6	3	(- -)	174	57	41	45	18	0	127	1	12	5	10	11	.48	12	.262	.287	.370
2001 High Desert	A+	89	346	105	21	6	15	(- -)	183	61	51	62	22	0	78	3	4	3	18	9	.67	3	.303	.348	.529
2001 Huntsville	AA	41	160	41	8	1	3	(- -)	60	14	14	15	5	0	46	0	3	0	5	3	.63	5	.256	.279	.375
2002 Indianapolis	AAA	134	465	106	20	1	4	(- -)	140	35	31	34	25	0	105	4	4	2	17	10	.63	12	.228	.272	.301
2002 Milwaukee	NL	19	36	7	1	1	1	(0 1)	13	3	5	3	3	0	13	0	0	0	0	1	.00	1	.194	.256	.361

Toby Hall

Bats: R **Throws:** R **Pos:** C-83; PH-2   **Ht:** 6'3" **Wt:** 240 **Born:** 10/21/75 **Age:** 27

								BATTING											BASERUNNING				AVERAGES		
Year Team	Lg	G	AB	H	2B	3B	HR	(Hm Rd)	TB	R	RBI	RC	TBB	IBB	SO	HBP	SH	SF	SB	CS	SB%	GDP	Avg	OBP	Slg
2002 Durham*	AAA	22	92	32	4	0	2	(- -)	42	13	20	16	3	0	10	4	0	3	0	0	-	3	.348	.382	.457
2000 Tampa Bay	AL	4	12	2	0	0	1	(0 1)	5	1	1	1	1	0	0	0	0	0	0	0	-	0	.167	.231	.417
2001 Tampa Bay	AL	49	188	56	16	0	4	(1 3)	84	28	30	25	4	0	16	3	0	1	2	2	.50	2	.298	.321	.447
2002 Tampa Bay	AL	85	330	85	19	1	6	(2 4)	124	37	42	39	17	3	27	1	2	3	0	1	.00	14	.258	.293	.376
3 ML YEARS		138	530	143	35	1	11	(3 8)	213	66	73	65	22	3	43	4	2	4	2	3	.40	19	.270	.302	.402

Roy Halladay

Pitches: R **Bats:** R **Pos:** SP-34   **Ht:** 6'6" **Wt:** 230 **Born:** 5/14/77 **Age:** 26

			HOW MUCH HE PITCHED						WHAT HE GAVE UP										THE RESULTS						
Year Team	Lg	G	GS	CG	GF	IP	BFP	H	R	ER	HR	SH	SF	HB	TBB	IBB	SO	WP	Bk	W	L	Pct	ShO	Sv-Op Hld	ERC	ERA
1998 Toronto	AL	2	2	1	0	14.0	53	9	4	3	2	0	0	0	2	0	13	0	0	1	0	1.000	0	0-0 0	1.61	1.93
1999 Toronto	AL	36	18	1	2	149.1	668	156	76	65	19	3	4	4	79	1	82	6	0	8	7	.533	1	1-1 2	5.19	3.92
2000 Toronto	AL	19	13	0	4	67.2	349	107	87	80	14	2	3	2	42	0	44	6	1	4	7	.364	0	0-0 0	9.70	10.64
2001 Toronto	AL	17	16	1	0	105.1	432	97	41	37	3	3	1	1	25	0	96	4	1	5	3	.625	1	0-0 0	2.61	3.16
2002 Toronto	AL	34	34	2	0	239.1	993	223	93	78	10	9	2	7	62	6	168	4	1	19	7	.731	1	0-0 0	2.85	2.93
5 ML YEARS		108	83	5	6	575.2	2495	592	301	263	48	17	10	14	210	7	403	20	3	37	24	.607	3	1-1 2	4.04	4.11

Shane Halter

Bats: R **Throws:** R **Pos:** SS-81; 3B-30; LF-8; 2B-4; PR-3; DH-2; PH-2; 1B-1   **Ht:** 6'0" **Wt:** 180 **Born:** 11/8/69 **Age:** 33

								BATTING											BASERUNNING				AVERAGES		
Year Team	Lg	G	AB	H	2B	3B	HR	(Hm Rd)	TB	R	RBI	RC	TBB	IBB	SO	HBP	SH	SF	SB	CS	SB%	GDP	Avg	OBP	Slg
1997 Kansas City	AL	74	123	34	5	1	2	(1 1)	47	16	10	16	10	0	28	2	4	0	4	3	.57	1	.276	.341	.382
1998 Kansas City	AL	86	204	45	12	0	2	(0 2)	63	17	13	15	12	0	38	1	7	2	2	5	.29	3	.221	.265	.309
2000 Detroit	AL	105	238	62	12	2	3	(0 3)	87	26	27	26	14	0	49	1	10	2	5	2	.71	5	.261	.302	.366
2001 Detroit	AL	136	450	128	32	7	12	(4 8)	210	53	65	69	37	2	100	7	7	6	3	3	.50	14	.284	.344	.467
2002 Detroit	AL	122	410	98	22	6	10	(4 6)	162	46	39	45	39	1	92	4	1	4	0	4	.00	12	.239	.309	.395
5 ML YEARS		523	1425	367	83	16	29	(9 20)	569	158	154	171	112	3	307	15	29	14	14	17	.45	35	.258	.315	.399

Joey Hamilton

Pitches: R **Bats:** R **Pos:** RP-22; SP-17   **Ht:** 6'4" **Wt:** 240 **Born:** 9/9/70 **Age:** 32

	HOW MUCH HE PITCHED						WHAT HE GAVE UP												THE RESULTS						
Year Team	Lg	G	GS	CG	GF	IP	BFP	H	R	ER	HR	SH	SF	HB	TBB	IBB	SO	WP	Bk	W	L	Pct	ShO	Sv-Op	Hld	ERC	ERA
2002 Louisville*	AAA	3	3	0	0	14.0	57	10	4	4	2	0	0	6	6	0	10	0	0	1	0	1.000	0	0- -	-	2.94	2.57
1994 San Diego	NL	16	16	1	0	108.2	447	98	40	36	7	4	2	6	29	3	61	6	0	9	6	.600	1	0-0	0	3.00	2.98
1995 San Diego	NL	31	30	2	1	204.1	850	189	89	70	17	12	4	11	56	5	123	2	0	6	9	.400	2	0-0	0	3.25	3.08
1996 San Diego	NL	34	33	3	0	211.2	908	206	100	98	19	6	5	9	83	3	184	14	1	15	9	.625	1	0-0	1	3.99	4.17
1997 San Diego	NL	31	29	1	1	192.2	831	199	100	91	22	8	8	12	69	2	124	7	0	12	7	.632	0	0-0	0	4.48	4.25
1998 San Diego	NL	34	34	0	0	217.1	958	220	113	103	15	13	6	8	106	10	147	4	0	13	13	.500	0	0-0	0	4.36	4.27
1999 Toronto	AL	22	18	0	1	98.0	440	118	73	71	13	0	2	3	39	0	56	4	1	7	8	.467	0	0-0	1	5.69	6.52
2000 Toronto	AL	6	6	0	0	33.0	135	28	13	13	3	0	1	2	12	0	15	0	0	2	1	.667	0	0-0	0	3.38	3.55
2001 Tor-Cin		26	26	0	0	139.2	633	193	100	92	20	6	8	4	44	1	92	5	0	6	10	.375	0	0-0	0	6.57	5.93
2002 Cincinnati	NL	39	17	0	9	124.2	554	136	78	73	11	7	3	6	50	2	85	5	0	4	10	.286	0	1-2	4	4.67	5.27
2001 Toronto	AL	22	22	0	0	122.1	554	170	88	80	17	4	8	3	38	1	82	5	0	5	8	.385	0	0-0	0	6.55	5.89
2001 Cincinnati	NL	4	4	0	0	17.1	79	23	12	12	3	2	0	1	6	0	10	0	0	1	2	.333	0	0-0	0	6.72	6.23
9 ML YEARS		239	209	7	12	1330.0	5756	1387	706	647	127	56	39	61	488	26	887	47	2	74	73	.503	4	1-2	6	4.34	4.38

Robby Hammock

Bats: R **Throws:** R **Pos:** C   **Ht:** 5'10" **Wt:** 187 **Born:** 5/13/77 **Age:** 26

	BATTING																BASERUNNING				AVERAGES		
Year Team	Lg	G	AB	H	2B	3B	HR	(Hm | Rd)	TB	R	RBI	RC	TBB	IBB	SO	HBP	SH	SF	SB	CS	SB%	GDP	Avg	OBP	Slg
1998 Lethbridge	R+	62	227	65	14	2	10	(- | -)	113	46	56	41	28	1	34	2	0	2	5	4	.56	3	.286	.367	.498
1999 High Desert	A+	114	379	26	20	7	9	(- | -)	87	80	72	6	47	2	63	2	0	6	3	6	.33	8	.069	.173	.230
2000 High Desert	A+	40	136	48	15	1	3	(- | -)	74	25	23	32	27	1	24	1	0	3	3	3	.50	5	.353	.455	.544
2000 El Paso	AA	45	140	35	5	1	1	(- | -)	45	22	15	14	11	1	25	1	0	2	1	2	.33	1	.250	.305	.321
2001 El Paso	AA	26	74	12	5	0	0	(- | -)	17	6	4	3	7	0	18	0	1	0	2	2	.50	1	.162	.235	.230
2001 South Bend	A	34	125	31	3	2	2	(- | -)	44	16	14	13	14	0	21	0	1	0	5	6	.45	2	.248	.324	.352
2001 Lancaster	A+	45	190	59	11	3	4	(- | -)	88	33	36	32	16	1	42	7	0	4	3	2	.60	6	.311	.378	.463
2002 El Paso	AA	122	441	128	28	4	11	(- | -)	197	68	73	69	43	0	68	8	1	8	5	4	.56	14	.290	.358	.447

Chris Hammond

Pitches: L **Bats:** L **Pos:** RP-63   **Ht:** 6'1" **Wt:** 195 **Born:** 1/21/66 **Age:** 37

	HOW MUCH HE PITCHED						WHAT HE GAVE UP												THE RESULTS						
Year Team	Lg	G	GS	CG	GF	IP	BFP	H	R	ER	HR	SH	SF	HB	TBB	IBB	SO	WP	Bk	W	L	Pct	ShO	Sv-Op	Hld	ERC	ERA
1990 Cincinnati	NL	3	3	0	0	11.1	56	13	9	8	2	1	0	0	12	1	4	1	3	0	2	.000	0	0-0	0	8.50	6.35
1991 Cincinnati	NL	20	18	0	0	99.2	425	92	51	45	4	6	1	2	48	3	50	3	0	7	7	.500	0	0-0	0	3.63	4.06
1992 Cincinnati	NL	28	26	0	1	147.1	627	149	75	69	13	5	3	3	55	6	79	6	0	7	10	.412	0	0-0	0	4.02	4.21
1993 Florida	NL	32	32	1	0	191.0	826	207	106	99	18	10	2	1	66	2	108	10	5	11	12	.478	1	0-0	0	4.31	4.66
1994 Florida	NL	13	13	1	0	73.1	312	79	30	25	5	5	2	1	23	1	40	3	0	4	4	.500	1	0-0	0	4.03	3.07
1995 Florida	NL	25	24	3	0	161.0	683	157	73	68	17	7	7	9	47	2	126	3	1	9	6	.600	2	0-0	0	3.75	3.80
1996 Florida	NL	38	9	0	6	81.0	368	104	65	59	14	3	4	4	27	3	50	1	0	5	8	.385	0	0-0	5	6.21	6.56
1997 Boston	AL	29	8	0	6	65.1	293	81	45	43	5	0	3	2	27	4	48	2	0	3	4	.429	0	1-2	4	5.47	5.92
1998 Florida	NL	3	3	0	0	13.2	67	20	11	10	3	2	0	1	8	0	8	0	0	0	2	.000	0	0-0	0	9.33	6.59
2002 Atlanta	NL	63	0	0	6	76.0	311	53	15	8	1	5	2	1	31	9	63	1	0	7	2	.778	0	0-2	17	1.85	0.95
10 ML YEARS		254	136	5	18	919.2	3968	955	480	434	82	44	24	24	344	31	576	30	9	53	57	.482	3	1-4	26	4.19	4.25

Jeffrey Hammonds

Bats: R **Throws:** R **Pos:** CF-78; RF-55; LF-2; PH-2; PR-1   **Ht:** 6'0" **Wt:** 200 **Born:** 3/5/71 **Age:** 32

	BATTING																BASERUNNING				AVERAGES		
Year Team	Lg	G	AB	H	2B	3B	HR	(Hm | Rd)	TB	R	RBI	RC	TBB	IBB	SO	HBP	SH	SF	SB	CS	SB%	GDP	Avg	OBP	Slg
1993 Baltimore	AL	33	105	32	8	0	3	(2 | 1)	49	10	19	15	2	1	16	0	1	2	4	0	1.00	3	.305	.312	.467
1994 Baltimore	AL	68	250	74	18	2	8	(6 | 2)	120	45	31	42	17	1	39	2	0	5	5	0	1.00	3	.296	.339	.480
1995 Baltimore	AL	57	178	43	9	1	4	(2 | 2)	66	18	23	18	9	0	30	1	1	2	4	2	.67	3	.242	.279	.371
1996 Baltimore	AL	71	248	56	10	1	9	(3 | 6)	95	38	27	27	23	1	53	4	6	1	3	3	.50	7	.226	.301	.383
1997 Baltimore	AL	118	397	105	19	3	21	(9 | 12)	193	71	55	64	32	1	73	3	0	2	15	1	.94	6	.264	.323	.486
1998 Bal-Cin		89	257	72	16	2	6	(1 | 5)	110	50	39	45	39	1	56	3	3	4	8	3	.73	2	.280	.376	.428
1999 Cincinnati	NL	123	262	73	13	0	17	(5 | 12)	137	43	41	45	27	0	64	1	2	1	3	6	.33	4	.279	.347	.523
2000 Colorado	NL	122	454	152	24	2	20	(14 | 6)	240	94	106	90	44	4	83	5	2	6	14	7	.67	11	.335	.395	.529
2001 Milwaukee	NL	49	174	43	11	1	6	(3 | 3)	74	20	21	23	14	1	42	4	0	2	5	3	.63	2	.247	.314	.425
2002 Milwaukee	NL	128	448	115	26	5	9	(2 | 7)	178	47	41	53	52	0	86	2	1	7	4	5	.44	13	.257	.332	.397
1998 Baltimore	AL	63	171	46	12	1	6	(1 | 5)	78	36	28	31	26	1	38	3	0	3	7	2	.78	2	.269	.369	.456
1998 Cincinnati	NL	26	86	26	4	1	0	(0 | 0)	32	14	11	14	13	0	18	0	3	1	1	1	.50	0	.302	.390	.372
10 ML YEARS		858	2773	765	154	17	103	(47 | 56)	1262	436	403	422	259	10	542	25	16	32	65	30	.68	54	.276	.340	.455

Mike Hampton

Pitches: L **Bats:** R **Pos:** SP-30   **Ht:** 5'10" **Wt:** 180 **Born:** 9/9/72 **Age:** 30

	HOW MUCH HE PITCHED						WHAT HE GAVE UP												THE RESULTS						
Year Team	Lg	G	GS	CG	GF	IP	BFP	H	R	ER	HR	SH	SF	HB	TBB	IBB	SO	WP	Bk	W	L	Pct	ShO	Sv-Op	Hld	ERC	ERA
1993 Seattle	AL	13	3	0	2	17.0	95	28	20	18	3	1	1	0	17	3	8	1	1	1	3	.250	0	1-1	2	11.09	9.53
1994 Houston	NL	44	0	0	7	41.1	181	46	19	17	4	0	0	2	16	1	24	5	1	2	1	.667	0	0-1	10	4.88	3.70
1995 Houston	NL	24	24	0	0	150.2	641	141	73	56	13	11	5	4	49	3	115	3	1	9	8	.529	0	0-0	0	3.37	3.35
1996 Houston	NL	27	27	2	0	160.1	691	175	79	64	12	10	3	4	49	1	101	7	2	10	10	.500	1	0-0	0	4.11	3.59
1997 Houston	NL	34	34	7	0	223.0	941	217	105	95	16	11	7	2	77	2	139	6	1	15	10	.600	2	0-0	0	3.56	3.83
1998 Houston	NL	32	32	1	0	211.2	917	227	92	79	18	7	5	5	81	1	137	4	2	11	7	.611	1	0-0	0	4.45	3.36
1999 Houston	NL	34	34	3	0	239.0	979	206	86	77	12	10	9	5	101	2	177	9	0	22	4	.846	2	0-0	0	3.25	2.90
2000 New York	NL	33	33	3	0	217.2	929	194	89	76	10	11	5	8	99	5	151	10	0	15	10	.600	1	0-0	0	3.44	3.14
2001 Colorado	NL	32	32	2	0	203.0	904	236	138	122	31	8	6	8	85	7	122	6	0	14	13	.519	0	0-0	0	5.69	5.41
2002 Colorado	NL	30	30	0	0	178.2	838	228	135	122	24	2	9	7	91	4	74	9	2	7	15	.318	0	0-0	0	6.61	6.15
10 ML YEARS		303	249	18	9	1642.1	7116	1698	836	726	143	71	52	44	665	29	1048	60	10	106	81	.567	8	1-2	12	4.31	3.98

Josh Hancock

Pitches: R **Bats:** R **Pos:** RP-2; SP-1 **Ht:** 6'3" **Wt:** 217 **Born:** 4/11/78 **Age:** 25

Year Team	Lg	G	GS	CG	GF	IP	BFP	H	R	ER	HR	SH	SF	HB	TBB	IBB	SO	WP	Bk	W	L	Pct	ShO	Sv-Op	Hld	ERC	ERA
1998 Red Sox	R	5	1	0	1	13.1	51	9	5	5	1	2	0	0	3	0	21	0	0	1	1	.500	0	0--	-	1.69	3.38
1998 Lowell	A-	1	1	0	0	4.0	20	5	2	1	0	0	1	0	4	0	4	1	0	0	1	.000	0	0--	-	7.36	2.25
1999 Augusta	A	25	25	0	0	139.2	607	154	79	59	12	4	2	4	46	0	106	10	1	6	8	.429	0	0--	-	4.41	3.80
2000 Sarasota	A+	26	24	1	0	143.2	628	164	89	71	9	5	6	6	37	0	95	8	2	5	10	.333	0	0--	-	4.17	4.45
2001 Trenton	AA	24	24	0	0	130.2	553	138	60	53	8	3	2	4	37	0	119	11	0	8	6	.571	0	0--	-	3.82	3.65
2002 Trenton	AA	15	14	2	1	84.2	351	82	40	34	9	0	0	5	18	0	69	5	0	4	4	.429	0	1--	-	3.46	3.61
2002 Pawtucket	AAA	8	8	0	0	44.1	198	39	20	17	2	2	2	2	26	0	29	3	0	4	2	.667	0	0--	-	3.85	3.45
2002 Boston	AL	3	1	0	2	7.1	28	5	3	3	1	1	0	0	2	0	6	0	0	0	1	.000	0	0-0	0	2.25	3.68

Chris Haney

Pitches: L **Bats:** L **Pos:** RP-24 **Ht:** 6'3" **Wt:** 210 **Born:** 11/16/68 **Age:** 34

Year Team	Lg	G	GS	CG	GF	IP	BFP	H	R	ER	HR	SH	SF	HB	TBB	IBB	SO	WP	Bk	W	L	Pct	ShO	Sv-Op	Hld	ERC	ERA
2002 Pawtucket*	AAA	25	0	0	14	29.0	124	27	10	9	1	0	0	2	10	0	31	5	0	2	0	1.000	0	4--	-	3.28	2.79
1991 Montreal	NL	16	16	0	0	84.2	387	94	49	38	6	6	1	1	43	1	51	9	0	3	7	.300	0	0-0	0	4.89	4.04
1992 Mon-KC		16	13	2	2	80.0	339	75	43	41	11	0	6	4	26	2	54	5	1	4	6	.400	2	0-0	0	3.84	4.61
1993 Kansas City	AL	23	23	1	0	124.0	556	141	87	83	13	3	4	3	53	2	65	6	1	9	9	.500	1	0-0	0	5.08	6.02
1994 Kansas City	AL	6	6	0	0	28.1	127	36	25	23	2	3	4	1	11	1	18	2	0	2	2	.500	0	0-0	0	5.59	7.31
1995 Kansas City	AL	16	13	1	0	81.1	338	78	35	33	7	1	4	2	33	0	31	2	0	3	4	.429	0	0-0	2	4.02	3.65
1996 Kansas City	AL	35	35	4	0	228.0	988	267	136	119	29	5	8	6	51	0	115	8	0	10	14	.417	1	0-0	0	4.63	4.70
1997 Kansas City	AL	8	3	0	1	24.2	110	29	16	12	1	2	1	2	5	2	16	1	0	1	2	.333	0	0-0	1	3.93	4.38
1998 KC-ChC		38	12	0	2	102.1	469	128	82	80	20	2	11	5	37	0	55	4	1	6	6	.500	0	0-1	0	6.31	7.04
1999 Cleveland	AL	13	4	0	1	40.1	178	43	22	21	3	0	0	3	16	0	22	0	0	0	2	.000	0	0-0	0	4.57	4.69
2000 Cleveland	AL	1	0	0	1	1.0	5	1	1	1	0	0	1	0	1	0	0	0	0	0	0	-	0	0-0	0	5.48	9.00
2002 Boston	AL	24	0	0	11	30.0	134	32	14	14	2	0	3	4	10	2	15	0	0	0	0	-	0	1-1	4	4.32	4.20
1992 Montreal	NL	9	6	1	2	38.0	165	40	25	23	6	0	3	4	10	0	27	5	1	2	3	.400	1	0-0	0	4.65	5.45
1992 Kansas City	AL	7	7	1	0	42.0	174	35	18	18	5	0	3	0	16	2	27	0	0	2	3	.400	1	0-0	0	3.15	3.86
1998 Kansas City	AL	33	12	0	2	97.1	450	125	78	76	18	2	11	5	36	0	51	4	1	6	6	.500	0	0-1	0	6.49	7.03
1998 Chicago	NL	5	0	0	1	5.0	19	3	4	4	2	0	0	0	1	0	4	0	0	0	0	-	0	0-0	0	2.77	7.20
11 ML YEARS		196	125	8	18	824.2	3631	924	510	465	94	22	43	31	286	10	442	37	3	38	52	.422	4	1-2	7	4.79	5.07

Dave Hansen

Bats: L **Throws:** R **Pos:** PH-65; 1B-27; 3B-11; DH-4 **Ht:** 6'0" **Wt:** 195 **Born:** 11/24/68 **Age:** 34

Year Team	Lg	G	AB	H	2B	3B	HR	(Hm	Rd)	TB	R	RBI	RC	TBB	IBB	SO	HBP	SH	SF	SB	CS	SB%	GDP	Avg	OBP	Slg
1990 Los Angeles	NL	5	7	1	0	0	0	(0	0)	1	0	1	0	0	0	3	0	0	0	0	0	-	0	.143	.143	.143
1991 Los Angeles	NL	53	56	15	4	0	1	(0	1)	22	3	5	6	2	0	12	0	0	0	1	0	1.00	0	.268	.293	.393
1992 Los Angeles	NL	132	341	73	11	0	6	(1	5)	102	30	22	27	34	3	49	1	0	2	0	2	.00	9	.214	.286	.299
1993 Los Angeles	NL	84	105	38	3	0	4	(2	2)	53	13	30	25	21	3	13	0	0	1	0	1	.00	0	.362	.465	.505
1994 Los Angeles	NL	40	44	15	3	0	0	(0	0)	18	3	5	8	5	0	5	0	0	0	0	0	-	0	.341	.408	.409
1995 Los Angeles	NL	100	181	52	10	0	1	(0	1)	65	19	14	26	28	4	28	1	0	1	0	0	-	4	.287	.384	.359
1996 Los Angeles	NL	80	104	23	1	0	0	(0	0)	24	7	6	6	11	1	22	0	0	4	0	0	-	4	.221	.293	.231
1997 Chicago	NL	90	151	47	8	2	3	(1	2)	68	19	21	31	31	1	32	1	2	1	1	2	.33	0	.311	.429	.450
1999 Los Angeles	NL	100	107	27	8	1	2	(2	0)	43	14	17	19	26	0	20	2	0	1	0	0	-	2	.252	.404	.402
2000 Los Angeles	NL	102	121	35	6	2	8	(4	4)	69	18	26	27	26	0	32	0	0	0	0	1	.00	3	.289	.415	.570
2001 Los Angeles	NL	92	140	33	10	0	2	(1	1)	49	13	20	20	32	5	29	0	0	3	0	1	.00	0	.236	.371	.350
2002 Los Angeles	NL	96	120	35	6	0	2	(0	2)	47	15	17	17	14	3	22	0	0	1	1	0	1.00	2	.292	.363	.392
12 ML YEARS		974	1477	394	70	5	29	(11	18)	561	154	184	212	230	20	267	5	2	11	3	7	.30	29	.267	.365	.380

Aaron Harang

Pitches: R **Bats:** R **Pos:** SP-15; RP-1 **Ht:** 6'7" **Wt:** 240 **Born:** 5/9/78 **Age:** 25

Year Team	Lg	G	GS	CG	GF	IP	BFP	H	R	ER	HR	SH	SF	HB	TBB	IBB	SO	WP	Bk	W	L	Pct	ShO	Sv-Op	Hld	ERC	ERA
1999 Pulaski	R+	16	10	1	6	78.1	309	64	22	20	5	2	3	4	17	1	87	2	1	9	2	.818	1	1--	-	2.44	2.30
2000 Charlotte	A+	28	27	3	0	157.0	642	128	68	58	10	1	3	7	50	0	136	5	1	13	5	.722	2	0--	-	2.73	3.32
2001 Midland	AA	27	27	0	0	150.0	654	173	81	69	9	0	3	6	37	1	112	3	0	10	8	.556	0	0--	-	4.17	4.14
2002 Midland	AA	3	3	0	0	16.2	66	12	3	2	0	1	0	3	7	0	21	1	0	2	0	1.000	0	0--	-	2.86	1.08
2002 Sacramento	AAA	8	8	0	0	38.2	165	41	17	14	1	0	0	2	9	0	39	2	0	3	3	.500	0	0--	-	3.43	3.26
2002 Oakland	AL	16	15	0	0	78.1	354	78	44	42	7	3	4	3	45	2	64	1	0	5	4	.556	0	0-0	0	4.76	4.83

Travis Harper

Pitches: R **Bats:** R **Pos:** RP-30; SP-7 **Ht:** 6'4" **Wt:** 192 **Born:** 5/21/76 **Age:** 27

Year Team	Lg	G	GS	CG	GF	IP	BFP	H	R	ER	HR	SH	SF	HB	TBB	IBB	SO	WP	Bk	W	L	Pct	ShO	Sv-Op	Hld	ERC	ERA
2002 Durham*	AAA	4	4	0	0	19.1	87	31	15	15	5	0	2	1	3	0	17	1	0	1	2	.333	0	0--	-	8.63	6.98
2000 Tampa Bay	AL	6	5	1	0	32.0	141	30	17	17	5	1	1	1	15	0	14	1	0	1	2	.333	1	0-0	0	4.46	4.78
2001 Tampa Bay	AL	2	2	0	0	7.0	36	15	11	6	5	0	0	0	3	0	2	1	0	0	2	.000	0	0-0	0	19.14	7.71
2002 Tampa Bay	AL	37	7	0	16	85.2	394	101	54	52	14	5	4	9	27	3	60	2	0	5	9	.357	0	1-2	3	5.49	5.46
3 ML YEARS		45	14	1	16	124.2	571	146	82	75	24	6	5	10	45	3	76	4	0	6	13	.316	1	1-2	3	5.81	5.41

Lenny Harris

Bats: L **Throws:** R **Pos:** PH-84; LF-16; 3B-14; 1B-12; DH-2; PR-1   **Ht:** 5'10" **Wt:** 220 **Born:** 10/28/64 **Age:** 38

							BATTING													BASERUNNING				AVERAGES		
Year	Team	Lg	G	AB	H	2B	3B	HR	(Hm | Rd)	TB	R	RBI	RC	TBB	IBB	SO	HBP	SH	SF	SB	CS	SB%	GDP	Avg	OBP	Slg
1988	Cincinnati	NL	16	43	16	1	0	0	(0 | 0)	17	7	8	8	5	0	4	0	1	2	4	1	.80	0	.372	.420	.395
1989	Cin-LA	NL	115	335	79	10	1	3	(1 | 2)	100	36	26	23	20	0	33	2	1	0	14	9	.61	14	.236	.283	.299
1990	Los Angeles	NL	137	431	131	16	4	2	(0 | 2)	161	61	29	55	29	2	31	1	3	1	15	10	.60	8	.304	.348	.374
1991	Los Angeles	NL	145	429	123	16	1	3	(1 | 2)	150	59	38	52	37	5	32	5	12	2	12	3	.80	16	.287	.349	.350
1992	Los Angeles	NL	135	347	94	11	0	0	(0 | 0)	105	28	30	33	24	3	24	1	6	2	19	7	.73	10	.271	.318	.303
1993	Los Angeles	NL	107	160	38	6	1	2	(0 | 2)	52	20	11	15	15	4	15	0	1	0	3	1	.75	4	.238	.303	.325
1994	Cincinnati	NL	66	100	31	3	1	0	(0 | 0)	36	13	14	13	5	0	13	0	0	1	7	2	.78	0	.310	.340	.360
1995	Cincinnati	NL	101	197	41	8	3	2	(0 | 2)	61	32	16	15	14	0	20	0	3	1	10	1	.91	6	.208	.259	.310
1996	Cincinnati	NL	125	302	86	17	2	5	(2 | 3)	122	33	32	41	21	1	31	1	6	3	14	6	.70	3	.285	.330	.404
1997	Cincinnati	NL	120	238	65	13	1	3	(2 | 1)	89	32	28	27	18	1	18	2	3	2	4	3	.57	10	.273	.327	.374
1998	Cin-NYM	NL	132	290	75	15	0	6	(2 | 4)	108	30	27	29	17	3	21	2	4	4	6	5	.55	13	.259	.300	.372
1999	Col-Ari	NL	110	187	58	13	0	1	(1 | 0)	74	17	20	23	6	0	7	0	0	1	2	1	.67	7	.310	.330	.396
2000	Ari-NYM	NL	112	223	58	7	4	4	(2 | 2)	85	31	26	28	20	2	22	0	2	3	13	1	.93	7	.260	.317	.381
2001	New York	NL	110	135	30	5	1	0	(0 | 0)	37	12	9	9	8	0	9	0	0	0	3	2	.60	3	.222	.266	.274
2002	Milwaukee	NL	122	197	60	8	2	3	(2 | 1)	81	23	17	25	14	1	17	2	1	1	4	1	.80	4	.305	.355	.411
1989	Cincinnati	NL	61	188	42	4	0	2	(0 | 2)	52	17	11	11	9	0	20	1	1	0	10	6	.63	5	.223	.263	.277
1989	Los Angeles	NL	54	147	37	6	1	1	(1 | 0)	48	19	15	12	11	0	13	1	0	0	4	3	.57	9	.252	.308	.327
1998	Cincinnati	NL	57	122	36	8	0	0	(0 | 0)	44	12	10	12	8	2	9	1	0	2	1	3	.25	8	.295	.338	.361
1998	New York	NL	75	168	39	7	0	6	(2 | 4)	64	18	17	17	9	1	12	1	4	2	5	2	.71	5	.232	.272	.381
1999	Colorado	NL	91	158	47	12	0	0	(0 | 0)	59	15	13	17	6	0	6	0	0	0	1	1	.50	7	.297	.323	.373
1999	Arizona	NL	19	29	11	1	0	1	(1 | 0)	15	2	7	6	0	0	1	0	0	1	1	0	1.00	0	.379	.367	.517
2000	Arizona	NL	36	85	16	1	1	1	(1 | 0)	22	9	13	4	3	1	5	0	0	3	5	0	1.00	3	.188	.209	.259
2000	New York	NL	76	138	42	6	3	3	(1 | 2)	63	22	13	24	17	1	17	0	2	0	8	1	.89	4	.304	.381	.457
	15 ML YEARS		1653	3614	985	149	21	34	(13 | 21)	1278	434	331	396	253	22	297	16	43	23	130	53	.71	105	.273	.321	.354

Willie Harris

Bats: L **Throws:** R **Pos:** 2B-38; CF-6; PH-3; PR-3   **Ht:** 5'9" **Wt:** 175 **Born:** 6/22/78 **Age:** 25

							BATTING													BASERUNNING				AVERAGES		
Year	Team	Lg	G	AB	H	2B	3B	HR	(Hm | Rd)	TB	R	RBI	RC	TBB	IBB	SO	HBP	SH	SF	SB	CS	SB%	GDP	Avg	OBP	Slg
1999	Bluefield	R+	5	22	6	1	0	0	(- | -)	7	3	3	3	4	0	2	0	0	1	1	0	1.00	1	.273	.370	.318
1999	Delmarva	A	66	272	72	13	3	2	(- | -)	97	42	32	30	20	0	41	1	4	4	17	11	.61	4	.265	.313	.357
2000	Delmarva	A	133	474	130	27	10	6	(- | -)	195	106	60	87	89	4	89	9	7	4	38	15	.72	3	.274	.396	.411
2001	Bowie	AA	133	525	160	27	4	9	(- | -)	222	83	49	86	46	3	71	5	10	4	54	16	.77	6	.305	.364	.423
2002	Charlotte	AAA	89	360	102	16	5	5	(- | -)	143	54	33	51	33	0	61	2	7	2	32	14	.70	4	.283	.345	.397
2001	Baltimore	AL	9	24	3	1	0	0	(0 | 0)	4	3	0	0	0	0	7	0	1	0	0	0	-	0	.125	.125	.167
2002	Chicago	AL	49	163	38	4	0	2	(2 | 0)	48	14	12	15	9	0	21	0	3	2	8	0	1.00	3	.233	.270	.294
	2 ML YEARS		58	187	41	5	0	2	(2 | 0)	52	17	12	15	9	0	28	0	4	2	8	0	1.00	3	.219	.253	.278

Jason Hart

Bats: R **Throws:** R **Pos:** LF-7; 1B-2; PH-2; PR-1   **Ht:** 6'4" **Wt:** 240 **Born:** 9/5/77 **Age:** 25

							BATTING													BASERUNNING				AVERAGES		
Year	Team	Lg	G	AB	H	2B	3B	HR	(Hm | Rd)	TB	R	RBI	RC	TBB	IBB	SO	HBP	SH	SF	SB	CS	SB%	GDP	Avg	OBP	Slg
1998	Sth Oregon	A-	75	295	76	19	1	20	(- | -)	157	58	69	51	36	2	67	3	0	8	0	1	.00	9	.258	.336	.532
1999	Modesto	A+	135	550	168	48	2	19	(- | -)	277	96	123	96	56	1	105	4	0	7	2	5	.29	18	.305	.370	.504
2000	Midland	AA	135	546	178	44	3	30	(- | -)	318	98	121	119	67	5	112	6	0	7	4	0	1.00	8	.326	.401	.582
2000	Sacramento	AAA	5	18	5	1	0	1	(- | -)	9	4	4	4	3	0	7	0	0	0	0	0	-	0	.278	.381	.500
2001	Sacramento	AAA	134	494	122	26	1	19	(- | -)	207	71	75	67	57	0	102	4	0	8	3	3	.50	11	.247	.325	.419
2002	Oklahoma	AAA	134	514	135	32	1	25	(- | -)	244	78	83	85	68	1	122	8	1	2	1	0	1.00	14	.263	.356	.475
2002	Texas	AL	10	15	4	3	0	0	(0 | 0)	7	2	0	2	2	0	7	0	0	0	0	0	-	0	.267	.353	.467

Ken Harvey

Bats: R **Throws:** R **Pos:** 1B   **Ht:** 6'2" **Wt:** 240 **Born:** 3/1/78 **Age:** 25

							BATTING													BASERUNNING				AVERAGES		
Year	Team	Lg	G	AB	H	2B	3B	HR	(Hm | Rd)	TB	R	RBI	RC	TBB	IBB	SO	HBP	SH	SF	SB	CS	SB%	GDP	Avg	OBP	Slg
1999	Spokane	A-	56	204	81	17	0	8	(- | -)	122	49	41	54	23	4	30	8	0	0	7	1	.88	3	.397	.477	.598
2000	Wilmington	A+	46	164	55	10	0	4	(- | -)	77	20	25	30	14	0	29	7	0	0	0	2	.00	4	.335	.410	.470
2001	Wilmington	A+	35	137	52	9	1	4	(- | -)	81	22	27	33	13	0	21	6	0	0	3	1	.75	5	.380	.455	.591
2001	Wichita	AA	79	314	106	20	3	9	(- | -)	159	54	63	55	18	0	60	4	0	8	3	0	1.00	12	.338	.372	.506
2002	Omaha	AAA	128	488	135	30	1	20	(- | -)	227	75	75	72	42	1	87	8	0	3	8	3	.73	22	.277	.342	.465
2001	Kansas City	AL	4	12	3	1	0	0	(0 | 0)	4	1	2	0	0	0	4	0	0	0	0	1	.00	1	.250	.250	.333

Shigetoshi Hasegawa

Pitches: R **Bats:** R **Pos:** RP-53   **Ht:** 5'11" **Wt:** 178 **Born:** 8/1/68 **Age:** 34

			HOW MUCH HE PITCHED							WHAT HE GAVE UP											THE RESULTS						
Year	Team	Lg	G	GS	CG	GF	IP	BFP	H	R	ER	HR	SH	SF	HB	TBB	IBB	SO	WP	Bk	W	L	Pct	ShO	Sv-Op	Hld	ERC	ERA
1997	Anaheim	AL	50	7	0	17	116.2	497	118	60	51	14	5	5	3	46	6	83	2	1	3	7	.300	0	0-1	3	4.37	3.93
1998	Anaheim	AL	61	0	0	20	97.1	401	86	37	34	14	4	6	2	32	2	73	5	2	8	3	.727	0	5-7	10	3.54	3.14
1999	Anaheim	AL	64	1	0	26	77.0	333	80	45	42	14	3	4	2	34	2	44	4	0	4	6	.400	0	2-5	6	5.25	4.91
2000	Anaheim	AL	66	0	0	26	95.2	415	100	43	38	11	2	3	2	38	6	59	2	1	10	6	.625	0	9-18	19	4.44	3.57
2001	Anaheim	AL	46	0	0	10	55.2	235	52	28	25	5	1	2	2	20	5	41	2	0	5	6	.455	0	0-6	12	3.50	4.04
2002	Seattle	AL	53	0	0	20	70.1	288	60	26	25	4	3	1	2	30	8	39	0	1	8	3	.727	0	1-5	8	3.13	3.20
	6 ML YEARS		340	8	0	119	512.2	2169	496	239	215	62	18	21	13	200	29	339	15	5	38	31	.551	0	17-42	58	4.08	3.77

Bill Haselman

Bats: R **Throws:** R **Pos:** C-67; PH-2; DH-1 **Ht:** 6'3" **Wt:** 225 **Born:** 5/25/66 **Age:** 37

Year Team	Lg	G	AB	H	2B	3B	HR	(Hm	Rd)	TB	R	RBI	RC	TBB	IBB	SO	HBP	SH	SF	SB	CS	SB%	GDP	Avg	OBP	Slg
1990 Texas	AL	7	13	2	0	0	0	(0	0)	2	0	3	0	1	0	5	0	0	0	0	0	-	0	.154	.214	.154
1992 Texas	AL	8	19	5	0	0	0	(0	0)	5	1	0	1	0	0	7	0	0	0	0	0	-	1	.263	.263	.263
1993 Seattle	AL	58	137	35	8	0	5	(3	2)	58	21	16	18	12	0	19	1	2	2	2	1	.67	5	.255	.316	.423
1994 Seattle	AL	38	83	16	7	1	1	(1	0)	28	11	8	6	3	0	11	1	1	0	1	0	1.00	2	.193	.230	.337
1995 Boston	AL	64	152	37	6	1	5	(3	2)	60	22	23	19	17	0	30	2	0	3	0	2	.00	4	.243	.322	.395
1996 Boston	AL	77	237	65	13	1	8	(5	3)	104	33	34	30	19	3	52	1	0	0	4	2	.67	13	.274	.331	.439
1997 Boston	AL	67	212	50	15	0	6	(3	3)	83	22	26	21	15	2	44	2	1	2	0	2	.00	8	.236	.290	.392
1998 Texas	AL	40	105	33	6	0	6	(4	2)	57	11	17	18	3	0	17	0	0	2	0	0	-	2	.314	.327	.543
1999 Detroit	AL	48	143	39	8	0	4	(2	2)	59	13	14	18	10	1	26	0	0	0	2	0	1.00	4	.273	.320	.413
2000 Texas	AL	62	193	53	18	0	6	(3	3)	89	23	26	29	15	0	36	1	0	1	0	1	.00	1	.275	.329	.461
2001 Texas	AL	47	130	37	6	0	3	(1	2)	52	12	25	15	8	0	27	1	1	0	0	1	.00	5	.285	.331	.400
2002 Texas	AL	69	179	44	7	0	3	(1	2)	60	16	18	15	11	1	25	2	1	0	0	0	-	6	.246	.297	.335
12 ML YEARS		585	1603	416	94	3	47	(27	20)	657	185	210	190	114	7	299	11	6	10	9	9	.50	51	.260	.311	.410

Scott Hatteberg

Bats: L **Throws:** R **Pos:** 1B-91; DH-42; PH-7 **Ht:** 6'1" **Wt:** 210 **Born:** 12/14/69 **Age:** 33

Year Team	Lg	G	AB	H	2B	3B	HR	(Hm	Rd)	TB	R	RBI	RC	TBB	IBB	SO	HBP	SH	SF	SB	CS	SB%	GDP	Avg	OBP	Slg
1995 Boston	AL	2	2	1	0	0	0	(0	0)	1	1	0	0	0	0	0	0	0	0	0	0	-	1	.500	.500	.500
1996 Boston	AL	10	11	2	1	0	0	(0	0)	3	3	0	1	3	0	2	0	0	0	0	0	-	2	.182	.357	.273
1997 Boston	AL	114	350	97	23	1	10	(5	5)	152	46	44	52	40	2	70	2	2	1	0	1	.00	11	.277	.354	.434
1998 Boston	AL	112	359	99	23	1	12	(4	8)	160	46	43	56	43	3	58	5	0	3	0	0	-	11	.276	.359	.446
1999 Boston	AL	30	80	22	5	0	1	(1	0)	30	12	11	14	18	0	14	1	0	1	0	0	-	2	.275	.410	.375
2000 Boston	AL	92	230	61	15	0	8	(2	6)	100	21	36	36	38	3	39	0	1	2	0	1	.00	8	.265	.367	.435
2001 Boston	AL	94	278	68	19	0	3	(2	1)	96	34	25	32	33	0	26	4	0	1	1	1	.50	7	.245	.332	.345
2002 Oakland	AL	136	492	138	22	4	15	(8	7)	213	58	61	76	68	1	56	6	1	1	0	0	-	8	.280	.374	.433
8 ML YEARS		590	1802	488	108	6	49	(22	27)	755	221	220	267	243	9	265	18	4	9	1	3	.25	50	.271	.361	.419

LaTroy Hawkins

Pitches: R **Bats:** R **Pos:** RP-65 **Ht:** 6'5" **Wt:** 204 **Born:** 12/21/72 **Age:** 30

Year Team	Lg	G	GS	CG	GF	IP	BFP	H	R	ER	HR	SH	SF	HB	TBB	IBB	SO	WP	Bk	W	L	Pct	ShO	Sv-Op	Hld	ERC	ERA
1995 Minnesota	AL	6	6	1	0	27.0	131	39	29	26	3	0	3	1	12	0	9	1	1	2	3	.400	0	0-0	0	7.14	8.67
1996 Minnesota	AL	7	6	0	1	26.1	124	42	24	24	8	1	1	0	9	0	24	1	1	1	1	.500	0	0-0	0	9.49	8.20
1997 Minnesota	AL	20	20	0	0	103.1	478	134	71	67	19	2	2	4	47	0	58	6	3	6	12	.333	0	0-0	0	7.01	5.84
1998 Minnesota	AL	33	33	0	0	190.1	840	227	126	111	27	4	10	5	61	1	105	10	2	7	14	.333	0	0-0	0	5.31	5.25
1999 Minnesota	AL	33	33	1	0	174.1	803	238	136	129	29	1	5	1	60	2	103	9	0	10	14	.417	0	0-0	0	6.55	6.66
2000 Minnesota	AL	66	0	0	38	87.2	370	85	34	33	7	4	1	1	32	1	59	6	0	2	5	.286	0	14-14	7	3.70	3.39
2001 Minnesota	AL	62	0	0	51	51.1	248	59	34	34	3	1	4	1	39	3	36	7	0	1	5	.167	0	28-31	7	6.02	5.96
2002 Minnesota	AL	65	0	0	15	80.1	310	63	23	19	5	2	3	0	15	1	63	5	0	6	0	1.000	0	0-3	13	1.99	2.13
8 ML YEARS		292	98	2	105	740.2	3304	887	477	443	101	15	29	13	275	8	457	45	7	35	54	.393	0	42-54	21	5.47	5.38

Jimmy Haynes

Pitches: R **Bats:** R **Pos:** SP-34 **Ht:** 6'4" **Wt:** 219 **Born:** 9/5/72 **Age:** 30

Year Team	Lg	G	GS	CG	GF	IP	BFP	H	R	ER	HR	SH	SF	HB	TBB	IBB	SO	WP	Bk	W	L	Pct	ShO	Sv-Op	Hld	ERC	ERA
1995 Baltimore	AL	4	3	0	0	24.0	94	11	6	6	2	1	0	0	12	1	22	0	0	2	1	.667	0	0-0	0	1.61	2.25
1996 Baltimore	AL	26	11	0	8	89.0	435	122	84	82	14	4	5	2	58	1	65	5	0	3	6	.333	0	1-1	0	8.05	8.29
1997 Oakland	AL	13	13	0	0	73.1	329	74	38	36	7	1	4	2	40	1	65	4	1	3	6	.333	0	0-0	0	4.75	4.42
1998 Oakland	AL	33	33	1	0	194.1	875	229	124	110	25	5	9	5	88	4	134	11	0	11	9	.550	1	0-0	0	5.69	5.09
1999 Oakland	AL	30	25	0	2	142.0	652	158	112	100	21	4	5	2	80	3	93	7	2	7	12	.368	0	0-0	0	5.79	6.34
2000 Milwaukee	NL	33	33	0	0	199.1	897	228	128	118	21	10	6	7	100	4	88	7	0	12	13	.480	0	0-0	0	5.54	5.33
2001 Milwaukee	NL	31	29	0	0	172.2	756	182	98	93	20	14	7	4	78	17	112	8	0	8	17	.320	0	0-0	0	4.69	4.85
2002 Cincinnati	NL	34	34	0	0	196.2	852	210	97	90	21	7	6	3	81	8	126	6	0	15	10	.600	0	0-0	0	4.66	4.12
8 ML YEARS		204	181	1	10	1091.1	4890	1214	687	635	131	46	42	25	537	38	705	48	3	61	74	.452	1	1-1	0	5.34	5.24

Rick Helling

Pitches: R **Bats:** R **Pos:** SP-30 **Ht:** 6'3" **Wt:** 220 **Born:** 12/15/70 **Age:** 32

Year Team	Lg	G	GS	CG	GF	IP	BFP	H	R	ER	HR	SH	SF	HB	TBB	IBB	SO	WP	Bk	W	L	Pct	ShO	Sv-Op	Hld	ERC	ERA
2002 Tucson*	AAA	1	1	0	0	7.0	25	4	1	1	1	0	1	0	0	1	7	0	0	1	0	1.000	0	0-	-	0.97	1.29
1994 Texas	AL	9	9	1	0	52.0	228	62	34	34	14	0	0	0	18	0	25	4	1	3	2	.600	1	0-0	0	6.33	5.88
1995 Texas	AL	3	3	0	0	12.1	62	17	11	9	2	0	2	2	8	0	5	0	0	0	2	.000	0	0-0	0	8.81	6.57
1996 Tex-Fla		11	6	0	2	48.0	198	37	23	23	9	1	1	0	16	0	42	1	1	3	3	.500	0	0-0	1	3.07	4.31
1997 Fla-Tex		41	16	0	9	131.0	550	108	67	65	17	3	9	6	69	2	99	3	0	5	9	.357	0	0-1	6	4.08	4.47
1998 Texas	AL	33	33	4	0	216.1	922	209	109	106	27	6	10	1	78	6	164	10	0	20	7	.741	2	0-0	0	3.86	4.41
1999 Texas	AL	35	35	3	0	219.1	943	228	127	118	41	5	10	6	85	5	131	8	0	13	11	.542	0	0-0	0	5.03	4.84
2000 Texas	AL	35	35	0	0	217.0	963	212	122	108	29	4	9	9	99	2	146	2	0	16	13	.552	0	0-0	0	4.50	4.48
2001 Texas	AL	34	34	2	0	215.2	941	256	134	124	38	3	10	4	63	2	154	6	0	12	11	.522	1	0-0	0	5.39	5.17
2002 Arizona	NL	30	30	0	0	175.2	751	180	94	88	31	10	6	6	48	6	120	7	1	10	12	.455	0	0-0	0	4.29	4.51
1996 Texas	AL	6	2	0	2	20.1	92	23	17	17	7	1	0	0	9	0	16	1	0	1	2	.333	0	0-0	1	6.80	7.52
1996 Florida	NL	5	4	0	0	27.2	106	14	6	6	2	1	0	0	7	0	26	0	1	2	1	.667	0	0-0	0	1.18	1.95
1997 Florida	NL	31	8	0	8	76.0	324	61	38	37	12	2	7	4	48	2	53	0	0	2	6	.250	0	0-1	6	4.62	4.38
1997 Texas	AL	10	8	0	0	55.0	226	47	29	28	5	1	2	4	21	0	46	3	0	3	3	.500	0	0-0	0	3.37	4.58
9 ML YEARS		231	201	10	11	1287.1	5558	1309	721	675	208	32	57	34	484	23	886	41	3	82	70	.539	4	0-1	7	4.60	4.72

Wes Helms

Bats: R **Throws:** R **Pos:** 1B-46; 3B-23; PH-20; LF-5; RF-4   **Ht:** 6'4" **Wt:** 230 **Born:** 5/12/76 **Age:** 27

								BATTING													BASERUNNING				AVERAGES		
Year Team	Lg	G	AB	H	2B	3B	HR	(Hm	Rd)	TB	R	RBI	RC	TBB	IBB	SO	HBP	SH	SF	SB	CS	SB%	GDP	Avg	OBP	Slg
1998 Atlanta	NL	7	13	4	1	0	1	(0	1)	8	2	2	2	0	0	4	0	0	0	0	0	-	0	.308	.308	.615
2000 Atlanta	NL	6	5	1	0	0	0	(0	0)	1	0	0	0	0	0	2	0	0	0	0	0	-	0	.200	.200	.200
2001 Atlanta	NL	100	216	48	10	3	10	(6	4)	94	28	36	27	21	2	56	1	0	1	1	1	.50	3	.222	.293	.435
2002 Atlanta	NL	85	210	51	16	0	6	(4	2)	85	20	22	16	11	2	57	3	1	6	1	1	.50	5	.243	.283	.405
4 ML YEARS		198	444	104	27	3	17	(10	7)	188	50	60	45	32	4	119	4	1	7	2	2	.50	8	.234	.287	.423

Todd Helton

Bats: L **Throws:** L **Pos:** 1B-156   **Ht:** 6'2" **Wt:** 204 **Born:** 8/20/73 **Age:** 29

								BATTING													BASERUNNING				AVERAGES		
Year Team	Lg	G	AB	H	2B	3B	HR	(Hm	Rd)	TB	R	RBI	RC	TBB	IBB	SO	HBP	SH	SF	SB	CS	SB%	GDP	Avg	OBP	Slg
1997 Colorado	NL	35	93	26	2	1	5	(3	2)	45	13	11	15	8	0	11	0	0	0	0	1	.00	1	.280	.337	.484
1998 Colorado	NL	152	530	167	37	1	25	(13	12)	281	78	97	101	53	5	54	6	1	5	3	3	.50	15	.315	.380	.530
1999 Colorado	NL	159	578	185	39	5	35	(23	12)	339	114	113	124	68	6	77	6	0	4	7	6	.54	14	.320	.395	.587
2000 Colorado	NL	160	580	**216**	**59**	2	42	(27	15)	**405**	138	**147**	**169**	103	22	61	4	0	10	5	3	.63	12	**.372**	**.463**	**.698**
2001 Colorado	NL	159	587	197	54	2	49	(27	22)	402	132	146	157	98	15	104	5	1	5	7	5	.58	14	.336	.432	.685
2002 Colorado	NL	156	553	182	39	4	30	(18	12)	319	107	109	128	99	21	91	5	0	10	5	1	.83	10	.329	.429	.577
6 ML YEARS		821	2921	973	230	15	186	(111	75)	1791	582	623	694	429	69	398	26	2	34	27	19	.59	66	.333	.419	.613

Rickey Henderson

Bats: R **Throws:** L **Pos:** LF-48; PR-17; PH-9; CF-4; DH-3; RF-1   **Ht:** 5'10" **Wt:** 190 **Born:** 12/25/58 **Age:** 44

								BATTING													BASERUNNING				AVERAGES		
Year Team	Lg	G	AB	H	2B	3B	HR	(Hm	Rd)	TB	R	RBI	RC	TBB	IBB	SO	HBP	SH	SF	SB	CS	SB%	GDP	Avg	OBP	Slg
1979 Oakland	AL	89	351	96	13	3	1	(1	0)	118	49	26	45	34	0	39	2	8	3	33	11	.75	4	.274	.338	.336
1980 Oakland	AL	158	591	179	22	4	9	(3	6)	236	111	53	119	117	7	54	5	6	3	100	26	.79	6	.303	.420	.399
1981 Oakland	AL	108	423	**135**	18	7	6	(5	1)	185	89	35	80	64	4	68	2	4	0	56	22	.72	7	.319	.408	.437
1982 Oakland	AL	149	536	143	24	4	10	(5	5)	205	119	51	100	116	1	94	2	0	2	130	42	.76	5	.267	.398	.382
1983 Oakland	AL	145	513	150	25	7	9	(5	4)	216	105	48	107	103	8	80	4	1	1	108	19	.85	11	.292	.414	.421
1984 Oakland	AL	142	502	147	27	4	16	(7	9)	230	113	58	101	86	1	81	5	1	3	66	18	.79	7	.293	.399	.458
1985 New York	AL	143	547	172	28	5	24	(8	16)	282	**146**	72	**130**	99	1	65	3	0	5	80	10	.89	8	.314	.419	.516
1986 New York	AL	153	608	160	31	5	28	(13	15)	285	**130**	74	112	89	2	81	2	0	4	87	18	.83	12	.263	.358	.469
1987 New York	AL	95	358	104	17	3	17	(10	7)	178	78	37	80	80	1	52	2	0	0	41	8	.84	10	.291	.423	.497
1988 New York	AL	140	554	169	30	2	6	(2	4)	221	118	50	106	82	1	54	3	2	6	93	13	.88	6	.305	.394	.399
1989 NYY-Oak	AL	150	541	148	26	3	12	(7	5)	216	119	57	108	**126**	5	68	3	0	4	77	14	.85	7	.274	.411	.399
1990 Oakland	AL	136	489	159	33	3	28	(8	20)	282	119	61	**127**	97	2	60	4	2	2	65	10	.87	13	.325	.439	.577
1991 Oakland	AL	134	470	126	17	1	18	(8	10)	199	105	57	90	98	7	73	7	0	3	58	18	.76	7	.268	.400	.423
1992 Oakland	AL	117	396	112	18	3	15	(10	5)	181	77	46	88	95	5	56	6	0	3	48	11	.81	5	.283	.426	.457
1993 Oak-Tor	AL	134	481	139	22	2	21	(10	11)	228	114	59	112	120	7	65	4	1	4	53	8	.87	9	.289	.432	.474
1994 Oakland	AL	87	296	77	13	0	6	(4	2)	108	66	20	55	72	1	45	5	1	2	22	7	.76	0	.260	.411	.365
1995 Oakland	AL	112	407	122	31	1	9	(3	6)	182	67	54	79	72	2	66	4	1	3	32	10	.76	8	.300	.407	.447
1996 San Diego	NL	148	465	112	17	2	9	(6	3)	160	110	29	81	125	2	90	10	0	2	37	15	.71	5	.241	.410	.344
1997 SD-Ana	AL	120	403	100	14	0	8	(6	2)	138	84	34	60	97	2	85	6	1	2	45	8	.85	10	.248	.400	.342
1998 Oakland	AL	152	542	128	16	1	14	(6	8)	188	101	57	89	118	0	114	5	2	3	66	13	.84	5	.236	.376	.347
1999 New York	NL	121	438	138	30	0	12	(1	11)	204	89	42	92	82	1	82	2	1	3	37	14	.73	4	.315	.423	.466
2000 NYM-Sea	NL	123	420	98	14	2	4	(3	1)	128	75	32	57	88	1	75	4	3	4	36	11	.77	11	.233	.368	.305
2001 San Diego	NL	123	379	86	17	3	8	(2	6)	133	70	42	56	81	0	84	3	0	2	25	7	.78	8	.227	.366	.351
2002 Boston	AL	72	179	40	6	1	5	(1	4)	63	40	16	24	38	0	47	4	0	1	8	2	.80	3	.223	.369	.352
1989 New York	AL	65	235	58	13	1	3	(1	2)	82	41	22	40	56	0	29	1	0	1	25	8	.76	0	.247	.392	.349
1989 Oakland	AL	85	306	90	13	2	9	(6	3)	134	72	35	68	70	5	39	2	0	3	52	6	.90	8	.294	.425	.438
1993 Oakland	AL	90	318	104	19	1	17	(8	9)	176	77	47	86	85	6	46	2	0	2	31	6	.84	8	.327	.469	.553
1993 Toronto	AL	44	163	35	3	1	4	(2	2)	52	37	12	26	35	1	19	2	1	2	22	2	.92	1	.215	.356	.319
1997 San Diego	NL	88	288	79	11	0	6	(5	1)	108	63	27	55	71	2	62	4	0	2	29	4	.88	7	.274	.422	.375
1997 Anaheim	AL	32	115	21	3	0	2	(1	1)	30	21	7	13	26	0	23	2	1	0	16	4	.80	3	.183	.343	.261
2000 New York	NL	31	96	21	1	0	0	(0	0)	22	17	2	12	25	1	20	2	0	1	5	2	.71	2	.219	.387	.229
2000 Seattle	AL	92	324	77	13	2	4	(2	1)	106	58	30	45	63	0	55	2	3	3	31	9	.78	9	.238	.362	.327
24 ML YEARS		3051	10889	3040	509	66	295	(133	162)	4566	2288	1110	2106	2179	61	1678	97	30	67	1403	335	.81	172	.279	.402	.419

Mark Hendrickson

Pitches: L **Bats:** L **Pos:** RP-12; SP-4   **Ht:** 6'9" **Wt:** 230 **Born:** 6/23/74 **Age:** 29

		HOW MUCH HE PITCHED						WHAT HE GAVE UP											THE RESULTS						
Year Team	Lg	G	GS	CG	GF	IP	BFP	H	R	ER	HR	SH	SF	HB	TBB	IBB	SO	WP	Bk	W	L	Pct	ShO	Sv-Op	Hld	ERC	ERA
1998 Dunedin	A+	16	5	0	1	49.1	207	44	16	13	2	2	2	0	26	1	38	2	0	4	3	.571	0	1--	-	3.64	2.37
1999 Knoxville	AA	12	11	0	0	55.2	254	73	46	41	4	2	0	2	21	0	39	2	1	2	7	.222	0	0--	-	5.81	6.63
2000 Dunedin	A+	12	12	1	0	51.1	235	63	34	32	7	1	5	0	29	0	38	1	0	2	2	.500	0	0--	-	6.56	5.61
2000 Tennessee	AA	6	6	0	0	39.2	161	32	17	16	5	1	0	0	12	0	29	4	0	3	1	.750	0	0--	-	2.83	3.63
2001 Syracuse	AAA	38	6	0	7	73.1	315	80	43	38	6	0	3	1	18	1	33	2	0	2	9	.182	0	0--	-	4.65	4.66
2002 Syracuse	AAA	19	14	0	3	92.0	385	90	38	36	12	4	4	1	22	0	68	2	2	7	5	.583	0	0--	-	3.54	3.52
2002 Toronto	AL	16	4	0	0	36.2	142	25	11	10	1	2	2	2	12	3	21	0	0	3	0	1.000	0	0-1	1	1.90	2.45

Oscar Henriquez

Pitches: R **Bats:** R **Pos:** RP-30   **Ht:** 6'6" **Wt:** 220 **Born:** 1/28/74 **Age:** 29

		HOW MUCH HE PITCHED						WHAT HE GAVE UP											THE RESULTS						
Year Team	Lg	G	GS	CG	GF	IP	BFP	H	R	ER	HR	SH	SF	HB	TBB	IBB	SO	WP	Bk	W	L	Pct	ShO	Sv-Op	Hld	ERC	ERA
2002 Toledo*	AAA	33	0	0	30	32.2	141	30	13	12	4	2	1	1	14	0	39	6	0	2	1	.667	0	17--	-	3.98	3.31
1997 Houston	NL	4	0	0	1	4.0	17	2	2	2	0	1	0	1	3	0	3	0	0	0	0	.000	0	0-0	1	2.99	4.50
1998 Florida	NL	15	0	0	4	20.0	100	26	22	19	4	0	2	1	12	0	19	1	0	0	0	-	0	0-0	0	7.53	8.55
2002 Detroit	AL	30	0	0	12	28.0	115	19	14	14	5	1	1	1	15	4	23	3	0	1	1	.500	0	2-2	9	3.37	4.50
3 ML YEARS		49	0	0	17	52.0	232	47	38	35	9	2	3	3	30	4	45	4	0	1	2	.333	0	2-2	10	4.85	6.06

Drew Henson

Bats: R **Throws:** R **Pos:** PR-2; PH-1   **Ht:** 6'5" **Wt:** 222 **Born:** 2/13/80 **Age:** 23

Year Team	Lg	G	AB	H	2B	3B	HR	Hm	Rd	TB	R	RBI	RC	TBB	IBB	SO	HBP	SH	SF	SB	CS	SB%	GDP	Avg	OBP	Slg
1998 Yankees	R	10	38	12	3	0	1	-	-	18	5	2	6	3	1	9	0	0	0	0	0	-	1	.316	.366	.474
1999 Tampa	A+	69	254	71	12	0	13	-	-	122	37	37	41	26	0	71	1	0	3	3	1	.75	6	.280	.345	.480
2000 Tampa	A+	5	21	7	2	0	1	-	-	12	4	1	4	1	0	7	0	0	0	0	1	.00	0	.333	.364	.571
2000 Norwich	AA	59	223	64	9	2	7	-	-	98	39	39	31	20	1	75	1	0	1	0	5	.00	6	.287	.347	.439
2000 Chattanooga	AA	16	64	11	8	0	1	-	-	22	7	9	4	4	0	25	0	0	0	2	0	1.00	2	.172	.221	.344
2001 Tampa	A+	5	14	2	0	0	1	-	-	5	2	3	2	2	0	7	2	0	1	1	0	1.00	0	.143	.316	.357
2001 Norwich	AA	5	19	7	1	0	0	-	-	8	2	2	3	1	1	4	1	0	0	0	1	.00	1	.368	.429	.421
2001 Columbus	AAA	71	270	60	6	0	11	-	-	99	29	38	21	10	1	85	0	0	0	2	1	.67	8	.222	.249	.367
2002 Columbus	AAA	128	471	113	30	4	18	-	-	205	68	65	60	37	0	151	6	2	5	2	1	.67	11	.240	.301	.435
2002 New York	AL	3	1	0	0	0	0	0	0	0	1	0	0	0	0	1	0	0	0	0	0	-	0	.000	.000	.000

Pat Hentgen

Pitches: R **Bats:** R **Pos:** SP-4   **Ht:** 6'2" **Wt:** 195 **Born:** 11/13/68 **Age:** 34

Year Team	Lg	G	GS	CG	GF	IP	BFP	H	R	ER	HR	SH	SF	HB	TBB	IBB	SO	WP	Bk	W	L	Pct	ShO	Sv-Op	Hld	ERC	ERA
2002 Orioles*	R	1	1	0	0	3.0	9	2	0	0	0		0	0	3	0	0	0	0	0	0	-	0	0--	-	1.12	0.00
2002 Delmarva*	A	1	1	0	0	5.0	21	4	1	1	0	2	0	1	1	0	4	0	0	0	1	.000	0	0--	-	2.31	1.80
2002 Aberdeen*	A-	2	2	0	0	11.2	51	16	8	4	1			1	0	10	0	0	1	1	.500	0	0--	-	4.36	3.09
2002 Bowie*	AA	1	1	0	0	6.0	24	5	2	1	1	0	0	0	2	0	3	0	0	0	0	-	0	0--	-	3.44	1.50
2002 Frederick*	A+	1	1	1	0	7.0	26	5	2	2	0	0	0	0	2	0	5	0	0	1	0	1.000	0	0--	-	1.76	2.57
1991 Toronto	AL	3	1	0	1	7.1	30	5	2	2	1	1	0	2	3	0	3	1	0	0	0	-	0	0-0	0	3.87	2.45
1992 Toronto	AL	28	2	0	10	50.1	229	49	30	30	7	2	2	0	32	5	39	2	1	5	2	.714	0	0-1	1	4.94	5.36
1993 Toronto	AL	34	32	3	0	216.1	926	215	103	93	27	6	5	7	74	0	122	11	1	19	9	.679	0	0-0	0	4.11	3.87
1994 Toronto	AL	24	24	6	0	174.2	728	158	74	66	21	6	3	3	59	1	147	5	1	13	8	.619	3	0-0	0	3.52	3.40
1995 Toronto	AL	30	30	2	0	200.2	913	236	129	114	24	2	1	5	90	6	135	7	2	10	14	.417	0	0-0	0	5.49	5.11
1996 Toronto	AL	35	35	10	0	265.2	1100	238	105	95	20	5	8	5	94	3	177	8	0	20	10	.667	3	0-0	0	3.26	3.22
1997 Toronto	AL	35	35	9	0	264.0	1085	253	116	108	31	9	3	7	71	2	160	6	2	15	10	.600	3	0-0	0	3.61	3.68
1998 Toronto	AL	29	29	0	0	177.2	795	208	109	102	28	5	7	5	69	1	94	7	1	12	11	.522	0	0-0	0	5.58	5.17
1999 Toronto	AL	34	34	1	0	199.0	869	225	115	106	32	3	11	3	65	1	118	8	1	11	12	.478	0	0-0	0	5.04	4.79
2000 St Louis	NL	33	33	1	0	194.1	846	202	107	102	24	13	8	3	89	4	118	4	0	15	12	.556	1	0-0	0	4.81	4.72
2001 Baltimore	AL	9	9	1	0	62.1	252	51	25	24	7	1	1	0	19	3	33	1	0	2	3	.400	0	0-0	0	2.77	3.47
2002 Baltimore	AL	4	4	0	0	22.0	103	31	20	19	6	0	1	0	10	0	11	1	0	0	4	.000	0	0-0	0	8.38	7.77
12 ML YEARS		298	268	33	11	1834.1	7876	1871	935	861	228	53	50	40	675	26	1157	61	9	122	95	.562	10	0-1	1	4.33	4.22

Felix Heredia

Pitches: L **Bats:** L **Pos:** RP-53   **Ht:** 6'0" **Wt:** 190 **Born:** 6/18/75 **Age:** 28

Year Team	Lg	G	GS	CG	GF	IP	BFP	H	R	ER	HR	SH	SF	HB	TBB	IBB	SO	WP	Bk	W	L	Pct	ShO	Sv-Op	Hld	ERC	ERA
1996 Florida	NL	21	0	0	5	16.2	78	21	8	8	1	0	1	0	10	1	10	2	0	1	1	.500	0	0-0	2	6.08	4.32
1997 Florida	NL	56	0	0	10	56.2	259	53	30	27	3	2	2	5	30	1	54	2	0	5	3	.625	0	0-1	7	4.06	4.29
1998 Fla-ChC	NL	71	2	0	18	58.2	268	57	33	33	2	1	2	1	38	3	54	6	1	3	3	.500	0	2-5	17	4.31	5.06
1999 Chicago	NL	69	0	0	15	52.0	237	56	35	28	7	1	4	1	25	2	50	2	0	3	1	.750	0	1-7	12	5.01	4.85
2000 Chicago	NL	74	0	0	24	58.2	250	46	31	31	6	4	2	2	33	4	52	5	0	7	3	.700	0	2-5	12	3.59	4.76
2001 Chicago	NL	48	0	0	9	35.0	165	45	27	24	6	1	3	2	16	1	28	3	0	2	2	.500	0	0-3	8	6.75	6.17
2002 Toronto	AL	53	0	0	15	52.1	232	51	29	21	5	3	2	2	26	3	31	5	0	2	4	.333	0	0-2	7	4.31	3.61
1998 Florida	NL	41	2	0	12	41.0	194	38	25	25	1	1	2	1	32	2	38	5	1	0	3	.000	0	2-3	9	4.44	5.49
1998 Chicago	NL	30	0	0	6	17.2	74	19	8	8	1	0	0	0	6	1	16	1	0	3	0	1.000	0	0-2	8	3.99	4.08
7 ML YEARS		392	2	0	96	330.0	1489	329	193	172	30	12	16	13	178	15	279	25	1	22	15	.595	0	5-23	65	4.58	4.69

Matt Herges

Pitches: R **Bats:** L **Pos:** RP-62   **Ht:** 6'0" **Wt:** 200 **Born:** 4/1/70 **Age:** 33

Year Team	Lg	G	GS	CG	GF	IP	BFP	H	R	ER	HR	SH	SF	HB	TBB	IBB	SO	WP	Bk	W	L	Pct	ShO	Sv-Op	Hld	ERC	ERA
1999 Los Angeles	NL	17	0	0	9	24.1	104	24	13	11	5	1	0	1	8	0	18	0	0	0	2	.000	0	0-2	1	4.61	4.07
2000 Los Angeles	NL	59	4	0	17	110.2	461	100	43	39	7	9	4	6	40	5	75	4	0	11	3	.786	0	1-3	4	3.35	3.17
2001 Los Angeles	NL	75	0	0	22	99.1	435	97	39	38	4	3		8	46	12	76	2	0	9	8	.529	0	1-8	15	4.20	3.44
2002 Montreal	NL	62	0	0	25	64.2	298	80	33	29	10	6	2	8	25	8	50	3	0	2	5	.286	0	6-14	9	5.74	4.04
4 ML YEARS		213	4	0	73	299.0	1298	301	128	117	30	20	9	17	120	25	219	9	0	22	18	.550	0	8-27	29	4.24	3.52

Chad Hermansen

Bats: R **Throws:** R **Pos:** CF-68; PH-21; RF-11; LF-6; PR-5   **Ht:** 6'2" **Wt:** 192 **Born:** 9/10/77 **Age:** 25

Year Team	Lg	G	AB	H	2B	3B	HR	Hm	Rd	TB	R	RBI	RC	TBB	IBB	SO	HBP	SH	SF	SB	CS	SB%	GDP	Avg	OBP	Slg
2002 Nashville*	AAA	16	56	11	2	0	4	-	-	25	11	9	9	8	0	23	2	0	0	1	0	1.00	0	.196	.318	.446
1999 Pittsburgh	NL	19	60	14	3	0	1	0	1	20	5	1	7	7	1	19	1	1	0	2	2	.50	0	.233	.324	.333
2000 Pittsburgh	NL	33	108	20	4	1	2	2	0	32	12	8	6	6	0	37	0	2	1	0	0	-	3	.185	.226	.296
2001 Pittsburgh	NL	22	55	9	1	0	2	1	1	16	5	5	2	1	0	18	0	0	0	0	1	.00	0	.164	.179	.291
2002 Pit-ChC	NL	100	237	49	14	1	8	4	4	89	25	18	20	22	0	82	1	4	1	7	5	.58	1	.207	.276	.376
2002 Pittsburgh	NL	65	194	40	11	1	7	4	3	74	22	15	17	17	0	68	1	3	1	7	5	.58	1	.206	.272	.381
2002 Chicago	NL	35	43	9	3	0	1	0	1	15	3	3	3	5	0	14	0	1	0	0	0	-	0	.209	.292	.349
4 ML YEARS		174	460	92	22	2	13	7	6	157	47	32	35	36	1	156	2	7	2	9	8	.53	4	.200	.260	.341

Dustin Hermanson

Pitches: R Bats: R Pos: RP-11; SP-1   Ht: 6'2" Wt: 200 Born: 12/21/72 Age: 30

Year Team	Lg	G	GS	CG	GF	IP	BFP	H	R	ER	HR	SH	SF	HB	TBB	IBB	SO	WP	Bk	W	L	Pct	ShO	Sv-Op	Hld	ERC	ERA
2002 Red Sox*	R	1	1	0	0	2.0	6	5	3	2	0				0	0	1	0	0	0	0		0	0--		20.38	9.00
2002 Pawtucket*	AAA	5	3	0	0	13.2	56	9	5	4	0	0	0	2	7	0	11	0	0	0	1	.000	0	0--		2.63	2.63
1995 San Diego	NL	26	0	0	6	31.2	151	35	26	24	8	3	0	1	22	1	19	3	0	3	1	.750	0	0-0	1	7.19	6.82
1996 San Diego	NL	8	0	0	4	13.2	62	18	15	13	3	2	3	0	4	0	11	0	1	1	0	1.000	0	0-0	0	6.37	8.56
1997 Montreal	NL	32	28	1	0	158.1	656	134	68	65	15	10	6	1	66	2	136	4	1	8	8	.500	1	0-0	0	3.32	3.69
1998 Montreal	NL	32	30	1	0	187.0	768	163	80	65	21	9	3	3	56	3	154	4	3	14	11	.560	0	0-0	1	3.12	3.13
1999 Montreal	NL	34	34	0	0	216.1	928	225	110	101	20	16	7	7	69	4	145	4	1	9	14	.391	0	0-0	0	4.03	4.20
2000 Montreal	NL	38	30	2	7	198.0	876	226	128	105	26	10	9	4	75	5	94	5	0	12	14	.462	1	4-7	1	5.10	4.77
2001 St Louis	NL	33	33	0	0	192.1	830	195	106	95	34	7	2	8	73	3	123	6	0	14	13	.519	0	0-0	0	4.80	4.45
2002 Boston	AL	12	1	0	4	22.0	107	35	19	19	3	0	1	0	7	0	13	2	0	1	1	.500	0	0-1	2	7.52	7.77
8 ML YEARS		215	156	4	21	1019.1	4378	1031	552	487	130	57	31	24	372	18	695	28	6	62	62	.500	2	4-8	5	4.28	4.30

Adrian Hernandez

Pitches: R Bats: R Pos: SP-1; RP-1   Ht: 6'2" Wt: 185 Born: 3/25/75 Age: 28

Year Team	Lg	G	GS	CG	GF	IP	BFP	H	R	ER	HR	SH	SF	HB	TBB	IBB	SO	WP	Bk	W	L	Pct	ShO	Sv-Op	Hld	ERC	ERA
2000 Tampa	A+	1	1	0	0	6.2	24	3	1	1	0	0	0	0	1	0	13	1	0	1	0	1.000	0	0--		0.66	1.35
2000 Norwich	AA	6	6	1	0	35.2	159	34	17	16	1	0	1	3	18	0	44	2	2	5	1	.833	0	0--		3.99	4.04
2000 Columbus	AAA	5	5	2	0	30.2	134	24	18	15	2	1	2	3	18	0	29	2	2	2	1	.667	1	0--		3.72	4.40
2001 Columbus	AAA	21	21	0	0	117.2	515	116	75	72	13	4	4	10	60	1	97	10	5	8	7	.533	0	0--		4.96	5.51
2002 Columbus	AAA	20	20	0	0	109.2	488	114	67	64	9	4	5	11	45	1	109	9	5	6	7	.462	0	0--		4.59	5.25
2001 New York	AL	6	3	0	1	22.0	91	15	10	9	7	0	0	2	10	1	10	4	0	0	3	.000	0	0-0	0	4.30	3.68
2002 New York	AL	2	1	0	0	6.0	34	10	8	8	2	0	0	0	6	0	9	1	0	0	1	.000	0	0-0	0	13.15	12.00
2 ML YEARS		8	4	0	1	28.0	125	25	18	17	9	0	0	2	16	1	19	5	0	0	4	.000	0	0-0	0	6.01	5.46

Carlos Hernandez

Pitches: L Bats: B Pos: SP-21; RP-2   Ht: 5'10" Wt: 185 Born: 4/22/80 Age: 23

Year Team	Lg	G	GS	CG	GF	IP	BFP	H	R	ER	HR	SH	SF	HB	TBB	IBB	SO	WP	Bk	W	L	Pct	ShO	Sv-Op	Hld	ERC	ERA
1999 Martinsville	R+	13	9	0	0	55.1	227	36	21	9	2	1	1	6	23	0	82	6	0	5	1	.833	0	0--		2.30	1.46
2000 Michigan	A	22	22	2	0	110.2	490	92	57	47	8	5	3	11	63	0	115	10	1	6	6	.500	1	0--		3.95	3.82
2001 Round Rock	AA	24	23	0	0	139.0	591	115	60	57	11	7	4	7	69	0	167	3	0	12	3	.800	0	0--		3.58	3.69
2002 New Orleans	AAA	1	1	0	0	3.0	11	1	0	0	0	0	0	0	1	0	2	0	0	0	0		0	0--		0.69	0.00
2002 Round Rock	AA	2	2	0	0	8.2	34	4	4	4	1	1	0	0	4	0	10	1	0	0	0		0	0--		1.68	4.15
2001 Houston	NL	3	3	0	0	17.2	70	11	2	2	1	1	0	0	7	0	17	2	0	1	0	1.000	0	0-0	0	1.88	1.02
2002 Houston	NL	23	21	0	0	111.0	495	112	56	54	11	2	0	3	61	5	93	1	2	7	5	.583	0	0-0	0	4.77	4.38
2 ML YEARS		26	24	0	0	128.2	565	123	58	56	12	3	0	3	68	5	110	3	2	8	5	.615	0	0-0	0	4.33	3.92

Jose Hernandez

Bats: R Throws: R Pos: SS-149; PH-3   Ht: 6'1" Wt: 188 Born: 7/14/69 Age: 33

Year Team	Lg	G	AB	H	2B	3B	HR	(Hm	Rd)	TB	R	RBI	RC	TBB	IBB	SO	HBP	SH	SF	SB	CS	SB%	GDP	Avg	OBP	Slg
1991 Texas	AL	45	98	18	2	1	0	(0	0)	22	8	4	2	3	0	31	0	6	0	0	1	.00	2	.184	.208	.224
1992 Cleveland	AL	3	4	0	0	0	0	(0	0)	0	0	0	0	0	0	2	0	0	0	0	0		0	.000	.000	.000
1994 Chicago	NL	56	132	32	2	3	1	(0	1)	43	18	9	11	8	0	29	1	5	0	2	2	.50	4	.242	.291	.326
1995 Chicago	NL	93	245	60	11	4	13	(6	7)	118	37	40	31	13	3	69	0	8	2	1	0	1.00	6	.245	.281	.482
1996 Chicago	NL	131	331	80	14	1	10	(4	6)	126	52	41	35	24	4	97	1	5	2	4	1	1.00	10	.242	.293	.381
1997 Chicago	NL	121	183	50	8	5	7	(4	3)	89	33	26	26	14	2	42	0	1	1	2	5	.29	5	.273	.323	.486
1998 Chicago	NL	149	488	124	23	7	23	(11	12)	230	76	75	67	40	3	140	1	2	2	4	6	.40	12	.254	.311	.471
1999 ChC-Atl	NL	147	508	135	20	2	19	(6	13)	216	79	62	73	52	6	145	5	2	1	11	3	.79	10	.266	.339	.425
2000 Milwaukee	NL	124	446	109	22	1	11	(8	3)	166	51	59	48	41	3	125	6	0	3	3	7	.30	12	.244	.315	.372
2001 Milwaukee	NL	152	542	135	26	2	25	(9	16)	240	67	78	69	39	8	185	2	5	4	5	4	.56	9	.249	.300	.443
2002 Milwaukee	NL	152	525	151	24	2	24	(13	11)	251	72	73	76	52	5	188	4	0	1	3	5	.38	19	.288	.356	.478
1999 Chicago	NL	99	342	93	12	2	15	(5	10)	154	57	43	55	40	3	101	5	1	0	7	2	.78	5	.272	.357	.450
1999 Atlanta	NL	48	166	42	8	0	4	(1	3)	62	22	19	18	12	3	44	0	1	1	4	1	.80	5	.253	.302	.373
11 ML YEARS		1173	3502	894	152	28	133	(61	72)	1501	493	467	438	286	34	1053	20	34	16	35	33	.51	91	.255	.314	.429

Livan Hernandez

Pitches: R Bats: R Pos: SP-33   Ht: 6'2" Wt: 240 Born: 2/20/75 Age: 28

Year Team	Lg	G	GS	CG	GF	IP	BFP	H	R	ER	HR	SH	SF	HB	TBB	IBB	SO	WP	Bk	W	L	Pct	ShO	Sv-Op	Hld	ERC	ERA
1996 Florida	NL	1	0	0	0	3.0	13	3	0	0	0	0	0	0	2	0	2	0	0	0	0	-	0	0-0	0	4.60	0.00
1997 Florida	NL	17	17	0	0	96.1	405	81	39	34	5	4	7	3	38	1	72	0	0	9	3	.750	0	0-0	0	2.96	3.18
1998 Florida	NL	33	33	9	0	234.1	1040	265	133	123	37	8	5	6	104	8	162	4	3	10	12	.455	0	0-0	0	5.58	4.72
1999 Fla-SF	NL	30	30	2	0	199.2	886	227	110	103	23	7	6	2	76	5	144	2	2	8	12	.400	0	0-0	0	4.88	4.64
2000 San Francisco	NL	33	33	5	0	240.0	1030	254	114	100	22	12	9	4	73	3	165	3	0	17	11	.607	2	0-0	0	4.01	3.75
2001 San Francisco	NL	34	34	2	0	226.2	1008	266	143	132	24	12	12	3	85	7	138	7	0	13	15	.464	0	0-0	0	5.03	5.24
2002 San Francisco	NL	33	33	5	0	216.0	921	233	113	105	19	14	8	4	71	5	134	1	1	12	16	.429	3	0-0	0	4.26	4.38
1999 Florida	NL	20	20	2	0	136.0	612	161	78	72	17	3	4	2	55	3	97	2	1	5	9	.357	0	0-0	0	5.37	4.76
1999 San Francisco	NL	10	10	0	0	63.2	274	66	32	31	6	4	2	0	21	2	47	0	1	3	3	.500	0	0-0	0	3.88	4.38
7 ML YEARS		181	180	23	0	1216.0	5303	1329	652	597	130	57	47	22	449	29	817	17	6	69	69	.500	5	0-0	0	4.59	4.42

Orlando Hernandez

Pitches: R **Bats:** R **Pos:** SP-22; RP-2 **Ht:** 6'2" **Wt:** 220 **Born:** 10/11/69 **Age:** 33

		HOW MUCH HE PITCHED						WHAT HE GAVE UP												THE RESULTS							
Year Team	Lg	G	GS	CG	GF	IP	BFP	H	R	ER	HR	SH	SF	HB	TBB	IBB	SO	WP	Bk	W	L	Pct	ShO	Sv-Op	Hld	ERC	ERA
2002 Columbus*	AAA	1	1	0	0	5.2	27	7	2	1	0	0	0	1	1	0	5	0	0	1	0	1.000	0	0--	-	4.17	1.59
1998 New York	AL	21	21	3	0	141.0	574	113	53	49	11	3	5	6	52	1	131	5	2	12	4	.750	1	0-0	0	2.96	3.13
1999 New York	AL	33	33	2	0	214.1	910	187	108	98	24	3	11	8	87	2	157	4	0	17	9	.654	1	0-0	0	3.60	4.12
2000 New York	AL	29	29	3	0	195.2	820	186	104	98	34	4	5	6	51	2	141	1	0	12	13	.480	0	0-0	0	3.82	4.51
2001 New York	AL	17	16	0	0	94.2	414	90	51	51	19	2	2	5	42	1	77	0	0	4	7	.364	0	0-0	0	4.87	4.85
2002 New York	AL	24	22	0	1	146.0	606	131	63	59	17	1	5	8	36	2	113	8	0	8	5	.615	0	1-1	1	3.20	3.64
5 ML YEARS		124	121	8	1	791.2	3324	707	379	355	105	13	28	33	268	8	619	18	2	53	38	.582	2	1-1	1	3.61	4.04

Ramon Hernandez

Bats: R **Throws:** R **Pos:** C-134; PH-3 **Ht:** 6'0" **Wt:** 210 **Born:** 5/20/76 **Age:** 27

		BATTING																		BASERUNNING				AVERAGES		
Year Team	Lg	G	AB	H	2B	3B	HR	Hm	Rd	TB	R	RBI	RC	TBB	IBB	SO	HBP	SH	SF	SB	CS	SB%	GDP	Avg	OBP	Slg
1999 Oakland	AL	40	136	38	7	0	3	1	2	54	13	21	20	18	0	11	1	1	2	1	0	1.00	5	.279	.363	.397
2000 Oakland	AL	143	419	101	19	0	14	7	7	162	52	62	49	38	1	64	7	10	5	1	0	1.00	14	.241	.311	.387
2001 Oakland	AL	136	453	115	25	0	15	5	10	185	55	60	58	37	3	68	6	9	4	1	1	.50	10	.254	.316	.408
2002 Oakland	AL	136	403	94	20	0	7	3	4	135	51	42	40	43	1	64	5	3	3	0	0	-	11	.233	.313	.335
4 ML YEARS		455	1411	348	71	0	39	16	23	536	171	185	167	136	5	207	19	23	14	3	1	.75	40	.247	.318	.380

Roberto Hernandez

Pitches: R **Bats:** R **Pos:** RP-53 **Ht:** 6'4" **Wt:** 250 **Born:** 11/11/64 **Age:** 38

		HOW MUCH HE PITCHED						WHAT HE GAVE UP												THE RESULTS							
Year Team	Lg	G	GS	CG	GF	IP	BFP	H	R	ER	HR	SH	SF	HB	TBB	IBB	SO	WP	Bk	W	L	Pct	ShO	Sv-Op	Hld	ERC	ERA
2002 Omaha*	AAA	2	0	0	1	2.0	10	0	1	0	0	0	0	0	3	0	3	1	0	0	0	-	0	0--	-	1.71	0.00
1991 Chicago	AL	9	3	0	1	15.0	69	18	15	13	1	0	0	0	7	0	6	1	0	1	0	1.000	0	0-0	0	5.19	7.80
1992 Chicago	AL	43	0	0	27	71.0	277	45	15	13	4	0	3	4	20	1	68	2	0	7	3	.700	0	12-16	6	1.74	1.65
1993 Chicago	AL	70	0	0	67	78.2	314	66	21	20	6	2	2	0	20	1	71	2	0	3	4	.429	0	38-44	0	2.54	2.29
1994 Chicago	AL	45	0	0	43	47.2	206	44	29	26	5	0	1	1	19	1	50	1	0	4	4	.500	0	14-20	0	3.66	4.91
1995 Chicago	AL	60	0	0	57	59.2	272	63	30	26	9	4	0	3	28	4	84	1	0	3	7	.300	0	32-42	0	5.04	3.92
1996 Chicago	AL	72	0	0	61	84.2	355	65	21	18	2	2	2	0	38	5	85	6	0	6	5	.545	0	38-46	0	2.40	1.91
1997 CWS-SF		74	0	0	50	80.2	340	67	24	22	7	2	1	1	38	5	82	3	0	10	3	.769	0	31-39	9	3.30	2.45
1998 Tampa Bay	AL	67	0	0	58	71.1	310	55	33	32	5	4	0	5	41	4	55	1	0	2	6	.250	0	26-35	0	3.43	4.04
1999 Tampa Bay	AL	72	0	0	66	73.1	321	68	27	25	1	2	3	4	33	1	69	3	0	2	3	.400	0	43-47	0	3.40	3.07
2000 Tampa Bay	AL	68	0	0	58	73.1	315	76	33	26	9	7	3	3	23	1	61	2	1	4	7	.364	0	32-40	1	4.24	3.19
2001 Kansas City	AL	63	0	0	55	67.2	287	69	34	31	7	1	0	1	26	3	46	6	0	5	6	.455	0	28-34	0	4.23	4.12
2002 Kansas City	AL	53	0	0	42	52.0	227	62	29	25	6	4	1	3	12	2	39	3	0	1	3	.250	0	26-33	0	4.79	4.33
1997 Chicago	AL	46	0	0	43	48.0	203	38	15	13	5	1	1	1	24	4	47	2	0	5	1	.833	0	27-31	0	3.30	2.44
1997 San Francisco	NL	28	0	0	7	32.2	137	29	9	9	2	1	0	0	14	1	35	1	0	5	2	.714	0	4-8	9	3.29	2.48
12 ML YEARS		696	3	0	585	775.0	3293	698	311	277	62	28	16	25	305	28	716	31	1	48	51	.485	0	320-396	16	3.43	3.22

Runelvys Hernandez

Pitches: R **Bats:** R **Pos:** SP-12 **Ht:** 6'1" **Wt:** 205 **Born:** 4/27/78 **Age:** 25

		HOW MUCH HE PITCHED						WHAT HE GAVE UP												THE RESULTS							
Year Team	Lg	G	GS	CG	GF	IP	BFP	H	R	ER	HR	SH	SF	HB	TBB	IBB	SO	WP	Bk	W	L	Pct	ShO	Sv-Op	Hld	ERC	ERA
2001 Burlington	A	17	17	0	0	100.2	426	94	46	38	5	2	3		29	0	100	6	3	7	5	.583	0	0--	-	3.01	3.40
2002 Wilmington	A+	2	2	0	0	12.0	46	12	6	5	0	1	0	0	1	0	9	0	0	1	1	.500	0	0--	-	2.40	3.75
2002 Wichita	AA	16	14	2	1	106.1	422	96	38	32	3	5	4		24	1	86	5	1	8	3	.727	0	0--	-	2.63	2.71
2002 Kansas City	AL	12	12	0	0	74.1	316	79	36	36	8	1	3	1	22	0	45	2	0	4	4	.500	0	0-0	0	4.16	4.36

Alex Herrera

Pitches: L **Bats:** L **Pos:** RP-5 **Ht:** 5'11" **Wt:** 175 **Born:** 11/5/76 **Age:** 26

		HOW MUCH HE PITCHED						WHAT HE GAVE UP												THE RESULTS							
Year Team	Lg	G	GS	CG	GF	IP	BFP	H	R	ER	HR	SH	SF	HB	TBB	IBB	SO	WP	Bk	W	L	Pct	ShO	Sv-Op	Hld	ERC	ERA
2000 Columbus	A	20	0	0	2	42.0	186	41	25	16	1	3	3	3	21	1	41	2	1	4	3	.571	0	0--	-	4.02	3.43
2000 Kinston	A+	17	0	0	6	31.0	138	28	11	8	1	0	1	1	19	0	40	3	1	0	1	.000	0	1--	-	3.98	2.32
2000 Akron	AA	2	0	0	1	1.1	6	2	1	0	0	0	0	0	1	0	1	0	0	0	0	-	0	0--	-	8.87	0.00
2001 Kinston	A+	28	0	0	8	59.2	231	36	6	4	1	0	0	2	18	0	83	2	0	4	0	1.000	0	3--	-	1.48	0.60
2001 Akron	AA	15	0	0	9	28.2	114	24	9	9	1	0	0	0	9	0	22	2	0	3	0	1.000	0	2--	-	2.56	2.83
2002 Akron	AA	30	0	0	9	61.1	261	47	24	23	8	3	0	6	30	1	65	3	0	0	2	.000	0	5--	-	3.72	3.38
2002 Buffalo	AAA	5	0	0	1	7.0	39	10	9	9	0	1	0	1	8	0	5	2	0	0	1	.000	0	0--	-	9.59	11.57
2002 Cleveland	AL	5	0	0	1	5.1	20	3	0	0	0	0	0	0	1	0	5	0	0	0	0	-	0	0-0	0	0.99	0.00

Richard Hidalgo

Bats: R **Throws:** R **Pos:** RF-110; PH-8; CF-1; PR-1 **Ht:** 6'3" **Wt:** 220 **Born:** 7/2/75 **Age:** 27

		BATTING																		BASERUNNING				AVERAGES		
Year Team	Lg	G	AB	H	2B	3B	HR	Hm	Rd	TB	R	RBI	RC	TBB	IBB	SO	HBP	SH	SF	SB	CS	SB%	GDP	Avg	OBP	Slg
1997 Houston	NL	19	62	19	5	0	2	0	2	30	8	6	11	4	0	18	1	0	0	1	0	1.00	0	.306	.358	.484
1998 Houston	NL	74	211	64	15	0	7	3	4	100	31	35	34	17	0	37	2	0	4	3	3	.50	5	.303	.355	.474
1999 Houston	NL	108	383	87	25	2	15	5	10	161	49	56	55	56	2	73	4	0	5	8	5	.62	5	.227	.328	.420
2000 Houston	NL	153	558	175	42	3	44	16	28	355	118	122	130	56	3	110	21	0	9	13	6	.68	13	.314	.391	.636
2001 Houston	NL	146	512	141	29	3	19	13	6	233	70	80	81	54	3	107	16	0	11	3	5	.38	15	.275	.356	.455
2002 Houston	NL	114	388	91	17	4	15	4	11	161	54	48	42	43	1	85	6	0	2	6	2	.75	13	.235	.319	.415
6 ML YEARS		614	2114	577	133	12	102	41	61	1040	330	347	353	230	9	430	50	0	31	34	21	.62	51	.273	.353	.492

Bobby Higginson

Bats: L Throws: R Pos: LF-117; DH-1; PH-1   Ht: 5'11" Wt: 202 Born: 8/18/70 Age: 32

Year Team	Lg	G	AB	H	2B	3B	HR	(Hm	Rd)	TB	R	RBI	RC	TBB	IBB	SO	HBP	SH	SF	SB	CS	SB%	GDP	Avg	OBP	Slg
1995 Detroit	AL	131	410	92	17	5	14	(10	4)	161	61	43	56	62	3	107	5	2	7	6	4	.60	5	.224	.329	.393
1996 Detroit	AL	130	440	141	35	0	26	(15	11)	254	75	81	99	65	7	66	1	3	6	6	3	.67	7	.320	.404	.577
1997 Detroit	AL	146	546	163	30	5	27	(16	11)	284	94	101	105	70	2	85	3	0	4	12	7	.63	10	.299	.379	.520
1998 Detroit	AL	157	612	174	37	4	25	(10	15)	294	92	85	100	63	2	101	6	0	4	3	3	.50	16	.284	.355	.480
1999 Detroit	AL	107	377	90	18	0	12	(8	4)	144	51	46	54	64	2	66	2	0	2	4	6	.40	2	.239	.351	.382
2000 Detroit	AL	154	597	179	44	4	30	(12	18)	321	104	102	121	74	6	99	2	2	3	15	3	.83	9	.300	.377	.538
2001 Detroit	AL	147	541	150	28	6	17	(7	10)	241	84	71	91	80	3	65	2	1	9	20	12	.63	8	.277	.367	.445
2002 Detroit	AL	119	444	125	24	3	10	(6	4)	185	50	63	72	41	3	45	6	1	7	12	5	.71	8	.282	.345	.417
8 ML YEARS		1091	3967	1114	233	27	161	(84	77)	1884	611	592	698	519	28	634	27	9	42	78	43	.64	61	.281	.364	.475

Erik Hiljus

Pitches: R Bats: R Pos: SP-9   Ht: 6'6" Wt: 222 Born: 12/25/72 Age: 30

Year Team	Lg	G	GS	CG	GF	IP	BFP	H	R	ER	HR	SH	SF	HB	TBB	IBB	SO	WP	Bk	W	L	Pct	ShO	Sv-Op	Hld	ERC	ERA
2002 Sacramento*	AAA	9	6	0	0	37.2	177	54	32	32	3	1	2	1	15	0	30	2	0	1	3	.250	0	0--	-	6.68	7.65
1999 Detroit	AL	6	0	0	0	8.2	35	7	5	4	2	0	1	0	5	0	1	0	0	0	0	-	0	0-0	1	4.96	4.15
2000 Detroit	AL	3	0	0	2	3.2	16	5	3	3	1	0	0	0	1	0	2	0	0	0	0	-	0	0-0	0	7.34	7.36
2001 Oakland	AL	16	11	0	3	66.0	290	70	29	25	7	2	1	0	21	1	67	2	1	5	0	1.000	0	0-0	0	4.00	3.41
2002 Oakland	AL	9	9	0	0	45.2	206	52	36	33	11	1	1	0	21	1	29	1	0	3	3	.500	0	0-0	0	6.16	6.50
4 ML YEARS		34	20	0	5	124.0	547	134	73	65	21	3	3	0	48	2	99	3	1	8	3	.727	0	0-0	1	4.92	4.72

Bobby Hill

Bats: B Throws: R Pos: 2B-55; PH-4; PR-2; SS-1   Ht: 5'10" Wt: 190 Born: 4/3/78 Age: 25

Year Team	Lg	G	AB	H	2B	3B	HR	(Hm	Rd)	TB	R	RBI	RC	TBB	IBB	SO	HBP	SH	SF	SB	CS	SB%	GDP	Avg	OBP	Slg
2000 Newark	IND	132	481	157	22	9	13	(-	-)	236	109	82	118	101	2	57	4	1	7	81	15	.84	8	.326	.442	.491
2001 W Tennessee	AA	57	209	63	8	1	3	(-	-)	82	30	21	34	32	1	39	2	1	2	20	8	.71	7	.301	.396	.392
2001 Cubs	R	3	9	2	0	0	0	(-	-)	2	1	1	1	2	0	3	0	0	0	1	0	1.00	0	.222	.364	.222
2002 Iowa	AAA	92	354	99	23	3	8	(-	-)	152	80	39	64	49	0	66	11	3	2	29	5	.85	7	.280	.382	.429
2002 Chicago	NL	59	190	48	7	2	4	(1	3)	71	26	20	24	17	4	42	4	4	0	6	1	.86	0	.253	.327	.374

Jeremy Hill

Pitches: R Bats: R Pos: RP-10   Ht: 5'10" Wt: 185 Born: 8/8/77 Age: 25

Year Team	Lg	G	GS	CG	GF	IP	BFP	H	R	ER	HR	SH	SF	HB	TBB	IBB	SO	WP	Bk	W	L	Pct	ShO	Sv-Op	Hld	ERC	ERA
2001 Burlington	A	40	0	0	31	47.2	190	22	11	8	2	2	0	3	25	0	66	6	0	0	2	.000	0	12--	-	1.68	1.51
2001 Wilmington	A+	9	0	0	7	12.1	52	10	2	1	0	1	0	0	8	1	13	2	0	4	0	1.000	0	2--	-	3.25	0.73
2002 Wichita	AA	56	0	0	46	76.1	317	61	26	20	4	6	2	1	32	5	80	3	0	4	7	.364	0	19--	-	2.71	2.36
2002 Kansas City	AL	10	0	0	6	9.1	43	8	4	4	1	0	1	0	8	1	7	1	0	0	1	.000	0	0-0	0	4.93	3.86

Shea Hillenbrand

Bats: R Throws: R Pos: 3B-156; PH-2   Ht: 6'1" Wt: 211 Born: 7/27/75 Age: 27

Year Team	Lg	G	AB	H	2B	3B	HR	(Hm	Rd)	TB	R	RBI	RC	TBB	IBB	SO	HBP	SH	SF	SB	CS	SB%	GDP	Avg	OBP	Slg
1996 Lowell	A-	72	279	88	18	2	2	(-	-)	116	33	38	42	18	1	32	8	0	2	4	3	.57	6	.315	.371	.416
1997 Michigan	A	64	224	65	13	3	3	(-	-)	93	28	39	29	9	1	20	1	0	4	1	3	.25	2	.290	.315	.415
1997 Sarasota	A+	57	220	65	12	0	2	(-	-)	83	25	28	24	7	1	29	2	1	2	9	8	.53	4	.295	.320	.377
1998 Michigan	A	129	498	174	33	4	19	(-	-)	272	80	92	96	19	2	49	10	1	3	13	7	.65	11	.349	.383	.546
1999 Trenton	AA	69	282	73	15	0	7	(-	-)	109	41	36	31	14	3	27	3	0	3	6	5	.55	6	.259	.298	.386
2000 Trenton	AA	135	529	171	35	3	11	(-	-)	245	77	79	81	19	0	39	6	3	3	3	3	.50	15	.323	.355	.463
2001 Boston	AL	139	468	123	20	2	12	(5	7)	183	52	49	49	13	3	61	7	1	4	3	4	.43	12	.263	.291	.391
2002 Boston	AL	156	634	186	43	4	18	(5	13)	291	94	83	88	25	4	95	12	0	5	4	2	.67	18	.293	.330	.459
2 ML YEARS		295	1102	309	63	6	30	(10	20)	474	146	132	137	38	7	156	19	1	9	7	6	.54	30	.280	.313	.430

A.J. Hinch

Bats: R Throws: R Pos: C-68; PH-4   Ht: 6'1" Wt: 205 Born: 5/15/74 Age: 29

Year Team	Lg	G	AB	H	2B	3B	HR	(Hm	Rd)	TB	R	RBI	RC	TBB	IBB	SO	HBP	SH	SF	SB	CS	SB%	GDP	Avg	OBP	Slg
1998 Oakland	AL	120	337	78	10	0	9	(4	5)	115	34	35	36	30	0	89	4	13	7	3	0	1.00	6	.231	.296	.341
1999 Oakland	AL	76	205	44	4	1	7	(3	4)	71	26	24	18	11	0	41	2	9	1	6	2	.75	4	.215	.260	.346
2000 Oakland	AL	6	8	2	0	0	0	(0	0)	2	1	0	1	1	0	1	0	0	0	0	0	-	0	.250	.333	.250
2001 Kansas City	AL	45	121	19	3	0	6	(4	2)	40	10	15	7	8	1	26	3	1	1	1	1	.50	5	.157	.226	.331
2002 Kansas City	AL	72	197	49	7	1	7	(6	1)	79	25	27	26	18	0	35	3	2	0	3	3	.50	2	.249	.321	.401
5 ML YEARS		319	868	192	24	2	29	(17	12)	307	96	101	88	68	1	192	12	25	9	13	6	.68	17	.221	.284	.354

Eric Hinske

Bats: L Throws: R Pos: 3B-148; PH-10   Ht: 6'2" Wt: 225 Born: 8/5/77 Age: 25

Year Team	Lg	G	AB	H	2B	3B	HR	(Hm	Rd)	TB	R	RBI	RC	TBB	IBB	SO	HBP	SH	SF	SB	CS	SB%	GDP	Avg	OBP	Slg
1998 Williamsport	A-	68	248	74	20	0	9	(-	-)	121	48	57	50	35	3	61	2	0	4	19	3	.86	2	.298	.384	.488
1998 Rockford	A	6	20	9	4	0	1	(-	-)	16	8	4	8	5	0	6	0	0	1	1	0	1.00	0	.450	.538	.800
1999 Daytona	A+	130	445	132	28	6	19	(-	-)	229	76	79	87	62	7	90	5	1	5	16	10	.62	5	.297	.385	.515

Year Team	Lg	G	AB	H	2B	3B	HR	(Hm	Rd)	TB	R	RBI	RC	TBB	IBB	SO	HBP	SH	SF	SB	CS	SB%	GDP	Avg	OBP	Slg
1999 Iowa	AAA	4	15	4	0	1	1	(-	-)	9	3	2	3	1	0	4	0	0	0	0	0	-	0	.267	.313	.600
2000 W Tennessee	AA	131	436	113	21	9	20	(-	-)	212	76	73	81	78	3	133	3	0	3	14	5	.74	7	.259	.373	.486
2001 Sacramento	AAA	121	436	123	27	1	25	(-	-)	227	71	79	85	54	3	113	10	2	2	20	7	.74	6	.282	.373	.521
2002 Toronto	AL	151	566	158	38	2	24	(15	9)	272	99	84	104	77	5	138	2	0	5	13	1	.93	12	.279	.365	.481

Sterling Hitchcock

Pitches: L **Bats:** L **Pos:** RP-18; SP-2   **Ht:** 6'0" **Wt:** 205 **Born:** 4/29/71 **Age:** 32

Year Team	Lg	HOW MUCH HE PITCHED						WHAT HE GAVE UP										THE RESULTS							
		G	GS	CG	GF	IP	BFP	H	R	ER	HR	SH	SF	HB	TBB	IBB	SO	WP	Bk	W	L	Pct	ShO	Sv-Op	Hld	ERC	ERA
2002 Yankees*	R	2	2	0	0	3.0	9	0	0	0	0				0	0	6	0	0	0	0	-	0	0--	-	-	0.00
2002 Tampa*	A+	1	1	0	0	6.0	22	3	1	1	0	1	0	1	0	0	3	0	0	0	0	-	0	0--	-	0.80	1.50
2002 Columbus*	AAA	2	2	0	0	7.1	42	19	11	11	2	0	0	0	3	0	3	0	1	0	0	-	0	0--	-	17.30	13.50
1992 New York	AL	3	3	0	0	13.0	68	23	12	12	2	0	0	1	6	0	6	0	0	0	2	.000	0	0-0	0	9.98	8.31
1993 New York	AL	6	6	0	0	31.0	135	32	18	16	4	0	2	1	14	1	26	3	2	1	2	.333	0	0-0	0	4.83	4.65
1994 New York	AL	23	5	1	4	49.1	218	48	24	23	3	1	7	0	29	1	37	5	0	4	1	.800	0	2-2	3	4.38	4.20
1995 New York	AL	27	27	4	0	168.1	719	155	91	88	22	5	9	5	68	1	121	5	2	11	10	.524	1	0-0	0	3.97	4.70
1996 Seattle	AL	35	35	0	0	196.2	885	245	131	117	27	3	8	7	73	4	132	4	1	13	9	.591	0	0-0	0	5.86	5.35
1997 San Diego	NL	32	28	1	1	161.0	693	172	102	93	24	7	4	4	55	2	106	6	2	10	11	.476	0	0-0	0	4.71	5.20
1998 San Diego	NL	39	27	2	3	176.1	743	169	83	77	29	9	3	9	48	2	158	11	1	9	7	.563	1	1-2	3	3.95	3.93
1999 San Diego	NL	33	33	1	0	205.2	892	202	99	94	29	9	6	5	76	6	194	15	2	12	14	.462	0	0-0	0	4.14	4.11
2000 San Diego	NL	11	11	0	0	65.2	292	69	38	36	12	2	1	5	26	1	61	4	0	1	6	.143	0	0-0	0	5.22	4.93
2001 SD-NYY	AL	13	12	1	0	70.1	323	89	46	44	6	2	4	3	21	0	43	3	1	6	5	.545	0	0-0	0	5.15	5.63
2002 New York	AL	20	2	0	11	39.1	193	57	29	24	4	1	1	1	15	3	31	1	0	1	2	.333	0	0-0	0	6.43	5.49
2001 San Diego	NL	3	3	0	0	19.0	85	22	9	7	1	1	0	1	3	0	15	1	0	2	1	.667	0	0-0	0	3.68	3.32
2001 New York	AL	10	9	1	0	51.1	238	67	37	37	5	1	4	2	18	0	28	2	1	4	4	.500	0	0-0	0	5.74	6.49
11 ML YEARS		242	189	10	19	1176.2	5161	1261	673	624	162	39	45	41	431	21	915	57	11	68	69	.496	2	3-4	6	4.72	4.77

Denny Hocking

Bats: B **Throws:** R **Pos:** 2B-56; SS-25; 3B-16; 1B-6; PH-6; PR-6; RF-4; CF-1   **Ht:** 5'10" **Wt:** 183 **Born:** 4/2/70 **Age:** 33

Year Team	Lg	G	AB	H	2B	3B	HR	(Hm	Rd)	TB	R	RBI	RC	TBB	IBB	SO	HBP	SH	SF	SB	CS	SB%	GDP	Avg	OBP	Slg
1993 Minnesota	AL	15	36	5	1	0	0	(0	0)	6	7	0	1	6	0	8	0	0	0	1	0	1.00	1	.139	.262	.167
1994 Minnesota	AL	11	31	10	3	0	0	(0	0)	13	3	2	4	0	0	4	0	0	0	2	0	1.00	1	.323	.323	.419
1995 Minnesota	AL	9	25	5	0	2	0	(0	0)	9	4	3	2	2	1	2	0	1	0	1	0	1.00	1	.200	.259	.360
1996 Minnesota	AL	49	127	25	6	0	1	(0	1)	34	16	10	6	8	0	24	0	1	1	3	3	.50	3	.197	.243	.268
1997 Minnesota	AL	115	253	65	12	4	2	(0	2)	91	28	25	26	18	0	51	1	5	1	3	5	.38	6	.257	.308	.360
1998 Minnesota	AL	110	198	40	6	1	3	(1	2)	57	32	15	14	16	1	44	0	3	2	2	1	.67	2	.202	.259	.288
1999 Minnesota	AL	136	386	103	18	2	7	(2	5)	146	47	41	43	22	1	54	3	4	6	11	7	.61	10	.267	.307	.378
2000 Minnesota	AL	134	373	111	24	4	4	(1	3)	155	52	47	61	48	1	77	0	7	5	7	5	.58	2	.298	.373	.416
2001 Minnesota	AL	112	327	82	16	2	3	(1	2)	111	34	25	35	29	1	67	2	4	6	6	1	.86	7	.251	.315	.339
2002 Minnesota	AL	102	260	65	13	0	2	(1	1)	84	28	25	25	24	0	44	1	4	5	0	2	.00	3	.250	.310	.323
10 ML YEARS		793	2016	511	99	15	22	(6	16)	706	251	193	217	173	5	375	7	29	21	36	24	.60	36	.253	.312	.350

Trey Hodges

Pitches: R **Bats:** R **Pos:** RP-4   **Ht:** 6'3" **Wt:** 187 **Born:** 6/29/78 **Age:** 25

Year Team	Lg	HOW MUCH HE PITCHED						WHAT HE GAVE UP										THE RESULTS							
		G	GS	CG	GF	IP	BFP	H	R	ER	HR	SH	SF	HB	TBB	IBB	SO	WP	Bk	W	L	Pct	ShO	Sv-Op	Hld	ERC	ERA
2000 Jamestown	A-	13	2	0	2	19.2	93	22	14	13	3	1	0	1	12	0	13	1	2	0	2	.000	0	0--	-	6.19	5.95
2001 Myrtle Beach	A+	26	26	1	0	173.0	686	156	64	53	13	4	2	5	18	0	139	7	0	15	8	.652	0	0--	-	2.41	2.76
2002 Richmond	AAA	28	28	1	0	172.1	716	158	66	61	9	7	5	8	56	1	116	2	1	15	9	.625	1	0--	-	3.22	3.19
2002 Atlanta	NL	4	0	0	0	11.2	53	16	7	7	2	2	2	1	2	0	6	1	0	2	0	1.000	0	0-0	0	6.20	5.40

Trevor Hoffman

Pitches: R **Bats:** R **Pos:** RP-61   **Ht:** 6'0" **Wt:** 205 **Born:** 10/13/67 **Age:** 35

Year Team	Lg	HOW MUCH HE PITCHED						WHAT HE GAVE UP										THE RESULTS							
		G	GS	CG	GF	IP	BFP	H	R	ER	HR	SH	SF	HB	TBB	IBB	SO	WP	Bk	W	L	Pct	ShO	Sv-Op	Hld	ERC	ERA
1993 Fla-SD	NL	67	0	0	26	90.0	391	80	43	39	10	4	5	1	39	13	79	5	0	4	6	.400	0	5-8	15	3.40	3.90
1994 San Diego	NL	47	0	0	41	56.0	225	39	16	16	4	1	2	0	20	6	68	3	0	4	4	.500	0	20-23	1	2.02	2.57
1995 San Diego	NL	55	0	0	51	53.1	218	48	25	23	10	0	0	0	14	3	52	1	0	7	4	.636	0	31-38	0	3.48	3.88
1996 San Diego	NL	70	0	0	62	88.0	348	50	23	22	6	2	2	2	31	5	111	2	0	9	5	.643	0	42-49	0	1.58	2.25
1997 San Diego	NL	70	0	0	59	81.1	322	59	25	24	9	2	1	0	24	4	111	7	0	6	4	.600	0	37-44	0	2.27	2.66
1998 San Diego	NL	66	0	0	61	73.0	274	41	12	12	2	3	0	1	21	2	86	8	0	4	2	.667	0	53-54	0	1.32	1.48
1999 San Diego	NL	64	0	0	54	67.1	263	48	23	16	5	1	3	0	15	2	73	4	0	2	3	.400	0	40-43	0	1.78	2.14
2000 San Diego	NL	70	0	0	59	72.1	291	61	29	24	7	3	5	0	11	4	85	4	0	4	7	.364	0	43-50	0	2.18	2.99
2001 San Diego	NL	62	0	0	55	60.1	248	48	23	23	10	2	2	1	21	2	63	3	0	3	4	.429	0	43-46	0	3.20	3.43
2002 San Diego	NL	61	0	0	52	59.1	245	52	20	18	2	2	0	1	18	2	69	3	0	2	5	.286	0	38-41	0	2.63	2.73
1993 Florida	NL	28	0	0	13	35.2	152	24	13	13	5	2	1	0	19	7	26	3	0	2	2	.500	0	2-3	8	2.71	3.28
1993 San Diego	NL	39	0	0	13	54.1	239	56	30	26	5	2	4	1	20	6	53	2	0	2	4	.333	0	3-5	7	3.88	4.31
10 ML YEARS		632	0	0	520	701.0	2825	526	241	217	65	20	22	6	214	43	797	40	0	45	44	.506	0	352-396	16	2.31	2.79

Todd Hollandsworth

Bats: L **Throws:** L **Pos:** LF-99; RF-24; PH-21; CF-17   **Ht:** 6'2" **Wt:** 207 **Born:** 4/20/73 **Age:** 30

Year Team	Lg	G	AB	H	2B	3B	HR	(Hm	Rd)	TB	R	RBI	RC	TBB	IBB	SO	HBP	SH	SF	SB	CS	SB%	GDP	Avg	OBP	Slg
1995 Los Angeles	NL	41	103	24	2	0	5	(3	2)	41	16	13	13	10	2	29	1	0	1	2	1	.67	1	.233	.304	.398
1996 Los Angeles	NL	149	478	139	26	4	12	(2	10)	209	64	59	76	41	1	93	2	3	2	21	6	.78	2	.291	.348	.437
1997 Los Angeles	NL	106	296	73	20	2	4	(1	3)	109	39	31	28	17	2	60	0	2	2	5	5	.50	8	.247	.286	.368
1998 Los Angeles	NL	55	175	47	6	4	3	(1	2)	70	23	20	21	9	0	42	1	2	0	4	3	.57	2	.269	.308	.400

105

Year Team	Lg	G	AB	H	2B	3B	HR	(Hm	Rd)	TB	R	RBI	RC	TBB	IBB	SO	HBP	SH	SF	SB	CS	SB%	GDP	Avg	OBP	Slg
1999 Los Angeles	NL	92	261	74	12	2	9	(5	4)	117	39	32	41	24	1	61	1	0	1	5	2	.71	2	.284	.345	.448
2000 LA-Col	NL	137	428	115	20	0	19	(13	6)	192	81	47	63	41	3	99	1	0	1	18	7	.72	8	.269	.333	.449
2001 Colorado	NL	33	117	43	15	1	6	(3	3)	78	21	19	30	8	2	20	0	0	1	5	0	1.00	1	.368	.408	.667
2002 Col-Tex	NL	134	430	122	27	1	16	(11	5)	199	55	67	68	40	4	98	1	3	3	8	8	.50	8	.284	.344	.463
2000 Los Angeles	NL	81	261	61	12	0	8	(6	2)	97	42	24	31	30	2	61	1	0	1	11	4	.73	4	.234	.314	.372
2000 Colorado	NL	56	167	54	8	0	11	(7	4)	95	39	23	32	11	1	38	0	0	0	7	3	.70	4	.323	.365	.569
2002 Colorado	NL	95	298	88	21	1	11	(9	2)	144	39	48	46	26	4	71	1	1	2	7	8	.47	8	.295	.352	.483
2002 Texas	AL	39	132	34	6	0	5	(2	3)	55	16	19	22	14	0	27	0	2	1	1	0	1.00	0	.258	.327	.417
8 ML YEARS		747	2288	637	128	14	74	(39	35)	1015	338	288	340	190	15	502	7	10	10	68	32	.68	32	.278	.334	.444

Dave Hollins

Bats: B Throws: R Pos: PH-6; 1B-5; PR-3   **Ht: 6'1" Wt: 232 Born: 5/25/66 Age: 37**

Year Team	Lg	G	AB	H	2B	3B	HR	(Hm	Rd)	TB	R	RBI	RC	TBB	IBB	SO	HBP	SH	SF	SB	CS	SB%	GDP	Avg	OBP	Slg
2002 Scrtn/WlksBr*	AAA	14	38	9	1	0	2	(-	-)	16	8	7	9	11	0	9	5	0	0	0	1	.00	0	.237	.463	.421
1990 Philadelphia	NL	72	114	21	0	0	5	(2	3)	36	14	15	9	10	3	28	1	0	1	0	0	-	1	.184	.252	.316
1991 Philadelphia	NL	56	151	45	10	2	6	(3	3)	77	18	21	29	17	1	26	3	0	1	1	1	.50	2	.298	.378	.510
1992 Philadelphia	NL	156	586	158	28	4	27	(14	13)	275	104	93	103	76	4	110	19	0	4	9	6	.60	8	.270	.369	.469
1993 Philadelphia	NL	143	543	148	30	4	18	(9	9)	240	104	93	89	85	5	109	5	0	7	2	3	.40	15	.273	.372	.442
1994 Philadelphia	NL	44	162	36	7	1	4	(1	3)	57	28	26	19	23	0	32	4	0	3	1	0	1.00	6	.222	.328	.352
1995 Phi-Bos		70	218	49	12	2	7	(5	2)	86	48	26	38	57	4	45	5	0	1	1	1	.50	4	.225	.391	.394
1996 Min-Sea	AL	149	516	135	29	0	16	(7	9)	212	88	78	82	84	7	117	13	1	2	6	6	.50	11	.262	.377	.411
1997 Anaheim	AL	149	572	165	29	2	16	(15	1)	246	101	85	90	62	2	124	8	1	5	16	6	.73	12	.288	.363	.430
1998 Anaheim	AL	101	363	88	16	2	11	(4	7)	141	60	39	50	44	2	69	7	2	2	11	3	.79	5	.242	.334	.388
1999 Anaheim	AL	27	99	22	5	0	2	(1	1)	33	12	6	8	5	0	22	0	0	0	0	0	-	2	.222	.260	.333
2001 Cleveland	AL	2	5	1	0	0	0	(0	0)	1	0	0	0	1	0	2	0	1	0	0	0	-	0	.200	.333	.200
2002 Philadelphia	NL	14	17	2	0	0	0	(0	0)	2	1	0	0	1	0	3	1	0	0	0	1	.00	0	.118	.167	.118
1995 Philadelphia	NL	65	205	47	12	2	7	(5	2)	84	46	25	37	53	4	38	5	0	4	1	1	.50	4	.229	.393	.410
1995 Boston	AL	5	13	2	0	0	0	(0	0)	2	2	1	1	4	0	7	0	0	0	0	0	-	0	.154	.353	.154
1996 Minnesota	AL	121	422	102	26	0	13	(6	7)	167	71	53	63	71	5	102	10	0	0	6	4	.60	9	.242	.364	.396
1996 Seattle	AL	28	94	33	3	0	3	(1	2)	45	17	25	19	13	2	15	3	1	2	0	2	.00	2	.351	.438	.479
12 ML YEARS		983	3346	870	166	17	112	(61	51)	1406	578	482	517	464	28	687	66	5	30	47	27	.64	66	.260	.358	.420

Darren Holmes

Pitches: R Bats: R Pos: RP-55   **Ht: 6'0" Wt: 202 Born: 4/25/66 Age: 37**

Year Team	Lg	G	GS	CG	GF	IP	BFP	H	R	ER	HR	SH	SF	HB	TBB	IBB	SO	WP	Bk	W	L	Pct	ShO	Sv-Op	Hld	ERC	ERA
1990 Los Angeles	NL	14	0	0	1	17.1	77	15	10	10	7	0	1	0	11	3	19	1	0	0	1	.000	0	0-0	0	3.59	5.19
1991 Milwaukee	NL	40	0	0	9	76.1	344	90	43	40	6	8	3	1	27	1	59	6	0	1	4	.200	0	3-6	3	4.71	4.72
1992 Milwaukee	NL	41	0	0	25	42.1	173	35	12	12	1	4	0	2	11	4	31	0	0	4	4	.500	0	6-8	2	2.19	2.55
1993 Colorado	NL	62	0	0	51	66.2	274	56	31	30	6	0	0	2	20	1	60	2	1	3	3	.500	0	25-29	3	2.86	4.05
1994 Colorado	NL	29	0	0	14	28.1	142	35	25	20	5	4	1	1	24	4	33	2	0	0	3	.000	0	3-8	3	7.90	6.35
1995 Colorado	NL	68	0	0	33	66.2	286	59	26	24	3	5	3	1	28	3	61	7	1	6	1	.857	0	14-18	13	3.09	3.24
1996 Colorado	NL	62	0	0	21	77.0	333	78	41	34	8	2	1	1	28	2	73	2	0	5	4	.556	0	1-8	7	4.01	3.97
1997 Colorado	NL	42	6	0	10	89.1	406	113	58	53	12	6	4	0	36	3	70	4	0	9	2	.818	0	3-4	5	5.87	5.34
1998 New York	NL	34	0	0	13	51.1	215	53	19	19	4	0	3	2	14	3	31	1	0	0	3	.000	0	2-3	2	3.73	3.33
1999 Arizona	NL	44	0	0	9	48.2	219	50	21	20	3	2	0	1	25	8	35	0	2	4	3	.571	0	0-2	4	4.14	3.70
2000 Ari-Stl-Bal		18	0	0	1	19.1	103	37	28	28	6	0	3	2	9	0	16	0	0	1	0	1.000	0	1-2	1	12.92	13.03
2002 Atlanta	NL	55	0	0	10	54.2	214	41	12	11	3	4	1	2	12	4	47	0	0	2	2	.500	0	1-2	7	1.92	1.81
2000 Arizona	NL	8	0	0	3	6.1	32	12	6	6	1	0	1	1	1	0	5	0	0	0	0	-	0	1-1	1	9.99	8.53
2000 St Louis	NL	5	0	0	1	8.1	39	12	9	9	2	0	2	1	3	0	5	0	0	0	1	.000	0	0-1	0	8.54	9.72
2000 Baltimore	AL	5	0	0	0	4.2	32	13	13	13	3	0	0	0	5	0	6	0	0	0	0	-	0	0-0	0	26.18	25.07
12 ML YEARS		509	6	0	200	638.0	2786	662	326	301	58	36	21	15	245	36	535	25	4	34	31	.523	0	59-90	49	4.14	4.25

Mike Holtz

Pitches: L Bats: L Pos: RP-49   **Ht: 5'9" Wt: 185 Born: 10/10/72 Age: 30**

Year Team	Lg	G	GS	CG	GF	IP	BFP	H	R	ER	HR	SH	SF	HB	TBB	IBB	SO	WP	Bk	W	L	Pct	ShO	Sv-Op	Hld	ERC	ERA
1996 Anaheim	AL	30	0	0	8	29.1	127	21	11	8	1	1	1	3	19	2	31	1	0	3	3	.500	0	0-0	5	3.29	2.45
1997 Anaheim	AL	66	0	0	11	43.1	187	38	21	16	7	1	2	2	15	4	40	1	0	3	4	.429	0	2-8	14	3.52	3.32
1998 Anaheim	AL	53	0	0	9	30.1	137	38	16	16	0	1	2	1	15	1	29	4	0	2	2	.500	0	1-2	13	5.39	4.75
1999 Anaheim	AL	28	0	0	9	22.1	106	26	20	20	3	1	0	2	15	1	17	3	0	2	3	.400	0	0-0	1	6.85	8.06
2000 Anaheim	AL	61	0	0	6	41.0	176	37	26	23	4	4	3	2	18	2	40	1	0	3	3	.500	0	0-0	10	3.79	5.05
2001 Anaheim	AL	63	0	0	11	37.0	167	40	24	20	5	3	1	2	15	4	38	5	0	1	2	.333	0	0-1	15	4.77	4.86
2002 Oak-SD		49	0	0	12	35.0	178	42	25	21	5	0	3	2	30	3	26	3	0	2	2	.500	0	0-4	5	7.50	5.40
2002 Oakland	AL	16	0	0	7	14.0	77	24	11	10	3	0	0	1	9	0	7	0	0	0	0	-	0	0-1	1	10.72	6.43
2002 San Diego	NL	33	0	0	5	21.0	101	18	14	11	2	0	3	1	21	3	19	3	0	2	2	.500	0	0-3	4	5.49	4.71
7 ML YEARS		350	0	0	66	238.1	1078	242	143	124	25	11	12	14	127	17	221	18	0	16	19	.457	0	3-15	63	4.82	4.68

Paul Hoover

Bats: R Throws: R Pos: C-4; PH-1   **Ht: 6'1" Wt: 211 Born: 4/14/76 Age: 27**

Year Team	Lg	G	AB	H	2B	3B	HR	(Hm	Rd)	TB	R	RBI	RC	TBB	IBB	SO	HBP	SH	SF	SB	CS	SB%	GDP	Avg	OBP	Slg
1997 Princeton	R+	55	201	56	16	4	4	(-	-)	92	55	37	41	20	0	37	6	3	4	7	4	.64	3	.303	.363	.446
1998 Chrlstn - SC	A	40	124	36	10	1	3	(-	-)	57	24	19	25	22	1	29	5	0	0	2	1	.67	0	.290	.417	.460
1998 Hudson Val	A-	73	269	76	20	1	4	(-	-)	110	51	37	50	39	3	44	11	0	6	26	3	.90	5	.283	.388	.409
1999 St.Pete	A+	118	408	111	13	6	8	(-	-)	160	66	49	54	53	3	81	16	0	4	23	7	.77	13	.272	.376	.392
2000 Orlando	AA	106	360	90	20	4	3	(-	-)	127	54	44	54	67	2	66	13	1	5	9	8	.53	5	.250	.382	.353
2000 Durham	AAA	4	10	3	0	0	0	(-	-)	3	0	0	1	1	0	5	1	0	0	1	0	1.00	0	.300	.364	.300
2001 Durham	AAA	89	293	63	18	4	3	(-	-)	98	37	21	23	11	0	66	7	8	1	5	3	.63	8	.215	.260	.334

Year Team	Lg	G	AB	H	2B	3B	HR	(Hm Rd)	TB	R	RBI	RC	TBB	IBB	SO	HBP	SH	SF	SB	CS	SB%	GDP	Avg	OBP	Slg
2002 Durham	AAA	69	227	50	12	3	5	(- -)	83	27	20	23	18	0	67	3	5	1	3	3	.60	5	.220	.285	.366
2001 Tampa Bay	AL	3	4	1	0	0	0	(0 0)	1	1	0	0	0	0	1	0	0	0	0	0	-	0	.250	.250	.250
2002 Tampa Bay	AL	5	17	3	0	0	0	(0 0)	3	1	2	1	0	0	5	0	0	0	0	0	-	0	.176	.176	.176
2 ML YEARS		8	21	4	0	0	0	(0 0)	4	2	2	1	0	0	6	0	0	0	0	0	-	0	.190	.190	.190

Tyler Houston

Bats: L **Throws:** R **Pos:** 3B-74; PH-29; 1B-13   **Ht:** 6'1" **Wt:** 218 **Born:** 1/17/71 **Age:** 32

Year Team	Lg	G	AB	H	2B	3B	HR	(Hm Rd)	TB	R	RBI	RC	TBB	IBB	SO	HBP	SH	SF	SB	CS	SB%	GDP	Avg	OBP	Slg
1996 Atl-ChC	NL	79	142	45	9	1	3	(1 2)	65	21	27	21	9	1	27	0	0	0	3	2	.60	5	.317	.358	.458
1997 Chicago	NL	72	196	51	10	0	2	(0 2)	67	15	28	19	9	1	35	0	0	2	1	0	1.00	4	.260	.290	.342
1998 Chicago	NL	95	255	65	7	1	9	(4 5)	101	26	33	27	13	1	53	0	1	1	2	2	.50	6	.255	.290	.396
1999 ChC-Cle		113	276	62	10	1	10	(2 8)	104	28	30	30	31	4	78	0	1	1	1	1	.50	7	.225	.302	.377
2000 Milwaukee	NL	101	284	71	15	0	18	(6 12)	140	30	43	37	17	3	72	0	4	0	2	1	.67	13	.250	.292	.493
2001 Milwaukee	NL	75	235	68	7	0	12	(6 6)	111	36	38	37	18	1	62	1	2	0	0	0	-	3	.289	.343	.472
2002 Mil-LA	NL	111	320	90	20	3	7	(6 1)	137	34	40	42	16	3	62	4	4	1	1	0	1.00	9	.281	.323	.428
1996 Atlanta	NL	33	27	6	2	1	1	(1 0)	13	3	8	3	1	0	9	0	0	0	0	0	-	1	.222	.250	.481
1996 Chicago	NL	46	115	39	7	0	2	(0 2)	52	18	19	18	8	1	18	0	0	0	3	2	.60	4	.339	.382	.452
1999 Chicago	NL	100	249	58	9	1	9	(2 7)	96	26	27	28	28	4	67	0	1	1	1	1	.50	7	.233	.309	.386
1999 Cleveland	AL	13	27	4	1	0	1	(0 1)	8	2	3	2	3	0	11	0	0	0	0	0	-	0	.148	.233	.296
2002 Milwaukee	NL	76	255	77	15	2	7	(6 1)	117	25	33	38	14	3	41	4	4	1	1	0	1.00	9	.302	.347	.459
2002 Los Angeles	NL	35	65	13	5	1	0	(0 0)	20	9	7	4	2	0	21	0	0	0	0	0	-	5	.200	.224	.308
7 ML YEARS		646	1708	452	78	6	61	(25 36)	725	190	239	213	113	14	389	5	12	5	10	6	.63	47	.265	.311	.424

Ben Howard

Pitches: R **Bats:** R **Pos:** SP-2; RP-1   **Ht:** 6'2" **Wt:** 190 **Born:** 1/15/79 **Age:** 24

Year Team	Lg	G	GS	CG	GF	IP	BFP	H	R	ER	HR	SH	SF	HB	TBB	IBB	SO	WP	Bk	W	L	Pct	ShO	Sv-Op	Hld	ERC	ERA
1997 Padres	R	13	12	0	1	54.1	281	54	53	45	3	1	0	2	63	0	59	19	7	1	4	.200	0	0- -	-	6.74	7.45
1998 Idaho Falls	R+	15	15	0	0	68.2	354	67	61	46	2	4	1	4	87	0	79	17	6	4	5	.444	0	0- -	-	7.08	6.03
1999 Fort Wayne	A	28	28	0	0	144.2	666	123	100	76	17	4	3	5	110	0	131	19	1	6	10	.375	0	0- -	-	4.85	4.73
2000 R Cucamnga	A+	32	19	0	4	107.1	506	88	87		8	2	2	2	111	1	150	14	1	5	11	.313	0	0- -	-		5.45
2001 Lk Elsinore	A+	18	18	0	0	101.2	414	86	37	32	4	3	2	1	32	0	107	3	0	8	2	.800	0	0- -	-	2.60	2.83
2001 Mobile	AA	7	5	0	1	30.0	117	17	9	8	3	0	0	0	15	0	29	3	0	2	0	1.000	0	0- -	-	2.29	2.40
2002 Mobile	AA	6	6	0	0	33.0	135	26	10	8	2	1	0	1	16	0	30	0	0	3	1	.750	0	0- -	-	3.21	2.18
2002 Portland	AAA	11	7	0	2	45.0	195	47	34	31	10	1	0	2	15	0	25	3	0	1	4	.000	0	0- -	-	5.11	6.20
2002 San Diego	NL	3	2	0	0	10.2	58	13	11	11	4	0	1	0	14	1	10	0	0	0	1	.000	0	0-0	0	11.84	9.28

Bob Howry

Pitches: R **Bats:** L **Pos:** RP-67   **Ht:** 6'5" **Wt:** 220 **Born:** 8/4/73 **Age:** 29

Year Team	Lg	G	GS	CG	GF	IP	BFP	H	R	ER	HR	SH	SF	HB	TBB	IBB	SO	WP	Bk	W	L	Pct	ShO	Sv-Op	Hld	ERC	ERA
1998 Chicago	AL	44	0	0	15	54.1	217	37	20	19	7	2	3	2	19	2	51	2	0	0	3	.000	0	9-11	19	2.50	3.15
1999 Chicago	AL	69	0	0	54	67.2	298	58	34	27	8	3	1	3	38	3	80	3	1	5	3	.625	0	28-34	1	4.11	3.59
2000 Chicago	AL	65	0	0	29	71.0	289	54	26	25	6	2	4	4	29	2	60	2	0	2	4	.333	0	7-12	14	2.96	3.17
2001 Chicago	AL	69	0	0	23	78.2	346	85	41	41	11	4	3	4	30	9	64	6	0	4	5	.444	0	5-11	21	4.78	4.69
2002 CWS-Bos	AL	67	0	0	28	68.2	292	67	37	32	9	4	6	5	21	4	45	2	0	3	5	.375	0	0-1	15	4.00	4.19
2002 Chicago	AL	47	0	0	19	50.2	209	45	22	22	7	1	4	3	17	2	31	1	0	2	2	.500	0	0-0	10	3.72	3.91
2002 Boston	AL	20	0	0	9	18.0	83	22	15	10	2	3	2	2	4	2	14	1	0	1	3	.250	0	0-1	5	4.79	5.00
5 ML YEARS		314	0	0	149	340.1	1442	301	158	144	41	15	17	18	137	20	300	15	1	14	20	.412	0	49-69	70	3.72	3.81

Trenidad Hubbard

Bats: R **Throws:** R **Pos:** RF-26; PH-26; LF-16; CF-16; PR-12; 3B-6; 2B-4; DH-1   **Ht:** 5'9" **Wt:** 203 **Born:** 5/11/66 **Age:** 37

Year Team	Lg	G	AB	H	2B	3B	HR	(Hm Rd)	TB	R	RBI	RC	TBB	IBB	SO	HBP	SH	SF	SB	CS	SB%	GDP	Avg	OBP	Slg
2002 Portland*	AAA	8	29	11	2	0	3	(- -)	22	9	6	8	2	0	3	0	0	1	2	2	.50	0	.379	.406	.759
1994 Colorado	NL	18	25	7	1	1	1	(1 0)	13	3	3	4	3	0	4	0	0	0	0	0	-	1	.280	.357	.520
1995 Colorado	NL	24	58	18	4	0	3	(2 1)	31	13	9	11	8	0	6	0	1	0	2	1	.67	2	.310	.394	.534
1996 Col-SF	NL	55	89	19	5	2	2	(2 0)	34	15	14	10	11	0	27	1	0	0	2	0	1.00	3	.213	.307	.382
1997 Cleveland	AL	7	12	3	1	0	0	(0 0)	4	3	0	2	1	0	3	0	0	0	2	0	1.00	0	.250	.308	.333
1998 Los Angeles	NL	94	208	62	9	1	7	(2 5)	94	29	18	33	18	0	46	3	3	3	9	5	.64	5	.298	.358	.452
1999 Los Angeles	NL	82	105	33	5	0	1	(0 1)	41	23	13	16	13	1	24	0	1	1	4	3	.57	2	.314	.387	.390
2000 Atl-Bal		92	108	20	2	2	1	(0 1)	29	18	6	7	11	0	23	1	3	0	4	2	.67	3	.185	.267	.269
2001 Kansas City	AL	5	12	3	0	1	0	(0 0)	5	2	0	1	0	0	2	0	0	0	0	0	-	0	.250	.250	.417
2002 San Diego	NL	89	129	27	5	0	1	(0 1)	35	16	7	9	14	0	28	0	0	1	9	6	.60	3	.209	.285	.271
1996 Colorado	NL	45	60	13	5	1	1	(1 0)	23	12	12	8	9	0	22	1	0	0	2	0	1.00	1	.217	.329	.383
1996 San Francisco	NL	10	29	6	0	1	1	(1 0)	11	3	2	2	2	0	5	0	0	0	0	0	-	2	.207	.258	.379
2000 Atlanta	NL	61	81	15	2	1	1	(0 1)	22	15	6	7	11	0	20	1	3	0	2	1	.67	1	.185	.290	.272
2000 Baltimore	AL	31	27	5	0	1	0	(0 0)	7	3	0	0	0	0	3	0	0	0	2	1	.67	2	.185	.185	.259
9 ML YEARS		466	746	192	32	7	16	(7 9)	286	122	70	93	79	1	163	5	8	5	32	17	.65	19	.257	.331	.383

Ken Huckaby

Bats: R **Throws:** R **Pos:** C-88; PH-1   **Ht:** 6'1" **Wt:** 205 **Born:** 1/27/71 **Age:** 32

Year Team	Lg	G	AB	H	2B	3B	HR	(Hm Rd)	TB	R	RBI	RC	TBB	IBB	SO	HBP	SH	SF	SB	CS	SB%	GDP	Avg	OBP	Slg
1991 Great Falls	R+	57	213	55	16	0	3	(- -)	80	39	37	26	17	0	38	4	1	3	3	2	.60	4	.258	.321	.376
1992 Vero Beach	A+	73	261	63	9	0	0	(- -)	72	14	21	16	7	0	42	1	2	2	1	1	.50	5	.241	.262	.276
1993 Vero Beach	A+	79	281	75	14	1	4	(- -)	103	22	41	30	11	1	35	2	3	2	2	1	.67	3	.267	.297	.367

Year Team	Lg	BATTING																		BASERUNNING				AVERAGES		
		G	AB	H	2B	3B	HR	(Hm	Rd)	TB	R	RBI	RC	TBB	IBB	SO	HBP	SH	SF	SB	CS	SB%	GDP	Avg	OBP	Slg
1993 San Antonio	AA	28	82	18	1	1	1	(-	-)	19	4	5	5	2	1	7	2	0	1	0	0	-	0	.220	.253	.232
1994 San Antonio	AA	11	41	11	1	0	1	(-	-)	15	3	9	4	1	1	1	0	0	0	1	0	1.00	1	.268	.286	.366
1994 Bakersfield	A+	77	270	81	18	1	2	(-	-)	107	29	30	32	10	0	37	2	0	1	2	3	.40	7	.300	.329	.396
1995 Albuquerque	AAA	89	278	90	16	2	1	(-	-)	113	30	40	36	12	1	26	4	3	1	3	1	.75	16	.324	.359	.406
1996 Albuquerque	AAA	103	286	79	16	2	3	(-	-)	108	37	41	32	17	1	35	2	3	1	0	0	-	10	.276	.320	.378
1997 Albuquerque	AAA	69	201	40	5	1	0	(-	-)	47	14	18	8	9	1	36	0	3	2	1	0	1.00	5	.199	.231	.234
1998 Tacoma	AAA	16	49	11	2	0	0	(-	-)	13	4	1	3	5	0	6	0	0	0	0	0	-	2	.224	.296	.265
1998 Columbus	AAA	36	101	21	3	1	1	(-	-)	29	13	10	7	11	0	14	0	3	0	0	2	.00	3	.208	.286	.287
1999 Tucson	AAA	107	355	107	20	1	2	(-	-)	135	44	42	41	13	2	33	2	4	5	0	0	-	11	.301	.325	.380
2000 Tucson	AAA	76	243	67	11	1	4	(-	-)	92	31	33	25	10	2	30	2	0	3	2	2	.50	10	.276	.306	.379
2001 El Paso	AA	30	104	36	4	0	2	(-	-)	46	14	14	17	3	0	16	3	1	4	0	0	-	3	.346	.368	.442
2001 Tucson	AAA	78	262	76	15	1	2	(-	-)	99	31	34	29	7	2	62	2	0	1	1	3	.25	3	.290	.313	.378
2002 Syracuse	AAA	21	81	22	2	0	0	(-	-)	24	7	9	4	2	1	15	0	0	1	0	2	.00	6	.272	.286	.296
2001 Arizona	NL	1	1	0	0	0	0	(0	0)	0	0	0	0	0	0	1	0	0	0	0	0	-	0	.000	.000	.000
2002 Toronto	AL	88	273	67	6	1	3	(1	2)	84	29	22	18	9	1	44	0	1	0	0	0	-	10	.245	.270	.308
2 ML YEARS		89	274	67	6	1	3	(1	2)	84	29	22	18	9	1	45	0	1	0	0	0	-	10	.245	.269	.307

Luke Hudson

Pitches: R Bats: R Pos: RP-3 **Ht: 6'3" Wt: 195 Born: 5/2/77 Age: 26**

Year Team	Lg	HOW MUCH HE PITCHED						WHAT HE GAVE UP												THE RESULTS							
		G	GS	CG	GF	IP	BFP	H	R	ER	HR	SH	SF	HB	TBB	IBB	SO	WP	Bk	W	L	Pct	ShO	Sv-Op	Hld	ERC	ERA
1998 Portland	A-	15	15	0	0	79.2	361	68	46	42	8	1	4	4	51	0	82	8	3	3	6	.333	0	0--	-	4.30	4.74
1999 Asheville	A	21	20	1	1	88.0	372	89	47	42	10	2	2	8	24	0	96	3	3	6	5	.545	0	0--	-	4.16	4.30
2000 Salem	A+	19	19	2	0	110.0	462	101	47	40	9	3	4	10	34	0	80	5	1	5	8	.385	2	0--	-	3.53	3.27
2001 Carolina	AA	29	28	1	0	165.0	729	159	90	77	19	5	4	15	68	0	145	18	1	7	12	.368	0	0--	-	4.34	4.20
2002 Louisville	AAA	30	17	0	6	117.2	518	102	64	59	6	4	4	16	57	1	129	10	1	5	9	.357	0	3--	-	3.80	4.51
2002 Cincinnati	NL	3	0	0	0	6.0	28	5	5	3	1	0	0	0	6	0	7	2	0	0	0	-	0	0-0	1	6.15	4.50

Orlando Hudson

Bats: B Throws: R Pos: 2B-52; PH-1; PR-1 **Ht: 6'0" Wt: 185 Born: 12/12/77 Age: 25**

Year Team	Lg	BATTING																		BASERUNNING				AVERAGES		
		G	AB	H	2B	3B	HR	(Hm	Rd)	TB	R	RBI	RC	TBB	IBB	SO	HBP	SH	SF	SB	CS	SB%	GDP	Avg	OBP	Slg
1998 Medicine Hat	R+	65	242	71	18	1	8	(-	-)	115	50	42	42	22	0	36	7	0	2	6	5	.55	3	.293	.366	.475
1999 Hagerstown	A	132	513	137	36	6	7	(-	-)	206	66	74	65	42	3	85	2	1	5	8	6	.57	10	.267	.322	.402
2000 Dunedin	A+	96	358	102	16	2	7	(-	-)	143	54	48	48	37	1	42	2	4	1	9	5	.64	15	.285	.354	.399
2000 Tennessee	AA	39	134	32	4	3	2	(-	-)	48	17	15	16	15	1	18	2	1	2	3	2	.60	3	.239	.320	.358
2001 Tennessee	AA	84	306	94	22	8	4	(-	-)	144	51	52	53	37	3	42	3	1	2	8	3	.73	12	.307	.385	.471
2001 Syracuse	AAA	55	194	59	14	3	4	(-	-)	91	31	27	36	23	1	34	2	2	3	11	3	.79	1	.304	.378	.469
2002 Syracuse	AAA	100	417	127	27	3	10	(-	-)	190	63	37	65	35	0	54	4	1	1	8	5	.62	14	.305	.363	.456
2002 Toronto	AL	54	192	53	10	5	4	(2	2)	85	20	23	30	11	0	27	2	0	2	0	1	.00	6	.276	.319	.443

Tim Hudson

Pitches: R Bats: R Pos: SP-34 **Ht: 6'1" Wt: 164 Born: 7/14/75 Age: 27**

Year Team	Lg	HOW MUCH HE PITCHED						WHAT HE GAVE UP												THE RESULTS							
		G	GS	CG	GF	IP	BFP	H	R	ER	HR	SH	SF	HB	TBB	IBB	SO	WP	Bk	W	L	Pct	ShO	Sv-Op	Hld	ERC	ERA
1999 Oakland	AL	21	21	1	0	136.1	580	121	56	49	8	1	2	4	62	2	132	6	0	11	2	.846	0	0-0	0	3.50	3.23
2000 Oakland	AL	32	32	2	0	202.1	847	169	100	93	24	5	7	7	82	5	169	7	0	20	6	.769	2	0-0	0	3.43	4.14
2001 Oakland	AL	35	35	3	0	235.0	980	216	100	88	20	12	8	6	71	5	181	9	1	18	9	.667	0	0-0	0	3.22	3.37
2002 Oakland	AL	34	34	4	0	238.1	983	237	87	79	19	6	6	6	62	9	152	7	1	15	9	.625	2	0-0	0	3.51	2.98
4 ML YEARS		122	122	10	0	812.0	3390	743	343	309	71	24	22	25	277	21	634	29	2	64	26	.711	4	0-0	0	3.41	3.42

Aubrey Huff

Bats: L Throws: R Pos: DH-53; 1B-45; 3B-14; PH-1 **Ht: 6'4" Wt: 231 Born: 12/20/76 Age: 26**

Year Team	Lg	BATTING																		BASERUNNING				AVERAGES		
		G	AB	H	2B	3B	HR	(Hm	Rd)	TB	R	RBI	RC	TBB	IBB	SO	HBP	SH	SF	SB	CS	SB%	GDP	Avg	OBP	Slg
2002 Durham*	AAA	32	126	41	9	0	3	(-	-)	59	18	20	21	12	5	13	1	0	1	0	0	-	4	.325	.386	.468
2000 Tampa Bay	AL	39	122	35	7	0	4	(3	1)	54	12	14	15	5	1	18	1	0	1	0	0	-	6	.287	.318	.443
2001 Tampa Bay	AL	111	411	102	25	1	8	(5	3)	153	42	45	37	23	2	72	0	0	0	1	3	.25	18	.248	.288	.372
2002 Tampa Bay	AL	113	454	142	25	0	23	(17	6)	236	67	59	59	37	7	55	1	0	2	4	1	.80	17	.313	.364	.520
3 ML YEARS		263	987	279	57	1	35	(25	10)	443	121	118	119	65	10	145	2	0	3	5	4	.56	41	.283	.327	.449

Todd Hundley

Bats: B Throws: R Pos: C-79; PH-17; DH-1 **Ht: 5'11" Wt: 200 Born: 5/27/69 Age: 34**

Year Team	Lg	BATTING																		BASERUNNING				AVERAGES		
		G	AB	H	2B	3B	HR	(Hm	Rd)	TB	R	RBI	RC	TBB	IBB	SO	HBP	SH	SF	SB	CS	SB%	GDP	Avg	OBP	Slg
2002 Iowa*	AAA	3	9	2	0	0	1	(-	-)	5	1	4	2	1	0	2	0	0	0	0	0	-	0	.222	.300	.556
1990 New York	NL	36	67	14	6	0	0	(0	0)	20	8	2	5	6	0	18	0	1	0	0	0	-	1	.209	.274	.299
1991 New York	NL	21	60	8	0	1	1	(1	0)	13	5	7	1	6	0	14	1	1	1	0	0	-	3	.133	.221	.217
1992 New York	NL	123	358	75	17	0	7	(2	5)	113	32	32	27	19	4	76	4	7	2	3	0	1.00	8	.209	.256	.316
1993 New York	NL	130	417	95	17	2	11	(5	6)	149	40	53	37	23	7	62	2	2	4	1	1	.50	10	.228	.269	.357
1994 New York	NL	91	291	69	10	1	16	(8	8)	129	45	42	39	25	4	73	3	3	1	2	1	.67	3	.237	.303	.443
1995 New York	NL	90	275	77	11	0	15	(6	9)	133	39	51	52	42	5	64	5	1	3	1	0	1.00	6	.280	.382	.484
1996 New York	NL	153	540	140	32	1	41	(20	21)	297	85	112	102	79	15	146	3	0	2	1	3	.25	9	.259	.356	.550
1997 New York	NL	132	417	114	21	2	30	(14	16)	229	78	86	87	83	16	116	3	0	5	2	3	.40	10	.273	.394	.549
1998 New York	NL	53	124	20	4	0	3	(1	2)	33	8	12	9	16	0	55	1	1	1	1	1	.50	0	.161	.261	.266
1999 Los Angeles	NL	114	376	78	14	0	24	(10	14)	164	49	55	50	44	3	113	4	1	3	3	0	1.00	1	.207	.295	.436
2000 Los Angeles	NL	90	299	85	16	0	24	(10	14)	173	49	70	63	45	6	69	2	1	6	0	1	.00	5	.284	.375	.579

Year Team	Lg	G	AB	H	2B	3B	HR	(Hm	Rd)	TB	R	RBI	RC	TBB	IBB	SO	HBP	SH	SF	SB	CS	SB%	GDP	Avg	OBP	Slg
2001 Chicago	NL	79	246	46	10	0	12	(4	8)	92	23	31	23	25	0	89	3	0	2	0	0	-	7	.187	.268	.374
2002 Chicago	NL	92	266	56	8	0	16	(8	8)	112	32	35	29	32	3	80	3	1	1	0	0	-	6	.211	.301	.421
13 ML YEARS		1204	3736	877	166	7	200	(89	111)	1657	493	588	524	445	63	975	34	18	31	14	10	.58	71	.235	.319	.444

Brian Hunter

Bats: R **Throws:** R **Pos:** CF-88; PH-18; PR-14   **Ht:** 6'3" **Wt:** 180 **Born:** 3/25/71 **Age:** 32

Year Team	Lg	G	AB	H	2B	3B	HR	(Hm	Rd)	TB	R	RBI	RC	TBB	IBB	SO	HBP	SH	SF	SB	CS	SB%	GDP	Avg	OBP	Slg
2002 New Orleans*	AAA	5	19	3	0	1	0	(-	-)	5	4	0	1	2	0	7	0	0	0	2	1	.67	1	.158	.238	.263
1994 Houston	NL	6	24	6	1	0	0	(0	0)	7	2	0	2	1	0	6	0	1	0	2	1	.67	0	.250	.280	.292
1995 Houston	NL	78	321	97	14	5	2	(0	2)	127	52	28	47	21	0	52	2	2	3	24	7	.77	2	.302	.346	.396
1996 Houston	NL	132	526	145	27	2	5	(1	4)	191	74	35	59	17	0	92	2	1	7	35	9	.80	6	.276	.297	.363
1997 Detroit	AL	162	658	177	29	7	4	(2	2)	232	112	45	86	66	1	121	1	8	5	74	18	.80	13	.269	.334	.353
1998 Detroit	AL	142	595	151	29	3	4	(1	3)	198	67	36	61	36	0	94	2	2	1	42	12	.78	8	.254	.298	.333
1999 Det-Sea	AL	139	539	125	13	6	4	(0	4)	162	79	34	50	37	0	91	2	3	4	44	8	.85	8	.232	.280	.301
2000 Col-Cin	NL	104	240	64	5	1	1	(0	1)	74	47	14	30	27	0	40	1	5	1	20	3	.87	3	.267	.342	.308
2001 Philadelphia	NL	83	145	40	6	0	2	(2	0)	52	22	16	20	16	0	25	0	3	2	14	3	.82	3	.276	.344	.359
2002 Houston	NL	98	201	54	16	3	3	(0	3)	85	32	20	27	16	0	39	2	1	0	5	0	1.00	3	.269	.329	.423
1999 Detroit	AL	18	55	13	2	1	0	(0	0)	17	8	0	5	5	0	11	1	1	0	0	3	.00	0	.236	.311	.309
1999 Seattle	AL	121	484	112	11	5	4	(0	4)	145	71	34	45	32	0	80	1	3	7	44	5	.90	8	.231	.277	.300
2000 Colorado	NL	72	200	55	4	1	1	(1	0)	64	36	13	25	21	0	31	1	4	0	15	3	.83	2	.275	.347	.320
2000 Cincinnati	NL	32	40	9	1	0	0	(0	0)	10	11	1	5	6	0	9	0	1	1	5	0	1.00	0	.225	.319	.250
9 ML YEARS		944	3249	859	140	27	25	(7	18)	1128	487	228	382	237	1	560	12	27	26	260	61	.81	45	.264	.314	.347

Torii Hunter

Bats: R **Throws:** R **Pos:** CF-146; DH-1; PH-1; PR-1   **Ht:** 6'2" **Wt:** 205 **Born:** 7/18/75 **Age:** 27

Year Team	Lg	G	AB	H	2B	3B	HR	(Hm	Rd)	TB	R	RBI	RC	TBB	IBB	SO	HBP	SH	SF	SB	CS	SB%	GDP	Avg	OBP	Slg
1998 Minnesota	AL	6	17	4	1	0	0	(0	0)	5	0	2	1	2	0	6	0	0	0	0	1	.00	1	.235	.316	.294
1999 Minnesota	AL	135	384	98	17	2	9	(2	7)	146	52	35	44	26	1	72	6	1	5	10	6	.63	9	.255	.309	.380
2000 Minnesota	AL	99	336	94	14	7	5	(4	1)	137	44	44	39	18	2	68	2	0	2	4	3	.57	13	.280	.318	.408
2001 Minnesota	AL	148	564	147	32	5	27	(13	14)	270	82	92	79	29	0	125	8	1	1	9	6	.60	12	.261	.306	.479
2002 Minnesota	AL	148	561	162	37	4	29	(13	16)	294	89	94	87	35	3	118	5	0	3	23	8	.74	17	.289	.334	.524
5 ML YEARS		536	1862	505	101	18	70	(32	38)	852	267	267	250	110	6	389	21	2	11	46	24	.66	52	.271	.317	.458

Adam Hyzdu

Bats: R **Throws:** R **Pos:** CF-36; RF-13; LF-10; PH-10; 1B-1   **Ht:** 6'2" **Wt:** 205 **Born:** 12/6/71 **Age:** 31

Year Team	Lg	G	AB	H	2B	3B	HR	(Hm	Rd)	TB	R	RBI	RC	TBB	IBB	SO	HBP	SH	SF	SB	CS	SB%	GDP	Avg	OBP	Slg
2002 Nashville*	AAA	65	243	59	17	0	10	(-	-)	106	33	50	34	29	0	59	0	0	5	1	2	.33	4	.243	.318	.436
2000 Pittsburgh	NL	12	18	7	2	0	1	(0	1)	12	2	4	4	0	0	4	0	0	0	0	0	-	0	.389	.389	.667
2001 Pittsburgh	NL	51	72	15	1	0	5	(0	5)	31	7	9	8	4	0	18	1	0	0	0	1	.00	1	.208	.260	.431
2002 Pittsburgh	NL	59	155	36	6	0	11	(6	5)	75	24	34	27	21	0	44	1	0	2	0	0	-	1	.232	.324	.484
3 ML YEARS		122	245	58	9	0	17	(6	11)	118	33	47	39	25	0	66	2	0	2	0	1	.00	2	.237	.310	.482

Raul Ibanez

Bats: L **Throws:** R **Pos:** 1B-50; LF-41; DH-36; RF-16; PH-7   **Ht:** 6'2" **Wt:** 200 **Born:** 6/2/72 **Age:** 31

Year Team	Lg	G	AB	H	2B	3B	HR	(Hm	Rd)	TB	R	RBI	RC	TBB	IBB	SO	HBP	SH	SF	SB	CS	SB%	GDP	Avg	OBP	Slg
1996 Seattle	AL	4	5	0	0	0	0	(0	0)	0	0	0	0	0	0	1	0	0	0	0	0	-	0	.000	.167	.000
1997 Seattle	AL	11	26	4	0	1	1	(1	0)	9	3	4	1	0	0	6	0	0	0	0	0	-	0	.154	.154	.346
1998 Seattle	AL	37	98	25	7	1	2	(1	1)	40	12	12	10	5	0	22	0	0	0	0	0	-	4	.255	.291	.408
1999 Seattle	AL	87	209	54	7	0	9	(3	6)	88	23	27	28	17	1	32	0	0	1	5	1	.83	4	.258	.313	.421
2000 Seattle	AL	92	140	32	8	0	2	(2	0)	46	21	15	15	14	1	25	1	0	1	2	0	1.00	1	.229	.301	.329
2001 Kansas City	AL	104	279	78	11	5	13	(5	8)	138	44	54	46	32	2	51	0	0	6	0	2	.00	6	.280	.353	.495
2002 Kansas City	AL	137	497	146	37	6	24	(14	10)	267	70	103	91	40	5	76	2	1	4	5	3	.63	11	.294	.346	.537
7 ML YEARS		472	1254	339	70	13	51	(26	25)	588	173	215	191	108	9	213	4	1	7	12	6	.67	26	.270	.328	.469

Omar Infante

Bats: R **Throws:** R **Pos:** SS-16; 2B-2   **Ht:** 5'9" **Wt:** 150 **Born:** 12/26/81 **Age:** 21

Year Team	Lg	G	AB	H	2B	3B	HR	(Hm	Rd)	TB	R	RBI	RC	TBB	IBB	SO	HBP	SH	SF	SB	CS	SB%	GDP	Avg	OBP	Slg
1999 Tigers	R	21	75	20	0	0	0	(-	-)	20	9	4	6	3	0	9	0	0	1	4	0	1.00	1	.267	.291	.267
2000 Lakeland	A+	79	259	71	11	0	2	(-	-)	88	35	24	30	20	0	29	1	5	4	11	5	.69	4	.274	.324	.340
2000 W Michigan	A	12	48	11	0	0	0	(-	-)	11	7	5	4	5	0	7	2	0	0	1	0	1.00	2	.229	.327	.229
2001 Erie	AA	132	540	163	21	4	2	(-	-)	198	86	62	73	46	1	87	2	4	7	27	12	.69	9	.302	.355	.367
2002 Toledo	AAA	120	436	117	16	8	4	(-	-)	161	49	51	48	28	0	49	0	5	5	19	15	.56	5	.268	.309	.369
2002 Detroit	AL	18	72	24	3	0	1	(0	1)	30	4	6	11	3	0	10	0	0	0	0	1	.00	0	.333	.360	.417

Brandon Inge

Bats: R **Throws:** R **Pos:** C-94; DH-1   **Ht:** 5'11" **Wt:** 189 **Born:** 5/19/77 **Age:** 26

								BATTING											BASERUNNING				AVERAGES		
Year	Team	Lg	G	AB	H	2B	3B	HR	(Hm | Rd)	TB	R	RBI	RC	TBB	IBB	SO	HBP	SH	SF	SB	CS	SB%	GDP	Avg	OBP	Slg
1998	Jamestown	A-	51	191	44	10	1	8	(- | -)	80	24	29	23	17	1	53	6	0	1	8	8	.50	4	.230	.312	.419
1999	W Michigan	A	100	352	86	25	2	9	(- | -)	142	54	46	48	39	0	87	3	2	6	15	3	.83	7	.244	.320	.403
2000	Jacksonville	AA	78	298	77	25	1	6	(- | -)	122	39	53	37	26	1	73	0	1	5	10	3	.77	10	.258	.313	.409
2000	Toledo	AAA	55	190	42	9	3	5	(- | -)	72	24	20	19	15	0	51	1	1	1	2	1	.67	5	.221	.280	.379
2001	Tigers	R	3	10	1	0	0	1	(- | -)	4	1	2	1	2	0	2	0	0	0	0	0	-	0	.100	.250	.400
2001	W Michigan	A	4	16	3	1	0	0	(- | -)	4	3	2	1	2	0	5	1	0	0	0	0	-	0	.188	.316	.250
2001	Toledo	AAA	27	90	26	11	1	2	(- | -)	45	11	15	15	7	0	24	1	1	3	1	0	1.00	2	.289	.337	.500
2002	Toledo	AAA	21	65	17	2	4	3	(- | -)	36	10	13	13	11	0	16	2	2	1	1	3	.25	2	.262	.380	.554
2001	Detroit	AL	79	189	34	11	0	0	(0 | 0)	45	13	15	6	9	0	41	0	2	2	1	4	.20	2	.180	.215	.238
2002	Detroit	AL	95	321	65	15	3	7	(3 | 4)	107	27	24	25	24	0	101	4	1	1	1	3	.25	7	.202	.266	.333
	2 ML YEARS		174	510	99	26	3	7	(3 | 4)	152	40	39	31	33	0	142	4	3	3	2	7	.22	9	.194	.247	.298

Hideki Irabu

Pitches: R **Bats:** R **Pos:** RP-36; SP-2   **Ht:** 6'4" **Wt:** 250 **Born:** 5/5/69 **Age:** 34

			HOW MUCH HE PITCHED					WHAT HE GAVE UP											THE RESULTS						
Year	Team	Lg	G	GS	CG	GF	IP	BFP	H	R	ER	HR	SH	SF	HB	TBB	IBB	SO	WP	Bk	W	L	Pct	ShO	Sv-Op	Hld	ERC	ERA
1997	New York	AL	13	9	0	0	53.1	246	69	47	42	15	1	2	1	20	0	56	4	3	5	4	.556	0	0-0	1	7.19	7.09
1998	New York	AL	29	28	2	0	173.0	732	148	78	78	27	6	6	9	76	1	126	6	1	13	9	.591	1	0-0	0	4.05	4.06
1999	New York	AL	32	27	2	2	169.1	733	180	98	91	26	2	4	6	46	0	133	7	0	11	7	.611	1	0-0	0	4.38	4.84
2000	Montreal	NL	11	11	0	0	54.2	247	77	45	44	9	3	2	1	14	0	42	5	2	2	5	.286	0	0-0	0	6.58	7.24
2001	Montreal	NL	3	3	0	0	16.2	74	22	9	9	3	0	1	0	3	0	18	0	0	2	0	.000	0	0-0	0	5.57	4.86
2002	Texas	AL	38	2	0	26	47.0	204	51	30	30	11	2	2	1	16	2	30	3	0	3	8	.273	0	16-20	2	5.33	5.74
	6 ML YEARS		126	80	4	28	514.0	2236	547	307	294	91	14	17	18	175	3	405	25	6	34	35	.493	2	16-20	3	4.89	5.15

Kazuhisa Ishii

Pitches: L **Bats:** L **Pos:** SP-28   **Ht:** 6'0" **Wt:** 190 **Born:** 9/9/73 **Age:** 29

			HOW MUCH HE PITCHED					WHAT HE GAVE UP											THE RESULTS						
Year	Team	Lg	G	GS	CG	GF	IP	BFP	H	R	ER	HR	SH	SF	HB	TBB	IBB	SO	WP	Bk	W	L	Pct	ShO	Sv-Op	Hld	ERC	ERA
2002	Los Angeles	NL	28	28	0	0	154.0	692	137	82	73	20	6	5	4	**106**	3	143	7	0	14	10	.583	0	0-0	0	4.90	4.27

Jason Isringhausen

Pitches: R **Bats:** R **Pos:** RP-60   **Ht:** 6'3" **Wt:** 230 **Born:** 9/7/72 **Age:** 30

			HOW MUCH HE PITCHED					WHAT HE GAVE UP											THE RESULTS						
Year	Team	Lg	G	GS	CG	GF	IP	BFP	H	R	ER	HR	SH	SF	HB	TBB	IBB	SO	WP	Bk	W	L	Pct	ShO	Sv-Op	Hld	ERC	ERA
1995	New York	NL	14	14	1	0	93.0	385	88	29	29	6	3	3	2	31	2	55	4	1	9	2	.818	0	0-0	0	3.40	2.81
1996	New York	NL	27	27	2	0	171.2	766	190	103	91	13	7	9	8	73	5	114	14	0	6	14	.300	1	0-0	0	4.75	4.79
1997	New York	NL	6	6	0	0	29.2	145	40	27	25	3	1	2	1	22	0	25	3	0	2	2	.500	0	0-0	0	7.99	7.58
1999	NYM-Oak		33	5	0	20	64.2	286	64	35	34	9	0	1	2	34	4	51	5	0	1	4	.200	0	9-9	0	4.86	4.73
2000	Oakland	AL	66	0	0	57	69.0	304	67	34	29	6	2	1	3	32	5	57	5	1	6	4	.600	0	33-40	0	4.09	3.78
2001	Oakland	AL	65	0	0	54	71.1	293	54	24	21	5	3	1	0	23	5	74	2	0	4	3	.571	0	34-43	0	2.18	2.65
2002	St Louis	NL	60	0	0	51	65.1	257	46	22	18	0	4	3	1	18	1	68	0	0	3	2	.600	0	32-37	0	1.61	2.48
1999	New York	NL	13	5	0	2	39.1	179	43	29	28	7	0	1	1	22	2	31	3	0	1	3	.250	0	1-1	0	5.93	6.41
1999	Oakland	AL	20	0	0	18	25.1	107	21	6	6	2	0	0	1	12	2	20	2	0	0	1	.000	0	8-8	0	3.33	2.13
	7 ML YEARS		271	52	3	182	564.2	2436	549	274	247	42	20	20	17	233	22	444	33	2	31	31	.500	1	108-129	0	3.85	3.94

Hansel Izquierdo

Pitches: R **Bats:** R **Pos:** RP-18; SP-2   **Ht:** 6'2" **Wt:** 205 **Born:** 1/2/77 **Age:** 26

			HOW MUCH HE PITCHED					WHAT HE GAVE UP											THE RESULTS						
Year	Team	Lg	G	GS	CG	GF	IP	BFP	H	R	ER	HR	SH	SF	HB	TBB	IBB	SO	WP	Bk	W	L	Pct	ShO	Sv-Op	Hld	ERC	ERA
1995	Marlins	R	1	0	0	0	2.0	10	3	3	0	0	1	0	0	2	0	0	1	0	0	0	-	0	0--	-	9.50	0.00
1996	Marlins	R	12	0	0	10	13.1	52	7	4	4	0	0	0	3	5	0	17	3	1	0	1	.000	0	3--	-	1.83	2.70
1997	White Sox	R	5	0	0	2	10.1	45	9	4	4	0	1	0	0	8	0	15	1	0	0	0	-	0	0--	-	4.22	3.48
1997	Bristol	R+	9	2	0	2	23.0	104	25	14	11	5	0	0	4	8	0	24	0	1	2	2	.500	0	0--	-	5.96	4.30
1998	Hickory	A	28	27	2	1	175.0	771	159	104	85	14	6	2	22	76	0	186	15	1	9	11	.450	1	0--	-	4.01	4.37
1998	Winstn-Salm	A+	1	0	0	1	2.0	7	1	0	0	0	0	0	0	1	0	2	0	0	0	0	-	0	1--	-	1.62	0.00
1999	Winstn-Salm	A+	18	13	0	4	82.2	371	76	46	38	5	5	2	8	46	1	72	13	1	3	5	.375	0	0--	-	4.28	4.14
2000	Birmingham	AA	8	0	0	5	12.0	53	12	11	10	2	1	1	0	5	1	5	1	0	1	2	.333	0	0--	-	4.38	7.50
2000	Kinston	A+	10	5	0	2	41.1	178	39	29	22	4	2	2	5	13	0	34	1	0	1	3	.250	0	1--	-	3.86	4.79
2000	SonomaCnty	IND	4	3	0	0	13.0	72	16	14	14	0	1	1	3	17	1	10	2	0	0	1	.000	0	0--	-	9.31	9.69
2001	Kane County	A	24	2	0	5	47.2	181	27	8	7	1	0	0	3	13	0	42	1	2	7	1	.875	0	2--	-	1.40	1.32
2001	Brevard Cnty	A+	4	4	0	0	26.2	105	15	8	8	3	1	0	4	6	0	22	0	0	2	0	1.000	0	0--	-	1.83	2.70
2001	Portland	AA	10	9	1	0	56.2	224	47	24	24	10	0	1	4	10	0	45	4	0	7	2	.778	1	0--	-	3.11	3.81
2002	Portland	AA	1	1	0	0	7.0	27	5	2	1	0	0	0	0	1	0	4	0	0	1	0	1.000	0	0--	-	1.32	1.29
2002	Calgary	AAA	13	13	0	0	71.0	323	90	55	42	11	3	4	2	23	0	36	2	1	4	5	.444	0	0--	-	5.82	5.32
2002	Florida	NL	20	2	0	5	29.2	143	33	17	15	2	1	3	5	21	3	20	0	0	2	0	1.000	0	0-0	1	6.28	4.55

Cesar Izturis

Bats: B **Throws:** R **Pos:** SS-128; PH-7; PR-6; 2B-1; DH-1   **Ht:** 5'9" **Wt:** 175 **Born:** 2/10/80 **Age:** 23

								BATTING											BASERUNNING				AVERAGES		
Year	Team	Lg	G	AB	H	2B	3B	HR	(Hm | Rd)	TB	R	RBI	RC	TBB	IBB	SO	HBP	SH	SF	SB	CS	SB%	GDP	Avg	OBP	Slg
1997	St. Ctharines	A-	70	231	44	3	0	1	(- | -)	50	32	11	10	15	0	27	1	8	3	6	3	.67	3	.190	.241	.216
1998	Hagerstown	A	130	413	108	13	1	1	(- | -)	126	56	38	38	20	0	43	2	9	2	20	9	.69	5	.262	.297	.305
1999	Dunedin	A+	131	536	165	28	4	3	(- | -)	226	77	77	75	22	4	58	6	17	9	32	16	.67	9	.308	.337	.422
2000	Syracuse	AAA	132	435	95	16	5	0	(- | -)	121	54	27	28	20	0	44	1	13	2	21	11	.66	5	.218	.253	.278
2001	Syracuse	AAA	87	342	100	16	3	2	(- | -)	128	32	35	41	10	0	22	1	4	5	24	9	.73	4	.292	.310	.374

Year Team	Lg	G	AB	H	2B	3B	HR	(Hm	Rd)	TB	R	RBI	RC	TBB	IBB	SO	HBP	SH	SF	SB	CS	SB%	GDP	Avg	OBP	Slg
2001 Toronto	AL	46	134	36	6	2	1	(1	1)	52	19	9	16	2	0	15	0	4	0	8	1	.89	0	.269	.279	.388
2002 Los Angeles	NL	135	439	102	24	2	1	(0	1)	133	43	31	26	14	1	39	0	10	5	7	7	.50	12	.232	.253	.303
2 ML YEARS		181	573	138	30	4	3	(1	2)	185	62	40	42	16	1	54	0	14	5	15	8	.65	12	.241	.259	.323

Damian Jackson

Bats: R Throws: R Pos: 2B-56; PR-9; SS-6; PH-5; LF-3; CF-3; DH-3; 3B-2 Ht: 5'11" Wt: 185 Born: 8/16/73 Age: 29

						BATTING														BASERUNNING				AVERAGES		
Year Team	Lg	G	AB	H	2B	3B	HR	(Hm	Rd)	TB	R	RBI	RC	TBB	IBB	SO	HBP	SH	SF	SB	CS	SB%	GDP	Avg	OBP	Slg
1996 Cleveland	AL	5	10	3	2	0	0	(0	0)	5	2	1	2	1	0	4	0	0	0	0	0	-	0	.300	.364	.500
1997 Cle-Cin		20	36	7	2	1	1	(0	1)	14	8	2	4	4	1	8	1	1	0	2	1	.67	0	.194	.293	.389
1998 Cincinnati	NL	13	38	12	5	0	0	(0	0)	17	4	7	7	6	0	4	0	0	0	2	0	1.00	1	.316	.400	.447
1999 San Diego	NL	133	388	87	20	2	9	(6	3)	138	56	39	50	53	3	105	3	0	3	34	10	.77	2	.224	.320	.356
2000 San Diego	NL	138	470	120	27	6	6	(5	1)	177	68	37	66	62	2	108	3	4	2	28	6	.82	7	.255	.345	.377
2001 San Diego	NL	122	440	106	21	6	4	(1	3)	151	67	38	51	44	2	128	6	2	3	23	6	.79	6	.241	.316	.343
2002 Detroit	AL	81	245	63	20	1	1	(0	1)	88	31	25	33	21	0	36	3	2	3	12	3	.80	3	.257	.320	.359
1997 Cleveland	AL	8	9	1	0	0	0	(0	0)	1	2	0	0	0	0	1	1	0	0	1	0	1.00	0	.111	.200	.111
1997 Cincinnati	NL	12	27	6	2	1	1	(0	1)	13	6	2	4	4	1	7	0	1	0	1	1	.50	0	.222	.323	.481
7 ML YEARS		512	1627	398	97	16	21	(12	9)	590	236	149	213	191	8	393	16	9	12	101	26	.80	19	.245	.328	.363

Mike Jackson

Pitches: R Bats: R Pos: RP-58 Ht: 6'2" Wt: 215 Born: 12/22/64 Age: 38

		HOW MUCH HE PITCHED						WHAT HE GAVE UP											THE RESULTS						
Year Team	Lg	G	GS	CG	GF	IP	BFP	H	R	ER	HR	SH	SF	HB	TBB	IBB	SO	WP	Bk	W	L	Pct	ShO	Sv-Op	Hld	ERC	ERA
1986 Philadelphia	NL	9	0	0	4	13.1	54	12	5	5	2	0	0	2	4	1	3	0	0	0	0	-	0	0-1	0	4.19	3.38
1987 Philadelphia	NL	55	7	0	8	109.1	468	88	55	51	16	3	4	3	56	6	93	6	8	3	10	.231	0	1-2	6	3.76	4.20
1988 Seattle	AL	62	0	0	29	99.1	412	74	37	29	10	3	10	2	43	10	76	6	6	6	5	.545	0	4-11	10	2.76	2.63
1989 Seattle	AL	65	0	0	27	99.1	431	81	43	35	8	6	2	6	54	6	94	1	2	4	6	.400	0	7-10	9	3.60	3.17
1990 Seattle	AL	63	0	0	28	77.1	338	64	42	39	8	6	8	5	44	12	69	9	2	5	7	.417	0	3-12	13	3.61	4.54
1991 Seattle	AL	72	0	0	35	88.2	363	64	35	32	5	4	0	6	34	11	74	3	0	7	7	.500	0	14-22	9	2.35	3.25
1992 San Francisco	NL	67	0	0	24	82.0	346	76	35	34	7	5	2	4	33	10	80	1	0	6	6	.500	0	2-3	9	3.64	3.73
1993 San Francisco	NL	81	0	0	17	77.1	317	58	28	26	7	4	2	3	24	6	70	2	2	6	6	.500	0	1-6	34	2.36	3.03
1994 San Francisco	NL	36	0	0	12	42.1	158	23	8	7	4	4	1	2	11	0	51	0	0	3	2	.600	0	4-6	9	1.55	1.49
1995 Cincinnati	NL	40	0	0	18	49.0	200	38	13	13	5	1	1	1	19	1	41	1	1	6	1	.857	0	2-4	9	2.92	2.39
1996 Seattle	AL	73	0	0	23	72.0	302	61	32	29	11	0	1	6	24	3	70	2	0	1	1	.500	0	6-8	15	3.59	3.63
1997 Cleveland	AL	71	0	0	38	75.0	313	59	33	27	3	3	3	4	29	5	74	2	0	2	5	.286	0	15-17	14	2.58	3.24
1998 Cleveland	AL	69	0	0	57	64.0	239	43	11	11	4	1	0	4	13	0	55	1	3	1	1	.500	0	40-45	1	1.82	1.55
1999 Cleveland	AL	72	0	0	65	68.2	291	60	32	31	11	2	2	2	26	1	55	0	1	3	4	.429	0	39-43	0	3.76	4.06
2001 Houston	NL	67	0	0	16	69.0	292	68	36	36	14	4	2	2	22	3	46	2	0	5	3	.625	0	4-9	19	4.45	4.70
2002 Minnesota	AL	58	0	0	17	55.0	232	59	20	20	5	4	3	4	13	3	29	2	0	2	3	.400	0	0-2	20	4.05	3.27
16 ML YEARS		960	7	0	410	1141.2	4756	928	465	425	120	52	38	53	449	78	980	38	25	60	67	.472	0	142-201	177	3.15	3.35

Ryan Jackson

Bats: L Throws: L Pos: LF-2; PH-2; CF-1 Ht: 6'2" Wt: 200 Born: 11/15/71 Age: 31

						BATTING														BASERUNNING				AVERAGES		
Year Team	Lg	G	AB	H	2B	3B	HR	(Hm	Rd)	TB	R	RBI	RC	TBB	IBB	SO	HBP	SH	SF	SB	CS	SB%	GDP	Avg	OBP	Slg
2002 Toledo*	AAA	104	420	114	35	1	8	(-	-)	175	40	50	47	13	1	84	3	2	1	5	3	.63	13	.271	.297	.417
1998 Florida	NL	111	260	65	15	1	5	(3	2)	97	26	31	29	20	0	73	1	2	1	1	1	.50	3	.250	.305	.373
1999 Seattle	AL	32	68	16	3	0	0	(0	0)	19	4	10	5	6	0	19	1	0	2	3	3	.50	3	.235	.299	.279
2001 Detroit	AL	79	118	25	4	2	2	(1	1)	39	19	11	9	5	0	26	1	2	0	3	1	.75	1	.212	.250	.331
2002 Detroit	AL	4	6	2	1	1	0	(0	0)	5	0	0	2	1	0	2	0	0	0	0	0	-	0	.333	.429	.833
4 ML YEARS		226	452	108	23	4	7	(4	3)	160	49	52	45	32	0	120	3	4	3	7	5	.58	7	.239	.292	.354

Delvin James

Pitches: R Bats: R Pos: SP-6; RP-2 Ht: 6'4" Wt: 240 Born: 1/3/78 Age: 25

		HOW MUCH HE PITCHED						WHAT HE GAVE UP											THE RESULTS						
Year Team	Lg	G	GS	CG	GF	IP	BFP	H	R	ER	HR	SH	SF	HB	TBB	IBB	SO	WP	Bk	W	L	Pct	ShO	Sv-Op	Hld	ERC	ERA
1996 Devil Rays	R	11	11	1	0	47.2	236	64	52	47	0	1	3	11	21	0	40	11	2	2	8	.200	0	0- -	-	6.31	8.87
1997 Princeton	R+	20	5	0	2	58.1	276	71	57	32	11	1	2	4	24	1	46	4	2	4	4	.500	0	0- -	-	6.15	4.94
1998 St.Pete	A+	1	0	0	0	1.2	7	2	2	2	0	0	0	0	1	0	0	0	0	0	0	-	0	0- -	-	5.91	10.80
1998 Chrlstn - SC	A	7	0	0	2	8.1	40	12	5	5	0	0	2	1	2	0	8	0	0	2	0	1.000	0	0- -	-	5.55	5.40
1998 Hudson Val	A-	15	15	0	0	81.2	345	71	39	27	2	1	1	5	32	0	64	6	0	7	4	.636	0	0- -	-	3.06	2.98
1999 Chrlstn - SC	A	25	25	1	0	158.1	654	142	76	64	13	9	4	8	33	1	106	8	1	8	8	.500	0	0- -	-	2.82	3.64
1999 St.Pete	A+	3	2	0	1	17.0	71	18	6	6	0	0	0	3	4	0	6	1	0	3	0	1.000	0	0- -	-	3.92	3.18
2000 St.Pete	A+	22	22	3	0	137.1	576	142	74	65	10	2	2	7	27	2	74	5	0	7	9	.438	1	0- -	-	3.46	4.26
2000 Orlando	AA	6	6	1	0	37.0	153	31	15	12	3	0	3	3	7	0	26	1	0	1	3	.250	0	0- -	-	2.54	2.92
2001 Orlando	AA	7	7	0	0	43.2	163	25	8	8	1	2	1	2	9	0	31	2	1	2	0	1.000	0	0- -	-	1.25	1.65
2001 Durham	AAA	31	9	1	8	84.1	373	99	51	45	8	4	2	5	27	1	51	6	0	3	7	.300	0	0- -	-	4.97	4.80
2002 Durham	AAA	7	7	0	0	34.1	146	41	16	15	4	0	1	2	4	0	26	5	0	2	1	.667	0	0- -	-	4.41	3.93
2002 Orlando	AA	3	1	0	0	12.2	53	12	7	5	2	0	0	0	4	0	13	0	0	1	2	.333	0	0- -	-	3.08	3.55
2002 Tampa Bay	AL	8	6	0	2	34.1	150	40	25	25	5	0	1	1	15	1	17	2	1	0	3	.000	0	0-0	0	5.83	6.55

Mike James

Pitches: R Bats: R Pos: RP-13 Ht: 6'3" Wt: 205 Born: 8/15/67 Age: 35

		HOW MUCH HE PITCHED						WHAT HE GAVE UP											THE RESULTS						
Year Team	Lg	G	GS	CG	GF	IP	BFP	H	R	ER	HR	SH	SF	HB	TBB	IBB	SO	WP	Bk	W	L	Pct	ShO	Sv-Op	Hld	ERC	ERA
2002 Co Springs*	AAA	24	0	0	7	31.0	146	38	31	28	5	2	0	2	16	0	25	3	0	1	1	.500	0	1- -	-	6.65	8.13
1995 Anaheim	AL	46	0	0	11	55.2	237	49	27	24	6	2	0	3	26	2	36	1	0	3	0	1.000	0	1-2	3	3.94	3.88
1996 Anaheim	AL	69	0	0	23	81.0	353	62	27	24	7	6	5	10	42	7	65	5	0	5	5	.500	0	1-6	18	3.44	2.67

Year Team	Lg	G	GS	CG	GF	IP	BFP	H	R	ER	HR	SH	SF	HB	TBB	IBB	SO	WP	Bk	W	L	Pct	ShO	Sv-Op	Hld	ERC	ERA
1997 Anaheim	AL	58	0	0	22	62.2	284	69	32	30	3	6	1	5	28	4	57	1	0	5	5	.500	0	7-13	12	4.63	4.31
1998 Anaheim	AL	11	0	0	3	14.0	55	10	3	3	0	0	0	0	7	0	12	0	0	0	0	-	0	0-0	2	2.44	1.93
2000 St Louis	NL	51	0	0	10	51.1	213	40	22	18	7	2	1	3	24	2	41	2	0	2	2	.500	0	2-5	12	3.62	3.16
2001 St Louis	NL	40	0	0	11	38.0	173	43	24	22	5	3	1	5	17	2	26	3	0	1	2	.333	0	0-0	4	5.80	5.21
2002 Colorado	NL	13	0	0	6	11.1	51	12	9	7	2	0	0	1	5	0	10	0	0	0	0	-	0	0-0	0	5.51	5.56
7 ML YEARS		288	0	0	86	314.0	1366	285	144	128	30	19	8	27	149	17	247	12	0	16	14	.533	0	11-26	51	4.09	3.67

Kevin Jarvis

Pitches: R **Bats:** L **Pos:** SP-7   **Ht:** 6'2" **Wt:** 200 **Born:** 8/1/69 **Age:** 33

Year Team	Lg	G	GS	CG	GF	IP	BFP	H	R	ER	HR	SH	SF	HB	TBB	IBB	SO	WP	Bk	W	L	Pct	ShO	Sv-Op	Hld	ERC	ERA
2002 Mobile*	AA	1	1	0	0	3.0	11	2	0	0	0	0	0	0	0	0	3	0	0	0	0	-	0	0--	-	0.91	0.00
2002 Lk Elsinore*	A+	1	1	0	0	5.0	17	2	0	0	0	1	0	0	1	0	1	0	0	0	1	1.000	0	0--	-	0.67	0.00
1994 Cincinnati	NL	6	3	0	0	17.2	79	22	14	14	4	1	0	0	5	0	10	1	0	1	1	.500	0	0-0	0	5.91	7.13
1995 Cincinnati	NL	19	11	1	2	79.0	354	91	56	50	13	2	5	3	32	2	33	2	0	3	4	.429	1	0-0	0	5.60	5.70
1996 Cincinnati	NL	24	20	2	2	120.1	552	152	93	80	17	6	2	2	43	5	63	3	0	8	9	.471	1	0-0	0	5.68	5.98
1997 Cin-Min-Det	NL	32	5	0	13	68.0	329	99	62	58	17	2	1	1	29	0	48	4	0	0	4	.000	0	1-1	0	8.21	7.68
1999 Oakland	AL	4	1	0	0	14.0	75	28	19	18	6	1	1	1	6	0	11	0	0	1	1	.500	0	0-0	0	14.40	11.57
2000 Colorado	NL	24	19	0	0	115.0	505	138	83	76	26	6	2	4	33	3	60	0	0	3	4	.429	0	0-0	0	5.86	5.95
2001 San Diego	NL	32	32	1	0	193.1	809	189	107	103	37	7	4	5	49	4	133	1	0	12	11	.522	1	0-0	0	4.05	4.79
2002 San Diego	NL	7	7	0	0	35.0	146	36	19	17	5	0	0	1	10	1	24	2	0	2	4	.333	0	0-0	0	4.24	4.37
1997 Cincinnati	NL	9	0	0	3	13.1	70	21	16	15	4	1	0	1	7	0	12	2	0	0	1	.000	0	1-1	0	9.98	10.13
1997 Minnesota	AL	6	2	0	1	13.0	70	23	18	18	4	0	0	0	8	0	9	2	0	0	0	-	0	0-0	0	11.69	12.46
1997 Detroit	AL	17	3	0	9	41.2	189	55	28	25	9	1	1	0	14	0	27	0	0	0	3	.000	0	0-0	0	6.64	5.40
8 ML YEARS		148	98	4	17	642.1	2849	755	453	416	125	24	16	17	207	15	382	15	0	29	38	.433	3	1-1	0	5.53	5.83

Geoff Jenkins

Bats: L **Throws:** R **Pos:** LF-66; PH-2   **Ht:** 6'1" **Wt:** 213 **Born:** 7/21/74 **Age:** 28

Year Team	Lg	G	AB	H	2B	3B	HR	(Hm	Rd)	TB	R	RBI	RC	TBB	IBB	SO	HBP	SH	SF	SB	CS	SB%	GDP	Avg	OBP	Slg
1998 Milwaukee	NL	84	262	60	12	1	9	(4	5)	101	33	28	26	20	4	61	2	0	1	1	3	.25	7	.229	.288	.385
1999 Milwaukee	NL	135	447	140	43	3	21	(10	11)	252	70	82	88	35	7	87	7	3	1	5	1	.83	10	.313	.371	.564
2000 Milwaukee	NL	135	512	155	36	4	34	(15	19)	301	100	94	104	33	6	135	15	0	4	11	1	.92	9	.303	.360	.588
2001 Milwaukee	NL	105	397	105	21	1	20	(11	9)	188	60	63	60	36	7	120	8	0	5	4	2	.67	11	.264	.334	.474
2002 Milwaukee	NL	67	243	59	17	1	10	(4	6)	108	35	29	29	22	1	60	6	0	1	1	2	.33	8	.243	.320	.444
5 ML YEARS		526	1861	519	129	10	94	(44	50)	950	298	296	307	146	25	463	38	3	12	22	9	.71	45	.279	.342	.510

Jason Jennings

Pitches: R **Bats:** L **Pos:** SP-32   **Ht:** 6'2" **Wt:** 242 **Born:** 7/17/78 **Age:** 24

Year Team	Lg	G	GS	CG	GF	IP	BFP	H	R	ER	HR	SH	SF	HB	TBB	IBB	SO	WP	Bk	W	L	Pct	ShO	Sv-Op	Hld	ERC	ERA
1999 Portland	A-	2	2	0	0	9.0	33	5	1	1	0	0	0	0	2	0	11	0	0	1	0	1.000	0	0--	-	1.07	1.00
1999 Asheville	A	12	12	0	0	58.1	242	55	27	24	3	3	2	6	8	0	69	4	0	2	2	.500	0	0--	-	2.81	3.70
2000 Salem	A+	22	22	3	0	150.1	632	136	66	58	6	3	5	2	42	0	133	8	1	7	10	.412	1	0--	-	2.70	3.47
2001 Carolina	AA	6	6	0	0	36.2	149	32	19	14	4	1	0	0	11	0	33	1	0	1	3	.250	0	0--	-	3.10	3.44
2001 Carolina	AA	4	4	0	0	25.0	106	25	9	8	1	0	0	1	8	0	24	0	0	2	0	1.000	0	0--	-	3.53	2.88
2001 Co Springs	AAA	22	22	4	0	131.2	572	145	80	69	9	6	2	7	41	0	110	3	2	7	8	.467	0	0--	-	4.30	4.72
2001 Colorado	NL	7	7	1	0	39.1	174	42	21	20	2	1	1	1	19	0	26	1	0	4	1	.800	1	0-0	0	4.58	4.58
2002 Colorado	NL	32	32	0	0	185.1	808	201	102	93	26	9	3	8	70	2	127	10	0	16	8	.667	0	0-0	0	4.98	4.52
2 ML YEARS		39	39	1	0	224.2	982	243	123	113	28	10	4	9	89	2	153	11	0	20	9	.690	1	0-0	0	4.92	4.53

Marcus Jensen

Bats: B **Throws:** R **Pos:** C-15; PH-1   **Ht:** 6'4" **Wt:** 204 **Born:** 12/14/72 **Age:** 30

Year Team	Lg	G	AB	H	2B	3B	HR	(Hm	Rd)	TB	R	RBI	RC	TBB	IBB	SO	HBP	SH	SF	SB	CS	SB%	GDP	Avg	OBP	Slg
2002 Indianapolis*	AAA	70	183	42	7	0	4	(-	-)	61	24	25	23	33	1	39	2	2	4	0	0	-	5	.230	.347	.333
1996 San Francisco	NL	9	19	4	1	0	0	(0	0)	5	4	4	3	8	0	7	0	0	0	0	0	-	1	.211	.444	.263
1997 SF-Det		38	85	13	2	0	1	(1	0)	18	6	4	2	8	1	28	0	0	0	0	0	-	2	.153	.226	.212
1998 Milwaukee	NL	2	2	0	0	0	0	(0	0)	0	0	0	0	0	0	2	0	0	0	0	0	-	0	.000	.000	.000
1999 St Louis	NL	16	34	8	5	0	1	(0	1)	16	5	1	6	6	1	12	0	2	0	0	0	-	1	.235	.350	.471
2000 Minnesota	AL	52	139	29	7	1	3	(2	1)	47	16	14	16	24	0	36	0	1	0	0	1	.00	3	.209	.325	.338
2001 Bos-Tex	AL	12	29	5	1	0	0	(0	0)	6	0	2	0	0	0	10	0	0	0	0	0	-	0	.172	.172	.207
2002 Milwaukee	NL	16	35	4	0	0	1	(1	0)	7	2	4	1	4	2	11	0	0	0	0	0	-	0	.114	.200	.200
1997 San Francisco	NL	30	74	11	2	0	1	(1	0)	16	5	3	2	7	1	23	0	0	0	0	0	-	2	.149	.222	.216
1997 Detroit	AL	8	11	2	0	0	0	(0	0)	2	1	1	0	1	0	5	0	0	0	0	0	-	0	.182	.250	.182
2001 Boston	AL	1	4	1	0	0	0	(0	0)	1	0	0	0	0	0	1	0	0	0	0	0	-	0	.250	.250	.250
2001 Texas	AL	11	25	4	1	0	0	(0	0)	5	0	2	0	0	0	9	0	0	0	0	0	-	1	.160	.160	.200
7 ML YEARS		145	343	63	16	1	6	(4	2)	99	33	29	28	50	4	106	0	3	1	0	1	.00	10	.184	.287	.289

Ryan Jensen

Pitches: R **Bats:** R **Pos:** SP-30; RP-2   **Ht:** 6'0" **Wt:** 205 **Born:** 9/17/75 **Age:** 27

Year Team	Lg	G	GS	CG	GF	IP	BFP	H	R	ER	HR	SH	SF	HB	TBB	IBB	SO	WP	Bk	W	L	Pct	ShO	Sv-Op	Hld	ERC	ERA
1996 Bellingham	A-	13	11	0	0	47.0	208	35	30	26	4	1	0	1	38	0	31	7	0	2	4	.333	0	0--	-	4.26	4.98
1997 Bakersfield	A+	1	1	0	0	1.1	7	3	2	2	1	0	1	0	0	0	2	0	0	0	0	-	0	0--	-	16.20	13.50
1997 Salem-Keizer	A-	16	16	0	0	80.1	353	87	55	46	10	2	2	4	32	0	67	2	1	7	3	.700	0	0--	-	4.97	5.15
1998 Bakersfield	A+	29	27	0	1	168.1	726	162	89	63	14	6	1	8	61	3	164	10	2	11	12	.478	0	0--	-	3.73	3.37
1998 Fresno	AAA	2	1	0	0	5.2	25	4	5	3	2	0	1	0	4	0	6	0	0	0	0	-	0	0--	-	5.33	4.76

Year Team		Lg	G	GS	CG	GF	IP	BFP	H	R	ER	HR	SH	SF	HB	TBB	IBB	SO	WP	Bk	W	L	Pct	ShO	Sv-Op	Hld	ERC	ERA
1999 Fresno		AAA	27	27	0	0	156.1	688	160	96	89	17	6	6	6	68	1	150	11	0	11	10	.524	0	0- -	-	4.55	5.12
2000 Fresno		AAA	26	26	1	0	135.1	628	167	106	87	18	4	9	4	63	0	114	3	1	5	8	.385	0	0- -	-	6.08	5.79
2001 Fresno		AAA	20	17	1	2	106.0	445	97	43	41	11	4	1	5	34	0	95	2	0	11	2	.846	1	0- -	-	3.52	3.48
2001 San Francisco		NL	10	7	0	2	42.1	193	44	21	20	5	0	0	4	25	0	26	2	0	1	2	.333	0	0-0	0	5.68	4.25
2002 San Francisco		NL	32	30	1	0	171.2	744	183	93	86	21	7	8	5	66	4	105	3	0	13	8	.619	0	0-0	0	4.69	4.51
2 ML YEARS			42	37	1	2	214.0	937	227	114	106	26	7	8	9	91	4	131	5	0	14	10	.583	0	0-0	0	4.88	4.46

Derek Jeter

Bats: R **Throws:** R **Pos:** SS-156; DH-1 **Ht:** 6'3" **Wt:** 195 **Born:** 6/26/74 **Age:** 29

Year Team		Lg	G	AB	H	2B	3B	HR	(Hm	Rd)	TB	R	RBI	RC	TBB	IBB	SO	HBP	SH	SF	SB	CS	SB%	GDP	Avg	OBP	Slg
1995 New York		AL	15	48	12	4	1	0	(0	0)	18	5	7	5	3	0	11	0	0	0	0	0	-	0	.250	.294	.375
1996 New York		AL	157	582	183	25	6	10	(3	7)	250	104	78	92	48	1	102	9	6	1	14	7	.67	13	.314	.370	.430
1997 New York		AL	159	654	190	31	7	10	(5	5)	265	116	70	99	74	0	125	10	8	2	23	12	.66	14	.291	.370	.405
1998 New York		AL	149	626	203	25	8	19	(9	10)	301	127	84	115	57	1	119	5	3	3	30	6	.83	13	.324	.384	.481
1999 New York		AL	158	627	**219**	37	9	24	(15	9)	346	134	102	146	91	5	116	12	3	6	19	8	.70	12	.349	.438	.552
2000 New York		AL	148	593	201	31	4	15	(8	7)	285	119	73	118	68	4	99	12	3	3	22	4	.85	14	.339	.416	.481
2001 New York		AL	150	614	191	35	3	21	(13	8)	295	110	74	112	56	3	99	10	5	1	27	3	.90	13	.311	.377	.480
2002 New York		AL	157	644	191	26	0	18	(8	10)	271	124	75	106	73	2	114	7	3	3	32	3	.91	14	.297	.373	.421
8 ML YEARS			1093	4388	1390	214	38	117	(61	56)	2031	839	563	793	470	16	785	65	31	27	167	43	.80	93	.317	.389	.463

D'Angelo Jimenez

Bats: B **Throws:** R **Pos:** 2B-71; 3B-33; SS-10; PH-1 **Ht:** 6'0" **Wt:** 194 **Born:** 12/21/77 **Age:** 25

Year Team		Lg	G	AB	H	2B	3B	HR	(Hm	Rd)	TB	R	RBI	RC	TBB	IBB	SO	HBP	SH	SF	SB	CS	SB%	GDP	Avg	OBP	Slg
2002 Charlotte*		AAA	42	157	44	11	1	6	(-	-)	75	24	18	29	24	1	14	0	1	2	6	2	.75	2	.280	.372	.478
1999 New York		AL	7	20	8	2	0	0	(0	0)	10	3	4	5	3	0	4	0	0	0	0	0	-	0	.400	.478	.500
2001 San Diego		NL	86	308	85	19	0	3	(2	1)	113	45	33	39	39	4	68	0	0	2	2	3	.40	9	.276	.355	.367
2002 SD-CWS			114	429	108	15	7	4	(3	1)	149	61	44	53	50	1	73	1	0	2	6	3	.67	11	.252	.330	.347
2002 San Diego		NL	87	321	77	11	4	3	(2	1)	105	39	33	34	34	1	63	0	0	2	4	2	.67	10	.240	.311	.327
2002 Chicago		AL	27	108	31	4	3	1	(1	0)	44	22	11	19	16	0	10	1	0	0	2	1	.67	1	.287	.384	.407
3 ML YEARS			207	757	201	36	7	7	(5	2)	272	109	81	97	92	5	145	1	0	4	8	6	.57	20	.266	.344	.359

Jason Jimenez

Pitches: L **Bats:** R **Pos:** RP-6 **Ht:** 6'2" **Wt:** 210 **Born:** 1/10/76 **Age:** 27

Year Team		Lg	G	GS	CG	GF	IP	BFP	H	R	ER	HR	SH	SF	HB	TBB	IBB	SO	WP	Bk	W	L	Pct	ShO	Sv-Op	Hld	ERC	ERA
1997 Hudson Val		A-	19	0	0	5	31.2	121	16	5	1	1	0	0	2	10	0	31	0	1	3	0	1.000	0	0- -	-	1.33	0.28
1998 St.Pete		A+	13	0	0	8	19.0	97	24	20	18	3	0	2	3	10	2	15	3	1	0	2	.000	0	0- -	-	6.72	8.53
1998 Hudson Val		A-	29	0	0	8	39.1	154	20	13	7	1	3	0	5	13	1	55	2	1	5	2	.714	0	4- -	-	1.45	1.60
1999 St.Pete		A+	41	1	0	19	56.2	229	46	23	15	2	2	0	3	21	2	47	2	0	4	4	.500	0	5- -	-	2.77	2.38
2000 Orlando		AA	30	1	0	8	46.1	185	29	13	10	4	0	1	2	12	0	53	3	0	5	1	.833	0	0- -	-	1.70	1.94
2000 Durham		AAA	19	1	0	7	31.2	147	33	17	17	4	0	0	1	25	0	28	1	0	1	1	.500	0	0- -	-	6.42	4.83
2001 Orlando		AA	35	4	0	22	51.0	218	46	20	18	2	2	1	3	24	1	46	2	0	3	3	.500	0	10- -	-	3.63	3.18
2001 Durham		AAA	15	0	0	8	23.0	102	23	12	12	4	0	0	0	14	0	25	0	0	1	0	1.000	0	1- -	-	5.59	4.70
2002 Durham		AAA	44	0	0	15	51.1	222	47	21	15	3	2	2	6	16	1	55	2	0	2	2	.500	0	3- -	-	3.34	2.63
2002 TB-Det		AL	6	0	0	4	7.1	36	12	8	6	2	0	1	0	2	0	5	0	0	0	0	-	0	0-0	0	8.70	7.36
2002 Tampa Bay		AL	5	0	0	4	6.2	29	9	4	4	2	0	1	0	1	0	5	0	0	0	0	-	0	0-0	0	6.65	5.40
2002 Detroit		AL	1	0	0	0	0.2	7	3	4	2	0	0	0	0	1	0	0	0	0	0	0	-	0	0-0	0	29.61	27.00

Jose Jimenez

Pitches: R **Bats:** R **Pos:** RP-74 **Ht:** 6'3" **Wt:** 228 **Born:** 7/7/73 **Age:** 29

Year Team		Lg	G	GS	CG	GF	IP	BFP	H	R	ER	HR	SH	SF	HB	TBB	IBB	SO	WP	Bk	W	L	Pct	ShO	Sv-Op	Hld	ERC	ERA
1998 St.Louis		NL	4	3	0	0	21.1	94	22	8	7	0	1	1	0	8	0	12	0	0	3	0	1.000	0	0-0	0	3.35	2.95
1999 St.Louis		NL	29	28	2	0	163.0	727	173	114	106	16	10	6	11	71	2	113	10	1	5	14	.263	2	0-1	0	4.81	5.85
2000 Colorado		NL	72	0	0	55	70.2	301	63	27	25	4	4	2	3	28	6	44	5	0	5	2	.714	0	24-30	2	3.18	3.18
2001 Colorado		NL	56	0	0	49	55.0	237	56	27	25	6	2	1	0	22	4	37	3	0	6	1	.857	0	17-22	0	4.14	4.09
2002 Colorado		NL	74	0	0	69	73.1	307	76	34	29	7	4	2	3	11	4	47	0	0	2	10	.167	0	41-47	0	3.31	3.56
5 ML YEARS			235	31	2	173	383.1	1666	390	210	192	33	21	12	17	140	16	253	18	1	21	27	.438	2	82-100	2	4.03	4.51

Charles Johnson

Bats: R **Throws:** R **Pos:** C-82; PH-1 **Ht:** 6'3" **Wt:** 250 **Born:** 7/20/71 **Age:** 31

Year Team		Lg	G	AB	H	2B	3B	HR	(Hm	Rd)	TB	R	RBI	RC	TBB	IBB	SO	HBP	SH	SF	SB	CS	SB%	GDP	Avg	OBP	Slg
2002 Jupiter*		A+	5	16	7	0	0	3	(-	-)	16	5	9	6	2	0	4	0	0	0	0	0	-	0	.438	.500	1.000
1994 Florida		NL	4	11	5	1	0	1	(1	0)	9	5	4	3	1	0	4	0	0	1	0	0	-	0	.455	.462	.818
1995 Florida		NL	97	315	79	15	1	11	(3	8)	129	40	39	44	46	2	71	4	4	2	0	2	.00	11	.251	.351	.410
1996 Florida		NL	120	386	84	13	1	13	(9	4)	138	34	37	35	40	6	91	2	2	4	1	0	1.00	20	.218	.292	.358
1997 Florida		NL	124	416	104	26	1	19	(7	12)	189	43	63	63	60	6	109	3	3	2	0	2	.00	13	.250	.347	.454
1998 Fla-LA		NL	133	459	100	18	0	19	(14	5)	175	44	58	48	45	1	129	1	0	1	0	2	.00	13	.218	.289	.381
1999 Baltimore		AL	135	426	107	19	1	16	(8	8)	176	58	54	59	55	2	107	4	4	3	0	0	-	13	.251	.340	.413
2000 Bal-CWS		AL	128	421	128	24	0	31	(19	12)	245	76	91	89	52	6	106	1	1	3	2	0	1.00	8	.304	.379	.582
2001 Florida		NL	128	451	117	32	0	18	(5	13)	203	51	75	64	38	2	133	4	0	3	0	0	-	8	.259	.321	.450
2002 Florida		NL	83	244	53	19	0	6	(2	4)	90	18	36	23	31	7	61	0	1	4	0	0	-	10	.217	.301	.369
1998 Florida		NL	31	113	25	5	0	7	(5	2)	51	13	23	16	16	0	30	0	0	1	0	0	.00	3	.221	.315	.451
1998 Los Angeles		NL	102	346	75	13	0	12	(9	3)	124	31	35	32	29	1	99	1	0	0	0	1	.00	0	.217	.279	.358

Year Team	Lg	G	AB	H	2B	3B	HR	(Hm	Rd)	TB	R	RBI	RC	TBB	IBB	SO	HBP	SH	SF	SB	CS	SB%	GDP	Avg	OBP	Slg
2000 Baltimore	AL	84	286	84	16	0	21	(12	9)	163	52	55	56	32	0	69	0	1	1	2	0	1.00	8	.294	.364	.570
2000 Chicago	AL	44	135	44	8	0	10	(7	3)	82	24	36	33	20	0	37	1	0	2	0	0	-	0	.326	.411	.607
9 ML YEARS		952	3129	777	167	4	134	(68	66)	1354	369	457	428	368	26	811	19	15	23	3	6	.33	96	.248	.329	.433

Jason Johnson

Pitches: R **Bats:** R **Pos:** SP-22

Ht: 6'6" **Wt:** 235 **Born:** 10/27/73 **Age:** 29

| | | HOW MUCH HE PITCHED | | | | | | WHAT HE GAVE UP | | | | | | | | | | | THE RESULTS | | | | | | |
Year Team	Lg	G	GS	CG	GF	IP	BFP	H	R	ER	HR	SH	SF	HB	TBB	IBB	SO	WP	Bk	W	L	Pct	ShO	Sv-Op	Hld	ERC	ERA
2002 Bowie*	AA	1	1	0	0	5.0	20	4	0	0	0	0	0	0	1	0	6	0	0	1	0	1.000	0	0--	-	1.70	0.00
1997 Pittsburgh	NL	3	0	0	0	6.0	27	10	4	4	2	0	1	0	1	0	3	0	0	0	0	-	0	0-0	0	9.59	6.00
1998 Tampa Bay	AL	13	13	0	0	60.0	274	74	38	38	9	1	1	3	27	0	36	2	0	2	5	.286	0	0-0	0	6.35	5.70
1999 Baltimore	AL	22	21	0	0	115.1	515	120	74	70	16	2	4	3	55	0	71	5	1	8	7	.533	0	0-0	0	4.99	5.46
2000 Baltimore	AL	25	13	0	3	107.2	501	119	95	84	21	3	5	4	61	2	79	3	0	1	10	.091	0	0-0	2	6.18	7.02
2001 Baltimore	AL	32	32	2	0	196.0	856	194	109	89	28	6	6	13	77	3	114	9	0	10	12	.455	0	0-0	0	4.53	4.09
2002 Baltimore	AL	22	22	1	0	131.1	561	141	68	67	19	0	3	6	41	2	97	4	0	5	14	.263	0	0-0	0	4.70	4.59
6 ML YEARS		117	101	3	3	616.1	2734	658	388	352	95	12	20	29	262	7	400	23	1	26	48	.351	0	0-0	2	5.15	5.14

Jonathan Johnson

Pitches: R **Bats:** R **Pos:** RP-16

Ht: 6'0" **Wt:** 180 **Born:** 7/16/74 **Age:** 28

| | | HOW MUCH HE PITCHED | | | | | | WHAT HE GAVE UP | | | | | | | | | | | THE RESULTS | | | | | | |
Year Team	Lg	G	GS	CG	GF	IP	BFP	H	R	ER	HR	SH	SF	HB	TBB	IBB	SO	WP	Bk	W	L	Pct	ShO	Sv-Op	Hld	ERC	ERA
2002 El Paso*	AA	3	1	0	0	11.1	49	14	7	7	1	0	0	0	3	0	9	3	0	0	1	.000	0	0--	-	4.88	5.56
2002 Tucson*	AAA	14	5	0	2	36.1	167	48	41	38	6	0	2	1	14	0	27	1	0	0	3	.000	0	0--	-	6.60	9.41
2002 Portland*	AAA	12	0	0	4	18.2	71	14	5	5	2	2	2	0	2	0	17	1	0	0	0	-	0	1--	-	1.79	2.41
1998 Texas	AL	1	1	0	0	4.1	22	5	4	4	0	0	1	0	5	0	3	0	0	0	0	-	0	0-0	0	7.36	8.31
1999 Texas	AL	1	0	0	0	3.0	21	9	5	5	0	0	1	1	2	0	3	0	0	0	0	-	0	0-0	0	19.55	15.00
2000 Texas	AL	15	0	0	3	29.0	144	34	23	20	3	0	2	6	19	2	23	2	0	1	1	.500	0	0-0	0	6.84	6.21
2001 Texas	AL	5	0	0	2	10.1	53	13	11	11	2	1	3	1	7	1	11	0	0	0	0	-	0	0-0	0	7.49	9.58
2002 San Diego	NL	16	0	0	5	15.1	67	15	8	7	2	1	0	1	5	1	21	0	0	1	2	.333	0	0-0	1	3.94	4.11
5 ML YEARS		38	1	0	10	62.0	307	76	51	47	7	2	7	9	38	4	61	2	0	2	3	.400	0	0-0	1	6.77	6.82

Mark L Johnson

Bats: L **Throws:** R **Pos:** C-85; PH-3

Ht: 6'0" **Wt:** 185 **Born:** 9/12/75 **Age:** 27

| | | BATTING | | | | | | | | | | | | | | | | | | BASERUNNING | | | | AVERAGES | | |
Year Team	Lg	G	AB	H	2B	3B	HR	(Hm	Rd)	TB	R	RBI	RC	TBB	IBB	SO	HBP	SH	SF	SB	CS	SB%	GDP	Avg	OBP	Slg
1998 Chicago	AL	7	23	2	0	2	0	(0	0)	6	2	1	0	1	0	8	0	0	0	0	0	-	0	.087	.125	.261
1999 Chicago	AL	73	207	47	11	0	4	(2	2)	70	27	16	27	36	0	58	2	1	2	3	1	.75	2	.227	.344	.338
2000 Chicago	AL	75	213	48	11	0	3	(2	1)	68	29	23	23	27	0	40	1	10	0	3	2	.60	3	.225	.315	.319
2001 Chicago	AL	61	173	43	6	1	5	(2	3)	66	21	18	23	23	1	31	2	10	3	2	1	.67	5	.249	.338	.382
2002 Chicago	AL	86	263	55	8	1	4	(1	3)	77	31	18	23	30	1	52	3	6	0	0	0	-	4	.209	.297	.293
5 ML YEARS		302	879	195	36	4	16	(7	9)	287	110	76	96	117	2	189	8	27	5	8	4	.67	14	.222	.317	.327

Mark P Johnson

Bats: L **Throws:** L **Pos:** PH-26; 1B-15; LF-1

Ht: 6'4" **Wt:** 230 **Born:** 10/17/67 **Age:** 35

| | | BATTING | | | | | | | | | | | | | | | | | | BASERUNNING | | | | AVERAGES | | |
Year Team	Lg	G	AB	H	2B	3B	HR	(Hm	Rd)	TB	R	RBI	RC	TBB	IBB	SO	HBP	SH	SF	SB	CS	SB%	GDP	Avg	OBP	Slg
2002 Norfolk*	AAA	77	270	70	17	1	14	(-	-)	131	45	37	46	32	4	53	4	0	3	1	0	1.00	2	.259	.343	.485
1995 Pittsburgh	NL	79	221	46	6	1	13	(7	6)	93	32	28	32	37	2	66	2	0	1	5	2	.71	2	.208	.326	.421
1996 Pittsburgh	NL	127	343	94	24	0	13	(10	3)	157	55	47	57	44	3	64	5	0	4	6	4	.60	5	.274	.361	.458
1997 Pittsburgh	NL	78	219	47	10	0	4	(2	2)	69	30	29	27	43	1	78	2	0	3	1	1	.50	1	.215	.345	.315
1998 Anaheim	AL	10	14	1	0	0	0	(0	0)	1	1	0	0	0	0	6	0	0	0	0	0	-	1	.071	.071	.071
2000 New York	NL	21	22	4	0	0	1	(1	0)	7	2	6	2	5	0	9	0	0	0	0	0	-	1	.182	.333	.318
2001 New York	NL	71	118	30	6	1	6	(2	4)	56	17	23	19	16	1	31	0	0	2	0	2	.00	0	.254	.338	.475
2002 New York	NL	42	51	7	4	0	1	(1	0)	14	5	4	4	9	0	18	0	1	0	0	0	-	0	.137	.267	.275
7 ML YEARS		428	988	229	50	2	38	(23	15)	397	142	137	141	154	7	272	9	1	10	12	9	.57	10	.232	.338	.402

Nick Johnson

Bats: L **Throws:** L **Pos:** 1B-78; DH-49; PR-5; PH-3; LF-2

Ht: 6'3" **Wt:** 224 **Born:** 9/19/78 **Age:** 24

| | | BATTING | | | | | | | | | | | | | | | | | | BASERUNNING | | | | AVERAGES | | |
Year Team	Lg	G	AB	H	2B	3B	HR	(Hm	Rd)	TB	R	RBI	RC	TBB	IBB	SO	HBP	SH	SF	SB	CS	SB%	GDP	Avg	OBP	Slg
1996 Yankees	R	47	157	45	11	1	2	(-	-)	64	31	33	29	30	0	35	9	0	3	0	0	-	5	.287	.422	.408
1997 Greensboro	A	127	433	118	23	1	16	(-	-)	191	77	75	84	76	1	99	18	0	6	16	3	.84	5	.273	.398	.441
1998 Tampa	A+	92	303	96	14	1	17	(-	-)	163	69	58	77	68	3	76	19	0	5	1	4	.20	5	.317	.466	.538
1999 Norwich	AA	132	420	145	33	5	14	(-	-)	230	114	87	125	123	6	88	37	0	1	8	6	.57	9	.345	.525	.548
2001 Columbus	AAA	110	359	92	20	0	18	(-	-)	166	68	49	74	81	3	105	14	0	5	9	2	.82	6	.256	.407	.462
2002 Columbus	AAA	3	11	1	0	0	0	(-	-)	1	1	0	1	1	0	4	0	0	0	0	0	-	1	.091	.167	.091
2001 New York	AL	23	67	13	2	0	2	(1	1)	21	6	8	6	7	0	15	4	0	0	0	0	-	3	.194	.308	.313
2002 New York	AL	129	378	92	15	0	15	(7	8)	152	56	58	58	48	5	98	12	3	0	1	3	.25	11	.243	.347	.402
2 ML YEARS		152	445	105	17	0	17	(8	9)	173	62	66	64	55	5	113	16	3	0	1	3	.25	14	.236	.341	.389

Randy Johnson

Pitches: L Bats: R Pos: SP-35   Ht: 6'10" Wt: 232 Born: 9/10/63 Age: 39

Year Team	Lg	G	GS	CG	GF	IP	BFP	H	R	ER	HR	SH	SF	HB	TBB	IBB	SO	WP	Bk	W	L	Pct	ShO	Sv-Op	Hld	ERC	ERA
1988 Montreal	NL	4	4	1	0	26.0	109	23	8	7	3	0	0	0	7	0	25	3	0	3	0	1.000	0	0-0	0	2.96	2.42
1989 Mon-Sea		29	28	2	1	160.2	715	147	100	86	13	10	13	3	96	2	130	7	7	7	13	.350	2	0-0	0	4.26	4.82
1990 Seattle	AL	33	33	5	0	219.2	944	174	103	89	26	7	6	5	120	2	194	4	2	14	11	.560	2	0-0	0	3.68	3.65
1991 Seattle	AL	33	33	2	0	201.1	889	151	96	89	15	9	8	12	152	0	228	12	2	13	10	.565	1	0-0	0	4.15	3.98
1992 Seattle	AL	31	31	6	0	210.1	922	154	104	88	13	3	8	18	144	1	241	13	1	12	14	.462	2	0-0	0	3.75	3.77
1993 Seattle	AL	35	34	10	1	255.1	1043	185	97	92	22	8	7	16	99	1	308	8	2	19	8	.704	3	1-1	0	2.73	3.24
1994 Seattle	AL	23	23	9	0	172.0	694	132	65	61	14	3	1	6	72	0	204	5	0	13	6	.684	4	0-0	0	2.99	3.19
1995 Seattle	AL	30	30	6	0	214.1	866	159	65	59	12	2	1	6	65	1	294	5	2	18	2	.900	3	0-0	0	2.18	2.48
1996 Seattle	AL	14	8	0	2	61.1	256	48	27	25	8	1	0	2	25	0	85	3	1	5	0	1.000	0	1-2	0	3.24	3.67
1997 Seattle	AL	30	29	5	0	213.0	850	147	60	54	20	4	1	10	77	2	291	4	0	20	4	.833	2	0-0	0	2.47	2.28
1998 Sea-Hou		34	34	10	0	244.1	1014	203	102	89	23	5	2	14	86	1	329	7	2	19	11	.633	5	0-0	0	3.16	3.28
1999 Arizona	NL	35	35	12	0	271.2	1079	207	86	75	30	4	3	9	70	3	364	4	2	17	9	.654	2	0-0	0	2.49	2.48
2000 Arizona	NL	35	35	8	0	248.2	1001	202	89	73	23	14	5	6	76	1	347	5	2	19	7	.731	3	0-0	0	2.80	2.64
2001 Arizona	NL	35	34	3	1	249.2	994	181	74	69	19	10	5	18	71	2	372	8	1	21	6	.778	2	0-0	0	2.35	2.49
2002 Arizona	NL	35	35	8	0	260.0	1035	197	78	67	26	4	2	13	71	1	334	3	2	24	5	.828	4	0-0	0	2.54	2.32
1989 Montreal	NL	7	6	0	1	29.2	143	29	25	22	2	3	4	0	26	1	26	2	2	0	4	.000	0	0-0	0	5.42	6.67
1989 Seattle	AL	22	22	2	0	131.0	572	118	75	64	11	7	9	3	70	1	104	5	5	7	9	.438	0	0-0	0	4.01	4.40
1998 Seattle	AL	23	23	6	0	160.0	685	146	90	77	19	5	1	11	60	0	213	7	2	9	10	.474	2	0-0	0	3.88	4.33
1998 Houston	NL	11	11	4	0	84.1	329	57	12	12	4	0	1	3	26	1	116	0	0	10	1	.909	4	0-0	0	1.93	1.28
15 ML YEARS		436	426	87	5	3008.1	12411	2310	1154	1023	267	84	62	138	1231	19	3746	91	26	224	106	.679	34	2-3	0	2.98	3.06

Russ Johnson

Bats: R Throws: R Pos: 3B-27; PH-15; DH-3; SS-2; 2B-1   Ht: 5'10" Wt: 198 Born: 2/22/73 Age: 30

Year Team	Lg	G	AB	H	2B	3B	HR	(Hm	Rd)	TB	R	RBI	RC	TBB	IBB	SO	HBP	SH	SF	SB	CS	SB%	GDP	Avg	OBP	Slg
2002 Orlando*	AA	12	43	12	5	0	0	(-	-)	17	10	3	6	8	0	7	0	0	0	1	0	1.00	4	.279	.392	.395
2002 Durham*	AAA	10	33	9	0	1	2	(-	-)	17	9	5	6	4	0	5	0	0	0	1	0	1.00	0	.273	.351	.515
1997 Houston	NL	21	60	18	1	0	2	(2	0)	25	7	9	8	6	0	14	0	1	0	1	1	.50	2	.300	.364	.417
1998 Houston	NL	8	13	3	1	0	0	(0	0)	4	2	0	1	1	0	5	1	0	0	1	0	1.00	1	.231	.333	.308
1999 Houston	NL	83	156	44	10	0	5	(2	3)	69	24	23	24	20	0	31	0	4	3	2	3	.40	3	.282	.358	.442
2000 Hou-TB		100	230	55	8	0	2	(2	0)	69	32	20	23	27	0	40	1	4	1	5	2	.71	5	.239	.320	.300
2001 Tampa Bay	AL	85	248	73	19	2	4	(1	3)	108	32	33	42	34	0	57	1	4	1	2	2	.50	2	.294	.380	.435
2002 Tampa Bay	AL	45	111	24	5	0	1	(0	1)	32	15	12	13	16	1	22	1	2	0	5	2	.71	2	.216	.320	.288
2000 Houston	NL	26	45	8	0	0	0	(0	0)	8	4	3	0	2	0	10	0	1	0	1	1	.50	3	.178	.213	.178
2000 Tampa Bay	AL	74	185	47	8	0	2	(2	0)	61	28	17	23	25	0	30	1	3	1	4	1	.80	4	.254	.344	.330
6 ML YEARS		342	818	217	44	2	14	(7	7)	307	112	97	111	104	1	169	4	15	5	16	10	.62	17	.265	.349	.375

Andruw Jones

Bats: R Throws: R Pos: CF-154; DH-1; PH-1   Ht: 6'1" Wt: 210 Born: 4/23/77 Age: 26

Year Team	Lg	G	AB	H	2B	3B	HR	(Hm	Rd)	TB	R	RBI	RC	TBB	IBB	SO	HBP	SH	SF	SB	CS	SB%	GDP	Avg	OBP	Slg
1996 Atlanta	NL	31	106	23	7	1	5	(3	2)	47	11	13	13	7	0	29	0	0	0	3	0	1.00	7	.217	.265	.443
1997 Atlanta	NL	153	399	92	18	1	18	(5	13)	166	60	70	54	56	2	107	4	5	3	20	11	.65	11	.231	.329	.416
1998 Atlanta	NL	159	582	158	33	8	31	(16	15)	300	89	90	97	40	8	129	4	1	4	27	4	.87	10	.271	.321	.515
1999 Atlanta	NL	162	592	163	35	5	26	(10	16)	286	97	84	103	76	11	103	9	0	2	24	12	.67	12	.275	.365	.483
2000 Atlanta	NL	161	656	199	36	6	36	(15	21)	355	122	104	127	59	0	100	9	0	5	21	6	.78	12	.303	.366	.541
2001 Atlanta	NL	161	625	157	25	2	34	(16	18)	288	104	104	90	56	3	142	9	0	9	11	4	.73	10	.251	.312	.461
2002 Atlanta	NL	154	560	148	34	0	35	(18	17)	287	91	94	97	83	4	135	10	0	6	8	3	.73	14	.264	.366	.513
7 ML YEARS		981	3520	940	188	23	185	(83	102)	1729	574	559	581	377	28	745	39	6	29	114	40	.74	70	.267	.342	.491

Bobby J Jones

Pitches: R Bats: R Pos: SP-18; RP-1   Ht: 6'4" Wt: 225 Born: 2/10/70 Age: 33

Year Team	Lg	G	GS	CG	GF	IP	BFP	H	R	ER	HR	SH	SF	HB	TBB	IBB	SO	WP	Bk	W	L	Pct	ShO	Sv-Op	Hld	ERC	ERA
1993 New York	NL	9	9	0	0	61.2	265	61	35	25	6	5	3	2	22	3	35	1	0	2	4	.333	0	0-0	0	3.87	3.65
1994 New York	NL	24	24	1	0	160.0	685	157	75	56	10	11	4	4	56	9	80	1	3	12	7	.632	1	0-0	0	3.51	3.15
1995 New York	NL	30	30	3	0	195.2	839	209	107	91	20	11	6	7	53	6	127	2	1	10	10	.500	1	0-0	0	4.05	4.19
1996 New York	NL	31	31	3	0	195.2	826	219	102	96	26	12	5	3	46	6	116	2	0	12	8	.600	1	0-0	0	4.40	4.42
1997 New York	NL	30	30	2	0	193.1	806	177	88	78	24	6	4	2	63	3	125	3	1	15	9	.625	1	0-0	0	3.51	3.63
1998 New York	NL	30	30	0	0	195.1	804	192	88	88	23	4	7	8	53	2	115	2	2	9	9	.500	0	0-0	0	3.84	4.05
1999 New York	NL	12	9	0	0	59.1	253	69	37	37	3	3	3	2	11	0	31	0	0	3	3	.500	0	0-0	0	3.95	5.61
2000 New York	NL	27	27	1	0	154.2	676	171	90	87	25	7	6	5	49	3	85	2	1	11	6	.647	0	0-0	0	4.88	5.06
2001 San Diego	NL	33	33	1	0	195.0	880	250	137	111	37	9	9	4	38	6	113	3	0	8	19	.296	0	0-0	0	5.41	5.12
2002 San Diego	NL	19	18	0	1	108.0	474	134	68	66	20	3	2	1	21	1	60	1	0	7	8	.467	0	0-0	0	5.21	5.50
10 ML YEARS		245	241	11	1	1518.2	6508	1639	827	735	194	71	49	38	412	39	887	17	8	89	83	.517	4	0-0	0	4.26	4.36

Bobby M Jones

Pitches: L Bats: R Pos: RP-14; SP-2   Ht: 6'0" Wt: 178 Born: 4/11/72 Age: 31

Year Team	Lg	G	GS	CG	GF	IP	BFP	H	R	ER	HR	SH	SF	HB	TBB	IBB	SO	WP	Bk	W	L	Pct	ShO	Sv-Op	Hld	ERC	ERA
2002 Norfolk*	AAA	13	6	0	1	40.1	187	42	25	18	4	1	1	5	15	0	35	1	0	1	4	.200	0	0--	-	4.46	4.02
1997 Colorado	NL	4	4	0	0	19.1	96	30	18	18	2	2	3	0	12	0	5	0	0	1	1	.500	0	0-0	0	8.63	8.38
1998 Colorado	NL	35	20	1	1	141.1	630	157	75	56	12	9	6	6	66	0	109	4	1	7	8	.467	0	0-0	1	4.91	5.22
1999 Colorado	NL	30	20	0	1	112.1	546	132	91	79	24	7	6	6	77	0	74	0	0	6	10	.375	0	0-0	0	7.41	6.33
2000 New York	NL	11	1	0	4	21.2	99	18	11	10	2	0	1	3	14	1	20	0	0	0	1	.000	0	0-0	0	4.43	4.15
2002 NYM-SD	NL	16	2	0	1	26.2	126	30	18	17	4	2	1	1	18	2	18	0	0	1	1	-	0	0-0	1	6.37	5.74

Year Team	Lg	G	GS	CG	GF	IP	BFP	H	R	ER	HR	SH	SF	HB	TBB	IBB	SO	WP	Bk	W	L	Pct	ShO	Sv-Op	Hld	ERC	ERA
2002 New York	NL	12	0	0	1	17.0	81	20	11	10	3	2	0	1	11	2	11	0	0	0	0	-	0	0-0	1	6.82	5.29
2002 San Diego	NL	4	2	0	0	9.2	45	10	7	7	1	0	1	0	7	0	7	0	0	0	0	-	0	0-0	0	5.61	6.52
5 ML YEARS		96	47	1	7	321.1	1497	363	225	206	44	20	15	16	187	3	226	8	1	14	20	.412	0	0-0	2	6.06	5.77

Chipper Jones

Bats: B **Throws:** R **Pos:** LF-152; PH-6   **Ht:** 6'4" **Wt:** 210 **Born:** 4/24/72 **Age:** 31

Year Team	Lg	G	AB	H	2B	3B	HR	(Hm	Rd)	TB	R	RBI	RC	TBB	IBB	SO	HBP	SH	SF	SB	CS	SB%	GDP	Avg	OBP	Slg
1993 Atlanta	NL	8	3	2	1	0	0	(0	0)	3	2	0	2	1	0	1	0	0	0	0	0	-	0	.667	.750	1.000
1995 Atlanta	NL	140	524	139	22	3	23	(15	8)	236	87	86	84	73	1	99	0	1	4	8	4	.67	10	.265	.353	.450
1996 Atlanta	NL	157	598	185	32	5	30	(18	12)	317	114	110	123	87	0	88	0	1	7	14	1	.93	14	.309	.393	.530
1997 Atlanta	NL	157	597	176	41	3	21	(7	14)	286	100	111	104	76	8	88	0	0	6	20	5	.80	19	.295	.371	.479
1998 Atlanta	NL	160	601	188	29	5	34	(17	17)	329	123	107	129	96	1	93	1	1	8	16	6	.73	17	.313	.404	.547
1999 Atlanta	NL	157	567	181	41	1	45	(25	20)	359	116	110	150	126	18	94	2	0	10	25	3	.89	20	.319	.441	.633
2000 Atlanta	NL	156	579	180	38	1	36	(18	18)	328	118	111	128	95	10	64	2	0	5	14	7	.67	14	.311	.404	.566
2001 Atlanta	NL	159	572	189	33	5	38	(19	19)	346	113	102	136	98	20	82	2	0	5	9	10	.47	13	.330	.427	.605
2002 Atlanta	NL	158	548	179	35	1	26	(17	9)	294	90	100	119	107	23	89	2	0	5	8	2	.80	18	.327	.435	.536
9 ML YEARS		1252	4589	1419	272	24	253	(136	117)	2498	863	837	975	759	81	698	9	3	51	114	38	.75	125	.309	.404	.544

Jacque Jones

Bats: L **Throws:** L **Pos:** LF-143; PH-10   **Ht:** 5'10" **Wt:** 176 **Born:** 4/25/75 **Age:** 28

Year Team	Lg	G	AB	H	2B	3B	HR	(Hm	Rd)	TB	R	RBI	RC	TBB	IBB	SO	HBP	SH	SF	SB	CS	SB%	GDP	Avg	OBP	Slg
1999 Minnesota	AL	95	322	93	24	2	9	(5	4)	148	54	44	46	17	1	63	4	1	3	4	4	.43	7	.289	.329	.460
2000 Minnesota	AL	154	523	149	26	5	19	(11	8)	242	66	76	70	26	4	111	0	1	0	7	5	.58	17	.285	.319	.463
2001 Minnesota	AL	149	475	131	25	0	14	(5	9)	198	57	49	63	39	2	92	3	2	0	12	9	.57	10	.276	.335	.417
2002 Minnesota	AL	149	577	173	37	2	27	(6	21)	295	96	85	100	37	2	129	2	4	6	6	7	.46	8	.300	.341	.511
4 ML YEARS		547	1897	546	112	9	69	(27	42)	883	273	254	279	119	9	395	9	8	9	28	25	.53	42	.288	.331	.465

Todd Jones

Pitches: R **Bats:** R **Pos:** RP-79   **Ht:** 6'3" **Wt:** 230 **Born:** 4/24/68 **Age:** 35

Year Team	Lg	G	GS	CG	GF	IP	BFP	H	R	ER	HR	SH	SF	HB	TBB	IBB	SO	WP	Bk	W	L	Pct	ShO	Sv-Op	Hld	ERC	ERA
1993 Houston	NL	27	0	0	8	37.1	150	28	14	13	4	2	1	1	15	2	25	1	1	1	2	.333	0	2-3	6	2.90	3.13
1994 Houston	NL	48	0	0	20	72.2	288	52	23	22	3	3	1	1	26	4	63	1	0	5	2	.714	0	5-9	8	2.10	2.72
1995 Houston	NL	68	0	0	40	99.2	442	89	38	34	8	5	4	6	52	17	96	5	0	6	5	.545	0	15-20	8	3.70	3.07
1996 Houston	NL	51	0	0	37	57.1	263	61	30	28	5	2	1	5	32	6	44	3	0	6	3	.667	0	17-23	5	5.16	4.40
1997 Detroit	AL	68	0	0	51	70.0	301	60	29	24	3	1	4	1	35	2	70	7	0	5	4	.556	0	31-36	5	3.27	3.09
1998 Detroit	AL	65	0	0	53	63.1	279	58	38	35	7	2	6	2	36	4	57	5	0	1	4	.200	0	28-32	0	4.37	4.97
1999 Detroit	AL	65	0	0	62	66.1	287	64	30	28	7	3	1	1	35	1	64	2	0	4	4	.500	0	30-35	0	4.55	3.80
2000 Detroit	AL	67	0	0	60	64.0	271	67	28	25	6	1	1	1	25	1	67	2	0	2	4	.333	0	42-46	0	4.43	3.52
2001 Det-Min	AL	69	0	0	36	68.0	314	87	39	32	9	3	3	0	29	1	54	3	0	5	5	.500	0	13-21	10	6.03	4.24
2002 Colorado	NL	79	0	0	20	82.1	352	84	43	43	10	6	3	3	28	3	73	1	0	1	4	.200	0	1-3	30	4.22	4.70
2001 Detroit	AL	45	0	0	28	48.2	225	60	31	25	6	2	3	0	22	1	39	3	0	4	5	.444	0	11-17	3	5.74	4.62
2001 Minnesota	AL	24	0	0	8	19.1	89	27	8	7	3	1	0	0	7	0	15	0	0	1	0	1.000	0	2-4	7	6.80	3.26
10 ML YEARS		607	0	0	387	681.0	2947	650	312	284	62	28	25	21	313	41	613	30	1	36	37	.493	0	184-228	68	4.04	3.75

Brian Jordan

Bats: R **Throws:** R **Pos:** LF-121; RF-4; DH-3; PH-2   **Ht:** 6'1" **Wt:** 205 **Born:** 3/29/67 **Age:** 36

Year Team	Lg	G	AB	H	2B	3B	HR	(Hm	Rd)	TB	R	RBI	RC	TBB	IBB	SO	HBP	SH	SF	SB	CS	SB%	GDP	Avg	OBP	Slg
1992 St Louis	NL	55	193	40	9	4	5	(3	2)	72	17	22	16	10	1	48	1	0	0	7	2	.78	6	.207	.250	.373
1993 St Louis	NL	67	223	69	10	6	10	(4	6)	121	33	44	39	12	0	35	4	0	3	6	6	.50	6	.309	.351	.543
1994 St Louis	NL	53	178	46	8	2	5	(4	1)	73	14	15	22	16	0	40	1	0	2	4	3	.57	6	.258	.320	.410
1995 St Louis	NL	131	490	145	20	4	22	(14	8)	239	83	81	80	22	4	79	11	0	2	24	9	.73	5	.296	.339	.488
1996 St Louis	NL	140	513	159	36	1	17	(3	14)	248	82	104	88	29	4	84	7	2	9	22	5	.81	6	.310	.349	.483
1997 St Louis	NL	47	145	34	5	0	0	(0	0)	39	17	10	13	10	1	21	6	0	0	6	1	.86	4	.234	.311	.269
1998 St Louis	NL	150	564	178	34	7	25	(9	16)	301	100	91	104	40	1	66	9	0	4	17	5	.77	18	.316	.368	.534
1999 Atlanta	NL	153	576	163	28	4	23	(11	12)	268	100	115	92	51	2	81	9	0	9	13	8	.62	9	.283	.346	.465
2000 Atlanta	NL	133	489	129	26	0	17	(7	10)	206	71	77	66	38	1	80	5	0	5	10	2	.83	12	.264	.320	.421
2001 Atlanta	NL	148	560	165	32	3	25	(14	11)	278	82	97	87	31	3	88	6	0	8	3	2	.60	18	.295	.334	.496
2002 Los Angeles	NL	128	471	134	27	3	18	(7	11)	221	65	80	73	34	3	86	6	0	4	2	2	.50	10	.285	.338	.469
11 ML YEARS		1205	4402	1262	235	34	167	(76	91)	2066	664	736	680	293	20	708	65	2	46	114	45	.72	100	.287	.337	.469

Felix Jose

Bats: B **Throws:** R **Pos:** PH-9; RF-4; LF-1   **Ht:** 6'1" **Wt:** 220 **Born:** 5/2/65 **Age:** 38

Year Team	Lg	G	AB	H	2B	3B	HR	(Hm	Rd)	TB	R	RBI	RC	TBB	IBB	SO	HBP	SH	SF	SB	CS	SB%	GDP	Avg	OBP	Slg
1988 Oakland	AL	8	6	2	1	0	0	(0	0)	3	2	1	1	0	0	1	0	0	0	1	0	1.00	0	.333	.333	.500
1989 Oakland	AL	20	57	11	2	0	0	(0	0)	13	3	5	2	4	0	13	0	0	0	0	1	.00	2	.193	.246	.228
1990 Oak-Stl	NL	126	426	113	16	1	11	(5	6)	164	54	52	49	24	0	81	5	2	1	12	6	.67	5	.265	.311	.385
1991 St Louis	NL	154	568	173	40	6	8	(3	5)	249	69	77	86	50	8	113	2	0	5	20	12	.63	12	.305	.360	.438
1992 St Louis	NL	131	509	150	22	3	14	(12	2)	220	62	75	75	40	8	100	1	0	7	28	12	.70	9	.295	.347	.432
1993 Kansas City	AL	149	499	126	24	3	6	(2	4)	174	64	43	54	36	5	95	1	1	2	31	13	.70	5	.253	.303	.349
1994 Kansas City	AL	99	366	111	28	1	11	(1	10)	174	56	55	57	35	6	75	0	0	4	10	12	.45	9	.303	.362	.475
1995 Kansas City	AL	9	30	4	1	0	0	(0	0)	5	2	1	1	2	0	6	0	0	0	0	0	-	0	.133	.188	.167
2000 New York	AL	20	29	7	0	0	1	(0	1)	10	4	5	2	2	0	9	0	0	1	0	1	.00	1	.241	.281	.345
2002 Arizona	NL	13	19	5	0	0	2	(2	0)	11	5	4	3	4	0	8	0	0	0	0	0	-	1	.263	.360	.579

Year Team	Lg	G	AB	H	2B	3B	HR	(Hm	Rd)	TB	R	RBI	RC	TBB	IBB	SO	HBP	SH	SF	SB	CS	SB%	GDP	Avg	OBP	Slg
1990 Oakland	AL	101	341	90	12	0	8	(3	5)	126	42	39	37	16	0	65	5	2	1	8	2	.80	8	.264	.306	.370
1990 St Louis	NL	25	85	23	4	1	3	(2	1)	38	12	13	12	8	0	16	0	0	0	4	4	.50	1	.271	.333	.447
10 ML YEARS		729	2509	702	134	14	53	(25	28)	1023	321	318	329	197	27	504	9	3	14	102	57	.64	49	.280	.333	.408

Kevin Joseph

Pitches: R **Bats:** R **Pos:** RP-11   **Ht:** 6'4" **Wt:** 200 **Born:** 8/1/76 **Age:** 26

Year Team	Lg	G	GS	CG	GF	IP	BFP	H	R	ER	HR	SH	SF	HB	TBB	IBB	SO	WP	Bk	W	L	Pct	ShO	Sv-Op	Hld	ERC	ERA
1997 Salem-Keizer	A-	17	6	0	5	45.0	208	44	35	27	4	1	2	2	26	0	45	10	3	3	5	.375	0	1--	-	4.60	5.40
1998 Bakersfield	A+	6	6	0	0	21.0	120	35	26	19	3	1	2	4	20	0	17	7	0	0	4	.000	0	0--	-	11.40	8.14
1998 Salem-Keizer	A-	23	0	0	0	43.1	194	36	25	21	3	1	3	5	27	0	37	8	1	1	1	.500	0	0--	-	4.21	4.36
1999 San Jose	A+	20	0	0	9	30.2	122	17	9	8	1	3	0	1	13	0	30	2	1	1	2	.333	0	2--	-	1.55	2.35
1999 Shreveport	AA	7	0	0	3	12.2	52	8	4	2	0	1	0	1	5	0	16	0	0	0	2	.000	0	0--	-	1.79	1.42
2000 Shreveport	AA	27	16	0	8	102.2	454	116	60	59	8	5	7	5	48	1	71	4	0	3	11	.214	0	1--	-	5.26	5.17
2001 Shreveport	AA	24	0	0	11	33.1	145	31	9	9	1	0	2	2	13	3	27	4	0	2	1	.667	0	1--	-	3.19	2.43
2001 San Jose	A+	9	0	0	4	13.1	53	12	6	5	0	0	3	2	1	0	15	2	0	0	0	-	0	3--	-	2.32	3.38
2001 Fresno	AAA	5	0	0	2	8.1	36	9	7	7	0	1	1	0	4	1	2	2	0	0	1	.000	0	0--	-	4.02	7.56
2001 Memphis	AAA	12	0	0	0	12.0	56	8	9	9	2	1	1	1	11	1	6	0	0	0	2	.000	0	0--	-	4.79	6.75
2002 Memphis	AAA	31	0	0	9	35.2	150	37	10	7	2	0	2	1	11	0	14	2	0	1	1	.500	0	2--	-	3.80	1.77
2002 St Louis	NL	11	0	0	6	11.0	52	16	7	6	1	0	0	2	6	0	2	0	0	0	1	.000	0	0-0	1	8.80	4.91

Jorge Julio

Pitches: R **Bats:** R **Pos:** RP-67   **Ht:** 6'1" **Wt:** 190 **Born:** 3/3/79 **Age:** 24

Year Team	Lg	G	GS	CG	GF	IP	BFP	H	R	ER	HR	SH	SF	HB	TBB	IBB	SO	WP	Bk	W	L	Pct	ShO	Sv-Op	Hld	ERC	ERA
1997 Expos	R	15	8	0	4	55.1	248	57	25	22	0	2	1		21	0	42	3	0	5	6	.455	0	1--	-	3.38	3.58
1997 W Palm Bch	A+	1	0	0	0	0.0	2	2	1	1	0	0	0	0	0	0	0	0	0	0	0	-	0	0--	-	-	-
1998 Vermont	A-	7	7	0	0	42.0	173	30	12	12	1	1	1	3	15	0	52	1	1	3	1	.750	0	0--	-	2.18	2.57
1998 Cape Fear	A	6	6	0	0	31.2	134	33	20	20	4	0	1	1	12	0	20	1	0	2	2	.500	0	0--	-	4.70	5.68
1999 Jupiter	A+	23	22	0	1	114.2	491	116	62	50	6	3	5	3	34	0	80	11	4	4	8	.333	0	0--	-	3.47	3.92
2000 Jupiter	A+	21	15	0	3	79.1	363	93	60	52	4	1	5	4	35	0	67	1	3	2	10	.167	0	1--	-	5.03	5.90
2001 Bowie	AA	12	0	0	12	12.1	44	5	1	1	0	0	1	0	2	1	14	0	0	0	0	-	0	7--	-	0.67	0.73
2001 Rochester	AAA	34	0	0	24	43.1	196	39	27	18	4	2	2	5	19	3	48	5	1	1	2	.333	0	12--	-	3.79	3.74
2001 Baltimore	AL	18	0	0	8	21.1	99	25	13	9	2	2	0	1	9	0	22	1	0	1	1	.500	0	0-3	1	5.17	3.80
2002 Baltimore	AL	67	0	0	61	68.0	289	55	22	15	5	1	1	2	27	3	55	8	0	5	6	.455	0	25-31	3	2.83	1.99
2 ML YEARS		85	0	0	69	89.1	388	80	35	24	7	3	1	3	36	3	77	9	0	6	7	.462	0	25-32	4	3.35	2.42

Eric Junge

Pitches: R **Bats:** R **Pos:** RP-3; SP-1   **Ht:** 6'5" **Wt:** 215 **Born:** 1/5/77 **Age:** 26

Year Team	Lg	G	GS	CG	GF	IP	BFP	H	R	ER	HR	SH	SF	HB	TBB	IBB	SO	WP	Bk	W	L	Pct	ShO	Sv-Op	Hld	ERC	ERA
1999 Yakima	A-	15	15	0	0	82.0	363	98	60	53	10	3	6	0	31	0	55	3	0	5	7	.417	0	0--	-	5.34	5.82
2000 Sn Brnardino	A+	29	24	0	2	158.0	666	159	69	59	8	3	5	9	53	0	116	8	2	8	1	.889	0	1--	-	3.82	3.36
2001 Jacksonville	AA	27	27	1	0	164.0	686	143	72	63	19	11	3	13	56	2	116	6	0	10	11	.476	1	0--	-	3.57	3.46
2002 Scrtn/WlksBr	AAA	29	29	1	0	180.2	766	170	77	71	16	8	4	5	67	1	126	10	0	12	6	.667	0	0--	-	3.67	3.54
2002 Philadelphia	NL	4	1	0	2	12.2	57	14	3	2	0	0	0	0	5	0	11	0	0	2	0	1.000	0	0-0	0	3.81	1.42

David Justice

Bats: L **Throws:** L **Pos:** LF-53; DH-36; RF-23; PH-10   **Ht:** 6'3" **Wt:** 215 **Born:** 4/14/66 **Age:** 37

Year Team	Lg	G	AB	H	2B	3B	HR	(Hm	Rd)	TB	R	RBI	RC	TBB	IBB	SO	HBP	SH	SF	SB	CS	SB%	GDP	Avg	OBP	Slg
1989 Atlanta	NL	16	51	12	3	0	1	(1	0)	18	7	3	5	3	1	9	1	1	0	2	1	.67	1	.235	.291	.353
1990 Atlanta	NL	127	439	124	23	2	28	(19	9)	235	76	78	87	64	4	92	0	0	1	11	6	.65	2	.282	.373	.535
1991 Atlanta	NL	109	396	109	25	1	21	(11	10)	199	67	87	75	65	9	81	3	0	5	8	8	.50	4	.275	.377	.503
1992 Atlanta	NL	144	484	124	19	5	21	(10	11)	216	78	72	81	79	8	85	2	0	6	2	4	.33	1	.256	.359	.446
1993 Atlanta	NL	157	585	158	15	4	40	(18	22)	301	90	120	105	78	12	90	3	0	4	3	5	.38	4	.270	.357	.515
1994 Atlanta	NL	104	352	110	16	2	19	(9	10)	187	61	59	77	69	5	45	2	0	1	2	4	.33	8	.313	.427	.531
1995 Atlanta	NL	120	411	104	17	2	24	(15	9)	197	73	78	74	73	5	68	2	0	5	4	2	.67	5	.253	.365	.479
1996 Atlanta	NL	40	140	45	9	0	6	(5	1)	72	23	25	28	21	1	22	1	0	2	1	1	.50	5	.321	.409	.514
1997 Cleveland	AL	139	495	163	31	1	33	(17	16)	295	84	101	115	80	11	79	0	0	7	3	5	.38	12	.329	.418	.596
1998 Cleveland	AL	146	540	151	39	2	21	(7	14)	257	94	88	95	76	7	98	0	0	9	9	3	.75	9	.280	.363	.476
1999 Cleveland	AL	133	429	123	18	0	21	(11	10)	204	75	88	84	94	11	90	2	0	5	1	3	.25	14	.287	.413	.476
2000 Cle-NYY	AL	146	524	150	31	1	41	(24	17)	306	89	118	110	77	3	91	1	0	3	2	1	.67	13	.286	.377	.584
2001 New York	AL	111	381	92	16	1	18	(8	10)	164	58	51	55	54	5	83	0	0	4	1	2	.33	6	.241	.333	.430
2002 Oakland	AL	118	398	106	18	3	11	(6	5)	163	54	49	57	70	1	66	1	0	2	4	1	.80	12	.266	.376	.410
2000 Cleveland	AL	68	249	66	14	1	21	(10	11)	145	46	58	50	38	2	49	0	0	1	1	1	.50	7	.265	.361	.582
2000 New York	AL	78	275	84	17	0	20	(14	6)	161	43	60	60	39	1	42	1	0	2	1	0	1.00	6	.305	.391	.585
14 ML YEARS		1610	5625	1571	280	24	305	(161	144)	2814	929	1017	1048	903	85	999	18	1	54	53	46	.54	101	.279	.378	.500

Gabe Kapler

Bats: R **Throws:** R **Pos:** LF-46; RF-41; CF-24; PH-17; PR-7; 1B-1   **Ht:** 6'2" **Wt:** 208 **Born:** 8/31/75 **Age:** 27

Year Team	Lg	G	AB	H	2B	3B	HR	(Hm	Rd)	TB	R	RBI	RC	TBB	IBB	SO	HBP	SH	SF	SB	CS	SB%	GDP	Avg	OBP	Slg
2002 Oklahoma*	AAA	5	17	8	2	0	1	(-	-)	13	6	5	6	3	0	2	0	0	0	1	0	1.00	0	.471	.550	.765
1998 Detroit	AL	7	25	5	0	1	0	(0	0)	7	3	0	2	1	0	4	0	0	0	2	0	1.00	0	.200	.231	.280
1999 Detroit	AL	130	416	102	22	4	18	(12	6)	186	60	49	59	42	0	74	2	4	4	11	5	.69	7	.245	.315	.447
2000 Texas	AL	116	444	134	32	1	14	(11	3)	210	59	66	72	42	2	57	0	2	3	8	4	.67	12	.302	.360	.473
2001 Texas	AL	134	483	129	29	1	17	(11	6)	211	72	77	77	61	2	70	3	2	7	23	6	.79	10	.267	.348	.437

Year Team	Lg	G	AB	H	2B	3B	HR	(Hm	Rd)	TB	R	RBI	RC	TBB	IBB	SO	HBP	SH	SF	SB	CS	SB%	GDP	Avg	OBP	Slg
2002 Tex-Col		112	315	88	16	4	11	(1	1)	118	37	34	43	16	1	53	1	7	3	11	4	.73	5	.279	.313	.375
2002 Texas	AL	72	196	51	12	1	0	(0	0)	65	25	17	20	8	0	30	0	7	3	5	2	.71	3	.260	.285	.332
2002 Colorado	NL	40	119	37	4	3	2	(1	1)	53	12	17	23	8	0	23	1	0	0	6	2	.75	2	.311	.359	.445
5 ML YEARS		499	1683	458	99	11	51	(35	16)	732	236	221	253	162	4	258	6	15	17	55	19	.74	34	.272	.335	.435

Eric Karros

Bats: R Throws: R Pos: 1B-142; PH-1; PR-1   Ht: 6'4" Wt: 226 Born: 11/4/67 Age: 35

Year Team	Lg	G	AB	H	2B	3B	HR	(Hm	Rd)	TB	R	RBI	RC	TBB	IBB	SO	HBP	SH	SF	SB	CS	SB%	GDP	Avg	OBP	Slg
1991 Los Angeles	NL	14	14	1	1	0	0	(0	0)	2	0	1	0	0	0	6	0	0	0	0	0	-	0	.071	.133	.143
1992 Los Angeles	NL	149	545	140	30	1	20	(6	14)	232	63	88	66	37	3	103	2	0	5	2	4	.33	15	.257	.304	.426
1993 Los Angeles	NL	158	619	153	27	2	23	(13	10)	253	74	80	68	34	1	82	2	0	3	0	1	.00	17	.247	.287	.409
1994 Los Angeles	NL	111	406	108	21	1	14	(5	9)	173	51	46	52	29	1	53	2	0	11	2	0	1.00	13	.266	.310	.426
1995 Los Angeles	NL	143	551	164	29	3	32	(19	13)	295	83	105	103	61	4	115	4	0	4	4	4	.50	14	.298	.369	.535
1996 Los Angeles	NL	154	608	158	29	1	34	(16	18)	291	84	111	86	53	2	121	1	0	8	8	0	1.00	27	.260	.316	.479
1997 Los Angeles	NL	162	628	167	28	0	31	(13	18)	288	86	104	95	61	2	116	2	0	9	15	7	.68	10	.266	.329	.459
1998 Los Angeles	NL	139	507	150	20	1	23	(9	14)	241	59	87	86	47	1	93	3	0	7	7	2	.78	7	.296	.355	.475
1999 Los Angeles	NL	153	578	176	40	0	34	(17	17)	318	74	112	107	53	0	119	2	0	6	8	5	.62	18	.304	.362	.550
2000 Los Angeles	NL	155	584	146	29	0	31	(16	15)	268	84	106	84	63	2	122	4	0	12	4	3	.57	18	.250	.321	.459
2001 Los Angeles	NL	121	438	103	22	0	15	(7	8)	170	42	63	49	41	2	101	3	0	3	3	1	.75	15	.235	.303	.388
2002 Los Angeles	NL	142	524	142	26	1	13	(9	4)	209	52	73	72	37	1	74	6	0	6	4	2	.67	11	.271	.323	.399
12 ML YEARS		1601	6002	1608	302	10	270	(130	140)	2740	752	976	868	517	19	1105	31	0	74	57	29	.66	165	.268	.325	.457

Steve Karsay

Pitches: R Bats: R Pos: RP-78   Ht: 6'3" Wt: 215 Born: 3/24/72 Age: 31

Year Team	Lg	G	GS	CG	GF	IP	BFP	H	R	ER	HR	SH	SF	HB	TBB	IBB	SO	WP	Bk	W	L	Pct	ShO	Sv-Op	Hld	ERC	ERA
1993 Oakland	AL	8	8	0	0	49.0	210	49	23	22	4	0	2	2	16	1	33	1	0	3	3	.500	0	0-0	0	3.78	4.04
1994 Oakland	AL	4	4	1	0	28.0	115	26	8	8	1	2	1	1	8	0	15	0	0	1	1	.500	0	0-0	0	3.01	2.57
1997 Oakland	AL	24	24	0	0	132.2	609	166	92	85	20	2	5	9	47	3	92	7	0	3	12	.200	0	0-0	0	5.97	5.77
1998 Cleveland	AL	11	1	0	4	24.1	111	31	16	16	3	1	2	2	6	1	13	2	0	0	2	.000	0	0-0	2	5.40	5.92
1999 Cleveland	AL	50	3	0	13	78.2	342	71	29	26	6	2	3	2	30	3	68	5	0	10	2	.833	0	1-3	9	3.45	2.97
2000 Cleveland	AL	72	0	0	46	76.2	329	79	33	32	5	2	2	3	25	4	66	0	0	5	9	.357	0	20-29	11	3.79	3.76
2001 Cle-Atl		74	0	0	29	88.0	356	73	27	23	5	6	4	1	25	10	83	3	0	3	5	.375	0	8-12	12	2.36	2.35
2002 New York	AL	78	0	0	38	88.1	379	87	33	32	7	7	3	2	30	14	65	0	0	6	4	.600	0	12-16	14	3.42	3.26
2001 Cleveland	AL	31	0	0	8	43.1	166	29	6	6	1	3	1	0	8	2	44	2	0	0	1	.000	0	1-1	8	1.33	1.25
2001 Atlanta	NL	43	0	0	21	44.2	190	44	21	17	4	3	3	1	17	8	39	1	0	3	4	.429	0	7-11	4	3.68	3.43
8 ML YEARS		321	40	1	130	565.2	2433	582	261	244	51	22	22	22	187	36	435	21	0	31	38	.449	0	41-60	48	3.95	3.88

Justin Kaye

Pitches: R Bats: R Pos: RP-3   Ht: 6'4" Wt: 195 Born: 6/9/76 Age: 27

Year Team	Lg	G	GS	CG	GF	IP	BFP	H	R	ER	HR	SH	SF	HB	TBB	IBB	SO	WP	Bk	W	L	Pct	ShO	Sv-Op	Hld	ERC	ERA
1995 Mariners	R	12	0	0	4	19.1	111	33	28	23	1	0	2	1	19	0	13	4	0	0	1	.000	0	0--	-	10.67	10.71
1996 Mariners	R	20	0	0	12	32.1	156	34	23	13	4	0	1	5	19	1	36	7	2	1	0	1.000	0	3--	-	5.71	3.62
1997 Wisconsin	A	28	26	0	2	127.0	618	129	113	103	13	6	5	16	104	0	115	21	6	8	12	.400	0	0--	-	6.38	7.30
1998 Wisconsin	A	28	0	0	23	47.1	196	25	11	9	2	6	0	2	30	4	79	6	0	6	2	.750	0	9--	-	2.12	1.71
1998 Lancaster	A+	16	0	0	7	30.1	139	37	24	23	4	2	1	0	13	2	34	9	0	1	2	.333	0	0--	-	5.55	6.82
1999 Lancaster	A+	53	0	0	46	61.0	289	68	42	39	4	2	3	5	40	1	66	6	0	3	5	.375	0	14--	-	5.81	5.75
2000 New Haven	AA	50	0	0	23	84.1	368	80	32	25	3	3	3	5	36	4	109	4	3	2	5	.286	0	8--	-	3.56	2.67
2001 Tacoma	AAA	56	0	0	15	77.0	332	51	27	25	5	6	1	6	46	2	107	3	1	3	2	.600	0	4--	-	2.96	2.92
2002 Tacoma	AAA	47	0	0	31	62.1	284	54	32	28	2	9	5	3	42	1	65	14	0	3	7	.300	0	6--	-	3.96	4.04
2002 Seattle	AL	3	0	0	2	3.0	15	6	4	4	0	0	0	0	1	0	3	0	0	0	0	-	0	0-0	0	9.61	12.00

Austin Kearns

Bats: R Throws: R Pos: RF-95; LF-13; PH-8; CF-6   Ht: 6'3" Wt: 220 Born: 5/20/80 Age: 23

Year Team	Lg	G	AB	H	2B	3B	HR	(Hm	Rd)	TB	R	RBI	RC	TBB	IBB	SO	HBP	SH	SF	SB	CS	SB%	GDP	Avg	OBP	Slg
1998 Billings	R+	30	108	34	9	0	1	(-	-)	46	17	14	21	23	0	22	1	0	2	1	1	.50	4	.315	.433	.426
1999 Rockford	A	124	426	110	36	5	13	(-	-)	195	72	48	68	50	3	120	9	0	3	21	8	.72	9	.258	.346	.458
2000 Dayton	A	136	484	148	37	2	27	(-	-)	270	110	104	111	90	5	93	7	0	9	18	5	.78	14	.306	.415	.558
2001 Chattanooga	AA	59	205	55	11	2	6	(-	-)	88	30	36	32	26	0	43	6	2	2	7	5	.58	4	.268	.364	.429
2001 Reds	R	6	17	3	2	0	0	(-	-)	5	2	4	1	2	0	7	0	0	3	0	0	-	0	.176	.227	.294
2002 Chattanooga	AA	12	41	11	2	0	5	(-	-)	28	10	13	12	9	0	9	3	0	0	1	0	1.00	0	.268	.434	.683
2002 Louisville	AAA	1	4	3	2	0	0	(-	-)	5	3	2	3	1	0	0	0	0	0	0	0	-	0	.750	.800	1.250
2002 Cincinnati	NL	107	372	117	24	3	13	(7	6)	186	66	56	69	54	3	81	6	0	3	6	3	.67	11	.315	.407	.500

Kris Keller

Pitches: R Bats: R Pos: RP-1   Ht: 6'2" Wt: 225 Born: 3/1/78 Age: 25

Year Team	Lg	G	GS	CG	GF	IP	BFP	H	R	ER	HR	SH	SF	HB	TBB	IBB	SO	WP	Bk	W	L	Pct	ShO	Sv-Op	Hld	ERC	ERA
1996 Tigers	R	8	6	0	0	34.0	143	23	12	9	0	1	2	0	21	0	23	7	1	1	1	.500	0	0--	-	2.49	2.38
1997 Jamestown	A-	16	0	0	10	27.0	143	37	33	26	3	1	3	3	20	0	18	5	2	0	2	.000	0	0--	-	8.05	8.67
1998 Jamestown	A-	27	0	0	24	33.0	141	29	12	12	3	1	2	1	16	0	41	3	0	1	3	.250	0	8--	-	3.82	3.27
1999 W Michigan	A	49	0	0	28	77.0	324	63	28	25	6	4	3	3	36	1	67	11	2	5	3	.625	0	8--	-	3.35	2.92
2000 Jacksonville	AA	62	0	0	58	68.0	299	58	24	22	0	1	5	0	44	3	60	9	0	2	3	.400	0	26--	-	3.40	2.91
2001 Toledo	AAA	52	0	0	23	68.1	302	64	42	34	10	0	4	3	38	3	60	10	0	5	2	.714	0	4--	-	4.81	4.48

Year	Team	Lg	G	GS	CG	GF	IP	BFP	H	R	ER	HR	SH	SF	HB	TBB	IBB	SO	WP	Bk	W	L	Pct	ShO	Sv-Op	Hld	ERC	ERA
			HOW MUCH HE PITCHED						WHAT HE GAVE UP												THE RESULTS						
2002	Toledo	AAA	17	0	0	4	26.0	113	20	10	6	1	1	0	0	17	1	20	6	0	2	0	1.000	0	0--	-	3.26	2.08
2002	Richmond	AAA	29	0	0	10	35.0	143	26	16	14	4	3	1	1	13	2	20	2	0	1	0	1.000	0	2--	-	2.72	3.60
2002	Detroit	AL	1	0	0	1	1.0	8	2	3	3	1	0	0	0	3	0	1	0	0	0	0	-	0	0-0	0	35.20	27.00

Jason Kendall

Bats: R **Throws:** R **Pos:** C-143; PH-4   **Ht:** 6'0" **Wt:** 195 **Born:** 6/26/74 **Age:** 29

Year	Team	Lg	G	AB	H	2B	3B	HR	(Hm	Rd)	TB	R	RBI	RC	TBB	IBB	SO	HBP	SH	SF	SB	CS	SB%	GDP	Avg	OBP	Slg
			BATTING																		BASERUNNING				AVERAGES		
1996	Pittsburgh	NL	130	414	124	23	5	3	(2	1)	166	54	42	63	35	11	30	15	3	4	5	2	.71	7	.300	.372	.401
1997	Pittsburgh	NL	144	486	143	36	4	8	(5	3)	211	71	49	86	49	2	53	31	1	5	18	6	.75	11	.294	.391	.434
1998	Pittsburgh	NL	149	535	175	36	3	12	(6	6)	253	95	75	110	51	3	51	31	2	8	26	5	.84	6	.327	.411	.473
1999	Pittsburgh	NL	78	280	93	20	3	8	(5	3)	143	61	41	63	38	3	32	12	0	4	22	3	.88	8	.332	.428	.511
2000	Pittsburgh	NL	152	579	185	33	6	14	(7	7)	272	112	58	112	79	3	79	15	1	4	22	12	.65	13	.320	.412	.470
2001	Pittsburgh	NL	157	606	161	22	2	10	(3	7)	217	84	53	68	44	4	48	20	0	2	13	14	.48	18	.266	.335	.358
2002	Pittsburgh	NL	145	545	154	25	3	3	(1	2)	194	59	44	63	49	1	29	9	0	2	15	8	.65	11	.283	.350	.356
7 ML YEARS			955	3445	1035	195	26	58	(29	29)	1456	536	362	565	345	27	322	133	7	29	121	50	.71	74	.300	.383	.423

Adam Kennedy

Bats: L **Throws:** R **Pos:** 2B-137; PH-14; PR-3; CF-1; DH-1   **Ht:** 6'1" **Wt:** 192 **Born:** 1/10/76 **Age:** 27

Year	Team	Lg	G	AB	H	2B	3B	HR	(Hm	Rd)	TB	R	RBI	RC	TBB	IBB	SO	HBP	SH	SF	SB	CS	SB%	GDP	Avg	OBP	Slg
			BATTING																		BASERUNNING				AVERAGES		
1999	St Louis	NL	33	102	26	10	1	1	(1	0)	41	12	16	12	3	0	8	2	1	0	0	1	.00	1	.255	.284	.402
2000	Anaheim	AL	156	598	159	33	11	9	(7	2)	241	82	72	72	28	5	73	3	8	4	22	8	.73	10	.266	.300	.403
2001	Anaheim	AL	137	478	129	25	3	6	(4	2)	178	48	40	57	27	3	71	11	7	9	12	7	.63	7	.270	.318	.372
2002	Anaheim	AL	144	474	148	32	6	7	(6	1)	213	65	52	70	19	1	80	7	5	4	17	4	.81	5	.312	.345	.449
4 ML YEARS			470	1652	462	100	21	23	(18	5)	673	207	180	211	77	9	232	23	21	19	51	20	.72	23	.280	.317	.407

Joe Kennedy

Pitches: L **Bats:** R **Pos:** SP-30   **Ht:** 6'4" **Wt:** 237 **Born:** 5/24/79 **Age:** 24

Year	Team	Lg	G	GS	CG	GF	IP	BFP	H	R	ER	HR	SH	SF	HB	TBB	IBB	SO	WP	Bk	W	L	Pct	ShO	Sv-Op	Hld	ERC	ERA
			HOW MUCH HE PITCHED						WHAT HE GAVE UP												THE RESULTS						
1998	Princeton	R+	13	13	0	0	67.1	282	66	37	28	5	1	2	3	26	0	44	4	2	6	4	.600	0	0--	-	4.04	3.74
1999	Hudson Val	A-	16	16	1	0	95.0	376	78	33	28	2	1	1	4	26	0	101	7	1	6	5	.545	1	0--	-	2.40	2.65
2000	Chrlstn - SC	A	22	22	3	0	136.1	546	122	59	50	6	2	6	4	29	1	142	9	2	11	6	.647	2	0--	-	2.60	3.30
2001	Orlando	AA	7	7	0	0	47.0	170	29	3	1	0	1	1	2	3	0	52	2	0	4	0	1.000	0	0--	-	1.01	0.19
2001	Durham	AA	4	4	0	0	26.0	109	24	9	7	2	1	0	2	9	0	23	7	0	2	0	1.000	0	0--	-	3.17	2.42
2001	Tampa Bay	AL	20	20	0	0	117.2	498	122	63	58	16	2	5	3	34	0	78	5	1	7	8	.467	0	0-0	0	4.23	4.44
2002	Tampa Bay	AL	30	30	5	0	196.2	840	204	114	99	23	2	9	16	55	0	109	4	0	8	11	.421	1	0-0	0	4.29	4.53
2 ML YEARS			50	50	5	0	314.1	1338	326	177	157	39	4	14	19	89	0	187	9	1	15	19	.441	1	0-0	0	4.27	4.50

Jeff Kent

Bats: R **Throws:** R **Pos:** 2B-149; 1B-9; PH-1   **Ht:** 6'1" **Wt:** 220 **Born:** 3/7/68 **Age:** 35

Year	Team	Lg	G	AB	H	2B	3B	HR	(Hm	Rd)	TB	R	RBI	RC	TBB	IBB	SO	HBP	SH	SF	SB	CS	SB%	GDP	Avg	OBP	Slg
			BATTING																		BASERUNNING				AVERAGES		
1992	Tor-NYM		102	305	73	21	2	11	(4	7)	131	52	50	40	27	0	76	7	0	4	2	3	.40	5	.239	.312	.430
1993	New York	NL	140	496	134	24	0	21	(9	12)	221	65	80	68	30	2	88	8	6	4	4	4	.50	11	.270	.320	.446
1994	New York	NL	107	415	121	24	5	14	(10	4)	197	53	68	64	23	3	84	10	1	3	1	4	.20	7	.292	.341	.475
1995	New York	NL	125	472	131	22	3	20	(11	9)	219	65	65	69	29	3	89	8	1	4	3	3	.50	9	.278	.327	.464
1996	NYM-Cle		128	437	124	27	1	12	(4	8)	189	61	55	61	31	1	78	2	1	6	6	4	.60	8	.284	.330	.432
1997	San Francisco	NL	155	580	145	38	2	29	(13	16)	274	90	121	86	48	6	133	13	0	10	11	3	.79	14	.250	.316	.472
1998	San Francisco	NL	137	526	156	37	3	31	(17	14)	292	94	128	100	48	4	110	9	1	10	9	4	.69	16	.297	.359	.555
1999	San Francisco	NL	138	511	148	40	2	23	(11	12)	261	86	101	93	61	3	112	5	0	8	13	6	.68	12	.290	.366	.511
2000	San Francisco	NL	159	587	196	41	7	33	(14	19)	350	114	125	138	90	6	107	9	0	9	12	9	.57	17	.334	.424	.596
2001	San Francisco	NL	159	607	181	49	6	22	(8	14)	308	84	106	112	65	4	96	11	0	13	7	6	.54	15	.298	.369	.507
2002	San Francisco	NL	152	623	195	42	2	37	(11	26)	352	102	108	106	52	3	101	4	0	3	5	1	.83	20	.313	.368	.565
1992	Toronto	AL	65	192	46	13	1	8	(2	6)	85	36	35	28	20	0	47	6	0	4	2	1	.67	3	.240	.324	.443
1992	New York	NL	37	113	27	8	1	3	(2	1)	46	16	15	12	7	0	29	1	0	0	0	2	.00	2	.239	.289	.407
1996	New York	NL	89	335	97	20	1	9	(2	7)	146	45	39	46	21	1	56	1	1	3	4	3	.57	7	.290	.331	.436
1996	Cleveland	AL	39	102	27	7	0	3	(2	1)	43	16	16	15	10	0	22	1	0	3	2	1	.67	1	.265	.328	.422
11 ML YEARS			1502	5559	1604	365	33	253	(112	141)	2794	866	1007	937	504	35	1074	86	10	74	73	47	.61	130	.289	.353	.503

Steve Kent

Pitches: L **Bats:** B **Pos:** RP-34   **Ht:** 5'11" **Wt:** 170 **Born:** 10/3/78 **Age:** 24

Year	Team	Lg	G	GS	CG	GF	IP	BFP	H	R	ER	HR	SH	SF	HB	TBB	IBB	SO	WP	Bk	W	L	Pct	ShO	Sv-Op	Hld	ERC	ERA
			HOW MUCH HE PITCHED						WHAT HE GAVE UP												THE RESULTS						
1999	Everett	A-	21	0	0	8	37.0	168	31	24	22	2	1	1	2	26	1	43	6	0	3	2	.600	0	4--	-	4.11	5.35
2000	Everett	A-	24	3	0	6	52.2	219	38	16	15	5	2	0	2	23	1	61	5	0	4	1	.800	0	0--	-	2.79	2.56
2001	Sn Brnardino	A+	51	0	0	12	65.1	285	50	21	16	2	3	2	2	34	0	73	4	1	0	3	.000	0	1--	-	2.80	2.20
2002	Tampa Bay	AL	34	0	0	10	57.1	272	67	41	36	6	1	2	3	38	0	41	2	3	0	2	.000	0	1-2	1	6.45	5.65

Jason Kershner

Pitches: L **Bats:** L **Pos:** RP-25   **Ht:** 6'2" **Wt:** 165 **Born:** 12/19/76 **Age:** 26

		HOW MUCH HE PITCHED						WHAT HE GAVE UP												THE RESULTS							
Year Team	Lg	G	GS	CG	GF	IP	BFP	H	R	ER	HR	SH	SF	HB	TBB	IBB	SO	WP	Bk	W	L	Pct	ShO	Sv-Op	Hld	ERC	ERA
1995 Martinsville	R+	13	13	0	0	63.0	278	67	42	36	10	0	2	5	29	0	64	4	2	0	0	-	0	0- -	-	5.58	5.14
1996 Piedmont	A	28	28	2	0	168.0	703	154	81	70	12	5	4	3	59	0	156	12	1	11	9	.550	1	0- -	-	3.33	3.75
1997 Clearwater	A+	22	16	0	3	99.1	417	113	49	43	9	2	4	4	21	0	51	2	0	5	10	.333	0	1- -	-	4.30	3.90
1998 Clearwater	A+	41	8	0	11	94.1	405	108	57	42	8	1	3	4	25	0	65	8	0	3	3	.500	0	3- -	-	4.60	4.01
1999 Reading	AA	57	2	0	30	92.2	412	99	67	59	14	3	6	5	40	3	86	5	0	4	4	.500	0	8- -	-	5.15	5.73
2000 Reading	AA	27	19	0	3	119.0	501	125	49	48	15	6	1	5	25	0	80	3	0	9	2	.818	0	1- -	-	3.96	3.63
2000 Clearwater	A+	2	2	0	0	14.0	52	7	1	1	1	0	0	0	5	0	15	0	0	1	0	1.000	0	0- -	-	1.45	0.64
2001 Reading	AA	26	19	0	2	123.2	525	147	75	66	18	5	5	3	26	1	70	4	0	5	9	.357	0	0- -	-	4.90	4.80
2001 Scrtn/WlksBr	AAA	6	1	0	1	15.0	63	12	8	6	3	0	2	0	3	0	7	0	0	1	1	.500	0	0- -	-	2.64	3.60
2002 Portland	AAA	31	12	0	3	86.0	339	65	30	29	8	3	0	1	26	0	83	2	0	7	2	.778	0	0- -	-	2.49	3.03
2002 SD-Tor		25	0	0	4	24.0	107	20	16	13	3	0	0	2	14	1	18	3	0	0	1	.000	0	1-2	1	4.24	4.88
2002 San Diego	NL	15	0	0	2	18.2	81	15	14	12	2	0	0	2	10	0	11	0	0	0	1	.000	0	0-0	0	4.00	5.79
2002 Toronto	AL	10	0	0	2	5.1	26	5	2	1	1	0	0	0	4	1	7	3	0	0	0	-	0	1-2	1	5.11	1.69

Bobby Kielty

Bats: B **Throws:** R **Pos:** RF-50; CF-34; PH-25; LF-9; DH-8; 1B-5; PR-4   **Ht:** 6'1" **Wt:** 215 **Born:** 8/5/76 **Age:** 26

		BATTING																			BASERUNNING				AVERAGES		
Year Team	Lg	G	AB	H	2B	3B	HR	(Hm	Rd)	TB	R	RBI	RC	TBB	IBB	SO	HBP	SH	SF		SB	CS	SB%	GDP	Avg	OBP	Slg
1999 Quad City	A	69	245	72	13	1	13	(-	-)	126	52	43	51	43	1	56	3	2	3		12	3	.80	7	.294	.401	.514
2000 New Britain	AA	129	451	118	30	3	14	(-	-)	196	79	65	79	98	4	109	5	0	4		6	4	.60	16	.262	.396	.435
2000 Salt Lake	AAA	9	33	8	0	0	0	(-	-)	12	8	2	5	7	0	10	0	0	0		0	0	-	0	.242	.375	.364
2001 Edmonton	AAA	94	341	98	25	2	12	(-	-)	163	58	50	63	53	1	76	6	2	2		5	0	1.00	11	.287	.391	.478
2002 Edmonton	AAA	2	7	3	1	0	0	(-	-)	4	0	0	2	1	0	1	0	1	0		0	0	-	1	.429	.500	.571
2001 Minnesota	AL	37	104	26	8	0	2	(1	1)	40	8	14	13	8	2	25	1	0	5		3	0	1.00	2	.250	.297	.385
2002 Minnesota	AL	112	289	84	14	3	12	(8	4)	140	49	46	58	52	4	66	5	0	2		4	1	.80	4	.291	.405	.484
2 ML YEARS		149	393	110	22	3	14	(9	5)	180	57	60	71	60	6	91	6	0	7		7	1	.88	6	.280	.378	.458

Darryl Kile

Pitches: R **Bats:** R **Pos:** SP-14   **Ht:** 6'5" **Wt:** 212 **Born:** 12/2/68

		HOW MUCH HE PITCHED						WHAT HE GAVE UP												THE RESULTS							
Year Team	Lg	G	GS	CG	GF	IP	BFP	H	R	ER	HR	SH	SF	HB	TBB	IBB	SO	WP	Bk	W	L	Pct	ShO	Sv-Op	Hld	ERC	ERA
1991 Houston	NL	37	22	0	5	153.2	689	144	81	63	16	9	5	6	84	4	100	5	4	7	11	.389	0	0-1	0	4.37	3.69
1992 Houston	NL	22	22	2	0	125.1	554	124	61	55	8	5	6	4	63	4	90	3	4	5	10	.333	0	0-0	0	4.23	3.95
1993 Houston	NL	32	26	4	0	171.2	733	152	73	67	12	5	7	15	69	1	141	9	3	15	8	.652	2	0-0	0	3.59	3.51
1994 Houston	NL	24	24	0	0	147.2	664	153	84	75	13	14	2	9	82	6	105	10	0	9	6	.600	0	0-0	0	5.04	4.57
1995 Houston	NL	25	21	0	1	127.0	570	114	81	70	5	7	3	12	73	2	113	11	1	4	12	.250	0	0-0	0	4.04	4.96
1996 Houston	NL	35	33	4	1	219.0	975	233	113	102	16	10	9	16	97	8	219	13	3	12	11	.522	0	0-0	0	4.66	4.19
1997 Houston	NL	34	34	6	0	255.2	1056	208	87	73	19	17	10	10	94	2	205	7	1	19	7	.731	4	0-0	0	2.93	2.57
1998 Colorado	NL	36	35	4	0	230.1	1020	257	141	133	28	15	8	7	96	4	158	12	0	13	17	.433	1	0-0	0	5.11	5.20
1999 Colorado	NL	32	32	1	0	190.2	888	225	150	140	33	9	9	6	109	5	116	13	1	8	13	.381	0	0-0	0	6.55	6.61
2000 St Louis	NL	34	34	5	0	232.1	960	215	109	101	33	11	8	13	58	1	192	8	1	20	9	.690	1	0-0	0	3.59	3.91
2001 St Louis	NL	34	34	2	0	227.1	956	228	83	78	22	13	5	11	65	3	179	6	1	16	11	.593	1	0-0	0	3.84	3.09
2002 St Louis	NL	14	14	0	0	84.2	364	82	36	35	9	6	3	8	28	1	50	5	0	5	4	.556	0	0-0	0	4.03	3.72
12 ML YEARS		359	331	28	8	2165.1	9429	2135	1099	992	214	121	75	117	918	41	1668	97	19	133	119	.528	9	0-1	0	4.28	4.12

Byung-Hyun Kim

Pitches: R **Bats:** R **Pos:** RP-72   **Ht:** 5'11" **Wt:** 177 **Born:** 1/19/79 **Age:** 24

		HOW MUCH HE PITCHED						WHAT HE GAVE UP												THE RESULTS							
Year Team	Lg	G	GS	CG	GF	IP	BFP	H	R	ER	HR	SH	SF	HB	TBB	IBB	SO	WP	Bk	W	L	Pct	ShO	Sv-Op	Hld	ERC	ERA
1999 Arizona	NL	25	0	0	10	27.1	121	20	15	14	2	1	0	5	20	2	31	4	1	1	2	.333	0	1-4	3	4.35	4.61
2000 Arizona	NL	61	1	0	30	70.2	320	52	39	35	9	2	3	9	46	5	111	3	2	6	6	.500	0	14-20	5	4.04	4.46
2001 Arizona	NL	78	0	0	44	98.0	392	58	32	32	10	5	0	8	44	3	113	5	1	5	6	.455	0	19-23	11	2.45	2.94
2002 Arizona	NL	72	0	0	66	84.0	343	64	20	19	5	1	2	6	26	2	92	2	0	8	3	.727	0	36-42	0	2.45	2.04
4 ML YEARS		236	1	0	150	280.0	1176	194	106	100	26	9	5	28	136	12	347	14	4	20	17	.541	0	70-89	19	3.01	3.21

Sun-Woo Kim

Pitches: R **Bats:** R **Pos:** RP-14; SP-5   **Ht:** 6'2" **Wt:** 188 **Born:** 9/4/77 **Age:** 25

		HOW MUCH HE PITCHED						WHAT HE GAVE UP												THE RESULTS							
Year Team	Lg	G	GS	CG	GF	IP	BFP	H	R	ER	HR	SH	SF	HB	TBB	IBB	SO	WP	Bk	W	L	Pct	ShO	Sv-Op	Hld	ERC	ERA
1998 Sarasota	A+	26	24	5	0	153.0	655	159	88	82	18	2	8	2	40	1	132	11	0	12	8	.600	0	0- -	-	3.85	4.82
1999 Trenton	AA	26	26	1	0	149.0	641	160	86	81	16	2	5	9	44	2	130	4	0	9	8	.529	1	0- -	-	4.38	4.89
2000 Pawtucket	AAA	25	25	0	0	134.1	603	170	98	90	17	2	4	5	42	1	116	5	0	11	7	.611	0	0- -	-	5.64	6.03
2001 Pawtucket	AAA	19	14	0	3	89.0	384	93	55	53	10	7	2	6	27	1	79	4	1	6	7	.462	0	0- -	-	4.29	5.36
2002 Pawtucket	AAA	8	8	1	0	45.1	186	34	18	16	4	0	2	3	16	0	37	1	0	4	2	.667	0	0- -	-	2.74	3.18
2002 Ottawa	AAA	7	7	1	0	43.2	167	29	11	6	2	1	1	0	16	0	28	0	0	3	0	1.000	1	0- -	-	2.01	1.24
2001 Boston	AL	20	2	0	7	41.2	201	54	27	27	1	3	0	4	21	5	27	5	0	0	2	.000	0	0-0	1	5.72	5.83
2002 Bos-Mon		19	5	0	7	49.1	208	52	26	26	5	0	2	2	14	2	29	2	0	3	0	1.000	0	0-0	2	4.10	4.74
2002 Boston	AL	15	2	0	7	29.0	128	34	24	24	5	0	2	1	7	1	18	2	0	2	0	1.000	0	0-0	2	5.01	7.45
2002 Montreal	NL	4	3	0	0	20.1	80	18	2	2	0	0	0	1	7	1	11	0	0	1	0	1.000	0	0-0	0	2.82	0.89
2 ML YEARS		39	7	0	14	91.0	409	106	53	53	6	3	2	6	35	7	56	7	0	3	2	.600	0	0-0	3	4.85	5.24

Ray King

Pitches: L Bats: L Pos: RP-76   **Ht: 6'1" Wt: 242 Born: 1/15/74 Age: 29**

Year Team	Lg	G	GS	CG	GF	IP	BFP	H	R	ER	HR	SH	SF	HB	TBB	IBB	SO	WP	Bk	W	L	Pct	ShO	Sv-Op	Hld	ERC	ERA
2002 Indianapolis*	AAA	1	1	0	0	1.0	4	1	0	0	0	0	0	0	1	0	1	0	0	0	0	-	0	0- -	-	6.99	0.00
1999 Chicago	NL	10	0	0	0	10.2	50	11	8	7	2	1	0	1	10	0	5	1	0	0	0	-	0	0-0	2	8.10	5.91
2000 Milwaukee	NL	36	0	0	8	28.2	111	18	7	4	1	0	1	0	10	1	19	1	0	3	2	.600	0	0-1	5	1.64	1.26
2001 Milwaukee	NL	82	0	0	19	55.0	234	49	22	22	5	3	2	1	25	7	49	2	0	4	0	.000	0	1-4	18	3.51	3.60
2002 Milwaukee	NL	76	0	0	15	65.0	273	61	24	22	5	5	2	3	24	6	50	0	1	3	2	.600	0	0-1	15	3.55	3.05
4 ML YEARS		204	0	0	42	159.1	668	139	61	55	13	9	5	5	69	14	123	4	1	6	8	.429	0	1-6	40	3.41	3.11

Gene Kingsale

Bats: B Throws: R Pos: RF-49; LF-26; CF-18; PH-17; PR-3   **Ht: 6'3" Wt: 190 Born: 8/20/76 Age: 26**

Year Team	Lg	G	AB	H	2B	3B	HR	(Hm	Rd)	TB	R	RBI	RC	TBB	IBB	SO	HBP	SH	SF	SB	CS	SB%	GDP	Avg	OBP	Slg
2002 Tacoma*	AAA	49	188	49	15	3	6	(-	-)	88	25	26	27	15	0	30	1	2	1	10	3	.77	6	.261	.317	.468
1998 Baltimore	AL	11	2	0	0	0	0	(0	0)	0	1	0	0	0	0	1	0	0	0	0	0	-	0	.000	.000	.000
1999 Baltimore	AL	28	85	21	2	0	0	(0	0)	23	9	7	6	5	0	13	2	2	1	1	3	.25	3	.247	.301	.271
2000 Baltimore	AL	26	88	21	2	1	0	(0	0)	25	13	9	4	2	0	14	0	0	1	1	2	.33	4	.239	.253	.284
2001 Bal-Sea	AL	13	19	5	0	0	0	(0	0)	5	4	1	3	2	0	4	1	0	0	3	1	.75	1	.263	.364	.263
2002 Sea-SD		91	219	62	10	3	2	(0	2)	84	27	28	36	20	0	47	3	3	1	9	2	.82	6	.283	.350	.384
2001 Baltimore	AL	3	4	0	0	0	0	(0	0)	0	0	0	0	0	0	2	0	0	0	1	1	.50	0	.000	.000	.000
2001 Seattle	AL	10	15	5	0	0	0	(0	0)	5	4	1	3	2	0	2	1	0	0	2	0	1.00	1	.333	.444	.333
2002 Seattle	AL	2	3	2	0	0	0	(0	0)	2	0	0	1	0	0	0	0	0	0	0	0	-	1	.667	.667	.667
2002 San Diego	NL	89	216	60	10	3	2	(0	2)	82	27	28	35	20	0	47	3	3	1	9	2	.82	5	.278	.346	.380
5 ML YEARS		169	413	109	14	4	2	(0	2)	137	54	45	49	29	0	79	6	5	3	14	8	.64	14	.264	.319	.332

Mike Kinkade

Bats: R Throws: R Pos: PH-23; 1B-11; LF-8; PR-1   **Ht: 6'1" Wt: 210 Born: 5/6/73 Age: 30**

Year Team	Lg	G	AB	H	2B	3B	HR	(Hm	Rd)	TB	R	RBI	RC	TBB	IBB	SO	HBP	SH	SF	SB	CS	SB%	GDP	Avg	OBP	Slg
2002 Las Vegas*	AAA	74	287	98	22	6	11	(-	-)	165	63	50	67	29	1	49	19	0	2	6	2	.75	9	.341	.433	.575
1998 New York	NL	3	2	0	0	0	0	(0	0)	0	2	0	0	0	0	0	0	0	0	0	0	-	0	.000	.000	.000
1999 New York	NL	28	46	9	2	1	2	(1	1)	19	3	6	5	3	0	9	2	0	0	1	0	1.00	1	.196	.275	.413
2000 NYM-Bal		5	9	3	1	0	0	(0	0)	4	0	1	2	0	0	1	1	0	0	0	0	-	0	.333	.400	.444
2001 Baltimore	AL	61	160	44	5	0	4	(2	2)	61	19	16	19	14	0	31	3	0	0	2	1	.67	8	.275	.345	.381
2002 Los Angeles	NL	37	50	19	5	0	2	(1	1)	30	7	11	12	4	0	10	6	0	0	1	0	1.00	2	.380	.483	.600
2000 New York	NL	2	2	0	0	0	0	(0	0)	0	0	0	0	0	0	1	0	0	0	0	0	-	0	.000	.000	.000
2000 Baltimore	AL	3	7	3	1	0	0	(0	0)	4	0	1	2	0	0	0	1	0	0	0	0	-	0	.429	.500	.571
5 ML YEARS		134	267	75	13	1	8	(4	4)	114	31	34	38	21	0	51	12	0	0	4	1	.80	11	.281	.360	.427

Matt Kinney

Pitches: R Bats: R Pos: SP-12; RP-2   **Ht: 6'5" Wt: 220 Born: 12/16/76 Age: 26**

Year Team	Lg	G	GS	CG	GF	IP	BFP	H	R	ER	HR	SH	SF	HB	TBB	IBB	SO	WP	Bk	W	L	Pct	ShO	Sv-Op	Hld	ERC	ERA
1995 Red Sox	R	8	2	0	4	27.2	119	29	13	9	0	1	2	2	10	0	11	5	0	1	3	.250	0	2- -	-	3.82	2.93
1996 Lowell	A-	15	15	0	0	87.1	387	68	51	26	0	3	3	9	44	2	72	13	1	3	9	.250	0	0- -	-	2.81	2.68
1997 Michigan	A	22	22	2	0	117.1	514	93	59	46	4	5	2	0	78	2	123	6	0	7	8	.615	1	0- -	-	3.43	3.53
1998 Sarasota	A+	22	20	2	1	121.1	536	109	70	54	5	5	2	2	75	3	96	19	2	9	6	.600	1	1- -	-	3.95	4.01
1998 Fort Myers	A+	7	7	0	0	37.1	162	31	18	13	0	2	1	0	18	0	39	6	0	3	2	.600	0	0- -	-	2.70	3.13
1999 New Britain	AA	14	13	0	0	60.2	284	69	54	48	8	2	3	4	36	0	50	6	1	4	7	.364	0	0- -	-	6.22	7.12
1999 Twins	R	3	3	0	0	5.2	24	6	4	3	0	0	0	0	3	0	8	0	0	1	0	1.000	0	0- -	-	4.43	4.76
2000 New Britain	AA	15	15	0	0	86.1	358	74	31	26	7	2	0	1	35	0	93	4	0	6	1	.857	0	0- -	-	3.28	2.71
2000 Salt Lake	AAA	9	9	0	0	55.0	228	42	26	26	5	1	1	1	26	0	59	2	1	5	2	.714	0	0- -	-	3.12	4.25
2001 Edmonton	AAA	29	29	2	0	161.2	727	178	101	91	25	2	8	7	74	0	146	11	0	6	11	.353	0	0- -	-	5.49	5.07
2002 Edmonton	AAA	5	5	0	0	27.1	125	42	27	27	9	1	0	0	4	0	21	0	0	2	1	.667	0	0- -	-	8.06	8.89
2002 Fort Myers	A+	1	1	0	0	5.0	22	4	2	0	0	0	0	1	3	0	5	0	0	0	0	-	0	0- -	-	3.83	0.00
2002 New Britain	AA	1	1	0	0	4.0	18	4	4	3	1	0	1	0	1	0	3	0	0	0	0	-	0	0- -	-	4.11	6.75
2002 Twins	R	2	2	0	0	6.0	22	2	2	2	1	0	0	0	4	0	7	0	0	0	0	-	0	0- -	-		3.00
2000 Minnesota	AL	8	8	0	0	42.1	186	41	26	24	7	0	4	0	25	1	24	4	0	2	2	.500	0	0-0	0	5.20	5.10
2002 Minnesota	AL	14	12	0	1	66.0	305	78	39	34	13	3	4	1	33	0	45	5	0	2	7	.222	0	0-0	0	6.35	4.64
2 ML YEARS		22	20	0	1	108.1	491	119	65	58	20	3	8	1	58	1	69	9	0	4	9	.308	0	0-0	0	5.89	4.82

Danny Klassen

Bats: R Throws: R Pos: 3B-2; PH-2; SS-1; PR-1   **Ht: 6'0" Wt: 190 Born: 9/22/75 Age: 27**

Year Team	Lg	G	AB	H	2B	3B	HR	(Hm	Rd)	TB	R	RBI	RC	TBB	IBB	SO	HBP	SH	SF	SB	CS	SB%	GDP	Avg	OBP	Slg
2002 El Paso*	AA	18	65	15	4	0	2	(-	-)	25	11	7	7	7	0	24	0	2	0	0	0	-	2	.231	.306	.385
2002 Tucson*	AAA	103	361	83	20	5	2	(-	-)	119	41	42	33	22	0	106	4	3	7	6	1	.86	7	.230	.277	.330
1998 Arizona	NL	29	108	21	2	1	3	(3	0)	34	12	8	7	9	0	33	1	0	1	1	1	.50	5	.194	.263	.315
1999 Arizona	NL	1	1	1	0	0	0	(0	0)	1	0	0	1	0	0	0	0	0	0	0	0	-	0	1.000	1.000	1.000
2000 Arizona	NL	29	76	18	3	0	2	(2	0)	27	13	8	9	8	0	24	1	2	0	1	1	.50	0	.237	.318	.355
2002 Arizona	NL	4	3	1	0	0	0	(0	0)	1	0	0	0	0	0	1	0	0	0	0	0	-	0	.333	.333	.333
4 ML YEARS		63	188	41	5	1	5	(5	0)	63	25	16	17	17	0	58	2	2	1	2	2	.50	5	.218	.290	.335

Ryan Klesko

Bats: L Throws: L Pos: 1B-112; RF-31; PH-3; DH-1   Ht: 6'3" Wt: 220 Born: 6/12/71 Age: 32

							BATTING													BASERUNNING				AVERAGES		
Year Team	Lg	G	AB	H	2B	3B	HR	(Hm	Rd)	TB	R	RBI	RC	TBB	IBB	SO	HBP	SH	SF	SB	CS	SB%	GDP	Avg	OBP	Slg
1992 Atlanta	NL	13	14	0	0	0	0	(0	0)	0	1	0	0	0	0	5	1	0	0	0	0	-	0	.000	.067	.000
1993 Atlanta	NL	22	17	6	1	0	2	(2	0)	13	3	5	5	3	1	4	0	0	0	0	0	-	0	.353	.450	.765
1994 Atlanta	NL	92	245	68	13	3	17	(7	10)	138	42	47	45	26	3	48	1	0	4	1	0	1.00	6	.278	.344	.563
1995 Atlanta	NL	107	329	102	25	2	23	(15	8)	200	48	70	73	47	10	72	2	0	3	5	4	.56	8	.310	.396	.608
1996 Atlanta	NL	153	528	149	21	4	34	(20	14)	280	90	93	99	68	10	129	2	0	4	6	3	.67	10	.282	.364	.530
1997 Atlanta	NL	143	467	122	23	6	24	(10	14)	229	67	84	73	48	5	130	4	1	2	4	4	.50	12	.261	.334	.490
1998 Atlanta	NL	129	427	117	29	1	18	(8	10)	202	69	70	72	56	5	66	3	0	4	5	3	.63	9	.274	.359	.473
1999 Atlanta	NL	133	404	120	28	2	21	(12	9)	215	55	80	80	53	8	69	2	0	7	5	2	.71	6	.297	.376	.532
2000 San Diego	NL	145	494	140	33	2	26	(9	17)	255	88	92	101	91	9	81	1	0	4	23	7	.77	10	.283	.393	.516
2001 San Diego	NL	146	538	154	34	6	30	(15	15)	290	105	113	111	88	7	89	3	0	9	23	4	.85	16	.286	.384	.539
2002 San Diego	NL	146	540	162	39	1	29	(11	18)	290	90	95	114	76	11	86	4	1	4	6	2	.75	7	.300	.388	.537
11 ML YEARS		1229	4003	1140	246	27	224	(109	115)	2112	657	750	773	556	69	779	23	2	41	78	29	.73	86	.285	.372	.528

Steve Kline

Pitches: L Bats: B Pos: RP-66   Ht: 6'1" Wt: 215 Born: 8/22/72 Age: 30

		HOW MUCH HE PITCHED						WHAT HE GAVE UP											THE RESULTS						
Year Team	Lg	G	GS	CG	GF	IP	BFP	H	R	ER	HR	SH	SF	HB	TBB	IBB	SO	WP	Bk	W	L	Pct	ShO	Sv-Op	Hld	ERC	ERA
2002 Peoria*	A	2	1	0	0	2.1	10	1	0	0	0	0	0	0	1	0	5	0	0	0	0	-	0	0- -	-	0.97	0.00
2002 New Haven*	AA	1	1	0	0	2.0	8	0	0	0	0	0	0	0	1	0	2	1	0	0	0	-	0	0- -	-	0.24	0.00
1997 Cle-Mon		46	1	0	7	52.2	248	73	37	35	10	4	2	2	23	4	37	4	1	4	4	.500	0	0-3	5	7.39	5.98
1998 Montreal	NL	78	0	0	18	71.2	319	62	25	22	4	1	2	3	41	7	76	5	0	3	6	.333	0	1-2	18	3.60	2.76
1999 Montreal	NL	82	0	0	18	69.2	297	56	32	29	8	3	1	3	33	6	69	2	0	7	4	.636	0	0-2	16	3.40	3.75
2000 Montreal	NL	83	0	0	42	82.1	349	88	36	32	8	2	1	3	27	2	64	4	0	1	5	.167	0	14-18	12	4.37	3.50
2001 St Louis	NL	89	0	0	26	75.0	303	53	16	15	3	4	5	4	29	7	54	1	0	3	3	.500	0	9-10	17	2.20	1.80
2002 St Louis	NL	66	0	0	17	58.1	241	54	23	22	3	2	2	1	21	2	41	1	0	2	1	.667	0	6-8	21	3.28	3.39
1997 Cleveland	AL	20	1	0	0	26.1	130	42	19	17	6	1	0	1	13	1	17	3	1	3	1	.750	0	0-2	4	9.58	5.81
1997 Montreal	AL	26	0	0	7	26.1	118	31	18	18	4	3	2	1	10	3	20	1	0	1	3	.250	0	0-1	5	5.39	6.15
6 ML YEARS		444	1	0	128	409.2	1757	386	169	155	36	16	13	16	174	28	341	17	1	20	23	.465	0	30-43	89	3.83	3.41

Brandon Knight

Pitches: R Bats: L Pos: RP-7   Ht: 6'0" Wt: 170 Born: 10/1/75 Age: 27

		HOW MUCH HE PITCHED						WHAT HE GAVE UP											THE RESULTS						
Year Team	Lg	G	GS	CG	GF	IP	BFP	H	R	ER	HR	SH	SF	HB	TBB	IBB	SO	WP	Bk	W	L	Pct	ShO	Sv-Op	Hld	ERC	ERA
1995 Rangers	R	3	2	0	0	12.0	54	12	7	7	0	0	1	0	6	0	11	2	0	2	1	.667	0	0- -	-	3.63	5.25
1995 Chrlstn - SC	A	9	9	0	0	54.2	218	37	22	19	5	0	4	0	21	0	52	4	1	4	2	.667	0	0- -	-	2.30	3.13
1996 Charlotte	A+	19	17	2	0	102.0	463	118	65	58	9	4	7	2	45	0	74	6	0	4	10	.286	0	0- -	-	5.10	5.12
1996 Hudson Val	A-	9	9	0	0	53.0	236	59	29	26	1	2	1	1	21	0	52	2	1	2	2	.500	0	0- -	-	4.14	4.42
1997 Charlotte	A+	14	13	3	1	92.2	380	82	33	23	9	3	2	1	22	0	91	0	2	7	4	.636	1	0- -	-	2.83	2.23
1997 Tulsa	AA	14	14	2	0	90.0	383	83	52	45	12	0	4	2	35	0	84	9	4	6	4	.600	1	0- -	-	3.91	4.50
1998 Tulsa	AA	14	14	0	0	86.1	379	94	54	49	11	1	3	0	37	0	87	12	0	6	6	.500	0	0- -	-	4.94	5.11
1998 Oklahoma	AAA	16	12	0	0	64.2	315	100	75	70	16	0	2	1	29	0	52	9	1	0	7	.000	0	0- -	-	9.07	9.74
1999 Oklahoma	AAA	27	26	5	0	163.0	706	173	96	89	23	1	3	10	47	2	97	9	3	8	9	.529	0	0- -	-	4.48	4.91
2000 Columbus	AAA	28	28	8	0	184.2	783	172	105	91	21	5	7	3	61	3	138	10	3	10	12	.455	1	0- -	-	3.52	4.44
2001 Columbus	AAA	25	25	3	0	162.1	681	174	77	66	16	4	1	2	45	0	173	9	1	12	7	.632	0	0- -	-	4.11	3.66
2002 Columbus	AAA	36	7	1	25	80.2	342	67	40	35	6	0	0	0	37	1	81	6	0	2	7	.222	0	12- -	-	3.16	3.90
2001 New York	AL	4	0	0	2	10.2	52	18	12	12	5	0	0	0	3	0	7	0	0	0	0	-	0	0-0	0	11.03	10.13
2002 New York	AL	7	0	0	5	8.2	41	11	12	11	2	0	0	0	5	0	7	1	0	0	0	-	0	0-0	0	7.53	11.42
2 ML YEARS		11	0	0	7	19.1	93	29	24	23	7	0	0	0	8	0	14	1	0	0	0	-	0	0-0	0	9.44	10.71

Chuck Knoblauch

Bats: R Throws: R Pos: LF-74; PR-3; DH-2; PH-2   Ht: 5'9" Wt: 175 Born: 7/7/68 Age: 34

							BATTING													BASERUNNING				AVERAGES		
Year Team	Lg	G	AB	H	2B	3B	HR	(Hm	Rd)	TB	R	RBI	RC	TBB	IBB	SO	HBP	SH	SF	SB	CS	SB%	GDP	Avg	OBP	Slg
2002 Wichita*	AA	5	16	5	2	0	0	(-	-)	7	3	0	4	6	1	4	0	0	0	1	0	1.00	0	.313	.500	.438
1991 Minnesota	AL	151	565	159	24	6	1	(1	0)	198	78	50	76	59	0	40	4	1	5	25	5	.83	8	.281	.351	.350
1992 Minnesota	AL	155	600	178	19	6	2	(0	2)	215	104	56	93	88	1	60	5	2	12	34	13	.72	8	.297	.384	.358
1993 Minnesota	AL	153	602	167	27	4	2	(2	0)	208	82	41	79	65	1	44	9	4	5	29	11	.73	11	.277	.354	.346
1994 Minnesota	AL	109	445	139	45	3	5	(1	4)	205	85	51	80	41	2	56	10	0	3	35	6	.85	13	.312	.381	.461
1995 Minnesota	AL	136	538	179	34	8	11	(4	7)	262	107	63	110	78	3	95	10	0	3	46	18	.72	15	.333	.424	.487
1996 Minnesota	A¦.	153	578	197	35	14	13	(7	6)	299	140	72	138	98	6	74	19	0	6	45	14	.76	9	.341	.448	.517
1997 Minnesota	AL	156	611	178	26	10	9	(2	7)	251	117	58	110	84	6	84	17	0	6	62	10	.86	11	.291	.390	.411
1998 New York	AL	150	603	160	25	4	17	(5	12)	244	117	64	93	76	1	70	18	2	7	31	12	.72	13	.265	.361	.405
1999 New York	AL	150	603	176	36	4	18	(11	7)	274	120	68	115	83	0	57	21	3	5	28	9	.76	7	.292	.393	.454
2000 New York	AL	102	400	113	22	2	5	(5	0)	154	75	26	68	46	0	45	8	1	2	15	7	.68	6	.283	.366	.385
2001 New York	AL	137	521	130	20	3	9	(6	3)	183	66	44	69	58	1	73	14	5	2	38	9	.81	10	.250	.339	.351
2002 Kansas City	AL	80	300	63	9	0	6	(3	3)	90	41	22	20	28	1	32	4	2	2	19	3	.86	5	.210	.284	.300
12 ML YEARS		1632	6366	1839	322	64	98	(47	51)	2583	1132	615	1042	804	22	730	139	20	56	407	117	.78	116	.289	.378	.406

Gary Knotts

Pitches: R Bats: R Pos: RP-28   Ht: 6'4" Wt: 200 Born: 2/12/77 Age: 26

		HOW MUCH HE PITCHED						WHAT HE GAVE UP											THE RESULTS						
Year Team	Lg	G	GS	CG	GF	IP	BFP	H	R	ER	HR	SH	SF	HB	TBB	IBB	SO	WP	Bk	W	L	Pct	ShO	Sv-Op	Hld	ERC	ERA
1996 Marlins	R	12	9	1	2	57.1	227	35	16	13	0	2	2	6	17	0	46	5	0	4	2	.667	1	0- -	-	1.56	2.04
1997 Kane County	A	7	7	0	0	20.0	113	33	34	29	2	2	0	3	17	0	19	8	1	1	5	.167	0	0- -	-	10.61	13.05
1997 Utica	A-	12	12	1	0	69.2	304	70	34	28	3	1	2	8	27	1	65	3	0	3	5	.375	0	0- -	-	4.11	3.62
1998 Kane County	A	27	27	3	0	158.1	686	144	84	68	11	4	6	11	66	1	148	7	0	8	8	.500	0	0- -	-	3.66	3.87
1999 Brevard Cnty	A+	16	16	3	0	94.0	402	101	52	48	7	1	3	6	29	0	65	1	0	9	6	.600	2	0- -	-	4.39	4.60

Year Team	Lg	G	GS	CG	GF	IP	BFP	H	R	ER	HR	SH	SF	HB	TBB	IBB	SO	WP	Bk	W	L	Pct	ShO	Sv-Op	Hld	ERC	ERA
1999 Portland	AA	12	12	1	0	81.2	358	79	39	34	12	4	3	8	33	0	63	4	0	6	3	.667	1	0--	-	4.63	3.75
2000 Portland	AA	27	27	2	0	156.1	687	161	102	81	15	3	5	7	63	1	113	8	0	9	8	.529	1	0--	-	4.38	4.66
2001 Calgary	AAA	21	21	1	0	118.2	528	136	77	72	16	3	3	2	43	0	104	5	0	6	7	.462	1	0--	-	5.06	5.46
2002 Calgary	AAA	42	0	0	14	53.0	236	53	29	25	4	2	0	5	32	2	44	7	0	5	3	.625	0	3--	5	5.18	4.25
2001 Florida	NL	2	1	0	0	6.0	28	7	4	4	1	0	0	2	1	0	9	0	0	0	1	.000	0	0-0	0	5.84	6.00
2002 Florida	NL	28	0	0	7	30.2	127	21	15	15	6	0	1	0	16	0	21	1	0	3	1	.750	0	0-1	5	3.62	4.40
2 ML YEARS		30	1	0	7	36.2	155	28	19	19	7	0	1	3	17	0	30	1	0	3	2	.600	0	0-1	5	3.97	4.66

Billy Koch

Pitches: R Bats: R Pos: RP-84 **Ht: 6'3" Wt: 215 Born: 12/14/74 Age: 28**

Year Team	Lg	G	GS	CG	GF	IP	BFP	H	R	ER	HR	SH	SF	HB	TBB	IBB	SO	WP	Bk	W	L	Pct	ShO	Sv-Op	Hld	ERC	ERA
1999 Toronto	AL	56	0	0	48	63.2	272	55	26	24	5	4	1	3	30	5	57	0	0	0	5	.000	0	31-35	0	3.53	3.39
2000 Toronto	AL	68	0	0	62	78.2	326	78	28	23	6	4	0	2	18	4	60	1	0	9	3	.750	0	33-38	0	3.25	2.63
2001 Toronto	AL	69	0	0	56	69.1	308	69	39	37	7	5	4	6	33	7	55	5	0	2	5	.286	0	36-44	0	4.54	4.80
2002 Oakland	AL	84	0	0	79	93.2	398	73	38	34	7	6	1	4	46	6	93	5	0	11	4	.733	0	44-50	0	3.10	3.27
4 ML YEARS		277	0	0	245	305.1	1304	275	131	118	25	19	6	15	127	22	265	11	0	22	17	.564	0	144-167	0	3.54	3.48

Danny Kolb

Pitches: R Bats: R Pos: RP-34 **Ht: 6'4" Wt: 215 Born: 3/29/75 Age: 28**

Year Team	Lg	G	GS	CG	GF	IP	BFP	H	R	ER	HR	SH	SF	HB	TBB	IBB	SO	WP	Bk	W	L	Pct	ShO	Sv-Op	Hld	ERC	ERA
2002 Charlotte*	A+	4	0	0	0	6.0	26	5	1	1	0	0	0	0	4	0	2	0	0	1	0	1.000	0	0--	-	3.50	1.50
2002 Tulsa*	AA	5	1	0	1	8.1	34	9	2	2	0	0	0	0	3	0	4	0	0	0	1	.000	0	0--	-	3.91	2.16
1999 Texas	AL	16	0	0	6	31.0	139	33	18	16	2	0	0	1	15	0	15	2	0	2	1	.667	0	0-0	0	4.63	4.65
2000 Texas	AL	1	0	0	0	0.2	9	5	5	5	0	0	1	0	2	0	0	0	0	0	0	-	0	0-0	0	69.84	67.50
2001 Texas	AL	17	0	0	1	15.1	70	15	8	8	2	1	1	0	10	1	15	3	0	0	0	-	0	0-0	7	5.03	4.70
2002 Texas	AL	34	0	0	14	32.0	145	27	17	15	1	1	2	1	22	2	20	6	0	3	6	.333	0	1-4	2	3.74	4.22
4 ML YEARS		68	0	0	21	79.0	363	80	48	44	5	2	4	2	49	3	50	11	0	5	7	.417	0	1-4	9	4.72	5.01

Satoru Komiyama

Pitches: R Bats: R Pos: RP-25 **Ht: 6'2" Wt: 195 Born: 9/15/65 Age: 37**

Year Team	Lg	G	GS	CG	GF	IP	BFP	H	R	ER	HR	SH	SF	HB	TBB	IBB	SO	WP	Bk	W	L	Pct	ShO	Sv-Op	Hld	ERC	ERA
2002 Norfolk	AAA	17	6	1	7	44.1	168	27	8	7	4	3	0	3	9	2	43	0	0	3	1	.750	0	0--	-	1.61	1.42
2002 New York	NL	25	0	0	13	43.1	194	53	29	27	7	0	3	3	12	4	33	1	0	0	3	.000	0	0-0	0	5.44	5.61

Paul Konerko

Bats: R Throws: R Pos: 1B-140; DH-7; PH-4 **Ht: 6'2" Wt: 215 Born: 3/5/76 Age: 27**

Year Team	Lg	G	AB	H	2B	3B	HR	(Hm	Rd)	TB	R	RBI	RC	TBB	IBB	SO	HBP	SH	SF	SB	CS	SB%	GDP	Avg	OBP	Slg
1997 Los Angeles	NL	6	7	1	0	0	0	(0	0)	1	0	0	0	1	0	2	0	0	0	0	0	-	1	.143	.250	.143
1998 LA-Cin	NL	75	217	47	4	0	7	(2	5)	72	21	29	17	16	0	40	3	0	3	0	1	.00	10	.217	.276	.332
1999 Chicago	AL	142	513	151	31	4	24	(16	8)	262	71	81	86	45	0	68	2	1	3	1	0	1.00	19	.294	.352	.511
2000 Chicago	AL	143	524	156	31	1	21	(10	11)	252	84	97	86	47	0	72	10	0	5	1	0	1.00	22	.298	.363	.481
2001 Chicago	AL	156	582	164	35	0	32	(19	13)	295	92	99	99	54	6	89	9	0	5	1	0	1.00	17	.282	.349	.507
2002 Chicago	AL	151	570	173	30	0	27	(13	14)	284	81	104	95	44	2	72	9	0	7	0	0	-	17	.304	.359	.498
1998 Los Angeles	NL	49	144	31	1	0	4	(2	2)	44	14	16	10	10	0	30	2	0	2	0	1	.00	5	.215	.272	.306
1998 Cincinnati	NL	26	73	16	3	0	3	(0	3)	28	7	13	7	6	0	10	1	0	1	0	0	-	5	.219	.284	.384
6 ML YEARS		673	2413	692	131	5	111	(60	51)	1166	349	410	383	207	8	343	33	1	23	3	1	.75	86	.287	.348	.483

Mike Koplove

Pitches: R Bats: R Pos: RP-55 **Ht: 6'0" Wt: 170 Born: 8/30/76 Age: 26**

Year Team	Lg	G	GS	CG	GF	IP	BFP	H	R	ER	HR	SH	SF	HB	TBB	IBB	SO	WP	Bk	W	L	Pct	ShO	Sv-Op	Hld	ERC	ERA
1998 Diamndbcks	R	2	0	0	0	4.0	19	4	4	4	0	0	0	1	2	0	5	0	0	0	0	-	0	0--	-	4.54	9.00
1998 Lethbridge	R+	12	1	0	4	28.0	114	23	12	11	2	0	1	4	3	0	22	0	0	1	2	.333	0	2--	-	2.36	3.54
1999 South Bend	A	45	0	0	19	84.0	351	70	23	19	5	3	0	11	29	0	98	4	0	5	2	.714	0	7--	-	3.23	2.04
2000 High Desert	A+	20	0	0	19	25.1	100	14	4	4	0	2	0	2	10	0	31	2	0	2	0	1.000	0	8--	-	1.45	1.42
2000 El Paso	AA	35	0	0	16	46.1	197	38	28	20	2	0	2	7	19	1	47	1	1	4	3	.571	0	6--	-	3.31	3.88
2001 El Paso	AA	34	0	0	14	44.0	193	44	18	13	3	3	2	2	19	3	43	0	0	3	2	.600	0	4--	-	4.02	2.66
2001 Tucson	AAA	17	0	0	13	22.1	92	17	7	7	1	0	0	0	10	1	22	2	0	4	1	.800	0	9--	-	2.57	2.82
2002 Tucson	AAA	23	0	0	14	30.2	115	21	5	4	1	0	2	2	4	0	31	3	0	1	2	.333	0	3--	-	1.51	1.17
2001 Arizona	NL	9	0	0	1	10.0	50	8	7	4	1	1	0	2	9	1	14	1	0	0	1	.000	0	0-0	1	5.25	3.60
2002 Arizona	NL	55	0	0	17	61.2	249	47	24	23	2	4	1	0	23	4	46	1	0	6	1	.857	0	0-0	10	2.23	3.36
2 ML YEARS		64	0	0	18	71.2	299	55	31	27	3	5	1	2	32	5	60	2	0	6	2	.750	0	0-0	11	2.62	3.39

Corey Koskie

Bats: L Throws: R Pos: 3B-138; PH-3; PR-1 **Ht: 6'3" Wt: 217 Born: 6/28/73 Age: 30**

Year Team	Lg	G	AB	H	2B	3B	HR	(Hm	Rd)	TB	R	RBI	RC	TBB	IBB	SO	HBP	SH	SF	SB	CS	SB%	GDP	Avg	OBP	Slg
1998 Minnesota	AL	11	29	4	0	0	1	(1	0)	7	2	2	1	2	0	10	0	0	0	0	0	-	0	.138	.194	.241
1999 Minnesota	AL	117	342	106	21	0	11	(4	7)	160	42	58	61	40	4	72	5	2	3	4	4	.50	6	.310	.387	.468
2000 Minnesota	AL	146	474	142	32	4	9	(1	8)	209	79	65	84	77	7	104	4	1	3	5	4	.56	11	.300	.400	.441

123

Year Team	Lg	G	AB	H	2B	3B	HR	(Hm	Rd)	TB	R	RBI	RC	TBB	IBB	SO	HBP	SH	SF	SB	CS	SB%	GDP	Avg	OBP	Slg
2001 Minnesota	AL	153	562	155	37	2	26	(11	15)	274	100	103	99	68	9	118	12	0	7	27	6	.82	16	.276	.362	.488
2002 Minnesota	AL	140	490	131	37	3	15	(6	9)	219	71	69	73	72	4	127	9	0	5	10	11	.48	14	.267	.368	.447
5 ML YEARS		567	1897	538	127	9	62	(23	39)	869	294	297	318	259	24	431	30	3	18	46	25	.65	47	.284	.375	.458

Mark Kotsay

Bats: L **Throws:** L **Pos:** CF-147; PH-7   **Ht:** 6'0" **Wt:** 201 **Born:** 12/2/75 **Age:** 27

Year Team	Lg	G	AB	H	2B	3B	HR	(Hm	Rd)	TB	R	RBI	RC	TBB	IBB	SO	HBP	SH	SF	SB	CS	SB%	GDP	Avg	OBP	Slg
1997 Florida	NL	14	52	10	1	1	0	(0	0)	13	5	4	3	4	0	7	0	1	0	3	0	1.00	1	.192	.250	.250
1998 Florida	NL	154	578	161	25	1	11	(5	6)	233	72	68	70	34	2	61	1	7	3	10	5	.67	17	.279	.318	.403
1999 Florida	NL	148	495	134	23	9	8	(5	3)	199	57	50	58	29	5	50	0	2	9	7	6	.54	11	.271	.306	.402
2000 Florida	NL	152	530	158	31	5	12	(5	7)	235	87	57	78	42	2	46	0	2	4	19	9	.68	11	.298	.347	.443
2001 San Diego	NL	109	406	118	29	1	10	(3	7)	179	67	58	65	48	1	58	2	1	3	13	5	.72	11	.291	.366	.441
2002 San Diego	NL	153	578	169	27	7	17	(11	6)	261	82	61	91	59	0	89	3	2	4	11	9	.55	10	.292	.359	.452
6 ML YEARS		740	2639	750	136	30	58	(29	29)	1120	370	298	365	216	10	311	6	15	23	63	34	.65	67	.284	.337	.424

Ben Kozlowski

Pitches: L **Bats:** L **Pos:** SP-2   **Ht:** 6'6" **Wt:** 220 **Born:** 8/16/80 **Age:** 22

		HOW MUCH HE PITCHED						WHAT HE GAVE UP											THE RESULTS						
Year Team	Lg	G	GS	CG	GF	IP	BFP	H	R	ER	HR	SH	SF	HB	TBB	IBB	SO	WP	Bk	W	L	Pct	ShO	Sv-Op	Hld	ERC	ERA
1999 Braves	R	15	0	0	7	33.2	132	28	9	7	0	0	0	6	0	29	2	0	1	1	.500	0	3--	-	1.82	1.87
2000 Macon	A	15	14	0	0	77.0	353	76	53	36	6	2	4	6	39	0	67	4	2	3	8	.273	0	0--	-	4.44	4.21
2001 Macon	A	26	23	1	1	145.1	588	134	60	40	8	8	2	10	27	0	147	7	1	10	7	.588	1	0--	-	2.86	2.48
2001 Myrtle Beach	A+	2	2	0	0	14.1	61	15	7	6	1	1	2	1	3	1	13	2	0	0	2	.000	0	0--	-	3.52	3.77
2002 Myrtle Beach	A+	1	1	0	0	4.0	21	4	5	2	0	1	0	0	3	0	3	0	1	1	0	1.000	0	0--	-	4.05	4.50
2002 Charlotte	A+	21	12	0	2	79.0	323	63	31	18	2	2	5	3	25	0	76	6	1	4	4	.500	0	0--	-	2.36	2.05
2002 Tulsa	AA	8	8	0	0	52.0	206	28	12	11	3	0	2	1	22	0	41	4	1	4	2	.667	0	0--	-	1.65	1.90
2002 Texas	AL	2	2	0	0	10.0	50	11	7	7	3	0	0	1	11	0	6	0	0	0	0	-	0	0-0	0	10.34	6.30

Chad Kreuter

Bats: B **Throws:** R **Pos:** C-41; PH-7   **Ht:** 6'2" **Wt:** 200 **Born:** 8/26/64 **Age:** 38

Year Team	Lg	G	AB	H	2B	3B	HR	(Hm	Rd)	TB	R	RBI	RC	TBB	IBB	SO	HBP	SH	SF	SB	CS	SB%	GDP	Avg	OBP	Slg
1988 Texas	AL	16	51	14	2	1	1	(0	1)	21	3	5	8	7	0	13	0	0	0	0	0	-	0	.275	.362	.412
1989 Texas	AL	87	158	24	3	0	5	(2	3)	42	16	9	11	27	0	40	0	6	1	0	1	.00	4	.152	.274	.266
1990 Texas	AL	22	22	1	1	0	0	(0	0)	2	2	2	1	8	0	9	0	1	1	0	0	-	0	.045	.290	.091
1991 Texas	AL	3	4	0	0	0	0	(0	0)	0	0	0	0	0	0	1	0	0	0	0	0	-	0	.000	.000	.000
1992 Detroit	AL	67	190	48	9	0	2	(2	0)	63	22	16	19	20	1	38	0	3	2	0	1	.00	5	.253	.321	.332
1993 Detroit	AL	119	374	107	23	3	15	(9	6)	181	59	51	67	49	4	92	3	2	3	2	1	.67	8	.286	.371	.484
1994 Detroit	AL	65	170	38	8	0	1	(1	0)	49	17	19	18	28	0	36	0	2	4	0	1	.00	3	.224	.327	.288
1995 Seattle	AL	26	75	17	5	0	1	(0	1)	25	12	8	8	5	0	22	2	1	0	0	0	-	0	.227	.293	.333
1996 Chicago	AL	46	114	25	8	0	3	(2	1)	42	14	18	13	13	0	29	2	2	1	0	0	-	2	.219	.308	.368
1997 CWS-Ana	AL	89	255	59	9	2	5	(3	2)	87	25	21	25	29	0	66	0	1	0	0	3	.00	7	.231	.310	.341
1998 CWS-Ana	AL	96	252	63	10	1	2	(2	0)	81	27	33	28	33	1	49	3	5	1	1	0	1.00	8	.250	.343	.321
1999 Kansas City	AL	107	324	73	15	0	5	(2	3)	103	31	35	29	34	1	65	6	2	2	0	0	-	16	.225	.309	.318
2000 Los Angeles	NL	80	212	56	13	0	6	(4	2)	87	32	28	40	54	0	48	2	2	1	1	0	1.00	6	.264	.416	.410
2001 Los Angeles	NL	73	191	41	11	1	6	(4	2)	72	21	17	27	41	2	52	1	0	1	0	0	-	5	.215	.355	.377
2002 Los Angeles	NL	41	95	25	5	0	2	(2	0)	36	8	12	13	10	4	31	1	0	2	1	0	1.00	3	.263	.333	.379
1997 Chicago	AL	19	37	8	2	1	1	(1	0)	15	6	3	6	8	0	9	0	0	0	0	1	.00	0	.216	.356	.405
1997 Anaheim	AL	70	218	51	7	1	4	(2	2)	72	19	18	19	21	0	57	0	1	0	0	2	.00	7	.234	.301	.330
1998 Chicago	AL	93	245	62	9	1	2	(2	0)	79	26	33	28	32	1	45	3	5	1	1	0	1.00	8	.253	.345	.322
1998 Anaheim	AL	3	7	1	1	0	0	(0	0)	2	1	0	0	1	0	4	0	0	0	0	0	-	0	.143	.250	.286
15 ML YEARS		937	2487	591	122	8	54	(33	21)	891	289	274	307	358	13	591	20	27	19	5	7	.42	68	.238	.336	.358

John Lackey

Pitches: R **Bats:** R **Pos:** SP-18   **Ht:** 6'6" **Wt:** 205 **Born:** 10/23/78 **Age:** 24

		HOW MUCH HE PITCHED						WHAT HE GAVE UP											THE RESULTS						
Year Team	Lg	G	GS	CG	GF	IP	BFP	H	R	ER	HR	SH	SF	HB	TBB	IBB	SO	WP	Bk	W	L	Pct	ShO	Sv-Op	Hld	ERC	ERA
1999 Boise	A-	15	15	1	0	81.1	372	81	59	45	7	5	2	8	50	1	77	14	1	6	2	.750	0	0--	-	5.21	4.98
2000 Cedar Rpds	A	5	5	0	0	30.1	115	20	7	7	1	0	0	2	5	0	21	4	0	3	2	.600	0	0--	-	1.50	2.08
2000 Lk Elsinore	A+	15	15	2	0	100.2	433	94	56	38	9	0	5	9	42	0	74	12	3	6	6	.500	1	0--	-	4.10	3.40
2000 Erie	AA	8	8	2	0	57.1	234	58	23	21	6	1	0	1	9	0	43	0	0	6	1	.857	0	0--	-	3.32	3.30
2001 Arkansas	AA	18	18	3	0	127.1	509	106	55	49	11	6	5	3	29	0	94	8	0	9	7	.563	2	0--	-	2.57	3.46
2001 Salt Lake	AAA	10	10	1	0	57.2	253	75	44	43	5	2	1	1	16	0	42	3	1	3	4	.429	0	0--	-	5.43	6.71
2002 Salt Lake	AAA	16	16	2	0	101.2	412	89	35	29	5	2	1	2	28	0	82	5	2	8	2	.800	1	0--	-	2.72	2.57
2002 Anaheim	AL	18	18	1	0	108.1	465	113	52	44	10	0	4	4	33	0	69	7	2	9	4	.692	0	0-0	0	4.03	3.66

Tim Laker

Bats: R **Throws:** R **Pos:** C   **Ht:** 6'3" **Wt:** 225 **Born:** 11/27/69 **Age:** 33

Year Team	Lg	G	AB	H	2B	3B	HR	(Hm	Rd)	TB	R	RBI	RC	TBB	IBB	SO	HBP	SH	SF	SB	CS	SB%	GDP	Avg	OBP	Slg
1992 Montreal	NL	28	46	10	3	0	0	(0	0)	13	8	4	2	2	0	14	0	0	0	1	1	.50	1	.217	.250	.283
1993 Montreal	NL	43	86	17	2	1	0	(0	0)	21	3	7	4	2	0	16	1	3	1	2	0	1.00	1	.198	.222	.244
1995 Montreal	NL	64	141	33	8	1	3	(1	2)	52	17	20	14	14	4	38	1	1	0	0	1	.00	5	.234	.306	.369
1997 Baltimore	AL	7	14	0	0	0	0	(0	0)	0	0	1	0	2	0	9	0	1	1	0	0	-	0	.000	.118	.000
1998 TB-Pit		17	29	10	1	0	1	(0	1)	14	3	2	5	2	0	4	0	0	1	0	0	.00	1	.345	.375	.483
1999 Pittsburgh	NL	6	9	3	0	0	0	(0	0)	3	0	0	1	0	0	2	0	0	0	0	0	-	0	.333	.333	.333
2001 Cleveland	AL	16	33	6	0	0	1	(0	1)	9	5	5	3	0	0	8	0	1	0	0	0	-	1	.182	.308	.273

Year Team		Lg	G	AB	H	2B	3B	HR	(Hm	Rd)	TB	R	RBI	RC	TBB	IBB	SO	HBP	SH	SF	SB	CS	SB%	GDP	Avg	OBP	Slg
							BATTING														**BASERUNNING**				**AVERAGES**		
1998 Tampa Bay		AL	3	5	1	0	0	0	(0	0)	1	1	0	0	1	0	1	0	0	0	0	1	.00	0	.200	.333	.200
1998 Pittsburgh		NL	14	24	9	1	0	1	(0	1)	13	2	2	5	1	0	3	0	0	1	0	0	-	1	.375	.385	.542
7 ML YEARS			181	358	79	14	2	5	(1	4)	112	36	39	29	28	4	91	2	6	4	3	3	.50	10	.221	.278	.313

David Lamb

Bats: L **Throws:** R **Pos:** SS-4; 2B-2; PH-2; 3B-1   **Ht:** 6'2" **Wt:** 165 **Born:** 6/6/75 **Age:** 28

Year Team		Lg	G	AB	H	2B	3B	HR	(Hm	Rd)	TB	R	RBI	RC	TBB	IBB	SO	HBP	SH	SF	SB	CS	SB%	GDP	Avg	OBP	Slg
							BATTING														**BASERUNNING**				**AVERAGES**		
2002 Edmonton*		AAA	123	440	136	25	3	10	(-	-)	197	72	72	70	45	0	57	6	5	5	2	6	.25	16	.309	.377	.448
1999 Tampa Bay		AL	55	124	28	5	1	1	(0	1)	38	18	13	9	10	0	18	0	0	0	0	1	.00	4	.226	.284	.306
2000 New York		NL	7	5	1	0	0	0	(0	0)	1	1	0	0	1	0	1	0	0	0	0	0	-	0	.200	.333	.200
2002 Minnesota		AL	7	10	1	0	0	0	(0	0)	1	0	0	0	0	0	2	0	0	1	0	0	-	1	.100	.100	.100
3 ML YEARS			69	139	30	5	1	1	(0	1)	40	19	13	9	11	0	21	0	0	1	0	1	.00	5	.216	.273	.288

Mike Lamb

Bats: L **Throws:** R **Pos:** 1B-51; PH-29; DH-21; 3B-14; LF-12; RF-4; C-3; 2B-1; PR-1   **Ht:** 6'1" **Wt:** 195 **Born:** 8/9/75 **Age:** 27

Year Team		Lg	G	AB	H	2B	3B	HR	(Hm	Rd)	TB	R	RBI	RC	TBB	IBB	SO	HBP	SH	SF	SB	CS	SB%	GDP	Avg	OBP	Slg
							BATTING														**BASERUNNING**				**AVERAGES**		
2002 Oklahoma*		AAA	6	28	11	1	0	0	(-	-)	12	3	4	5	1	0	4	0	0	0	0	0	-	1	.393	.414	.429
2000 Texas		AL	138	493	137	25	2	6	(4	2)	184	65	47	59	34	6	60	4	5	2	0	2	.00	10	.278	.324	.373
2001 Texas		AL	76	284	87	18	0	4	(1	3)	117	42	35	40	14	1	27	5	1	2	2	1	.67	6	.306	.348	.412
2002 Texas		AL	115	314	89	13	0	9	(7	2)	129	54	33	45	33	5	48	3	2	3	0	0	-	7	.283	.354	.411
3 ML YEARS			329	1091	313	56	2	19	(12	7)	430	161	115	144	81	12	135	12	8	7	2	3	.40	23	.287	.341	.394

Tom Lampkin

Bats: L **Throws:** R **Pos:** C-94; PH-15; PR-2   **Ht:** 5'11" **Wt:** 198 **Born:** 3/4/64 **Age:** 39

Year Team		Lg	G	AB	H	2B	3B	HR	(Hm	Rd)	TB	R	RBI	RC	TBB	IBB	SO	HBP	SH	SF	SB	CS	SB%	GDP	Avg	OBP	Slg
							BATTING														**BASERUNNING**				**AVERAGES**		
1988 Cleveland		AL	4	4	0	0	0	0	(0	0)	0	0	0	0	1	0	0	0	0	0	0	0	-	0	.000	.200	.000
1990 San Diego		NL	26	63	14	0	1	1	(1	0)	19	4	4	4	4	1	9	0	0	0	0	1	.00	2	.222	.269	.302
1991 San Diego		NL	38	58	11	3	1	0	(0	0)	16	4	3	3	3	0	9	0	0	0	0	0	-	0	.190	.230	.276
1992 San Diego		NL	9	17	4	0	0	0	(0	0)	4	3	0	3	6	0	1	1	0	0	2	0	1.00	0	.235	.458	.235
1993 Milwaukee		NL	73	162	32	8	0	4	(1	3)	52	22	25	15	20	3	26	0	2	4	7	3	.70	2	.198	.280	.321
1995 San Francisco		NL	65	76	21	2	0	1	(1	0)	26	8	9	10	9	1	8	1	0	0	2	0	1.00	1	.276	.360	.342
1996 San Francisco		NL	66	177	41	8	0	6	(5	1)	67	26	29	21	20	2	22	5	0	2	1	5	.17	2	.232	.324	.379
1997 St Louis		NL	108	229	56	8	1	7	(2	5)	87	28	22	29	28	5	30	4	4	2	1	1	.67	8	.245	.335	.380
1998 St Louis		NL	93	216	50	12	1	6	(4	2)	82	25	28	27	24	5	32	7	1	0	3	2	.60	5	.231	.328	.380
1999 Seattle		AL	76	206	60	11	2	9	(5	4)	102	29	34	34	13	1	32	5	1	2	1	3	.25	2	.291	.345	.495
2000 Seattle		AL	36	103	26	6	1	7	(3	4)	55	15	23	16	9	1	17	3	0	2	0	0	-	7	.252	.325	.534
2001 Seattle		AL	79	204	46	10	0	5	(1	4)	71	28	22	22	18	1	41	7	1	1	1	0	1.00	4	.225	.309	.348
2002 San Diego		NL	104	281	61	10	1	10	(5	5)	103	32	37	32	38	7	59	3	1	4	2	1	.67	4	.217	.313	.367
13 ML YEARS			777	1796	422	78	8	56	(28	28)	684	224	236	216	193	27	286	36	10	17	23	17	.58	38	.235	.319	.381

Jason Lane

Bats: R **Throws:** L **Pos:** RF-27; LF-12; PH-8; PR-4; CF-1   **Ht:** 6'2" **Wt:** 215 **Born:** 12/22/76 **Age:** 26

Year Team		Lg	G	AB	H	2B	3B	HR	(Hm	Rd)	TB	R	RBI	RC	TBB	IBB	SO	HBP	SH	SF	SB	CS	SB%	GDP	Avg	OBP	Slg
							BATTING														**BASERUNNING**				**AVERAGES**		
1999 Auburn		A-	74	283	79	18	5	13	(-	-)	146	46	59	54	38	2	46	3	0	4	6	4	.60	2	.279	.366	.516
2000 Michigan		A	133	511	153	38	6	23	(-	-)	260	98	104	99	62	7	91	8	0	13	20	7	.74	9	.299	.375	.509
2001 Round Rock		AA	137	526	166	36	2	38	(-	-)	320	103	124	126	61	11	98	21	1	1	14	2	.88	6	.316	.407	.608
2002 New Orleans		AAA	111	426	116	36	2	15	(-	-)	201	65	83	67	31	0	90	7	0	6	13	3	.81	6	.272	.328	.472
2002 Houston		NL	44	69	20	3	1	4	(2	2)	37	12	10	11	10	1	12	0	0	1	1	1	.50	0	.290	.375	.536

Ryan Langerhans

Bats: L **Throws:** L **Pos:** LF-1   **Ht:** 6'3" **Wt:** 195 **Born:** 2/20/80 **Age:** 23

Year Team		Lg	G	AB	H	2B	3B	HR	(Hm	Rd)	TB	R	RBI	RC	TBB	IBB	SO	HBP	SH	SF	SB	CS	SB%	GDP	Avg	OBP	Slg
							BATTING														**BASERUNNING**				**AVERAGES**		
1998 Braves		R	43	148	41	10	4	2	(-	-)	65	15	19	23	19	1	38	0	0	1	2	5	.29	0	.277	.357	.439
1999 Macon		A	121	448	120	30	1	9	(-	-)	179	66	49	64	52	2	99	7	2	2	19	11	.63	8	.268	.352	.400
2000 Myrtle Beach		A+	116	392	83	14	7	6	(-	-)	129	55	37	38	32	1	104	9	4	0	25	11	.69	3	.212	.289	.329
2001 Myrtle Beach		A+	125	450	129	30	3	7	(-	-)	186	66	48	71	55	3	104	8	2	0	22	13	.63	9	.287	.374	.413
2002 Greenville		AA	109	391	98	23	2	9	(-	-)	152	57	62	59	68	3	83	6	4	5	10	5	.67	9	.251	.366	.389
2002 Atlanta		NL	1	1	0	0	0	0	(0	0)	0	0	0	0	0	0	0	0	0	0	0	0	-	0	.000	.000	.000

Ray Lankford

Bats: L **Throws:** L **Pos:** LF-59; PH-23; CF-3; DH-1   **Ht:** 5'11" **Wt:** 200 **Born:** 6/5/67 **Age:** 36

Year Team		Lg	G	AB	H	2B	3B	HR	(Hm	Rd)	TB	R	RBI	RC	TBB	IBB	SO	HBP	SH	SF	SB	CS	SB%	GDP	Avg	OBP	Slg
							BATTING														**BASERUNNING**				**AVERAGES**		
1990 St Louis		NL	39	126	36	10	1	3	(2	1)	57	12	12	21	13	0	27	0	0	0	8	2	.80	1	.286	.353	.452
1991 St Louis		NL	151	566	142	23	**15**	9	(4	5)	222	83	69	68	41	1	114	1	4	3	44	20	.69	4	.251	.301	.392
1992 St Louis		NL	153	598	175	40	6	20	(13	7)	287	87	86	106	72	6	**147**	5	2	5	42	**24**	.64	5	.293	.371	.480
1993 St Louis		NL	127	407	97	17	3	7	(6	1)	141	64	45	55	81	7	111	3	1	3	14	14	.50	5	.238	.366	.346
1994 St Louis		NL	109	416	111	25	5	19	(8	11)	203	89	57	74	58	3	113	4	0	4	11	10	.52	0	.267	.359	.488
1995 St Louis		NL	132	483	134	35	2	25	(16	9)	248	81	82	89	63	6	110	2	0	5	24	8	.75	10	.277	.360	.513
1996 St Louis		NL	149	545	150	36	8	21	(8	13)	265	100	86	100	79	10	133	3	1	7	35	7	.83	12	.275	.366	.486

Year Team	Lg	G	AB	H	2B	3B	HR	(Hm	Rd)	TB	R	RBI	RC	TBB	IBB	SO	HBP	SH	SF	SB	CS	SB%	GDP	Avg	OBP	Slg
1997 St Louis	NL	133	465	137	36	3	31	(10	21)	272	94	98	108	95	10	125	0	0	5	21	11	.66	9	.295	.411	.585
1998 St Louis	NL	154	533	156	37	1	31	(20	11)	288	94	105	115	86	5	151	3	0	4	26	5	.84	4	.293	.391	.540
1999 St Louis	NL	122	422	129	32	1	15	(8	7)	208	77	63	79	49	3	110	3	0	2	14	4	.78	6	.306	.380	.493
2000 St Louis	NL	128	392	99	16	3	26	(18	8)	199	73	65	73	70	1	148	4	0	6	5	6	.45	6	.253	.367	.508
2001 Stl-SD	NL	131	389	98	28	4	19	(10	9)	191	58	58	69	62	9	145	4	1	3	10	2	.83	6	.252	.358	.491
2002 San Diego	NL	81	205	46	7	1	6	(3	3)	73	20	26	25	30	3	61	2	1	2	2	2	.50	3	.224	.326	.356
2001 St Louis	NL	91	264	62	18	3	15	(7	8)	131	38	39	45	44	8	105	2	1	3	4	2	.67	4	.235	.345	.496
2001 San Diego	NL	40	125	36	10	1	4	(3	1)	60	20	19	24	18	1	40	2	0	0	6	0	1.00	2	.288	.386	.480
13 ML YEARS		1609	5547	1510	342	53	232	(126	106)	2654	932	852	982	799	64	1495	34	10	49	256	115	.69	71	.272	.364	.478

Barry Larkin

Bats: R Throws: R Pos: SS-135; PH-12; PR-1   Ht: 6'0" Wt: 185 Born: 4/28/64 Age: 39

Year Team	Lg	G	AB	H	2B	3B	HR	(Hm	Rd)	TB	R	RBI	RC	TBB	IBB	SO	HBP	SH	SF	SB	CS	SB%	GDP	Avg	OBP	Slg
1986 Cincinnati	NL	41	159	45	4	3	3	(3	0)	64	27	19	22	9	1	21	0	0	1	8	0	1.00	2	.283	.320	.403
1987 Cincinnati	NL	125	439	107	16	2	12	(6	6)	163	64	43	52	36	3	52	5	5	3	21	6	.78	8	.244	.306	.371
1988 Cincinnati	NL	151	588	174	32	5	12	(9	3)	252	91	56	94	41	3	24	8	10	5	40	7	.85	7	.296	.347	.429
1989 Cincinnati	NL	97	325	111	14	4	4	(1	3)	145	47	36	53	20	5	23	2	2	8	10	5	.67	7	.342	.375	.446
1990 Cincinnati	NL	158	614	185	25	6	7	(4	3)	243	85	67	90	49	3	49	7	7	4	30	5	.86	14	.301	.358	.396
1991 Cincinnati	NL	123	464	140	27	4	20	(16	4)	235	88	69	90	55	1	64	3	3	2	24	6	.80	7	.302	.378	.506
1992 Cincinnati	NL	140	533	162	32	6	12	(8	4)	242	76	78	92	63	8	58	4	2	7	15	4	.79	13	.304	.377	.454
1993 Cincinnati	NL	100	384	121	20	3	8	(4	4)	171	57	51	68	51	6	33	1	1	3	14	1	.93	13	.315	.394	.445
1994 Cincinnati	NL	110	427	119	23	5	9	(3	6)	179	78	52	73	64	3	58	0	5	5	26	2	.93	6	.279	.369	.419
1995 Cincinnati	NL	131	496	158	29	6	15	(8	7)	244	98	66	104	61	2	49	3	3	4	51	5	.91	6	.319	.394	.492
1996 Cincinnati	NL	152	517	154	32	4	33	(14	19)	293	117	89	118	96	3	52	7	0	7	36	10	.78	20	.298	.410	.567
1997 Cincinnati	NL	73	224	71	17	3	4	(0	4)	106	34	20	50	47	6	24	3	1	1	14	3	.82	3	.317	.440	.473
1998 Cincinnati	NL	145	538	166	34	10	17	(8	9)	271	93	72	109	79	5	69	2	4	3	26	3	.90	12	.309	.397	.504
1999 Cincinnati	NL	161	583	171	30	4	12	(7	5)	245	108	75	102	93	5	57	2	5	4	30	8	.79	12	.293	.390	.420
2000 Cincinnati	NL	102	396	124	26	5	11	(6	5)	193	71	41	73	48	0	31	1	2	0	14	6	.70	10	.313	.389	.487
2001 Cincinnati	NL	45	156	40	12	0	2	(1	1)	58	29	17	23	27	2	25	2	0	0	3	2	.60	2	.256	.373	.372
2002 Cincinnati	NL	145	507	124	37	2	7	(4	3)	186	72	47	54	44	9	57	3	6	7	13	4	.76	13	.245	.305	.367
17 ML YEARS		1999	7350	2172	410	72	188	(102	86)	3290	1235	898	1267	883	65	746	53	56	64	375	77	.83	155	.296	.372	.448

Greg LaRocca

Bats: R Throws: R Pos: 3B-15; PH-4; 2B-3; PR-3   Ht: 5'11" Wt: 185 Born: 11/10/72 Age: 30

Year Team	Lg	G	AB	H	2B	3B	HR	(Hm	Rd)	TB	R	RBI	RC	TBB	IBB	SO	HBP	SH	SF	SB	CS	SB%	GDP	Avg	OBP	Slg
1994 Spokane	A-	42	158	46	9	2	0	(-	-)	59	20	14	21	14	0	18	2	2	0	7	2	.78	4	.291	.356	.373
1994 R Cucamnga	A+	28	85	14	5	1	1	(-	-)	24	7	8	5	7	0	11	2	1	1	3	1	.75	2	.165	.242	.282
1995 R Cucamnga	A+	125	466	150	36	5	8	(-	-)	220	77	74	85	44	0	77	12	0	2	15	4	.79	13	.322	.393	.472
1995 Memphis	AA	2	7	1	0	0	0	(-	-)	1	0	0	0	0	0	1	0	0	0	0	1	.00	1	.143	.143	.143
1996 Memphis	AA	128	445	122	22	5	6	(-	-)	172	66	42	61	51	4	58	10	5	5	5	9	.36	9	.274	.358	.387
1997 Mobile	AA	76	300	80	16	2	3	(-	-)	109	44	31	39	26	0	46	8	0	5	8	3	.73	4	.267	.336	.363
1998 Las Vegas	AAA	95	304	94	22	5	8	(-	-)	150	55	39	55	19	0	48	12	2	2	7	4	.64	3	.309	.345	.493
1999 Las Vegas	AAA	14	51	14	2	0	0	(-	-)	16	3	2	5	2	0	10	4	0	1	2	2	.50	3	.275	.345	.314
2000 Las Vegas	AAA	137	482	142	42	7	9	(-	-)	225	90	80	86	54	1	62	12	1	2	13	4	.76	9	.295	.378	.467
2001 Akron	AA	31	104	33	9	0	3	(-	-)	51	16	19	22	18	1	11	2	0	2	2	0	.00	1	.317	.421	.490
2001 Buffalo	AAA	61	216	67	12	1	12	(-	-)	117	39	37	40	12	0	35	6	2	1	2	1	.67	4	.310	.362	.542
2002 Buffalo	AAA	107	382	112	28	2	7	(-	-)	165	70	41	72	48	0	48	23	2	2	17	4	.81	4	.293	.402	.432
2000 San Diego	NL	13	27	6	2	0	0	(0	0)	8	1	2	2	1	0	4	0	2	0	0	0	-	1	.222	.250	.296
2002 Cleveland	AL	21	52	14	3	1	0	(0	0)	19	12	4	8	6	0	6	2	0	0	1	0	1.00	1	.269	.367	.365
2 ML YEARS		34	79	20	5	1	0	(0	0)	27	13	6	10	7	0	10	2	2	0	1	0	1.00	2	.253	.330	.342

Brandon Larson

Bats: R Throws: R Pos: PH-11; LF-9; 3B-5; 1B-2   Ht: 6'0" Wt: 210 Born: 5/24/76 Age: 27

Year Team	Lg	G	AB	H	2B	3B	HR	(Hm	Rd)	TB	R	RBI	RC	TBB	IBB	SO	HBP	SH	SF	SB	CS	SB%	GDP	Avg	OBP	Slg
1997 Chattanooga	AA	11	41	11	5	1	0	(-	-)	18	4	6	5	1	0	10	0	0	1	0	0	-	1	.268	.279	.439
1998 Burlington	A	18	68	15	3	0	2	(-	-)	24	5	9	6	4	0	16	0	0	0	2	1	.67	1	.221	.264	.353
1999 Rockford	A	69	250	75	18	1	13	(-	-)	134	38	52	48	25	1	67	3	0	3	12	2	.86	7	.300	.367	.536
1999 Chattanooga	AA	43	172	49	10	0	12	(-	-)	95	28	42	29	10	1	51	1	0	2	4	5	.44	3	.285	.332	.552
2000 Chattanooga	AA	111	427	116	26	0	20	(-	-)	202	61	64	66	31	5	122	8	0	3	15	5	.75	8	.272	.330	.473
2000 Louisville	AAA	17	63	18	7	1	2	(-	-)	33	11	4	10	4	0	16	0	0	0	0	0	-	0	.286	.328	.524
2001 Louisville	AAA	115	424	108	22	2	14	(-	-)	176	61	55	50	24	1	123	12	0	2	5	6	.45	15	.255	.312	.415
2002 Louisville	AAA	80	297	101	20	1	25	(-	-)	198	47	69	71	24	2	70	3	1	2	1	1	.50	9	.340	.393	.667
2001 Cincinnati	NL	14	33	4	2	0	0	(0	0)	6	2	1	0	2	0	10	0	0	0	0	0	-	1	.121	.171	.182
2002 Cincinnati	NL	23	51	14	2	0	4	(4	0)	28	8	13	9	6	1	10	1	0	0	1	0	1.00	1	.275	.362	.549
2 ML YEARS		37	84	18	4	0	4	(4	0)	34	10	14	9	8	1	20	1	0	0	1	0	1.00	2	.214	.290	.405

Jason LaRue

Bats: R Throws: R Pos: C-110; PH-4; PR-3   Ht: 5'11" Wt: 200 Born: 3/19/74 Age: 29

Year Team	Lg	G	AB	H	2B	3B	HR	(Hm	Rd)	TB	R	RBI	RC	TBB	IBB	SO	HBP	SH	SF	SB	CS	SB%	GDP	Avg	OBP	Slg
1999 Cincinnati	NL	36	90	19	7	0	3	(1	2)	35	12	10	10	11	1	32	2	0	0	4	1	.80	4	.211	.311	.389
2000 Cincinnati	NL	31	98	23	3	0	5	(1	4)	41	12	12	12	5	2	19	4	0	0	0	0	-	1	.235	.299	.418
2001 Cincinnati	NL	121	364	86	21	2	12	(3	9)	147	39	43	42	27	4	106	9	1	2	3	3	.50	11	.236	.303	.404
2002 Cincinnati	NL	113	353	88	17	1	12	(5	7)	143	42	52	44	27	6	117	13	2	2	1	2	.33	13	.249	.324	.405
4 ML YEARS		301	905	216	48	3	32	(10	22)	366	105	117	108	70	13	274	28	3	4	8	6	.57	29	.239	.312	.404

Chris Latham

Bats: B **Throws:** R **Pos:** LF   **Ht:** 6'0" **Wt:** 205 **Born:** 5/26/73 **Age:** 30

Year Team	Lg	G	AB	H	2B	3B	HR	(Hm	Rd)	TB	R	RBI	RC	TBB	IBB	SO	HBP	SH	SF	SB	CS	SB%	GDP	Avg	OBP	Slg
2002 Norfolk*	AAA	117	405	94	22	6	6	(--	--)	146	60	43	54	62	2	103	4	0	3	26	9	.74	6	.232	.338	.360
1997 Minnesota	AL	15	22	4	1	0	0	(0	0)	5	4	1	0	0	0	8	0	0	0	0	0	--	0	.182	.182	.227
1998 Minnesota	AL	34	94	15	1	0	1	(1	0)	19	14	5	5	13	0	36	0	1	0	4	2	.67	1	.160	.262	.202
1999 Minnesota	AL	14	22	2	0	0	0	(0	0)	2	1	3	0	0	0	13	0	0	2	0	0	--	0	.091	.083	.091
2001 Toronto	AL	43	73	20	3	1	2	(1	1)	31	12	10	12	10	1	28	1	0	0	4	1	.80	1	.274	.369	.425
4 ML YEARS		106	211	41	5	1	3	(2	1)	57	31	19	17	23	1	85	1	1	2	8	3	.73	1	.194	.274	.270

Brian Lawrence

Pitches: R **Bats:** R **Pos:** SP-31; RP-4   **Ht:** 6'0" **Wt:** 195 **Born:** 5/14/76 **Age:** 27

Year Team	Lg	G	GS	CG	GF	IP	BFP	H	R	ER	HR	SH	SF	HB	TBB	IBB	SO	WP	Bk	W	L	Pct	ShO	Sv-Op	Hld	ERC	ERA
1998 Idaho Falls	R+	4	4	2	0	22.0	92	22	7	6	1	0	1	2	5	0	21	0	0	3	0	1.000	1	0--	-	3.43	2.45
1998 Clinton	A	12	12	0	0	80.1	323	67	34	25	5	2	1	4	13	0	79	0	0	5	3	.625	0	0--	-	2.25	2.80
1999 R Cucamnga	A+	27	27	4	0	175.1	723	178	72	66	6	7	5	10	30	1	166	7	5	12	8	.600	3	0--	-	3.08	3.39
2000 Mobile	AA	21	21	0	0	126.2	496	99	40	34	6	1	0	10	28	0	119	1	0	7	6	.538	0	0--	-	2.32	2.42
2000 Las Vegas	AAA	8	8	0	0	46.2	193	48	13	10	6	0	0	4	7	0	46	0	0	4	0	1.000	0	0--	-	3.83	1.93
2001 Portland	AAA	9	8	0	1	45.0	196	42	22	19	3	1	2	2	17	2	42	2	0	1	3	.250	0	1--	-	3.41	3.80
2001 San Diego	NL	27	15	1	5	114.2	484	107	53	44	10	4	3	5	34	5	84	1	0	5	5	.500	0	0-0	0	3.30	3.45
2002 San Diego	NL	35	31	2	0	210.0	894	230	97	86	16	8	4	11	52	6	149	2	1	12	12	.500	2	0-0	1	4.05	3.69
2 ML YEARS		62	46	3	5	324.2	1378	337	150	130	26	12	7	16	86	11	233	3	1	17	17	.500	2	0-0	1	3.78	3.60

Joe Lawrence

Bats: R **Throws:** R **Pos:** 2B-49; PH-3; PR-3   **Ht:** 6'2" **Wt:** 200 **Born:** 2/13/77 **Age:** 26

Year Team	Lg	G	AB	H	2B	3B	HR	(Hm	Rd)	TB	R	RBI	RC	TBB	IBB	SO	HBP	SH	SF	SB	CS	SB%	GDP	Avg	OBP	Slg
1996 St. Ctharines	A-	29	98	22	7	2	0	(--	--)	33	23	11	12	14	1	17	2	1	3	1	1	.50	1	.224	.325	.337
1997 Hagerstown	A	116	446	102	24	1	8	(--	--)	152	63	38	47	49	0	107	5	3	2	10	12	.45	3	.229	.311	.341
1998 Dunedin	A+	125	454	140	31	6	11	(--	--)	216	102	44	97	105	2	88	4	5	1	15	12	.56	11	.308	.441	.476
1999 Knoxville	AA	70	250	66	16	2	7	(--	--)	107	52	24	43	56	0	48	3	0	2	7	6	.54	10	.264	.402	.428
2000 Dunedin	A+	101	375	113	32	1	13	(--	--)	186	69	67	78	69	6	74	5	0	3	21	7	.75	9	.301	.414	.496
2000 Tennessee	AA	39	133	35	9	0	0	(--	--)	44	22	9	22	30	0	27	3	1	1	7	1	.88	2	.263	.407	.331
2001 Syracuse	AAA	93	318	70	11	4	1	(--	--)	92	27	26	27	36	0	62	6	1	1	6	9	.40	6	.220	.310	.289
2002 Syracuse	AAA	29	108	18	4	1	2	(--	--)	30	13	12	8	14	0	23	0	0	0	3	0	1.00	1	.167	.262	.278
2002 Toronto	AL	55	150	27	4	0	2	(0	2)	37	16	15	7	16	0	38	2	2	4	2	1	.67	1	.180	.262	.247

Matt Lawton

Bats: L **Throws:** R **Pos:** RF-85; LF-23; PH-4; DH-3   **Ht:** 5'10" **Wt:** 186 **Born:** 11/3/71 **Age:** 31

Year Team	Lg	G	AB	H	2B	3B	HR	(Hm	Rd)	TB	R	RBI	RC	TBB	IBB	SO	HBP	SH	SF	SB	CS	SB%	GDP	Avg	OBP	Slg
2002 Akron*	AA	3	10	0	0	0	0	(--	--)	0	1	0	0	3	0	1	0	0	0	0	0	--	0	.000	.231	.000
1995 Minnesota	AL	21	60	19	4	1	1	(1	0)	28	11	12	11	7	0	11	3	0	0	1	1	.50	1	.317	.414	.467
1996 Minnesota	AL	79	252	65	7	1	6	(1	5)	92	34	42	31	28	1	28	4	0	2	4	4	.50	6	.258	.339	.365
1997 Minnesota	AL	142	460	114	29	3	14	(8	6)	191	74	60	73	76	3	81	10	1	1	7	4	.64	7	.248	.366	.415
1998 Minnesota	AL	152	557	155	36	6	21	(11	10)	266	91	77	105	86	6	64	15	0	4	16	8	.67	10	.278	.387	.478
1999 Minnesota	AL	118	406	105	18	0	7	(2	5)	144	58	54	57	57	7	42	6	0	7	26	4	.87	11	.259	.353	.355
2000 Minnesota	AL	156	561	171	44	2	13	(8	5)	258	84	88	109	91	8	63	7	0	5	23	7	.77	10	.305	.405	.460
2001 Min-NYM		151	559	155	36	1	13	(5	8)	232	95	64	92	85	6	80	11	0	2	29	8	.78	16	.277	.382	.415
2002 Cleveland	AL	114	416	98	19	2	15	(8	7)	166	71	57	59	59	0	34	8	1	0	8	9	.47	13	.236	.342	.399
2001 Minnesota	AL	103	376	110	25	0	10	(4	6)	165	71	51	66	63	6	46	3	0	2	19	6	.76	14	.293	.396	.439
2001 New York	NL	48	183	45	11	1	3	(1	2)	67	24	13	26	22	0	34	8	0	0	10	2	.83	2	.246	.352	.366
8 ML YEARS		933	3271	882	193	16	90	(44	46)	1377	518	454	537	489	31	403	64	2	21	114	45	.72	74	.270	.373	.421

Matt LeCroy

Bats: R **Throws:** R **Pos:** DH-39; PH-17; 1B-8; C-6   **Ht:** 6'2" **Wt:** 225 **Born:** 12/13/75 **Age:** 27

Year Team	Lg	G	AB	H	2B	3B	HR	(Hm	Rd)	TB	R	RBI	RC	TBB	IBB	SO	HBP	SH	SF	SB	CS	SB%	GDP	Avg	OBP	Slg
2002 Edmonton*	AAA	46	174	61	7	1	12	(--	--)	106	36	50	42	17	0	34	4	0	4	2	0	1.00	1	.351	.412	.609
2000 Minnesota	AL	56	167	29	10	0	5	(2	3)	54	18	17	12	17	2	38	2	1	3	0	0	--	6	.174	.254	.323
2001 Minnesota	AL	15	40	17	5	0	3	(0	3)	31	6	12	11	0	0	8	1	0	1	0	1	.00	0	.425	.429	.775
2002 Minnesota	AL	63	181	47	11	1	7	(2	5)	81	19	27	24	13	1	38	0	0	2	0	2	.00	5	.260	.306	.448
3 ML YEARS		134	388	93	26	1	15	(4	11)	166	43	56	47	30	3	84	3	1	6	0	3	.00	11	.240	.295	.428

Ricky Ledee

Bats: L **Throws:** L **Pos:** PH-51; CF-40; LF-10; RF-5   **Ht:** 6'1" **Wt:** 190 **Born:** 11/22/73 **Age:** 29

Year Team	Lg	G	AB	H	2B	3B	HR	(Hm	Rd)	TB	R	RBI	RC	TBB	IBB	SO	HBP	SH	SF	SB	CS	SB%	GDP	Avg	OBP	Slg
1998 New York	AL	42	79	19	5	2	1	(--	--)	31	13	12	9	7	0	29	0	0	1	3	1	.75	1	.241	.299	.392
1999 New York	AL	88	250	69	13	5	9	(4	5)	119	45	40	41	28	5	73	0	0	2	4	3	.57	2	.276	.346	.476
2000 NYY-Cle-Tex		137	467	110	19	5	13	(6	7)	178	59	77	56	59	4	98	2	0	3	13	6	.68	17	.236	.322	.381
2001 Texas	AL	78	242	56	21	1	2	(1	1)	85	33	36	26	23	0	58	3	1	3	3	3	.50	3	.231	.303	.351
2002 Philadelphia	NL	96	203	46	13	1	8	(4	4)	85	33	23	24	35	0	50	1	1	1	1	2	.33	3	.227	.342	.419
2000 New York	AL	62	191	46	11	1	7	(2	5)	80	23	31	26	26	2	39	1	0	1	7	3	.70	7	.241	.332	.419
2000 Cleveland	AL	17	63	14	2	1	2	(2	0)	24	13	8	7	8	0	9	0	0	0	0	0	--	3	.222	.310	.381
2000 Texas	AL	58	213	50	6	3	4	(2	2)	74	23	38	23	25	2	50	1	0	1	6	3	.67	7	.235	.317	.347
5 ML YEARS		441	1241	300	71	14	33	(15	18)	498	183	188	156	152	9	308	6	2	10	24	15	.62	26	.242	.325	.401

Carlos Lee

Bats: R **Throws:** R **Pos:** LF-137; PH-3; DH-2   **Ht:** 6'2" **Wt:** 235 **Born:** 6/20/76 **Age:** 27

Year Team	Lg	G	AB	H	2B	3B	HR	(Hm	Rd)	TB	R	RBI	RC	TBB	IBB	SO	HBP	SH	SF	SB	CS	SB%	GDP	Avg	OBP	Slg
1999 Chicago	AL	127	492	144	32	2	16	(10	6)	228	66	84	68	13	0	72	1	1	7	4	2	.67	11	.293	.312	.463
2000 Chicago	AL	152	572	172	29	2	24	(12	12)	277	107	92	91	38	1	94	3	1	5	13	4	.76	17	.301	.345	.484
2001 Chicago	AL	150	558	150	33	3	24	(12	12)	261	75	84	81	38	2	85	6	1	2	17	7	.71	15	.269	.321	.468
2002 Chicago	AL	140	492	130	26	2	26	(14	12)	238	82	80	86	75	4	73	2	0	7	1	4	.20	5	.264	.359	.484
4 ML YEARS		569	2114	596	120	9	90	(48	42)	1004	330	340	326	164	7	324	15	3	21	35	17	.67	48	.282	.335	.475

Cliff Lee

Pitches: L **Bats:** L **Pos:** SP-2   **Ht:** 6'3" **Wt:** 190 **Born:** 8/30/78 **Age:** 24

		HOW MUCH HE PITCHED						WHAT HE GAVE UP										THE RESULTS						
Year Team	Lg	G	GS	CG	GF	IP	BFP	H	R	ER	HR	SH	SF	HB	TBB	IBB	SO	WP	Bk	W	L	Pct	ShO	Sv-Op	Hld	ERC	ERA
2000 Cape Fear	A	11	11	0	0	44.2	217	50	39	26	1	1	1	1	36	0	63	3	2	1	4	.200	0	0--	5.82	5.24
2001 Jupiter	A+	21	20	0	1	109.2	451	78	43	34	13	5	5	4	46	0	129	2	3	6	7	.462	0	0--	2.86	2.79
2002 Harrisburg	AA	15	15	0	0	86.1	336	61	31	31	12	1	1	1	23	0	105	2	0	7	2	.778	0	0--	2.36	3.23
2002 Akron	AA	3	3	0	0	16.2	72	11	11	10	1	0	0	1	10	0	18	1	0	2	1	.667	0	0--	2.89	5.40
2002 Buffalo	AAA	8	8	0	0	43.0	180	36	18	18	7	0	0	1	22	0	30	1	1	3	2	.600	0	0--	4.26	3.77
2002 Cleveland	AL	2	2	0	0	10.1	44	6	2	2	1	0	0	0	8	1	6	0	1	0	1	.000	0	0-0	0	2.38	1.74

Derrek Lee

Bats: R **Throws:** R **Pos:** 1B-162   **Ht:** 6'5" **Wt:** 248 **Born:** 9/6/75 **Age:** 27

Year Team	Lg	G	AB	H	2B	3B	HR	(Hm	Rd)	TB	R	RBI	RC	TBB	IBB	SO	HBP	SH	SF	SB	CS	SB%	GDP	Avg	OBP	Slg
1997 San Diego	NL	22	54	14	3	0	1	(0	1)	20	9	4	8	9	0	24	0	0	0	0	0	-	1	.259	.365	.370
1998 Florida	NL	141	454	106	29	1	17	(4	13)	188	62	74	59	47	1	120	10	0	2	5	2	.71	12	.233	.318	.414
1999 Florida	NL	70	218	45	9	1	5	(0	5)	71	21	20	18	17	1	70	0	0	1	2	1	.67	3	.206	.263	.326
2000 Florida	NL	158	477	134	18	3	28	(9	19)	242	70	70	84	63	6	123	4	0	2	0	3	.00	14	.281	.368	.507
2001 Florida	NL	158	561	158	37	4	21	(8	13)	266	83	75	88	50	1	126	8	0	6	4	2	.67	18	.282	.346	.474
2002 Florida	NL	**162**	581	157	35	7	27	(9	18)	287	95	86	98	98	8	164	5	0	4	19	9	.68	14	.270	.378	.494
6 ML YEARS		711	2345	614	131	16	99	(30	69)	1074	340	329	355	284	17	627	27	0	15	30	17	.64	62	.262	.346	.458

Travis Lee

Bats: L **Throws:** L **Pos:** 1B-148; PH-13   **Ht:** 6'3" **Wt:** 210 **Born:** 5/26/75 **Age:** 28

Year Team	Lg	G	AB	H	2B	3B	HR	(Hm	Rd)	TB	R	RBI	RC	TBB	IBB	SO	HBP	SH	SF	SB	CS	SB%	GDP	Avg	OBP	Slg
1998 Arizona	NL	146	562	151	20	2	22	(12	10)	241	71	72	83	67	5	123	0	0	1	8	1	.89	13	.269	.346	.429
1999 Arizona	NL	120	375	89	16	2	9	(7	2)	136	57	50	49	58	4	50	0	0	3	17	3	.85	10	.237	.337	.363
2000 Ari-Phi	NL	128	404	95	24	1	9	(2	7)	148	53	54	53	65	1	79	2	0	2	8	1	.89	12	.235	.342	.366
2001 Philadelphia	NL	157	555	143	34	2	20	(11	9)	241	75	90	81	71	5	109	4	1	9	3	4	.43	15	.258	.341	.434
2002 Philadelphia	NL	153	536	142	26	2	13	(8	5)	211	55	70	64	54	10	104	0	0	2	5	3	.63	12	.265	.331	.394
2000 Arizona	NL	72	224	52	13	0	8	(1	7)	89	34	40	27	25	1	46	0	0	1	5	1	.83	6	.232	.308	.397
2000 Philadelphia	NL	56	180	43	11	1	1	(1	0)	59	19	14	26	40	0	33	2	0	1	3	0	1.00	6	.239	.381	.328
5 ML YEARS		704	2432	620	120	9	73	(40	33)	977	311	336	330	315	25	465	6	1	17	41	12	.77	62	.255	.340	.402

Al Leiter

Pitches: L **Bats:** L **Pos:** SP-33   **Ht:** 6'3" **Wt:** 220 **Born:** 10/23/65 **Age:** 37

		HOW MUCH HE PITCHED						WHAT HE GAVE UP										THE RESULTS						
Year Team	Lg	G	GS	CG	GF	IP	BFP	H	R	ER	HR	SH	SF	HB	TBB	IBB	SO	WP	Bk	W	L	Pct	ShO	Sv-Op	Hld	ERC	ERA
1987 New York	AL	4	4	0	0	22.2	104	24	16	16	2	1	0	0	15	0	28	4	0	2	2	.500	0	0-0	0	5.41	6.35
1988 New York	AL	14	14	0	0	57.1	251	49	27	25	7	1	0	5	33	0	60	1	4	4	4	.500	0	0-0	0	4.51	3.92
1989 NYY-Tor	AL	5	5	0	0	33.1	154	32	23	21	2	1	1	2	23	0	26	2	1	1	2	.333	0	0-0	0	4.90	5.67
1990 Toronto	AL	4	0	0	2	6.1	22	1	0	0	0	0	0	0	2	0	5	0	0	0	0	-	0	0-0	0	0.33	0.00
1991 Toronto	AL	3	0	0	1	1.2	13	3	5	5	0	1	0	0	5	0	1	0	0	0	0	-	0	0-0	0	19.88	27.00
1992 Toronto	AL	1	0	0	0	1.0	7	1	1	1	0	0	0	0	2	0	0	0	0	0	0	-	0	0-0	0	8.07	9.00
1993 Toronto	AL	34	12	1	4	105.0	454	93	52	48	8	3	3	4	56	2	66	2	2	9	6	.600	1	2-3	5	3.94	4.11
1994 Toronto	AL	20	20	1	0	111.2	516	125	68	63	6	3	8	2	65	3	100	7	**5**	6	7	.462	0	0-0	0	5.14	5.08
1995 Toronto	AL	28	28	2	0	183.0	805	162	80	74	15	6	4	6	**108**	1	153	**14**	0	11	11	.500	1	0-0	0	4.18	3.64
1996 Florida	NL	33	33	2	0	215.1	896	153	74	70	14	7	3	11	**119**	3	200	5	0	16	12	.571	1	0-0	0	3.09	2.93
1997 Florida	NL	27	27	0	0	151.1	668	133	78	73	13	10	3	12	91	4	132	2	0	11	9	.550	0	0-0	0	4.39	4.34
1998 New York	NL	28	28	4	0	193.0	789	151	55	53	8	6	2	11	71	2	174	4	1	17	6	.739	2	0-0	0	2.65	2.47
1999 New York	NL	32	32	1	0	213.0	923	209	107	100	19	13	10	9	93	8	162	4	1	13	12	.520	0	0-0	0	4.17	4.23
2000 New York	NL	31	31	2	0	208.0	874	176	84	74	19	10	6	11	76	1	200	4	1	16	8	.667	1	0-0	0	3.23	3.20
2001 New York	NL	29	29	0	0	187.1	772	178	81	69	18	9	6	4	46	3	142	5	2	11	11	.500	0	0-0	0	3.26	3.31
2002 New York	NL	33	33	2	0	204.1	868	194	99	79	23	12	2	8	69	5	172	1	1	13	13	.500	2	0-0	0	3.75	3.48
1989 New York	AL	4	4	0	0	26.2	123	23	20	18	1	1	1	2	21	0	22	1	1	1	2	.333	0	0-0	0	4.62	6.08
1989 Toronto	AL	1	1	0	0	6.2	31	9	3	3	1	0	0	0	2	0	4	1	0	0	0	-	0	0-0	0	5.96	4.05
16 ML YEARS		326	296	15	7	1894.1	8116	1684	850	771	154	83	48	85	874	32	1621	55	18	130	103	.558	9	2-3	3	3.74	3.66

Jose Leon

Bats: R **Throws:** R **Pos:** 1B-17; 3B-12; PH-5; LF-2; DH-1   **Ht:** 6'0" **Wt:** 175 **Born:** 12/8/76 **Age:** 26

Year Team	Lg	G	AB	H	2B	3B	HR	(Hm	Rd)	TB	R	RBI	RC	TBB	IBB	SO	HBP	SH	SF	SB	CS	SB%	GDP	Avg	OBP	Slg
1994 Cardinals	R	46	161	37	3	2	0	(-	-)	44	16	17	11	11	0	51	3	1	4	1	4	.20	4	.230	.285	.273
1995 Savannah	A	41	133	22	4	1	0	(-	-)	28	15	11	3	10	1	46	1	1	0	0	1	.00	6	.165	.229	.211
1996 Johnson City	R+	59	222	55	9	3	10	(-	-)	100	29	36	31	17	0	92	2	2	1	5	3	.63	1	.248	.306	.450
1996 New Jersey	A-	7	28	8	3	1	1	(-	-)	16	4	3	5	0	0	7	2	0	0	0	0	-	0	.286	.333	.571
1997 Peoria	A	118	399	92	21	2	20	(-	-)	177	50	54	51	32	1	122	9	2	2	6	5	.55	10	.231	.301	.444

Year Team	Lg	G	AB	H	2B	3B	HR	(Hm	Rd)	TB	R	RBI	RC	TBB	IBB	SO	HBP	SH	SF	SB	CS	SB%	GDP	Avg	OBP	Slg
1998 Prnc William	A+	124	436	127	31	3	21	(-	-)	227	77	74	84	53	4	137	9	2	4	5	3	.63	6	.291	.376	.521
1999 Arkansas	AA	112	335	78	17	0	18	(-	-)	149	37	54	43	25	0	114	6	1	1	3	3	.50	5	.233	.297	.445
2000 Arkansas	AA	90	297	80	16	3	14	(-	-)	144	41	41	44	16	0	66	5	2	0	2	1	.67	7	.269	.318	.485
2000 Bowie	AA	18	68	17	1	0	1	(-	-)	21	7	6	6	4	0	13	2	0	0	5	2	.71	2	.250	.311	.309
2001 Bowie	AA	26	95	34	9	1	4	(-	-)	57	18	20	21	8	0	21	1	0	0	1	1	.50	2	.358	.413	.600
2001 Rochester	AAA	109	416	116	20	4	12	(-	-)	180	54	53	55	25	0	96	4	2	1	7	3	.70	14	.279	.325	.433
2002 Rochester	AAA	83	312	87	16	1	8	(-	-)	129	39	40	39	18	1	54	2	1	3	0	0	-	9	.279	.319	.413
2002 Baltimore	AL	36	89	22	2	0	3	(1	2)	33	8	10	9	3	0	20	1	0	0	1	0	1.00	2	.247	.280	.371

Brian Lesher

Bats: R **Throws:** L **Pos:** 1B-12; PH-6; LF-3; RF-2; DH-2; PR-2   **Ht:** 6'5" **Wt:** 222 **Born:** 3/5/71 **Age:** 32

Year Team	Lg	G	AB	H	2B	3B	HR	(Hm	Rd)	TB	R	RBI	RC	TBB	IBB	SO	HBP	SH	SF	SB	CS	SB%	GDP	Avg	OBP	Slg
2002 Syracuse*	AAA	66	248	65	13	1	7	(-	-)	101	34	28	33	20	0	55	1	1	4	6	1	.86	4	.262	.315	.407
1996 Oakland	AL	26	82	19	3	0	5	(2	3)	37	11	16	10	5	0	17	1	1	1	0	0	-	2	.232	.281	.451
1997 Oakland	AL	46	131	30	4	1	4	(2	2)	48	17	16	13	9	0	30	0	0	2	4	1	.80	2	.229	.275	.366
1998 Oakland	AL	7	7	1	1	0	0	(0	0)	2	0	1	0	0	0	3	0	0	0	0	0	-	0	.143	.143	.286
2000 Seattle	AL	5	5	4	1	1	0	(0	0)	7	1	3	4	1	0	0	0	0	0	1	0	1.00	0	.800	.833	1.400
2002 Toronto	AL	24	38	5	1	0	0	(0	0)	6	2	2	0	4	0	15	0	0	1	0	0	-	2	.132	.209	.158
5 ML YEARS		108	263	59	10	2	9	(4	5)	100	31	38	27	19	0	65	1	1	4	5	1	.83	8	.224	.275	.380

Curtis Leskanic

Pitches: R **Bats:** R **Pos:** RP   **Ht:** 6'0" **Wt:** 196 **Born:** 4/2/68 **Age:** 35

Year Team	Lg	G	GS	CG	GF	IP	BFP	H	R	ER	HR	SH	SF	HB	TBB	IBB	SO	WP	Bk	W	L	Pct	ShO	Sv-Op	Hld	ERC	ERA
2002 Indianapolis*	AAA	5	1	0	0	6.2	28	5	1	0	1	0	0	1	0	7	0	0	0	0	-	0	0--	-	1.33	1.35
2002 Huntsville*	AA	3	0	0	0	3.0	14	4	2	1	0	0	0	0	2	0	2	0	0	0	0	-	0	0--	-	6.62	3.00
1993 Colorado	NL	18	8	0	1	57.0	260	59	40	34	7	5	4	2	27	1	30	8	2	1	5	.167	0	0-0	0	4.71	5.37
1994 Colorado	NL	8	3	0	2	22.1	98	27	14	14	2	2	0	0	10	0	17	2	0	1	1	.500	0	0-0	0	5.62	5.64
1995 Colorado	NL	76	0	0	27	98.0	406	83	38	37	7	3	2	0	33	1	107	6	1	6	3	.667	0	10-16	19	2.79	3.40
1996 Colorado	NL	70	0	0	32	73.2	334	82	51	51	13	3	2	0	38	1	76	6	2	7	5	.583	0	6-10	9	5.81	6.23
1997 Colorado	NL	55	0	0	23	58.1	248	59	36	36	8	2	4	0	24	0	53	4	0	4	0	1.000	0	2-4	6	4.55	5.55
1998 Colorado	NL	66	0	0	20	75.2	332	75	37	37	9	0	0	1	40	2	55	3	1	6	4	.600	0	2-5	12	4.74	4.40
1999 Colorado	NL	63	0	0	5	85.0	382	87	54	48	7	5	3	5	49	4	77	5	0	6	2	.750	0	0-3	8	5.00	5.08
2000 Milwaukee	NL	73	0	0	39	77.1	333	58	23	22	7	1	4	3	51	5	75	5	0	9	3	.750	0	12-13	11	3.72	2.56
2001 Milwaukee	NL	70	0	0	58	69.1	297	63	30	28	11	3	0	2	31	5	64	2	0	2	6	.250	0	17-24	2	4.18	3.63
9 ML YEARS		499	11	0	207	616.2	2690	593	323	307	70	24	20	15	303	19	554	41	6	42	29	.592	0	49-75	67	4.39	4.48

Al Levine

Pitches: R **Bats:** L **Pos:** RP-52   **Ht:** 6'3" **Wt:** 190 **Born:** 5/22/68 **Age:** 35

Year Team	Lg	G	GS	CG	GF	IP	BFP	H	R	ER	HR	SH	SF	HB	TBB	IBB	SO	WP	Bk	W	L	Pct	ShO	Sv-Op	Hld	ERC	ERA
2002 Salt Lake*	AAA	2	0	0	0	3.0	13	5	1	1	0	0	0	0	1	0	0	0	0	0	0	-	0	0--	-	5.88	3.00
1996 Chicago	AL	16	0	0	5	18.1	85	22	14	11	1	0	1	1	7	1	12	0	0	0	1	.000	0	0-1	0	4.80	5.40
1997 Chicago	AL	25	0	0	6	27.1	133	35	22	21	4	1	2	2	16	1	22	2	0	2	2	.500	0	0-1	3	7.10	6.91
1998 Texas	AL	30	0	0	11	58.0	251	68	30	29	6	1	3	0	16	1	19	5	0	1	1	.000	0	0-0	4	4.58	4.50
1999 Anaheim	AL	50	1	0	12	85.0	349	76	40	32	13	2	7	3	29	2	37	3	0	1	1	.500	0	0-1	3	3.81	3.39
2000 Anaheim	AL	51	5	0	12	95.1	426	98	44	41	10	3	3	2	49	5	42	1	0	3	4	.429	0	2-2	5	4.71	3.87
2001 Anaheim	AL	64	1	0	21	75.2	316	71	25	20	7	5	5	2	28	4	40	6	0	8	10	.444	0	2-6	17	3.66	2.38
2002 Anaheim	AL	52	0	0	21	63.2	286	61	35	30	8	2	7	2	34	3	40	2	0	4	4	.500	0	5-7	10	4.53	4.24
7 ML YEARS		288	7	0	88	423.1	1846	431	210	184	49	14	28	12	179	17	212	19	0	18	23	.439	0	9-18	38	4.44	3.91

Allen Levrault

Pitches: R **Bats:** R **Pos:** RP   **Ht:** 6'3" **Wt:** 241 **Born:** 8/15/77 **Age:** 25

Year Team	Lg	G	GS	CG	GF	IP	BFP	H	R	ER	HR	SH	SF	HB	TBB	IBB	SO	WP	Bk	W	L	Pct	ShO	Sv-Op	Hld	ERC	ERA
1996 Helena	R+	18	11	0	2	71.0	302	70	43	42	9	0	0	8	22	0	68	4	3	4	3	.571	0	1--	-	4.35	5.32
1997 Beloit	A	24	24	1	0	131.1	561	141	89	77	18	1	2	6	40	1	112	3	12	3	10	.231	0	0--	-	4.62	5.28
1998 Stockton	A+	16	15	4	0	97.1	388	76	33	31	8	4	3	2	27	0	96	2	1	9	3	.750	1	0--	-	2.46	2.87
1998 El Paso	AA	11	11	0	0	62.2	281	97	51	41	7	2	1	1	17	0	46	1	1	5	1	.167	0	0--	-	4.94	5.89
1999 Huntsville	AA	16	16	2	0	99.2	404	77	44	38	11	3	2	5	33	0	82	3	3	9	2	.818	1	0--	-	2.89	3.43
1999 Louisville	AAA	9	5	0	1	34.1	169	48	37	33	9	1	2	3	16	0	33	1	0	1	3	.250	0	0--	-	8.40	8.65
2000 Indianapolis	AAA	21	18	1	1	108.1	460	98	55	51	9	7	5	6	46	3	78	5	2	6	8	.429	0	0--	-	3.74	4.24
2002 Sacramento	AAA	24	23	0	0	111.1	526	145	91	79	15	0	11	9	45	0	81	4	3	7	8	.467	0	0--	-	6.44	6.39
2000 Milwaukee	NL	5	1	0	2	12.0	51	10	7	6	1	1	1	0	7	0	9	0	0	0	1	.000	0	0-0	0	3.21	4.50
2001 Milwaukee	NL	32	20	1	0	130.2	593	146	93	88	27	3	4	7	59	7	80	2	1	6	10	.375	0	0-0	0	5.89	6.06
2 ML YEARS		37	21	1	2	142.2	644	156	100	94	27	4	5	7	66	7	89	2	1	6	11	.353	0	0-0	0	5.66	5.93

Colby Lewis

Pitches: R **Bats:** R **Pos:** RP-11; SP-4   **Ht:** 6'4" **Wt:** 215 **Born:** 8/2/79 **Age:** 23

Year Team	Lg	G	GS	CG	GF	IP	BFP	H	R	ER	HR	SH	SF	HB	TBB	IBB	SO	WP	Bk	W	L	Pct	ShO	Sv-Op	Hld	ERC	ERA
1999 Pulaski	R+	14	11	1	0	64.2	280	46	24	14	3	0	3	7	27	0	84	3	4	7	3	.700	0	0--	-	2.53	1.95
2000 Charlotte	A+	28	27	3	0	163.2	692	169	83	74	11	4	7	10	45	0	153	11	2	11	10	.524	1	0--	-	3.83	4.07
2001 Charlotte	A+	1	0	0	0	4.1	13	3	0	0	0	0	0	0	0	0	8	0	0	1	0	1.000	0	0--	-	0.00	0.00
2001 Tulsa	AA	25	25	1	0	156.0	686	150	85	78	15	8	6	16	62	2	162	16	0	10	10	.500	0	0--	-	4.17	4.50
2002 Oklahoma	AAA	20	20	0	0	106.2	448	100	49	43	4	1	4	7	28	0	99	5	0	5	6	.455	0	0--	-	3.03	3.63
2002 Texas	AL	15	4	0	4	34.1	168	42	26	24	4	2	0	2	26	2	28	3	1	1	3	.250	0	0-2	0	7.22	6.29

Darren Lewis

Bats: R **Throws:** R **Pos:** LF-22; CF-18; PH-11; RF-9; PR-6 **Ht:** 6'0" **Wt:** 200 **Born:** 8/28/67 **Age:** 35

Year Team	Lg	G	AB	H	2B	3B	HR	(Hm	Rd)	TB	R	RBI	RC	TBB	IBB	SO	HBP	SH	SF	SB	CS	SB%	GDP	Avg	OBP	Slg
1990 Oakland	AL	25	35	8	0	0	0	(0	0)	8	4	1	4	7	0	4	1	3	0	2	0	1.00	2	.229	.372	.229
1991 San Francisco	NL	72	222	55	5	3	1	(0	1)	69	41	15	28	36	0	30	2	7	0	13	7	.65	1	.248	.358	.311
1992 San Francisco	NL	100	320	74	8	1	1	(1	0)	87	38	18	29	29	0	46	1	10	2	28	8	.78	5	.231	.295	.272
1993 San Francisco	NL	136	522	132	17	7	2	(2	0)	169	84	48	55	30	0	40	7	12	1	46	15	.75	4	.253	.302	.324
1994 San Francisco	NL	114	451	116	15	9	4	(4	0)	161	70	29	58	53	0	50	4	4	1	30	13	.70	6	.257	.340	.357
1995 SF-Cin	NL	132	472	118	13	3	1	(1	0)	140	66	24	43	34	0	57	8	12	1	32	18	.64	9	.250	.311	.297
1996 Chicago	AL	141	337	77	12	2	4	(0	4)	105	55	53	38	45	1	40	3	15	5	21	5	.81	9	.228	.321	.312
1997 CWS-LA	NL	107	154	41	4	1	1	(0	1)	50	22	15	18	17	0	31	0	7	0	14	6	.70	3	.266	.339	.325
1998 Boston	AL	155	585	157	25	3	8	(5	3)	212	95	63	79	70	0	94	8	2	5	29	12	.71	12	.268	.352	.362
1999 Boston	AL	135	470	113	14	6	2	(1	1)	145	63	40	47	45	0	52	5	14	4	16	10	.62	5	.240	.311	.309
2000 Boston	AL	97	270	65	12	0	2	(0	2)	83	44	17	27	22	0	34	3	8	0	10	5	.67	2	.241	.305	.307
2001 Boston	AL	81	164	46	9	1	1	(0	1)	60	18	12	19	8	0	25	3	5	0	5	5	.50	2	.280	.326	.366
2002 NY	NL	58	79	19	3	1	0	(0	0)	24	7	7	8	7	0	11	3	2	0	1	3	.25	0	.241	.326	.304
1995 San Francisco	NL	74	309	78	10	3	1	(1	0)	97	47	16	30	17	0	37	6	7	1	21	7	.75	6	.252	.303	.314
1995 Cincinnati	NL	58	163	40	3	0	0	(0	0)	43	19	8	13	17	0	20	2	5	0	11	11	.50	3	.245	.324	.264
1997 Chicago	AL	81	77	18	1	0	0	(0	0)	19	15	5	7	11	0	14	0	5	0	11	4	.73	2	.234	.330	.247
1997 Los Angeles	NL	26	77	23	3	1	1	(0	1)	31	7	10	11	6	0	17	0	2	0	3	2	.60	1	.299	.349	.403
13 ML YEARS		1353	4081	1021	137	37	27	(14	13)	1313	607	342	453	403	1	514	48	101	19	247	107	.70	58	.250	.323	.322

Brad Lidge

Pitches: R **Bats:** R **Pos:** RP-5; SP-1 **Ht:** 6'5" **Wt:** 200 **Born:** 12/23/76 **Age:** 26

Year Team	Lg	G	GS	CG	GF	IP	BFP	H	R	ER	HR	SH	SF	HB	TBB	IBB	SO	WP	Bk	W	L	Pct	ShO	Sv-Op	Hld	ERC	ERA
1998 Quad City	A	4	4	0	0	11.0	50	10	5	4	0	0	0	1	5	0	6	1	0	0	1	.000	0	0--	-	3.24	3.27
1999 Kissimmee	A+	6	6	0	0	21.1	82	13	8	8	0	0	0	0	11	0	19	2	0	0	2	.000	0	0--	-	1.99	3.38
2000 Kissimmee	A+	8	8	0	0	41.2	164	28	14	13	3	1	0	1	15	0	46	1	2	4	2	.667	0	0--	-	2.20	2.81
2001 Round Rock	AA	5	5	0	0	26.0	107	21	5	5	1	1	1	2	7	0	42	1	0	2	0	1.000	0	0--	-	2.44	1.73
2002 Round Rock	AA	5	0	0	1	11.0	44	9	4	3	0	0	0	0	3	0	18	0	0	1	1	.500	0	0--	-	2.06	2.45
2002 New Orleans	AAA	24	19	0	1	111.2	459	83	47	42	9	1	2	7	47	0	110	5	1	5	5	.500	0	0--	-	2.93	3.39
2002 Houston	NL	6	1	0	2	8.2	48	12	6	6	0	1	0	2	9	1	12	0	0	1	0	1.000	0	0-0	0	8.90	6.23

Cory Lidle

Pitches: R **Bats:** R **Pos:** SP-30; RP-1 **Ht:** 5'11" **Wt:** 192 **Born:** 3/22/72 **Age:** 31

Year Team	Lg	G	GS	CG	GF	IP	BFP	H	R	ER	HR	SH	SF	HB	TBB	IBB	SO	WP	Bk	W	L	Pct	ShO	Sv-Op	Hld	ERC	ERA
2002 Sacramento*	AAA	1	1	0	0	4.0	16	2	1	1	0	0	0	1	3	0	3	0	0	0	0	-	0	0--	-	3.21	2.25
1997 New York	NL	54	2	0	20	81.2	345	86	38	32	7	4	4	3	20	4	54	2	0	7	2	.778	0	2-3	9	3.75	3.53
1999 Tampa Bay	AL	5	1	0	1	5.0	24	8	4	4	0	0	0	0	2	0	4	0	0	1	0	1.000	0	0-0	0	6.98	7.20
2000 Tampa Bay	AL	31	11	0	5	96.2	424	114	61	54	13	3	1	3	29	3	62	6	0	4	6	.400	0	0-0	2	5.06	5.03
2001 Oakland	AL	29	29	1	0	188.0	762	170	84	75	23	2	1	10	47	7	118	5	0	13	6	.684	0	0-0	0	3.35	3.59
2002 Oakland	AL	31	30	2	0	192.0	796	191	90	83	17	5	6	6	39	3	111	6	1	8	10	.444	2	0-0	0	3.31	3.89
5 ML YEARS		150	73	3	26	563.1	2351	569	277	248	60	14	12	22	137	17	349	19	1	33	24	.579	2	2-3	11	3.70	3.96

Jon Lieber

Pitches: R **Bats:** L **Pos:** SP-21 **Ht:** 6'2" **Wt:** 230 **Born:** 4/2/70 **Age:** 33

Year Team	Lg	G	GS	CG	GF	IP	BFP	H	R	ER	HR	SH	SF	HB	TBB	IBB	SO	WP	Bk	W	L	Pct	ShO	Sv-Op	Hld	ERC	ERA
1994 Pittsburgh	NL	17	17	1	0	108.2	460	116	62	45	12	3	3	1	25	3	71	2	3	6	7	.462	0	0-0	0	3.83	3.73
1995 Pittsburgh	NL	21	12	0	3	72.2	327	103	56	51	7	5	6	4	14	0	45	3	0	4	7	.364	0	0-1	3	5.96	6.32
1996 Pittsburgh	NL	51	15	0	6	142.0	600	156	70	63	19	7	2	3	28	2	94	0	0	9	5	.643	0	1-4	9	4.12	3.99
1997 Pittsburgh	NL	33	32	1	0	188.1	799	193	102	94	23	6	7	1	51	8	160	3	1	11	14	.440	0	0-0	0	3.78	4.49
1998 Pittsburgh	NL	29	28	2	1	171.0	731	182	93	78	23	7	4	3	40	4	138	0	3	8	14	.364	0	1-1	0	4.00	4.11
1999 Chicago	NL	31	31	0	0	203.1	875	226	107	92	28	7	11	1	46	6	186	2	2	10	11	.476	1	0-0	0	4.19	4.07
2000 Chicago	NL	35	35	6	0	251.0	1047	248	130	123	36	9	7	10	54	3	192	2	2	12	11	.522	0	0-0	0	3.70	4.41
2001 Chicago	NL	34	34	5	0	232.1	958	226	104	98	25	13	9	7	41	4	148	4	1	20	6	.769	1	0-0	0	3.19	3.80
2002 Chicago	NL	21	21	3	0	141.0	582	153	64	58	15	10	6	1	12	2	87	0	0	6	8	.429	0	0-0	0	3.33	3.70
9 ML YEARS		272	225	21	10	1510.1	6379	1603	788	702	188	67	55	31	311	32	1121	16	12	86	83	.509	3	2-6	12	3.84	4.18

Mike Lieberthal

Bats: R **Throws:** R **Pos:** C-129; PH-3 **Ht:** 6'0" **Wt:** 190 **Born:** 1/18/72 **Age:** 31

Year Team	Lg	G	AB	H	2B	3B	HR	(Hm	Rd)	TB	R	RBI	RC	TBB	IBB	SO	HBP	SH	SF	SB	CS	SB%	GDP	Avg	OBP	Slg
1994 Philadelphia	NL	24	79	21	3	1	1	(1	0)	29	6	5	8	3	0	5	1	1	0	0	0	-	4	.266	.301	.367
1995 Philadelphia	NL	16	47	12	2	0	0	(0	0)	14	1	4	5	5	0	5	0	2	0	0	0	-	4	.255	.327	.298
1996 Philadelphia	NL	50	166	42	8	0	7	(4	3)	71	21	23	21	10	0	30	2	0	4	0	0	-	4	.253	.297	.428
1997 Philadelphia	NL	134	455	112	27	1	20	(11	9)	201	59	77	62	44	1	76	4	0	7	3	4	.43	10	.246	.314	.442
1998 Philadelphia	NL	86	313	80	15	3	8	(5	3)	125	39	45	39	17	1	44	7	0	5	2	1	.67	4	.256	.304	.399
1999 Philadelphia	NL	145	510	153	33	1	31	(10	21)	281	84	96	96	44	7	86	11	1	8	0	0	-	9	.300	.363	.551
2000 Philadelphia	NL	108	389	108	30	0	15	(8	7)	183	55	71	62	40	3	53	6	0	3	2	0	1.00	12	.278	.352	.470
2001 Philadelphia	NL	34	121	28	8	0	2	(0	2)	42	21	11	13	12	2	21	3	0	0	0	0	-	3	.231	.316	.347
2002 Philadelphia	NL	130	476	133	29	2	15	(7	8)	211	46	52	55	38	2	58	14	0	2	0	1	.00	16	.279	.349	.443
9 ML YEARS		727	2556	689	155	8	99	(46	53)	1157	332	384	361	213	16	378	48	4	29	7	6	.54	68	.270	.334	.453

Jeff Liefer

Bats: L **Throws:** R **Pos:** 1B-31; LF-25; RF-12; PH-12; DH-4; PR-3   **Ht:** 6'3" **Wt:** 210 **Born:** 8/17/74 **Age:** 28

Year Team	Lg	G	AB	H	2B	3B	HR	(Hm	Rd)	TB	R	RBI	RC	TBB	IBB	SO	HBP	SH	SF	SB	CS	SB%	GDP	Avg	OBP	Slg
1999 Chicago	AL	45	113	28	7	1	0	(0	0)	37	8	14	11	8	0	28	0	0	1	2	0	1.00	3	.248	.295	.327
2000 Chicago	AL	5	11	2	0	0	0	(0	0)	2	0	0	0	0	0	4	0	0	0	0	0	-	0	.182	.182	.182
2001 Chicago	AL	83	254	65	13	0	18	(10	8)	132	36	39	40	20	1	69	2	1	2	0	1	.00	6	.256	.313	.520
2002 Chicago	AL	76	204	47	8	0	7	(4	3)	76	28	26	24	19	2	60	0	0	1	0	0	-	3	.230	.295	.373
4 ML YEARS		209	582	142	28	1	25	(14	11)	247	72	79	75	47	3	161	2	1	4	2	1	.67	12	.244	.301	.424

Kerry Ligtenberg

Pitches: R **Bats:** R **Pos:** RP-52   **Ht:** 6'2" **Wt:** 215 **Born:** 5/11/71 **Age:** 32

Year Team	Lg	G	GS	CG	GF	IP	BFP	H	R	ER	HR	SH	SF	HB	TBB	IBB	SO	WP	Bk	W	L	Pct	ShO	Sv-Op	Hld	ERC	ERA
1997 Atlanta	NL	15	0	0	9	15.0	61	12	5	5	4	0	0	0	4	2	19	0	0	1	0	1.000	0	1-1	0	3.26	3.00
1998 Atlanta	NL	75	0	0	56	73.0	290	51	24	22	6	1	1	0	24	1	79	3	0	3	2	.600	0	30-34	11	2.13	2.71
2000 Atlanta	NL	59	0	0	19	52.1	217	43	21	21	7	2	1	0	24	5	51	0	0	2	3	.400	0	12-14	12	3.46	3.61
2001 Atlanta	NL	53	0	0	24	59.2	254	50	22	20	4	1	2	0	30	8	56	3	0	3	3	.500	0	1-2	0	3.14	3.02
2002 Atlanta	NL	52	0	0	25	66.2	281	52	23	22	6	3	1	0	33	3	51	1	1	3	4	.429	0	0-0	2	3.10	2.97
5 ML YEARS		254	0	0	133	266.2	1103	208	95	90	27	7	5	0	115	19	256	7	1	12	12	.500	0	44-51	25	2.92	3.04

Ted Lilly

Pitches: L **Bats:** L **Pos:** SP-16; RP-6   **Ht:** 6'0" **Wt:** 185 **Born:** 1/4/76 **Age:** 27

Year Team	Lg	G	GS	CG	GF	IP	BFP	H	R	ER	HR	SH	SF	HB	TBB	IBB	SO	WP	Bk	W	L	Pct	ShO	Sv-Op	Hld	ERC	ERA
1999 Montreal	NL	9	3	0	1	23.2	110	30	20	20	7	0	1	3	9	0	28	1	0	0	1	.000	0	0-0	0	7.76	7.61
2000 New York	AL	7	0	0	1	8.0	39	8	6	5	1	0	0	0	5	0	11	1	0	0	0	-	0	0-0	0	4.76	5.63
2001 New York	AL	26	21	0	2	120.2	537	126	81	72	20	2	5	7	51	1	112	9	2	5	6	.455	0	0-0	0	5.10	5.37
2002 NYY-Oak	AL	22	16	2	1	100.0	413	80	43	41	15	0	3	6	31	3	77	6	1	5	7	.417	1	0-0	0	3.14	3.69
2002 New York	AL	16	11	2	1	76.2	314	57	31	29	10	0	3	5	24	3	59	6	0	3	6	.333	1	0-0	0	2.74	3.40
2002 Oakland	AL	6	5	0	0	23.1	99	23	12	12	5	0	0	1	7	0	18	0	1	2	1	.667	0	0-0	0	4.56	4.63
4 ML YEARS		64	40	2	5	252.1	1099	244	150	138	43	2	9	16	96	4	228	17	4	10	14	.417	1	0-0	0	4.50	4.92

Jose Lima

Pitches: R **Bats:** R **Pos:** SP-12; RP-8   **Ht:** 6'2" **Wt:** 205 **Born:** 9/30/72 **Age:** 30

Year Team	Lg	G	GS	CG	GF	IP	BFP	H	R	ER	HR	SH	SF	HB	TBB	IBB	SO	WP	Bk	W	L	Pct	ShO	Sv-Op	Hld	ERC	ERA
1994 Detroit	AL	3	1	0	1	6.2	34	11	10	10	2	0	0	0	3	1	7	1	0	0	1	.000	0	0-0	0	9.61	13.50
1995 Detroit	AL	15	15	0	0	73.2	320	85	52	50	10	2	1	4	18	4	37	5	0	3	9	.250	0	0-0	0	4.73	6.11
1996 Detroit	AL	39	4	0	15	72.2	329	87	48	46	13	5	3	5	22	4	59	3	0	5	6	.455	0	3-7	6	5.53	5.70
1997 Houston	NL	52	1	0	15	75.0	321	79	45	44	9	6	3	5	16	2	63	2	0	1	6	.143	0	2-2	3	3.96	5.28
1998 Houston	NL	33	33	3	0	233.1	950	229	100	96	34	11	5	7	32	1	169	4	0	16	8	.667	1	0-0	0	3.36	3.70
1999 Houston	NL	35	35	3	0	246.1	1024	256	108	98	30	5	7	2	44	2	187	8	0	21	10	.677	0	0-0	0	3.58	3.58
2000 Houston	NL	33	33	0	0	196.1	895	251	152	145	48	12	12	2	68	3	124	3	0	7	16	.304	0	0-0	0	6.59	6.65
2001 Hou-Det	AL	32	27	2	3	165.2	719	197	114	102	35	5	9	9	38	3	84	4	0	6	12	.333	0	0-0	0	5.53	5.54
2002 Detroit	AL	20	12	0	3	68.1	304	86	60	59	12	1	6	2	21	0	33	2	0	4	6	.400	0	0-0	0	5.97	7.77
2001 Houston	NL	14	9	0	3	53.0	249	77	48	43	12	4	4	5	16	1	41	3	0	1	2	.333	0	0-0	0	7.90	7.30
2001 Detroit	AL	18	18	2	0	112.2	470	120	66	59	23	1	5	4	22	2	43	1	0	5	10	.333	0	0-0	0	4.49	4.71
9 ML YEARS		262	161	8	37	1138.0	4896	1281	689	650	193	47	46	36	262	20	763	32	0	63	74	.460	1	5-9	9	4.69	5.14

Mike Lincoln

Pitches: R **Bats:** R **Pos:** RP-55   **Ht:** 6'2" **Wt:** 203 **Born:** 4/10/75 **Age:** 28

Year Team	Lg	G	GS	CG	GF	IP	BFP	H	R	ER	HR	SH	SF	HB	TBB	IBB	SO	WP	Bk	W	L	Pct	ShO	Sv-Op	Hld	ERC	ERA
2002 Nashville*	AAA	10	0	0	7	14.2	61	14	2	2	0	0	0	0	2	0	15	1	0	0	0	-	0	2--	-	2.14	1.23
1999 Minnesota	AL	18	15	0	0	76.1	353	102	59	58	11	2	6	1	26	0	27	4	0	3	10	.231	0	0-0	0	6.16	6.84
2000 Minnesota	AL	8	4	0	1	20.2	109	36	25	25	10	0	0	2	13	0	15	1	0	0	3	.000	0	0-0	0	14.32	10.89
2001 Pittsburgh	NL	31	0	0	5	40.1	168	34	16	12	3	1	1	4	11	0	24	2	0	2	1	.667	0	0-2	7	2.94	2.68
2002 Pittsburgh	NL	55	0	0	9	72.1	309	80	28	25	7	2	4	0	27	8	50	2	0	2	4	.333	0	0-3	11	4.49	3.11
4 ML YEARS		112	19	0	15	209.2	939	252	128	120	31	5	11	7	77	8	116	9	0	7	18	.280	0	0-5	19	5.58	5.15

Scott Linebrink

Pitches: R **Bats:** R **Pos:** RP-22   **Ht:** 6'2" **Wt:** 200 **Born:** 8/4/76 **Age:** 26

Year Team	Lg	G	GS	CG	GF	IP	BFP	H	R	ER	HR	SH	SF	HB	TBB	IBB	SO	WP	Bk	W	L	Pct	ShO	Sv-Op	Hld	ERC	ERA
2002 New Orleans*	AAA	13	0	0	3	15.0	71	17	11	10	1	1	0	1	11	3	16	2	0	1	1	.500	0	0--	-	5.93	6.00
2002 Round Rock*	AA	2	2	0	0	2.0	9	2	0	0	0	0	0	0	2	0	1	0	0	0	0	-	0	0--	-	6.15	0.00
2000 SF-Hou	NL	11	0	0	4	12.0	63	18	8	8	4	0	0	3	8	0	6	0	0	0	0	-	0	0-0	0	11.88	6.00
2001 Houston	NL	9	0	0	2	10.1	44	6	4	3	0	1	1	2	6	0	9	1	0	0	0	-	0	0-0	0	2.54	2.61
2002 Houston	NL	22	0	0	4	24.1	119	31	21	19	2	0	2	1	13	4	24	0	0	0	0	-	0	0-0	1	5.75	7.03
2000 San Francisco	NL	3	0	0	1	2.1	16	7	3	3	1	0	0	0	2	0	0	0	0	0	0	-	0	0-0	0	24.13	11.57
2000 Houston	NL	8	0	0	3	9.2	47	11	5	5	3	0	0	3	6	0	6	0	0	0	0	-	0	0-0	0	9.21	4.66
3 ML YEARS		42	0	0	10	46.2	226	55	33	30	6	1	3	6	27	4	39	1	0	0	0	-	0	0-0	1	6.37	5.79

Doug Linton

Pitches: R **Bats:** R **Pos:** RP **Ht:** 6'1" **Wt:** 190 **Born:** 2/9/65 **Age:** 38

			HOW MUCH HE PITCHED					WHAT HE GAVE UP											THE RESULTS						
Year Team	Lg	G	GS	CG	GF	IP	BFP	H	R	ER	HR	SH	SF	HB	TBB	IBB	SO	WP	Bk	W	L	Pct	ShO	Sv-Op	Hld	ERC	ERA
2002 Richmond*	AAA	28	28	1	0	174.0	709	167	63	49	14	4	3	7	26	0	160	9	1	9	11	.450	0	0- -	-	2.93	2.53
1992 Toronto	AL	8	3	0	2	24.0	116	31	23	23	5	1	2	0	17	0	16	2	0	1	3	.250	0	0-0	0	8.19	8.63
1993 Tor-Ana	AL	23	1	0	6	36.2	178	46	30	30	8	0	3	1	23	1	23	2	0	2	1	.667	0	0-1	0	7.53	7.36
1994 New York	NL	32	3	0	8	50.1	241	74	27	25	4	3	1	0	20	3	29	2	0	6	2	.750	0	0-0	0	6.55	4.47
1995 Kansas City	AL	7	2	0	0	22.1	98	22	21	18	4	0	0	2	10	1	13	0	0	0	1	.000	0	0-0	0	5.10	7.25
1996 Kansas City	AL	21	18	0	0	104.0	452	111	65	58	13	6	2	8	26	1	87	3	1	7	9	.438	0	0-0	1	4.28	5.02
1999 Baltimore	AL	14	8	0	0	59.0	264	69	41	39	14	4	0	2	25	1	31	4	0	1	4	.200	0	0-0	0	6.42	5.95
1993 Toronto	AL	4	1	0	0	11.0	55	11	8	8	0	0	2	1	9	0	4	0	0	0	1	.000	0	0-0	0	5.03	6.55
1993 Anaheim	AL	19	0	0	6	25.2	123	35	22	22	8	0	1	0	14	1	19	2	0	2	0	1.000	0	0-1	0	8.65	7.71
6 ML YEARS		105	35	0	16	296.1	1349	353	207	193	48	14	8	13	121	7	199	13	1	17	20	.459	0	0-1	1	5.83	5.86

Mark Little

Bats: R **Throws:** R **Pos:** PH-29; RF-24; LF-20; CF-13; PR-9 **Ht:** 6'0" **Wt:** 195 **Born:** 7/11/72 **Age:** 30

					BATTING														BASERUNNING				AVERAGES		
Year Team	Lg	G	AB	H	2B	3B	HR	(Hm	Rd)	TB	R	RBI	RC	TBB	IBB	SO	HBP	SH	SF	SB	CS	SB%	GDP	Avg	OBP	Slg
2002 Norfolk*	AAA	2	10	5	0	0	0	(-	-)	5	1	2	3	1	0	3	0	0	0	0	0	-	0	.500	.545	.500
2002 Tucson*	AAA	13	54	17	3	1	2	(-	-)	28	6	8	8	0	0	11	0	0	2	2	1	.67	0	.315	.304	.519
1998 St Louis	NL	7	12	1	0	0	0	(0	0)	1	0	0	0	2	0	5	0	1	0	1	0	1.00	0	.083	.214	.083
2001 Colorado	NL	51	85	29	6	0	3	(3	0)	44	18	13	16	1	1	20	4	0	0	5	2	.71	0	.341	.378	.518
2002 Col-NYM-Ari	NL	79	130	27	5	3	0	(0	0)	38	28	7	16	15	0	34	8	1	0	2	2	.50	1	.208	.327	.292
2002 Colorado	NL	61	105	21	5	2	0	(0	0)	30	20	5	11	13	0	28	4	1	0	2	1	.67	1	.200	.311	.286
2002 New York	NL	3	3	0	0	0	0	(0	0)	0	0	0	0	0	0	1	0	0	0	0	1	.00	0	.000	.000	.000
2002 Arizona	NL	15	22	6	0	1	0	(0	0)	8	8	2	5	2	0	5	4	0	0	0	0	-	0	.273	.429	.364
3 ML YEARS		137	227	57	11	3	3	(3	0)	83	46	20	32	18	1	59	12	2	0	8	4	.67	1	.251	.339	.366

Graeme Lloyd

Pitches: L **Bats:** L **Pos:** RP-66 **Ht:** 6'7" **Wt:** 225 **Born:** 4/9/67 **Age:** 36

				HOW MUCH HE PITCHED					WHAT HE GAVE UP											THE RESULTS						
Year Team	Lg	G	GS	CG	GF	IP	BFP	H	R	ER	HR	SH	SF	HB	TBB	IBB	SO	WP	Bk	W	L	Pct	ShO	Sv-Op	Hld	ERC	ERA
1993 Milwaukee	NL	55	0	0	12	63.2	269	64	24	20	5	1	2	3	13	3	31	4	0	3	4	.429	0	0-4	6	3.26	2.83
1994 Milwaukee	NL	43	0	0	21	47.0	203	49	28	27	4	1	2	3	15	6	31	2	0	2	3	.400	0	3-6	3	3.94	5.17
1995 Milwaukee	NL	33	0	0	14	32.0	127	28	16	16	4	1	4	0	8	2	13	3	0	0	5	.000	0	4-6	9	2.98	4.50
1996 Mil-NYY		65	0	0	15	56.2	252	61	30	27	4	5	3	1	22	4	30	4	0	2	6	.250	0	0-5	17	4.13	4.29
1997 New York	AL	46	0	0	17	49.0	217	55	24	18	6	3	5	1	20	7	26	3	0	1	1	.500	0	1-1	2	4.84	3.31
1998 New York	AL	50	0	0	8	37.2	145	26	10	7	3	0	1	2	6	2	20	2	0	3	0	1.000	0	0-2	9	1.67	1.67
1999 Toronto	AL	74	0	0	25	72.0	301	68	36	29	11	1	1	4	23	4	47	1	0	5	3	.625	0	3-9	22	4.00	3.63
2001 Montreal	AL	84	0	0	28	70.1	303	74	38	34	6	2	2	6	21	2	44	1	0	9	5	.643	0	1-3	11	4.19	4.35
2002 Mon-Fla	NL	66	0	0	19	57.0	253	67	34	33	6	4	3	2	19	4	37	2	0	4	5	.444	0	5-8	11	4.88	5.21
1996 Milwaukee	NL	52	0	0	15	51.0	217	49	19	16	3	5	1	1	17	3	24	0	0	2	4	.333	0	0-3	15	3.28	2.82
1996 New York	AL	13	0	0	0	5.2	35	12	11	11	1	0	2	0	5	1	6	4	0	0	2	.000	0	0-2	2	13.39	17.47
2002 Montreal	NL	41	0	0	14	30.2	138	41	21	20	5	2	1	1	8	3	17	1	0	2	3	.400	0	5-7	9	5.97	5.87
2002 Florida	NL	25	0	0	5	26.1	115	26	13	13	1	2	2	1	11	1	20	1	0	2	2	.500	0	0-1	2	3.69	4.44
9 ML YEARS		516	0	0	159	485.1	2070	492	240	211	49	18	23	22	147	34	279	22	0	29	32	.475	0	17-44	90	3.85	3.91

Paul Lo Duca

Bats: R **Throws:** R **Pos:** C-137; 1B-18; LF-9; PH-8 **Ht:** 5'10" **Wt:** 185 **Born:** 4/12/72 **Age:** 31

					BATTING														BASERUNNING				AVERAGES		
Year Team	Lg	G	AB	H	2B	3B	HR	(Hm	Rd)	TB	R	RBI	RC	TBB	IBB	SO	HBP	SH	SF	SB	CS	SB%	GDP	Avg	OBP	Slg
1998 Los Angeles	NL	6	14	4	1	0	0	(0	0)	5	2	1	1	0	0	1	0	0	0	0	0	-	0	.286	.286	.357
1999 Los Angeles	NL	36	95	22	1	0	3	(1	2)	32	11	11	9	10	4	9	2	1	2	1	2	.33	3	.232	.312	.337
2000 Los Angeles	NL	34	65	16	2	0	2	(0	2)	24	6	8	6	6	0	8	0	2	2	0	2	.00	2	.246	.301	.369
2001 Los Angeles	NL	125	460	147	28	0	25	(11	14)	250	71	90	89	39	2	30	6	5	9	2	4	.33	11	.320	.374	.543
2002 Los Angeles	NL	149	580	163	38	1	10	(5	5)	233	74	64	72	34	2	31	10	4	4	3	1	.75	20	.281	.330	.402
5 ML YEARS		350	1214	352	70	1	40	(17	23)	544	164	174	177	89	8	79	18	12	17	6	9	.40	36	.290	.343	.448

Esteban Loaiza

Pitches: R **Bats:** R **Pos:** SP-25 **Ht:** 6'3" **Wt:** 205 **Born:** 12/31/71 **Age:** 31

				HOW MUCH HE PITCHED					WHAT HE GAVE UP											THE RESULTS						
Year Team	Lg	G	GS	CG	GF	IP	BFP	H	R	ER	HR	SH	SF	HB	TBB	IBB	SO	WP	Bk	W	L	Pct	ShO	Sv-Op	Hld	ERC	ERA
2002 Dunedin*	A+	2	2	0	0	5.0	18	2	0	0	0	0	0	0	2	0	2	0	0	0	0	-	0	0- -	-	1.01	0.00
2002 Syracuse*	AAA	1	1	0	0	4.1	18	4	1	1	0	0	0	0	0	0	4	0	0	0	0	-	0	0- -	-	1.55	2.08
2002 Tennessee*	AA	2	2	0	0	14.1	49	10	3	3	0	0	0	0	1	0	13	0	0	2	0	1.000	0	0- -	-	1.24	1.88
1995 Pittsburgh	NL	32	31	1	0	172.2	762	205	115	99	21	10	9	5	55	3	85	6	1	8	9	.471	0	0-0	0	5.10	5.16
1996 Pittsburgh	NL	10	10	1	0	52.2	236	65	32	29	11	3	1	2	19	2	32	0	0	2	3	.400	1	0-0	0	6.30	4.96
1997 Pittsburgh	NL	33	32	1	0	196.1	851	214	99	90	17	10	7	12	56	9	122	2	3	11	11	.500	0	0-0	0	4.20	4.13
1998 Pit-Tex		35	28	1	3	171.0	751	199	107	98	28	7	12	5	52	4	108	4	2	9	11	.450	0	0-1	0	5.19	5.16
1999 Texas	AL	30	15	0	4	120.1	517	128	65	61	10	7	4	0	40	2	77	2	0	9	5	.643	0	0-0	0	4.03	4.56
2000 Tex-Tor		34	31	1	2	199.1	871	228	112	101	29	4	5	13	57	1	137	1	0	10	13	.435	1	1-1	0	5.07	4.56
2001 Toronto	AL	36	30	1	0	190.0	837	239	113	106	27	6	4	9	40	1	110	1	1	11	11	.500	0	0-0	0	5.30	5.02
2002 Toronto	AL	25	25	3	0	151.1	670	192	102	96	18	1	6	4	38	3	87	1	0	9	10	.474	1	0-0	0	5.26	5.71
1998 Pittsburgh	NL	21	14	0	3	91.2	394	96	50	46	13	5	7	3	30	1	53	1	2	6	5	.545	0	0-1	0	4.48	4.52
1998 Texas	AL	14	14	1	0	79.1	357	103	57	52	15	2	5	2	22	3	55	3	0	3	6	.333	0	0-0	0	6.04	5.90
2000 Texas	AL	20	17	0	2	107.1	480	133	67	64	21	2	4	3	31	1	75	1	0	5	6	.455	0	1-1	0	5.81	5.37
2000 Toronto	AL	14	14	1	0	92.0	391	95	45	37	8	2	1	10	26	0	62	0	0	5	7	.417	1	0-0	0	4.22	3.62
8 ML YEARS		235	202	9	10	1253.2	5495	1470	745	680	161	48	48	50	357	25	758	17	7	69	73	.486	4	1-2	0	4.96	4.88

Keith Lockhart

Bats: L **Throws:** R **Pos:** 2B-88; PH-45; 3B-1

Ht: 5'10" **Wt:** 170 **Born:** 11/10/64 **Age:** 38

Year Team	Lg	G	AB	H	2B	3B	HR	(Hm	Rd)	TB	R	RBI	RC	TBB	IBB	SO	HBP	SH	SF	SB	CS	SB%	GDP	Avg	OBP	Slg
1994 San Diego	NL	27	43	9	0	0	2	(2	0)	15	4	6	4	4	0	10	1	1	1	1	0	1.00	2	.209	.286	.349
1995 Kansas City	AL	94	274	88	19	3	6	(3	3)	131	41	33	48	14	2	21	4	1	7	8	1	.89	2	.321	.355	.478
1996 Kansas City	AL	138	433	118	33	3	7	(4	3)	178	49	55	56	30	4	40	2	1	5	11	6	.65	7	.273	.319	.411
1997 Atlanta	NL	96	147	41	5	3	6	(3	3)	70	25	32	23	14	0	17	1	3	4	0	0	-	4	.279	.337	.476
1998 Atlanta	NL	109	366	94	21	0	9	(4	5)	142	50	37	45	29	0	37	1	2	3	2	2	.50	2	.257	.311	.388
1999 Atlanta	NL	108	161	42	3	1	1	(0	1)	50	20	21	19	19	0	21	1	0	3	3	1	.75	2	.261	.337	.311
2000 Atlanta	NL	113	275	73	12	3	2	(1	1)	97	32	32	31	29	7	31	0	5	4	4	1	.80	10	.265	.331	.353
2001 Atlanta	NL	104	178	39	6	0	3	(0	3)	54	17	12	16	16	1	22	2	2	1	1	2	.33	1	.219	.289	.303
2002 Atlanta	NL	128	296	64	13	3	5	(3	2)	98	34	32	31	27	9	50	1	5	2	0	1	.00	2	.216	.282	.331
9 ML YEARS		917	2173	568	112	16	41	(20	21)	835	272	260	273	182	23	249	13	20	30	30	14	.68	34	.261	.318	.384

Carlton Loewer

Pitches: R **Bats:** R **Pos:** SP

Ht: 6'6" **Wt:** 211 **Born:** 9/24/73 **Age:** 29

Year Team	Lg	G	GS	CG	GF	IP	BFP	H	R	ER	HR	SH	SF	HB	TBB	IBB	SO	WP	Bk	W	L	Pct	ShO	Sv-Op	Hld	ERC	ERA
1998 Philadelphia	NL	21	21	1	0	122.2	549	154	86	83	18	5	8	3	39	1	58	4	0	7	8	.467	0	0-0	0	5.70	6.09
1999 Philadelphia	NL	20	13	2	2	89.2	385	100	54	51	9	5	6	0	26	0	48	3	0	2	6	.250	1	0-0	1	4.31	5.12
2001 San Diego	NL	2	2	0	0	4.1	29	13	12	12	2	1	0	0	3	0	1	0	0	0	2	.000	0	0-0	0	23.60	24.92
3 ML YEARS		43	36	3	2	216.2	963	267	152	146	29	11	14	3	68	1	107	7	0	9	16	.360	1	0-0	1	5.39	6.06

Kenny Lofton

Bats: L **Throws:** L **Pos:** CF-136; PH-6

Ht: 6'0" **Wt:** 180 **Born:** 5/31/67 **Age:** 36

Year Team	Lg	G	AB	H	2B	3B	HR	(Hm	Rd)	TB	R	RBI	RC	TBB	IBB	SO	HBP	SH	SF	SB	CS	SB%	GDP	Avg	OBP	Slg
1991 Houston	NL	20	74	15	1	0	0	(0	0)	16	9	0	4	5	0	19	0	0	0	2	1	.67	0	.203	.253	.216
1992 Cleveland	AL	148	576	164	15	8	5	(3	2)	210	96	42	88	68	3	54	2	4	1	66	12	.85	7	.285	.362	.365
1993 Cleveland	AL	148	569	185	28	8	1	(1	0)	232	116	42	107	81	6	83	1	2	4	70	14	.83	8	.325	.408	.408
1994 Cleveland	AL	112	459	160	32	9	12	(10	2)	246	105	57	105	52	5	56	2	4	6	60	12	.83	5	.349	.412	.536
1995 Cleveland	AL	118	481	149	22	13	7	(5	2)	218	93	53	83	40	6	49	1	4	3	54	15	.78	6	.310	.362	.453
1996 Cleveland	AL	154	662	210	35	4	14	(7	7)	295	132	67	118	61	3	82	0	7	6	75	17	.82	7	.317	.372	.446
1997 Atlanta	NL	122	493	164	20	6	5	(3	2)	211	90	48	84	64	5	83	2	2	3	27	20	.57	10	.333	.409	.428
1998 Cleveland	AL	154	600	169	31	6	12	(6	6)	248	101	64	103	87	1	80	2	3	6	54	10	.84	7	.282	.371	.413
1999 Cleveland	AL	120	465	140	28	6	7	(1	6)	201	110	39	89	79	2	84	6	5	5	25	6	.81	6	.301	.405	.432
2000 Cleveland	AL	137	543	151	23	5	15	(10	5)	229	107	73	91	79	3	72	4	6	8	30	7	.81	11	.278	.369	.422
2001 Cleveland	AL	133	517	135	21	4	14	(9	5)	206	91	66	67	47	1	69	2	5	5	16	8	.67	8	.261	.322	.398
2002 CWS-SF		139	532	139	30	9	11	(3	8)	220	98	51	84	72	0	73	1	5	1	29	11	.73	1	.261	.350	.414
2002 Chicago	AL	93	352	91	20	6	8	(3	5)	147	68	42	58	49	0	51	0	4	1	22	8	.73	0	.259	.348	.418
2002 San Francisco	NL	46	180	48	10	3	3	(0	3)	73	30	9	26	23	0	22	1	1	0	7	3	.70	1	.267	.353	.406
12 ML YEARS		1505	5971	1781	286	78	103	(58	45)	2532	1148	602	1023	735	35	804	23	47	48	508	133	.79	76	.298	.375	.424

Kyle Lohse

Pitches: R **Bats:** R **Pos:** SP-31; RP-1

Ht: 6'2" **Wt:** 190 **Born:** 10/4/78 **Age:** 24

Year Team	Lg	G	GS	CG	GF	IP	BFP	H	R	ER	HR	SH	SF	HB	TBB	IBB	SO	WP	Bk	W	L	Pct	ShO	Sv-Op	Hld	ERC	ERA
1997 Cubs	R	12	11	0	0	47.2	210	46	22	16	0	1	1	1	22	0	49	3	0	2	2	.500	0	0--	-	3.43	3.02
1998 Rockford	A	28	26	3	1	170.2	712	158	76	61	8	8	5	11	45	1	121	13	1	13	8	.619	1	0--	-	3.04	3.22
1999 Daytona	A+	9	9	1	0	53.0	217	48	21	17	4	2	1	0	16	0	41	1	0	5	3	.625	1	0--	-	3.06	2.89
1999 Fort Myers	A+	7	7	0	0	41.2	180	47	28	24	5	2	4	4	9	0	33	1	0	2	3	.400	0	0--	-	4.62	5.18
1999 New Britain	AA	11	11	1	0	70.1	311	87	49	46	9	3	4	5	23	0	41	2	0	3	4	.429	0	0--	-	5.82	5.89
2000 New Britain	AA	28	28	0	0	167.0	744	196	123	112	23	5	6	3	55	0	124	6	0	3	18	.143	0	0--	-	5.10	6.04
2001 New Britain	AA	6	6	0	0	38.0	145	32	10	10	5	0	0	2	4	0	32	0	0	3	1	.750	0	0--	-	2.63	2.37
2001 Edmonton	AAA	8	8	1	0	49.0	208	50	21	17	3	0	0	4	13	0	48	3	0	4	2	.667	1	0--	-	3.74	3.12
2001 Minnesota	AL	19	16	0	2	90.1	402	102	60	57	16	1	5	8	29	0	64	5	0	4	7	.364	0	0-0	0	5.43	5.68
2002 Minnesota	AL	32	31	1	0	180.2	783	181	92	85	26	3	3	9	70	2	124	8	0	13	8	.619	1	0-1	0	4.55	4.23
2 ML YEARS		51	47	1	2	271.0	1185	283	152	142	42	4	8	17	99	2	188	13	0	17	15	.531	1	0-1	0	4.84	4.72

George Lombard

Bats: L **Throws:** R **Pos:** CF-40; LF-29; PH-3; RF-1; DH-1; PR-1

Ht: 6'0" **Wt:** 212 **Born:** 9/14/75 **Age:** 27

Year Team	Lg	G	AB	H	2B	3B	HR	(Hm	Rd)	TB	R	RBI	RC	TBB	IBB	SO	HBP	SH	SF	SB	CS	SB%	GDP	Avg	OBP	Slg
2002 Greenville*	AA	8	25	7	0	0	3	(-	-)	16	4	5	7	5	0	6	1	1	0	2	0	1.00	0	.280	.419	.640
2002 Richmond*	AAA	11	39	12	4	1	1	(-	-)	21	10	5	9	5	1	12	1	0	0	2	0	1.00	0	.308	.400	.538
1998 Atlanta	NL	6	6	2	0	0	1	(0	1)	5	2	1	2	0	0	1	0	0	0	1	0	1.00	0	.333	.333	.833
1999 Atlanta	NL	6	6	2	0	0	0	(0	0)	2	1	0	1	1	0	2	0	0	0	2	0	1.00	0	.333	.429	.333
2000 Atlanta	NL	27	39	4	0	0	0	(0	0)	8	2	0	1	0	0	14	1	0	0	4	0	1.00	2	.103	.146	.103
2002 Detroit	AL	72	241	58	11	3	5	(2	3)	90	34	13	26	20	1	78	1	7	1	13	2	.87	0	.241	.300	.373
4 ML YEARS		111	292	66	11	3	6	(2	4)	101	45	16	29	22	1	95	2	7	1	20	2	.91	2	.226	.284	.346

Terrence Long

Bats: L **Throws:** L **Pos:** CF-162; PR-2; PH-1

Ht: 6'1" **Wt:** 202 **Born:** 2/29/76 **Age:** 27

Year Team	Lg	G	AB	H	2B	3B	HR	(Hm	Rd)	TB	R	RBI	RC	TBB	IBB	SO	HBP	SH	SF	SB	CS	SB%	GDP	Avg	OBP	Slg
1999 New York	NL	3	3	0	0	0	0	(0	0)	0	0	0	0	0	0	2	0	0	0	0	0	-	1	.000	.000	.000
2000 Oakland	AL	138	584	168	34	4	18	(9	9)	264	104	80	85	43	1	77	1	0	3	5	0	1.00	18	.288	.336	.452

Year Team	Lg	G	AB	H	2B	3B	HR	(Hm	Rd)	TB	R	RBI	RC	TBB	IBB	SO	HBP	SH	SF	SB	CS	SB%	GDP	Avg	OBP	Slg
2001 Oakland	AL	**162**	629	178	37	4	12	(6	6)	259	90	85	84	52	8	103	0	0	6	9	3	.75	17	.283	.335	.412
2002 Oakland	AL	**162**	587	141	32	4	16	(9	7)	229	71	67	62	48	6	96	2	0	3	3	6	.33	17	.240	.298	.390
4 ML YEARS		465	1803	487	103	12	46	(24	22)	752	265	232	231	143	15	278	3	0	12	17	9	.65	53	.270	.323	.417

Braden Looper

Pitches: R **Bats:** R **Pos:** RP-78   **Ht:** 6'3" **Wt:** 220 **Born:** 10/28/74 **Age:** 28

Year Team	Lg	G	GS	CG	GF	IP	BFP	H	R	ER	HR	SH	SF	HB	TBB	IBB	SO	WP	Bk	W	L	Pct	ShO	Sv-Op	Hld	ERC	ERA
1998 St Louis	NL	4	0	0	3	3.1	16	5	4	2	1	0	1	0	1	0	4	1	0	0	1	.000	0	0-2	0	8.14	5.40
1999 Florida	NL	72	0	0	22	83.0	370	96	43	35	7	5	5	1	31	5	50	2	1	3	3	.500	0	0-4	8	4.67	3.80
2000 Florida	NL	73	0	0	23	67.1	311	71	41	33	3	3	2	5	36	6	29	5	0	5	1	.833	0	2-5	18	4.55	4.41
2001 Florida	NL	71	0	0	21	71.0	295	63	28	28	8	0	3	2	30	3	52	0	0	3	3	.500	0	3-6	16	3.77	3.55
2002 Florida	NL	78	0	0	40	86.0	349	73	31	30	8	3	0	1	28	3	55	1	0	2	5	.286	0	13-16	16	2.98	3.14
5 ML YEARS		298	0	0	109	310.2	1341	308	147	128	27	11	11	9	126	17	190	9	2	13	13	.500	0	18-33	58	4.00	3.71

Albie Lopez

Pitches: R **Bats:** R **Pos:** RP-26; SP-4   **Ht:** 6'2" **Wt:** 240 **Born:** 8/18/71 **Age:** 31

Year Team	Lg	G	GS	CG	GF	IP	BFP	H	R	ER	HR	SH	SF	HB	TBB	IBB	SO	WP	Bk	W	L	Pct	ShO	Sv-Op	Hld	ERC	ERA
2002 Greenville*	AA	1	1	0	0	4.0	18	2	2	2	0	0	0	0	4	0	4	0	0	0	0		0	0- -		2.80	4.50
1993 Cleveland	AL	9	9	0	0	49.2	222	49	34	33	7	1	1	1	32	1	25	0	0	3	1	.750	0	0-0	0	5.45	5.98
1994 Cleveland	AL	4	4	1	0	17.0	76	20	11	8	3	0	0	1	6	0	18	3	0	1	2	.333	1	0-0	0	5.76	4.24
1995 Cleveland	AL	6	2	0	0	23.0	92	17	8	8	4	0	1	1	7	1	22	2	0	0	0		0	0-0	0	2.91	3.13
1996 Cleveland	AL	13	10	0	0	62.0	282	80	47	44	14	0	1	1	22	1	45	2	0	5	4	.556	0	0-0	0	6.74	6.39
1997 Cleveland	AL	37	6	0	0	76.2	364	101	61	59	11	3	2	4	40	9	63	5	0	3	7	.300	0	0-1	4	6.89	6.93
1998 Tampa Bay	AL	54	0	0	12	79.2	335	73	31	23	7	4	3	3	32	4	62	5	0	7	4	.636	0	1-5	4	3.66	2.60
1999 Tampa Bay	AL	51	0	0	14	64.0	281	66	40	33	8	1	4	1	24	2	37	3	0	3	2	.600	0	1-3	12	4.27	4.64
2000 Tampa Bay	AL	45	24	4	10	185.1	798	199	95	85	24	6	3	1	70	3	96	4	1	11	13	.458	1	2-4	1	4.68	4.13
2001 TB-Ari		33	33	3	0	205.2	896	226	123	110	26	8	5	4	75	3	136	2	1	9	19	.321	3	0-0	0	4.78	4.81
2002 Atlanta	NL	30	4	0	14	55.2	242	66	29	27	1	1	3	0	18	3	39	5	0	1	4	.200	0	0-0	1	4.19	4.37
2001 Tampa Bay	AL	20	20	1	0	124.2	567	152	87	74	16	5	3	4	51	1	67	1	1	5	12	.294	1	0-0	0	5.74	5.34
2001 Arizona	NL	13	13	2	0	81.0	329	74	36	36	10	3	2	0	24	2	69	1	0	4	7	.364	2	0-0	0	3.39	4.00
10 ML YEARS		282	92	8	60	818.2	3588	897	479	430	105	24	23	18	326	27	543	31	2	43	56	.434	5	4-13	22	4.90	4.73

Aquilino Lopez

Pitches: R **Bats:** R **Pos:** RP   **Ht:** 6'3" **Wt:** 165 **Born:** 4/21/75 **Age:** 28

Year Team	Lg	G	GS	CG	GF	IP	BFP	H	R	ER	HR	SH	SF	HB	TBB	IBB	SO	WP	Bk	W	L	Pct	ShO	Sv-Op	Hld	ERC	ERA
1999 Everett	A-	15	15	1	0	87.2	365	76	44	37	8	1	2	3	30	2	93	2	0	7	6	.538	0	0- -	-	3.12	3.80
2000 Wisconsin	A	39	5	1	29	68.0	268	47	16	14	1	0	1	4	20	4	67	3	0	6	1	.857	1	17- -	-	1.76	1.85
2001 San Antonio	AA	42	0	0	13	62.2	265	48	24	21	4	2	2	6	25	2	79	5	0	4	3	.571	0	2- -	-	2.85	3.02
2002 Tacoma	AAA	34	11	0	10	109.1	438	89	33	29	6	3	4	2	27	1	103	4	4	4	4	.500	0	5- -	-	2.30	2.39

Felipe Lopez

Bats: B **Throws:** R **Pos:** SS-79; PH-5; 3B-2; PR-2   **Ht:** 6'0" **Wt:** 185 **Born:** 5/12/80 **Age:** 23

Year Team	Lg	G	AB	H	2B	3B	HR	(Hm	Rd)	TB	R	RBI	RC	TBB	IBB	SO	HBP	SH	SF	SB	CS	SB%	GDP	Avg	OBP	Slg
1998 St. Ctharines	A-	19	83	31	5	2	1	(-	-)	43	14	11	16	3	0	14	0	0	0	4	2	.67	1	.373	.395	.518
1998 Dunedin	A+	4	13	5	0	1	1	(-	-)	10	3	1	3	0	0	3	0	0	0	0	0	-	1	.385	.385	.769
1999 Hagerstown	A	134	537	149	27	4	14	(-	-)	226	87	80	80	61	0	157	3	0	6	21	14	.60	7	.277	.351	.421
2000 Tennessee	AA	127	463	119	18	4	9	(-	-)	172	52	41	50	31	0	110	1	8	3	12	11	.52	6	.257	.303	.371
2001 Tennessee	AA	19	72	16	2	1	2	(-	-)	26	12	4	7	9	0	23	0	0	0	4	4	.50	1	.222	.309	.361
2001 Syracuse	AAA	89	358	100	19	7	16	(-	-)	181	65	44	60	30	4	94	3	2	4	13	5	.72	5	.279	.337	.506
2002 Syracuse	AAA	43	173	55	11	2	3	(-	-)	79	35	16	36	29	1	37	1	1	0	13	0	1.00	3	.318	.419	.457
2001 Toronto	AL	49	177	46	5	4	5	(3	2)	74	21	23	22	12	1	39	0	1	2	4	3	.57	2	.260	.304	.418
2002 Toronto	AL	85	282	64	15	3	8	(5	3)	109	35	34	32	23	1	90	1	2	1	5	4	.56	4	.227	.287	.387
2 ML YEARS		134	459	110	20	7	13	(8	5)	183	56	57	54	35	2	129	1	3	3	9	7	.56	6	.240	.293	.399

Javier Lopez

Pitches: L **Bats:** L **Pos:** RP   **Ht:** 6'4" **Wt:** 200 **Born:** 7/11/77 **Age:** 25

Year Team	Lg	G	GS	CG	GF	IP	BFP	H	R	ER	HR	SH	SF	HB	TBB	IBB	SO	WP	Bk	W	L	Pct	ShO	Sv-Op	Hld	ERC	ERA
1998 South Bend	A	16	9	0	1	44.0	218	60	36	32	2	2	3	0	30	0	31	7	0	2	4	.333	0	0- -	-	6.93	6.55
1999 South Bend	A	20	20	0	0	99.0	458	122	74	66	9	1	4	3	43	0	70	9	0	4	6	.400	0	0- -	-	5.58	6.00
2000 High Desert	A+	30	21	0	4	136.1	602	152	87	79	14	4	7	6	57	0	98	8	2	4	8	.333	0	2- -	-	5.08	5.22
2001 Lancaster	A+	17	0	0	10	24.0	103	30	9	7	2	2	0	0	5	0	18	1	1	1	3	.250	0	1- -	-	4.69	2.63
2001 El Paso	AA	22	1	0	4	40.0	191	64	39	33	6	2	1	0	14	2	21	1	0	1	0	1.000	0	0- -	-	7.97	7.43
2002 El Paso	AA	61	0	0	25	46.1	186	34	16	14	3	2	1	0	15	1	47	1	0	2	2	.500	0	6- -	-	2.16	2.72
2002 Vero Beach	A+	1	0	0	0	0.1	7	2	4	2	0	0	0	0	3	0	0	0	0	0	0	-	0	0- -	-	74.92	54.00

Javy Lopez

Bats: R **Throws:** R **Pos:** C-103; PH-14   **Ht:** 6'3" **Wt:** 225 **Born:** 11/5/70 **Age:** 32

							BATTING												BASERUNNING				AVERAGES		
Year Team	Lg	G	AB	H	2B	3B	HR	(Hm | Rd)	TB	R	RBI	RC	TBB	IBB	SO	HBP	SH	SF	SB	CS	SB%	GDP	Avg	OBP	Slg
1992 Atlanta	NL	9	16	6	2	0	0	(0 | 0)	8	3	2	3	0	0	1	0	0	0	0	0	-	0	.375	.375	.500
1993 Atlanta	NL	8	16	6	1	1	1	(0 | 1)	12	1	2	4	0	0	2	1	0	0	0	0	-	0	.375	.412	.750
1994 Atlanta	NL	80	277	68	9	0	13	(4 | 9)	116	27	35	31	17	0	61	5	2	2	0	2	.00	12	.245	.299	.419
1995 Atlanta	NL	100	333	105	11	4	14	(8 | 6)	166	37	51	51	14	0	57	2	0	3	0	1	.00	13	.315	.344	.498
1996 Atlanta	NL	138	489	138	19	1	23	(10 | 13)	228	56	69	66	28	5	84	3	1	5	1	6	.14	18	.282	.322	.466
1997 Atlanta	NL	123	414	122	28	1	23	(11 | 12)	221	52	68	76	40	10	82	5	1	4	1	1	.50	9	.295	.361	.534
1998 Atlanta	NL	133	489	139	21	1	34	(18 | 16)	264	73	106	79	30	1	85	6	1	8	5	3	.63	22	.284	.328	.540
1999 Atlanta	NL	65	246	78	18	1	11	(1 | 10)	131	34	45	45	20	2	41	3	0	0	0	3	.00	6	.317	.375	.533
2000 Atlanta	NL	134	481	138	21	0	24	(12 | 12)	233	60	89	72	35	3	80	4	0	5	0	0	-	20	.287	.337	.484
2001 Atlanta	NL	128	438	117	16	1	17	(10 | 7)	186	45	66	58	28	3	82	10	1	5	1	0	1.00	12	.267	.322	.425
2002 Atlanta	NL	109	347	81	15	0	11	(1 | 10)	129	31	52	40	26	8	63	8	0	4	0	1	.00	15	.233	.299	.372
11 ML YEARS		1027	3546	998	161	11	171	(75 | 96)	1694	419	585	525	238	32	638	47	6	36	8	17	.32	126	.281	.332	.478

Luis Lopez

Bats: B **Throws:** R **Pos:** PH-27; SS-25; 2B-12; 1B-1; DH-1; PR-1   **Ht:** 5'11" **Wt:** 175 **Born:** 9/4/70 **Age:** 32

							BATTING												BASERUNNING				AVERAGES		
Year Team	Lg	G	AB	H	2B	3B	HR	(Hm	Rd)	TB	R	RBI	RC	TBB	IBB	SO	HBP	SH	SF	SB	CS	SB%	GDP	Avg	OBP	Slg
2002 Indianapolis*	AAA	6	22	5	0	0	0	(-	-)	5	2	0	1	0	0	4	1	0	0	0	0	-	0	.227	.261	.227
2002 Rochester*	AAA	17	68	22	6	0	3	(-	-)	37	12	8	13	3	0	11	1	3	0	0	0	-	1	.324	.361	.544
1993 San Diego	NL	17	43	5	1	0	0	(0	0)	6	1	1	0	0	0	8	0	1	0	0	0	-	0	.116	.114	.140
1994 San Diego	NL	77	235	65	16	1	2	(2	0)	89	29	20	27	15	2	39	3	2	2	3	2	.60	7	.277	.325	.379
1996 San Diego	NL	63	139	25	3	0	2	(1	1)	34	10	11	5	9	1	35	1	1	1	0	0	-	7	.180	.233	.245
1997 New York	NL	78	178	48	12	1	1	(1	0)	65	19	19	21	12	2	42	4	2	0	2	4	.33	2	.270	.330	.365
1998 New York	NL	117	266	67	13	2	2	(1	1)	90	37	22	26	20	3	60	4	3	2	2	2	.50	10	.252	.312	.338
1999 New York	NL	68	104	22	4	0	2	(1	1)	32	11	13	10	12	0	33	3	1	1	1	1	.50	1	.212	.308	.308
2000 Milwaukee	NL	78	201	53	14	0	6	(3	3)	85	24	27	26	9	1	35	5	8	2	1	2	.33	2	.264	.309	.423
2001 Milwaukee	NL	92	222	60	8	3	4	(2	2)	86	22	18	24	14	2	44	5	5	1	0	1	.00	6	.270	.326	.387
2002 Mil-Bal		58	117	23	6	0	2	(1	1)	35	11	10	7	5	0	21	0	0	0	1	0	1.00	3	.197	.230	.299
2002 Milwaukee	NL	6	8	0	0	0	0	(0	0)	0	1	1	0	2	0	1	0	0	0	0	0	-	0	.000	.200	.000
2002 Baltimore	AL	52	109	23	6	0	2	(1	1)	35	10	9	7	3	0	20	0	0	0	1	0	1.00	3	.211	.232	.321
9 ML YEARS		648	1505	368	77	7	21	(12	9)	522	164	141	149	96	11	317	25	22	10	10	12	.45	38	.245	.299	.347

Mendy Lopez

Bats: R **Throws:** R **Pos:** PH-3   **Ht:** 6'2" **Wt:** 200 **Born:** 10/15/74 **Age:** 28

							BATTING												BASERUNNING				AVERAGES		
Year Team	Lg	G	AB	H	2B	3B	HR	(Hm	Rd)	TB	R	RBI	RC	TBB	IBB	SO	HBP	SH	SF	SB	CS	SB%	GDP	Avg	OBP	Slg
2002 Nashville*	AAA	101	385	97	26	0	11	(-	-)	156	60	72	48	34	3	99	2	0	9	4	1	.80	10	.252	.309	.405
1998 Kansas City	AL	74	206	50	10	2	1	(1	0)	67	18	15	18	12	0	40	1	5	1	5	2	.71	6	.243	.286	.325
1999 Kansas City	AL	7	20	8	0	1	0	(0	0)	10	2	3	4	0	0	5	1	0	0	0	0	-	0	.400	.429	.500
2000 Florida	NL	4	3	0	0	0	0	(0	0)	0	0	0	0	1	0	1	0	0	0	0	0	-	0	.000	.250	.000
2001 Hou-Pit	NL	32	58	14	3	1	1	(0	1)	22	8	7	8	6	1	20	1	0	1	0	0	-	0	.241	.318	.379
2002 Pittsburgh	NL	3	3	0	0	0	0	(0	0)	0	0	0	0	0	0	3	0	0	0	0	0	-	0	.000	.000	.000
2001 Houston	NL	10	15	4	0	0	1	(0	1)	7	3	3	3	2	0	4	1	0	0	0	0	-	0	.267	.389	.467
2001 Pittsburgh	NL	22	43	10	3	1	0	(0	0)	15	5	4	5	4	1	16	0	0	1	0	0	-	0	.233	.292	.349
5 ML YEARS		120	290	72	13	4	2	(1	1)	99	28	25	30	19	1	69	3	5	2	5	2	.71	6	.248	.299	.341

Rodrigo Lopez

Pitches: R **Bats:** R **Pos:** SP-28; RP-5   **Ht:** 6'1" **Wt:** 180 **Born:** 12/14/75 **Age:** 27

		HOW MUCH HE PITCHED						WHAT HE GAVE UP												THE RESULTS						
Year Team	Lg	G	GS	CG	GF	IP	BFP	H	R	ER	HR	SH	SF	HB	TBB	IBB	SO	WP	Bk	W	L	Pct	ShO	Sv-Op	Hld	ERC	ERA
1995 Padres	R	11	7	0	3	34.2	162	41	29	21	0	1	2	12	14	0	33	3	1	1	1	.500	0	1--	-	4.44	5.45
1996 Idaho Falls	R+	15	14	0	1	71.0	314	76	52	45	3	4	3	4	34	0	72	8	4	4	4	.500	0	1--	-	4.66	5.70
1997 Clinton	A	37	14	2	19	121.2	508	103	49	43	6	7	4	3	42	1	123	3	4	6	8	.429	0	9--	-	2.77	3.18
1998 Mobile	AA	4	4	0	0	25.2	101	21	11	4	1	0	1	0	4	0	20	0	0	3	0	1.000	0	0--	-	1.88	1.40
1999 Mobile	AA	28	28	2	0	169.1	728	187	91	83	14	4	6	7	58	3	138	5	1	10	8	.556	1	0--	-	4.55	4.41
2000 Las Vegas	AAA	20	20	1	0	109.1	483	123	66	57	9	3	7	2	45	1	100	0	0	8	7	.533	0	0--	-	4.80	4.69
2001 Lk Elsinore	A+	9	0	0	2	13.0	60	15	7	1	1	1	1	0	4	0	9	0	0	1	0	1.000	0	0--	-	4.14	0.69
2001 Portland	AAA	11	8	0	1	52.1	214	45	22	20	7	1	1	1	15	0	37	1	0	2	2	.500	0	0--	-	3.18	3.44
2000 San Diego	NL	6	6	0	0	24.2	120	40	24	24	5	0	1	0	13	0	17	0	0	3	0	.000	0	0-0	0	9.78	8.76
2002 Baltimore	AL	33	28	1	0	196.2	809	172	83	78	23	2	4	5	62	4	136	2	1	15	9	.625	0	0-0	0	3.27	3.57
2 ML YEARS		39	34	1	0	221.1	929	212	107	102	28	2	5	5	75	4	153	2	1	15	12	.556	0	0-0	0	3.88	4.15

Mark Loretta

Bats: R **Throws:** R **Pos:** 3B-57; PH-29; SS-18; 2B-6; 1B-5; DH-1   **Ht:** 6'0" **Wt:** 186 **Born:** 8/14/71 **Age:** 31

							BATTING												BASERUNNING				AVERAGES		
Year Team	Lg	G	AB	H	2B	3B	HR	(Hm	Rd)	TB	R	RBI	RC	TBB	IBB	SO	HBP	SH	SF	SB	CS	SB%	GDP	Avg	OBP	Slg
1995 Milwaukee	NL	19	50	13	3	0	1	(0	1)	19	13	3	6	4	0	7	1	1	0	1	1	.50	1	.260	.327	.380
1996 Milwaukee	NL	73	154	43	3	0	1	(1	0)	49	20	13	16	14	0	15	0	2	0	2	1	.67	7	.279	.339	.318
1997 Milwaukee	NL	132	418	120	17	5	5	(2	3)	162	56	47	56	47	2	60	2	5	10	5	5	.50	15	.287	.354	.388
1998 Milwaukee	NL	140	434	137	29	0	6	(3	3)	184	55	54	68	42	1	47	7	4	4	9	6	.60	14	.316	.382	.424
1999 Milwaukee	NL	153	587	170	34	5	5	(2	3)	229	93	67	82	52	1	59	10	9	6	4	1	.80	14	.290	.354	.390
2000 Milwaukee	NL	91	352	99	21	1	7	(3	4)	143	49	40	48	37	2	38	1	8	1	0	3	.00	9	.281	.350	.406
2001 Milwaukee	NL	102	384	111	14	2	2	(0	2)	135	40	29	48	28	0	46	7	7	3	1	2	.33	6	.289	.346	.352
2002 Mil-Hou	NL	107	283	86	18	0	4	(1	3)	116	33	27	48	32	1	37	5	6	3	1	1	.50	7	.304	.381	.410
2002 Milwaukee	NL	86	217	58	14	0	2	(1	1)	78	23	19	32	23	1	32	5	6	1	0	0	-	6	.267	.350	.359
2002 Houston	NL	21	66	28	4	0	2	(1	2)	38	10	8	16	9	0	5	0	0	2	1	1	.50	1	.424	.481	.576
8 ML YEARS		817	2662	779	139	13	31	(12	19)	1037	359	280	372	256	7	309	33	42	27	23	20	.53	73	.293	.359	.390

Andrew Lorraine

Pitches: L **Bats:** L **Pos:** RP-4; SP-1   **Ht:** 6'3" **Wt:** 200 **Born:** 8/11/72 **Age:** 30

Year Team	Lg	G	GS	CG	GF	IP	BFP	H	R	ER	HR	SH	SF	HB	TBB	IBB	SO	WP	Bk	W	L	Pct	ShO	Sv-Op	Hld	ERC	ERA
2002 Indianapolis*	AAA	25	24	2	1	165.0	677	157	65	56	14	10	3	1	42	7	86	1	1	7	11	.389	0	0--	0	3.14	3.05
1994 Anaheim	AL	4	3	0	0	18.2	96	30	23	22	7	2	1	0	11	0	10	0	0	0	2	.000	0	0-0	0	11.13	10.61
1995 Chicago	AL	5	0	0	2	8.0	30	3	3	3	0	0	0	1	2	0	5	0	0	0	0	-	0	0-0	1	0.85	3.38
1997 Oakland	AL	12	6	0	0	29.2	146	45	22	21	2	0	3	1	15	0	18	0	0	3	1	.750	0	0-0	0	7.57	6.37
1998 Seattle	AL	4	0	0	1	3.2	16	3	1	1	0	0	0	0	4	0	0	1	0	0	0	-	0	0-0	1	5.44	2.45
1999 Chicago	NL	11	11	2	0	61.2	272	71	42	38	9	6	2	0	22	3	40	3	0	2	5	.286	1	0-0	0	5.03	5.55
2000 ChC-Cle		18	5	0	3	41.1	189	44	29	27	6	2	2	0	23	1	30	0	1	1	2	.333	0	0-1	1	5.32	5.88
2002 Milwaukee	NL	5	1	0	3	12.0	65	22	18	15	7	1	0	0	6	0	10	0	0	1	0	1.000	0	0-0	0	13.99	11.25
2000 Chicago	NL	8	5	0	0	32.0	148	36	25	23	5	2	2	0	18	1	25	0	1	1	2	.333	0	0-1	0	5.80	6.47
2000 Cleveland	AL	10	0	0	3	9.1	41	8	4	4	1	0	0	0	5	0	5	0	0	0	0	-	0	0-0	1	3.78	3.86
7 ML YEARS		59	26	2	10	175.0	814	218	138	127	31	11	8	2	83	4	113	4	1	6	11	.353	1	0-1	3	6.42	6.53

Shane Loux

Pitches: R **Bats:** R **Pos:** SP-3   **Ht:** 6'2" **Wt:** 205 **Born:** 8/13/79 **Age:** 23

Year Team	Lg	G	GS	CG	GF	IP	BFP	H	R	ER	HR	SH	SF	HB	TBB	IBB	SO	WP	Bk	W	L	Pct	ShO	Sv-Op	Hld	ERC	ERA
1997 Tigers	R	10	9	1	0	43.0	158	19	7	4	0	0	1	0	10	0	33	2	1	4	1	.800	1	0--	-	0.82	0.84
1998 W Michigan	A	28	28	2	0	157.0	698	184	96	81	13	2	4	8	52	0	88	12	2	7	13	.350	1	0--	-	4.87	4.64
1999 W Michigan	A	8	8	0	0	47.1	215	55	39	33	5	1	2	8	16	1	43	4	0	1	3	.250	0	0--	-	5.49	6.27
1999 Lakeland	A+	17	17	0	0	91.0	412	92	48	41	8	2	5	10	47	0	52	7	1	6	5	.545	0	0--	-	4.96	4.05
2000 Lakeland	A+	1	1	0	0	5.0	19	2	1	1	0	1	0	0	3	0	6	0	0	0	1	.000	0	0--	-	1.39	1.80
2000 Jacksonville	AA	26	26	2	0	157.2	670	150	78	67	12	3	7	14	55	0	130	7	0	12	9	.571	0	0--	-	3.83	3.82
2001 Toledo	AAA	28	27	2	1	151.0	727	203	111	97	22	4	10	15	73	0	72	14	1	10	11	.476	0	0--	-	7.31	5.78
2002 Toledo	AAA	26	26	5	0	158.1	696	196	94	83	11	4	4	10	38	1	87	9	2	11	10	.524	3	0--	-	4.86	4.72
2002 Detroit	AL	3	3	0	0	14.0	64	19	16	14	4	0	0	1	3	0	7	1	0	0	3	.000	0	0-0	0	7.12	9.00

Derek Lowe

Pitches: R **Bats:** R **Pos:** SP-32   **Ht:** 6'6" **Wt:** 214 **Born:** 6/1/73 **Age:** 30

Year Team	Lg	G	GS	CG	GF	IP	BFP	H	R	ER	HR	SH	SF	HB	TBB	IBB	SO	WP	Bk	W	L	Pct	ShO	Sv-Op	Hld	ERC	ERA
1997 Sea-Bos	AL	20	9	0	1	69.0	298	74	49	47	11	4	2	4	23	3	52	2	0	2	6	.250	0	0-2	1	4.88	6.13
1998 Boston	AL	63	10	0	8	123.0	527	126	65	55	5	4	5	4	42	5	77	8	0	3	9	.250	0	4-9	12	3.64	4.02
1999 Boston	AL	74	0	0	32	109.1	436	84	35	32	7	1	2	4	25	1	80	1	0	6	3	.667	0	15-20	22	2.14	2.63
2000 Boston	AL	74	0	0	64	91.1	379	90	27	26	6	4	1	2	22	5	79	1	1	4	4	.500	0	42-47	0	3.17	2.56
2001 Boston	AL	67	3	0	50	91.2	404	103	39	36	7	5	1	5	29	9	82	4	0	5	10	.333	0	24-30	4	4.31	3.53
2002 Boston	AL	32	32	1	0	219.2	854	166	65	63	12	5	2	12	48	0	127	5	0	21	8	.724	1	0-0	0	2.13	2.58
1997 Seattle	AL	12	9	0	1	53.0	234	59	43	41	11	2	1	2	20	2	39	2	0	2	4	.333	0	0-0	0	5.55	6.96
1997 Boston	AL	8	0	0	0	16.0	64	15	6	6	0	2	1	2	3	1	13	0	0	0	2	.000	0	0-2	1	2.78	3.38
6 ML YEARS		330	54	1	155	704.0	2898	643	280	259	48	23	13	31	189	23	497	21	1	41	40	.506	1	85-108	39	3.04	3.31

Sean Lowe

Pitches: R **Bats:** R **Pos:** RP-50; SP-1   **Ht:** 6'2" **Wt:** 225 **Born:** 3/29/71 **Age:** 32

Year Team	Lg	G	GS	CG	GF	IP	BFP	H	R	ER	HR	SH	SF	HB	TBB	IBB	SO	WP	Bk	W	L	Pct	ShO	Sv-Op	Hld	ERC	ERA
2002 Nashville*	AAA	5	5	0	0	22.0	96	29	14	14	0	0	2	0	3	0	21	0	0	1	1	.500	0	0--	-	4.09	5.73
1997 St Louis	NL	6	4	0	1	17.1	89	27	21	18	2	1	2	1	10	0	8	0	0	0	2	.000	0	0-0	0	8.57	9.35
1998 St Louis	NL	4	1	0	2	5.1	31	11	9	9	1	1	0	0	5	0	2	0	0	0	3	.000	0	0-0	0	14.71	15.19
1999 Chicago	AL	64	0	0	13	91.1	379	90	39	39	10	3	9	4	46	1	62	4	0	4	1	.800	0	0-3	6	4.38	3.67
2000 Chicago	AL	50	5	0	8	70.2	325	78	47	43	10	4	1	6	39	3	53	3	0	4	1	.800	0	0-0	6	5.95	5.48
2001 Chicago	AL	45	11	0	9	127.0	529	123	55	51	12	3	7	7	32	2	71	6	0	9	4	.692	0	3-3	3	3.51	3.61
2002 Pit-Col	NL	51	1	0	8	79.1	379	101	58	51	9	5	3	7	41	6	64	1	1	5	3	.625	0	0-2	10	6.50	5.79
2002 Pittsburgh	NL	43	1	0	8	69.0	326	85	45	41	8	5	3	7	34	6	57	1	1	2	2	.667	0	0-2	9	6.20	5.35
2002 Colorado	NL	8	0	0	0	10.1	53	16	13	10	1	0	0	0	7	0	7	0	0	1	1	.500	0	0-0	1	8.60	8.71
6 ML YEARS		220	22	0	41	395.1	1759	430	229	211	44	17	22	25	173	12	260	14	1	22	14	.611	0	3-8	25	5.06	4.80

Mike Lowell

Bats: R **Throws:** R **Pos:** 3B-159; PH-1   **Ht:** 6'3" **Wt:** 217 **Born:** 2/24/74 **Age:** 29

Year Team	Lg	G	AB	H	2B	3B	HR	(Hm	Rd)	TB	R	RBI	RC	TBB	IBB	SO	HBP	SH	SF	SB	CS	SB%	GDP	Avg	OBP	Slg
1998 New York	AL	8	15	4	0	0	0	(0	0)	4	1	0	1	0	0	1	0	0	0	0	0	-	0	.267	.267	.267
1999 Florida	NL	97	308	78	15	0	12	(7	5)	129	32	47	40	26	1	69	5	0	5	0	0	-	8	.253	.317	.419
2000 Florida	NL	140	508	137	38	0	22	(11	11)	241	73	91	86	54	4	75	9	0	11	4	0	1.00	6	.270	.344	.474
2001 Florida	NL	146	551	156	37	0	18	(12	6)	247	65	100	84	43	3	79	10	0	10	1	2	.33	9	.283	.340	.448
2002 Florida	NL	160	597	165	44	0	24	(13	11)	281	88	92	86	65	5	92	4	0	11	4	3	.57	16	.276	.346	.471
5 ML YEARS		551	1979	540	134	0	76	(43	33)	902	259	330	297	188	13	316	28	0	37	9	5	.64	37	.273	.339	.456

Ryan Ludwick

Bats: R **Throws:** L **Pos:** CF-21; LF-2; RF-1; PH-1   **Ht:** 6'3" **Wt:** 203 **Born:** 7/13/78 **Age:** 24

Year Team	Lg	G	AB	H	2B	3B	HR	(Hm	Rd)	TB	R	RBI	RC	TBB	IBB	SO	HBP	SH	SF	SB	CS	SB%	GDP	Avg	OBP	Slg
1999 Modesto	A+	43	171	47	11	3	4	(-	-)	76	28	34	28	19	0	45	3	0	5	2	1	.67	0	.275	.348	.444
2000 Modesto	A+	129	493	130	26	3	29	(-	-)	249	86	102	90	68	0	128	9	1	7	10	6	.63	6	.264	.359	.505
2001 Midland	AA	119	443	119	23	3	25	(-	-)	223	82	96	78	56	1	113	7	1	5	9	10	.47	6	.269	.356	.503

Year Team	Lg	G	AB	H	2B	3B	HR	(Hm	Rd)	TB	R	RBI	RC	TBB	IBB	SO	HBP	SH	SF	SB	CS	SB%	GDP	Avg	OBP	Slg
								BATTING												BASERUNNING				AVERAGES		
2001 Sacramento	AAA	17	57	13	3	0	1	(-	-)	19	10	7	5	2	0	16	0	1	2	2	0	1.00	0	.228	.246	.333
2002 Oklahoma	AAA	78	305	87	27	4	15	(-	-)	167	62	52	60	38	1	76	5	1	3	2	2	.50	6	.285	.370	.548
2002 Texas	AL	23	81	19	6	0	1	(1	0)	28	10	9	6	7	0	24	0	0	0	2	1	.67	4	.235	.295	.346

Julio Lugo

Bats: R **Throws:** R **Pos:** SS-84; PH-4   **Ht:** 6'1" **Wt:** 170 **Born:** 11/16/75 **Age:** 27

Year Team	Lg	G	AB	H	2B	3B	HR	(Hm	Rd)	TB	R	RBI	RC	TBB	IBB	SO	HBP	SH	SF	SB	CS	SB%	GDP	Avg	OBP	Slg
								BATTING												BASERUNNING				AVERAGES		
2000 Houston	NL	116	420	119	22	5	10	(6	4)	181	78	40	62	37	0	93	4	3	1	22	9	.71	9	.283	.346	.431
2001 Houston	NL	140	513	135	20	3	10	(6	4)	191	93	37	63	46	0	116	5	15	7	12	11	.52	7	.263	.326	.372
2002 Houston	NL	88	322	84	15	1	8	(6	2)	125	45	35	43	28	3	74	2	4	2	9	3	.75	6	.261	.322	.388
3 ML YEARS		344	1255	338	57	9	28	(18	10)	497	216	112	168	111	3	283	11	22	10	43	23	.65	22	.269	.332	.396

Mark Lukasiewicz

Pitches: L **Bats:** L **Pos:** RP-17   **Ht:** 6'5" **Wt:** 240 **Born:** 3/8/73 **Age:** 30

Year Team	Lg	G	GS	CG	GF	IP	BFP	H	R	ER	HR	SH	SF	HB	TBB	IBB	SO	WP	Bk	W	L	Pct	ShO	Sv-Op	Hld	ERC	ERA
		HOW MUCH HE PITCHED						WHAT HE GAVE UP												THE RESULTS							
1994 Hagerstown	A	29	17	0	5	98.0	449	108	70	52	8	6	4	7	51	0	84	8	0	3	6	.333	0	0- -	-	5.30	4.78
1995 Dunedin	A+	31	13	0	11	88.1	383	80	62	55	13	1	2	7	42	0	71	7	0	3	6	.333	0	1- -	-	4.54	5.60
1996 Dunedin	A+	23	0	0	5	31.1	144	28	20	16	1	1	1	4	22	1	31	1	0	2	1	.667	0	1- -	-	4.58	4.60
1996 Bakersfield	A+	7	0	0	3	12.2	66	17	14	13	2	1	0	1	11	0	9	1	0	0	2	.000	0	0- -	-	8.99	9.24
1996 Hagerstown	A	9	1	0	4	15.2	63	8	5	4	0	0	0	1	7	0	20	1	0	2	0	1.000	0	0- -	-	1.47	2.30
1997 Knoxville	AA	27	0	0	8	37.0	149	26	17	15	2	1	1	1	14	1	43	4	0	2	0	1.000	0	7- -	-	2.24	3.65
1997 Syracuse	AAA	30	0	0	9	31.1	146	37	22	18	7	1	2	2	13	1	31	1	0	2	3	.400	0	0- -	-	6.22	5.17
1998 Syracuse	AAA	22	4	0	3	47.2	201	38	18	18	8	0	0	3	24	1	30	3	0	2	2	.500	0	1- -	-	4.11	3.40
1998 Knoxville	AA	5	0	0	2	9.1	33	6	2	2	0	0	0	0	1	0	16	0	0	1	0		0	1- -	-	1.11	1.93
1998 Dunedin	A+	9	0	0	1	10.2	42	7	2	1	0	0	1	0	4	0	8	0	0	1	1	.500	0	0- -	-	1.67	0.84
1999 Syracuse	AAA	37	9	1	6	97.2	431	109	59	58	20	1	2	0	40	1	77	5	1	4	4	.500	0	3- -	-	5.57	5.34
2000 Syracuse	AAA	42	0	0	12	41.1	176	34	17	16	7	2	0	0	25	1	52	3	0	2	1	.667	0	0- -	-	4.44	3.48
2000 Tennessee	AA	3	0	0	1	4.2	22	4	3	3	1	0	0	0	4	0	6	0	0	0	0		0	0- -	-	5.86	5.79
2001 Salt Lake	AAA	20	0	0	8	30.1	105	12	5	5	4	0	0	0	2	0	41	0	0	3	0	1.000	0	2- -	-	0.72	1.48
2002 Salt Lake	AAA	35	0	0	8	43.0	193	46	26	19	6	3	5	2	17	0	48	2	0	3	2	.600	0	0- -	-	4.85	3.98
2001 Anaheim	AL	24	0	0	11	22.1	98	21	17	15	6	1	1	2	9	2	25	2	0	0	2	.000	0	0-0	0	5.12	6.04
2002 Anaheim	AL	17	0	0	4	14.0	67	17	6	6	0	0	1	0	9	0	15	0	0	2	0	1.000	0	0-0	2	5.43	3.86
2 ML YEARS		41	0	0	15	36.1	165	38	23	21	6	1	2	2	18	2	40	2	0	2	2	.500	0	0-0	2	5.29	5.20

Fernando Lunar

Bats: R **Throws:** R **Pos:** C-2   **Ht:** 6'1" **Wt:** 190 **Born:** 5/25/77 **Age:** 26

Year Team	Lg	G	AB	H	2B	3B	HR	(Hm	Rd)	TB	R	RBI	RC	TBB	IBB	SO	HBP	SH	SF	SB	CS	SB%	GDP	Avg	OBP	Slg
								BATTING												BASERUNNING				AVERAGES		
2002 Rochester*	AAA	42	145	28	1	0	2	(-	-)	35	7	8	4	4	0	27	4	0	1	1	0	1.00	9	.193	.234	.241
2000 Atl-Bal		31	70	12	1	0	0	(0	0)	13	5	6	1	3	1	19	4	0	1	0	2	.00	2	.171	.247	.186
2001 Baltimore	AL	64	167	41	7	0	0	(0	0)	48	8	16	11	7	0	32	3	2	1	0	0	-	8	.246	.287	.287
2002 Baltimore	AL	2	0	0	0	0	0	(0	0)	0	0	0	0	0	0	0	0	0	0	0	0	-	0			
2000 Atlanta	NL	22	54	10	1	0	0	(0	0)	11	5	5	1	3	1	15	3	0	0	0	2	.00	2	.185	.267	.204
2000 Baltimore	AL	9	16	2	0	0	0	(0	0)	2	0	1	0	0	0	4	1	0	1	0	0	-	0	.125	.176	.125
3 ML YEARS		97	237	53	8	0	0	(0	0)	61	13	22	12	10	1	51	7	2	1	0	2	.00	10	.224	.275	.257

David Lundquist

Pitches: R **Bats:** R **Pos:** RP-3   **Ht:** 6'2" **Wt:** 200 **Born:** 6/4/73 **Age:** 30

Year Team	Lg	G	GS	CG	GF	IP	BFP	H	R	ER	HR	SH	SF	HB	TBB	IBB	SO	WP	Bk	W	L	Pct	ShO	Sv-Op	Hld	ERC	ERA
		HOW MUCH HE PITCHED						WHAT HE GAVE UP												THE RESULTS							
2002 Portland*	AAA	30	0	0	29	32.0	138	28	21	20	6	2	0	0	15	1	31	0	0	1	4	.200	0	21- -	-	4.15	5.63
1999 Chicago	AL	17	0	0	7	22.0	106	28	21	21	3	2	2	1	12	0	18	0	0	1	1	.500	0	0-0	0	6.70	8.59
2001 San Diego	NL	17	0	0	9	19.2	86	20	13	13	1	0	1	1	7	1	19	2	1	0	1	.000	0	0-1	0	3.72	5.95
2002 San Diego	NL	3	0	0	2	2.2	19	8	5	5	0	0	0	1	5	2	0	0	0	0	0	-	0	0-1	0	27.23	16.88
3 ML YEARS		37	0	0	18	44.1	211	56	39	39	4	2	3	3	24	3	37	2	1	1	2	.333	0	0-2	0	6.29	7.92

Trey Lunsford

Bats: R **Throws:** R **Pos:** C-3   **Ht:** 6'1" **Wt:** 195 **Born:** 5/25/79 **Age:** 24

Year Team	Lg	G	AB	H	2B	3B	HR	(Hm	Rd)	TB	R	RBI	RC	TBB	IBB	SO	HBP	SH	SF	SB	CS	SB%	GDP	Avg	OBP	Slg
								BATTING												BASERUNNING				AVERAGES		
2000 Salem-Keizer	A-	120	438	110	24	2	15	(-	-)	183	61	61	63	43	1	106	10	3	2	10	1	.91	7	.251	.331	.418
2001 Hagerstown	A	114	396	94	19	0	5	(-	-)	128	53	50	41	45	1	89	5	4	4	10	5	.67	12	.237	.320	.323
2002 San Jose	A+	16	51	13	3	0	1	(-	-)	19	7	5	6	3	0	15	2	1	0	2	0	1.00	3	.255	.321	.373
2002 Shreveport	AA	66	210	59	13	0	1	(-	-)	75	26	20	31	29	1	42	4	5	0	5	2	.71	3	.281	.379	.357
2002 Fresno	AAA	19	57	10	0	0	2	(-	-)	16	3	9	4	6	0	15	1	0	2	0	0	-	2	.175	.258	.281
2002 San Francisco	NL	3	3	2	1	0	0	(0	0)	3	0	1	1	0	0	1	0	0	0	0	0	-	0	.667	.667	1.000

Brandon Lyon

Pitches: R Bats: R Pos: SP-10; RP-5
Ht: 6'1" Wt: 185 Born: 8/10/79 Age: 23

Year Team	Lg	G	GS	CG	GF	IP	BFP	H	R	ER	HR	SH	SF	HB	TBB	IBB	SO	WP	Bk	W	L	Pct	ShO	Sv-Op	Hld	ERC	ERA
2000 Queens	A-	15	13	0	0	60.1	230	43	20	16	1	2	3	2	6	0	55	1	1	5	3	.625	0	0--	-	1.36	2.39
2001 Tennessee	AA	9	9	0	0	58.2	241	57	25	24	7	2	1	3	9	0	45	1	0	5	0	1.000	0	0--	-	3.28	3.68
2001 Syracuse	AAA	11	11	2	0	68.1	279	68	33	28	7	1	2	1	10	0	53	0	0	5	3	.625	1	0--	-	3.14	3.69
2002 Syracuse	AAA	14	14	0	0	75.2	344	99	54	43	4	2	6	3	19	0	35	1	0	4	9	.308	0	0--	-	4.99	5.11
2001 Toronto	AL	11	11	0	0	63.0	261	63	31	30	6	2	1	6	15	0	35	0	1	5	4	.556	0	0-0	0	3.50	4.29
2002 Toronto	AL	15	10	0	0	62.0	279	78	47	45	14	3	2	2	19	2	30	2	0	1	4	.200	0	0-1	0	6.24	6.53
2 ML YEARS		26	21	0	0	125.0	540	141	78	75	20	5	8	3	34	2	65	2	1	6	8	.429	0	0-1	0	4.80	5.40

John Mabry

Bats: L Throws: R Pos: 1B-51; LF-34; PH-33; RF-20
Ht: 6'4" Wt: 210 Born: 10/17/70 Age: 32

Year Team	Lg	G	AB	H	2B	3B	HR	(Hm Rd)	TB	R	RBI	RC	TBB	IBB	SO	HBP	SH	SF	SB	CS	SB%	GDP	Avg	OBP	Slg
1994 St Louis	NL	6	23	7	3	0	0	(0 0)	10	2	3	4	2	0	4	0	0	0	0	0	-	0	.304	.360	.435
1995 St Louis	NL	129	388	119	21	1	5	(2 3)	157	35	41	53	20	4	45	2	0	4	0	3	.00	6	.307	.347	.405
1996 St Louis	NL	151	543	161	30	2	13	(3 10)	234	63	74	74	37	11	84	3	3	5	3	2	.60	21	.297	.342	.431
1997 St Louis	NL	116	388	110	19	0	5	(5 0)	144	40	36	49	39	9	77	3	2	2	0	1	.00	11	.284	.352	.371
1998 St Louis	NL	142	377	94	22	0	9	(4 5)	143	41	46	42	30	6	76	1	3	2	0	2	.00	6	.249	.305	.379
1999 Seattle	AL	87	262	64	14	0	9	(5 4)	105	34	33	30	20	1	60	0	2	1	2	1	.67	6	.244	.297	.401
2000 Sea-SD		95	226	53	13	0	8	(3 5)	90	35	32	25	15	0	69	2	0	1	0	1	.00	4	.235	.287	.398
2001 Stl-Fla	NL	87	154	32	7	0	6	(2 4)	57	14	20	16	13	1	46	5	0	2	1	0	1.00	6	.208	.287	.370
2002 Phi-Oak		110	214	59	13	1	11	(8 3)	107	28	43	35	15	2	42	1	0	4	1	1	.50	7	.276	.321	.500
2000 Seattle	AL	47	103	25	5	0	1	(0 1)	33	18	7	11	10	0	31	2	0	0	0	1	.00	1	.243	.322	.320
2000 San Diego	NL	48	123	28	8	0	7	(3 4)	57	17	25	14	5	0	38	0	0	1	0	0	-	3	.228	.256	.463
2001 St Louis	NL	5	7	0	0	0	0	(0 0)	0	0	0	0	0	0	2	0	0	0	0	0	-	0	.000	.000	.000
2001 Florida	NL	82	147	32	7	0	6	(2 4)	57	14	20	16	13	1	44	5	0	2	1	0	1.00	6	.218	.299	.388
2002 Philadelphia	NL	21	21	6	0	0	0	(0 0)	6	1	3	3	1	1	5	0	0	1	0	0	-	0	.286	.304	.286
2002 Oakland	AL	89	193	53	13	1	11	(8 3)	101	27	40	32	14	1	37	1	0	3	1	1	.50	7	.275	.322	.523
9 ML YEARS		923	2575	699	142	4	66	(32 34)	1047	292	328	328	195	35	503	17	10	21	7	11	.39	67	.271	.324	.407

Mike MacDougal

Pitches: R Bats: B Pos: RP-6
Ht: 6'4" Wt: 195 Born: 3/5/77 Age: 26

Year Team	Lg	G	GS	CG	GF	IP	BFP	H	R	ER	HR	SH	SF	HB	TBB	IBB	SO	WP	Bk	W	L	Pct	ShO	Sv-Op	Hld	ERC	ERA
1999 Spokane	A-	11	11	0	0	46.1	196	43	25	23	3	1	1	6	17	0	57	8	1	2	2	.500	0	0--	-	3.90	4.47
2000 Wilmington	A+	26	25	0	1	144.2	620	115	79	63	5	5	1	14	76	0	129	21	4	9	7	.563	0	1--	-	3.37	3.92
2000 Wichita	AA	2	2	0	0	11.2	54	16	10	10	0	0	1	1	7	0	9	1	0	0	1	.000	0	0--	-	7.10	7.71
2001 Omaha	AAA	28	27	1	0	144.1	649	144	90	75	13	3	2	11	76	0	110	15	2	8	8	.500	0	0--	-	4.80	4.68
2002 Omaha	AAA	12	10	0	0	53.0	260	52	42	33	4	1	3	5	55	0	30	15	0	3	5	.375	0	0--	-	6.86	5.60
2002 Wichita	AA	4	4	1	0	17.2	85	11	12	6	1	1	1	2	24	0	14	7	0	1	1	.500	0	0--	-	5.94	3.06
2002 Royals	R	1	1	0	0	3.0	13	3	1	1	0				0	0	3	0	0	0	0	-	0	0--	-	2.79	3.00
2002 Wilmington	A+	5	0	0	4	8.1	33	3	4	1	1	0	0	0	5	0	10	3	0	0	1	.000	0	2--	-	1.69	1.08
2001 Kansas City	AL	3	3	0	0	15.1	67	18	10	8	2	0	0	1	4	0	7	3	0	1	1	.500	0	0-0	0	5.04	4.70
2002 Kansas City	AL	6	0	0	1	9.0	38	5	5	5	0	0	0	0	7	1	10	1	0	0	1	.000	0	0-0	0	2.26	5.00
2 ML YEARS		9	3	0	1	24.1	105	23	15	13	2	0	0	1	11	1	17	4	0	1	2	.333	0	0-0	0	3.97	4.81

Robert Machado

Bats: R Throws: R Pos: C-69; PH-6; 1B-2
Ht: 6'1" Wt: 210 Born: 6/3/73 Age: 30

Year Team	Lg	G	AB	H	2B	3B	HR	(Hm Rd)	TB	R	RBI	RC	TBB	IBB	SO	HBP	SH	SF	SB	CS	SB%	GDP	Avg	OBP	Slg
1996 Chicago	AL	4	6	4	1	0	0	(0 0)	5	1	2	2	0	0	0	0	0	0	0	0	-	1	.667	.667	.833
1997 Chicago	AL	10	15	3	0	1	0	(0 0)	5	1	2	1	1	0	6	0	1	0	0	0	-	0	.200	.250	.333
1998 Chicago	AL	34	111	23	6	0	3	(2 1)	38	14	15	9	7	0	22	0	3	0	0	0	-	3	.207	.254	.342
1999 Montreal	NL	17	22	4	1	0	0	(0 0)	5	3	0	1	2	0	6	0	0	0	0	0	-	0	.182	.250	.227
2000 Seattle	AL	8	14	3	0	0	1	(1 0)	6	2	1	2	1	0	4	0	0	0	0	0	-	0	.214	.267	.429
2001 Chicago	NL	52	135	30	10	0	2	(2 0)	46	13	13	11	7	3	26	1	3	0	0	0	-	4	.222	.266	.341
2002 ChC-Mil	NL	73	211	55	14	1	3	(1 2)	80	19	22	22	17	4	41	1	2	2	0	0	-	7	.261	.316	.379
2002 Chicago	NL	22	58	16	4	0	1	(0 1)	23	5	5	7	5	0	11	0	1	0	0	0	-	2	.276	.333	.397
2002 Milwaukee	NL	51	153	39	10	1	2	(1 1)	57	14	17	15	12	4	30	1	1	2	0	0	-	5	.255	.310	.373
7 ML YEARS		198	514	122	32	2	9	(6 3)	185	53	55	48	35	7	105	2	9	2	0	0	-	15	.237	.288	.360

Jose Macias

Bats: B Throws: R Pos: CF-58; 3B-30; 2B-23; PH-18; PR-11; SS-4; RF-1
Ht: 5'10" Wt: 189 Born: 1/25/72 Age: 31

Year Team	Lg	G	AB	H	2B	3B	HR	(Hm Rd)	TB	R	RBI	RC	TBB	IBB	SO	HBP	SH	SF	SB	CS	SB%	GDP	Avg	OBP	Slg
1999 Detroit	AL	5	4	1	0	0	1	(1 0)	4	2	2	1	0	0	1	0	0	0	0	0	-	0	.250	.250	1.000
2000 Detroit	AL	73	173	44	3	5	2	(2 0)	63	25	24	21	18	0	24	1	4	0	2	0	1.00	3	.254	.328	.364
2001 Detroit	AL	137	488	131	24	6	8	(7 1)	191	62	51	62	32	0	54	3	8	3	21	6	.78	7	.268	.316	.391
2002 Det-Mon		123	338	84	21	1	7	(4 3)	128	43	39	40	21	0	57	2	8	4	8	8	.50	4	.249	.293	.379
2002 Detroit	AL	33	107	25	4	0	0	(0 0)	29	10	6	7	8	0	13	1	4	1	3	2	.60	4	.234	.291	.271
2002 Montreal	NL	90	231	59	17	1	7	(4 3)	99	33	33	33	13	0	44	1	4	3	5	6	.45	2	.255	.294	.429
4 ML YEARS		338	1003	260	48	12	18	(14 4)	386	132	116	124	71	0	136	6	20	7	31	14	.69	16	.259	.310	.385

Rob Mackowiak

Bats: L **Throws:** R **Pos:** RF-75; CF-41; PH-29; 3B-26; 2B-3; LF-2; PR-1 **Ht:** 5'10" **Wt:** 190 **Born:** 6/20/76 **Age:** 27

						BATTING															BASERUNNING				AVERAGES		
Year Team	Lg	G	AB	H	2B	3B	HR	(Hm	Rd)	TB	R	RBI	RC	TBB	IBB	SO	HBP	SH	SF		SB	CS	SB%	GDP	Avg	OBP	Slg
1996 Pirates	R	27	86	23	6	1	0	(-	-)	31	8	14	12	13	1	11	1	0	1		3	1	.75	3	.267	.366	.360
1997 Erie	A-	61	203	58	14	2	1	(-	-)	79	26	25	27	21	0	47	7	3	1		1	7	.13	5	.286	.371	.389
1998 Augusta	A	25	70	17	4	0	1	(-	-)	24	16	8	9	13	0	19	1	1	0		4	2	.67	2	.243	.369	.343
1998 Lynchburg	A+	86	292	80	24	6	3	(-	-)	125	30	31	40	17	0	65	4	4	2		6	3	.67	4	.274	.321	.428
1999 Lynchburg	A+	74	263	80	7	4	7	(-	-)	116	51	30	41	18	0	57	6	4	0		9	4	.69	5	.304	.362	.441
1999 Altoona	AA	53	195	51	15	3	3	(-	-)	81	21	27	23	8	1	34	7	2	4		0	2	.00	6	.262	.308	.415
2000 Altoona	AA	134	526	156	33	4	13	(-	-)	236	82	87	79	22	0	96	9	4	7		18	5	.78	8	.297	.332	.449
2001 Nashville	AAA	32	118	31	5	0	4	(-	-)	48	14	14	15	7	0	39	0	2	1		1	1	.50	0	.263	.302	.407
2001 Pittsburgh	NL	83	214	57	15	2	4	(3	1)	88	30	21	28	15	5	52	3	2	3		4	3	.57	3	.266	.319	.411
2002 Pittsburgh	NL	136	385	94	22	0	16	(9	7)	164	57	48	58	42	5	120	7	3	2		9	3	.75	0	.244	.328	.426
2 ML YEARS		219	599	151	37	2	20	(12	8)	252	87	69	86	57	10	172	10	5	5		13	6	.68	3	.252	.325	.421

Greg Maddux

Pitches: R **Bats:** R **Pos:** SP-34 **Ht:** 6'0" **Wt:** 185 **Born:** 4/14/66 **Age:** 37

		HOW MUCH HE PITCHED						WHAT HE GAVE UP												THE RESULTS						
Year Team	Lg	G	GS	CG	GF	IP	BFP	H	R	ER	HR	SH	SF	HB	TBB	IBB	SO	WP	Bk		W	L	Pct	ShO	Sv-Op	Hld	ERC	ERA
1986 Chicago	NL	6	5	1	1	31.0	144	44	20	19	3	1	0	1	11	2	20	2	0		2	4	.333	0	0-0	0	6.45	5.52
1987 Chicago	NL	30	27	1	2	155.2	701	181	111	97	17	7	1	4	74	13	101	4	7		6	14	.300	1	0-0	0	5.42	5.61
1988 Chicago	NL	34	34	9	0	249.0	1047	230	97	88	13	11	2	9	81	16	140	3	6		18	8	.692	3	0-0	0	3.09	3.18
1989 Chicago	NL	35	35	7	0	238.1	1002	222	90	78	13	18	6	6	82	13	135	5	3		19	12	.613	1	0-0	0	3.20	2.95
1990 Chicago	NL	35	35	8	0	237.0	1011	242	116	91	11	18	6	6	71	10	144	3	3		15	15	.500	2	0-0	0	3.41	3.46
1991 Chicago	NL	37	37	7	0	263.0	1070	232	113	98	18	16	3	6	66	9	198	6	3		15	11	.577	2	0-0	0	2.73	3.35
1992 Chicago	NL	35	35	9	0	268.0	1061	201	68	65	7	15	3	14	70	7	199	5	0		20	11	.645	4	0-0	0	2.01	2.18
1993 Atlanta	NL	36	36	8	0	267.0	1064	228	85	70	14	15	7	6	52	7	197	5	1		20	10	.667	1	0-0	0	2.32	2.36
1994 Atlanta	NL	25	25	10	0	202.0	774	150	44	35	4	6	5	6	31	3	156	3	1		16	6	.727	3	0-0	0	1.59	1.56
1995 Atlanta	NL	28	28	10	0	209.2	785	147	39	38	8	9	1	4	23	3	181	1	0		19	2	.905	3	0-0	0	1.41	1.63
1996 Atlanta	NL	35	35	5	0	245.0	978	225	85	74	11	8	5	3	28	11	172	4	0		15	11	.577	1	0-0	0	2.22	2.72
1997 Atlanta	NL	33	33	5	0	232.2	893	200	58	57	9	11	7	6	20	6	177	0	0		19	4	.826	2	0-0	0	1.95	2.20
1998 Atlanta	NL	34	34	9	0	251.0	987	201	75	62	13	15	5	7	45	10	204	4	0		18	9	.667	5	0-0	0	2.01	2.22
1999 Atlanta	NL	33	33	4	0	219.1	940	258	103	87	16	15	5	4	37	8	136	1	0		19	9	.679	0	0-0	0	3.95	3.57
2000 Atlanta	NL	35	35	6	0	249.1	1012	225	91	83	19	8	5	10	42	12	190	1	2		19	9	.679	3	0-0	0	2.60	3.00
2001 Atlanta	NL	34	34	3	0	233.0	927	220	86	79	20	12	11	7	27	10	173	2	0		17	11	.607	3	0-0	0	2.70	3.05
2002 Atlanta	NL	34	34	0	0	199.1	820	194	67	58	14	13	4	4	45	7	118	1	0		16	6	.727	0	0-0	0	3.11	2.62
17 ML YEARS		539	535	102	3	3750.1	15216	3400	1348	1179	210	198	75	101	805	147	2641	50	26		273	152	.642	34	0-0	0	2.66	2.83

Calvin Maduro

Pitches: R **Bats:** R **Pos:** SP-10; RP-2 **Ht:** 6'0" **Wt:** 180 **Born:** 9/5/74 **Age:** 28

		HOW MUCH HE PITCHED						WHAT HE GAVE UP												THE RESULTS						
Year Team	Lg	G	GS	CG	GF	IP	BFP	H	R	ER	HR	SH	SF	HB	TBB	IBB	SO	WP	Bk		W	L	Pct	ShO	Sv-Op	Hld	ERC	ERA
1996 Philadelphia	NL	4	2	0	0	15.1	62	13	6	6	1	1	0	2	3	0	11	1	0		1	0	1.000	0	0-0	0	2.81	3.52
1997 Philadelphia	NL	15	13	0	0	71.0	331	83	59	57	12	1	4	3	41	5	31	6	2		3	7	.300	0	0-0	0	6.44	7.23
2000 Baltimore	AL	15	2	0	6	23.1	113	29	25	25	8	1	2	2	16	1	18	1	0		0	0	-	0	0-0	1	9.30	9.64
2001 Baltimore	AL	22	12	0	2	93.2	386	83	44	44	10	0	0	4	36	0	51	1	0		5	6	.455	0	0-0	0	3.71	4.23
2002 Baltimore	AL	12	10	0	2	56.2	252	64	37	35	12	0	1	1	22	1	29	1	0		2	5	.286	0	0-0	0	5.64	5.56
5 ML YEARS		68	39	0	11	260.0	1144	272	171	167	43	3	7	12	118	7	140	10	2		10	19	.345	0	0-0	2	5.25	5.78

Wendell Magee

Bats: R **Throws:** R **Pos:** CF-78; RF-9; LF-5; PH-5; DH-3; PR-3 **Ht:** 6'0" **Wt:** 227 **Born:** 8/3/72 **Age:** 30

						BATTING															BASERUNNING				AVERAGES		
Year Team	Lg	G	AB	H	2B	3B	HR	(Hm	Rd)	TB	R	RBI	RC	TBB	IBB	SO	HBP	SH	SF		SB	CS	SB%	GDP	Avg	OBP	Slg
1996 Philadelphia	NL	38	142	29	7	0	2	(2	0)	42	9	14	10	9	0	33	0	0	0		0	0	-	2	.204	.252	.296
1997 Philadelphia	NL	38	115	23	4	0	1	(0	1)	30	7	9	3	9	1	20	0	1	0		1	4	.20	8	.200	.254	.261
1998 Philadelphia	NL	20	75	22	6	1	1	(0	1)	33	9	11	10	7	0	11	0	0	2		0	0	-	4	.293	.354	.440
1999 Philadelphia	NL	12	14	5	1	0	2	(1	1)	12	4	5	4	1	0	4	0	0	0		0	0	-	1	.357	.400	.857
2000 Detroit	AL	91	186	51	4	2	7	(2	5)	80	31	31	23	10	0	28	0	0	1		1	0	1.00	8	.274	.310	.430
2001 Detroit	AL	90	207	44	11	4	5	(3	2)	78	26	17	22	23	1	44	1	1	1		3	0	1.00	8	.213	.293	.377
2002 Detroit	AL	97	347	94	19	1	6	(3	3)	133	34	35	34	10	0	64	1	1	5		2	4	.33	9	.271	.289	.383
7 ML YEARS		386	1086	268	52	8	24	(11	13)	408	120	122	106	69	2	204	2	2	9		7	8	.47	39	.247	.291	.376

Mike Magnante

Pitches: L **Bats:** L **Pos:** RP-32 **Ht:** 6'2" **Wt:** 212 **Born:** 6/17/65 **Age:** 38

		HOW MUCH HE PITCHED						WHAT HE GAVE UP												THE RESULTS						
Year Team	Lg	G	GS	CG	GF	IP	BFP	H	R	ER	HR	SH	SF	HB	TBB	IBB	SO	WP	Bk		W	L	Pct	ShO	Sv-Op	Hld	ERC	ERA
2002 Las Vegas*	AAA	7	0	0	1	6.0	27	5	3	2	1	0	1	0	2	0	4	0	0		1	0	1.000	0	0--	-	3.00	3.00
1991 Kansas City	AL	38	0	0	10	55.0	236	55	19	15	3	2	1	0	23	3	42	1	0		0	1	.000	0	0-0	2	3.76	2.45
1992 Kansas City	AL	44	12	0	11	89.1	403	115	53	49	5	5	7	2	35	5	31	2	0		4	9	.308	0	0-3	4	5.47	4.94
1993 Kansas City	AL	7	6	0	0	35.1	145	37	16	16	3	1	1	0	11	1	16	1	0		1	2	.333	0	0-0	0	4.16	4.08
1994 Kansas City	AL	36	1	0	10	47.0	211	55	27	24	5	2	3	0	16	1	21	3	0		2	3	.400	0	0-0	6	4.73	4.60
1995 Kansas City	AL	28	0	0	7	44.2	190	45	23	21	6	2	2	2	16	1	28	2	0		1	1	.500	0	0-1	5	4.41	4.23
1996 Kansas City	AL	38	0	0	9	54.0	238	58	38	34	5	0	4	4	24	1	32	3	0		2	2	.500	0	0-1	5	4.99	5.67
1997 Houston	NL	40	0	0	14	47.2	191	39	16	12	2	3	2	0	11	2	43	2	2		3	1	.750	0	1-5	3	2.08	2.27
1998 Houston	NL	48	0	0	20	51.2	237	56	28	28	2	3	1	4	26	4	39	3	0		4	7	.364	0	2-4	5	4.62	4.88
1999 Anaheim	AL	53	0	0	13	69.1	299	68	30	26	2	0	7	3	29	4	44	3	1		5	2	.714	0	0-3	4	3.63	3.38
2000 Oakland	AL	55	0	0	15	39.2	189	50	22	19	4	6	0	3	19	7	17	1	0		1	1	.500	0	0-1	8	5.49	4.31
2001 Oakland	AL	65	0	0	10	55.1	223	50	23	17	7	0	4	1	13	3	23	3	0		3	1	.750	0	0-1	18	3.13	2.77
2002 Oakland	AL	32	0	0	13	28.2	134	38	22	19	2	0	4	2	11	1	11	2	1		0	2	.000	0	0-1	3	5.71	5.97
12 ML YEARS		484	19	0	123	617.2	2696	666	317	280	45	24	34	20	234	33	347	26	4		26	32	.448	0	3-22	67	4.30	4.08

Chris Magruder

Bats: B **Throws:** R **Pos:** LF-45; RF-26; CF-20; PH-5; PR-5 **Ht:** 5'11" **Wt:** 200 **Born:** 4/26/77 **Age:** 26

Year Team	Lg	G	AB	H	2B	3B	HR	(Hm	Rd)	TB	R	RBI	RC	TBB	IBB	SO	HBP	SH	SF	SB	CS	SB%	GDP	Avg	OBP	Slg
1998 Salem-Keizer	A-	47	177	59	8	5	3	(-	-)	86	43	18	42	37	1	21	8	2	2	14	7	.67	2	.333	.464	.486
1998 Bakersfield	A+	22	92	28	7	0	1	(-	-)	38	21	4	16	13	1	16	0	0	0	3	0	1.00	0	.304	.390	.413
1999 Shreveport	AA	133	476	122	21	4	6	(-	-)	169	78	60	61	69	4	85	8	2	3	17	12	.59	15	.256	.358	.355
2000 Shreveport	AA	134	496	140	33	3	4	(-	-)	191	85	39	74	67	2	75	8	6	3	18	10	.64	11	.282	.375	.385
2001 Fresno	AAA	54	214	60	7	1	10	(-	-)	99	37	30	36	18	0	45	7	0	1	3	1	.75	2	.280	.354	.463
2001 Shreveport	AA	40	149	38	6	3	2	(-	-)	56	22	11	19	15	2	27	3	4	0	5	3	.63	2	.255	.335	.376
2001 Oklahoma	AAA	33	127	46	14	4	5	(-	-)	83	28	21	35	21	3	19	4	4	1	1	2	.33	3	.362	.464	.654
2002 Buffalo	AAA	54	191	51	10	2	5	(-	-)	80	28	16	30	26	2	34	3	4	0	3	2	.60	2	.267	.364	.419
2001 Texas	AL	17	29	5	0	0	0	(0	0)	5	3	1	0	1	0	5	1	0	0	0	0	-	1	.172	.226	.172
2002 Cleveland	AL	87	258	56	15	1	6	(3	3)	91	34	29	21	15	2	55	1	2	2	2	0	1.00	7	.217	.261	.353
2 ML YEARS		104	287	61	15	1	6	(3	3)	96	37	30	21	16	2	60	2	2	2	2	0	1.00	8	.213	.257	.334

Ron Mahay

Pitches: L **Bats:** L **Pos:** RP-11 **Ht:** 6'2" **Wt:** 190 **Born:** 6/28/71 **Age:** 32

		HOW MUCH HE PITCHED						WHAT HE GAVE UP												THE RESULTS							
Year Team	Lg	G	GS	CG	GF	IP	BFP	H	R	ER	HR	SH	SF	HB	TBB	IBB	SO	WP	Bk	W	L	Pct	ShO	Sv-Op	Hld	ERC	ERA
2002 Iowa*	AAA	39	1	0	13	46.2	186	32	11	10	3	2	0	0	15	1	50	4	0	0	1	.000	0	2--	-	1.92	1.93
1997 Boston	AL	28	0	0	7	25.0	105	19	7	7	3	1	0	0	11	0	22	3	0	3	0	1.000	0	0-2	6	3.01	2.52
1998 Boston	AL	29	0	0	6	26.0	120	26	16	10	2	0	4	2	15	1	14	3	0	1	1	.500	0	1-2	7	4.76	3.46
1999 Oakland	AL	6	1	0	2	19.1	68	8	4	4	2	0	0	0	3	0	15	0	0	2	0	1.000	0	1-1	0	0.88	1.86
2000 Oak-Fla		23	2	0	7	41.1	199	57	35	33	10	1	2	0	25	1	32	4	0	1	1	.500	0	0-0	2	8.55	7.19
2001 Chicago	NL	17	0	0	4	20.2	86	14	6	6	4	0	0	0	15	1	24	1	0	0	0	-	0	0-0	2	4.32	2.61
2002 Chicago	NL	11	0	0	1	14.2	65	13	14	14	6	0	0	0	8	0	14	0	0	2	0	1.000	0	0-0	6	6.11	8.59
2000 Oakland	AL	5	2	0	1	16.0	82	26	18	16	4	1	1	0	9	0	5	2	0	0	1	.000	0	0-0	0	9.97	9.00
2000 Florida	NL	18	0	0	6	25.1	117	31	17	17	6	0	1	0	16	1	27	2	0	1	0	1.000	0	0-0	2	7.67	6.04
6 ML YEARS		114	3	0	27	147.0	643	137	82	74	27	2	6	2	77	3	121	11	0	9	2	.818	0	2-5	17	4.82	4.53

Pat Mahomes

Pitches: R **Bats:** R **Pos:** RP-14; SP-2 **Ht:** 6'4" **Wt:** 212 **Born:** 8/9/70 **Age:** 32

		HOW MUCH HE PITCHED						WHAT HE GAVE UP												THE RESULTS							
Year Team	Lg	G	GS	CG	GF	IP	BFP	H	R	ER	HR	SH	SF	HB	TBB	IBB	SO	WP	Bk	W	L	Pct	ShO	Sv-Op	Hld	ERC	ERA
2002 Iowa*	AAA	44	5	0	34	72.1	291	57	30	28	11	3	2	0	20	1	70	1	1	4	5	.444	0	14--	-	2.77	3.48
1992 Minnesota	AL	14	13	0	1	69.2	302	73	41	39	5	0	3	0	37	0	44	2	1	3	4	.429	0	0-0	0	4.83	5.04
1993 Minnesota	AL	12	5	0	4	37.1	173	47	34	32	8	1	3	1	16	0	23	3	0	1	5	.167	0	0-0	0	6.71	7.71
1994 Minnesota	AL	21	21	0	0	120.0	517	121	68	63	22	1	4	1	62	1	53	0	0	9	5	.643	0	0-0	0	5.41	4.73
1995 Minnesota	AL	47	7	0	16	94.2	423	100	74	67	22	3	2	2	47	1	67	6	0	4	10	.286	0	3-7	9	5.88	6.37
1996 Min-Bos	AL	31	5	0	10	57.1	271	72	46	44	13	2	2	0	33	0	36	2	0	3	4	.429	0	2-2	4	7.39	6.91
1997 Boston	AL	10	0	0	2	10.0	54	15	10	9	2	0	1	2	10	1	5	0	0	0	1	.000	0	0-0	1	11.95	8.10
1999 New York	NL	39	0	0	12	63.2	265	44	26	26	7	1	2	2	37	5	51	2	0	8	0	1.000	0	0-1	3	3.22	3.68
2000 New York	NL	53	5	0	12	94.0	439	96	63	57	15	3	3	2	66	4	76	5	0	5	3	.625	0	0-1	3	5.87	5.46
2001 Texas	AL	56	4	0	14	107.1	475	115	71	68	17	2	7	0	55	9	61	3	0	7	6	.538	0	0-1	6	5.31	5.70
2002 Chicago	NL	16	2	0	2	32.2	147	36	15	14	3	3	0	1	17	3	23	1	0	1	1	.500	0	0-1	2	5.10	3.86
1996 Minnesota	AL	20	5	0	5	45.0	220	63	38	36	10	0	2	0	27	0	30	2	0	1	4	.200	0	0-0	3	8.43	7.20
1996 Boston	AL	11	0	0	5	12.1	51	9	8	8	3	2	0	0	6	0	6	0	0	2	0	1.000	0	2-2	1	3.89	5.84
10 ML YEARS		299	62	0	73	686.2	3066	719	448	419	114	16	27	11	380	24	439	28	1	42	38	.525	0	5-13	26	5.55	5.49

Mike Mahoney

Bats: R **Throws:** R **Pos:** C-16; PH-1 **Ht:** 6'1" **Wt:** 200 **Born:** 12/5/72 **Age:** 30

Year Team	Lg	G	AB	H	2B	3B	HR	(Hm	Rd)	TB	R	RBI	RC	TBB	IBB	SO	HBP	SH	SF	SB	CS	SB%	GDP	Avg	OBP	Slg
1995 Eugene	A-	43	112	27	6	0	1	(-	-)	36	14	15	13	15	1	17	3	1	1	6	2	.75	5	.241	.344	.321
1996 Durham	A+	101	363	94	24	2	9	(-	-)	149	52	46	45	23	0	64	7	4	4	4	3	.57	8	.259	.312	.410
1997 Greenville	AA	87	298	68	17	0	8	(-	-)	109	46	46	31	28	1	75	3	5	2	1	0	1.00	10	.228	.299	.366
1998 Greenville	AA	20	74	16	5	0	1	(-	-)	24	3	6	5	1	0	20	2	0	2	1	1	.50	1	.216	.241	.324
1998 Richmond	AAA	71	208	44	10	0	5	(-	-)	69	26	28	19	24	3	49	5	6	5	1	1	.50	10	.212	.302	.332
1999 Richmond	AAA	55	145	33	7	0	2	(-	-)	46	10	20	11	6	1	25	1	2	3	0	1	.00	2	.228	.258	.317
2000 W Tennessee	AA	24	76	23	7	0	0	(-	-)	30	12	7	12	7	0	16	2	0	1	0	0	-	0	.303	.372	.395
2000 Iowa	AAA	63	181	55	14	0	6	(-	-)	87	29	28	33	16	0	28	6	1	3	2	1	.67	2	.304	.374	.481
2001 Iowa	AAA	95	289	65	14	1	3	(-	-)	90	22	27	23	22	0	63	4	6	2	1	3	.25	8	.225	.287	.311
2002 Iowa	AAA	78	223	57	12	1	2	(-	-)	77	33	18	25	17	1	44	1	5	0	1	1	.50	4	.256	.311	.345
2000 Chicago	NL	4	7	2	1	0	0	(0	0)	3	1	1	2	1	0	1	1	0	0	0	0	-	0	.286	.444	.429
2002 Chicago	NL	16	29	6	3	0	0	(0	0)	9	2	3	0	1	1	10	0	1	0	0	0	-	1	.207	.233	.310
2 ML YEARS		20	36	8	4	0	0	(0	0)	12	3	4	2	2	1	10	1	1	0	0	0	-	1	.222	.282	.333

Oswaldo Mairena

Pitches: L **Bats:** L **Pos:** RP-31 **Ht:** 5'11" **Wt:** 165 **Born:** 6/30/74 **Age:** 29

		HOW MUCH HE PITCHED						WHAT HE GAVE UP												THE RESULTS							
Year Team	Lg	G	GS	CG	GF	IP	BFP	H	R	ER	HR	SH	SF	HB	TBB	IBB	SO	WP	Bk	W	L	Pct	ShO	Sv-Op	Hld	ERC	ERA
1997 Greensboro	A	49	0	0	20	60.1	241	43	24	17	2	3	1	1	16	3	75	0	3	6	1	.857	0	8--	-	1.70	2.54
1997 Tampa	A+	3	0	0	0	4.1	19	6	2	2	1	0	0	0	0	0	6	0	0	0	0	-	0	0--	-	5.44	4.15
1998 Tampa	A+	52	0	0	11	54.0	238	53	24	19	5	2	2	3	23	3	50	0	2	1	5	.167	0	0--	-	4.10	3.17
1999 Norwich	AA	49	0	0	16	57.1	252	48	24	17	3	4	4	1	27	4	47	4	0	4	3	.571	0	2--	-	2.96	2.67
2000 Norwich	AA	35	0	0	5	32.1	137	29	16	10	0	1	2	1	11	3	30	0	0	4	0	.000	0	0--	-	2.56	2.78
2000 Columbus	AAA	5	1	0	2	9.0	43	12	3	3	2	1	0	0	5	1	4	0	0	1	1	.500	0	0--	-	7.56	3.00
2000 W Tennessee	AA	2	0	0	1	2.0	10	3	1	0	0	1	0	1	1	1	1	0	0	0	1	.000	0	0--	-	8.24	0.00
2000 Iowa	AAA	11	0	0	3	14.2	62	13	9	8	1	1	0	0	2	0	4	3	0	1	0	1.000	0	0--	-	2.12	4.91
2001 Portland	AA	22	0	0	7	34.1	134	27	12	6	3	5	0	0	8	0	21	2	0	4	2	.667	0	3--	-	2.31	1.57

Year Team	Lg	G	GS	CG	GF	IP	BFP	H	R	ER	HR	SH	SF	HB	TBB	IBB	SO	WP	Bk	W	L	Pct	ShO	Sv-Op	Hld	ERC	ERA
2001 Calgary	AAA	31	0	0	8	39.1	179	52	33	33	4	2	2	0	13	5	44	2	0	3	2	.600	0	0--	-	5.45	7.55
2002 Marlins	R	1	1	0	0	1.1	4	1	0	0	0	0	0	0	0	0	1	0	0	0	0	-	0	0--	-	1.41	0.00
2002 Calgary	AAA	25	0	0	8	29.0	139	39	20	16	2	1	0	1	13	0	19	1	0	3	0	1.000	0	1--	-	6.10	4.97
2000 Chicago	NL	2	0	0	1	2.0	14	7	4	4	1	0	0	0	2	0	0	0	0	0	0	-	0	0-0	0	32.37	18.00
2002 Florida	NL	31	0	0	10	33.2	148	38	21	20	7	3	1	0	12	0	21	3	1	2	3	.400	0	0-0	3	5.42	5.35
2 ML YEARS		33	0	0	11	35.2	162	45	25	24	8	3	1	0	14	0	21	3	1	2	3	.400	0	0-0	3	6.58	6.06

Brian Mallette

Pitches: R Bats: R Pos: RP-5   **Ht: 6'0" Wt: 185 Born: 1/19/75 Age: 28**

Year Team	Lg	G	GS	CG	GF	IP	BFP	H	R	ER	HR	SH	SF	HB	TBB	IBB	SO	WP	Bk	W	L	Pct	ShO	Sv-Op	Hld	ERC	ERA
1997 Helena	R+	23	0	0	13	35.1	156	33	19	17	1	3	2	1	20	2	58	7	0	6	2	.750	0	5--	-	3.84	4.33
1998 Beloit	A	50	0	0	44	55.1	234	40	23	19	2	1	0	3	29	1	76	2	0	2	1	.667	0	23--	-	2.76	3.09
1999 Stockton	A+	28	0	0	14	36.0	162	38	16	6	1	0	1	3	16	1	34	0	0	2	0	1.000	0	4--	-	4.28	1.50
2000 Mudville	A+	50	0	0	15	71.0	316	52	35	26	6	1	3	5	52	1	94	11	0	4	4	.500	0	2--	-	3.99	3.30
2001 Huntsville	AA	44	0	0	39	55.0	232	43	13	12	4	4	1	3	23	4	71	4	0	7	2	.778	0	17--	-	2.85	1.96
2001 Indianapolis	AAA	12	0	0	6	17.0	69	10	4	2	2	0	1	1	8	0	23	1	0	0	1	.000	0	2--	-	2.52	1.06
2002 Indianapolis	AAA	45	0	0	38	45.1	191	39	15	14	4	3	2	3	17	1	50	0	0	3	2	.600	0	25--	-	3.36	2.78
2002 Milwaukee	NL	5	0	0	2	5.0	26	7	6	6	3	2	0	1	3	1	5	1	0	0	0	-	0	0-0	0	12.26	10.80

Marty Malloy

Bats: L Throws: R Pos: PH-18; 2B-3; PR-3; 3B-2   **Ht: 5'10" Wt: 165 Born: 4/6/72 Age: 31**

Year Team	Lg	G	AB	H	2B	3B	HR	(Hm	Rd)	TB	R	RBI	RC	TBB	IBB	SO	HBP	SH	SF	SB	CS	SB%	GDP	Avg	OBP	Slg
1992 Idaho Falls	R+	62	251	79	18	1	2	(-	-)	105	45	28	36	11	0	43	2	0	1	8	4	.67	2	.315	.347	.418
1993 Macon	A	109	376	110	19	3	2	(-	-)	141	55	36	54	39	3	70	2	3	3	24	8	.75	4	.293	.360	.375
1994 Durham	A+	118	428	113	22	1	6	(-	-)	155	53	35	54	52	2	69	2	2	3	18	12	.60	9	.264	.344	.362
1995 Greenville	AA	124	461	128	20	3	10	(-	-)	184	73	59	60	39	1	58	0	7	8	11	12	.48	6	.278	.329	.399
1996 Greenville	AA	111	429	134	27	2	4	(-	-)	177	82	36	68	54	6	50	4	6	2	11	10	.52	11	.312	.393	.413
1996 Richmond	AAA	18	64	13	2	1	0	(-	-)	17	7	8	5	5	1	7	0	2	1	3	0	1.00	1	.203	.257	.266
1997 Richmond	AAA	108	414	118	19	5	2	(-	-)	153	66	25	55	41	1	61	1	5	0	17	7	.71	6	.285	.351	.370
1998 Richmond	AAA	124	483	140	25	3	7	(-	-)	192	75	54	71	51	2	65	5	5	4	20	7	.74	12	.290	.361	.398
1999 Richmond	AAA	114	407	119	23	1	7	(-	-)	165	58	36	64	53	2	52	2	4	3	19	15	.56	2	.292	.374	.405
2000 Toledo	AAA	30	115	27	8	0	4	(-	-)	47	16	16	14	7	0	18	0	1	1	0	0	-	0	.235	.276	.409
2000 Tigers	R	2	1	1	0	0	0	(-	-)	1	0	1	1	2	0	0	0	0	1	0	0	-	0	1.000	1.000	1.000
2000 Lakeland	A+	7	26	6	1	0	1	(-	-)	10	4	4	3	1	0	1	1	0	0	1	0	1.00	0	.231	.286	.385
2001 Louisville	AAA	126	468	142	36	4	6	(-	-)	204	69	49	67	27	0	51	2	2	7	8	7	.53	8	.303	.340	.436
2002 Louisville	AAA	56	180	44	7	1	4	(-	-)	65	25	16	22	21	0	24	2	2	0	7	4	.64	7	.244	.330	.361
1998 Atlanta	NL	11	28	5	1	0	1	(0	1)	9	3	1	2	2	0	2	0	0	0	0	0	-	0	.179	.233	.321
2002 Florida	NL	24	25	3	0	0	0	(0	0)	3	1	1	0	2	0	8	0	1	0	0	0	-	1	.120	.185	.120
2 ML YEARS		35	53	8	1	0	1	(0	1)	12	4	2	2	4	0	10	0	1	0	0	0	-	1	.151	.211	.226

Jim Mann

Pitches: R Bats: R Pos: RP-17   **Ht: 6'3" Wt: 225 Born: 11/17/74 Age: 28**

Year Team	Lg	G	GS	CG	GF	IP	BFP	H	R	ER	HR	SH	SF	HB	TBB	IBB	SO	WP	Bk	W	L	Pct	ShO	Sv-Op	Hld	ERC	ERA
1994 Blue Jays	R	11	9	0	0	53.0	236	54	28	22	1	3	1	3	26	1	41	0	1	3	2	.600	0	0--	-	4.12	3.74
1995 Medicine Hat	R+	14	14	1	0	77.2	347	78	47	37	5	3	2	7	37	0	66	6	0	5	4	.556	1	0--	-	4.49	4.29
1996 St. Ctharines	A-	26	0	0	23	27.1	117	22	12	11	3	2	3	3	10	1	37	0	1	2	1	.667	0	17--	-	3.24	3.62
1997 Hagerstown	A	19	0	0	16	26.2	122	35	18	15	4	0	1	1	11	0	90	2	0	0	1	.000	0	4--	-	6.67	5.06
1997 Dunedin	A+	12	0	0	4	18.0	88	27	12	12	2	0	1	1	6	1	13	1	0	1	0	1.000	0	0--	-	6.86	6.00
1998 Dunedin	A+	51	0	0	47	50.1	206	31	19	17	4	0	2	0	24	1	59	2	0	2	2	.000	0	25--	-	2.17	3.04
1999 Knoxville	AA	6	0	0	4	9.2	39	6	2	1	1	3	1	2	1	0	12	0	0	1	2	.333	0	0--	-	1.77	0.93
1999 Syracuse	AAA	47	0	0	20	66.0	287	53	35	34	11	1	1	2	39	1	72	6	0	6	5	.545	0	5--	-	4.28	4.64
2000 Norfolk	AAA	49	0	0	19	81.2	326	61	27	27	8	3	2	2	33	3	74	3	1	3	4	.429	0	3--	-	2.87	2.98
2001 New Orleans	AAA	53	0	0	50	68.0	272	52	21	19	7	5	2	2	17	2	81	4	0	6	3	.667	0	27--	-	2.37	2.51
2002 New Orleans	AAA	33	0	0	28	34.2	142	33	20	16	6	2	1	1	8	1	29	3	0	0	3	.000	0	22--	-	3.74	4.15
2002 Round Rock	AA	1	0	0	1	2.0	7	1	1	1	1	0	0	0	0	0	2	0	0	0	0	-	0	0--	-	1.73	4.50
2000 New York	NL	2	0	0	2	2.2	15	6	3	3	1	0	0	0	1	0	0	0	0	0	0	-	0	0-0	0	14.72	10.13
2001 Houston	NL	4	0	0	1	5.1	23	3	2	2	0	0	0	2	4	0	5	0	0	0	0	-	0	0-0	0	3.87	3.38
2002 Houston	NL	17	0	0	12	22.0	94	19	10	10	3	1	0	5	7	1	19	0	0	0	1	.000	0	0-0	0	4.12	4.09
3 ML YEARS		23	0	0	15	30.0	132	28	15	15	4	1	0	7	12	1	24	0	0	0	1	.000	0	0-0	0	4.90	4.50

Matt Mantei

Pitches: R Bats: R Pos: RP-31   **Ht: 6'1" Wt: 200 Born: 7/7/73 Age: 29**

Year Team	Lg	G	GS	CG	GF	IP	BFP	H	R	ER	HR	SH	SF	HB	TBB	IBB	SO	WP	Bk	W	L	Pct	ShO	Sv-Op	Hld	ERC	ERA
2002 El Paso*	AA	4	3	0	0	4.0	16	3	1	1	0	0	0	0	1	0	5	0	0	0	1	.000	0	0--	-	1.65	2.25
2002 Tucson*	AAA	9	1	0	2	10.0	44	8	1	0	0	1	0	1	4	0	9	1	0	0	1	1.000	0	0--	-	2.56	0.00
1995 Florida	NL	12	0	0	3	13.1	64	12	8	7	1	1	0	1	13	0	15	1	0	0	1	.000	0	0-0	0	5.54	4.73
1996 Florida	NL	14	0	0	1	18.1	89	13	13	13	2	1	0	1	21	1	25	2	0	1	0	1.000	0	0-1	0	5.46	6.38
1998 Florida	NL	42	0	0	23	54.2	224	38	19	18	1	3	4	7	23	3	63	0	0	3	4	.429	0	9-12	2	2.44	2.96
1999 Fla-Ari	NL	65	0	0	60	65.1	284	44	21	20	5	1	1	5	44	1	99	2	0	1	3	.250	0	32-37	0	3.42	2.76
2000 Arizona	NL	47	0	0	38	45.1	200	31	24	23	4	2	0	2	35	1	53	5	0	1	1	.500	0	17-20	0	3.80	4.57
2001 Arizona	NL	8	0	0	7	7.0	31	6	2	2	2	0	0	0	4	0	12	1	0	0	0	-	0	2-2	1	5.18	2.57
2002 Arizona	NL	31	0	0	6	26.2	122	28	15	14	3	0	0	1	12	0	26	1	0	1	2	.500	0	4-4	2	4.64	4.73
1999 Florida	NL	35	0	0	32	36.1	157	24	11	11	4	0	1	2	25	1	50	0	0	1	2	.333	0	10-12	0	3.55	2.72
1999 Arizona	NL	30	0	0	28	29.0	127	20	10	9	1	1	0	3	19	0	49	2	0	0	1	.000	0	22-25	0	3.25	2.79
7 ML YEARS		219	0	0	138	230.2	1014	172	102	97	18	8	6	16	152	6	293	13	0	8	11	.421	0	60-73	5	3.72	3.78

Josias Manzanillo

Pitches: R **Bats:** R **Pos:** RP-13   **Ht:** 6'0" **Wt:** 205 **Born:** 10/16/67 **Age:** 35

Year Team	Lg	G	GS	CG	GF	IP	BFP	H	R	ER	HR	SH	SF	HB	TBB	IBB	SO	WP	Bk	W	L	Pct	ShO	Sv-Op	Hld	ERC	ERA
2002 Nashville*	AAA	15	1	0	4	20.1	79	18	6	6	3	0	0	0	2	1	14	1	0	1	0	1.000	0	1--	-	2.58	2.66
2002 Hickory*	A	1	0	0	0	2.0	12	5	3	2	1	0	0	0	0	0	1	0	0	0	0	-	0	0--	-	14.49	9.00
1991 Boston	AL	1	0	0	1	1.0	8	2	2	2	0	0	0	0	2	0	0	0	0	0	0	-	0	0-0	0	21.46	18.00
1993 Mil-NYM	NL	16	1	0	6	29.0	140	30	27	22	2	3	3	2	19	3	21	1	0	1	1	.500	0	1-2	0	4.92	6.83
1994 New York	NL	37	0	0	14	47.1	186	34	15	14	4	0	0	3	13	2	48	2	0	3	2	.600	0	2-5	11	2.28	2.66
1995 NYM-NYY	NL	23	0	0	8	33.1	154	37	19	18	4	2	1	2	15	4	25	6	0	1	2	.333	0	0-0	0	4.97	4.86
1997 Seattle	AL	16	0	0	4	18.1	88	19	13	11	3	0	2	0	17	1	18	2	0	0	1	.000	0	0-1	1	6.97	5.40
1999 New York	NL	12	0	0	1	18.2	80	19	12	12	5	1	1	2	4	1	25	0	0	0	0	-	0	0-0	1	4.90	5.79
2000 Pittsburgh	NL	43	0	0	11	58.2	246	50	23	22	6	4	2	0	32	4	39	1	0	2	2	.500	0	0-2	5	3.85	3.38
2001 Pittsburgh	NL	71	0	0	25	79.2	329	60	32	30	4	5	8	5	26	3	80	4	0	3	2	.600	0	2-7	9	2.33	3.39
2002 Pittsburgh	NL	13	0	0	5	13.0	61	20	11	11	5	0	0	1	5	0	4	0	0	0	1	.000	0	0-1	0	10.63	7.62
1993 Milwaukee	NL	10	1	0	4	17.0	86	22	20	18	1	2	2	2	10	3	10	1	0	1	1	.500	0	1-2	0	6.15	9.53
1993 New York	NL	6	0	0	2	12.0	54	8	7	4	1	1	1	0	9	0	11	0	0	0	0	-	0	0-0	0	3.32	3.00
1995 New York	NL	12	0	0	4	16.0	73	18	15	14	3	0	1	0	6	2	14	5	0	1	2	.333	0	0-0	0	4.93	7.88
1995 New York	AL	11	0	0	4	17.1	81	19	4	4	1	2	0	2	9	2	11	1	0	0	0	-	0	0-0	0	4.96	2.08
9 ML YEARS		232	1	0	75	299.0	1292	271	154	142	33	15	17	15	134	18	261	16	0	10	10	.500	0	5-18	27	3.91	4.27

Mike Maroth

Pitches: L **Bats:** L **Pos:** SP-21   **Ht:** 6'0" **Wt:** 180 **Born:** 8/17/77 **Age:** 25

Year Team	Lg	G	GS	CG	GF	IP	BFP	H	R	ER	HR	SH	SF	HB	TBB	IBB	SO	WP	Bk	W	L	Pct	ShO	Sv-Op	Hld	ERC	ERA
1998 Red Sox	R	4	2	0	1	12.2	49	9	3	0	0	0	0	0	2	0	14	0	0	1	1	.500	0	0--	-	1.34	0.00
1998 Lowell	A-	6	6	0	0	31.0	127	22	13	10	1	0	1	3	13	0	34	3	0	2	3	.400	0	0--	-	2.57	2.90
1999 Sarasota	A+	20	19	0	0	111.1	497	124	65	50	3	6	4	10	35	1	64	11	2	11	6	.647	0	0--	-	4.13	4.04
1999 Lakeland	A+	3	3	0	0	16.2	71	18	7	6	1	1	0	0	7	0	11	2	0	2	1	.667	0	0--	-	4.47	3.24
1999 Jacksonville	AA	4	4	0	0	20.2	96	27	15	11	2	1	1	0	7	0	10	1	0	1	2	.333	0	0--	-	5.45	4.79
2000 Jacksonville	AA	27	26	2	0	164.1	689	176	79	72	14	9	9	3	58	0	85	6	1	9	14	.391	1	0--	-	4.43	3.94
2001 Toledo	AAA	24	23	0	0	131.2	587	158	80	68	11	5	5	4	50	1	63	4	0	7	10	.412	0	0--	-	5.19	4.65
2002 Toledo	AAA	11	11	1	0	73.1	289	53	25	23	7	1	2	0	22	0	51	2	0	8	1	.889	1	0--	-	2.26	2.82
2002 Detroit	AL	21	21	0	0	128.2	538	136	68	64	7	5	3	2	36	1	58	4	0	6	10	.375	0	0-0	0	3.73	4.48

Jason Marquis

Pitches: R **Bats:** L **Pos:** SP-22   **Ht:** 6'1" **Wt:** 210 **Born:** 8/21/78 **Age:** 24

Year Team	Lg	G	GS	CG	GF	IP	BFP	H	R	ER	HR	SH	SF	HB	TBB	IBB	SO	WP	Bk	W	L	Pct	ShO	Sv-Op	Hld	ERC	ERA
2002 Richmond*	AAA	1	1	0	0	5.0	21	5	2	2	0	1	0	0	1	0	6	1	0	0	1	.000	0	0--	-	2.60	3.60
2000 Atlanta	NL	15	0	0	7	23.1	103	23	16	13	4	1	1	1	12	1	17	1	0	1	0	1.000	0	0-1	1	5.13	5.01
2001 Atlanta	NL	38	16	0	9	129.1	556	113	62	50	14	6	5	4	59	4	98	1	2	5	6	.455	0	0-2	2	3.70	3.48
2002 Atlanta	NL	22	22	0	0	114.1	507	127	66	64	19	4	3	3	49	3	84	4	0	8	9	.471	0	0-0	0	5.43	5.04
3 ML YEARS		75	38	0	16	267.0	1166	263	144	127	37	11	9	8	120	8	199	6	2	14	15	.483	0	0-3	3	4.54	4.28

Eli Marrero

Bats: R **Throws:** R **Pos:** RF-46; C-44; LF-39; CF-36; PH-12; PR-5; 1B-4   **Ht:** 6'1" **Wt:** 180 **Born:** 11/17/73 **Age:** 29

Year Team	Lg	G	AB	H	2B	3B	HR	(Hm	Rd)	TB	R	RBI	RC	TBB	IBB	SO	HBP	SH	SF	SB	CS	SB%	GDP	Avg	OBP	Slg
1997 St Louis	NL	17	45	11	2	0	2	(0	2)	19	4	7	6	2	1	13	0	0	1	4	0	1.00	1	.244	.271	.422
1998 St Louis	NL	83	254	62	18	1	4	(2	2)	94	28	20	30	28	5	42	0	0	1	6	2	.75	5	.244	.318	.370
1999 St Louis	NL	114	317	61	13	1	6	(3	3)	94	32	34	18	18	4	56	1	4	3	11	2	.85	14	.192	.236	.297
2000 St Louis	NL	53	102	23	3	1	5	(2	3)	43	21	17	14	9	0	16	3	0	2	5	0	1.00	4	.225	.302	.422
2001 St Louis	NL	86	203	54	11	3	6	(2	4)	89	37	23	27	15	2	36	0	3	3	6	3	.67	4	.266	.312	.438
2002 St Louis	NL	131	397	104	19	1	18	(9	9)	179	63	66	60	40	11	72	0	5	4	14	2	.88	5	.262	.327	.451
6 ML YEARS		484	1318	315	66	7	41	(18	23)	518	185	167	155	112	23	235	4	13	14	46	9	.84	32	.239	.298	.393

Damaso Marte

Pitches: L **Bats:** L **Pos:** RP-68   **Ht:** 6'2" **Wt:** 200 **Born:** 2/14/75 **Age:** 28

Year Team	Lg	G	GS	CG	GF	IP	BFP	H	R	ER	HR	SH	SF	HB	TBB	IBB	SO	WP	Bk	W	L	Pct	ShO	Sv-Op	Hld	ERC	ERA
1999 Seattle	AL	5	0	0	2	16.9	89	16	9	9	3	0	0	0	6	0	3	0	0	0	1	.000	0	0-0	0	13.32	9.35
2001 Pittsburgh	NL	23	0	0	4	36.1	154	34	21	19	5	1	2	3	12	3	39	1	0	0	1	.000	0	0-0	0	3.93	4.71
2002 Chicago	AL	68	0	0	22	60.1	240	44	19	19	5	1	1	4	18	2	72	3	1	1	1	.500	0	10-12	16	2.42	2.83
3 ML YEARS		96	0	0	28	105.1	441	94	49	47	13	2	3	7	36	5	114	4	1	1	3	.250	0	10-12	16	3.63	4.02

Al Martin

Bats: L **Throws:** L **Pos:** RF   **Ht:** 6'2" **Wt:** 214 **Born:** 11/24/67 **Age:** 35

Year Team	Lg	G	AB	H	2B	3B	HR	(Hm	Rd)	TB	R	RBI	RC	TBB	IBB	SO	HBP	SH	SF	SB	CS	SB%	GDP	Avg	OBP	Slg
1992 Pittsburgh	NL	12	12	2	0	0	0	(0	0)	4	1	2	1	0	0	5	0	0	1	0	0	-	0	.167	.154	.333
1993 Pittsburgh	NL	143	480	135	26	8	18	(15	3)	231	85	64	77	42	5	122	1	2	3	16	9	.64	5	.281	.338	.481
1994 Pittsburgh	NL	82	276	79	12	4	9	(6	3)	126	48	33	47	34	3	56	2	0	1	15	6	.71	3	.286	.367	.457
1995 Pittsburgh	NL	124	439	124	25	3	13	(8	5)	194	70	41	60	44	6	92	2	1	5	20	11	.65	5	.282	.351	.442
1996 Pittsburgh	NL	155	630	189	40	1	18	(8	10)	285	101	72	103	54	2	116	2	1	7	38	12	.76	9	.300	.354	.452
1997 Pittsburgh	NL	113	423	123	24	7	13	(8	5)	200	64	59	73	45	7	83	3	1	5	23	7	.77	7	.291	.359	.473
1998 Pittsburgh	NL	125	440	105	15	2	12	(5	7)	160	57	47	47	32	2	91	5	0	2	20	3	.87	13	.239	.296	.364
1999 Pittsburgh	NL	143	541	150	36	8	24	(12	12)	274	97	63	93	49	5	119	1	0	2	20	3	.87	8	.277	.337	.506
2000 SD-Sea		135	480	137	15	10	15	(10	5)	217	81	36	73	36	5	85	4	0	3	10	9	.53	3	.285	.338	.452

								BATTING											BASERUNNING				AVERAGES		
Year Team	Lg	G	AB	H	2B	3B	HR	(Hm | Rd)	TB	R	RBI	RC	TBB	IBB	SO	HBP	SH	SF	SB	CS	SB%	GDP	Avg	OBP	Slg
2001 Seattle	AL	100	283	68	15	2	7	(2 | 5)	108	41	42	38	37	4	59	2	0	2	9	3	.75	2	.240	.330	.382
2000 San Diego	NL	93	346	106	13	6	11	(8 | 3)	164	62	27	57	28	5	54	2	0	2	6	8	.43	2	.306	.360	.474
2000 Seattle	AL	42	134	31	2	4	4	(2 | 2)	53	19	9	16	8	0	31	2	0	1	4	1	.80	1	.231	.283	.396
10 ML YEARS		1132	4004	1112	208	46	129	(74 | 55)	1799	645	459	619	373	39	828	22	5	26	171	63	.73	55	.278	.341	.449

Tom Martin

Pitches: L Bats: L Pos: RP-2 **Ht: 6'1" Wt: 206 Born: 5/21/70 Age: 33**

		HOW MUCH HE PITCHED						WHAT HE GAVE UP										THE RESULTS							
Year Team	Lg	G	GS	CG	GF	IP	BFP	H	R	ER	HR	SH	SF	HB	TBB	IBB	SO	WP	Bk	W	L	Pct	ShO	Sv-Op	Hld	ERC	ERA
2002 Durham*	AAA	4	0	0	3	3.1	14	3	0	0	0	0	0	0	1	0	6	0	0	0	0	—	0	2- --		2.46	0.00
1997 Houston	NL	55	0	0	18	56.0	236	52	13	13	2	6	1	1	23	2	36	3	0	5	3	.625	0	2-3	9	3.34	2.09
1998 Cleveland	AL	14	0	0	1	14.2	85	29	21	21	3	1	1	0	12	0	9	2	0	1	1	.500	0	0-0	3	13.19	12.89
1999 Cleveland	AL	6	0	0	0	9.1	44	13	9	9	2	0	1	0	3	1	8	0	0	0	1	.000	0	0-0	0	6.64	8.68
2000 Cleveland	AL	31	0	0	7	33.1	143	32	16	15	3	0	1	1	15	2	21	1	0	1	0	1.000	0	0-0	0	4.05	4.05
2001 New York	NL	14	0	0	2	17.0	85	23	22	19	4	1	1	1	10	2	12	0	0	1	0	1.000	0	0-0	1	8.02	10.06
2002 Tampa Bay	AL	2	0	0	2	1.2	11	5	3	3	0	0	0	0	1	0	1	0	0	0	0	—	0	0-0	0	17.54	16.20
6 ML YEARS		122	0	0	30	132.0	604	154	84	80	14	8	5	3	64	7	87	6	0	8	5	.615	0	2-3	11	5.42	5.45

Edgar Martinez

Bats: R Throws: R Pos: DH-91; PH-6 **Ht: 5'11" Wt: 210 Born: 1/2/63 Age: 40**

								BATTING											BASERUNNING				AVERAGES		
Year Team	Lg	G	AB	H	2B	3B	HR	(Hm	Rd)	TB	R	RBI	RC	TBB	IBB	SO	HBP	SH	SF	SB	CS	SB%	GDP	Avg	OBP	Slg
1987 Seattle	AL	13	43	16	5	2	0	(0	0)	25	6	5	10	2	0	5	1	0	0	0	0	—	0	.372	.413	.581
1988 Seattle	AL	14	32	9	4	0	0	(0	0)	13	0	5	5	4	0	7	0	1	1	0	0	—	0	.281	.351	.406
1989 Seattle	AL	65	171	41	5	0	2	(0	2)	52	20	20	17	17	1	26	3	2	3	2	1	.67	3	.240	.314	.304
1990 Seattle	AL	144	487	147	27	2	11	(3	8)	211	71	49	83	74	3	62	5	1	3	1	4	.20	13	.302	.397	.433
1991 Seattle	AL	150	544	167	35	1	14	(8	6)	246	98	52	97	84	9	72	8	2	4	0	3	.00	19	.307	.405	.452
1992 Seattle	AL	135	528	181	46	3	18	(11	7)	287	100	73	110	54	2	61	4	1	5	14	4	.78	15	.343	.404	.544
1993 Seattle	AL	42	135	32	7	0	4	(1	3)	51	20	13	20	28	1	19	0	1	1	0	0	—	4	.237	.366	.378
1994 Seattle	AL	89	326	93	23	1	13	(4	9)	157	47	51	63	53	3	42	3	2	3	6	2	.75	2	.285	.387	.482
1995 Seattle	AL	145	511	182	52	0	29	(16	13)	321	121	113	144	116	19	87	8	0	4	4	3	.57	11	.356	.479	.628
1996 Seattle	AL	139	499	163	52	2	26	(14	12)	297	121	103	132	123	12	84	8	0	4	3	3	.50	15	.327	.464	.595
1997 Seattle	AL	155	542	179	35	1	28	(12	16)	300	104	108	130	119	11	86	11	0	6	2	4	.33	21	.330	.456	.554
1998 Seattle	AL	154	556	179	46	1	29	(17	12)	314	86	102	130	106	4	96	3	0	7	1	1	.50	13	.322	.429	.565
1999 Seattle	AL	142	502	169	35	1	24	(12	12)	278	86	86	121	97	6	99	6	0	3	7	2	.78	12	.337	.447	.554
2000 Seattle	AL	153	556	180	31	0	37	(19	18)	322	100	145	131	96	8	95	5	0	8	3	0	1.00	13	.324	.423	.579
2001 Seattle	AL	132	470	144	40	1	23	(10	13)	255	80	116	108	93	9	90	9	0	6	4	1	.80	11	.306	.423	.543
2002 Seattle	AL	97	328	91	23	0	15	(9	6)	159	42	59	61	67	8	69	6	0	6	1	1	.50	6	.277	.403	.485
16 ML YEARS		1769	6230	1973	466	15	273	(136	137)	3288	1102	1100	1362	1133	96	1000	80	10	67	48	29	.62	158	.317	.424	.528

Pedro Martinez

Pitches: R Bats: R Pos: SP-30 **Ht: 5'11" Wt: 180 Born: 10/25/71 Age: 31**

		HOW MUCH HE PITCHED						WHAT HE GAVE UP										THE RESULTS							
Year Team	Lg	G	GS	CG	GF	IP	BFP	H	R	ER	HR	SH	SF	HB	TBB	IBB	SO	WP	Bk	W	L	Pct	ShO	Sv-Op	Hld	ERC	ERA
1992 Los Angeles	NL	2	1	0	1	8.0	31	6	2	2	0	0	0	0	1	0	8	0	0	0	1	.000	0	0-0	0	1.38	2.25
1993 Los Angeles	NL	65	2	0	20	107.0	444	76	34	31	5	0	5	4	57	4	119	3	1	10	5	.667	0	2-3	14	2.79	2.61
1994 Montreal	NL	24	23	1	1	144.2	584	115	58	55	11	2	3	11	45	3	142	6	0	11	5	.688	1	1-1	0	2.81	3.42
1995 Montreal	NL	30	30	2	0	194.2	784	158	79	76	21	7	3	11	66	1	174	5	2	14	10	.583	2	0-0	0	3.19	3.51
1996 Montreal	NL	33	33	4	0	216.2	901	189	100	89	19	9	6	3	70	3	222	6	0	13	10	.565	1	0-0	0	3.02	3.70
1997 Montreal	NL	31	31	13	0	241.1	947	158	65	56	16	9	1	9	67	5	305	3	1	17	8	.680	4	0-0	0	1.79	1.90
1998 Boston	AL	33	33	3	0	233.2	951	188	82	75	26	4	7	8	67	3	251	9	0	19	7	.731	2	0-0	0	2.78	2.89
1999 Boston	AL	31	29	5	1	213.1	835	160	56	49	9	3	6	9	37	1	313	6	0	23	4	.852	1	0-0	0	1.79	2.07
2000 Boston	AL	29	29	7	0	217.0	817	128	44	42	17	2	1	14	32	0	284	1	0	18	6	.750	4	0-0	0	1.39	1.74
2001 Boston	AL	18	18	1	0	116.2	456	84	33	31	5	2	0	6	25	0	163	4	0	7	3	.700	0	0-0	0	1.84	2.39
2002 Boston	AL	30	30	2	0	199.1	787	144	62	50	13	2	4	15	40	1	239	3	0	20	4	.833	0	0-0	0	1.98	2.26
11 ML YEARS		326	259	38	23	1892.1	7537	1406	615	551	142	40	36	90	507	21	2220	46	4	152	63	.707	15	3-4	14	2.27	2.62

Ramon Martinez

Bats: R Throws: R Pos: SS-40; 2B-17; PH-8; 1B-4; LF-3; 3B-2; PR-2 **Ht: 6'1" Wt: 183 Born: 10/10/72 Age: 30**

								BATTING											BASERUNNING				AVERAGES		
Year Team	Lg	G	AB	H	2B	3B	HR	(Hm	Rd)	TB	R	RBI	RC	TBB	IBB	SO	HBP	SH	SF	SB	CS	SB%	GDP	Avg	OBP	Slg
1998 San Francisco	NL	19	19	6	1	0	0	(0	0)	7	4	0	4	4	0	2	0	1	0	0	0	—	0	.316	.435	.368
1999 San Francisco	NL	61	144	38	6	0	5	(3	2)	59	21	19	19	14	0	17	0	6	1	1	2	.33	2	.264	.327	.410
2000 San Francisco	NL	88	189	57	13	2	6	(4	2)	92	30	25	31	15	1	22	1	4	1	3	2	.60	6	.302	.354	.487
2001 San Francisco	NL	128	391	99	18	3	5	(1	4)	138	48	37	44	38	6	52	5	6	6	1	2	.33	11	.253	.323	.353
2002 San Francisco	NL	72	181	49	10	2	4	(4	0)	75	26	25	32	14	2	26	4	0	1	2	0	1.00	1	.271	.335	.414
5 ML YEARS		368	924	249	48	7	20	(12	8)	371	129	106	130	85	9	119	10	17	9	7	6	.54	20	.269	.335	.402

Tino Martinez

Bats: L Throws: R Pos: 1B-149; PH-4 **Ht: 6'2" Wt: 210 Born: 12/7/67 Age: 35**

								BATTING											BASERUNNING				AVERAGES		
Year Team	Lg	G	AB	H	2B	3B	HR	(Hm	Rd)	TB	R	RBI	RC	TBB	IBB	SO	HBP	SH	SF	SB	CS	SB%	GDP	Avg	OBP	Slg
1990 Seattle	AL	24	68	15	4	0	0	(0	0)	19	4	5	7	9	0	9	0	0	0	0	0	—	0	.221	.308	.279
1991 Seattle	AL	36	112	23	2	0	4	(3	1)	37	11	9	10	11	0	24	0	0	2	0	0	—	0	.205	.272	.330
1992 Seattle	AL	136	460	118	19	2	16	(10	6)	189	53	66	54	42	9	77	2	1	8	2	1	.67	24	.257	.316	.411
1993 Seattle	AL	109	408	108	25	1	17	(8	9)	186	48	60	62	45	9	56	5	3	3	0	1	.00	7	.265	.343	.456
1994 Seattle	AL	97	329	86	21	0	20	(8	12)	167	42	61	51	29	2	52	1	4	3	1	2	.33	9	.261	.320	.508
1995 Seattle	AL	141	519	152	35	3	31	(14	17)	286	92	111	102	62	15	91	4	2	6	0	0	—	10	.293	.369	.551

Year Team	Lg	G	AB	H	2B	3B	HR	(Hm	Rd)	TB	R	RBI	RC	TBB	IBB	SO	HBP	SH	SF	SB	CS	SB%	GDP	Avg	OBP	Slg
1996 New York	AL	155	595	174	28	0	25	(9	16)	277	82	117	97	68	4	85	2	1	5	2	1	.67	18	.292	.364	.466
1997 New York	AL	158	594	176	31	2	44	(18	26)	343	96	141	122	75	14	75	3	0	13	3	1	.75	15	.296	.371	.577
1998 New York	AL	142	531	149	33	1	28	(12	16)	268	92	123	92	61	3	83	6	0	10	2	1	.67	18	.281	.355	.505
1999 New York	AL	159	589	155	27	2	28	(7	21)	270	95	105	90	69	7	86	3	0	4	3	4	.43	14	.263	.341	.458
2000 New York	AL	155	569	147	37	4	16	(12	4)	240	69	91	76	52	9	74	8	0	3	4	1	.80	16	.258	.328	.422
2001 New York	AL	154	589	165	24	2	34	(22	12)	295	89	113	93	42	2	89	2	0	2	1	2	.33	12	.280	.329	.501
2002 St Louis	NL	150	511	134	25	1	21	(12	9)	224	63	75	70	58	9	71	2	1	4	3	2	.60	12	.262	.337	.438
13 ML YEARS		1616	5874	1602	311	18	284	(136	148)	2801	836	1077	926	623	83	872	38	12	64	21	18	.54	157	.273	.343	.477

Victor Martinez

Bats: B **Throws:** R **Pos:** C-9; PH-5   **Ht:** 6'2" **Wt:** 170 **Born:** 12/23/78 **Age:** 24

Year Team	Lg	G	AB	H	2B	3B	HR	(Hm	Rd)	TB	R	RBI	RC	TBB	IBB	SO	HBP	SH	SF	SB	CS	SB%	GDP	Avg	OBP	Slg
1999 Mahning VI	A-	64	235	65	9	0	4	(-	-)	86	37	36	31	27	0	31	1	0	6	0	1	.00	4	.277	.346	.366
2000 Kinston	A+	26	83	18	7	0	0	(-	-)	25	9	8	8	11	0	5	1	3	1	1	1	.50	3	.217	.313	.301
2000 Columbus	A	21	70	26	9	1	2	(-	-)	43	11	12	19	11	0	6	1	0	2	0	0	-	1	.371	.452	.614
2001 Kinston	A+	114	420	138	33	2	10	(-	-)	205	59	57	76	39	1	60	8	0	3	3	3	.50	12	.329	.394	.488
2002 Akron	AA	121	443	149	40	0	22	(-	-)	255	84	85	100	58	6	62	8	0	6	3	3	.50	10	.336	.417	.576
2002 Cleveland	AL	12	32	9	1	0	1	(1	0)	13	2	5	5	3	0	2	0	0	1	0	0	-	1	.281	.333	.406

Henry Mateo

Bats: B **Throws:** R **Pos:** PH-13; PR-5; 2B-3; SS-2   **Ht:** 5'11" **Wt:** 170 **Born:** 10/14/76 **Age:** 26

Year Team	Lg	G	AB	H	2B	3B	HR	(Hm	Rd)	TB	R	RBI	RC	TBB	IBB	SO	HBP	SH	SF	SB	CS	SB%	GDP	Avg	OBP	Slg
1995 Expos	R	38	122	18	0	0	0	(-	-)	18	11	6	2	14	0	47	5	5	1	2	7	.22	2	.148	.261	.148
1996 Expos	R	14	44	11	3	0	0	(-	-)	14	8	3	7	5	0	11	3	2	0	5	1	.83	0	.250	.365	.318
1997 Vermont	A-	67	228	56	9	3	1	(-	-)	74	32	31	28	30	1	44	7	3	2	21	11	.66	4	.246	.348	.325
1998 Cape Fear	A	114	416	115	20	5	4	(-	-)	157	72	41	57	40	2	111	13	15	4	22	16	.58	5	.276	.355	.377
1998 Jupiter	A+	12	43	12	3	1	0	(-	-)	17	11	6	7	2	0	6	2	1	1	3	0	1.00	6	.279	.333	.395
1999 Jupiter	A+	118	447	116	27	7	4	(-	-)	169	69	58	60	44	3	112	10	17	6	32	16	.67	4	.260	.335	.378
2000 Harrisburg	AA	140	530	152	25	11	5	(-	-)	214	91	63	84	58	0	97	6	4	2	48	16	.75	4	.287	.362	.404
2001 Ottawa	AAA	118	500	134	14	12	5	(-	-)	187	71	43	66	33	1	89	7	11	1	47	14	.77	2	.268	.322	.374
2002 Ottawa	AAA	74	285	73	10	6	5	(-	-)	110	35	25	33	18	0	53	3	7	1	15	6	.71	6	.256	.306	.386
2001 Montreal	NL	5	9	3	1	0	0	(0	0)	4	1	0	1	0	0	1	0	0	0	0	0	-	0	.333	.333	.444
2002 Montreal	NL	22	23	4	0	1	0	(0	0)	6	1	0	1	2	1	6	0	0	0	2	0	1.00	0	.174	.240	.261
2 ML YEARS		27	32	7	1	1	0	(0	0)	10	2	0	2	2	1	7	0	0	0	2	0	1.00	0	.219	.265	.313

Julio Mateo

Pitches: R **Bats:** R **Pos:** RP-12   **Ht:** 6'0" **Wt:** 177 **Born:** 8/2/77 **Age:** 25

		HOW MUCH HE PITCHED						WHAT HE GAVE UP										THE RESULTS						
Year Team	Lg	G	GS	CG	GF	IP	BFP	H	R	ER	HR	SH	SF	HB	TBB	IBB	SO	WP	Bk	W	L	Pct	ShO	Sv-Op	Hld	ERC	ERA
1997 Mariners	R	13	6	0	4	60.0	254	45	32	22	1	2	2	8	23	0	54	10	1	3	1	.750	0	1--	-	2.58	3.30
1998 Lancaster	A+	1	0	0	0	1.1	6	1	1	1	0	0	1	1	1	0	1	0	0	0	0	-	0	0--	-	15.24	6.75
1998 Everett	A-	28	0	0	13	38.1	170	40	25	20	6	3	2	2	17	1	37	6	0	3	3	.500	0	4--	-	5.10	4.70
1999 Wisconsin	A	20	0	0	10	29.0	131	31	18	14	2	2	1	1	8	2	27	2	0	1	3	.250	0	4--	-	3.56	4.34
2000 Wisconsin	A	36	1	0	15	68.2	295	63	38	32	12	4	1	6	23	1	73	9	0	4	8	.333	0	4--	-	4.16	4.19
2001 Sn Brnardino	A+	56	0	0	47	66.0	273	58	28	21	5	2	1	2	16	5	79	1	1	5	4	.556	0	26--	-	2.64	2.86
2002 San Antonio	AA	12	0	0	4	17.1	61	7	3	1	2	0	0	0	3	0	18	0	0	1	0	1.000	0	0--	-	0.92	0.52
2002 Tacoma	AAA	20	0	0	16	31.0	137	39	15	14	2	1	2	4	7	1	23	2	0	4	2	.667	0	6--	-	5.17	4.06
2002 Seattle	AL	12	0	0	7	21.0	94	20	10	10	2	0	1	0	12	0	15	1	0	0	0	-	0	0-0	2	4.63	4.29

Ruben Mateo

Bats: R **Throws:** R **Pos:** PH-25; RF-23; CF-2; PR-1   **Ht:** 6'0" **Wt:** 185 **Born:** 2/10/78 **Age:** 25

Year Team	Lg	G	AB	H	2B	3B	HR	(Hm	Rd)	TB	R	RBI	RC	TBB	IBB	SO	HBP	SH	SF	SB	CS	SB%	GDP	Avg	OBP	Slg
2002 Louisville*	AAA	52	209	63	14	0	6	(-	-)	104	37	23	35	11	1	40	3	0	2	6	2	.75	2	.301	.342	.498
1999 Texas	AL	32	122	29	9	1	5	(2	3)	55	16	18	15	4	0	28	1	0	0	3	0	1.00	2	.238	.268	.451
2000 Texas	AL	52	206	60	11	0	7	(3	4)	92	32	19	31	10	1	34	5	1	0	6	0	1.00	5	.291	.339	.447
2001 Texas	AL	40	129	32	5	2	1	(0	1)	44	18	13	14	9	0	28	6	1	0	1	0	1.00	4	.248	.322	.341
2002 Cincinnati	NL	46	86	22	6	0	2	(2	0)	34	11	7	7	6	0	20	2	0	0	0	0	-	1	.256	.319	.395
4 ML YEARS		170	543	143	31	3	15	(7	8)	225	77	57	67	29	1	110	14	2	2	10	0	1.00	12	.263	.316	.414

Mike Matheny

Bats: R **Throws:** R **Pos:** C-106; PH-4; 1B-1   **Ht:** 6'3" **Wt:** 205 **Born:** 9/22/70 **Age:** 32

Year Team	Lg	G	AB	H	2B	3B	HR	(Hm	Rd)	TB	R	RBI	RC	TBB	IBB	SO	HBP	SH	SF	SB	CS	SB%	GDP	Avg	OBP	Slg
1994 Milwaukee	NL	28	53	12	3	0	1	(1	0)	18	3	2	5	3	0	13	2	1	0	0	1	.00	1	.226	.293	.340
1995 Milwaukee	NL	80	166	41	9	1	0	(0	0)	52	13	21	16	12	0	28	2	1	0	2	1	.67	3	.247	.306	.313
1996 Milwaukee	NL	106	313	64	15	2	8	(5	3)	107	31	46	23	14	0	80	3	7	4	3	2	.60	9	.204	.243	.342
1997 Milwaukee	NL	123	320	78	16	1	4	(2	2)	108	29	32	30	17	0	68	7	9	3	0	1	.00	9	.244	.294	.338
1998 Milwaukee	NL	108	320	76	13	0	6	(4	2)	107	24	27	28	11	0	63	7	3	0	1	0	1.00	9	.238	.278	.334
1999 Toronto	AL	57	163	35	6	0	3	(1	2)	50	16	11	13	12	0	37	1	2	1	0	0	-	6	.215	.271	.307
2000 St Louis	NL	128	417	109	22	1	6	(2	4)	151	43	47	46	32	8	96	4	7	0	0	0	-	11	.261	.317	.362
2001 St Louis	NL	121	381	83	12	0	7	(4	3)	116	40	42	29	28	5	76	4	8	3	0	1	.00	11	.218	.276	.304
2002 St Louis	NL	110	315	77	12	1	3	(1	2)	100	31	35	35	32	6	49	2	8	6	1	3	.25	3	.244	.313	.317
9 ML YEARS		861	2448	575	108	6	38	(20	18)	809	230	269	225	161	19	510	32	46	21	7	9	.44	56	.235	.289	.330

T.J. Mathews

Pitches: R **Bats:** R **Pos:** RP-12   **Ht:** 6'1" **Wt:** 225 **Born:** 1/19/70 **Age:** 33

		HOW MUCH HE PITCHED						WHAT HE GAVE UP											THE RESULTS						
Year Team	Lg	G	GS	CG	GF	IP	BFP	H	R	ER	HR	SH	SF	HB	TBB	IBB	SO	WP	Bk	W	L	Pct	ShO	Sv-Op	Hld	ERC	ERA
2002 New Orleans*	AAA	4	0	0	1	5.0	20	3	1	1	0	0	0	0	1	0	3	1	0	0	0	-	0	0- -		1.06	1.80
2002 Round Rock*	AA	1	0	0	0	1.0	5	1	0	0	0	0	0	0	0	0	1	0	0	0	0	-	0	0- -		1.51	0.00
2002 Memphis*	AAA	4	0	0	1	4.0	17	3	2	2	1	0	0	0	2	0	3	0	0	0	0	-	0	0- -		4.02	4.50
1995 St Louis	NL	23	0	0	12	29.2	120	21	7	5	1	4	0	0	11	1	28	2	0	1	1	.500	0	2-2	7	1.99	1.52
1996 St Louis	NL	67	0	0	23	83.2	345	62	32	28	8	5	0	2	32	4	80	1	0	2	6	.250	0	6-11	9	2.60	3.01
1997 Stl-Oak		64	0	0	26	74.2	329	75	32	25	9	8	1	2	30	4	70	1	0	10	6	.625	0	3-9	12	4.20	3.01
1998 Oakland	AL	66	0	0	15	72.2	319	71	44	37	6	2	9	4	29	3	53	1	0	7	4	.636	0	1-4	19	3.91	4.58
1999 Oakland	AL	50	0	0	15	59.0	242	46	28	25	9	5	1	2	20	4	42	2	0	9	5	.643	0	3-5	17	3.02	3.81
2000 Oakland	AL	50	0	0	19	59.2	273	73	40	40	10	1	4	2	25	5	42	2	0	2	3	.400	0	0-1	5	5.98	6.03
2001 Oak-Stl		30	0	0	7	37.2	164	39	20	18	4	2	1	0	12	3	29	1	0	1	1	.500	0	1-1	5	3.78	4.30
2002 Houston	NL	12	0	0	4	18.1	76	19	7	7	2	1	0	0	5	3	13	0	0	0	0	-	0	0-0	2	3.66	3.44
1997 St Louis	NL	40	0	0	12	46.0	197	41	14	11	4	6	0	1	18	3	46	1	0	4	4	.500	0	0-3	8	3.29	2.15
1997 Oakland	AL	24	0	0	14	28.2	132	34	18	14	5	2	1	1	12	1	24	0	0	6	2	.750	0	3-6	4	5.80	4.40
2001 Oakland	AL	20	0	0	4	23.0	108	28	14	13	2	2	0	0	11	3	19	1	0	0	1	.000	0	1-1	3	5.18	5.09
2001 St Louis	NL	10	0	0	3	14.2	56	11	6	5	2	0	1	0	1	0	10	0	0	1	0	1.000	0	0-0	2	1.77	3.07
8 ML YEARS		362	0	0	121	435.1	1868	406	210	185	49	28	16	12	164	27	357	10	0	32	26	.552	0	16-33	80	3.67	3.82

Julius Matos

Bats: R **Throws:** R **Pos:** 2B-49; 3B-17; PH-7; SS-4; PR-4; RF-3; 1B-2; DH-1   **Ht:** 5'11" **Wt:** 170 **Born:** 12/12/74 **Age:** 28

		BATTING																BASERUNNING				AVERAGES		
Year Team	Lg	G	AB	H	2B	3B	HR	(Hm | Rd)	TB	R	RBI	RC	TBB	IBB	SO	HBP	SH	SF	SB	CS	SB%	GDP	Avg	OBP	Slg
1994 Watertown	A-	43	138	34	2	2	0	(- | -)	40	13	18	11	13	0	33	1	0	2	3	2	.60	6	.246	.307	.290
1995 Columbus	A	52	155	38	7	3	0	(- | -)	51	16	13	13	11	1	21	3	1	0	2	2	.50	8	.245	.308	.329
1996 Thunder Bay	IND	82	295	81	13	0	3	(- | -)	103	33	32	29	14	0	48	2	5	1	8	7	.53	9	.275	.311	.349
1997 Sioux City	IND	83	353	94	12	3	6	(- | -)	130	64	44	40	20	0	38	4	1	2	8	7	.53	4	.266	.311	.368
1998 High Desert	A+	111	439	132	27	4	4	(- | -)	179	70	60	58	23	0	40	2	7	8	19	13	.59	9	.301	.333	.408
1999 El Paso	AA	120	425	119	17	5	5	(- | -)	161	54	41	46	13	0	37	1	4	3	5	2	.71	10	.280	.301	.379
2000 Mobile	AA	135	546	144	30	0	5	(- | -)	189	61	35	54	31	0	57	2	7	0	11	9	.55	13	.264	.306	.346
2001 Mobile	AA	19	67	22	6	0	0	(- | -)	28	13	2	9	1	0	5	1	2	1	1	2	.33	2	.328	.343	.418
2001 Portland	AAA	106	383	107	12	2	7	(- | -)	144	40	34	43	15	2	48	6	3	3	6	8	.43	6	.279	.314	.376
2002 Portland	AAA	50	186	58	17	0	4	(- | -)	87	20	26	28	9	0	20	2	5	3	1	2	.33	6	.312	.345	.468
2002 San Diego	NL	76	185	44	3	0	2	(0 | 2)	53	19	19	13	9	0	33	2	3	1	1	1	.50	5	.238	.279	.286

Luis Matos

Bats: R **Throws:** R **Pos:** RF-7; CF-6; PH-4; LF-2; PR-2   **Ht:** 6'0" **Wt:** 179 **Born:** 10/30/78 **Age:** 24

		BATTING																BASERUNNING				AVERAGES		
Year Team	Lg	G	AB	H	2B	3B	HR	(Hm | Rd)	TB	R	RBI	RC	TBB	IBB	SO	HBP	SH	SF	SB	CS	SB%	GDP	Avg	OBP	Slg
2002 Frederick*	A+	3	12	4	1	0	0	(- | -)	5	2	1	2	2	0	3	0	0	0	0	0	-	0	.333	.429	.417
2002 Bowie*	AA	62	218	60	14	2	9	(- | -)	105	34	40	39	32	1	45	2	1	3	14	4	.78	6	.275	.370	.482
2000 Baltimore	AL	72	182	41	6	3	1	(1 | 0)	56	21	17	15	12	0	30	3	2	2	13	4	.76	7	.225	.281	.308
2001 Baltimore	AL	31	98	21	7	0	4	(1 | 3)	40	16	12	14	11	0	30	1	2	0	7	0	1.00	1	.214	.300	.408
2002 Baltimore	AL	17	31	4	1	0	0	(0 | 0)	5	0	1	0	1	0	6	0	1	0	1	0	1.00	1	.129	.156	.161
3 ML YEARS		120	311	66	14	3	5	(2 | 3)	101	37	30	29	24	0	66	4	5	2	21	4	.84	9	.212	.276	.325

Hideki Matsui

Bats: L **Throws:** R **Pos:** LF   **Ht:** 6'2" **Wt:** 210 **Born:** 6/12/74 **Age:** 29

		BATTING																BASERUNNING				AVERAGES		
Year Team	Lg	G	AB	H	2B	3B	HR	(Hm | Rd)	TB	R	RBI	RC	TBB	IBB	SO	HBP	SH	SF	SB	CS	SB%	GDP	Avg	OBP	Slg
1993 Yomiuri	Jap	57	184	41	9	0	11	(- | -)	83	27	27	25	17	0	50	2	0	1	1	0	1.00	1	.223	.296	.451
1994 Yomiuri	Jap	130	503	148	23	4	20	(- | -)	239	70	66	86	57	1	101	4	1	4	6	3	.67	12	.294	.368	.475
1995 Yomiuri	Jap	131	501	142	31	1	22	(- | -)	241	76	80	85	62	1	93	2	2	2	9	7	.56	12	.283	.363	.481
1996 Yomiuri	Jap	130	487	153	34	1	38	(- | -)	303	97	99	118	71	1	98	4	0	7	7	2	.78	5	.314	.401	.622
1997 Yomiuri	Jap	135	484	144	18	0	37	(- | -)	273	93	103	115	100	10	84	6	0	6	9	3	.75	5	.298	.419	.564
1998 Yomiuri	Jap	135	487	142	24	3	34	(- | -)	274	103	100	114	104	2	101	8	0	4	3	5	.38	7	.292	.421	.563
1999 Yomiuri	Jap	135	471	143	24	2	42	(- | -)	297	100	95		93	-	99	4	0	6	0	4	.00	9	.304	.416	.631
2000 Yomiuri	Jap	135	474	150	32	1	42	(- | -)	310	116	108	133	106	5	108	2	0	7	5	2	.71	1	.316	.438	.654
2001 Yomiuri	Jap	140	481	160	23	3	36	(- | -)	297	107	104	133	120	6	96	3	0	7	3	3	.50	9	.333	.463	.617
2002 Yomiuri	Jap	140	500	167	27	1	50	(- | -)	346	112	107	148	114	17	104	6	0	3	3	4	.43	4	.334	.461	.692

Mike Matthews

Pitches: L **Bats:** L **Pos:** RP-47   **Ht:** 6'2" **Wt:** 175 **Born:** 10/24/73 **Age:** 29

		HOW MUCH HE PITCHED						WHAT HE GAVE UP											THE RESULTS						
Year Team	Lg	G	GS	CG	GF	IP	BFP	H	R	ER	HR	SH	SF	HB	TBB	IBB	SO	WP	Bk	W	L	Pct	ShO	Sv-Op	Hld	ERC	ERA
2000 St Louis	NL	14	0	0	4	9.1	54	15	12	12	2	0	0	1	10	2	8	0	0	0	0	-	0	0-0	2	11.83	11.57
2001 St Louis	NL	51	10	0	7	89.0	368	74	32	32	11	4	1	4	33	4	72	4	1	3	4	.429	0	1-3	3	3.34	3.24
2002 Stl-Mil	NL	47	0	0	10	45.2	205	43	23	20	5	2	4	2	29	3	34	5	1	2	1	.667	0	0-2	4	4.84	3.94
2002 St Louis	NL	43	0	0	10	41.2	184	40	21	18	5	2	4	2	22	2	32	5	0	2	1	.667	0	0-2	4	4.64	3.89
2002 Milwaukee	NL	4	0	0	0	4.0	21	3	2	2	0	0	0	0	7	1	2	0	1	0	0	-	0	0-0	0	6.63	4.50
3 ML YEARS		112	10	0	21	144.0	627	132	67	64	18	6	5	7	72	9	114	9	2	5	5	.500	0	1-5	9	4.29	4.00

Gary Matthews Jr

Bats: B **Throws:** R **Pos:** RF-76; LF-16; CF-16; PH-11; PR-3; DH-1   **Ht:** 6'3" **Wt:** 210 **Born:** 8/25/74 **Age:** 28

Year Team	Lg	G	AB	H	2B	3B	HR	(Hm	Rd)	TB	R	RBI	RC	TBB	IBB	SO	HBP	SH	SF	SB	CS	SB%	GDP	Avg	OBP	Slg
1999 San Diego	NL	23	36	8	0	0	0	(0	0)	8	4	7	4	9	0	9	0	0	0	2	1	1.00	1	.222	.378	.222
2000 Chicago	NL	80	158	30	1	2	4	(2	2)	47	24	14	13	15	1	28	1	1	0	3	0	1.00	2	.190	.264	.297
2001 ChC-Pit	NL	152	405	92	15	2	14	(4	10)	153	63	44	51	62	2	100	1	5	1	8	5	.62	8	.227	.328	.378
2002 NYM-Bal		111	345	95	25	3	7	(6	1)	147	54	38	55	43	1	69	1	5	4	15	5	.75	4	.275	.354	.426
2001 Chicago	NL	106	258	56	9	1	9	(2	7)	94	41	30	31	38	2	55	1	5	0	5	3	.63	4	.217	.320	.364
2001 Pittsburgh	NL	46	147	36	6	1	5	(2	3)	59	22	14	20	22	0	45	0	0	1	3	2	.60	4	.245	.341	.401
2002 New York	NL	2	1	0	0	0	0	(0	0)	0	0	0	0	0	0	0	0	0	0	0	0	-	0	.000	.000	.000
2002 Baltimore	AL	109	344	95	25	3	7	(6	1)	147	54	38	55	43	1	69	1	5	4	15	5	.75	4	.276	.355	.427
4 ML YEARS		366	944	225	41	7	25	(12	13)	355	145	103	123	127	4	206	3	11	5	28	10	.74	15	.238	.329	.376

Dave Maurer

Pitches: L **Bats:** R **Pos:** RP-2   **Ht:** 6'2" **Wt:** 205 **Born:** 2/23/75 **Age:** 28

Year Team	Lg	G	GS	CG	GF	IP	BFP	H	R	ER	HR	SH	SF	HB	TBB	IBB	SO	WP	Bk	W	L	Pct	ShO	Sv-Op	Hld	ERC	ERA
2002 Buffalo*	AAA	36	3	0	12	68.1	274	50	27	22	6	2	0	3	24	0	73	2	0	5	1	.833	0	5--	-	2.61	2.90
2000 San Diego	NL	14	0	0	1	14.2	64	15	8	6	2	0	0	2	5	1	13	1	0	0	1	.000	0	0-1	2	4.71	3.68
2001 San Diego	NL	3	0	0	1	5.0	27	8	6	6	1	0	0	0	4	0	4	1	0	0	0	-	0	0-0	0	10.33	10.80
2002 Cleveland	AL	2	0	0	2	1.1	7	3	2	2	1	0	0	0	0	0	0	0	0	1	0	1.000	0	0-0	0	16.20	13.50
3 ML YEARS		19	0	0	4	21.0	98	26	16	14	4	0	0	2	9	1	17	2	0	1	1	.500	0	0-1	2	6.63	6.00

Darrell May

Pitches: L **Bats:** L **Pos:** SP-21; RP-9   **Ht:** 6'2" **Wt:** 184 **Born:** 6/13/72 **Age:** 31

Year Team	Lg	G	GS	CG	GF	IP	BFP	H	R	ER	HR	SH	SF	HB	TBB	IBB	SO	WP	Bk	W	L	Pct	ShO	Sv-Op	Hld	ERC	ERA
2002 Omaha*	AAA	2	2	0	0	12.0	41	8	1	1	0	0	1	0	0	0	9	0	0	1	0	1.000	0	0--	-	0.98	0.75
2002 Wichita*	AA	1	1	0	0	4.1	18	4	1	1	0	0	0	0	1	0	5	0	0	0	0	-	0	0--	-	2.34	2.08
1995 Atlanta	NL	2	0	0	1	4.0	21	10	5	5	0	0	1	0	0	0	1	0	0	0	0	-	0	0-0	0	11.41	11.25
1996 Pit-Ana		10	2	0	2	11.1	60	18	13	12	6	0	2	1	6	0	6	0	0	0	1	.000	0	0-0	1	12.24	9.53
1997 Anaheim	AL	29	2	0	7	51.2	234	56	31	30	6	3	4	0	25	2	42	2	0	2	1	.667	0	0-1	2	4.87	5.23
2002 Kansas City	AL	30	21	2	3	131.1	579	144	83	78	28	3	5	1	50	3	95	2	0	4	10	.286	1	0-1	0	5.35	5.35
1996 Pittsburgh	NL	5	2	0	0	8.2	47	15	10	9	5	0	0	0	4	0	5	0	0	0	1	.000	0	0-0	1	13.48	9.35
1996 Anaheim	AL	5	0	0	2	2.2	13	3	3	3	1	0	2	1	2	0	1	0	0	0	0	-	0	0-0	0	8.41	10.13
4 ML YEARS		71	25	2	13	198.1	894	228	132	125	40	6	12	2	81	5	144	4	0	6	12	.333	1	0-2	3	5.69	5.67

Brent Mayne

Bats: L **Throws:** R **Pos:** C-99; PH-7   **Ht:** 6'1" **Wt:** 190 **Born:** 4/19/68 **Age:** 35

Year Team	Lg	G	AB	H	2B	3B	HR	(Hm	Rd)	TB	R	RBI	RC	TBB	IBB	SO	HBP	SH	SF	SB	CS	SB%	GDP	Avg	OBP	Slg
2002 Wichita*	AA	2	4	2	0	0	0	(-	-)	2	0	1	1	1	0	0	0	0	0	0	0	-	1	.500	.600	.500
1990 Kansas City	AL	5	13	3	0	0	0	(0	0)	3	2	1	1	3	0	3	0	0	0	0	1	.00	1	.231	.375	.231
1991 Kansas City	AL	85	231	58	8	0	3	(2	1)	75	22	31	22	23	4	42	0	2	3	2	4	.33	6	.251	.315	.325
1992 Kansas City	AL	82	213	48	10	0	0	(0	0)	58	16	18	12	11	0	26	0	4	2	0	4	.00	5	.225	.260	.272
1993 Kansas City	AL	71	205	52	9	1	2	(0	2)	69	22	22	20	18	7	31	1	3	0	3	2	.60	6	.254	.317	.337
1994 Kansas City	AL	46	144	37	5	1	2	(1	1)	50	19	20	16	14	1	27	0	0	1	1	0	1.00	3	.257	.323	.347
1995 Kansas City	AL	110	307	77	18	1	1	(1	0)	100	23	27	24	25	1	41	3	11	1	0	1	.00	16	.251	.313	.326
1996 New York	NL	70	99	26	6	0	1	(0	1)	35	9	6	11	12	1	22	0	2	0	0	1	.00	4	.263	.342	.354
1997 Oakland	AL	85	256	74	12	0	6	(4	2)	104	29	22	35	18	1	33	4	2	2	1	0	1.00	5	.289	.343	.406
1998 San Francisco	NL	94	275	75	15	0	3	(0	3)	99	26	32	36	37	3	47	1	2	2	2	1	.67	8	.273	.359	.360
1999 San Francisco	NL	117	322	97	32	0	2	(1	1)	135	39	39	50	43	5	65	5	1	3	2	2	.50	16	.301	.389	.419
2000 Colorado	NL	117	335	101	21	0	6	(3	3)	140	36	64	52	47	13	48	1	4	8	1	3	.25	12	.301	.381	.418
2001 Col-KC		100	326	93	11	1	2	(1	1)	112	28	40	35	26	5	41	1	0	6	1	2	.33	12	.285	.334	.344
2002 Kansas City	AL	101	326	77	8	2	4	(2	2)	101	35	30	31	34	1	54	2	4	4	4	4	.50	8	.236	.309	.310
2001 Colorado	NL	49	160	53	7	0	0	(0	0)	60	15	20	23	16	3	24	0	0	3	0	0	-	4	.331	.385	.375
2001 Kansas City	AL	51	166	40	4	1	2	(1	1)	52	13	20	12	10	2	17	1	0	3	1	2	.33	8	.241	.283	.313
13 ML YEARS		1083	3052	818	155	6	32	(15	17)	1081	306	352	348	311	42	480	18	33	32	17	25	.40	102	.268	.336	.354

Joe Mays

Pitches: R **Bats:** B **Pos:** SP-17   **Ht:** 6'1" **Wt:** 185 **Born:** 12/10/75 **Age:** 27

Year Team	Lg	G	GS	CG	GF	IP	BFP	H	R	ER	HR	SH	SF	HB	TBB	IBB	SO	WP	Bk	W	L	Pct	ShO	Sv-Op	Hld	ERC	ERA
2002 Fort Myers*	A+	3	3	0	0	8.2	36	9	2	2	0	0	0	0	3	0	7	1	0	1	0	1.000	0	0--	-	3.50	2.08
2002 New Britain*	AA	1	1	0	0	7.0	25	2	1	1	1	0	0	1	1	0	5	1	0	1	0	1.000	0	0--	-	0.89	1.29
1999 Minnesota	AL	49	20	2	8	171.0	746	179	92	83	24	7	6	2	67	2	115	6	0	6	11	.353	1	0-0	2	4.62	4.37
2000 Minnesota	AL	31	28	2	1	160.1	723	193	105	99	20	3	5	2	67	1	102	11	0	7	15	.318	1	0-0	0	5.59	5.56
2001 Minnesota	AL	34	34	4	0	233.2	957	205	87	82	25	8	8	5	64	2	123	11	0	17	13	.567	2	0-0	0	3.05	3.16
2002 Minnesota	AL	17	17	1	0	95.1	418	113	60	57	14	2	2	2	25	0	38	6	0	4	8	.333	1	0-0	0	4.99	5.38
4 ML YEARS		131	99	9	9	660.1	2844	690	344	321	83	20	21	11	223	5	378	34	0	34	47	.420	5	0-0	2	4.32	4.38

Dave McCarty

Bats: R **Throws:** R **Pos:** LF-11; 1B-9; PH-6; PR-1   **Ht:** 6'5" **Wt:** 215 **Born:** 11/23/69 **Age:** 33

Year Team	Lg	G	AB	H	2B	3B	HR	(Hm	Rd)	TB	R	RBI	RC	TBB	IBB	SO	HBP	SH	SF	SB	CS	SB%	GDP	Avg	OBP	Slg
2002 Durham*	AAA	29	114	37	7	1	8	(-	-)	70	25	22	26	14	1	33	0	0	0	0	1	.00	1	.325	.398	.614
1993 Minnesota	AL	98	350	75	15	2	2	(2	0)	100	36	21	18	19	0	80	1	1	0	2	6	.25	13	.214	.257	.286
1994 Minnesota	AL	44	131	34	8	2	1	(1	0)	49	21	12	15	7	1	32	5	0	0	2	1	.67	3	.260	.322	.374

Year Team	Lg	G	AB	H	2B	3B	HR	(Hm Rd)	TB	R	RBI	RC	TBB	IBB	SO	HBP	SH	SF	SB	CS	SB%	GDP	Avg	OBP	Slg
1995 Min-SF		37	75	17	4	1	0	(0 0)	23	11	6	6	6	0	22	1	0	1	1	1	.50	1	.227	.289	.307
1996 San Francisco	NL	91	175	38	3	0	6	(5 1)	59	16	24	17	18	0	43	2	0	2	2	1	.67	5	.217	.294	.337
1998 Seattle	AL	8	18	5	0	0	1	(1 0)	8	1	2	4	5	0	4	0	0	0	1	0	1.00		.278	.435	.444
2000 Kansas City	AL	103	270	75	14	2	12	(6 6)	129	34	53	41	22	1	68	0	0	3	0	0	-	6	.278	.329	.478
2001 Kansas City	AL	98	200	50	10	0	7	(5 2)	81	26	26	26	24	1	45	1	1	4	0	0	-	8	.250	.328	.405
2002 KC-TB	AL	25	66	9	1	0	2	(0 2)	16	5	4	2	6	0	19	2	0	0	0	0	-		.136	.230	.242
1995 Minnesota	AL	25	55	12	3	1	0	(0 0)	17	10	4	4	4	0	18	1	0	1	0	1	.00		.218	.279	.309
1995 San Francisco	NL	12	20	5	1	0	0	(0 0)	6	1	2	2	2	0	4	0	0	0	1	0	1.00		.250	.318	.300
2002 Kansas City	AL	13	32	3	1	0	1	(0 1)	7	3	2	0	2	0	10	0	0	0	0	0	-		.094	.147	.219
2002 Tampa Bay	AL	12	34	6	0	0	1	(0 1)	9	2	2	2	4	0	9	2	0	0	0	0	-		.176	.300	.265
8 ML YEARS		504	1285	303	55	7	31	(20 11)	465	150	148	129	107	3	313	12	2	10	8	9	.47	37	.236	.298	.362

Seth McClung

Pitches: R Bats: L Pos: SP; RP **Ht: 6'6" Wt: 235 Born: 2/7/81 Age: 22**

Year Team	Lg	G	GS	CG	GF	IP	BFP	H	R	ER	HR	SH	SF	HB	TBB	IBB	SO	WP	Bk	W	L	Pct	ShO	Sv-Op	Hld	ERC	ERA
1999 Princeton	R+	13	6	0	0	45.2	244	53	47	39	3	0	1	9	48	0	46	20	0	2	4	.333	0	0--	-	8.19	7.69
2000 Hudson Val	A-	8	8	0	0	43.2	186	37	18	9	0	1	2	3	17	0	38	6	1	2	2	.500	0	0--	-	2.76	1.85
2000 Chrlstn - SC	A	6	6	0	0	31.0	145	30	14	11	0	1	0	3	19	0	26	8	0	2	1	.667	0	0--	-	4.21	3.19
2001 Chrlstn - SC	A	28	28	2	0	164.1	683	142	72	51	6	4	1	11	53	1	165	3	2	10	11	.476	1	0--	-	2.88	2.79
2002 Bakersfield	A+	7	7	0	0	37.0	158	35	16	12	1	1	0	2	11	0	48	0	1	3	2	.600	0	0--	-	3.05	2.92
2002 Orlando	AA	20	19	0	1	114.0	533	138	74	68	12	2	7	9	53	0	64	7	1	5	7	.417	0	0--	-	5.90	5.37

Quinton McCracken

Bats: B Throws: R Pos: RF-68; PH-34; CF-31; LF-7; PR-1 **Ht: 5'7" Wt: 173 Born: 3/16/70 Age: 33**

Year Team	Lg	G	AB	H	2B	3B	HR	(Hm Rd)	TB	R	RBI	RC	TBB	IBB	SO	HBP	SH	SF	SB	CS	SB%	GDP	Avg	OBP	Slg
1995 Colorado	NL	3	1	0	0	0	0	(0 0)	0	0	0	0	0	0	1	0	0	0	0	0	-	0	.000	.000	.000
1996 Colorado	NL	124	283	82	13	6	3	(2 1)	116	50	40	43	32	4	62	1	12	1	17	6	.74	5	.290	.363	.410
1997 Colorado	NL	147	325	95	11	1	3	(1 2)	117	69	36	47	42	0	62	1	6	1	28	11	.72	6	.292	.374	.360
1998 Tampa Bay	AL	155	614	179	38	7	7	(5 2)	252	77	59	83	41	1	107	3	9	8	19	10	.66	12	.292	.335	.410
1999 Tampa Bay	AL	40	148	37	6	1	1	(1 0)	48	20	18	13	14	0	23	1	1	1	6	5	.55	7	.250	.317	.324
2000 Tampa Bay	AL	15	31	4	0	0	0	(0 0)	4	5	2	0	6	0	4	0	0	0	0	1	.00	3	.129	.270	.129
2001 Minnesota	AL	24	64	14	2	2	0	(0 0)	20	7	3	5	5	0	13	0	1	0	0	1	.00	2	.219	.275	.313
2002 Arizona	NL	123	349	108	27	8	3	(1 2)	160	60	40	62	32	0	68	2	13	4	5	4	.56	3	.309	.367	.458
8 ML YEARS		631	1815	519	97	25	17	(10 7)	717	288	198	253	172	5	340	8	42	15	75	38	.66	38	.286	.348	.395

Donzell McDonald

Bats: B Throws: R Pos: LF-7; PH-3; PR-1 **Ht: 5'11" Wt: 180 Born: 2/20/75 Age: 28**

Year Team	Lg	G	AB	H	2B	3B	HR	(Hm Rd)	TB	R	RBI	RC	TBB	IBB	SO	HBP	SH	SF	SB	CS	SB%	GDP	Avg	OBP	Slg
1995 Yankees	R	28	110	26	5	1	0	(- -)	33	23	9	14	16	0	24	2	0	1	11	2	.85	1	.236	.341	.300
1996 Oneonta	A-	74	282	78	8	10	2	(- -)	112	57	30	54	43	0	62	2	3	2	54	4	.93	1	.277	.374	.397
1997 Tampa	A+	77	297	88	23	8	3	(- -)	136	69	23	57	48	0	75	4	4	1	39	18	.68	3	.296	.400	.458
1998 Norwich	AA	134	495	125	20	7	6	(- -)	177	80	36	59	55	1	127	4	7	4	35	22	.61	8	.253	.330	.358
1998 Tampa	A+	5	18	6	1	2	0	(- -)	11	6	2	5	2	0	7	1	1	0	2	0	1.00	0	.333	.429	.611
1999 Norwich	AA	137	533	145	19	10	4	(- -)	196	95	33	86	90	0	110	6	11	1	54	20	.73	5	.272	.383	.368
2000 Columbus	AAA	24	77	19	4	4	1	(- -)	34	17	6	19	23	0	11	2	2	0	12	0	1.00	0	.247	.431	.442
2000 Norwich	AA	44	170	41	7	2	2	(- -)	58	23	10	24	35	1	36	0	0	0	13	7	.65	1	.241	.371	.341
2001 Columbus	AAA	105	374	96	11	9	8	(- -)	149	59	36	56	42	1	79	7	1	1	20	4	.83	5	.257	.342	.398
2002 Omaha	AAA	112	452	118	15	15	7	(- -)	184	63	35	69	56	0	102	4	1	2	30	6	.83	5	.261	.346	.407
2001 New York	AL	5	3	1	0	0	0	(0 0)	1	0	0	0	0	0	2	0	1	0	0	0	-	0	.333	.333	.333
2002 Kansas City	AL	10	22	4	2	0	0	(0 0)	6	3	1	2	4	0	5	0	0	1	1	0	1.00	0	.182	.296	.273
2 ML YEARS		15	25	5	2	0	0	(0 0)	7	3	1	2	4	0	7	0	1	1	1	0	1.00	0	.200	.300	.280

John McDonald

Bats: R Throws: R Pos: 2B-64; SS-21; 3B-9; PH-5; PR-5 **Ht: 5'11" Wt: 175 Born: 9/24/74 Age: 28**

Year Team	Lg	G	AB	H	2B	3B	HR	(Hm Rd)	TB	R	RBI	RC	TBB	IBB	SO	HBP	SH	SF	SB	CS	SB%	GDP	Avg	OBP	Slg
1999 Cleveland	AL	18	21	7	0	0	0	(0 0)	7	2	0	1	0	0	3	0	0	0	0	1	.00	2	.333	.333	.333
2000 Cleveland	AL	9	9	4	1	0	0	(0 0)	4	0	0	2	0	0	1	0	0	0	0	0	-	0	.444	.444	.444
2001 Cleveland	AL	17	22	2	1	0	0	(0 0)	3	1	0	0	1	0	7	1	1	0	0	0	-	0	.091	.167	.136
2002 Cleveland	AL	93	264	66	11	3	1	(0 1)	86	35	12	23	10	0	50	5	7	2	3	0	1.00	4	.250	.288	.326
4 ML YEARS		137	316	79	12	3	1	(0 1)	100	38	12	26	11	0	61	6	8	2	3	1	.75	6	.250	.287	.316

Joe McEwing

Bats: R Throws: R Pos: PH-31; RF-24; SS-21; 1B-20; 2B-13; PR-13; 3B-10; LF-10; CF-1 **Ht: 5'11" Wt: 170 Born: 10/19/72 Age: 30**

Year Team	Lg	G	AB	H	2B	3B	HR	(Hm Rd)	TB	R	RBI	RC	TBB	IBB	SO	HBP	SH	SF	SB	CS	SB%	GDP	Avg	OBP	Slg
2002 Brooklyn*	A-	1	4	1	0	0	0	(- -)	1	0	1	0	0	0	0	0	0	0	0	0	-	0	.250	.250	.250
2002 Binghamton*	AA	1	5	0	0	0	0	(- -)	0	0	0	0	0	0	1	0	0	0	0	0	-	0	.000	.000	.000
1998 St Louis	NL	10	20	4	1	0	0	(0 0)	5	5	1	1	1	0	3	1	1	0	0	1	.00	0	.200	.273	.250
1999 St Louis	NL	152	513	141	28	4	9	(5 4)	204	65	44	70	41	8	87	6	9	5	7	4	.64	3	.275	.333	.398
2000 New York	NL	87	153	34	14	1	2	(1 1)	56	20	19	14	5	0	29	1	8	2	3	1	.75	2	.222	.248	.366
2001 New York	NL	116	283	80	17	3	8	(3 5)	127	41	30	44	17	0	57	10	6	3	8	5	.62	2	.283	.342	.449
2002 New York	NL	105	196	39	8	1	3	(2 1)	58	22	26	14	9	0	50	3	3	3	4	4	.50	0	.199	.242	.296
5 ML YEARS		470	1165	298	68	9	22	(11 11)	450	153	120	143	73	8	226	21	27	13	22	15	.59	7	.256	.308	.386

Fred McGriff

Bats: L **Throws:** L **Pos:** 1B-137; PH-8; DH-2   **Ht:** 6'3" **Wt:** 225 **Born:** 10/31/63 **Age:** 39

Year Team	Lg	G	AB	H	2B	3B	HR	(Hm	Rd)	TB	R	RBI	RC	TBB	IBB	SO	HBP	SH	SF	SB	CS	SB%	GDP	Avg	OBP	Slg
1986 Toronto	AL	3	5	1	0	0	0	(0	0)	1	1	0	0	0	0	2	0	0	0	0	0	-	0	.200	.200	.200
1987 Toronto	AL	107	295	73	16	0	20	(7	13)	149	58	43	57	60	4	104	1	0	0	3	2	.60	3	.247	.376	.505
1988 Toronto	AL	154	536	151	35	4	34	(18	16)	296	100	82	107	79	3	149	4	0	4	6	1	.86	15	.282	.376	.552
1989 Toronto	AL	161	551	148	27	3	36	(18	18)	289	98	92	115	119	12	132	4	1	5	7	4	.64	14	.269	.399	.525
1990 Toronto	AL	153	557	167	21	1	35	(14	21)	295	91	88	117	94	12	108	2	1	4	5	3	.63	7	.300	.400	.530
1991 San Diego	NL	153	528	147	19	1	31	(18	13)	261	84	106	102	105	26	135	2	0	7	4	1	.80	14	.278	.396	.494
1992 San Diego	NL	152	531	152	30	4	35	(21	14)	295	79	104	110	96	23	108	1	0	4	8	6	.57	14	.286	.394	.556
1993 SD-Atl	NL	151	557	162	29	2	37	(15	22)	306	111	101	110	76	6	106	2	0	5	5	3	.63	14	.291	.375	.549
1994 Atlanta	NL	113	424	135	25	1	34	(13	21)	264	81	94	96	50	8	76	1	0	3	7	3	.70	8	.318	.389	.623
1995 Atlanta	NL	144	528	148	27	1	27	(15	12)	258	85	93	87	65	6	99	5	0	6	3	6	.33	19	.280	.361	.489
1996 Atlanta	NL	159	617	182	37	1	28	(17	11)	305	81	107	105	68	12	116	2	0	4	7	3	.70	20	.295	.365	.494
1997 Atlanta	NL	152	564	156	25	1	22	(8	14)	249	77	97	85	68	4	112	4	0	5	5	0	1.00	22	.277	.356	.441
1998 Tampa Bay	AL	151	564	160	33	0	19	(14	5)	250	73	81	93	79	9	118	2	0	4	7	2	.78	14	.284	.371	.443
1999 Tampa Bay	AL	144	529	164	30	1	32	(14	18)	292	75	104	114	86	11	107	1	0	4	1	0	1.00	12	.310	.405	.552
2000 Tampa Bay	AL	158	566	157	18	0	27	(10	17)	256	82	106	95	91	10	120	0	0	7	2	0	1.00	16	.277	.373	.452
2001 TB-ChC		146	513	157	25	2	31	(17	14)	279	67	102	101	66	13	106	3	0	4	1	2	.33	13	.306	.386	.544
2002 Chicago	NL	146	523	143	27	2	30	(11	19)	264	67	103	88	63	6	99	4	0	5	1	2	.33	13	.273	.353	.505
1993 San Diego	NL	83	302	83	11	1	18	(7	11)	150	52	46	52	42	4	55	1	0	4	4	3	.57	9	.275	.361	.497
1993 Atlanta	NL	68	255	79	18	1	19	(8	11)	156	59	55	58	34	2	51	1	0	1	1	0	1.00	5	.310	.392	.612
2001 Tampa Bay	NL	97	343	109	18	0	19	(10	9)	184	40	61	67	40	9	69	0	0	2	1	1	.50	7	.318	.387	.536
2001 Chicago	NL	49	170	48	7	2	12	(7	5)	95	27	41	34	26	4	37	3	0	2	0	1	.00	6	.282	.383	.559
17 ML YEARS		2347	8388	2403	424	24	478	(234	244)	4309	1310	1503	1582	1265	165	1797	38	2	71	72	38	.65	218	.286	.380	.514

Ryan McGuire

Bats: L **Throws:** L **Pos:** PH-10; 1B-7; DH-1   **Ht:** 6'0" **Wt:** 215 **Born:** 11/23/71 **Age:** 31

Year Team	Lg	G	AB	H	2B	3B	HR	(Hm	Rd)	TB	R	RBI	RC	TBB	IBB	SO	HBP	SH	SF	SB	CS	SB%	GDP	Avg	OBP	Slg
2002 Rochester*	AAA	81	315	90	15	2	11	(-	-)	142	44	46	46	29	4	69	0	1	3	0	1	.00	10	.286	.343	.451
1997 Montreal	NL	84	199	51	15	2	3	(2	1)	79	22	17	24	19	1	34	0	3	1	1	4	.20	3	.256	.320	.397
1998 Montreal	NL	130	210	39	9	0	1	(1	0)	51	17	10	13	32	0	55	0	1	1	0	0	-	9	.186	.292	.243
1999 Montreal	NL	88	140	31	7	2	2	(1	1)	48	17	18	16	27	0	33	0	3	0	1	1	.50	9	.221	.347	.343
2000 New York	NL	1	2	0	0	0	0	(0	0)	0	0	0	0	1	0	1	0	0	0	0	0	-	1	.000	.333	.000
2001 Florida	NL	48	54	10	2	0	1	(1	0)	15	8	4	5	7	0	15	0	0	2	1	0	1.00	0	.185	.270	.278
2002 Baltimore	AL	17	26	2	1	0	0	(0	0)	3	0	2	0	2	0	7	0	0	0	0	0	-	2	.077	.143	.115
6 ML YEARS		368	631	133	34	4	7	(5	2)	196	64	55	58	88	1	144	0	7	4	3	5	.38	24	.211	.306	.311

Cody McKay

Bats: L **Throws:** R **Pos:** C-1; PH-1   **Ht:** 6'0" **Wt:** 208 **Born:** 1/11/74 **Age:** 29

Year Team	Lg	G	AB	H	2B	3B	HR	(Hm	Rd)	TB	R	RBI	RC	TBB	IBB	SO	HBP	SH	SF	SB	CS	SB%	GDP	Avg	OBP	Slg
1996 Sth Oregon	A-	69	254	68	13	0	3	(-	-)	90	33	30	30	25	0	42	6	1	3	0	5	.00	7	.268	.344	.354
1997 Modesto	A+	125	390	97	20	1	7	(-	-)	140	47	50	51	46	2	69	16	3	4	4	2	.67	9	.249	.349	.359
1998 Modesto	A+	107	402	114	25	1	6	(-	-)	159	59	58	58	40	1	62	17	3	3	2	4	.33	12	.284	.370	.396
1998 Huntsville	AA	9	21	6	0	0	1	(-	-)	9	5	1	5	6	0	5	2	0	0	0	0	-	0	.286	.483	.429
1998 Edmonton	AAA	19	57	13	3	0	0	(-	-)	16	6	5	6	7	0	5	3	2	0	1	0	1.00	0	.228	.343	.281
1999 Midland	AA	94	333	98	21	1	6	(-	-)	139	59	43	51	38	5	40	8	1	5	1	2	.33	11	.294	.375	.417
2000 Midland	AA	115	427	136	35	2	5	(-	-)	190	70	89	78	67	6	54	10	0	10	1	5	.17	15	.319	.414	.445
2000 Sacramento	AAA	16	58	13	4	0	1	(-	-)	20	8	7	6	5	1	14	1	0	0	0	0	-	0	.224	.297	.345
2001 Sacramento	AAA	99	350	92	19	0	6	(-	-)	129	36	41	40	27	1	64	5	2	1	1	0	1.00	12	.263	.324	.369
2002 Sacramento	AAA	108	378	109	16	1	13	(-	-)	166	55	57	57	21	0	59	10	4	6	2	1	.67	4	.288	.337	.439
2002 Oakland	AL	2	3	2	0	0	0	(0	0)	2	0	2	1	0	0	1	0	0	1	0	0	-	0	.667	.500	.667

Walt McKeel

Bats: R **Throws:** R **Pos:** C-5   **Ht:** 6'0" **Wt:** 200 **Born:** 1/17/72 **Age:** 31

Year Team	Lg	G	AB	H	2B	3B	HR	(Hm	Rd)	TB	R	RBI	RC	TBB	IBB	SO	HBP	SH	SF	SB	CS	SB%	GDP	Avg	OBP	Slg
2002 Co Springs	AAA	49	130	32	7	0	2	(-	-)	45	10	11	15	16	0	27	0	0	1	0	0	-	2	.246	.327	.346
1997 Boston	AL	5	3	0	0	0	0	(0	0)	0	0	0	0	0	0	1	0	0	0	0	0	-	0	.000	.000	.000
2002 Colorado	NL	5	13	4	0	0	0	(0	0)	4	1	0	1	0	0	3	0	0	0	0	0	-	0	.308	.308	.308
2 ML YEARS		10	16	4	0	0	0	(0	0)	4	1	0	1	0	0	4	0	0	0	0	0	-	0	.250	.250	.250

Mark McLemore

Bats: B **Throws:** R **Pos:** LF-82; 3B-14; CF-13; PH-8; DH-4; 2B-1; SS-1; RF-1   **Ht:** 5'11" **Wt:** 207 **Born:** 10/4/64 **Age:** 38

Year Team	Lg	G	AB	H	2B	3B	HR	(Hm	Rd)	TB	R	RBI	RC	TBB	IBB	SO	HBP	SH	SF	SB	CS	SB%	GDP	Avg	OBP	Slg
1986 Anaheim	AL	5	4	0	0	0	0	(0	0)	0	0	0	0	1	0	2	0	1	0	0	1	.00	0	.000	.200	.000
1987 Anaheim	AL	138	433	102	13	3	3	(3	0)	130	61	41	44	48	0	72	0	15	3	25	8	.76	7	.236	.310	.300
1988 Anaheim	AL	77	233	56	11	2	2	(1	1)	77	38	16	24	25	0	28	0	5	2	13	7	.65	6	.240	.312	.330
1989 Anaheim	AL	32	103	25	3	1	0	(0	0)	30	12	14	9	7	0	19	1	3	1	6	1	.86	2	.243	.295	.291
1990 Ana-Cle	AL	28	60	9	2	0	0	(0	0)	11	6	2	1	4	0	15	0	1	0	1	0	1.00	1	.150	.203	.183
1991 Houston	NL	21	61	9	1	0	0	(0	0)	10	6	2	1	6	0	13	0	0	1	0	1	.00	1	.148	.221	.164
1992 Baltimore	AL	101	228	56	7	2	0	(0	0)	67	40	27	20	21	1	26	0	6	1	11	5	.69	6	.246	.308	.294
1993 Baltimore	AL	148	581	165	27	5	4	(2	2)	214	81	72	72	64	4	92	1	11	6	21	15	.58	21	.284	.353	.368
1994 Baltimore	AL	104	343	88	11	1	3	(2	1)	110	44	29	44	51	3	50	1	4	1	20	5	.80	7	.257	.354	.321
1995 Texas	AL	129	467	122	20	5	5	(3	2)	167	73	41	59	59	6	71	3	10	3	21	11	.66	10	.261	.346	.358
1996 Texas	AL	147	517	150	23	4	5	(3	2)	196	84	46	81	87	5	69	0	2	5	27	10	.73	16	.290	.389	.379
1997 Texas	AL	89	349	91	17	2	1	(0	1)	115	47	25	41	40	1	54	2	6	2	7	5	.58	5	.261	.338	.330

Year Team	Lg	G	AB	H	2B	3B	HR	(Hm	Rd)	TB	R	RBI	RC	TBB	IBB	SO	HBP	SH	SF	SB	CS	SB%	GDP	Avg	OBP	Slg
								BATTING												**BASERUNNING**				**AVERAGES**		
1998 Texas	AL	126	461	114	15	1	5	(4	1)	146	79	53	60	89	1	64	2	12	3	12	4	.75	15	.247	.369	.317
1999 Texas	AL	144	566	155	20	7	6	(2	4)	207	105	45	81	83	2	79	0	9	6	16	8	.67	8	.274	.363	.366
2000 Seattle	AL	138	481	118	23	1	3	(2	1)	152	72	46	59	81	2	78	1	11	4	30	14	.68	12	.245	.353	.316
2001 Seattle	AL	125	409	117	16	9	5	(2	3)	166	78	57	73	69	0	84	1	0	3	39	7	.85	6	.286	.384	.406
2002 Seattle	AL	104	337	91	17	2	7	(4	3)	133	54	41	60	61	1	63	1	4	4	18	10	.64	3	.270	.380	.395
1990 Anaheim	AL	20	48	7	2	0	0	(0	0)	9	4	2	1	4	0	9	0	1	0	1	0	1.00	1	.146	.212	.188
1990 Cleveland	AL	8	12	2	0	0	0	(0	0)	2	2	0	0	0	0	6	0	0	0	0	0	-	0	.167	.167	.167
17 ML YEARS		1656	5633	1468	226	45	49	(28	21)	1931	880	557	729	796	26	879	12	103	48	267	112	.70	126	.261	.351	.343

Billy McMillon

Bats: L Throws: L Pos: OF

Ht: 5'11" Wt: 195 Born: 11/17/71 Age: 31

Year Team	Lg	G	AB	H	2B	3B	HR	(Hm	Rd)	TB	R	RBI	RC	TBB	IBB	SO	HBP	SH	SF	SB	CS	SB%	GDP	Avg	OBP	Slg
								BATTING												**BASERUNNING**				**AVERAGES**		
2002 Columbus*	AAA	115	442	133	32	3	8	(-	-)	195	72	46	76	59	2	71	6	1	3	2	5	.29	6	.301	.388	.441
1996 Florida	NL	28	51	11	0	0	0	(0	0)	11	4	4	3	5	1	14	0	0	0	0	0	-	0	.216	.286	.216
1997 Phi-Fla	NL	37	90	23	5	1	2	(0	2)	36	10	14	11	6	0	24	0	0	3	2	1	.67	0	.256	.293	.400
2000 Detroit	AL	46	123	37	7	1	4	(1	3)	58	20	24	24	19	0	19	1	2	4	1	0	1.00	2	.301	.388	.472
2001 Det-Oak	AL	40	92	20	8	1	1	(1	0)	33	7	14	10	7	0	25	2	0	1	1	0	1.00	1	.217	.284	.359
1997 Philadelphia	NL	24	72	21	4	1	2	(0	2)	33	10	13	11	6	0	17	0	0	3	2	1	.67	0	.292	.333	.458
1997 Florida	NL	13	18	2	1	0	0	(0	0)	3	0	1	0	0	0	7	0	0	0	0	0	-	0	.111	.111	.167
2001 Detroit	AL	20	34	3	1	0	1	(1	0)	7	1	4	0	2	0	12	1	0	0	0	0	-	0	.088	.162	.206
2001 Oakland	AL	20	58	17	7	1	0	(0	0)	26	6	10	10	5	0	13	1	0	1	1	0	1.00	1	.293	.354	.448
4 ML YEARS		151	356	91	20	3	7	(2	5)	138	41	56	48	37	1	82	3	2	8	4	1	.80	5	.256	.324	.388

Brian Meadows

Pitches: R Bats: R Pos: SP-11

Ht: 6'4" Wt: 220 Born: 11/21/75 Age: 27

Year Team	Lg	G	GS	CG	GF	IP	BFP	H	R	ER	HR	SH	SF	HB	TBB	IBB	SO	WP	Bk	W	L	Pct	ShO	Sv-Op	Hld	ERC	ERA
				HOW MUCH HE PITCHED							**WHAT HE GAVE UP**											**THE RESULTS**				
2002 Nashville*	AAA	23	22	1	0	126.1	530	132	69	60	15	3	2	5	26	1	98	2	0	9	8	.529	1	0--	-	3.84	4.27
1998 Florida	NL	31	31	1	0	174.1	772	222	106	101	20	14	4	3	46	3	88	5	1	11	13	.458	0	0-0	0	5.29	5.21
1999 Florida	NL	31	31	0	0	178.1	795	214	117	111	31	16	8	5	57	5	72	4	1	11	15	.423	0	0-0	0	5.51	5.60
2000 SD-KC		33	32	2	0	196.1	869	234	119	112	32	7	5	8	64	6	79	3	0	13	10	.565	0	0-0	0	5.52	5.13
2001 Kansas City	AL	10	10	0	0	50.1	224	73	41	39	12	1	2	1	12	2	21	1	0	1	6	.143	0	0-0	0	7.47	6.97
2002 Pittsburgh	NL	11	11	0	0	62.2	259	62	29	27	7	2	0	1	14	8	31	2	0	1	6	.143	0	0-0	0	3.29	3.88
2000 San Diego	NL	22	22	0	0	124.2	565	150	80	74	24	7	2	8	50	6	53	3	0	7	8	.467	0	0-0	0	6.23	5.34
2000 Kansas City	AL	11	10	2	0	71.2	304	84	39	38	8	0	3	0	14	0	26	0	0	6	2	.750	0	0-0	0	4.35	4.77
5 ML YEARS		116	115	3	0	662.0	2919	805	412	390	102	40	19	18	193	24	291	15	2	37	50	.425	0	0-0	0	5.37	5.30

Gil Meche

Pitches: R Bats: R Pos: SP

Ht: 6'3" Wt: 200 Born: 9/8/78 Age: 24

Year Team	Lg	G	GS	CG	GF	IP	BFP	H	R	ER	HR	SH	SF	HB	TBB	IBB	SO	WP	Bk	W	L	Pct	ShO	Sv-Op	Hld	ERC	ERA
				HOW MUCH HE PITCHED							**WHAT HE GAVE UP**											**THE RESULTS**				
1996 Peoria	A	2	0	0	0	3.0	13	4	2	2	0	0	0	1	0	4	0	0	0	1	.000	0	0--	-	5.24	6.00
1997 Everett	A-	12	12	1	0	74.2	316	75	40	33	7	3	2	3	24	0	62	7	0	3	4	.429	0	0--	-	3.95	3.98
1997 Wisconsin	A	2	2	0	0	12.0	51	12	5	4	1	0	0	1	4	0	14	2	1	0	2	.000	0	0--	-	4.10	3.00
1998 Wisconsin	A	26	26	0	0	149.0	643	136	77	57	9	2	3	5	63	0	168	12	2	8	7	.533	4	0--	-	3.50	3.44
1999 New Haven	AA	10	10	0	0	59.0	250	51	24	20	3	2	1	0	26	0	56	4	0	3	4	.429	0	0--	-	3.14	3.05
1999 Tacoma	AAA	6	6	0	0	31.0	135	31	12	11	3	0	2	1	13	0	24	2	0	2	2	.500	0	0--	-	4.26	3.19
2000 Tacoma	AAA	3	3	0	0	14.0	61	10	7	6	1	0	1	0	10	0	15	0	0	1	1	.500	0	0--	-	3.49	3.86
2000 Wisconsin	A	1	1	0	0	5.0	17	1	0	0	0	0	0	0	2	0	6	0	0	0	0	-	0	0--	-	0.53	0.00
2000 Everett	A-	1	1	0	0	1.0	5	3	1	1	0	0	0	0	0	0	0	0	0	0	1	.000	0	0--	-	17.53	9.00
2002 San Antonio	AA	25	13	0	1	65.0	290	68	49	47	8	0	3	4	32	0	56	0	0	4	6	.400	0	0--	-	5.18	6.51
1999 Seattle	AL	16	15	0	0	85.2	375	73	48	45	9	5	3	2	57	1	47	1	0	8	4	.667	0	0-0	0	4.47	4.73
2000 Seattle	AL	15	15	1	0	85.2	363	75	37	36	7	5	4	1	40	0	60	2	0	4	4	.500	1	0-0	0	3.60	3.78
2 ML YEARS		31	30	1	0	171.1	738	148	85	81	16	10	7	3	97	1	107	3	0	12	8	.600	1	0-0	0	4.03	4.25

Jim Mecir

Pitches: R Bats: B Pos: RP-61

Ht: 6'1" Wt: 230 Born: 5/16/70 Age: 33

Year Team	Lg	G	GS	CG	GF	IP	BFP	H	R	ER	HR	SH	SF	HB	TBB	IBB	SO	WP	Bk	W	L	Pct	ShO	Sv-Op	Hld	ERC	ERA
				HOW MUCH HE PITCHED							**WHAT HE GAVE UP**											**THE RESULTS**				
1995 Seattle	AL	2	0	0	1	4.2	21	5	1	0	0	0	0	0	2	0	3	0	0	0	0	-	0	0-0	0	3.75	0.00
1996 New York	AL	26	0	0	10	40.1	185	42	24	23	6	5	4	0	23	4	38	6	0	1	1	.500	0	0-0	0	5.10	5.13
1997 New York	AL	25	0	0	11	33.2	142	36	23	22	5	0	1	2	10	1	25	1	0	0	4	.000	0	0-1	1	4.73	5.88
1998 Tampa Bay	AL	68	0	0	23	84.0	343	68	30	29	6	3	2	3	33	5	77	2	0	7	2	.778	0	0-3	14	2.95	3.11
1999 Tampa Bay	AL	17	0	0	3	20.2	91	15	7	6	0	0	2	1	14	5	15	0	0	0	1	.000	0	0-2	6	3.05	2.61
2000 TB-Oak	AL	63	0	0	17	85.0	352	70	31	28	4	1	2	2	36	2	70	2	0	10	3	.769	0	5-13	21	2.95	2.96
2001 Oakland	AL	54	0	0	14	63.0	264	54	25	24	4	3	0	1	26	7	61	0	0	2	8	.200	0	3-8	17	3.00	3.43
2002 Oakland	AL	61	0	0	10	67.2	304	68	38	32	5	4	4	4	29	4	53	4	1	6	4	.600	0	1-6	20	4.05	4.26
2000 Tampa Bay	AL	38	0	0	10	49.2	199	35	17	17	2	1	1	2	22	0	33	0	0	7	2	.778	0	1-4	11	2.44	3.08
2000 Oakland	AL	25	0	0	7	35.1	153	35	14	11	2	0	1	0	14	2	37	2	0	3	1	.750	0	4-9	10	3.71	2.80
8 ML YEARS		316	0	0	89	399.0	1702	358	177	164	30	16	15	13	173	23	342	17	1	26	23	.531	0	9-33	79	3.51	3.70

Mitch Meluskey

Bats: B Throws: R Pos: C-8   Ht: 6'0" Wt: 185 Born: 9/18/73 Age: 29

Year Team	Lg	G	AB	H	2B	3B	HR	(Hm	Rd)	TB	R	RBI	RC	TBB	IBB	SO	HBP	SH	SF	SB	CS	SB%	GDP	Avg	OBP	Slg
1998 Houston	NL	8	8	2	1	0	0	(0	0)	3	1	0	1	1	0	4	0	0	0	0	0	-	1	.250	.333	.375
1999 Houston	NL	10	33	7	1	0	1	(0	1)	11	4	3	4	5	1	6	0	0	0	1	0	1.00	1	.212	.316	.333
2000 Houston	NL	117	337	101	21	0	14	(11	3)	164	47	69	65	55	10	74	4	1	3	1	0	1.00	7	.300	.401	.487
2002 Detroit	AL	8	27	6	0	0	0	(0	0)	6	3	1	3	5	0	3	1	0	1	0	0	-	0	.222	.353	.222
4 ML YEARS		143	405	116	23	0	15	(11	4)	184	55	73	73	66	11	87	5	1	4	2	0	1.00	9	.286	.390	.454

Kevin Mench

Bats: R Throws: R Pos: RF-61; LF-57; PH-6; PR-3; CF-1   Ht: 6'0" Wt: 215 Born: 1/7/78 Age: 25

Year Team	Lg	G	AB	H	2B	3B	HR	(Hm	Rd)	TB	R	RBI	RC	TBB	IBB	SO	HBP	SH	SF	SB	CS	SB%	GDP	Avg	OBP	Slg
1999 Pulaski	R+	65	260	94	22	1	16	(-	-)	166	63	60	67	28	0	48	2	0	5	12	2	.86	2	.362	.420	.638
1999 Savannah	A	6	23	7	1	1	2	(-	-)	16	4	8	6	2	0	4	2	0	0	0	0	-	1	.304	.407	.696
2000 Charlotte	A+	132	491	164	39	9	27	(-	-)	302	118	121	124	78	3	72	7	0	7	19	7	.73	9	.334	.427	.615
2001 Tulsa	AA	120	475	126	34	2	26	(-	-)	242	78	83	75	34	0	76	6	0	6	4	6	.40	7	.265	.319	.509
2002 Oklahoma	AAA	26	98	21	8	0	6	(-	-)	47	17	15	14	17	0	33	2	0	0	0	0	-	7	.214	.342	.480
2002 Texas	AL	110	366	95	20	2	15	(8	7)	164	52	60	59	31	0	83	8	2	5	1	1	.50	4	.260	.327	.448

Ramiro Mendoza

Pitches: R Bats: R Pos: RP-62   Ht: 6'2" Wt: 195 Born: 6/15/72 Age: 31

Year Team	Lg	G	GS	CG	GF	IP	BFP	H	R	ER	HR	SH	SF	HB	TBB	IBB	SO	WP	Bk	W	L	Pct	ShO	Sv-Op	Hld	ERC	ERA
1996 New York	AL	12	11	0	0	53.0	249	80	43	40	5	1	1	4	10	1	34	2	1	4	5	.444	0	0-0	6	6.42	6.79
1997 New York	AL	39	15	0	9	133.2	578	157	67	63	15	3	5	5	28	2	82	2	1	8	6	.571	0	2-4	4	4.52	4.24
1998 New York	AL	41	14	1	6	130.1	548	131	50	47	9	6	7	9	30	6	56	3	0	10	2	.833	1	1-4	5	3.44	3.25
1999 New York	AL	53	6	0	15	123.2	536	141	68	59	13	6	4	3	27	3	80	2	0	9	9	.500	0	3-6	4	4.19	4.29
2000 New York	AL	14	9	1	0	65.2	281	66	32	31	9	1	2	4	20	1	30	0	0	7	4	.636	1	0-1	0	4.21	4.25
2001 New York	AL	56	2	0	11	100.2	401	89	44	42	9	4	3	2	23	3	70	2	0	8	4	.667	0	6-8	13	2.84	3.75
2002 New York	AL	62	0	0	14	91.2	394	102	43	35	8	1	4	2	16	2	61	1	0	8	4	.667	0	4-8	12	3.70	3.44
7 ML YEARS		277	57	2	55	698.2	2987	766	347	317	68	22	26	29	154	18	413	12	2	54	34	.614	2	16-31	38	4.00	4.08

Frank Menechino

Bats: R Throws: R Pos: 2B-32; 3B-4; SS-2; PH-2   Ht: 5'8" Wt: 198 Born: 1/7/71 Age: 32

Year Team	Lg	G	AB	H	2B	3B	HR	(Hm	Rd)	TB	R	RBI	RC	TBB	IBB	SO	HBP	SH	SF	SB	CS	SB%	GDP	Avg	OBP	Slg
2002 Sacramento*	AAA	84	314	78	12	0	6	(-	-)	108	50	50	41	46	0	58	8	0	3	10	3	.77	10	.248	.356	.344
1999 Oakland	AL	9	9	2	0	0	0	(0	0)	2	0	0	0	1	0	4	0	0	0	0	0	-	0	.222	.222	.222
2000 Oakland	AL	66	145	37	9	1	6	(3	3)	66	31	26	22	20	0	45	1	1	2	1	4	.20	1	.255	.345	.455
2001 Oakland	AL	139	471	114	22	2	12	(4	8)	176	82	60	69	79	0	97	19	3	6	2	3	.40	13	.242	.369	.374
2002 Oakland	AL	38	132	27	7	0	3	(2	1)	43	22	15	14	20	0	32	1	0	1	0	0	-	4	.205	.312	.326
4 ML YEARS		252	757	180	38	3	21	(9	12)	287	135	101	105	119	0	178	21	4	9	3	7	.30	18	.238	.353	.379

Hector Mercado

Pitches: L Bats: L Pos: RP-28; SP-3   Ht: 6'3" Wt: 235 Born: 4/29/74 Age: 29

Year Team	Lg	G	GS	CG	GF	IP	BFP	H	R	ER	HR	SH	SF	HB	TBB	IBB	SO	WP	Bk	W	L	Pct	ShO	Sv-Op	Hld	ERC	ERA
2002 Scrtn/WlksBr*	AAA	26	0	0	12	33.1	131	22	6	6	2	0	0	1	12	1	43	2	0	3	1	.750	0	3- -	-	2.05	1.62
2000 Cincinnati	NL	12	0	0	4	14.0	60	12	7	7	2	1	1	0	8	0	13	2	0	0	0	-	0	0-0	1	4.32	4.50
2001 Cincinnati	NL	56	0	0	10	53.0	240	55	27	24	6	1	2	0	30	1	59	4	0	3	2	.600	0	0-2	5	4.99	4.08
2002 Philadelphia	NL	31	3	0	7	39.0	173	32	21	20	2	1	1	3	25	2	40	3	1	2	2	.500	0	0-0	3	3.86	4.62
3 ML YEARS		99	3	0	21	106.0	473	99	55	51	10	3	4	3	63	3	112	9	1	5	4	.556	0	0-2	9	4.48	4.33

Orlando Merced

Bats: L Throws: R Pos: PH-62; RF-44; LF-20; 1B-7; 3B-1; DH-1; PR-1   Ht: 6'1" Wt: 195 Born: 11/2/66 Age: 36

Year Team	Lg	G	AB	H	2B	3B	HR	(Hm	Rd)	TB	R	RBI	RC	TBB	IBB	SO	HBP	SH	SF	SB	CS	SB%	GDP	Avg	OBP	Slg
1990 Pittsburgh	NL	25	24	5	1	0	0	(0	0)	6	3	0	1	1	0	9	0	0	0	0	0	-	1	.208	.240	.250
1991 Pittsburgh	NL	120	411	113	17	2	10	(5	5)	164	83	50	64	64	4	81	1	1	1	8	4	.67	6	.275	.373	.399
1992 Pittsburgh	NL	134	405	100	28	5	6	(4	2)	156	50	60	53	52	8	63	2	1	5	5	4	.56	6	.247	.332	.385
1993 Pittsburgh	NL	137	447	140	26	4	8	(3	5)	198	68	70	83	77	10	64	1	0	2	3	3	.50	9	.313	.414	.443
1994 Pittsburgh	NL	108	386	105	21	3	9	(4	5)	159	48	51	51	42	5	58	1	0	2	4	1	.80	17	.272	.343	.412
1995 Pittsburgh	NL	132	487	146	29	4	15	(8	7)	228	75	83	82	52	9	74	1	0	5	7	2	.78	9	.300	.365	.468
1996 Pittsburgh	NL	120	453	130	24	1	17	(9	8)	207	69	80	73	51	5	74	0	0	3	8	4	.67	9	.287	.357	.457
1997 Toronto	AL	98	368	98	23	2	9	(3	6)	152	45	40	55	47	1	62	3	0	2	7	3	.70	6	.266	.352	.413
1998 Min-Bos-ChC		84	223	62	12	0	6	(4	2)	92	24	40	29	20	3	34	1	0	3	1	4	.20	6	.278	.336	.413
1999 Montreal	NL	93	194	52	12	1	6	(3	3)	90	25	26	31	26	0	27	0	0	1	2	1	.67	5	.268	.353	.464
2001 Houston	NL	94	137	36	6	1	6	(3	3)	62	19	29	29	14	1	32	1	0	1	5	1	.83	3	.263	.333	.453
2002 Houston	NL	123	251	72	13	3	6	(4	2)	109	35	30	36	26	5	50	0	1	3	4	0	1.00	9	.287	.350	.434
1998 Minnesota	AL	63	204	59	12	0	5	(3	2)	86	22	33	28	17	3	29	1	0	1	1	4	.20	4	.289	.345	.422
1998 Boston	AL	9	9	0	0	0	0	(0	0)	0	0	2	0	2	0	3	0	0	1	0	0	-	0	.000	.167	.000
1998 Chicago	NL	12	10	3	0	0	1	(1	0)	6	2	5	1	1	0	2	0	0	1	0	0	-	2	.300	.333	.600
12 ML YEARS		1268	3786	1059	212	26	100	(50	50)	1623	544	559	579	472	51	628	11	3	28	54	27	.67	86	.280	.359	.429

Kent Mercker

Pitches: L Bats: L Pos: RP-58

Ht: 6'2" Wt: 195 Born: 2/1/68 Age: 35

Year Team	Lg	G	GS	CG	GF	IP	BFP	H	R	ER	HR	SH	SF	HB	TBB	IBB	SO	WP	Bk	W	L	Pct	ShO	Sv-Op	Hld	ERC	ERA
2002 Co Springs*	AAA	2	0	0	2	1.2	10	3	4	4	2	0	1	0	2	0	0	0	0	0	0	-	0	0- -	0	24.70	21.60
1989 Atlanta	NL	2	1	0	1	4.1	26	8	6	6	0	1	0	0	6	0	4	0	0	0	0	-	0	0-0	0	13.19	12.46
1990 Atlanta	NL	36	0	0	28	48.1	211	43	22	17	6	1	2	2	24	3	39	2	0	4	7	.364	0	7-10	0	4.04	3.17
1991 Atlanta	NL	50	4	0	28	73.1	306	56	23	21	5	2	2	1	35	3	62	4	1	5	3	.625	0	6-8	3	2.88	2.58
1992 Atlanta	NL	53	0	0	18	68.1	289	51	27	26	4	4	1	3	35	1	49	6	0	3	2	.600	0	6-9	6	2.99	3.42
1993 Atlanta	NL	43	6	0	9	66.0	283	52	24	21	2	0	0	2	36	3	59	5	1	3	1	.750	0	0-3	4	3.02	2.86
1994 Atlanta	NL	20	17	2	0	112.1	461	90	46	43	16	4	3	0	45	3	111	4	1	9	4	.692	1	0-0	0	3.27	3.45
1995 Atlanta	NL	29	26	0	1	143.0	622	140	73	66	16	8	7	3	61	2	102	6	2	7	8	.467	0	0-0	0	4.19	4.15
1996 Bal-Cle	AL	24	12	0	0	69.2	329	83	60	54	13	3	6	3	38	2	29	3	1	4	6	.400	0	0-0	2	6.56	6.98
1997 Cincinnati	NL	28	25	0	0	144.2	616	135	65	63	16	8	4	2	62	6	75	2	1	8	11	.421	0	0-0	0	3.91	3.92
1998 St Louis	NL	30	29	0	1	161.2	716	199	99	91	11	10	9	3	53	4	72	6	4	11	11	.500	0	0-0	0	4.96	5.07
1999 Stl-Bos	NL	30	23	0	2	129.1	589	148	85	69	16	8	3	3	64	3	81	3	1	6	5	.615	0	0-0	0	5.54	4.80
2000 Anaheim	AL	21	7	0	2	48.1	225	57	35	35	12	3	1	2	29	3	30	2	0	1	3	.250	0	0-0	1	7.35	6.52
2002 Colorado	NL	58	0	0	8	44.0	208	55	33	30	12	0	0	2	22	2	37	1	0	3	1	.750	0	0-3	9	7.45	6.14
1996 Baltimore	AL	14	12	0	0	58.0	283	73	56	50	12	3	4	3	35	1	22	3	1	3	6	.333	0	0-0	0	7.45	7.76
1996 Cleveland	AL	10	0	0	2	11.2	46	10	4	4	1	0	2	0	3	1	7	0	0	1	0	1.000	0	0-0	2	2.65	3.09
1999 St Louis	NL	25	18	0	0	103.2	476	125	73	59	16	8	3	2	51	3	64	3	1	6	5	.545	0	0-0	0	6.15	5.12
1999 Boston	AL	5	5	0	0	25.2	113	23	12	10	0	0	1	1	13	0	17	0	0	2	0	1.000	0	0-0	0	3.29	3.51
13 ML YEARS		424	150	2	100	1113.1	4881	1117	598	542	129	51	39	26	510	35	750	44	12	66	62	.516	1	19-33	25	4.49	4.38

Lou Merloni

Bats: R Throws: R Pos: 2B-66; 3B-8; PR-7; SS-5; PH-4; 1B-3; LF-1; RF-1

Ht: 5'10" Wt: 201 Born: 4/6/71 Age: 32

								BATTING												BASERUNNING				AVERAGES		
Year Team	Lg	G	AB	H	2B	3B	HR	(Hm	Rd)	TB	R	RBI	RC	TBB	IBB	SO	HBP	SH	SF	SB	CS	SB%	GDP	Avg	OBP	Slg
2002 Pawtucket*	AAA	8	25	5	2	0	0	(-	-)	7	1	2	1	1	0	3	1	0	1	0	0	-	2	.200	.250	.280
1998 Boston	AL	39	96	27	6	0	1	(1	0)	36	10	15	13	7	1	20	2	1	0	1	0	1.00	1	.281	.343	.375
1999 Boston	AL	43	126	32	7	0	1	(0	1)	42	18	13	12	8	0	16	2	3	1	0	0	-	6	.254	.307	.333
2000 Boston	AL	40	128	41	11	2	0	(0	0)	56	10	18	17	4	1	22	1	4	2	1	0	1.00	8	.320	.341	.438
2001 Boston	AL	52	146	39	10	0	3	(0	3)	58	21	13	16	6	0	31	3	2	2	2	1	.67	5	.267	.306	.397
2002 Boston	AL	84	194	48	12	2	4	(1	3)	76	28	18	25	20	0	35	5	2	1	1	2	.33	4	.247	.332	.392
5 ML YEARS		258	690	187	46	4	9	(2	7)	268	87	77	83	45	2	124	13	12	6	5	3	.63	25	.271	.325	.388

Jose Mesa

Pitches: R Bats: R Pos: RP-74

Ht: 6'3" Wt: 225 Born: 5/22/66 Age: 37

Year Team	Lg	G	GS	CG	GF	IP	BFP	H	R	ER	HR	SH	SF	HB	TBB	IBB	SO	WP	Bk	W	L	Pct	ShO	Sv-Op	Hld	ERC	ERA
1987 Baltimore	AL	6	5	0	0	31.1	143	38	23	21	7	0	0	0	15	0	17	4	0	1	3	.250	0	0-0	1	6.67	6.03
1990 Baltimore	AL	7	7	0	0	46.2	202	37	20	20	2	2	2	1	27	2	24	1	1	3	2	.600	0	0-0	0	3.21	3.86
1991 Baltimore	AL	23	23	2	0	123.2	566	151	86	82	11	5	4	3	62	2	64	3	0	6	11	.353	1	0-0	0	5.85	5.97
1992 Bal-Cle	AL	28	27	1	1	160.2	700	169	86	82	14	2	5	4	70	1	62	2	0	7	12	.368	1	0-0	0	4.57	4.59
1993 Cleveland	AL	34	33	3	0	208.2	897	232	122	114	21	9	9	7	62	2	118	8	2	10	12	.455	0	0-0	0	4.48	4.92
1994 Cleveland	AL	51	0	0	22	73.0	315	71	33	31	3	3	4	3	26	7	63	3	0	7	5	.583	0	2-6	8	3.31	3.82
1995 Cleveland	AL	62	0	0	57	64.0	250	49	9	8	3	4	2	0	17	2	58	5	0	3	0	1.000	0	46-48	0	2.06	1.13
1996 Cleveland	AL	69	0	0	60	72.1	304	69	32	30	6	2	2	3	28	4	64	4	0	2	7	.222	0	39-44	0	3.81	3.73
1997 Cleveland	AL	66	0	0	38	82.1	356	83	28	22	7	2	2	3	28	3	69	1	0	4	4	.500	0	16-21	9	3.83	2.40
1998 Cle-SF		76	0	0	36	84.2	383	91	50	43	8	6	2	4	38	5	63	10	0	8	7	.533	0	1-4	13	4.68	4.57
1999 Seattle	AL	68	0	0	60	68.2	325	84	42	38	11	2	4	4	40	4	42	7	0	3	6	.333	0	33-38	1	6.83	4.98
2000 Seattle	AL	66	0	0	29	80.2	372	89	48	48	11	2	6	5	41	0	84	3	0	4	6	.400	0	1-3	11	5.60	5.36
2001 Philadelphia	NL	71	0	0	59	69.1	291	65	26	18	4	2	3	2	20	2	59	2	1	3	3	.500	0	42-46	0	3.07	2.34
2002 Philadelphia	NL	74	0	0	64	75.2	331	65	26	25	5	6	1	4	39	7	64	9	0	4	6	.400	0	45-54	0	3.51	2.97
1992 Baltimore	AL	13	12	0	1	67.2	300	77	41	39	9	0	3	2	27	1	22	2	0	3	8	.273	0	0-0	0	5.25	5.19
1992 Cleveland	AL	15	15	1	0	93.0	400	92	45	43	5	2	2	2	43	0	40	0	0	4	4	.500	1	0-0	0	4.09	4.16
1998 Cleveland	AL	44	0	0	18	54.0	244	61	36	31	7	2	2	4	20	3	35	2	0	3	4	.429	0	1-3	7	5.07	5.17
1998 San Francisco	NL	32	0	0	18	30.2	139	30	14	12	1	4	0	0	18	2	28	8	0	5	3	.625	0	0-1	6	3.99	3.52
14 ML YEARS		701	95	6	426	1241.2	5435	1293	631	582	113	47	46	43	513	41	851	62	4	65	84	.436	2	225-264	44	4.39	4.22

Dan Miceli

Pitches: R Bats: R Pos: RP-9

Ht: 6'0" Wt: 216 Born: 9/9/70 Age: 32

Year Team	Lg	G	GS	CG	GF	IP	BFP	H	R	ER	HR	SH	SF	HB	TBB	IBB	SO	WP	Bk	W	L	Pct	ShO	Sv-Op	Hld	ERC	ERA
1993 Pittsburgh	NL	9	0	0	1	5.1	25	6	3	3	0	0	0	0	3	0	4	0	1	0	0	-	0	0-0	0	4.53	5.06
1994 Pittsburgh	NL	28	0	0	9	27.1	121	28	19	18	5	1	2	2	11	2	27	2	0	2	1	.667	0	2-3	4	4.98	5.93
1995 Pittsburgh	NL	58	0	0	51	58.0	264	61	30	30	7	2	4	4	28	5	56	4	0	4	4	.500	0	21-27	2	4.93	4.66
1996 Pittsburgh	NL	44	9	0	17	85.2	398	99	65	55	15	3	7	3	45	5	66	9	0	2	10	.167	0	1-1	4	6.09	5.78
1997 Detroit	AL	71	0	0	24	82.2	357	77	49	46	13	5	3	1	38	4	79	3	0	3	2	.600	0	3-8	11	4.30	5.01
1998 San Diego	NL	67	0	0	18	72.2	302	64	28	26	6	3	2	1	27	4	70	5	1	10	5	.667	0	2-8	20	3.20	3.22
1999 San Diego	NL	66	0	0	28	68.2	296	67	39	34	7	4	2	2	36	5	59	2	0	4	5	.444	0	2-4	9	4.57	4.46
2000 Florida	NL	45	0	0	9	48.2	207	45	23	23	4	1	1	1	18	2	40	3	0	6	4	.600	0	0-3	11	3.42	4.25
2001 Fla-Col	NL	51	0	0	15	45.0	199	47	29	24	7	2	2	0	16	2	48	4	0	2	5	.286	0	1-4	8	4.34	4.80
2002 Texas	AL	9	0	0	5	8.1	42	13	8	8	1	0	0	0	3	0	5	0	0	0	2	.000	0	0-1	0	7.11	8.64
2001 Florida	NL	29	0	0	9	24.2	114	29	21	19	5	1	1	0	11	2	31	3	0	0	5	.000	0	0-3	8	5.80	6.93
2001 Colorado	NL	22	0	0	6	20.1	85	18	8	5	2	1	1	0	5	0	17	1	0	2	0	1.000	0	1-1	0	2.77	2.21
10 ML YEARS		448	9	0	177	502.1	2211	507	293	267	65	21	23	14	225	29	454	32	3	33	38	.465	0	32-59	69	4.53	4.78

Jason Michaels

Bats: R **Throws:** R **Pos:** PH-59; CF-14; RF-7; LF-6; DH-2; 3B-1; PR-1   **Ht:** 6'0" **Wt:** 204 **Born:** 5/4/76 **Age:** 27

							BATTING												BASERUNNING				AVERAGES		
Year Team	Lg	G	AB	H	2B	3B	HR	(Hm | Rd)	TB	R	RBI	RC	TBB	IBB	SO	HBP	SH	SF	SB	CS	SB%	GDP	Avg	OBP	Slg
1998 Batavia	A-	67	235	63	14	3	11	(- | -)	116	45	49	44	40	3	69	4	0	2	4	2	.67	5	.268	.381	.494
1999 Clearwater	A+	122	451	138	31	6	14	(- | -)	223	91	65	88	68	2	103	3	1	6	10	7	.59	7	.306	.396	.494
2000 Reading	AA	113	437	129	30	4	10	(- | -)	197	71	74	65	28	1	87	3	3	7	7	4	.64	9	.295	.337	.451
2001 Scrtn/WlksBr	AAA	109	418	109	19	3	17	(- | -)	185	58	69	61	37	2	126	8	0	1	11	3	.79	7	.261	.332	.443
2002 Scrtn/WlksBr	AAA	9	32	9	2	0	0	(- | -)	11	3	7	4	5	0	5	0	0	2	1	3	.25	0	.281	.359	.344
2001 Philadelphia	NL	6	6	1	0	0	0	(0 | 0)	1	0	1	0	0	0	2	0	0	0	0	0	-	0	.167	.167	.167
2002 Philadelphia	NL	81	105	28	10	3	2	(0 | 2)	50	16	11	15	13	1	33	1	0	2	1	1	.50	2	.267	.347	.476
2 ML YEARS		87	111	29	10	3	2	(0 | 2)	51	16	12	15	13	1	35	1	0	2	1	1	.50	1	.261	.339	.459

Chris Michalak

Pitches: L **Bats:** L **Pos:** RP-13   **Ht:** 6'2" **Wt:** 195 **Born:** 1/4/71 **Age:** 32

		HOW MUCH HE PITCHED						WHAT HE GAVE UP												THE RESULTS						
Year Team	Lg	G	GS	CG	GF	IP	BFP	H	R	ER	HR	SH	SF	HB	TBB	IBB	SO	WP	Bk	W	L	Pct	ShO	Sv-Op	Hld	ERC	ERA
2002 Oklahoma*	AAA	1	0	0	0	1.0	3	0	0	0	0	0	0	0	0	0	1	0	0	0	0	-	0	0--	-	0.00	0.00
2002 Pawtucket*	AAA	17	16	0	0	93.2	432	125	66	60	15	3	2	9	31	0	52	2	4	5	9	.357	0	0--	-	6.73	5.77
1998 Arizona	NL	5	0	0	2	5.1	29	9	7	7	1	0	1	0	4	0	5	0	0	0	0	-	0	0-0	0	10.59	11.81
2001 Tor-Tex	AL	35	18	0	4	136.2	610	157	74	67	19	3	4	13	55	5	67	1	6	8	9	.471	0	1-2	0	5.68	4.41
2002 Texas	AL	13	0	0	4	14.1	71	20	7	7	1	0	1	1	10	2	5	1	0	0	0	-	0	0-0	2	7.62	4.40
2001 Toronto	AL	24	18	0	2	115.0	517	133	66	59	14	3	4	12	49	5	57	0	5	6	7	.462	0	0-0	0	5.73	4.62
2001 Texas	AL	11	0	0	2	21.2	93	24	8	8	5	0	0	1	6	0	10	1	1	2	2	.500	0	1-2	0	5.39	3.32
3 ML YEARS		53	18	0	10	156.1	710	186	88	81	21	3	6	14	69	7	77	2	6	8	11	.421	0	1-2	2	6.02	4.66

Jason Middlebrook

Pitches: R **Bats:** R **Pos:** RP-10; SP-5   **Ht:** 6'3" **Wt:** 215 **Born:** 6/26/75 **Age:** 28

		HOW MUCH HE PITCHED						WHAT HE GAVE UP												THE RESULTS						
Year Team	Lg	G	GS	CG	GF	IP	BFP	H	R	ER	HR	SH	SF	HB	TBB	IBB	SO	WP	Bk	W	L	Pct	ShO	Sv-Op	Hld	ERC	ERA
1997 R Cucamnga	A+	6	6	0	0	22.1	105	29	15	10	1	1	3	0	12	1	18	2	1	0	2	.000	0	0--	-	5.89	4.03
1997 Clinton	A	14	14	2	0	81.1	353	76	46	36	4	3	1	1	39	0	86	6	5	6	4	.600	1	0--	-	3.70	3.98
1998 R Cucamnga	A+	28	28	0	0	150.0	665	162	99	82	10	1	9	4	63	0	132	17	4	10	12	.455	0	0--	-	4.46	4.92
1999 Padres	R	1	1	0	0	5.0	25	9	5	4	0	0	0	0	1	0	3	0	0	0	1	.000	0	0--	-	7.08	7.20
1999 Mobile	AA	13	13	0	0	63.2	302	78	59	57	9	1	5	8	30	1	38	5	0	4	6	.400	0	0--	-	6.49	8.06
2000 Mobile	AA	24	24	0	0	120.0	533	133	89	82	15	5	4	4	52	0	75	3	0	5	13	.278	0	0--	-	5.20	6.15
2000 Las Vegas	AAA	1	1	0	0	0.1	9	8	8	8	1	0	1	0	0	0	0	0	0	1	0	1.000	0	0--	-	272.5	216.0
2001 Mobile	AA	10	9	0	0	52.2	200	36	10	7	1	0	2	1	9	0	51	0	0	3	0	1.000	0	0--	-	1.42	1.20
2001 Portland	AAA	15	15	0	0	90.1	374	86	34	33	5	2	3	2	23	1	66	3	0	7	4	.636	0	0--	-	3.04	3.29
2002 Portland	AAA	10	7	0	1	36.2	166	42	27	23	6	2	0	0	13	0	32	0	0	2	5	.286	0	0--	-	5.04	5.65
2002 Norfolk	AA	5	5	0	0	23.2	84	13	7	7	1	0	1	1	1	0	22	0	0	2	1	.667	0	0--	-	0.92	2.66
2001 San Diego	NL	4	3	0	0	19.1	85	18	11	11	6	1	0	1	10	1	10	0	0	2	1	.667	0	0-0	0	5.85	5.12
2002 SD-NYM	NL	15	5	0	5	51.1	216	44	27	27	2	4	3	1	22	2	42	2	1	2	3	.400	0	0-0	1	3.02	4.73
2002 San Diego	NL	12	2	0	5	35.1	149	31	20	20	1	3	3	1	15	2	28	2	0	1	3	.250	0	0-0	0	3.05	5.09
2002 New York	NL	3	3	0	0	16.0	67	13	7	7	1	1	0	0	7	0	14	0	1	1	0	1.000	0	0-0	1	2.95	3.94
2 ML YEARS		19	8	0	5	70.2	301	62	38	38	8	5	3	2	32	3	52	2	1	4	4	.500	0	0-0	1	3.75	4.84

Doug Mientkiewicz

Bats: L **Throws:** R **Pos:** 1B-143; PR-2; PH-1   **Ht:** 6'2" **Wt:** 200 **Born:** 6/19/74 **Age:** 29

							BATTING												BASERUNNING				AVERAGES		
Year Team	Lg	G	AB	H	2B	3B	HR	(Hm	Rd)	TB	R	RBI	RC	TBB	IBB	SO	HBP	SH	SF	SB	CS	SB%	GDP	Avg	OBP	Slg
1998 Minnesota	AL	8	25	5	1	0	0	(0	0)	6	1	2	2	4	0	3	0	0	0	1	1	.50	0	.200	.310	.240
1999 Minnesota	AL	118	327	75	21	3	2	(0	2)	108	34	32	34	43	3	51	4	3	2	1	1	.50	13	.229	.324	.330
2000 Minnesota	AL	3	14	6	0	0	0	(0	0)	6	0	4	2	0	0	0	0	0	1	0	0	-	1	.429	.400	.429
2001 Minnesota	AL	151	543	166	39	1	15	(11	4)	252	77	74	96	67	6	92	9	0	7	2	6	.25	10	.306	.387	.464
2002 Minnesota	AL	143	467	122	29	1	10	(6	4)	183	60	64	75	74	8	69	6	0	7	1	2	.33	7	.261	.365	.392
5 ML YEARS		423	1376	374	90	5	27	(17	10)	555	172	176	209	188	17	215	19	3	17	5	10	.33	31	.272	.363	.403

Kevin Millar

Bats: R **Throws:** R **Pos:** LF-89; RF-22; PH-10; DH-6; 1B-2; 3B-2   **Ht:** 6'0" **Wt:** 210 **Born:** 9/24/71 **Age:** 31

							BATTING												BASERUNNING				AVERAGES		
Year Team	Lg	G	AB	H	2B	3B	HR	(Hm	Rd)	TB	R	RBI	RC	TBB	IBB	SO	HBP	SH	SF	SB	CS	SB%	GDP	Avg	OBP	Slg
1998 Florida	NL	2	2	1	0	0	0	(0	0)	1	1	0	1	1	0	0	0	0	0	0	0	-	0	.500	.667	.500
1999 Florida	NL	105	351	100	17	4	9	(3	6)	152	48	67	57	40	2	64	7	1	8	1	0	1.00	7	.285	.362	.433
2000 Florida	NL	123	259	67	14	3	14	(6	8)	129	36	42	47	36	0	47	8	0	2	0	0	-	5	.259	.364	.498
2001 Florida	NL	144	449	141	39	5	20	(13	7)	250	62	85	89	39	2	70	5	0	2	0	0	-	8	.314	.374	.557
2002 Florida	NL	126	438	134	41	0	16	(11	5)	223	58	57	64	40	0	74	5	0	6	0	2	.00	15	.306	.366	.509
5 ML YEARS		500	1499	443	111	12	59	(33	26)	755	205	251	258	156	4	255	25	1	18	1	2	.33	35	.296	.367	.504

Corky Miller

Bats: R **Throws:** R **Pos:** C-38; PH-1   **Ht:** 6'1" **Wt:** 225 **Born:** 3/18/76 **Age:** 27

							BATTING												BASERUNNING				AVERAGES		
Year Team	Lg	G	AB	H	2B	3B	HR	(Hm	Rd)	TB	R	RBI	RC	TBB	IBB	SO	HBP	SH	SF	SB	CS	SB%	GDP	Avg	OBP	Slg
1998 Billings	R+	45	129	35	8	0	5	(-	-)	58	28	24	29	24	0	24	2	2	1	4	2	.20	2	.271	.455	.450
1999 Rockford	A	66	196	56	10	1	10	(-	-)	98	43	40	42	33	1	42	20	1	0	3	6	.33	5	.286	.436	.500
1999 Chattanooga	AA	33	104	23	10	0	4	(-	-)	45	20	16	16	11	0	30	11	0	1	0	0	-	0	.221	.354	.433
2000 Chattanooga	AA	103	317	74	18	0	9	(-	-)	119	40	44	44	41	1	51	30	1	5	0	8	.38	12	.233	.373	.375
2001 Chattanooga	AA	59	170	47	12	0	9	(-	-)	86	25	42	38	25	1	32	19	1	0	1	2	.33	1	.276	.425	.506
2001 Louisville	AAA	44	144	50	11	0	7	(-	-)	82	30	28	34	10	0	19	12	0	1	2	0	1.00	2	.347	.431	.569

BATTING																			BASERUNNING				AVERAGES		
Year Team	Lg	G	AB	H	2B	3B	HR	(Hm Rd)	TB	R	RBI	RC	TBB	IBB	SO	HBP	SH	SF	SB	CS	SB%	GDP	Avg	OBP	Slg
2002 Louisville	AAA	43	134	31	5	0	6	(- -)	54	14	21	17	16	2	21	6	3	0	1	2	.33	6	.231	.340	.403
2001 Cincinnati	NL	17	49	9	2	0	3	(1 2)	20	5	7	4	4	0	16	2	0	2	1	0	1.00	1	.184	.263	.408
2002 Cincinnati	NL	39	114	29	10	0	3	(2 1)	48	9	15	15	9	2	20	4	1	1	0	0	-	7	.254	.328	.421
2 ML YEARS		56	163	38	12	0	6	(3 3)	68	14	22	21	13	2	36	6	1	3	1	0	1.00	8	.233	.308	.417

Damian Miller

Bats: R **Throws:** R **Pos:** C-100; PH-4 **Ht:** 6'2" **Wt:** 218 **Born:** 10/13/69 **Age:** 33

BATTING																			BASERUNNING				AVERAGES		
Year Team	Lg	G	AB	H	2B	3B	HR	(Hm Rd)	TB	R	RBI	RC	TBB	IBB	SO	HBP	SH	SF	SB	CS	SB%	GDP	Avg	OBP	Slg
2002 Tucson*	AAA	3	9	3	1	0	0	(- -)	4	1	0	1	0	0	1	0	0	0	0	0	-	1	.333	.333	.444
1997 Minnesota	AL	25	66	18	1	0	2	(1 1)	25	5	13	7	2	0	12	0	0	3	0	0	-	2	.273	.282	.379
1998 Arizona	NL	57	168	48	14	2	3	(2 1)	75	17	14	25	11	2	43	2	2	0	1	0	1.00	2	.286	.337	.446
1999 Arizona	NL	86	296	80	19	0	11	(3 8)	132	35	47	40	19	3	78	2	0	0	0	0	-	6	.270	.316	.446
2000 Arizona	NL	100	324	89	24	0	10	(6 4)	143	43	44	49	36	4	74	1	1	2	2	2	.50	6	.275	.347	.441
2001 Arizona	NL	123	380	103	19	0	13	(9 4)	161	45	47	52	35	9	80	4	4	2	0	1	.00	9	.271	.337	.424
2002 Arizona	NL	101	297	74	22	0	11	(4 7)	129	40	42	36	38	5	88	3	2	0	0	0	-	14	.249	.340	.434
6 ML YEARS		492	1531	412	99	2	50	(25 25)	665	185	207	209	141	23	375	12	9	10	3	3	.50	39	.269	.334	.434

Justin Miller

Pitches: R **Bats:** R **Pos:** SP-18; RP-7 **Ht:** 6'2" **Wt:** 195 **Born:** 8/27/77 **Age:** 25

HOW MUCH HE PITCHED							WHAT HE GAVE UP											THE RESULTS						
Year Team	Lg	G	GS	CG	GF	IP	BFP	H	R	ER	HR	SH	SF	HB	TBB	IBB	SO	WP	Bk	W	L	Pct	ShO	Sv-Op	Hld	ERC	ERA
1997 Portland	A-	14	11	0	1	67.1	288	68	26	16	3	2	2	4	20	0	54	6	0	4	2	.667	0	0- -	-	3.57	2.14
1998 Asheville	A	27	27	3	0	163.1	705	177	89	67	14	4	3	15	40	0	142	5	0	13	8	.619	1	0- -	-	4.20	3.69
1999 Salem	A+	8	8	0	0	37.0	159	35	18	17	3	0	0	5	11	0	35	5	0	2	3	.333	0	0- -	-	3.76	4.14
2000 Midland	AA	18	18	0	0	87.0	371	74	49	44	8	2	0	6	41	1	82	9	1	5	4	.556	0	0- -	-	3.76	4.55
2000 Sacramento	AAA	9	9	0	0	54.2	217	42	18	15	3	0	1	3	13	0	34	2	0	4	1	.800	0	0- -	-	2.22	2.47
2001 Sacramento	AAA	29	28	1	0	165.0	718	174	94	87	26	4	4	16	64	1	134	11	0	7	10	.412	0	0- -	-	5.27	4.75
2002 Syracuse	AAA	8	8	0	0	44.2	183	34	11	8	0	1	2	0	16	0	29	1	0	3	2	.600	0	0- -	-	2.02	1.61
2002 Toronto	AL	25	18	0	2	102.1	469	103	70	63	12	1	6	11	66	2	68	6	0	9	5	.643	0	0-0	1	5.73	5.54

Matt Miller

Pitches: L **Bats:** L **Pos:** RP-2 **Ht:** 6'3" **Wt:** 190 **Born:** 8/2/74 **Age:** 28

HOW MUCH HE PITCHED							WHAT HE GAVE UP											THE RESULTS						
Year Team	Lg	G	GS	CG	GF	IP	BFP	H	R	ER	HR	SH	SF	HB	TBB	IBB	SO	WP	Bk	W	L	Pct	ShO	Sv-Op	Hld	ERC	ERA
1996 Jamestown	A-	6	6	0	0	25.1	115	33	16	13	0	1	0	5	13	0	21	6	2	1	3	.250	0	0- -	-	6.38	4.62
1996 Greenville	IND	19	6	0	5	69.2	331	77	51	47	2	1	3	8	50	0	54	3	2	5	2	.714	0	1- -	-	5.94	6.07
1997 Greenville	IND	15	15	5	0	107.1	433	76	34	27	0	3	2	4	49	0	129	10	1	12	3	.800	3	0- -	-	2.30	2.26
1998 Greenville	IND	8	8	4	0	53.2	228	46	26	17	1	6	2	1	19	1	49	2	0	1	7	.125	0	0- -	-	2.57	2.85
1998 W Michigan	A	14	14	3	0	95.0	366	59	20	16	1	5	0	4	26	0	102	4	1	7	4	.636	1	0- -	-	1.47	1.52
1998 Savannah	A	17	0	0	10	35.1	137	25	9	9	0	2	0	2	10	0	46	2	0	3	1	.750	0	3- -	-	1.82	2.29
1998 Jacksonville	AA	13	13	0	0	61.1	297	70	49	48	6	0	2	2	50	1	49	3	1	3	7	.300	0	0- -	-	6.76	7.04
1999 Charlotte	A+	22	0	0	20	29.2	132	27	12	10	0	0	1	1	13	1	39	2	0	1	2	.333	0	8- -	-	2.97	3.03
1999 Lakeland	A+	19	19	1	0	108.1	473	108	58	50	9	5	2	2	45	0	82	0	1	4	9	.308	0	0- -	-	4.04	4.15
1999 Jacksonville	AA	7	7	0	0	40.2	176	43	23	20	3	3	1	2	12	0	25	0	0	4	1	.800	0	0- -	-	3.97	4.43
1999 Tulsa	AA	34	0	0	25	56.0	235	42	24	21	2	4	5	1	28	2	83	5	0	6	4	.600	0	7- -	-	2.69	3.38
2000 Jacksonville	AA	20	20	1	0	121.2	513	126	50	43	10	4	3	5	32	1	99	4	0	8	5	.615	0	0- -	-	3.80	3.18
2000 Rangers	R	1	0	0	0	2.0	9	2	1	1	0	0	0	1	0	0	4	0	0	0	0	-	0	0- -	-	3.63	4.50
2000 Tulsa	AA	3	0	0	0	3.2	22	7	7	6	0	0	1	0	4	0	4	1	0	0	0	-	0	0- -	-	11.78	14.73
2000 Oklahoma	AAA	39	0	0	25	60.1	276	61	29	24	6	4	4	3	34	4	69	4	0	3	3	.500	0	4- -	-	4.80	3.58
2001 Toledo	AAA	50	0	0	20	62.2	260	60	26	20	3	5	1	4	18	3	49	1	0	1	2	.333	0	4- -	-	3.29	2.87
2001 Portland	AAA	44	0	0	31	44.2	192	44	22	18	1	3	0	2	14	2	43	5	0	1	7	.125	0	17- -	-	3.18	3.63
2001 Detroit	AL	13	0	0	5	9.2	48	16	8	8	0	0	0	0	4	0	6	1	0	0	0	-	0	0-0	3	7.86	7.45
2002 Detroit	AL	2	0	0	0	0.2	8	4	2	1	1	0	0	0	1	0	1	0	0	0	0	-	0	0-1	0	62.48	13.50
2 ML YEARS		15	0	0	5	10.1	56	20	10	9	1	0	0	1	5	0	7	1	0	0	0	-	0	0-1	3	10.82	7.84

Travis Miller

Pitches: L **Bats:** R **Pos:** RP-5 **Ht:** 6'3" **Wt:** 215 **Born:** 11/2/72 **Age:** 30

HOW MUCH HE PITCHED							WHAT HE GAVE UP											THE RESULTS						
Year Team	Lg	G	GS	CG	GF	IP	BFP	H	R	ER	HR	SH	SF	HB	TBB	IBB	SO	WP	Bk	W	L	Pct	ShO	Sv-Op	Hld	ERC	ERA
2002 Edmonton*	AAA	24	0	0	3	29.1	122	35	15	13	3	0	0	0	9	0	24	1	0	0	1	.000	0	1- -	-	4.39	3.99
2002 Iowa*	AAA	9	0	0	5	11.2	53	13	8	8	1	1	5	0	5	1	8	3	0	0	1	.000	0	0- -	-	4.47	6.17
2002 Buffalo*	AAA	7	0	0	3	14.2	66	15	9	4	1	3	1	0	8	3	5	1	0	1	1	.500	0	0- -	-	4.14	2.45
1996 Minnesota	AL	7	7	0	0	26.1	126	45	29	27	7	1	0	0	9	0	15	0	0	1	2	.333	0	0-0	0	10.05	9.23
1997 Minnesota	AL	13	7	0	1	48.1	227	64	49	41	8	1	2	1	23	2	26	5	0	1	5	.167	0	0-0	0	6.90	7.63
1998 Minnesota	AL	14	0	0	2	23.1	104	25	10	10	0	0	1	0	11	1	23	2	0	0	2	.000	0	0-0	0	3.92	3.86
1999 Minnesota	AL	52	0	0	12	49.2	214	55	18	15	3	2	2	0	16	3	40	6	0	2	2	.500	0	0-2	8	4.01	2.72
2000 Minnesota	AL	67	0	0	12	67.0	316	83	35	29	4	1	3	1	32	2	62	2	0	2	3	.400	0	1-4	10	5.35	3.90
2001 Minnesota	AL	45	0	0	14	48.2	216	54	30	26	5	0	4	1	20	1	30	1	0	1	4	.200	0	0-0	5	4.82	4.81
2002 Minnesota	AL	5	0	0	3	4.0	19	5	2	2	0	0	0	0	2	2	3	0	0	0	0	-	0	0-0	1	4.07	4.50
7 ML YEARS		203	14	0	44	267.1	1222	331	173	150	27	5	12	3	113	11	199	16	0	7	18	.280	0	1-6	23	5.53	5.05

Trever Miller

Pitches: L Bats: R Pos: RP   Ht: 6'4" Wt: 195 Born: 5/29/73 Age: 30

Year Team	Lg	G	GS	CG	GF	IP	BFP	H	R	ER	HR	SH	SF	HB	TBB	IBB	SO	WP	Bk	W	L	Pct	ShO	Sv-Op	Hld	ERC	ERA
1996 Detroit	AL	5	4	0	0	16.2	88	28	17	17	3	2	2	2	9	0	8	0	0	0	4	.000	0	0-0	0	10.15	9.18
1998 Houston	NL	37	1	0	15	53.1	235	57	21	18	4	0	0	1	20	1	30	1	0	2	0	1.000	0	1-2	1	4.18	3.04
1999 Houston	NL	47	0	0	11	49.2	232	58	29	28	6	2	2	5	29	1	37	4	0	3	2	.600	0	1-1	4	6.48	5.07
2000 Phi-LA	NL	16	0	0	2	16.1	90	27	22	19	3	1	1	2	12	1	11	1	0	0	0	-	0	0-0	0	10.68	10.47
2000 Philadelphia	NL	14	0	0	2	14.0	72	19	16	13	3	1	1	1	9	1	10	1	0	0	0	-	0	0-0	0	8.14	8.36
2000 Los Angeles	NL	2	0	0	0	2.1	18	8	6	6	0	0	0	1	3	0	1	0	0	0	0	-	0	0-0	0	28.18	23.14
4 ML YEARS		105	5	0	28	136.0	645	170	89	82	16	5	5	10	70	3	86	6	0	5	6	.455	0	2-3	5	6.42	5.43

Wade Miller

Pitches: R Bats: R Pos: SP-26   Ht: 6'2" Wt: 210 Born: 9/13/76 Age: 26

Year Team	Lg	G	GS	CG	GF	IP	BFP	H	R	ER	HR	SH	SF	HB	TBB	IBB	SO	WP	Bk	W	L	Pct	ShO	Sv-Op	Hld	ERC	ERA
2002 New Orleans*	AAA	2	2	0	0	8.0	34	10	4	2	0	0	1	1	1	0	9	0	0	0	0	-	0	0--	-	4.32	2.25
1999 Houston	NL	5	1	0	2	10.1	52	17	11	11	4	0	0	0	5	0	8	0	0	0	1	.000	0	0-0	0	11.07	9.58
2000 Houston	NL	16	16	2	0	105.0	453	104	66	60	14	3	1	3	42	1	89	1	0	6	6	.500	0	0-0	0	4.37	5.14
2001 Houston	NL	32	32	1	0	212.0	873	183	91	80	31	7	5	4	76	3	183	8	0	16	8	.667	0	0-0	0	3.57	3.40
2002 Houston	NL	26	26	1	0	164.2	688	151	63	60	14	8	5	6	62	9	144	4	0	15	4	.789	1	0-0	0	3.54	3.28
4 ML YEARS		79	75	4	2	492.0	2066	455	231	211	63	18	11	13	185	13	424	13	0	37	19	.661	1	0-0	0	3.87	3.86

Kevin Millwood

Pitches: R Bats: R Pos: SP-34; RP-1   Ht: 6'4" Wt: 220 Born: 12/24/74 Age: 28

Year Team	Lg	G	GS	CG	GF	IP	BFP	H	R	ER	HR	SH	SF	HB	TBB	IBB	SO	WP	Bk	W	L	Pct	ShO	Sv-Op	Hld	ERC	ERA
1997 Atlanta	NL	12	8	0	2	51.1	227	55	26	23	1	3	5	2	21	1	42	1	0	5	3	.625	0	0-0	0	4.03	4.03
1998 Atlanta	NL	31	29	3	1	174.1	748	175	86	79	18	8	3	3	56	3	163	6	1	17	8	.680	1	0-0	1	3.81	4.08
1999 Atlanta	NL	33	33	2	0	228.0	906	168	80	68	24	9	3	4	59	2	205	5	0	18	7	.720	0	0-0	0	2.26	2.68
2000 Atlanta	NL	36	35	0	0	212.2	903	213	115	110	26	8	5	3	62	2	168	4	0	10	13	.435	0	0-0	0	3.83	4.66
2001 Atlanta	NL	21	21	0	0	121.0	515	121	66	58	20	7	2	1	40	6	84	5	1	7	7	.500	0	0-0	0	4.20	4.31
2002 Atlanta	NL	35	34	1	0	217.0	895	186	83	78	16	9	4	8	65	7	178	4	0	18	8	.692	1	0-0	0	2.85	3.24
6 ML YEARS		168	160	6	3	1004.1	4194	918	456	416	105	44	22	21	303	21	840	25	2	75	46	.620	2	0-0	1	3.29	3.73

Eric Milton

Pitches: L Bats: L Pos: SP-29   Ht: 6'3" Wt: 220 Born: 8/4/75 Age: 27

Year Team	Lg	G	GS	CG	GF	IP	BFP	H	R	ER	HR	SH	SF	HB	TBB	IBB	SO	WP	Bk	W	L	Pct	ShO	Sv-Op	Hld	ERC	ERA
1998 Minnesota	AL	32	32	1	0	172.1	772	195	113	108	28	1	3	5	70	0	107	1	0	8	14	.364	0	0-0	0	5.21	5.64
1999 Minnesota	AL	34	34	4	0	206.1	858	190	111	103	28	3	6	3	63	2	163	2	0	7	11	.389	2	0-0	0	3.56	4.49
2000 Minnesota	AL	33	33	0	0	200.0	849	205	123	108	35	4	6	7	44	0	160	5	0	13	10	.565	0	0-0	0	4.09	4.86
2001 Minnesota	AL	35	34	2	0	220.2	944	222	109	106	35	8	6	5	61	0	157	2	0	15	7	.682	1	0-0	0	4.05	4.32
2002 Minnesota	AL	29	29	2	0	171.0	707	173	96	92	24	0	4	3	30	0	121	4	0	13	9	.591	1	0-0	0	3.59	4.84
5 ML YEARS		163	162	9	0	970.1	4130	985	552	517	147	17	28	20	268	2	708	14	0	56	51	.523	4	0-0	0	4.07	4.80

Damon Minor

Bats: L Throws: L Pos: 1B-43; PH-39; DH-3   Ht: 6'7" Wt: 230 Born: 1/5/74 Age: 29

Year Team	Lg	G	AB	H	2B	3B	HR	(Hm	Rd)	TB	R	RBI	RC	TBB	IBB	SO	HBP	SH	SF	SB	CS	SB%	GDP	Avg	OBP	Slg
2002 Fresno*	AAA	9	29	15	6	1	0	(-	-)	23	8	5	11	5	0	5	0	0	0	0	0	-	0	.517	.588	.793
2000 San Francisco	NL	10	9	4	0	0	3	(2	1)	13	3	6	5	2	0	1	0	0	0	0	0	-	0	.444	.545	1.444
2001 San Francisco	NL	19	45	7	1	0	0	(0	0)	8	3	3	1	3	1	8	0	0	0	0	0	-	1	.156	.208	.178
2002 San Francisco	NL	83	173	41	6	0	10	(3	7)	77	21	24	18	24	6	34	2	0	2	0	0	-	8	.237	.333	.445
3 ML YEARS		112	227	52	7	0	13	(5	8)	98	27	33	24	29	7	43	2	0	2	0	0	-	9	.229	.319	.432

Doug Mirabelli

Bats: R Throws: R Pos: C-50; PH-7; DH-3   Ht: 6'1" Wt: 227 Born: 10/18/70 Age: 32

Year Team	Lg	G	AB	H	2B	3B	HR	(Hm	Rd)	TB	R	RBI	RC	TBB	IBB	SO	HBP	SH	SF	SB	CS	SB%	GDP	Avg	OBP	Slg
1996 San Francisco	NL	9	18	4	1	0	0	(0	0)	5	2	1	2	3	0	4	0	0	0	0	0	-	0	.222	.333	.278
1997 San Francisco	NL	6	7	1	0	0	0	(0	0)	1	0	0	0	1	0	3	0	0	0	0	0	-	0	.143	.250	.143
1998 San Francisco	NL	10	17	4	2	0	1	(1	0)	9	2	4	3	2	0	6	0	0	0	0	0	-	0	.235	.316	.529
1999 San Francisco	NL	33	87	22	6	0	1	(1	0)	31	10	10	10	9	1	25	1	0	1	0	0	-	1	.253	.327	.356
2000 San Francisco	NL	82	230	53	10	2	6	(2	4)	85	23	28	30	36	2	57	2	3	2	1	0	1.00	6	.230	.337	.370
2001 Tex-Bos	AL	77	190	43	10	0	11	(5	6)	86	20	29	29	27	2	57	4	1	2	0	0	-	3	.226	.332	.453
2002 Boston	AL	57	151	34	7	0	7	(5	2)	62	17	25	19	17	0	33	3	0	2	0	0	-	6	.225	.312	.411
2001 Texas	AL	23	49	5	2	0	2	(1	1)	13	4	3	3	10	0	21	0	0	0	0	0	-	1	.102	.254	.265
2001 Boston	AL	54	141	38	8	0	9	(4	5)	73	16	26	26	17	2	36	4	1	2	0	0	-	2	.270	.360	.518
7 ML YEARS		274	700	161	36	2	26	(14	12)	279	74	97	93	95	5	185	10	4	7	1	0	1.00	16	.230	.328	.399

Dave Mlicki

Pitches: R **Bats:** R **Pos:** SP-16; RP-6   **Ht:** 6'4" **Wt:** 200 **Born:** 6/8/68 **Age:** 35

Year Team	Lg	G	GS	CG	GF	IP	BFP	H	R	ER	HR	SH	SF	HB	TBB	IBB	SO	WP	Bk	W	L	Pct	ShO	Sv-Op	Hld	ERC	ERA
2002 New Orleans*	AAA	1	1	0	0	3.0	11	2	0	0	0	0	0	0	1	0	2	0	0	0	0	-	0	0- -	-	1.73	0.00
2002 Round Rock*	AA	2	2	0	0	9.0	37	8	3	3	0	1	0	0	2	0	7	0	0	1	1	.500	0	0- -	-	2.16	3.00
1992 Cleveland	AL	4	4	0	0	21.2	101	23	14	12	3	2	0	1	16	0	16	1	0	0	2	.000	0	0-0	0	6.44	4.98
1993 Cleveland	AL	3	3	0	0	13.1	58	11	6	5	2	0	0	2	6	0	7	2	0	0	0	-	0	0-0	0	4.23	3.38
1995 New York	NL	29	25	0	1	160.2	696	160	82	76	23	8	5	4	54	2	123	5	1	9	7	.563	0	0-0	0	4.11	4.26
1996 New York	NL	51	2	0	16	90.0	393	95	46	33	9	8	3	6	33	8	83	7	0	6	7	.462	0	1-3	8	4.40	3.30
1997 New York	NL	32	32	1	0	193.2	838	194	89	86	21	3	6	5	76	7	157	5	1	8	12	.400	1	0-0	0	4.16	4.00
1998 NYM-LA	NL	30	30	3	0	181.1	789	188	102	92	23	8	7	7	63	5	117	10	0	8	7	.533	1	0-0	0	4.35	4.57
1999 LA-Det		33	31	2	0	199.0	883	219	112	102	25	3	8	12	72	1	120	1	0	14	13	.519	0	0-0	1	4.91	4.61
2000 Detroit	AL	24	21	0	1	119.1	547	143	79	74	17	3	6	3	44	1	57	4	0	6	11	.353	0	0-0	0	5.39	5.58
2001 Det-Hou		34	29	0	1	167.2	772	203	122	115	37	8	9	15	74	3	97	8	0	11	11	.500	0	0-0	0	6.86	6.17
2002 Houston	NL	22	16	0	1	86.0	391	101	57	51	11	3	3	3	34	5	57	3	0	4	10	.286	0	0-0	0	5.26	5.34
1998 New York	NL	10	10	1	0	57.0	264	68	38	36	8	2	3	5	25	4	39	4	0	1	4	.200	0	0-0	0	5.89	5.68
1998 Los Angeles	NL	20	20	2	0	124.1	525	120	64	56	15	6	4	2	38	1	78	6	0	7	3	.700	1	0-0	0	3.69	4.05
1999 Los Angeles	NL	2	0	0	0	7.1	33	10	4	4	1	0	0	0	2	0	1	1	0	0	1	.000	0	0-0	1	6.01	4.91
1999 Detroit	AL	31	31	2	0	191.2	850	209	108	98	24	3	8	12	70	1	119	0	0	14	12	.538	0	0-0	0	4.86	4.60
2001 Detroit	AL	15	15	0	0	81.0	391	118	69	66	19	2	3	6	41	2	48	3	0	4	8	.333	0	0-0	0	8.98	7.33
2001 Houston	NL	19	14	0	1	86.2	381	85	53	49	18	6	6	9	33	1	49	5	0	7	3	.700	0	0-0	0	5.04	5.09
10 ML YEARS		**262**	**193**	**6**	**20**	**1232.2**	**5468**	**1337**	**709**	**646**	**171**	**46**	**47**	**58**	**472**	**32**	**834**	**46**	**2**	**66**	**80**	**.452**	**2**	**1-3**	**9**	**4.90**	**4.72**

Brian Moehler

Pitches: R **Bats:** R **Pos:** SP-12; RP-1   **Ht:** 6'3" **Wt:** 235 **Born:** 12/31/71 **Age:** 31

Year Team	Lg	G	GS	CG	GF	IP	BFP	H	R	ER	HR	SH	SF	HB	TBB	IBB	SO	WP	Bk	W	L	Pct	ShO	Sv-Op	Hld	ERC	ERA
2002 Lakeland*	A+	2	2	0	0	12.1	51	10	9	4	2	1	0	1	0	7	2	0	1	1	.500	0	0- -	-	2.39	2.92
2002 Toledo*	AAA	4	4	0	0	24.0	104	28	15	13	3	0	0	0	3	0	7	0	0	2	1	.667	0	0- -	-	3.94	4.88
1996 Detroit	AL	2	2	0	0	10.1	51	11	10	5	1	1	0	0	8	1	2	1	0	0	1	.000	0	0-0	0	5.49	4.35
1997 Detroit	AL	31	31	2	0	175.1	770	198	97	91	22	1	8	5	61	1	97	3	0	11	12	.478	1	0-0	0	4.92	4.67
1998 Detroit	AL	33	33	4	0	221.1	912	220	103	96	30	3	3	2	56	1	123	4	0	14	13	.519	3	0-0	0	3.79	3.90
1999 Detroit	AL	32	32	2	0	196.1	859	229	116	110	22	8	5	7	59	5	106	4	0	10	**16**	.385	2	0-0	0	4.85	5.04
2000 Detroit	AL	29	29	2	0	178.0	776	222	99	89	20	3	4	2	40	0	103	2	1	12	9	.571	0	0-0	0	4.95	4.50
2001 Detroit	AL	1	1	0	0	8.0	30	6	3	3	0	0	0	0	1	0	2	0	0	0	0	-	0	0-0	0	1.43	3.38
2002 Det-Cin		13	12	0	0	63.0	278	78	39	34	11	4	2	1	13	0	31	0	0	3	5	.375	0	0-0	0	5.20	4.86
2002 Detroit	AL	3	3	0	0	19.2	77	17	5	5	3	1	1	0	2	0	13	0	0	1	1	.500	0	0-0	0	2.54	2.29
2002 Cincinnati	NL	10	9	0	0	43.1	201	61	34	29	8	3	1	1	11	0	18	0	0	2	4	.333	0	0-0	0	6.56	6.02
7 ML YEARS		**141**	**140**	**10**	**0**	**852.1**	**3676**	**964**	**467**	**428**	**106**	**20**	**22**	**17**	**238**	**8**	**464**	**14**	**1**	**50**	**56**	**.472**	**6**	**0-0**	**0**	**4.60**	**4.52**

Chad Moeller

Bats: R **Throws:** R **Pos:** C-35; PH-3   **Ht:** 6'3" **Wt:** 210 **Born:** 2/18/75 **Age:** 28

Year Team	Lg	G	AB	H	2B	3B	HR	(Hm	Rd)	TB	R	RBI	RC	TBB	IBB	SO	HBP	SH	SF	SB	CS	SB%	GDP	Avg	OBP	Slg
2002 Tucson*	AAA	60	211	67	8	2	10	(-	-)	109	37	48	43	29	1	46	3	2	4	1	0	1.00	4	.318	.401	.517
2000 Minnesota	AL	48	128	27	3	1	1	(1	0)	35	13	9	8	9	0	33	0	1	1	1	0	1.00	4	.211	.261	.273
2001 Arizona	NL	25	56	13	0	1	1	(1	0)	18	8	2	5	6	1	12	0	1	0	0	0	-	2	.232	.306	.321
2002 Arizona	NL	37	105	30	11	1	2	(2	0)	49	10	16	18	17	3	23	0	1	0	0	1	.00	6	.286	.385	.467
3 ML YEARS		**110**	**289**	**70**	**14**	**3**	**4**	**(4**	**0)**	**102**	**31**	**27**	**31**	**32**	**4**	**68**	**0**	**3**	**1**	**1**	**1**	**.50**	**12**	**.242**	**.317**	**.353**

Dustan Mohr

Bats: R **Throws:** R **Pos:** RF-94; LF-28; PH-10; PR-3; CF-1; DH-1   **Ht:** 6'0" **Wt:** 210 **Born:** 6/19/76 **Age:** 27

Year Team	Lg	G	AB	H	2B	3B	HR	(Hm	Rd)	TB	R	RBI	RC	TBB	IBB	SO	HBP	SH	SF	SB	CS	SB%	GDP	Avg	OBP	Slg
1997 Watertown	A-	74	275	80	20	2	7	(-	-)	125	52	53	46	31	1	76	4	0	4	3	6	.33	1	.291	.366	.455
1998 Kinston	A+	134	491	119	23	9	19	(-	-)	217	60	65	66	39	3	146	9	2	2	8	4	.67	7	.242	.309	.442
1999 Akron	AA	12	42	7	2	1	0	(-	-)	11	3	2	2	5	0	7	0	1	0	0	1	.00	1	.167	.255	.262
1999 Kinston	A+	112	429	120	29	3	8	(-	-)	179	46	60	52	26	2	104	1	1	1	6	6	.50	13	.280	.322	.417
2000 Fort Myers	A+	101	370	98	19	2	11	(-	-)	154	58	75	51	35	1	65	8	1	4	7	4	.64	11	.265	.338	.416
2001 New Britain	AA	135	518	174	41	3	24	(-	-)	293	90	91	108	49	4	111	4	0	3	9	9	.50	6	.336	.395	.566
2001 Minnesota	AL	20	51	12	2	0	0	(0	0)	14	6	4	4	5	0	17	0	0	1	1	1	.50	0	.235	.298	.275
2002 Minnesota	AL	120	383	103	23	2	12	(3	9)	166	55	45	51	31	3	86	1	2	0	6	3	.67	5	.269	.325	.433
2 ML YEARS		**140**	**434**	**115**	**25**	**2**	**12**	**(3**	**9)**	**180**	**61**	**49**	**55**	**36**	**3**	**103**	**1**	**2**	**1**	**7**	**4**	**.64**	**5**	**.265**	**.322**	**.415**

Ben Molina

Bats: R **Throws:** R **Pos:** C-121; PH-7   **Ht:** 5'11" **Wt:** 210 **Born:** 7/20/74 **Age:** 28

Year Team	Lg	G	AB	H	2B	3B	HR	(Hm	Rd)	TB	R	RBI	RC	TBB	IBB	SO	HBP	SH	SF	SB	CS	SB%	GDP	Avg	OBP	Slg
2002 R Cucamnga*	A+	1	2	1	0	0	0	(-	-)	1	0	0	1	1	0	0	1	0	0	0	0	-	0	.500	.750	.500
1998 Anaheim	AL	2	1	0	0	0	0	(0	0)	0	0	0	0	0	0	0	0	0	0	0	0	-	0	.000	.000	.000
1999 Anaheim	AL	31	101	26	5	0	1	(0	1)	34	8	10	9	6	0	6	2	0	0	0	1	.00	5	.257	.312	.337
2000 Anaheim	AL	130	473	133	20	2	14	(11	3)	199	59	71	60	23	0	33	6	4	7	1	0	1.00	17	.281	.318	.421
2001 Anaheim	AL	96	325	85	11	0	6	(6	0)	114	31	40	34	16	3	51	8	2	4	0	1	.00	8	.262	.309	.351
2002 Anaheim	AL	122	428	105	18	0	5	(2	3)	138	34	47	32	15	3	34	4	6	6	0	0	-	15	.245	.274	.322
5 ML YEARS		**381**	**1328**	**349**	**54**	**2**	**26**	**(19**	**7)**	**485**	**132**	**168**	**135**	**60**	**6**	**124**	**20**	**12**	**17**	**1**	**2**	**.33**	**45**	**.263**	**.301**	**.365**

Gabe Molina

Pitches: R **Bats:** R **Pos:** RP-12   **Ht:** 6'1" **Wt:** 220 **Born:** 5/3/75 **Age:** 28

		HOW MUCH HE PITCHED						WHAT HE GAVE UP										THE RESULTS							
Year Team	Lg	G	GS	CG	GF	IP	BFP	H	R	ER	HR	SH	SF	HB	TBB	IBB	SO	WP	Bk	W	L	Pct	ShO	Sv-Op	Hld	ERC	ERA
2002 Memphis*	AAA	56	0	0	31	71.0	293	59	21	17	7	1	1	3	24	1	54	1	0	5	4	.556	0	12- -	-	3.07	2.15
1999 Baltimore	AL	20	0	0	7	23.0	102	22	19	17	4	0	0	0	16	1	14	4	0	1	2	.333	0	0-1	2	5.67	6.65
2000 Bal-Atl		11	0	0	4	15.0	85	28	18	15	3	0	3	1	10	0	9	0	0	0	0	-	0	0-0	1	11.76	9.00
2002 St Louis	NL	12	0	0	3	11.1	43	6	2	2	1	0	0	0	6	0	4	0	0	1	0	1.000	0	0-0	2	2.21	1.59
2000 Baltimore	AL	9	0	0	3	13.0	74	25	14	13	2	0	2	0	9	0	8	0	0	0	0	-	0	0-0	1	11.48	9.00
2000 Atlanta	NL	2	0	0	1	2.0	11	3	4	2	1	0	1	1	1	0	1	0	0	0	0	-	0	0-0	0	13.58	9.00
3 ML YEARS		43	0	0	14	49.1	230	56	39	34	8	0	3	1	32	1	27	4	0	2	2	.500	0	0-1	5	6.50	6.20

Izzy Molina

Bats: R **Throws:** R **Pos:** C-1   **Ht:** 6'1" **Wt:** 224 **Born:** 6/3/71 **Age:** 32

		BATTING																	BASERUNNING				AVERAGES		
Year Team	Lg	G	AB	H	2B	3B	HR	(Hm	Rd)	TB	R	RBI	RC	TBB	IBB	SO	HBP	SH	SF	SB	CS	SB%	GDP	Avg	OBP	Slg
2002 Rochester*	AAA	42	146	25	4	0	2	(-	-)	35	11	15	6	9	0	24	3	0	2	1	1	.50	5	.171	.231	.240
2002 Bowie*	AA	57	196	51	7	0	5	(-	-)	73	23	18	24	19	0	34	2	0	3	1	0	1.00	4	.260	.327	.372
1996 Oakland	AL	14	25	5	2	0	0	(0	0)	7	0	1	1	1	0	3	0	0	0	0	0	-	0	.200	.231	.280
1997 Oakland	AL	48	111	22	3	1	3	(1	2)	36	6	7	7	3	0	17	0	1	0	0	0	-	1	.198	.219	.324
1998 Oakland	AL	6	2	1	0	0	0	(0	0)	1	1	0	0	0	0	0	0	0	0	0	0	-	0	.500	.500	.500
2002 Baltimore	AL	1	3	1	0	0	0	(0	0)	1	1	0	1	0	0	0	0	0	0	0	0	-	0	.333	.333	.333
4 ML YEARS		69	141	29	5	1	3	(1	2)	45	8	8	9	4	0	20	0	1	0	0	0	-	1	.206	.228	.319

Jose Molina

Bats: R **Throws:** R **Pos:** C-29   **Ht:** 6'1" **Wt:** 215 **Born:** 6/3/75 **Age:** 28

		BATTING																	BASERUNNING				AVERAGES		
Year Team	Lg	G	AB	H	2B	3B	HR	(Hm	Rd)	TB	R	RBI	RC	TBB	IBB	SO	HBP	SH	SF	SB	CS	SB%	GDP	Avg	OBP	Slg
2002 Salt Lake*	AAA	79	290	89	14	2	4	(-	-)	119	30	43	39	12	1	60	4	7	2	0	3	.00	4	.307	.341	.410
1999 Chicago	NL	10	19	5	1	0	0	(0	0)	6	3	1	2	2	1	4	0	0	0	0	0	-	0	.263	.333	.316
2001 Anaheim	AL	15	37	10	3	0	2	(0	2)	19	8	4	6	3	0	8	0	2	0	0	0	-	2	.270	.325	.514
2002 Anaheim	AL	29	70	19	3	0	0	(0	0)	22	5	5	4	5	0	15	0	4	2	0	2	.00	2	.271	.312	.314
3 ML YEARS		54	126	34	7	0	2	(0	2)	47	16	10	12	10	1	27	0	6	2	0	2	.00	4	.270	.319	.373

Raul Mondesi

Bats: R **Throws:** R **Pos:** RF-121; DH-14; CF-11   **Ht:** 5'11" **Wt:** 230 **Born:** 3/12/71 **Age:** 32

		BATTING																	BASERUNNING				AVERAGES		
Year Team	Lg	G	AB	H	2B	3B	HR	(Hm	Rd)	TB	R	RBI	RC	TBB	IBB	SO	HBP	SH	SF	SB	CS	SB%	GDP	Avg	OBP	Slg
1993 Los Angeles	NL	42	86	25	3	1	4	(2	2)	42	13	10	14	4	0	16	0	1	0	4	1	.80	1	.291	.322	.488
1994 Los Angeles	NL	112	434	133	27	8	16	(10	6)	224	63	56	69	16	5	78	2	0	2	11	8	.58	9	.306	.333	.516
1995 Los Angeles	NL	139	536	153	23	6	26	(13	13)	266	91	88	89	33	4	96	4	0	7	27	4	.87	7	.285	.328	.496
1996 Los Angeles	NL	157	634	188	40	7	24	(11	13)	314	98	88	102	32	9	122	5	0	2	14	7	.67	6	.297	.334	.495
1997 Los Angeles	NL	159	616	191	42	5	30	(16	14)	333	95	87	114	44	7	105	6	1	3	32	15	.68	11	.310	.360	.541
1998 Los Angeles	NL	148	580	162	26	5	30	(13	17)	288	85	90	88	30	4	112	3	0	4	16	10	.62	8	.279	.316	.497
1999 Los Angeles	NL	159	601	152	29	5	33	(18	15)	290	98	99	102	71	6	134	3	0	5	36	9	.80	3	.253	.332	.483
2000 Toronto	AL	96	388	105	22	2	24	(10	14)	203	78	67	67	32	0	73	3	0	3	22	6	.79	5	.271	.329	.523
2001 Toronto	AL	149	572	144	26	4	27	(10	17)	259	88	84	89	73	3	128	6	0	4	30	11	.73	13	.252	.342	.453
2002 Tor-NYY	AL	146	569	132	34	1	26	(16	10)	246	90	88	75	59	3	103	5	0	4	15	6	.71	11	.232	.308	.432
2002 Toronto	AL	75	299	67	16	1	15	(10	5)	130	51	45	39	31	1	57	3	0	2	9	2	.82	8	.224	.301	.435
2002 New York	AL	71	270	65	18	0	11	(6	5)	116	39	43	36	28	2	46	2	0	2	6	4	.60	3	.241	.315	.430
10 ML YEARS		1307	5016	1385	272	44	240	(119	121)	2465	799	757	809	394	41	967	37	2	32	207	77	.73	77	.276	.331	.491

Craig Monroe

Bats: R **Throws:** R **Pos:** RF-5; LF-4; PR-4; DH-1   **Ht:** 6'1" **Wt:** 195 **Born:** 2/27/77 **Age:** 26

		BATTING																	BASERUNNING				AVERAGES		
Year Team	Lg	G	AB	H	2B	3B	HR	(Hm	Rd)	TB	R	RBI	RC	TBB	IBB	SO	HBP	SH	SF	SB	CS	SB%	GDP	Avg	OBP	Slg
1995 Rangers	R	54	193	48	6	2	0	(-	-)	58	22	33	22	18	0	25	2	1	2	13	2	.87	1	.249	.316	.301
1996 Chrlstn - SC	A	49	153	23	11	1	0	(-	-)	36	11	9	8	18	0	48	3	0	0	2	2	.50	3	.150	.253	.235
1996 Hudson Val	A-	67	268	74	16	6	5	(-	-)	117	53	29	40	23	0	63	2	0	2	21	7	.75	4	.276	.336	.437
1997 Charlotte	A+	92	328	77	23	1	7	(-	-)	123	54	41	45	44	1	80	0	0	6	24	1	.96	5	.235	.320	.375
1998 Charlotte	A+	132	472	114	26	7	17	(-	-)	205	73	76	72	66	0	102	3	0	7	50	13	.79	15	.242	.334	.434
1999 Charlotte	A+	130	480	125	21	1	17	(-	-)	199	77	81	66	42	2	102	4	3	7	40	16	.71	8	.260	.321	.415
1999 Oklahoma	AAA	6	16	4	1	0	0	(-	-)	5	2	1	2	1	0	4	0	0	0	0	0	-	0	.250	.294	.313
2000 Tulsa	AA	120	464	131	34	5	20	(-	-)	235	89	89	82	64	4	91	2	1	8	12	13	.48	12	.282	.366	.506
2001 Oklahoma	AAA	114	410	115	25	5	20	(-	-)	210	60	75	71	46	2	85	5	1	3	10	8	.56	11	.280	.358	.512
2002 Toledo	AAA	99	358	115	30	4	10	(-	-)	183	61	49	67	35	4	57	2	1	6	7	3	.70	8	.321	.379	.511
2001 Texas	AL	27	52	11	1	0	2	(1	1)	18	8	5	6	6	0	18	0	0	0	2	0	1.00	1	.212	.293	.346
2002 Detroit	AL	13	25	3	1	0	1	(0	1)	7	3	1	0	0	0	5	1	0	0	0	2	.00	1	.120	.154	.280
2 ML YEARS		40	77	14	2	0	3	(1	2)	25	11	6	6	6	0	23	1	0	0	2	2	.50	2	.182	.250	.325

Melvin Mora

Bats: R **Throws:** R **Pos:** LF-74; SS-41; CF-31; 2B-12; RF-5; DH-3; PH-3   **Ht:** 5'10" **Wt:** 180 **Born:** 2/2/72 **Age:** 31

		BATTING																	BASERUNNING				AVERAGES		
Year Team	Lg	G	AB	H	2B	3B	HR	(Hm	Rd)	TB	R	RBI	RC	TBB	IBB	SO	HBP	SH	SF	SB	CS	SB%	GDP	Avg	OBP	Slg
1999 New York	NL	66	31	5	0	0	0	(0	0)	5	6	1	2	4	0	7	1	3	0	2	1	.67	0	.161	.278	.161
2000 NYM-Bal		132	414	114	22	5	8	(5	3)	170	60	47	56	35	3	80	6	4	5	12	11	.52	5	.275	.337	.411
2001 Baltimore	AL	128	436	109	28	0	7	(6	1)	158	49	48	55	41	2	91	14	5	7	11	4	.73	6	.250	.329	.362
2002 Baltimore	AL	149	557	130	30	4	19	(8	11)	225	86	64	78	70	2	108	20	1	4	16	10	.62	7	.233	.338	.404

156

Year Team	Lg	G	AB	H	2B	3B	HR	(Hm	Rd)	TB	R	RBI	RC	TBB	IBB	SO	HBP	SH	SF	SB	CS	SB%	GDP	Avg	OBP	Slg
2000 New York	NL	79	215	56	13	2	6	(4	2)	91	35	30	29	18	3	48	2	2	5	7	3	.70	3	.260	.317	.423
2000 Baltimore	AL	53	199	58	9	3	2	(1	1)	79	25	17	27	17	0	32	4	2	0	5	8	.38	2	.291	.359	.397
4 ML YEARS		475	1438	358	80	9	34	(19	15)	558	201	160	191	150	7	286	41	13	16	41	26	.61	18	.249	.334	.388

Mike Mordecai

Bats: R Throws: R Pos: 3B-34; PH-30; SS-26; PR-6; 1B-4; 2B-4; LF-1 **Ht: 5'10" Wt: 185 Born: 12/13/67 Age: 35**

Year Team	Lg	G	AB	H	2B	3B	HR	(Hm	Rd)	TB	R	RBI	RC	TBB	IBB	SO	HBP	SH	SF	SB	CS	SB%	GDP	Avg	OBP	Slg
1994 Atlanta	NL	4	4	1	0	0	1	(1	0)	4	1	3	1	1	0	0	0	0	0	0	0	-	0	.250	.400	1.000
1995 Atlanta	NL	69	75	21	6	0	3	(1	2)	36	10	11	13	9	0	16	0	2	1	0	0	-	0	.280	.353	.480
1996 Atlanta	NL	66	108	26	5	0	2	(0	2)	37	12	8	11	9	1	24	0	4	1	1	0	1.00	1	.241	.297	.343
1997 Atlanta	NL	61	81	14	2	1	0	(0	0)	18	8	3	2	6	0	16	0	1	1	0	1	.00	4	.173	.227	.222
1998 Montreal	NL	73	119	24	4	2	3	(1	2)	41	12	10	10	9	0	20	0	2	0	1	0	1.00	1	.202	.258	.345
1999 Montreal	NL	109	226	53	10	2	5	(4	1)	82	29	25	24	20	0	31	1	1	2	2	5	.29	1	.235	.297	.363
2000 Montreal	NL	86	169	48	16	0	4	(2	2)	76	20	16	25	12	0	34	1	1	0	2	2	.50	1	.284	.335	.450
2001 Montreal	NL	96	254	71	17	2	3	(1	2)	101	28	32	32	19	1	53	1	1	2	2	2	.50	6	.280	.330	.398
2002 Mon-Fla	NL	93	151	37	8	0	0	(0	0)	45	19	11	15	13	4	27	2	10	0	2	2	.50	3	.245	.313	.298
2002 Montreal	NL	55	74	15	4	0	0	(0	0)	19	9	4	6	8	3	14	1	7	0	1	1	.50	2	.203	.289	.257
2002 Florida	NL	38	77	22	4	0	0	(0	0)	26	10	7	9	5	1	13	1	3	0	1	1	.50	1	.286	.337	.338
9 ML YEARS		657	1187	295	68	7	21	(10	11)	440	139	119	133	98	6	221	5	22	7	10	12	.45	18	.249	.307	.371

Juan Moreno

Pitches: L Bats: L Pos: RP-4 **Ht: 6'1" Wt: 205 Born: 2/28/75 Age: 28**

Year Team	Lg	G	GS	CG	GF	IP	BFP	H	R	ER	HR	SH	SF	HB	TBB	IBB	SO	WP	Bk	W	L	Pct	ShO	Sv-Op	Hld	ERC	ERA
1995 Athletics	R	20	0	0	8	44.2	181	36	10	6	1	1	1	0	20	0	49	2	5	6	2	.750	0	0- -	-	2.80	1.21
1996 W Michigan	A	38	11	0	5	107.0	475	98	60	52	6	6	6	2	69	5	97	6	2	4	6	.400	0	0- -	-	4.26	4.37
1999 Tulsa	AA	42	0	0	27	62.2	255	33	20	16	5	2	3	3	32	2	83	6	0	4	3	.571	0	3- -	-	2.03	2.30
2000 Charlotte	A+	1	1	0	0	2.0	7	0	0	0	0	0	0	0	1	0	0	0	0	0	0	-	0	0- -	-	0.27	0.00
2000 Tulsa	AA	5	0	0	3	6.2	30	6	4	4	0	0	1	0	5	0	12	1	0	0	0	-	0	1- -	-	4.14	5.40
2001 Tulsa	AA	6	0	0	6	8.2	34	6	1	0	0	3	1	0	3	0	10	1	0	1	1	.500	0	1- -	-	1.74	0.00
2001 Oklahoma	AAA	7	0	0	2	9.2	35	4	2	2	1	0	0	0	2	0	13	0	0	0	0	-	0	0- -	-	0.96	1.86
2002 Red Sox	R	3	3	0	0	5.0	15	4	2	1	0			0	0	0	10	0	0	0	1	.000	0	0- -	-		1.80
2002 Pawtucket	AAA	3	0	0	2	2.2	14	2	4	3	1	1	0	0	3	0	1	0	0	0	0	-	0	0- -	-	7.10	10.13
2001 Texas	AL	45	0	0	6	41.1	173	22	21	18	6	1	0	0	28	2	36	5	3	3	3	.500	0	0-2	8	2.83	3.92
2002 San Diego	NL	4	0	0	1	6.0	34	6	6	5	1	0	1	0	10	1	3	0	0	0	0	-	0	0-0	0	9.45	7.50
2 ML YEARS		49	0	0	7	47.1	207	28	27	23	7	1	1	0	38	3	39	5	3	3	3	.500	0	0-2	8	3.56	4.37

Mike Morgan

Pitches: R Bats: R Pos: RP-29 **Ht: 6'2" Wt: 226 Born: 10/8/59 Age: 43**

Year Team	Lg	G	GS	CG	GF	IP	BFP	H	R	ER	HR	SH	SF	HB	TBB	IBB	SO	WP	Bk	W	L	Pct	ShO	Sv-Op	Hld	ERC	ERA
2002 Tucson*	AAA	2	0	0	0	3.0	12	3	1	0	0	1	1	0	0	0	2	0	0	0	0	-	0	0- -	-	1.95	0.00
1978 Oakland	AL	3	3	1	0	12.1	60	19	12	10	1	0	0	0	8	0	0	0	0	0	3	.000	0	0-0	-	8.68	7.30
1979 Oakland	AL	13	13	2	0	77.1	368	102	57	51	7	4	4	3	50	0	17	7	0	2	10	.167	0	0-0	-	7.32	5.94
1982 New York	AL	30	23	2	2	150.1	661	167	77	73	15	2	4	2	67	5	71	6	0	7	11	.389	0	0-0	-	4.98	4.37
1983 Toronto	AL	16	4	0	2	45.1	198	48	26	26	6	0	1	0	21	0	22	3	0	0	3	.000	0	0-0	-	4.98	5.16
1985 Seattle	AL	2	2	0	0	6.0	33	11	8	8	2	0	0	0	5	0	2	1	0	1	1	.500	0	0-0	-	13.97	12.00
1986 Seattle	AL	37	33	9	2	216.1	951	243	122	109	24	7	3	4	86	3	116	8	1	11	17	.393	1	1-1	-	4.96	4.53
1987 Seattle	AL	34	31	8	2	207.0	898	245	117	107	25	8	5	5	53	3	85	11	0	12	17	.414	2	0-0	-	4.80	4.65
1988 Baltimore	AL	22	10	2	6	71.1	299	70	45	43	6	1	0	1	23	1	29	5	0	1	6	.143	0	1-1	-	3.63	5.43
1989 Los Angeles	NL	40	19	0	7	152.2	604	130	51	43	6	8	6	2	33	8	72	6	0	8	11	.421	0	0-1	1	2.26	2.53
1990 Los Angeles	NL	33	33	6	0	211.0	891	216	100	88	19	11	4	5	60	5	106	4	1	11	15	.423	4	0-0	-	3.76	3.75
1991 Los Angeles	NL	34	33	5	1	236.1	949	197	85	73	12	10	4	3	61	10	140	6	0	14	10	.583	1	1-1	-	2.37	2.78
1992 Chicago	NL	34	34	6	0	240.0	966	203	80	68	14	10	5	7	79	10	123	11	0	16	8	.667	1	0-0	-	2.77	2.55
1993 Chicago	NL	32	32	1	0	207.2	883	206	100	93	15	11	5	7	74	8	111	8	2	10	15	.400	1	0-0	-	3.77	4.03
1994 Chicago	NL	15	15	1	0	80.2	412	111	65	60	12	7	6	4	35	2	57	5	0	2	10	.167	0	0-0	-	7.10	6.69
1995 ChC-Stl	NL	21	21	1	0	131.1	548	133	56	52	12	12	5	6	34	2	61	6	0	7	7	.500	0	0-0	-	3.75	3.56
1996 Stl-Cin	NL	23	23	0	0	130.1	567	146	72	67	16	6	7	1	47	0	74	2	0	6	11	.353	0	0-0	-	4.85	4.63
1997 Cincinnati	NL	31	30	1	0	162.0	688	165	91	86	13	9	2	8	49	6	103	7	0	9	12	.429	0	0-0	-	3.83	4.78
1998 Min-ChC		23	22	0	0	120.2	524	138	62	56	21	3	3	8	39	2	60	1	0	4	3	.571	0	0-0	-	5.51	4.18
1999 Texas	AL	35	0	0	13	140.0	632	184	108	97	25	3	5	7	48	2	61	3	1	13	10	.565	0	0-0	-	6.64	6.24
2000 Arizona	NL	60	4	0	15	101.2	448	123	55	55	10	7	4	1	40	5	56	0	0	5	5	.500	0	5-6	5	5.34	4.87
2001 Arizona	NL	31	1	0	9	38.0	168	45	20	18	2	2	2	0	17	4	24	2	0	1	0	1.000	0	0-1	5	4.90	4.26
2002 Arizona	NL	29	0	0	4	34.0	156	41	22	20	7	2	0	3	9	1	13	3	0	1	1	.500	0	0-1	2	5.65	5.29
1995 Chicago	NL	4	4	0	0	24.2	100	19	8	6	2	2	0	1	9	1	15	0	0	2	1	.667	0	0-0	-	2.74	2.19
1995 St Louis	NL	17	17	1	0	106.2	448	114	48	46	10	10	5	5	25	1	46	6	0	5	6	.455	0	0-0	-	4.00	3.88
1996 St Louis	NL	18	18	0	0	103.0	452	118	63	60	14	5	6	0	40	0	55	2	0	4	8	.333	0	0-0	-	5.19	5.24
1996 Cincinnati	NL	5	5	0	0	27.1	115	28	9	7	2	1	1	1	7	0	19	0	0	2	3	.400	0	0-0	-	3.63	2.30
1998 Minnesota	AL	18	17	0	0	98.0	412	108	41	38	13	0	3	7	24	1	50	1	0	4	2	.667	0	0-0	-	4.68	3.49
1998 Chicago	NL	5	5	0	0	22.2	112	30	21	18	8	3	0	1	15	1	10	0	0	0	1	.000	0	0-0	-	9.46	7.15
22 ML YEARS		597	411	46	56	2772.1	11872	2943	1431	1303	270	124	75	73	938	77	1403	105	5	141	186	.431	10	8-13	14	4.27	4.23

Mike Moriarty

Bats: R Throws: R Pos: SS-4; 2B-2; PH-2; 3B-1; PR-1 **Ht: 6'0" Wt: 188 Born: 3/8/74 Age: 29**

Year Team	Lg	G	AB	H	2B	3B	HR	(Hm	Rd)	TB	R	RBI	RC	TBB	IBB	SO	HBP	SH	SF	SB	CS	SB%	GDP	Avg	OBP	Slg
1995 Fort Wayne	A	62	203	46	6	3	4	(-	-)	70	26	26	26	27	1	44	2	2	3	8	0	1.00	1	.227	.319	.345
1996 Fort Myers	A+	133	428	107	18	2	3	(-	-)	138	76	39	52	59	0	67	8	5	4	14	15	.48	2	.250	.349	.322
1997 New Britain	AA	135	421	93	22	5	6	(-	-)	143	60	48	46	53	1	68	3	10	5	12	5	.71	10	.221	.309	.340

Year Team	Lg	G	AB	H	2B	3B	HR	(Hm	Rd)	TB	R	RBI	RC	TBB	IBB	SO	HBP	SH	SF	SB	CS	SB%	GDP	Avg	OBP	Slg
1998 New Britain	AA	38	112	32	8	0	4	(-	-)	52	22	15	20	17	0	16	3	3	1	0	4	.00	1	.286	.391	.464
1998 Salt Lake	AAA	64	161	36	8	2	3	(-	-)	57	21	19	20	22	0	39	1	2	1	2	1	.67	1	.224	.319	.354
1999 Salt Lake	AAA	128	380	98	21	7	4	(-	-)	145	63	51	54	56	1	62	6	11	5	6	4	.60	9	.258	.358	.382
2000 Salt Lake	AAA	127	390	97	23	4	13	(-	-)	167	73	55	61	63	0	58	5	9	4	1	2	.33	9	.249	.357	.428
2001 Edmonton	AAA	131	404	98	17	2	13	(-	-)	158	66	50	57	58	0	94	13	5	2	5	4	.56	12	.243	.354	.391
2002 Rochester	AAA	90	311	86	18	1	4	(-	-)	118	48	26	44	37	0	50	4	3	4	4	1	.80	6	.277	.357	.379
2002 Baltimore	AL	8	16	3	1	0	0	(0	0)	4	0	3	0	0	0	2	0	0	0	0	1	.00	3	.188	.188	.250

Matt Morris

Pitches: R **Bats:** R **Pos:** SP-32 **Ht:** 6'5" **Wt:** 210 **Born:** 8/9/74 **Age:** 28

Year Team	Lg	G	GS	CG	GF	IP	BFP	H	R	ER	HR	SH	SF	HB	TBB	IBB	SO	WP	Bk	W	L	Pct	ShO	Sv-Op	Hld	ERC	ERA
1997 St Louis	NL	33	33	3	0	217.0	900	208	88	77	12	11	7	7	69	2	149	5	3	12	9	.571	1	0-0	0	3.41	3.19
1998 St Louis	NL	17	17	2	0	113.2	468	101	37	32	8	6	1	3	42	6	79	3	0	7	5	.583	1	0-0	0	3.25	2.53
2000 St Louis	NL	31	0	0	12	53.0	226	53	22	21	3	3	1	2	17	1	34	0	0	3	3	.500	0	4-7	7	3.58	3.57
2001 St Louis	NL	34	34	2	0	216.1	909	218	86	76	13	14	5	13	54	3	185	5	1	**22**	8	.733	1	0-0	0	3.50	3.16
2002 St Louis	NL	32	32	1	0	210.1	890	210	86	80	16	7	8	6	64	3	171	3	0	17	9	.654	1	0-0	0	3.63	3.42
5 ML YEARS		147	116	8	12	810.1	3393	790	319	286	52	41	22	31	246	15	618	16	4	61	34	.642	3	4-7	7	3.48	3.18

Warren Morris

Bats: L **Throws:** R **Pos:** 2B-4; PH-1 **Ht:** 5'11" **Wt:** 180 **Born:** 1/11/74 **Age:** 29

Year Team	Lg	G	AB	H	2B	3B	HR	(Hm	Rd)	TB	R	RBI	RC	TBB	IBB	SO	HBP	SH	SF	SB	CS	SB%	GDP	Avg	OBP	Slg
2002 Edmonton*	AAA	27	92	24	6	2	2	(-	-)	40	15	10	10	3	0	16	0	1	1	2	1	.67	3	.261	.281	.435
2002 Memphis*	AAA	29	100	26	4	1	2	(-	-)	38	16	14	10	8	0	12	0	0	3	0	1	.00	5	.260	.306	.380
2002 Pawtucket*	AAA	43	164	50	11	2	3	(-	-)	74	21	21	25	11	0	22	3	0	4	2	1	.67	6	.305	.352	.451
1999 Pittsburgh	NL	147	511	147	20	3	15	(9	6)	218	65	73	76	59	3	88	2	4	5	3	7	.30	12	.288	.360	.427
2000 Pittsburgh	NL	144	528	137	31	2	3	(3	0)	181	68	43	63	65	3	78	2	8	3	7	10	.41	7	.259	.341	.343
2001 Pittsburgh	NL	48	103	21	6	0	2	(2	0)	33	6	11	6	3	0	9	2	0	1	2	3	.40	2	.204	.239	.320
2002 Minnesota	AL	4	7	0	0	0	0	(0	0)	0	0	0	0	0	0	1	0	0	0	0	0	-	0	.000	.000	.000
4 ML YEARS		343	1149	305	57	5	20	(14	6)	432	139	127	145	127	6	176	6	12	9	12	20	.38	21	.265	.339	.376

Damian Moss

Pitches: L **Bats:** R **Pos:** SP-29; RP-4 **Ht:** 6'0" **Wt:** 187 **Born:** 11/24/76 **Age:** 26

Year Team	Lg	G	GS	CG	GF	IP	BFP	H	R	ER	HR	SH	SF	HB	TBB	IBB	SO	WP	Bk	W	L	Pct	ShO	Sv-Op	Hld	ERC	ERA
1994 Danville	R+	12	12	1	0	60.1	265	30	28	24	1	1	0	14	55	0	77	12	3	2	5	.286	1	0--	-	3.60	3.58
1995 Macon	A	27	27	0	0	149.1	653	134	73	59	13	0	2	12	70	0	177	14	5	9	10	.474	0	0--	-	3.97	3.56
1996 Durham	A+	14	14	0	0	84.0	333	52	25	21	9	3	3	2	40	0	89	7	2	9	1	.900	0	0--	-	2.57	2.25
1996 Greenville	AA	11	10	0	0	58.0	262	57	41	32	5	0	3		35	0	48	12	0	2	5	.286	0	0--	-	4.91	4.97
1997 Greenville	AA	21	19	1	0	112.2	498	111	73	67	13	1	8	9	58	0	116	14	2	6	8	.429	0	0--	-	4.96	5.35
1999 Macon	A	12	12	0	0	41.2	172	33	20	20	8	1	0	4	15	0	19	4	2	0	3	.000	0	0--	-	3.82	4.32
1999 Macon	AA	7	7	0	0	32.2	171	50	33	31	6	0	3	2	21	0	22	8	0	1	3	.250	0	0--	-	9.25	8.54
2000 Richmond	AAA	29	28	0	0	160.2	710	130	67	56	14	8	5	6	106	0	123	10	2	9	6	.600	0	0--	-	4.06	3.14
2001 Richmond	AAA	17	16	0	0	88.2	372	75	34	31	10	5	2	3	38	1	94	5	0	5	4	.556	0	0--	-	3.57	3.15
2001 Greenville	AA	3	2	0	1	9.0	34	7	3	3	3	0	0	0	0	0	10	0	0	0	1	.000	0	0--	-	2.56	3.00
2001 Atlanta	NL	5	1	0	2	9.0	41	3	3	3	1	1	0	1	9	0	8	1	0	0	0	-	0	0-0	0	2.61	3.00
2002 Atlanta	NL	33	29	0	2	179.0	743	140	80	68	20	12	3	6	89	5	111	13	2	12	6	.667	0	0-0	0	3.51	3.42
2 ML YEARS		38	30	0	4	188.0	784	143	83	71	21	13	3	6	98	5	119	14	2	12	6	.667	0	0-0	0	3.46	3.40

Guillermo Mota

Pitches: R **Bats:** R **Pos:** RP-43 **Ht:** 6'4" **Wt:** 205 **Born:** 7/25/73 **Age:** 29

Year Team	Lg	G	GS	CG	GF	IP	BFP	H	R	ER	HR	SH	SF	HB	TBB	IBB	SO	WP	Bk	W	L	Pct	ShO	Sv-Op	Hld	ERC	ERA
2002 Las Vegas*	AAA	20	0	0	6	36.2	145	34	13	12	1	3	1	2	8	1	38	3	1	1	3	.250	0	1--	-	2.83	2.95
1999 Montreal	NL	51	0	0	18	55.1	243	54	24	18	5	3	3	2	25	3	27	1	1	2	4	.333	0	0-1	3	4.10	2.93
2000 Montreal	NL	29	0	0	7	30.0	126	27	21	20	3	1	1	2	12	0	24	1	1	1	1	.500	0	0-0	5	3.86	6.00
2001 Montreal	NL	53	0	0	12	49.2	212	51	30	29	9	3	2	2	18	1	31	1	0	1	3	.250	0	0-3	12	4.77	5.26
2002 Los Angeles	NL	43	0	0	11	60.2	256	45	30	28	4	3	1	2	27	6	49	3	0	1	3	.250	0	0-1	3	2.57	4.15
4 ML YEARS		176	0	0	48	195.2	837	177	105	95	21	10	7	7	82	10	131	6	2	5	11	.313	0	0-5	24	3.73	4.37

Jamie Moyer

Pitches: L **Bats:** L **Pos:** SP-34 **Ht:** 6'0" **Wt:** 175 **Born:** 11/18/62 **Age:** 40

Year Team	Lg	G	GS	CG	GF	IP	BFP	H	R	ER	HR	SH	SF	HB	TBB	IBB	SO	WP	Bk	W	L	Pct	ShO	Sv-Op	Hld	ERC	ERA
1986 Chicago	NL	16	16	1	0	87.1	395	107	52	49	10	3	3	3	42	1	45	3	3	7	4	.636	1	0-0	0	6.13	5.05
1987 Chicago	NL	35	33	1	1	201.0	899	210	127	**114**	28	14	7	5	97	9	147	11	2	12	15	.444	0	0-0	0	4.96	5.10
1988 Chicago	NL	34	30	3	1	202.0	855	212	84	78	20	14	4	4	55	7	121	4	0	9	15	.375	1	0-2	0	3.89	3.48
1989 Texas	AL	15	15	1	0	76.0	337	84	51	41	10	1	4	2	33	0	44	1	0	4	9	.308	0	0-0	0	5.20	4.86
1990 Texas	AL	33	10	1	6	102.1	447	115	59	53	6	1	7	4	39	4	58	1	0	2	6	.250	0	0-0	0	4.57	4.66
1991 St Louis	NL	8	7	0	0	31.1	142	38	21	20	5	4	2	1	16	0	20	2	1	0	5	.000	0	0-0	0	6.58	5.74
1993 Baltimore	AL	25	25	3	0	152.0	630	154	63	58	11	3	1	6	38	2	90	1	1	12	9	.571	1	0-0	0	3.58	3.43
1994 Baltimore	AL	23	23	0	0	149.0	631	158	81	79	23	5	2	2	38	3	87	1	0	5	7	.417	0	0-0	0	4.24	4.77
1995 Baltimore	AL	27	18	0	3	115.2	483	117	70	67	18	5	3	3	30	0	65	0	0	8	6	.571	0	0-0	0	4.11	5.21
1996 Bos-Sea	AL	34	21	0	1	160.2	703	177	86	71	23	7	4	2	46	5	79	3	1	13	3	**.813**	0	0-0	0	4.42	3.98
1997 Seattle	AL	30	30	2	0	188.2	787	187	82	81	21	6	1	7	43	2	113	3	0	17	5	.773	0	0-0	0	3.56	3.86
1998 Seattle	AL	34	34	4	0	234.1	974	234	99	92	23	4	3	10	42	2	158	3	1	15	9	.625	0	0-0	0	3.34	3.53
1999 Seattle	AL	32	32	4	0	228.0	945	235	108	98	23	4	6	5	48	1	137	3	0	14	8	.636	0	0-0	0	3.71	3.87

Year Team	Lg	HOW MUCH HE PITCHED						WHAT HE GAVE UP												THE RESULTS							
		G	GS	CG	GF	IP	BFP	H	R	ER	HR	SH	SF	HB	TBB	IBB	SO	WP	Bk	W	L	Pct	ShO	Sv-Op	Hld	ERC	ERA
2000 Seattle	AL	26	26	0	0	154.0	678	173	103	94	22	3	3	3	53	2	98	4	1	13	10	.565	0	0-0	0	4.91	5.49
2001 Seattle	AL	33	33	1	0	209.2	851	187	84	80	24	5	11	10	44	4	119	1	0	20	6	.769	0	0-0	0	3.03	3.43
2002 Seattle	AL	34	34	4	0	230.2	931	198	89	85	28	5	7	9	50	4	147	1	0	13	8	.619	2	0-0	0	2.89	3.32
1996 Boston	AL	23	10	0	0	90.0	405	111	50	45	14	4	3	1	27	2	50	2	1	7	1	.875	0	0-0	1	5.37	4.50
1996 Seattle	AL	11	11	0	0	70.2	298	66	36	26	9	3	3	1	19	3	29	1	0	6	2	.750	0	0-0	0	3.31	3.31
16 ML YEARS		439	387	25	13	2522.2	10688	2586	1259	1160	295	86	66	80	714	46	1528	44	10	164	125	.567	8	0-2	2	3.98	4.14

Bill Mueller

Bats: B Throws: R Pos: 3B-104; PH-14

Ht: 5'10" Wt: 180 Born: 3/17/71 Age: 32

Year Team	Lg	BATTING																	BASERUNNING				AVERAGES		
		G	AB	H	2B	3B	HR	(Hm	Rd)	TB	R	RBI	RC	TBB	IBB	SO	HBP	SH	SF	SB	CS	SB%	GDP	Avg	OBP	Slg
2002 Iowa*	AAA	6	16	6	1	0	1	(-	-)	10	2	5	4	3	0	1	0	0	0	0	1	.00	0	.375	.474	.625
1996 San Francisco	NL	55	200	66	15	1	0	(0	0)	83	31	19	35	24	0	26	1	1	2	0	0	-	1	.330	.401	.415
1997 San Francisco	NL	128	390	114	26	3	7	(5	2)	167	51	44	62	48	1	71	3	6	6	4	3	.57	10	.292	.369	.428
1998 San Francisco	NL	145	534	157	27	0	9	(1	8)	211	93	59	83	79	1	83	1	3	5	3	3	.50	12	.294	.383	.395
1999 San Francisco	NL	116	414	120	24	0	2	(1	1)	150	61	36	62	65	1	52	3	8	2	4	2	.67	11	.290	.388	.362
2000 San Francisco	NL	153	560	150	29	4	10	(3	7)	217	97	55	72	52	0	62	6	7	6	4	2	.67	16	.268	.333	.388
2001 Chicago	NL	70	210	62	12	1	6	(3	3)	94	38	23	39	37	3	19	3	4	1	1	1	.50	4	.295	.403	.448
2002 ChC-SF	NL	111	366	96	19	4	7	(4	3)	144	51	38	55	52	2	42	0	4	5	0	0	-	9	.262	.350	.393
2002 Chicago	NL	103	353	94	19	4	7	(4	3)	142	51	37	55	51	2	41	0	4	5	0	0	-	8	.266	.355	.402
2002 San Francisco	NL	8	13	2	0	0	0	(0	0)	2	0	1	0	1	0	1	0	0	0	0	0	-	1	.154	.214	.154
7 ML YEARS		778	2674	765	152	13	41	(17	24)	1066	422	274	408	357	8	355	17	33	29	16	11	.59	63	.286	.370	.399

Mark Mulder

Pitches: L Bats: L Pos: SP-30

Ht: 6'6" Wt: 215 Born: 8/5/77 Age: 25

Year Team	Lg	HOW MUCH HE PITCHED						WHAT HE GAVE UP												THE RESULTS							
		G	GS	CG	GF	IP	BFP	H	R	ER	HR	SH	SF	HB	TBB	IBB	SO	WP	Bk	W	L	Pct	ShO	Sv-Op	Hld	ERC	ERA
2000 Oakland	AL	27	27	0	0	154.0	705	191	106	93	22	3	8	4	69	3	88	6	0	9	10	.474	0	0-0	0	6.14	5.44
2001 Oakland	AL	34	34	6	0	229.1	927	214	92	88	16	8	3	5	51	4	153	4	0	21	8	.724	4	0-0	0	2.95	3.45
2002 Oakland	AL	30	30	2	0	207.1	862	182	88	80	21	6	4	11	55	3	159	7	1	19	7	.731	1	0-0	0	3.06	3.47
3 ML YEARS		91	91	8	0	590.2	2494	587	286	261	59	17	15	20	175	10	400	17	1	49	25	.662	5	0-0	0	3.76	3.98

Terry Mulholland

Pitches: L Bats: R Pos: RP-34; SP-3

Ht: 6'3" Wt: 220 Born: 3/9/63 Age: 40

Year Team	Lg	HOW MUCH HE PITCHED						WHAT HE GAVE UP												THE RESULTS							
		G	GS	CG	GF	IP	BFP	H	R	ER	HR	SH	SF	HB	TBB	IBB	SO	WP	Bk	W	L	Pct	ShO	Sv-Op	Hld	ERC	ERA
1986 San Francisco	NL	15	10	0	1	54.2	245	51	33	30	3	5	1	1	35	2	27	6	0	1	7	.125	0	0-0	0	4.31	4.94
1988 San Francisco	NL	9	6	2	1	46.0	191	50	20	19	3	5	0	1	7	0	18	1	0	2	1	.667	1	0-0	1	3.46	3.72
1989 SF-Phi	NL	25	18	2	4	115.1	513	137	66	63	8	7	1	4	36	3	66	3	0	4	7	.364	1	0-0	1	4.64	4.92
1990 Philadelphia	NL	33	26	6	2	180.2	746	172	78	67	15	7	12	2	42	7	75	7	2	9	10	.474	1	0-1	0	3.04	3.34
1991 Philadelphia	NL	34	34	8	0	232.0	956	231	100	93	15	11	6	3	49	2	142	3	0	16	13	.552	3	0-0	0	3.15	3.61
1992 Philadelphia	NL	32	32	12	0	229.0	937	227	101	97	14	10	7	3	46	3	125	3	0	13	11	.542	2	0-0	0	3.07	3.81
1993 Philadelphia	NL	29	28	7	0	191.0	786	177	80	69	20	5	4	3	40	2	116	5	0	12	9	.571	2	0-0	0	2.99	3.25
1994 New York	AL	24	19	2	4	120.2	542	150	94	87	24	3	4	3	37	1	72	5	0	6	7	.462	0	0-0	0	5.92	6.49
1995 San Francisco	NL	29	24	2	2	149.0	666	190	112	96	25	11	6	4	38	1	65	4	0	5	13	.278	0	0-0	0	5.67	5.80
1996 Phi-Sea		33	33	3	0	202.2	871	232	112	105	22	11	8	5	49	4	86	6	0	13	11	.542	0	0-0	0	4.41	4.66
1997 Chicago	NL	70	6	0	14	112.0	476	100	49	36	7	5	3	4	39	7	72	4	0	6	5	.545	0	3-5	19	3.04	2.89
1998 ChC-SF	NL	40	27	1	5	186.2	794	190	100	88	24	17	4	11	51	3	99	3	0	6	13	.316	0	0-0	1	4.09	4.24
1999 ChC-Atl	NL	42	24	0	7	170.1	736	201	95	83	21	9	4	1	45	6	83	3	0	10	8	.556	0	1-1	4	4.73	4.39
2000 Atlanta	NL	54	20	1	14	156.2	702	198	96	89	24	10	5	4	41	7	78	3	0	9	9	.500	0	1-3	2	5.43	5.11
2001 Pit-LA	NL	41	4	0	8	65.2	285	78	35	34	12	1	1	2	17	1	42	1	0	1	1	.500	0	0-0	7	5.34	4.66
2002 LA-Cle		37	3	0	17	79.0	358	101	56	50	15	2	6	6	21	3	38	1	0	3	2	.600	0	0-2	2	6.08	5.70
1989 San Francisco	NL	5	1	0	2	11.0	51	15	5	5	0	0	0	0	4	0	6	0	0	0	0	-	0	0-0	1	5.23	4.09
1989 Philadelphia	NL	20	17	2	2	104.1	462	122	61	58	8	7	1	4	32	3	60	3	0	4	7	.364	1	0-0	0	4.58	5.00
1996 Philadelphia	NL	21	21	3	0	133.1	571	157	74	69	17	6	5	3	21	1	52	5	0	8	7	.533	0	0-0	0	4.36	4.66
1996 Seattle	AL	12	12	0	0	69.1	300	75	38	36	5	5	3	2	28	3	34	1	0	5	4	.556	0	0-0	0	4.49	4.67
1997 Chicago	NL	25	25	1	0	157.0	668	162	79	71	20	13	3	9	45	2	74	2	0	6	12	.333	0	0-0	0	4.24	4.07
1997 San Francisco	NL	15	2	0	5	29.2	126	28	21	17	4	4	1	2	6	1	25	1	0	0	1	.000	0	0-0	1	3.34	5.16
1999 Chicago	NL	26	16	0	4	110.0	485	137	71	63	16	6	3	1	32	4	44	2	0	6	6	.500	0	0-0	1	5.42	5.15
1999 Atlanta	NL	16	8	0	3	60.1	251	64	24	20	5	3	1	0	13	2	39	1	0	4	2	.667	0	1-1	3	3.55	2.98
2001 Pittsburgh	NL	22	1	0	3	36.1	150	38	15	15	5	1	1	1	10	1	17	1	0	0	0	-	0	0-0	3	4.32	3.72
2001 Los Angeles	NL	19	3	0	5	29.1	135	40	20	19	7	0	0	1	7	0	25	0	0	1	1	.500	0	0-0	4	6.67	5.83
2002 Los Angeles	NL	21	0	0	12	32.0	148	45	29	26	10	0	2	2	7	0	17	1	0	0	0	-	0	0-0	0	7.62	7.31
2002 Cleveland	AL	16	3	0	5	47.0	210	56	27	24	5	2	4	4	14	3	21	0	0	3	2	.600	0	0-2	2	5.05	4.60
16 ML YEARS		547	314	46	79	2291.1	9804	2485	1227	1106	252	119	72	57	593	52	1204	58	2	116	127	.477	10	5-10	37	4.12	4.34

Scott Mullen

Pitches: L Bats: R Pos: RP-44

Ht: 6'2" Wt: 195 Born: 1/17/75 Age: 28

Year Team	Lg	HOW MUCH HE PITCHED						WHAT HE GAVE UP												THE RESULTS							
		G	GS	CG	GF	IP	BFP	H	R	ER	HR	SH	SF	HB	TBB	IBB	SO	WP	Bk	W	L	Pct	ShO	Sv-Op	Hld	ERC	ERA
2002 Omaha*	AAA	19	1	0	6	31.0	130	32	16	9	0	3	1	0	9	3	21	0	0	1	2	.333	0	0- -		3.02	2.61
2000 Kansas City	AL	11	0	0	5	10.1	44	10	5	5	2	0	1	0	3	0	7	0	0	0	0	-	0	0-0	2	4.00	4.35
2001 Kansas City	AL	17	0	0	2	10.0	52	13	6	5	0	0	1	0	9	0	3	0	0	0	0	-	0	0-0	1	6.89	4.50
2002 Kansas City	AL	44	0	0	10	40.0	171	40	16	14	5	4	2	2	13	2	21	1	0	4	5	.444	0	0-2	6	4.08	3.15
3 ML YEARS		72	0	0	17	60.1	267	63	27	24	7	4	3	2	25	2	31	1	0	4	5	.444	0	0-2	9	4.54	3.58

Pete Munro

Pitches: R Bats: R Pos: SP-14; RP-5   Ht: 6'2" Wt: 200 Born: 6/14/75 Age: 28

Year Team	Lg		HOW MUCH HE PITCHED						WHAT HE GAVE UP										THE RESULTS						
		G	GS	CG	GF	IP	BFP	H	R	ER	HR	SH	SF	HB	TBB	IBB	SO	WP	Bk	W	L	Pct	ShO	Sv-Op	Hld	ERC	ERA
2002 New Orleans*	AAA	19	13	1	3	94.1	367	68	30	25	3	2	1	9	15	1	73	2	0	7	1	.875	1	0--	-	1.74	2.39
1999 Toronto	AL	31	2	0	9	55.1	250	70	38	37	6	1	4	2	23	0	38	3	0	0	1	.000	0	0-1	4	6.04	6.02
2000 Toronto	AL	9	3	0	2	25.2	127	38	22	17	1	1	0	3	16	0	16	1	0	1	1	.500	0	0-0	0	8.18	5.96
2002 Houston	NL	19	14	0	0	80.2	347	89	37	32	5	7	0	3	23	3	45	2	0	5	5	.500	0	0-0	1	4.04	3.57
3 ML YEARS		59	19	0	11	161.2	724	197	97	86	12	9	4	8	62	3	99	6	0	6	8	.429	0	0-1	5	5.33	4.79

Eric Munson

Bats: L Throws: R Pos: DH-14; 1B-4; PH-1   Ht: 6'3" Wt: 228 Born: 10/3/77 Age: 25

Year Team	Lg		BATTING																BASERUNNING				AVERAGES		
		G	AB	H	2B	3B	HR	(Hm	Rd)	TB	R	RBI	RC	TBB	IBB	SO	HBP	SH	SF	SB	CS	SB%	GDP	Avg	OBP	Slg
1999 Lakeland	A+	2	6	2	0	0	0	(-	-)	2	0	1	1	1	0	1	0	0	0	0	0	-	0	.333	.429	.333
1999 W Michigan	A	67	252	67	16	1	14	(-	-)	127	42	44	49	37	3	47	9	0	1	3	1	.75	4	.266	.378	.504
2000 Jacksonville	AA	98	365	92	21	4	15	(-	-)	166	52	68	59	39	5	96	18	0	6	5	2	.71	6	.252	.348	.455
2001 Erie	AA	142	519	135	35	1	26	(-	-)	250	88	102	94	84	6	141	11	0	6	0	3	.00	6	.260	.371	.482
2002 Toledo	AAA	136	477	125	30	4	24	(-	-)	235	77	84	87	77	5	114	7	0	8	1	3	.25	9	.262	.367	.493
2000 Detroit	AL	3	5	0	0	0	0	(0	0)	0	0	0	0	0	0	1	0	0	0	0	0	-	0	.000	.000	.000
2001 Detroit	AL	17	66	10	3	1	1	(1	0)	18	4	6	2	3	0	21	0	0	0	0	1	.00	2	.152	.188	.273
2002 Detroit	AL	18	59	11	0	0	2	(0	2)	17	3	5	2	6	0	11	1	0	1	0	0	-	1	.186	.269	.288
3 ML YEARS		38	130	21	3	1	3	(1	2)	35	7	12	4	9	0	33	1	0	1	0	1	.00	3	.162	.220	.269

Calvin Murray

Bats: R Throws: R Pos: CF-37; PR-9; LF-5; RF-4; PH-1   Ht: 5'11" Wt: 184 Born: 7/30/71 Age: 31

Year Team	Lg		BATTING																BASERUNNING				AVERAGES		
		G	AB	H	2B	3B	HR	(Hm	Rd)	TB	R	RBI	RC	TBB	IBB	SO	HBP	SH	SF	SB	CS	SB%	GDP	Avg	OBP	Slg
2002 Oklahoma*	AAA	33	139	37	7	1	2	(-	-)	52	23	14	17	11	0	20	0	4	1	4	0	1.00	0	.266	.318	.374
1999 San Francisco	NL	15	19	5	2	0	0	(0	0)	7	1	5	3	2	0	4	0	0	0	1	0	1.00	0	.263	.333	.368
2000 San Francisco	NL	108	194	47	12	1	2	(1	1)	67	35	22	27	29	0	33	3	2	1	9	3	.75	0	.242	.348	.345
2001 San Francisco	NL	106	326	80	14	2	6	(3	3)	116	54	25	36	32	0	57	3	3	0	8	8	.50	5	.245	.319	.356
2002 SF-Tex		48	89	13	5	1	0	(0	0)	20	16	1	5	7	0	17	1	2	0	4	0	1.00	0	.146	.216	.225
2002 San Francisco	NL	11	12	0	0	0	0	(0	0)	0	0	0	0	1	0	2	0	0	0	0	0	-	0	.000	.077	.000
2002 Texas	AL	37	77	13	5	1	0	(0	0)	20	16	1	5	6	0	15	1	2	0	4	0	1.00	0	.169	.238	.260
4 ML YEARS		277	628	145	33	4	8	(4	4)	210	106	53	71	70	0	111	7	7	1	22	11	.67	5	.231	.314	.334

Heath Murray

Pitches: L Bats: L Pos: RP-9   Ht: 6'4" Wt: 205 Born: 4/19/73 Age: 30

Year Team	Lg		HOW MUCH HE PITCHED						WHAT HE GAVE UP										THE RESULTS						
		G	GS	CG	GF	IP	BFP	H	R	ER	HR	SH	SF	HB	TBB	IBB	SO	WP	Bk	W	L	Pct	ShO	Sv-Op	Hld	ERC	ERA
2002 Buffalo*	AAA	21	2	0	8	29.2	114	23	10	10	2	2	0	2	6	0	32	1	0	1	2	.333	0	5- -	-	2.33	3.03
1997 San Diego	NL	17	3	0	1	33.1	162	50	25	25	3	3	1	4	21	3	16	1	1	1	2	.333	0	0-0	1	8.88	6.75
1999 San Diego	NL	22	8	0	1	50.0	234	60	33	32	7	3	2	1	26	4	25	1	1	0	4	.000	0	0-0	0	5.93	5.76
2001 Detroit	AL	40	4	0	10	63.1	301	82	48	46	11	2	1	3	40	5	42	1	0	1	7	.125	0	0-2	2	7.69	6.54
2002 Cleveland	AL	9	0	0	2	12.0	55	12	10	10	3	1	0	2	7	0	11	1	0	0	2	.000	0	0-0	0	6.82	7.50
4 ML YEARS		88	15	0	14	158.2	752	204	116	113	24	9	4	10	94	12	94	4	2	2	15	.118	0	0-2	3	7.29	6.41

Mike Mussina

Pitches: R Bats: L Pos: SP-33   Ht: 6'2" Wt: 185 Born: 12/8/68 Age: 34

Year Team	Lg		HOW MUCH HE PITCHED						WHAT HE GAVE UP										THE RESULTS						
		G	GS	CG	GF	IP	BFP	H	R	ER	HR	SH	SF	HB	TBB	IBB	SO	WP	Bk	W	L	Pct	ShO	Sv-Op	Hld	ERC	ERA
1991 Baltimore	AL	12	12	2	0	87.2	349	77	31	28	7	3	2	1	21	0	52	3	1	4	5	.444	0	0-0	0	2.80	2.87
1992 Baltimore	AL	32	32	8	0	241.0	957	212	70	68	16	13	6	2	48	2	130	6	0	18	5	.783	4	0-0	0	2.54	2.54
1993 Baltimore	AL	25	25	3	0	167.2	693	163	84	83	20	6	4	3	44	2	117	5	0	14	6	.700	2	0-0	0	3.61	4.46
1994 Baltimore	AL	24	24	3	0	176.1	712	163	63	60	19	3	9	1	42	1	99	0	0	16	5	.762	0	0-0	0	3.16	3.06
1995 Baltimore	AL	32	32	7	0	221.2	882	187	86	81	24	2	2	1	50	4	158	2	0	19	9	.679	4	0-0	0	2.66	3.29
1996 Baltimore	AL	36	36	4	0	243.1	1039	264	137	130	31	4	4	3	69	0	204	3	0	19	11	.633	1	0-0	0	4.36	4.81
1997 Baltimore	AL	33	33	4	0	224.2	905	197	87	80	27	3	2	3	54	3	218	5	0	15	8	.652	1	0-0	0	3.00	3.20
1998 Baltimore	AL	29	29	4	0	206.1	835	189	85	80	22	6	3	4	41	3	175	10	0	13	10	.565	2	0-0	0	2.96	3.49
1999 Baltimore	AL	31	31	4	0	203.1	842	207	88	79	16	9	7	1	52	0	172	2	0	18	7	.720	0	0-0	0	3.54	3.50
2000 Baltimore	AL	34	34	6	0	237.2	987	236	100	100	28	8	6	3	46	0	210	3	0	11	15	.423	1	0-0	0	3.37	3.79
2001 New York	AL	34	34	4	0	228.2	909	202	87	80	20	5	6	4	42	2	214	6	0	17	11	.607	3	0-0	0	2.65	3.15
2002 New York	AL	33	33	2	0	215.2	886	208	103	97	27	5	5	5	48	1	182	7	0	18	10	.643	2	0-0	0	3.46	4.05
12 ML YEARS		355	355	51	0	2454.0	9996	2305	1026	966	257	67	56	31	557	18	1931	52	1	182	102	.641	20	0-0	0	3.18	3.54

Brett Myers

Pitches: R Bats: R Pos: SP-12   Ht: 6'4" Wt: 215 Born: 8/17/80 Age: 22

Year Team	Lg		HOW MUCH HE PITCHED						WHAT HE GAVE UP										THE RESULTS						
		G	GS	CG	GF	IP	BFP	H	R	ER	HR	SH	SF	HB	TBB	IBB	SO	WP	Bk	W	L	Pct	ShO	Sv-Op	Hld	ERC	ERA
1999 Phillies	R	7	5	0	0	27.0	105	17	8	7	0	0	2	7	0	30	2	0	2	1	.667	0	0- -	-	1.49	2.33
2000 Piedmont	A	27	27	2	0	175.1	738	165	78	62	7	1	4	9	69	0	140	8	0	13	7	.650	0	0- -	-	3.58	3.18
2001 Reading	AA	26	23	1	0	156.0	661	156	71	67	21	3	1	10	43	1	130	5	0	13	4	.765	1	0- -	-	4.09	3.87
2002 Scrtn/WlksBr	AAA	19	19	4	0	128.0	509	121	54	51	9	3	3	3	20	0	97	1	0	9	6	.600	1	0- -	-	2.82	3.59
2002 Philadelphia	NL	12	12	1	0	72.0	307	73	38	34	11	6	2	6	29	1	34	2	1	4	5	.444	0	0-0	0	5.04	4.25

Greg Myers

Bats: L Throws: R Pos: C-54; PH-22   Ht: 6'2" Wt: 225 Born: 4/14/66 Age: 37

Year Team	Lg	G	AB	H	2B	3B	HR	(Hm	Rd)	TB	R	RBI	RC	TBB	IBB	SO	HBP	SH	SF	SB	CS	SB%	GDP	Avg	OBP	Slg
1987 Toronto	AL	7	9	1	0	0	0	(0	0)	1	1	0	0	0	0	3	0	0	0	0	0	-	2	.111	.111	.111
1989 Toronto	AL	17	44	5	2	0	0	(0	0)	7	0	1	0	2	0	9	0	0	0	0	1	.00	2	.114	.152	.159
1990 Toronto	AL	87	250	59	7	1	5	(3	2)	83	33	22	21	22	0	33	0	1	4	0	1	.00	12	.236	.293	.332
1991 Toronto	AL	107	309	81	22	0	8	(5	3)	127	25	36	35	21	4	45	0	1	3	0	0	-	13	.262	.306	.411
1992 Tor-Ana	AL	30	78	18	7	0	1	(0	1)	28	4	13	7	5	0	11	0	1	2	0	0	-	2	.231	.271	.359
1993 Anaheim	AL	108	290	74	10	0	7	(4	3)	105	27	40	29	17	2	47	2	3	3	3	3	.50	3	.255	.298	.362
1994 Anaheim	AL	45	126	31	6	0	2	(1	1)	43	10	8	12	10	3	27	0	5	1	0	2	.00	3	.246	.299	.341
1995 Anaheim	AL	85	273	71	12	2	9	(6	3)	114	35	38	34	17	3	49	1	1	2	0	1	.00	4	.260	.304	.418
1996 Minnesota	AL	97	329	94	22	3	6	(3	3)	140	37	47	42	19	3	52	0	0	5	0	0	-	11	.286	.320	.426
1997 Min-Atl	AL	71	174	45	11	1	5	(3	2)	73	24	29	23	17	2	32	0	0	2	0	0	-	4	.259	.321	.420
1998 San Diego	NL	69	171	42	10	0	4	(1	3)	64	19	20	18	17	1	36	0	0	1	0	1	.00	6	.246	.312	.374
1999 SD-Atl	NL	84	200	53	6	0	3	(3	2)	74	19	24	26	26	4	30	0	0	1	0	0	-	6	.265	.348	.370
2000 Baltimore	AL	43	125	28	6	0	3	(1	2)	43	9	12	13	9	0	29	0	1	0	0	0	-	7	.224	.271	.344
2001 Bal-Oak	AL	58	161	36	3	0	11	(5	6)	72	24	31	22	21	1	38	0	0	0	0	0	-	5	.224	.313	.447
2002 Oakland	AL	65	144	32	5	0	6	(2	4)	55	15	21	17	26	3	36	0	0	0	0	0	-	4	.222	.341	.382
1992 Toronto	AL	22	61	14	6	0	1	(0	1)	23	4	13	6	5	0	5	0	0	2	0	0	-	2	.230	.279	.377
1992 Anaheim	AL	8	17	4	1	0	0	(0	1)	5	0	0	1	0	0	6	0	1	0	0	0	-	2	.235	.235	.294
1997 Minnesota	AL	62	165	44	11	1	5	(3	2)	72	24	28	23	16	2	29	0	0	2	0	0	-	4	.267	.328	.436
1997 Atlanta	NL	9	9	1	0	0	0	(0	0)	1	0	1	0	1	0	3	0	0	0	0	0	-	0	.111	.200	.111
1999 San Diego	NL	50	128	37	4	0	3	(2	1)	50	9	15	17	13	2	14	0	0	0	0	0	-	5	.289	.355	.391
1999 Atlanta	NL	34	72	16	2	0	2	(1	1)	24	10	9	9	13	2	16	0	0	1	0	0	-	1	.222	.337	.333
2001 Baltimore	AL	25	74	20	2	0	4	(3	1)	34	11	18	11	8	0	17	0	0	0	0	0	-	3	.270	.341	.459
2001 Oakland	AL	33	87	16	1	0	7	(2	5)	38	13	13	11	13	1	21	0	0	0	0	0	-	2	.184	.290	.437
15 ML YEARS		973	2683	670	129	7	72	(37	35)	1029	282	342	295	228	26	477	3	12	24	3	9	.25	89	.250	.307	.384

Mike Myers

Pitches: L Bats: L Pos: RP-69   Ht: 6'4" Wt: 212 Born: 6/26/69 Age: 34

Year Team	Lg	G	GS	CG	GF	IP	BFP	H	R	ER	HR	SH	SF	HB	TBB	IBB	SO	WP	Bk	W	L	Pct	ShO	Sv-Op	Hld	ERC	ERA
1995 Fla-Det		13	0	0	5	8.1	42	11	7	7	1	0	1	2	7	0	4	0	0	1	0	1.000	0	0-1		9.61	7.56
1996 Detroit	AL	83	0	0	25	64.2	298	70	41	36	6	2	1	4	34	8	69	2	0	1	5	.167	0	6-8	17	4.97	5.01
1997 Detroit	AL	88	0	0	23	53.2	246	58	36	34	12	4	3	2	25	2	50	0	0	0	4	.000	0	2-5	18	5.70	5.70
1998 Milwaukee	NL	70	0	0	14	50.0	211	44	19	15	5	4	2	6	22	1	40	2	1	2	2	.500	0	1-3	23	4.14	2.70
1999 Milwaukee	NL	71	0	0	14	41.1	179	46	24	24	7	5	0	3	13	1	35	1	0	2	1	.667	0	0-3	14	5.24	5.23
2000 Colorado	NL	78	0	0	22	45.1	177	24	10	10	2	1	0	2	24	3	41	1	0	1	0	1.000	0	1-2	15	1.94	1.99
2001 Colorado	NL	73	0	0	14	40.0	169	32	17	16	2	1	1	1	24	7	36	0	0	2	3	.400	0	0-2	10	3.29	3.60
2002 Arizona	NL	69	0	0	15	37.0	171	39	18	18	2	3	1	8	17	0	31	0	0	4	3	.571	0	4-9	17	5.13	4.38
1995 Florida	NL	2	0	0	1	2.0	9	1	0	0	0	0	0	0	3	0	0	0	0	0	0	-	0	0-0		5.03	0.00
1995 Detroit	AL	11	0	0	3	6.1	33	10	7	7	1	0	1	2	4	0	4	0	0	1	0	1.000	0	0-1	1	11.13	9.95
8 ML YEARS		545	0	0	132	340.1	1493	324	172	160	37	20	9	28	166	22	306	6	1	12	19	.387	0	14-33	115	4.47	4.23

Rodney Myers

Pitches: R Bats: R Pos: RP-14   Ht: 6'1" Wt: 215 Born: 6/26/69 Age: 34

Year Team	Lg	G	GS	CG	GF	IP	BFP	H	R	ER	HR	SH	SF	HB	TBB	IBB	SO	WP	Bk	W	L	Pct	ShO	Sv-Op	Hld	ERC	ERA
2002 Portland*	AAA	42	0	0	17	48.2	203	48	23	20	2	2	1	2	13	1	35	1	1	5	2	.714	0	4--	-	3.25	3.70
1996 Chicago	NL	45	0	0	8	67.1	298	61	38	35	6	1	5	3	38	3	50	4	1	2	1	.667	0	0-0	1	4.20	4.68
1997 Chicago	NL	5	1	0	2	9.0	44	12	6	6	1	0	0	1	7	1	6	0	0	0	0	-	0	0-0	0	8.42	6.00
1998 Chicago	NL	12	0	0	3	18.0	82	26	14	14	3	0	0	0	6	0	15	1	0	0	0	-	0	0-1	0	7.19	7.00
1999 Chicago	NL	46	0	0	5	63.2	278	71	34	31	10	4	2	1	25	2	41	2	0	3	1	.750	0	0-1	8	5.22	4.38
2000 San Diego	NL	3	0	0	1	2.0	8	2	1	1	0	0	0	0	0	0	3	1	0	0	0	-	0	0-0	0	1.95	4.50
2001 San Diego	NL	37	0	0	16	47.1	211	53	31	28	6	1	4	4	20	0	29	2	0	1	2	.333	0	1-2	3	5.50	5.32
2002 San Diego	NL	14	0	0	4	21.1	101	29	20	14	1	1	0	3	10	0	11	2	0	1	1	.500	0	0-0	2	6.83	5.91
7 ML YEARS		162	1	0	39	228.2	1022	254	144	129	27	7	11	12	106	6	155	12	1	7	5	.583	0	1-4	14	5.35	5.08

Aaron Myette

Pitches: R Bats: R Pos: SP-12; RP-3   Ht: 6'4" Wt: 210 Born: 9/26/77 Age: 25

Year Team	Lg	G	GS	CG	GF	IP	BFP	H	R	ER	HR	SH	SF	HB	TBB	IBB	SO	WP	Bk	W	L	Pct	ShO	Sv-Op	Hld	ERC	ERA
2002 Oklahoma*	AAA	16	16	2	0	106.0	444	86	41	37	5	1	5	7	44	0	106	7	0	7	4	.636	1	0--	-	3.02	3.14
1999 Chicago	AL	4	3	0	0	15.2	80	17	11	11	2	0	0	2	14	1	11	2	0	0	2	.000	0	0-0		7.09	6.32
2000 Chicago	AL	2	0	0	1	2.2	12	0	0	0	0	0	0	0	4	0	1	0	0	0	0	-	0	0-0		1.96	0.00
2001 Texas	AL	19	15	0	1	80.2	376	94	65	64	12	3	4	11	37	0	67	2	0	4	5	.444	0	0-0		6.23	7.14
2002 Texas	AL	15	12	0	2	48.1	248	64	57	54	11	1	4	6	41	0	48	5	0	2	5	.286	0	0-0		9.83	10.06
4 ML YEARS		40	30	0	4	147.1	716	175	133	129	25	4	8	19	96	1	127	9	0	6	12	.333	0	0-0		7.37	7.88

Xavier Nady

Bats: R Throws: R Pos: RF   Ht: 6'0" Wt: 180 Born: 11/14/78 Age: 24

Year Team	Lg	G	AB	H	2B	3B	HR	(Hm	Rd)	TB	R	RBI	RC	TBB	IBB	SO	HBP	SH	SF	SB	CS	SB%	GDP	Avg	OBP	Slg
2001 Lk Elsinore	A+	137	524	158	38	1	26	(-	-)	276	96	100	102	62	7	109	10	0	8	6	0	1.00	14	.302	.381	.527
2002 Lk Elsinore	A+	45	169	47	6	3	13	(-	-)	98	41	37	37	28	4	40	1	0	1	2	0	1.00	2	.278	.382	.580
2002 Portland	AAA	85	315	89	12	1	10	(-	-)	133	46	43	41	20	0	60	3	0	2	0	1	.00	11	.283	.329	.422
2000 San Diego	NL	1	1	1	0	0	0	(0	0)	1	1	0	1	0	0	0	0	0	0	0	0	-	0	1.000	1.000	1.000

Charles Nagy

Pitches: R Bats: L Pos: RP-12; SP-7   Ht: 6'3" Wt: 200 Born: 5/5/67 Age: 36

Year Team	Lg	G	GS	CG	GF	IP	BFP	H	R	ER	HR	SH	SF	HB	TBB	IBB	SO	WP	Bk	W	L	Pct	ShO	Sv-Op	Hld	ERC	ERA
2002 Buffalo*	AAA	5	5	2	0	36.2	150	38	18	13	6	1	2	1	4	0	18	2	0	1	2	.333	0	0--	0	3.65	3.19
1990 Cleveland	AL	9	8	0	1	45.2	208	58	31	30	7	1	1	1	21	1	26	1	1	2	4	.333	0	0-0	0	6.54	5.91
1991 Cleveland	AL	33	33	6	0	211.1	914	228	103	97	15	5	9	6	66	7	109	6	2	10	15	.400	1	0-0	0	4.02	4.13
1992 Cleveland	AL	33	33	10	0	252.0	1018	245	91	83	11	6	9	2	57	1	169	7	0	17	10	.630	3	0-0	0	2.99	2.96
1993 Cleveland	AL	9	9	1	0	48.2	223	66	38	34	6	2	1	2	13	1	30	2	0	2	6	.250	0	0-0	0	5.90	6.29
1994 Cleveland	AL	23	23	3	0	169.1	717	175	76	65	15	2	2	5	48	1	108	5	1	10	8	.556	0	0-0	0	3.86	3.45
1995 Cleveland	AL	29	29	2	0	178.0	771	194	95	90	20	2	5	6	61	0	139	2	0	16	6	.727	1	0-0	0	4.63	4.55
1996 Cleveland	AL	32	32	5	0	222.0	921	217	89	84	21	2	4	3	61	2	167	7	0	17	5	.773	0	0-0	0	3.50	3.41
1997 Cleveland	AL	34	34	1	0	227.0	991	253	115	108	27	5	6	7	77	4	149	5	0	15	11	.577	0	0-0	0	4.74	4.28
1998 Cleveland	AL	33	33	2	0	210.1	930	250	139	122	34	8	6	9	66	12	120	3	0	15	10	.600	0	0-0	0	5.39	5.22
1999 Cleveland	AL	33	32	1	0	202.0	887	238	120	111	26	5	4	6	59	4	126	3	0	17	11	.607	0	0-0	0	4.97	4.95
2000 Cleveland	AL	11	11	0	0	57.0	267	71	53	52	15	5	2	2	21	2	41	1	0	2	7	.222	0	0-0	0	6.54	8.21
2001 Cleveland	AL	15	13	0	1	70.1	325	102	53	50	10	3	4	0	20	1	29	2	0	5	6	.455	0	0-0	0	6.60	6.40
2002 Cleveland	AL	19	7	0	7	48.2	231	76	51	48	10	2	2	2	13	1	22	1	0	1	4	.200	0	0-0	0	7.98	8.88
13 ML YEARS		313	297	31	9	1942.1	8403	2173	1054	974	217	48	55	51	583	37	1235	45	4	129	103	.556	6	0-0	0	4.53	4.51

Shane Nance

Pitches: L Bats: L Pos: RP-4   Ht: 5'8" Wt: 180 Born: 9/7/77 Age: 25

Year Team	Lg	G	GS	CG	GF	IP	BFP	H	R	ER	HR	SH	SF	HB	TBB	IBB	SO	WP	Bk	W	L	Pct	ShO	Sv-Op	Hld	ERC	ERA
2000 Yakima	A-	12	9	0	0	58.0	228	41	19	16	1	2	0	2	22	0	66	2	0	2	4	.333	0	0--	-	2.17	2.48
2001 Vero Beach	A+	21	0	0	13	48.0	196	28	15	14	3	1	0	3	21	1	63	2	0	6	3	.667	0	4--	-	2.00	2.63
2001 Jacksonville	AA	28	0	0	11	45.1	179	31	11	8	4	2	1	0	17	1	44	1	0	7	0	1.000	0	1--	-	2.28	1.59
2002 Las Vegas	AAA	37	0	0	10	58.1	255	58	32	27	5	2	2	2	26	1	53	1	0	11	3	.786	0	1--	-	4.23	4.17
2002 Indianapolis	AAA	9	0	0	4	16.2	67	12	0	0	0	0	0	3	6	0	10	0	2	3	0	1.000	0	0--	-	2.56	0.00
2002 Milwaukee	NL	4	0	0	1	6.1	27	4	3	3	1	0	0	0	4	0	5	0	0	0	0	-	0	0-0	0	3.29	4.26

Joe Nathan

Pitches: R Bats: R Pos: RP-4   Ht: 6'4" Wt: 195 Born: 11/22/74 Age: 28

Year Team	Lg	G	GS	CG	GF	IP	BFP	H	R	ER	HR	SH	SF	HB	TBB	IBB	SO	WP	Bk	W	L	Pct	ShO	Sv-Op	Hld	ERC	ERA
2002 Fresno*	AAA	31	25	1	0	146.1	673	167	97	91	20	2	4	3	74	0	117	9	0	6	12	.333	0	0--	-	5.65	5.60
1999 San Francisco	NL	19	14	0	2	90.1	395	84	45	42	17	2	0	1	46	0	54	2	0	7	4	.636	0	1-1	0	4.78	4.18
2000 San Francisco	NL	20	15	0	0	93.1	426	89	63	54	12	5	5	4	63	4	61	5	0	5	2	.714	0	0-1	0	5.23	5.21
2002 San Francisco	NL	4	0	0	3	3.2	12	1	0	0	0	0	0	0	0	0	2	0	0	0	0	-	0	0-0	0	0.17	0.00
3 ML YEARS		43	29	0	5	187.1	833	174	108	96	29	7	5	5	109	4	117	7	0	12	6	.667	0	1-2	0	4.87	4.61

Denny Neagle

Pitches: L Bats: L Pos: SP-28; RP-7   Ht: 6'3" Wt: 225 Born: 9/13/68 Age: 34

Year Team	Lg	G	GS	CG	GF	IP	BFP	H	R	ER	HR	SH	SF	HB	TBB	IBB	SO	WP	Bk	W	L	Pct	ShO	Sv-Op	Hld	ERC	ERA
1991 Minnesota	AL	7	3	0	2	20.0	92	28	9	9	3	0	0	0	7	2	14	1	0	0	1	.000	0	0-0	0	6.53	4.05
1992 Pittsburgh	NL	55	6	0	8	86.1	380	81	46	43	9	4	3	2	43	8	77	3	2	4	6	.400	0	2-4	5	4.04	4.48
1993 Pittsburgh	NL	50	7	0	13	81.1	360	82	49	48	10	1	1	3	37	3	73	5	0	3	5	.375	0	1-1	0	4.57	5.31
1994 Pittsburgh	NL	24	24	2	0	137.0	587	135	80	78	18	7	6	3	49	3	122	2	0	9	10	.474	0	0-0	0	4.09	5.12
1995 Pittsburgh	NL	31	31	5	0	209.2	876	221	91	80	20	13	6	3	45	3	150	6	0	13	8	.619	1	0-0	0	3.67	3.43
1996 Pit-Atl	NL	33	33	2	0	221.1	910	226	93	86	26	10	4	3	48	2	149	3	1	16	9	.640	0	0-0	0	3.69	3.50
1997 Atlanta	NL	34	34	4	0	233.1	947	204	87	77	18	12	6	6	49	5	172	3	0	20	5	.800	4	0-0	0	2.60	2.97
1998 Atlanta	NL	32	31	5	0	210.1	861	196	91	83	25	7	3	6	60	3	165	6	1	16	11	.593	2	0-0	0	3.55	3.55
1999 Cincinnati	NL	20	19	0	0	111.2	467	95	54	53	23	3	5	4	40	3	76	4	0	9	5	.643	0	0-0	0	3.88	4.27
2000 Cin-NYY	NL	34	33	1	0	209.0	906	210	109	105	31	8	6	5	81	4	146	7	1	15	9	.625	0	0-0	0	4.45	4.52
2001 Colorado	NL	30	30	0	0	170.2	760	192	107	102	29	8	9	7	60	3	139	2	0	9	8	.529	0	0-0	0	5.21	5.38
2002 Colorado	NL	35	28	1	0	164.1	724	170	101	96	26	5	6	10	63	5	111	4	1	8	11	.421	0	0-0	2	4.80	5.26
1996 Pittsburgh	NL	27	27	1	0	182.2	745	186	67	62	21	9	3	3	34	2	131	2	1	14	6	.700	0	0-0	0	3.55	3.05
1996 Atlanta	NL	6	6	1	0	38.2	165	40	26	24	5	1	1	0	14	0	18	1	0	2	3	.400	0	0-0	0	4.37	5.59
2000 Cincinnati	NL	18	18	0	0	117.2	506	111	48	46	15	2	1	3	50	3	88	3	0	8	2	.800	0	0-0	0	4.12	3.52
2000 New York	AL	16	15	1	0	91.1	400	99	61	59	16	6	5	2	31	1	58	4	1	7	7	.500	0	0-0	0	4.89	5.81
12 ML YEARS		385	279	20	23	1855.0	7870	1840	917	860	238	78	55	52	582	44	1394	46	6	122	88	.581	7	3-5	13	3.97	4.17

Blaine Neal

Pitches: R Bats: L Pos: RP-32   Ht: 6'5" Wt: 240 Born: 4/6/78 Age: 25

Year Team	Lg	G	GS	CG	GF	IP	BFP	H	R	ER	HR	SH	SF	HB	TBB	IBB	SO	WP	Bk	W	L	Pct	ShO	Sv-Op	Hld	ERC	ERA
1996 Marlins	R	7	5	0	1	29.1	126	32	18	15	1	0	0	3	6	0	15	3	3	1	1	.500	0	1--	-	3.76	4.60
1997 Marlins	R	10	0	0	5	22.1	102	24	11	9	1	0	0	1	11	0	19	2	0	4	1	.800	0	1--	-	4.56	3.63
1999 Kane County	A	26	0	0	18	31.0	117	21	8	8	2	2	0	0	10	0	31	1	0	4	2	.667	0	6--	-	2.05	2.32
2000 Brevard Cnty	A+	41	0	0	34	54.1	231	40	27	13	1	1	2	4	24	3	65	1	0	2	2	.500	0	11--	-	2.42	2.15
2001 Portland	AA	54	0	0	44	53.1	225	43	17	14	1	4	1	2	21	3	45	2	0	2	3	.400	0	21--	-	2.49	2.36
2002 Calgary	AAA	29	0	0	25	31.0	134	27	11	10	2	0	1	2	15	1	26	1	0	3	1	.750	0	11--	-	3.63	2.90
2001 Florida	NL	4	0	0	0	5.1	28	7	4	4	0	0	0	0	5	0	3	1	0	0	0	-	0	0-0	0	7.12	6.75
2002 Florida	NL	32	0	0	6	33.0	144	32	12	10	1	1	0	0	14	2	33	4	0	3	0	1.000	0	0-0	2	3.35	2.73
2 ML YEARS		36	0	0	6	38.1	172	39	16	14	1	1	0	0	19	2	36	5	0	3	0	1.000	0	0-0	2	3.84	3.29

Bry Nelson

Bats: B **Throws:** R **Pos:** 2B-11; LF-7; PR-6; PH-4; CF-2; RF-2; DH-1   **Ht:** 5'10" **Wt:** 205 **Born:** 1/27/74 **Age:** 29

Year Team	Lg	G	AB	H	2B	3B	HR	(Hm	Rd)	TB	R	RBI	RC	TBB	IBB	SO	HBP	SH	SF	SB	CS	SB%	GDP	Avg	OBP	Slg
1994 Quad City	A	45	156	38	6	0	1	(-	-)	47	20	6	12	11	0	15	0	0	0	3	5	.38	3	.244	.293	.301
1994 Auburn	A-	65	261	84	16	7	6	(-	-)	132	53	35	42	11	0	13	1	3	1	2	1	.67	9	.322	.350	.506
1995 Kissimmee	A+	105	395	129	34	5	3	(-	-)	182	47	52	61	20	0	37	1	1	6	14	10	.58	8	.327	.355	.461
1995 Quad City	A	6	26	1	1	0	0	(-	-)	2	1	2	0	0	0	3	0	0	0	0	0	-	2	.038	.038	.077
1996 Kissimmee	A+	89	345	87	21	6	3	(-	-)	129	38	52	35	19	3	27	1	1	4	8	2	.80	13	.252	.290	.374
1997 Orlando	AA	110	382	110	33	2	8	(-	-)	171	51	58	57	45	4	43	1	1	6	5	7	.42	15	.288	.359	.448
1998 W Tennesse	AA	32	102	29	6	2	2	(-	-)	45	10	18	15	12	2	12	0	0	1	4	2	.67	5	.284	.357	.441
1999 W Tennesse	AA	129	471	126	24	5	16	(-	-)	208	66	78	65	42	4	52	2	1	4	10	7	.59	13	.268	.328	.442
2000 Tucson	AAA	69	261	81	21	0	5	(-	-)	117	34	31	38	16	0	20	0	0	2	4	2	.67	8	.310	.348	.448
2001 Tucson	AAA	85	326	98	15	0	6	(-	-)	131	37	41	40	16	2	20	1	1	3	9	5	.64	12	.301	.332	.402
2001 Nashville	AAA	49	185	58	7	0	5	(-	-)	80	23	15	25	10	0	16	1	4	2	3	3	.50	7	.314	.348	.432
2002 Pawtucket	AAA	60	223	66	8	3	8	(-	-)	104	25	24	33	14	1	19	1	2	0	1	5	.17	3	.296	.340	.466
2002 Boston	AL	25	34	9	3	0	0	(0	0)	12	6	2	2	4	0	1	0	1	0	1	1	.50	1	.265	.342	.353

Jeff Nelson

Pitches: R **Bats:** R **Pos:** RP-41   **Ht:** 6'8" **Wt:** 235 **Born:** 11/17/66 **Age:** 36

Year Team	Lg	G	GS	CG	GF	IP	BFP	H	R	ER	HR	SH	SF	HB	TBB	IBB	SO	WP	Bk	W	L	Pct	ShO	Sv-Op	Hld	ERC	ERA
2002 Everett*	A-	1	1	0	0	1.1	5	1	1	0	0	0	0	0	0	0	0	0	0	0	1	.000	0	0- -	-	1.13	0.00
1992 Seattle	AL	66	0	0	27	81.0	352	71	34	31	7	9	3	6	44	12	46	2	0	1	7	.125	0	6-14	6	3.93	3.44
1993 Seattle	AL	71	0	0	13	60.0	269	57	30	29	5	2	4	8	34	10	61	2	0	5	3	.625	0	1-11	17	4.62	4.35
1994 Seattle	AL	28	0	0	7	42.1	185	35	18	13	3	1	1	8	20	4	44	2	0	0	0	-	0	0-0	2	3.77	2.76
1995 Seattle	AL	62	0	0	22	78.2	318	58	21	19	4	5	3	6	27	5	96	1	0	7	3	.700	0	2-4	14	2.39	2.17
1996 New York	AL	73	0	0	27	74.1	328	75	38	36	6	3	1	2	36	1	91	4	0	4	4	.500	0	2-4	10	4.41	4.36
1997 New York	AL	77	0	0	22	78.2	327	53	32	25	7	7	2	4	37	12	81	4	0	3	7	.300	0	2-8	22	2.48	2.86
1998 New York	AL	45	0	0	13	40.1	192	44	18	17	1	1	3	8	22	4	35	2	0	5	3	.625	0	3-6	10	5.13	3.79
1999 New York	AL	39	0	0	8	30.1	139	27	14	14	2	2	2	3	22	2	35	2	1	2	1	.667	0	1-2	10	4.76	4.15
2000 New York	AL	73	0	0	13	69.2	296	44	24	19	2	6	2	2	45	1	71	4	0	8	4	.667	0	0-4	15	2.61	2.45
2001 Seattle	AL	69	0	0	16	65.1	273	30	21	20	3	2	0	6	44	1	88	2	0	4	3	.571	0	4-5	26	2.20	2.76
2002 Seattle	AL	41	0	0	12	45.2	199	36	20	20	4	2	4	3	27	3	55	5	0	3	2	.600	0	2-4	12	3.70	3.94
11 ML YEARS		**644**	**0**	**0**	**182**	**666.1**	**2878**	**530**	**270**	**243**	**44**	**40**	**25**	**56**	**358**	**55**	**703**	**30**	**1**	**42**	**37**	**.532**	**0**	**23-62**	**144**	**3.43**	**3.28**

Robb Nen

Pitches: R **Bats:** R **Pos:** RP-68   **Ht:** 6'5" **Wt:** 222 **Born:** 11/28/69 **Age:** 33

Year Team	Lg	G	GS	CG	GF	IP	BFP	H	R	ER	HR	SH	SF	HB	TBB	IBB	SO	WP	Bk	W	L	Pct	ShO	Sv-Op	Hld	ERC	ERA
1993 Tex-Fla		24	4	0	5	56.0	272	63	45	42	6	1	2	0	46	0	39	6	1	1	5	.667	0	0-0	0	6.58	6.75
1994 Florida	NL	44	0	0	28	58.0	228	46	20	19	6	3	1	0	17	2	60	3	2	5	5	.500	0	15-15	1	2.63	2.95
1995 Florida	NL	62	0	0	54	65.2	279	62	26	24	6	0	1	1	23	3	68	2	0	0	7	.000	0	23-29	3	3.48	3.29
1996 Florida	NL	75	0	0	65	83.0	326	67	21	18	2	5	1	1	21	6	92	4	0	5	1	.833	0	35-42	0	2.07	1.95
1997 Florida	NL	73	0	0	65	74.0	332	72	35	32	7	1	3	0	40	7	81	5	0	9	3	.750	0	35-42	0	4.20	3.89
1998 San Francisco	NL	78	0	0	67	88.2	357	59	21	15	4	2	2	1	25	5	110	3	0	7	7	.500	0	40-45	0	1.58	1.52
1999 San Francisco	NL	72	0	0	64	72.1	320	79	36	32	8	5	1	0	27	3	77	5	0	3	8	.273	0	37-46	0	4.44	3.98
2000 San Francisco	NL	68	0	0	63	66.0	256	37	15	11	4	4	3	2	19	1	92	5	0	4	3	.571	0	41-46	0	1.44	1.50
2001 San Francisco	NL	79	0	0	71	77.2	312	58	28	26	6	0	3	1	22	6	93	2	0	4	5	.444	0	45-52	0	2.12	3.01
2002 San Francisco	NL	68	0	0	66	73.2	301	64	19	18	2	4	0	1	20	8	81	1	0	6	2	.750	0	43-51	0	2.33	2.20
1993 Texas	AL	9	3	0	3	22.2	113	28	17	16	1	0	1	0	26	0	12	2	1	1	1	.500	0	0-0	0	8.60	6.35
1993 Florida	NL	15	1	0	2	33.1	159	35	28	26	5	1	1	0	20	0	27	4	0	1	0	1.000	0	0-0	0	5.28	7.02
10 ML YEARS		**643**	**4**	**0**	**549**	**715.0**	**2983**	**607**	**266**	**237**	**51**	**25**	**17**	**7**	**260**	**41**	**793**	**36**	**3**	**45**	**42**	**.517**	**0**	**314-368**	**1**	**2.87**	**2.98**

Mike Neu

Pitches: R **Bats:** B **Pos:** RP   **Ht:** 5'10" **Wt:** 175 **Born:** 3/9/78 **Age:** 25

Year Team	Lg	G	GS	CG	GF	IP	BFP	H	R	ER	HR	SH	SF	HB	TBB	IBB	SO	WP	Bk	W	L	Pct	ShO	Sv-Op	Hld	ERC	ERA
1999 Rockford	A	9	0	0	2	18.0	84	17	10	9	1	0	1	2	12	1	23	4	0	0	1	.000	0	1- -	-	4.74	4.50
2000 Clinton	A	58	0	0	54	69.0	306	47	27	24	5	4	3	1	52	8	95	10	0	7	7	.500	0	24- -	-	3.27	3.13
2001 Mudville	A+	53	0	0	46	64.2	277	50	21	17	3	4	1	3	30	4	102	5	1	3	2	.600	0	21- -	-	2.75	2.37
2002 Louisville	AAA	40	0	0	34	40.1	172	35	19	18	4	2	1	0	18	0	47	1	0	2	3	.400	0	16- -	-	3.49	4.02
2002 Chattanooga	AA	21	0	0	12	27.0	113	22	4	4	1	1	1	1	9	1	38	3	0	1	0	1.000	0	7- -	-	2.24	1.33

Nick Neugebauer

Pitches: R **Bats:** R **Pos:** SP-12   **Ht:** 6'3" **Wt:** 235 **Born:** 7/15/80 **Age:** 22

Year Team	Lg	G	GS	CG	GF	IP	BFP	H	R	ER	HR	SH	SF	HB	TBB	IBB	SO	WP	Bk	W	L	Pct	ShO	Sv-Op	Hld	ERC	ERA
1999 Beloit	A	18	18	0	0	80.2	372	50	41	35	4	2	3	6	80	0	125	10	2	7	5	.583	0	0- -	-	4.08	3.90
2000 Mudville	A+	18	18	0	0	77.1	349	43	40	36	0	0	2	4	87	0	117	10	1	4	4	.500	0	0- -	-	3.86	4.19
2000 Huntsville	AA	10	10	0	0	50.2	229	35	28	21	2	0	0	3	47	0	57	1	0	1	3	.250	0	0- -	-	4.19	3.73
2001 Huntsville	AA	21	21	1	0	106.2	453	94	46	41	6	5	3	2	52	0	149	13	0	5	6	.455	1	0- -	-	3.57	3.46
2001 Indianapolis	AAA	4	4	0	0	24.0	89	10	5	4	1	1	1	0	9	0	26	1	0	2	1	.667	0	0- -	-	1.21	1.50
2002 Indianapolis	AAA	5	5	0	0	19.1	90	20	13	11	4	1	0	0	12	0	18	1	0	0	3	.000	0	0- -	-	5.87	5.12
2001 Milwaukee	NL	2	2	0	0	6.0	30	6	5	5	1	0	0	0	6	0	11	0	0	1	1	.500	0	0-0	0	6.94	7.50
2002 Milwaukee	NL	12	12	0	0	55.1	260	56	33	29	10	3	1	0	44	3	47	5	2	1	7	.125	0	0-0	0	6.32	4.72
2 ML YEARS		**14**	**14**	**0**	**0**	**61.1**	**290**	**62**	**38**	**34**	**11**	**3**	**1**	**0**	**50**	**3**	**58**	**5**	**2**	**2**	**8**	**.200**	**0**	**0-0**	**0**	**6.38**	**4.99**

Phil Nevin

Bats: R Throws: R Pos: 3B-71; 1B-36   Ht: 6'2" Wt: 231 Born: 1/19/71 Age: 32

Year Team	Lg	G	AB	H	2B	3B	HR	(Hm	Rd)	TB	R	RBI	RC	TBB	IBB	SO	HBP	SH	SF	SB	CS	SB%	GDP	Avg	OBP	Slg
2002 Lk Elsinore*	A+	2	6	2	1	0	1	(-	-)	6	2	6	2	1	0	2	0	0	0	0	0	-	0	.333	.375	1.000
1995 Hou-Det		47	156	28	4	1	2	(2	0)	40	13	13	10	18	1	40	4	1	0	1	0	1.00	5	.179	.281	.256
1996 Detroit	AL	38	120	35	5	0	8	(3	5)	64	15	19	21	8	0	39	1	0	1	1	0	1.00	1	.292	.338	.533
1997 Detroit	AL	93	251	59	16	1	9	(4	5)	104	32	35	31	25	1	68	1	0	1	0	1	.00	5	.235	.306	.414
1998 Anaheim	AL	75	237	54	8	1	8	(3	5)	88	27	27	25	17	0	67	5	0	2	0	0	-	6	.228	.291	.371
1999 San Diego	NL	128	383	103	27	0	24	(12	12)	202	52	85	71	51	1	82	1	1	5	1	0	1.00	7	.269	.352	.527
2000 San Diego	NL	143	538	163	34	1	31	(13	18)	292	87	107	102	59	9	121	4	0	4	2	0	1.00	17	.303	.374	.543
2001 San Diego	NL	149	546	167	31	0	41	(19	22)	321	97	126	116	71	7	147	4	0	3	4	4	.50	13	.306	.388	.588
2002 San Diego	NL	107	407	116	16	0	12	(5	7)	168	53	57	51	38	4	87	1	0	4	4	0	1.00	12	.285	.344	.413
1995 Houston	NL	18	60	7	1	0	0	(0	0)	8	4	1	0	7	1	13	1	1	0	1	0	1.00	2	.117	.221	.133
1995 Detroit	AL	29	96	21	3	1	2	(2	0)	32	9	12	10	11	0	27	3	0	0	0	0	-	3	.219	.318	.333
8 ML YEARS		780	2638	725	141	4	135	(61	74)	1279	376	469	427	287	23	651	21	2	20	13	5	.72	66	.275	.348	.485

Chris Nichting

Pitches: R Bats: R Pos: RP-29   Ht: 6'2" Wt: 220 Born: 5/13/66 Age: 37

Year Team	Lg	G	GS	CG	GF	IP	BFP	H	R	ER	HR	SH	SF	HB	TBB	IBB	SO	WP	Bk	W	L	Pct	ShO	Sv-Op	Hld	ERC	ERA
2002 Co Springs*	AAA	23	0	0	7	32.2	171	53	40	37	7	2	2	1	22	1	23	3	0	1	4	.200	0	1--	-	10.29	10.19
1995 Texas	AL	13	0	0	3	24.1	122	36	19	19	1	1	2	1	13	1	6	3	0	0	0	-	0	0-0	1	7.01	7.03
2000 Cleveland	AL	7	0	0	1	9.0	46	13	7	7	0	0	1	2	5	1	7	1	0	0	0	-	0	0-1	0	7.21	7.00
2001 Cin-Col	NL	43	0	0	11	42.1	189	55	27	21	8	3	2	0	8	1	40	2	0	0	3	.000	0	1-3	4	5.46	4.46
2002 Colorado	NL	29	0	0	5	36.1	151	40	18	18	7	1	1	1	5	0	25	1	0	1	1	.500	0	0-0	1	4.36	4.46
2001 Cincinnati	NL	36	0	0	11	36.1	162	46	24	18	6	2	2	0	8	1	33	2	0	0	3	.000	0	1-3	4	5.22	4.46
2001 Colorado	NL	7	0	0	0	6.0	27	9	3	3	2	1	0	0	0	0	7	0	0	0	0	-	0	0-0	0	6.91	4.50
4 ML YEARS		92	0	0	20	112.0	508	144	71	65	16	5	6	4	31	3	78	7	0	1	4	.200	0	1-4	6	5.61	5.22

Doug Nickle

Pitches: R Bats: R Pos: RP-14   Ht: 6'4" Wt: 230 Born: 10/2/74 Age: 28

Year Team	Lg	G	GS	CG	GF	IP	BFP	H	R	ER	HR	SH	SF	HB	TBB	IBB	SO	WP	Bk	W	L	Pct	ShO	Sv-Op	Hld	ERC	ERA
2002 Scrtn/WlksBr*	AAA	34	1	0	22	60.2	250	58	24	20	4	3	2	4	16	4	37	2	0	3	5	.375	0	7--	-	3.31	2.97
2002 Memphis*	AAA	14	0	0	7	15.2	66	13	8	8	3	0	0	1	7	0	10	1	0	3	1	.750	0	3--	-	4.25	4.60
2000 Philadelphia	NL	4	0	0	3	2.2	15	5	4	4	0	0	0	1	2	0	0	0	0	0	0	-	0	0-0	0	12.52	13.50
2001 Philadelphia	NL	2	0	0	2	2.0	7	1	0	0	0	0	0	0	0	0	1	0	0	0	0	-	0	0-0	0	0.54	0.00
2002 Phi-SD	NL	14	0	0	6	16.0	90	26	16	14	3	0	1	1	13	0	9	0	0	1	0	1.000	0	0-0	0	10.49	7.88
2002 Philadelphia	NL	4	0	0	4	4.1	23	6	3	3	2	0	0	0	4	0	2	0	0	0	0	-	0	0-0	0	11.93	6.23
2002 San Diego	NL	10	0	0	2	11.2	67	20	13	11	1	0	1	1	9	0	7	0	0	1	0	1.000	0	0-0	0	9.93	8.49
3 ML YEARS		20	0	0	11	20.2	112	32	20	18	3	0	1	2	15	0	10	0	0	1	0	1.000	0	0-0	0	9.46	7.84

Jose Nieves

Bats: R Throws: R Pos: 2B-18; SS-13; PH-8; PR-5; 3B-4; 1B-3; CF-1; RF-1   Ht: 6'0" Wt: 180 Born: 6/16/75 Age: 28

Year Team	Lg	G	AB	H	2B	3B	HR	(Hm	Rd)	TB	R	RBI	RC	TBB	IBB	SO	HBP	SH	SF	SB	CS	SB%	GDP	Avg	OBP	Slg
2002 Salt Lake*	AAA	15	63	18	3	1	4	(-	-)	35	12	13	11	4	0	6	0	0	0	2	1	.67	1	.286	.328	.556
1998 Chicago	NL	2	1	0	0	0	0	(0	0)	0	0	0	0	0	0	0	0	0	1	0	0	-	0	.000	.000	.000
1999 Chicago	NL	54	181	45	9	1	2	(2	0)	62	16	18	17	8	0	25	4	3	3	0	2	.00	5	.249	.291	.343
2000 Chicago	NL	82	198	42	6	3	5	(1	4)	69	17	24	14	11	1	43	0	1	2	1	1	.50	8	.212	.251	.348
2001 Anaheim	AL	29	53	13	3	1	2	(2	0)	24	5	3	7	2	0	20	2	2	0	0	1	.00	1	.245	.298	.453
2002 Anaheim	AL	45	97	28	2	0	0	(0	0)	30	17	6	9	2	0	14	0	1	0	1	1	.50	3	.289	.303	.309
5 ML YEARS		212	530	128	20	5	9	(5	4)	185	55	51	47	23	1	102	6	9	5	2	5	.29	17	.242	.278	.349

Wil Nieves

Bats: R Throws: R Pos: C-27; PH-3   Ht: 5'11" Wt: 190 Born: 9/25/77 Age: 25

Year Team	Lg	G	AB	H	2B	3B	HR	(Hm	Rd)	TB	R	RBI	RC	TBB	IBB	SO	HBP	SH	SF	SB	CS	SB%	GDP	Avg	OBP	Slg
1996 Padres	R	43	113	39	5	0	2	(-	-)	50	23	22	20	13	0	19	0	2	0	3	4	.43	1	.345	.413	.442
1997 Clinton	A	18	55	12	1	1	1	(-	-)	18	6	7	6	6	0	10	0	1	1	2	1	.67	0	.218	.290	.327
1997 Padres	R	8	27	8	2	0	0	(-	-)	10	2	2	5	5	0	5	0	1	0	1	0	1.00	0	.296	.406	.370
1998 Clinton	A	115	380	97	22	0	3	(-	-)	128	47	55	42	47	4	69	7	4	6	7	9	.44	16	.255	.343	.337
1999 R Cucamnga	A+	120	427	140	26	2	7	(-	-)	191	58	61	70	40	1	54	5	1	4	2	7	.22	12	.328	.389	.447
2000 Las Vegas	AAA	1	1	0	0	0	0	(-	-)	0	0	0	0	0	0	0	0	0	0	0	0	-	0	.000	.000	.000
2000 Mobile	AA	68	214	57	4	0	4	(-	-)	73	18	30	21	16	4	22	1	2	1	1	1	.50	9	.266	.319	.341
2000 R Cucamnga	A+	31	101	26	5	0	0	(-	-)	31	16	9	12	15	0	17	0	2	1	2	0	1.00	3	.257	.350	.307
2001 Mobile	AA	95	330	99	24	0	3	(-	-)	132	28	41	43	18	2	40	2	2	4	1	0	1.00	8	.300	.336	.400
2002 Portland	AAA	70	237	73	20	2	7	(-	-)	118	24	29	35	5	0	40	0	2	1	0	0	-	7	.308	.321	.498
2002 San Diego	NL	28	72	13	3	1	0	(0	0)	18	7	4	4	4	4	15	0	0	0	1	0	1.00	1	.181	.224	.250

C.J. Nitkowski

Pitches: L Bats: L Pos: RP-12   Ht: 6'3" Wt: 205 Born: 3/9/73 Age: 30

Year Team	Lg	G	GS	CG	GF	IP	BFP	H	R	ER	HR	SH	SF	HB	TBB	IBB	SO	WP	Bk	W	L	Pct	ShO	Sv-Op	Hld	ERC	ERA
2002 New Orleans*	AAA	24	0	0	7	22.2	95	21	7	7	1	2	0	0	7	1	20	1	1	1	2	.333	0	2--	-	2.86	2.78
2002 Memphis*	AAA	16	1	0	7	14.2	82	24	18	16	3	0	0	1	9	0	12	1	0	1	2	.333	0	0--	-	10.91	9.82
2002 Oklahoma*	AAA	9	0	0	3	10.0	43	8	3	2	0	0	0	1	4	0	11	0	0	1	1	.500	0	0--	-	2.63	1.80
1995 Cin-Det		20	18	0	0	71.2	338	94	57	53	11	2	4	5	35	3	31	2	2	2	7	.222	0	0-1	0	7.04	6.66

Year Team	Lg	G	GS	CG	GF	IP	BFP	H	R	ER	HR	SH	SF	HB	TBB	IBB	SO	WP	Bk	W	L	Pct	ShO	Sv-Op	Hld	ERC	ERA
1996 Detroit	AL	11	8	0	0	45.2	234	62	44	41	7	0	2	7	38	1	36	2	0	2	3	.400	0	0-0	0	9.44	8.08
1998 Houston	NL	43	0	0	11	59.2	250	49	27	25	4	4	2	6	23	2	44	3	1	3	3	.500	0	3-5	8	3.19	3.77
1999 Detroit	AL	68	7	0	7	81.2	349	63	44	39	11	1	4	3	45	3	66	4	3	5	4	.444	0	0-0	11	3.73	4.30
2000 Detroit	AL	67	11	0	7	109.2	497	124	79	64	13	3	8	4	49	3	81	3	1	4	9	.308	0	0-2	15	5.23	5.25
2001 Det-NYM		61	0	0	14	51.0	241	54	30	28	7	3	1	5	34	8	42	1	0	1	3	.250	0	0-6	6	5.89	4.94
2002 Texas	AL	12	0	0	2	13.2	63	11	4	4	0	1	0	0	13	0	14	0	0	0	1	.000	0	0-0	1	4.35	2.63
1995 Cincinnati	NL	9	7	0	0	32.1	154	41	25	22	4	2	1	2	15	1	18	1	2	1	3	.250	0	0-1	0	6.20	6.12
1995 Detroit	AL	11	11	0	0	39.1	184	53	32	31	7	0	3	3	20	2	13	1	0	1	4	.200	0	0-0	0	7.76	7.09
2001 Detroit	AL	56	0	0	12	45.1	220	51	30	28	7	3	1	5	31	7	38	1	0	0	3	.000	0	0-6	6	6.53	5.56
2001 New York	NL	5	0	0	2	5.2	21	3	0	0	0	0	0	0	3	1	4	0	0	1	0	1.000	0	0-0	0	1.52	0.00
7 ML YEARS		282	44	0	41	433.0	1972	457	285	254	53	14	21	30	237	20	314	15	7	16	31	.340	0	3-14	41	5.38	5.28

Trot Nixon

Bats: L **Throws:** L **Pos:** RF-145; CF-13; PH-2; PR-1   **Ht:** 6'2" **Wt:** 211 **Born:** 4/11/74 **Age:** 29

Year Team	Lg	G	AB	H	2B	3B	HR	(Hm	Rd)	TB	R	RBI	RC	TBB	IBB	SO	HBP	SH	SF	SB	CS	SB%	GDP	Avg	OBP	Slg
1996 Boston	AL	2	4	2	1	0	0	(0	0)	3	2	0	1	0	0	1	0	0	0	1	0	1.00	0	.500	.500	.750
1998 Boston	AL	13	27	7	1	0	0	(0	0)	8	3	0	2	1	0	3	0	0	0	0	0	-	0	.259	.286	.296
1999 Boston	AL	124	381	103	22	5	15	(3	12)	180	67	52	66	53	1	75	3	2	8	3	1	.75	7	.270	.357	.472
2000 Boston	AL	123	427	118	27	8	12	(4	8)	197	66	60	74	63	2	85	2	5	5	8	1	.89	11	.276	.368	.461
2001 Boston	AL	148	535	150	31	4	27	(14	13)	270	100	88	102	79	1	113	7	6	6	7	4	.64	8	.280	.376	.505
2002 Boston	AL	152	532	136	36	3	24	(8	16)	250	81	94	86	65	2	109	5	3	7	4	2	.67	7	.256	.338	.470
6 ML YEARS		562	1906	516	118	20	78	(29	49)	908	319	294	331	261	6	386	17	16	26	23	8	.74	33	.271	.359	.476

Hideo Nomo

Pitches: R **Bats:** R **Pos:** SP-34   **Ht:** 6'2" **Wt:** 210 **Born:** 8/31/68 **Age:** 34

Year Team	Lg	G	GS	CG	GF	IP	BFP	H	R	ER	HR	SH	SF	HB	TBB	IBB	SO	WP	Bk	W	L	Pct	ShO	Sv-Op	Hld	ERC	ERA
1995 Los Angeles	NL	28	28	4	0	191.1	780	124	63	54	14	11	4	5	78	2	236	19	5	13	6	.684	3	0-0	0	2.16	2.54
1996 Los Angeles	NL	33	33	3	0	228.1	932	180	93	81	23	12	6	2	85	6	234	11	3	16	11	.593	2	0-0	0	2.86	3.19
1997 Los Angeles	NL	33	33	1	0	207.1	904	193	104	98	23	7	1	9	92	2	233	10	4	14	12	.538	0	0-0	0	4.06	4.25
1998 LA-NYM	NL	29	28	3	0	157.1	687	130	88	86	19	8	5	4	94	2	167	13	4	6	12	.333	0	0-0	0	4.10	4.92
1999 Milwaukee	NL	28	28	0	0	176.1	767	173	96	89	27	5	5	3	78	2	161	10	1	12	8	.600	0	0-0	0	4.57	4.54
2000 Detroit	AL	32	31	1	0	190.0	828	191	102	100	31	6	3	3	89	1	181	16	0	8	12	.400	0	0-0	0	4.95	4.74
2001 Boston	AL	33	33	2	0	198.0	849	171	105	99	26	4	7	3	96	2	220	6	0	13	10	.565	2	0-0	0	3.90	4.50
2002 Los Angeles	NL	34	34	0	0	220.1	926	189	92	83	26	17	4	2	101	5	193	6	0	16	6	.727	0	0-0	0	3.68	3.39
1998 Los Angeles	NL	12	12	2	0	67.2	295	57	39	38	8	2	2	3	38	0	73	4	1	2	7	.222	0	0-0	0	4.13	5.05
1998 New York	NL	17	16	1	0	89.2	392	73	49	48	11	6	3	1	56	2	94	9	3	4	5	.444	0	0-0	0	4.07	4.82
8 ML YEARS		250	248	14	0	1569.0	6673	1351	743	690	189	70	35	31	713	22	1625	91	17	98	77	.560	7	0-0	0	3.72	3.96

Takahito Nomura

Pitches: L **Bats:** L **Pos:** RP-21   **Ht:** 5'7" **Wt:** 175 **Born:** 1/10/69 **Age:** 34

Year Team	Lg	G	GS	CG	GF	IP	BFP	H	R	ER	HR	SH	SF	HB	TBB	IBB	SO	WP	Bk	W	L	Pct	ShO	Sv-Op	Hld	ERC	ERA
2002 Indianapolis	AAA	31	0	0	12	33.0	146	38	24	21	4	1	0	2	11	1	23	0	0	1	2	.333	0	0- -	-	5.05	5.73
2002 Milwaukee	NL	21	0	0	2	13.2	71	11	14	13	2	0	2	2	18	4	9	2	1	0	0	-	0	0-1	2	6.95	8.56

Greg Norton

Bats: B **Throws:** R **Pos:** PH-78; 3B-22; 1B-15; LF-2; DH-1   **Ht:** 6'1" **Wt:** 200 **Born:** 7/6/72 **Age:** 30

Year Team	Lg	G	AB	H	2B	3B	HR	(Hm	Rd)	TB	R	RBI	RC	TBB	IBB	SO	HBP	SH	SF	SB	CS	SB%	GDP	Avg	OBP	Slg
2002 Co Springs*	AAA	3	12	1	0	0	0	(-	-)	1	2	0	0	3	0	5	0	0	0	0	0	-	0	.083	.267	.083
1996 Chicago	AL	11	23	5	0	0	2	(0	2)	11	4	3	3	4	0	6	0	0	0	0	1	.00	0	.217	.333	.478
1997 Chicago	AL	18	34	9	2	2	0	(0	0)	15	5	1	5	2	0	8	0	1	0	0	0	-	0	.265	.306	.441
1998 Chicago	AL	105	299	71	17	2	9	(6	3)	119	38	36	33	26	1	77	2	1	2	3	3	.50	11	.237	.301	.398
1999 Chicago	AL	132	436	111	26	0	16	(5	11)	185	62	50	66	69	3	93	1	1	2	4	4	.50	11	.255	.358	.424
2000 Chicago	AL	71	201	49	6	1	6	(2	4)	75	25	28	27	26	0	47	2	0	2	1	0	1.00	2	.244	.333	.373
2001 Colorado	NL	117	225	60	13	2	13	(7	6)	116	30	40	36	19	2	65	0	0	2	1	0	1.00	1	.267	.321	.516
2002 Colorado	NL	113	168	37	8	1	7	(3	4)	68	19	37	22	24	0	52	0	1	2	2	3	.40	4	.220	.314	.405
7 ML YEARS		567	1386	342	72	8	53	(25	28)	589	183	195	192	170	6	348	6	4	10	11	11	.50	34	.247	.330	.425

Abraham Nunez

Bats: B **Throws:** R **Pos:** CF-12; PR-4; PH-3; LF-2; RF-1   **Ht:** 6'2" **Wt:** 186 **Born:** 2/5/77 **Age:** 26

Year Team	Lg	G	AB	H	2B	3B	HR	(Hm	Rd)	TB	R	RBI	RC	TBB	IBB	SO	HBP	SH	SF	SB	CS	SB%	GDP	Avg	OBP	Slg
1997 Diamndbcks	R	54	213	65	17	4	0	(-	-)	90	52	21	35	26	0	40	2	2	1	3	3	.50	4	.305	.384	.423
1997 Lethbridge	R+	2	6	1	0	0	0	(-	-)	1	2	1	0	1	0	0	0	0	0	0	0	-	0	.167	.286	.167
1998 South Bend	A	110	364	93	14	2	9	(-	-)	138	44	47	53	67	4	81	3	3	5	12	14	.46	4	.255	.371	.379
1999 High Desert	A+	130	488	133	29	6	22	(-	-)	240	106	93	95	86	2	122	2	1	8	40	13	.75	10	.273	.378	.492
2000 Portland	AA	74	221	61	17	3	6	(-	-)	102	39	42	41	44	1	64	0	0	3	8	6	.57	3	.276	.392	.462
2000 Brevard Cnty	A+	31	103	20	4	0	1	(-	-)	27	17	9	13	28	1	34	2	0	0	11	3	.79	3	.194	.376	.262
2001 Portland	AA	136	467	112	14	9	17	(-	-)	195	75	53	72	83	3	155	3	5	2	26	19	.58	4	.240	.357	.418
2002 Calgary	AAA	129	428	107	24	5	21	(-	-)	204	68	60	72	51	3	112	1	0	4	31	6	.84	4	.250	.329	.477
2002 Florida	NL	19	17	2	0	0	0	(0	0)	2	2	1	0	0	0	5	0	0	0	0	1	.00	1	.118	.118	.118

Abraham O Nunez

Bats: B **Throws:** R **Pos:** PH-54; 2B-45; SS-21; DH-1; PR-1   **Ht:** 5'11" **Wt:** 185 **Born:** 3/16/76 **Age:** 27

Year Team	Lg	G	AB	H	2B	3B	HR	(Hm	Rd)	TB	R	RBI	RC	TBB	IBB	SO	HBP	SH	SF	SB	CS	SB%	GDP	Avg	OBP	Slg
2002 Nashville*	AAA	5	18	4	0	0	0	(-	-)	4	3	0	2	2	0	7	0	0	0	4	1	.80	0	.222	.300	.222
1997 Pittsburgh	NL	19	40	9	2	2	0	(0	0)	15	3	6	4	3	0	10	1	0	1	1	0	1.00	1	.225	.289	.375
1998 Pittsburgh	NL	24	52	10	2	0	1	(0	1)	15	6	2	6	12	0	14	0	3	0	4	2	.67	1	.192	.344	.288
1999 Pittsburgh	NL	90	259	57	8	0	0	(0	0)	65	25	17	22	28	0	54	1	13	0	9	1	.90	2	.220	.299	.251
2000 Pittsburgh	NL	40	91	20	1	0	1	(0	1)	24	10	8	6	8	1	14	0	0	0	0	0	-	3	.220	.283	.264
2001 Pittsburgh	NL	115	301	79	11	4	1	(0	1)	101	30	21	36	28	1	53	1	4	1	8	2	.80	0	.262	.326	.336
2002 Pittsburgh	NL	112	253	59	14	1	2	(2	0)	81	28	15	25	27	1	44	2	3	1	3	4	.43	2	.233	.311	.320
6 ML YEARS		400	996	234	38	7	5	(2	3)	301	102	69	99	106	3	189	5	23	3	25	9	.74	9	.235	.311	.302

Jose Nunez

Pitches: L **Bats:** L **Pos:** RP-1   **Ht:** 6'2" **Wt:** 173 **Born:** 3/14/79 **Age:** 24

Year Team	Lg	G	GS	CG	GF	IP	BFP	H	R	ER	HR	SH	SF	HB	TBB	IBB	SO	WP	Bk	W	L	Pct	ShO	Sv-Op	Hld	ERC	ERA
1998 Mets	R	13	11	1	0	68.0	267	60	26	18	6	1	3	2	12	0	69	0	1	3	7	.300	0	0- -	-	2.72	2.38
1999 Kingsport	R+	13	13	0	0	69.2	296	75	36	29	6	0	2	4	15	0	63	4	0	3	4	.429	0	0- -	-	3.91	3.75
2000 Capital City	A	34	5	0	16	95.1	396	82	36	32	6	2	7	10	23	0	112	4	2	3	4	.429	0	8- -	-	2.86	3.02
2001 LA-SD	NL	62	0	0	10	59.0	265	62	35	30	7	2	2	4	25	3	60	5	0	4	2	.667	0	0-2	11	4.73	4.58
2002 San Diego	NL	1	0	0	1	1.0	4	0	0	0	0	0	0	0	1	0	0	0	0	0	0	-	0	0-0	0	0.95	0.00
2001 Los Angeles	NL	6	0	0	2	7.1	42	14	15	11	4	1	0	0	5	0	11	0	0	0	1	.000	0	0-1	0	15.10	13.50
2001 San Diego	NL	56	0	0	8	51.2	223	48	20	19	3	1	2	4	20	3	49	5	0	4	1	.800	0	0-1	11	3.53	3.31
2 ML YEARS		63	0	0	11	60.0	269	62	35	30	7	2	2	4	26	3	60	5	0	4	2	.667	0	0-2	11	4.65	4.50

Vladimir Nunez

Pitches: R **Bats:** R **Pos:** RP-77   **Ht:** 6'4" **Wt:** 240 **Born:** 3/15/75 **Age:** 28

Year Team	Lg	G	GS	CG	GF	IP	BFP	H	R	ER	HR	SH	SF	HB	TBB	IBB	SO	WP	Bk	W	L	Pct	ShO	Sv-Op	Hld	ERC	ERA
1998 Arizona	NL	4	0	0	2	5.1	25	7	6	6	0	0	0	0	2	0	2	0	1	0	0	-	0	0-0	0	4.87	10.13
1999 Ari-Fla	NL	44	12	0	12	108.2	463	95	63	49	11	7	6	4	54	6	86	8	1	7	10	.412	0	1-3	4	3.88	4.06
2000 Florida	NL	17	12	0	3	68.1	322	88	63	60	12	5	5	2	34	2	45	5	0	0	6	.000	0	0-0	1	6.88	7.90
2001 Florida	NL	52	3	0	13	92.0	380	79	33	28	9	2	5	5	30	5	64	1	1	4	5	.444	0	0-1	4	3.17	2.74
2002 Florida	NL	77	0	0	43	97.2	404	80	38	37	8	6	4	0	37	1	73	2	0	6	5	.545	0	20-28	11	2.88	3.41
1999 Arizona	NL	27	0	0	11	34.0	146	29	15	11	2	2	3	1	20	5	28	3	0	3	2	.600	0	1-2	3	3.63	2.91
1999 Florida	NL	17	12	0	1	74.2	317	66	48	38	9	5	3	3	34	1	58	5	1	4	8	.333	0	0-1	1	3.98	4.58
5 ML YEARS		194	27	0	73	372.0	1594	349	203	180	40	20	21	11	157	14	270	16	3	17	26	.395	0	21-32	20	3.94	4.35

Wes Obermueller

Pitches: R **Bats:** R **Pos:** SP-2   **Ht:** 6'2" **Wt:** 195 **Born:** 12/22/76 **Age:** 26

Year Team	Lg	G	GS	CG	GF	IP	BFP	H	R	ER	HR	SH	SF	HB	TBB	IBB	SO	WP	Bk	W	L	Pct	ShO	Sv-Op	Hld	ERC	ERA
1999 Royals	R	11	7	0	2	38.1	159	33	16	11	2	0	1	1	12	1	39	2	1	2	1	.667	0	0- -	-	2.73	2.58
2000 Chrlstn - WV	A	8	7	0	0	31.2	117	19	6	4	0	0	0	3	5	0	29	1	0	3	0	1.000	0	0- -	-	1.26	1.14
2001 Wilmington	A+	20	6	0	1	38.0	163	38	15	13	3	2	1	1	16	1	28	2	0	0	2	.000	0	0- -	-	4.13	3.08
2002 Wilmington	A+	8	4	0	1	45.2	182	38	14	14	1	1	0	1	14	0	44	4	0	5	0	1.000	0	0- -	-	2.41	2.76
2002 Wichita	AA	17	17	0	0	105.2	443	98	39	34	6	3	3	4	40	3	65	6	2	9	5	.643	0	0- -	-	3.46	2.90
2002 Kansas City	AL	2	2	0	0	7.2	39	14	10	10	3	0	0	0	2	0	5	0	0	0	2	.000	0	0-0	0	11.04	11.74

Alex Ochoa

Bats: R **Throws:** R **Pos:** RF-91; PH-26; LF-25; PR-5; CF-2   **Ht:** 6'0" **Wt:** 200 **Born:** 3/29/72 **Age:** 31

Year Team	Lg	G	AB	H	2B	3B	HR	(Hm	Rd)	TB	R	RBI	RC	TBB	IBB	SO	HBP	SH	SF	SB	CS	SB%	GDP	Avg	OBP	Slg
1995 New York	NL	11	37	11	1	0	0	(0	0)	12	7	0	4	2	0	10	0	0	0	1	0	1.00	1	.297	.333	.324
1996 New York	NL	82	282	83	19	3	4	(1	3)	120	37	33	40	17	0	30	2	0	3	4	3	.57	2	.294	.336	.426
1997 New York	NL	113	238	58	14	1	3	(1	2)	83	31	22	23	18	0	32	2	2	2	3	4	.43	7	.244	.300	.349
1998 Minnesota	AL	94	249	64	14	2	2	(1	1)	88	35	25	23	10	0	35	1	0	0	6	3	.67	7	.257	.288	.353
1999 Milwaukee	NL	119	277	83	16	3	8	(8	0)	129	47	40	53	45	2	43	5	0	2	6	4	.60	4	.300	.404	.466
2000 Cincinnati	NL	118	244	77	21	3	13	(9	4)	143	50	58	51	24	3	27	3	0	4	8	4	.67	7	.316	.378	.586
2001 Cin-Col	NL	148	536	148	30	7	8	(5	3)	216	73	52	71	45	0	76	4	4	4	17	13	.57	10	.276	.334	.403
2002 Mil-Ana		122	280	73	16	0	8	(4	4)	113	40	31	37	42	2	35	2	1	0	10	7	.59	7	.261	.361	.404
2001 Cincinnati	NL	90	349	101	20	4	7	(5	2)	150	48	35	50	24	0	53	2	2	3	12	9	.57	3	.289	.337	.430
2001 Colorado	NL	58	187	47	10	3	1	(0	1)	66	25	17	21	21	0	23	2	2	1	5	4	.56	7	.251	.330	.353
2002 Milwaukee	NL	85	215	55	9	0	6	(3	3)	82	32	21	26	32	2	30	2	1	0	8	5	.62	7	.256	.357	.381
2002 Anaheim	AL	37	65	18	7	0	2	(1	1)	31	8	10	11	10	0	5	0	0	0	2	2	.50	0	.277	.373	.477
8 ML YEARS		807	2143	597	131	19	46	(29	17)	904	320	261	302	203	7	288	19	7	15	55	38	.59	45	.279	.344	.422

Jose Offerman

Bats: B **Throws:** R **Pos:** 1B-51; DH-26; PH-17; PR-8; LF-4; RF-3; 2B-1   **Ht:** 6'0" **Wt:** 192 **Born:** 11/11/68 **Age:** 34

Year Team	Lg	G	AB	H	2B	3B	HR	(Hm	Rd)	TB	R	RBI	RC	TBB	IBB	SO	HBP	SH	SF	SB	CS	SB%	GDP	Avg	OBP	Slg
1990 Los Angeles	NL	29	58	9	0	0	1	(1	0)	12	7	7	2	4	1	14	0	1	0	1	0	1.00	1	.155	.210	.207
1991 Los Angeles	NL	52	113	22	2	0	0	(0	0)	24	10	3	9	25	2	32	1	1	0	3	2	.60	5	.195	.345	.212
1992 Los Angeles	NL	149	534	139	20	8	1	(1	0)	178	67	30	60	57	4	98	0	5	2	23	16	.59	5	.260	.331	.333
1993 Los Angeles	NL	158	590	159	21	6	1	(1	0)	195	77	62	72	71	7	75	2	25	1	30	13	.70	12	.269	.346	.331
1994 Los Angeles	NL	72	243	51	8	4	1	(0	1)	70	27	25	23	38	4	38	0	6	2	2	1	.67	6	.210	.314	.288
1995 Los Angeles	NL	119	429	123	14	6	4	(2	2)	161	69	33	66	69	0	67	3	10	0	2	7	.22	5	.287	.389	.375
1996 Kansas City	AL	151	561	170	33	8	5	(1	4)	234	85	47	93	74	3	98	1	7	2	24	10	.71	9	.303	.384	.417

Year Team	Lg	G	AB	H	2B	3B	HR	(Hm	Rd)	TB	R	RBI	RC	TBB	IBB	SO	HBP	SH	SF	SB	CS	SB%	GDP	Avg	OBP	Slg
1997 Kansas City	AL	106	424	126	23	6	2	(2	0)	167	59	39	59	41	3	64	0	6	1	9	10	.47	5	.297	.359	.394
1998 Kansas City	AL	158	607	191	28	13	7	(4	3)	266	102	66	116	89	1	96	5	2	6	45	12	.79	7	.315	.403	.438
1999 Boston	AL	149	586	172	37	11	8	(5	3)	255	107	69	102	96	5	79	2	2	7	18	12	.60	11	.294	.391	.435
2000 Boston	AL	116	451	115	14	3	9	(3	6)	162	73	41	58	70	0	70	1	2	3	0	8	.00	9	.255	.354	.359
2001 Boston	AL	128	524	140	23	3	9	(4	5)	196	76	49	69	61	2	97	1	3	5	5	2	.71	9	.267	.342	.374
2002 Bos-Sea	AL	101	284	66	12	1	5	(2	3)	95	48	31	33	37	0	38	1	1	3	9	6	.60	12	.232	.320	.335
2002 Boston	AL	72	237	55	10	0	4	(1	3)	77	39	27	30	33	0	29	1	1	3	8	5	.62	9	.232	.325	.325
2002 Seattle	AL	29	47	11	2	1	1	(1	0)	18	9	4	3	4	0	9	0	0	0	1	1	.50	3	.234	.294	.383
13 ML YEARS		1488	5404	1483	235	69	53	(26	27)	2015	807	502	762	732	32	866	17	71	38	171	99	.63	95	.274	.361	.373

Tomo Ohka

Pitches: R Bats: R Pos: SP-31; RP-1　　Ht: 6'1" Wt: 180 Born: 3/18/76 Age: 27

Year Team	Lg	G	GS	CG	GF	IP	BFP	H	R	ER	HR	SH	SF	HB	TBB	IBB	SO	WP	Bk	W	L	Pct	ShO	Sv-Op	Hld	ERC	ERA
1999 Boston	AL	8	2	0	3	13.0	65	21	12	9	2	0	0	0	8	0	8	0	0	1	2	.333	0	0-0	0	8.56	6.23
2000 Boston	AL	13	12	0	1	69.1	297	70	25	24	7	1	2	2	26	0	40	3	0	3	6	.333	0	0-0	0	4.19	3.12
2001 Bos-Mon		22	21	0	1	107.0	469	134	70	65	15	2	2	3	29	0	68	2	1	3	9	.250	0	0-0	0	5.52	5.47
2002 Montreal	NL	32	31	2	1	192.2	806	194	83	68	19	13	6	7	45	7	118	2	1	13	8	.619	0	0-0	0	3.55	3.18
2001 Boston	AL	12	11	0	1	52.1	241	69	40	36	7	1	1	2	19	0	37	1	1	2	5	.286	0	0-0	0	6.24	6.19
2001 Montreal	NL	10	10	0	0	54.2	228	65	30	29	8	1	1	1	10	0	31	1	0	1	4	.200	0	0-0	0	4.83	4.77
4 ML YEARS		75	66	2	6	382.0	1637	419	190	166	43	16	11	12	106	7	234	7	2	20	25	.444	0	0-0	0	4.35	3.91

Augie Ojeda

Bats: B Throws: R Pos: SS-16; 2B-10; 3B-5; PH-2　　Ht: 5'8" Wt: 170 Born: 12/20/74 Age: 28

Year Team	Lg	G	AB	H	2B	3B	HR	(Hm	Rd)	TB	R	RBI	RC	TBB	IBB	SO	HBP	SH	SF	SB	CS	SB%	GDP	Avg	OBP	Slg
2002 Iowa*	AAA	73	291	67	20	4	1	(-	-)	98	54	27	34	31	0	30	9	0	5	5	3	.63	2	.230	.318	.337
2000 Chicago	NL	28	77	17	3	1	2	(1	1)	28	10	8	9	10	1	9	0	1	1	0	1	.00	1	.221	.307	.364
2001 Chicago	NL	78	144	29	5	1	1	(1	0)	39	16	12	10	12	1	20	2	2	2	1	0	1.00	2	.201	.269	.271
2002 Chicago	NL	30	70	13	4	0	0	(0	0)	17	4	4	4	5	0	5	1	4	1	1	0	1.00	2	.186	.247	.243
3 ML YEARS		136	291	59	12	2	3	(2	1)	84	30	24	23	27	2	34	3	7	4	2	1	.67	5	.203	.274	.289

Troy O'Leary

Bats: L Throws: L Pos: LF-69; PH-25; DH-3; RF-1　　Ht: 6'0" Wt: 208 Born: 8/4/69 Age: 33

Year Team	Lg	G	AB	H	2B	3B	HR	(Hm	Rd)	TB	R	RBI	RC	TBB	IBB	SO	HBP	SH	SF	SB	CS	SB%	GDP	Avg	OBP	Slg
2002 Ottawa*	AAA	23	86	29	6	0	3	(-	-)	44	11	16	16	7	2	15	0	0	0	0	1	.00	1	.337	.387	.512
1993 Milwaukee	NL	19	41	12	3	0	0	(0	0)	15	3	3	6	5	0	9	0	3	0	0	0	-	1	.293	.370	.366
1994 Milwaukee	NL	27	66	18	1	1	2	(0	2)	27	9	7	9	5	0	12	1	0	1	1	1	.50	0	.273	.329	.409
1995 Boston	AL	112	399	123	31	6	10	(5	5)	196	60	49	66	29	4	64	1	3	2	5	3	.63	8	.308	.355	.491
1996 Boston	AL	149	497	129	28	5	15	(10	5)	212	68	81	67	47	3	80	4	1	3	3	2	.60	13	.260	.327	.427
1997 Boston	AL	146	499	154	32	4	15	(5	10)	239	65	80	79	39	7	70	2	1	4	0	5	.00	13	.309	.358	.479
1998 Boston	AL	156	611	165	36	8	23	(12	11)	286	95	83	85	36	2	108	4	5	5	2	2	.50	17	.270	.314	.468
1999 Boston	AL	157	596	167	36	4	28	(13	15)	295	84	103	95	56	5	91	4	0	5	1	2	.33	21	.280	.343	.495
2000 Boston	AL	138	513	134	30	4	13	(7	6)	211	68	70	65	44	2	76	2	0	4	0	2	.00	12	.261	.320	.411
2001 Boston	AL	104	341	82	16	6	13	(9	4)	149	50	50	42	25	2	73	5	0	5	1	3	.25	9	.240	.298	.437
2002 Montreal	NL	97	273	78	12	2	3	(1	2)	103	27	37	40	34	5	47	3	4	0	1	2	.33	6	.286	.371	.377
10 ML YEARS		1105	3836	1062	225	40	122	(62	60)	1733	529	563	554	320	30	630	27	12	29	14	22	.39	100	.277	.335	.452

John Olerud

Bats: L Throws: L Pos: 1B-152; DH-2; PH-1　　Ht: 6'5" Wt: 220 Born: 8/5/68 Age: 34

Year Team	Lg	G	AB	H	2B	3B	HR	(Hm	Rd)	TB	R	RBI	RC	TBB	IBB	SO	HBP	SH	SF	SB	CS	SB%	GDP	Avg	OBP	Slg
1989 Toronto	AL	6	8	3	0	0	0	(0	0)	3	2	0	1	0	0	1	0	0	0	0	0	-	0	.375	.375	.375
1990 Toronto	AL	111	358	95	15	1	14	(11	3)	154	43	48	57	57	6	75	1	1	4	0	2	.00	5	.265	.364	.430
1991 Toronto	AL	139	454	116	30	1	17	(7	10)	199	64	68	71	68	9	84	6	3	10	0	2	.00	13	.256	.353	.438
1992 Toronto	AL	138	458	130	28	0	16	(4	12)	206	68	66	76	70	11	61	1	1	7	0	1	1.00	15	.284	.375	.450
1993 Toronto	AL	158	551	200	54	2	24	(9	15)	330	109	107	146	114	33	65	7	0	7	0	2	.00	12	.363	.473	.599
1994 Toronto	AL	108	384	114	29	2	12	(6	6)	183	47	67	70	61	12	53	3	0	5	1	2	.33	11	.297	.393	.477
1995 Toronto	AL	135	492	143	32	0	8	(1	7)	199	72	54	80	84	10	54	4	0	1	0	0	-	17	.291	.398	.404
1996 Toronto	AL	125	398	109	25	0	18	(9	9)	188	59	61	72	60	6	37	10	0	1	1	0	1.00	10	.274	.382	.472
1997 New York	NL	154	524	154	34	1	22	(13	9)	256	90	102	101	85	5	67	13	0	8	0	0	-	19	.294	.400	.489
1998 New York	NL	160	557	197	36	4	22	(13	9)	307	91	93	131	96	11	73	4	1	7	2	5	.29	15	.354	.447	.551
1999 New York	NL	162	581	173	39	0	19	(11	8)	269	107	96	118	125	5	66	11	0	6	3	0	1.00	22	.298	.427	.463
2000 Seattle	AL	159	565	161	45	0	14	(8	6)	248	84	103	98	102	11	96	4	2	10	0	2	.00	17	.285	.392	.439
2001 Seattle	AL	159	572	173	32	1	21	(15	6)	270	91	95	106	94	19	70	5	1	7	3	1	.75	21	.302	.401	.472
2002 Seattle	AL	154	553	166	39	0	22	(9	13)	271	85	102	108	98	6	66	5	0	12	0	0	-	19	.300	.403	.490
14 ML YEARS		1868	6455	1934	438	12	229	(116	113)	3083	1012	1062	1235	1114	144	868	74	9	85	11	13	.46	195	.300	.404	.478

Darren Oliver

Pitches: L Bats: R Pos: SP-9; RP-5　　Ht: 6'2" Wt: 220 Born: 10/6/70 Age: 32

Year Team	Lg	G	GS	CG	GF	IP	BFP	H	R	ER	HR	SH	SF	HB	TBB	IBB	SO	WP	Bk	W	L	Pct	ShO	Sv-Op	Hld	ERC	ERA
2002 Memphis*	AAA	5	5	0	0	16.0	78	17	16	14	1	3	1	0	17	0	9	2	0	0	2	.000	0	0- -	-	7.03	7.88
1993 Texas	AL	2	0	0	0	3.1	14	2	1	1	1	0	0	0	4	0	0	0	0	0	0	-	0	0-0	0	2.15	2.70
1994 Texas	AL	43	0	0	10	50.0	226	40	24	19	4	6	0	6	35	4	50	2	2	4	0	1.000	0	2-3	9	4.29	3.42
1995 Texas	AL	17	7	0	2	49.0	222	47	25	23	3	5	1	1	32	1	39	4	0	4	2	.667	0	0-0	0	4.59	4.22
1996 Texas	AL	30	30	1	0	173.2	777	190	97	90	20	2	7	10	76	3	112	5	1	14	6	.700	0	0-0	0	5.10	4.66

			HOW MUCH HE PITCHED					WHAT HE GAVE UP											THE RESULTS							
Year Team	Lg	G	GS	CG	GF	IP	BFP	H	R	ER	HR	SH	SF	HB	TBB	IBB	SO	WP	Bk	W	L	Pct	ShO	Sv-Op	Hld	ERC	ERA
1997 Texas	AL	32	32	3	0	201.1	887	213	111	94	29	2	5	11	82	3	104	7	0	13	12	.520	1	0-0	0	4.98	4.20
1998 Tex-Stl	NL	29	29	2	0	160.1	749	204	115	102	18	8	8	10	66	2	87	7	4	10	11	.476	0	0-0	0	6.01	5.73
1999 St Louis	NL	30	30	2	0	196.1	842	197	96	93	16	11	4	11	74	4	119	6	2	9	9	.500	1	0-0	0	4.11	4.26
2000 Texas	AL	21	21	0	0	108.0	501	151	95	89	16	5	4	4	42	3	49	4	1	2	9	.182	0	0-0	0	7.04	7.42
2001 Texas	AL	28	28	1	0	154.0	696	189	109	103	23	1	5	6	65	0	104	8	2	11	11	.500	0	0-0	0	6.14	6.02
2002 Boston	AL	14	9	1	0	58.0	258	70	30	30	7	1	3	6	27	0	32	1	0	4	5	.444	1	0-0	0	6.49	4.66
1998 Texas	AL	19	19	2	0	103.1	493	140	84	75	11	3	6	10	43	1	58	6	1	6	7	.462	0	0-0	0	6.68	6.53
1998 St Louis	NL	10	10	0	0	57.0	256	64	31	27	7	5	2	0	23	1	29	1	3	4	4	.500	0	0-0	0	4.85	4.26
10 ML YEARS		246	186	10	12	1154.0	5172	1303	703	644	137	41	37	65	500	21	700	44	12	71	65	.522	4	2-3	9	5.34	5.02

Miguel Olivo

Bats: R **Throws:** R **Pos:** C-6   **Ht:** 6'0" **Wt:** 180 **Born:** 7/15/78 **Age:** 24

								BATTING													BASERUNNING				AVERAGES		
Year Team	Lg	G	AB	H	2B	3B	HR	(Hm	Rd)	TB	R	RBI	RC	TBB	IBB	SO	HBP	SH	SF	SB	CS	SB%	GDP	Avg	OBP	Slg
1998 Athletics	R	46	164	51	11	3	2	(-	-)	74	30	23	24	8	0	43	4	0	1	2	2	.50	5	.311	.356	.451
1999 Modesto	A+	73	243	74	13	6	9	(-	-)	126	46	42	42	21	1	60	2	1	1	4	5	.44	6	.305	.363	.519
2000 Modesto	A+	58	227	64	11	5	5	(-	-)	100	40	35	31	16	0	53	2	0	2	5	2	.71	8	.282	.332	.441
2000 Midland	AA	19	59	14	2	0	1	(-	-)	19	8	9	5	5	0	15	0	1	0	0	0	-	3	.237	.297	.322
2001 Birmingham	AA	93	316	82	23	1	14	(-	-)	149	45	55	53	37	4	62	7	5	3	6	3	.67	4	.259	.347	.472
2002 Birmingham	AA	106	359	110	24	10	6	(-	-)	172	51	49	63	40	5	66	5	4	3	29	13	.69	11	.306	.381	.479
2002 Chicago	AL	6	19	4	1	0	1	(0	1)	8	2	5	4	2	0	5	0	0	0	0	0	-	1	.211	.286	.421

Kevin Olsen

Pitches: R **Bats:** R **Pos:** RP-9; SP-8   **Ht:** 6'2" **Wt:** 196 **Born:** 7/26/76 **Age:** 26

				HOW MUCH HE PITCHED					WHAT HE GAVE UP											THE RESULTS							
Year Team	Lg	G	GS	CG	GF	IP	BFP	H	R	ER	HR	SH	SF	HB	TBB	IBB	SO	WP	Bk	W	L	Pct	ShO	Sv-Op	Hld	ERC	ERA
1998 Utica	A-	21	4	0	8	45.0	181	37	21	13	3	1	0	1	10	1	56	1	1	4	3	.571	0	2- -	-	2.32	2.60
1999 Brevard Cnty	A+	11	11	0	0	57.0	253	70	37	32	8	1	1	1	13	0	45	3	0	2	5	.286	0	0- -	-	4.97	5.05
1999 Kane County	A	10	9	0	0	61.1	257	65	25	23	3	0	3	2	16	0	52	2	0	5	2	.714	0	0- -	-	3.71	3.38
2000 Brevard Cnty	A+	18	18	1	0	110.0	436	93	40	35	2	2	4	6	25	2	77	4	0	4	8	.333	0	0- -	-	2.35	2.86
2000 Portland	AA	9	9	0	0	54.0	234	54	30	29	8	1	0	2	21	0	47	3	0	3	4	.429	0	0- -	-	4.53	4.83
2001 Portland	AA	26	26	2	0	154.2	611	123	56	46	11	2	3	10	21	1	144	0	0	10	3	.769	1	0- -	-	2.10	2.68
2002 Calgary	AAA	8	8	1	0	49.0	201	45	22	21	6	1	1	1	14	0	25	0	0	2	5	.286	1	0- -	-	3.46	3.86
2001 Florida	NL	4	2	0	0	15.0	56	11	2	2	0	0	0	0	2	1	13	0	0	0	0	-	0	0-0	0	1.34	1.20
2002 Florida	NL	17	8	0	3	55.2	250	57	31	28	5	5	2	1	31	1	38	3	1	0	5	.000	0	0-0	1	4.81	4.53
2 ML YEARS		21	10	0	3	70.2	306	68	33	30	5	5	2	1	33	2	51	3	1	0	5	.000	0	0-0	1	3.94	3.82

Luis Ordaz

Bats: R **Throws:** R **Pos:** 2B-28; 3B-6; SS-2; PH-1   **Ht:** 5'11" **Wt:** 170 **Born:** 8/12/75 **Age:** 27

								BATTING													BASERUNNING				AVERAGES		
Year Team	Lg	G	AB	H	2B	3B	HR	(Hm	Rd)	TB	R	RBI	RC	TBB	IBB	SO	HBP	SH	SF	SB	CS	SB%	GDP	Avg	OBP	Slg
2002 Iowa*	AAA	61	194	53	10	0	1	(-	-)	66	22	14	21	9	1	21	1	4	0	5	2	.71	2	.273	.309	.340
2002 Omaha*	AAA	35	136	42	11	4	2	(-	-)	67	25	19	22	9	0	16	1	2	2	4	1	.80	6	.309	.351	.493
1997 St Louis	NL	12	22	6	1	0	0	(0	0)	7	3	1	3	1	0	2	0	0	0	3	0	1.00	0	.273	.304	.318
1998 St Louis	NL	57	153	31	5	0	0	(0	0)	36	9	8	9	12	1	18	0	4	0	2	0	1.00	3	.203	.261	.235
1999 St Louis	NL	10	9	1	0	0	0	(0	0)	1	3	2	0	1	0	2	0	1	0	1	0	1.00	0	.111	.200	.111
2000 Kansas City	AL	65	104	23	2	0	0	(0	0)	25	17	11	5	5	0	10	1	4	3	4	2	.67	6	.221	.257	.240
2001 Kansas City	AL	28	56	14	3	0	0	(0	0)	17	8	4	5	3	0	8	1	2	1	0	0	-	1	.250	.295	.304
2002 Kansas City	AL	33	94	21	2	0	0	(0	0)	23	11	4	6	12	0	13	0	4	1	2	3	.40	2	.223	.308	.245
6 ML YEARS		205	438	96	13	0	0	(0	0)	109	51	30	28	34	1	53	2	15	5	12	5	.71	12	.219	.276	.249

Magglio Ordonez

Bats: R **Throws:** R **Pos:** RF-150; PH-3; DH-1   **Ht:** 6'0" **Wt:** 210 **Born:** 1/28/74 **Age:** 29

								BATTING													BASERUNNING				AVERAGES		
Year Team	Lg	G	AB	H	2B	3B	HR	(Hm	Rd)	TB	R	RBI	RC	TBB	IBB	SO	HBP	SH	SF	SB	CS	SB%	GDP	Avg	OBP	Slg
1997 Chicago	AL	21	69	22	6	0	4	(2	2)	40	12	11	12	2	0	8	0	1	0	1	2	.33	1	.319	.338	.580
1998 Chicago	AL	145	535	151	25	2	14	(8	6)	222	70	65	67	28	1	53	9	2	4	9	7	.56	19	.282	.326	.415
1999 Chicago	AL	157	624	188	34	3	30	(16	14)	318	100	117	102	47	4	64	1	0	5	13	6	.68	24	.301	.349	.510
2000 Chicago	AL	153	588	185	34	3	32	(21	11)	321	102	126	102	60	3	64	2	0	15	18	4	.82	28	.315	.371	.546
2001 Chicago	AL	160	593	181	40	1	31	(17	14)	316	97	113	117	70	7	70	5	0	3	25	7	.78	14	.305	.382	.533
2002 Chicago	AL	153	590	189	47	1	38	(24	14)	352	116	135	122	53	2	77	7	0	3	7	5	.58	21	.320	.381	.597
6 ML YEARS		789	2999	916	186	10	149	(88	61)	1569	497	567	532	260	17	336	24	3	30	73	31	.70	107	.305	.362	.523

Rey Ordonez

Bats: R **Throws:** R **Pos:** SS-142; PH-3; PR-1   **Ht:** 5'9" **Wt:** 159 **Born:** 1/11/71 **Age:** 32

								BATTING													BASERUNNING				AVERAGES		
Year Team	Lg	G	AB	H	2B	3B	HR	(Hm	Rd)	TB	R	RBI	RC	TBB	IBB	SO	HBP	SH	SF	SB	CS	SB%	GDP	Avg	OBP	Slg
1996 New York	NL	151	502	129	12	4	1	(0	1)	152	51	30	39	22	12	53	1	4	1	1	3	.25	12	.257	.289	.303
1997 New York	NL	120	356	77	5	3	1	(1	0)	91	35	33	19	18	3	36	1	14	2	11	5	.69	10	.216	.255	.256
1998 New York	NL	153	505	134	20	2	1	(0	1)	151	46	42	37	23	7	60	1	15	4	3	6	.33	11	.265	.278	.299
1999 New York	NL	154	520	134	24	2	1	(1	0)	165	49	60	41	49	12	59	1	11	7	8	4	.67	16	.258	.319	.317
2000 New York	NL	45	133	25	5	0	0	(0	0)	30	10	9	8	17	2	16	0	4	1	0	0	-	4	.188	.278	.226
2001 New York	NL	149	461	114	24	4	3	(0	3)	155	31	44	41	34	17	43	1	7	2	3	2	.60	17	.247	.299	.336
2002 New York	NL	144	460	117	25	2	1	(0	1)	149	53	42	36	24	11	46	2	9	4	2	2	.50	19	.254	.292	.324
7 ML YEARS		916	2937	720	115	17	8	(2	6)	893	275	260	231	187	64	313	7	64	21	28	22	.56	89	.245	.290	.304

Kevin Orie

Bats: R **Throws:** R **Pos:** 3B-12; PH-1   **Ht:** 6'4" **Wt:** 215 **Born:** 9/1/72 **Age:** 30

								BATTING												BASERUNNING				AVERAGES		
Year Team		Lg	G	AB	H	2B	3B	HR	(Hm | Rd)	TB	R	RBI	RC	TBB	IBB	SO	HBP	SH	SF	SB	CS	SB%	GDP	Avg	OBP	Slg
2002 Iowa*		AAA	86	294	88	16	3	20	(- | -)	170	51	63	56	25	1	40	2	0	0	0	1	.00	10	.299	.358	.578
1997 Chicago		NL	114	364	100	23	5	8	(6 | 2)	157	40	44	53	39	3	57	5	3	4	2	2	.50	13	.275	.350	.431
1998 ChC-Fla		NL	112	379	83	22	1	8	(2 | 6)	131	47	38	37	32	2	59	8	2	4	2	1	.67	8	.219	.291	.346
1999 Florida		NL	77	240	61	16	0	6	(1 | 5)	95	26	29	30	22	1	43	3	0	2	1	0	1.00	8	.254	.322	.396
2002 Chicago		NL	13	32	9	3	0	0	(0 | 0)	12	4	5	5	1	0	4	1	0	2	0	0	-	1	.281	.306	.375
1998 Chicago		NL	64	204	37	14	0	2	(1 | 1)	57	24	21	13	18	0	35	3	1	4	1	1	.50	4	.181	.253	.279
1998 Florida		NL	48	175	46	8	1	6	(1 | 5)	74	23	17	24	14	2	24	5	1	0	1	0	1.00	4	.263	.335	.423
4 ML YEARS			316	1015	253	64	6	22	(9 | 13)	395	117	116	125	94	6	163	17	5	12	5	3	.63	30	.249	.320	.389

Eddie Oropesa

Pitches: L **Bats:** L **Pos:** RP-32   **Ht:** 6'3" **Wt:** 215 **Born:** 11/23/71 **Age:** 31

			HOW MUCH HE PITCHED						WHAT HE GAVE UP											THE RESULTS						
Year Team		Lg	G	GS	CG	GF	IP	BFP	H	R	ER	HR	SH	SF	HB	TBB	IBB	SO	WP	Bk	W	L	Pct	ShO	Sv-Op	Hld	ERC	ERA
1993 St.Paul		IND	4	3	0	0	18.2	0	6	4	4	0	0	0	0	9	0	19	0	0	3	1	.750	0	0- -	-	-	1.93
1994 Vero Beach		A+	19	10	1	3	72.0	285	54	24	17	2	3	2	4	25	2	67	2	0	4	3	.571	1	0- -	-	2.36	2.13
1995 San Antonio		AA	16	0	0	7	17.1	87	22	8	6	2	1	2	3	12	1	16	0	1	1	1	.500	0	1- -	-	7.68	3.12
1995 Vero Beach		A+	19	1	0	7	28.1	120	25	12	12	0	1	2	3	10	0	23	4	2	3	1	.750	0	1- -	-	2.98	3.81
1995 Sn Brnardino		A+	1	0	0	1	1.0	3	0	0	0	0	0	0	0	0	0	0	0	0	0	0	-	0	1- -	-	0.00	0.00
1996 Sn Brnardino		A+	33	19	0	2	156.1	669	133	74	58	8	1	3	6	77	1	133	8	4	11	6	.647	0	1- -	-	3.42	3.34
1997 Shreveport		AA	43	9	1	12	124.0	531	122	58	54	7	7	4	4	64	0	65	6	6	7	7	.500	0	0- -	-	4.41	3.92
1998 Shreveport		AA	32	20	2	3	143.0	623	143	71	60	6	7	5	7	67	36	104	15	2	7	11	.389	0	0- -	-	3.73	3.78
1999 Bakersfield		A+	2	1	0	0	10.0	41	13	5	4	2	0	0	0	1	0	10	2	0	2	0	1.000	0	0- -	-	5.58	3.60
1999 Fresno		AAA	21	18	1	0	102.0	460	113	69	55	15	3	1	3	49	0	61	13	4	6	5	.545	0	0- -	-	5.52	4.85
2000 Shreveport		AA	59	2	0	23	76.1	341	70	38	26	6	3	1	3	40	6	76	3	2	2	4	.333	0	4- -	-	3.88	3.07
2001 Scrtn/WlksBr		AAA	14	1	0	3	15.1	61	14	5	4	1	0	0	0	4	1	11	1	0	1	1	.500	0	0- -	-	2.86	2.35
2001 Clearwater		A+	2	0	0	1	2.0	10	2	0	0	0	0	0	1	1	0	3	0	0	0	0	-	0	0- -	-	5.48	0.00
2002 Tucson		AAA	29	0	0	4	25.2	111	23	11	11	2	2	0	1	13	2	26	1	0	1	0	1.000	0	0- -	-	3.80	3.86
2001 Philadelphia		NL	30	0	0	4	19.0	87	16	10	10	1	1	0	0	17	6	15	1	0	1	0	1.000	0	0-1	6	4.20	4.74
2002 Arizona		NL	32	0	0	5	25.1	132	39	30	29	6	2	1	2	15	0	18	1	1	2	0	1.000	0	0-1	7	9.65	10.30
2 ML YEARS			62	0	0	9	44.1	219	55	40	39	7	3	1	2	32	6	33	2	1	3	0	1.000	0	0-2	13	7.21	7.92

Jesse Orosco

Pitches: L **Bats:** R **Pos:** RP-56   **Ht:** 6'2" **Wt:** 205 **Born:** 4/21/57 **Age:** 46

			HOW MUCH HE PITCHED						WHAT HE GAVE UP											THE RESULTS						
Year Team		Lg	G	GS	CG	GF	IP	BFP	H	R	ER	HR	SH	SF	HB	TBB	IBB	SO	WP	Bk	W	L	Pct	ShO	Sv-Op	Hld	ERC	ERA
1979 New York		NL	18	2	0	6	35.0	154	33	20	19	4	3	0	2	22	0	22	0	0	1	2	.333	0	0-0	0	5.16	4.89
1981 New York		NL	8	0	0	4	17.1	69	13	4	3	2	2	0	0	6	2	18	0	1	1	0	1.000	0	1-1	0	2.53	1.56
1982 New York		NL	54	2	0	22	109.1	451	92	37	33	7	5	4	2	40	2	89	3	2	4	10	.286	0	4-5	5	2.92	2.72
1983 New York		NL	62	0	0	42	110.0	432	76	27	18	3	4	3	1	38	7	84	1	2	13	7	.650	0	17-22	1	1.84	1.47
1984 New York		NL	60	0	0	52	87.0	355	58	29	25	7	3	3	2	34	6	85	1	1	10	6	.625	0	31-39	0	2.14	2.59
1985 New York		NL	54	0	0	39	79.0	331	66	26	24	6	1	1	0	34	7	68	4	0	8	6	.571	0	17-25	1	3.00	2.73
1986 New York		NL	58	0	0	40	81.0	338	64	23	21	6	2	3	0	35	3	62	2	0	8	6	.571	0	21-29	1	2.99	2.33
1987 New York		NL	58	0	0	41	77.0	335	78	41	38	5	5	4	2	31	9	78	2	0	3	9	.250	0	16-22	4	3.81	4.44
1988 Los Angeles		NL	55	0	0	21	53.0	229	41	18	16	4	3	3	2	30	3	43	1	0	3	2	.600	0	9-15	11	3.33	2.72
1989 Cleveland		AL	69	0	0	29	78.0	312	54	20	18	7	8	3	2	26	4	79	0	0	3	4	.429	0	3-7	11	2.20	2.08
1990 Cleveland		AL	55	0	0	28	64.2	289	58	35	28	9	5	3	0	38	7	55	1	0	5	4	.556	0	2-3	2	4.25	3.90
1991 Cleveland		AL	47	0	0	20	45.2	202	52	20	19	4	1	3	1	15	6	36	1	1	2	0	1.000	0	0-0	3	4.24	3.74
1992 Milwaukee		NL	59	0	0	14	39.0	158	33	15	14	5	0	2	1	13	1	40	2	0	3	1	.750	0	1-2	11	3.31	3.23
1993 Milwaukee		NL	57	0	0	27	56.2	233	47	25	20	2	1	2	3	17	3	67	3	1	3	5	.375	0	8-13	11	2.50	3.18
1994 Milwaukee		NL	40	0	0	5	39.0	174	32	26	22	4	0	2	2	26	2	36	0	0	3	1	.750	0	0-4	8	4.22	5.08
1995 Baltimore		AL	65	0	0	23	49.2	200	28	19	18	4	2	4	1	27	7	58	2	1	2	4	.333	0	3-6	15	2.12	3.26
1996 Baltimore		AL	66	0	0	10	55.2	236	42	22	21	5	2	1	2	28	4	52	2	0	3	1	.750	0	0-3	19	3.07	3.40
1997 Baltimore		AL	71	0	0	12	50.1	205	29	13	13	6	1	2	0	30	0	46	1	1	6	3	.667	0	0-4	21	2.73	2.32
1998 Baltimore		AL	69	0	0	26	56.2	243	46	20	20	6	4	2	1	28	1	50	3	1	4	1	.800	0	7-9	9	3.45	3.18
1999 Baltimore		AL	65	0	0	12	32.0	144	28	21	19	5	2	3	2	20	3	35	2	0	0	2	.000	0	1-4	12	4.73	5.34
2000 St Louis		NL	6	0	0	0	2.1	16	3	3	1	1	0	0	2	3	2	4	0	0	0	0	-	0	0-0	3	13.85	3.86
2001 Los Angeles		NL	35	0	0	7	16.0	69	17	7	7	3	0	1	0	7	1	21	0	0	1	0	1.000	0	0-2	10	5.25	3.94
2002 Los Angeles		NL	56	0	0	8	27.0	119	24	10	9	4	1	1	0	12	1	22	2	0	1	2	.333	0	1-1	17	3.75	3.00
23 ML YEARS			1187	4	0	488	1261.1	5294	1014	481	426	109	55	50	31	560	83	1150	33	11	85	78	.521	0	142-216	175	3.08	3.04

David Ortiz

Bats: L **Throws:** L **Pos:** DH-94; PH-17; 1B-15   **Ht:** 6'4" **Wt:** 230 **Born:** 11/18/75 **Age:** 27

								BATTING												BASERUNNING				AVERAGES		
Year Team		Lg	G	AB	H	2B	3B	HR	(Hm	Rd)	TB	R	RBI	RC	TBB	IBB	SO	HBP	SH	SF	SB	CS	SB%	GDP	Avg	OBP	Slg
1997 Minnesota		AL	15	49	16	3	0	1	(0	1)	22	10	6	7	2	0	19	0	0	0	0	0	-	1	.327	.353	.449
1998 Minnesota		AL	86	278	77	20	0	9	(2	7)	124	47	46	46	39	3	72	5	0	4	1	0	1.00	8	.277	.371	.446
1999 Minnesota		AL	10	20	0	0	0	0	(0	0)	0	1	0	0	5	0	12	0	0	0	0	0	-	2	.000	.200	.000
2000 Minnesota		AL	130	415	117	36	1	10	(7	3)	185	59	63	66	57	2	81	0	0	6	1	0	1.00	13	.282	.364	.446
2001 Minnesota		AL	89	303	71	17	1	18	(6	12)	144	46	48	46	40	8	68	1	1	2	1	0	1.00	6	.234	.324	.475
2002 Minnesota		AL	125	412	112	32	1	20	(5	15)	206	52	75	63	43	0	87	3	0	8	1	2	.33	5	.272	.339	.500
6 ML YEARS			455	1477	393	108	3	58	(20	38)	681	215	238	228	186	13	339	9	1	20	4	2	.67	35	.266	.348	.461

Hector Ortiz

Bats: R **Throws:** R **Pos:** C-7; PH-1 **Ht:** 6'0" **Wt:** 205 **Born:** 10/14/69 **Age:** 33

Year Team	Lg	G	AB	H	2B	3B	HR	(Hm	Rd)	TB	R	RBI	RC	TBB	IBB	SO	HBP	SH	SF	SB	CS	SB%	GDP	Avg	OBP	Slg
2002 Omaha*	AAA	35	99	25	5	0	1	(-	-)	33	10	5	12	11	0	15	2	6	0	1	0	1.00	2	.253	.339	.333
2002 Oklahoma*	AAA	25	82	17	2	0	0	(-	-)	19	3	7	5	11	0	16	0	1	1	0	1	.00	3	.207	.298	.232
1998 Kansas City	AL	4	4	0	0	0	0	(0	0)	0	1	0	0	0	0	0	0	0	0	0	0	-	0	.000	.000	.000
2000 Kansas City	AL	26	88	34	6	0	0	(0	0)	40	15	5	18	8	1	8	1	2	0	0	0	-	0	.386	.443	.455
2001 Kansas City	AL	56	154	38	6	1	0	(0	0)	46	12	11	11	9	0	24	1	2	0	1	3	.25	4	.247	.293	.299
2002 Texas	AL	7	14	3	1	0	1	(1	0)	7	1	2	1	0	1	0	0	0	0	0	0	-	1	.214	.267	.500
4 ML YEARS		93	260	75	13	1	1	(1	0)	93	29	18	30	18	1	33	2	4	0	1	3	.25	6	.288	.339	.358

Jose Ortiz

Bats: R **Throws:** R **Pos:** 2B-54; PH-11; 3B-1 **Ht:** 5'10" **Wt:** 182 **Born:** 6/13/77 **Age:** 26

Year Team	Lg	G	AB	H	2B	3B	HR	(Hm	Rd)	TB	R	RBI	RC	TBB	IBB	SO	HBP	SH	SF	SB	CS	SB%	GDP	Avg	OBP	Slg
2002 Co Springs*	AAA	26	111	37	9	2	6	(-	-)	68	23	18	22	4	0	13	0	0	1	1	1	.50	3	.333	.353	.613
2000 Oakland	AL	11	11	2	0	0	0	(0	0)	2	4	1	1	2	0	3	0	0	0	0	0	-	0	.182	.308	.182
2001 Oak-Col		64	246	59	8	1	13	(9	4)	108	42	38	31	17	0	41	4	1	2	4	1	.80	9	.240	.297	.439
2002 Colorado	NL	65	192	48	7	1	1	(1	0)	60	22	12	18	16	0	30	3	2	2	2	0	1.00	3	.250	.315	.313
2001 Oakland	AL	11	42	7	0	0	0	(0	0)	7	4	3	0	3	0	5	0	0	1	1	0	1.00	4	.167	.217	.167
2001 Colorado	NL	53	204	52	8	1	13	(9	4)	101	38	35	31	14	0	36	4	1	1	3	1	.75	5	.255	.314	.495
3 ML YEARS		136	449	109	15	2	14	(10	4)	170	68	51	50	35	0	74	7	3	4	6	1	.86	12	.243	.305	.379

Ramon Ortiz

Pitches: R **Bats:** R **Pos:** SP-32 **Ht:** 6'0" **Wt:** 170 **Born:** 3/23/73 **Age:** 30

Year Team	Lg	G	GS	CG	GF	IP	BFP	H	R	ER	HR	SH	SF	HB	TBB	IBB	SO	WP	Bk	W	L	Pct	ShO	Sv-Op	Hld	ERC	ERA
1999 Anaheim	AL	9	9	0	0	48.1	218	50	35	35	7	0	2	2	25	0	44	2	2	2	3	.400	0	0-0	0	5.23	6.52
2000 Anaheim	AL	18	18	2	0	111.1	472	96	69	63	18	4	4	4	55	0	73	7	4	8	6	.571	0	0-0	0	4.24	5.09
2001 Anaheim	AL	32	32	2	0	208.2	916	223	114	101	25	9	6	12	76	6	135	7	0	13	11	.542	0	0-0	0	4.65	4.36
2002 Anaheim	AL	32	32	4	0	217.1	896	188	97	91	40	2	5	5	68	0	162	7	3	15	9	.625	1	0-0	0	3.64	3.77
4 ML YEARS		91	91	8	0	585.2	2502	557	315	290	90	15	17	21	224	6	414	23	9	38	29	.567	1	0-0	0	4.25	4.46

Russ Ortiz

Pitches: R **Bats:** R **Pos:** SP-33 **Ht:** 6'1" **Wt:** 208 **Born:** 6/5/74 **Age:** 29

Year Team	Lg	G	GS	CG	GF	IP	BFP	H	R	ER	HR	SH	SF	HB	TBB	IBB	SO	WP	Bk	W	L	Pct	ShO	Sv-Op	Hld	ERC	ERA
1998 San Francisco	NL	22	13	0	3	88.1	394	90	51	49	11	5	4	4	46	1	75	3	0	4	4	.500	0	0-0	1	5.05	4.99
1999 San Francisco	NL	33	33	3	0	207.2	922	189	109	88	24	11	6	6	125	5	164	13	0	18	9	.667	0	0-0	0	4.56	3.81
2000 San Francisco	NL	33	32	0	0	195.2	871	192	117	109	28	10	6	7	112	1	167	8	0	14	12	.538	0	0-0	0	5.17	5.01
2001 San Francisco	NL	33	33	1	0	218.2	911	187	90	80	13	10	4	0	91	3	169	8	1	17	9	.654	1	0-0	0	3.08	3.29
2002 San Francisco	NL	33	33	2	0	214.1	911	191	89	86	15	15	6	4	94	5	137	5	0	14	10	.583	0	0-0	0	3.46	3.61
5 ML YEARS		154	144	6	3	924.2	4009	849	456	412	91	51	26	21	468	15	712	37	1	67	44	.604	1	0-0	1	4.10	4.01

Donovan Osborne

Pitches: L **Bats:** L **Pos:** RP-11 **Ht:** 6'2" **Wt:** 210 **Born:** 6/21/69 **Age:** 34

Year Team	Lg	G	GS	CG	GF	IP	BFP	H	R	ER	HR	SH	SF	HB	TBB	IBB	SO	WP	Bk	W	L	Pct	ShO	Sv-Op	Hld	ERC	ERA
1992 St Louis	NL	34	29	0	2	179.0	754	193	91	75	14	7	4	2	38	2	104	6	0	11	9	.550	0	0-0	1	3.65	3.77
1993 St Louis	NL	26	26	1	0	155.2	657	153	73	65	18	6	2	7	47	4	83	4	0	10	7	.588	0	0-0	0	3.86	3.76
1995 St Louis	NL	19	19	0	0	113.1	477	112	58	48	17	8	3	2	34	2	82	0	0	4	6	.400	0	0-0	0	4.01	3.81
1996 St Louis	NL	30	30	2	0	198.2	822	191	87	78	22	7	4	1	57	5	134	6	1	13	9	.591	0	0-0	0	3.51	3.53
1997 St Louis	NL	14	14	0	0	80.1	337	84	46	44	10	3	3	1	23	2	51	0	0	3	7	.300	0	0-0	0	4.13	4.93
1998 St Louis	NL	14	14	1	0	83.2	358	84	42	38	11	3	4	1	22	2	60	1	0	5	4	.556	1	0-0	0	3.70	4.09
1999 St Louis	NL	6	6	0	0	29.1	130	34	18	18	4	3	1	2	10	0	21	1	0	1	3	.250	0	0-0	0	5.35	5.52
2002 Chicago	NL	11	0	0	1	16.0	77	19	11	11	1	2	1	0	10	2	13	0	0	0	1	.000	0	0-0	0	5.40	6.19
8 ML YEARS		154	138	4	3	856.0	3612	870	426	377	97	39	22	16	241	19	548	19	1	47	46	.505	2	0-0	1	3.84	3.96

Keith Osik

Bats: R **Throws:** R **Pos:** C-27; PH-19; 3B-4; 1B-3; 2B-1; LF-1 **Ht:** 6'0" **Wt:** 200 **Born:** 10/22/68 **Age:** 34

Year Team	Lg	G	AB	H	2B	3B	HR	(Hm	Rd)	TB	R	RBI	RC	TBB	IBB	SO	HBP	SH	SF	SB	CS	SB%	GDP	Avg	OBP	Slg
1996 Pittsburgh	NL	48	140	41	14	1	1	(0	1)	60	18	14	21	14	1	22	1	1	0	1	0	1.00	3	.293	.361	.429
1997 Pittsburgh	NL	49	105	27	9	1	0	(0	0)	38	10	7	12	9	1	21	1	2	0	0	1	.00	1	.257	.322	.362
1998 Pittsburgh	NL	39	98	21	4	0	0	(0	0)	25	8	7	7	13	2	16	2	2	1	1	2	.33	4	.214	.316	.255
1999 Pittsburgh	NL	66	167	31	3	1	2	(1	1)	42	12	13	7	11	0	30	1	1	0	0	0	-	8	.186	.239	.251
2000 Pittsburgh	NL	46	123	36	6	1	4	(1	3)	56	11	22	23	14	0	11	5	1	0	3	0	1.00	2	.293	.387	.455
2001 Pittsburgh	NL	56	120	25	4	0	2	(0	2)	35	9	13	11	13	0	24	3	0	1	1	0	1.00	1	.208	.299	.292
2002 Pittsburgh	NL	55	100	16	3	0	2	(1	1)	25	6	11	4	6	0	25	1	2	2	0	0	-	2	.160	.211	.250
7 ML YEARS		359	853	197	43	4	11	(3	8)	281	74	87	85	80	4	149	14	9	5	6	3	.67	21	.231	.306	.329

Jimmy Osting

Pitches: L **Bats:** R **Pos:** SP-3 **Ht:** 6'5" **Wt:** 190 **Born:** 4/7/77 **Age:** 26

Year Team	Lg	G	GS	CG	GF	IP	BFP	H	R	ER	HR	SH	SF	HB	TBB	IBB	SO	WP	Bk	W	L	Pct	ShO	Sv-Op	Hld	ERC	ERA
1995 Danville	R+	11	10	0	0	39.0	190	46	34	31	1	0	1	0	25	0	43	12	0	2	7	.222	0	0- -		5.29	7.15
1996 Eugene	A-	5	5	0	0	24.1	99	14	11	7	1	0	0	0	13	0	35	1	0	2	1	.667	0	0- -		2.00	2.59
1997 Macon	A	15	15	0	0	57.2	251	54	28	21	3	1	0	2	29	0	62	5	0	2	3	.400	0	0- -		3.93	3.28
1999 Macon	A	27	22	0	5	147.0	581	130	52	47	13	2	1	5	30	0	131	2	0	14	4	.778	0	2- -		2.86	2.88
2000 Myrtle Beach	A+	4	4	0	0	23.0	94	25	8	8	0	0	1	0	5	0	17	0	0	2	2	.500	0	0- -		3.28	3.13
2000 Greenville	AA	11	11	0	0	71.1	302	67	30	21	6	2	1	0	29	1	52	1	0	2	6	.250	0	0- -		3.66	2.65
2000 Richmond	AAA	3	3	0	0	9.1	52	15	12	12	2	1	1	0	11	1	2	1	0	0	2	.000	0	0- -		12.57	11.57
2000 Reading	AA	10	9	1	0	56.2	245	53	17	15	1	6	2	4	26	2	31	2	0	4	2	.667	1	0- -		3.60	2.38
2001 Carolina	AA	1	1	0	0	5.0	22	3	1	1	1	0	0	0	3	0	3	0	0	1	0	1.000	0	0- -		3.11	1.80
2001 Mobile	AA	18	18	0	0	97.2	414	85	41	39	6	4	3	5	42	1	69	7	0	9	4	.692	0	0- -		3.42	3.59
2001 Portland	AAA	5	5	0	0	25.1	124	41	27	27	5	0	0	1	10	0	15	0	0	1	4	.200	0	0- -		9.00	9.59
2002 Indianapolis	AAA	22	22	3	0	126.2	529	115	52	49	7	6	5	6	38	1	112	2	1	5	7	.417	1	0- -		3.06	3.48
2001 San Diego	NL	3	0	0	1	2.0	9	1	0	0	0	0	0	0	2	1	3	0	0				0		0	1.96	0.00
2002 Milwaukee	NL	3	3	0	0	12.0	64	18	11	10	3	1	0	0	10	0	7	0	0	0	2	.000	0	0-0	0	10.28	7.50
2 ML YEARS		6	3	0	1	14.0	73	19	11	10	3	1	0	0	12	1	10	0	0	0	2	.000	0	0-0	0	8.92	6.43

Antonio Osuna

Pitches: R **Bats:** R **Pos:** RP-59 **Ht:** 5'11" **Wt:** 205 **Born:** 4/12/73 **Age:** 30

Year Team	Lg	G	GS	CG	GF	IP	BFP	H	R	ER	HR	SH	SF	HB	TBB	IBB	SO	WP	Bk	W	L	Pct	ShO	Sv-Op	Hld	ERC	ERA
1995 Los Angeles	NL	39	0	0	8	44.2	186	39	22	22	5	2	1	1	20	2	46	1	0	2	4	.333	0	0-2	11	3.76	4.43
1996 Los Angeles	NL	73	0	0	21	84.0	342	65	33	28	6	7	5	2	32	12	85	3	2	9	6	.600	0	4-9	16	2.53	3.00
1997 Los Angeles	NL	48	0	0	18	61.2	245	46	15	15	6	4	1	1	19	2	68	2	0	3	4	.429	0	0-0	10	2.43	2.19
1998 Los Angeles	NL	54	0	0	25	64.2	272	50	26	22	8	2	2	2	32	0	72	1	0	7	1	.875	0	6-11	12	3.50	3.06
1999 Los Angeles	NL	5	0	0	1	4.2	22	4	5	4	0	0	0	1	3	0	5	1	0	0	0	-	0	0-0	2	4.14	7.71
2000 Los Angeles	NL	46	0	0	16	67.1	293	57	30	28	7	4	3	2	35	2	70	1	2	3	6	.333	0	0-3	4	3.74	3.74
2001 Chicago	AL	4	0	0	4	4.1	23	8	10	10	3	0	1	1	2	1	6	0	0	0	0	-	0	0-1	0	16.71	20.77
2002 Chicago	AL	59	0	0	28	67.2	296	64	32	29	1	5	3	4	28	4	66	0	1	8	2	.800	0	11-16	9	3.31	3.86
8 ML YEARS		328	0	0	117	399.0	1679	333	173	158	36	24	16	14	171	23	418	9	5	32	23	.582	0	21-42	64	3.27	3.56

Roy Oswalt

Pitches: R **Bats:** R **Pos:** SP-34; RP-1 **Ht:** 6'0" **Wt:** 175 **Born:** 8/29/77 **Age:** 25

Year Team	Lg	G	GS	CG	GF	IP	BFP	H	R	ER	HR	SH	SF	HB	TBB	IBB	SO	WP	Bk	W	L	Pct	ShO	Sv-Op	Hld	ERC	ERA
1997 Astros	R	5	5	0	0	28.1	117	25	7	2	2	0	0	0	7	0	28	0	0	1	1	.500	0	0- -		2.63	0.64
1997 Auburn	A-	9	9	1	0	51.2	220	50	29	26	1	0	1	6	15	1	44	3	1	2	4	.333	1	0- -		3.35	4.53
1998 Astros	R	4	4	0	0	16.0	62	10	6	4	2	1	1	3	1	0	27	0	1	1	1	.500	0	0- -		1.76	2.25
1998 Auburn	A-	11	11	0	0	70.1	289	49	24	17	3	1	2	3	31	0	67	2	1	4	5	.444	0	0- -		2.42	2.18
1999 Michigan	A	22	22	2	0	151.1	643	144	78	75	8	2	5	7	54	0	143	8	4	13	4	.765	0	0- -		3.51	4.46
2000 Kissimmee	A+	8	8	0	0	45.1	191	52	15	15	1	1	1	1	11	0	47	0	1	4	3	.571	0	0- -		3.91	2.98
2000 Round Rock	AA	19	18	2	0	129.2	521	106	37	28	5	4	2	3	22	1	141	4	1	11	4	.733	2	0- -		1.95	1.94
2001 New Orleans	AAA	5	5	0	0	31.0	128	32	16	15	4	0	0	2	6	0	34	0	1	2	3	.400	0	0- -		3.98	4.35
2001 Houston	NL	28	20	3	4	141.2	575	126	48	43	13	4	4	6	24	2	144	0	0	14	3	.824	1	0-0	0	2.68	2.73
2002 Houston	NL	35	34	0	0	233.0	956	215	86	78	17	12	7	5	62	4	208	3	0	19	9	.679	0	0-0	0	3.05	3.01
2 ML YEARS		63	54	3	4	374.2	1531	341	134	121	30	16	11	11	86	6	352	3	0	33	12	.733	1	0-0	0	2.91	2.91

Lyle Overbay

Bats: L **Throws:** L **Pos:** PH-10 **Ht:** 6'2" **Wt:** 215 **Born:** 1/28/77 **Age:** 26

Year Team	Lg	G	AB	H	2B	3B	HR	(Hm	Rd)	TB	R	RBI	RC	TBB	IBB	SO	HBP	SH	SF	SB	CS	SB%	GDP	Avg	OBP	Slg
1999 Missoula	R+	75	306	105	25	7	12	(-	-)	180	66	101	69	40	2	53	2	0	4	10	3	.77	14	.343	.418	.588
2000 South Bend	A	71	259	86	19	3	6	(-	-)	129	47	47	52	27	0	36	2	0	2	9	2	.82	2	.332	.397	.498
2000 El Paso	AA	62	244	86	16	2	8	(-	-)	130	43	49	51	28	0	39	2	0	2	3	2	.60	6	.352	.420	.533
2001 El Paso	AA	138	532	187	49	3	13	(-	-)	281	82	100	115	67	11	92	5	0	8	5	4	.56	6	.352	.423	.528
2002 Tucson	AAA	134	525	180	40	0	19	(-	-)	277	83	109	103	42	3	86	7	0	5	0	0	-	12	.343	.396	.528
2001 Arizona	NL	2	2	1	0	0	0	(0	0)	1	0	0	0	0	0	1	0	0	0	0	0	-	0	.500	.500	.500
2002 Arizona	NL	10	10	1	0	0	0	(0	0)	1	0	1	0	0	0	5	0	0	0	0	0	-	0	.100	.100	.100
2 ML YEARS		12	12	2	0	0	0	(0	0)	2	0	1	0	0	0	6	0	0	0	0	0	-	0	.167	.167	.167

Eric Owens

Bats: R **Throws:** R **Pos:** LF-75; RF-39; CF-22; PH-17; PR-1 **Ht:** 6'0" **Wt:** 208 **Born:** 2/3/71 **Age:** 32

Year Team	Lg	G	AB	H	2B	3B	HR	(Hm	Rd)	TB	R	RBI	RC	TBB	IBB	SO	HBP	SH	SF	SB	CS	SB%	GDP	Avg	OBP	Slg
1995 Cincinnati	NL	2	2	2	0	0	0	(0	0)	2	0	1	1	0	0	0	0	1	0	0	0	-	0	1.000	1.000	1.000
1996 Cincinnati	NL	88	205	41	6	0	0	(0	0)	47	26	9	16	23	1	38	1	1	2	16	2	.89	2	.200	.281	.229
1997 Cincinnati	NL	27	57	15	0	0	0	(0	0)	15	8	3	4	4	0	11	0	0	0	3	2	.60	2	.263	.311	.263
1998 Milwaukee	NL	34	40	5	2	0	1	(0	1)	10	5	4	0	2	0	6	0	1	0	0	0	-	3	.125	.167	.250
1999 San Diego	NL	149	440	117	22	3	9	(2	7)	172	55	61	58	38	2	50	3	2	5	33	7	.83	12	.266	.327	.391
2000 San Diego	NL	145	583	171	19	7	6	(4	2)	222	87	51	75	45	4	63	4	0	4	29	14	.67	16	.293	.346	.381
2001 Florida	NL	119	400	101	16	1	5	(4	1)	134	51	28	37	29	2	59	0	4	1	8	6	.57	13	.253	.302	.335
2002 Florida	NL	131	385	104	15	5	4	(2	2)	141	44	37	42	31	1	33	0	8	1	26	9	.74	11	.270	.324	.366
8 ML YEARS		695	2112	556	80	16	25	(12	13)	743	276	194	233	172	10	260	8	17	10	115	40	.74	59	.263	.320	.352

Pablo Ozuna

Bats: R Throws: R Pos: PH-18; 2B-10; PR-8; CF-1   Ht: 6'0" Wt: 160 Born: 8/25/74 Age: 28

Year Team	Lg	G	AB	H	2B	3B	HR	(Hm	Rd)	TB	R	RBI	RC	TBB	IBB	SO	HBP	SH	SF	SB	CS	SB%	GDP	Avg	OBP	Slg
1997 Johnson City	R+	56	232	75	13	1	5	(-	-)	105	40	24	39	10	0	24	1	6	2	23	5	.82	2	.323	.351	.453
1998 Peoria	A	133	538	192	27	10	9	(-	-)	266	122	62	104	29	3	56	11	12	2	62	26	.70	6	.357	.400	.494
1999 Portland	AA	117	502	141	25	7	7	(-	-)	201	62	46	62	13	0	50	13	7	3	31	15	.67	8	.281	.315	.400
2000 Portland	AA	118	464	143	25	6	7	(-	-)	201	74	59	69	40	40	55	7	5	5	35	24	.59	9	.308	.368	.433
2002 Calgary	AAA	77	261	85	16	1	7	(-	-)	124	37	33	47	17	0	37	3	7	2	16	3	.84	5	.326	.371	.475
2000 Florida	NL	14	24	8	1	0	0	(0	0)	9	2	0	3	0	0	2	0	2	0	1	0	1.00	0	.333	.333	.375
2002 Florida	NL	34	47	13	2	2	0	(0	0)	19	4	3	4	1	0	3	1	0	1	1	1	.50	2	.277	.300	.404
2 ML YEARS		48	71	21	3	2	0	(0	0)	28	6	3	7	1	0	5	1	2	1	2	1	.67	2	.296	.311	.394

Vicente Padilla

Pitches: R Bats: B Pos: SP-32   Ht: 6'2" Wt: 200 Born: 9/27/77 Age: 25

Year Team	Lg	G	GS	CG	GF	IP	BFP	H	R	ER	HR	SH	SF	HB	TBB	IBB	SO	WP	Bk	W	L	Pct	ShO	Sv-Op	Hld	ERC	ERA
1999 Arizona	NL	5	0	0	2	2.2	19	7	5	5	1	1	0	0	3	0	0	0	0	0	1	.000	0	0-1	1	20.65	16.88
2000 Ari-Phi	NL	55	0	0	16	65.1	291	72	33	27	3	5	3	1	28	7	51	1	0	4	7	.364	0	2-7	15	4.22	3.72
2001 Philadelphia	NL	23	0	0	5	34.0	144	36	18	16	1	0	0	0	12	0	29	1	0	3	1	.750	0	0-3	1	3.80	4.24
2002 Philadelphia	NL	32	32	1	0	206.0	861	198	83	75	16	10	3	15	53	5	128	6	2	14	11	.560	1	0-0	0	3.43	3.28
2000 Arizona	NL	27	0	0	12	35.0	143	32	10	9	0	0	1	0	10	2	30	0	0	2	1	.667	0	0-1	7	2.48	2.31
2000 Philadelphia	NL	28	0	0	4	30.1	148	40	23	18	3	5	2	1	18	5	21	1	0	2	6	.250	0	2-6	8	6.52	5.34
4 ML YEARS		115	32	1	23	308.0	1315	313	139	123	21	16	6	16	96	12	208	8	2	21	20	.512	1	2-11	17	3.76	3.59

Lance Painter

Pitches: L Bats: L Pos: RP   Ht: 6'1" Wt: 200 Born: 7/21/67 Age: 35

Year Team	Lg	G	GS	CG	GF	IP	BFP	H	R	ER	HR	SH	SF	HB	TBB	IBB	SO	WP	Bk	W	L	Pct	ShO	Sv-Op	Hld	ERC	ERA
1993 Colorado	NL	10	6	1	2	39.0	166	52	26	26	5	1	0	0	9	0	16	2	0	2	2	.500	0	0-0	0	5.83	6.00
1994 Colorado	NL	15	14	0	1	73.2	336	91	51	50	9	3	5	1	26	2	41	3	1	4	6	.400	0	0-0	0	5.35	6.11
1995 Colorado	NL	33	1	0	7	45.1	198	55	23	22	9	0	0	2	10	0	36	4	1	3	0	1.000	0	1-1	4	5.50	4.37
1996 Colorado	NL	34	1	0	4	50.2	234	56	37	33	12	3	3	3	25	3	48	1	0	4	2	.667	0	0-1	4	6.19	5.86
1997 St Louis	NL	14	0	0	4	17.0	69	13	9	9	1	0	0	0	8	2	11	0	0	1	1	.500	0	0-0	3	2.71	4.76
1998 St Louis	NL	65	0	0	9	47.1	207	42	24	21	5	4	2	4	28	3	39	2	0	4	0	1.000	0	1-2	21	4.56	3.99
1999 St Louis	NL	56	4	0	10	63.1	272	63	37	34	6	4	3	2	25	1	56	4	0	4	5	.444	0	1-3	10	4.12	4.83
2000 Toronto	AL	42	2	0	11	66.2	285	69	37	35	9	5	1	2	22	1	53	4	0	2	0	1.000	0	0-1	5	4.37	4.73
2001 Tor-Mil		23	0	0	7	29.0	139	38	22	21	7	0	0	1	18	2	20	0	0	1	1	.500	0	0-0	0	8.23	6.52
2001 Toronto	AL	10	0	0	3	18.1	91	27	17	16	4	0	0	1	11	0	14	0	0	0	1	.000	0	0-0	0	9.25	7.85
2001 Milwaukee	NL	13	0	0	4	10.2	48	11	5	5	3	0	0	0	7	2	6	0	0	1	0	1.000	0	0-0	0	6.53	4.22
9 ML YEARS		292	28	1	55	432.0	1906	479	266	251	63	20	14	15	171	14	320	20	2	25	17	.595	0	3-8	47	5.15	5.23

Orlando Palmeiro

Bats: L Throws: L Pos: RF-47; LF-33; PH-32; CF-11; DH-4; PR-3   Ht: 5'10" Wt: 182 Born: 1/19/69 Age: 34

Year Team	Lg	G	AB	H	2B	3B	HR	(Hm	Rd)	TB	R	RBI	RC	TBB	IBB	SO	HBP	SH	SF	SB	CS	SB%	GDP	Avg	OBP	Slg
1995 Anaheim	AL	15	20	7	0	0	0	(0	0)	7	3	1	3	1	0	1	0	0	0	0	0	-	0	.350	.381	.350
1996 Anaheim	AL	50	87	25	6	1	0	(0	0)	33	6	6	12	8	1	13	2	1	0	0	1	.00	1	.287	.361	.379
1997 Anaheim	AL	74	134	29	2	2	0	(0	0)	35	19	8	10	17	1	11	1	3	1	2	2	.50	4	.216	.307	.261
1998 Anaheim	AL	75	165	53	7	2	0	(0	0)	64	28	21	26	20	1	11	0	7	0	5	4	.56	2	.321	.395	.388
1999 Anaheim	AL	109	317	88	12	1	1	(0	1)	105	46	23	41	39	1	30	6	6	3	5	5	.50	4	.278	.364	.331
2000 Anaheim	AL	108	243	73	20	2	0	(0	0)	97	38	25	42	38	0	20	2	10	3	4	1	.80	4	.300	.395	.399
2001 Anaheim	AL	104	230	56	10	1	2	(0	2)	74	29	23	25	25	2	24	3	7	5	6	6	.50	3	.243	.319	.322
2002 Anaheim	AL	110	263	79	12	1	0	(0	0)	93	35	31	38	30	1	22	0	4	3	7	2	.78	7	.300	.368	.354
8 ML YEARS		645	1459	410	69	10	3	(0	3)	508	204	138	197	178	7	132	14	38	15	29	21	.58	25	.281	.361	.348

Rafael Palmeiro

Bats: L Throws: L Pos: 1B-97; DH-55; PH-5   Ht: 6'0" Wt: 190 Born: 9/24/64 Age: 38

Year Team	Lg	G	AB	H	2B	3B	HR	(Hm	Rd)	TB	R	RBI	RC	TBB	IBB	SO	HBP	SH	SF	SB	CS	SB%	GDP	Avg	OBP	Slg
1986 Chicago	NL	22	73	18	4	0	3	(1	2)	31	9	12	8	4	0	6	1	0	0	1	1	.50	4	.247	.295	.425
1987 Chicago	NL	84	221	61	15	1	14	(5	9)	120	32	30	39	20	1	26	1	0	2	2	2	.50	4	.276	.336	.543
1988 Chicago	NL	152	580	178	41	5	8	(8	0)	253	75	53	88	38	6	34	3	2	6	12	2	.86	11	.307	.349	.436
1989 Texas	AL	156	559	154	23	4	8	(4	4)	209	76	64	73	63	3	48	6	2	2	4	3	.57	18	.275	.354	.374
1990 Texas	AL	154	598	191	35	6	14	(9	5)	280	72	89	93	40	6	59	3	2	8	3	3	.50	24	.319	.361	.468
1991 Texas	AL	159	631	203	49	3	26	(12	14)	336	115	88	123	68	10	72	6	2	7	4	3	.57	17	.322	.389	.532
1992 Texas	AL	159	608	163	27	4	22	(8	14)	264	84	85	94	72	8	83	10	5	6	2	3	.40	10	.268	.352	.434
1993 Texas	AL	160	597	176	40	2	37	(22	15)	331	124	105	123	73	22	85	5	2	9	22	3	.88	8	.295	.371	.554
1994 Baltimore	AL	111	436	139	32	0	23	(11	12)	240	82	76	90	54	1	63	2	0	6	7	3	.70	11	.319	.392	.550
1995 Baltimore	AL	143	554	172	30	2	39	(21	18)	323	89	104	116	62	5	65	3	0	5	3	1	.75	12	.310	.380	.583
1996 Baltimore	AL	162	626	181	40	2	39	(21	18)	342	110	142	130	95	12	96	3	0	8	8	0	1.00	9	.289	.381	.546
1997 Baltimore	AL	158	614	156	24	2	38	(20	18)	298	95	110	97	67	7	109	5	0	6	5	2	.71	14	.254	.329	.485
1998 Baltimore	AL	162	619	183	36	1	43	(25	18)	350	98	121	126	79	8	91	7	0	4	11	7	.61	14	.296	.379	.565
1999 Texas	AL	158	565	183	30	1	47	(28	19)	356	96	148	139	97	14	69	3	0	9	2	4	.33	13	.324	.420	.630
2000 Texas	AL	158	565	163	29	3	39	(26	13)	315	102	120	121	103	17	77	3	0	7	2	1	.67	14	.288	.397	.558
2001 Texas	AL	160	600	164	33	0	47	(23	24)	338	98	123	124	101	8	90	7	0	6	1	1	.50	8	.273	.381	.563
2002 Texas	AL	155	546	149	34	0	43	(23	20)	312	99	105	106	104	16	94	6	0	7	2	0	1.00	10	.273	.391	.571
17 ML YEARS		2413	8992	2634	522	36	490	(267	223)	4698	1456	1575	1694	1140	144	1167	74	15	98	91	39	.70	201	.293	.373	.522

Dean Palmer

Bats: R **Throws:** R **Pos:** DH-3; PH-1 **Ht:** 6'1" **Wt:** 219 **Born:** 12/27/68 **Age:** 34

Year Team	Lg	G	AB	H	2B	3B	HR	(Hm	Rd)	TB	R	RBI	RC	TBB	IBB	SO	HBP	SH	SF	SB	CS	SB%	GDP	Avg	OBP	Slg
1989 Texas	AL	16	19	2	2	0	0	(0	0)	4	0	1	0	0	0	12	0	0	1	0	0	-	0	.105	.100	.211
1991 Texas	AL	81	268	50	9	2	15	(6	9)	108	38	37	30	32	0	98	3	1	0	0	2	.00	4	.187	.281	.403
1992 Texas	AL	152	541	124	25	0	26	(11	15)	227	74	72	71	62	2	154	4	2	4	10	4	.71	9	.229	.311	.420
1993 Texas	AL	148	519	127	31	2	33	(12	21)	261	88	96	83	53	4	154	8	0	5	11	10	.52	5	.245	.321	.503
1994 Texas	AL	93	342	84	14	2	19	(11	8)	159	50	59	46	26	0	89	2	0	1	3	4	.43	7	.246	.302	.465
1995 Texas	AL	36	119	40	6	0	9	(5	4)	73	30	24	31	21	1	21	4	0	1	1	1	.50	2	.336	.448	.613
1996 Texas	AL	154	582	163	26	2	38	(19	19)	307	98	107	103	59	4	145	5	0	6	2	0	1.00	15	.280	.348	.527
1997 Tex-KC	AL	143	542	139	31	1	23	(10	13)	241	70	86	74	41	2	134	3	1	5	2	2	.50	7	.256	.310	.445
1998 Kansas City	AL	152	572	159	27	2	34	(21	13)	292	84	119	94	48	3	134	6	0	13	8	2	.80	18	.278	.333	.510
1999 Detroit	AL	150	560	147	25	2	38	(24	14)	290	92	100	95	57	3	153	10	0	4	3	3	.50	12	.263	.339	.518
2000 Detroit	AL	145	524	134	22	2	29	(15	14)	247	73	102	84	66	2	146	4	0	10	4	2	.67	9	.256	.338	.471
2001 Detroit	AL	57	216	48	11	0	11	(5	6)	92	34	40	30	27	0	59	3	0	0	4	1	.80	3	.222	.317	.426
2002 Detroit	AL	4	12	0	0	0	0	(0	0)	0	0	0	0	1	0	5	0	0	0	0	0	-	1	.000	.077	.000
1997 Texas	AL	94	355	87	21	0	14	(6	8)	150	47	55	45	26	2	84	1	1	3	1	0	1.00	4	.245	.296	.423
1997 Kansas City	AL	49	187	52	10	1	9	(4	5)	91	23	31	29	15	0	50	2	0	2	1	2	.33	3	.278	.335	.487
13 ML YEARS		1331	4816	1217	229	15	275	(139	136)	2301	731	843	741	493	21	1304	52	4	50	48	31	.61	92	.253	.326	.478

Jose Paniagua

Pitches: R **Bats:** R **Pos:** RP-41 **Ht:** 6'2" **Wt:** 195 **Born:** 8/20/73 **Age:** 29

Year Team	Lg	G	GS	CG	GF	IP	BFP	H	R	ER	HR	SH	SF	HB	TBB	IBB	SO	WP	Bk	W	L	Pct	ShO	Sv-Op	Hld	ERC	ERA
2002 Toledo*	AAA	12	0	0	2	15.2	59	10	2	2	1	0	1	1	4	1	13	1	0	2	0	1.000	0	1- -	-	1.76	1.15
1996 Montreal	NL	13	11	0	0	51.0	223	55	24	20	7	1	1	3	23	0	27	2	2	2	4	.333	0	0-0	0	5.41	3.53
1997 Montreal	NL	9	3	0	0	18.0	100	29	24	24	2	1	1	4	16	1	8	1	0	1	2	.333	0	0-0	0	11.18	12.00
1998 Seattle	AL	18	0	0	2	22.0	83	15	5	5	3	0	0	3	5	0	16	2	0	2	0	1.000	0	1-2	6	2.68	2.05
1999 Seattle	AL	59	0	0	16	77.2	350	75	37	35	5	4	3	7	52	4	74	6	0	6	11	.353	0	3-12	16	5.06	4.06
2000 Seattle	AL	69	0	0	26	80.1	344	68	31	31	6	3	5	7	38	3	71	4	1	3	0	1.000	0	5-8	14	3.64	3.47
2001 Seattle	AL	60	0	0	24	66.0	296	59	35	32	7	0	4	4	38	2	46	3	0	4	3	.571	0	3-4	16	4.34	4.36
2002 Detroit	AL	41	0	0	15	41.2	191	50	30	27	10	0	3	3	15	1	34	2	0	1	1	.000	0	1-2	7	6.35	5.83
7 ML YEARS		269	14	0	83	356.2	1587	351	186	174	40	9	14	31	187	11	276	20	3	18	21	.462	0	13-28	59	4.92	4.39

Craig Paquette

Bats: R **Throws:** R **Pos:** 3B-49; 1B-14; DH-5; LF-4; RF-4; PH-3; PR-1 **Ht:** 6'0" **Wt:** 190 **Born:** 3/28/69 **Age:** 34

Year Team	Lg	G	AB	H	2B	3B	HR	(Hm	Rd)	TB	R	RBI	RC	TBB	IBB	SO	HBP	SH	SF	SB	CS	SB%	GDP	Avg	OBP	Slg
1993 Oakland	AL	105	393	86	20	4	12	(8	4)	150	35	46	34	14	2	108	0	1	1	4	2	.67	7	.219	.245	.382
1994 Oakland	AL	14	49	7	2	0	0	(0	0)	9	0	0	0	2	0	14	0	1	0	1	0	1.00	0	.143	.143	.184
1995 Oakland	AL	105	283	64	13	1	13	(8	5)	118	42	49	30	12	0	88	1	3	5	5	2	.71	5	.226	.256	.417
1996 Kansas City	AL	118	429	111	15	1	22	(12	10)	194	61	67	55	23	2	101	2	3	5	5	3	.63	11	.259	.296	.452
1997 Kansas City	AL	77	252	58	15	1	8	(7	1)	99	26	33	21	10	0	57	2	1	2	2	2	.50	13	.230	.263	.393
1998 New York	NL	7	19	5	2	0	0	(0	0)	7	3	0	1	0	0	6	0	0	0	1	0	1.00	3	.263	.263	.368
1999 St Louis	NL	48	157	45	6	0	10	(7	3)	81	21	37	23	6	0	38	0	1	2	1	0	1.00	6	.287	.309	.516
2000 St Louis	NL	134	384	94	24	2	15	(13	2)	167	47	61	49	27	1	83	2	1	6	4	3	.57	5	.245	.294	.435
2001 St Louis	NL	123	340	96	17	0	15	(8	7)	158	47	64	48	18	1	67	5	5	2	3	1	.75	11	.282	.326	.465
2002 Detroit	AL	72	252	49	14	1	4	(0	4)	77	20	20	13	10	0	53	0	1	3	1	0	1.00	7	.194	.223	.306
10 ML YEARS		803	2558	615	128	10	99	(63	36)	1060	302	377	274	120	6	615	12	17	26	27	13	.68	68	.240	.275	.414

Chan Ho Park

Pitches: R **Bats:** R **Pos:** SP-25 **Ht:** 6'2" **Wt:** 204 **Born:** 6/30/73 **Age:** 30

Year Team	Lg	G	GS	CG	GF	IP	BFP	H	R	ER	HR	SH	SF	HB	TBB	IBB	SO	WP	Bk	W	L	Pct	ShO	Sv-Op	Hld	ERC	ERA
2002 Oklahoma*	AAA	1	1	0	0	3.0	21	9	9	9	0	0	0	0	3	0	3	1	0	0	1	.000	0	0- -	-	19.55	27.00
1994 Los Angeles	NL	2	0	0	1	4.0	23	5	5	5	1	0	0	1	5	0	6	0	0	0	0	-	0	0-0	0	11.69	11.25
1995 Los Angeles	NL	2	1	0	0	4.0	16	2	2	2	1	0	0	0	2	0	7	0	1	0	0	-	0	0-0	0	2.70	4.50
1996 Los Angeles	NL	48	10	0	7	108.2	477	82	48	44	7	8	1	4	71	3	119	4	3	5	5	.500	0	0-0	4	3.50	3.64
1997 Los Angeles	NL	32	29	2	1	192.0	792	149	80	72	24	9	5	8	70	1	166	4	1	14	8	.636	0	0-0	0	3.04	3.38
1998 Los Angeles	NL	34	34	2	0	220.2	946	199	101	91	16	11	10	11	97	1	191	6	2	15	9	.625	0	0-0	0	3.69	3.71
1999 Los Angeles	NL	33	33	0	0	194.1	883	208	120	113	31	10	5	14	100	4	174	11	1	13	11	.542	0	0-0	0	5.68	5.23
2000 Los Angeles	NL	34	34	3	0	226.0	963	173	92	82	21	12	5	12	124	4	217	13	0	18	10	.643	1	0-0	0	3.51	3.27
2001 Los Angeles	NL	36	35	2	0	234.0	981	183	98	91	23	16	7	20	91	1	218	3	3	15	11	.577	0	0-0	0	3.15	3.50
2002 Texas	AL	25	25	0	0	145.2	666	154	95	93	20	4	3	17	78	2	121	9	0	9	8	.529	0	0-0	0	5.75	5.75
9 ML YEARS		246	201	9	9	1329.1	5747	1155	641	593	144	70	36	87	638	16	1219	50	11	89	62	.589	2	0-0	4	3.96	4.01

Chad Paronto

Pitches: R **Bats:** R **Pos:** RP-29 **Ht:** 6'5" **Wt:** 250 **Born:** 7/28/75 **Age:** 27

Year Team	Lg	G	GS	CG	GF	IP	BFP	H	R	ER	HR	SH	SF	HB	TBB	IBB	SO	WP	Bk	W	L	Pct	ShO	Sv-Op	Hld	ERC	ERA
1996 Bluefield	R+	9	2	0	1	21.1	82	16	4	4	0	0	0	0	5	0	24	0	1	1	1	.500	0	1- -	-	1.68	1.69
1996 Frederick	A+	8	1	0	2	15.0	63	11	9	8	0	2	0	0	8	0	6	2	0	0	1	.000	0	0- -	-	2.47	4.80
1997 Delmarva	A	28	23	0	2	127.1	569	133	95	67	9	5	5	1	56	1	93	5	0	6	9	.400	0	0- -	-	4.21	4.74
1998 Frederick	A+	18	18	0	0	103.2	451	116	44	36	4	3	2	3	39	0	87	8	0	7	6	.538	0	0- -	-	4.39	3.13
1998 Bowie	AA	8	7	0	1	35.2	165	38	30	23	1	0	1	3	23	0	28	4	0	1	3	.250	0	1- -	-	5.26	5.80
1999 Bowie	AA	15	9	0	0	41.0	209	59	39	37	3	1	4	1	32	1	27	3	0	0	4	.000	0	0- -	-	8.70	8.12
1999 Frederick	A+	13	13	0	0	72.1	323	81	46	38	7	2	1	5	26	1	55	2	0	3	5	.375	0	0- -	-	4.81	4.73
2000 Rochester	AAA	12	6	0	2	36.0	162	40	26	23	5	0	3	1	15	0	18	2	0	1	1	.500	0	0- -	-	5.13	5.75
2000 Bowie	AA	8	8	1	0	47.0	183	29	19	15	2	1	2	4	16	0	31	0	0	4	2	.667	0	0- -	-	1.77	2.87
2001 Rochester	AAA	33	0	0	10	43.1	199	44	28	22	5	2	1	4	24	4	39	2	0	3	3	.500	0	1- -	-	5.06	4.57

Year Team	Lg	G	GS	CG	GF	IP	BFP	H	R	ER	HR	SH	SF	HB	TBB	IBB	SO	WP	Bk	W	L	Pct	ShO	Sv-Op	Hld	ERC	ERA
2002 Buffalo	AAA	8	0	0	5	13.0	49	10	0	0	0	1	0	0	1	1	7	0	0	0	0	-	0	1--	5	1.30	0.00
2002 Akron	AA	1	1	0	0	0.1	3	1	1	1	0	0	0	0	1	0	0	0	0	0	0	-	0	0--	-	29.63	27.00
2001 Baltimore	AL	24	0	0	9	27.0	128	33	24	15	5	1	1	1	11	0	16	1	0	1	3	.250	0	0-1	5	5.98	5.00
2002 Cleveland	AL	29	0	0	11	35.2	154	34	19	16	3	0	4	2	11	1	23	2	0	0	2	.000	0	0-0	0	3.45	4.04
2 ML YEARS		53	0	0	20	62.2	282	67	43	31	8	1	5	3	22	1	39	3	0	1	5	.167	0	0-1	5	4.49	4.45

Jim Parque

Pitches: L Bats: L Pos: SP-4; RP-4 **Ht: 5'11" Wt: 170 Born: 2/8/76 Age: 27**

Year Team	Lg	G	GS	CG	GF	IP	BFP	H	R	ER	HR	SH	SF	HB	TBB	IBB	SO	WP	Bk	W	L	Pct	ShO	Sv-Op	Hld	ERC	ERA
2002 Charlotte*	AAA	20	20	0	0	105.2	472	131	80	76	21	2	5	4	38	0	63	5	1	7	9	.438	0	0--	-	6.34	6.47
1998 Chicago	AL	21	21	0	0	113.0	507	135	72	64	14	1	0	6	49	0	77	0	3	7	5	.583	0	0-0	0	5.88	5.10
1999 Chicago	AL	31	30	1	0	173.2	804	210	111	99	23	5	8	10	79	2	111	3	2	9	15	.375	0	0-0	0	5.98	5.13
2000 Chicago	AL	33	32	0	0	187.0	828	208	105	89	21	5	5	11	71	1	111	2	5	13	6	.684	0	0-0	0	4.99	4.28
2001 Chicago	AL	5	5	1	0	28.0	132	36	26	25	7	2	1	2	10	1	15	0	0	0	3	.000	0	0-0	0	6.86	8.04
2002 Chicago	AL	8	4	0	0	25.1	126	34	29	28	11	0	2	1	16	0	13	0	0	1	4	.200	0	0-0	0	10.13	9.95
5 ML YEARS		98	92	2	0	527.0	2397	623	343	305	76	13	16	30	225	4	327	5	10	30	33	.476	0	0-0	0	5.83	5.21

Jose Parra

Pitches: R Bats: R Pos: RP-16 **Ht: 5'11" Wt: 175 Born: 11/28/72 Age: 30**

Year Team	Lg	G	GS	CG	GF	IP	BFP	H	R	ER	HR	SH	SF	HB	TBB	IBB	SO	WP	Bk	W	L	Pct	ShO	Sv-Op	Hld	ERC	ERA
2002 Tucson*	AAA	7	0	0	3	9.1	36	3	0	0	0	0	0	2	2	0	10	0	0	0	0	-	0	1--	-	0.79	0.00
1995 LA-Min		20	12	0	0	72.0	339	93	64	57	13	0	4	3	28	1	36	3	1	1	5	.167	0	0-0	0	6.41	7.13
1996 Minnesota	AL	27	5	0	7	70.0	320	88	48	47	15	1	3	3	27	0	50	4	1	5	5	.500	0	0-1	0	6.63	6.04
2000 Pittsburgh	NL	6	2	0	1	11.2	57	17	9	9	3	1	0	1	7	0	9	0	0	0	1	.000	0	0-0	0	9.86	6.94
2002 Arizona	NL	16	0	0	3	14.0	63	13	5	5	0	0	0	1	11	2	8	1	0	0	1	.000	0	0-0	4	4.57	3.21
1995 Los Angeles	NL	8	0	0	0	10.1	47	10	8	5	2	0	1	1	6	1	7	0	1	0	0	-	0	0-0	0	5.56	4.35
1995 Minnesota	AL	12	12	0	0	61.2	292	83	59	52	11	0	3	2	22	0	29	3	0	1	5	.167	0	0-0	0	6.55	7.59
4 ML YEARS		69	19	0	11	167.2	779	211	129	118	31	2	7	8	73	3	103	8	2	6	12	.333	0	0-1	4	6.58	6.33

Steve Parris

Pitches: R Bats: R Pos: SP-14 **Ht: 6'0" Wt: 195 Born: 12/17/67 Age: 35**

Year Team	Lg	G	GS	CG	GF	IP	BFP	H	R	ER	HR	SH	SF	HB	TBB	IBB	SO	WP	Bk	W	L	Pct	ShO	Sv-Op	Hld	ERC	ERA
2002 Dunedin*	A+	3	3	0	0	16.1	68	19	10	8	1	0	1	1	1	0	8	0	0	0	1	.000	0	0--	-	3.66	4.41
2002 Tennessee*	AA	1	1	0	0	6.0	28	7	2	2	0	0	0	1	2	0	5	0	0	0	0	-	0	0--	-	3.75	3.00
2002 Syracuse*	AAA	2	2	0	0	14.0	54	10	6	2	0	0	0	0	2	0	5	0	0	1	1	.500	0	0--	-	1.32	1.29
1995 Pittsburgh	NL	15	15	1	0	82.0	360	89	49	49	12	3	2	7	33	1	61	4	0	6	6	.500	1	0-0	0	5.36	5.38
1996 Pittsburgh	NL	8	4	0	3	26.1	123	35	22	21	4	1	1	1	11	0	27	2	0	0	3	.000	0	0-0	0	6.70	7.18
1998 Cincinnati	NL	18	16	1	0	99.0	421	89	44	41	9	7	1	4	32	3	77	1	1	6	5	.545	1	0-0	0	3.22	3.73
1999 Cincinnati	NL	22	21	2	0	128.2	545	124	59	50	16	7	3	6	52	4	86	3	0	11	4	.733	1	0-0	0	4.29	3.50
2000 Cincinnati	NL	33	33	0	0	192.2	861	227	109	103	30	10	3	4	71	5	117	9	1	12	17	.414	0	0-0	0	5.44	4.81
2001 Toronto	AL	19	19	1	0	105.2	471	126	60	54	18	4	2	2	41	4	49	3	0	4	6	.400	0	0-0	0	5.75	4.60
2002 Toronto	AL	14	14	0	0	75.1	348	96	50	50	13	2	2	3	35	5	48	3	0	5	5	.500	0	0-0	0	6.68	5.97
7 ML YEARS		129	122	5	3	709.2	3129	786	393	368	102	34	14	27	275	22	465	25	2	44	46	.489	3	0-0	0	5.10	4.67

Corey Patterson

Bats: L Throws: R Pos: CF-147; PH-10; PR-2 **Ht: 5'9" Wt: 175 Born: 8/13/79 Age: 23**

Year Team	Lg	G	AB	H	2B	3B	HR	(Hm	Rd)	TB	R	RBI	RC	TBB	IBB	SO	HBP	SH	SF	SB	CS	SB%	GDP	Avg	OBP	Slg
2000 Chicago	NL	11	42	7	1	0	2	(1	1)	14	9	2	3	3	0	14	1	1	0	1	1	.50	0	.167	.239	.333
2001 Chicago	NL	59	131	29	3	0	4	(1	3)	44	26	14	13	6	0	33	3	2	3	4	0	1.00	1	.221	.266	.336
2002 Chicago	NL	153	592	150	30	5	14	(7	7)	232	71	54	61	19	1	142	8	4	5	18	3	.86	8	.253	.284	.392
3 ML YEARS		223	765	186	34	5	20	(9	11)	290	106	70	77	28	1	189	12	7	8	23	4	.85	9	.243	.278	.379

Danny Patterson

Pitches: R Bats: R Pos: RP-6 **Ht: 6'0" Wt: 185 Born: 2/17/71 Age: 32**

Year Team	Lg	G	GS	CG	GF	IP	BFP	H	R	ER	HR	SH	SF	HB	TBB	IBB	SO	WP	Bk	W	L	Pct	ShO	Sv-Op	Hld	ERC	ERA
2002 Toledo*	AAA	5	1	0	0	5.0	15	1	0	0	0	0	0	0	0	0	3	0	0	0	0	-	0	0--	0	0.10	0.00
1996 Texas	AL	7	0	0	5	8.2	38	10	4	0	0	0	0	0	3	1	5	0	0	0	0	-	0	0-0	0	3.81	0.00
1997 Texas	AL	54	0	0	17	71.0	296	70	29	27	3	4	3	0	23	4	69	7	1	10	6	.625	0	1-8	9	3.27	3.42
1998 Texas	AL	56	0	0	21	60.2	257	64	31	30	11	1	1	2	19	2	33	3	0	2	5	.286	0	2-2	19	4.79	4.45
1999 Texas	AL	53	0	0	18	60.1	275	77	38	38	5	0	2	1	19	3	43	2	0	2	0	1.000	0	0-1	4	5.11	5.67
2000 Detroit	AL	58	0	0	12	56.2	244	69	26	25	4	3	2	2	14	2	29	1	0	5	1	.833	0	0-2	12	4.68	3.97
2001 Detroit	AL	60	0	0	16	64.2	258	64	24	22	4	5	3	4	12	5	27	2	0	5	4	.556	0	1-5	16	3.21	3.06
2002 Detroit	AL	6	0	0	1	3.0	17	5	5	5	0	0	0	1	2	0	1	0	0	0	2	.000	0	0-1	0	9.70	15.00
7 ML YEARS		294	0	0	90	325.0	1385	359	157	147	27	13	11	10	92	17	207	15	1	24	18	.571	0	4-19	60	4.18	4.07

John Patterson

Pitches: R Bats: R Pos: SP-5; RP-2   Ht: 6'5" Wt: 183 Born: 1/30/78 Age: 25

Year Team	Lg	G	GS	CG	GF	IP	BFP	H	R	ER	HR	SH	SF	HB	TBB	IBB	SO	WP	Bk	W	L	Pct	ShO	Sv-Op	Hld	ERC	ERA
1997 South Bend	A	18	18	0	0	78.0	327	63	32	28	3	1	2	5	34	0	95	8	0	1	9	.100	0	0--	-	3.02	3.23
1998 High Desert	A+	25	25	0	0	127.0	519	102	54	40	12	0	3	4	42	0	148	5	0	8	7	.533	0	0--	-	2.86	2.83
1999 El Paso	AA	18	18	2	0	100.0	429	98	61	53	16	3	1	0	42	0	117	3	0	8	6	.571	0	0--	-	4.49	4.77
1999 Tucson	AAA	7	6	0	0	30.2	148	43	26	24	3	0	0	0	18	0	29	0	0	1	5	.167	0	0--	-	7.36	7.04
2000 Tucson	AAA	3	2	0	0	15.0	76	21	14	13	1	1	1	0	9	0	10	2	0	0	2	.000	0	0--	-	6.77	7.80
2001 Lancaster	A+	2	2	0	0	9.1	40	9	6	6	3	0	0	0	3	0	9	0	0	0	0	-	0	0--	-	4.95	5.79
2001 El Paso	AA	5	5	0	0	25.1	112	30	15	12	2	0	0	2	9	0	19	1	0	1	2	.333	0	0--	-	5.23	4.26
2001 Tucson	AAA	13	12	0	0	67.2	313	82	50	44	9	2	5	3	31	3	40	2	1	2	7	.222	0	0--	-	5.89	5.85
2002 Tucson	AAA	19	18	0	0	112.2	496	117	59	53	14	3	3	4	45	1	104	6	0	10	5	.667	0	0--	-	4.57	4.23
2002 Arizona	NL	7	5	0	1	30.2	123	27	11	11	7	0	0	1	7	0	31	2	0	2	0	1.000	0	0-0	0	3.76	3.23

Josh Paul

Bats: R Throws: R Pos: C-32; LF-1   Ht: 6'1" Wt: 200 Born: 5/19/75 Age: 28

Year Team	Lg	G	AB	H	2B	3B	HR	(Hm	Rd)	TB	R	RBI	RC	TBB	IBB	SO	HBP	SH	SF	SB	CS	SB%	GDP	Avg	OBP	Slg
2002 Charlotte*	AAA	65	231	63	15	2	0	(-	-)	82	18	17	26	17	1	45	1	6	2	10	4	.71	7	.273	.323	.355
1999 Chicago	AL	6	18	4	1	0	0	(0	0)	5	2	1	1	0	0	4	0	0	0	0	0	-	0	.222	.222	.278
2000 Chicago	AL	36	71	20	3	2	1	(1	0)	30	15	8	9	5	0	17	1	2	0	1	0	1.00	3	.282	.338	.423
2001 Chicago	AL	57	139	37	11	0	3	(0	3)	57	20	18	19	13	0	25	0	1	1	6	2	.75	3	.266	.327	.410
2002 Chicago	AL	33	104	25	4	0	0	(0	0)	29	11	11	11	9	0	22	1	2	2	2	0	1.00	1	.240	.302	.279
4 ML YEARS		132	332	86	19	2	4	(1	3)	121	48	38	40	27	0	68	2	5	3	9	2	.82	7	.259	.316	.364

Carl Pavano

Pitches: R Bats: R Pos: SP-22; RP-15   Ht: 6'5" Wt: 230 Born: 1/8/76 Age: 27

Year Team	Lg	G	GS	CG	GF	IP	BFP	H	R	ER	HR	SH	SF	HB	TBB	IBB	SO	WP	Bk	W	L	Pct	ShO	Sv-Op	Hld	ERC	ERA
2002 Ottawa*	AAA	3	3	0	0	20.1	82	23	8	7	2	0	2	0	2	0	9	1	0	3	0	1.000	0	0--	-	3.72	3.10
1998 Montreal	NL	24	23	0	0	134.2	580	130	70	63	18	5	6	8	43	1	83	1	0	6	9	.400	0	0-0	0	3.97	4.21
1999 Montreal	NL	19	18	1	0	104.0	457	117	66	65	8	5	2	4	35	1	70	1	3	6	8	.429	1	0-0	0	4.51	5.63
2000 Montreal	NL	15	15	0	0	97.0	408	89	40	33	8	4	3	8	34	1	64	1	1	8	4	.667	0	0-0	0	3.67	3.06
2001 Montreal	NL	8	8	0	0	42.2	199	59	33	30	7	2	1	2	16	1	36	0	1	1	6	.143	0	0-0	0	6.99	6.33
2002 Mon-Fla	NL	37	22	0	2	136.0	618	174	88	78	19	4	4	10	45	8	92	3	2	6	10	.375	0	0-0	3	5.99	5.16
2002 Montreal	NL	15	14	0	0	74.1	349	98	55	52	14	2	2	7	31	5	51	2	1	3	8	.273	0	0-0	0	7.09	6.30
2002 Florida	NL	22	8	0	2	61.2	269	76	33	26	5	2	2	3	14	3	41	1	1	3	2	.600	0	0-0	3	4.74	3.79
5 ML YEARS		103	86	1	2	514.1	2262	569	297	269	60	20	16	32	173	12	345	6	7	27	37	.422	1	0-0	3	4.77	4.71

Jay Payton

Bats: R Throws: R Pos: CF-97; LF-33; PH-18; RF-2   Ht: 5'10" Wt: 185 Born: 11/22/72 Age: 30

Year Team	Lg	G	AB	H	2B	3B	HR	(Hm	Rd)	TB	R	RBI	RC	TBB	IBB	SO	HBP	SH	SF	SB	CS	SB%	GDP	Avg	OBP	Slg
1998 New York	NL	15	22	7	1	0	0	(0	0)	8	2	0	3	1	0	4	0	0	0	0	0	-	0	.318	.348	.364
1999 New York	NL	13	8	2	1	0	0	(0	0)	3	1	1	0	0	0	2	1	0	0	1	2	.33	1	.250	.333	.375
2000 New York	NL	149	488	142	23	1	17	(9	8)	218	63	62	68	30	0	60	3	0	5	5	11	.31	9	.291	.331	.447
2001 New York	NL	104	361	92	16	1	8	(6	2)	134	44	34	37	18	1	52	5	0	2	4	3	.57	11	.255	.298	.371
2002 NYM-Col	NL	134	445	135	20	7	16	(9	7)	217	69	59	71	29	0	54	4	2	1	7	4	.64	11	.303	.351	.488
2002 New York	NL	87	275	78	6	3	8	(4	4)	114	33	31	37	21	0	34	1	2	1	4	1	.80	8	.284	.336	.415
2002 Colorado	NL	47	170	57	14	4	8	(5	3)	103	36	28	34	8	0	20	3	0	0	3	3	.50	3	.335	.376	.606
5 ML YEARS		415	1324	378	61	9	41	(24	17)	580	179	156	179	78	1	172	13	2	11	17	20	.46	31	.285	.329	.438

Josh Pearce

Pitches: R Bats: R Pos: SP-3   Ht: 6'3" Wt: 215 Born: 8/20/77 Age: 25

Year Team	Lg	G	GS	CG	GF	IP	BFP	H	R	ER	HR	SH	SF	HB	TBB	IBB	SO	WP	Bk	W	L	Pct	ShO	Sv-Op	Hld	ERC	ERA
1999 New Jersey	A-	14	14	1	0	77.2	336	78	45	43	8	2	6	5	20	0	78	14	1	3	7	.300	1	0--	-	3.73	4.98
2000 Potomac	A+	10	10	1	0	62.2	259	70	25	24	5	0	1	1	10	0	42	0	0	5	3	.625	0	0--	-	3.78	3.45
2000 Arkansas	AA	17	17	0	0	97.1	441	117	68	59	13	6	2	6	35	2	63	5	1	5	6	.455	0	0--	-	5.54	5.46
2001 New Haven	AA	18	18	0	0	115.1	484	111	55	48	11	4	2	6	34	1	96	5	0	6	8	.429	0	0--	-	3.64	3.75
2001 Memphis	AAA	10	10	0	0	69.2	291	72	43	33	11	2	5	1	12	1	36	3	0	4	4	.500	0	0--	-	3.74	4.26
2002 Memphis	AAA	4	4	0	0	20.0	91	28	18	17	8	1	0	0	3	0	17	1	0	0	4	.000	0	0--	-	7.49	7.65
2002 St Louis	NL	3	3	0	0	13.0	66	20	13	11	1	3	1	1	8	0	1	0	0	0	0	-	0	0-0	0	8.51	7.62

Jason Pearson

Pitches: L Bats: L Pos: RP-2   Ht: 6'0" Wt: 195 Born: 12/29/75 Age: 27

Year Team	Lg	G	GS	CG	GF	IP	BFP	H	R	ER	HR	SH	SF	HB	TBB	IBB	SO	WP	Bk	W	L	Pct	ShO	Sv-Op	Hld	ERC	ERA
1998 Marlins	R	11	3	0	5	34.1	134	28	8	6	0	0	1	1	5	0	36	2	0	4	0	1.000	0	2--	-	1.74	1.57
1998 Kane County	A	2	0	0	2	2.2	14	3	3	1	0	0	1	1	1	0	1	0	0	0	0	-	0	0--	-	4.83	3.38
1999 Sioux Falls	IND	27	2	0	11	63.1	271	57	29	21	6	3	5	3	28	2	48	2	0	2	3	.400	0	0--	-	3.80	2.98
2000 Fargo-Mh	IND	18	16	1	0	107.2	455	90	45	36	6	3	2	3	49	1	82	4	1	10	2	.833	0	0--	-	3.19	3.01
2001 Mobile	AA	54	5	0	16	86.1	371	88	40	40	5	4	6	2	30	3	67	3	0	5	5	.500	0	1--	-	3.77	4.17
2002 Portland	AAA	23	0	0	5	30.0	125	25	5	5	3	0	0	2	9	0	18	0	0	3	0	1.000	0	0--	-	3.02	1.50
2002 Fresno	AAA	34	0	0	8	36.0	155	35	20	15	5	2	1	2	16	1	28	3	0	0	1	.000	0	0--	-	4.64	3.75
2002 San Diego	NL	2	0	0	1	1.2	6	1	0	0	0	0	0	0	0	0	3	0	0	0	0	-	0	0-0	0	0.75	0.00

Terry Pearson

Pitches: R **Bats:** R **Pos:** RP-4   **Ht:** 6'0" **Wt:** 200 **Born:** 11/10/71 **Age:** 31

Year Team	Lg	G	GS	CG	GF	IP	BFP	H	R	ER	HR	SH	SF	HB	TBB	IBB	SO	WP	Bk	W	L	Pct	ShO	Sv-Op	Hld	ERC	ERA
1995 Zanesville	IND	14	14	0	0	83.2	367	80	45	30	5	5	4	5	37	0	55	2	0	6	2	.750	0	0--	-	3.91	3.23
1996 Zanesville	IND	31	0	0	30	35.2	152	30	12	2	0	2	0	3	8	0	43	2	0	4	1	.800	0	20--	-	2.14	0.50
1997 Sioux Falls	IND	41	0	0	15	62.2	298	85	54	29	5	4	4	3	30	3	46	6	0	2	3	.400	0	1--	-	6.49	4.16
2000 Sioux Falls	IND	19	0	0	13	22.1	103	27	17	11	1	2	0	2	7	2	14	4	0	2	2	.500	0	6--	-	4.58	4.43
2000 Duluth-Sup	IND	18	0	0	8	20.1	94	28	18	15	0	4	0	0	4	0	18	6	0	2	2	.500	0	3--	-	4.49	6.64
2001 Erie	AA	59	0	0	47	61.1	273	65	26	20	1	4	1	3	16	2	62	5	1	4	4	.500	0	23--	-	3.26	2.93
2002 Toledo	AAA	40	0	0	11	47.0	210	52	29	25	1	5	0	3	18	4	30	4	0	3	8	.273	0	2--	-	4.10	4.79
2002 Erie	AA	15	0	0	13	14.2	70	25	7	6	1	0	0	1	2	0	11	4	0	0	0	-	0	4--	-	7.31	3.68
2002 Detroit	AL	4	0	0	3	6.0	27	8	7	7	2	0	0	0	2	1	4	0	0	0	0	-	0	0-0	0	7.43	10.50

Jake Peavy

Pitches: R **Bats:** R **Pos:** SP-17   **Ht:** 6'1" **Wt:** 180 **Born:** 5/31/81 **Age:** 22

Year Team	Lg	G	GS	CG	GF	IP	BFP	H	R	ER	HR	SH	SF	HB	TBB	IBB	SO	WP	Bk	W	L	Pct	ShO	Sv-Op	Hld	ERC	ERA
1999 Padres	R	13	11	1	0	73.2	286	52	16	11	4	2	0	3	23	0	90	5	3	7	1	.875	0	0--	-	2.19	1.34
1999 Idaho Falls	R+	2	2	0	0	11.0	40	5	0	0	0	0	0	0	1	0	13	0	0	2	0	1.000	0	0--	-	0.57	0.00
2000 Fort Wayne	A	26	25	0	0	133.2	565	107	61	43	6	4	3	9	53	0	164	8	2	13	8	.619	0	0--	-	2.84	2.90
2001 Lk Elsinore	A+	19	19	0	0	105.1	422	76	41	36	6	2	1	6	33	1	144	5	0	7	5	.583	0	0--	-	2.25	3.08
2001 Mobile	AA	5	5	0	0	28.0	114	19	8	8	3	0	0	3	12	1	44	1	0	2	1	.667	0	0--	-	2.93	2.57
2002 Mobile	AA	14	14	0	0	80.1	335	65	26	25	4	3	1	5	30	0	89	1	1	4	5	.444	0	0--	-	2.85	2.80
2002 San Diego	NL	17	17	0	0	97.2	430	106	54	49	11	5	2	3	33	4	90	4	1	6	7	.462	0	0-0	0	4.41	4.52

Alex Pelaez

Bats: R **Throws:** R **Pos:** 1B-1; 2B-1; 3B-1; PH-1   **Ht:** 5'9" **Wt:** 190 **Born:** 4/6/76 **Age:** 27

Year Team	Lg	G	AB	H	2B	3B	HR	(Hm	Rd)	TB	R	RBI	RC	TBB	IBB	SO	HBP	SH	SF	SB	CS	SB%	GDP	Avg	OBP	Slg
1998 Idaho Falls	R+	63	262	89	17	1	8	(-	-)	132	52	51	50	29	0	32	1	0	2	3	1	.75	10	.340	.405	.504
1999 R Cucamnga	A+	117	443	132	21	4	4	(-	-)	173	62	54	54	35	3	53	1	1	2	7	3	.70	24	.298	.349	.391
1999 Las Vegas	AAA	5	13	4	0	0	0	(-	-)	4	1	0	1	0	0	2	0	0	0	0	0	-	1	.308	.308	.308
2000 R Cucamnga	A+	62	235	66	20	0	2	(-	-)	92	29	28	29	23	0	27	0	0	4	2	2	.50	11	.281	.340	.391
2000 Las Vegas	AAA	34	108	27	3	0	1	(-	-)	33	13	15	9	4	1	20	1	5	1	0	0	-	2	.250	.281	.306
2000 Mobile	AA	28	90	24	3	0	2	(-	-)	33	8	11	10	10	0	15	0	0	1	0	0	-	5	.267	.337	.367
2001 Mobile	AA	114	416	117	22	1	10	(-	-)	171	44	53	54	32	3	52	2	2	5	2	0	1.00	14	.281	.332	.411
2002 Portland	AAA	112	411	127	31	1	11	(-	-)	193	47	64	60	20	3	40	0	0	3	0	1	.00	15	.309	.339	.470
2002 San Diego	NL	3	8	2	0	0	0	(0	0)	2	0	0	0	0	0	0	0	0	0	0	0	-	2	.250	.250	.250

Kit Pellow

Bats: R **Throws:** R **Pos:** 3B-12; 1B-10; PH-5; DH-4; PR-1   **Ht:** 6'1" **Wt:** 200 **Born:** 8/28/73 **Age:** 29

Year Team	Lg	G	AB	H	2B	3B	HR	(Hm	Rd)	TB	R	RBI	RC	TBB	IBB	SO	HBP	SH	SF	SB	CS	SB%	GDP	Avg	OBP	Slg
1996 Spokane	A-	71	279	80	18	2	18	(-	-)	156	48	66	53	20	0	52	8	1	7	8	3	.73	5	.287	.344	.559
1997 Lansing	A	65	256	76	17	2	11	(-	-)	130	39	52	47	24	1	74	6	0	4	2	0	1.00	5	.297	.366	.508
1997 Wichita	AA	68	241	60	12	1	10	(-	-)	104	40	41	32	21	1	72	2	2	3	5	2	.71	5	.249	.311	.432
1998 Wichita	AA	103	374	100	24	3	29	(-	-)	217	70	73	70	27	2	107	6	1	3	4	3	.57	2	.267	.324	.580
1998 Omaha	AAA	14	54	10	3	0	2	(-	-)	19	8	6	4	2	0	19	0	0	2	2	0	1.00	1	.185	.207	.352
1999 Omaha	AAA	131	475	136	28	4	35	(-	-)	277	88	99	88	20	3	117	18	1	7	6	5	.55	11	.286	.335	.583
2000 Omaha	AAA	117	421	105	17	3	22	(-	-)	194	61	75	65	38	1	89	16	1	5	6	4	.60	7	.249	.331	.461
2001 Omaha	AAA	129	484	141	15	0	20	(-	-)	216	81	81	78	37	1	101	13	2	7	4	3	.57	3	.291	.353	.446
2002 Omaha	AAA	105	402	116	25	2	27	(-	-)	226	65	76	76	21	1	82	19	0	4	4	2	.67	7	.289	.350	.562
2002 Kansas City	AL	29	63	15	1	0	1	(0	1)	19	6	5	7	9	0	21	1	0	0	1	1	.50	2	.238	.342	.302

Dave Pember

Pitches: R **Bats:** R **Pos:** RP-3; SP-1   **Ht:** 6'5" **Wt:** 225 **Born:** 5/24/78 **Age:** 25

Year Team	Lg	G	GS	CG	GF	IP	BFP	H	R	ER	HR	SH	SF	HB	TBB	IBB	SO	WP	Bk	W	L	Pct	ShO	Sv-Op	Hld	ERC	ERA
2000 Beloit	A	17	16	0	0	98.0	434	118	56	51	9	3	4	8	25	2	70	5	2	2	10	.167	0	0--	-	4.91	4.68
2001 Beloit	A	8	8	0	0	44.0	185	49	20	16	3	0	2	1	10	0	39	5	0	3	4	.429	0	0--	-	3.97	3.27
2001 High Desert	A+	20	20	0	0	121.1	533	135	73	65	12	2	7	7	35	1	96	14	0	9	6	.600	0	0--	-	4.44	4.82
2002 Huntsville	AA	27	27	2	0	156.0	669	157	69	55	13	9	2	6	53	1	111	13	1	10	6	.625	0	0--	-	3.90	3.17
2002 Milwaukee	NL	4	1	0	1	8.2	40	7	6	5	1	1	1	0	6	0	5	1	0	0	1	.000	0	0-0	0	4.04	5.19

Carlos Pena

Bats: L **Throws:** L **Pos:** 1B-113; DH-2; PH-1   **Ht:** 6'2" **Wt:** 210 **Born:** 5/17/78 **Age:** 25

Year Team	Lg	G	AB	H	2B	3B	HR	(Hm	Rd)	TB	R	RBI	RC	TBB	IBB	SO	HBP	SH	SF	SB	CS	SB%	GDP	Avg	OBP	Slg
1998 Rangers	R	2	5	2	0	0	0	(-	-)	2	1	0	2	3	0	1	0	0	0	1	1	.50	0	.400	.625	.400
1998 Savannah	A	30	117	38	14	0	6	(-	-)	70	22	20	26	8	0	26	4	0	1	3	2	.60	0	.325	.385	.598
1998 Charlotte	A+	7	22	6	1	0	0	(-	-)	7	1	3	2	2	0	8	1	0	0	0	1	.00	0	.273	.360	.318
1999 Charlotte	A+	136	501	128	31	8	18	(-	-)	229	85	103	85	74	2	135	16	0	6	2	5	.29	7	.255	.365	.457
2000 Tulsa	AA	138	529	158	36	2	28	(-	-)	282	117	105	120	101	10	108	9	1	8	12	0	1.00	7	.299	.414	.533
2001 Oklahoma	AAA	119	431	124	38	3	23	(-	-)	237	71	74	97	80	1	127	8	0	0	11	3	.79	6	.288	.408	.550
2002 Sacramento	AAA	44	175	42	10	1	10	(-	-)	84	30	33	30	24	0	49	4	0	3	3	0	1.00	3	.240	.340	.480
2001 Texas	AL	22	62	16	4	1	3	(2	1)	31	6	12	11	10	0	17	0	0	0	0	0	-	1	.258	.361	.500
2002 Oak-Det	AL	115	397	96	17	4	19	(10	9)	178	43	52	57	41	0	111	3	0	2	2	2	.50	7	.242	.316	.448

Year Team	Lg	G	AB	H	2B	3B	HR	(Hm	Rd)	TB	R	RBI	RC	TBB	IBB	SO	HBP	SH	SF	SB	CS	SB%	GDP	Avg	OBP	Slg
2002 Oakland	AL	40	124	27	4	0	7	(5	2)	52	12	16	17	15	1	38	1	0	1	0	0	-	2	.218	.305	.419
2002 Detroit	AL	75	273	69	13	4	12	(5	7)	126	31	36	40	26	0	73	2	0	1	2	2	.50	5	.253	.321	.462
2 ML YEARS		137	459	112	21	5	22	(12	10)	209	49	64	68	51	0	128	3	0	2	2	2	.50	8	.244	.322	.455

Wily Mo Pena

Bats: R **Throws:** R **Pos:** PH-6; LF-3; PR-3; RF-1   **Ht:** 6'3" **Wt:** 215 **Born:** 1/23/82 **Age:** 21

Year Team	Lg	G	AB	H	2B	3B	HR	(Hm	Rd)	TB	R	RBI	RC	TBB	IBB	SO	HBP	SH	SF	SB	CS	SB%	GDP	Avg	OBP	Slg
1999 Yankees	R	45	166	41	10	1	7	(-	-)	74	21	26	24	12	0	54	7	0	1	3	2	.60	2	.247	.323	.446
2000 Greensboro	A	67	249	51	7	1	10	(-	-)	90	41	28	21	18	1	91	6	5	5	6	5	.55	9	.205	.268	.361
2000 Staten Island	A-	20	73	22	1	2	0	(-	-)	27	7	10	10	2	0	23	4	0	0	2	0	1.00	1	.301	.354	.370
2001 Dayton	A	135	511	135	25	5	26	(-	-)	248	87	113	82	33	1	177	17	0	4	26	10	.72	6	.264	.327	.485
2002 Chattanooga	AA	105	388	99	23	1	11	(-	-)	157	47	47	53	36	2	126	9	0	3	8	0	1.00	9	.255	.330	.405
2002 Cincinnati	NL	13	18	4	0	0	1	(1	0)	7	1	1	1	0	0	11	0	0	0	0	0	-	0	.222	.222	.389

Brad Penny

Pitches: R **Bats:** R **Pos:** SP-24   **Ht:** 6'4" **Wt:** 247 **Born:** 5/24/78 **Age:** 25

	HOW MUCH HE PITCHED						WHAT HE GAVE UP												THE RESULTS						
Year Team	Lg	G	GS	CG	GF	IP	BFP	H	R	ER	HR	SH	SF	HB	TBB	IBB	SO	WP	Bk	W	L	Pct	ShO	Sv-Op	Hld	ERC	ERA
2002 Jupiter*	A+	2	2	0	0	7.2	28	5	0	0	0	0	0	0	0	0	9	0	0	-	-	-	-	0-0	0	0.88	0.00
2000 Florida	NL	23	22	0	0	119.2	529	120	70	64	13	6	2	5	60	4	80	4	1	8	7	.533	0	0-0	0	4.70	4.81
2001 Florida	NL	31	31	1	0	205.0	833	183	92	84	15	8	2	7	54	3	154	2	0	10	10	.500	1	0-0	0	2.96	3.69
2002 Florida	NL	24	24	1	0	129.1	574	148	76	67	18	6	4	1	50	7	93	4	0	8	7	.533	1	0-0	0	5.08	4.66
3 ML YEARS		78	77	2	0	454.0	1936	451	238	215	46	20	8	13	164	14	327	10	1	26	24	.520	2	0-0	0	3.99	4.26

Troy Percival

Pitches: R **Bats:** R **Pos:** RP-58   **Ht:** 6'3" **Wt:** 235 **Born:** 8/9/69 **Age:** 33

	HOW MUCH HE PITCHED						WHAT HE GAVE UP												THE RESULTS						
Year Team	Lg	G	GS	CG	GF	IP	BFP	H	R	ER	HR	SH	SF	HB	TBB	IBB	SO	WP	Bk	W	L	Pct	ShO	Sv-Op	Hld	ERC	ERA
1995 Anaheim	AL	62	0	0	16	74.0	284	37	19	16	6	4	1	1	26	2	94	2	2	3	2	.600	0	3-6	29	1.44	1.95
1996 Anaheim	AL	62	0	0	52	74.0	291	38	20	19	8	2	1	2	31	4	100	2	0	0	2	.000	0	36-39	2	1.76	2.31
1997 Anaheim	AL	55	0	0	46	52.0	224	40	20	20	6	1	2	4	22	2	72	5	0	5	5	.500	0	27-31	0	3.15	3.46
1998 Anaheim	AL	67	0	0	60	66.2	287	45	31	27	5	3	2	3	37	4	87	3	0	2	7	.222	0	42-48	0	2.74	3.65
1999 Anaheim	AL	60	0	0	50	57.0	230	38	24	24	9	0	1	3	22	0	58	3	0	4	6	.400	0	31-39	0	2.83	3.79
2000 Anaheim	AL	54	0	0	45	50.0	221	42	27	25	7	3	2	2	30	4	49	1	0	5	5	.500	0	32-42	0	4.24	4.50
2001 Anaheim	AL	57	0	0	50	57.2	230	39	19	17	3	1	0	2	18	1	71	2	0	4	2	.667	0	39-42	0	1.90	2.65
2002 Anaheim	AL	58	0	0	50	56.1	226	38	12	12	5	0	1	0	25	1	68	5	0	4	1	.800	0	40-44	0	2.47	1.92
8 ML YEARS		475	0	0	369	487.2	1993	317	172	160	49	14	10	17	211	18	599	23	2	27	30	.474	0	250-291	31	2.42	2.95

Eddie Perez

Bats: R **Throws:** R **Pos:** C-42; PH-1   **Ht:** 6'1" **Wt:** 220 **Born:** 5/4/68 **Age:** 35

Year Team	Lg	G	AB	H	2B	3B	HR	(Hm	Rd)	TB	R	RBI	RC	TBB	IBB	SO	HBP	SH	SF	SB	CS	SB%	GDP	Avg	OBP	Slg
1995 Atlanta	NL	7	13	4	1	0	1	(0	1)	8	1	4	2	0	0	2	0	0	0	0	0	-	0	.308	.308	.615
1996 Atlanta	NL	68	156	40	9	1	4	(2	2)	63	19	17	17	8	0	19	1	0	2	0	0	-	6	.256	.293	.404
1997 Atlanta	NL	73	191	41	5	0	6	(4	2)	64	20	18	14	10	0	35	2	1	2	0	1	.00	6	.215	.259	.335
1998 Atlanta	NL	61	149	50	12	0	6	(3	3)	80	18	32	30	15	0	28	2	1	0	1	1	.50	3	.336	.404	.537
1999 Atlanta	NL	104	309	77	17	0	7	(0	7)	115	30	30	32	17	4	40	6	4	3	0	1	.00	9	.249	.299	.372
2000 Atlanta	NL	7	22	4	1	0	0	(0	0)	5	0	3	1	0	0	2	0	0	0	0	0	-	0	.182	.182	.227
2001 Atlanta	NL	5	10	3	0	0	0	(0	0)	3	0	1	0	1	0	2	0	0	0	0	0	-	0	.300	.300	.300
2002 Cleveland	AL	42	117	25	9	0	0	(0	0)	34	6	4	4	5	0	25	1	2	0	0	0	-	6	.214	.252	.291
8 ML YEARS		367	967	244	54	1	24	(9	15)	372	94	108	101	55	4	153	12	8	7	1	3	.25	32	.252	.299	.385

Eduardo Perez

Bats: R **Throws:** R **Pos:** PH-59; RF-29; 1B-10; LF-7; 3B-6; DH-1   **Ht:** 6'4" **Wt:** 215 **Born:** 9/11/69 **Age:** 33

Year Team	Lg	G	AB	H	2B	3B	HR	(Hm	Rd)	TB	R	RBI	RC	TBB	IBB	SO	HBP	SH	SF	SB	CS	SB%	GDP	Avg	OBP	Slg
1993 Anaheim	AL	52	180	45	6	2	4	(2	2)	67	16	30	18	9	0	39	2	0	1	5	4	.56	4	.250	.292	.372
1994 Anaheim	AL	38	129	27	7	0	5	(3	2)	49	10	16	13	12	1	29	0	1	1	3	0	1.00	5	.209	.275	.380
1995 Anaheim	AL	29	71	12	4	1	1	(0	1)	21	9	7	6	12	0	9	2	0	1	0	2	.00	2	.169	.302	.296
1996 Cincinnati	NL	18	36	8	0	0	3	(3	0)	17	8	5	5	5	1	9	0	0	0	0	0	-	2	.222	.317	.472
1997 Cincinnati	NL	106	297	75	18	0	16	(7	9)	141	44	52	45	29	1	76	2	0	2	5	1	.83	6	.253	.321	.475
1998 Cincinnati	NL	84	172	41	4	0	4	(1	3)	57	20	30	19	21	2	45	2	1	2	0	1	.00	2	.238	.325	.331
1999 St Louis	NL	21	32	11	2	0	1	(0	1)	16	6	9	8	7	0	6	0	0	0	0	0	-	0	.344	.462	.500
2000 St Louis	NL	35	91	27	4	0	3	(3	0)	40	9	10	14	5	0	19	3	2	1	1	0	1.00	3	.297	.350	.440
2002 St Louis	NL	96	154	31	9	0	10	(4	6)	70	22	26	18	17	0	36	3	1	2	0	0	-	7	.201	.290	.455
9 ML YEARS		479	1162	277	54	3	47	(20	27)	478	144	185	146	117	5	268	14	5	10	14	8	.64	31	.238	.313	.411

Neifi Perez

Bats: B **Throws:** R **Pos:** SS-139; 2B-5; PH-1; PR-1   **Ht:** 6'0" **Wt:** 175 **Born:** 6/2/73 **Age:** 30

Year Team	Lg	G	AB	H	2B	3B	HR	(Hm	Rd)	TB	R	RBI	RC	TBB	IBB	SO	HBP	SH	SF	SB	CS	SB%	GDP	Avg	OBP	Slg
1996 Colorado	NL	17	45	7	2	0	0	(0	0)	9	4	3	0	0	0	8	0	1	0	2	2	.50	2	.156	.156	.200
1997 Colorado	NL	83	313	91	13	10	5	(3	2)	139	46	31	46	21	4	43	1	5	4	4	3	.57	3	.291	.333	.444
1998 Colorado	NL	162	647	177	25	9	9	(6	3)	247	80	59	77	38	0	70	1	22	4	5	6	.45	8	.274	.313	.382

Year Team	Lg	G	AB	H	2B	3B	HR	(Hm	Rd)	TB	R	RBI	RC	TBB	IBB	SO	HBP	SH	SF	SB	CS	SB%	GDP	Avg	OBP	Slg
1999 Colorado	NL	157	**690**	193	27	**11**	12	(8	4)	278	108	70	87	28	0	54	1	9	4	13	5	.72	4	.280	.307	.403
2000 Colorado	NL	**162**	651	187	39	11	10	(7	3)	278	92	71	85	30	6	63	0	7	11	3	6	.33	9	.287	.314	.427
2001 Col-KC		136	581	162	26	9	8	(7	1)	230	83	59	69	26	1	68	1	11	4	9	6	.60	10	.279	.309	.396
2002 Kansas City	AL	145	554	131	20	4	3	(1	2)	168	65	37	36	20	2	53	0	5	6	8	9	.47	11	.236	.260	.303
2001 Colorado	NL	87	382	114	19	8	7	(7	0)	170	65	47	53	16	1	49	0	4	1	6	2	.75	8	.298	.326	.445
2001 Kansas City	AL	49	199	48	7	1	1	(0	1)	60	18	12	16	10	0	19	1	1	3	3	4	.43	2	.241	.277	.302
7 ML YEARS		862	3481	948	152	54	47	(32	15)	1349	478	330	400	163	13	359	4	60	33	44	37	.54	47	.272	.303	.388

Odalis Perez

Pitches: L **Bats:** L **Pos:** SP-32   **Ht:** 6'0" **Wt:** 150 **Born:** 6/11/77 **Age:** 26

Year Team	Lg	G	GS	CG	GF	IP	BFP	H	R	ER	HR	SH	SF	HB	TBB	IBB	SO	WP	Bk	W	L	Pct	ShO	Sv-Op	Hld	ERC	ERA
1998 Atlanta	NL	10	0	0	0	10.2	45	10	5	5	1	0	4	0	5	0	5	0	0	0	1	.000	0	0-1	5	3.60	4.22
1999 Atlanta	NL	18	17	0	0	93.0	424	100	65	62	12	3	4	1	53	2	82	5	3	4	6	.400	0	0-0	0	5.42	6.00
2001 Atlanta	NL	24	16	0	1	95.1	418	108	55	52	7	3	3	1	39	0	71	2	3	7	8	.467	0	0-0	0	4.79	4.91
2002 Los Angeles	NL	32	32	4	0	222.1	869	182	76	74	21	13	7	4	38	5	155	2	3	15	10	.600	2	0-0	0	**2.31**	3.00
4 ML YEARS		84	65	4	1	421.1	1756	400	201	193	41	19	14	6	134	7	313	9	9	26	25	.510	2	0-1	5	3.52	4.12

Oliver Perez

Pitches: L **Bats:** L **Pos:** SP-15; RP-1   **Ht:** 6'3" **Wt:** 160 **Born:** 8/15/81 **Age:** 21

Year Team	Lg	G	GS	CG	GF	IP	BFP	H	R	ER	HR	SH	SF	HB	TBB	IBB	SO	WP	Bk	W	L	Pct	ShO	Sv-Op	Hld	ERC	ERA
1999 Padres	R	15	2	0	7	28.1	133	28	20	16	1	1	0	1	16	0	37	0	2	1	2	.333	0	3- -	-	4.09	5.08
2000 Idaho Falls	R+	5	5	0	0	24.1	100	24	14	11	1	0	1	1	9	0	27	3	0	3	1	.750	0	0- -	-	3.82	4.07
2001 Fort Wayne	A	19	19	0	0	101.1	415	84	46	39	9	0	5	1	43	0	98	1	2	8	5	.615	0	0- -	-	3.29	3.46
2001 Lk Elsinore	A+	9	9	0	0	53.0	231	45	22	16	4	3	2	1	25	0	62	6	0	2	4	.333	0	0- -	-	3.33	2.72
2002 Lk Elsinore	A+	9	8	0	0	48.2	201	36	13	10	0	1	2	2	24	0	66	0	0	3	3	.500	0	0- -	-	2.56	1.85
2002 Mobile	AA	4	4	0	0	23.0	93	11	3	3	1	2	0	0	16	0	34	4	0	1	0	1.000	0	0- -	-	2.13	1.17
2002 San Diego	NL	16	15	0	0	90.0	387	71	37	35	13	5	3	5	48	1	94	3	0	4	5	.444	0	0-0	0	3.93	3.50

Timo Perez

Bats: L **Throws:** L **Pos:** CF-93; LF-24; PH-20; RF-17; PR-3   **Ht:** 5'9" **Wt:** 167 **Born:** 4/8/75 **Age:** 28

Year Team	Lg	G	AB	H	2B	3B	HR	(Hm	Rd)	TB	R	RBI	RC	TBB	IBB	SO	HBP	SH	SF	SB	CS	SB%	GDP	Avg	OBP	Slg
2002 Norfolk*	AAA	5	21	12	2	1	1	(-	-)	19	5	5	9	2	0	2	0	0	0	3	1	.75	1	.571	.609	.905
2000 New York	NL	24	49	14	4	1	1	(0	1)	23	11	3	8	3	0	5	1	0	1	1	1	.50	0	.286	.333	.469
2001 New York	NL	85	239	59	9	1	5	(2	3)	85	26	22	23	12	0	25	2	6	1	1	6	.14	1	.247	.287	.356
2002 New York	NL	136	444	131	27	6	8	(3	5)	194	52	47	63	23	2	36	2	10	2	10	6	.63	10	.295	.331	.437
3 ML YEARS		245	732	204	40	8	14	(5	9)	302	89	72	94	38	2	66	5	16	4	12	13	.48	11	.279	.317	.413

Tomas Perez

Bats: B **Throws:** R **Pos:** 2B-50; PH-23; 3B-14; SS-13; 1B-3   **Ht:** 5'11" **Wt:** 177 **Born:** 12/29/73 **Age:** 29

Year Team	Lg	G	AB	H	2B	3B	HR	(Hm	Rd)	TB	R	RBI	RC	TBB	IBB	SO	HBP	SH	SF	SB	CS	SB%	GDP	Avg	OBP	Slg
2002 Reading*	AA	2	9	4	0	0	0	(-	-)	4	2	1	2	0	0	1	0	0	0	0	0	-	0	.444	.444	.444
1995 Toronto	AL	41	98	24	3	1	1	(1	0)	32	12	8	7	7	0	18	0	0	1	0	1	.00	6	.245	.292	.327
1996 Toronto	AL	91	295	74	13	4	1	(1	0)	98	24	19	28	25	0	29	1	6	1	1	2	.33	10	.251	.311	.332
1997 Toronto	AL	40	123	24	3	2	0	(0	0)	31	9	9	8	11	0	28	1	3	0	1	1	.50	2	.195	.267	.252
1998 Toronto	AL	6	9	1	0	0	0	(0	0)	1	1	0	0	1	0	3	0	1	0	0	0	-	1	.111	.200	.111
2000 Philadelphia	NL	45	140	31	7	1	1	(0	1)	43	17	13	11	11	2	30	0	1	0	1	1	.50	3	.221	.278	.307
2001 Philadelphia	NL	62	135	41	7	1	3	(2	1)	59	11	19	20	7	1	22	2	1	0	0	1	.00	2	.304	.347	.437
2002 Philadelphia	NL	92	212	53	13	1	5	(2	3)	83	22	20	20	21	6	40	1	2	1	1	0	1.00	5	.250	.319	.392
7 ML YEARS		377	1012	248	46	10	11	(6	5)	347	96	88	94	83	9	170	5	14	3	4	6	.40	29	.245	.305	.343

Yorkis Perez

Pitches: L **Bats:** B **Pos:** RP-23   **Ht:** 6'0" **Wt:** 213 **Born:** 9/30/67 **Age:** 35

Year Team	Lg	G	GS	CG	GF	IP	BFP	H	R	ER	HR	SH	SF	HB	TBB	IBB	SO	WP	Bk	W	L	Pct	ShO	Sv-Op	Hld	ERC	ERA
2002 Rochester*	AAA	28	0	0	4	40.1	181	42	20	17	4	1	2	0	20	1	44	3	0	1	1	.500	0	0- -	-	4.59	3.79
1991 Chicago	NL	3	0	0	0	4.1	16	2	1	1	0	0	2	0	2	0	3	2	0	1	0	1.000	0	0-1	0	1.31	2.08
1994 Florida	NL	44	0	0	11	40.2	167	33	18	16	4	2	0	1	14	3	41	4	1	3	0	1.000	0	0-2	15	2.83	3.54
1995 Florida	NL	69	0	0	11	46.2	205	35	29	27	6	2	1	2	28	4	47	2	0	2	6	.250	0	1-4	16	3.62	5.21
1996 Florida	NL	64	0	0	15	47.2	222	51	28	28	2	2	2	1	31	4	47	2	0	3	4	.429	0	0-2	10	4.91	5.29
1997 New York	NL	9	0	0	1	8.2	45	15	8	8	2	0	1	0	4	0	7	1	0	0	1	.000	0	0-1	1	9.91	8.31
1998 Philadelphia	NL	57	0	0	7	52.0	221	40	23	22	3	2	3	0	25	0	42	7	0	0	2	.000	0	0-0	13	2.80	3.81
1999 Philadelphia	NL	35	0	0	4	32.0	137	29	15	14	4	2	1	0	15	1	26	5	0	3	1	.750	0	0-1	5	3.96	3.94
2000 Houston	NL	33	0	0	9	22.2	111	25	18	13	4	1	2	0	14	2	21	1	0	2	1	.667	0	0-2	3	5.64	5.16
2002 Baltimore	AL	23	0	0	8	27.1	121	21	12	10	4	0	0	0	14	1	25	3	0	0	0	-	0	1-1	1	3.30	3.29
9 ML YEARS		337	0	0	66	282.0	1245	251	152	139	29	11	12	4	147	15	259	27	1	14	15	.483	0	2-14	64	3.84	4.44

Matt Perisho

Pitches: L Bats: L Pos: RP-5   Ht: 6'0" Wt: 205 Born: 6/8/75 Age: 28

		HOW MUCH HE PITCHED					WHAT HE GAVE UP											THE RESULTS					
Year Team*	Lg	G	GS	CG	GF	IP	BFP	H	R	ER	HR	SH	SF	HB	TBB	IBB	SO	WP	Bk	W	L	Pct	ShO	Sv-Op	Hld	ERC	ERA
2002 Toledo*	AAA	51	2	0	8	66.0	279	62	20	18	4	1	5	2	19	4	44	3	0	4	4	.500	0	1- -	-	3.03	2.45
1997 Anaheim	AL	11	8	0	2	45.0	217	59	34	30	6	2	2	3	28	0	35	5	2	0	2	.000	0	0-0	0	7.56	6.00
1998 Texas	AL	2	2	0	0	5.0	40	15	17	15	2	0	0	2	8	0	2	0	0	0	2	.000	0	0-0	0	30.09	27.00
1999 Texas	AL	4	1	0	3	10.1	40	8	3	3	0	0	0	2	2	1	17	1	0	0	0	-	0	0-0	0	1.55	2.61
2000 Texas	AL	34	13	0	4	105.0	515	136	99	86	20	6	5	6	67	3	74	4	0	2	7	.222	0	0-1	0	7.79	7.37
2001 Detroit	AL	30	4	0	5	39.1	186	54	29	25	5	2	1	4	14	1	19	0	0	2	3	.400	0	0-2	4	6.71	5.72
2002 Detroit	AL	5	0	0	1	10.1	50	16	11	10	2	0	1	0	6	0	3	0	0	0	0	-	0	0-0	0	9.45	8.71
6 ML YEARS		86	28	0	15	215.0	1048	288	193	169	35	10	9	15	125	5	150	10	2	4	14	.222	0	0-3	4	7.69	7.07

Chan Perry

Bats: R Throws: R Pos: 1B-5   Ht: 6'2" Wt: 200 Born: 9/13/72 Age: 30

		BATTING																		BASERUNNING				AVERAGES		
Year Team	Lg	G	AB	H	2B	3B	HR	(Hm	Rd)	TB	R	RBI	RC	TBB	IBB	SO	HBP	SH	SF	SB	CS	SB%	GDP	Avg	OBP	Slg
1994 Burlington	R+	52	185	58	16	1	5	(-	-)	91	28	32	32	18	0	28	1	0	4	6	0	1.00	9	.314	.370	.492
1995 Columbus	A	113	411	117	30	4	9	(-	-)	182	64	50	69	53	1	49	2	4	7	7	2	.78	6	.285	.366	.443
1996 Kinston	A+	96	358	104	27	1	10	(-	-)	163	44	62	56	36	3	33	2	3	3	2	3	.40	9	.291	.356	.455
1997 Akron	AA	119	476	150	34	2	20	(-	-)	248	74	96	82	28	0	61	5	1	6	3	3	.50	14	.315	.355	.521
1998 Buffalo	AAA	13	49	11	4	0	0	(-	-)	15	8	3	6	6	0	10	2	0	0	1	0	1.00	0	.224	.333	.306
1998 Akron	AA	54	203	57	17	2	5	(-	-)	93	36	27	33	23	1	43	0	0	1	3	2	.60	2	.281	.352	.458
1999 Buffalo	AAA	79	273	77	17	0	10	(-	-)	124	44	59	40	19	0	34	3	3	7	5	1	.83	9	.282	.328	.454
1999 Akron	AA	37	154	43	14	0	7	(-	-)	78	24	30	25	11	0	27	1	0	1	1	0	1.00	5	.279	.329	.506
2000 Buffalo	AAA	92	362	107	18	1	10	(-	-)	157	48	65	50	21	0	55	3	0	4	1	2	.33	9	.296	.336	.434
2001 Richmond	AAA	98	350	96	15	3	8	(-	-)	141	38	39	39	19	2	60	3	1	1	1	6	.14	13	.274	.316	.403
2002 Wichita	AA	105	399	126	20	2	14	(-	-)	192	59	73	65	29	3	44	1	0	6	6	5	.55	11	.316	.359	.481
2000 Cleveland	AL	13	14	1	0	0	0	(0	0)	1	1	0	0	0	0	5	0	0	0	0	0	-	1	.071	.071	.071
2002 Kansas City	AL	5	11	1	0	0	0	(0	0)	1	0	3	0	0	0	1	0	0	0	0	0	-	1	.091	.091	.091
2 ML YEARS		18	25	2	0	0	0	(0	0)	2	1	3	0	0	0	6	0	0	0	0	0	-	2	.080	.080	.080

Herbert Perry

Bats: R Throws: R Pos: 3B-112; PH-14; 1B-12; DH-2; LF-1   Ht: 6'2" Wt: 225 Born: 9/15/69 Age: 33

		BATTING																		BASERUNNING				AVERAGES		
Year Team	Lg	G	AB	H	2B	3B	HR	(Hm	Rd)	TB	R	RBI	RC	TBB	IBB	SO	HBP	SH	SF	SB	CS	SB%	GDP	Avg	OBP	Slg
1994 Cleveland	AL	4	9	1	0	0	0	(0	0)	1	1	1	1	3	1	1	1	0	1	0	0	-	0	.111	.357	.111
1995 Cleveland	AL	52	162	51	13	1	3	(3	0)	75	23	23	26	13	0	28	4	3	2	1	3	.25	5	.315	.376	.463
1996 Cleveland	AL	7	12	1	1	0	0	(0	0)	2	1	0	0	1	0	2	0	0	0	1	0	1.00	0	.083	.154	.167
1999 Tampa Bay	AL	66	209	53	10	1	6	(5	1)	83	29	32	25	16	1	42	10	0	4	0	0	-	13	.254	.331	.397
2000 TB-CWS	AL	116	411	124	30	1	12	(7	5)	192	71	62	64	24	1	75	9	2	4	4	1	.80	13	.302	.350	.467
2001 Chicago	AL	92	285	73	21	1	7	(5	2)	117	38	32	35	23	1	55	7	0	1	2	2	.50	11	.256	.326	.411
2002 Texas	AL	132	450	124	24	1	22	(9	13)	216	64	77	64	34	1	66	6	4	2	4	2	.67	17	.276	.333	.480
2000 Tampa Bay	AL	7	28	6	1	0	0	(0	0)	7	2	1	2	2	0	7	0	0	0	0	0	-	0	.214	.267	.250
2000 Chicago	AL	109	383	118	29	1	12	(7	5)	185	69	61	62	22	1	68	9	2	4	4	1	.80	13	.308	.356	.483
7 ML YEARS		469	1538	427	99	5	50	(29	21)	686	227	227	215	114	5	269	37	9	14	12	8	.60	59	.278	.339	.446

Robert Person

Pitches: R Bats: R Pos: SP-16   Ht: 6'0" Wt: 193 Born: 10/6/69 Age: 33

		HOW MUCH HE PITCHED						WHAT HE GAVE UP												THE RESULTS					
Year Team	Lg	G	GS	CG	GF	IP	BFP	H	R	ER	HR	SH	SF	HB	TBB	IBB	SO	WP	Bk	W	L	Pct	ShO	Sv-Op	Hld	ERC	ERA
2002 Scrtn/WlksBr*	AAA	2	2	0	0	8.1	32	8	4	4	2	1	0	0	1	0	7	1	0	0	1	.000	0	0- -	-	3.81	4.32
1995 New York	NL	3	1	0	1	12.0	44	5	1	1	1	0	0	0	2	0	10	0	1	1	0	1.000	0	0-0	0	0.82	0.75
1996 New York	NL	27	13	0	1	89.2	390	86	50	45	16	1	4	2	35	3	76	3	0	4	5	.444	0	0-0	1	4.32	4.52
1997 Toronto	AL	23	22	0	0	128.1	566	125	86	80	19	4	6	5	60	2	99	7	0	5	10	.333	0	0-0	0	4.65	5.61
1998 Toronto	AL	27	0	0	14	38.1	184	45	31	30	9	2	5	2	22	1	31	0	0	3	1	.750	0	6-8	6	6.94	7.04
1999 Tor-Phi		42	22	0	8	148.0	659	139	84	77	24	7	6	6	85	2	139	5	1	10	7	.588	0	2-2	1	5.04	4.68
2000 Philadelphia	NL	28	28	1	0	173.1	743	144	73	70	13	4	9	6	95	1	164	10	1	9	7	.563	1	0-0	0	3.70	3.63
2001 Philadelphia	NL	33	33	3	0	208.1	867	179	103	97	34	8	6	8	80	3	183	10	1	15	7	.682	1	0-0	0	3.84	4.19
2002 Philadelphia	NL	16	16	0	0	87.2	388	79	58	53	13	2	2	5	51	0	61	2	0	4	5	.444	0	0-0	0	4.85	5.44
1999 Toronto	AL	11	0	0	7	11.0	60	9	12	12	1	0	2	4	15	1	12	2	0	0	2	.000	0	2-2	1	8.06	9.82
1999 Philadelphia	NL	31	22	0	1	137.0	599	130	72	65	23	7	4	2	70	1	127	3	1	10	5	.667	0	0-0	0	4.78	4.27
8 ML YEARS		199	135	4	23	885.2	3841	802	486	453	129	28	38	34	430	12	763	37	3	51	42	.548	2	8-10	2	4.34	4.60

Ben Petrick

Bats: R Throws: R Pos: LF-15; C-14; PH-9; CF-2   Ht: 6'0" Wt: 200 Born: 4/7/77 Age: 26

		BATTING																		BASERUNNING				AVERAGES		
Year Team	Lg	G	AB	H	2B	3B	HR	(Hm	Rd)	TB	R	RBI	RC	TBB	IBB	SO	HBP	SH	SF	SB	CS	SB%	GDP	Avg	OBP	Slg
2002 Co Springs*	AAA	79	265	85	18	4	16	(-	-)	159	51	54	61	40	1	77	1	1	4	10	6	.63	4	.321	.406	.600
1999 Colorado	NL	19	62	20	3	0	4	(4	0)	35	13	12	14	10	0	13	0	0	0	1	0	1.00	1	.323	.417	.565
2000 Colorado	NL	52	146	47	10	1	3	(2	1)	68	32	20	28	20	2	33	2	1	4	1	2	.33	1	.322	.401	.466
2001 Colorado	NL	85	244	58	15	3	11	(7	4)	112	41	39	36	31	3	67	3	1	3	3	3	.50	5	.238	.327	.459
2002 Colorado	NL	38	95	20	3	1	5	(4	1)	40	10	11	6	9	0	33	1	0	1	0	1	.00	1	.211	.283	.421
4 ML YEARS		194	547	145	31	5	23	(17	6)	255	96	82	84	70	5	146	6	2	8	5	6	.45	8	.265	.350	.466

179

Andy Pettitte

Pitches: L Bats: L Pos: SP-22   Ht: 6'5" Wt: 225 Born: 6/15/72 Age: 31

Year Team	Lg	G	GS	CG	GF	IP	BFP	H	R	ER	HR	SH	SF	HB	TBB	IBB	SO	WP	Bk	W	L	Pct	ShO	Sv-Op	Hld	ERC	ERA
2002 Tampa*	A+	2	2	0	0	5.0	18	3	0	0	0	0	0	0	0	0	4	0	0	0	0	-	0	0--	-	0.75	0.00
2002 Norwich*	AA	1	1	0	0	6.1	21	2	1	1	0	0	0	0	0	0	5	0	0	0	0	-	0	0--	-	0.23	1.42
1995 New York	AL	31	26	3	1	175.0	745	183	86	81	15	4	5	1	63	3	114	8	1	12	9	.571	0	0-0	0	4.13	4.17
1996 New York	AL	35	34	2	1	221.0	929	229	105	95	23	7	3	3	72	2	162	6	1	21	8	.724	0	0-0	0	4.14	3.87
1997 New York	AL	35	35	4	0	240.1	986	233	86	77	7	6	2	3	65	0	166	7	0	18	7	.720	1	0-0	0	3.05	2.88
1998 New York	AL	33	32	5	0	216.1	932	226	110	102	20	6	7	6	87	1	146	5	0	16	11	.593	0	0-0	0	4.46	4.24
1999 New York	AL	31	31	0	0	191.2	851	216	105	100	20	6	6	3	89	3	121	3	1	14	11	.560	0	0-0	0	5.22	4.70
2000 New York	AL	32	32	3	0	204.2	903	219	111	99	17	7	4	4	80	4	125	2	3	19	9	.679	1	0-0	0	4.32	4.35
2001 New York	AL	31	31	2	0	200.2	858	224	103	89	14	8	7	6	41	3	164	2	2	15	10	.600	0	0-0	0	3.82	3.99
2002 New York	AL	22	22	3	0	134.2	570	144	58	49	6	3	2	4	32	2	97	2	1	13	5	.722	1	0-0	0	3.55	3.27
8 ML YEARS		250	243	22	2	1584.1	6774	1674	764	692	122	47	36	30	529	18	1095	35	9	128	70	.646	3	0-0	0	4.07	3.93

Josh Phelps

Bats: R Throws: R Pos: DH-70; 1B-2; PH-2   Ht: 6'3" Wt: 220 Born: 5/12/78 Age: 25

Year Team	Lg	G	AB	H	2B	3B	HR	(Hm	Rd)	TB	R	RBI	RC	TBB	IBB	SO	HBP	SH	SF	SB	CS	SB%	GDP	Avg	OBP	Slg
2002 Syracuse*	AAA	70	257	75	20	1	24	(-	-)	169	50	64	59	32	6	83	5	0	1	0	0	-	6	.292	.380	.658
2000 Toronto	AL	1	1	0	0	0	0	(0	0)	0	0	0	0	0	0	1	0	0	0	0	0	-	0	.000	.000	.000
2001 Toronto	AL	8	12	0	0	0	0	(0	0)	0	3	1	0	2	0	5	0	0	0	1	0	1.00	1	.000	.143	.000
2002 Toronto	AL	74	265	82	20	1	15	(6	9)	149	41	58	53	19	0	82	3	0	0	0	0	-	7	.309	.362	.562
3 ML YEARS		83	278	82	20	1	15	(6	9)	149	44	59	53	21	0	88	3	0	0	1	0	1.00	8	.295	.351	.536

Tommy Phelps

Pitches: L Bats: L Pos: SP; RP   Ht: 6'3" Wt: 192 Born: 3/4/74 Age: 29

Year Team	Lg	G	GS	CG	GF	IP	BFP	H	R	ER	HR	SH	SF	HB	TBB	IBB	SO	WP	Bk	W	L	Pct	ShO	Sv-Op	Hld	ERC	ERA
1993 Burlington	A	8	8	0	0	41.0	173	36	18	17	4	1	1	1	13	0	33	2	0	2	4	.333	0	0--	-	3.11	3.73
1993 Jamestown	A-	16	15	1	0	92.1	416	102	62	47	4	4	3	5	37	1	74	7	1	3	8	.273	0	0--	-	4.39	4.58
1994 Burlington	A	23	23	1	0	118.1	534	143	91	73	9	7	7	5	48	1	82	7	0	8	8	.500	1	0--	-	5.33	5.55
1995 W Palm Bch	A+	2	2	0	0	5.0	33	10	10	9	0	0	0	0	11	0	5	2	0	0	2	.000	0	0--	-	19.29	16.20
1995 Albany	A	24	24	1	0	135.1	597	142	76	50	6	0	4	5	45	0	119	5	1	10	9	.526	0	0--	-	3.74	3.33
1996 W Palm Bch	A+	18	18	1	0	112.0	468	105	42	36	5	4	1	2	35	0	71	8	0	10	2	.833	1	0--	-	3.10	2.89
1996 Harrisburg	AA	8	8	2	0	47.1	195	43	16	13	3	2	0	1	19	2	23	0	0	2	2	.500	2	0--	-	3.46	2.47
1997 Harrisburg	AA	18	18	0	0	101.1	462	115	68	53	14	8	5	5	39	1	86	3	1	10	6	.625	0	0--	-	5.15	4.71
1998 Jupiter	A+	7	7	0	0	41.0	181	42	21	20	3	0	2	2	15	0	21	1	0	2	2	.500	0	0--	-	4.00	4.39
1998 Harrisburg	AA	12	10	0	0	59.2	247	57	29	24	5	4	3	0	26	0	26	2	0	5	4	.556	0	0--	-	4.02	3.62
1999 Harrisburg	AA	13	13	1	0	64.2	306	76	53	41	13	3	6	7	26	0	36	2	0	3	6	.333	0	0--	-	6.14	5.71
2000 Jacksonville	AA	38	11	0	7	102.0	435	111	59	56	17	1	0	7	26	2	62	1	0	6	6	.500	0	0--	-	4.78	4.94
2001 Toledo	AAA	29	0	0	8	59.2	271	74	30	24	4	0	1	3	19	3	53	1	0	3	2	.600	0	1--	-	4.95	3.62
2001 Erie	AA	15	2	0	5	32.2	139	33	14	13	1	3	2	3	8	2	31	2	0	1	1	.500	0	2--	-	3.31	3.58
2002 Calgary	AAA	51	0	0	10	74.1	314	76	27	26	8	4	1	2	21	3	62	3	0	4	2	.667	0	2--	-	3.85	3.15

Travis Phelps

Pitches: R Bats: R Pos: RP-26   Ht: 6'2" Wt: 166 Born: 7/25/77 Age: 25

Year Team	Lg	G	GS	CG	GF	IP	BFP	H	R	ER	HR	SH	SF	HB	TBB	IBB	SO	WP	Bk	W	L	Pct	ShO	Sv-Op	Hld	ERC	ERA
1997 Princeton	R+	14	13	1	0	62.2	279	73	42	34	4	3	1	2	23	0	60	4	1	4	3	.571	0	0--	-	4.75	4.88
1998 Chrlstn - SC	A	18	18	0	0	91.0	401	100	54	49	4	1	1	3	35	0	96	7	3	5	8	.385	0	0--	-	4.30	4.85
1999 St.Pete	A+	24	23	1	0	133.2	574	148	70	63	6	4	4	11	39	0	101	2	0	10	8	.556	1	0--	-	4.27	4.24
2000 Orlando	AA	21	21	2	0	108.0	448	85	44	36	5	1	1	13	46	0	106	5	0	7	8	.467	0	0--	-	3.20	3.00
2000 Durham	AAA	6	6	0	0	29.2	131	29	17	16	6	2	0	0	16	0	21	0	0	3	1	.750	0	0--	-	5.28	4.85
2001 Durham	AAA	9	0	0	1	15.2	57	11	0	0	1	0	1	1	1	0	12	1	0	2	0	1.000	0	0--	-	1.32	0.00
2002 Durham	AAA	27	0	0	17	31.0	134	29	15	15	2	1	2	0	14	1	34	2	0	3	2	.600	0	8--	-	3.59	4.35
2001 Tampa Bay	AL	49	0	0	15	62.0	268	53	30	24	6	2	4	3	24	1	54	2	1	2	2	.500	0	5-6	13	3.27	3.48
2002 Tampa Bay	AL	26	0	0	9	37.2	169	30	20	20	7	0	2	5	27	0	36	6	2	1	2	.333	0	0-0	3	5.45	4.78
2 ML YEARS		75	0	0	24	99.2	437	83	50	44	13	2	6	8	51	1	90	8	3	3	4	.429	0	5-6	16	4.05	3.97

Brandon Phillips

Bats: R Throws: R Pos: 2B-11   Ht: 5'11" Wt: 185 Born: 6/28/81 Age: 22

Year Team	Lg	G	AB	H	2B	3B	HR	(Hm	Rd)	TB	R	RBI	RC	TBB	IBB	SO	HBP	SH	SF	SB	CS	SB%	GDP	Avg	OBP	Slg
1999 Expos	R	47	169	49	11	3	1	(-	-)	69	23	21	25	15	0	35	3	0	0	12	3	.80	6	.290	.358	.408
2000 Cape Fear	A	126	484	117	17	8	11	(-	-)	183	74	72	56	38	3	97	9	0	5	23	8	.74	11	.242	.306	.378
2001 Jupiter	A+	55	194	55	12	2	4	(-	-)	83	36	23	39	38	0	45	6	0	1	17	3	.85	3	.284	.414	.428
2001 Harrisburg	AA	67	265	79	19	0	7	(-	-)	119	35	36	37	12	0	42	4	1	1	13	6	.68	9	.298	.337	.449
2002 Harrisburg	AA	60	245	80	18	2	9	(-	-)	124	40	35	44	16	2	33	5	1	0	6	3	.67	7	.327	.380	.506
2002 Ottawa	AAA	10	35	9	4	0	1	(-	-)	16	1	5	5	2	0	6	0	0	0	0	0	-	0	.257	.297	.457
2002 Buffalo	AAA	55	223	63	14	0	8	(-	-)	101	30	27	32	14	0	39	1	4	5	8	2	.80	6	.283	.321	.453
2002 Cleveland	AL	11	31	8	3	1	0	(0	0)	13	5	4	5	3	0	6	1	1	0	0	0	-	0	.258	.343	.419

Jason Phillips

Bats: R **Throws:** R **Pos:** C-7; PH-6 **Ht:** 6'1" **Wt:** 177 **Born:** 9/27/76 **Age:** 26

Year Team	Lg	G	AB	H	2B	3B	HR	(Hm	Rd)	TB	R	RBI	RC	TBB	IBB	SO	HBP	SH	SF	SB	CS	SB%	GDP	Avg	OBP	Slg
1997 Pittsfield	A-	48	155	32	9	0	2	(-	-)	47	15	17	14	13	0	24	4	1	2	4	0	1.00	2	.206	.282	.303
1998 Capital City	A	69	251	68	15	1	5	(-	-)	100	36	37	35	23	1	35	5	1	1	5	2	.71	3	.271	.343	.398
1998 St.Lucie	A+	8	28	13	2	0	0	(-	-)	15	4	2	7	2	0	1	0	1	0	0	0	-	1	.464	.500	.536
1999 St.Lucie	A+	81	283	73	12	1	9	(-	-)	114	36	48	36	23	0	28	8	0	4	0	1	.00	10	.258	.327	.403
1999 Binghamton	AA	39	141	32	5	0	7	(-	-)	58	13	23	17	13	0	20	3	2	1	0	0	-	4	.227	.304	.411
2000 St.Lucie	A+	80	297	82	21	0	6	(-	-)	121	53	41	39	23	2	19	8	1	1	1	1	.50	12	.276	.343	.407
2000 Binghamton	AA	27	98	38	4	0	0	(-	-)	42	16	13	18	7	0	9	2	0	1	0	0	-	3	.388	.435	.429
2001 Binghamton	AA	93	317	93	21	0	11	(-	-)	147	42	55	51	31	3	25	5	1	3	0	1	.00	9	.293	.362	.464
2001 Norfolk	AAA	19	66	20	2	0	2	(-	-)	28	8	14	10	7	0	8	0	0	1	0	0	-	3	.303	.365	.424
2002 Norfolk	AAA	88	323	91	22	1	13	(-	-)	154	35	65	49	24	3	29	2	0	9	1	0	1.00	10	.282	.327	.477
2001 New York	NL	6	7	1	1	0	0	(0	0)	2	2	0	0	0	0	1	0	0	0	0	0	-	0	.143	.143	.286
2002 New York	NL	11	19	7	0	0	1	(0	1)	10	4	3	3	1	0	1	1	0	1	0	0	-	1	.368	.409	.526
2 ML YEARS		17	26	8	1	0	1	(0	1)	12	6	3	3	1	0	2	1	0	1	0	0	-	1	.308	.345	.462

Jason C Phillips

Pitches: R **Bats:** R **Pos:** SP-6; RP-2 **Ht:** 6'6" **Wt:** 225 **Born:** 3/22/74 **Age:** 29

Year Team	Lg	G	GS	CG	GF	IP	BFP	H	R	ER	HR	SH	SF	HB	TBB	IBB	SO	WP	Bk	W	L	Pct	ShO	Sv-Op	Hld	ERC	ERA
1992 Pirates	R	4	4	0	0	17.0	88	21	21	16	0	1	1	0	13	0	10	4	4	1	2	.333	0	0--	-	5.73	8.47
1993 Welland	A-	14	14	0	0	71.1	323	60	44	28	2	1	2	9	36	66	15	4	4	4	6	.400	0	0--	-	1.91	3.53
1994 Augusta	A	23	23	1	0	108.1	531	118	97	81	4	3	4	12	88	1	108	21	3	6	12	.333	0	0--	-	6.16	6.73
1995 Augusta	A	30	6	0	3	80.0	354	76	46	32	2	2	2	0	53	1	65	10	0	4	3	.571	0	0--	-	4.31	3.60
1996 Augusta	A	14	14	1	0	89.2	366	79	35	24	3	2	3	6	29	1	75	9	1	5	4	.556	1	0--	-	3.02	2.41
1996 Lynchburg	A+	13	13	1	0	73.2	343	82	47	37	3	2	2	5	35	0	63	6	1	5	6	.455	1	0--	-	4.71	4.52
1997 Lynchburg	A+	23	23	2	0	138.2	577	129	66	58	10	4	2	6	35	0	140	9	1	11	6	.647	1	0--	-	3.10	3.76
1997 Carolina	AA	4	4	2	0	31.0	127	21	8	8	1	1	2	4	9	0	22	2	0	1	2	.333	1	0--	-	2.02	2.32
1998 Carolina	AA	25	25	1	0	151.0	663	161	89	79	14	8	1	9	52	3	114	10	3	7	13	.350	1	0--	-	4.36	4.71
1998 Nashville	AAA	5	5	0	0	31.1	136	38	10	9	3	3	0	1	12	0	21	3	0	2	0	1.000	0	0--	-	5.59	2.59
1999 Nashville	AAA	1	1	0	0	3.0	19	6	6	5	0	0	0	0	5	1	5	1	0	0	0	-	0	0--	-	14.97	15.00
2000 Nashville	AAA	6	6	0	0	30.2	138	30	20	16	4	2	0	3	18	0	18	0	0	2	4	.333	0	0--	-	5.41	4.70
2001 Altoona	AA	6	1	0	2	9.0	48	18	11	10	0	0	0	1	4	0	4	2	0	1	0	.000	0	0--	-	10.42	10.00
2001 Akron	AA	10	3	0	1	24.0	102	18	11	11	2	0	2	1	15	0	20	2	0	2	1	.667	0	0--	-	3.68	4.13
2001 Buffalo	AAA	8	6	1	1	35.0	138	27	15	13	3	0	1	2	8	0	25	0	0	2	2	.500	0	0--	-	2.41	3.34
2002 Buffalo	AAA	16	16	1	0	98.1	392	88	37	37	8	4	1	7	17	0	71	0	0	7	4	.636	0	0--	-	2.87	3.39
1999 Pittsburgh	NL	6	0	0	0	7.0	37	11	9	9	2	2	1	0	6	1	7	2	0	0	0	-	0	0-0	0	11.24	11.57
2002 Cleveland	AL	8	6	0	0	41.2	185	41	24	23	7	1	2	4	20	0	23	0	1	1	3	.250	0	0-0	0	5.23	4.97
2 ML YEARS		14	6	0	0	48.2	222	52	33	32	9	3	3	4	26	1	30	2	1	1	3	.250	0	0-0	0	6.02	5.92

Adam Piatt

Bats: R **Throws:** R **Pos:** LF-40; RF-12; PH-11; PR-3; 1B-1 **Ht:** 6'2" **Wt:** 205 **Born:** 2/8/76 **Age:** 27

Year Team	Lg	G	AB	H	2B	3B	HR	(Hm	Rd)	TB	R	RBI	RC	TBB	IBB	SO	HBP	SH	SF	SB	CS	SB%	GDP	Avg	OBP	Slg
2002 Sacramento*	AAA	62	234	69	15	0	8	(-	-)	108	46	44	39	35	0	30	1	0	3	4	3	.57	12	.295	.385	.462
2000 Oakland	AL	60	157	47	5	5	5	(3	2)	77	24	23	30	23	0	44	1	1	0	0	1	.00	1	.299	.392	.490
2001 Oakland	AL	36	95	20	5	1	0	(0	0)	27	9	6	7	13	0	26	0	1	2	0	0	-	5	.211	.300	.284
2002 Oakland	AL	55	137	32	8	0	5	(3	2)	55	18	18	16	12	0	33	2	0	1	2	1	.67	1	.234	.303	.401
3 ML YEARS		151	389	99	18	6	10	(6	4)	159	51	47	53	48	0	103	3	2	3	2	2	.50	7	.254	.339	.409

Mike Piazza

Bats: R **Throws:** R **Pos:** C-121; PH-10; DH-6 **Ht:** 6'3" **Wt:** 215 **Born:** 9/4/68 **Age:** 34

Year Team	Lg	G	AB	H	2B	3B	HR	(Hm	Rd)	TB	R	RBI	RC	TBB	IBB	SO	HBP	SH	SF	SB	CS	SB%	GDP	Avg	OBP	Slg
1992 Los Angeles	NL	21	69	16	3	0	1	(1	0)	22	5	7	6	4	0	12	1	0	0	0	0	-	1	.232	.284	.319
1993 Los Angeles	NL	149	547	174	24	2	35	(21	14)	307	81	112	107	46	6	86	3	0	6	3	4	.43	10	.318	.370	.561
1994 Los Angeles	NL	107	405	129	18	0	24	(13	11)	219	64	92	74	33	10	65	1	0	2	1	3	.25	11	.319	.370	.541
1995 Los Angeles	NL	112	434	150	17	0	32	(9	23)	263	82	93	96	39	10	80	1	0	1	1	0	1.00	10	.346	.400	.606
1996 Los Angeles	NL	148	547	184	16	0	36	(14	22)	308	87	105	117	81	21	93	1	0	2	0	3	.00	21	.336	.422	.563
1997 Los Angeles	NL	152	556	201	32	1	40	(22	18)	355	104	124	137	69	11	77	3	0	5	5	1	.83	19	.362	.431	.638
1998 LA-Fla-NYM	NL	151	561	184	38	1	32	(15	17)	320	88	111	116	58	14	80	2	0	5	1	0	1.00	15	.328	.390	.570
1999 New York	NL	141	534	162	25	0	40	(18	22)	307	100	124	99	51	11	70	1	0	7	2	2	.50	27	.303	.361	.575
2000 New York	NL	136	482	156	26	0	38	(17	21)	296	90	113	107	58	10	69	3	0	4	4	2	.67	15	.324	.398	.614
2001 New York	NL	141	503	151	29	0	36	(14	22)	288	81	94	100	67	19	87	2	0	1	0	2	.00	20	.300	.384	.573
2002 New York	NL	135	478	134	23	2	33	(12	21)	260	69	98	84	57	9	82	3	0	3	0	3	.00	15	.280	.359	.544
1998 Los Angeles	NL	37	149	42	5	0	9	(5	4)	74	20	30	23	11	4	27	0	0	1	0	0	-	3	.282	.329	.497
1998 Florida	NL	5	18	5	0	1	0	(0	0)	7	1	5	2	0	0	0	0	0	0	0	0	-	0	.278	.263	.389
1998 New York	NL	109	394	137	33	0	23	(10	13)	239	67	76	91	47	10	53	2	0	3	1	0	1.00	12	.348	.417	.607
11 ML YEARS		1393	5116	1641	251	6	347	(158	189)	2945	851	1073	1043	563	121	801	21	0	34	17	20	.46	175	.321	.388	.576

Hipolito Pichardo

Pitches: R **Bats:** R **Pos:** RP-1 **Ht:** 6'1" **Wt:** 195 **Born:** 8/22/69 **Age:** 33

Year Team	Lg	G	GS	CG	GF	IP	BFP	H	R	ER	HR	SH	SF	HB	TBB	IBB	SO	WP	Bk	W	L	Pct	ShO	Sv-Op	Hld	ERC	ERA
2002 New Orleans*	AAA	5	1	0	3	6.2	24	6	0	0	0	0	0	0	1	0	4	0	0	0	0	-	0	0--	-	2.30	0.00
1992 Kansas City	AL	31	24	1	0	143.2	615	148	71	63	9	4	5	3	49	1	59	3	1	9	6	.600	1	0-0	0	3.84	3.95
1993 Kansas City	AL	30	25	2	2	165.0	720	183	85	74	10	3	8	6	53	2	70	5	3	7	8	.467	0	0-0	1	4.22	4.04
1994 Kansas City	AL	45	0	0	19	67.2	303	82	42	37	4	4	2	7	24	5	36	3	0	5	3	.625	0	3-5	6	5.19	4.92
1995 Kansas City	AL	44	0	0	16	64.0	287	66	34	31	4	3	1	4	30	7	43	4	1	8	4	.667	0	1-2	7	4.27	4.36

Year Team	Lg	G	GS	CG	GF	IP	BFP	H	R	ER	HR	SH	SF	HB	TBB	IBB	SO	WP	Bk	W	L	Pct	ShO	Sv-Op	Hld	ERC	ERA
1996 Kansas City	AL	57	0	0	28	68.0	294	74	41	41	5	3	2	2	26	5	43	4	0	3	5	.375	0	3-5	15	4.39	5.43
1997 Kansas City	AL	47	0	0	26	49.0	215	51	24	23	7	2	0	1	24	8	34	2	1	3	5	.375	0	11-13	4	4.87	4.22
1998 Kansas City	AL	27	18	0	2	112.1	503	126	73	64	11	3	3	4	43	2	55	2	0	7	8	.467	0	1-1	2	4.75	5.13
2000 Boston	AL	38	1	0	5	65.0	275	63	29	25	1	2	3	3	26	2	37	2	0	6	3	.667	0	1-2	5	3.51	3.46
2001 Boston	AL	30	0	0	5	34.2	159	42	23	19	3	2	2	5	10	3	17	3	0	2	1	.667	0	0-3	2	5.11	4.93
2002 Houston	NL	1	0	0	0	0.1	6	3	3	3	0	0	0	0	2	1	0	1	0	0	1	.000	0	0-0	0	87.43	81.00
10 ML YEARS		350	68	3	103	769.2	3377	838	425	380	54	26	25	35	287	36	394	29	6	50	44	.532	1	20-31	41	4.37	4.44

Kevin Pickford

Pitches: L Bats: L Pos: RP-12; SP-4   **Ht: 6'4" Wt: 200 Born: 3/12/75 Age: 28**

Year Team	Lg	G	GS	CG	GF	IP	BFP	H	R	ER	HR	SH	SF	HB	TBB	IBB	SO	WP	Bk	W	L	Pct	ShO	Sv-Op	Hld	ERC	ERA
1993 Pirates	R	9	7	0	1	34.1	151	24	19	13	1	2		3	20	0	28	0	2	0	4	.000	0	0--	-	2.88	3.41
1994 Augusta	A	2	2	0	0	8.2	37	9	6	4	1	0	0	0	5	0	7	1	0	0	1	.000	0	0--	-	5.45	4.15
1994 Welland	A-	15	15	1	0	84.2	377	86	52	46	7	1	6	5	36	0	52	2	2	5	8	.385	1	0--	-	4.31	4.89
1995 Augusta	A	16	16	0	0	85.2	354	85	28	19	5	2	1	5	16	1	59	2	0	7	3	.700	0	0--	-	3.16	2.00
1995 Lynchburg	A+	4	4	0	0	27.1	110	31	15	15	5	0	1	0	0	0	15	2	1	0	3	.000	0	0--	-	3.79	4.94
1996 Lynchburg	A+	28	28	4	0	172.1	749	195	99	78	15	7	6	11	25	0	100	4	1	11	11	.500	1	0--	-	3.86	4.07
1997 Carolina	AA	21	1	0	0	29.1	152	48	29	24	3	1	1	3	15	3	24	0	0	1	2	.333	0	1--	-	8.68	7.36
1997 Lynchburg	A+	14	10	0	1	73.1	296	72	31	29	3	4	1	2	11	0	50	2	0	3	4	.429	0	0--	-	2.79	3.56
1998 Carolina	AA	13	8	1	2	57.2	228	48	26	25	7	1	0	3	15	1	43	2	0	5	1	.833	0	1--	-	3.06	3.90
1998 Nashville	AAA	13	12	0	0	80.0	336	84	33	31	7	4	2	0	20	2	59	4	0	6	1	.857	0	0--	-	3.65	3.49
2000 Altoona	AA	10	4	0	1	21.2	115	38	29	24	2	3	3	2	14	0	9	1	1	0	5	.000	0	0--	-	10.42	9.97
2000 Lynchburg	A+	10	6	0	1	30.2	153	42	30	21	3	1	2	8	14	0	13	1	0	2	3	.333	0	0--	-	7.61	6.16
2001 SonomaCnty	IND	9	9	0	0	38.0	190	51	45	35	2	2	4	5	23	1	19	1	1	3	5	.375	0	0--	-	7.02	8.29
2002 Portland	AAA	20	12	1	2	69.2	313	79	50	46	5	2	5	3	31	1	40	3	0	4	7	.364	0	1--	-	4.99	5.94
2002 San Diego	NL	16	4	0	3	30.0	144	37	23	20	3	2	1	3	20	1	18	1	0	0	2	.000	0	0-0	0	7.06	6.00

Juan Pierre

Bats: L Throws: L Pos: CF-149; PH-9; PR-1   **Ht: 6'0" Wt: 180 Born: 8/14/77 Age: 25**

Year Team	Lg	G	AB	H	2B	3B	HR	(Hm	Rd)	TB	R	RBI	RC	TBB	IBB	SO	HBP	SH	SF	SB	CS	SB%	GDP	Avg	OBP	Slg
2000 Colorado	NL	51	200	62	2	0	0	(0	0)	64	26	20	23	13	0	15	1	4	1	7	6	.54	2	.310	.353	.320
2001 Colorado	NL	156	617	202	26	11	2	(0	2)	256	108	55	101	41	1	29	10	14	1	46	17	.73	6	.327	.378	.415
2002 Colorado	NL	152	592	170	20	5	1	(0	1)	203	90	35	77	31	0	52	9	8	0	47	12	.80	7	.287	.332	.343
3 ML YEARS		359	1409	434	48	16	3	(0	3)	523	224	110	201	85	1	96	20	26	2	100	35	.74	15	.308	.356	.371

A.J. Pierzynski

Bats: L Throws: R Pos: C-124; PH-11   **Ht: 6'3" Wt: 220 Born: 12/30/76 Age: 26**

Year Team	Lg	G	AB	H	2B	3B	HR	(Hm	Rd)	TB	R	RBI	RC	TBB	IBB	SO	HBP	SH	SF	SB	CS	SB%	GDP	Avg	OBP	Slg
1998 Minnesota	AL	7	10	3	0	0	0	(0	0)	3	1	1	2	1	0	2	1	0	1	0	0	-	0	.300	.385	.300
1999 Minnesota	AL	9	22	6	2	0	0	(0	0)	8	3	3	3	1	0	4	1	0	0	0	0	-	0	.273	.333	.364
2000 Minnesota	AL	33	88	27	5	1	2	(1	1)	40	12	11	14	5	0	14	2	0	1	1	0	1.00	1	.307	.354	.455
2001 Minnesota	AL	114	381	110	33	2	7	(3	4)	168	51	55	50	16	4	57	4	1	3	1	7	.13	7	.289	.322	.441
2002 Minnesota	AL	130	440	132	31	6	6	(2	4)	193	54	49	59	13	1	61	11	2	3	1	2	.33	14	.300	.334	.439
5 ML YEARS		293	941	278	71	9	15	(6	9)	412	121	119	128	36	5	138	19	3	8	3	9	.25	22	.295	.332	.438

Luis Pineda

Pitches: R Bats: R Pos: RP-24; SP-2   **Ht: 6'1" Wt: 178 Born: 10/17/74 Age: 28**

Year Team	Lg	G	GS	CG	GF	IP	BFP	H	R	ER	HR	SH	SF	HB	TBB	IBB	SO	WP	Bk	W	L	Pct	ShO	Sv-Op	Hld	ERC	ERA
1996 Rangers	R	11	11	1	0	71.2	306	67	31	28	6	3	1	3	25	0	66	10	5	6	3	.667	0	0--	-	3.54	3.52
1999 W Michigan	A	24	3	0	19	40.1	175	30	18	16	2	2	5	1	26	2	55	5	0	0	2	.000	0	7--	-	3.25	3.57
1999 Lakeland	A+	8	0	0	8	8.2	39	6	2	1	0	0	0	0	7	0	8	0	0	0	1	.000	0	0--	-	3.12	1.04
2000 Lakeland	A+	18	0	0	13	26.2	122	23	13	10	3	2	1	1	19	0	42	4	1	1	3	.250	0	4--	-	4.70	3.38
2001 Erie	AA	16	12	2	2	85.2	340	68	33	29	8	3	5	2	28	0	92	3	0	6	2	.750	1	0--	-	2.84	3.05
2001 Toledo	AAA	2	0	0	0	8.0	27	3	0	0	0	0	0	0	0	0	6	0	0	1	0	1.000	0	0--	-	0.31	0.00
2002 Louisville	AAA	3	3	0	0	12.2	50	9	6	6	1	0	0	1	4	0	12	0	0	1	0	1.000	0	0--	-	2.48	4.26
2001 Detroit	AL	16	0	0	4	18.1	82	16	10	10	2	0	1	0	14	2	13	0	0	0	1	.000	0	0-0	2	4.73	4.91
2002 Cincinnati	NL	26	2	0	9	32.1	143	25	16	15	4	3	2	2	24	1	31	4	0	1	3	.250	0	0-0	4	4.57	4.18
2 ML YEARS		42	2	0	13	50.2	225	41	26	25	6	3	3	2	38	3	44	4	0	1	4	.200	0	0-0	6	4.63	4.44

Joel Pineiro

Pitches: R Bats: R Pos: SP-28; RP-9   **Ht: 6'1" Wt: 180 Born: 9/25/78 Age: 24**

Year Team	Lg	G	GS	CG	GF	IP	BFP	H	R	ER	HR	SH	SF	HB	TBB	IBB	SO	WP	Bk	W	L	Pct	ShO	Sv-Op	Hld	ERC	ERA
2000 Seattle	AL	8	1	0	5	19.1	94	25	13	12	3	0	2	0	13	0	10	0	0	1	0	1.000	0	0-0	0	7.44	5.59
2001 Seattle	AL	17	11	0	1	75.1	289	50	24	17	2	1	2	3	21	0	56	2	0	6	2	.750	0	0-0	2	1.71	2.03
2002 Seattle	AL	37	28	2	4	194.1	812	189	95	70	24	5	7	7	54	1	136	8	0	14	7	.667	1	0-0	3	3.77	3.24
3 ML YEARS		62	40	2	10	289.0	1195	264	112	99	29	6	11	10	88	1	202	10	0	21	9	.700	1	0-0	5	3.40	3.08

Dan Plesac

Pitches: L **Bats:** L **Pos:** RP-60 **Ht:** 6'5" **Wt:** 217 **Born:** 2/4/62 **Age:** 41

Year Team	Lg	G	GS	CG	GF	IP	BFP	H	R	ER	HR	SH	SF	HB	TBB	IBB	SO	WP	Bk	W	L	Pct	ShO	Sv-Op	Hld	ERC	ERA
1986 Milwaukee	NL	51	0	0	33	91.0	377	81	34	30	5	6	5	0	29	1	75	4	0	10	7	.588	0	14-18	6	2.86	2.97
1987 Milwaukee	NL	57	0	0	47	79.1	325	63	30	23	8	1	2	3	23	1	89	6	0	5	6	.455	0	23-36	6	2.67	2.61
1988 Milwaukee	NL	50	0	0	48	52.1	211	46	14	14	2	2	0	0	12	2	52	4	6	1	2	.333	0	30-35	0	2.36	2.41
1989 Milwaukee	NL	52	0	0	51	61.1	242	47	16	16	6	0	4	0	17	1	52	0	0	3	4	.429	0	33-40	0	2.39	2.35
1990 Milwaukee	NL	66	0	0	52	69.0	299	67	36	34	5	2	2	3	31	6	65	2	0	3	7	.300	0	24-34	2	3.97	4.43
1991 Milwaukee	NL	45	10	0	25	92.1	402	92	49	44	12	3	7	3	39	1	61	2	1	2	7	.222	0	8-12	1	4.48	4.29
1992 Milwaukee	NL	44	4	0	13	79.0	330	64	28	26	5	8	4	3	35	5	54	3	1	5	4	.556	0	1-3	1	3.04	2.96
1993 Chicago	NL	57	0	0	12	62.2	276	74	37	33	10	4	3	0	21	6	47	5	2	2	1	.667	0	0-2	12	5.15	4.74
1994 Chicago	NL	54	0	0	14	54.2	235	61	30	28	9	1	1	1	13	0	53	0	0	2	3	.400	0	1-3	14	4.59	4.61
1995 Pittsburgh	NL	58	0	0	16	60.1	259	53	26	24	3	4	3	1	27	7	57	1	0	4	4	.500	0	3-5	11	3.09	3.58
1996 Pittsburgh	NL	73	0	0	30	70.1	300	67	35	32	4	2	3	0	24	6	76	4	0	6	5	.545	0	11-17	11	3.12	4.09
1997 Toronto	AL	73	0	0	18	50.1	215	47	22	20	8	2	1	0	19	4	61	2	0	2	4	.333	0	1-5	27	3.86	3.58
1998 Toronto	AL	78	0	0	16	50.0	203	41	23	21	4	0	3	1	16	1	55	0	0	4	3	.571	0	4-5	27	2.76	3.78
1999 Tor-Ari		64	0	0	11	44.1	198	50	30	29	7	4	1	0	17	2	53	3	0	4	3	.333	0	1-3	15	5.03	5.89
2000 Arizona	NL	62	0	0	14	40.0	182	34	21	14	4	6	1	0	26	2	45	3	0	5	1	.833	0	0-4	9	3.98	3.15
2001 Toronto	AL	62	0	0	5	45.1	190	34	18	18	4	0	1	1	24	5	68	1	0	4	5	.444	0	1-2	16	3.07	3.57
2002 Tor-Phi		60	0	0	8	36.1	154	27	17	17	6	0	1	0	18	3	41	0	0	3	3	.500	0	1-4	18	3.29	4.21
1999 Toronto	AL	30	0	0	5	22.2	104	28	21	21	4	3	1	0	9	1	26	2	0	0	3	.000	0	0-2	9	5.87	8.34
1999 Arizona		34	0	0	6	21.2	94	22	9	8	3	1	0	0	8	1	27	1	0	2	1	.667	0	1-1	6	4.19	3.32
2002 Toronto	AL	19	0	0	3	13.1	58	11	5	5	1	0	1	0	6	0	14	0	0	1	2	.333	0	0-1	5	3.02	3.38
2002 Philadelphia	NL	41	0	0	5	23.0	96	16	12	12	5	0	0	0	12	3	27	0	0	2	1	.667	0	1-3	13	3.45	4.70
17 ML YEARS		1006	14	0	413	1038.2	4398	948	466	423	102	45	42	16	391	53	1004	40	10	63	70	.474	0	156-228	170	3.46	3.67

Scott Podsednik

Bats: L **Throws:** L **Pos:** LF-9; PH-3; PR-3; RF-2; CF-1 **Ht:** 6'0" **Wt:** 170 **Born:** 3/18/76 **Age:** 27

Year Team	Lg	G	AB	H	2B	3B	HR	(Hm	Rd)	TB	R	RBI	RC	TBB	IBB	SO	HBP	SH	SF	SB	CS	SB%	GDP	Avg	OBP	Slg
1994 Rangers	R	60	211	48	7	1	1	(-	-)	60	34	17	28	41	0	34	3	2	3	18	5	.78	1	.227	.357	.284
1995 Hudson Val	A-	65	252	67	3	0	0	(-	-)	70	42	20	28	35	3	31	1	1	2	20	6	.77	9	.266	.355	.278
1996 Brevard Cnty	A+	108	383	100	9	2	0	(-	-)	113	39	30	41	45	0	65	3	7	0	20	10	.67	8	.261	.343	.295
1997 Kane County	A	135	531	147	23	4	3	(-	-)	187	80	49	72	60	2	72	3	14	3	28	11	.72	5	.277	.352	.352
1998 Charlotte	A+	81	302	86	12	4	4	(-	-)	118	55	39	50	44	0	32	0	4	6	26	8	.76	2	.285	.369	.391
1998 Tulsa	AA	17	75	18	4	1	0	(-	-)	24	9	4	6	6	0	11	0	0	0	5	2	.71	3	.240	.296	.320
1999 Rangers	R	5	17	7	2	0	0	(-	-)	9	6	5	4	2	0	3	0	0	0	1	0	1.00	1	.412	.474	.529
1999 Tulsa	AA	37	116	18	4	0	0	(-	-)	22	10	1	1	5	0	13	0	2	0	6	2	.75	3	.155	.190	.190
2000 Tulsa	AA	49	169	42	7	2	2	(-	-)	59	20	13	25	30	1	33	1	1	2	19	4	.83	4	.249	.361	.349
2001 Tacoma	AAA	66	269	78	15	4	3	(-	-)	110	46	30	37	13	0	46	2	4	0	12	5	.71	5	.290	.327	.409
2002 Tacoma	AAA	125	438	122	25	6	9	(-	-)	186	63	61	64	43	5	70	9	4	11	35	13	.73	18	.279	.347	.425
2001 Seattle	AL	5	6	1	0	1	0	(0	0)	3	1	3	0	0	0	1	0	0	0	0	0	-	1	.167	.167	.500
2002 Seattle	AL	14	20	4	0	0	1	(0	1)	7	2	5	3	4	0	6	0	0	0	0	0	-	1	.200	.320	.350
2 ML YEARS		19	26	5	0	1	1	(0	1)	10	3	8	3	4	0	7	0	0	1	0	0	-	2	.192	.290	.385

Placido Polanco

Bats: R **Throws:** R **Pos:** 3B-131; SS-13; PH-9; 2B-6 **Ht:** 5'10" **Wt:** 168 **Born:** 10/10/75 **Age:** 27

Year Team	Lg	G	AB	H	2B	3B	HR	(Hm	Rd)	TB	R	RBI	RC	TBB	IBB	SO	HBP	SH	SF	SB	CS	SB%	GDP	Avg	OBP	Slg
1998 St Louis	NL	45	114	29	3	2	1	(1	0)	39	10	11	12	5	0	9	1	2	0	2	0	1.00	1	.254	.292	.342
1999 St Louis	NL	88	220	61	9	3	1	(0	1)	79	24	19	23	15	1	24	0	3	2	1	3	.25	7	.277	.321	.359
2000 St Louis	NL	118	323	102	12	3	5	(2	3)	135	50	39	44	16	0	26	1	7	3	4	4	.50	8	.316	.347	.418
2001 St Louis	NL	144	564	173	26	4	3	(1	2)	216	87	38	70	25	0	43	6	14	1	12	3	.80	22	.307	.342	.383
2002 Stl-Phi	NL	147	548	158	32	2	9	(8	1)	221	75	49	64	26	1	41	8	13	0	5	3	.63	15	.288	.330	.403
2002 St Louis	NL	94	342	97	19	1	5	(5	0)	133	47	27	38	12	1	27	4	9	0	3	1	.75	12	.284	.316	.389
2002 Philadelphia	NL	53	206	61	13	1	4	(3	1)	88	28	22	26	14	0	14	4	4	0	2	2	.50	3	.296	.353	.427
5 ML YEARS		542	1769	523	82	14	19	(12	7)	690	246	156	213	87	2	143	16	39	6	24	13	.65	53	.296	.333	.390

Cliff Politte

Pitches: R **Bats:** R **Pos:** RP-68 **Ht:** 5'11" **Wt:** 185 **Born:** 2/27/74 **Age:** 29

Year Team	Lg	G	GS	CG	GF	IP	BFP	H	R	ER	HR	SH	SF	HB	TBB	IBB	SO	WP	Bk	W	L	Pct	ShO	Sv-Op	Hld	ERC	ERA
1998 St Louis	NL	8	8	0	0	37.0	172	45	32	26	6	3	1	1	18	0	22	2	1	2	3	.400	0	0-0	1	6.28	6.32
1999 Philadelphia	NL	13	0	0	0	17.2	85	19	14	14	2	1	0	0	15	0	15	2	0	1	0	1.000	0	0-0	1	6.47	7.13
2000 Philadelphia	NL	12	8	0	1	59.0	251	55	24	24	8	1	1	0	27	1	50	3	0	4	3	.571	0	0-0	4	4.20	3.66
2001 Philadelphia	NL	23	0	0	7	26.0	109	24	8	7	2	1	3	1	8	3	23	1	0	2	3	.400	0	0-0	1	3.11	2.42
2002 Phi-Tor		68	0	0	20	73.2	304	57	33	30	5	3	1	2	28	2	72	2	0	3	3	.500	0	1-4	25	2.64	3.67
2002 Philadelphia	NL	13	0	0	7	16.1	77	19	10	7	0	1	0	1	9	1	15	1	0	2	0	1.000	0	0-1	0	4.89	3.86
2002 Toronto	AL	55	0	0	13	57.1	227	38	23	23	5	2	1	1	19	1	57	1	0	1	3	.250	0	1-3	25	2.06	3.61
5 ML YEARS		124	16	0	28	213.1	921	200	111	101	23	9	6	4	96	6	182	10	1	12	12	.500	0	1-4	27	4.01	4.26

Sidney Ponson

Pitches: R **Bats:** R **Pos:** SP-28 **Ht:** 6'1" **Wt:** 225 **Born:** 11/2/76 **Age:** 26

Year Team	Lg	G	GS	CG	GF	IP	BFP	H	R	ER	HR	SH	SF	HB	TBB	IBB	SO	WP	Bk	W	L	Pct	ShO	Sv-Op	Hld	ERC	ERA
1998 Baltimore	AL	31	20	0	5	135.0	588	157	79	79	19	3	4	3	42	2	85	4	1	8	9	.471	0	1-2	0	5.07	5.27
1999 Baltimore	AL	32	32	2	0	210.0	897	227	118	110	35	4	7	1	80	2	112	4	0	12	12	.500	0	0-0	0	5.08	4.71
2000 Baltimore	AL	32	32	6	0	222.0	953	223	125	119	30	3	3	1	83	0	152	5	0	9	13	.409	1	0-0	0	4.26	4.82

Year Team	Lg	G	GS	CG	GF	IP	BFP	H	R	ER	HR	SH	SF	HB	TBB	IBB	SO	WP	Bk	W	L	Pct	ShO	Sv-Op	Hld	ERC	ERA
2001 Baltimore	AL	23	23	3	0	138.1	605	161	83	76	21	3	2	6	37	0	84	2	0	5	10	.333	0	0-0	0	5.04	4.94
2002 Baltimore	AL	28	28	3	0	176.0	736	172	84	80	26	2	3	2	63	1	120	3	0	7	9	.438	0	0-0	0	4.24	4.09
5 ML YEARS		146	135	18	5	881.1	3779	940	492	464	131	15	19	13	305	5	553	18	1	41	53	.436	2	1-2	0	4.69	4.74

Mike Porzio

Pitches: L Bats: L Pos: RP-32 | **Ht: 6'3" Wt: 190 Born: 8/20/72 Age: 30**

Year Team	Lg	G	GS	CG	GF	IP	BFP	H	R	ER	HR	SH	SF	HB	TBB	IBB	SO	WP	Bk	W	L	Pct	ShO	Sv-Op	Hld	ERC	ERA
1993 Cubs	R	10	8	0	2	42.1	200	42	26	18	1	3	2	3	30	0	30	1	2	1	3	.250	0	0- -		4.85	3.83
1994 Cubs	R	7	0	0	6	13.2	64	19	10	9	0	0	0	1	6	0	5	0	0	0	3	.000	0	1- -		6.17	5.93
1995 Mobile	IND	16	2	0	4	28.1	131	32	19	17	2	4	1	3	13	2	15	2	0	0	3	.000	0	0- -		5.08	5.40
1995 Ogden	R+	8	8	2	0	48.0	220	66	39	34	4	0	3	2	15	0	26	6	0	4	3	.571	0	0- -		6.02	6.38
1996 Tennessee	IND	15	15	3	0	98.2	428	94	55	40	9	2	4	9	30	1	54	4	0	7	4	.636	0	0- -		3.64	3.65
1997 Sioux Falls	IND	27	5	1	6	61.1	284	75	32	29	6	0	3	5	27	1	63	2	0	2	2	.500	1	0- -		5.84	4.26
1998 Danville	A+	26	11	1	8	97.0	384	74	34	27	7	5	3	1	30	5	95	1	0	3	2	.600	0	2- -		2.34	2.51
1998 Salem	A+	7	7	0	0	42.1	173	40	20	13	6	1	0	2	12	0	46	1	0	2	3	.400	0	0- -		3.90	2.76
1999 Co Springs	AAA	35	0	0	6	42.2	198	44	16	16	5	3	0	3	30	4	33	4	1	5	1	.833	0	0- -		5.81	3.38
2000 Carolina	AA	20	18	1	2	121.1	502	111	53	46	11	5	4	5	31	0	90	5	0	7	4	.636	1	0- -		3.15	3.41
2000 Co Springs	AAA	6	6	0	0	26.0	133	39	30	29	7	3	2	0	20	0	26	0	1	0	3	.000	0	0- -		10.47	10.04
2001 Birmingham	AA	2	2	0	0	13.0	49	3	2	2	1	0	0	1	5	0	10	2	0	0	1	1.000	0	0- -		0.87	1.38
2001 Charlotte	AAA	31	23	0	2	134.1	592	138	76	65	14	6	6	8	55	2	107	9	1	6	6	.500	0	0- -		4.50	4.35
2002 Charlotte	AAA	14	13	0	0	75.2	332	83	43	38	9	1	5	6	29	0	59	1	0	6	5	.545	0	0- -		5.12	4.52
1999 Colorado	NL	16	0	0	3	14.2	75	21	14	14	5	1	0	0	10	0	10	0	0	0	0	-	0	0-0	0	9.91	8.59
2002 Chicago	AL	32	0	0	8	43.0	190	40	25	23	10	0	3	3	23	2	33	3	1	2	2	.500	0	0-0	3	5.44	4.81
2 ML YEARS		48	0	0	11	57.2	265	61	39	37	15	1	3	3	33	2	43	3	1	2	2	.500	0	0-0	3	6.51	5.77

Jorge Posada

Bats: B Throws: R Pos: C-138; PH-7; DH-5 | **Ht: 6'2" Wt: 205 Born: 8/17/71 Age: 31**

Year Team	Lg	G	AB	H	2B	3B	HR	(Hm	Rd)	TB	R	RBI	RC	TBB	IBB	SO	HBP	SH	SF	SB	CS	SB%	GDP	Avg	OBP	Slg
1996 New York	AL	8	14	1	0	0	0	(0	0)	1	1	0	0	1	0	6	0	0	0	0	0	-	1	.071	.133	.071
1997 New York	AL	60	188	47	12	0	6	(2	4)	77	29	25	29	30	2	33	3	1	2	1	2	.33	2	.250	.359	.410
1998 New York	AL	111	358	96	23	0	17	(6	11)	170	56	63	56	47	7	92	0	1	4	0	1	.00	14	.268	.350	.475
1999 New York	AL	112	379	93	19	2	12	(4	8)	152	50	57	52	53	2	91	3	0	2	1	0	1.00	9	.245	.341	.401
2000 New York	AL	151	505	145	35	1	28	(18	10)	266	92	86	110	107	10	151	8	0	4	2	2	.50	11	.287	.417	.527
2001 New York	AL	138	484	134	28	1	22	(14	8)	230	59	95	80	62	10	132	6	0	5	2	6	.25	10	.277	.363	.475
2002 New York	AL	143	511	137	40	1	20	(12	8)	239	79	99	92	81	9	143	3	0	3	1	0	1.00	23	.268	.370	.468
7 ML YEARS		723	2439	653	157	5	105	(56	49)	1135	366	425	419	381	40	648	23	1	20	7	11	.39	70	.268	.369	.465

Lou Pote

Pitches: R Bats: R Pos: RP-31 | **Ht: 6'3" Wt: 208 Born: 8/21/71 Age: 31**

Year Team	Lg	G	GS	CG	GF	IP	BFP	H	R	ER	HR	SH	SF	HB	TBB	IBB	SO	WP	Bk	W	L	Pct	ShO	Sv-Op	Hld	ERC	ERA
2002 Salt Lake*	AAA	7	7	0	0	39.0	170	42	26	26	3	0	2	1	10	0	43	4	0	2	1	.667	0	0- -		3.79	6.00
1999 Anaheim	AL	20	0	0	10	29.1	118	23	9	7	1	1	0	0	12	1	20	1	0	1	1	.500	0	3-3	3	2.56	2.15
2000 Anaheim	AL	32	1	0	12	50.1	214	52	23	19	4	1	1	0	17	1	44	3	0	1	1	.500	0	1-1	2	3.87	3.40
2001 Anaheim	AL	44	1	0	15	86.2	380	88	41	40	11	1	3	3	32	5	66	3	0	2	0	1.000	0	2-3	0	4.21	4.15
2002 Anaheim	AL	31	0	0	13	50.1	206	33	20	18	7	2	5	3	26	2	32	3	0	0	2	.000	0	0-1	1	3.16	3.22
4 ML YEARS		127	2	0	50	216.2	918	196	93	84	23	5	9	6	87	9	162	10	0	4	4	.500	0	6-8	6	3.65	3.49

Brian Powell

Pitches: R Bats: R Pos: SP-9; RP-4 | **Ht: 6'2" Wt: 205 Born: 10/10/73 Age: 29**

Year Team	Lg	G	GS	CG	GF	IP	BFP	H	R	ER	HR	SH	SF	HB	TBB	IBB	SO	WP	Bk	W	L	Pct	ShO	Sv-Op	Hld	ERC	ERA
2002 Toledo*	AAA	20	20	0	0	119.1	503	127	54	52	8	0	4	3	26	0	82	6	0	10	3	.769	0	0- -		3.59	3.92
1998 Detroit	AL	18	16	0	1	83.2	383	101	67	59	17	1	1	2	36	2	46	3	0	3	8	.273	0	0-0	0	6.25	6.35
2000 Houston	NL	9	5	0	1	31.1	140	34	21	20	8	2	2	1	13	0	14	0	0	1	2	.667	0	0-0	0	5.88	5.74
2001 Houston	NL	1	1	0	0	3.0	17	5	6	6	1	0	0	0	3	0	3	0	0	0	1	.000	0	0-0	0	13.15	18.00
2002 Detroit	AL	13	9	0	1	57.2	254	64	34	31	11	0	2	1	21	0	30	2	0	2	4	.167	0	0-0	0	5.29	4.84
4 ML YEARS		41	31	0	3	175.2	794	204	128	116	37	3	5	4	73	2	93	5	0	6	15	.286	0	0-0	0	5.97	5.94

Jay Powell

Pitches: R Bats: R Pos: RP-51 | **Ht: 6'4" Wt: 225 Born: 1/9/72 Age: 31**

Year Team	Lg	G	GS	CG	GF	IP	BFP	H	R	ER	HR	SH	SF	HB	TBB	IBB	SO	WP	Bk	W	L	Pct	ShO	Sv-Op	Hld	ERC	ERA
2002 Tulsa*	AA	2	0	0	0	2.0	7	0	0	0	0	0	0	0	1	0	0	0	0	0	0	-	0	0- -		0.27	0.00
2002 Oklahoma*	AAA	8	0	0	0	8.0	43	14	11	11	2	0	0	1	3	1	8	0	0	2	0	1.000	0	0- -		9.90	12.38
1995 Florida	NL	9	0	0	1	8.1	38	7	2	1	0	1	0	2	6	1	4	0	0	0	0	-	0	0-0	2	4.44	1.08
1996 Florida	NL	67	0	0	16	71.1	321	71	41	36	5	2	1	4	36	1	52	3	0	4	3	.571	0	2-5	10	4.39	4.54
1997 Florida	NL	74	0	0	23	79.2	337	71	35	29	3	6	4	4	30	3	65	3	0	7	2	.778	0	2-4	24	3.10	3.28
1998 Fla-Hou	NL	62	0	0	35	70.1	302	58	28	26	6	3	1	3	37	9	62	1	0	7	7	.500	0	7-11	3	3.46	3.33
1999 Houston	NL	67	0	0	26	75.0	341	82	38	36	3	5	2	3	40	4	77	5	0	5	4	.556	0	4-7	16	4.75	4.32
2000 Houston	NL	29	0	0	10	27.0	127	29	18	17	1	1	0	2	19	1	16	0	0	1	1	.500	0	0-0	5	5.10	5.67
2001 Hou-Col	NL	74	0	0	29	75.0	327	75	36	27	9	5	1	2	31	3	54	0	1	5	3	.625	0	7-13	8	4.30	3.24
2002 Texas	AL	51	0	0	5	49.2	224	50	28	19	5	1	1	1	24	4	35	2	0	3	4	.429	0	0-4	12	4.28	3.44
1998 Florida	NL	33	0	0	26	36.1	165	36	19	17	5	3	1	2	22	6	24	1	0	4	4	.500	0	3-6	0	5.07	4.21
1998 Houston	NL	29	0	0	9	34.0	137	22	9	9	1	0	0	1	15	3	38	0	0	3	3	.500	0	4-5	3	1.96	2.38

Year Team	Lg	HOW MUCH HE PITCHED						WHAT HE GAVE UP											THE RESULTS							
		G	GS	CG	GF	IP	BFP	H	R	ER	HR	SH	SF	HB	TBB	IBB	SO	WP	Bk	W	L	Pct	ShO	Sv-Op	Hld	ERC	ERA
2001 Houston	NL	35	0	0	5	36.1	170	41	18	15	4	1	1	0	19	0	28	0	1	2	2	.500	0	0-5	5	5.23	3.72
2001 Colorado	NL	39	0	0	15	38.2	157	34	18	12	5	4	0	2	12	3	26	0	0	3	1	.750	0	7-8	5	3.45	2.79
8 ML YEARS		433	0	0	136	456.1	2017	443	226	191	32	24	9	19	223	26	365	14	1	32	22	.593	0	22-44	80	4.09	3.77

Andy Pratt

Pitches: L Bats: L Pos: RP-1

Ht: 5'11" Wt: 160 Born: 8/27/79 Age: 23

Year Team	Lg	HOW MUCH HE PITCHED						WHAT HE GAVE UP											THE RESULTS							
		G	GS	CG	GF	IP	BFP	H	R	ER	HR	SH	SF	HB	TBB	IBB	SO	WP	Bk	W	L	Pct	ShO	Sv-Op	Hld	ERC	ERA
1998 Rangers	R	12	8	0	1	56.0	225	49	25	24	4	1	3	1	14	0	49	0	1	4	3	.571	0	0- -	-	2.77	3.86
1999 Savannah	A	13	13	1	0	71.2	299	66	30	23	4	4	2	4	16	0	100	4	0	4	4	.500	1	0- -	-	2.86	2.89
2000 Charlotte	A+	16	16	2	0	92.2	365	68	37	28	8	1	2	1	26	0	95	1	2	7	4	.636	1	0- -	-	2.24	2.72
2000 Tulsa	AA	11	11	0	0	52.1	255	66	48	42	7	0	2	2	33	0	42	5	1	1	6	.143	0	0- -	-	6.96	7.22
2001 Tulsa	AA	27	26	3	0	168.0	730	175	99	86	18	8	5	6	57	0	132	9	1	8	10	.444	1	0- -	-	4.24	4.61
2002 Greenville	AA	20	18	1	0	93.0	404	92	54	44	5	4	3	2	44	0	67	6	0	4	9	.308	1	0- -	-	4.09	4.26
2002 Richmond	AAA	6	6	1	0	40.2	163	35	15	14	2	2	1	0	9	0	36	3	0	4	2	.667	1	0- -	-	2.37	3.10
2002 Atlanta	NL	1	0	0	0	1.1	9	1	1	1	0	0	0	0	4	0	1	0	0	0	0	-	0	0-0	0	12.03	6.75

Todd Pratt

Bats: R Throws: R Pos: C-34; PH-3; 1B-2

Ht: 6'3" Wt: 230 Born: 2/9/67 Age: 36

Year Team	Lg	BATTING																		BASERUNNING				AVERAGES		
		G	AB	H	2B	3B	HR	(Hm	Rd)	TB	R	RBI	RC	TBB	IBB	SO	HBP	SH	SF	SB	CS	SB%	GDP	Avg	OBP	Slg
1992 Philadelphia	NL	16	46	13	1	0	2	(2	0)	20	6	10	6	4	0	12	0	0	0	0	0	-	2	.283	.340	.435
1993 Philadelphia	NL	33	87	25	6	0	5	(4	1)	46	8	13	15	5	0	19	1	1	1	0	0	-	2	.287	.330	.529
1994 Philadelphia	NL	28	102	20	6	1	2	(1	1)	34	10	9	9	12	0	29	0	0	0	0	1	.00	3	.196	.281	.333
1995 Chicago	NL	25	60	8	2	0	0	(0	0)	10	3	4	1	6	1	21	0	0	1	0	0	-	1	.133	.209	.167
1997 New York	NL	39	106	30	6	0	2	(1	1)	42	12	19	16	13	0	32	2	0	0	0	1	.00	1	.283	.372	.396
1998 New York	NL	41	69	19	9	1	2	(1	1)	36	9	18	11	2	0	20	0	0	0	0	0	-	0	.275	.296	.522
1999 New York	NL	71	140	41	4	0	3	(1	2)	54	18	21	22	15	0	32	3	0	2	2	0	1.00	4	.293	.369	.386
2000 New York	NL	80	160	44	6	0	8	(2	6)	74	33	25	28	22	1	31	5	2	1	0	0	-	5	.275	.378	.463
2001 NYM-Phi	NL	80	173	32	8	0	4	(0	4)	52	18	11	18	34	3	61	3	1	1	1	0	1.00	6	.185	.327	.301
2002 Philadelphia	NL	39	106	33	11	0	3	(1	2)	53	14	16	21	24	6	28	4	0	2	2	0	1.00	3	.311	.449	.500
2001 New York	NL	45	80	13	5	0	2	(0	2)	24	6	4	7	15	1	36	2	0	1	1	0	1.00	4	.163	.306	.300
2001 Philadelphia	NL	35	93	19	3	0	2	(0	2)	28	12	7	11	19	2	25	1	1	0	0	0	-	2	.204	.345	.301
10 ML YEARS		452	1049	265	59	2	31	(14	17)	421	131	146	147	137	11	285	18	4	8	5	2	.71	24	.253	.347	.401

Tom Prince

Bats: R Throws: R Pos: C-50; PH-1

Ht: 5'11" Wt: 206 Born: 8/13/64 Age: 38

Year Team	Lg	BATTING																		BASERUNNING				AVERAGES		
		G	AB	H	2B	3B	HR	(Hm	Rd)	TB	R	RBI	RC	TBB	IBB	SO	HBP	SH	SF	SB	CS	SB%	GDP	Avg	OBP	Slg
1987 Pittsburgh	NL	4	9	2	1	0	1	(0	1)	6	1	2	1	0	0	2	0	0	0	0	0	-	0	.222	.222	.667
1988 Pittsburgh	NL	29	74	13	2	0	0	(0	0)	15	3	6	1	4	0	15	0	2	0	0	0	-	5	.176	.218	.203
1989 Pittsburgh	NL	21	52	7	4	0	0	(0	0)	11	1	5	1	6	1	12	0	0	1	1	1	.50	1	.135	.220	.212
1990 Pittsburgh	NL	4	10	1	0	0	0	(0	0)	1	1	0	0	1	0	2	0	0	0	0	1	.00	0	.100	.182	.100
1991 Pittsburgh	NL	26	34	9	3	0	1	(0	1)	15	4	2	6	7	0	3	1	0	0	0	0	-	3	.265	.405	.441
1992 Pittsburgh	NL	27	44	4	2	0	0	(0	0)	6	1	5	0	6	0	9	0	0	2	1	1	.50	0	.091	.192	.136
1993 Pittsburgh	NL	66	179	35	14	0	2	(2	0)	55	14	24	14	13	2	38	7	2	3	1	1	.50	5	.196	.272	.307
1994 Los Angeles	NL	3	6	2	0	0	0	(0	0)	2	2	1	1	1	0	3	0	0	0	0	0	-	0	.333	.429	.333
1995 Los Angeles	NL	18	40	8	2	1	1	(0	1)	15	3	4	4	4	0	10	0	0	0	0	0	-	0	.200	.273	.375
1996 Los Angeles	NL	40	64	19	6	0	1	(0	1)	28	6	11	11	6	2	15	2	3	2	0	0	-	2	.297	.365	.438
1997 Los Angeles	NL	47	100	22	5	0	3	(2	1)	36	17	14	10	5	0	15	3	4	1	0	0	-	0	.220	.275	.360
1998 Los Angeles	NL	37	81	15	5	1	0	(0	0)	22	7	5	6	7	1	24	2	2	0	0	0	-	0	.185	.267	.272
1999 Philadelphia	NL	4	6	1	0	0	0	(0	0)	1	1	0	0	1	0	1	0	0	0	0	0	-	0	.167	.286	.167
2000 Philadelphia	NL	46	122	29	9	0	2	(0	2)	44	14	16	13	13	0	31	2	3	0	1	0	1.00	6	.238	.321	.361
2001 Minnesota	AL	64	196	43	4	1	7	(3	4)	70	19	23	19	12	0	39	6	0	1	3	1	.75	5	.219	.284	.357
2002 Minnesota	AL	51	125	28	7	1	4	(3	1)	49	14	16	17	14	0	26	4	3	2	1	3	.25	4	.224	.317	.392
16 ML YEARS		487	1142	238	64	4	22	(10	12)	376	108	134	104	100	6	245	27	19	12	8	8	.50	34	.208	.285	.329

Bret Prinz

Pitches: R Bats: R Pos: RP-20

Ht: 6'3" Wt: 185 Born: 6/15/77 Age: 26

Year Team	Lg	HOW MUCH HE PITCHED						WHAT HE GAVE UP											THE RESULTS							
		G	GS	CG	GF	IP	BFP	H	R	ER	HR	SH	SF	HB	TBB	IBB	SO	WP	Bk	W	L	Pct	ShO	Sv-Op	Hld	ERC	ERA
1998 Diamndbcks	R	4	0	0	4	5.1	24	7	3	2	0	0	0	1	0	0	3	0	0	0	0	-	0	0- -	-	4.15	3.38
1998 Lethbridge	R+	11	10	0	0	46.2	204	49	26	16	2	1	0	3	13	0	30	8	0	4	2	.667	0	0- -	-	3.65	3.09
1999 South Bend	A	30	23	0	3	138.2	594	129	82	69	16	5	7	8	52	0	98	10	4	6	10	.375	0	0- -	-	3.92	4.48
2000 South Bend	A	6	0	0	5	7.1	26	2	2	0	0	0	0	0	1	0	10	1	0	1	0	1.000	0	1- -	-	0.47	0.00
2000 El Paso	AA	53	0	0	42	60.2	265	71	24	24	6	1	1	5	16	3	69	3	0	9	1	.900	0	26- -	-	4.80	3.56
2001 Tucson	AAA	5	0	0	5	5.2	18	1	0	0	0	0	0	0	0	0	6	0	0	0	0	-	0	3- -	-	0.07	0.00
2002 Tucson	AAA	37	0	0	32	39.1	165	42	14	13	4	0	0	0	9	1	34	3	0	1	0	1.000	0	18- -	-	3.77	2.97
2002 Lancaster	A+	5	0	0	1	7.0	25	2	0	0	0	0	0	1	0	0	6	0	0	1	0	1.000	0	0- -	-	0.32	0.00
2001 Arizona	NL	46	0	0	26	41.0	174	33	13	12	4	3	1	1	19	1	27	1	1	4	1	.800	0	9-12	6	3.27	2.63
2002 Arizona	NL	20	0	0	5	13.1	71	23	14	14	1	2	1	1	10	1	10	3	0	0	2	.000	0	0-2	5	10.34	9.45
2 ML YEARS		66	0	0	31	54.1	245	56	27	26	5	5	2	2	29	2	37	4	1	4	3	.571	0	9-14	11	4.79	4.31

Mark Prior

Pitches: R **Bats:** R **Pos:** SP-19   **Ht:** 6'5" **Wt:** 225 **Born:** 9/7/80 **Age:** 22

		HOW MUCH HE PITCHED						WHAT HE GAVE UP												THE RESULTS							
Year Team	Lg	G	GS	CG	GF	IP	BFP	H	R	ER	HR	SH	SF	HB	TBB	IBB	SO	WP	Bk	W	L	Pct	ShO	Sv-Op	Hld	ERC	ERA
2002 W Tennese	AA	6	6	0	0	34.2	145	26	16	10	0	2	0	2	10	0	55	3	1	4	1	.800	0	0--	-	1.87	2.60
2002 Iowa	AAA	3	3	0	0	16.1	75	13	10	3	1	1	1	1	8	0	24	0	1	1	1	.500	0	0--	-	3.00	1.65
2002 Chicago	NL	19	19	1	0	116.2	486	98	45	43	14	3	4	7	38	0	147	1	0	6	6	.500	0	0-0	0	3.27	3.32

Luke Prokopec

Pitches: R **Bats:** L **Pos:** SP-12; RP-10   **Ht:** 5'11" **Wt:** 175 **Born:** 2/23/78 **Age:** 25

		HOW MUCH HE PITCHED						WHAT HE GAVE UP												THE RESULTS							
Year Team	Lg	G	GS	CG	GF	IP	BFP	H	R	ER	HR	SH	SF	HB	TBB	IBB	SO	WP	Bk	W	L	Pct	ShO	Sv-Op	Hld	ERC	ERA
2002 Syracuse*	AAA	2	0	0	0	2.0	6	0	0	0	0	0	0	0	0	0	2	0	0	0	0	-	0	0--	-	0.00	0.00
2000 Los Angeles	NL	5	3	0	0	21.0	88	19	10	7	2	1	1	2	9	0	12	0	0	1	1	.500	0	0--	0	4.15	3.00
2001 Los Angeles	NL	29	22	0	2	138.1	596	146	80	75	27	4	3	4	40	1	91	3	2	8	7	.533	0	0-0	0	4.69	4.88
2002 Toronto	AL	22	12	0	4	71.2	336	90	57	54	19	1	5	7	25	2	41	3	1	2	9	.182	0	0-0	0	6.91	6.78
3 ML YEARS		56	37	0	7	231.0	1020	255	147	136	48	6	9	13	74	3	144	6	3	11	17	.393	0	0-0	0	5.31	5.30

Brandon Puffer

Pitches: R **Bats:** R **Pos:** RP-55   **Ht:** 6'3" **Wt:** 190 **Born:** 10/5/75 **Age:** 27

		HOW MUCH HE PITCHED						WHAT HE GAVE UP												THE RESULTS							
Year Team	Lg	G	GS	CG	GF	IP	BFP	H	R	ER	HR	SH	SF	HB	TBB	IBB	SO	WP	Bk	W	L	Pct	ShO	Sv-Op	Hld	ERC	ERA
1994 Twins	R	18	0	0	16	35.1	157	33	18	12	1	0	1	4	19	0	40	6	1	2	2	.500	0	2--	-	4.18	3.06
1995 Twins	R	14	5	0	6	40.2	175	29	21	13	0	0	0	2	21	0	35	5	0	0	3	.000	0	1--	-	2.42	2.88
1996 Angels	R	1	1	0	0	5.0	23	7	2	2	0	0	0	0	1	0	3	1	0	0	1	.000	0	0--	-	4.69	3.60
1996 Boise	A-	16	0	0	8	30.1	129	27	19	15	3	1	3	1	11	0	22	3	0	2	0	1.000	0	1--	-	3.41	4.45
1997 Boise	A-	6	0	0	2	15.1	63	10	5	4	0	0	1	1	2	0	15	1	0	0	0	-	0	1--	-	1.17	2.35
1997 Cedar Rpds	A	10	0	0	2	17.1	66	8	6	5	0	0	0	0	10	0	11	3	1	0	0	-	0	1--	-	1.54	2.60
1998 Chrlstn - WV	A	29	0	0	12	50.2	242	68	45	39	4	2	1	7	23	4	36	5	0	2	7	.222	0	1--	-	6.65	6.93
1998 Chattanooga	AA	7	0	0	4	8.2	32	2	3	3	2	0	0	1	3	0	6	0	0	0	0	-	0	0--	-	1.37	3.12
1999 Clinton	A	59	0	0	55	63.1	277	53	20	14	2	2	2	11	24	3	60	4	1	1	2	.333	0	34--	-	3.14	1.99
2000 Asheville	A	14	0	0	9	14.1	75	19	16	13	3	2	0	3	11	3	15	3	0	0	0	-	0	5--	-	9.03	8.16
2000 Somerset	IND	15	0	0	7	23.0	104	25	12	9	1	0	1	1	9	2	21	2	1	2	2	.500	0	1--	-	4.03	3.52
2000 Kissimmee	A+	18	0	0	18	21.1	95	18	6	3	0	3	0	1	11	4	26	3	0	2	3	.400	0	9--	-	2.72	1.27
2001 Round Rock	AA	56	0	0	33	82.2	331	52	19	19	4	1	1	7	35	2	91	3	0	6	1	.857	0	8--	-	2.23	2.07
2002 New Orleans	AAA	11	0	0	4	15.0	57	8	3	3	1	0	0	2	4	0	13	1	0	2	1	.667	0	0--	-	1.63	1.80
2002 Houston	NL	55	0	0	19	69.0	311	67	37	34	3	5	2	5	38	8	48	2	0	3	3	.500	0	0-0	2	4.13	4.43

Albert Pujols

Bats: R **Throws:** R **Pos:** LF-117; 3B-41; 1B-21; DH-2; SS-1; RF-1; PH-1   **Ht:** 6'3" **Wt:** 210 **Born:** 1/16/80 **Age:** 23

		BATTING																	BASERUNNING				AVERAGES		
Year Team	Lg	G	AB	H	2B	3B	HR	(Hm Rd)	TB	R	RBI	RC	TBB	IBB	SO	HBP	SH	SF	SB	CS	SB%	GDP	Avg	OBP	Slg
2000 Peoria	A	109	395	128	32	6	17	(- -)	223	62	84	80	38	7	37	5	0	2	2	4	.33	10	.324	.389	.565
2000 Potomac	A+	21	81	23	8	1	2	(- -)	39	11	10	12	7	0	8	0	1	0	1	1	.50	3	.284	.341	.481
2000 Memphis	AAA	3	14	3	1	0	0	(- -)	4	1	2	1	1	0	2	0	0	0	0	1	1.00	0	.214	.267	.286
2001 St Louis	NL	161	590	194	47	4	37	(18 19)	360	112	130	132	69	6	93	9	1	7	1	3	.25	21	.329	.403	.610
2002 St Louis	NL	157	590	185	40	2	34	(14 20)	331	118	127	122	72	13	69	9	0	4	2	4	.33	20	.314	.394	.561
2 ML YEARS		318	1180	379	87	6	71	(32 39)	691	230	257	254	141	19	162	18	1	11	3	7	.30	41	.321	.399	.586

Nick Punto

Bats: B **Throws:** R **Pos:** PH-6; PR-2; 2B-1; SS-1   **Ht:** 5'9" **Wt:** 170 **Born:** 11/8/77 **Age:** 25

		BATTING																	BASERUNNING				AVERAGES		
Year Team	Lg	G	AB	H	2B	3B	HR	(Hm Rd)	TB	R	RBI	RC	TBB	IBB	SO	HBP	SH	SF	SB	CS	SB%	GDP	Avg	OBP	Slg
1998 Batavia	A-	72	279	69	9	4	1	(- -)	89	51	20	35	42	0	48	1	0	1	19	7	.73	4	.247	.347	.319
1999 Clearwater	A+	106	400	122	18	6	1	(- -)	155	65	48	66	67	3	53	3	3	5	16	7	.70	13	.305	.404	.388
2000 Reading	AA	121	456	116	15	4	5	(- -)	154	77	47	63	69	0	71	2	14	6	33	10	.77	5	.254	.351	.338
2001 Scrtn/WlksBr	AAA	123	463	106	19	5	1	(- -)	138	57	39	48	68	3	114	0	3	3	33	9	.79	15	.229	.327	.298
2002 Scrtn/WlksBr	AAA	115	443	120	12	5	1	(- -)	145	74	29	67	76	0	84	2	6	3	42	8	.84	5	.271	.378	.327
2001 Philadelphia	NL	4	5	2	0	0	0	(0 0)	2	0	1	0	0	0	0	0	0	0	0	0	-	0	.400	.400	.400
2002 Philadelphia	NL	9	6	1	0	0	0	(0 0)	1	0	0	0	0	0	3	0	1	0	0	0	-	0	.167	.167	.167
2 ML YEARS		13	11	3	0	0	0	(0 0)	3	0	1	0	0	0	3	0	1	0	0	0	-	0	.273	.273	.273

Paul Quantrill

Pitches: R **Bats:** L **Pos:** RP-86   **Ht:** 6'1" **Wt:** 195 **Born:** 11/3/68 **Age:** 34

		HOW MUCH HE PITCHED						WHAT HE GAVE UP												THE RESULTS							
Year Team	Lg	G	GS	CG	GF	IP	BFP	H	R	ER	HR	SH	SF	HB	TBB	IBB	SO	WP	Bk	W	L	Pct	ShO	Sv-Op	Hld	ERC	ERA
1992 Boston	AL	27	0	0	10	49.1	213	55	18	12	1	4	2	1	15	5	24	1	0	2	3	.400	0	1-5	3	3.70	2.19
1993 Boston	AL	49	14	1	8	138.0	594	151	73	60	13	4	2	2	44	14	66	0	1	6	12	.333	1	1-2	3	4.16	3.91
1994 Bos-Phi		35	1	0	9	53.0	236	64	31	29	7	5	3	5	15	4	28	0	2	3	3	.500	0	1-4	3	5.34	4.92
1995 Philadelphia	NL	33	29	0	1	179.1	784	212	102	93	20	9	6	6	44	3	103	0	3	11	12	.478	0	0-0	0	4.67	4.67
1996 Toronto	AL	38	20	0	7	134.1	609	172	90	81	27	5	7	2	51	3	86	1	1	5	14	.263	0	0-2	1	6.52	5.43
1997 Toronto	AL	77	0	0	29	88.0	373	103	25	19	5	5	3	1	17	3	56	1	0	6	7	.462	0	5-10	16	3.94	1.94
1998 Toronto	AL	82	0	0	32	80.0	345	88	26	24	5	7	4	3	22	6	59	1	0	3	4	.429	0	7-14	27	3.90	2.59
1999 Toronto	AL	41	0	0	13	48.2	212	53	19	18	5	1	2	4	17	1	28	0	0	3	2	.600	0	0-4	8	4.77	3.33
2000 Toronto	AL	68	0	0	24	83.2	367	100	45	42	7	1	3	2	25	1	47	1	0	2	5	.286	0	1-3	13	4.78	4.52
2001 Toronto	AL	80	0	0	20	83.0	341	86	29	28	6	7	2	6	12	7	58	0	0	11	2	.846	0	2-9	21	3.31	3.04
2002 Los Angeles	NL	86	0	0	22	76.2	330	80	27	25	5	5	7	2	16	7	53	0	0	5	4	.556	0	1-3	34	3.42	2.70

Year Team	Lg	HOW MUCH HE PITCHED						WHAT HE GAVE UP												THE RESULTS						
		G	GS	CG	GF	IP	BFP	H	R	ER	HR	SH	SF	HB	TBB	IBB	SO	WP	Bk	W	L	Pct	ShO	Sv-Op	Hld	ERC	ERA
1994 Boston	AL	17	0	0	4	23.0	101	25	10	9	4	2	2	2	5	1	15	0	0	1	1	.500	0	0-2	2	4.53	3.52
1994 Philadelphia	NL	18	1	0	5	30.0	135	39	21	20	3	3	1	3	10	3	13	0	2	2	2	.500	0	1-2	1	5.97	6.00
11 ML YEARS		616	64	1	175	1014.0	4404	1164	485	428	97	49	35	35	287	54	608	5	7	57	68	.456	1	19-56	129	4.49	3.80

Ruben Quevedo

Pitches: R **Bats:** R **Pos:** SP-25; RP-1   **Ht:** 6'1" **Wt:** 257 **Born:** 1/5/79 **Age:** 24

Year Team	Lg	HOW MUCH HE PITCHED						WHAT HE GAVE UP												THE RESULTS						
		G	GS	CG	GF	IP	BFP	H	R	ER	HR	SH	SF	HB	TBB	IBB	SO	WP	Bk	W	L	Pct	ShO	Sv-Op	Hld	ERC	ERA
2002 Indianapolis*	AAA	1	1	0	0	2.0	8	1	0	0	0	0	0	0	1	0	3	0	0	0	0	-	0	0--	-	1.41	0.00
2000 Chicago	NL	21	15	1	1	88.0	418	96	81	73	21	4	3	3	54	4	65	2	0	3	10	.231	0	0-0	0	6.49	7.47
2001 Milwaukee	NL	10	10	0	0	56.2	253	56	30	29	9	3	2	0	30	4	60	1	0	4	5	.444	0	0-0	0	4.79	4.61
2002 Milwaukee	NL	26	25	1	0	139.0	634	159	100	89	28	6	3	4	68	3	93	6	0	6	11	.353	1	0-0	0	6.16	5.76
3 ML YEARS		57	50	2	1	283.2	1305	311	211	191	58	13	8	7	152	11	218	9	0	13	26	.333	1	0-0	0	5.98	6.06

Mark Quinn

Bats: R **Throws:** R **Pos:** RF-15; DH-7; PH-1   **Ht:** 6'1" **Wt:** 195 **Born:** 5/21/74 **Age:** 29

Year Team	Lg	BATTING																		BASERUNNING				AVERAGES		
		G	AB	H	2B	3B	HR	(Hm	Rd)	TB	R	RBI	RC	TBB	IBB	SO	HBP	SH	SF	SB	CS	SB%	GDP	Avg	OBP	Slg
2002 Omaha*	AAA	12	39	7	2	1	0	(-	-)	11	4	2	3	4	1	7	2	0	0	0	0	-	1	.179	.289	.282
2002 Wichita*	AA	2	8	2	1	0	0	(-	-)	3	0	1	1	0	0	1	0	0	0	0	0	-	0	.250	.250	.375
1999 Kansas City	AL	17	60	20	4	1	6	(2	4)	44	11	18	15	4	0	11	1	0	0	1	0	1.00	1	.333	.385	.733
2000 Kansas City	AL	135	500	147	33	2	20	(12	8)	244	76	78	80	35	1	91	3	3	3	5	2	.71	11	.294	.342	.488
2001 Kansas City	AL	118	453	122	31	2	17	(10	7)	208	57	60	56	12	1	69	7	0	1	9	5	.64	16	.269	.298	.459
2002 Kansas City	AL	23	76	18	4	0	2	(2	0)	28	9	11	7	5	0	15	2	1	0	2	1	.67	3	.237	.301	.368
4 ML YEARS		293	1089	307	72	5	45	(26	19)	524	153	167	158	56	2	186	13	4	4	17	8	.68	31	.282	.324	.481

Brad Radke

Pitches: R **Bats:** R **Pos:** SP-21   **Ht:** 6'2" **Wt:** 188 **Born:** 10/27/72 **Age:** 30

Year Team	Lg	HOW MUCH HE PITCHED						WHAT HE GAVE UP												THE RESULTS						
		G	GS	CG	GF	IP	BFP	H	R	ER	HR	SH	SF	HB	TBB	IBB	SO	WP	Bk	W	L	Pct	ShO	Sv-Op	Hld	ERC	ERA
2002 Twins*	R	1	1	0	0	3.0	9	2	0	0	0	0	0	0	0	0	4	0	0	0	0	-	0	0--	-	1.12	0.00
2002 Fort Myers*	A+	2	2	0	0	8.2	39	11	6	3	1	0	1	0	0	0	6	1	0	0	1	.000	0	0--	-	3.75	3.12
1995 Minnesota	AL	29	28	2	0	181.0	772	195	112	107	32	2	9	4	47	0	75	4	0	11	14	.440	1	0-0	0	4.58	5.32
1996 Minnesota	AL	35	35	3	0	232.0	973	231	125	115	40	5	6	4	57	2	148	1	0	11	16	.407	1	0-0	0	3.97	4.46
1997 Minnesota	AL	35	35	4	0	239.2	989	238	114	103	28	2	9	3	48	1	174	1	1	20	10	.667	1	0-0	0	3.41	3.87
1998 Minnesota	AL	32	32	5	0	213.2	904	238	109	102	23	9	3	9	43	1	146	3	1	12	14	.462	1	0-0	0	4.18	4.30
1999 Minnesota	AL	33	33	4	0	218.2	910	239	97	91	28	5	5	1	44	0	121	4	0	12	14	.462	0	0-0	0	4.07	3.75
2000 Minnesota	AL	34	34	4	0	226.2	978	261	119	112	27	7	4	5	51	1	141	5	0	12	16	.429	1	0-0	0	4.44	4.45
2001 Minnesota	AL	33	33	6	0	226.0	919	235	105	99	24	10	6	10	26	0	137	4	0	15	11	.577	2	0-0	0	3.45	3.94
2002 Minnesota	AL	21	21	2	0	118.1	490	124	64	62	12	2	5	7	20	0	62	0	0	9	5	.643	1	0-0	0	3.73	4.72
8 ML YEARS		252	251	30	0	1656.0	6935	1761	845	791	214	42	47	43	336	5	1004	22	3	102	100	.505	7	0-0	0	3.97	4.30

Tim Raines

Bats: B **Throws:** R **Pos:** PH-86; LF-14; RF-1; DH-1   **Ht:** 5'9" **Wt:** 202 **Born:** 9/16/59 **Age:** 43

Year Team	Lg	BATTING																		BASERUNNING				AVERAGES		
		G	AB	H	2B	3B	HR	(Hm	Rd)	TB	R	RBI	RC	TBB	IBB	SO	HBP	SH	SF	SB	CS	SB%	GDP	Avg	OBP	Slg
1980 Montreal	NL	15	20	1	0	0	0	(0	0)	1	5	0	1	6	0	3	0	1	0	5	0	1.00	0	.050	.269	.050
1981 Montreal	NL	88	313	95	13	7	5	(3	2)	137	61	37	63	45	5	31	2	0	3	71	11	.87	7	.304	.391	.438
1982 Montreal	NL	156	647	179	32	8	4	(1	3)	239	90	43	97	75	9	83	2	6	1	78	16	.83	6	.277	.353	.369
1983 Montreal	NL	156	615	183	32	8	11	(5	6)	264	133	71	118	97	9	70	2	2	4	90	14	.87	12	.298	.393	.429
1984 Montreal	NL	160	622	192	38	9	8	(2	6)	272	106	60	121	87	7	69	2	3	4	75	10	.88	9	.309	.393	.437
1985 Montreal	NL	150	575	184	30	13	11	(4	7)	273	115	41	120	81	13	60	3	3	3	70	9	.89	9	.320	.405	.475
1986 Montreal	NL	151	580	194	35	10	9	(4	5)	276	91	62	124	78	9	60	2	1	3	70	9	.89	9	.334	.413	.476
1987 Montreal	NL	139	530	175	34	8	18	(9	9)	279	123	68	124	90	26	52	4	0	3	50	5	.91	9	.330	.429	.526
1988 Montreal	NL	109	429	116	19	7	12	(5	7)	185	66	48	68	53	14	44	2	0	4	33	7	.83	8	.270	.350	.431
1989 Montreal	NL	145	517	148	29	6	9	(6	3)	216	76	60	94	93	18	48	3	0	5	41	9	.82	8	.286	.395	.418
1990 Montreal	NL	130	457	131	11	5	9	(6	3)	179	65	62	75	70	8	43	3	0	8	49	16	.75	9	.287	.379	.392
1991 Chicago	AL	155	609	163	20	6	5	(1	4)	210	102	50	85	83	9	68	5	9	3	51	15	.77	7	.268	.359	.345
1992 Chicago	AL	144	551	162	22	9	7	(4	3)	223	102	54	97	81	4	48	0	4	8	45	6	.88	5	.294	.380	.405
1993 Chicago	AL	115	415	127	16	4	16	(7	9)	199	75	54	82	64	4	35	3	2	2	21	7	.75	7	.306	.401	.480
1994 Chicago	AL	101	384	102	15	5	10	(5	5)	157	80	52	61	61	3	43	1	4	3	13	0	1.00	10	.266	.365	.409
1995 Chicago	AL	133	502	143	25	4	12	(6	6)	212	81	67	84	70	3	52	3	3	3	13	2	.87	5	.285	.374	.422
1996 New York	AL	59	201	57	10	0	9	(7	2)	94	45	33	38	34	1	29	1	0	4	10	1	.91	5	.284	.383	.468
1997 New York	AL	74	271	87	20	2	4	(3	1)	123	56	38	51	41	0	34	0	0	6	8	5	.62	4	.321	.403	.454
1998 New York	AL	109	321	93	13	1	5	(2	3)	123	53	47	53	55	1	49	3	0	3	8	3	.73	5	.290	.395	.383
1999 Oakland	AL	58	135	29	5	0	4	(2	2)	46	20	17	17	26	1	17	0	1	2	4	1	.80	5	.215	.337	.341
2001 Mon-Bal		51	89	27	8	1	1	(1	0)	40	14	9	18	18	0	9	0	0	2	1	0	1.00	2	.303	.413	.449
2002 Florida	NL	98	89	17	3	0	1	(0	1)	23	9	7	6	22	4	19	1	0	2	0	0	-	3	.191	.351	.258
2001 Montreal	NL	47	78	24	8	1	0	(1	0)	34	13	4	16	18	0	6	0	0	1	1	0	1.00	2	.308	.433	.436
2001 Baltimore	AL	4	11	3	0	0	1	(1	0)	6	1	5	2	0	0	3	0	0	1	0	0	-	0	.273	.250	.545
22 ML YEARS		2496	8872	2605	430	113	170	(83	87)	3771	1568	980	1597	1330	148	966	42	39	76	806	146	.85	142	.294	.385	.425

Aramis Ramirez

Bats: R **Throws:** R **Pos:** 3B-131; PH-9; DH-3   **Ht:** 6'1" **Wt:** 211 **Born:** 6/25/78 **Age:** 25

								BATTING												BASERUNNING				AVERAGES		
Year Team	Lg	G	AB	H	2B	3B	HR	(Hm	Rd)	TB	R	RBI	RC	TBB	IBB	SO	HBP	SH	SF	SB	CS	SB%	GDP	Avg	OBP	Slg
1998 Pittsburgh	NL	72	251	59	9	1	6	(3	3)	88	23	24	26	18	0	72	4	1	1	0	1	.00	3	.235	.296	.351
1999 Pittsburgh	NL	18	56	10	2	1	0	(0	0)	14	2	7	4	6	0	9	1	0	1	0	0	-	0	.179	.254	.250
2000 Pittsburgh	NL	73	254	65	15	2	6	(4	2)	102	19	35	28	10	0	36	5	1	4	0	0	-	9	.256	.293	.402
2001 Pittsburgh	NL	158	603	181	40	4	34	(16	18)	323	83	112	108	40	4	100	8	0	4	5	4	.56	3	.300	.350	.536
2002 Pittsburgh	NL	142	522	122	26	0	18	(7	11)	202	51	71	49	29	3	95	8	0	11	2	0	1.00	17	.234	.279	.387
5 ML YEARS		463	1686	437	92	4	64	(30	34)	729	178	249	215	103	7	312	25	3	21	7	5	.58	38	.259	.308	.432

Horacio Ramirez

Pitches: L **Bats:** L **Pos:** SP   **Ht:** 6'1" **Wt:** 170 **Born:** 11/24/79 **Age:** 23

		HOW MUCH HE PITCHED						WHAT HE GAVE UP												THE RESULTS					
Year Team	Lg	G	GS	CG	GF	IP	BFP	H	R	ER	HR	SH	SF	HB	TBB	IBB	SO	WP	Bk	W	L	Pct	ShO	Sv-Op	Hld	ERC	ERA
1997 Braves	R	11	8	0	2	44.0	175	30	13	11	1	0	1	0	18	0	61	4	0	3	3	.500	0	0- -	-	2.02	2.25
1998 Macon	A	12	12	0	0	55.1	249	70	50	36	8	2	3	2	16	0	38	2	0	1	7	.125	0	0- -	-	5.64	5.86
1998 Eugene	A-	16	8	0	3	55.2	273	84	51	39	4	3	6	4	17	0	39	4	2	2	7	.222	0	0- -	-	6.61	6.31
1999 Macon	A	17	14	1	0	77.2	316	70	30	23	6	2	5	2	25	0	43	1	1	6	3	.667	1	0- -	-	3.28	2.67
2000 Myrtle Beach	A+	27	26	3	0	148.1	609	136	57	53	14	1	1	2	42	0	125	6	4	15	8	.652	2	0- -	-	3.22	3.22
2001 Greenville	AA	3	3	0	0	14.2	66	17	8	8	2	2	0	1	8	0	17	0	0	1	1	.500	0	0- -	-	6.43	4.91
2002 Greenville	AA	16	16	0	0	92.0	376	85	41	31	5	1	7	0	32	0	64	3	1	9	5	.643	0	0- -	-	3.25	3.03

Julio Ramirez

Bats: R **Throws:** R **Pos:** CF-15; PR-10; RF-9; PH-4; DH-1   **Ht:** 5'11" **Wt:** 170 **Born:** 8/10/77 **Age:** 25

								BATTING												BASERUNNING				AVERAGES		
Year Team	Lg	G	AB	H	2B	3B	HR	(Hm	Rd)	TB	R	RBI	RC	TBB	IBB	SO	HBP	SH	SF	SB	CS	SB%	GDP	Avg	OBP	Slg
2002 Salt Lake*	AAA	39	139	38	3	5	2	(-	-)	57	17	10	17	4	0	31	1	1	0	8	3	.73	2	.273	.299	.410
1999 Florida	NL	15	21	3	1	0	0	(0	0)	4	3	2	0	1	0	6	0	0	0	0	1	.00	0	.143	.182	.190
2001 Chicago	AL	22	37	3	0	0	0	(0	0)	3	2	1	0	2	0	15	0	0	0	2	0	1.00	0	.081	.128	.081
2002 Anaheim	AL	29	32	9	0	1	1	(1	0)	14	6	7	5	2	0	14	1	0	0	0	2	.00	0	.281	.343	.438
3 ML YEARS		66	90	15	1	1	1	(1	0)	21	11	10	5	5	0	35	1	0	0	2	3	.40	0	.167	.219	.233

Manny Ramirez

Bats: R **Throws:** R **Pos:** LF-64; DH-50; RF-7; PH-2   **Ht:** 6'0" **Wt:** 213 **Born:** 5/30/72 **Age:** 31

								BATTING												BASERUNNING				AVERAGES		
Year Team	Lg	G	AB	H	2B	3B	HR	(Hm	Rd)	TB	R	RBI	RC	TBB	IBB	SO	HBP	SH	SF	SB	CS	SB%	GDP	Avg	OBP	Slg
2002 Pawtucket*	AAA	11	30	3	1	0	1	(-	-)	7	2	2	2	8	0	9	1	0	0	0	0	-	1	.100	.308	.233
1993 Cleveland	AL	22	53	9	1	0	2	(0	2)	16	5	5	2	2	0	8	0	0	0	0	0	-	3	.170	.200	.302
1994 Cleveland	AL	91	290	78	22	0	17	(9	8)	151	51	60	53	42	4	72	0	0	4	4	2	.67	6	.269	.357	.521
1995 Cleveland	AL	137	484	149	26	1	31	(12	19)	270	85	107	103	75	6	112	5	2	5	6	6	.50	13	.308	.402	.558
1996 Cleveland	AL	152	550	170	45	3	33	(19	14)	320	94	112	120	85	8	104	3	0	9	8	5	.62	18	.309	.399	.582
1997 Cleveland	AL	150	561	184	40	0	26	(14	12)	302	99	88	117	79	5	115	7	0	4	2	3	.40	19	.328	.415	.538
1998 Cleveland	AL	150	571	168	35	2	45	(25	20)	342	108	145	121	76	6	121	6	0	10	5	3	.63	18	.294	.377	.599
1999 Cleveland	AL	147	522	174	34	3	44	(21	23)	346	131	165	141	96	9	131	13	0	9	2	4	.33	12	.333	.442	.663
2000 Cleveland	AL	118	439	154	34	2	38	(22	16)	306	92	122	127	86	9	117	3	0	4	1	1	.50	9	.351	.457	.697
2001 Boston	AL	142	529	162	33	2	41	(21	20)	322	93	125	122	81	25	147	8	0	2	0	1	.00	9	.306	.405	.609
2002 Boston	AL	120	436	152	31	0	33	(18	15)	282	84	107	126	73	14	85	8	0	1	0	0	-	13	.349	.450	.647
10 ML YEARS		1229	4435	1400	301	13	310	(161	149)	2657	842	1036	1032	695	86	1012	53	2	48	28	25	.53	120	.316	.411	.599

Joe Randa

Bats: R **Throws:** R **Pos:** 3B-129; DH-19; PH-6   **Ht:** 5'11" **Wt:** 190 **Born:** 12/18/69 **Age:** 33

								BATTING												BASERUNNING				AVERAGES		
Year Team	Lg	G	AB	H	2B	3B	HR	(Hm	Rd)	TB	R	RBI	RC	TBB	IBB	SO	HBP	SH	SF	SB	CS	SB%	GDP	Avg	OBP	Slg
1995 Kansas City	AL	34	70	12	2	0	1	(1	0)	17	6	5	3	6	0	17	0	0	0	0	1	.00	2	.171	.237	.243
1996 Kansas City	AL	110	337	102	24	1	6	(2	4)	146	36	47	50	26	4	47	1	2	4	13	4	.76	10	.303	.351	.433
1997 Pittsburgh	NL	126	443	134	27	9	7	(5	2)	200	58	60	72	41	1	64	6	4	5	4	2	.67	10	.302	.366	.451
1998 Detroit	AL	138	460	117	21	2	9	(3	6)	169	56	50	54	41	1	70	7	3	3	8	7	.53	9	.254	.323	.367
1999 Kansas City	AL	156	628	197	36	8	16	(7	9)	297	92	84	103	50	4	80	3	1	7	5	4	.56	15	.314	.363	.473
2000 Kansas City	AL	158	612	186	29	4	15	(9	6)	268	88	106	88	36	3	66	6	1	10	6	3	.67	19	.304	.343	.438
2001 Kansas City	AL	151	581	147	34	2	13	(8	5)	224	59	83	67	42	2	80	6	1	6	3	2	.60	15	.253	.307	.386
2002 Kansas City	AL	151	549	155	36	5	11	(6	5)	234	63	80	77	46	1	69	9	2	11	2	1	.67	13	.282	.341	.426
8 ML YEARS		1024	3680	1050	209	31	78	(41	37)	1555	458	515	514	288	16	493	38	14	46	41	24	.63	93	.285	.340	.423

Stephen Randolph

Pitches: L **Bats:** L **Pos:** RP   **Ht:** 6'3" **Wt:** 202 **Born:** 5/1/74 **Age:** 29

		HOW MUCH HE PITCHED						WHAT HE GAVE UP												THE RESULTS					
Year Team	Lg	G	GS	CG	GF	IP	BFP	H	R	ER	HR	SH	SF	HB	TBB	IBB	SO	WP	Bk	W	L	Pct	ShO	Sv-Op	Hld	ERC	ERA
1995 Yankees	R	8	3	0	1	24.1	94	11	7	6	1	0	0	1	16	0	34	3	1	4	0	1.000	0	0- -	-	2.11	2.22
1995 Oneonta	A-	6	6	0	0	21.2	109	19	22	18	0	0	2	1	23	0	31	5	0	0	3	.000	0	0- -	-	5.12	7.48
1996 Greensboro	A	32	17	1	6	100.1	451	64	46	42	8	4	5	5	96	1	111	13	3	4	7	.364	0	0- -	-	4.27	3.77
1997 Tampa	A+	34	13	1	6	95.1	417	74	55	41	8	7	3	3	63	5	108	4	1	4	7	.364	0	1- -	-	3.76	3.87
1998 High Desert	A+	17	17	0	0	85.1	357	71	44	34	6	3	2	3	42	0	104	0	0	4	4	.500	0	0- -	-	3.52	3.59
1998 Tucson	AAA	17	1	0	3	22.2	99	16	11	8	1	0	2	0	19	2	23	3	0	1	3	.250	0	0- -	-	3.63	3.18
1999 El Paso	AA	8	8	0	0	44.1	186	39	14	13	1	2	0	1	23	0	38	1	1	2	2	.500	0	0- -	-	3.53	2.64
1999 Tucson	AAA	11	10	1	0	41.2	204	47	37	32	7	1	2	2	32	1	26	1	0	0	7	.000	0	0- -	-	6.99	6.91
1999 Diamndbcks	R	2	2	0	0	6.0	25	5	3	3	0	0	0	0	2	0	7	0	0	0	0	-	0	0- -	-	2.26	4.50
2000 Tucson	AAA	5	3	0	1	13.1	69	11	13	13	3	1	1	0	19	0	6	0	0	0	0	-	0	0- -	-	8.32	8.78

Year Team	Lg	HOW MUCH HE PITCHED						WHAT HE GAVE UP												THE RESULTS							
		G	GS	CG	GF	IP	BFP	H	R	ER	HR	SH	SF	HB	TBB	IBB	SO	WP	Bk	W	L	Pct	ShO	Sv-Op	Hld	ERC	ERA
2001 El Paso	AA	18	14	1	0	75.0	342	69	50	43	11	1	2	3	53	1	66	7	1	5	6	.455	1	0--	-	5.35	5.16
2001 Tucson	AAA	18	0	0	7	21.1	109	24	15	15	2	1	2	2	19	1	16	2	0	2	0	1.000	0	0--	-	6.91	6.33
2002 Tucson	AAA	28	27	1	1	163.1	704	151	70	63	15	6	7	6	81	2	129	6	0	15	7	.682	1	0--	-	4.15	3.47

Cody Ransom

Bats: R **Throws:** R **Pos:** PR-5; SS-3　　　　**Ht:** 6'2" **Wt:** 196 **Born:** 2/17/76 **Age:** 27

Year Team	Lg	BATTING																		BASERUNNING				AVERAGES		
		G	AB	H	2B	3B	HR	(Hm	Rd)	TB	R	RBI	RC	TBB	IBB	SO	HBP	SH	SF	SB	CS	SB%	GDP	Avg	OBP	Slg
1998 Salem-Keizer	A-	71	236	55	12	7	6	(-	-)	99	52	27	38	43	1	56	2	3	4	19	6	.76	4	.233	.351	.419
1999 Bakersfield	A+	99	356	98	12	6	11	(-	-)	155	69	47	62	54	0	108	8	1	1	15	8	.65	2	.275	.382	.435
1999 Shreveport	AA	14	41	5	0	0	2	(-	-)	11	6	4	2	4	0	22	1	1	2	0	0	-	0	.122	.208	.268
2000 Shreveport	AA	130	459	92	21	2	7	(-	-)	138	58	47	34	40	1	141	0	3	3	9	3	.75	9	.200	.263	.301
2001 Fresno	AAA	134	469	113	21	6	23	(-	-)	215	77	78	66	44	1	137	0	3	5	17	2	.89	10	.241	.303	.458
2002 Fresno	AAA	135	449	93	18	4	13	(-	-)	158	53	46	46	47	0	151	3	12	6	6	4	.60	5	.207	.283	.352
2001 San Francisco	NL	9	7	0	0	0	0	(0	0)	0	1	0	0	0	0	5	0	0	0	0	0	-	0	.000	.000	.000
2002 San Francisco	NL	7	3	2	0	0	0	(0	0)	2	2	1	1	1	1	1	0	0	0	0	0	-	0	.667	.750	.667
2 ML YEARS		16	10	2	0	0	0	(0	0)	2	3	1	1	1	1	6	0	0	0	0	0	-	0	.200	.273	.200

Jon Rauch

Pitches: R **Bats:** R **Pos:** SP-6; RP-2　　　　**Ht:** 6'10" **Wt:** 230 **Born:** 9/27/78 **Age:** 24

Year Team	Lg	HOW MUCH HE PITCHED						WHAT HE GAVE UP												THE RESULTS							
		G	GS	CG	GF	IP	BFP	H	R	ER	HR	SH	SF	HB	TBB	IBB	SO	WP	Bk	W	L	Pct	ShO	Sv-Op	Hld	ERC	ERA
1999 Bristol	R+	14	9	0	3	56.2	264	65	44	28	4	1	2	3	16	1	66	6	2	4	4	.500	0	2--	-	4.11	4.45
1999 Winstn-Salm	A+	1	1	0	0	6.0	26	4	3	2	1	0	0	0	3	0	7	1	0	0	0	-	0	0--	-	2.91	3.00
2000 Winstn-Salm	A+	18	18	1	0	110.0	456	102	49	35	10	4	3	5	33	0	124	4	1	11	3	.786	0	0--	-	3.45	2.86
2000 Birmingham	AA	8	8	2	0	56.0	220	36	18	14	4	1	0	2	16	0	63	2	0	5	1	.833	2	0--	-	1.81	2.25
2001 Charlotte	AAA	6	6	0	0	28.0	121	28	20	18	8	0	0	1	7	0	27	1	0	1	3	.250	0	0--	-	4.73	5.79
2002 Charlotte	AAA	19	19	1	0	109.1	451	91	60	52	14	2	1	3	42	2	97	2	0	7	8	.467	0	0--	-	3.41	4.28
2002 Chicago	AL	8	6	0	1	28.2	130	28	26	21	7	0	1	2	14	2	19	1	1	2	1	.667	0	0-0	0	5.41	6.59

Britt Reames

Pitches: R **Bats:** R **Pos:** RP-36; SP-6　　　　**Ht:** 5'11" **Wt:** 175 **Born:** 8/19/73 **Age:** 29

Year Team	Lg	HOW MUCH HE PITCHED						WHAT HE GAVE UP												THE RESULTS							
		G	GS	CG	GF	IP	BFP	H	R	ER	HR	SH	SF	HB	TBB	IBB	SO	WP	Bk	W	L	Pct	ShO	Sv-Op	Hld	ERC	ERA
2002 Ottawa*	AAA	7	7	0	0	42.0	170	31	16	13	3	3	1	2	14	0	26	1	0	3	2	.600	0	0--	-	2.46	2.79
2000 St Louis	NL	8	7	0	0	40.2	170	30	17	13	4	0	1	1	23	1	31	2	1	2	1	.667	0	0-0	0	3.39	2.88
2001 Montreal	NL	41	13	0	3	95.0	432	101	68	59	16	7	2	5	48	3	86	2	0	4	8	.333	0	0-1	6	5.52	5.59
2002 Montreal	NL	42	6	0	7	68.0	308	70	42	38	8	3	1	3	38	6	76	2	0	1	4	.200	0	0-1	6	5.04	5.03
3 ML YEARS		91	26	0	10	203.2	910	201	127	110	28	10	4	9	109	10	193	6	1	7	13	.350	0	0-2	12	4.91	4.86

Jeff Reboulet

Bats: R **Throws:** R **Pos:** PH-25; 2B-11; SS-5; 3B-3; DH-1　　　　**Ht:** 6'0" **Wt:** 175 **Born:** 4/30/64 **Age:** 39

Year Team	Lg	BATTING																		BASERUNNING				AVERAGES		
		G	AB	H	2B	3B	HR	(Hm	Rd)	TB	R	RBI	RC	TBB	IBB	SO	HBP	SH	SF	SB	CS	SB%	GDP	Avg	OBP	Slg
2002 Las Vegas*	AAA	18	63	16	2	0	1	(-	-)	21	10	3	7	6	0	9	0	2	1	2	0	1.00	1	.254	.314	.333
1992 Minnesota	AL	73	137	26	7	1	1	(1	0)	38	15	16	14	23	0	26	1	7	0	3	2	.60	1	.190	.311	.277
1993 Minnesota	AL	109	240	62	8	0	1	(0	1)	73	33	15	27	35	0	37	2	5	1	5	5	.50	6	.258	.356	.304
1994 Minnesota	AL	74	189	49	11	1	3	(2	1)	71	28	23	22	18	0	23	1	2	0	0	0	-	6	.259	.327	.376
1995 Minnesota	AL	87	216	63	11	0	4	(1	3)	86	39	23	33	27	0	34	1	2	0	1	2	.33	3	.292	.373	.398
1996 Minnesota	AL	107	234	52	9	0	0	(0	0)	61	20	23	16	25	1	34	1	4	2	4	2	.67	10	.222	.298	.261
1997 Baltimore	AL	99	228	54	9	4	4	(2	2)	75	26	27	25	23	0	44	1	11	2	3	0	1.00	3	.237	.307	.329
1998 Baltimore	AL	79	126	31	6	0	1	(1	0)	40	20	8	15	19	0	34	2	7	1	0	1	.00	3	.246	.351	.317
1999 Baltimore	AL	99	154	25	4	0	0	(0	0)	29	25	4	12	33	0	29	2	3	0	1	0	1.00	1	.162	.317	.188
2000 Kansas City	AL	66	182	44	7	0	0	(0	0)	51	29	14	16	23	0	32	0	6	1	3	1	.75	8	.242	.325	.280
2001 Los Angeles	NL	94	214	57	15	2	3	(3	0)	85	35	22	32	33	1	48	1	5	0	0	1	.00	3	.266	.367	.397
2002 Los Angeles	NL	38	48	10	3	0	0	(0	0)	13	3	2	2	6	0	13	0	3	1	0	0	-	1	.208	.291	.271
11 ML YEARS		925	1968	473	90	4	17	(10	7)	622	273	177	214	265	2	354	12	55	8	20	14	.59	44	.240	.333	.316

Tim Redding

Pitches: R **Bats:** R **Pos:** SP-14; RP-4　　　　**Ht:** 6'0" **Wt:** 195 **Born:** 2/12/78 **Age:** 25

Year Team	Lg	HOW MUCH HE PITCHED						WHAT HE GAVE UP												THE RESULTS							
		G	GS	CG	GF	IP	BFP	H	R	ER	HR	SH	SF	HB	TBB	IBB	SO	WP	Bk	W	L	Pct	ShO	Sv-Op	Hld	ERC	ERA
1998 Auburn	A-	16	15	0	1	73.2	323	49	44	37	2	2	3	7	50	0	98	10	4	7	3	.700	0	1--	-	3.11	4.52
1999 Michigan	A	43	11	0	24	105.0	470	84	69	58	4	6	5	3	76	1	141	19	2	8	6	.571	0	14--	-	3.82	4.97
2000 Kissimmee	A+	24	24	0	0	154.2	649	125	62	46	5	4	6	9	57	1	170	13	0	12	5	.706	0	0--	-	2.66	2.68
2000 Round Rock	AA	5	5	0	0	26.0	111	14	12	10	4	2	2	1	22	0	22	4	0	2	0	1.000	0	0--	-	3.86	3.46
2001 Round Rock	AA	14	14	1	0	90.2	364	64	26	22	5	1	0	3	25	0	113	1	0	10	2	.833	1	0--	-	1.93	2.18
2001 New Orleans	AAA	6	6	0	0	37.2	153	22	21	19	4	0	1	5	19	0	42	1	0	4	1	.800	0	0--	-	2.87	4.54
2002 New Orleans	AAA	11	7	0	2	38.0	158	32	22	22	6	3	1	3	13	1	50	5	0	3	3	.500	0	0--	-	3.67	5.21
2001 Houston	NL	13	9	0	1	55.2	249	62	38	34	11	2	3	3	24	0	55	2	0	3	1	.750	0	0-0	0	5.87	5.50
2002 Houston	NL	18	14	0	1	73.1	325	78	49	44	10	4	3	0	35	3	63	5	1	3	6	.333	0	0-0	0	4.96	5.40
2 ML YEARS		31	23	0	2	129.0	574	140	87	78	21	6	6	3	59	3	118	7	1	6	7	.462	0	0-0	0	5.35	5.44

Mark Redman

Pitches: L **Bats:** L **Pos:** SP-30   **Ht:** 6'5" **Wt:** 245 **Born:** 1/5/74 **Age:** 29

Year Team	Lg	HOW MUCH HE PITCHED						WHAT HE GAVE UP										THE RESULTS						
		G	GS	CG	GF	IP	BFP	H	R	ER	HR	SH	SF	HB	TBB	IBB	SO	WP	Bk	W	L	Pct	ShO	Sv-Op	Hld	ERC	ERA
1999 Minnesota	AL	5	1	0	0	12.2	65	17	13	12	3	0	1	0	7	0	11	0	0	1	0	1.000	0	0-0	0	7.86	8.53
2000 Minnesota	AL	32	24	0	3	151.1	651	168	81	80	22	3	2	3	45	0	117	6	0	12	9	.571	0	0-0	0	4.73	4.76
2001 Min-Det	AL	11	11	0	0	58.0	261	68	32	29	7	2	0	1	23	0	33	6	0	2	6	.250	0	0-0	0	5.26	4.50
2002 Detroit	AL	30	30	3	0	203.0	858	211	107	95	15	5	8	6	51	2	109	11	1	8	15	.348	0	0-0	0	3.64	4.21
2001 Minnesota	AL	9	9	0	0	49.0	219	57	26	23	6	1	0	0	19	0	29	6	0	2	4	.333	0	0-0	0	5.11	4.22
2001 Detroit	AL	2	2	0	0	9.0	42	11	6	6	1	1	0	1	4	0	4	0	0	0	2	.000	0	0-0	0	6.12	6.00
4 ML YEARS		78	66	3	3	425.0	1835	464	233	216	47	10	10	11	126	2	270	23	1	23	30	.434	0	0-0	0	4.36	4.57

Mike Redmond

Bats: R **Throws:** R **Pos:** C-80; PH-7; 1B-2   **Ht:** 5'11" **Wt:** 208 **Born:** 5/5/71 **Age:** 32

Year Team	Lg	BATTING																	BASERUNNING				AVERAGES		
		G	AB	H	2B	3B	HR	(Hm	Rd)	TB	R	RBI	RC	TBB	IBB	SO	HBP	SH	SF	SB	CS	SB%	GDP	Avg	OBP	Slg
1998 Florida	NL	37	118	39	9	0	1	(1	1)	54	10	12	18	5	2	16	2	4	0	0	0	-	6	.331	.368	.458
1999 Florida	NL	84	242	73	9	0	1	(0	1)	85	22	27	33	26	2	34	5	5	0	0	0	-	8	.302	.381	.351
2000 Florida	NL	87	210	53	8	1	0	(0	0)	63	17	15	20	13	3	19	8	1	3	0	0	-	5	.252	.316	.300
2001 Florida	NL	48	141	44	4	0	4	(3	1)	60	19	14	21	13	4	13	2	1	1	0	0	-	6	.312	.376	.426
2002 Florida	NL	89	256	78	15	0	2	(1	1)	99	19	28	36	21	8	34	8	2	3	0	2	.00	4	.305	.372	.387
5 ML YEARS		345	967	287	45	1	9	(5	4)	361	87	96	128	78	19	116	25	13	7	0	2	.00	29	.297	.362	.373

Rick Reed

Pitches: R **Bats:** R **Pos:** SP-32; RP-1   **Ht:** 6'1" **Wt:** 195 **Born:** 8/16/65 **Age:** 37

Year Team	Lg	HOW MUCH HE PITCHED						WHAT HE GAVE UP										THE RESULTS						
		G	GS	CG	GF	IP	BFP	H	R	ER	HR	SH	SF	HB	TBB	IBB	SO	WP	Bk	W	L	Pct	ShO	Sv-Op	Hld	ERC	ERA
1988 Pittsburgh	NL	2	2	0	0	12.0	47	10	4	4	1	2	0	0	2	0	6	0	0	1	0	1.000	0	0-0	0	2.26	3.00
1989 Pittsburgh	NL	15	7	0	2	54.2	232	62	35	34	5	2	3	2	11	3	34	0	3	1	4	.200	0	0-0	0	4.07	5.60
1990 Pittsburgh	NL	13	8	1	2	53.2	238	62	32	26	6	2	1	1	12	6	27	0	0	2	3	.400	1	1-1	1	4.08	4.36
1991 Pittsburgh	NL	1	1	0	0	4.1	21	8	6	5	1	0	0	0	1	0	2	0	0	0	0	-	0	0-0	0	10.07	10.38
1992 Kansas City	AL	19	18	1	0	100.1	419	105	47	41	10	2	5	5	20	3	49	0	0	3	7	.300	1	0-0	0	3.73	3.68
1993 KC-Tex	AL	3	0	0	2	7.2	36	12	5	5	1	0	0	2	2	0	5	0	0	1	0	1.000	0	0-0	0	8.88	5.87
1994 Texas	AL	4	3	0	0	16.2	75	17	13	11	3	0	0	1	7	0	12	0	0	1	1	.500	0	0-0	0	4.98	5.94
1995 Cincinnati	NL	4	3	0	1	17.0	70	18	12	11	5	1	0	0	3	0	10	0	0	0	0	-	0	0-0	0	4.84	5.82
1997 New York	NL	33	31	2	0	208.1	824	186	76	67	19	7	3	5	31	4	113	0	0	13	9	.591	0	0-0	0	2.61	2.89
1998 New York	NL	31	31	2	0	212.1	845	208	84	82	30	8	5	6	29	2	153	1	0	16	11	.593	0	0-0	0	3.39	3.48
1999 New York	NL	26	26	1	0	149.1	637	163	77	76	23	6	3	1	47	2	104	1	0	11	5	.688	0	0-0	0	4.71	4.58
2000 New York	NL	30	30	0	0	184.0	768	192	90	84	28	3	5	5	34	3	121	2	1	11	5	.688	0	0-0	0	3.90	4.11
2001 NYM-Min		32	32	3	0	202.1	834	211	98	91	28	8	3	5	31	3	142	3	0	12	12	.500	1	0-0	0	3.69	4.05
2002 Minnesota	AL	33	32	2	0	188.0	778	192	89	79	32	1	5	6	26	0	121	1	1	15	7	.682	1	0-0	1	3.72	3.78
1993 Kansas City	AL	1	0	0	0	3.2	18	6	4	4	0	0	0	1	1	0	3	0	0	0	0	-	0	0-0	0	7.97	9.82
1993 Texas	AL	2	0	0	0	4.0	18	6	1	1	1	0	0	1	1	0	2	0	0	1	0	1.000	0	0-0	0	9.70	2.25
2001 New York	NL	20	20	3	0	134.2	531	119	53	52	16	8	1	1	17	3	99	2	0	8	6	.571	1	0-0	0	2.55	3.48
2001 Minnesota	AL	12	12	0	0	67.2	303	92	45	39	12	0	2	4	14	0	43	1	0	4	6	.400	0	0-0	0	6.30	5.19
14 ML YEARS		246	224	12	5	1410.2	5824	1446	668	616	192	42	33	39	256	26	899	8	5	87	64	.576	6	1-1	2	3.70	3.93

Steve Reed

Pitches: R **Bats:** R **Pos:** RP-64   **Ht:** 6'2" **Wt:** 212 **Born:** 3/11/66 **Age:** 37

Year Team	Lg	HOW MUCH HE PITCHED						WHAT HE GAVE UP										THE RESULTS						
		G	GS	CG	GF	IP	BFP	H	R	ER	HR	SH	SF	HB	TBB	IBB	SO	WP	Bk	W	L	Pct	ShO	Sv-Op	Hld	ERC	ERA
1992 San Francisco	NL	18	0	0	2	15.2	63	13	5	4	2	0	0	1	3	0	11	0	0	1	0	1.000	0	0-0	1	2.80	2.30
1993 Colorado	NL	64	0	0	14	84.1	347	80	47	42	13	2	3	3	30	5	51	1	0	9	5	.643	0	3-6	9	4.19	4.48
1994 Colorado	NL	61	0	0	11	64.0	297	79	33	28	9	0	7	6	26	3	51	1	0	3	2	.600	0	3-10	14	6.09	3.94
1995 Colorado	NL	71	0	0	15	84.0	327	61	24	20	8	3	1	1	21	3	79	0	2	5	2	.714	0	3-6	11	2.11	2.14
1996 Colorado	NL	70	0	0	7	75.0	322	66	38	33	11	2	4	6	19	0	51	1	0	4	3	.571	0	0-6	22	3.52	3.96
1997 Colorado	NL	63	0	0	23	62.1	260	49	28	28	10	3	1	5	27	1	43	0	0	4	6	.400	0	6-13	10	3.78	4.04
1998 SF-Cle		70	0	0	19	80.1	322	56	29	28	8	2	0	5	27	5	73	0	0	4	3	.571	0	1-6	21	2.42	3.14
1999 Cleveland	AL	63	0	0	15	61.2	274	69	33	29	10	4	5	3	20	5	44	2	0	3	2	.600	0	0-3	8	4.91	4.23
2000 Cleveland	AL	57	0	0	16	56.0	243	58	30	27	7	4	1	1	21	4	39	2	1	2	0	1.000	0	0-1	9	4.31	4.34
2001 Cle-Atl		70	0	0	14	58.1	250	52	25	23	6	3	1	3	23	5	46	0	0	3	3	.500	0	1-2	11	3.51	3.55
2002 SD-NYM	NL	64	0	0	15	67.0	269	56	15	15	2	6	0	8	14	3	50	2	0	2	5	.286	0	1-4	17	2.48	2.01
1998 San Francisco	NL	50	0	0	14	54.2	213	30	10	9	4	2	0	4	19	5	50	0	0	2	1	.667	0	1-5	13	1.64	1.48
1998 Cleveland	AL	20	0	0	5	25.2	109	26	19	19	4	0	0	1	8	0	23	0	0	2	2	.500	0	0-1	8	4.38	6.66
2001 Cleveland	AL	31	0	0	8	27.1	116	22	11	11	3	0	0	2	10	2	21	0	0	1	1	.500	0	0-1	6	3.06	3.62
2001 Atlanta	NL	39	0	0	6	31.0	134	30	14	12	3	3	1	1	13	3	25	0	0	2	2	.500	0	1-1	5	3.92	3.48
2002 San Diego	NL	40	0	0	11	41.0	166	33	9	9	2	5	0	6	10	2	36	1	0	2	4	.333	0	1-3	11	2.65	1.98
2002 New York	NL	24	0	0	4	26.0	103	23	6	6	0	1	0	2	4	1	14	1	0	0	1	.000	0	0-1	6	2.22	2.08
11 ML YEARS		671	0	0	151	708.2	2959	639	307	277	86	29	23	42	231	34	538	9	3	40	31	.563	0	18-57	133	3.58	3.52

Pokey Reese

Bats: R **Throws:** R **Pos:** 2B-117; PH-1; PR-1   **Ht:** 5'11" **Wt:** 188 **Born:** 6/10/73 **Age:** 30

Year Team	Lg	BATTING																	BASERUNNING				AVERAGES		
		G	AB	H	2B	3B	HR	(Hm	Rd)	TB	R	RBI	RC	TBB	IBB	SO	HBP	SH	SF	SB	CS	SB%	GDP	Avg	OBP	Slg
1997 Cincinnati	NL	128	397	87	15	0	4	(3	1)	114	48	26	35	31	2	82	5	4	0	25	7	.78	5	.219	.284	.287
1998 Cincinnati	NL	59	133	34	2	2	1	(0	1)	43	20	16	14	14	1	28	0	2	2	3	2	.60	3	.256	.322	.323
1999 Cincinnati	NL	149	585	167	37	5	10	(5	5)	244	85	52	84	35	3	81	6	5	5	38	7	.84	9	.285	.330	.417
2000 Cincinnati	NL	135	518	132	26	6	12	(3	9)	200	76	46	69	45	5	86	6	3	6	29	3	.91	6	.255	.319	.386
2001 Cincinnati	NL	133	428	96	20	2	9	(4	5)	147	50	40	44	34	4	82	3	5	5	25	4	.86	7	.224	.284	.343
2002 Pittsburgh	NL	119	421	111	20	0	4	(3	1)	148	46	50	60	41	4	81	3	5	5	12	1	.92	4	.264	.330	.352
6 ML YEARS		723	2482	627	119	15	40	(18	22)	896	325	230	306	200	19	440	23	24	21	132	24	.85	32	.253	.312	.361

Dan Reichert

Pitches: R **Bats:** R **Pos:** RP-24; SP-6 **Ht:** 6'3" **Wt:** 175 **Born:** 7/12/76 **Age:** 26

Year Team	Lg	G	GS	CG	GF	IP	BFP	H	R	ER	HR	SH	SF	HB	TBB	IBB	SO	WP	Bk	W	L	Pct	ShO	Sv-Op	Hld	ERC	ERA
2002 Omaha*	AAA	5	0	0	1	5.0	24	6	3	3	0	0	2	1	4	1	3	0	0	0	0	-	0	0- -	-	6.82	5.40
2002 Wichita*	AA	8	0	0	2	11.0	58	16	15	14	0	1	1	0	9	0	11	0	0	0	1	.000	0	0- -	-	7.52	11.45
1999 Kansas City	AL	8	8	0	0	36.2	183	48	38	37	2	1	1	2	32	1	20	1	0	2	2	.500	0	0-0	0	7.91	9.08
2000 Kansas City	AL	44	18	1	11	153.1	690	157	92	80	15	5	7	7	91	1	94	18	0	8	10	.444	1	2-6	4	5.22	4.70
2001 Kansas City	AL	27	19	0	4	123.0	554	131	83	77	14	3	4	8	67	2	77	12	0	8	8	.500	0	0-0	1	5.46	5.63
2002 Kansas City	AL	30	6	0	3	66.0	290	77	48	39	10	6	3	4	25	2	36	3	0	3	5	.375	0	0-0	6	5.70	5.32
4 ML YEARS		109	51	1	18	379.0	1717	413	261	233	41	15	15	21	215	6	227	34	0	21	25	.457	1	2-6	11	5.64	5.53

Chris Reitsma

Pitches: R **Bats:** R **Pos:** SP-21; RP-11 **Ht:** 6'5" **Wt:** 215 **Born:** 12/31/77 **Age:** 25

Year Team	Lg	G	GS	CG	GF	IP	BFP	H	R	ER	HR	SH	SF	HB	TBB	IBB	SO	WP	Bk	W	L	Pct	ShO	Sv-Op	Hld	ERC	ERA
1996 Red Sox	R	7	6	0	0	26.2	109	24	7	4	0	1	0	2	1	0	32	3	0	3	1	.750	0	0- -	-	1.82	1.35
1997 Michigan	A	9	9	0	0	49.2	217	57	23	16	4	0	2	2	13	0	41	3	0	4	1	.800	0	0- -	-	4.36	2.90
1998 Sarasota	A+	8	8	0	0	12.2	55	12	6	4	0	0	1	0	5	0	9	0	0	0	0	-	0	0- -	-	3.00	2.84
1999 Sarasota	A+	19	19	0	0	96.1	440	116	71	60	11	1	4	10	31	1	79	7	3	4	10	.286	0	0- -	-	5.40	5.61
2000 Sarasota	A+	11	11	0	0	64.0	267	57	29	26	3	4	1	5	17	0	47	0	0	3	4	.429	0	0- -	-	2.91	3.66
2001 Trenton	AA	14	14	1	0	90.2	361	78	28	26	7	1	1	2	21	1	58	1	0	7	2	.778	0	0- -	-	2.68	2.58
2002 Louisville	AAA	3	3	1	0	21.0	86	17	10	9	2	1	1	0	8	1	13	1	0	2	0	1.000	0	0- -	-	2.90	3.86
2001 Cincinnati	NL	36	29	0	1	182.0	800	209	121	107	23	13	8	5	49	6	96	5	0	7	15	.318	0	0-0	1	4.59	5.29
2002 Cincinnati	NL	32	21	1	6	138.1	598	144	73	56	17	4	4	5	45	5	84	4	0	6	12	.333	1	0-0	0	4.24	3.64
2 ML YEARS		68	50	1	7	320.1	1398	353	194	163	40	17	12	10	94	11	180	9	0	13	27	.325	1	0-0	1	4.44	4.58

Bryan Rekar

Pitches: R **Bats:** R **Pos:** SP-2 **Ht:** 6'3" **Wt:** 220 **Born:** 6/3/72 **Age:** 31

Year Team	Lg	G	GS	CG	GF	IP	BFP	H	R	ER	HR	SH	SF	HB	TBB	IBB	SO	WP	Bk	W	L	Pct	ShO	Sv-Op	Hld	ERC	ERA
2002 Omaha*	AAA	5	4	0	1	24.0	105	30	16	12	4	1	0	1	5	0	20	1	0	0	0	-	0	0- -	-	5.44	4.50
2002 Co Springs*	AAA	20	20	0	0	123.0	573	173	91	81	14	5	3	8	35	1	88	7	1	7	10	.412	0	0- -	-	6.36	5.93
1995 Colorado	NL	15	14	1	0	85.0	375	95	51	47	11	7	4	3	24	2	60	3	2	4	6	.400	0	0-0	1	4.50	4.98
1996 Colorado	NL	14	11	0	0	58.1	289	87	61	58	11	3	3	5	26	1	25	4	0	2	4	.333	0	0-1	0	8.31	8.95
1997 Colorado	NL	2	2	0	0	9.1	46	11	7	6	3	1	0	0	6	0	4	0	0	1	0	1.000	0	0-0	0	7.63	5.79
1998 Tampa Bay	AL	16	15	1	1	86.2	369	95	56	48	16	1	8	2	21	0	55	1	0	2	8	.200	0	0-0	1	4.69	4.98
1999 Tampa Bay	AL	27	12	0	2	94.2	437	121	68	61	14	3	2	5	41	2	55	4	0	6	6	.500	0	0-0	1	6.49	5.80
2000 Tampa Bay	AL	30	27	2	2	173.1	743	200	92	85	22	3	9	4	39	0	95	5	0	7	10	.412	0	0-0	0	4.56	4.41
2001 Tampa Bay	AL	25	25	0	0	140.2	630	167	104	92	21	4	7	6	45	2	87	6	1	3	13	.188	0	0-0	0	5.31	5.89
2002 Kansas City	AL	2	2	0	0	7.0	38	12	12	12	1	0	1	0	6	0	2	1	0	0	2	.000	0	0-0	0	11.14	15.43
8 ML YEARS		131	108	4	5	655.0	2927	788	451	409	99	22	34	25	208	7	383	24	3	25	49	.338	0	0-1	2	5.42	5.62

Desi Relaford

Bats: B **Throws:** R **Pos:** SS-40; 3B-38; LF-25; PH-12; 2B-11; RF-10; PR-8; DH-1 **Ht:** 5'9" **Wt:** 174 **Born:** 9/16/73 **Age:** 29

Year Team	Lg	G	AB	H	2B	3B	HR	(Hm	Rd)	TB	R	RBI	RC	TBB	IBB	SO	HBP	SH	SF	SB	CS	SB%	GDP	Avg	OBP	Slg
1996 Philadelphia	NL	15	40	7	2	0	0	(0	0)	9	2	1	2	3	0	9	0	1	0	1	0	1.00	1	.175	.233	.225
1997 Philadelphia	NL	15	38	7	1	2	0	(0	0)	12	3	6	4	5	0	6	0	1	0	3	0	1.00	0	.184	.279	.316
1998 Philadelphia	NL	142	494	121	25	3	5	(4	1)	167	45	41	48	33	4	87	3	10	6	9	5	.64	9	.245	.293	.338
1999 Philadelphia	NL	65	211	51	11	2	1	(0	1)	69	31	26	22	19	2	34	6	6	0	4	3	.57	5	.242	.322	.327
2000 Phi-SD	NL	128	410	88	14	3	5	(0	5)	123	55	46	51	75	7	71	12	3	2	13	0	1.00	10	.215	.351	.300
2001 New York	NL	120	301	91	27	0	8	(4	4)	142	43	36	52	27	1	65	5	2	5	13	5	.72	4	.302	.364	.472
2002 Seattle	AL	112	329	88	13	2	6	(1	5)	123	55	43	42	33	2	51	6	1	7	10	3	.77	6	.267	.339	.374
2000 Philadelphia	NL	83	253	56	12	3	3	(0	3)	83	29	30	34	48	7	45	9	2	1	5	0	1.00	7	.221	.363	.328
2000 San Diego	NL	45	157	32	2	0	2	(0	2)	40	26	16	17	27	0	26	3	1	1	8	0	1.00	3	.204	.330	.255
7 ML YEARS		597	1823	453	93	12	25	(9	16)	645	234	199	221	195	16	323	32	24	20	53	16	.77	35	.248	.329	.354

Mike Remlinger

Pitches: L **Bats:** L **Pos:** RP-73 **Ht:** 6'1" **Wt:** 210 **Born:** 3/23/66 **Age:** 37

Year Team	Lg	G	GS	CG	GF	IP	BFP	H	R	ER	HR	SH	SF	HB	TBB	IBB	SO	WP	Bk	W	L	Pct	ShO	Sv-Op	Hld	ERC	ERA
1991 San Francisco	NL	8	6	1	1	35.0	155	36	17	17	5	1	1	0	20	1	19	2	1	2	1	.667	1	0-0	0	5.30	4.37
1994 New York	NL	10	9	0	0	54.2	252	55	30	28	9	2	3	1	35	4	33	3	0	1	5	.167	0	0-0	1	5.46	4.61
1995 NYM-Cin	NL	7	0	0	4	6.2	34	9	6	5	1	1	0	0	5	0	7	0	0	0	1	.000	0	0-1	0	7.94	6.75
1996 Cincinnati	NL	19	4	0	2	27.1	125	24	17	17	4	3	1	3	19	2	19	2	2	0	1	.000	0	0-0	1	5.23	5.60
1997 Cincinnati	NL	69	12	2	10	124.0	525	100	61	57	11	6	4	7	60	6	145	12	2	8	8	.500	0	2-2	14	3.43	4.14
1998 Cincinnati	NL	35	28	1	0	164.1	727	164	96	88	23	12	7	5	87	1	144	11	1	8	15	.348	1	0-0	0	5.04	4.82
1999 Atlanta	NL	73	0	0	14	83.2	346	66	24	22	9	2	1	1	35	5	81	5	0	10	1	.909	0	1-3	21	3.03	2.37
2000 Atlanta	NL	71	0	0	18	72.2	311	55	29	28	6	3	2	3	37	1	72	3	0	5	3	.625	0	12-16	23	3.15	3.47
2001 Atlanta	NL	74	0	0	6	75.0	313	67	25	23	9	2	0	2	23	4	93	4	0	3	3	.500	0	1-5	31	3.27	2.76
2002 Atlanta	NL	73	0	0	7	68.0	275	48	17	15	3	4	0	1	28	3	69	0	0	7	3	.700	0	0-5	30	2.24	1.99
1995 New York	NL	5	0	0	4	5.2	27	7	5	4	1	1	0	0	2	0	6	0	0	0	1	.000	0	0-1	0	5.47	6.35
1995 Cincinnati	NL	2	0	0	0	1.0	7	2	1	1	0	0	0	0	3	0	1	0	0	0	0	-	0	0-0	0	24.60	9.00
10 ML YEARS		439	59	4	62	711.1	3063	624	322	300	80	36	19	23	349	27	682	42	6	44	41	.518	2	16-32	121	3.91	3.80

Edgar Renteria

Bats: R **Throws:** R **Pos:** SS-149; PH-3; PR-1   **Ht:** 6'1" **Wt:** 180 **Born:** 8/7/75 **Age:** 27

Year Team	Lg	G	AB	H	2B	3B	HR	(Hm	Rd)	TB	R	RBI	RC	TBB	IBB	SO	HBP	SH	SF	SB	CS	SB%	GDP	Avg	OBP	Slg
1996 Florida	NL	106	431	133	18	3	5	(2	3)	172	68	31	62	33	0	68	2	2	3	16	2	.89	12	.309	.358	.399
1997 Florida	NL	154	617	171	21	3	4	(3	1)	210	90	52	68	45	1	108	4	19	6	32	15	.68	17	.277	.327	.340
1998 Florida	NL	133	517	146	18	2	3	(2	1)	177	79	31	61	48	1	78	4	9	2	41	22	.65	13	.282	.347	.342
1999 St Louis	NL	154	585	161	36	2	11	(6	5)	234	92	63	81	53	0	82	2	6	7	37	8	.82	16	.275	.334	.400
2000 St Louis	NL	150	562	156	32	1	16	(4	12)	238	94	76	80	63	3	77	1	8	9	21	13	.62	19	.278	.346	.423
2001 St Louis	NL	141	493	128	19	3	10	(3	7)	183	54	57	57	39	4	73	3	8	6	17	4	.81	15	.260	.314	.371
2002 St Louis	NL	152	544	166	36	2	11	(4	7)	239	77	83	94	49	2	57	4	7	5	22	7	.76	17	.305	.364	.439
7 ML YEARS		990	3749	1061	180	16	60	(24	36)	1453	554	393	503	330	16	543	20	59	38	186	71	.72	109	.283	.341	.388

Michael Restovich

Bats: R **Throws:** R **Pos:** LF-4; PR-3; PH-2; RF-1   **Ht:** 6'4" **Wt:** 233 **Born:** 1/3/79 **Age:** 24

Year Team	Lg	G	AB	H	2B	3B	HR	(Hm	Rd)	TB	R	RBI	RC	TBB	IBB	SO	HBP	SH	SF	SB	CS	SB%	GDP	Avg	OBP	Slg
1998 Elizabethton	R+	65	242	86	20	1	13	(-	-)	147	68	64	67	54	0	58	9	0	0	5	2	.71	10	.355	.489	.607
1998 Fort Wayne	A	11	45	20	5	2	0	(-	-)	29	9	6	12	4	0	12	0	0	0	0	0	-	1	.444	.490	.644
1999 Quad City	A	131	493	154	30	6	19	(-	-)	253	91	107	101	74	4	100	13	0	5	7	9	.44	9	.312	.412	.513
2000 Fort Myers	A+	135	475	125	27	9	8	(-	-)	194	73	64	69	61	1	100	4	0	3	7	2	.73	11	.263	.350	.408
2001 New Britain	AA	140	501	135	33	4	23	(-	-)	245	69	84	84	54	8	125	6	0	4	15	7	.68	8	.269	.345	.489
2002 Edmonton	AAA	138	518	148	32	7	29	(-	-)	281	95	98	95	53	2	151	4	0	5	11	7	.61	10	.286	.353	.542
2002 Minnesota	AL	8	13	4	0	0	1	(0	1)	7	3	1	0	1	0	4	0	0	0	1	0	1.00	2	.308	.357	.538

Al Reyes

Pitches: R **Bats:** R **Pos:** RP-15   **Ht:** 6'1" **Wt:** 206 **Born:** 4/10/71 **Age:** 32

Year Team	Lg	G	GS	CG	GF	IP	BFP	H	R	ER	HR	SH	SF	HB	TBB	IBB	SO	WP	Bk	W	L	Pct	ShO	Sv-Op	Hld	ERC	ERA
2002 Nashville*	AAA	43	0	0	10	66.2	270	40	21	20	5	0	0	9	22	2	90	5	0	7	3	.700	0	1- -	-	2.04	2.70
1995 Milwaukee	NL	27	0	0	13	33.1	138	19	9	9	1	4	2	3	18	2	29	0	0	1	1	.500	0	1-1	4	2.51	2.43
1996 Milwaukee	NL	5	0	0	2	5.2	27	8	5	5	1	0	0	0	2	0	2	2	0	1	0	1.000	0	0-0	0	6.79	7.94
1997 Milwaukee	NL	19	0	0	7	29.2	131	32	19	18	4	2	0	3	9	0	28	1	0	1	2	.333	0	1-1	1	4.76	5.46
1998 Milwaukee	NL	50	0	0	13	57.0	253	55	26	25	9	2	1	2	31	1	58	2	0	5	1	.833	0	0-1	10	5.01	3.95
1999 Mil-Bal		53	0	0	12	65.2	287	50	33	33	9	4	3	6	41	3	67	3	0	4	3	.571	0	0-4	6	4.19	4.52
2000 Bal-LA		19	0	0	6	19.2	86	15	10	10	2	1	2	0	12	1	18	0	0	1	0	1.000	0	0-1	3	3.43	4.58
2001 Los Angeles	NL	19	0	0	9	25.2	120	28	13	11	3	0	2	1	13	1	23	0	1	2	1	.667	0	1-2	5	5.07	3.86
2002 Pittsburgh	NL	15	0	0	6	17.0	67	9	5	5	1	1	1	2	7	0	21	1	0	0	0	-	0	0-1	3	1.93	2.65
1999 Milwaukee	NL	26	0	0	6	36.0	161	27	17	17	5	1	1	3	25	1	39	2	0	2	0	1.000	0	0-1	2	4.35	4.25
1999 Baltimore	AL	27	0	0	6	29.2	126	23	16	16	4	3	2	3	16	2	28	1	0	2	3	.400	0	0-3	4	3.99	4.85
2000 Baltimore	AL	13	0	0	2	13.0	62	13	10	10	2	1	2	0	11	1	10	0	0	1	0	1.000	0	0-1	2	6.14	6.92
2000 Los Angeles	NL	6	0	0	4	6.2	24	2	0	0	0	0	0	0	1	0	8	0	0	0	0	-	0	0-0	1	0.35	0.00
8 ML YEARS		207	0	0	68	253.2	1109	216	120	116	32	11	11	17	133	8	246	9	1	15	8	.652	0	3-11	27	4.11	4.12

Carlos Reyes

Pitches: R **Bats:** B **Pos:** SP   **Ht:** 6'0" **Wt:** 190 **Born:** 4/4/69 **Age:** 34

Year Team	Lg	G	GS	CG	GF	IP	BFP	H	R	ER	HR	SH	SF	HB	TBB	IBB	SO	WP	Bk	W	L	Pct	ShO	Sv-Op	Hld	ERC	ERA
1994 Oakland	AL	27	9	0	8	78.0	344	71	38	36	10	2	3	2	44	1	57	3	0	0	3	.000	0	1-1	0	4.50	4.15
1995 Oakland	AL	40	1	0	19	69.0	306	71	43	39	10	4	0	5	28	4	48	5	0	4	6	.400	0	0-1	4	4.76	5.09
1996 Oakland	AL	46	10	0	14	122.1	550	134	71	65	19	2	8	2	61	8	78	2	1	7	10	.412	0	0-0	1	5.42	4.78
1997 Oakland	AL	37	6	0	9	77.1	352	101	52	50	13	3	2	2	25	2	43	2	1	3	4	.429	0	0-1	1	6.15	5.82
1998 SD-Bos		46	0	0	18	66.0	267	58	26	26	6	2	2	3	20	2	47	3	1	3	3	.500	0	1-2	3	3.21	3.55
1999 San Diego	NL	65	0	0	23	77.1	331	76	38	32	11	5	3	0	24	4	57	7	1	2	4	.333	0	1-2	6	3.76	3.72
2000 Phi-SD	NL	22	0	0	9	28.1	121	25	18	18	7	2	0	1	13	0	17	1	1	1	3	.250	0	1-3	2	4.85	5.72
1998 San Diego	NL	22	0	0	8	27.2	109	23	11	11	4	2	1	2	6	0	24	0	1	2	2	.500	0	1-2	1	3.14	3.58
1998 Boston	AL	24	0	0	10	38.1	158	35	15	15	2	0	1	1	14	2	23	3	0	1	1	.500	0	0-0	2	3.25	3.52
2000 Philadelphia	NL	10	0	0	5	10.1	44	10	6	6	2	2	0	0	5	0	4	1	0	0	2	.000	0	0-0	0	5.04	5.23
2000 San Diego	NL	12	0	0	4	18.0	77	15	12	12	5	0	0	1	8	0	13	0	1	1	1	.500	0	1-3	2	4.74	6.00
7 ML YEARS		283	26	0	100	518.1	2271	536	286	266	76	20	18	15	215	21	347	23	5	20	33	.377	0	4-10	17	4.72	4.62

Dennys Reyes

Pitches: L **Bats:** R **Pos:** RP-53; SP-5   **Ht:** 6'3" **Wt:** 246 **Born:** 4/19/77 **Age:** 26

Year Team	Lg	G	GS	CG	GF	IP	BFP	H	R	ER	HR	SH	SF	HB	TBB	IBB	SO	WP	Bk	W	L	Pct	ShO	Sv-Op	Hld	ERC	ERA
1997 Los Angeles	NL	14	5	0	0	47.0	207	51	21	20	4	5	1	1	18	3	36	2	1	2	3	.400	0	0-0	0	4.34	3.83
1998 LA-Cin	NL	19	10	0	4	67.1	300	62	36	34	3	7	2	1	47	5	77	6	1	3	5	.375	0	0-0	0	4.37	4.54
1999 Cincinnati	NL	65	1	0	12	61.2	277	53	30	26	5	4	3	3	39	1	72	5	1	2	2	.500	0	2-3	14	4.16	3.79
2000 Cincinnati	NL	62	0	0	15	43.2	200	43	31	22	5	3	3	1	29	0	36	6	0	2	1	.667	0	0-1	10	5.24	4.53
2001 Cincinnati	NL	35	6	0	2	53.0	246	51	35	29	5	2	2	1	35	1	52	5	0	2	6	.250	0	0-0	6	4.77	4.92
2002 Col-Tex		58	5	0	15	82.2	378	98	52	49	10	3	2	0	45	4	59	10	1	4	4	.500	0	0-0	4	5.90	5.33
1998 Los Angeles	NL	11	3	0	4	28.2	130	27	17	15	1	3	1	0	20	4	33	1	1	0	4	.000	0	0-0	0	4.16	4.71
1998 Cincinnati	NL	8	7	0	0	38.2	170	35	19	19	2	4	1	1	27	1	44	5	0	3	1	.750	0	0-0	0	4.54	4.42
2002 Colorado	NL	43	0	0	13	40.1	182	43	19	19	1	2	2	0	24	3	30	4	0	1	1	.000	0	0-0	4	4.55	4.24
2002 Texas	AL	15	5	0	2	42.1	196	55	33	30	9	1	0	0	21	1	29	6	1	4	3	.571	0	0-0	0	7.24	6.38
6 ML YEARS		253	27	0	48	355.1	1608	358	205	180	32	24	13	7	213	14	332	34	4	15	21	.417	0	2-4	34	4.84	4.56

Shane Reynolds

Pitches: R **Bats:** R **Pos:** SP-13 **Ht:** 6'3" **Wt:** 215 **Born:** 3/26/68 **Age:** 35

		HOW MUCH HE PITCHED						WHAT HE GAVE UP												THE RESULTS							
Year Team	Lg	G	GS	CG	GF	IP	BFP	H	R	ER	HR	SH	SF	HB	TBB	IBB	SO	WP	Bk	W	L	Pct	ShO	Sv-Op	Hld	ERC	ERA
1992 Houston	NL	8	5	0	0	25.1	122	42	22	20	2	6	1	0	6	1	10	1	1	1	3	.250	0	0-0	0	7.07	7.11
1993 Houston	NL	5	1	0	0	11.0	49	11	4	1	0	0	0	0	1	1	10	0	0	0	0	-	0	0-0	0	3.72	0.82
1994 Houston	NL	33	14	1	5	124.0	517	128	46	42	10	4	0	6	21	3	110	3	2	8	5	.615	1	0-0	5	3.38	3.05
1995 Houston	NL	30	30	3	0	189.1	792	196	87	73	15	8	0	2	37	6	175	7	1	10	11	.476	2	0-0	0	3.31	3.47
1996 Houston	NL	35	35	4	0	239.0	981	227	103	97	20	11	7	8	44	3	204	5	1	16	10	.615	1	0-0	0	2.97	3.65
1997 Houston	NL	30	30	2	0	181.0	773	189	92	85	19	9	5	3	47	5	152	5	2	9	10	.474	0	0-0	0	3.79	4.23
1998 Houston	NL	35	35	3	0	233.1	986	257	91	91	25	5	7	2	53	2	209	5	0	19	8	.704	1	0-0	0	4.05	3.51
1999 Houston	NL	35	35	4	0	231.2	963	250	108	99	23	11	5	1	37	0	197	4	0	16	14	.533	2	0-0	0	3.58	3.85
2000 Houston	NL	22	22	0	0	131.0	588	150	86	76	20	6	8	6	45	2	93	5	0	7	8	.467	0	0-0	0	5.17	5.22
2001 Houston	NL	28	28	3	0	182.2	772	208	95	88	24	13	2	4	36	2	102	2	0	14	11	.560	0	0-0	0	4.38	4.34
2002 Houston	NL	13	13	0	0	74.0	322	80	43	40	13	2	1	1	26	2	47	1	0	3	6	.333	0	0-0	0	4.90	4.86
11 ML YEARS		274	248	20	5	1622.1	6865	1738	785	712	171	75	36	33	358	27	1309	38	7	103	86	.545	7	0-0	5	3.85	3.95

Armando Reynoso

Pitches: R **Bats:** R **Pos:** RP-2 **Ht:** 6'0" **Wt:** 210 **Born:** 5/1/66 **Age:** 37

		HOW MUCH HE PITCHED						WHAT HE GAVE UP												THE RESULTS							
Year Team	Lg	G	GS	CG	GF	IP	BFP	H	R	ER	HR	SH	SF	HB	TBB	IBB	SO	WP	Bk	W	L	Pct	ShO	Sv-Op	Hld	ERC	ERA
2002 Tucson*	AAA	6	6	0	0	27.2	119	29	16	16	2	1	2	2	9	0	16	1	0	1	2	.333	0	0--	-	4.19	5.20
1991 Atlanta	NL	6	5	0	1	23.1	103	26	18	16	4	3	0	3	10	1	10	2	0	2	1	.667	0	0-0	0	6.09	6.17
1992 Atlanta	NL	3	1	0	1	7.2	32	11	4	4	2	1	0	1	2	1	2	0	0	1	0	1.000	0	1-1	0	8.83	4.70
1993 Colorado	NL	30	30	4	0	189.0	830	206	101	84	22	5	8	9	63	7	117	7	6	12	11	.522	0	0-0	0	4.55	4.00
1994 Colorado	NL	9	9	1	0	52.1	226	54	30	28	5	2	2	6	22	1	25	2	2	3	4	.429	0	0-0	0	4.91	4.82
1995 Colorado	NL	20	18	0	0	93.0	418	116	61	55	12	8	2	5	36	3	40	2	0	7	7	.500	0	0-0	0	5.99	5.32
1996 Colorado	NL	30	30	0	0	168.2	733	195	97	93	27	3	3	9	49	0	88	4	3	8	9	.471	0	0-0	0	5.26	4.96
1997 New York	NL	16	16	1	0	91.1	388	95	47	46	7	3	5	6	29	4	47	4	1	6	3	.667	1	0-0	0	4.08	4.53
1998 New York	NL	11	11	0	0	68.1	292	64	31	29	4	4	1	5	32	3	40	2	2	7	3	.700	0	0-0	0	4.01	3.82
1999 Arizona	NL	31	27	0	1	167.0	730	178	90	81	20	6	6	6	67	7	79	7	1	10	6	.625	0	0-0	1	4.71	4.37
2000 Arizona	NL	31	30	2	0	170.2	730	179	102	100	22	11	5	6	52	5	89	3	0	11	12	.478	0	0-0	0	4.29	5.27
2001 Arizona	NL	9	9	0	0	46.2	207	58	32	31	13	2	2	4	13	2	15	1	0	1	6	.143	0	0-0	0	6.77	5.98
2002 Arizona	NL	2	0	0	1	1.2	9	3	2	2	0	0	0	0	1	0	2	1	0	0	0	-	0	0-0	0	8.83	10.80
12 ML YEARS		198	186	8	4	1079.2	4698	1185	615	569	138	48	34	60	376	34	554	35	15	68	62	.523	1	1-1	1	4.86	4.74

Arthur Rhodes

Pitches: L **Bats:** L **Pos:** RP-66 **Ht:** 6'2" **Wt:** 205 **Born:** 10/24/69 **Age:** 33

		HOW MUCH HE PITCHED						WHAT HE GAVE UP												THE RESULTS							
Year Team	Lg	G	GS	CG	GF	IP	BFP	H	R	ER	HR	SH	SF	HB	TBB	IBB	SO	WP	Bk	W	L	Pct	ShO	Sv-Op	Hld	ERC	ERA
1991 Baltimore	AL	8	8	0	0	36.0	174	47	35	32	4	1	3	0	23	0	23	2	0	0	3	.000	0	0-0	0	7.00	8.00
1992 Baltimore	AL	15	15	2	0	94.1	394	87	39	38	6	5	1	1	38	2	77	2	1	7	5	.583	1	0-0	0	3.48	3.63
1993 Baltimore	AL	17	17	0	0	85.2	387	91	62	62	16	2	3	1	49	1	49	2	0	5	6	.455	0	0-0	0	5.88	6.51
1994 Baltimore	AL	10	10	3	0	52.2	238	51	34	34	8	2	3	2	30	1	47	3	0	3	5	.375	2	0-0	0	5.03	5.81
1995 Baltimore	AL	19	9	0	3	75.1	336	68	53	52	13	4	0	0	48	1	77	3	1	2	5	.286	0	0-1	0	4.97	6.21
1996 Baltimore	AL	28	2	0	5	53.0	224	48	28	24	6	1	1	0	23	3	62	0	0	9	1	.900	0	1-1	2	3.72	4.08
1997 Baltimore	AL	53	0	0	6	95.1	378	75	32	32	9	0	4	4	26	5	102	2	0	10	3	.769	0	1-2	9	2.58	3.02
1998 Baltimore	AL	45	0	0	10	77.0	321	65	30	30	8	2	5	1	34	2	83	1	1	4	4	.500	0	4-8	10	3.47	3.51
1999 Baltimore	AL	43	0	0	11	53.0	244	43	37	32	9	2	2	0	45	6	59	4	0	3	4	.429	0	3-5	5	5.07	5.43
2000 Seattle	AL	72	0	0	9	69.1	281	51	34	33	6	1	2	0	29	3	77	4	0	5	8	.385	0	0-7	24	2.62	4.28
2001 Seattle	AL	71	0	0	16	68.0	258	46	14	13	5	1	0	1	12	0	83	3	0	8	0	1.000	0	3-7	32	1.61	1.72
2002 Seattle	AL	66	0	0	9	69.2	257	45	18	18	4	2	1	0	13	1	81	2	0	10	4	.714	0	2-7	27	1.46	2.33
12 ML YEARS		447	61	5	69	829.1	3492	717	416	400	94	23	25	10	370	25	820	28	3	66	48	.579	3	14-38	109	3.63	4.34

Chris Richard

Bats: L **Throws:** L **Pos:** DH-36; 1B-9; PH-5 **Ht:** 6'2" **Wt:** 190 **Born:** 6/7/74 **Age:** 29

		BATTING																		BASERUNNING				AVERAGES		
Year Team	Lg	G	AB	H	2B	3B	HR	(Hm	Rd)	TB	R	RBI	RC	TBB	IBB	SO	HBP	SH	SF	SB	CS	SB%	GDP	Avg	OBP	Slg
2002 Orioles*	R	1	1	1	0	0	0	(-	-)	1	1	0	1	1	0	0	0	0	0	0	0	-	0	1.000	1.000	1.000
2002 Bowie*	AA	2	6	2	1	0	0	(-	-)	3	0	1	1	1	0	2	0	0	1	0	0	-	0	.333	.375	.500
2002 Aberdeen*	A-	1	5	3	1	0	1	(-	-)	7	2	3	3	0	0	1	0	0	0	0	0	-	0	.600	.600	1.400
2002 Rochester*	AAA	14	53	17	6	0	6	(-	-)	41	10	18	15	6	1	14	2	0	2	0	0	-	2	.321	.397	.774
2000 Stl-Bal		62	215	57	14	2	14	(4	10)	117	39	37	36	17	3	40	4	0	3	7	5	.58	5	.265	.326	.544
2001 Baltimore	AL	136	483	128	31	3	15	(6	9)	210	74	61	66	45	4	100	8	2	4	11	9	.55	15	.265	.335	.435
2002 Baltimore	AL	50	155	36	11	0	4	(2	2)	59	15	21	16	12	0	30	2	0	2	0	3	.00	2	.232	.292	.381
2000 St Louis	NL	6	16	2	0	0	1	(0	1)	5	1	1	1	2	0	2	0	0	0	0	0	-	0	.125	.222	.313
2000 Baltimore	AL	56	199	55	14	2	13	(4	9)	112	38	36	35	15	3	38	4	0	3	7	5	.58	5	.276	.335	.563
3 ML YEARS		248	853	221	56	5	33	(12	21)	386	128	119	118	74	7	170	14	2	9	18	17	.51	22	.259	.325	.453

John Riedling

Pitches: R **Bats:** R **Pos:** RP-33 **Ht:** 5'11" **Wt:** 190 **Born:** 8/29/75 **Age:** 27

		HOW MUCH HE PITCHED						WHAT HE GAVE UP												THE RESULTS							
Year Team	Lg	G	GS	CG	GF	IP	BFP	H	R	ER	HR	SH	SF	HB	TBB	IBB	SO	WP	Bk	W	L	Pct	ShO	Sv-Op	Hld	ERC	ERA
2002 Chattanooga*	AA	6	0	0	0	7.1	42	13	11	9	0	1	2	0	5	2	5	0	0	1	1	.500	0	0--	-	7.96	11.05
2002 Louisville*	AAA	7	0	0	4	9.2	43	10	6	5	0	0	0	0	4	0	10	1	0	0	1	1.000	0	0--	-	3.50	4.66
2000 Cincinnati	NL	13	0	0	5	15.1	63	11	7	4	1	1	0	1	8	0	18	1	0	3	1	.750	0	1-2	2	3.12	2.35
2001 Cincinnati	NL	29	0	0	14	33.2	136	22	9	9	1	2	0	2	14	0	23	5	0	1	1	.500	0	1-3	5	2.13	2.41
2002 Cincinnati	NL	33	0	0	7	46.2	202	39	16	14	2	6	1	3	26	6	30	1	0	2	4	.333	0	0-0	8	3.42	2.70
3 ML YEARS		75	0	0	26	95.2	401	72	32	27	4	9	1	6	48	6	71	7	0	6	6	.500	0	2-5	15	2.90	2.54

Jerrod Riggan

Pitches: R **Bats:** R **Pos:** RP-29 — **Ht:** 6'3" **Wt:** 197 **Born:** 5/16/74 **Age:** 29

Year Team	Lg	G	GS	CG	GF	IP	BFP	H	R	ER	HR	SH	SF	HB	TBB	IBB	SO	WP	Bk	W	L	Pct	ShO	Sv-Op	Hld	ERC	ERA
2002 Buffalo*	AAA	27	0	0	18	45.1	178	40	12	12	3	2	1	2	11	2	37	3	0	4	1	.800	0	3- -	-	2.88	2.38
2000 New York	NL	1	0	0	0	2.0	10	3	2	0	0	0	0	0	0	0	1	0	0	0	0	-	0	0-0	0	3.96	0.00
2001 New York	NL	35	0	0	12	47.2	202	42	19	18	5	2	3	0	24	7	41	4	0	3	3	.500	0	0-1	4	3.67	3.40
2002 Cleveland	AL	29	0	0	9	33.0	165	53	28	28	3	1	4	0	18	4	22	4	1	2	1	.667	0	0-0	0	8.17	7.64
3 ML YEARS		65	0	0	21	82.2	377	98	49	46	8	3	7	0	42	11	64	8	1	5	4	.556	0	0-1	4	5.36	5.01

Jose Rijo

Pitches: R **Bats:** R **Pos:** RP-22; SP-9 — **Ht:** 6'3" **Wt:** 200 **Born:** 5/13/65 **Age:** 38

Year Team	Lg	G	GS	CG	GF	IP	BFP	H	R	ER	HR	SH	SF	HB	TBB	IBB	SO	WP	Bk	W	L	Pct	ShO	Sv-Op	Hld	ERC	ERA
1984 New York	AL	24	5	0	8	62.1	289	74	40	33	5	6	1	1	33	1	47	2	1	2	8	.200	0	2-3	1	5.56	4.76
1985 Oakland	AL	12	9	0	1	63.2	272	57	26	25	6	5	0	1	28	2	65	0	0	6	4	.600	0	0-1	0	3.62	3.53
1986 Oakland	AL	39	26	4	9	193.2	856	172	116	100	24	10	9	4	108	7	176	6	4	9	11	.450	0	1-3	0	4.21	4.65
1987 Oakland	AL	21	14	1	3	82.1	394	106	67	54	10	0	3	2	41	1	67	5	2	2	7	.222	0	0-0	0	6.32	5.90
1988 Cincinnati	NL	49	19	0	12	162.0	653	120	47	43	7	8	5	3	63	7	160	1	4	13	8	.619	0	0-2	1	2.35	2.39
1989 Cincinnati	NL	19	19	1	0	111.0	464	101	39	35	6	3	6	2	48	3	86	4	3	7	6	.538	1	0-0	0	3.50	2.84
1990 Cincinnati	NL	29	29	7	0	197.0	801	151	65	59	10	8	1	2	78	1	152	2	5	14	8	.636	1	0-0	0	2.57	2.70
1991 Cincinnati	NL	30	30	3	0	204.1	825	165	69	57	8	4	8	3	55	4	172	2	4	15	6	.714	1	0-0	0	2.23	2.51
1992 Cincinnati	NL	33	33	2	0	211.0	836	185	67	60	15	9	4	3	44	1	171	2	1	15	10	.600	0	0-0	0	2.62	2.56
1993 Cincinnati	NL	36	36	2	0	257.1	1029	218	76	71	19	13	3	2	62	2	227	0	1	14	9	.609	1	0-0	0	2.55	2.48
1994 Cincinnati	NL	26	26	2	0	172.1	733	177	73	59	16	7	2	4	52	1	171	1	2	9	6	.600	0	0-0	0	3.88	3.08
1995 Cincinnati	NL	14	14	0	0	69.0	295	76	33	32	6	3	3	0	22	1	62	3	0	5	4	.556	0	0-0	0	4.26	4.17
2001 Cincinnati	NL	13	0	0	4	17.0	80	19	6	4	2	1	0	0	9	2	12	1	1	0	0	-	0	0-0	2	5.00	2.12
2002 Cincinnati	NL	31	9	0	6	77.0	340	89	48	44	13	4	0	1	20	1	38	1	0	5	4	.556	0	0-0	0	4.82	5.14
14 ML YEARS		376	269	22	43	1880.0	7867	1710	772	676	147	81	45	28	663	34	1606	30	28	116	91	.560	4	3-9	4	3.29	3.24

Juan Rincon

Pitches: R **Bats:** R **Pos:** RP-7; SP-3 — **Ht:** 5'11" **Wt:** 190 **Born:** 1/23/79 **Age:** 24

Year Team	Lg	G	GS	CG	GF	IP	BFP	H	R	ER	HR	SH	SF	HB	TBB	IBB	SO	WP	Bk	W	L	Pct	ShO	Sv-Op	Hld	ERC	ERA
1997 Twins	R	11	10	1	1	58.0	245	55	21	19	0	2	3	4	24	0	46	7	1	3	3	.500	0	0- -	1	3.49	2.95
1997 Elizabethton	R+	2	1	0	0	9.1	41	11	4	4	0	0	0	0	3	0	7	2	0	1	0	1.000	0	0- -	0	4.04	3.86
1998 Fort Wayne	A	37	13	0	17	96.1	427	84	51	41	6	5	1	5	54	1	74	12	0	6	4	.600	0	6- -	5	3.85	3.83
1999 Quad City	A	28	28	0	0	163.1	683	146	67	53	8	1	3	2	66	3	153	11	0	14	8	.636	0	0- -	0	3.22	2.92
2000 Fort Myers	A+	13	13	0	0	76.1	309	67	26	18	3	1	0	4	23	2	55	10	0	5	3	.625	0	0- -	0	2.89	2.12
2000 New Britain	AA	15	15	2	0	89.0	399	96	55	46	9	0	0	1	39	0	79	9	1	3	9	.250	0	0- -	0	4.67	4.65
2001 New Britain	AA	29	23	3	1	153.1	645	130	60	49	9	3	3	8	57	5	133	9	1	14	6	.700	1	0- -	0	3.00	2.88
2002 Edmonton	AAA	19	16	3	1	101.2	444	111	56	54	12	2	1	6	35	0	75	4	0	7	4	.636	0	0- -	0	4.78	4.78
2001 Minnesota	AL	4	0	0	1	5.2	28	7	5	4	1	1	0	0	5	0	4	0	0	0	0	-	0	0-0	0	8.33	6.35
2002 Minnesota	AL	10	3	0	0	28.2	135	44	23	20	5	0	1	0	9	0	21	2	0	0	2	.000	0	0-1	0	7.62	6.28
2 ML YEARS		14	3	0	1	34.1	163	51	28	24	6	1	1	0	14	0	25	2	0	0	2	.000	0	0-1	0	7.75	6.29

Ricardo Rincon

Pitches: L **Bats:** L **Pos:** RP-71 — **Ht:** 5'9" **Wt:** 187 **Born:** 4/13/70 **Age:** 33

Year Team	Lg	G	GS	CG	GF	IP	BFP	H	R	ER	HR	SH	SF	HB	TBB	IBB	SO	WP	Bk	W	L	Pct	ShO	Sv-Op	Hld	ERC	ERA
1997 Pittsburgh	NL	62	0	0	23	60.0	254	51	26	23	5	5	1	2	24	6	71	2	3	4	8	.333	0	4-6	18	3.10	3.45
1998 Pittsburgh	NL	60	0	0	27	65.0	272	50	31	21	6	1	2	0	29	2	64	2	0	0	2	.000	0	14-17	11	2.88	2.91
1999 Cleveland	AL	59	0	0	14	44.2	193	41	22	22	6	2	1	1	24	5	30	2	1	2	3	.400	0	0-2	11	4.38	4.43
2000 Cleveland	AL	35	0	0	4	20.0	90	17	7	6	1	0	0	1	13	1	20	1	0	2	0	1.000	0	0-0	10	3.89	2.70
2001 Cleveland	AL	67	0	0	19	54.0	223	44	18	17	3	2	3	0	21	5	50	1	0	2	1	.667	0	2-4	12	2.62	2.83
2002 Cle-Oak	AL	71	0	0	9	56.0	222	47	28	26	4	2	4	1	11	1	49	0	0	1	4	.200	0	1-5	27	2.36	4.18
2002 Cleveland	AL	46	0	0	6	35.2	150	36	21	19	3	2	2	1	8	1	30	0	0	1	4	.200	0	0-3	11	3.38	4.79
2002 Oakland	AL	25	0	0	3	20.1	72	11	7	7	1	0	2	0	3	0	19	0	0	0	0	-	0	1-2	16	1.06	3.10
6 ML YEARS		354	0	0	96	299.2	1254	250	132	115	25	12	11	5	122	20	284	8	4	11	18	.379	0	21-34	89	3.05	3.45

Armando Rios

Bats: L **Throws:** L **Pos:** RF-47; PH-21; LF-11 — **Ht:** 5'9" **Wt:** 185 **Born:** 9/13/71 **Age:** 31

Year Team	Lg	G	AB	H	2B	3B	HR	(Hm	Rd)	TB	R	RBI	RC	TBB	IBB	SO	HBP	SH	SF	SB	CS	SB%	GDP	Avg	OBP	Slg
2002 Altoona*	AA	1	2	0	0	0	0	(-	-)	0	0	0	0	1	0	0	0	0	0	0	0	-	0	.000	.333	.000
2002 Nashville*	AAA	15	52	13	2	0	0	(-	-)	15	6	6	5	5	0	10	1	0	1	1	2	.33	1	.250	.322	.288
1998 San Francisco	NL	12	7	4	0	0	2	(0	2)	10	3	3	5	3	0	2	0	0	0	0	0	-	0	.571	.700	1.429
1999 San Francisco	NL	72	150	49	9	0	7	(4	3)	79	32	29	32	24	1	35	1	1	1	7	4	.64	3	.327	.420	.527
2000 San Francisco	NL	115	233	62	15	5	10	(2	8)	117	38	50	38	31	4	43	0	1	4	3	2	.60	9	.266	.347	.502
2001 SF-Pit	NL	95	319	83	17	3	14	(3	11)	148	38	50	50	36	6	74	0	1	3	3	2	.60	5	.260	.332	.464
2002 Pittsburgh	NL	76	208	55	11	0	1	(0	1)	69	20	24	17	16	1	39	1	0	1	1	1	.50	8	.264	.319	.332
2001 San Francisco	NL	93	316	82	17	3	14	(3	11)	147	38	49	49	34	6	73	0	1	2	3	2	.60	2	.259	.330	.465
2001 Pittsburgh	NL	2	3	1	0	0	0	(0	0)	1	0	1	1	2	0	1	0	0	1	0	0	-	1	.333	.500	.333
5 ML YEARS		370	917	253	52	8	34	(9	25)	423	131	156	142	110	12	193	2	3	9	14	9	.61	23	.276	.352	.461

David Riske

Pitches: R **Bats:** R **Pos:** RP-51   **Ht:** 6'2" **Wt:** 175 **Born:** 10/23/76 **Age:** 26

Year Team	Lg	G	GS	CG	GF	IP	BFP	H	R	ER	HR	SH	SF	HB	TBB	IBB	SO	WP	Bk	W	L	Pct	ShO	Sv-Op	Hld	ERC	ERA
2002 Akron*	AA	4	2	0	2	6.0	24	5	2	2	1	0	0	1	1	0	10	0	0	0	0	-	0	0--	-	2.66	3.00
2002 Buffalo*	AAA	9	0	0	8	9.2	40	6	4	4	2	2	0	1	4	0	17	0	0	0	1	.000	0	3--	-	3.12	3.72
1999 Cleveland	AL	12	0	0	3	14.0	68	20	15	13	2	1	1	0	6	0	16	0	0	1	1	.500	0	0-1	0	6.96	8.36
2001 Cleveland	AL	26	0	0	6	27.1	118	20	7	6	3	0	1	2	18	3	29	1	0	2	0	1.000	0	1-1	3	3.81	1.98
2002 Cleveland	AL	51	0	0	17	51.1	237	49	32	30	8	4	3	4	35	4	65	1	0	2	2	.500	0	1-1	5	5.55	5.26
3 ML YEARS		89	0	0	26	92.2	423	89	54	49	13	5	5	6	59	7	110	2	0	5	3	.625	0	2-3	8	5.23	4.76

Todd Ritchie

Pitches: R **Bats:** R **Pos:** SP-23; RP-3   **Ht:** 6'3" **Wt:** 210 **Born:** 11/7/71 **Age:** 31

Year Team	Lg	G	GS	CG	GF	IP	BFP	H	R	ER	HR	SH	SF	HB	TBB	IBB	SO	WP	Bk	W	L	Pct	ShO	Sv-Op	Hld	ERC	ERA
1997 Minnesota	AL	42	0	0	19	74.2	331	87	41	38	11	0	1	2	28	0	44	11	0	2	3	.400	0	0-2	3	5.44	4.58
1998 Minnesota	AL	15	0	0	7	24.0	113	30	17	15	1	0	0	0	9	0	21	3	0	0	0	-	0	0-0	0	4.75	5.63
1999 Pittsburgh	NL	28	26	3	0	172.2	715	169	79	67	17	3	2	4	54	3	107	7	0	15	9	.625	0	0-0	1	3.76	3.49
2000 Pittsburgh	NL	31	31	1	0	187.0	804	208	111	100	26	8	5	3	51	1	124	5	1	9	8	.529	1	0-0	0	4.55	4.81
2001 Pittsburgh	NL	33	33	4	0	207.1	887	211	118	103	23	9	5	5	52	5	124	7	0	11	15	.423	2	0-0	0	3.68	4.47
2002 Chicago	AL	26	23	0	1	133.2	623	176	104	90	18	6	7	5	52	2	77	10	0	5	15	.250	0	0-0	0	6.27	6.06
6 ML YEARS		175	113	7	27	799.1	3473	881	470	413	96	26	20	21	246	13	497	43	1	42	50	.457	3	0-2	4	4.50	4.65

Luis Rivas

Bats: R **Throws:** R **Pos:** 2B-93   **Ht:** 5'11" **Wt:** 175 **Born:** 8/30/79 **Age:** 23

Year Team	Lg	G	AB	H	2B	3B	HR	(Hm	Rd)	TB	R	RBI	RC	TBB	IBB	SO	HBP	SH	SF	SB	CS	SB%	GDP	Avg	OBP	Slg
2002 Fort Myers*	A+	6	22	2	0	1	0	(-	-)	4	1	3	0	2	0	2	0	0	0	1	0	1.00	0	.091	.167	.182
2000 Minnesota	AL	16	58	18	4	1	0	(0	0)	24	8	6	8	2	0	4	0	0	2	2	0	1.00	0	.310	.323	.414
2001 Minnesota	AL	153	563	150	21	6	8	(3	4)	204	70	47	65	40	0	99	6	5	5	31	11	.74	15	.266	.319	.362
2002 Minnesota	AL	93	316	81	23	4	4	(2	2)	124	46	35	35	19	2	51	3	8	0	9	4	.69	12	.256	.305	.392
3 ML YEARS		262	937	249	48	11	11	(5	6)	352	124	88	108	61	2	154	9	15	7	42	15	.74	29	.266	.315	.376

Juan Rivera

Bats: R **Throws:** R **Pos:** LF-15; RF-15; PH-1; PR-1   **Ht:** 6'2" **Wt:** 170 **Born:** 7/3/78 **Age:** 24

Year Team	Lg	G	AB	H	2B	3B	HR	(Hm	Rd)	TB	R	RBI	RC	TBB	IBB	SO	HBP	SH	SF	SB	CS	SB%	GDP	Avg	OBP	Slg
1998 Yankees	R	57	210	70	9	1	12	(-	-)	117	43	45	42	26	2	27	1	0	1	8	5	.62	10	.333	.408	.557
1998 Oneonta	A-	6	18	5	0	0	1	(-	-)	8	2	3	2	1	0	4	0	0	0	1	1	.50	0	.278	.316	.444
1999 Tampa	A+	109	426	112	20	2	14	(-	-)	178	50	77	52	26	3	67	5	0	8	5	4	.56	13	.263	.308	.418
1999 Yankees	R	5	18	6	0	0	1	(-	-)	9	7	4	4	4	0	1	0	0	0	0	0	-	1	.333	.455	.500
2000 Norwich	AA	17	62	14	5	0	2	(-	-)	25	9	12	7	6	0	15	0	0	0	0	0	-	2	.226	.294	.403
2000 Tampa	A+	115	409	113	26	1	14	(-	-)	183	62	69	60	33	1	56	6	0	5	11	7	.61	9	.276	.336	.447
2001 Norwich	AA	77	316	101	18	3	14	(-	-)	167	50	58	53	15	2	50	3	0	3	5	7	.42	10	.320	.353	.528
2001 Columbus	AAA	55	199	65	11	1	14	(-	-)	120	39	40	39	15	1	31	1	0	3	4	5	.44	7	.327	.372	.603
2002 Columbus	AAA	65	265	86	21	1	8	(-	-)	133	40	47	46	13	1	39	1	1	3	5	1	.83	4	.325	.355	.502
2002 Yankees	R	4	13	4	2	0	0	(-	-)	6	1	4	2	0	0	3	1	0	0	0	0	-	1	.308	.438	.462
2001 New York	AL	3	4	0	0	0	0	(0	0)	0	0	0	0	0	0	0	0	0	0	0	0	-	0	.000	.000	.000
2002 New York	AL	28	83	22	5	0	1	(0	1)	30	9	6	8	6	0	10	0	1	1	1	1	.50	4	.265	.311	.361
2 ML YEARS		31	87	22	5	0	1	(0	1)	30	9	6	8	6	0	10	0	1	1	1	1	.50	4	.253	.298	.345

Mariano Rivera

Pitches: R **Bats:** R **Pos:** RP-45   **Ht:** 6'2" **Wt:** 185 **Born:** 11/29/69 **Age:** 33

Year Team	Lg	G	GS	CG	GF	IP	BFP	H	R	ER	HR	SH	SF	HB	TBB	IBB	SO	WP	Bk	W	L	Pct	ShO	Sv-Op	Hld	ERC	ERA
2002 Yankees*	R	1	1	0	0	2.0	7	2	0	0	0	0	0	0	1	0	2	0	0	0	0	-	0	0--	-	1.14	0.00
1995 New York	AL	19	10	0	2	67.0	301	71	43	41	11	0	2	2	30	0	51	0	1	5	3	.625	0	0-1	0	5.14	5.51
1996 New York	AL	61	0	0	14	107.2	425	73	25	25	1	2	1	2	34	3	130	1	0	8	3	.727	0	5-8	27	1.65	2.09
1997 New York	AL	66	0	0	56	71.2	301	65	17	15	5	3	4	0	20	6	68	2	0	6	4	.600	0	43-52	0	2.73	1.88
1998 New York	AL	54	0	0	49	61.1	246	48	13	13	3	2	3	1	17	1	36	0	0	3	0	1.000	0	36-41	0	2.21	1.91
1999 New York	AL	66	0	0	63	69.0	268	43	15	14	2	0	2	3	18	3	52	2	1	4	3	.571	0	45-49	0	1.47	1.83
2000 New York	AL	66	0	0	61	75.2	311	58	26	24	4	5	2	0	25	3	58	2	0	7	4	.636	0	36-41	0	2.20	2.85
2001 New York	AL	71	0	0	66	80.2	310	61	24	21	5	4	1	1	12	2	83	1	0	4	6	.400	0	50-57	0	1.74	2.34
2002 New York	AL	45	0	0	37	46.0	187	35	16	14	3	2	0	2	11	2	41	1	1	1	4	.200	0	28-32	2	2.08	2.74
8 ML YEARS		448	10	0	348	579.0	2349	454	179	167	34	18	15	11	167	20	519	9	3	38	27	.585	0	243-281	29	2.28	2.60

Mike Rivera

Bats: R **Throws:** R **Pos:** C-37; DH-1; PH-1   **Ht:** 6'0" **Wt:** 210 **Born:** 9/8/76 **Age:** 26

Year Team	Lg	G	AB	H	2B	3B	HR	(Hm	Rd)	TB	R	RBI	RC	TBB	IBB	SO	HBP	SH	SF	SB	CS	SB%	GDP	Avg	OBP	Slg
1997 Tigers	R	47	154	44	9	2	10	(-	-)	87	34	36	31	18	2	25	3	0	2	0	0	-	2	.286	.367	.565
1998 W Michigan	A	108	403	111	34	3	9	(-	-)	178	40	67	51	15	0	68	2	1	5	0	2	.00	9	.275	.301	.442
1999 Lakeland	A+	104	370	103	20	2	14	(-	-)	169	44	72	51	20	0	59	3	0	8	1	1	.50	10	.278	.314	.457
1999 Jacksonville	AA	7	23	4	1	0	2	(-	-)	11	3	6	3	2	0	5	0	0	0	0	0	-	0	.174	.240	.478
2000 Lakeland	A+	64	243	71	19	4	11	(-	-)	131	30	53	41	16	3	45	1	0	2	2	0	1.00	8	.292	.336	.539
2000 Toledo	AAA	4	13	3	3	0	0	(-	-)	6	0	1	1	0	0	2	0	0	0	0	0	-	0	.231	.231	.462
2000 Jacksonville	AA	39	150	29	8	1	2	(-	-)	45	10	9	8	7	0	30	0	0	1	0	0	-	6	.193	.228	.300
2001 Erie	AA	112	415	120	19	1	33	(-	-)	240	76	101	84	44	2	96	10	0	4	2	2	.50	9	.289	.368	.578
2002 Toledo	AAA	74	265	66	11	1	20	(-	-)	139	43	53	46	35	3	64	3	0	2	0	1	.00	6	.249	.341	.525

Year Team	Lg	G	AB	H	2B	3B	HR	(Hm	Rd)	TB	R	RBI	RC	TBB	IBB	SO	HBP	SH	SF	SB	CS	SB%	GDP	Avg	OBP	Slg
2001 Detroit	AL	4	12	4	2	0	0	(0	0)	6	2	1	2	0	0	2	0	0	0	0	0	-	0	.333	.333	.500
2002 Detroit	AL	39	132	30	8	1	1	(0	1)	43	11	11	8	4	0	35	1	0	1	0	0	-	5	.227	.254	.326
2 ML YEARS		43	144	34	10	1	1	(0	1)	49	13	12	10	4	0	37	1	0	1	0	0	-	5	.236	.260	.340

Ruben Rivera

Bats: R **Throws:** R **Pos:** CF-66; PR-3; PH-2; DH-1   **Ht:** 6'3" **Wt:** 200 **Born:** 11/14/73 **Age:** 29

Year Team	Lg	G	AB	H	2B	3B	HR	(Hm	Rd)	TB	R	RBI	RC	TBB	IBB	SO	HBP	SH	SF	SB	CS	SB%	GDP	Avg	OBP	Slg
2002 Tulsa*	AA	59	205	64	17	4	10	(-	-)	119	38	43	44	23	2	46	5	0	4	4	3	.57	5	.312	.388	.580
2002 Oklahoma*	AAA	27	98	27	2	4	7	(-	-)	58	19	23	21	13	1	23	1	0	0	2	0	1.00	2	.276	.366	.592
1995 New York	AL	5	1	0	0	0	0	(0	0)	0	0	0	0	0	0	1	0	0	0	0	0	-	0	.000	.000	.000
1996 New York	AL	46	88	25	6	1	2	(0	2)	39	17	16	16	13	0	26	2	1	2	6	2	.75	1	.284	.381	.443
1997 San Diego	NL	17	20	5	1	0	0	(0	0)	6	2	1	2	2	0	9	0	0	0	2	1	.67	0	.250	.318	.300
1998 San Diego	NL	95	172	36	7	2	6	(2	4)	65	31	29	23	28	0	52	2	1	1	5	1	.83	1	.209	.325	.378
1999 San Diego	NL	147	411	80	16	1	23	(10	13)	167	65	48	50	55	1	143	5	0	4	18	7	.72	9	.195	.295	.406
2000 San Diego	NL	135	423	88	18	6	17	(8	9)	169	62	57	50	44	1	137	10	0	2	8	4	.67	8	.208	.296	.400
2001 Cincinnati	NL	117	263	67	13	1	10	(6	4)	112	37	34	34	21	1	83	5	0	1	6	3	.67	7	.255	.321	.426
2002 Texas	AL	69	158	33	4	0	4	(2	2)	49	17	14	15	17	0	45	5	4	2	4	2	.67	2	.209	.302	.310
8 ML YEARS		631	1536	334	65	11	62	(28	34)	607	231	199	190	180	3	496	29	6	12	49	20	.71	28	.217	.309	.395

Joe Roa

Pitches: R **Bats:** R **Pos:** SP-11; RP-3   **Ht:** 6'1" **Wt:** 194 **Born:** 10/11/71 **Age:** 31

	HOW MUCH HE PITCHED						WHAT HE GAVE UP									THE RESULTS						
Year Team	Lg	G	GS	CG	GF	IP	BFP	H	R	ER	HR	SH	SF	HB	TBB	IBB	SO	WP	Bk	W	L	Pct	ShO	Sv-Op	Hld	ERC	ERA
2002 Scrtn/WlksBr*	AAA	17	17	1	0	111.0	422	83	24	23	4	4	1	4	16	2	74	0	2	14	0	1.000	0	0--	-	1.67	1.86
1995 Cleveland	AL	1	1	0	0	6.0	28	9	4	4	1	1	0	0	2	0	0	0	0	0	1	.000	0	0-0	0	7.46	6.00
1996 Cleveland	AL	1	0	0	0	1.2	11	4	2	2	0	0	0	0	3	0	0	0	0	0	0	-	0	0-0	0	20.57	10.80
1997 San Francisco	NL	28	3	0	4	65.2	289	86	40	38	8	5	4	2	20	5	34	0	1	2	5	.286	0	0-0	2	5.85	5.21
2002 Philadelphia	NL	14	11	0	1	71.1	298	78	33	32	11	1	3	1	13	2	35	0	1	4	4	.500	0	0-0	0	4.14	4.04
4 ML YEARS		44	15	0	5	144.2	626	177	79	76	20	7	7	3	38	7	69	0	2	6	10	.375	0	0-0	2	5.19	4.73

Brian Roberts

Bats: B **Throws:** R **Pos:** 2B-25; DH-7; PH-4; PR-2   **Ht:** 5'9" **Wt:** 170 **Born:** 10/9/77 **Age:** 25

Year Team	Lg	G	AB	H	2B	3B	HR	(Hm	Rd)	TB	R	RBI	RC	TBB	IBB	SO	HBP	SH	SF	SB	CS	SB%	GDP	Avg	OBP	Slg
1999 Delmarva	A	47	167	40	12	1	0	(-	-)	54	22	21	23	27	0	42	1	5	1	17	5	.77	0	.240	.347	.323
2000 Frederick	A+	48	163	49	6	3	0	(-	-)	61	27	16	25	27	1	24	1	7	0	13	10	.57	4	.301	.403	.374
2000 Orioles	R	9	29	9	1	2	1	(-	-)	17	8	3	9	7	0	4	0	0	1	7	1	.88	0	.310	.432	.586
2001 Bowie	AA	22	81	24	7	0	1	(-	-)	34	12	7	15	9	0	12	1	2	2	10	0	1.00	2	.296	.366	.420
2001 Rochester	AAA	44	161	43	4	1	1	(-	-)	52	16	12	26	28	0	22	0	1	0	23	3	.88	0	.267	.376	.323
2002 Rochester	AAA	78	313	86	9	7	3	(-	-)	118	49	30	48	40	1	46	3	2	1	22	4	.85	3	.275	.361	.377
2001 Baltimore	AL	75	273	69	12	3	2	(0	2)	93	42	17	27	13	0	36	0	3	3	12	3	.80	3	.253	.284	.341
2002 Baltimore	AL	38	128	29	6	0	1	(1	0)	38	18	11	12	15	0	21	1	3	2	9	2	.82	3	.227	.308	.297
2 ML YEARS		113	401	98	18	3	3	(1	2)	131	60	28	39	28	0	57	1	6	5	21	5	.81	6	.244	.292	.327

Dave Roberts

Bats: L **Throws:** L **Pos:** CF-116; PH-9; PR-4; LF-3   **Ht:** 5'10" **Wt:** 180 **Born:** 5/31/72 **Age:** 31

Year Team	Lg	G	AB	H	2B	3B	HR	(Hm	Rd)	TB	R	RBI	RC	TBB	IBB	SO	HBP	SH	SF	SB	CS	SB%	GDP	Avg	OBP	Slg
1999 Cleveland	AL	41	143	34	4	0	2	(1	1)	44	26	12	14	9	0	16	0	3	1	11	3	.79	0	.238	.281	.308
2000 Cleveland	AL	19	10	2	0	0	0	(0	0)	2	1	0	1	2	0	2	0	1	0	1	1	.50	0	.200	.333	.200
2001 Cleveland	AL	15	12	4	1	0	0	(0	0)	5	3	2	2	1	0	2	0	0	0	0	1	.00	0	.333	.385	.417
2002 Los Angeles	NL	127	422	117	14	7	3	(0	3)	154	63	34	66	48	0	51	2	6	1	45	10	.82	1	.277	.353	.365
4 ML YEARS		202	587	157	19	7	5	(1	4)	205	93	48	83	60	0	71	2	10	2	57	15	.79	1	.267	.336	.349

Grant Roberts

Pitches: R **Bats:** R **Pos:** RP-34   **Ht:** 6'3" **Wt:** 205 **Born:** 9/13/77 **Age:** 25

	HOW MUCH HE PITCHED						WHAT HE GAVE UP									THE RESULTS						
Year Team	Lg	G	GS	CG	GF	IP	BFP	H	R	ER	HR	SH	SF	HB	TBB	IBB	SO	WP	Bk	W	L	Pct	ShO	Sv-Op	Hld	ERC	ERA
2002 Binghamton*	AA	1	1	0	0	1.0	3	0	0	0	0	0	0	0	0	0	1	0	0	0	0	-	0	0--	0	0.00	0.00
2000 New York	NL	4	1	0	0	7.0	38	11	10	9	0	0	2	0	4	1	6	0	0	0	0	-	0	0-0	0	6.53	11.57
2001 New York	NL	16	0	0	2	26.0	110	24	11	11	2	1	1	0	8	1	29	0	1	1	0	1.000	0	0-1	1	3.03	3.81
2002 New York	NL	34	0	0	6	45.0	192	43	12	11	3	3	2	1	16	7	31	0	0	3	1	.750	0	0-0	0	3.25	2.20
3 ML YEARS		54	1	0	8	78.0	340	78	33	31	5	4	5	1	28	9	66	0	1	4	1	.800	0	0-1	1	3.45	3.58

Willis Roberts

Pitches: R **Bats:** R **Pos:** RP-66   **Ht:** 6'3" **Wt:** 175 **Born:** 6/19/75 **Age:** 28

	HOW MUCH HE PITCHED						WHAT HE GAVE UP									THE RESULTS						
Year Team	Lg	G	GS	CG	GF	IP	BFP	H	R	ER	HR	SH	SF	HB	TBB	IBB	SO	WP	Bk	W	L	Pct	ShO	Sv-Op	Hld	ERC	ERA
1999 Detroit	AL	1	0	0	0	1.1	8	3	4	2	0	0	1	1	0	0	0	0	0	0	0	-	0	0-0	0	12.64	13.50
2001 Baltimore	AL	46	18	1	20	132.0	593	142	75	72	15	5	4	11	55	1	95	3	2	9	10	.474	0	6-10	1	4.98	4.91
2002 Baltimore	AL	66	0	0	24	75.0	334	79	34	28	5	1	4	4	32	3	51	7	0	5	4	.556	0	1-3	13	4.35	3.36
3 ML YEARS		113	18	1	44	208.1	935	224	113	102	20	6	9	16	87	4	146	10	2	14	14	.500	0	7-13	14	4.80	4.41

Jeriome Robertson

Pitches: L **Bats:** L **Pos:** RP-10; SP-1   **Ht:** 6'1" **Wt:** 190 **Born:** 3/30/77 **Age:** 26

Year Team	Lg	G	GS	CG	GF	IP	BFP	H	R	ER	HR	SH	SF	HB	TBB	IBB	SO	WP	Bk	W	L	Pct	ShO	Sv-Op	Hld	ERC	ERA
1996 Astros	R	13	13	1	0	78.1	304	51	20	15	2	3	0	4	15	0	98	6	2	5	3	.625	1	0--	-	1.44	1.72
1996 Kissimmee	A+	1	1	0	0	7.0	27	4	4	2	0	0	0	0	1	0	2	0	0	0	0	-	0	0--	-	0.90	2.57
1997 Quad City	A	26	25	2	1	146.0	647	151	86	66	12	1	4	8	56	1	135	5	3	11	8	.579	1	1--	-	4.22	4.07
1998 Kissimmee	A+	28	28	2	0	175.0	740	185	83	72	13	3	5	7	53	3	131	5	6	10	10	.500	1	0--	-	4.04	3.70
1999 Jackson	AA	28	28	1	0	191.0	791	184	81	65	22	6	4	8	45	2	133	5	7	15	7	.682	0	0--	-	3.50	3.06
2000 Kissimmee	A+	5	5	1	0	29.0	121	28	19	15	1	1	0	2	5	0	13	0	0	1	2	.667	1	0--	-	2.82	4.66
2000 Round Rock	AA	11	10	0	0	61.0	265	62	36	28	8	3	1	2	18	1	30	4	1	2	2	.500	0	0--	-	3.98	4.13
2000 New Orleans	AAA	9	9	0	0	49.2	228	64	42	39	10	2	2	3	23	1	27	1	0	1	7	.125	0	0--	-	7.30	7.07
2001 Round Rock	AA	57	0	0	11	73.2	326	89	33	32	10	2	1	1	21	0	72	6	0	5	1	.833	0	3--	-	5.10	3.91
2002 New Orleans	AAA	27	27	2	0	180.0	734	160	59	51	13	4	4	9	45	0	114	4	0	12	8	.600	1	0--	-	2.95	2.55
2002 Houston	NL	11	1	0	1	9.2	46	13	8	7	4	5	3	0	5	3	6	2	0	0	2	.000	0	0-0	0	8.70	6.52

Nate Robertson

Pitches: L **Bats:** R **Pos:** RP-5; SP-1   **Ht:** 6'2" **Wt:** 215 **Born:** 9/3/77 **Age:** 25

Year Team	Lg	G	GS	CG	GF	IP	BFP	H	R	ER	HR	SH	SF	HB	TBB	IBB	SO	WP	Bk	W	L	Pct	ShO	Sv-Op	Hld	ERC	ERA
1999 Utica	A-	9	9	0	0	26.0	101	22	9	8	0	1	2	0	8	0	26	0	0	2	0	1.000	0	0--	-	2.43	2.77
1999 Kane County	A	8	8	1	0	51.0	197	42	14	13	1	0	2	0	12	0	33	0	0	6	1	.857	1	0--	-	2.15	2.29
2000 Kane County	A	6	6	0	0	17.2	81	24	13	10	0	0	1	0	6	0	15	0	0	0	2	.000	0	0--	-	5.43	5.09
2001 Brevard Cnty	A+	19	19	2	0	106.1	445	95	44	34	3	6	2	5	43	1	67	5	1	11	4	.733	0	0--	-	3.24	2.88
2002 Portland	AA	27	27	3	0	163.0	670	156	77	62	12	6	8	7	50	2	109	0	2	10	9	.526	0	0--	-	3.55	3.42
2002 Florida	NL	6	1	0	1	8.1	46	15	11	11	3	0	0	2	4	1	3	0	0	0	1	.000	0	0-0	0	12.69	11.88

Kerry Robinson

Bats: L **Throws:** L **Pos:** PH-71; LF-49; RF-17; CF-10; PR-10; DH-1   **Ht:** 6'0" **Wt:** 175 **Born:** 10/3/73 **Age:** 29

Year Team	Lg	G	AB	H	2B	3B	HR	(Hm	Rd)	TB	R	RBI	RC	TBB	IBB	SO	HBP	SH	SF	SB	CS	SB%	GDP	Avg	OBP	Slg
1998 Tampa Bay	AL	2	3	0	0	0	0	(0	0)	0	0	0	0	0	0	1	0	0	0	0	0	-	0	.000	.000	.000
1999 Cincinnati	NL	9	1	0	0	0	0	(0	0)	0	0	0	0	0	0	1	0	0	0	1	0	1.00	0	.000	.000	.000
2001 St Louis	NL	114	186	53	6	1	1	(1	0)	64	34	15	24	12	0	20	2	4	3	11	2	.85	1	.285	.330	.344
2002 St Louis	NL	124	181	47	7	4	1	(0	1)	65	27	15	20	11	3	29	0	2	1	7	4	.64	1	.260	.301	.359
4 ML YEARS		249	371	100	13	5	2	(1	1)	129	65	30	44	23	3	51	2	6	4	18	7	.72	2	.270	.313	.348

John Rocker

Pitches: L **Bats:** R **Pos:** RP-30   **Ht:** 6'4" **Wt:** 225 **Born:** 10/17/74 **Age:** 28

Year Team	Lg	G	GS	CG	GF	IP	BFP	H	R	ER	HR	SH	SF	HB	TBB	IBB	SO	WP	Bk	W	L	Pct	ShO	Sv-Op	Hld	ERC	ERA
2002 Oklahoma*	AAA	6	0	0	1	8.2	32	4	0	0	0	0	0	0	2	0	14	0	0	1	0	1.000	0	0--	-	0.82	0.00
2002 Tulsa*	AA	3	0	0	0	2.2	12	3	4	4	0	0	0	0	2	0	5	1	0	0	1	.000	0	0--	-	5.73	13.50
1998 Atlanta	NL	47	0	0	16	38.0	156	22	10	9	4	3	0	3	22	4	42	6	0	1	3	.250	0	2-4	15	2.73	2.13
1999 Atlanta	NL	74	0	0	61	72.1	301	47	24	20	5	2	0	1	37	4	104	7	0	4	5	.444	0	38-45	3	2.38	2.49
2000 Atlanta	NL	59	0	0	41	53.0	251	42	25	17	5	1	0	2	48	4	77	5	2	1	2	.333	0	24-27	4	4.72	2.89
2001 Atl-Cle	NL	68	0	0	48	66.2	300	58	36	32	4	4	2	5	41	4	79	11	2	5	9	.357	0	23-30	7	4.03	4.32
2002 Texas	AL	30	0	0	10	24.1	114	29	19	18	5	1	3	0	13	1	30	0	0	2	3	.400	0	1-4	10	6.43	6.66
2001 Atlanta	NL	30	0	0	28	32.0	135	25	13	11	2	0	1	2	16	1	36	5	0	2	2	.500	0	19-23	0	3.23	3.09
2001 Cleveland	AL	38	0	0	20	34.2	165	33	23	21	2	4	1	3	25	3	43	6	2	3	7	.300	0	4-7	7	4.79	5.45
5 ML YEARS		278	0	0	176	254.1	1122	198	114	96	23	11	5	11	161	17	332	29	4	13	22	.371	0	88-110	36	3.69	3.40

Fernando Rodney

Pitches: R **Bats:** R **Pos:** RP-20   **Ht:** 5'11" **Wt:** 170 **Born:** 3/18/77 **Age:** 26

Year Team	Lg	G	GS	CG	GF	IP	BFP	H	R	ER	HR	SH	SF	HB	TBB	IBB	SO	WP	Bk	W	L	Pct	ShO	Sv-Op	Hld	ERC	ERA
1999 Tigers	R	22	0	0	20	30.0	129	20	8	8	1	3	2	3	21	0	39	1	1	3	3	.500	0	9--	-	3.35	2.40
1999 Lakeland	A+	4	0	0	4	6.1	25	7	1	1	0	0	0	1	1	0	5	0	0	1	0	1.000	0	2--	-	4.01	1.42
2000 W Michigan	A	22	10	0	1	82.2	353	74	34	27	2	5	0	2	35	0	56	3	0	6	4	.600	0	0--	-	3.15	2.94
2001 Lakeland	A+	16	9	0	4	55.1	235	53	26	21	2	2	0	1	19	1	44	1	1	4	2	.667	0	0--	-	3.22	3.42
2001 Tigers	R	1	1	0	0	1.0	3	0	0	0	0	0	0	0	1	0	1	0	0	0	0	-	0	0--	-	1.26	0.00
2001 Erie	AA	4	0	0	2	6.1	30	7	3	3	1	0	1	2	3	0	8	0	0	0	0	-	0	0--	-	6.86	4.26
2002 Erie	AA	21	0	0	19	20.1	77	14	4	3	0	0	0	0	5	0	18	3	0	1	0	1.000	0	11--	-	1.51	1.33
2002 Toledo	AAA	20	0	0	11	22.1	90	13	4	2	1	1	3	1	9	0	25	2	2	1	1	.500	0	4--	-	1.76	0.81
2002 Detroit	AL	20	0	0	10	18.0	89	25	15	12	2	2	1	0	10	2	10	0	1	1	3	.250	0	0-4	-	6.77	6.00

Alex Rodriguez

Bats: R **Throws:** R **Pos:** SS-162; PH-2   **Ht:** 6'3" **Wt:** 210 **Born:** 7/27/75 **Age:** 27

Year Team	Lg	G	AB	H	2B	3B	HR	(Hm	Rd)	TB	R	RBI	RC	TBB	IBB	SO	HBP	SH	SF	SB	CS	SB%	GDP	Avg	OBP	Slg
1994 Seattle	AL	17	54	11	0	0	0	(0	0)	11	4	2	3	3	0	20	0	1	1	3	0	1.00	0	.204	.241	.204
1995 Seattle	AL	48	142	33	6	2	5	(1	4)	58	15	19	15	6	0	42	0	1	0	4	2	.67	0	.232	.264	.408
1996 Seattle	AL	146	601	215	54	1	36	(18	18)	379	141	123	144	59	1	104	4	6	7	15	4	.79	15	.358	.414	.631
1997 Seattle	AL	141	587	176	40	3	23	(16	7)	291	100	84	100	41	1	99	5	4	1	29	6	.83	14	.300	.350	.496
1998 Seattle	AL	161	686	213	35	5	42	(18	24)	384	123	124	135	45	0	121	10	3	4	46	13	.78	12	.310	.360	.560
1999 Seattle	AL	129	502	143	25	0	42	(20	22)	294	110	111	102	56	2	109	5	1	8	21	7	.75	12	.285	.357	.586
2000 Seattle	AL	148	554	175	34	2	41	(13	28)	336	134	132	138	100	5	121	7	0	11	15	4	.79	10	.316	.420	.606

Year Team	Lg	G	AB	H	2B	3B	HR	(Hm	Rd)	TB	R	RBI	RC	TBB	IBB	SO	HBP	SH	SF	SB	CS	SB%	GDP	Avg	OBP	Slg
									BATTING											BASERUNNING				AVERAGES		
2001 Texas	AL	**162**	632	201	34	1	**52**	(26	**26)**	393	**133**	135	148	75	6	131	16	0	9	18	3	.86	17	.318	.399	.622
2002 Texas	AL	**162**	624	187	27	2	**57**	(34	23)	389	125	**142**	153	87	12	122	10	0	4	9	4	.69	14	.300	.392	.623
9 ML YEARS		1114	4382	1354	255	16	298	(146	152)	2535	885	872	938	472	27	869	57	16	45	160	43	.79	94	.309	.380	.579

Felix Rodriguez

Pitches: R **Bats:** R **Pos:** RP-71   **Ht:** 6'1" **Wt:** 198 **Born:** 9/9/72 **Age:** 30

Year Team	Lg	G	GS	CG	GF	IP	BFP	H	R	ER	HR	SH	SF	HB	TBB	IBB	SO	WP	Bk	W	L	Pct	ShO	Sv-Op	Hld	ERC	ERA
				HOW MUCH HE PITCHED						WHAT HE GAVE UP												THE RESULTS					
1995 Los Angeles	NL	11	0	0	5	10.2	45	11	3	3	2	0	0	0	5	0	5	0	0	1	1	.500	0	0-1	0	5.43	2.53
1997 Cincinnati	NL	26	1	0	13	46.0	212	48	23	22	2	0	1	6	28	2	34	4	1	0	0	-	0	0-0	0	5.22	4.30
1998 Arizona	NL	43	0	0	23	44.0	207	44	31	30	5	4	3	1	29	1	36	5	2	0	2	.000	0	5-8	0	5.11	6.14
1999 San Francisco	NL	47	0	0	26	66.1	292	67	32	28	6	2	3	2	29	2	55	2	0	2	3	.400	0	0-1	3	4.25	3.80
2000 San Francisco	NL	76	0	0	19	81.2	346	65	29	24	6	2	3	3	42	2	95	3	1	4	2	.667	0	3-8	30	3.26	2.64
2001 San Francisco	NL	80	0	0	13	80.1	314	53	16	15	5	1	3	1	27	2	91	1	0	9	1	.900	0	0-3	32	1.92	1.68
2002 San Francisco	NL	71	0	0	12	69.0	288	53	33	32	4	2	3	4	29	1	58	4	0	8	6	.571	0	0-6	24	2.92	4.17
7 ML YEARS		354	1	0	111	398.0	1704	341	167	154	30	11	16	17	189	10	374	19	4	24	15	.615	0	8-27	89	3.53	3.48

Francisco Rodriguez

Pitches: R **Bats:** R **Pos:** RP-5   **Ht:** 6'0" **Wt:** 175 **Born:** 1/7/82 **Age:** 21

Year Team	Lg	G	GS	CG	GF	IP	BFP	H	R	ER	HR	SH	SF	HB	TBB	IBB	SO	WP	Bk	W	L	Pct	ShO	Sv-Op	Hld	ERC	ERA
				HOW MUCH HE PITCHED						WHAT HE GAVE UP												THE RESULTS					
1999 Butte	R+	12	9	1	0	51.2	211	33	21	19	1	3	0	3	21	1	69	10	3	1	1	.500	1	0--	-	1.90	3.31
1999 Boise	A-	1	1	0	0	5.0	22	3	4	3	0	0	1	0	1	0	6	0	0	1	0	1.000	0	0--	-	0.96	5.40
2000 Lk Elsinore	A+	13	12	0	0	64.0	265	43	29	20	2	2	2	1	32	0	79	12	1	4	4	.500	0	0--	-	2.32	2.81
2001 R Cucamnga	A+	20	20	1	0	113.2	523	127	72	68	13	2	1	6	55	1	147	17	4	5	7	.417	1	0--	-	5.34	5.38
2002 Arkansas	AA	23	0	0	16	41.1	170	32	13	9	2	0	0	0	15	0	61	7	1	3	3	.500	0	9--	-	2.39	1.96
2002 Salt Lake	AAA	27	0	0	23	42.0	164	30	13	12	1	1	0	3	13	0	59	2	0	2	3	.400	0	6--	-	2.14	2.57
2002 Anaheim	AL	5	0	0	4	5.2	21	3	0	0	0	0	0	1	2	1	13	0	0	0	0	-	0	0-0	0	1.52	0.00

Henry Rodriguez

Bats: L **Throws:** L **Pos:** PH-16; LF-4; RF-1   **Ht:** 6'2" **Wt:** 225 **Born:** 11/8/67 **Age:** 35

Year Team	Lg	G	AB	H	2B	3B	HR	(Hm	Rd)	TB	R	RBI	RC	TBB	IBB	SO	HBP	SH	SF	SB	CS	SB%	GDP	Avg	OBP	Slg
									BATTING											BASERUNNING				AVERAGES		
1992 Los Angeles	NL	53	146	32	7	0	3	(2	1)	48	11	14	12	8	0	30	0	1	1	0	0	-	2	.219	.258	.329
1993 Los Angeles	NL	76	176	39	10	0	8	(5	3)	73	20	23	20	11	2	39	0	0	1	1	0	1.00	1	.222	.266	.415
1994 Los Angeles	NL	104	306	82	14	2	8	(5	3)	124	33	49	36	17	2	58	2	1	4	0	1	.00	9	.268	.307	.405
1995 LA-Mon	NL	45	138	33	4	1	2	(1	1)	45	13	15	12	11	2	28	0	0	1	0	1	.00	5	.239	.293	.326
1996 Montreal	NL	145	532	147	42	1	36	(20	16)	299	81	103	93	37	7	**160**	3	0	4	2	0	1.00	10	.276	.325	.562
1997 Montreal	NL	132	476	116	28	3	26	(14	12)	228	55	83	69	42	5	149	2	0	3	3	3	.50	6	.244	.306	.479
1998 Chicago	NL	128	415	104	21	1	31	(16	15)	220	56	85	72	54	7	113	0	0	4	1	3	.25	6	.251	.334	.530
1999 Chicago	NL	130	447	136	29	0	26	(14	12)	243	72	87	87	56	6	113	0	0	4	2	4	.33	9	.304	.381	.544
2000 ChC-Fla	NL	112	367	94	21	1	20	(7	13)	177	47	61	57	36	2	99	4	0	3	1	2	.33	5	.256	.327	.482
2001 New York	AL	5	8	0	0	0	0	(0	0)	0	0	0	0	0	0	6	0	0	0	0	0	-	0	.000	.000	.000
2002 Montreal	NL	20	20	1	0	0	0	(0	0)	1	1	3	0	4	0	8	0	0	0	0	0	-	0	.050	.200	.050
1995 Los Angeles	NL	21	80	21	4	1	1	(0	1)	30	6	10	8	5	2	17	0	0	0	0	1	.00	3	.263	.306	.375
1995 Montreal	NL	24	58	12	0	0	1	(1	0)	15	7	5	4	6	0	11	0	0	1	0	0	-	2	.207	.277	.259
2000 Chicago	NL	76	259	65	15	1	18	(6	12)	136	37	51	42	22	2	76	3	0	3	1	2	.33	4	.251	.314	.525
2000 Florida	NL	36	108	29	6	0	2	(1	1)	41	10	10	15	14	0	23	1	0	0	0	0	-	1	.269	.358	.380
11 ML YEARS		950	3031	784	176	9	160	(84	76)	1458	389	523	458	276	33	803	11	2	23	10	14	.42	53	.259	.321	.481

Ivan Rodriguez

Bats: R **Throws:** R **Pos:** C-100; DH-6; PH-3   **Ht:** 5'9" **Wt:** 205 **Born:** 11/30/71 **Age:** 31

Year Team	Lg	G	AB	H	2B	3B	HR	(Hm	Rd)	TB	R	RBI	RC	TBB	IBB	SO	HBP	SH	SF	SB	CS	SB%	GDP	Avg	OBP	Slg
									BATTING											BASERUNNING				AVERAGES		
2002 Charlotte*	A+	3	9	3	0	0	0	(-	-)	3	1	0	1	0	0	3	0	0	0	0	0	-	0	.333	.333	.333
1991 Texas	AL	88	280	74	16	0	3	(3	0)	99	24	27	23	5	0	42	0	2	1	0	1	.00	10	.264	.276	.354
1992 Texas	AL	123	420	109	16	1	8	(4	4)	151	39	37	41	24	2	73	1	7	2	0	0	-	15	.260	.300	.360
1993 Texas	AL	137	473	129	28	4	10	(7	3)	195	56	66	57	29	3	70	4	5	8	8	7	.53	16	.273	.315	.412
1994 Texas	AL	99	363	108	19	1	16	(7	9)	177	56	57	61	31	5	42	7	0	4	6	3	.67	10	.298	.360	.488
1995 Texas	AL	130	492	149	32	2	12	(5	7)	221	56	67	68	16	2	48	4	0	5	0	2	.00	11	.303	.327	.449
1996 Texas	AL	153	639	192	47	3	19	(10	9)	302	116	86	99	38	4	55	4	0	5	5	0	1.00	15	.300	.342	.473
1997 Texas	AL	150	597	187	34	4	20	(12	8)	289	98	77	98	38	7	89	8	1	4	7	3	.70	18	.313	.360	.484
1998 Texas	AL	145	579	186	40	4	21	(12	9)	297	88	91	100	32	4	88	3	0	3	9	1	.90	16	.321	.358	.513
1999 Texas	AL	144	600	199	29	1	35	(12	23)	335	116	113	104	24	2	64	1	0	5	25	12	.68	**31**	.332	.356	.558
2000 Texas	AL	91	363	126	27	4	27	(16	11)	242	66	83	78	19	5	48	1	0	6	5	5	.50	17	.347	.375	.667
2001 Texas	AL	111	442	136	24	2	25	(16	9)	239	70	65	77	23	3	73	4	0	1	10	3	.77	13	.308	.347	.541
2002 Texas	AL	108	408	128	32	2	19	(15	4)	221	67	60	64	25	2	71	2	1	4	5	4	.56	13	.314	.353	.542
12 ML YEARS		1479	5656	1723	344	28	215	(119	96)	2768	852	829	870	304	42	763	39	16	47	80	40	.67	187	.305	.342	.489

Jose Rodriguez

Pitches: L **Bats:** L **Pos:** RP-6   **Ht:** 6'1" **Wt:** 215 **Born:** 12/18/74 **Age:** 28

Year Team	Lg	G	GS	CG	GF	IP	BFP	H	R	ER	HR	SH	SF	HB	TBB	IBB	SO	WP	Bk	W	L	Pct	ShO	Sv-Op	Hld	ERC	ERA
				HOW MUCH HE PITCHED						WHAT HE GAVE UP												THE RESULTS					
1997 Johnson City	R+	4	0	0	1	6.2	27	8	3	3	1	1	0	1	3	1	8	1	0	0	0	-	0	0--	-	2.88	4.05
1998 Peoria	A	40	0	0	12	39.1	191	47	32	20	0	6	1	2	19	1	30	3	0	2	4	.333	0	0--	-	4.63	4.58
1999 Arkansas	AA	30	0	0	9	36.0	173	38	16	13	6	2	0	0	25	0	30	4	0	1	2	.333	0	0--	-	5.91	3.25
1999 Peoria	A	15	0	0	2	16.1	74	14	7	6	1	3	0	0	8	0	15	0	0	2	3	.400	0	1--	-	3.14	3.31
2000 Arkansas	AA	10	0	0	2	11.0	47	7	3	3	0	2	0	0	4	2	8	0	0	1	0	1.000	0	1--	-	1.28	2.45

Year Team	Lg	G	GS	CG	GF	IP	BFP	H	R	ER	HR	SH	SF	HB	TBB	IBB	SO	WP	Bk	W	L	Pct	ShO	Sv-Op	Hld	ERC	ERA
2000 Memphis	AAA	40	0	0	17	47.1	200	48	21	20	4	5	1	0	19	1	37	0	1	4	2	.667	0	3--	-	4.12	3.80
2001 Memphis	AAA	54	0	0	17	60.2	262	52	25	24	7	2	2	2	31	0	54	0	0	2	1	.667	0	1--	-	3.95	3.56
2002 Memphis	AAA	22	0	0	14	18.1	85	26	13	7	2	0	2	0	7	0	14	2	1	2	1	.667	0	2--	-	6.65	3.44
2002 Edmonton	AAA	4	0	0	2	5.2	21	4	0	0	0	0	0	0	1	0	6	0	0	0	0	-	0	1--	-	1.43	0.00
2000 St Louis	NL	6	0	0	1	4.0	19	2	2	0	0	0	1	1	3	0	2	0	0	0	0	-	0	0-0	1	2.62	0.00
2002 Stl-Min		6	0	0	1	4.0	30	12	8	8	0	0	0	0	6	1	1	0	0	0	1	.000	0	0-0	0	21.31	18.00
2002 St Louis	NL	2	0	0	0	0.1	7	4	2	2	0	0	0	0	2	0	0	0	0	0	0	-	0	0-0	0	128.8	54.00
2002 Minnesota	AL	4	0	0	1	3.2	23	8	6	6	0	0	0	0	4	1	1	0	0	0	1	.000	0	0-0	0	13.03	14.73
2 ML YEARS		12	0	0	2	8.0	49	14	10	8	0	0	1	1	9	1	3	0	0	0	1	.000	0	0-0	1	10.83	9.00

Nerio Rodriguez

Pitches: R Bats: R Pos: RP-3 **Ht: 6'1" Wt: 205 Born: 3/4/71 Age: 32**

Year Team	Lg	G	GS	CG	GF	IP	BFP	H	R	ER	HR	SH	SF	HB	TBB	IBB	SO	WP	Bk	W	L	Pct	ShO	Sv-Op	Hld	ERC	ERA
2002 Buffalo*	AAA	13	10	1	0	74.1	286	55	20	15	6	2	0	1	12	0	44	0	0	4	2	.667	0	0--	-	1.84	1.82
2002 Memphis*	AAA	8	8	0	0	51.2	206	42	22	16	7	1	1	2	10	0	43	6	1	3	1	.750	0	0--	-	2.67	2.79
1996 Baltimore	AL	8	1	0	2	16.2	77	18	11	8	2	0	1	1	7	0	12	0	0	1	0	1.000	0	0-0	0	4.81	4.32
1997 Baltimore	AL	6	2	0	1	22.0	98	21	15	12	2	1	4	1	8	0	11	1	0	2	1	.667	0	0-1	0	3.62	4.91
1998 Bal-Tor	AL	13	4	0	3	27.1	133	35	26	26	1	0	2	1	17	0	11	1	0	2	3	.400	0	0-0	0	6.21	8.56
1999 Toronto	AL	2	0	0	1	2.0	10	2	3	3	2	0	0	0	2	0	2	0	0	0	1	.000	0	0-0	0	14.27	13.50
2002 Cle-Stl		3	0	0	3	4.2	20	4	3	2	1	0	0	0	1	0	2	0	0	0	0	-	0	0-0	0	3.04	3.86
1998 Baltimore	AL	6	4	0	0	19.0	89	25	17	17	0	0	2	0	9	0	8	1	0	1	3	.250	0	0-0	0	5.41	8.05
1998 Toronto	AL	7	0	0	3	8.1	44	10	9	9	1	0	0	1	8	0	3	0	0	1	0	1.000	0	0-0	0	8.14	9.72
2002 Cleveland	AL	1	0	0	1	0.1	1	0	0	0	0	0	0	0	0	0	0	0	0	0	0	-	0	0-0	0	0.00	0.00
2002 St Louis	NL	2	0	0	2	4.1	19	4	3	2	1	0	0	0	1	0	2	0	0	0	0	-	0	0-0	0	3.52	4.15
5 ML YEARS		32	7	0	10	72.2	338	80	58	51	8	1	7	3	35	0	38	2	0	4	6	.400	0	0-1	0	5.07	6.32

Ricardo Rodriguez

Pitches: R Bats: R Pos: SP-7 **Ht: 6'3" Wt: 165 Born: 5/21/78 Age: 25**

Year Team	Lg	G	GS	CG	GF	IP	BFP	H	R	ER	HR	SH	SF	HB	TBB	IBB	SO	WP	Bk	W	L	Pct	ShO	Sv-Op	Hld	ERC	ERA
2000 Great Falls	R+	15	15	2	0	95.2	374	66	32	20	2	3	3	1	23	0	129	4	0	10	3	.769	0	0--	-	1.56	1.88
2001 Vero Beach	A+	26	26	2	0	154.1	645	133	67	55	13	7	2	3	60	0	154	18	1	14	6	.700	0	0--	-	3.26	3.21
2002 Jacksonville	AA	11	11	2	0	68.0	268	56	21	15	4	2	1	2	13	0	44	5	0	5	4	.556	0	0--	-	2.27	1.99
2002 Las Vegas	AAA	2	2	0	0	11.2	51	13	5	5	1	0	1	1	5	0	7	0	0	1	0	1.000	0	0--	-	5.28	3.86
2002 Buffalo	AAA	4	4	0	0	25.0	106	26	10	10	1	1	0	2	7	0	14	0	0	3	1	.750	0	0--	-	3.78	3.60
2002 Cleveland	AL	7	7	0	0	41.1	183	40	27	26	5	0	0	8	18	3	24	1	0	2	2	.500	0	0-0	0	4.92	5.66

Rich Rodriguez

Pitches: L Bats: L Pos: RP-36 **Ht: 6'0" Wt: 205 Born: 3/1/63 Age: 40**

Year Team	Lg	G	GS	CG	GF	IP	BFP	H	R	ER	HR	SH	SF	HB	TBB	IBB	SO	WP	Bk	W	L	Pct	ShO	Sv-Op	Hld	ERC	ERA
2002 Tulsa*	AA	3	0	0	0	2.2	14	4	2	2	0	0	0	0	2	0	3	1	0	0	0	-	0	0--	-	7.52	6.75
2002 Oklahoma*	AAA	3	0	0	0	2.2	14	6	4	4	0	0	0	0	0	0	1	0	0	0	0	-	0	0--	-	9.13	13.50
1990 San Diego	NL	32	0	0	15	47.2	201	52	17	15	2	2	1	1	16	4	22	1	1	1	1	.500	0	1-1	3	3.99	2.83
1991 San Diego	NL	64	1	0	15	80.0	335	66	31	29	8	7	2	0	44	8	40	4	1	3	1	.750	0	0-2	8	3.63	3.26
1992 San Diego	NL	61	1	0	15	91.0	369	77	28	24	4	2	2	0	29	4	64	1	1	6	3	.667	0	0-1	5	2.56	2.37
1993 SD-Fla		70	0	0	21	76.0	331	73	38	32	10	5	0	2	33	8	43	3	0	2	4	.333	0	3-7	10	4.12	3.79
1994 St Louis	NL	56	0	0	15	60.1	260	62	30	27	6	2	1	1	26	4	43	4	0	3	5	.375	0	0-3	15	4.38	4.03
1995 St Louis	NL	1	0	0	0	1.2	4	0	0	0	0	0	0	0	0	0	0	0	0	0	0	-	0	0-0	0	0.00	0.00
1997 San Francisco	NL	71	0	0	15	65.1	271	65	24	23	7	3	0	1	21	4	32	0	0	4	3	.571	0	1-5	14	3.85	3.17
1998 San Francisco	NL	68	0	0	11	65.2	278	69	28	27	7	2	2	0	20	5	44	3	0	4	0	1.000	0	2-6	22	3.94	3.70
1999 San Francisco	NL	62	0	0	8	56.2	255	60	33	33	8	5	2	1	28	5	44	1	0	3	0	1.000	0	0-2	11	4.98	5.24
2000 New York	NL	32	0	0	13	37.0	185	59	40	32	7	0	5	3	15	0	18	2	1	1	0	1.000	0	0-0	0	8.86	7.78
2001 Cleveland	AL	53	0	0	6	39.0	174	41	24	18	2	2	1	2	17	3	31	1	1	2	2	.500	0	0-2	8	4.19	4.15
2002 Texas	AL	36	0	0	6	16.2	72	14	10	10	1	1	0	1	11	1	12	0	0	3	2	.600	0	1-3	6	4.17	5.40
1993 San Diego	NL	34	0	0	10	30.0	133	34	15	11	2	2	0	1	9	3	22	1	0	2	3	.400	0	2-5	8	4.08	3.30
1993 Florida	NL	36	0	0	11	46.0	198	39	23	21	8	3	0	1	24	5	21	2	0	0	1	.000	0	1-2	2	4.14	4.11
12 ML YEARS		606	2	0	144	637.0	2735	638	303	270	62	31	16	12	260	46	393	20	5	31	22	.585	0	8-32	100	4.10	3.81

Eddie Rogers

Bats: R Throws: R Pos: SS-4; PH-1 **Ht: 6'1" Wt: 172 Born: 8/29/78 Age: 24**

Year Team	Lg	G	AB	H	2B	3B	HR	(Hm	Rd)	TB	R	RBI	RC	TBB	IBB	SO	HBP	SH	SF	SB	CS	SB%	GDP	Avg	OBP	Slg
1999 Orioles	R	53	177	51	5	1	1	(-	-)	61	34	19	28	23	0	22	4	4	2	20	3	.87	2	.288	.379	.345
2000 Delmarva	A	80	332	91	14	5	5	(-	-)	130	46	42	45	22	0	63	0	10	3	27	6	.82	3	.274	.317	.392
2000 Bowie	AA	13	49	14	3	0	1	(-	-)	20	4	8	6	3	0	15	0	0	1	1	1	.50	2	.286	.321	.408
2001 Bowie	AA	53	191	38	10	1	0	(-	-)	50	11	13	10	6	0	40	2	4	0	10	2	.83	4	.199	.231	.262
2001 Frederick	A+	73	292	76	20	3	8	(-	-)	126	39	41	39	14	0	47	8	2	2	18	6	.75	8	.260	.310	.432
2002 Bowie	AA	112	422	110	26	2	11	(-	-)	173	59	57	52	16	1	70	10	5	6	14	4	.78	9	.261	.300	.410
2002 Baltimore	AL	5	3	0	0	0	0	(0	0)	0	0	0	0	0	0	0	0	0	0	0	0	-	1	.000	.000	.000

Kenny Rogers

Pitches: L **Bats:** L **Pos:** SP-33   **Ht:** 6'1" **Wt:** 217 **Born:** 11/10/64 **Age:** 38

Year Team	Lg	G	GS	CG	GF	IP	BFP	H	R	ER	HR	SH	SF	HB	TBB	IBB	SO	WP	Bk	W	L	Pct	ShO	Sv-Op	Hld	ERC	ERA
1989 Texas	AL	73	0	0	24	73.2	314	60	28	24	2	6	3	4	42	9	63	6	0	3	4	.429	0	2-5	15	3.26	2.93
1990 Texas	AL	69	3	0	46	97.2	428	93	40	34	6	7	4	1	42	5	74	5	0	10	6	.625	0	15-23	6	3.53	3.13
1991 Texas	AL	63	9	0	20	109.2	511	121	80	66	14	9	5	6	61	7	73	3	1	10	10	.500	0	5-6	11	5.57	5.42
1992 Texas	AL	81	0	0	38	78.2	337	80	32	27	7	4	1	0	26	8	70	4	1	3	6	.333	0	6-10	16	3.63	3.09
1993 Texas	AL	35	33	5	0	208.1	885	210	108	95	18	7	5	4	71	2	140	6	5	16	10	.615	0	0-0	1	3.88	4.10
1994 Texas	AL	24	24	6	0	167.1	714	169	93	83	24	3	6	3	52	1	120	3	1	11	8	.579	2	0-0	0	4.12	4.46
1995 Texas	AL	31	31	3	0	208.0	877	192	87	78	26	3	5	2	76	1	140	8	1	17	7	.708	1	0-0	0	3.72	3.38
1996 New York	AL	30	30	2	0	179.0	786	179	97	93	16	6	3	8	83	2	92	5	0	12	8	.600	1	0-0	0	4.43	4.68
1997 New York	AL	31	22	1	4	145.0	651	161	100	91	18	2	4	7	62	1	78	2	2	6	7	.462	0	0-0	1	5.18	5.65
1998 Oakland	AL	34	34	7	0	238.2	970	215	96	84	19	4	5	7	67	0	138	5	2	16	8	.667	0	0-0	0	3.13	3.17
1999 Oak-NYM	AL	31	31	5	0	195.1	845	206	100	91	16	7	7	13	69	1	126	4	1	10	4	.714	1	0-0	0	4.38	4.19
2000 Texas	AL	34	34	2	0	227.1	998	257	126	115	20	3	4	11	78	2	127	1	1	13	13	.500	0	0-0	0	4.72	4.55
2001 Texas	AL	20	20	0	0	120.2	552	150	88	83	18	1	6	8	49	2	74	4	1	5	7	.417	0	0-0	0	6.22	6.19
2002 Texas	AL	33	33	2	0	210.2	892	212	101	90	21	3	1	6	70	1	107	5	1	13	8	.619	1	0-0	0	3.99	3.84
1999 Oakland	AL	19	19	3	0	119.1	528	135	66	57	8	4	6	9	41	0	68	3	1	5	3	.625	0	0-0	0	4.68	4.30
1999 New York	NL	12	12	2	0	76.0	317	71	35	34	8	3	1	4	28	1	58	1	0	5	1	.833	1	0-0	0	3.91	4.03
14 ML YEARS		589	304	33	132	2260.0	9760	2305	1177	1054	225	65	59	80	848	42	1422	61	17	145	106	.578	7	28-44	50	4.22	4.20

Scott Rolen

Bats: R **Throws:** R **Pos:** 3B-155; PH-1   **Ht:** 6'4" **Wt:** 226 **Born:** 4/4/75 **Age:** 28

Year Team	Lg	G	AB	H	2B	3B	HR	(Hm	Rd)	TB	R	RBI	RC	TBB	IBB	SO	HBP	SH	SF	SB	CS	SB%	GDP	Avg	OBP	Slg
1996 Philadelphia	NL	37	130	33	7	0	4	(2	2)	52	10	18	16	13	0	27	1	0	2	0	2	.00	4	.254	.322	.400
1997 Philadelphia	NL	156	561	159	35	3	21	(11	10)	263	93	92	103	76	4	138	13	0	7	16	6	.73	6	.283	.377	.469
1998 Philadelphia	NL	160	601	174	45	4	31	(19	12)	320	120	110	124	93	6	141	11	0	6	14	7	.67	10	.290	.391	.532
1999 Philadelphia	NL	112	421	113	28	1	26	(9	17)	221	74	77	83	67	2	114	3	0	6	12	2	.86	8	.268	.368	.525
2000 Philadelphia	NL	128	483	144	32	6	26	(12	14)	266	88	89	97	51	9	99	5	0	2	8	1	.89	4	.298	.370	.551
2001 Philadelphia	NL	151	554	160	39	1	25	(12	13)	276	96	107	108	74	6	127	13	0	12	16	5	.76	6	.289	.378	.498
2002 Phi-Stl	NL	155	580	154	29	8	31	(14	17)	292	89	110	99	72	4	102	12	0	3	8	4	.67	22	.266	.357	.503
2002 Philadelphia	NL	100	375	97	21	4	17	(8	9)	177	52	66	60	52	2	68	8	0	3	5	2	.71	12	.259	.358	.472
2002 St Louis	NL	55	205	57	8	4	14	(6	8)	115	37	44	39	20	2	34	4	0	0	3	2	.60	10	.278	.354	.561
7 ML YEARS		899	3330	937	215	23	164	(79	85)	1690	570	603	630	446	31	748	58	0	38	74	27	.73	60	.281	.372	.508

Jimmy Rollins

Bats: B **Throws:** R **Pos:** SS-152; PH-3; 2B-1   **Ht:** 5'8" **Wt:** 165 **Born:** 11/27/78 **Age:** 24

Year Team	Lg	G	AB	H	2B	3B	HR	(Hm	Rd)	TB	R	RBI	RC	TBB	IBB	SO	HBP	SH	SF	SB	CS	SB%	GDP	Avg	OBP	Slg
2000 Philadelphia	NL	14	53	17	1	1	0	(0	0)	20	5	5	8	2	0	7	0	0	0	3	0	1.00	0	.321	.345	.377
2001 Philadelphia	NL	158	656	180	29	12	14	(8	6)	275	97	54	96	48	2	108	2	9	5	46	8	.85	5	.274	.323	.419
2002 Philadelphia	NL	154	637	156	33	10	11	(3	8)	242	82	60	71	54	3	103	4	6	4	31	13	.70	14	.245	.306	.380
3 ML YEARS		326	1346	353	63	23	25	(11	14)	537	184	119	175	104	5	218	6	15	9	80	21	.79	19	.262	.316	.399

Damian Rolls

Bats: R **Throws:** R **Pos:** RF-13; LF-4; CF-4   **Ht:** 6'2" **Wt:** 215 **Born:** 9/15/77 **Age:** 25

Year Team	Lg	G	AB	H	2B	3B	HR	(Hm	Rd)	TB	R	RBI	RC	TBB	IBB	SO	HBP	SH	SF	SB	CS	SB%	GDP	Avg	OBP	Slg
2002 Orlando*	AA	2	7	3	0	1	0	(-	-)	5	1	0	2	1	0	0	0	0	0	0	1	.00	0	.429	.500	.714
2002 Durham*	AAA	67	244	65	6	4	6	(-	-)	97	41	35	36	21	0	43	5	6	4	15	0	1.00	0	.266	.332	.398
2000 Tampa Bay	AL	4	3	1	0	0	0	(0	0)	1	0	0	0	0	0	1	0	0	0	0	0	-	0	.333	.333	.333
2001 Tampa Bay	AL	81	237	62	11	1	2	(2	0)	81	33	12	23	10	0	47	0	2	0	12	4	.75	5	.262	.291	.342
2002 Tampa Bay	AL	21	89	26	6	1	0	(0	0)	34	15	6	7	3	0	16	2	1	0	2	5	.29	1	.292	.330	.382
3 ML YEARS		106	329	89	17	2	2	(2	0)	116	48	18	30	13	0	64	2	3	0	14	9	.61	6	.271	.302	.353

Jason Romano

Bats: R **Throws:** R **Pos:** 2B-20; PR-13; LF-11; CF-11; SS-5; PH-3; 3B-2   **Ht:** 6'0" **Wt:** 185 **Born:** 6/24/79 **Age:** 24

Year Team	Lg	G	AB	H	2B	3B	HR	(Hm	Rd)	TB	R	RBI	RC	TBB	IBB	SO	HBP	SH	SF	SB	CS	SB%	GDP	Avg	OBP	Slg
1997 Rangers	R	34	109	28	5	3	2	(-	-)	45	27	11	18	13	0	19	3	1	1	13	4	.76	1	.257	.349	.413
1998 Savannah	A	134	524	142	19	4	7	(-	-)	190	72	52	68	46	1	94	8	5	5	40	17	.70	6	.271	.336	.363
1998 Charlotte	A+	7	24	5	1	0	0	(-	-)	6	3	1	1	2	0	2	0	1	1	1	2	.33	0	.208	.259	.250
1999 Charlotte	A+	120	459	143	27	14	13	(-	-)	237	84	71	89	39	2	72	13	4	7	34	16	.68	4	.312	.376	.516
2000 Tulsa	AA	131	535	145	35	2	8	(-	-)	208	87	70	73	56	0	84	6	16	7	25	10	.71	13	.271	.343	.389
2001 Tulsa	AA	46	186	45	9	1	1	(-	-)	59	19	19	17	16	0	31	1	3	1	8	3	.73	8	.242	.304	.317
2001 Oklahoma	AAA	41	149	47	6	1	4	(-	-)	67	32	13	25	20	1	28	0	6	1	3	4	.43	4	.315	.394	.450
2001 Rangers	R	5	21	3	0	0	0	(-	-)	3	2	0	0	1	0	8	0	0	0	1	0	1.00	0	.143	.182	.143
2001 Charlotte	A+	3	10	4	2	0	0	(-	-)	6	3	1	4	4	0	1	0	0	0	1	0	1.00	0	.400	.571	.600
2002 Oklahoma	AAA	48	196	53	8	1	4	(-	-)	75	28	28	29	19	0	41	0	8	4	10	3	.77	5	.270	.329	.383
2002 Co Springs	AAA	31	129	40	7	2	0	(-	-)	51	20	9	18	6	0	27	0	3	1	8	3	.73	1	.310	.338	.395
2002 Tex-Col		47	91	23	4	1	0	(0	0)	29	17	5	10	7	0	24	0	2	1	6	1	.86	1	.253	.303	.319
2002 Texas	AL	29	54	11	4	0	0	(0	0)	15	8	4	5	4	0	13	0	1	1	2	0	1.00	0	.204	.254	.278
2002 Colorado	NL	18	37	12	0	1	0	(0	0)	14	9	1	5	3	0	11	0	1	0	4	1	.80	1	.324	.375	.378

J.C. Romero

Pitches: L **Bats:** B **Pos:** RP-81   **Ht:** 5'11" **Wt:** 195 **Born:** 6/4/76 **Age:** 27

Year Team		HOW MUCH HE PITCHED						WHAT HE GAVE UP										THE RESULTS						
	Lg	G	GS	CG	GF	IP	BFP	H	R	ER	HR	SH	SF	HB	TBB	IBB	SO	WP	Bk	W	L	Pct	ShO	Sv-Op	Hld	ERC	ERA
1999 Minnesota	AL	5	0	0	3	9.2	39	13	4	4	0	0	0	0	0	0	4	0	0	0	0	.000	0	0-0	0	3.95	3.72
2000 Minnesota	AL	12	11	0	0	57.2	268	72	51	45	8	4	2	1	30	0	50	2	1	2	7	.222	0	0-0	0	6.48	7.02
2001 Minnesota	AL	14	11	0	1	65.0	286	71	48	45	10	3	2	1	24	1	39	1	0	4	4	.200	0	0-0	0	4.89	6.23
2002 Minnesota	AL	81	0	0	15	81.0	332	62	17	17	3	1	0	4	36	4	76	9	0	9	2	.818	0	1-5	**33**	2.74	1.89
4 ML YEARS		112	22	0	19	213.1	925	218	120	111	21	8	4	6	90	5	169	12	1	12	13	.480	0	1-5	33	4.39	4.68

Matt Roney

Pitches: R **Bats:** R **Pos:** RP   **Ht:** 6'3" **Wt:** 230 **Born:** 1/10/80 **Age:** 23

Year Team		HOW MUCH HE PITCHED						WHAT HE GAVE UP										THE RESULTS						
	Lg	G	GS	CG	GF	IP	BFP	H	R	ER	HR	SH	SF	HB	TBB	IBB	SO	WP	Bk	W	L	Pct	ShO	Sv-Op	Hld	ERC	ERA
1998 Rockies	R	9	9	1	0	40.1	187	50	31	26	1	1	0	3	11	0	49	4	2	1	1	.500	1	0- --	-	4.49	5.80
2000 Portland	A-	15	15	0	0	80.1	360	75	35	28	6	1	1	7	44	0	85	8	2	7	5	.583	0	0- --	-	4.42	3.14
2001 Asheville	A	23	23	1	0	121.0	540	131	74	67	16	2	5	13	43	0	115	6	1	8	10	.444	0	0- --	-	5.02	4.98
2002 Asheville	A	14	14	1	0	82.2	349	82	39	32	7	3	2	5	25	1	88	1	1	4	6	.400	1	0- --	-	3.80	3.48
2002 Carolina	AA	13	13	0	0	70.2	312	73	52	48	6	1	1	2	33	0	61	2	1	3	6	.333	0	0- --	-	4.54	6.11

Dave Ross

Bats: R **Throws:** R **Pos:** C-6; PH-3   **Ht:** 6'2" **Wt:** 205 **Born:** 3/19/77 **Age:** 26

Year Team		BATTING																BASERUNNING				AVERAGES		
	Lg	G	AB	H	2B	3B	HR	(Hm | Rd)	TB	R	RBI	RC	TBB	IBB	SO	HBP	SH	SF	SB	CS	SB%	GDP	Avg	OBP	Slg
1998 Yakima	A-	59	191	59	14	1	6	(- | -)	93	31	25	38	34	0	49	1	2	2	2	2	.50	5	.309	.412	.487
1999 Vero Beach	A+	114	375	85	19	1	7	(- | -)	127	47	39	38	46	1	111	7	1	6	5	10	.33	10	.227	.318	.339
2000 Sn Brnardino	A+	51	191	49	11	1	7	(- | -)	83	27	21	26	17	1	43	1	3	1	3	2	.60	3	.257	.319	.435
2000 San Antonio	AA	24	67	14	2	1	3	(- | -)	27	11	12	9	9	1	17	1	1	1	1	0	1.00	0	.209	.308	.403
2001 Jacksonville	AA	74	146	65	13	1	11	(- | -)	113	35	45	55	34	0	72	10	0	3	1	1	.50	4	.445	.565	.774
2002 Las Vegas	AAA	92	293	87	16	2	15	(- | -)	152	48	68	58	35	0	86	9	5	4	1	1	.50	4	.297	.384	.519
2002 Los Angeles	NL	8	10	2	1	0	1	(0 | 1)	6	2	2	2	2	0	4	1	0	0	0	0	-	0	.200	.385	.600

Aaron Rowand

Bats: R **Throws:** R **Pos:** CF-76; LF-39; PH-9; RF-8; PR-1   **Ht:** 6'1" **Wt:** 200 **Born:** 8/29/77 **Age:** 25

Year Team		BATTING																BASERUNNING				AVERAGES		
	Lg	G	AB	H	2B	3B	HR	(Hm | Rd)	TB	R	RBI	RC	TBB	IBB	SO	HBP	SH	SF	SB	CS	SB%	GDP	Avg	OBP	Slg
1998 Hickory	A	61	222	76	13	3	5	(- | -)	110	42	32	44	21	0	36	6	5	2	7	3	.70	5	.342	.410	.495
1999 Winstn-Salm	A+	133	512	143	37	3	24	(- | -)	258	96	88	82	33	2	94	13	2	5	15	10	.60	13	.279	.336	.504
2000 Birmingham	AA	139	532	137	26	5	20	(- | -)	233	80	98	75	38	4	117	14	4	4	22	7	.76	12	.258	.321	.438
2001 Charlotte	AAA	82	329	97	28	0	16	(- | -)	173	54	48	58	21	3	47	9	2	1	8	2	.80	9	.295	.353	.526
2001 Chicago	AL	63	123	36	5	0	4	(3 | 1)	53	21	20	22	15	0	28	4	5	1	5	1	.83	2	.293	.385	.431
2002 Chicago	AL	126	302	78	16	2	7	(5 | 2)	119	41	29	37	12	1	54	6	9	2	0	1	.00	8	.258	.298	.394
2 ML YEARS		189	425	114	21	2	11	(8 | 3)	172	62	49	59	27	1	82	10	14	3	5	2	.71	10	.268	.325	.405

Wilkin Ruan

Bats: R **Throws:** R **Pos:** PR-8; CF-5; PH-3   **Ht:** 6'0" **Wt:** 170 **Born:** 11/18/79 **Age:** 23

Year Team		BATTING																BASERUNNING				AVERAGES		
	Lg	G	AB	H	2B	3B	HR	(Hm | Rd)	TB	R	RBI	RC	TBB	IBB	SO	HBP	SH	SF	SB	CS	SB%	GDP	Avg	OBP	Slg
1998 Jupiter	A+	5	18	3	0	0	0	(- | -)	3	2	0	1	1	0	3	0	0	0	2	0	1.00	0	.167	.211	.167
1998 Expos	R	54	201	48	9	3	1	(- | -)	66	22	19	15	5	0	43	2	3	2	13	13	.50	1	.239	.262	.328
1999 Cape Fear	A	112	397	89	16	4	1	(- | -)	116	43	47	28	18	0	79	6	7	0	29	17	.63	5	.224	.268	.292
2000 Cape Fear	A	134	574	165	29	10	0	(- | -)	214	95	51	78	24	1	75	8	2	3	64	10	.86	4	.287	.323	.373
2001 Jupiter	A+	72	293	83	8	2	2	(- | -)	101	41	26	31	10	2	35	3	7	1	25	14	.64	3	.283	.313	.345
2001 Harrisburg	AA	30	117	29	7	0	0	(- | -)	36	14	6	11	3	0	18	2	1	0	6	0	1.00	1	.248	.279	.308
2002 Jacksonville	AA	78	324	82	16	6	3	(- | -)	119	44	34	40	17	0	33	8	5	1	23	3	.88	4	.253	.306	.367
2002 Las Vegas	AAA	40	153	50	7	3	0	(- | -)	63	18	29	21	2	0	17	0	2	0	12	0	1.00	7	.327	.335	.412
2002 Los Angeles	NL	12	11	3	1	0	0	(0 | 0)	4	2	3	2	0	0	2	0	0	0	0	0	-	0	.273	.273	.364

Kirk Rueter

Pitches: L **Bats:** L **Pos:** SP-33   **Ht:** 6'3" **Wt:** 212 **Born:** 12/1/70 **Age:** 32

Year Team		HOW MUCH HE PITCHED						WHAT HE GAVE UP										THE RESULTS						
	Lg	G	GS	CG	GF	IP	BFP	H	R	ER	HR	SH	SF	HB	TBB	IBB	SO	WP	Bk	W	L	Pct	ShO	Sv-Op	Hld	ERC	ERA
1993 Montreal	NL	14	14	1	0	85.2	341	85	33	26	5	1	0	0	18	1	31	0	0	8	0	1.000	0	0-0	0	3.14	2.73
1994 Montreal	NL	20	20	0	0	92.1	397	106	60	53	11	6	6	2	23	1	50	2	0	7	3	.700	0	0-0	0	4.54	5.17
1995 Montreal	NL	9	9	1	0	47.1	184	38	17	17	3	4	0	1	9	0	28	0	0	5	3	.625	1	0-0	0	2.19	3.23
1996 Mon-SF	NL	20	19	0	0	102.0	430	109	50	45	12	4	1	2	27	0	46	2	0	6	8	.429	0	0-0	0	4.18	3.97
1997 San Francisco	NL	32	32	0	0	190.2	802	194	83	73	17	10	6	1	51	8	115	3	0	13	6	.684	0	0-0	0	3.54	3.45
1998 San Francisco	NL	33	33	1	0	187.2	806	193	100	91	27	5	8	7	57	3	102	6	0	16	9	.640	0	0-0	0	4.27	4.36
1999 San Francisco	NL	33	33	1	0	184.2	804	219	118	111	28	6	4	2	55	2	94	2	0	15	10	.600	0	0-0	0	5.19	5.41
2000 San Francisco	NL	32	31	0	0	184.0	799	205	92	81	23	**19**	9	2	62	5	71	1	0	11	9	.550	0	0-0	0	4.68	3.96
2001 San Francisco	NL	34	34	0	0	195.1	840	213	105	96	25	11	6	4	66	4	83	1	0	14	12	.538	0	0-0	0	4.65	4.42
2002 San Francisco	NL	33	33	0	0	203.2	846	204	83	73	22	6	6	6	54	7	76	3	0	14	8	.636	0	0-0	0	3.61	3.23
1996 San Francisco	NL	16	16	0	0	78.2	338	91	44	40	12	4	1	2	22	0	30	0	0	5	6	.455	0	0-0	0	5.06	4.58
1996 San Francisco	NL	4	3	0	0	23.1	92	18	6	5	0	0	0	0	5	0	16	2	0	1	2	.333	0	0-0	0	1.66	1.93
10 ML YEARS		260	258	4	0	1473.1	6249	1566	741	666	173	72	46	22	422	31	696	20	0	109	68	.616	1	0-0	0	4.16	4.07

Ryan Rupe

Pitches: R **Bats:** R **Pos:** SP-15   **Ht:** 6'5" **Wt:** 248 **Born:** 3/31/75 **Age:** 28

Year Team	Lg	G	GS	CG	GF	IP	BFP	H	R	ER	HR	SH	SF	HB	TBB	IBB	SO	WP	Bk	W	L	Pct	ShO	Sv-Op	Hld	ERC	ERA
1999 Tampa Bay	AL	24	24	0	0	142.1	614	136	81	72	17	1	7	12	57	2	97	4	1	8	9	.471	0	0-0	0	4.32	4.55
2000 Tampa Bay	AL	18	18	0	0	91.0	425	121	75	70	19	2	6	9	31	3	61	4	0	5	6	.455	0	0-0	0	7.02	6.92
2001 Tampa Bay	AL	28	26	0	0	143.1	635	161	111	105	30	3	5	11	48	0	123	7	1	5	12	.294	0	0-1	0	5.67	6.59
2002 Tampa Bay	AL	15	15	2	0	90.0	382	83	60	56	11	2	4	10	25	0	67	6	0	5	10	.333	0	0-0	0	3.74	5.60
4 ML YEARS		85	83	2	0	466.2	2056	501	327	303	77	8	22	42	161	5	348	21	2	23	37	.383	0	0-1	0	5.11	5.84

Glendon Rusch

Pitches: L **Bats:** L **Pos:** SP-34   **Ht:** 6'1" **Wt:** 200 **Born:** 11/7/74 **Age:** 28

Year Team	Lg	G	GS	CG	GF	IP	BFP	H	R	ER	HR	SH	SF	HB	TBB	IBB	SO	WP	Bk	W	L	Pct	ShO	Sv-Op	Hld	ERC	ERA
1997 Kansas City	AL	30	27	1	0	170.1	758	206	111	104	28	8	7	7	52	0	116	0	1	6	9	.400	0	0-0	0	5.56	5.50
1998 Kansas City	AL	29	24	1	2	154.2	686	191	104	101	22	1	2	4	50	0	94	1	0	6	15	.286	1	1-1	0	5.62	5.88
1999 KC-NYM		4	0	0	2	5.0	26	8	7	7	1	0	0	1	3	0	4	0	0	0	1	.000	0	0-0	0	10.75	12.60
2000 New York	NL	31	30	2	0	190.2	802	196	91	85	18	10	7	6	44	2	157	2	0	11	11	.500	0	0-0	0	3.64	4.01
2001 New York	NL	33	33	1	0	179.0	785	216	101	92	23	11	5	7	43	2	156	3	2	8	12	.400	0	0-0	0	4.97	4.63
2002 Milwaukee	NL	34	34	4	0	210.2	913	227	118	110	30	14	5	5	76	1	140	6	0	10	16	.385	1	0-0	0	4.80	4.70
1999 Kansas City	AL	3	0	0	1	4.0	23	7	7	7	1	0	0	1	3	0	4	0	0	0	1	.000	0	0-0	0	12.89	15.75
1999 New York	NL	1	0	0	1	1.0	3	1	0	0	0	0	0	0	0	0	0	0	0	0	0	-	0	0-0	0	2.79	0.00
6 ML YEARS		161	148	9	4	910.1	3970	1044	532	499	122	44	26	30	268	5	667	12	3	41	64	.390	2	1-1	0	4.88	4.93

Jim Rushford

Bats: L **Throws:** L **Pos:** RF-21; PH-2; LF-1   **Ht:** 6'1" **Wt:** 190 **Born:** 3/24/74 **Age:** 29

Year Team	Lg	G	AB	H	2B	3B	HR	(Hm	Rd)	TB	R	RBI	RC	TBB	IBB	SO	HBP	SH	SF	SB	CS	SB%	GDP	Avg	OBP	Slg
1996 Dubois Cty	IND	40	44	15	2	0	2	(-	-)	23	9	6	11	6	0	10	3	1	1	6	0	1.00	1	.341	.444	.523
1997 Mission Viejo	IND	8	0	0	0	0	0	(-	-)	0	0	0	0	0	0	0	0	0	0	0	0	-	0	-	-	-
1999 Schaumburg	IND	47	166	48	12	2	2	(-	-)	70	26	28	28	23	3	27	3	2	3	7	2	.78	3	.289	.379	.422
2000 Duluth-Sup	IND	75	289	95	16	3	12	(-	-)	153	53	53	57	25	2	32	4	0	4	13	5	.72	6	.329	.390	.529
2001 High Desert	A+	65	259	94	22	2	14	(-	-)	162	68	61	67	38	4	35	5	0	3	3	3	.50	5	.363	.449	.625
2001 Huntsville	AA	57	187	64	16	1	7	(-	-)	103	35	30	42	23	0	22	5	0	3	3	2	.60	3	.342	.422	.551
2002 Indianapolis	AAA	117	405	128	33	3	7	(-	-)	188	54	68	74	45	0	41	7	1	3	0	2	.00	4	.316	.391	.464
2002 Milwaukee	NL	23	77	11	2	0	1	(0	1)	16	8	6	3	6	0	9	1	0	0	0	0	-	3	.143	.214	.208

B.J. Ryan

Pitches: L **Bats:** L **Pos:** RP-67   **Ht:** 6'6" **Wt:** 230 **Born:** 12/28/75 **Age:** 27

Year Team	Lg	G	GS	CG	GF	IP	BFP	H	R	ER	HR	SH	SF	HB	TBB	IBB	SO	WP	Bk	W	L	Pct	ShO	Sv-Op	Hld	ERC	ERA
1999 Cin-Bal		14	0	0	3	20.1	82	13	7	7	0	0	1	0	13	1	29	1	0	1	0	1.000	0	0-0	0	2.42	3.10
2000 Baltimore	AL	42	0	0	9	42.2	193	36	29	28	7	1	1	0	31	1	41	2	1	2	3	.400	0	0-3	7	4.87	5.91
2001 Baltimore	AL	61	0	0	9	53.0	237	47	31	25	6	1	2	2	30	4	54	0	0	2	4	.333	0	2-4	14	4.13	4.25
2002 Baltimore	AL	67	0	0	13	57.2	252	51	31	30	7	3	0	4	33	4	56	4	0	2	1	.667	0	1-2	12	4.48	4.68
1999 Cincinnati	NL	1	0	0	0	2.0	9	4	1	1	0	0	0	0	1	0	1	0	0	0	0	-	0	0-0	0	12.01	4.50
1999 Baltimore	AL	13	0	0	3	18.1	73	9	6	6	0	0	1	0	12	1	28	1	0	1	0	1.000	0	0-0	0	1.73	2.95
4 ML YEARS		184	0	0	34	173.2	764	147	98	90	20	5	4	6	107	10	180	7	1	7	8	.467	0	3-9	33	4.21	4.66

Mike Ryan

Bats: L **Throws:** R **Pos:** LF-4; CF-3; PR-2   **Ht:** 6'0" **Wt:** 185 **Born:** 7/6/77 **Age:** 25

Year Team	Lg	G	AB	H	2B	3B	HR	(Hm	Rd)	TB	R	RBI	RC	TBB	IBB	SO	HBP	SH	SF	SB	CS	SB%	GDP	Avg	OBP	Slg
1996 Twins	R	43	157	31	8	2	0	(-	-)	43	12	13	11	13	1	20	1	1	2	3	0	1.00	3	.197	.260	.274
1997 Elizabethton	R+	62	220	66	10	3	0	(-	-)	85	44	29	35	38	3	39	3	1	4	2	2	.50	8	.300	.404	.386
1998 Fort Wayne	A	113	412	131	24	6	9	(-	-)	194	69	71	73	44	2	92	2	3	5	7	3	.70	8	.318	.382	.471
1999 Fort Myers	A+	131	507	139	26	5	8	(-	-)	199	85	71	72	63	2	60	5	4	6	3	4	.43	11	.274	.356	.393
2000 New Britain	AA	122	481	133	23	8	11	(-	-)	205	64	69	64	34	1	79	2	3	6	4	3	.57	13	.277	.323	.426
2000 Salt Lake	AAA	3	9	2	0	0	0	(-	-)	2	1	2	1	3	0	0	0	0	0	0	0	-	0	.222	.417	.222
2001 Edmonton	AAA	135	527	152	36	7	18	(-	-)	256	89	73	83	52	1	121	2	1	3	1	6	.14	17	.288	.353	.486
2002 Edmonton	AAA	131	540	141	36	6	31	(-	-)	282	92	101	90	55	6	124	2	0	3	4	5	.44	9	.261	.330	.522
2002 Minnesota	AL	7	11	1	0	0	0	(0	0)	1	3	0	0	0	0	2	0	0	0	0	0	-	0	.091	.091	.091

Kirk Saarloos

Pitches: R **Bats:** R **Pos:** SP-17   **Ht:** 6'0" **Wt:** 185 **Born:** 5/23/79 **Age:** 24

Year Team	Lg	G	GS	CG	GF	IP	BFP	H	R	ER	HR	SH	SF	HB	TBB	IBB	SO	WP	Bk	W	L	Pct	ShO	Sv-Op	Hld	ERC	ERA
2001 Lexington	A	22	0	0	19	30.2	119	18	5	4	1	2	0	1	7	0	40	2	0	1	1	.500	0	11--	1	1.30	1.17
2002 Round Rock	AA	13	13	1	0	83.1	315	48	17	13	1	3	2	4	21	0	82	1	0	10	1	.909	1	0--	0	1.32	1.40
2002 New Orleans	AAA	4	2	0	2	16.0	65	12	4	4	1	1	0	5	2	0	19	0	0	2	0	1.000	0	0--	0	2.69	2.25
2002 Houston	NL	17	17	1	0	85.1	372	100	59	57	12	5	2	6	27	5	54	1	0	6	7	.462	1	0-0	0	5.35	6.01

C.C. Sabathia

Pitches: L Bats: L Pos: SP-33   **Ht: 6'7" Wt: 270 Born: 7/21/80 Age: 22**

Year Team	Lg	G	GS	CG	GF	IP	BFP	H	R	ER	HR	SH	SF	HB	TBB	IBB	SO	WP	Bk	W	L	Pct	ShO	Sv-Op	Hld	ERC	ERA
1998 Burlington	R+	5	5	0	0	18.0	83	20	14	9	1	0	1	1	8	0	35	1	1	1	0	1.000	0	0- -	-	4.65	4.50
1999 Mahning VI	A-	6	6	0	0	19.2	77	9	5	4	0	0	2	0	12	0	27	0	0	0	0	-	0	0- -	-	1.57	1.83
1999 Columbus	A	3	3	0	0	16.2	64	8	2	2	1	1	0	1	5	0	20	1	0	2	0	1.000	0	0- -	-	1.31	1.08
1999 Kinston	A+	7	7	0	0	32.0	143	30	22	19	3	3	3	1	19	0	29	6	0	3	3	.500	0	0- -	-	4.56	5.34
2000 Kinston	A+	10	10	2	0	56.0	232	48	23	22	4	0	1	2	24	0	69	2	1	3	2	.600	2	0- -	-	3.44	3.54
2000 Akron	AA	17	17	0	0	90.1	394	75	41	36	6	2	1	7	48	0	90	2	1	3	7	.300	0	0- -	-	3.69	3.59
2001 Cleveland	AL	33	33	0	0	180.1	763	149	93	88	19	3	5	7	95	1	171	7	3	17	5	.773	0	0-0	0	3.86	4.39
2002 Cleveland	AL	33	33	2	0	210.0	891	198	109	102	17	5	10	1	88	2	149	6	3	13	11	.542	0	0-0	0	3.74	4.37
2 ML YEARS		66	66	2	0	390.1	1654	347	202	190	36	8	15	8	183	3	320	13	6	30	16	.652	0	0-0	0	3.80	4.38

Erik Sabel

Pitches: R Bats: R Pos: RP-1   **Ht: 6'3" Wt: 195 Born: 10/14/74 Age: 28**

Year Team	Lg	G	GS	CG	GF	IP	BFP	H	R	ER	HR	SH	SF	HB	TBB	IBB	SO	WP	Bk	W	L	Pct	ShO	Sv-Op	Hld	ERC	ERA
2002 Tucson*	AAA	25	7	0	4	66.2	282	67	37	32	7	2	1	4	19	1	46	0	0	4	5	.444	0	1- -	-	3.93	4.32
2002 Toledo*	AAA	14	0	0	3	11.0	52	15	8	8	0	1	0	0	4	0	7	0	0	2	0	1.000	0	0- -	-	5.12	6.55
1999 Arizona	NL	7	0	0	1	9.2	48	12	7	7	1	0	0	2	6	2	6	1	0	0	0	-	0	0- -	0	6.89	6.52
2001 Arizona	NL	42	0	0	11	51.1	218	57	26	25	8	1	0	3	12	3	25	1	0	3	2	.600	0	0-0	4	4.65	4.38
2002 Detroit	AL	1	0	0	0	0.0	2	2	2	1	1	0	0	0	0	0	0	0	0	0	0	-	0	0-0	0		
3 ML YEARS		50	0	0	12	61.0	268	71	35	34	10	1	0	5	18	5	31	2	0	3	2	.600	0	0-0	4	5.33	5.02

Carl Sadler

Pitches: L Bats: L Pos: RP-24   **Ht: 6'2" Wt: 180 Born: 10/11/76 Age: 26**

Year Team	Lg	G	GS	CG	GF	IP	BFP	H	R	ER	HR	SH	SF	HB	TBB	IBB	SO	WP	Bk	W	L	Pct	ShO	Sv-Op	Hld	ERC	ERA
1996 Expos	R	17	3	0	6	37.0	170	41	24	16	2	2	0	2	12	0	24	3	3	2	2	.500	0	1- -	-	4.05	3.89
1997 Expos	R	9	3	0	0	20.2	91	26	11	10	0	0	1	2	5	0	14	2	0	0	2	.000	0	0- -	-	4.65	4.35
1997 Vermont	A-	7	6	0	0	36.1	167	33	20	17	2	1	2	2	23	0	27	4	1	2	2	.500	0	0- -	-	4.24	4.21
1999 Burlington	R+	5	5	0	0	23.0	93	18	10	8	1	0	1	0	10	0	22	5	0	1	0	1.000	0	0- -	-	2.47	3.13
1999 Mahning VI	A-	1	1	0	0	2.0	17	8	7	7	0	0	0	0	3	0	3	1	0	1	0	1.000	0	0- -	-	30.35	31.50
2000 Mahning VI	A-	5	0	0	1	6.0	25	5	2	2	0	1	0	0	3	0	3	0	0	0	0	-	0	0- -	-	2.93	3.00
2000 Columbus	A	10	0	0	3	16.1	73	20	13	12	0	0	1	0	7	0	21	5	0	1	3	.250	0	0- -	-	4.79	6.61
2001 Kinston	A+	27	2	0	10	62.1	258	51	19	13	2	0	0	3	18	1	78	1	0	6	0	1.000	0	2- -	-	2.38	1.88
2001 Akron	AA	11	0	0	6	18.0	85	23	16	13	1	0	0	0	9	0	14	0	1	2	3	.400	0	0- -	-	5.68	6.50
2002 Akron	AA	21	0	0	7	46.1	185	39	12	12	0	0	1	2	12	1	37	2	0	4	1	.800	0	2- -	-	2.27	2.33
2002 Buffalo	AAA	12	0	0	8	18.2	81	19	7	4	1	2	0	0	8	1	13	0	0	1	1	.500	0	1- -	-	3.87	1.93
2002 Cleveland	AL	24	0	0	5	20.1	82	15	10	10	2	0	0	0	11	0	23	3	0	1	2	.333	0	0-1	5	3.34	4.43

Donnie Sadler

Bats: R Throws: R Pos: PR-22; SS-16; 3B-15; CF-14; LF-12; RF-7; PH-7; 2B-6; DH-1   **Ht: 5'6" Wt: 175 Born: 6/17/75 Age: 28**

Year Team	Lg	G	AB	H	2B	3B	HR	(Hm	Rd)	TB	R	RBI	RC	TBB	IBB	SO	HBP	SH	SF	SB	CS	SB%	GDP	Avg	OBP	Slg
2002 Omaha*	AAA	5	21	7	0	0	0	(-	-)	7	6	0	3	2	0	3	1	0	0	0	2	.00	0	.333	.417	.333
2002 Oklahoma*	AAA	12	43	10	3	1	0	(-	-)	15	7	4	6	6	0	7	1	0	0	2	1	.67	0	.233	.340	.349
1998 Boston	AL	58	124	28	4	4	3	(0	3)	49	21	15	15	6	0	28	3	5	1	4	0	1.00	1	.226	.276	.395
1999 Boston	AL	49	107	30	5	1	0	(0	0)	37	18	4	12	5	0	20	0	3	0	2	1	.67	1	.280	.313	.346
2000 Boston	AL	49	99	22	5	0	1	(0	1)	30	14	10	9	5	0	18	1	5	2	3	1	.75	1	.222	.262	.303
2001 Cin-KC		93	185	30	6	0	1	(0	1)	39	28	5	8	18	0	37	2	5	1	7	4	.64	3	.162	.243	.211
2002 KC-Tex	AL	73	98	16	2	1	0	(0	0)	20	16	7	3	7	0	19	2	1	1	5	3	.63	1	.163	.231	.204
2001 Cincinnati	NL	39	84	17	3	0	1	(0	1)	23	9	3	5	9	0	20	0	2	0	3	3	.50	3	.202	.280	.274
2001 Kansas City	AL	54	101	13	3	0	0	(0	0)	16	19	2	3	9	0	17	2	3	1	4	1	.80	0	.129	.212	.158
2002 Kansas City	AL	35	68	13	1	1	0	(0	0)	16	10	5	3	4	0	12	0	1	0	3	1	.75	0	.191	.233	.235
2002 Texas	AL	38	30	3	1	0	0	(0	0)	4	6	2	0	3	0	7	2	0	1	2	2	.50	1	.100	.229	.133
5 ML YEARS		322	613	126	22	6	5	(0	5)	175	97	41	46	41	0	122	8	19	5	21	9	.70	7	.206	.262	.285

Olmedo Saenz

Bats: R Throws: R Pos: 1B-34; PH-26; 3B-15; DH-6   **Ht: 5'11" Wt: 221 Born: 10/8/70 Age: 32**

Year Team	Lg	G	AB	H	2B	3B	HR	(Hm	Rd)	TB	R	RBI	RC	TBB	IBB	SO	HBP	SH	SF	SB	CS	SB%	GDP	Avg	OBP	Slg
1994 Chicago	AL	5	14	2	0	1	0	(0	0)	4	2	0	0	0	0	5	0	1	0	0	0	-	1	.143	.143	.286
1999 Oakland	AL	97	255	70	18	0	11	(8	3)	121	41	41	44	22	1	47	15	0	3	1	1	.50	6	.275	.363	.475
2000 Oakland	AL	76	214	67	12	2	9	(3	6)	110	40	33	42	25	2	40	7	0	1	1	0	1.00	6	.313	.401	.514
2001 Oakland	AL	106	305	67	21	1	9	(6	3)	117	33	32	32	19	1	64	13	1	3	0	1	.00	9	.220	.291	.384
2002 Oakland	AL	68	156	43	10	1	6	(3	3)	73	15	18	23	13	1	31	7	0	2	1	1	.50	2	.276	.354	.468
5 ML YEARS		352	944	249	61	5	35	(20	15)	425	131	124	141	79	5	187	42	2	9	3	3	.50	24	.264	.345	.450

Oscar Salazar

Bats: R Throws: R Pos: 2B-6; 3B-1; SS-1; PH-1; PR-1   **Ht: 5'11" Wt: 178 Born: 6/27/78 Age: 25**

Year Team	Lg	G	AB	H	2B	3B	HR	(Hm	Rd)	TB	R	RBI	RC	TBB	IBB	SO	HBP	SH	SF	SB	CS	SB%	GDP	Avg	OBP	Slg
1998 Athletics	R	26	102	33	7	5	2	(-	-)	56	29	18	22	12	0	15	1	0	0	4	1	.80	1	.324	.400	.549
1998 Sth Oregon	A-	28	101	32	4	1	5	(-	-)	53	19	28	22	16	0	22	0	1	3	5	2	.71	0	.317	.400	.525
1999 Modesto	A+	130	525	155	26	18	18	(-	-)	271	100	105	90	39	1	106	1	0	9	14	6	.70	10	.295	.340	.516
2000 Midland	AA	111	427	128	27	1	13	(-	-)	196	70	57	68	39	0	71	2	2	3	4	4	.50	9	.300	.359	.459
2000 Sacramento	AAA	4	13	2	1	0	0	(-	-)	3	0	1	0	1	0	1	0	0	0	1	0	1.00	2	.154	.214	.231

Year Team	Lg	G	AB	H	2B	3B	HR	(Hm	Rd)	TB	R	RBI	RC	TBB	IBB	SO	HBP	SH	SF	SB	CS	SB%	GDP	Avg	OBP	Slg
2001 Midland	AA	130	521	139	31	4	18	(-	-)	232	75	95	76	49	2	100	2	1	6	10	3	.77	11	.267	.329	.445
2001 Sacramento	AAA	5	16	1	0	0	0	(-	-)	1	0	1	0	1	0	5	0	0	0	0	0	-		.063	.118	.063
2002 Toledo	AAA	8	19	6	0	0	0	(-	-)	6	0	1	3	3	0	1	0	0	0	0	1	.00		.316	.409	.316
2002 Erie	AA	53	191	41	18	1	6	(-	-)	79	16	26	21	14	0	36	3	0	0	2	1	.67	6	.215	.279	.414
2002 Binghamton	AA	28	75	13	2	0	1	(-	-)	18	6	5	3	5	0	19	1	0	1	0	1	.00	2	.173	.232	.240
2002 Detroit	AL	8	21	4	1	0	1	(0	1)	8	2	3	3	1	0	2	0	1	0	0	0	-	0	.190	.227	.381

Tim Salmon

Bats: R **Throws:** R **Pos:** RF-111; DH-21; PH-6; PR-1   **Ht:** 6'3" **Wt:** 225 **Born:** 8/24/68 **Age:** 34

Year Team	Lg	G	AB	H	2B	3B	HR	(Hm	Rd)	TB	R	RBI	RC	TBB	IBB	SO	HBP	SH	SF	SB	CS	SB%	GDP	Avg	OBP	Slg
1992 Anaheim	AL	23	79	14	1	0	2	(1	1)	21	8	6	6	11	1	23	1	0	1	1	1	.50	1	.177	.283	.266
1993 Anaheim	AL	142	515	146	35	1	31	(23	8)	276	93	95	104	82	5	135	5	0	8	5	6	.45	5	.283	.382	.536
1994 Anaheim	AL	100	373	107	18	2	23	(12	11)	198	67	70	75	54	2	102	5	0	3	1	3	.25	3	.287	.382	.531
1995 Anaheim	AL	143	537	177	34	3	34	(15	19)	319	111	105	130	91	2	111	6	0	4	5	5	.50	9	.330	.429	.594
1996 Anaheim	AL	156	581	166	27	4	30	(18	12)	291	90	98	113	93	7	125	4	0	3	4	2	.67	8	.286	.386	.501
1997 Anaheim	AL	157	582	172	28	1	33	(17	16)	301	95	129	117	95	5	142	7	0	11	9	12	.43	7	.296	.394	.517
1998 Anaheim	AL	136	463	139	28	1	26	(13	13)	247	84	88	103	90	5	100	3	0	10	0	1	.00	4	.300	.410	.533
1999 Anaheim	AL	98	353	94	24	2	17	(7	10)	173	60	69	66	63	2	82	6	0	7	4	1	.80	7	.266	.372	.490
2000 Anaheim	AL	158	568	165	36	2	34	(17	17)	307	108	97	120	104	5	139	6	0	2	0	2	.00	14	.290	.404	.540
2001 Anaheim	AL	137	475	108	21	1	17	(11	6)	182	63	49	72	96	4	121	8	0	2	9	3	.75	11	.227	.365	.383
2002 Anaheim	AL	138	483	138	37	1	22	(10	12)	243	84	88	100	71	3	102	7	0	7	6	3	.67	6	.286	.380	.503
11 ML YEARS		1388	5009	1426	289	18	269	(144	125)	2558	863	894	1006	850	41	1182	52	0	57	44	39	.53	76	.285	.390	.511

Alex Sanchez

Bats: L **Throws:** L **Pos:** CF-86; LF-16; PH-10; PR-3   **Ht:** 5'10" **Wt:** 159 **Born:** 8/26/76 **Age:** 26

Year Team	Lg	G	AB	H	2B	3B	HR	(Hm	Rd)	TB	R	RBI	RC	TBB	IBB	SO	HBP	SH	SF	SB	CS	SB%	GDP	Avg	OBP	Slg
1996 Devil Rays	R	56	227	64	7	6	1	(-	-)	86	36	22	28	10	0	35	6	1	1	20	12	.63	2	.282	.328	.379
1997 Chrlstn - SC	A	131	537	155	15	6	0	(-	-)	182	73	34	65	37	2	72	3	12	4	92	40	.70	7	.289	.336	.339
1998 St.Pete	A+	128	545	180	17	9	1	(-	-)	218	77	50	80	31	1	70	1	4	12	66	33	.67	5	.330	.360	.400
1999 Orlando	AA	121	500	127	12	4	2	(-	-)	153	68	29	41	26	1	88	0	10	2	48	27	.64	8	.254	.290	.306
1999 Durham	AAA	3	10	2	1	0	0	(-	-)	3	2	0	1	1	0	0	0	0	0	0	0	-		.200	.273	.300
2000 Durham	AAA	107	446	130	18	3	2	(-	-)	160	76	33	58	30	1	66	5	3	2	52	20	.72	6	.291	.342	.359
2000 Orlando	AA	20	86	25	2	1	0	(-	-)	29	12	4	7	1	0	13	1	1	0	2	6	.25	1	.291	.307	.337
2001 Indianapolis	AAA	83	335	105	14	5	1	(-	-)	132	52	26	50	22	1	44	2	2	0	27	8	.77	2	.313	.359	.394
2001 Milwaukee	NL	30	68	14	3	2	0	(0	0)	21	7	4	6	5	0	13	0	0	0	6	2	.75	0	.206	.260	.309
2002 Milwaukee	NL	112	394	114	10	7	1	(0	1)	141	55	33	53	31	0	62	2	6	2	37	14	.73	4	.289	.343	.358
2 ML YEARS		142	462	128	13	9	1	(0	1)	162	62	37	59	36	0	75	2	6	2	43	16	.73	4	.277	.331	.351

Duaner Sanchez

Pitches: R **Bats:** R **Pos:** RP-9   **Ht:** 6'0" **Wt:** 190 **Born:** 10/14/79 **Age:** 23

Year Team	Lg	G	GS	CG	GF	IP	BFP	H	R	ER	HR	SH	SF	HB	TBB	IBB	SO	WP	Bk	W	L	Pct	ShO	Sv-Op	Hld	ERC	ERA
1999 High Desert	A+	3	3	0	0	14.1	63	15	13	12	2	0	1	1	9	0	9	0	0	0	0	-	0	0--	-	6.23	7.53
1999 Missoula	R+	13	11	0	0	63.1	269	54	34	22	3	1	1	3	23	0	51	8	0	5	3	.625	0	0--	-	2.91	3.13
2000 South Bend	A	28	28	4	0	165.1	700	152	80	67	6	5	5	11	54	1	121	6	2	8	9	.471	0	0--	-	3.16	3.65
2001 El Paso	AA	13	13	0	0	70.1	323	92	56	53	5	1	7	6	25	1	41	5	0	3	7	.300	0	0--	-	5.86	6.78
2001 Lancaster	A+	10	10	1	0	59.0	270	65	44	30	7	4	4	7	18	0	49	3	4	2	4	.333	0	0--	-	4.71	4.58
2002 El Paso	AA	31	0	0	29	35.2	155	31	16	12	1	0	1	2	13	1	37	3	0	4	3	.571	0	13--	-	2.80	3.03
2002 Tucson	AAA	4	0	0	4	5.1	24	6	4	4	1	0	0	0	1	0	9	0	0	1	1	.500	0	1--	-	4.22	6.75
2002 Nashville	AAA	20	0	0	17	22.2	100	23	12	12	2	2	2	1	11	2	20	2	0	0	3	.000	0	6--	-	4.47	4.76
2002 Ari-Pit	NL	9	0	0	5	6.0	31	6	6	6	2	0	0	0	7	0	6	0	0	0	0	-	0	0-1	1	9.19	9.00
2002 Arizona	NL	6	0	0	3	3.2	19	3	2	2	1	0	0	0	5	0	4	0	0	0	0	-	0	0-1	1	8.32	4.91
2002 Pittsburgh	NL	3	0	0	2	2.1	12	3	4	4	1	0	0	0	2	0	2	0	0	0	0	-	0	0-0	0	10.55	15.43

Freddy Sanchez

Bats: R **Throws:** R **Pos:** 2B-5; SS-5; PR-4; PH-2   **Ht:** 5'11" **Wt:** 185 **Born:** 12/21/77 **Age:** 25

Year Team	Lg	G	AB	H	2B	3B	HR	(Hm	Rd)	TB	R	RBI	RC	TBB	IBB	SO	HBP	SH	SF	SB	CS	SB%	GDP	Avg	OBP	Slg
2000 Lowell	A-	34	132	38	13	2	1	(-	-)	58	24	14	19	9	0	16	3	2	0	2	4	.33	1	.288	.347	.439
2000 Augusta	A	30	109	33	7	0	0	(-	-)	40	17	15	16	11	0	19	1	4	0	4	0	1.00	1	.303	.372	.367
2001 Sarasota	A+	69	280	95	19	4	1	(-	-)	125	40	24	48	22	1	30	2	3	3	5	3	.63	3	.339	.388	.446
2001 Trenton	AA	44	178	58	20	0	2	(-	-)	84	25	19	29	9	0	21	2	2	1	3	1	.75	6	.326	.363	.472
2002 Trenton	AA	80	311	102	23	1	3	(-	-)	136	60	38	57	37	0	45	5	5	4	19	3	.86	9	.328	.403	.437
2002 Pawtucket	AAA	45	183	55	10	1	4	(-	-)	79	25	28	28	12	0	21	3	5	2	5	3	.63	3	.301	.350	.432
2002 Boston	AL	12	16	3	0	0	0	(0	0)	3	3	2	1	2	0	3	0	0	0	0	0	-	0	.188	.278	.188

Jesus Sanchez

Pitches: L **Bats:** L **Pos:** RP-8   **Ht:** 5'11" **Wt:** 175 **Born:** 10/11/74 **Age:** 28

Year Team	Lg	G	GS	CG	GF	IP	BFP	H	R	ER	HR	SH	SF	HB	TBB	IBB	SO	WP	Bk	W	L	Pct	ShO	Sv-Op	Hld	ERC	ERA
2002 Iowa*	AAA	26	24	0	0	125.0	570	144	90	82	27	8	3	6	65	3	94	7	0	7	8	.471	0	0--	-	6.63	5.90
1998 Florida	NL	35	29	0	1	173.0	765	178	98	86	18	12	4	4	91	2	137	8	5	7	9	.438	0	0-1	0	4.91	4.47
1999 Florida	NL	59	10	0	8	76.1	362	84	53	51	16	2	7	4	60	11	62	5	2	5	7	.417	0	0-2	11	7.28	6.01
2000 Florida	NL	32	32	2	0	182.0	805	197	118	108	32	9	**12**	4	76	4	123	4	0	9	12	.429	2	0-0	0	5.24	5.34

		HOW MUCH HE PITCHED		WHAT HE GAVE UP		THE RESULTS	

Year Team	Lg	G GS CG GF	IP BFP	H R ER HR SH SF HB	TBB IBB SO WP Bk	W L Pct ShO	Sv-Op Hld ERC ERA
2001 Florida	NL	16 9 0 3	62.2 274	61 33 33 7 2 1 2	31 2 46 0 0	2 4 .333 0	0-0 0 4.49 4.74
2002 Chicago	NL	8 0 0 2	8.1 51	15 12 12 4 0 2 1	10 1 6 3 0	0 0 - 0	0-0 0 17.13 12.96
5 ML YEARS		150 80 2 14	502.1 2257	535 314 290 77 25 26 15	268 20 374 20 7	23 32 .418 2	0-3 11 5.50 5.20

Rey Sanchez

Bats: R **Throws:** R **Pos:** 2B-100; SS-10; PH-2   **Ht:** 5'9" **Wt:** 175 **Born:** 10/5/67 **Age:** 35

								BATTING											BASERUNNING				AVERAGES		
Year Team	Lg	G	AB	H	2B	3B	HR	(Hm Rd)	TB	R	RBI	RC	TBB	IBB	SO	HBP	SH	SF	SB	CS	SB%	GDP	Avg	OBP	Slg
1991 Chicago	NL	13	23	6	0	0	0	(0 0)	6	1	2	3	4	0	3	0	0	0	0	0	-	0	.261	.370	.261
1992 Chicago	NL	74	255	64	14	3	1	(1 0)	87	24	19	23	10	1	17	3	5	2	1	2	.67	7	.251	.285	.341
1993 Chicago	NL	105	344	97	11	2	0	(0 0)	112	35	28	34	15	7	22	3	9	2	1	1	.50	8	.282	.316	.326
1994 Chicago	NL	96	291	83	13	1	0	(0 0)	98	26	24	32	20	4	29	7	4	1	2	5	.29	9	.285	.345	.337
1995 Chicago	NL	114	428	119	22	2	3	(0 3)	154	57	27	44	14	2	48	1	8	2	6	4	.60	9	.278	.301	.360
1996 Chicago	NL	95	289	61	9	0	1	(1 0)	73	28	12	19	22	6	42	3	8	2	7	1	.88	6	.211	.272	.253
1997 ChC-NYY		135	343	94	21	0	2	(1 1)	121	35	27	34	16	2	47	1	9	1	4	6	.40	8	.274	.307	.353
1998 San Francisco	NL	109	316	90	14	2	2	(0 2)	114	44	30	35	16	0	47	4	1	2	0	0	-	11	.285	.325	.361
1999 Kansas City	AL	134	479	141	18	6	2	(1 1)	177	66	56	56	22	2	48	4	10	3	11	5	.69	14	.294	.329	.370
2000 Kansas City	AL	143	509	139	18	2	1	(1 0)	164	68	38	49	28	0	55	4	11	3	7	3	.70	17	.273	.314	.322
2001 KC-Atl		149	544	153	18	6	0	(0 0)	183	56	37	52	15	1	49	2	13	5	11	1	.92	20	.281	.300	.336
2002 Boston	AL	107	357	102	12	3	1	(1 0)	123	46	38	40	17	1	31	2	5	5	2	2	.50	9	.286	.318	.345
1997 Chicago	NL	97	205	51	9	0	1	(1 0)	63	14	12	16	11	2	26	0	4	0	4	2	.67	7	.249	.287	.307
1997 New York	AL	38	138	43	12	0	1	(0 1)	58	21	15	18	5	0	21	1	5	1	0	4	.00	1	.312	.338	.420
2001 Kansas City	AL	100	390	118	14	5	0	(0 0)	142	46	28	45	11	0	34	2	9	1	9	1	.90	11	.303	.322	.364
2001 Atlanta	NL	49	154	35	4	1	0	(0 0)	41	10	9	7	4	1	15	0	4	1	2	0	1.00	9	.227	.245	.266
12 ML YEARS		1274	4178	1149	170	27	13	(6 7)	1412	486	338	421	199	26	438	34	83	28	53	29	.65	118	.275	.311	.338

Jared Sandberg

Bats: R **Throws:** R **Pos:** 3B-97; 1B-3; DH-2; PH-1   **Ht:** 6'3" **Wt:** 226 **Born:** 3/2/78 **Age:** 25

								BATTING											BASERUNNING				AVERAGES		
Year Team	Lg	G	AB	H	2B	3B	HR	(Hm Rd)	TB	R	RBI	RC	TBB	IBB	SO	HBP	SH	SF	SB	CS	SB%	GDP	Avg	OBP	Slg
1996 Devil Rays	R	22	77	13	2	1	0	(- -)	17	6	7	4	9	0	26	0	3	0	1	0	1.00	1	.169	.256	.221
1997 St.Pete	A+	2	3	1	0	0	0	(- -)	1	1	2	1	2	0	2	0	0	0	0	0	-	0	.333	.600	.333
1997 Princeton	R+	67	268	81	15	5	17	(- -)	157	61	68	61	42	5	94	2	0	0	12	3	.80	4	.302	.401	.586
1998 Chrstn - SC	A	56	191	35	11	0	3	(- -)	55	31	25	16	27	0	76	3	0	1	4	0	1.00	6	.183	.293	.288
1998 Hudson Val	A-	73	271	78	15	2	12	(- -)	133	49	54	53	42	1	76	5	0	4	13	3	.81	6	.288	.388	.491
1999 St.Pete	A+	136	504	139	24	1	22	(- -)	231	73	96	80	51	0	133	9	1	5	8	2	.80	12	.276	.350	.458
2000 Orlando	AA	67	244	63	15	1	5	(- -)	95	30	35	34	33	0	55	2	0	3	5	3	.63	6	.258	.348	.389
2000 Durham	AAA	3	15	6	3	0	2	(- -)	15	2	7	5	0	0	6	0	0	0	0	0	-	1	.400	.400	1.000
2001 Orlando	AA	8	28	8	2	0	1	(- -)	13	4	4	5	6	0	10	0	0	0	0	0	-	1	.286	.412	.464
2001 Durham	AAA	93	322	77	16	0	16	(- -)	141	39	50	44	38	0	81	6	2	0	0	1	.00	13	.239	.331	.438
2002 Durham	AAA	30	114	32	9	0	4	(- -)	53	20	21	19	14	1	42	2	0	0	1	0	1.00	2	.281	.369	.465
2001 Tampa Bay	AL	39	136	28	7	0	1	(1 0)	38	13	15	9	10	0	45	1	2	0	1	0	1.00	2	.206	.265	.279
2002 Tampa Bay	AL	102	358	82	21	1	18	(10 8)	159	55	54	47	39	3	139	1	1	2	3	2	.60	7	.229	.305	.444
2 ML YEARS		141	494	110	28	1	19	(11 8)	197	68	69	56	49	3	184	2	3	2	4	2	.67	9	.223	.294	.399

Reggie Sanders

Bats: R **Throws:** R **Pos:** RF-137; PH-3   **Ht:** 6'1" **Wt:** 205 **Born:** 12/1/67 **Age:** 35

								BATTING											BASERUNNING				AVERAGES		
Year Team	Lg	G	AB	H	2B	3B	HR	(Hm Rd)	TB	R	RBI	RC	TBB	IBB	SO	HBP	SH	SF	SB	CS	SB%	GDP	Avg	OBP	Slg
1991 Cincinnati	NL	9	40	8	0	0	1	(0 1)	11	6	3	1	0	0	9	0	0	0	1	1	.50	1	.200	.200	.275
1992 Cincinnati	NL	116	385	104	26	6	12	(6 6)	178	62	36	64	48	2	98	4	0	1	16	7	.70	6	.270	.356	.462
1993 Cincinnati	NL	138	496	136	16	4	20	(8 12)	220	90	83	76	51	7	118	5	3	8	27	10	.73	10	.274	.343	.444
1994 Cincinnati	NL	107	400	105	20	8	17	(10 7)	192	66	62	65	41	1	114	2	1	3	21	9	.70	2	.263	.332	.480
1995 Cincinnati	NL	133	484	148	36	6	28	(9 19)	280	91	99	109	69	4	122	8	0	6	36	12	.75	9	.306	.397	.579
1996 Cincinnati	NL	81	287	72	17	1	14	(7 7)	133	49	33	47	44	4	86	2	0	1	24	8	.75	8	.251	.353	.463
1997 Cincinnati	NL	86	312	79	17	2	19	(11 8)	159	52	56	53	42	3	93	3	1	0	13	7	.65	9	.253	.347	.510
1998 Cincinnati	NL	135	481	129	18	6	14	(7 7)	201	83	59	69	51	2	137	7	4	2	20	9	.69	10	.268	.346	.418
1999 San Diego	NL	133	478	136	24	7	26	(11 15)	252	92	72	94	65	1	108	6	0	1	36	13	.73	10	.285	.376	.527
2000 Atlanta	NL	103	340	79	23	1	11	(4 7)	137	43	37	42	32	2	78	2	3	0	21	4	.84	9	.232	.302	.403
2001 Arizona	NL	126	441	116	21	3	33	(19 14)	242	84	90	80	46	7	126	5	1	3	14	10	.58	2	.263	.337	.549
2002 San Francisco	NL	140	505	126	23	6	23	(12 11)	230	75	85	66	47	3	121	12	0	7	18	6	.75	10	.250	.324	.455
12 ML YEARS		1307	4649	1238	243	50	218	(104 114)	2235	793	715	766	536	36	1210	56	13	32	247	96	.72	86	.266	.347	.481

Johan Santana

Pitches: L **Bats:** L **Pos:** SP-14; RP-13   **Ht:** 6'0" **Wt:** 195 **Born:** 3/13/79 **Age:** 24

		HOW MUCH HE PITCHED		WHAT HE GAVE UP		THE RESULTS	
Year Team	Lg	G GS CG GF	IP BFP	H R ER HR SH SF HB	TBB IBB SO WP Bk	W L Pct ShO	Sv-Op Hld ERC ERA
2002 Edmonton*	AAA	11 9 0 0	48.2 212	37 24 17 7 2 0 2	27 0 75 2 0	5 2 .714 0	0-- - 3.55 3.14
2000 Minnesota	AL	30 5 0 9	86.0 398	102 64 62 11 1 3 2	54 0 64 5 2	2 3 .400 0	0-0 0 6.59 6.49
2001 Minnesota	AL	15 4 0 5	43.2 195	50 25 23 6 2 3 3	16 0 28 3 0	1 0 1.000 0	0-0 0 5.36 4.74
2002 Minnesota	AL	27 14 0 2	108.1 452	84 41 36 7 3 3 1	49 0 137 15 2	8 6 .571 0	1-1 3 2.86 2.99
3 ML YEARS		72 23 0 16	238.0 1045	236 130 121 24 6 9 6	119 0 229 23 4	11 9 .550 0	1-1 3 4.56 4.58

Julio Santana

Pitches: R **Bats:** R **Pos:** RP-38   **Ht:** 6'0" **Wt:** 225 **Born:** 1/20/74 **Age:** 29

Year Team	Lg	G	GS	CG	GF	IP	BFP	H	R	ER	HR	SH	SF	HB	TBB	IBB	SO	WP	Bk	W	L	Pct	ShO	Sv-Op	Hld	ERC	ERA
2002 Toledo*	AAA	7	0	0	4	12.2	52	12	5	3	1	0	1	0	3	0	12	1	0	0	1	.000	0	1- --	1	3.03	2.13
1997 Texas	AL	30	14	0	3	104.0	496	141	86	78	16	1	5	4	49	2	64	8	1	4	6	.400	0	0-1	1	7.06	6.75
1998 Tex-TB	AL	35	19	1	5	145.2	630	151	77	71	18	2	5	5	62	3	61	3	0	5	6	.455	0	0-0	0	4.75	4.39
1999 Tampa Bay	AL	22	5	0	7	55.1	261	66	49	45	10	1	1	7	32	0	34	0	0	1	4	.200	0	0-0	0	7.29	7.32
2000 Montreal	NL	36	4	0	9	66.2	293	69	45	42	11	1	2	2	33	2	58	2	0	1	5	.167	0	0-2	1	5.31	5.67
2002 Detroit	AL	38	0	0	8	57.0	239	49	19	18	8	3	0	2	28	2	38	3	1	3	5	.375	0	0-1	7	4.13	2.84
1998 Texas	AL	3	0	0	0	5.1	27	7	5	5	0	0	0	0	4	1	1	0	0	0	0	-	0	0-0	0	5.97	8.44
1998 Tampa Bay	AL	32	19	1	5	140.1	603	144	72	66	18	2	5	5	58	2	60	3	0	5	6	.455	0	0-0	0	4.70	4.23
5 ML YEARS		161	42	1	32	428.2	1919	476	276	254	63	8	13	20	204	9	255	16	2	14	26	.350	0	0-4	9	5.61	5.33

Benito Santiago

Bats: R **Throws:** R **Pos:** C-125; PH-3   **Ht:** 6'1" **Wt:** 200 **Born:** 3/9/65 **Age:** 38

Year Team	Lg	G	AB	H	2B	3B	HR	(Hm	Rd)	TB	R	RBI	RC	TBB	IBB	SO	HBP	SH	SF	SB	CS	SB%	GDP	Avg	OBP	Slg
1986 San Diego	NL	17	62	18	2	0	3	(2	1)	29	10	6	9	2	0	12	0	0	1	0	1	.00	0	.290	.308	.468
1987 San Diego	NL	146	546	164	33	2	18	(11	7)	255	64	79	77	16	2	112	5	1	4	21	12	.64	12	.300	.324	.467
1988 San Diego	NL	139	492	122	22	2	10	(3	7)	178	49	46	45	24	2	82	1	5	5	15	7	.68	18	.248	.282	.362
1989 San Diego	NL	129	462	109	16	3	16	(8	8)	179	50	62	47	26	6	89	1	3	2	11	6	.65	9	.236	.277	.387
1990 San Diego	NL	100	344	93	8	5	11	(5	6)	144	42	53	47	27	2	55	3	1	7	5	5	.50	4	.270	.323	.419
1991 San Diego	NL	152	580	155	22	3	17	(6	11)	234	60	87	61	23	5	114	4	0	7	8	10	.44	21	.267	.296	.403
1992 San Diego	NL	106	386	97	21	0	10	(2	8)	148	37	42	37	21	1	52	0	0	4	2	5	.29	14	.251	.287	.383
1993 Florida	NL	139	469	108	19	6	13	(6	7)	178	49	50	50	37	2	88	5	0	4	10	7	.59	9	.230	.291	.380
1994 Florida	NL	101	337	92	14	2	11	(4	7)	143	35	41	43	25	1	57	1	2	4	1	2	.33	11	.273	.322	.424
1995 Cincinnati	NL	81	266	76	20	0	11	(7	4)	129	40	44	44	24	1	48	4	0	2	2	2	.50	7	.286	.351	.485
1996 Philadelphia	NL	136	481	127	21	2	30	(8	22)	242	71	85	79	49	7	104	1	0	2	2	0	1.00	8	.264	.332	.503
1997 Toronto	AL	97	341	83	10	0	13	(7	6)	132	31	42	35	17	1	80	2	1	5	1	0	1.00	10	.243	.279	.387
1998 Toronto	AL	15	29	9	5	0	0	(0	0)	14	3	4	4	1	0	6	0	0	0	0	0	-	1	.310	.333	.483
1999 Chicago	NL	109	350	87	18	3	7	(2	5)	132	28	36	39	32	6	71	2	0	2	1	1	.50	12	.249	.313	.377
2000 Cincinnati	NL	89	252	66	11	1	8	(7	1)	103	22	45	30	19	8	45	1	0	5	2	2	.50	7	.262	.310	.409
2001 San Francisco	NL	133	477	125	25	4	6	(3	3)	176	39	45	46	23	0	78	2	7	6	5	4	.56	19	.262	.295	.369
2002 San Francisco	NL	126	478	133	24	5	16	(6	10)	215	56	74	57	27	8	73	2	3	7	4	2	.67	19	.278	.315	.450
17 ML YEARS		1815	6352	1664	291	38	200	(93	107)	2631	686	841	749	393	52	1166	34	23	67	90	66	.58	181	.262	.305	.414

Jose Santiago

Pitches: R **Bats:** R **Pos:** RP-42   **Ht:** 6'3" **Wt:** 215 **Born:** 11/5/74 **Age:** 28

Year Team	Lg	G	GS	CG	GF	IP	BFP	H	R	ER	HR	SH	SF	HB	TBB	IBB	SO	WP	Bk	W	L	Pct	ShO	Sv-Op	Hld	ERC	ERA
2002 Scrtn/WlksBr*	AAA	22	0	0	20	28.0	117	28	6	4	0	3	0	1	7	1	21	1	0	3	2	.600	0	7- --	-	2.92	1.29
1997 Kansas City	AL	4	0	0	3	4.2	24	7	2	1	0	0	0	1	2	1	1	0	0	0	0	-	0	0-0	0	6.62	1.93
1998 Kansas City	AL	2	0	0	2	2.0	9	4	2	2	0	0	0	0	0	0	2	0	0	0	0	-	0	0-0	0	8.38	9.00
1999 Kansas City	AL	34	0	0	15	47.1	203	46	23	18	7	1	3	2	14	2	15	2	1	3	4	.429	0	2-3	4	3.87	3.42
2000 Kansas City	AL	45	0	0	20	69.0	302	70	33	30	7	1	3	3	26	3	44	0	0	8	6	.571	0	2-8	5	4.14	3.91
2001 KC-Phi		73	0	0	11	91.2	397	106	47	47	5	4	5	3	22	2	43	1	0	4	6	.400	0	0-2	9	4.09	4.61
2002 Philadelphia	NL	42	0	0	7	47.0	214	56	35	35	7	1	2	3	15	1	30	1	0	1	3	.250	0	0-1	9	5.34	6.70
2001 Kansas City	AL	20	0	0	6	29.1	136	40	22	22	2	3	3	1	9	1	15	1	0	2	2	.500	0	0-1	0	5.60	6.75
2001 Philadelphia	NL	53	0	0	5	62.1	261	66	25	25	3	1	2	2	13	1	28	0	0	2	4	.333	0	0-1	9	3.42	3.61
6 ML YEARS		200	0	0	58	261.2	1149	289	142	133	26	7	13	12	79	9	135	4	1	16	19	.457	0	4-14	27	4.36	4.57

Ramon Santiago

Bats: B **Throws:** R **Pos:** SS-63; PR-2   **Ht:** 5'11" **Wt:** 150 **Born:** 8/31/79 **Age:** 23

Year Team	Lg	G	AB	H	2B	3B	HR	(Hm	Rd)	TB	R	RBI	RC	TBB	IBB	SO	HBP	SH	SF	SB	CS	SB%	GDP	Avg	OBP	Slg
1999 Tigers	R	35	134	43	9	2	0	(-	-)	56	25	11	21	9	0	17	1	4	3	20	7	.74	3	.321	.361	.418
1999 Oneonta	A-	12	50	17	1	2	1	(-	-)	25	9	8	10	2	0	12	1	1	0	5	0	1.00	0	.340	.377	.500
2000 W Michigan	A	98	379	103	15	1	1	(-	-)	123	69	42	47	34	1	60	12	15	6	39	12	.76	11	.272	.346	.325
2001 Lakeland	A+	120	429	115	15	3	2	(-	-)	142	64	46	60	54	0	60	11	14	4	34	8	.81	7	.268	.361	.331
2002 Erie	AA	22	75	21	0	2	1	(-	-)	28	9	7	10	3	0	12	3	2	1	6	0	1.00	0	.280	.329	.373
2002 Toledo	AAA	9	28	12	1	0	2	(-	-)	19	8	6	8	3	0	4	2	0	0	0	2	.00	0	.429	.515	.679
2002 Detroit	AL	65	222	54	5	5	4	(3	1)	81	33	20	23	13	0	48	8	4	2	8	5	.62	2	.243	.306	.365

Victor Santos

Pitches: R **Bats:** R **Pos:** RP-22; SP-2   **Ht:** 6'3" **Wt:** 195 **Born:** 10/2/76 **Age:** 26

Year Team	Lg	G	GS	CG	GF	IP	BFP	H	R	ER	HR	SH	SF	HB	TBB	IBB	SO	WP	Bk	W	L	Pct	ShO	Sv-Op	Hld	ERC	ERA
1996 Lakeland	A+	5	4	0	0	28.1	114	19	11	7	2	2	1	4	9	0	25	2	0	2	2	.500	0	0- --	-	2.42	2.22
1996 Tigers	R	9	9	0	0	50.0	199	44	12	11	1	3	1	1	13	0	39	3	0	3	2	.600	0	0- --	-	3.07	1.98
1997 Lakeland	A+	26	26	4	0	145.0	623	136	74	52	10	4	6	6	59	1	108	12	1	10	5	.667	2	0- --	-	3.69	3.23
1998 Lakeland	A+	16	15	0	1	100.1	408	88	38	28	9	5	2	3	24	1	74	3	0	5	2	.714	0	1- --	-	2.85	2.51
1998 Toledo	AAA	5	3	0	1	14.2	80	24	22	18	5	0	0	0	10	0	12	0	0	1	2	.333	0	0- --	-	11.57	11.05
1998 Jacksonville	AA	6	6	0	0	36.2	159	40	20	17	2	1	3	1	15	1	37	1	0	4	2	.667	0	0- --	-	4.45	4.17
1999 Jacksonville	AA	28	28	2	0	173.0	722	150	86	67	16	1	5	7	58	2	146	3	0	12	6	.667	1	0- --	-	3.19	3.49
2000 Tigers	R	1	1	0	0	3.0	13	2	1	0	0	0	0	0	2	0	5	0	0	0	0	-	0	0- --	-	2.54	0.00
2000 Lakeland	A+	1	1	0	0	5.0	20	5	0	0	0	0	0	0	1	0	4	0	0	1	0	1.000	0	0- --	-	2.76	0.00
2000 Toledo	AAA	2	2	0	0	6.1	33	7	8	8	4	2	0	0	6	0	2	0	0	1	0	.000	0	0- --	-	11.17	11.37
2001 Toledo	AAA	6	6	0	0	35.1	162	50	27	25	6	1	1	0	12	0	22	0	0	2	1	.667	0	0- --	-	7.15	6.37
2002 Co Springs	AAA	21	21	1	0	118.0	535	147	81	75	17	2	6	4	43	0	134	5	0	4	9	.308	1	0- --	-	5.86	5.72

Year Team	Lg	G	GS	CG	GF	IP	BFP	H	R	ER	HR	SH	SF	HB	TBB	IBB	SO	WP	Bk	W	L	Pct	ShO	Sv-Op	Hld	ERC	ERA
2001 Detroit	AL	33	7	0	6	76.1	335	62	33	28	9	1	3	3	49	4	52	0	0	2	2	.500	0	0-0	2	4.18	3.30
2002 Colorado	NL	24	2	0	6	26.0	140	41	30	30	3	3	1	0	22	3	25	2	0	0	4	.000	0	0-0	1	9.37	10.38
2 ML YEARS		57	9	0	12	102.1	475	103	63	58	12	4	4	3	71	7	77	2	0	2	6	.250	0	0-0	3	5.40	5.10

Kazuhiro Sasaki

Pitches: R **Bats:** R **Pos:** RP-61 **Ht:** 6'4" **Wt:** 220 **Born:** 2/22/68 **Age:** 35

		HOW MUCH HE PITCHED						WHAT HE GAVE UP												THE RESULTS							
Year Team	Lg	G	GS	CG	GF	IP	BFP	H	R	ER	HR	SH	SF	HB	TBB	IBB	SO	WP	Bk	W	L	Pct	ShO	Sv-Op	Hld	ERC	ERA
2000 Seattle	AL	63	0	0	58	62.2	265	42	25	22	10	2	2	2	31	5	78	1	0	2	5	.286	0	37-40	0	2.98	3.16
2001 Seattle	AL	69	0	0	63	66.2	261	48	24	24	6	0	0	4	11	2	62	4	0	0	4	.000	0	45-52	0	1.90	3.24
2002 Seattle	AL	61	0	0	55	60.2	249	44	24	17	6	3	5	2	20	4	73	6	0	4	5	.444	0	37-45	0	2.35	2.52
3 ML YEARS		193	0	0	176	190.0	775	134	73	63	22	5	7	8	62	11	213	11	0	6	14	.300	0	119-137	0	2.39	2.98

Scott Sauerbeck

Pitches: L **Bats:** R **Pos:** RP-78 **Ht:** 6'3" **Wt:** 197 **Born:** 11/9/71 **Age:** 31

		HOW MUCH HE PITCHED						WHAT HE GAVE UP												THE RESULTS							
Year Team	Lg	G	GS	CG	GF	IP	BFP	H	R	ER	HR	SH	SF	HB	TBB	IBB	SO	WP	Bk	W	L	Pct	ShO	Sv-Op	Hld	ERC	ERA
1999 Pittsburgh	NL	65	0	0	16	67.2	287	53	19	15	6	4	0	4	38	5	55	3	0	4	1	.800	0	2-5	10	3.60	2.00
2000 Pittsburgh	NL	75	0	0	13	75.2	349	76	36	34	4	3	3	1	61	8	83	9	2	5	4	.556	0	1-4	13	5.31	4.04
2001 Pittsburgh	NL	70	0	0	14	62.2	281	61	41	39	4	2	0	2	40	6	79	3	0	2	2	.500	0	2-4	19	4.60	5.60
2002 Pittsburgh	NL	78	0	0	21	62.2	255	50	18	16	4	0	0	1	27	4	70	2	1	5	4	.556	0	0-0	28	2.91	2.30
4 ML YEARS		288	0	0	64	268.2	1172	240	114	104	18	9	3	8	166	23	287	17	3	16	11	.593	0	5-13	70	4.13	3.48

Curt Schilling

Pitches: R **Bats:** R **Pos:** SP-35; RP-1 **Ht:** 6'4" **Wt:** 231 **Born:** 11/14/66 **Age:** 36

		HOW MUCH HE PITCHED						WHAT HE GAVE UP												THE RESULTS							
Year Team	Lg	G	GS	CG	GF	IP	BFP	H	R	ER	HR	SH	SF	HB	TBB	IBB	SO	WP	Bk	W	L	Pct	ShO	Sv-Op	Hld	ERC	ERA
1988 Baltimore	AL	4	4	0	0	14.2	76	22	19	16	3	0	3	1	10	1	4	2	0	0	3	.000	0	0-0	0	9.43	9.82
1989 Baltimore	AL	5	1	0	0	8.2	38	10	6	6	2	0	0	0	3	0	6	1	0	0	1	.000	0	0-0	0	5.74	6.23
1990 Baltimore	AL	35	0	0	16	46.0	191	38	13	13	1	2	4	0	19	0	32	0	0	1	2	.333	0	3-9	5	2.68	2.54
1991 Houston	NL	56	0	0	34	75.2	336	79	35	32	2	5	1	0	39	7	71	4	1	3	5	.375	0	8-11	5	4.08	3.81
1992 Philadelphia	NL	42	26	10	10	226.1	895	165	67	59	11	7	8	5	59	4	147	4	0	14	11	.560	4	2-3	0	1.86	2.35
1993 Philadelphia	NL	34	34	7	0	235.1	982	234	114	105	23	9	7	4	57	6	186	9	3	16	7	.696	2	0-0	0	3.44	4.02
1994 Philadelphia	NL	13	13	1	0	82.1	360	87	42	41	10	6	1	3	28	3	58	3	1	2	8	.200	0	0-0	0	4.36	4.48
1995 Philadelphia	NL	17	17	1	0	116.0	473	96	52	46	12	5	2	3	26	2	114	0	1	7	5	.583	0	0-0	0	2.55	3.57
1996 Philadelphia	NL	26	26	8	0	183.1	732	149	69	65	16	6	4	3	50	5	182	5	0	9	10	.474	2	0-0	0	2.59	3.19
1997 Philadelphia	NL	35	35	7	0	254.1	1009	208	96	84	25	8	8	5	58	3	319	5	1	17	11	.607	2	0-0	0	2.55	2.97
1998 Philadelphia	NL	35	35	15	0	268.2	1089	236	101	97	23	14	7	6	61	3	300	12	0	15	14	.517	2	0-0	0	2.75	3.25
1999 Philadelphia	NL	24	24	8	0	180.1	735	159	74	71	25	11	3	6	44	0	152	4	0	15	6	.714	1	0-0	0	3.20	3.54
2000 Phi-Ari	NL	29	29	8	0	210.1	862	204	90	89	27	11	4	1	45	4	168	4	0	11	12	.478	2	0-0	0	3.38	3.81
2001 Arizona	NL	35	35	6	0	256.2	1021	237	86	85	37	8	5	1	39	0	293	4	0	22	6	.786	1	0-0	0	3.03	2.98
2002 Arizona	NL	36	35	5	0	259.1	1017	218	95	93	29	4	3	3	33	1	316	6	0	23	7	.767	1	0-0	0	2.33	3.23
2000 Philadelphia	NL	16	16	4	0	112.2	474	110	49	49	17	5	1	1	32	4	96	4	0	6	6	.500	1	0-0	0	3.79	3.91
2000 Arizona	NL	13	13	4	0	97.2	388	94	41	40	10	6	3	0	13	0	72	0	0	5	6	.455	1	0-0	0	2.91	3.69
15 ML YEARS		426	314	76	60	2418.0	9816	2142	959	902	246	96	60	36	571	39	2348	63	7	155	108	.589	17	13-23	10	2.89	3.36

Jason Schmidt

Pitches: R **Bats:** R **Pos:** SP-29 **Ht:** 6'5" **Wt:** 205 **Born:** 1/29/73 **Age:** 30

		HOW MUCH HE PITCHED						WHAT HE GAVE UP												THE RESULTS							
Year Team	Lg	G	GS	CG	GF	IP	BFP	H	R	ER	HR	SH	SF	HB	TBB	IBB	SO	WP	Bk	W	L	Pct	ShO	Sv-Op	Hld	ERC	ERA
2002 Fresno*	AAA	2	2	0	0	12.0	46	11	4	4	0	2	0	0	2	0	12	2	0	2	0	1.000	0	0- -	-	2.28	3.00
1995 Atlanta	NL	9	2	0	1	25.0	119	27	17	16	2	2	4	1	18	3	19	1	0	2	2	.500	0	0-1	0	5.56	5.76
1996 Atl-Pit	NL	19	17	1	0	96.1	445	108	67	61	10	4	9	2	53	0	74	8	1	5	6	.455	0	0-0	0	5.46	5.70
1997 Pittsburgh	NL	32	32	2	0	187.2	825	193	106	96	16	10	3	9	76	2	136	8	0	10	9	.526	0	0-0	0	4.31	4.60
1998 Pittsburgh	NL	33	33	0	0	214.1	916	228	106	97	24	10	3	4	71	3	158	15	1	11	14	.440	0	0-0	0	4.35	4.07
1999 Pittsburgh	NL	33	33	2	0	212.2	937	219	110	99	24	7	7	3	85	4	148	6	4	13	11	.542	0	0-0	0	4.30	4.19
2000 Pittsburgh	NL	11	11	0	0	63.1	295	71	43	38	6	1	2	1	41	2	51	1	0	2	5	.286	0	0-0	0	5.77	5.40
2001 Pit-SF	NL	25	25	1	0	150.1	641	138	75	69	13	5	3	7	61	3	142	8	1	13	7	.650	0	0-0	0	3.72	4.07
2002 San Francisco	NL	29	29	2	0	185.1	769	148	78	71	15	11	5	2	73	1	196	12	0	13	8	.619	2	0-0	0	2.87	3.45
1996 Atlanta	NL	13	11	0	0	58.2	274	69	48	44	8	3	6	0	32	0	48	5	1	3	4	.429	0	0-0	0	5.92	6.75
1996 Pittsburgh	NL	6	6	1	0	37.2	171	39	19	17	2	1	3	2	21	0	26	3	0	2	2	.500	0	0-0	0	4.75	4.06
2001 Pittsburgh	NL	14	14	1	0	84.0	357	81	46	43	11	3	2	5	28	2	77	3	1	6	6	.500	0	0-0	0	4.17	4.61
2001 San Francisco	NL	11	11	0	0	66.1	284	57	29	25	2	2	1	2	33	1	65	5	0	7	1	.875	0	0-0	0	3.16	3.39
8 ML YEARS		191	182	8	1	1135.0	4947	1132	602	546	110	50	36	29	478	18	924	59	7	69	62	.527	2	0-1	0	4.19	4.33

Brian Schneider

Bats: L **Throws:** R **Pos:** C-65; PH-7; PR-3; LF-1; RF-1 **Ht:** 6'1" **Wt:** 200 **Born:** 11/26/76 **Age:** 26

		BATTING																BASERUNNING				AVERAGES		
Year Team	Lg	G	AB	H	2B	3B	HR	(Hm | Rd)	TB	R	RBI	RC	TBB	IBB	SO	HBP	SH	SF	SB	CS	SB%	GDP	Avg	OBP	Slg
2000 Montreal	NL	45	115	27	6	0	0	(0 | 0)	33	6	11	8	7	2	24	0	0	1	0	1	.00	1	.235	.276	.287
2001 Montreal	NL	27	41	13	3	0	1	(1 | 0)	19	4	6	8	6	1	3	0	0	0	0	0	-	0	.317	.396	.463
2002 Montreal	NL	73	207	57	19	2	5	(3 | 2)	95	21	29	30	21	8	41	0	2	2	1	2	.33	7	.275	.339	.459
3 ML YEARS		145	363	97	28	2	6	(4 | 2)	147	31	46	46	34	11	68	0	2	4	1	3	.25	8	.267	.327	.405

Scott Schoeneweis

Pitches: L Bats: L Pos: RP-39; SP-15   Ht: 6'0" Wt: 185 Born: 10/2/73 Age: 29

| | | HOW MUCH HE PITCHED | | | | WHAT HE GAVE UP | | | | | | | | | | THE RESULTS | | | | | | |
Year Team	Lg	G	GS	CG	GF	IP	BFP	H	R	ER	HR	SH	SF	HB	TBB	IBB	SO	WP	Bk	W	L	Pct	ShO	Sv-Op	Hld	ERC	ERA
1999 Anaheim	AL	31	0	0	6	39.1	175	47	27	24	4	0	1	0	14	1	22	1	0	1	1	.500	0	0-0	3	4.99	5.49
2000 Anaheim	AL	27	27	1	0	170.0	742	183	112	103	21	2	5	6	67	2	78	4	3	7	10	.412	1	0-0	0	4.84	5.45
2001 Anaheim	AL	32	32	1	0	205.1	910	227	122	116	21	3	8	14	77	2	104	4	1	10	11	.476	0	0-0	0	4.87	5.08
2002 Anaheim	AL	54	15	0	4	118.0	510	119	68	64	17	1	5	5	49	4	65	1	1	9	8	.529	0	1-4	11	4.68	4.88
4 ML YEARS		144	74	2	10	532.2	2337	576	329	307	63	6	19	25	207	9	269	10	5	27	30	.474	1	1-4	14	4.83	5.19

Marco Scutaro

Bats: R Throws: R Pos: 2B-11; PH-10; SS-5; 3B-2; PR-2; LF-1   Ht: 5'10" Wt: 170 Born: 10/30/75 Age: 27

| | | BATTING | | | | | | | | | | | | | | | | | BASERUNNING | | | | AVERAGES | | |
Year Team	Lg	G	AB	H	2B	3B	HR	(Hm	Rd)	TB	R	RBI	RC	TBB	IBB	SO	HBP	SH	SF	SB	CS	SB%	GDP	Avg	OBP	Slg
1996 Columbus	A	85	315	79	12	3	10	(-	-)	127	66	45	44	38	0	86	4	4	5	6	3	.67	6	.251	.334	.403
1997 Kinston	A+	97	378	103	17	6	10	(-	-)	162	58	59	60	35	0	72	9	2	3	23	7	.77	3	.272	.346	.429
1997 Buffalo	AAA	21	57	15	3	0	1	(-	-)	21	8	6	6	6	0	8	0	1	1	0	1	.00	4	.263	.328	.368
1998 Akron	AA	124	462	146	27	6	11	(-	-)	218	68	62	84	47	0	71	10	4	6	33	16	.67	8	.316	.387	.472
1998 Buffalo	AAA	8	26	6	3	0	0	(-	-)	9	3	4	2	0	0	2	0	1	0	0	0	-	0	.231	.231	.346
1999 Buffalo	AAA	129	462	126	24	2	8	(-	-)	178	76	51	71	61	2	69	6	6	4	21	6	.78	5	.273	.362	.385
2000 Buffalo	AAA	124	425	117	20	5	5	(-	-)	162	67	54	65	61	0	53	9	7	7	9	6	.60	8	.275	.373	.381
2000 Indianapolis	AAA	4	13	7	1	1	1	(-	-)	13	5	3	5	1	0	2	0	0	0	1	0	1.00	1	.538	.571	1.000
2001 Indianapolis	AAA	132	495	146	29	3	11	(-	-)	214	87	50	81	62	2	83	10	5	3	11	11	.50	9	.295	.382	.432
2002 Norfolk	AAA	97	354	113	22	6	7	(-	-)	168	48	28	59	30	3	61	2	7	1	7	8	.47	7	.319	.375	.475
2002 New York	NL	27	36	8	0	1	1	(1	0)	13	2	6	2	0	0	11	0	1	0	0	1	.00	1	.222	.216	.361

Rudy Seanez

Pitches: R Bats: R Pos: RP-33   Ht: 5'11" Wt: 205 Born: 10/20/68 Age: 34

| | | HOW MUCH HE PITCHED | | | | WHAT HE GAVE UP | | | | | | | | | | THE RESULTS | | | | | | |
Year Team	Lg	G	GS	CG	GF	IP	BFP	H	R	ER	HR	SH	SF	HB	TBB	IBB	SO	WP	Bk	W	L	Pct	ShO	Sv-Op	Hld	ERC	ERA
2002 Oklahoma*	AAA	4	0	0	1	4.0	15	4	2	2	0	0	0	0	0	0	3	0	0	0	0	-	0	0--	-	2.12	4.50
1989 Cleveland	AL	5	0	0	2	5.0	20	1	2	2	0	0	2	0	4	1	7	1	1	0	0	-	0	0-0	0	0.94	3.60
1990 Cleveland	AL	24	0	0	12	27.1	127	22	17	17	2	0	1	1	25	1	24	5	0	2	1	.667	0	0-0	3	4.85	5.60
1991 Cleveland	AL	5	0	0	0	5.0	33	10	12	9	2	0	0	0	7	0	7	2	0	0	0	-	0	0-1	0	17.96	16.20
1993 San Diego	NL	3	0	0	3	3.1	20	8	6	5	1	1	0	0	2	0	1	0	0	0	0	-	0	0-0	0	16.31	13.50
1994 Los Angeles	NL	17	0	0	6	23.2	104	24	7	7	2	4	2	1	9	1	18	3	0	1	1	.500	0	0-1	1	4.01	2.66
1995 Los Angeles	NL	37	0	0	12	34.2	159	39	27	26	5	3	0	1	18	3	29	0	0	1	3	.250	0	3-4	6	5.57	6.75
1998 Atlanta	NL	34	0	0	8	36.0	148	25	13	11	2	1	2	1	16	0	50	2	0	4	1	.800	0	2-4	8	2.44	2.75
1999 Atlanta	NL	56	0	0	13	53.2	225	47	21	20	3	0	2	1	21	1	41	3	0	6	1	.857	0	3-8	18	3.12	3.35
2000 Atlanta	NL	23	0	0	8	21.0	89	15	11	10	3	1	0	1	9	1	20	0	0	2	4	.333	0	2-3	6	2.95	4.29
2001 SD-Atl	NL	38	0	0	8	36.0	150	23	12	11	4	1	1	0	19	0	41	4	0	0	2	.000	0	1-3	9	2.78	2.75
2002 Texas	AL	33	0	0	4	33.0	150	28	25	21	5	3	1	0	24	1	40	6	0	1	3	.250	0	0-4	10	4.77	5.73
2001 San Diego	NL	26	0	0	8	24.0	102	15	8	7	3	0	1	1	15	0	24	1	0	0	2	.000	0	1-3	5	3.21	2.63
2001 Atlanta	NL	12	0	0	0	12.0	48	8	4	4	1	0	0	0	4	0	17	3	0	0	0	-	0	0-0	4	1.99	3.00
11 ML YEARS		275	0	0	76	278.2	1225	242	153	139	29	13	11	7	154	9	278	26	1	17	16	.515	0	11-28	61	3.97	4.49

Todd Sears

Bats: L Throws: R Pos: 1B-6; PH-1   Ht: 6'5" Wt: 215 Born: 10/23/75 Age: 27

| | | BATTING | | | | | | | | | | | | | | | | | BASERUNNING | | | | AVERAGES | | |
Year Team	Lg	G	AB	H	2B	3B	HR	(Hm	Rd)	TB	R	RBI	RC	TBB	IBB	SO	HBP	SH	SF	SB	CS	SB%	GDP	Avg	OBP	Slg
1997 Portland	A-	55	200	54	13	1	2	(-	-)	75	37	29	32	41	7	49	0	1	1	2	0	1.00	4	.270	.393	.375
1998 Asheville	A	130	459	133	26	2	11	(-	-)	196	71	82	79	72	1	89	5	1	6	10	4	.71	9	.290	.387	.427
1999 Salem	A+	109	385	108	21	0	14	(-	-)	171	58	59	66	58	1	99	4	0	1	11	2	.85	9	.281	.379	.444
2000 Carolina	AA	86	299	90	21	0	12	(-	-)	147	54	72	66	72	11	76	2	0	5	12	3	.80	7	.301	.434	.492
2000 New Britain	AA	40	140	44	8	1	3	(-	-)	63	15	15	24	18	1	40	1	0	0	1	0	1.00	5	.314	.396	.450
2000 Salt Lake	AAA	3	11	4	1	0	1	(-	-)	8	2	4	3	1	0	2	0	0	0	0	0	-	1	.364	.417	.727
2001 Edmonton	AAA	118	408	127	25	2	13	(-	-)	195	61	50	68	41	2	71	3	1	3	2	1	.67	16	.311	.376	.478
2002 Edmonton	AAA	129	484	150	36	4	20	(-	-)	254	88	100	96	59	4	142	5	0	4	2	1	.67	6	.310	.388	.525
2002 Minnesota	AL	7	12	4	2	0	0	(0	0)	6	2	0	1	0	0	1	0	0	0	0	0	-		.333	.333	.500

Shawn Sedlacek

Pitches: R Bats: R Pos: SP-14; RP-2   Ht: 6'4" Wt: 200 Born: 6/29/77 Age: 26

| | | HOW MUCH HE PITCHED | | | | WHAT HE GAVE UP | | | | | | | | | | THE RESULTS | | | | | | |
Year Team	Lg	G	GS	CG	GF	IP	BFP	H	R	ER	HR	SH	SF	HB	TBB	IBB	SO	WP	Bk	W	L	Pct	ShO	Sv-Op	Hld	ERC	ERA
1998 Spokane	A-	16	16	0	0	86.0	371	89	43	33	2	1	4	6	18	0	62	4	5	9	2	.818	0	0--	-	3.19	3.45
1999 Wilmington	A+	17	17	1	0	92.0	411	111	61	54	7	6	3	6	26	0	69	4	0	4	6	.400	0	0--	-	4.85	5.28
2000 Wichita	AA	35	16	1	11	140.1	612	153	69	57	10	5	2	12	43	4	81	8	2	5	6	.714	0	3--	-	4.32	3.66
2001 Wichita	AA	14	14	1	0	86.2	360	85	37	35	7	1	2	8	14	1	66	3	0	6	7	.462	1	0--	-	3.26	3.63
2001 Omaha	AAA	14	13	0	1	81.0	348	98	49	45	13	4	2	3	22	2	44	3	1	5	4	.556	0	0--	-	5.49	5.00
2002 Wichita	AA	3	3	0	0	18.1	78	14	6	3	0	1	2	2	4	0	16	0	0	1	2	.667	0	0--	-	1.83	1.47
2002 Omaha	AAA	11	11	2	0	80.1	326	67	37	33	6	1	3	5	15	0	66	1	0	6	5	.545	1	0--	-	2.45	3.70
2002 Kansas City	AL	16	14	0	1	84.1	381	99	64	63	16	5	7	6	36	2	52	5	0	3	5	.375	0	0-0	0	6.24	6.72

David Segui

Bats: B Throws: L Pos: DH-19; 1B-7   Ht: 6'1" Wt: 202 Born: 7/19/66 Age: 36

								BATTING											BASERUNNING				AVERAGES		
Year Team	Lg	G	AB	H	2B	3B	HR	(Hm	Rd)	TB	R	RBI	RC	TBB	IBB	SO	HBP	SH	SF	SB	CS	SB%	GDP	Avg	OBP	Slg
1990 Baltimore	AL	40	123	30	7	0	2	(1	1)	43	14	15	10	11	1	15	1	1	0	0	0	-	12	.244	.311	.350
1991 Baltimore	AL	86	212	59	7	0	2	(1	1)	72	15	22	21	12	2	19	0	3	1	1	1	.50	7	.278	.316	.340
1992 Baltimore	AL	115	189	44	9	0	1	(1	0)	56	21	17	17	20	3	23	0	2	0	1	0	1.00	4	.233	.306	.296
1993 Baltimore	AL	146	450	123	27	0	10	(6	4)	180	54	60	62	58	4	53	0	3	8	2	1	.67	18	.273	.351	.400
1994 New York	NL	92	336	81	17	1	10	(5	5)	130	46	43	40	33	6	43	1	1	3	0	0	-	6	.241	.308	.387
1995 NYM-Mon	NL	130	456	141	25	4	12	(6	6)	210	68	68	73	40	5	47	3	8	3	2	7	.22	10	.309	.367	.461
1996 Montreal	NL	115	416	119	30	1	11	(6	5)	184	69	58	69	60	4	54	0	0	4	4	4	.50	8	.286	.375	.442
1997 Montreal	NL	125	449	141	22	3	21	(10	11)	232	75	68	86	57	12	66	1	0	6	1	0	1.00	9	.307	.380	.505
1998 Seattle	AL	143	522	159	36	1	19	(10	9)	254	79	84	89	49	4	80	0	0	9	3	1	.75	12	.305	.359	.487
1999 Sea-Tor	AL	121	440	131	27	3	14	(5	9)	206	57	52	70	40	4	60	1	1	4	1	2	.33	10	.298	.355	.468
2000 Tex-Cle	AL	150	574	192	42	1	19	(8	11)	293	93	103	105	53	2	84	1	0	6	0	1	.00	20	.334	.388	.510
2001 Baltimore	AL	82	292	88	18	1	10	(5	5)	138	48	46	57	49	5	61	4	0	2	1	1	.50	4	.301	.406	.473
2002 Baltimore	AL	26	95	25	4	0	2	(1	1)	35	10	16	14	11	0	22	0	0	1	0	0	-	0	.263	.336	.368
1995 New York	NL	33	73	24	3	1	2	(2	0)	35	9	11	14	12	1	9	1	4	2	1	3	.25	2	.329	.420	.479
1995 Montreal	NL	97	383	117	22	3	10	(4	6)	175	59	57	59	28	4	38	2	4	1	1	4	.20	8	.305	.355	.457
1999 Seattle	AL	90	345	101	22	3	9	(4	5)	156	43	39	52	32	4	43	1	1	3	1	2	.33	9	.293	.352	.452
1999 Toronto	AL	31	95	30	5	0	5	(1	4)	50	14	13	18	8	0	17	0	0	1	0	0	-	1	.316	.365	.526
2000 Texas	AL	93	351	118	29	1	11	(4	7)	182	52	57	66	34	1	51	0	0	4	0	1	.00	12	.336	.391	.519
2000 Cleveland	AL	57	223	74	13	0	8	(4	4)	111	41	46	39	19	1	33	1	0	2	0	0	-	8	.332	.384	.498
13 ML YEARS		1371	4564	1333	271	15	133	(65	68)	2033	649	652	713	493	53	627	12	19	44	16	18	.47	120	.292	.359	.445

Bill Selby

Bats: L Throws: R Pos: 3B-33; PH-22; LF-13; 2B-6; RF-5; SS-1; PR-1   Ht: 5'10" Wt: 195 Born: 6/11/70 Age: 33

								BATTING											BASERUNNING				AVERAGES		
Year Team	Lg	G	AB	H	2B	3B	HR	(Hm	Rd)	TB	R	RBI	RC	TBB	IBB	SO	HBP	SH	SF	SB	CS	SB%	GDP	Avg	OBP	Slg
2002 Buffalo*	AAA	51	184	55	14	2	5	(-	-)	88	28	22	33	20	2	33	0	0	2	4	1	.80	3	.299	.364	.478
1996 Boston	AL	40	95	26	4	0	3	(0	3)	39	12	6	12	9	1	11	0	1	0	1	1	.50	3	.274	.337	.411
2000 Cleveland	AL	30	46	11	1	0	0	(0	0)	12	8	4	3	1	0	9	1	0	0	0	0	-	1	.239	.271	.261
2001 Cincinnati	NL	36	92	21	7	1	2	(1	1)	36	7	12	10	5	1	13	1	1	1	0	0	-	1	.228	.273	.391
2002 Cleveland	AL	65	159	34	7	2	6	(2	4)	63	15	21	21	15	2	27	0	0	2	0	1	.00	4	.214	.278	.396
4 ML YEARS		171	392	92	19	3	11	(3	8)	150	42	43	46	30	4	60	2	2	3	1	2	.33	9	.235	.290	.383

Aaron Sele

Pitches: R Bats: R Pos: SP-26   Ht: 6'5" Wt: 220 Born: 6/25/70 Age: 33

		HOW MUCH HE PITCHED						WHAT HE GAVE UP												THE RESULTS						
Year Team	Lg	G	GS	CG	GF	IP	BFP	H	R	ER	HR	SH	SF	HB	TBB	IBB	SO	WP	Bk	W	L	Pct	ShO	Sv-Op	Hld	ERC	ERA
1993 Boston	AL	18	18	0	0	111.2	484	100	42	34	5	2	5	7	48	2	93	5	0	7	2	.778	0	0-0	0	3.40	2.74
1994 Boston	AL	22	22	2	0	143.1	615	140	68	61	13	4	5	9	60	2	105	4	0	8	7	.533	0	0-0	0	4.26	3.83
1995 Boston	AL	6	6	0	0	32.1	146	32	14	11	3	1	3		14	0	21	3	0	3	1	.750	0	0-0	0	4.35	3.06
1996 Boston	AL	29	29	1	0	157.1	722	192	110	93	14	6	7	8	67	2	137	2	0	7	11	.389	0	0-0	0	5.56	5.32
1997 Boston	AL	33	33	1	0	177.1	810	196	115	106	25	5	7	15	80	4	122	7	0	13	12	.520	0	0-0	0	5.47	5.38
1998 Texas	AL	33	33	3	0	212.2	954	239	116	100	14	5	7	13	84	6	167	4	0	19	11	.633	0	0-0	0	4.69	4.23
1999 Texas	AL	33	33	2	0	205.0	920	244	115	109	21	1	3	12	70	3	186	4	0	18	9	.667	2	0-0	0	5.17	4.79
2000 Seattle	AL	34	34	2	0	211.2	908	221	110	106	17	5	8	5	74	7	137	5	0	17	10	.630	2	0-0	0	4.06	4.51
2001 Seattle	AL	34	33	2	0	215.0	899	216	93	86	25	5	9	7	51	2	114	1	0	15	5	.750	0	0-0	0	3.70	3.60
2002 Anaheim	AL	26	26	1	0	160.0	706	190	92	87	21	5	10	7	49	2	82	5	0	8	9	.471	1	0-0	0	5.20	4.89
10 ML YEARS		268	267	14	0	1626.1	7164	1770	875	793	158	39	62	86	597	30	1164	40	0	115	77	.599	8	0-0	0	4.61	4.39

Jae Seo

Pitches: R Bats: R Pos: RP-1   Ht: 6'1" Wt: 215 Born: 5/24/77 Age: 26

		HOW MUCH HE PITCHED						WHAT HE GAVE UP												THE RESULTS						
Year Team	Lg	G	GS	CG	GF	IP	BFP	H	R	ER	HR	SH	SF	HB	TBB	IBB	SO	WP	Bk	W	L	Pct	ShO	Sv-Op	Hld	ERC	ERA
1998 St.Lucie	A+	8	7	0	0	35.0	141	26	13	9	2	2	0	3	10	0	37	1	6	3	1	.750	0	0--	-	2.37	2.31
1998 Mets	R	2	0	0	0	5.0	17	4	0	0	0	0	0	0	0	0	5	0	0	0	0	-	0	0--	-	1.42	0.00
1999 St.Lucie	A+	3	3	0	0	14.2	55	8	3	3	0	0	1	0	2	0	14	0	0	2	0	1.000	0	0--	-	0.84	1.84
2001 St.Lucie	A+	6	5	0	0	25.1	104	21	11	10	2	0	1	1	6	0	19	0	0	2	3	.400	0	0--	-	2.53	3.55
2001 Binghamton	AA	12	10	0	0	60.1	235	44	14	13	3	3	1	6	11	1	47	0	0	5	1	.833	0	0--	-	1.97	1.94
2001 Norfolk	AAA	9	9	0	0	47.1	191	53	18	18	4	4	0	2	6	1	25	0	0	2	2	.500	0	0--	-	3.87	3.42
2002 Binghamton	AA	1	0	0	0	5.0	21	5	3	3	1	0	0	0	1	0	6	0	0	0	0	-	0	0--	-	3.86	5.40
2002 Norfolk	AAA	26	24	1	0	128.2	548	145	66	57	14	6	6	3	22	1	87	0	0	6	9	.400	0	0--	-	3.99	3.99
2002 New York	NL	1	0	0	1	1.0	3	0	0	0	0	0	0	0	0	0	1	0	0	0	0	-	0	0-0	0	0.00	0.00

Scott Service

Pitches: R Bats: R Pos: RP   Ht: 6'6" Wt: 240 Born: 2/26/67 Age: 36

		HOW MUCH HE PITCHED						WHAT HE GAVE UP												THE RESULTS						
Year Team	Lg	G	GS	CG	GF	IP	BFP	H	R	ER	HR	SH	SF	HB	TBB	IBB	SO	WP	Bk	W	L	Pct	ShO	Sv-Op	Hld	ERC	ERA
1988 Philadelphia	NL	5	0	0	1	5.1	23	7	1	1	0	0	0	1	1	0	6	0	0	0	0	-	0	0-0	0	5.34	1.69
1992 Montreal	NL	5	0	0	0	7.0	41	15	11	11	1	0	0	0	5	0	11	0	0	0	0	-	0	0-0	1	13.24	14.14
1993 Col-Cin	NL	29	0	0	7	46.0	197	44	24	22	6	2	4	2	16	4	43	0	0	2	2	.500	0	2-2	3	3.85	4.30
1994 Cincinnati	NL	6	0	0	2	7.1	35	8	9	6	2	2	0	0	3	0	5	0	0	1	2	.333	0	0-0	3	5.42	7.36
1995 San Francisco	NL	28	0	0	6	31.0	129	18	11	11	4	3	2	2	20	4	30	3	0	3	1	.750	0	0-0	7	3.04	3.19
1996 Cincinnati	NL	34	1	0	5	48.0	213	51	21	21	7	4	1	6	18	4	46	5	0	1	0	1.000	0	0-0	3	5.07	3.94
1997 Cin-KC		16	0	0	3	22.1	95	28	16	16	2	2	1	0	6	0	22	2	0	0	3	.000	0	0-1	3	5.14	6.45
1998 Kansas City	AL	73	0	0	26	82.2	353	70	36	32	7	2	5	9	34	4	95	10	6	4	6	.400	0	4-8	18	3.52	3.48
1999 Kansas City	AL	68	0	0	29	75.1	352	87	51	51	13	4	7	3	42	8	68	3	0	5	5	.500	0	8-15	6	6.14	6.09
2000 Oakland	AL	20	0	0	6	36.2	172	45	31	26	5	1	2	1	19	1	35	0	0	1	2	.333	0	1-1	1	6.22	6.38
1993 Colorado	NL	3	0	0	0	4.2	24	8	5	5	1	0	2	1	1	0	3	0	0	0	0	-	0	0-0	0	9.48	9.64

Year Team	Lg		HOW MUCH HE PITCHED							WHAT HE GAVE UP											THE RESULTS						
		G	GS	CG	GF	IP	BFP	H	R	ER	HR	SH	SF	HB	TBB	IBB	SO	WP	Bk	W	L	Pct	ShO	Sv-Op	Hld	ERC	ERA
1993 Cincinnati	NL	26	0	0	7	41.1	173	36	19	17	5	2	2	1	15	4	40			2	2	.500	0	2-2	3	3.31	3.70
1997 Cincinnati	NL	4	0	0	2	5.1	26	11	7	7	1	1	0	0	1	0	3	2	0	0	0	-	0	0-0	1	11.35	11.81
1997 Kansas City	AL	12	0	0	1	17.0	69	17	9	9	1	4	1	0	5	0	19	0	0	0	3	.000	0	0-1	2	3.53	4.76
10 ML YEARS		284	1	0	85	361.2	1610	373	210	197	47	20	22	24	164	25	361	23	1	19	19	.500	0	15-27	44	4.84	4.90

Richie Sexson

Bats: R **Throws:** R **Pos:** 1B-155; PH-2; DH-1   **Ht:** 6'8" **Wt:** 227 **Born:** 12/29/74 **Age:** 28

Year Team	Lg				BATTING															BASERUNNING				AVERAGES		
		G	AB	H	2B	3B	HR	(Hm	Rd)	TB	R	RBI	RC	TBB	IBB	SO	HBP	SH	SF	SB	CS	SB%	GDP	Avg	OBP	Slg
1997 Cleveland	AL	5	11	3	0	0	0	(0	0)	3	1	0	0	0	0	2	0	0	0	0	0	-	2	.273	.273	.273
1998 Cleveland	AL	49	174	54	14	1	11	(9	2)	103	28	35	33	6	0	42	3	0	0	1	1	.50	3	.310	.344	.592
1999 Cleveland	AL	134	479	122	17	7	31	(18	13)	246	72	116	70	34	0	117	4	0	8	3	3	.50	19	.255	.305	.514
2000 Cle-Mil		148	537	146	30	1	30	(15	15)	268	89	91	91	59	2	159	7	0	4	2	0	1.00	11	.272	.349	.499
2001 Milwaukee	NL	158	598	162	24	3	45	(28	17)	327	94	125	103	60	5	178	6	0	3	2	4	.33	20	.271	.342	.547
2002 Milwaukee	NL	157	570	159	37	2	29	(13	16)	287	86	102	100	70	7	136	8	0	4	0	0	-	17	.279	.363	.504
2000 Cleveland	AL	91	324	83	16	1	16	(8	8)	149	45	44	45	25	0	96	4	0	3	1	0	1.00	8	.256	.315	.460
2000 Milwaukee	NL	57	213	63	14	0	14	(7	7)	119	44	47	46	34	2	63	3	0	1	1	0	1.00	3	.296	.398	.559
6 ML YEARS		651	2369	646	122	14	146	(83	63)	1234	370	469	397	229	14	634	28	0	19	8	8	.50	72	.273	.341	.521

Andy Sheets

Bats: R **Throws:** R **Pos:** 2B-26; SS-11; 3B-4   **Ht:** 6'2" **Wt:** 192 **Born:** 11/19/71 **Age:** 31

Year Team	Lg				BATTING															BASERUNNING				AVERAGES		
		G	AB	H	2B	3B	HR	(Hm	Rd)	TB	R	RBI	RC	TBB	IBB	SO	HBP	SH	SF	SB	CS	SB%	GDP	Avg	OBP	Slg
2002 Durham*	AAA	98	374	110	25	6	14	(-	-)	189	55	69	63	28	1	72	3	2	4	7	2	.78	9	.294	.345	.505
1996 Seattle	AL	47	110	21	8	0	0	(0	0)	29	18	9	7	10	0	41	1	2	1	2	0	1.00	5	.191	.262	.264
1997 Seattle	AL	32	89	22	3	0	4	(2	2)	37	18	9	12	7	0	34	0	5	1	2	0	1.00	1	.247	.299	.416
1998 San Diego	NL	88	194	47	5	3	7	(2	5)	79	31	29	25	21	3	62	1	2	1	7	2	.78	4	.242	.318	.407
1999 Anaheim	AL	87	244	48	10	0	3	(3	0)	67	22	29	13	14	0	59	0	6	5	1	2	.33	6	.197	.236	.275
2000 Boston	AL	12	21	2	0	0	0	(0	0)	2	1	1	0	0	0	3	0	0	0	0	0	-	1	.095	.095	.095
2001 Tampa Bay	AL	49	153	30	8	0	1	(1	0)	41	10	14	11	12	0	35	0	7	2	2	0	1.00	0	.196	.251	.268
2002 Tampa Bay	AL	41	149	37	4	0	4	(1	3)	53	18	22	18	12	0	41	0	1	2	2	3	.40	1	.248	.301	.356
7 ML YEARS		356	960	207	38	3	19	(9	10)	308	118	113	86	76	3	275	2	23	12	16	7	.70	15	.216	.271	.321

Ben Sheets

Pitches: R **Bats:** R **Pos:** SP-34   **Ht:** 6'1" **Wt:** 203 **Born:** 7/18/78 **Age:** 24

Year Team	Lg		HOW MUCH HE PITCHED							WHAT HE GAVE UP										THE RESULTS						
		G	GS	CG	GF	IP	BFP	H	R	ER	HR	SH	SF	HB	TBB	IBB	SO	WP	Bk	W	L	Pct	ShO	Sv-Op	Hld	ERC	ERA
1999 Ogden	R+	2	2	0	0	8.0	33	8	5	5	2	0	0	1	2	0	12	0	0	0	1	.000	0	0--	-	5.25	5.63
1999 Stockton	A+	5	5	0	0	27.2	115	23	11	11	1	0	1	1	14	0	28	1	0	1	0	1.000	0	0--	-	3.37	3.58
2000 Huntsville	AA	13	13	0	0	72.0	288	55	17	15	4	1	4	2	25	0	60	2	0	5	3	.625	0	0--	-	2.51	1.88
2000 Indianapolis	AAA	14	13	1	0	81.2	346	77	31	26	4	1	3	4	31	0	59	3	1	5	5	.375	0	0--	-	3.56	2.87
2001 Indianapolis	AAA	2	2	0	0	10.2	49	14	5	4	0	2	0	0	3	0	6	0	0	1	1	.500	0	0--	-	4.51	3.38
2001 Milwaukee	NL	25	25	1	0	151.1	653	166	89	80	23	8	5	5	48	6	94	3	0	11	10	.524	1	0-0	0	4.78	4.76
2002 Milwaukee	NL	34	34	1	0	216.2	934	237	105	100	21	10	0	10	70	10	170	9	0	11	16	.407	0	0-0	0	4.45	4.15
2 ML YEARS		59	59	2	0	368.0	1587	403	194	180	44	18	5	15	118	16	264	12	0	22	26	.458	1	0-0	0	4.59	4.40

Gary Sheffield

Bats: R **Throws:** R **Pos:** RF-127; DH-4; PH-4   **Ht:** 6'0" **Wt:** 205 **Born:** 11/18/68 **Age:** 34

Year Team	Lg				BATTING															BASERUNNING				AVERAGES		
		G	AB	H	2B	3B	HR	(Hm	Rd)	TB	R	RBI	RC	TBB	IBB	SO	HBP	SH	SF	SB	CS	SB%	GDP	Avg	OBP	Slg
1988 Milwaukee	NL	24	80	19	1	0	4	(1	3)	32	12	12	8	7	0	7	0	1	1	3	1	.75	5	.238	.295	.400
1989 Milwaukee	NL	95	368	91	18	0	5	(2	3)	124	34	32	38	27	0	33	4	3	3	10	6	.63	4	.247	.303	.337
1990 Milwaukee	NL	125	487	143	30	1	10	(3	7)	205	67	67	73	44	1	41	3	4	9	25	10	.71	11	.294	.350	.421
1991 Milwaukee	NL	50	175	34	12	2	2	(2	0)	56	25	22	15	19	1	15	3	1	5	5	5	.50	3	.194	.277	.320
1992 San Diego	NL	146	557	184	34	3	33	(23	10)	323	87	100	113	48	5	40	6	0	7	5	6	.45	19	.330	.385	.580
1993 SD-Fla	NL	140	494	145	20	5	20	(10	10)	235	67	73	84	47	6	64	9	0	7	17	5	.77	11	.294	.361	.476
1994 Florida	NL	87	322	89	16	1	27	(15	12)	188	61	78	68	51	11	50	6	0	5	12	6	.67	10	.276	.380	.584
1995 Florida	NL	63	213	69	8	0	16	(4	12)	125	46	46	60	55	8	45	4	0	2	19	4	.83	3	.324	.467	.587
1996 Florida	NL	161	519	163	33	1	42	(19	23)	324	118	120	144	142	19	66	10	0	6	16	9	.64	16	.314	.465	.624
1997 Florida	NL	135	444	111	22	1	21	(13	8)	198	86	71	92	121	11	79	15	0	2	11	7	.61	7	.250	.424	.446
1998 Fla-LA	NL	130	437	132	27	2	22	(11	11)	229	73	85	102	95	12	46	8	0	9	22	7	.76	7	.302	.428	.524
1999 Los Angeles	NL	152	549	165	20	0	34	(15	19)	287	103	101	118	101	4	64	4	0	9	11	5	.69	10	.301	.407	.523
2000 Los Angeles	NL	141	501	163	24	3	43	(23	20)	322	105	109	131	101	7	71	4	0	6	4	6	.40	13	.325	.438	.643
2001 Los Angeles	NL	143	515	160	28	2	36	(16	20)	300	98	100	125	94	13	67	4	0	5	10	4	.71	9	.311	.417	.583
2002 Atlanta	NL	135	492	151	26	0	25	(10	15)	252	82	84	102	72	2	53	11	0	4	12	2	.86	16	.307	.404	.512
1993 San Diego	NL	68	258	76	12	2	10	(6	4)	122	34	36	40	18	0	30	3	0	3	5	1	.83	9	.295	.344	.473
1993 Florida	NL	72	236	69	8	3	10	(4	6)	113	33	37	44	29	6	34	6	0	4	12	4	.75	2	.292	.378	.479
1998 Florida	NL	40	136	37	11	1	6	(6	0)	68	21	28	27	26	1	16	2	0	2	4	2	.67	3	.272	.392	.500
1998 Los Angeles	NL	90	301	95	16	1	16	(5	11)	161	52	57	75	69	11	30	6	0	7	18	5	.78	4	.316	.444	.535
15 ML YEARS		1727	6153	1819	319	21	340	(167	173)	3200	1064	1100	1268	1024	100	741	91	9	80	182	83	.69	147	.296	.399	.520

Scot Shields

Pitches: R **Bats:** R **Pos:** RP-28; SP-1   **Ht:** 6'1" **Wt:** 175 **Born:** 7/22/75 **Age:** 27

Year Team	Lg		HOW MUCH HE PITCHED							WHAT HE GAVE UP										THE RESULTS						
		G	GS	CG	GF	IP	BFP	H	R	ER	HR	SH	SF	HB	TBB	IBB	SO	WP	Bk	W	L	Pct	ShO	Sv-Op	Hld	ERC	ERA
1997 Boise	A-	30	0	0	13	52.0	225	45	20	17	1	3	2	3	24	4	61	9	1	7	2	.778	0	2--	-	3.07	2.94
1998 Cedar Rpds	A	58	0	0	38	74.0	311	62	33	30	5	5	2	8	29	0	81	9	1	6	5	.545	0	7--	-	3.40	3.65
1999 Lk Elsinore	A+	24	9	2	6	107.1	443	91	37	30	4	4	4	5	39	4	113	6	1	10	3	.769	1	1--	-	2.67	2.52

Year Team	Lg	G	GS	CG	GF	IP	BFP	H	R	ER	HR	SH	SF	HB	TBB	IBB	SO	WP	Bk	W	L	Pct	ShO	Sv-Op	Hld	ERC	ERA
1999 Erie	AA	10	10	1	0	74.2	300	57	26	24	10	4	0	6	26	0	81	2	0	4	4	.500	1	0--	-	3.23	2.89
2000 Edmonton	AAA	27	27	4	0	163.0	734	158	114	98	16	1	6	14	82	0	156	7	0	7	13	.350	1	0--	-	4.59	5.41
2001 Salt Lake	AAA	21	21	4	0	137.2	578	141	84	76	24	4	4	10	31	0	104	7	1	6	11	.353	0	0--	-	4.36	4.97
2002 Salt Lake	AAA	28	1	0	5	47.0	185	39	18	16	5	0	1	3	6	0	50	3	0	2	2	.500	0	1--	-	2.46	3.06
2001 Anaheim	AL	8	0	0	6	11.0	48	8	1	0	0	0	0	1	7	0	7	2	0	0	0	-	0	0-0	0	3.10	0.00
2002 Anaheim	AL	29	1	0	13	49.0	188	31	13	12	4	1	0	1	21	1	30	3	0	5	3	.625	0	0-0	3	2.35	2.20
2 ML YEARS		37	1	0	19	60.0	236	39	14	12	4	1	0	2	28	1	37	5	0	5	3	.625	0	0-0	3	2.49	1.80

Jason Shiell

Pitches: R Bats: R Pos: RP-3 Ht: 6'0" Wt: 180 Born: 10/19/76 Age: 26

Year Team	Lg	G	GS	CG	GF	IP	BFP	H	R	ER	HR	SH	SF	HB	TBB	IBB	SO	WP	Bk	W	L	Pct	ShO	Sv-Op	Hld	ERC	ERA
1995 Braves	R	12	0	0	9	22.1	101	23	16	11	0	0	0	2	10	1	13	3	0	1	3	.250	0	2--	-	3.89	4.43
1996 Danville	R+	12	12	0	0	59.1	231	44	14	13	1	0	1	1	19	0	57	3	0	3	1	.750	0	0--	-	2.08	1.97
1997 Macon	A	27	24	0	0	129.0	523	113	53	41	12	3	5	8	32	0	101	6	0	10	5	.667	0	0--	-	3.07	2.86
1998 Macon	A	4	3	0	0	8.0	32	7	4	4	2	0	0	0	1	0	8	1	0	1	0	1.000	0	0--	-	3.17	4.50
1999 Myrtle Beach	A+	26	17	0	1	114.2	485	118	51	48	5	4	2	3	36	0	90	9	0	6	7	.462	0	0--	-	3.65	3.77
2000 R Cucamnga	A+	16	14	0	0	81.0	356	73	54	48	9	0	3	6	41	0	80	10	2	7	5	.583	0	0--	-	4.30	5.33
2001 Mobile	AA	45	2	0	8	81.0	353	91	46	40	5	4	8	1	32	2	60	4	0	2	3	.400	0	0--	-	4.56	4.44
2002 Portland	AAA	56	0	0	22	74.1	315	62	26	23	6	0	1	2	29	0	74	2	1	4	3	.571	0	6--	-	3.06	2.78
2002 San Diego	NL	3	0	0	0	1.1	13	7	4	4	0	0	0	0	3	0	1	0	0	0	0	-	0	0-0	0	48.76	27.00

Tsuyoshi Shinjo

Bats: R Throws: R Pos: CF-108; RF-10; PH-2; LF-1; PR-1 Ht: 6'1" Wt: 185 Born: 1/28/72 Age: 31

Year Team	Lg	G	AB	H	2B	3B	HR	(Hm	Rd)	TB	R	RBI	RC	TBB	IBB	SO	HBP	SH	SF	SB	CS	SB%	GDP	Avg	OBP	Slg
2001 Brooklyn	A-	2	7	2	0	0	0	(-	-)	2	0	1	1	1	0	2	0	0	0	0	0	-	1	.286	.375	.286
2002 Fresno	AAA	2	7	0	0	0	0	(-	-)	0	0	0	0	1	0	1	0	0	0	0	0	-	0	.000	.125	.000
2001 New York	NL	123	400	107	23	1	10	(4	6)	162	46	56	50	25	3	70	7	4	2	4	5	.44	8	.268	.320	.405
2002 San Francisco	NL	118	362	86	15	3	9	(4	5)	134	42	37	36	24	2	46	6	3	3	5	0	1.00	5	.238	.294	.370
2 ML YEARS		241	762	193	38	4	19	(8	11)	296	88	93	86	49	5	116	13	7	5	9	5	.64	13	.253	.308	.388

Brian Shouse

Pitches: L Bats: L Pos: RP-23 Ht: 5'11" Wt: 180 Born: 9/26/68 Age: 34

Year Team	Lg	G	GS	CG	GF	IP	BFP	H	R	ER	HR	SH	SF	HB	TBB	IBB	SO	WP	Bk	W	L	Pct	ShO	Sv-Op	Hld	ERC	ERA
2002 Omaha*	AAA	5	0	0	2	2.1	16	7	3	3	0	0	1	1	1	0	2	0	1	0	0	-	0	0--	-	18.83	11.57
2002 New Orleans*	AAA	19	0	0	4	21.0	83	17	10	8	2	0	1	0	3	0	20	0	0	1	0	1.000	0	0--	-	2.08	3.43
1993 Pittsburgh	NL	6	0	0	0	4.0	22	7	4	4	1	0	1	0	2	0	3	1	0	0	0	-	0	0-0	0	9.92	9.00
1998 Boston	AL	7	0	0	4	8.0	36	9	5	5	2	0	0	0	4	0	5	0	0	0	1	.000	0	0-0	1	6.42	5.63
2002 Kansas City	AL	23	0	0	7	14.2	71	15	10	10	3	1	1	2	9	1	11	2	0	0	0	-	0	0-0	0	6.11	6.14
3 ML YEARS		36	0	0	12	26.2	129	31	19	19	6	1	2	2	15	1	19	3	0	0	1	.000	0	0-0	3	6.75	6.41

Paul Shuey

Pitches: R Bats: R Pos: RP-67 Ht: 6'3" Wt: 215 Born: 9/16/70 Age: 32

Year Team	Lg	G	GS	CG	GF	IP	BFP	H	R	ER	HR	SH	SF	HB	TBB	IBB	SO	WP	Bk	W	L	Pct	ShO	Sv-Op	Hld	ERC	ERA
2002 Akron*	AA	2	2	0	0	2.0	8	2	1	1	0	0	0	0	0	0	3	0	0	0	0	-	0	0--	-	1.95	4.50
1994 Cleveland	AL	14	0	0	11	11.2	62	14	11	11	1	0	0	0	12	1	16	4	0	0	1	.000	0	5-5	1	7.28	8.49
1995 Cleveland	AL	7	0	0	3	6.1	28	5	4	3	0	0	2	0	5	0	5	1	0	0	2	.000	0	0-0	0	3.70	4.26
1996 Cleveland	AL	42	0	0	18	53.2	225	45	19	17	6	1	3	0	26	3	44	3	1	5	2	.714	0	4-7	7	3.56	2.85
1997 Cleveland	AL	40	0	0	16	45.0	212	52	31	31	5	4	2	1	28	3	46	2	0	4	2	.667	0	2-3	4	5.92	6.20
1998 Cleveland	AL	43	0	0	16	51.0	222	44	19	17	6	2	0	3	25	5	58	3	0	5	4	.556	0	2-5	12	3.83	3.00
1999 Cleveland	AL	72	0	0	28	81.2	351	68	37	32	8	4	1	1	40	7	103	8	0	8	5	.615	0	6-12	19	3.36	3.53
2000 Cleveland	AL	57	0	0	12	63.2	270	51	25	24	4	1	3	3	30	3	69	0	0	4	2	.667	0	0-5	28	3.11	3.39
2001 Cleveland	AL	47	0	0	18	54.1	244	53	25	17	1	4	2	1	26	5	70	6	0	5	3	.625	0	2-5	9	3.46	2.82
2002 Cle-LA		67	0	0	18	68.0	288	56	29	25	3	1	2	1	31	2	63	3	0	8	2	.800	0	1-5	19	2.95	3.31
2002 Cleveland	AL	39	0	0	12	37.1	150	31	11	10	1	1	1	0	10	1	39	2	0	3	0	1.000	0	0-2	12	2.21	2.41
2002 Los Angeles	NL	28	0	0	6	30.2	138	25	18	15	2	0	1	1	21	1	24	1	0	5	2	.714	0	1-3	7	3.89	4.40
9 ML YEARS		389	0	0	133	435.1	1902	388	200	177	34	19	13	10	223	29	474	30	1	39	23	.629	0	22-47	99	3.70	3.66

Terry Shumpert

Bats: R Throws: R Pos: 2B-60; PH-41; LF-7; SS-2; PR-2; 3B-1; RF-1 Ht: 6'0" Wt: 198 Born: 8/16/66 Age: 36

Year Team	Lg	G	AB	H	2B	3B	HR	(Hm	Rd)	TB	R	RBI	RC	TBB	IBB	SO	HBP	SH	SF	SB	CS	SB%	GDP	Avg	OBP	Slg
1990 Kansas City	AL	32	91	25	6	1	0	(0	0)	33	7	8	8	2	0	17	1	0	2	3	3	.50	4	.275	.292	.363
1991 Kansas City	AL	144	369	80	16	4	5	(1	4)	119	45	34	31	30	0	75	5	10	3	17	11	.61	10	.217	.283	.322
1992 Kansas City	AL	36	94	14	5	1	1	(0	1)	24	6	11	2	3	0	17	0	2	0	2	2	.50	2	.149	.175	.255
1993 Kansas City	AL	8	10	1	0	0	0	(0	0)	1	0	0	0	2	0	2	0	0	0	1	0	1.00	0	.100	.250	.100
1994 Kansas City	AL	64	183	44	6	2	8	(2	6)	78	28	24	26	13	0	39	0	5	1	18	3	.86	5	.240	.289	.426
1995 Boston	AL	21	47	11	3	0	0	(0	0)	14	6	3	4	4	0	13	0	0	0	3	1	.75	0	.234	.294	.298
1996 Chicago	NL	27	31	7	1	0	2	(2	0)	14	5	6	4	2	0	11	1	0	1	0	1	.00	0	.226	.286	.452
1997 San Diego	NL	13	33	9	3	0	1	(0	1)	15	4	6	5	3	0	4	0	0	1	0	0	-	0	.273	.324	.455
1998 Colorado	NL	23	26	6	1	0	1	(0	1)	10	3	2	3	2	0	8	0	0	0	0	0	-	0	.231	.286	.385
1999 Colorado	NL	92	262	91	26	3	10	(8	2)	153	58	37	64	31	2	41	2	4	5	14	0	1.00	2	.347	.413	.584
2000 Colorado	NL	115	263	68	11	7	9	(7	2)	120	52	40	42	28	1	40	6	0	3	8	4	.67	3	.259	.340	.456

Year	Team	Lg	G	AB	H	2B	3B	HR	(Hm	Rd)	TB	R	RBI	RC	TBB	IBB	SO	HBP	SH	SF	SB	CS	SB%	GDP	Avg	OBP	Slg
2001	Colorado	NL	114	242	70	14	5	4	(3	1)	106	37	24	37	15	2	44	3	4	1	14	3	.82	2	.289	.337	.438
2002	Colorado	NL	106	234	55	12	1	6	(4	2)	87	30	21	21	21	0	41	4	5	4	4	1	.80	9	.235	.304	.372
	13 ML YEARS		795	1885	481	104	24	47	(27	20)	774	281	216	247	156	5	352	22	30	21	84	29	.74	33	.255	.316	.411

Ruben Sierra

Bats: B **Throws:** R **Pos:** LF-59; DH-49; PH-17; SS-1; RF-1   **Ht:** 6'1" **Wt:** 215 **Born:** 10/6/65 **Age:** 37

			BATTING																		BASERUNNING				AVERAGES		
Year	Team	Lg	G	AB	H	2B	3B	HR	(Hm	Rd)	TB	R	RBI	RC	TBB	IBB	SO	HBP	SH	SF	SB	CS	SB%	GDP	Avg	OBP	Slg
1986	Texas	AL	113	382	101	13	10	16	(8	8)	182	50	55	52	22	3	65	1	1	5	7	8	.47	8	.264	.302	.476
1987	Texas	AL	158	643	169	35	4	30	(15	15)	302	97	109	86	39	4	114	2	0	12	16	11	.59	18	.263	.302	.470
1988	Texas	AL	156	615	156	32	2	23	(15	8)	261	77	91	78	44	10	91	1	0	8	18	4	.82	15	.254	.301	.424
1989	Texas	AL	162	634	194	35	14	29	(21	8)	344	101	119	118	43	2	82	2	0	10	8	2	.80	7	.306	.347	.543
1990	Texas	AL	159	608	170	37	2	16	(10	6)	259	70	96	84	49	13	86	1	0	8	9	0	1.00	15	.280	.330	.426
1991	Texas	AL	161	661	203	44	5	25	(12	13)	332	110	116	114	56	7	91	0	0	9	16	4	.80	17	.307	.357	.502
1992	Tex-Oak	AL	151	601	167	34	7	17	(10	7)	266	83	87	86	45	12	68	0	0	10	14	4	.78	11	.278	.323	.443
1993	Oakland	AL	158	630	147	23	5	22	(9	13)	246	77	101	70	52	16	97	0	0	10	25	5	.83	17	.233	.288	.390
1994	Oakland	AL	110	426	114	21	1	23	(11	12)	206	71	92	58	23	4	64	0	0	11	8	5	.62	15	.268	.298	.484
1995	Oak-NYY	AL	126	479	126	32	0	19	(8	11)	215	73	86	69	46	4	76	0	0	8	5	4	.56	8	.263	.323	.449
1996	NYY-Det	AL	142	518	128	26	2	12	(4	8)	194	61	72	62	60	12	83	0	0	9	4	4	.50	12	.247	.320	.375
1997	Cin-Tor		39	138	32	5	3	3	(3	0)	52	10	12	14	9	2	34	0	0	1	0	0	-	1	.232	.277	.377
1998	Chicago	AL	27	74	16	4	1	4	(0	4)	34	7	11	8	3	0	11	0	0	0	2	0	1.00	0	.216	.247	.459
2000	Texas	AL	20	60	14	0	0	1	(0	1)	17	5	7	5	4	0	9	0	0	0	1	0	1.00	1	.233	.281	.283
2001	Texas	AL	94	344	100	22	1	23	(13	10)	193	55	67	58	19	0	52	0	0	6	2	0	1.00	13	.291	.322	.561
2002	Seattle	AL	122	419	113	23	0	13	(6	7)	175	47	60	47	31	5	66	0	0	2	4	0	1.00	17	.270	.319	.418
1992	Texas	AL	124	500	139	30	6	14	(8	6)	223	66	70	70	31	6	59	0	0	8	12	4	.75	9	.278	.315	.446
1992	Oakland	AL	27	101	28	4	1	3	(2	1)	43	17	17	16	14	6	9	0	0	2	2	0	1.00	2	.277	.359	.426
1995	Oakland	AL	70	264	70	17	0	12	(3	9)	123	40	42	40	24	2	42	0	0	3	4	4	.50	2	.265	.323	.466
1995	New York	AL	56	215	56	15	0	7	(5	2)	92	33	44	29	22	2	34	0	0	5	1	0	1.00	6	.260	.322	.428
1996	New York	AL	96	360	93	17	1	11	(4	7)	145	39	52	46	40	11	58	0	0	7	1	3	.25	10	.258	.327	.403
1996	Detroit	AL	46	158	35	9	1	1	(0	1)	49	22	20	16	20	1	25	0	0	2	3	1	.75	2	.222	.306	.310
1997	Cincinnati	NL	25	90	22	5	1	2	(2	0)	35	6	7	10	6	1	21	0	0	0	0	0	-	1	.244	.292	.389
1997	Toronto	AL	14	48	10	0	2	1	(1	0)	17	4	5	4	3	1	13	0	0	1	0	0	-	0	.208	.250	.354
	16 ML YEARS		1898	7232	1950	386	57	276	(145	131)	3278	994	1181	1009	545	94	1089	7	1	109	139	51	.73	177	.270	.317	.453

Carlos Silva

Pitches: R **Bats:** R **Pos:** RP-68   **Ht:** 6'4" **Wt:** 225 **Born:** 4/23/79 **Age:** 24

			HOW MUCH HE PITCHED						WHAT HE GAVE UP										THE RESULTS						
Year	Team	Lg	G	GS	CG	GF	IP	BFP	H	R	ER	HR	SH	SF	HB	TBB	IBB	SO	WP	Bk	W	L	Pct	ShO	Sv-Op	Hld	ERC	ERA
1996	Martinsville	R+	7	1	0	1	18.0	78	20	11	8	1	4	1	1	5	0	16	0	0	0	0	-	0	0--	-	4.13	4.00
1997	Martinsville	R+	11	11	0	0	57.2	252	66	46	33	9	3	2	1	14	0	31	6	3	2	2	.500	0	0--	-	4.66	5.15
1998	Martinsville	R+	7	7	1	0	41.0	180	48	24	23	2	2	3	2	4	0	21	3	2	1	4	.200	0	0--	-	3.51	5.05
1998	Batavia	A-	9	7	0	0	45.1	206	61	37	32	4	0	1	2	9	0	27	2	0	2	3	.400	0	0--	-	5.27	6.35
1999	Piedmont	A	26	26	3	0	164.1	708	176	79	57	6	8	6	9	41	2	99	8	2	11	8	.579	1	0--	-	3.60	3.12
2000	Clearwater	A+	26	24	4	0	176.1	778	229	99	70	7	6	5	11	26	1	82	4	2	8	13	.381	0	0--	-	4.55	3.57
2001	Reading	AA	28	28	4	0	180.0	740	197	85	78	20	6	2	11	27	0	100	3	0	15	8	.652	1	0--	-	4.05	3.90
2002	Reading	AA	2	0	0	0	3.0	10	0	0	0	0	0	0	0	0	0	1	0	0	0	0	-	0	1--	-	0.00	0.00
2002	Philadelphia	NL	68	0	0	21	84.0	350	88	34	30	4	9	3	4	22	6	41	3	0	5	0	1.000	0	1-5	8	3.60	3.21

Jose Silva

Pitches: R **Bats:** R **Pos:** RP-12   **Ht:** 6'6" **Wt:** 235 **Born:** 12/19/73 **Age:** 29

			HOW MUCH HE PITCHED						WHAT HE GAVE UP										THE RESULTS						
Year	Team	Lg	G	GS	CG	GF	IP	BFP	H	R	ER	HR	SH	SF	HB	TBB	IBB	SO	WP	Bk	W	L	Pct	ShO	Sv-Op	Hld	ERC	ERA
2002	Louisville*	AAA	20	3	0	4	35.2	151	41	15	9	1	2	1	0	4	0	28	3	0	1	2	.333	0	1--	-	3.24	2.27
1996	Toronto	AL	2	0	0	0	2.0	11	5	3	3	1	0	0	0	0	0	0	0	0	0	0	-	0	0-0	0	15.86	13.50
1997	Pittsburgh	NL	11	4	0	0	36.1	174	52	26	24	4	4	3	1	16	3	30	0	1	2	1	.667	0	0-0	0	6.88	5.94
1998	Pittsburgh	NL	18	18	1	0	100.1	425	104	55	49	7	5	5	1	30	2	64	2	2	6	7	.462	0	0-0	0	3.70	4.40
1999	Pittsburgh	NL	34	12	0	9	97.1	433	108	70	62	10	3	3	3	39	0	77	4	3	2	8	.200	0	4-5	2	4.84	5.73
2000	Pittsburgh	NL	51	19	1	12	136.0	631	178	96	84	16	9	5	5	50	7	98	6	1	11	9	.550	0	0-2	1	5.91	5.56
2001	Pittsburgh	NL	26	0	0	10	32.0	160	35	24	24	6	2	0	0	9	1	23	0	0	3	3	.500	0	0-2	2	4.59	6.75
2002	Cincinnati	NL	12	0	0	1	23.1	100	25	11	11	3	2	1	3	10	3	6	2	0	1	0	1.000	0	0-0	0	5.43	4.24
	7 ML YEARS		154	53	2	32	427.1	1914	507	285	257	47	25	17	13	154	16	298	14	7	25	28	.472	0	4-9	5	5.12	5.41

Randall Simon

Bats: L **Throws:** L **Pos:** DH-65; 1B-59; PH-6   **Ht:** 6'0" **Wt:** 230 **Born:** 5/26/75 **Age:** 28

			BATTING																		BASERUNNING				AVERAGES		
Year	Team	Lg	G	AB	H	2B	3B	HR	(Hm	Rd)	TB	R	RBI	RC	TBB	IBB	SO	HBP	SH	SF	SB	CS	SB%	GDP	Avg	OBP	Slg
1997	Atlanta	NL	13	14	6	1	0	0	(0	0)	7	2	1	3	1	0	2	0	0	0	0	0	-	1	.429	.467	.500
1998	Atlanta	NL	7	16	3	0	0	0	(0	0)	3	2	4	0	0	0	1	0	0	1	0	0	-	0	.188	.176	.188
1999	Atlanta	NL	90	218	69	16	0	5	(2	3)	100	26	25	33	17	6	25	1	0	1	2	2	.50	10	.317	.367	.459
2001	Detroit	AL	81	256	78	14	2	6	(1	5)	114	28	37	36	15	2	28	0	1	2	0	1	.00	9	.305	.341	.445
2002	Detroit	AL	130	482	145	17	1	19	(13	6)	221	51	82	68	13	5	30	4	0	7	0	1	.00	13	.301	.320	.459
	5 ML YEARS		321	986	301	48	3	30	(16	14)	445	109	149	140	46	13	86	5	1	11	2	4	.33	33	.305	.336	.451

Jason Simontacchi

Pitches: R **Bats:** R **Pos:** SP-24   **Ht:** 6'2" **Wt:** 185 **Born:** 11/13/73 **Age:** 29

			HOW MUCH HE PITCHED						WHAT HE GAVE UP									THE RESULTS						
Year Team	Lg	G	GS	CG	GF	IP	BFP	H	R	ER	HR	SH	SF	HB	TBB	IBB	SO	WP	Bk	W	L	Pct	ShO	Sv-Op	Hld	ERC	ERA
1996 Spokane	A-	14	6	0	3	47.0	214	59	37	27	8	3	3	3	15	0	43	1	0	2	5	.286	0	2--	-	6.02	5.17
1997 Lansing	A	29	1	0	11	60.2	295	93	56	47	7	3	4	4	15	1	38	1	2	3	7	.300	0	2--	-	6.82	6.97
1998 Springfield	IND	16	16	3	0	110.0	451	103	43	36	14	7	0	6	21	3	92	4	1	10	2	.833	1	0--	-	3.28	2.95
1999 Hickory	A	23	7	0	8	69.1	297	71	34	31	8	2	1	6	19	1	66	5	3	4	6	.400	0	1--	-	4.15	4.02
2001 Edmonton	AAA	32	18	2	3	143.1	627	192	97	85	21	3	7	6	23	1	83	4	0	7	13	.350	0	0--	-	5.67	5.34
2002 Memphis	AAA	6	6	0	0	42.1	170	44	12	11	2	3	0	1	5	1	28	0	0	5	1	.833	0	0--	-	2.99	2.34
2002 St Louis	NL	24	24	0	0	143.1	600	134	68	64	18	6	4	6	54	4	72	1	0	11	5	.688	0	0-0	0	4.01	4.02

Chris Singleton

Bats: L **Throws:** L **Pos:** CF-126; PH-9; PR-8; DH-1   **Ht:** 6'2" **Wt:** 210 **Born:** 8/15/72 **Age:** 30

					BATTING															BASERUNNING				AVERAGES		
Year Team	Lg	G	AB	H	2B	3B	HR	(Hm	Rd)	TB	R	RBI	RC	TBB	IBB	SO	HBP	SH	SF	SB	CS	SB%	GDP	Avg	OBP	Slg
1999 Chicago	AL	133	496	149	31	6	17	(5	12)	243	72	72	79	22	1	45	1	4	6	20	5	.80	10	.300	.328	.490
2000 Chicago	AL	147	511	130	22	5	11	(5	6)	195	83	62	61	35	2	85	1	12	4	22	7	.76	6	.254	.301	.382
2001 Chicago	AL	140	392	117	21	5	7	(4	3)	169	57	45	54	20	2	61	1	14	4	12	11	.52	5	.298	.331	.431
2002 Baltimore	AL	136	466	122	30	6	9	(4	5)	191	67	50	56	21	0	83	4	6	5	20	2	.91	8	.262	.296	.410
4 ML YEARS		556	1865	518	104	22	44	(18	26)	798	279	229	250	98	5	274	7	36	19	74	25	.75	29	.278	.313	.428

Aaron Small

Pitches: R **Bats:** R **Pos:** RP-1   **Ht:** 6'5" **Wt:** 237 **Born:** 11/23/71 **Age:** 31

					HOW MUCH HE PITCHED						WHAT HE GAVE UP								THE RESULTS						
Year Team	Lg	G	GS	CG	GF	IP	BFP	H	R	ER	HR	SH	SF	HB	TBB	IBB	SO	WP	Bk	W	L	Pct	ShO	Sv-Op	Hld	ERC	ERA
2002 Richmond*	AAA	14	4	0	3	31.0	154	48	27	22	2	2	4	2	14	1	19	1	0	0	3	.000	0	0--	-	7.51	6.39
2002 Braves*	R	5	5	0	0	6.0	18	9	4	4	0		0	0	0	0	3	1	0	0	0	-	0	0--	-	6.98	6.00
1994 Toronto	AL	1	0	0	1	2.0	13	5	2	2	1	0	1	0	2		0	0	0	0	0	-	0	0-0	0	21.61	9.00
1995 Florida	NL	7	0	0	1	6.1	32	7	2	1	1	0	0	0	6	0	5	0	0	1	0	1.000	0	0-0	0	7.30	1.42
1996 Oakland	AL	12	3	0	4	28.2	144	37	28	26	3	0	1	1	22	1	17	2	0	1	3	.250	0	0-0	0	7.42	8.16
1997 Oakland	AL	71	0	0	22	96.2	425	109	50	46	6	5	6	3	40	6	57	4	0	9	5	.643	0	4-6	8	4.67	4.28
1998 Oak-Ari	AL	47	0	0	13	67.2	304	83	48	42	8	5	1	4	22	4	33	4	0	4	2	.667	0	0-2	4	5.38	5.59
2002 Atlanta	NL	1	0	0	1	0.1	5	2	1	1	0	0	0	0	0	0	0	0	0	0	0	-	0	0-0	0	71.88	27.00
1998 Oakland	AL	24	0	0	4	36.0	174	51	34	29	3	3	1	3	14	3	19	4	0	1	1	.500	0	0-0	3	6.49	7.25
1998 Arizona	NL	23	0	0	9	31.2	130	32	14	13	5	2	0	1	8	1	14	0	0	3	1	.750	0	0-2	1	4.14	3.69
6 ML YEARS		139	3	0	42	201.2	923	243	131	118	19	10	9	8	94	11	113	11	0	15	10	.600	0	4-8	12	5.59	5.27

Bobby Smith

Bats: R **Throws:** R **Pos:** 3B-10; 1B-6; LF-1; RF-1; DH-1; PR-1   **Ht:** 6'3" **Wt:** 199 **Born:** 5/10/74 **Age:** 29

					BATTING															BASERUNNING				AVERAGES		
Year Team	Lg	G	AB	H	2B	3B	HR	(Hm	Rd)	TB	R	RBI	RC	TBB	IBB	SO	HBP	SH	SF	SB	CS	SB%	GDP	Avg	OBP	Slg
2002 Indianapolis*	AAA	80	293	70	21	0	7	(-	-)	112	26	31	34	25	0	57	4	2	1	11	2	.85	8	.239	.307	.382
1998 Tampa Bay	AL	117	370	102	15	3	11	(4	7)	156	44	55	52	34	0	110	6	2	4	5	3	.63	9	.276	.343	.422
1999 Tampa Bay	AL	68	199	36	4	1	3	(1	2)	51	18	19	8	16	0	64	1	2	1	4	4	.50	8	.181	.244	.256
2000 Tampa Bay	AL	49	175	41	8	0	6	(2	4)	67	21	26	18	14	1	59	1	0	1	2	2	.50	6	.234	.293	.383
2001 Tampa Bay	AL	6	19	2	0	0	0	(0	0)	2	1	1	0	3	0	10	0	0	0	0	0	-	1	.105	.227	.105
2002 Tampa Bay	AL	18	63	11	2	0	1	(1	0)	16	4	6	4	3	0	25	0	0	0	0	0	-	0	.175	.212	.254
5 ML YEARS		258	826	192	29	4	21	(8	13)	292	88	107	82	70	1	268	8	4	6	11	9	.55	24	.232	.297	.354

Bud Smith

Pitches: L **Bats:** L **Pos:** SP-10; RP-1   **Ht:** 6'0" **Wt:** 170 **Born:** 10/23/79 **Age:** 23

					HOW MUCH HE PITCHED						WHAT HE GAVE UP								THE RESULTS						
Year Team	Lg	G	GS	CG	GF	IP	BFP	H	R	ER	HR	SH	SF	HB	TBB	IBB	SO	WP	Bk	W	L	Pct	ShO	Sv-Op	Hld	ERC	ERA
1998 Johnson City	R+	14	14	0	0	64.1	305	85	47	37	9	2	3	2	34	1	65	2	0	3	3	.500	0	0--	-	7.02	5.18
1999 Peoria	A	9	9	0	0	54.0	219	53	20	17	4	1	3	2	16	0	59	2	1	4	1	.800	0	0--	-	3.71	2.83
1999 Potomac	A+	18	18	0	0	103.1	433	91	47	34	2	3	2	9	32	0	93	4	0	4	9	.308	0	0--	-	2.88	2.96
2000 Arkansas	AA	18	18	3	0	108.2	439	93	32	28	5	2	3	4	27	1	102	5	0	12	1	.923	3	0--	-	2.55	2.32
2000 Memphis	AAA	9	8	0	0	54.1	213	40	24	13	4	2	1	1	15	0	34	0	0	5	1	.833	0	0--	-	2.20	2.15
2001 Memphis	AAA	17	17	0	0	108.0	462	114	38	33	6	6	5	4	28	2	78	1	1	8	5	.615	0	0--	-	3.62	2.75
2002 Memphis	AAA	6	6	0	0	38.0	158	33	10	9	1	0	1	2	13	0	34	0	0	3	0	1.000	0	0--	-	2.87	2.13
2002 Scrtn/WlksBr	AAA	3	3	0	0	17.1	74	21	8	8	0	0	0	1	6	0	11	0	0	1	0	1.000	0	0--	-	4.82	4.15
2001 St Louis	NL	16	14	1	1	84.2	351	79	40	36	12	9	1	1	24	5	59	0	0	6	3	.667	1	0-0	0	3.50	3.83
2002 St Louis	NL	11	10	0	1	48.0	229	67	39	37	4	2	4	3	22	2	22	0	1	1	5	.167	0	0-0	0	6.78	6.94
2 ML YEARS		27	24	1	2	132.2	580	146	79	73	16	11	5	4	46	7	81	0	1	7	8	.467	1	0-0	0	4.63	4.95

Dan Smith

Pitches: R **Bats:** R **Pos:** RP-33   **Ht:** 6'3" **Wt:** 210 **Born:** 9/15/75 **Age:** 27

					HOW MUCH HE PITCHED						WHAT HE GAVE UP								THE RESULTS						
Year Team	Lg	G	GS	CG	GF	IP	BFP	H	R	ER	HR	SH	SF	HB	TBB	IBB	SO	WP	Bk	W	L	Pct	ShO	Sv-Op	Hld	ERC	ERA
2002 Ottawa*	AAA	14	14	1	0	83.1	335	72	30	30	10	4	2	2	18	1	61	0	0	5	4	.556	0	0--	-	2.90	3.24
1999 Montreal	NL	20	17	0	0	89.2	407	104	64	60	12	7	2	4	39	2	72	3	0	4	9	.308	0	0-1	0	5.59	6.02
2000 Boston	AL	2	0	0	0	3.1	15	2	3	3	0	1	3	0	3	0	1	0	0	0	0	-	0	0-0	0	2.96	8.10
2002 Montreal	NL	33	0	0	13	46.2	188	34	18	18	6	2	2	1	21	0	34	1	0	1	1	.500	0	2-2	2	3.17	3.47
3 ML YEARS		55	17	0	13	139.2	610	140	85	81	18	10	7	5	63	0	107	4	0	5	10	.333	0	2-3	2	4.68	5.22

Jason Smith

Bats: L Throws: R Pos: 3B-12; SS-9; PH-5; PR-3; 2B-1; DH-1 Ht: 6'3" Wt: 199 Born: 7/24/77 Age: 25

Year Team	Lg	G	AB	H	2B	3B	HR	Hm	Rd	TB	R	RBI	RC	TBB	IBB	SO	HBP	SH	SF	SB	CS	SB%	GDP	Avg	OBP	Slg
1997 Williamsport	A-	51	205	59	5	2	0	-	-	68	25	11	23	10	0	44	0	0	0	9	2	.82	0	.288	.321	.332
1997 Rockford	A	9	33	6	0	1	0	-	-	8	4	3	1	2	0	11	0	0	0	1	0	1.00	1	.182	.229	.242
1998 Rockford	A	126	464	111	15	9	7	-	-	165	67	60	50	31	1	122	1	1	6	23	6	.79	2	.239	.286	.356
1999 Daytona	A+	39	142	37	5	2	5	-	-	61	22	26	21	12	3	29	3	0	1	9	3	.75	2	.261	.329	.430
2000 W Tennessee	AA	119	481	114	22	7	12	-	-	186	55	61	48	22	3	130	2	2	1	16	10	.62	7	.237	.273	.387
2001 Iowa	AAA	70	240	56	8	6	4	-	-	88	31	15	22	12	4	71	1	1	2	6	3	.67	4	.233	.271	.367
2001 Durham	AAA	8	31	6	1	0	0	-	-	7	2	3	1	0	0	11	0	1	0	0	0	--	0	.194	.194	.226
2002 Durham	AAA	54	206	57	11	2	4	-	-	84	29	28	27	10	1	44	1	2	1	5	1	.83	2	.277	.312	.408
2001 Chicago	NL	2	1	0	0	0	0	0	0	0	0	0	0	0	0	1	0	0	0	0	0	--	0	.000	.000	.000
2002 Tampa Bay	AL	26	65	13	1	2	1	0	1	21	9	6	5	2	0	24	0	2	0	3	0	1.00	0	.200	.224	.323
2 ML YEARS		28	66	13	1	2	1	0	1	21	9	6	5	2	0	25	0	2	0	3	0	1.00	0	.197	.221	.318

Mike Smith

Pitches: R Bats: R Pos: RP-8; SP-6 Ht: 5'11" Wt: 195 Born: 9/19/77 Age: 25

Year Team	Lg	G	GS	CG	GF	IP	BFP	H	R	ER	HR	SH	SF	HB	TBB	IBB	SO	WP	Bk	W	L	Pct	ShO	Sv-Op	Hld	ERC	ERA
2000 Queens	A-	14	12	0	0	51.0	205	41	18	13	1	1	2	2	17	0	55	9	1	2	2	.500	0	0--	-	2.48	2.29
2001 Chrlstn - WV	A	14	14	2	0	94.1	378	78	32	22	2	1	2	6	21	0	85	6	0	5	5	.500	1	0--	-	2.28	2.10
2001 Tennessee	AA	14	14	1	0	93.0	393	80	32	25	7	4	1	8	26	2	77	6	0	6	2	.750	0	0--	-	2.93	2.42
2002 Syracuse	AAA	20	20	1	0	121.2	505	106	51	47	10	0	3	6	43	0	76	3	0	8	4	.667	1	0--	-	3.31	3.48
2002 Toronto	AL	14	6	0	3	35.1	174	43	28	26	3	3	1	7	20	0	16	2	0	0	3	.000	0	0-0	0	6.66	6.62

Roy Smith

Pitches: R Bats: R Pos: RP-3; SP-1 Ht: 6'6" Wt: 235 Born: 5/18/76 Age: 27

Year Team	Lg	G	GS	CG	GF	IP	BFP	H	R	ER	HR	SH	SF	HB	TBB	IBB	SO	WP	Bk	W	L	Pct	ShO	Sv-Op	Hld	ERC	ERA
1994 Mariners	R	11	5	0	1	45.0	164	30	9	8	2	1	1	4	0	35	2	0	3	1	.750	0	0--	-	1.32	1.60	
1995 Wisconsin	A	27	27	1	0	149.0	669	179	100	89	9	5	2	3	54	2	109	10	2	7	14	.333	0	0--	-	4.82	5.38
1996 Wisconsin	A	27	27	0	0	146.0	679	164	113	83	9	6	4	8	73	3	99	11	2	6	13	.316	0	0--	-	4.98	5.12
1997 Wisconsin	A	18	11	0	0	66.0	304	81	50	41	3	1	2	2	31	0	38	14	2	4	4	.429	0	0--	-	5.39	5.59
1997 Memphis	AA	4	0	0	3	4.1	20	6	5	5	0	0	1	0	1	0	6	1	0	0	0	--	0	0--	-	4.72	10.38
1998 St.Paul	IND	18	18	1	0	105.2	467	119	75	59	10	3	3	1	36	0	74	6	0	6	7	.462	1	0--	-	4.51	5.03
1999 St.Paul	IND	8	7	1	0	42.0	182	38	18	15	3	1	0	1	23	0	43	1	0	4	2	.667	1	0--	-	4.05	3.21
2000 Kinston	A+	21	0	0	9	45.0	183	35	15	14	0	0	1	3	21	1	45	3	0	2	2	.500	0	2--	-	2.79	2.80
2000 Akron	AA	18	0	0	15	55.0	217	36	14	12	0	4	0	1	22	2	50	6	0	5	1	.833	0	6--	-	1.75	1.96
2001 Buffalo	AAA	48	0	0	31	74.0	307	59	25	18	2	6	1	8	29	4	86	3	0	0	5	.000	0	18--	-	2.83	2.19
2002 Buffalo	AAA	36	3	0	12	70.1	305	65	37	30	2	2	4	6	29	0	65	3	0	5	4	.556	0	1--	-	3.51	3.84
2001 Cleveland	AL	9	0	0	2	16.1	80	16	14	11	3	0	0	2	13	1	17	0	0	0	0	--	0	0-0	1	6.49	6.06
2002 Cleveland	AL	4	1	0	1	6.0	35	9	4	2	1	0	0	1	5	0	2	0	0	0	0	--	0	0-0	0	9.63	3.00
2 ML YEARS		13	1	0	3	22.1	115	25	18	13	4	0	0	3	18	1	19	0	0	0	0	--	0	0-0	1	7.32	5.24

Travis Smith

Pitches: R Bats: R Pos: SP-10; RP-2 Ht: 5'10" Wt: 165 Born: 11/7/72 Age: 30

Year Team	Lg	G	GS	CG	GF	IP	BFP	H	R	ER	HR	SH	SF	HB	TBB	IBB	SO	WP	Bk	W	L	Pct	ShO	Sv-Op	Hld	ERC	ERA
1995 Helena	R+	20	7	0	11	56.0	224	41	16	15	4	0	0	7	19	0	63	4	2	4	2	.667	0	5--	-	2.81	2.41
1996 Stockton	A+	14	6	0	3	58.2	241	56	17	12	4	1	0	4	21	0	48	2	4	7	1	.857	0	1--	-	3.89	1.84
1996 El Paso	AA	17	17	3	0	107.2	478	119	56	50	6	4	5	6	39	0	68	2	0	7	4	.636	1	0--	-	4.40	4.18
1997 El Paso	AA	28	28	5	0	184.1	805	210	106	85	12	7	5	7	58	2	107	7	3	16	3	.842	1	0--	-	4.43	4.15
1998 Louisville	AAA	12	11	0	0	67.2	296	77	44	40	9	3	4	2	25	1	36	3	0	4	6	.400	0	0--	-	5.17	5.32
1999 Ogden	R+	1	1	0	0	1.0	5	1	0	0	0	0	0	1	0	0	3	0	0	0	0	--	0	0--	-	0.76	0.00
1999 Stockton	A+	3	3	0	0	7.1	35	9	6	5	1	1	0	1	3	0	8	0	0	0	2	.000	0	0--	-	6.16	6.14
1999 Huntsville	AA	7	7	0	0	38.1	171	40	27	25	3	2	2	0	18	0	23	3	1	3	2	.600	0	0--	-	4.38	5.87
2000 Huntsville	AA	27	24	1	1	154.1	631	141	77	64	13	4	2	5	37	0	113	3	1	12	7	.632	1	0--	-	3.04	3.73
2000 Indianapolis	AAA	3	3	0	0	10.2	58	19	18	15	6	1	1	1	9	1	5	0	0	1	1	.500	0	0--	-	16.70	12.66
2001 Round Rock	AA	29	22	1	1	160.1	653	154	66	55	7	5	4	5	26	0	85	2	0	15	8	.652	0	1--	-	2.72	3.09
2001 New Orleans	AAA	1	0	0	0	2.0	10	3	0	0	0	0	0	0	1	0	0	0	0	0	0	--	0	0--	-	6.48	0.00
2002 Memphis	AAA	16	13	1	0	85.2	341	76	24	22	7	4	3	1	14	1	62	0	0	4	7	.364	0	0--	-	2.52	2.31
1998 Milwaukee	NL	1	0	0	0	2.0	7	1	0	0	0	0	0	0	0	0	1	1	0	0	0	--	0	0-0	0	0.54	0.00
2002 St Louis	NL	12	10	0	0	54.0	244	69	44	43	10	7	0	3	20	0	32	2	0	4	2	.667	0	0-0	0	6.63	7.17
2 ML YEARS		13	10	0	0	56.0	251	70	44	43	10	7	0	3	20	0	33	2	0	4	2	.667	0	0-0	0	6.32	6.91

John Smoltz

Pitches: R Bats: R Pos: RP-75 Ht: 6'3" Wt: 220 Born: 5/15/67 Age: 36

Year Team	Lg	G	GS	CG	GF	IP	BFP	H	R	ER	HR	SH	SF	HB	TBB	IBB	SO	WP	Bk	W	L	Pct	ShO	Sv-Op	Hld	ERC	ERA
1988 Atlanta	NL	12	12	0	0	64.0	297	74	40	39	10	2	0	2	33	4	37	2	1	2	7	.222	0	0-0	0	5.86	5.48
1989 Atlanta	NL	29	29	5	0	208.0	847	160	79	68	15	10	7	2	72	2	168	8	3	12	11	.522	0	0-0	0	2.50	2.94
1990 Atlanta	NL	34	34	6	0	231.1	966	206	109	99	20	9	8	1	90	3	170	14	3	14	11	.560	2	0-0	0	3.37	3.85
1991 Atlanta	NL	36	36	5	0	229.2	947	206	101	97	16	9	9	3	77	1	148	20	2	14	13	.519	2	0-0	0	3.15	3.80
1992 Atlanta	NL	35	35	9	0	246.2	1021	206	90	78	17	7	8	5	80	5	215	17	1	15	12	.556	3	0-0	0	2.73	2.85
1993 Atlanta	NL	35	35	3	0	243.2	1028	208	104	98	23	13	4	6	100	12	208	13	1	15	11	.577	3	0-0	0	3.29	3.62
1994 Atlanta	NL	21	21	1	0	134.2	568	120	69	62	15	7	6	4	48	4	113	7	0	6	10	.375	0	0-0	0	3.44	4.14
1995 Atlanta	NL	29	29	2	0	192.2	808	166	76	68	15	13	5	4	72	8	193	13	0	12	7	.632	1	0-0	0	3.08	3.18
1996 Atlanta	NL	35	35	6	0	253.2	995	199	93	83	19	12	4	2	55	5	276	10	1	24	8	.750	2	0-0	0	2.17	2.94
1997 Atlanta	NL	35	35	7	0	256.0	1043	234	97	86	21	10	3	1	63	9	241	10	1	15	12	.556	2	0-0	0	2.89	3.02
1998 Atlanta	NL	26	26	3	0	167.2	681	145	58	54	10	4	2	4	44	2	173	3	1	17	3	.850	2	0-0	0	2.67	2.90

Year Team	Lg	G	GS	CG	GF	IP	BFP	H	R	ER	HR	SH	SF	HB	TBB	IBB	SO	WP	Bk	W	L	Pct	ShO	Sv-Op	Hld	ERC	ERA
1999 Atlanta	NL	29	29	1	0	186.1	746	168	70	66	14	10	5	4	40	2	156	2	0	11	8	.579	1	0-0	0	2.81	3.19
2001 Atlanta	NL	36	5	0	20	59.0	238	53	24	22	7	1	2	2	10	2	57	0	0	3	3	.500	0	10-11	5	2.85	3.36
2002 Atlanta	NL	75	0	0	68	80.1	314	59	30	29	4	2	1	1	24	1	85	1	1	3	2	.600	0	55-59	0	2.06	3.25
14 ML YEARS		467	361	47	88	2553.2	10499	2204	1040	949	206	109	64	40	808	58	2240	120	15	163	118	.580	14	65-70	5	2.93	3.34

Steve Smyth

Pitches: L Bats: L Pos: SP-7; RP-1

Ht: 6'1" Wt: 195 Born: 6/3/78 Age: 25

Year Team	Lg	G	GS	CG	GF	IP	BFP	H	R	ER	HR	SH	SF	HB	TBB	IBB	SO	WP	Bk	W	L	Pct	ShO	Sv-Op	Hld	ERC	ERA
1999 Eugene	A-	5	5	0	0	24.2	110	29	17	12	2	1	3	0	7	0	14	2	1	1	1	.500	0	0- -	-	4.36	4.38
1999 Lansing	A	10	10	0	0	50.2	238	68	40	39	5	0	2	2	30	0	46	6	0	5	3	.625	0	0- -	-	7.36	6.93
2000 Daytona	A+	24	23	1	0	138.1	589	134	62	50	9	0	2	5	57	0	100	9	1	8	8	.500	0	0- -	-	3.91	3.25
2001 W Tennessee	AA	18	18	3	0	120.1	497	110	38	34	9	4	1	5	40	1	93	6	0	3	1	.750	1	0- -	-	3.39	2.54
2002 W Tennessee	AA	11	11	0	0	73.0	304	62	34	29	7	6	2	6	18	0	74	0	0	4	4	.500	0	0- -	-	2.92	3.58
2002 Iowa	AAA	6	6	0	0	31.0	135	35	21	20	4	1	2	0	10	0	25	0	0	3	2	.600	0	0- -	-	4.71	5.81
2002 Chicago	NL	8	7	0	0	26.0	122	34	28	27	9	1	4	1	10	0	16	2	0	1	3	.250	0	0-0	0	7.88	9.35

Esix Snead

Bats: B Throws: R Pos: PR-10; CF-5; PH-4; LF-1

Ht: 5'10" Wt: 175 Born: 6/7/76 Age: 27

Year Team	Lg	G	AB	H	2B	3B	HR	Hm	Rd	TB	R	RBI	RC	TBB	IBB	SO	HBP	SH	SF	SB	CS	SB%	GDP	Avg	OBP	Slg
1998 New Jersey	A-	58	193	45	4	4	1	-	-	60	38	16	29	33	0	54	7	1	0	42	11	.79	3	.233	.365	.311
1999 Potomac	A+	67	249	45	8	5	0	-	-	63	37	14	21	32	0	57	4	3	3	35	12	.74	2	.181	.281	.253
1999 Peoria	A	59	181	35	7	1	2	-	-	50	35	18	21	35	0	42	2	7	1	29	9	.76	3	.193	.329	.276
2000 Potomac	A+	132	493	116	14	3	1	-	-	139	82	34	60	72	1	98	7	9	1	109	35	.76	7	.235	.340	.282
2001 New Haven	AA	133	520	121	21	6	1	-	-	157	71	33	54	44	0	115	12	5	1	64	23	.74	4	.233	.307	.302
2002 Binghamton	AA	125	401	101	9	6	3	-	-	131	62	42	53	45	0	72	6	16	2	66	18	.79	4	.252	.335	.327
2002 New York	NL	17	13	4	0	0	1	1	0	7	3	3	3	1	0	4	0	0	0	4	3	.57	0	.308	.357	.538

Chris Snelling

Bats: L Throws: L Pos: LF-6; RF-2

Ht: 5'10" Wt: 165 Born: 12/3/81 Age: 21

Year Team	Lg	G	AB	H	2B	3B	HR	Hm	Rd	TB	R	RBI	RC	TBB	IBB	SO	HBP	SH	SF	SB	CS	SB%	GDP	Avg	OBP	Slg
1999 Everett	A-	12	40	11	0	1	0	-	-	13	9	2	3	1	0	4	0	0	0	2	1	.67	1	.275	.293	.325
2000 Wisconsin	A	72	259	79	9	5	9	-	-	125	44	56	50	34	3	34	6	1	9	7	4	.64	2	.305	.386	.483
2001 Sn Brnardino	A+	114	450	151	29	10	7	-	-	221	90	73	92	45	4	63	21	2	3	12	5	.71	7	.336	.418	.491
2002 San Antonio	AA	23	89	29	9	2	1	-	-	45	10	12	20	12	3	11	4	3	0	5	1	.83	5	.326	.429	.506
2002 Seattle	AL	8	27	4	0	0	1	0	1	7	2	3	2	2	0	4	0	0	0	0	0	-	2	.148	.207	.259

J.T. Snow

Bats: L Throws: L Pos: 1B-135; PH-13

Ht: 6'2" Wt: 209 Born: 2/26/68 Age: 35

Year Team	Lg	G	AB	H	2B	3B	HR	Hm	Rd	TB	R	RBI	RC	TBB	IBB	SO	HBP	SH	SF	SB	CS	SB%	GDP	Avg	OBP	Slg
1992 New York	AL	7	14	2	1	0	0	0	0	3	1	2	2	5	1	5	0	0	0	0	0	-	0	.143	.368	.214
1993 Anaheim	AL	129	419	101	18	2	16	10	6	171	60	57	57	55	4	88	2	7	6	3	0	1.00	10	.241	.328	.408
1994 Anaheim	AL	61	223	49	4	0	8	7	1	77	22	30	22	19	1	48	3	2	1	0	1	.00	7	.220	.289	.345
1995 Anaheim	AL	143	544	157	22	1	24	14	10	253	80	102	85	52	4	91	3	5	2	2	1	.67	16	.289	.353	.465
1996 Anaheim	AL	155	575	148	20	1	17	8	9	221	69	67	67	56	6	96	5	2	3	1	6	.14	19	.257	.327	.384
1997 San Francisco	NL	157	531	149	36	1	28	14	14	271	81	104	105	96	13	124	1	2	7	6	4	.60	8	.281	.387	.510
1998 San Francisco	NL	138	435	108	29	1	15	9	6	184	65	79	60	58	3	84	0	0	7	1	2	.33	12	.248	.332	.423
1999 San Francisco	NL	161	570	156	25	2	24	7	17	257	93	98	93	86	7	121	5	1	6	0	4	.00	16	.274	.370	.451
2000 San Francisco	NL	155	536	152	33	2	19	10	9	246	82	96	87	66	6	129	11	0	14	1	3	.25	20	.284	.365	.459
2001 San Francisco	NL	101	285	70	12	1	8	5	3	108	43	34	44	55	10	81	4	0	4	0	0	-	9	.246	.371	.379
2002 San Francisco	NL	143	422	104	26	2	6	1	5	152	47	53	53	59	5	90	7	0	6	0	0	-	11	.246	.344	.360
11 ML YEARS		1350	4554	1196	226	13	165	83	82	1943	643	722	675	607	60	957	41	19	56	14	21	.40	116	.263	.351	.427

Earl Snyder

Bats: R Throws: R Pos: 1B-12; PH-3; 3B-2; DH-1

Ht: 6'0" Wt: 207 Born: 5/6/76 Age: 27

Year Team	Lg	G	AB	H	2B	3B	HR	Hm	Rd	TB	R	RBI	RC	TBB	IBB	SO	HBP	SH	SF	SB	CS	SB%	GDP	Avg	OBP	Slg
1998 Pittsfield	A-	71	262	66	8	1	11	-	-	109	39	40	33	23	0	60	2	0	1	0	1	.00	6	.252	.316	.416
1999 Capital City	A	136	486	130	25	4	28	-	-	247	73	97	84	55	0	117	2	0	9	2	2	.50	5	.267	.339	.508
2000 St.Lucie	A+	134	514	145	36	0	25	-	-	256	84	93	90	57	6	127	8	0	8	4	4	.50	8	.282	.358	.498
2001 Binghamton	AA	114	405	114	35	2	20	-	-	213	69	75	79	58	5	111	4	0	3	4	2	.67	5	.281	.374	.526
2001 Norfolk	AAA	6	19	9	3	0	0	-	-	12	5	3	6	3	0	1	1	0	0	0	1	.00	0	.474	.565	.632
2002 Buffalo	AAA	110	400	105	29	1	19	-	-	193	69	66	65	43	2	96	6	1	3	0	2	.00	5	.263	.341	.483
2002 Cleveland	AL	18	55	11	2	0	1	1	0	16	5	4	3	6	0	21	0	1	0	0	0	-	1	.200	.279	.291

Kyle Snyder

Pitches: R Bats: B Pos: SP

Ht: 6'8" Wt: 220 Born: 9/9/77 Age: 25

Year Team	Lg	G	GS	CG	GF	IP	BFP	H	R	ER	HR	SH	SF	HB	TBB	IBB	SO	WP	Bk	W	L	Pct	ShO	Sv-Op	Hld	ERC	ERA
1999 Spokane	A-	7	7	0	0	24.0	103	20	13	11	1	2	1	2	7	0	25	1	0	1	0	1.000	0	0- -	-	2.59	4.13
2000 Royals	R	1	1	0	0	2.0	7	1	0	0	0	0	0	0	0	0	4	0	0	0	0	-	0	0- -	-	0.54	0.00

Year Team	Lg	G	GS	CG	GF	IP	BFP	H	R	ER	HR	SH	SF	HB	TBB	IBB	SO	WP	Bk	W	L	Pct	ShO	Sv-Op	Hld	ERC	ERA
2000 Wilmington	A+	1	1	0	0	0.0	1	0	1	0	0	0	0	0	1	0	0	0	0	0	0	.000	0	0--	-	3.31	2.98
2002 Wilmington	A+	15	15	0	0	48.1	207	49	19	16	1	1	2	5	11	0	48	2	0	0	2	.000	0	0--	-	3.31	2.98
2002 Wichita	AA	6	6	0	0	25.2	101	21	12	12	4	0	0	1	7	1	18	3	0	2	2	.500	0	0--	-	3.18	4.21

Alfonso Soriano

Bats: R **Throws:** R **Pos:** 2B-155; PR-2; DH-1 **Ht:** 6'1" **Wt:** 180 **Born:** 1/7/78 **Age:** 25

Year Team	Lg	G	AB	H	2B	3B	HR	(Hm	Rd)	TB	R	RBI	RC	TBB	IBB	SO	HBP	SH	SF	SB	CS	SB%	GDP	Avg	OBP	Slg
1999 New York	AL	9	8	1	0	0	1	(1	0)	4	2	1	0	0	0	3	0	0	0	0	1	.00	0	.125	.125	.500
2000 New York	AL	22	50	9	3	0	2	(0	2)	18	5	3	4	1	0	15	0	0	0	2	0	1.00	0	.180	.196	.360
2001 New York	AL	158	574	154	34	3	18	(8	10)	248	77	73	77	29	0	125	3	3	5	43	14	.75	7	.268	.304	.432
2002 New York	AL	156	696	209	51	2	39	(17	22)	381	128	102	125	23	1	157	14	1	7	41	13	.76	8	.300	.332	.547
4 ML YEARS		345	1328	373	88	5	60	(26	34)	651	212	179	206	53	1	300	17	6	12	86	28	.75	15	.281	.314	.490

Rafael Soriano

Pitches: R **Bats:** R **Pos:** SP-8; RP-2 **Ht:** 6'1" **Wt:** 175 **Born:** 12/19/79 **Age:** 23

Year Team	Lg	G	GS	CG	GF	IP	BFP	H	R	ER	HR	SH	SF	HB	TBB	IBB	SO	WP	Bk	W	L	Pct	ShO	Sv-Op	Hld	ERC	ERA
1999 Everett	A-	14	14	0	0	75.1	323	56	34	26	8	1	0	4	49	0	83	2	0	5	4	.556	0	0--	-	3.95	3.11
2000 Wisconsin	A	21	21	1	0	122.1	500	97	41	39	3	2	5	12	50	0	90	5	2	8	4	.667	0	0--	-	2.96	2.87
2001 Sn Brnardino	A+	15	15	2	0	89.0	346	49	28	25	4	2	2	4	39	0	98	2	0	6	3	.667	1	0--	-	1.82	2.53
2001 San Antonio	AA	8	8	0	0	48.1	193	34	18	18	5	0	0	2	14	0	53	2	1	2	2	.500	0	0--	-	2.29	3.35
2002 San Antonio	AA	10	8	0	0	46.2	185	32	13	12	6	0	1	1	15	0	52	0	0	2	3	.400	0	0--	-	2.41	2.31
2002 Seattle	AL	10	8	0	1	47.1	202	45	25	24	8	1	0	0	16	1	32	2	0	0	3	.000	0	1-1	0	3.93	4.56

Jorge Sosa

Pitches: R **Bats:** B **Pos:** RP-17; SP-14 **Ht:** 6'2" **Wt:** 177 **Born:** 4/28/77 **Age:** 26

Year Team	Lg	G	GS	CG	GF	IP	BFP	H	R	ER	HR	SH	SF	HB	TBB	IBB	SO	WP	Bk	W	L	Pct	ShO	Sv-Op	Hld	ERC	ERA
2001 Everett	A-	21	7	0	11	58.2	247	45	22	11	2	2	3	2	19	0	57	8	1	3	1	.750	0	7--	-	2.18	1.69
2001 Wisconsin	A	2	0	0	0	2.0	9	3	2	2	1	0	0	0	0	0	4	0	0	0	0	-	0	0--	-	8.13	9.00
2002 Orlando	AA	2	2	0	0	7.0	25	4	2	0	1	0	0	0	1	0	3	0	0	0	0	-	0	0--	-	1.44	0.00
2002 Tampa Bay	AL	31	14	0	10	99.1	434	88	63	61	16	0	5	2	54	0	48	5	0	2	7	.222	0	0-0	1	4.51	5.53

Sammy Sosa

Bats: R **Throws:** R **Pos:** RF-150 **Ht:** 6'0" **Wt:** 220 **Born:** 11/12/68 **Age:** 34

Year Team	Lg	G	AB	H	2B	3B	HR	(Hm	Rd)	TB	R	RBI	RC	TBB	IBB	SO	HBP	SH	SF	SB	CS	SB%	GDP	Avg	OBP	Slg
1989 Tex-CWS	AL	58	183	47	8	0	4	(1	3)	67	27	13	18	11	2	47	2	5	2	7	5	.58	6	.257	.303	.366
1990 Chicago	AL	153	532	124	26	10	15	(10	5)	215	72	70	59	33	4	150	6	2	5	32	16	.67	10	.233	.282	.404
1991 Chicago	AL	116	316	64	10	1	10	(3	7)	106	39	33	23	14	2	98	2	5	1	13	6	.68	5	.203	.240	.335
1992 Chicago	NL	67	262	68	7	2	8	(4	4)	103	41	25	33	19	1	63	4	4	2	15	7	.68	4	.260	.317	.393
1993 Chicago	NL	159	598	156	25	5	33	(23	10)	290	92	93	88	38	6	135	4	0	1	36	11	.77	14	.261	.309	.485
1994 Chicago	NL	105	426	128	17	6	25	(11	14)	232	59	70	75	25	1	92	2	1	4	22	13	.63	7	.300	.339	.545
1995 Chicago	NL	144	564	151	17	3	36	(19	17)	282	89	119	98	58	11	134	5	0	2	34	7	.83	8	.268	.340	.500
1996 Chicago	NL	124	498	136	21	2	40	(26	14)	281	84	100	87	34	6	134	5	0	4	18	5	.78	14	.273	.323	.564
1997 Chicago	NL	162	642	161	31	4	36	(25	11)	308	90	119	88	45	9	174	2	0	5	22	12	.65	16	.251	.300	.480
1998 Chicago	NL	159	643	198	20	0	66	(35	31)	416	134	158	142	73	14	171	1	0	5	18	9	.67	20	.308	.377	.647
1999 Chicago	NL	162	625	180	24	2	63	(33	30)	397	114	141	134	78	8	171	3	0	6	7	8	.47	17	.288	.367	.635
2000 Chicago	NL	156	604	193	38	1	50	(22	28)	383	106	138	144	91	19	168	2	0	8	7	4	.64	12	.320	.406	.634
2001 Chicago	NL	160	577	189	34	5	64	(34	30)	425	146	160	170	116	37	153	6	0	12	0	2	.00	6	.328	.437	.737
2002 Chicago	NL	150	556	160	19	2	49	(24	25)	330	122	108	122	103	15	144	3	0	4	2	0	1.00	14	.288	.399	.594
1989 Texas	AL	25	84	20	3	0	1	(0	1)	26	8	3	4	0	0	20	0	4	0	0	2	.00	3	.238	.238	.310
1989 Chicago	AL	33	99	27	5	0	3	(1	2)	41	19	10	14	11	2	27	2	1	2	7	3	.70	3	.273	.351	.414
14 ML YEARS		1875	7026	1955	297	43	499	(270	229)	3835	1215	1347	1281	738	135	1834	47	17	62	233	105	.69	153	.278	.348	.546

Steve Sparks

Pitches: R **Bats:** R **Pos:** SP-30; RP-2 **Ht:** 6'0" **Wt:** 195 **Born:** 7/2/65 **Age:** 37

Year Team	Lg	G	GS	CG	GF	IP	BFP	H	R	ER	HR	SH	SF	HB	TBB	IBB	SO	WP	Bk	W	L	Pct	ShO	Sv-Op	Hld	ERC	ERA
1995 Milwaukee	NL	33	27	3	2	202.0	875	210	111	104	17	5	12	5	86	1	96	5	1	9	11	.450	0	0-0	0	4.44	4.63
1996 Milwaukee	NL	20	13	1	2	88.2	406	103	66	65	19	3	1	3	52	0	21	6	0	4	7	.364	0	0-0	0	7.03	6.60
1998 Anaheim	AL	22	20	0	1	128.2	562	130	66	62	14	2	3	5	58	0	90	6	0	9	4	.692	0	0-0	0	4.60	4.34
1999 Anaheim	AL	28	26	0	1	147.2	688	165	101	89	21	2	8	9	82	0	73	8	0	5	11	.313	0	0-0	0	5.94	5.42
2000 Detroit	AL	20	15	1	5	104.0	446	108	59	47	7	1	4	1	29	0	53	6	0	7	5	.583	0	1-1	0	3.71	4.07
2001 Detroit	AL	35	33	8	2	232.0	982	244	110	94	22	4	9	6	64	1	116	8	2	14	9	.609	1	0-0	0	3.97	3.65
2002 Detroit	AL	32	30	3	0	189.0	868	238	134	116	23	3	8	12	67	3	98	8	3	8	16	.333	0	0-0	0	5.78	5.52
7 ML YEARS		190	164	16	13	1092.0	4827	1198	643	577	123	20	42	44	438	5	547	47	6	56	63	.471	2	1-1	0	4.91	4.76

Justin Speier

Pitches: R **Bats:** R **Pos:** RP-63 **Ht:** 6'4" **Wt:** 205 **Born:** 11/6/73 **Age:** 29

Year Team	Lg	G	GS	CG	GF	IP	BFP	H	R	ER	HR	SH	SF	HB	TBB	IBB	SO	WP	Bk	W	L	Pct	ShO	Sv-Op	Hld	ERC	ERA
2002 Co Springs*	AAA	12	0	0	5	14.0	64	20	7	6	2	0	0	1	3	1	14	1	0	2	0	1.000	0	2--	-	6.41	3.86
1998 ChC-Fla	NL	19	0	0	10	20.2	99	27	20	20	7	2	1	0	13	1	17	3	0	0	3	.000	0	0-1	1	8.94	8.71
1999 Atlanta	NL	19	0	0	8	28.2	127	28	18	18	8	0	1	0	13	1	22	0	0	0	0	-	0	0-0	0	5.27	5.65
2000 Cleveland	AL	47	0	0	12	68.1	290	57	27	25	9	2	4	4	28	3	69	7	1	5	2	.714	0	0-1	6	3.56	3.29
2001 Cle-Col		54	0	0	10	76.2	324	71	40	39	13	2	7	8	20	3	62	6	1	6	3	.667	0	0-1	4	3.93	4.58
2002 Colorado	NL	63	0	0	7	62.1	259	51	31	30	9	0	1	3	19	4	47	1	2	5	1	.833	0	1-4	18	3.06	4.33
1998 Chicago	NL	1	0	0	0	1.1	7	2	2	2	0	0	0	0	1	0	2	1	0	0	0	-	0	0-0	0	7.52	13.50
1998 Florida	NL	18	0	0	10	19.1	92	25	18	18	7	2	1	0	12	1	15	2	0	0	3	.000	0	0-1	1	9.02	8.38
2001 Cleveland	AL	12	0	0	2	20.2	96	24	16	16	5	0	3	3	8	0	15	2	0	2	0	1.000	0	0-0	0	6.61	6.97
2001 Colorado	NL	42	0	0	8	56.0	228	47	24	23	8	2	4	5	12	3	47	4	1	4	3	.571	0	0-1	4	3.04	3.70
5 ML YEARS		202	0	0	47	256.2	1099	234	136	132	46	6	14	15	93	12	217	17	4	16	9	.640	0	1-7	29	4.10	4.63

Shane Spencer

Bats: R **Throws:** R **Pos:** RF-54; LF-40; PH-10; DH-1; PR-1 **Ht:** 5'11" **Wt:** 225 **Born:** 2/20/72 **Age:** 31

Year Team	Lg	G	AB	H	2B	3B	HR	(Hm	Rd)	TB	R	RBI	RC	TBB	IBB	SO	HBP	SH	SF	SB	CS	SB%	GDP	Avg	OBP	Slg
1998 New York	AL	27	67	25	6	0	10	(8	2)	61	18	27	22	5	0	12	0	0	1	0	1	.00	1	.373	.411	.910
1999 New York	AL	71	205	48	8	0	8	(2	6)	80	25	20	23	18	0	51	2	0	1	0	4	.00	1	.234	.301	.390
2000 New York	AL	73	248	70	11	3	9	(4	5)	114	33	40	37	19	0	45	2	0	7	1	2	.33	4	.282	.330	.460
2001 New York	AL	80	283	73	14	2	10	(6	4)	121	40	46	39	21	0	58	4	0	3	4	1	.80	4	.258	.315	.428
2002 New York	AL	94	288	71	15	2	6	(5	1)	108	32	34	34	31	4	62	4	2	4	0	3	.00	5	.247	.324	.375
5 ML YEARS		345	1091	287	54	7	43	(25	18)	484	148	167	155	94	4	228	12	2	16	5	11	.31	14	.263	.324	.444

Scott Spiezio

Bats: B **Throws:** R **Pos:** 1B-143; 3B-20; LF-8; PH-8; RF-2; 2B-1 **Ht:** 6'2" **Wt:** 225 **Born:** 9/21/72 **Age:** 30

Year Team	Lg	G	AB	H	2B	3B	HR	(Hm	Rd)	TB	R	RBI	RC	TBB	IBB	SO	HBP	SH	SF	SB	CS	SB%	GDP	Avg	OBP	Slg
1996 Oakland	AL	9	29	9	2	0	2	(1	1)	17	6	8	6	4	1	4	0	2	0	0	1	.00	0	.310	.394	.586
1997 Oakland	AL	147	538	131	28	4	14	(6	8)	209	58	65	61	44	2	75	1	3	6	9	3	.75	13	.243	.300	.388
1998 Oakland	AL	114	406	105	19	1	9	(6	3)	153	54	50	50	43	3	56	2	7	2	1	3	.25	10	.259	.333	.377
1999 Oakland	AL	89	247	60	24	0	8	(3	5)	108	31	33	35	29	3	36	2	1	3	0	0	-	5	.243	.324	.437
2000 Anaheim	AL	123	297	72	11	2	17	(10	7)	138	47	49	47	40	2	56	3	1	4	1	2	.33	5	.242	.334	.465
2001 Anaheim	AL	139	457	124	29	4	13	(8	5)	200	57	54	65	34	4	65	5	3	4	5	2	.71	6	.271	.326	.438
2002 Anaheim	AL	153	491	140	34	2	12	(7	5)	214	80	82	86	67	7	52	4	3	6	6	7	.46	12	.285	.371	.436
7 ML YEARS		774	2465	641	147	13	75	(41	34)	1039	333	341	350	262	22	344	17	20	23	22	18	.55	51	.260	.332	.422

Junior Spivey

Bats: R **Throws:** R **Pos:** 2B-143; PH-1 **Ht:** 6'0" **Wt:** 185 **Born:** 1/28/75 **Age:** 28

Year Team	Lg	G	AB	H	2B	3B	HR	(Hm	Rd)	TB	R	RBI	RC	TBB	IBB	SO	HBP	SH	SF	SB	CS	SB%	GDP	Avg	OBP	Slg
1996 Diamndbcks	R	20	69	23	0	0	0	(-	-)	23	13	3	14	12	0	16	4	1	1	11	2	.85	0	.333	.453	.333
1996 Lethbridge	R+	31	107	36	3	4	2	(-	-)	53	30	25	26	23	0	24	3	1	2	8	3	.73	2	.336	.459	.495
1997 High Desert	A+	136	491	134	24	6	6	(-	-)	188	88	53	73	69	2	115	11	2	3	14	9	.61	9	.273	.373	.383
1998 High Desert	A+	79	285	80	14	5	5	(-	-)	119	64	35	56	64	0	61	3	0	1	34	12	.74	4	.281	.416	.418
1998 Tulsa	AA	34	119	37	10	1	3	(-	-)	58	26	16	28	28	1	25	3	1	1	8	4	.67	1	.311	.450	.487
1999 El Paso	AA	44	164	48	10	4	3	(-	-)	75	40	19	32	36	0	27	2	1	1	14	10	.58	5	.293	.424	.457
2000 Tucson	AAA	28	117	33	8	4	3	(-	-)	58	21	16	19	11	0	17	0	1	1	3	1	.75	4	.282	.341	.496
2000 El Paso	AA	6	19	8	5	0	1	(-	-)	16	5	2	5	0	0	5	0	1	0	0	0	-	1	.421	.421	.842
2001 Tucson	AAA	54	194	45	6	4	6	(-	-)	69	25	27	22	27	1	32	0	0	0	9	6	.60	4	.232	.326	.356
2001 Arizona	NL	72	163	42	6	3	5	(4	1)	69	33	21	26	23	0	47	2	6	1	3	0	1.00	3	.258	.354	.423
2002 Arizona	NL	143	538	162	34	6	16	(9	7)	256	103	78	94	65	5	100	16	1	6	11	6	.65	10	.301	.389	.476
2 ML YEARS		215	701	204	40	9	21	(13	8)	325	136	99	120	88	5	147	18	7	7	14	6	.70	13	.291	.381	.464

Tim Spooneybarger

Pitches: R **Bats:** R **Pos:** RP-51 **Ht:** 6'3" **Wt:** 190 **Born:** 10/21/79 **Age:** 23

Year Team	Lg	G	GS	CG	GF	IP	BFP	H	R	ER	HR	SH	SF	HB	TBB	IBB	SO	WP	Bk	W	L	Pct	ShO	Sv-Op	Hld	ERC	ERA
1999 Danville	R+	12	0	0	2	24.1	103	15	11	7	0	0	0	2	14	0	36	5	0	3	0	1.000	0	0--	-	2.30	2.59
1999 Macon	A	7	0	0	3	10.0	47	7	4	4	1	1	0	0	10	1	17	2	0	1	0	1.000	0	0--	-	4.42	3.60
2000 Myrtle Beach	A+	19	6	0	5	49.2	187	18	7	5	0	4	0	1	19	0	57	6	0	3	0	1.000	0	0--	-	0.86	0.91
2001 Greenville	AA	15	0	0	6	21.0	86	20	12	12	1	1	0	0	4	0	24	5	0	1	1	.500	0	0--	-	2.67	5.14
2001 Richmond	AAA	42	0	0	18	50.2	202	33	5	4	1	1	0	2	21	1	58	5	0	3	0	1.000	0	5--	-	1.98	0.71
2002 Richmond	AAA	18	0	0	17	20.0	82	13	2	2	1	0	0	1	8	0	21	4	0	1	0	1.000	0	11--	-	2.10	0.90
2001 Atlanta	NL	4	0	0	3	4.0	19	5	1	1	0	0	1	0	2	1	3	0	0	0	0	1.000	0	0-0	0	4.53	2.25
2002 Atlanta	NL	51	0	0	14	51.1	214	38	16	15	4	1	1	2	26	5	33	4	0	1	0	1.000	0	1-1	11	2.96	2.63
2 ML YEARS		55	0	0	17	55.1	233	43	17	16	4	1	2	2	28	6	36	4	0	1	1	.500	0	1-1	11	3.07	2.60

Dennis Springer

Pitches: R **Bats:** R **Pos:** RP-1 **Ht:** 5'10" **Wt:** 185 **Born:** 2/12/65 **Age:** 38

Year Team	Lg	G	GS	CG	GF	IP	BFP	H	R	ER	HR	SH	SF	HB	TBB	IBB	SO	WP	Bk	W	L	Pct	ShO	Sv-Op	Hld	ERC	ERA
2002 Las Vegas*	AAA	26	22	1	2	143.0	642	203	100	93	21	3	9	4	37	0	38	7	0	7	8	.467	1	1--	-	6.64	5.85
1995 Philadelphia	NL	4	4	0	0	22.1	94	21	15	12	3	2	0	1	9	1	15	1	0	0	3	.000	0	0-0	0	4.20	4.84
1996 Anaheim	AL	20	15	2	3	94.2	413	91	65	58	24	0	1	6	43	0	64	1	0	5	6	.455	0	0-0	1	5.49	5.51
1997 Anaheim	AL	32	28	3	0	194.2	846	199	118	112	32	4	13	10	73	0	75	7	0	9	9	.500	1	0-0	0	4.79	5.18

Year Team	Lg	G	GS	CG	GF	IP	BFP	H	R	ER	HR	SH	SF	HB	TBB	IBB	SO	WP	Bk	W	L	Pct	ShO	Sv-Op	Hld	ERC	ERA
1998 Tampa Bay	AL	29	17	1	8	115.2	517	120	77	70	21	1	2	12	60	1	46	6	0	3	11	.214	0	0-0	2	5.94	5.45
1999 Florida	NL	38	29	3	3	196.1	855	231	121	106	23	12	10	7	64	3	83	2	0	6	16	.273	2	1-1	1	5.14	4.86
2000 New York	NL	2	2	0	0	11.1	59	20	11	11	2	0	0	1	5	0	5	2	0	0	1	.000	0	0-0	0	10.14	8.74
2001 Los Angeles	NL	4	3	0	1	19.0	75	19	7	7	3	1	0	3	2	0	7	2	0	1	1	.500	0	0-0	0	4.19	3.32
2002 Los Angeles	NL	1	0	0	1	1.1	7	1	1	1	0	0	0	0	2	0	1	0	0	0	1	.000	0	0-0	0	5.91	6.75
8 ML YEARS		130	98	9	16	655.1	2866	702	415	377	108	20	26	40	258	5	296	21	0	24	48	.333	4	1-1	2	5.25	5.18

Russ Springer

Pitches: R **Bats:** R **Pos:** RP   **Ht:** 6'4" **Wt:** 211 **Born:** 11/7/68 **Age:** 34

Year Team	Lg	G	GS	CG	GF	IP	BFP	H	R	ER	HR	SH	SF	HB	TBB	IBB	SO	WP	Bk	W	L	Pct	ShO	Sv-Op	Hld	ERC	ERA
1992 New York	AL	14	0	0	5	16.0	75	18	11	11	0	0	0	1	10	0	12	0	0	0	0	-	0	0-0	2	5.15	6.19
1993 Anaheim	AL	14	9	1	3	60.0	278	73	48	48	11	1	1	3	32	1	31	6	0	1	6	.143	0	0-0	0	6.87	7.20
1994 Anaheim	AL	18	5	0	6	45.2	198	53	28	28	9	1	1	0	14	0	28	2	0	2	2	.500	0	2-3	5	5.38	5.52
1995 Ana-Phi		33	6	0	6	78.1	350	82	48	46	16	2	2	7	35	4	70	2	0	1	2	.333	0	1-2	0	5.63	5.29
1996 Philadelphia	NL	51	7	0	12	96.2	437	106	60	50	12	5	3	1	38	6	94	5	0	3	10	.231	0	0-3	6	4.57	4.66
1997 Houston	NL	54	0	0	13	55.1	241	48	28	26	4	1	2	4	27	2	74	4	0	3	3	.500	0	3-7	9	3.69	4.23
1998 Ari-Atl	NL	48	0	0	14	52.2	232	51	26	24	4	2	1	1	30	4	56	5	0	5	4	.556	0	0-4	7	4.38	4.10
1999 Atlanta	NL	49	0	0	8	47.1	194	31	20	18	5	0	2	2	22	2	49	0	0	2	1	.667	0	1-1	8	2.63	3.42
2000 Arizona	NL	52	0	0	10	62.0	282	63	36	35	11	2	3	2	34	6	59	3	0	2	4	.333	0	0-2	3	5.25	5.08
2001 Arizona	NL	18	0	0	9	17.2	79	20	16	14	5	1	1	0	4	0	12	2	0	0	0	-	0	1-1	2	5.13	7.13
1995 Anaheim	AL	19	6	0	3	51.2	238	60	37	35	11	1	0	5	25	1	38	1	0	1	2	.333	0	1-2	0	6.69	6.10
1995 Philadelphia	NL	14	0	0	3	26.2	112	22	11	11	5	1	2	2	10	3	32	1	0	0	0	-	0	0-0	0	3.73	3.71
1998 Arizona	NL	26	0	0	13	32.2	140	29	16	15	4	0	0	1	14	1	37	3	0	4	3	.571	0	0-3	1	3.77	4.13
1998 Atlanta	NL	22	0	0	1	20.0	92	22	10	9	0	2	1	0	16	3	19	2	0	1	1	.500	0	0-1	6	5.36	4.05
10 ML YEARS		351	27	1	86	531.2	2366	545	321	300	77	15	16	21	246	25	485	29	0	19	32	.373	0	8-23	38	4.86	5.08

Matt Stairs

Bats: L **Throws:** R **Pos:** RF-51; LF-35; PH-28; PR-1   **Ht:** 5'9" **Wt:** 215 **Born:** 2/27/68 **Age:** 35

								BATTING											BASERUNNING				AVERAGES		
Year Team	Lg	G	AB	H	2B	3B	HR	(Hm | Rd)	TB	R	RBI	RC	TBB	IBB	SO	HBP	SH	SF	SB	CS	SB%	GDP	Avg	OBP	Slg
1992 Montreal	NL	13	30	5	2	0	0	(0 | 0)	7	2	5	3	7	0	7	0	0	1	0	0	-	0	.167	.316	.233
1993 Montreal	NL	6	8	3	1	0	0	(0 | 0)	4	1	2	1	0	0	1	0	0	0	0	0	-	1	.375	.375	.500
1995 Boston	AL	39	88	23	7	1	1	(0 | 1)	35	8	17	9	4	0	14	1	1	1	0	1	.00	4	.261	.298	.398
1996 Oakland	AL	61	137	38	5	1	10	(5 | 5)	75	21	23	27	19	2	23	1	0	1	1	1	.50	2	.277	.367	.547
1997 Oakland	AL	133	352	105	19	0	27	(20 | 7)	205	62	73	77	50	1	60	3	1	4	3	2	.60	6	.298	.386	.582
1998 Oakland	AL	149	523	154	33	1	26	(16 | 10)	267	88	106	96	59	4	93	6	1	4	8	3	.73	13	.294	.370	.511
1999 Oakland	AL	146	531	137	26	3	38	(15 | 23)	283	94	102	101	89	6	124	2	0	1	2	7	.22	8	.258	.366	.533
2000 Oakland	AL	143	476	108	26	0	21	(9 | 12)	197	74	81	69	78	4	122	1	1	6	5	2	.71	7	.227	.333	.414
2001 Chicago	NL	128	340	85	21	0	17	(5 | 12)	157	48	61	57	52	7	76	7	1	3	2	3	.40	4	.250	.358	.462
2002 Milwaukee	NL	107	270	66	15	0	16	(6 | 10)	129	41	41	39	36	4	50	8	0	1	2	0	1.00	7	.244	.349	.478
10 ML YEARS		925	2755	724	155	6	156	(76 | 80)	1359	439	511	479	394	28	570	29	5	22	23	19	.55	52	.263	.358	.493

Jason Standridge

Pitches: R **Bats:** R **Pos:** RP-1   **Ht:** 6'4" **Wt:** 230 **Born:** 11/9/78 **Age:** 24

Year Team	Lg	G	GS	CG	GF	IP	BFP	H	R	ER	HR	SH	SF	HB	TBB	IBB	SO	WP	Bk	W	L	Pct	ShO	Sv-Op	Hld	ERC	ERA
1997 Devil Rays	R	13	13	0	0	57.2	246	56	30	23	3	2	5	2	13	1	55	2	2	0	6	.000	0	0--	-	2.94	3.59
1998 Princeton	R+	12	12	0	0	63.0	298	82	61	49	4	2	4	3	28	0	47	9	0	4	4	.500	0	---	-	5.87	7.00
1999 Chrlstn - SC	A	18	18	3	0	116.0	455	80	35	26	5	5	5	7	31	0	84	9	2	9	1	.900	3	0--	-	1.91	2.02
1999 St.Pete	A+	8	8	0	0	48.1	208	49	21	21	0	1	0	4	20	0	26	6	1	4	4	.500	0	0--	-	3.90	3.91
2000 St.Pete	A+	10	10	1	0	56.0	243	45	28	21	4	0	1	1	31	0	41	6	0	2	4	.333	0	0--	-	3.41	3.38
2000 Orlando	AA	17	17	2	0	97.0	416	85	46	39	4	2	2	11	43	0	55	4	0	6	8	.429	0	0--	-	3.62	3.62
2001 Durham	AAA	20	20	0	0	102.1	475	130	73	60	13	2	7	3	50	0	48	6	0	5	10	.333	0	0--	-	6.44	5.28
2001 Orlando	AA	2	2	0	0	9.2	44	12	6	6	0	0	0	0	4	0	7	0	0	0	2	.000	0	0--	-	4.74	5.59
2002 Durham	AAA	29	29	0	0	173.0	732	168	71	60	12	2	7	10	64	1	111	2	2	10	9	.526	0	0--	-	3.87	3.12
2001 Tampa Bay	AL	9	1	0	6	19.1	87	19	10	10	5	0	0	0	14	1	9	0	0	0	0	-	0	0-0	0	6.63	4.66
2002 Tampa Bay	AL	1	0	0	0	3.0	18	7	3	3	1	0	0	0	4	0	1	0	0	0	0	-	0	0-0	0	22.36	9.00
2 ML YEARS		10	1	0	6	22.1	105	26	13	13	6	0	0	0	18	1	10	0	0	0	0	-	0	0-0	0	8.43	5.24

Mike Stanton

Pitches: L **Bats:** L **Pos:** RP-79   **Ht:** 6'1" **Wt:** 215 **Born:** 6/2/67 **Age:** 36

Year Team	Lg	G	GS	CG	GF	IP	BFP	H	R	ER	HR	SH	SF	HB	TBB	IBB	SO	WP	Bk	W	L	Pct	ShO	Sv-Op	Hld	ERC	ERA
1989 Atlanta	NL	20	0	0	10	24.0	94	17	4	4	0	4	0	0	8	1	27	1	0	0	1	.000	0	7-8	2	1.72	1.50
1990 Atlanta	NL	7	0	0	4	7.0	42	16	16	14	1	1	0	1	4	2	7	1	0	0	3	.000	0	2-3	0	13.58	18.00
1991 Atlanta	NL	74	0	0	20	78.0	314	62	27	25	6	6	0	1	21	6	54	0	0	5	5	.500	0	7-10	15	2.31	2.88
1992 Atlanta	NL	65	0	0	23	63.2	264	59	32	29	6	1	2	2	20	2	44	3	0	5	4	.556	0	8-11	15	3.42	4.10
1993 Atlanta	NL	63	0	0	41	52.0	236	51	35	27	4	5	2	0	29	7	43	1	0	4	6	.400	0	27-33	5	4.08	4.67
1994 Atlanta	NL	49	0	0	15	45.2	197	41	18	18	2	2	1	3	26	3	35	1	0	3	1	.750	0	3-4	10	4.01	3.55
1995 Atl-Bos		48	0	0	22	40.1	178	48	23	19	6	2	1	1	14	2	31	2	1	2	1	.667	0	1-3	8	5.41	4.24
1996 Bos-Tex		81	0	0	28	78.2	327	78	32	32	11	4	2	0	27	5	60	3	2	4	4	.500	0	1-6	22	4.08	3.66
1997 New York	AL	64	0	0	15	66.2	283	50	19	19	3	2	0	3	34	2	70	3	2	6	1	.857	0	3-5	26	2.88	2.57
1998 New York	AL	67	0	0	26	79.0	330	71	51	48	13	1	2	4	26	1	69	0	0	4	1	.800	0	6-10	18	3.88	5.47
1999 New York	AL	73	1	0	20	62.1	271	71	30	30	5	4	2	1	18	4	59	2	0	2	2	.500	0	0-5	11	4.23	4.33
2000 New York	AL	69	0	0	20	68.0	291	68	32	31	5	2	4	2	24	2	75	1	0	2	3	.400	0	0-4	15	3.78	4.10
2001 New York	AL	76	0	0	16	80.1	342	80	25	23	9	4	4	4	29	9	78	3	1	9	4	.692	0	0-1	23	3.61	2.58
2002 New York	AL	79	0	0	25	78.0	324	73	29	26	4	4	7	0	28	3	44	4	0	7	1	.875	0	6-9	17	3.23	3.00
1995 Atlanta	NL	26	0	0	10	19.1	94	31	14	12	3	2	1	1	6	2	13	1	1	1	1	.500	0	1-2	4	7.86	5.59
1995 Boston	AL	22	0	0	12	21.0	84	17	9	7	3	0	0	0	8	0	18	1	0	1	0	1.000	0	0-1	4	3.37	3.00

Year Team	Lg	G	GS	CG	GF	IP	BFP	H	R	ER	HR	SH	SF	HB	TBB	IBB	SO	WP	Bk	W	L	Pct	ShO	Sv-Op	Hld	ERC	ERA
1996 Boston	AL	59	0	0	19	56.1	239	58	24	24	9	3	2	0	23	4	46	3	2	4	3	.571	0	1-5	15	4.71	3.83
1996 Texas	AL	22	0	0	9	22.1	88	20	8	8	2	1	0	0	4	1	14	0	0	0	1	.000	0	0-1	7	2.62	3.22
14 ML YEARS		835	1	0	275	823.2	3493	785	373	345	70	40	26	22	308	49	688	25	6	53	37	.589	0	71-112	197	3.64	3.77

Denny Stark

Pitches: R **Bats:** R **Pos:** SP-20; RP-12   **Ht:** 6'2" **Wt:** 210 **Born:** 10/27/74 **Age:** 28

Year Team	Lg	G	GS	CG	GF	IP	BFP	H	R	ER	HR	SH	SF	HB	TBB	IBB	SO	WP	Bk	W	L	Pct	ShO	Sv-Op	Hld	ERC	ERA
2002 Co Springs*	AAA	7	7	0	0	37.2	163	35	20	16	4	1	2	4	14	0	38	0	0	1	2	.333	0	0--	-	4.02	3.82
1999 Seattle	AL	5	0	0	2	6.1	31	10	8	7	0	0	0	0	4	0	4	0	0	0	0	-	0	0-0	0	8.05	9.95
2001 Seattle	AL	4	3	0	0	14.2	68	21	15	15	5	0	1	0	4	0	12	0	0	1	1	.500	0	0-0	0	7.99	9.20
2002 Colorado	NL	32	20	0	1	128.1	554	108	69	57	25	2	4	5	64	4	64	2	0	11	4	.733	0	0-1	1	4.33	4.00
3 ML YEARS		41	23	0	3	149.1	653	139	92	79	30	2	5	5	72	4	80	2	0	12	5	.706	0	0-1	1	4.81	4.76

Gene Stechschulte

Pitches: R **Bats:** R **Pos:** RP-29   **Ht:** 6'5" **Wt:** 210 **Born:** 8/12/73 **Age:** 29

Year Team	Lg	G	GS	CG	GF	IP	BFP	H	R	ER	HR	SH	SF	HB	TBB	IBB	SO	WP	Bk	W	L	Pct	ShO	Sv-Op	Hld	ERC	ERA
2002 Memphis*	AAA	10	0	0	10	10.0	43	8	2	2	0	1	0	2	2	0	7	1	0	1	0	1.000	0	5--	-	2.25	1.80
2000 St Louis	NL	20	0	0	7	25.2	116	24	22	18	6	0	2	0	17	1	12	2	0	1	0	1.000	0	0-1	3	5.69	6.31
2001 St Louis	NL	67	0	0	18	70.0	301	71	35	30	10	4	3	4	30	2	51	2	0	1	5	.167	0	6-8	13	4.90	3.86
2002 St Louis	NL	29	0	0	5	32.0	138	27	19	17	4	1	4	1	17	1	21	3	0	6	2	.750	0	0-2	5	3.98	4.78
3 ML YEARS		116	0	0	30	127.2	555	122	76	65	20	5	9	5	64	4	84	7	0	8	7	.533	0	6-11	21	4.81	4.58

Blake Stein

Pitches: R **Bats:** R **Pos:** RP-25; SP-2   **Ht:** 6'7" **Wt:** 240 **Born:** 8/3/73 **Age:** 29

Year Team	Lg	G	GS	CG	GF	IP	BFP	H	R	ER	HR	SH	SF	HB	TBB	IBB	SO	WP	Bk	W	L	Pct	ShO	Sv-Op	Hld	ERC	ERA
2002 Wichita*	AA	6	3	0	0	10.1	46	11	4	4	1	0	0	0	7	0	7	2	0	0	1	.000	0	0--	-	5.80	3.48
1998 Oakland	AL	24	20	1	0	117.1	538	117	92	83	22	1	2	5	71	3	89	15	0	5	9	.357	1	0-0	0	5.64	6.37
1999 Oak-KC	AL	13	12	0	0	73.0	327	65	38	37	11	2	1	7	47	1	47	2	0	1	2	.333	0	0-0	0	5.23	4.56
2000 Kansas City	AL	17	17	1	0	107.2	464	98	57	56	19	3	4	3	57	1	78	7	0	8	5	.615	0	0-0	0	4.82	4.68
2001 Kansas City	AL	36	15	0	5	131.0	568	112	73	69	20	1	4	3	79	2	113	10	0	7	8	.467	0	1-2	1	4.57	4.74
2002 Kansas City	AL	27	2	0	7	46.2	227	59	41	41	6	1	3	3	27	1	42	1	0	0	4	.000	0	1-2	1	6.76	7.91
1999 Oakland	AL	1	1	0	0	2.2	19	6	5	5	1	0	0	0	6	0	4	1	0	0	0	-	0	0-0	0	26.09	16.88
1999 Kansas City	AL	12	11	0	0	70.1	308	59	33	32	10	2	1	7	41	1	43	1	0	1	2	.333	0	0-0	0	4.63	4.09
5 ML YEARS		117	66	2	12	475.2	2124	451	301	286	78	8	14	21	281	8	369	35	0	21	28	.429	1	2-4	2	5.20	5.41

John Stephens

Pitches: R **Bats:** R **Pos:** SP-11; RP-1   **Ht:** 6'1" **Wt:** 204 **Born:** 11/15/79 **Age:** 23

Year Team	Lg	G	GS	CG	GF	IP	BFP	H	R	ER	HR	SH	SF	HB	TBB	IBB	SO	WP	Bk	W	L	Pct	ShO	Sv-Op	Hld	ERC	ERA
1997 Orioles	R	9	3	0	0	33.0	121	15	3	3	1	3	2	0	9	0	43	0	0	3	0	1.000	0	1--	-	0.98	0.82
1997 Bluefield	R+	4	4	0	0	24.0	93	17	6	6	4	0	0	1	5	0	34	1	1	2	0	1.000	0	0--	-	2.42	2.25
1998 Delmarva	A	6	6	1	0	34.2	141	25	11	10	3	1	0	1	13	0	40	3	0	1	2	.333	1	0--	-	2.53	2.60
1999 Delmarva	A	28	27	4	0	170.1	702	148	75	61	10	5	4	10	36	1	217	4	0	10	8	.556	2	0--	-	2.59	3.22
2000 Frederick	A+	20	20	0	0	118.0	497	119	45	40	5	3	4	8	22	1	121	6	0	7	6	.538	0	0--	-	3.13	3.05
2001 Bowie	AA	18	17	3	0	132.0	502	95	32	27	10	2	1	6	21	1	130	2	0	11	4	.733	3	0--	-	1.84	1.84
2001 Rochester	AAA	9	9	0	0	58.0	247	52	31	26	5	2	3	3	19	1	61	4	0	2	5	.286	0	0--	-	3.25	4.03
2002 Rochester	AAA	21	21	1	0	142.2	571	126	51	48	10	4	3	8	23	0	118	1	0	11	5	.688	0	0--	-	2.61	3.03
2002 Baltimore	AL	12	11	0	0	65.0	281	68	44	44	13	1	4	3	22	2	56	2	0	2	5	.286	0	0-0	0	4.97	6.09

Garrett Stephenson

Pitches: R **Bats:** R **Pos:** SP-10; RP-2   **Ht:** 6'5" **Wt:** 208 **Born:** 1/2/72 **Age:** 31

Year Team	Lg	G	GS	CG	GF	IP	BFP	H	R	ER	HR	SH	SF	HB	TBB	IBB	SO	WP	Bk	W	L	Pct	ShO	Sv-Op	Hld	ERC	ERA
2002 Peoria*	A	2	2	0	0	8.2	26	0	0	0	0	0	0	0	0	0	11	0	0	0	0	-	0	0--	-	0.00	0.00
2002 Memphis*	AAA	3	3	0	0	12.2	49	12	5	5	0	1	0	0	2	0	12	1	0	0	1	.000	0	0--	-	2.39	3.55
1996 Baltimore	AL	3	0	0	2	6.1	35	13	9	9	1	0	1	0	3	1	3	0	0	0	1	.000	0	0-0	0	12.31	12.79
1997 Philadelphia	NL	20	18	2	0	117.0	474	104	45	41	11	2	5	3	38	0	81	1	0	8	6	.571	0	0-0	0	3.35	3.15
1998 Philadelphia	NL	6	6	0	0	23.0	118	31	24	23	3	1	0	0	19	0	17	0	1	0	2	.000	0	0-0	0	8.16	9.00
1999 St Louis	NL	18	12	0	1	85.1	371	90	43	40	11	5	5	5	29	1	59	0	0	6	3	.667	0	0-0	0	4.58	4.22
2000 St Louis	NL	32	31	3	0	200.1	858	209	105	100	31	6	7	7	63	0	123	2	2	16	9	.640	2	0-0	1	4.53	4.49
2002 St Louis	NL	12	10	0	0	45.0	205	48	27	27	4	4	1	5	25	0	34	2	0	2	5	.286	0	0-0	0	5.54	5.40
6 ML YEARS		91	77	5	3	477.0	2061	495	253	240	61	19	18	21	177	2	317	5	3	32	26	.552	2	0-0	1	4.59	4.53

Lee Stevens

Bats: L **Throws:** L **Pos:** 1B-83; PH-19; LF-11; RF-5; DH-2   **Ht:** 6'4" **Wt:** 235 **Born:** 10/3/67 **Age:** 35

Year Team	Lg	G	AB	H	2B	3B	HR	(Hm	Rd)	TB	R	RBI	RC	TBB	IBB	SO	HBP	SH	SF	SB	CS	SB%	GDP	Avg	OBP	Slg
1990 Anaheim	AL	67	248	53	10	0	7	(4	3)	84	28	32	21	22	3	75	0	2	3	1	1	.50	8	.214	.275	.339
1991 Anaheim	AL	18	58	17	7	0	0	(0	0)	24	8	9	8	6	2	12	0	1	1	1	2	.33	6	.293	.354	.414
1992 Anaheim	AL	106	312	69	19	0	7	(2	5)	109	25	37	30	29	6	64	1	1	2	1	4	.20	4	.221	.288	.349
1996 Texas	AL	27	78	18	2	3	3	(2	1)	35	6	12	10	6	0	22	1	0	1	0	0	-	2	.231	.291	.449
1997 Texas	AL	137	426	128	24	2	21	(12	9)	219	58	74	65	23	2	83	1	1	3	1	3	.25	18	.300	.336	.514

Year Team	Lg	G	AB	H	2B	3B	HR	(Hm Rd)	TB	R	RBI	RC	TBB	IBB	SO	HBP	SH	SF	SB	CS	SB%	GDP	Avg	OBP	Slg
1998 Texas	AL	120	344	91	17	4	20	(13 7)	176	52	59	55	31	4	93	0	0	1	0	2	.00	6	.265	.324	.512
1999 Texas	AL	146	517	146	31	1	24	(10 14)	251	76	81	80	52	10	132	0	0	7	2	3	.40	19	.282	.344	.485
2000 Montreal	NL	123	449	119	27	2	22	(14 8)	216	60	75	71	48	6	105	2	0	2	0	0	-	10	.265	.337	.481
2001 Montreal	NL	152	542	133	35	1	25	(12 13)	245	77	95	80	74	12	157	5	0	7	2	1	.67	17	.245	.338	.452
2002 Mon-Cle		116	358	73	13	2	15	(7 8)	135	50	57	48	54	5	89	0	0	5	1	0	1.00	9	.204	.305	.377
2002 Montreal	NL	63	205	39	6	1	10	(6 4)	77	28	31	27	39	5	57	0	0	1	1	0	1.00	4	.190	.318	.376
2002 Cleveland	AL	53	153	34	7	1	5	(1 4)	58	22	26	21	15	0	32	0	0	4	0	0	-	5	.222	.285	.379
10 ML YEARS		1012	3332	847	185	15	144	(76 68)	1494	440	531	468	345	50	832	10	5	32	9	16	.36	93	.254	.323	.448

Josh Stewart

Pitches: L **Bats:** L **Pos:** SP · **Ht:** 6'3" **Wt:** 205 **Born:** 12/5/78 **Age:** 24

Year Team	Lg	G	GS	CG	GF	IP	BFP	H	R	ER	HR	SH	SF	HB	TBB	IBB	SO	WP	Bk	W	L	Pct	ShO	Sv-Op	Hld	ERC	ERA
1999 Bristol	R+	5	0	0	2	18.0	71	13	5	3	0	1	0	0	5	0	25	0	1	1	0	1.000	0	1- -	-	2.04	1.50
1999 Burlington	A	16	0	0	3	29.2	138	32	25	24	6	0	2	2	21	0	35	1	0	2	0	1.000	0	1- -	-	7.09	7.28
2000 Burlington	A	25	25	1	0	138.0	617	157	84	70	14	5	3	10	58	2	82	9	0	9	9	.500	1	0- -	-	5.30	4.57
2001 Winstn-Salm	A+	12	12	1	0	63.2	287	64	41	27	6	3	4	4	28	1	38	3	0	4	6	.400	0	0- -	-	4.33	3.82
2001 Birmingham	AA	16	16	0	0	82.1	388	110	68	61	7	2	3	8	42	0	47	2	2	3	4	.429	0	0- -	-	7.01	6.67
2002 Birmingham	AA	26	26	1	0	150.1	630	145	65	59	11	2	0	2	56	1	92	7	0	11	7	.611	1	0- -	-	3.70	3.53

Scott Stewart

Pitches: L **Bats:** R **Pos:** RP-67 · **Ht:** 6'2" **Wt:** 225 **Born:** 8/14/75 **Age:** 27

Year Team	Lg	G	GS	CG	GF	IP	BFP	H	R	ER	HR	SH	SF	HB	TBB	IBB	SO	WP	Bk	W	L	Pct	ShO	Sv-Op	Hld	ERC	ERA
1994 Rangers	R	14	8	0	3	54.1	221	47	22	17	1	1	0	2	12	0	62	7	9	4	1	.800	0	1- -	-	2.31	2.82
1995 Chrlstn - SC	A	11	11	1	0	75.2	302	76	38	31	6	1	4	0	14	1	47	3	5	1	7	.125	0	0- -	-	3.23	3.69
1995 Twins	R	3	1	0	0	5.2	29	7	4	4	0	0	0	1	4	0	9	1	0	0	0	-	0	0- -	-	6.42	6.35
1996 St.Paul	IND	19	18	0	0	86.1	417	121	70	56	13	5	3	1	42	2	54	14	1	6	8	.429	0	0- -	-	7.22	5.84
1997 St.Lucie	A+	22	18	4	1	123.1	496	114	62	55	8	3	7	4	18	1	64	4	7	5	10	.333	0	0- -	-	2.61	4.01
1998 Binghamton	AA	24	13	0	3	90.0	382	91	44	37	12	4	2	1	29	2	65	2	4	8	5	.615	0	2- -	-	4.08	3.70
1998 Norfolk	AAA	9	9	0	0	51.2	235	60	43	38	12	3	2	1	22	0	32	0	0	0	6	.000	0	0- -	-	6.16	6.62
1999 Norfolk	AAA	35	14	0	3	99.2	442	109	55	49	9	5	2	2	36	1	85	5	3	6	4	.600	0	0- -	-	4.38	4.42
1999 Binghamton	AA	1	1	0	0	5.0	18	3	0	0	0	0	0	0	0	0	5	0	0	1	0	1.000	0	0- -	-	0.75	0.00
2000 Norfolk	AAA	53	1	0	18	72.0	313	80	32	28	3	5	2	3	18	2	57	8	0	3	5	.375	0	5- -	-	3.77	3.50
2001 Ottawa	AAA	4	0	0	3	5.0	21	5	1	1	0	1	0	0	1	0	4	0	0	0	0	-	0	0- -	-	2.76	1.80
2001 Montreal	NL	62	0	0	9	47.2	199	43	20	20	5	2	4	3	13	0	39	2	0	3	1	.750	0	3-4	8	3.31	3.78
2002 Montreal	NL	67	0	0	28	64.0	263	49	29	22	4	2	2	1	22	5	67	1	0	4	2	.667	0	17-19	14	2.31	3.09
2 ML YEARS		129	0	0	37	111.2	462	92	49	42	9	4	6	4	35	5	106	3	0	7	3	.700	0	20-23	22	2.73	3.39

Shannon Stewart

Bats: R **Throws:** R **Pos:** LF-100; DH-38; PH-2; PR-1 · **Ht:** 6'1" **Wt:** 210 **Born:** 2/25/74 **Age:** 29

Year Team	Lg	G	AB	H	2B	3B	HR	(Hm Rd)	TB	R	RBI	RC	TBB	IBB	SO	HBP	SH	SF	SB	CS	SB%	GDP	Avg	OBP	Slg
1995 Toronto	AL	12	38	8	0	0	0	(0 0)	8	2	1	3	5	0	5	1	0	0	2	0	1.00	0	.211	.318	.211
1996 Toronto	AL	7	17	3	1	0	0	(0 0)	4	2	2	1	1	0	4	0	0	0	1	0	1.00	1	.176	.222	.235
1997 Toronto	AL	44	168	48	13	7	0	(0 0)	75	25	22	29	19	1	24	4	0	2	10	3	.77	3	.286	.368	.446
1998 Toronto	AL	144	516	144	29	3	12	(6 6)	215	90	55	88	67	1	77	15	6	1	51	18	.74	5	.279	.371	.417
1999 Toronto	AL	145	608	185	28	2	11	(4 7)	250	102	67	95	59	0	83	8	3	4	37	14	.73	12	.304	.371	.411
2000 Toronto	AL	136	583	186	43	5	21	(12 9)	302	107	69	106	37	1	79	6	1	4	20	5	.80	12	.319	.363	.518
2001 Toronto	AL	155	640	202	44	7	12	(6 6)	296	103	60	109	46	1	72	11	0	1	27	10	.73	9	.316	.371	.463
2002 Toronto	AL	141	577	175	38	6	10	(4 6)	255	103	45	91	54	2	60	9	0	1	14	2	.88	17	.303	.371	.442
8 ML YEARS		784	3147	951	196	30	66	(32 34)	1405	534	321	522	288	6	404	54	10	13	162	52	.76	59	.302	.369	.446

Kelly Stinnett

Bats: R **Throws:** R **Pos:** C-30; PH-4 · **Ht:** 5'11" **Wt:** 225 **Born:** 2/4/70 **Age:** 33

Year Team	Lg	G	AB	H	2B	3B	HR	(Hm Rd)	TB	R	RBI	RC	TBB	IBB	SO	HBP	SH	SF	SB	CS	SB%	GDP	Avg	OBP	Slg
2002 Louisville*	AAA	30	86	17	6	0	0	(- -)	23	6	5	4	3	0	24	0	0	0	0	0	-	1	.198	.225	.267
1994 New York	NL	47	150	38	6	2	2	(0 2)	54	20	14	18	11	1	28	5	0	1	2	0	1.00	5	.253	.323	.360
1995 New York	NL	77	196	43	8	1	4	(1 3)	65	23	18	24	29	3	65	4	0	1	2	0	1.00	3	.219	.338	.332
1996 Milwaukee	NL	14	26	2	0	0	0	(0 0)	2	1	0	0	2	0	11	1	0	0	0	0	-	0	.077	.172	.077
1997 Milwaukee	NL	30	36	9	4	0	0	(0 0)	13	2	3	4	3	0	9	0	0	0	0	0	-	0	.250	.308	.361
1998 Arizona	NL	92	274	71	14	1	11	(5 6)	120	35	34	41	35	3	74	6	1	2	0	1	.00	9	.259	.353	.438
1999 Arizona	NL	88	284	66	13	0	14	(3 11)	121	36	38	37	24	2	83	5	2	2	2	1	.67	4	.232	.302	.426
2000 Arizona	NL	76	240	52	7	0	8	(2 6)	83	22	33	23	19	4	56	6	0	1	0	0	.00	5	.217	.291	.346
2001 Cincinnati	NL	63	187	48	11	0	9	(6 3)	86	27	25	27	17	3	61	5	1	1	2	2	.50	5	.257	.333	.460
2002 Cincinnati	NL	34	93	21	5	0	3	(1 2)	35	10	13	13	15	1	25	0	0	0	2	0	1.00	5	.226	.333	.376
9 ML YEARS		521	1486	350	68	4	51	(18 33)	579	176	178	187	155	17	412	34	4	6	10	5	.67	30	.236	.321	.390

Ricky Stone

Pitches: R **Bats:** R **Pos:** RP-78 · **Ht:** 6'1" **Wt:** 190 **Born:** 2/28/75 **Age:** 28

Year Team	Lg	G	GS	CG	GF	IP	BFP	H	R	ER	SH	SF	HB	TBB	IBB	SO	WP	Bk	W	L	Pct	ShO	Sv-Op	Hld	ERC	ERA
1994 Great Falls	R+	13	7	0	4	50.2	232	55	40	25	5	0	1	24	0	48	9	0	2	2	.500	0	2- -	-	4.91	4.44
1995 Sn Brnardino	A+	12	12	0	0	58.0	273	79	50	42	7	6	3	25	0	31	5	0	3	5	.375	0	0- -	-	6.70	6.52
1995 Yakima	A-	16	6	0	7	48.0	213	54	31	28	5	2	2	20	0	28	4	1	4	4	.500	0	2- -	-	5.12	5.25
1996 Savannah	A	5	5	0	0	31.2	130	34	15	14	2	2	1	9	0	31	5	0	4	2	.667	0	0- -	-	3.94	3.98
1996 Vero Beach	A+	21	21	1	0	112.2	488	115	58	48	9	4	3	46	0	74	10	0	8	6	.571	0	0- -	-	4.22	3.83

Year Team	Lg	G	GS	CG	GF	IP	BFP	H	R	ER	HR	SH	SF	HB	TBB	IBB	SO	WP	Bk	W	L	Pct	ShO	Sv-Op	Hld	ERC	ERA
1997 San Antonio	AA	25	5	0	10	52.2	245	63	33	32	4	4	1	3	30	0	46	3	0	0	3	.000	0	3- -	-	6.04	5.47
1997 Sn Brnardino	A+	8	8	0	0	53.2	206	40	22	20	4	2	1	2	10	0	40	2	0	3	3	.500	0	0- -	-	2.03	3.35
1998 San Antonio	AA	13	13	1	0	82.0	336	76	40	35	7	5	1	1	26	0	69	6	0	7	2	.778	1	0- -	-	3.38	3.84
1998 Albuquerque	AAA	18	16	0	0	105.1	465	120	69	63	13	2	1	3	41	0	85	9	1	5	5	.500	0	0- -	-	5.18	5.38
1999 Albuquerque	AAA	27	27	2	0	167.0	764	205	123	102	23	8	7	8	71	4	132	11	1	6	10	.375	0	0- -	-	5.99	5.50
2000 Albuquerque	AAA	48	7	0	22	120.1	535	146	79	66	9	7	6	7	42	3	75	10	0	5	3	.643	0	5- -	-	5.19	4.94
2001 New Orleans	AAA	51	8	0	15	95.1	404	98	42	38	8	4	1	8	27	4	78	6	1	6	3	.667	0	2- -	-	3.99	3.59
2001 Houston	NL	6	0	0	3	7.2	33	8	3	2	1	0	0	0	2	1	4	0	0	0	0	-	0	0-0	-	3.69	2.35
2002 Houston	NL	78	0	0	16	77.1	335	78	36	31	9	5	2	1	34	3	63	1	0	3	3	.500	0	1-2	12	4.43	3.61
2 ML YEARS		84	0	0	19	85.0	368	86	39	33	10	5	2	1	36	4	67	1	0	3	3	.500	0	1-2	12	4.36	3.49

Todd Stottlemyre

Pitches: R **Bats:** L **Pos:** SP-4; RP-1

Ht: 6'2" **Wt:** 210 **Born:** 5/20/65 **Age:** 38

Year Team	Lg	G	GS	CG	GF	IP	BFP	H	R	ER	HR	SH	SF	HB	TBB	IBB	SO	WP	Bk	W	L	Pct	ShO	Sv-Op	Hld	ERC	ERA
2002 Tucson*	AAA	11	0	0	5	15.2	66	13	6	6	0	0	1	0	4	1	12	0	0	1	1	.500	0	1- -	-	1.84	3.45
1988 Toronto	AL	28	16	0	2	98.0	443	109	70	62	15	5	3	4	46	5	67	2	3	4	8	.333	0	0-1	0	5.49	5.69
1989 Toronto	AL	27	18	0	4	127.2	545	137	56	55	11	3	7	5	44	4	63	4	1	7	7	.500	0	0-0	0	4.37	3.88
1990 Toronto	AL	33	33	4	0	203.0	866	214	101	98	18	3	5	8	69	4	115	6	1	13	17	.433	0	0-0	0	4.27	4.34
1991 Toronto	AL	34	34	1	0	219.0	921	194	97	92	21	0	8	12	75	3	116	4	0	15	8	.652	0	0-0	0	3.39	3.78
1992 Toronto	AL	28	27	6	0	174.0	755	175	99	87	20	2	11	10	63	4	98	7	0	12	11	.522	2	0-0	0	4.25	4.50
1993 Toronto	AL	30	28	1	0	176.2	786	204	107	95	11	5	11	3	69	5	98	7	1	11	12	.478	1	0-0	0	4.67	4.84
1994 Toronto	AL	26	19	3	5	140.2	605	149	67	66	19	4	5	7	48	2	105	0	0	7	7	.500	1	1-3	0	4.67	4.22
1995 Oakland	AL	31	31	2	0	209.2	920	228	117	106	26	4	4	6	80	7	205	11	0	14	7	.667	0	0-0	0	4.75	4.55
1996 St Louis	NL	34	33	5	0	223.1	944	191	100	96	30	12	9	4	93	8	194	8	1	14	11	.560	2	0-0	0	3.58	3.87
1997 St Louis	NL	28	28	0	0	181.0	761	155	86	78	16	8	5	12	65	3	160	6	0	12	9	.571	0	0-0	0	3.29	3.88
1998 Stl-Tex		33	33	3	0	221.2	949	214	107	92	25	8	6	4	81	1	204	5	2	14	13	.519	0	0-0	0	3.88	3.74
1999 Arizona	NL	17	17	0	0	101.1	446	106	51	46	12	3	1	6	40	1	74	2	0	6	3	.667	0	0-0	0	4.67	4.09
2000 Arizona	NL	18	18	0	0	95.1	408	98	55	52	18	3	2	2	36	2	76	2	1	9	6	.600	0	0-0	0	4.90	4.91
2002 Arizona	NL	5	4	0	1	20.1	92	26	17	17	4	1	1	0	7	0	12	0	0	0	2	.000	0	0-0	0	6.22	7.52
1998 St Louis	NL	23	23	3	0	161.1	674	146	74	63	20	7	3	4	51	0	147	4	2	9	9	.500	0	0-0	0	3.48	3.51
1998 Texas	AL	10	10	0	0	60.1	275	68	33	29	5	1	3	0	30	1	57	1	0	5	4	.556	0	0-0	0	4.99	4.33
14 ML YEARS		372	339	25	12	2191.2	9441	2200	1130	1042	246	61	78	83	816	49	1587	64	10	138	121	.533	6	1-4	0	4.20	4.28

Pat Strange

Pitches: R **Bats:** R **Pos:** RP-5

Ht: 6'5" **Wt:** 243 **Born:** 8/23/80 **Age:** 22

Year Team	Lg	G	GS	CG	GF	IP	BFP	H	R	ER	HR	SH	SF	HB	TBB	IBB	SO	WP	Bk	W	L	Pct	ShO	Sv-Op	Hld	ERC	ERA
1998 Mets	R	4	4	0	0	18.0	79	18	3	3	0	0	0	1	7	0	19	0	0	1	1	.500	0	0- -	-	3.49	1.50
1999 Capital City	A	28	21	2	1	154.0	627	138	57	45	4	4	3	10	29	1	113	7	0	12	5	.706	0	1- -	-	2.50	2.63
2000 St.Lucie	A+	19	13	2	1	88.0	374	78	48	35	4	2	5	9	32	0	77	9	1	10	1	.909	0	0- -	-	3.34	3.58
2000 Binghamton	AA	10	10	0	0	55.1	252	62	30	28	2	3	2	1	30	0	36	3	0	4	3	.571	0	0- -	-	4.93	4.55
2001 Binghamton	AA	26	24	1	1	153.1	669	171	94	83	18	5	6	12	52	1	106	7	0	11	6	.647	0	0- -	-	5.01	4.87
2001 Norfolk	AAA	1	1	0	0	6.0	23	4	0	0	0	0	0	0	1	0	6	0	0	1	0	1.000	0	0- -	-	1.23	0.00
2002 Norfolk	AAA	29	25	2	1	165.0	699	165	77	70	12	6	4	7	59	2	109	3	0	10	10	.500	0	0- -	-	3.94	3.82
2002 New York	NL	5	0	0	4	8.0	30	6	1	1	0	0	0	0	1	1	4	0	1	0	0	-	0	0-0	0	1.32	1.13

Scott Strickland

Pitches: R **Bats:** R **Pos:** RP-69

Ht: 5'11" **Wt:** 180 **Born:** 4/26/76 **Age:** 27

Year Team	Lg	G	GS	CG	GF	IP	BFP	H	R	ER	HR	SH	SF	HB	TBB	IBB	SO	WP	Bk	W	L	Pct	ShO	Sv-Op	Hld	ERC	ERA
1999 Montreal	NL	17	0	0	5	18.0	78	15	10	9	3	2	0	0	11	0	23	0	0	0	1	.000	0	0-0	2	4.48	4.50
2000 Montreal	NL	49	0	0	20	48.0	200	38	18	16	3	3	3	1	16	2	48	2	0	4	3	.571	0	9-13	6	2.44	3.00
2001 Montreal	NL	77	0	0	31	81.1	351	67	36	29	9	3	1	4	41	5	85	4	0	2	6	.250	0	9-12	12	3.65	3.21
2002 Mon-NYM	NL	69	0	0	21	68.2	299	61	29	27	7	1	2	2	33	9	69	3	0	6	9	.400	0	2-6	15	3.64	3.54
2002 Montreal	NL	1	0	0	0	1.0	3	0	0	0	0	0	0	0	0	0	2	0	0	0	0	-	0	0-0	0	0.00	0.00
2002 New York	NL	68	0	0	21	67.2	296	61	29	27	7	1	2	2	33	9	67	3	0	6	9	.400	0	2-6	15	3.74	3.59
4 ML YEARS		212	0	0	77	216.0	928	181	93	81	22	9	6	7	101	16	225	9	0	12	19	.387	0	20-31	35	3.43	3.38

Everett Stull

Pitches: R **Bats:** R **Pos:** SP-2

Ht: 6'3" **Wt:** 200 **Born:** 8/24/71 **Age:** 31

Year Team	Lg	G	GS	CG	GF	IP	BFP	H	R	ER	HR	SH	SF	HB	TBB	IBB	SO	WP	Bk	W	L	Pct	ShO	Sv-Op	Hld	ERC	ERA
2002 Indianapolis*	AAA	24	24	0	0	151.0	644	149	72	65	13	4	3	8	49	2	119	4	1	11	11	.500	0	0- -	-	3.81	3.87
1997 Montreal	NL	3	0	0	1	3.1	21	7	7	6	1	1	0	0	4	0	2	0	0	0	1	.000	0	0-0	0	17.12	16.20
1999 Atlanta	NL	1	0	0	0	0.2	7	2	3	1	0	0	1	0	2	0	0	0	0	0	0	-	0	0-0	0	25.31	13.50
2000 Milwaukee	NL	20	4	0	3	43.1	199	41	30	28	7	2	3	4	30	3	33	5	0	2	3	.400	0	0-0	0	5.72	5.82
2002 Milwaukee	NL	2	2	0	0	10.0	53	15	7	7	0	1	0	1	9	2	7	0	0	0	1	.000	0	0-0	0	8.45	6.30
4 ML YEARS		26	6	0	4	57.1	280	65	47	42	8	4	4	5	45	5	42	5	0	2	5	.286	0	0-0	0	7.01	6.59

Tanyon Sturtze

Pitches: R **Bats:** R **Pos:** SP-33

Ht: 6'5" **Wt:** 221 **Born:** 10/12/70 **Age:** 32

Year Team	Lg	G	GS	CG	GF	IP	BFP	H	R	ER	HR	SH	SF	HB	TBB	IBB	SO	WP	Bk	W	L	Pct	ShO	Sv-Op	Hld	ERC	ERA
1995 Chicago	NL	2	0	0	0	2.0	9	2	2	2	1	0	0	0	1	0	0	0	0	0	0	-	0	0-0	0	7.30	9.00
1996 Chicago	NL	6	0	0	3	11.0	51	16	11	11	3	0	0	0	5	0	7	0	0	1	0	1.000	0	0-0	0	8.87	9.00
1997 Texas	AL	9	5	0	1	32.2	155	45	30	30	6	0	4	0	18	0	18	1	1	1	1	.500	0	0-0	0	7.84	8.27
1999 Chicago	AL	1	1	0	0	6.0	22	4	0	0	0	0	0	0	2	0	2	0	0	0	0	-	0	0-0	0	1.73	0.00

			HOW MUCH HE PITCHED						WHAT HE GAVE UP												THE RESULTS							
Year Team	Lg	G	GS	CG	GF	IP	BFP	H	R	ER	HR	SH	SF	HB	TBB	IBB	SO	WP	Bk	W	L	Pct	ShO	Sv-Op	Hld	ERC	ERA
2000 CWS-TB	AL	29	6	0	9	68.1	300	72	39	36	8	1	2	3	29	1	44	2	0	5	2	.714	0	0-0	0	4.80	4.74
2001 Tampa Bay	AL	39	27	0	6	195.1	837	200	98	96	23	2	10	9	79	0	110	11	0	11	12	.478	0	1-3	3	4.65	4.42
2002 Tampa Bay	AL	33	33	4	0	224.0	1008	271	141	129	33	7	6	9	89	2	137	7	2	4	18	.182	0	0-0	0	5.87	5.18
2000 Chicago	AL	10	1	0	2	15.2	85	25	23	21	4	0	2	2	15	0	6	1	0	1	2	.333	0	0-0	0	12.84	12.06
2000 Tampa Bay	AL	19	5	0	7	52.2	215	47	16	15	4	1	0	1	14	1	38	1	0	4	0	1.000	0	0-0	0	2.89	2.56
7 ML YEARS		119	72	4	19	539.1	2382	610	321	304	74	10	22	21	223	3	318	21	3	22	33	.400	0	1-3	3	5.41	5.07

Chris Stynes

Bats: R **Throws:** R **Pos:** PH-44; 3B-40; 2B-20; PR-1   **Ht:** 5'10" **Wt:** 205 **Born:** 1/19/73 **Age:** 30

							BATTING												BASERUNNING				AVERAGES		
Year Team	Lg	G	AB	H	2B	3B	HR	(Hm	Rd)	TB	R	RBI	RC	TBB	IBB	SO	HBP	SH	SF	SB	CS	SB%	GDP	Avg	OBP	Slg
1995 Kansas City	AL	22	35	6	1	0	0	(0	0)	7	7	2	1	4	0	3	0	0	0	0	0	-	3	.171	.256	.200
1996 Kansas City	AL	36	92	27	6	0	0	(0	0)	33	8	6	10	2	0	5	0	1	0	5	2	.71	1	.293	.309	.359
1997 Cincinnati	NL	49	198	69	7	1	6	(2	4)	96	31	28	37	11	1	13	4	2	0	11	2	.85	5	.348	.394	.485
1998 Cincinnati	NL	123	347	88	10	1	6	(3	3)	118	52	27	42	32	1	36	4	4	1	15	1	.94	5	.254	.323	.340
1999 Cincinnati	NL	73	113	27	1	0	2	(1	1)	34	18	14	11	12	1	13	0	3	1	5	2	.71	2	.239	.310	.301
2000 Cincinnati	NL	119	380	127	24	1	12	(8	4)	189	71	40	71	32	2	54	2	3	3	5	2	.71	5	.334	.386	.497
2001 Boston	AL	96	361	101	19	2	8	(3	5)	148	52	33	43	20	0	56	3	1	1	4	5	.44	12	.280	.322	.410
2002 Chicago	NL	98	195	47	9	1	5	(1	4)	73	25	26	27	21	1	29	1	5	3	1	1	.50	5	.241	.314	.374
8 ML YEARS		616	1721	492	77	6	39	(18	21)	698	264	176	242	134	6	209	14	19	9	46	15	.75	38	.286	.341	.406

Scott Sullivan

Pitches: R **Bats:** R **Pos:** RP-71   **Ht:** 6'3" **Wt:** 210 **Born:** 3/13/71 **Age:** 32

			HOW MUCH HE PITCHED						WHAT HE GAVE UP												THE RESULTS							
Year Team	Lg	G	GS	CG	GF	IP	BFP	H	R	ER	HR	SH	SF	HB	TBB	IBB	SO	WP	Bk	W	L	Pct	ShO	Sv-Op	Hld	ERC	ERA
1995 Cincinnati	NL	3	0	0	1	3.2	17	4	2	2	0	1	0	0	2	0	2	0	0	0	0	-	0	0-0	0	4.28	4.91
1996 Cincinnati	NL	7	0	0	4	8.0	35	7	2	2	0	1	0	1	5	0	3	1	0	0	0	-	0	0-0	0	4.11	2.25
1997 Cincinnati	NL	59	0	0	15	97.1	402	79	36	35	12	3	3	7	30	8	96	7	1	5	3	.625	0	1-2	13	3.01	3.24
1998 Cincinnati	NL	67	0	0	13	102.0	440	98	62	59	14	3	4	9	36	4	86	4	0	5	5	.500	0	1-4	5	4.22	5.21
1999 Cincinnati	NL	79	0	0	16	113.2	470	88	41	38	10	4	4	8	47	4	78	6	1	5	4	.556	0	3-5	13	3.08	3.01
2000 Cincinnati	NL	79	0	0	22	106.1	439	87	44	41	14	2	5	9	38	8	96	7	0	3	6	.333	0	3-6	22	3.40	3.47
2001 Cincinnati	NL	79	0	0	16	103.1	437	94	44	38	10	1	5	8	36	8	82	0	0	7	1	.875	0	0-3	20	3.55	3.31
2002 Cincinnati	NL	71	0	0	16	78.2	358	93	60	53	15	2	3	5	31	11	78	2	0	6	5	.545	0	1-3	19	5.81	6.06
8 ML YEARS		444	0	0	103	613.0	2598	550	291	268	75	17	24	47	225	43	521	27	2	31	24	.564	0	9-23	92	3.74	3.93

Jeff Suppan

Pitches: R **Bats:** R **Pos:** SP-33   **Ht:** 6'2" **Wt:** 210 **Born:** 1/2/75 **Age:** 28

			HOW MUCH HE PITCHED						WHAT HE GAVE UP												THE RESULTS							
Year Team	Lg	G	GS	CG	GF	IP	BFP	H	R	ER	HR	SH	SF	HB	TBB	IBB	SO	WP	Bk	W	L	Pct	ShO	Sv-Op	Hld	ERC	ERA
1995 Boston	AL	8	3	0	1	22.2	100	29	15	15	4	1	1	0	5	1	19	0	0	1	2	.333	0	0-0	0	5.43	5.96
1996 Boston	AL	8	4	0	2	22.2	107	29	19	19	3	1	4	1	13	0	13	3	0	1	1	.500	0	0-0	0	7.03	7.54
1997 Boston	AL	23	22	0	1	112.1	503	140	75	71	12	0	4	4	36	1	67	5	0	7	3	.700	0	0-0	0	5.39	5.69
1998 Ari-KC		17	14	1	2	78.2	345	91	56	50	13	3	2	1	22	1	51	2	0	1	7	.125	0	0-0	0	4.95	5.72
1999 Kansas City	AL	32	32	4	0	208.2	887	222	110	105	28	7	5	3	62	4	103	5	1	10	12	.455	1	0-0	0	4.33	4.53
2000 Kansas City	AL	35	33	3	0	217.0	948	240	121	119	36	5	6	7	84	3	128	7	1	10	9	.526	1	0-0	0	5.31	4.94
2001 Kansas City	AL	34	34	1	0	218.1	946	227	120	106	26	5	6	12	74	3	120	6	0	10	14	.417	0	0-0	0	4.40	4.37
2002 Kansas City	AL	33	33	3	0	208.0	912	229	134	123	32	4	11	7	68	3	109	10	1	9	16	.360	1	0-0	0	4.84	5.32
1998 Arizona	NL	13	13	1	0	66.0	299	82	55	49	12	3	2	1	21	1	39	2	0	1	7	.125	0	0-0	0	5.73	6.68
1998 Kansas City	AL	4	1	0	2	12.2	46	9	1	1	1	0	0	0	1	0	12	0	0	0	0	-	0	0-0	0	1.51	0.71
8 ML YEARS		190	175	12	6	1088.1	4748	1207	653	608	154	26	39	35	364	16	610	38	3	49	64	.434	3	0-0	1	4.86	5.03

B.J. Surhoff

Bats: L **Throws:** R **Pos:** 1B-10; RF-9; PH-6; 3B-1   **Ht:** 6'1" **Wt:** 200 **Born:** 8/4/64 **Age:** 38

							BATTING												BASERUNNING				AVERAGES		
Year Team	Lg	G	AB	H	2B	3B	HR	(Hm	Rd)	TB	R	RBI	RC	TBB	IBB	SO	HBP	SH	SF	SB	CS	SB%	GDP	Avg	OBP	Slg
1987 Milwaukee	NL	115	395	118	22	3	7	(5	2)	167	50	68	56	36	1	30	0	5	9	11	10	.52	13	.299	.350	.423
1988 Milwaukee	NL	139	493	121	21	0	5	(2	3)	157	47	38	45	31	9	49	3	11	3	21	6	.78	12	.245	.292	.318
1989 Milwaukee	NL	126	436	108	17	4	5	(3	2)	148	42	55	41	25	1	29	3	3	10	14	12	.54	8	.248	.287	.339
1990 Milwaukee	NL	135	474	131	21	4	6	(4	2)	178	55	59	61	41	5	37	1	7	7	18	7	.72	8	.276	.331	.376
1991 Milwaukee	NL	143	505	146	19	4	5	(3	2)	188	57	68	53	26	2	33	0	13	9	5	8	.38	21	.289	.319	.372
1992 Milwaukee	NL	139	480	121	19	1	4	(3	1)	154	63	62	50	46	8	41	2	5	10	14	8	.64	9	.252	.314	.321
1993 Milwaukee	NL	148	552	151	38	3	7	(4	3)	216	66	79	67	36	5	47	2	4	5	12	9	.57	9	.274	.318	.391
1994 Milwaukee	NL	40	134	35	11	2	5	(2	3)	65	20	22	21	16	0	14	0	2	2	0	1	.00	5	.261	.336	.485
1995 Milwaukee	NL	117	415	133	26	3	13	(7	6)	204	72	73	75	37	4	43	4	2	4	7	3	.70	7	.320	.378	.492
1996 Baltimore	AL	143	537	157	27	6	21	(12	9)	259	74	82	89	47	8	79	3	2	1	0	1	.00	7	.292	.352	.482
1997 Baltimore	AL	147	528	150	30	4	18	(10	8)	242	80	88	84	49	14	60	5	3	10	1	1	.50	7	.284	.345	.458
1998 Baltimore	AL	162	573	160	34	1	22	(9	13)	262	79	92	84	49	9	81	1	1	10	9	7	.56	13	.279	.332	.457
1999 Baltimore	AL	162	673	207	38	1	28	(9	19)	331	104	107	111	43	1	78	2	1	8	5	1	.83	15	.308	.347	.492
2000 Bal-Atl		147	539	157	36	2	14	(7	7)	239	69	68	81	41	3	58	3	2	2	10	2	.83	10	.291	.344	.443
2001 Atlanta	NL	141	484	131	33	4	10	(5	5)	196	68	58	65	38	5	48	1	1	1	9	3	.75	5	.271	.321	.405
2002 Atlanta	NL	25	75	22	5	0	0	(0	0)	27	9	9	9	9	0	5	0	1	0	1	3	.25	1	.293	.369	.360
2000 Baltimore	AL	103	411	120	27	0	13	(6	7)	186	56	57	63	29	3	46	2	1	1	7	2	.78	5	.292	.341	.453
2000 Atlanta	NL	44	128	37	9	2	1	(1	0)	53	13	11	18	12	0	12	1	1	1	3	0	1.00	5	.289	.352	.414
16 ML YEARS		2029	7293	2048	397	39	170	(85	85)	3033	951	1028	992	570	75	732	30	63	97	137	82	.63	150	.281	.331	.416

Larry Sutton

Bats: L **Throws:** L **Pos:** 1B-6; LF-2; PR-2; RF-1   **Ht:** 6'0" **Wt:** 185 **Born:** 5/14/70 **Age:** 33

Year Team	Lg	G	AB	H	2B	3B	HR	(Hm	Rd)	TB	R	RBI	RC	TBB	IBB	SO	HBP	SH	SF	SB	CS	SB%	GDP	Avg	OBP	Slg
2002 Sacramento*	AAA	116	431	126	40	2	12	(-	-)	206	83	81	88	93	1	108	1	0	3	2	1	1.00	9	.292	.417	.478
1997 Kansas City	AL	27	69	20	2	0	2	(1	1)	28	9	8	10	5	0	12	0	1	0	0	0	-	0	.290	.338	.406
1998 Kansas City	AL	111	310	76	14	2	5	(3	2)	109	29	42	34	29	3	46	3	4	5	3	3	.50	5	.245	.311	.352
1999 Kansas City	AL	43	102	23	6	0	2	(1	1)	35	14	15	11	13	0	17	0	1	2	1	0	1.00	4	.225	.308	.343
2000 St Louis	NL	23	25	8	0	0	1	(0	1)	11	5	6	5	5	0	7	0	1	2	0	0	-	0	.320	.406	.440
2001 St Louis	NL	33	42	5	1	0	1	(1	0)	9	3	3	0	1	0	10	0	1	0	0	0	-	0	.119	.140	.214
2002 Oakland	AL	7	19	2	0	0	1	(1	0)	5	3	3	1	1	0	8	0	0	0	0	0	-	1	.105	.150	.263
6 ML YEARS		244	567	134	23	2	12	(8	4)	197	63	77	61	54	3	100	3	8	9	4	3	.57	10	.236	.302	.347

Ichiro Suzuki

Bats: L **Throws:** R **Pos:** RF-150; DH-4; CF-3; PH-3   **Ht:** 5'9" **Wt:** 160 **Born:** 10/22/73 **Age:** 29

Year Team	Lg	G	AB	H	2B	3B	HR	(Hm	Rd)	TB	R	RBI	RC	TBB	IBB	SO	HBP	SH	SF	SB	CS	SB%	GDP	Avg	OBP	Slg
2001 Seattle	AL	157	692	242	34	8	8	(5	3)	316	127	69	124	30	10	53	4	8	4	56	14	.80	3	.350	.381	.457
2002 Seattle	AL	157	647	208	27	8	8	(4	4)	275	111	51	108	68	27	62	5	3	5	31	15	.67	8	.321	.388	.425
2 ML YEARS		314	1339	450	61	16	16	(9	7)	591	238	120	232	98	37	115	13	7	9	87	29	.75	11	.336	.385	.441

Mac Suzuki

Pitches: R **Bats:** R **Pos:** RP-6; SP-1   **Ht:** 6'3" **Wt:** 205 **Born:** 5/31/75 **Age:** 28

Year Team	Lg	G	GS	CG	GF	IP	BFP	H	R	ER	HR	SH	SF	HB	TBB	IBB	SO	WP	Bk	W	L	Pct	ShO	Sv-Op	Hld	ERC	ERA
2002 Wichita*	AA	1	1	0	0	5.0	18	0	0	0	0	0	0	0	2	0	3	0	0	0	0	-	0	0-0	-	0.17	0.00
2002 Omaha*	AAA	29	1	0	10	53.2	237	63	30	27	6	4	1	1	21	2	46	4	0	0	4	.000	0	0- -	-	5.23	4.53
1996 Seattle	AL	1	0	0	0	1.1	8	2	3	3	0	0	0	0	2	1	1	0	0	0	0	-	0	0-0	0	8.87	20.25
1998 Seattle	AL	6	5	0	0	26.1	127	34	23	21	3	0	0	0	15	0	19	0	0	1	2	.333	0	0-0	0	6.52	7.18
1999 Sea-KC	AL	38	13	0	6	110.0	510	124	92	83	16	2	3	7	64	3	68	11	0	2	5	.286	0	0-0	6	6.19	6.79
2000 Kansas City	AL	32	29	1	0	188.2	839	195	100	91	26	2	3	3	94	6	135	11	0	8	10	.444	1	0-0	0	4.96	4.34
2001 KC-Col-Mil	AL	33	19	0	4	118.1	542	122	87	77	20	4	3	8	73	4	89	16	0	5	12	.294	0	0-0	1	5.94	5.86
2002 Kansas City	AL	7	1	0	1	21.0	100	24	21	21	2	1	1	0	17	2	15	6	1	0	2	.000	0	0-0	0	6.48	9.00
1999 Seattle	AL	16	4	0	3	42.0	207	47	47	44	7	0	3	4	34	2	32	2	0	0	2	.000	0	0-0	0	7.34	9.43
1999 Kansas City	AL	22	9	0	3	68.0	303	77	45	39	9	2	0	3	30	1	36	9	0	2	3	.400	0	0-0	0	5.49	5.16
2001 Kansas City	AL	15	9	0	0	56.0	251	61	38	33	12	0	3	0	25	1	37	6	0	2	5	.286	0	0-0	0	5.85	5.30
2001 Colorado	NL	3	1	0	0	6.1	39	9	12	11	3	0	0	1	11	0	5	2	0	0	2	.000	0	0-0	0	17.88	15.63
2001 Milwaukee	NL	15	7	0	1	56.0	252	52	37	33	5	4	0	4	37	3	47	8	0	3	5	.375	0	0-0	1	4.87	5.30
6 ML YEARS		117	67	1	11	465.2	2126	501	326	296	67	9	10	18	265	16	327	44	1	16	31	.340	1	0-0	-	5.66	5.72

Pedro Swann

Bats: L **Throws:** R **Pos:** PH-9; PR-3; RF-1; DH-1   **Ht:** 6'0" **Wt:** 200 **Born:** 10/27/70 **Age:** 32

Year Team	Lg	G	AB	H	2B	3B	HR	(Hm	Rd)	TB	R	RBI	RC	TBB	IBB	SO	HBP	SH	SF	SB	CS	SB%	GDP	Avg	OBP	Slg
1991 Idaho Falls	R+	55	174	48	6	1	3	(-	-)	65	35	28	27	33	0	45	2	1	2	8	5	.62	4	.276	.393	.374
1992 Pulaski	R+	59	203	61	18	1	5	(-	-)	96	36	34	39	32	3	33	7	0	1	13	6	.68	5	.300	.412	.473
1993 Durham	A+	61	182	63	8	2	6	(-	-)	93	27	27	33	19	0	38	1	0	0	6	12	.33	2	.346	.411	.511
1993 Greenville	AA	44	157	48	9	2	3	(-	-)	70	19	21	22	9	0	23	1	1	0	2	2	.50	5	.306	.347	.446
1994 Greenville	AA	126	428	121	25	2	10	(-	-)	180	55	49	61	46	2	85	4	0	2	16	9	.64	14	.283	.356	.421
1995 Richmond	AAA	15	38	8	1	0	0	(-	-)	9	2	3	1	1	0	2	1	0	0	0	2	.00	0	.211	.250	.237
1995 Greenville	AA	102	339	110	24	2	11	(-	-)	171	57	64	66	45	2	63	3	0	3	14	11	.56	8	.324	.405	.504
1996 Greenville	AA	35	129	40	5	0	3	(-	-)	54	15	20	22	18	2	23	3	1	1	4	4	.50	3	.310	.404	.419
1996 Richmond	AAA	93	296	74	11	4	4	(-	-)	105	42	35	31	22	2	56	4	2	3	7	7	.50	5	.250	.308	.355
1997 Greenville	AA	124	465	133	29	2	24	(-	-)	238	78	83	80	49	5	75	4	0	1	5	5	.50	14	.286	.358	.512
1998 Toledo	AAA	120	419	122	28	2	15	(-	-)	199	56	66	68	41	4	74	3	1	4	6	3	.67	11	.291	.355	.475
1999 Toledo	AAA	103	332	86	14	2	10	(-	-)	134	51	37	46	36	0	67	6	0	5	3	1	.75	7	.259	.338	.404
2000 Richmond	AAA	125	442	135	22	2	9	(-	-)	188	70	57	72	54	6	68	5	2	1	6	5	.55	10	.305	.386	.425
2001 Richmond	AAA	139	488	142	33	5	8	(-	-)	209	66	72	75	52	3	95	8	1	10	12	6	.67	14	.291	.362	.428
2002 Syracuse	AAA	97	368	102	17	4	14	(-	-)	169	52	62	56	37	2	77	8	1	3	1	3	.25	14	.277	.353	.459
2000 Atlanta	NL	4	2	0	0	0	0	(0	0)	0	0	0	0	0	0	2	0	0	0	0	0	-	0	.000	.000	.000
2002 Toronto	AL	13	12	1	0	0	0	(0	0)	1	3	1	0	1	0	6	0	0	0	0	0	-	0	.083	.154	.083
2 ML YEARS		17	14	1	0	0	0	(0	0)	1	3	1	0	1	0	8	0	0	0	0	0	-	0	.071	.133	.071

Mark Sweeney

Bats: L **Throws:** L **Pos:** PH-35; 1B-11; RF-5; DH-1   **Ht:** 6'1" **Wt:** 215 **Born:** 10/26/69 **Age:** 33

Year Team	Lg	G	AB	H	2B	3B	HR	(Hm	Rd)	TB	R	RBI	RC	TBB	IBB	SO	HBP	SH	SF	SB	CS	SB%	GDP	Avg	OBP	Slg
2002 Portland*	AAA	1	1	1	0	0	0	(-	-)	1	0	0	1	0	0	0	0	0	0	0	0	-	0	1.000	1.000	1.000
1995 St Louis	NL	37	77	21	2	0	2	(0	2)	29	5	13	10	10	0	15	0	1	2	1	1	.50	3	.273	.348	.377
1996 St Louis	NL	98	170	45	9	0	3	(0	3)	63	32	22	27	33	2	29	1	5	0	3	0	1.00	4	.265	.387	.371
1997 Stl-SD	NL	115	164	46	7	0	2	(2	0)	59	16	23	22	20	1	32	1	1	2	2	3	.40	3	.280	.358	.360
1998 San Diego	NL	122	192	45	8	3	2	(1	1)	65	17	15	21	26	0	37	1	0	3	1	2	.33	5	.234	.324	.339
1999 Cincinnati	NL	37	31	11	3	0	2	(1	1)	20	6	7	7	4	1	9	0	0	0	0	0	-	2	.355	.429	.645
2000 Milwaukee	NL	71	73	16	6	0	1	(0	1)	25	9	6	9	12	1	18	1	1	0	0	0	-	1	.219	.337	.342
2001 Milwaukee	NL	48	89	23	3	1	3	(1	2)	37	9	11	14	12	0	23	0	2	0	2	1	.67	3	.258	.347	.416
2002 San Diego	NL	48	65	11	3	0	1	(0	1)	17	3	4	1	4	0	19	0	0	1	0	0	-	1	.169	.217	.262
1997 St Louis	NL	44	61	13	3	0	0	(0	0)	16	5	4	5	9	1	14	1	1	1	0	1	.00	2	.213	.319	.262
1997 San Diego	NL	71	103	33	4	0	2	(2	0)	43	11	19	17	11	0	18	0	0	1	2	2	.50	1	.320	.383	.417
8 ML YEARS		576	861	218	41	4	16	(5	11)	315	97	101	111	121	5	182	4	10	7	9	7	.56	19	.253	.345	.366

Mike Sweeney

Bats: R **Throws:** R **Pos:** 1B-102; DH-24; PH-1   **Ht:** 6'3" **Wt:** 225 **Born:** 7/22/73 **Age:** 29

						BATTING												BASERUNNING				AVERAGES		
Year Team	Lg	G	AB	H	2B	3B	HR	(Hm | Rd)	TB	R	RBI	RC	TBB	IBB	SO	HBP	SH	SF	SB	CS	SB%	GDP	Avg	OBP	Slg
2002 Omaha*	AAA	3	12	3	1	0	1	(- | -)	7	2	4	2	1	1	2	0	0	1	0	0	-	1	.250	.286	.583
1995 Kansas City	AL	4	4	1	0	0	0	(0 | 0)	1	1	0	0	0	0	0	0	0	0	0	0	-	0	.250	.250	.250
1996 Kansas City	AL	50	165	46	10	0	4	(1 | 3)	68	23	24	23	18	0	21	4	0	3	1	2	.33	7	.279	.358	.412
1997 Kansas City	AL	84	240	58	8	0	7	(5 | 2)	87	30	31	25	17	0	33	6	1	2	3	2	.60	8	.242	.306	.363
1998 Kansas City	AL	92	282	73	18	0	8	(6 | 2)	115	32	35	35	24	1	38	2	2	1	2	3	.40	7	.259	.320	.408
1999 Kansas City	AL	150	575	185	44	2	22	(10 | 12)	299	101	102	109	54	0	48	10	0	4	6	1	.86	21	.322	.387	.520
2000 Kansas City	AL	159	618	206	30	0	29	(17 | 12)	323	105	144	128	71	5	67	15	0	13	8	3	.73	15	.333	.407	.523
2001 Kansas City	AL	147	559	170	46	0	29	(14 | 15)	303	97	99	109	64	13	64	2	1	6	10	3	.77	13	.304	.374	.542
2002 Kansas City	AL	126	471	160	31	1	24	(14 | 10)	265	81	86	113	61	10	46	6	0	7	9	7	.56	9	.340	.417	.563
8 ML YEARS		812	2914	899	187	3	123	(67 | 56)	1461	470	521	542	309	29	317	45	4	36	39	21	.65	80	.309	.379	.501

Greg Swindell

Pitches: L **Bats:** R **Pos:** RP-34   **Ht:** 6'3" **Wt:** 239 **Born:** 1/2/65 **Age:** 38

		HOW MUCH HE PITCHED						WHAT HE GAVE UP											THE RESULTS						
Year Team	Lg	G	GS	CG	GF	IP	BFP	H	R	ER	HR	SH	SF	HB	TBB	IBB	SO	WP	Bk	W	L	Pct	ShO	Sv-Op	Hld	ERC	ERA
2002 Tucson*	AAA	1	1	0	0	1.0	3	0	0	0	0	0	0	0	0	0	0	0	0	0	0	-	0	0- -	-	0.00	0.00
1986 Cleveland	AL	9	9	1	0	61.2	255	57	35	29	9	3	1	1	15	0	46	3	2	5	2	.714	0	0-0	0	3.39	4.23
1987 Cleveland	AL	16	15	4	0	102.1	441	112	62	58	18	4	3	1	37	1	97	0	1	3	8	.273	1	0-0	1	5.12	5.10
1988 Cleveland	AL	33	33	12	0	242.0	988	234	97	86	18	9	5	1	45	3	180	5	0	18	14	.563	4	0-0	0	2.91	3.20
1989 Cleveland	AL	28	28	5	0	184.1	749	170	71	69	16	4	4	0	51	1	129	3	1	13	6	.684	2	0-0	0	3.14	3.37
1990 Cleveland	AL	34	34	3	0	214.2	912	245	110	105	27	8	6	1	47	2	135	3	2	12	9	.571	0	0-0	0	4.36	4.40
1991 Cleveland	AL	33	33	7	0	238.0	971	241	112	92	21	13	8	3	31	1	169	3	1	9	16	.360	0	0-0	0	3.07	3.48
1992 Cincinnati	NL	31	30	5	0	213.2	867	210	72	64	14	9	7	2	41	4	138	3	2	12	8	.600	3	0-0	0	3.01	2.70
1993 Houston	NL	31	30	1	0	190.1	818	215	98	88	24	13	3	1	40	3	124	2	2	12	13	.480	1	0-0	0	4.18	4.16
1994 Houston	NL	24	24	1	0	148.1	623	175	80	72	20	9	7	1	26	2	74	1	1	8	9	.471	0	0-0	0	4.52	4.37
1995 Houston	NL	33	26	1	3	153.0	659	180	86	76	21	4	8	2	39	2	96	3	0	10	9	.526	1	0-2	0	4.85	4.47
1996 Hou-Cle		21	6	0	4	51.2	237	66	46	41	13	1	2	1	19	0	36	0	0	1	4	.200	0	0-2	1	6.82	7.14
1997 Minnesota	AL	65	1	0	12	115.2	460	102	46	46	12	2	3	2	25	3	75	0	0	7	4	.636	0	1-7	12	2.86	3.58
1998 Min-Bos		81	0	0	15	90.1	385	92	40	36	13	4	2	3	31	3	63	3	0	5	6	.455	0	2-5	24	4.39	3.59
1999 Arizona	NL	63	0	0	15	64.2	261	54	19	18	8	4	0	1	21	1	51	0	0	4	0	1.000	0	1-2	19	3.15	2.51
2000 Arizona	NL	64	0	0	21	76.0	318	71	29	27	7	6	3	1	20	5	64	0	0	2	6	.250	0	1-1	9	3.05	3.20
2001 Arizona	NL	64	0	0	18	53.2	214	51	27	27	12	1	1	0	8	2	42	1	0	2	6	.250	0	2-5	11	3.58	4.53
2002 Arizona	NL	34	0	0	5	33.0	153	38	23	23	9	0	2	0	5	1	23	0	0	0	2	.000	0	0-1	2	4.91	6.27
1996 Houston	NL	8	4	0	3	23.0	116	35	25	20	5	0	1	1	11	0	15	0	0	0	3	.000	0	0-2	0	8.64	7.83
1996 Cleveland	AL	13	2	0	1	28.2	121	31	21	21	8	1	1	0	8	0	21	0	0	1	1	.500	0	0-0	1	5.37	6.59
1998 Minnesota	AL	52	0	0	12	66.1	281	67	27	27	10	3	2	3	18	2	45	3	0	3	3	.500	0	2-4	18	4.11	3.66
1998 Boston	AL	29	0	0	3	24.0	104	25	13	9	3	1	0	0	13	1	18	0	0	2	3	.400	0	0-1	6	5.19	3.38
17 ML YEARS		664	269	40	93	2233.1	9301	2313	1053	957	262	94	65	21	501	34	1542	30	12	123	122	.502	12	7-25	79	3.74	3.86

So Taguchi

Bats: R **Throws:** R **Pos:** LF-8; PH-8; CF-6; PR-2   **Ht:** 5'10" **Wt:** 163 **Born:** 7/2/69 **Age:** 33

						BATTING												BASERUNNING				AVERAGES		
Year Team	Lg	G	AB	H	2B	3B	HR	(Hm	Rd)	TB	R	RBI	RC	TBB	IBB	SO	HBP	SH	SF	SB	CS	SB%	GDP	Avg	OBP	Slg
2002 Memphis	AAA	91	304	75	17	0	5	(-	-)	107	37	36	30	13	0	44	5	11	3	6	3	.67	5	.247	.286	.352
2002 New Haven	AA	26	107	33	10	0	1	(-	-)	46	21	15	18	9	0	15	3	0	1	3	1	.75	1	.308	.375	.430
2002 St Louis	NL	19	15	6	0	0	0	(0	0)	6	4	2	4	2	0	1	0	2	0	1	0	1.00	0	.400	.471	.400

Brian Tallet

Pitches: L **Bats:** L **Pos:** SP-2   **Ht:** 6'7" **Wt:** 208 **Born:** 9/21/77 **Age:** 25

		HOW MUCH HE PITCHED						WHAT HE GAVE UP											THE RESULTS						
Year Team	Lg	G	GS	CG	GF	IP	BFP	H	R	ER	HR	SH	SF	HB	TBB	IBB	SO	WP	Bk	W	L	Pct	ShO	Sv-Op	Hld	ERC	ERA
2000 Mahning VI	A-	6	6	0	0	15.2	62	10	2	2	0	0	0	1	3	0	20	0	0	0	0	-	0	0- -	-	1.30	1.15
2001 Kinston	A+	27	27	2	0	160.0	644	134	62	54	12	3	2	4	38	0	164	2	0	9	7	.563	0	0- -	-	2.55	3.04
2002 Akron	AA	18	16	1	0	102.1	425	93	41	35	9	1	1	9	32	0	73	2	1	10	1	.909	0	0- -	-	3.57	3.08
2002 Buffalo	AAA	8	7	0	1	44.0	189	47	17	15	1	3	2	1	16	0	25	4	0	2	3	.400	0	0- -	-	3.90	3.07
2002 Cleveland	AL	2	2	0	0	12.0	47	9	3	2	0	0	0	1	4	0	5	0	0	1	0	1.000	0	0-0	0	2.31	1.50

Jeff Tam

Pitches: R **Bats:** R **Pos:** RP-40   **Ht:** 6'1" **Wt:** 219 **Born:** 8/19/70 **Age:** 32

		HOW MUCH HE PITCHED						WHAT HE GAVE UP											THE RESULTS						
Year Team	Lg	G	GS	CG	GF	IP	BFP	H	R	ER	HR	SH	SF	HB	TBB	IBB	SO	WP	Bk	W	L	Pct	ShO	Sv-Op	Hld	ERC	ERA
2002 Sacramento*	AAA	20	0	0	6	29.0	125	31	20	18	2	3	2	3	5	0	26	1	0	1	3	.250	0	2- -	-	3.70	5.59
1998 New York	NL	15	0	0	5	14.1	62	13	10	10	2	0	0	2	4	1	8	0	0	1	1	.500	0	0-1	1	3.86	6.28
1999 NYM-Cle		10	0	0	3	11.2	47	8	7	7	3	1	0	0	4	1	8	0	0	0	0	-	0	0-0	0	2.97	5.40
2000 Oakland	AL	72	0	0	23	85.2	351	86	30	25	3	2	4	1	23	8	46	3	0	3	3	.500	0	3-6	19	3.14	2.63
2001 Oakland	AL	70	0	0	15	74.2	310	68	27	25	3	3	3	3	29	9	44	0	0	2	4	.333	0	3-6	25	3.18	3.01
2002 Oakland	AL	40	0	0	14	40.1	188	56	25	23	2	3	2	2	13	5	14	3	0	1	2	.333	0	0-4	3	5.59	5.13
1999 New York	NL	9	0	0	3	11.1	43	6	4	4	3	0	0	0	3	0	8	0	0	0	0	-	0	0-0	0	2.05	3.18
1999 Cleveland	AL	1	0	0	0	0.1	4	2	3	3	0	1	0	0	1	1	0	0	0	0	0	-	0	0-0	0	44.68	81.00
5 ML YEARS		207	0	0	60	226.2	956	231	99	90	13	9	9	8	73	24	120	6	0	7	10	.412	0	6-17	48	3.61	3.57

Dennis Tankersley

Pitches: R Bats: R Pos: SP-9; RP-8   Ht: 6'2" Wt: 185 Born: 2/24/79 Age: 24

				HOW MUCH HE PITCHED					WHAT HE GAVE UP												THE RESULTS						
Year Team	Lg	G	GS	CG	GF	IP	BFP	H	R	ER	HR	SH	SF	HB	TBB	IBB	SO	WP	Bk	W	L	Pct	ShO	Sv-Op	Hld	ERC	ERA
1999 Red Sox	R	11	6	0	2	35.2	133	14	7	3	2	0	0	3	9	1	57	0	0	1	0	1.000	0	1--	-	0.99	0.76
2000 Augusta	A	15	15	1	0	75.1	326	73	41	34	4	0	0	4	32	0	74	1	1	5	3	.625	1	0--	-	3.89	4.06
2000 Fort Wayne	A	12	12	0	0	66.1	265	48	25	21	5	2	2	2	25	0	87	2	0	5	2	.714	0	0--	-	2.55	2.85
2001 Lk Elsinore	A+	9	8	0	0	52.1	196	29	5	3	1	1	0	0	12	0	68	0	0	5	1	.833	0	0--	-	1.12	0.52
2001 Mobile	AA	13	13	0	0	69.2	282	44	23	16	6	1	0	4	24	1	89	2	1	4	1	.800	0	0--	-	2.04	2.07
2001 Portland	AAA	3	3	0	0	14.1	68	16	13	11	2	2	2	0	8	0	16	0	0	1	2	.333	0	0--	-	5.48	6.91
2002 Mobile	AA	10	10	0	0	50.2	218	47	20	17	1	2	1	2	21	0	56	0	1	3	3	.500	0	0--	-	3.31	3.02
2002 Portland	AAA	9	9	0	0	51.0	223	43	29	22	6	2	2	1	30	0	51	2	1	3	4	.429	0	0--	-	4.13	3.88
2002 San Diego	NL	17	9	0	3	51.1	245	59	46	46	10	3	2	6	40	3	39	3	0	1	4	.200	0	0-0	0	8.04	8.06

Tony Tarasco

Bats: L Throws: R Pos: PH-32; LF-18; RF-13; 1B-7; CF-2; DH-2; PR-1   Ht: 6'0" Wt: 205 Born: 12/9/70 Age: 32

					BATTING																BASERUNNING				AVERAGES		
Year Team	Lg	G	AB	H	2B	3B	HR	(Hm	Rd)	TB	R	RBI	RC	TBB	IBB	SO	HBP	SH	SF	SB	CS	SB%	GDP	Avg	OBP	Slg
2002 Norfolk*	AAA	42	153	43	7	1	1	(-	-)	55	21	18	18	9	0	15	1	0	1	5	3	.63	0	.281	.323	.359
1993 Atlanta	NL	24	35	8	2	0	0	(0	0)	10	6	2	2	0	0	5	1	0	1	0	1	.00	1	.229	.243	.286
1994 Atlanta	NL	87	132	36	6	0	5	(0	3)	57	16	19	18	9	1	17	0	0	3	5	0	1.00	5	.273	.313	.432
1995 Montreal	NL	126	438	109	18	4	14	(7	7)	177	64	40	64	51	12	78	2	3	1	24	3	.89	5	.249	.329	.404
1996 Baltimore	AL	31	84	20	3	0	1	(1	0)	26	14	9	8	7	0	15	0	1	0	5	3	.63	1	.238	.297	.310
1997 Baltimore	AL	100	166	34	8	1	7	(4	3)	65	26	26	20	25	1	33	1	1	0	2	2	.50	3	.205	.313	.392
1998 Cincinnati	NL	15	24	5	2	0	1	(1	0)	10	5	4	3	3	0	5	0	1	0	0	0	-	0	.208	.296	.417
1999 New York	AL	14	31	5	2	0	0	(0	0)	7	5	3	1	3	0	5	0	1	0	1	0	1.00	1	.161	.229	.226
2002 New York	NL	60	96	24	5	0	6	(4	2)	47	15	15	12	8	0	13	0	0	1	2	1	.67	1	.250	.305	.490
8 ML YEARS		457	1006	241	46	5	34	(19	15)	399	151	118	128	106	14	171	4	6	7	39	10	.80	15	.240	.313	.397

Fernando Tatis

Bats: R Throws: R Pos: 3B-99; PH-11; DH-4   Ht: 5'10" Wt: 180 Born: 1/1/75 Age: 28

					BATTING																BASERUNNING				AVERAGES		
Year Team	Lg	G	AB	H	2B	3B	HR	(Hm	Rd)	TB	R	RBI	RC	TBB	IBB	SO	HBP	SH	SF	SB	CS	SB%	GDP	Avg	OBP	Slg
2002 Brevard Cnty*	A+	6	17	4	1	0	0	(-	-)	5	2	2	2	3	1	4	2	0	1	0	0	-	1	.235	.391	.294
1997 Texas	AL	60	223	57	9	0	8	(6	2)	90	29	29	26	14	0	42	0	2	2	3	0	1.00	6	.256	.297	.404
1998 Tex-Stl		150	532	147	33	4	11	(6	5)	221	69	58	69	36	3	123	6	4	1	13	5	.72	16	.276	.329	.415
1999 St Louis	NL	149	537	160	31	2	34	(16	18)	297	104	107	117	82	4	128	16	0	4	21	9	.70	11	.298	.404	.553
2000 St Louis	NL	96	324	82	21	1	18	(11	7)	159	59	64	58	57	1	94	10	1	2	2	3	.40	13	.253	.379	.491
2001 Montreal	NL	41	145	37	9	0	2	(0	2)	52	20	11	18	16	0	43	4	0	3	0	0	-	5	.255	.339	.359
2002 Montreal	NL	114	381	87	18	1	15	(5	10)	152	43	55	39	35	1	90	8	1	5	2	2	.50	15	.228	.303	.399
1998 Texas	AL	95	330	89	17	2	3	(1	2)	119	41	32	33	12	2	66	4	4	0	6	2	.75	10	.270	.303	.361
1998 St Louis	NL	55	202	58	16	2	8	(5	3)	102	28	26	36	24	1	57	2	0	1	7	3	.70	6	.287	.367	.505
6 ML YEARS		610	2142	570	121	8	88	(44	44)	971	324	324	327	240	9	520	44	8	17	41	19	.68	66	.266	.350	.453

Julian Tavarez

Pitches: R Bats: L Pos: SP-27; RP-2   Ht: 6'2" Wt: 195 Born: 5/22/73 Age: 30

				HOW MUCH HE PITCHED					WHAT HE GAVE UP												THE RESULTS						
Year Team	Lg	G	GS	CG	GF	IP	BFP	H	R	ER	HR	SH	SF	HB	TBB	IBB	SO	WP	Bk	W	L	Pct	ShO	Sv-Op	Hld	ERC	ERA
1993 Cleveland	AL	8	7	0	0	37.0	172	53	29	27	7	0	1	2	13	2	19	3	1	2	2	.500	0	0-0	0	7.48	6.57
1994 Cleveland	AL	1	1	0	0	1.2	14	6	8	4	1	0	1	0	1	1	0	0	0	0	1	.000	0	0-0	0	24.13	21.60
1995 Cleveland	AL	57	0	0	15	85.0	350	76	36	23	7	0	2	3	21	0	68	3	2	10	2	.833	0	0-4	19	2.93	2.44
1996 Cleveland	AL	51	4	0	13	80.2	353	101	49	48	9	5	4	1	22	5	46	1	0	4	7	.364	0	0-0	13	5.12	5.36
1997 San Francisco	NL	89	0	0	13	88.1	378	91	43	38	6	3	8	4	34	5	38	4	0	6	4	.600	0	0-3	26	4.13	3.87
1998 San Francisco	NL	60	0	0	12	85.1	374	96	41	36	5	5	3	8	36	11	52	1	1	5	3	.625	0	1-6	10	4.89	3.80
1999 San Francisco	NL	47	0	0	12	54.2	258	65	38	36	7	3	2	8	25	3	33	4	1	2	0	1.000	0	0-2	5	6.10	5.93
2000 Colorado	NL	51	12	1	8	120.0	530	124	68	59	11	3	4	7	53	9	62	2	1	11	5	.688	0	1-1	6	4.49	4.43
2001 Chicago	NL	34	28	0	1	161.1	712	172	98	81	13	8	4	11	69	4	107	2	1	10	9	.526	0	0-0	2	4.70	4.52
2002 Florida	NL	29	27	0	1	153.2	714	188	100	92	9	13	2	15	74	7	67	7	2	10	12	.455	0	0-1	0	5.75	5.39
10 ML YEARS		427	79	1	75	867.2	3855	972	510	444	75	40	31	59	348	47	492	27	9	60	45	.571	0	2-17	81	4.90	4.61

Aaron Taylor

Pitches: R Bats: R Pos: RP-5   Ht: 6'7" Wt: 230 Born: 8/20/77 Age: 25

				HOW MUCH HE PITCHED					WHAT HE GAVE UP												THE RESULTS						
Year Team	Lg	G	GS	CG	GF	IP	BFP	H	R	ER	HR	SH	SF	HB	TBB	IBB	SO	WP	Bk	W	L	Pct	ShO	Sv-Op	Hld	ERC	ERA
1996 Braves	R	13	9	0	3	52.1	259	68	54	45	0	7	2	6	28	0	33	14	2	0	9	.000	0	0--	-	5.87	7.74
1997 Danville	R+	15	7	0	2	55.1	261	65	49	34	4	1	1	2	31	0	38	11	1	1	8	.111	0	0--	-	5.60	5.53
1998 Danville	R+	14	14	1	0	72.0	334	87	60	50	9	1	3	3	36	0	55	3	1	3	6	.333	0	0--	-	6.09	6.25
1999 Macon	A	27	8	0	6	79.1	360	86	56	43	9	2	5	7	27	2	78	17	0	6	7	.462	0	1--	-	4.58	4.88
2000 Everett	A-	15	14	0	1	63.0	298	76	54	52	5	0	2	9	37	0	57	10	1	1	4	.200	0	0--	-	6.63	7.43
2001 Wisconsin	A	28	0	0	26	29.1	119	19	9	8	1	2	1	2	11	2	50	4	2	3	1	.750	0	9--	-	1.90	2.45
2002 San Antonio	AA	61	0	0	48	77.0	323	51	28	20	5	3	3	6	34	0	93	2	0	4	3	.571	0	24--	-	2.46	2.34
2002 Seattle	AL	5	0	0	2	5.0	23	8	5	5	2	0	0	0	0	0	6	0	0	0	0	-	0	0-1	-	8.09	9.00

Reggie Taylor

Bats: L **Throws:** R **Pos:** CF-69; PH-40; LF-33; PR-12; RF-6   **Ht:** 6'1" **Wt:** 178 **Born:** 1/12/77 **Age:** 26

							BATTING												BASERUNNING				AVERAGES		
Year Team	Lg	G	AB	H	2B	3B	HR	(Hm | Rd)	TB	R	RBI	RC	TBB	IBB	SO	HBP	SH	SF	SB	CS	SB%	GDP	Avg	OBP	Slg
2000 Philadelphia	NL	9	11	1	0	0	0	(0 | 0)	1	1	0	0	0	0	8	0	0	0	1	0	1.00	0	.091	.091	.091
2001 Philadelphia	NL	5	7	0	0	0	0	(0 | 0)	0	1	0	1	0	1	1	0	0	0	0	0	-	0	.000	.125	.000
2002 Cincinnati	NL	135	287	73	15	4	9	(6 | 3)	123	41	38	33	14	3	79	2	5	3	11	8	.58	6	.254	.291	.429
3 ML YEARS		149	305	74	15	4	9	(6 | 3)	124	43	38	33	15	3	88	2	5	3	12	8	.60	6	.243	.280	.407

Mark Teixeira

Bats: B **Throws:** R **Pos:** 1B; 3B   **Ht:** 6'2" **Wt:** 215 **Born:** 4/11/80 **Age:** 23

							BATTING												BASERUNNING				AVERAGES		
Year Team	Lg	G	AB	H	2B	3B	HR	(Hm | Rd)	TB	R	RBI	RC	TBB	IBB	SO	HBP	SH	SF	SB	CS	SB%	GDP	Avg	OBP	Slg
2002 Charlotte	A+	38	150	48	10	2	9	(- | -)	89	32	41	35	21	2	24	3	0	1	2	0	1.00	4	.320	.411	.593
2002 Tulsa	AA	48	171	54	11	3	10	(- | -)	101	31	28	40	25	0	36	4	0	0	3	2	.60	2	.316	.415	.591

Miguel Tejada

Bats: R **Throws:** R **Pos:** SS-162; PH-1   **Ht:** 5'9" **Wt:** 200 **Born:** 5/25/76 **Age:** 27

							BATTING												BASERUNNING				AVERAGES		
Year Team	Lg	G	AB	H	2B	3B	HR	(Hm | Rd)	TB	R	RBI	RC	TBB	IBB	SO	HBP	SH	SF	SB	CS	SB%	GDP	Avg	OBP	Slg
1997 Oakland	AL	26	99	20	3	2	2	(1 | 1)	33	10	10	7	2	0	22	3	0	0	2	0	1.00	3	.202	.240	.333
1998 Oakland	AL	105	365	85	20	1	11	(5 | 6)	140	53	45	40	28	0	86	7	4	3	5	6	.45	8	.233	.298	.384
1999 Oakland	AL	159	593	149	33	4	21	(12 | 9)	253	93	84	82	57	3	94	10	9	5	8	7	.53	11	.251	.325	.427
2000 Oakland	AL	160	607	167	32	1	30	(16 | 14)	291	105	115	99	66	6	102	4	2	2	6	0	1.00	15	.275	.349	.479
2001 Oakland	AL	162	622	166	31	3	31	(17 | 14)	296	107	113	94	43	5	89	13	1	4	11	5	.69	14	.267	.326	.476
2002 Oakland	AL	162	662	204	30	0	34	(17 | 17)	336	108	131	122	38	3	84	11	0	4	7	2	.78	21	.308	.354	.508
6 ML YEARS		774	2948	791	149	11	129	(68 | 61)	1349	476	498	444	234	17	477	48	16	18	39	20	.66	72	.268	.330	.458

Michael Tejera

Pitches: L **Bats:** L **Pos:** RP-29; SP-18   **Ht:** 5'9" **Wt:** 175 **Born:** 10/18/76 **Age:** 26

		HOW MUCH HE PITCHED						WHAT HE GAVE UP												THE RESULTS						
Year Team	Lg	G	GS	CG	GF	IP	BFP	H	R	ER	HR	SH	SF	HB	TBB	IBB	SO	WP	Bk	W	L	Pct	ShO	Sv-Op	Hld	ERC	ERA
1995 Marlins	R	11	3	0	4	34.0	142	28	13	10	2	4	1	2	16	1	28	3	0	3	1	.750	0	2- -	-	3.36	2.65
1996 Marlins	R	2	0	0	0	5.0	21	6	2	2	0	0	0	0	0	0	2	0	0	1	0	1.000	0	0- -	-	2.89	3.60
1997 Utica	A-	12	12	0	0	69.1	279	65	36	29	8	3	1	2	11	0	67	6	0	3	3	.500	0	0- -	-	3.05	3.76
1998 Kane County	A	10	10	0	0	55.1	218	44	20	17	3	3	1	2	13	0	47	2	0	6	1	.857	0	0- -	-	2.30	2.77
1998 Portland	AA	18	18	2	0	107.1	466	113	55	49	15	3	1	4	36	2	97	4	0	9	5	.643	2	0- -	-	4.51	4.11
1999 Portland	AA	25	25	0	0	154.2	640	137	55	45	13	9	3	7	45	1	152	6	1	13	4	.765	0	0- -	-	3.11	2.62
1999 Calgary	AAA	2	2	0	0	9.0	49	19	14	12	2	1	1	1	4	0	5	1	0	0	2	.000	0	0- -	-	13.60	12.00
2001 Portland	AA	25	25	0	0	141.0	595	143	61	56	17	7	1	8	41	0	131	6	0	9	8	.529	0	0- -	-	4.15	3.57
1999 Florida	NL	3	1	0	1	6.1	31	10	8	8	1	0	0	0	5	0	7	0	0	0	0	-	0	0-0	0	10.73	11.37
2002 Florida	NL	47	18	0	2	139.2	611	144	71	69	17	5	4	6	60	3	95	3	0	8	8	.500	0	1-3	8	4.70	4.45
2 ML YEARS		50	19	0	3	146.0	642	154	79	77	18	5	4	6	65	3	102	3	0	8	8	.500	0	1-3	8	4.93	4.75

Anthony Telford

Pitches: R **Bats:** R **Pos:** RP-20   **Ht:** 6'0" **Wt:** 195 **Born:** 3/6/66 **Age:** 37

		HOW MUCH HE PITCHED						WHAT HE GAVE UP												THE RESULTS						
Year Team	Lg	G	GS	CG	GF	IP	BFP	H	R	ER	HR	SH	SF	HB	TBB	IBB	SO	WP	Bk	W	L	Pct	ShO	Sv-Op	Hld	ERC	ERA
2002 Oklahoma*	AAA	35	0	0	25	50.1	217	47	19	19	3	4	1	3	21	2	35	2	0	8	2	.800	0	5- -	-	3.66	3.40
1990 Baltimore	AL	8	8	0	0	36.1	168	43	22	20	4	0	2	1	19	0	20	1	0	3	3	.500	0	0-0	0	5.85	4.95
1991 Baltimore	AL	9	1	0	4	26.2	109	27	12	12	3	0	1	0	6	1	24	1	0	0	0	-	0	0-0	0	3.56	4.05
1993 Baltimore	AL	3	0	0	2	7.1	34	11	8	8	3	0	0	1	1	0	6	1	0	0	0	-	0	0-0	0	9.17	9.82
1997 Montreal	NL	65	0	0	17	89.0	369	77	34	32	11	4	1	5	33	4	61	6	0	4	6	.400	0	1-5	11	3.60	3.24
1998 Montreal	NL	77	0	0	24	91.0	398	85	45	39	9	10	4	4	36	1	59	8	1	5	10	.333	0	1-5	8	3.75	3.86
1999 Montreal	NL	79	0	0	21	96.0	429	112	52	42	3	3	5	3	38	3	69	3	1	5	4	.556	0	2-9	18	4.58	3.94
2000 Montreal	NL	64	0	0	18	78.1	330	76	38	33	10	2	4	5	23	1	68	4	1	5	4	.556	0	3-5	11	3.95	3.79
2001 Montreal	NL	8	0	0	0	7.0	41	14	12	8	2	1	0	1	5	1	5	1	0	0	1	.000	0	0-0	1	14.07	10.29
2002 Texas	AL	20	0	0	4	23.2	117	30	18	17	3	1	2	4	15	2	19	0	0	2	1	.667	0	1-2	4	7.46	6.46
9 ML YEARS		333	9	0	90	455.1	1995	475	241	211	48	21	19	24	176	13	331	25	3	22	25	.468	0	8-26	53	4.47	4.17

Jay Tessmer

Pitches: R **Bats:** R **Pos:** RP-2   **Ht:** 6'3" **Wt:** 188 **Born:** 12/26/71 **Age:** 31

		HOW MUCH HE PITCHED						WHAT HE GAVE UP												THE RESULTS						
Year Team	Lg	G	GS	CG	GF	IP	BFP	H	R	ER	HR	SH	SF	HB	TBB	IBB	SO	WP	Bk	W	L	Pct	ShO	Sv-Op	Hld	ERC	ERA
2002 Columbus*	AAA	63	0	0	28	78.1	353	109	42	38	6	2	1	3	14	4	54	2	0	5	4	.556	0	4- -	-	5.33	4.37
1998 New York	AL	7	0	0	3	8.2	33	4	3	3	1	0	0	0	4	0	6	1	0	1	0	1.000	0	0-0	1	1.74	3.12
1999 New York	AL	6	0	0	4	6.2	41	16	11	11	1	0	0	1	4	2	3	0	0	0	0	-	0	0-0	0	14.65	14.85
2000 New York	AL	7	0	0	5	6.2	31	9	6	5	3	0	0	0	1	1	5	0	0	0	0	-	0	0-0	0	7.01	6.75
2002 New York	AL	2	0	0	0	1.1	6	0	1	1	0	0	0	0	2	0	0	0	0	0	0	-	0	0-0	0	1.96	6.75
4 ML YEARS		22	0	0	12	23.1	111	29	21	20	5	0	1	1	11	3	14	1	0	1	0	1.000	0	0-0	1	6.51	7.71

Nate Teut

Pitches: L **Bats:** R **Pos:** SP-1; RP-1 **Ht:** 6'6" **Wt:** 225 **Born:** 3/11/76 **Age:** 27

Year Team	Lg	G	GS	CG	GF	IP	BFP	H	R	ER	HR	SH	SF	HB	TBB	IBB	SO	WP	Bk	W	L	Pct	ShO	Sv-Op	Hld	ERC	ERA
1997 Williamsport	A-	9	9	0	0	49.0	203	55	23	14	0	1	2	4	6	1	37	2	1	3	4	.429	0	0--	-	2.99	2.57
1997 Rockford	A	2	2	0	0	10.2	52	18	12	12	1	0	0	1	2	0	6	0	0	0	1	.000	0	0--	-	7.70	10.13
1998 Rockford	A	16	16	1	0	103.1	434	99	49	38	9	3	6	23	0	67	3	1	8	5	0	1.000	0	0--	-	2.08	3.31
1998 Daytona	A+	11	11	1	0	65.2	302	88	48	40	7	0	0	3	19	0	54	5	1	5	3	.625	0	0--	-	5.82	5.48
1999 Daytona	A+	26	26	1	0	132.2	613	180	113	94	16	3	9	9	41	0	91	13	1	5	12	.294	0	0--	-	6.27	6.38
2000 W Tennesse	AA	27	21	1	2	138.1	583	133	53	47	13	4	2	10	44	0	106	4	0	11	6	.647	1	0--	-	3.83	3.06
2001 Iowa	AAA	29	29	0	0	167.0	753	184	109	95	28	4	6	5	69	3	125	3	1	13	8	.619	0	0--	-	5.23	5.12
2002 Calgary	AAA	27	19	0	3	116.0	530	132	81	68	19	5	4	8	52	2	82	12	1	5	6	.455	0	0--	-	5.80	5.28
2002 Florida	NL	2	1	0	0	7.1	36	13	8	8	0	0	0	0	3	1	4	0	0	0	1	.000	0	0-0	0	7.97	9.82

Marcus Thames

Bats: R **Throws:** R **Pos:** RF-4; LF-3; PH-1 **Ht:** 6'2" **Wt:** 205 **Born:** 3/6/77 **Age:** 26

								BATTING										BASERUNNING				AVERAGES		
Year Team	Lg	G	AB	H	2B	3B	HR	(Hm | Rd)	TB	R	RBI	RC	TBB	IBB	SO	HBP	SH	SF	SB	CS	SB%	GDP	Avg	OBP	Slg
1997 Yankees	R	57	195	67	17	4	7	(- | -)	113	51	36	42	16	0	26	3	1	4	6	4	.60	3	.344	.394	.579
1997 Greensboro	A	4	16	5	1	0	0	(- | -)	6	2	2	2	0	0	3	0	0	0	1	0	1.00	0	.313	.313	.375
1998 Tampa	A+	122	457	130	18	3	11	(- | -)	187	62	59	62	24	1	78	8	1	5	13	6	.68	5	.284	.328	.409
1999 Norwich	AA	51	182	41	6	2	4	(- | -)	63	25	26	21	22	0	40	3	1	2	0	1	.00	2	.225	.316	.346
1999 Tampa	A+	69	266	65	12	4	11	(- | -)	118	47	38	42	33	1	58	3	1	2	3	0	1.00	1	.244	.332	.444
2000 Norwich	AA	131	474	114	30	2	15	(- | -)	193	72	79	58	50	1	89	4	0	8	1	5	.17	13	.241	.313	.407
2001 Norwich	AA	139	520	167	43	4	31	(- | -)	311	114	97	122	73	8	101	7	0	3	10	4	.71	6	.321	.410	.598
2002 Columbus	AAA	107	386	80	21	3	13	(- | -)	146	51	45	43	43	0	71	7	0	2	5	4	.56	8	.207	.297	.378
2002 New York	AL	7	13	3	1	0	1	(1 | 0)	7	2	2	2	0	0	4	0	0	0	0	0	-	0	.231	.231	.538

Frank Thomas

Bats: R **Throws:** R **Pos:** DH-139; PH-5; 1B-4 **Ht:** 6'5" **Wt:** 275 **Born:** 5/27/68 **Age:** 35

								BATTING										BASERUNNING				AVERAGES		
Year Team	Lg	G	AB	H	2B	3B	HR	(Hm	Rd)	TB	R	RBI	RC	TBB	IBB	SO	HBP	SH	SF	SB	CS	SB%	GDP	Avg	OBP	Slg
1990 Chicago	AL	60	191	63	11	3	7	(2	5)	101	39	31	46	44	0	54	2	0	3	0	1	.00	5	.330	.454	.529
1991 Chicago	AL	158	559	178	31	2	32	(24	8)	309	104	109	134	138	13	112	1	0	2	1	2	.33	20	.318	.453	.553
1992 Chicago	AL	160	573	185	46	2	24	(10	14)	307	108	115	132	122	6	88	5	0	11	6	3	.67	19	.323	.439	.536
1993 Chicago	AL	153	549	174	36	0	41	(26	15)	333	106	128	137	112	23	54	2	0	13	4	2	.67	15	.317	.426	.607
1994 Chicago	AL	113	399	141	34	1	38	(22	16)	291	106	101	127	109	12	61	2	0	7	2	3	.40	15	.353	.487	.729
1995 Chicago	AL	145	493	152	27	0	40	(15	25)	299	102	111	132	136	29	74	6	0	12	3	2	.60	14	.308	.454	.606
1996 Chicago	AL	141	527	184	26	0	40	(16	24)	330	110	134	137	109	26	70	5	0	8	1	1	.50	25	.349	.459	.626
1997 Chicago	AL	146	530	184	35	0	35	(16	19)	324	110	125	139	109	9	69	3	0	7	1	1	.50	15	.347	.456	.611
1998 Chicago	AL	160	585	155	35	2	29	(15	14)	281	109	109	111	110	2	93	6	0	11	7	0	1.00	14	.265	.381	.480
1999 Chicago	AL	135	486	148	36	0	15	(9	6)	229	74	77	95	87	13	66	9	0	8	3	3	.50	15	.305	.414	.471
2000 Chicago	AL	159	582	191	44	0	43	(30	13)	364	115	143	148	112	18	94	5	0	8	1	3	.25	13	.328	.436	.625
2001 Chicago	AL	20	68	15	3	0	4	(2	2)	30	8	10	10	10	2	12	0	0	1	0	0	-	2	.221	.316	.441
2002 Chicago	AL	148	523	132	29	1	28	(24	4)	247	77	92	96	88	2	115	7	0	10	3	0	1.00	10	.252	.361	.472
13 ML YEARS		1698	6065	1902	393	11	376	(211	165)	3445	1168	1285	1444	1286	155	962	53	0	101	32	21	.60	175	.314	.432	.568

Jim Thome

Bats: L **Throws:** R **Pos:** 1B-128; DH-18; PH-1 **Ht:** 6'4" **Wt:** 220 **Born:** 8/27/70 **Age:** 32

								BATTING										BASERUNNING				AVERAGES		
Year Team	Lg	G	AB	H	2B	3B	HR	(Hm	Rd)	TB	R	RBI	RC	TBB	IBB	SO	HBP	SH	SF	SB	CS	SB%	GDP	Avg	OBP	Slg
1991 Cleveland	AL	27	98	25	4	2	1	(0	1)	36	7	9	9	5	1	16	1	0	0	1	1	.50	4	.255	.298	.367
1992 Cleveland	AL	40	117	24	3	1	2	(1	1)	35	8	12	9	10	2	34	2	0	2	2	0	1.00	3	.205	.275	.299
1993 Cleveland	AL	47	154	41	11	0	7	(5	2)	73	28	22	30	29	1	36	4	0	5	2	1	.67	3	.266	.385	.474
1994 Cleveland	AL	98	321	86	20	1	20	(10	10)	168	58	52	56	46	5	84	0	1	1	3	3	.50	11	.268	.359	.523
1995 Cleveland	AL	137	452	142	29	3	25	(13	12)	252	92	73	109	97	3	113	5	0	3	4	3	.57	3	.314	.438	.558
1996 Cleveland	AL	151	505	157	28	5	38	(18	20)	309	122	116	132	123	8	141	6	0	2	2	2	.50	13	.311	.450	.612
1997 Cleveland	AL	147	496	142	25	0	40	(17	23)	287	104	102	120	120	9	146	3	0	4	1	1	.50	9	.286	.423	.579
1998 Cleveland	AL	123	440	129	34	2	30	(18	12)	257	89	85	104	89	8	141	4	0	4	1	0	1.00	8	.293	.413	.584
1999 Cleveland	AL	146	494	137	27	2	33	(14	19)	267	101	108	116	127	13	171	4	0	4	0	0	-	6	.277	.426	.540
2000 Cleveland	AL	158	557	150	33	1	37	(21	16)	296	106	106	119	118	4	171	4	0	5	1	0	1.00	4	.269	.398	.531
2001 Cleveland	AL	156	526	153	26	1	49	(30	19)	328	101	124	130	111	14	185	4	0	3	0	1	.00	9	.291	.416	.624
2002 Cleveland	AL	147	480	146	19	2	52	(30	22)	325	101	118	140	122	18	139	5	0	5	1	2	.33	5	.304	.445	.677
12 ML YEARS		1377	4640	1332	259	20	334	(182	152)	2633	917	927	1074	997	86	1377	42	1	43	18	14	.56	86	.287	.414	.567

Ryan Thompson

Bats: R **Throws:** R **Pos:** LF-34; PH-20; RF-14; CF-5; PR-4 **Ht:** 6'3" **Wt:** 215 **Born:** 11/4/67 **Age:** 35

								BATTING										BASERUNNING				AVERAGES		
Year Team	Lg	G	AB	H	2B	3B	HR	(Hm	Rd)	TB	R	RBI	RC	TBB	IBB	SO	HBP	SH	SF	SB	CS	SB%	GDP	Avg	OBP	Slg
2002 Indianapolis*	AAA	70	273	80	12	3	12	(-	-)	134	36	40	39	11	1	46	4	0	5	0	4	.00	9	.293	.324	.491
1992 New York	NL	30	108	24	7	1	3	(3	0)	42	15	10	11	8	0	24	0	0	1	2	2	.50	5	.222	.274	.389
1993 New York	NL	80	288	72	19	2	11	(6	5)	128	34	26	35	19	4	81	3	5	1	2	7	.22	5	.250	.302	.444
1994 New York	NL	98	334	75	14	1	18	(5	13)	145	39	59	42	28	7	94	10	3	4	1	1	.50	4	.225	.301	.434
1995 New York	NL	75	267	67	13	0	7	(3	4)	101	39	31	28	19	1	77	4	0	4	3	1	.75	12	.251	.306	.378
1996 Cleveland	NL	8	22	7	0	0	1	(1	0)	10	2	5	3	1	0	6	0	0	0	0	0	-	0	.318	.348	.455
1999 Houston	NL	12	20	4	1	0	1	(0	1)	8	2	5	2	2	0	7	0	0	0	0	0	-	1	.200	.273	.400
2000 New York	NL	33	50	13	3	0	3	(2	1)	25	12	14	8	5	0	12	1	0	0	0	1	.00	0	.260	.339	.500
2001 Florida	NL	18	31	9	5	0	0	(0	0)	14	6	2	4	1	0	8	0	0	0	0	0	-	3	.290	.313	.452
2002 Milwaukee	NL	62	137	34	9	2	8	(4	4)	71	16	24	15	7	0	38	2	0	0	1	0	1.00	7	.248	.295	.518
9 ML YEARS		416	1257	305	71	6	52	(23	29)	544	165	176	148	90	12	347	20	8	10	9	12	.43	37	.243	.301	.433

John Thomson

Pitches: R **Bats:** R **Pos:** SP-30   **Ht:** 6'3" **Wt:** 190 **Born:** 10/1/73 **Age:** 29

		HOW MUCH HE PITCHED					WHAT HE GAVE UP										THE RESULTS						
Year Team	Lg	G	GS	CG	GF	IP	BFP	H	R	ER	HR	SH	SF	HB	TBB	IBB	SO	WP Bk	W	L	Pct	ShO	Sv-Op	Hld	ERC	ERA
1997 Colorado	NL	27	27	2	0	166.1	721	193	94	87	15	10	3	5	51	0	106	2 0	7	9	.438	1	0-0	0	4.74	4.71
1998 Colorado	NL	26	26	2	0	161.0	680	174	86	86	21	8	5	0	49	0	106	4 2	8	11	.421	0	0-0	0	4.45	4.81
1999 Colorado	NL	14	13	1	1	62.2	305	85	62	56	11	4	2	1	36	1	34	2 0	1	10	.091	0	0-0	0	7.60	8.04
2001 Colorado	NL	14	14	1	0	93.2	386	84	46	42	15	3	3	4	25	3	68	1 0	4	5	.444	1	0-0	0	3.52	4.04
2002 Col-NYM	NL	30	30	0	0	181.2	800	201	116	95	28	13	10	2	44	9	107	2 0	9	14	.391	0	0-0	0	4.24	4.71
2002 Colorado	NL	21	21	0	0	127.1	550	136	77	69	21	7	7	2	27	6	76	2 0	7	8	.467	0	0-0	0	4.02	4.88
2002 New York	NL	9	9	0	0	54.1	250	65	39	26	7	6	3	0	17	3	31	0 0	2	6	.250	0	0-0	0	4.74	4.31
5 ML YEARS		111	110	6	1	665.1	2892	737	404	366	90	38	23	12	205	13	421	11 2	29	49	.372	2	0-0	0	4.60	4.95

Corey Thurman

Pitches: R **Bats:** R **Pos:** RP-42; SP-1   **Ht:** 6'1" **Wt:** 215 **Born:** 11/5/78 **Age:** 24

		HOW MUCH HE PITCHED					WHAT HE GAVE UP										THE RESULTS						
Year Team	Lg	G	GS	CG	GF	IP	BFP	H	R	ER	HR	SH	SF	HB	TBB	IBB	SO	WP Bk	W	L	Pct	ShO	Sv-Op	Hld	ERC	ERA
1996 Royals	R	11	11	0	0	47.1	221	53	32	32	2	0	2	3	28	0	52	8 1	1	6	.143	0	0--	-	5.33	6.08
1997 Royals	R	8	8	1	0	34.0	149	28	12	9	1	1	0	2	22	0	42	1 0	2	1	.667	0	0--	-	3.80	2.38
1997 Spokane	A-	5	5	0	0	22.2	106	23	19	13	2	0	2	2	13	0	24	2 1	1	2	.333	0	0--	-	4.99	5.16
1998 Lansing	A	14	11	0	2	62.1	261	47	31	25	6	0	1	4	30	0	61	10 0	5	6	.455	0	0--	-	3.30	3.61
1998 Spokane	A-	12	11	0	0	60.0	278	72	35	27	3	1	3	5	31	0	49	6 0	3	3	.500	0	0--	-	5.73	4.05
1999 Wilmington	A+	27	27	0	0	149.1	667	160	89	81	11	4	5	9	64	0	131	11 1	8	11	.421	0	0--	-	4.63	4.88
2000 Wilmington	A+	19	19	1	0	115.2	468	97	33	29	6	1	5	4	46	0	96	7 0	10	5	.667	0	0--	-	3.13	2.26
2000 Wichita	AA	9	9	0	0	50.1	222	46	34	27	10	2	1	3	24	0	47	4 1	5	4	.444	0	0--	-	4.79	4.83
2001 Wichita	AA	25	25	0	0	155.0	636	117	66	58	16	2	2	1	65	1	148	8 0	13	5	.722	0	0--	-	2.88	3.37
2001 Omaha	AAA	1	1	0	0	5.0	24	6	4	3	0	0	0	0	2	0	4	1 0	0	0	—	0	0--	-	4.13	5.40
2002 Toronto	AL	43	1	0	5	68.0	310	65	34	33	11	1	0	2	45	2	56	4 0	2	3	.400	0	0-2	4	5.40	4.37

Mike Thurman

Pitches: R **Bats:** R **Pos:** RP-10; SP-2   **Ht:** 6'5" **Wt:** 210 **Born:** 7/22/73 **Age:** 29

		HOW MUCH HE PITCHED					WHAT HE GAVE UP										THE RESULTS						
Year Team	Lg	G	GS	CG	GF	IP	BFP	H	R	ER	HR	SH	SF	HB	TBB	IBB	SO	WP Bk	W	L	Pct	ShO	Sv-Op	Hld	ERC	ERA
2002 Columbus*	AAA	12	12	0	0	76.2	327	83	34	30	8	3	0	3	14	0	51	1 0	7	3	.700	0	0--	-	3.81	3.52
1997 Montreal	NL	5	2	0	1	11.2	48	8	9	7	3	0	0	1	4	0	8	0 0	1	0	1.000	0	0-0	0	3.42	5.40
1998 Montreal	NL	14	13	0	1	67.0	287	60	38	35	7	2	4	3	26	2	32	3 0	5	4	.444	0	0-0	0	3.57	4.70
1999 Montreal	NL	29	27	0	1	146.2	627	140	84	66	17	8	3	7	52	4	85	4 1	7	11	.389	0	0-0	0	3.89	4.05
2000 Montreal	NL	17	17	0	0	88.1	415	112	69	63	9	5	6	3	46	4	52	2 0	4	9	.308	0	0-0	0	6.25	6.42
2001 Montreal	NL	28	26	0	0	147.0	658	172	90	87	21	8	9	6	50	7	96	8 0	9	11	.450	0	0-0	0	5.19	5.33
2002 New York	AL	12	2	0	6	33.0	152	45	21	19	2	2	0	1	12	1	23	0 0	1	0	1.000	0	0-1	0	5.88	5.18
6 ML YEARS		105	87	0	9	493.2	2187	537	311	277	59	25	22	21	190	18	296	17 1	26	36	.419	0	0-1	0	4.75	5.05

Joe Thurston

Bats: L **Throws:** R **Pos:** PH-5; 2B-4   **Ht:** 5'11" **Wt:** 175 **Born:** 9/29/79 **Age:** 23

		BATTING																	BASERUNNING				AVERAGES		
Year Team	Lg	G	AB	H	2B	3B	HR	(Hm Rd)	TB	R	RBI	RC	TBB	IBB	SO	HBP	SH	SF	SB	CS	SB%	GDP	Avg	OBP	Slg
1999 Yakima	A-	71	277	79	10	3	0	(- -)	95	48	32	41	27	1	34	21	6	3	27	17	.61	3	.285	.387	.343
1999 Sn Brnardino	A+	2	3	0	0	0	0	(- -)	0	0	0	0	0	0	1	1	0	0	0	0	-	0	.000	.250	.000
2000 Sn Brnardino	A+	138	551	167	31	8	4	(- -)	226	97	70	89	56	1	61	17	9	8	43	25	.63	8	.303	.380	.410
2001 Jacksonville	AA	134	544	145	25	7	7	(- -)	205	80	46	70	48	0	65	12	9	3	20	18	.53	5	.267	.338	.377
2002 Las Vegas	AAA	136	587	196	39	13	12	(- -)	297	106	55	106	25	1	60	12	5	2	22	9	.71	10	.334	.372	.506
2002 Los Angeles	NL	8	13	6	1	0	0	(0 0)	7	1	1	2	0	0	1	0	1	1	0	0	-	0	.462	.429	.538

Mike Timlin

Pitches: R **Bats:** R **Pos:** RP-71; SP-1   **Ht:** 6'4" **Wt:** 210 **Born:** 3/10/66 **Age:** 37

		HOW MUCH HE PITCHED					WHAT HE GAVE UP										THE RESULTS						
Year Team	Lg	G	GS	CG	GF	IP	BFP	H	R	ER	HR	SH	SF	HB	TBB	IBB	SO	WP Bk	W	L	Pct	ShO	Sv-Op	Hld	ERC	ERA
1991 Toronto	AL	63	3	0	17	108.1	463	94	43	38	6	6	2	1	50	11	85	5 0	11	6	.647	0	3-8	9	3.14	3.16
1992 Toronto	AL	26	0	0	14	43.2	190	45	23	20	0	2	1	1	20	5	35	0 0	0	2	.000	0	1-1	1	3.68	4.12
1993 Toronto	AL	54	0	0	27	55.2	254	63	32	29	7	1	3	1	27	3	49	1 0	4	2	.667	0	1-4	9	5.32	4.69
1994 Toronto	AL	34	0	0	16	40.0	179	41	25	23	5	0	0	2	20	0	38	3 0	0	1	.000	0	2-4	5	5.01	5.18
1995 Toronto	AL	31	0	0	19	42.0	179	38	13	10	1	3	0	2	17	5	36	3 1	4	3	.571	0	5-9	4	3.04	2.14
1996 Toronto	AL	59	0	0	56	56.2	230	47	25	23	4	2	3	2	18	4	52	3 0	1	6	.143	0	31-38	2	2.74	3.65
1997 Tor-Sea	AL	64	0	0	31	72.2	297	69	30	26	8	6	1	1	20	5	45	1 1	6	4	.600	0	10-18	9	3.40	3.22
1998 Seattle	AL	70	0	0	40	79.1	321	78	26	26	5	4	2	3	16	2	60	0 0	3	3	.500	0	19-24	5	3.17	2.95
1999 Baltimore	AL	62	0	0	52	63.0	261	51	30	25	9	1	1	5	23	3	50	1 0	3	9	.250	0	27-36	0	3.46	3.57
2000 Bal-Stl		62	0	0	40	64.2	295	67	33	30	8	7	2	4	35	6	52	0 0	5	4	.556	0	12-18	6	5.08	4.18
2001 St Louis	NL	67	0	0	19	72.2	307	78	35	33	6	1	2	3	19	4	47	3 1	4	5	.444	0	3-7	12	3.95	4.09
2002 Stl-Phi	NL	72	1	0	17	96.2	376	75	35	32	15	2	1	5	14	2	50	3 0	4	6	.400	0	0-4	20	2.46	2.98
1997 Toronto	AL	38	0	0	26	47.0	190	41	17	15	6	4	1	1	15	4	36	1 1	3	2	.600	0	9-13	9	3.30	2.87
1997 Seattle	AL	26	0	0	5	25.2	107	28	13	11	2	2	0	0	5	1	9	0 0	3	2	.600	0	1-5	7	3.59	3.86
2000 Baltimore	AL	37	0	0	31	35.0	157	37	22	19	6	5	1	2	15	3	26	0 0	2	3	.400	0	11-15	1	5.08	4.89
2000 St Louis	NL	25	0	0	9	29.2	138	30	11	11	2	2	1	2	20	3	26	0 0	3	1	.750	0	1-3	5	5.05	3.34
2002 St Louis	NL	42	1	0	10	61.0	236	48	19	17	9	2	0	4	7	2	35	1 0	1	3	.250	0	0-2	12	2.41	2.51
2002 Philadelphia	NL	30	0	0	7	35.2	140	27	16	15	6	0	1	1	7	0	15	2 0	3	3	.500	0	0-2	8	2.55	3.79
12 ML YEARS		664	4	0	348	795.1	3352	746	350	315	74	35	18	30	279	50	599	23 3	45	51	.469	0	114-171	83	3.57	3.56

Kevin Tolar

Pitches: L **Bats:** R **Pos:** RP
Ht: 6'3" **Wt:** 230 **Born:** 1/28/71 **Age:** 32

Year Team	Lg	G	GS	CG	GF	IP	BFP	H	R	ER	HR	SH	SF	HB	TBB	IBB	SO	WP	Bk	W	L	Pct	ShO	Sv-Op	Hld	ERC	ERA
1989 White Sox	R	13	12	1	0	60.0	256	29	16	11	0	1	1	1	54	0	58	10	0	6	2	.750	0	0--	-	2.55	1.65
1990 Utica	A-	15	15	1	0	90.1	407	80	44	33	2	1	3	4	61	1	69	9	1	4	6	.400	0	0--	-	4.06	3.29
1991 South Bend	A	30	19	0	6	114.2	510	87	54	35	3	5	5	8	85	0	87	6	0	5	.615	4	0	1--	-	3.78	2.75
1992 Salinas	A	14	8	3	3	53.1	255	55	43	36	4	1	7	5	46	0	24	6	0	1	8	.111	0	0--	-	6.44	6.08
1992 South Bend	A	18	10	0	6	81.1	339	59	34	26	5	7	4	2	41	0	81	5	1	6	5	.545	0	0--	-	2.84	2.88
1993 Sarasota	A+	23	11	0	8	77.1	358	75	55	46	1	5	7	6	51	1	60	8	0	2	6	.250	0	1--	-	4.49	5.35
1995 Lynchburg	A+	18	0	0	4	19.1	77	13	7	6	1	0	1	1	6	0	19	3	0	2	0	1.000	0	0--	-	1.97	2.79
1995 Carolina	AA	12	0	0	3	12.1	59	16	5	5	0	0	2	0	7	0	9	2	0	1	0	1.000	0	0--	-	5.64	3.65
1996 Cantn-Akrn	AA	50	0	0	15	44.2	201	42	19	13	1	4	2	3	26	2	39	5	0	1	3	.250	0	1--	-	4.03	2.62
1997 Binghamton	AA	22	0	0	9	31.2	157	38	20	18	3	4	1	2	22	1	26	6	0	1	1	.500	0	1--	-	6.47	5.12
1997 St.Lucie	A+	9	0	0	3	13.1	54	9	3	3	0	0	0	0	6	0	8	1	0	0	0	-	0	1--	-	1.95	2.03
1998 Carolina	AA	42	0	0	15	48.2	211	35	12	12	1	4	1	2	33	0	48	1	0	1	2	.333	0	1--	-	3.19	2.22
1998 Nashville	AAA	1	0	0	0	3.0	14	2	2	2	0	0	0	0	4	0	1	1	0	0	0	-	0	0--	-	5.19	6.00
1998 Indianapolis	AAA	19	0	0	3	14.2	82	21	18	17	3	1	0	0	17	1	19	3	0	0	1	.000	0	0--	-	10.74	10.43
1999 Chattanooga	AA	47	1	0	16	54.1	262	61	32	30	2	2	2	0	45	4	60	4	0	4	4	.500	0	1--	-	5.87	4.97
1999 Indianapolis	AAA	8	1	0	1	13.0	53	8	4	3	1	0	0	0	7	1	18	1	0	1	0	1.000	0	1--	-	2.33	2.08
2000 Jacksonville	AA	9	0	0	2	17.1	66	7	3	1	0	0	0	0	8	0	19	1	0	2	0	1.000	0	0--	-	1.09	0.52
2000 Toledo	AAA	33	0	0	12	46.1	203	37	23	17	4	0	3	0	26	1	42	4	0	4	2	.667	0	2--	-	3.36	3.30
2001 Toledo	AAA	44	0	0	32	56.0	234	49	18	17	3	4	1	1	21	2	73	9	0	3	4	.429	0	7--	-	3.01	2.73
2002 Nashville	AAA	44	7	1	12	78.0	328	66	23	22	5	3	2	2	27	0	82	2	1	6	1	.857	1	1--	-	2.85	2.54

Brian Tollberg

Pitches: R **Bats:** R **Pos:** SP-11; RP-1
Ht: 6'3" **Wt:** 195 **Born:** 9/16/72 **Age:** 30

Year Team	Lg	G	GS	CG	GF	IP	BFP	H	R	ER	HR	SH	SF	HB	TBB	IBB	SO	WP	Bk	W	L	Pct	ShO	Sv-Op	Hld	ERC	ERA
2000 San Diego	NL	19	19	1	0	118.0	506	126	58	47	13	6	0	5	35	4	76	2	1	4	5	.444	0	0-0	0	4.26	3.58
2001 San Diego	NL	19	19	0	0	117.1	503	133	58	56	15	5	7	2	25	3	71	1	0	10	4	.714	0	0-0	0	4.29	4.30
2002 San Diego	NL	12	11	0	0	61.2	288	88	47	42	11	5	6	1	19	2	33	4	0	1	5	.167	0	0-0	0	6.84	6.13
3 ML YEARS		50	49	1	0	297.0	1297	347	163	145	39	16	13	8	79	9	180	7	1	15	14	.517	0	0-0	0	4.78	4.39

Brett Tomko

Pitches: R **Bats:** R **Pos:** SP-32
Ht: 6'4" **Wt:** 215 **Born:** 4/7/73 **Age:** 30

Year Team	Lg	G	GS	CG	GF	IP	BFP	H	R	ER	HR	SH	SF	HB	TBB	IBB	SO	WP	Bk	W	L	Pct	ShO	Sv-Op	Hld	ERC	ERA
1997 Cincinnati	NL	22	19	0	1	126.0	519	106	50	48	14	5	9	4	47	4	95	5	0	11	7	.611	0	0-0	0	3.31	3.43
1998 Cincinnati	NL	34	34	1	0	210.2	887	198	111	104	22	12	2	7	64	3	162	9	1	13	12	.520	0	0-0	0	3.50	4.44
1999 Cincinnati	NL	33	26	1	1	172.0	744	175	103	94	31	9	5	4	60	10	132	8	0	5	7	.417	0	0-0	1	4.51	4.92
2000 Seattle	AL	32	8	0	10	92.1	401	92	53	48	12	5	5	3	40	4	59	1	1	7	5	.583	0	1-2	3	4.49	4.68
2001 Seattle	AL	11	4	0	1	34.2	164	42	24	20	9	1	2	0	15	2	22	1	0	3	1	.750	0	0-1	0	6.31	5.19
2002 San Diego	NL	32	32	3	0	204.1	871	212	107	102	31	6	8	2	60	9	126	3	0	10	10	.500	0	0-0	0	4.18	4.49
6 ML YEARS		164	123	5	13	840.0	3586	825	448	416	119	38	31	20	286	32	596	27	2	49	42	.538	0	1-3	4	4.05	4.46

Tony Torcato

Bats: L **Throws:** R **Pos:** RF-3; PH-3
Ht: 6'1" **Wt:** 195 **Born:** 10/25/79 **Age:** 23

Year Team	Lg	G	AB	H	2B	3B	HR	(Hm	Rd)	TB	R	RBI	RC	TBB	IBB	SO	HBP	SH	SF	SB	CS	SB%	GDP	Avg	OBP	Slg
1998 Salem-Keizer	A-	59	220	64	15	2	3	(-	-)	92	31	43	32	14	0	38	3	0	6	4	2	.67	0	.291	.333	.418
1999 Bakersfield	A+	110	422	123	25	0	4	(-	-)	160	50	58	55	30	3	67	3	1	7	2	1	.67	6	.291	.338	.379
2000 San Jose	A+	119	490	159	37	2	7	(-	-)	221	77	88	87	41	8	62	6	0	7	19	4	.83	2	.324	.379	.451
2000 Shreveport	AA	2	8	4	0	0	0	(-	-)	4	1	2	2	0	0	1	0	0	0	0	0	-	0	.500	.500	.500
2001 San Jose	A+	67	258	88	21	2	2	(-	-)	119	38	47	45	17	3	40	4	0	7	9	3	.75	5	.341	.381	.461
2001 Shreveport	AA	36	147	43	9	1	1	(-	-)	57	13	23	18	9	3	15	4	0	3	0	1	.00	6	.293	.344	.388
2001 Fresno	AAA	35	150	48	8	1	2	(-	-)	64	20	8	19	2	0	20	0	0	0	1	0	1.00	0	.320	.329	.427
2002 Fresno	AAA	130	490	142	23	3	13	(-	-)	210	64	64	67	29	3	65	2	2	4	4	6	.40	8	.290	.330	.429
2002 San Francisco	NL	5	11	3	1	0	0	(0	0)	4	0	0	0	0	0	2	0	0	0	0	0	-	0	.273	.273	.364

Steve Torrealba

Bats: R **Throws:** R **Pos:** C-12; PH-1
Ht: 6'0" **Wt:** 175 **Born:** 2/24/78 **Age:** 25

Year Team	Lg	G	AB	H	2B	3B	HR	(Hm	Rd)	TB	R	RBI	RC	TBB	IBB	SO	HBP	SH	SF	SB	CS	SB%	GDP	Avg	OBP	Slg
1995 Braves	R	30	92	19	4	0	0	(-	-)	23	3	10	6	11	0	20	2	0	1	0	1	.00	3	.207	.302	.250
1996 Braves	R	52	146	25	2	0	0	(-	-)	27	9	7	6	16	0	19	2	5	0	1	2	.33	3	.171	.262	.185
1996 Danville	R+	2	5	1	0	0	0	(-	-)	1	1	0	0	0	0	2	0	0	0	0	1	.00	0	.200	.200	.200
1997 Danville	R+	44	150	34	9	0	2	(-	-)	49	17	18	14	15	0	27	2	2	2	0	1	.00	6	.227	.302	.327
1998 Macon	A	67	209	57	10	0	10	(-	-)	97	28	37	33	20	0	31	3	1	6	3	0	1.00	7	.273	.336	.464
1999 Myrtle Beach	A+	52	175	37	9	0	6	(-	-)	64	23	23	17	13	0	47	2	3	0	1	0	1.00	4	.211	.274	.366
2000 Myrtle Beach	A+	99	334	90	16	0	7	(-	-)	127	43	35	41	31	0	79	1	4	6	5	1	.83	12	.269	.328	.380
2001 Greenville	AA	90	295	80	21	0	8	(-	-)	125	37	34	42	33	0	54	4	0	4	0	0	-	8	.271	.347	.424
2002 Richmond	AAA	61	191	45	11	0	3	(-	-)	65	19	18	20	19	2	31	3	1	1	0	0	-	5	.236	.313	.340
2001 Atlanta	NL	2	2	1	0	0	0	(0	0)	1	0	0	0	0	0	0	0	0	0	0	0	-	1	.500	.500	.500
2002 Atlanta	NL	13	17	1	0	0	0	(0	0)	1	1	1	0	3	0	4	0	1	0	0	0	-	0	.059	.200	.059
2 ML YEARS		15	19	2	0	0	0	(0	0)	2	1	1	0	3	0	4	0	1	0	0	0	-	1	.105	.227	.105

Yorvit Torrealba

Bats: R Throws: R Pos: C-53; PH-1; PR-1   Ht: 5'11" Wt: 180 Born: 7/19/78 Age: 24

							BATTING													BASERUNNING				AVERAGES		
Year Team	Lg	G	AB	H	2B	3B	HR	(Hm Rd)	TB	R	RBI	RC	TBB	IBB	SO	HBP	SH	SF	SB	CS	SB%	GDP	Avg	OBP	Slg
1995 Bellingham	A-	26	71	11	3	0	0	(- -)	14	2	8	1	2	0	14	1	0	1	0	1	.00	1	.155	.187	.197
1996 San Jose	A+	2	5	0	0	0	0	(- -)	0	0	0	0	1	0	1	0	0	0	0	0	-	0	.000	.167	.000
1996 Burlington	A	1	4	0	0	0	0	(- -)	0	0	0	0	0	0	1	0	0	0	0	0	-	1	.000	.000	.000
1996 Bellingham	A-	48	150	40	4	0	1	(- -)	47	23	10	13	9	0	27	0	4	2	4	1	.80	5	.267	.304	.313
1997 Bakersfield	A+	119	446	122	15	3	4	(- -)	155	52	40	51	31	0	58	5	1	3	4	2	.67	8	.274	.326	.348
1998 Shreveport	AA	59	196	46	7	0	0	(- -)	53	18	13	15	18	3	30	4	3	1	0	5	.00	3	.235	.311	.270
1998 San Jose	A+	21	70	20	2	0	0	(- -)	22	10	10	6	1	0	6	0	2	1	2	2	.50	2	.286	.292	.314
1998 Fresno	AAA	4	11	2	1	0	0	(- -)	3	1	1	1	1	1	4	0	0	0	0	0	-	0	.182	.250	.273
1999 Shreveport	AA	65	217	53	10	1	4	(- -)	77	25	19	19	9	0	34	2	2	2	2	2	.00	6	.244	.278	.355
1999 Fresno	AAA	17	63	16	2	0	2	(- -)	24	9	10	7	4	0	11	2	0	0	1	1	.00	2	.254	.319	.381
1999 San Jose	A+	19	73	23	3	0	2	(- -)	32	10	14	12	6	0	15	1	0	1	0	0	-	2	.315	.370	.438
2000 Shreveport	AA	108	398	114	21	1	4	(- -)	149	50	32	49	34	2	55	6	10	2	2	3	.40	17	.286	.350	.374
2001 Fresno	AAA	115	394	108	23	3	8	(- -)	161	56	36	47	19	0	65	4	3	2	2	3	.40	11	.274	.313	.409
2001 San Francisco	NL	3	4	2	0	1	0	(0 0)	4	0	2	2	0	0	0	0	0	0	0	0	-	0	.500	.500	1.000
2002 San Francisco	NL	53	136	38	10	0	2	(0 2)	54	17	14	15	14	2	20	2	3	0	0	0	-	11	.279	.355	.397
2 ML YEARS		56	140	40	10	1	2	(0 2)	58	17	16	17	14	2	20	2	3	0	0	0	-	11	.286	.359	.414

Andres Torres

Bats: B Throws: R Pos: CF-19   Ht: 5'10" Wt: 175 Born: 1/26/78 Age: 25

							BATTING													BASERUNNING				AVERAGES		
Year Team	Lg	G	AB	H	2B	3B	HR	(Hm Rd)	TB	R	RBI	RC	TBB	IBB	SO	HBP	SH	SF	SB	CS	SB%	GDP	Avg	OBP	Slg
1998 Jamestown	A-	48	192	45	2	6	1	(- -)	62	28	21	24	25	0	50	1	1	1	13	2	.87	1	.234	.323	.323
1999 W Michigan	A	117	407	96	20	5	2	(- -)	132	72	34	63	92	1	116	10	9	5	39	18	.68	2	.236	.385	.324
2000 Lakeland	A+	108	398	118	11	11	3	(- -)	160	82	33	72	63	2	82	5	10	0	65	16	.80	10	.296	.399	.402
2000 Jacksonville	AA	14	54	8	0	0	0	(- -)	8	3	0	1	5	0	14	0	0	0	2	0	1.00	1	.148	.220	.148
2001 Erie	AA	64	252	74	16	3	1	(- -)	99	54	23	41	36	1	50	5	0	1	19	11	.63	1	.294	.391	.393
2002 Toledo	AAA	115	462	123	17	8	4	(- -)	168	80	42	66	53	0	116	5	14	4	42	12	.78	3	.266	.345	.364
2002 Detroit	AL	19	70	14	1	1	0	(0 0)	17	7	3	3	6	0	16	1	0	2	2	2	.50	2	.200	.266	.243

Salomon Torres

Pitches: R Bats: R Pos: SP-5   Ht: 5'11" Wt: 165 Born: 3/11/72 Age: 31

			HOW MUCH HE PITCHED					WHAT HE GAVE UP												THE RESULTS						
Year Team	Lg	G	GS	CG	GF	IP	BFP	H	R	ER	HR	SH	SF	HB	TBB	IBB	SO	WP	Bk	W	L	Pct	ShO	Sv-Op	Hld	ERC	ERA
2002 Nashville*	AAA	26	24	2	0	162.1	686	169	78	69	12	6	4	11	39	2	136	3	0	8	5	.615	1	0--	-	3.78	3.83
1993 San Francisco	NL	8	8	0	0	44.2	196	37	21	20	5	7	1	1	27	3	23	3	1	3	5	.375	0	0-0	-	3.95	4.03
1994 San Francisco	NL	16	14	1	2	84.1	378	95	55	51	10	4	8	7	34	2	42	4	1	2	8	.200	0	0-0	0	5.29	5.44
1995 SF-Sea		20	14	1	4	80.0	384	100	61	56	16	1	0	2	49	3	47	1	2	3	9	.250	0	0-0	0	7.30	6.30
1996 Seattle	AL	10	7	1	1	49.0	212	44	27	25	5	3	1	3	23	2	36	1	0	3	3	.500	1	0-0	0	3.98	4.59
1997 Sea-Mon		14	0	0	4	25.2	127	32	29	28	2	3	1	3	15	0	11	3	0	0	0	-	0	0-0	0	6.44	9.82
2002 Pittsburgh	NL	5	5	0	0	30.0	127	28	10	9	2	2	0	3	13	1	12	0	0	2	1	.667	0	0-0	0	4.07	2.70
1995 San Francisco	NL	4	1	0	2	8.0	40	13	8	8	4	0	0	0	7	0	2	0	0	0	1	.000	0	0-0	0	15.31	9.00
1995 Seattle	AL	16	13	1	2	72.0	344	87	53	48	12	1	0	2	42	3	45	1	2	3	8	.273	0	0-0	0	6.55	6.00
1997 Seattle	AL	2	0	1	0	3.1	21	7	10	10	0	0	0	1	3	0	0	0	0	0	0	-	0	0-0	0	13.67	27.00
1997 Montreal	NL	12	0	0	3	22.1	106	25	19	18	2	3	0	3	12	0	11	3	0	0	0	-	0	0-0	0	5.47	7.25
6 ML YEARS		73	48	3	11	313.2	1424	336	203	189	40	20	11	19	161	11	171	12	4	13	26	.333	1	0-0	0	5.34	5.42

Josh Towers

Pitches: R Bats: R Pos: SP-3; RP-2   Ht: 6'1" Wt: 165 Born: 2/26/77 Age: 26

			HOW MUCH HE PITCHED					WHAT HE GAVE UP												THE RESULTS						
Year Team	Lg	G	GS	CG	GF	IP	BFP	H	R	ER	HR	SH	SF	HB	TBB	IBB	SO	WP	Bk	W	L	Pct	ShO	Sv-Op	Hld	ERC	ERA
1996 Bluefield	R+	14	9	0	1	55.0	234	63	35	32	9	0	1	1	5	0	61	4	1	0	0	-	0	0--	-	4.06	5.24
1997 Delmarva	A	9	1	0	5	18.1	73	18	8	7	1	1	1	0	2	0	16	0	0	0	0	-	0	1--	-	2.62	3.44
1997 Frederick	A+	25	3	0	8	53.2	252	74	36	29	4	1	1	3	18	0	64	2	1	6	2	.750	0	1--	-	6.03	4.86
1998 Frederick	A+	25	20	3	3	145.1	583	137	58	54	11	6	3	11	9	0	122	5	2	8	7	.533	0	1--	-	2.63	3.34
1998 Bowie	AA	5	2	0	1	18.0	80	20	9	7	1	0	0	2	4	0	7	1	0	2	1	.667	0	0--	-	4.01	3.50
1999 Bowie	AA	29	28	5	1	189.0	786	204	86	79	26	12	4	5	26	1	106	5	3	12	7	.632	2	0--	-	3.83	3.76
2000 Rochester	AAA	24	24	5	0	148.0	618	157	63	57	17	2	4	8	21	0	102	1	1	8	6	.571	1	0--	-	3.71	3.47
2001 Rochester	AAA	6	6	1	0	41.0	168	40	18	16	2	0	1	2	8	2	27	0	0	3	1	.750	0	0--	-	2.97	3.51
2002 Rochester	AAA	15	13	1	1	69.0	329	109	65	58	16	1	3	2	14	0	43	1	0	9	0	.000	0	0--	-	7.85	7.57
2001 Baltimore	AL	24	20	1	2	140.1	586	165	74	70	21	3	4	6	16	0	58	1	0	8	10	.444	1	0-0	0	4.51	4.49
2002 Baltimore	AL	5	3	0	1	27.1	124	42	24	24	11	1	2	0	5	0	13	1	0	0	3	.000	0	0-0	0	9.00	7.90
2 ML YEARS		29	23	1	3	167.2	710	207	98	94	32	4	6	6	21	0	71	2	0	8	13	.381	1	0-0	0	5.18	5.05

Billy Traber

Pitches: L Bats: L Pos: RP   Ht: 6'5" Wt: 205 Born: 9/18/79 Age: 23

			HOW MUCH HE PITCHED					WHAT HE GAVE UP												THE RESULTS						
Year Team	Lg	G	GS	CG	GF	IP	BFP	H	R	ER	HR	SH	SF	HB	TBB	IBB	SO	WP	Bk	W	L	Pct	ShO	Sv-Op	Hld	ERC	ERA
2001 St.Lucie	A+	18	18	0	0	101.2	415	85	30	30	2	3	2	5	23	0	79	4	1	6	5	.545	0	0--	-	2.22	2.66
2001 Binghamton	AA	8	8	0	0	42.2	188	50	25	21	4	1	3	2	13	1	45	4	1	4	3	.571	0	0--	-	4.80	4.43
2001 Norfolk	AAA	1	1	0	0	7.0	26	5	3	1	0	0	0	0	0	0	9	1	1	1	0	1.000	0	0--	-	1.04	1.29
2002 Akron	AA	18	17	2	0	107.2	436	99	38	33	8	1	0	7	20	0	82	2	0	13	4	.867	2	0--	-	2.95	2.76
2002 Buffalo	AAA	9	9	0	0	54.2	229	58	22	20	3	1	4	2	12	0	33	1	1	4	3	.571	0	0--	-	3.58	3.29

Steve Trachsel

Pitches: R Bats: R Pos: SP-30

Ht: 6'4" **Wt:** 205 **Born:** 10/31/70 **Age:** 32

		HOW MUCH HE PITCHED						WHAT HE GAVE UP												THE RESULTS							
Year Team	Lg	G	GS	CG	GF	IP	BFP	H	R	ER	HR	SH	SF	HB	TBB	IBB	SO	WP	Bk	W	L	Pct	ShO	Sv-Op	Hld	ERC	ERA
2002 Binghamton*	AA	1	1	0	0	5.2	25	3	1	0	0	0	1	0	4	0	5	0	0	1	0	1.000	0	0--	0	1.93	0.00
1993 Chicago	NL	3	3	0	0	19.2	78	16	10	10	4	1	1	0	3	0	14	1	0	0	2	.000	0	0-0	0	2.71	4.58
1994 Chicago	NL	22	22	1	0	146.0	612	133	57	52	19	3	3	3	54	4	108	6	0	9	7	.563	0	0-0	0	3.74	3.21
1995 Chicago	NL	30	29	2	0	160.2	722	174	104	92	25	12	5	0	76	8	117	2	1	7	13	.350	0	0-0	0	5.13	5.15
1996 Chicago	NL	31	31	3	0	205.0	845	181	82	69	30	3	3	8	62	3	132	5	2	13	9	.591	2	0-0	0	3.52	3.03
1997 Chicago	NL	34	34	0	0	201.1	878	225	110	101	32	8	11	5	69	6	160	4	1	8	12	.400	0	0-0	0	5.04	4.51
1998 Chicago	NL	33	33	1	0	208.0	894	204	107	103	27	9	7	8	84	5	149	3	2	15	8	.652	0	0-0	0	4.35	4.46
1999 Chicago	NL	34	34	4	0	205.2	894	226	133	127	32	6	14	3	64	4	149	8	3	8	18	.308	0	0-0	0	4.69	5.56
2000 TB-Tor	AL	34	34	3	0	200.2	882	232	116	107	26	6	6	6	74	2	110	4	0	8	15	.348	1	0-0	0	5.25	4.80
2001 New York	NL	28	28	1	0	173.2	726	168	90	86	28	8	7	3	47	7	144	4	0	11	13	.458	1	0-0	0	3.80	4.46
2002 New York	NL	30	30	1	0	173.2	741	170	80	65	16	9	3	0	69	4	105	4	0	11	11	.500	1	0-0	0	3.88	3.37
2000 Tampa Bay	AL	23	23	3	0	137.2	606	160	76	70	16	2	5	6	49	1	78	3	0	6	10	.375	1	0-0	0	5.19	4.58
2000 Toronto	AL	11	11	0	0	63.0	276	72	40	37	10	4	1	0	25	1	32	1	0	2	5	.286	0	0-0	0	5.38	5.29
10 ML YEARS		279	278	16	0	1694.1	7272	1729	889	812	239	65	60	36	602	43	1188	41	9	90	108	.455	5	0-0	0	4.36	4.31

Bubba Trammell

Bats: R Throws: R Pos: RF-104; LF-23; PH-14; DH-2

Ht: 6'2" **Wt:** 220 **Born:** 11/6/71 **Age:** 31

		BATTING																	BASERUNNING				AVERAGES		
Year Team	Lg	G	AB	H	2B	3B	HR	(Hm	Rd)	TB	R	RBI	RC	TBB	IBB	SO	HBP	SH	SF	SB	CS	SB%	GDP	Avg	OBP	Slg
1997 Detroit	AL	44	123	28	5	0	4	(2	2)	45	14	13	14	15	0	35	0	0	2	3	1	.75	2	.228	.307	.366
1998 Tampa Bay	AL	59	199	57	18	1	12	(6	6)	113	28	35	36	16	0	45	0	0	1	0	2	.00	4	.286	.338	.568
1999 Tampa Bay	AL	82	283	82	19	0	14	(6	8)	143	49	39	53	43	1	37	1	0	1	0	2	.00	7	.290	.384	.505
2000 TB-NYM		102	245	65	13	2	10	(6	4)	112	28	45	38	29	0	49	2	0	2	4	0	1.00	8	.265	.345	.457
2001 San Diego	NL	142	490	128	20	3	25	(11	14)	229	66	92	74	48	2	78	4	0	4	2	2	.50	10	.261	.330	.467
2002 San Diego	NL	133	403	98	16	1	17	(5	12)	167	54	56	55	53	2	71	3	3	3	1	3	.25	6	.243	.333	.414
2000 Tampa Bay	AL	66	189	52	11	2	7	(5	2)	88	19	33	31	21	0	30	2	0	1	3	0	1.00	5	.275	.352	.466
2000 New York	NL	36	56	13	2	0	3	(1	2)	24	9	12	7	8	0	19	0	0	1	1	0	1.00	3	.232	.323	.429
6 ML YEARS		562	1743	458	91	7	82	(36	46)	809	239	280	270	204	5	315	10	3	13	10	10	.50	37	.263	.341	.464

Mike Trombley

Pitches: R Bats: R Pos: RP-5

Ht: 6'2" **Wt:** 204 **Born:** 4/14/67 **Age:** 36

		HOW MUCH HE PITCHED						WHAT HE GAVE UP												THE RESULTS							
Year Team	Lg	G	GS	CG	GF	IP	BFP	H	R	ER	HR	SH	SF	HB	TBB	IBB	SO	WP	Bk	W	L	Pct	ShO	Sv-Op	Hld	ERC	ERA
2002 Fort Myers*	A+	10	1	0	0	2.0	8	2	1	0	0	0	0	0	0	0	3	0	0	0	0	-	0	0--	-	1.95	0.00
2002 Edmonton*	AAA	9	0	0	3	8.2	37	11	6	5	1	0	0	0	2	0	13	0	0	0	1	.000	0	0--	-	5.22	5.19
1992 Minnesota	AL	10	7	0	0	46.1	194	43	20	17	5	2	0	1	17	0	38	0	0	3	2	.600	0	0-0	0	3.74	3.30
1993 Minnesota	AL	44	10	0	0	114.1	506	131	72	62	15	3	7	3	41	4	85	5	0	6	6	.500	0	2-5	8	5.03	4.88
1994 Minnesota	AL	24	0	0	8	48.1	219	56	36	34	10	1	2	3	18	2	32	3	0	2	0	1.000	0	0-1	1	5.83	6.33
1995 Minnesota	AL	20	18	0	0	97.2	442	107	68	61	18	3	2	3	42	1	68	4	0	4	8	.333	0	0-0	0	5.40	5.62
1996 Minnesota	AL	43	0	0	19	68.2	292	61	24	23	2	0	3	5	25	8	57	4	0	5	1	.833	0	6-9	4	2.93	3.01
1997 Minnesota	AL	67	0	0	21	82.1	349	77	43	40	7	2	3	2	31	4	74	5	0	2	3	.400	0	1-1	11	3.55	4.37
1998 Minnesota	AL	77	1	0	17	96.2	413	90	41	39	16	2	1	5	41	3	89	6	1	6	5	.545	0	1-4	23	4.46	3.63
1999 Minnesota	AL	75	0	0	56	87.1	377	93	42	42	15	2	3	2	28	2	82	6	0	2	8	.200	0	24-30	4	4.69	4.33
2000 Baltimore	AL	75	0	0	32	72.0	322	67	34	33	15	7	2	4	38	8	72	8	0	4	5	.444	0	4-11	18	4.96	4.13
2001 Bal-LA		69	0	0	31	78.0	334	65	40	40	8	9	8	4	37	5	72	1	0	8	3	.273	0	6-9	13	3.52	4.38
2002 Minnesota	AL	5	0	0	3	4.0	23	10	7	7	2	0	0	0	1	0	3	0	0	0	1	.000	0	0-1	2	17.32	15.75
2001 Baltimore	AL	50	0	0	21	54.2	226	38	23	21	4	4	3	2	27	2	45	1	0	3	4	.429	0	6-9	11	2.73	3.46
2001 Los Angeles	NL	19	0	0	10	23.1	108	27	17	17	5	4	1	0	10	3	27	0	0	0	0	.000	0	0-0	2	5.56	6.56
11 ML YEARS		509	36	0	195	795.2	3471	800	427	396	114	30	27	30	319	37	672	42	1	37	47	.440	0	44-71	83	4.48	4.48

Chris Truby

Bats: R Throws: R Pos: 3B-120; PH-4; 1B-2; LF-1; PR-1

Ht: 6'2" **Wt:** 215 **Born:** 12/9/73 **Age:** 29

		BATTING																	BASERUNNING				AVERAGES		
Year Team	Lg	G	AB	H	2B	3B	HR	(Hm	Rd)	TB	R	RBI	RC	TBB	IBB	SO	HBP	SH	SF	SB	CS	SB%	GDP	Avg	OBP	Slg
2002 Toledo*	AAA	3	12	4	0	2	1	(-	-)	11	2	1	4	2	0	1	0	0	0	0	0	-	1	.333	.429	.917
2000 Houston	NL	78	258	67	15	4	11	(9	2)	123	28	59	36	10	1	56	5	1	5	2	1	.67	4	.260	.295	.477
2001 Houston	NL	48	136	28	6	1	8	(4	4)	60	11	23	17	13	2	38	1	0	2	1	2	.33	1	.206	.276	.441
2002 Mon-Det		124	382	82	18	4	4	(1	3)	120	35	22	17	10	1	98	3	4	5	2	2	.50	7	.215	.238	.314
2002 Montreal	NL	35	105	27	5	2	2	(1	1)	42	12	7	8	5	1	27	1	1	0	1	1	.50	2	.257	.297	.400
2002 Detroit	AL	89	277	55	13	2	2	(0	2)	78	23	15	9	5	0	71	2	3	5	1	1	.50	5	.199	.215	.282
3 ML YEARS		250	776	177	39	9	23	(14	9)	303	74	104	70	33	4	192	9	5	12	5	5	.50	12	.228	.264	.390

J.J. Trujillo

Pitches: R Bats: R Pos: RP-4

Ht: 6'0" **Wt:** 180 **Born:** 10/9/75 **Age:** 27

		HOW MUCH HE PITCHED						WHAT HE GAVE UP												THE RESULTS							
Year Team	Lg	G	GS	CG	GF	IP	BFP	H	R	ER	HR	SH	SF	HB	TBB	IBB	SO	WP	Bk	W	L	Pct	ShO	Sv-Op	Hld	ERC	ERA
1999 Johnstown	IND	39	0	0	29	45.2	192	33	11	8	0	2	2	3	21	1	60	4	0	1	3	.250	0	14--	-	2.35	1.58
2000 Fort Wayne	A	63	0	0	59	742.0	286	39	16	11	3	3	0	5	25	1	85	4	2	3	4	.429	0	42--	-	0.15	0.13
2001 Lk Elsinore	A+	23	0	0	21	29.0	119	20	7	6	1	0	0	2	13	2	31	1	0	4	1	.800	0	13--	-	2.37	1.86
2001 Mobile	AA	43	0	0	21	51.0	217	44	20	15	1	3	4	4	20	2	44	4	1	3	3	.500	0	6--	-	2.97	2.65
2002 Mobile	AA	31	0	0	26	41.0	159	25	3	3	1	1	0	3	12	0	49	1	0	3	0	1.000	0	20--	-	1.61	0.66
2002 Portland	AAA	18	1	0	2	27.0	121	30	14	13	2	0	0	4	8	0	28	2	1	2	0	1.000	0	0--	-	4.66	4.33
2002 San Diego	NL	4	0	0	1	2.2	18	4	3	3	1	0	0	1	6	0	3	0	0	0	1	.000	0	0-0	0	21.78	10.13

Michael Tucker

Bats: L **Throws:** R **Pos:** RF-68; LF-33; DH-21; PH-15; CF-14; 1B-5; PR-4; 2B-2 **Ht:** 6'2" **Wt:** 195 **Born:** 6/25/71 **Age:** 32

							BATTING												BASERUNNING				AVERAGES		
Year Team	Lg	G	AB	H	2B	3B	HR	(Hm | Rd)	TB	R	RBI	RC	TBB	IBB	SO	HBP	SH	SF	SB	CS	SB%	GDP	Avg	OBP	Slg
1995 Kansas City	AL	62	177	46	10	0	4	(1 | 3)	68	23	17	22	18	2	51	1	2	0	2	3	.40	3	.260	.332	.384
1996 Kansas City	AL	108	339	88	18	4	12	(2 | 10)	150	55	53	53	40	1	69	7	3	4	10	4	.71	7	.260	.346	.442
1997 Atlanta	NL	138	499	141	25	7	14	(5 | 9)	222	80	56	76	44	0	116	6	4	1	12	7	.63	7	.283	.347	.445
1998 Atlanta	NL	130	414	101	27	3	13	(10 | 3)	173	54	46	58	49	10	112	3	1	2	8	3	.73	4	.244	.327	.418
1999 Cincinnati	NL	133	296	75	8	5	11	(5 | 6)	126	55	44	44	37	3	81	3	0	4	11	4	.73	5	.253	.338	.426
2000 Cincinnati	NL	148	270	72	13	4	15	(7 | 8)	138	55	36	53	44	1	64	7	0	2	13	6	.68	6	.267	.381	.511
2001 Cin-ChC	NL	149	436	110	19	8	12	(4 | 8)	181	62	61	59	46	4	102	2	10	6	16	8	.67	8	.252	.322	.415
2002 Kansas City	AL	144	475	118	27	6	12	(10 | 2)	193	65	56	64	56	1	105	3	7	2	23	9	.72	5	.248	.330	.406
2001 Cincinnati	NL	86	231	56	10	1	7	(1 | 6)	89	31	30	28	23	1	55	1	5	5	12	5	.71	4	.242	.308	.385
2001 Chicago	NL	63	205	54	9	7	5	(3 | 2)	92	31	31	31	23	3	47	1	5	1	4	3	.57	4	.263	.339	.449
8 ML YEARS		1012	2906	751	147	37	93	(44 | 49)	1251	449	369	429	334	22	700	32	27	21	95	44	.68	45	.258	.339	.430

T.J. Tucker

Pitches: R **Bats:** R **Pos:** RP-57 **Ht:** 6'3" **Wt:** 245 **Born:** 8/20/78 **Age:** 24

		HOW MUCH HE PITCHED						WHAT HE GAVE UP										THE RESULTS						
Year Team	Lg	G	GS	CG	GF	IP	BFP	H	R	ER	HR	SH	SF	HB	TBB	IBB	SO	WP	Bk	W	L	Pct	ShO	Sv-Op	Hld	ERC	ERA
1997 Expos	R	3	2	0	0	4.2	19	5	1	1	0	0	0	0	1	0	11	0	0	1	0	1.000	0	0- -		3.18	1.93
1998 Expos	R	7	7	0	0	36.0	134	23	5	3	1	0	0	0	5	0	40	0	0	1	0	1.000	0	0- -		1.21	0.75
1998 Vermont	A-	6	6	0	0	33.0	135	24	9	8	0	1	0	2	15	0	34	3	0	3	1	.750	0	0- -		2.45	2.18
1998 Jupiter	A+	2	1	0	1	9.0	32	5	1	1	0	1	1	0	0	0	10	1	0	1	1	.500	0	0- -		0.65	1.00
1999 Jupiter	A+	7	7	0	0	44.0	171	24	7	6	2	0	1	0	16	0	35	1	0	5	1	.833	0	0- -		1.46	1.23
1999 Harrisburg	AA	19	19	1	0	116.1	489	110	55	53	12	4	1	4	38	0	85	5	1	8	5	.615	1	0- -		3.67	4.10
2000 Harrisburg	AA	8	8	0	0	45.0	182	33	19	18	7	2	1	3	17	0	24	1	0	2	1	.667	0	0- -		3.24	3.60
2001 Harrisburg	AA	13	13	0	0	82.0	348	77	38	34	10	4	2	3	37	0	57	4	2	5	5	.500	0	0- -		4.34	3.73
2001 Ottawa	AAA	14	14	1	0	84.0	354	68	42	29	11	6	2	4	33	0	63	3	2	3	5	.375	0	0- -		3.37	3.11
2000 Montreal	NL	2	2	0	0	7.0	35	11	9	9	5	0	0	0	3	0	2	1	0	0	1	.000	0	0-0	0	12.90	11.57
2002 Montreal	NL	57	0	0	19	61.1	278	69	32	28	5	5	2	0	31	9	42	4	0	6	3	.667	0	4-7	17	4.80	4.11
2 ML YEARS		59	2	0	19	68.1	313	80	41	37	10	5	2	0	34	9	44	5	0	6	4	.600	0	4-7	17	5.57	4.87

Jason Tyner

Bats: L **Throws:** L **Pos:** LF-41; PH-2; CF-1 **Ht:** 6'1" **Wt:** 168 **Born:** 4/23/77 **Age:** 26

							BATTING												BASERUNNING				AVERAGES		
Year Team	Lg	G	AB	H	2B	3B	HR	(Hm	Rd)	TB	R	RBI	RC	TBB	IBB	SO	HBP	SH	SF	SB	CS	SB%	GDP	Avg	OBP	Slg
2002 Durham*	AAA	88	351	102	12	4	0	(-	-)	122	59	27	49	34	2	27	6	10	1	20	7	.74	3	.291	.362	.348
2000 NYM-TB		50	124	28	4	0	0	(0	0)	32	9	13	9	5	0	16	2	8	3	7	2	.78	2	.226	.261	.258
2001 Tampa Bay	AL	105	396	111	8	5	0	(0	0)	129	51	21	43	15	0	42	3	5	1	31	6	.84	6	.280	.311	.326
2002 Tampa Bay	AL	44	168	36	2	1	0	(0	0)	40	17	9	7	7	0	19	1	3	1	7	1	.88	1	.214	.249	.238
2000 New York	NL	13	41	8	2	0	0	(0	0)	10	3	5	2	1	0	4	1	3	2	1	1	.50	1	.195	.222	.244
2000 Tampa Bay	AL	37	83	20	2	0	0	(0	0)	22	6	8	7	4	0	12	1	5	1	6	1	.86	1	.241	.281	.265
3 ML YEARS		199	688	175	14	6	0	(0	0)	201	77	43	59	27	0	77	6	16	5	45	9	.83	9	.254	.287	.292

Luis Ugueto

Bats: B **Throws:** R **Pos:** PR-43; 2B-11; SS-8; DH-8; PH-3; 3B-1 **Ht:** 5'11" **Wt:** 170 **Born:** 2/15/79 **Age:** 24

							BATTING												BASERUNNING				AVERAGES		
Year Team	Lg	G	AB	H	2B	3B	HR	(Hm	Rd)	TB	R	RBI	RC	TBB	IBB	SO	HBP	SH	SF	SB	CS	SB%	GDP	Avg	OBP	Slg
1998 Brevard Cnty	A+	3	11	2	0	0	0	(-	-)	2	0	0	0	0	0	5	0	1	0	0	0	-	0	.182	.182	.182
1998 Marlins	R	50	166	38	8	2	0	(-	-)	50	20	15	14	8	0	37	2	2	2	7	1	.88	2	.229	.270	.301
1999 Brevard Cnty	A+	12	30	4	0	0	0	(-	-)	4	1	3	1	7	0	5	0	1	0	1	0	1.00	3	.133	.297	.133
1999 Marlins	R	1	3	0	0	0	0	(-	-)	0	0	2	0	1	0	0	0	0	0	0	0	-	0	.000	.200	.000
1999 Utica	A-	56	217	60	11	2	0	(-	-)	78	33	26	26	18	0	46	1	3	0	9	4	.69	4	.276	.335	.359
2000 Kane County	A	114	393	92	13	2	1	(-	-)	112	43	32	28	28	0	83	5	7	4	12	14	.46	10	.234	.291	.285
2001 Brevard Cnty	A+	121	392	103	12	5	3	(-	-)	134	53	43	46	38	0	96	2	9	1	22	7	.76	7	.263	.330	.342
2002 Tacoma	AAA	12	51	13	1	0	0	(-	-)	14	5	5	4	3	0	13	0	0	1	2	1	.67	0	.255	.291	.275
2002 Seattle	AL	62	23	5	0	0	1	(0	1)	8	19	1	2	2	0	8	0	0	0	8	4	.67	0	.217	.280	.348

Ugueth Urbina

Pitches: R **Bats:** R **Pos:** RP-61 **Ht:** 6'0" **Wt:** 205 **Born:** 2/15/74 **Age:** 29

		HOW MUCH HE PITCHED						WHAT HE GAVE UP										THE RESULTS						
Year Team	Lg	G	GS	CG	GF	IP	BFP	H	R	ER	HR	SH	SF	HB	TBB	IBB	SO	WP	Bk	W	L	Pct	ShO	Sv-Op	Hld	ERC	ERA
1995 Montreal	NL	7	4	0	0	23.1	109	26	17	16	6	2	0	0	14	1	15	2	0	2	2	.500	0	0-0	0	6.66	6.17
1996 Montreal	NL	33	17	0	2	114.0	484	102	54	47	18	1	3	1	44	4	108	3	1	10	5	.667	0	0-1	6	3.78	3.71
1997 Montreal	NL	63	0	0	50	64.1	276	52	29	27	9	3	0	1	29	2	84	2	0	5	8	.385	0	27-32	1	3.42	3.78
1998 Montreal	NL	64	0	0	59	69.1	272	37	11	10	2	2	1	0	33	2	94	3	2	6	3	.667	0	34-38	1	1.59	1.30
1999 Montreal	NL	71	0	0	62	75.2	323	59	35	31	6	1	2	0	36	6	100	6	0	6	6	.500	0	41-50	2	2.85	3.69
2000 Montreal	NL	13	0	0	11	13.1	54	11	6	6	1	0	0	0	5	0	22	1	0	1	0	1.000	0	8-10	0	2.95	4.05
2001 Mon-Bos		64	0	0	53	66.2	278	58	29	27	9	2	1	0	24	1	89	2	1	2	2	.500	0	24-28	3	3.41	3.65
2002 Boston	AL	61	0	0	55	60.0	242	44	21	20	8	1	3	0	20	5	71	3	1	1	6	.143	0	40-46	0	2.50	3.00
2001 Montreal	NL	45	0	0	40	46.2	201	42	24	22	8	1	1	0	21	1	57	2	1	2	1	.667	0	15-18	1	4.13	4.24
2001 Boston	AL	19	0	0	13	20.0	77	16	5	5	1	1	0	0	3	0	32	0	0	0	1	.000	0	9-10	2	1.88	2.25
8 ML YEARS		376	21	0	292	486.2	2038	389	202	184	59	12	10	2	205	21	583	22	5	32	33	.492	0	174-205	10	3.13	3.40

Juan Uribe

Bats: R Throws: R Pos: SS-155; PH-1; PR-1   Ht: 5'11" Wt: 173 Born: 7/22/79 Age: 23

Year Team	Lg	G	AB	H	2B	3B	HR	(Hm	Rd)	TB	R	RBI	RC	TBB	IBB	SO	HBP	SH	SF	SB	CS	SB%	GDP	Avg	OBP	Slg
1998 Rockies	R	40	148	41	5	3	0	(-	-)	52	25	17	20	12	0	25	3	3	2	8	1	.89	1	.277	.339	.351
1999 Asheville	A	125	430	115	28	3	9	(-	-)	176	57	46	51	20	0	79	6	11	4	11	7	.61	12	.267	.307	.409
2000 Salem	A+	134	485	124	22	7	13	(-	-)	199	64	65	63	38	0	100	4	4	2	22	5	.81	11	.256	.314	.410
2001 Carolina	AA	3	13	3	1	0	0	(-	-)	4	1	1	1	0	0	4	0	0	0	1	0	1.00	1	.231	.231	.308
2001 Co Springs	AAA	74	281	87	27	7	7	(-	-)	149	40	48	46	12	1	43	2	0	2	11	8	.58	8	.310	.340	.530
2001 Colorado	NL	72	273	82	15	11	8	(3	5)	143	32	53	44	8	1	55	2	0	0	3	0	1.00	6	.300	.325	.524
2002 Colorado	NL	155	566	136	25	7	6	(4	2)	193	69	49	53	34	1	120	5	7	6	9	2	.82	17	.240	.286	.341
2 ML YEARS		227	839	218	40	18	14	(7	7)	336	101	102	97	42	2	175	7	7	6	12	2	.86	23	.260	.299	.400

Chase Utley

Bats: L Throws: R Pos: 2B   Ht: 6'1" Wt: 170 Born: 12/17/78 Age: 24

Year Team	Lg	G	AB	H	2B	3B	HR	(Hm	Rd)	TB	R	RBI	RC	TBB	IBB	SO	HBP	SH	SF	SB	CS	SB%	GDP	Avg	OBP	Slg
2000 Batavia	A-	40	153	47	13	1	2	(-	-)	68	21	22	26	18	1	23	2	0	2	5	3	.63	3	.307	.383	.444
2001 Clearwater	A+	122	467	120	25	2	16	(-	-)	197	65	59	65	37	4	88	12	1	6	19	8	.70	6	.257	.324	.422
2002 Scrtn/WlksBr	AAA	125	464	122	39	1	17	(-	-)	214	73	70	78	46	2	89	20	0	4	8	3	.73	5	.263	.352	.461

Ismael Valdes

Pitches: R Bats: R Pos: SP-31   Ht: 6'4" Wt: 225 Born: 8/21/73 Age: 29

Year Team	Lg	G	GS	CG	GF	IP	BFP	H	R	ER	HR	SH	SF	HB	TBB	IBB	SO	WP	Bk	W	L	Pct	ShO	Sv-Op	Hld	ERC	ERA
1994 Los Angeles	NL	21	1	0	7	28.1	115	21	10	10	2	3	0	0	10	2	28	1	2	3	1	.750	0	0-0	4	2.25	3.18
1995 Los Angeles	NL	33	27	6	1	197.2	804	168	76	67	17	10	5	1	51	5	150	1	3	13	11	.542	2	1-1	2	2.62	3.05
1996 Los Angeles	NL	33	33	0	0	225.0	945	219	94	83	20	7	7	3	54	10	173	1	5	15	7	.682	0	0-0	0	3.18	3.32
1997 Los Angeles	NL	30	30	0	0	196.2	795	171	68	58	16	11	3	3	47	1	140	3	2	10	11	.476	0	0-0	0	2.72	2.65
1998 Los Angeles	NL	27	27	2	0	174.0	745	171	82	77	17	5	3	2	66	4	122	4	2	11	10	.524	2	0-0	0	3.89	3.98
1999 Los Angeles	NL	32	32	2	0	203.1	871	213	97	90	32	9	8	6	58	2	143	6	0	9	14	.391	1	0-0	0	4.38	3.98
2000 ChC-LA	NL	21	20	0	1	107.0	469	124	69	67	22	0	4	3	40	2	74	0	0	2	7	.222	0	0-0	0	5.89	5.64
2001 Anaheim	AL	27	27	1	0	163.2	699	177	82	81	20	3	0	8	50	3	100	3	0	9	13	.409	0	0-0	0	4.57	4.45
2002 Tex-Sea	AL	31	31	1	0	196.0	818	194	94	91	26	2	4	9	47	1	102	0	2	8	12	.400	0	0-0	0	3.80	4.18
2000 Chicago	NL	12	12	0	0	67.0	291	71	40	40	17	0	2	2	27	2	45	0	0	2	4	.333	0	0-0	0	5.72	5.37
2000 Los Angeles	NL	9	8	0	1	40.0	178	53	29	27	5	0	2	1	13	0	29	0	0	0	3	.000	0	0-0	0	6.15	6.08
2002 Texas	AL	23	23	0	0	146.2	608	135	65	64	19	2	2	9	36	1	75	0	2	6	9	.400	0	0-0	0	3.47	3.93
2002 Seattle	AL	8	8	1	0	49.1	210	59	29	27	7	0	2	0	11	0	27	0	0	2	3	.400	0	0-0	0	4.86	4.93
9 ML YEARS		255	228	12	9	1491.2	6261	1458	672	624	172	50	34	35	423	30	1032	19	16	80	86	.482	5	1-1	6	3.67	3.76

Eric Valent

Bats: L Throws: L Pos: PH-5; RF-2; 1B-1   Ht: 6'0" Wt: 191 Born: 4/4/77 Age: 26

Year Team	Lg	G	AB	H	2B	3B	HR	(Hm	Rd)	TB	R	RBI	RC	TBB	IBB	SO	HBP	SH	SF	SB	CS	SB%	GDP	Avg	OBP	Slg
1998 Piedmont	A	22	89	38	12	0	8	(-	-)	74	24	28	32	14	2	19	0	0	1	0	0	-	0	.427	.500	.831
1998 Clearwater	A+	34	125	33	8	1	5	(-	-)	58	24	25	20	16	0	29	3	0	1	1	2	.33	4	.264	.359	.464
1999 Clearwater	A+	134	520	150	31	9	20	(-	-)	259	91	106	92	58	5	110	5	1	10	5	3	.63	10	.288	.359	.498
2000 Reading	AA	128	469	121	22	5	22	(-	-)	219	81	90	80	70	4	89	5	0	6	2	3	.40	7	.258	.356	.467
2001 Scrtn/WlksBr	AAA	117	448	122	30	2	21	(-	-)	219	65	78	74	49	4	105	4	0	8	0	1	.00	13	.272	.352	.489
2002 Scrtn/WlksBr	AAA	140	546	137	34	2	9	(-	-)	202	69	84	61	49	1	94	1	1	5	0	2	.00	13	.251	.311	.370
2001 Philadelphia	NL	22	41	4	2	0	0	(0	0)	6	3	1	0	4	0	11	1	0	0	0	0	-	0	.098	.196	.146
2002 Philadelphia	NL	7	10	2	0	0	0	(0	0)	2	1	0	0	0	0	3	0	0	0	0	0	-	1	.200	.200	.200
2 ML YEARS		29	51	6	2	0	0	(0	0)	8	4	1	0	4	0	14	1	0	0	0	0	-	1	.118	.196	.157

Javier Valentin

Bats: B Throws: R Pos: C-4   Ht: 5'10" Wt: 192 Born: 9/19/75 Age: 27

Year Team	Lg	G	AB	H	2B	3B	HR	(Hm	Rd)	TB	R	RBI	RC	TBB	IBB	SO	HBP	SH	SF	SB	CS	SB%	GDP	Avg	OBP	Slg
2002 Edmonton*	AAA	127	455	130	33	1	21	(-	-)	228	69	80	75	41	2	96	5	0	8	0	1	.00	15	.286	.346	.501
1997 Minnesota	AL	4	7	2	0	0	0	(0	0)	2	1	0	1	0	0	3	0	0	0	0	0	-	0	.286	.286	.286
1998 Minnesota	AL	55	162	32	7	1	3	(1	2)	50	11	18	10	11	1	30	0	3	1	0	0	-	7	.198	.247	.309
1999 Minnesota	AL	78	218	54	12	1	5	(2	3)	83	22	28	27	22	0	39	1	1	5	0	0	-	2	.248	.313	.381
2002 Minnesota	AL	4	4	2	0	0	0	(0	0)	2	0	0	0	0	0	0	0	0	0	0	0	-	0	.500	.500	.500
4 ML YEARS		141	391	90	19	2	8	(3	5)	137	34	46	38	33	1	72	1	4	6	0	0	-	9	.230	.288	.350

John Valentin

Bats: R Throws: R Pos: PH-63; SS-24; 1B-23; 3B-18; 2B-3; DH-1   Ht: 6'0" Wt: 185 Born: 2/18/67 Age: 36

Year Team	Lg	G	AB	H	2B	3B	HR	(Hm	Rd)	TB	R	RBI	RC	TBB	IBB	SO	HBP	SH	SF	SB	CS	SB%	GDP	Avg	OBP	Slg
1992 Boston	AL	58	185	51	13	0	5	(1	4)	79	21	25	28	20	0	17	2	4	1	1	0	1.00	5	.276	.351	.427
1993 Boston	AL	144	468	130	40	3	11	(7	4)	209	50	66	71	49	2	77	2	16	4	3	4	.43	9	.278	.346	.447
1994 Boston	AL	84	301	95	26	2	9	(6	3)	152	53	49	62	42	1	38	3	5	4	3	1	.75	3	.316	.400	.505
1995 Boston	AL	135	520	155	37	2	27	(11	16)	277	108	102	113	81	2	67	10	4	6	20	5	.80	7	.298	.399	.533
1996 Boston	AL	131	527	156	29	3	13	(11	2)	230	84	59	84	63	0	59	7	2	7	9	10	.47	15	.296	.374	.436
1997 Boston	AL	143	575	176	47	5	18	(11	7)	287	95	77	100	58	5	66	5	1	5	7	4	.64	21	.306	.372	.499
1998 Boston	AL	153	588	145	44	1	23	(11	12)	260	113	73	90	77	3	82	9	2	5	4	5	.44	9	.247	.340	.442
1999 Boston	AL	113	450	114	27	1	12	(5	7)	179	58	70	56	40	2	68	4	1	8	0	1	.00	11	.253	.315	.398
2000 Boston	AL	10	35	9	1	0	2	(0	2)	16	6	2	4	2	0	5	0	1	0	1	0	1.00	1	.257	.297	.457

(continued)

Year Team	Lg	G	AB	H	2B	3B	HR	Hm	Rd	TB	R	RBI	RC	TBB	IBB	SO	HBP	SH	SF	SB	CS	SB%	GDP	Avg	OBP	Slg
2001 Boston	AL	20	60	12	2	0	1	(0	1)	17	8	5	5	9	0	8	1	0	0	0	0	-	4	.200	.314	.283
2002 New York	NL	114	208	50	15	0	3	(2	1)	74	18	30	32	22	0	37	10	0	2	0	0	-	6	.240	.339	.356
11 ML YEARS		1105	3917	1093	281	17	124	(63	61)	1780	614	558	645	463	15	524	53	36	42	47	31	.60	91	.279	.360	.454

Jose Valentin

Bats: B Throws: R Pos: 3B-83; SS-50; PH-12; DH-1

Ht: 5'10" Wt: 185 Born: 10/12/69 Age: 33

Year Team	Lg	G	AB	H	2B	3B	HR	Hm	Rd	TB	R	RBI	RC	TBB	IBB	SO	HBP	SH	SF	SB	CS	SB%	GDP	Avg	OBP	Slg
1992 Milwaukee	NL	4	3	0	0	0	0	(0	0)	0	0	0	0	0	0	0	0	0	0	0	0	-	0	.000	.000	.000
1993 Milwaukee	NL	19	53	13	1	2	1	(1	0)	21	10	7	8	7	1	16	1	2	0	1	0	1.00	1	.245	.344	.396
1994 Milwaukee	NL	97	285	68	19	0	11	(8	3)	120	47	46	43	38	1	75	2	4	2	12	3	.80	1	.239	.330	.421
1995 Milwaukee	NL	112	338	74	23	3	11	(8	3)	136	62	49	42	37	0	83	0	7	4	16	8	.67	0	.219	.293	.402
1996 Milwaukee	NL	154	552	143	33	7	24	(10	14)	262	90	95	91	66	9	145	0	6	4	17	4	.81	4	.259	.336	.475
1997 Milwaukee	NL	136	494	125	23	1	17	(4	13)	201	58	58	64	39	4	109	4	4	5	19	8	.70	5	.253	.310	.407
1998 Milwaukee	NL	151	428	96	24	0	16	(7	9)	168	65	49	57	63	8	105	1	2	3	10	7	.59	2	.224	.323	.393
1999 Milwaukee	NL	89	256	58	9	5	10	(3	7)	107	45	38	40	48	7	52	2	2	5	3	2	.60	3	.227	.347	.418
2000 Chicago	AL	144	568	136	37	6	25	(11	14)	279	107	92	97	59	1	106	4	13	4	19	2	.90	11	.273	.343	.491
2001 Chicago	AL	124	438	113	22	2	28	(14	14)	223	74	68	74	50	2	114	3	8	3	9	6	.60	7	.258	.336	.509
2002 Chicago	AL	135	474	118	26	4	25	(15	10)	227	70	75	76	43	2	99	2	3	5	3	3	.50	9	.249	.311	.479
11 ML YEARS		1165	3889	963	217	30	168	(81	87)	1744	629	578	592	450	35	904	19	51	36	109	43	.72	43	.248	.326	.448

Jose Valverde

Pitches: R Bats: R Pos: RP

Ht: 6'4" Wt: 254 Born: 7/24/79 Age: 23

Year Team	Lg	G	GS	CG	GF	IP	BFP	H	R	ER	HR	SH	SF	HB	TBB	IBB	SO	WP	Bk	W	L	Pct	ShO	Sv-Op	Hld	ERC	ERA
1999 Diamndbcks	R	20	0	0	17	28.2	138	34	21	13	1	0	0	4	10	0	47	1	1	1	2	.333	0	8--	-	4.71	4.08
1999 South Bend	A	2	0	0	0	2.2	11	2	0	0	0	0	0	0	2	0	3	1	1	0	0	-	0	0--	-	5.44	0.00
2000 South Bend	A	31	0	0	21	31.2	152	31	20	19	1	2	0	3	25	0	39	8	0	1	5	.000	0	14--	-	5.26	5.40
2000 Missoula	R+	12	0	0	11	11.2	44	3	0	0	0	0	0	0	4	0	24	2	0	1	0	1.000	0	4--	-	0.51	0.00
2001 El Paso	AA	39	0	0	28	41.1	193	36	19	18	1	1	1	4	27	0	72	6	1	2	2	.500	0	13--	-	3.98	3.92
2002 Tucson	AAA	49	0	0	24	47.2	214	45	33	31	8	3	5	5	23	2	65	4	2	2	4	.333	0	5--	-	4.91	5.85

Andy Van Hekken

Pitches: L Bats: R Pos: SP-5

Ht: 6'3" Wt: 175 Born: 7/31/79 Age: 23

Year Team	Lg	G	GS	CG	GF	IP	BFP	H	R	ER	HR	SH	SF	HB	TBB	IBB	SO	WP	Bk	W	L	Pct	ShO	Sv-Op	Hld	ERC	ERA
1998 Mariners	R	11	8	0	0	40.2	179	34	23	20	1	0	0	2	18	0	55	7	1	6	3	.667	0	0--	-	2.89	4.43
1999 Oneonta	A-	11	10	0	0	50.1	210	44	17	12	3	0	0	3	16	0	50	1	0	4	2	.667	0	0--	-	3.04	2.15
2000 W Michigan	A	26	25	3	1	158.0	648	139	48	43	3	3	2	7	37	0	126	3	0	16	6	.727	1	1--	-	2.45	2.45
2001 Lakeland	A+	19	19	2	0	110.2	460	105	43	39	8	3	2	5	33	0	82	1	0	10	4	.714	0	0--	-	3.44	3.17
2001 Erie	AA	8	8	0	0	48.0	210	63	29	25	5	1	3	1	8	0	29	1	0	5	0	1.000	0	0--	-	5.07	4.69
2002 Erie	AA	21	21	1	0	134.0	565	138	69	57	10	6	7	7	34	0	97	7	2	4	7	.364	0	0--	-	3.73	3.83
2002 Toledo	AAA	7	7	1	0	49.1	194	41	14	10	4	1	0	2	11	0	19	2	0	5	0	1.000	0	0--	-	2.63	1.82
2002 Detroit	AL	5	5	1	0	30.0	131	38	13	10	2	2	1	0	6	0	5	1	0	1	3	.250	1	0-0	0	4.55	3.00

Todd Van Poppel

Pitches: R Bats: R Pos: RP-50

Ht: 6'5" Wt: 240 Born: 12/9/71 Age: 31

Year Team	Lg	G	GS	CG	GF	IP	BFP	H	R	ER	HR	SH	SF	HB	TBB	IBB	SO	WP	Bk	W	L	Pct	ShO	Sv-Op	Hld	ERC	ERA
1991 Oakland	AL	1	1	0	0	4.2	21	7	5	5	1	0	0	0	2	0	6	0	0	0	0	-	0	0-0	0	8.85	9.64
1993 Oakland	AL	16	16	0	0	84.0	380	76	50	47	10	1	2	2	62	0	47	3	0	6	6	.500	0	0-0	0	5.17	5.04
1994 Oakland	AL	23	23	0	0	116.2	532	108	80	79	20	4	4	3	89	2	83	3	1	7	10	.412	0	0-0	0	5.82	6.09
1995 Oakland	AL	36	14	1	10	138.1	582	125	77	75	16	3	6	4	56	1	122	4	0	8	8	.333	0	0-0	1	3.82	4.88
1996 Oak-Det	AL	37	15	1	8	99.1	491	139	107	100	24	4	7	3	62	3	53	7	0	3	9	.250	1	1-2	0	8.80	9.06
1998 Tex-Pit		22	11	0	3	66.1	303	79	52	47	9	3	3	1	28	3	42	3	0	2	4	.333	0	0-0	0	5.47	6.38
2000 Chicago	NL	51	2	0	13	86.1	378	80	38	36	10	4	3	2	48	2	77	5	0	4	5	.444	0	2-5	7	4.48	3.75
2001 Chicago	NL	59	0	0	18	75.0	324	63	22	21	9	4	0	0	38	4	90	5	1	4	1	.800	0	0-0	5	3.61	2.52
2002 Texas	AL	50	0	0	19	72.2	326	80	44	44	14	1	1	3	29	1	85	8	0	3	2	.600	0	1-2	3	5.44	5.45
1996 Oakland	AL	28	6	0	8	63.0	301	86	56	54	13	3	5	2	33	3	37	4	0	1	5	.167	0	1-2	0	7.81	7.71
1996 Detroit	AL	9	9	1	0	36.1	190	53	51	46	11	1	2	1	29	0	16	3	0	2	4	.333	1	0-0	0	10.57	11.39
1998 Texas	AL	4	4	0	0	19.1	95	26	20	19	5	0	1	1	10	0	10	2	0	1	2	.333	0	0-0	0	8.04	8.84
1998 Pittsburgh	NL	18	7	0	3	47.0	208	53	32	28	4	3	2	0	18	3	32	5	3	1	2	.333	0	0-0	0	4.50	5.36
9 ML YEARS		295	82	2	71	743.1	3337	757	475	454	113	24	26	18	414	16	605	42	5	33	45	.423	1	4-9	16	5.28	5.50

Cory Vance

Pitches: L Bats: L Pos: SP-1; RP-1

Ht: 6'1" Wt: 195 Born: 6/20/79 Age: 24

Year Team	Lg	G	GS	CG	GF	IP	BFP	H	R	ER	HR	SH	SF	HB	TBB	IBB	SO	WP	Bk	W	L	Pct	ShO	Sv-Op	Hld	ERC	ERA
2000 Portland	A-	7	3	0	1	24.1	93	11	5	3	1	3	2		8	0	26	1	0	0	2	.000	0	0--	-	1.27	1.11
2001 Salem	A+	26	26	1	0	154.0	641	129	65	53	9	3	2	14	65	0	142	4	4	10	8	.556	0	0--	-	3.43	3.10
2002 Carolina	AA	25	25	1	0	150.1	646	142	73	63	8	9	5	2	76	1	114	5	1	10	8	.556	0	0--	-	3.95	3.77
2002 Colorado	NL	2	1	0	0	4.0	20	4	3	3	2	0	0	1	4	0	1	0	0	0	0	-	0	0-0	0	11.75	6.75

John Vander Wal

Bats: L **Throws:** L **Pos:** RF-49; PH-17; DH-10; LF-8; 1B-6; PR-1   **Ht:** 6'1" **Wt:** 197 **Born:** 4/29/66 **Age:** 37

Year Team	Lg	G	AB	H	2B	3B	HR	Hm	Rd	TB	R	RBI	RC	TBB	IBB	SO	HBP	SH	SF	SB	CS	SB%	GDP	Avg	OBP	Slg
1991 Montreal	NL	21	61	13	4	1	1	(0	1)	22	4	8	4	1	0	18	0	0		0	0	-	2	.213	.222	.361
1992 Montreal	NL	105	213	51	8	2	4	(2	2)	75	21	20	25	24	2	36	0	0	0	3	0	1.00	2	.239	.316	.352
1993 Montreal	NL	106	215	50	7	4	5	(1	4)	80	34	30	26	27	2	30	1	0	1	6	3	.67	4	.233	.320	.372
1994 Colorado	NL	91	110	27	3	1	5	(1	4)	47	12	15	15	16	0	31	0	0	0	2	1	.67	4	.245	.339	.427
1995 Colorado	NL	105	101	35	8	1	5	(2	3)	60	15	21	24	16	5	23	0	0	1	1	1	.50	2	.347	.432	.594
1996 Colorado	NL	104	151	38	6	2	5	(5	0)	63	20	31	22	19	2	38	1	0	2	1	1	.50	2	.252	.335	.417
1997 Colorado	NL	76	92	16	2	0	1	(0	1)	21	7	11	4	10	0	33	0	0	0	1	1	.50	2	.174	.255	.228
1998 Col-SD	NL	109	129	36	13	1	5	(3	2)	66	21	20	26	22	0	34	0	0	1	0	0	-	2	.279	.382	.512
1999 San Diego	NL	132	246	67	18	0	6	(2	4)	103	26	41	39	37	1	59	2	0	3	2	1	.67	5	.272	.368	.419
2000 Pittsburgh	NL	134	384	115	29	0	24	(13	11)	216	74	94	88	72	5	92	2	0	3	11	2	.85	7	.299	.410	.563
2001 Pit-SF	NL	146	452	122	28	4	14	(6	8)	200	58	70	72	68	9	122	1	2	4	8	6	.57	10	.270	.364	.442
2002 New York	AL	84	219	57	17	1	6	(2	4)	94	30	20	20	23	3	58	1	0	1	1	1	.50	7	.260	.327	.429
1998 Colorado	NL	89	104	30	10	1	5	(3	2)	57	18	20	22	16	0	29	0	0	1	0	0	-	1	.288	.380	.548
1998 San Diego	NL	20	25	6	3	0	0	(0	0)	9	3	0	4	6	0	5	0	0	0	0	0	-	1	.240	.387	.360
2001 Pittsburgh	NL	97	313	87	22	3	11	(5	6)	148	39	50	52	42	6	84	1	0	4	7	4	.64	7	.278	.361	.473
2001 San Francisco	NL	49	139	35	6	1	3	(1	2)	52	19	20	20	26	3	38	0	2	0	1	2	.33	3	.252	.370	.374
12 ML YEARS		1213	2373	627	143	17	81	(37	44)	1047	322	381	365	335	29	574	7	2	20	37	18	.67	48	.264	.354	.441

Claudio Vargas

Pitches: R **Bats:** R **Pos:** SP   **Ht:** 6'3" **Wt:** 225 **Born:** 6/19/78 **Age:** 25

Year Team	Lg	G	GS	CG	GF	IP	BFP	H	R	ER	HR	SH	SF	HB	TBB	IBB	SO	WP	Bk	W	L	Pct	ShO	Sv-Op	Hld	ERC	ERA
1998 Brevard Cnty	A+	2	2	0	0	9.2	46	15	5	5	5	1	1	0	2	1	9	0	0	0	1	.000	0	0--	-	11.23	4.66
1998 Marlins	R	5	4	0	0	28.2	117	24	15	13	1	0	1	3	7	0	27	2	0	0	4	.000	0	0--	-	2.62	4.08
1999 Kane County	A	19	19	1	0	99.2	426	97	47	43	8	2	3	0	41	0	88	2	2	5	5	.500	0	0--	-	3.85	3.88
2000 Brevard Cnty	A+	24	23	0	0	145.1	596	126	64	53	10	4	2	7	44	3	143	3	0	10	5	.667	0	0--	-	2.97	3.28
2000 Portland	AA	3	2	0	0	15.0	68	16	9	6	1	1	2	1	6	0	13	0	0	1	1	.500	0	0--	-	4.36	3.60
2001 Portland	AA	27	27	0	0	159.0	666	122	77	74	25	8	2	11	67	1	151	2	1	9	9	.471	0	0--	-	3.53	4.19
2002 Calgary	AAA	17	16	1	0	76.1	346	88	63	57	18	6	2	4	35	0	61	3	1	4	11	.267	0	0--	-	6.54	6.72
2002 Harrisburg	AA	8	8	0	0	33.0	146	38	17	17	2	1	0	3	9	0	34	3	0	2	2	.500	0	0--	-	4.49	4.64

Jason Varitek

Bats: B **Throws:** R **Pos:** C-127; PH-6; LF-1; DH-1   **Ht:** 6'2" **Wt:** 237 **Born:** 4/11/72 **Age:** 31

Year Team	Lg	G	AB	H	2B	3B	HR	Hm	Rd	TB	R	RBI	RC	TBB	IBB	SO	HBP	SH	SF	SB	CS	SB%	GDP	Avg	OBP	Slg
1997 Boston	AL	1	1	1	0	0	0	(0	0)	1	0	0	1	0	0	0	0	0	0	0	0	-	0	1.000	1.000	1.000
1998 Boston	AL	86	221	56	13	0	7	(1	6)	90	31	33	26	17	1	45	2	4	3	2	2	.50	8	.253	.309	.407
1999 Boston	AL	144	483	130	39	2	20	(12	8)	233	70	76	75	46	2	85	2	5	8	1	2	.33	13	.269	.330	.482
2000 Boston	AL	139	448	111	31	1	10	(2	8)	174	55	65	59	60	3	84	6	1	4	1	1	.50	16	.248	.342	.388
2001 Boston	AL	51	174	51	11	1	7	(2	5)	85	19	25	30	21	3	35	1	1	1	0	0	-	6	.293	.371	.489
2002 Boston	AL	132	467	124	27	1	10	(6	4)	183	58	61	52	41	3	95	7	1	3	4	3	.57	13	.266	.332	.392
6 ML YEARS		553	1794	473	121	5	54	(23	31)	766	233	260	243	185	12	344	18	12	19	8	8	.50	56	.264	.335	.427

Greg Vaughn

Bats: R **Throws:** R **Pos:** DH-38; LF-31; PH-1   **Ht:** 6'0" **Wt:** 206 **Born:** 7/3/65 **Age:** 37

Year Team	Lg	G	AB	H	2B	3B	HR	Hm	Rd	TB	R	RBI	RC	TBB	IBB	SO	HBP	SH	SF	SB	CS	SB%	GDP	Avg	OBP	Slg
1989 Milwaukee	AL	38	113	30	3	0	5	(1	4)	48	18	23	18	13	0	23	0	0	2	4	1	.80	6	.265	.336	.425
1990 Milwaukee	AL	120	382	84	26	2	17	(9	8)	165	51	61	45	33	1	91	1	7	6	7	4	.64	11	.220	.280	.432
1991 Milwaukee	AL	145	542	132	24	5	27	(16	11)	247	81	98	81	62	2	125	1	2	7	2	2	.50	5	.244	.319	.456
1992 Milwaukee	AL	141	501	114	18	2	23	(13	10)	205	77	78	63	60	1	123	5	2	5	15	15	.50	8	.228	.313	.409
1993 Milwaukee	AL	154	569	152	28	2	30	(12	18)	274	97	97	102	89	14	118	5	0	4	10	7	.59	6	.267	.369	.482
1994 Milwaukee	AL	95	370	94	24	1	19	(9	10)	177	59	55	61	51	6	93	1	0	1	9	5	.64	6	.254	.345	.478
1995 Milwaukee	AL	108	392	88	19	1	17	(8	9)	160	67	59	55	55	3	89	0	0	4	10	4	.71	10	.224	.317	.408
1996 Mil-SD	NL	145	516	134	19	1	41	(22	19)	278	98	117	101	82	6	130	6	0	4	9	3	.75	7	.260	.365	.539
1997 San Diego	NL	120	361	78	10	0	18	(11	7)	142	60	57	47	56	1	110	2	0	3	7	4	.64	7	.216	.322	.393
1998 San Diego	NL	158	573	156	28	4	50	(23	27)	342	112	119	122	79	6	121	5	0	4	11	4	.73	7	.272	.363	.597
1999 Cincinnati	NL	153	550	135	20	2	45	(20	25)	294	104	118	104	85	3	137	3	0	5	15	2	.88	9	.245	.347	.535
2000 Tampa Bay	AL	127	461	117	27	1	28	(13	15)	230	83	74	85	80	3	128	2	0	2	8	1	.89	10	.254	.365	.499
2001 Tampa Bay	AL	136	485	113	25	0	24	(12	12)	210	74	82	70	71	7	130	3	0	3	11	5	.69	7	.233	.333	.433
2002 Tampa Bay	AL	69	251	41	12	0	8	(1	7)	77	28	29	23	41	1	82	3	0	2	3	2	.60	5	.163	.286	.307
1996 Milwaukee	AL	102	375	105	16	0	31	(16	15)	214	78	95	79	58	4	99	4	0	5	5	2	.71	6	.280	.378	.571
1996 San Diego	NL	43	141	29	3	1	10	(6	4)	64	20	22	22	24	2	31	2	0	0	4	1	.80	1	.206	.329	.454
14 ML YEARS		1709	6066	1468	281	23	352	(168	184)	2851	1009	1067	973	857	54	1500	37	11	53	121	59	.67	101	.242	.337	.470

Mo Vaughn

Bats: L **Throws:** R **Pos:** 1B-134; PH-6   **Ht:** 6'1" **Wt:** 275 **Born:** 12/15/67 **Age:** 35

Year Team	Lg	G	AB	H	2B	3B	HR	Hm	Rd	TB	R	RBI	RC	TBB	IBB	SO	HBP	SH	SF	SB	CS	SB%	GDP	Avg	OBP	Slg
1991 Boston	AL	74	219	57	12	0	4	(1	3)	81	21	32	27	26	2	43	2	0	4	2	1	.67	7	.260	.339	.370
1992 Boston	AL	113	355	83	16	2	13	(8	5)	142	42	57	46	47	7	67	3	0	3	3	3	.50	8	.234	.326	.400
1993 Boston	AL	152	539	160	34	1	29	(13	16)	283	86	101	106	79	23	130	8	0	7	4	3	.57	14	.297	.390	.525
1994 Boston	AL	111	394	122	25	1	26	(15	11)	227	65	82	87	57	20	112	10	0	2	4	4	.50	7	.310	.408	.576
1995 Boston	AL	140	550	165	28	3	39	(15	24)	316	98	126	115	68	17	150	14	0	14	11	4	.73	7	.300	.388	.575
1996 Boston	AL	161	635	207	29	1	44	(27	17)	370	118	143	146	95	19	154	14	0	8	2	0	1.00	17	.326	.420	.583
1997 Boston	AL	141	527	166	24	0	35	(20	15)	295	91	96	118	86	17	154	12	0	3	2	2	.50	10	.315	.420	.560
1998 Boston	AL	154	609	205	31	2	40	(19	21)	360	107	115	134	61	13	144	8	0	9	0	0	-	13	.337	.402	.591

Year Team	Lg	G	AB	H	2B	3B	HR	(Hm Rd)	TB	R	RBI	RC	TBB	IBB	SO	HBP	SH	SF	SB	CS	SB%	GDP	Avg	OBP	Slg
1999 Anaheim	AL	139	524	147	20	0	33	(16 17)	266	63	108	92	54	7	127	11	0	3	0	0	-	11	.281	.358	.508
2000 Anaheim	AL	161	614	167	31	0	36	(18 18)	306	93	117	110	79	11	181	14	0	5	2	0	1.00	14	.272	.365	.498
2002 New York	NL	139	487	126	18	0	26	(16 10)	222	67	72	74	59	6	145	10	0	2	0	1	.00	15	.259	.349	.456
11 ML YEARS		1485	5453	1605	268	10	325	(168 157)	2868	851	1049	1055	711	142	1407	106	0	44	30	18	.63	133	.294	.384	.526

Javier Vazquez

Pitches: R **Bats:** R **Pos:** SP-34 **Ht:** 6'2" **Wt:** 195 **Born:** 7/25/76 **Age:** 26

Year Team	Lg	G	GS	CG	GF	IP	BFP	H	R	ER	HR	SH	SF	HB	TBB	IBB	SO	WP	Bk	W	L	Pct	ShO	Sv-Op	Hld	ERC	ERA
1998 Montreal	NL	33	32	0	1	172.1	764	196	121	116	31	9	4	11	68	2	139	2	0	5	15	.250	1	0-0	0	5.79	6.06
1999 Montreal	NL	26	26	3	0	154.2	667	154	98	86	20	3	3	4	52	4	113	2	0	9	8	.529	1	0-0	0	4.02	5.00
2000 Montreal	NL	33	33	2	0	217.2	945	247	104	98	24	11	3	5	61	10	196	3	0	11	9	.550	1	0-0	0	4.45	4.05
2001 Montreal	NL	32	32	5	0	223.2	898	197	92	85	24	9	2	3	44	4	208	3	1	16	11	.593	3	0-0	0	2.75	3.42
2002 Montreal	NL	34	34	2	0	230.1	971	243	111	100	28	15	7	4	49	6	179	3	0	10	13	.435	0	0-0	0	3.80	3.91
5 ML YEARS		158	157	12	1	998.2	4245	1037	526	485	127	47	19	27	274	26	835	13	1	51	56	.477	5	0-0	0	4.05	4.37

Ramon Vazquez

Bats: L **Throws:** R **Pos:** 2B-81; SS-41; 3B-19; PH-11 **Ht:** 5'11" **Wt:** 170 **Born:** 8/21/76 **Age:** 26

Year Team	Lg	G	AB	H	2B	3B	HR	(Hm Rd)	TB	R	RBI	RC	TBB	IBB	SO	HBP	SH	SF	SB	CS	SB%	GDP	Avg	OBP	Slg
1995 Mariners	R	39	141	29	3	1	0	(- -)	34	20	11	11	19	0	27	2	0	0	4	3	.57	2	.206	.309	.241
1996 Everett	A-	33	126	35	5	2	1	(- -)	47	25	18	22	26	0	26	1	2	5	7	2	.78	3	.278	.392	.373
1996 Tacoma	AAA	18	49	11	2	1	0	(- -)	15	7	4	4	4	0	12	1	0	0	0	0	-	2	.224	.296	.306
1996 Wisconsin	A	3	10	3	1	0	0	(- -)	4	1	1	1	2	0	2	0	0	0	0	0	-	1	.300	.417	.400
1997 Wisconsin	A	131	479	129	25	5	8	(- -)	188	79	49	74	78	2	93	3	4	3	16	10	.62	6	.269	.373	.392
1998 Lancaster	A+	121	468	129	26	4	2	(- -)	169	77	72	70	81	5	66	2	4	1	15	11	.58	6	.276	.384	.361
1999 New Haven	AA	127	428	113	27	3	5	(- -)	161	58	45	61	62	4	77	5	6	3	8	1	.89	11	.264	.361	.376
2000 New Haven	AA	124	405	116	25	4	8	(- -)	173	58	59	63	52	4	76	2	8	4	1	6	.14	6	.286	.367	.427
2001 Tacoma	AAA	127	466	140	28	1	10	(- -)	200	85	79	79	76	3	84	1	4	3	9	7	.56	13	.300	.397	.429
2001 Seattle	AL	17	35	8	0	0	0	(0 0)	8	5	4	2	0	0	3	0	1	1	0	0	-	0	.229	.222	.229
2002 San Diego	NL	128	423	116	21	5	2	(0 2)	153	50	32	54	45	3	79	1	3	2	7	2	.78	6	.274	.344	.362
2 ML YEARS		145	458	124	21	5	2	(0 2)	161	55	36	56	45	3	82	1	4	3	7	2	.78	6	.271	.335	.352

Randy Velarde

Bats: R **Throws:** R **Pos:** 2B-38; PH-10; PR-10; 1B-5; 3B-1; DH-1 **Ht:** 6'0" **Wt:** 200 **Born:** 11/24/62 **Age:** 40

Year Team	Lg	G	AB	H	2B	3B	HR	(Hm Rd)	TB	R	RBI	RC	TBB	IBB	SO	HBP	SH	SF	SB	CS	SB%	GDP	Avg	OBP	Slg
2002 Sacramento*	AAA	4	17	8	3	0	1	(- -)	14	3	4	6	1	1	3	1	0	0	1	0	1.00	0	.471	.526	.824
1987 New York	AL	8	22	4	0	0	0	(0 0)	4	1	1	0	0	0	6	0	0	0	0	0	-	1	.182	.182	.182
1988 New York	AL	48	115	20	6	0	5	(2 3)	41	18	12	9	8	0	24	2	0	0	1	1	.50	3	.174	.240	.357
1989 New York	AL	33	100	34	4	2	2	(1 1)	48	12	11	17	7	0	14	1	3	0	0	3	.00	0	.340	.389	.480
1990 New York	AL	95	229	48	6	2	5	(1 4)	73	21	19	18	20	0	53	1	2	1	0	3	.00	0	.210	.275	.319
1991 New York	AL	80	184	45	11	1	1	(0 1)	61	19	15	19	18	0	43	3	5	0	3	1	.75	6	.245	.322	.332
1992 New York	AL	121	412	112	24	1	7	(2 5)	159	57	46	52	38	1	78	2	4	5	7	2	.78	13	.272	.333	.386
1993 New York	AL	85	226	68	13	2	7	(4 3)	106	28	24	34	18	2	39	4	3	2	2	2	.50	12	.301	.360	.469
1994 New York	AL	77	280	78	16	1	9	(3 6)	123	47	34	40	22	0	61	4	2	2	4	2	.67	7	.279	.338	.439
1995 New York	AL	111	367	102	19	1	7	(2 5)	144	60	46	57	55	0	64	4	3	3	5	1	.83	9	.278	.375	.392
1996 Anaheim	AL	136	530	151	27	3	14	(8 6)	226	82	54	85	70	0	118	5	4	2	7	7	.50	7	.285	.372	.426
1998 Anaheim	AL	51	188	49	13	1	4	(1 3)	76	29	26	29	34	0	42	1	0	1	7	2	.78	8	.261	.375	.404
1999 Ana-Oak	AL	156	631	200	25	7	16	(8 8)	287	105	76	110	70	2	98	6	4	0	24	8	.75	19	.317	.390	.455
2000 Oakland	AL	122	485	135	23	0	12	(11 1)	194	82	41	68	54	0	95	3	3	1	9	3	.75	15	.278	.354	.400
2001 Tex-NYY	AL	93	342	95	19	2	9	(3 6)	145	50	32	51	34	0	86	8	4	1	6	2	.75	8	.278	.356	.424
2002 Oakland	AL	56	133	30	8	0	2	(0 2)	44	22	8	18	15	1	32	5	1	1	3	0	1.00	4	.226	.325	.331
1999 Anaheim	AL	95	376	115	15	4	9	(4 5)	165	57	48	64	43	1	56	4	2	0	13	4	.76	8	.306	.383	.439
1999 Oakland	AL	61	255	85	10	3	7	(4 3)	122	48	28	46	27	1	42	2	2	0	11	4	.73	11	.333	.401	.478
2001 Texas	AL	78	296	88	16	2	9	(3 6)	135	46	31	48	29	0	73	5	3	1	4	2	.67	8	.297	.369	.456
2001 New York	AL	15	46	7	3	0	0	(0 0)	10	4	1	3	5	0	13	3	1	0	2	0	1.00	0	.152	.278	.217
15 ML YEARS		1272	4244	1171	214	23	100	(46 54)	1731	633	445	604	463	6	853	49	38	19	78	37	.68	118	.276	.352	.408

Mike Venafro

Pitches: L **Bats:** L **Pos:** RP-47 **Ht:** 5'10" **Wt:** 180 **Born:** 8/2/73 **Age:** 29

Year Team	Lg	G	GS	CG	GF	IP	BFP	H	R	ER	HR	SH	SF	HB	TBB	IBB	SO	WP	Bk	W	L	Pct	ShO	Sv-Op	Hld	ERC	ERA
2002 Sacramento*	AAA	8	0	0	2	10.1	46	12	8	8	2	1	1	2	1	0	14	0	0	0	0	.000	0	0- -	-	5.11	6.97
1999 Texas	AL	65	0	0	11	68.1	283	63	29	25	4	5	2	3	22	0	37	0	0	3	2	.600	0	0-1	19	3.30	3.29
2000 Texas	AL	77	0	0	21	56.1	248	64	27	24	2	2	4	4	21	4	32	1	0	3	1	.750	0	1-2	17	4.49	3.83
2001 Texas	AL	70	0	0	20	60.0	266	54	35	32	2	2	4	7	28	4	29	3	0	5	5	.500	0	4-8	21	3.58	4.80
2002 Oakland	AL	47	0	0	8	37.0	168	45	23	19	5	4	2	2	14	2	16	1	0	2	2	.500	0	0-0	15	5.65	4.62
4 ML YEARS		259	0	0	60	221.2	965	226	114	100	13	13	12	16	85	10	114	5	0	13	10	.565	0	5-11	72	4.05	4.06

Robin Ventura

Bats: L **Throws:** R **Pos:** 3B-138; PH-10; 1B-5 **Ht:** 6'1" **Wt:** 198 **Born:** 7/14/67 **Age:** 35

Year Team	Lg	G	AB	H	2B	3B	HR	(Hm Rd)	TB	R	RBI	RC	TBB	IBB	SO	HBP	SH	SF	SB	CS	SB%	GDP	Avg	OBP	Slg
1989 Chicago	AL	16	45	8	3	0	0	(0 0)	11	5	7	4	8	0	6	1	1	3	0	0	-	1	.178	.298	.244
1990 Chicago	AL	150	493	123	17	1	5	(2 3)	157	48	54	53	55	2	53	1	13	3	1	4	.20	9	.249	.324	.318
1991 Chicago	AL	157	606	172	25	1	23	(16 7)	268	92	100	95	80	3	67	4	8	7	2	4	.33	22	.284	.367	.442
1992 Chicago	AL	157	592	167	38	1	16	(7 9)	255	85	93	96	93	9	71	0	1	8	2	4	.33	14	.282	.375	.431

BATTING / BASERUNNING / AVERAGES

Year Team	Lg	G	AB	H	2B	3B	HR	(Hm	Rd)	TB	R	RBI	RC	TBB	IBB	SO	HBP	SH	SF	SB	CS	SB%	GDP	Avg	OBP	Slg
1993 Chicago	AL	157	554	145	27	1	22	(12	10)	240	85	94	90	105	16	82	3	1	6	1	6	.14	18	.262	.379	.433
1994 Chicago	AL	109	401	113	15	1	18	(8	10)	184	57	78	70	61	15	69	2	2	8	3	1	.75	8	.282	.373	.459
1995 Chicago	AL	135	492	145	22	0	26	(8	18)	245	79	93	94	75	11	98	1	1	8	4	3	.57	8	.295	.384	.498
1996 Chicago	AL	158	586	168	31	2	34	(13	21)	305	96	105	107	78	10	81	2	0	8	1	3	.25	18	.287	.368	.520
1997 Chicago	AL	54	183	48	10	1	6	(2	4)	78	27	26	31	34	5	21	0	0	3	0	0	-	3	.262	.373	.426
1998 Chicago	AL	161	590	155	31	4	21	(15	6)	257	84	91	90	79	15	111	1	1	3	1	1	.50	10	.263	.349	.436
1999 New York	NL	161	588	177	38	0	32	(13	19)	311	88	120	113	74	10	109	3	1	5	1	1	.50	14	.301	.379	.529
2000 New York	NL	141	469	109	23	1	24	(12	12)	206	61	84	68	75	12	91	2	1	4	3	5	.38	14	.232	.338	.439
2001 New York	NL	142	456	108	20	0	21	(9	12)	191	70	61	68	88	10	101	1	0	4	2	5	.29	13	.237	.359	.419
2002 New York	AL	141	465	115	17	0	27	(9	18)	213	68	93	78	90	9	101	2	0	5	3	1	.75	14	.247	.368	.458
14 ML YEARS		1839	6520	1753	317	13	275	(126	149)	2921	945	1099	1057	995	127	1061	23	30	75	24	38	.39	162	.269	.364	.448

Dave Veres

Pitches: R **Bats:** R **Pos:** RP-71   **Ht:** 6'2" **Wt:** 220 **Born:** 10/19/66 **Age:** 36

HOW MUCH HE PITCHED / WHAT HE GAVE UP / THE RESULTS

Year Team	Lg	G	GS	CG	GF	IP	BFP	H	R	ER	HR	SH	SF	HB	TBB	IBB	SO	WP	Bk	W	L	Pct	ShO	Sv-Op	Hld	ERC	ERA
1994 Houston	NL	32	0	0	7	41.0	168	39	13	11	4	0	2	1	7	3	28	2	0	3	3	.500	0	1-1	3	2.89	2.41
1995 Houston	NL	72	0	0	15	103.1	418	89	29	26	5	6	8	4	30	6	94	4	0	5	1	.833	0	1-3	19	2.70	2.26
1996 Montreal	NL	68	0	0	22	77.2	351	85	39	36	10	3	3	6	32	2	81	3	2	6	3	.667	0	4-6	15	5.11	4.17
1997 Montreal	NL	53	0	0	11	62.0	281	68	28	24	5	6	1	2	27	3	47	7	0	2	3	.400	0	1-4	10	4.59	3.48
1998 Colorado	NL	63	0	0	26	76.1	319	67	26	24	6	0	2	2	27	2	74	2	2	3	1	.750	0	8-13	8	3.15	2.83
1999 Colorado	NL	73	0	0	63	77.0	349	88	46	44	14	5	2	2	37	7	71	8	1	4	8	.333	0	31-39	1	5.84	5.14
2000 St Louis	NL	71	0	0	61	75.2	310	65	26	24	6	5	2	6	25	2	67	3	1	3	5	.375	0	29-36	1	3.25	2.85
2001 St Louis	NL	71	0	0	44	65.2	279	57	29	27	12	2	1	2	28	1	61	6	0	3	2	.600	0	15-19	8	4.11	3.70
2002 St Louis	NL	71	0	0	26	82.2	346	67	34	32	12	3	3	2	39	4	68	7	0	5	8	.385	0	4-8	16	3.68	3.48
9 ML YEARS		574	0	0	275	661.1	2821	625	270	248	74	30	24	27	252	30	591	42	6	34	34	.500	0	94-129	80	3.88	3.38

Jose Vidro

Bats: B **Throws:** R **Pos:** 2B-152; PH-1   **Ht:** 5'11" **Wt:** 195 **Born:** 8/27/74 **Age:** 28

BATTING / BASERUNNING / AVERAGES

Year Team	Lg	G	AB	H	2B	3B	HR	(Hm	Rd)	TB	R	RBI	RC	TBB	IBB	SO	HBP	SH	SF	SB	CS	SB%	GDP	Avg	OBP	Slg
1997 Montreal	NL	67	169	42	12	1	2	(0	2)	62	19	17	19	11	0	20	2	0	3	1	0	1.00	1	.249	.297	.367
1998 Montreal	NL	83	205	45	12	0	0	(0	0)	57	24	18	19	27	0	33	4	6	3	2	2	.50	5	.220	.318	.278
1999 Montreal	NL	140	494	150	45	2	12	(5	7)	235	67	59	76	29	2	51	4	2	2	0	4	.00	12	.304	.346	.476
2000 Montreal	NL	153	606	200	51	2	24	(11	13)	327	101	97	115	49	4	69	2	0	6	5	4	.56	17	.330	.379	.540
2001 Montreal	NL	124	486	155	34	1	15	(6	9)	236	82	59	81	31	2	49	10	2	2	4	1	.80	18	.319	.371	.486
2002 Montreal	NL	152	604	190	43	3	19	(11	8)	296	103	96	112	60	1	70	3	11	3	2	1	.67	12	.315	.378	.490
6 ML YEARS		719	2564	782	197	9	72	(33	39)	1213	396	346	422	207	9	292	25	21	19	14	12	.54	65	.305	.360	.473

Brandon Villafuerte

Pitches: R **Bats:** R **Pos:** RP-31   **Ht:** 5'11" **Wt:** 165 **Born:** 12/17/75 **Age:** 27

HOW MUCH HE PITCHED / WHAT HE GAVE UP / THE RESULTS

Year Team	Lg	G	GS	CG	GF	IP	BFP	H	R	ER	HR	SH	SF	HB	TBB	IBB	SO	WP	Bk	W	L	Pct	ShO	Sv-Op	Hld	ERC	ERA
1995 Kingsport	R+	20	0	0	6	32.0	144	28	21	20	0	1	1	1	26	0	42	8	0	5	1	.833	0	0--	-	4.42	5.63
1996 Pittsfield	A-	18	7	1	4	62.2	267	53	21	21	5	2	3	6	27	0	59	4	0	3	1	.727	0	1--	-	3.60	3.02
1997 Capital City	A	47	3	0	31	75.2	308	58	23	20	6	2	1	4	33	0	88	12	0	3	1	.750	0	7--	-	3.11	2.38
1998 Brevard Cnty	A+	3	0	0	0	9.2	34	7	3	1	0	0	0	0	1	0	6	0	0	1	0	1.000	0	0--	-	1.38	0.93
1998 Portland	AA	30	0	0	11	54.1	262	68	35	30	3	6	0	4	33	2	52	3	0	2	2	.000	0	1--	-	6.27	4.97
1998 Charlotte	AAA	10	0	0	1	11.1	55	15	8	8	2	1	0	1	8	0	9	1	0	1	0	1.000	0	0--	-	8.69	6.35
1999 Portland	AA	22	12	0	4	100.1	422	97	45	39	11	4	2	5	40	3	85	2	1	6	8	.429	0	0--	-	4.23	3.50
1999 Jacksonville	AA	15	0	0	10	24.0	101	17	6	5	0	2	1	1	12	0	20	1	0	0	2	.000	0	5--	-	2.37	1.88
2000 Toledo	AAA	46	6	0	21	87.2	417	112	70	65	7	2	3	1	49	1	85	12	1	4	9	.308	0	4--	-	6.21	6.67
2001 Oklahoma	AAA	38	0	0	28	63.2	275	63	21	20	4	4	3	6	26	1	65	2	0	5	5	.500	0	10--	-	4.20	2.83
2002 Portland	AAA	47	0	0	19	58.0	234	43	17	13	2	3	1	0	22	1	54	2	0	8	4	.667	0	1--	-	2.23	2.02
2000 Detroit	AL	3	0	0	2	4.1	20	4	5	5	0	0	1	0	4	0	1	1	0	0	0		0	0-0	0	5.01	10.38
2001 Texas	AL	6	0	0	4	5.2	35	12	9	9	3	0	1	1	4	0	4	1	0	0	0		-	0-0	0	17.59	14.29
2002 San Diego	NL	31	0	0	11	32.0	133	29	5	5	2	1	1	2	12	2	25	0	0	1	2	.333	0	1-1	8	3.44	1.41
3 ML YEARS		40	0	0	17	42.0	188	45	19	19	5	1	2	3	20	2	30	2	0	1	2	.333	0	1-1	8	5.19	4.07

Oscar Villarreal

Pitches: R **Bats:** L **Pos:** RP   **Ht:** 6'0" **Wt:** 205 **Born:** 11/22/81 **Age:** 21

HOW MUCH HE PITCHED / WHAT HE GAVE UP / THE RESULTS

Year Team	Lg	G	GS	CG	GF	IP	BFP	H	R	ER	HR	SH	SF	HB	TBB	IBB	SO	WP	Bk	W	L	Pct	ShO	Sv-Op	Hld	ERC	ERA
1999 Diamndbcks	R	14	11	0	1	64.1	286	64	39	27	1	2	3	10	25	0	51	6	4	1	5	.167	0	0--	-	3.97	3.78
2000 Tucson	AAA	2	0	0	0	4.1	19	6	1	1	0	0	0	0	2	0	4	0	0	1	0	1.000	0	0--	-	6.28	2.08
2000 South Bend	A	13	5	0	5	32.2	155	37	19	16	0	0	0	3	17	3	30	2	1	1	3	.250	0	0--	-	4.59	4.41
2000 Diamndbcks	R	1	0	0	0	1.0	5	2	1	1	0	0	0	0	0	0	1	0	0	0	0		0	0--	-	7.48	9.00
2000 High Desert	A+	9	4	0	0	24.2	117	24	20	10	4	4	3	1	14	0	18	2	0	0	2	.000	0	0--	-	5.33	3.65
2001 El Paso	AA	27	27	0	0	140.2	644	154	86	69	10	4	7	8	63	1	108	14	11	6	9	.400	0	0--	-	4.71	4.41
2002 El Paso	AA	14	12	1	0	84.1	344	73	36	35	2	0	1	4	26	0	85	5	2	6	3	.667	0	0--	-	2.74	3.74
2002 Tucson	AAA	10	10	0	0	64.0	272	68	33	31	8	0	1	4	22	0	40	5	2	3	3	.500	0	0--	-	4.79	4.36

Ron Villone

Pitches: L **Bats:** L **Pos:** RP-38; SP-7   **Ht:** 6'4" **Wt:** 235 **Born:** 1/16/70 **Age:** 33

Year Team	Lg	G	GS	CG	GF	IP	BFP	H	R	ER	HR	SH	SF	HB	TBB	IBB	SO	WP	Bk	W	L	Pct	ShO	Sv-Op	Hld	ERC	ERA
1995 Sea-SD		38	0	0	15	45.0	212	44	31	29	11	3	1	1	34	0	63	3	0	2	3	.400	0	1-5	6	6.57	5.80
1996 SD-Mil	NL	44	0	0	19	43.0	182	31	15	15	6	0	2	5	25	0	38	2	0	1	1	.500	0	2-3	9	4.08	3.14
1997 Milwaukee	NL	50	0	0	15	52.2	238	54	23	20	4	2	0	1	36	2	40	3	0	1	0	1.000	0	0-2	8	5.30	3.42
1998 Cleveland	AL	25	0	0	6	27.0	129	30	18	18	3	2	2	2	22	0	15	0	0	0	0	-	0	0-0	1	7.01	6.00
1999 Cincinnati	NL	29	22	0	2	142.2	610	114	70	67	8	9	3	5	73	2	97	6	0	9	7	.563	0	2-2	0	3.20	4.23
2000 Cincinnati	NL	35	23	2	5	141.0	643	154	95	85	22	10	8	9	78	3	77	7	0	10	10	.500	0	0-0	1	5.97	5.43
2001 Col-Hou	NL	53	12	0	12	114.2	523	133	81	75	18	1	1	5	53	5	113	4	1	6	10	.375	0	0-0	6	5.81	5.89
2002 Pittsburgh	NL	45	7	0	6	93.0	399	95	63	60	8	5	3	5	34	3	55	1	0	4	6	.400	0	0-1	4	4.18	5.81
1995 Seattle	AL	19	0	0	7	19.1	101	20	19	17	6	3	0	1	23	0	26	1	0	0	2	.000	0	0-3	3	9.67	7.91
1995 San Diego	NL	19	0	0	8	25.2	111	24	12	12	5	0	1	0	11	0	37	2	0	2	1	.667	0	1-2	3	4.44	4.21
1996 San Diego	NL	21	0	0	9	18.1	78	17	6	6	2	0	0	1	7	0	19	0	0	1	1	.500	0	0-1	4	3.90	2.95
1996 Milwaukee	NL	23	0	0	10	24.2	104	14	9	9	4	0	2	4	18	0	19	2	0	0	0	-	0	2-2	5	4.21	3.28
2001 Colorado	NL	22	6	0	6	46.2	222	56	35	33	6	1	1	1	29	4	48	2	0	1	3	.250	0	0-0	2	6.30	6.36
2001 Houston	NL	31	6	0	6	68.0	301	77	46	42	12	0	0	4	24	1	65	2	1	5	7	.417	0	0-0	4	5.46	5.56
8 ML YEARS		319	64	2	80	659.0	2936	655	396	369	80	32	20	33	355	15	498	26	1	33	37	.471	0	5-13	31	4.95	5.04

Fernando Vina

Bats: L **Throws:** R **Pos:** 2B-150   **Ht:** 5'9" **Wt:** 174 **Born:** 4/16/69 **Age:** 34

Year Team	Lg	G	AB	H	2B	3B	HR	(Hm	Rd)	TB	R	RBI	RC	TBB	IBB	SO	HBP	SH	SF	SB	CS	SB%	GDP	Avg	OBP	Slg
1993 Seattle	AL	24	45	10	2	0	0	(0	0)	12	5	2	6	4	0	3	3	1	0	6	0	1.00	0	.222	.327	.267
1994 New York	NL	79	124	31	6	0	0	(0	0)	37	20	6	15	12	0	11	12	2	0	3	1	.75	4	.250	.372	.298
1995 Milwaukee	NL	113	288	74	7	7	3	(1	2)	104	46	29	35	22	0	28	9	4	2	6	3	.67	6	.257	.327	.361
1996 Milwaukee	NL	140	554	157	19	10	7	(3	4)	217	94	46	73	38	3	35	13	6	4	16	7	.70	15	.283	.342	.392
1997 Milwaukee	NL	79	324	89	12	2	4	(1	3)	117	37	28	36	12	1	23	7	2	3	8	7	.53	4	.275	.312	.361
1998 Milwaukee	NL	159	637	198	39	7	7	(2	5)	272	101	45	106	54	2	46	25	5	1	22	16	.58	7	.311	.386	.427
1999 Milwaukee	NL	37	154	41	7	0	1	(0	1)	51	17	16	19	14	0	6	4	3	2	5	2	.71	1	.266	.339	.331
2000 St Louis	NL	123	487	146	24	6	4	(1	3)	194	81	31	76	36	0	36	28	2	1	10	8	.56	5	.300	.380	.398
2001 St Louis	NL	154	631	191	30	8	9	(5	4)	264	95	56	96	32	3	35	22	3	2	17	7	.71	7	.303	.357	.418
2002 St Louis	NL	150	622	168	29	5	1	(0	1)	210	75	54	70	44	2	36	18	1	7	17	11	.61	11	.270	.333	.338
10 ML YEARS		1058	3866	1105	175	45	36	(13	23)	1478	571	313	532	268	11	259	141	29	22	110	62	.64	60	.286	.352	.382

Jose Vizcaino

Bats: B **Throws:** R **Pos:** SS-58; 3B-30; PH-26; 2B-25; 1B-5; PR-2   **Ht:** 6'1" **Wt:** 185 **Born:** 3/26/68 **Age:** 35

Year Team	Lg	G	AB	H	2B	3B	HR	(Hm	Rd)	TB	R	RBI	RC	TBB	IBB	SO	HBP	SH	SF	SB	CS	SB%	GDP	Avg	OBP	Slg
1989 Los Angeles	NL	7	10	2	0	0	0	(0	0)	2	2	0	0	0	0	1	0	1	0	0	0	-	0	.200	.200	.200
1990 Los Angeles	NL	37	51	14	1	1	0	(0	0)	17	3	2	5	4	1	8	0	0	0	1	1	.50	1	.275	.327	.333
1991 Chicago	NL	93	145	38	5	0	0	(0	0)	43	7	10	12	5	0	18	0	2	2	2	1	.67	1	.262	.283	.297
1992 Chicago	NL	86	285	64	10	4	1	(0	1)	85	25	17	21	14	2	35	0	5	1	3	0	1.00	4	.225	.260	.298
1993 Chicago	NL	151	551	158	19	4	4	(1	3)	197	74	54	68	46	2	71	3	8	9	12	9	.57	9	.287	.340	.358
1994 New York	NL	103	410	105	13	3	3	(1	2)	133	47	33	39	33	3	62	2	5	6	1	11	.08	5	.256	.310	.324
1995 New York	NL	135	509	146	21	5	3	(2	1)	186	66	56	60	35	4	76	1	13	3	8	3	.73	14	.287	.332	.365
1996 NYM-Cle		144	542	161	17	8	1	(1	0)	197	70	45	68	35	0	82	3	10	3	15	7	.68	8	.297	.341	.363
1997 San Francisco	NL	151	568	151	19	7	5	(1	4)	199	77	50	62	48	1	87	0	13	1	8	8	.50	13	.266	.323	.350
1998 Los Angeles	NL	67	237	62	9	0	3	(1	0)	80	30	29	25	17	0	35	1	10	2	7	3	.70	4	.262	.311	.338
1999 Los Angeles	NL	94	266	67	9	0	1	(1	0)	79	27	29	23	20	0	23	1	9	2	2	1	.67	9	.252	.304	.297
2000 LA-NYY		113	267	67	10	2	0	(0	0)	81	32	14	23	22	3	43	1	5	2	6	7	.46	6	.251	.308	.303
2001 Houston	NL	107	256	71	8	3	1	(1	0)	88	38	14	28	15	0	33	2	9	0	3	2	.60	6	.277	.322	.344
2002 Houston	NL	125	406	123	19	2	5	(4	1)	161	53	37	52	24	2	40	1	5	2	3	5	.38	5	.303	.342	.397
1996 New York	NL	96	363	110	12	6	1	(1	0)	137	47	32	49	28	0	58	3	6	2	9	5	.64	6	.303	.356	.377
1996 Cleveland	AL	48	179	51	5	2	0	(0	0)	60	23	13	19	7	0	24	0	4	1	6	2	.75	2	.285	.310	.335
2000 Los Angeles	NL	40	93	19	2	1	0	(0	0)	23	9	4	6	10	3	15	1	2	0	1	0	1.00	3	.204	.288	.247
2000 New York	AL	73	174	48	8	1	0	(0	0)	58	23	10	17	12	0	28	0	3	2	5	7	.42	3	.276	.319	.333
14 ML YEARS		1413	4503	1229	160	39	27	(12	15)	1548	551	390	486	318	18	614	15	95	33	71	58	.55	85	.273	.321	.344

Luis Vizcaino

Pitches: R **Bats:** R **Pos:** RP-76   **Ht:** 5'11" **Wt:** 174 **Born:** 8/6/74 **Age:** 28

Year Team	Lg	G	GS	CG	GF	IP	BFP	H	R	ER	HR	SH	SF	HB	TBB	IBB	SO	WP	Bk	W	L	Pct	ShO	Sv-Op	Hld	ERC	ERA
1999 Oakland	AL	1	0	0	1	3.1	16	3	2	2	1	0	0	0	3	0	2	1	0	0	0	-	0	0-0	0	7.01	5.40
2000 Oakland	AL	12	0	0	1	19.1	96	25	17	16	2	0	1	2	11	0	18	1	0	0	1	.000	0	0-0	0	6.83	7.45
2001 Oakland	AL	36	0	0	15	36.2	156	38	19	19	8	0	1	0	12	1	31	3	0	2	1	.667	0	1-1	3	4.80	4.66
2002 Milwaukee	NL	76	0	0	31	81.1	326	55	27	27	6	3	3	3	30	4	79	3	2	5	3	.625	0	5-6	19	2.20	2.99
4 ML YEARS		125	0	0	48	140.2	594	121	65	64	17	3	5	5	56	5	130	8	2	7	5	.583	0	6-7	22	3.52	4.09

Omar Vizquel

Bats: B **Throws:** R **Pos:** SS-150; PH-1   **Ht:** 5'9" **Wt:** 175 **Born:** 4/24/67 **Age:** 36

Year Team	Lg	G	AB	H	2B	3B	HR	(Hm	Rd)	TB	R	RBI	RC	TBB	IBB	SO	HBP	SH	SF	SB	CS	SB%	GDP	Avg	OBP	Slg
1989 Seattle	AL	143	387	85	7	3	1	(1	0)	101	45	20	25	28	0	40	1	13	2	1	4	.20	6	.220	.273	.261
1990 Seattle	AL	81	255	63	3	2	2	(0	2)	76	19	18	22	18	0	22	0	10	2	4	1	.80	7	.247	.295	.298
1991 Seattle	AL	142	426	98	16	4	1	(1	0)	125	42	41	39	45	0	37	0	8	3	7	2	.78	8	.230	.302	.293
1992 Seattle	AL	136	483	142	20	4	0	(0	0)	170	49	21	54	32	0	38	2	9	1	15	13	.54	14	.294	.340	.352
1993 Seattle	AL	158	560	143	14	2	2	(1	1)	167	68	31	53	50	2	71	4	13	3	12	14	.46	7	.255	.319	.298
1994 Cleveland	AL	69	286	78	10	1	1	(0	1)	93	39	33	32	23	0	23	0	11	2	13	4	.76	4	.273	.325	.325
1995 Cleveland	AL	136	542	144	28	0	6	(3	3)	190	87	56	70	59	0	59	1	10	10	29	11	.73	4	.266	.333	.351

238

BATTING

Year Team	Lg	G	AB	H	2B	3B	HR	(Hm	Rd)	TB	R	RBI	RC	TBB	IBB	SO	HBP	SH	SF	SB	CS	SB%	GDP	Avg	OBP	Slg
1996 Cleveland	AL	151	542	161	36	1	9	(2	7)	226	98	64	87	56	0	42	4	12	9	35	9	.80	10	.297	.362	.417
1997 Cleveland	AL	153	565	158	23	6	5	(3	2)	208	89	49	75	57	1	58	2	16	2	43	12	.78	16	.280	.347	.368
1998 Cleveland	AL	151	576	166	30	6	2	(0	2)	214	86	50	82	62	1	64	4	12	6	37	12	.76	10	.288	.358	.372
1999 Cleveland	AL	144	574	191	36	4	5	(3	2)	250	112	66	106	65	0	50	1	17	7	42	9	.82	8	.333	.397	.436
2000 Cleveland	AL	156	613	176	27	3	7	(1	6)	230	101	66	92	87	0	72	5	7	5	22	10	.69	13	.287	.377	.375
2001 Cleveland	AL	155	611	156	26	8	2	(2	0)	204	84	50	66	61	0	72	2	15	4	13	9	.59	14	.255	.323	.334
2002 Cleveland	AL	151	582	160	31	5	14	(9	5)	243	85	72	91	56	3	64	8	7	10	18	10	.64	7	.275	.341	.418
14 ML YEARS		1926	7002	1921	307	49	57	(26	31)	2497	1004	637	894	699	7	712	34	160	66	291	120	.71	128	.274	.340	.357

Ed Vosberg

Pitches: L Bats: L Pos: RP-4

Ht: 6'1" Wt: 208 Born: 9/28/61 Age: 41

Year Team	Lg	G	GS	CG	GF	IP	BFP	H	R	ER	HR	SH	SF	HB	TBB	IBB	SO	WP	Bk	W	L	Pct	ShO	Sv-Op	Hld	ERC	ERA
1986 San Diego	NL	5	3	0	0	13.2	65	17	11	10	1	0	0	0	9	1	8	0	1	0	1	.000	0	0-0	0	6.27	6.59
1990 San Francisco	NL	18	0	0	5	24.1	113	21	16	15	3	2	0	0	12	2	12	0	0	1	1	.500	0	0-0	0	3.71	5.55
1994 Oakland	AL	16	0	0	2	13.2	56	16	7	6	2	1	0	0	5	0	12	1	1	0	2	.000	0	0-1	5	5.75	3.95
1995 Texas	AL	44	0	0	20	36.0	154	32	15	12	3	2	3	0	16	1	36	3	2	5	5	.500	0	4-8	5	3.45	3.00
1996 Texas	AL	52	0	0	21	44.0	195	51	17	16	4	2	1	0	21	4	32	1	2	1	1	.500	0	8-9	11	5.20	3.27
1997 Tex-Fla	NL	59	0	0	22	53.0	239	59	30	26	3	2	4	5	21	6	37	2	1	2	3	.400	0	1-3	15	4.54	4.42
1999 SD-Ari	NL	19	0	0	3	11.0	60	22	12	10	1	2	2	2	3	0	8	1	0	0	1	.000	0	0-2	4	10.42	8.18
2000 Philadelphia	NL	31	0	0	5	24.0	106	21	11	11	4	1	0	0	18	0	23	1	0	1	1	.500	0	0-0	11	5.42	4.13
2001 Philadelphia	NL	18	0	0	4	12.2	46	8	4	4	0	0	0	0	3	0	11	0	1	0	0	-	0	0-0	6	1.35	2.84
2002 Montreal	NL	4	0	0	0	1.0	8	3	3	2	1	0	0	0	1	0	0	1	0	0	0	-	0	0-0	0	28.03	18.00
1997 Texas	AL	42	0	0	16	41.0	180	44	23	21	3	1	3	2	15	6	29	1	0	1	2	.333	0	0-1	5	4.10	4.61
1997 Florida	NL	17	0	0	6	12.0	59	15	7	5	0	1	1	3	6	0	8	1	1	1	1	.500	0	1-2	3	6.09	3.75
1999 San Diego	NL	15	0	0	3	8.1	47	16	11	9	1	2	2	2	3	0	6	1	0	0	0	-	0	0-2	4	10.59	9.72
1999 Arizona	NL	4	0	0	0	2.2	13	6	1	1	0	0	0	0	0	0	2	0	0	0	1	.000	0	0-0	0	9.88	3.38
10 ML YEARS		266	3	0	82	233.1	1033	250	126	112	22	12	10	7	109	14	179	10	8	10	15	.400	0	13-23	41	4.77	4.32

Brad Voyles

Pitches: R Bats: R Pos: RP-22

Ht: 6'0" Wt: 195 Born: 12/30/76 Age: 26

Year Team	Lg	G	GS	CG	GF	IP	BFP	H	R	ER	HR	SH	SF	HB	TBB	IBB	SO	WP	Bk	W	L	Pct	ShO	Sv-Op	Hld	ERC	ERA
1998 Eugene	A-	7	0	0	4	11.2	57	9	5	4	0	1	1	2	10	1	22	2	0	0	0	-	0	0--	-	4.05	3.09
1999 Macon	A	38	0	0	26	51.1	226	27	21	17	0	1	2	5	39	2	65	7	2	3	3	.500	0	14--	-	2.40	2.98
1999 Myrtle Beach	A+	5	0	0	2	12.0	50	7	3	3	1	1	0	0	9	1	13	1	0	1	1	.500	0	0--	-	2.98	2.25
2000 Myrtle Beach	A+	39	0	0	36	56.2	212	21	8	7	1	1	3	0	25	2	70	8	0	5	2	.714	0	19--	-	1.00	1.11
2001 Myrtle Beach	A+	2	0	0	2	1.2	6	0	0	0	0	0	0	0	1	0	3	0	0	0	0	-	0	1--	-	0.38	0.00
2001 Greenville	AA	15	0	0	8	16.2	72	11	3	2	0	2	2	1	10	1	25	6	0	0	0	-	0	6--	-	2.39	1.08
2001 Wichita	AA	11	0	0	8	15.1	63	8	0	0	0	2	1	1	10	1	19	1	0	1	0	1.000	0	4--	-	2.01	0.00
2002 Omaha	AAA	26	0	0	12	32.1	145	29	15	15	2	0	2	4	22	1	34	4	0	3	4	.429	0	5--	-	4.85	4.18
2001 Kansas City	AL	7	0	0	3	9.1	40	5	4	4	1	0	0	1	8	0	6	0	0	0	0	-	0	0-0	1	3.85	3.86
2002 Kansas City	AL	22	0	0	6	27.2	131	31	21	20	5	2	0	2	18	1	26	1	0	0	2	.000	0	1-2	1	6.72	6.51
2 ML YEARS		29	0	0	9	37.0	171	36	25	24	6	2	0	3	26	1	32	1	0	0	2	.000	0	1-2	2	5.96	5.84

Billy Wagner

Pitches: L Bats: L Pos: RP-70

Ht: 5'11" Wt: 195 Born: 7/25/71 Age: 31

Year Team	Lg	G	GS	CG	GF	IP	BFP	H	R	ER	HR	SH	SF	HB	TBB	IBB	SO	WP	Bk	W	L	Pct	ShO	Sv-Op	Hld	ERC	ERA
1995 Houston	NL	1	0	0	0	0.1	1	0	0	0	0	0	0	0	0	0	0	0	0	0	0	-	0	0-0	0	0.00	0.00
1996 Houston	NL	37	0	0	20	51.2	212	28	16	14	6	7	2	3	30	2	67	1	0	2	2	.500	0	9-13	3	2.61	2.44
1997 Houston	NL	62	0	0	49	66.1	277	49	23	21	5	3	1	3	30	1	106	3	0	7	8	.467	0	23-29	1	2.85	2.85
1998 Houston	NL	58	0	0	50	60.0	247	46	19	18	6	4	0	0	25	1	97	2	0	4	3	.571	0	30-35	1	2.87	2.70
1999 Houston	NL	66	0	0	55	74.2	286	35	14	13	5	2	1	1	23	1	124	2	0	4	1	.800	0	39-42	1	1.20	1.57
2000 Houston	NL	28	0	0	19	27.2	129	28	19	19	6	0	0	1	18	0	28	7	0	2	4	.333	0	6-15	0	6.15	6.18
2001 Houston	NL	64	0	0	58	62.2	251	44	19	19	5	3	1	5	20	0	79	3	0	2	5	.286	0	39-41	0	2.42	2.73
2002 Houston	NL	70	0	0	61	75.0	289	51	21	21	7	2	3	2	22	5	88	6	0	4	2	.667	0	35-41	0	2.08	2.52
8 ML YEARS		386	0	0	312	418.1	1692	281	131	125	40	21	8	15	168	10	589	24	0	25	25	.500	0	181-216	6	2.44	2.69

Tim Wakefield

Pitches: R Bats: R Pos: RP-30; SP-15

Ht: 6'2" Wt: 214 Born: 8/2/66 Age: 36

Year Team	Lg	G	GS	CG	GF	IP	BFP	H	R	ER	HR	SH	SF	HB	TBB	IBB	SO	WP	Bk	W	L	Pct	ShO	Sv-Op	Hld	ERC	ERA
1992 Pittsburgh	NL	13	13	4	0	92.0	373	76	26	22	3	6	4	1	35	1	51	3	1	8	1	.889	1	0-0	0	2.72	2.15
1993 Pittsburgh	NL	24	20	3	1	128.1	595	145	83	80	14	7	5	9	75	2	59	6	0	6	11	.353	2	0-0	0	5.97	5.61
1995 Boston	AL	27	27	6	0	195.1	804	163	76	64	22	3	7	9	68	0	119	11	0	16	8	.667	1	0-0	0	3.28	2.95
1996 Boston	AL	32	32	6	0	211.2	963	238	151	121	38	1	9	12	90	0	140	4	1	14	13	.519	0	0-0	0	5.68	5.14
1997 Boston	AL	35	29	4	2	201.1	866	193	109	95	24	3	7	16	87	5	151	6	0	12	15	.444	2	0-0	1	4.47	4.25
1998 Boston	AL	36	33	2	1	216.0	939	211	123	110	30	1	8	14	79	1	146	6	1	17	8	.680	0	0-0	0	4.30	4.58
1999 Boston	AL	49	17	0	28	140.0	635	146	93	79	19	1	8	5	72	2	104	1	0	6	11	.353	0	15-18	0	5.12	5.08
2000 Boston	AL	51	17	0	13	159.1	706	170	107	97	31	4	4	8	65	3	102	4	0	6	10	.375	0	0-1	3	5.23	5.48
2001 Boston	AL	45	17	0	5	168.2	732	156	84	73	13	3	9	18	73	5	148	5	1	9	12	.429	0	3-5	3	4.02	3.90
2002 Boston	AL	45	15	0	10	163.1	657	121	57	51	15	1	4	9	51	2	134	5	2	11	5	.688	0	3-5	5	2.54	2.81
10 ML YEARS		357	220	25	60	1676.0	7270	1619	909	792	209	30	69	97	695	21	1154	51	6	105	94	.528	6	21-29	12	4.34	4.25

Matt Walbeck

Bats: B Throws: R Pos: C-27

Ht: 5'11" Wt: 188 Born: 10/2/69 Age: 33

Year Team	Lg	G	AB	H	2B	3B	HR	(Hm	Rd)	TB	R	RBI	RC	TBB	IBB	SO	HBP	SH	SF	SB	CS	SB%	GDP	Avg	OBP	Slg
2002 Toledo*	AAA	21	75	16	3	0	1	(-	-)	22	4	6	3	4	0	10	0	1	0	0	0	-	6	.213	.250	.293
1993 Chicago	NL	11	30	6	2	0	1	(1	0)	11	2	6	2	1	0	6	0	0	0	0	0	-	0	.200	.226	.367
1994 Minnesota	AL	97	338	69	12	0	5	(0	5)	96	31	35	20	17	1	37	2	1	1	1	1	.50	7	.204	.246	.284
1995 Minnesota	AL	115	393	101	18	1	1	(1	0)	124	40	44	35	25	2	71	1	1	2	3	1	.75	11	.257	.302	.316
1996 Minnesota	AL	63	215	48	10	0	2	(1	1)	64	25	24	14	9	0	34	0	1	2	3	1	.75	6	.223	.252	.298
1997 Detroit	AL	47	137	38	3	0	3	(1	2)	50	18	10	16	12	0	19	0	0	2	3	3	.50	4	.277	.331	.365
1998 Anaheim	AL	108	338	87	15	2	6	(3	3)	124	41	46	39	30	0	68	2	5	5	1	1	.50	9	.257	.317	.367
1999 Anaheim	AL	107	288	69	8	1	3	(1	2)	88	26	22	24	26	1	46	3	3	1	2	3	.40	12	.240	.308	.306
2000 Anaheim	AL	47	146	29	5	0	6	(2	4)	52	17	12	11	7	0	22	1	1	0	0	1	.00	2	.199	.240	.356
2001 Philadelphia	NL	1	1	1	0	0	0	(0	0)	1	0	0	1	0	0	0	0	0	0	0	0	-	0	1.000	1.000	1.000
2002 Detroit	AL	27	85	20	2	0	0	(0	0)	22	4	3	4	3	0	14	0	0	1	0	0	-	2	.235	.258	.259
10 ML YEARS		623	1971	468	75	4	27	(10	17)	632	204	202	166	130	4	317	9	12	14	13	11	.54	53	.237	.286	.321

Jamie Walker

Pitches: L Bats: L Pos: RP-57

Ht: 6'2" Wt: 190 Born: 7/1/71 Age: 31

		HOW MUCH HE PITCHED						WHAT HE GAVE UP											THE RESULTS						
Year Team	Lg	G	GS	CG	GF	IP	BFP	H	R	ER	HR	SH	SF	HB	TBB	IBB	SO	WP	Bk	W	L	Pct	ShO	Sv-Op	Hld	ERC	ERA
2002 Toledo*	AAA	10	0	0	4	13.2	49	7	3	3	2	1	0	0	3	0	9	0	0	0	1	.000	0	1--	1	1.45	1.98
1997 Kansas City	AL	50	0	0	15	43.0	197	46	28	26	6	2	2	3	20	3	24	2	0	3	3	.500	0	0-1	3	5.10	5.44
1998 Kansas City	AL	6	2	0	2	17.1	86	30	20	19	5	1	1	2	3	0	15	0	0	0	1	.000	0	0-0	1	9.69	9.87
2002 Detroit	AL	57	0	0	16	43.2	175	32	19	18	9	0	1	4	9	1	40	1	1	1	1	.500	0	1-4	5	2.86	3.71
3 ML YEARS		113	2	0	33	104.0	458	108	67	63	20	3	4	9	32	4	79	3	1	4	5	.444	0	1-5	9	4.80	5.45

Kevin Walker

Pitches: L Bats: L Pos: RP-11

Ht: 6'4" Wt: 190 Born: 9/20/76 Age: 26

		HOW MUCH HE PITCHED						WHAT HE GAVE UP											THE RESULTS						
Year Team	Lg	G	GS	CG	GF	IP	BFP	H	R	ER	HR	SH	SF	HB	TBB	IBB	SO	WP	Bk	W	L	Pct	ShO	Sv-Op	Hld	ERC	ERA
2002 Lk Elsinore*	A+	5	1	0	0	7.0	22	3	0	0	0	0	0	0	0	0	10	0	0	0	0	-	0	0--	-	0.44	0.00
2002 Portland*	AAA	3	0	0	0	3.0	10	1	1	1	1	0	0	0	0	0	4	0	0	0	0	-	0	0--	-	0.80	3.00
2000 San Diego	NL	70	0	0	14	66.2	287	49	35	31	5	4	2	5	38	6	56	2	1	7	1	.875	0	0-0	19	3.23	4.19
2001 San Diego	NL	16	0	0	5	12.0	49	5	4	4	0	1	0	0	8	2	17	0	1	0	0	-	0	0-1	4	1.33	3.00
2002 San Diego	NL	11	0	0	1	8.0	42	12	6	5	2	1	0	0	5	1	11	1	0	0	1	.000	0	0-1	1	8.79	5.63
3 ML YEARS		97	0	0	20	86.2	378	66	45	40	7	5	2	5	51	9	84	3	2	7	2	.778	0	0-2	24	3.37	4.15

Larry Walker

Bats: L Throws: R Pos: RF-123; DH-7; PH-7

Ht: 6'3" Wt: 233 Born: 12/1/66 Age: 36

Year Team	Lg	G	AB	H	2B	3B	HR	(Hm	Rd)	TB	R	RBI	RC	TBB	IBB	SO	HBP	SH	SF	SB	CS	SB%	GDP	Avg	OBP	Slg
1989 Montreal	NL	20	47	8	0	0	0	(0	0)	8	4	4	2	5	0	13	1	3	0	1	1	.50	0	.170	.264	.170
1990 Montreal	NL	133	419	101	18	3	19	(9	10)	182	59	51	60	49	5	112	5	3	2	21	7	.75	8	.241	.326	.434
1991 Montreal	NL	137	487	141	30	2	16	(5	11)	223	59	64	77	42	2	102	5	1	4	14	9	.61	7	.290	.349	.458
1992 Montreal	NL	143	528	159	31	4	23	(13	10)	267	85	93	93	41	10	97	6	0	8	18	6	.75	9	.301	.353	.506
1993 Montreal	NL	138	490	130	24	5	22	(13	9)	230	85	86	89	80	20	76	6	0	6	29	7	.81	8	.265	.371	.469
1994 Montreal	NL	103	395	127	44	2	19	(7	12)	232	76	86	88	47	5	74	4	0	6	15	5	.75	8	.322	.394	.587
1995 Colorado	NL	131	494	151	31	5	36	(24	12)	300	96	101	108	49	13	72	14	0	5	16	3	.84	13	.306	.381	.607
1996 Colorado	NL	83	272	75	18	4	18	(12	6)	155	58	58	53	20	2	58	9	0	3	18	2	.90	7	.276	.342	.570
1997 Colorado	NL	153	568	208	46	4	49	(20	29)	409	143	130	166	78	14	90	14	0	4	33	8	.80	15	.366	.452	.720
1998 Colorado	NL	130	454	165	46	3	23	(17	6)	286	113	67	117	64	2	61	4	0	2	14	4	.78	11	.363	.445	.630
1999 Colorado	NL	127	438	166	26	4	37	(26	11)	311	108	115	127	57	8	52	12	0	6	11	4	.73	12	.379	.458	.710
2000 Colorado	NL	87	314	97	21	7	9	(7	2)	159	64	51	61	46	4	40	9	0	3	5	5	.50	12	.309	.409	.506
2001 Colorado	NL	142	497	174	35	3	38	(20	18)	329	107	123	138	82	6	103	14	0	8	14	5	.74	9	.350	.449	.662
2002 Colorado	NL	136	477	161	40	4	26	(18	8)	287	95	104	114	65	6	73	7	0	4	6	5	.55	8	.338	.421	.602
14 ML YEARS		1663	5880	1863	410	50	335	(191	144)	3378	1152	1133	1293	725	97	1023	110	7	61	215	71	.75	127	.317	.398	.574

Pete Walker

Pitches: R Bats: R Pos: SP-20; RP-18

Ht: 6'2" Wt: 195 Born: 4/8/69 Age: 34

		HOW MUCH HE PITCHED						WHAT HE GAVE UP											THE RESULTS						
Year Team	Lg	G	GS	CG	GF	IP	BFP	H	R	ER	HR	SH	SF	HB	TBB	IBB	SO	WP	Bk	W	L	Pct	ShO	Sv-Op	Hld	ERC	ERA
2002 Norfolk*	AAA	2	2	0	0	9.0	38	9	3	3	1	0	0	0	1	0	6	0	0	0	0	-	0	0--	-	2.88	3.00
1995 New York	NL	13	0	0	10	17.2	79	24	9	9	3	0	1	0	5	0	5	0	0	1	0	1.000	0	0-0	1	6.35	4.58
1996 San Diego	NL	1	0	0	0	0.2	5	0	0	0	0	0	0	0	3	0	1	0	0	0	0	-	0	0-0	0	13.05	0.00
2000 Colorado	NL	3	0	0	1	4.2	27	10	9	9	1	0	0	0	4	0	2	0	0	0	0	-	0	0-0	0	15.29	17.36
2001 New York	NL	2	0	0	1	6.2	25	6	2	2	0	0	0	0	4	0	4	0	0	0	0	-	0	0-0	0	1.63	2.70
2002 NYM-Tor		38	20	0	4	140.1	599	145	73	68	18	4	6	3	51	5	80	2	1	10	5	.667	0	1-1	3	4.41	4.36
2002 New York	NL	1	0	0	0	1.0	5	2	1	1	0	0	0	0	0	0	0	0	0	0	0	-	0	0-0	0	7.48	9.00
2002 Toronto	AL	37	20	0	4	139.1	594	143	72	67	18	4	6	3	51	5	80	2	1	10	5	.667	0	1-1	3	4.39	4.33
5 ML YEARS		57	20	0	16	170.0	735	185	93	88	22	4	7	3	63	5	92	2	1	11	5	.688	0	1-1	4	4.77	4.66

Todd Walker

Bats: L Throws: R Pos: 2B-154; PH-5

Ht: 6'0" Wt: 190 Born: 5/25/73 Age: 30

Year Team	Lg	G	AB	H	2B	3B	HR	(Hm	Rd)	TB	R	RBI	RC	TBB	IBB	SO	HBP	SH	SF	SB	CS	SB%	GDP	Avg	OBP	Slg
1996 Minnesota	AL	25	82	21	6	0	0	(0	0)	27	8	6	7	4	0	13	0	0	3	2	0	1.00	4	.256	.281	.329
1997 Minnesota	AL	52	156	37	7	1	3	(1	2)	55	15	16	16	11	1	30	1	1	2	7	0	1.00	5	.237	.288	.353
1998 Minnesota	AL	143	528	167	41	3	12	(7	5)	250	85	62	90	47	9	65	2	0	4	19	7	.73	13	.316	.372	.473

Year Team	Lg	G	AB	H	2B	3B	HR	(Hm	Rd)	TB	R	RBI	RC	TBB	IBB	SO	HBP	SH	SF	SB	CS	SB%	GDP	Avg	OBP	Slg
1999 Minnesota	AL	143	531	148	37	4	6	(4	2)	211	62	46	70	52	5	83	1	1	2	18	10	.64	15	.279	.343	.397
2000 Min-Col	AL	80	248	72	11	4	9	(5	4)	118	42	44	43	27	0	29	1	1	4	7	1	.88	5	.290	.355	.476
2001 Col-Cin	NL	151	565	163	35	2	17	(13	4)	253	93	75	84	51	1	82	1	4	3	8	1	.11	14	.296	.355	.459
2002 Cincinnati	NL	155	612	183	42	3	11	(7	4)	264	79	64	89	50	7	81	3	7	3	8	5	.62	9	.299	.353	.435
2000 Minnesota	AL	23	77	18	1	0	2	(0	2)	25	14	8	7	7	0	10	0	0	3	3	0	1.00	3	.234	.287	.325
2000 Colorado	NL	57	171	54	10	4	7	(5	2)	93	28	36	36	20	0	19	1	1	3	4	1	.80	2	.316	.385	.544
2001 Colorado	NL	85	290	86	18	2	12	(10	2)	144	52	43	47	25	1	40	0	0	3	1	3	.25	8	.297	.349	.497
2001 Cincinnati	NL	66	261	77	17	0	5	(3	2)	109	41	32	37	26	0	42	1	1	0	0	5	.00	6	.295	.361	.418
7 ML YEARS		749	2708	791	179	17	58	(37	21)	1178	384	313	399	242	23	383	9	13	23	62	31	.67	65	.292	.349	.435

Tyler Walker

Pitches: R Bats: R Pos: RP-4; SP-1   Ht: 6'3" Wt: 255 Born: 5/15/76 Age: 27

Year Team	Lg	G	GS	CG	GF	IP	BFP	H	R	ER	HR	SH	SF	HB	TBB	IBB	SO	WP	Bk	W	L	Pct	ShO	Sv-Op	Hld	ERC	ERA
1997 Mets	R	5	0	0	5	9.0	37	8	1	1	1	0	0	0	2	1	9	0	0	0	0	-	0	3--	-	2.01	1.00
1997 Pittsfield	A-	1	0	0	0	0.2	6	2	2	1	1	0	0	0	1	0	1	1	0	0	0	-	0	0--	-	34.79	13.50
1998 Capital City	A	34	13	0	3	115.2	503	122	63	53	9	3	4	3	38	0	110	8	1	5	5	.500	0	1--	-	4.01	4.12
1999 St.Lucie	A+	13	13	2	0	79.2	329	64	31	26	6	3	2	3	29	2	64	4	1	6	5	.545	0	0--	-	2.83	2.94
1999 Binghamton	AA	13	13	0	0	68.0	306	78	49	47	11	3	2	2	32	0	59	4	3	6	4	.600	0	0--	-	5.88	6.22
2000 Binghamton	AA	22	22	0	0	121.0	495	82	43	37	3	2	4	2	55	1	111	9	1	7	6	.538	0	0--	-	2.16	2.75
2000 Norfolk	AAA	5	5	0	0	26.1	111	29	7	7	0	0	0	0	9	0	17	1	0	1	3	.250	0	0--	-	3.82	2.39
2001 St.Lucie	A+	4	4	0	0	15.2	69	19	14	14	0	0	0	0	3	0	11	3	0	2	0	1.000	0	0--	-	3.63	8.04
2001 Binghamton	AA	4	3	0	0	22.1	88	9	2	1	1	3	1	0	13	1	13	1	0	0	1	.000	0	0--	-	1.45	0.40
2001 Norfolk	AAA	8	5	0	0	40.1	160	34	19	18	7	2	1	1	8	0	35	1	0	3	2	.600	0	0--	-	3.05	4.02
2002 Norfolk	AAA	28	25	1	3	142.0	603	152	65	63	13	3	5	4	38	3	109	2	3	10	5	.667	1	1--	-	3.99	3.99
2002 New York	NL	5	1	0	3	10.2	49	11	7	7	3	0	0	0	5	1	7	0	0	1	0	1.000	0	0-0	0	5.46	5.91

Donne Wall

Pitches: R Bats: R Pos: RP-17   Ht: 6'1" Wt: 205 Born: 7/11/67 Age: 35

Year Team	Lg	G	GS	CG	GF	IP	BFP	H	R	ER	HR	SH	SF	HB	TBB	IBB	SO	WP	Bk	W	L	Pct	ShO	Sv-Op	Hld	ERC	ERA
2002 Salt Lake*	AAA	1	1	0	0	1.2	6	1	1	1	0	0	0	0	0	0	2	0	0	0	1	.000	0	0--	-	2.64	5.40
2002 Co Springs*	AAA	14	0	0	4	17.1	70	16	10	10	1	1	3	1	4	0	11	0	0	1	2	.333	0	0--	-	3.04	5.19
1995 Houston	NL	6	5	0	0	24.1	110	33	19	15	5	0	2	0	5	0	16	1	0	3	1	.750	0	0-0	1	6.07	5.55
1996 Houston	NL	26	23	2	1	150.0	643	170	84	76	17	4	5	6	34	3	99	3	2	9	8	.529	1	0-0	0	4.38	4.56
1997 Houston	NL	8	8	0	0	41.2	186	53	31	29	8	0	0	2	16	0	25	2	1	2	5	.286	0	0-0	0	6.76	6.26
1998 San Diego	NL	46	1	0	14	70.1	287	50	20	19	6	4	2	1	32	2	56	3	1	5	4	.556	0	1-4	16	2.69	2.43
1999 San Diego	NL	55	0	0	12	70.1	290	58	31	24	11	1	1	0	23	3	53	6	0	7	4	.636	0	0-6	18	3.12	3.07
2000 San Diego	NL	44	0	0	14	53.2	211	36	20	20	4	3	0	0	21	1	29	1	0	5	2	.714	0	1-5	12	2.21	3.35
2001 New York	NL	32	0	0	14	42.2	193	51	24	23	8	3	2	1	17	6	31	1	0	0	4	.000	0	0-0	5	5.72	4.85
2002 Anaheim	AL	17	0	0	8	21.0	86	17	15	15	3	0	1	1	7	1	13	2	0	0	0	-	0	0-0	1	3.21	6.43
8 ML YEARS		234	37	2	63	474.0	2006	468	244	221	62	15	13	11	155	16	322	19	4	31	28	.525	1	2-15	48	3.99	4.20

Daryle Ward

Bats: L Throws: L Pos: LF-122; PH-16; DH-1   Ht: 6'2" Wt: 240 Born: 6/27/75 Age: 28

Year Team	Lg	G	AB	H	2B	3B	HR	(Hm	Rd)	TB	R	RBI	RC	TBB	IBB	SO	HBP	SH	SF	SB	CS	SB%	GDP	Avg	OBP	Slg
1998 Houston	NL	4	3	1	0	0	0	(0	0)	1	1	0	1	1	0	2	0	0	0	0	0	-	0	.333	.500	.333
1999 Houston	NL	64	150	41	6	0	8	(2	6)	71	11	30	21	9	0	31	0	0	2	0	0	-	3	.273	.311	.473
2000 Houston	NL	119	264	68	10	2	20	(13	7)	142	36	47	40	15	2	61	0	0	2	0	0	-	3	.258	.295	.538
2001 Houston	NL	95	213	56	15	0	9	(5	4)	98	21	39	31	19	4	48	1	0	2	0	0	-	3	.263	.323	.460
2002 Houston	NL	136	453	125	31	0	12	(9	3)	192	41	72	61	33	5	82	1	0	4	1	3	.25	9	.276	.324	.424
5 ML YEARS		418	1083	291	62	2	49	(29	20)	504	110	188	154	77	11	224	2	0	10	1	3	.25	21	.269	.316	.465

Jarrod Washburn

Pitches: L Bats: L Pos: SP-32   Ht: 6'1" Wt: 187 Born: 8/13/74 Age: 28

Year Team	Lg	G	GS	CG	GF	IP	BFP	H	R	ER	HR	SH	SF	HB	TBB	IBB	SO	WP	Bk	W	L	Pct	ShO	Sv-Op	Hld	ERC	ERA
1998 Anaheim	AL	15	11	0	0	74.0	317	70	40	38	11	2	3	3	27	1	48	0	0	6	3	.667	0	0-0	1	4.09	4.62
1999 Anaheim	AL	16	10	0	3	61.2	264	61	36	36	6	1	2	1	26	0	39	2	0	4	5	.444	0	0-0	1	4.20	5.25
2000 Anaheim	AL	14	14	0	0	84.1	340	64	38	35	16	1	3	1	37	0	49	1	0	7	2	.778	0	0-0	0	3.66	3.74
2001 Anaheim	AL	30	30	1	0	193.1	813	196	89	81	25	4	4	7	54	4	126	3	0	11	10	.524	0	0-0	0	4.03	3.77
2002 Anaheim	AL	32	32	1	0	206.0	852	183	75	72	19	4	7	3	59	1	139	5	1	18	6	.750	0	0-0	0	3.02	3.15
5 ML YEARS		107	97	2	3	619.1	2586	574	278	262	77	12	19	15	203	6	401	11	1	46	26	.639	0	0-0	2	3.66	3.81

Dusty Wathan

Bats: R Throws: R Pos: C-3   Ht: 6'4" Wt: 215 Born: 8/22/73 Age: 29

Year Team	Lg	G	AB	H	2B	3B	HR	(Hm	Rd)	TB	R	RBI	RC	TBB	IBB	SO	HBP	SH	SF	SB	CS	SB%	GDP	Avg	OBP	Slg
1994 Mariners	R	35	86	18	2	0	1	(-	-)	23	14	7	9	11	0	13	3	0	0	0	0	-	0	.209	.320	.267
1995 Wisconsin	A	5	11	1	0	0	1	(-	-)	4	1	3	1	0	0	3	1	0	0	0	0	-	-	.091	.167	.364
1995 Everett	A-	53	181	49	9	1	6	(-	-)	78	32	25	28	17	0	26	7	1	0	2	1	.67	4	.271	.356	.431
1996 Lancaster	A+	74	246	64	10	1	8	(-	-)	100	41	40	35	26	0	65	6	3	1	1	1	.50	5	.260	.344	.407
1997 Lancaster	A+	56	202	60	17	0	4	(-	-)	89	27	35	32	21	0	51	7	1	1	1	1	.50	4	.297	.381	.441
1997 Memphis	AA	49	149	40	4	1	4	(-	-)	58	20	19	22	19	0	28	5	0	1	1	1	.50	4	.268	.368	.389
1998 Tacoma	AAA	19	51	15	1	1	0	(-	-)	18	6	8	6	6	0	10	2	2	0	0	0	-	2	.294	.390	.353
1998 Orlando	AA	69	234	60	10	2	8	(-	-)	98	32	21	30	28	2	39	15	2	2	3	1	.75	8	.256	.369	.325
1999 New Haven	AA	96	333	93	16	2	4	(-	-)	125	37	37	43	24	1	60	12	4	1	4	1	.80	11	.279	.349	.375

BATTING

Year Team	Lg	G	AB	H	2B	3B	HR	(Hm Rd)	TB	R	RBI	RC	TBB	IBB	SO	HBP	SH	SF	SB	CS	SB%	GDP	Avg	OBP	Slg
2000 Tacoma	AAA	64	203	66	12	0	3	(- -)	87	25	29	35	15	1	28	12	4	1	0	2	.00	4	.325	.403	.429
2001 Portland	AA	55	134	36	10	0	2	(- -)	52	24	21	22	13	1	28	17	1	0	0	1	.00	3	.269	.402	.388
2002 Huntsville	AA	9	25	4	2	0	0	(- -)	6	2	2	2	2	0	4	2	0	0	0	0	-	0	.160	.276	.240
2002 Omaha	AAA	49	160	46	9	1	1	(- -)	60	22	26	22	16	0	36	10	3	1	1	1	.50	9	.288	.385	.375
2002 Kansas City	AL	3	5	3	1	0	0	(0 0)	4	1	1	3	0	0	1	1	0	0	0	0	-	0	.600	.667	.800

Mark Watson

Pitches: L **Bats:** R **Pos:** RP-3   **Ht:** 6'4" **Wt:** 215 **Born:** 1/23/74 **Age:** 29

		HOW MUCH HE PITCHED						WHAT HE GAVE UP										THE RESULTS							
Year Team	Lg	G	GS	CG	GF	IP	BFP	H	R	ER	HR	SH	SF	HB	TBB	IBB	SO	WP	Bk	W	L	Pct	ShO	Sv-Op	Hld	ERC	ERA
1996 Helena	R+	13	13	0	0	60.1	262	59	43	32	2	1	2	1	28	0	68	7	0	5	2	.714	0	0--	-	3.80	4.77
1997 Beloit	A	8	7	0	0	32.1	153	40	33	24	3	0	3	1	20	0	33	3	0	0	3	.000	0	0--	-	6.52	6.68
1997 Ogden	R+	10	10	1	0	47.2	202	44	26	22	4	1	2	0	19	0	49	2	0	4	3	.571	0	0--	-	3.54	4.15
1998 Columbus	A	31	12	1	8	97.2	408	95	53	44	10	3	3	3	32	0	77	6	2	3	4	.429	0	0--	-	3.85	4.05
1998 Kinston	A+	1	1	0	0	6.1	26	3	4	0	0	0	1	0	2	0	8	0	0	1	0	1.000	0	0--	-	0.92	0.00
1999 Kinston	A+	11	4	0	1	43.1	163	28	7	5	1	0	0	0	10	0	40	1	1	6	0	1.000	0	0--	-	1.43	1.04
1999 Akron	AA	19	17	0	1	110.0	500	143	64	53	9	6	7	6	38	0	57	6	2	9	8	.529	0	0--	-	5.75	4.34
2000 Buffalo	AAA	16	0	0	3	20.1	91	18	11	10	1	1	2	0	12	6	16	1	0	1	2	.333	0	1--	-	3.22	4.43
2000 Tacoma	AAA	16	0	0	4	25.0	111	30	16	11	3	0	3	0	6	0	17	0	1	2	1	.667	0	0--	-	4.60	3.96
2001 Tacoma	AAA	3	0	0	2	4.0	20	4	2	1	1	0	0	0	2	0	1	0	0	0	1	.000	0	1--	-	4.86	2.25
2001 Akron	AA	30	0	0	21	39.1	166	34	19	18	2	1	1	1	13	0	34	2	0	3	1	.750	0	4--	-	2.79	4.12
2001 Buffalo	AAA	3	0	0	0	4.0	25	9	7	6	1	0	0	0	3	1	3	0	0	1	0	1.000	0	0--	-	14.14	13.50
2002 Iowa	AAA	28	0	0	6	37.2	162	35	22	18	3	3	1	2	19	3	25	0	0	4	0	1.000	0	1--	-	4.11	4.30
2002 Tacoma	AAA	6	0	0	3	12.1	50	10	2	1	0	0	0	0	3	0	8	0	0	2	0	1.000	0	2--	-	1.88	0.73
2002 Co Springs	AAA	10	0	0	4	10.2	65	22	19	19	3	1	0	1	11	1	10	1	0	0	0	-	0	0--	-	16.24	16.03
2000 Cleveland	AL	6	0	0	1	6.1	33	12	7	6	0	0	0	1	2	0	4	0	0	0	1	.000	0	0-0	0	9.18	8.53
2002 Seattle	AL	3	0	0	1	4.0	24	8	8	8	1	0	1	0	4	0	1	1	0	1	0	1.000	0	0-0	0	14.76	18.00
2 ML YEARS		9	0	0	2	10.1	57	20	15	14	1	0	1	1	6	0	5	1	0	1	1	.500	0	0-0	0	11.28	12.19

Justin Wayne

Pitches: R **Bats:** R **Pos:** SP-5   **Ht:** 6'3" **Wt:** 200 **Born:** 4/16/79 **Age:** 24

		HOW MUCH HE PITCHED						WHAT HE GAVE UP										THE RESULTS							
Year Team	Lg	G	GS	CG	GF	IP	BFP	H	R	ER	HR	SH	SF	HB	TBB	IBB	SO	WP	Bk	W	L	Pct	ShO	Sv-Op	Hld	ERC	ERA
2000 Jupiter	A+	5	5	0	0	26.1	112	26	22	17	2	1	1	0	11	0	24	1	0	0	3	.000	0	0--	-	3.97	5.81
2001 Jupiter	A+	8	7	0	0	41.2	166	31	16	14	0	0	2	3	9	0	35	2	0	2	3	.400	0	0--	-	1.75	3.02
2001 Harrisburg	AA	14	14	2	0	92.2	398	87	28	27	4	3	1	9	34	0	70	5	0	9	2	.818	0	0--	-	3.60	2.62
2002 Harrisburg	AA	17	17	0	0	98.2	401	74	41	26	7	6	9	6	32	0	47	5	2	5	2	.714	0	0--	-	2.52	2.37
2002 Portland	AAA	7	7	1	0	42.2	184	43	26	23	3	2	4	5	13	0	30	2	0	3	3	.500	1	0--	-	4.02	4.85
2002 Calgary	AAA	2	2	0	0	11.1	48	8	8	8	3	0	0	1	6	0	10	0	0	0	1	.000	0	0--	-	4.45	6.35
2002 Florida	NL	5	5	0	0	23.2	105	22	16	14	3	0	2	0	13	0	16	2	1	2	3	.400	0	0-0	0	4.41	5.32

David Weathers

Pitches: R **Bats:** R **Pos:** RP-71   **Ht:** 6'3" **Wt:** 230 **Born:** 9/25/69 **Age:** 33

		HOW MUCH HE PITCHED						WHAT HE GAVE UP										THE RESULTS							
Year Team	Lg	G	GS	CG	GF	IP	BFP	H	R	ER	HR	SH	SF	HB	TBB	IBB	SO	WP	Bk	W	L	Pct	ShO	Sv-Op	Hld	ERC	ERA
1991 Toronto	AL	15	0	0	4	14.2	79	15	9	8	1	2	1	2	17	3	13	0	0	1	0	1.000	0	0-0	1	6.88	4.91
1992 Toronto	AL	2	0	0	0	3.1	15	5	3	3	1	0	0	0	2	0	3	0	0	0	0	-	0	0-0	0	10.97	8.10
1993 Florida	NL	14	6	0	2	45.2	202	57	26	26	3	2	0	1	13	1	34	6	0	2	3	.400	0	0-0	0	4.86	5.12
1994 Florida	NL	24	24	0	0	135.0	621	166	87	79	13	12	4	4	59	9	72	7	1	8	12	.400	0	0-0	0	5.52	5.27
1995 Florida	NL	28	15	0	0	90.1	419	104	68	60	8	7	3	5	52	3	60	3	0	4	5	.444	0	0-0	1	5.79	5.98
1996 Fla-NYY		42	12	0	9	88.2	408	108	60	54	8	5	2	6	42	5	53	3	0	2	4	.333	0	0-0	3	5.80	5.48
1997 NYY-Cle		19	1	0	5	25.2	126	38	24	24	3	2	1	1	15	0	18	3	0	1	3	.250	0	0-1	3	8.27	8.42
1998 Cin-Mil	NL	44	9	0	9	110.0	492	130	69	60	6	6	2	3	41	3	94	7	2	6	5	.545	0	0-1	3	4.73	4.91
1999 Milwaukee	NL	63	0	0	14	93.0	414	102	49	48	14	4	4	2	38	3	74	1	1	7	4	.636	0	2-6	9	5.04	4.65
2000 Milwaukee	NL	69	0	0	23	76.1	320	73	29	26	7	4	1	2	32	8	50	0	0	3	5	.375	0	1-7	14	3.90	3.07
2001 Mil-ChC	NL	80	0	0	25	86.0	351	65	24	23	6	6	3	3	34	8	66	0	0	4	5	.444	0	4-10	16	2.59	2.41
2002 New York	NL	71	0	0	12	77.1	331	69	30	25	6	6	4	3	36	7	61	2	0	6	3	.667	0	0-5	18	3.60	2.91
1996 Florida	NL	31	8	0	8	71.1	319	85	41	36	7	5	1	4	28	4	40	2	0	2	2	.500	0	0-0	3	5.35	4.54
1996 New York	AL	11	4	0	1	17.1	89	23	19	18	1	0	1	2	14	1	13	1	0	0	2	.000	0	0-0	0	7.66	9.35
1997 New York	AL	10	0	0	3	9.0	47	15	10	10	1	0	0	0	7	0	4	2	0	1	0	1.000	0	0-1	0	10.26	10.00
1997 Cleveland	AL	9	1	0	2	16.2	79	23	14	14	2	2	1	1	8	0	14	1	0	0	3	.000	0	0-0	3	7.23	7.56
1998 Cincinnati	NL	16	9	0	0	62.1	294	86	47	43	3	4	1	1	27	2	51	5	1	2	4	.333	0	0-0	0	6.04	6.21
1998 Milwaukee	NL	28	0	0	9	47.2	198	44	22	17	3	2	1	2	14	1	43	2	1	4	1	.800	0	0-1	3	3.15	3.21
2001 Milwaukee	NL	52	0	0	21	57.2	233	37	14	13	3	8	1	2	25	7	46	0	0	3	4	.429	0	4-7	10	2.01	2.03
2001 Chicago	NL	28	0	0	4	28.1	118	28	10	10	3	2	2	1	9	1	20	0	0	1	1	.500	0	0-3	6	3.90	3.18
12 ML YEARS		471	67	0	103	846.0	3779	932	478	436	76	60	25	32	381	50	598	32	4	44	49	.473	0	7-30	65	4.85	4.64

Jeff Weaver

Pitches: R **Bats:** R **Pos:** SP-25; RP-7   **Ht:** 6'5" **Wt:** 200 **Born:** 8/22/76 **Age:** 26

		HOW MUCH HE PITCHED						WHAT HE GAVE UP										THE RESULTS							
Year Team	Lg	G	GS	CG	GF	IP	BFP	H	R	ER	HR	SH	SF	HB	TBB	IBB	SO	WP	Bk	W	L	Pct	ShO	Sv-Op	Hld	ERC	ERA
1999 Detroit	AL	30	29	0	1	163.2	717	176	104	101	27	5	5	17	56	2	114	0	0	9	12	.429	0	0-0	0	5.21	5.55
2000 Detroit	AL	31	30	2	0	200.0	849	205	102	96	26	3	9	15	52	2	136	3	2	11	15	.423	0	0-0	0	4.18	4.32
2001 Detroit	AL	33	33	5	0	229.1	985	235	116	104	19	12	7	14	68	4	152	3	0	13	16	.448	0	0-0	0	3.89	4.08
2002 Det-NYY	AL	32	25	3	3	199.2	840	193	88	78	16	6	3	11	48	4	132	6	0	11	11	.500	3	2-2	0	3.30	3.52
2002 Detroit	AL	17	17	3	0	121.2	509	112	50	43	4	2	2	8	33	1	75	4	0	6	8	.429	3	0-0	0	2.94	3.18
2002 New York	AL	15	8	0	3	78.0	331	81	38	35	12	1	1	3	15	3	57	2	0	5	3	.625	0	2-2	0	3.86	4.04
4 ML YEARS		126	117	10	4	792.2	3391	809	410	379	88	26	24	57	224	12	534	12	2	44	54	.449	3	2-2	0	4.07	4.30

Brandon Webb

Pitches: R Bats: R Pos: SP   Ht: 6'2" Wt: 228 Born: 5/9/79 Age: 24

Year Team	Lg	G	GS	CG	GF	IP	BFP	H	R	ER	HR	SH	SF	HB	TBB	IBB	SO	WP	Bk	W	L	Pct	ShO	Sv-Op	Hld	ERC	ERA
2000 Diamndbcks	R	1	1	0	0	1.0	5	2	1	1	0	0	0	0	0	0	3	0	0	0	0	-	0	0--	-	7.48	9.00
2000 South Bend	A	12	0	0	7	16.2	69	10	7	6	0	0	0	2	9	1	18	1	0	0	0	-	0	2--	-	2.20	3.24
2001 Lancaster	A+	29	28	0	0	162.1	711	174	90	72	9	3	5	27	44	0	158	11	1	6	10	.375	0	0--	-	4.33	3.99
2002 El Paso	AA	26	25	1	1	152.0	647	141	66	53	4	2	3	13	59	1	122	12	1	10	6	.625	1	0--	-	3.48	3.14
2002 Tucson	AAA	1	1	0	0	7.0	31	5	3	3	0	1	0	1	4	0	5	0	0	0	1	.000	0	0--	-	2.92	3.86

Ben Weber

Pitches: R Bats: R Pos: RP-63   Ht: 6'4" Wt: 210 Born: 11/17/69 Age: 33

Year Team	Lg	G	GS	CG	GF	IP	BFP	H	R	ER	HR	SH	SF	HB	TBB	IBB	SO	WP	Bk	W	L	Pct	ShO	Sv-Op	Hld	ERC	ERA
2000 SF-Ana		19	0	0	3	22.2	103	28	19	16	0	0	1	0	6	1	14	2	0	1	1	.500	0	0-2	2	3.91	6.35
2001 Anaheim	AL	56	0	0	19	68.1	299	66	28	26	4	0	0	5	31	8	40	0	1	6	2	.750	0	0-1	6	3.90	3.42
2002 Anaheim	AL	63	0	0	16	78.0	314	70	25	22	4	4	2	3	22	3	43	2	0	7	2	.778	0	7-11	18	2.94	2.54
2000 San Francisco	NL	9	0	0	2	8.0	44	16	13	13	0	0	0	0	4	0	6	1	0	0	1	.000	0	0-2	1	9.72	14.63
2000 Anaheim	AL	10	0	0	1	14.2	59	12	6	3	0	0	1	0	2	1	8	1	0	1	0	1.000	0	0-0	1	1.52	1.84
3 ML YEARS		138	0	0	38	169.0	716	164	72	64	8	4	3	8	59	12	97	4	1	14	5	.737	0	7-14	26	3.45	3.41

Todd Wellemeyer

Pitches: R Bats: R Pos: RP   Ht: 6'3" Wt: 205 Born: 8/30/78 Age: 24

Year Team	Lg	G	GS	CG	GF	IP	BFP	H	R	ER	HR	SH	SF	HB	TBB	IBB	SO	WP	Bk	W	L	Pct	ShO	Sv-Op	Hld	ERC	ERA
2000 Eugene	A-	15	15	0	0	76.0	315	62	35	31	3	1	1	4	33	2	85	3	1	4	4	.500	0	0--	-	3.02	3.67
2001 Lansing	A	27	27	1	0	147.0	667	165	85	68	14	4	5	11	74	0	167	10	1	13	9	.591	0	0--	-	5.55	4.16
2002 Daytona	A+	14	14	0	0	73.2	301	63	33	31	7	1	3	4	19	1	87	3	0	2	4	.333	0	0--	-	2.92	3.79
2002 W Tennesse	AA	8	8	1	0	46.0	187	33	25	24	2	0	4	3	18	0	37	2	0	3	3	.500	1	0--	-	2.46	4.70

Bob Wells

Pitches: R Bats: R Pos: RP-48   Ht: 6'0" Wt: 200 Born: 11/1/66 Age: 36

Year Team	Lg	G	GS	CG	GF	IP	BFP	H	R	ER	HR	SH	SF	HB	TBB	IBB	SO	WP	Bk	W	L	Pct	ShO	Sv-Op	Hld	ERC	ERA
1994 Phi-Sea		7	0	0	2	9.0	38	8	2	2	0	0	0	1	4	0	6	0	0	2	0	1.000	0	0-0	0	3.45	2.00
1995 Seattle	AL	30	4	0	3	76.2	358	88	51	49	11	1	5	3	39	3	38	1	0	4	3	.571	0	0-1	0	5.71	5.75
1996 Seattle	AL	36	16	1	6	130.2	574	141	78	77	25	3	4	6	46	5	94	0	0	12	7	.632	1	0-0	1	5.11	5.30
1997 Seattle	AL	46	1	0	19	67.1	304	88	49	43	11	1	2	3	18	1	51	1	0	2	0	1.000	0	2-4	5	5.98	5.75
1998 Seattle	AL	30	0	0	4	51.2	228	54	38	35	12	2	1	2	16	1	29	1	0	2	2	.500	0	0-1	1	4.89	6.10
1999 Minnesota	AL	76	0	0	18	87.1	364	79	41	37	8	5	3	5	28	4	44	4	0	8	3	.727	0	1-5	17	3.37	3.81
2000 Minnesota	AL	76	0	0	25	86.1	351	80	39	35	14	3	5	4	15	2	76	1	0	0	7	.000	0	10-20	11	3.35	3.65
2001 Minnesota	AL	65	0	0	18	68.2	299	72	39	39	12	3	4	10	18	2	49	0	0	8	5	.615	0	2-4	16	4.89	5.11
2002 Minnesota	AL	48	0	0	16	58.0	261	78	41	38	8	2	2	1	16	1	30	0	0	2	1	.667	0	0-0	0	5.97	5.90
1994 Philadelphia	NL	6	0	0	2	5.0	21	4	1	1	0	0	0	1	3	0	3	0	0	1	0	1.000	0	0-0	0	4.04	1.80
1994 Seattle		1	0	0	0	4.0	17	4	1	1	0	0	0	0	1	0	3	0	0	1	0	1.000	0	0-0	0	2.77	2.25
9 ML YEARS		414	21	1	111	635.2	2777	688	378	355	101	20	26	35	200	19	417	8	0	40	28	.588	1	15-35	57	4.79	5.03

David Wells

Pitches: L Bats: L Pos: SP-31   Ht: 6'4" Wt: 240 Born: 5/20/63 Age: 40

Year Team	Lg	G	GS	CG	GF	IP	BFP	H	R	ER	HR	SH	SF	HB	TBB	IBB	SO	WP	Bk	W	L	Pct	ShO	Sv-Op	Hld	ERC	ERA
1987 Toronto	AL	18	2	0	6	29.1	132	37	14	13	4	0	1	0	12	0	32	4	0	4	3	.571	0	1-2	2	4.91	3.99
1988 Toronto	AL	41	0	0	15	64.1	279	65	36	33	12	2	2	2	31	9	56	6	2	3	5	.375	0	4-6	8	5.11	4.62
1989 Toronto	AL	54	0	0	19	86.1	352	66	25	23	5	3	2	0	28	7	78	6	3	7	4	.636	0	2-9	8	2.16	2.40
1990 Toronto	AL	43	25	0	8	189.0	759	165	72	66	14	9	2	4	45	3	115	7	1	11	6	.647	0	3-3	3	2.67	3.14
1991 Toronto	AL	40	28	2	3	198.1	811	188	88	82	24	6	6	2	49	1	106	10	3	15	10	.600	0	1-2	3	3.41	3.72
1992 Toronto	AL	41	14	0	14	120.0	529	138	84	72	16	3	4	9	36	6	62	3	1	7	9	.438	0	2-4	3	4.98	5.40
1993 Detroit	AL	32	30	0	0	187.0	776	183	93	87	26	3	3	7	42	6	139	13	0	11	9	.550	0	0-0	1	3.64	4.19
1994 Detroit	AL	16	16	5	0	111.1	464	113	54	49	13	3	1	2	24	6	71	5	0	5	7	.417	1	0-0	0	3.54	3.96
1995 Det-Cin		29	29	6	0	203.0	839	194	88	73	23	7	3	2	53	9	133	7	2	16	8	.667	1	0-0	0	3.37	3.24
1996 Baltimore	AL	34	34	3	0	224.1	946	247	132	128	32	8	14	7	51	7	130	4	2	11	14	.440	0	0-0	0	4.39	5.14
1997 New York	AL	32	32	5	0	218.0	922	239	109	102	24	7	3	6	45	0	156	8	0	16	10	.615	2	0-0	0	4.04	4.21
1998 New York	AL	30	30	8	0	214.1	851	195	86	83	29	2	2	1	29	0	163	2	0	18	4	.818	5	0-0	0	2.83	3.49
1999 Toronto	AL	34	34	7	0	231.2	987	246	132	124	32	6	6	0	62	2	169	1	0	17	10	.630	1	0-0	0	4.26	4.82
2000 Toronto	AL	35	35	9	0	229.2	972	266	115	105	23	6	7	8	31	0	166	9	1	20	8	.714	0	0-0	0	4.69	4.47
2001 Chicago	AL	16	16	1	0	100.2	432	120	55	50	12	2	2	3	21	1	59	2	0	5	7	.417	0	0-0	0	4.05	4.47
2002 New York	AL	31	31	2	0	206.1	873	210	100	86	21	6	5	5	45	2	137	4	0	19	7	.731	1	0-0	0	3.50	3.75
1995 Detroit	AL	18	18	3	0	130.1	539	120	54	44	17	3	2	2	37	5	83	6	1	10	3	.769	0	0-0	0	3.40	3.04
1995 Cincinnati	NL	11	11	3	0	72.2	300	74	34	29	6	4	1	0	16	4	50	1	1	6	5	.545	1	0-0	0	3.31	3.59
16 ML YEARS		526	356	48	65	2613.2	10924	2672	1283	1176	306	74	62	61	604	59	1772	91	15	185	121	.605	11	13-26	28	3.72	4.05

Kip Wells

Pitches: R Bats: R Pos: SP-33   Ht: 6'3" Wt: 205 Born: 4/21/77 Age: 26

Year Team	Lg	G	GS	CG	GF	IP	BFP	H	R	ER	HR	SH	SF	HB	TBB	IBB	SO	WP	Bk	W	L	Pct	ShO	Sv-Op	Hld	ERC	ERA
1999 Chicago	AL	7	7	0	0	35.2	153	33	17	16	2	0	2	3	15	0	29	1	2	4	1	.800	0	0-0	0	3.80	4.04
2000 Chicago	AL	20	20	0	0	98.2	468	126	76	66	15	1	3	2	58	4	71	7	0	6	9	.400	0	0-0	0	7.01	6.02

Year Team	Lg	G	GS	CG	GF	IP	BFP	H	R	ER	HR	SH	SF	HB	TBB	IBB	SO	WP	Bk	W	L	Pct	ShO	Sv-Op	Hld	ERC	ERA
2001 Chicago	AL	40	20	0	3	133.1	603	145	80	71	14	8	6	12	61	5	99	14	0	10	11	.476		0-2	6	5.16	4.79
2002 Pittsburgh	NL	33	33	1	0	198.1	844	197	92	79	21	7	5	7	71	11	134	7	0	12	14	.462	1	0-0	0	4.01	3.58
4 ML YEARS		100	80	1	3	466.0	2068	501	265	232	52	16	16	24	205	20	333	29	2	32	35	.478	1	0-2	6	4.92	4.48

Vernon Wells

Bats: R **Throws:** R **Pos:** CF-146; RF-13; PH-1   **Ht:** 6'1" **Wt:** 225 **Born:** 12/8/78 **Age:** 24

Year Team	Lg	G	AB	H	2B	3B	HR	(Hm	Rd)	TB	R	RBI	RC	TBB	IBB	SO	HBP	SH	SF	SB	CS	SB%	GDP	Avg	OBP	Slg
1999 Toronto	AL	24	88	23	5	0	1	(1	0)	31	8	8	7	4	0	18	0	0	0	1	1	.50	6	.261	.293	.352
2000 Toronto	AL	3	2	0	0	0	0	(0	0)	0	0	0	0	0	0	0	0	0	0	0	0	-	0	.000	.000	.000
2001 Toronto	AL	30	96	30	8	0	1	(1	0)	41	14	6	16	5	0	15	1	0	1	5	0	1.00	0	.313	.350	.427
2002 Toronto	AL	159	608	167	34	4	23	(10	13)	278	87	100	89	27	0	85	3	2	8	9	4	.69	15	.275	.305	.457
4 ML YEARS		216	794	220	47	4	25	(12	13)	350	109	114	112	36	0	118	4	2	9	15	5	.75	21	.277	.308	.441

Turk Wendell

Pitches: R **Bats:** L **Pos:** RP   **Ht:** 6'2" **Wt:** 205 **Born:** 5/19/67 **Age:** 36

Year Team	Lg	G	GS	CG	GF	IP	BFP	H	R	ER	HR	SH	SF	HB	TBB	IBB	SO	WP	Bk	W	L	Pct	ShO	Sv-Op	Hld	ERC	ERA
1993 Chicago	NL	7	4	0	1	22.2	98	24	13	11	0	2	0	0	8	1	15	1	1	1	2	.333	0	0-0	0	3.42	4.37
1994 Chicago	NL	6	2	0	1	14.1	76	22	20	19	3	2	1	0	10	1	9	1	0	0	1	.000	0	0-0	0	9.21	11.93
1995 Chicago	NL	43	0	0	17	60.1	270	71	35	33	11	3	3	2	24	4	50	1	0	3	1	.750	0	0-0	3	5.79	4.92
1996 Chicago	NL	70	0	0	49	79.1	339	58	26	25	8	3	1	3	44	4	75	3	2	4	5	.444	0	18-21	6	3.25	2.84
1997 ChC-NYM	NL	65	0	0	21	76.1	345	68	42	37	7	4	3	2	53	6	64	4	0	3	5	.375	0	5-7	2	4.51	4.36
1998 New York	NL	66	0	0	17	76.2	319	62	25	25	4	2	1	2	33	9	58	1	0	5	1	.833	0	4-8	11	2.78	2.93
1999 New York	NL	80	0	0	14	85.2	369	80	31	29	9	2	1	2	37	8	77	2	1	5	4	.556	0	3-6	21	3.80	3.05
2000 New York	NL	77	0	0	17	82.2	346	60	36	33	9	6	3	5	41	7	73	0	1	8	6	.571	0	1-5	16	3.14	3.59
2001 NYM-Phi	NL	70	0	0	22	67.0	297	63	36	33	12	2	4	4	34	9	56	2	0	4	5	.444	0	1-3	8	4.74	4.43
1997 Chicago	NL	52	0	0	18	60.0	269	53	32	28	4	3	3	1	39	5	54	4	0	3	5	.375	0	4-5	2	4.03	4.20
1997 New York	NL	13	0	0	3	16.1	76	15	10	9	3	1	0	1	14	1	10	0	0	0	0	-	0	1-2	0	6.38	4.96
2001 New York	NL	49	0	0	14	51.1	218	42	23	20	8	2	3	3	22	6	41	1	0	4	3	.571	0	1-3	6	3.59	3.51
2001 Philadelphia	NL	21	0	0	8	15.2	79	21	13	13	4	0	1	1	12	3	15	1	0	0	2	.000	0	0-0	2	9.04	7.47
9 ML YEARS		484	6	0	159	565.0	2459	508	264	245	63	26	17	20	284	49	477	15	5	33	30	.524	0	32-50	67	3.99	3.90

Jayson Werth

Bats: R **Throws:** R **Pos:** RF-10; LF-4; CF-1   **Ht:** 6'5" **Wt:** 190 **Born:** 5/20/79 **Age:** 24

Year Team	Lg	G	AB	H	2B	3B	HR	(Hm	Rd)	TB	R	RBI	RC	TBB	IBB	SO	HBP	SH	SF	SB	CS	SB%	GDP	Avg	OBP	Slg
1997 Orioles	R	32	88	26	6	0	1	(-	-)	35	16	8	19	22	0	22	0	0	1	7	1	.88	0	.295	.432	.398
1998 Delmarva	A	120	408	108	20	3	8	(-	-)	158	71	53	59	50	0	92	15	1	2	21	6	.78	14	.265	.364	.387
1998 Bowie	AA	5	19	3	2	0	0	(-	-)	5	2	1	1	2	0	6	0	0	0	1	0	1.00	0	.158	.238	.263
1999 Frederick	A+	66	236	72	10	1	3	(-	-)	93	41	30	42	37	2	37	3	1	2	16	3	.84	4	.305	.403	.394
1999 Bowie	AA	35	121	33	5	1	1	(-	-)	43	18	11	18	17	0	26	2	1	3	7	1	.88	1	.273	.364	.355
2000 Bowie	AA	85	276	63	16	2	5	(-	-)	98	47	26	38	54	1	50	4	4	1	9	3	.75	10	.228	.361	.355
2000 Frederick	A+	24	83	23	3	0	2	(-	-)	32	16	18	12	10	1	15	0	1	2	5	1	.83	5	.277	.347	.386
2001 Dunedin	A+	85	70	14	3	0	2	(-	-)	23	9	14	9	17	0	19	0	0	0	1	1	.50	2	.200	.356	.329
2001 Tennessee	AA	104	369	105	23	1	18	(-	-)	184	51	69	74	63	0	93	3	1	7	12	3	.80	5	.285	.387	.499
2002 Syracuse	AAA	127	443	114	25	2	18	(-	-)	197	65	82	74	67	2	125	4	0	9	24	7	.77	7	.257	.354	.445
2002 Toronto	AL	15	46	12	2	1	0	(0	0)	16	4	6	5	6	0	11	0	0	1	1	0	1.00	4	.261	.340	.348

Barry Wesson

Bats: R **Throws:** R **Pos:** CF-9; LF-3; RF-3; PH-2   **Ht:** 6'2" **Wt:** 210 **Born:** 4/6/77 **Age:** 26

Year Team	Lg	G	AB	H	2B	3B	HR	(Hm	Rd)	TB	R	RBI	RC	TBB	IBB	SO	HBP	SH	SF	SB	CS	SB%	GDP	Avg	OBP	Slg
1995 Astros	R	45	138	26	2	2	2	(-	-)	38	14	18	12	19	0	40	1	1	1	4	0	1.00	2	.188	.289	.275
1995 Jackson	AA	4	3	2	0	1	0	(-	-)	4	2	1	2	0	0	0	0	0	0	0	0	-	0	.667	.667	1.333
1996 Auburn	A-	55	176	28	7	0	0	(-	-)	35	11	12	4	12	1	46	1	1	1	5	3	.63	5	.159	.214	.199
1997 Auburn	A-	58	208	54	7	3	3	(-	-)	76	24	26	23	10	0	45	1	1	1	8	4	.67	1	.260	.295	.365
1998 Quad City	A	138	493	124	21	2	7	(-	-)	170	71	43	49	32	1	90	5	2	2	22	12	.65	10	.252	.304	.345
1999 Kissimmee	A+	115	352	76	15	1	4	(-	-)	105	32	34	28	26	0	84	4	1	2	8	7	.53	3	.216	.276	.298
2000 Round Rock	AA	39	110	26	1	2	2	(-	-)	37	12	15	11	10	0	32	0	0	2	6	2	.75	2	.236	.295	.336
2000 Kissimmee	A+	81	308	84	21	3	5	(-	-)	126	50	35	48	33	0	66	2	4	1	24	5	.83	2	.273	.346	.409
2001 Round Rock	AA	133	472	119	23	7	16	(-	-)	204	67	54	66	41	0	135	6	7	4	20	10	.67	4	.252	.317	.432
2002 New Orleans	AAA	111	413	121	25	5	11	(-	-)	189	43	61	57	16	0	100	5	2	3	4	7	.36	9	.293	.325	.458
2002 Houston	NL	15	20	4	0	1	0	(0	0)	6	1	1	1	1	0	5	0	0	0	0	0	-	2	.200	.238	.300

Jake Westbrook

Pitches: R **Bats:** R **Pos:** RP-7; SP-4   **Ht:** 6'3" **Wt:** 185 **Born:** 9/29/77 **Age:** 25

Year Team	Lg	G	GS	CG	GF	IP	BFP	H	R	ER	HR	SH	SF	HB	TBB	IBB	SO	WP	Bk	W	L	Pct	ShO	Sv-Op	Hld	ERC	ERA
2002 Akron*	AA	3	3	0	0	15.0	62	13	8	8	0	0	2	0	2	1	0	8	1	0	0	1	.000	0	0--	-	1.95	4.80
2002 Buffalo*	AAA	1	1	0	0	6.0	26	8	4	4	1	0	1	1	0	0	2	0	0	0	1	0	1.000	0	0--	-	5.64	6.00
2000 New York	AL	3	2	0	1	6.2	35	15	10	10	1	0	2	0	4	1	1	0	0	0	2	.000	0	0-0	0	13.53	13.50
2001 Cleveland	AL	23	6	0	3	64.2	290	79	43	42	6	1	5	4	22	4	48	4	0	4	4	.500	0	0-0	5	5.25	5.85
2002 Cleveland	AL	11	4	0	1	41.2	185	50	30	27	6	2	1	1	12	1	20	1	0	1	3	.250	0	0-2	1	5.12	5.83
3 ML YEARS		37	12	0	5	113.0	513	144	83	79	13	3	8	5	38	6	69	5	0	5	9	.357	0	0-2	6	5.63	6.29

Gabe White

Pitches: L **Bats:** L **Pos:** RP-62   **Ht:** 6'2" **Wt:** 204 **Born:** 11/20/71 **Age:** 31

Year Team	Lg	G	GS	CG	GF	IP	BFP	H	R	ER	HR	SH	SF	HB	TBB	IBB	SO	WP	Bk	W	L	Pct	ShO	Sv-Op	Hld	ERC	ERA
1994 Montreal	NL	7	5	0	2	23.2	106	24	16	16	4	1	1	1	11	0	17	0	0	1	1	.500	0	1-1	0	5.03	6.08
1995 Montreal	NL	19	1	0	8	25.2	115	26	21	20	7	2	3	1	9	0	25	0	0	1	2	.333	0	0-0	1	5.12	7.01
1997 Cincinnati	NL	12	6	0	2	41.0	168	39	20	20	6	3	2	1	8	1	25	0	0	2	2	.500	0	1-1	3	3.37	4.39
1998 Cincinnati	NL	69	3	0	29	98.2	404	86	46	44	17	2	2	1	27	6	83	3	0	5	5	.500	0	9-13	6	3.30	4.01
1999 Cincinnati	NL	50	0	0	18	61.0	261	68	31	30	13	2	1	2	14	1	61	0	0	1	2	.333	0	0-1	3	4.95	4.43
2000 Cin-Col	NL	68	0	0	17	84.0	329	64	23	22	6	2	6	3	15	2	84	1	0	11	2	.846	0	5-9	19	1.98	2.36
2001 Colorado	NL	69	0	0	16	67.2	290	70	47	47	18	2	2	1	26	5	47	1	0	1	7	.125	0	0-2	8	5.42	6.25
2002 Cincinnati	NL	62	0	0	7	54.1	220	49	19	18	3	1	0	2	10	2	41	0	0	6	1	.857	0	0-1	19	2.55	2.98
2000 Cincinnati	NL	1	0	0	0	1.0	6	2	2	2	1	0	0	0	1	0	2	0	0	0	0	-	0	0-0	0	23.01	18.00
2000 Colorado	NL	67	0	0	17	83.0	323	62	21	20	5	2	6	3	14	2	82	1	0	11	2	.846	0	5-9	19	1.82	2.17
8 ML YEARS		356	15	0	99	456.0	1893	426	223	217	74	15	17	12	120	17	383	5	0	28	22	.560	0	16-28	58	3.63	4.28

Rick White

Pitches: R **Bats:** R **Pos:** RP-61   **Ht:** 6'4" **Wt:** 230 **Born:** 12/23/68 **Age:** 34

Year Team	Lg	G	GS	CG	GF	IP	BFP	H	R	ER	HR	SH	SF	HB	TBB	IBB	SO	WP	Bk	W	L	Pct	ShO	Sv-Op	Hld	ERC	ERA
1994 Pittsburgh	NL	43	5	0	23	75.1	317	79	35	32	9	7	5	6	17	3	38	2	2	4	5	.444	0	6-9	3	4.11	3.82
1995 Pittsburgh	NL	15	9	0	2	55.0	247	66	33	29	3	3	3	2	18	0	29	2	0	2	3	.400	0	0-0	0	4.70	4.75
1998 Tampa Bay	AL	38	3	0	12	68.2	289	66	32	29	8	0	3	2	23	2	39	3	0	2	6	.250	0	0-0	2	3.82	3.80
1999 Tampa Bay	AL	63	1	0	11	99.2	480	132	56	49	8	2	5	1	38	5	81	3	0	5	3	.625	0	0-2	4	4.96	4.08
2000 TB-NYM		66	0	0	14	99.2	420	83	44	39	9	1	3	7	38	5	67	3	0	5	9	.357	0	3-7	4	3.21	3.52
2001 New York	NL	55	0	0	15	69.2	299	71	38	30	7	2	2	2	17	4	51	1	0	4	5	.444	0	2-4	10	3.52	3.88
2002 Col-Stl	NL	61	0	0	10	62.2	264	62	33	30	4	3	4	1	21	5	41	3	0	5	7	.417	0	0-1	16	3.49	4.31
2000 Tampa Bay	AL	44	0	0	8	71.1	293	57	30	27	7	1	2	5	26	3	47	3	0	3	6	.333	0	2-5	2	3.09	3.41
2000 New York	NL	22	0	0	6	28.1	127	26	14	12	2	0	1	2	12	2	20	0	0	2	3	.400	0	1-2	2	3.51	3.81
2002 Colorado	NL	41	0	0	8	40.2	182	49	30	28	4	1	4	1	18	4	27	3	0	2	6	.250	0	0-1	9	5.47	6.20
2002 St Louis	NL	20	0	0	2	22.0	82	13	3	2	0	2	0	0	3	1	14	0	0	3	1	.750	0	0-0	7	0.94	0.82
7 ML YEARS		341	18	0	87	539.0	2316	559	271	238	48	18	25	21	172	24	346	17	2	27	38	.415	0	11-23	39	3.97	3.97

Rondell White

Bats: R **Throws:** R **Pos:** LF-113; DH-11; PH-8; CF-1   **Ht:** 6'1" **Wt:** 225 **Born:** 2/23/72 **Age:** 31

Year Team	Lg	G	AB	H	2B	3B	HR	(Hm	Rd)	TB	R	RBI	RC	TBB	IBB	SO	HBP	SH	SF	SB	CS	SB%	GDP	Avg	OBP	Slg
1993 Montreal	NL	23	73	19	3	1	2	(1	1)	30	9	15	9	7	0	16	0	2	1	1	2	.33	2	.260	.321	.411
1994 Montreal	NL	40	97	27	10	1	2	(1	1)	45	16	13	16	9	0	18	3	0	0	1	1	.50	1	.278	.358	.464
1995 Montreal	NL	130	474	140	33	4	13	(6	7)	220	87	57	79	41	1	87	6	0	4	25	5	.83	11	.295	.356	.464
1996 Montreal	NL	88	334	98	19	4	6	(2	4)	143	35	41	46	22	0	53	2	0	1	14	6	.70	11	.293	.340	.428
1997 Montreal	NL	151	592	160	29	5	28	(9	19)	283	84	82	84	31	3	111	10	1	4	16	8	.67	18	.270	.316	.478
1998 Montreal	NL	97	357	107	21	2	17	(8	9)	183	54	58	65	30	2	57	7	0	3	16	7	.70	9	.300	.363	.513
1999 Montreal	NL	138	539	168	26	6	22	(10	12)	272	83	64	91	32	2	85	11	0	6	10	6	.63	17	.312	.359	.505
2000 Mon-ChC	NL	94	357	111	26	0	13	(3	10)	176	59	61	64	33	0	79	4	0	2	5	3	.63	4	.311	.374	.493
2001 Chicago	NL	95	323	99	19	1	17	(7	10)	171	43	50	57	26	4	56	7	1	0	1	0	1.00	14	.307	.371	.529
2002 New York	AL	126	455	109	21	0	14	(5	9)	172	59	62	42	25	1	86	8	1	5	1	2	.33	11	.240	.288	.378
2000 Montreal	NL	75	290	89	24	0	11	(3	8)	146	52	54	53	28	0	67	2	0	2	5	1	.83	4	.307	.370	.503
2000 Chicago	NL	19	67	22	2	0	2	(0	2)	30	7	7	11	5	0	12	2	0	0	0	2	.00	0	.328	.392	.448
10 ML YEARS		982	3601	1038	207	24	134	(53	81)	1695	529	503	553	256	13	648	58	5	26	90	40	.69	96	.288	.343	.471

Bob Wickman

Pitches: R **Bats:** R **Pos:** RP-36   **Ht:** 6'1" **Wt:** 240 **Born:** 2/6/69 **Age:** 34

Year Team	Lg	G	GS	CG	GF	IP	BFP	H	R	ER	HR	SH	SF	HB	TBB	IBB	SO	WP	Bk	W	L	Pct	ShO	Sv-Op	Hld	ERC	ERA
1992 New York	AL	8	8	0	0	50.1	213	51	25	23	2	1	3	2	20	0	21	3	0	6	1	.857	0	0-0	0	3.99	4.11
1993 New York	AL	41	19	1	9	140.0	629	156	82	72	13	4	1	5	69	0	70	2	0	14	4	.778	1	4-8	2	5.16	4.63
1994 New York	AL	53	0	0	19	70.0	286	54	26	24	3	6	0	5	27	3	56	2	0	5	4	.556	0	6-10	11	2.45	3.09
1995 New York	AL	63	1	0	14	80.0	347	77	38	36	6	4	1	5	33	3	51	2	0	2	4	.333	0	1-10	21	3.92	4.05
1996 NYY-Mil		70	0	0	18	95.2	429	106	50	47	10	2	4	5	44	3	75	4	0	7	1	.875	0	0-4	10	5.17	4.42
1997 Milwaukee	NL	74	0	0	20	95.2	405	89	32	29	8	6	2	3	41	7	78	8	0	7	6	.538	0	1-5	28	3.76	2.73
1998 Milwaukee	NL	72	0	0	51	82.1	357	79	38	34	5	10	3	4	39	2	71	1	0	6	9	.400	0	25-32	5	4.05	3.72
1999 Milwaukee	NL	71	0	0	63	74.1	331	75	31	28	6	3	2	2	38	6	60	2	0	3	8	.273	0	37-45	0	4.38	3.39
2000 Mil-Cle		69	0	0	60	72.2	309	64	30	25	1	3	1	1	32	5	55	2	0	5	5	.375	0	30-37	0	2.92	3.10
2001 Cleveland	AL	70	0	0	56	67.2	270	61	18	18	4	0	0	2	14	2	66	2	0	5	0	1.000	0	32-35	4	2.69	2.39
2002 Cleveland	AL	36	0	0	30	34.1	159	42	22	17	3	0	1	0	10	0	36	0	0	1	3	.250	0	20-22	0	4.72	4.46
1996 New York	AL	58	0	0	14	79.0	358	94	41	41	7	1	4	5	34	1	61	3	0	4	1	.800	0	0-3	6	5.51	4.67
1996 Milwaukee	NL	12	0	0	4	16.2	71	12	9	6	3	1	0	0	10	2	14	1	0	3	0	1.000	0	0-1	4	3.66	3.24
2000 Milwaukee	NL	43	0	0	36	46.0	194	37	18	15	1	0	1	1	20	2	44	2	0	2	2	.500	0	16-20	0	2.62	2.93
2000 Cleveland	AL	26	0	0	24	26.2	115	27	12	10	0	3	0	0	12	3	11	0	0	3	3	.250	0	14-17	0	3.47	3.38
11 ML YEARS		627	28	1	340	863.0	3735	854	392	353	61	33	22	31	367	38	639	28	0	59	45	.567	1	156-208	85	4.00	3.68

Chris Widger

Bats: R **Throws:** R **Pos:** C-21   **Ht:** 6'3" **Wt:** 215 **Born:** 5/21/71 **Age:** 32

Year Team	Lg	G	AB	H	2B	3B	HR	(Hm	Rd)	TB	R	RBI	RC	TBB	IBB	SO	HBP	SH	SF	SB	CS	SB%	GDP	Avg	OBP	Slg
2002 Columbus*	AAA	61	217	53	14	1	10	(-	-)	99	26	39	29	17	0	31	1	1	2	0	3	.00	3	.244	.300	.456
1995 Seattle	AL	23	45	9	0	0	1	(1	0)	12	2	2	3	3	0	11	0	0	1	0	0	-	0	.200	.245	.267
1996 Seattle	AL	8	11	2	0	0	0	(0	0)	2	1	0	0	0	0	5	1	0	0	0	0	-	0	.182	.250	.182
1997 Montreal	NL	91	278	65	20	3	7	(4	3)	112	30	37	32	22	1	59	1	2	2	2	0	1.00	7	.234	.290	.403
1998 Montreal	NL	125	417	97	18	1	15	(6	9)	162	36	53	46	29	2	85	0	0	5	6	1	.86	5	.233	.281	.388

Year Team	Lg	G	AB	H	2B	3B	HR	(Hm	Rd)	TB	R	RBI	RC	TBB	IBB	SO	HBP	SH	SF	SB	CS	SB%	GDP	Avg	OBP	Slg
1999 Montreal	NL	124	383	101	24	1	14	(11	3)	169	42	56	53	28	0	86	7	0	1	1	4	.20	5	.264	.325	.441
2000 Mon-Sea		96	292	68	17	2	13	(6	7)	128	32	35	39	30	3	63	1	0	1	1	2	.33	5	.233	.306	.438
2002 New York	AL	21	64	19	5	0	0	(0	0)	24	4	5	8	2	0	9	2	0	0	0	0	--	0	.297	.338	.375
2000 Montreal	NL	86	281	67	17	2	12	(6	6)	124	31	34	38	29	3	61	1	0	1	1	2	.33	5	.238	.311	.441
2000 Seattle	AL	10	11	1	0	0	1	(0	1)	4	1	1	1	1	0	2	0	0	0	0	0	--	0	.091	.167	.364
7 ML YEARS		488	1490	361	84	7	50	(28	22)	609	147	188	181	114	6	318	12	2	7	10	7	.59	22	.242	.300	.409

Scott Wiggins

Pitches: L **Bats:** L **Pos:** RP-3   **Ht:** 6'3" **Wt:** 205 **Born:** 3/24/76 **Age:** 27

Year Team	Lg	G	GS	CG	GF	IP	BFP	H	R	ER	HR	SH	SF	HB	TBB	IBB	SO	WP	Bk	W	L	Pct	ShO	Sv-Op	Hld	ERC	ERA
1997 Oneonta	A-	13	13	1	0	63.1	261	58	25	18	1	0	0	2	22	0	44	0	0	6	2	.750	1	0--	-	3.04	2.56
1998 Greensboro	A	14	4	0	6	42.1	171	37	17	14	4	0	0	2	11	0	56	0	0	2	2	.500	0	1--	-	3.07	2.98
1998 Tampa	A+	11	5	0	1	33.2	136	19	12	7	1	2	0	0	17	1	36	2	0	1	1	.500	0	0--	-	1.75	1.87
1998 Yankees	R	1	1	0	0	1.2	7	2	1	0	0	0	0	0	0	0	2	0	0	0	0	-	0	0--	-	2.89	0.00
1999 Greensboro	A	17	17	0	0	93.1	395	84	45	41	15	1	0	6	32	0	110	7	0	7	1	.875	0	0--	-	3.96	3.95
2000 Tampa	A+	28	15	1	1	100.2	444	106	61	46	4	2	3	5	46	0	68	4	1	2	8	.200	1	0--	-	4.39	4.11
2001 Tampa	A+	36	5	0	9	68.1	302	72	29	23	5	1	2	10	23	1	77	8	0	4	3	.571	0	0--	-	4.50	3.03
2001 Norwich	AA	4	0	0	3	4.0	12	0	0	0	0	0	0	0	1	0	5	0	0	0	0	-	0	0--	-	0.08	0.00
2002 Norwich	AA	24	0	0	12	27.2	112	19	8	7	1	1	1	2	9	1	26	2	0	2	1	.667	0	0--	-	1.99	2.28
2002 Tennessee	AA	16	0	0	6	19.1	82	18	3	2	0	2	2	1	5	1	19	0	0	1	0	1.000	0	1--	-	2.56	0.93
2002 Syracuse	AAA	12	0	0	3	14.0	60	11	6	4	0	0	1	2	7	0	14	3	0	2	0	1.000	0	0--	-	3.15	2.57
2002 Toronto	AL	3	0	0	0	2.2	13	5	1	1	1	0	0	0	1	0	3	1	0	0	0	-	0	0-0	0	12.82	3.38

Ty Wigginton

Bats: R **Throws:** R **Pos:** 3B-14; 1B-13; 2B-12; PH-12; LF-1; RF-1; PR-1   **Ht:** 6'0" **Wt:** 200 **Born:** 10/11/77 **Age:** 25

Year Team	Lg	G	AB	H	2B	3B	HR	(Hm	Rd)	TB	R	RBI	RC	TBB	IBB	SO	HBP	SH	SF	SB	CS	SB%	GDP	Avg	OBP	Slg
1998 Pittsfield	A-	70	272	65	14	4	8	(-	-)	111	39	29	32	16	0	72	1	1	0	11	2	.85	4	.239	.284	.408
1999 St.Lucie	A+	123	456	133	23	5	21	(-	-)	229	69	73	82	56	4	82	4	4	2	9	12	.43	5	.292	.373	.502
2000 Binghamton	AA	122	453	129	27	3	20	(-	-)	222	64	77	70	24	0	107	2	1	7	5	5	.50	4	.285	.319	.490
2001 Norfolk	AAA	78	260	65	12	0	7	(-	-)	98	29	24	32	27	0	66	2	1	2	3	3	.50	4	.250	.323	.377
2001 St.Lucie	A+	3	9	3	1	0	0	(-	-)	4	1	1	3	4	0	2	1	0	0	0	0	-	0	.333	.571	.444
2001 Binghamton	AA	8	28	8	3	0	0	(-	-)	11	5	0	5	5	0	5	0	1	0	1	0	1.00	0	.286	.394	.393
2002 Norfolk	AAA	104	383	115	26	3	6	(-	-)	165	49	48	61	43	4	50	1	0	8	5	3	.63	7	.300	.366	.431
2002 New York	NL	46	116	35	8	0	6	(4	2)	61	18	18	16	8	0	19	2	0	1	2	1	.67	4	.302	.354	.526

Brad Wilkerson

Bats: L **Throws:** L **Pos:** CF-73; LF-72; 1B-23; PH-9; RF-3   **Ht:** 6'0" **Wt:** 200 **Born:** 6/1/77 **Age:** 26

Year Team	Lg	G	AB	H	2B	3B	HR	(Hm	Rd)	TB	R	RBI	RC	TBB	IBB	SO	HBP	SH	SF	SB	CS	SB%	GDP	Avg	OBP	Slg
1999 Harrisburg	AA	138	422	99	21	3	8	(-	-)	150	66	49	63	88	3	100	7	1	5	3	5	.38	3	.235	.372	.355
2000 Harrisburg	AA	66	229	77	36	2	6	(-	-)	135	53	44	58	42	1	38	4	1	3	8	4	.67	4	.336	.442	.590
2000 Ottawa	AAA	63	212	53	11	1	12	(-	-)	102	40	35	42	45	1	60	3	0	1	5	4	.56	0	.250	.387	.481
2001 Jupiter	A+	6	26	6	3	0	0	(-	-)	9	3	1	3	3	0	10	0	0	0	0	0	-	0	.231	.310	.346
2001 Ottawa	AAA	69	233	63	10	0	12	(-	-)	109	43	48	51	60	0	68	3	2	2	12	5	.71	2	.270	.423	.468
2001 Montreal	NL	47	117	24	7	2	1	(1	0)	38	11	5	12	17	1	41	0	1	0	2	1	.67	2	.205	.304	.325
2002 Montreal	NL	153	507	135	27	8	20	(12	8)	238	92	59	83	81	7	161	5	6	4	7	8	.47	5	.266	.370	.469
2 ML YEARS		200	624	159	34	10	21	(13	8)	276	103	64	95	98	8	202	5	7	5	9	9	.50	7	.255	.358	.442

Bernie Williams

Bats: B **Throws:** R **Pos:** CF-147; DH-7; PH-1   **Ht:** 6'2" **Wt:** 205 **Born:** 9/13/68 **Age:** 34

Year Team	Lg	G	AB	H	2B	3B	HR	(Hm	Rd)	TB	R	RBI	RC	TBB	IBB	SO	HBP	SH	SF	SB	CS	SB%	GDP	Avg	OBP	Slg
1991 New York	AL	85	320	76	19	4	3	(1	2)	112	43	34	41	48	0	57	1	2	3	10	5	.67	4	.238	.336	.350
1992 New York	AL	62	261	73	14	2	5	(3	2)	106	39	26	37	29	1	36	1	2	0	7	6	.54	5	.280	.354	.406
1993 New York	AL	139	567	152	31	4	12	(5	7)	227	67	68	71	53	4	106	4	1	3	9	9	.50	17	.268	.333	.400
1994 New York	AL	108	408	118	29	1	12	(4	8)	185	80	57	70	61	2	54	3	1	2	16	9	.64	11	.289	.384	.453
1995 New York	AL	144	563	173	29	9	18	(7	11)	274	93	82	105	75	1	98	5	2	3	8	6	.57	12	.307	.392	.487
1996 New York	AL	143	551	168	26	7	29	(12	17)	295	108	102	113	82	8	72	0	1	7	17	4	.81	15	.305	.391	.535
1997 New York	AL	129	509	167	35	6	21	(13	8)	277	107	100	109	73	7	80	1	0	8	15	8	.65	10	.328	.408	.544
1998 New York	AL	128	499	169	30	5	26	(14	12)	287	101	97	110	74	9	81	1	0	4	15	9	.63	19	.339	.422	.575
1999 New York	AL	158	591	202	28	6	25	(11	14)	317	116	115	131	100	17	95	1	0	5	9	10	.47	11	.342	.435	.536
2000 New York	AL	141	537	165	37	6	30	(15	15)	304	108	121	112	71	11	84	5	0	3	13	5	.72	11	.307	.391	.566
2001 New York	AL	146	540	166	38	0	26	(14	12)	282	102	94	109	78	11	67	6	0	9	11	5	.69	15	.307	.395	.522
2002 New York	AL	154	612	204	37	2	19	(13	6)	302	102	102	122	83	7	97	3	0	1	8	4	.67	19	.333	.415	.493
12 ML YEARS		1537	5958	1833	353	52	226	(112	114)	2968	1066	998	1129	827	78	927	31	9	48	138	80	.63	153	.308	.392	.498

Dave Williams

Pitches: L **Bats:** L **Pos:** SP-9   **Ht:** 6'2" **Wt:** 213 **Born:** 3/12/79 **Age:** 24

Year Team	Lg	G	GS	CG	GF	IP	BFP	H	R	ER	HR	SH	SF	HB	TBB	IBB	SO	WP	Bk	W	L	Pct	ShO	Sv-Op	Hld	ERC	ERA
1998 Erie	A-	22	2	0	4	47.1	203	45	24	17	6	2	0	3	14	0	38	2	0	2	2	.500	0	0--	-	3.76	3.23
1999 Williamsport	A-	7	7	1	0	45.2	180	33	17	13	2	0	0	2	11	0	47	0	0	4	2	.667	0	0--	-	1.91	2.56
1999 Hickory	A	9	9	1	0	59.0	228	42	22	21	5	0	2	6	11	0	46	2	0	3	1	.750	0	0--	-	2.15	3.20
2000 Hickory	A	24	24	1	0	170.0	687	145	66	56	14	11	2	9	39	0	193	4	0	11	9	.550	0	0--	-	2.74	2.96
2000 Lynchburg	A+	2	2	0	0	11.0	51	18	8	8	2	1	0	0	3	0	8	2	0	1	0	1.000	0	0--	-	8.43	6.55
2001 Altoona	AA	9	8	1	1	58.2	228	45	17	17	8	1	1	2	12	0	39	0	0	5	2	.714	0	0--	-	2.45	2.61

Year Team	Lg	G	GS	CG	GF	IP	BFP	H	R	ER	HR	SH	SF	HB	TBB	IBB	SO	WP	Bk	W	L	Pct	ShO	Sv-Op	Hld	ERC	ERA
2001 Nashville	AAA	2	2	0	0	10.2	45	9	5	4	3	0		1	5	0	6	0	0	1	1	.500	0	0--	-	4.74	3.38
2001 Pittsburgh	NL	22	18	0	1	114.0	472	100	53	47	15	3	8	7	45	4	57	0	0	3	7	.300	0	0-0	1	3.89	3.71
2002 Pittsburgh	NL	9	9	0	0	43.1	195	38	26	24	9	2	1	4	24	2	33	2	2	2	5	.286	0	0-0	0	4.99	4.98
2 ML YEARS		31	27	0	1	157.1	667	138	79	71	24	5	9	11	69	6	90	2	2	5	12	.294	0	0-0	1	4.19	4.06

Gerald Williams

Bats: R **Throws:** R **Pos:** RF-16; PR-13; LF-7; CF-6; PH-3   **Ht:** 6'2" **Wt:** 187 **Born:** 8/10/66 **Age:** 36

Year Team	Lg	G	AB	H	2B	3B	HR	(Hm	Rd)	TB	R	RBI	RC	TBB	IBB	SO	HBP	SH	SF	SB	CS	SB%	GDP	Avg	OBP	Slg
2002 Memphis*	AAA	21	73	11	3	0	1	(-	-)	17	11	3	2	3	0	8	1	1	0	2	0	1.00	2	.151	.195	.233
2002 Louisville*	AAA	48	205	54	10	3	2	(-	-)	76	29	12	22	11	0	36	2	1	0	6	4	.60	4	.263	.307	.371
1992 New York	AL	15	27	8	2	0	3	(2	1)	19	7	6	6	0	0	3	0	0	0	2	0	1.00	0	.296	.296	.704
1993 New York	AL	42	67	10	2	3	0	(0	0)	18	11	6	2	1	0	14	2	0	1	2	0	1.00	2	.149	.183	.269
1994 New York	AL	57	86	25	8	0	4	(2	2)	45	19	13	11	4	0	17	2	0	1	1	3	.25	6	.291	.319	.523
1995 New York	AL	100	182	45	18	2	6	(4	2)	85	33	28	28	22	1	34	1	0	3	4	2	.67	4	.247	.327	.467
1996 NYY-Mil		125	325	82	19	4	5	(3	2)	124	43	34	34	19	3	57	5	3	5	10	9	.53	8	.252	.299	.382
1997 Milwaukee	NL	155	566	143	32	2	10	(3	7)	209	73	41	58	19	1	90	6	5	5	23	9	.72	9	.253	.282	.369
1998 Atlanta	NL	129	266	81	19	2	10	(5	5)	134	46	44	45	17	1	48	3	2	1	11	5	.69	5	.305	.352	.504
1999 Atlanta	NL	143	422	116	24	1	17	(7	10)	193	76	68	63	33	1	67	6	4	2	19	11	.63	8	.275	.335	.457
2000 Tampa Bay	AL	146	632	173	30	2	21	(6	15)	270	87	89	83	34	0	103	3	9	4	12	12	.50	5	.274	.312	.427
2001 TB-NYY	AL	100	279	56	18	0	4	(3	1)	86	42	19	20	18	0	55	5	4	0	13	5	.72	9	.201	.262	.308
2002 New York	AL	33	17	0	0	0	0	(0	0)	0	6	0	0	2	0	4	0	0	0	2	0	1.00	1	.000	.105	.000
1996 New York	AL	99	233	63	15	4	5	(3	2)	101	37	30	29	15	2	39	4	1	5	7	8	.47	7	.270	.319	.433
1996 Milwaukee	NL	26	92	19	4	0	0	(0	0)	23	6	4	5	4	1	18	1	2	0	3	1	.75	1	.207	.247	.250
2001 Tampa Bay	AL	62	232	48	17	0	4	(3	1)	77	30	17	18	13	0	42	4	3	0	10	4	.71	8	.207	.261	.332
2001 New York	AL	38	47	8	1	0	0	(0	0)	9	12	2	2	5	0	13	1	1	0	3	1	.75	1	.170	.264	.191
11 ML YEARS		1045	2869	739	172	16	80	(35	45)	1183	443	348	350	169	7	492	31	27	22	99	56	.64	57	.258	.304	.412

Jeff Williams

Pitches: L **Bats:** R **Pos:** RP-10   **Ht:** 6'0" **Wt:** 185 **Born:** 6/6/72 **Age:** 31

Year Team	Lg	G	GS	CG	GF	IP	BFP	H	R	ER	HR	SH	SF	HB	TBB	IBB	SO	WP	Bk	W	L	Pct	ShO	Sv-Op	Hld	ERC	ERA
2002 Las Vegas*	AAA	56	0	0	48	79.2	334	80	25	23	3	4	0	5	22	0	75	0	0	6	4	.600	0	28--	-	3.49	2.60
1999 Los Angeles	NL	5	3	0	1	17.2	73	12	10	8	2	1	0	0	9	0	7	0	0	2	0	1.000	0	0-0	0	2.86	4.08
2000 Los Angeles	NL	7	0	0	0	5.2	35	12	11	10	1	0	1	0	8	0	3	0	0	0	0	-	0	0-1	1	17.89	15.88
2001 Los Angeles	NL	15	1	0	2	24.1	109	26	18	17	5	1	2	1	17	1	9	1	0	2	1	.667	0	0-0	1	7.02	6.29
2002 Los Angeles	NL	10	0	0	7	10.0	54	15	13	13	2	0	1	1	7	0	11	1	0	0	0	-	0	0-0	0	9.45	11.70
4 ML YEARS		37	4	0	10	57.2	271	65	52	48	10	2	4	2	41	1	30	2	0	4	1	.800	0	0-1	2	6.94	7.49

Jerome Williams

Pitches: R **Bats:** R **Pos:** SP   **Ht:** 6'1" **Wt:** 189 **Born:** 12/4/81 **Age:** 21

Year Team	Lg	G	GS	CG	GF	IP	BFP	H	R	ER	HR	SH	SF	HB	TBB	IBB	SO	WP	Bk	W	L	Pct	ShO	Sv-Op	Hld	ERC	ERA
1999 Salem-Keizer	A-	7	7	1	0	37.0	151	29	13	9	1	0	1	3	19	0	34	1	0	1	1	.500	1	0--	-	2.40	2.19
2000 San Jose	A+	23	19	0	2	125.2	512	89	53	41	6	5	6	10	48	3	115	9	2	7	6	.538	1	0--	-	2.42	2.94
2001 Shreveport	AA	23	23	2	0	130.0	542	116	69	57	14	2	3	9	34	0	84	6	1	9	7	.563	1	0--	-	3.26	3.95
2002 Fresno	AAA	28	28	0	0	160.2	671	140	76	64	16	8	5	9	50	1	130	5	3	6	11	.353	0	--	-	3.23	3.59

Matt Williams

Bats: R **Throws:** R **Pos:** 3B-56; PH-6   **Ht:** 6'2" **Wt:** 219 **Born:** 11/28/65 **Age:** 37

Year Team	Lg	G	AB	H	2B	3B	HR	(Hm	Rd)	TB	R	RBI	RC	TBB	IBB	SO	HBP	SH	SF	SB	CS	SB%	GDP	Avg	OBP	Slg
2002 Tucson*	AAA	5	15	3	0	0	1	(-	-)	6	1	3	0	0	0	0	0	0	0	0	0	-	2	.200	.200	.400
2002 Lancaster*	A+	4	12	4	1	0	1	(-	-)	8	2	5	3	2	0	1	0	0	0	0	0	-	0	.333	.429	.667
1987 San Francisco	NL	84	245	46	9	2	8	(5	3)	83	28	21	17	16	4	68	1	3	1	4	3	.57	5	.188	.240	.339
1988 San Francisco	NL	52	156	32	6	1	8	(7	1)	64	17	19	14	8	0	41	2	3	1	0	1	.00	7	.205	.251	.410
1989 San Francisco	NL	84	292	59	18	1	18	(10	8)	133	31	50	31	14	1	72	2	1	2	1	2	.33	7	.202	.242	.455
1990 San Francisco	NL	159	617	171	27	2	33	(20	13)	301	87	122	92	33	9	138	7	2	5	7	4	.64	13	.277	.319	.488
1991 San Francisco	NL	157	589	158	24	5	34	(17	17)	294	72	98	88	33	6	128	6	0	7	5	5	.50	11	.268	.310	.499
1992 San Francisco	NL	146	529	120	13	5	20	(9	11)	203	58	66	53	39	11	109	6	0	2	7	7	.50	15	.227	.286	.384
1993 San Francisco	NL	145	579	170	33	4	38	(19	19)	325	105	110	100	27	4	80	4	0	9	1	3	.25	12	.294	.325	.561
1994 San Francisco	NL	112	445	119	16	3	43	(20	23)	270	74	96	82	33	7	87	2	0	3	1	0	1.00	11	.267	.319	.607
1995 San Francisco	NL	76	283	95	17	1	23	(9	14)	183	53	65	66	30	8	58	2	0	3	2	0	1.00	8	.336	.399	.647
1996 San Francisco	NL	105	404	122	16	1	22	(13	9)	206	69	85	72	39	9	91	6	0	6	1	2	.33	10	.302	.367	.510
1997 Cleveland	AL	151	596	157	32	3	32	(7	25)	291	86	105	86	34	4	108	4	0	2	12	4	.75	14	.263	.307	.488
1998 Arizona	NL	135	510	136	26	1	20	(19	1)	224	72	71	68	43	8	102	3	0	1	5	1	.83	19	.267	.327	.439
1999 Arizona	NL	154	627	190	37	2	35	(17	18)	336	98	142	109	41	9	93	2	0	8	2	0	1.00	8	.303	.344	.536
2000 Arizona	NL	96	371	102	18	2	12	(5	7)	160	43	47	47	20	1	51	0	0	3	1	2	.33	11	.275	.315	.431
2001 Arizona	NL	106	408	112	30	0	16	(7	9)	190	58	65	55	22	3	70	3	0	3	1	0	1.00	8	.275	.314	.466
2002 Arizona	NL	60	215	56	7	2	12	(7	5)	103	29	40	31	21	1	41	0	0	2	3	1	.75	8	.260	.324	.479
16 ML YEARS		1822	6866	1845	329	35	374	(183	191)	3366	980	1202	1011	453	85	1337	53	9	58	53	35	.60	181	.269	.316	.490

Mike Williams

Pitches: R **Bats:** R **Pos:** RP-59 | **Ht:** 6'2" **Wt:** 200 **Born:** 7/29/68 **Age:** 34

Year Team	Lg	G	GS	CG	GF	IP	BFP	H	R	ER	HR	SH	SF	HB	TBB	IBB	SO	WP	Bk	W	L	Pct	ShO	Sv-Op	Hld	ERC	ERA
2002 Kannapolis*	A	22	0	0	6	41.0	170	28	15	7	4	2	1	2	23	0	37	1	0	1	0	1.000	0	1--	-	3.21	1.54
1992 Philadelphia	NL	5	5	1	0	28.2	121	29	20	17	3	1	1	0	7	0	5	0	0	1	1	.500	0	0-0	0	3.52	5.34
1993 Philadelphia	NL	17	4	0	2	51.0	221	50	32	30	5	1	0	0	22	2	33	2	0	1	3	.250	0	0-0	0	4.00	5.29
1994 Philadelphia	NL	12	8	0	2	50.1	222	61	31	28	7	2	3	0	20	3	29	0	0	2	4	.333	0	0-0	0	5.62	5.01
1995 Philadelphia	NL	33	8	0	7	87.2	367	78	37	32	10	5	3	3	29	2	57	7	0	3	3	.500	0	0-0	1	3.39	3.29
1996 Philadelphia	NL	32	29	0	1	167.0	732	188	107	101	25	6	5	6	67	6	103	16	1	6	14	.300	0	0-0	0	5.37	5.44
1997 Kansas City	AL	10	0	0	4	14.0	70	20	11	10	1	0	1	0	8	1	10	0	0	0	2	.000	0	1-1	0	7.23	6.43
1998 Pittsburgh	NL	37	1	0	9	51.0	204	39	12	11	1	1	2	0	16	4	59	3	0	4	2	.667	0	0-1	7	1.95	1.94
1999 Pittsburgh	NL	58	0	0	50	58.1	269	63	36	33	9	2	1	1	37	7	76	4	0	3	4	.429	0	23-28	6	5.80	5.09
2000 Pittsburgh	NL	72	0	0	63	72.0	307	56	34	28	8	2	4	4	40	3	71	1	0	3	4	.429	0	24-29	4	3.72	3.50
2001 Pit-Hou	NL	65	0	0	48	64.0	285	60	28	27	9	3	1	0	35	3	59	2	0	6	4	.600	0	22-25	3	4.45	3.80
2002 Pittsburgh	NL	59	0	0	59	61.1	258	54	24	20	6	4	0	1	21	3	43	2	0	2	6	.250	0	46-50	0	3.14	2.93
2001 Pittsburgh	NL	40	0	0	38	41.2	183	39	18	17	6	2	0	0	21	2	43	1	0	2	4	.333	0	22-24	0	4.32	3.67
2001 Houston	NL	25	0	0	10	22.1	102	21	10	10	3	1	1	0	14	1	16	1	0	4	0	1.000	0	0-1	3	4.70	4.03
11 ML YEARS		400	55	1	245	705.1	3056	698	372	337	84	27	21	16	302	34	545	37	1	31	47	.397	0	116-134	13	4.29	4.30

Woody Williams

Pitches: R **Bats:** R **Pos:** SP-17 | **Ht:** 6'0" **Wt:** 195 **Born:** 8/19/66 **Age:** 36

Year Team	Lg	G	GS	CG	GF	IP	BFP	H	R	ER	HR	SH	SF	HB	TBB	IBB	SO	WP	Bk	W	L	Pct	ShO	Sv-Op	Hld	ERC	ERA
2002 Memphis*	AAA	1	1	0	0	5.0	16	1	1	1	0	0	0	0	1	0	7	0	0	1	0	1.000	0	0--	-	0.28	1.80
1993 Toronto	AL	30	0	0	9	37.0	172	40	18	18	2	2	1	1	22	3	24	2	1	3	1	.750	0	0-2	4	4.85	4.38
1994 Toronto	AL	38	0	0	14	59.1	253	44	24	24	5	1	2	2	33	1	56	4	0	1	3	.250	0	0-0	5	3.25	3.64
1995 Toronto	AL	23	3	0	10	53.2	232	44	23	22	6	2	0	2	28	1	41	0	0	1	2	.333	0	0-1	1	3.72	3.69
1996 Toronto	AL	12	10	1	0	59.0	255	64	33	31	8	2	1	1	21	1	43	2	0	4	5	.444	0	0-0	0	4.73	4.73
1997 Toronto	AL	31	31	0	0	194.2	833	201	99	94	31	6	8	5	66	3	124	7	0	9	14	.391	0	0-0	0	4.55	4.35
1998 Toronto	AL	32	32	1	0	209.2	894	196	112	104	36	5	6	2	81	3	151	2	1	10	9	.526	1	0-0	0	4.15	4.46
1999 San Diego	NL	33	33	0	0	208.1	887	213	106	102	33	9	9	2	73	5	137	9	0	12	12	.500	0	0-0	0	4.46	4.41
2000 San Diego	NL	23	23	4	0	168.0	700	152	74	70	23	4	3	3	54	2	111	4	0	10	8	.556	0	0-0	0	3.55	3.75
2001 SD-Stl	NL	34	34	3	0	220.0	922	224	110	99	35	13	8	8	56	5	154	5	0	15	9	.625	1	0-0	0	4.15	4.05
2002 St Louis	NL	17	17	1	0	103.1	412	84	30	29	10	3	1	4	25	2	76	2	0	9	4	.692	0	0-0	0	2.63	2.53
2001 San Diego	NL	23	23	0	0	145.0	632	170	88	80	28	8	8	5	37	4	102	4	0	8	8	.500	0	0-0	0	5.26	4.97
2001 St Louis	NL	11	11	3	0	75.0	290	54	22	19	7	5	0	3	19	1	52	1	0	7	1	.875	1	0-0	0	2.24	2.28
10 ML YEARS		273	183	10	33	1313.0	5560	1262	628	593	189	47	39	30	459	26	917	37	2	74	67	.525	2	0-3	10	4.04	4.06

Scott Williamson

Pitches: R **Bats:** R **Pos:** RP-63 | **Ht:** 6'0" **Wt:** 185 **Born:** 2/17/76 **Age:** 27

Year Team	Lg	G	GS	CG	GF	IP	BFP	H	R	ER	HR	SH	SF	HB	TBB	IBB	SO	WP	Bk	W	L	Pct	ShO	Sv-Op	Hld	ERC	ERA
1999 Cincinnati	NL	62	0	0	40	93.1	366	54	29	25	8	5	2	1	43	6	107	13	0	12	7	.632	0	19-26	5	2.05	2.41
2000 Cincinnati	NL	48	10	0	13	112.0	495	92	45	41	7	4	2	3	75	7	136	21	1	5	8	.385	0	6-8	6	3.85	3.29
2001 Cincinnati	NL	2	0	0	0	2.0	6	1	0	0	0	0	0	0	2	0	0	1	0	0	0	-	0	0-0	1	24.61	0.00
2002 Cincinnati	NL	63	0	0	23	74.0	299	46	27	24	5	5	2	2	36	5	84	8	1	3	4	.429	0	8-12	8	2.24	2.92
4 ML YEARS		175	10	0	76	280.0	1166	193	101	90	20	14	6	7	156	18	327	43	2	20	19	.513	0	33-46	20	2.83	2.89

Dontrelle Willis

Pitches: L **Bats:** L **Pos:** SP | **Ht:** 6'4" **Wt:** 200 **Born:** 1/12/82 **Age:** 21

Year Team	Lg	G	GS	CG	GF	IP	BFP	H	R	ER	HR	SH	SF	HB	TBB	IBB	SO	WP	Bk	W	L	Pct	ShO	Sv-Op	Hld	ERC	ERA
2000 Cubs	R	9	1	0	3	28.0	118	26	15	12	0	1	22	1	8	1	22	0	0	3	1	.750	0	0--	-	2.64	3.86
2001 Boise	A-	15	15	0	0	93.2	374	76	36	31	1	0	1	3	19	0	77	5	1	8	2	.800	0	0--	-	1.95	2.98
2002 Kane County	A	19	19	3	0	127.2	491	91	29	26	3	5	2	3	21	0	101	9	3	10	2	.833	2	0--	-	1.52	1.83
2002 Jupiter	A+	5	5	0	0	30.0	115	24	7	6	2	0	0	1	3	0	27	0	0	2	0	1.000	0	0--	-	1.92	1.80

Craig Wilson

Bats: R **Throws:** R **Pos:** RF-74; 1B-42; PH-17; C-5; DH-3; LF-1 | **Ht:** 6'2" **Wt:** 225 **Born:** 11/30/76 **Age:** 26

Year Team	Lg	G	AB	H	2B	3B	HR	(Hm	Rd)	TB	R	RBI	RC	TBB	IBB	SO	HBP	SH	SF	SB	CS	SB%	GDP	Avg	OBP	Slg
1995 Medicine Hat	R+	49	184	52	14	1	7	(-	-)	89	33	35	35	24	1	41	3	0	4	8	2	.80	1	.283	.367	.484
1996 Hagerstown	A	131	495	129	27	5	11	(-	-)	199	66	70	60	32	1	120	10	0	4	17	11	.61	12	.261	.316	.402
1997 Lynchburg	A+	117	401	106	26	1	19	(-	-)	191	54	69	67	39	6	98	15	1	2	6	5	.55	3	.264	.350	.476
1998 Lynchburg	A+	61	219	59	12	2	12	(-	-)	111	26	45	38	22	1	53	5	0	1	2	1	.67	3	.269	.348	.507
1998 Carolina	AA	45	148	49	11	0	5	(-	-)	75	21	31	30	14	0	32	4	0	2	4	1	.80	2	.331	.399	.507
1999 Altoona	AA	111	362	97	21	3	20	(-	-)	184	57	69	66	40	0	104	19	1	4	1	3	.25	8	.268	.367	.508
2000 Nashville	AAA	124	396	112	24	2	33	(-	-)	239	83	86	89	44	2	121	25	0	7	1	2	.33	7	.283	.383	.604
2001 Nashville	AAA	11	45	13	2	1	1	(-	-)	20	4	3	6	2	0	14	1	0	0	0	0	-	1	.289	.333	.444
2001 Pittsburgh	NL	88	158	49	3	1	13	(8	5)	93	27	32	34	15	1	53	7	1	2	3	1	.75	4	.310	.390	.589
2002 Pittsburgh	NL	131	368	97	16	1	16	(3	13)	163	48	57	54	32	0	116	21	1	2	2	3	.40	10	.264	.355	.443
2 ML YEARS		219	526	146	19	2	29	(11	18)	256	75	89	88	47	1	169	28	2	4	5	4	.56	14	.278	.365	.487

Dan Wilson

Bats: R Throws: R Pos: C-113; 1B-4; PH-2   Ht: 6'3" Wt: 214 Born: 3/25/69 Age: 34

Year Team	Lg	G	AB	H	2B	3B	HR	(Hm	Rd)	TB	R	RBI	RC	TBB	IBB	SO	HBP	SH	SF	SB	CS	SB%	GDP	Avg	OBP	Slg
1992 Cincinnati	NL	12	25	9	1	0	0	(0	0)	10	2	3	4	3	0	8	0	0	0	0	0	-	2	.360	.429	.400
1993 Cincinnati	NL	36	76	17	3	0	0	(0	0)	20	6	8	6	9	4	16	0	2	1	0	0	-	3	.224	.302	.263
1994 Seattle	AL	91	282	61	14	2	3	(1	2)	88	24	27	17	10	0	57	1	8	2	1	2	.33	11	.216	.244	.312
1995 Seattle	AL	119	399	111	22	3	9	(5	4)	166	40	51	53	33	1	63	2	5	1	2	1	.67	12	.278	.336	.416
1996 Seattle	AL	138	491	140	24	0	18	(7	11)	218	51	83	68	32	2	88	3	9	5	1	2	.33	15	.285	.330	.444
1997 Seattle	AL	146	508	137	31	1	15	(9	6)	215	66	74	69	39	1	72	5	8	3	7	2	.78	12	.270	.326	.423
1998 Seattle	AL	96	325	82	17	1	9	(6	3)	128	39	44	40	24	0	56	5	8	6	2	1	.67	6	.252	.308	.394
1999 Seattle	AL	123	414	110	23	2	7	(3	4)	158	46	38	49	29	4	83	2	10	2	5	0	1.00	6	.266	.315	.382
2000 Seattle	AL	90	268	63	12	0	5	(2	3)	90	31	27	24	22	0	51	0	11	2	1	2	.33	8	.235	.291	.336
2001 Seattle	AL	123	377	100	20	1	10	(4	6)	152	44	42	45	20	0	69	2	8	1	3	2	.60	6	.265	.305	.403
2002 Seattle	AL	115	359	106	16	1	6	(3	3)	142	35	44	41	18	1	81	2	7	8	1	0	1.00	8	.295	.326	.396
11 ML YEARS		1089	3524	936	183	11	82	(40	42)	1387	384	441	416	239	13	644	22	76	31	23	12	.66	92	.266	.314	.394

Enrique Wilson

Bats: B Throws: R Pos: 3B-25; PR-20; SS-14; PH-10; 2B-7; RF-2; DH-2   Ht: 5'11" Wt: 195 Born: 7/27/73 Age: 29

Year Team	Lg	G	AB	H	2B	3B	HR	(Hm	Rd)	TB	R	RBI	RC	TBB	IBB	SO	HBP	SH	SF	SB	CS	SB%	GDP	Avg	OBP	Slg
1997 Cleveland	AL	5	15	5	0	0	0	(0	0)	5	2	1	2	0	0	2	0	0	0	0	0	-	0	.333	.333	.333
1998 Cleveland	AL	32	90	29	6	0	2	(1	1)	41	13	12	13	4	0	8	1	1	1	2	4	.33	1	.322	.354	.456
1999 Cleveland	AL	113	332	87	22	1	2	(1	1)	117	41	24	34	25	1	41	1	4	6	5	4	.56	12	.262	.310	.352
2000 Cle-Pit		80	239	70	15	1	5	(3	2)	102	27	27	34	18	2	24	0	4	2	2	2	.50	6	.293	.340	.427
2001 Pit-NYY		94	228	48	8	1	2	(1	1)	64	17	20	9	9	0	37	0	2	2	0	5	.00	10	.211	.238	.281
2002 New York	AL	60	105	19	2	2	2	(1	1)	31	17	11	9	8	0	22	0	6	0	1	1	.50	2	.181	.239	.295
2000 Cleveland	AL	40	117	38	9	0	2	(2	0)	53	16	12	19	7	0	11	0	2	2	2	1	.67	2	.325	.360	.453
2000 Pittsburgh	NL	40	122	32	6	1	3	(1	2)	49	11	15	15	11	2	13	0	2	0	0	1	.00	4	.262	.321	.402
2001 Pittsburgh	NL	46	129	24	3	0	1	(0	1)	30	7	8	1	3	0	23	0	0	1	0	3	.00	7	.186	.203	.233
2001 New York	AL	48	99	24	5	1	1	(1	0)	34	10	12	8	6	0	14	0	2	1	0	2	.00	3	.242	.283	.343
6 ML YEARS		384	1009	258	53	5	13	(8	5)	360	117	95	101	64	3	134	2	17	11	10	16	.38	31	.256	.298	.357

Jack Wilson

Bats: R Throws: R Pos: SS-143; PH-3; PR-3   Ht: 6'0" Wt: 195 Born: 12/29/77 Age: 25

Year Team	Lg	G	AB	H	2B	3B	HR	(Hm	Rd)	TB	R	RBI	RC	TBB	IBB	SO	HBP	SH	SF	SB	CS	SB%	GDP	Avg	OBP	Slg
1998 Johnson City	R+	61	241	90	18	4	4	(-	-)	128	50	29	53	18	0	30	3	1	0	22	6	.79	4	.373	.424	.531
1999 Peoria	A	64	251	86	22	4	3	(-	-)	125	47	28	47	15	0	23	2	3	0	11	5	.69	2	.343	.384	.498
1999 Potomac	A+	64	257	76	10	1	2	(-	-)	94	44	18	33	19	1	31	1	3	1	7	4	.64	2	.296	.345	.366
2000 Potomac	A+	13	47	13	0	1	2	(-	-)	21	7	7	6	5	0	10	0	1	1	2	3	.40	1	.277	.340	.447
2000 Arkansas	AA	88	343	101	20	8	6	(-	-)	155	65	34	57	36	0	59	5	5	2	2	3	.40	5	.294	.368	.452
2000 Altoona	AA	33	139	35	7	2	1	(-	-)	49	17	16	15	14	1	17	2	2	2	1	3	.25	3	.252	.325	.353
2001 Nashville	AAA	27	103	38	6	1	1	(-	-)	49	20	6	20	9	0	13	2	1	0	2	2	.50	1	.369	.430	.476
2001 Pittsburgh	NL	108	390	87	17	1	3	(0	3)	115	44	25	27	16	2	70	1	17	1	1	3	.25	4	.223	.255	.295
2002 Pittsburgh	NL	147	527	133	22	4	4	(2	2)	175	77	47	58	37	2	74	4	17	1	5	2	.71	7	.252	.306	.332
2 ML YEARS		255	917	220	39	5	7	(2	5)	290	121	72	85	53	4	144	5	34	2	6	5	.55	11	.240	.285	.316

Kris Wilson

Pitches: R Bats: R Pos: RP-12   Ht: 6'4" Wt: 225 Born: 8/6/76 Age: 26

Year Team	Lg	G	GS	CG	GF	IP	BFP	H	R	ER	HR	SH	SF	HB	TBB	IBB	SO	WP	Bk	W	L	Pct	ShO	Sv-Op	Hld	ERC	ERA
2002 Omaha*	AAA	8	3	0	1	26.1	115	38	9	9	0	2	1	0	1	0	17	0	0	2	0	1.000	0	1--	-	4.42	3.08
2002 Wichita*	AA	13	7	1	1	48.0	192	47	17	10	4	3	0	4	4	1	33	1	0	3	3	.500	0	0--	-	3.00	1.88
2000 Kansas City	AL	20	0	0	5	34.1	145	38	16	16	3	1	1	0	11	3	17	0	0	0	1	.000	0	0-1	0	4.25	4.19
2001 Kansas City	AL	29	15	0	6	109.1	487	132	78	63	26	1	3	7	32	0	67	1	0	6	5	.545	0	1-1	0	6.17	5.19
2002 Kansas City	AL	12	0	0	4	18.2	91	29	18	17	7	0	2	2	5	0	10	0	0	2	0	1.000	0	0-2	0	9.63	8.20
3 ML YEARS		61	15	0	15	162.1	723	199	112	96	36	2	6	9	48	3	94	1	0	8	6	.571	0	1-4	0	6.12	5.32

Paul Wilson

Pitches: R Bats: R Pos: SP-30   Ht: 6'5" Wt: 214 Born: 3/28/73 Age: 30

Year Team	Lg	G	GS	CG	GF	IP	BFP	H	R	ER	HR	SH	SF	HB	TBB	IBB	SO	WP	Bk	W	L	Pct	ShO	Sv-Op	Hld	ERC	ERA
1996 New York	NL	26	26	1	0	149.0	677	157	102	89	15	7	3	10	71	11	109	3	3	5	12	.294	0	0-0	0	4.77	5.38
2000 Tampa Bay	AL	11	7	0	0	51.0	206	38	20	19	1	2	2	4	16	2	40	1	0	1	4	.200	0	0-0	1	2.17	3.35
2001 Tampa Bay	AL	37	24	0	6	151.1	674	165	94	82	21	3	12	13	52	2	119	7	0	8	9	.471	0	0-1	0	4.94	4.88
2002 Tampa Bay	AL	30	30	1	0	193.2	851	219	113	104	29	2	6	13	67	2	111	4	1	6	12	.333	0	0-0	0	5.30	4.83
4 ML YEARS		104	87	2	6	545.0	2408	579	329	294	66	14	23	40	206	17	379	15	4	20	37	.351	0	0-1	1	4.74	4.86

Preston Wilson

Bats: R Throws: R Pos: CF-138; PH-3; PR-2   Ht: 6'2" Wt: 213 Born: 7/19/74 Age: 28

Year Team	Lg	G	AB	H	2B	3B	HR	(Hm	Rd)	TB	R	RBI	RC	TBB	IBB	SO	HBP	SH	SF	SB	CS	SB%	GDP	Avg	OBP	Slg
1998 NYM-Fla	NL	22	51	8	2	0	1	(1	0)	13	7	3	3	6	0	21	1	2	0	1	1	.50	0	.157	.259	.255
1999 Florida	NL	149	482	135	21	4	26	(8	18)	242	67	71	81	46	3	156	9	0	6	11	4	.73	15	.280	.350	.502
2000 Florida	NL	161	605	160	35	3	31	(12	19)	294	94	121	97	55	1	187	8	0	6	36	14	.72	11	.264	.331	.486
2001 Florida	NL	123	468	128	24	0	23	(9	14)	221	70	71	73	36	2	107	6	0	3	20	8	.71	14	.274	.331	.494
2002 Florida	NL	141	510	124	22	2	23	(8	15)	219	80	65	59	58	3	140	9	2	5	20	11	.65	17	.243	.329	.429

BATTING																			BASERUNNING				AVERAGES		
Year Team	Lg	G	AB	H	2B	3B	HR	(Hm Rd)	TB	R	RBI	RC	TBB	IBB	SO	HBP	SH	SF	SB	CS	SB%	GDP	Avg	OBP	Slg
1998 New York	NL	8	20	6	2	0	0	(0 0)	8	3	2	3	2	0	8	0	0	0	1	1	.50	0	.300	.364	.400
1998 Florida	NL	14	31	2	0	0	1	(1 0)	5	4	1	0	4	0	13	1	2	0	0	0	-	0	.065	.194	.161
5 ML YEARS		596	2116	555	110	11	104	(38 66)	999	318	331	313	201	9	611	33	4	18	88	38	.70	57	.262	.333	.472

Tom Wilson

Bats: R **Throws:** R **Pos:** C-65; PH-16; DH-12; 1B-11

Ht: 6'3" **Wt:** 220 **Born:** 12/19/70 **Age:** 32

BATTING																			BASERUNNING				AVERAGES		
Year Team	Lg	G	AB	H	2B	3B	HR	(Hm Rd)	TB	R	RBI	RC	TBB	IBB	SO	HBP	SH	SF	SB	CS	SB%	GDP	Avg	OBP	Slg
1991 Oneonta	A-	70	243	59	12	2	4	(- -)	87	38	42	30	34	2	71	3	0	5	4	4	.50	6	.243	.337	.358
1992 Greensboro	A	117	395	83	22	0	6	(- -)	123	50	48	43	68	0	128	3	1	8	2	1	.67	8	.210	.325	.311
1993 Greensboro	A	120	394	98	20	10	10	(- -)	168	55	63	71	91	0	112	4	3	8	2	5	.29	5	.249	.388	.426
1994 Albany-Col	AA	123	408	100	20	1	7	(- -)	143	54	42	51	58	2	100	6	4	4	4	6	.40	8	.245	.345	.350
1995 Columbus	AAA	22	62	16	3	1	0	(- -)	21	11	9	8	9	0	10	0	2	0	0	0	-	0	.258	.352	.339
1995 Norwich	AA	28	84	12	4	0	0	(- -)	16	6	4	4	17	0	22	0	0	0	0	0	-	3	.143	.287	.190
1995 Tampa	A+	17	48	8	0	0	0	(- -)	8	3	2	4	11	0	13	0	1	1	1	0	1.00	0	.167	.317	.167
1996 Columbus	AAA	1	1	0	0	0	0	(- -)	0	0	0	0	0	0	0	0	0	0	0	0	-	0	.000	.000	.000
1996 Buffalo	AAA	72	208	56	14	2	9	(- -)	101	28	30	39	35	0	66	6	1	0	0	1	.00	4	.269	.390	.486
1997 Norwich	AA	124	419	124	21	4	21	(- -)	216	88	80	89	86	0	126	4	0	5	1	4	.20	8	.296	.416	.516
1997 Columbus	AAA	1	3	0	0	0	0	(- -)	0	0	0	0	1	0	0	0	0	0	0	0	-	0	.000	.250	.000
1998 Tucson	AAA	111	370	112	17	3	12	(- -)	171	59	54	63	41	3	81	7	0	3	3	1	.75	10	.303	.380	.462
1999 Durham	AAA	67	215	60	19	0	16	(- -)	127	41	44	48	49	1	59	0	1	1	0	2	.00	9	.279	.411	.591
1999 Orlando	AA	30	104	30	2	0	7	(- -)	53	12	23	22	18	0	34	3	0	1	0	0	-	2	.288	.405	.510
2000 Columbus	AAA	104	330	91	20	0	20	(- -)	171	63	71	69	73	1	114	3	0	1	2	2	.50	9	.276	.410	.518
2001 Sacramento	AAA	77	259	73	15	1	8	(- -)	114	43	48	48	49	1	62	4	0	8	1	0	.00	5	.282	.394	.440
2001 Oakland	AL	9	21	4	0	0	2	(1 1)	10	4	4	2	1	0	5	1	0	1	0	0	-	1	.190	.250	.476
2002 Toronto	AL	96	265	68	10	0	8	(6 2)	102	33	37	37	28	0	79	5	0	4	0	0	-	6	.257	.334	.385
2 ML YEARS		105	286	72	10	0	10	(7 3)	112	37	41	39	29	0	84	6	0	5	0	0	-	7	.252	.328	.392

Vance Wilson

Bats: R **Throws:** R **Pos:** C-65; PH-11; 1B-1; PR-1

Ht: 5'11" **Wt:** 190 **Born:** 3/17/73 **Age:** 30

BATTING																			BASERUNNING				AVERAGES		
Year Team	Lg	G	AB	H	2B	3B	HR	(Hm Rd)	TB	R	RBI	RC	TBB	IBB	SO	HBP	SH	SF	SB	CS	SB%	GDP	Avg	OBP	Slg
2000 New York	NL	4	4	0	0	0	0	(0 0)	0	0	0	0	0	0	2	0	0	0	0	0	-	0	.000	.000	.000
2001 New York	NL	32	57	17	3	0	0	(0 0)	20	3	6	6	2	0	16	2	0	1	0	1	.00	1	.298	.339	.351
2002 New York	NL	74	163	40	7	0	5	(3 2)	62	19	26	21	5	0	32	8	2	0	0	1	.00	4	.245	.301	.380
3 ML YEARS		110	224	57	10	0	5	(3 2)	82	22	32	27	7	0	50	10	2	1	0	2	.00	5	.254	.306	.366

Randy Winn

Bats: B **Throws:** R **Pos:** CF-138; RF-8; PH-6; DH-4

Ht: 6'2" **Wt:** 197 **Born:** 6/9/74 **Age:** 29

BATTING																			BASERUNNING				AVERAGES		
Year Team	Lg	G	AB	H	2B	3B	HR	(Hm Rd)	TB	R	RBI	RC	TBB	IBB	SO	HBP	SH	SF	SB	CS	SB%	GDP	Avg	OBP	Slg
1998 Tampa Bay	AL	109	338	94	9	9	1	(0 1)	124	51	17	44	29	0	69	1	11	0	26	12	.68	2	.278	.337	.367
1999 Tampa Bay	AL	79	303	81	16	4	2	(2 0)	111	44	24	32	17	0	63	1	1	3	9	9	.50	3	.267	.307	.366
2000 Tampa Bay	AL	51	159	40	5	0	1	(1 0)	48	28	16	18	26	0	25	2	2	1	6	7	.46	2	.252	.362	.302
2001 Tampa Bay	AL	128	429	117	25	6	6	(3 3)	172	54	50	56	38	0	81	6	5	2	12	10	.55	10	.273	.339	.401
2002 Tampa Bay	AL	152	607	181	39	9	14	(9 5)	280	87	75	105	55	3	109	6	1	5	27	8	.77	9	.298	.360	.461
5 ML YEARS		519	1836	513	94	28	24	(15 9)	735	264	182	255	165	3	347	16	20	10	80	46	.63	26	.279	.342	.400

Dewayne Wise

Bats: L **Throws:** L **Pos:** RF-26; PR-9; LF-6; CF-3; PH-3; DH-1

Ht: 6'1" **Wt:** 180 **Born:** 2/24/78 **Age:** 25

BATTING																			BASERUNNING				AVERAGES		
Year Team	Lg	G	AB	H	2B	3B	HR	(Hm Rd)	TB	R	RBI	RC	TBB	IBB	SO	HBP	SH	SF	SB	CS	SB%	GDP	Avg	OBP	Slg
1997 Billings	R+	62	268	84	13	9	7	(- -)	136	53	41	45	9	0	47	2	1	3	18	8	.69	2	.313	.337	.507
1998 Burlington	A	127	496	111	15	9	2	(- -)	150	61	44	42	41	1	111	1	7	9	27	17	.61	4	.224	.280	.302
1999 Rockford	A	131	502	127	20	13	11	(- -)	206	70	81	68	42	2	81	7	5	14	35	13	.73	6	.253	.312	.410
2000 Tennessee	AA	15	56	14	5	2	2	(- -)	29	10	8	9	7	0	13	0	0	0	3	2	.60	2	.250	.333	.518
2001 Tennessee	AA	87	351	84	13	6	8	(- -)	133	44	44	37	21	1	58	1	4	2	13	5	.72	6	.239	.283	.379
2001 Syracuse	AAA	3	13	3	0	0	0	(- -)	3	1	0	0	0	0	8	0	0	0	0	1	.00	0	.231	.231	.231
2001 Dunedin	A+	25	103	23	3	1	2	(- -)	34	9	16	9	5	0	13	0	0	3	5	0	1.00	3	.223	.252	.330
2002 Tennessee	AA	86	340	101	21	4	10	(- -)	160	59	49	56	29	5	49	1	6	4	15	8	.65	4	.297	.350	.471
2000 Toronto	AL	28	22	3	0	0	0	(0 0)	3	3	0	0	1	0	5	1	0	0	1	0	1.00	0	.136	.208	.136
2002 Toronto	AL	42	112	20	4	1	3	(2 1)	35	14	13	8	4	0	15	0	0	0	5	0	1.00	0	.179	.207	.313
2 ML YEARS		70	134	23	4	1	3	(2 1)	38	17	13	8	5	0	20	1	0	0	6	0	1.00	0	.172	.207	.284

Matt Wise

Pitches: R **Bats:** R **Pos:** RP-7

Ht: 6'4" **Wt:** 195 **Born:** 11/18/75 **Age:** 27

HOW MUCH HE PITCHED							WHAT HE GAVE UP											THE RESULTS						
Year Team	Lg	G	GS	CG	GF	IP	BFP	H	R	ER	HR	SH	SF	HB	TBB	IBB	SO	WP	Bk	W	L	Pct	ShO	Sv-Op	Hld	ERC	ERA
2002 Salt Lake*	AAA	16	16	0	0	78.0	340	102	51	47	12	2	3	5	15	0	76	0	0	3	4	.429	0	0- -		5.83	5.42
2000 Anaheim	AL	8	6	0	0	37.1	163	40	23	23	7	0	2	1	13	1	20	1	0	3	3	.500	0	0-0	0	4.96	5.54
2001 Anaheim	AL	11	9	0	2	49.1	211	47	27	24	11	2	1	2	18	1	50	0	0	1	4	.200	0	-	0	4.65	4.38
2002 Anaheim	AL	7	0	0	6	8.1	33	7	3	3	0	1	0	1	1	0	6	0	0	0	0	-	0	0-0	0	2.07	3.24
3 ML YEARS		26	15	0	8	95.0	407	94	53	50	18	3	3	4	32	2	76	1	0	4	7	.364	0	0-0	0	4.52	4.74

Jay Witasick

Pitches: R **Bats:** R **Pos:** RP-44

Ht: 6'4" **Wt:** 235 **Born:** 8/28/72 **Age:** 30

		HOW MUCH HE PITCHED					WHAT HE GAVE UP										THE RESULTS							
Year Team	Lg	G	GS	CG	GF	IP	BFP	H	R	ER	HR	SH	SF	HB	TBB	IBB	SO	WP	Bk	W	L	Pct	ShO	Sv-Op	Hld	ERC	ERA
2002 Fresno*	AAA	2	2	0	0	2.0	8	1	1	1	0	0	0	0	1	0	2	1	0	0	0	-	0	0- -	-	1.41	4.50
1996 Oakland	AL	12	0	0	6	13.0	55	12	9	9	5	0	1	0	5	0	12	2	0	1	1	.500	0	0-1	0	5.52	6.23
1997 Oakland	AL	8	0	0	1	11.0	53	14	7	7	2	1	0	0	6	0	8	0	0	0	0	-	0	0-0	1	6.81	5.73
1998 Oakland	AL	7	3	0	1	27.0	131	36	24	19	9	0	0	0	15	1	29	2	0	1	3	.250	0	0-0	0	8.53	6.33
1999 Kansas City	AL	32	28	1	2	158.1	732	191	108	98	23	4	8	8	83	1	102	4	2	9	12	.429	1	0-0	0	6.45	5.57
2000 KC-SD		33	25	2	2	150.0	697	178	107	97	24	8	4	7	73	5	121	5	1	6	10	.375	0	0-0	0	6.09	5.82
2001 SD-NYY		63	0	0	17	79.0	352	78	41	29	8	3	2	6	33	4	106	4	0	8	2	.800	0	1-4	10	4.22	3.30
2002 San Francisco	NL	44	0	0	9	68.1	276	58	19	18	3	2	1	4	21	3	54	3	0	1	0	1.000	0	0-0	4	2.78	2.37
2000 Kansas City	AL	22	14	2	2	89.1	410	109	65	59	15	3	3	4	38	0	67	3	0	3	8	.273	0	0-0	0	6.19	5.94
2000 San Diego	NL	11	11	0	0	60.2	287	69	42	38	9	5	1	3	35	5	54	2	1	3	2	.600	0	0-0	0	5.94	5.64
2001 San Diego	NL	31	0	0	9	38.2	164	31	14	8	3	3	0	4	15	3	53	3	0	5	2	.714	0	1-3	5	3.05	1.86
2001 New York	AL	32	0	0	8	40.1	188	47	27	21	5	0	2	2	18	1	53	1	0	3	0	1.000	0	0-1	5	5.43	4.69
7 ML YEARS		199	56	3	38	506.2	2296	567	315	277	74	18	16	25	236	14	432	20	3	26	28	.481	1	1-5	15	5.54	4.92

Kevin Witt

Bats: L **Throws:** R **Pos:** 1B

Ht: 6'4" **Wt:** 220 **Born:** 1/5/76 **Age:** 27

		BATTING																		BASERUNNING				AVERAGES		
Year Team	Lg	G	AB	H	2B	3B	HR	(Hm	Rd)	TB	R	RBI	RC	TBB	IBB	SO	HBP	SH	SF	SB	CS	SB%	GDP	Avg	OBP	Slg
2002 Louisville*	AAA	131	509	134	32	1	24	(-	-)	240	77	107	70	34	5	140	6	0	5	0	1	.00	18	.263	.314	.472
1998 Toronto	AL	5	7	1	0	0	0	(0	0)	1	0	0	0	0	0	3	0	0	0	0	0	-	0	.143	.143	.143
1999 Toronto	AL	15	34	7	1	0	1	(1	0)	11	3	5	3	2	0	9	0	1	0	0	0	-	0	.206	.250	.324
2001 San Diego	NL	14	27	5	0	0	2	(1	1)	11	5	5	3	2	0	7	0	0	1	0	0	-	0	.185	.233	.407
3 ML YEARS		34	68	13	1	0	3	(2	1)	23	8	10	6	4	0	19	0	1	1	0	0	-	0	.191	.233	.338

Mark Wohlers

Pitches: R **Bats:** R **Pos:** RP-64

Ht: 6'4" **Wt:** 207 **Born:** 1/23/70 **Age:** 33

		HOW MUCH HE PITCHED						WHAT HE GAVE UP											THE RESULTS							
Year Team	Lg	G	GS	CG	GF	IP	BFP	H	R	ER	HR	SH	SF	HB	TBB	IBB	SO	WP	Bk	W	L	Pct	ShO	Sv-Op	Hld	ERC	ERA
1991 Atlanta	NL	17	0	0	4	19.2	89	17	7	7	1	2	1	2	13	3	13	0	0	3	1	.750	0	2-4	2	4.07	3.20
1992 Atlanta	NL	32	0	0	16	35.1	140	28	11	10	0	5	1	1	14	4	17	1	0	1	2	.333	0	4-6	2	2.37	2.55
1993 Atlanta	NL	46	0	0	13	48.0	199	37	25	24	2	5	1	1	22	3	45	0	0	6	2	.750	0	0-0	12	2.69	4.50
1994 Atlanta	NL	51	0	0	15	51.0	236	51	35	26	1	4	6	0	33	9	58	2	0	7	2	.778	0	1-2	7	4.02	4.59
1995 Atlanta	NL	65	0	0	49	64.2	269	51	16	15	2	2	0	1	24	3	90	4	0	7	3	.700	0	25-29	2	2.36	2.09
1996 Atlanta	NL	77	0	0	64	77.1	323	71	30	26	8	2	2	2	21	3	100	10	0	2	4	.333	0	39-44	0	3.17	3.03
1997 Atlanta	NL	71	0	0	55	69.1	300	57	29	27	4	4	4	0	38	0	92	6	0	5	7	.417	0	33-40	1	3.33	3.50
1998 Atlanta	NL	27	0	0	17	20.1	113	18	23	23	2	1	0	1	33	0	22	7	0	0	1	.000	0	8-8	0	8.41	10.18
1999 Atlanta	NL	2	0	0	0	0.2	10	1	2	2	1	0	0	0	6	0	0	2	0	0	0	-	0	0-0	0	41.75	27.00
2000 Cincinnati	NL	20	0	0	7	28.0	119	19	14	14	3	2	1	0	17	0	20	2	0	1	2	.333	0	0-0	0	3.14	4.50
2001 Cin-NYY		61	0	0	25	67.2	298	69	40	32	8	5	3	2	25	2	54	11	0	4	1	.800	0	0-1	13	4.18	4.26
2002 Cleveland	AL	64	0	0	28	71.1	304	71	41	38	6	1	2	3	26	3	46	7	0	3	4	.429	0	7-11	10	3.94	4.79
2001 Cincinnati	NL	30	0	0	11	32.0	139	36	20	14	5	4	1	1	7	2	21	4	0	3	1	.750	0	0-1	8	4.41	3.94
2001 New York	AL	31	0	0	14	35.2	159	33	20	18	3	1	2	1	18	0	33	7	0	1	0	1.000	0	0-0	5	3.96	4.54
12 ML YEARS		533	0	0	293	553.1	2400	490	273	244	37	34	21	13	272	30	557	50	0	39	29	.574	0	119-145	49	3.54	3.97

Randy Wolf

Pitches: L **Bats:** L **Pos:** SP-31

Ht: 6'0" **Wt:** 194 **Born:** 8/22/76 **Age:** 26

		HOW MUCH HE PITCHED						WHAT HE GAVE UP											THE RESULTS							
Year Team	Lg	G	GS	CG	GF	IP	BFP	H	R	ER	HR	SH	SF	HB	TBB	IBB	SO	WP	Bk	W	L	Pct	ShO	Sv-Op	Hld	ERC	ERA
2002 Clearwater*	A+	1	1	0	0	5.0	15	1	0	0	0	0	0	1	0	8	0	0	0	0	-	0	0- -	-	0.30	0.00
1999 Philadelphia	NL	22	21	0	0	121.2	552	126	78	75	20	5	1	5	67	0	116	4	0	6	9	.400	0	0-0	0	5.54	5.55
2000 Philadelphia	NL	32	32	1	0	206.1	889	210	107	100	21	10	8	8	83	2	160	1	0	11	9	.550	0	0-0	0	4.54	4.36
2001 Philadelphia	NL	28	25	4	1	163.0	684	150	74	67	15	11	7	10	51	4	152	1	0	10	11	.476	2	0-0	0	3.46	3.70
2002 Philadelphia	NL	31	31	3	0	210.2	855	172	77	75	23	7	6	7	63	5	172	4	0	11	9	.550	2	0-0	0	2.88	3.20
4 ML YEARS		113	109	8	1	701.2	2980	658	336	317	83	33	22	30	264	11	600	10	0	38	38	.500	4	0-0	0	3.93	4.07

Tony Womack

Bats: L **Throws:** R **Pos:** SS-149; PH-6; PR-2; RF-1

Ht: 5'9" **Wt:** 170 **Born:** 9/25/69 **Age:** 33

		BATTING																		BASERUNNING				AVERAGES		
Year Team	Lg	G	AB	H	2B	3B	HR	(Hm	Rd)	TB	R	RBI	RC	TBB	IBB	SO	HBP	SH	SF	SB	CS	SB%	GDP	Avg	OBP	Slg
1993 Pittsburgh	NL	15	24	2	0	0	0	(0	0)	2	5	0	0	3	0	3	0	1	0	2	0	1.00	0	.083	.185	.083
1994 Pittsburgh	NL	5	12	4	0	0	0	(0	0)	4	4	1	2	2	0	3	0	0	0	0	0	-	0	.333	.429	.333
1996 Pittsburgh	NL	17	30	10	3	1	0	(0	0)	15	11	7	8	6	0	1	1	3	0	2	0	1.00	0	.333	.459	.500
1997 Pittsburgh	NL	155	641	178	26	9	6	(5	1)	240	85	50	87	43	2	109	3	2	0	60	7	.90	6	.278	.326	.374
1998 Pittsburgh	NL	159	655	185	26	7	3	(2	1)	234	85	45	84	38	1	94	0	6	5	58	8	.88	6	.282	.319	.357
1999 Arizona	NL	144	614	170	25	10	4	(1	3)	227	111	41	88	52	0	68	2	9	7	72	13	.85	4	.277	.332	.370
2000 Arizona	NL	146	617	167	21	14	7	(4	3)	237	95	57	78	30	0	74	5	2	5	45	11	.80	4	.271	.307	.384
2001 Arizona	NL	125	481	128	19	5	3	(2	1)	166	66	30	54	23	2	54	6	7	1	28	7	.80	4	.266	.307	.345
2002 Arizona	NL	153	590	160	23	5	5	(4	1)	208	90	57	74	46	2	80	4	6	6	29	12	.71	9	.271	.325	.353
9 ML YEARS		919	3664	1004	143	51	28	(18	10)	1333	552	288	475	243	7	486	21	36	24	296	58	.84	33	.274	.321	.364

Kerry Wood

Pitches: R **Bats:** R **Pos:** SP-33   **Ht:** 6'5" **Wt:** 230 **Born:** 6/16/77 **Age:** 26

Year Team	Lg	G	GS	CG	GF	IP	BFP	H	R	ER	HR	SH	SF	HB	TBB	IBB	SO	WP	Bk	W	L	Pct	ShO	Sv-Op	Hld	ERC	ERA
1998 Chicago	NL	26	26	1	0	166.2	699	117	69	63	14	2	4	11	85	1	233	6	3	13	6	.684	1	0-0	0	3.03	3.40
2000 Chicago	NL	23	23	1	0	137.0	603	112	77	73	17	7	5	9	87	0	132	5	1	8	7	.533	0	0-0	0	4.43	4.80
2001 Chicago	NL	28	28	1	0	174.1	740	127	70	65	16	4	5	10	92	3	217	9	0	12	6	.667	1	0-0	0	3.22	3.36
2002 Chicago	NL	33	33	4	0	213.2	895	169	92	87	22	13	6	16	97	5	217	8	1	12	11	.522	1	0-0	0	3.46	3.66
4 ML YEARS		110	110	7	0	691.2	2937	525	308	288	69	26	19	46	361	9	799	28	5	45	30	.600	3	0-0	0	3.48	3.75

Steve Woodard

Pitches: R **Bats:** L **Pos:** RP-14   **Ht:** 6'4" **Wt:** 217 **Born:** 5/15/75 **Age:** 28

Year Team	Lg	G	GS	CG	GF	IP	BFP	H	R	ER	HR	SH	SF	HB	TBB	IBB	SO	WP	Bk	W	L	Pct	ShO	Sv-Op	Hld	ERC	ERA
2002 Scrtn/WlksBr*	AAA	15	1	0	10	25.0	97	17	6	6	1	2	0	6	6	1	13	1	0	3	1	.750	0	5--	1	1.55	2.16
2002 Memphis*	AAA	7	6	1	0	40.0	173	53	28	28	7	2	1	1	3	0	42	2	0	2	3	.400	0	0--		5.26	6.30
1997 Milwaukee	NL	7	7	0	0	36.2	153	39	25	21	5	0	0	2	6	0	32	0	0	3	3	.500	0	0-0	0	3.98	5.15
1998 Milwaukee	NL	34	26	0	2	165.2	692	170	83	77	19	2	4	9	33	4	135	3	2	10	12	.455	0	0-0	0	3.73	4.18
1999 Milwaukee	NL	31	29	2	0	185.0	801	219	101	93	23	9	4	6	36	7	119	4	1	11	8	.579	0	0-0	0	4.52	4.52
2000 Mil-Cle		40	22	1	7	147.2	659	182	105	96	26	8	4	6	44	5	100	8	0	4	10	.286	0	0-0	0	5.71	5.85
2001 Cleveland	AL	29	10	0	2	97.0	429	129	59	56	10	7	3	5	17	1	52	4	3	3	3	.500	0	0-0	1	5.33	5.20
2002 Texas	AL	14	0	0	4	17.2	83	20	13	13	4	0	0	2	8	1	14	0	1	0	0	–	0	0-1	1	6.28	6.62
2000 Milwaukee	NL	27	11	1	6	93.2	432	125	70	62	16	7	3	4	33	4	65	5	0	1	7	.125	0	0-0	0	6.55	5.96
2000 Cleveland	AL	13	11	0	1	54.0	227	57	35	34	10	1	1	2	11	1	35	3	0	3	3	.500	0	0-0	0	4.31	5.67
6 ML YEARS		155	94	3	15	649.2	2817	759	386	356	87	26	15	30	144	18	452	19	7	31	36	.463	0	0-1	2	4.71	4.93

Chris Woodward

Bats: R **Throws:** R **Pos:** SS-79; 2B-6; 1B-3; 3B-2; PR-2; DH-1; PH-1   **Ht:** 6'0" **Wt:** 185 **Born:** 6/27/76 **Age:** 27

Year Team	Lg	G	AB	H	2B	3B	HR	(Hm	Rd)	TB	R	RBI	RC	TBB	IBB	SO	HBP	SH	SF	SB	CS	SB%	GDP	Avg	OBP	Slg
2002 Dunedin*	A+	2	6	2	0	0	0	(-	-)	2	1	0	1	0	0	0	1	0	0	0	0	-	0	.333	.429	.333
1999 Toronto	AL	14	26	6	1	0	0	(0	0)	7	1	2	2	2	0	6	0	0	1	0	0	-	1	.231	.276	.269
2000 Toronto	AL	37	104	19	7	0	3	(1	2)	35	16	14	9	10	3	28	0	1	0	1	0	1.00	1	.183	.254	.337
2001 Toronto	AL	37	63	12	3	2	2	(2	0)	25	9	5	4	1	0	14	0	2	0	0	1	.00	1	.190	.203	.397
2002 Toronto	AL	90	312	86	13	4	13	(9	4)	146	48	45	45	26	0	72	3	1	8	3	0	1.00	8	.276	.330	.468
4 ML YEARS		178	505	123	24	6	18	(12	6)	213	74	66	60	39	3	120	3	4	9	4	1	.80	11	.244	.297	.422

Shawn Wooten

Bats: R **Throws:** R **Pos:** DH-21; 1B-16; PH-15; C-2; 3B-1; PR-1   **Ht:** 5'10" **Wt:** 225 **Born:** 7/24/72 **Age:** 30

Year Team	Lg	G	AB	H	2B	3B	HR	(Hm	Rd)	TB	R	RBI	RC	TBB	IBB	SO	HBP	SH	SF	SB	CS	SB%	GDP	Avg	OBP	Slg
2002 Salt Lake*	AAA	10	42	11	2	0	0	(-	-)	13	2	7	3	0	0	11	1	0	0	0	0	-	1	.262	.279	.310
2002 R Cucamnga*	A+	6	18	4	3	0	0	(-	-)	7	2	3	3	4	0	4	0	0	1	0	0	-	0	.222	.348	.389
2000 Anaheim	AL	7	9	5	1	0	0	(0	0)	6	2	1	3	0	0	0	0	0	0	0	0	-	0	.556	.556	.667
2001 Anaheim	AL	79	221	69	8	1	8	(3	5)	103	24	32	33	5	0	42	3	0	3	2	0	1.00	5	.312	.342	.466
2002 Anaheim	AL	49	113	33	8	0	3	(2	1)	50	13	19	17	6	1	24	1	0	1	2	0	1.00	3	.292	.331	.442
3 ML YEARS		135	343	107	17	1	11	(5	6)	159	39	52	53	11	1	66	4	0	4	4	0	1.00	8	.312	.337	.464

Tim Worrell

Pitches: R **Bats:** R **Pos:** RP-80   **Ht:** 6'4" **Wt:** 230 **Born:** 7/5/67 **Age:** 35

Year Team	Lg	G	GS	CG	GF	IP	BFP	H	R	ER	HR	SH	SF	HB	TBB	IBB	SO	WP	Bk	W	L	Pct	ShO	Sv-Op	Hld	ERC	ERA
1993 San Diego	NL	21	16	0	1	100.2	443	104	63	55	11	8	5	0	43	5	52	3	0	2	7	.222	0	0-0	1	4.31	4.92
1994 San Diego	NL	3	3	0	0	14.2	59	9	7	6	0	0	1	0	5	0	14	0	0	0	1	.000	0	0-0	0	1.40	3.68
1995 San Diego	NL	9	0	0	4	13.1	63	16	7	7	2	1	0	1	6	0	13	1	0	1	0	1.000	0	0-0	0	6.01	4.73
1996 San Diego	NL	50	11	0	8	121.0	510	109	45	41	9	3	1	6	39	1	99	0	0	9	7	.563	0	1-2	10	3.22	3.05
1997 San Diego	NL	60	10	0	14	106.1	483	116	67	61	14	6	6	7	50	2	81	2	1	4	8	.333	0	3-7	16	5.34	5.16
1998 Det-Cle-Oak	AL	43	9	0	5	103.0	440	106	62	60	16	2	3	1	29	3	82	2	0	2	7	.222	0	0-3	6	4.10	5.24
1999 Oakland	AL	53	0	0	17	69.1	309	69	38	32	6	1	1	3	34	1	62	1	0	2	2	.500	0	0-5	5	4.42	4.15
2000 Bal-ChC		59	0	0	29	69.1	307	72	26	23	10	4	1	3	29	11	57	1	0	5	6	.455	0	3-6	12	4.42	2.99
2001 San Francisco	NL	73	0	0	12	78.1	339	71	33	30	4	3	4	3	33	4	63	2	0	2	5	.286	0	0-3	13	3.32	3.45
2002 San Francisco	NL	80	0	0	23	72.0	296	55	21	18	3	3	4	0	30	2	55	0	0	8	2	.800	0	0-1	23	2.47	2.25
1998 Detroit	AL	15	9	0	0	61.2	265	66	42	41	11	0	1	1	19	2	47	2	0	2	6	.250	0	0-1	0	4.68	5.98
1998 Cleveland	AL	3	0	0	1	5.1	24	6	3	3	0	0	2	0	2	0	2	0	0	0	0	–	0	0-0	0	3.84	5.06
1998 Oakland	AL	25	0	0	4	36.0	151	34	17	16	5	2	0	0	8	1	33	2	0	0	1	.000	0	0-2	6	3.20	4.00
2000 Baltimore	AL	5	0	0	2	7.1	39	12	6	6	3	0	0	0	5	3	5	0	0	2	2	.500	0	0-0	0	11.13	7.36
2000 Chicago	NL	54	0	0	27	62.0	268	60	20	17	7	4	1	3	24	8	52	1	0	3	4	.429	0	3-6	12	3.75	2.47
10 ML YEARS		451	49	0	113	748.0	3249	727	369	333	75	31	26	22	298	29	578	12	1	35	45	.438	0	7-27	86	3.93	4.01

Dan Wright

Pitches: R **Bats:** R **Pos:** SP-33   **Ht:** 6'5" **Wt:** 225 **Born:** 12/14/77 **Age:** 25

Year Team	Lg	G	GS	CG	GF	IP	BFP	H	R	ER	HR	SH	SF	HB	TBB	IBB	SO	WP	Bk	W	L	Pct	ShO	Sv-Op	Hld	ERC	ERA
1999 Bristol	R+	10	0	0	3	18.0	79	14	8	2	1	0	0	1	9	1	18	3	0	2	0	1.000	0	1--	1	2.95	1.00
1999 Burlington	A	2	0	0	0	6.0	26	5	4	4	1	0	0	1	3	0	3	0	0	0	0	–	0	0--	0	4.77	6.00
2000 Winstn-Salm	A+	21	21	1	0	132.1	577	135	64	55	4	4	5	10	50	0	106	18	2	9	8	.529	0	0--	0	3.90	3.74
2000 Birmingham	AA	7	7	0	0	43.1	175	28	15	12	3	0	0	1	24	0	31	3	0	2	4	.333	0	0--	0	2.75	2.49
2001 Birmingham	AA	20	20	0	0	134.0	548	112	54	42	6	3	7	6	41	0	128	6	2	7	7	.500	0	0--	0	2.68	2.82

Year Team	Lg	G	GS	CG	GF	IP	BFP	H	R	ER	HR	SH	SF	HB	TBB	IBB	SO	WP	Bk	W	L	Pct	ShO	Sv-Op	Hld	ERC	ERA
2001 Chicago	AL	13	12	0	1	66.1	307	78	45	42	12	1	5	2	39	1	36	5	0	5	3	.625	0	0-0	0	6.74	5.70
2002 Chicago	AL	33	33	1	0	196.1	855	200	124	113	32	7	10	6	71	1	136	10	1	14	12	.538	1	0-0	0	4.55	5.18
2 ML YEARS		46	45	1	1	262.2	1162	278	169	155	44	8	15	8	110	2	172	15	1	19	15	.559	1	0-0	0	5.08	5.31

Jamey Wright

Pitches: R **Bats:** R **Pos:** SP-22; RP-1

Ht: 6'5" **Wt:** 234 **Born:** 12/24/74 **Age:** 28

Year Team	Lg	G	GS	CG	GF	IP	BFP	H	R	ER	HR	SH	SF	HB	TBB	IBB	SO	WP	Bk	W	L	Pct	ShO	Sv-Op	Hld	ERC	ERA
2002 Indianapolis*	AAA	3	3	0	0	15.1	64	16	7	7	3	0	0	0	5	0	13	0	0	1	1	.500	0	0--	-	4.83	4.11
1996 Colorado	NL	16	15	0	0	91.1	406	105	60	50	8	4	2	7	41	1	45	1	2	4	4	.500	0	0-0	1	5.50	4.93
1997 Colorado	NL	26	26	1	0	149.2	698	198	113	104	19	8	3	11	71	3	59	6	2	8	12	.400	0	0-0	0	6.96	6.25
1998 Colorado	NL	34	34	1	0	206.1	919	235	143	130	24	8	6	11	95	3	86	6	3	9	14	.391	0	0-0	0	5.57	5.67
1999 Colorado	NL	16	16	0	0	94.1	423	110	52	51	10	3	4	4	54	3	49	3	0	4	3	.571	0	0-0	0	6.19	4.87
2000 Milwaukee	NL	26	25	0	1	164.2	718	157	81	75	12	4	6	18	88	5	96	9	2	7	9	.438	0	0-0	0	4.67	4.10
2001 Milwaukee	NL	33	33	1	0	194.2	868	201	115	100	26	7	5	20	98	10	129	6	1	11	12	.478	1	0-0	0	5.36	4.90
2002 Mil-Stl	NL	23	22	1	0	129.1	585	130	80	76	17	9	6	11	75	9	77	9	0	7	13	.350	1	0-0	0	5.35	5.29
2002 Milwaukee	NL	19	19	1	0	114.1	515	115	72	68	15	9	6	11	63	8	69	8	0	5	13	.278	1	0-0	0	5.28	5.35
2002 St Louis	NL	4	3	0	0	15.0	70	15	8	8	2	0	0	0	12	1	8	1	0	2	0	1.000	0	0-0	0	5.87	4.80
7 ML YEARS		174	171	4	1	1030.1	4617	1136	644	592	116	43	32	82	522	34	541	40	10	50	67	.427	2	0-0	1	5.60	5.17

Jaret Wright

Pitches: R **Bats:** R **Pos:** SP-6; RP-2

Ht: 6'2" **Wt:** 230 **Born:** 12/29/75 **Age:** 27

Year Team	Lg	G	GS	CG	GF	IP	BFP	H	R	ER	HR	SH	SF	HB	TBB	IBB	SO	WP	Bk	W	L	Pct	ShO	Sv-Op	Hld	ERC	ERA
2002 Buffalo*	AAA	10	10	1	0	55.2	244	57	27	24	5	1	1	4	24	0	43	4	1	5	3	.625	0	0--	-	4.60	3.88
1997 Cleveland	AL	16	16	0	0	90.1	388	81	45	44	9	3	4	5	35	0	63	1	0	8	3	.727	0	0-0	0	3.63	4.38
1998 Cleveland	AL	32	32	1	0	192.2	855	207	109	101	22	4	6	11	87	4	140	6	0	12	10	.545	1	0-0	0	5.07	4.72
1999 Cleveland	AL	26	26	0	0	133.2	609	144	99	90	18	3	3	7	77	1	91	4	0	8	10	.444	0	0-0	0	5.77	6.06
2000 Cleveland	AL	9	9	1	0	51.2	217	44	27	27	6	0	1	1	28	0	36	2	0	3	4	.429	1	0-0	0	4.13	4.70
2001 Cleveland	AL	7	7	0	0	29.0	140	36	23	21	2	2	1	0	22	0	18	1	1	2	2	.500	0	0-0	0	6.82	6.52
2002 Cleveland	AL	8	6	0	1	18.1	116	40	34	32	3	0	3	2	19	0	12	1	0	2	3	.400	0	0-0	0	15.90	15.71
6 ML YEARS		98	96	2	1	515.2	2325	552	337	315	60	12	18	26	268	5	360	15	1	35	32	.522	2	0-0	0	5.31	5.50

Ron Wright

Bats: R **Throws:** R **Pos:** DH-1

Ht: 6'1" **Wt:** 230 **Born:** 1/21/76 **Age:** 27

										BATTING														BASERUNNING				AVERAGES		
Year Team	Lg	G	AB	H	2B	3B	HR	(Hm	Rd)	TB	R	RBI	RC	TBB	IBB	SO	HBP	SH	SF			SB	CS	SB%	GDP	Avg	OBP	Slg
1994 Braves	R	45	169	29	9	0	1	(-	-)	41	10	16	7	10	0	21	0	0	0			1	0	1.00	3	.172	.218	.243
1995 Macon	A	135	527	143	23	1	32	(-	-)	264	93	104	90	62	1	118	2	0	3			2	0	1.00	11	.271	.348	.501
1996 Durham	A+	66	240	66	15	2	20	(-	-)	145	47	62	52	37	2	71	0	0	7			1	0	1.00	5	.275	.363	.604
1996 Greenville	AA	63	232	59	11	1	16	(-	-)	120	39	52	44	38	5	73	2	0	3			1	0	1.00	2	.254	.360	.517
1996 Carolina	AA	4	14	2	0	0	0	(-	-)	2	1	0	0	2	0	7	0	0	0			0	1	.00	0	.143	.250	.143
1997 Calgary	AAA	91	336	102	31	0	16	(-	-)	181	50	63	61	24	2	81	2	0	6			0	2	.00	4	.304	.348	.539
1998 Nashville	AAA	17	56	12	3	0	0	(-	-)	15	6	9	5	9	0	18	1	0	1			0	0	-	0	.214	.328	.268
1998 Pirates	R	3	10	6	0	0	2	(-	-)	12	4	5	6	2	0	0	0	0	1			0	0	-	0	.600	.615	1.200
1999 Altoona	AA	24	80	17	6	0	0	(-	-)	23	2	4	7	9	0	27	1	0	0			0	0	-	1	.213	.300	.288
2000 Chattanooga	AA	79	237	63	18	0	12	(-	-)	117	36	50	43	37	0	70	2	0	2			2	2	.50	3	.266	.367	.494
2000 Louisville	AAA	18	60	12	5	0	2	(-	-)	23	10	13	7	8	0	18	0	0	0			0	0	-	3	.200	.294	.383
2001 Durham	AAA	121	439	115	27	0	20	(-	-)	202	63	75	67	51	3	103	3	0	4			2	2	.50	11	.262	.340	.460
2002 Tacoma	AAA	99	359	98	20	1	15	(-	-)	165	52	57	57	39	2	89	5	0	2			0	1	.00	6	.273	.351	.460
2002 Seattle	AL	1	3	0	0	0	0	(0	0)	0	0	0	0	0	0	1	0	0	0			0	0	-	1	.000	.000	.000

Kelly Wunsch

Pitches: L **Bats:** L **Pos:** RP-50

Ht: 6'5" **Wt:** 225 **Born:** 7/12/72 **Age:** 30

Year Team	Lg	G	GS	CG	GF	IP	BFP	H	R	ER	HR	SH	SF	HB	TBB	IBB	SO	WP	Bk	W	L	Pct	ShO	Sv-Op	Hld	ERC	ERA
2002 Charlotte*	AAA	10	2	0	0	12.0	49	13	3	3	0	0	0	0	5	0	9	0	0	1	0	1.000	0	0--	-	4.21	2.25
2000 Chicago	AL	83	0	0	12	61.1	259	50	22	20	4	0	2	2	29	1	51	0	0	6	3	.667	0	1-5	25	3.22	2.93
2001 Chicago	AL	33	0	0	2	22.1	105	21	19	19	4	3	2	6	9	1	16	0	0	2	1	.667	0	0-2	3	5.11	7.66
2002 Chicago	AL	50	0	0	9	31.2	138	26	12	12	3	1	0	5	19	1	22	1	0	2	1	.667	0	0-1	9	4.51	3.41
3 ML YEARS		166	0	0	23	115.1	502	97	53	51	11	4	4	13	57	3	89	1	0	10	5	.667	0	1-8	37	3.92	3.98

Esteban Yan

Pitches: R **Bats:** R **Pos:** RP-55

Ht: 6'4" **Wt:** 255 **Born:** 6/22/75 **Age:** 28

Year Team	Lg	G	GS	CG	GF	IP	BFP	H	R	ER	HR	SH	SF	HB	TBB	IBB	SO	WP	Bk	W	L	Pct	ShO	Sv-Op	Hld	ERC	ERA
1996 Baltimore	AL	4	0	0	2	9.1	42	13	7	6	3	0	0	0	3	1	7	0	0	0	0	-	0	0-0	0	7.88	5.79
1997 Baltimore	AL	3	2	0	0	9.2	58	20	18	17	3	0	1	2	7	0	4	1	0	0	1	.000	0	0-0	0	15.60	15.83
1998 Tampa Bay	AL	64	0	0	18	88.2	381	78	41	38	11	1	3	5	41	2	77	6	0	5	4	.556	0	1-5	8	4.02	3.86
1999 Tampa Bay	AL	50	1	0	15	61.0	286	77	41	40	8	6	3	9	32	4	46	2	0	3	4	.429	0	0-3	7	7.13	5.90
2000 Tampa Bay	AL	43	20	0	8	137.2	618	158	98	95	26	4	6	11	42	0	111	7	1	7	8	.467	0	0-2	3	5.46	6.21
2001 Tampa Bay	AL	54	0	0	51	62.1	264	64	34	27	7	3	1	5	11	1	64	5	0	4	6	.400	0	22-31	0	3.68	3.90
2002 Tampa Bay	AL	55	0	0	47	69.0	305	70	35	33	10	2	1	3	29	1	53	5	1	7	8	.467	0	19-27	0	4.67	4.30
7 ML YEARS		273	23	0	141	437.2	1954	480	274	256	68	16	15	35	165	9	362	26	2	26	31	.456	0	42-68	18	5.23	5.26

Masato Yoshii

Pitches: R **Bats:** R **Pos:** SP-20; RP-11 **Ht:** 6'2" **Wt:** 215 **Born:** 4/20/65 **Age:** 38

			HOW MUCH HE PITCHED					WHAT HE GAVE UP										THE RESULTS						
Year Team	Lg	G	GS	CG	GF	IP	BFP	H	R	ER	HR	SH	SF	HB	TBB	IBB	SO	WP	Bk	W	L	Pct	ShO	Sv-Op	Hld	ERC	ERA
1998 New York	NL	29	29	1	0	171.2	724	166	79	75	22	9	4	6	53	5	117	5	1	6	8	.429	0	0-0	0	3.83	3.93
1999 New York	NL	31	29	1	1	174.0	723	168	86	85	25	7	6	6	58	3	105	1	0	12	8	.600	0	0-0	0	4.14	4.40
2000 Colorado	NL	29	29	0	0	167.1	726	201	112	109	32	8	7	2	53	5	88	2	1	6	15	.286	0	0-0	0	5.71	5.86
2001 Montreal	NL	42	11	0	4	113.0	493	127	65	60	18	4	3	5	26	2	63	4	0	4	7	.364	0	0-0	0	4.60	4.78
2002 Montreal	NL	31	20	1	4	131.1	553	143	66	60	15	4	5	4	32	2	74	5	0	4	9	.308	0	0-0	1	4.22	4.11
5 ML YEARS		162	118	3	9	757.1	3219	805	408	389	112	32	25	23	222	17	447	17	2	32	47	.405	0	0-0	1	4.48	4.62

Dmitri Young

Bats: B **Throws:** R **Pos:** DH-35; 1B-15; PH-2; 3B-1; LF-1 **Ht:** 6'2" **Wt:** 235 **Born:** 10/11/73 **Age:** 29

								BATTING												BASERUNNING				AVERAGES		
Year Team	Lg	G	AB	H	2B	3B	HR	(Hm	Rd)	TB	R	RBI	RC	TBB	IBB	SO	HBP	SH	SF	SB	CS	SB%	GDP	Avg	OBP	Slg
1996 St Louis	NL	16	29	7	0	0	0	(0	0)	7	3	2	2	4	0	5	1	0	0	0	1	.00	1	.241	.353	.241
1997 St Louis	NL	110	333	86	14	3	5	(2	3)	121	38	34	40	38	3	63	2	1	3	6	5	.55	8	.258	.335	.363
1998 Cincinnati	NL	144	536	166	48	1	14	(3	11)	258	81	83	88	47	4	94	2	0	5	2	4	.33	16	.310	.364	.481
1999 Cincinnati	NL	127	373	112	30	2	14	(9	5)	188	63	56	63	30	1	71	2	0	4	3	1	.75	11	.300	.352	.504
2000 Cincinnati	NL	152	548	166	37	6	18	(6	12)	269	68	88	86	36	6	80	3	1	5	0	3	.00	16	.303	.346	.491
2001 Cincinnati	NL	142	540	163	28	3	21	(8	13)	260	68	69	83	37	10	77	5	1	3	8	5	.62	22	.302	.350	.481
2002 Detroit	AL	54	201	57	14	0	7	(5	2)	92	25	27	28	12	5	39	2	0	1	2	0	1.00	12	.284	.329	.458
7 ML YEARS		745	2560	757	171	15	79	(33	46)	1195	346	359	390	204	29	429	17	3	21	21	19	.53	86	.296	.349	.467

Eric Young

Bats: R **Throws:** R **Pos:** 2B-123; PH-7; PR-7; DH-2; LF-1; RF-1 **Ht:** 5'8" **Wt:** 180 **Born:** 5/18/67 **Age:** 36

								BATTING												BASERUNNING				AVERAGES		
Year Team	Lg	G	AB	H	2B	3B	HR	(Hm	Rd)	TB	R	RBI	RC	TBB	IBB	SO	HBP	SH	SF	SB	CS	SB%	GDP	Avg	OBP	Slg
1992 Los Angeles	NL	49	132	34	1	0	1	(0	1)	38	9	11	12	8	0	9	0	4	0	6	1	.86	3	.258	.300	.288
1993 Colorado	NL	144	490	132	16	8	3	(3	0)	173	82	42	66	63	3	41	4	4	4	42	19	.69	9	.269	.355	.353
1994 Colorado	NL	90	228	62	13	1	7	(6	1)	98	37	30	40	38	1	17	2	5	2	18	7	.72	3	.272	.378	.430
1995 Colorado	NL	120	366	116	21	9	6	(5	1)	173	68	36	73	49	3	29	5	3	1	35	12	.74	4	.317	.404	.473
1996 Colorado	NL	141	568	184	23	4	8	(7	1)	239	113	74	99	47	1	31	21	2	5	53	19	.74	9	.324	.393	.421
1997 Col-LA	NL	155	622	174	33	4	8	(2	6)	247	106	61	93	71	1	54	9	10	6	45	14	.76	18	.280	.359	.397
1998 Los Angeles	NL	117	452	129	24	1	8	(7	1)	179	78	43	70	45	0	32	5	9	2	42	13	.76	4	.285	.355	.396
1999 Los Angeles	NL	119	456	128	24	2	2	(2	0)	162	73	41	65	63	0	26	5	6	4	51	22	.70	12	.281	.371	.355
2000 Chicago	NL	153	607	180	40	2	6	(5	1)	242	98	47	99	63	1	39	8	7	5	54	7	.89	12	.297	.367	.399
2001 Chicago	NL	149	603	168	43	4	6	(4	2)	237	98	42	78	42	1	45	9	15	3	31	14	.69	15	.279	.333	.393
2002 Milwaukee	NL	138	496	139	29	3	3	(2	1)	183	57	28	52	39	0	38	6	8	4	31	11	.74	14	.280	.338	.369
1997 Colorado	NL	118	468	132	29	6	6	(2	4)	191	78	45	71	57	0	37	5	8	5	32	12	.73	16	.282	.363	.408
1997 Los Angeles	NL	37	154	42	4	2	2	(0	2)	56	28	16	22	14	1	17	4	2	1	13	2	.87	2	.273	.347	.364
11 ML YEARS		1375	5020	1446	267	42	58	(43	15)	1971	819	455	747	528	11	361	74	73	36	408	139	.75	103	.288	.362	.393

Kevin Young

Bats: R **Throws:** R **Pos:** 1B-144; PH-5 **Ht:** 6'3" **Wt:** 225 **Born:** 6/16/69 **Age:** 34

								BATTING												BASERUNNING				AVERAGES		
Year Team	Lg	G	AB	H	2B	3B	HR	(Hm	Rd)	TB	R	RBI	RC	TBB	IBB	SO	HBP	SH	SF	SB	CS	SB%	GDP	Avg	OBP	Slg
1992 Pittsburgh	NL	10	7	4	0	0	0	(0	0)	4	2	4	3	2	0	0	0	0	0	1	0	1.00	0	.571	.667	.571
1993 Pittsburgh	NL	141	449	106	24	3	6	(6	0)	154	38	47	46	36	3	82	9	5	9	2	2	.50	10	.236	.300	.343
1994 Pittsburgh	NL	59	122	25	7	2	1	(1	0)	39	15	11	8	8	2	34	1	2	1	0	2	.00	3	.205	.258	.320
1995 Pittsburgh	NL	56	181	42	9	0	6	(5	1)	69	13	22	16	8	0	53	2	1	3	1	3	.25	5	.232	.268	.381
1996 Kansas City	AL	55	132	32	6	0	8	(4	4)	62	20	23	18	11	0	32	0	0	0	3	3	.50	2	.242	.301	.470
1997 Pittsburgh	NL	97	333	100	18	3	18	(11	7)	178	59	74	59	16	1	89	4	1	8	11	2	.85	6	.300	.332	.535
1998 Pittsburgh	NL	159	592	160	40	2	27	(15	12)	285	88	108	89	44	1	127	11	0	9	15	7	.68	20	.270	.328	.481
1999 Pittsburgh	NL	156	584	174	41	6	26	(16	10)	305	103	106	115	75	5	124	12	0	4	22	10	.69	13	.298	.387	.522
2000 Pittsburgh	NL	132	496	128	27	0	20	(11	9)	215	77	88	64	32	1	96	8	0	3	8	3	.73	15	.258	.311	.433
2001 Pittsburgh	NL	142	449	104	33	0	14	(7	7)	179	53	65	51	42	3	119	11	0	5	15	11	.58	17	.232	.310	.399
2002 Pittsburgh	NL	146	468	115	26	1	6	(7	9)	191	60	51	55	50	2	101	6	0	4	6	4	.60	13	.246	.322	.408
11 ML YEARS		1153	3813	990	231	17	142	(83	59)	1681	528	599	520	324	18	857	62	9	47	82	49	.63	104	.260	.324	.441

Michael Young

Bats: R **Throws:** R **Pos:** 2B-153; SS-11; 3B-4; PH-4; PR-3 **Ht:** 6'1" **Wt:** 190 **Born:** 10/19/76 **Age:** 26

								BATTING												BASERUNNING				AVERAGES		
Year Team	Lg	G	AB	H	2B	3B	HR	(Hm	Rd)	TB	R	RBI	RC	TBB	IBB	SO	HBP	SH	SF	SB	CS	SB%	GDP	Avg	OBP	Slg
2000 Texas	AL	2	2	0	0	0	0	(0	0)	0	0	0	0	0	0	1	0	0	0	0	0	-	0	.000	.000	.000
2001 Texas	AL	106	386	96	18	4	11	(7	4)	155	57	49	45	26	0	91	3	9	5	3	1	.75	9	.249	.298	.402
2002 Texas	AL	156	573	150	26	8	9	(3	6)	219	77	62	62	41	1	112	0	13	6	6	7	.46	14	.262	.308	.382
3 ML YEARS		264	961	246	44	12	20	(10	10)	374	134	111	107	67	1	204	3	22	11	9	8	.53	23	.256	.303	.389

Carlos Zambrano

Pitches: R **Bats:** B **Pos:** SP-16; RP-16 **Ht:** 6'5" **Wt:** 250 **Born:** 6/1/81 **Age:** 22

			HOW MUCH HE PITCHED					WHAT HE GAVE UP											THE RESULTS							
Year Team	Lg	G	GS	CG	GF	IP	BFP	H	R	ER	HR	SH	SF	HB	TBB	IBB	SO	WP	Bk	W	L	Pct	ShO	Sv-Op	Hld	ERC	ERA
1998 Cubs	R	14	2	0	4	40.0	177	39	17	14	0	0	0	0	25	3	36	3	1	1	0	.000	0	1--	0	3.99	3.15
1999 Lansing	A	27	24	2	2	153.1	663	150	87	71	9	5	4	10	62	1	98	10	2	13	7	.650	1	0--	0	3.95	4.17
2000 W Tennesse	AA	9	9	0	0	60.1	241	39	14	9	2	1	0	3	21	0	43	4	0	3	1	.750	0	0--	0	1.85	1.34
2000 Iowa	AAA	34	0	0	17	56.2	259	54	30	25	3	5	4	2	40	2	46	3	0	2	5	.286	0	6--	0	4.74	3.97
2001 Iowa	AAA	26	25	1	1	150.2	639	124	73	65	9	5	3	14	68	1	155	10	1	10	5	.667	0	0--	0	3.40	3.88
2002 Iowa	AAA	3	3	0	0	9.0	35	2	0	0	0	0	0	0	6	0	11	0	0	0	0	-	0	0--	0	0.96	0.00

Year Team		Lg	G	GS	CG	GF	IP	BFP	H	R	ER	HR	SH	SF	HB	TBB	IBB	SO	WP	Bk	W	L	Pct	ShO	Sv-Op	Hld	ERC	ERA
2001 Chicago		NL	6	1	0	1	7.2	42	11	13	13	2	1	1	1	8	0	4	1	0	1	2	.333	0	0-1	0	11.86	15.26
2002 Chicago		NL	32	16	0	3	108.1	477	94	53	44	9	9	1	4	63	2	93	6	0	4	8	.333	0	0-0	0	4.02	3.66
2 ML YEARS			38	17	0	4	116.0	519	105	66	57	11	10	2	5	71	2	97	7	0	5	10	.333	0	0-1	0	4.46	4.42

Victor Zambrano

Pitches: R **Bats:** R **Pos:** RP-31; SP-11

Ht: 6'0" Wt: 203 Born: 8/6/75 Age: 27

Year Team		Lg	G	GS	CG	GF	IP	BFP	H	R	ER	HR	SH	SF	HB	TBB	IBB	SO	WP	Bk	W	L	Pct	ShO	Sv-Op	Hld	ERC	ERA
1996 Devil Rays		R	1	0	0	3.1	16.0	4	4	3	0	0	0	0	0	0	0	6	0	0	0	0	-	0	0--	-	1.95	0.00
1997 Devil Rays		R	2	0	0	0	3.0	10	1	0	0	0	0	0	0	0	0	2	0	0	0	0	-	0	0--	-	0.25	0.00
1997 Princeton		R+	20	0	0	60	29.2	126	18	13	6	1	0	0	4	9	1	36	2	1	0	2	.000	0	0--	-	1.64	1.82
1998 Chrlstn - SC		A	48	2	0	15	77.1	330	72	32	29	5	5	0	12	20	1	89	7	1	6	4	.600	0	0--	-	3.47	3.38
1999 St.Pete		A+	7	0	0	1	9.0	43	10	5	4	1	0	1	1	5	0	15	1	0	2	0	.000	0	0--	-	5.76	4.00
1999 Orlando		AA	40	4	0	12	82.1	379	92	55	42	5	1	2	9	38	2	81	6	1	7	2	.778	0	1--	-	5.06	4.59
2000 Durham		AAA	53	0	0	27	62.2	290	72	38	35	9	4	0	4	29	2	55	6	0	0	6	.000	0	5--	-	5.67	5.03
2001 Durham		AAA	29	0	0	27	30.1	126	26	10	7	2	0	1	1	12	1	29	4	0	1	2	.333	0	12--	-	3.17	2.08
2002 Durham		AAA	10	0	0	6	14.0	55	9	4	3	2	0	0	1	4	0	15	0	0	1	0	.000	0	1--	-	2.34	1.93
2001 Tampa Bay		AL	36	0	0	19	51.1	212	38	21	18	6	2	0	3	18	0	58	4	0	6	2	.750	0	2-6	5	2.80	3.16
2002 Tampa Bay		AL	42	11	0	11	114.0	519	120	77	70	15	7	8	4	68	5	73	10	0	8	8	.500	0	1-3	6	5.52	5.53
2 ML YEARS			78	11	0	30	165.1	731	158	98	88	21	9	8	7	86	5	131	14	0	14	10	.583	0	3-9	11	4.62	4.79

Gregg Zaun

Bats: B **Throws:** R **Pos:** C-44; PH-34

Ht: 5'10" Wt: 190 Born: 4/14/71 Age: 32

Year Team		Lg	G	AB	H	2B	3B	HR	(Hm	Rd)	TB	R	RBI	RC	TBB	IBB	SO	HBP	SH	SF	SB	CS	SB%	GDP	Avg	OBP	Slg
1995 Baltimore		AL	40	104	27	5	0	3	(1	2)	41	18	14	15	16	0	14	0	2	0	1	1	.50	2	.260	.358	.394
1996 Bal-Fla			60	139	34	9	1	2	(1	1)	51	20	15	16	14	3	20	2	1	2	1	0	1.00	5	.245	.318	.367
1997 Florida		NL	58	143	43	10	2	2	(0	2)	63	21	20	27	26	4	18	2	1	0	1	0	1.00	1	.301	.415	.441
1998 Florida		NL	106	298	56	12	2	5	(2	3)	87	19	29	23	35	2	52	1	2	2	5	2	.71	7	.188	.274	.292
1999 Texas		AL	43	93	23	2	1	1	(0	1)	30	12	12	10	10	0	7	0	1	2	1	0	1.00	4	.247	.314	.323
2000 Kansas City		AL	83	234	64	11	0	7	(2	5)	96	36	33	40	43	3	34	3	0	2	7	3	.70	4	.274	.390	.410
2001 Kansas City		AL	39	125	40	9	0	6	(1	5)	67	15	18	24	12	0	16	0	0	1	1	2	.33	2	.320	.377	.536
2002 Houston		NL	76	185	41	7	1	3	(3	0)	59	18	24	16	12	1	36	2	2	1	1	0	1.00	4	.222	.275	.319
1996 Baltimore		AL	50	108	25	8	1	1	(1	0)	38	16	13	12	11	2	15	2	0	2	0	0	-	3	.231	.309	.352
1996 Florida		NL	10	31	9	1	0	1	(0	1)	13	4	2	4	3	1	5	0	1	0	1	0	1.00	1	.290	.353	.419
8 ML YEARS			505	1321	328	65	7	29	(10	19)	494	159	165	171	168	13	197	10	9	10	18	8	.69	29	.248	.335	.374

Todd Zeile

Bats: R **Throws:** R **Pos:** 3B-139; PH-4

Ht: 6'1" Wt: 200 Born: 9/9/65 Age: 37

Year Team		Lg	G	AB	H	2B	3B	HR	(Hm	Rd)	TB	R	RBI	RC	TBB	IBB	SO	HBP	SH	SF	SB	CS	SB%	GDP	Avg	OBP	Slg
1989 St Louis		NL	28	82	21	3	1	1	(0	1)	29	7	8	10	9	1	14	0	1	1	0	0	-	1	.256	.326	.354
1990 St Louis		NL	144	495	121	25	3	15	(8	7)	197	62	57	66	67	3	77	2	0	6	2	4	.33	11	.244	.333	.398
1991 St Louis		NL	155	565	158	36	3	11	(7	4)	233	76	81	81	62	3	94	5	0	6	17	11	.61	15	.280	.353	.412
1992 St Louis		NL	126	439	113	18	4	7	(4	3)	160	51	48	56	68	4	70	0	0	7	7	10	.41	11	.257	.352	.364
1993 St Louis		NL	157	571	158	36	1	17	(8	9)	247	82	103	86	70	5	76	0	0	6	5	4	.56	15	.277	.352	.433
1994 St Louis		NL	113	415	111	25	1	19	(9	10)	195	62	75	66	52	3	56	3	0	7	1	3	.25	13	.267	.348	.470
1995 Stl-ChC		NL	113	426	105	22	0	14	(8	6)	169	50	52	50	34	1	76	4	4	5	1	0	1.00	13	.246	.305	.397
1996 Phi-Bal			163	617	162	32	0	25	(10	15)	269	78	99	92	82	4	104	1	0	4	1	1	.50	18	.263	.348	.436
1997 Los Angeles		NL	160	575	154	17	0	31	(17	14)	264	89	90	94	85	7	112	6	0	6	8	7	.53	18	.268	.365	.459
1998 LA-Fla-Tex			158	572	155	32	3	19	(7	12)	250	85	94	87	69	2	90	4	1	7	4	4	.50	12	.271	.350	.437
1999 Texas		AL	156	588	172	41	1	24	(13	11)	287	80	98	96	56	3	94	4	1	7	1	2	.33	20	.293	.354	.488
2000 New York		NL	153	544	146	36	3	22	(8	14)	254	67	79	88	74	4	85	2	0	3	3	4	.43	15	.268	.356	.467
2001 New York		NL	151	531	141	25	1	10	(4	6)	198	66	62	72	73	3	102	6	0	2	1	0	1.00	16	.266	.359	.373
2002 Colorado		NL	144	506	138	23	0	18	(11	7)	215	61	87	76	66	3	92	1	0	7	1	1	.50	27	.273	.353	.425
1995 St Louis		NL	34	127	37	6	0	5	(2	3)	58	16	22	23	18	1	23	1	0	2	1	0	1.00	2	.291	.378	.457
1995 Chicago		NL	79	299	68	16	0	9	(6	3)	111	34	30	27	16	0	53	3	4	3	0	0	-	11	.227	.271	.371
1996 Philadelphia		NL	134	500	134	24	0	20	(9	11)	218	61	80	75	67	4	88	1	0	4	1	1	.50	16	.268	.353	.436
1996 Baltimore		AL	29	117	28	8	0	5	(1	4)	51	17	19	17	15	0	16	0	0	0	0	0	-	2	.239	.326	.436
1998 Los Angeles		NL	40	158	40	6	1	7	(1	6)	69	22	27	19	10	0	24	1	0	1	1	1	.50	5	.253	.300	.437
1998 Florida		NL	66	234	68	12	1	6	(2	4)	100	37	39	38	31	2	34	2	0	3	2	3	.40	4	.291	.374	.427
1998 Texas		AL	52	180	47	14	1	6	(4	2)	81	26	28	30	28	0	32	1	1	3	1	0	1.00	3	.261	.358	.450
14 ML YEARS			1921	6926	1855	371	21	233	(114	119)	2967	916	1033	1020	867	46	1142	38	7	74	52	51	.50	204	.268	.349	.428

Chad Zerbe

Pitches: L **Bats:** L **Pos:** RP-50

Ht: 6'0" Wt: 200 Born: 4/27/72 Age: 31

Year Team		Lg	G	GS	CG	GF	IP	BFP	H	R	ER	HR	SH	SF	HB	TBB	IBB	SO	WP	Bk	W	L	Pct	ShO	Sv-Op	Hld	ERC	ERA
2002 Fresno*		AAA	3	3	0	0	10.1	42	8	0	0	0	1	0	1	3	0	5	0	0	0	0	-	0	0--	-	2.22	0.00
2000 San Francisco		NL	4	0	0	2	6.0	24	6	3	3	1	1	0	1	3	0	5	0	0	0	0	-	0	0-0	0	3.69	4.50
2001 San Francisco		NL	27	1	0	9	39.0	162	41	21	17	3	3	2	1	10	0	22	2	0	3	0	1.000	0	0-0	0	3.83	3.92
2002 San Francisco		NL	50	0	0	16	56.1	240	52	22	19	3	4	1	4	21	2	26	1	0	2	0	1.000	0	0-1	5	3.45	3.04
3 ML YEARS			81	1	0	27	101.1	426	99	46	39	7	8	3	5	32	2	53	3	0	5	0	1.000	0	0-1	5	3.62	3.46

Alan Zinter

Bats: B **Throws:** R **Pos:** PH-34; 1B-7; C-1   **Ht:** 6'2" **Wt:** 200 **Born:** 5/19/68 **Age:** 35

					BATTING																BASERUNNING				AVERAGES		
Year	Team	Lg	G	AB	H	2B	3B	HR	(Hm	Rd)	TB	R	RBI	RC	TBB	IBB	SO	HBP	SH	SF	SB	CS	SB%	GDP	Avg	OBP	Slg
1989	Pittsfield	A-	12	41	15	2	1	2	(-	-)	25	11	12	12	12	0	4	0	0	1	0	1	.00	0	.366	.500	.610
1989	St.Lucie	A+	48	159	38	10	0	3	(-	-)	57	17	32	17	18	2	31	1	1	5	0	1	.00	5	.239	.311	.358
1990	St.Lucie	A+	98	333	97	19	6	7	(-	-)	149	63	63	59	54	1	70	1	0	6	8	1	.89	10	.291	.386	.447
1990	Jackson	AA	6	20	4	1	0	0	(-	-)	5	2	1	1	3	0	11	0	0	0	1	0	1.00	1	.200	.304	.250
1991	Williamsport	AA	124	422	93	13	6	9	(-	-)	145	44	54	46	59	1	106	3	2	2	3	3	.50	10	.220	.319	.344
1992	Binghamton	AA	128	431	96	13	5	16	(-	-)	167	63	50	58	70	5	117	4	0	0	0	0	-	7	.223	.337	.387
1993	Binghamton	AA	134	432	113	24	4	24	(-	-)	217	68	87	87	90	7	105	1	0	5	1	0	1.00	4	.262	.386	.502
1994	Toledo	AAA	134	471	112	29	5	21	(-	-)	214	66	58	76	69	4	185	7	0	0	13	5	.72	3	.238	.344	.454
1995	Toledo	AAA	101	334	74	15	4	13	(-	-)	136	42	48	41	36	1	102	2	2	5	4	1	.80	5	.222	.297	.407
1996	Pawtucket	AAA	108	357	96	19	5	26	(-	-)	203	78	69	76	58	2	123	4	0	5	5	1	.83	3	.269	.373	.569
1997	Tacoma	AAA	110	404	116	19	4	20	(-	-)	203	69	70	78	64	9	113	3	1	1	3	1	.75	7	.287	.388	.502
1998	Iowa	AAA	129	419	130	23	1	23	(-	-)	224	82	81	89	75	1	116	3	0	3	3	5	.38	10	.310	.416	.535
1999	Iowa	AAA	14	51	13	2	0	3	(-	-)	24	7	8	8	5	0	13	0	0	0	0	0	-	0	.255	.321	.471
2000	Iowa	AAA	90	233	53	12	2	14	(-	-)	111	27	35	39	39	2	78	2	0	3	0	0	-	3	.227	.339	.476
2000	Tucson	AAA	11	36	13	5	1	1	(-	-)	23	9	5	10	8	1	8	0	0	0	0	0	-	1	.361	.477	.639
2001	New Orleans	AAA	104	332	88	16	0	19	(-	-)	161	58	65	50	33	1	85	3	0	3	1	1	.50	13	.265	.334	.485
2002	New Orleans	AAA	63	225	52	14	0	11	(-	-)	99	30	39	30	22	0	64	0	0	1	2	0	1.00	3	.231	.298	.440
2002	Houston	NL	39	44	6	2	0	2	(0	2)	14	5	3	2	0	0	19	0	0	0	0	0	-	0	.136	.136	.318

Barry Zito

Pitches: L **Bats:** L **Pos:** SP-35   **Ht:** 6'4" **Wt:** 215 **Born:** 5/13/78 **Age:** 25

			HOW MUCH HE PITCHED						WHAT HE GAVE UP												THE RESULTS					
Year	Team	Lg	G	GS	CG	GF	IP	BFP	H	R	ER	HR	SH	SF	HB	TBB	IBB	SO	WP	Bk	W	L	Pct	ShO	Sv-Op	Hld	ERC	ERA
2000	Oakland	AL	14	14	1	0	92.2	376	64	30	28	6	1	0	2	45	2	78	2	0	7	4	.636	1	0-0	0	2.63	2.72
2001	Oakland	AL	35	35	3	0	214.1	902	184	92	83	18	5	4	13	80	0	205	6	1	17	8	.680	2	0-0	0	3.33	3.49
2002	Oakland	AL	35	35	1	0	229.1	939	182	79	70	24	9	7	9	78	2	182	2	1	23	5	.821	0	0-0	0	2.92	2.75
	3 ML YEARS		84	84	5	0	536.1	2217	430	201	181	48	15	11	24	203	4	465	10	2	47	17	.734	3	0-0	0	3.03	3.04

2002 Fielding Statistics

Due to our late release date, we were able to include official fielding statistics in this edition. In the future, this book will be out much sooner when therefore only unofficial fielding statistics are available.

SBA is Total Stolen Bases Attempted.
CS is Total Caught Stealing.
PCS is Number of the Total Caught Stealing attributed to the pitcher, not the catcher in question.
CS% is the percentage of runners caught stealing not including PCS.

In other words, the formula for CS% is:

$$\frac{(CS - PCS)}{(SBA - PCS)}$$

You will find many of our catcher ERAs (CERA - which, like pitcher ERAs, tracks runs each catcher "gave up" while he was behind the plate) to be different from other sources. However, we have solid statistical reasons to believe ours are the most accurate catcher ERAs available.

First Basemen - Regulars

Player	Tm	G	GS	Inn	PO	A	E	DP	Pct.	Rng
Spiezio,Scott	Ana	143	125	1106.1	1078	59	3	101	.997	-
Karros,Eric	LA	142	141	1191.0	1175	106	4	101	.997	-
Pena,Carlos	TOT	113	111	977.2	1010	71	4	96	.996	-
Martinez,Tino	Stl	149	141	1218.0	1220	86	5	119	.996	-
Olerud,John	Sea	152	150	1317.2	1169	101	5	122	.996	-
Mientkiewicz,D	Min	143	132	1177.1	1073	69	5	92	.996	-
Lee,Travis	Phi	148	130	1231.0	1262	75	6	120	.996	-
Helton,Todd	Col	156	155	1342.0	1357	113	7	138	.995	-
Giambi,Jason	NYY	92	92	781.2	761	35	4	53	.995	-
Bagwell,Jeff	Hou	153	153	1348.0	1254	112	7	119	.995	-
Sexson,Richie	Mil	154	153	1325.1	1224	119	7	134	.995	-
Hatteberg,S	Oak	91	88	721.1	768	74	5	77	.994	-
Palmeiro,R	Tex	97	95	836.1	739	84	5	83	.994	-
Konerko,Paul	CWS	140	140	1201.0	1146	75	8	113	.993	-
McGriff,Fred	ChC	137	136	1149.1	1005	60	7	84	.993	-
Snow,J.T.	SF	135	111	1015.0	939	79	7	104	.993	-
Casey,Sean	Cin	108	106	935.0	927	70	7	93	.993	-
Klesko,Ryan	SD	112	111	967.2	918	73	7	92	.993	-
Cox,Steve	TB	110	110	967.2	852	85	7	101	.993	-
Lee,Derrek	Fla	162	161	1441.1	1312	121	12	138	.992	-
Clark,Tony	Bos	85	70	638.0	653	58	6	54	.992	-
Thome,Jim	Cle	128	128	1109.1	1063	75	10	118	.991	-
Stevens,Lee	TOT	83	77	682.0	728	55	7	66	.991	-
Delgado,Carlos	Tor	140	140	1229.0	1232	95	12	121	.991	-
Young,Kevin	Pit	144	127	1130.2	1277	89	13	119	.991	-
Sweeney,Mike	KC	102	101	872.0	838	105	9	94	.991	-
Conine,Jeff	Bal	103	102	917.2	947	58	10	99	.990	-
Grace,Mark	Ari	98	70	682.0	649	34	7	58	.990	-
Franco,Julio	Atl	95	70	696.0	717	59	8	79	.990	-
Vaughn,Mo	NYM	134	131	1124.2	1085	47	18	95	.984	-
Galarraga,A	Mon	89	72	664.2	629	59	11	55	.981	-

First Basemen - The Rest

Player	Tm	G	GS	Inn	PO	A	E	DP	Pct.	Rng
Alcantara,Izzy	Mil	2	1	13.0	13	0	1	1	.929	-
Alicea,Luis	KC	2	0	5.0	8	0	0	0	1.000	-
Andrews,Shane	Bos	2	1	12.0	6	1	0	1	1.000	-
Banks,Brian	Fla	1	0	2.0	2	0	1	1	.667	-
Barajas,Rod	Ari	1	0	2.1	2	0	0	0	1.000	-
Barker,Kevin	SD	6	5	45.1	49	1	0	5	1.000	-
Barrett,M	Mon	6	2	21.2	27	1	0	4	1.000	-
Bell,David	SF	2	2	15.0	13	4	0	2	1.000	-
Bell,Jay	Ari	5	3	25.0	16	0	0	0	1.000	-
Bellhorn,Mark	ChC	22	7	88.0	90	3	1	10	.989	-
Bellinger,Clay	Ana	2	0	3.0	2	0	0	0	1.000	-
Benjamin,Mike	Pit	1	0	4.0	4	0	0	1	1.000	-
Berg,Dave	Tor	10	7	66.1	61	2	1	5	.984	-
Berger,Brandon	KC	1	0	1.0	1	0	0	0	1.000	-
Blake,Casey	Min	3	0	9.1	12	0	0	0	1.000	-
Blum,Geoff	Hou	1	0	2.0	1	0	0	1	1.000	-
Branyan,R	Cin	18	18	161.2	170	14	1	23	.995	-
Broussard,Ben	Cle	4	3	28.2	27	1	0	2	1.000	-
Buchanan,Brian	SD	15	7	73.2	74	6	0	6	1.000	-
Cairo,Miguel	Stl	4	1	10.0	10	0	0	0	1.000	-
Castro,Juan	Cin	1	0	1.0	0	1	0	0	1.000	-
Catalanotto,F	Tex	15	9	85.2	87	5	0	6	1.000	-
Choi,Hee Seop	ChC	22	12	125.2	106	8	2	16	.983	-
Cirillo,Jeff	Sea	11	4	44.1	32	7	0	2	1.000	-
Clark,Howie	Bal	1	1	8.0	7	0	0	2	1.000	-
Colbrunn,Greg	Ari	40	36	267.2	260	12	2	16	.993	-
Coomer,Ron	NYY	11	6	59.0	60	6	1	5	.985	-
Cordero,Wil	Cle	1	0	2.0	1	0	0	0	1.000	-
Cordero,Wil	Mon	10	8	63.0	66	5	0	6	1.000	-
Cruz,Deivi	SD	1	0	2.0	4	0	0	0	1.000	-
Cruz,Ivan	Stl	7	0	14.0	12	1	0	0	1.000	-
Cruz,Jacob	Det	4	2	24.0	26	2	0	1	1.000	-
Cuddyer,Mike	Min	6	5	38.0	28	5	0	0	1.000	-
Daubach,Brian	Bos	60	54	455.2	443	30	5	37	.990	-
Davis,Ben	Sea	2	0	6.0	8	0	0	0	1.000	-
Diaz,Juan	Bos	1	1	6.0	8	0	0	0	1.000	-
Donnels,Chris	Ari	1	0	1.0	1	0	0	0	1.000	-
Dunn,Adam	Cin	44	37	352.0	360	22	6	30	.985	-
Dunston,Shawon	SF	1	1	7.0	6	0	0	0	1.000	-

Player	Tm	G	GS	Inn	PO	A	E	DP	Pct.	Rng
Durazo,Erubiel	Ari	56	53	468.2	409	26	7	29	.984	-
Echevarria,A	ChC	13	7	77.1	61	4	1	12	.985	-
Erstad,Darin	Ana	5	0	8.2	9	0	0	2	1.000	-
Franco,Matt	Atl	51	49	382.2	353	30	4	31	.990	-
Fullmer,Brad	Ana	29	27	210.1	176	8	1	22	.995	-
Giambi,Jeremy	Phi	21	21	142.2	169	8	2	16	.989	-
Gibbons,Jay	Bal	30	28	243.0	208	17	1	26	.996	-
Gil,Benji	Ana	10	5	40.2	33	3	1	6	.973	-
Gload,Ross	Col	4	2	20.2	20	3	0	1	1.000	-
Greene,Todd	Tex	15	10	86.1	92	13	2	11	.981	-
Greer,Rusty	Tex	1	1	8.0	8	0	0	0	1.000	-
Hafner,Travis	Tex	3	3	22.0	7	3	1	0	.909	-
Halter,Shane	Det	1	0	5.0	8	1	0	0	1.000	-
Hansen,Dave	LA	27	7	86.0	76	5	0	3	1.000	-
Harris,Lenny	Mil	12	5	66.0	49	7	0	1	1.000	-
Hart,Jason	Tex	2	0	2.0	2	0	0	0	1.000	-
Helms,Wes	Atl	45	31	293.0	285	27	4	34	.987	-
Hocking,Denny	Min	6	0	10.0	9	0	0	0	1.000	-
Hollins,Dave	Phi	5	5	30.0	37	1	0	3	1.000	-
Houston,Tyler	Mil	1	0	2.0	4	0	0	0	1.000	-
Houston,Tyler	LA	12	9	89.0	98	3	2	9	.981	-
Huff,Aubrey	TB	45	45	402.2	354	21	5	41	.987	-
Hyzdu,Adam	Pit	1	0	1.1	3	0	0	0	1.000	-
Ibanez,Raul	KC	49	45	406.0	362	30	2	36	.995	-
Johnson,Mark P	NYM	15	10	87.2	84	6	1	7	.989	-
Johnson,Nick	NYY	78	59	550.2	519	44	7	46	.988	-
Kapler,Gabe	Tex	1	0	1.0	1	0	0	0	1.000	-
Kent,Jeff	SF	9	9	66.2	55	2	0	7	1.000	-
Kielty,Bobby	Min	5	4	35.0	27	2	0	4	1.000	-
Kinkade,Mike	LA	11	3	46.0	39	4	0	3	1.000	-
Lamb,Mike	Tex	52	38	335.1	358	28	5	36	.987	-
Larson,Brandon	Cin	2	0	4.0	5	0	0	1	1.000	-
LeCroy,Matt	Min	8	5	45.0	39	1	1	8	.976	-
Leon,Jose	Bal	17	13	122.1	135	9	0	15	1.000	-
Lesher,Brian	Tor	12	4	42.0	34	4	0	1	1.000	-
Liefer,Jeff	CWS	31	18	191.0	187	10	2	23	.990	-
Lo Duca,Paul	LA	18	2	45.2	45	1	1	3	.979	-
Lopez,Luis	Bal	1	0	5.0	5	0	0	0	1.000	-
Loretta,Mark	Mil	5	2	21.0	20	1	0	2	1.000	-
Mabry,John	Phi	1	1	7.0	6	1	0	0	1.000	-
Mabry,John	Oak	50	7	133.2	136	14	0	10	1.000	-
Machado,Robert	ChC	1	0	1.0	0	0	0	0	-	-
Machado,Robert	Mil	2	0	5.0	8	1	0	1	1.000	-
Marrero,Eli	Stl	4	0	11.1	13	0	0	2	1.000	-
Martinez,Ramon	SF	4	4	31.0	30	3	0	3	1.000	-
Matheny,Mike	Stl	1	0	1.0	1	0	0	1	1.000	-
Matos,Julius	SD	2	0	2.0	3	0	0	0	1.000	-
McCarty,Dave	KC	9	8	68.0	66	5	0	5	1.000	-
McEwing,Joe	NYM	20	2	50.1	45	4	0	5	1.000	-
McGuire,Ryan	Bal	7	4	37.2	36	3	0	4	1.000	-
Merced,Orlando	Hou	7	6	54.0	53	3	0	8	1.000	-
Merloni,Lou	Bos	3	0	3.0	1	0	0	0	1.000	-
Millar,Kevin	Fla	2	1	6.0	6	1	0	0	1.000	-
Minor,Damon	SF	44	35	302.2	310	20	1	29	.997	-
Mordecai,Mike	Mon	3	2	18.0	20	2	0	1	1.000	-
Mordecai,Mike	Fla	1	0	3.0	1	0	0	0	1.000	-
Munson,Eric	Det	4	4	34.0	29	3	1	3	.970	-
Nevin,Phil	SD	36	36	295.0	269	22	4	30	.986	-
Nieves,Jose	Ana	3	0	16.1	16	1	0	3	1.000	-
Norton,Greg	Col	15	5	64.0	55	3	0	5	1.000	-
Offerman,Jose	Bos	41	36	331.1	309	29	2	35	.994	-
Offerman,Jose	Sea	11	7	63.1	56	8	0	3	1.000	-
Ortiz,David	Min	15	13	103.0	90	6	1	8	.990	-
Osik,Keith	Pit	3	0	8.2	7	2	0	1	1.000	-
Paquette,Craig	Det	14	11	98.1	96	9	1	5	.991	-
Pelaez,Alex	SD	1	1	9.0	12	1	0	3	1.000	-
Pellow,Kit	KC	10	3	39.1	36	3	0	5	1.000	-
Pena,Carlos	Oak	40	39	339.0	351	42	1	25	.997	-
Pena,Carlos	Det	73	72	638.2	659	29	3	71	.996	-
Perez,Eduardo	Stl	10	4	48.0	52	1	0	5	1.000	-
Perez,Tomas	Phi	3	2	16.0	10	0	0	1	1.000	-
Perry,Chan	KC	5	3	26.2	35	2	0	2	1.000	-
Perry,Herbert	Tex	12	6	63.0	55	7	0	6	1.000	-
Phelps,Josh	Tor	2	1	9.0	9	0	0	1	1.000	-
Piatt,Adam	Oak	1	0	3.0	4	0	0	1	1.000	-
Pratt,Todd	Phi	2	2	18.0	19	1	0	1	1.000	-
Pujols,Albert	Stl	21	16	144.0	140	13	1	24	.994	-
Redmond,Mike	Fla	2	0	4.0	4	0	0	0	1.000	-
Richard,Chris	Bal	9	7	60.0	63	3	0	0	1.000	-

Player	Tm	G	GS	Inn	PO	A	E	DP	Pct.	Rng
Saenz,Olmedo	Oak	34	23	204.0	190	12	0	17	1.000	-
Sandberg,Jared	TB	3	3	26.0	23	2	1	4	.962	-
Sears,Todd	Min	6	2	27.0	26	2	0	3	1.000	-
Segui,David	Bal	7	7	57.0	61	5	0	12	1.000	-
Simon,Randall	Det	59	57	490.2	541	27	7	48	.988	-
Smith,Bobby	TB	6	3	44.0	47	6	1	4	.981	-
Snyder,Earl	Cle	12	10	92.2	98	8	2	3	.981	-
Stevens,Lee	Mon	58	56	490.0	512	47	4	47	.993	-
Stevens,Lee	Cle	25	21	192.0	216	8	3	19	.987	-
Surhoff,B.J.	Atl	11	11	95.2	72	7	0	12	1.000	-
Sutton,Larry	Oak	6	2	25.0	29	0	0	0	1.000	-
Sweeney,Mark	SD	11	2	41.2	32	3	2	5	.946	-
Tarasco,Tony	NYM	7	0	10.0	11	0	0	0	1.000	-
Thomas,Frank	CWS	4	4	31.0	38	4	2	5	.955	-
Truby,Chris	Mon	2	1	7.0	10	0	0	2	1.000	-
Tucker,Michael	KC	5	2	23.0	22	3	1	2	.962	-
Valent,Eric	Phi	1	0	5.0	3	0	1	2	.750	-
Valentin,John	NYM	22	11	104.0	106	6	3	12	.974	-
Vander Wal,J	NYY	6	4	40.0	32	0	0	3	1.000	-
Velarde,Randy	Oak	5	3	26.0	25	0	1	2	.962	-
Ventura,Robin	NYY	5	0	20.2	19	2	0	1	1.000	-
Vizcaino,Jose	Hou	5	1	14.0	10	1	0	2	1.000	-
Wigginton,Ty	NYM	13	7	64.0	56	5	0	4	1.000	-
Wilkerson,Brad	Mon	23	21	188.2	179	15	0	25	1.000	-
Wilson,Craig	Pit	42	34	268.0	277	21	3	35	.990	-
Wilson,Dan	Sea	4	1	14.0	17	1	0	0	1.000	-
Wilson,Tom	Tor	11	9	82.0	79	2	0	12	1.000	-
Wilson,Vance	NYM	1	0	2.0	2	0	0	0	1.000	-
Woodward,Chris	Tor	3	1	10.0	9	0	0	1	1.000	-
Wooten,Shawn	Ana	16	5	67.0	62	4	0	3	1.000	-
Young,Dmitri	Det	15	15	123.1	117	16	4	5	.971	-
Zinter,Alan	Hou	8	2	27.0	24	2	0	3	1.000	-

Second Basemen - Regulars

Player	Tm	G	GS	Inn	PO	A	E	DP	Pct.	Rng
Reese,Pokey	Pit	117	116	991.1	283	363	8	84	.988	5.86
Easley,Damion	Det	84	84	731.1	181	253	9	54	.980	5.34
Vidro,Jose	Mon	152	151	1323.0	314	448	11	93	.986	5.18
Kennedy,Adam	Ana	139	123	1112.0	273	367	11	90	.983	5.18
Lockhart,Keith	Atl	89	72	646.2	141	230	8	46	.979	5.16
Durham,Ray	TOT	103	103	884.2	209	298	17	73	.968	5.16
Hairston Jr.,J	Bal	119	118	1043.2	232	365	11	75	.982	5.15
Young,Michael	Tex	152	144	1258.0	298	420	9	97	.988	5.13
Walker,Todd	Cin	154	150	1319.1	314	438	8	93	.989	5.13
Abernathy,B	TB	116	115	1016.0	253	316	12	85	.979	5.05
Kent,Jeff	SF	149	142	1259.1	293	411	16	113	.978	5.03
Gutierrez,R	Cle	93	92	797.1	167	277	11	66	.976	5.01
Young,Eric	Mil	123	120	1034.1	249	323	12	79	.979	4.98
Febles,Carlos	KC	116	103	918.0	193	312	15	76	.971	4.95
Ellis,Mark	Oak	85	83	732.2	170	232	9	48	.978	4.94
Anderson,Mar	Phi	143	140	1198.2	272	382	20	90	.970	4.91
Biggio,Craig	Hou	142	140	1236.2	313	352	8	88	.988	4.84
Spivey,Junior	Ari	143	138	1230.2	288	358	15	64	.977	4.72
Castillo,Luis	Fla	144	143	1257.2	269	391	13	93	.981	4.72
Vina,Fernando	Stl	150	149	1312.1	287	401	13	104	.981	4.72
Sanchez,Rey	Bos	100	97	817.2	151	272	4	61	.991	4.66
Soriano,A	NYY	155	154	1388.0	300	402	23	86	.968	4.55
Grudzielanek,M	LA	147	145	1226.1	253	366	7	76	.989	4.54
Alomar,Roberto	NYM	147	146	1265.2	273	348	11	94	.983	4.42
Boone,Bret	Sea	153	154	1317.1	251	387	7	84	.989	4.36
Rivas,Luis	Min	93	91	811.1	147	205	5	51	.986	3.90

Second Basemen - The Rest

Player	Tm	G	GS	Inn	PO	A	E	DP	Pct.	Rng
Alicea,Luis	KC	32	23	202.0	56	90	2	21	.986	6.50
Baerga,Carlos	Bos	17	10	88.0	25	32	1	4	.983	5.83
Bell,David	SF	12	10	87.0	21	29	3	6	.943	5.17
Bell,Jay	Ari	2	0	3.1	1	2	0	0	1.000	8.10
Bellhorn,Mark	ChC	77	63	569.2	121	175	6	42	.980	4.68
Belliard,R	Mil	49	40	380.0	86	106	5	27	.975	4.55
Benjamin,Mike	Pit	11	7	72.1	23	23	0	6	1.000	5.72
Berg,Dave	Tor	52	43	378.1	71	126	7	34	.966	4.69
Bloomquist,W	Sea	4	2	27.0	5	10	0	1	1.000	5.00
Blum,Geoff	Hou	1	0	5.0	2	2	0	0	1.000	7.20

Player	Tm	G	GS	Inn	PO	A	E	DP	Pct.	Rng
Bocachica,H	Det	2	1	8.0	1	4	0	0	1.000	5.63
Burroughs,Sean	SD	13	11	77.1	26	23	1	8	.980	5.70
Bush,Homer	Tor	22	21	182.0	38	58	1	12	.990	4.75
Bush,Homer	Fla	12	6	67.2	11	14	1	2	.962	3.33
Butler,Brent	Col	72	67	570.1	121	178	8	46	.974	4.72
Cabrera,Jol	Cle	3	2	18.0	3	7	0	2	1.000	5.00
Cabrera,Jol	LA	1	1	7.0	2	1	0	0	1.000	3.86
Cairo,Miguel	Stl	18	8	88.0	25	31	1	8	.982	5.73
Canizaro,Jay	Min	30	25	211.2	39	62	1	13	.990	4.29
Carroll,Jamey	Mon	1	0	2.0	0	0	0	0	-	.00
Caruso,Mike	KC	4	2	25.0	10	4	1	1	.933	5.04
Castro,Juan	Cin	17	8	74.0	15	24	0	7	1.000	4.74
Catalanotto,F	Tex	23	15	139.1	24	47	1	8	.986	4.59
Cintron,Alex	Ari	18	14	131.2	27	31	0	9	1.000	3.96
Collier,Lou	Mon	2	0	5.0	1	1	0	0	1.000	3.60
Cora,Alex	LA	40	10	153.0	30	53	2	11	.976	4.88
Counsell,Craig	Ari	13	10	81.0	24	23	0	5	1.000	5.22
Crespo,Cesar	SD	4	0	9.1	1	2	0	0	1.000	2.89
Dawkins,Gookie	Cin	3	0	5.0	0	0	1	0	.000	.00
DeRosa,Mark	Atl	32	27	250.0	59	89	4	23	.974	5.33
DeShields,D	ChC	41	34	297.2	65	98	5	15	.970	4.93
Durham,Ray	CWS	92	92	786.1	188	261	15	61	.968	5.14
Durham,Ray	Oak	11	11	98.1	21	37	2	12	.967	5.31
Escalona,Felix	TB	25	20	191.1	46	61	4	12	.964	5.03
Figgins,Chone	Ana	8	1	29.0	7	9	1	2	.941	4.97
Flores,Jose	Oak	2	1	6.0	0	0	0	0	-	.00
Fox,Andy	Fla	7	7	59.0	18	23	1	7	.976	6.25
Furcal,Rafael	Atl	4	4	30.0	7	12	0	5	1.000	5.70
Garcia,Jesse	Atl	21	11	116.0	28	42	1	10	.986	5.43
German,Esteban	Oak	8	8	77.0	22	23	1	6	.978	5.26
Gil,Benji	Ana	26	22	181.2	41	58	1	11	.990	4.90
Giles,Marcus	Atl	52	47	424.2	118	139	6	35	.977	5.45
Graffanino,T	CWS	25	17	163.1	33	58	5	17	.948	5.01
Guerrero,W	Cin	10	4	55.1	11	22	0	5	1.000	5.37
Guerrero,W	Mon	5	4	47.2	9	12	0	2	1.000	3.97
Halter,Shane	Det	4	2	19.0	6	8	2	2	.875	6.63
Harris,Willie	CWS	38	37	323.1	87	104	3	21	.985	5.32
Hill,Bobby	ChC	55	48	419.2	96	117	2	31	.991	4.57
Hocking,Denny	Min	56	42	393.2	69	115	7	22	.963	4.21
Hubbard,T	SD	4	1	12.0	0	4	0	1	1.000	3.00
Hudson,Orlando	Tor	52	51	450.2	117	157	4	49	.986	5.47
Infante,Omar	Det	2	2	18.0	5	9	0	4	1.000	7.00
Izturis,Cesar	LA	1	0	3.0	1	3	0	0	1.000	12.00
Jackson,Damian	Det	56	53	471.2	110	146	5	37	.981	4.88
Jimenez,D	SD	54	52	444.2	116	159	7	44	.975	5.57
Jimenez,D	CWS	17	17	150.0	31	53	1	16	.988	5.04
Johnson,Russ	TB	1	0	1.0	0	0	0	0	-	.00
Lamb,David	Min	2	1	12.0	6	2	0	1	1.000	6.00
Lamb,Mike	Tex	1	0	2.0	0	2	0	0	1.000	9.00
LaRocca,Greg	Cle	3	1	13.0	3	4	0	1	1.000	4.85
Lawrence,Joe	Tor	49	44	401.1	73	131	7	20	.967	4.57
Lopez,Luis	Bal	12	8	84.0	12	19	1	3	.969	3.32
Loretta,Mark	Mil	3	2	18.0	7	6	0	2	1.000	6.50
Loretta,Mark	Hou	3	3	22.0	7	8	0	2	1.000	6.14
Macias,Jose	Det	17	15	130.0	26	54	3	5	.964	5.54
Macias,Jose	Mon	6	4	44.0	13	15	0	5	1.000	5.73
Mackowiak,Rob	Pit	3	1	11.0	2	3	1	1	.833	4.09
Malloy,Marty	Fla	3	0	13.0	5	3	0	1	1.000	5.54
Martinez,Ramon	SF	17	10	91.0	17	25	1	6	.977	4.15
Mateo,Henry	Mon	3	1	12.0	2	8	0	1	1.000	7.50
Matos,Julius	SD	49	32	318.0	72	110	7	26	.963	5.15
McDonald,John	Cle	64	56	486.2	94	184	4	42	.986	5.14
McEwing,Joe	NYM	13	4	54.0	15	14	0	2	1.000	4.83
McLemore,Mark	Sea	2	1	9.0	2	2	0	0	1.000	4.00
Menechino,F	Oak	32	31	278.0	37	90	1	10	.992	4.11
Merloni,Lou	Bos	66	47	455.1	99	142	3	28	.988	4.76
Mora,Melvin	Bal	12	9	82.2	22	41	2	10	.969	6.86
Mordecai,Mike	Mon	4	1	19.1	6	6	2	2	.857	5.59
Moriarty,Mike	Bal	2	2	18.0	4	10	0	4	1.000	7.00
Morris,Warren	Min	4	2	16.0	2	6	0	1	1.000	4.50
Nelson,Bry	Bos	11	5	56.0	11	16	1	2	.964	4.34
Nieves,Jose	Ana	18	16	129.0	30	31	4	8	.938	4.26
Nunez,A O	Pit	46	37	336.0	84	133	2	35	.991	5.81
Offerman,Jose	Sea	1	0	2.0	1	2	0	0	1.000	13.50
Ojeda,Augie	ChC	10	7	61.0	18	13	1	4	.969	4.57
Ordaz,Luis	KC	28	26	227.2	43	68	2	14	.982	4.39
Ortiz,Jose	Col	53	52	428.0	103	133	3	24	.987	4.96
Osik,Keith	Pit	1	0	2.0	0	0	0	0	-	.00
Ozuna,Pablo	Fla	10	6	59.0	13	16	1	3	.967	4.42

Player	Tm	G	GS	Inn	PO	A	E	DP	Pct.	Rng
Pelaez,Alex	SD	1	0	1.0	0	0	0	0	-	.00
Perez,Neifi	KC	5	5	41.0	14	13	1	2	.964	5.93
Perez,Tomas	Phi	50	21	249.2	67	90	1	22	.994	5.66
Phillips,B	Cle	11	8	80.2	16	28	2	4	.957	4.91
Polanco,P	Stl	6	5	46.0	11	17	1	7	.966	5.48
Punto,Nick	Phi	1	0	1.0	1	1	0	1	1.000	18.00
Reboulet,Jeff	LA	11	5	49.1	6	22	2	2	.933	5.11
Relaford,Desi	Sea	11	5	53.0	14	21	0	6	1.000	5.94
Roberts,Brian	Bal	25	25	222.1	43	80	3	19	.976	4.98
Rollins,Jimmy	Phi	1	0	0.1	0	0	0	0	-	.00
Romano,Jason	Tex	8	2	29.2	10	8	1	2	.947	5.46
Romano,Jason	Col	12	2	37.2	6	14	1	2	.952	4.78
Sadler,Donnie	KC	4	2	19.1	9	5	0	0	1.000	6.52
Sadler,Donnie	Tex	2	1	10.0	2	4	0	1	1.000	5.40
Salazar,Oscar	Det	6	4	36.0	7	8	1	3	.938	3.75
Sanchez,Freddy	Bos	5	3	29.0	4	9	0	1	1.000	4.03
Scutaro,Marco	NYM	12	1	27.0	4	7	0	0	1.000	3.67
Selby,Bill	Cle	6	3	29.0	5	10	0	3	1.000	4.66
Sheets,Andy	TB	26	26	232.0	55	72	1	26	.992	4.93
Shumpert,Terry	Col	60	40	390.2	95	126	6	30	.974	5.09
Smith,Jason	TB	1	0	1.0	0	0	0	0	-	.00
Spiezio,Scott	Ana	1	0	0.2	0	0	0	0	-	.00
Stynes,Chris	ChC	20	10	93.1	22	33	0	12	1.000	5.30
Thurston,Joe	LA	4	1	19.0	4	6	0	3	1.000	4.74
Tucker,Michael	KC	2	1	8.0	2	3	1	1	.833	5.63
Ugueto,Luis	Sea	11	2	37.0	10	14	1	3	.960	5.84
Valentin,John	NYM	3	1	12.0	4	3	0	2	1.000	5.25
Vazquez,Ramon	SD	81	66	574.0	131	190	5	46	.985	5.03
Velarde,Randy	Oak	38	28	260.0	70	88	3	22	.981	5.47
Vizcaino,Jose	Hou	25	19	181.1	38	57	0	15	1.000	4.72
Wigginton,Ty	NYM	12	9	84.0	22	34	2	4	.966	6.00
Wilson,Enrique	NYY	7	7	64.0	15	18	0	5	1.000	4.64
Woodward,Chris	Tor	6	3	26.0	8	14	2	4	.917	7.62

Third Basemen - Regulars

Player	Tm	G	GS	Inn	PO	A	E	DP	Pct.	Rng
Rolen,Scott	TOT	155	154	1360.0	133	335	16	41	.967	3.10
Polanco,P	TOT	131	115	1066.2	90	272	8	33	.978	3.05
Counsell,Craig	Ari	94	88	774.2	66	194	7	13	.974	3.02
Chavez,Eric	Oak	143	143	1262.0	120	301	17	24	.961	3.00
Ventura,Robin	NYY	137	130	1129.1	109	261	23	22	.941	2.95
Valentin,Jose	CWS	83	76	667.1	65	152	11	14	.952	2.93
Blum,Geoff	Hou	104	91	824.0	68	199	8	27	.971	2.92
Truby,Chris	TOT	120	108	967.0	84	229	16	26	.951	2.91
Boone,Aaron	Cin	154	141	1277.2	89	324	20	42	.954	2.91
Alfonzo,E	NYM	134	131	1154.0	95	278	12	22	.969	2.91
Koskie,Corey	Min	138	136	1180.1	117	254	12	16	.969	2.83
Ramirez,Aramis	Pit	131	130	1066.2	78	255	19	32	.946	2.81
Lowell,Mike	Fla	159	159	1400.1	150	286	14	36	.969	2.80
Randa,Joe	KC	129	128	1110.2	108	234	10	12	.972	2.77
Sandberg,Jared	TB	97	94	841.2	83	174	14	19	.948	2.75
Beltre,Adrian	LA	157	154	1372.0	120	294	20	18	.954	2.72
Cirillo,Jeff	Sea	141	126	1107.1	112	217	9	23	.973	2.67
Perry,Herbert	Tex	112	105	921.0	83	190	14	17	.951	2.67
Zeile,Todd	Col	139	138	1173.1	87	257	21	23	.942	2.64
Batista,Tony	Bal	154	154	1373.2	111	290	16	35	.962	2.63
Tatis,Fernando	Mon	99	99	832.2	59	180	13	17	.948	2.58
Glaus,Troy	Ana	156	153	1335.1	101	281	20	30	.950	2.57
Bell,David	SF	139	128	1137.0	78	244	9	21	.973	2.55
Hillenbrand,B	Bos	156	154	1366.0	100	283	23	27	.943	2.52
Hinske,Eric	Tor	148	141	1259.1	103	245	20	14	.946	2.49
Castilla,Vinny	Atl	139	138	1222.0	75	256	6	23	.982	2.44
Mueller,Bill	TOT	104	90	834.2	62	159	6	19	.974	2.38
Fryman,Travis	Cle	113	107	928.1	53	185	10	27	.960	2.31

Third Basemen - The Rest

Player	Tm	G	GS	Inn	PO	A	E	DP	Pct.	Rng
Alicea,Luis	KC	32	20	192.2	8	39	6	1	.887	2.20
Andrews,Shane	Bos	4	2	20.0	3	6	0	1	1.000	4.05
Arias,Alex	NYY	4	1	11.0	0	3	1	1	.750	2.45
Baerga,Carlos	Bos	1	0	2.0	0	0	0	0	-	.00
Banks,Brian	Fla	1	0	2.0	1	1	0	0	1.000	9.00
Bell,Jay	Ari	6	5	42.2	4	8	0	2	1.000	2.53
Bellhorn,Mark	ChC	36	29	252.2	16	33	3	3	.942	1.75

Player	Tm	G	GS	Inn	PO	A	E	DP	Pct.	Rng
Belliard,R	Mil	42	20	215.0	22	43	5	5	.929	2.72
Benjamin,Mike	Pit	62	5	141.1	13	33	1	3	.979	2.93
Berg,Dave	Tor	20	18	152.2	10	35	0	2	1.000	2.65
Blake,Casey	Min	5	5	44.0	5	6	2	1	.846	2.25
Blalock,Hank	Tex	46	42	383.2	28	72	6	7	.943	2.35
Branyan,R	Cle	8	6	59.0	3	10	1	1	.929	1.98
Branyan,R	Cin	16	13	108.0	10	21	3	1	.912	2.58
Burroughs,Sean	SD	48	39	339.0	33	68	7	5	.935	2.68
Butler,Brent	Col	33	3	85.2	4	16	0	0	1.000	2.10
Cabrera,Jol	LA	3	1	13.0	2	4	0	1	1.000	4.15
Cairo,Miguel	Stl	7	5	41.0	5	2	1	1	.875	1.54
Canizaro,Jay	Min	8	7	67.1	3	16	2	3	.905	2.54
Carroll,Jamey	Mon	13	13	125.0	7	26	3	2	.917	2.38
Caruso,Mike	KC	2	0	4.0	1	0	0	0	1.000	2.25
Castro,Juan	Cin	1	1	11.0	2	4	1	1	.857	4.91
Cintron,Alex	Ari	9	1	22.2	2	7	0	1	1.000	3.57
Colbrunn,Greg	Ari	5	3	27.0	1	3	0	0	1.000	1.33
Collier,Lou	Mon	1	0	1.0	0	0	0	0	-	.00
Coolbaugh,Mike	Stl	4	3	26.0	0	8	0	3	1.000	2.77
Coomer,Ron	NYY	26	22	193.0	12	33	6	2	.882	2.10
Crede,Joe	CWS	53	53	461.2	33	87	8	12	.938	2.34
Crespo,Cesar	SD	4	2	27.1	1	5	1	1	.857	1.98
Cuddyer,Mike	Min	10	4	57.0	5	10	0	2	1.000	2.37
DeRosa,Mark	Atl	4	3	28.0	1	4	0	0	1.000	1.61
Donnels,Chris	Ari	26	11	104.2	10	16	0	0	1.000	2.24
Ellis,Mark	Oak	7	7	63.0	7	18	2	0	.926	3.57
Ensberg,Morgan	Hou	43	37	328.1	28	76	8	5	.929	2.85
Escalona,Felix	TB	4	4	34.0	1	8	2	1	.818	2.38
Feliz,Pedro	SF	44	32	280.1	29	57	3	9	.966	2.76
Fox,Andy	Fla	4	0	10.0	2	1	0	0	1.000	2.70
Giles,Marcus	Atl	8	6	62.1	6	13	2	2	.905	2.74
Ginter,Keith	Hou	4	1	13.0	3	4	1	1	.875	4.85
Ginter,Keith	Mil	21	21	186.0	18	31	2	3	.961	2.37
Gipson,Charles	Sea	4	1	10.1	1	1	0	0	1.000	1.74
Graffanino,T	CWS	35	32	285.0	19	61	4	5	.952	2.53
Guerrero,W	Cin	3	2	16.0	1	2	1	0	.750	1.69
Guerrero,W	Mon	2	2	18.0	1	3	1	0	.800	2.00
Hall,Bill	Mil	2	0	5.0	2	0	0	0	1.000	3.60
Halter,Shane	Det	30	24	213.0	21	45	4	9	.943	2.79
Hansen,Dave	LA	11	5	51.2	4	13	2	0	.895	2.96
Harris,Lenny	Mil	14	10	80.0	7	14	0	3	1.000	2.36
Helms,Wes	Atl	24	14	151.1	8	24	1	0	.970	1.90
Hocking,Denny	Min	16	9	95.0	10	20	0	2	1.000	2.84
Houston,Tyler	Mil	72	67	573.1	43	101	8	8	.947	2.26
Houston,Tyler	LA	2	2	13.1	0	4	1	0	.800	2.70
Hubbard,T	SD	6	3	30.0	4	5	1	1	.900	2.70
Huff,Aubrey	TB	14	13	115.2	14	25	3	1	.929	3.03
Jackson,Damian	Det	2	0	5.0	0	3	0	0	1.000	5.40
Jimenez,D	SD	32	30	258.0	19	70	5	9	.947	3.10
Jimenez,D	CWS	1	1	9.0	0	2	0	0	1.000	2.00
Johnson,Russ	TB	27	27	239.0	23	38	1	5	.984	2.30
Klassen,Danny	Ari	2	0	3.0	0	1	0	0	1.000	3.00
Lamb,David	Min	1	0	1.0	0	0	0	0	-	.00
Lamb,Mike	Tex	14	13	108.0	12	20	3	0	.914	2.67
LaRocca,Greg	Cle	15	13	112.0	9	15	6	1	.800	1.93
Larson,Brandon	Cin	5	5	41.0	2	10	0	3	1.000	2.63
Leon,Jose	Bal	12	8	76.0	7	16	0	2	1.000	2.72
Lockhart,Keith	Atl	1	0	3.2	1	0	0	0	1.000	2.45
Lopez,Felipe	Tor	2	2	17.0	2	1	0	0	1.000	1.59
Loretta,Mark	Mil	47	44	373.0	37	73	1	6	.991	2.65
Loretta,Mark	Hou	10	10	78.0	6	11	1	1	.944	1.96
Macias,Jose	Det	8	7	61.2	4	8	2	0	.857	1.75
Macias,Jose	Mon	22	15	137.0	10	38	3	0	.941	3.15
Mackowiak,Rob	Pit	26	22	176.1	13	50	3	4	.955	3.22
Malloy,Marty	Fla	2	0	6.0	0	1	0	0	1.000	1.50
Martinez,Ramon	SF	2	0	2.0	2	0	0	0	1.000	9.00
Matos,Julius	SD	17	6	80.0	9	18	2	3	.931	3.04
McDonald,John	Cle	10	6	61.0	4	11	2	0	.882	2.21
McEwing,Joe	NYM	10	5	54.2	5	13	2	2	.900	2.96
McLemore,Mark	Sea	14	10	83.2	7	13	2	1	.909	2.15
Menechino,F	Oak	4	1	18.0	1	5	1	1	.857	3.00
Merced,Orlando	Hou	1	0	2.1	0	1	0	0	1.000	3.86
Merloni,Lou	Bos	8	6	58.0	5	24	1	1	.967	4.50
Michaels,Jason	Phi	1	0	0.1	0	0	0	0	.000	.00
Millar,Kevin	Fla	2	1	11.0	1	5	1	0	.857	4.91
Mordecai,Mike	Mon	28	8	101.1	6	21	0	3	.931	2.40
Mordecai,Mike	Fla	7	2	27.0	5	4	0	2	1.000	3.00
Moriarty,Mike	Bal	1	0	1.0	0	1	0	0	1.000	9.00
Mueller,Bill	ChC	101	88	816.2	60	156	6	19	.973	2.38

Player	Tm	G	GS	Inn	PO	A	E	DP	Pct.	Rng
Mueller,Bill	SF	3	2	18.0	2	3	0	0	1.000	2.50
Nevin,Phil	SD	71	71	592.2	49	131	14	17	.928	2.73
Nieves,Jose	Ana	5	1	16.0	0	5	0	0	1.000	2.81
Norton,Greg	Col	22	20	154.2	16	27	5	4	.896	2.50
Ojeda,Augie	ChC	5	0	13.0	1	5	0	0	1.000	4.15
Ordaz,Luis	KC	6	0	12.1	0	2	0	0	1.000	1.46
Orie,Kevin	ChC	12	9	81.0	4	13	2	1	.895	1.89
Ortiz,Jose	Col	1	1	9.0	1	1	0	0	1.000	2.00
Osik,Keith	Pit	4	4	28.1	2	16	0	1	1.000	5.72
Paquette,Craig	Det	49	45	388.1	35	82	8	5	.936	2.71
Pelaez,Alex	SD	1	1	9.0	1	1	0	0	1.000	2.00
Pellow,Kit	KC	12	10	79.1	5	22	5	3	.844	3.06
Perez,Eduardo	Stl	6	0	13.1	0	0	1	0	.000	.00
Perez,Tomas	Phi	14	9	95.2	5	25	3	0	.909	2.82
Polanco,P	Stl	78	63	587.0	52	139	5	18	.974	2.93
Polanco,P	Phi	53	52	479.2	38	133	3	15	.983	3.21
Pujols,Albert	Stl	41	37	293.0	25	66	6	6	.938	2.80
Reboulet,Jeff	LA	3	0	7.2	0	0	0	0	-	.00
Relaford,Desi	Sea	38	25	243.0	25	41	3	2	.957	2.44
Rolen,Scott	Phi	100	100	874.0	81	206	8	23	.973	2.96
Rolen,Scott	Stl	55	54	486.0	52	129	8	18	.958	3.35
Romano,Jason	Tex	1	0	1.0	0	1	0	0	1.000	9.00
Romano,Jason	Col	1	0	2.0	0	0	0	0	-	.00
Sadler,Donnie	KC	11	4	42.0	4	6	1	0	.909	2.14
Sadler,Donnie	Tex	4	2	18.0	2	5	0	0	1.000	3.50
Saenz,Olmedo	Oak	15	10	100.0	14	28	5	1	.894	3.78
Salazar,Oscar	Det	1	1	8.0	0	3	0	0	1.000	3.38
Scutaro,Marco	NYM	3	0	7.0	1	2	0	0	1.000	3.86
Selby,Bill	Cle	33	28	245.1	20	50	5	3	.933	2.57
Sheets,Andy	TB	4	4	37.0	3	10	0	1	1.000	3.16
Shumpert,Terry	Col	1	0	2.0	0	2	0	0	1.000	9.00
Smith,Bobby	TB	10	10	89.0	7	19	3	3	.897	2.63
Smith,Jason	TB	12	9	84.0	7	18	1	3	.962	2.68
Snyder,Earl	Cle	2	2	19.0	1	4	0	0	1.000	2.37
Spiezio,Scott	Ana	20	8	94.0	14	19	2	2	.943	3.16
Stynes,Chris	ChC	40	36	278.0	15	43	5	3	.921	1.88
Truby,Chris	Mon	31	25	238.0	13	48	5	4	.924	2.31
Truby,Chris	Det	89	83	729.0	71	181	11	22	.958	3.11
Ugueto,Luis	Sea	1	0	1.0	0	1	0	0	1.000	9.00
Valentin,John	NYM	18	14	126.1	9	27	5	3	.878	2.56
Vazquez,Ramon	SD	20	10	100.1	7	27	0	5	1.000	3.05
Velarde,Randy	Oak	1	1	9.0	0	1	0	0	1.000	1.00
Vizcaino,Jose	Hou	30	23	199.1	18	44	0	3	1.000	2.80
Wigginton,Ty	NYM	14	11	100.2	7	29	3	3	.900	2.41
Williams,Matt	Ari	56	54	472.0	29	94	4	7	.969	2.35
Wilson,Enrique	NYY	26	8	118.2	15	26	3	1	.932	3.11
Woodward,Chris	Tor	2	1	9.1	2	3	0	0	1.000	4.82
Wooten,Shawn	Ana	1	0	7.0	0	0	0	0	-	.00
Young,Dmitri	Det	1	1	9.0	2	2	0	0	1.000	4.00
Young,Michael	Tex	4	0	8.0	0	3	0	0	1.000	3.38

Shortstops - Regulars

Player	Tm	G	GS	Inn	PO	A	E	DP	Pct.	Rng
Uribe,Juan	Col	155	150	1316.0	261	504	27	118	.966	5.23
Bordick,Mike	Bal	117	115	1007.2	197	372	1	92	.998	5.08
Wilson,Jack	Pit	143	135	1180.1	187	463	15	90	.977	4.96
Halter,Shane	Det	81	78	683.1	122	253	15	37	.962	4.94
Hernandez,Jose	Mil	149	148	1268.1	244	451	19	107	.973	4.93
Cabrera,O	Mon	153	150	1352.1	237	498	29	102	.962	4.89
Furcal,Rafael	Atl	150	147	1314.1	245	466	27	111	.963	4.87
Perez,Neifi	KC	139	137	1208.2	251	400	19	107	.972	4.85
Woodward,Chris	Tor	79	77	678.0	131	231	13	63	.965	4.81
Rodriguez,Alex	Tex	162	160	1390.2	259	472	10	108	.987	4.73
Gomez,Chris	TB	130	128	1113.1	229	356	12	94	.973	4.73
Vizquel,Omar	Cle	150	148	1291.0	239	431	7	98	.990	4.67
Clayton,Royce	CWS	109	100	883.1	166	292	5	72	.989	4.67
Tejada,Miguel	Oak	162	161	1424.0	229	504	19	106	.975	4.63
Larkin,Barry	Cin	135	131	1090.1	191	370	12	89	.979	4.63
Garciaparra,N	Bos	154	153	1341.0	220	467	25	92	.965	4.61
Ordonez,Rey	NYM	142	134	1164.2	208	388	19	82	.969	4.61
Rollins,Jimmy	Phi	152	149	1343.1	226	455	14	90	.980	4.56
Fox,Andy	Fla	112	103	940.1	187	279	17	73	.965	4.46
Aurilia,Rich	SF	131	130	1126.0	213	334	11	97	.980	4.37
Guzman,C	Min	147	143	1262.2	247	360	12	84	.981	4.33
Renteria,Edgar	Stl	149	147	1287.1	202	410	19	72	.970	4.28
Eckstein,David	Ana	147	146	1276.1	205	397	14	91	.977	4.24

Player	Tm	G	GS	Inn	PO	A	E	DP	Pct.	Rng
Gonzalez,A S	ChC	142	139	1236.0	220	360	21	84	.965	4.22
Lopez,Felipe	Tor	79	74	668.0	112	200	8	51	.975	4.20
Cruz,Deivi	SD	147	133	1161.2	169	372	15	83	.973	4.19
Izturis,Cesar	LA	128	109	992.2	155	306	10	69	.979	4.18
Lugo,Julio	Hou	84	81	716.0	121	205	8	32	.976	4.10
Guillen,Carlos	Sea	130	127	1113.0	200	304	18	68	.966	4.08
Womack,Tony	Ari	149	145	1271.2	175	364	20	66	.964	3.81
Jeter,Derek	NYY	156	156	1383.1	219	367	14	69	.977	3.81

Shortstops - The Rest

Player	Tm	G	GS	Inn	PO	A	E	DP	Pct.	Rng
Alicea,Luis	KC	1	0	0.1	0	0	0	0	-	.00
Amezaga,A	Ana	5	3	34.0	7	11	0	1	1.000	4.76
Arias,Alex	NYY	1	1	9.0	0	3	0	0	1.000	3.00
Bell,David	SF	3	3	27.0	4	7	0	1	1.000	3.67
Bell,Jay	Ari	2	1	9.0	1	4	0	0	1.000	5.00
Bellhorn,Mark	ChC	12	10	83.1	15	22	1	7	.974	4.00
Benjamin,Mike	Pit	15	11	88.2	18	35	1	5	.981	5.38
Berg,Dave	Tor	13	11	92.1	23	25	2	8	.960	4.68
Berroa,Angel	KC	20	20	178.2	41	67	4	13	.964	5.44
Blum,Geoff	Hou	2	0	1.2	0	0	0	0	-	.00
Boone,Aaron	Cin	16	13	106.2	24	35	2	6	.967	4.98
Bush,Homer	Fla	4	1	14.0	0	0	0	0	-	.00
Butler,Brent	Col	13	8	71.1	15	24	1	5	.975	4.92
Cairo,Miguel	Stl	6	2	22.1	7	6	0	3	1.000	5.24
Carroll,Jamey	Mon	3	3	26.2	6	10	1	2	.941	5.40
Caruso,Mike	KC	5	2	23.1	4	10	0	0	1.000	5.40
Castro,Juan	Cin	25	7	105.2	20	33	2	10	.964	4.51
Cintron,Alex	Ari	8	5	47.0	7	18	1	5	.962	4.79
Cora,Alex	LA	61	53	453.0	67	144	5	32	.977	4.19
Counsell,Craig	Ari	22	11	117.0	23	37	1	8	.984	4.62
Crespo,Cesar	SD	1	0	1.1	0	0	0	0	-	.00
Dawkins,Gookie	Cin	21	9	124.2	18	33	3	6	.944	3.68
Delgado,Wilson	Stl	8	4	44.0	8	9	0	1	1.000	3.48
DeRosa,Mark	Atl	19	14	139.1	30	52	2	17	.976	5.30
Dunston,Shawon	SF	1	0	2.0	0	0	0	0	-	.00
Ellis,Mark	Oak	8	1	19.0	3	13	0	4	1.000	7.58
Escalona,Felix	TB	26	16	168.0	28	58	5	16	.945	4.61
Everett,Adam	Hou	34	29	252.2	34	93	5	22	.962	4.52
Febles,Carlos	KC	1	0	1.0	0	0	0	0	-	.00
Feliz,Pedro	SF	1	0	1.0	0	0	0	0	-	.00
Flores,Jose	Oak	1	0	3.0	1	1	0	0	1.000	6.00
Garcia,Jesse	Atl	5	0	13.2	4	7	0	4	1.000	7.24
Gil,Benji	Ana	14	7	71.1	16	32	2	5	.960	6.06
Ginter,Keith	Hou	1	0	2.1	2	1	0	1	1.000	11.57
Glaus,Troy	Ana	2	2	20.0	1	1	0	1	1.000	.00
Gonzalez,Alex	Fla	42	41	348.1	72	113	3	32	.984	4.78
Graffanino,T	CWS	8	6	53.1	13	19	1	1	.970	5.40
Guerrero,W	Cin	7	2	26.1	7	7	1	3	.933	4.78
Hall,Bill	Mil	13	9	86.0	15	22	2	5	.949	3.87
Hill,Bobby	ChC	1	0	2.0	0	0	1	0	.000	.00
Hocking,Denny	Min	25	18	172.0	32	43	3	8	.962	3.92
Infante,Omar	Det	16	16	140.0	18	54	5	10	.935	4.63
Jackson,Damian	Det	6	4	36.2	4	11	2	0	.882	3.68
Jimenez,D	CWS	10	9	77.1	13	31	1	8	.978	5.12
Johnson,Russ	TB	2	0	2.0	0	0	0	0	-	.00
Klassen,Danny	Ari	1	0	2.0	0	0	0	0	-	.00
Lamb,David	Min	4	0	10.0	4	1	0	1	1.000	4.50
Lopez,Luis	Mil	4	0	14.1	3	1	0	0	1.000	2.51
Lopez,Luis	Bal	22	10	114.0	18	41	2	5	.967	4.66
Loretta,Mark	Mil	12	5	63.2	14	10	2	3	.923	3.39
Loretta,Mark	Hou	6	5	43.0	6	16	1	2	.957	4.60
Macias,Jose	Mon	4	4	34.0	3	13	1	2	.941	4.24
Martinez,Ramon	SF	40	28	269.1	52	82	7	26	.950	4.48
Mateo,Henry	Mon	2	2	17.0	2	7	1	0	.900	4.76
Matos,Julius	SD	4	1	17.1	3	3	0	1	1.000	3.12
McDonald,John	Cle	21	14	133.2	31	42	2	10	.973	4.92
McEwing,Joe	NYM	21	10	109.0	18	40	5	4	.921	4.79
McLemore,Mark	Sea	1	0	2.0	0	1	0	0	1.000	4.50
Menechino,F	Oak	2	0	6.0	2	1	0	1	1.000	4.50
Merloni,Lou	Bos	5	1	17.0	2	4	1	1	.857	3.18
Mora,Melvin	Bal	41	36	309.0	57	108	7	17	.959	4.81
Mordecai,Mike	Mon	3	3	23.0	3	9	0	1	1.000	4.70
Mordecai,Mike	Fla	24	17	153.2	26	53	1	11	.988	4.63
Moriarty,Mike	Bal	1	1	13.0	2	6	0	0	1.000	5.54
Nieves,Jose	Ana	13	6	68.2	11	20	2	4	.939	4.06

Player	Tm	G	GS	Inn	PO	A	E	DP	Pct.	Rng
Nunez,A O	Pit	24	15	143.2	19	57	5	15	.938	4.76
Ojeda,Augie	ChC	16	13	120.0	15	41	2	4	.966	4.20
Ordaz,Luis	KC	2	2	16.0	4	5	0	2	1.000	5.06
Perez,Tomas	Phi	13	12	103.1	30	33	0	11	1.000	5.49
Polanco,P	Stl	13	9	90.2	19	24	0	7	1.000	4.27
Pujols,Albert	Stl	1	0	2.0	0	0	0	0	-	.00
Punto,Nick	Phi	1	0	3.0	1	0	1	0	.500	3.00
Ransom,Cody	SF	3	1	12.0	3	3	0	0	1.000	4.50
Reboulet,Jeff	LA	5	0	12.0	3	2	2	0	.714	3.75
Relaford,Desi	Sea	40	34	303.0	46	87	5	24	.964	3.95
Rogers,Eddie	Bal	4	0	7.0	2	5	0	1	1.000	9.00
Romano,Jason	Col	5	3	29.0	6	5	3	1	.786	3.41
Sadler,Donnie	KC	4	1	13.0	2	2	1	0	.800	2.77
Sadler,Donnie	Tex	12	1	24.0	3	5	0	1	1.000	3.00
Salazar,Oscar	Det	1	0	6.0	1	1	0	1	1.000	3.00
Sanchez,Freddy	Bos	5	1	17.0	5	3	0	1	1.000	4.24
Sanchez,Rey	Bos	10	7	71.0	9	26	1	3	.972	4.44
Santiago,Ramon	Det	63	63	548.0	97	205	7	41	.977	4.96
Scutaro,Marco	NYM	6	4	36.0	5	11	1	3	.941	4.00
Sheets,Andy	TB	11	10	92.0	19	34	0	9	1.000	5.18
Shumpert,Terry	Col	3	1	10.1	2	4	0	0	1.000	5.23
Smith,Jason	TB	9	7	65.0	15	17	5	4	.865	4.43
Ugueto,Luis	Sea	8	1	27.1	1	10	2	4	.846	3.62
Valentin,John	NYM	24	13	133.0	20	48	2	9	.971	4.60
Valentin,Jose	CWS	50	47	409.0	81	124	8	38	.962	4.51
Vazquez,Ramon	SD	41	28	256.0	32	97	2	16	.985	4.54
Vizcaino,Jose	Hou	58	47	429.1	59	135	4	35	.980	4.07
Wilson,Enrique	NYY	14	4	59.2	11	21	2	5	.941	4.83
Young,Michael	Tex	11	1	25.0	2	10	0	2	1.000	4.32

Left Fielders - Regulars

Player	Tm	G	GS	Inn	PO	A	E	DP	Pct.	Rng
Jones,Jacque	Min	143	134	1179.0	330	11	5	1	.986	2.60
White,Rondell	NYY	113	105	944.2	246	3	0	0	1.000	2.37
Higginson,B	Det	117	116	1002.1	241	15	7	3	.973	2.30
Knoblauch,C	KC	74	73	618.1	145	5	3	0	.980	2.18
Anderson,G	Ana	137	135	1177.2	262	6	2	2	.993	2.05
Lee,Carlos	CWS	137	134	1133.2	249	8	1	1	.996	2.04
Millar,Kevin	Fla	89	87	737.0	161	4	3	0	.982	2.01
Dunn,Adam	Cin	113	105	905.0	193	9	8	2	.962	2.01
Stewart,Sh	Tor	99	99	861.2	189	3	2	1	.990	2.01
Bonds,Barry	SF	135	133	1115.0	241	4	8	2	.968	1.98
Cordova,Marty	Bal	72	72	620.1	132	2	4	1	.971	1.94
Jordan,Brian	LA	121	119	1020.2	205	10	4	4	.982	1.90
Cedeno,Roger	NYM	132	125	1087.1	225	2	8	0	.966	1.88
Jones,Chipper	Atl	152	152	1341.1	268	8	7	0	.975	1.85
Gonzalez,Luis	Ari	146	143	1246.1	252	4	4	1	.985	1.85
Pujols,Albert	Stl	117	101	870.2	173	4	4	0	.978	1.83
Burrell,Pat	Phi	157	154	1383.0	273	8	6	1	.979	1.83
Alou,Moises	ChC	122	120	1012.2	198	6	2	1	.990	1.81
Giles,Brian	Pit	151	149	1278.2	243	13	7	5	.973	1.80
Hollandsworth,T	TOT	99	79	715.0	135	6	4	0	.972	1.77
Ward,Daryle	Hou	122	117	936.2	146	9	3	3	.981	1.49

Left Fielders - The Rest

Player	Tm	G	GS	Inn	PO	A	E	DP	Pct.	Rng
Agbayani,Benny	Col	37	31	235.2	53	1	0	0	1.000	2.06
Agbayani,Benny	Bos	11	7	76.0	20	1	1	0	.955	2.49
Alcantara,Izzy	Mil	2	2	15.0	1	0	0	0	1.000	.60
Alicea,Luis	KC	1	0	2.2	0	0	0	0	-	.00
Allen,Chad	Cle	3	3	27.0	4	0	0	0	1.000	1.33
Alvarez,Tony	Pit	2	1	15.0	4	0	0	0	1.000	2.40
Anderson,Bra	Cle	14	6	74.0	15	0	1	0	.938	1.82
Andrews,Shane	Bos	1	0	2.0	0	0	0	0	-	.00
Aven,Bruce	Cle	5	5	41.0	10	0	0	0	1.000	2.20
Banks,Brian	Fla	3	1	11.0	3	0	0	0	1.000	2.45
Bellhorn,Mark	ChC	1	0	2.0	0	0	0	0	-	.00
Benard,Marvin	SF	14	6	68.2	14	1	0	0	1.000	1.97
Berg,Dave	Tor	3	1	11.0	4	0	0	0	1.000	3.27
Berger,Brandon	KC	14	8	81.2	23	2	0	1	1.000	2.76
Berkman,Lance	Hou	76	31	351.1	47	1	3	0	.941	1.23
Bigbie,Larry	Bal	6	5	44.0	12	0	0	0	1.000	2.45
Biggio,Craig	Hou	1	1	9.0	1	0	0	0	1.000	1.00
Bloomquist,W	Sea	6	6	43.0	12	0	0	0	1.000	2.51

Player	Tm	G	GS	Inn	PO	A	E	DP	Pct.	Rng
Blum,Geoff	Hou	9	2	22.1	3	0	0	0	1.000	1.21
Bocachica,H	LA	19	10	100.0	21	0	1	0	.955	1.89
Bocachica,H	Det	1	0	2.0	0	0	0	0	-	.00
Borchard,Joe	CWS	10	3	39.0	12	0	0	0	1.000	2.77
Bragg,Darren	Atl	12	6	62.0	12	1	1	0	.929	1.89
Branyan,R	Cle	42	39	334.2	66	4	1	1	.986	1.88
Branyan,R	Cin	25	21	173.1	36	3	2	0	.951	2.03
Broussard,Ben	Cle	32	29	228.2	47	1	2	0	.960	1.89
Brown,Dee	KC	8	8	69.0	12	0	1	0	.923	1.57
Brown,R	ChC	48	32	290.1	60	1	1	1	.984	1.89
Burks,Ellis	Cle	6	6	40.1	6	0	0	0	1.000	1.34
Byrnes,Eric	Oak	52	10	150.1	24	0	1	0	.960	1.44
Cabrera,Jol	Cle	5	1	16.0	4	0	0	0	1.000	2.25
Cabrera,Jol	LA	3	0	7.2	4	0	0	0	1.000	4.70
Cairo,Miguel	Stl	19	10	85.1	17	0	1	0	.944	1.79
Catalanotto,F	Tex	26	19	173.2	34	0	1	0	.971	1.76
Cepicky,Matt	Mon	16	14	127.0	21	0	0	0	1.000	1.49
Chavez,Eric	Oak	1	0	4.0	0	0	0	0	-	.00
Chen,Chin-Feng	LA	1	1	9.0	3	0	0	0	1.000	3.00
Christensen,M	NYM	2	0	5.1	3	0	0	0	1.000	5.06
Christenson,R	Mil	6	3	30.0	10	0	0	0	1.000	3.00
Clark,Brady	Cin	15	3	48.1	6	0	0	0	1.000	1.12
Clark,Brady	NYM	1	0	4.0	1	0	0	0	1.000	2.25
Clark,Howie	Bal	4	4	34.0	10	0	0	0	1.000	2.65
Colangelo,Mike	Oak	14	1	39.0	7	0	0	0	1.000	1.62
Collier,Lou	Mon	3	1	12.0	4	0	0	0	1.000	3.00
Conine,Jeff	Bal	6	6	48.0	8	0	0	0	1.000	1.50
Conti,Jason	TB	21	14	138.2	39	2	2	0	.953	2.66
Cordero,Wil	Cle	4	4	33.0	8	2	0	1	1.000	2.73
Cordero,Wil	Mon	24	21	169.1	42	1	1	0	.977	2.29
Crawford,Carl	TB	63	63	561.1	160	5	1	1	.994	2.65
Crespo,Cesar	SD	6	0	13.1	1	0	0	0	1.000	.68
Crisp,Coco	Cle	2	1	9.0	2	0	0	0	1.000	2.00
Cruz,Jacob	Det	3	2	19.0	2	0	1	0	.667	.95
Cruz,Jose	Tor	56	52	469.2	124	3	0	0	1.000	2.43
Cust,Jack	Col	18	15	121.1	24	0	1	0	.960	1.78
Daubach,Brian	Bos	35	31	273.0	45	1	0	0	1.000	1.52
DaVanon,Jeff	Ana	2	0	3.0	1	0	0	0	1.000	3.00
DeHaan,Kory	SD	2	2	22.2	5	0	0	0	1.000	1.99
Dellucci,David	Ari	20	12	130.1	30	1	2	1	.939	2.14
DeRosa,Mark	Atl	2	1	14.0	1	0	0	0	1.000	.64
Dunston,Shawon	SF	18	10	99.2	15	0	0	0	1.000	1.35
Dunwoody,Todd	Cle	1	1	5.2	1	0	0	0	1.000	1.59
Echevarria,A	ChC	8	5	50.1	16	1	1	1	.944	3.04
Encarnacion,M	ChC	2	2	13.0	5	0	0	0	1.000	3.46
Everett,Carl	Tex	18	18	151.0	20	0	3	0	.870	1.19
Feliz,Pedro	SF	1	0	1.0	0	0	0	0	-	.00
Floyd,Cliff	Fla	20	20	183.2	49	2	1	0	.981	2.50
Floyd,Cliff	Mon	13	13	113.0	14	2	1	0	.941	1.27
Floyd,Cliff	Bos	21	19	166.0	31	1	1	1	.970	1.73
Franco,Matt	Atl	2	0	12.0	3	0	0	0	1.000	2.25
Gant,Ron	SD	78	70	597.2	138	6	3	0	.980	2.17
Garcia,Jesse	Atl	2	0	7.0	2	0	0	0	1.000	2.57
Garcia,Karim	NYY	1	1	9.0	1	0	0	0	1.000	1.00
Garcia,Karim	Cle	1	1	9.0	3	0	0	0	1.000	3.00
Giambi,Jeremy	Oak	40	40	323.0	62	0	1	0	.984	1.73
Giambi,Jeremy	Phi	2	2	13.0	4	0	0	0	1.000	2.77
Gipson,Charles	Sea	57	8	153.0	41	2	0	1	1.000	2.53
Gload,Ross	Col	2	0	4.0	0	1	0	0	1.000	2.25
Gonzalez,Raul	Col	1	0	2.0	1	0	0	0	1.000	4.50
Gonzalez,Raul	NYM	11	9	71.0	15	1	0	0	1.000	2.03
Goodwin,Tom	SF	28	11	118.2	32	0	1	0	.970	2.43
Grabowski,J	Oak	4	3	27.0	6	0	0	0	1.000	2.00
Greene,Todd	Tex	1	1	7.0	0	0	0	0	-	.00
Greer,Rusty	Tex	22	18	167.1	27	0	1	0	.964	1.45
Griffey Jr.,K	Cin	1	1	8.0	1	0	0	0	1.000	1.13
Grissom,M	LA	36	25	237.2	51	3	1	0	.982	2.04
Guerrero,W	Mon	4	0	7.0	1	0	0	0	1.000	1.29
Guillen,Jose	Ari	2	2	15.2	2	0	0	0	1.000	1.15
Guillen,Jose	Cin	4	3	21.2	4	1	1	0	.833	2.08
Halter,Shane	Det	8	6	59.0	15	2	0	1	1.000	2.59
Hammonds,J	Mil	2	2	11.0	3	0	0	0	1.000	2.45
Harris,Lenny	Mil	16	12	110.1	26	0	0	0	1.000	2.12
Hart,Jason	Tex	7	4	39.2	9	0	0	0	1.000	2.04
Helms,Wes	Atl	5	2	29.0	7	1	0	0	1.000	2.48
Henderson,R	Bos	49	42	378.1	78	4	4	0	.953	1.95
Hermansen,Chad	Pit	2	0	6.0	0	0	0	0	-	.00
Hermansen,Chad	ChC	4	0	9.0	2	0	0	0	1.000	2.00
Hollandsworth,T	Col	74	60	552.1	107	6	4	0	.966	1.84

Player	Tm	G	GS	Inn	PO	A	E	DP	Pct.	Rng
Hollandsworth,T	Tex	25	19	162.2	28	0	0	0	1.000	1.55
Hubbard,T	SD	16	5	70.1	17	0	0	0	1.000	2.18
Hyzdu,Adam	Pit	10	2	32.0	5	0	0	0	1.000	1.41
Ibanez,Raul	KC	42	33	302.2	67	2	1	0	.986	2.05
Jackson,Damian	Det	3	1	11.0	2	0	1	0	.667	1.64
Jackson,Ryan	Det	2	1	10.0	2	0	0	0	1.000	1.80
Jenkins,Geoff	Mil	66	65	570.1	124	7	1	1	.992	2.07
Johnson,Mark P	NYM	1	0	3.0	0	0	0	0	-	.00
Johnson,Nick	NYY	2	1	7.2	2	0	0	0	1.000	2.35
Jose,Felix	Ari	1	0	1.0	0	0	0	0	-	.00
Justice,David	Oak	53	49	390.2	75	3	2	0	.975	1.80
Kapler,Gabe	Tex	31	23	206.1	57	2	1	0	.983	2.57
Kapler,Gabe	Col	15	8	81.2	17	1	0	0	1.000	1.98
Kearns,Austin	Cin	13	10	83.0	17	1	0	0	1.000	1.95
Kielty,Bobby	Min	9	5	54.0	9	0	0	0	1.000	1.50
Kingsale,Gene	SD	26	19	177.1	43	0	0	0	1.000	2.18
Kinkade,Mike	LA	8	4	44.2	4	0	0	0	1.000	.81
Lamb,Mike	Tex	12	5	51.2	10	0	1	0	.909	1.74
Lane,Jason	Hou	11	1	22.1	4	0	0	0	1.000	1.61
Langerhans,R	Atl	1	0	2.0	0	0	0	0	-	.00
Lankford,Ray	SD	59	53	425.0	98	4	4	1	.962	2.16
Larson,Brandon	Cin	9	7	58.0	13	0	0	0	1.000	2.02
Lawton,Matt	Cle	23	23	202.2	45	2	0	0	1.000	2.09
Ledee,Ricky	Phi	10	5	41.0	8	0	0	0	1.000	1.76
Leon,Jose	Bal	2	2	17.0	4	0	1	0	.800	2.12
Lesher,Brian	Tor	3	2	26.0	11	0	0	0	1.000	3.81
Lewis,Darren	ChC	22	3	64.0	17	0	0	0	1.000	2.39
Liefer,Jeff	CWS	24	22	163.1	35	0	0	0	1.000	1.93
Little,Mark	Col	16	1	46.0	5	0	1	0	.833	.98
Little,Mark	Ari	4	3	27.0	8	0	0	0	1.000	2.67
Lo Duca,Paul	LA	9	3	34.0	4	1	0	0	1.000	1.32
Lombard,George	Det	29	24	215.2	46	2	1	0	.980	2.00
Ludwick,Ryan	Tex	2	0	2.0	0	0	0	0	-	.00
Mabry,John	Oak	33	28	225.0	57	1	1	0	.983	2.32
Mackowiak,Rob	Pit	2	0	2.0	1	0	0	0	1.000	4.50
Magee,Wendell	Det	5	3	30.0	9	1	0	0	1.000	3.00
Magruder,Chris	Cle	45	26	270.2	73	1	0	0	1.000	2.46
Marrero,Eli	Stl	39	29	237.0	41	1	1	0	.977	1.59
Martinez,Ramon	SF	3	2	25.0	8	0	0	0	1.000	2.88
Matos,Luis	Bal	2	0	2.0	1	0	0	0	1.000	4.50
Matthews Jr,G	Bal	16	10	96.2	15	1	1	0	.941	1.49
McCarty,Dave	TB	11	9	81.0	20	1	0	0	1.000	2.33
McCracken,Q	Ari	7	2	26.1	5	0	0	0	1.000	1.71
McDonald,D	KC	7	6	49.2	3	0	0	0	1.000	.54
McEwing,Joe	NYM	10	4	39.1	11	0	0	1	1.000	2.52
McLemore,Mark	Sea	82	69	588.0	148	2	5	0	.968	2.30
Mench,Kevin	Tex	57	49	417.0	87	6	1	0	.989	2.01
Merced,Orlando	Hou	20	10	96.1	28	1	0	1	1.000	2.71
Merloni,Lou	Bos	1	0	1.0	0	0	0	0	-	.00
Michaels,Jason	Phi	6	0	12.2	3	0	0	0	1.000	2.13
Mohr,Dustan	Min	28	19	178.2	44	1	0	0	1.000	2.27
Monroe,Craig	Det	4	3	29.0	7	1	1	0	.889	2.48
Mora,Melvin	Bal	74	63	588.2	159	6	2	3	.988	2.52
Mordecai,Mike	Mon	1	0	0.1	0	0	0	0	-	.00
Murray,Calvin	SF	5	0	8.1	2	0	0	0	1.000	2.16
Nelson,Bry	Bos	7	1	20.1	7	0	0	0	1.000	3.10
Norton,Greg	Col	2	2	14.0	4	0	0	0	1.000	2.57
Nunez,Abraham	Fla	2	0	4.0	1	0	0	0	1.000	2.25
Ochoa,Alex	Mil	18	12	113.2	28	1	0	0	1.000	2.30
Ochoa,Alex	Ana	7	5	48.0	12	0	1	0	.923	2.25
Offerman,Jose	Sea	5	4	28.0	8	0	0	0	1.000	2.57
O'Leary,Troy	Mon	69	68	561.1	126	1	3	0	.977	2.04
Osik,Keith	Pit	1	0	1.0	0	0	0	0	-	.00
Owens,Eric	Fla	75	50	476.1	122	7	2	0	.985	2.44
Palmeiro,O	Ana	33	22	208.2	50	1	0	0	1.000	2.20
Paquette,Craig	Det	4	4	32.0	11	0	0	0	1.000	3.09
Paul,Josh	CWS	1	1	8.0	3	0	0	0	1.000	3.38
Payton,Jay	Col	32	25	225.2	44	2	0	0	1.000	1.83
Pena,Wily Mo	Cin	3	3	21.1	4	0	0	0	1.000	1.69
Perez,Eduardo	Stl	7	3	34.0	9	3	0	0	1.000	3.18
Perez,Timo	NYM	24	16	143.2	42	3	2	1	.957	2.82
Perry,Herbert	Tex	1	0	1.0	0	0	0	0	-	.00
Petrick,Ben	Col	15	13	95.0	18	0	1	0	.947	1.71
Piatt,Adam	Oak	40	29	277.0	55	1	0	0	1.000	1.82
Podsednik,S	Sea	9	2	40.0	11	0	0	0	1.000	2.48
Raines,Tim	Fla	14	4	44.1	10	1	1	0	.917	2.23
Ramirez,Manny	Bos	64	62	529.1	98	4	5	0	.953	1.73
Relaford,Desi	Sea	25	14	132.0	27	3	0	0	1.000	2.05
Restovich,M	Min	4	1	18.0	5	0	0	0	1.000	2.50

Player	Tm	G	GS	Inn	PO	A	E	DP	Pct.	Rng
Rios,Armando	Pit	11	8	75.1	13	1	0	0	1.000	1.67
Rivera,Juan	NYY	15	13	115.0	21	2	2	1	.920	1.80
Roberts,Dave	LA	3	0	4.0	1	0	0	0	1.000	2.25
Robinson,Kerry	Stl	52	19	207.2	55	0	2	0	.965	2.38
Rodriguez,H	Mon	4	2	19.0	0	0	0	0	-	.00
Rolls,Damian	TB	4	4	36.0	17	0	1	0	.944	4.25
Romano,Jason	Tex	11	6	58.1	17	0	0	0	1.000	2.62
Rowand,Aaron	CWS	40	22	79.0	12	1	0	0	1.000	1.48
Rushford,Jim	Mil	1	1	8.0	3	0	1	0	.750	3.38
Ryan,Mike	Min	4	2	15.0	2	0	0	0	1.000	1.20
Sadler,Donnie	KC	11	8	72.0	19	0	1	0	.950	2.38
Sadler,Donnie	Tex	2	0	2.0	0	0	0	0	-	.00
Sanchez,Alex	Mil	16	14	121.1	37	1	0	0	1.000	2.82
Schneider,Mon	Mon	1	0	1.0	0	0	0	0	-	.00
Scutaro,Marco	NYM	1	0	2.0	0	0	0	0	-	.00
Selby,Bill	Cle	13	6	60.0	11	0	0	0	1.000	1.65
Shinjo,T	SF	1	0	1.0	1	0	0	0	1.000	9.00
Shumpert,Terry	Col	7	7	51.0	9	0	0	0	1.000	1.59
Sierra,Ruben	Sea	59	53	417.1	91	1	1	0	.989	1.98
Smith,Bobby	TB	1	1	8.0	1	1	0	0	1.000	2.25
Snead,Esix	NYM	1	1	9.0	1	0	0	0	1.000	1.00
Snelling,Chris	Sea	6	6	44.0	13	0	0	0	1.000	2.66
Spencer,Shane	NYY	40	34	309.2	64	2	0	0	.971	1.92
Spiezio,Scott	Ana	8	0	15.0	3	0	0	0	1.000	1.80
Stairs,Matt	Mil	35	32	261.1	59	2	1	1	.984	2.10
Stevens,Lee	Cle	11	10	73.0	24	1	0	0	1.000	3.08
Sutton,Larry	Oak	2	2	16.0	5	1	0	0	1.000	3.38
Taguchi,So	Stl	8	0	11.2	3	0	1	0	.750	2.31
Tarasco,Tony	NYM	18	7	75.0	17	1	0	0	1.000	2.16
Taylor,Reggie	Cin	34	9	133.0	29	0	1	0	.967	1.96
Thames,Marcus	NYY	3	0	5.0	2	0	0	0	1.000	3.60
Thompson,Ryan	Mil	34	18	184.1	42	1	0	0	1.000	2.10
Trammell,Bubba	SD	23	13	130.0	26	2	1	0	.966	1.94
Truby,Chris	Mon	1	0	2.2	0	0	0	0	-	.00
Tucker,Michael	KC	33	26	245.0	57	2	0	1	1.000	2.17
Tyner,Jason	TB	41	40	356.1	96	2	1	0	.990	2.48
Vander Wal,J	NYY	8	7	49.0	12	0	0	0	1.000	2.20
Vaughn,Greg	TB	31	30	259.0	75	2	1	0	.987	2.68
Werth,Jayson	Tor	4	2	22.0	5	0	0	0	1.000	2.05
Wesson,Barry	Hou	3	0	7.0	1	0	0	0	1.000	1.29
Wigginton,Ty	NYM	1	0	3.0	0	0	0	0	-	.00
Wilkerson,Brad	Mon	72	43	440.1	72	8	2	0	.976	1.64
Williams,G	NYY	7	0	12.0	2	0	0	0	1.000	1.50
Wilson,Craig	Pit	1	0	2.2	1	0	0	0	1.000	3.38
Wise,Dewayne	Tor	6	5	48.0	13	1	0	0	1.000	2.63
Young,Dmitri	Det	1	1	4.0	1	0	0	0	1.000	2.25
Young,Eric	Mil	1	1	7.0	0	0	0	0	-	.00

Center Fielders - Regulars

Player	Tm	G	GS	Inn	PO	A	E	DP	Pct.	Rng
Erstad,Darin	Ana	143	142	1227.2	452	11	1	3	.998	3.39
Magee,Wendell	Det	78	75	660.2	242	3	5	1	.980	3.34
Shinjo,T	SF	108	93	821.0	275	10	6	3	.979	3.12
Rowand,Aaron	CWS	76	67	601.2	203	3	3	3	.986	3.08
Sanchez,Alex	Mil	86	78	694.1	234	0	5	0	.979	3.03
Winn,Randy	TB	138	134	1203.0	379	10	3	2	.992	2.91
Cameron,Mike	Sea	155	146	1318.0	415	7	5	0	.988	2.88
Lofton,Kenny	TOT	136	130	1114.2	346	6	0	0	1.000	2.84
Beltran,Carlos	KC	149	149	1308.1	398	12	7	0	.983	2.82
Edmonds,Jim	Stl	139	132	1160.0	347	11	5	4	.986	2.78
Pierre,Juan	Col	149	133	1197.2	363	2	2	1	.995	2.74
Jones,Andruw	Atl	154	152	1357.0	404	5	3	1	.993	2.71
Hunter,Torii	Min	146	144	1234.2	364	7	3	0	.992	2.70
Bradley,Milton	Cle	94	86	749.1	214	9	4	2	.982	2.68
Wells,Vernon	Tor	146	139	1240.1	357	11	2	1	.995	2.67
Perez,Timo	NYM	93	83	709.0	203	5	4	1	.981	2.64
Kotsay,Mark	SD	147	143	1228.1	349	11	4	3	.989	2.64
Payton,Jay	TOT	98	83	745.2	206	7	1	1	.995	2.57
Long,Terrence	Oak	162	158	1410.0	384	5	8	1	.980	2.48
Finley,Steve	Ari	142	141	1171.1	319	4	2	1	.994	2.48
Roberts,Dave	LA	115	111	935.0	252	4	0	1	1.000	2.46
Damon,Johnny	Bos	151	150	1319.1	351	7	1	0	.997	2.44
Singleton,C	Bal	126	111	1023.1	274	3	4	0	.986	2.44
Williams,B	NYY	147	141	1317.1	350	2	5	1	.986	2.40
Wilson,Preston	Fla	138	132	1178.2	300	8	6	2	.981	2.35
Glanville,Doug	Phi	117	95	891.1	220	8	0	4	1.000	2.30

263

Player	Tm	G	GS	Inn	PO	A	E	DP	Pct.	Rng
Patterson,C	ChC	147	136	1217.1	303	5	3	1	.990	2.28
Berkman,Lance	Hou	122	118	955.0	229	4	4	0	.983	2.20

Center Fielders - The Rest

Player	Tm	G	GS	Inn	PO	A	E	DP	Pct.	Rng
Abreu,Bobby	Phi	18	17	128.2	30	1	0	1	1.000	2.17
Agbayani,Benny	Bos	1	0	2.0	1	0	0	0	1.000	4.50
Alou,Moises	ChC	1	0	2.0	0	0	0	0	-	.00
Alvarez,Tony	Pit	6	5	41.2	5	0	0	0	1.000	1.08
Anderson,Bra	Cle	16	13	115.2	37	0	0	0	1.000	2.88
Anderson,G	Ana	14	12	99.0	40	1	0	1	1.000	3.73
Aven,Cle	Cle	1	0	1.0	0	0	0	0	-	.00
Bautista,Danny	Ari	5	4	34.0	9	0	0	0	1.000	2.38
Benard,Marvin	SF	6	3	29.2	8	1	0	0	1.000	2.73
Berger,Brandon	KC	1	0	5.0	1	0	0	0	1.000	1.80
Bergeron,Peter	Mon	31	30	277.1	76	0	2	0	.974	2.47
Bigbie,Larry	Bal	1	1	8.0	2	0	0	0	1.000	2.25
Bocachica,H	LA	3	1	11.0	3	0	0	0	1.000	2.45
Bocachica,H	Det	27	17	165.2	48	1	2	0	.961	2.66
Borchard,Joe	CWS	5	5	38.0	8	0	0	0	1.000	1.89
Bragg,Darren	Atl	18	9	110.1	30	0	1	0	.968	2.45
Brown,Adrian	Pit	64	41	402.0	104	1	3	0	.972	2.35
Brown,R	ChC	13	8	74.2	18	0	1	0	.947	2.17
Byrd,Marlon	Phi	8	8	66.0	15	0	0	0	1.000	2.05
Byrnes,Eric	Oak	10	3	35.0	10	1	0	0	1.000	2.83
Cabrera,Jol	Cle	16	15	130.2	35	0	0	0	1.000	2.41
Chavez,Endy	Mon	35	27	274.0	82	7	1	2	.989	2.92
Christensen,M	NYM	1	0	2.1	0	0	0	0	-	.00
Christensen,R	Mil	16	11	111.2	28	0	0	0	1.000	2.26
Clark,Brady	Cin	3	3	22.0	6	0	1	0	.857	2.45
Clark,Brady	NYM	2	0	2.0	0	0	0	0	-	.00
Colangelo,Mike	Oak	1	1	7.0	1	0	0	0	1.000	1.29
Collier,Lou	Mon	3	2	13.2	1	0	0	0	1.000	.66
Conti,Jason	TB	28	23	201.1	79	3	2	1	.976	3.67
Crespo,Cesar	SD	1	0	2.0	2	0	0	0	1.000	9.00
Crisp,Coco	Cle	31	30	269.1	80	1	1	1	.988	2.71
Cruz,Jose	Tor	21	20	175.0	50	1	1	0	.981	2.62
DaVanon,Jeff	Ana	4	1	16.0	2	0	0	0	1.000	1.13
DeHaan,Kory	SD	2	0	2.0	1	0	0	0	1.000	4.50
Dellucci,David	Ari	2	1	10.0	3	0	0	0	1.000	2.70
Drew,J.D.	Stl	6	1	15.0	3	0	0	0	1.000	1.80
Dunston,Shawon	SF	9	7	61.1	10	0	0	0	1.000	1.47
Encarnacion,J	Cin	59	57	498.0	162	2	2	1	.988	2.96
Encarnacion,J	Fla	12	12	87.1	20	0	0	0	1.000	2.06
Everett,Carl	Tex	33	24	217.1	61	0	1	0	.984	2.53
Gant,Ron	SD	1	0	2.0	1	0	0	0	1.000	4.50
Garcia,Karim	Cle	3	2	20.0	3	0	0	0	1.000	1.35
Garcia,Luis	Bal	1	0	1.0	0	0	0	0	-	.00
Giles,Brian	Pit	3	1	12.0	1	0	0	0	1.000	.75
Gipson,Charles	Sea	5	2	21.0	5	0	0	0	1.000	2.14
Gonzalez,Raul	Cin	5	5	40.0	10	1	0	0	1.000	2.48
Gonzalez,Raul	NYM	13	9	75.1	25	0	0	0	1.000	2.99
Goodwin,Tom	SF	22	13	134.2	50	0	0	0	1.000	3.34
Griffey Jr.,K	Cin	54	50	423.2	94	4	3	1	.970	2.08
Grissom,M	LA	72	48	491.2	115	1	3	0	.975	2.12
Guerrero,W	Mon	5	4	32.0	9	1	0	0	1.000	2.81
Guiel,Aaron	KC	1	0	4.0	2	0	0	0	1.000	4.50
Guillen,Jose	Ari	2	2	12.2	4	0	0	0	1.000	2.84
Hammonds,J	Mil	78	70	597.1	166	2	1	0	.994	2.53
Harris,Willie	CWS	6	4	39.0	19	1	0	0	1.000	4.62
Henderson,R	Bos	4	3	27.0	5	0	1	0	.833	1.67
Hermansen,Chad	Pit	59	46	401.1	106	5	2	1	.982	2.49
Hermansen,Chad	ChC	9	6	53.0	12	0	2	0	.857	2.04
Hidalgo,R	Hou	1	0	1.0	0	0	0	0	-	.00
Hocking,Denny	Min	1	0	1.0	1	0	0	0	1.000	9.00
Hollandsworth,T	Col	1	0	1.0	1	0	0	0	1.000	9.00
Hollandsworth,T	Tex	16	13	111.0	34	0	0	0	1.000	2.76
Hubbard,T	SD	16	9	92.2	20	1	1	0	.955	2.04
Hunter,Brian	Hou	88	40	440.0	121	4	0	1	1.000	2.56
Hyzdu,Adam	Pit	36	31	261.0	67	4	0	0	1.000	2.34
Jackson,Damian	Det	3	3	24.0	6	0	0	0	1.000	2.25
Jackson,Ryan	Det	1	0	1.0	0	0	0	0	-	.00
Kapler,Gabe	Tex	23	16	154.0	41	4	0	0	1.000	2.63
Kapler,Gabe	Col	1	0	2.0	1	0	0	0	1.000	4.50
Kearns,Austin	Cin	6	2	14.0	3	0	0	0	1.000	1.93
Kennedy,Adam	Ana	1	0	0.2	0	0	0	0	-	.00
Kielty,Bobby	Min	34	16	193.0	48	2	0	0	1.000	2.33
Kingsale,Gene	Sea	1	1	9.0	4	0	0	0	1.000	4.00
Kingsale,Gene	SD	17	9	94.1	40	1	0	0	1.000	3.91
Lane,Jason	Hou	1	1	12.0	4	0	0	0	1.000	3.00
Lankford,Ray	SD	3	1	15.0	0	0	0	1	.000	.00
Ledee,Ricky	Phi	40	35	297.2	83	0	0	0	1.000	2.51
Lewis,Darren	ChC	18	12	94.1	27	2	0	1	1.000	2.77
Little,Mark	Col	11	11	79.0	25	1	0	0	1.000	2.96
Little,Mark	Ari	2	1	10.0	4	0	0	0	1.000	3.60
Lofton,Kenny	CWS	92	86	744.1	230	3	0	0	1.000	2.82
Lofton,Kenny	SF	44	44	370.1	116	3	0	0	1.000	2.89
Lombard,George	Det	40	40	333.1	111	0	2	0	.982	3.00
Ludwick,Ryan	Tex	21	21	183.2	41	0	0	0	1.000	2.01
Macias,Jose	Det	9	8	71.1	24	0	0	0	1.000	3.03
Macias,Jose	Mon	49	29	274.1	83	4	2	1	.978	2.85
Mackowiak,Rob	Pit	42	37	294.2	68	2	1	0	.986	2.14
Magruder,Chris	Cle	20	16	138.2	42	0	1	0	.977	2.73
Marrero,Eli	Stl	36	24	207.1	72	3	0	1	1.000	3.26
Mateo,Ruben	Cin	2	2	13.1	5	0	0	0	1.000	3.38
Matos,Luis	Bal	6	4	36.0	11	0	0	0	1.000	2.75
Matthews Jr,G	Bal	16	15	125.0	34	3	2	0	.949	2.66
McCracken,Q	Ari	31	23	208.2	64	1	0	1	1.000	2.80
McEwing,Joe	NYM	1	1	9.0	4	0	0	0	1.000	4.00
McLemore,Mark	Sea	12	9	71.1	23	0	0	0	1.000	2.90
Mench,Kevin	Tex	1	0	2.0	0	0	0	0	-	.00
Michaels,Jason	Phi	14	6	66.0	11	2	0	0	1.000	1.77
Mohr,Dustan	Min	1	1	8.0	1	0	0	0	1.000	1.13
Mondesi,Raul	NYY	11	11	99.2	22	0	1	0	.957	1.99
Mora,Melvin	Bal	31	31	257.1	86	3	1	2	.989	3.11
Murray,Calvin	SF	4	2	20.1	6	1	1	0	.875	3.10
Murray,Calvin	Tex	33	24	220.2	69	2	0	1	1.000	2.90
Nelson,Bry	Bos	2	1	11.0	4	0	0	0	1.000	3.27
Nieves,Jose	Ana	1	0	1.0	1	0	1	0	.500	9.00
Nixon,Trot	Bos	13	8	87.0	21	3	0	0	1.000	2.48
Nunez,Abraham	Fla	12	2	38.0	10	0	0	0	1.000	2.37
Ochoa,Alex	Mil	2	0	6.0	3	0	0	0	1.000	4.50
Owens,Eric	Fla	22	16	150.1	47	1	1	1	.980	2.87
Ozuna,Pablo	Fla	1	0	2.0	0	0	0	0	-	.00
Palmeiro,O	Ana	15	5	62.0	23	0	1	0	.958	3.34
Payton,Jay	NYM	82	68	625.2	163	6	1	0	.994	2.43
Payton,Jay	Col	16	15	120.0	43	1	0	1	1.000	3.30
Petrick,Ben	Col	2	0	8.0	2	0	0	0	1.000	2.25
Podsednik,S	Sea	1	0	2.0	1	0	0	0	1.000	4.50
Ramirez,Julio	Ana	15	2	46.0	11	0	0	0	1.000	2.15
Rivera,Ruben	Tex	67	56	471.2	167	2	3	1	.983	3.22
Robinson,Kerry	Stl	10	3	39.0	15	0	0	0	1.000	3.46
Rolls,Damian	TB	4	4	35.0	10	1	0	1	1.000	2.83
Romano,Jason	Tex	8	4	36.2	15	0	0	0	1.000	3.68
Romano,Jason	Col	3	3	19.0	7	1	0	0	1.000	3.79
Ruan,Wilkin	LA	5	1	20.0	5	0	0	0	1.000	2.25
Ryan,Mike	Min	3	0	8.0	1	0	0	0	1.000	1.13
Sadler,Donnie	Tex	14	4	42.2	16	1	0	0	1.000	3.59
Snead,Esix	NYM	5	0	14.0	4	0	0	0	1.000	2.57
Suzuki,Ichiro	Sea	3	3	24.0	8	0	0	0	1.000	3.00
Taguchi,So	Stl	6	2	25.0	8	2	0	0	1.000	3.60
Tarasco,Tony	NYM	2	0	5.0	2	0	0	0	1.000	3.60
Taylor,Reggie	Cin	68	43	442.2	142	2	4	0	.973	2.93
Thompson,Ryan	Mil	5	3	23.0	4	0	0	0	1.000	1.57
Torres,Andres	Det	19	18	158.0	51	0	1	0	.981	2.91
Tucker,Michael	KC	14	13	123.2	46	2	0	0	1.000	3.49
Tyner,Jason	TB	1	0	1.0	2	0	0	0	1.000	18.00
Werth,Jayson	Tor	1	1	9.0	6	0	0	0	1.000	6.00
Wesson,Barry	Hou	9	3	37.0	9	0	0	0	1.000	2.19
White,Rondell	NYY	1	1	7.0	0	0	0	0	-	.00
Wilkerson,Brad	Mon	73	70	581.2	151	5	5	3	.969	2.41
Williams,G	NYY	6	2	28.0	6	0	0	0	1.000	1.93
Wise,Dewayne	Tor	3	2	14.0	9	0	0	0	1.000	5.79

Right Fielders - Regulars

Player	Tm	G	GS	Inn	PO	A	E	DP	Pct.	Rng
Mohr,Dustan	Min	94	78	718.0	195	3	2	2	.990	2.48
Kearns,Austin	Cin	95	87	774.2	203	7	4	2	.981	2.44
Lawton,Matt	Cle	85	84	699.1	184	5	6	2	.969	2.43
Sanders,Reggie	SF	137	133	1135.2	290	12	5	2	.984	2.39
Suzuki,Ichiro	Sea	150	146	1284.1	325	8	3	0	.991	2.33
Fick,Robert	Det	140	139	1202.2	288	21	12	5	.963	2.31

Player	Tm	G	GS	Inn	PO	A	E	DP	Pct.	Rng
Grieve,Ben	TB	118	117	1038.2	249	6	3	2	.988	2.21
Green,Shawn	LA	156	156	1388.2	333	7	2	3	.994	2.20
Encarnacion,J	TOT	92	78	710.1	165	7	4	5	.977	2.18
Drew,J.D.	Stl	119	107	931.2	220	4	3	1	.987	2.16
Hidalgo,R	Hou	110	101	913.1	209	6	1	3	.995	2.12
Walker,Larry	Col	123	122	1037.0	229	14	4	5	.984	2.11
Gibbons,Jay	Bal	92	91	787.2	174	6	1	2	.994	2.06
Nixon,Trot	Bos	145	137	1223.0	273	4	5	3	.982	2.04
Ordonez,M	CWS	150	149	1289.0	283	8	4	0	.986	2.03
Burnitz,Jeromy	NYM	140	131	1148.0	251	8	9	0	.966	2.03
Sosa,Sammy	ChC	150	150	1294.1	284	7	6	1	.980	2.02
Salmon,Tim	Ana	111	109	918.2	201	4	3	0	.986	2.01
Guerrero,V	Mon	161	160	1409.1	298	14	10	4	.969	1.99
Sheffield,Gary	Atl	127	127	1102.0	232	7	4	0	.984	1.95
Abreu,Bobby	Phi	148	136	1225.1	252	9	5	1	.981	1.92
Mondesi,Raul	TOT	121	121	1087.1	218	7	5	1	.978	1.86
Trammell,Bubba	SD	104	94	761.1	148	3	4	1	.974	1.79
Dye,Jermaine	Oak	111	109	956.1	170	4	5	2	.972	1.62

Right Fielders - The Rest

Player	Tm	G	GS	Inn	PO	A	E	DP	Pct.	Rng
Agbayani,Benny	Bos	3	2	19.0	3	0	0	0	1.000	1.42
Alcantara,Izzy	Mil	5	3	27.0	6	0	0	0	1.000	2.00
Alicea,Luis	KC	1	0	0.1	0	0	0	0	-	.00
Allen,Chad	Cle	1	0	2.0	0	0	0	0	-	.00
Allen,Luke	LA	3	1	16.0	4	0	0	0	1.000	2.25
Alou,Moises	ChC	4	4	29.0	5	0	0	0	1.000	1.55
Alvarez,Tony	Pit	1	0	4.0	1	0	0	0	1.000	2.25
Anderson,Bra	Cle	2	2	18.2	0	0	0	0	-	.00
Aven,Bruce	Cle	1	1	8.0	2	0	0	0	1.000	2.25
Banks,Brian	Fla	5	4	27.0	5	0	0	0	1.000	1.67
Bautista,Danny	Ari	37	35	293.1	56	0	1	0	.982	1.72
Benard,Marvin	SF	20	8	92.1	28	1	0	0	1.000	2.83
Benjamin,Mike	Pit	1	0	1.0	0	0	0	0	-	.00
Berg,Dave	Tor	10	9	83.0	16	0	0	0	1.000	1.73
Berger,Brandon	KC	21	19	163.2	36	2	0	0	1.000	2.09
Berkman,Lance	Hou	12	6	58.0	18	1	0	1	1.000	2.95
Bigbie,Larry	Bal	6	1	13.0	5	0	0	0	1.000	3.46
Blum,Geoff	Hou	3	2	18.0	5	0	0	0	1.000	2.50
Bocachica,H	LA	2	0	4.0	0	0	0	0	-	.00
Bocachica,H	Det	4	2	29.0	6	2	0	0	1.000	2.48
Borchard,Joe	CWS	3	1	12.0	1	0	0	0	1.000	.75
Bragg,Darren	Atl	36	22	228.1	56	2	1	0	.983	2.29
Brown,Adrian	Pit	9	3	38.2	7	0	0	0	1.000	1.63
Brown,R	ChC	4	1	10.1	0	0	0	0	-	.00
Buchanan,Brian	Min	24	20	166.1	48	0	0	0	1.000	2.60
Buchanan,Brian	SD	14	13	95.1	18	1	1	0	.950	1.79
Byrd,Marlon	Phi	2	1	11.0	2	0	0	0	1.000	1.64
Byrnes,Eric	Oak	22	6	75.2	19	0	0	0	1.000	2.26
Cabrera,Jol	Cle	13	1	26.0	3	0	0	0	1.000	1.04
Cabrera,Jol	LA	1	0	4.0	0	0	0	0	-	.00
Cairo,Miguel	Stl	5	0	7.0	2	0	1	0	.667	2.57
Cepicky,Matt	Mon	1	0	1.0	0	0	0	0	-	.00
Clark,Brady	Cin	6	0	10.1	3	0	0	0	1.000	2.61
Clark,Brady	NYM	3	1	13.0	3	0	0	0	1.000	2.08
Colangelo,Mike	Oak	5	3	29.0	9	0	0	0	1.000	2.79
Collier,Lou	Mon	1	0	1.0	1	0	0	0	1.000	9.00
Conti,Jason	TB	28	22	206.1	45	3	2	0	.960	2.09
Cordero,Wil	Mon	5	1	22.0	3	0	1	0	.750	1.23
Crespo,Cesar	SD	1	0	0.2	0	0	0	0	-	.00
Cruz,Jacob	Det	9	8	67.1	11	0	0	0	1.000	1.47
Cruz,Jose	Tor	47	46	390.2	81	5	1	2	.989	1.98
Cuddyer,Mike	Min	25	20	165.1	47	1	1	0	.980	2.61
Daubach,Brian	Bos	13	8	74.0	19	2	0	0	1.000	2.55
DaVanon,Jeff	Ana	4	3	32.0	10	0	0	0	1.000	2.81
Davis,J.J.	Pit	4	2	18.2	3	0	0	0	1.000	1.45
DeHaan,Kory	SD	1	0	1.0	0	0	0	0	-	.00
Dellucci,David	Ari	45	40	335.2	52	1	1	1	.981	1.42
DeRosa,Mark	Atl	5	1	15.0	3	0	0	0	1.000	1.80
DeShields,D	ChC	1	0	2.2	2	0	0	0	1.000	6.75
Dunn,Adam	Cin	17	9	82.1	8	2	1	0	.909	1.09
Dunston,Shawon	SF	22	8	91.0	22	0	0	0	1.000	2.18
Dunwoody,Todd	Cle	1	1	8.0	0	0	0	0	-	.00
Durazo,Erubiel	Ari	2	2	15.0	3	0	0	0	1.000	1.80
Echevarria,A	ChC	11	7	69.0	17	1	0	0	1.000	2.35
Encarnacion,J	Cin	31	24	206.2	50	3	3	3	.946	2.31

Player	Tm	G	GS	Inn	PO	A	E	DP	Pct.	Rng
Encarnacion,J	Fla	61	54	503.2	115	4	1	2	.992	2.13
Everett,Carl	Tex	39	38	325.2	76	0	1	0	.987	2.10
Floyd,Cliff	Fla	60	60	522.2	124	3	2	1	.984	2.19
Floyd,Cliff	Bos	6	6	49.0	10	0	0	0	1.000	1.84
Fox,Andy	Fla	1	0	1.0	0	0	0	0	-	.00
Franco,Matt	Atl	2	1	12.0	0	0	0	0	-	.00
Gant,Ron	SD	5	3	25.0	3	0	0	0	1.000	1.08
Garcia,Jesse	Atl	2	0	7.0	4	0	0	0	1.000	5.14
Garcia,Karim	NYY	1	0	1.0	0	0	0	0	-	.00
Garcia,Karim	Cle	48	46	414.0	91	2	1	0	.989	2.02
Garcia,Luis	Bal	1	0	2.0	1	0	0	0	1.000	4.50
Giambi,Jeremy	Phi	18	17	132.2	22	0	2	0	.917	1.49
Gipson,Charles	Sea	13	7	70.0	19	0	2	0	.905	2.44
Gomez,Alexis	KC	2	2	15.0	4	1	0	1	1.000	3.00
Gonzalez,Juan	Tex	62	61	515.2	117	9	1	1	.992	2.20
Gonzalez,Raul	NYM	0	0	15.0	3	0	0	0	1.000	1.80
Goodwin,Tom	SF	7	7	56.0	16	0	0	0	1.000	2.57
Greer,Rusty	Tex	6	6	51.2	9	0	1	0	.900	1.57
Griffey Jr.,K	Cin	1	0	4.0	1	0	0	0	1.000	2.25
Grissom,M	LA	2	1	11.0	3	1	0	0	1.000	3.27
Guerrero,W	Mon	3	0	3.1	1	0	0	0	1.000	2.70
Guiel,Aaron	KC	61	53	488.0	112	5	6	1	.951	2.16
Guillen,Jose	Ari	34	26	239.2	48	2	0	0	1.000	1.88
Guillen,Jose	Cin	26	22	204.1	40	2	0	0	1.000	1.85
Hammonds,J	Mil	55	49	428.0	78	2	1	1	.988	1.68
Helms,Wes	Atl	4	1	23.0	8	0	0	0	1.000	3.13
Henderson,R	Bos	1	0	1.0	0	0	0	0	-	.00
Hermansen,Chad	Pit	2	0	3.0	1	0	0	0	1.000	3.00
Hermansen,Chad	ChC	9	0	25.0	3	0	0	0	1.000	1.08
Hocking,Denny	Min	4	0	11.0	3	0	0	0	1.000	2.45
Hollandsworth,T	Col	20	13	120.1	30	1	0	0	1.000	2.32
Hollandsworth,T	Tex	4	1	6.0	2	0	0	0	1.000	3.00
Hubbard,T	SD	26	2	65.1	12	1	0	0	1.000	1.79
Hyzdu,Adam	Pit	13	6	63.2	13	1	0	0	1.000	1.98
Ibanez,Raul	KC	16	14	116.1	21	1	0	0	1.000	1.70
Jordan,Brian	LA	4	4	34.0	8	0	0	0	1.000	2.12
Jose,Felix	Ari	4	4	33.1	5	0	0	0	1.000	1.35
Justice,David	Oak	23	23	195.0	50	0	0	0	1.000	2.31
Kapler,Gabe	Tex	18	9	83.1	21	1	2	0	.917	2.38
Kapler,Gabe	Col	23	16	172.0	44	2	0	0	1.000	2.41
Kielty,Bobby	Min	50	42	375.0	102	2	0	0	1.000	2.50
Kingsale,Gene	Sea	1	0	2.0	0	0	0	0	-	.00
Kingsale,Gene	SD	50	18	217.0	44	3	2	0	.959	1.95
Klesko,Ryan	SD	31	30	239.0	39	0	0	0	1.000	1.47
Lamb,Mike	Tex	5	0	6.0	1	0	0	0	1.000	1.50
Lane,Jason	Hou	27	16	150.2	39	3	1	1	.977	2.51
Ledee,Ricky	Phi	5	2	33.0	6	0	0	0	1.000	1.64
Lesher,Brian	Tor	2	1	8.0	0	0	0	0	-	.00
Lewis,Darren	ChC	9	0	11.0	2	0	0	0	1.000	1.64
Liefer,Jeff	CWS	12	9	84.0	18	1	0	0	1.000	2.04
Little,Mark	Col	16	9	87.0	32	1	1	1	.971	3.41
Little,Mark	NYM	1	0	2.0	0	0	0	0	-	.00
Little,Mark	Ari	7	2	21.2	2	0	0	0	1.000	.83
Lombard,George	Det	1	1	9.0	1	0	0	0	1.000	1.00
Ludwick,Ryan	Tex	1	0	0.1	0	0	0	0	-	.00
Mabry,John	Phi	1	1	5.0	1	0	0	0	1.000	1.80
Mabry,John	Oak	24	15	131.0	30	0	1	0	.968	2.06
Macias,Jose	Det	1	0	2.0	0	0	0	0	-	.00
Mackowiak,Rob	Pit	76	40	397.1	82	5	1	2	.989	1.97
Magee,Wendell	Det	9	6	57.0	11	2	0	0	1.000	2.05
Magruder,Chris	Cle	27	21	190.2	31	1	1	0	.970	1.51
Marrero,Eli	Stl	46	33	301.0	72	5	2	3	.975	2.30
Mateo,Ruben	Cin	23	16	138.2	28	1	0	0	1.000	1.88
Matos,Julius	SD	3	0	6.1	1	0	0	0	1.000	1.42
Matos,Luis	Bal	7	4	38.2	5	0	0	0	1.000	1.16
Matthews Jr,G	Bal	76	63	579.1	130	2	3	1	.978	2.05
McCracken,Q	Ari	68	53	506.0	113	4	1	0	.992	2.08
McEwing,Joe	NYM	24	15	118.2	33	0	0	0	1.000	2.50
McLemore,Mark	Sea	1	1	8.0	1	0	0	0	1.000	1.13
Mench,Kevin	Tex	62	47	445.0	106	1	1	0	.991	2.16
Merced,Orlando	Hou	44	36	293.0	61	6	2	0	.971	2.06
Merloni,Lou	Bos	1	0	0.0	0	0	0	0	-	
Michaels,Jason	Phi	7	4	35.0	8	0	0	0	1.000	2.06
Millar,Kevin	Fla	22	21	162.2	26	2	0	1	1.000	1.55
Mondesi,Raul	Tor	62	62	551.0	119	3	2	1	.984	1.99
Mondesi,Raul	NYY	59	59	536.1	99	4	3	0	.972	1.73
Monroe,Craig	Det	5	3	27.0	11	0	0	0	1.000	3.67
Mora,Melvin	Bal	5	3	30.0	6	0	0	0	1.000	1.80
Murray,Calvin	SF	3	0	4.0	2	0	0	0	1.000	4.50

Player	Tm	G	GS	Inn	PO	A	E	DP	Pct.	Rng
Murray,Calvin	Tex	1	0	1.0	0	0	0	0	-	.00
Nelson,Bry	Bos	2	1	10.0	3	1	0	0	1.000	3.60
Nieves,Jose	Ana	1	0	3.0	0	0	0	0	-	.00
Nunez,Abraham	Fla	1	0	3.0	1	0	0	0	1.000	3.00
Ochoa,Alex	Mil	61	41	390.0	104	4	1	1	.991	2.49
Ochoa,Alex	Ana	31	10	136.0	25	2	0	1	1.000	1.79
Offerman,Jose	Bos	2	2	18.0	2	0	1	0	.667	1.00
Offerman,Jose	Sea	1	0	1.0	0	0	0	0	-	.00
O'Leary,Troy	Mon	1	0	0.1	0	0	0	0	-	.00
Owens,Eric	Fla	39	23	236.1	54	2	3	0	.949	2.13
Palmeiro,O	Ana	47	35	313.0	73	2	0	1	1.000	2.16
Paquette,Craig	Det	4	2	20.0	4	0	0	0	1.000	1.80
Payton,Jay	Col	2	1	3.1	1	0	0	0	1.000	2.70
Pena,Wily Mo	Cin	1	1	5.0	0	0	0	0	-	.00
Perez,Eduardo	Stl	29	18	143.0	41	1	1	1	.977	2.64
Perez,Timo	NYM	17	8	80.2	20	1	0	1	1.000	2.34
Piatt,Adam	Oak	12	6	61.0	11	0	0	0	1.000	1.62
Podsednik,S	Sea	2	1	9.0	3	0	1	0	.750	3.00
Pujols,Albert	Stl	1	0	3.0	0	0	0	0	-	.00
Quinn,Mark	KC	15	15	123.0	25	0	0	0	1.000	1.83
Ramirez,Julio	Ana	9	5	46.2	15	1	0	0	1.000	3.09
Ramirez,Manny	Bos	7	6	52.0	13	2	0	1	1.000	2.60
Relaford,Desi	Sea	10	4	50.0	14	0	0	0	1.000	2.52
Restovich,M	Min	1	1	9.0	2	0	0	0	1.000	2.00
Rios,Armando	Pit	47	45	348.2	76	4	0	1	1.000	2.07
Rivera,Juan	NYY	15	12	119.2	33	0	0	0	1.000	2.48
Robinson,Kerry	Stl	17	4	60.2	15	0	0	0	1.000	2.23
Rodriguez,H	Mon	1	0	3.0	0	0	0	0	-	.00
Rolls,Damian	TB	13	13	114.0	26	0	2	0	.929	2.05
Rowand,Aaron	CWS	7	3	38.0	9	1	1	0	.909	2.37
Rushford,Jim	Mil	21	20	173.0	40	0	1	0	.976	2.08
Sadler,Donnie	KC	4	1	12.0	3	0	0	0	1.000	2.25
Sadler,Donnie	Tex	3	0	5.0	2	0	0	0	1.000	3.60
Schneider,B	Mon	1	0	3.0	0	0	0	0	-	.00
Selby,Bill	Cle	5	1	18.0	4	0	0	0	1.000	2.00
Shinjo,T	SF	10	4	36.1	10	0	0	0	1.000	2.48
Shumpert,Terry	Col	1	1	7.0	1	0	0	0	1.000	1.29
Sierra,Ruben	Sea	1	1	3.0	0	0	1	0	.000	.00
Smith,Bobby	TB	1	1	9.0	2	0	0	0	1.000	2.00
Snelling,Chris	Sea	2	2	18.0	3	0	0	0	1.000	1.50
Spencer,Shane	NYY	55	42	385.0	88	3	2	1	.978	2.13
Spiezio,Scott	Ana	2	0	3.0	0	0	0	0	-	.00
Stairs,Matt	Mil	51	43	341.0	70	4	0	0	1.000	1.95
Stevens,Lee	Cle	5	5	40.0	8	0	0	0	1.000	1.80
Surhoff,B.J.	Atl	9	9	80.0	27	2	0	0	1.000	3.26
Sutton,Larry	Oak	1	0	4.0	0	0	0	0	-	.00
Swann,Pedro	Tor	1	0	2.0	0	0	0	0	-	.00
Sweeney,Mark	SD	5	2	25.1	8	0	0	0	1.000	2.84
Tarasco,Tony	NYM	13	6	64.1	21	2	1	1	.958	3.22
Taylor,Reggie	Cin	6	3	27.2	5	0	0	0	1.000	1.63
Thames,Marcus	NYY	4	2	25.0	5	0	0	0	1.000	1.80
Thompson,Ryan	Mil	14	6	71.2	16	1	1	0	.944	2.13
Torcato,Tony	SF	3	2	22.0	2	0	0	0	1.000	.82
Tucker,Michael	KC	67	58	522.2	121	5	2	0	.984	2.17
Valent,Eric	Phi	2	0	7.2	0	0	0	0	-	.00
Vander Wal,J	NYY	49	45	343.0	75	0	2	0	.974	1.97
Wells,Vernon	Tor	13	13	118.0	24	0	1	0	.960	1.83
Werth,Jayson	Tor	10	10	90.0	22	1	0	0	1.000	2.30
Wesson,Barry	Hou	3	1	12.0	1	0	0	0	1.000	.75
Wigginton,Ty	NYM	1	0	1.0	0	0	0	0	-	.00
Wilkerson,Brad	Mon	3	1	10.0	3	0	0	0	1.000	2.70
Williams,G	NYY	17	0	33.0	4	1	0	1	1.000	1.36
Wilson,Craig	Pit	74	65	537.2	106	6	2	0	.982	1.87
Wilson,Enrique	NYY	1	1	9.0	0	0	0	0	-	.00
Winn,Randy	TB	8	8	72.1	15	3	0	1	1.000	2.24
Wise,Dewayne	Tor	26	21	195.2	57	4	0	3	1.000	2.81
Womack,Tony	Ari	1	0	2.0	0	0	0	0	-	.00
Young,Eric	Mil	1	0	1.2	1	0	0	0	1.000	5.40

Catchers - Regulars

Player	Tm	G	GS	Inn	PO	A	E	DP	PB	Pct.
Molina,Ben	Ana	121	114	1014.1	707	60	1	6	5	.999
Inge,Brandon	Det	94	94	820.1	484	46	1	3	10	.998
Miller,Damian	Ari	100	90	763.0	716	49	2	8	8	.997
Wilson,Dan	Sea	113	107	902.2	692	27	2	4	2	.997
Ausmus,Brad	Hou	129	121	1079.0	942	65	3	9	2	.997

Player	Tm	G	GS	Inn	PO	A	E	DP	PB	Pct.
Pierzynski,A	Min	124	118	1035.2	757	41	3	3	2	.996
Alomar Jr.,S	TOT	88	76	676.2	483	22	2	4	5	.996
Varitek,Jason	Bos	127	121	1064.2	912	54	4	8	10	.996
Gil,Geronimo	Bal	125	122	1068.2	740	60	4	14	19	.995
Santiago,B	SF	125	122	1066.2	738	54	4	10	7	.995
Johnson,C	Fla	82	77	638.1	488	49	3	9	5	.994
LaRue,Jason	Cin	110	100	906.1	626	56	4	5	20	.994
Johnson,Mark L	CWS	85	80	707.1	484	27	3	3	3	.994
Matheny,Mike	Stl	106	96	830.1	562	64	4	6	5	.994
Lieberthal,M	Phi	129	126	1127.1	840	56	6	8	7	.993
Mayne,Brent	KC	99	94	836.2	552	39	4	4	5	.993
Redmond,Mike	Fla	80	68	615.2	492	50	4	9	1	.993
Lo Duca,Paul	LA	137	136	1184.0	965	76	8	9	12	.992
Bennett,Gary	Col	90	85	726.2	453	32	4	5	6	.992
Hernandez,Ra	Oak	135	125	1100.2	788	58	7	12	6	.992
Flaherty,John	TB	75	74	669.0	450	33	4	8	7	.992
Lampkin,Tom	SD	94	79	710.1	553	42	5	7	7	.992
Girardi,Joe	ChC	88	67	615.2	554	43	6	6	6	.990
Rodriguez,Ivan	Tex	100	97	836.1	632	45	7	6	6	.990
Kendall,Jason	Pit	143	140	1191.2	797	64	9	13	8	.990
Hall,Toby	TB	83	83	737.1	506	34	6	5	4	.989
Barrett,M	Mon	110	105	931.1	751	55	9	9	9	.989
Diaz,Einar	Cle	100	97	833.1	640	75	8	4	8	.989
Huckaby,Ken	Tor	88	77	683.0	494	31	6	10	13	.989
Posada,Jorge	NYY	138	131	1190.2	965	66	12	5	7	.988
Piazza,Mike	NYM	121	119	1006.2	811	46	12	3	8	.986
Lopez,Javy	Atl	103	92	815.1	635	54	10	8	5	.986
Hundley,Todd	ChC	79	71	604.1	622	40	11	8	7	.984

Catchers - The Rest

Player	Tm	G	GS	Inn	PO	A	E	DP	PB	Pct.
Alomar Jr.,S	CWS	50	46	404.0	293	14	2	3	2	.994
Alomar Jr.,S	Col	38	30	272.2	190	8	0	1	3	1.000
Bako,Paul	Mil	76	65	587.2	420	33	4	2	5	.991
Barajas,Rod	Ari	69	41	406.0	293	18	1	1	4	.997
Bard,Josh	Cle	24	24	209.1	153	13	2	4	2	.988
Blanco,Henry	Atl	79	64	594.2	417	38	3	1	6	.993
Borders,Pat	Sea	2	0	4.0	2	0	0	0	0	1.000
Brito,Juan	KC	9	8	63.0	42	3	1	1	1	.978
Brown,Kevin L	Bos	2	0	3.0	1	0	0	0	0	1.000
Cardona,Javier	SD	14	11	101.0	76	5	2	2	0	.976
Casanova,Raul	Mil	28	25	218.1	166	13	1	0	2	.994
Casanova,Raul	Bal	2	0	2.0	3	0	0	0	0	1.000
Cash,Kevin	Tor	7	4	38.0	26	4	1	1	2	.968
Castillo,A	NYY	14	12	104.0	93	9	1	0	2	.990
Castro,Ramon	Fla	37	17	202.1	148	12	0	0	0	1.000
Chavez,Raul	Hou	2	1	14.0	10	0	0	0	0	1.000
Cota,Humberto	Pit	7	4	40.1	33	1	0	1	0	1.000
Davis,Ben	Sea	77	55	538.2	416	23	1	5	5	.998
DiFelice,Mike	Stl	51	51	435.1	313	32	3	5	2	.991
Estalella,B	Col	38	32	289.1	203	9	1	2	2	.995
Estrada,Johnny	Phi	10	3	40.2	34	2	0	0	1	1.000
Fabregas,Jorge	Ana	32	23	214.0	156	8	1	1	1	.994
Fabregas,Jorge	Mil	20	17	149.0	118	9	1	0	1	.992
Fasano,Sal	Ana	2	0	7.0	10	2	0	0	0	1.000
Fletcher,D	Tor	36	29	253.2	181	12	1	1	0	.995
Fordyce,Brook	Bal	55	39	369.0	267	8	4	1	3	.986
Gonzalez,Wiki	SD	54	52	442.2	367	27	6	4	6	.985
Greene,Todd	Tex	15	11	104.2	87	7	1	2	2	.989
Haselman,Bill	Tex	67	49	453.2	310	19	3	0	2	.991
Hinch,A.J.	KC	68	60	527.1	349	23	4	2	2	.989
Hoover,Paul	TB	4	4	34.0	16	2	0	0	2	1.000
Jensen,Marcus	Mil	15	10	95.1	73	9	2	1	2	.976
Kreuter,Chad	LA	41	24	247.2	197	16	3	1	0	.986
Lamb,Mike	Tex	3	1	7.0	10	1	0	0	1	1.000
LeCroy,Matt	Min	6	3	27.0	20	1	0	0	2	1.000
Lunar,Fernando	Bal	2	0	2.0	2	0	0	0	0	1.000
Lunsford,Trey	SF	3	0	7.0	4	0	1	0	0	.800
Machado,Robert	ChC	21	15	138.0	110	25	2	2	1	.985
Machado,Robert	Mil	48	45	382.0	277	31	4	5	2	.987
Mahoney,Mike	ChC	15	9	83.1	76	7	0	0	1	1.000
Marrero,Eli	Stl	44	15	180.2	151	9	4	2	2	.976
Martinez,V	Cle	9	7	69.0	55	2	1	0	1	.983
McKay,Cody	Oak	1	1	8.0	6	0	0	0	0	1.000
McKeel,Walt	Col	5	3	28.1	22	0	0	0	1	1.000
Meluskey,Mitch	Det	8	8	71.1	34	3	0	0	1	1.000

Player	Tm	G	GS	Inn	PO	A	E	DP	PB	Pct.
Miller,Corky	Cin	38	35	301.0	220	23	2	4	1	.992
Mirabelli,Doug	Bos	50	41	378.1	285	30	0	3	10	1.000
Moeller,Chad	Ari	35	31	277.2	310	7	1	0	1	.997
Molina,Izzy	Bal	1	1	9.0	7	1	0	0	0	1.000
Molina,Jose	Ana	29	24	210.0	154	16	3	3	1	.983
Myers,Greg	Oak	53	36	343.1	264	21	1	0	3	.997
Nieves,Wil	SD	27	20	182.1	160	8	5	0	1	.971
Olivo,Miguel	CWS	6	6	48.1	31	1	0	0	2	1.000
Ortiz,Hector	Tex	7	4	38.0	22	0	1	0	0	.957
Osik,Keith	Pit	27	17	171.2	118	15	1	1	2	.993
Paul,Josh	CWS	32	30	263.1	200	6	2	1	2	.990
Perez,Eddie	Cle	42	34	313.0	235	19	3	7	4	.988
Petrick,Ben	Col	14	12	109.2	89	3	2	0	0	.979
Phillips,Jason	NYM	7	2	37.0	27	1	0	0	0	1.000
Pratt,Todd	Phi	34	32	281.2	239	10	0	3	4	1.000
Prince,Tom	Min	50	40	371.0	272	14	1	2	1	.997
Rivera,Mike	Det	37	35	303.0	189	19	2	1	10	.990
Ross,Dave	LA	6	2	26.0	19	2	0	0	0	1.000
Schneider,B	Mon	65	57	521.2	382	34	3	6	3	.993
Stinnett,Kelly	Cin	30	27	246.1	189	14	2	3	7	.990
Torrealba,S	Atl	12	5	57.1	40	2	0	1	1	1.000
Torrealba,Y	SF	53	40	363.2	269	20	2	3	0	.993
Valentin,Ja	Min	4	0	11.0	14	1	0	0	0	1.000
Walbeck,Matt	Det	27	24	219.1	127	8	1	2	2	.993
Wathan,Dusty	KC	3	1	14.0	14	0	0	0	0	1.000
Widger,Chris	NYY	21	18	157.1	111	6	2	1	1	.983
Wilson,Craig	Pit	5	0	9.0	10	0	0	0	2	1.000
Wilson,Tom	Tor	65	52	463.2	318	20	4	4	3	.988
Wilson,Vance	NYM	66	40	399.0	315	38	6	5	3	.983
Wooten,Shawn	Ana	2	1	7.0	2	1	0	0	0	1.000
Zaun,Gregg	Hou	44	40	351.0	307	18	5	3	3	.985
Zinter,Alan	Hou	1	0	1.0	2	0	0	0	0	1.000

Catchers Special - Regulars

Player	Tm	G	GS	Inn	SBA	CS	PCS	CS%	ER	CERA
Lopez,Javy	Atl	103	92	815.1	87	33	8	.32	302	3.33
Matheny,Mike	Stl	106	96	830.1	66	23	1	.34	322	3.49
Santiago,B	SF	125	122	1066.2	83	25	3	.28	415	3.50
Hernandez,Ra	Oak	134	125	1100.2	75	30	8	.33	431	3.52
Molina,Ben	Ana	121	114	1014.1	78	35	3	.43	404	3.58
Lo Duca,Paul	LA	137	136	1184.0	135	42	12	.24	491	3.73
Varitek,Jason	Bos	127	121	1064.2	112	31	2	.26	442	3.74
Barrett,M	Mon	110	105	931.1	83	24	3	.26	388	3.75
Posada,Jorge	NYY	138	131	1190.2	107	31	8	.23	502	3.79
Ausmus,Brad	Hou	129	121	1079.0	96	31	1	.32	461	3.85
Piazza,Mike	NYM	121	119	1006.2	152	27	6	.14	433	3.87
Girardi,Joe	ChC	88	67	615.2	65	20	0	.31	275	4.02
Hundley,Todd	ChC	78	71	604.1	77	20	0	.26	270	4.02
Redmond,Mike	Fla	80	68	615.2	69	29	3	.39	278	4.06
Pierzynski,A	Min	123	118	1035.2	64	19	4	.25	469	4.08
Miller,Damian	Ari	100	90	763.0	66	25	2	.36	350	4.13
Kendall,Jason	Pit	143	140	1191.2	117	39	13	.25	547	4.13
Wilson,Dan	Sea	113	107	902.2	60	17	3	.25	416	4.15
Gil,Geronimo	Bal	125	122	1068.2	96	35	3	.34	507	4.27
Lieberthal,M	Phi	129	126	1127.1	79	28	2	.34	536	4.28
Huckaby,Ken	Tor	88	77	683.0	57	20	2	.33	325	4.28
Johnson,Mark L	CWS	85	80	707.1	66	24	8	.28	346	4.40
Flaherty,John	TB	75	74	669.0	74	26	6	.29	337	4.53
Johnson,C	Fla	82	77	638.1	62	25	4	.36	328	4.62
LaRue,Jason	Cin	110	100	906.1	62	28	3	.42	474	4.71
Inge,Brandon	Det	94	94	820.1	61	17	4	.23	436	4.78
Alomar Jr.,S	TOT	87	76	676.2	64	15	2	.21	368	4.89
Lampkin,Tom	SD	94	79	710.1	57	18	0	.32	405	5.13
Mayne,Brent	KC	99	93	836.2	66	23	2	.33	479	5.15
Diaz,Einar	Cle	100	97	833.1	118	36	4	.28	480	5.18
Rodriguez,Ivan	Tex	100	97	836.1	41	15	2	.33	485	5.22
Bennett,Gary	Col	90	85	726.2	54	12	1	.21	438	5.42
Hall,Toby	TB	83	83	737.1	64	24	5	.32	486	5.93

Catchers Special - The Rest

Player	Tm	G	GS	Inn	SBA	CS	PCS	CS%	ER	CERA
Alomar Jr.,S	CWS	50	46	404.0	46	10	1	.20	199	4.43
Alomar Jr.,S	Col	37	30	272.2	18	5	1	.25	169	5.58
Bako,Paul	Mil	76	65	587.2	61	16	2	.25	311	4.76

Player	Tm	G	GS	Inn	SBA	CS	PCS	CS%	ER	CERA
Barajas,Rod	Ari	68	41	406.0	28	10	3	.32	199	4.41
Bard,Josh	Cle	24	24	209.1	16	7	0	.44	117	5.03
Blanco,Henry	Atl	79	64	594.2	58	21	2	.35	194	2.94
Borders,Pat	Sea	2	0	4.0	0	0	0	-	2	4.50
Brito,Juan	KC	9	8	63.0	11	4	2	.29	34	4.86
Brown,Kevin L	Bos	2	0	3.0	0	0	0	-	0	0.00
Cardona,Javier	SD	14	11	101.0	9	4	0	.44	38	3.39
Casanova,Raul	Mil	28	25	218.1	30	9	2	.27	107	4.41
Casanova,Raul	Bal	2	0	2.0	0	0	0	-	4	18.00
Cash,Kevin	Tor	7	4	38.0	4	1	0	.25	24	5.68
Castillo,A	NYY	14	12	104.0	13	5	1	.36	45	3.89
Castro,Ramon	Fla	37	17	202.1	23	7	0	.30	100	4.45
Chavez,Raul	Hou	1	1	14.0	0	0	0	-	6	3.86
Cota,Humberto	Pit	7	4	40.1	2	1	0	.50	21	4.69
Davis,Ben	Sea	76	55	538.2	41	18	6	.41	236	3.94
DiFelice,Mike	Stl	61	51	435.1	32	9	0	.28	195	4.03
Estalella,B	Col	37	32	289.1	23	5	0	.22	140	4.35
Estrada,Johnny	Phi	10	3	40.2	5	0	0	.00	8	1.77
Fabregas,Jorge	Ana	32	23	214.0	23	5	0	.22	113	4.75
Fabregas,Jorge	Mil	20	17	149.0	12	5	1	.40	70	4.23
Fasano,Sal	Ana	2	0	7.0	3	2	0	.67	5	6.43
Fletcher,D	Tor	36	29	253.2	30	7	1	.21	160	5.68
Fordyce,Brook	Bal	55	39	369.0	49	8	2	.13	199	4.85
Gonzalez,Wiki	SD	54	52	442.2	37	15	0	.41	214	4.35
Greene,Todd	Tex	15	11	104.2	15	3	1	.15	71	6.11
Haselman,Bill	Tex	49	47	453.2	43	10	2	.21	255	5.06
Hinch,A.J.	KC	68	60	527.1	48	8	2	.16	316	5.39
Hoover,Paul	TB	4	4	34.0	7	3	1	.40	24	6.35
Jensen,Marcus	Mil	15	10	95.1	9	5	0	.56	47	4.44
Kreuter,Chad	LA	41	24	247.2	27	10	4	.32	100	3.63
Lamb,Mike	Tex	3	1	7.0	3	0	0	.00	7	9.00
LeCroy,Matt	Min	6	3	27.0	0	0	0	-	18	6.00
Lunar,Fernando	Bal	2	0	2.0	0	0	0	-	0	0.00
Lunsford,Trey	SF	3	0	7.0	1	0	0	.00	1	1.29
Machado,Robert	ChC	21	15	138.0	20	10	1	.50	91	5.93
Machado,Robert	Mil	48	45	382.0	46	14	1	.30	222	5.23
Mahoney,Mike	ChC	16	9	83.1	4	4	0	1.00	54	5.83
Marrero,Eli	Stl	44	15	180.2	22	2	0	.09	78	3.89
Martinez,V	Cle	9	7	69.0	13	2	0	.15	28	3.65
McKay,Cody	Oak	1	1	8.0	0	0	0	-	8	9.00
McKeel,Walt	Col	5	3	28.1	7	0	0	.00	23	7.31
Meluskey,Mitch	Det	8	8	71.1	5	3	1	.67	52	6.56
Miller,Corky	Cin	38	35	301.0	21	7	1	.32	125	3.74
Mirabelli,Doug	Bos	50	41	378.1	56	19	1	.33	161	3.83
Moeller,Chad	Ari	35	31	277.2	26	8	5	.19	82	2.66
Molina,Izzy	Bal	1	1	9.0	2	1	1	-	9	9.00
Molina,Jose	Ana	29	24	210.0	24	9	0	.38	70	3.00
Myers,Greg	Oak	53	36	343.1	39	16	5	.38	156	4.09
Nieves,Wil	SD	27	20	182.1	13	3	0	.23	85	4.20
Olivo,Miguel	CWS	6	6	48.1	2	1	0	.50	22	4.10
Ortiz,Hector	Tex	7	4	38.0	0	0	0	-	8	1.89
Osik,Keith	Pit	27	17	171.2	19	4	1	.18	93	4.88
Paul,Josh	CWS	32	30	263.1	23	3	1	.10	156	5.33
Perez,Eddie	Cle	42	34	313.0	38	14	0	.37	152	4.37
Petrick,Ben	Col	13	12	109.2	8	1	0	.13	56	4.60
Phillips,Jason	NYM	7	2	37.0	1	1	0	.00	7	1.70
Pratt,Todd	Phi	34	32	281.2	24	6	1	.23	127	4.06
Prince,Tom	Min	50	40	371.0	20	8	0	.40	169	4.10
Rivera,Mike	Det	37	35	303.0	32	12	2	.36	185	5.50
Ross,Dave	LA	6	2	26.0	1	1	0	1.00	7	2.42
Schneider,B	Mon	65	57	521.2	46	20	1	.43	254	4.38
Stinnett,Kelly	Cin	30	27	246.1	26	7	1	.25	94	3.43
Torrealba,S	Atl	12	5	57.1	6	1	0	.17	15	2.35
Torrealba,Y	SF	53	40	363.2	39	11	1	.27	151	3.74
Valentin,Ja	Min	4	0	11.0	0	0	0	-	6	4.91
Walbeck,Matt	Det	27	24	219.1	8	2	0	.25	103	4.23
Wathan,Dusty	KC	3	1	14.0	1	0	0	.00	6	3.86
Widger,Chris	NYY	21	18	157.1	11	3	0	.27	80	4.58
Wilson,Craig	Pit	5	0	9.0	0	0	0	-	4	4.00
Wilson,Tom	Tor	65	52	463.2	57	13	2	.21	259	5.03
Wilson,Vance	NYM	65	40	399.0	51	25	3	.49	186	4.20
Wooten,Shawn	Ana	2	1	7.0	1	0	0	.00	3	3.86
Zaun,Gregg	Hou	44	40	351.0	44	5	0	.11	175	4.49
Zinter,Alan	Hou	1	0	1.0	0	0	0	-	1	9.00

Pitchers Hitting, Fielding & Holding Runners,

and Hitters Pitching

Pitchers Hitting, Fielding and Holding Runners

Pitcher	2002 Hitting						Career Hitting										2002 Fielding and Holding Runners											
	Avg	AB	H	HR	RBI	SH	Avg	AB	H	2B	3B	HR	RBI	BB	SO	SH	G	Inn	PO	A	E	DP	Pct	SBA	CS	PCS	PPO	CS%
Abbott,Paul, Sea	-	0	0	0	0	0	.333	9	3	1	0	0	0	0	2	2	7	26.1	2	6	0	0	1.000	5	1	0	0	.20
Acevedo,Jose, Cin	.143	7	1	0	2	2	.122	41	5	2	0	0	3	1	24	4	6	23.2	2	1	0	0	1.000	2	0	0	0	.00
Acevedo,Juan, Det	-	0	0	0	0	0	.092	65	6	2	0	0	0	3	33	6	65	74.2	4	11	1	0	.938	7	2	1	0	.29
Adams,Terry, Phi	.080	25	2	0	1	6	.052	77	4	1	0	0	2	7	40	12	46	136.2	11	24	4	1	.897	8	3	1	0	.38
Affeldt,Jeremy, KC	-	0	0	0	0	0	-	0	0	0	0	0	0	0	0	0	34	77.2	4	14	2	1	.900	7	3	3	0	.43
Ainsworth,Kurt, SF	.167	6	1	0	0	1	.167	6	1	1	0	0	0	0	1	1	6	25.2	1	8	0	0	1.000	3	1	0	0	.33
Alfonseca,A, ChC	.667	3	2	0	2	0	.167	12	2	0	0	0	2	0	7	0	66	74.1	4	13	1	1	.944	10	2	0	0	.20
Almanza,A, Fla	-	0	0	0	0	0	.000	4	0	0	0	0	0	0	2	1	51	45.2	3	5	0	0	1.000	3	2	0	1	.67
Almanzar,C, Cin	-	0	0	0	0	0	.000	4	0	0	0	0	0	0	3	0	8	11.2	0	3	0	1	1.000	0	0	0	0	-
Alvarez,Juan, Tex	-	0	0	0	0	0	-	0	0	0	0	0	0	0	0	0	52	39.2	5	4	0	1	1.000	5	1	0	0	.20
Alvarez,Victor, LA	.000	2	0	0	0	0	.000	2	0	0	0	0	0	0	2	0	4	10.1	0	1	0	0	1.000	0	0	0	0	-
Alvarez,Wilson, TB	.000	4	0	0	0	0	.083	36	3	0	0	0	1	2	11	1	23	75.0	2	6	0	0	1.000	4	2	2	1	.50
Anderson,Bri, Ari	.116	43	5	0	2	5	.138	253	35	5	3	1	10	6	57	21	35	156.0	5	36	2	4	.953	7	3	3	5	.43
Anderson,Ji, Pit	.119	42	5	0	1	3	.138	160	22	3	0	0	6	6	40	13	28	140.2	6	34	1	4	.976	28	7	7	1	.25
Anderson,Mat, Det	-	0	0	0	0	0	-	0	0	0	0	0	0	0	0	0	12	11.0	1	1	0	1	1.000	2	0	0	0	.00
Appier,Kevin, Ana	.000	2	0	0	0	2	.103	78	8	0	0	0	4	1	35	5	32	188.1	18	14	0	1	1.000	24	13	1	1	.54
Armas Jr.,Tony, Mon	.100	50	5	0	2	5	.107	131	14	1	1	0	7	2	46	14	29	164.1	15	22	0	4	1.000	25	7	0	0	.28
Arrojo,Rolando, Bos	.000	2	0	0	0	1	.081	37	3	1	0	0	3	1	20	2	29	81.1	13	6	2	2	.905	4	2	0	0	.50
Arroyo,Bronson, Pit	.000	6	0	0	0	0	.083	48	4	2	0	0	1	1	27	2	9	27.0	3	7	0	0	1.000	2	0	0	0	.00
Asencio,Miguel, KC	.000	2	0	0	0	0	.000	2	0	0	0	0	0	0	0	1	31	123.1	14	11	1	1	.962	11	2	0	0	.18
Ashby,Andy, LA	.125	48	6	1	4	6	.138	507	70	13	0	1	26	16	210	80	30	181.2	16	18	1	2	.971	22	5	1	0	.23
Astacio,Pedro, NYM	.161	62	10	0	1	6	.133	623	83	7	1	0	27	4	241	74	31	191.2	6	28	1	0	.971	16	6	1	0	.38
Austin,Jeff, KC	-	0	0	0	0	0	-	0	0	0	0	0	0	0	0	0	10	11.0	0	0	0	0	-	1	1	0	0	1.00
Avery,Steve,	-	0	0	0	0	0	.172	436	75	14	4	4	32	12	135	41	0	0.0	0	0	0	0	-	0	0	0	0	-
Aybar,Manny, SF	.000	1	0	0	0	0	.186	70	13	0	0	1	5	2	28	4	15	14.1	2	1	0	0	1.000	0	0	0	0	-
Backe,Brandon, TB	-	0	0	0	0	0	-	0	0	0	0	0	0	0	0	0	9	13.0	0	0	0	0	-	2	0	0	0	.00
Bacsik,Mike, NYM	.111	18	2	0	2	3	.111	18	2	1	0	0	2	0	3	3	11	55.2	4	15	1	0	.950	4	2	1	0	.50
Baez,Danys, Cle	.000	2	0	0	0	0	.000	2	0	0	0	0	0	0	0	0	39	165.1	12	17	2	1	.935	22	11	0	0	.50
Bailey,Cory, KC	-	0	0	0	0	0	.500	2	1	0	0	0	0	0	0	1	37	46.0	7	7	0	0	1.000	5	2	0	0	.40
Baldwin,James, Sea	.500	2	1	0	0	0	.098	41	4	1	1	0	2	0	19	1	30	150.0	9	25	0	2	1.000	7	5	0	1	.71
Banks,Willie, Bos	-	0	0	0	0	0	.176	68	12	2	0	0	1	2	23	8	29	39.0	3	8	1	0	.917	5	2	1	0	.40
Barcelo,L, CWS	-	0	0	0	0	0	-	0	0	0	0	0	0	0	0	0	4	6.0	0	3	0	1	1.000	0	0	0	0	-
Batista,Miguel, Ari	.157	51	8	1	2	2	.105	162	17	3	0	2	5	8	93	10	36	184.2	8	33	1	2	.976	14	2	0	0	.14
Bauer,Rick, Bal	-	0	0	0	0	0	-	0	0	0	0	0	0	0	0	0	56	83.2	1	15	0	2	1.000	7	2	0	0	.29
Bechler,Steve, Bal	-	0	0	0	0	0	-	0	0	0	0	0	0	0	0	0	3	4.2	1	0	0	0	1.000	0	0	0	0	-
Beck,Rod,	-	0	0	0	0	0	.211	19	4	0	0	0	1	0	10	1	0	0	0	0	0	0	-	0	0	0	0	-
Beckett,Josh, Fla	.032	31	1	0	0	5	.079	38	3	2	0	0	0	0	22	7	23	107.2	11	9	1	0	.952	17	5	0	0	.29
Bedard,Erik, Bal	-	0	0	0	0	0	-	0	0	0	0	0	0	0	0	0	2	0.2	0	0	0	0	-	0	0	0	0	-
Beimel,Joe, Pit	.300	10	3	0	1	2	.278	36	10	1	0	0	1	2	13	6	53	85.1	1	12	3	1	.813	11	3	0	1	.27
Beirne,Kevin, LA	.400	5	2	0	0	1	.400	5	2	0	0	0	0	0	0	1	12	29.0	1	3	0	0	1.000	2	2	1	0	1.00
Bell,Rob, Tex	.000	1	0	0	0	0	.075	53	4	1	0	0	3	3	31	5	17	94.0	18	13	1	0	.969	5	0	0	0	.00
Beltran,F, ChC	.000	1	0	0	0	0	.000	1	0	0	0	0	0	0	0	0	11	12.0	0	4	0	1	1.000	2	0	0	0	.00
Benes,Alan, ChC	.077	13	1	0	0	0	.159	138	22	6	0	0	8	3	53	9	7	39.1	2	4	0	2	1.000	4	1	0	0	.25
Benes,Andy, Stl	.206	34	7	1	2	2	.143	741	106	21	0	8	50	34	307	95	18	97.0	5	10	1	1	.938	12	7	0	0	.58
Benitez,A, NYM	-	0	0	0	0	0	.000	6	0	0	0	0	2	0	2	0	62	67.1	2	8	2	0	.833	8	1	0	1	.13
Benoit,Joaquin, Tex	-	0	0	0	0	0	-	0	0	0	0	0	0	0	0	0	17	84.2	4	4	0	1	1.000	8	1	0	0	.13
Benson,Kris, Pit	.175	40	7	0	1	4	.135	170	23	6	0	0	9	7	64	19	25	130.1	12	11	2	2	.920	13	8	1	1	.62
Bere,Jason, ChC	.125	24	3	0	0	7	.186	161	30	6	1	0	5	3	60	17	16	85.2	4	11	2	1	.882	15	4	0	0	.27
Bernero,Adam, Det	.000	4	0	0	0	0	.000	4	0	0	0	0	0	0	4	1	28	101.2	4	10	1	1	.933	7	3	0	0	.43
Beverlin,Jason, Cle-Det	-	0	0	0	0	0	-	0	0	0	0	0	0	0	0	0	7	19.2	0	0	0	0	-	2	0	0	0	.00
Biddle,Rocky, CWS	.000	1	0	0	0	0	.000	2	0	0	0	0	0	0	2	1	44	77.2	8	8	0	0	1.000	12	4	1	0	.33
Bierbrodt,Nick,	-	0	0	0	0	0	.667	6	4	1	0	0	2	0	2	0	0	0.0	0	0	0	0	-	0	0	0	0	-
Boehringer,B, Pit	-	0	0	0	0	0	.067	30	2	0	0	0	2	3	15	3	70	79.2	7	0	0	0	1.000	3	0	0	0	.60
Bong,Jung, Atl	.000	2	0	0	0	0	.000	2	0	0	0	0	0	0	1	0	1	6.0	0	1	0	1	1.000	1	0	0	0	.00
Borbon,Pedro, Tor-Hou	.000	3	0	0	0	0	.143	7	1	0	0	0	0	0	4	1	72	50.1	6	6	0	1	1.000	5	1	0	0	.20
Borland,Toby, Fla	-	0	0	0	0	0	.083	12	1	0	0	0	2	0	3	1	15	13.2	1	2	0	0	1.000	2	1	0	0	.50
Borowski,Joe, ChC	.286	7	2	0	0	0	.222	9	2	0	0	0	0	0	7	1	73	95.2	5	9	1	3	.933	17	4	0	0	.24
Bottalico,R, Phi	-	0	0	0	0	0	.133	15	2	2	0	0	1	0	8	1	30	27.1	2	3	0	0	1.000	6	0	0	0	.00
Bowie,Micah, Oak	-	0	0	0	0	0	.214	14	3	0	0	0	3	1	3	0	13	12.0	1	2	0	0	1.000	0	0	0	0	-
Bowles,Brian, Tor	-	0	0	0	0	0	-	0	0	0	0	0	0	0	0	0	17	20.0	1	3	0	0	1.000	2	0	0	0	.00
Boyd,Jason, SD	-	0	0	0	0	0	.000	1	0	0	0	0	0	0	1	0	23	28.1	3	7	0	0	1.000	1	1	0	0	1.00
Bradford,Chad, Oak	-	0	0	0	0	0	-	0	0	0	0	0	0	0	0	0	75	75.1	10	10	1	1	.952	5	2	0	0	.40
Brazelton,D, TB	-	0	0	0	0	0	-	0	0	0	0	0	0	0	0	0	2	13.0	1	1	0	0	1.000	0	0	0	0	-
Brock,Chris, Bal	.000	2	0	0	0	0	.190	63	12	1	0	1	7	3	13	6	22	44.0	2	6	1	2	.889	3	0	0	0	.00
Brohawn,Troy, SF	-	0	0	0	0	0	.000	1	0	0	0	0	0	0	0	0	11	5.2	1	0	0	0	1.000	0	0	0	0	-
Brower,Jim, Cin-Mon	.000	9	0	0	0	0	.211	38	8	1	0	0	3	0	13	3	52	80.1	9	12	0	1	1.000	8	1	0	0	.13
Brown,Kevin, LA	.250	20	5	1	2	2	.123	430	53	6	0	2	27	19	158	48	17	63.2	8	6	1	0	.933	10	5	0	0	.50
Buddie,Mike, Mil	.000	2	0	0	0	0	.167	6	1	0	0	0	0	0	4	0	25	39.2	5	10	2	0	.882	4	1	0	0	.25
Buehrle,Mark, CWS	.167	6	1	0	0	0	.111	9	1	0	0	0	0	1	6	0	34	239.0	6	46	2	2	.963	14	10	7	1	.71
Bukvich,Ryan, KC	-	0	0	0	0	0	-	0	0	0	0	0	0	0	0	0	26	25.2	2	4	3	0	.667	0	0	0	0	-
Burba,Dave, Tex-Cle	.200	5	1	0	0	0	.144	180	26	1	0	3	12	10	76	21	35	145.1	10	10	1	2	.952	18	5	0	0	.28
Burkett,John, Bos	.000	3	0	0	0	1	.093	539	50	6	0	0	18	26	226	61	29	173.0	8	11	1	0	.950	17	6	1	1	.35

269

Pitchers Hitting, Fielding and Holding Runners

Pitcher	2002 Hitting						Career Hitting										2002 Fielding and Holding Runners											
	Avg	AB	H	HR	RBI	SH	Avg	AB	H	2B	3B	HR	RBI	BB	SO	SH	G	Inn	PO	A	E	DP	Pct	SBA	CS	PCS	PPO	CS%
Burnett,A.J., Fla	.105	57	6	1	3	7	.128	149	19	4	1	2	6	9	75	16	31	204.1	12	19	4	3	.886	20	10	1	0	.50
Bynum,Mike, SD	.000	8	0	0	0	0	.000	8	0	0	0	0	0	0	3	0	14	27.1	0	4	0	0	1.000	3	1	0	0	.33
Byrd,Paul, KC	.000	2	0	0	0	0	.144	111	16	0	0	0	6	7	30	17	33	228.1	18	15	1	1	.971	15	6	0	0	.40
Cabrera,Jose, Mil	.105	19	2	0	0	1	.087	23	2	0	0	0	0	0	12	1	50	103.1	8	10	2	2	.900	17	6	1	0	.35
Callaway,M, Ana	-	0	0	0	0	0	.667	3	2	0	0	0	1	0	0	0	6	34.1	4	4	2	1	.800	2	1	0	0	.50
Carpenter,C, Tor	1.000	1	1	0	0	1	.182	11	2	0	0	0	0	1	5	2	13	73.1	7	3	0	0	1.000	8	4	0	0	.50
Carrara,G, LA	.000	6	0	0	0	1	.107	28	3	0	0	0	0	1	9	3	63	90.2	8	18	0	1	1.000	7	2	1	0	.29
Carter,Lance, TB	-	0	0	0	0	0	-	0	0	0	0	0	0	0	0	0	8	20.1	1	3	0	1	1.000	0	0	0	0	
Cassidy,Scott, Tor	-	0	0	0	0	0	-	0	0	0	0	0	0	0	0	0	58	66.0	0	8	1	0	.889	10	4	0	0	.40
Castillo,Frank, Bos	.000	1	0	0	0	1	.110	337	37	0	0	0	13	13	111	42	36	163.1	10	18	0	0	1.000	32	8	0	1	.25
Cerda,Jaime, NYM	.000	1	0	0	0	0	.000	1	0	0	0	0	0	0	0	0	32	25.2	1	1	1	0	.667	2	0	0	0	.00
Chacon,Shawn, Col	.257	35	9	0	2	2	.134	82	11	1	0	0	3	0	36	9	21	119.1	18	15	2	1	.943	6	1	0	3	.17
Chen,Bruce, NYM-Mon-Cin	.333	15	5	0	1	2	.118	110	13	1	0	0	3	1	53	17	55	77.2	6	6	0	0	1.000	5	2	0	0	.40
Chiasson,Scott, ChC	-	0	0	0	0	0	-	0	0	0	0	0	0	0	0	0	4	4.2	0	1	0	0	1.000	1	0	0	0	.00
Childers,Matt, Mil	.000	1	0	0	0	0	.000	1	0	0	0	0	0	0	0	0	8	9.0	0	2	0	1	1.000	0	0	0	0	
Choate,Randy, NYY	.000	1	0	0	0	0	.000	4	0	0	0	0	0	0	2	0	18	22.1	1	2	0	0	1.000	0	0	0	0	
Christiansen,J, SF	-	0	0	0	0	0	.100	10	1	0	0	0	1	0	7	1	6	5.0	0	0	0	0	-	1	1	0	0	1.00
Clemens,Roger, NYY	.667	3	2	0	1	0	.211	19	4	2	0	0	1	2	7	2	29	180.0	12	17	0	0	1.000	28	5	0	3	.18
Clement,Matt, ChC	.049	61	3	0	4	10	.067	225	15	2	1	0	7	12	115	31	32	205.0	8	23	2	1	.939	11	5	0	0	.45
Coco,Pasqual, Tor	-	0	0	0	0	0	-	0	0	0	0	0	0	0	0	0	2	1.0	0	0	0	0	-	0	0	0	0	
Coggin,Dave, Phi	.000	8	0	0	0	2	.042	48	2	1	0	0	1	3	23	4	38	77.0	5	8	0	0	1.000	8	3	1	0	.38
Colome,Jesus, TB	-	0	0	0	0	0	-	0	0	0	0	0	0	0	0	0	32	41.1	4	8	0	0	1.000	13	4	0	0	.31
Colon,Bartolo, Cle-Mon	.133	45	6	0	3	2	.134	67	9	0	0	0	4	0	40	3	33	233.1	13	32	3	4	.938	12	7	0	4	.58
Condrey,Clay, SD	.000	6	0	0	0	0	.000	6	0	0	0	0	0	0	0	0	9	26.2	3	2	0	1	1.000	2	1	0	0	.50
Cone,David,	-	0	0	0	0	0	.154	408	63	9	0	0	22	16	90	38							-					
Cook,Aaron, Col	.091	11	1	0	1	1	.091	11	1	0	0	0	1	0	0	1	9	35.2	4	9	1	3	.929	1	1	0	1	1.00
Cook,Dennis, Ana	-	0	0	0	0	0	.264	110	29	2	1	2	9	3	13	9	37	24.0	2	0	1	0	.667	2	1	0	0	.50
Cooper,Brian, Tor	-	0	0	0	0	0	.000	4	0	0	0	0	0	0	3	0	2	8.1	2	0	0	0	1.000	1	1	0	0	1.00
Cordero,F, Tex	.000	1	0	0	0	0	.000	1	0	0	0	0	0	0	0	1	39	45.1	5	5	0	0	1.000	4	4	0	0	1.00
Corey,Bryan, LA	-	0	0	0	0	0	-	0	0	0	0	0	0	0	0	0	1	1.0	0	0	0	0	-	0	0	0	0	
Corey,Mark, NYM-Col	.000	2	0	0	0	0	.000	2	0	0	0	0	0	0	2	0	26	22.0	0	1	0	0	1.000	0	0	0	0	.00
Cormier,Rheal, Phi	.333	3	1	0	0	0	.186	188	35	4	1	0	12	4	43	28	54	60.0	3	14	0	3	1.000	2	1	0	0	.50
Cornejo,Nate, Det	-	0	0	0	0	0	-	0	0	0	0	0	0	0	0	0	9	50.0	1	8	0	0	1.000	4	2	0	0	.50
Creek,Doug, TB-Sea	.000	1	0	0	0	0	.200	5	1	0	0	0	0	0	3	3	52	55.2	3	5	0	0	1.000	2	1	0	0	.50
Cressend,Jack, Min	-	0	0	0	0	0	-	0	0	0	0	0	0	0	0	0	23	32.0	2	3	0	0	1.000	3	0	0	0	.00
Crudale,Mike, Stl	.000	2	0	0	0	0	.000	2	0	0	0	0	0	0	0	1	49	52.2	8	2	1	0	.909	5	1	0	0	.20
Cruz,Juan, ChC	.143	14	2	0	0	2	.133	30	4	0	0	0	1	0	9	4	45	97.1	3	12	3	0	.833	20	9	0	0	.45
Cruz,Nelson, Hou	.000	13	0	0	1	2	.050	20	1	0	0	0	1	1	10	2	43	78.1	5	12	0	0	1.000	3	1	0	0	.17
Cunnane,Will, ChC	.250	4	1	0	0	1	.200	35	7	1	1	0	4	3	9	1	16	26.1	1	2	0	1	1.000	2	1	0	0	.50
Cyr,Eric, SD	.000	1	0	0	0	0	.000	1	0	0	0	0	0	0	1	0	5	6.0	0	0	0	0	-	1	0	0	0	.00
Daal,Omar, LA	.154	39	6	1	4	8	.196	275	54	8	0	2	22	14	61	31	39	161.1	10	33	0	5	1.000	4	2	0	0	.50
D'Amico,Jeff, NYM	.108	37	4	0	0	5	.090	100	9	1	1	1	2	7	49	12	29	145.2	5	18	0	0	1.000	14	2	0	0	.14
Darensbourg,V, Fla	.000	1	0	0	0	1	.118	17	2	0	0	0	0	2	5	1	42	48.1	2	4	1	0	.857	4	0	0	0	.00
Davey,Tom, SD	-	0	0	0	0	0	-	0	0	0	0	0	0	0	1	0	19	21.0	0	1	0	0	1.000	2	0	0	0	.00
Davis,Doug, Tex	-	0	0	0	0	0	.000	3	0	0	0	0	0	0	2	1	10	59.2	3	6	1	0	.900	6	2	1	0	.33
Davis,Jason, Cle	-	0	0	0	0	0	-	0	0	0	0	0	0	0	0	0	3	14.2	2	4	0	0	1.000	4	0	0	0	.00
Davis,Kane, NYM	-	0	0	0	0	0	.000	6	0	0	0	0	0	0	6	0	16	14.0	0	1	0	0	1.000	4	0	0	0	.00
Dawley,Joey, Atl	-	0	0	0	0	0	-	0	0	0	0	0	0	0	0	0	1	0.1	0	0	0	0	-	0	0	0	0	
Day,Zach, Mon	.167	6	1	0	0	2	.167	6	1	0	0	0	0	1	4	2	19	37.1	6	6	0	1	1.000	4	2	0	0	.50
de los Santos,L, TB	-	0	0	0	0	0	-	0	0	0	0	0	0	0	0	0	3	14.0	2	2	1	0	.800	4	1	1	0	.25
de los Santos,V, Mil	.000	2	0	0	0	2	.000	8	0	0	0	0	0	1	5	2	51	57.2	3	3	0	1	1.000	9	2	0	0	.22
DeJean,Mike, Mil	.000	1	0	0	0	0	.063	16	1	1	0	0	0	0	9	1	68	75.0	9	8	0	0	1.000	6	2	0	0	.33
Dempster,Ryan, Fla-Cin	.127	63	8	0	3	9	.084	263	22	5	1	0	7	5	108	31	33	209.0	19	26	0	4	1.000	20	13	2	0	.65
DePaula,Sean, Cle	-	0	0	0	0	0	-	0	0	0	0	0	0	0	0	0	5	6.1	2	0	0	0	1.000	1	0	0	0	.00
Dessens,Elmer, Cin	.200	45	9	0	5	9	.168	155	26	1	0	0	10	14	43	23	30	178.0	12	27	1	3	.975	16	8	1	0	.50
DeWitt,Matt, SD	-	0	0	0	0	0	-	0	0	0	0	0	0	0	0	0	5	7.1	1	0	0	0	1.000	1	0	0	0	.00
Dickey,R.A.,	-	0	0	0	0	0	-	0	0	0	0	0	0	0	0	0	0	0.0	0	0	0	0	-	0	0	0	0	
Diggins,Ben, Mil	.143	7	1	0	0	1	.143	7	1	0	0	0	0	0	1	1	5	24.0	0	2	0	0	1.000	2	0	0	0	.00
Donnelly,B, Ana	-	0	0	0	0	0	-	0	0	0	0	0	0	0	0	0	46	49.2	3	3	0	0	1.000	2	0	0	0	.00
Dotel,Octavio, Hou	.000	1	0	0	0	0	.074	68	5	0	0	0	1	5	38	9	83	97.1	8	0	0	0	1.000	8	2	0	0	.25
Douglass,Sean, Bal	-	0	0	0	0	0	-	0	0	0	0	0	0	0	0	0	15	53.1	3	8	0	2	1.000	6	2	0	0	.33
Dreifort,D,	-	0	0	0	0	0	.188	223	42	9	0	6	22	7	97	14							-					
Drese,Ryan, Cle	.000	3	0	0	0	1	.000	3	0	0	0	0	0	1	0	1	26	137.1	11	25	2	2	.947	16	9	1	1	.56
Drew,Tim, Mon	.000	4	0	0	0	0	.000	4	0	0	0	0	0	0	4	0	7	16.0	1	3	0	0	1.000	2	0	0	0	.00
Driskill,T, Bal	.000	3	0	0	0	0	.000	3	0	0	0	0	0	1	3	0	29	132.2	7	13	0	1	1.000	7	5	1	1	.71
DuBose,Eric, Bal	-	0	0	0	0	0	-	0	0	0	0	0	0	0	0	0	4	6.0	0	1	0	0	1.000	0	0	0	0	
Duckworth,B, Phi	.188	48	9	0	4	6	.200	70	14	2	0	0	5	7	15	8	30	163.0	4	15	0	1	1.000	27	3	0	1	.11
Duff,Matt, Stl	-	0	0	0	0	0	-	0	0	0	0	0	0	0	0	0	7	5.2	0	1	0	0	1.000	1	0	0	0	.00
Duncan,C, ChC	-	0	0	0	0	0	.000	3	0	0	0	0	1	2	1	0	2	2.1	0	0	0	0	-	0	0	0	0	
Durbin,Chad, KC	-	0	0	0	0	0	.000	1	0	0	0	0	0	0	1	0	2	8.1	1	1	1	0	.667	5	0	0	0	.00
Durocher,J, Mil	.000	2	0	0	0	0	.000	2	0	0	0	0	0	0	1	0	39	48.0	1	5	0	0	1.000	7	2	0	0	.29
Eaton,Adam, SD	.111	9	1	0	0	0	.188	85	16	3	0	0	6	11	26	2	6	33.1	1	4	0	0	1.000	4	2	0	0	.50
Eckenstahler,E, Det	-	0	0	0	0	0	-	0	0	0	0	0	0	0	0	0	7	3.0	1	0	0	0	1.000	0	0	0	0	
Eischen,Joey, Mon	.125	8	1	0	0	0	.063	16	1	1	0	0	0	1	6	0	59	53.2	3	8	1	0	.917	5	3	0	0	.60
Elder,Dave, Cle	-	0	0	0	0	0	-	0	0	0	0	0	0	0	0	0	15	23.0	3	1	0	0	1.000	1	0	0	0	.00

Pitchers Hitting, Fielding and Holding Runners

Pitcher	2002 Hitting						Career Hitting										2002 Fielding and Holding Runners											
	Avg	AB	H	HR	RBI	SH	Avg	AB	H	2B	3B	HR	RBI	BB	SO	SH	G	Inn	PO	A	E	DP	Pct	SBA	CS	PCS	PPO	CS%
Eldred,Cal,	-	0	0	0	0	0	.111	63	7	2	0	0	4	6	33	10	0	0.0	0	0	0	0	-	0	0	0	0	-
Ellis,Robert, LA	-	0	0	0	0	0	.154	26	4	0	0	0	1	1	12	1	3	2.2	0	0	0	0	-	1	0	0	0	.00
Embree,Alan, SD-Bos	-	0	0	0	0	0	.000	2	0	0	0	0	0	1	1	0	68	62.0	4	7	1	0	.917	12	1	0	0	.08
Ennis,John, Atl	.000	1	0	0	0	0	.000	1	0	0	0	0	0	0	0	0	1	4.0	1	2	0	1	1.000	1	1	0	0	1.00
Erickson,Scott, Bal	.000	4	0	0	0	0	.105	19	2	1	0	0	1	4	8	4	29	160.2	14	22	3	2	.923	26	9	0	0	.35
Escobar,Kelvim, Tor	-	0	0	0	0	0	.000	8	0	0	0	0	0	0	5	0	76	78.0	1	9	0	0	1.000	11	3	0	0	.27
Estes,Shawn, NYM-Cin	.070	43	3	1	3	7	.147	348	51	10	0	3	23	11	128	55	29	160.2	3	24	3	2	.900	26	6	2	1	.23
Estrella,Leo,	-	0	0	0	0	0	-	0	0	0	0	0	0	0	0	0	0	0.0	0	0	0	0	-	0	0	0	0	-
Eyre,Scott, Tor-SF	-	0	0	0	0	0	.200	5	1	0	0	0	0	0	3	0	70	74.2	3	9	0	0	1.000	8	2	1	0	.25
Farnsworth,J, Det	-	0	0	0	0	0	-	0	0	0	0	0	0	0	0	0	44	70.0	6	8	2	0	.875	4	0	0	0	.00
Farnsworth,K, ChC	.000	1	0	0	1	0	.077	52	4	1	0	0	3	2	18	8	45	46.2	5	10	0	0	1.000	14	3	0	0	.21
Fassero,Jeff, ChC-Stl	.333	3	1	0	0	0	.079	229	18	2	1	0	5	17	131	40	73	69.0	4	10	0	0	1.000	5	3	1	0	.60
Feliciano,P, NYM	-	0	0	0	0	0	-	0	0	0	0	0	0	0	0	0	6	6.0	0	0	0	0	-	0	0	0	0	-
Fernandez,J, Cin	.200	10	2	0	1	2	.167	12	2	0	0	0	1	1	7	2	14	50.2	3	12	0	0	1.000	10	1	0	2	.10
Fetters,Mike, Pit-Ari	-	0	0	0	0	0	-	0	0	0	0	0	0	0	0	0	65	55.0	4	8	2	0	.857	10	4	2	3	.40
Field,Nate, KC	-	0	0	0	0	0	-	0	0	0	0	0	0	0	0	0	5	5.0	1	0	0	0	1.000	1	0	0	0	.00
Figueroa,N, Mil	.133	15	2	0	3	4	.214	42	9	1	0	0	4	2	18	6	30	93.0	4	12	2	0	.889	8	2	1	0	.25
Fikac,Jeremy, SD	.000	2	0	0	0	0	.000	2	0	0	0	0	0	0	1	0	65	69.0	4	6	0	0	1.000	4	0	0	0	.00
File,Bob, Tor	-	0	0	0	0	0	-	0	0	0	0	0	0	0	0	0	5	3.1	0	0	0	0	-	0	0	0	0	-
Finley,Chuck, Cle-Stl	.094	32	3	0	1	5	.057	53	3	1	0	0	1	0	26	6	32	190.2	4	23	3	2	.900	27	10	0	0	.37
Fiore,Tony, Min	.000	3	0	0	0	0	.000	3	0	0	0	0	0	0	1	0	48	91.0	4	14	0	1	1.000	9	5	0	0	.56
Fitzgerald,B, Sea	-	0	0	0	0	0	-	0	0	0	0	0	0	0	0	0	6	6.1	0	1	1	0	.500	0	0	0	0	-
Flores,Randy, Tex-Col	.000	4	0	0	0	0	.000	4	0	0	0	0	0	0	3	0	28	29.0	2	6	0	2	1.000	3	2	2	0	.67
Fogg,Josh, Pit	.121	58	7	0	1	2	.121	58	7	0	0	0	1	2	22	2	33	194.1	9	29	1	2	.974	11	4	1	1	.36
Fossum,Casey, Bos	-	0	0	0	0	0	-	0	0	0	0	0	0	0	0	0	43	106.2	8	5	0	2	1.000	14	7	0	0	.50
Foster,John, Atl	-	0	0	0	0	0	-	0	0	0	0	0	0	0	0	0	5	5.0	0	0	0	0	-	0	0	0	0	-
Foulke,Keith, CWS	.000	1	0	0	0	0	.125	16	2	0	0	0	0	0	5	2	65	77.2	6	6	0	1	1.000	7	0	0	0	.00
Fox,Chad, Mil	-	0	0	0	0	0	.000	7	0	0	0	0	0	0	3	1	3	4.2	0	0	0	0	-	0	0	0	0	-
Franklin,Ryan, Sea	-	0	0	0	0	0	-	0	0	0	0	0	0	0	0	0	41	118.2	9	13	1	0	.957	11	5	1	0	.45
Franklin,Wayne, Mil	.000	6	0	0	0	0	.000	8	0	0	0	0	0	2	4	0	4	24.0	1	4	0	0	1.000	4	0	0	0	.00
Frederick,K, Min	-	0	0	0	0	0	-	0	0	0	0	0	0	0	0	0	8	11.2	3	0	0	0	1.000	0	0	0	0	-
Fuentes,Brian, Col	-	0	0	0	0	0	-	0	0	0	0	0	0	0	0	0	31	26.2	2	2	1	0	.800	1	0	0	0	.00
Fultz,Aaron, SF	.000	1	0	0	0	0	.333	12	4	0	0	0	0	0	1	1	43	41.1	2	6	0	0	1.000	0	0	1	0	-
Fyhrie,Mike, Oak	-	0	0	0	0	0	.000	2	0	0	0	0	0	0	0	0	16	48.2	4	6	0	1	1.000	7	3	0	0	.43
Gagne,Eric, LA	.000	1	0	0	0	0	.145	83	12	2	1	1	3	1	22	12	77	82.1	4	10	0	1	1.000	5	3	0	0	.60
Garces,Rich, Bos	-	0	0	0	0	0	.000	3	0	0	0	0	0	0	1	0	26	21.1	0	5	0	0	1.000	2	0	0	0	.00
Garcia,Freddy, Sea	.333	6	2	0	0	1	.300	20	6	1	0	0	1	0	6	8	34	223.2	12	30	3	2	.933	10	1	0	0	.10
Garcia,R, Tex	-	0	0	0	0	0	-	0	0	0	0	0	0	0	0	0	3	2.0	0	0	0	0	-	0	0	0	0	-
Gardner,Lee, TB	-	0	0	0	0	0	-	0	0	0	0	0	0	0	0	0	12	13.1	0	3	1	0	.750	0	0	0	0	-
Garland,Jon, CWS	.000	2	0	0	0	1	.000	4	0	0	0	0	0	0	1	1	33	192.2	10	21	0	3	1.000	12	6	1	0	.50
George,Chris, KC	-	0	0	0	0	0	-	0	0	0	0	0	0	0	0	0	6	27.1	2	8	0	0	1.000	6	3	2	1	.50
German,F, Det	-	0	0	0	0	0	-	0	0	0	0	0	0	0	0	0	6	6.2	1	1	0	0	1.000	1	1	0	0	1.00
Ginter,Matt, CWS	-	0	0	0	0	0	-	0	0	0	0	0	0	0	0	0	33	54.1	4	2	0	1	1.000	7	2	1	0	.29
Glavine,Tom, Atl	.103	68	7	0	3	13	.187	1024	191	20	2	1	69	69	265	168	36	224.2	22	49	0	3	1.000	29	16	3	1	.55
Glover,Gary, CWS	.000	1	0	0	0	0	.000	1	0	0	0	0	0	0	1	0	41	138.1	10	19	0	0	1.000	19	4	0	0	.21
Gomes,Wayne, Bos	-	0	0	0	0	0	.167	6	1	0	0	0	1	2	4	0	20	21.1	0	0	1	0	.000	0	0	0	0	.00
Gonzalez,J,	-	0	0	0	0	0	.139	72	10	1	0	0	3	3	23	16	0	0.0	0	0	0	0	-	0	0	0	0	-
Gordon,Tom, ChC-Hou	.000	1	0	0	0	0	.000	1	0	0	0	0	0	0	0	0	34	42.2	1	6	1	1	.875	5	2	0	1	.40
Graves,Danny, Cin	.000	6	0	0	0	2	.091	22	2	0	0	2	3	1	10	2	68	98.2	13	20	0	1	1.000	4	3	0	1	.75
Greisinger,S, Det	-	0	0	0	0	0	.250	4	1	0	0	0	1	0	0	0	8	37.2	2	6	0	0	1.000	6	1	0	0	.17
Grimsley,Jason, KC	-	0	0	0	0	0	.103	39	4	0	0	0	2	5	11	5	70	71.1	6	10	1	1	.941	5	1	0	0	.20
Groom,Buddy, Bal	-	0	0	0	0	0	-	0	0	0	0	0	0	0	0	0	70	62.0	3	4	0	0	1.000	5	0	0	0	.00
Gryboski,Kevin, Atl	-	0	0	0	0	0	-	0	0	0	0	0	0	0	0	0	57	51.2	2	4	0	0	1.000	11	5	0	0	.45
Guardado,Eddie, Min	-	0	0	0	0	0	-	0	0	0	0	0	0	0	0	0	68	67.2	2	8	0	0	1.000	6	2	2	0	.33
Guthrie,Mark, NYM	.000	2	0	0	0	0	.077	13	1	0	0	0	0	0	1	1	68	48.0	1	6	0	0	1.000	12	5	2	0	.42
Hackman,Luther, Stl	.063	16	1	0	0	0	.091	22	2	0	0	0	0	1	9	2	43	81.0	1	11	1	1	.923	11	4	0	0	.36
Halama,John, Sea	-	0	0	0	0	0	.111	18	2	1	0	0	0	3	10	3	31	101.0	8	20	2	1	.933	6	3	3	1	.50
Halladay,Roy, Tor	.000	6	0	0	0	0	.000	9	0	0	0	0	0	0	3	2	34	239.1	22	41	2	1	.969	28	7	1	0	.25
Hamilton,Joey, Cin	.250	28	7	0	1	4	.128	336	43	8	1	4	22	8	164	36	39	124.2	7	14	3	0	.875	2	2	0	0	1.00
Hammond,Chris, Atl	.000	1	0	0	0	0	.204	235	48	7	1	4	14	28	95	19	63	76.0	2	17	0	2	1.000	3	1	0	0	.33
Hampton,Mike, Col	.344	64	22	3	5	1	.254	515	131	13	4	10	52	35	131	43	30	178.2	12	35	1	1	.979	7	2	0	0	.29
Hancock,Josh, Bos	-	0	0	0	0	0	-	0	0	0	0	0	0	0	0	0	3	7.1	0	0	0	0	-	0	0	0	0	-
Haney,Chris, Bos	-	0	0	0	0	0	.111	36	4	0	0	0	4	0	4	3	24	30.0	3	3	0	0	1.000	0	0	0	0	-
Harang,Aaron, Oak	.000	3	0	0	0	0	.000	3	0	0	0	0	0	0	0	0	16	78.1	6	7	1	0	.929	2	1	0	0	.50
Harper,Travis, TB	-	0	0	0	0	0	-	0	0	0	0	0	0	0	0	0	37	85.2	1	5	1	0	.857	6	2	0	0	.33
Hasegawa,S, Sea	-	0	0	0	0	0	.000	1	0	0	0	0	0	0	0	0	53	70.1	5	10	0	3	1.000	1	1	0	0	1.00
Hawkins,LaTroy, Min	-	0	0	0	0	0	.000	5	0	0	0	0	0	0	4	0	65	80.1	4	12	0	1	1.000	9	3	0	0	.33
Haynes,Jimmy, Cin	.164	61	10	0	6	10	.140	186	26	8	0	0	10	5	63	21	34	196.2	10	28	3	4	.927	9	5	0	2	.56
Helling,Rick, Ari	.043	46	2	0	1	6	.063	96	6	0	0	1	8	36	9	30	175.2	4	17	1	1	.955	12	8	1	0	.67
Hendrickson,M, Tor	-	0	0	0	0	0	-	0	0	0	0	0	0	0	0	0	16	36.2	0	5	0	0	1.000	2	1	0	0	.50
Henriquez,O, Det	-	0	0	0	0	0	.000	1	0	0	0	0	0	0	0	0	30	28.0	0	2	0	0	1.000	6	2	1	0	.33
Hentgen,Pat, Bal	-	0	0	0	0	0	.115	78	9	0	0	0	4	25	9	4	22.0	4	2	0	0	1.000	0	0	0	1	-
Heredia,Felix, Tor	-	0	0	0	0	0	.250	12	3	0	0	0	1	0	4	1	53	52.1	3	9	0	2	1.000	7	2	1	0	.29
Herges,Matt, Mon	.000	1	0	0	0	0	.208	24	5	0	0	0	1	1	13	2	62	64.2	5	7	0	0	1.000	8	2	1	0	.25
Hermanson,D, Bos	-	0	0	0	0	0	.096	281	27	5	0	2	9	19	143	31	12	22.0	0	0	0	0	-	0	0	0	0	-

Pitchers Hitting, Fielding and Holding Runners

Pitcher	2002 Hitting Avg	AB	H	HR	RBI	SH	Career Hitting Avg	AB	H	2B	3B	HR	RBI	BB	SO	SH	2002 Fielding and Holding Runners G	Inn	PO	A	E	DP	Pct	SBA	CS	PCS	PPO	CS%
Hernandez,A, NYY	-	0	0	0	0	0	-	0	0	0	0	0	0	0	0	0	2	6.0	0	0	0	0	-	0	0	0	0	-
Hernandez,C, Hou	.171	35	6	0	1	4	.175	40	7	0	0	0	1	2	13	5	23	111.0	7	22	0	1	1.000	7	3	0	1	.43
Hernandez,L, SF	.234	64	15	0	6	10	.242	409	99	18	1	4	39	3	63	34	33	216.0	18	53	3	7	.959	25	3	1	3	.12
Hernandez,O, NYY	-	0	0	0	0	0	.053	19	1	0	0	0	0	0	12	2	24	146.0	8	22	0	0	1.000	21	7	1	0	.33
Hernandez,Ro, KC	-	0	0	0	0	0	.500	2	1	0	0	0	0	0	1	0	53	52.0	6	4	1	1	.909	3	0	0	0	.00
Hernandez,Ru, KC	-	0	0	0	0	0	-	0	0	0	0	0	0	0	0	0	12	74.1	9	12	0	1	1.000	3	0	0	0	.00
Herrera,Alex, Cle	-	0	0	0	0	0	-	0	0	0	0	0	0	0	0	0	5	5.1	0	0	0	0	-	0	0	0	0	-
Hiljus,Erik, Oak	-	0	0	0	0	0	-	0	0	0	0	0	0	0	0	0	9	45.2	3	5	1	0	.889	5	1	0	0	.20
Hill,Jeremy, KC	-	0	0	0	0	0	-	0	0	0	0	0	0	0	0	0	10	9.1	1	1	0	0	1.000	1	0	0	0	.00
Hitchcock,S, NYY	-	0	0	0	0	0	.094	191	18	0	0	0	5	7	103	21	20	39.1	1	5	0	0	1.000	2	1	1	0	.50
Hodges,Trey, Atl	.000	3	0	0	0	0	.000	3	0	0	0	0	0	0	2	0	4	11.2	0	2	0	0	1.000	0	0	0	0	-
Hoffman,Trevor, SD	-	0	0	0	0	0	.121	33	4	2	0	0	5	0	10	2	61	59.1	5	2	1	0	.875	5	1	0	0	.20
Holmes,Darren, Atl	.000	2	0	0	0	0	.107	28	3	0	0	1	2	1	14	6	55	54.2	4	9	3	1	.813	7	4	0	0	.57
Holtz,Mike, Oak-SD	.000	2	0	0	0	0	.000	3	0	0	0	0	0	0	2	0	49	35.0	4	3	0	0	1.000	2	1	0	0	.50
Howard,Ben, SD	.000	4	0	0	0	1	.000	4	0	0	0	0	0	0	2	1	3	10.2	0	1	0	0	1.000	2	1	0	0	.50
Howry,Bob, CWS-Bos	-	0	0	0	0	0	-	0	0	0	0	0	0	0	0	0	67	68.2	3	9	1	1	.923	5	0	0	0	.00
Hudson,Luke, Cin	-	0	0	0	0	1	-	0	0	0	0	0	0	0	0	0	3	6.0	0	0	0	0	-	0	0	0	0	-
Hudson,Tim, Oak	.200	5	1	0	0	0	.100	20	2	1	0	0	0	2	7	0	34	238.1	26	27	0	2	1.000	13	8	0	0	.62
Irabu,Hideki, Tex	-	0	0	0	0	0	.107	28	3	0	0	0	1	1	13	5	38	47.0	2	9	0	1	1.000	8	1	0	0	.13
Ishii,Kazuhisa, LA	.100	50	5	0	2	4	.100	50	5	0	0	0	2	2	21	4	28	154.0	3	21	1	1	.960	27	11	3	0	.41
Isringhausen,J, Stl	-	0	0	0	0	0	.196	97	19	4	0	2	11	5	33	8	60	65.1	3	6	2	0	.818	11	2	0	0	.18
Izquierdo,H, Fla	.000	2	0	0	0	0	.000	2	0	0	0	0	0	0	0	0	20	29.2	1	4	1	0	.833	2	1	0	0	.50
Jackson,Mike, Min	-	0	0	0	0	0	.179	28	5	2	0	0	1	1	4	4	58	55.0	2	10	0	1	1.000	3	0	0	0	.00
James,Bill, KC	.143	7	1	0	0	1	.143	7	1	1	0	0	0	1	3	1	5	18.1	1	2	0	0	1.000	2	0	0	0	.00
James,Delvin, TB	-	0	0	0	0	0	-	0	0	0	0	0	0	0	0	0	8	34.1	1	2	0	0	1.000	0	0	0	0	-
James,Mike, Col	-	0	0	0	0	0	.000	2	0	0	0	0	0	0	0	0	13	11.1	0	1	0	0	1.000	0	0	0	0	-
Jarvis,Kevin, SD	.333	9	3	0	0	1	.163	166	27	6	0	1	12	9	55	20	7	35.0	1	2	1	0	.750	3	1	0	0	.33
Jennings,Jason, Col	.306	62	19	0	11	2	.299	77	23	5	0	1	13	4	16	3	32	185.1	14	28	1	1	.977	16	4	0	3	.25
Jensen,Ryan, SF	.107	56	6	0	2	9	.118	68	8	2	0	0	4	1	21	9	32	171.2	11	19	0	4	1.000	27	8	2	0	.30
Jimenez,Jason, TB-Det	-	0	0	0	0	0	-	0	0	0	0	0	0	0	0	0	6	7.1	0	0	0	0	-	0	0	0	0	-
Jimenez,Jose, Col	-	0	0	0	0	0	.109	64	7	0	1	0	4	0	28	5	74	73.1	11	15	1	2	.963	3	0	0	0	.00
Johnson,Jason, Bal	.000	3	0	0	0	0	.071	14	1	0	0	0	0	1	10	2	22	131.1	8	12	0	4	1.000	15	3	0	1	.20
Johnson, Jon, SD	-	0	0	0	0	0	-	0	0	0	0	0	0	0	0	0	16	15.1	0	0	1	0	.000	3	1	0	0	.33
Johnson,Randy, Ari	.135	89	12	0	8	6	.124	404	50	10	0	0	26	9	187	30	35	260.0	5	20	2	2	.926	34	15	3	0	.44
Jones,Bobby J, SD	.152	33	5	0	2	1	.133	442	59	8	0	1	16	15	164	64	19	108.0	7	14	0	1	1.000	8	2	0	1	.25
Jones,Bobby M, NYM-SD	.000	2	0	0	0	1	.173	81	14	2	0	0	8	4	23	12	16	26.2	0	3	0	0	1.000	1	0	0	0	.00
Jones,Todd, Col	.000	3	0	0	0	0	.214	14	3	1	0	0	0	0	3	0	79	82.1	11	13	0	1	1.000	9	4	0	0	.44
Joseph,Kevin, Stl	-	0	0	0	0	0	-	0	0	0	0	0	0	0	0	0	11	11.0	0	1	0	0	1.000	0	0	0	0	-
Julio,Jorge, Bal	-	0	0	0	0	0	-	0	0	0	0	0	0	0	0	0	67	68.0	5	5	0	0	1.000	7	0	0	1	.00
Junge,Eric, Phi	.000	3	0	0	0	0	.000	3	0	0	0	0	0	0	0	0	4	12.2	1	2	0	0	1.000	1	0	0	0	.00
Karsay,Steve, NYY	.000	1	0	0	0	0	.000	4	0	0	0	0	0	0	0	0	78	88.1	6	15	0	1	1.000	11	0	0	0	.00
Kaye,Justin, Sea	-	0	0	0	0	0	-	0	0	0	0	0	0	0	0	0	3	3.1	1	0	0	0	1.000	0	0	0	0	-
Keller,Kris, Det	-	0	0	0	0	0	-	0	0	0	0	0	0	0	0	0	1	1.0	0	0	0	0	-	0	0	0	0	-
Kennedy,Joe, TB	.429	7	3	0	1	0	.364	11	4	0	0	0	1	0	3	0	30	196.2	10	21	10	2	.756	21	9	6	2	.43
Kent,Steve, TB	-	0	0	0	0	0	-	0	0	0	0	0	0	0	0	0	34	57.1	2	7	2	2	.818	4	3	1	0	.75
Kershner,Jason, SD-Tor	-	0	0	0	0	1	-	0	0	0	0	0	0	0	0	0	25	24.0	3	2	1	1	.833	2	1	0	0	.50
Kile,Darryl, Stl	.091	22	2	0	0	3	.132	657	87	23	0	2	40	43	300	81	14	84.2	3	18	1	2	.955	11	4	1	0	.36
Kim,Byung-Hyun, Ari	.500	2	1	0	0	0	.167	12	2	0	0	0	2	1	4	0	72	84.0	3	12	1	2	.938	6	1	0	0	.17
Kim,Sun-Woo, Bos-Mon	.250	8	2	0	0	0	.250	8	2	0	0	0	0	0	2	0	19	49.1	2	4	0	0	1.000	5	2	0	0	.40
King,Ray, Mil	-	0	0	0	0	0	.000	3	0	0	0	0	0	0	0	0	76	65.0	10	21	2	1	.939	5	0	0	0	.00
Kinney,Matt, Min	.000	2	0	0	0	0	.000	2	0	0	0	0	0	0	1	0	14	66.0	5	6	0	1	1.000	8	1	0	1	.13
Kline,Steve, Stl	.000	1	0	0	0	0	.091	11	1	0	0	0	0	0	5	2	66	58.1	4	6	0	1	1.000	3	2	0	0	.67
Knight,Brandon, NYY	-	0	0	0	0	0	-	0	0	0	0	0	0	0	0	0	7	8.2	1	0	0	0	1.000	0	0	0	0	-
Knotts,Gary, Fla	.000	1	0	0	0	0	.333	3	1	0	0	0	0	0	0	0	28	30.2	1	3	0	0	1.000	2	0	0	0	.00
Koch,Billy, Oak	-	0	0	0	0	0	.000	2	0	0	0	0	0	0	2	0	84	93.2	14	12	0	2	1.000	14	4	2	0	.29
Kolb,Danny, Tex	-	0	0	0	0	0	-	0	0	0	0	0	0	0	0	0	34	32.0	2	6	0	0	1.000	3	1	0	0	.33
Komiyama,S, NYM	.000	1	0	0	0	1	.000	1	0	0	0	0	0	1	1	1	25	43.1	3	1	0	0	1.000	3	1	0	0	.33
Koplove,Mike, Ari	.000	1	0	0	0	0	.000	2	0	0	0	0	0	0	1	0	55	61.2	2	12	0	2	1.000	6	2	0	0	.33
Kozlowski,Ben, Tex	-	0	0	0	0	0	-	0	0	0	0	0	0	0	0	0	2	10.0	2	0	0	0	1.000	3	2	1	0	.67
Lackey,John, Ana	-	0	0	0	0	0	-	0	0	0	0	0	0	0	0	0	18	108.1	4	16	0	2	1.000	16	4	0	0	.25
Lawrence,Brian, SD	.095	63	6	0	6	3	.101	89	9	4	0	0	9	5	21	5	35	210.0	22	31	0	1	1.000	19	8	0	0	.42
Lee,Cliff, Cle	-	0	0	0	0	0	-	0	0	0	0	0	0	0	0	0	2	10.1	1	2	0	0	1.000	3	1	0	0	.33
Leiter,Al, NYM	.151	53	8	0	2	3	.096	405	39	6	1	0	16	30	220	37	33	204.1	1	31	3	2	.914	41	12	3	0	.29
Leskanic,C,	-	0	0	0	0	0	.179	39	7	3	0	1	7	1	17	5	0	0	0	0	0	0	-	0	0	0	0	-
Levine,Al, Ana	-	0	0	0	0	0	-	0	0	0	0	0	0	0	0	0	52	63.2	2	12	0	0	1.000	5	0	0	0	.00
Levrault,Allen,	-	0	0	0	0	0	.056	36	2	0	0	0	1	1	16	6	0	0	0	0	0	0	-	0	0	0	0	-
Lewis,Colby, Tex	-	0	0	0	0	0	-	0	0	0	0	0	0	0	0	0	15	34.1	5	7	0	2	1.000	1	0	0	0	.00
Lidge,Brad, Hou	1.000	2	2	0	2	0	1.000	2	2	1	0	0	2	0	0	0	6	8.2	0	2	0	0	1.000	2	0	0	0	.00
Lidle,Cory, Oak	.000	1	0	0	0	1	.000	10	0	0	0	0	0	1	7	1	31	192.0	15	42	2	5	.966	14	5	0	0	.36
Lieber,Jon, ChC	.163	43	7	0	0	4	.154	461	71	15	0	0	20	21	165	44	21	141.0	5	19	0	1	1.000	5	2	0	0	.40
Ligtenberg,K, Atl	-	0	0	0	0	0	-	0	0	0	0	0	0	0	0	0	52	66.2	1	8	1	1	.900	9	2	0	0	.22
Lilly,Ted, NYY-Oak	.000	3	0	0	0	0	.111	9	1	0	0	0	0	0	4	3	22	100.0	4	12	0	1	1.000	8	2	1	0	.25
Lima,Jose, Det	-	0	0	0	0	0	.115	234	27	4	0	0	8	6	77	33	20	68.1	4	5	0	0	1.000	9	3	0	0	.33
Lincoln,Mike, Pit	.000	5	0	0	0	0	.100	10	1	0	0	0	0	0	5	1	55	72.1	4	11	0	2	1.000	2	1	0	1	.50
Linebrink,S, Hou	-	0	0	0	0	0	1.000	1	1	0	0	0	0	0	0	0	22	24.1	1	2	0	0	1.000	6	0	0	0	.00

Pitchers Hitting, Fielding and Holding Runners

Pitcher	2002 Hitting						Career Hitting											2002 Fielding and Holding Runners											
	Avg	AB	H	HR	RBI	SH	Avg	AB	H	2B	3B	HR	RBI	BB	SO	SH	G	Inn	PO	A	E	DP	Pct	SBA	CS	PCS	PPO	CS%
Linton,Doug,	-	0	0	0	0	0	.000	7	0	0	0	0	0	0	3	2	0	0.0	0	0	0	0	-	0	0	0	0	
Lloyd,Graeme, Mon-Fla	.000	4	0	0	0	0	.000	6	0	0	0	0	0	1	2	0	66	57.0	3	2	0	2	1.000	5	0	0	0	.00
Loaiza,Esteban, Tor	.167	6	1	0	0	0	.178	169	30	2	1	0	11	3	36	23	25	151.1	12	22	1	1	.971	6	1	0	1	.17
Loewer,Carlton,	-	0	0	0	0	0	.140	57	8	0	0	0	2	4	19	7	0	0.0	0	0	0	0	-	0	0	0	0	
Lohse,Kyle, Min	.250	4	1	0	0	0	.333	9	3	1	0	0	1	0	3	0	32	180.2	10	18	0	0	1.000	16	5	0	2	.31
Looper,Braden, Fla	.000	1	0	0	0	0	.000	5	0	0	0	0	0	0	4	0	78	86.0	3	14	0	2	1.000	9	5	0	0	.56
Lopez,Albie, Atl	.111	9	1	0	0	0	.043	46	2	0	0	0	0	2	25	3	30	55.2	4	3	0	1	1.000	4	2	0	0	.50
Lopez,Rodrigo, Bal	.000	3	0	0	0	0	.083	12	1	0	0	0	0	0	6	0	33	196.2	6	25	1	2	.969	18	4	1	3	.22
Lorraine,A, Mil	.000	1	0	0	0	1	.125	24	3	1	0	0	0	2	14	7	5	12.0	0	1	1	0	.500	1	0	0	0	.00
Loux,Shane, Det	-	0	0	0	0	0	-	0	0	0	0	0	0	0	0	0	3	14.0	1	3	0	0	1.000	0	0	0	0	-
Lowe,Derek, Bos	.333	3	1	0	0	1	.083	12	1	0	0	0	0	2	7	1	32	219.2	18	31	0	2	1.000	26	7	0	0	.27
Lowe,Sean, Pit-Col	.071	14	1	0	0	2	.136	22	3	0	0	0	0	0	8	2	51	79.1	6	15	0	2	1.000	8	3	2	1	.38
Lukasiewicz,M, Ana	-	0	0	0	0	0	-	0	0	0	0	0	0	0	0	0	17	14.0	1	0	1	0	.500	0	0	0	0	-
Lundquist,D, SD	-	0	0	0	0	0	-	0	0	0	0	0	0	0	0	0	3	2.2	0	0	0	0	-	0	0	0	0	-
Lyon,Brandon, Tor	-	0	0	0	0	0	-	0	0	0	0	0	0	0	0	0	15	62.0	5	12	1	1	.944	9	1	0	0	.11
MacDougal,Mike, KC	-	0	0	0	0	0	-	0	0	0	0	0	0	0	0	0	6	9.0	1	0	0	0	1.000	2	0	0	0	.00
Maddux,Greg, Atl	.186	59	11	0	2	9	.179	1193	214	28	2	4	62	28	315	135	34	199.1	21	48	1	3	.986	28	4	0	2	.14
Maduro,Calvin, Bal	-	0	0	0	0	0	.042	24	1	0	0	0	0	0	14	1	12	56.2	7	4	0	0	1.000	8	1	0	0	.13
Magnante,Mike, Oak	-	0	0	0	0	0	.333	6	2	0	0	0	1	0	2	0	32	28.2	3	4	0	0	1.000	1	0	0	0	.00
Mahay,Ron, ChC	-	0	0	0	0	0	.333	6	2	1	0	0	0	0	2	0	11	14.2	1	1	1	0	.667	0	0	0	0	-
Mahomes,Pat, ChC	.000	5	0	0	0	0	.256	39	10	4	0	0	4	1	14	2	16	32.2	1	6	0	0	1.000	4	1	0	1	.25
Mairena,O, Fla	-	0	0	0	0	0	-	0	0	0	0	0	0	0	0	0	31	33.2	0	5	0	0	1.000	3	1	0	0	.33
Mallette,Brian, Mil	-	0	0	0	0	0	-	0	0	0	0	0	0	0	0	0	5	5.0	0	2	0	0	1.000	1	0	0	0	.00
Mann,Jim, Hou	.000	1	0	0	0	0	.000	1	0	0	0	0	0	0	1	0	17	22.0	0	2	0	0	1.000	3	1	0	0	.33
Mantei,Matt, Ari	-	0	0	0	0	0	.200	5	1	0	0	0	0	0	2	0	31	26.2	0	2	0	0	1.000	1	0	0	0	.00
Manzanillo,J, Pit	-	0	0	0	0	0	.091	11	1	0	0	0	0	0	5	2	13	13.0	2	1	0	0	1.000	0	0	0	0	-
Maroth,Mike, Det	.167	6	1	0	0	0	.167	6	1	0	0	0	0	0	5	0	21	128.2	5	13	0	0	1.000	6	4	1	0	.67
Marquis,Jason, Atl	.132	38	5	1	1	3	.085	71	6	0	0	1	1	2	26	5	22	114.1	18	10	1	1	.966	7	4	0	0	.57
Marte,Damaso, CWS	-	0	0	0	0	0	.000	4	0	0	0	0	0	0	1	0	68	60.1	0	10	0	0	1.000	8	2	0	0	.25
Martin,Tom, TB	-	0	0	0	0	0	.000	6	0	0	0	0	0	0	2	0	2	1.2	0	0	0	0	-	0	0	0	0	-
Martinez,Pedro, Bos	.000	5	0	0	0	1	.096	260	25	3	2	0	11	11	120	38	30	199.1	16	16	2	1	.941	13	5	0	2	.38
Mateo,Julio, Sea	-	0	0	0	0	0	-	0	0	0	0	0	0	0	0	0	12	21.0	0	1	0	0	1.000	3	1	0	0	.33
Mathews,T.J., Hou	.000	1	0	0	0	0	.000	11	0	0	0	0	0	1	7	0	12	18.1	0	4	0	1	1.000	5	1	0	0	.20
Matthews,Mike, Stl-Mil	.167	6	1	0	0	1	.130	23	3	0	0	1	1	0	8	2	47	45.2	0	9	1	1	.900	3	0	0	0	.00
Maurer,Dave, Cle	-	0	0	0	0	0	.000	1	0	0	0	0	0	0	1	0	2	1.1	0	0	0	0	-	0	0	0	0	-
May,Darrell, KC	.000	4	0	0	0	0	.111	9	1	0	0	0	0	1	5	0	30	131.1	13	14	2	1	.931	14	1	0	0	.07
Mays,Joe, Min	-	0	0	0	0	0	.222	9	2	1	0	0	0	2	4	2	17	95.1	8	13	2	4	.913	2	0	0	1	.00
Meadows,Brian, Pit	.000	18	0	0	1	3	.123	162	20	3	0	0	7	6	67	16	11	62.2	3	12	2	1	.882	7	2	0	1	.29
Meche,Gil,	-	0	0	0	0	0	-	0	0	0	0	0	0	0	0	0	0	0.0	0	0	0	0	-	0	0	0	0	-
Mecir,Jim, Oak	-	0	0	0	0	0	.000	1	0	0	0	0	0	0	0	0	61	67.2	7	15	0	0	1.000	10	1	1	0	.10
Mendoza,Ramiro, NYY	.000	1	0	0	0	0	.000	3	0	0	0	0	0	0	3	1	62	91.2	7	22	1	0	.967	3	1	0	0	.33
Mercado,Hector, Phi	.250	4	1	0	0	0	.143	7	1	0	0	0	0	0	4	0	31	39.0	1	3	0	0	1.000	5	0	0	1	.00
Mercker,Kent, Col	.000	1	0	0	0	0	.114	245	28	5	2	1	18	11	114	22	58	44.0	3	2	1	0	.833	2	0	0	0	.00
Mesa,Jose, Phi	-	0	0	0	0	0	-	0	0	0	0	0	0	0	1	0	74	75.2	4	16	0	0	1.000	2	0	0	0	.00
Miceli,Dan, Tex	-	0	0	0	0	0	.053	19	1	0	0	0	0	0	8	0	9	8.1	0	1	0	0	1.000	1	0	0	0	.00
Michalak,Chris, Tex	-	0	0	0	0	0	.333	3	1	0	1	0	0	0	1	2	13	14.1	0	4	0	0	1.000	1	1	0	0	1.00
Middlebrook,J, SD-NYM	.182	11	2	0	0	1	.167	18	3	0	0	0	1	1	9	1	15	51.1	0	4	0	0	1.000	4	1	0	0	.25
Miller,Justin, Tor	.000	2	0	0	0	0	.000	2	0	0	0	0	0	0	1	0	25	102.1	8	10	0	0	1.000	15	4	1	1	.27
Miller,Matt, Det	-	0	0	0	0	0	-	0	0	0	0	0	0	0	0	0	2	0.2	0	0	0	0	-	0	0	0	0	-
Miller,Travis, Min	-	0	0	0	0	0	-	0	0	0	0	0	0	0	0	0	5	4.0	0	0	0	0	-	0	0	0	0	-
Miller,Trever,	-	0	0	0	0	0	.167	6	1	1	0	0	0	0	1	2	0	0.0	0	0	0	0	-	0	0	0	0	-
Miller,Wade, Hou	.177	62	11	0	4	6	.154	169	26	6	0	0	8	2	58	17	26	164.2	22	19	2	1	.953	12	5	0	1	.42
Millwood,Kevin, Atl	.200	70	14	1	11	11	.131	312	41	10	0	2	22	12	132	39	35	217.0	8	25	2	2	.943	22	1	0	0	.05
Milton,Eric, Min	.400	5	2	0	1	0	.300	20	6	0	0	0	2	1	7	0	29	171.0	5	12	1	1	.944	3	1	0	0	.33
Mlicki,Dave, Hou	.185	27	5	0	1	0	.125	208	26	5	0	0	6	18	76	31	22	86.0	4	8	1	0	.923	13	2	0	0	.15
Moehler,Brian, Det-Cin	.000	14	0	0	0	1	.000	26	0	0	0	0	0	2	10	1	13	63.0	4	13	0	0	1.000	5	2	0	0	.40
Molina,Gabe, Stl	-	0	0	0	0	0	-	0	0	0	0	0	0	0	0	0	12	11.1	0	2	0	1	1.000	0	0	0	0	-
Moreno,Juan, SD	-	0	0	0	0	0	-	0	0	0	0	0	0	0	0	0	4	6.0	0	0	0	0	-	0	0	0	0	-
Morgan,Mike, Ari	-	0	0	0	0	0	.109	497	54	3	1	0	15	13	151	59	29	34.0	1	3	1	0	.800	3	0	0	0	.00
Morris,Matt, Stl	.169	71	12	0	3	5	.161	248	40	8	0	0	17	15	109	28	32	210.1	11	22	0	0	1.000	22	4	0	0	.18
Moss,Damian, Atl	.100	50	5	0	2	6	.098	51	5	1	0	0	2	5	25	6	33	179.0	5	37	2	3	.955	19	11	6	3	.58
Mota,Guillermo, LA	.250	4	1	0	0	0	.333	9	3	0	0	1	3	0	3	0	43	60.2	2	7	0	0	1.000	5	1	0	1	.20
Moyer,Jamie, Sea	.200	5	1	0	0	0	.145	166	24	2	0	0	4	15	55	21	34	230.2	22	34	1	5	.982	18	6	4	0	.33
Mulder,Mark, Oak	.000	5	0	0	0	0	.071	14	1	0	0	0	0	0	5	0	30	207.1	10	36	0	3	1.000	16	9	6	0	.56
Mulholland,T, LA-Cle	.000	1	0	0	0	0	.112	616	69	13	1	2	23	13	280	53	37	79.0	10	13	2	2	.920	0	0	0	0	-
Mullen,Scott, KC	-	0	0	0	0	0	-	0	0	0	0	0	0	0	0	0	44	40.0	1	3	2	1	.667	4	1	0	0	.25
Munro,Pete, Hou	.136	22	3	0	2	1	.130	23	3	0	0	0	2	1	7	1	19	80.2	14	18	1	1	.970	3	1	0	1	.33
Murray,Heath, Cle	-	0	0	0	0	0	.105	19	2	0	0	0	0	1	10	1	9	12.0	0	3	0	0	1.000	1	1	0	0	1.00
Mussina,Mike, NYY	.600	5	3	0	0	1	.229	35	8	1	0	0	5	0	6	1	33	215.2	16	32	1	3	.980	16	10	1	0	.63
Myers,Brett, Phi	.130	23	3	0	1	3	.130	23	3	1	0	0	1	1	9	3	12	72.0	6	11	0	2	1.000	4	3	0	0	.75
Myers,Mike, Ari	-	0	0	0	0	0	.000	1	0	0	0	0	0	0	0	1	69	37.0	2	11	0	0	1.000	4	2	2	0	.50
Myers,Rodney, SD	.000	1	0	0	0	0	.188	16	3	1	0	0	1	0	7	0	14	21.1	3	2	0	1	1.000	0	0	0	0	-
Myette,Aaron, Tex	-	0	0	0	0	0	-	0	0	0	0	0	0	0	0	0	15	48.1	3	2	1	0	.833	3	0	0	0	.00
Nagy,Charles, Cle	-	0	0	0	0	0	.118	17	2	0	0	0	0	0	10	0	19	48.2	2	4	0	0	1.000	6	0	0	0	.00
Nance,Shane, Mil	.333	3	1	0	1	0	.333	3	1	0	0	0	1	0	2	0	4	6.1	1	1	0	0	1.000	0	0	0	0	-

Pitchers Hitting, Fielding and Holding Runners

Pitcher	2002 Hitting						Career Hitting										2002 Fielding and Holding Runners											
	Avg	AB	H	HR	RBI	SH	Avg	AB	H	2B	3B	HR	RBI	BB	SO	SH	G	Inn	PO	A	E	DP	Pct	SBA	CS	PCS	PPO	CS%
Nathan,Joe, SF	-	0	0	0	0	0	.167	60	10	3	0	2	4	3	15	9	4	3.2	0	2	0	0	1.000	0	0	0	0	-
Neagle,Denny, Col	.267	45	12	0	1	5	.167	520	87	17	0	5	44	19	151	73	35	164.1	8	25	1	1	.971	22	3	0	0	.14
Neal,Blaine, Fla	-	0	0	0	0	0	-	0	0	0	0	0	0	0	0	0	32	33.0	3	1	0	0	1.000	4	1	0	0	.25
Nelson,Jeff, Sea	-	0	0	0	0	0	.000	2	0	0	0	0	0	0	0	1	41	45.2	2	4	0	0	1.000	6	1	1	0	.17
Nen,Robb, SF	.500	2	1	0	0	0	.067	15	1	0	0	0	0	0	4	0	68	73.2	7	5	0	0	1.000	6	0	0	0	.00
Neugebauer,N, Mil	.105	19	2	0	1	1	.091	22	2	1	0	0	1	0	5	1	12	55.1	4	4	0	0	1.000	14	3	0	0	.21
Nichting,Chris, Col	.333	3	1	0	0	0	.250	4	1	0	0	0	0	0	1	1	29	36.1	2	3	0	1	1.000	1	0	0	0	.00
Nickle,Doug, Phi-SD	.000	1	0	0	0	0	.000	1	0	0	0	0	0	0	0	0	14	16.0	1	2	1	0	.750	0	0	0	0	-
Nitkowski,C.J., Tex	-	0	0	0	0	0	.133	15	2	0	0	0	1	0	10	1	12	13.2	0	2	0	0	1.000	3	1	0	0	.33
Nomo,Hideo, LA	.063	63	4	1	3	6	.136	390	53	13	1	2	22	10	179	37	34	220.1	10	21	4	2	.886	38	10	0	0	.26
Nomura,T, Mil	-	0	0	0	0	0	-	0	0	0	0	0	0	0	0	0	21	13.2	0	1	0	0	1.000	0	0	0	0	.00
Norton,Phil,	-	0	0	0	0	0	-										0	0.0	0	0	0	0	-	0	0	0	0	-
Nunez,Jose, SD	-	0	0	0	0	0	.000	3	0	0	0	0	0	0	2	0	1	1.0	0	0	0	0	-	0	0	0	0	-
Nunez,Vladimir, Fla	.200	5	1	0	0	0	.136	59	8	0	0	1	5	1	19	8	77	97.2	4	13	0	1	1.000	9	2	0	1	.22
Obermueller,W, KC	-	0	0	0	0	0	-	0	0	0	0	0	0	0	0	0	2	7.2	0	0	0	0	-	0	0	0	0	-
Ohka,Tomo, Mon	.127	55	7	0	2	7	.137	73	10	1	0	0	3	4	36	10	32	192.2	24	30	0	2	1.000	9	4	1	1	.44
Oliver,Darren, Bos	.000	1	0	0	0	0	.230	113	26	7	0	0	9	4	41	10	14	58.0	2	6	0	0	1.000	7	3	1	0	.43
Olsen,Kevin, Fla	.083	12	1	0	0	0	.067	15	1	0	0	0	0	0	10	1	17	55.2	8	4	1	0	.923	11	0	0	0	.00
Oropesa,Eddie, Ari	-	0	0	0	0	0	-	0	0	0	0	0	0	0	0	0	32	25.1	1	4	1	0	.833	0	0	0	0	-
Orosco,Jesse, LA	-	0	0	0	0	0	.169	59	10	0	0	0	4	8	25	7	56	27.0	2	3	0	0	1.000	2	0	0	0	.00
Ortiz,Ramon, Ana	.000	7	0	0	0	0	.000	14	0	0	0	0	0	0	5	0	32	217.1	8	19	4	1	.871	20	9	0	0	.45
Ortiz,Russ, SF	.246	69	17	2	9	7	.215	293	63	15	0	4	30	24	78	33	33	214.1	15	47	1	2	.984	14	7	0	0	.50
Osborne,D, ChC	.000	3	0	0	0	0	.162	259	42	10	1	1	19	12	87	28	11	16.0	0	2	0	0	1.000	3	0	0	0	.00
Osting,Jimmy, Mil	.000	3	0	0	0	1	.000	3	0	0	0	0	0	0	1	1	3	12.0	1	3	0	0	1.000	2	1	1	0	.50
Osuna,Antonio, CWS	-	0	0	0	0	0	.111	9	1	0	0	0	1	1	1	0	59	67.2	7	10	0	2	1.000	4	1	0	1	.25
Oswalt,Roy, Hou	.130	77	10	0	4	7	.153	124	19	3	0	0	7	5	38	10	35	233.0	13	38	1	3	.981	17	7	0	1	.41
Padilla,V, Phi	.052	58	3	0	5	7	.081	62	5	2	0	0	5	1	33	8	32	206.0	10	32	1	1	.977	8	3	0	0	.38
Painter,Lance,	-	0	0	0	0	0	.156	64	10	2	1	0	5	2	33	8	0	0.0	0	0	0	0	-	0	0	0	0	-
Paniagua,Jose, Det	-	0	0	0	0	0	.000	18	0	0	0	0	0	2	11	1	41	41.2	1	5	0	0	1.000	4	1	0	0	.25
Park,Chan Ho, Tex	.000	4	0	0	0	0	.168	345	58	15	1	2	23	16	125	39	25	145.2	12	15	1	3	.964	9	3	0	0	.33
Paronto,Chad, Cle	-	0	0	0	0	0	-	0	0	0	0	0	0	0	0	0	29	35.2	2	5	0	1	1.000	4	0	0	0	.00
Parque,Jim, CWS	-	0	0	0	0	0	.200	10	2	0	0	0	0	0	4	3	8	25.1	0	2	0	0	1.000	4	1	0	0	.25
Parra,Jose, Ari	-	0	0	0	0	0	-	0	0	0	0	0	0	2	0	2	16	14.0	1	1	0	0	1.000	2	1	0	0	.50
Parris,Steve, Tor	.000	4	0	0	0	0	.155	161	25	4	0	0	15	3	53	16	14	75.1	6	7	0	0	1.000	3	1	0	0	.33
Patterson,D, Det	-	0	0	0	0	0	.000	1	0	0	0	0	0	0	0	0	6	3.0	0	1	0	0	1.000	0	0	0	0	-
Patterson,John, Ari	.100	10	1	0	0	1	.100	10	1	0	0	0	0	1	4	1	7	30.2	1	5	0	0	1.000	2	0	0	0	.00
Pavano,Carl, Mon-Fla	.200	40	8	0	2	5	.138	159	22	3	1	0	7	1	61	20	37	136.0	3	19	1	4	.957	21	7	0	0	.33
Pearce,Josh, Stl	.250	4	1	0	1	2	.250	4	1	0	0	0	1	0	0	2	3	13.0	2	1	0	1	1.000	3	0	0	0	.00
Pearson,Jason, SD	-	0	0	0	0	0	-	0	0	0	0	0	0	0	0	0	2	1.2	0	0	0	0	-	0	0	0	0	-
Pearson,Terry, Det	-	0	0	0	0	0	-	0	0	0	0	0	0	0	0	0	4	6.0	0	0	0	0	-	1	0	0	0	.00
Peavy,Jake, SD	.212	33	7	0	2	2	.212	33	7	3	0	0	2	0	13	2	17	97.2	9	19	0	0	1.000	3	0	0	0	.00
Pember,Dave, Mil	.000	1	0	0	0	0	.000	1	0	0	0	0	0	0	0	0	4	8.2	1	0	0	0	1.000	0	0	0	0	-
Penny,Brad, Fla	.167	48	8	0	1	1	.148	155	23	3	1	0	4	1	50	5	24	129.1	12	14	0	1	1.000	14	4	0	0	.29
Percival,Troy, Ana	-	0	0	0	0	0	.000	1	0	0	0	0	0	0	1	0	58	56.1	1	3	0	0	1.000	6	1	0	0	.17
Perez,Odalis, LA	.156	64	10	1	4	10	.158	120	19	6	0	1	8	1	29	16	32	222.1	23	51	2	3	.974	27	10	9	0	.37
Perez,Oliver, SD	.133	30	4	0	0	3	.133	30	4	0	0	0	0	0	11	3	16	90.0	2	9	1	1	.917	2	1	0	0	.50
Perez,Yorkis, Bal	-	0	0	0	0	0	.000	11	0	0	0	0	0	0	8	0	23	27.1	2	3	2	0	.714	6	0	0	0	.00
Perisho,Matt, Det	-	0	0	0	0	0	.000	5	0	0	0	0	0	0	0	0	5	10.1	0	1	0	0	1.000	6	0	0	0	.00
Person,Robert, Phi	.083	24	2	2	7	3	.117	213	25	5	0	4	16	10	118	25	16	87.2	4	9	0	0	1.000	12	5	0	1	.42
Pettitte,Andy, NYY	.333	3	1	0	1	0	.095	21	2	1	0	0	1	1	9	3	22	134.2	8	27	2	0	.946	11	4	3	3	.36
Phelps,Travis, TB	-	0	0	0	0	0	-	0	0	0	0	0	0	0	0	0	26	37.2	0	6	0	0	1.000	5	0	0	1	.00
Phillips,J C, Cle	-	0	0	0	0	0	-	0	0	0	0	0	0	0	0	0	8	41.2	2	7	0	0	1.000	11	4	0	1	.36
Pichardo,H, Hou	-	0	0	0	0	0	.000	5	0	0	0	0	0	0	0	3	1	0.1	0	0	0	0	-	3	0	0	0	.00
Pickford,Kevin, SD	.000	5	0	0	0	0	.000	5	0	0	0	0	0	0	0	3	16	30.0	3	5	1	1	.889	6	3	0	0	.50
Pineda,Luis, Cin	.000	3	0	0	0	0	.000	3	0	0	0	0	0	0	0	2	26	32.1	1	1	0	1	1.000	1	0	0	0	.00
Pineiro,Joel, Sea	.143	7	1	0	2	0	.143	7	1	0	0	0	2	0	2	0	37	194.1	14	34	2	4	.960	17	4	0	0	.24
Plesac,Dan, Tor-Phi	-	0	0	0	0	0	.067	15	1	0	0	0	0	0	10	0	60	36.1	0	3	0	0	1.000	8	1	0	0	.13
Politte,Cliff, Phi-Tor	.000	1	0	0	0	0	.094	32	3	1	0	0	2	3	14	3	68	73.2	1	5	0	0	1.000	11	3	0	0	.27
Ponson,Sidney, Bal	.333	3	1	0	0	0	.214	14	3	1	0	0	0	0	5	3	28	176.0	20	21	0	3	1.000	11	5	0	3	.45
Porzio,Mike, CWS	-	0	0	0	0	0	-	0	0	0	0	0	0	0	0	0	32	43.0	3	3	0	1	1.000	2	1	0	0	.50
Pote,Lou, Ana	-	0	0	0	0	0	-	0	0	0	0	0	0	0	0	0	31	50.1	4	11	1	0	.938	8	3	0	0	.38
Powell,Brian, Det	-	0	0	0	0	0	.182	11	2	1	0	0	0	1	6	0	13	57.2	6	3	0	0	1.000	6	2	0	0	.33
Powell,Jay, Tex	-	0	0	0	0	0	.167	12	2	0	0	0	1	0	8	1	51	49.2	4	9	0	0	1.000	0	0	0	0	-
Pratt,Andy, Atl	-	0	0	0	0	0	-	0	0	0	0	0	0	0	0	0	1	1.1	0	1	0	0	1.000	0	0	0	0	-
Prinz,Bret, Ari	-	0	0	0	0	0	-	0	0	0	0	0	0	0	0	0	20	13.1	0	2	0	0	1.000	2	0	0	0	.00
Prior,Mark, ChC	.171	35	6	0	4	2	.171	35	6	1	0	0	4	2	15	2	19	116.2	1	8	0	0	1.000	19	6	0	0	.32
Prokopec,Luke, Tor	-	0	0	0	0	0	.171	41	7	1	0	0	0	0	15	8	12	72.1	4	6	1	0	.909	3	1	0	0	.33
Puffer,Brandon, Hou	.000	6	0	0	0	1	.000	6	0	0	0	0	0	1	5	1	55	69.0	10	13	0	0	1.000	4	0	0	0	.00
Quantrill,Paul, LA	.333	3	1	0	0	0	.109	64	7	0	0	0	0	4	28	7	86	76.2	4	13	0	2	1.000	7	2	1	0	.29
Quevedo,Ruben, Mil	.095	42	4	0	3	3	.136	88	12	0	0	0	5	2	39	8	26	139.0	2	13	1	1	.938	17	3	0	1	.18
Radke,Brad, Min	-	0	0	0	0	0	.125	16	2	0	0	0	0	0	5	0	21	118.1	10	9	0	0	1.000	4	2	0	1	.33
Rauch,Jon, CWS	-	0	0	0	0	0	-	0	0	0	0	0	0	0	0	0	8	28.2	0	3	1	0	.750	2	1	0	0	.50
Reames,Britt, Mon	.111	9	1	0	1	2	.132	38	5	0	0	1	3	4	11	6	42	68.0	2	10	0	2	1.000	10	4	1	0	.40
Redding,Tim, Hou	.100	20	2	0	2	1	.147	34	5	0	0	0	0	0	23	3	18	73.1	4	15	2	1	.905	9	2	0	0	.22
Redman,Mark, Det	.200	5	1	0	0	0	.111	9	1	0	0	0	0	0	3	1	30	203.0	7	23	6	1	.833	6	3	3	1	.50

274

Pitchers Hitting, Fielding and Holding Runners

Pitcher	2002 Hitting						Career Hitting										2002 Fielding and Holding Runners											
	Avg	AB	H	HR	RBI	SH	Avg	AB	H	2B	3B	HR	RBI	BB	SO	SH	G	Inn	PO	A	E	DP	Pct	SBA	CS	PCS	PPO	CS%
Reed,Rick, Min	.250	4	1	0	0	1	.172	297	51	9	0	2	24	13	93	47	33	188.0	8	20	2	1	.933	9	2	0	3	.22
Reed,Steve, SD-NYM	.000	2	0	0	0	0	.154	26	4	0	0	0	0	0	8	2	64	67.0	4	13	0	1	1.000	5	3	0	0	.60
Reichert,Dan, KC	-	0	0	0	0	0	.111	9	1	0	0	0	0	0	6	1	30	66.0	17	13	1	0	.968	5	4	0	0	.80
Reith,Brian,	-	0	0	0	0	0	-	0	0	0	0	0	0	0	0	0	0	0.0	0	0	0	0	-	0	0	0	0	-
Reitsma,Chris, Cin	.100	30	3	0	2	7	.103	78	8	1	0	0	3	3	36	14	32	138.1	9	19	1	1	.966	8	3	0	1	.38
Rekar,Bryan, KC	-	0	0	0	0	0	.145	55	8	2	0	0	1	4	25	5	2	7.0	2	1	0	0	1.000	1	0	0	0	.00
Remlinger,Mike, Atl	.000	2	0	0	0	0	.074	108	8	3	0	0	8	8	35	19	73	68.0	1	10	0	1	1.000	2	2	2	0	1.00
Reyes,Al, Pit	-	0	0	0	0	0	.200	10	2	0	0	0	0	0	5	1	15	17.0	1	3	0	0	1.000	3	2	0	0	.67
Reyes,Carlos,	-	0	0	0	0	0	.000	2	0	0	0	0	0	0	1	1	0	0.0	0	0	0	0	-	0	0	0	0	-
Reyes,Dennys, Col-Tex	-	0	0	0	0	0	.070	43	3	1	0	0	0	2	20	2	58	82.2	1	11	1	1	.923	9	2	1	0	.22
Reynolds,Shane, Hou	.048	21	1	0	3	9	.146	492	72	15	0	5	40	13	221	87	13	74.0	2	16	1	0	.947	13	4	0	0	.31
Reynoso,A, Ari	-	0	0	0	0	0	.148	337	50	6	0	3	13	16	149	38	2	1.2	0	0	0	0	-	0	0	0	0	-
Rhodes,Arthur, Sea	-	0	0	0	0	0	.250	4	1	0	0	0	0	0	3	0	66	69.2	6	5	0	1	1.000	4	3	0	0	.75
Riedling,John, Cin	.000	1	0	0	0	0	.000	4	0	0	0	0	0	0	4	0	33	46.2	4	12	2	1	.889	6	0	0	0	.00
Riggan,Jerrod, Cle	-	0	0	0	0	0	.000	2	0	0	0	0	0	0	2	0	29	33.0	3	3	0	1	1.000	6	2	0	0	.33
Rijo,Jose, Cin	.125	16	2	0	0	3	.191	445	85	13	0	2	29	8	101	58	31	77.0	4	14	0	0	1.000	7	0	0	0	.00
Rincon,Juan, Min	-	0	0	0	0	0	1.000	1	1	0	0	0	0	0	0	0	10	28.2	2	5	1	1	.875	1	0	0	1	.00
Rincon,Ricardo, Cle-Oak	.000	1	0	0	0	0	.000	4	0	0	0	0	0	0	1	1	71	56.0	1	7	0	1	1.000	6	3	2	0	.50
Riske,David, Cle	-	0	0	0	0	0	-	0	0	0	0	0	0	0	0	0	51	51.1	0	8	0	1	1.000	8	2	0	0	.25
Ritchie,Todd, CWS	.250	4	1	0	0	0	.174	178	31	5	0	0	6	7	67	18	26	133.2	12	18	3	1	.909	17	2	0	0	.12
Rivera,Mariano, NYY	-	0	0	0	0	0	-	0	0	0	0	0	0	0	0	0	45	46.0	3	6	2	1	.818	3	0	0	0	.00
Roa,Joe, Phi	.240	25	6	0	2	3	.200	40	8	1	0	0	2	2	10	3	14	71.1	2	4	0	1	1.000	4	1	0	0	.25
Roberts,Grant, NYM	1.000	1	1	0	0	0	.250	4	1	0	0	0	0	0	3	1	34	45.0	4	5	0	0	1.000	5	0	0	0	.00
Roberts,Willis, Bal	-	0	0	0	0	0	.250	4	1	0	0	0	0	0	3	1	66	75.0	4	10	2	0	.875	10	3	0	1	.30
Robertson,J, Hou	-	0	0	0	0	0	-	0	0	0	0	0	0	0	0	0	11	9.2	1	4	0	1	1.000	1	0	0	0	.00
Robertson,Nate, Fla	.000	2	0	0	0	0	.000	2	0	0	0	0	0	0	1	0	6	8.1	0	1	1	0	.500	0	0	0	0	-
Rocker,John, Tex	-	0	0	0	0	0	-	0	0	0	0	0	0	0	0	0	30	24.1	1	2	1	1	.750	2	1	0	0	.50
Rodney,F, Det	-	0	0	0	0	0	-	0	0	0	0	0	0	0	0	0	20	18.0	1	1	0	0	1.000	2	0	0	0	.00
Rodriguez,Fe, SF	1.000	1	1	0	0	0	.214	14	3	1	0	1	3	0	4	2	71	69.0	1	5	0	0	1.000	8	3	0	0	.38
Rodriguez,Fr, Ana	-	0	0	0	0	0	-	0	0	0	0	0	0	0	0	0	5	5.2	0	1	0	0	1.000	5	2	0	0	.40
Rodriguez,Jose, Stl-Min	-	0	0	0	0	0	.000	1	0	0	0	0	0	0	1	0	6	4.0	0	0	0	0	-	0	0	0	0	-
Rodriguez,N, Cle-Stl	.000	1	0	0	0	0	.000	1	0	0	0	0	0	0	1	0	3	4.2	0	0	0	0	-	1	0	0	0	.00
Rodriguez,Rica, Cle	-	0	0	0	0	0	-	0	0	0	0	0	0	0	0	0	7	41.1	5	2	0	0	1.000	6	1	0	0	.17
Rodriguez,Rich, Tex	-	0	0	0	0	0	.107	28	3	0	0	0	1	3	9	4	36	16.2	1	4	1	0	.833	1	1	1	0	1.00
Rogers,Kenny, Tex	.667	3	2	0	1	0	.159	44	7	0	0	0	3	3	16	4	33	210.2	22	40	3	5	.954	1	1	0	1	1.00
Romero,J.C., Min	-	0	0	0	0	0	.500	2	1	1	0	0	0	0	0	0	81	81.0	5	9	0	2	1.000	7	3	0	0	.43
Rueter,Kirk, SF	.177	62	11	0	3	13	.157	478	75	6	0	0	34	21	88	71	33	203.2	15	37	0	5	1.000	7	5	0	1	.71
Rupe,Ryan, TB	.000	1	0	0	0	0	.111	9	1	0	0	0	0	0	3	0	15	90.0	3	7	0	0	1.000	11	3	0	0	.27
Rusch,Glendon, Mil	.288	66	19	1	8	14	.142	176	25	0	0	1	14	5	68	24	34	210.2	3	35	2	1	.950	7	6	3	0	.86
Ryan,B.J., Bal	.000	1	0	0	0	0	.000	2	0	0	0	0	0	0	0	0	67	57.2	1	8	0	1	1.000	9	5	0	0	.56
Saarloos,Kirk, Hou	.067	30	2	0	2	5	.067	30	2	1	0	0	2	0	11	5	17	85.1	8	14	1	3	.957	8	1	0	1	.13
Sabathia,C.C., Cle	.200	5	1	0	0	0	.111	9	1	0	0	0	1	1	1	1	33	210.0	2	19	1	2	.955	28	9	1	0	.32
Sabel,Erik, Det	-	0	0	0	0	0	.000	2	0	0	0	0	0	0	0	2	1	0.0	0	0	0	0	-	0	0	0	0	-
Sadler,Carl, Cle	-	0	0	0	0	0	-	0	0	0	0	0	0	0	0	0	24	20.1	0	2	0	0	1.000	0	0	0	0	-
Sanchez,Duaner, Ari-Pit	-	0	0	0	0	0	-	0	0	0	0	0	0	0	0	0	9	6.0	1	0	0	0	1.000	0	0	0	0	-
Sanchez,Jesus, ChC	.000	1	0	0	0	0	.181	138	25	0	1	0	6	3	38	11	8	8.1	0	1	2	0	.333	0	0	0	0	-
Santana,Johan, Min	.250	4	1	0	0	0	.200	5	1	0	0	0	0	0	0	0	27	108.1	4	9	2	0	.867	6	3	2	0	.50
Santana,Julio, Det	-	0	0	0	0	0	.111	18	2	0	0	0	0	1	10	0	38	57.0	0	3	2	0	.600	7	2	0	0	.29
Santiago,Jose, Phi	.000	2	0	0	0	0	.000	5	0	0	0	0	0	2	4	0	42	47.0	3	4	0	1	1.000	1	0	0	0	.00
Santos,Victor, Col	.500	2	1	0	0	0	.500	2	1	0	0	0	0	0	0	0	24	26.0	1	2	0	0	1.000	6	2	0	0	.33
Sasaki,K, Sea	-	0	0	0	0	0	-	0	0	0	0	0	0	0	0	0	61	60.2	1	13	2	0	.875	3	1	0	0	.33
Sauerbeck,S, Pit	.000	2	0	0	0	0	.000	6	0	0	0	0	0	0	0	3	78	62.2	2	12	0	2	1.000	8	1	1	0	.13
Schilling,Curt, Ari	.174	86	15	0	3	8	.156	710	111	13	1	0	29	22	245	98	36	259.1	9	16	0	1	1.000	15	6	0	0	.40
Schmidt,Jason, SF	.125	56	7	0	2	4	.101	338	34	6	0	2	14	16	160	48	29	185.1	5	15	0	0	1.000	14	2	0	0	.14
Schoeneweis,S, Ana	.000	2	0	0	0	0	.200	5	1	0	0	0	1	2	2	0	54	118.0	3	17	1	2	.952	8	2	0	0	.25
Seanez,Rudy, Tex	-	0	0	0	0	0	.000	4	0	0	0	0	0	1	4	0	33	33.0	5	2	0	0	1.000	5	0	0	0	.00
Seay,Bobby,	-	0	0	0	0	0	-	0	0	0	0	0	0	0	0	0	0	0.0	0	0	0	0	-	0	0	0	0	-
Sedlacek,Shawn, KC	.000	6	0	0	0	0	.000	6	0	0	0	0	0	0	4	0	16	84.1	11	7	0	1	1.000	8	3	0	0	.38
Sele,Aaron, Ana	.500	2	1	0	0	0	.143	21	3	1	0	0	1	1	4	4	26	160.0	3	12	0	1	1.000	13	7	0	0	.54
Seo,Jae, NYM	-	0	0	0	0	0	-	0	0	0	0	0	0	0	0	0	1	1.0	0	0	0	0	-	0	0	0	0	-
Service,Scott,	-	0	0	0	0	0	.063	16	1	0	0	0	1	0	9	0	0	0.0	0	0	0	0	-	0	0	0	0	-
Sheets,Ben, Mil	.088	68	6	0	3	4	.082	110	9	1	0	0	4	8	68	6	34	216.2	28	36	1	6	.985	26	12	0	1	.46
Shields,Scot, Ana	-	0	0	0	0	0	-	0	0	0	0	0	0	0	0	0	29	49.0	2	6	0	0	1.000	2	0	0	0	.00
Shiell,Jason, SD	-	0	0	0	0	0	-	0	0	0	0	0	0	0	0	0	3	1.1	0	0	0	0	-	0	0	0	0	-
Shouse,Brian, KC	-	0	0	0	0	0	-	0	0	0	0	0	0	0	0	0	23	14.2	1	5	0	0	1.000	1	1	1	0	1.00
Shuey,Paul, Cle-LA	.333	3	1	0	0	0	.200	5	1	0	0	0	0	0	3	0	67	68.0	7	17	0	0	1.000	7	0	0	0	.00
Silva,Carlos, Phi	.000	2	0	0	0	0	.000	2	0	0	0	0	0	1	1	0	68	84.0	4	19	1	2	.958	9	5	0	0	.56
Silva,Jose, Cin	-	0	0	0	0	1	.111	90	10	1	0	0	5	3	38	16	12	23.1	3	8	0	1	1.000	3	2	0	1	.67
Simontacchi,J, Stl	.240	50	12	0	2	4	.240	50	12	0	0	0	2	2	15	4	24	143.1	12	25	0	4	1.000	2	1	0	0	.50
Small,Aaron, Atl	-	0	0	0	0	0	1.000	1	1	0	0	0	0	0	0	0	3	0.1	0	0	0	0	-	0	0	0	0	-
Smith,Bud, Stl	.214	14	3	0	1	3	.179	39	7	1	0	0	2	2	9	5	11	48.0	0	3	0	0	1.000	4	0	0	1	.00
Smith,Dan, Mon	.000	3	0	0	0	0	.074	27	2	0	0	0	1	3	18	3	33	46.2	2	2	0	0	1.000	1	1	0	1	1.00
Smith,Mike, Tor	-	0	0	0	0	0	-	0	0	0	0	0	0	0	0	0	14	35.1	2	5	1	1	.875	2	0	0	0	.00
Smith,Roy, Cle	-	0	0	0	0	0	-	0	0	0	0	0	0	0	0	0	4	6.0	1	3	0	0	1.000	0	0	0	0	-
Smith,Travis, Stl	.167	18	3	0	2	2	.158	19	3	0	0	0	2	0	6	2	12	54.0	4	7	0	1	1.000	5	1	0	0	.20

Pitchers Hitting, Fielding and Holding Runners

Pitcher	2002 Hitting Avg	AB	H	HR	RBI	SH	Career Hitting Avg	AB	H	2B	3B	HR	RBI	BB	SO	SH	2002 Fielding and Holding Runners G	Inn	PO	A	E	DP	Pct	SBA	CS	PCS	PPO	CS%
Smoltz,John, Atl	.000	2	0	0	0	0	.173	736	127	20	1	5	51	70	282	92	75	80.1	11	11	0	0	1.000	3	1	0	0	.33
Smyth,Steve, ChC	.222	9	2	0	1	1	.222	9	2	0	0	0	1	0	1	1	8	26.0	1	1	1	0	.667	1	1	0	0	1.00
Soriano,Rafael, Sea	.000	4	0	0	0	0	.000	4	0	0	0	0	0	0	1	0	10	47.1	2	4	1	0	.857	4	2	0	0	.50
Sosa,Jorge, TB	-	0	0	0	0	0	-	0	0	0	0	0	0	0	0	0	31	99.1	7	4	0	0	1.000	16	4	1	0	.25
Sparks,Steve, Det	.000	2	0	0	0	0	.100	10	1	1	0	0	2	1	3	1	32	189.0	15	41	2	3	.966	13	4	1	1	.31
Speier,Justin, Col	.333	3	1	0	0	0	.200	15	3	0	0	0	0	0	7	0	63	62.1	0	2	0	0	1.000	2	0	0	0	.00
Spooneybarger,T, Atl	.000	1	0	0	0	0	.000	1	0	0	0	0	0	0	1	0	51	51.1	3	9	1	0	.923	5	1	0	0	.20
Springer,D, LA	-	0	0	0	0	0	.097	72	7	1	0	0	2	0	30		1	1.1	1	0	0	0	1.000	0	0	0	0	-
Springer,Russ,	-	0	0	0	0	0	.080	25	2	0	0	0	0	0	15	3	0	0.0	0	0	0	0	-	0	0	0	0	-
Standridge,J, TB	-	0	0	0	0	0	-	0	0	0	0	0	0	0	0	0	1	3.0	1	0	0	0	1.000	0	0	0	0	-
Stanton,Mike, NYY	.000	2	0	0	0	0	.438	16	7	1	0	0	2	1	2	1	79	78.0	4	9	2	1	.867	6	4	2	0	.67
Stark,Denny, Col	.171	41	7	1	4	3	.171	41	7	3	0	1	4	0	19	3	32	128.1	6	15	0	1	1.000	12	1	0	0	.08
Stechschulte,G, Stl	.000	2	0	0	0	0	.400	5	2	0	0	1	3	1	3	0	29	32.0	2	4	0	0	1.000	2	1	0	0	.50
Stein,Blake, KC	-	0	0	0	0	0	.000	9	0	0	0	0	0	0	6	1	27	46.2	2	1	0	0	1.000	8	2	0	0	.25
Stephens,John, Bal	-	0	0	0	0	0	-	0	0	0	0	0	0	0	0	0	12	65.0	2	10	1	1	.923	9	4	0	0	.44
Stephenson,G, Stl	.000	12	0	0	0	2	.066	136	9	2	0	0	5	6	53	24	12	45.0	1	9	0	0	1.000	3	2	0	0	.67
Stewart,Scott, Mon	.000	2	0	0	0	0	.000	2	0	0	0	0	0	0	2	0	67	64.0	1	9	1	0	.909	6	2	1	0	.33
Stone,Ricky, Hou	.000	4	0	0	0	1	.000	4	0	0	0	0	0	0	1	0	78	77.1	2	11	0	0	1.000	8	2	0	0	.25
Stottlemyre,T, Ari	.000	4	0	0	0	1	.207	242	50	7	1	1	11	28	93	26	5	20.1	1	3	0	0	1.000	3	0	0	0	.00
Strange,Pat, NYM	-	0	0	0	0	0	-	0	0	0	0	0	0	0	0	0	5	8.0	0	1	1	0	.500	2	0	0	0	-
Strickland,S, Mon-NYM	-	0	0	0	0	0	.000	5	0	0	0	0	0	4	4	0	69	68.2	4	8	2	1	.857	15	4	1	0	.27
Stull,Everett, Mil	.333	3	1	0	0	0	.083	12	1	0	0	0	0	1	10	1	2	10.0	1	4	0	0	1.000	3	1	0	0	.33
Sturtze,Tanyon, TB	.000	4	0	0	0	1	.077	13	1	0	0	0	0	0	4	2	33	224.0	11	23	2	4	.944	32	15	1	1	.47
Sullivan,Scott, Cin	.333	3	1	0	0	0	.083	48	4	0	0	0	1	0	28	3	71	78.2	3	5	3	0	.727	4	3	0	0	.75
Suppan,Jeff, KC	.000	1	0	0	0	3	.237	38	9	0	0	0	2	1	10	4	33	208.0	23	31	3	0	.947	10	5	0	3	.50
Suzuki,Mac, KC	.500	2	1	0	0	0	.080	25	2	0	0	0	0	1	13	4	7	21.0	2	2	1	0	.800	7	0	0	0	.00
Swindell,Greg, Ari	-	0	0	0	0	0	.188	245	46	10	0	0	13	4	57	36	34	33.0	1	3	0	1	1.000	2	0	0	0	.00
Tallet,Brian, Cle	-	0	0	0	0	0	-	0	0	0	0	0	0	0	0	0	2	12.0	1	0	1	0	.500	1	1	0	0	1.00
Tam,Jeff, Oak	-	0	0	0	0	0	.000	1	0	0	0	0	0	0	0	0	40	40.1	9	8	0	1	1.000	1	0	0	0	.00
Tankersley,D, SD	.308	13	4	1	1	0	.308	13	4	1	0	1	1	0	2	0	17	51.1	3	5	0	0	1.000	10	5	0	1	.50
Tavarez,Julian, Fla	.125	40	5	0	4	5	.115	131	15	0	0	0	8	5	55	20	29	153.2	15	30	4	2	.918	16	5	1	0	.31
Taylor,Aaron, Sea	-	0	0	0	0	0	-	0	0	0	0	0	0	0	0	0	5	5.0	0	0	0	0	-	0	0	0	0	-
Tejera,Michael, Fla	.189	37	7	1	5	2	.189	37	7	0	0	1	5	1	6	2	47	139.2	9	24	1	4	.971	10	6	3	0	.60
Telford,A, Tex	-	0	0	0	0	0	.174	23	4	1	0	0	3	1	4	4	20	23.2	4	3	1	1	.875	0	0	0	0	-
Tessmer,Jay, NYY	-	0	0	0	0	0	-	0	0	0	0	0	0	0	0	0	2	1.1	0	0	0	0	-	0	0	0	0	-
Teut,Nate, Fla	.000	2	0	0	0	0	.000	2	0	0	0	0	0	0	2	0	2	7.1	0	0	0	0	-	1	1	0	0	1.00
Thomson,John, Col-NYM	.212	52	11	0	3	6	.189	196	37	1	1	0	12	10	87	27	30	181.2	20	36	1	0	.982	23	4	0	0	.17
Thurman,Corey, Tor	.000	1	0	0	0	1	.000	1	0	0	0	0	0	0	0	0	43	68.0	3	6	0	0	1.000	9	1	0	0	.11
Thurman,Mike, NYY	-	0	0	0	0	0	.031	131	4	0	0	0		7	93	16	12	33.0	3	3	0		1.000	4	1	0	0	.25
Timlin,Mike, Stl-Phi	.000	6	0	0	0	0	.000	7	0	0	0	0	0	0	4	0	72	96.2	9	15	1	2	.960	2	1	0	0	.50
Tolar,Kevin,	-	0	0	0	0	0	-										0	0.0	0	0	0	0	-	0	0	0	0	-
Tollberg,Brian, SD	.158	19	3	0	0	1	.154	91	14	1	0	0	2	4	33	12	12	61.2	4	6	0	1	1.000	11	5	0	0	.45
Tomko,Brett, SD	.182	66	12	0	6	7	.159	214	34	6	0	0	14	9	80	27	32	204.1	19	26	1	1	.978	13	3	0	1	.23
Torres,Salomon, Pit	.154	13	2	0	0	0	.153	59	9	0	0	0	0	0	24	6	5	30.0	4	2	0	0	1.000	1	1	0	0	1.00
Towers,Josh, Bal	-	0	0	0	0	0	.000	2	0	0	0	0	0	0	0	0	5	27.1	5	7	0	1	1.000	4	1	0	1	.25
Trachsel,Steve, NYM	.109	46	5	0	4	9	.164	457	75	13	1	2	29	19	143	61	30	173.2	12	37	2	3	.961	32	11	1	0	.34
Trombley,Mike, Min	-	0	0	0	0	0	.000	2	0	0	0	0	0	0	2	0	5	4.0	0	0	0	0	-	0	0	0	0	-
Trujillo,J.J., SD	-	0	0	0	0	0	-	0	0	0	0	0	0	0	0	0	4	2.2	0	0	0	0	-	1	0	0	0	.00
Tucker,T.J., Mon	.750	4	3	0	0	0	.800	5	4	0	0	0	0	0	0	0	57	61.1	6	8	5	2	.737	5	2	0	0	.40
Turnbow,D,	-	0	0	0	0	0	-										0	0.0	0	0	0	0	-	0	0	0	0	-
Urbina,Ugueth, Bos	-	0	0	0	0	0	.094	53	5	0	0	0	1	2	32	3	61	60.0	7	1	0	1	1.000	8	2	0	0	.25
Valdes,Ismael, Tex-Sea	.000	3	0	0	1	1	.121	330	40	5	0	1	12	10	107	53	31	190.2	12	32	1	2	.978	8	3	0	0	.38
Van Hekken,A, Det	-	0	0	0	0	0	-	0	0	0	0	0	0	0	0	0	5	30.0	2	4	0	1	1.000	0	0	0	0	-
Van Poppel,T, Tex	.000	1	0	0	0	0	.161	31	5	1	0	0	1	1	12	5	50	72.2	4	4	0	0	1.000	12	1	0	1	.08
Vance,Cory, Col	.000	1	0	0	0	0	.000	1	0	0	0	0	0	0	1	0	2	4.0	1	1	0	0	1.000	2	1	1	0	.50
Vazquez,Javier, Mon	.178	73	13	0	4	10	.221	294	65	8	1	0	16	12	50	53	34	230.1	14	33	1	6	.979	13	3	0	2	.23
Venafro,Mike, Oak	-	0	0	0	0	0	-	0	0	0	0	0	0	0	0	0	47	37.0	1	11	0	1	1.000	4	2	0	0	.50
Veres,Dave, Stl	.333	3	1	0	0	0	.259	27	7	1	0	0	5	1	12	3	71	82.2	3	10	2	3	.867	3	1	0	0	.33
Villafuerte,B, SD	-	0	0	0	0	0	-	0	0	0	0	0	0	0	0	0	31	32.0	2	4	0	0	1.000	0	0	0	0	-
Villone,Ron, Pit	.250	16	4	0	0	1	.119	126	15	2	1	0	5	1	32	11	45	93.0	6	20	2	2	.929	3	1	1	0	.33
Vizcaino,Luis, Mil	.000	2	0	0	0	0	.000	2	0	0	0	0	0	0	2	0	76	81.1	3	7	0	0	1.000	10	3	0	0	.30
Vosberg,Ed, Mon	-	0	0	0	0	0	.000	2	0	0	0	0	0	0	1	0	4	1.0	0	0	0	0	-	0	0	0	0	-
Voyles,Brad, KC	-	0	0	0	0	0	-	0	0	0	0	0	0	0	0	0	22	27.2	3	3	0		1.000	1	1	0	0	1.00
Wagner,Billy, Hou	.000	2	0	0	0	0	.077	13	1	0	0	0	0	0	8	0	70	75.0	5	9	0	0	1.000	6	2	1	1	.33
Wakefield,Tim, Bos	-	0	0	0	0	0	.122	82	10	2	0	1	3	2	29	12	45	163.1	9	9	1	4	.947	28	7	0	0	.25
Walker,Jamie, Det	-	0	0	0	0	0	-	0	0	0	0	0	0	0	0	0	57	43.2	0	3	0	0	1.000	7	0	0	0	.00
Walker,Kevin, SD	-	0	0	0	0	0	.250	4	1	0	0	0	0	0	1	0	11	8.0	1	0	0	0	1.000	0	0	0	0	-
Walker,Pete, NYM-Tor	-	0	0	0	0	0	.000	1	0	0	0	0	0	0	1	1	38	140.1	11	22	2	3	.943	14	6	1	1	.43
Walker,Tyler, NYM	.000	2	0	0	0	0	.000	2	0	0	0	0	0	0	1	0	5	10.2	1	1	0	0	1.000	0	0	0	0	-
Wall,Donne, Ana	-	0	0	0	0	0	.176	68	12	1	0	1		3	22	13	17	21.0	0	6	0	0	1.000	2	0	0	0	.00
Washburn,J, Ana	.200	5	1	0	0	0	.357	14	5	0	0	0	2	2	6	4	32	206.0	6	15	1	1	.955	10	5	2	0	.50
Watson,Mark, Sea	-	0	0	0	0	0	-	0	0	0	0	0	0	0	0	0	3	4.0	0	1	0	0	1.000	1	0	0	0	.00
Wayne,Justin, Fla	.000	7	0	0	0	1	.000	7	0	0	0	0	0	0	3	1	5	23.2	5	3	0	1	1.000	1	1	0	0	1.00
Weathers,David, NYM	.000	1	0	0	0	0	.106	132	14	0	0	2	4	7	82	16	71	77.1	1	14	0	2	1.000	8	2	0	0	.25
Weaver,Jeff, Det-NYY	.286	7	2	0	1	0	.211	19	4	1	0	0	1	0	7	2	32	199.2	13	32	3	3	.938	5	4	0	2	.80

Pitchers Hitting, Fielding and Holding Runners

Pitcher	2002 Hitting						Career Hitting										2002 Fielding and Holding Runners											
	Avg	AB	H	HR	RBI	SH	Avg	AB	H	2B	3B	HR	RBI	BB	SO	SH	G	Inn	PO	A	E	DP	Pct	SBA	CS	PCS	PPO	CS%
Weber,Ben, Ana	-	0	0	0	0	0	-	0	0	0	0	0	0	0	0	0	63	78.0	4	15	0	1	1.000	4	3	0	0	.75
Wells,Bob, Min	-	0	0	0	0	0	-	0	0	0	0	0	0	1	0	0	48	58.0	5	5	0	1	1.000	1	1	0	0	1.00
Wells,David, NYY	.000	4	0	0	0	1	.120	50	6	0	0	0	0	0	12	3	31	206.1	6	24	1	2	.968	18	4	1	0	.22
Wells,Kip, Pit	.190	63	12	1	5	13	.183	71	13	2	0	1	5	0	35	13	33	198.1	12	30	3	1	.933	25	7	0	2	.28
Wendell,Turk,	-	0	0	0	0	0	.077	39	3	0	0	0	0	5	17	1	0	0.0	0	0	0	0	-	0	0	0	0	-
Westbrook,Jake, Cle	-	0	0	0	0	0	.000	1	0	0	0	0	0	0	1	1	11	41.2	4	6	0	0	1.000	2	0	0	0	.00
White,Gabe, Cin	.000	2	0	0	0	1	.111	36	4	0	0	1	3	1	24	10	62	54.1	3	5	0	0	1.000	9	2	2	1	.22
White,Rick, Col-Stl	.000	1	0	0	0	0	.100	40	4	1	0	0	1	0	12	2	61	62.2	2	9	0	2	1.000	2	1	0	1	.50
Wickman,Bob, Cle	-	0	0	0	0	0	.000	2	0	0	0	0	0	0	0	0	36	34.1	1	3	1	0	.800	4	0	0	0	.00
Wiggins,Scott, Tor	-	0	0	0	0	0	-	0	0	0	0	0	0	0	0	0	3	2.2	0	1	0	0	1.000	0	0	0	0	-
Williams,Dave, Pit	.125	16	2	1	3	0	.120	50	6	2	0	1	5	0	31	3	9	43.1	1	12	2	1	.867	3	0	0	0	.00
Williams,Jeff, LA	.500	2	1	0	0	0	.182	11	2	0	0	0	0	1	7	1	10	10.0	1	3	0	0	1.000	0	0	0	0	-
Williams,Mike, Pit	.000	1	0	0	0	0	.157	108	17	2	0	0	7	3	33	24	59	61.1	8	15	1	2	.958	6	0	0	0	.00
Williams,Woody, Stl	.207	29	6	1	3	5	.212	250	53	16	0	2	25	9	78	12	17	103.1	7	19	0	2	1.000	9	2	0	2	.22
Williamson,S, Cin	-	0	0	0	0	0	.043	23	1	0	0	0	0	3	14	7	63	74.0	2	7	1	0	.900	12	6	1	0	.50
Wilson,Kris, KC	-	0	0	0	0	0	.333	3	1	0	0	0	0	0	1	0	12	18.2	1	1	1	0	.667	2	0	0	0	.00
Wilson,Paul, TB	.000	5	0	0	0	1	.073	55	4	0	0	1	4	1	37	5	30	193.2	16	21	2	4	.949	10	2	0	0	.20
Wise,Matt, Ana	-	0	0	0	0	0	-	0	0	0	0	0	0	0	0	0	7	8.1	0	0	0	0	-	0	0	0	0	-
Witasick,Jay, SF	.000	5	0	0	0	0	.081	37	3	0	0	0	3	1	21	2	44	68.1	2	5	0	0	1.000	6	4	0	0	.67
Wohlers,Mark, Cle	-	0	0	0	0	0	.083	12	1	0	0	0	0	0	11	1	64	71.1	7	7	2	0	.875	17	2	0	0	.12
Wolf,Randy, Phi	.136	59	8	1	4	12	.178	191	34	7	0	1	10	12	64	34	31	210.2	9	23	2	2	.941	8	4	1	1	.50
Wood,Kerry, ChC	.167	72	12	1	5	6	.178	214	38	1	0	4	19	7	69	31	33	213.2	14	20	0	3	1.000	19	6	0	1	.32
Woodard,Steve, Tex	-	0	0	0	0	0	.119	126	15	3	0	0	6	7	34	14	14	17.2	0	3	0	0	1.000	2	0	0	0	.00
Worrell,Tim, SF	.000	3	0	0	0	0	.105	76	8	1	0	0	4	4	39	10	80	72.0	2	10	0	0	1.000	8	2	0	0	.25
Wright,Dan, CWS	.000	4	0	0	0	0	.000	4	0	0	0	0	0	0	2	0	33	196.1	10	28	0	1	1.000	23	4	0	1	.17
Wright,Jamey, Mil-Stl	.132	38	5	0	0	7	.137	314	43	11	1	1	13	11	130	34	23	129.1	12	23	1	3	.972	13	5	0	1	.38
Wright,Jaret, Cle	-	0	0	0	0	0	.286	14	4	0	0	0	1	0	6	3	8	18.1	0	2	0	0	1.000	8	0	0	0	.00
Wunsch,Kelly, CWS	-	0	0	0	0	0	-	0	0	0	0	0	0	0	0	0	50	31.2	1	3	0	1	1.000	2	0	0	0	.00
Yan,Esteban, TB	-	0	0	0	0	0	1.000	1	1	0	0	1	1	0	0	1	55	69.0	3	7	0	1	1.000	3	2	0	0	.67
Yoshii,Masato, Mon	.057	35	2	0	0	5	.123	204	25	3	0	1	13	9	76	33	31	131.1	9	19	0	3	1.000	9	4	0	0	.44
Zambrano,C, ChC	.033	30	1	0	0	2	.031	32	1	1	0	0	0	0	15	2	32	108.1	8	26	0	4	1.000	12	5	0	0	.42
Zambrano,V, TB	.000	1	0	0	0	0	.000	1	0	0	0	0	0	0	1	0	42	114.0	9	9	2	1	.900	13	5	0	0	.38
Zerbe,Chad, SF	.167	6	1	0	1	1	.200	15	3	0	0	0	2	0	3	3	50	56.1	4	7	0	0	1.000	2	0	0	0	.00
Zito,Barry, Oak	.000	4	0	0	0	2	.000	9	0	0	0	0	0	0	7	2	35	229.1	11	31	3	3	.933	19	9	5	0	.47

Hitters Pitching

Player	2002 Pitching											Career Pitching										
	G	W	L	Sv	IP	H	R	ER	BB	SO	ERA	G	W	L	Sv	IP	H	R	ER	BB	SO	ERA
Benjamin,Mike, Pit	0	0	0	0	0.0	0	0	0	0	0	–	1	0	0	0	1.0	0	0	0	0	0	0.00
Donnels,Chris, Ari	0	0	0	0	0.0	0	0	0	0	0	–	1	0	0	0	0.1	0	0	0	0	0	0.00
Finley,Steve, Ari	0	0	0	0	0.0	0	0	0	0	0	–	1	0	0	0	1.0	0	0	0	1	0	0.00
Franco,Matt, Atl	0	0	0	0	0.0	0	0	0	0	0	–	2	0	0	0	1.1	3	2	2	3	2	13.50
Grace,Mark, Ari	1	0	0	0	1.0	1	1	1	0	0	9.00	1	0	0	0	1.0	1	1	1	0	0	9.00
Halter,Shane, Det	0	0	0	0	0.0	0	0	0	0	0	–	2	0	0	0	1.0	1	0	0	1	0	0.00
Harris,Lenny, Mil	0	0	0	0	0.0	0	0	0	0	0	–	1	0	0	0	1.0	0	0	0	0	1	0.00
Jimenez,D, SD-CWS	1	0	0	0	1.1	0	0	0	0	0	0.00	1	0	0	0	1.1	0	0	0	0	0	0.00
Laker,Tim,	0	0	0	0	0.0	0	0	0	0	0	–	1	0	0	0	1.0	1	0	0	1	1	0.00
Loretta,Mark, Mil-Hou	0	0	0	0	0.0	0	0	0	0	0	–	1	0	0	0	1.0	1	0	0	1	2	0.00
Mabry,John, Phi-Oak	0	0	0	0	0.0	0	0	0	0	0	–	2	0	0	0	1.0	6	7	7	4	0	63.00
Mayne,Brent, KC	0	0	0	0	0.0	0	0	0	0	0	–	1	1	0	0	1.0	1	0	0	1	0	0.00
Menechino,F, Oak	0	0	0	0	0.0	0	0	0	0	0	–	1	0	0	0	1.0	6	4	4	0	0	36.00
Osik,Keith, Pit	0	0	0	0	0.0	0	0	0	0	0	–	2	0	0	0	2.0	7	9	9	2	2	40.50
Perez,Tomas, Phi	1	0	0	0	0.1	0	0	0	0	0	0.00	1	0	0	0	0.1	0	0	0	0	0	0.00
Relaford,Desi, Sea	0	0	0	0	0.0	0	0	0	0	0	–	1	0	0	0	1.0	0	0	0	0	1	0.00
Zeile,Todd, Col	1	0	0	0	1.0	1	0	0	0	1	0.00	1	0	0	0	1.0	1	0	0	0	1	0.00

2002 Park Data

Sammy Sosa took back the National League Home Run title from Barry Bonds in 2002. However, in the context of their home parks, Bonds' 46 long balls may be more impressive than Sosa's 49.

Check out the relevant Park Indices: Sosa played his home games at Wrigley Field, where the Home Run Index for right-handed batters was 148. That means there were 48% more home runs by right-handed hitters in Wrigley than in other National League ballparks. Bonds, on the other hand, played his home games at Pacific Bell Park, where the Home Run Index for lefties was a mere 55 - meaning lefthanders are barely half as likely to hit the ball out in San Francisco as compared with other National League parks.

There are certainly other factors to consider in any situation to which you can apply Park Indices, but if all else were equal, and we recast Sosa's and Bonds' home games into neutral parks (i.e. Park Index of 100), Sosa's 24 home runs become 16, while Bonds' 19 become 35, giving Sosa a new total of 41 and Bonds a new total of 62!

Park Indices are calculated in a way that neutralizes the effect of a team's makeup and isolates the effects of the park. This isolation is accomplished by comparing what both the team and its opponents accomplished at home, and comparing that to what the same team and its opponents accomplished on the road. To calculate the Park Index for Home Runs in Bank One Ballpark, take the total Home Runs of the Diamondbacks and their opponents at Bank One (79+73=152), and compare it to the total Home Runs of the Diamondbacks and their opponents in other games (70+71=141). We divide each of these totals by the At Bats in the equivalent situations (4962 and 4846) so that if there are more at bats in either situation, the index is not skewed. The result, (152/4962) / (141/4846) = 1.05, is multiplied by 100 to yield the familiar form, 105. In 2002, it was 5% easier to hit home runs in Bank One Ballpark than in other National League parks.

The Park Indices for Doubles, Triples, Walks, Strikeouts and Home Runs by Lefties and Righties are determined like Home Runs, above - relative to At Bats. Indices of At Bats, Runs, Hits, Errors, and Infield Fielding Errors (E-Infield) are calculated relative to Games. The three Batting Average Indices are calculated as-is, as these are already relative to At Bats.

Additionally, interleague games are not included in the underlying Park Index data, both because the interleague schedules are significantly imbalanced, and because the Designated Hitter rule, only used in the American League parks, would artificially skew AL parks towards appearing to be Hitters' Parks and all NL parks towards appearing to be Pitchers' Parks.

Anaheim Angels
Edison International Field
Surface: Grass

	Home Games			Away Games			
	Angels	Opp	Total	Angels	Opp	Total	Index
G	72	72	144	72	72	144	
Avg	.277	.242	.259	.286	.244	.266	97
AB	2467	2489	4956	2603	2353	4956	100
R	358	284	642	399	284	683	94
H	683	603	1286	745	574	1319	97
2B	142	114	256	156	98	254	101
3B	17	4	21	9	12	21	100
HR	62	67	129	73	81	154	84
BB	198	234	432	210	229	439	98
SO	352	459	811	364	434	798	102
E	40	46	86	43	62	105	82
E-Infield	18	18	36	23	21	44	82
LHB-Avg	.280	.240	.261	.294	.234	.269	97
LHB-HR	28	30	58	35	34	69	83
RHB-Avg	.274	.244	.258	.278	.251	.264	98
RHB-HR	34	37	71	38	47	85	85

Baltimore Orioles
Oriole Park at Camden Yards
Surface: Grass

	Home Games			Away Games			
	Orioles	Opp	Total	Orioles	Opp	Total	Index
G	72	72	144	72	72	144	
Avg	.246	.260	.253	.247	.280	.263	96
AB	2406	2543	4949	2483	2461	4944	100
R	292	331	623	300	374	674	92
H	592	661	1253	614	688	1302	96
2B	111	109	220	160	129	289	76
3B	10	5	15	12	19	31	48
HR	81	101	182	66	91	157	116
BB	207	241	448	195	242	437	102
SO	425	426	851	432	448	880	97
E	42	54	96	36	38	74	130
E-Infield	15	20	35	12	16	28	125
LHB-Avg	.253	.248	.250	.260	.281	.272	92
LHB-HR	30	47	77	20	49	69	109
RHB-Avg	.243	.272	.256	.242	.279	.257	99
RHB-HR	51	54	105	46	42	88	121

Arizona Diamondbacks
Bank One Ballpark
Surface: Grass

	Home Games			Away Games			
	D'Backs	Opp	Total	D'Backs	Opp	Total	Index
G	72	72	144	72	72	144	
Avg	.284	.248	.266	.248	.247	.248	107
AB	2413	2549	4962	2485	2361	4846	102
R	415	313	728	319	284	603	121
H	686	632	1318	617	584	1201	110
2B	131	127	258	116	101	217	116
3B	25	22	47	14	8	22	209
HR	79	73	152	70	71	141	105
BB	331	195	526	255	179	434	118
SO	432	623	1055	486	541	1027	100
E	43	45	88	37	59	96	92
E-Infield	25	21	46	14	29	43	107
LHB-Avg	.286	.263	.277	.260	.260	.260	106
LHB-HR	45	25	70	41	32	73	98
RHB-Avg	.282	.240	.256	.233	.239	.237	108
RHB-HR	34	48	82	29	39	68	114

Boston Red Sox
Fenway Park
Surface: Grass

	Home Games			Away Games			
	Red Sox	Opp	Total	Red Sox	Opp	Total	Index
G	72	72	144	72	72	144	
Avg	.280	.251	.265	.287	.236	.263	101
AB	2415	2478	4893	2634	2379	5013	98
R	365	312	677	431	283	714	95
H	676	621	1297	755	562	1317	98
2B	159	145	304	163	97	260	120
3B	14	6	20	14	16	30	68
HR	71	58	129	91	76	167	79
BB	248	173	421	249	202	451	96
SO	400	544	944	420	488	908	107
E	53	54	107	38	47	85	126
E-Infield	25	17	42	16	19	35	120
LHB-Avg	.276	.230	.252	.272	.244	.259	97
LHB-HR	29	21	50	44	42	86	63
RHB-Avg	.283	.268	.276	.300	.229	.266	104
RHB-HR	42	37	79	47	34	81	95

Atlanta Braves
Turner Field
Surface: Grass

	Home Games			Away Games			
	Braves	Opp	Total	Braves	Opp	Total	Index
G	72	72	144	71	71	142	
Avg	.261	.243	.252	.252	.244	.248	102
AB	2361	2480	4841	2496	2350	4846	99
R	321	257	578	286	258	544	105
H	617	603	1220	628	573	1201	100
2B	118	119	237	122	95	217	109
3B	13	12	25	9	16	25	100
HR	74	58	132	68	55	123	107
BB	243	236	479	250	268	518	93
SO	433	450	883	485	469	954	93
E	52	52	104	50	48	98	105
E-Infield	26	31	57	23	11	34	165
LHB-Avg	.274	.250	.262	.259	.236	.248	106
LHB-HR	24	16	40	12	17	29	138
RHB-Avg	.254	.240	.247	.248	.248	.248	100
RHB-HR	50	42	92	56	38	94	98

Chicago Cubs
Wrigley Field
Surface: Grass

	Home Games			Away Games			
	Cubs	Opp	Total	Cubs	Opp	Total	Index
G	75	75	150	75	75	150	
Avg	.236	.243	.240	.253	.266	.259	92
AB	2467	2568	5035	2618	2473	5091	99
R	305	342	647	336	358	694	93
H	583	623	1206	662	659	1321	91
2B	107	125	232	129	130	259	91
3B	13	10	23	16	19	35	66
HR	88	93	181	90	58	148	124
BB	286	265	551	255	289	544	102
SO	580	680	1260	591	549	1140	112
E	58	42	100	49	51	100	100
E-Infield	22	22	44	25	28	53	83
LHB-Avg	.235	.247	.241	.251	.277	.263	91
LHB-HR	36	35	71	43	30	73	99
RHB-Avg	.238	.239	.238	.255	.258	.256	93
RHB-HR	52	58	110	47	28	75	148

Chicago White Sox
Comiskey Park
Surface: Grass

	Home Games			Away Games			
	White Sox	Opp	Total	White Sox	Opp	Total	Index
G	72	72	144	72	72	144	
Avg	.284	.255	.269	.262	.264	.263	102
AB	2392	2447	4839	2519	2393	4912	99
R	427	331	758	342	368	710	107
H	679	623	1302	661	631	1292	101
2B	120	127	247	140	124	264	95
3B	10	7	17	15	9	24	72
HR	120	79	199	74	85	159	127
BB	237	241	478	233	229	462	105
SO	387	415	802	435	416	851	96
E	32	49	81	53	49	102	79
E-Infield	17	21	38	22	14	36	106
LHB-Avg	.293	.266	.277	.232	.286	.265	105
LHB-HR	30	46	76	22	43	65	123
RHB-Avg	.279	.244	.264	.276	.241	.262	101
RHB-HR	90	33	123	52	42	94	130

Colorado Rockies
Coors Field
Surface: Grass

	Home Games			Away Games			
	Rockies	Opp	Total	Rockies	Opp	Total	Index
G	72	72	144	72	72	144	
Avg	.310	.279	.294	.236	.270	.253	116
AB	2442	2543	4985	2447	2405	4852	103
R	435	419	854	259	361	620	138
H	756	709	1465	577	649	1226	119
2B	141	142	283	108	121	229	120
3B	26	17	43	12	16	28	149
HR	83	120	203	51	80	131	151
BB	232	243	475	204	267	471	98
SO	403	424	827	541	381	922	87
E	49	51	100	42	39	81	123
E-Infield	24	20	44	21	16	37	119
LHB-Avg	.332	.286	.309	.265	.285	.274	113
LHB-HR	41	48	89	27	30	57	147
RHB-Avg	.294	.274	.284	.215	.262	.239	119
RHB-HR	42	72	114	24	50	74	153

Cincinnati Reds
Cinergy Field
Surface: Grass

	Home Games			Away Games			
	Reds	Opp	Total	Reds	Opp	Total	Index
G	75	75	150	75	75	150	
Avg	.267	.279	.273	.244	.259	.252	109
AB	2487	2681	5168	2586	2505	5091	102
R	372	383	755	302	321	623	121
H	664	747	1411	632	649	1281	110
2B	165	148	313	114	127	241	128
3B	3	11	14	18	13	31	44
HR	83	103	186	79	57	136	135
BB	316	241	557	236	271	507	108
SO	522	486	1008	588	430	1018	98
E	49	43	92	64	50	114	81
E-Infield	20	14	34	28	18	46	74
LHB-Avg	.277	.283	.280	.263	.266	.264	106
LHB-HR	36	44	80	34	31	65	125
RHB-Avg	.260	.275	.268	.230	.254	.242	111
RHB-HR	47	59	106	45	26	71	144

Detroit Tigers
Comerica Park
Surface: Grass

	Home Games			Away Games			
	Tigers	Opp	Total	Tigers	Opp	Total	Index
G	71	71	142	72	72	144	
Avg	.247	.280	.264	.252	.293	.272	97
AB	2347	2550	4897	2465	2436	4901	101
R	249	356	605	279	436	715	86
H	579	713	1292	621	713	1334	98
2B	92	144	236	153	162	315	75
3B	26	31	57	6	21	27	211
HR	57	55	112	56	97	153	73
BB	162	192	354	167	223	390	91
SO	396	363	759	503	352	855	89
E	63	33	96	71	35	106	92
E-Infield	24	13	37	32	17	49	77
LHB-Avg	.266	.281	.273	.268	.298	.282	97
LHB-HR	43	34	77	30	43	73	104
RHB-Avg	.225	.279	.256	.236	.288	.263	97
RHB-HR	14	21	35	26	54	80	44

Cleveland Indians
Jacobs Field
Surface: Grass

	Home Games			Away Games			
	Indians	Opp	Total	Indians	Opp	Total	Index
G	72	72	144	72	72	144	
Avg	.248	.274	.261	.257	.276	.266	98
AB	2372	2533	4905	2490	2397	4887	100
R	337	388	725	341	375	716	101
H	588	694	1282	639	661	1300	99
2B	120	151	271	114	135	249	108
3B	8	13	21	14	25	39	54
HR	85	71	156	93	60	153	102
BB	209	287	496	264	256	520	95
SO	435	533	968	453	398	851	113
E	43	65	108	55	32	87	124
E-Infield	20	34	54	21	17	38	142
LHB-Avg	.251	.288	.268	.252	.278	.264	102
LHB-HR	58	35	93	63	25	88	103
RHB-Avg	.245	.263	.255	.261	.274	.268	95
RHB-HR	27	36	63	30	35	65	99

Florida Marlins
Pro Player Stadium
Surface: Grass

	Home Games			Away Games			
	Marlins	Opp	Total	Marlins	Opp	Total	Index
G	72	72	144	72	72	144	
Avg	.270	.255	.262	.252	.273	.262	100
AB	2398	2522	4920	2488	2402	4890	101
R	342	322	664	278	373	651	102
H	647	644	1291	627	656	1283	101
2B	130	133	263	117	130	247	106
3B	22	20	42	8	16	24	174
HR	63	58	121	67	84	151	80
BB	294	291	585	226	277	503	116
SO	497	556	1053	517	437	954	110
E	43	47	90	49	56	105	86
E-Infield	15	18	33	23	16	39	85
LHB-Avg	.259	.254	.256	.255	.301	.284	90
LHB-HR	11	20	31	12	36	48	61
RHB-Avg	.274	.256	.266	.251	.253	.252	105
RHB-HR	52	38	90	55	48	103	89

Houston Astros
Minute Maid Park
Surface: Grass

	Home Games			Away Games			
	Astros	Opp	Total	Astros	Opp	Total	Index
G	75	75	150	75	75	150	
Avg	.284	.256	.270	.238	.259	.248	109
AB	2524	2596	5120	2558	2458	5016	102
R	380	312	692	318	314	632	109
H	717	665	1382	608	637	1245	111
2B	142	143	285	132	143	275	102
3B	18	10	28	13	22	35	78
HR	83	60	143	73	72	145	97
BB	289	218	507	251	275	526	94
SO	488	575	1063	549	539	1088	96
E	41	49	90	38	43	81	111
E-Infield	16	19	35	16	23	39	90
LHB-Avg	.300	.273	.286	.262	.269	.266	107
LHB-HR	42	25	67	26	32	58	114
RHB-Avg	.275	.246	.260	.225	.252	.237	110
RHB-HR	41	35	76	47	40	87	85

Milwaukee Brewers
Miller Park
Surface: Grass

	Home Games			Away Games			
	Brewers	Opp	Total	Brewers	Opp	Total	Index
G	75	75	150	75	75	150	
Avg	.249	.255	.252	.252	.277	.264	96
AB	2417	2579	4996	2580	2473	5053	99
R	277	354	631	305	388	693	91
H	603	658	1261	649	684	1333	95
2B	122	141	263	126	127	253	105
3B	12	14	26	14	13	27	97
HR	58	95	153	71	88	159	97
BB	242	284	526	238	340	578	92
SO	485	519	1004	550	431	981	104
E	46	40	86	53	44	97	89
E-Infield	21	18	39	18	15	33	118
LHB-Avg	.249	.267	.259	.247	.284	.265	98
LHB-HR	20	47	67	21	41	62	104
RHB-Avg	.250	.247	.248	.254	.272	.263	94
RHB-HR	38	48	86	50	47	97	92

Kansas City Royals
Ewing M. Kauffman Stadium
Surface: Grass

	Home Games			Away Games			
	Royals	Opp	Total	Royals	Opp	Total	Index
G	72	72	144	72	72	144	
Avg	.272	.291	.282	.236	.266	.251	112
AB	2466	2637	5103	2444	2397	4841	105
R	372	433	805	276	347	623	129
H	671	767	1438	577	638	1215	118
2B	132	159	291	114	130	244	113
3B	23	14	37	16	16	32	110
HR	75	109	184	47	84	131	133
BB	236	243	479	229	244	473	96
SO	339	399	738	475	437	912	77
E	52	55	107	62	42	104	103
E-Infield	13	24	37	26	22	48	77
LHB-Avg	.273	.296	.285	.229	.268	.248	115
LHB-HR	36	49	85	25	36	61	132
RHB-Avg	.271	.287	.279	.243	.265	.254	110
RHB-HR	39	60	99	22	48	70	135

Minnesota Twins
Hubert H. Humphrey Metrodome
Surface: AstroTurf

	Home Games			Away Games			
	Twins	Opp	Total	Twins	Opp	Total	Index
G	72	72	144	71	71	142	
Avg	.279	.251	.265	.271	.274	.272	97
AB	2432	2521	4953	2523	2435	4958	99
R	357	287	644	336	348	684	93
H	678	634	1312	684	666	1350	96
2B	174	132	306	137	122	259	118
3B	22	17	39	9	13	22	177
HR	63	66	129	89	96	185	70
BB	217	195	412	204	197	401	103
SO	452	472	924	505	417	922	100
E	30	51	81	39	53	92	87
E-Infield	14	16	30	20	19	39	76
LHB-Avg	.287	.254	.272	.276	.294	.284	96
LHB-HR	30	35	65	54	49	103	65
RHB-Avg	.268	.250	.258	.264	.257	.260	99
RHB-HR	33	31	64	35	47	82	76

Los Angeles Dodgers
Dodger Stadium
Surface: Grass

	Home Games			Away Games			
	Dodgers	Opp	Total	Dodgers	Opp	Total	Index
G	72	72	144	72	72	144	
Avg	.251	.233	.242	.279	.249	.265	91
AB	2372	2463	4835	2597	2365	4962	97
R	270	265	535	363	300	663	81
H	596	574	1170	725	588	1313	89
2B	103	98	201	154	127	281	73
3B	11	3	14	15	15	30	48
HR	60	75	135	77	66	143	97
BB	202	251	453	187	264	451	103
SO	400	530	930	448	488	936	102
E	45	57	102	32	56	88	116
E-Infield	16	30	46	15	19	34	135
LHB-Avg	.237	.222	.229	.268	.252	.260	88
LHB-HR	16	21	37	28	23	51	78
RHB-Avg	.259	.239	.249	.286	.246	.267	93
RHB-HR	44	54	98	49	43	92	106

Montreal Expos
Olympic Stadium
Surface: AstroTurf

	Home Games			Away Games			
	Expos	Opp	Total	Expos	Opp	Total	Index
G	72	72	144	72	72	144	
Avg	.271	.260	.265	.252	.273	.262	101
AB	2396	2520	4916	2492	2434	4926	100
R	341	309	650	315	341	656	99
H	649	656	1305	627	664	1291	101
2B	145	150	295	128	123	251	118
3B	15	15	30	16	16	32	94
HR	76	71	147	69	79	148	100
BB	266	201	467	253	256	509	92
SO	458	492	950	545	467	1012	94
E	64	60	124	61	54	115	108
E-Infield	23	22	45	28	23	51	88
LHB-Avg	.289	.267	.277	.245	.270	.257	108
LHB-HR	34	31	65	25	34	59	108
RHB-Avg	.259	.256	.257	.256	.275	.266	97
RHB-HR	42	40	82	44	45	89	93

New York Mets
Shea Stadium
Surface: Grass

	Home Games			Away Games			Index
	Mets	Opp	Total	Mets	Opp	Total	
G	72	72	144	71	71	142	
Avg	.244	.254	.249	.267	.260	.264	94
AB	2392	2555	4947	2496	2352	4848	101
R	290	311	601	326	313	639	93
H	583	648	1231	666	612	1278	95
2B	96	104	200	119	122	241	81
3B	11	13	24	8	17	25	94
HR	72	74	146	67	68	135	106
BB	222	230	452	222	244	466	95
SO	459	515	974	476	460	936	102
E	68	46	114	63	52	115	98
E-Infield	31	24	55	23	23	46	118
LHB-Avg	.254	.261	.257	.257	.246	.252	102
LHB-HR	39	30	69	23	20	43	162
RHB-Avg	.236	.249	.243	.274	.269	.272	90
RHB-HR	33	44	77	44	48	92	80

Philadelphia Phillies
Veterans Stadium
Surface: NexTurf

	Home Games			Away Games			Index
	Phillies	Opp	Total	Phillies	Opp	Total	
G	71	71	142	72	72	144	
Avg	.251	.233	.242	.270	.274	.272	89
AB	2338	2402	4740	2571	2452	5023	96
R	295	287	582	347	365	712	83
H	588	560	1148	695	673	1368	85
2B	134	110	244	160	147	307	84
3B	20	13	33	16	19	35	100
HR	73	67	140	77	73	150	99
BB	274	242	516	291	264	555	99
SO	487	524	1011	488	425	913	117
E	33	39	72	45	52	97	75
E-Infield	9	11	20	23	20	43	47
LHB-Avg	.240	.238	.239	.283	.289	.285	84
LHB-HR	32	25	57	33	31	64	94
RHB-Avg	.262	.230	.245	.259	.266	.262	93
RHB-HR	41	42	83	44	42	86	102

New York Yankees
Yankee Stadium
Surface: Grass

	Home Games			Away Games			Index
	Yankees	Opp	Total	Yankees	Opp	Total	
G	71	71	142	72	72	144	
Avg	.274	.245	.259	.276	.262	.269	96
AB	2407	2506	4913	2579	2488	5067	98
R	386	298	684	411	305	716	97
H	660	614	1274	711	653	1364	95
2B	125	133	258	149	141	290	92
3B	6	9	15	4	13	17	91
HR	95	66	161	104	57	161	103
BB	281	154	435	288	190	478	94
SO	494	550	1044	537	473	1010	107
E	50	54	104	60	38	98	108
E-Infield	17	23	40	24	16	40	101
LHB-Avg	.275	.233	.254	.276	.239	.259	98
LHB-HR	52	32	84	57	22	79	106
RHB-Avg	.274	.254	.263	.275	.277	.276	95
RHB-HR	43	34	77	47	35	82	99

Pittsburgh Pirates
PNC Park
Surface: Grass

	Home Games			Away Games			Index
	Pirates	Opp	Total	Pirates	Opp	Total	
G	74	74	148	75	75	150	
Avg	.250	.272	.262	.236	.263	.249	105
AB	2389	2576	4965	2523	2430	4953	102
R	317	362	679	286	321	607	113
H	598	701	1299	595	639	1234	107
2B	122	145	267	121	126	247	108
3B	6	16	22	14	12	26	84
HR	57	81	138	78	71	149	92
BB	269	254	523	243	278	521	100
SO	451	445	896	593	423	1016	88
E	59	50	109	51	40	91	121
E-Infield	28	24	52	23	15	38	139
LHB-Avg	.265	.278	.273	.253	.269	.262	104
LHB-HR	25	29	54	31	34	65	82
RHB-Avg	.244	.268	.256	.229	.259	.242	106
RHB-HR	32	52	84	47	37	84	100

Oakland Athletics
Network Associates Coliseum
Surface: Grass

	Home Games			Away Games			Index
	Athletics	Opp	Total	Athletics	Opp	Total	
G	72	72	144	72	72	144	
Avg	.263	.248	.255	.254	.260	.257	99
AB	2401	2476	4877	2547	2442	4989	98
R	363	302	665	334	300	634	105
H	631	613	1244	647	636	1283	97
2B	123	123	246	117	123	240	105
3B	15	9	24	11	17	28	88
HR	104	61	165	79	62	141	120
BB	287	196	483	252	232	484	102
SO	434	483	917	447	427	874	107
E	43	49	92	45	39	84	110
E-Infield	15	28	43	17	13	30	143
LHB-Avg	.278	.253	.267	.243	.256	.248	107
LHB-HR	59	25	84	44	25	69	125
RHB-Avg	.247	.244	.245	.267	.263	.265	93
RHB-HR	45	36	81	35	37	72	115

San Diego Padres
Qualcomm Stadium
Surface: Grass

	Home Games			Away Games			Index
	Padres	Opp	Total	Padres	Opp	Total	
G	72	72	144	72	72	144	
Avg	.270	.261	.265	.239	.290	.264	101
AB	2440	2531	4971	2479	2412	4891	102
R	307	312	619	277	419	696	89
H	658	661	1319	592	699	1291	102
2B	102	120	222	113	159	272	80
3B	16	17	33	10	19	29	112
HR	57	73	130	64	91	155	83
BB	249	227	476	227	283	510	92
SO	427	524	951	526	466	992	94
E	53	52	105	58	48	106	99
E-Infield	25	19	44	22	29	51	86
LHB-Avg	.295	.275	.285	.240	.310	.272	105
LHB-HR	31	28	59	34	45	79	73
RHB-Avg	.245	.250	.248	.237	.275	.257	96
RHB-HR	26	45	71	30	46	76	92

San Francisco Giants
Pacific Bell Park
Surface: Grass

	Home Games			Away Games			Index
	Giants	Opp	Total	Giants	Opp	Total	
G	72	72	144	72	72	144	
Avg	.258	.245	.251	.275	.255	.265	95
AB	2329	2443	4772	2545	2346	4891	98
R	320	249	569	388	300	688	83
H	601	599	1200	700	598	1298	92
2B	119	105	224	149	108	257	89
3B	22	17	39	11	10	21	190
HR	62	34	96	116	67	183	54
BB	277	216	493	284	253	537	94
SO	399	440	839	460	411	871	99
E	44	56	100	41	45	86	116
E-Infield	22	22	44	21	21	42	105
LHB-Avg	.261	.249	.254	.299	.264	.278	91
LHB-HR	23	13	36	39	27	66	55
RHB-Avg	.257	.242	.250	.266	.248	.258	97
RHB-HR	39	21	60	77	40	117	53

Tampa Bay Devil Rays
Tropicana Field
Surface: NexTurf

	Home Games			Away Games			Index
	Devil Rays	Opp	Total	Devil Rays	Opp	Total	
G	72	72	144	71	71	142	
Avg	.264	.268	.266	.239	.293	.266	100
AB	2492	2585	5077	2445	2383	4828	104
R	308	406	714	287	421	708	99
H	659	694	1353	585	698	1283	104
2B	125	148	273	126	150	276	94
3B	16	14	30	13	8	21	136
HR	54	88	142	63	105	168	80
BB	206	288	494	201	270	471	100
SO	488	455	943	503	364	867	103
E	49	39	88	60	45	105	83
E-Infield	20	16	36	19	17	36	99
LHB-Avg	.275	.291	.282	.252	.309	.278	102
LHB-HR	35	50	85	32	50	82	98
RHB-Avg	.255	.251	.253	.227	.281	.256	99
RHB-HR	19	38	57	31	55	86	63

Seattle Mariners
Safeco Field
Surface: Grass

	Home Games			Away Games			Index
	Mariners	Opp	Total	Mariners	Opp	Total	
G	72	72	144	72	72	144	
Avg	.265	.255	.260	.288	.265	.277	94
AB	2391	2511	4902	2554	2435	4989	98
R	327	306	633	403	348	751	84
H	633	641	1274	736	646	1382	92
2B	105	126	231	145	135	280	84
3B	17	3	20	10	11	21	97
HR	55	73	128	78	91	169	77
BB	308	217	525	257	190	447	120
SO	442	506	948	446	434	880	110
E	37	56	93	40	52	92	101
E-Infield	17	25	42	15	21	36	117
LHB-Avg	.274	.265	.269	.308	.276	.292	92
LHB-HR	21	41	62	40	37	77	81
RHB-Avg	.257	.246	.251	.271	.255	.263	95
RHB-HR	34	32	66	38	54	92	74

Texas Rangers
The Ballpark in Arlington
Surface: Grass

	Home Games			Away Games			Index
	Rangers	Opp	Total	Rangers	Opp	Total	
G	72	72	144	72	72	144	
Avg	.282	.278	.280	.253	.265	.259	108
AB	2440	2579	5019	2549	2417	4966	101
R	421	425	846	322	364	686	123
H	689	718	1407	645	640	1285	109
2B	141	167	308	132	145	277	110
3B	13	20	33	12	19	31	105
HR	123	99	222	83	72	155	142
BB	258	286	544	231	308	539	100
SO	429	486	915	482	431	913	99
E	39	44	83	48	47	95	87
E-Infield	13	16	29	20	21	41	71
LHB-Avg	.285	.268	.275	.254	.268	.262	105
LHB-HR	43	43	86	28	37	65	126
RHB-Avg	.281	.287	.284	.252	.262	.257	111
RHB-HR	80	56	136	55	35	90	153

St Louis Cardinals
Busch Stadium
Surface: Grass

	Home Games			Away Games			Index
	Cardinals	Opp	Total	Cardinals	Opp	Total	
G	75	75	150	75	75	150	
Avg	.265	.242	.253	.268	.263	.266	95
AB	2495	2568	5063	2615	2442	5057	100
R	362	273	635	365	333	698	91
H	661	622	1283	702	643	1345	95
2B	126	134	260	136	117	253	103
3B	8	1	9	17	10	27	33
HR	80	63	143	81	68	149	96
BB	276	259	535	231	260	491	109
SO	439	500	939	440	443	883	106
E	42	53	95	49	52	101	94
E-Infield	14	25	39	17	31	48	81
LHB-Avg	.274	.244	.259	.267	.255	.261	99
LHB-HR	37	22	59	30	29	59	101
RHB-Avg	.258	.241	.249	.270	.268	.269	93
RHB-HR	43	41	84	51	39	90	93

Toronto Blue Jays
SkyDome
Surface: NexTurf

	Home Games			Away Games			Index
	Blue Jays	Opp	Total	Blue Jays	Opp	Total	
G	72	72	144	72	72	144	
Avg	.270	.267	.269	.256	.274	.265	102
AB	2432	2533	4965	2553	2444	4997	99
R	370	374	744	372	379	751	99
H	657	677	1334	653	669	1322	101
2B	151	154	305	126	129	255	120
3B	19	9	28	16	17	33	85
HR	92	78	170	75	80	155	110
BB	226	263	489	230	268	498	99
SO	483	455	938	544	437	981	96
E	47	51	98	50	41	91	108
E-Infield	21	22	43	26	16	42	102
LHB-Avg	.261	.279	.271	.260	.287	.276	98
LHB-HR	42	43	85	37	44	81	110
RHB-Avg	.275	.256	.267	.254	.259	.256	104
RHB-HR	50	35	85	38	36	74	112

2002 American League Ballpark Index Rankings - Runs

Team	TOTALS											LHB		RHB	
	Avg	AB	R	H	2B	3B	HR	BB	SO	E	E-Inf	Avg	HR	Avg	HR
Kansas City - Ewing M. Kauffman Stadium	112	105	129	118	113	110	133	96	77	103	77	115	132	110	135
Texas - The Ballpark in Arlington	108	101	123	109	110	105	142	100	99	87	71	105	126	111	153
Chicago - Comiskey Park	102	99	107	101	95	72	127	105	96	79	106	105	123	101	130
Oakland - Network Associates Coliseum	99	98	105	97	105	88	120	102	107	110	143	107	125	93	115
Cleveland - Jacobs Field	98	100	101	99	108	54	102	95	113	124	142	102	103	95	99
Tampa Bay - Tropicana Field	100	104	99	104	94	136	80	100	103	83	99	102	98	99	63
Toronto - SkyDome	102	99	99	101	120	85	110	99	96	108	102	98	110	104	112
New York - Yankee Stadium	96	98	97	95	92	91	103	94	107	108	101	98	106	95	99
Boston - Fenway Park	101	98	95	98	120	68	79	96	107	126	120	97	63	104	95
Anaheim - Edison International Field	97	100	94	97	101	100	84	98	102	82	82	97	83	98	85
Minnesota - Hubert H. Humphrey Metrodome	97	99	93	96	118	177	70	103	100	87	76	96	65	99	76
Baltimore - Oriole Park at Camden Yards	96	100	92	96	76	48	116	102	97	130	125	92	109	99	121
Detroit - Comerica Park	97	101	86	98	75	211	73	91	89	92	77	97	104	97	44
Seattle - Safeco Field	94	98	84	92	84	97	77	120	110	101	117	92	81	95	74

2002 American League Ballpark Index Rankings - Home Runs

Team	TOTALS											LHB		RHB	
	Avg	AB	R	H	2B	3B	HR	BB	SO	E	E-Inf	Avg	HR	Avg	HR
Texas - The Ballpark in Arlington	108	101	123	109	110	105	142	100	99	87	71	105	126	111	153
Kansas City - Ewing M. Kauffman Stadium	112	105	129	118	113	110	133	96	77	103	77	115	132	110	135
Chicago - Comiskey Park	102	99	107	101	95	72	127	105	96	79	106	105	123	101	130
Oakland - Network Associates Coliseum	99	98	105	97	105	88	120	102	107	110	143	107	125	93	115
Baltimore - Oriole Park at Camden Yards	96	100	92	96	76	48	116	102	97	130	125	92	109	99	121
Toronto - SkyDome	102	99	99	101	120	85	110	99	96	108	102	98	110	104	112
New York - Yankee Stadium	96	98	97	95	92	91	103	94	107	108	101	98	106	95	99
Cleveland - Jacobs Field	98	100	101	99	108	54	102	95	113	124	142	102	103	95	99
Anaheim - Edison International Field	97	100	94	97	101	100	84	98	102	82	82	97	83	98	85
Tampa Bay - Tropicana Field	100	104	99	104	94	136	80	100	103	83	99	102	98	99	63
Boston - Fenway Park	101	98	95	98	120	68	79	96	107	126	120	97	63	104	95
Seattle - Safeco Field	94	98	84	92	84	97	77	120	110	101	117	92	81	95	74
Detroit - Comerica Park	97	101	86	98	75	211	73	91	89	92	77	97	104	97	44
Minnesota - Hubert H. Humphrey Metrodome	97	99	93	96	118	177	70	103	100	87	76	96	65	99	76

2002 National League Ballpark Index Rankings - Runs

Team	TOTALS											LHB		RHB	
	Avg	AB	R	H	2B	3B	HR	BB	SO	E	E-Inf	Avg	HR	Avg	HR
Colorado - Coors Field	116	103	138	119	120	149	151	98	87	123	119	113	147	119	153
Cincinnati - Cinergy Field	109	102	121	110	128	44	135	108	98	81	74	106	125	111	144
Arizona - Bank One Ballpark	107	102	121	110	116	209	105	118	100	92	107	106	98	108	114
Pittsburgh - PNC Park	105	102	113	107	108	84	92	100	88	121	139	104	82	106	100
Houston - Minute Maid Park	109	102	109	111	102	78	97	94	96	111	90	107	114	110	85
Atlanta - Turner Field	102	99	105	100	109	100	107	93	93	105	165	106	138	100	98
Florida - Pro Player Stadium	100	101	102	101	106	174	80	116	110	86	85	90	61	105	89
Montreal - Olympic Stadium	101	100	99	101	118	94	100	92	94	108	88	108	108	97	93
Chicago - Wrigley Field	92	99	93	91	91	66	124	102	112	100	83	91	99	93	148
New York - Shea Stadium	94	101	93	95	81	94	106	95	102	98	118	102	162	90	80
Milwaukee - Miller Park	96	99	91	95	105	97	97	92	104	89	118	98	104	94	92
St Louis - Busch Stadium	95	100	91	95	103	33	96	109	106	94	81	99	101	93	93
San Diego - Qualcomm Stadium	101	102	89	102	80	112	83	92	94	99	86	105	73	96	92
Philadelphia - Veterans Stadium	89	96	83	85	84	100	99	99	117	75	47	84	94	93	102
San Francisco - Pacific Bell Park	95	98	83	92	89	190	54	94	99	116	105	91	55	97	53
Los Angeles - Dodger Stadium	91	97	81	89	73	48	97	103	102	116	135	88	78	93	106

2002 National League Ballpark Index Rankings - Home Runs

Team	TOTALS											LHB		RHB	
	Avg	AB	R	H	2B	3B	HR	BB	SO	E	E-Inf	Avg	HR	Avg	HR
Colorado - Coors Field	116	103	138	119	120	149	151	98	87	123	119	113	147	119	153
Cincinnati - Cinergy Field	109	102	121	110	128	44	135	108	98	81	74	106	125	111	144
Chicago - Wrigley Field	92	99	93	91	91	66	124	102	112	100	83	91	99	93	148
Atlanta - Turner Field	102	99	105	100	109	100	107	93	93	105	165	106	138	100	98
New York - Shea Stadium	94	101	93	95	81	94	106	95	102	98	118	102	162	90	80
Arizona - Bank One Ballpark	107	102	121	110	116	209	105	118	100	92	107	106	98	108	114
Montreal - Olympic Stadium	101	100	99	101	118	94	100	92	94	108	88	108	108	97	93
Philadelphia - Veterans Stadium	89	96	83	85	84	100	99	99	117	75	47	84	94	93	102
Milwaukee - Miller Park	96	99	91	95	105	97	97	92	104	89	118	98	104	94	92
Los Angeles - Dodger Stadium	91	97	81	89	73	48	97	103	102	116	135	88	78	93	106
Houston - Minute Maid Park	109	102	109	111	102	78	97	94	96	111	90	107	114	110	85
St Louis - Busch Stadium	95	100	91	95	103	33	96	109	106	94	81	99	101	93	93
Pittsburgh - PNC Park	105	102	113	107	108	84	92	100	88	121	139	104	82	106	100
San Diego - Qualcomm Stadium	101	102	89	102	80	112	83	92	94	99	86	105	73	96	92
Florida - Pro Player Stadium	100	101	102	101	106	174	80	116	110	86	85	90	61	105	89
San Francisco - Pacific Bell Park	95	98	83	92	89	190	54	94	99	116	105	91	55	97	53

2002 Lefty/Righty Statistics

Batters vs. Left-Handed and Right-Handed Pitchers

Batter	vs	Avg	AB	H	2B	3B	HR	RBI	BB	SO	OBP	Slg
Abernathy,Brent	L	.203	79	16	6	0	1	8	5	11	.259	.316
Bats Right	R	.250	384	96	12	4	1	32	20	35	.294	.310
Abreu,Bobby	L	.302	162	49	17	0	0	22	29	47	.411	.407
Bats Left	R	.310	410	127	33	6	20	63	75	70	.414	.566
Agbayani,Benny	L	.209	67	14	3	0	1	12	7	14	.284	.299
Bats Right	R	.241	87	21	3	0	3	15	9	26	.309	.379
Alcantara,Izzy	L	.313	16	5	1	0	2	4	0	4	.313	.750
Bats Right	R	.188	16	3	0	0	0	1	0	2	.188	.188
Alfonzo,Edgardo	L	.364	121	44	10	0	4	18	25	13	.477	.545
Bats Right	R	.290	369	107	16	0	12	38	37	42	.361	.431
Alicea,Luis	L	.205	44	9	1	0	0	2	4	3	.271	.227
Bats Both	R	.233	193	45	7	2	1	21	28	31	.333	.306
Allen,Chad	L	.125	8	1	1	0	0	0	0	2	.125	.250
Bats Right	R	.000	2	0	0	0	0	0	0	0	.000	.000
Allen,Luke	L	.200	5	1	1	0	0	0	0	3	.200	.400
Bats Left	R	.000	2	0	0	0	0	0	2	0	.500	.000
Alomar,Roberto	L	.204	162	33	4	1	4	14	12	36	.259	.315
Bats Both	R	.290	428	124	20	3	7	39	45	47	.358	.400
Alomar Jr.,Sandy	L	.247	81	20	4	1	1	10	4	12	.279	.358
Bats Right	R	.292	202	59	10	0	6	27	5	21	.311	.431
Alou,Moises	L	.322	115	37	9	1	2	12	16	13	.402	.470
Bats Right	R	.260	369	96	14	0	13	49	31	48	.316	.404
Alvarez,Tony	L	.333	3	1	0	0	0	0	2	1	.600	.333
Bats Right	R	.304	23	7	2	0	1	2	1	4	.333	.522
Amezaga,Alfredo	L	.800	5	4	1	0	0	1	0	0	.800	1.000
Bats Both	R	.375	8	3	1	0	0	1	0	1	.375	.500
Anderson,Brady	L	.111	9	1	1	0	0	0	1	5	.333	.222
Bats Left	R	.169	71	12	3	0	1	5	17	18	.326	.254
Anderson,Garret	L	.284	208	59	15	0	11	41	7	37	.301	.514
Bats Left	R	.316	430	136	41	3	18	82	23	43	.346	.551
Anderson,Marlon	L	.220	123	27	4	0	0	10	6	20	.267	.252
Bats Left	R	.269	416	112	26	6	8	38	36	51	.330	.418
Andrews,Shane	L	.000	4	0	0	0	0	0	1	0	.333	.000
Bats Right	R	.111	9	1	1	0	0	0	0	3	.111	.222
Arias,Alex	L	.000	2	0	0	0	0	0	0	1	.000	.000
Bats Right	R	.000	5	0	0	0	0	0	1	1	.167	.000
Aurilia,Rich	L	.241	116	28	5	0	2	16	7	18	.276	.336
Bats Right	R	.261	422	110	30	2	13	45	30	72	.314	.434
Ausmus,Brad	L	.307	88	27	4	0	3	12	9	7	.390	.455
Bats Right	R	.245	359	88	15	3	3	38	29	64	.305	.329
Aven,Bruce	L	.182	11	2	0	0	0	0	2	2	.308	.182
Bats Right	R	.000	6	0	0	0	0	0	2	2	.250	.000
Baerga,Carlos	L	.224	49	11	3	0	0	3	1	6	.235	.286
Bats Both	R	.308	133	41	8	0	2	16	6	14	.345	.414
Bagwell,Jeff	L	.333	108	36	6	1	10	24	26	25	.459	.685
Bats Right	R	.281	463	130	27	1	21	74	75	105	.387	.479
Bako,Paul	L	.167	30	5	1	0	0	2	1	8	.194	.200
Bats Left	R	.245	204	50	7	1	4	18	19	38	.309	.348
Banks,Brian	L	.500	8	4	0	0	1	3	0	2	.500	.875
Bats Both	R	.250	20	5	1	0	0	1	1	4	.286	.300
Barajas,Rod	L	.196	51	10	1	0	1	5	6	5	.276	.275
Bats Right	R	.252	103	26	9	0	2	18	4	20	.295	.398
Bard,Josh	L	.229	35	8	3	0	2	5	1	5	.250	.486
Bats Both	R	.218	55	12	2	0	1	7	3	8	.259	.309
Barker,Kevin	L	.000	6	0	0	0	0	0	1	4	.143	.000
Bats Left	R	.231	13	3	0	0	0	0	0	2	.231	.231
Barrett,Michael	L	.261	111	29	9	0	1	6	11	20	.325	.369
Bats Right	R	.264	265	70	11	1	11	43	29	45	.334	.438
Batista,Tony	L	.234	158	37	10	0	3	11	13	30	.295	.354
Bats Right	R	.247	457	113	26	1	28	76	37	77	.314	.492
Bautista,Danny	L	.362	47	17	0	0	4	11	4	6	.412	.617
Bats Right	R	.308	107	33	5	2	2	12	7	15	.348	.449
Bell,David	L	.263	137	36	6	0	5	22	16	20	.333	.416
Bats Right	R	.260	415	108	23	2	15	51	38	60	.333	.434
Bell,Jay	L	.130	23	3	1	0	0	2	4	4	.259	.174
Bats Right	R	.192	26	5	0	0	2	9	1	5	.241	.423
Bellhorn,Mark	L	.303	122	37	11	2	10	24	18	41	.397	.672
Bats Both	R	.241	323	78	13	2	17	32	58	103	.365	.452
Belliard,Ronnie	L	.200	100	20	2	0	3	9	5	16	.238	.310
Bats Right	R	.217	189	41	11	0	0	17	13	30	.267	.275
Bellinger,Clay	L	-	0	0	0	0	0	0	0	0	-	-
Bats Right	R	.000	1	0	0	0	0	0	0	1	.000	.000
Beltran,Carlos	L	.245	163	40	12	1	8	24	15	31	.307	.479
Bats Both	R	.283	474	134	32	6	21	81	56	104	.359	.508
Beltre,Adrian	L	.302	126	38	4	1	6	18	2	19	.305	.492
Bats Right	R	.245	461	113	22	4	15	57	35	77	.302	.408

Batter	vs	Avg	AB	H	2B	3B	HR	RBI	BB	SO	OBP	Slg
Benard,Marvin	L	.389	18	7	1	1	0	2	1	2	.421	.556
Bats Left	R	.257	105	27	8	1	1	11	6	24	.304	.381
Benjamin,Mike	L	.128	39	5	0	0	0	0	4	8	.209	.128
Bats Right	R	.160	81	13	2	1	0	3	3	23	.198	.210
Bennett,Gary	L	.365	63	23	2	0	1	7	5	6	.412	.444
Bats Right	R	.237	228	54	8	2	3	19	10	39	.287	.329
Berg,Dave	L	.264	106	28	5	0	2	10	8	14	.310	.368
Bats Right	R	.272	268	73	21	2	2	29	18	43	.327	.388
Berger,Brandon	L	.214	56	12	3	0	3	5	4	16	.267	.429
Bats Right	R	.192	78	15	2	1	3	12	4	16	.247	.359
Bergeron,Peter	L	.200	20	4	0	1	0	1	4	7	.333	.300
Bats Left	R	.184	103	19	3	1	0	6	18	37	.306	.233
Berkman,Lance	L	.240	129	31	8	1	2	14	22	20	.351	.364
Bats Both	R	.307	449	138	27	1	40	114	85	98	.420	.639
Berroa,Angel	L	.261	23	6	2	0	0	1	2	4	.320	.348
Bats Right	R	.212	52	11	5	1	0	4	5	6	.293	.346
Bigbie,Larry	L	.000	2	0	0	0	0	0	0	1	.000	.000
Bats Left	R	.188	32	6	1	0	0	3	1	10	.206	.219
Biggio,Craig	L	.183	115	21	2	1	2	8	16	19	.291	.270
Bats Right	R	.271	462	125	34	2	13	50	34	92	.340	.437
Blake,Casey	L	.143	7	1	0	0	0	0	2	2	.333	.143
Bats Right	R	.231	13	3	1	0	0	1	0	5	.231	.308
Blalock,Hank	L	.067	30	2	0	0	0	3	3	11	.176	.067
Bats Left	R	.248	117	29	8	0	3	14	17	32	.338	.393
Blanco,Henry	L	.211	38	8	0	0	2	7	4	10	.273	.368
Bats Right	R	.202	183	37	9	1	4	15	16	41	.266	.328
Bloomquist,Willie	L	.571	14	8	3	0	0	5	2	0	.625	.786
Bats Right	R	.368	19	7	1	0	0	2	3	2	.455	.421
Blum,Geoff	L	.185	65	12	4	0	1	6	6	19	.254	.292
Bats Both	R	.304	303	92	16	4	9	46	43	51	.390	.472
Bocachica,Hiram	L	.275	69	19	4	0	3	9	6	13	.333	.464
Bats Right	R	.182	99	18	3	0	5	8	4	28	.214	.364
Bonds,Barry	L	.384	125	48	9	1	21	45	45	16	.556	.976
Bats Left	R	.363	278	101	22	1	25	65	153	31	.592	.719
Boone,Aaron	L	.233	150	35	13	1	4	24	24	26	.341	.413
Bats Right	R	.243	456	111	25	1	22	63	32	85	.304	.447
Boone,Bret	L	.295	149	44	10	1	8	26	17	23	.363	.537
Bats Right	R	.272	459	125	24	2	16	81	36	79	.331	.438
Borchard,Joe	L	.250	8	2	0	0	0	0	0	4	.250	.250
Bats Both	R	.214	28	6	0	0	2	5	1	10	.241	.429
Borders,Pat	L	.500	2	1	0	0	0	0	0	1	.500	.500
Bats Right	R	.500	2	1	1	0	0	1	0	0	.500	1.000
Bordick,Mike	L	.236	110	26	6	0	3	6	11	14	.306	.373
Bats Right	R	.230	257	59	13	3	5	30	24	49	.301	.362
Bradley,Milton	L	.293	99	29	6	1	1	11	13	16	.375	.404
Bats Both	R	.230	226	52	12	2	8	27	19	42	.290	.407
Bragg,Darren	L	.308	26	8	0	0	0	0	5	6	.438	.308
Bats Left	R	.263	186	49	15	2	3	15	19	46	.333	.414
Branyan,Russell	L	.233	60	14	0	0	7	13	2	25	.258	.583
Bats Left	R	.226	318	72	13	1	17	43	49	126	.330	.434
Brito,Juan	L	.000	1	0	0	0	0	0	0	0	.000	.000
Bats Right	R	.318	22	7	2	0	0	1	0	3	.318	.409
Broussard,Ben	L	.167	18	3	1	0	1	3	0	4	.167	.389
Bats Left	R	.255	94	24	3	0	3	6	7	21	.314	.383
Brown,Adrian	L	.154	52	8	1	0	0	4	1	7	.167	.173
Bats Both	R	.237	156	37	9	2	1	17	18	27	.320	.340
Brown,Dee	L	.091	11	1	0	0	0	0	0	6	.091	.091
Bats Left	R	.275	40	11	3	1	1	7	4	14	.341	.475
Brown,Kevin L	L	-	0	0	0	0	0	0	0	0	-	-
Bats Right	R	.000	1	0	0	0	0	0	0	0	.000	.000
Brown,Roosevelt	L	.200	20	4	1	0	0	3	3	7	.292	.250
Bats Left	R	.212	184	39	11	0	3	20	20	43	.300	.321
Buchanan,Brian	L	.225	102	23	6	1	6	14	7	22	.282	.480
Bats Right	R	.304	125	38	4	0	5	14	8	37	.356	.456
Burks,Ellis	L	.316	136	43	9	0	9	19	19	22	.400	.581
Bats Right	R	.296	382	113	19	0	23	72	25	86	.348	.526
Burnitz,Jeromy	L	.174	121	21	4	0	3	9	8	39	.242	.281
Bats Left	R	.229	358	82	11	0	16	45	50	96	.333	.394
Burrell,Pat	L	.311	122	38	7	0	12	29	37	32	.469	.664
Bats Right	R	.274	464	127	32	2	25	87	52	121	.347	.513
Burroughs,Sean	L	.218	55	12	0	0	0	2	1	11	.246	.218
Bats Left	R	.292	137	40	5	1	1	9	11	19	.345	.365
Bush,Homer	L	.196	46	9	1	0	0	2	1	11	.229	.217
Bats Right	R	.244	86	21	1	0	1	5	4	14	.286	.291
Butler,Brent	L	.237	76	18	7	1	1	7	4	10	.275	.395
Bats Right	R	.265	268	71	11	3	8	35	6	30	.290	.418

Batters vs. Left-Handed and Right-Handed Pitchers

Batter	vs	Avg	AB	H	2B	3B	HR	RBI	BB	SO	OBP	Slg
Byrd,Marlon	L	.222	9	2	1	0	1	1	0	1	.222	.667
Bats Right	R	.231	26	6	1	0	0	0	1	7	.259	.269
Byrnes,Eric	L	.279	43	12	2	0	1	5	0	8	.273	.395
Bats Right	R	.216	51	11	2	2	2	6	4	9	.305	.451
Cabrera,Jolbert	L	.256	39	10	2	0	0	5	5	6	.341	.308
Bats Right	R	.044	45	2	0	0	0	3	2	9	.102	.044
Cabrera,Orlando	L	.264	125	33	6	0	1	14	14	10	.338	.336
Bats Right	R	.263	438	115	37	1	6	42	34	43	.316	.393
Cairo,Miguel	L	.273	66	18	5	0	2	9	5	7	.342	.439
Bats Right	R	.237	118	28	4	2	0	14	8	29	.287	.305
Cameron,Mike	L	.239	142	34	10	1	10	29	20	40	.343	.535
Bats Right	R	.238	403	96	16	4	15	51	59	136	.338	.409
Canizaro,Jay	L	.205	39	8	2	1	0	7	7	5	.313	.308
Bats Right	R	.219	73	16	6	0	0	4	3	17	.260	.301
Cardona,Javier	L	.067	30	2	1	0	0	2	1	9	.094	.100
Bats Right	R	.222	9	2	0	0	0	0	1	1	.300	.222
Carroll,Jamey	L	.400	10	4	2	0	0	0	0	1	.400	.600
Bats Right	R	.295	61	18	3	3	1	6	4	11	.338	.492
Caruso,Mike	L	-	0	0	0	0	0	0	0	0	-	-
Bats Left	R	.100	20	2	0	0	0	0	1	2	.143	.100
Casanova,Raul	L	.154	26	4	0	0	0	0	0	6	.154	.154
Bats Both	R	.194	62	12	1	0	1	8	10	13	.311	.258
Casey,Sean	L	.231	130	30	6	0	2	16	12	17	.299	.323
Bats Left	R	.275	295	81	19	0	4	26	31	30	.349	.380
Cash,Kevin	L	.000	6	0	0	0	0	0	0	2	.000	.000
Bats Right	R	.250	8	2	0	0	0	0	1	2	.333	.250
Castilla,Vinny	L	.224	76	17	1	0	2	10	5	7	.268	.316
Bats Right	R	.233	467	109	22	2	10	51	17	62	.268	.353
Castillo,Alberto	L	.000	10	0	0	0	0	0	1	1	.091	.000
Bats Right	R	.185	27	5	1	1	0	4	0	11	.185	.296
Castillo,Luis	L	.329	158	52	8	2	1	10	9	20	.369	.424
Bats Both	R	.297	448	133	10	3	1	29	46	56	.363	.339
Castro,Juan	L	.222	36	8	1	0	0	4	3	4	.282	.250
Bats Right	R	.217	46	10	2	0	2	7	4	14	.275	.391
Castro,Ramon	L	.160	25	4	2	0	0	3	2	5	.214	.240
Bats Right	R	.263	76	20	2	0	6	15	12	19	.356	.526
Catalanotto,Frank	L	.231	26	6	1	1	0	4	3	5	.364	.346
Bats Left	R	.274	186	51	15	5	3	19	22	22	.364	.457
Cedeno,Roger	L	.231	156	36	6	1	3	8	10	45	.275	.340
Bats Both	R	.273	355	97	13	1	4	33	32	47	.336	.349
Cepicky,Matt	L	.182	11	2	0	0	1	2	1	1	.250	.455
Bats Left	R	.222	63	14	3	0	2	13	3	20	.258	.365
Chavez,Endy	L	.316	19	6	1	0	0		4	3	.435	.368
Bats Left	R	.292	106	31	7	5	1	9	1	13	.296	.481
Chavez,Eric	L	.209	163	34	7	0	6	27	11	37	.261	.362
Bats Left	R	.301	422	127	24	3	28	82	54	82	.379	.571
Chavez,Raul	L	.500	2	1	1	0	0	0	0	0	.500	1.000
Bats Right	R	.000	2	0	0	0	0	0	1	0	.500	.000
Chen,Chin-Feng	L	.000	3	0	0	0	0	0	1	2	.250	.000
Bats Right	R	.000	2	0	0	0	0	0	0	1	.000	.000
Choi,Hee Seop	L	.000	4	0	0	0	0	0	1	2	.200	.000
Bats Left	R	.196	46	9	1	0	2	4	6	13	.288	.348
Christensen,McKay	L	.000	1	0	0	0	0	0	0	0	.000	.000
Bats Left	R	.500	2	1	0	0	0	0	1	1	.667	.500
Christenson,Ryan	L	.118	17	2	2	0	0	1	2	3	.211	.235
Bats Right	R	.171	41	7	2	0	1	2	3	10	.227	.293
Cintron,Alex	L	.182	22	4	1	0	0	4	4	4	.308	.227
Bats Both	R	.226	53	12	5	0	0	4	8	9	.328	.321
Cirillo,Jeff	L	.304	148	45	6	0	4	20	10	17	.362	.426
Bats Right	R	.226	337	76	14	0	2	34	21	50	.275	.285
Clark,Brady	L	.143	28	4	0	0	0	2	6	1	.314	.143
Bats Right	R	.220	50	11	4	0	0	8	1	10	.235	.300
Clark,Howie	L	.000	3	0	0	0	0	0	0	1	.000	.000
Bats Left	R	.320	50	16	5	0	0	4	3	5	.382	.420
Clark,Tony	L	.159	82	13	3	1	1	6	3	24	.188	.256
Bats Both	R	.228	193	44	9	0	2	23	18	33	.296	.306
Clayton,Royce	L	.238	101	24	2	0	3	10	3	20	.257	.347
Bats Right	R	.257	241	62	12	2	4	25	17	47	.311	.373
Colangelo,Mike	L	.143	14	2	1	0	0	0	0	2	.200	.214
Bats Right	R	.222	9	2	0	0	0	0	1	0	.300	.222
Colbrunn,Greg	L	.368	117	43	14	0	7	21	10	8	.414	.667
Bats Right	R	.259	54	14	2	2	3	6	3	11	.298	.537
Collier,Lou	L	.125	8	1	1	0	0	0	1	0	.300	.250
Bats Right	R	.000	3	0	0	0	0	0	0	0	.000	.000
Conine,Jeff	L	.292	113	33	4	1	6	20	10	21	.336	.504
Bats Right	R	.266	338	90	22	3	9	43	15	45	.297	.429
Conti,Jason	L	.367	30	11	3	2	1	3	1	7	.387	.700
Bats Left	R	.240	192	46	12	0	2	18	17	48	.305	.333
Coolbaugh,Mike	L	.100	10	1	0	0	0	0	0	3	.100	.100
Bats Right	R	.000	2	0	0	0	0	0	1	0	.333	.000
Coomer,Ron	L	.288	80	23	4	0	2	10	3	13	.313	.413
Bats Right	R	.235	68	16	3	0	1	7	3	10	.264	.324
Cora,Alex	L	.318	22	7	1	1	0	2	2	3	.375	.455
Bats Left	R	.288	236	68	13	3	5	26	24	35	.371	.432
Cordero,Wil	L	.258	93	24	6	0	4	15	12	11	.339	.452
Bats Right	R	.279	68	19	3	0	2	15	5	18	.333	.412
Cordova,Marty	L	.274	135	37	6	1	7	19	13	27	.340	.489
Bats Right	R	.245	323	79	19	1	11	45	34	84	.319	.412
Cota,Humberto	L	.000	4	0	0	0	0	0	0	1	.000	.000
Bats Right	R	.385	13	5	1	0	0	0	1	3	.429	.462
Counsell,Craig	L	.269	145	39	9	0	0	20	18	25	.348	.331
Bats Left	R	.289	291	84	13	1	2	31	27	27	.349	.361
Cox,Steve	L	.197	152	30	8	0	4	22	12	39	.260	.329
Bats Left	R	.275	408	112	22	1	12	50	48	77	.356	.422
Crawford,Carl	L	.200	60	12	2	2	0	7	3	10	.250	.300
Bats Left	R	.276	199	55	9	4	2	23	6	31	.303	.392
Crede,Joe	L	.259	54	14	6	0	3	9	2	15	.286	.537
Bats Right	R	.295	146	43	4	0	9	26	6	25	.320	.507
Crespo,Cesar	L	.273	11	3	1	0	0	0	1	1	.333	.364
Bats Both	R	.111	18	2	1	0	0	0	2	5	.200	.167
Crisp,Coco	L	.270	37	10	3	0	1	3	2	4	.308	.432
Bats Both	R	.256	90	23	6	2	0	6	9	15	.317	.367
Cruz,Deivi	L	.242	161	39	6	0	3	11	9	20	.285	.335
Bats Right	R	.272	353	96	22	2	4	36	13	38	.298	.380
Cruz,Ivan	L	-	0	0	0	0	0	0	0	0	-	-
Bats Left	R	.357	14	5	0	0	1	3	1	3	.400	.571
Cruz,Jacob	L	.400	10	4	1	0	0	1	3	4	.500	.500
Bats Left	R	.256	78	20	2	1	2	5	10	16	.359	.385
Cruz,Jose	L	.225	142	32	8	0	3	15	10	24	.275	.345
Bats Both	R	.253	324	82	18	5	15	55	41	82	.334	.478
Cuddyer,Mike	L	.256	43	11	3	0	1	3	3	13	.304	.395
Bats Right	R	.261	69	18	4	0	3	10	5	17	.316	.449
Cust,Jack	L	.000	5	0	0	0	0	0	0	3	.000	.000
Bats Left	R	.183	60	11	2	0	1	8	12	29	.315	.267
Damon,Johnny	L	.306	157	48	12	4	3	14	10	14	.357	.490
Bats Left	R	.279	466	130	22	7	11	49	55	56	.356	.427
Daubach,Brian	L	.242	62	15	2	0	3	16	6	20	.314	.419
Bats Left	R	.270	382	103	22	2	17	62	45	106	.353	.471
DaVanon,Jeff	L	.091	11	1	1	0	0	0	1	4	.167	.182
Bats Both	R	.211	19	4	2	0	1	4	1	2	.250	.474
Davis,Ben	L	.235	51	12	2	0	0	6	2	13	.278	.275
Bats Both	R	.266	177	47	8	1	7	37	16	45	.323	.441
Davis,J.J.	L	.000	2	0	0	0	0	0	0	2	.000	.000
Bats Right	R	.125	8	1	0	0	0	0	0	2	.222	.125
Dawkins,Gookie	L	.125	8	1	0	0	0	0	2	4	.300	.125
Bats Right	R	.125	40	5	2	0	0	0	4	17	.205	.175
DeHaan,Kory	L	.000	1	0	0	0	0	0	0	0	.000	.000
Bats Left	R	.100	10	1	0	0	0	0	0	6	.100	.100
Delgado,Carlos	L	.238	172	41	9	0	4	29	20	50	.325	.360
Bats Left	R	.297	333	99	25	2	29	79	82	76	.444	.646
Delgado,Wilson	L	.500	4	2	1	0	1	3	0	2	.500	1.500
Bats Both	R	.125	16	2	1	0	1	2	0	4	.125	.375
Dellucci,David	L	.111	27	3	1	0	0	3	2	11	.167	.148
Bats Left	R	.262	202	53	10	2	7	26	26	44	.346	.436
DeRosa,Mark	L	.293	58	17	4	1	1	5	6	5	.369	.448
Bats Right	R	.299	154	46	5	1	4	18	6	19	.327	.422
DeShields,Delino	L	.105	19	2	1	0	0	0	5	6	.292	.158
Bats Left	R	.205	127	26	5	1	3	10	16	32	.292	.331
Diaz,Einar	L	.225	71	16	5	0	1	4	6	4	.286	.338
Bats Right	R	.201	249	50	14	0	1	12	11	23	.250	.269
Diaz,Juan	L	.200	5	1	1	0	0	0	0	2	.200	.400
Bats Right	R	.500	2	1	0	0	1	2	1	0	.667	2.000
DiFelice,Mike	L	.216	51	11	5	0	1	6	7	14	.310	.373
Bats Right	R	.236	123	29	6	0	3	13	10	28	.292	.358
Donnels,Chris	L	.222	9	2	0	0	2	4	0	2	.200	.889
Bats Left	R	.239	71	17	4	1	1	12	10	12	.325	.366
Drew,J.D.	L	.262	84	22	4	0	3	13	10	23	.351	.417
Bats Left	R	.250	340	85	15	1	15	43	47	81	.348	.432
Dunn,Adam	L	.254	169	43	12	0	11	27	31	55	.385	.521
Bats Left	R	.246	366	90	16	2	15	44	97	115	.406	.423
Dunston,Shawon	L	.229	48	11	3	0	0	1	0	11	.245	.292
Bats Right	R	.232	99	23	2	0	1	8	3	22	.252	.283

Batters vs. Left-Handed and Right-Handed Pitchers

Batter	vs	Avg	AB	H	2B	3B	HR	RBI	BB	SO	OBP	Slg
Dunwoody,Todd	L	-	0	0	0	0	0	0	0	0	-	-
Bats Left	R	.000	6	0	0	0	0	0	0	3	.000	.000
Durazo,Erubiel	L	.167	54	9	1	0	2	5	7	14	.274	.296
Bats Left	R	.292	168	49	11	2	14	43	42	46	.430	.631
Durham,Ray	L	.255	145	37	7	0	3	16	14	22	.327	.366
Bats Both	R	.301	419	126	27	6	12	54	59	71	.390	.480
Dye,Jermaine	L	.212	99	21	5	0	1	5	12	28	.304	.293
Bats Right	R	.262	389	102	22	1	23	81	40	80	.341	.501
Easley,Damion	L	.313	67	21	2	0	4	9	4	8	.370	.522
Bats Right	R	.198	237	47	12	1	4	21	23	35	.290	.308
Echevarria,Angel	L	.408	49	20	4	0	3	10	3	7	.426	.673
Bats Right	R	.204	49	10	3	0	0	11	5	10	.281	.265
Eckstein,David	L	.302	172	52	9	2	4	23	16	5	.387	.448
Bats Right	R	.289	436	126	13	4	4	40	29	39	.354	.365
Edmonds,Jim	L	.262	130	34	7	0	7	23	16	40	.357	.477
Bats Left	R	.329	346	114	24	2	21	60	70	94	.443	.592
Ellis,Mark	L	.296	54	16	2	1	2	9	10	9	.415	.481
Bats Right	R	.268	291	78	14	3	4	26	34	45	.347	.378
Encarnacion,Juan	L	.233	133	31	3	0	5	15	9	23	.276	.368
Bats Right	R	.282	451	127	19	5	19	70	37	90	.339	.472
Encarnacion,Mario	L	.000	4	0	0	0	0	0	2	3	.333	.000
Bats Right	R	.000	3	0	0	0	0	0	0	0	.000	.000
Ensberg,Morgan	L	.320	25	8	2	0	2	7	6	3	.469	.640
Bats Right	R	.224	107	24	5	2	1	12	12	22	.314	.336
Erstad,Darin	L	.280	193	54	7	1	2	26	6	28	.305	.358
Bats Left	R	.285	432	123	21	3	8	47	21	39	.316	.403
Escalona,Felix	L	.172	29	5	2	0	0	2	0	11	.219	.241
Bats Right	R	.227	128	29	6	2	0	7	3	33	.272	.305
Estalella,Bobby	L	.136	22	3	0	0	1	5	6	7	.300	.273
Bats Right	R	.222	90	20	8	0	7	20	8	26	.280	.544
Estrada,Johnny	L	.250	4	1	0	0	0	1	1	0	.400	.250
Bats Both	R	.077	13	1	1	0	0	1	1	2	.143	.154
Everett,Adam	L	.261	23	6	1	0	0	2	2	4	.320	.304
Bats Right	R	.169	65	11	2	0	0	2	10	15	.289	.200
Everett,Carl	L	.220	91	20	2	0	4	11	6	20	.280	.374
Bats Both	R	.283	283	80	14	0	12	51	27	57	.350	.459
Fabregas,Jorge	L	.188	16	3	0	0	0	1	1	3	.222	.188
Bats Left	R	.180	139	25	4	0	3	21	7	10	.215	.273
Fasano,Sal	L	.000	1	0	0	0	0	0	0	1	.000	.000
Bats Right	R	-	0	0	0	0	0	0	0	0	-	-
Febles,Carlos	L	.229	83	19	2	0	1	4	16	21	.354	.289
Bats Right	R	.250	268	67	14	4	3	22	25	42	.330	.366
Feliz,Pedro	L	.184	49	9	1	0	0	3	1	7	.200	.204
Bats Right	R	.289	97	28	3	1	2	10	5	20	.320	.402
Fick,Robert	L	.281	171	48	8	1	5	14	13	31	.342	.427
Bats Left	R	.265	385	102	28	1	12	49	33	59	.325	.436
Figgins,Chone	L	.125	8	1	1	0	0	0	0	4	.125	.250
Bats Both	R	.250	4	1	0	0	0	1	0	1	.250	.250
Finley,Steve	L	.297	158	47	8	2	9	30	16	27	.371	.544
Bats Left	R	.282	347	98	16	2	16	59	49	46	.369	.478
Flaherty,John	L	.250	56	14	4	0	1	4	1	10	.254	.375
Bats Right	R	.262	225	59	16	0	3	29	14	40	.306	.373
Fletcher,Darrin	L	.375	16	6	0	0	2	8	2	2	.421	.750
Bats Left	R	.198	111	22	6	0	1	14	2	11	.209	.279
Flores,Jose	L	.000	1	0	0	0	0	0	1	0	.667	.000
Bats Right	R	.000	2	0	0	0	0	0	0	0	.000	.000
Floyd,Cliff	L	.247	154	38	10	0	10	24	10	41	.304	.506
Bats Left	R	.306	366	112	33	0	18	55	66	65	.420	.544
Fordyce,Brook	L	.103	29	3	1	0	0	1	2	6	.188	.138
Bats Right	R	.267	101	27	7	0	1	7	7	13	.333	.366
Fox,Andy	L	.148	88	13	4	0	0	6	7	30	.208	.193
Bats Left	R	.277	347	96	10	5	4	35	42	64	.369	.369
Franco,Julio	L	.382	76	29	2	0	3	14	9	16	.442	.526
Bats Right	R	.256	262	67	11	1	3	16	30	59	.332	.340
Franco,Matt	L	.333	6	2	0	1	0	0	1	1	.429	.667
Bats Left	R	.317	199	63	15	3	6	30	26	30	.394	.513
Fryman,Travis	L	.281	128	36	4	1	5	20	8	26	.328	.445
Bats Right	R	.186	269	50	10	2	6	35	32	56	.275	.305
Fullmer,Brad	L	.222	63	14	3	0	2	7	1	12	.231	.365
Bats Left	R	.301	366	110	32	6	17	52	31	32	.377	.560
Furcal,Rafael	L	.288	111	32	6	2	1	12	8	19	.336	.405
Bats Both	R	.272	525	143	25	6	7	35	35	95	.320	.383
Galarraga,Andres	L	.294	85	25	3	0	0	8	9	19	.368	.329
Bats Right	R	.246	207	51	9	0	9	32	21	62	.335	.420
Gant,Ron	L	.294	109	32	9	0	7	25	17	23	.383	.569
Bats Right	R	.245	200	49	5	1	11	34	19	36	.313	.445

Batter	vs	Avg	AB	H	2B	3B	HR	RBI	BB	SO	OBP	Slg
Garcia,Jesse	L	.154	26	4	0	0	0	2	0	5	.154	.154
Bats Right	R	.229	35	8	1	0	0	3	0	9	.229	.257
Garcia,Karim	L	.278	72	20	5	0	5	21	5	20	.325	.556
Bats Left	R	.308	130	40	3	0	11	31	1	21	.308	.585
Garcia,Luis	L	1.000	1	1	0	0	0	0	0	0	1.000	1.000
Bats Right	R	.000	2	0	0	0	0	0	0	1	.000	.000
Garciaparra,Nomar	L	.305	118	36	14	2	3	21	10	15	.364	.534
Bats Right	R	.311	517	161	42	3	21	99	31	48	.349	.526
German,Esteban	L	.000	5	0	0	0	0	0	1	1	.286	.000
Bats Right	R	.233	30	7	0	0	0	0	3	10	.303	.233
Giambi,Jason	L	.299	154	46	8	0	9	32	23	39	.400	.526
Bats Left	R	.320	406	130	26	1	32	90	86	73	.448	.626
Giambi,Jeremy	L	.286	70	20	5	0	1	8	14	19	.432	.400
Bats Left	R	.251	243	61	12	0	19	37	65	75	.409	.535
Gibbons,Jay	L	.235	98	23	8	0	2	10	5	11	.272	.378
Bats Left	R	.250	392	98	21	1	26	59	40	55	.320	.508
Gil,Benji	L	.310	87	27	7	0	3	13	5	25	.344	.494
Bats Right	R	.233	43	10	1	1	0	7	0	8	.227	.302
Gil,Geronimo	L	.239	109	26	6	0	4	10	6	15	.276	.404
Bats Right	R	.230	313	72	13	0	8	35	15	73	.267	.348
Giles,Brian	L	.231	143	33	9	1	8	29	26	26	.355	.476
Bats Left	R	.325	354	115	28	4	30	74	109	48	.485	.681
Giles,Marcus	L	.158	38	6	1	0	1	1	3	9	.238	.263
Bats Right	R	.246	175	43	9	1	7	22	22	32	.332	.429
Ginter,Keith	L	.154	13	2	1	0	0	0	4	4	.353	.231
Bats Right	R	.250	68	17	8	0	1	8	13	11	.378	.412
Gipson,Charles	L	.175	40	7	2	2	0	4	7	4	.313	.325
Bats Right	R	.313	32	10	3	0	0	4	2	10	.353	.406
Girardi,Joe	L	.172	64	11	3	0	0	5	6	9	.239	.219
Bats Right	R	.247	170	42	7	1	1	8	10	26	.289	.318
Glanville,Doug	L	.250	128	32	6	1	4	11	8	16	.292	.406
Bats Right	R	.248	294	73	10	2	2	18	17	41	.292	.316
Glaus,Troy	L	.298	161	48	8	0	10	41	24	39	.389	.534
Bats Right	R	.230	408	94	16	1	20	70	64	105	.337	.422
Gload,Ross	L	.143	7	1	0	0	0	0	1	2	.250	.143
Bats Left	R	.292	24	7	1	0	1	4	2	5	.346	.458
Gomez,Alexis	L	.000	1	0	0	0	0	0	0	0	.000	.000
Bats Left	R	.222	9	2	0	0	0	0	0	2	.222	.222
Gomez,Chris	L	.172	87	15	2	1	1	8	3	14	.200	.253
Bats Right	R	.286	374	107	29	2	9	38	18	44	.328	.447
Gonzalez,Alex	L	.200	30	6	1	0	1	7	2	5	.242	.333
Bats Right	R	.231	121	28	6	1	1	11	10	27	.309	.322
Gonzalez,Alex S	L	.237	114	27	5	2	5	16	18	21	.338	.447
Bats Right	R	.251	399	100	22	3	13	45	28	115	.304	.419
Gonzalez,Juan	L	.358	81	29	9	0	3	10	4	13	.384	.580
Bats Right	R	.250	196	49	12	1	5	25	13	43	.300	.398
Gonzalez,Luis	L	.272	191	52	4	0	10	41	29	32	.377	.450
Bats Left	R	.297	333	99	15	3	18	62	68	44	.412	.523
Gonzalez,Raul	L	.273	33	9	1	0	1	2	4	7	.351	.394
Bats Right	R	.254	71	18	2	0	2	10	2	15	.270	.366
Gonzalez,Wiki	L	.310	42	13	3	0	1	8	11	6	.453	.452
Bats Right	R	.189	122	23	5	1	0	12	16	18	.284	.246
Goodwin,Tom	L	.053	19	1	0	0	0	1	0	8	.053	.053
Bats Left	R	.289	135	39	5	2	1	16	14	17	.356	.378
Grabowski,Jason	L	.667	3	2	0	1	0	1	0	0	.667	1.333
Bats Left	R	.200	5	1	1	0	0	0	3	1	.500	.400
Grace,Mark	L	.321	81	26	5	0	3	16	7	7	.382	.494
Bats Left	R	.226	217	49	14	0	4	32	39	23	.340	.346
Graffanino,Tony	L	.261	92	24	5	0	4	10	15	13	.361	.446
Bats Right	R	.263	137	36	7	4	2	21	7	25	.306	.416
Green,Shawn	L	.270	163	44	13	0	11	35	18	43	.351	.552
Bats Left	R	.291	419	122	18	1	31	79	75	69	.398	.561
Greene,Todd	L	.271	48	13	3	0	4	9	1	10	.286	.583
Bats Right	R	.266	64	17	2	0	6	10	1	13	.279	.578
Greer,Rusty	L	.293	58	17	1	1	0	5	3	4	.328	.345
Bats Left	R	.298	141	42	8	1	1	12	16	13	.367	.390
Grieve,Ben	L	.221	131	29	6	0	2	14	15	45	.320	.313
Bats Left	R	.262	351	92	24	0	17	50	54	76	.365	.476
Griffey Jr.,Ken	L	.217	60	13	2	0	1	7	6	17	.294	.300
Bats Left	R	.285	137	39	6	0	7	16	22	22	.384	.482
Grissom,Marquis	L	.293	133	39	6	2	11	29	11	25	.354	.617
Bats Right	R	.267	210	56	15	2	6	31	11	43	.299	.443
Grudzielanek,Mark	L	.257	109	28	5	0	3	15	9	14	.317	.385
Bats Right	R	.274	427	117	18	0	6	35	13	75	.297	.358
Guerrero,Vladimir	L	.290	124	36	8	0	6	20	34	8	.443	.500
Bats Right	R	.347	490	170	29	2	33	91	50	62	.410	.616

Batters vs. Left-Handed and Right-Handed Pitchers

Batter	vs	Avg	AB	H	2B	3B	HR	RBI	BB	SO	OBP	Slg
Guerrero,Wilton	L	.136	44	6	1	0	0	3	1	4	.156	.159
Bats Both	R	.260	96	25	1	1	0	2	6	28	.304	.292
Guiel,Aaron	L	.169	59	10	2	0	2	14	3	17	.219	.305
Bats Left	R	.254	181	46	11	0	2	24	16	44	.320	.348
Guillen,Carlos	L	.221	122	27	4	0	3	16	10	21	.280	.328
Bats Both	R	.275	353	97	20	6	6	40	36	70	.341	.416
Guillen,Jose	L	.252	107	27	3	0	3	9	5	19	.283	.364
Bats Right	R	.226	133	30	4	0	5	22	9	24	.290	.368
Gutierrez,Ricky	L	.371	89	33	3	0	1	14	7	6	.417	.438
Bats Right	R	.242	264	64	10	0	3	24	13	42	.295	.314
Guzman,Cristian	L	.257	214	55	12	3	5	25	6	29	.279	.411
Bats Both	R	.281	409	115	19	3	4	34	11	50	.298	.372
Hafner,Travis	L	.333	6	2	0	1	0	1	1	1	.429	.667
Bats Left	R	.232	56	13	4	0	1	5	7	14	.317	.357
Hairston Jr.,Jerry	L	.263	118	31	7	0	1	4	5	16	.290	.347
Bats Right	R	.269	308	83	18	3	4	28	29	39	.343	.386
Hall,Bill	L	.125	8	1	0	0	0	0	0	2	.125	.125
Bats Right	R	.214	28	6	1	1	1	5	3	11	.290	.429
Hall,Toby	L	.200	65	13	4	0	1	4	6	2	.264	.308
Bats Right	R	.272	265	72	15	1	5	38	11	25	.301	.392
Halter,Shane	L	.243	107	26	8	1	2	7	5	24	.281	.393
Bats Right	R	.238	303	72	14	5	8	32	34	68	.318	.396
Hammonds,Jeffrey	L	.298	84	25	5	2	3	10	12	18	.381	.512
Bats Right	R	.247	364	90	21	3	6	31	40	68	.320	.371
Hansen,Dave	L	.125	8	1	0	0	0	0	2	2	.300	.125
Bats Left	R	.304	112	34	6	0	2	17	12	20	.368	.411
Harris,Lenny	L	.467	15	7	1	0	0	3	0	2	.467	.533
Bats Left	R	.291	182	53	7	2	3	14	14	15	.347	.401
Harris,Willie	L	.237	38	9	0	0	0	2	3	6	.293	.237
Bats Left	R	.232	125	29	4	0	2	10	6	15	.263	.312
Hart,Jason	L	.200	10	2	2	0	0	0	1	4	.273	.400
Bats Right	R	.400	5	2	1	0	0	0	1	3	.500	.600
Haselman,Bill	L	.362	47	17	2	0	1	8	4	5	.434	.468
Bats Right	R	.205	132	27	5	0	2	10	7	20	.245	.288
Hatteberg,Scott	L	.233	86	20	2	0	4	12	11	12	.333	.395
Bats Left	R	.291	406	118	20	4	11	49	57	44	.382	.441
Helms,Wes	L	.167	54	9	5	0	1	5	4	14	.217	.315
Bats Right	R	.269	156	42	11	0	5	17	7	43	.306	.436
Helton,Todd	L	.327	199	65	12	2	11	46	36	38	.437	.573
Bats Left	R	.331	354	117	27	2	19	63	63	53	.424	.579
Henderson,Rickey	L	.200	85	17	4	0	2	6	20	24	.364	.318
Bats Right	R	.245	94	23	2	1	3	10	18	23	.374	.383
Henson,Drew	L	.000	1	0	0	0	0	0	0	1	.000	.000
Bats Right	R	-	0	0	0	0	0	0	0	0	-	-
Hermansen,Chad	L	.178	45	8	1	0	1	4	6	17	.275	.267
Bats Right	R	.214	192	41	13	1	7	14	16	65	.276	.401
Hernandez,Jose	L	.253	99	25	4	0	8	16	10	39	.321	.535
Bats Right	R	.296	426	126	20	2	16	57	42	149	.364	.465
Hernandez,Ramon	L	.257	109	28	10	0	3	11	12	11	.325	.431
Bats Right	R	.224	294	66	10	0	4	31	31	53	.308	.299
Hidalgo,Richard	L	.263	76	20	5	1	3	11	14	16	.378	.474
Bats Right	R	.228	312	71	12	3	12	37	29	69	.304	.401
Higginson,Bobby	L	.241	133	32	3	0	1	15	9	19	.293	.286
Bats Left	R	.299	311	93	21	3	9	48	32	26	.368	.473
Hill,Bobby	L	.327	52	17	4	0	0	5	8	9	.426	.404
Bats Both	R	.225	138	31	3	2	4	15	9	33	.287	.362
Hillenbrand,Shea	L	.269	119	32	10	0	1	12	6	16	.323	.378
Bats Right	R	.299	515	154	33	4	17	71	19	79	.332	.478
Hinch,A.J.	L	.276	76	21	3	0	2	6	6	13	.345	.395
Bats Right	R	.231	121	28	4	1	5	21	12	22	.306	.405
Hinske,Eric	L	.202	124	25	5	0	4	17	15	38	.293	.339
Bats Left	R	.301	442	133	33	2	20	67	62	100	.384	.520
Hocking,Denny	L	.342	76	26	7	0	0	12	10	16	.404	.434
Bats Both	R	.212	184	39	6	0	2	13	14	28	.269	.277
Hollandsworth,Todd	L	.228	57	13	2	0	1	5	6	16	.302	.316
Bats Left	R	.292	373	109	25	1	15	62	34	82	.350	.485
Hollins,Dave	L	.125	16	2	0	0	0	0	0	3	.176	.125
Bats Both	R	.000	1	0	0	0	0	0	0	0	.000	.000
Hoover,Paul	L	.500	4	2	0	0	0	2	0	1	.500	.500
Bats Right	R	.077	13	1	0	0	0	0	0	4	.077	.077
Houston,Tyler	L	.259	27	7	0	1	0	2	0	5	.259	.333
Bats Left	R	.283	293	83	20	2	7	38	16	57	.328	.437
Hubbard,Trenidad	L	.204	54	11	2	0	1	3	8	12	.302	.296
Bats Right	R	.213	75	16	3	0	0	4	6	16	.272	.253
Huckaby,Ken	L	.274	62	17	1	0	0	3	4	9	.318	.290
Bats Right	R	.237	211	50	5	1	3	19	5	35	.255	.313

Batter	vs	Avg	AB	H	2B	3B	HR	RBI	BB	SO	OBP	Slg
Hudson,Orlando	L	.184	49	9	3	1	0	4	0	8	.184	.286
Bats Both	R	.308	143	44	7	4	4	19	11	19	.361	.497
Huff,Aubrey	L	.307	127	39	13	0	4	15	12	20	.362	.504
Bats Left	R	.315	327	103	12	0	19	44	25	35	.365	.526
Hundley,Todd	L	.217	46	10	1	0	2	6	8	14	.345	.370
Bats Both	R	.209	220	46	7	0	14	29	24	66	.291	.432
Hunter,Brian	L	.241	108	26	7	2	1	12	11	17	.311	.370
Bats Right	R	.301	93	28	9	1	2	8	5	22	.350	.484
Hunter,Torii	L	.296	169	50	16	1	6	23	12	38	.346	.509
Bats Right	R	.286	392	112	21	3	23	71	23	80	.329	.531
Hyzdu,Adam	L	.204	49	10	2	0	4	13	7	16	.298	.490
Bats Right	R	.245	106	26	4	0	7	21	14	28	.336	.481
Ibanez,Raul	L	.274	124	34	9	2	1	23	2	28	.291	.403
Bats Left	R	.300	373	112	28	4	23	80	38	48	.363	.582
Infante,Omar	L	.417	12	5	1	0	0	1	0	2	.417	.500
Bats Right	R	.317	60	19	2	0	1	5	3	8	.349	.400
Inge,Brandon	L	.229	70	16	4	0	3	6	4	23	.270	.414
Bats Right	R	.195	251	49	11	3	4	18	20	78	.264	.311
Izturis,Cesar	L	.306	147	45	9	1	1	13	6	9	.331	.401
Bats Both	R	.195	292	57	15	1	0	18	8	30	.214	.253
Jackson,Damian	L	.217	60	13	4	0	0	7	8	7	.309	.283
Bats Right	R	.270	185	50	16	1	1	18	13	29	.324	.384
Jackson,Ryan	L	-	0	0	0	0	0	0	0	0	-	-
Bats Left	R	.333	6	2	1	1	0	0	1	2	.429	.833
Jenkins,Geoff	L	.200	65	13	3	1	2	7	2	23	.232	.369
Bats Left	R	.258	178	46	14	0	8	22	20	37	.350	.472
Jensen,Marcus	L	.133	15	2	0	0	0	0	2	2	.235	.133
Bats Both	R	.100	20	2	0	0	1	4	2	9	.174	.250
Jeter,Derek	L	.315	124	39	4	0	5	13	18	23	.410	.468
Bats Right	R	.292	520	152	22	0	13	62	55	91	.364	.410
Jimenez,D'Angelo	L	.261	138	36	6	1	0	11	15	20	.331	.319
Bats Both	R	.247	291	72	9	6	4	33	35	53	.329	.361
Johnson,Charles	L	.275	51	14	7	0	1	9	5	11	.333	.471
Bats Right	R	.202	193	39	12	0	5	27	26	50	.293	.342
Johnson,Mark L	L	.095	21	2	1	0	0	0	1	6	.136	.143
Bats Left	R	.219	242	53	7	1	4	18	29	46	.310	.306
Johnson,Mark P	L	.000	6	0	0	0	0	0	0	4	.000	.000
Bats Left	R	.156	45	7	4	0	1	4	9	14	.296	.311
Johnson,Nick	L	.175	63	11	2	0	2	13	9	23	.316	.302
Bats Left	R	.257	315	81	13	0	13	45	39	75	.354	.422
Johnson,Russ	L	.208	24	5	2	0	1	3	5	1	.345	.417
Bats Right	R	.218	87	19	3	0	0	9	11	21	.313	.253
Jones,Andruw	L	.228	79	18	5	0	2	14	19	22	.370	.367
Bats Right	R	.270	481	130	29	0	33	80	64	113	.365	.536
Jones,Chipper	L	.320	100	32	7	0	4	15	14	16	.400	.510
Bats Both	R	.328	448	147	28	1	22	85	93	73	.442	.542
Jones,Jacque	L	.213	160	34	8	1	3	17	10	50	.259	.331
Bats Left	R	.333	417	139	29	1	24	68	27	79	.372	.580
Jordan,Brian	L	.303	109	33	10	0	6	28	7	18	.347	.560
Bats Right	R	.279	362	101	17	3	12	52	27	68	.335	.442
Jose,Felix	L	.143	7	1	0	0	1	1	2	4	.333	.571
Bats Both	R	.333	12	4	0	0	1	3	2	4	.375	.583
Justice,David	L	.257	105	27	6	1	1	8	10	21	.328	.362
Bats Left	R	.270	293	79	12	2	10	41	60	45	.392	.427
Kapler,Gabe	L	.250	100	25	8	2	0	7	7	16	.296	.370
Bats Right	R	.293	215	63	8	2	2	27	9	37	.322	.377
Karros,Eric	L	.317	101	32	8	0	3	17	13	6	.397	.485
Bats Right	R	.260	423	110	18	1	10	56	24	68	.304	.378
Kearns,Austin	L	.330	91	30	4	0	2	9	25	17	.474	.440
Bats Right	R	.310	281	87	20	3	11	47	29	64	.382	.520
Kendall,Jason	L	.275	109	30	4	1	1	9	23	4	.403	.358
Bats Right	R	.284	436	124	21	2	2	35	26	25	.335	.356
Kennedy,Adam	L	.275	69	19	3	0	3	9	2	16	.320	.449
Bats Left	R	.319	405	129	29	6	4	43	17	64	.350	.449
Kent,Jeff	L	.366	145	53	11	0	11	24	18	14	.439	.669
Bats Right	R	.297	478	142	31	2	26	84	34	87	.346	.533
Kielty,Bobby	L	.264	91	24	6	0	4	14	16	18	.380	.462
Bats Both	R	.303	198	60	8	3	8	32	36	48	.417	.495
Kingsale,Gene	L	.293	41	12	1	0	1	3	3	9	.356	.390
Bats Both	R	.281	178	50	9	3	1	25	17	38	.348	.382
Kinkade,Mike	L	.400	30	12	4	0	2	7	1	7	.486	.733
Bats Right	R	.350	20	7	1	0	0	4	3	3	.480	.400
Klassen,Danny	L	.000	1	0	0	0	0	0	0	1	.000	.000
Bats Right	R	.500	2	1	0	0	0	0	0	0	.500	.500
Klesko,Ryan	L	.287	157	45	8	0	8	32	20	32	.372	.490
Bats Left	R	.305	383	117	31	1	21	63	56	54	.394	.556

Batters vs. Left-Handed and Right-Handed Pitchers

Batter	vs	Avg	AB	H	2B	3B	HR	RBI	BB	SO	OBP	Slg
Knoblauch,Chuck	L	.231	78	18	1	0	1	2	10	8	.315	.282
Bats Right	R	.203	222	45	8	0	5	20	18	24	.273	.306
Konerko,Paul	L	.279	122	34	3	0	5	19	9	10	.328	.426
Bats Right	R	.310	448	139	27	0	22	85	35	62	.367	.518
Koskie,Corey	L	.253	162	41	11	1	5	15	24	55	.361	.426
Bats Left	R	.274	328	90	26	2	10	54	48	72	.371	.457
Kotsay,Mark	L	.324	188	61	11	3	5	20	14	34	.372	.495
Bats Left	R	.277	390	108	16	4	12	41	45	55	.352	.431
Kreuter,Chad	L	.462	26	12	2	0	2	6	4	7	.533	.769
Bats Both	R	.188	69	13	3	0	0	6	6	24	.256	.232
Lamb,David	L	.000	2	0	0	0	0	0	0	1	.000	.000
Bats Left	R	.125	8	1	0	0	0	0	0	1	.125	.125
Lamb,Mike	L	.211	38	8	2	0	0	4	6	4	.326	.263
Bats Left	R	.293	276	81	11	0	9	29	27	44	.358	.431
Lampkin,Tom	L	.167	48	8	1	0	1	3	1	9	.184	.250
Bats Left	R	.227	233	53	9	1	9	34	37	50	.336	.391
Lane,Jason	L	.349	43	15	2	1	4	10	7	5	.431	.721
Bats Right	R	.192	26	5	1	0	0	3	3	7	.276	.231
Langerhans,Ryan	L	-	0	0	0	0	0	0	0	0	-	-
Bats Left	R	.000	1	0	0	0	0	0	0	0	.000	.000
Lankford,Ray	L	.194	31	6	2	0	0	2	6	10	.359	.258
Bats Left	R	.230	174	40	5	1	6	24	24	51	.320	.374
Larkin,Barry	L	.189	122	23	10	1	3	11	20	13	.299	.361
Bats Right	R	.262	385	101	27	1	4	36	24	44	.307	.369
LaRocca,Greg	L	.333	18	6	1	0	0	2	3	2	.455	.389
Bats Right	R	.235	34	8	2	1	0	2	3	4	.316	.353
Larson,Brandon	L	.308	26	8	1	0	4	9	4	5	.419	.808
Bats Right	R	.240	25	6	1	0	0	4	2	5	.296	.280
LaRue,Jason	L	.207	92	19	4	0	2	5	6	30	.291	.315
Bats Right	R	.264	261	69	13	1	10	47	21	87	.336	.437
Lawrence,Joe	L	.171	41	7	1	0	2	5	5	10	.271	.341
Bats Right	R	.183	109	20	3	0	0	10	11	28	.258	.211
Lawton,Matt	L	.178	118	21	2	1	5	16	19	13	.297	.339
Bats Left	R	.258	298	77	17	1	10	41	40	21	.359	.423
LeCroy,Matt	L	.289	90	26	6	0	5	16	8	12	.347	.522
Bats Right	R	.231	91	21	5	1	2	11	5	26	.265	.374
Ledee,Ricky	L	.080	25	2	1	0	0	1	9		.115	.120
Bats Left	R	.247	178	44	12	1	8	23	34	41	.369	.461
Lee,Carlos	L	.295	112	33	6	1	3	13	20	11	.400	.446
Bats Right	R	.255	380	97	20	1	23	67	55	62	.347	.495
Lee,Derrek	L	.264	125	33	5	2	6	18	25	35	.391	.480
Bats Right	R	.272	456	124	30	5	21	68	73	129	.374	.498
Lee,Travis	L	.282	142	40	3	2	6	20	12	28	.338	.458
Bats Left	R	.259	394	102	23	0	7	50	42	76	.329	.371
Leon,Jose	L	.290	62	18	1	0	3	8	1	16	.302	.452
Bats Right	R	.148	27	4	1	0	0	2	2	4	.233	.185
Lesher,Brian	L	.200	20	4	1	0	0	0	3	10	.304	.250
Bats Right	R	.056	18	1	0	0	0	2	1	5	.100	.056
Lewis,Darren	L	.264	53	14	2	1	0	7	3	9	.328	.340
Bats Right	R	.192	26	5	1	0	0	0	4	2	.323	.231
Lieberthal,Mike	L	.346	107	37	9	1	6	12	12	8	.426	.617
Bats Right	R	.260	369	96	20	1	9	40	26	50	.326	.393
Liefer,Jeff	L	.300	10	3	0	0	1	4	2	6	.417	.600
Bats Left	R	.227	194	44	8	0	6	22	17	54	.288	.361
Little,Mark	L	.187	75	14	2	2	0	5	8	18	.307	.267
Bats Right	R	.236	55	13	3	1	0	2	7	16	.354	.327
Lo Duca,Paul	L	.307	137	42	13	1	2	20	9	5	.351	.460
Bats Right	R	.273	443	121	25	0	8	44	25	26	.323	.384
Lockhart,Keith	L	.067	15	1	0	0	0	1	0	1	.125	.267
Bats Left	R	.224	281	63	13	3	4	30	27	43	.290	.335
Lofton,Kenny	L	.248	109	27	6	2	0	8	11	12	.322	.339
Bats Left	R	.265	423	112	24	7	11	43	61	61	.357	.433
Lombard,George	L	.152	33	5	1	0	0	2	1	13	.200	.182
Bats Left	R	.255	208	53	10	3	5	11	19	65	.316	.404
Long,Terrence	L	.250	156	39	9	1	3	15	9	29	.295	.378
Bats Left	R	.237	431	102	23	3	13	52	39	67	.300	.394
Lopez,Felipe	L	.303	66	20	5	0	3	14	3	17	.338	.515
Bats Both	R	.204	216	44	10	3	5	20	20	73	.271	.347
Lopez,Javy	L	.255	51	13	3	0	2	11	6	11	.333	.431
Bats Right	R	.230	296	68	12	0	9	41	20	52	.293	.361
Lopez,Luis	L	.208	24	5	1	0	0	0	1	1	.240	.250
Bats Both	R	.194	93	18	5	0	2	10	4	20	.227	.312
Lopez,Mendy	L	.000	1	0	0	0	0	0	0	1	.000	.000
Bats Right	R	.000	2	0	0	0	0	0	0	2	.000	.000
Loretta,Mark	L	.309	94	29	7	0	2	8	19	13	.421	.447
Bats Right	R	.302	189	57	11	0	2	19	13	24	.359	.392
Lowell,Mike	L	.255	145	37	9	0	4	13	15	16	.323	.400
Bats Right	R	.283	452	128	35	0	20	79	50	76	.353	.493
Ludwick,Ryan	L	.167	18	3	0	0	1	3	1	5	.211	.333
Bats Right	R	.254	63	16	6	0	0	6	6	19	.319	.349
Lugo,Julio	L	.270	74	20	1	0	3	10	5	18	.313	.405
Bats Right	R	.258	248	64	14	1	5	25	23	56	.325	.383
Lunar,Fernando	L	-	0	0	0	0	0	0	0	0	-	-
Bats Right	R	-	0	0	0	0	0	0	0	0	-	-
Lunsford,Trey	L	-	0	0	0	0	0	0	0	0	-	-
Bats Right	R	.667	3	2	1	0	0	1	0	1	.667	1.000
Mabry,John	L	.192	26	5	1	0	1	2	0	7	.185	.346
Bats Left	R	.287	188	54	12	1	10	41	15	35	.338	.521
Machado,Robert	L	.226	62	14	2	1	1	7	6	15	.290	.339
Bats Right	R	.275	149	41	12	0	2	15	11	26	.327	.396
Macias,Jose	L	.250	108	27	10	0	0	8	6	15	.291	.343
Bats Both	R	.248	230	57	11	1	7	31	15	42	.294	.396
Mackowiak,Rob	L	.302	43	13	2	0	4	7	6	8	.400	.628
Bats Left	R	.237	342	81	20	0	12	41	36	112	.319	.401
Magee,Wendell	L	.236	89	21	6	0	1	6	1	16	.242	.337
Bats Right	R	.283	258	73	13	1	5	29	9	48	.305	.399
Magruder,Chris	L	.275	91	25	5	0	3	11	11	16	.283	.429
Bats Both	R	.186	167	31	10	1	3	18	14	39	.250	.311
Mahoney,Mike	L	.300	10	3	2	0	0	3	0	2	.300	.500
Bats Right	R	.158	19	3	1	0	0	0	1	8	.200	.211
Malloy,Marty	L	.000	4	0	0	0	0	0	0	2	.000	.000
Bats Left	R	.143	21	3	0	0	0	1	2	6	.217	.143
Marrero,Eli	L	.227	97	22	8	1	1	19	14	14	.321	.361
Bats Right	R	.273	300	82	11	0	17	47	26	58	.328	.480
Martinez,Edgar	L	.306	85	26	8	0	6	14	26	14	.469	.612
Bats Right	R	.267	243	65	15	0	9	45	41	55	.378	.440
Martinez,Ramon	L	.254	59	15	4	2	1	8	8	7	.348	.441
Bats Right	R	.279	122	34	6	0	3	17	6	19	.328	.402
Martinez,Tino	L	.207	111	23	3	0	4	12	14	21	.294	.342
Bats Left	R	.278	400	111	22	1	17	63	44	50	.350	.465
Martinez,Victor	L	.444	9	4	0	0	1	3	1	0	.455	.778
Bats Both	R	.217	23	5	1	0	0	2	2	2	.280	.261
Mateo,Henry	L	.000	3	0	0	0	0	0	0	1	.000	.000
Bats Both	R	.200	20	4	0	1	0	0	2	5	.273	.300
Mateo,Ruben	L	.161	31	5	2	0	0	1	2	10	.257	.226
Bats Right	R	.309	55	17	4	0	2	6	4	10	.356	.491
Matheny,Mike	L	.265	68	18	5	0	0	6	7	9	.333	.338
Bats Right	R	.239	247	59	7	1	3	29	25	40	.307	.312
Matos,Julius	L	.200	75	15	0	0	0	4	5	16	.259	.200
Bats Right	R	.264	110	29	3	0	2	15	4	17	.293	.345
Matos,Luis	L	.160	25	4	1	0	0	1	1	4	.192	.200
Bats Right	R	.000	6	0	0	0	0	0	0	2	.000	.000
Matthews Jr,Gary	L	.239	109	26	7	1	1	10	10	23	.303	.349
Bats Both	R	.292	236	69	18	2	6	28	33	46	.376	.462
Mayne,Brent	L	.162	68	11	0	0	1	2	2	20	.208	.206
Bats Left	R	.256	258	66	8	2	3	28	32	34	.333	.337
McCarty,Dave	L	.188	32	6	1	0	2	4	2	8	.257	.406
Bats Right	R	.088	34	3	0	0	0	0	4	11	.205	.088
McCracken,Quinton	L	.306	144	44	10	3	0	11	13	22	.367	.417
Bats Both	R	.312	205	64	17	5	3	29	19	46	.367	.488
McDonald,Donzell	L	.286	7	2	1	0	0	0	0	2	.286	.429
Bats Both	R	.133	15	2	1	0	0	1	4	3	.300	.200
McDonald,John	L	.232	69	16	2	2	1	8	4	11	.280	.362
Bats Right	R	.256	195	50	9	1	0	4	6	39	.291	.313
McEwing,Joe	L	.204	93	19	4	0	2	12	3	28	.232	.312
Bats Right	R	.194	103	20	4	1	1	14	6	22	.250	.282
McGriff,Fred	L	.213	141	30	8	1	2	22	16	39	.294	.326
Bats Left	R	.296	382	113	19	1	28	81	47	60	.375	.571
McGuire,Ryan	L	-	0	0	0	0	0	0	0	0	-	-
Bats Left	R	.077	26	2	1	0	0	2	2	7	.143	.115
McKay,Cody	L	.500	2	1	0	0	0	0	0	1	.500	.500
Bats Left	R	1.000	1	1	0	0	0	2	0	0	.500	1.000
McKeel,Walt	L	.000	1	0	0	0	0	0	0	1	.000	.000
Bats Right	R	.333	12	4	0	0	0	0	2	5	.333	.333
McLemore,Mark	L	.152	33	5	1	0	1	10	11	8	.348	.273
Bats Both	R	.283	304	86	16	2	6	31	50	55	.384	.408
Meluskey,Mitch	L	.143	7	1	0	0	0	0	0	0	.143	.143
Bats Both	R	.250	20	5	0	0	0	1	5	2	.407	.250
Mench,Kevin	L	.269	108	29	2	0	8	21	7	16	.316	.509
Bats Right	R	.256	258	66	18	2	7	39	24	67	.331	.422
Menechino,Frank	L	.185	54	10	3	0	1	6	8	9	.290	.296
Bats Right	R	.218	78	17	4	0	2	9	12	23	.326	.346

291

Batters vs. Left-Handed and Right-Handed Pitchers

Batter	vs	Avg	AB	H	2B	3B	HR	RBI	BB	SO	OBP	Slg
Merced,Orlando	L	.231	39	9	1	1	2	6	2	10	.262	.462
Bats Left	R	.297	212	63	12	2	4	24	24	40	.366	.429
Merloni,Lou	L	.321	56	18	6	1	1	8	7	8	.406	.518
Bats Right	R	.217	138	30	6	1	3	10	13	27	.301	.341
Michaels,Jason	L	.242	62	15	8	0	1	5	7	17	.314	.419
Bats Right	R	.302	43	13	2	3	1	6	6	16	.392	.558
Mientkiewicz,Doug	L	.257	152	39	11	0	4	22	21	24	.361	.408
Bats Left	R	.263	315	83	18	1	6	42	53	45	.366	.384
Millar,Kevin	L	.317	104	33	8	0	3	9	12	12	.390	.481
Bats Right	R	.302	334	101	33	0	13	48	28	62	.358	.518
Miller,Corky	L	.412	17	7	5	0	1	3	1	1	.444	.882
Bats Right	R	.227	97	22	5	0	2	12	8	19	.309	.340
Miller,Damian	L	.275	91	25	10	0	2	11	18	27	.394	.451
Bats Right	R	.238	206	49	12	0	9	31	20	61	.314	.427
Minor,Damon	L	.250	44	11	2	0	3	10	5	10	.327	.500
Bats Left	R	.233	129	30	4	0	7	14	19	24	.336	.426
Mirabelli,Doug	L	.364	44	16	2	0	5	12	5	9	.440	.750
Bats Right	R	.168	107	18	5	0	2	13	12	24	.260	.271
Moeller,Chad	L	.120	25	3	0	0	1	1	6	7	.290	.240
Bats Right	R	.338	80	27	11	1	1	15	11	16	.418	.538
Mohr,Dustan	L	.203	133	27	9	0	3	11	17	34	.293	.338
Bats Right	R	.304	250	76	14	2	9	34	14	52	.343	.484
Molina,Ben	L	.248	125	31	7	0	1	12	5	4	.278	.328
Bats Right	R	.244	303	74	11	0	4	35	10	30	.272	.320
Molina,Izzy	L	-	0	0	0	0	0	0	0	0		
Bats Right	R	.333	3	1	0	0	0	0	0	0	.333	.333
Molina,Jose	L	.100	20	2	0	0	0	0	2	4	.182	.100
Bats Right	R	.340	50	17	3	0	0	5	3	11	.364	.400
Mondesi,Raul	L	.244	135	33	8	1	8	20	22	21	.346	.496
Bats Right	R	.228	434	99	26	0	18	68	37	82	.295	.412
Monroe,Craig	L	.000	6	0	0	0	0	0	0	1	.000	.000
Bats Right	R	.158	19	3	1	0	1	1	0	4	.200	.368
Mora,Melvin	L	.240	146	35	8	0	4	12	18	24	.329	.377
Bats Right	R	.231	411	95	22	4	15	52	52	84	.341	.414
Mordecai,Mike	L	.282	78	22	5	0	5	8	13	13	.356	.346
Bats Right	R	.205	73	15	3	0	0	6	5	14	.266	.247
Moriarty,Mike	L	.333	3	1	1	0	0	2	0	0	.333	.667
Bats Right	R	.154	13	2	0	0	0	1	0	2	.154	.154
Morris,Warren	L	-	0	0	0	0	0	0	0	0		
Bats Left	R	.000	7	0	0	0	0	0	0	1	.000	.000
Mueller,Bill	L	.221	68	15	3	1	3	11	8	15	.295	.426
Bats Both	R	.272	298	81	16	3	4	27	44	27	.362	.386
Munson,Eric	L	.200	15	3	0	0	0	0	1	5	.250	.200
Bats Left	R	.182	44	8	0	0	2	5	5	6	.275	.318
Murray,Calvin	L	.190	21	4	2	0	0	1	1	5	.227	.286
Bats Both	R	.132	68	9	3	1	0	0	6	12	.213	.206
Myers,Greg	L	.200	25	5	1	0	0	2	2	8	.259	.240
Bats Left	R	.227	119	27	4	0	6	19	24	28	.357	.412
Nelson,Bry	L	.500	12	6	2	0	0	0	0	0	.500	.667
Bats Both	R	.136	22	3	1	0	0	2	4	1	.269	.182
Nevin,Phil	L	.337	101	34	5	0	5	22	14	12	.407	.535
Bats Right	R	.268	306	82	11	0	7	35	24	75	.322	.373
Nieves,Jose	L	.353	51	18	2	0	0	3	2	6	.377	.392
Bats Right	R	.217	46	10	0	0	0	3	0	8	.217	.217
Nieves,Wil	L	.188	32	6	3	1	0	3	3	7	.257	.344
Bats Right	R	.175	40	7	0	0	0	0	1	8	.195	.175
Nixon,Trot	L	.233	116	27	5	0	3	15	11	39	.303	.353
Bats Left	R	.262	416	109	31	3	21	79	54	70	.348	.502
Norton,Greg	L	.167	30	5	1	0	0	0	5	8	.278	.200
Bats Both	R	.232	138	32	7	1	7	33	19	44	.323	.449
Nunez,Abraham	L	.143	7	1	0	0	0	1	0	3	.143	.143
Bats Both	R	.100	10	1	0	0	0	0	0	2	.100	.100
Nunez,Abraham O	L	.176	34	6	2	0	0	2	4	10	.282	.235
Bats Both	R	.242	219	53	12	1	2	13	23	34	.316	.333
Ochoa,Alex	L	.272	114	31	4	0	3	14	15	13	.362	.386
Bats Right	R	.253	166	42	12	0	5	17	27	22	.361	.416
Offerman,Jose	L	.216	74	16	3	0	0	5	12	10	.322	.257
Bats Both	R	.238	210	50	9	1	5	26	25	28	.319	.362
Ojeda,Augie	L	.130	23	3	1	0	0	1	1	2	.200	.174
Bats Both	R	.213	47	10	3	0	0	3	4	3	.269	.277
O'Leary,Troy	L	.351	37	13	2	0	0	8	8	2	.467	.405
Bats Left	R	.275	236	65	10	2	3	29	26	45	.355	.373
Olerud,John	L	.287	164	47	14	0	3	33	25	20	.376	.427
Bats Left	R	.306	389	119	25	0	19	69	73	46	.414	.517
Olivo,Miguel	L	.143	7	1	0	0	1	3	1	2	.250	.571
Bats Right	R	.250	12	3	1	0	0	2	1	3	.308	.333

Batter	vs	Avg	AB	H	2B	3B	HR	RBI	BB	SO	OBP	Slg
Ordaz,Luis	L	.200	25	5	1	0	0	1	2	3	.250	.240
Bats Right	R	.232	69	16	1	0	0	3	10	10	.329	.246
Ordonez,Magglio	L	.288	125	36	13	1	9	28	13	23	.357	.624
Bats Right	R	.329	465	153	34	0	29	107	40	54	.388	.589
Ordonez,Rey	L	.193	119	23	4	0	0	3	7	9	.236	.227
Bats Right	R	.276	341	94	21	2	1	39	17	37	.311	.358
Orie,Kevin	L	1.000	1	1	0	0	0	1	0	0	1.000	1.000
Bats Right	R	.258	31	8	3	0	0	4	1	4	.286	.355
Ortiz,David	L	.203	118	24	6	0	5	18	6	30	.256	.381
Bats Left	R	.299	294	88	26	1	15	57	37	57	.371	.548
Ortiz,Hector	L	-	0	0	0	0	0	0	0	0		
Bats Right	R	.214	14	3	1	0	1	2	1	1	.267	.500
Ortiz,Jose	L	.233	43	10	2	1	0	1	4	7	.298	.326
Bats Right	R	.255	149	38	5	0	1	11	12	23	.319	.309
Osik,Keith	L	.091	22	2	0	0	1	4	1	7	.125	.227
Bats Right	R	.179	78	14	3	0	1	7	5	18	.235	.256
Overbay,Lyle	L	-	0	0	0	0	0	0	0	0	-	-
Bats Left	R	.100	10	1	0	0	0	1	0	5	.100	.100
Owens,Eric	L	.266	94	25	0	2	1	6	10	7	.337	.340
Bats Right	R	.271	291	79	15	3	3	31	21	26	.319	.375
Ozuna,Pablo	L	.071	14	1	0	0	0	0	0	1	.133	.071
Bats Right	R	.364	33	12	2	2	0	3	1	2	.371	.545
Palmeiro,Orlando	L	.412	34	14	1	0	0	2	6	3	.500	.441
Bats Left	R	.284	225	65	11	1	0	29	24	19	.348	.341
Palmeiro,Rafael	L	.220	159	35	9	0	10	33	22	29	.315	.465
Bats Left	R	.295	387	114	25	0	33	72	82	65	.420	.615
Palmer,Dean	L	.000	7	0	0	0	0	0	0	3	.000	.000
Bats Right	R	.000	5	0	0	0	0	0	1	2	.167	.000
Paquette,Craig	L	.271	59	16	4	0	0	3	3	10	.306	.339
Bats Right	R	.171	193	33	10	1	4	17	7	43	.197	.295
Patterson,Corey	L	.188	149	28	3	1	2	14	2	40	.215	.262
Bats Left	R	.275	443	122	27	4	12	40	17	102	.307	.436
Paul,Josh	L	.250	44	11	2	0	0	6	5	8	.327	.295
Bats Right	R	.233	60	14	2	0	0	5	4	14	.284	.267
Payton,Jay	L	.252	135	34	5	2	4	13	9	15	.308	.407
Bats Right	R	.326	310	101	15	5	12	46	20	39	.369	.523
Pelaez,Alex	L	.333	6	2	0	0	0	0	0	0	.333	.333
Bats Right	R	.000	2	0	0	0	0	0	0	0	.000	.000
Pellow,Kit	L	.225	40	9	0	0	0	2	3	14	.295	.225
Bats Right	R	.261	23	6	1	0	1	3	6	7	.414	.435
Pena,Carlos	L	.265	132	35	8	2	8	23	12	41	.333	.538
Bats Left	R	.230	265	61	9	2	11	29	29	70	.307	.404
Pena,Wily Mo	L	.143	7	1	0	0	1	1	0	6	.143	.571
Bats Right	R	.273	11	3	0	0	0	0	0	5	.273	.273
Perez,Eddie	L	.222	45	10	4	0	0	3	1	9	.239	.311
Bats Right	R	.208	72	15	5	0	0	1	4	16	.260	.278
Perez,Eduardo	L	.271	70	19	0	0	6	13	9	13	.354	.643
Bats Right	R	.143	84	12	1	0	4	13	8	23	.237	.298
Perez,Neifi	L	.227	154	35	7	0	2	10	5	15	.250	.312
Bats Both	R	.240	400	96	13	4	1	27	15	38	.264	.300
Perez,Timo	L	.156	64	10	2	0	0	3	4	8	.206	.188
Bats Left	R	.318	380	121	25	6	8	44	19	28	.352	.479
Perez,Tomas	L	.250	92	23	6	0	2	5	6	13	.296	.380
Bats Both	R	.250	120	30	7	1	3	15	15	27	.336	.400
Perry,Chan	L	.000	4	0	0	0	0	0	1	0	.000	.000
Bats Right	R	.143	7	1	0	0	0	0	0	0	.143	.143
Perry,Herbert	L	.260	127	33	8	0	6	22	10	21	.324	.465
Bats Right	R	.282	323	91	16	1	16	55	24	45	.337	.486
Petrick,Ben	L	.250	52	13	0	0	4	5	5	14	.316	.481
Bats Right	R	.163	43	7	3	1	1	6	4	19	.245	.349
Phelps,Josh	L	.286	49	14	4	0	1	10	6	18	.364	.429
Bats Right	R	.315	216	68	16	1	14	48	13	64	.362	.593
Phillips,Brandon	L	.444	9	4	1	0	0	0	2	1	.545	.556
Bats Right	R	.182	22	4	2	1	0	4	1	5	.250	.364
Phillips,Jason	L	.000	2	0	0	0	0	0	1	0	.333	.000
Bats Right	R	.412	17	7	0	0	1	3	0	1	.421	.588
Piatt,Adam	L	.233	43	10	3	0	2	6	4	12	.298	.442
Bats Right	R	.234	94	22	5	0	3	12	8	21	.305	.383
Piazza,Mike	L	.286	126	36	11	0	8	26	22	18	.396	.563
Bats Right	R	.278	352	98	12	2	25	72	35	64	.344	.537
Pierre,Juan	L	.294	126	37	1	0	0	3	1	7	.326	.302
Bats Left	R	.285	466	133	19	5	1	32	30	45	.334	.354
Pierzynski,A.J.	L	.270	89	24	3	1	2	13	1	15	.280	.393
Bats Right	R	.308	351	108	28	5	4	36	12	46	.348	.450
Podsednik,Scott	L	.000	2	0	0	0	0	0	0	0	.000	.000
Bats Left	R	.222	18	4	0	0	1	4	4	6	.348	.389

Batter	vs	Avg	AB	H	2B	3B	HR	RBI	BB	SO	OBP	Slg
Polanco,Placido	L	.338	151	51	12	1	3	12	10	7	.390	.490
Bats Right	R	.270	397	107	20	1	6	37	16	34	.306	.370
Posada,Jorge	L	.326	135	44	16	0	5	25	22	33	.420	.556
Bats Both	R	.247	376	93	24	1	15	74	59	110	.351	.436
Pratt,Todd	L	.417	24	10	4	0	1	4	7	3	.563	.708
Bats Right	R	.280	82	23	7	0	2	12	17	25	.413	.439
Prince,Tom	L	.224	76	17	5	1	0	6	8	15	.326	.316
Bats Right	R	.224	49	11	2	0	4	10	6	11	.304	.510
Pujols,Albert	L	.309	152	47	15	1	8	32	20	17	.391	.579
Bats Right	R	.315	438	138	25	1	26	95	52	52	.395	.555
Punto,Nick	L	.000	2	0	0	0	0	0	0	1	.000	.000
Bats Both	R	.250	4	1	0	0	0	0	0	2	.250	.250
Quinn,Mark	L	.348	23	8	1	0	1	6	2	2	.423	.522
Bats Right	R	.189	53	10	3	0	1	5	3	13	.246	.302
Raines,Tim	L	.333	12	4	1	0	0	2	3	2	.438	.417
Bats Both	R	.169	77	13	2	0	1	5	19	17	.337	.234
Ramirez,Aramis	L	.260	123	32	5	0	9	20	8	24	.303	.520
Bats Right	R	.226	399	90	21	0	9	51	21	71	.272	.346
Ramirez,Julio	L	.304	23	7	0	1	1	5	1	9	.360	.522
Bats Right	R	.222	9	2	0	0	0	2	1	5	.300	.222
Ramirez,Manny	L	.438	73	32	10	0	6	21	15	9	.534	.822
Bats Right	R	.331	363	120	21	0	27	86	58	76	.433	.612
Randa,Joe	L	.321	131	42	10	1	2	19	14	14	.378	.458
Bats Right	R	.270	418	113	26	4	9	61	32	55	.330	.416
Ransom,Cody	L	-	0	0	0	0	0	0	0	0	-	-
Bats Right	R	.667	3	2	0	0	0	1	1	1	.750	.667
Reboulet,Jeff	L	.375	24	9	3	0	0	0	3	5	.444	.500
Bats Right	R	.042	24	1	0	0	0	2	3	8	.143	.042
Redmond,Mike	L	.286	70	20	2	0	1	6	4	10	.346	.357
Bats Right	R	.312	186	58	13	0	1	22	17	24	.381	.398
Reese,Pokey	L	.282	85	24	6	0	1	7	8	19	.340	.388
Bats Right	R	.259	336	87	19	0	3	43	33	62	.327	.342
Relaford,Desi	L	.202	89	18	1	0	1	7	12	13	.301	.247
Bats Both	R	.292	240	70	12	2	5	36	21	38	.353	.421
Renteria,Edgar	L	.288	125	36	9	0	3	12	17	19	.378	.432
Bats Right	R	.310	419	130	27	2	8	71	32	38	.359	.442
Restovich,Michael	L	.667	6	4	0	0	1	1	0	2	.667	1.167
Bats Right	R	.000	7	0	0	0	0	0	1	2	.125	.000
Richard,Chris	L	.250	16	4	0	0	0	1	1	3	.278	.250
Bats Left	R	.230	139	32	11	0	4	20	11	27	.294	.396
Rios,Armando	L	.300	30	9	1	0	1	6	2	6	.333	.433
Bats Left	R	.258	178	46	10	0	0	18	14	33	.316	.315
Rivas,Luis	L	.234	107	25	7	2	3	10	7	24	.287	.421
Bats Right	R	.268	209	56	16	2	1	25	12	27	.314	.378
Rivera,Juan	L	.200	10	2	0	0	0	0	2	1	.333	.200
Bats Right	R	.274	73	20	5	0	1	6	4	9	.308	.384
Rivera,Mike	L	.273	33	9	3	1	0	3	0	13	.273	.424
Bats Right	R	.212	99	21	5	0	1	8	4	22	.248	.293
Rivera,Ruben	L	.200	55	11	1	0	2	5	11	16	.338	.327
Bats Right	R	.214	103	22	3	0	2	9	6	29	.281	.301
Roberts,Brian	L	.146	41	6	1	0	0	3	1	8	.163	.171
Bats Both	R	.264	87	23	5	0	1	8	14	13	.369	.356
Roberts,Dave	L	.400	25	10	1	2	0	4	7	3	.531	.600
Bats Left	R	.270	397	107	13	5	3	30	41	48	.340	.350
Robinson,Kerry	L	.222	9	2	0	0	0	0	1	0	.300	.222
Bats Left	R	.262	172	45	7	4	1	15	10	29	.301	.366
Rodriguez,Alex	L	.239	159	38	8	1	8	24	22	34	.331	.453
Bats Right	R	.320	465	149	19	1	49	118	65	88	.412	.682
Rodriguez,Henry	L	.000	3	0	0	0	0	0	1	3	.250	.000
Bats Left	R	.059	17	1	0	0	0	3	3	5	.190	.059
Rodriguez,Ivan	L	.306	108	33	9	0	4	15	11	15	.372	.500
Bats Right	R	.317	300	95	23	2	15	45	14	56	.346	.557
Rogers,Eddie	L	-	0	0	0	0	0	0	0	0	-	-
Bats Right	R	.000	3	0	0	0	0	0	0	0	.000	.000
Rolen,Scott	L	.288	118	34	4	1	6	22	25	18	.413	.492
Bats Right	R	.260	462	120	25	7	25	88	47	84	.342	.506
Rollins,Jimmy	L	.243	173	42	6	4	3	15	13	22	.302	.376
Bats Both	R	.246	464	114	27	6	8	45	41	81	.308	.381
Rolls,Damian	L	.500	12	6	3	0	0	1	1	2	.538	.750
Bats Right	R	.260	77	20	3	1	0	5	2	14	.296	.325
Romano,Jason	L	.138	29	4	2	0	0	1	3	6	.219	.207
Bats Right	R	.306	62	19	2	1	0	4	4	18	.343	.371
Ross,Dave	L	.333	6	2	1	0	1	2	0	2	.429	1.000
Bats Right	R	.000	4	0	0	0	0	0	2	2	.333	.000
Rowand,Aaron	L	.265	98	26	4	1	5	13	8	15	.327	.480
Bats Right	R	.255	204	52	12	1	2	16	4	39	.284	.353
Ruan,Wilkin	L	.333	9	3	1	0	0	3	0	1	.333	.444
Bats Right	R	.000	2	0	0	0	0	0	0	1	.000	.000
Rushford,Jim	L	.182	11	2	1	0	0	1	0	3	.182	.273
Bats Left	R	.136	66	9	1	0	1	5	6	6	.219	.197
Ryan,Mike	L	.000	1	0	0	0	0	0	0	0	.000	.000
Bats Left	R	.100	10	1	0	0	0	0	0	2	.100	.100
Sadler,Donnie	L	.071	28	2	0	0	0	2	0	5	.069	.071
Bats Right	R	.200	70	14	2	1	0	5	7	14	.291	.257
Saenz,Olmedo	L	.317	63	20	2	1	4	10	5	15	.366	.571
Bats Right	R	.247	93	23	8	0	2	8	8	16	.346	.398
Salazar,Oscar	L	.200	10	2	1	0	0	1	0	1	.200	.300
Bats Right	R	.182	11	2	0	0	1	2	1	1	.250	.455
Salmon,Tim	L	.299	137	41	11	1	5	23	27	29	.411	.504
Bats Right	R	.280	346	97	26	0	17	65	44	73	.368	.503
Sanchez,Alex	L	.267	45	12	0	1	0	4	4	6	.327	.311
Bats Left	R	.292	349	102	10	6	1	29	27	56	.345	.364
Sanchez,Freddy	L	.333	3	1	0	0	0	2	1	0	.500	.333
Bats Right	R	.154	13	2	0	0	0	0	1	3	.214	.154
Sanchez,Rey	L	.273	77	21	3	3	0	7	3	4	.296	.390
Bats Right	R	.289	280	81	9	0	1	31	14	27	.323	.332
Sandberg,Jared	L	.209	86	18	4	1	4	6	10	30	.299	.419
Bats Right	R	.235	272	64	17	0	14	48	29	109	.307	.452
Sanders,Reggie	L	.289	121	35	4	1	8	19	13	20	.358	.537
Bats Right	R	.237	384	91	19	5	15	66	34	101	.313	.430
Santiago,Benito	L	.276	116	32	9	1	4	20	12	15	.341	.474
Bats Right	R	.279	362	101	15	4	12	54	15	58	.306	.442
Santiago,Ramon	L	.222	54	12	2	0	0	2	3	17	.276	.259
Bats Both	R	.250	168	42	3	5	4	18	10	31	.316	.399
Schneider,Brian	L	.280	25	7	1	1	0	2	2	7	.333	.400
Bats Left	R	.275	182	50	18	1	5	27	19	34	.340	.467
Scutaro,Marco	L	.000	7	0	0	0	0	0	0	4	.000	.000
Bats Right	R	.276	29	8	0	1	1	6	0	7	.267	.448
Sears,Todd	L	1.000	2	2	1	0	0	0	0	0	1.000	1.500
Bats Left	R	.200	10	2	1	0	0	0	0	1	.200	.300
Segui,David	L	.192	26	5	0	0	0	3	4	6	.300	.192
Bats Both	R	.290	69	20	4	0	2	13	7	16	.351	.435
Selby,Bill	L	.160	25	4	0	0	0	1	1	6	.192	.160
Bats Left	R	.224	134	30	7	2	6	20	14	21	.293	.440
Sexson,Richie	L	.238	101	24	8	0	3	18	14	28	.330	.406
Bats Right	R	.288	469	135	29	2	26	84	56	108	.371	.525
Sheets,Andy	L	.268	41	11	1	0	0	3	3	7	.311	.293
Bats Right	R	.241	108	26	3	0	4	19	9	34	.297	.380
Sheffield,Gary	L	.293	82	24	4	0	2	8	13	4	.408	.415
Bats Right	R	.310	410	127	22	0	23	76	59	49	.403	.532
Shinjo,Tsuyoshi	L	.291	110	32	4	3	4	20	6	11	.328	.491
Bats Right	R	.214	252	54	11	0	5	17	18	35	.279	.317
Shumpert,Terry	L	.294	85	25	6	1	3	11	9	8	.354	.494
Bats Right	R	.201	149	30	6	0	3	10	12	33	.275	.302
Sierra,Ruben	L	.266	143	38	10	0	1	14	4	20	.312	.357
Bats Both	R	.272	276	75	13	0	12	46	21	42	.322	.449
Simon,Randall	L	.255	141	36	2	0	3	14	2	7	.266	.333
Bats Left	R	.320	341	109	15	1	16	68	11	23	.342	.510
Singleton,Chris	L	.208	72	15	2	1	2	12	3	22	.250	.347
Bats Left	R	.272	394	107	28	5	7	38	18	61	.305	.421
Smith,Bobby	L	.154	13	2	0	0	0	2	0	3	.154	.154
Bats Right	R	.180	50	9	2	0	1	4	3	22	.226	.280
Smith,Jason	L	.000	5	0	0	0	0	0	0	0	.000	.000
Bats Left	R	.217	60	13	1	2	1	6	2	22	.242	.350
Snead,Esix	L	1.000	1	1	0	0	0	0	0	0	1.000	1.000
Bats Both	R	.250	12	3	0	0	1	3	1	4	.308	.500
Snelling,Chris	L	.000	3	0	0	0	0	0	0	0	.000	.000
Bats Left	R	.167	24	4	0	0	1	3	2	4	.231	.292
Snow,J.T.	L	.229	70	16	6	1	2	10	14	22	.382	.429
Bats Left	R	.250	352	88	20	1	4	43	45	68	.336	.347
Snyder,Earl	L	.192	26	5	1	0	1	3	1	11	.222	.346
Bats Right	R	.207	29	6	1	0	0	1	5	10	.324	.241
Soriano,Alfonso	L	.316	133	42	10	0	8	19	7	32	.359	.571
Bats Right	R	.297	563	167	41	2	31	83	16	125	.326	.542
Sosa,Sammy	L	.366	101	37	2	1	11	19	34	24	.526	.733
Bats Right	R	.270	455	123	17	1	38	89	69	120	.367	.563
Spencer,Shane	L	.267	75	20	6	0	1	8	13	15	.363	.387
Bats Right	R	.239	213	51	9	2	5	26	18	47	.309	.371
Spiezio,Scott	L	.368	152	56	8	0	6	35	24	16	.448	.539
Bats Both	R	.248	339	84	26	2	6	47	30	36	.336	.389
Spivey,Junior	L	.324	170	55	10	3	11	29	33	22	.441	.612
Bats Right	R	.291	368	107	24	3	5	49	32	78	.362	.413

Batters vs. Left-Handed and Right-Handed Pitchers

Batter	vs	Avg	AB	H	2B	3B	HR	RBI	BB	SO	OBP	Slg
Stairs,Matt	L	.154	13	2	0	0	0	1	1	2	.214	.154
Bats Left	R	.249	257	64	15	0	16	40	35	48	.355	.494
Stevens,Lee	L	.137	73	10	1	0	3	9	5	22	.192	.274
Bats Left	R	.221	285	63	12	2	12	48	49	67	.330	.404
Stewart,Shannon	L	.302	129	39	7	1	3	10	16	16	.392	.442
Bats Right	R	.304	448	136	31	5	7	35	38	44	.365	.442
Stinnett,Kelly	L	.286	21	6	1	0	1	5	5	7	.423	.476
Bats Right	R	.208	72	15	4	0	2	8	10	18	.305	.347
Stynes,Chris	L	.240	96	23	3	0	3	12	12	17	.321	.365
Bats Right	R	.242	99	24	6	1	2	14	9	12	.306	.384
Surhoff,B.J.	L	1.000	1	1	0	0	0	0	0	0	1.000	1.000
Bats Left	R	.284	74	21	5	0	0	9	9	5	.361	.351
Sutton,Larry	L	-	0	0	0	0	0	0	0	0	-	-
Bats Left	R	.105	19	2	0	0	1	3	1	8	.150	.263
Suzuki,Ichiro	L	.356	180	64	8	3	3	19	19	11	.416	.483
Bats Left	R	.308	467	144	19	5	5	32	49	51	.377	.403
Swann,Pedro	L	.000	1	0	0	0	0	0	0	1	.000	.000
Bats Left	R	.091	11	1	0	0	0	1	1	5	.167	.091
Sweeney,Mark	L	.083	12	1	1	0	0	1	1	3	.154	.167
Bats Left	R	.189	53	10	2	0	1	3	3	16	.232	.283
Sweeney,Mike	L	.357	112	40	6	0	6	19	11	10	.411	.571
Bats Right	R	.334	359	120	25	1	18	67	50	36	.418	.560
Taguchi,So	L	.500	10	5	0	0	0	2	1	0	.545	.500
Bats Right	R	.200	5	1	0	0	0	1	1	1	.333	.200
Tarasco,Tony	L	.333	9	3	0	0	0	2	1	1	.400	.333
Bats Right	R	.241	87	21	5	0	6	13	7	12	.295	.506
Tatis,Fernando	L	.230	87	20	5	0	5	15	9	19	.307	.460
Bats Right	R	.228	294	67	13	1	10	40	26	71	.302	.381
Taylor,Reggie	L	.184	38	7	0	1	0	1	1	13	.205	.237
Bats Left	R	.265	249	66	15	3	9	37	13	66	.303	.458
Tejada,Miguel	L	.285	137	39	5	0	9	26	11	15	.342	.518
Bats Right	R	.314	525	165	25	0	25	105	27	69	.357	.505
Thames,Marcus	L	.200	5	1	0	0	1	2	0	2	.200	.800
Bats Right	R	.250	8	2	1	0	0	0	0	2	.250	.375
Thomas,Frank	L	.214	117	25	5	0	6	19	25	22	.352	.410
Bats Right	R	.264	406	107	24	1	22	73	63	93	.364	.490
Thome,Jim	L	.245	159	39	4	0	12	32	27	55	.358	.497
Bats Left	R	.333	321	107	15	2	40	86	95	84	.485	.766
Thompson,Ryan	L	.300	50	15	3	1	2	8	3	8	.352	.520
Bats Right	R	.218	87	19	6	1	6	16	4	30	.261	.517
Thurston,Joe	L	.833	6	5	0	0	0	1	0	1	.714	.833
Bats Left	R	.143	7	1	1	0	0	0	0	0	.143	.286
Torcato,Tony	L	-	0	0	0	0	0	0	0	0	-	-
Bats Left	R	.273	11	3	1	0	0	0	0	2	.273	.364
Torrealba,Steve	L	.000	4	0	0	0	0	1	1	1	.200	.000
Bats Right	R	.077	13	1	0	0	0	0	2	3	.077	.077
Torrealba,Yorvit	L	.385	26	10	3	0	0	2	4	5	.484	.500
Bats Right	R	.255	110	28	7	0	2	12	10	15	.322	.373
Torres,Andres	L	.235	17	4	0	1	0	1	1	2	.278	.353
Bats Both	R	.189	53	10	1	0	0	2	5	14	.262	.208
Trammell,Bubba	L	.305	131	40	9	0	7	20	18	21	.387	.534
Bats Right	R	.213	272	58	7	1	10	36	35	50	.308	.357
Truby,Chris	L	.206	68	14	4	2	1	5	4	20	.260	.368
Bats Right	R	.217	314	68	14	2	3	17	6	78	.232	.303
Tucker,Michael	L	.208	77	16	5	0	3	10	10	21	.299	.390
Bats Left	R	.256	398	102	22	6	9	46	46	84	.336	.410
Tyner,Jason	L	.189	37	7	0	0	0	2	2	6	.231	.189
Bats Left	R	.221	131	29	2	1	0	9	5	13	.254	.252
Ugueto,Luis	L	.250	4	1	0	0	0	0	0	1	.250	.250
Bats Both	R	.211	19	4	0	0	1	1	2	7	.286	.368
Uribe,Juan	L	.241	141	34	5	2	1	18	8	28	.281	.326
Bats Right	R	.240	425	102	20	5	5	31	26	92	.288	.346
Valent,Eric	L	-	0	0	0	0	0	0	0	0	-	-
Bats Left	R	.200	10	2	0	0	0	0	0	3	.200	.200
Valentin,Javier	L	.333	3	1	0	0	0	0	0	0	.333	.333
Bats Both	R	1.000	1	1	0	0	0	0	0	0	1.000	1.000
Valentin,John	L	.178	73	13	3	0	1	5	12	17	.315	.260
Bats Right	R	.274	135	37	12	0	2	25	10	20	.353	.407
Valentin,Jose	L	.152	46	7	2	0	1	4	3	11	.204	.261
Bats Both	R	.259	428	111	24	4	24	71	40	88	.322	.502
Vander Wal,John	L	.238	21	5	2	0	0	1	0	8	.238	.333
Bats Left	R	.263	198	52	15	1	6	19	23	50	.335	.439
Varitek,Jason	L	.263	118	31	7	0	2	21	7	19	.318	.373
Bats Both	R	.266	349	93	20	1	8	40	34	76	.337	.398
Vaughn,Greg	L	.080	50	4	0	0	1	1	13	14	.281	.140
Bats Right	R	.184	201	37	10	2	7	28	28	68	.288	.358
Vaughn,Mo	L	.272	136	37	7	0	7	20	20	47	.381	.478
Bats Left	R	.254	351	89	11	0	19	52	39	98	.337	.447
Vazquez,Ramon	L	.157	70	11	2	0	0	4	2	17	.181	.186
Bats Left	R	.297	353	105	19	5	2	28	43	62	.373	.397
Velarde,Randy	L	.162	37	6	2	0	1	2	8	7	.311	.297
Bats Right	R	.250	96	24	6	0	1	6	7	25	.330	.344
Ventura,Robin	L	.218	101	22	2	0	8	23	14	33	.310	.475
Bats Left	R	.255	364	93	15	0	19	70	76	68	.383	.453
Vidro,Jose	L	.297	155	46	12	0	3	18	20	21	.375	.432
Bats Both	R	.321	449	144	31	3	16	78	40	49	.379	.510
Vina,Fernando	L	.238	143	34	4	0	0	13	16	9	.345	.266
Bats Left	R	.280	479	134	25	5	1	41	28	27	.329	.359
Vizcaino,Jose	L	.337	101	34	6	0	1	17	8	10	.378	.426
Bats Both	R	.292	305	89	13	2	4	20	16	30	.329	.387
Vizquel,Omar	L	.281	171	48	12	1	3	22	10	16	.319	.415
Bats Both	R	.273	411	112	19	4	11	50	46	48	.350	.418
Walbeck,Matt	L	.286	21	6	0	0	0	2	0	4	.273	.286
Bats Both	R	.219	64	14	2	0	0	1	3	10	.254	.250
Walker,Larry	L	.337	166	56	15	1	5	40	12	27	.390	.530
Bats Left	R	.338	311	105	25	3	21	64	53	46	.437	.640
Walker,Todd	L	.278	158	44	7	1	2	17	8	17	.315	.373
Bats Left	R	.306	454	139	35	2	9	47	42	64	.366	.452
Ward,Daryle	L	.204	54	11	0	0	1	7	3	17	.246	.259
Bats Left	R	.286	399	114	31	0	11	65	30	65	.334	.446
Wathan,Dusty	L	-	0	0	0	0	0	0	0	0	-	-
Bats Right	R	.600	5	3	1	0	0	1	0	1	.667	.800
Wells,Vernon	L	.260	154	40	10	0	4	29	9	18	.297	.403
Bats Right	R	.280	454	127	24	4	19	71	18	67	.308	.476
Werth,Jayson	L	.167	12	2	0	0	0	1	1	1	.231	.167
Bats Right	R	.294	34	10	2	1	0	6	5	10	.375	.412
Wesson,Barry	L	.214	14	3	0	1	0	0	1	3	.267	.357
Bats Right	R	.167	6	1	0	0	0	0	0	2	.167	.167
White,Rondell	L	.286	105	30	9	0	3	14	8	23	.347	.457
Bats Right	R	.226	350	79	12	0	11	48	17	63	.269	.354
Widger,Chris	L	.294	17	5	2	0	0	2	1	1	.368	.412
Bats Right	R	.298	47	14	3	0	0	3	1	8	.327	.362
Wigginton,Ty	L	.314	35	11	3	0	2	5	2	5	.351	.571
Bats Right	R	.296	81	24	5	0	4	13	6	14	.356	.506
Wilkerson,Brad	L	.230	87	20	5	1	5	18	17	29	.352	.483
Bats Left	R	.274	420	115	22	7	15	41	64	132	.374	.467
Williams,Bernie	L	.354	164	58	10	0	4	22	21	25	.430	.488
Bats Both	R	.326	448	146	27	2	15	80	62	72	.409	.496
Williams,Gerald	L	.000	5	0	0	0	0	0	0	3	.000	.000
Bats Right	R	.000	12	0	0	0	0	0	2	1	.143	.000
Williams,Matt	L	.289	83	24	4	1	8	18	6	17	.337	.651
Bats Right	R	.242	132	32	3	1	4	22	15	24	.315	.371
Wilson,Craig	L	.313	112	35	4	0	5	14	10	28	.376	.482
Bats Right	R	.242	256	62	12	1	11	43	22	88	.346	.426
Wilson,Dan	L	.288	104	30	5	0	3	14	9	26	.336	.423
Bats Right	R	.298	255	76	11	1	3	30	9	55	.321	.384
Wilson,Enrique	L	.105	38	4	1	1	0	2	1	10	.128	.184
Bats Both	R	.224	67	15	1	1	2	9	7	12	.297	.358
Wilson,Jack	L	.360	114	41	9	2	2	11	8	14	.402	.526
Bats Right	R	.223	413	92	13	2	2	36	29	60	.280	.278
Wilson,Preston	L	.242	120	29	4	1	8	18	15	34	.328	.492
Bats Right	R	.244	390	95	18	1	15	47	43	106	.330	.410
Wilson,Tom	L	.337	83	28	5	0	3	17	12	23	.412	.506
Bats Right	R	.220	182	40	5	0	5	20	16	56	.298	.330
Wilson,Vance	L	.125	32	4	0	0	1	5	0	7	.176	.219
Bats Right	R	.275	131	36	7	0	4	21	5	25	.331	.420
Winn,Randy	L	.347	144	50	9	4	4	16	10	19	.387	.549
Bats Both	R	.283	463	131	30	5	10	59	45	90	.351	.434
Wise,Dewayne	L	.136	22	3	0	0	0	3	0	4	.136	.136
Bats Left	R	.189	90	17	4	1	3	10	4	11	.223	.356
Womack,Tony	L	.214	182	39	7	0	0	10	16	30	.292	.253
Bats Left	R	.297	408	121	16	5	5	47	30	50	.340	.397
Woodward,Chris	L	.149	74	11	2	1	2	8	5	16	.247	.203
Bats Right	R	.315	238	75	11	3	13	42	16	53	.356	.550
Wooten,Shawn	L	.282	71	20	3	0	3	14	5	16	.329	.451
Bats Right	R	.310	42	13	5	0	0	5	1	8	.333	.429
Wright,Ron	L	.000	3	0	0	0	0	0	0	1	.000	.000
Bats Right	R	-	0	0	0	0	0	0	0	0	-	-
Young,Dmitri	L	.296	54	16	3	0	1	7	4	12	.345	.407
Bats Both	R	.279	147	41	11	0	6	20	8	27	.323	.476
Young,Eric	L	.292	89	26	7	0	1	3	10	7	.364	.404
Bats Right	R	.278	407	113	22	3	2	25	29	31	.332	.361

Batters vs. Left-handed and Right-Handed Pitchers

Batter	vs	Avg	AB	H	2B	3B	HR	RBI	BB	SO	OBP	Slg
Young,Kevin	L	.283	106	30	4	0	7	17	14	17	.377	.519
Bats Right	R	.235	362	85	22	1	9	34	36	84	.305	.376
Young,Michael	L	.290	155	45	7	2	2	11	9	21	.327	.400
Bats Right	R	.251	418	105	19	6	7	51	32	91	.301	.376
Zaun,Gregg	L	.316	38	12	3	0	0	7	3	4	.366	.395
Bats Both	R	.197	147	29	4	1	3	17	9	32	.252	.299
Zeile,Todd	L	.274	146	40	7	0	4	23	24	16	.372	.404
Bats Right	R	.272	360	98	16	0	14	64	42	76	.346	.433
Zinter,Alan	L	.000	11	0	0	0	0	0	0	4	.000	.000
Bats Both	R	.182	33	6	2	0	2	3	0	15	.182	.424

Pitchers vs. Left-Handed and Right-Handed Batters

Pitcher	vs	Avg	AB	H	2B	3B	HR	RBI	BB	SO	OBP	Slg
Abbott,Paul	L	.383	60	23	2	0	3	14	13	10	.486	.567
Throws Right	R	.315	54	17	8	0	2	18	7	12	.403	.574
Acevedo,Jose	L	.348	46	16	3	1	4	10	8	7	.455	.717
Throws Right	R	.240	50	12	1	0	4	10	4	7	.309	.500
Acevedo,Juan	L	.263	137	36	5	2	3	20	16	23	.333	.394
Throws Right	R	.230	139	32	7	3	1	13	7	20	.288	.345
Adams,Terry	L	.247	231	57	7	1	5	30	35	44	.346	.351
Throws Right	R	.262	286	75	13	2	4	33	23	52	.322	.364
Affeldt,Jeremy	L	.283	92	26	7	0	3	15	12	29	.365	.457
Throws Left	R	.271	218	59	13	0	5	25	25	38	.352	.399
Ainsworth,Kurt	L	.236	55	13	3	0	1	5	10	10	.364	.345
Throws Right	R	.237	38	9	0	1	0	2	2	5	.275	.289
Alfonseca,Antonio	L	.304	125	38	5	2	3	24	13	17	.362	.448
Throws Right	R	.220	159	35	7	0	2	18	23	44	.330	.302
Almanza,Armando	L	.255	55	14	4	1	0	5	15	20	.408	.364
Throws Left	R	.208	106	22	2	1	8	19	8	37	.259	.472
Almanzar,Carlos	L	.154	13	2	0	0	0	1	0	3	.154	.154
Throws Right	R	.160	25	4	1	0	0	2	5	4	.281	.200
Alvarez,Juan	L	.233	73	17	5	2	4	18	11	22	.356	.521
Throws Left	R	.250	72	18	3	2	3	17	10	8	.333	.472
Alvarez,Victor	L	.118	17	2	0	0	0	1	0	6	.118	.118
Throws Left	R	.333	21	7	0	0	1	3	2	1	.391	.476
Alvarez,Wilson	L	.299	77	23	5	1	4	17	11	18	.396	.545
Throws Left	R	.263	217	57	12	2	9	25	25	38	.341	.461
Anderson,Brian	L	.302	159	48	14	0	6	18	11	23	.343	.503
Throws Left	R	.278	453	126	27	1	17	59	21	58	.308	.455
Anderson,Jimmy	L	.273	128	35	3	0	7	15	11	20	.340	.461
Throws Left	R	.306	431	132	31	2	13	70	52	27	.382	.478
Anderson,Matt	L	.455	22	10	0	1	1	9	6	3	.567	.682
Throws Right	R	.304	23	7	0	0	0	3	2	5	.370	.304
Appier,Kevin	L	.250	376	94	14	1	11	30	38	68	.321	.380
Throws Right	R	.286	339	97	23	0	12	50	26	64	.341	.460
Armas Jr.,Tony	L	.308	273	84	19	4	10	37	47	42	.412	.516
Throws Right	R	.192	339	65	13	3	12	40	31	89	.269	.354
Arrojo,Rolando	L	.313	163	51	10	1	3	22	18	22	.380	.442
Throws Right	R	.221	145	32	4	2	4	25	9	29	.288	.359
Arroyo,Bronson	L	.294	34	10	2	0	0	3	6	3	.390	.353
Throws Right	R	.278	72	20	6	0	1	10	9	19	.358	.403
Asencio,Miguel	L	.264	250	66	17	4	7	25	39	33	.366	.448
Throws Right	R	.302	232	70	9	1	10	35	25	25	.365	.478
Ashby,Andy	L	.285	372	106	21	3	7	33	45	47	.363	.414
Throws Right	R	.233	313	73	14	0	13	45	20	60	.289	.403
Astacio,Pedro	L	.239	339	81	14	1	15	45	40	85	.324	.419
Throws Right	R	.281	395	111	17	1	17	52	23	67	.336	.458
Austin,Jeff	L	.278	18	5	1	0	0	2	3	1	.364	.333
Throws Right	R	.346	26	9	2	0	0	4	3	5	.400	.423
Aybar,Manny	L	.429	14	6	1	0	0	2	3	2	.529	.500
Throws Right	R	.222	45	10	3	0	1	3	0	9	.239	.356
Backe,Brandon	L	.292	24	7	2	0	0	1	3	4	.370	.375
Throws Right	R	.286	28	8	0	0	3	9	4	2	.412	.607
Bacsik,Mike	L	.216	37	8	3	1	1	4	5	6	.341	.432
Throws Left	R	.304	181	55	11	1	7	19	14	24	.359	.492
Baez,Danys	L	.278	324	90	23	3	5	37	48	58	.373	.414
Throws Right	R	.233	301	70	14	1	9	40	34	72	.318	.375
Bailey,Cory	L	.282	71	20	5	0	2	12	21	7	.452	.437
Throws Right	R	.324	102	33	3	0	3	20	10	17	.383	.441
Baldwin,James	L	.323	297	96	21	1	11	36	29	45	.382	.512
Throws Right	R	.274	303	83	22	1	15	51	20	43	.332	.502
Banks,Willie	L	.246	69	17	3	0	3	10	4	17	.303	.420
Throws Right	R	.200	75	15	4	0	2	7	10	9	.302	.333
Barcelo,Lorenzo	L	.600	10	6	0	0	1	4	0	0	.600	.900
Throws Right	R	.176	17	3	0	0	0	1	1	1	.222	.176
Batista,Miguel	L	.269	334	90	18	4	7	43	39	47	.347	.410
Throws Right	R	.223	367	82	18	2	5	41	31	65	.287	.324
Bauer,Rick	L	.286	133	38	5	1	5	12	15	14	.358	.451
Throws Right	R	.254	181	46	2	0	7	23	21	31	.341	.381
Bechler,Steve	L	.200	10	2	0	0	2	5	2	2	.385	.800
Throws Right	R	.400	10	4	1	0	1	1	2	1	.500	.800
Beckett,Josh	L	.246	195	48	7	4	9	27	29	51	.347	.462
Throws Right	R	.218	206	45	7	1	4	25	15	62	.268	.320
Bedard,Erik	L	.667	3	2	0	0	0	1	0	1	.667	.667
Throws Left	R	.000	1	0	0	0	0	0	0	0	.000	.000
Beimel,Joe	L	.262	103	27	5	1	3	21	9	18	.330	.417
Throws Left	R	.269	227	61	17	0	6	33	36	35	.371	.423
Beirne,Kevin	L	.208	48	10	3	0	1	4	10	9	.356	.333
Throws Right	R	.276	58	16	2	1	3	7	7	8	.358	.500

Pitcher	vs	Avg	AB	H	2B	3B	HR	RBI	BB	SO	OBP	Slg
Bell,Rob	L	.307	205	63	19	2	8	30	22	41	.372	.537
Throws Right	R	.282	177	50	13	2	8	30	13	29	.326	.514
Beltran,Francis	L	.286	14	4	2	0	0	0	9	3	.565	.429
Throws Right	R	.323	31	10	0	0	2	7	7	8	.436	.516
Benes,Alan	L	.239	67	16	4	0	1	7	6	16	.297	.343
Throws Right	R	.306	85	26	3	0	2	10	6	16	.348	.412
Benes,Andy	L	.250	156	39	7	1	3	14	27	27	.360	.365
Throws Right	R	.210	195	41	9	0	7	18	24	37	.305	.364
Benitez,Armando	L	.160	119	19	3	0	6	12	19	41	.277	.336
Throws Right	R	.220	123	27	7	0	2	10	6	38	.267	.325
Benoit,Joaquin	L	.275	171	47	8	2	5	29	32	30	.391	.433
Throws Right	R	.268	164	44	10	2	1	17	26	29	.376	.372
Benson,Kris	L	.310	229	71	18	2	10	40	30	27	.389	.537
Throws Right	R	.283	286	81	18	1	8	32	20	52	.333	.437
Bere,Jason	L	.326	141	46	9	3	5	22	13	20	.392	.539
Throws Right	R	.264	197	52	14	1	8	33	15	45	.307	.467
Bernero,Adam	L	.321	224	72	16	4	10	42	19	39	.375	.563
Throws Right	R	.295	190	56	10	0	7	28	12	30	.346	.458
Beverlin,Jason	L	.348	46	16	5	0	3	13	4	9	.400	.652
Throws Right	R	.275	40	11	2	1	0	3	5	7	.356	.375
Biddle,Rocky	L	.287	143	41	9	1	9	25	21	31	.393	.552
Throws Right	R	.205	151	31	9	1	4	20	18	33	.292	.358
Boehringer,Brian	L	.250	96	24	5	0	1	10	15	19	.348	.333
Throws Right	R	.218	188	41	7	1	4	23	18	46	.290	.330
Bong,Jung	L	.182	11	2	1	0	0	2	1	2	.250	.273
Throws Left	R	.429	14	6	4	0	0	3	1	2	.467	.714
Borbon,Pedro	L	.240	121	29	9	0	4	21	10	36	.291	.413
Throws Left	R	.324	74	24	8	0	6	21	15	14	.442	.676
Borland,Toby	L	.304	23	7	1	0	2	5	2	5	.360	.609
Throws Right	R	.241	29	7	1	0	1	6	3	6	.351	.379
Borowski,Joe	L	.209	148	31	7	1	4	11	12	51	.273	.351
Throws Right	R	.260	204	53	10	1	6	31	17	46	.313	.407
Bottalico,Ricky	L	.311	45	14	2	0	1	6	9	8	.429	.422
Throws Right	R	.292	65	19	5	2	2	16	4	16	.343	.523
Bowie,Micah	L	.273	22	6	2	0	1	5	3	3	.385	.500
Throws Left	R	.250	24	6	5	0	0	2	5	5	.379	.458
Bowles,Brian	L	.222	27	6	2	0	0	8	7	5	.389	.296
Throws Right	R	.159	44	7	3	0	0	3	7	14	.302	.227
Boyd,Jason	L	.235	51	12	2	0	3	12	7	11	.317	.451
Throws Right	R	.356	59	21	6	1	3	17	8	7	.426	.644
Bradford,Chad	L	.267	90	24	4	1	0	11	9	14	.346	.333
Throws Right	R	.247	198	49	9	0	2	25	5	42	.273	.323
Brazelton,Dewon	L	.267	15	4	0	0	2	5	2	1	.389	.667
Throws Right	R	.286	28	8	2	0	1	2	4	4	.394	.464
Brock,Chris	L	.253	83	21	4	1	4	13	8	15	.315	.470
Throws Right	R	.337	92	31	8	1	2	14	6	6	.380	.511
Brohawn,Troy	L	.250	12	3	1	0	0	0	0	2	.308	.333
Throws Left	R	.200	10	2	0	0	1	2	1	1	.333	.500
Brower,Jim	L	.254	126	32	9	0	2	14	17	21	.347	.373
Throws Right	R	.251	179	45	8	1	5	24	15	36	.318	.391
Brown,Kevin	L	.245	106	26	3	0	4	16	12	23	.322	.387
Throws Right	R	.296	142	42	5	2	5	14	11	35	.367	.465
Buddie,Mike	L	.324	71	23	5	0	4	10	11	9	.415	.563
Throws Right	R	.267	86	23	6	0	1	12	10	19	.347	.372
Buehrle,Mark	L	.228	241	55	11	0	10	37	14	43	.275	.398
Throws Left	R	.271	667	181	42	2	15	55	47	91	.319	.408
Bukvich,Ryan	L	.171	41	7	1	0	0	6	11	12	.327	.195
Throws Right	R	.358	53	19	7	0	2	16	8	8	.452	.604
Burba,Dave	L	.247	295	73	18	4	7	31	33	45	.333	.407
Throws Right	R	.294	279	82	30	1	9	51	24	50	.355	.505
Burkett,John	L	.278	352	98	15	1	15	53	28	66	.332	.455
Throws Right	R	.296	341	101	20	3	10	31	22	58	.349	.460
Burnett,A.J.	L	.242	359	87	19	3	5	34	46	100	.335	.354
Throws Right	R	.177	373	66	12	0	7	44	44	103	.270	.265
Bynum,Mike	L	.375	24	9	0	0	2	8	2	5	.444	.625
Throws Left	R	.289	83	24	4	2	1	19	13	12	.390	.422
Byrd,Paul	L	.269	472	127	28	6	17	48	18	59	.294	.462
Throws Right	R	.241	403	97	18	1	19	54	20	70	.281	.432
Cabrera,Jose	L	.284	183	52	14	2	13	32	22	26	.371	.596
Throws Right	R	.338	234	79	17	2	10	53	14	35	.383	.556
Callaway,Mickey	L	.215	65	14	0	0	1	6	7	13	.292	.262
Throws Right	R	.254	67	17	3	0	3	10	4	10	.324	.433
Carpenter,Chris	L	.327	165	54	7	1	8	24	15	22	.377	.527
Throws Right	R	.278	126	35	8	0	3	16	12	23	.357	.413
Carrara,Giovanni	L	.248	137	34	10	0	6	22	11	17	.313	.453
Throws Right	R	.240	204	49	9	1	8	27	21	39	.320	.412

Pitchers vs. Left-handed and Right-Handed Batters

Pitcher	vs	Avg	AB	H	2B	3B	HR	RBI	BB	SO	OBP	Slg
Carter,Lance	L	.212	33	7	1	0	1	1	2	4	.257	.333
Throws Right	R	.195	41	8	3	0	1	2	3	10	.250	.341
Cassidy,Scott	L	.242	95	23	9	0	5	17	21	21	.380	.495
Throws Right	R	.209	139	29	3	1	7	27	11	27	.287	.396
Castillo,Frank	L	.281	288	81	16	0	9	49	41	62	.372	.431
Throws Right	R	.269	346	93	15	1	10	44	17	50	.305	.405
Cerda,Jaime	L	.268	41	11	2	1	0	9	9	9	.385	.366
Throws Left	R	.204	54	11	1	0	0	4	5	12	.279	.222
Chacon,Shawn	L	.319	204	65	9	3	14	36	29	29	.409	.598
Throws Right	R	.220	259	57	17	1	11	37	31	38	.313	.421
Chen,Bruce	L	.252	115	29	5	0	2	17	17	35	.343	.348
Throws Left	R	.287	195	56	15	0	14	35	26	45	.375	.579
Chiasson,Scott	L	.500	10	5	2	0	1	6	3	2	.615	1.000
Throws Right	R	.400	15	6	2	0	1	5	3	1	.500	.733
Childers,Matt	L	.533	15	8	3	1	1	11	6	1	.667	1.067
Throws Right	R	.217	23	5	1	0	1	5	2	5	.308	.391
Choate,Randy	L	.107	28	3	0	0	0	3	6	12	.265	.107
Throws Left	R	.273	55	15	6	0	1	12	9	5	.403	.436
Christiansen,Jason	L	.143	7	1	0	0	0	0	2	1	.333	.143
Throws Left	R	.417	12	5	2	0	1	2	0	0	.417	.833
Clemens,Roger	L	.220	363	80	15	2	9	31	47	104	.313	.347
Throws Right	R	.283	325	92	28	0	9	47	16	88	.322	.452
Clement,Matt	L	.220	341	75	16	2	7	34	53	81	.322	.340
Throws Right	R	.212	411	87	23	0	11	40	32	134	.278	.348
Coco,Pasqual	L	.500	4	2	1	0	0	1	1	0	.600	.750
Throws Right	R	.667	3	2	0	0	0	1	2	0	.800	.667
Coggin,Dave	L	.287	122	35	7	4	2	21	23	18	.400	.459
Throws Right	R	.189	159	30	5	0	2	21	28	46	.321	.258
Colome,Jesus	L	.414	70	29	3	0	4	21	14	12	.506	.629
Throws Right	R	.287	94	27	5	2	2	17	19	21	.417	.447
Colon,Bartolo	L	.242	409	99	14	4	11	31	37	77	.307	.377
Throws Right	R	.261	460	120	30	2	9	45	33	72	.307	.393
Condrey,Clay	L	.250	44	11	2	0	0	2	6	4	.333	.295
Throws Right	R	.188	48	9	2	0	1	4	2	12	.245	.292
Cook,Aaron	L	.295	61	18	2	1	0	5	6	2	.368	.361
Throws Right	R	.295	78	23	3	0	4	13	7	12	.360	.487
Cook,Dennis	L	.264	53	14	4	1	1	9	7	6	.349	.434
Throws Left	R	.206	34	7	0	0	1	5	3	7	.270	.294
Cooper,Brian	L	.391	23	9	1	0	3	7	3	2	.462	.826
Throws Right	R	.417	12	5	1	0	2	5	1	1	.429	1.000
Cordero,Francisco	L	.189	74	14	2	0	1	9	8	22	.277	.257
Throws Right	R	.216	88	19	5	0	1	6	5	19	.266	.307
Corey,Bryan	L	.000	2	0	0	0	0	0	0	0	.000	.000
Throws Right	R	.000	1	0	0	0	0	0	0	0	.000	.000
Corey,Mark	L	.342	38	13	1	0	3	12	4	8	.432	.605
Throws Right	R	.333	57	19	3	0	6	10	12	13	.457	.702
Cormier,Rheal	L	.295	78	23	3	2	1	16	11	20	.391	.423
Throws Left	R	.252	151	38	8	1	5	20	21	29	.349	.417
Cornejo,Nate	L	.269	108	29	6	1	2	11	11	12	.333	.398
Throws Right	R	.340	100	34	8	0	4	18	7	11	.394	.540
Creek,Doug	L	.239	88	21	2	0	5	18	11	25	.340	.432
Throws Left	R	.277	130	36	13	0	5	23	24	31	.405	.492
Cressend,Jack	L	.355	62	22	7	1	1	15	12	11	.453	.548
Throws Right	R	.261	69	18	1	0	5	12	7	11	.333	.493
Crudale,Mike	L	.247	73	18	5	0	1	7	6	15	.304	.356
Throws Right	R	.216	116	25	7	0	2	18	8	32	.260	.328
Cruz,Juan	L	.250	148	37	4	1	3	22	31	37	.388	.351
Throws Right	R	.234	201	47	5	1	8	28	28	44	.331	.388
Cruz,Nelson	L	.299	147	44	11	2	5	29	13	27	.362	.503
Throws Right	R	.272	169	46	14	1	7	31	16	34	.346	.491
Cunnane,Will	L	.395	38	15	1	0	4	7	7	8	.500	.737
Throws Right	R	.194	62	12	3	0	1	9	6	22	.265	.290
Cyr,Eric	L	.273	11	3	1	0	0	2	3	3	.400	.364
Throws Left	R	.300	10	3	0	0	0	2	3	1	.462	.300
Daal,Omar	L	.248	149	37	6	0	6	18	15	33	.319	.409
Throws Left	R	.235	446	105	22	1	14	51	39	72	.299	.383
D'Amico,Jeff	L	.249	269	67	15	3	5	30	28	44	.322	.383
Throws Right	R	.283	300	85	19	3	15	46	9	57	.304	.517
Darensbourg,Vic	L	.254	67	17	3	0	3	11	8	15	.351	.433
Throws Left	R	.331	133	44	5	4	7	26	18	18	.403	.586
Davey,Tom	L	.281	32	9	2	0	2	8	6	10	.410	.531
Throws Right	R	.292	48	14	3	0	0	11	5	11	.362	.354
Davis,Doug	L	.240	75	18	4	2	2	11	5	10	.293	.427
Throws Left	R	.314	156	49	11	1	5	23	17	18	.384	.494
Davis,Jason	L	.231	39	9	4	0	1	3	2	9	.268	.410
Throws Right	R	.188	16	3	0	0	0	0	2	2	.278	.188

Pitcher	vs	Avg	AB	H	2B	3B	HR	RBI	BB	SO	OBP	Slg
Davis,Kane	L	.364	22	8	3	0	2	10	6	7	.483	.773
Throws Right	R	.212	33	7	2	0	0	3	5	17	.333	.273
Dawley,Joey	L	.000	1	0	0	0	0	0	0	1	.000	.000
Throws Right	R	-	0	0	0	0	0	0	0	0	-	-
Day,Zach	L	.158	57	9	3	1	0	4	9	7	.284	.246
Throws Right	R	.244	78	19	5	0	3	12	6	18	.294	.423
de los Santos,Luis	L	.414	29	12	3	0	3	8	3	3	.441	.828
Throws Right	R	.364	33	12	3	0	2	8	1	4	.432	.636
de los Santos,Valerio	L	.219	64	14	1	0	1	10	8	14	.316	.281
Throws Left	R	.207	135	28	11	0	3	12	18	24	.291	.356
DeJean,Mike	L	.262	141	37	5	1	2	14	21	39	.356	.355
Throws Right	R	.210	138	29	5	1	5	14	18	26	.308	.370
Dempster,Ryan	L	.332	358	119	24	6	14	56	68	57	.444	.550
Throws Right	R	.248	439	109	18	5	14	59	25	96	.293	.408
DePaula,Sean	L	.563	16	9	0	0	3	8	0	4	.563	1.125
Throws Right	R	.143	14	2	1	0	0	1	3	4	.294	.214
Dessens,Elmer	L	.247	316	78	14	1	8	30	19	39	.304	.373
Throws Right	R	.266	357	95	19	0	16	37	30	54	.322	.454
DeWitt,Matt	L	.300	10	3	0	0	1	3	2	0	.385	.600
Throws Right	R	.188	16	3	0	0	0	1	1	5	.235	.188
Diggins,Ben	L	.316	38	12	1	0	2	9	11	4	.451	.500
Throws Right	R	.286	56	16	4	0	2	8	7	11	.375	.464
Donnelly,Brendan	L	.242	66	16	3	0	2	10	7	9	.320	.379
Throws Right	R	.148	108	16	2	0	0	5	12	45	.240	.167
Dotel,Octavio	L	.190	153	29	7	0	2	10	20	48	.292	.275
Throws Right	R	.159	182	29	4	1	5	18	7	70	.190	.275
Douglass,Sean	L	.269	104	28	5	0	8	22	20	28	.392	.548
Throws Right	R	.297	101	30	6	1	2	13	15	16	.390	.436
Drese,Ryan	L	.333	309	103	24	7	7	53	39	55	.410	.524
Throws Right	R	.297	246	73	13	1	8	35	23	47	.355	.455
Drew,Tim	L	.273	22	6	1	0	0	2	1	4	.304	.318
Throws Right	R	.158	38	6	0	0	1	2	1	6	.175	.237
Driskill,Travis	L	.290	279	81	16	0	11	32	27	33	.363	.466
Throws Right	R	.276	250	69	14	2	10	32	21	45	.337	.468
DuBose,Eric	L	.333	6	2	1	0	1	1	0	2	.429	1.000
Throws Left	R	.294	17	5	1	0	0	1	1	2	.333	.353
Duckworth,Brandon	L	.249	297	74	22	0	10	38	36	79	.335	.424
Throws Right	R	.272	342	93	21	4	16	57	33	88	.341	.497
Duff,Matt	L	.000	5	0	0	0	0	0	5	0	.500	.000
Throws Right	R	.200	15	3	0	0	0	1	3	4	.333	.200
Duncan,Courtney	L	.333	3	1	0	0	0	2	0	0	.333	.333
Throws Right	R	.167	6	1	0	0	0	0	1	1	.286	.167
Durbin,Chad	L	.250	16	4	1	0	0	1	2	2	.368	.313
Throws Right	R	.409	22	9	2	0	3	9	2	3	.458	.909
Durocher,Jayson	L	.187	75	14	3	1	1	2	15	25	.319	.293
Throws Right	R	.144	90	13	3	1	2	12	6	19	.214	.267
Eaton,Adam	L	.333	51	17	3	1	4	11	12	9	.462	.667
Throws Right	R	.162	68	11	4	1	1	7	5	16	.227	.294
Eckenstahler,Eric	L	.400	15	6	1	0	0	4	1	5	.438	.467
Throws Left	R	.364	22	8	3	1	1	5	1	8	.391	.727
Eischen,Joey	L	.173	81	14	3	0	1	8	6	27	.247	.247
Throws Left	R	.261	111	29	5	0	0	12	12	24	.328	.306
Elder,Dave	L	.243	37	9	2	1	0	5	6	8	.341	.351
Throws Right	R	.200	45	9	3	1	1	5	8	15	.327	.378
Ellis,Robert	L	.333	3	1	0	0	0	1	0	0	.333	.333
Throws Right	R	.500	10	5	0	1	1	2	0	0	.500	1.000
Embree,Alan	L	.155	97	15	2	1	3	14	8	44	.215	.289
Throws Left	R	.246	130	32	5	1	3	13	12	37	.315	.369
Ennis,John	L	.375	8	3	2	0	0	0	1	1	.444	.625
Throws Right	R	.400	5	2	1	0	0	2	2	0	.500	.600
Erickson,Scott	L	.304	342	104	21	1	13	54	45	32	.386	.485
Throws Right	R	.302	291	88	15	1	7	45	23	42	.360	.433
Escobar,Kelvim	L	.245	163	40	6	1	5	20	34	48	.382	.387
Throws Right	R	.246	142	35	5	0	5	21	10	37	.310	.387
Estes,Shawn	L	.300	130	39	8	1	2	19	15	32	.409	.423
Throws Left	R	.276	478	132	28	4	11	67	68	77	.362	.421
Eyre,Scott	L	.233	146	34	7	0	2	21	17	32	.309	.322
Throws Left	R	.317	145	46	8	2	2	23	19	26	.392	.441
Farnsworth,Jeff	L	.364	129	47	9	2	4	24	15	12	.435	.558
Throws Right	R	.317	167	53	18	0	2	21	14	16	.370	.461
Farnsworth,Kyle	L	.388	80	31	7	3	5	31	11	19	.452	.738
Throws Right	R	.218	101	22	4	2	4	18	13	27	.305	.416
Fassero,Jeff	L	.318	110	35	3	1	1	14	11	22	.390	.391
Throws Left	R	.275	167	46	8	1	8	26	16	34	.341	.479
Feliciano,Pedro	L	.444	9	4	1	0	0	2	0	1	.444	.556
Throws Left	R	.313	16	5	2	0	0	3	1	3	.353	.438

Pitchers vs. Left-Handed and Right-Handed Batters

Pitcher	vs	Avg	AB	H	2B	3B	HR	RBI	BB	SO	OBP	Slg
Fernandez,Jared	L	.191	68	13	2	0	1	7	11	16	.309	.265
Throws Right	R	.346	133	46	12	1	4	22	13	20	.409	.541
Fetters,Mike	L	.311	61	19	5	0	1	8	17	10	.450	.443
Throws Right	R	.228	149	34	3	0	3	23	20	43	.331	.309
Field,Nate	L	.455	11	5	2	0	0	0	0	1	.455	.636
Throws Right	R	.273	11	3	0	0	2	4	3	2	.429	.818
Figueroa,Nelson	L	.273	154	42	5	1	12	27	21	23	.362	.552
Throws Right	R	.269	201	54	16	0	6	30	16	28	.326	.438
Fikac,Jeremy	L	.274	117	32	10	2	3	19	21	23	.388	.470
Throws Right	R	.263	160	42	9	2	10	33	13	43	.322	.531
File,Bob	L	.500	8	4	1	0	0	3	0	0	.500	.625
Throws Right	R	.444	9	4	1	0	0	4	2	2	.545	.556
Finley,Chuck	L	.180	122	22	4	0	1	14	17	34	.277	.238
Throws Left	R	.271	595	161	33	4	12	70	61	140	.337	.400
Fiore,Tony	L	.247	154	38	7	2	3	17	25	21	.350	.377
Throws Right	R	.203	177	36	4	0	7	16	18	34	.294	.345
Fitzgerald,Brian	L	.231	13	3	1	0	0	1	0	2	.286	.308
Throws Left	R	.421	19	8	1	0	2	5	2	1	.455	.789
Flores,Randy	L	.326	43	14	2	0	3	15	2	4	.340	.581
Throws Left	R	.351	74	26	6	2	4	18	14	10	.473	.649
Fogg,Josh	L	.293	358	105	16	6	16	45	36	42	.361	.506
Throws Right	R	.242	388	94	18	2	12	48	33	71	.309	.392
Fossum,Casey	L	.277	112	31	7	1	1	18	6	27	.311	.384
Throws Left	R	.265	309	82	18	1	11	33	24	74	.324	.437
Foster,John	L	.286	7	2	0	0	1	1	3	4	.500	.714
Throws Left	R	.286	14	4	0	0	2	5	3	2	.444	.714
Foulke,Keith	L	.268	142	38	4	1	3	12	10	31	.316	.373
Throws Right	R	.184	147	27	3	0	4	12	3	27	.211	.286
Fox,Chad	L	.182	11	2	1	0	0	2	1	2	.250	.273
Throws Right	R	.500	8	4	1	0	0	1	4	1	.667	.625
Franklin,Ryan	L	.265	219	58	9	2	6	27	10	33	.299	.406
Throws Right	R	.247	239	59	12	1	8	33	12	32	.290	.406
Franklin,Wayne	L	.000	4	0	0	0	0	0	0	0	.000	.000
Throws Left	R	.198	81	16	2	0	1	4	17	17	.337	.259
Frederick,Kevin	L	.250	24	6	1	0	2	4	4	3	.357	.542
Throws Right	R	.318	22	7	3	0	1	9	6	2	.464	.591
Fuentes,Brian	L	.386	44	17	3	0	3	10	5	14	.481	.659
Throws Left	R	.143	56	8	1	0	1	7	8	24	.242	.214
Fultz,Aaron	L	.310	87	27	5	2	2	16	8	14	.375	.483
Throws Left	R	.274	73	20	1	1	2	11	11	17	.379	.397
Fyhrie,Mike	L	.203	79	16	2	0	1	13	9	13	.308	.266
Throws Right	R	.278	108	30	10	0	2	13	11	16	.350	.426
Gagne,Eric	L	.213	150	32	7	2	2	12	11	52	.268	.327
Throws Right	R	.163	141	23	4	0	4	7	5	62	.197	.277
Garces,Rich	L	.364	33	12	1	0	2	11	7	8	.442	.576
Throws Right	R	.205	44	9	3	0	2	9	5	8	.327	.409
Garcia,Freddy	L	.255	482	123	27	1	17	58	37	85	.313	.421
Throws Right	R	.265	392	104	18	1	13	43	26	96	.310	.416
Garcia,Reynaldo	L	.600	5	3	0	0	1	3	0	1	.600	1.200
Throws Right	R	.500	8	4	2	0	2	5	1	1	.556	1.500
Gardner,Lee	L	.286	21	6	0	0	2	4	3	1	.375	.571
Throws Right	R	.200	30	6	0	0	1	5	5	7	.350	.300
Garland,Jon	L	.288	413	119	30	0	14	53	54	53	.374	.462
Throws Right	R	.219	315	69	12	1	9	38	29	59	.293	.349
George,Chris	L	.138	29	4	1	0	0	1	3	8	.242	.172
Throws Left	R	.388	85	33	9	0	2	14	5	5	.418	.565
German,Franklyn	L	.100	10	1	0	0	0	0	2	5	.308	.100
Throws Right	R	.200	10	2	1	0	0	0	0	1	.200	.300
Ginter,Matt	L	.336	110	37	8	0	2	23	8	16	.383	.464
Throws Right	R	.216	102	22	2	0	4	21	13	21	.302	.353
Glavine,Tom	L	.247	166	41	11	0	6	21	17	18	.324	.422
Throws Left	R	.254	666	169	38	2	15	50	61	109	.319	.384
Glover,Gary	L	.281	303	85	19	0	17	45	35	38	.360	.512
Throws Right	R	.218	234	51	11	1	4	33	17	32	.280	.325
Gomes,Wayne	L	.103	39	4	1	0	1	7	6	6	.222	.205
Throws Right	R	.364	44	16	6	0	1	6	6	9	.472	.568
Gordon,Tom	L	.269	67	18	2	2	2	11	11	20	.372	.448
Throws Right	R	.255	94	24	7	0	1	8	5	28	.300	.362
Graves,Danny	L	.268	149	40	7	1	3	19	13	29	.325	.389
Throws Right	R	.261	226	59	6	1	4	37	12	29	.301	.350
Greisinger,Seth	L	.333	72	24	8	0	3	11	8	7	.407	.569
Throws Right	R	.275	80	22	5	0	1	11	5	7	.314	.375
Grimsley,Jason	L	.248	129	32	2	2	3	15	21	23	.353	.364
Throws Right	R	.225	142	32	10	0	1	25	16	36	.308	.317
Groom,Buddy	L	.181	94	17	2	0	2	7	6	25	.238	.266
Throws Left	R	.208	130	27	3	1	2	13	6	23	.246	.292

Pitcher	vs	Avg	AB	H	2B	3B	HR	RBI	BB	SO	OBP	Slg
Gryboski,Kevin	L	.171	70	12	0	1	1	3	21	9	.363	.243
Throws Right	R	.304	125	38	5	0	5	25	16	24	.404	.464
Guardado,Eddie	L	.263	57	15	2	0	1	6	2	18	.288	.351
Throws Left	R	.200	190	38	9	0	8	17	16	52	.263	.374
Guthrie,Mark	L	.187	75	14	0	0	2	6	10	25	.287	.267
Throws Left	R	.223	94	21	4	0	1	6	9	19	.291	.298
Hackman,Luther	L	.298	124	37	8	1	3	21	14	11	.371	.452
Throws Right	R	.279	190	53	13	1	4	24	25	35	.363	.421
Halama,John	L	.248	133	33	7	0	5	13	5	24	.281	.414
Throws Left	R	.297	266	79	9	0	4	25	28	46	.361	.376
Halladay,Roy	L	.259	475	123	20	2	6	51	36	79	.313	.347
Throws Right	R	.228	438	100	23	2	4	35	26	89	.279	.317
Hamilton,Joey	L	.300	227	68	11	3	8	37	21	40	.370	.480
Throws Right	R	.261	261	68	15	2	3	35	29	45	.334	.368
Hammond,Chris	L	.174	92	16	0	1	1	8	6	26	.232	.228
Throws Left	R	.206	180	37	11	1	0	11	25	37	.300	.278
Hampton,Mike	L	.376	170	64	7	0	10	38	19	22	.442	.594
Throws Left	R	.293	559	164	32	2	14	85	72	52	.374	.433
Hancock,Josh	L	.083	12	1	0	0	0	0	1	2	.154	.083
Throws Right	R	.308	13	4	1	0	1	3	1	4	.357	.615
Haney,Chris	L	.286	49	14	6	1	0	7	4	7	.368	.449
Throws Left	R	.265	68	18	3	0	2	10	6	8	.325	.397
Harang,Aaron	L	.237	156	37	9	0	1	19	28	30	.349	.314
Throws Right	R	.287	143	41	8	0	6	17	17	34	.370	.469
Harper,Travis	L	.302	162	49	11	0	10	33	15	32	.372	.556
Throws Right	R	.278	187	52	7	0	4	24	12	28	.335	.380
Hasegawa,Shigetoshi	L	.284	116	33	9	1	1	19	15	19	.366	.405
Throws Right	R	.199	136	27	7	0	3	11	15	20	.286	.316
Hawkins,LaTroy	L	.220	127	28	7	0	3	16	9	34	.270	.346
Throws Right	R	.215	163	35	4	0	2	15	6	29	.240	.276
Haynes,Jimmy	L	.280	328	92	14	1	10	46	44	55	.365	.421
Throws Right	R	.276	427	118	21	2	11	36	37	71	.334	.412
Helling,Rick	L	.283	315	89	20	3	14	43	32	63	.348	.498
Throws Right	R	.249	366	91	15	3	17	45	16	57	.288	.445
Hendrickson,Mark	L	.194	31	6	1	0	0	5	1	5	.242	.226
Throws Left	R	.204	93	19	5	0	1	8	11	16	.290	.290
Henriquez,Oscar	L	.164	55	9	1	0	3	5	10	15	.292	.345
Throws Right	R	.238	42	10	2	0	2	8	5	8	.327	.429
Hentgen,Pat	L	.333	48	16	5	2	2	7	8	7	.429	.646
Throws Right	R	.341	44	15	2	0	4	11	2	4	.362	.659
Heredia,Felix	L	.224	85	19	5	0	3	14	11	14	.309	.388
Throws Left	R	.281	114	32	9	0	2	19	15	17	.371	.412
Herges,Matt	L	.319	91	29	7	0	3	13	13	16	.404	.495
Throws Right	R	.298	171	51	5	1	7	26	13	34	.351	.462
Hermanson,Dustin	L	.325	40	13	5	0	0	4	4	4	.378	.450
Throws Right	R	.373	59	22	7	0	3	13	3	9	.403	.644
Hernandez,Adrian	L	.364	11	4	1	0	1	5	4	4	.533	.727
Throws Right	R	.353	17	6	2	0	1	3	2	5	.421	.647
Hernandez,Carlos	L	.265	83	22	5	0	2	10	16	14	.384	.398
Throws Left	R	.260	346	90	24	2	9	33	45	79	.350	.419
Hernandez,Livan	L	.296	371	110	26	4	8	46	37	59	.361	.453
Throws Right	R	.272	453	123	14	3	11	55	34	75	.322	.389
Hernandez,Orlando	L	.224	286	64	14	0	12	37	18	57	.282	.399
Throws Right	R	.248	270	67	10	2	5	20	18	56	.297	.356
Hernandez,Roberto	L	.282	103	29	6	1	2	16	8	21	.333	.417
Throws Right	R	.317	104	33	5	0	4	12	4	18	.357	.481
Hernandez,Runelvys	L	.302	162	49	10	1	6	19	18	23	.368	.488
Throws Right	R	.236	127	30	5	0	2	13	4	22	.263	.323
Herrera,Alex	L	.000	9	0	0	0	0	0	0	4	.000	.000
Throws Left	R	.300	10	3	2	0	0	0	1	1	.364	.500
Hiljus,Erik	L	.274	106	29	6	0	5	20	15	17	.361	.472
Throws Right	R	.299	77	23	7	0	6	13	6	12	.349	.623
Hill,Jeremy	L	.263	19	5	1	0	1	3	4	6	.391	.474
Throws Right	R	.200	15	3	0	1	0	4	4	1	.350	.333
Hitchcock,Sterling	L	.316	57	18	4	0	1	8	3	10	.355	.439
Throws Left	R	.331	118	39	7	0	3	18	12	21	.392	.466
Hodges,Trey	L	.273	11	3	0	0	0	1	2	1	.385	.273
Throws Right	R	.371	35	13	0	0	2	7	0	5	.368	.543
Hoffman,Trevor	L	.186	102	19	4	1	2	7	13	35	.278	.304
Throws Right	R	.275	120	33	4	1	0	12	5	34	.305	.325
Holmes,Darren	L	.230	74	17	3	2	1	6	8	15	.313	.365
Throws Right	R	.198	121	24	2	0	2	6	4	32	.228	.264
Holtz,Mike	L	.306	62	19	6	2	3	19	10	12	.395	.613
Throws Left	R	.284	81	23	5	0	2	8	20	14	.431	.420
Howard,Ben	L	.333	15	5	3	0	2	6	10	4	.577	.933
Throws Right	R	.286	28	8	1	0	2	5	4	6	.375	.536

Pitchers vs. Left-handed and Right-Handed Batters

Pitcher	vs	Avg	AB	H	2B	3B	HR	RBI	BB	SO	OBP	Slg
Howry,Bob	L	.241	112	27	11	0	6	22	14	18	.328	.500
Throws Right	R	.278	144	40	8	1	3	25	7	27	.318	.410
Hudson,Luke	L	.222	9	2	0	0	0	0	3	3	.417	.222
Throws Right	R	.231	13	3	0	0	1	2	3	4	.375	.462
Hudson,Tim	L	.283	484	137	27	4	15	53	38	76	.337	.448
Throws Right	R	.239	418	100	16	3	4	23	24	76	.288	.321
Irabu,Hideki	L	.269	93	25	8	1	3	12	7	11	.317	.473
Throws Right	R	.289	90	26	3	0	8	16	9	19	.356	.589
Ishii,Kazuhisa	L	.223	130	29	2	0	3	12	12	47	.290	.308
Throws Left	R	.245	441	108	20	0	17	61	94	96	.379	.406
Isringhausen,Jason	L	.247	97	24	3	0	0	11	12	25	.333	.278
Throws Right	R	.164	134	22	7	0	0	7	6	43	.197	.216
Izquierdo,Hansel	L	.356	45	16	7	1	1	9	14	6	.492	.622
Throws Right	R	.246	69	17	4	0	1	7	7	14	.354	.348
Jackson,Mike	L	.275	69	19	4	0	2	9	8	10	.342	.420
Throws Right	R	.288	139	40	8	1	3	13	5	19	.329	.424
James,Delvin	L	.299	67	20	8	0	2	9	10	6	.397	.507
Throws Right	R	.303	66	20	6	1	3	11	5	11	.347	.561
James,Mike	L	.158	19	3	0	0	1	3	1	6	.238	.316
Throws Right	R	.346	26	9	3	1	1	6	4	4	.433	.654
Jarvis,Kevin	L	.218	55	12	3	2	3	6	4	13	.279	.509
Throws Right	R	.304	79	24	8	0	2	11	6	11	.353	.481
Jennings,Jason	L	.300	297	89	19	2	8	40	34	32	.374	.458
Throws Right	R	.266	421	112	14	0	18	52	36	95	.331	.428
Jensen,Ryan	L	.288	306	88	16	2	12	47	43	46	.371	.471
Throws Right	R	.270	352	95	20	3	9	41	23	59	.320	.420
Jimenez,Jason	L	.250	8	2	0	1	0	1	2	2	.400	.500
Throws Left	R	.400	25	10	0	1	2	6	0	3	.385	.720
Jimenez,Jose	L	.268	138	37	3	2	4	16	7	18	.301	.406
Throws Right	R	.262	149	39	9	0	3	19	4	29	.293	.383
Johnson,Jason	L	.261	249	65	8	2	7	30	16	48	.319	.394
Throws Right	R	.290	262	76	15	1	12	32	25	49	.351	.492
Johnson,Jonathan	L	.261	23	6	0	0	1	1	0	6	.261	.391
Throws Right	R	.243	37	9	3	1	1	6	5	15	.349	.459
Johnson,Randy	L	.221	140	31	6	2	5	11	11	47	.310	.400
Throws Left	R	.206	805	166	36	3	21	62	60	287	.266	.337
Jones,Bobby J	L	.273	205	56	9	2	10	27	15	25	.323	.483
Throws Right	R	.322	242	78	20	3	10	37	6	35	.339	.554
Jones,Bobby M	L	.314	35	11	4	0	0	4	5	7	.400	.429
Throws Left	R	.275	69	19	6	0	4	14	13	11	.393	.536
Jones,Todd	L	.233	146	34	7	0	2	14	12	38	.289	.322
Throws Right	R	.301	166	50	10	2	8	34	16	35	.369	.530
Joseph,Kevin	L	.600	10	6	0	0	1	1	1	0	.636	.900
Throws Right	R	.294	34	10	1	0	0	6	5	2	.415	.324
Julio,Jorge	L	.213	127	27	8	0	2	12	15	23	.299	.323
Throws Right	R	.214	131	28	9	0	3	11	12	32	.285	.351
Junge,Eric	L	.167	12	2	0	0	0	0	3	4	.333	.167
Throws Right	R	.324	37	12	4	0	0	2	2	7	.359	.432
Karsay,Steve	L	.243	136	33	4	3	6	20	15	39	.316	.449
Throws Right	R	.269	201	54	8	0	1	20	15	26	.323	.323
Kaye,Justin	L	.429	7	3	2	0	0	3	0	3	.429	.714
Throws Right	R	.429	7	3	1	0	0	1	1	0	.500	.571
Keller,Kris	L	.500	2	1	0	0	0	0	1	1	.667	.500
Throws Right	R	.333	3	1	0	0	1	3	2	0	.600	1.333
Kennedy,Joe	L	.273	172	47	14	1	7	28	6	25	.309	.488
Throws Left	R	.268	586	157	33	1	16	75	49	84	.333	.410
Kent,Steve	L	.308	78	24	3	0	3	19	9	16	.386	.462
Throws Left	R	.287	150	43	8	0	3	26	29	25	.404	.400
Kershner,Jason	L	.256	39	10	2	0	2	6	6	11	.383	.462
Throws Left	R	.192	52	10	2	0	1	7	8	7	.300	.288
Kile,Darryl	L	.246	126	31	5	0	4	14	10	19	.301	.381
Throws Right	R	.264	193	51	14	1	5	20	18	31	.347	.425
Kim,Byung-Hyun	L	.220	141	31	3	0	3	12	16	46	.317	.305
Throws Right	R	.198	167	33	3	0	2	14	10	46	.249	.251
Kim,Sun-Woo	L	.247	89	22	6	0	4	12	5	18	.284	.449
Throws Right	R	.297	101	30	6	2	1	11	9	11	.363	.426
King,Ray	L	.227	97	22	2	0	2	10	8	17	.303	.309
Throws Left	R	.275	142	39	6	1	3	16	16	33	.346	.394
Kinney,Matt	L	.336	146	49	7	3	9	23	16	18	.402	.610
Throws Right	R	.246	118	29	3	0	4	15	17	27	.333	.373
Kline,Steve	L	.230	87	20	4	1	1	7	11	20	.313	.333
Throws Left	R	.266	128	34	6	0	2	13	10	21	.321	.359
Knight,Brandon	L	.357	14	5	1	0	0	2	3	2	.471	.429
Throws Right	R	.273	22	6	2	0	2	9	2	5	.333	.636
Knotts,Gary	L	.196	46	9	1	1	4	9	6	6	.288	.522
Throws Right	R	.190	63	12	3	0	2	7	10	15	.307	.333

Pitcher	vs	Avg	AB	H	2B	3B	HR	RBI	BB	SO	OBP	Slg
Koch,Billy	L	.235	153	36	5	1	3	14	22	38	.335	.340
Throws Right	R	.197	188	37	4	0	4	24	24	55	.296	.282
Kolb,Danny	L	.291	55	16	2	1	1	8	13	8	.420	.418
Throws Right	R	.172	64	11	2	0	0	9	9	12	.280	.203
Komiyama,Satoru	L	.305	82	25	7	0	4	11	6	10	.344	.537
Throws Right	R	.298	94	28	9	0	3	16	6	23	.356	.489
Koplove,Mike	L	.174	69	12	4	1	0	3	21	18	.367	.261
Throws Right	R	.230	152	35	2	0	2	15	2	28	.239	.283
Kozlowski,Ben	L	.444	9	4	0	0	0	2	1	2	.500	.444
Throws Left	R	.241	29	7	2	0	3	5	10	4	.450	.621
Lackey,John	L	.211	194	41	1	1	1	18	15	22	.269	.242
Throws Right	R	.313	230	72	18	0	9	25	18	47	.368	.509
Lawrence,Brian	L	.324	413	134	18	4	7	45	28	61	.371	.438
Throws Right	R	.236	406	96	16	1	9	38	24	88	.289	.347
Lee,Cliff	L	.000	9	0	0	0	0	0	2	4	.182	.000
Throws Left	R	.231	26	6	1	0	0	1	6	2	.375	.269
Leiter,Al	L	.221	154	34	4	0	4	14	11	45	.281	.325
Throws Left	R	.257	623	160	31	1	19	70	58	127	.325	.401
Levine,Al	L	.240	104	25	5	0	4	15	21	11	.362	.404
Throws Right	R	.263	137	36	6	2	4	20	13	29	.325	.423
Lewis,Colby	L	.320	75	24	4	0	3	12	13	12	.427	.493
Throws Right	R	.286	63	18	2	1	1	11	13	16	.416	.397
Lidge,Brad	L	.500	14	7	2	0	0	3	3	2	.611	.643
Throws Right	R	.227	22	5	2	0	0	2	6	10	.414	.318
Lidle,Cory	L	.248	391	97	26	0	11	36	22	66	.288	.399
Throws Right	R	.269	349	94	17	1	6	36	17	45	.310	.375
Lieber,Jon	L	.308	273	84	15	0	11	36	8	33	.325	.484
Throws Right	R	.246	280	69	11	2	4	22	4	54	.255	.343
Ligtenberg,Kerry	L	.214	98	21	3	2	3	11	27	23	.384	.378
Throws Right	R	.212	146	31	7	1	3	12	6	28	.242	.336
Lilly,Ted	L	.154	78	12	5	0	2	6	7	20	.221	.295
Throws Left	R	.231	295	68	17	3	13	33	24	57	.300	.441
Lima,Jose	L	.319	144	46	8	3	7	31	13	16	.377	.563
Throws Right	R	.308	130	40	14	2	5	24	8	17	.340	.562
Lincoln,Mike	L	.279	86	24	3	1	2	9	14	20	.380	.407
Throws Right	R	.295	190	56	11	1	5	25	13	30	.333	.442
Linebrink,Scott	L	.265	49	13	4	0	0	3	5	11	.321	.347
Throws Right	R	.327	55	18	6	1	2	12	8	13	.422	.582
Lloyd,Graeme	L	.326	86	28	6	0	2	14	4	17	.355	.465
Throws Left	R	.281	139	39	7	0	4	25	15	20	.353	.417
Loaiza,Esteban	L	.308	325	100	24	1	8	44	26	41	.361	.462
Throws Right	R	.311	296	92	15	5	10	46	12	46	.338	.497
Lohse,Kyle	L	.308	341	105	24	4	13	44	45	51	.394	.516
Throws Right	R	.213	357	76	14	0	13	38	25	73	.272	.361
Looper,Braden	L	.275	142	39	7	1	4	17	11	21	.327	.423
Throws Right	R	.194	175	34	5	1	4	15	17	34	.269	.303
Lopez,Albie	L	.344	93	32	5	1	1	12	7	18	.382	.452
Throws Right	R	.268	127	34	6	2	0	12	11	21	.324	.346
Lopez,Rodrigo	L	.228	386	88	19	1	10	38	31	74	.291	.360
Throws Right	R	.241	349	84	11	4	13	37	31	62	.303	.407
Lorraine,Andrew	L	.167	12	2	1	0	0	1	1	3	.231	.250
Throws Left	R	.435	46	20	3	0	7	17	5	7	.490	.957
Loux,Shane	L	.361	36	13	3	1	2	7	2	6	.395	.667
Throws Right	R	.250	24	6	1	0	2	6	1	1	.308	.542
Lowe,Derek	L	.209	407	85	17	3	6	31	33	63	.275	.310
Throws Right	R	.213	380	81	13	0	6	27	15	64	.256	.295
Lowe,Sean	L	.351	111	39	4	2	6	18	18	19	.442	.586
Throws Right	R	.292	212	62	10	0	3	33	23	45	.376	.382
Lukasiewicz,Mark	L	.300	30	9	1	0	0	3	5	7	.389	.333
Throws Left	R	.296	27	8	0	0	0	2	4	8	.387	.296
Lundquist,David	L	.429	7	3	1	0	0	2	3	0	.600	.571
Throws Right	R	.833	6	5	1	0	0	5	2	0	.889	1.000
Lyon,Brandon	L	.321	156	50	9	3	9	22	8	18	.354	.590
Throws Right	R	.289	97	28	7	0	5	14	11	12	.366	.515
MacDougal,Mike	L	.176	17	3	0	0	0	0	4	6	.333	.176
Throws Right	R	.143	14	2	0	0	0	2	3	4	.294	.143
Maddux,Greg	L	.232	327	76	11	1	6	29	26	52	.291	.327
Throws Right	R	.276	427	118	19	1	8	31	19	66	.310	.382
Maduro,Calvin	L	.243	103	25	4	1	4	10	7	18	.295	.417
Throws Right	R	.310	126	39	11	1	8	25	15	11	.383	.603
Magnante,Mike	L	.256	39	10	1	1	1	8	5	5	.348	.410
Throws Left	R	.346	81	28	6	3	1	14	6	6	.386	.531
Mahay,Ron	L	.231	26	6	2	0	3	6	1	7	.259	.654
Throws Left	R	.226	31	7	1	0	3	8	7	7	.368	.548
Mahomes,Pat	L	.308	39	12	2	0	0	3	10	7	.460	.359
Throws Right	R	.276	87	24	7	0	3	8	7	16	.330	.460

Pitchers vs. Left-Handed and Right-Handed Batters

Pitcher	vs	Avg	AB	H	2B	3B	HR	RBI	BB	SO	OBP	Slg
Mairena,Oswaldo	L	.315	54	17	5	0	3	9	7	9	.393	.574
Throws Left	R	.269	78	21	4	1	4	13	5	12	.310	.500
Mallette,Brian	L	.500	8	4	1	0	3	5	2	1	.600	1.750
Throws Right	R	.250	12	3	0	0	0	1	1	4	.357	.250
Mann,Jim	L	.243	37	9	2	0	2	7	4	7	.317	.459
Throws Right	R	.227	44	10	3	0	1	3	3	12	.346	.364
Mantei,Matt	L	.250	32	8	2	0	2	5	2	7	.314	.500
Throws Right	R	.260	77	20	3	1	1	7	10	19	.345	.364
Manzanillo,Josias	L	.353	17	6	0	0	2	3	4	2	.500	.706
Throws Right	R	.368	38	14	4	0	3	9	1	2	.385	.711
Maroth,Mike	L	.250	116	29	9	1	1	13	7	15	.293	.371
Throws Left	R	.285	376	107	32	3	6	41	29	43	.337	.434
Marquis,Jason	L	.292	209	61	8	4	7	21	29	35	.379	.469
Throws Right	R	.276	239	66	14	1	12	39	20	49	.335	.494
Marte,Damaso	L	.149	101	15	1	0	2	11	9	35	.237	.218
Throws Left	R	.252	115	29	4	0	3	14	9	37	.312	.365
Martin,Tom	L	.000	2	0	0	0	0	0	0	0	.000	.000
Throws Left	R	.625	8	5	5	0	0	4	1	1	.667	1.250
Martinez,Pedro	L	.203	428	87	20	3	7	32	20	136	.253	.313
Throws Right	R	.191	298	57	15	0	6	23	20	103	.255	.302
Mateo,Julio	L	.333	39	13	5	0	2	8	10	6	.469	.615
Throws Right	R	.167	42	7	1	0	0	4	2	9	.222	.190
Mathews,T.J.	L	.357	28	10	2	0	0	2	2	5	.400	.429
Throws Right	R	.214	42	9	3	0	2	6	3	8	.267	.429
Matthews,Mike	L	.208	72	15	3	0	2	8	8	23	.286	.333
Throws Left	R	.292	96	28	5	0	3	17	21	11	.420	.438
Maurer,Dave	L	.500	4	2	1	0	1	2	0	0	.500	1.500
Throws Left	R	.333	3	1	0	0	0	0	0	0	.333	.333
May,Darrell	L	.288	139	40	13	0	6	24	12	32	.340	.511
Throws Left	R	.273	381	104	27	1	22	53	38	63	.338	.522
Mays,Joe	L	.275	222	61	12	0	10	33	14	23	.322	.464
Throws Right	R	.315	165	52	7	0	4	19	11	15	.356	.430
Meadows,Brian	L	.267	105	28	7	0	3	10	11	17	.336	.419
Throws Right	R	.248	137	34	8	0	4	13	3	14	.270	.394
Mecir,Jim	L	.204	108	22	5	1	3	14	15	21	.305	.352
Throws Right	R	.297	155	46	6	2	2	21	14	32	.360	.400
Mendoza,Ramiro	L	.261	165	43	9	2	4	18	6	24	.283	.412
Throws Right	R	.286	206	59	9	0	4	31	10	37	.323	.388
Mercado,Hector	L	.125	32	4	1	0	0	1	11	11	.349	.156
Throws Left	R	.252	111	28	8	1	2	20	14	29	.349	.396
Mercker,Kent	L	.206	68	14	6	0	3	9	9	20	.299	.426
Throws Left	R	.353	116	41	11	0	9	24	13	17	.427	.681
Mesa,Jose	L	.225	142	32	9	0	3	11	21	29	.337	.352
Throws Right	R	.237	139	33	6	0	2	12	18	35	.327	.324
Miceli,Dan	L	.409	22	9	1	0	1	6	2	1	.458	.591
Throws Right	R	.235	17	4	0	0	0	3	1	4	.278	.235
Michalak,Chris	L	.217	23	5	0	0	0	0	5	1	.357	.217
Throws Left	R	.417	36	15	2	0	1	6	5	4	.488	.556
Middlebrook,Jason	L	.235	68	16	2	1	1	11	14	14	.361	.338
Throws Right	R	.237	118	28	6	1	1	18	8	28	.287	.331
Miller,Justin	L	.296	189	56	9	3	7	41	34	25	.405	.487
Throws Right	R	.240	196	47	9	0	5	24	32	43	.364	.362
Miller,Matt	L	.750	4	3	1	0	0	2	0	1	.750	1.000
Throws Left	R	.333	3	1	0	0	1	4	1	0	.500	1.333
Miller,Travis	L	.000	3	0	0	0	0	0	0	0	.000	.000
Throws Left	R	.357	14	5	1	0	0	0	2	3	.438	.429
Miller,Wade	L	.254	260	66	16	3	8	25	37	56	.349	.431
Throws Right	R	.245	347	85	18	1	6	33	25	88	.301	.354
Millwood,Kevin	L	.248	379	94	15	1	8	35	38	89	.325	.356
Throws Right	R	.214	430	92	18	2	8	40	27	89	.262	.321
Milton,Eric	L	.307	114	35	4	2	10	28	7	19	.344	.640
Throws Left	R	.248	556	138	29	4	14	62	23	102	.280	.390
Mlicki,Dave	L	.354	147	52	10	2	5	23	13	22	.414	.551
Throws Right	R	.244	201	49	11	1	6	24	21	35	.314	.398
Moehler,Brian	L	.296	125	37	6	1	7	18	6	15	.328	.528
Throws Right	R	.308	133	41	13	1	4	16	7	16	.343	.511
Molina,Gabe	L	.200	15	3	0	0	1	2	3	1	.333	.400
Throws Right	R	.136	22	3	0	0	0	0	3	3	.240	.136
Moreno,Juan	L	.400	5	2	2	0	0	1	6	1	.727	.800
Throws Left	R	.222	18	4	0	1	1	5	4	2	.348	.500
Morgan,Mike	L	.328	58	19	2	0	2	6	4	7	.381	.466
Throws Right	R	.262	84	22	4	0	5	14	5	6	.319	.488
Morris,Matt	L	.267	374	100	16	2	11	49	31	78	.324	.409
Throws Right	R	.255	431	110	20	0	5	37	33	93	.311	.336
Moss,Damian	L	.165	103	17	3	2	2	7	19	27	.298	.291
Throws Left	R	.232	530	123	28	3	18	65	70	84	.326	.398

Pitcher	vs	Avg	AB	H	2B	3B	HR	RBI	BB	SO	OBP	Slg
Mota,Guillermo	L	.188	96	18	5	2	1	12	18	31	.319	.313
Throws Right	R	.213	127	27	9	0	3	17	9	18	.270	.354
Moyer,Jamie	L	.280	293	82	8	0	12	38	20	35	.339	.430
Throws Left	R	.205	567	116	25	0	16	45	30	112	.245	.333
Mulder,Mark	L	.244	172	42	8	1	5	18	9	46	.301	.390
Throws Left	R	.228	614	140	31	1	16	61	46	113	.287	.360
Mulholland,Terry	L	.312	125	39	5	2	5	22	5	17	.343	.504
Throws Left	R	.315	197	62	16	0	10	34	16	21	.371	.548
Mullen,Scott	L	.263	76	20	3	0	4	13	4	12	.309	.461
Throws Left	R	.270	74	20	3	0	1	11	9	9	.349	.351
Munro,Pete	L	.328	122	40	9	2	3	15	7	16	.374	.508
Throws Right	R	.255	192	49	10	0	2	16	16	29	.316	.339
Murray,Heath	L	.125	24	3	0	0	0	2	4	7	.300	.125
Throws Left	R	.429	21	9	0	0	3	5	3	4	.500	.857
Mussina,Mike	L	.257	444	114	20	3	16	53	34	109	.310	.423
Throws Right	R	.248	379	94	19	3	11	40	14	73	.280	.401
Myers,Brett	L	.225	111	25	5	2	5	13	14	14	.320	.441
Throws Right	R	.314	153	48	5	0	6	18	15	20	.387	.464
Myers,Mike	L	.244	78	19	6	0	0	11	10	24	.362	.321
Throws Left	R	.313	64	20	2	0	2	10	7	7	.405	.438
Myers,Rodney	L	.471	34	16	4	0	1	13	4	3	.538	.676
Throws Right	R	.245	53	13	4	0	0	7	6	8	.344	.321
Myette,Aaron	L	.396	96	38	11	1	6	26	26	20	.520	.719
Throws Right	R	.257	101	26	5	3	5	23	15	28	.376	.515
Nagy,Charles	L	.415	118	49	10	1	6	24	5	12	.439	.669
Throws Right	R	.287	94	27	6	1	4	22	8	10	.349	.500
Nance,Shane	L	.200	5	1	0	0	1	1	1	2	.333	.800
Throws Left	R	.167	18	3	1	0	0	3	3	3	.286	.222
Nathan,Joe	L	.000	4	0	0	0	0	0	0	1	.000	.000
Throws Right	R	.125	8	1	1	0	0	0	0	1	.125	.250
Neagle,Denny	L	.315	149	47	10	0	10	29	15	31	.388	.584
Throws Left	R	.251	491	123	26	5	16	66	48	80	.322	.422
Neal,Blaine	L	.266	64	17	3	0	1	11	4	14	.309	.359
Throws Right	R	.231	65	15	4	1	0	10	10	19	.333	.323
Nelson,Jeff	L	.224	76	17	6	0	1	6	15	22	.351	.342
Throws Right	R	.218	87	19	1	0	3	12	12	33	.320	.333
Nen,Robb	L	.224	152	34	9	1	1	12	10	42	.272	.316
Throws Right	R	.242	124	30	1	1	1	14	10	39	.304	.290
Neugebauer,Nick	L	.318	88	28	3	3	4	11	26	16	.474	.557
Throws Right	R	.226	124	28	6	0	6	18	18	31	.322	.419
Nichting,Chris	L	.167	60	10	2	0	0	6	4	12	.219	.200
Throws Right	R	.361	83	30	3	2	7	15	1	13	.372	.699
Nickle,Doug	L	.290	31	9	2	0	0	6	6	4	.405	.355
Throws Right	R	.386	44	17	3	0	3	11	7	5	.472	.659
Nitkowski,C.J.	L	.190	21	4	0	0	0	1	2	8	.261	.190
Throws Left	R	.250	28	7	1	0	0	1	11	6	.462	.286
Nomo,Hideo	L	.218	395	86	19	3	8	38	42	99	.293	.342
Throws Right	R	.254	406	103	19	2	18	47	59	94	.348	.443
Nomura,Takahito	L	.185	27	5	2	1	1	8	8	4	.395	.444
Throws Left	R	.273	22	6	1	0	1	4	10	5	.485	.455
Nunez,Jose	L	.000	1	0	0	0	0	0	1	0	.500	.000
Throws Left	R	.000	2	0	0	0	0	0	0	0	.000	.000
Nunez,Vladimir	L	.191	162	31	9	0	2	14	23	49	.286	.284
Throws Right	R	.251	195	49	12	1	6	26	14	24	.301	.415
Obermueller,Wes	L	.409	22	9	2	1	2	4	2	2	.458	.864
Throws Right	R	.333	15	5	1	0	1	5	0	3	.333	.600
Ohka,Tomo	L	.218	316	69	15	1	6	25	19	42	.260	.329
Throws Right	R	.298	419	125	21	6	13	48	26	76	.347	.470
Oliver,Darren	L	.462	52	24	4	0	1	8	9	8	.563	.596
Throws Left	R	.272	169	46	6	0	6	18	18	24	.347	.414
Olsen,Kevin	L	.292	106	31	7	2	2	11	15	17	.385	.453
Throws Right	R	.248	105	26	6	0	3	17	16	21	.341	.390
Oropesa,Eddie	L	.340	53	18	0	1	2	15	5	14	.397	.491
Throws Left	R	.356	59	21	4	0	4	16	10	4	.458	.627
Orosco,Jesse	L	.238	63	15	3	0	3	9	6	13	.300	.429
Throws Left	R	.214	42	9	2	0	1	3	6	9	.313	.333
Ortiz,Ramon	L	.217	406	88	12	6	22	46	39	68	.290	.438
Throws Right	R	.244	410	100	17	1	18	42	29	94	.294	.422
Ortiz,Russ	L	.247	397	98	14	4	4	39	50	65	.330	.332
Throws Right	R	.235	395	93	21	2	11	39	44	72	.315	.382
Osborne,Donovan	L	.261	23	6	2	0	0	3	4	6	.357	.348
Throws Left	R	.317	41	13	3	1	1	6	6	7	.404	.512
Osting,Jimmy	L	.400	10	4	1	0	1	2	2	1	.500	.800
Throws Left	R	.326	43	14	2	1	2	9	8	6	.431	.558
Osuna,Antonio	L	.250	120	30	7	1	0	17	21	28	.366	.325
Throws Right	R	.250	136	34	9	0	1	16	7	38	.295	.338

Pitchers vs. Left-handed and Right-Handed Batters

Pitcher	vs	Avg	AB	H	2B	3B	HR	RBI	BB	SO	OBP	Slg
Oswalt,Roy	L	.251	391	98	16	3	11	37	29	90	.306	.391
Throws Right	R	.244	479	117	23	5	6	42	33	118	.293	.351
Padilla,Vicente	L	.272	379	103	19	0	9	37	35	53	.336	.393
Throws Right	R	.236	402	95	18	2	7	36	18	75	.290	.343
Paniagua,Jose	L	.276	76	21	1	4	4	19	10	14	.360	.553
Throws Right	R	.309	94	29	3	2	6	19	5	20	.353	.574
Park,Chan Ho	L	.287	328	94	28	4	12	55	53	61	.395	.506
Throws Right	R	.254	236	60	12	1	8	33	25	60	.349	.415
Paronto,Chad	L	.226	53	12	4	1	2	11	7	7	.317	.453
Throws Right	R	.262	84	22	2	1	1	13	4	16	.297	.345
Parque,Jim	L	.394	33	13	1	0	3	8	4	5	.462	.697
Throws Left	R	.284	74	21	2	0	8	18	12	8	.379	.635
Parra,Jose	L	.214	14	3	0	0	0	1	5	1	.421	.214
Throws Right	R	.270	37	10	4	0	0	4	6	7	.386	.378
Parris,Steve	L	.341	164	56	9	0	6	21	23	21	.421	.506
Throws Right	R	.282	142	40	8	2	7	23	12	27	.346	.514
Patterson,Danny	L	.333	6	2	0	1	0	1	2	0	.500	.667
Throws Right	R	.375	8	3	1	0	0	3	0	1	.444	.500
Patterson,John	L	.236	55	13	2	0	5	6	3	13	.288	.545
Throws Right	R	.233	60	14	2	0	2	5	4	18	.281	.367
Pavano,Carl	L	.353	252	89	16	1	8	30	24	42	.411	.520
Throws Right	R	.280	304	85	17	0	11	38	21	50	.340	.444
Pearce,Josh	L	.381	21	8	1	0	1	5	3	0	.480	.571
Throws Right	R	.375	32	12	6	0	0	6	5	1	.447	.563
Pearson,Jason	L	.250	4	1	1	0	0	0	0	2	.250	.500
Throws Left	R	.000	2	0	0	0	0	0	0	1	.000	.000
Pearson,Terry	L	.308	13	4	1	1	0	2	1	0	.357	.538
Throws Right	R	.333	12	4	1	0	2	3	1	4	.385	.917
Peavy,Jake	L	.325	194	63	19	1	8	32	24	39	.405	.557
Throws Right	R	.223	193	43	7	0	3	17	9	51	.256	.306
Pember,Dave	L	.286	14	4	0	0	0	1	5	1	.450	.286
Throws Right	R	.167	18	3	2	0	1	5	1	4	.211	.444
Penny,Brad	L	.294	231	68	19	1	9	30	32	42	.379	.502
Throws Right	R	.284	282	80	10	3	9	41	18	51	.326	.436
Percival,Troy	L	.247	93	23	3	0	5	15	18	30	.366	.441
Throws Right	R	.138	109	15	2	1	0	6	7	38	.190	.174
Perez,Odalis	L	.223	179	40	4	1	4	13	9	25	.276	.324
Throws Left	R	.226	628	142	29	0	17	61	29	130	.258	.354
Perez,Oliver	L	.294	85	25	3	1	1	5	12	29	.390	.388
Throws Left	R	.191	241	46	6	1	12	29	36	65	.301	.373
Perez,Yorkis	L	.204	49	10	2	0	1	4	5	8	.278	.306
Throws Left	R	.193	57	11	4	0	3	6	9	17	.303	.421
Perisho,Matt	L	.444	9	4	0	0	0	3	3	2	.583	.444
Throws Left	R	.353	34	12	1	1	2	8	3	1	.395	.618
Person,Robert	L	.243	144	35	12	2	6	20	25	28	.370	.479
Throws Right	R	.239	184	44	14	1	7	33	26	33	.333	.440
Pettitte,Andy	L	.255	102	26	4	1	2	12	5	24	.294	.373
Throws Left	R	.276	427	118	25	0	4	39	27	73	.323	.363
Phelps,Travis	L	.267	60	16	4	0	4	11	13	12	.429	.533
Throws Right	R	.187	75	14	2	0	3	11	14	24	.315	.333
Phillips,Jason C	L	.247	93	23	4	0	5	14	13	16	.340	.452
Throws Right	R	.277	65	18	1	0	2	8	7	7	.372	.385
Pichardo,Hipolito	L	.667	3	2	1	0	0	2	1	0	.750	1.000
Throws Right	R	1.000	1	1	0	0	0	0	1	0	1.000	1.000
Pickford,Kevin	L	.375	32	12	5	1	1	9	3	5	.432	.688
Throws Left	R	.291	86	25	6	0	2	9	17	13	.419	.430
Pineda,Luis	L	.250	48	12	4	0	1	2	8	14	.379	.396
Throws Right	R	.200	65	13	4	0	3	11	16	17	.349	.400
Pineiro,Joel	L	.270	396	107	22	1	14	41	35	78	.328	.437
Throws Right	R	.239	343	82	15	2	10	30	19	58	.288	.382
Plesac,Dan	L	.120	75	9	1	0	4	12	6	28	.183	.293
Throws Left	R	.300	60	18	6	0	2	7	12	13	.417	.500
Politte,Cliff	L	.272	125	34	4	0	4	16	18	24	.361	.400
Throws Right	R	.159	145	23	6	0	1	13	10	48	.223	.221
Ponson,Sidney	L	.243	325	79	11	1	12	28	42	74	.330	.394
Throws Right	R	.273	341	93	18	1	14	47	21	46	.316	.455
Porzio,Mike	L	.269	78	21	3	0	4	13	8	16	.337	.462
Throws Left	R	.229	83	19	4	1	6	19	15	17	.356	.518
Pote,Lou	L	.221	77	17	1	0	4	10	9	16	.315	.390
Throws Right	R	.172	93	16	2	0	3	11	17	16	.295	.290
Powell,Brian	L	.293	123	36	8	1	8	15	11	18	.353	.569
Throws Right	R	.262	107	28	4	0	3	13	10	12	.322	.383
Powell,Jay	L	.222	72	16	3	0	2	12	9	14	.309	.347
Throws Right	R	.270	126	34	5	0	3	20	15	21	.352	.381
Pratt,Andy	L	1.000	1	1	0	0	0	0	0	0	1.000	1.000
Throws Left	R	.000	4	0	0	0	0	0	4	1	.500	.000

Pitcher	vs	Avg	AB	H	2B	3B	HR	RBI	BB	SO	OBP	Slg
Prinz,Bret	L	.429	14	6	3	0	0	4	3	4	.529	.643
Throws Right	R	.395	43	17	4	0	1	13	7	6	.481	.558
Prior,Mark	L	.204	186	38	9	0	7	19	22	69	.294	.366
Throws Right	R	.242	248	60	15	1	7	23	16	78	.298	.395
Prokopec,Luke	L	.346	162	56	12	1	12	33	19	22	.426	.654
Throws Right	R	.250	136	34	9	1	7	19	6	19	.283	.485
Puffer,Brandon	L	.324	71	23	7	1	1	13	27	17	.510	.493
Throws Right	R	.233	189	44	6	1	2	26	11	31	.288	.307
Quantrill,Paul	L	.258	124	32	13	0	1	11	18	25	.359	.387
Throws Right	R	.273	176	48	6	0	0	11	7	28	.304	.307
Quevedo,Ruben	L	.271	247	67	17	3	17	46	24	43	.339	.571
Throws Right	R	.302	305	92	19	2	11	48	44	50	.391	.485
Radke,Brad	L	.247	239	59	13	3	7	32	14	35	.290	.414
Throws Right	R	.300	217	65	17	2	5	30	6	27	.332	.465
Rauch,Jon	L	.258	66	17	4	0	4	11	10	10	.372	.500
Throws Right	R	.234	47	11	2	0	3	10	4	9	.288	.468
Reames,Britt	L	.342	79	27	4	1	3	13	25	17	.500	.532
Throws Right	R	.234	184	43	10	1	5	37	13	59	.294	.380
Redding,Tim	L	.258	128	33	7	1	2	13	20	30	.358	.375
Throws Right	R	.290	155	45	14	1	8	27	15	33	.347	.548
Redman,Mark	L	.289	190	55	11	4	4	26	11	32	.329	.453
Throws Left	R	.261	598	156	33	4	11	66	40	77	.310	.385
Reed,Rick	L	.262	405	106	16	4	25	56	15	85	.290	.506
Throws Right	R	.257	335	86	17	4	7	26	11	36	.286	.394
Reed,Steve	L	.181	83	15	3	0	0	5	8	9	.261	.217
Throws Right	R	.259	158	41	7	0	2	12	6	41	.316	.342
Reichert,Dan	L	.297	111	33	5	2	3	17	16	10	.380	.459
Throws Right	R	.312	141	44	7	0	7	25	9	26	.368	.511
Reitsma,Chris	L	.265	230	61	15	1	10	28	21	32	.323	.470
Throws Right	R	.268	310	83	21	1	7	38	24	52	.329	.410
Rekar,Bryan	L	.400	15	6	2	0	1	4	0	1	.400	.733
Throws Right	R	.375	16	6	0	0	0	3	6	1	.522	.375
Remlinger,Mike	L	.235	68	16	2	1	1	8	6	20	.297	.338
Throws Left	R	.184	174	32	4	1	2	11	22	49	.279	.253
Reyes,Al	L	.158	19	3	2	0	0	1	4	10	.304	.263
Throws Right	R	.162	37	6	1	0	1	7	3	11	.256	.270
Reyes,Dennys	L	.299	107	32	9	1	3	15	20	22	.409	.486
Throws Left	R	.299	221	66	15	3	7	36	25	37	.367	.489
Reynolds,Shane	L	.257	109	28	4	2	2	9	16	19	.357	.385
Throws Right	R	.284	183	52	10	1	11	29	10	28	.320	.530
Reynoso,Armando	L	.333	3	1	0	0	0	1	1	1	.500	.333
Throws Right	R	.400	5	2	1	0	0	1	0	1	.400	.600
Rhodes,Arthur	L	.158	120	19	5	1	1	20	3	41	.177	.242
Throws Left	R	.215	121	26	2	0	3	10	10	40	.275	.306
Riedling,John	L	.320	75	24	6	0	2	9	13	11	.427	.480
Throws Right	R	.163	92	15	1	0	0	1	13	19	.278	.174
Riggan,Jerrod	L	.371	70	26	2	0	2	19	9	7	.443	.486
Throws Right	R	.375	72	27	3	0	1	17	9	15	.424	.458
Rijo,Jose	L	.286	133	38	7	1	6	26	16	15	.362	.489
Throws Right	R	.280	182	51	8	1	7	23	4	23	.299	.451
Rincon,Juan	L	.283	60	17	4	1	2	13	6	9	.343	.483
Throws Right	R	.415	65	27	4	0	3	7	3	12	.441	.615
Rincon,Ricardo	L	.203	118	24	6	0	2	12	5	34	.240	.305
Throws Left	R	.267	86	23	6	0	2	16	6	15	.305	.407
Riske,David	L	.253	75	19	4	0	4	19	16	22	.394	.467
Throws Right	R	.259	116	30	5	1	4	20	19	43	.367	.422
Ritchie,Todd	L	.349	301	105	19	4	13	72	26	44	.398	.568
Throws Right	R	.282	252	71	14	1	5	25	26	33	.353	.405
Rivera,Mariano	L	.177	79	14	1	0	1	13	5	18	.244	.228
Throws Right	R	.226	93	21	4	0	2	10	6	23	.273	.333
Roa,Joe	L	.328	116	38	5	2	7	19	8	16	.371	.586
Throws Right	R	.244	164	40	7	2	4	16	5	19	.266	.384
Roberts,Grant	L	.261	69	18	2	0	1	7	7	10	.329	.333
Throws Right	R	.248	101	25	4	3	2	8	9	21	.310	.406
Roberts,Willis	L	.276	116	32	3	1	1	18	13	15	.353	.345
Throws Right	R	.266	177	47	7	0	4	23	19	36	.340	.373
Robertson,Jeriome	L	.357	14	5	1	0	2	5	0	4	.294	.857
Throws Left	R	.421	19	8	0	0	2	4	5	2	.542	.737
Robertson,Nate	L	.444	9	4	1	0	2	5	1	1	.545	1.222
Throws Left	R	.355	31	11	1	0	1	6	3	2	.429	.484
Rocker,John	L	.364	33	12	2	1	3	15	9	8	.488	.758
Throws Left	R	.266	64	17	2	0	2	7	4	22	.300	.391
Rodney,Fernando	L	.241	29	7	1	1	1	10	6	5	.361	.448
Throws Right	R	.383	47	18	3	0	1	7	4	5	.431	.511
Rodriguez,Felix	L	.236	106	25	4	0	3	18	13	27	.325	.358
Throws Right	R	.194	144	28	6	0	2	16	16	31	.282	.278

Pitchers vs. Left-Handed and Right-Handed Batters

Pitcher	vs	Avg	AB	H	2B	3B	HR	RBI	BB	SO	OBP	Slg
Rodriguez,Francisco	L	.286	7	2	0	0	0	0	1	4	.375	.286
Throws Right	R	.091	11	1	0	0	0	1	1	9	.231	.091
Rodriguez,Jose	L	.455	11	5	3	0	0	4	1	1	.500	.727
Throws Left	R	.538	13	7	3	0	0	4	5	0	.667	.769
Rodriguez,Nerio	L	.091	11	1	0	0	0	0	0	2	.091	.091
Throws Right	R	.375	8	3	0	0	1	3	1	0	.444	.750
Rodriguez,Ricardo	L	.278	72	20	3	2	3	13	11	9	.395	.500
Throws Right	R	.235	85	20	5	0	2	10	7	15	.330	.365
Rodriguez,Rich	L	.214	42	9	2	0	1	5	9	8	.365	.333
Throws Left	R	.294	17	5	3	0	0	1	2	4	.368	.471
Rogers,Kenny	L	.193	176	34	7	2	6	17	25	40	.297	.358
Throws Left	R	.280	636	178	39	3	15	69	45	67	.332	.421
Romero,J.C.	L	.214	126	27	1	0	0	8	11	44	.298	.222
Throws Left	R	.212	165	35	12	0	3	16	25	32	.316	.339
Rueter,Kirk	L	.243	177	43	3	0	3	14	15	19	.301	.311
Throws Left	R	.267	602	161	30	1	19	63	39	57	.311	.415
Rupe,Ryan	L	.246	183	45	14	0	7	32	14	25	.300	.437
Throws Right	R	.241	158	38	13	1	4	23	11	42	.322	.411
Rusch,Glendon	L	.235	187	44	6	0	10	33	13	30	.289	.428
Throws Left	R	.292	626	183	29	3	20	75	63	110	.358	.444
Ryan,B.J.	L	.192	99	19	3	0	5	15	16	35	.322	.374
Throws Left	R	.283	113	32	6	1	2	15	17	21	.382	.407
Saarloos,Kirk	L	.301	143	43	8	0	8	23	14	23	.365	.524
Throws Right	R	.302	189	57	11	1	4	26	13	31	.361	.434
Sabathia,C.C.	L	.241	195	47	8	2	3	16	19	30	.309	.349
Throws Left	R	.255	592	151	34	6	14	81	69	119	.329	.404
Sabel,Erik	L	1.000	1	1	0	0	1	1	0	0	1.000	4.000
Throws Right	R	1.000	1	1	1	0	0	0	0	0	1.000	2.000
Sadler,Carl	L	.205	39	8	2	0	0	4	4	15	.279	.256
Throws Left	R	.219	32	7	1	0	2	6	7	8	.359	.438
Sanchez,Duaner	L	.200	10	2	0	0	1	3	1	2	.273	.500
Throws Right	R	.286	14	4	2	0	1	4	6	4	.500	.643
Sanchez,Jesus	L	.222	18	4	1	0	1	8	1	3	.263	.444
Throws Left	R	.550	20	11	2	0	3	9	9	3	.656	1.100
Santana,Johan	L	.195	77	15	5	0	0	7	7	18	.256	.260
Throws Left	R	.216	319	69	11	1	7	25	42	119	.309	.323
Santana,Julio	L	.256	90	23	3	1	3	12	15	15	.374	.411
Throws Right	R	.224	116	26	2	1	5	12	13	23	.302	.388
Santiago,Jose	L	.304	69	21	6	1	1	16	6	6	.355	.464
Throws Right	R	.282	124	35	4	2	6	21	9	24	.343	.492
Santos,Victor	L	.277	47	13	4	0	0	8	10	12	.397	.362
Throws Right	R	.418	67	28	5	0	3	21	12	13	.506	.627
Sasaki,Kazuhiro	L	.205	117	24	5	0	2	13	10	41	.264	.299
Throws Right	R	.196	102	20	2	1	4	9	10	32	.274	.353
Sauerbeck,Scott	L	.146	96	14	2	0	2	9	6	33	.196	.229
Throws Left	R	.275	131	36	9	0	2	14	21	37	.379	.389
Schilling,Curt	L	.243	449	109	22	5	14	46	17	140	.270	.408
Throws Right	R	.208	525	109	10	3	15	44	16	176	.234	.324
Schmidt,Jason	L	.259	328	85	12	1	11	43	46	88	.350	.402
Throws Right	R	.180	350	63	16	0	4	30	27	108	.239	.260
Schoeneweis,Scott	L	.202	129	26	3	0	5	13	10	25	.270	.341
Throws Left	R	.290	321	93	19	1	12	53	39	40	.367	.467
Seanez,Rudy	L	.220	59	13	0	0	2	9	17	19	.390	.322
Throws Right	R	.238	63	15	5	0	3	10	7	21	.314	.460
Sedlacek,Shawn	L	.324	173	56	11	0	10	31	22	21	.393	.561
Throws Right	R	.279	154	43	10	0	6	26	14	31	.354	.461
Sele,Aaron	L	.315	317	100	20	1	7	40	30	44	.374	.451
Throws Right	R	.283	318	90	14	1	14	41	19	38	.328	.465
Seo,Jae	L	-	0	0	0	0	0	0	0	0	-	-
Throws Right	R	.000	3	0	0	0	0	0	0	1	.000	.000
Sheets,Ben	L	.318	406	129	33	3	13	58	39	61	.382	.510
Throws Right	R	.247	438	108	22	1	8	37	31	109	.307	.356
Shields,Scot	L	.184	76	14	1	0	3	3	10	16	.279	.316
Throws Right	R	.191	89	17	2	0	1	8	11	14	.287	.247
Shiell,Jason	L	.600	5	3	0	0	0	2	2	1	.714	.600
Throws Right	R	.800	5	4	0	0	0	0	1	0	.833	.800
Shouse,Brian	L	.276	29	8	1	0	2	10	3	10	.364	.517
Throws Left	R	.241	29	7	3	0	1	6	6	1	.378	.448
Shuey,Paul	L	.226	115	26	3	1	1	15	16	27	.318	.296
Throws Right	R	.217	138	30	8	1	2	18	15	36	.297	.333
Silva,Carlos	L	.294	119	35	10	1	0	9	12	15	.364	.395
Throws Right	R	.275	193	53	11	1	4	30	10	26	.316	.404
Silva,Jose	L	.276	29	8	3	0	2	6	8	3	.447	.586
Throws Right	R	.304	56	17	2	0	1	6	2	3	.344	.393
Simontacchi,Jason	L	.248	226	56	15	0	9	22	27	31	.333	.434
Throws Right	R	.257	304	78	20	1	9	37	27	41	.321	.418

Pitcher	vs	Avg	AB	H	2B	3B	HR	RBI	BB	SO	OBP	Slg
Small,Aaron	L	.000	1	0	0	0	0	0	2	1	.667	.000
Throws Right	R	1.000	2	2	2	0	0	4	0	0	1.000	2.000
Smith,Bud	L	.326	46	15	3	0	0	4	1	9	.353	.391
Throws Left	R	.342	152	52	11	1	4	29	21	13	.420	.507
Smith,Dan	L	.151	53	8	2	0	2	6	8	13	.254	.302
Throws Right	R	.239	109	26	4	1	4	10	13	21	.325	.404
Smith,Mike	L	.378	74	28	2	2	1	18	9	4	.447	.500
Throws Right	R	.217	69	15	4	0	2	8	11	12	.372	.362
Smith,Roy	L	.375	16	6	0	0	1	3	1	1	.412	.563
Throws Right	R	.231	13	3	1	0	0	0	4	1	.444	.308
Smith,Travis	L	.273	88	24	4	0	3	11	6	14	.319	.420
Throws Right	R	.357	126	45	8	0	7	27	14	18	.434	.587
Smoltz,John	L	.214	140	30	9	1	1	17	10	43	.267	.314
Throws Right	R	.197	147	29	3	1	3	14	14	42	.265	.293
Smyth,Steve	L	.241	29	7	2	1	2	6	3	5	.313	.586
Throws Left	R	.351	77	27	6	1	7	21	7	11	.393	.727
Soriano,Rafael	L	.297	101	30	6	1	5	14	8	14	.349	.525
Throws Right	R	.179	84	15	5	0	3	10	8	18	.250	.345
Sosa,Jorge	L	.290	186	54	10	1	6	30	32	19	.392	.452
Throws Right	R	.182	187	34	7	0	10	29	22	29	.269	.380
Sparks,Steve	L	.301	372	112	17	4	10	61	25	48	.350	.449
Throws Right	R	.310	406	126	38	4	13	69	42	50	.381	.520
Speier,Justin	L	.240	104	25	5	0	4	11	6	22	.282	.404
Throws Right	R	.197	132	26	6	0	5	19	13	25	.282	.356
Spooneybarger,Tim	L	.150	60	9	4	0	0	2	14	16	.316	.217
Throws Right	R	.234	124	29	1	0	4	15	12	17	.307	.339
Springer,Dennis	L	.333	3	1	1	0	0	1	2	0	.600	.667
Throws Right	R	.000	2	0	0	0	0	0	0	1	.000	.000
Standridge,Jason	L	.444	9	4	1	0	1	3	3	1	.583	.889
Throws Right	R	.600	5	3	0	0	0	0	1	0	.667	.600
Stanton,Mike	L	.264	125	33	6	0	2	19	11	27	.312	.360
Throws Left	R	.250	160	40	8	2	2	15	17	17	.318	.363
Stark,Denny	L	.228	184	42	9	0	13	34	39	28	.361	.489
Throws Right	R	.224	295	66	9	2	12	32	25	36	.292	.390
Stechschulte,Gene	L	.263	38	10	0	0	2	10	5	6	.341	.421
Throws Right	R	.221	77	17	4	0	2	10	12	15	.323	.351
Stein,Blake	L	.319	94	30	3	1	3	20	15	19	.409	.468
Throws Right	R	.293	99	29	7	3	3	17	12	23	.379	.515
Stephens,John	L	.268	123	33	7	0	6	20	12	32	.328	.472
Throws Right	R	.273	128	35	3	1	7	24	10	24	.336	.477
Stephenson,Garrett	L	.355	76	27	7	0	2	16	10	11	.444	.526
Throws Right	R	.223	94	21	8	0	2	7	15	23	.342	.372
Stewart,Scott	L	.157	89	14	1	0	1	5	3	32	.194	.202
Throws Left	R	.236	148	35	8	3	3	19	19	35	.320	.392
Stone,Ricky	L	.291	79	23	3	0	5	14	13	13	.391	.519
Throws Right	R	.257	214	55	7	1	4	34	21	50	.324	.355
Stottlemyre,Todd	L	.310	42	13	1	1	3	11	5	5	.375	.595
Throws Right	R	.317	41	13	2	1	1	6	2	7	.349	.488
Strange,Pat	L	.154	13	2	1	0	0	0	0	2	.154	.231
Throws Right	R	.250	16	4	0	1	0	0	1	2	.294	.375
Strickland,Scott	L	.316	95	30	2	4	3	14	16	11	.414	.516
Throws Right	R	.187	166	31	5	2	4	21	17	58	.267	.313
Stull,Everett	L	.417	24	10	2	0	0	4	6	3	.533	.500
Throws Right	R	.278	18	5	2	0	0	3	3	4	.409	.389
Sturtze,Tanyon	L	.323	443	143	28	1	22	68	60	64	.404	.540
Throws Right	R	.282	454	128	29	1	11	64	29	73	.333	.423
Sullivan,Scott	L	.357	126	45	8	2	7	26	12	26	.414	.619
Throws Right	R	.253	190	48	5	0	8	30	19	52	.330	.405
Suppan,Jeff	L	.275	425	117	21	3	12	54	40	49	.335	.424
Throws Right	R	.282	397	112	21	2	20	58	28	60	.335	.496
Suzuki,Mac	L	.371	35	13	4	0	0	8	10	4	.511	.486
Throws Right	R	.239	46	11	3	0	2	15	7	11	.333	.435
Swindell,Greg	L	.339	59	20	3	0	6	16	0	10	.333	.695
Throws Left	R	.234	77	18	6	1	3	13	5	13	.277	.455
Tallet,Brian	L	.222	9	2	1	0	0	1	1	2	.364	.333
Throws Left	R	.212	33	7	5	0	0	1	3	3	.278	.364
Tam,Jeff	L	.300	60	18	2	0	0	6	9	3	.386	.333
Throws Right	R	.352	108	38	8	3	2	30	4	11	.383	.537
Tankersley,Dennis	L	.363	80	29	5	0	6	21	18	12	.475	.650
Throws Right	R	.263	114	30	10	0	4	21	22	27	.406	.456
Tavarez,Julian	L	.333	300	100	27	2	3	39	55	32	.437	.467
Throws Right	R	.284	310	88	27	2	6	50	19	35	.352	.442
Taylor,Aaron	L	.444	9	4	0	0	1	2	0	1	.444	.778
Throws Right	R	.286	14	4	1	0	1	4	0	5	.286	.571
Tejera,Michael	L	.228	114	26	6	0	4	15	20	22	.350	.386
Throws Left	R	.280	422	118	28	3	13	48	40	73	.345	.453

Pitchers vs. Left-Handed and Right-Handed Batters

Pitcher	vs	Avg	AB	H	2B	3B	HR	RBI	BB	SO	OBP	Slg
Telford,Anthony	L	.273	44	12	3	0	2	4	9	9	.396	.477
Throws Right	R	.353	51	18	3	2	1	13	6	10	.444	.549
Tessmer,Jay	L	-	0	0	0	0	0	0	1	0	1.000	-
Throws Right	R	.000	4	0	0	0	0	0	1	0	.200	.000
Teut,Nate	L	.286	7	2	0	0	0	0	1	2	.375	.286
Throws Left	R	.423	26	11	4	0	0	7	2	2	.464	.577
Thomson,John	L	.285	368	105	20	1	13	42	26	58	.328	.451
Throws Right	R	.264	363	96	29	4	15	62	18	49	.299	.490
Thurman,Corey	L	.236	123	29	10	0	5	17	23	32	.365	.439
Throws Right	R	.259	139	36	6	1	6	16	22	24	.360	.446
Thurman,Mike	L	.361	61	22	5	0	1	9	7	9	.426	.492
Throws Right	R	.303	76	23	5	1	1	14	5	14	.354	.434
Timlin,Mike	L	.208	125	26	1	1	4	10	10	12	.272	.328
Throws Right	R	.214	229	49	12	0	11	29	4	38	.239	.410
Tollberg,Brian	L	.373	118	44	11	0	5	19	11	12	.414	.593
Throws Right	R	.317	139	44	14	1	6	21	8	21	.353	.561
Tomko,Brett	L	.270	374	101	24	4	9	35	31	56	.327	.428
Throws Right	R	.264	421	111	23	3	22	62	29	70	.308	.489
Torres,Salomon	L	.241	54	13	1	0	0	4	9	4	.349	.259
Throws Right	R	.273	55	15	2	1	2	5	4	8	.355	.455
Towers,Josh	L	.404	57	23	3	0	7	14	5	7	.444	.825
Throws Right	R	.322	59	19	2	0	4	10	0	6	.317	.559
Trachsel,Steve	L	.233	318	74	11	1	9	34	34	46	.305	.358
Throws Right	R	.281	342	96	17	1	7	33	35	59	.347	.398
Trombley,Mike	L	.444	9	4	2	0	1	4	1	1	.500	1.000
Throws Right	R	.462	13	6	3	0	1	3	0	2	.462	.923
Trujillo,J.J.	L	.200	5	1	0	0	0	1	5	2	.600	.200
Throws Right	R	.500	6	3	1	0	1	2	1	1	.625	1.167
Tucker,T.J.	L	.263	76	20	4	1	1	7	15	8	.380	.382
Throws Right	R	.302	162	49	16	1	4	24	16	34	.363	.488
Urbina,Ugueth	L	.257	113	29	6	0	6	15	14	26	.333	.469
Throws Right	R	.143	105	15	4	2	2	8	6	45	.188	.276
Valdes,Ismael	L	.255	411	105	20	1	15	44	32	52	.315	.418
Throws Right	R	.259	344	89	20	2	11	41	15	50	.297	.424
Van Hekken,Andy	L	.364	11	4	0	0	1	2	5	0	.563	.636
Throws Left	R	.306	111	34	10	0	1	10	1	5	.310	.423
Van Poppel,Todd	L	.291	127	37	8	0	6	16	17	37	.375	.496
Throws Right	R	.262	164	43	13	0	8	36	12	48	.322	.488
Vance,Cory	L	.333	3	1	0	0		1	3	0	.714	1.333
Throws Left	R	.250	12	3	0	0	1	2	1	1	.308	.500
Vazquez,Javier	L	.283	417	118	24	4	19	49	40	84	.346	.496
Throws Right	R	.261	479	125	32	3	9	54	9	95	.276	.397
Venafro,Mike	L	.262	65	17	2	1	1	7	8	10	.351	.369
Throws Left	R	.346	81	28	3	1	4	20	6	6	.389	.556
Veres,Dave	L	.190	116	22	3	0	4	11	24	27	.324	.319
Throws Right	R	.246	183	45	7	2	8	26	15	41	.308	.437
Villafuerte,Brandon	L	.286	56	16	3	0	0	5	7	13	.369	.339
Throws Right	R	.213	61	13	0	0	2	7	5	12	.284	.311
Villone,Ron	L	.233	120	28	6	0	2	15	8	24	.301	.333
Throws Left	R	.289	232	67	17	5	6	40	26	31	.360	.483
Vizcaino,Luis	L	.225	111	25	7	0	1	13	11	32	.296	.315
Throws Right	R	.170	176	30	5	0	5	14	19	47	.258	.284
Vosberg,Ed	L	.600	5	3	1	0	1	4	1	0	.667	1.400
Throws Left	R	.000	2	0	0	0	0	0	0	0	.000	.000
Voyles,Brad	L	.318	44	14	2	1	2	9	10	11	.444	.545
Throws Right	R	.262	65	17	5	1	3	11	8	15	.360	.508
Wagner,Billy	L	.180	61	11	1	0	1	4	4	21	.231	.246
Throws Left	R	.201	199	40	7	0	6	18	18	67	.270	.327
Wakefield,Tim	L	.197	269	53	18	1	6	25	32	57	.283	.338
Throws Right	R	.211	323	68	11	0	9	33	19	77	.270	.328
Walker,Jamie	L	.200	90	18	1	0	7	18	3	26	.242	.444
Throws Left	R	.197	71	14	1	1	2	8	6	14	.275	.324
Walker,Kevin	L	.238	21	5	2	0	1	2	4	8	.304	.476
Throws Left	R	.467	15	7	1	1	1	3	3	3	.556	.867
Walker,Pete	L	.288	271	78	19	1	11	41	35	36	.371	.487
Throws Right	R	.254	264	67	20	0	7	35	16	44	.295	.409
Walker,Tyler	L	.235	17	4	2	0	1	3	3	4	.350	.529
Throws Right	R	.259	27	7	0	0	2	5	2	3	.310	.481
Wall,Donne	L	.139	36	5	0	1	0	4	4	9	.220	.194
Throws Right	R	.293	41	12	3	0	3	12	3	4	.356	.585
Washburn,Jarrod	L	.199	181	36	13	0	5	15	15	35	.264	.354
Throws Left	R	.246	598	147	37	1	14	50	44	104	.297	.381
Watson,Mark	L	.222	9	2	0	0	0	1	1	1	.273	.222
Throws Left	R	.600	10	6	1	0	1	6	3	0	.692	1.000
Wayne,Justin	L	.214	42	9	3	0	1	5	8	7	.333	.357
Throws Right	R	.271	48	13	4	0	2	7	5	9	.333	.479
Weathers,David	L	.267	105	28	4	1	0	16	16	26	.360	.324
Throws Right	R	.232	177	41	5	1	6	20	20	35	.315	.373
Weaver,Jeff	L	.233	387	90	26	3	6	29	28	71	.296	.362
Throws Right	R	.268	385	103	21	1	10	47	20	61	.308	.405
Weber,Ben	L	.245	102	25	8	1	1	13	15	13	.336	.373
Throws Right	R	.251	179	45	10	0	3	15	7	30	.291	.358
Wells,Bob	L	.355	110	39	7	0	3	16	11	20	.413	.500
Throws Right	R	.300	130	39	4	0	5	26	5	10	.326	.446
Wells,David	L	.213	202	43	12	0	5	19	14	35	.271	.347
Throws Left	R	.274	610	167	39	3	16	68	31	102	.310	.426
Wells,Kip	L	.274	361	99	14	3	11	39	40	45	.347	.421
Throws Right	R	.249	394	98	21	1	10	42	31	89	.310	.383
Westbrook,Jake	L	.292	89	26	6	1	4	22	10	11	.364	.517
Throws Right	R	.300	80	24	4	1	2	15	2	9	.321	.450
White,Gabe	L	.200	90	18	4	1	1	8	5	21	.258	.300
Throws Left	R	.270	115	31	8	2	2	12	5	20	.300	.426
White,Rick	L	.302	86	26	6	3	2	6	10	12	.371	.512
Throws Right	R	.242	149	36	7	2	2	21	11	29	.293	.356
Wickman,Bob	L	.275	80	22	5	0	2	12	6	18	.326	.413
Throws Right	R	.294	68	20	4	0	1	6	4	18	.342	.397
Wiggins,Scott	L	.250	8	2	0	0	0	1	0	3	.250	.250
Throws Left	R	.750	4	3	1	0	1	1	1	0	.800	1.750
Williams,Dave	L	.086	35	3	1	0	0	4	2	11	.200	.114
Throws Left	R	.271	129	35	8	1	9	17	22	22	.379	.558
Williams,Jeff	L	.250	16	4	0	0	0	3	2	5	.333	.250
Throws Left	R	.379	29	11	2	0	2	7	5	6	.472	.655
Williams,Mike	L	.283	120	34	7	0	1	12	14	22	.358	.367
Throws Right	R	.179	112	20	1	1	5	14	7	21	.233	.339
Williams,Woody	L	.182	176	32	3	0	6	10	14	41	.250	.301
Throws Right	R	.256	203	52	9	1	4	17	11	35	.300	.369
Williamson,Scott	L	.198	101	20	5	1	3	12	18	29	.328	.356
Throws Right	R	.170	153	26	4	0	2	14	18	55	.256	.235
Wilson,Kris	L	.378	37	14	4	0	4	11	1	6	.385	.811
Throws Right	R	.333	45	15	5	1	3	12	4	4	.404	.689
Wilson,Paul	L	.309	359	111	28	5	13	50	40	46	.379	.524
Throws Right	R	.267	404	108	19	1	16	56	27	65	.327	.438
Wise,Matt	L	.375	8	3	0	0	0	2	0	2	.375	.375
Throws Right	R	.182	22	4	1	0	0	1	1	4	.250	.227
Witasick,Jay	L	.228	101	23	5	1	0	5	13	27	.322	.297
Throws Right	R	.238	147	35	7	0	3	11	8	27	.289	.347
Wohlers,Mark	L	.259	116	30	5	0	5	21	13	26	.333	.431
Throws Right	R	.263	156	41	8	0	1	20	13	20	.327	.333
Wolf,Randy	L	.258	120	31	8	1	4	12	18	34	.357	.442
Throws Left	R	.216	652	141	24	3	19	60	45	138	.271	.350
Wood,Kerry	L	.223	363	81	19	0	8	34	61	100	.340	.342
Throws Right	R	.219	401	88	20	1	14	47	36	117	.301	.379
Woodard,Steve	L	.323	31	10	2	1	2	7	2	5	.364	.645
Throws Right	R	.238	42	10	2	0	2	8	6	9	.360	.429
Worrell,Tim	L	.204	103	21	4	2	1	17	18	29	.320	.311
Throws Right	R	.218	156	34	9	0	2	9	12	26	.269	.314
Wright,Dan	L	.257	413	106	23	0	18	58	42	83	.327	.443
Throws Right	R	.270	348	94	20	2	14	47	29	53	.326	.440
Wright,Jamey	L	.271	229	62	12	0	9	31	51	38	.406	.441
Throws Right	R	.267	255	68	14	0	8	44	24	39	.345	.416
Wright,Jaret	L	.458	48	22	7	0	1	15	13	4	.578	.667
Throws Right	R	.409	44	18	4	0	2	17	6	8	.462	.636
Wunsch,Kelly	L	.208	72	15	2	0	1	13	8	15	.313	.278
Throws Left	R	.268	41	11	2	0	2	9	11	7	.444	.463
Yan,Esteban	L	.273	128	35	7	2	8	27	20	23	.369	.547
Throws Right	R	.246	142	35	5	0	2	8	9	30	.305	.324
Yoshii,Masato	L	.251	223	56	5	0	5	22	22	32	.319	.341
Throws Right	R	.306	284	87	22	1	10	36	10	42	.333	.496
Zambrano,Carlos	L	.209	163	34	8	2	2	19	35	38	.355	.319
Throws Right	R	.253	237	60	7	0	7	28	28	55	.336	.371
Zambrano,Victor	L	.292	195	57	13	1	6	28	41	31	.416	.462
Throws Right	R	.266	237	63	14	2	9	48	27	42	.339	.456
Zerbe,Chad	L	.247	85	21	5	0	0	8	9	13	.333	.306
Throws Left	R	.248	125	31	1	2	3	16	12	13	.321	.360
Zito,Barry	L	.275	171	47	5	1	7	14	20	34	.352	.439
Throws Left	R	.203	665	135	19	2	17	54	58	148	.273	.314

2002 Leader Boards

You'll find a higher quantity and higher quality of Leader Boards in this section than you've ever seen before in print. Each Board has the Top 10 players, giving a more complete picture of the best (or worst) players in each category.

You'll also find some Boards containing the complex pitching data we charted in 2002. There's more of this in the Pitch Data Analysis Section. Look out for a lot more of it from Baseball Info Solutions in the future.

And what the heck is "Best BPS on POSZ" you're very likely to ask?

POSZ stands for "Pitches Outside The Strike Zone" and BPS is Batting Average Plus Slugging, a combination we felt made more sense than OPS (On-Base Plus Slugging) when evaluating a player's hitting abilities outside the strike zone. (In this case, we're not all that interested in knowing who walks the most - we know that already. OPS outside the strike zone would be heavily populated with the league's most frequent walkers.)

2002 American League Batting Leaders

Batting Average (minimum 502 PA)		On Base Percentage (minimum 502 PA)		Slugging Average (minimum 502 PA)		Home Runs	
Ramirez,Manny, Bos	.349	Ramirez,Manny, Bos	.450	Thome,Jim, Cle	.677	Rodriguez,Alex, Tex	57
Sweeney,Mike, KC	.340	Thome,Jim, Cle	.445	Ramirez,Manny, Bos	.647	Thome,Jim, Cle	52
Williams,B, NYY	.333	Giambi,Jason, NYY	.435	Rodriguez,Alex, Tex	.623	Palmeiro,R, Tex	43
Suzuki,Ichiro, Sea	.321	Sweeney,Mike, KC	.417	Giambi,Jason, NYY	.598	Giambi,Jason, NYY	41
Ordonez,M, CWS	.320	Williams,B, NYY	.415	Ordonez,M, CWS	.597	Soriano,A, NYY	39
Giambi,Jason, NYY	.314	Delgado,Carlos, Tor	.406	Palmeiro,R, Tex	.571	Ordonez,M, CWS	38
Kennedy,Adam, Ana	.312	Olerud,John, Sea	.403	Sweeney,Mike, KC	.563	Chavez,Eric, Oak	34
Garciaparra,N, Bos	.310	Rodriguez,Alex, Tex	.392	Delgado,Carlos, Tor	.549	Tejada,Miguel, Oak	34
Tejada,Miguel, Oak	.308	Palmeiro,R, Tex	.391	Soriano,A, NYY	.547	Delgado,Carlos, Tor	33
Anderson,G, Ana	.306	Suzuki,Ichiro, Sea	.388	Burks,Ellis, Cle	.541	Ramirez,Manny, Bos	33

Games		Plate Appearances		At Bats		Hits	
Beltran,Carlos, KC	162	Soriano,A, NYY	741	Soriano,A, NYY	696	Soriano,A, NYY	209
Long,Terrence, Oak	162	Jeter,Derek, NYY	730	Tejada,Miguel, Oak	662	Suzuki,Ichiro, Sea	208
Rodriguez,Alex, Tex	162	Suzuki,Ichiro, Sea	728	Suzuki,Ichiro, Sea	647	Tejada,Miguel, Oak	204
Tejada,Miguel, Oak	162	Rodriguez,Alex, Tex	725	Jeter,Derek, NYY	644	Williams,B, NYY	204
Batista,Tony, Bal	161	Beltran,Carlos, KC	722	Anderson,G, Ana	638	Garciaparra,N, Bos	197
Wells,Vernon, Tor	159	Tejada,Miguel, Oak	715	Beltran,Carlos, KC	637	Anderson,G, Ana	195
Anderson,G, Ana	158	Damon,Johnny, Bos	702	Garciaparra,N, Bos	635	Jeter,Derek, NYY	191
Cameron,Mike, Sea	158	Eckstein,David, Ana	702	Hillenbrand,S, Bos	634	Ordonez,M, CWS	189
Jeter,Derek, NYY	157	Williams,B, NYY	699	Erstad,Darin, Ana	625	Rodriguez,Alex, Tex	187
Suzuki,Ichiro, Sea	157	Garciaparra,N, Bos	693	Rodriguez,Alex, Tex	624	Hillenbrand,S, Bos	186

Singles		Doubles		Triples		Total Bases	
Suzuki,Ichiro, Sea	165	Anderson,G, Ana	56	Damon,Johnny, Bos	11	Rodriguez,Alex, Tex	389
Jeter,Derek, NYY	147	Garciaparra,N, Bos	56	Winn,Randy, TB	9	Soriano,A, NYY	381
Williams,B, NYY	146	Soriano,A, NYY	51	Suzuki,Ichiro, Sea	8	Ordonez,M, CWS	352
Eckstein,David, Ana	142	Ordonez,M, CWS	47	Young,Michael, Tex	8	Anderson,G, Ana	344
Tejada,Miguel, Oak	140	Beltran,Carlos, KC	44	Beltran,Carlos, KC	7	Tejada,Miguel, Oak	336
Erstad,Darin, Ana	135	Hillenbrand,S, Bos	43	15 tied with	6	Garciaparra,N, Bos	335
Guzman,C, Min	124	Posada,Jorge, NYY	40			Giambi,Jason, NYY	335
Hillenbrand,S, Bos	121	Olerud,John, Sea	39			Thome,Jim, Cle	325
Stewart,Sh, Tor	121	Winn,Randy, TB	39			Beltran,Carlos, KC	319
2 tied with	119	2 tied with	38			Palmeiro,R, Tex	312

Runs Scored		RBI		Walks		Strikeouts	
Soriano,A, NYY	128	Rodriguez,Alex, Tex	142	Thome,Jim, Cle	122	Cameron,Mike, Sea	176
Rodriguez,Alex, Tex	125	Ordonez,M, CWS	135	Giambi,Jason, NYY	109	Soriano,A, NYY	157
Jeter,Derek, NYY	124	Tejada,Miguel, Oak	131	Palmeiro,R, Tex	104	Glaus,Troy, Ana	144
Giambi,Jason, NYY	120	Anderson,G, Ana	123	Delgado,Carlos, Tor	102	Posada,Jorge, NYY	143
Damon,Johnny, Bos	118	Giambi,Jason, NYY	122	Olerud,John, Sea	98	Sandberg,Jared, TB	139
Ordonez,M, CWS	116	Garciaparra,N, Bos	120	Ventura,Robin, NYY	90	Thome,Jim, Cle	139
Beltran,Carlos, KC	114	Thome,Jim, Cle	118	Glaus,Troy, Ana	88	Hinske,Eric, Tor	138
Durham,Ray, CWS-Oak	114	Glaus,Troy, Ana	111	Thomas,Frank, CWS	88	Beltran,Carlos, KC	135
Suzuki,Ichiro, Sea	111	Chavez,Eric, Oak	109	Rodriguez,Alex, Tex	87	Jones,Jacque, Min	129
Tejada,Miguel, Oak	108	Delgado,Carlos, Tor	108	Williams,B, NYY	83	Koskie,Corey, Min	127

2002 American League Batting Leaders

Sacrifice Hits		Sacrifice Flies		Stolen Bases		Caught Stealing	
Eckstein,David, Ana	14	Olerud,John, Sea	12	Soriano,A, NYY	41	Suzuki,Ichiro, Sea	15
Cirillo,Jeff, Sea	13	Garciaparra,N, Bos	11	Beltran,Carlos, KC	35	Eckstein,David, Ana	13
Young,Michael, Tex	13	Randa,Joe, KC	11	Jeter,Derek, NYY	32	Guzman,C, Min	13
Durham,Ray, CWS-Oak	10	Anderson,G, Ana	10	Cameron,Mike, Sea	31	Soriano,A, NYY	13
Rowand,Aaron, CWS	9	Conine,Jeff, Bal	10	Damon,Johnny, Bos	31	Koskie,Corey, Min	11
Abernathy,B, TB	8	Thomas,Frank, CWS	10	Suzuki,Ichiro, Sea	31	McLemore,Mark, Sea	10
Ellis,Mark, Oak	8	Vizquel,Omar, Cle	10	Winn,Randy, TB	27	Mora,Melvin, Bal	10
Guzman,C, Min	8	Cirillo,Jeff, Sea	9	Durham,Ray, CWS-Oak	26	Vizquel,Omar, Cle	10
Hairston Jr.,J, Bal	8	7 tied with	8	3 tied with	23	3 tied with	9
Rivas,Luis, Min	8						

Intentional Walks		Hit By Pitch		Grounded Into DP		Grounded Into DP Pct	
						(minimum 50 GIDP Ops)	
Suzuki,Ichiro, Sea	27	Eckstein,David, Ana	27	Posada,Jorge, NYY	23	Lofton,Kenny, CWS	0.00
Delgado,Carlos, Tor	18	Mora,Melvin, Bal	20	Ordonez,M, CWS	21	McLemore,Mark, Sea	0.03
Thome,Jim, Cle	18	Fullmer,Brad, Ana	15	Tejada,Miguel, Oak	21	Damon,Johnny, Bos	0.04
Palmeiro,R, Tex	16	Giambi,Jason, NYY	15	Olerud,John, Sea	19	Thome,Jim, Cle	0.04
Ramirez,Manny, Bos	14	Soriano,A, NYY	14	Williams,B, NYY	19	Ellis,Mark, Oak	0.04
Chavez,Eric, Oak	13	Delgado,Carlos, Tor	13	Giambi,Jason, NYY	18	Lee,Carlos, CWS	0.05
Rodriguez,Alex, Tex	12	Hillenbrand,S, Bos	12	Hillenbrand,S, Bos	18	Mench,Kevin, Tex	0.05
Anderson,G, Ana	11	Johnson,Nick, NYY	12	11 tied with	17	Tucker,Michael, KC	0.05
Sweeney,Mike, KC	10	4 tied with	11			Matthews Jr,G, Bal	0.05
3 tied with	9					Guiel,Aaron, KC	0.05

Leadoff Hitters OBP		Cleanup Hitters SLG		BA vs. LHP		BA vs. RHP	
(minimum 150 PA)		(minimum 150 PA)		(minimum 125 PA)		(minimum 377 PA)	
Suzuki,Ichiro, Sea	.383	Thome,Jim, Cle	.707	Spiezio,Scott, Ana	.368	Sweeney,Mike, KC	.334
Giambi,Jeremy, Oak	.380	Giambi,Jason, NYY	.640	Suzuki,Ichiro, Sea	.356	Jones,Jacque, Min	.333
Stewart,Sh, Tor	.379	Ordonez,M, CWS	.628	Williams,B, NYY	.354	Thome,Jim, Cle	.333
Winn,Randy, TB	.375	Ramirez,Manny, Bos	.621	Winn,Randy, TB	.347	Ramirez,Manny, Bos	.331
Henderson,R, Bos	.368	Sweeney,Mike, KC	.602	Posada,Jorge, NYY	.326	Ordonez,M, CWS	.329
Catalanotto,F, Tex	.366	Palmeiro,R, Tex	.582	Randa,Joe, KC	.321	Williams,B, NYY	.326
Eckstein,David, Ana	.364	Konerko,Paul, CWS	.580	Burks,Ellis, Cle	.316	Rodriguez,Alex, Tex	.320
Durham,Ray, CWS-Oak	.357	Anderson,G, Ana	.554	Soriano,A, NYY	.316	Giambi,Jason, NYY	.320
Lofton,Kenny, CWS	.349	Delgado,Carlos, Tor	.549	Jeter,Derek, NYY	.315	Kennedy,Adam, Ana	.319
Ellis,Mark, Oak	.347	Ibanez,Raul, KC	.530	Huff,Aubrey, TB	.307	Anderson,G, Ana	.316

Home BA		Away BA		OBP vs. LHP		OBP vs. RHP	
(minimum 251 PA)		(minimum 251 PA)		(minimum 125 PA)		(minimum 377 PA)	
Thome,Jim, Cle	.350	Ramirez,Manny, Bos	.360	Spiezio,Scott, Ana	.448	Thome,Jim, Cle	.485
Ramirez,Manny, Bos	.336	Williams,B, NYY	.354	Williams,B, NYY	.430	Giambi,Jason, NYY	.448
Hunter,Torii, Min	.334	Sweeney,Mike, KC	.349	Posada,Jorge, NYY	.420	Delgado,Carlos, Tor	.444
Giambi,Jason, NYY	.333	Burks,Ellis, Cle	.341	Suzuki,Ichiro, Sea	.416	Ramirez,Manny, Bos	.433
Sweeney,Mike, KC	.331	Tejada,Miguel, Oak	.336	Salmon,Tim, Ana	.411	Palmeiro,R, Tex	.420
Garciaparra,N, Bos	.328	Suzuki,Ichiro, Sea	.334	Jeter,Derek, NYY	.410	Sweeney,Mike, KC	.418
Tucker,Michael, KC	.328	Jones,Jacque, Min	.329	Burks,Ellis, Cle	.400	Olerud,John, Sea	.414
Huff,Aubrey, TB	.328	Olerud,John, Sea	.325	Giambi,Jason, NYY	.400	Rodriguez,Alex, Tex	.412
Ordonez,M, CWS	.326	Hillenbrand,S, Bos	.322	Lee,Carlos, CWS	.400	Williams,B, NYY	.409
Winn,Randy, TB	.325	Soriano,A, NYY	.319	Stewart,Sh, Tor	.392	Durham,Ray, CWS-Oak	.390

2002 American League Batting Leaders

BA Close & Late
(minimum 50 PA)

Spiezio,Scott, Ana	.420
Williams,B, NYY	.393
Matthews Jr,G, Bal	.383
Sweeney,Mike, KC	.382
Hillenbrand,S, Bos	.375
Winn,Randy, TB	.368
Posada,Jorge, NYY	.354
Erstad,Darin, Ana	.348
Huff,Aubrey, TB	.347
Martinez,Edgar, Sea	.347

BA Bases Loaded
(minimum 10 PA)

Glaus,Troy, Ana	.600
Posada,Jorge, NYY	.579
Hall,Toby, TB	.571
Relaford,Desi, Sea	.571
Davis,Ben, Sea	.545
Phelps,Josh, Tor	.545
Ordonez,M, CWS	.529
6 tied with	.500

SLG vs. LHP
(minimum 125 PA)

Ordonez,M, CWS	.624
Burks,Ellis, Cle	.581
Soriano,A, NYY	.571
Posada,Jorge, NYY	.556
Winn,Randy, TB	.549
Spiezio,Scott, Ana	.539
Pena,Carlos, Oak-Det	.538
Boone,Bret, Sea	.537
Cameron,Mike, Sea	.535
Glaus,Troy, Ana	.534

SLG vs. RHP
(minimum 377 PA)

Thome,Jim, Cle	.766
Rodriguez,Alex, Tex	.682
Delgado,Carlos, Tor	.646
Giambi,Jason, NYY	.626
Palmeiro,R, Tex	.615
Ramirez,Manny, Bos	.612
Ordonez,M, CWS	.589
Ibanez,Raul, KC	.582
Jones,Jacque, Min	.580
Chavez,Eric, Oak	.571

Batting Average w/ RISP
(minimum 100 PA)

Ramirez,Manny, Bos	.435
Sweeney,Mike, KC	.398
Tejada,Miguel, Oak	.375
Williams,B, NYY	.374
Burks,Ellis, Cle	.369
Rodriguez,Alex, Tex	.366
Higginson,B, Det	.366
Suzuki,Ichiro, Sea	.361
Jones,Jacque, Min	.352
Valentin,Jose, CWS	.351

At Bats Per Home Run
(minimum 502 PA)

Thome,Jim, Cle	9.2
Rodriguez,Alex, Tex	10.9
Palmeiro,R, Tex	12.7
Ramirez,Manny, Bos	13.2
Giambi,Jason, NYY	13.7
Delgado,Carlos, Tor	15.3
Ordonez,M, CWS	15.5
Burks,Ellis, Cle	16.2
Chavez,Eric, Oak	17.2
Ventura,Robin, NYY	17.2

Pitches Seen

Giambi,Jason, NYY	2904
Beltran,Carlos, KC	2869
Rodriguez,Alex, Tex	2857
Batista,Tony, Bal	2764
Tejada,Miguel, Oak	2757
Jeter,Derek, NYY	2741
Damon,Johnny, Bos	2739
Palmeiro,R, Tex	2715
Durham,Ray, CWS-Oak	2687
Thomas,Frank, CWS	2686

Pitches Per Plate App
(minimum 502 PA)

Thomas,Frank, CWS	4.28
Giambi,Jason, NYY	4.21
Thome,Jim, Cle	4.17
Dye,Jermaine, Oak	4.17
Hatteberg,S, Oak	4.14
Cameron,Mike, Sea	4.10
Daubach,Brian, Bos	4.10
Palmeiro,R, Tex	4.10
Ventura,Robin, NYY	4.08
Durham,Ray, CWS-Oak	4.08

Pct Pitches Taken
(minimum 1500 Pitches)

Olerud,John, Sea	66.5
McLemore,Mark, Sea	65.0
Hatteberg,S, Oak	64.4
Martinez,Edgar, Sea	63.0
Thomas,Frank, CWS	62.8
Giambi,Jason, NYY	62.8
Lawton,Matt, Cle	62.2
Grieve,Ben, TB	62.0
Vizquel,Omar, Cle	61.3
Johnson,Nick, NYY	61.2

Highest GB/FB Ratio
(minimum 502 PA)

Suzuki,Ichiro, Sea	2.59
Jeter,Derek, NYY	2.30
Grieve,Ben, TB	2.21
Guzman,C, Min	2.14
Jones,Jacque, Min	2.09
Williams,B, NYY	1.96
Boone,Bret, Sea	1.90
Simon,Randall, Det	1.68
Young,Michael, Tex	1.65
Erstad,Darin, Ana	1.57

Lowest GB/FB Ratio
(minimum 502 PA)

Thomas,Frank, CWS	0.39
Palmeiro,R, Tex	0.50
Batista,Tony, Bal	0.53
Lee,Carlos, CWS	0.67
Giambi,Jason, NYY	0.67
Garciaparra,N, Bos	0.71
Spiezio,Scott, Ana	0.71
Mora,Melvin, Bal	0.76
Chavez,Eric, Oak	0.77
Delgado,Carlos, Tor	0.78

Stolen Base Success Pct
(minimum 20 SBA)

Jeter,Derek, NYY	91.4
Singleton,C, Bal	90.9
Erstad,Darin, Ana	88.5
Knoblauch,C, KC	86.4
Damon,Johnny, Bos	83.8
Beltran,Carlos, KC	83.3
Kennedy,Adam, Ana	81.0
Cameron,Mike, Sea	79.5
Durham,Ray, CWS-Oak	78.8
Hairston Jr.,J, Bal	77.8

Steals of Third

Soriano,A, NYY	9
Suzuki,Ichiro, Sea	9
Knoblauch,C, KC	8
Singleton,C, Bal	7
Winn,Randy, TB	6
Beltran,Carlos, KC	5
Jeter,Derek, NYY	5
10 tied with	3

Pct CS by Catchers
(minimum 50 SBA)

Molina,Ben, Ana	42.7
Gil,Geronimo, Bal	34.4
Mayne,Brent, KC	32.8
Huckaby,Ken, Tor	32.7
Mirabelli,Doug, Bos	32.7
Hernandez,Ra, Oak	31.8
Hall,Toby, TB	31.0
Flaherty,John, TB	29.4
Diaz,Einar, Cle	28.1
Johnson,Mark L, CWS	27.6

Best BPS on POSZ
(minimum 502 PA)

Eckstein,David, Ana	.667
Cruz,Jose, Tor	.591
Lee,Carlos, CWS	.578
Damon,Johnny, Bos	.538
Durham,Ray, CWS-Oak	.488
Sweeney,Mike, KC	.485
Hinske,Eric, Tor	.484
Anderson,G, Ana	.471
Chavez,Eric, Oak	.464
Ramirez,Manny, Bos	.450

Worst BPS on POSZ
(minimum 502 PA)

Dye,Jermaine, Oak	.000
Daubach,Brian, Bos	.042
Posada,Jorge, NYY	.044
Valentin,Jose, CWS	.052
Vizquel,Omar, Cle	.065
Salmon,Tim, Ana	.071
Erstad,Darin, Ana	.080
Nixon,Trot, Bos	.105
Abernathy,B, TB	.118
Koskie,Corey, Min	.118

2002 American League Batting Leaders

Best OPS vs Fastballs
(minimum 251 PA)

Thome,Jim, Cle	1.254
Ramirez,Manny, Bos	1.134
Ordonez,M, CWS	1.057
Giambi,Jason, NYY	1.035
Rodriguez,Alex, Tex	1.023
Burks,Ellis, Cle	1.001
Palmeiro,R, Tex	.986
Rodriguez,Ivan, Tex	.942
Phelps,Josh, Tor	.937
Ortiz,David, Min	.935

Best OPS vs Curveballs
(minimum 50 PA)

Thome,Jim, Cle	1.060
Hunter,Torii, Min	.998
Giambi,Jason, NYY	.996
Anderson,G, Ana	.920
Salmon,Tim, Ana	.915
Mohr,Dustan, Min	.909
Konerko,Paul, CWS	.906
Ordonez,M, CWS	.853
Suzuki,Ichiro, Sea	.818
Tejada,Miguel, Oak	.811

Best OPS vs Changeups
(minimum 50 PA)

Hillenbrand,S, Bos	1.174
Ramirez,Manny, Bos	1.149
Tejada,Miguel, Oak	1.132
Giambi,Jason, NYY	1.115
Burks,Ellis, Cle	1.109
Rodriguez,Alex, Tex	1.083
Garciaparra,N, Bos	1.068
Winn,Randy, TB	1.052
Anderson,G, Ana	.995
Wells,Vernon, Tor	.984

Best OPS vs Sliders
(minimum 32 PA)

Spiezio,Scott, Ana	1.140
Gibbons,Jay, Bal	1.093
Chavez,Eric, Oak	.952
Hunter,Torii, Min	.951
Crede,Joe, CWS	.938
Pena,Carlos, Oak-Det	.930
Guzman,C, Min	.914
Ordonez,M, CWS	.912
Giambi,Jason, NYY	.908
Perry,Herbert, Tex	.877

OPS
(minimum 502 PA)

Thome,Jim, Cle	1.122
Ramirez,Manny, Bos	1.097
Giambi,Jason, NYY	1.034
Rodriguez,Alex, Tex	1.015
Sweeney,Mike, KC	.979
Ordonez,M, CWS	.978
Palmeiro,R, Tex	.962
Delgado,Carlos, Tor	.955
Williams,B, NYY	.908
Burks,Ellis, Cle	.903

OPS First Half
(minimum 251 PA)

Sweeney,Mike, KC	1.044
Giambi,Jason, NYY	1.032
Thome,Jim, Cle	1.021
Rodriguez,Alex, Tex	1.008
Olerud,John, Sea	.965
Konerko,Paul, CWS	.949
Palmeiro,R, Tex	.938
Soriano,A, NYY	.918
Hunter,Torii, Min	.911
Ordonez,M, CWS	.909

OPS Second Half
(minimum 251 PA)

Thome,Jim, Cle	1.254
Ramirez,Manny, Bos	1.134
Ordonez,M, CWS	1.057
Giambi,Jason, NYY	1.035
Rodriguez,Alex, Tex	1.023
Burks,Ellis, Cle	1.001
Palmeiro,R, Tex	.986
Rodriguez,Ivan, Tex	.942
Phelps,Josh, Tor	.937
Ortiz,David, Min	.935

2002 National League Batting Leaders

Batting Average (minimum 502 PA)		On Base Percentage (minimum 502 PA)		Slugging Average (minimum 502 PA)		Home Runs	
Bonds,Barry, SF	.370	Bonds,Barry, SF	.582	Bonds,Barry, SF	.799	Sosa,Sammy, ChC	49
Walker,Larry, Col	.338	Giles,Brian, Pit	.450	Giles,Brian, Pit	.622	Bonds,Barry, SF	46
Guerrero,V, Mon	.336	Jones,Chipper, Atl	.435	Walker,Larry, Col	.602	Berkman,Lance, Hou	42
Helton,Todd, Col	.329	Helton,Todd, Col	.429	Sosa,Sammy, ChC	.594	Green,Shawn, LA	42
Jones,Chipper, Atl	.327	Walker,Larry, Col	.421	Guerrero,V, Mon	.593	Guerrero,V, Mon	39
Vidro,Jose, Mon	.315	Edmonds,Jim, Stl	.420	Berkman,Lance, Hou	.578	Giles,Brian, Pit	38
Pujols,Albert, Stl	.314	Guerrero,V, Mon	.417	Helton,Todd, Col	.577	Burrell,Pat, Phi	37
Kent,Jeff, SF	.313	Abreu,Bobby, Phi	.413	Kent,Jeff, SF	.565	Kent,Jeff, SF	37
Edmonds,Jim, Stl	.311	Berkman,Lance, Hou	.405	Pujols,Albert, Stl	.561	Jones,Andruw, Atl	35
Alfonzo,E, NYM	.308	Sheffield,Gary, Atl	.404	Edmonds,Jim, Stl	.561	Pujols,Albert, Stl	34

Games		Plate Appearances		At Bats		Hits	
Boone,Aaron, Cin	162	Guerrero,V, Mon	709	Rollins,Jimmy, Phi	637	Guerrero,V, Mon	206
Lee,Derrek, Fla	162	Rollins,Jimmy, Phi	705	Furcal,Rafael, Atl	636	Kent,Jeff, SF	195
Guerrero,V, Mon	161	Furcal,Rafael, Atl	693	Kent,Jeff, SF	623	Vidro,Jose, Mon	190
Lowell,Mike, Fla	160	Berkman,Lance, Hou	692	Vina,Fernando, Stl	622	Castillo,Luis, Fla	185
Beltre,Adrian, LA	159	Vina,Fernando, Stl	692	Guerrero,V, Mon	614	Pujols,Albert, Stl	185
Bagwell,Jeff, Hou	158	Bagwell,Jeff, Hou	691	Walker,Todd, Cin	612	Walker,Todd, Cin	183
Berkman,Lance, Hou	158	Lee,Derrek, Fla	688	Boone,Aaron, Cin	606	Helton,Todd, Col	182
Dunn,Adam, Cin	158	Abreu,Bobby, Phi	685	Castillo,Luis, Fla	606	Jones,Chipper, Atl	179
Green,Shawn, LA	158	Boone,Aaron, Cin	685	Vidro,Jose, Mon	604	Abreu,Bobby, Phi	176
Jones,Chipper, Atl	158	Green,Shawn, LA	685	Lowell,Mike, Fla	597	Furcal,Rafael, Atl	175

Singles		Doubles		Triples		Total Bases	
Castillo,Luis, Fla	160	Abreu,Bobby, Phi	50	Rollins,Jimmy, Phi	10	Guerrero,V, Mon	364
Pierre,Juan, Col	144	Lowell,Mike, Fla	44	Furcal,Rafael, Atl	8	Kent,Jeff, SF	352
Vina,Fernando, Stl	133	Cabrera,O, Mon	43	McCracken,Q, Ari	8	Berkman,Lance, Hou	334
Furcal,Rafael, Atl	128	Vidro,Jose, Mon	43	Rolen,Scott, Phi-Stl	8	Pujols,Albert, Stl	331
Guerrero,V, Mon	128	Kent,Jeff, SF	42	Wilkerson,Brad, Mon	8	Sosa,Sammy, ChC	330
Walker,Todd, Cin	127	Walker,Todd, Cin	42	6 tied with	7	Green,Shawn, LA	325
Womack,Tony, Ari	127	Millar,Kevin, Fla	41			Bonds,Barry, SF	322
Vidro,Jose, Mon	125	Pujols,Albert, Stl	40			Burrell,Pat, Phi	319
Kendall,Jason, Pit	123	Walker,Larry, Col	40			Helton,Todd, Col	319
2 tied with	118	3 tied with	39			Giles,Brian, Pit	309

Runs Scored		RBI		Walks		Strikeouts	
Sosa,Sammy, ChC	122	Berkman,Lance, Hou	128	Bonds,Barry, SF	198	Hernandez,Jose, Mil	188
Pujols,Albert, Stl	118	Pujols,Albert, Stl	127	Giles,Brian, Pit	135	Dunn,Adam, Cin	170
Bonds,Barry, SF	117	Burrell,Pat, Phi	116	Dunn,Adam, Cin	128	Lee,Derrek, Fla	164
Green,Shawn, LA	110	Green,Shawn, LA	114	Berkman,Lance, Hou	107	Wilkerson,Brad, Mon	161
Helton,Todd, Col	107	Guerrero,V, Mon	111	Jones,Chipper, Atl	107	Burrell,Pat, Phi	153
Berkman,Lance, Hou	106	Bonds,Barry, SF	110	Abreu,Bobby, Phi	104	Vaughn,Mo, NYM	145
Guerrero,V, Mon	106	Rolen,Scott, Phi-Stl	110	Sosa,Sammy, ChC	103	Bellhorn,Mark, ChC	144
Spivey,Junior, Ari	103	Helton,Todd, Col	109	Bagwell,Jeff, Hou	101	Sosa,Sammy, ChC	144
Vidro,Jose, Mon	103	Kent,Jeff, SF	108	Helton,Todd, Col	99	Patterson,C, ChC	142
2 tied with	102	Sosa,Sammy, ChC	108	Lee,Derrek, Fla	98	Wilson,Preston, Fla	140

2002 National League Batting Leaders

Sacrifice Hits		Sacrifice Flies		Stolen Bases		Caught Stealing	
Wilson,Jack, Pit	17	Lowell,Mike, Fla	11	Castillo,Luis, Fla	48	Guerrero,V, Mon	20
Rusch,Glendon, Mil	14	Ramirez,Aramis, Pit	11	Pierre,Juan, Col	47	Castillo,Luis, Fla	15
Glavine,Tom, Atl	13	Helton,Todd, Col	10	Roberts,Dave, LA	45	Furcal,Rafael, Atl	15
McCracken,Q, Ari	13	Bagwell,Jeff, Hou	9	Guerrero,V, Mon	40	Sanchez,Alex, Mil	14
Polanco,P, Stl-Phi	13	10 tied with	7	Sanchez,Alex, Mil	37	Rollins,Jimmy, Phi	13
Rueter,Kirk, SF	13			Boone,Aaron, Cin	32	Abreu,Bobby, Phi	12
Wells,Kip, Pit	13			Abreu,Bobby, Phi	31	Pierre,Juan, Col	12
Wolf,Randy, Phi	12			Fox,Andy, Fla	31	Womack,Tony, Ari	12
Millwood,Kevin, Atl	11			Rollins,Jimmy, Phi	31	3 tied with	11
Vidro,Jose, Mon	11			Young,Eric, Mil	31		

Intentional Walks		Hit By Pitch		Grounded Into DP		Grounded Into DP Pct (minimum 50 GIDP Ops)	
Bonds,Barry, SF	68	Wilson,Craig, Pit	21	Ausmus,Brad, Hou	30	Floyd,Cliff, Fla-Mon	0.00
Guerrero,V, Mon	32	Vina,Fernando, Stl	18	Zeile,Todd, Col	27	Mackowiak,Rob, Pit	0.00
Giles,Brian, Pit	24	Biggio,Craig, Hou	17	Green,Shawn, LA	26	Durazo,Erubiel, Ari	0.02
Jones,Chipper, Atl	23	Spivey,Junior, Ari	16	Piazza,Mike, NYM	26	Bonds,Barry, SF	0.04
Green,Shawn, LA	22	Lieberthal,M, Phi	14	Castilla,Vinny, Atl	22	McCracken,Q, Ari	0.04
Helton,Todd, Col	21	LaRue,Jason, Cin	13	Rolen,Scott, Phi-Stl	22	Drew,J.D., Stl	0.04
Berkman,Lance, Hou	20	Rolen,Scott, Phi-Stl	12	5 tied with	20	Matheny,Mike, Stl	0.04
Floyd,Cliff, Fla-Mon	19	Sanders,Reggie, SF	12			Klesko,Ryan, SD	0.05
Sosa,Sammy, ChC	15	Sheffield,Gary, Atl	11			Alfonzo,E, NYM	0.05
2 tied with	14	8 tied with	10			2 tied with	0.06

Leadoff Hitters OBP (minimum 150 PA)		Cleanup Hitters SLG (minimum 150 PA)		BA vs. LHP (minimum 125 PA)		BA vs. RHP (minimum 377 PA)	
Kotsay,Mark, SD	.396	Bonds,Barry, SF	.730	Bonds,Barry, SF	.384	Bonds,Barry, SF	.363
Bellhorn,Mark, ChC	.389	Guerrero,V, Mon	.612	Colbrunn,Greg, Ari	.368	Guerrero,V, Mon	.347
Wilkerson,Brad, Mon	.373	Berkman,Lance, Hou	.596	Sosa,Sammy, ChC	.366	Helton,Todd, Col	.331
Alomar,Roberto, NYM	.371	Dunn,Adam, Cin	.595	Kent,Jeff, SF	.366	Edmonds,Jim, Stl	.329
Lofton,Kenny, SF	.364	Giles,Brian, Pit	.582	Alfonzo,E, NYM	.364	Jones,Chipper, Atl	.328
Castillo,Luis, Fla	.363	Pujols,Albert, Stl	.573	Polanco,P, Stl-Phi	.338	Giles,Brian, Pit	.325
Vazquez,Ramon, SD	.354	Floyd,Cliff, Fla-Mon	.571	Walker,Larry, Col	.337	Vidro,Jose, Mon	.321
Counsell,Craig, Ari	.349	Jones,Chipper, Atl	.566	Bagwell,Jeff, Hou	.333	Perez,Timo, NYM	.318
Sanchez,Alex, Mil	.349	Green,Shawn, LA	.556	Castillo,Luis, Fla	.329	Pujols,Albert, Stl	.315
Kendall,Jason, Pit	.349	Piazza,Mike, NYM	.555	Helton,Todd, Col	.327	Renteria,Edgar, Stl	.310

Home BA (minimum 251 PA)		Away BA (minimum 251 PA)		OBP vs. LHP (minimum 125 PA)		OBP vs. RHP (minimum 377 PA)	
Helton,Todd, Col	.378	Bonds,Barry, SF	.386	Bonds,Barry, SF	.556	Bonds,Barry, SF	.592
Walker,Larry, Col	.362	Pujols,Albert, Stl	.340	Sosa,Sammy, ChC	.526	Giles,Brian, Pit	.485
Bonds,Barry, SF	.351	Sheffield,Gary, Atl	.336	Alfonzo,E, NYM	.477	Edmonds,Jim, Stl	.443
Guerrero,V, Mon	.348	Alfonzo,E, NYM	.335	Burrell,Pat, Phi	.469	Jones,Chipper, Atl	.442
Jones,Chipper, Atl	.346	Abreu,Bobby, Phi	.327	Bagwell,Jeff, Hou	.459	Helton,Todd, Col	.424
Vidro,Jose, Mon	.335	Guerrero,V, Mon	.324	Guerrero,V, Mon	.443	Berkman,Lance, Hou	.420
Millar,Kevin, Fla	.333	Kent,Jeff, SF	.323	Spivey,Junior, Ari	.441	Abreu,Bobby, Phi	.414
Pierre,Juan, Col	.328	Edmonds,Jim, Stl	.316	Kent,Jeff, SF	.439	Gonzalez,Luis, Ari	.412
Giles,Brian, Pit	.323	Walker,Larry, Col	.312	Helton,Todd, Col	.437	Guerrero,V, Mon	.410
Berkman,Lance, Hou	.320	Sosa,Sammy, ChC	.310	Colbrunn,Greg, Ari	.414	Dunn,Adam, Cin	.406

2002 National League Batting Leaders

BA Close & Late
(minimum 50 PA)

Walker,Larry, Col	.468
Castillo,Luis, Fla	.379
Vizcaino,Jose, Hou	.377
Ramirez,Aramis, Pit	.377
Alfonzo,E, NYM	.364
Sheffield,Gary, Atl	.357
Karros,Eric, LA	.355
Durazo,Erubiel, Ari	.349
Kearns,Austin, Cin	.348
Alomar,Roberto, NYM	.343

BA Bases Loaded
(minimum 10 PA)

Perez,Timo, NYM	.625
Pujols,Albert, Stl	.538
Alou,Moises, ChC	.500
Bonds,Barry, SF	.500
Cruz,Deivi, SD	.500
Nevin,Phil, SD	.500
Reese,Pokey, Pit	.500
Trammell,Bubba, SD	.500
Vazquez,Ramon, SD	.500
Ward,Daryle, Hou	.467

SLG vs. LHP
(minimum 125 PA)

Bonds,Barry, SF	.976
Sosa,Sammy, ChC	.733
Bagwell,Jeff, Hou	.685
Bellhorn,Mark, ChC	.672
Kent,Jeff, SF	.669
Colbrunn,Greg, Ari	.667
Burrell,Pat, Phi	.664
Grissom,M, LA	.617
Spivey,Junior, Ari	.612
Pujols,Albert, Stl	.579

SLG vs. RHP
(minimum 377 PA)

Bonds,Barry, SF	.719
Giles,Brian, Pit	.681
Berkman,Lance, Hou	.639
Guerrero,V, Mon	.616
Edmonds,Jim, Stl	.592
Helton,Todd, Col	.579
McGriff,Fred, ChC	.571
Abreu,Bobby, Phi	.566
Sosa,Sammy, ChC	.563
Green,Shawn, LA	.561

Batting Average w/ RISP
(minimum 100 PA)

Bonds,Barry, SF	.376
Vidro,Jose, Mon	.372
Renteria,Edgar, Stl	.372
Sheffield,Gary, Atl	.367
Counsell,Craig, Ari	.364
Berkman,Lance, Hou	.361
Walker,Larry, Col	.360
Gonzalez,Luis, Ari	.351
Pujols,Albert, Stl	.340
Pierre,Juan, Col	.336

At Bats Per Home Run
(minimum 502 PA)

Bonds,Barry, SF	8.8
Sosa,Sammy, ChC	11.3
Giles,Brian, Pit	13.1
Berkman,Lance, Hou	13.8
Green,Shawn, LA	13.9
Piazza,Mike, NYM	14.5
Guerrero,V, Mon	15.7
Burrell,Pat, Phi	15.8
Jones,Andruw, Atl	16.0
Bellhorn,Mark, ChC	16.5

Pitches Seen

Abreu,Bobby, Phi	2960
Dunn,Adam, Cin	2942
Lee,Derrek, Fla	2924
Burrell,Pat, Phi	2827
Bagwell,Jeff, Hou	2768
Helton,Todd, Col	2745
Sosa,Sammy, ChC	2744
Berkman,Lance, Hou	2735
Rollins,Jimmy, Phi	2726
Rolen,Scott, Phi-Stl	2689

Pitches Per Plate App
(minimum 502 PA)

Dunn,Adam, Cin	4.35
Zeile,Todd, Col	4.35
Abreu,Bobby, Phi	4.32
Wilkerson,Brad, Mon	4.29
Lee,Derrek, Fla	4.25
Burnitz,Jeromy, NYM	4.23
Bellhorn,Mark, ChC	4.22
Burrell,Pat, Phi	4.13
Sosa,Sammy, ChC	4.12
Helton,Todd, Col	4.11

Pct Pitches Taken
(minimum 1500 Pitches)

Bonds,Barry, SF	68.4
Giles,Brian, Pit	66.2
Zeile,Todd, Col	65.2
Abreu,Bobby, Phi	64.5
Dunn,Adam, Cin	62.7
Roberts,Dave, LA	62.7
Counsell,Craig, Ari	62.6
Bellhorn,Mark, ChC	61.3
Castillo,Luis, Fla	61.0
Wilkerson,Brad, Mon	60.3

Highest GB/FB Ratio
(minimum 502 PA)

Castillo,Luis, Fla	3.32
Pierre,Juan, Col	3.14
Cedeno,Roger, NYM	2.00
Furcal,Rafael, Atl	1.97
Polanco,P, Stl-Phi	1.95
Kendall,Jason, Pit	1.87
Hernandez,Jose, Mil	1.67
Green,Shawn, LA	1.66
Vidro,Jose, Mon	1.64
Zeile,Todd, Col	1.63

Lowest GB/FB Ratio
(minimum 502 PA)

Young,Kevin, Pit	0.62
Giles,Brian, Pit	0.63
Lowell,Mike, Fla	0.63
Bonds,Barry, SF	0.64
Aurilia,Rich, SF	0.68
Alfonzo,E, NYM	0.70
Burrell,Pat, Phi	0.71
Bellhorn,Mark, ChC	0.78
Rolen,Scott, Phi-Stl	0.82
Kent,Jeff, SF	0.84

Stolen Base Success Pct
(minimum 20 SBA)

Glanville,Doug, Phi	90.5
Cedeno,Roger, NYM	86.2
Patterson,C, ChC	85.7
Roberts,Dave, LA	81.8
Fox,Andy, Fla	81.6
Alomar,Roberto, NYM	80.0
Boone,Aaron, Cin	80.0
Finley,Steve, Ari	80.0
Pierre,Juan, Col	79.7
Cabrera,O, Mon	78.1

Steals of Third

Fox,Andy, Fla	8
Boone,Aaron, Cin	7
Rollins,Jimmy, Phi	7
Guerrero,V, Mon	6
Cabrera,O, Mon	5
Castillo,Luis, Fla	5
Giles,Brian, Pit	5
Womack,Tony, Ari	5
5 tied with	4

Pct CS by Catchers
(minimum 50 SBA)

LaRue,Jason, Cin	42.4
Redmond,Mike, Fla	39.4
Johnson,C, Fla	36.2
Miller,Damian, Ari	35.9
Machado,Rbrt, ChC-Mil	34.4
Blanco,Henry, Atl	33.9
Matheny,Mike, Stl	33.8
Lieberthal,M, Phi	33.8
Ausmus,Brad, Hou	31.6
Lampkin,Tom, SD	31.6

Best BPS on POSZ
(minimum 502 PA)

Giles,Brian, Pit	1.000
Aurilia,Rich, SF	.906
Kendall,Jason, Pit	.650
Karros,Eric, LA	.595
Klesko,Ryan, SD	.551
Guerrero,V, Mon	.546
Alou,Moises, ChC	.500
Sanders,Reggie, SF	.500
Walker, Todd, Cin	.486
Lo Duca,Paul, LA	.485

Worst BPS on POSZ
(minimum 502 PA)

Boone,Aaron, Cin	.000
Lee,Travis, Phi	.000
Vaughn,Mo, NYM	.000
Wilson,Preson, Fla	.034
McGriff,Fred, ChC	.045
Cedeno,Roger, NYM	.051
Dunn,Adam, Cin	.054
Jones,Andruw, Atl	.070
Lee,Derrek, Fla	.071
Womack,Tony, Ari	.073

2002 National League Batting Leaders

Best OPS vs Fastballs
(minimum 251 PA)

Bonds,Barry, SF	1.432
Jones,Chipper, Atl	1.130
Giles,Brian, Pit	1.113
Guerrero,V, Mon	1.071
Sheffield,Gary, Atl	1.031
Kent,Jeff, SF	.989
Bagwell,Jeff, Hou	.977
Abreu,Bobby, Phi	.956
Millar,Kevin, Fla	.951
Helton,Todd, Col	.951

Best OPS vs Curveballs
(minimum 50 PA)

Helton,Todd, Col	1.127
Karros,Eric, LA	.973
Bagwell,Jeff, Hou	.955
Lo Duca,Paul, LA	.949
Rolen,Scott, Phi-Stl	.913
Piazza,Mike, NYM	.903
Edmonds,Jim, Stl	.900
Giles,Brian, Pit	.880
Anderson,Mar, Phi	.878
Lee,Travis, Phi	.873

Best OPS vs Changeups
(minimum 50 PA)

Bonds,Barry, SF	1.740
Walker,Larry, Col	1.309
Giles,Brian, Pit	1.175
Finley,Steve, Ari	1.154
Alfonzo,E, NYM	1.078
Beltre,Adrian, LA	1.028
Sosa,Sammy, ChC	1.016
Sheffield,Gary, Atl	1.011
Millar,Kevin, Fla	1.005
Berkman,Lance, Hou	.915

Best OPS vs Sliders
(minimum 32 PA)

Bonds,Barry, SF	1.376
Edmonds,Jim, Stl	1.085
Snow,J.T., SF	1.080
Berkman,Lance, Hou	1.067
Young,Eric, Mil	1.066
Guerrero,V, Mon	1.055
Lowell,Mike, Fla	1.013
Kendall,Jason, Pit	.988
Sexson,Richie, Mil	.962
Wilson,Craig, Pit	.925

OPS
(minimum 502 PA)

Bonds,Barry, SF	1.381
Giles,Brian, Pit	1.072
Walker,Larry, Col	1.023
Guerrero,V, Mon	1.010
Helton,Todd, Col	1.006
Sosa,Sammy, ChC	.993
Berkman,Lance, Hou	.982
Edmonds,Jim, Stl	.981
Jones,Chipper, Atl	.972
Pujols,Albert, Stl	.955

OPS First Half
(minimum 251 PA)

Bonds,Barry, SF	1.342
Walker,Larry, Col	1.082
Sosa,Sammy, ChC	1.059
Berkman,Lance, Hou	1.053
Helton,Todd, Col	1.050
Edmonds,Jim, Stl	1.038
Giles,Brian, Pit	1.038
Dunn,Adam, Cin	.996
Pujols,Albert, Stl	.973
Green,Shawn, LA	.970

OPS Second Half
(minimum 251 PA)

Bonds,Barry, SF	1.432
Jones,Chipper, Atl	1.130
Giles,Brian, Pit	1.113
Guerrero,V, Mon	1.071
Sheffield,Gary, Atl	1.031
Kent,Jeff, SF	.989
Bagwell,Jeff, Hou	.977
Abreu,Bobby, Phi	.956
Millar,Kevin, Fla	.951
Helton,Todd, Col	.951

2002 American League Pitching Leaders

Earned Run Average (minimum 162 IP)			Winning Percentage (minimum 15 Decisions)			Opponent Batting Average (minimum 162 IP)			Baserunners Per 9 IP (minimum 162 IP)		
Martinez,Pedro, Bos		2.26	Martinez,Pedro, Bos		.833	Martinez,Pedro, Bos		.198	Martinez,Pedro, Bos		8.98
Lowe,Derek, Bos		2.58	Zito,Barry, Oak		.821	Wakefield,Tim, Bos		.204	Lowe,Derek, Bos		9.26
Zito,Barry, Oak		2.75	Washburn,J, Ana		.750	Lowe,Derek, Bos		.211	Wakefield,Tim, Bos		9.97
Wakefield,Tim, Bos		2.81	Koch,Billy, Oak		.733	Zito,Barry, Oak		.218	Moyer,Jamie, Sea		10.03
Halladay,Roy, Tor		2.93	Halladay,Roy, Tor		.731	Moyer,Jamie, Sea		.230	Zito,Barry, Oak		10.56
Hudson,Tim, Oak		2.98	Mulder,Mark, Oak		.731	Ortiz,Ramon, Ana		.230	Byrd,Paul, KC		10.60
Washburn,J, Ana		3.15	Wells,David, NYY		.731	Mulder,Mark, Oak		.232	Washburn,J, Ana		10.70
Pineiro,Joel, Sea		3.24	Lowe,Derek, Bos		.724	Lopez,Rodrigo, Bal		.234	Reed,Rick, Min		10.72
Moyer,Jamie, Sea		3.32	Pettitte,Andy, NYY		.722	Washburn,J, Ana		.235	Mulder,Mark, Oak		10.77
Mulder,Mark, Oak		3.47	Wakefield,Tim, Bos		.688	Halladay,Roy, Tor		.244	Ortiz,Ramon, Ana		10.81

Games			Games Started			Complete Games			Shutouts		
Koch,Billy, Oak		84	Zito,Barry, Oak		35	Byrd,Paul, KC		7	Weaver,Jeff, Det-NYY		3
Romero,J.C., Min		81	Buehrle,Mark, CWS		34	Buehrle,Mark, CWS		5	Buehrle,Mark, CWS		2
Stanton,Mike, NYY		79	Garcia,Freddy, Sea		34	Kennedy,Joe, TB		5	Byrd,Paul, KC		2
Karsay,Steve, NYY		78	Halladay,Roy, Tor		34	Colon,Bartolo, Cle		4	Colon,Bartolo, Cle		2
Escobar,Kelvim, Tor		76	Hudson,Tim, Oak		34	Hudson,Tim, Oak		4	Hudson,Tim, Oak		2
Bradford,Chad, Oak		75	Moyer,Jamie, Sea		34	Moyer,Jamie, Sea		4	Lidle,Cory, Oak		2
Rincon,Ricrdo, Cle-Oak		71	8 tied with		33	Ortiz,Ramon, Ana		4	Moyer,Jamie, Sea		2
Grimsley,Jason, KC		70				Sturtze,Tanyon, TB		4	Mussina,Mike, NYY		2
Groom,Buddy, Bal		70				8 tied with		3	26 tied with		1
2 tied with		68									

Wins			Losses			Innings Pitched			Batters Faced		
Zito,Barry, Oak		23	Sturtze,Tanyon, TB		18	Halladay,Roy, Tor		239.1	Sturtze,Tanyon, TB		1008
Lowe,Derek, Bos		21	Sparks,Steve, Det		16	Buehrle,Mark, CWS		239.0	Halladay,Roy, Tor		993
Martinez,Pedro, Bos		20	Suppan,Jeff, KC		16	Hudson,Tim, Oak		238.1	Buehrle,Mark, CWS		984
Buehrle,Mark, CWS		19	Castillo,Frank, Bos		15	Moyer,Jamie, Sea		230.2	Hudson,Tim, Oak		983
Halladay,Roy, Tor		19	Redman,Mark, Det		15	Zito,Barry, Oak		229.1	Garcia,Freddy, Sea		955
Mulder,Mark, Oak		19	Ritchie,Todd, CWS		15	Byrd,Paul, KC		228.1	Zito,Barry, Oak		939
Wells,David, NYY		19	Johnson,Jason, Bal		14	Sturtze,Tanyon, TB		224.0	Byrd,Paul, KC		935
Mussina,Mike, NYY		18	7 tied with		12	Garcia,Freddy, Sea		223.2	Moyer,Jamie, Sea		931
Washburn,J, Ana		18				Lowe,Derek, Bos		219.2	Suppan,Jeff, KC		912
Byrd,Paul, KC		17				Ortiz,Ramon, Ana		217.1	Ortiz,Ramon, Ana		896

Strikeouts			Walks Allowed			Hit Batters			Wild Pitches		
Martinez,Pedro, Bos		239	Sturtze,Tanyon, TB		89	Park,Chan Ho, Tex		17	Santana,Johan, Min		15
Clemens,Roger, NYY		192	Sabathia,C.C., Cle		88	Kennedy,Joe, TB		16	Clemens,Roger, NYY		14
Mussina,Mike, NYY		182	Garland,Jon, CWS		83	Martinez,Pedro, Bos		15	Drese,Ryan, Cle		11
Zito,Barry, Oak		182	Baez,Danys, Cle		82	Wilson,Paul, TB		13	Redman,Mark, Det		11
Garcia,Freddy, Sea		181	Park,Chan Ho, Tex		78	Lowe,Derek, Bos		12	Ritchie,Todd, CWS		10
Halladay,Roy, Tor		168	Zito,Barry, Oak		78	Sparks,Steve, Det		12	Suppan,Jeff, KC		10
Ortiz,Ramon, Ana		162	Wright,Dan, CWS		71	Miller,Justin, Tor		11	Wright,Dan, CWS		10
Mulder,Mark, Oak		159	Lohse,Kyle, Min		70	Mulder,Mark, Oak		11	Zambrano,V, TB		10
Hudson,Tim, Oak		152	Rogers,Kenny, Tex		70	Weaver,Jeff, Det-NYY		11	3 tied with		9
Sabathia,C.C., Cle		149	4 tied with		68	Rupe,Ryan, TB		10			

2002 American League Pitching Leaders

Runs Allowed

Sturtze,Tanyon, TB	141
Sparks,Steve, Det	134
Suppan,Jeff, KC	134
Wright,Dan, CWS	124
Kennedy,Joe, TB	114
Wilson,Paul, TB	113
Byrd,Paul, KC	111
Garcia,Freddy, Sea	110
3 tied with	109

Hits Allowed

Sturtze,Tanyon, TB	271
Sparks,Steve, Det	238
Hudson,Tim, Oak	237
Buehrle,Mark, CWS	236
Suppan,Jeff, KC	229
Garcia,Freddy, Sea	227
Byrd,Paul, KC	224
Halladay,Roy, Tor	223
Wilson,Paul, TB	219
Rogers,Kenny, Tex	212

Doubles Allowed

Sturtze,Tanyon, TB	57
Sparks,Steve, Det	55
Buehrle,Mark, CWS	53
Wells,David, NYY	51
Washburn,J, Ana	50
Burba,Dave, Tex-Cle	48
Kennedy,Joe, TB	47
Weaver,Jeff, Det-NYY	47
Wilson,Paul, TB	47
2 tied with	46

Home Runs Allowed

Ortiz,Ramon, Ana	40
Byrd,Paul, KC	36
Sturtze,Tanyon, TB	33
Reed,Rick, Min	32
Suppan,Jeff, KC	32
Wright,Dan, CWS	32
Garcia,Freddy, Sea	30
Wilson,Paul, TB	29
May,Darrell, KC	28
Moyer,Jamie, Sea	28

Run Support Per Nine IP
(minimum 162 IP)

Wells,David, NYY	7.46
Lowe,Derek, Bos	6.84
Zito,Barry, Oak	6.79
Ortiz,Ramon, Ana	6.67
Buehrle,Mark, CWS	6.55
Burkett,John, Bos	6.45
Mussina,Mike, NYY	6.30
Martinez,Pedro, Bos	6.23
Lopez,Rodrigo, Bal	6.22
Reed,Rick, Min	6.13

% Pitches In Strike Zone
(minimum 162 IP)

Byrd,Paul, KC	71.2
Wells,David, NYY	68.8
Reed,Rick, Min	67.5
Milton,Eric, Min	66.8
Valdes,Ismael, Tex-Sea	66.6
Martinez,Pedro, Bos	66.4
Washburn,Jarrod, Ana	65.9
Halladay,Roy, Tor	65.8
Castillo,Frank, Bos	65.6
Burkett,John, Bos	65.5

Pitches Per Start
(minimum 30 GS)

Sturtze,Tanyon, TB	108.5
Garcia,Freddy, Sea	106.1
Zito,Barry, Oak	105.7
Redman,Mark, Det	105.7
Washburn,J, Ana	104.8
Suppan,Jeff, KC	104.4
Wilson,Paul, TB	103.8
Kennedy,Joe, TB	103.6
Martinez,Pedro, Bos	103.2
Buehrle,Mark, CWS	103.2

Pitches Per Batter
(minimum 162 IP)

Byrd,Paul, KC	3.44
Mulder,Mark, Oak	3.50
Hudson,Tim, Oak	3.51
Halladay,Roy, Tor	3.53
Sparks,Steve, Det	3.54
Burkett,John, Bos	3.55
Sturtze,Tanyon, TB	3.55
Buehrle,Mark, CWS	3.57
Wells,David, NYY	3.59
Lowe,Derek, Bos	3.60

Quality Starts

Zito,Barry, Oak	27
Halladay,Roy, Tor	26
Hudson,Tim, Oak	24
Lowe,Derek, Bos	24
Buehrle,Mark, CWS	23
Washburn,J, Ana	23
Martinez,Pedro, Bos	21
Rogers,Kenny, Tex	21
5 tied with	20

Easy Saves

Urbina,Ugueth, Bos	31
Guardado,Eddie, Min	29
Koch,Billy, Oak	26
Escobar,Kelvim, Tor	22
Percival,Troy, Ana	22
Sasaki,K, Sea	22
Hernandez,Ro, KC	19
Wickman,Bob, Cle	18
Rivera,Mariano, NYY	15
Julio,Jorge, Bal	13

Regular Saves

Guardado,Eddie, Min	16
Koch,Billy, Oak	16
Percival,Troy, Ana	16
Escobar,Kelvim, Tor	14
Sasaki,K, Sea	14
Acevedo,Juan, Det	12
Rivera,Mariano, NYY	11
Julio,Jorge, Bal	9
Urbina,Ugueth, Bos	8
4 tied with	7

Tough Saves

Acevedo,Juan, Det	4
Julio,Jorge, Bal	3
Escobar,Kelvim, Tor	2
Groom,Buddy, Bal	2
Koch,Billy, Oak	2
Nelson,Jeff, Sea	2
Percival,Troy, Ana	2
Rivera,Mariano, NYY	2
13 tied with	1

Stolen Bases Allowed

Castillo,Frank, Bos	24
Clemens,Roger, NYY	23
Halladay,Roy, Tor	21
Wakefield,Tim, Bos	21
Lowe,Derek, Bos	19
Sabathia,C.C., Cle	19
Wright,Dan, CWS	19
Erickson,Scott, Bal	17
Sturtze,Tanyon, TB	17
3 tied with	15

Caught Stealing Off

Sturtze,Tanyon, TB	15
Appier,Kevin, Ana	13
Baez,Danys, Cle	11
Buehrle,Mark, CWS	10
Mussina,Mike, NYY	10
8 tied with	9

Stolen Base Pct Allowed
(minimum 162 IP)

Rogers,Kenny, Tex	0.0
Weaver,Jeff, Det-NYY	20.0
Buehrle,Mark, CWS	28.6
Mussina,Mike, NYY	37.5
Hudson,Tim, Oak	38.5
Mulder,Mark, Oak	43.8
Appier,Kevin, Ana	45.8
5 tied with	50.0

Pickoffs

Buehrle,Mark, CWS	8
Kennedy,Joe, TB	8
Pettitte,Andy, NYY	6
Mulder,Mark, Oak	5
Zito,Barry, Oak	5
Halama,John, Sea	4
Lopez,Rodrigo, Bal	4
Moyer,Jamie, Sea	4
Redman,Mark, Det	4
7 tied with	3

2002 American League Pitching Leaders

Strikeouts Per 9 IP
(minimum 162 IP)

Martinez,Pedro, Bos	10.79
Clemens,Roger, NYY	9.60
Mussina,Mike, NYY	7.60
Wakefield,Tim, Bos	7.38
Garcia,Freddy, Sea	7.28
Zito,Barry, Oak	7.14
Baez,Danys, Cle	7.08
Mulder,Mark, Oak	6.90
Ortiz,Ramon, Ana	6.71
Burkett,John, Bos	6.45

Opp On-Base Percentage
(minimum 162 IP)

Martinez,Pedro, Bos	.254
Lowe,Derek, Bos	.266
Wakefield,Tim, Bos	.276
Moyer,Jamie, Sea	.278
Reed,Rick, Min	.288
Byrd,Paul, KC	.288
Washburn,J, Ana	.289
Zito,Barry, Oak	.289
Mulder,Mark, Oak	.290
Milton,Eric, Min	.291

Opp Slugging Average
(minimum 162 IP)

Lowe,Derek, Bos	.302
Martinez,Pedro, Bos	.309
Wakefield,Tim, Bos	.333
Halladay,Roy, Tor	.333
Zito,Barry, Oak	.340
Moyer,Jamie, Sea	.366
Mulder,Mark, Oak	.366
Washburn,J, Ana	.375
Lopez,Rodrigo, Bal	.382
Weaver,Jeff, Det-NYY	.383

Hits Per Nine Innings
(minimum 162 IP)

Martinez,Pedro, Bos	6.50
Wakefield,Tim, Bos	6.67
Lowe,Derek, Bos	6.80
Zito,Barry, Oak	7.14
Moyer,Jamie, Sea	7.73
Ortiz,Ramon, Ana	7.79
Lopez,Rodrigo, Bal	7.87
Mulder,Mark, Oak	7.90
Washburn,J, Ana	8.00
Halladay,Roy, Tor	8.39

Home Runs Per Nine IP
(minimum 162 IP)

Halladay,Roy, Tor	0.38
Lowe,Derek, Bos	0.49
Martinez,Pedro, Bos	0.59
Redman,Mark, Det	0.67
Hudson,Tim, Oak	0.72
Weaver,Jeff, Det-NYY	0.72
Sabathia,C.C., Cle	0.73
Baez,Danys, Cle	0.76
Lidle,Cory, Oak	0.80
Wakefield,Tim, Bos	0.83

Batting Average vs. LHB
(minimum 125 BF)

Rhodes,Arthur, Sea	.158
Rogers,Kenny, Tex	.193
Wakefield,Tim, Bos	.197
Washburn,J, Ana	.199
Schoeneweis,S, Ana	.202
Martinez,Pedro, Bos	.203
Rincon,Ricrdo, Cle-Oak	.203
Mecir,Jim, Oak	.204
Sasaki,K, Sea	.205
Lowe,Derek, Bos	.209

Batting Average vs. RHB
(minimum 225 BF)

Martinez,Pedro, Bos	.191
Zito,Barry, Oak	.203
Moyer,Jamie, Sea	.205
Wakefield,Tim, Bos	.211
Lohse,Kyle, Min	.213
Lowe,Derek, Bos	.213
Santana,Johan, Min	.216
Glover,Gary, CWS	.218
Garland,Jon, CWS	.219
Mulder,Mark, Oak	.228

Opp BA w/ RISP
(minimum 125 BF)

Zito,Barry, Oak	.185
Pineiro,Joel, Sea	.193
Koch,Billy, Oak	.196
Martinez,Pedro, Bos	.196
Hernandez,O, NYY	.208
Ortiz,Ramon, Ana	.210
Karsay,Steve, NYY	.212
Lohse,Kyle, Min	.212
Lowe,Derek, Bos	.220
Fossum,Casey, Bos	.230

OBP vs. Leadoff Hitter
(minimum 150 BF)

Mulder,Mark, Oak	.221
Martinez,Pedro, Bos	.236
Milton,Eric, Min	.243
Moyer,Jamie, Sea	.253
Lowe,Derek, Bos	.253
Wakefield,Tim, Bos	.259
Weaver,Jeff, Det-NYY	.262
Lopez,Rodrigo, Bal	.264
Reed,Rick, Min	.268
Lidle,Cory, Oak	.269

Strikeouts / Walks Ratio
(minimum 162 IP)

Martinez,Pedro, Bos	5.98
Reed,Rick, Min	4.65
Milton,Eric, Min	4.03
Mussina,Mike, NYY	3.79
Byrd,Paul, KC	3.39
Clemens,Roger, NYY	3.05
Wells,David, NYY	3.04
Moyer,Jamie, Sea	2.94
Mulder,Mark, Oak	2.89
Garcia,Freddy, Sea	2.87

Highest GB/FB Ratio
(minimum 162 IP)

Lowe,Derek, Bos	3.36
Halladay,Roy, Tor	2.84
Hudson,Tim, Oak	2.22
Rogers,Kenny, Tex	2.07
Mulder,Mark, Oak	1.68
Lidle,Cory, Oak	1.59
Buehrle,Mark, CWS	1.48
Ponson,Sidney, Bal	1.46
Pineiro,Joel, Sea	1.41
Sparks,Steve, Det	1.33

Lowest GB/FB Ratio
(minimum 162 IP)

Washburn,J, Ana	0.63
Milton,Eric, Min	0.69
Zito,Barry, Oak	0.76
Appier,Kevin, Ana	0.78
Byrd,Paul, KC	0.80
Moyer,Jamie, Sea	0.85
Kennedy,Joe, TB	0.89
Lohse,Kyle, Min	0.89
Sturtze,Tanyon, TB	0.91
Wakefield,Tim, Bos	0.91

Rel Opp BA w/ Runners On
(minimum 50 IP)

Percival,Troy, Ana	.170
Sasaki,K, Sea	.179
Urbina,Ugueth, Bos	.184
Julio,Jorge, Bal	.195
Jackson,Mike, Min	.196
Fiore,Tony, Min	.197
Romero,J.C., Min	.199
Acevedo,Juan, Det	.200
Groom,Buddy, Bal	.202
Politte,Cliff, Tor	.210

Relief Opp BA w/ RISP
(minimum 50 IP)

Jackson,Mike, Min	.167
Romero,J.C., Min	.170
Fiore,Tony, Min	.171
Sasaki,K, Sea	.174
Bauer,Rick, Bal	.176
Urbina,Ugueth, Bos	.176
Pote,Lou, Ana	.189
Thurman,Corey, Tor	.190
Mecir,Jim, Oak	.196
Koch,Billy, Oak	.196

GIDP Induced

Hudson,Tim, Oak	35
Garland,Jon, CWS	32
Lowe,Derek, Bos	28
Rogers,Kenny, Tex	27
Sturtze,Tanyon, TB	26
Buehrle,Mark, CWS	24
Halladay,Roy, Tor	24
Sabathia,C.C., Cle	24
Pineiro,Joel, Sea	23
3 tied with	22

GIDP Per Nine IP
(minimum 162 IP)

Garland,Jon, CWS	1.49
Hudson,Tim, Oak	1.32
Rogers,Kenny, Tex	1.15
Lowe,Derek, Bos	1.15
Pineiro,Joel, Sea	1.07
Sturtze,Tanyon, TB	1.04
Sabathia,C.C., Cle	1.03
Wilson,Paul, TB	1.02
Kennedy,Joe, TB	1.01
Ponson,Sidney, Bal	0.92

2002 American League Pitching Leaders

Saves

Guardado,Eddie, Min	45
Koch,Billy, Oak	44
Percival,Troy, Ana	40
Urbina,Ugueth, Bos	40
Escobar,Kelvim, Tor	38
Sasaki,K, Sea	37
Acevedo,Juan, Det	28
Rivera,Mariano, NYY	28
Hernandez,Ro, KC	26
Julio,Jorge, Bal	25

Blown Saves

Escobar,Kelvim, Tor	8
Sasaki,K, Sea	8
Yan,Esteban, TB	8
Acevedo,Juan, Det	7
Cassidy,Scott, Tor	7
Hernandez,Ro, KC	7
5 tied with	6

Save Pct
(minimum 20 Save Ops)

Percival,Troy, Ana	90.9
Wickman,Bob, Cle	90.9
Guardado,Eddie, Min	88.2
Koch,Billy, Oak	88.0
Rivera,Mariano, NYY	87.5
Urbina,Ugueth, Bos	87.0
Escobar,Kelvim, Tor	82.6
Sasaki,K, Sea	82.2
Julio,Jorge, Bal	80.6
2 tied with	80.0

Relief Earned Run Average
(minimum 50 IP)

Groom,Buddy, Bal	1.60
Romero,J.C., Min	1.89
Percival,Troy, Ana	1.92
Julio,Jorge, Bal	1.99
Hawkins,LaTroy, Min	2.13
Halama,John, Sea	2.31
Rhodes,Arthur, Sea	2.33
Sasaki,K, Sea	2.52
Weber,Ben, Ana	2.54
Acevedo,Juan, Det	2.65

Relief Wins

Koch,Billy, Oak	11
Rhodes,Arthur, Sea	10
Fiore,Tony, Min	9
Romero,J.C., Min	9
Hasegawa,S, Sea	8
Mendoza,Ramiro, NYY	8
Osuna,Antonio, CWS	8
Stanton,Mike, NYY	7
Weber,Ben, Ana	7
Yan,Esteban, TB	7

Relief Losses

Yan,Esteban, TB	8
Colome,Jesus, TB	7
Escobar,Kelvim, Tor	7
Grimsley,Jason, KC	7
Bauer,Rick, Bal	6
Irabu,Hideki, Tex	6
Julio,Jorge, Bal	6
Kolb,Danny, Tex	6
Urbina,Ugueth, Bos	6
6 tied with	5

Holds

Romero,J.C., Min	33
Rhodes,Arthur, Sea	27
Rincon,Ricrdo, Cle-Oak	27
Politte,Cliff, Tor	25
Bradford,Chad, Oak	24
Jackson,Mike, Min	20
Mecir,Jim, Oak	20
Groom,Buddy, Bal	19
Weber,Ben, Ana	18
Stanton,Mike, NYY	17

Relief Games

Koch,Billy, Oak	84
Romero,J.C., Min	81
Stanton,Mike, NYY	79
Karsay,Steve, NYY	78
Escobar,Kelvim, Tor	76
Bradford,Chad, Oak	75
Rincon,Ricrdo, Cle-Oak	71
Grimsley,Jason, KC	70
Groom,Buddy, Bal	70
2 tied with	68

Relief Innings

Koch,Billy, Oak	93.2
Mendoza,Ramiro, NYY	91.2
Karsay,Steve, NYY	88.1
Romero,J.C., Min	81.0
Fiore,Tony, Min	80.2
Hawkins,LaTroy, Min	80.1
Escobar,Kelvim, Tor	78.0
Stanton,Mike, NYY	78.0
Weber,Ben, Ana	78.0
2 tied with	77.2

Relief Opp Batting Average
(minimum 50 IP)

Politte,Cliff, Tor	.186
Rhodes,Arthur, Sea	.187
Percival,Troy, Ana	.188
Pote,Lou, Ana	.194
Groom,Buddy, Bal	.196
Sasaki,K, Sea	.201
Urbina,Ugueth, Bos	.202
Marte,Damaso, CWS	.204
Fiore,Tony, Min	.211
2 tied with	.213

Relief Opp On Base Pct
(minimum 50 IP)

Rhodes,Arthur, Sea	.227
Groom,Buddy, Bal	.243
Hawkins,LaTroy, Min	.253
Politte,Cliff, Tor	.258
Foulke,Keith, CWS	.263
Urbina,Ugueth, Bos	.266
Rincon,Ricrdo, Cle-Oak	.268
Sasaki,K, Sea	.268
Guardado,Eddie, Min	.269
2 tied with	.276

Relief Opp Slugging Avg
(minimum 50 IP)

Rhodes,Arthur, Sea	.274
Groom,Buddy, Bal	.281
Politte,Cliff, Tor	.284
Romero,J.C., Min	.289
Marte,Damaso, CWS	.296
Percival,Troy, Ana	.297
Hawkins,LaTroy, Min	.307
Koch,Billy, Oak	.308
Halama,John, Sea	.314
Sasaki,K, Sea	.324

Inherited Runners Scrd %
(minimum 30 IR)

Rodriguez,Rich, Tex	13.2
Donnelly,B, Ana	15.6
Mecir,Jim, Oak	17.9
Romero,J.C., Min	18.5
Eyre,Scott, Tor	20.8
Ryan,B.J., Bal	22.0
Rincon,Ricrdo, Cle-Oak	22.6
Venafro,Mike, Oak	22.7
Cook,Dennis, Ana	26.7
Karsay,Steve, NYY	27.8

Rel OBP 1st Batter Faced
(minimum 40 BF)

Donnelly,B, Ana	.156
Wohlers,Mark, Cle	.188
Fiore,Tony, Min	.196
Rhodes,Arthur, Sea	.200
Rivera,Mariano, NYY	.200
Groom,Buddy, Bal	.214
Bradford,Chad, Oak	.227
Walker,Jamie, Det	.228
Foulke,Keith, CWS	.231
Politte,Cliff, Tor	.236

Relief Opp BA Vs LHB
(minimum 50 AB)

Marte,Damaso, CWS	.149
Rhodes,Arthur, Sea	.158
Groom,Buddy, Bal	.181
Ryan,B.J., Bal	.192
Rincon,Ricrdo, Cle-Oak	.203
Mecir,Jim, Oak	.204
Sasaki,K, Sea	.205
Julio,Jorge, Bal	.213
Romero,J.C., Min	.214
3 tied with	.220

Relief Opp BA Vs RHB
(minimum 50 AB)

Percival,Troy, Ana	.138
Urbina,Ugueth, Bos	.143
Politte,Cliff, Tor	.154
Pote,Lou, Ana	.172
Foulke,Keith, CWS	.184
Fiore,Tony, Min	.184
Sasaki,K, Sea	.196
Koch,Billy, Oak	.197
Wakefield,Tim, Bos	.197
Hasegawa,S, Sea	.199

2002 American League Pitching Leaders

Fastest Average Fastball
(minimum 162 IP)

Clemens,Roger, NYY	93.2
Garcia,Freddy, Sea	92.9
Ponson,Sidney, Bal	92.6
Sabathia,C.C., Cle	92.3
Ortiz,Ramon, Ana	92.3
Weaver,Jeff, Det-NYY	92.2
Halladay,Roy, Tor	91.7
Lohse,Kyle, Min	91.7
Hudson,Tim, Oak	91.5
Lopez,Rodrigo, Bal	91.2

Slowest Average Fastball
(minimum 162 IP)

Wakefield,Tim, Bos	76.4
Sparks,Steve, Det	79.5
Moyer,Jamie, Sea	82.7
Burkett,John, Bos	83.8
Rogers,Kenny, Tex	85.1
Castillo,Frank, Bos	85.4
Byrd,Paul, KC	86.5
Buehrle,Mark, CWS	86.5
Redman,Mark, Det	86.7
Zito,Barry, Oak	87.1

Pitches 100+ Velocity

Colon,Bartolo, Cle	6
Hernandez,Ro, KC	4
Anderson,Mat, Det	3
Garcia,Freddy, Sea	2
Julio,Jorge, Bal	2
Koch,Billy, Oak	2
Santana,Julio, Det	2
Wohlers,Mark, Cle	2
4 tied with	1

Pitches 95+ Velocity

Koch,Billy, Oak	754
Percival,Troy, Ana	482
Julio,Jorge, Bal	441
Colon,Bartolo, Cle	381
Rhodes,Arthur, Sea	328
Santana,Julio, Det	324
Clemens,Roger, NYY	314
Garcia,Freddy, Sea	300
Cordero,F, Tex	296
Hernandez,Ro, KC	291

Pitches Less Than 80 MPH

Sparks,Steve, Det	1953
Wakefield,Tim, Bos	1510
Moyer,Jamie, Sea	1234
Zito,Barry, Oak	1188
Redman,Mark, Det	761
Appier,Kevin, Ana	757
Rogers,Kenny, Tex	716
Weaver,Jeff, Det-NYY	654
Burkett,John, Bos	606
Sele,Aaron, Ana	574

Lowest % Fastballs
(minimum 162 IP)

Wakefield,Tim, Bos	7.0
Sparks,Steve, Det	14.4
Rogers,Kenny, Tex	43.6
Moyer,Jamie, Sea	45.6
Appier,Kevin, Ana	45.8
Byrd,Paul, KC	48.6
Zito,Barry, Oak	52.3
Mulder,Mark, Oak	53.9
Ortiz,Ramon, Ana	54.0
Pineiro,Joel, Sea	54.6

Highest % Fastballs
(minimum 162 IP)

Lowe,Derek, Bos	76.4
Washburn,J, Ana	70.6
Baez,Danys, Cle	70.5
Burkett,John, Bos	66.8
Wilson,Paul, TB	66.2
Suppan,Jeff, KC	65.7
Hudson,Tim, Oak	65.3
Reed,Rick, Min	64.8
Clemens,Roger, NYY	64.8
Kennedy,Joe, TB	64.7

Highest % Curveballs
(minimum 162 IP)

Mussina,Mike, NYY	30.4
Appier,Kevin, Ana	26.6
Wells,David, NYY	25.6
Zito,Barry, Oak	24.3
Halladay,Roy, Tor	24.2
Wright,Dan, CWS	22.9
Garcia,Freddy, Sea	22.9
Weaver,Jeff, Det-NYY	22.3
Sabathia,C.C., Cle	21.0
Rogers,Kenny, Tex	20.5

Highest % Changeups
(minimum 162 IP)

Moyer,Jamie, Sea	32.4
Redman,Mark, Det	24.3
Rogers,Kenny, Tex	23.6
Martinez,Pedro, Bos	18.6
Castillo,Frank, Bos	17.7
Zito,Barry, Oak	14.2
Mulder,Mark, Oak	14.2
Buehrle,Mark, CWS	13.8
Ortiz,Ramon, Ana	13.4
Suppan,Jeff, KC	13.1

Highest % Sliders
(minimum 162 IP)

Ortiz,Ramon, Ana	32.5
Lopez,Rodrigo, Bal	23.9
Ponson,Sidney, Bal	19.3
Byrd,Paul, KC	16.1
Pineiro,Joel, Sea	14.7
Sturtze,Tanyon, TB	13.4
Lohse,Kyle, Min	13.4
Redman,Mark, Det	13.3
Weaver,Jeff, Det-NYY	13.3
Hudson,Tim, Oak	12.9

2002 National League Pitching Leaders

Earned Run Average
(minimum 162 IP)

Johnson,Randy, Ari	2.32
Maddux,Greg, Atl	2.62
Glavine,Tom, Atl	2.96
Perez,Odalis, LA	3.00
Oswalt,Roy, Hou	3.01
Dessens,Elmer, Cin	3.03
Ohka,Tomo, Mon	3.18
Wolf,Randy, Phi	3.20
Rueter,Kirk, SF	3.23
Schilling,Curt, Ari	3.23

Winning Percentage
(minimum 15 Decisions)

Johnson,Randy, Ari	.828
Miller,Wade, Hou	.789
Schilling,Curt, Ari	.767
Stark,Denny, Col	.733
Maddux,Greg, Atl	.727
Nomo,Hideo, LA	.727
Millwood,Kevin, Atl	.692
Simontacchi,J, Stl	.688
Oswalt,Roy, Hou	.679
2 tied with	.667

Opponent Batting Average
(minimum 162 IP)

Johnson,Randy, Ari	.208
Burnett,A.J., Fla	.209
Clement,Matt, ChC	.215
Schmidt,Jason, SF	.218
Moss,Damian, Atl	.221
Wood,Kerry, ChC	.221
Wolf,Randy, Phi	.223
Schilling,Curt, Ari	.224
Perez,Odalis, LA	.226
Millwood,Kevin, Atl	.230

Baserunners Per 9 IP
(minimum 162 IP)

Schilling,Curt, Ari	8.81
Perez,Odalis, LA	9.07
Johnson,Randy, Ari	9.73
Wolf,Randy, Phi	10.34
Millwood,Kevin, Atl	10.74
Schmidt,Jason, SF	10.83
Oswalt,Roy, Hou	10.89
Maddux,Greg, Atl	10.97
Burnett,A.J., Fla	11.10
Clement,Matt, ChC	11.11

Games

Quantrill,Paul, LA	86
Dotel,Octavio, Hou	83
Worrell,Tim, SF	80
Jones,Todd, Col	79
Looper,Braden, Fla	78
Sauerbeck,S, Pit	78
Stone,Ricky, Hou	78
Gagne,Eric, LA	77
Nunez,Vladimir, Fla	77
2 tied with	76

Games Started

Glavine,Tom, Atl	36
Johnson,Randy, Ari	35
Schilling,Curt, Ari	35
8 tied with	34

Complete Games

Johnson,Randy, Ari	8
Burnett,A.J., Fla	7
Hernandez,L, SF	5
Schilling,Curt, Ari	5
Colon,Bartolo, Mon	4
Dempster,Ryan, Fla-Cin	4
Perez,Odalis, LA	4
Rusch,Glendon, Mil	4
Wood,Kerry, ChC	4
5 tied with	3

Shutouts

Burnett,A.J., Fla	5
Johnson,Randy, Ari	4
Hernandez,L, SF	3
Clement,Matt, ChC	2
Lawrence,Brian, SD	2
Leiter,Al, NYM	2
Perez,Odalis, LA	2
Schmidt,Jason, SF	2
Wolf,Randy, Phi	2
20 tied with	1

Wins

Johnson,Randy, Ari	24
Schilling,Curt, Ari	23
Oswalt,Roy, Hou	19
Glavine,Tom, Atl	18
Millwood,Kevin, Atl	18
Morris,Matt, Stl	17
Jennings,Jason, Col	16
Maddux,Greg, Atl	16
Nomo,Hideo, LA	16
3 tied with	15

Losses

Hernandez,L, SF	16
Rusch,Glendon, Mil	16
Sheets,Ben, Mil	16
Hampton,Mike, Col	15
Thomson,J, Col-NYM	14
Wells,Kip, Pit	14
6 tied with	13

Innings Pitched

Johnson,Randy, Ari	260.0
Schilling,Curt, Ari	259.1
Oswalt,Roy, Hou	233.0
Vazquez,Javier, Mon	230.1
Glavine,Tom, Atl	224.2
Perez,Odalis, LA	222.1
Nomo,Hideo, LA	220.1
Millwood,Kevin, Atl	217.0
Sheets,Ben, Mil	216.2
Hernandez,L, SF	216.0

Batters Faced

Johnson,Randy, Ari	1035
Schilling,Curt, Ari	1017
Vazquez,Javier, Mon	971
Oswalt,Roy, Hou	956
Glavine,Tom, Atl	936
Sheets,Ben, Mil	934
Nomo,Hideo, LA	926
Hernandez,L, SF	921
Dempster,Ryan, Fla-Cin	915
Rusch,Glendon, Mil	913

Strikeouts

Johnson,Randy, Ari	334
Schilling,Curt, Ari	316
Wood,Kerry, ChC	217
Clement,Matt, ChC	215
Oswalt,Roy, Hou	208
Burnett,A.J., Fla	203
Schmidt,Jason, SF	196
Nomo,Hideo, LA	193
Vazquez,Javier, Mon	179
Millwood,Kevin, Atl	178

Walks Allowed

Ishii,Kazuhisa, LA	106
Nomo,Hideo, LA	101
Wood,Kerry, ChC	97
Ortiz,Russ, SF	94
Dempster,Ryan, Fla-Cin	93
Hampton,Mike, Col	91
Burnett,A.J., Fla	90
Moss,Damian, Atl	89
Clement,Matt, ChC	85
Estes,Shawn, NYM-Cin	83

Hit Batters

Astacio,Pedro, NYM	16
Wood,Kerry, ChC	16
Padilla,V, Phi	15
Tavarez,Julian, Fla	15
Johnson,Randy, Ari	13
Lawrence,Brian, SD	11
Wright,Jamey, Mil-Stl	11
4 tied with	10

Wild Pitches

Armas Jr.,Tony, Mon	14
Burnett,A.J., Fla	14
Moss,Damian, Atl	13
Schmidt,Jason, SF	12
Coggin,Dave, Phi	11
Duckworth,B, Phi	10
Jennings,Jason, Col	10
5 tied with	9

2002 National League Pitching Leaders

Runs Allowed

Hampton,Mike, Col	135
Dempster,Ryan, Fla-Cin	127
Rusch,Glendon, Mil	118
Thomson,J, Col-NYM	116
Hernandez,L, SF	113
Vazquez,Javier, Mon	111
Tomko,Brett, SD	107
Astacio,Pedro, NYM	106
Sheets,Ben, Mil	105
Duckworth,B, Phi	103

Hits Allowed

Vazquez,Javier, Mon	243
Sheets,Ben, Mil	237
Hernandez,L, SF	233
Lawrence,Brian, SD	230
Dempster,Ryan, Fla-Cin	228
Hampton,Mike, Col	228
Rusch,Glendon, Mil	227
Schilling,Curt, Ari	218
Oswalt,Roy, Hou	215
Tomko,Brett, SD	212

Doubles Allowed

Vazquez,Javier, Mon	56
Sheets,Ben, Mil	55
Tavarez,Julian, Fla	54
Glavine,Tom, Atl	49
Thomson,J, Col-NYM	49
Tomko,Brett, SD	47
Duckworth,B, Phi	43
Dempster,Ryan, Fla-Cin	42
Johnson,Randy, Ari	42
Anderson,Bri, Ari	41

Home Runs Allowed

Astacio,Pedro, NYM	32
Helling,Rick, Ari	31
Tomko,Brett, SD	31
Rusch,Glendon, Mil	30
Schilling,Curt, Ari	29
Dempster,Ryan, Fla-Cin	28
Fogg,Josh, Pit	28
Quevedo,Ruben, Mil	28
Thomson,J, Col-NYM	28
Vazquez,Javier, Mon	28

Run Support Per Nine IP
(minimum 162 IP)

Jensen,Ryan, SF	6.55
Jennings,Jason, Col	6.51
Miller,Wade, Hou	6.12
Johnson,Randy, Ari	5.99
Schilling,Curt, Ari	5.93
Wood,Kerry, ChC	5.85
Helling,Rick, Ari	5.69
Dempster,Ryan, Fla-Cin	5.64
Oswalt,Roy, Hou	5.52
Hampton,Mike, Col	5.44

% Pitches In Strike Zone
(minimum 162 IP)

Millwood,Kevin, Atl	69.2
Oswalt,Roy, Hou	69.1
Padilla,V, Phi	68.6
Schilling,Curt, Ari	68.5
Maddux,Greg, Atl	68.0
Astacio,Pedro, NYM	67.6
Thomson,J, Col-NYM	67.1
Helling,Rick, Ari	65.9
Morris,Matt, Stl	65.8
Rusch,Glendon, Mil	65.3

Pitches Per Start
(minimum 30 GS)

Johnson,Randy, Ari	114.1
Ortiz,Russ, SF	109.1
Rusch,Glendon, Mil	106.4
Schilling,Curt, Ari	105.8
Hernandez,L, SF	105.3
Vazquez,Javier, Mon	104.6
Leiter,Al, NYM	103.5
Wolf,Randy, Phi	103.5
Sheets,Ben, Mil	103.4
Wood,Kerry, ChC	102.5

Pitches Per Batter
(minimum 162 IP)

Maddux,Greg, Atl	3.27
Lawrence,Brian, SD	3.48
Perez,Odalis, LA	3.48
Tomko,Brett, SD	3.53
Padilla,V, Phi	3.53
Fogg,Josh, Pit	3.55
Batista,Miguel, Ari	3.55
Ohka,Tomo, Mon	3.55
Ashby,Andy, LA	3.55
Hampton,Mike, Col	3.58

Quality Starts

Johnson,Randy, Ari	30
Schilling,Curt, Ari	27
Nomo,Hideo, LA	25
Ortiz,Russ, SF	24
Oswalt,Roy, Hou	24
Perez,Odalis, LA	23
Glavine,Tom, Atl	22
Sheets,Ben, Mil	22
Wolf,Randy, Phi	22
Wood,Kerry, ChC	22

Easy Saves

Smoltz,John, Atl	36
Mesa,Jose, Phi	33
Hoffman,Trevor, SD	27
Williams,Mike, Pit	27
Gagne,Eric, LA	26
Wagner,Billy, Hou	26
Jimenez,Jose, Col	25
Nen,Robb, SF	25
Benitez,A, NYM	19
2 tied with	18

Regular Saves

Gagne,Eric, LA	21
Williams,Mike, Pit	19
Jimenez,Jose, Col	15
Isringhausen,J, Stl	14
Nen,Robb, SF	14
Smoltz,John, Atl	14
DeJean,Mike, Mil	12
Kim,Byung-Hyun, Ari	12
Mesa,Jose, Phi	12
3 tied with	11

Tough Saves

Kim,Byung-Hyun, Ari	6
Gagne,Eric, LA	5
Smoltz,John, Atl	5
Nen,Robb, SF	4
Stewart,Scott, Mon	4
Benitez,A, NYM	3
Graves,Danny, Cin	3
5 tied with	2

Stolen Bases Allowed

Leiter,Al, NYM	29
Nomo,Hideo, LA	28
Duckworth,B, Phi	24
Maddux,Greg, Atl	24
Hernandez,L, SF	22
Anderson,Ji, Pit	21
Millwood,Kevin, Atl	21
Trachsel,Steve, NYM	21
Estes,Shawn, NYM-Cin	20
4 tied with	19

Caught Stealing Off

Glavine,Tom, Atl	16
Johnson,Randy, Ari	15
Dempster,Ryan, Fla-Cin	13
Leiter,Al, NYM	12
Sheets,Ben, Mil	12
Ishii,Kazuhisa, LA	11
Moss,Damian, Atl	11
Trachsel,Steve, NYM	11
3 tied with	10

Stolen Base Pct Allowed
(minimum 162 IP)

Rusch,Glendon, Mil	14.3
Rueter,Kirk, SF	28.6
Helling,Rick, Ari	33.3
Dempster,Ryan, Fla-Cin	35.0
Moss,Damian, Atl	42.1
Haynes,Jimmy, Cin	44.4
Glavine,Tom, Atl	44.8
4 tied with	50.0

Pickoffs

Moss,Damian, Atl	9
Perez,Odalis, LA	9
Anderson,Bri, Ari	8
Anderson,Ji, Pit	8
Fetters,Mike, Pit-Ari	5
Glavine,Tom, Atl	4
Hernandez,L, SF	4
10 tied with	3

2002 National League Pitching Leaders

Strikeouts Per 9 IP
(minimum 162 IP)

Johnson,Randy, Ari	11.56
Schilling,Curt, Ari	10.97
Schmidt,Jason, SF	9.52
Clement,Matt, ChC	9.44
Duckworth,B, Phi	9.22
Wood,Kerry, ChC	9.14
Burnett,A.J., Fla	8.94
Oswalt,Roy, Hou	8.03
Nomo,Hideo, LA	7.88
Miller,Wade, Hou	7.87

Opp On-Base Percentage
(minimum 162 IP)

Schilling,Curt, Ari	.251
Perez,Odalis, LA	.262
Johnson,Randy, Ari	.273
Wolf,Randy, Phi	.285
Millwood,Kevin, Atl	.292
Schmidt,Jason, SF	.294
Clement,Matt, ChC	.299
Oswalt,Roy, Hou	.299
Maddux,Greg, Atl	.301
Burnett,A.J., Fla	.302

Opp Slugging Average
(minimum 162 IP)

Burnett,A.J., Fla	.309
Schmidt,Jason, SF	.329
Millwood,Kevin, Atl	.337
Clement,Matt, ChC	.344
Johnson,Randy, Ari	.346
Perez,Odalis, LA	.347
Ortiz,Russ, SF	.357
Maddux,Greg, Atl	.358
Wood,Kerry, ChC	.361
Schilling,Curt, Ari	.362

Hits Per Nine Innings
(minimum 162 IP)

Burnett,A.J., Fla	6.74
Johnson,Randy, Ari	6.82
Moss,Damian, Atl	7.04
Clement,Matt, ChC	7.11
Wood,Kerry, ChC	7.12
Schmidt,Jason, SF	7.19
Wolf,Randy, Phi	7.35
Perez,Odalis, LA	7.37
Schilling,Curt, Ari	7.57
Millwood,Kevin, Atl	7.71

Home Runs Per Nine IP
(minimum 162 IP)

Burnett,A.J., Fla	0.53
Batista,Miguel, Ari	0.58
Ortiz,Russ, SF	0.63
Maddux,Greg, Atl	0.63
Oswalt,Roy, Hou	0.66
Millwood,Kevin, Atl	0.66
Morris,Matt, Stl	0.68
Lawrence,Brian, SD	0.69
Padilla,V, Phi	0.70
Schmidt,Jason, SF	0.73

Batting Average vs. LHB
(minimum 125 BF)

Benitez,A, NYM	.160
Moss,Damian, Atl	.165
Williams,Woody, Stl	.182
Dotel,Octavio, Hou	.190
Veres,Dave, Stl	.190
Nunez,Vladimir, Fla	.191
Gagne,Eric, LA	.204
Prior,Mark, ChC	.204
Timlin,Mike, Stl-Phi	.208
Zambrano,C, ChC	.209

Batting Average vs. RHB
(minimum 225 BF)

Burnett,A.J., Fla	.177
Schmidt,Jason, SF	.180
Perez,Oliver, SD	.191
Armas Jr.,Tony, Mon	.192
Johnson,Randy, Ari	.206
Schilling,Curt, Ari	.208
Benes,Andy, Stl	.210
Clement,Matt, ChC	.212
Millwood,Kevin, Atl	.214
Timlin,Mike, Stl-Phi	.214

Opp BA w/ RISP
(minimum 125 BF)

Johnson,Randy, Ari	.146
Wood,Kerry, ChC	.182
Glavine,Tom, Atl	.193
Moss,Damian, Atl	.204
Wolf,Randy, Phi	.207
Armas Jr.,Tony, Mon	.208
Ashby,Andy, LA	.214
Maddux,Greg, Atl	.216
Hernandez,C, Hou	.219
Colon,Bartolo, Mon	.221

OBP vs. Leadoff Hitter
(minimum 150 BF)

Schilling,Curt, Ari	.223
Tomko,Brett, SD	.242
Wolf,Randy, Phi	.243
Millwood,Kevin, Atl	.254
Daal,Omar, LA	.262
Clement,Matt, ChC	.263
Johnson,Randy, Ari	.264
Ortiz,Russ, SF	.268
Simontacchi,J, Stl	.270
Lawrence,Brian, SD	.276

Strikeouts / Walks Ratio
(minimum 162 IP)

Schilling,Curt, Ari	9.58
Johnson,Randy, Ari	4.70
Perez,Odalis, LA	4.08
Vazquez,Javier, Mon	3.65
Oswalt,Roy, Hou	3.35
Lawrence,Brian, SD	2.87
Millwood,Kevin, Atl	2.74
Wolf,Randy, Phi	2.73
Schmidt,Jason, SF	2.68
Morris,Matt, Stl	2.67

Highest GB/FB Ratio
(minimum 162 IP)

Maddux,Greg, Atl	2.30
Lawrence,Brian, SD	2.28
Wells,Kip, Pit	2.06
Padilla,V, Phi	1.97
Morris,Matt, Stl	1.74
Batista,Miguel, Ari	1.72
Sheets,Ben, Mil	1.58
Hampton,Mike, Col	1.57
Clement,Matt, ChC	1.57
Oswalt,Roy, Hou	1.55

Lowest GB/FB Ratio
(minimum 162 IP)

Helling,Rick, Ari	0.72
Wood,Kerry, ChC	0.81
Schmidt,Jason, SF	0.82
Thomson,J, Col-NYM	0.83
Duckworth,B, Phi	0.85
Jensen,Ryan, SF	0.89
Nomo,Hideo, LA	0.95
Neagle,Denny, Col	1.00
Vazquez,Javier, Mon	1.00
Wolf,Randy, Phi	1.00

Rel Opp BA w/ Runners On
(minimum 50 IP)

Holmes,Darren, Atl	.133
Dotel,Octavio, Hou	.144
Benitez,A, NYM	.149
Gagne,Eric, LA	.157
Hammond,Chris, Atl	.173
Reed,Steve, SD-NYM	.179
Mota,Guillermo, LA	.183
Ligtenberg,K, Atl	.183
Vizcaino,Luis, Mil	.185
Remlinger,Mike, Atl	.186

Relief Opp BA w/ RISP
(minimum 50 IP)

Holmes,Darren, Atl	.122
Gagne,Eric, LA	.123
Ligtenberg,K, Atl	.130
Dotel,Octavio, Hou	.147
Witasick,Jay, SF	.148
Hammond,Chris, Atl	.156
Vizcaino,Luis, Mil	.161
Crudale,Mike, Stl	.167
de los Santos,V, Mil	.167
Worrell,Tim, SF	.171

GIDP Induced

Hernandez,L, SF	29
Lawrence,Brian, SD	29
Hampton,Mike, Col	28
Rusch,Glendon, Mil	27
Estes,Shawn, NYM-Cin	26
Padilla,V, Phi	26
Rueter,Kirk, SF	26
Haynes,Jimmy, Cin	25
Jennings,Jason, Col	25
Maddux,Greg, Atl	24

GIDP Per Nine IP
(minimum 162 IP)

Hampton,Mike, Col	1.41
Lawrence,Brian, SD	1.24
Jennings,Jason, Col	1.21
Hernandez,L, SF	1.21
Rusch,Glendon, Mil	1.15
Rueter,Kirk, SF	1.15
Haynes,Jimmy, Cin	1.14
Padilla,V, Phi	1.14
Maddux,Greg, Atl	1.08
Moss,Damian, Atl	1.01

2002 National League Pitching Leaders

Saves

Smoltz,John, Atl	55
Gagne,Eric, LA	52
Williams,Mike, Pit	46
Mesa,Jose, Phi	45
Nen,Robb, SF	43
Jimenez,Jose, Col	41
Hoffman,Trevor, SD	38
Kim,Byung-Hyun, Ari	36
Wagner,Billy, Hou	35
Benitez,A, NYM	33

Blown Saves

Alfonseca,A, ChC	9
Mesa,Jose, Phi	9
Herges,Matt, Mon	8
Nen,Robb, SF	8
Nunez,Vladimir, Fla	8
Graves,Danny, Cin	7
6 tied with	6

Save Pct
(minimum 20 Save Ops)

Smoltz,John, Atl	93.2
Gagne,Eric, LA	92.9
Hoffman,Trevor, SD	92.7
Williams,Mike, Pit	92.0
DeJean,Mike, Mil	90.0
Benitez,A, NYM	89.2
Jimenez,Jose, Col	87.2
Isringhausen,J, Stl	86.5
Kim,Byung-Hyun, Ari	85.7
Wagner,Billy, Hou	85.4

Relief Earned Run Average
(minimum 50 IP)

Hammond,Chris, Atl	0.95
Eischen,Joey, Mon	1.34
Holmes,Darren, Atl	1.81
Dotel,Octavio, Hou	1.85
Crudale,Mike, Stl	1.95
Gagne,Eric, LA	1.97
Remlinger,Mike, Atl	1.99
Reed,Steve, SD-NYM	2.01
Kim,Byung-Hyun, Ari	2.04
Nen,Robb, SF	2.20

Relief Wins

Fassero,Jeff, ChC-Stl	8
Kim,Byung-Hyun, Ari	8
Rodriguez,Fe, SF	8
Worrell,Tim, SF	8
Hammond,Chris, Atl	7
Remlinger,Mike, Atl	7
13 tied with	6

Relief Losses

Jimenez,Jose, Col	10
Strickland,S, Mon-NYM	9
Veres,Dave, Stl	8
Fikac,Jeremy, SD	7
White,Rick, Col-Stl	7
6 tied with	6

Holds

Quantrill,Paul, LA	33
Dotel,Octavio, Hou	31
Jones,Todd, Col	30
Remlinger,Mike, Atl	30
Boehringer,B, Pit	28
Sauerbeck,S, Pit	28
Rodriguez,Fe, SF	24
Worrell,Tim, SF	23
Kline,Steve, Stl	21
Timlin,Mike, Stl-Phi	20

Relief Games

Quantrill,Paul, LA	86
Dotel,Octavio, Hou	83
Worrell,Tim, SF	80
Jones,Todd, Col	79
Looper,Braden, Fla	78
Sauerbeck,S, Pit	78
Stone,Ricky, Hou	78
Gagne,Eric, LA	77
Nunez,Vladimir, Fla	77
2 tied with	76

Relief Innings

Nunez,Vladimir, Fla	97.2
Dotel,Octavio, Hou	97.1
Borowski,Joe, ChC	95.2
Timlin,Mike, Stl-Phi	92.1
Looper,Braden, Fla	86.0
Carrara,G, LA	85.2
Kim,Byung-Hyun, Ari	84.0
Silva,Carlos, Phi	84.0
Veres,Dave, Stl	82.2
2 tied with	82.1

Relief Opp Batting Average
(minimum 50 IP)

Dotel,Octavio, Hou	.173
Williamson,S, Cin	.181
Gagne,Eric, LA	.189
Benitez,A, NYM	.190
Vizcaino,Luis, Mil	.192
Hammond,Chris, Atl	.195
Wagner,Billy, Hou	.196
Remlinger,Mike, Atl	.198
Isringhausen,J, Stl	.199
Mota,Guillermo, LA	.202

Relief Opp On Base Pct
(minimum 50 IP)

Gagne,Eric, LA	.235
Dotel,Octavio, Hou	.239
Timlin,Mike, Stl-Phi	.246
Isringhausen,J, Stl	.257
Wagner,Billy, Hou	.261
Holmes,Darren, Atl	.262
Smoltz,John, Atl	.266
Benitez,A, NYM	.272
Vizcaino,Luis, Mil	.272
Crudale,Mike, Stl	.274

Relief Opp Slugging Avg
(minimum 50 IP)

Isringhausen,J, Stl	.242
Hammond,Chris, Atl	.261
Dotel,Octavio, Hou	.275
Kim,Byung-Hyun, Ari	.276
Koplove,Mike, Ari	.276
Remlinger,Mike, Atl	.277
Eischen,Joey, Mon	.281
Williamson,S, Cin	.283
Vizcaino,Luis, Mil	.296
2 tied with	.299

Inherited Runners Scrd %
(minimum 30 IR)

Speier,Justin, Col	5.7
Orosco,Jesse, LA	12.8
Stewart,Scott, Mon	14.7
Vizcaino,Luis, Mil	15.0
Guthrie,Mark, NYM	16.2
White,Rick, Col-Stl	17.1
Hammond,Chris, Atl	18.2
Lowe,Sean, Pit-Col	18.8
Sauerbeck,S, Pit	20.4
2 tied with	20.6

Rel OBP 1st Batter Faced
(minimum 40 BF)

Koplove,Mike, Ari	.185
Plesac,Dan, Phi	.195
Boehringer,B, Pit	.203
Timlin,Mike, Stl-Phi	.214
White,Rick, Col-Stl	.220
Gagne,Eric, LA	.221
Stewart,Scott, Mon	.224
White,Gabe, Cin	.230
Fikac,Jeremy, SD	.231
Smoltz,John, Atl	.240

Relief Opp BA Vs LHB
(minimum 50 AB)

Sauerbeck,S, Pit	.146
Spooneybarger,T, Atl	.150
Stewart,Scott, Mon	.157
Benitez,A, NYM	.160
Gryboski,Kevin, Atl	.171
Eischen,Joey, Mon	.173
Hammond,Chris, Atl	.174
Koplove,Mike, Ari	.174
Cruz,Juan, ChC	.178
Wagner,Billy, Hou	.180

Relief Opp BA Vs RHB
(minimum 50 AB)

Dotel,Octavio, Hou	.159
Gagne,Eric, LA	.163
Isringhausen,J, Stl	.164
Williamson,S, Cin	.170
Vizcaino,Luis, Mil	.170
Williams,Mike, Pit	.179
Remlinger,Mike, Atl	.184
Strickland,S, Mon-NYM	.187
Looper,Braden, Fla	.194
Rodriguez,Fe, SF	.194

2002 National League Pitching Leaders

Fastest Average Fastball (minimum 162 IP)	
Burnett,A.J., Fla	94.9
Johnson,Randy, Ari	94.5
Wood,Kerry, ChC	94.3
Oswalt,Roy, Hou	93.7
Schilling,Curt, Ari	93.4
Schmidt,Jason, SF	93.0
Miller,Wade, Hou	92.6
Sheets,Ben, Mil	92.6
Wells,Kip, Pit	92.1
Armas Jr.,Tony, Mon	91.8

Slowest Average Fastball (minimum 162 IP)	
Lawrence,Brian, SD	85.0
Rueter,Kirk, SF	85.1
Glavine,Tom, Atl	85.3
Maddux,Greg, Atl	85.8
Neagle,Denny, Col	86.4
Helling,Rick, Ari	87.0
Nomo,Hideo, LA	87.3
Wolf,Randy, Phi	87.4
Rusch,Glendon, Mil	87.8
Ashby,Andy, LA	87.9

Pitches 100+ Velocity	
Wagner,Billy, Hou	42
Benitez,A, NYM	9
Farnsworth,K, ChC	6
Johnson,Randy, Ari	6
Oswalt,Roy, Hou	5
Nen,Robb, SF	2
Wood,Kerry, ChC	2
8 tied with	1

Pitches 95+ Velocity	
Wood,Kerry, ChC	1043
Burnett,A.J., Fla	979
Johnson,Randy, Ari	898
Rodriguez,Fe, SF	751
Oswalt,Roy, Hou	673
Wagner,Billy, Hou	644
Looper,Braden, Fla	628
Dotel,Octavio, Hou	564
Schilling,Curt, Ari	531
Schmidt,Jason, SF	512

Pitches Less Than 80 MPH	
Nomo,Hideo, LA	807
Morris,Matt, Stl	707
Astacio,Pedro, NYM	705
Tejera,Michael, Fla	704
Wolf,Randy, Phi	682
Fernandez,J, Cin	639
Ishii,Kazuhisa, LA	628
D'Amico,Jeff, NYM	615
Estes,Shawn, NYM-Cin	615
Glavine,Tom, Atl	601

Lowest % Fastballs (minimum 162 IP)	
Ohka,Tomo, Mon	44.3
Perez,Odalis, LA	45.0
Haynes,Jimmy, Cin	46.6
Fogg,Josh, Pit	48.5
Lawrence,Brian, SD	49.9
Vazquez,Javier, Mon	50.4
Nomo,Hideo, LA	50.7
Schilling,Curt, Ari	52.6
Neagle,Denny, Col	52.8
Tomko,Brett, SD	53.6

Highest % Fastballs (minimum 162 IP)	
Padilla,V, Phi	77.1
Maddux,Greg, Atl	76.3
Ashby,Andy, LA	72.7
Rueter,Kirk, SF	70.7
Millwood,Kevin, Atl	70.4
Leiter,Al, NYM	70.2
Ortiz,Russ, SF	69.1
Wood,Kerry, ChC	68.6
Duckworth,B, Phi	68.2
Rusch,Glendon, Mil	68.2

Highest % Curveballs (minimum 162 IP)	
Astacio,Pedro, NYM	32.4
Morris,Matt, Stl	27.4
Haynes,Jimmy, Cin	25.0
Burnett,A.J., Fla	23.4
Wolf,Randy, Phi	22.9
Duckworth,B, Phi	22.4
Wood,Kerry, ChC	22.0
Sheets,Ben, Mil	21.3
Wells,Kip, Pit	20.2
Oswalt,Roy, Hou	19.6

Highest % Changeups (minimum 162 IP)	
Glavine,Tom, Atl	33.6
Moss,Damian, Atl	30.2
Neagle,Denny, Col	19.4
Maddux,Greg, Atl	19.4
Vazquez,Javier, Mon	15.9
Fogg,Josh, Pit	15.5
Trachsel,Steve, NYM	14.9
Perez,Odalis, LA	14.1
Rusch,Glendon, Mil	14.1
Ohka,Tomo, Mon	12.7

Highest % Sliders (minimum 162 IP)	
Johnson,Randy, Ari	40.9
Clement,Matt, ChC	36.9
Lawrence,Brian, SD	32.5
Fogg,Josh, Pit	29.7
Armas Jr.,Tony, Mon	29.6
Perez,Odalis, LA	29.6
Dempster,Ryan, Fla-Cin	26.2
Jennings,Jason, Col	22.5
Leiter,Al, NYM	21.7
Hampton,Mike, Col	19.0

2002 Active Career Batting Leaders

Batting Average (minimum 1000 PA)		On Base Percentage (minimum 1000 PA)		Slugging Average (minimum 1000 PA)		Home Runs	
Suzuki,Ichiro	.336	Thomas,Frank	.432	Helton,Todd	.613	Bonds,Barry	613
Helton,Todd	.333	Bonds,Barry	.428	Ramirez,Manny	.599	Sosa,Sammy	499
Garciaparra,N	.328	Martinez,Edgar	.424	Bonds,Barry	.595	Palmeiro,R	490
Guerrero,V	.322	Helton,Todd	.419	Guerrero,V	.588	McGriff,Fred	478
Pujols,Albert	.321	Giles,Brian	.416	Pujols,Albert	.586	Griffey Jr.,K	468
Piazza,Mike	.321	Giambi,Jason	.416	Rodriguez,Alex	.579	Gonzalez,Juan	405
Walker,Larry	.317	Thome,Jim	.414	Berkman,Lance	.578	Galarraga,A	386
Jeter,Derek	.317	Bagwell,Jeff	.414	Piazza,Mike	.576	Bagwell,Jeff	380
Martinez,Edgar	.317	Ramirez,Manny	.411	Walker,Larry	.574	Thomas,Frank	376
Ramirez,Manny	.316	Abreu,Bobby	.409	Giles,Brian	.570	Williams,Matt	374

Games		At Bats		Hits		Total Bases	
Henderson,R	3051	Henderson,R	10889	Henderson,R	3040	Bonds,Barry	4961
Raines,Tim	2502	Palmeiro,R	8992	Palmeiro,R	2634	Palmeiro,R	4698
Bonds,Barry	2439	Raines,Tim	8872	Raines,Tim	2605	Henderson,R	4566
Palmeiro,R	2413	McGriff,Fred	8388	Alomar,Roberto	2546	McGriff,Fred	4309
McGriff,Fred	2347	Alomar,Roberto	8386	Bonds,Barry	2462	Galarraga,A	3899
Alomar,Roberto	2183	Bonds,Barry	8335	Grace,Mark	2418	Griffey Jr.,K	3883
Grace,Mark	2179	Biggio,Craig	7960	McGriff,Fred	2403	Sosa,Sammy	3835
Galarraga,A	2140	Grace,Mark	7930	Franco,Julio	2300	Alomar,Roberto	3771
Biggio,Craig	2100	Galarraga,A	7814	Biggio,Craig	2295	Raines,Tim	3771
Franco,Julio	2041	Franco,Julio	7672	Galarraga,A	2248	Burks,Ellis	3599

Doubles		Triples		Runs Scored		RBI	
Palmeiro,R	522	Raines,Tim	113	Henderson,R	2288	Bonds,Barry	1652
Bonds,Barry	514	Finley,Steve	98	Bonds,Barry	1830	Palmeiro,R	1575
Henderson,R	509	Lofton,Kenny	78	Raines,Tim	1571	McGriff,Fred	1503
Grace,Mark	506	Alomar,Roberto	76	Palmeiro,R	1456	Galarraga,A	1381
Biggio,Craig	473	DeShields,D	74	Alomar,Roberto	1414	Griffey Jr.,K	1358
Alomar,Roberto	470	Bonds,Barry	73	Biggio,Craig	1401	Sosa,Sammy	1347
Martinez,Edgar	466	Larkin,Barry	72	McGriff,Fred	1310	Bagwell,Jeff	1321
Olerud,John	438	Offerman,Jose	69	Bagwell,Jeff	1293	Gonzalez,Juan	1317
Raines,Tim	430	Anderson,Bra	67	Griffey Jr.,K	1237	Thomas,Frank	1285
Galarraga,A	429	Bell,Jay	67	Larkin,Barry	1235	Williams,Matt	1202

Walks		Intentional Walks		Hit By Pitch		Strikeouts	
Henderson,R	2179	Bonds,Barry	423	Biggio,Craig	214	Galarraga,A	1939
Bonds,Barry	1922	Griffey Jr.,K	199	Galarraga,A	175	Sosa,Sammy	1834
Raines,Tim	1330	McGriff,Fred	165	Anderson,Bra	154	McGriff,Fred	1797
Thomas,Frank	1286	Thomas,Frank	155	Vina,Fernando	141	Henderson,R	1678
McGriff,Fred	1265	Raines,Tim	148	Knoblauch,C	139	Vaughn,Greg	1500
Bagwell,Jeff	1199	Bagwell,Jeff	145	Kendall,Jason	133	Lankford,Ray	1495
Palmeiro,R	1140	Olerud,John	144	Bagwell,Jeff	113	Vaughn,Mo	1407
Martinez,Edgar	1133	Palmeiro,R	144	Walker,Larry	110	Bell,Jay	1405
Olerud,John	1114	Vaughn,Mo	142	Vaughn,Mo	106	Gant,Ron	1402
Grace,Mark	1059	Sosa,Sammy	135	Easley,Damion	103	Thome,Jim	1377

2002 Active Career Batting Leaders

Sacrifice Hits

Glavine,Tom	168
Vizquel,Omar	160
Bell,Jay	158
Maddux,Greg	135
Alomar,Roberto	133
McLemore,Mark	103
Lewis,Darren	101
Schilling,Curt	98
Bordick,Mike	97
2 tied with	95

Sacrifice Flies

Sierra,Ruben	109
Thomas,Frank	101
Palmeiro,R	98
Surhoff,B.J.	97
Grace,Mark	96
Bagwell,Jeff	92
Alomar,Roberto	88
Olerud,John	85
Bonds,Barry	82
Sheffield,Gary	80

Stolen Bases

Henderson,R	1403
Raines,Tim	808
Lofton,Kenny	508
Bonds,Barry	493
DeShields,D	463
Alomar,Roberto	462
Grissom,M	414
Young,Eric	408
Knoblauch,C	407
Biggio,Craig	381

Seasons Played

Henderson,R	24
Orosco,Jesse	23
Raines,Tim	23
Morgan,Mike	22
Clemens,Roger	19
Dunston,Shawon	18
Franco,Julio	18
12 tied with	17

At Bats Per Home Run
(minimum 1000 AB)

Bonds,Barry	13.6
Thome,Jim	13.9
Sosa,Sammy	14.1
Ramirez,Manny	14.3
Rodriguez,Alex	14.7
Piazza,Mike	14.7
Griffey Jr.,K	14.8
Gonzalez,Juan	15.1
Delgado,Carlos	15.2
Helton,Todd	15.7

Grounded Into DP

Franco,Julio	271
McGriff,Fred	218
Zeile,Todd	204
Palmeiro,R	201
Olerud,John	195
Rodriguez,Ivan	187
Grace,Mark	186
Alomar,Roberto	185
Bagwell,Jeff	182
2 tied with	181

Stolen Base Success Pct
(minimum 100 SBA)

Beltran,Carlos	87.2
Raines,Tim	84.7
Reese,Pokey	84.6
Womack,Tony	83.6
Larkin,Barry	83.0
Glanville,Doug	81.7
Hunter,Brian	81.0
Alomar,Roberto	80.8
Henderson,R	80.7
Cruz,Jose	80.4

At Bats Per RBI
(minimum 1000 AB)

Ramirez,Manny	4.3
Pujols,Albert	4.6
Gonzalez,Juan	4.6
Helton,Todd	4.7
Thomas,Frank	4.7
Berkman,Lance	4.8
Piazza,Mike	4.8
Delgado,Carlos	4.9
Bagwell,Jeff	4.9
4 tied with	5.0

Strikeouts / Walks Ratio
(minimum 1000 AB)

Grace,Mark	.592
Young,Eric	.684
Bonds,Barry	.691
Sheffield,Gary	.724
Raines,Tim	.726
Giles,Brian	.728
Palmeiro,O	.742
Thomas,Frank	.748
Henderson,R	.770
Olerud,John	.779

At Bats Per GIDP
(minimum 1000 AB)

Maddux,Greg	170.4
McEwing,Joe	166.4
Suzuki,Ichiro	121.7
Bergeron,Peter	117.9
Womack,Tony	111.0
Glavine,Tom	102.4
Anderson,Bra	100.0
Damon,Johnny	98.3
Furcal,Rafael	94.3
Pierre,Juan	93.9

OPS
(minimum 1000 PA)

Helton,Todd	1.032
Bonds,Barry	1.023
Ramirez,Manny	1.010
Thomas,Frank	1.000
Giles,Brian	.986
Pujols,Albert	.984
Berkman,Lance	.984
Thome,Jim	.982
Guerrero,V	.973
Walker,Larry	.973

2002 Active Career Pitching Leaders

Earned Run Average
(minimum 750 IP)

Martinez,Pedro	2.62
Maddux,Greg	2.83
Orosco,Jesse	3.04
Johnson,Randy	3.06
Clemens,Roger	3.15
Morris,Matt	3.18
Hernandez,Ro	3.22
Brown,Kevin	3.22
Rijo,Jose	3.24
Smoltz,John	3.34

Winning Percentage
(minimum 100 Decisions)

Martinez,Pedro	.707
Johnson,Randy	.679
Clemens,Roger	.660
Pettitte,Andy	.646
Maddux,Greg	.642
Mussina,Mike	.641
Colon,Bartolo	.634
Glavine,Tom	.629
Millwood,Kevin	.620
Rueter,Kirk	.616

Opponent Batting Average
(minimum 750 IP)

Martinez,Pedro	.205
Johnson,Randy	.212
Orosco,Jesse	.221
Jackson,Mike	.223
Clemens,Roger	.230
Nomo,Hideo	.232
Smoltz,John	.233
Rhodes,Arthur	.234
Park,Chan Ho	.235
Schilling,Curt	.237

Baserunners Per 9 IP
(minimum 750 IP)

Martinez,Pedro	9.53
Schilling,Curt	10.23
Maddux,Greg	10.33
Mussina,Mike	10.61
Smoltz,John	10.76
Clemens,Roger	10.92
Johnson,Randy	11.01
Reed,Rick	11.11
Millwood,Kevin	11.13
Jackson,Mike	11.27

Games

Orosco,Jesse	1187
Plesac,Dan	1006
Jackson,Mike	960
Stanton,Mike	835
Mesa,Jose	701
Guthrie,Mark	700
Hernandez,Ro	696
Reed,Steve	671
Cook,Dennis	665
2 tied with	664

Games Started

Clemens,Roger	573
Maddux,Greg	535
Glavine,Tom	505
Finley,Chuck	467
Johnson,Randy	426
Morgan,Mike	411
Brown,Kevin	409
Burkett,John	393
Benes,Andy	387
Moyer,Jamie	387

Complete Games

Clemens,Roger	116
Maddux,Greg	102
Johnson,Randy	87
Schilling,Curt	76
Brown,Kevin	72
Finley,Chuck	63
Glavine,Tom	52
Erickson,Scott	51
Mussina,Mike	51
Wells,David	48

Shutouts

Clemens,Roger	45
Johnson,Randy	34
Maddux,Greg	34
Glavine,Tom	22
Mussina,Mike	20
Brown,Kevin	17
Erickson,Scott	17
Schilling,Curt	17
Finley,Chuck	15
Martinez,Pedro	15

Wins

Clemens,Roger	293
Maddux,Greg	273
Glavine,Tom	242
Johnson,Randy	224
Finley,Chuck	200
Wells,David	185
Brown,Kevin	183
Mussina,Mike	182
Moyer,Jamie	164
Smoltz,John	163

Losses

Morgan,Mike	186
Finley,Chuck	173
Maddux,Greg	152
Clemens,Roger	151
Glavine,Tom	143
Benes,Andy	139
Erickson,Scott	128
Appier,Kevin	127
Burkett,John	127
Mulholland,T	127

Innings Pitched

Clemens,Roger	4067.0
Maddux,Greg	3750.1
Glavine,Tom	3344.2
Finley,Chuck	3197.1
Johnson,Randy	3008.1
Brown,Kevin	2840.0
Morgan,Mike	2772.1
Wells,David	2613.2
Smoltz,John	2553.2
Moyer,Jamie	2522.2

Batters Faced

Clemens,Roger	16775
Maddux,Greg	15216
Glavine,Tom	14030
Finley,Chuck	13638
Johnson,Randy	12411
Morgan,Mike	11872
Brown,Kevin	11788
Wells,David	10924
Moyer,Jamie	10688
Benes,Andy	10645

Strikeouts

Clemens,Roger	3909
Johnson,Randy	3746
Maddux,Greg	2641
Finley,Chuck	2610
Schilling,Curt	2348
Smoltz,John	2240
Martinez,Pedro	2220
Brown,Kevin	2079
Glavine,Tom	2054
Benes,Andy	2000

Walks Allowed

Finley,Chuck	1332
Clemens,Roger	1321
Johnson,Randy	1231
Glavine,Tom	1140
Morgan,Mike	938
Benes,Andy	909
Appier,Kevin	887
Leiter,Al	874
Rogers,Kenny	848
Gordon,Tom	839

Hit Batters

Johnson,Randy	138
Clemens,Roger	136
Brown,Kevin	124
Astacio,Pedro	105
Maddux,Greg	101
Wakefield,Tim	97
Erickson,Scott	96
Martinez,Pedro	90
Park,Chan Ho	87
Sele,Aaron	86

Wild Pitches

Finley,Chuck	130
Clemens,Roger	120
Smoltz,John	120
Morgan,Mike	105
Appier,Kevin	98
Gordon,Tom	93
Brown,Kevin	91
Johnson,Randy	91
Nomo,Hideo	91
Wells,David	91

2002 Active Career Pitching Leaders

Saves			Save Pct (minimum 50 Save Ops)			Home Runs Allowed			Strikeouts Per 9 IP (minimum 750 IP)	
Hoffman,Trevor	352		Gagne,Eric	92.9		Wells,David	306		Johnson,Randy	11.21
Hernandez,Ro	320		Smoltz,John	92.9		Finley,Chuck	304		Martinez,Pedro	10.56
Nen,Robb	314		Hoffman,Trevor	88.9		Clemens,Roger	297		Nomo,Hideo	9.32
Percival,Troy	250		Sasaki,K	86.9		Moyer,Jamie	295		Rhodes,Arthur	8.90
Rivera,Mariano	243		Benitez,A	86.7		Benes,Andy	289		Schilling,Curt	8.74
Mesa,Jose	225		Williams,Mike	86.6		Morgan,Mike	270		Plesac,Dan	8.70
Jones,Todd	184		Rivera,Mariano	86.5		Johnson,Randy	267		Clemens,Roger	8.65
Wagner,Billy	181		Ligtenberg,K	86.3		Swindell,Greg	262		Hernandez,Ro	8.31
Benitez,A	176		Koch,Billy	86.2		Mussina,Mike	257		Park,Chan Ho	8.25
Urbina,Ugueth	174		Percival,Troy	85.9		Mulholland,T	252		Orosco,Jesse	8.21

Opp On-Base Percentage (minimum 750 IP)			Opp Slugging Average (minimum 750 IP)			Hits Per Nine Innings (minimum 750 IP)			Home Runs Per Nine IP (minimum 750 IP)	
Martinez,Pedro	.267		Martinez,Pedro	.315		Martinez,Pedro	6.69		Maddux,Greg	0.50
Schilling,Curt	.283		Orosco,Jesse	.332		Johnson,Randy	6.91		Brown,Kevin	0.56
Maddux,Greg	.287		Johnson,Randy	.334		Orosco,Jesse	7.24		Morris,Matt	0.58
Mussina,Mike	.291		Maddux,Greg	.335		Jackson,Mike	7.32		Pichardo,H	0.63
Smoltz,John	.294		Clemens,Roger	.341		Clemens,Roger	7.70		Wickman,Bob	0.64
Clemens,Roger	.296		Hernandez,Ro	.343		Nomo,Hideo	7.75		Clemens,Roger	0.66
Johnson,Randy	.298		Brown,Kevin	.345		Smoltz,John	7.77		Glavine,Tom	0.66
Millwood,Kevin	.299		Smoltz,John	.353		Rhodes,Arthur	7.78		Martinez,Pedro	0.68
Reed,Rick	.301		Jackson,Mike	.354		Park,Chan Ho	7.82		Estes,Shawn	0.68
Jackson,Mike	.304		Rijo,Jose	.361		Schilling,Curt	7.97		Pettitte,Andy	0.69

Strikeouts / Walks Ratio (minimum 750 IP)			Stolen Base Pct Allowed (minimum 750 IP)			GIDP Induced			GIDP Per Nine IP (minimum 750 IP)	
Martinez,Pedro	4.38		Rueter,Kirk	34.5		Morgan,Mike	331		Wright,Jamey	1.23
Schilling,Curt	4.11		Mulholland,T	41.3		Maddux,Greg	318		Estes,Shawn	1.20
Reynolds,Shane	3.66		Rogers,Kenny	41.4		Glavine,Tom	313		Tavarez,Julian	1.19
Lieber,Jon	3.60		Daal,Omar	41.7		Finley,Chuck	306		Hampton,Mike	1.18
Reed,Rick	3.51		Carpenter,C	42.7		Erickson,Scott	297		Erickson,Scott	1.18
Mussina,Mike	3.47		Park,Chan Ho	49.1		Brown,Kevin	286		Wickman,Bob	1.15
Maddux,Greg	3.28		Weaver,Jeff	49.1		Clemens,Roger	273		Pettitte,Andy	1.10
Swindell,Greg	3.08		Alvarez,Wilson	50.3		Rogers,Kenny	232		Pichardo,H	1.10
Vazquez,Javier	3.05		Helling,Rick	51.5		Mulholland,T	227		Morgan,Mike	1.07
Johnson,Randy	3.04		Hammond,Chris	51.7		Hampton,Mike	216		Timlin,Mike	1.01

Complete Game % (minimum 100 GS)			Quality Start Pct (minimum 100 GS)			Walks Per 9 IP (minimum 750 IP)			Games Finished	
Schilling,Curt	0.24		Martinez,Pedro	70.7		Reed,Rick	1.63		Hernandez,Ro	585
Johnson,Randy	0.20		Johnson,Randy	70.0		Radke,Brad	1.83		Nen,Robb	549
Clemens,Roger	0.20		Maddux,Greg	69.0		Anderson,Bri	1.85		Hoffman,Trevor	520
Maddux,Greg	0.19		Schilling,Curt	68.2		Lieber,Jon	1.85		Orosco,Jesse	488
Brown,Kevin	0.18		Morris,Matt	68.1		Maddux,Greg	1.93		Mesa,Jose	426
Swindell,Greg	0.15		Brown,Kevin	67.0		Reynolds,Shane	1.99		Plesac,Dan	413
Martinez,Pedro	0.15		Wood,Kerry	66.4		Swindell,Greg	2.02		Jackson,Mike	410
Mulholland,T	0.15		Clemens,Roger	65.1		Mussina,Mike	2.04		Jones,Todd	387
Erickson,Scott	0.15		Hudson,Tim	64.8		Lima,Jose	2.07		Percival,Troy	369
Mussina,Mike	0.14		Glavine,Tom	64.4		Wells,David	2.08		2 tied with	348

2002 American League Bill James Leaders

Top Game Scores of the Year

Pitcher	Date	Opp	IP	H	R	ER	BB	SO	GS
Weaver,Jeff, Det	5/22	Cle	9.0	1	0	0	2	11	94
Mussina,Mike, NYY	9/24	TB	9.0	2	0	0	2	12	93
Lidle,Cory, Oak	8/21	Cle	9.0	1	0	0	1	8	92
Lowe,Derek, Bos	4/27	TB	9.0	0	0	0	1	6	92
Milton,Eric, Min	8/1	CWS	9.0	3	0	0	0	11	92
Lidle,Cory, Oak	7/19	Tex	9.0	1	0	0	1	6	90
Lilly,Ted, NYY	6/22	SD	9.0	3	0	0	2	11	90
Loaiza,Esteban, Tor	5/19	Oak	9.0	2	0	0	0	7	90
Mulder,Mark, Oak	9/17	Ana	9.0	5	0	0	0	12	89
Mussina,Mike, NYY	8/28	Bos	9.0	3	0	0	1	9	89

Worst Game Scores of the Year

Pitcher	Date	Opp	IP	H	R	ER	BB	SO	GS
Lima,Jose, Det	8/24	Oak	2.2	9	11	11	2	1	-5
Garcia,Freddy, Sea	6/24	Oak	3.0	9	10	10	5	3	-1
Bernero,Adam, Det	6/5	Bos	2.2	10	9	9	3	2	1
Park,Chan Ho, Tex	6/7	Atl	1.1	8	9	9	1	1	2
Arrojo,Rolando, Bos	6/23	LA	2.1	9	9	9	2	2	3
Milton,Eric, Min	9/13	Cle	1.2	8	9	9	1	1	3
Stephens,John, Bal	7/30	TB	3.0	10	9	9	1	1	3
Drese,Ryan, Cle	7/13	NYY	1.1	8	8	8	3	1	4
Drese,Ryan, Cle	7/24	NYY	1.0	7	8	8	2	0	5
Ortiz,Ramon, Ana	7/14	KC	2.0	7	9	9	2	1	5

Runs Created

Rodriguez,Alex, Tex	153
Giambi,Jason, NYY	140
Thome,Jim, Cle	140
Ramirez,Manny, Bos	126
Soriano,A, NYY	125
Ordonez,M, CWS	122
Tejada,Miguel, Oak	122
Williams,B, NYY	122
Beltran,Carlos, KC	120
Delgado,Carlos, Tor	118

Runs Created Per 27 Outs

Ramirez,Manny, Bos	11.3
Thome,Jim, Cle	10.8
Giambi,Jason, NYY	9.1
Sweeney,Mike, KC	9.0
Rodriguez,Alex, Tex	8.9
Delgado,Carlos, Tor	8.3
Ordonez,M, CWS	7.6
Williams,B, NYY	7.5
Salmon,Tim, Ana	7.4
Burks,Ellis, Cle	7.4

Offensive Winning %

Ramirez,Manny, Bos	.846
Thome,Jim, Cle	.834
Giambi,Jason, NYY	.783
Sweeney,Mike, KC	.779
Rodriguez,Alex, Tex	.774
Delgado,Carlos, Tor	.747
Ordonez,M, CWS	.713
Williams,B, NYY	.711
Salmon,Tim, Ana	.703
Burks,Ellis, Cle	.702

Secondary Average
(minimum 502 PA)

Thome,Jim, Cle	.625
Palmeiro,R, Tex	.493
Giambi,Jason, NYY	.479
Delgado,Carlos, Tor	.475
Rodriguez,Alex, Tex	.471
Ramirez,Manny, Bos	.466
Ventura,Robin, NYY	.409
Thomas,Frank, CWS	.394
Cameron,Mike, Sea	.391
Beltran,Carlos, KC	.383

Isolated Power
(minimum 502 PA)

Thome,Jim, Cle	.373
Rodriguez,Alex, Tex	.324
Palmeiro,R, Tex	.299
Ramirez,Manny, Bos	.298
Giambi,Jason, NYY	.284
Ordonez,M, CWS	.276
Delgado,Carlos, Tor	.271
Soriano,A, NYY	.247
Ibanez,Raul, KC	.243
Burks,Ellis, Cle	.239

Power / Speed Number

Soriano,A, NYY	40.0
Beltran,Carlos, KC	31.7
Cameron,Mike, Sea	27.7
Hunter,Torii, Min	25.7
Jeter,Derek, NYY	23.0
Damon,Johnny, Bos	19.3
Durham,Ray, CWS-Oak	19.0
Mondesi,Raul, Tor-NYY	19.0
Winn,Randy, TB	18.4
Mora,Melvin, Bal	17.4

Speed Scores (2001-2002)

Beltran,Carlos, KC	8.09
Lofton,Kenny, CWS	7.87
Damon,Johnny, Bos	7.69
Suzuki,Ichiro, Sea	7.60
Erstad,Darin, Ana	7.50
Guzman,C, Min	7.43
Cameron,Mike, Sea	7.36
Singleton,C, Bal	7.31
Soriano,A, NYY	7.29
Durham,Ray, CWS-Oak	6.95

Cheap Wins

Mussina,Mike, NYY	5
Burkett,John, Bos	4
Drese,Ryan, Cle	4
Garcia,Freddy, Sea	4
Garland,Jon, CWS	4
Lohse,Kyle, Min	4
Washburn,J, Ana	4
Wells,David, NYY	4
17 tied with	3

Tough Losses

Buehrle,Mark, CWS	6
Suppan,Jeff, KC	6
Erickson,Scott, Bal	5
Johnson,Jason, Bal	5
Maroth,Mike, Det	5
Ponson,Sidney, Bal	5
Valdes,Ismael, Tex-Sea	5
10 tied with	4

2002 National League Bill James Leaders

Top Game Scores of the Year

Pitcher	Date	Opp	IP	H	R	ER	BB	SO	GS
Schilling,Curt, Ari	4/7	Mil	9.0	1	0	0	2	17	100
Johnson,Randy, Ari	4/21	Col	9.0	2	1	0	1	17	97
Johnson,Randy, Ari	9/14	Mil	9.0	3	0	0	2	17	96
Estes,Shawn, NYM	4/26	Mil	9.0	1	0	0	1	8	92
Johnson,Randy, Ari	8/5	NYM	9.0	2	0	0	2	11	92
Perez,Odalis, LA	4/26	ChC	9.0	1	0	0	0	6	91
Astacio,Pedro, NYM	5/14	LA	9.0	2	0	0	2	9	90
Miller,Wade, Hou	9/15	Stl	9.0	3	0	0	0	9	90
Perez,Odalis, LA	6/25	Col	9.0	1	0	0	1	6	90
Schmidt,Jason, SF	8/20	NYM	9.0	5	0	0	0	13	90

Worst Game Scores of the Year

Pitcher	Date	Opp	IP	H	R	ER	BB	SO	GS
Neagle,Denny, Col	7/2	SF	2.0	10	10	10	3	0	-7
Dempster,Ryan, Fla	6/7	Min	4.0	11	10	10	4	0	-4
Simontacchi,J, Stl	8/2	Atl	1.0	7	9	9	4	0	-1
Tollberg,Brian, SD	4/2	Ari	2.2	9	9	9	3	0	1
Hampton,Mike, Col	7/17	Ari	5.0	13	10	9	2	1	2
Tomko,Brett, SD	8/9	Cin	3.1	9	10	10	3	3	2
Astacio,Pedro, NYM	8/17	LA	3.0	12	8	8	2	2	3
Rusch,Glendon, Mil	5/23	LA	1.2	9	8	8	2	0	3
Tavarez,Julian, Fla	5/16	Col	4.0	9	10	10	4	3	3
3 tied with									5

Runs Created

Bonds,Barry, SF	161
Berkman,Lance, Hou	131
Giles,Brian, Pit	131
Helton,Todd, Col	128
Guerrero,V, Mon	125
Pujols,Albert, Stl	122
Sosa,Sammy, ChC	122
Jones,Chipper, Atl	119
Abreu,Bobby, Phi	115
2 tied with	114

Runs Created Per 27 Outs

Bonds,Barry, SF	16.5
Giles,Brian, Pit	9.5
Walker,Larry, Col	9.2
Helton,Todd, Col	8.7
Berkman,Lance, Hou	8.2
Jones,Chipper, Atl	8.1
Edmonds,Jim, Stl	7.9
Sosa,Sammy, ChC	7.9
Klesko,Ryan, SD	7.8
Gonzalez,Luis, Ari	7.7

Offensive Winning %

Bonds,Barry, SF	.932
Giles,Brian, Pit	.820
Walker,Larry, Col	.809
Helton,Todd, Col	.794
Berkman,Lance, Hou	.774
Jones,Chipper, Atl	.768
Edmonds,Jim, Stl	.759
Sosa,Sammy, ChC	.759
Klesko,Ryan, SD	.754
Gonzalez,Luis, Ari	.749

Secondary Average
(minimum 502 PA)

Bonds,Barry, SF	.938
Giles,Brian, Pit	.614
Sosa,Sammy, ChC	.495
Berkman,Lance, Hou	.478
Dunn,Adam, Cin	.464
Green,Shawn, LA	.438
Helton,Todd, Col	.434
Edmonds,Jim, Stl	.433
Bellhorn,Mark, ChC	.429
Abreu,Bobby, Phi	.428

Isolated Power
(minimum 502 PA)

Bonds,Barry, SF	.429
Giles,Brian, Pit	.324
Sosa,Sammy, ChC	.306
Berkman,Lance, Hou	.285
Green,Shawn, LA	.273
Walker,Larry, Col	.264
Piazza,Mike, NYM	.264
Burrell,Pat, Phi	.263
Guerrero,V, Mon	.257
Bellhorn,Mark, ChC	.254

Power / Speed Number

Guerrero,V, Mon	39.5
Boone,Aaron, Cin	28.7
Abreu,Bobby, Phi	24.3
Encarnacion,J, Cin-Fla	22.4
Lee,Derrek, Fla	22.3
Dunn,Adam, Cin	22.0
Giles,Brian, Pit	21.5
Wilson,Preston, Fla	21.4
Sanders,Reggie, SF	20.2
Finley,Steve, Ari	19.5

Speed Scores (2001-2002)

Pierre,Juan, Col	7.94
Rollins,Jimmy, Phi	7.61
Glanville,Doug, Phi	7.41
Womack,Tony, Ari	7.11
Castillo,Luis, Fla	7.07
Furcal,Rafael, Atl	6.94
Reese,Pokey, Pit	6.88
Uribe,Juan, Col	6.77
Sanders,Reggie, SF	6.71
Floyd,Cliff, Fla-Mon	6.52

Cheap Wins

Haynes,Jimmy, Cin	7
Batista,Miguel, Ari	6
Jennings,Jason, Col	6
Ishii,Kazuhisa, LA	5
Helling,Rick, Ari	4
Penny,Brad, Fla	4
Rueter,Kirk, SF	4
Tavarez,Julian, Fla	4
Thomson,John, Col-NYM	4
10 tied with	3

Tough Losses

Hernandez,L, SF	6
Wood,Kerry, ChC	6
Ashby,Andy, LA	5
Dempster,Ryan, Fla-Cin	5
Helling,Rick, Ari	5
Ishii,Kazuhisa, LA	5
Ortiz,Russ, SF	5
Sheets,Ben, Mil	5
Wells,Kip, Pit	5
Zambrano,C, ChC	5

Pitch Data Introduction

What follows is one of the facets of Baseball Info Solutions that makes us most excited. For the 2002 season, we charted 96 percent of all pitches for location, 93 percent of all pitches for pitch type and 70 percent of all pitches for velocity. Considering the 2002 season was our initial venture, those percentages will grow larger for 2003.

The possibilities of combining traditional baseball statistics and splits with pitch-charting data are still mostly "uncharted" territory. The reports you see on Barry Bonds and Barry Zito are intended as simply a taste of what we can do and further things to come.

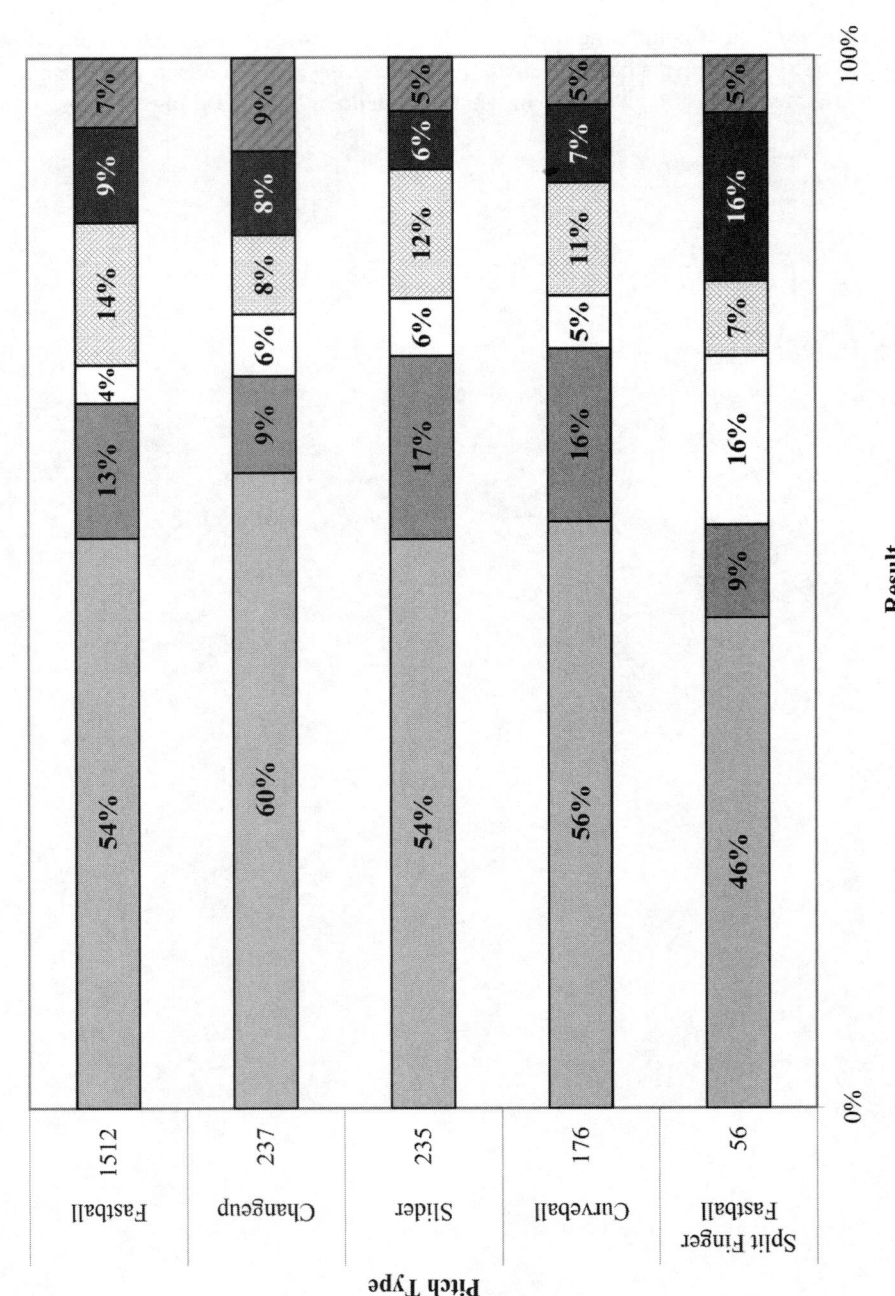

Barry Bonds: Batting By Pitch Type, 2002 Season

Legend: Balls, Taken Strikes, Swinging Strikes, Fouls, In Play Outs, Hits

Pitch Type							
Fastball	1512	54%	13%	4%	14%	9%	7%
Changeup	237	60%	9%	6%	8%	8%	9%
Slider	235	54%	17%	6%	12%	6%	5%
Curveball	176	56%	16%	5%	11%	7%	5%
Split Finger Fastball	56	46%	9%	16%	7%	16%	5%

Result

330

Barry Zito: Pitch Selection By Count, 2002 Season

Career Assessments

Just as the excitement around Barry Bonds breaking the single-season home-run record started to subside, the buzz around Bonds passing hitting greats on the career list increased. In 2002, Bonds passed Harmon Killebrew, Mark McGwire and Frank Robinson to leap into fourth place on the list. The Bonds watch continues this season, where Bonds stands 47 home runs shy of his godfather, Willie Mays.

While passing a baseball great like Mays is quite an accomplishment, the ultimate holy grail of any home run hitter is to supplant Hammerin' Hank Aaron as baseball's all-time home-run king. Bonds, Sammy Sosa and Alex Rodriguez are the only active players with a greater than 40% chance of surpassing Aaron by the end of their careers. Bonds is the most likely to achieve the milestone at 47%, while Sosa and Rodriguez are at 45% and 42% respectively. But while Bonds and Sosa have held somewhat steady from last year, Rodriguez surged 15% from the 27% chance he had last season.

While Aaron's home-run record may nearly be on life-support, his RBI record of 2,297 can breathe a little easier. It is nearly a toss-up whether or not an active player will achieve 2,298 RBI at 47%. A few of the same players chasing Aaron's home-run total are also endangering his RBI record. Rodriguez (27%) and Sosa (12%) lead the way, but younger players such as Tejada (4%), Guerrero (3%) and Pujols (2%) could see their percentages grow considerably if they keep up the high RBI production that they have achieved over the early part of their career.

Only one active player, who appears to be at a record pace in the early part of his career, has any chance at all of breaking Pete Rose's record of 4,256 career hits. A-Rod, hitting at an astonishing rate, has a 2% chance of surpassing Rose's hit total. While the chance of Rodriguez breaking the record is low, it marks an increase from last year, when no active player had any established chance of reaching the hit record.

While it is exciting to speculate on the possibilities that Alex Rodriguez has to smash career records, it is also important to remember that anything can happen. Rodriguez has a career beginning similar to that of Ken Griffey Jr. In fact, Rodriguez is hitting home runs at a pace that exceeded that of Griffey at the same point in his career. Griffey, who as late as 2000 had a 44% chance to surpass Aaron's home-run record, fell upon a few tough seasons with injuries. These seasons have caused Griffey to no longer have a reasonable chance at chasing Aaron.

The assault on Aaron's records does not seem to be ending in the near future. If established superstars like Bonds and Sosa do not surpass Aaron, there will still be plenty of young stars like Rodriguez, Guerrero and Pujols to challenge Aaron's marks. While the climb towards career records may not create the burst of excitement that a pennant race would create, the chase for Aaron will keep fans interested in years to come.

-- Ryan Galla

Career Assessments

Player	Age	CURRENT TOTALS H	HR	RBI	HOME RUN GOALS 500	600	700	756	800	HIT GOALS 3000	4000	4257	RBI GOALS 2000	2298
Barry Bonds	37	2462	613	1652	4/17/2001	8/9/2002	95%	47%	24%	20%	0%	0%	35%	0%
Sammy Sosa	33	1955	499	1347	100%	94%	71%	45%	31%	25%	0%	0%	40%	12%
Rafael Palmeiro	37	2634	490	1575	99%	49%	2%	0%	0%	57%	0%	0%	17%	0%
Fred McGriff	38	2403	478	1503	98%	0%	0%	0%	0%	0%	0%	0%	0%	0%
Ken Griffey Jr.	32	2039	468	1358	95%	18%	0%	0%	0%	0%	0%	0%	0%	0%
Jim Thome	31	1332	334	927	90%	50%	23%	13%	7%	0%	0%	0%	10%	0%
Alex Rodriguez	26	1354	298	872	89%	84%	55%	42%	34%	42%	7%	2%	48%	27%
Jeff Bagwell	34	1969	380	1321	71%	16%	0%	0%	0%	16%	0%	0%	17%	0%
Manny Ramirez	30	1400	310	1036	65%	26%	6%	0%	0%	8%	0%	0%	22%	5%
Vladimir Guerrero	26	1085	209	623	55%	28%	12%	6%	2%	32%	4%	0%	15%	3%
Juan Gonzalez	32	1805	405	1317	52%	0%	0%	0%	0%	0%	0%	0%	5%	0%
Shawn Green	29	1232	234	714	51%	23%	8%	1%	0%	13%	0%	0%	8%	0%
Andruw Jones	25	940	185	559	44%	21%	7%	2%	0%	16%	0%	0%	8%	0%
Carlos Delgado	30	1118	262	814	42%	14%	0%	0%	0%	0%	0%	0%	6%	0%
Gary Sheffield	33	1819	340	1100	39%	5%	0%	0%	0%	9%	0%	0%	0%	0%
Troy Glaus	25	617	148	423	38%	19%	6%	1%	0%	2%	0%	0%	8%	0%
Todd Helton	28	973	186	623	35%	15%	2%	0%	0%	17%	0%	0%	15%	3%
Jason Giambi	31	1224	228	797	32%	10%	0%	0%	0%	4%	0%	0%	7%	0%
Chipper Jones	30	1419	253	837	27%	5%	0%	0%	0%	19%	0%	0%	3%	0%
Richie Sexson	27	646	146	469	23%	7%	0%	0%	0%	0%	0%	0%	3%	0%
Eric Chavez	24	561	105	365	23%	8%	0%	0%	0%	8%	0%	0%	9%	0%
Frank Thomas	34	1902	376	1285	23%	0%	0%	0%	0%	0%	0%	0%	0%	0%
Lance Berkman	26	487	101	336	22%	7%	0%	0%	0%	3%	0%	0%	6%	0%
Mike Piazza	33	1641	347	1073	22%	0%	0%	0%	0%	0%	0%	0%	0%	0%
Miguel Tejada	26	791	129	498	20%	5%	0%	0%	0%	17%	0%	0%	15%	4%
Magglio Ordonez	28	916	149	567	19%	4%	0%	0%	0%	12%	0%	0%	12%	1%
Albert Pujols	22	379	71	257	18%	5%	0%	0%	0%	10%	0%	0%	11%	2%
Brian Giles	31	909	188	593	16%	0%	0%	0%	0%	0%	0%	0%	0%	0%
Scott Rolen	27	937	164	603	13%	0%	0%	0%	0%	6%	0%	0%	7%	0%
Tony Batista	28	784	156	472	12%	0%	0%	0%	0%	0%	0%	0%	0%	0%
Pat Burrell	25	410	82	284	12%	0%	0%	0%	0%	0%	0%	0%	0%	0%
Luis Gonzalez	34	1783	249	1020	11%	0%	0%	0%	0%	7%	0%	0%	0%	0%
Alfonso Soriano	24	373	60	179	10%	0%	0%	0%	0%	4%	0%	0%	0%	0%
Larry Walker	35	1863	335	1133	8%	0%	0%	0%	0%	0%	0%	0%	0%	0%
Ryan Klesko	31	1140	224	750	7%	0%	0%	0%	0%	0%	0%	0%	0%	0%
Paul Konerko	26	692	111	410	7%	0%	0%	0%	0%	8%	0%	0%	1%	0%
Jim Edmonds	32	1223	221	709	6%	0%	0%	0%	0%	0%	0%	0%	0%	0%
Raul Mondesi	31	1385	240	757	5%	0%	0%	0%	0%	0%	0%	0%	0%	0%
Garret Anderson	30	1432	164	756	3%	0%	0%	0%	0%	24%	0%	0%	9%	0%
Jeff Kent	34	1604	253	1007	1%	0%	0%	0%	0%	5%	0%	0%	5%	0%
Derek Lee	26	614	99	329	0%	0%	0%	0%	0%	1%	0%	0%	0%	0%
Rickey Henderson	43	3040	295	1110	0%	0%	0%	0%	0%	10/8/2001	0%	0%	0%	0%
Roberto Alomar	34	2546	201	1071	0%	0%	0%	0%	0%	92%	0%	0%	0%	0%
Derek Jeter	28	1390	117	563	0%	0%	0%	0%	0%	34%	2%	0%	0%	0%
Johnny Damon	28	1237	88	464	0%	0%	0%	0%	0%	21%	0%	0%	0%	0%
Bernie Williams	33	1833	226	998	0%	0%	0%	0%	0%	21%	0%	0%	0%	0%
John Olerud	33	1934	229	1062	0%	0%	0%	0%	0%	21%	0%	0%	0%	0%
Darin Erstad	28	1107	96	468	0%	0%	0%	0%	0%	18%	0%	0%	0%	0%
Craig Biggio	36	2295	195	869	0%	0%	0%	0%	0%	14%	0%	0%	0%	0%
Shannon Stewart	28	951	66	321	0%	0%	0%	0%	0%	13%	0%	0%	0%	0%
Edgar Renteria	26	1061	60	393	0%	0%	0%	0%	0%	13%	0%	0%	0%	0%
Luis Castillo	26	790	8	155	0%	0%	0%	0%	0%	11%	0%	0%	0%	0%
Jose Vidro	27	782	72	346	0%	0%	0%	0%	0%	11%	0%	0%	0%	0%
Carlos Beltran	25	665	82	365	0%	0%	0%	0%	0%	10%	0%	0%	0%	0%
Cristian Guzman	24	570	28	190	0%	0%	0%	0%	0%	10%	0%	0%	0%	0%
Bobby Abreu	28	918	116	468	0%	0%	0%	0%	0%	9%	0%	0%	0%	0%
Ray Durham	30	1306	112	506	0%	0%	0%	0%	0%	8%	0%	0%	0%	0%
Juan Pierre	24	434	3	110	0%	0%	0%	0%	0%	7%	0%	0%	0%	0%
Mike Sweeney	28	899	123	521	0%	0%	0%	0%	0%	7%	0%	0%	0%	0%
Adrian Beltre	23	615	76	309	0%	0%	0%	0%	0%	7%	0%	0%	0%	0%
Mark Kotsay	26	750	58	298	0%	0%	0%	0%	0%	3%	0%	0%	0%	0%
Edgardo Alfonzo	28	1136	120	538	0%	0%	0%	0%	0%	3%	0%	0%	0%	0%
Nomar Garciaparra	28	1033	145	564	0%	0%	0%	0%	0%	3%	0%	0%	0%	0%
Omar Vizquel	35	1921	57	637	0%	0%	0%	0%	0%	2%	0%	0%	0%	0%
Ichiro Suzuki	28	450	16	120	0%	0%	0%	0%	0%	1%	0%	0%	0%	0%
Jimmy Rollins	23	353	25	119	0%	0%	0%	0%	0%	1%	0%	0%	0%	0%

Baseball Glossary

% Inherited Scored
The percentage of inherited baserunners a relief pitcher allows to score.

% Pitches Taken
The percentage of pitches that a batter does not swing at out of the total number of pitches thrown to him.

1st Batter Average
The Batting Average that a relief pitcher allows to the first batter he faces when he enters a game.

1st Batter OBP
The On-Base Percentage that a relief pitcher allows to the first batter he faces when he enters a game.

Active Career Batting Leaders
A list of batting leaders among active (appearing in 2002) players. An active player is eligible when he meets the minimum requirements for the following categories:

1,000 At Bats - Batting Average, On-Base Percentage, Slugging Average, At Bats Per HR, At Bats Per GDP, At Bats Per RBI, Strikeout to Walk Ratio
100 Stolen Base Attempts - Stolen Base Success Percentage

Active Career Pitching Leaders
A list of pitching leaders among active (appearing in 2002) players. An active player is eligible when he meets the minimum requirements for the following categories:

750 Innings Pitched - Earned Run Average, Opponent Batting Average, all "Per 9 Innings" categories, Strikeout to Walk Ratio
250 Games Started - Complete Game Frequency
100 Decisions - Win-Loss Percentage

AVG Allowed ScPos
The Batting Average allowed by a pitcher while pitching with runners in scoring position.

AVG Bases Loaded
The Batting Average of a hitter while batting with the bases loaded.

Batting Average
Hits divided by at bats.

Blown Save
When a relief pitcher enters a game in a Save Situation (see definition for Save Situation) and allows the other team to score the tying or go-ahead run.

Career Assessments

This method, once called the Favorite Toy, is a way to estimate the probability that a player will achieve a specific career goal. In this example, 3,000 hits will be used. The four components of the formula are Needed Hits, Years Remaining, Established Hit Level and Projected Remaining Hits.

Needed Hits: This is the number of Hits (or any statistic) that a player needs to reach a desired goal.

Years Remaining. This is the estimated number of years remaining in the player's career. It is determined using the player's age (on June 30th of the previous year; use 2002 when making the calculation after the 2002 season is complete). The formula is (42 - age) divided by two. This means a player who is 20 years old will have 11 remaining seasons, a player who is 25 years old will have 8.5 remaining seasons and a player who is 35 years old will have 3.5 remaining seasons. If the player is a catcher, than multiply his remaining seasons by .7. If a player is older than 39 (the Years Remaining calculation yields less than 1.5), consult the player's statistics for the most recent year. If the player either had 100 Hits or an Offensive Winning Percentage of .500 or greater, then the player will have 1.0 remaining seasons. If the player has both, he has 1.5 remaining seasons. If he has neither, he has .5 remaining seasons.

Established Hit Level. The Established Hit Level is a weighted average of the player's hits over the past three seasons. To calculate the Established Hit Level after the 2002 season is complete, add 2000 Hits, (2001 Hits multiplied by two) and (2002 Hits multiplied by three), then divide by six. If the Established Hit Level is less than 75% of the most recent performance (2002 Hits in this case), then the Established Hit Level is equal to .75 times the most recent performance.

Projected Remaining Hits. This is calculated by multiplying Years Remaining by the Established Hit Level.

The probability of achieving the specified goal is found by dividing Projected Remaining Hits by Need Hits, then subtracting .5. The maximum chance that any player has of achieving a goal is .97 raised to the power of (Need Hits / Established Hit Level). This prevents the possibility of a player reaching a goal from being higher than 100 percent, which is impossible.

Catcher's ERA

The ERA for a catcher is equal to the ERA of pitchers pitching while the catcher is playing behind the plate. It is calculated exactly like ERA for pitchers. Take the number of earned runs allowed while the catcher is playing, multiply it by 9 and then divide it by the total number of defensive innings that the catcher was behind the plate.

Cleanup Slugging Average

The Slugging Average of a batter when he bats in the cleanup spot, or fourth, in the batting order.

Component ERA (ERC)

A statistic that estimates what a pitcher's ERA should have been, based on his pitching performance. The ERC formula is calculated as follows:

1. Subtract the pitcher's Home Runs Allowed from his Hits Allowed.
2. Multiply Step 1 by 1.255.
3. Multiply his Home Runs Allowed by four.
4. Add Steps 2 and 3 together.
5. Multiply Step 4 by .89.
6. Add his Walks and Hit Batsmen.
7. Multiply Step 6 by .475.
8. Add Steps 5 and 7 together.

This yields the pitcher's total base estimate (PTB), which is:

$$PTB = 0.89 \times (1.255 \times (H - HR) + 4 \times HR) + 0.475 \times (BB + HB)$$

For those pitchers for whom there is intentional walk data, use this formula instead:

$$PTB = 0.89 \times (1.255 \times (H - HR) + 4 \times HR) + 0.56 \times (BB + HB - IBB)$$

9. Add Hits and Walks and Hit Batsmen.
10. Multiply Step 9 by PTB.
11. Divide Step 10 by Batters Facing Pitcher. If BFP data is unavailable, approximate it by multiplying Innings Pitched by 2.9, then adding Step 9.
12. Multiply Step 11 by 9.
13. Divide Step 12 by Innings Pitched.
14. Subtract .56 from Step 13.

This is the pitcher's ERC, which is:

$$\frac{(H + BB + HBP) \times PTB}{BFP \times IP} \times 9 - 0.56$$

If the result after Step 13 is less than 2.24, adjust the formula as follows:

$$\frac{(H + BB + HBP) \times PTB}{BFP \times IP} \times 9 \times 0.75$$

Earned Run Average

The number of earned runs that a pitcher surrenders per nine innings that he pitches. It is calculated by multiplying the total earned runs allowed by nine and dividing by the total number of innings pitched.

Easy Save

This label is used to separate Saves by difficulty level (Easy or Tough). A Save is considered Easy if the relief pitcher enters the game, pitches one inning or less, and the first batter he faces does not at least represent the tying run.

Fielding Percentage

The percentage of plays a player makes in the field without making an error out of the total number of opportunities. It is calculated by adding (Putouts plus Assists) and dividing by (Putouts plus Assists plus Errors).

Games Finished

The relief pitcher who is in the game for each team when the game ends is credited with a Game Finished.

Game Score

To determine the starting pitcher's Game Score:
Start with 50.
Add 1 point for each out recorded by the starting pitcher.
Add 2 points for each inning the pitcher completes after the fourth inning.
Add 1 point for each strikeout.
Subtract 2 points for each hit allowed.
Subtract 4 points for each earned run allowed.
Subtract 2 points for an unearned run.
Subtract 1 point for each walk.

GDP

Grounded into Double Play

GDP Opportunity

This is a situation where the batter has a chance to ground into a double play. It occurs with at least a runner on first base and less than two outs.

Ground / Fly Ratio (Grd/Fly, GB/FB)

Calculated for both batters and pitchers. For batters, it is the number of groundballs hit divided by the number of flyballs hit. For pitchers, it is exactly the same but uses the number of groundballs and flyballs allowed. Every fair batted ball is included except for bunts and line drives.

Hold

A relief pitcher is given a Hold anytime he enters a game in a Save Situation (see definition for Save Situation), records one out or more, and exits the game without giving up the lead. If the pitcher finishes the game, then he will only earn credit for a Save. He cannot receive credit for both a Hold and a Save.

Inherited Runner

When a relief pitcher enters the game, any runner who is on base at the time is considered an Inherited Runner.

Isolated Power
Slugging Average minus Batting Average.

K/BB Ratio
Strikeouts divided by Walks.

Late & Close
A situation in a game that is very similar to a Save Situation. The following requirements are necessary for a Late & Close game:
1. The game is in the seventh inning or later AND
2. The batting team is either leading by one run or tied OR
3. The tying run is on base, at bat, or on deck.

Leadoff On-Base Percentage
The On-Base Percentage of a batter when he bats leadoff, or first, in the batting order.

Offensive Winning Percentage (OWP)
A player's Offensive Winning Percentage is the winning percentage of a hypothetical team which has an offense consisting of nine of that player, and pitching and defense which is average for the player's league. It is calculated by taking the square of RC/27 (see the definition for Runs Created per 27 Outs), dividing it by the sum of RC/27 and the square of the average runs scored per game in the league.

On-Base Percentage
(Hits plus Walks plus Hit by Pitcher) divided by (At Bats plus Walks plus Hit by Pitcher plus Sacrifice Flies).

$$\frac{H + BB + HBP}{AB + BB + HBP + SF}$$

Opponent Batting Average
Hits Allowed divided by (Batters Faced minus Walks minus Hit Batsmen minus Sacrifice Hits minus Sacrifice Flies minus Catcher's Interference).

$$\frac{H}{BFP - BB - HBP - SH - SF - CI}$$

PA*
Used in the denominator for the calculation of On-Base Percentage. It is calculated by subtracting (Sacrifice Hits plus Times Reached Base on Defensive Interference) from Plate Appearances (see definition for Plate Appearances).

Park Index

The Park Index of a given ballpark is the amount that the ballpark influences a given statistic. The following is a calculation of a park index using runs as the statistic:

1. Add Runs and Opponent Runs in home games.
2. Add At Bats and Opponent At Bats in home games. (If At Bats are unavailable, use home games.)
3. Divide Step 1 by Step 2.
4. Add Runs and Opponent Runs in road games.
5. Add At Bats and Opponent At Bats in road games. (if At Bats are unavailable, use road games.)
6. Divide Step 4 by Step 5.
7. Divide Step 3 by Step 6.
8. Multiply Step 7 by 100.

An index of 100 means the park is completely neutral and does not influence the particular statistic at all. A park index of 112 for runs indicates that teams score 12 percent more runs in this ballpark than a neutral park. A park index of 92 for runs means that teams tend to score 8 percent fewer runs in this ballpark than a neutral park.

PCS (Pitchers' Caught Stealing)

The number of runners officially scored as Caught Stealing where the pitcher initiated the play. The normal Caught Stealing is when a runner is out attempting to steal a base but the play was initiated by the catcher. PCS plays are often referred to as pickoffs, but differ when the runner breaks towards the next base as opposed to returning to the base he was currently on. Pickoffs occur when the pitcher throws to a base that a runner is leading from, and the runner is out attempting to return to that base. Pickoffs are not an official statistic.

Pitches per PA

The total number of pitches a hitter sees divided by his total Plate Appearances.

Plate Appearances

At Bats plus Total Walks plus Hit By Pitcher plus Sacrifice Hits plus Sacrifice Flies plus Times Reached on Defensive Interference.

Power/Speed Number

A single number that reflects a combination of power and speed. To achieve a high Power/Speed Number, a player must score high in both power and speed. To calculate the Power/Speed Number, multiply Home Runs by Stolen Bases by two, and divide by the sum of Home Runs and Stolen Bases.

$$\frac{2 \times HR \times SB}{HR + SB}$$

PPO (Pitcher Pickoff)

The number of baserunners thrown out when a pitcher throws to a base with a leading baserunner, and the runner is tagged out attempting to return to the base. PPO is not an official statistic and does not count toward Caught Stealing totals.

Quality Start

A game where the starting pitcher pitches for at least six innings and allows no more than three earned runs.

Quality Start Percentage

Quality Starts divided by Games Started (see the definition for Quality Start).

Range Factor

The number of Successful Chances (Putouts plus Assists) times nine divided by the number of Defensive Innings Played. The average for a Regular Player at each position in 2002:

Second Base: 4.93
Third Base: 2.69
Shortstop: 4.54
Left Field: 2.02
Center Field: 2.67
Right Field: 2.09

RHS

Righthanded Starting Pitcher.

Run Support Per 9 IP

The total number of runs scored by a pitcher's team while he is in the game multiplied by nine and divided by total Innings Pitched.

Runs Created

Bill James has devised many different Runs Created formulas, based on the statistics available and the time period of the statistics. The current method is as follows:

  1. Add hits plus walks plus hit by pitcher.
  2. Subtract caught stealings and grounded into double plays from Step 1. This is the A factor.
  3. Add unintentional walks plus hit by pitcher.
  4. Multiply Step 3 by .24.
  5. Multiply stolen bases by .62.
  6. Add sacrifice hits plus sacrifice flies.
  7. Multiply Step 6 by .5.
  8. Add total bases plus Step 4 plus Step 5 plus Step 7.
  9. Multiply strikeouts by .03.
10. Subtract Step 9 from Step 8. This is the B factor.
11. Add at-bats plus walks plus hit by pitcher plus sacrifice hits plus sacrifice flies. This is the C factor.

To summarize:

$$A = H + BB + HBP - CS - GDP$$
$$B = 0.24 \times (BB - IBB + HBP) + 0.62 \times SB + 0.5 \times (SH + SF) + TB - 0.03 \times SO$$
$$C = AB + BB + HBP + SH + SF$$

Each player's runs created is determined as if he were operating in a context of eight other players of average skill. The final steps are:

12. Multiply C by 2.4.
13. Add A plus Step 12.
14. Multiply C by 3.
15. Add B plus Step 14.
16. Multiply Step 13 by Step 15.
17. Multiply C by 9.
18. Divide Step 16 by Step 17.
19. Multiply C by .9.
20. Subtract Step 19 from Step 18.

Expressed as an equation, that's:

$$\frac{(2.4 \times C + A) \times (3 \times C + B)}{9 \times C} - (0.9 \times C)$$

When there is available data for home runs with men on base (HRmob) and batting average with runners in scoring position (AVGrsp), we can make further adjustments to the Runs Created formula.

The first adjustment deals with HRmob. It comes from the fact that the Runs Created formula assumes that a player hits home runs at the same frequency with men on base as he does with no men on base. If a player hits home runs at a higher frequency with men on base, then he creates more runs. If he hits home runs at a lower frequency, he will have created less runs than the original formula gives him. To figure out the HRmob adjustment, first divide home runs by total at bats to calculate the player's overall home run frequency. Then, multiply the frequency by the player's at bats with men on base (ABmob) to get the expected number of home runs with men on base. Subtract this expected number from the players actual HRmob and add the result to the player's Runs Created.

The other adjustment deals with AVGrsp. The adjustment is needed to deal with the fact that the Runs Created formula assumes that a player has the same batting average with runners in scoring position as he does without. If this is not the case, Runs Created needs to be adjusted. The calculation is similar to the HRmob adjustment. First multiply the player's overall batting average by at bats with runners in scoring position (ABrsp) to get the number of expected hits with runners in scoring position. Then subtract the expected hits from the actual hits with runners in scoring position (AVGrsp * ABrsp) and add it to Runs Created.

The adjustment formulas written are:

$$HRmob - \frac{HR \times ABmob}{AB}$$

$$(AVGrsp \times ABrsp) - (AVG \times ABrsp)$$

The last step is an adjustment to reconcile the results of the Runs Created formula with actual runs scored. Add up all of a team's players' runs created and compare it to the team's actual number of runs scored and reconcile the difference proportionally. For example, if the sum of the Runs Created for the team is 800 runs and the team in reality scored 848 runs, increase each player's Runs Created by 6 percent (848 / 800 = 1.06). Finally, each player's Runs Created can be rounded to the nearest integer value.

Runs Created per 27 Outs (RC/27)
This statistic estimates the number of runs per game that a team made up of nine of the same player would score. The name is a bit deceiving, because Bill James' current formula is based upon each league's average outs per team game instead of the standard 27. To calculate RC/27, multiply Runs Created by league outs per team game, divide the result by outs made by the player (the sum of at bats plus sacrifice hits plus sacrifice flies plus caught stealing plus grounded into double plays, minus hits). The formula written out is:

$$\frac{\frac{RC \times 3 \times LgIP}{2 \times LgG}}{AB - H + SH + SF + CS + GDP}$$

Save Percentage
A pitcher's Saves divided by the total number of Save Situations he faces (see definition for Save Situation).

Save Situation
A relief pitcher is in a Save Situation when he enters the game with his team in the lead, has the opportunity to finish the game, is not the winning pitcher of record at the time, and meets any one of the three following conditions:
   1. The pitcher's team is leading by no more than three runs and the pitcher has the chance to pitch for at least one inning, OR
   2. The pitcher enters the game with the potential tying run on base, at bat, or on deck, OR
   3. The pitcher pitches three or more effective innings regardless of the lead. The determination of a save in this situation is made by the official scorer.
It is not possible to have more than one save credited to a single team in a game.

SB Success Percentage

Stolen Bases divided by the number of Stolen Base attempts (Stolen Bases plus Caught Stealing).

$$\frac{SB}{SB + CS}$$

Secondary Average

A number meant to reflect everything else except for batting average. A player will have a high Secondary Average if he hits for power, takes walks and steals bases. It is calculated with the following formula:

$$\frac{TB - H + BB + SB - CS}{AB}$$

Similarity Score

A number which reflects the similarity between two different statistical lines, either for a player or for a team. A score of 1,000 means that the statistical lines are identical.

Slugging Average

Total Bases divided by At Bats.

$$\frac{TB}{AB}$$

Speed Score

Speed Score is a number which evaluates how fast a player is. To calculate the Speed Score, start with the player's statistics over the last two seasons combined. A value will be found for each of the following six categories and will be combined for a final score at the end:

1. Stolen Base Percentage. The value of this category is:

$$\left(\frac{SB + 3}{SB + CS + 7} - 0.4 \right) \times 20$$

2. Frequency of Stolen Base Attempts. The value of this category is:

$$\frac{\sqrt{\dfrac{SB + CS}{Singles + BB + HBP}}}{0.07}$$

3. Percentage of Triples. This is calculated by taking the percentage of triples out of the number of balls put in play. To get the percentage, use this formula:

$$\frac{3B}{AB - HR - SO}$$

From this assign an integer from 0 to 10, based on the following chart:

Less than .001	0
.001 - .0023	1
.0023 - .0039	2
.0039 - .0058	3
.0058 - .0080	4
.0080 - .0105	5
.0105 - .013	6
.013 - .0158	7
.0158 - .0189	8
.0189 - .0223	9
.0223 or more	10

4. Runs Scored Percentage. This is calculated by taking the percentage of times the player scores a run out of the number of times the player is on base. To get the percentage, use this formula:

$$\frac{\left(\dfrac{R - HR}{H + HBP + BB - HR} - 0.1\right)}{0.04}$$

5. Grounded Into Double Play Frequency. To get the frequency, use this formula:

$$\frac{0.055 - \left(\dfrac{GIDP}{AB - HR - SO}\right)}{0.005}$$

6. Range Factor. The value of this category depends on the players position:

Catcher - 1
First Baseman - 2
Designated Hitter - 1.5
Second Baseman - 1.25 * Range Factor
Third Baseman - 1.51 * Range Factor
Shortstop - 1.52 * Range Factor
Outfield - 3 * Range Factor
For an explanation on Range Factor, consult the definition in this glossary. Remember to figure range factors over a two-year period.